Avery Index to Architectural Periodicals

Eleventh Supplement 1990

an operating program of The Getty Art History Information Program at Columbia University

Volume 4: S—Z

G.K. Hall & Co.
70 Lincoln Street
Boston, Massachusetts
1991

ISBN 0-8161-0519-7 (set)
      0-8161-0529-4 (vol. 1)
      0-8161-0530-8 (vol. 2)
      0-8161-0531-6 (vol. 3)
      0-8161-0532-4 (vol. 4)
ISSN 0196-0008

Avery Index to Architectural Periodicals

an operating program of the J. Paul Getty Trust's Art History Information Program

S. ISHIDA & ASSOCIATES
Le grand souffle: stade de
Carbonara, Bari, Italie.
Architects: Renzo Piano, Building
Workshop with Ishida & Associates.
English summary, p.48. Spanish
summary, p.153.
TECHNIQUES ET ARCHITECTURE 1990
Dec.-1991 Jan., no.393, p.44-49,
elevs., photos., plans, secns.,
site plan.
Renzo Piano: stadio di calcio e
atletica leggera, Bari / Ermanno
Ranzani.
Architects: Renzo Piano/Building
Workshop; associated architect:
Shinji Ishida. In Italian and
English.
DOMUS 1990 May, no.716, p.[33-39],
dets., elev., map, photos., plans,
secns., site plans, aerial photos.

SAALMAN, HOWARD
Goodness and value in the structure
of cognitive processes / Howard
Saalman.
JOURNAL OF ARCHITECTURAL EDUCATION
1990 Summer, v.43, no.4, p.3-7,
refs.

SAARINEN, EERO, 1910-1961
Gateway Arch wins 25-year award.
Jefferson National Expansion
Memorial, St. Louis. Architect:
Eero Saarinen.
PROGRESSIVE ARCHITECTURE 1990
Mar., v.71, no.3, p.25, photo.

SAARINEN, EERO, 1910-1961--EXHIBITIONS
Preservation: the Saarinens in
Buffalo [exhibition review] /
Mathew Ginal.
On the exhibition and symposium,
Kleinhans Music Hall: the
Saarinens in Buffalo, 1940- a
streamline vision, at Buffalo
State College's Burchfield Center.
PROGRESSIVE ARCHITECTURE 1990
June, v.71, no.6, p.28, photo.

SAARINEN, EERO, 1910-1961--INFLUENCE
RDA lectures survey the Saarinen
legacy / Gerald Moorhead.
Lecture series at Rice Design
Alliance, Houston, Oct.1989.
TEXAS ARCHITECT 1990 Jan.-Feb.,
v.40, no.1, p.20, photos.

SAARINEN, ELIEL, 1873-1950
L'accademia Cranbrook = The academy:
Cranbrook / Juliana Balint.
A visit to the American design
school near Detroit, including the
house of Eliel Saarinen, recently
restored.
ABITARE 1990 Jan., no.281,
p.108-[115], ill., photos., aerial
photo.

SAARINEN, ELIEL, 1873-1950--
EXHIBITIONS
Preservation: the Saarinens in
Buffalo [exhibition review] /
Mathew Ginal.
On the exhibition and symposium,
Kleinhans Music Hall: the
Saarinens in Buffalo, 1940- a
streamline vision, at Buffalo
State College's Burchfield Center.
PROGRESSIVE ARCHITECTURE 1990
June, v.71, no.6, p.28, photo.

SAAVEDRA, RUBEN DE, 1933-1990
Ruben de Saavedra 1933-1990
[obituary].
INTERIOR DESIGN 1990 Nov., v.61,
no.15, p.[51], port.

SABADY, PIERRE
Bio-Solar-Haus: Entwurf und
Konstruktion / T. Koncz.
Part of the Basel Mustermesse.
Architect: Pierre Sabady.
DEUTSCHE BAUZEITSCHRIFT 1990 Aug.,
v.38, no.8, p.1117-1120, dets.,
photos., plans.

SABATE, JOAQUIM
"En noviembre de 1934...": Van
Eesteren y el Plan de Extension de
Amsterdam = "In November 1934..."
Van Eesteren and the Amsterdam
Extension Plan / Joaquim Sabate.
In Spanish and English.
URBANISMO REVISTA 1989, no.8,
p.28-39, axonometric views,
models, maps, photos., plans,
secns., aerial photos.

SABATELLO, DAVID
Merzbau U.S.A.,1983-1989.
Competition entry for Harvard
Gate. Architect: David Sabatello.
English summary, p.90.
METAMORFOSI 1989, no.12, p.89-90,
axonometric views, dwgs., elevs.,
plans, secns.

SABATIER, PIERRE
Hotel du Departement de l'Allier: le
Jardin des Metamorphoses.
A grotto-like outdoor sculpture.
Sculptor: Pierre Sabatier.
LE MUR VIVANT 1990, no.97,
p.73-74, photos.

SABBAGH, KARL. SKYSCRAPER
Brute force and ignorance:
Skyscraper [by] Karl Sabbagh [book
review] / Hugh Aldersey-Williams.
BLUEPRINT (LONDON, ENGLAND) 1990
Feb., no.64, p.51, port.

SABIKHI, RANJIT
The Aga Khan Award for Architecture
1989.
Publishes the 11 winning projects
in the categories of Restoration
and rehabilitation, Social
development, and Architecture,
followed by commentary by Ranjit
Sabikhi, Satish Grover, and Romi
Khosla.
ARCHITECTURE + DESIGN 1990
Jan.-Feb., v.7, no.1, p.61-76,
elevs., photos., plans, secn.,
site plan.

SABIKHI, RANJIT , 1935?-
The Indira Gandhi Institute of
Development Research, Bombay /
Ranjit Sabikhi.
Located on a hillside in Goregoan.
Architect: Uttam C. Jain.
Completed in Dec.1987.
MIMAR: ARCHITECTURE IN DEVELOPMENT
1990 Dec., v.10, no.4(37),
p.24-29, dwgs., photos., plan,
secns.
Modernism redefined: place making in
the architecture of The Design
Group / Abhimanyu Dalal.
Feature section, on Ajoy Choudhury
nd Ranjit Sabikhi and five
(Continued next column)

SABIKHI, RANJIT , 1935?- (CONTINUED)
Modernism redefined:...(CONTINUED)
projects, in Jalandhar, Uttar
Pradesh, New Delhi, and the Taj
Bengal Hotel in Calcutta.
ARCHITECTURE + DESIGN 1990
July-Aug., v.7, no.4, p.21-47,
dets., ports., elevs., models,
photos., plans, secns.
Urban design in India.
Theme of issue. Contents: Making
legible city form, by Rahul J.
Mehrotra --The urban explosion and
urban design, by Ranjit Sabikhi --
Urban form, by The National
Commission on Urbanization --Inner
city areas, by Martyn D --Urban
transformations, by Ramesh Kumar
Biswas --Simulations in urban
architecture, by Bharat M. Gami --
Papankala (Dwarka) sub-city, by
Delhi Development Authority.
ARCHITECTURE + DESIGN 1990
Sept.-Oct., v.7, no.5, p.18-99,
dwgs., elev., model, maps,
photos., plans, tables, aerial
photos., biblio., refs.

SABIN, PALMER, 1892-1956
Realizing aromantic vision: a wave
of Spanish Revival architecture
swept across Southern California
during the 1920s, and Architect
Palmer Sabin rode it to success /
Christopher Weeks.
METROPOLIS 1990 Mar., v.9, no.7,
p.[44]-49,77,79,81, photos., ill.,
dwgs.

SABISCH, CHRISTIAN
Aus der Reihe getantzt / Christian
Sabisch.
Interiors of renovated house in
Kerpen, near Cologne. Architects:
Baucoop Koln.
ARCHITEKTUR & WOHNEN 1990
Oct.-Nov., no.5, p.68-72, photos.,
plan.

SACCHI, ANDREA, CALLED OUCHE,
1599?-1661
Il rinnovamento seicentesco della
Villa Mattei al Celio: Francesco
Peparelli, Andrea Saachi, Andrea
Lilli ed altri artisti / Carla
Benocci.
STORIA DELL'ARTE 1989, no.66,
p.[187]-196,pl.1-9, photos, plan,
engrs., refs.

SACCONI, ANNA MARIA, 1948-
Une ellipse funebre en Italie
[interview] / E. Doutriaux, M. C.
Devillers.
Interview with Massimiliano
Fuksas, on the Civita Castellana
cemetery. Architects: Fuksas with
Anna Maria Sacconi.
ARCHITECTURE D'AUJOURD'HUI 1990
June, no.269, p.92-95, elevs.,
photos., plan, secn., sketch.

SACCOPOULAS, CHRISTOS A.
Roadside monuments in Greece /
Christos A. Saccopoulos.
EKISTICS 1986 May-Aug., v.53,
no.318-319, p.144-148, photos,
refs.

SACHNER, PAUL M.
Anything but standard: American Standard Showroom, Long Island City, New York, Tigerman McCurry Architects / Paul M. Sachner.
ARCHITECTURAL RECORD 1990 Sept., v.178, no.10, p.[94-97], photos., plan.
The coastal condition: regional portfolio: California housing / Paul M. Sachner.
The first of a series of regional portfolios, on 5 multifamily projects: Armacost Duplex, Los Angeles [Rebecca Binder]; 14-16 Leroy Pl., San Francisco (Hood Miller); 1150 Lombard St., San Francisco (Hood Miller); Meadow Court, San Mateo (David Baker Assoc.); and Seacliff, Malibu (Kanner Associates).
ARCHITECTURAL RECORD 1990 Jan., v.178, no.1, p.90-99, elevs., photos., plans, secns., site plans.
Collective memory: a unique building ensemble that seems molded by the forces of nature, Douglas Cardinal's Canadian Museum of Civilization / Paul M. Sachner.
ARCHITECTURAL RECORD 1990 Feb., v.178, no.2, p.88-93, photos., plans, secns., site plans, aerial photo.
Harlem heritage: some of Manhattan's finest landmarks stand on the island's historic heights / Paul M. Sachner.
HOUSE & GARDEN 1990 Oct., v.162, no.10, p.118,[120], port., photos.
High-risk high rises: Building Types Study 685: high-rise office buildings / Paul M. Sachner.
Presents 3 recent speculative office buildings, each indexed separately.
ARCHITECTURAL RECORD 1990 Oct., v.178, no.11, p.87-[101], dwg., photos.
Rich as Rockefeller: the NBC Tower in Chicago's Cityfront Center... / Paul M. Sachner.
Architect: Adrian Smith of SOM.
ARCHITECTURAL RECORD 1990 Apr., v.178, no.4, p.68-[73], photos., plans, secn., site plan.
To gather together: Andover Town Hall restoration / Paul M. Sachner.
In Andover, Mass. Architects: Ann Beha Associates. Original architect (1855): Theodore Voelker.
ARCHITECTURAL RECORD 1990 Nov., v.178, no.12, p.62-65, photos., plans, secn.
Villa Carolina: Croffead House, Charleston, North Carolina / Paul M. Sachner.
Architect: Clark & Menefee Architects.
ARCHITECTURAL RECORD 1990 Mid-Apr., v.178, no.5, p.42-[47], photos., plans, secn., site plan.

SACHS, NORBERT, 1964-
Bibliothek fur Alexandria.
Student projects by Maria D. Hirschmann, Universitat Karlsruhe, and Norbert Sachs, Universitat Hannover.
DEUTSCHE BAUZEITUNG 1990 May,
(Continued next column)

SACHS, NORBERT, 1964- (CONTINUED)
Bibliothek fur...(CONTINUED)
v.124, no.5, p.154-155, dwgs., elevs., plan, site plan.

SACK, MANFRED
Der Flaneur in der Stadt, oder, Das Klobige Inventar der Strasse / Manfred Sack.
DER ARCHITEKT 1990 July-Aug., no.7-8, p.344-345, ill., photos.

SACKVILLE-WEST, V. (VICTORIA) 1892-1962
Sissinghurst grows up / Nigel Nicolson.
On the garden designed by Vita Sackville-West and Harold Nicolson.
HOUSE & GARDEN 1990 Nov., v.162, no.11, p.104-108, photos.

SACRED SITES
Nel territorio del sacro = In the sacred territory: an itinerary / Giovanni Chiaramonte.
LOTUS INTERNATIONAL 1990, no.65, p.132-144, photos.
Il territorio secolarizzato = The secularized territory / Pierluigi Nicolin.
LOTUS INTERNATIONAL 1990, no.65, p.4-15, photos.

SACRED SITES--BUDDHIST--CONSERVATION AND RESTORATION--THAILAND-- SUKKHOTHAI HISTORICAL PARK
Reflections on a "golden age": restorer's of Thailand's ancient city of Sukhothai appear to have sacrificed historical accuracy for an idealized version of the past / Betty Gosling.
Sukhothai Historical Park.
ARCHAEOLOGY 1990 July-Aug., v.43, no.4, p.24-31, ill., map, photos.

SACRED SITES--UNITED STATES--NEW MEXICO
Sacred places of the Southwest / Laura Sue Sanborn.
On camposantos, burial grounds of Hispanic Catholics in the American Southwest.
PLACES 1990 Fall, v.7, no.1, p.[42]-49, photos.

SACRISTE, EDUARDO, 1905-
Cien anos de soledad?: identidad y modernidad en la cultura arquitectonica latinoamerica / Adrian Gorelik.
Includes discussion of Luis Barragan, Eduardo Sacriste, and Lucio Costa.
ARQ 1990 Aug., no.15, p.32-[39], photos., plans, secns., refs.

SACRISTIES
See also DIACONICA

SAEE, MICHELE
Le corps en morceaux d'architecture. Features Ecru Clothing store, Marina del Rey, Calif. Architect: Michele Saee.
ARCHITECTURE INTERIEURE CREE 1990 Oct.-Nov., no.239, p.138-[139], photos.

SAEE, MICHELE (CONTINUED)
Kitchens that cook: hot news, cool choices / Julie V. Iovine.
Five projects, including an expansion of the Sprecher house, Los Angeles (architect: Michele Saee); a Connecticut kitchen renovation (architect: Louis Mackall); Reichel-Singer house conversion, Los Angeles (designer: Josh Schweitzer); Sagalyn kitchen (architect: Scott Simons); Laurie and Maurie Williams' kitchen renovation, Ore.
METROPOLITAN HOME 1990 May, v.22, no.5, p.[123-136], det., photos.
Out on a limb / Ziva Freiman.
Focus on two Marina del Rey projects by Michele Saee of Building: Ecru clothing store, and Angeli Mare restaurant. Includes selected detail article on the ceiling structure of the restaurant.
PROGRESSIVE ARCHITECTURE 1990 Apr., v.71, no.4, p.108-116, dets., photos., plans, secns.

SAEKS, DIANE DORRANS
Style's fairest trader [Sandra Sakata] / Diane Dorrans Saeks.
Includes views of the designer's San Francisco apartment and her boutique, Obiko.
METROPOLITAN HOME 1990 Sept., v.22, no.9, p.120-123, port., photos.

SAENZ DE OIZA, FRANCISCO JAVIER, 1918-1988
346 Sozialwohnungen in Moratalaz, Madrid.
Architect: Fransisco Javier Saenz de Oiza.
BAUWELT 1990 July 6, v.81, no.25, p.1302-1303, photos., plan, site plan.
Atlantic cries - Mediterranean whispers / Luis Fernandez-Galiano.
On the Centro Atlantico de Arte Moderno, Las Palmas, Canary Islands, architect: Francisco Javier Saenz de Oiza and the Juan and Pilar Miro Foundation, Son Abrines, Majorca, architect: Jose Rafael Moneo.
ARCHITECTURAL REVIEW 1990 July, v.188, no.1121, p.44-[51], models, photos., plans, secn., site plan.
Centro Atlantico de Arte Moderno = Modern art centre, Las Palmas de Gran Canaria, 1958-1989.
Architect: F. Javier Saenz de Oiza.
EL CROQUIS 1990 Mar., v.9, no.42, p.124-137, dets., photos., plans, secns.
Il concorso per il centro culturale della Difesa a Madrid / Antonio Velez Catrain.
Publishes the entries by Juan Navarro Baldeweg, Lluis Clotet Ballus and Ignacio Paricio, Francisco Javier Saenz de Oiza, and Alvaro Siza, and contains an interview with Eduardo Mangada. Includes English summary, captions, and translation.
CASABELLA 1990 May, v.54, no.568, p.40-51, 61-63, axonometric view, models, map, plans, secns., sketches, aerial photos.

SAENZ DE OIZA, FRANCISCO JAVIER, 1918-1988 (CONTINUED)
El odeon varado: Teatro de Festivales, Santander = The beached odeon.
Architect: Francisco Javier Saenz de Oiza. English text, p.92.
A & V 1990, no.24, p.68-75, elevs., photos., plans, secns., sketches.
Un paso al frente: el Centro Cultural de la Defensa / Juan Miguel Hernandez Leon.
Four entries in the competition for Madrid cultural center.
ARQUITECTURA VIVA 1990 Mar.-Apr., no.11, p.34-36, axonometric view, dwgs., models, plans, secns., sketches.
Proyectar para una arquitectura dada: analogia y diversidad = To design for a given architecture: analogy and diversity / Anton Capitel.
Discusses 4 recent projects in Spain.
EL CROQUIS 1990 Mar., v.9, no.42, p.64-79, photos.

SAFAVID
See "SAFAVID" AS A SUBHEADING AFTER SPECIFIC BUILDING TYPES OR OTHER MAIN HEADINGS.

SAFDIE, MOSHE, 1938-
Moshe Safdie: defining a language of architecture.
Reports on a lecture given on Nov. 15, 1989.
GSD NEWS / HARVARD UNIVERSITY. GRADUATE SCHOOL OF DESIGN 1990 Spring, v.18, no.4, p.17-18, photos.
The National Gallery of Canada, Ottawa, Ontario, Canada, 1982-1988 / Moshe Safdie.
Architects: Moshe Safdie and Associates. Text in Japanese and English. Includes essay: Fortuitous triangular amalgam / Dennis Sharp.
ARCHITECTURE AND URBANISM 1990 Sept., no.9(240), p.[3]-[36], axonometric view, photos., plans, secns., site plan.
Reading Herod's purpose / Christopher Hume.
Focus on two projects in Jerusalem by Moshe Safdie: the plaza at the Western Wall and the Mamilla complex, outside the Jaffa Gate.
LANDSCAPE ARCHITECTURE 1990 Sept., v.80, no.9, p.39-40, elev., photo., site plan.

SAFETY, OCCUPATIONAL
See OCCUPATIONAL SAFETY

SAFFRAN, ELKE
Gluckspiele im Untergrund: Diplomarbeit uber eine Spielbank unter der Erde.
Student project by Elke Saffran, FH Lippe.
ARCHITEKTUR, INNENARCHITEKTUR, TECHNISCHER AUSBAU 1990 July-Aug., v.98, no.7-8, p.56-60, dwgs., plans.

SAFRAN, YEHUDA
Adolf Loos: Graphischen Sammlung Albertina, Vienna 2 December 1989-25 February 1990 [exhibition review] / Yehuda Safran.
AA FILES 1990 Autumn, no.20, p.89-94, ports., refs.
Frederick Kiesler 1890-1965: AA Exhibitions Gallery, Members' Room & Bar 8 November-9 December 1989 [exhibition review] / Yehuda Safran.
AA FILES 1990 Autumn, no.20, p.83-88, dwgs., port., photos.
Ornamento e tempo = Ornament and time / Yehuda Safran.
Refers to A. Loos' 1908 essay "Ornament and crime". In Italian and English.
OTTAGONO 1990 Dec., no.97, p.3-10, dwgs., ports., photos., sketches, refs.
La pelle / Yehuda Safran.
9H 1989, no.8, p.154-163, elevs., photos., plans, secns.

SAGA, TAKESHI
Temperature and velocity distribution of fire gas from a belt-shaped heat source / Takeshi Saga.
Subtitle: Study on flame of big fire in urban area. In Japanese; English summary, p.165.
NIHON KENCHIKU GAKKAI KEIKAKUKEI RONBUN HOKOKU SHU = JOURNAL OF ARCHITECTURE, PLANNING AND ENVIRONMENTAL ENGINEERING 1990 May, no.5(411), p.165-176, figs., graphs, tables, refs.

SAGALYN, LYNNE B. DOWNTOWN, INC.
Urban renewal: Downtown inc.: how America rebuilds cities, by Bernard J. Frieden and Lynne B. Sagalyn [book review] / Francis Tibbalds.
ROYAL SOCIETY OF ARTS, LONDON. RSA JOURNAL 1990 Dec., v.139, no.5413, p.947.

SAGE, SEBASTIAN
Stadt und Verkehr.
Special issue on towns and traffic. 22 projects illustrated. English summary, p.53.
BAUMEISTER 1990 Aug., v.87, no.8, p.13-53, dwgs., models, photos., plans, secns., site plans, aerial photos.

SAGGIO, ANTONINO, 1955-
Villa a Sutri.
Architects: Luigi Franciosini, Antonino Saggio. English summary, p.76.
METAMORFOSI 1989, no.12, p.76-78, photos., plan.

SAGLAMER, GULSUN
The analysis of layout patterns in squatter settlements / Gulsun Saglamer, Halil Dincel.
INTERNATIONAL JOURNAL FOR HOUSING SCIENCE AND ITS APPLICATIONS 1990, v.14, no.2, p.107-113, graphs, plans, tables, refs.

SAGOT, MARIETTE
400.000 nouveau menages a loger d'ici l'an 2000 / Mariette Sagot.
Smaller, changing households reflecting the needs of single, divorced, handicapped and elderly are needed by the year 2000. French, English and Spanish summaries, p.3, English translation p.57-58.
CAHIERS DE L'INSTITUT D'AMENAGEMENT ET D'URBANISME DE LA REGION D'ILE-DE-FRANCE 1990 June, no.93, p.49-58, graphs, ports., photos.

SAHIN, SPENCER
Das Grabmal von Konig Antiochos 1. von Kommagene duf dem Nemrud Dag / Spencer Sahin, Jorg Wagner.
ANTIKE WELT 1989, v.20, no.1, p.55-58, dwg., photos, refs.

SAHLIN, BO
Tidsfaktorn-dolt styrmedal / Bo Sahlin.
ARKITEKTUR: THE SWEDISH REVIEW OF ARCHITECTURE 1990 Oct., v.90, no.8, p.36-43, maps, photo., site plans, sketches.

SAHNER, G. A.
Kunsthalle Heilbronn.
First prize (shared): G.A. Sahner; Buro Heckmann, Christel + Jung.
BAUWELT 1990 July 13, v.81, no.26, p.1324-1325, models.

SAIA ET BARBARESE
Complexe scientifique et multifonctionnel de l'UQAM / Julia Bourke.
Architects, planners: Saia et Barbarese; Birtz, Bastien, architectes; Blouin et associes.
ARQ: ARCHITECTURE/QUEBEC 1990 Dec., no.58, p.22, model, site plans.

SAILBOATS--CONSERVATION AND RESTORATION--UNITED STATES--MAINE
Windjammer days / Christina Tree.
The preservation of Maine's windjammer fleets.
HISTORIC PRESERVATION 1990 July-Aug., v.42, no.4, p.[22-29], photos.

SAILBOATS--INTERIOR DESIGN
In barca come a casa = A life on the ocean wave.
Interiors of a 28-meter ketch. Architect: Carlo Santi.
ABITARE 1990 May, no.285, p.176-185, dets., photos, plans, secns.

SAINI, B. S.
Training professionals for slum improvement and rural development in the Third World / B. S. Saini.
EKISTICS 1988 Jan.-June, v.55, no.328-330, p.85-87, refs.

SAINSBURY, MELANIE
Building bloc / Jose Manser.
On the original members of NATO, Narrative Architecture Today: Nigel Coates, Mark Prizeman, Carlos Villanueva, Robert Mull, Catrina Beevor, Peter Fleissig, Melanie Sainsbury, Martin Benson
(Continued next page)

SAINSBURY, MELANIE (CONTINUED)
Building bloc / Jose...(CONTINUED)
and Christina Norton.
DESIGNERS' JOURNAL 1990 June,
no.58, p.33-38, ports.
Highway revisited.
On five designs for the redesign
of Birmingham's "Spaghetti
Junction", sponsored by a British
television show.
BUILDING DESIGN 1990 June 15,
no.990, p.14-16, sketches.

SAINT, ANDREW
Chi dimensionava le travi? / Andrew
Saint.
CASABELLA 1990 Dec., v.54, no.574,
p.25-26, dets., secn.
First impressions of London: or, Sir
Edwin in wonderland / Steen Eiler
Rasmussen.
Translation of article which
appeared in "Wasmuths Monatshefte
fur Baukunst," vol.12,1928,
p.304-312. Foreword by Andrew
Saint.
AA FILES 1990 Autumn, no.20,
p.16-21, photos., refs.
Gothic revisionism: the Gothic
cathedral, by Christopher Wilson
[book review] / Andrew Saint.
Review of the Gothic cathedral, by
C. Wilson.
ARCHITECTS' JOURNAL 1990 Mar.28,
v.191, no.13, p.90-91, photos.
Strasbourg Cathedral / Andrew Saint.
ARCHITECTS' JOURNAL 1990 May 9,
v.191. no.19, p.38-55, dets.,
bill., dwgs., photos.. plans, site
plan, engrs., refs.
The Unromantic castle by John
Summerson [book review] / Andrew
Saint.
AA FILES 1990 Autumn, no.20,
p.109-110,

SAINT ANDREW. POLITICS AND THE PEOPLE
OF LONDON: THE LONDON COUNTY COUNCIL
1889-1965
Running London: Politics and the
people of London: the London
County Council 1889-1965, edited
by Andrew Saint [book review] /
Hermione Hobhouse.
ARCHITECTS' JOURNAL 1990 Feb.28,
v.191, no.9, p.77-78, photo.

SAINT-AUBIN, JEAN-PAUL
The image of built architecture =
L'Image de l'architecture batie /
Jean-Paul Saint-Aubin.
ASSOCIATION FOR PRESERVATION
TECHNOLOGY BULLETIN 1990, v.22,
no.1-2, p.44-54, photos., plan,
isometric dwgs., refs.

SAINT BARTHELEMY--VACATION HOUSES--
BARYSHNIKOV HOUSE
Mikhail Baryshnikov on St.
Barthelemy / Philippe Seulliet.
Features the interiors of
neighboring Mexican vernacular
style vacation houses owned by the
dancer. Architect: Rob Miles
Reincke. Interior designer: Bille
du Mesnil.
ARCHITECTURAL DIGEST 1990 Aug.,
v.47, no.8, p.132-137, photos.

SAINT BLANQUAT, TESSA DE
Siege social a Levallois / Brigitte
Fitoussi.
Auguste Thouard corporate office
building, Levallois-Perret.
Architects: Tessa de Saint
Blanquat, Christian Varroquier,
David Mary.
ARCHITECTURE D'AUJOURD'HUI 1990
Sept., no.270, p.197-198, photos.,
plans.

SAINTY, JEAN
Le Centre Experimental de
Prehistoire Alsacienne / Jean
Sainty.
Shows reconstructions of pre- and
proto-historic buildings based on
archaeological excavations
organized by CEPA.
ARCHEOLOGIA 1989 Nov., no.251,
p.40, photos.

SAINZ, JORGE
Aduana con peneita: OMA en
Checkpoint Charlie / Jorge Sainz.
Architects: M. Sauerbruch, E.
Zenghelis.
ARQUITECTURA VIVA 1990 July-Aug.,
no.13, p.20-23, dwgs., elevs.,
photos., plans, secns.
El color del dibujo: de la
convencion al virtuosismo / Jorge
Sainz.
Excerpt from the book: El dibujo
de arquitectura.
ARQUITECTURA VIVA 1990 Mar.-Apr.,
no.11, p.44-45, ill., elevs.
Esperando a Colon: La ilusion de
Genova 92 / Jorge Sainz.
ARQUITECTURA VIVA 1990 Sept.-Oct.,
no.14, p.12-15, dwg., elev.,
models, photos.
Pel de azoque: Angulema, rede del
"comic" / Jorge Sainz.
Centre national de la bande
dessinee et de l'image, Angouleme,
France. Architect: Roland Castro.
ARQUITECTURA VIVA 1990 Nov.-Dec.,
no.15, p.29-31, photos., plan,
secn.
Renzo Piano Building Workshop.
Entire issue on Piano. Includes
fifteen projects, a bibliography,
and three essays. English texts,
p.81-88.
A & V 1990, no.23, entire issue,
axonometric views, dets., ill.,
dwgs., elevs., models, maps,
photos., plans, secns., site
plans, sketches.

SAITO, SHIKIKO
Journey in African savanna:
recollections of an unrecorded
continent / Shikiko Saito.
Text in Japanese.
SPACE DESIGN 1990 Dec.,
no.12(315), p.53-60, photos.

SAITO, TADASHI
Fascinating moulded concrete block
structure / Tadashi Saito.
Two concrete block structures by
Tadashi Saito and Atelier R:
Aoyama Cemetery office, Tokyo and
Villa Shiomisaki. English summary,
p.19.
KENCHIKU BUNKA 1990 Oct., v.45,
no.520, p.73-90, axonometric view,
dwgs., ports., photos., plans,
site plan.

SAITO, YUTAKA, 1947-
Chimenkanoya / Yutaka Saito.
House, Nakano Ward, Tokyo,
nicknamed by architect, "Beaver
House." Architects: Yutaka Saito,
Architect and Associates.
JAPAN ARCHITECT 1990 Jan., v.65,
no.1(393), p.[54]-60, photos.,
plans, secns.
The "Transfiguration" exhibition in
Europalia Japan.
Special feature. Works by Kazuyo
Seijima + Noriyuki Tanaka, Toyo
Ito, Keiichi Irie, Hiromi Fujii,
Shin Takamatsu, and Yutaka Saito.
Essays by Riichi Miyake; Toyo Ito,
Alvin Boyarsky, and Nigel Coates;
Keiichi Irie and Kobun ito; Hiromi
Fujii and Shusaku Arakawa; Shin
Takamatsu and Daniel Libeskind;
Yutaka Saito and Issei Miyake.
Text in Japanese.
SPACE DESIGN 1990 Feb., no.305,
p.13-44, dets., dwgs., models,
photos., sketches.

SAITOWITZ, STANLEY, 1948-
Critical mass [DiNapoli residence,
Los Gatos, Calif.] / Ziva Freiman.
Architects: Stanley Saitowitz
Office.
PROGRESSIVE ARCHITECTURE 1990
Nov., v.71, no.12, p.64-69,
axonometric view, photos., plan.
A different wavelength: the curves
of a California beach house
express architect Stanley
Saitowitz's sense of place / Pilar
Viladas.
The McDonald house, Stinson Beach.
HOUSE & GARDEN 1990 Aug., v.162,
no.8, p.[108]-111, photos.
Grewal Residence, Oakland,
California, design: 1988.
Architect: Stanley Saitowitz. Text
in Japanese and English.
GA HOUSES 1990 Mar., no.28, p.82,
elevs., model, plan, secns.
In the mind's eye / Ziva Freiman.
Former Kress dept. store in
Riverside, Calif. converted into
the California Museum of
Photography. Architect: Stanley
Saitowitz. Includes Selected
Detail article on the steel
staircase in the museum.
PROGRESSIVE ARCHITECTURE 1990
Sept., v.71, no.9, p.130-136,
dets., ill., dwgs., photos.,
plans.
McDonald residence, Stinson Beach,
California, 1987-88.
Architect: Stanley Saitowitz.
Text in Japanese and English.
GA HOUSES 1990 July, no.29,
p.[120]-125, elevs., photos.,
plan.
The perfect wave: McDonald House,
Stinson Beach, California / Donald
J. Canty.
Architect: The Stanley Saitowitz
Office.
ARCHITECTURAL RECORD 1990
Mid-Apr., v.178, no.5, p.[52]-57,
elev., photos., plan.
Stanley Saitowitz.
Features two projects: Di Napoli,
Los Gatos, Calif. and McDonald
beach house, Stinson Beach, Calif.
English summary.
ARCHITECTURE D'AUJOURD'HUI 1990
Oct., no.271, p.168-170,
(Continued next page)

SAITOWITZ, STANLEY, 1948-
(CONTINUED)
Stanley Saitowitz. (CONTINUED)
axonometric views, photos., site
plan.

SAIZ, DENIS
Bordeaux: l'avenir a quai / Pascale
Joffroy.
Proposed urban renewal projects.
Contents: La Bastide district;
architect: Ricardo Bofill.--
Riverfront esplanade; architects:
Bernard Nivelle & Denis Saiz.--
Hangar no.17 for Crus et Domaines
de France; architects: Bernard
Reichen & Philippe Robert.--River
pier; architect: Christian de
Portzamparc.--Axis plan;
architect: Rem Koolhaas.--Bridge
project; architect: Santiago
Calatrava.--Bridge project:
architects: William Alsop & John
Lyall.
LE MONITEUR ARCHITECTURE AMC 1990
Feb., no.8, p.28-36, models,
plans, site plans.

SAJOUS D'ORIA, MICHELE
Parigi: i teatri negli anni della
Rivoluzione / Giuseppe Radicchio,
Michele Sajous D'Oria.
In Italian; English, French,
German and Spanish summaries,
p.127. Also includes index of
theaters.
STORIA DELLA CITTA 1988
Jul.-Sept., v.13, no.47, p.7-118,
127, axonometric views, dwgs.,
elevs., plans, secns., sketches,
engrs., biblio., refs.

SAKAKURA ASSOCIATES, ARCHITECTS AND
ENGINEERS
Arakawa-Sommerschule in Shimoda.
Architects: Sakakura Associates,
Architects and Engineers.
DEUTSCHE BAUZEITSCHRIFT 1990 Nov.,
v.38, no.11, p.1587-1590, photos.,
isometric dwgs.
Mie Children's Castle / Takanobu
Ota.
Children's museum/play center,
Matsusaka, Mie Prefecture.
Architects: Sakakura Associates,
Architects and Engineers.
JAPAN ARCHITECT 1990 Feb., v.65,
no.2(394), p.38-41, elevs.,
photos., plans.
Mie-Schloss der Kinder.
Mie Children's Castle, Matsusaka
Architects: Sakakura Associates,
Architects and Engineers.
DEUTSCHE BAUZEITSCHRIFT 1990 Nov.,
v.38, no.11, p.1583-1586, elevs.,
photos., plans, secns., site plan.
Sakakura Associates / Seizo Sakata.
Tokyo Salesian Boy's Home (phase
1-3), design: 1984-87 -- Tokyo
Salesian Boy's Home gymnasium
(phase 4), design: 1988-89. Text
in Japanese and English.
GA DOCUMENT 1990 Apr., no.25,
p.[156]-160, model, photos., plan,
secn., site plan.

SAKAMOTO, KAZUNARI, 1943-
Doppia struttura fluidificante = A
fluidifying double structure.
"F House", Tokyo. Architect:
Kazunari Sakamoto.
ARCHITETTURA: CRONACHE E STORIA
1990 Dec., v.36, no.12(422),
p.886, photos., plan, secn.
Maison F a Tokyo.
3-level house. Architect:
Kazunari Sakamoto. Includes
English summary.
TECHNIQUES ET ARCHITECTURE 1990
June-July, no.390, p.144-[147],
photos., plans, secn.

SAKAMOTO, NOBUYUKI
Commercial vitality and the parking
problem in regional cities /
Nobuyuki Sakamoto.
Three examples in Japan.
THE WHEEL EXTENDED 1990, no.74,
p.24-32, graph, maps, photos.,
plans, secn., table.

SAKAMURA, KEN, 1951-
TRON-concept intelligent house / Ken
Sakamura.
Intelligent house, Tokyo.
Architect: Ken Sakamura.
JAPAN ARCHITECT 1990 Apr., v.65,
no.4(396), p.35-40, diagrs.,
photos., plans.

SAKATA, SEIZO
Sakakura Associates / Seizo Sakata.
Tokyo Salesian Boy's Home (phase
1-3), design: 1984-87 -- Tokyo
Salesian Boy's Home gymnasium
(phase 4), design: 1988-89. Text
in Japanese and English.
GA DOCUMENT 1990 Apr., no.25,
p.[156]-160, model, photos., plan,
secn., site plan.

SAKKARA
See SAQQARAH

SAKURAI, YASUHIRO
The room composition and space
zoning of community assembly
facilities / Yasuhiro Sakurai.
In Japanese; English summary,
p.57.
NIHON KENCHIKU GAKKAI KEIKAKUKEI
RONBUN HOKOKU SHU = JOURNAL OF
ARCHITECTURE, PLANNING AND
ENVIRONMENTAL ENGINEERING 1990
May, no.5(411), p.57-68, charts,
graphs, elevs., plans, tables,
refs.

SALADIN, HUBERT
Profils: les elus 1989: Albums de
la jeune architecture.
Contents: Epinard Bleu, Pascal
Marchant, Philtre Avant-Travaux,
Patricia Leboucq, Shinobu Akahori,
Pascal Quintard Hofstein, and
Herve Daridan.
LE MONITEUR ARCHITECTURE AMC 1990
Mar., no.9, p.55, ports.

SALADINO, JOHN F.
Classical order / Charles Gandee.
Las Tejas, Montecito, Calif., was
inspired by the Villa Farnese.
Interior designer: John Saladino.
HOUSE & GARDEN 1990 Sept., v.162,
no.9, p.186-[195], port., photos.

SALADINO, JOHN F. (CONTINUED)
Library for living / Edie Lee Cohen.
Interiors of small Manhattan
apartment designed by John
Saladino.
INTERIOR DESIGN 1990 Dec., v.61,
no.16, p.138-[141], photos., plan.

SALAS, JULIAN
An analysis of Latin American
auto-construction: a plural and
mass phenomenon / Julian Salas.
OPEN HOUSE INTERNATIONAL 1988,
v.13, no.4, p.2-11, axonometric
view, graphs, dwgs., photos.,
refs.

SALAU, M. A.
Shear resistance of reinforced
laterized concrete beams without
shear reinforcement / M.A. Salau,
L.A. Balogun.
BUILDING AND ENVIRONMENT 1990,
v.25, no.1, p.71-76, graphs,
photos., tables, refs.

SALES, JOHN
Garden of many parts / John Sales.
At Dunster Castle.
COUNTRY LIFE 1990 May 31, v.184,
no.22, p.152-155, photos.
Themes on a Londonderry air [gardens
of Mount Stewart] / John Sales.
Site: on A20 five mi. from
Newtonards, County Down.
COUNTRY LIFE 1990 May 17, v.184,
no.20, p.180-187, photos, site
plan.
Unfaithful but honest / John Sales.
Garden at Little Moreton Hall,
Cheshire.
COUNTRY LIFE 1990 Aug.23, v.184,
no.34, p.48-49, photos.

SALGUQS
See SELJUKS

SALINAS, FERNANDO
Dialogo com Salinas, Segre, Tosca e
Calventi, em Havana / Nildo Carlos
Oliveira.
PROJETO 1989 Apr., no.120,
p.127-129, port.

SALIOU, CATHERINE
Maison et paysage urbain dans les
villes du Proche-Orient (IIe-Ve
siecles ap. J.-C.) / Catherine
Saliou.
HISTOIRE DE L'ART 1990 May,
no.9-10, p.9-20, photos., site
plans, refs.

SALISBURY, WILMA
Cleveland grows up and up / Wilma
Salisbury.
Recent projects by Cesar Pelli,
Kohn Pedersen Fox, Frank Gehry,
I.M. Pei, and others.
INLAND ARCHITECT 1990 Jan.-Feb.,
v.34, no.1, p.22-25, aerial photo.
The spirit of invention in Akron /
Wilma Salisbury.
The National Inventors Hall of
Fame. Architect: James Stewart
Polshek & Partners.
INLAND ARCHITECT 1990 Sept.-Oct.,
v.34, no.5, p.10, dwg., models.

SALIVA, ERNESTO
La progettazione dell'E42: la prima
fase = The planning of the E42:
the first phase / Riccardo
Mariani.
The planning of the E42:
Esposizione Universale in Roma
1941-1942; architects: Giuseppe
Pagano, Marcello Piacentini, Luigi
Piccinato, Ettore Rossi, Luigi
Vietti, Adalberto Libera, Giuseppe
Terragni, Pietro Lingeri, Cesare
Cattaneo, Giovanni Guerrini,
Ernesto La Padula, Mario Romano,
Gian Luigi Banfi, Ludovico B. di
Belgioso, Gaetano Ciocca, Enrico
Peressutti, Ernesto N. Rogers,
Franco Albini, Ignazio Gardella,
Giancarlo Palanti, Giovanna
Romano, Luciano Baldessari,
Ernesto Saliva, Luigi Moretti,
Gino Pollini, Luigi Figini, and
Giuseppe Vaccaro.
LOTUS INTERNATIONAL 1990, no.67,
p.90-125, elevs., models, photos.,
plans, secns., site plans,
sketches, aerial photos.

SALK, JONAS, 1914-
Horizons into the future / Jonas
Salk.
A personal reminiscence about the
author's collaboration with Kahn
on the design of the Salk
Institute for Biological Studies,
La Jolla, Calif.
ART & ANTIQUES 1990 Dec., v.7,
no.10, p.[66]-67,116-117, port.

SALLE, ALIX
L'archeologie urbaine autour du
monastere de Saint-Denis / Alix
Salle.
ARCHEOLOGIA 1989 Nov., no.251,
p.6-8, dets., photos.
Archeologie de la Bastille
[exhibition review] / Alix Salle.
On the exhibition on view at the
Hotel de Sully, Paris, Oct.12,
1989-Jan.7, 1990.
ARCHEOLOGIA 1989 Dec., no.252,
p.18-19, ill., dwgs., plan, engr.
Patrimoine parisien pendant la
Revolution [exhibition review] /
Alix Salle.
Exhibition at the Bibliotheque
historique de la ville de Paris, 8
Nov.-8 Dec. 1989.
ARCHEOLOGIA 1989 Nov., no.251,
p.[19], ill., engr.

SALMAN, KAREN
Of mice and men / Callum Murray,
Karen Salman, Charlotte Ellis.
Profiles of British firms John
Winter and Associates, YRM
Partnership, Eric Parry: EP
Associates, Troughton McAslan, Eva
Jiricna, Richard Rogers, and Jean
Nouvel and their approaches to
architectural design for the
series "How architects design."
ARCHITECTS' JOURNAL 1990
Dec.19-26, v.192, no.25-26,
p.24-37, axonometric views, dets.,
dwgs., ports., model, photos.,
secn.

SALMELA, DAVID
Learning from Lundie: a north-woods
house reinterprets its
Scandanavian roots / Adelheid
Fischer.
Thompson house, Lake Pokegama,
Minn. Architect: David Salmela.
ARCHITECTURE MINNESOTA 1990
July-Aug., v.16, no.4, p.40-43,
dwg., photos.

SALMI, MARKKU
Kehitysta ilmassa / Markku Salmi.
ARKKITEHTI 1989, v.86, no.8,
p.64-69, diagrs., graphs, plans,
tables.

SALMOIRAGHI, RENZO
Ampliamento di edificio per uffici a
Ravenna / Renzo Salmoiraghi.
Englargement of S.A.R. offices.
Architect: Bruno Minardi.
Summaries in English, French and
Spanish.
ABACUS 1990 July-Sept., v.6,
no.23, p.38-45, dets., dwgs.,
elevs., photos., plans, secns.
Ristratturazione a Vico Morcote
(Canton Ticino) / Renzo
Salmoiraghi.
On the renovation of Villa Ruggia,
the seat of the Southern
California Institute of
Architecture (SCI-ARC) school.
Architect: Martin Wagner.
English, French and Spanish
summaries.
ABACUS 1990 Apr.-June, v.6, no.22,
p.34-43, axonometric views, dets.,
photos., plans, secns.

SALMON, FRANK
The site of Michelangelo's
Laurentian Library / Frank Salmon.
The Medici Library in Florence and
documents from c.1524, includes
abstract, and an appendix citing
documents for properties in the
borgo and for the Macciagnini and
Calcagni houses.
SOCIETY OF ARCHITECTURAL
HISTORIANS. JOURNAL 1990 Dec.,
v.49, no.4, p.407-429, dwgs.,
photos., plans, refs.

SALMON, JAMES, 1874-1924
Acquiring a taste for Salmon /
Raymond O'Donnell.
On the work of the Glasgow
architect James Salmon
(1874-1924).
RIBA JOURNAL 1990 Aug., v.97,
no.8, p.34-40, dwgs., port.,
photos.

SALMONES, VICTOR
Parks with a purpose [Bloch Cancer
Survivor Park] / Leonard Ehrler.
The Richard and Annette Bloch
Cancer Survivor Park in Kansas
City, Mo.; designed by
LandCorp-Ehrler (landscape
architects) and Milosav Cekic
Architects. Sculptures by Victor
Salmones.
PARKS & RECREATION 1990 July,
v.25, no.7, p.50-52,79, dwgs.,
elevs., plans.

SALOCCHI, CLAUDIO
National Guard Sports Center, Khashm
Alaan / Maurizio Vitta.
Architect: Claudio Salocchi. Text
in Italian and English.
L'ARCA 1990 May, no.38, p.26-33,
photos., plans, secns., site
plans.

SALOMON, ALAIN
An American in Paris / Suzanne
Stephens.
Focus on the offices of James
Stewart Polshek and Partner, Alain
Salomon.
ARCHITECTURAL DIGEST 1990 Oct.,
v.47, no.11, p.134,138,142, port.,
photos.
French revolution / Amy Dana.
Interiors of Omnilogic offices
located in a renovated 19th cent.
warehouse, Paris. Architects:
James Stewart Polshek, Alain
Salomon.
INTERIORS 1990 Aug., v.149, no.13,
p.18, photos.

SALOMON, ANDRE
Reference: le Musee des Beaux-Arts
du Havre / Joseph Abram.
Built from 1958 to 1961:
architects: Guy Lagneau, Michel
Weill, Jean Dimitrijevic, Raymond
Audigier, with Jean Prouve.
LE MONITEUR ARCHITECTURE AMC 1990
Oct., no.15, p.50-64, model,
photos., plans, secn.

SALOMON, DAVID
Beachside fantasy / Glenn Harrell.
Summer house of New York decorator
David Salomon in Southampton, N.Y.
HOUSE BEAUTIFUL 1990 July, v.132,
no.7, p.[44]-49, port., photos.
Decorators' private domains / Amy
Fine Collins.
The New York apartments of five
young interior decorators.
HOUSE & GARDEN 1990 Sept., v.162,
no.9, p.[118]-125, ports., photos.

SALOMON, LAURENT
Le Portique de Saint-Priest /
Pascale Joffroy.
Municipal building. Architects:
Laurent Salomon, Anne Chabert.
LE MONITEUR ARCHITECTURE AMC 1990
Mar., no.9, p.24-26, axonometric
views, photos.

SALOMON, PIERRE
Architecte dans les Alpes-Maritimes
/ Christine Lippens.
Architect: Yves Bayard, Marc
Barani, Pierre Salomon, Pierre
Fauroux, Jean-Paul Gomis &
Christian Mace, Renaud
d'Hauteserre and Brante et
Vollweider.
LE MONITEUR ARCHITECTURE AMC 1990
June, no.12, p.26-31, photos.

SALOMONI, CARLO
Das Museum der Industriegesellschaft
in Battiferro.
Refurbishment of a late 19th-cent.
brickyard for the city of Bologna,
1984-1989. Architect: Carlo
Salomoni.
BAUWELT 1990 Apr.6, v.81, no.13,
p.672-673, photos., plans, secns.

SALOONS--UNITED STATES--GREAT SALT
LAKE (UTAH)--SALOON FOR JESSE JAMES
Ins Gewicht fallend. Zwei
Balanceakte von Douglas Darden =
Tipping scales. Two balancing acts
by Douglas Darden.
Contents: Project for saloon,
Great Salt Lake, Utah --Project
for Temple Forgetful, at Romun
Romanum, Rome. Architect: Douglas
Darden.
DAIDALOS 1990 Sept.15, no.37,
p.102-105, dwg., elevs., model,
plans, secn.

SALSANO ASSOCIATES
ARC West / Monica Geran.
Interiors of renovated and
expanded addiction recovery center
in Yorktown, NY. Architects/
Interior designers: Salsano
Associates.
INTERIOR DESIGN 1990 Nov., v.61,
no.15, p.184-[187], photos.,
plans.
Chartwell Group in New York / Monica
Geran.
Furniture showroom in the New York
Design Center, better known as 200
Lex. Designers: Salsano
Associates.
INTERIOR DESIGN 1990 Jan., v.61,
no.1, p.188-[191], axonometric
view, photos., plans.
Kravet Fabrics / Monica Geran.
Interiors of New York showroom in
the New York Design Center.
Interior designers: Salsano
Associates.
INTERIOR DESIGN 1990 June, v.61,
no.9, p.254-[257], diagr., photos.

SALT, HENRY, 1780-1827
The travels of Henry Salt and Lord
Valentia in India / Pheroza
Godrej.
Published journals include
illustrations by Salt.
MARG [1989?], v.40, no.4, p.71-88,
engrs., biblio.

SALTBOX HOUSES--18TH CENTURY--UNITED
STATES--CONNECTICUT
East Hampton, N. Y.: Connecticut
transplant.
Goldman house, a 1787 saltbox
moved from Conn.
COLONIAL HOMES 1990 Apr., v.16,
no.2, p.[80]-89,136, photo.

SALTBOX HOUSES--18TH CENTURY--UNITED
STATES--EAST HAMPTON (NEW YORK)--
GOLDMAN HOUSE
East Hampton, N. Y.: Connecticut
transplant.
Goldman house, a 1787 saltbox
moved from Conn.
COLONIAL HOMES 1990 Apr., v.16,
no.2, p.[80]-89,136, photo.

SALTBOX HOUSES--COLONIAL--UNITED
STATES--EAST HAMPTON (NEW YORK)--
PAYNE HOUSE
Home Sweet Home [Payne house, East
Hampton, N.Y.].
Saltbox house, built ca. 1715, now
a museum.
COLONIAL HOMES 1990 June, v.16,
no.3, p.76-[81], port., photos.

SALTER, PETER
AA diploma honours 1989-90 / Raoul
Bunschoten, Wiel Arets, Stefano de
Martino, Peter Salter, Ron Herron,
Andrew Holmes and John Frazer.
Diploma prizes to Joel Segal, Voon
Yee Wong, Simon Hart, Toru Ogata,
Bobby Desai, Shin Egashira and
Matthew Waltman.
AA FILES 1990 Autumn, no.20,
p.95-101, dwgs., models, photo.
Folly 13 [part 2]: Expo '90.
Contents: Zaha Hadid, Chris
Macdonald + Peter Salter, Hajime
Yatsuka, Eleni Gigantes + Elia
Zenghelis.--Folly 13 story [2], by
Hajime Yatsuka.
SPACE DESIGN 1990 Mar., no.306,
p.129-136, axonometric views,
diagrs., dwgs., models, site
plans.
Technical studies: intuition &
process: AA Exhibition Gallery,
Members Room and Bar 23
February-17 March 1989 [exhibition
review].
Peter Salter in conversation with
Alvin Boyarsky.
AA FILES 1990 Spring, no.19,
p.91-100, dwgs., elevs., plans,
secns.

SALTER, PETER--EXHIBITIONS
Technical studies: intuition &
process: AA Exhibition Gallery,
Members Room and Bar 23
February-17 March 1989 [exhibition
review].
Peter Salter in conversation with
Alvin Boyarsky.
AA FILES 1990 Spring, no.19,
p.91-100, dwgs., elevs., plans,
secns.

SALTMAN, STEVEN
Bryant Park plans proceed / Albert
Amateau, Steven Saltzman.
Restoration to enter final phase
in winter of 1990, to be completed
in spring of 1991. Landscape
architects: Hanna/Olin.
METROPOLIS 1990 Jan.-Feb., v.9,
no.6, p.13-14, elev., photos.

SALTWATER AQUARIUMS
See MARINE AQUARIUMS

SALTZMAN, STEVEN
Divine light ... Louis Comfort
Tiffany / Steven Saltzman.
Tiffany windows in New York City.
METROPOLIS 1990 May, v.9, no.9,
p.92-95,119-123, photos.
Immigration returns to Ellis Island
/ Jeffrey Hoff, Steven Saltzman.
On the new National Museum of
Immigration, which opens Sept.10,
1990. Original architects: Boring
& Tilton; restoration architects:
Notter Finegold & Alexander, Beyer
Blinder Belle.
METROPOLIS 1990 Sept., v.10 no.2,
p.19-22, photos.
Latest city additions / Steven
Saltzman.
On the New York City Panorama, a
9000 sq. ft. model made in 1965,
now at the Queens Museum.
METROPOLIS 1990 Nov., v.10, no.4,
p.22, models.

SALVADORES NAVARRO, CARLOS
Caja Juerte: Instituto Valenciano de
Arte Moderno, Valencia.
Architects: Emilio Gimenez Julian,
Vicent Garcia, Jose Francisco
Murcia Vidal, Carlos Salvadores
Navarro, Joaquin Vicente Sanchis
Serrano. English summary, p.90.
A & V 1990, no.26, p.32-34,
elevs., photos., plans, secns.

SALVAGE
See also ARCHITECTURAL ELEMENTS -
REMOVAL OF
See also RECYCLING (WASTE, ETC.)
Architectural salvage to the rescue
/ J. Randall Cotton, Matt Schultz.
Includes list of sources.
OLD-HOUSE JOURNAL 1990 Mar.-Apr.,
v.18, no.2, p.28-39, photos.
Urban icon: Norwest Center refines
and enervates - and is haunted by
- an historical type / Edward W.
Wolner.
A 57-story tower in Minneapolis,
incorporating fragments form the
former Norwest Bank Building.
Architect: Cesar Pelli.
INLAND ARCHITECT 1990 Jan.-Feb.,
v.34, no.1, p.44-48, elev.,
photos.

SALVAGE--DIRECTORIES
Architectural salvage to the rescue
/ J. Randall Cotton, Matt Schultz.
Includes list of sources.
OLD-HOUSE JOURNAL 1990 Mar.-Apr.,
v.18, no.2, p.28-39, photos.

SALVAGE--ENGLAND--COLLECTIONS--
BROOKING COLLECTION
The Brooking Collection / Charles
Brooking.
A private museum of salvaged
historic building details from
G.B., begun in the 1960s. It is
now being transferred to Thames
Polytechnic's collections.
TRADITIONAL HOMES 1990 July, v.6,
no.10, p.[101], photo.

SALVAING, BERNARD
Los mosquees peules du Fouta-Djalon,
l'exemple de Kamsa-Gawol /
Fracoise Doutreuwe, Bernard
Salvaing.
Discussion of 1980 mud mosque
complex in the Fouta Djallon
region of Guinea. Summaries in
English, Italian and Spanish.
ICOMOS INFORMATION 1990 Apr.-June,
no.2, p.17-29, maps, photos.,
plans, secns., site plan, biblio.,
refs.

SALVAT, JORDI
Vivienda unifamiliar en Alella:
Jordi Salvat y Joan Carles Vert,
arquitectos.
Spanish and English text.
ON DISENO 1989, no.106, p.110-117,
photos., plans, secns.

SALVESEN, DAVID
Growth management Tempe style /
David Salvesen.
Third in series on growth
management.
URBAN LAND 1990 Aug., v.49, no.8,
p.20-23, map, photo.

SALVESEN, DAVID (CONTINUED)
Lizards, blind invertebrates, and development / David Salvesen.
Preserving wildlife in the face of development.
URBAN LAND 1990 Dec., v.49, no.12, p.36-37, photo.

SALVIN, ANTHONY, 1799-1881
Arley Hall, Cheshire: the property of the Hon. Michael and Mrs. Flower / Michael Hall.
Site: 5 mi. north of Northwich; architect: George Latham; chapel architects: Anthony Salvin, George E. Street.
COUNTRY LIFE 1990 June 7, v.184, no.23, p.140-145, elevs., photos.
Salving Salvin's mess: Marcus Binney on the property market / Marcus Binney.
Proposed conversion of former Officers' Mess at Dover Castle, Kent for use as a hotel; architect: Anthony Salvin.
COUNTRY LIFE 1990 Nov.15, v.184, no.46, p.70, photo.

SALVIONI, ANDREAS
Stadtischer Park auf dem Gelande einer ehemaligen Tabakfabrik in Bologna, Italien = Urban park on the area of a former tobacco factory in Bologna, Italy.
Architects: Alessandro Anselmi, Francesco Cellini, Andrea Salvioni, Roberto Ugolini.
ARCHITEKTUR + WETTBEWERBE 1990 Dec., no.144, p.17, dwgs.

SALZMANN, BRUNO
Mimikry: zum ersten Preis im Wettbewerb "Schulhauserweiterung Buren" / Bruno Salzmann.
Architects: Marques & Zurkirchen.
ARCHITHESE 1990 July-Aug., v.20, no.4, p.78-80, elevs., models, plans, site plan.

SAMALAVICIUS, ALMANTAS
The realm of Lithuanian Baroque: SS Peter and Paul, Vilnius / Almantas Samalavicius, Stasys Samalavicius.
Built between 1668 and 1675, with stucco decorations by Pietro Perti and Giovanni Maria Galli.
APOLLO 1990 July, v.132, no.341, p.17-21,67, photos., refs.
Restoration in Vilnius: reviving the Lithuanian capital / Stasys and Almantas Samalavicius.
APOLLO 1990 Nov., v.132, no.345, p.333-335, photos.

SAMALAVICIUS, STASYS
The realm of Lithuanian Baroque: SS Peter and Paul, Vilnius / Almantas Samalavicius, Stasys Samalavicius.
Built between 1668 and 1675, with stucco decorations by Pietro Perti and Giovanni Maria Galli.
APOLLO 1990 July, v.132, no.341, p.17-21,67, photos., refs.
Restoration in Vilnius; reviving the Lithuanian capital / Stasys and Almantas Samalavicius.
APOLLO 1990 Nov., v.132, no.345, p.333-335, photos.

SAMBA, ROBERTO
Bologna arte architettura / R. Gamba.
On a new initiative in Bologna and the 1990 exhibit in Milan.
L'INDUSTRIA DELLE COSTRUZIONI 1990 Oct., v.24, no.228, p.70, photos.

SAMBRICIO, CARLOS
Corso storico di un canale: il canale di Castiglia = Historic course of a canal: the canal of Castile / Carlos Sambricio.
LOTUS INTERNATIONAL 1986, no.52, p.[6]-12, photos., secn.

SAMEC, ERNIE
Negotiation and mediation in urban design and development: Forrest Place/City Station Redevelopment, Perth, Western Australia / Ernie Samec, Barrie Melotte.
AUSTRALIAN PLANNER: JOURNAL OF THE ROYAL AUSTRALIAN PLANNING INSTITUTE 1989 Mar., v.27, no.1, p.12-20, photos., site plans, refs.

SAMONA, GIUSEPPE, 1898-
Una casa [Alberto Samona villa] / Franco Purini.
Designed between 1948 and 1950; located in Gibilmanna. Architect: Giuseppe Samona. Includes English summary; captions in Italian and English.
CASABELLA 1990 Feb., v.54, no.565, p.40-43,60-61, dwg., elevs., plan.

SAMOYAULT, JEAN-PIERRE
Ameublement des appartements royaux a Fontainbleau en 1749 / Colombe Samoyault-Verlet, Jean-Pierre Samoyault.
ANTOLOGIA DI BELLE ARTI 1988, new ser., no.27-28, p.111-122, plans, refs.
Louis Poisson, peintre d'Henri IV: ses travaux aux chateaux de Fontainebleau et de Saint-Germain-en-Laye / Jean-Pierre Samoyault.
SOCIETE DE L'HISTOIRE DE L'ART FRANCAIS. BULLETIN 1990, p.[21]-42, ill., photos., plans, engrs., refs.

SAMOYAULT-VERLET, COLOMBE
Ameublement des appartements royaux a Fontainbleau en 1749 / Colombe Samoyault-Verlet, Jean-Pierre Samoyault.
ANTOLOGIA DI BELLE ARTI 1988, new ser., no.27-28, p.111-122, plans, refs.

SAMPSON, BARRY W.
Ah Montreal! Reflections on differing views of public space, past and present / Barry W. Sampson.
French summary.
ARCHITECTURE & COMPORTEMENT = ARCHITECTURE & BEHAVIOR 1990, v.6, no.4, p.[293]-306, photos., engr., aerial pohto., biblio.

SAMSO, EDUARD, 1956-
Eduardo Samso.
Includes criticism by Josep Maria Montaner and four projects by the architect. Text in Spanish and English.
E_ CROQUIS 1990 Nov., v.9, no.45, p.125-162, axonometric views, dets., port., elevs., models, photos., plans, secns., site plans.
Raume des Alltags: Einkaufszentrum in Parma und Interieurs in Barcelona.
Torri center (1989), architect: Aldo Rossi, Gianni Braghieri; and Ekseption interiors (1989); architect: Eduard Samso. Text in German; summaries in German, French, and English.
WERK, BAUEN + WOHNEN 1990 June, no.6, p.54-65, axonometric views, elevs., photos., plans, site plans, sketches.
Special feature: Commercial interiors in Barcelona.
Contents: Between minimalism and Movid, by Naoki Inagawa -- Alfredo Arribas -- Josep Val and Xavier Vendrell -- Dani Freixes and Vicente Miranda -- Tonet Sunyer and Jordi Badia -- Eduard Samso -- Ventura Valcarce and Carlos Valls. Includes interviews and biographical information and features 13 individual commercial projects. Text in Japanese.
SPACE DESIGN 1990 Nov., no.11(314), p.005-072, dets., ports., photos., plans, secns., refs.

SAMTON, PETER
Oculus Special Feature Committee on Zoning on the Upper East Side: Part II.
Shows interpretations for 4 sites, by James Gauer, Marilyn Taylor, Peter Samton, and Peter De Witt.
OCULUS 1990 Sept., v.53, no.1, p.6-10, dwgs., ports., elevs., models, map, plans.

SAMUEL, MARK
Fifteenth-century garner at Leadenhall, London / Mark Samuel.
ANTIQUARIES JOURNAL 1989, v.69, pt.1, p.119-153, axonometric view, dets., dwgs., elevs., map, photos., plans, site plans, sketches, engrs., refs.

SAMUEL, RICHARD
At a crossroad in care and repair / June Eccles, Richard Samuel, Janice Casey.
British efforts at maintenance and repair of elderly housing.
HOUSING 1990 Feb., v.26, no.1, p.18-21, ports.

SAMUELSON, STEPHEN
Gene Hackman: Santa Fe spaces for The French Connections's Best Actor / Joan Chatfield-Taylor.
Features interiors of home redesigned by Stephen Samuelson and Harry Daple. Interior designers; Ken Figueredo and Glynn Gomez.
ARCHITECTURAL DIGEST 1990 Apr., v.47, no.4, p.250-251,312, port., photos.

SAMWORTH, JOE
Tomorrow's landscape architects:
Manchester Polytechnic [part 2] /
Joe Samworth.
Review of graduate work in
landscape architecture.
LANDSCAPE DESIGN 1989 Oct.,
no.184, p.53-54, dwgs., site
plans.

SAMYN ET ASSOCIES
Architetture sotto la tenda = Tent
architecture / Lucia Bisi.
Lightweight metal arch and cable
tensile structure for Sinco
research center, Venafro, Italy;
architects: Samyn et Associes.
L'ARCA 1990 Oct., no.42,
p.48-[55], elevs., models, plans,
secns.
Beyond technical finesse: [graphic
studio annex, Brussels] / Philip
Arcidi.
Modernist addition to Behaeghel &
Partners' villa in suburban
Brussels. Architects: Samyn et
Associes.
PROGRESSIVE ARCHITECTURE 1990
Dec., v.71, no.13, p.76-77,
photos., site plans.
Una immagine per l'Europa: Samyn in
Seville / Fabrizio Bonomo.
Competition project by Samyn et
Associes architects. Text in
Italian and English.
L'ARCA 1990 June, no.39
suppl.l'Arca 2, p.99, dwg., plans,
secn.
Lo spettacolo del lavoro = Work on
display / Lucia Bisi.
Architects: Philippe Samyn et
Associes.
L'ARCA 1990 Apr., no.37, p.48-55,
elevs., model, plans, secns., site
plan.
Una tenda per la rete d'acqua di
Nouakchott = a tent for the
Nouakchott water system / Fabrizio
Bonomo.
Architects: Samyn et Associes.
Text in Italian and English.
L'ARCA 1990 Sept., no.41 suppl.
l'Arca 2, p.97-98.
Gli uffici nel parco = Parkland
offices / Frederick Boorman.
Office of Eric Boulanger,
Waterloo, Belgium; architects:
Samyn et Associes.
L'ARCA 1990 Oct., no.42 suppl.
l'Arca 2, p.102, elev., model,
plan, secn.

SAMYN, PHILIPPE, 1948-
Aanbouw als meubel: uitbreiding
Design Board in Ukkel / Helene
Damen.
Addition to a traditional villa in
Uccle, a Brussels suburb, for
design offices. Architect:
Philippe Samyn.
DE ARCHITECT 1990 Mar., v.21,
no.3, p.41-45, dwgs., photos.,
secn., site plans.

**SAN FRANCISCO MUSEUM OF MODERN ART--
EXHIBITIONS**
Artists afraid of their city:
Visionary San Francisco, San
Francisco Museum of Modern Art
[exhibition review] / Diana
Ketcham.
BLUEPRINT (LONDON, ENGLAND) 1990
(Continued next column)

**SAN FRANCISCO MUSEUM OF MODERN ART--
EXHIBITIONS (CONTINUED)**
Artists afraid of...(CONTINUED)
Sept., no.70, p.57, ill.
California dreamers: an exhibition
looks backward and forward at
visionary schemes for San
Francisco [exhibition review] /
Thomas Hine.
"Visionary San Francisco", at the
San Francisco Museum of Modern
Art, June 14-Aug. 26.
HOUSE & GARDEN 1990 July, v.162,
no.7, p.[32],34, ill.
Dreaming by the Bay [exhibition
review] / Michael Webb.
"Visionary San Francisco", at the
San Francisco Musuem of Modern
Art, June 14-Aug. 26.
METROPOLIS 1990 July-Aug., v.10,
no.1, p.50-55,75, ill., dwgs.
"Visionary San Francisco": una
mostra tra sogno e realta
[exhibition review] / L.
Prestinenza Puglisi.
Exhibition at the Museum of Modern
Art, in San Francisco.
L'INDUSTRIA DELLE COSTRUZIONI 1990
Dec., v.24, no.230, p.60-61,
axonometric view, ill., models,
aerial photo.

SAN JOSE MARQUES, JAVIER
Dos interiores para el metro de
Barcelona: Javier San Jose,
arquitecto.
Spanish, English text.
ON DISENO 1990, no.110, p.85-99,
dets., photos., plans, secns.
Estacion de metro Urgell, Linea 1:
Javier San Jose, arquitecto.
In Barcelona.
ON DISENO 1990, no.116, p.174-175,
photos.

**SAN MARINO--ARCHITECTURE--CONSERVATION
AND RESTORATION**
Medievale e moderno: Gino Zani e il
rifacimento di San Marino / Guido
Zucconi.
URBANISTICA 1990 Mar., no.98,
p.19-32, ill., dwgs., elevs.,
plans, secns., refs.

SAN MARINO--BANKS--CASSA DI RISPARMIO
Tra progetto e didattica: Vicenzo
Giuseppe Berti, 1980-90 / Glauco
Gresleri.
Four projects: Cassa di Risparmio,
San Marino -- Railroad station,
Bologna -- City walls, Florence --
Teatro Amintore Galli, Rimini.
PARAMETRO 1990 Jan.-Feb., no.176,
p.70-81, axonometric views.,
elevs., photos., plans, secns.,
site plans.

SAN MARINO--SCHOOLS--ELEMENTARY
Scuola elementare e materna a San
Marino / Renato Pedio.
Architect: Gilberto Rossini.
Summaries in English, French,
German, and Spanish.
ARCHITETTURA; CRONACHE E STORIA
1990 Mar., v.36, no.3(413),
p.[166]-173, dets., elevs.,
photos, plans, secns., site plans.

SAN MARTIN MORA, PEDRO ANTONIO
Rehabilitacion de Colegio de San
Esteban de Murcia: J. Plaza, E.
Sancho, V. Perez, M. de la Villa,
P. Sanmartin y S. Moreno.
Spanish, English text.
ON DISENO 1990, no.105, p.128-135,
photos., plans.

**SAN PIETRO, SILVIO. 1990 STADI IN
ITALIA**
A sporting advantage: 1990 stadiums
in Italy, edited by Silvio San
Pietro [book review] / Simon
Inglis.
ARCHITECTS' JOURNAL 1990 Oct.24,
v.192, no.17, p.82, photos.

**SAN SADURNI DE NOYA--WINERIES--SPAIN--
CAVAS RAVENTOS BLANC**
Archaic in Arcadia.
Features two wine-related projects
in Sant-Sadurni d'Anoia by Jaume
Bach and Gabriel Mora: Raventos
Blanc winery, and the school of
viticulture and enology.
ARCHITECTURAL REVIEW 1990 July,
v.188, no.1121, p.60-67, elevs.,
photos., plans, secns., site
plans, aerial photos.

SANABRIA, SERGIO LUIS
Techniques de l'architecture
ancienne: construction et
restauration [by] Yves-Marie
Froidevaux [book review] / Sergio
Luis Sanabria.
SOCIETY OF ARCHITECTURAL
HISTORIANS. JOURNAL 1990 Dec.,
v.49 no.4, p.443-445.

SANATARIUMS
See SANATORIUMS

SANATORIUMS
See also HEALTH RESORTS

SANATORIUMS--HISTORY--SCOTLAND
"Declined into a profitable
consumption": the tuberculosis
sanatorium in Scotland / Harriet
Richardson.
THE JOURNAL AND ANNUAL REPORT /
THE SCOTTISH GEORGIAN SOCIETY FOR
THE STUDY AND PROTECTION OF
SCOTTISH ARCHITECTURE 1989, no.16,
p.55-58, photo., refs.

SANBORN, LAURA SUE
Sacred places of the Southwest /
Laura Sue Sanborn.
On camposantos, burial grounds of
Hispanic Catholics in the American
Southwest.
PLACES 1990 Fall, v.7, no.1,
p.[42]-49, photos.

SANCHEZ ARQUITECTOS Y ASOCIADOS
Mexican architecture: new directions
/ John V. Mutlow.
Profiles works by: Agustin
Hernandez, David Munoz Suarez,
Enrique Norten and Associates S.C.
Workshop (T.E.N.), Gutierrez
Cortina, Sanchez Arquitectos Y
Asociados, Legorreta Arquitectos,
and Teodoro Gonzalez de Leon.
L. A. ARCHITECT 1990 Jan., p.7-11,

SANCHEZ DE LA BLANCA, ADOLFO
Concurso de anteproyectos museo del
espacio en Madrid.
First prize: Manuel J. Fernandez
Iglesias and Adolfo Sanchez de la
Blanca.
ARQUITECTURA 1990 Jan.-Feb., v.72,
no.282, p.12-15, axonometric
views, elevs., plans, secns.

SANCHEZ DE LEON, FRANCISCO
Concurso internacional europeo de
puente sobre el Rio Guadiana,
Badajoz 1990.
First prize project by Francisco
Sanchez de Leon, architect, and
Ramon Alfonso Sanchez de Leon,
engineer.
ARQUITECTURA 1990 July-Aug., v.72,
no.285, p.26-27, elevs., models,
secns.

SANCHEZ DE LEON, RAMON ALFONSO
Concurso internacional europeo de
puente sobre el Rio Guadiana,
Badajoz 1990.
First prize project by Francisco
Sanchez de Leon, architect, and
Ramon Alfonso Sanchez de Leon,
engineer.
ARQUITECTURA 1990 July-Aug., v.72,
no.285, p.26-27, elevs., models,
secns.

SANCHEZ HEVIA, GINES
Contradecoradores: del confort y los
espacios / Gines Sanchez Hevia.
ARQUITECTURA VIVA 1990 Nov.-Dec.,
no.15, p.12-13, dwgs., photos.
Historia de una escalera: Eva
Jiricna para Joseph / Gines
Sanchez Hevia.
Store in London.
ARQUITECTURA VIVA 1990 Jan.-Feb.,
no.10, p.62-63, photos., plan.

SANCHEZ LOPEZ, EDUARDO
Guarderia infantil en Palomeras,
Madrid: J. Frechilla, C. Herrero,
J. M. Lopez-Pelaez, E. Rodriguez,
y E. Sanchez, arquitectos.
Nursery school. Spanish, English
text.
ON DISENO 1989, no.104, p.111-117,
photos., plan.

SANCHEZ, PEDRO SUPELANO
O mapa tecnologico do evidente.
Equipe Minga, a research facility
in Cali, Colombia. Architects:
Alvaro Thomas Mosquera, Pedro
Supelano Sanchez.
PROJETO 1990 Oct., no.135,
p.92-100, photos., plans, secns.,
site plans.

SANCHIS SERRANO, JOAQUIN VICENTE
Caja Juerte: Instituto Valenciano de
Arte Moderno, Valencia.
Architects: Emilio Gimenez Julian,
Vicent Garcia, Jose Francisco
Murcia Vidal, Carlos Salvadores
Navarro, Joaquin Vicente Sanchis
Serrano, English summary, p.90.
A & V 1990, no.26, p.32-34,
elevs., photos., plans, secns.

SANCHO, JOSE LUIS
El palacio mudejar de Tordesillas /
Maria Luisa Bujarrabal, Jose Luis
Sancho.
REALES SITIOS 1990, v.27, no.106,
p.29-36, elev., photos., plans.
Reconstruccion del Monasterio de El
Escorial despues del incendio de
1671 / Jose Luis Sancho, Maria
Teresa Fernandez Talaya.
REALES SITIOS 1990, v.27, no.103,
p.57-64, elevs., secns.

SANCHO RUANO, ENRIQUE
Rehabilitacion de Colegio de San
Esteban de Murcia: J. Plaza, E.
Sancho, V. Perez, M. de la Villa,
P. Sanmartin y S. Moreno.
Spanish, English text.
ON DISENO 1990, no.109, p.128-135,
photos., plans.

SANCTUARIES (SHRINES)
See SHRINES

SANDAKER, BJORN NORMANN. ARKITEKTURENS
KONSTRUKTIVE GRUNNLAG
Det konstruktive grundlag er
arkitekturen [book review]/ Karl
Christiansen, Per Dombernowsky.
Review of Arkitekturens
konstruktive grunnlag, by Bjorn
Normann Sandaker and Arne Eggen.
ARKITEKTEN 1990 Aug., v.92, no.10,
p.346-347, diagr., model, sketch.

SANDBECK, PETER B. HISTORIC
ARCHITECTURE OF NEW BERN AND CRAVEN
COUNTY, NORTH CAROLINA
The historic architecture of New
Bern and Craven County, North
Carolina [by] Peter B. Sandbeck
[book review] / Carl Lounsbury.
SOCIETY OF ARCHITECTURAL
HISTORIANS. JOURNAL 1990 Sept.,
v.49, no.3, p.344-345,

SANDE, BRIGITTE VAN DER
Toefjes cultuur in het landschap:
Beeldenparken en -tuinen in
Nederland en Belgie / Brigitte van
der Sande.
ARCHIS 1990 Sept., no.9, p.8-10,
photos.

SANDEEN, ERIC J.
Public sculpture and the civic ideal
in New York City [by] Michele H.
Bogart [book review] / Eric J.
Sandeen.
WINTERTHUR PORTFOLIO 1990 Autumn,
v.25, no.2-3, p.209-212, refs.

SANDELIN, EJVIND
Carta desde Bucarest: la herencia de
Ceausescu / Ejvind Sandelin.
ARQUITECTURA VIVA 1990 July-Aug.,
no.13, p.78, photos.
L'urbanisme selon Ceaucescu / Ejvind
Sandelin, Gilles Antier.
English translation, p.22-24.
French, English and Spanish
summaries, p.3.
CAHIERS DE L'INSTITUT
D'AMENAGEMENT ET D'URBANISME DE LA
REGION D'ILE-DE-FRANCE. 1990 June,
no.93, p.9-24, model, photos.,
plans, site plan, aerial photo.,
refs.

SANDELING, EJVIND
The new Europeans. Part one: Soviet
Union, Czechoslovakia, Bulgaria /
Peter Cooper, Penny Guest, Ejvind
Sandeling.
Analysis of market conditions for
construction in each country.
Includes "Economic overview," an
interview with Peter Wiles.
BUILDING 1990 June 29, v.255,
no.26, p.35-43, graphs, dwgs.,
ports., tables, photos.

SANDERS, BRUCE G.
Source of civic pride: stunning
addition for a well-loved
Greensboro home / Susannah M.
Wilson.
Rapp house. Architect: Bruce G.
Sanders, interior designer Lindsay
Henderson.
SOUTHERN ACCENTS 1990 Oct., v.13,
no.8, p.106-111, port., photos.

SANDERS, G. D. R.
Central places and major roads in
the Peloponnese / G.D.R. Sanders,
I.K. Whitbread.
THE ANNUAL OF THE BRITISH SCHOOL
AT ATHENS 1990, no.85,
p.[333]-361, charts, maps, tables,
refs.

SANDERS GUENZBURGER ARCHITECTS
Spotlight: the younger generation:
Sanders/Guenzburger Architects.
4-person firm in New York City.
OCULUS 1990 Oct., v.53, no.2, p.5,
ports., photos.

SANDERSON, WARREN
Romanische Baukunst an Rhein und
Maas [by] Hans Erich Kubach [and]
Albert Vaerbeek [book review] /
Warren Sanderson.
Review of the final interpretative
volume (4) of
Architekturgeschichte und
Kunstland-schaft.
SOCIETY OF ARCHITECTURAL
HISTORIANS. JOURNAL 1990 Dec.,
v.49, no.4, p.441-443,

SANDORI, PAUL
Air spaces and insulation / Paul
Sandori.
CANADIAN ARCHITECT 1990 July,
v.35, no.7, p.33,37, det.
Practical buildability [book review]
/ Paul Sandori.
Review of a book entitled Practial
Buildability, based on research by
British engineers.
CANADIAN ARCHITECT 1990 Apr.,
v.35, no.4, p.53,66, diagrs.
Sails in the light / Paul Sandori.
Lightweight fabric roof at Sherway
Gardens, Toronto. Architects:
Zeidler Roberts.
CANADIAN ARCHITECT 1990 June,
v.35, no.6, p.26-28, dets.,
photos., sketch.
Why blame the building inspector? /
Paul Sandori.
CANADIAN ARCHITECT 1990 Oct.,
v.35, no.10, p.41,69,

SANDOVAL ROMERO, JORGE ALBERTO
Arquitetura e paisagem em centro cultural no Mexico: Centro Cultural Mexicano, Toluca, Mexico. Architects: Garduno, Maldonado, Romero (Grupo de Diseno Urbano). PROJETO 1989 Apr., no.120, p.60-65, elevs., photos., plans, secns.

SANDRI, DOMENICO
Edificio postale a Villa Falletto. Architects: Massimo Fazzino, Domenico Sandri. CASABELLA 1990 July-Aug., v.54, no.570, p.36-37, photos., plan, secn.

SANDSTONE
See also "SANDSTONE" AS A SUBHEADING AFTER SPECIFIC BUILDING TYPES OR OTHER MAIN HEADINGS.
Maritime Training Institute, Powai, Bombay / CP Kukreja. Located on the site of an abandoned quarry and built partially with red sandstone. Completed in 1990. Architect: C.P. Kukreja Associates. ARCHITECTURE + DESIGN 1990 May-June, v.7, no.3, p.38-45, axonometric views, dets., photos., plans, site plan.

SANDSTROM, BIRGITTA
Landsorten Kontra centraïstyret / Birgitta Sandstrom. Attitudes of rural parishes in Smaland, Sweden (Urshult and Almundsryd) toward the Swedish Board of Public Works, 1794-1917. Includes English summary. BEBYGGELSEHISTORISK TIDSKRIFT 1989, no.17-18, p.114-124, elevs., photos., plans, secns., biblio.

SANDY & BABCOCK ARCHITECTS & PLANNERS
1990 AIA Component Awards: San Francisco Chapter. Three awards, one photo each. ARCHITECTURE: THE MAGAZINE OF THE AMERICAN INSTITUTE OF ARCHITECTS 1990 May, v.79, no.5, p.52, photos.
Pueblo for two / Kate Simonne. Sonoma, Calif., house resembles adobe village. Architect: Don Sandy of Sandy & Babcock; landscape architects: Garden Design. HOUSE BEAUTIFUL 1990 May, v.132, no.5, p.70-[77], dets., ports., photos., plan.

SANDYS, FRANCIS, FL. 1796-1814
The Beautiful and the Sublime: two neoclassical houses compared / Gervase Jackson-Stops. Castle Coole, near Enniskillen, Northern Ireland, begun in 1790 (architects: Richard Johnston, James Wyatt), and Ickworth, near Bury St. Edmunds, ca. 1796 (architect: Francis Sandys). ANTIQUES 1990 June, v.137, no.6, p.[1356]-1367, dets., ill., dwg., elevs., model, photos., secns., engr., refs.

SANFORD HANAUER
Green point Savings Bank [Massapequa, N.Y.] / Mayer, Kus. Interior designers: Sanford Hanauer. INTERIOR DESIGN 1990 Feb., v.61, no.3, p.178-[179], photos., plan.

SANGALLO, ANTONIO DA, CA. 1455-1534 OR 5
Italy's finest renaissance church / Dan Hofstadter. On the Madonna di San Biagio, Montepulciano. Architect: Antonio da Sangallo. CONNOISSEUR 1990 Oct., v.220, no.945, p.138-141,167-168, port., photos.

SANGALLO, FRANCESCO DA, 1494-1576
Francesco da Sangallo's tomb of Leonardo Bonafede in the Certosa del Galluzzo / Rona Roisman. THE RUTGERS ART REVIEW 1988-1989, v.9-10, p.17-41, dwgs., photos., plans, refs.

SANGWIRE, TONY
Roadside horticulture / Tony Sangwine. LANDSCAPE DESIGN 1990 May, no.190, p.38-40, photos.

SANITARIUMS
See SANATORIUMS

SANITARY ENGINEERING
See also DRAINAGE
See also LANDFILLS
See also SEWERS

SANITARY ENGINEERING--18TH CENTURY--FRANCE--PARIS
Cities and environmental decline: elites and the sewage problem in Paris from the mid-eighteenth to the mid-nineteenth century / Barrie M. Ratcliffe. PLANNING PERSPECTIVES PP 1990 May, v.5, no.2, p.189-192, refs.

SANITARY ENGINEERING--19TH CENTURY--FRANCE--PARIS
Cities and environmental decline: elites and the sewage problem in Paris from the mid-eighteenth to the mid-nineteenth century / Barrie M. Ratcliffe. PLANNING PERSPECTIVES PP 1990 May, v.5, no.2, p.189-192, refs.
Les galeries souterraines d'Haussmann: le systeme des egouts parisiens, prototype ou exception? / Pierre-Yves Mauguen. French, English, Spanish and German summaries, p.247-252. LES ANNALES DE LA RECHERCHE URBAINE 1989 Dec., no.44-45, p.163-175, 247-248, 250, 252, graph, ill., photo., plans, secns., refs.

SANITARY ENGINEERING--19TH CENTURY--ITALY
Igiene e urbanistica in Italia nella seconda meta del XIX secolo / Giorgio Piccinato. STORIA URBANA 1989 Apr.-June, v.13, no.47, p.[47]-66, refs.

SANITARY ENGINEERING--19TH CENTURY--ITALY--CATANIA
Ingegneria sanitaria e citta meridionale: il contributo di Filadelfo Fichera / Giuseppe Dato. Sanitary engineering in late 19th cent. Catania, with a profile of Filadelfo Fichera, a pioneer in the field. URBANISTICA 1988 Nov., no.93, p.31-39, ill, maps, plans, secn., refs.

SANITARY ENGINEERING--STANDARDS--CHINA
Standards. Contents: XXI. Public transport in cities. -- XXII.Road and bridge engineering in urban areas. -- XXIII. Gardens and parks in urban areas. -- XXIV.Urban environmental sanitation. -- XXV. Urban disaster mitigation. BUILDING IN CHINA 1990 Mar., v.3, no.1, p.46-48, tables.

SANITARY LANDFILLS
See LANDFILLS

SANITORIUMS
See SANATORIUMS

SANMICHELI, MICHELI, 1484-1559
The Italian Renaissance [book review] / David Hemsoll. Review of Michele Sanmicheli architetto: opera completa, by Lionello Puppi. SOCIETY OF ARCHITECTURAL HISTORIANS. JOURNAL 1990 June, v.49, no.2, p.216-217,

SANNA, ANTONELLO
Una piazza come opera d'arte: Costantino Nivola a Nuoro / Antonello Sanna. Plaza with big granite block sculptures as a monument to the poet Sebastiano Satta. English, French, German, Spanish summaries, p.138. STORIA DELLA CITTA 1988 Oct.-Dec., v.13, no.48, p.87-92, dwgs., photos., refs.

SANNAZZARO, GIOVANNI BATTISTA
Un nuovo documento per la cascina Pozzobonelli / Giovanni Battista Sannazzaro, Grazioso Sironi. 15th cent. chapel and portico, Milan. ARTE CRISTIANA 1990 July-Aug., v.78, no.739, p.280, plan.

SANO, YUKIO
Herald city / Yukio Sano. Four "domed" tent structure buildings by Kajima Kensetsu Kabushiki Kaisha. English summary, p.19. KENCHIKU BUNKA 1990 Oct., v.45, no.528, p.91-102, dwgs., models, maps, photos., plans, aerial photos.

SANOVICZ, ABRAHAO
Recorrendo a linguagem da historia presente: Sede regional Banespa, Recife. Architect: A. Sanovicz. PROJETO 1989 Oct., no.126, p.78-81, elevs., photos., plans, secns.

SANSOT, PIERRE
Memoire collective et perdurances urbaines: Nimes inondee / Pierre Sansot.
Flooding in Nimes. French, English, Spanish and German summaries, p.[122]-124.
LES ANNALES DE LA RECHERCHE URBAINE 1989 [Mar.-Apr.], no.42, p.[5]-10, [123]-124, photos.

SANTA FE STYLE
See "SANTA FE STYLE" AS A SUBHEADING AFTER SPECIFIC BUILDING TYPES OR OTHER MAIN HEADINGS.
The city different: Santa Fe has charm, and Old-world feel--and an identity crisis / Joy Waldron Murphy.
HISTORIC PRESERVATION 1990 Mar.-Apr., v.42, no.2, p.16-19, photo.

SANTACHIARA, DENIS, 1950-
Il museo dei designers = The designers' museum.
Emblematic images and products by six designers: Achille Castiglioni, Michele de Lucchi, Denis Santachiara, Franco Raggi, Alberto Meda, and 02.
OTTAGONO 1990 June, no.95, p.[89-104], dwgs., photos.

SANTACROCE, PAOLO
Atlante dei comuni d'Italia = Atlas of Italian municipalities / Paolo Santacroce, Bernardo Secchi.
In Italian; English summary, p.30.
URBANISTICA 1988 Nov., no.93, p.22-30, maps, tables.

SANTANGUEDA, BENJAMIN JUAN
La Provisoria, Toledo: Benjamin Juan y J. Gomez-Escalonilla, arquitectos.
Spanish, English text.
ON DISENO 1989, no.104, p.146-151, photos., plan.

SANTASIERO, ANTHONY
A stargazer's garden: decorator Anthony Santasiero went through the roof of his Central Park West penthouse to open a view of trees and sky / Anthony Santasiero.
Landscape architect: Bruce Kelly.
HOUSE & GARDEN 1990 Oct., v.162, no.10, p.[176]-179,251, photos.

SANT'ELIA, ANTONIO, 1888-1916
Briefing: the confusion of a Futurist: Antonio Sant'Elia, Accademia Italiana, London [exhibition review] / Brian Hatton.
Architect: Antonio Sant'Elia.
BLUEPRINT (LONDON, ENGLAND) 1990 Mar., no.65, p.51-52, dwg.
Field of vision [exhibition review] / Clare Melhuish.
Review of the show, Futurism and the architecture of Sant'Elia, at the Accademia Italiana, London, until Feb.24, 1990.
BUILDING DESIGN 1990 Feb.2, no.971, p.20-21, dwgs.

SANT'ELIA, ANTONIO, 1888-1916-- EXHIBITIONS
The future that was: Futurism and the architecture of Sant'Elia [exhibition review] / James Dunnett.
Exhibition at the Accademia Italiana, London, through 24 Feb.1990.
ARCHITECTS' JOURNAL 1990 Jan.24, v.191, no.4, p.72-73, dwgs.

SANTELLI, SERGE, 1944-
The Aga Khan Award for Architecture 1989 Winners.
Contents: A search for solutions with no beginning or end, by Romi Khosla.-- The two traditions of the Aga Khan Award for Architecture, by Serge Santelli.-- [winning projects].
MIMAR: ARCHITECTURE IN DEVELOPMENT 1989 Dec., v.33, p.8-33, ports., maps, photos., plans, site plan.
Revisiter Benares / Serge Santelli.
On the architecture of Benares, India on the occasion of the travelling exhibition, Benares: an urban space, organized by the author.
CONNAISSANCE DES ARTS 1990 June, no.460, p.[118-127], photos.
Village Club Aquarius, Senegal / Serge Santelli.
A coastal resort in the Casamance region, for developer Aquarius International. Expected completion date: Sept.1991. Architect: Serge Santelli.
MIMAR: ARCHITECTURE IN DEVELOPMENT 1990 Sept., v.10, no.3(36), p.60-62, ill., elevs., map, plan, site plan, sketch.

SANTI, CARLO, 1925-
[Amenagement interieur]: bureaux.
Contents: Office of president, Region Champagne-Ardennes, Chalons-sur-Marne, France; architect: Henri Ciriani-- Office, Ministere de Finances, Paris; architect: Isabelle Hebey-- Office, 5 place de la Pergola, Toulouse, France; architect: Jean-Pierre Estrampes-- Office, 181 avenue Joliot-Curie, Nanterre, France; architect: Alain Richard-- Bank interior, Bruges; architect: Stephane Beel-- Office, Green Movie, Milan, Italy; architect: Carlo Santi.
LE MONITEUR ARCHITECTURE AMC 1990 July-Aug., no.13, p.46-57, axonometric views, photos., plans.
In barca come a casa = A life on the ocean wave.
Interiors of a 28-meter ketch. Architect: Carlo Santi.
ABITARE 1990 May, no.285, p.176-185, dets., photos, plans, secns.
Studi di post-produzione televisiva Green Movie, Milano: Carlo Santi / Marco Romanelli.
Text in Italian and English.
DOMUS 1990 Apr., no.715, p.[58-62],xxiii, photos, plan, secns.

SANTI, GIANCARLO
Il "riuso" delle chiese nella Diocesi di Milano / Giancarlo Santi.
Paper presented at Qualita ecclesiale nell'arte conference in 1989.
ARTE CRISTIANA 1990 Mar.-July, v.78, no.737-738, p.187-194, map, refs.

SANTIER, GILLES
Capote et transparent: Gymnase des Droits de l'Homme, Guyancourt.
Architects: Gilles Bouchez, Gilles Santier. English summary, p.54.
TECHNIQUES ET ARCHITECTURE 1990 Dec.-1991 Jan., no.393, p.52-54, elev., photos., plan.

SANTINI & ROCHA ARQUITETOS
Residencia dos irmaos maristas.
In Viamao, Brazil. Architects: Santini & Rocha Arquitetos.
PROJETO 1990 Dec.-1991 Jan., no.137, p.38-41, elev., photos., plans, site plan.

SANTINI, PIER CARLO
Ai piedi delle mura di Lucca = The new Banco di Napoli building in Lucca / Pier Carlo Santini.
Architects: Raffaello Lotti, Angela Chiantelli.
L'ARCA 1990 Feb., no.35, p.59-61, elevs., photos, plans, secns.
Sede del Banco di Napoli a Lucca = New offices for a bank in Lucca / Pier Carlo Santini.
On the outskirts of the old town and influenced by the city view. Architects: Raffaello Lotti, Angela Chiantelli. Includes English translation; French, German, and Spanish summaries, p.3.
L'INDUSTRIA DELLE COSTRUZIONI 1990 Feb., v.24, no.220, p.6-11, photos., plans, secsn., site plan, aerial photo.

SANTINI, RINALDO
Traffico e monumenti / Rinaldo Santini.
L'URBE: RIVISTA ROMANA DI STORIA, ARTE, LETTERE, COSTUMANZE 1989 May-Aug., v.52, nos.3-4, p.3-17, map, photos., plan.

SANTIS, FRANCESCO DE, 1679-1731
Notizie d'archivio sull'opera di Francesco de Sanctis architetto del primo settecento romano / Emanuela Settimi.
English, French, German and Spanish summaries, p.158.
PALLADIO 1989 July-Dec., v.2, no.4, p.113-126, photos., plans, engrs., refs.

SANTIS, MICHAEL DE
American playhouse: inventive solutions for a Long Island guest cottage / Brooks Peters.
Interiors of Kings Point guest house with interior pool. Interior designer: Michael de Santis.
ARCHITECTURAL DIGEST 1990 Sept., v.47, no.10, p.202-205, photos.

SANTOS, ADELE NAUDE
Adele Naude Santos: Ninomiya seaside house, Ninomiya, Kanagawa, Japan, 1986-88.
Architect: Adele Naude Santos. Text in Japanese and English.
GA HOUSES 1990 Dec., no.30, p.110-117, axonometric views, photos., plan.
The Los Angeles Arts Park / Philip Arcidi.
Features five projects by the following architects: Tod Williams, Billie Tsien & Associates, Mark Mack, Hodgetts and Fung Design Associates, Adele Naude Santos and Morphosis.
PROGRESSIVE ARCHITECTURE 1990 Sept., v.71, no.9, p.143-146., axonometric views, ill., models, plans, secns., site plan.
New case study housing: MoCA housing competition, Franklin and La Brea, Hollywood, 1988.
Competition for design of 40 units of housing. Architects: Adele Naude Santos (first prize), Hodgetts & Fung, Eric Owen Moss. Text in Japanese and English.
GA HOUSES 1990 July, no.29, p.16-21, elevs., plan, secn., site plan.
Projects: Adele Naude Santos in Tokyo / Philip Arcidi.
Features three projects: Fantasia office building, Harajuku Illuminacion and a duplex house.
PROGRESSIVE ARCHITECTURE 1990 Nov., v.71, no.12, p.102-104, elevs., models, plans, secns., site plan.
Urbanist without Portfolio: Notes on a career / by Jane Thompson.
One of four sections in a special feature on "Women in American Architecture". Contents: Marion G. Weiss.-- Inea Elskop/1100 Architect. Billie Tsien.-- Patricia Sapinsley.--Alison Sky+Michelle Stone/SITE Projects, Inc.--Karen Bausman+Leslie Gill.-- Deborah Berke.--Amy Weinstein.-- Adele Naude Santos. English translation, p.73.
SPACE DESIGN 1990 June, no.309, p.36-53,73, axonometric views, dwgs., ports., elevs., models, photos., plans, secns.
Utopia in the Suburbs [exhibition review] / Douglas R. Suisman.
Exhibition "Blueprints for Modern Living," MOCA, Los Angeles, Oct. 17, 1989-Feb. 17, 1990.
ART IN AMERICA 1990 Mar., v.78, no.3, p.184-193, models, photos.

SANTOS, CECILIA RODRIGUES DOS
Uma nova postura para o planejamento de cidades / Cecilia Rodrigues dos Santos.
PROJETO 1989 Oct., no.126, p.86-[102], dets., ill., elevs., maps, photos., site plans.

SANTOS, GERARDO
Libros monumentales: La Gran Biblioteca de Francia / Gerardo Santos.
Illustrates the models by 20 entrants in the competition. First prize: Dominique Perrault.
ARQUITECTURA VIVA 1990 May-June,
(Continued next column)

SANTOS, GERARDO (CONTINUED)
Libros monumentales:...(CONTINUED)
no.12, p.22-27, axonometric views, dwgs., models, sketches.

SANTOS, PAULO
Espace: identite et alterite des mobiles: la perspective du retour au Portugal / Pierre Pellegrino, Paulo Santos.
French, English, and Spanish summaries.
ESPACES ET SOCIETES 1988, no.54-55, p.[141]-155, graphs, table, biblio.

SANTOS, PAULO F.
Paulo F. Santos, um mestre da historia da arquitetura [obituary] / Augusto C. da Silva Telles.
PROJETO 1988 Nov., no.116, p.152.

SANVILLE, PHILIPPE
Histoire de faux.
On the faux French chateau built in Tokyo for Sapporo Breweries. Architects: Jacques Cossin, Philippe Sanville.
ARCHITECTURE D'AUJOURD'HUI 1990 Oct., no.271, p.83, axonometric views, elev., models, photos., plans.

SANYAL, BISHWAPRIYA
Poor countries' students in rich countries' universities: possibilities of planning education for the twenty-first century / Bishwapriya Sanyal.
JOURNAL OF PLANNING EDUCATION AND RESEARCH 1989 Summer, v.8, no.3, p.139-155, refs.

SANZ SANZ, JUAN MANUEL
Rehabilitacion del antiguo Hospital de San Rafael en Santander: Juan Manuel Sanz y Juan Lopez-Rioboo, arquitectos.
Spanish, English text.
ON DISENO 1990, no.109, p.136-147, photos., plans, secn.

SAPERS, CARL
The ins and outs of living with lawyers / Carl Sapers.
ARCHITECTURAL RECORD 1990 Feb., v.178, no.2, p.55-[57], ill.
Why go for conventional project delivery? / Carl Sapers.
An argument against using a general-contractor construction manager.
ARCHITECTURAL RECORD 1990 Aug., v.178, no.9, p.43-44.

SAPINSLEY, PATRICIA
Urbanist without Portfolio: Notes on a career / by Jane Thompson.
One of four sections in a special feature on "Women in American Architecture". Contents: Marion G. Weiss.-- Inea Elskop/1100 Architect. Billie Tsien.-- Patricia Sapinsley.--Alison Sky+Michelle Stone/SITE Projects, Inc.--Karen Bausman+Leslie Gill.-- Deborah Berke.--Amy Weinstein.-- Adele Naude Santos. English translation, p.73.
SPACE DESIGN 1990 June, no.309, p.36-53,73, axonometric views, dwgs., ports., elevs., models, photos., plans, secns.

SAPOLIN, DONNA
High-rise heaven / Donna Sapolin.
Studio apartment of designer Carey Maloney of the M (Group).
METROPOLITAN HOME 1990 Dec., v.22, no.12, p.120-[121], photos.
The "pique" of perfection / Donna Sapolin.
On the revival of a folk art technique (pique assiette) using pottery and glass fragments. Work shown includes that of Robert Bellamy, a Dallas landscape designer.
METROPOLITAN HOME 1990 July, v.21, no.7, p.76-80,106, port., photos.
Poetry in a box / Donna Sapolin.
Renovation of apartment for Jay Adlersberg. Architect: Margaret Helfand.
METROPOLITAN HOME 1990 Oct., v.22, no.10, p.[156]-160, port., photos.

SARASIN, CARL, 1815-1886
Carl Sarasin(-Vischer)-Sauvain (1815-1886): Industriepatriarch, Politiker und Auftraggeber Arnold Bocklins / Nikolaus Meier.
The paintings in a Basel garden pavillion, built 1868.
ZEITSCHRIFT FUR SCHWEIZERISCHE ARCHAOLOGIE UND KUNSTGESCHICHTE 1990, v.47, no.1, p.55-62, ill., photo., secn., refs.

SARAVIA MADRIGAL, MANUEL
Cesar Cort Boti / Manuel Saravia Madrigal.
Biography and chronology of the Spanish architect and city planner.
URBANISMO / COAM 1990 May, no.10, p.128-137, diagrs., ports., plans, refs.

SARCOPHAGI
See also COFFINS
See also TOMBS

SARDNAL, THEO
Auguste Perret e Le Havre: utopie e compromessi di una ricostruzione = Auguste Perret and Le Havre: utopias and compromises of a reconstruction / Joseph Abram.
Reconstruction of Le Havre, France, after World War II destruction. Architects: Auguste Perret, with Theo Sardnal, Jacques Guilbert, Pierre Edouard Lambert, A. Le Donne, Andre Hermant, Jose Imbert and others.
LOTUS INTERNATIONAL 1989, no.64, p.108-127, dwgs., model, maps, photos., site plans, refs.

SARFATI, ALAIN, 1937-
Actualites: un concours hors du commun / Elisabeth Allain-Dupre.
Contents: Interview with Christian Cleret, director of the Etablissement public du Centre international de Conferences-- Competition projects by architects Stanislas Fiszer & Philippe Guyard, Yves Lion & Alan Levitt, Claude Vasconi, Jean Nouvel & Emmanuel Cattani, Alain Domingo, Bernard Dufournet, Alain Rihn, Franck Hammoutene, Olivier Arene, Christine Edeikins, Olivier Chaslin, Alain Le Houedec, Luc
(Continued next page)

SARFATI, ALAIN, 1937- (CONTINUED)
Actualites: un...(CONTINUED)
Weizmann, Alain Sarfati, Jean
Dubus, Jean-Pierre Loth, Christian
de Portzamparc, and Bertrand
Bonnier.
LE MONITEUR ARCHITECTURE AMC 1990
May, no.11, p.6-9, elevs., models,
plans, secns., site plans.
Coquillage blanc: piscine, sports,
loisirs, Quimper.
English summary, p.89. Spanish
summary, p.155.
TECHNIQUES ET ARCHITECTURE 1990
Dec.-1991 Jan., no.393, p.88-89,
plans, secn., elevs., models.
Details: garde-corps et serrurerie /
Pascale Joffroy.
Includes commentary by Stanislas
Fiszer, Francois Leclercq, Fabrice
Dusapin, Paul Chemetov, Alain
Sarfati.
LE MONITEUR ARCHITECTURE AMC 1990
May, no.11, p.55-59, ports.,
elevs., photos, secns.
France: des modeles aux methodes
[interview] / Marie-Helene Contal.
Interview with Alain Sarfati on
housing in France. Includes two
projects: student housing, rue
Saint-Jacques, Paris, architect:
Georges Maurios; public housing,
Belleville, architect: Fernando
Montes. English summaries, p.138,
142.
ARCHITECTURE INTERIEURE CREE 1990
June-July, no.237, p.132-143.
Pavillon francais de Seville: cinq
projets pour l'exposition
universelle de 1992.
Winning architects: Jean-Paul
Viquier, Jean-Francois Jodry,
Francois Seigneur. English
summary, p.68. Spanish summary,
p.148.
TECHNIQUES ET ARCHITECTURE 1990
Mar., no.388, p.64-69, axonometric
view, dets., ill., dwgs., models,
plans, site plans..

SARFATI, ALAIN, 1937---EXHIBITIONS
Actualites: Alain Sarfati a l'IFA
[exhibition review].
Exhibition held at l'Institut
francais d'architecture from 20
June to 9 Sept., 1990.
LE MONITEUR ARCHITECTURE AMC 1990
July-Aug., no.13, p.8, port.,
photo. site plan.
Building promotions [exhibition
review] / Charlotte Ellis.
Review of two exhibitions held at
the Institut Francais
d'Architecture in Paris through
early Sept. 1990: "Architecture et
Publicite" and "Alain Sarfati,
Architectures".
ARCHITECTS' JOURNAL 1990 July 25,
v.192, no.4, p.60-61, ill.,
models, photos.

SARFATI, CHRISTIAN
Details: logements: la
rehabilitation / Jean-Pierre
Menard.
Contents: Restoration of Jean Zay
Universite residence, Antony,
France, built 1955-1958; original
architect: Eugene Baudoin;
renovation architect: Pierre
Grandveaud-- Renovation of
apartment complex "Les Buffets",
(Continued next column)

SARFATI, CHRISTIAN (CONTINUED)
Details: Logements: la (CONTINUED)
Fontenay-aux-Roses, France, built
1958; original architects: Guy
Lagneau, Michel Weill, Jean
Dimitrijevic, Jean Perrottet;
renovation architect: Jean
Perrottet-- Renovation of la Viste
housing complex, Marseille,
France, built in 1959; original
architect : Georges Candilis;
renovaiton architect: Pierre
Gangnet-- Renovation of apartment
house, quartier du Haut-du-Lievre,
Nancy, France, built 1956-62;
original architect: Bernard
Zehrfuss; renovation architect:
Christian Sarfati.
LE MONITEUR ARCHITECTURE AMC 1990
Nov., no.16, p.37-44, axonometric
views, dets., ports., photos.

SARGENT & POTIRIADIS
Buildings update: swimming pools 2:
case studies.
Second in series on British
swimming pools. Case studies of
The Rapids, Romsey, architects:
Sargent & Potiriadis; Ainslie
Park, architects: Faulkner Browns;
and Coral Reef, Bracknell,
architects: Sargent & Potiriadis.
ARCHITECTS' JOURNAL 1990 Oct.17,
v.192, no.16, p.69-75, photos.,
plans, site plans.

SARGENT, ANDREW
The Greater London excavation index
/ Andrew Sargent.
The National Archaeological Record
of the Royal Commission on the
Historical Monuments of England is
compiling an index of
archaeological excavations carried
out in England. Begun in 1978, the
Greater London index completed
national coverage in 1989.
LONDON ARCHAEOLOGIST 1990 Autumn,
v.6, no.8, p.216-221, graph, maps,
table, refs.

SARGENT, LAWRENCE
Campamento de exploracion:
asentamiento minero temporal para
la alta cordillera / Lawrence
Sargent.
Project for mining facilities in
northern Chile, designed by the
author. Commentary by Sergio
Miranda R.
ARQ 1990 Aug., no.15, p.20-27,
dets., dwgs., elevs., models,
plans, secns.

SARGER, RENE, 1917-1988
Reference: le Musee des Beaux-Arts
du Havre / Joseph Abram.
Built from 1958 to 1961:
architects: Guy Lagneau, Michel
Weill, Jean Dimitrijevic, Raymond
Audigier, with Jean Prouve.
LE MONITEUR ARCHITECTURE AMC 1990
Oct., no.15, p.50-64, model,
photos., plans, secn.

SARGIANI, FRANCO, 1940-
Scultura abitabile: sul Lago
Maggiore / Gilberto Oneto.
House with outdoor sculptures.
Architect: Franco Sargiani.
VILLE GIARDINI 1990 Jan., no.244,
p.[54]-59, photos.

SARIAN, ANNIG C.
Annig C. Sarian: interno per una
collezionista, Milano / Marta
Laudani.
Apartment interiors. Text in
Italian and English.
DOMUS 1990 Dec., no.722,
p.[72]-75, elev., photos., plans.

SARJE, KIMMO
Struktuurista myohaisstalinistisen
idyllin erittelyyn [exhibition
review] / Kimmo Sarje.
Review of Struktuuri/Metafysiika,
at three Finnish museums,
Feb.-June 1989.
ARKKITEHTI 1989, v.86, no.7,
p.90-91, ill.

SARKISSIAN, WENDY
Remembering the essentials:
medium-density housing from the
users perspective / Wendy
Sarkissian.
PLANNING QUARTERLY 1989 Mar.,
no.93, p.34-39, refs.

SAROS, LASZLO, 1947-
Special feature: Contemporary
Hungarian architecture / edited by
Botond Bognar.
Works illustrated by architects:
Imre Makovecz, Gabor Mezei, Andras
Erdei, Sandor Devenyi, Attila
Kovacs, Laszlo Saros, Tamas Nagy,
Gyorgy Csete, Peter Oltai, Istvan
Kistelegdi, Tibor Jankovics, Csasa
Bodonyi, Istvan Ferencz, Tamas
Noll, Beno Taba, Janos Golda,
Agnes Thoma, Jozsef Kerenyi,
Gyorgy Vadasz, Gyorgy Keves, Adam
Sylvester and Gabor Turanyi. Text
in Japanese and English.
ARCHITECTURE AND URBANISM 1990
Mar., no.3(234), p.7-126,
axonometric views, dwgs., elevs.,
photos., plans, secns.

SARRING, KEVIN LEE
Restoring Trajan's Forum / James E.
Packer, Kevin Lee Sarring.
Review of 19th and 20th-cent.
excavations and of a recent survey
and documentation of the site.
Excavation architect 1928-1933:
Italo Gismondi.
INLAND ARCHITECT 1990 Sept.-Oct.,
v.34, no.5, p.57-65, dwgs.,
elevs., model, plans, secns., site
plan.

SARSFIELD, BRENDAN
Short-but not always sweet / Brendan
Sarsfield.
"Short-life housing", temporary,
substandard housing accomodation.
VOLUNTARY HOUSING 1990 May, v.23,
no.4, p.18-19, ports., photo.

SARTI, ANTONIO, 1797-1880
Evoking a Roman past in the family
palazzo / Charlotte Aillaud.
Focus on the home of Prince
Giovanni Torlonia, Palazzo
Torlonia, Rome, built in the
second half of the 17th cent.
Architect: Giovanni Antonio de
Rossi. Remodeled in mid-19th
cent. by Antonio Sarti.
ARCHITECTURAL DIGEST 1990 Jan.,
v.47, no.1, p.46,52,60. port.,
photos.

SARTOGO, PIERO, 1934-
730 Fifth Avenue, New York = Il
nuovo negozio Bulgari / Paul
Goldberger.
Architects: Piero Sartogo
Architetti Associati: Piero
Sartogo and Nathalie Grenon.
L'ARCA 1990 Apr., no.37, p.72-79,
elevs., photos., plans, secn.
730 Fifth Avenue, New York / Paul
Goldberger and Richard Reid.
Bulgari shop, Crown Building.
Architect: Piero Sartogo.
L'ARCA 1990 June, no.39 suppl.,
p.[1]-61, dets., elevs., photos.
La Roma industriale in mostra =
Industrial Rome on show
[exhibition review] / Piero
Sartogo.
Exhibition at Palazzo dei
Congressi, Rome, Nov.1989. Piero
Sartogo Architetti: Piero Sartogo,
Nathalie Grenon, Giovanni
D'Ambrosio, Sergio Micheli.
L'ARCA 1990 Mar., no.36, p.88-93,
ill., model, photos., plan.

SARTORIS, ALBERTO, 1901-
Alberto Sartoris, che avra cent'anni
nel 2000 = Alberto Sartoris who
will be 100 in the year 2000 /
Fulvio Irace.
ABITARE 1990 Nov., no.290,
p.206-210, axonometric views,
ill., dwgs., ports.
Quand la tradition permet la
modernite, l'Abbaye de
Saint-Maurice et la chapelle de
Lourtier / Bernard Wyder.
Chapel built 1932. Architect:
Alberto Sartoris. German and
Italian summaries.
UNSERE KUNSTDENKMALER 1989, v.40,
no.3, p.268-276, axonometric view,
dwg., photos., refs.

SARTORIS, ALBERTO, 1901---EXHIBITIONS
Omaggio di Roma a Sartoris
[exhibition review].
Exhibit at the Biblioteca
nazionale centrale entitled
"Alberto Sartoris e il '900".
L'INDUSTRIA DELLE COSTRUZIONI 1990
Sept., v.24, no.227, p.54-55,
axonometric views, photos.

SARTORY, BARNA VON
Wohnungsbau in Berlin.
IBA apartment building in the
Kreuzberg section, built 1989.
Architects: G. Kohlmaier, B. von
Sartory. Includes English summary.
BAUMEISTER 1990 July, v.87, no.7,
p.50-53, axonometric views,
elevs., photos., plans, secn.,
site plan.

SASAKI ASSOCIATES
The Ames plan: insights in action /
Martha Huntington.
On a community planning effort
assisted by Alan Fujimori of
Sasaki Associates.
IOWA ARCHITECT 1990 Winter, v.39,
no.4, p.24-25, site plans.
Brambleton.
On the new town to be located in a
375-acre core of a 1200-acre rural
site in Loudoun County, Va.
Architects: Sasaki Associates.
PROGRESSIVE ARCHITECTURE 1990
Jan., v.71, no.1, p.118-119,
plans, site plans.

SASAKI ASSOCIATES (CONTINUED)
Desert blooms: a trio of engaging
buildings breaks Arizona State
University's arid architectural
tradition / Lawrence W. Cheek.
Fine Arts Center (Antoine Predock
Architect); Hayden Library
Expansion (Sasaki Associates); and
College of Architecture and
Environmental Design (Hillier
Group).
ARCHITECTURE: THE AIA JOURNAL 1990
Jan., v.79, no.1, p.92-97,
photos., plan, secn., site plan,
aerial photo.
Kuwait City waterfront development /
Brian Brace Taylor.
Completed in 1988. Consultants:
Ghazi Sultan, architect, Kuwait
Engineers Office; Sasaki
Associates, Boston.
MIMAR: ARCHITECTURE IN DEVELOPMENT
1990 Mar., v.10, no.1(34),
p.[12]-20,cover, map, photos.,
plans, secns., site plans.
The search continues: building types
study 681, multifamily housing /
Donald J. Canty.
Four low-rise condominium
projects: The Waterworks, New
Hope, Penn. (Cecil Baker &
Associates, Architects); Back of
the Hill Rowhouses, Boston
(William Rawn Associates,
Architects); Samoset Resort and
Village, Rockport, Me. (Sasaki
Associates, Architects); and
Parkview Commons, San Francisco
(David Baker Architects).
ARCHITECTURAL RECORD 1990 July,
v.178, no.8, p.15-87, axonometric
views, elev., photos., plans, site
plans.

SASAKI, MIKIRO
On the contemporary landscape, Part
1: Structure without design.
"Special series." Contents:
Photographs by Toshiharu Kitajima.
Text in Japanese.
SPACE DESIGN 1990 Sept., no.312,
p.005-076, photos., map.

SASANIAN
See "SASANIAN" AS A SUBHEADING AFTER
SPECIFIC BUILDING TYPES OR OTHER
MAIN HEADINGS.

SASANID
See SASANIAN

SASANO, SHIRO
The relation between the aesthetic
principle and architectural idea
of interior composition in
centralized ecclesiastical
buildings of the early Christian
period / Shiro Sasano.
From the 4th to the 6th cents.,
and covering the influence of
Plotinus' aesthetic principles.
Text in Japanese; English summary,
p.125.
NIHON KENCHIKU GAKKAI KEIKAKUKEI
RONBUN HOKOKU SHU = JOURNAL OF
ARCHITECTURE, PLANNING AND
ENVIRONMENTAL ENGINEERING 1990
Apr., no.4(410), p.125-133, refs.

SASSANIAN
See SASANIAN

SASSI, CLAUDIO
Piano della mobilita per la citta di
Bologna / Bernhard Winkler.
Article forms most of this issue.
Presents the traffic scheme for
Bologna proposed by Prof. Winkler.
Summaries in French, English,
German, and Spanish, p.1. Captions
in Italian and English. Includes
commentary by Claudio Sassi, and
German text on p.88-89.
PARAMETRO 1990 Mar.-Apr., no.177,
p.19-67,cover, dwgs., port., maps,
photos., site plans, tables,
engrs., aerial photos.

SASSI, LAURO
Mensa aziendale a Moncalerio, Torino
= An office cafeteria in
Moncalerio, Turin / Domenico
Bagliani, Lauro Sassi.
For the D.E.A. Company. Architect:
Giuseppe Varaldo. In English and
Italian; summaries in French,
German and Spanish, p.3.
L'INDUSTRIA DELLE COSTRUZIONI 1990
Nov., v.24, no.229, p.22-27,
axonometric views, photos.

SASTRE, JUAN CABEZA
Espaco publico em ambiente fechado.
Shopping. Interlagos, Sao Paulo.
Architect: Juan Cabeza Sastre.
PROJETO 1990 Mar., no.130,
p.72-73, photos., plans.

SATKOWSKI, LEON
On the iconography of the Uffizi
facade [letter].
Comments by Leon Satkowski on an
article published in Art Bulletin,
v.71, no.2 (June 1989), p.237-253
and a reply by author Roger J.
Crum.
ART BULLETIN 1990 Mar., v.72,
no.1, p.[131]-135, elev., site
plan, refs.

SATO, KEIJI
A study on the move of the aged from
inner ring / Keiji Sato, Yuka
Hasegawa.
Subtitle: Especially small site
housing areas for housing and
environmental renewals in Nagoya.
Text in Japanese. Includes English
summary.
NIHON KENCHIKU GAKKAI KEIKAKUKEI
RONBUN HOKOKU SHU = JOURNAL OF
ARCHITECTURE, PLANNING AND
ENVIRONMENTAL ENGINEERING 1990
Sept., no.9(415), p.89-99, graphs,
maps, tables.

SATO, MASATO
A study on effects of visual
environmental factors on human
psychology in an office space
(continued report) / Masato Sato,
Masao Inui, Yoshiki Nakamura.
Text in Japanese; includes English
summary.
NIHON KENCHIKU GAKKAI KEIKAKUKEI
RONBUN HOKOKU SHU = JOURNAL OF
ARCHITECTURE, PLANNING AND
ENVIRONMENTAL ENGINEERING 1990
Nov., no.11(417), p.11-17,
photos., tables,

SATO, SHIMPEI, 1953-
Shimpei Sato / Jorg Metzinger.
Japanese glass artist (b.1953) and
a 1990 window at the Oberin middle
school.
KUNST UND KIRCHE 1990, no.3,
p.143, photo.

SATO, TOSHIRO
Conversations with Women Architects
/ Toshira Sato.
One of four sections in a special
feature on "Women in American
Architecture". Contents: Julie
Eizenberg.--Norma Sklarek/The
Jerda Partnership.--Deborah
Sussman.--Diane M. Caughey.--
Pamela Burton+Katherine Spitz.--
Dolores Hayden.--Sheila Levrant de
Bretteville.
SPACE DESIGN 1990 June, no.309,
p.06-22, dwgs., ports., elev.,
models, phgotos., plans, secn.
Special feature: Women in American
architecture / Toshiro Sato, guest
editor.
The four sections are indexed
separately.
SPACE DESIGN 1990 June, no.309,
p.05-76, ill.

SATOH, KATUYUKI
A study on standardization of a
composite evaluation scale for an
elderly's escape ability in a fire
emergency at nursing home /
Katuyuki Satoh.
Text in Japanese; includes English
summary.
NIHON KENCHIKU GAKKAI KEIKAKUKEI
RONBUN HOKOKU SHU = JOURNAL OF
ARCHITECTURE, PLANNING AND
ENVIRONMENTAL ENGINEERING 1990
Aug., no.8(414), p.59-68, graphs,
plans, tables, refs.

SATOH, MASARU
Discussion: streets as dramatic
space / Osamu Hirao, Motoko Ishii,
Masaru Satoh.
THE WHEEL EXTENDED 1990, v.19,
no.4, p.16-23, ports., photos.

SAUBOT ET JULLIEN
Gehry goes to Paris / John Morris
Dixon.
American Center, Paris.
Architects: Frank O. Gehry with
Saubot & Jullien.
PROGRESSIVE ARCHITECTURE 1990
July, v.71, no.7, p.21, model,
site plan.
L'Opera de la Bastille a Parigi.
Architect: Carlos Ott, with Saubot
et Jullien. Summaries in English,
French, German, and Spanish.
ARCHITETTURA; CRONACHE E STORIA
1990 Apr., v.36, no.4(414),
p.[270-282], axonometric views,
photos., plans, secns., aerial
photos.

SAUBOUA, MICHEL
Dans le Luberon, un bastion au fil
du temps / Gilles Dalliere.
Home of interior designer Michel
Sauboua, which he created out part
of a 12th cent. rampart in
Luberon. English summary, p.III.
MAISON FRANCAISE 1990 Apr.,
no.435, p.82-[91], port., photos.

SAUCIER & PERROTTE ARCHITECTES
The Canadian Architect 1990 22nd
Annual Awards of Excellence.
Eight awards. Architects: Steven
Fong, A.J. Diamond, Donald Schmitt
& Co. with Kolker Kolker Epstein
Architects, Meltzer Igra
Architects, Bugod Figueiredo
Krendel Architects, Peter Cardew
Architects, Richard Henriquez
Architect, Laszlo Nemeth Assoc.,
Kearns Mancini Architects, Patkan
Architects, Saucier + Perrotte,
and Kuwabara Payne McKenna
Blumberg.
CANADIAN ARCHITECT 1990 Dec.,
v.35, no.12, p.9-24,29, dwgs.,
elevs., models, plans, secns.,
site plans.
Eight young firms / Bronwen Ledger.
Saucier & Perrotte; Stephen R.
Teeple; Jenkins & Sturgess; Brian
Allsopp; Natale Scott Browne; Ruth
Cawker Architect; Busby Bridger;
and Brian MacKay-Lyons
Architecture and Urban Design.
CANADIAN ARCHITECT 1990 Sept.,
v.35, no.9, p.19-35, axonometric
views, dwgs., ports., elevs.,
models, photos., plans.

SAUDI ARABIA--AIR BASES
Value engineering in master planning
/ Humoud A. Al-Salmi.
Applied to aviation center in
Saudi Arabia.
EKISTICS 1989 May-Aug., v.56,
no.336-337, p.198-201, plan,
tables.

SAUDI ARABIA--CONSTRUCTION MANAGEMENT
A study of the interface problems
between owners and contractors
over the construction of
residential houses in Saudi Arabia
/ Abdul-Muhsen al-Hammad.
INTERNATIONAL JOURNAL FOR HOUSING
SCIENCE AND ITS APPLICATIONS 1990,
v.14, no.4, p.245-257, table,
refs.

SAUDI ARABIA--HOUSING
A study of the interface problems
between owners and contractors
over the construction of
residential houses in Saudi Arabia
/ Abdul-Muhsen al-Hammad.
INTERNATIONAL JOURNAL FOR HOUSING
SCIENCE AND ITS APPLICATIONS 1990,
v.14, no.4, p.245-257, table,
refs.

SAUDI ARABIA--JEDDAH--ARCHITECTURE
Transformations in the built
environment in Saudi Arabia /
Farooq A. Mofti.
Riyadh and Jeddah.
URBAN FUTURES 1989 Winter, v.2,
no.4, p.17-26, dwgs., elevs.,
maps, plans, secns., sketches,
refs.

SAUDI ARABIA--JEDDAH--CITIES AND TOWNS
Transformations in the built
environment in Saudi Arabia /
Farooq A. Mofti.
Riyadh and Jeddah.
URBAN FUTURES 1989 Winter, v.2,
no.4, p.17-26, dwgs., elevs.,
maps, plans, secns., sketches,
refs.

SAUDI ARABIA--MEDINA--CITIES AND
TOWNS--GROWTH
Implications of subdivision activity
for the urban growth of Madina /
Walead Abdulaal.
Medina, Saudi Arabia.
URBAN STUDIES 1990 Oct., v.27,
no.5, p.725-738, graph, maps,
plan, refs.

SAUDI ARABIA--MEDINA--LAND SUBDIVISION
Implications of subdivision activity
for the urban growth of Madina /
Walead Abdulaal.
Medina, Saudi Arabia.
URBAN STUDIES 1990 Oct., v.27,
no.5, p.725-738, graph, maps,
plan, refs.

SAUDI ARABIA--RIYADH--ARCHITECTURE
Transformations in the built
environment in Saudi Arabia /
Farooq A. Mofti.
Riyadh and Jeddah.
URBAN FUTURES 1989 Winter, v.2,
no.4, p.17-26, dwgs., elevs.,
maps, plans, secns., sketches,
refs.

SAUDI ARABIA--RIYADH--CITIES AND TOWNS
Transformations in the built
environment in Saudi Arabia /
Farooq A. Mofti.
Riyadh and Jeddah.
URBAN FUTURES 1989 Winter, v.2,
no.4, p.17-26, dwgs., elevs.,
maps, plans, secns., sketches,
refs.

SAUDI ARABIA--RIYADH--EMBASSIES--
AUSTRALIAN CHANCERY
Daryl Jackson: four projects / Daryl
Jackson.
The Australian Film, Television
and Radio School, North Ryde, NSW;
Bond University, Queensland;
Penguin Parade, Phillip Island,
Victoria; and Australian Chancery,
Riyadh, Saudi Arabia.
ARCHITECTURE AUSTRALIA 1990 Mar.,
v.79, no.2, p.27-42, dets., dwgs.,
photos., plans, secns., site
plans, aerial photo.

SAUDI ARABIA--RIYADH--EMBASSIES--
DEUTSCHE BOTSCHAFT
Oase fur Deutsche: Neubau eines
Dienst- und eines
Dienst-Wohngebaudes der Deutschen
Botschaft in Riyadh/Saudi-Arabien.
Architect: Kurt Schentke.
ARCHITEKTUR, INNENARCHITEKTUR,
TECHNISCHER AUSBAU 1990 May, v.98,
no.5, p.58-59, photos., site plan.

SAUDI ARABIA--RIYADH--NEW TOWNS--
KHASHM-AL-AAN
Uma cicade nova no deserto: cidade
nova de Khashm-Al-Aan, Riad,
Arabia Saudita.
Architects: Dumez S.A.
PROJETO 1989 Oct., no.126,
p.115-117, photos., site plan,
aerial photo.

SAUDI ARABIA--RIYADH--SPORTS
FACILITIES--KHASHM ALAAN NATIONAL
GUARD SPORTS CENTER
National Guard Sports Center, Khashm
Alaan / Maurizio Vitta.
Architect: Claudio Salocchi. Text
in Italian and English.
L'ARCA 1990 May, no.38, p.26-33,
photos., plans, secns., site
plans.

SAUDI ARABIA--RIYADH--UNIVERSITIES AND
COLLEGES--BUILDINGS--KING SAUD
UNIVERSITY
King Saud University, Riyadh, Saudi
Arabia, 1984.
Architects: Gyo Obata of Hellmuth,
Obata & Kassabaum, with Gollins
Melvin Ward Partnership. Text in
Japanese and English.
ARCHITECTURE AND URBANISM 1990
Dec., no.12 extra edition,
p.40-[47], photos., secn., site
plan.

SAUER, LOUIS
Streetscapes in an American city
[Boulder, CO] / Louis Sauer.
ARCHITECTURE & COMPORTEMENT =
ARCHITECTURE & BEHAVIOR 1990, v.6,
no.4, p.[357]-371, photos., map,
site plan, biblio.

SAUER, SILVIA
Assoziativer Raum: Diplomarbeit zu
einer raumlichen Analogie.
Student project by Silvia Sauer,
FH Mainz.
ARCHITEKTUR, INNENARCHITEKTUR,
TECHNISCHER AUSBAU 1990 Nov.,
v.98, no.11, p.76-79, dwgs.,
plans, secns., isometric dwgs.

SAUERBRUCH, MATTHIAS
Aduana con peneita: OMA en
Checkpoint Charlie / Jorge Sainz.
Architects: M. Sauerbruch, E.
Zenghelis.
ARQUITECTURA VIVA 1990 July-Aug.,
no.13, p.20-23, dwgs., elevs.,
photos., plans, secns.
Metropolitan sophistication:
Burohaus Riverside Three /
Matthias Sauerbruch.
Located at 22 Hester Road, London.
Architects: Foster Association
[sic].
BAUWELT 1990 Sept.7, v.81, no.34,
p.1662-1665, axonometric view,
photos., plan, elev., secn.

SAUMAREZ SMITH, CHARLES. BUILDING OF
CASTLE HOWARD
Anatomy of a country house:
Building of Castle Howard [book
review] / Julian Bicknell.
BLUEPRINT (LONDON, ENGLAND) 1990
Apr., no.66, p.66,68,

SAUNDERS, ANDREW
The historical development of the
martello tower in the Channel
Islands, by E.J. Grimsley [book
review] / Andrew Saunders.
POST-MEDIEVAL ARCHAEOLOGY 1989,
v.23, p.77,

SAUNDERS, ANN
Citisights guide to London [by]
Kevin Flude and Paul Herbert [book
review] / Ann Saunders.
LONDON JOURNAL 1990, v.15, no.2,
p.[178]-179,

SAUNDERS, MATTHEW
Monstrous carbuncles and all that:
the extension and adaptation of
historic buildings, 1988-9 /
Matthew Saunders.
Twelve historic buildings in
Britain about which the Society
was consulted during 1988-1989.
ANCIENT MONUMENTS SOCIETY.
TRANSACTIONS 1990, new ser., v.34,
p.[171]-186, dwgs., elevs., plans,
site plan.

SAUNIER, ERIC, 1952-
De l'hotel de police a l'hotel
industriel.
Features two projects by Jerome
Brunet and Eric Saunier: police
station, Herouville-Saint-Clair
and an industrial building, Paris.
English summary, p.117. Spanish
summary, p.173.
TECHNIQUES ET ARCHITECTURE 1990
Oct.-Nov., no.392, p.115-117,
elev., photos., plans, secn., site
plans.
Industrial appeal: nel giardino del
sindaco = Industrial appeal: in a
mayor's garden.
Addition to house of Francois
Geindre, Herouville Saint-Clair,
France. Architects: J. Brunet, E.
Saunier.
ABITARE 1990 Dec., no.291,
p.88-91, axonometric view,
photos., site plan.
Round study.
Stainless steel tower addition to
home in Herouville Saint-Clair.
Architects: Jerome Brunet, Eric
Saunier.
ARCHITECTURAL REVIEW 1990 June,
v.187, no.1120, p.96-[97],
axonometric view, elevs., photos.,
plans, secns., site plan.

SAUNUS, CRISTOPH
Vermeidung von Baufehlern und
Bauschaden bei
Stahlbeton-Schwimmbecken /
Cristoph Saunus.
DEUTSCHES ARCHITEKTENBLATT 1990
Nov.1, v.22, no.11, p.1745-1749,
dets., photos., refs.

SAURA, MAGDA
Modernismo modernized / Magda Saura.
On the remodeling of 1905-1908
Palau de la Musiça Catalana,
Barcelona. Original architect:
Lluis Domenechi Montaner.
Renovation architects: Tusquets,
Diaz & Associates. Includes
interview with Tusquets.
PROGRESSIVE ARCHITECTURE 1990
June, v.71, no.6, p.84-[91],
elevs., photos., plans, secns.,
site plan.

SAURON, GILLES
Les monstres, au coeur des conflits
esthetiques a Rome au Ier siecle
avant J.-C. / Gilles Sauron.
REVUE DE L'ART 1990, no.90,
p.34-35, photos., refs.

SAUTER, PATRICK
Kein Brett vor dem Kopf:
Standarchitekter unterstutzt
Imagewandel.
Designers: Patrick Sauter,
Eberhard Kappler.
ARCHITEKTUR, INNENARCHITEKTUR,
TECHNISCHER AUSBAU 1990 Sept.,
v.98, no.9, p.107, model, plan.

SAUVAGE, HENRI, 1873-1932
Stepped apartment building, rue
Vavin, Paris, 1912.
Architect: Henri Sauvage. Text in
Japanese and English.
ARCHITECTURE AND URBANISM 1990
Sept., no.9 Extra edition,
p.50-57,262, photos., plans,
secns.

SAUVESTRE, STEPHEN, 1847-
Architecture on the edge: Stephen
Sauvestre, the Ecole centrale
d'architecture, and marginalist
practice / Shelley
Hornstein-Rabinovitch.
Includes abstract.
JOURNAL OF ARCHITECTURAL AND
PLANNING RESEARCH 1990 Autumn,
v.7, no.3, p.209-221, elevs.,
photos.

SAUX, ALAIN LE
Les inondations en region
d'Ile-de-France: prevenir ou
pallier / Alain Le Saux.
On flood prevention or alleviation
in the Paris and Seine River area,
with reference to the 1983 and
earlier floods. Includes English
abstract. English, French, and
Spanish summaries, p.3.
CAHIERS DE L'INSTITUT
D'AMENAGEMENT ET D'URBANISME DE LA
REGION D'ILE-DE-FRANCE 1989 Oct.,
no.91, p.47-64, photos., tables.

SAUZE, ELIZABETH
Le chateau d'Uchaux / Elizabeth
Sauze.
Now in ruins, castle dates back to
the early 13th cent.
MONUMENTS HISTORIQUES 1990
Sept.-Oct., no.170, p.24-27,
photos., refs.
Le groupe episcopal de Cavaillon /
Francois Fray, Rollin Guild,
Elizabeth Sauze.
Dates from the 11th century.
MONUMENTS HISTORIQUES 1990
Sept.-Oct., no.170, p.77-[79],
photos., refs.

SAUZET, MAURICE
L'eapace des sens / Maurice Sauzet.
On the work of Sauzet and the
influence of Buddhist temple
architecture. Includes English and
Spanish summaries.
TECHNIQUES ET ARCHITECTURE 1990
June-July, no.390, p.96-100,180,
photos., plans.

SAUZET, MAURICE (CONTINUED)

SAVAGE, BYRON
Lighting: American Home Video Store in Granada Hills, Ca. / Justin Henderson, Peter Barna.
Interior designer: Byron B. Savage III.
INTERIORS 1989 Feb., v.148, no.7, p.54-55, photos., plan.

SAVARE, CARLA
Un servizio privato di trasporto su diligenza in Lombardia: l'impresas franchetti, 1813-1870 / Carla Savare.
STORIA URBANA 1990 July-Sept., v.14, no.52, p.[49]-73, refs.

SAVARESE, SILVERANA
La presenza dei Teatini sulla collina di Pizzofalcone / Silvana Savarese.
PROSPETTIVA 1989 Apr.-1990 Oct., no.57-60, p.146-152, dwgs., maps, photos., plans, refs.

SAVE BRITAIN'S HERITAGE (ASSOCIATION)
Mills and boom / Peter Weatherhead.
SAVE Britain's Heritage is campaigning to promote adaptive reuse of old industrial buildings.
BUILDING 1990 June 29, v.255, no.26, p.46-49, photos.

SAVE SURVEYING ARCHITECTURE VALUES IN THE ENVIRONMENT
"Besvarelsen vil fortrinsvis have for Oje de store Helheder..." / Gregers Algreen-Ussing.
Presented at a SAVE Seminar on Physical Planning, Lisbon, Nov.6-11, 1989. Discusses a planning case study in Evora and Danish planning methodology in Nakslov and Roskilde.
ARKITEKTEN 1990 Apr., v.92, no.5, p.149-151, dwg., photo., table, refs.

SAVI, VITTORIO
Das neue Teatro Carlo Felice in Genua / Vittorio Savi.
Architects: Aldo Rossi, Ignazio Gardella, Fabio Reinhart.
WERK, BAUEN + WOHNEN 1990 Dec., no.12, p.2-9, dwgs., maps, photos., plans, secns., aerial photos.
Nuovo Teatro Carlo Felice , Genova: Ignazio Gardella, Aldo Rossi / Vittorio Savi.
Text in Italian and English.
DOMUS 1990 Sept., no.719, p.[33-49], dets., dwgs., elevs., models, maps, photos., plans, secns., site plans, sketches, aerial photos.
Progetti recenti di Francesco Venezia / Vittorio Savi, Giordano Tirani.
Includes restoration of Buida Oli waterfront, Alcoy, Spain; renovation to Palazzo Falna museum, Orvieto; competition entry for gardens, Park de la Fontaine, Nimes; and urban center alterations, San Pietro a Patierno, Naples. Includes English captions and summary.
CASABELLA 1990 Mar., v.54, no.566, p.4-17,59-60, axonometric view,
(Continued next column)

SAVI, VITTORIO (CONTINUED)
Progetti recenti di...(CONTINUED) models, photos., plans, secns., site plans, sketches.

SAVINI, FRANCESCO, 1846-1940
Restauri di Francesco Savini e Guido Cirilli in Abruzzo / Maria Antonietta Adorante.
STORIA ARCHITETTURA 1987 Jan.-Dec., v.10, no.1-2, p.127-152, dets., dwgs., map, photos., plans, secns., sketches, refs.

SAVITCH, H. V.
Post-industrial planning in New York, Paris, and London / H. V. Savitch.
AMERICAN PLANNING ASSOCIATION. JOURNAL 1987 Winter, v.53, no.1, p.80-91, maps, biblio., refs.

SAVITCH, H.V. POST-INDUSTRIAL CITIES: POLITICS AND PLANNING IN NEW YORK, PARIS AND LONDON
Post-industrial cities: politics and planning in New York, Paris and London [by] H.V. Savitch [book review] / Anthony Sutcliffe.
LONDON JOURNAL 1990, v.15, no.1, p.74-77,

SAVOURET, HUBERT
Quatre ans de protection des monuments historiques en Ile-de-France.
"Catalogue de l'exposition presentee a la Rotonde de la Villette 8 novembre-3decembre 1989, organisee par la Prefecture..., Direction regionale des Affaires culturelles, Conservation regionale des monuments historiques." Includes 13 signed essays and indexes of place names and architects. Authors: Charles Bourely, Bruno Girveau, Odile Herbert, Hubert Savouret, Monique Mahaux, Christine Lorre, Michele Matthieussent, Claudine Cartier, Rosine de Charon, and Francois Loyer.
CAHIERS DE LA ROTONDE 1989, no.12, p.[1]-96, ill., elev., photos., secn., engrs., aerial photos.

SAW MILLS--SWITZERLAND--ALTISHOFEN
Werkstattgebaude in Altishofen, LU, Projekt, 1989.
Architects: Marcel Meili, Markus Peter.
WERK, BAUEN + WOHNEN 1990 Apr., no.4, p.48-53, elevs., models, photos., plans, secns., site plan.

SAWADE, JURGEN
Nachdenken uber die Akademie der Kunste / Hans Meyer ... [et al.].
Presents the winning entry for addition to the Berlin Art School, by Jurgen Sawade, followed by commentary by East and West Berliners on the Academy's role.
BAUWELT 1990 Jan.5, v.81, no.1, p.16-21, model., photos.

SAWICKI, DAVID S.
Demographic analysis in planning: a graduate course and alternative paradigm / David S. Sawicki.
JOURNAL OF PLANNING EDUCATION AND RESEARCH 1989 Fall, v.9, no.1, p.45-56, refs.

SAWICKI, RICHARD
Southampton character study: updating a historic summer estate on Long Island / John Taylor.
Interiors of Brue and Joann Hackett's renovated ca. 1913 weekend house. Interior designer: Mary Meehan. Renavation architect: Richard Sawicki. Landscape architect: Elise DeBoeck Deans.
ARCHITECTURAL DIGEST 1990 May, v.47, no.5, p.[178-185], port., photos.

SAWMILLS
See SAW MILLS

SAX, JOSEPH L.
Olmsted's Yosemite, a vision betrayed / Joseph L. Sax.
PLACES 1990 Spring, v.6, no.3, p.60,

SAX, ULRIKA. VITA STADEN: HAMMARBYHOJDEN UNDER FEMTIO AR
Den vita staden [book review] / Eva Rudberg.
Review of Den vita staden - Hammarbyhojden under femtio ar, by Ulrika Sax.
ARKITEKTUR: THE SWEDISH REVIEW OF ARCHITECTURE 1990 Aug., v.90, no.6, p.50-51, photo., aerial photo.

SAXE, HANS
Alte Bader neu genutzt: Beispiele fur die Umgestaltung von Hallenbadern der Jahrhundertwende.
Five examples of bath halls converted to other uses.
BAUMEISTER 1990 Mar., v.87, no.3, p.52-57, photos., plans, secns.

SAXELBYE, HAROLD
Epping Forest Yacht Club / Judith Nasatir.
1926 du Pont mansion converted to yacht club, Jacksonville, Fla. Original architect: Harold Saxelbye. Conversion architects: Pappa Associates. Interior designers: Catlin Interiors.
INTERIOR DESIGN 1990 June, v.61, no.9, p.208-[213], photos., plan.

SAXENIAN, ANNALEE
Silicon Valley y Route 128: i prototipos regionales o excepciones historicas? / Annalee Saxenian.
Concentrations of technology-based industries in northern California and suburban Boston. In Spanish; English summary p.57.
URBANISMO / COAM 1990 Sept., no.11, p.46-57, maps, photos., aerial photos.

SAXER, MATTHIAS
Neuer Kern in alter Schale: Umbau des Amtshauses Baden, Schweiz / Matthias Saxer.
Architects: H. Eppler, L. Maraini.
DEUTSCHE BAUZEITUNG 1990 Apr., v.124, no.4, p.58-60, axonometric views, photos., plan, site plan.

SAXON, RICHARD
Clearing the smoke: fire safety in atria / Richard Saxon.
Discusses forthcoming British code.
ARCHITECTS' JOURNAL 1990 Sept.5, v.192, no.10, p.65,67, photos., table, ref.

SAYAH, AMBER
Gestrandet oder gerade vom Stapel gelaufen? / Amber Sayah.
A kindergarten in Stuttgart-Luginsland. Architect: Behnisch & Partner. Project architect: Sibylle Kappel-Klieber.
BAUWELT 1990 Aug.24, v.81, no.32, p.1570-1576, photos., plans, secns.
Landesmuseum fur Technik und Arbeit in Mannheim / Amber Sayah.
Architect: Ingeborg Kuhler.
BAUWELT 1990 Nov.16, v.81, no.42-43, p.2131-2139, photos., plan, secn.
Neubau Volkshochschule / Amber Sayah.
Located on the Spendhausstrasse on the outskirts of Reutlingen. Architect: Rossmann + Partner. Interior designers: Herta Maria Witzemann, Robert Haussmann.
BAUWELT 1990 Jan.19, v.81, no.2-3, p.103-107, elevs., photos., plans, secns., site plan.
Parkhaus Lederstrasse / Amber Sayah. In Reutlingen. Architect: Dieter Herrmann.
BAUWELT 1990 Jan.19, v.81, no.2-3, p.108-110, elevs., photos., plans, site plan.
Reutlingen / Amber Sayah.
BAUWELT 1990 Jan.19, v.81, no.2-3, p.100-103, photos.

SAYERS, PATRICIA
Somptuous suite.
Showroom bedroom designed by Patricia Sayers.
COLONIAL HOMES 1990 Aug., v.16, no.4, p.44-47,115, photos.

SAZATORNIL RUIZ, LUIS
Sematica de la Ciudad-Balneario: el Caso del Sardinero en Santander (1840-1900) / Luis Sazatornil Ruiz.
ARCHIVO ESPANOL DE ARTE 1989 Oct.-Dec., v.62, no.248, p.[421]-434, On the history of El Sardinero, Spain. English summary, p.434.

SBS
See SICK BUILDING SYNDROME

SBT KEPPIE
Religious conversion / Heather Rose. 1929 John Ross Memorial Church, Glasgow, converted into offices for the architectural firm, SBT Keppie. Original architect: Norman A. Dick.

(Continued next column)

SBT KEPPIE (CONTINUED)
Religious conversion...(CONTINUED)
BUILDING DESIGN 1990 Aug., suppl., p.V, photos.

SCAFFOLDING
See SCAFFOLDS

SCAGLIOLA--CONSERVATION AND RESTORATION
"Proud of what I've done": Romanian emigre blossoms in new world / Thomas W. Sweeney.
Aurelian Ilie, a specialist in marbleizing, scagliola and stenciling, has restored the painted interior finish of Union Station, Wahington, D.C., and the Riggs Bank (formerly Farmers and Mechanics Bank), Georgetown, D.C.
PRESERVATION NEWS 1990 Feb., v.30, no.2, p.14-15, ports., photos.

SCALA, ANDREA, 1820-1892
Conservazione e restauro = A conserving restoration / Massimo Carmassi.
Restoration of 1867 Teatro Verdi, Pisa. Original architect: Andrea Scala. Restoration architect: Massimo Carmassi.
SPAZIO E SOCIETA 1990 Apr.-June, v.13, no.50, p.66-79, ports., maps, photos., plans, secns.

SCALE (ARCHITECTURE)
See ARCHITECTURE - COMPOSITION, PROPORTION, ETC.

SCALER, CHANTAL
Suisse: le credo de l'habitat groupe.
Feature four projects: Castel Schmitten, Fribourg, architects: Martin Wagner, David and Samuel Spycher; Merzenacker project, Bern, architects: ARB Arbeitsgruppe; Habitat industriel, Givisiez, architect: Rodolphe Luscher and a multi-use building, Geneva, architect: Rodolpke Luscher and a multi-use building, Geneva, architect: Chantal Scaler. English summary, p.180.
ARCHITECTURE INTERIEURE CREE 1990 June-July, no.237, p.[108]-119, dwgs., photos., secns.

SCALI, FRANCOIS
Quai Branly / Jean-Paul Robert.
Entries by 7 French firms in the competition to design an international conference center in Paris near the Eiffel Tower. Winning architect: Francois Soler. Includes English summaries.
ARCHITECTURE D'AUJOURD'HUI 1990 Apr., no.268, p.[20]-38, axonometric views, dwgs., ports., elev., models, photos., plans, secns., aerial photo.
Sept projets pour le Quai Branly: Centre de conferences internationales.
Includes seven entries in the competition for an international conference center near the Quai Branly, Paris. Winning architect: Francis Soler.
TECHNIQUES ET ARCHITECTURE 1990 Apr.-May, no.389, p.17-26, dwgs., models, plans, secns., site plans, aerial photo.

SCALISI, LUCIA
A room for all seasons / Lucia Scalisi.
Cabinet from house at 106 rue Vielle du Temple, Paris, 1778 which became the Hotel de Serilly now in Victoria & Albert Museum; architect: attributed to Claude N. Ledoux; decoration: Jean-Simeon Rousseau de la Rottiere; chimneypiece: Philippe-Laurent Roland.
COUNTRY LIFE 1990 Jan.4, v.184, no.1, p.54-56, photos.

SCAMOZZI, VINCENZO, 1552-1616. IDEA DELL'ARCHITETTURA UNIVERSALE
A secret semiotic skiagraphy: the corporal theatre of meanings in Vincenzo Scamozzi's idea of architecture / Marco Frascari.
On the symbolic use of shadows in Scamozzi's treatise.
VIA 1990, no.11, p.32-51, elevs., photos., plans, secns., refs.

SCANDANAVIA--APARTMENT HOUSES--20TH CENTURY--EXHIBITIONS
Bo i Nord: Skandinavische Wohnungsbau-Ausstellungen [exhibition review] / Wilfried Dechau.
Exhibited in 3 Scandanavian countries in 1990.
DEUTSCHE BAUZEITUNG 1990 Aug., v.124, no.8, p.116-118, photos.

SCANDINAVIA--ARCHITECTURE--19TH CENTURY
Stone, style and truth: The vogue for natural stone in Nordic architecture 1880-1910 [by] Sixten Ringbom [book review] / Ingrid Sjostrom.
KONSTHISTORISK TIDSKRIFT 1989, v.58, no.4, p.181-182,

SCANDINAVIA--ARCHITECTURE--20TH CENTURY
Nordisk klassicisme og Italien [book review] / Fredrik Fogh.
Review of Classicismo nordico: architettura nel paesi scandinavi 1910-1930, published in conjunction with a 1982 exhibition.
ARKITEKTEN 1990 Feb., v.92, no.2, p.72, dwgs., elevs., photos., refs.
Scandinavian architecture during the late 1930s: Asplund and Aalto vs. Functionalism / William C. Miller.
REFLECTIONS: THE JOURNAL OF THE SCHOOL OF ARCHITECTURE UNIVERSITY OF ILLINOIS AT URBANA-CHAMPAIGN 1990 Spring, no.7, p.4-13, photos., biblio., refs.

SCANDINAVIA--ARCHITECTURE--INFLUENCE
Barcelona / Peder Boas Jensen ... [et al.].
Theme of issue. Contents: By eller OL, by Peder Boas Jensen and Elith Juul Moller.-- Idraettens arenaer, by Ebbe Melgaard.-- Kataloniens hovedstad, by Jorgen Sestoft.-- Gensyn med Gaudi, by Nils-Ole Lund.-- Parkerne i Barcelona, by Jorgen Peder Hansen and Anna Maria Indrio.-- Den nordiske inspiration, by Nils-Ole Lund.-- Ny katalansk arkitektur,

(Continued next page)

SCANDINAVIA--ARCHITECTURE--INFLUENCE
(CONTINUED)
Barcelona / Peder... (CONTINUED)
by Jan Christiansen and Gosta
Knudsen.-- Miralles og Pinos, by
Thomas Wiesner.
ARKITEKTEN 1990 May, v.92, no.7,
p.[212]-249,cover, axonometric
views, diagrs., maps, photos.,
secns., aerial photos., biblios.

SCANDINAVIA--ART--19TH CENTURY
Norden kring 1800 / Goran Lindahl.
Introduction to issue devoted to
Nordic culture at the beginning of
the 19th cent. The 11 articles are
indexed separately.
BEBYGGELSEHISTORISK TIDSKRIFT
1989, no.17-18, p.5-14,cover,
ill., dwgs., sketches, biblio.,
ref.

SCANDINAVIA--BUILDINGS--STONE
Stone, style and truth: The vogue
for natural stone in Nordic
architecture 1880-1910 [by] Sixten
Ringbom [book review] / Ingrid
Sjostrom.
KONSTHISTORISK TIDSKRIFT 1989,
v.58, no.4, p.181-182,

SCANDINAVIA DESIGN COUNCIL--
EXHIBITIONS
NordForm 90 [exhibition review] /
Mike Romer.
Scandinavian design exhibit in
Malmo, Sweden, 1 June-2 Sept.1990,
sponsored by the Scandinavian
Design Council.
ARKITEKTEN 1990 Nov., v.92, no.17,
p.[536]-539, photos., site plans.

SCANDINAVIA--DESIGN--EXHIBITIONS
Design in Skandinavien NordForm 90
[exhibition review].
Exhibition through 2 Sept.1990.
BAUWELT 1990 July 20, v.81, no.27,
p.1386-1391, photos., plans,
secns.
Malmo och NordForm.
Report on exhibition on
Hjalmarekajen in Malmo.
ARKITEKTUR: THE SWEDISH REVIEW OF
ARCHITECTURE 1990 May, v.90, no.4,
p.54-55, dwg., models, plans.
Nordform 90 [exhibition review] /
Gunnar Ericson.
Summer 1990, in Malmo, Sweden.
Includes English summary and
captions.
LANDSKAB 1990 Dec., v.71, no.8,
p.142-149,152, dwg., photos.,
plans.
NordForm 90 [exhibition review] /
Mike Romer.
Scandinavian design exhibit in
Malmo, Sweden, 1 June-2 Sept.1990,
sponsored by the Scandinavian
Design Council.
ARKITEKTEN 1990 Nov., v.92, no.17,
p.[536]-539, photos., site plans.
NordForm 90 / Gunilla Lundahl.
Photographs by Olof Hultin of the
1990 Scandinavian design
exhibition, Malmo.
ARKITEKTUR: THE SWEDISH REVIEW OF
ARCHITECTURE 1990 Oct., v.90,
no.8, p.44-51, photos., site plan.

SCANDINAVIA--DESIGN--EXHIBITIONS
(CONTINUED)
Nordic but nice / John Welsh.
On the NordForm 90 exhibitions,
Malmo.
BUILDING DESIGN 1990 May 25,
no.987, p.36-39, ill., dwgs.,
secns.

SCANDINAVIA--INDUSTRIAL BUILDINGS
Industribyggandets metaforer /
Anders Tornqvist, Peter Ullmark.
In conjunction with an
international congress in
Stockholm and a related
publication entitled "When people
matter".
ARKITEKTUR: THE SWEDISH REVIEW OF
ARCHITECTURE 1990 Sept., v.90,
no.7, p.28-35, model, photo.,
secns., site plan.

SCANDINAVIA--LANDSCAPE ARCHITECTURE
Landscape on the edge / Marc Treib.
An essay on landscape architecture
in Scandinavia, from a global
perspective.
LANDSKAB 1990 May, v.71, no.3-4,
p.I-VIII, port., photos., plan,
refs.

SCANDINAVIA--LANDSCAPE ARCHITECTURE--
EXHIBITIONS
Nordform 90 [exhibition review] /
Gunnar Ericson.
Summer 1990, in Malmo, Sweden.
Includes English summary and
captions.
LANDSKAB 1990 Dec., v.71, no.8,
p.142-149,152, dwg., photos.,
plans.

SCANDINAVIA--MODEL HOUSES
Arkitektur pa NordForm / Kim
Dirckinck-Holmfeld, Lard Nevald.
Model town houses for the summer
1990 exhibit in Malmo, by
Tegnestuen Vandkunsten, Gudrun
Molden and Per Hojgaard, Ori Merom
and Peter Hesselgren, Kari Kousma
and Esko Valkama, and Gudmundur
Jonsson.
ARKITEKTEN 1990 Nov., v.92, no.17,
p.540-545, photos., model, plans,
secns.

SCANDINAVIA--PALACES--EMPIRE--INTERIOR
DESIGN
I tidens sonak: om kungliga miljoer
i Danmark, Norge och Sverige under
empiren / Goran Alm.
Royal patronage in the early 19th
cent. Includes English summary.
BEBYGGELSEHISTORISK TIDSKRIFT
1989, no.17-18, p.91-102, dwgs.,
elevs., photos. plans, secns.,
refs.

SCANDINAVIA--PROTOTYPE BUILDINGS--
CONGRESSES
Experiment, fara, erfarenhet / Claes
Caldenby.
Report on a symposium held at CTH
in Gothenburg entitled
"Experimentbyggande i nordiskt
perspektiv".
ARKITEKTUR: THE SWEDISH REVIEW OF
ARCHITECTURE 1990 Sept., v.90,
no.7, p.57-58, ill., photo.

SCANDINAVIA--SCULPTURE--20TH CENTURY
Nordisk rumkunst.
Installation works at the Volvo
Personvagnar AB office in
Torslanda, outside of Gothenburg,
Sweden. In Danish and English.
SKALA 1990, no.22, p.10, photos.

SCANDINAVIAN DESIGN COUNCIL--
EXHIBITIONS
Design in Skandinavien NordForm 90
[exhibition review].
Exhibition through 2 Sept.1990.
BAUWELT 1990 July 20, v.81, no.27,
p.1386-1391, photos., plans,
secns.
Malmo och NordForm.
Report on exhibition on
Hjalmarekajen in Malmo.
ARKITEKTUR: THE SWEDISH REVIEW OF
ARCHITECTURE 1990 May, v.90, no.4,
p.54-55, dwg., models, plans.

SCANLON, GEORGE T.
The Rajput palaces [book review] /
George T. Scanlon.
Review of a 1987 book by G.H.R.
Tillotson.
APOLLO 1990 Feb., v.131, no.336,
p.132,

SCARBOROUGH, KAREN
Uptown District, San Diego: looking
at the future of mixed-use
development in American cities /
Janice Fillip.
Residential and commercial project
in the Hillcrest section.
Architects: SGPA Planning and
Architecture and Lorimer-Case;
landscape architects Karen
Scarborough, with Roger Deweese,
Inc.
URBAN LAND 1990 June, v.49, no.6,
p.2-7, photos., site plan, aerial
photo.

SCARISBRICK, DIANA
Piranesi and the 'Dactyliotheca
Zanettiana' / Diana Scarisbrick.
Miniature engraved hardstones as
sources for illustrations in
Piranesi's "Parere su
l'Architettura" of 1765.
BURLINGTON MAGAZINE 1990 June,
v.132, no.1047, p.413-414, dwg.,
photo., engr., refs.

SCARLATTA, MARINA
La Sicilia del cinquecento nella
"Descrittione in diseguo" di
Camillo Camiliani / Marina
Scarlatta.
On the 300 16th cent. watercolor
and India ink drawings by
Camilliani which comprise the
historical and geographic
treatise, Descrittione della
Sicilia. Summaries in English,
French, German and Spanish.
PALLADIO 1988 Dec., v.1, no.2,
p.15-36, ill., dwgs., refs.

SCARPA, AFRA
[Amenagement interieur]: commerces.
Contents: Boutique Koshino, Paris
Ville; architect: Jean-Michel
Wilmotte-- Apple showroom, ave. de
la Grande Armee, Paris; architect:
Berbesson Racine et Associes--
Castelli showroom, Paris;
designer: Ronald Cecil Sportes--
(Continued next page)

SCARPA, AFRA (CONTINUED)
[Amenagement...(CONTINUED)
Unifor furniture showroom, Milan,
Italy; architects: Afra & Tobia
Scarpa-- Boutique Jean-Louis
Imbert, Marseille, France;
architect: Rudy Ricciotti--
Recorded music store, Nantes,
France; architect: Studio Naco.
LE MONITEUR ARCHITECTURE AMC 1990
July-Aug., no.13, p.36-45,
axonometric views, photos., plans.
Etat, prospectives et
representations de l'industrie
europeenne du bureau.
On the office furniture industry.
Features four showrooms and a
factory by the following
architects: Frank Gehry, Afra and
Tobia Scarpa, Pierluigi Cerri and
Paolo Ferrari. English summary,
p.182-183.
ARCHITECTURE INTERIEURE CREE 1990
Apr.-May, no.236, p.[138-157],153,
ports., elev., photos., plans,
site plan.
Paesaggi attorno al lavoro: Ponzano
Veneto, Italia: Benetton =
Landscapes of labour: Benetton, at
Ponzano Veneto, Italy.
Corporate headquarters and
factory. Architects: Afra and
Tobia Scarpa.
ABITARE 1990 Oct., no.289,
p.230-243, model, photos., site
plan, sketches.
Showroom Unifor, Milan.
Furniture showroom. Architects:
Afra and Tobia Scarpa.
TECHNIQUES ET ARCHITECTURE 1990
Mar., no.388, p.126-129, photos.,
plans.

SCARPA, CARLO, 1906-1978
L'invitation au voyage / Guido
Pietropoli.
On the Cimitero Briori Vega, San
Vito di Altivole, Italy.
Architect: Carlo Scarpa.
SPAZIO E SOCIETA 1990 Apr.-June,
v.13, no.50, p.90-97, ports.,
plans, sketches.

SCARPA, CARLO, 1906-1978--EXHIBITIONS
Architectuur en poezie bij Carlo
Scarpa: tentoonstelling in Wenen
[exhibition review] / Bart
Lootsma.
"Die andere Stadt", at the
Osterreichisches Museum fur
Angewandte Kunst, Fall 1989.
DE ARCHITECT 1990 Apr., v.21,
no.4, p.52-57, dwgs., ports.,
sketches, refs.
Lo Scarpa che non vedremo = The
Scarpa we shan't be seeing
[exhibition review] / Manolo de
Giorgi.
An exhibition of Carlo Scarpa's
work entitled "Die andere Stadt,"
at the Osterreichishches Museum
fur Angewandte Kunst, Vienna,
Oct.12, 1989-Jan.15, 1990.
DOMUS 1990 Feb., no.713,
p.[14-15], photo, sketches.

SCARPA, CARLO, 1906-1978--INFLUENCE
Scarpa and the mothers of invention
/ John Welsh.
Barn in North Wales converted into
house for architect's parents.
Architects: Ar.drew Taylor, Pankaj
Patel.
BUILDING DESIGN 1990 Mar.2,
no.975, p.12, axonometric view,
det., elevs., plans, site plan.

SCARPA, TOBIA
[Amenagement interieur]: commerces.
Contents: Boutique Koshino, Paris
VIIIe; architect: Jean-Michel
Wilmotte-- Apple showroom, ave. de
la Grande Armee, Paris; architect:
Berbesson Racine et Associes--
Castelli showroom, Paris;
designer: Ronald Cecil Sportes--
Unifor furniture showroom, Milan,
Italy; architects: Afra & Tobia
Scarpa-- Boutique Jean-Louis
Imbert, Marseille, France;
architect: Rudy Ricciotti--
Recorded music store, Nantes,
France; architect: Studio Naco.
LE MONITEUR ARCHITECTURE AMC 1990
July-Aug., no.13, p.36-45,
axonometric views, photos., plans.
Etat, prospectives et
representations de l'industrie
europeenne du bureau.
On the office furniture industry.
Features four showrooms and a
factory by the following
architects: Frank Gehry, Afra and
Tobia Scarpa, Pierluigi Cerri and
Paolo Ferrari. English summary,
p.182-183.
ARCHITECTURE INTERIEURE CREE 1990
Apr.-May, no.236, p.[138-157],153,
ports., elev., photos., plans,
site plan.
Paesaggi attorno al lavoro: Ponzano
Veneto, Italia: Benetton =
Landscapes of labour: Benetton, at
Ponzano Veneto, Italy.
Corporate headquarters and
factory. Architects: Afra and
Tobia Scarpa.
ABITARE 1990 Oct., no.289,
p.230-243, model, photos., site
plan, sketches.
Showroom Unifor, Milan.
Furniture showroom. Architects:
Afra and Tobia Scarpa.
TECHNIQUES ET ARCHITECTURE 1990
Mar., no.388, p.126-129, photos.,
plans.

SCASSELLATI, FABRIZIA, 1953-
Fabrizia Scassellati Sforzolini: un
bancone in vetro.
Text in Italian and English.
DOMUS 1990 Nov., no.721, p.8-[9],
dwgs., photos.

SCATASTA, RAFFAELLO
Cassa Rurale e Artigiana di
Castelferretti (Ancona) /
Raffaello Scatasta.
Bank located in renovated house.
Architects: Danilo Guerri, Stefano
Gidoni. Summaries in English,
French and Spanish.
ABACUS 1990 Oct.-Dec., v.6, no.24,
p.58-71, dets., dwgs., photos.,
plans, secns.

SCATASTA, RAFFAELLO (CONTINUED)
Complesso residenziale ad Ancona =
Housing in Ancona / Raffaello
Scatasta.
A semicircular garden apartment
complex built by the "Galileo
cooperative". Architect: Danilo
Guerri. In Italian and English;
French, German and Spanish
summaries, p.4.
L'INDUSTRIA DELLE COSTRUZIONI 1990
Dec., v.24, no.230, p.28-[35],
elev., photos., plan, secns.,
aerial photo.

SCATTERGOOD, D.
John Dennis Haslam [obituary] / D.
Scattergood.
RIBA JOURNAL 1990 Nov., v.97,
no.11, p.98,

SCENERY (STAGE)
See THEATERS - STAGE-SETTING AND
SCENERY

SCEUOPHYLACIA
See DIACONICA

SCHAARSCHMIDT-RICHTER, IRMTRAUD
Wege und Schritisteine im
japanischen Garten / Irmtraud
Schaarschmidt-Richter.
BAUWELT 1990 Feb.23, v.81, no.7-8,
p.303-305, photos.

SCHACHE, WOLFGANG
Asbest.
Introduction to issue devoted to
asbestos problems and removal from
buildings. Includes 11 articles
(one indexed separately), by Peter
Munchhoff, Werner Hildebrandt et
al., Wolfgang Schache, Paul
Bornemann, Bernard Schneider,
Frank M. Ruff, Klaus Dierks, and
Karlheinz Pfarr.
BAUWELT 1990 Dec.14, v.81, no.47,
p.2329,2338-2371, graphs, photos.,
tables, refs.
Herrscher Tod. Kreig, Zerstorung,
Opfer- und Todeskult in der
NS-Architektur = Sovereign death.
War, destruction, sacrifice and
death cult in Nazi architecture /
Wolfgang Schache.
DAIDALOS 1990 Dec.15, no.38,
p.52-59, ill., models, photos.,
refs.

SCHADEL, HANS, 1910-
Aufbruch im Kirchenbau: Hans Schadel
zum 80. Geburtstag / Richard
Schomig.
The work of this German church
architect.
DAS MUNSTER 1990, v.43, no.1,
p.29-36, ill., photos.

SCHADLER, ULRICH
Ionisches und Atlisches am
sogenannten Erechtheion in Athen /
Ulrich Schadler.
ARCHAOLOGISCHER ANZEIGER 1990,
no.3, p.[361]-378, dwg., photos.,
plans, refs.

SCHAFER, PETER
Ohne Unterbruch: ausgewahlte Bauten aus dem Werk von Peter Schafer. Text in German; summaries in German, French and English.
WERK, BAUEN + WOHNEN 1990 Oct., no.10, p.34-47, axonometric views, elevs., photos., plans, secns., aerial photos.

SCHAFFEL, GUNTER
Interview mit Ministerialdirektor Dipl.-Ing. Gunter Schaffel, Bundesministerium fur Raumordnung, Bauwesen und Stadtebau / Ingeborg Flagge.
DER ARCHITEKT 1990 Dec., no.12, p.558-561, photos.
Weiterkommen mit Rucksichtnahme - oder: wie Bauverwaltung und freie Architekten gemeinsam die Zukunft bewaltigen / Gunter Schaffel.
DEUTSCHES ARCHITEKTENBLATT 1990 Dec.1, v.22, no.12, p.1839-1844, dwg., photos., plan.

SCHAFFER, ALBERT
The Houston growth coalition in "boom" and "bust" / Albert Schaffer.
JOURNAL OF URBAN AFFAIRS 1989, v.11, no.1, p.[21]-38, refs.

SCHAFFER, DANIEL
Benton MacKaye: the TVA years / Daniel Schaffer.
Regional planner and sometime associate of Lewis Mumford.
PLANNING PERSPECTIVES: PP 1990 Jan., v.5, no.1, p.5-21, refs.

SCHAFFER, RICHARD L., 1947-
The planning man [Richard Schaffer] / Eve Heyn.
New York's first professional planner to head the City Planning Commission was formerly dean of Columbia University's school of urban planning. Also profiled are the members of the City Planning Commission.
CITY LIMITS 1990 Nov., v.15, no.9, p.20-23, ports.

SCHAIBLE, MICHAEL
Park Avenue thoroughbred / Judith Thurman.
1929 New York apartment interiors designed by Robert Bray and Michael Schaible.
ARCHITECTURAL DIGEST 1990 Mar., v.47, no.3, p.[158]-165, photos.

SCHAICH, DIETER, 1939-
Perfekte Prasentation: Sussman's Presse- und Buchladen im Ostbahnhof Munchen.
Architect: Dieter Schaich.
ARCHITEKTUR, INNENARCHITEKTUR, TECHNISCHER AUSBAU 1989 Sept., v.97, no.9, p.[24-33], dets., photos., plans, secns.

SCHAIK, LEON VAN
Architects and firms: a sociological perspective on architectural practice [book review] / Leon van Schaik.
Review of 1984 book by Judith R. Blau.
ARCHITECTURE AUSTRALIA 1990 Apr., v.79, no.3, p.29-30, photo., plan.

SCHAIK, LEON VAN (CONTINUED)
Participation in Architecture: fact or fraud? / Leon van Schaik.
Criticism of the Charles Joseph La Trobe Design for Living Award, which acknowledges socially responsive and liveable residential environments in Victoria, Australia.
TRANSITION 1990, no.33, p.[68-75], photos., plan, refs.
A survival manual for the 90's [book review] / Leon van Schaik.
Review of Architectural practice, a critical view, by Robert Gutman.
ARCHITECTURE AUSTRALIA 1990 Apr., v.79, no.3, p.30-32, port.

SCHALIN, MONA
J.S. Sirenin elamantyo nayttelyna: J. S. Siren arkkitehti-architect 1889-1961 [exhibition review] / Mona Schalin.
Exhibition at Helsingen Jugendsalissa, Mar.31-Apr.28, 1989.
ARKKITEHTI 1989, v.86, no.4, p.20, elevs.

SCHARFENORTH, HEINER
Gehry was here .... / Heiner Scharfenorth.
The Vitra Design Museum, Weil am Rhein. Architect: Frank O. Gehry.
ARCHITEKTUR & WOHNEN 1990 Feb.-Mar., no.1, p.110-114,116, port., elev., photos.

SCHARLACH, WOLFGANG
Wohnungspolitische Konzepte: Wohnungsbauprojekte / Rudi Kujath.
Section on many new housing projects in Germany. Contents: Berlin, by Rudi Kujath.--Koln, by Uwe Kessler.--Bayern, by Dieter Gutekunst.--Frankfurt, by Martin Wentz.--Hannover, by Hanns Adrian.--Der LEG Nordrhein-Westfalen, by Roswitha Sinz.--Anmerkungen..., by Hartmut Grosshans. Among the architects represented are Otto Steidle + Partner; Andreas Brandt & Rudolf Bottcher; Joachim Ganz, Walter Rolfes; Axel Schultes; Wolfgang Scharlach und Rainer Wischhusen; Rebecca Chestnutt et al; Hubertus Hoffmann; Paul Petry; Hermann Schroder; Sampo Widmann; Gerhart Laage; Freed Ahrens.
BAUWELT 1990 Mar.30, v.81, no.12, p.572-598, elevs., plans, secns., site plans, tables.

SCHAROUN, HANS, 1893-1972
Cranked, curled and cantilevered / Pilar Viladas.
On the Vitra Design Museum, Weil am Rhein, Architect: Frank O. Gehry. Includes short article by Philip Arcidi which compares Gehry and Hans Scharoun (1893-1972).
PROGRESSIVE ARCHITECTURE 1990 May, v.71, no.5, p.94-[99], model, photos., plans, secn., site plan.
Ideenwettbewerb fur das Hygiene-Museum in Dresden 1920 / Volker Welter.
Architect: Wilhelm Kreis.
Publishes competition entries by Hans Scharoun, Carl Krayl, and Hans Luckhardt.
(Continued next column)

SCHAROUN, HANS, 1893-1972 (CONTINUED)
Ideenwettbewerb fur das (CONTINUED) BAUWELT 1990 Nov.23, v.81, no.44, p.2214-2219, axonometric view, dwgs., photos., plans, site plan, biblic.
Luxury country houses / Vladimir Slapeta.
Features four houses: Dr. Rabe's house, Zwenkau, Leipzig, 1928-30, architect: Adolf Rading; Hasek house, Jablonec, Czechoslovakia, 1930-31 and the Schmelowsky house, Jablonec, 1931-32, architect: Heinrich Lauterbach and Schminke house, Lobau, E. Germany, 1930-33, architect: Hans Scharoun.
RASSEGNA 1989 Dec., v.11, no.40/4, p.78-88, dwg., photos., plans, refs.
Neues Bauen in Breslau / Vladimir Slapeta.
On the work of Ernst May, Hans Poelzig, Max Berg and Adolf Rading, Erich Mendelsohn, and others in Breslau during the early part of the 20th cent.
RASSEGNA 1989 Dec., v.11, no.40/4, p.14-62, ill., dwgs., ports., elevs., models, photos, plans, site plans, aerial photo., refs.
Romeo and Juliet in middle age / Peter Blundell Jones.
On the high rise housing blocks, Romeo and Juliet, built between 1956 and 1959 in Zuffenhausen, a suburb of Stuttgart. Architect: Hans Scharoun.
ARCHITECTURAL REVIEW 1990 Oct., v.188, no.1124, p.90-95, photos., plans, secns., site plans.

SCHATTNER, KARLJOSEF, 1924-
Architectural lessons of a Bavarian town / Larry Doll.
Architect Karljosef Schattner has reconstructed, remodeled, or built 18 major public buildings in the town of Eichstatt.
TEXAS ARCHITECT 1990 July-Aug., v.40, no.4, p.56, photos.
Des Bischofs Architekt / Falk Jaeger.
On the work of Karljosef Schattner.
DEUTSCHE BAUZEITSCHRIFT 1990 Aug., v.38, no.8, p.1052-1055, port., photos.
Restauro e trasformazione dell storico orfanotrofio di Eichstatt: karljosef Schattner / Gilberto Botti.
Text in Italian and English.
DOMUS 1990 Apr., no.715, p.[52-57], axonometric view, elev., photos, plans, site plan.
Salonatmosphare: Stadien in Barcelona, Sportanlagen in Eichstatt, Multihallestadion bei London, Amphitheater in Nimes.
Architects: Esteve Bonell and Francesc Rius, Karljosef Schattner with Wilhelm Huber, Michael Hopkins and Partner, Finn Geipel and Nicolas Michelin. Text in German, French and English.
WERK, BAUEN + WOHNEN 1990 Sept., no.9, p.46-65, dets., elevs., models, photos., plans, secns., site plans.

SCHATTNER, KARLJOSEF, 1924-
(CONTINUED)
Schutzdacher Kaiserpfalz,
Gelnhausen, Projekt 1989.
Project for a new roof to cover a
medieval fort. Architect:
Karljosef Schattner with Jorg
Homeier.
WERK, BAUEN + WOHNEN 1990 Apr.,
no.4, p.44-45, elevs., model.
Treppenhaus in ehemaligen Waisenhaus
in Eichstatt = Staircase in a
former orphanage in Eichstatt,
Bavaria.
Architect: K. Schattner.
DETAIL 1990 Apr.-May, v.30, no.2,
p.162-164, axonometric views,
det., photos., plans, secn.
Der Ulmer Hof in Eichstatt / Karl
Josef Schattner.
Room in a college library.
Architect: K. Schattner.
DER ARCHITEKT 1990 Sept., no.9,
p.400, photos.

SCHATZL, LOTHAR
Militarflug: der ehemalige
Militarflughafen Schleissheim /
Lothar Schatzl.
Architects: Reichert, Pranschke,
Maluche.
DEUTSCHE BAUZEITUNG 1990 Aug.,
v.124, no.11, p.133-134, model,
site plans, aerial photos.

SCHAUDT, HERBERT, 1933-
High-technisches Rathaus:
Erweiterung Verwaltungsgebaude
Laube in Konstanz.
Architect: Herbert Schaudt.
BAUWELT 1990 May 4, v.81, no.4,
p.848-850, photos., plans, secn.
Das Rathaus in Dorf Lassen: Umbau
und Sanierung Rathaus in
Dunningen.
Architect: Herbert Schaudt.
BAUWELT 1990 May 4, v.81, no.4,
p.857-859, photos., plans, secns.

SCHAUR, EDA
Architetture per la gente =
Architectures for the people /
Yona Friedman, Eda Schaur.
Includes essay by Friedman
entitled, convivial monuments and
an article on the Museum of Simple
Technology, Madras, India.
Architects: Eda Schaur, Yona
Friedman.
SPAZIO E SOCIETA 1990 Apr.-June,
v.13, no.50, p.56-65, ports.,
photos., sketches.
Tecnologie semplici a Madras =
Madras Museum of Simple Technology
/ Albert Stevens.
Architects: Yona Friedman, Eda
Schaur.
L'ARCA 1990 Feb., no.35, p.44-51,
axonometric view, elevs., photos,
plans, secns.

SCHAWELKA, KARL
Ut hortus poesis. Die Gartenkunst
des Ian Finlay = Ut hortus poesis.
The garden art of Ian Hamilton
Finlay / Karl Schawelka.
Stonypath (Little Sparta) garden,
Lanarkshire, Scotland.
DAIDALOS 1990 Dec.15, no.38,
p.80-89, photos.

SCHECHNER, RICHARD
Behavior, performance, and
performance space: an interview
with Richard Schechner.
Conducted by the editors of
Perspecta in New York, Spring
1988.
PERSPECTA 1990, no.26, p.97-102.

SCHEDIVY, EWALD
Osterreichische Konservatorentagung
vom 18. bis 22. September 1989 in
Tirol / Wolfgang Czerny, Eqald
Schedivy.
OSTERREICHISCHE ZEITSCHRIFT FUR
KUNST UND DENKMALPFLEGE 1990,
v.44, no.1-2, p.118-125, ill.,
photo., engr.

SCHEELE, PETER
Regierungsprasidium und
Staatstheater Kassel / Jurgen
Noll.
Results of competition, for
addition to a public building,
announced in Dec.1989. First
prize: Bieling und Bieling.
Second prize: Gerber und Partner.
Third prize: Peter Scheele.
BAUWELT 1990 Jan.19, v.81, no.2-3,
p.63, models.
Zentralbetriebshof Dortmund.
Competition. First prize: Peter
Scheele.
BAUWELT 1990 July 27, v.81, no.28,
p.1408, secn., model, site plans.

SCHEEMAKERS, PETER, 1691-1781
Lord Shelburne's 'costly fabrick':
Scheemakers, Roubiliac and Taylor
as rivals / Malcolm Baker.
"The monument by Peter Scheemakers
to Henry Petty, 1st Earl of
Shelburne at High Wycombe is among
the largest and most costly
monuments to have been erected in
an English parish church in the
18th century."
BURLINGTON MAGAZINE 1990 Dec.,
v.132, no.1053, p.841-848, ill.,
dwg., photos., refs.

SCHEERBART, PAUL, 1863-1915
Architetture di luce = Architectures
of light / Marino Ferrari.
On glass architecture. Includes
text of a letter from Paul
Scheerbart to Bruno Taut on the
"house of glass", dated 1914.
FRAMES, PORTE & FINESTRE 1990
July-Sept., no.28, p.68-73,
photos.
Lektionen uber das Gleichgewicht:
Luftvergnugen um 1920 = Lectures
on the Equilibrium: aerial
pleasures at around 1920 / Ulrich
Conrads.
DAIDALOS 1990 Sept.15, no.37,
p.72-77, ill., refs.

SCHEEREN, DIETER
Im spitzen Winkel: eine Apotheke in
Karlsruhe.
Architect: Andreas Winkler with
Dieter Scheeren.
ARCHITEKTUR, INNENARCHITEKTUR,
TECHNISCHER AUSBAU 1990 Nov.,
v.98, no.11, p.58-60, photos.,
plan, isometric dwg.

SCHEFFLER & WARSCHAUER
Liebieghaus in Frankfurt/Main:
Museum alter Plastik.
Architects: Scheffler &
Warschauer. Includes English
summary.
BAUMEISTER 1990 Sept., v.87, no.9,
p.30-35, elevs., photos., secns.,
site plans, isometric dwgs.

SCHEFFLER, GISELHER
Futuristische Bau- und Burotechnik:
Werndls EOS in der neuen
Hauptverwaltung der EVT / Halina
Noll.
Architects: G. Scheffler, R.
Zinsmeister.
ARCHITEKTUR, INNENARCHITEKTUR,
TECHNISCHER AUSBAU 1990 Apr.,
v.98, no.4, p.108-110, photos.

SCHEIBER, DAEN
Kitchen strategies / Sally Clark.
Customized kitchen in 1902 San
Francisco house. Designer: Daen
Scheiber.
HOUSE BEAUTIFUL 1990 Dec., v.132,
no.12, p.64-67, ports., photos.,
plan.

SCHEIBLAUER, CHRISTINE
Entwicklungskonzept Hasenbergl /
Christine Scheiblauer, Reiner
Schmidt.
Large scale housing development
built in the 1960s in Munich.
Architects: E.M. Lang and
Wertz/Ottow. Includes English
summary and captions.
GARTEN UND LANDSCHAFT 1990, v.100,
no.4, p.39-45, axonometric views,
model, photos., secn., site plans,
aerial photos.

SCHEITLIN + SYFRIG
Wohn-und Geschaftshaus "Emmenbaum",
Emmenbrucke LU.
Architects: A. Scheitlin + M.
Syfrig.
WERK, BAUEN + WOHNEN 1990 May,
no.5, p.1-4, photos., plans,
secn., table, aerial photo.

SCHELL, HEINRICH
Gestaltung von Strassen, Gassen und
Platzen im Altstadtbereich von
Passau = Design of streets, alleys
and squares in the old town of
Passau.
Competition. Winning architects:
Werner Roth, Heinrich Schell,
Harald Wicke. Text in German.
ARCHITEKTUR + WETTBEWERBE 1990
Dec., no.144, p.64-67, site plans,
photos.

SCHEMMARI, ATTILIO
A proposito di un libro su Milano
[interview and review] / Stefano
Boeri.
Interview with Attilio Schemmari
and discussion of a supplement to
Domus, no.711 (Dec.1989) edited by
Luca Basso Peressut and Ilaria
Valente, "Milano: architetture per
la citta 1980-1990".
CASABELLA 1990 Apr., v.54, no.567,
p.34-36, ill.

SCHEMNITZ, PHILIP
  Feminism's cultural commodity:
    assessing the Frida Kahlo Bar /
    Brenda Marshall.
  On the appropriation of Kahlo's
    paintings in the example of the
    1990 bar in the Santa Fe
    Restaurant Bar, Melbourne,
    Australia, designed by Dale
    Jones-Evans and Philip Schemnitz.
    The murals were painted by Sara
    Curtis.
  TRANSITION 1990, no.33, p.60-67,
    ill., photos., refs.

SCHEMPP, DIETER
  Konzentrierte Energie: Wettbewerb:
    Energie-Informations centrum (EIC)
    der Stadtwerke Rottweil.
  1st prize: LOG ID, D. Schempp, K.
    Miebach.
  ARCH PLUS 1990 July, no.104, p.45,
    model, plan, secns.

SCHENCK, FREYA S.
  El puerto de Hamburgo, centro
    dinamico de mercancias para la
    Europa septentrional / W. Becker,
    F. S. Schenck.
  URBANISMO / COAM 1990 May, no.10,
    p.104-117, chart, graphs, maps,
    photos., plans, secns., site
    plans, tables, aerial photos.

SCHENDEL, MARK
  Karlsruhe: Centre des Arts et des
    Technologies / Dominique Boudet.
    Architects: Rem Koolhaas, with
    Xaveer de Geyter, Heike Lohmann,
    Rients Dijtestra, Alex Wall,
    Christophe Cornubert, Georges
    Heintz, Mark Schendel, Ron
    Steiner.
  LE MONITEUR ARCHITECTURE AMC 1990
    Feb., no.8, p.12-13, dwgs., plans,
    secns.

SCHENTKE, KURT
  Oase fur Deutsche: Neubau eines
    Dienst- und eines
    Dienst-Wohngebaudes der Deutschen
    Botschaft in Riyadh/Saudi-Arabien.
    Architect: Kurt Schentke.
  ARCHITEKTUR, INNENARCHITEKTUR,
    TECHNISCHER AUSBAU 1990 May, v.98,
    no.5, p.58-59, photos., site plan.

SCHERF, GUILHEM
  Un monument meconnu: le mausolee de
    Charles-Joseph de Pollinchove par
    Christophe-Gabriel Allegrain
    (1710-1795) / Guilhem Scherf.
    Located in the Eglise
    Saint-Pierre, Douai.
  SOCIETE DE L'HISTOIRE DE L'ART
    FRANCAIS. BULLETIN 1990,
    p.[117]-130, dwgs., photos.

SCHERRER, OLIVIER
  Afghan refugee housing / Olivier
    Scherrer.
  The author, a French architect,
    went to Afgan refugee camps in
    northern Pakistan to assess a
    program begun in 1987 by
    ACROTERRE.
  MIMAR: ARCHITECTURE IN DEVELOPMENT
    1990 Mar., v.10, no.1 (34),
    p.[42]-49, axonometric views, map,
    photos., plans, secns.

SCHEUER, JOAN G.
  Searching for the Phoenicians in
    Sardinia / Joan G. Scheuer.
  BIBLICAL ARCHAEOLOGY REVIEW 1990
    Jan.-Feb., v.16, no.1, p.[52]-60,
    map, photos., refs.

SCHEUNER, BRUNO
  Hexenturm Sarnen, Obwalden.
  Built 1985-86. Architect: Bruno
    Scheuner.
  WERK, BAUEN + WOHNEN 1990 Dec.,
    no.12, p.1-4, axonometric view,
    photos., plans, secn.

SCHEVING, HANS
  "Jerusalem in England"/ Hans
    Schering.
  ARKITEKTEN 1990 Sept., v.92,
    no.13, p.[412]-421, ill., dwgs.,
    port., elevs., models, maps,
    photos., secns., site plans.

SCHICK, AUGUST
  Larm.
  Issue features ten articles on
    aspects of sound, including
    standards, psychological factors,
    insulation, sound sculpture
    (including one 45 rpm record, "Mut
    zur Fuge"), noise in housing
    units, and noise pollution.
    Authors: Joachim-Ernst Berendt,
    Dorothea Baumann, Gerd Jansen,
    August Schick, Jurgen Becker,
    Gustav Kilian Ringel, Wolfgang
    Moll, Ralf Kurer, and Martin
    Kirchner.
  BAUWELT 1990 May 25, v.81, no.20,
    p.980-1014, graphs, map, photos.,
    tables, refs.

SCHICK, LESLIE MERAL
  A note on the dating of the mosque
    of Rustem Pasa in Istanbul /
    Leslie Meral Schick.
  Argues that the mosque was
    constructed in 1561 under Sinan
    and may have been completed in or
    after 1562.
  ARTIBUS ASIAE 1990, v.50, no.3-4,
    p.285-288, refs.

SCHICKEL, RICHARD
  James Cagney: Yankee doodle dandy's
    Best Actor / Richard Schickel.
  Features interiors of his 1939
    home in Coldwater Canyon.
  ARCHITECTURAL DIGEST 1990 Apr.,
    v.47, no.4, p.184-185,290, ports.,
    photos.
  Mary Pickford and Douglas Fairbanks,
    Sr.: the fabled house of
    Hollywood's royal couple / Richard
    Schickel.
  Pickfair, Beverly Hills, was
    remodeled in 1925 by Wallace Neff.
  ARCHITECTURAL DIGEST 1990 Apr.,
    v.47, no.4, p.148-149, ports.,
    photo, aerial photo.
  Norma Shearer and Irving G.
    Thalberg: the Santa Monica beach
    house of a Hollywood genius and
    his leading lady / Richard
    Schickel.
  ARCHITECTURAL DIGEST 1990 Apr.,
    v.47, no.4, p.218-[221],300,
    ports., photos.

SCHICKEL, RICHARD (CONTINUED)
  Warner Baxter: Bel-Air mansion of
    enigmatic best actor for In old
    Arizona / Richard Schickel.
  Tudor revival home built in 1933.
  ARCHITECTURAL DIGEST 1990 Apr.,
    v.47, no.4, p.170-172, port.,
    photos.
  William Powell: sophisticated wit of
    My man Godfrey and The thin man /
    Richard Schickel.
  Features Beverly Hills mansion
    designed by James Dolena.
  ARCHITECTURAL DIGEST 1990 Apr.,
    v.47, no.4, p.152-155, port.,
    photos.

SCHIEDHELM, MANFRED, 1934-
  Sanierung des Alten Chemiegebaudes
    der TU-Berlin = Refurbishment of
    old chemistry building, Technical
    University, Berlin.
    Architects: Manfred Schiedhelm,
    Karen Axelrad.
  DETAIL 1990 Oct.-Nov., v.30, no.5,
    p.490-493, axonometric views,
    dets., photos., plans.
  Sparsam: Wohnungsbau in
    Berlin-Lichtenrade, Loptener
    Strasse.
  Sections 2 and 3 of an apartment
    complex between Bahnhof Strasse
    and Loptener Strasse. Architects:
    Manfred Schiedhelm, Karen S.
    Axelrad.
  BAUWELT 1990 Oct.26, v.81, no.40,
    p.2050-2053, axonometric view,
    photos., plans, secn., site plan.

SCHIERLE, GOTTHILF G.
  Frei Otto at USC / Gotthilf G.
    Schierle.
  Report on his address entitled:
    The new plurality in architecture.
  L. A. ARCHITECT 1990 Apr., p.1,
    photo.

SCHIFFMAN, BONNIE, B.1951?-
  Portrait of a home / Michael Small.
  Four American photographers' views
    of the interior of their homes:
    Erica Lennard, Barbara Kasten,
    Jean Pagliuso, and Bonnie
    Schiffman. Three are in New York,
    one is in West Hollywood, Calif.
  METROPOLITAN HOME 1990 May, v.22,
    no.5, p.[111-121], dets., ports.,
    photos.

SCHIJNDEL, MART VAN
  Uitbreiding Centraal Museum
    [Utrecht].
  Addition to 1921 building.
    Architect: Mart van Schijndel.
  DE ARCHITECT 1990 Jan., v.21,
    no.1, p.12-13, axonometric view,
    photo., site plan.

SCHILT, JEROEN
  Banaler's maken vorst tegen
    kunststoframen: Dudoks Witte Dorp
    in Eindhoven [exhibition review] /
    Jeroen Schilt.
  Exhibition in the Van Abbemuseum,
    until 6 Nov.1989; sponsored by
    Witte Dorp De Burgh. Architect:
    W.M. Dudok.
  ARCHIS 1989 Oct., no.10, p.4,
    dwgs., photos.

SCHILT, JEROEN (CONTINUED)
Docomomo and conventions: een
enthousiaste waakhond / Jeroen
Schilt.
Report on international conference
held Sept.14, 1990, in Eindhoven.
Sponsor: International working
party for documentation and
conservation of buildings, sites
and neighborhoods of the Modern
Movement.
ARCHIS 1990 Oct., no.10, p.2,
photos.
Eindhoven hoed u!: Bakema's woonwijk
't Hool bedreigd / Jeroen Schilt.
In conjunction with an exhibition
in Eindhoven, discusses the design
(1961-1972) of the apartment
complex in Eindhoven-Noord.
ARCHIS 1990 Sept., no.9, p.2,
photo., site plan, sketches.
Gooiland: verplichte kost
[exhibition review] / Jeroen
Schilt.
On the restoration of Modern
Movement buildings in the
Netherlands, including Duiker's
Gooiland in Hilversum (restoration
architects: Van Klooster and Van
Velsen). Exhibition opened on
Sept. 27, 1990.
ARCHIS 1990 Nov., no.11, p.3,
photo.

SCHIMMELSCHMIDT, MICHAEL
Breathing life into housing /
Michael Schimmelschmidt.
On the ecological, self-build,
timber-frame houses designed by
Keystone Architects & Designers
Co-operative for the Findhorn
Foundation, Scotland.
RIBA JOURNAL 1990 Nov., v.97,
no.11, p.56-58, photo., plan,
secn.

SCHINDEL UND KAHLE
Umbau eines Wasserturmes in Hamburg
Lokstedt = Conversion of a water
tower in Hamburg Lokstedt.
Conversion of water tower into a
house. Architects: Siegfried
Geisler, Schindel und Kahle.
ARCHITEKTUR + WETTBEWERBE 1989
Dec., no.140, p.25, photos., plan.

SCHINDLER, NORBERT
Ein Garten als Museumsobjekt:
Probleme und Gedanken am Beispiel
eines chinesischen Gartens im
Metropolitan Museum of Art in New
York / Norbert Schindler.
GARTEN UND LANDSCHAFT 1990, v.100,
no.4, p.4-6, photos.
Der Skulpturengarten des "Museum of
Modern Art" in New York: ein
Garten als Museumsmitte / Norbert
Schindler.
GARTEN UND LANDSCHAFT 1990, v.100,
no.10, p.5-6, photo., plan.

SCHINKEL, KARL FRIEDRICH, 1781-1841
Classical exemplar: Collection of
architectural designs including
designs which have been executed
and objects whose execution was
intended, by Karl Friedrich
Schinkel [book review] / James
Stevens Curl.
Translation and reprint of
Sammlung Architektonischer
Entwurfe, Berlin, 1866.
(Continued next column)

SCHINKEL, KARL FRIEDRICH, 1781-1841
(CONTINUED)
Classical exemplar:... (CONTINUED)
ROYAL SOCIETY OF ARTS, LONDON. RSA
JOURNAL 1990 Apr., v.138, no.5405,
p.377.
Die Einrichtung des Alten Museums in
Berlin anmerkungen zu einem neu
entdeckten Schinkel-Dokument /
Reinhard Wegner.
JAHRBUCH DER BERLINER MUSEEN 1989,
v.31, p.[265]-287, plans, engrs.,
refs.
Farbfassung und Raumerlebnis /
Gottfried Grafe.
Restoration of interior and glass
of Schinkel's Wedersche Kirche,
Berlin. German, Russian, English
and French summaries, p.55-56.
ARCHITEKTUR DER DDR 1990 Jan.,
v.38, no.1, p.17-20, photos.,
dwg., elev., refs.
Karl Friedrich Schinkel Lebenswerk
[book review] / Erik Forssman.
1989 book edited by Margarethe
Kuhn.
ZEITSCHRIFT FUR KUNSTGESCHICHTE
1990, v.55, no.30, p.408-413.
Quality vs. history: Schinkel's
Altes Museum and Prussian arts
policy / Steven Moyano.
ART BULLETIN 1990 Dec., v.72,
no.4, p.[585]-608, dwgs., elevs.,
photos., plans, secns., engrs.,
biblio., refs.
Zur Restaurierung der Werderschen
Kirche Berlin / Peter Brenn.
Original architect: K.F. Schinkel.
German, Russian, English and
French summaries, p.55-56.
ARCHITEKTUR DER DDR 1990 Jan.,
v.38, no.1, p.15-16, dwgs.,
photos., plan, secn.

SCHINKEL, KARL FRIEDRICH, 1781-1841.
COLLECTION OF ARCHITECTURAL DESIGNS
INCLUDING DESIGNS WHICH HAVE BEEN
EXECUTED AND OBJECTS WHOSE EXECUTION
WAS INTENDED
Classical exemplar: Collection of
architectural designs including
designs which have been executed
and objects whose execution was
intended, by Karl Friedrich
Schinkel [book review] / James
Stevens Curl.
Translation and reprint of
Sammlung Architektonischer
Entwurfe, Berlin, 1866.
ROYAL SOCIETY OF ARTS, LONDON. RSA
JOURNAL 1990 Apr., v.138, no.5405,
p.377.

SCHINKEL, KARL FRIEDRICH, 1781-1841.
SAMMLUNG ARCHITEKTONISCHER ENTWURFE
Classical exemplar: Collection of
architectural designs including
designs which have been executed
and objects whose execution was
intended, by Karl Friedrich
Schinkel [book review] / James
Stevens Curl.
Translation and reprint of
Sammlung Architektonischer
Entwurfe, Berlin, 1866.
ROYAL SOCIETY OF ARTS, LONDON. RSA
JOURNAL 1990 Apr., v.138, no.5405,
p.377.

SCHIPPERS, JO
Hofhaus in Kralingen.
Architects: Rem Koolhaas, et al.
Includes English summary.
BAUMEISTER 1990 Nov., v.87, no.11,
p.56-57, photos., plans.

SCHIRMER, WULF
Some aspects of building at the
'aceramic-neolithic' settlement of
Cayonu Tepesi [Turkey] / Wulf
Schirmer.
WORLD ARCHAEOLOGY 1990 Feb., v.21,
no.3, p.[363]-387, axonometric
view, dets., figs., photos.,
plans, site plans, reconst. dwgs.,
isometric dwgs., aerial photos.,
refs.

SCHJETNAN GARDUNO, MARIO
Arquitetura e paisagem em centro
cultural no Mexico: Centro
Cultural Mexicano, Toluca, Mexico.
Architects: Garduno, Maldonado,
Romero (Grupo de Diseno Urbano).
PROJETO 1989 Apr., no.120,
p.60-65, elevs., photos., plans,
secns.
Centro Cultural Mexiquense: un
proyecto integral de arquitectura,
urbanismo y paisaje.
In Toluca, Mexico. Architects:
Grupo de Diseno Urbano, M.
Schjetnan Garduno, J.L. Perez
Maldonado, G. Gomez Palacio, V.
Monsivais Rodriguez, P. Ramirez
Vasquez, A. Giovanini Garcia.
PROA 1988 Nov., no.377, p.22-25,
elevs., photos., plans, site
plans.

SCHLEDER MACHADO, NINO ROBERTO
Forum municipal de Passo Fundo.
Architects: Machado, Nobre,
Tramontini.
PROJETO 1990 [June]., no.132,
p.40-41, photos., plans, secns.

SCHLEE, HANNAH
Character references / Hannah
Schlee.
Interiors of Bernard Van Meer's
London apartment. Interior
designer: Carlos Villanueva
Brandt.
THE WORLD OF INTERIORS 1990 May,
p.112-119, photos.

SCHLEPER, THOMAS
Architekturgeschichte rigoros:
Rathauser fur Burger als
Sprechblasenbabys -- Martin Damus
uber gemeindliche Bauten
vermeintlicher Selbstverwaltung
[book review] / Thomas Schleper.
Review of Martin Damus, Das
Rathaus: Architektur und
Sozialgeschichte von der
Grunderzeit zur Postmoderne.
KRITISCHE BERICHTE 1989, v.17,
no.1, p.90-95, refs.

SCHLIEBITZ, HANS-WERNER
Erste Preise: Kirchen.
Three projects: plans for chapel,
Stiftung Kloster Frenswegen,
Nordhorn (architect: Hans Busso
von Busse); Catholic church and
parish hall, Mossingen (architect:
Wolfgang Liese-Grasser); Catholic
church and regional offices,
Ravensburg-Sonnenbuchel
(Continued next page)

SCHLIEBITZ, HANS-WERNER (CONTINUED)
Erste Preise: Kirchen. (CONTINUED)
(architects: Bert Perlia,
Hans-Werner Schliebitz, Jurgen
Schwarz).
DEUTSCHES ARCHITEKTENBLATT 1990
Dec.1, v.22, no.12, p.1831-1834,
elevs., models, plans, secn., site
plans.

SCHLOSSER
See CASTLES

SCHMERTZ, MILDRED F.
Japanese imports / Mildred F.
Schmertz.
Eight recent projects in Japan
designed by American architects.
ARCHITECTURE: THE AIA JOURNAL 1990
Sept., v.79, no.9, p.72-[75], 154,
ill., elevs., models.
Pride of place: the Humboldt Library
by Moore Ruble Yudell / Mildred F.
Schmertz.
In the Tegel Harbor development of
West Berlin.
ARCHITECTURAL RECORD 1990 Jan.,
v.178, no.1, p.100-107, dets.,
dwg., elev., photos., plan,
secns., site plans.
Urban realism: Landsman/Holzman
Loft, New York City, Andrea
Landsman/Malcolm Holzman,
Architects / Mildred F. Schmertz.
ARCHITECTURE: THE MAGAZINE OF THE
AMERICAN INSTITUTE OF ARCHITECTS
1990 June, v.79, no.6, p.[86-89],
photos., plan.

SCHMID, ANDREAS
Place du Marche in Bex, Schweiz =
Place du Marche in Bex,
Switzerland.
Competition. First prize winners:
Pierre Plancherel, Andreas Schmid.
Text in German.
ARCHITEKTUR + WETTBEWERBE 1990
Dec., no.144, p.88-89, dwg.,
elev., model, site plans.

SCHMIDHUBER, KLAUS
Zooabteilung Niederurseler Hang in
Frankfurt = Zoological district
Niederurseler Hang in Frankfurt.
Competition. Winning architects:
Gottfried Hansjakob, Anton
Hansjakob, Klaus Schmidhuber. Text
in German.
ARCHITEKTUR + WETTBEWERBE 1990
Mar., no.141, p.23-31, axonometric
views, dwgs., plans, secns., site
plans, isometric dwgs.

SCHMIDT, ALBERT J.
Masterpieces in wood: houses of
worship in Ukraine [by] Titus D.
Hewryk [and] the wooden
architecture of Russia; houses,
fortifications, churches [by]
Alexander Opolovnikov, Yelena
Opolovnikova [book review] /
Albert J. Schmidt.
SOCIETY OF ARCHITECTURAL
HISTORIANS, JOURNAL 1990 Dec.,
v.49, no.4, p.460-462.

SCHMIDT, CLAUS M.
Det kinesiske Lysthus.
The late 18th cent. Chinese
pavilion in the garden at
Frederiksberg Castle (architect:
Andreas Kirkerup). Restoration
architects: Ole Priskorn, Vilhelm
Wohlert. Includes an
art-historical commentary on the
restoration (by Claus M. Schmidt)
and English and German summaries.
ARKITEKTUR DK 1990, v.34, no.7,
p.344-350, elevs., photos., plans,
secns., site plans.

SCHMIDT, DIETRICH
Das Haus der jungen Pioniere in
Kalinin: zur Wiederentdeckung
eines Gebaudes von Iwan Leonidow /
Dietrich Schmidt.
Built 1937-39, in Estonia.
ARCHITHESE 1990 July-Aug., v.20,
no.4, p.37-39, elev., photos.,
plans, biblio.

SCHMIDT, EIKE
Friedhof Neuried bei Munchen / Eike
Schmidt, Gerrit Stahr.
Competition for a chapel and
landscaped cemetery. Winners:
Christoph Brandt and Schmidt and
Stahr. Includes English summary.
GARTEN UND LANDSCHAFT 1989, v.99,
no.12, p.40-43, dwgs., photos.,
site plan.

SCHMIDT, GORM, 1939-
Gravminder: konkurrence om
udformning af nye gravmindetyper /
Susanne Guldager.
Results of a 1989 competition
sponsored by the Danish Society
for Graveyard Culture. First
prize: Lene Lunghoj. Second
prizes: Gorm Schmidt, and others.
Includes English summary and
captions.
LANDSKAB 1990 Dec., v.71, no.8,
p.129-132,152, dwgs., photos.

SCHMIDT, GOTZ
Filigrane Raumbegrenzung:
Erweiterung und Umbau der
Raiffeisenbank Hassfurt.
Architect: Gotz Schmidt.
ARCHITEKTUR, INNENARCHITEKTUR,
TECHNISCHER AUSBAU 1990 Apr.,
v.98, no.4, p.58-63, photos.,
plans, secns.

SCHMIDT, HAMMER OG LASSEN
Tre jyske trykkerier.
Three printing plants: Aarhuus
Stiftsbogtrykkerie, Hasselager;
Scanoprint, Viby J; Stibo Graphic,
Horsens. Architects: Sohmidt,
Hammer & Lassen. Includes English
and German summaries.
ARKITEKTUR DK 1990, v.34, no.3,
p.89-101, dwg., elevs., photos.,
plans, site plans.

SCHMIDT, HANS, 1893 1972
"Das Werk dieses Kommunisten lohnt
sich nicht zu erhalten / Ursula
Suter.
On the renovation of the 1928 Haus
"zum Neuen Singer," in Basel.
Original architects: Artaria &
Schmidt.
ARCHITHESE 1990 July-Aug., v.20,
no.4, p.73-74, photos.

SCHMIDT, HANS-PETER
Ideenwettbewerb "Weiterentwicklung
des industriellen Wohnungsbaus" /
Carl Krause.
Presents 18 projects, including
winning ones by Hans-Georg
Vollmar, Ch. Dielitzsch,
Hans-Peter Schmidt, and Jorg
Bohringer. German, Russian,
English and French summaries,
p.55-56.
ARCHITEKTUR DER DDR 1990 Feb.,
v.38, no.2, p.17-33, axonometric
views, elevs., photos., plans,
secns., site plans.

SCHMIDT, J. MARK
Tailored to suit: Johnston residence
/ J. Mark Schmidt.
West Des Moines, Iowa. Architect:
Lon Sinclair.
IOWA ARCHITECT 1990 Summer, v.39,
no.2, p.18-[19], photos., plan.

SCHMIDT, JOACHIM
Der Kreuznimbus im Christusbild /
Joachim Schmidt.
Includes the 15th cent. wall
paintings in San Nicolao in
Giornico, Switzerland.
DAS MUNSTER 1990, v.43, no.1,
p.20-28, photos.

SCHMIDT, JORN PALLE, 1923-
Gronne strukturer.
Several Danish landscape projects
since the 1950s by Aksel Andersen,
J. P. Schmidt, C.Th. Sorensen,
Michael Bellham, and Norgard,
Harboe, Ginman and others.
ARKITEKTUR DK 1990, v.34, no.4,
p.199-205, dwgs., photos., plans,
site plans.
Haver til huse.
A sculpture garden, Andreas
Brunn's own garden and one at a
farmhouse in Ulkerup by J. P.
Schmidt and Agnete Muusfeldt.
ARKITEKTUR DK 1990, v.34, no.4,
p.208-213, dwg., photos., plans,
site plans, isometric dwg.
Lovvaerk [Foliage] / Agnete
Muusfeldt, J.Palle Schmidt.
Photographic views and commentary
on several Danish gardens from the
late 1970s and 1980s. Includes
English summary and captions.
LANDSKAB 1990 Dec., v.71, no.8,
p.133-141,152, photos.
Mindesteder.
Memorial cemeteries in Naestved,
Skansebakken, and Frederikshaven;
the Ryvang military cemetery
(architect: Kaj Gottlob, landscape
architect: Aksel Andersen); the
1964 Herning cemetery (architect:
K. Joos, landscape architect: J.
P. Schmidt); the 1984 cemetry
extension in Greve (landscape
architect: Andreas Bruun). In
Danish and English.
ARKITEKTUR DK 1990, v.34, no.4,
p.188-198, dwgs., models, photos.,
plans, site plans.

SCHMIDT-KIRCHBERG, BARBARA, 1936-
Stadtmuseum Steinfurt: historische
Perspektiven in begrentztem Raum.
Architect: Barbara
Schmidt-Kirchberg.
DEUTSCHE BAUZEITUNG 1990 Jan.,
v.124, no.1, p.56-53, photos.,
plans, isometric dwg.

SCHMIDT, KURT
Technologiepark Universitat Bremen.
Architects: Gert Schulze and
Heinrich Campe; Hochbauamt Bremen;
Wolfram Dahms; Haslob Hartlich
Schutz; Oswald M. Ungers;
Rosengart + Partner; Kurt Schmidt.
Includes English summary.
BAUMEISTER 1990 Dec., v.87, no.12,
p.32-41, photos., plans, secns.,
site plans, aerial photos.

SCHMIDT, REINER
Entwicklungskonzept Hasenbergl /
Christine Scheiblauer, Reiner
Schmidt.
Large scale housing development
built in the 1960s in Munich.
Architects: E.M. Lang and
Wertz/Ottow. Includes English
summary and captions.
GARTEN UND LANDSCHAFT 1990, v.100,
no.4, p.39-45, axonometric views,
model, photos., secn., site plans,
aerial photos.

SCHMIDT, ROLF
Kontrapunkt: Museum und Stadtarchiv
der Stadt Eschborn/Taunus.
Architect: Rolf Schmidt.
ARCHITEKTUR, INNENARCHITEKTUR,
TECHNISCHER AUSBAU 1990 July-Aug.,
v.98, no.7-8, p.44-46, model,
photos., plans.

SCHMIDT, SCHICKETANZ UND PARTNER
Energiezentrale Flughafen Munchen II
= Services Centre Airport Munich
II.
Architects: Schmidt-Schicketanz
und Partner.
DETAIL 1990 Dec.-1991 Jan., v.30,
no.6, p.594-596, dets., dwgs.,
photos., plan, site plans.
Famose Grosse: Zwischenbericht vom
Flughafen Munchen II im Erdinger
Moos / Ursula Baus.
Architects: von Busse & Partner
Blees, Buch, Kampmann; Auer und
Weber; Schmidt, Schicketanz und
Partner; Planungsburo Buschl.
DEUTSCHE BAUZEITUNG 1990 Nov.,
v.124, no.11, p.28-39, dets.,
models, maps, photos., plan,
secns., site plans, aerial photo.
Stadt und Verkehr.
Special issue on towns and
traffic. 22 projects illustrated.
English summary, p.53.
BAUMEISTER 1990 Aug., v.87, no.8,
p.13-53, dwgs., models, photos.,
plans, secns., site plans, aerial
photos.

SCHMIDT, THOMAS
Grundtypen und Elemente der
Olympia-Stadien: eine
chronologische Ubersicht / Thomas
Schmidt.
BAUWELT 1990 June 29, v.81, no.24,
p.1208-1214, photos., secns.,
aerial photos.

SCHMIDT, ULRICH
Vom "Optiker-Laden" zum Augenoptiker
- Fachgeschaft: Zeitgemasse
Modernisierung in Wesel.
Architects: Ulrich Schmidt, Roland
Viehl.
ARCHITEKTUR, INNENARCHITEKTUR,
TECHNISCHER AUSBAU 1989 Sept.,
v.97, no.9, p.74-76, photos.,
plan.

SCHMIEDEL, KARLHEINZ
Der Preis des Deutschen Stahlbaues
'90 / Karlheinz Schmiedel.
DEUTSCHE BAUZEITUNG 1990 Nov.,
v.124, no.11, p.141-144, photos.

SCHMIKL, ROBERT, 1903-1977
Robert Schmikl I.A. L.I.A. argitek /
Anton E. du Toit.
Viennse architect who worked in
Pretoria, 1940-80. In Africaans,
with English summary.
ARCHITECTUUR SA = ARGITEKTUUR SA
1989 May-June, no.5-6, p.37-38,
port., photos., biblio., refs.

SCHMIT, JEAN-FRANCOIS
Fins de Chantier.
Contents: Commercial building,
Pau, France; architect:
Jean-Jacques Cachau -- Post
office, Saint-Germain-les-Corbeil,
France; architect: Jean-Francois
Schmit -- Extension of L'Institut
Universitaire de Technologie,
Cergy-Pontoise, France; architect:
Michel Remon, Laura Carducci,
Rodolphe Picollet -- Exhibition
installation, Hamburg, West
Germany; architect: Josef Paul
Kleihues -- Vitra museum, Weil am
Rhein, West Germany; architects:
Frank O. Gehry & Associates.
LE MONITEUR ARCHITECTURE AMC 1990
Feb., no.8, p.14-19, elevs.,
photos., plans, secns.
Petits projets in the provinces /
Marie-Helene Contal.
10 new projects in the French
provinces.
ARCHITECTURAL REVIEW 1990 May,
v.187, no.1119, p.44-64,
axonometric views, elevs.,
photos., plans, secns., site
plans.
La Porte, une strategie de
l'accueil.
Features four new French post
offices in various areas: Charmes,
Saint-Germain-les-Corbeil,
Chaville and Puteaux.
TECHNIQUES ET ARCHITECTURE 1990
Aug.-Sept., no.391, p.50-54,
axonometric view, photos., plans.

SCHMIT, JEAN PHILIPPE, 1790-
The "Gothic", the revolution and the
abyss: Jean-Philippe Schmit's
aesthetic of authority / Michael
Paul Driskel.
ART HISTORY 1990 June, v.13, no.2,
p.193-211, dwgs., engrs., refs.

SCHMITGES, HORST, 1939-
The green house effect / Anthony
Paine.
Features two projects by Horst
Schmitges: social housing,
Monchengladbach-Ronneter and the
Reisen house, Viersen.
ARCHITECTURAL REVIEW 1990 Sept.,
(Continued next column)

SCHMITGES, HORST, 1939- (CONTINUED)
The green house...(CONTINUED)
v.188, no.1123, p.54-58,
axonometric view, photos., plans.

SCHMITT, ADOLF
Stadt - Teil der Landschaft.
Okologischer stadtumbau fur die
Zukunft / Adolf Schmitt.
Introductory remarks given early
in 1990 by the president of the
BDLA at the Landestag NW.
DEUTSCHES ARCHITEKTENBLATT 1990
Oct.1, v.22, no.10, p.1547,

SCHMITT, ARMIN
Wohin mit dem Schrott?: Denkmaler
der Industriekultur im Saarland /
Armin Schmitt.
Introduction to theme issue on
this industrial region of Germany.
11 articles indexed separately.
DEUTSCHE BAUZEITUNG 1990 Mar.,
v.124, no.3, p.14-23, ill.,
photos., site plans.

SCHMITT, FREDERICK
Additions and alterations / Regan
Young, Robert Cerutti.
On the architect's job of adding
to existing structures. Examples
of 12 projects in and near New
Jersey by New Jersey architects:
Katz Novoa Architects and
Planners; John DeFazio; Michael
Burns; Frederick Schmitt; Michael
Ryan Architects; Sykes O'Connor
Salerno Hazaveh; Parette and
Associates; Nadaskay Kopelson;
Michael Graves; Carla Bonacci;
Robert N. Auld; and Albert F.
Zaccone.
ARCHITECTURE NEW JERSEY 1990,
v.26, no.5, p.9-22, axonometric
view, ill., elevs., models,
photos., plans, secn.
Design awards [New Jersey Society of
Architects 1989 Design Awards
Competition].
Excellence in architecture awards
to The Hillier Group; Frederick
Schmitt; Michael Graves; Short and
Ford; Venturi, Rauch and Scott
Brown. Other awards also included.
ARCHITECTURE NEW JERSEY 1990,
v.26, no.1, p.9-24, axonometric
view, dwgs., elevs., models,
photos., plans, secns.

SCHMITT, GERHARD
Design support systems: die nachste
Generation des Computer Aided
Architectural Design / Gerhard
Schmitt, Ulrich Flemming, Leandro
Madrazo.
ARCHITHESE 1990 May-June, v.20,
no.3, p.28-31, ill.

SCHMITT, HARALD
Behindertengerechter Wohnbau /
Harald Schmitt.
Features pilot project to be built
in Berlin this summer.
DEUTSCHE BAUZEITSCHRIFT 1990 June,
v.38, no.6, p.879-880,883-804,
elevs., plans, site plans, refs.

AVERY INDEX TO ARCHITECTURAL PERIODICALS

SCHMITT, KASIMIR UND PARTNER
Noch ist alles offen - Raum als
Instrument: katholische Kirche St.
Judas Thaddaus in Karlsruhe -
Neureut / Ottokar Uhl, Bernd
Selbmann.
Architects: Ottokar Uhl, and
Schmitt, Kasimir und Partner.
KUNST UND KIRCHE 1990, no.1,
p.20-25, models, photos., plans.

SCHMITT, MARILYN. OBJECT-IMAGE-INQUIRY
Object-image inquiry: the art
historian at work [book review] /
Dora P. Crouch.
Authors: Elizabeth Bakewell,
William O. Beeman and Carol McM.
Reese. Editor: Marilyn Schmitt.
SOCIETY OF ARCHITECTURAL
HISTORIANS. JOURNAL 1990 Mar.,
v.49, no.1, p.120-122,

SCHMITZ, HEINZ
Anpassung von vorhandenen Bauteilen
an das Baurecht / Heinz Schmitz,
Norbert Stannek.
DEUTSCHES ARCHITEKTENBLATT 1990
Mar.1, v.22, no.1, p.389-392,
photos., refs.
Ausschreibung und Vergabe fur
Bauleistungen im Bestand (II) /
Heinz Schmitz.
Part I appeared in the Nov.1, 1989
issue of this journal.
DEUTSCHES ARCHITEKTENBLATT 1989
Dec.1, v.21, no.12, p.1849-1852,
photos.
Bauvorbereitung und
Bauleitungsempfehlungen / Heinz
Schmitz.
Advice on ways to prepare and
tools to use in renovation of
older buildings, from an architect
in Aachen.
DEUTSCHES ARCHITEKTENBLATT 1990
June 1, v.22, no.6, p.961-964,
966-967, photos., tables.
Geschosswohnungsbau (II): hohe
Qualitat, niedrige Kosten,
weitgehende Flexibilitat / Heinz
Schmitz.
Part I appeared in the Nov.1, 1989
issue of this journal.
DEUTSCHES ARCHITEKTENBLATT 1989
Dec.1, v.21, no.12, p.1841-1843,
photos.
Letzte Rettung?:
Altbaumodernisierung in der DDR /
Heinz Schmitz, Claus Sieverding.
DEUTSCHE BAUZEITUNG 1990 June,
v.124, no.6, p.110-126, elev.,
photos., plan, secns., tables.
Recycling von Abbruchmassen bei
Modernisierung / Heinz Schmitz,
Norbert Stannek.
On the disposal and recycling of
building materials removed during
renovations.
DEUTSCHES ARCHITEKTENBLATT 1990
July 1, v.22, no.7, p.1123-1126,
photos., tables, refs.
Schutz von Bauteilen bei
Modernisierungsmassnahmen / Heinz
Schmitz, Norbert Stannek.
Ways to protect building details
and parts during renovations.
DEUTSCHES ARCHITEKTENBLATT 1990
Apr.1, v.22, no.4, p.567-570,
photos.

SCHMITZ, HEINZ (CONTINUED)
Sinn und Zweck von Untersuchungen
zur Althaussanierung / Heinz
Schmitz.
DEUTSCHES ARCHITEKTENBLATT 1990
May 1, v.22, no.5, p.777-779,
photos., tables.
Weiterverwendung von elektrischen
Installationen / Heinz Schmitz,
Norbert Stannek.
DEUTSCHES ARCHITEKTENBLATT 1990
Nov.1, v.22, no.11, p.1725-1726,
photos.
Weiterverwendung von Heizungsanlagen
und Schornsteinen / Heinz Schmitz,
Norbert Stannek.
DEUTSCHES ARCHITEKTENBLATT 1990
Oct.1, v.22, no.10, p.1573-1574,
photos.
Weiterverwendung von sanitaren
Installationen / Heinz Schmitz,
Norbert Stannek.
DEUTSCHES ARCHITEKTENBLATT 1990
Sept.1, v.22, no.9, p.1337-1338,
photos.

SCHMITZ, JOSEPH
Fachhochschule Koblenz.
Report on competition. First
prize: Karl Eichler. Second
prize: Joseph Schmitz.
BAUWELT 1990 Mar.2, v.81, no.9,
p.366, models.

SCHMOLL, FRITZ
Metropolis Berlin? Prospects and
problems of post-November 1989
urban developments / Fritz
Schmoll.
INTERNATIONAL JOURNAL OF URBAN AND
REGIONAL RESEARCH 1990 Dec., v.14,
no.4, p.[676]-686, refs.

SCHMUCK, FRIEDRICH
Rekonstruktion des Cafe de Unie von
J.J.P. Oud / Friedrich Schmuck.
DEUTSCHE BAUZEITSCHRIFT 1990 Jan.,
v.38, no.1, p.101-104, axonometric
view, dwgs., photos., refs.

SCHMUTZ, LUKAS
Die Bruckenhaftigkeit eines Bahnhofs
= Une gare au caractere de pont /
Lukas Schmutz.
Bridges by Santiago Calatrava, in
relation to the Zurich Bahnhof
Stadelhofen.
ARCHITHESE 1990 Mar.-Apr., v.20,
no.2, p.70-83, photos.

SCHNARE, SUSAN E.
Lawrence Weaver,1876-1930: an
annotated bibliography [by]
Lawrence Trevelyan Weaver [book
review] / Susan E. Schnare.
SOCIETY OF ARCHITECTURAL
HISTORIANS. JOURNAL 1990 Dec.,
v.49, no.4, p.448-449,

SCHNEBLI + AMMANN + PARTNER
Svizzera anni '90: tre culture, tre
architetture = Switzerland 1990:
three cultures, three
architectures / Paolo Fumagalli.
Features projects by Jacques
Herzog and Pierre de Meuron; Livio
Vacchini; Atelier 5; Willi Egli;
Mario Botta; Jean-Jacques Oberson;
Giancarlo Durisch; Aurelio
Galfetti; Luigi Snozzi; Roger
Diener; Atelier Cube; Matti,
Burgi, Ragaz; Schnebli, Ammann &
(Continued next column)

SCHNEBLI + AMMANN + PARTNER
(CONTINUED)
Svizzera anni '90:...(CONTINUED)
Partner; R. Luscher; V. Mangeat;
S. Calatrava, A. Amsler, and W.
Rueger; Mario Campi and Franco
Pessina; and Peter Zumthor.
Includes an article by Werner
Jehle, "The mountain: painters,
engineers, and architects." Text
in Italian and English.
ABITARE 1990 Nov., no.290,
p.150-191, axonometric views,
dets., ill., elevs., maps,
photos., plans, secns., site
plans, sketch, aerial photo.
Wohnbebauung "im Buel" in Baar, CH =
Residential housing "Im Buel" in
Baar, CH.
Architects: Werner Egli + Hans
Rohr; Dolf Schnebli, Tobias Ammann
und Partner.
DETAIL 1990 Feb.-Mar., v.30, no.1,
p.34-37, dets., elevs., photos.,
plans, secns., site plans.
Wohnuberbauung "Unter der Halde",
Wurenlingen, 1988.
Architects: Schnebli und Ammann.
WERK, BAUEN + WOHNEN 1989 Dec.,
no.12, p.48, photo., plans, secn.,
site plan.

SCHNEBLI, DOLF, 1928-
Dolf Schnebli.
Most of issue devoted to the work
of this Swiss architect.
Introduction by Paolo Fumagalli.
Text in German, French and
English.
WERK, BAUEN + WOHNEN 1990 Dec.,
no.12, p.20-69, axonometric views,
dets., dwgs., port., elevs.,
models, photos., plans, secns.,
site plans, sketches, aerial
photo.

SCHNEIDER, BERNARD
Asbest.
Introduction to issue devoted to
asbestos problems and removal from
buildings. Includes 11 articles
(one indexed separately), by Peter
Munchhoff, Werner Hildebrandt et
al., Wolfgang Schache, Paul
Bornemann, Bernard Schneider,
Frank M. Ruff, Klaus Dierks, and
Karlheinz Pfarr.
BAUWELT 1990 Dec.14, v.81, no.47,
p.2329,2338-2371, graphs, photos.,
tables, refs.

SCHNEIDER, HEINRICH
Erste Preise: Stadt- und Ortskerne.
Three projects: Innenstadt
Grevenbroich (architects: Ruth
Paffrath-Baureis, Heinrich
Schneider); Neckarstrasse
Stuttgart (architect: Gunter H.
Telian); Innenstadt Puttlingen
(architect: Hubertus Wandel).
DEUTSCHES ARCHITEKTENBLATT 1990
Nov.1, v.22, no.11, p.1699-1702,
dwgs., models, site plans.

SCHNEIDER, JOHN C.
Homeless men and housing policy in
urban America, 1850-1920 / John C.
Schneider.
URBAN STUDIES 1989 Feb., v.26,
no.1, p.90-99, refs.

SCHNEIDER, JURG E.
Zurichs Rindermarkt und Neumarkt:
Entstehung und Entwicklung eines
Quartiers / Jurg E. Schneider.
Monograph.
MITTEILUNGEN DER ANTIQUARISCHEN
GESELLSCHAFT IN ZURICH 1989, v.56,
p.5-171, dets., dwgs., elevs.,
maps, photos., site plans, biblio.

SCHNEIDER, LAURIE
Leon Battista Alberti: some
biographical implications of the
winged eye / Laurie Schneider.
An interpretation of Alberti's
literary themes based on
literature, iconography, and
mythology.
ART BULLETIN 1990 June, v.72,
no.2, p.261-270, photos., engr.,
biblio., refs.

SCHNEIDER, RICHARD H.
Searching for substandard housing in
Alachua County: a case study /
Paul D. Zwick, Richard H.
Schneider.
Computer automated methodology for
the inventory and identification
of substandard housing.
COMPUTERS, ENVIRONMENT AND URBAN
SYSTEMS 1990, v.14, no.4,
p.273-282, chart, plans, refs.

SCHNEIDER, ROLAND
Dokumente der Architektur des 20.
Jahrhunderts: Die Bundesschule des
ADGB in Bernau / Roland Schneider.
Built late 1920s. Architects:
Hannes Meyer, Hans Wittwer.
DER ARCHITEKT 1990 July-Aug.,
no.7-8, p.330, photos.

SCHNEIDER, ROMANA
Metropolis in vitro / Paola
Antonelli, Romana Schneider.
On Fritz Lang's 1926 film
"Metropolis."
DOMUS 1990 June, no.717,
p.[74]-80, ill., photos.

SCHNEIDER, SABINE
Aufgefrischt: Stadtsanierung in
Fellbach / Sabine Schneider.
Architects: Arno Lederer, Jorunn
Ragnarsdottir.
DEUTSCHE BAUZEITUNG 1990 Apr.,
v.124, no.4, p.44-49, photos.,
plans, secns., site plan.
Schlicht, schon und weiss: das
Designmuseum in London / Sabine
Schneider.
Architects: Conran Roche
Architects.
DEUTSCHE BAUZEITUNG 1990 Jan.,
v.124, no.1, p.36-41, axonometric
views, photos., maps, secn.
Seite an Seite: Okumenisches
Kirchenzentrum in
Nurnberg-Langwasser / Sabibe
Schneider.
Architects: Eberhard Schunck,
Dieter Ullrich.
DEUTSCHE BAUZEITUNG 1990 Apr.,
v.124, no.4, p.[30]-35, photos.,
secn., site plans.

SCHNEIDER-WESSLING, ERICH, 1931-
Solitar, nicht elitar: Wohnhaus in
Berlin-Tiergarten, Lutzowufer.
Architect: Erich
Schneider-Wessling.
BAUWELT 1990 Oct.26, v.81, no.40,
p.2030-2035, photos., plans, site
plan.

SCHNITGERHANS, HOLGER
"Das Buro wird ein menschlicher Ort"
/ Holger Schnitgerhans.
Mario Bellini's views on the
office of the future.
ARCHITEKTUR & WOHNEN 1990
Aug.-Sept., no.4, p.108, port.
Zwischen Licht und Schatten / Holger
Schnitgerhans.
Lighting fixtures designed by
Harry Mayer. English summary,
p.2-3.
ARCHITEKTUR & WOHNEN 1990
Dec.-1991 Jan., no.6, p.68-72,
photos.

SCHOBERL, GERHARD
Architektentag im Herzen einer
europaischen Region / Gerhard
Schoberl.
Report on Architektentag 1990,
held in Kaiserslautern, Sept.1990.
Includes text of a talk given by
Wolfgang Pehnt, "Die Architektur
des europaischen Hauses".
DEUTSCHES ARCHITEKTENBLATT 1990
Nov.1, v.22, no.11, p.291-296,
ports.

SCHOCH, RAINER
Palast und Hutte: zum
Bedeutungswandel eines
kunstlerischen Motivs zwischen
Aufklarung und Romantik / Rainer
Schoch.
KRITISCHE BERICHTE 1989, v.17,
no.4, p.42-59, ill., engrs., refs.

SCHODEK, DANIEL
Hypermedia in akademischer
Ausbildung und Forschung: die
Kuppel von Santa Maria del Fiore /
Spiro Pollalis, Daniel Schodek,
Howard Burns.
ARCHITHESE 1990 May-June, v.20,
no.3, p.49-53, ill., biblio.,
refs.

SCHOELLER, FREDERIC
Tadao Ando.
Special issue devoted to Ando's
work from 1983-1990. Includes
essay by Ando; criticism by J.L.
Gonzalez Cobelo, Alain
Bretagnolle, and Frederic
Schoeller. Pages 21-188 are
devoted to 20 works and projects.
Text in Spanish and English.
EL CROQUIS 1990 July-Sept., v.9,
no.44, entire issue, axonometric
views, dwgs., port., elevs.,
photos., plans, secns., site
plans, sketches, aerial photo.

SCHOELLKOPF, GEORGE E.
Simple virtues: in Connecticut's
quiet northwest corner, garden
designer Nancy McCabe cultivates
the art of understatement / George
E. Schoellkopf.
HOUSE & GARDEN 1990 June, v.162,
no.6, p.[100-107],172, dets.,
port., photos.

SCHOEMAKER, C. P. WOLF
Grand Hotel Preanger, Bandung.
Renovation of hotel on Java opened
in 1897 and expanded in the 1920s
by architect C.P. Wolf Schoemaker.
Architects: Atelier 6.
MIMAR: ARCHITECTURE IN DEVELOPMENT
1990 Sept., v.10, no.3(36),
p.30-33, dwg., map, photos.,
plans.

SCHOEMEHL, VINCENT C.
Economics, politics and city design
/ Vincent C. Schoemehl.
The Mayor of St. Louis describes
his experiences in planning and
development after participating in
the Mayors' Institute for City
Design.
PLACES 1990 Summer, v.6, no.4,
p.14-21, photos.

SCHOEN, DAVID A.
Using microcomputer CAD packages in
planning / David F. Brown, David
A. Shoen.
AMERICAN PLANNING ASSOCIATION.
JOURNAL 1987 Spring, v.53, no.2,
p.249-258, graphs, maps, tables,
biblio.

SCHOFFLER, SCHLOENBACH UND JACOBI
Titania Palast, Berlin, Germany /
Ray Gingell.
Movie theater built 1928;
Schoffler, Schloenbach and Jacobi,
architects. Includes an English
translation of the description of
the Titania-Palast from
"Lichtspielhauser und
Tonfilmtheater", by Paul Zucker
and G.O. Stindt (Berlin, 1931).
MARQUEE 1990, v.22, no.3, p.11-15,
photos.

SCHOFIELD, JOHN
Practical repair / John Schofield.
Repair of an early 18th century
house at 29 Queen Sq. Bristol.
Restoration architects:
Architectron.
ARCHITECTS' JOURNAL 1990 May 2,
v.191, no.18, p.26-31, dets.,
photos., plans, secn.

SCHOLER, KLAUSJURGEN, 1943-
Strasse der Befreiung: Neugestaltung
des Platzes der Einheit in
Prestlen.
Public housing project.
Architects: Wolfgang Steinbruck,
Klausjurgen Scholer.
DEUTSCHE BAUZEITUNG 1990 June,
v.124, no.6, p.17-21, photos.,
plans, site plan.

SCHOLLHAMMER, GEORG
Formgewordene Neurose: Hans Holleins
Haas-Haus in Wien / Georg
Schollhammer.
Apartment building, located at
Stock-im-Eisen-Platz. Reprinted
from "Der Standard".
BAUWELT 1990 Oct. 19, v.81, no.39,
p.1958-1959, photos.
Siebenfacher Blick auf einen Seligen
[exhibition review] / Georg
Schollhammer.
Reviews the recent exhibition, in
three locations in Vienna, of the
work of Adolf Loos.
BAUWELT 1990 Feb.9, v.81, no.6,
(Continued next page)

SCHOLLHAMMER, GEORG (CONTINUED)
Siebenfacher Blick...(CONTINUED)
p.248, model, secns.

SCHOLTEN, H.J.
Working with geographic information
systems in a policy environment /
H.J. Scholten, P. Padding.
ENVIRONMENT AND PLANNING B 1990
Oct., v.17, no.4, p.405-416,
chart, diagr., table, refs.

SCHOLTEN, HENK J.
Application of geographic
information systems in Europe /
Henk J. Scholten, Maurits van der
Vlugt.
EKISTICS 1989 Sept.-Dec., v.56,
no.338-339, p.304-311, chart,
table, biblio.

SCHOLZ, HARTMUT
Der zentralaustralische Nationalpark
Uluru / Hartmut Scholz.
Landscape planning in Australia's
Uluru National Park. English
summary, p.37.
GARTEN UND LANDSCHAFT 1990 v.100,
no.7, p.32-37, maps, photos.

SCHOLZ,, JOHN
The Eugene Field House and Toy
Mansion in St. Louis, Missouri /
John Scholz.
Federal-style row house, built in
1845.
VICTORIAN HOMES 1990 Holidays,
v.9, no.5, p.26, photos.

SCHOLZ, STEFAN JAN, 1938-
Erweiterung der
Albert-Einstein-Schule in
Berlin-Neukolln.
Architect: Stefan Scholz, of
Bangert, Jansen, Scholz, Schultes.
BAUWELT 1990 Sept.28, v.81, no.36,
p.1752-1753, dwg., photos.

SCHOLZE, MANFRED
Ausdruck einer neuen Einheit der
Kunste zu Oskar Kokoschkas
Entwurfen fur ein Krematorium in
Breslau (Worclaw) / Manfred
Scholze.
Date: 1914.
JAHRBUCH DER STAATLICHEN
KUNSTSAMMLUNGEN DRESDEN 1986,
v.18, p.123-131, dwgs., sketch,
refs.

SCHOMERS, MANFRED
Das Silberwerk: Kraftwerk
Bremen-Hastedt, Block 15.
Architects: Manfred Schomers,
Rainer Schurmann, Walter Stridde.
BAUWELT 1990 Oct.5, v.81, no.37,
p.1874-1881 cover, dets., elev.,
photos., site plan.

SCHOMIG, RICHARD
Aufbruch im Kirchenbau: Hans Schadel
zum 80. Geburtstag / Richard
Schomig.
The work of this German church
architect.
DAS MUNSTER 1990, v.43, no.1,
p.29-36, ill., photos.

SCHONHERR, TORBEN
Pigen som ligger ved soen / Torben
Schonherr.
Garden for Liselotte Haman and
Henning Overgaard, Langeso,
Silkeborg (1985) in the shape of a
female torso. Article includes a
fictionalized presentation by the
designer. Includes English
translation.
LANDSKAB 1990 Nov., v.71, no.7,
p.118-119, plan.

SCHOOL BUILDINGS - COMMUNITY USE
See COMMUNITY CENTERS

SCHOOL GROUNDS
See CAMPUSES

SCHOOL HOUSES
See SCHOOLS

SCHOOL PLAYGROUNDS
See PLAYGROUNDS

SCHOOLEY CALDWELL ASSOCIATES
Answering a capitol question: atrium
proposed for Ohio Statehouse
raises preservation eyebrows /
Arnold Berke.
Architects: Schooley Caldwell.
PRESERVATION NEWS 1990 June, v.30,
no.6, p.7,20, diagr., photo.

SCHOOLS
See also ART SCHOOLS
See also CAMPUSES
See also CLASSROOMS
See also COMMUNITY SCHOOLS
See also KINDERGARTENS
See also LAW SCHOOLS
See also MIDDLE SCHOOLS
See also MILITARY ACADEMIES
See also NURSERY SCHOOLS
See also NURSING SCHOOLS
See also VETERINARY COLLEGES
See also YESHIVAS
Eine zweite Chance zur baulichen
Verwirklichung der Bildungsreform
/ Jen C. Bassenge.
The introductory article in issue
entitled "Schulen" Other articles
are indexed separately.
BAUWELT 1990 Apr.27, v.81, no.16,
p.792-793, photo.

SCHOOLS--19TH CENTURY--ALTERATIONS AND
ADDITIONS--GERMANY (WEST)--
PFAFFENHOFEN--STILLING HOUSE
Eigene Klasse: Umbau eines
Dorfschulhauses in
Pfaffenhofen/Heilbronn in ein
Atelier mit Wohnung.
Architects: Hans-Peter Glucker,
Marija Glucker.
ARCHITEKTUR, INNENARCHITEKTUR,
TECHNISCHER AUSBAU 1990 Jan.-Feb.,
v.98, no.1-2, p.22-25, elevs.,
photos., plans.

SCHOOLS--19TH CENTURY--UNITED STATES--
GILLESPIE COUNTY (TEXAS)--MORRIS
RANCH SCHOOLHOUSE
The best little schoolhouse in Texas
/ Nancy Holmes.
On the Morris Ranch Schoolhouse,
built in 1893, near
Fredericksburg, TX. Architect:
Alfred Giles. The school is now
home to Frances Billup.
CONNOISSEUR 1990 May, v.220,
no.940, p.92-[97],148, port.,
photos.

SCHOOLS--ALTERATIONS AND ADDITIONS--
COMPETITIONS--GERMANY (WEST)--
RODINGSHAUSEN--GESAMTSCHULE
Erste Preise: Schulen.
Four projects: Kaufmannische
Berufsschule, Ohringen (winner:
Architekten Behnisch & Partner);
addition to Realschule, Markt
Indersdorf (winner: Peter Kaup,
Helmut M. Scholz & Partner);
addition and double gymnasium,
Gesamtschule, Rodingshausen
(winner: Gunter Schmidt +
Friedrich Schmersahl); new
gymnasium and sports building, Bad
Neuenahr-Ahrweiler (winner: Georg
A. Schutz).
DEUTSCHES ARCHITEKTENBLATT 1990
Jan.1, v.22, no.1, p.55-58, dwgs.,
models, plan, secns., site plans.

SCHOOLS--ALTERATIONS AND ADDITIONS--
COMPETITIONS--SWITZERLAND--BUREN
Mimikry: zum ersten Preis im
Wettbewerb "Schulhauserweiterung
Buren" / Bruno Salzmann.
Architects: Marques & Zurkirchen.
ARCHITHESE 1990 July-Aug., v.20,
no.4, p.78-80, elevs., models,
plans, site plan.

SCHOOLS--ALTERATIONS AND ADDITIONS--
SPAIN--MURCIA--COLEGIO DE SAN
ESTEBAN
Rehabilitacion de Colegio de San
Esteban de Murcia: J. Plaza, E.
Sancho, V. Perez, M. de la Villa,
P. Sanmartin y S. Moreno.
Spanish, English text.
ON DISENO 1990, no.109, p.128-135,
photos., plans.

SCHOOLS--ALTERATIONS AND ADDITIONS--
SWITZERLAND--WINTERTHUR--
KANTONSSCHULE BUELRAIN
Erweiterung Kantonsschule Buelrain,
Winterthur, 1987.
Architect: Arnold Amsler.
WERK, BAUEN + WOHNEN 1989 Dec.,
no.12, p.49, plan, elev., secns.

SCHOOLS--ALTERATIONS AND ADDITIONS--
UNITED STATES--COLUMBUS (INDIANA)--
NORTHSIDE MIDDLE SCHOOL
Hoosier patron: Cummins Engine
Foundation continues to foster
design in Columbus, Indiana.
Two projects under development:
Northside Middle School (Leers,
Weinzapfel Associates) and
Bartholemew Co. Hospital (Robert
A. M. Stern Architects and
Falick/Klein Partnership).
ARCHITECTURE: THE AIA JOURNAL 1990
Dec., v.79, no.12, p.41, elevs.,
secn.

SCHOOLS--ALTERATIONS AND ADDITIONS--
UNITED STATES--NEW YORK (NEW YORK)
New York City schools: small is
better / Abby Bussel.
On the hypothetical design study
project and exhibition, New
Schools for New York, sponsored by
the Architectrual League of New
York and the Public Education
Association.
PROGRESSIVE ARCHITECTURE 1990
Mar., v.71, no.3, p.24-25, secn.

SCHOOLS AS SOCIAL CENTERS
See COMMUNITY CENTERS

SCHOOLS--AUSTRALIA--MENINDEE--MENINDEE
CENTRAL SCHOOL
New educational buildings.
Three projects designed by the New
South Wales Government Architect,
L.D. Kelly, for small communities.
ARCHITECTURE AUSTRALIA 1990 July,
v.79, no.6, p.48-50, photos.,
plans.

SCHOOLS--AUSTRIA--SALZBURG--LEHRBAUHOF
SALZBURG-GLANEGG
Auslander rein / Friedrich
Achleitner.
Three projects in Salzburg:
Heating plant (architects: Marie
Claude Betrix, Eraldo
Consolascio); Hans-Sachs-Hof
(architects: Drener + Drener); and
Lehrbauhof Salzburg-Glanegg
(architect: Michael Ander).
DER ARCHITEKT 1990 May, no.5,
p.242-244, photos.

SCHOOLS--BOARDING--SPAIN--MORELLA
Provocative and participatory
places.
Features seven projects in the
Barcelona area by Enric Miralles
and Carme Pinos.
ARCHITECTURAL REVIEW 1990 July,
v.188, no.1121, p.74-89, dets.,
ill., elevs., plans, secns., site
plans, sketches.

SCHOOLS--BOARDING--UNITED STATES--
WALLINGFORD (CONNECTICUT)--CHOATE
ROSEMARY HALL--SCIENCE CENTER
Bridging science with art: Science
Center, Choate Rosemary Hall,
Wallingford, Connecticut, Pei Cobb
Freed & Partners, Architects /
Michael J. Crosbie.
ARCHITECTURE: THE AIA JOURNAL 1990
Feb., v.79, no.2, p.[50-55],
axonometric view, elev., photos,
plans, secns., site plans.
Pei Cobb Freed & Partners: un
legamento dinamico = a dynamic
ligament.
Science Center, Wallingford, Ct.
ARCHITETTURA: CRONACHE E STORIA
1990 Sept., v.36, no.9(419),
p.640-641, axonometric view,
photos., secn., site plan.

SCHOOLS--BRAZIL--BELO HORIZONTE--
NUCLEO DE ENSINO
Escolas de aco com varandao, a
proposta arquitetonica e
pedagogica mineira.
Nucleo Ensino e Extensao
Comunitaria, Belo Horizonte,
Brazil. Architect: Gustavo A.
Penna.
PROJETO 1989 June, no.122,
p.51-56, photos, elevs., map,
plans, site plans.

SCHOOLS--CHINA
En dansk arkitekt i Kina: Johannes
Prip-Moller (1889-1943) / Tobias
Faber.
ARCHITECTURA: ARKITEKTURHISTORISK
ARSSKRIFT 1989, v.11, p.7-66,
dets., ill., dwgs., ports.,
elevs., maps, photos., plans,
secns., biblio.

SCHOOLS - COMMUNITY USE
See COMMUNITY CENTERS

SCHOOLS--CONSERVATION AND
RESTORATION--NETHERLANDS--AALSMEER--
NAAI- EN KNIPSCHOOL
Gered en toch verloren: restauratie
school Wiebenga Aalsmeer / Arjen
Oosterman, Dick Kuhn.
Built in 1930, restored in 1989.
DE ARCHITECT 1989 Oct., v.20,
no.10, p.95-99, port., photos.,
plans.

SCHOOLS--DANCE--AUSTRALIA--MELBOURNE--
AUSTRALIAN BALLET CENTRE
Hassell Architects: two projects.
The Australian Ballet Centre,
Melbourne; and an extension to the
Ballarat Fine Art Gallery.
Includes a review, by Hamish Lyon.
ARCHITECTURE AUSTRALIA 1990 Mar.,
v.79, no.2, p.49-53, photos,
plans, site plan.

SCHOOLS--DANCE--ENGLAND--LEEDS--
YORKSHIRE DANCE CENTRE
Take your partners [Yorkshire Dance
Centre] / Peter Weatherhead.
Conversion of an Edwardian
warehouse in inner Leeds.
Architects: Allen Tod.
BUILDING 1990 Feb.23, v.255, no.8,
p.51-53, photos.

SCHOOLS--DANCE--STUDENT PROJECTS--
NETHERLANDS--AMSTERDAM--DANSACADEMIE
Staalprijs voor afstudeeontwerp
dansopleiding: resultaten
twee-fasenopleiding van hoog
niveau / Joop Niesten.
Student projects at the TU-Delft
for the Dansacademie Amsterdam.
DE ARCHITECT 1989 Nov., v.20,
no.11, p.143-147, axonometric
view, dets., elev., model, plans,
secn.

SCHOOLS--DANCE--UNITED STATES--NEW
YORK (NEW YORK)--ALVIN AILEY
AMERICAN DANCE CENTER
A sensuous space / Jean Gorman.
Features the Alvin Ailey American
Dance Center, New York, NY.
Architects: R.M. Kliment & Frances
Halsband Architects.
INTERIORS 1990 Dec., v.150, no.5,
p.78-81, axonometric view, photos.

SCHOOLS--DANCE--UNITED STATES--
OKLAHOMA CITY (OKLAHOMA)--BALLET
OKLAHOMA
Ballet fairy tale / Kristen
Richards.
Oklahoma City industrial building
converted into dance school for
the Ballet Oklahoma. Renovation
architects: Elliott + Associates
Architects.
INTERIORS 1990 Dec., v.150, no.5,
p.84-[87], photos., plan.

SCHOOLS--ELEMENTARY--ALTERATIONS AND
ADDITIONS--NETHERLANDS--AERDENHOUT
Herman Hertzberger.
Focus on three projects: Ministry
of Social Welfare, the Hague;
elementary school, Aerdenhout; and
competition entry for the
Bibliotheque de France.
ARCHITECTURAL REVIEW 1990 Feb.,
v.187, no.1116, p.58-69,
(Continued next column)

SCHOOLS--ELEMENTARY--ALTERATIONS AND
ADDITIONS--NETHERLANDS--AERDENHOUT
(CONTINUED)
Herman Hertzberger. (CONTINUED)
axonometric views, dwgs., elevs.,
model, photos., plans, secns.,
site plans.
Scuola elementare a Aerdenhout di
Herman Hertzberger / Pierre-Alain
Croset.
An 1988-1989 addition to an old
brick schoolhouse. Includes
English summary and captions.
CASABELLA 1990 May, v.54, no.568,
p.4-11, axonometric views,
photos., plans, secns., site plan.
Scuola elementare Aerdenhout =
Primary school, Aerdenhout /
Herman Hertzberger.
Architect: Herman Hertzberger.
SPAZIO E SOCIETA 1990 Apr.-June,
v.13, no.50, p.28-33, axonometric
views, port., photos., plans,
secns.

SCHOOLS--ELEMENTARY--ALTERATIONS AND
ADDITIONS--UNITED STATES--NASHUA
(NEW HAMPSHIRE)--MOUNT PLEASANT
ELEMENTARY SCHOOL
A lesson in tectonics / Thomas
Fisher.
On the gymnasium and classroom
additions to the 1920s Mount
Pleasant Elementary School,
Nashua, N.H. Architects: TAMS
Consultants. Includes Selected
Detail article on a wall section
of the addition.
PROGRESSIVE ARCHITECTURE 1990
Aug., v.71, no.8, p.110-112, det.,
photos., plans.

SCHOOLS--ELEMENTARY--ALTERATIONS AND
ADDITIONS--UNITED STATES--ROCHESTER
(MICHIGAN)--GAGE ELEMENTARY SCHOOL
Making the grade: ATS & R advances a
1950's elementary school to the
head of its class.
Gage Elementary School, Rochester,
Minn.
ARCHITECTURE MINNESOTA 1990
Sept.-Oct., v.16, no.5, p.24-25,
photos.

SCHOOLS--ELEMENTARY--ALTERATIONS AND
ADDITIONS--UNITED STATES--SAN
FRANCISCO (CALIFORNIA)--WALDORF
SCHOOL
Lessons in civility: two schools in
San Francisco exemplify the
multiple challenges of melding new
construction and existing
buildings into a single entity /
Donald J. Canty.
The Waldorf School, by Tanner
Leddy Maytum Stacy Architects; and
the San Francisco Day School, by
Simon Martin-Vegue Winkelstein
Moris.
ARCHITECTURAL RECORD 1990 Mar.,
v.178, no.3, p.84-91, elevs.,
photos., plans, secn., site plans.

(Continued next page)

SCHOOLS--ELEMENTARY--JAPAN--TSUKUBA--
TAKEZONO-NISHI (CONTINUED)
  Special edition I:...(CONTINUED)
    no.527, p.25-56, axonometric
    views, elevs., photos., plans,
    secns., site plans.

SCHOOLS--ELEMENTARY--LAOS--NAXATHONG
  Scuola elementare a Naxathong, Laos
  = Primary school in Naxathong,
  Laos.
    Architects: Four professors from
    the Ecole des Techniciens
    Superieurs du Batiment, Vientiane
    and architects from the Groupe de
    Recherche et d'Echanges
    Technologiques, Paris. Article is
    reprinted from Mimar, 1989 Mar.,
    no.31, p.16-20.
    SPAZIO E SOCIETA 1990 Jan.-Mar.,
    v.13, no.49, p.114-117, det.,
    photos., plan, secn., site plan.

SCHOOLS--ELEMENTARY--NETHERLANDS--
AMSTERDAM--DE EVENAAR
  Primarschule "De Evenaar" in
  Amsterdam / NL.
    Architect: Herman Hertzberger.
    DEUTSCHE BAUZEITSCHRIFT 1990 Jan.,
    v.38, no.1, p.79-84, dets.,
    photos., secns., site plan.

SCHOOLS--ELEMENTARY--NETHERLANDS--
VEGHEL
  Basisschool te Veghel / Gerard van
  Asperen.
    Built 1988. Architectenbureau BAS;
    G. van Asperen.
    BOUW 1989 Nov.3, v.44, no.22,
    p.46-49, dwg., elevs., photos.,
    plans, site plan.

SCHOOLS--ELEMENTARY--ROUND--GERMANY
(WEST)--STUTTGART--STAMMHEIM
  Green school of thought / Peter
  Blundell Jones.
    Elementary school, Stammheim, a
    northern suburb of Stuttgart.
    Architect: Peter Hubner.
    ARCHITECTURAL REVIEW 1990 Sept.,
    v.188, no.1123, p.49-53, models,
    photos., plan, secns., site plans.
  Stuttgart-Stammheim:
    Grundschulpavillon.
    Architect: Peter Hubner.
    BAUWELT 1990 Apr.27, v.81, no.16,
    p.804-807, dets., photos., plan,
    site plan.

SCHOOLS--ELEMENTARY--SAN MARINO
  Scuola elementare e materna a San
  Marino / Renato Pedio.
    Architect: Gilberto Rossini.
    Summaries in English, French,
    German, and Spanish.
    ARCHITETTURA; CRONACHE E STORIA
    1990 Mar., v.36, no.3(413),
    p.[166]-173, dets., elevs.,
    photos, plans, secns., site plans.

SCHOOLS--ELEMENTARY--SPAIN--
CERDANYOLA--COLEGIO PUBLICO SANTA
ROSA
  Las arquitectural publicas de Mario
  Luis Corea, Francisco Gallardo y
  Edgardo Manino.
    Six articles. Includes the
    Boardwalk and beach at Badalona;
    Public Health center, Badalona;
    Plaza, Badalona; San Roc community
    center and residence for the
    elderly handicapped, Badalona;
        (Continued next column)

SCHOOLS--ELEMENTARY--SPAIN--
CERDANYOLA--COLEGIO PUBLICO SANTA
ROSA (CONTINUED)
  Las arquitectural...(CONTINUED)
    Primary school Santa Rosa,
    Cerdanyola. Spanish and English
    text.
    ON DISENO 1990, no.107,
    p.[100]-141, elevs., photos.,
    plans, secns., site plan,
    sketches.

SCHOOLS--ELEMENTARY--SWEDEN--TABY--
MYRANGEN
  Teori och praktik / Lis Hogdahl.
    Features two elementary schools,
    in Vastervik and Taby (architects:
    ATRIO Arkitekter; Dranger och
    Kvant Arkitektkontor); a parish
    secondary school in Osterfarnebo
    (architect: Carlson Fernberg
    Arkitektkontor); and a crafts
    school in Stockholm (architect:
    Asmussens arkitektkontor).
    ARKITEKTUR: THE SWEDISH REVIEW OF
    ARCHITECTURE 1990 Dec., v.90,
    no.10, p.10-21,cover, photos.,
    plans, site plans.

SCHOOLS--ELEMENTARY--SWEDEN--UPPSALA--
VAKSALASKOLAN
  Skolhusets betydelse / Ann Skantze.
    Theoretical aspects of school
    design, with reference to the 1925
    Vaksalaskolan in Uppsala
    (architect: Gunnar Leche).
    ARKITEKTUR: THE SWEDISH REVIEW OF
    ARCHITECTURE 1990 Dec., v.90,
    no.10, p.22-25, photos., biblio.

SCHOOLS--ELEMENTARY--SWEDEN--
VASTERVIK--KVANNAREN
  Teori och praktik / Lis Hogdahl.
    Features two elementary schools,
    in Vastervik and Taby (architects:
    ATRIO Arkitekter; Dranger och
    Kvant Arkitektkontor); a parish
    secondary school in Osterfarnebo
    (architect: Carlson Fernberg
    Arkitektkontor); and a crafts
    school in Stockholm (architect:
    Asmussens arkitektkontor).
    ARKITEKTUR: THE SWEDISH REVIEW OF
    ARCHITECTURE 1990 Dec., v.90,
    no.10, p.10-21,cover, photos.,
    plans, site plans.

SCHOOLS--ELEMENTARY--SWITZERLAND--
MONTAGNOLA
  Escola primaria cria a praca
  principal da cidade.
    In Montagnola, Switzerland.
    Architect: Civio Vacchini.
    PROJETO 1989 June, no.122,
    p.44-50, elev, photos, plans,
    secns., site plan.

SCHOOLS--ELEMENTARY--UNITED STATES--
SAN FRANCISCO (CALIFORNIA)--SAN
FRANCISCO DAY SCHOOL
  Lessons in civility: two schools in
  San Francisco exemplify the
  multiple challenges of melding new
  construction and existing
  buildings into a single entity /
  Donald J. Canty.
    The Waldorf School, by Tanner
    Leddy Maytum Stacy Architects; and
    the San Francisco Day School, by
    Simon Martin-Vegue Winkelstein
    Moris.
    ARCHITECTURAL RECORD 1990 Mar.,
        (Continued next column)

SCHOOLS--ELEMENTARY--UNITED STATES--
SAN FRANCISCO (CALIFORNIA)--SAN
FRANCISCO DAY SCHOOL (CONTINUED)
  Lessons in civility:...(CONTINUED)
    v.178, no.3, p.84-91, elevs.,
    photos., plans, secn., site plans.

SCHOOLS--ENGLAND--WINCHESTER--SAINT
SWITHUN'S SCHOOL
  St. Swithun's School wins Beta
  Award.
    "Swedish-style" dormitory and
    refrectory for St. Swithun's
    School, Winchester, wins award for
    energy efficiency. Sponsored by
    the Electricity Supply Industry.
    THE PLANNER 1990 June 1, v.76,
    no.21, p.9, photo.

SCHOOLS FOR THE HANDICAPPED
  See also ADULT DAY CARE CENTERS

SCHOOLS FOR THE HANDICAPPED--ENGLAND--
LONDON--CHOLMELEY PARK--HARINGTON
SCHEME
  Highgate haven / David Jenkins.
    Multi-purpose garden building
    serves as tool shed, changing
    room, offices, and storage for the
    training of handicapped gardeners
    in Highgate, London. Architect:
    Tim Ronalds Architects. Includes
    second article: Roof, gardeners'
    centre, Tim Ronalds Architects,
    p.59-61.
    ARCHITECTS' JOURNAL 1990 Sept.12,
    v.192, no.11, p.[46]-51,59-61,
    det., elev., photos., plans,
    secns., isometric dwg.

SCHOOLS FOR THE HANDICAPPED--GERMANY
(WEST)--MUNICH
  Eine Schule zum Entspannen / Gerrit
  Confurius.
    School complex for hearing and
    speech-disabled children, in
    Johanneskirchen, Munich.
    Architect: Utz-Peter Strehle.
    BAUWELT 1990 June 15, v.81, no.23,
    p.1136-1143, photos., plans,
    secns., site plans.
  Zum Wohl-Fuhlen und Lernen: Neubau
    der Schwerhorigen- und
    Sprachheilschule in
    Munchen-Johanneskirchen.
    Architect: Utz-Peter Strehle.
    ARCHITEKTUR, INNENARCHITEKTUR,
    TECHNISCHER AUSBAU 1990 May, v.98,
    no.5, p.36-41, photos., plans,
    secns., site plans.

SCHOOLS--FRANCE--CLAMART
  Fins de chantier.
    Contents: Parking garage, rue
    Notre-Dame, Saint-Brieuc, France;
    architect: Jean Guervilly --
    Ecole maternelle, rue Sovignet,
    Saint-Etienne, France; architect:
    Christian Kock -- Factory,
    Hathersage, Derbyshire, England;
    architect: Michael Hopkins &
    Partners -- School, Zac
    Pierre-Corby, Clamart, France;
    architect: Pierre Lombard & Agnes
    Bertholon.
    LE MONITEUR ARCHITECTURE AMC 1990
    Mar., no.9, p.12-17, elev.,
    photos., plans, secns., site
    plans.

SCHOOLS--FRANCE--POITIERS--
FUTUROSCOPE--LYCEE DU FUTUR
Des formes pour l'information /
Denis Picard.
On the Futuroscope theme park.
Poitiers, France. Architect: Denis
Laming. Architects for the Lycee
du futur: Architecture Studio.
CONNAISSANCE DES ARTS 1990 Jan.,
no.455, p.108-[115], photos.

SCHOOLS--FRANCE--TANNAY
Monumentalitat und Demokratie:
Schulhauser in Nyon, Arzler und
Tannay / Paolo Fumagalli.
Architect: Vincent Mangeat. French
text, p.67.
WERK, BAUEN + WOHNEN 1989 Oct.,
no.10, p.4-11, axonometric views,
elev., photos., plans, secns.,
site plan, isometric dwg., aerial
photo.

SCHOOLS--FRENCH COLONIAL--CONSERVATION
AND RESTORATION--INDIA--
PONIDCHERRY--ECOLE FRANCAISE
D'EXTREME-ORIENT
Restoration / Smita Dutla Makhija,
Pierre Pichard.
Two projects: Rajmahal, Chanderi:
Ecole francaise d'extreme-orient,
20 rue Dumas, Pondicherry.
ARCHITECTURE + DESIGN 1989
Nov.-Dec., v.6, no.1, p.115-118,
photos, plan, secns., site plan.

SCHOOLS--GERMANY (WEST)
Soziale Aufgaben.
Issue features school projects
meeting specific social needs.
Individual articles are indexed
separately.
BAUWELT 1990 June 15, v.81, no.23,
p.1136-1151, ill., photos.

SCHOOLS--GERMANY (WEST)--DULMEN--
VOLKHOCHSCHULE DULMEN
Fur offene Kulturarbeit: die neue
Passage der VHS-Dulmen in der
ehemaligen Kassenhalle der
Stadtsparkasse.
Architects: Geller + Muller.
ARCHITEKTUR, INNENARCHITEKTUR,
TECHNISCHER AUSBAU 1990 May, v.98,
no.5, p.46-47, phoots., plan.

SCHOOLS--GERMANY (WEST)--GOTTINGEN--
FREIE WALDORFSCHULE
Anthroposophische Architektur - ein
Akademiethema? / Paulgerd Jesberg.
Discusses Meinhard von Gerkan,
Gundolf Bockemuhl, the Freie
Waldorfschule Gottingen by
Nikolaus Ruff, and the NMB-Zentrum
in Amsterdam by Tom Alberts and
Max von Huut.
DEUTSCHES ARCHITEKTENBLATT 1990
Aug.1, v.22, no.8, p.199-200,
photos.

SCHOOLS--GERMANY (WEST)--HEIDENHEIM--
FREIE WALDORFSCHULE
Das Geschehen gestalten: adaquate
Form In der Architektur der
Waldorfschule / Peter Ferger.
Built 1974. Architect: Werner
Seyfert.
ARCHITHESE 1990 Sept.-Oct., v.20,
no.5, p.56-59, photos., plans.

SCHOOLS--GERMANY (WEST)--MUNICH
Zwischen-Chaos und Zwischen-Ordnung,
in ubler Lage? / Utz-Peter
Strehle.
DER ARCHITEKT 1990 Jan., no.1,
p.30-31, models, photos.

SCHOOLS--HEATING AND VENTILATION--
RESEARCH
Second order system identification
in the thermal response of a
working school / J.M. Penman.
BUILDING AND ENVIRONMENT 1990,
v.25, no.2, p.105-110, graphs,
tables, refs.

SCHOOLS--HISTORY--UNITED STATES--NEW
YORK (NEW YORK)
Learning from history [New York City
public schools] / Frank
Sommerfield.
METROPOLIS 1990 Dec., v.10, no.5,
p.[56]-61, photos.

SCHOOLS--INDIA--AHMADABAD--INDIAN
INSTITUTE OF MANAGEMENT
L'Indian Institute of Management ad
Ahmedabad 1962-1974 di Louis I.
Kahn / Christian Devillers.
English translation,p.60-62.
CASABELLA 1990 Sept., v.54,
no.571, p.36-58, elevs., photos.,
plans, site plans, sketches, refs.

SCHOOLS--ITALY--NAPLES--TRAIANO A
SOCCAVO
Due scuole a Napoli di Salvatore
Bisogni / Kenneth Frampton.
Built 1987-1989. Also includes
design for piazza, Villa di
Briano.
CASABELLA 1990 Jan., v.54, no.564,
p.16-24,60, axonometric view,
dwgs., elevs., photos., plans,
secns., site plan.

SCHOOLS--ITALY--NAPLES--VIA AQUILEIA -
VIA POGGIOREALE
Due scuole a Napoli di Salvatore
Bisogni / Kenneth Frampton.
Built 1987-1989. Also includes
design for piazza, Villa di
Briano.
CASABELLA 1990 Jan., v.54, no.564,
p.16-24,60, axonometric view,
dwgs., elevs., photos., plans,
secns., site plan.

SCHOOLS--ITALY--ROME--CASA DELLA GIL
Luigi Moretti: due architetture =
Luigi Moretti: two architectures /
Giancarlo Rosa.
The Casa della Cooperativa Astrea,
and the Casa della GIL, Rome.
FRAMES, PORTE & FINESTRE 1990
Oct.-Dec., no.29, p.30-35,
photos., plan.

SCHOOLS--JAPAN--SHIMODA--ARAKAWA
Arakawa-Sommerschule in Shimoda.
Architects: Sakakura Associates,
Architects and Engineers.
DEUTSCHE BAUZEITSCHRIFT 1990 Nov.,
v.38, no.11, p.1587-1590, photos.,
isometric dwgs.

SCHOOLS--MAINTENANCE AND REPAIR--LAW
AND LEGISLATION--ENGLAND
School reports / Sarah Kitchen.
Changes in maintenance of British
primary and secondary schools
resulting from the Education
Reform Act.
BUILDING 1990 Mar.16, v.255,
no.11, p.26-27, chart, graph,
port.

SCHOOLS - MEDICAL
See MEDICAL SCHOOLS

SCHOOLS--NETHERLANDS--AMSTERDAM--
ASVO-SCHOOL
Passen en meten binnen de
Londo-norm: twee basisscholen van
Tom van de Pol. / Egbert Koster.
The ASVO-School (1989) and Dr.
Rijk Kramerschool (1989), both in
Amsterdam. Architect: Tom van de
Pol.
DE ARCHITECT 1990 Sept., v.21,
no.9, p.108-115, photos., plans,
secns., site plans.

SCHOOLS--NETHERLANDS--AMSTERDAM--DR.
RIJK KRAMERSCHOOL
Passen en meten binnen de
Londo-norm: twee basisscholen van
Tom van de Pol. / Egbert Koster.
The ASVO-School (1989) and Dr.
Rijk Kramerschool (1989), both in
Amsterdam. Architect: Tom van de
Pol.
DE ARCHITECT 1990 Sept., v.21,
no.9, p.108-115, photos., plans,
secns., site plans.

SCHOOLS--NORWAY--BERGEN--STEINERSKOLEN
BARNEHAGE
Spieltrieb / Espen Tharaldsen.
Work by the Arbeidsgruppen HUS in
Bergen and Stavanger, Norway.
ARCHITHESE 1990 Sept.-Oct., v.20,
no.5, p.28-33,66, elevs., photos.,
plans, secns., refs.

SCHOOLS--NORWAY--STAVANGER--
STEINERSKOLEN
Spieltrieb / Espen Tharaldsen.
Work by the Arbeidsgruppen HUS in
Bergen and Stavanger, Norway.
ARCHITHESE 1990 Sept.-Oct., v.20,
no.5, p.28-33,66, elevs., photos.,
plans, secns., refs.

SCHOOLS OF ARCHITECTURE
See also ARCHITECTURE - STUDY AND
TEACHING
The architecture of architecture
schools / Alan J. Plattus.
"Discusses various images or
models that have guided the design
of architecture schools."
PROGRESSIVE ARCHITECTURE 1990
Apr., v.71, no.4, p.92-93, elev.,
photos.

SCHOOLS OF ARCHITECTURE--ALTERATIONS
AND ADDITIONS--ENGLAND--LIVERPOOL--
LIVERPOOL UNIVERSITY SCHOOL OF
ARCHITECTURE
Un nuovo edificio per la Liverpool
School of Architecture = New
addition to the Liverpool School
of Architecture / Silvano Stucchi.
Architects: Dave King, Rod
McAllister. Includes English
translation; French, German, and
Spanish summaries, p.3-4.
(Continued next page)

SCHOOLS OF ARCHITECTURE--ALTERATIONS
AND ADDITIONS--ENGLAND--LIVERPOOL--
LIVERPOOL UNIVERSITY SCHOOL OF
ARCHITECTURE (CONTINUED)
Un nuovo edificio per...(CONTINUED)
L'INDUSTRIA DELLE COSTRUZIONI 1990
Jan., v.24, no.219, p.22-31,
axonometric view, dets., photos.,
plans, secns., site plan.

SCHOOLS OF ARCHITECTURE--ALTERATIONS
AND ADDITIONS--FRANCE--TOULOUSE--
ECOLE D'ARCHITECTURE DE TOULOUSE
Ecole d'architecture de Toulouse.
Architects: Joseph Almudever,
Christian Lefebvre. English
summary, p.114; Spanish summary,
p.173.
TECHNIQUES ET ARCHITECTURE 1990
Oct.-Nov., no.392, p.114, dwgs.,
plans.

SCHOOLS OF ARCHITECTURE--ALTERATIONS
AND ADDITIONS--SWITZERLAND--VICO
MORCOTE--VILLA RUGGIA (SCI-ARC)
Ristratturazione a Vico Morcote
(Canton Ticino) / Renzo
Salmoiraghi.
On the renovation of Villa Ruggia,
the seat of the Southern
California Institute of
Architecture (SCI-ARC) school.
Architect: Martin Wagner.
English, French and Spanish
summaries.
ABACUS 1990 Apr.-June, v.6, no.22,
p.34-43, axonometric views, dets.,
photos., plans, secns.

SCHOOLS OF ARCHITECTURE--ALTERATIONS
AND ADDITIONS--UNITED STATES--
MINNEAPOLIS (MINNESOTA)--UNIVERSITY
OF MINNESOTA--SCHOOL OF ARCHITECTURE
AND LANDSCAPE ARCHITECTURE
School of Architecture.
Addition and renovation of the
School of Architecture and
Landscape Architecture, University
of Minnesota, Minneapolis. Design
architects: Steven Holl
Architects. Project architects:
Ellerbe Becket.
PROGRESSIVE ARCHITECTURE 1990
Jan., v.71, no.1, p.83-85,
axonometric view, models, plans,
secn., site plan.
Steven Holl.
Features four projects: P House,
Dallas; apartment house, Fukuoka,
Japan; American Memorial Library
extension competition entry,
Berlin; and the addition to the
School of Architecture, Univ. of
Minn., Minneapolis. English
summaries.
ARCHITECTURE D'AUJOURD'HUI 1990
Oct., no.271, p.122-126, dwgs.,
models, plan, secns., site plan.

SCHOOLS OF ARCHITECTURE--
COMPETITIONS--SPAIN--LERIDA--COLEGIO
DE ARQUITECTOS DE CATALUNA
Concurso de ideas para la nueva sede
colegial de C.O.A. de Cataluna en
Lerida.
First prize: Francisco Burgos,
Luis de Pereda. Also shows 2nd &
3rd prize entries.
ARQUITECTURA 1990 Mar.-June, v.72,
no.283-284, p.16-19, axonometric
view, elevs., plans, secns.

SCHOOLS OF ARCHITECTURE--ENGLAND--
LONDON--ARCHITECTURAL ASSOCIATION
Developing the network / Colin
Davies.
Chairman of the Architectural
Association School of
Architecture, London: Alvin
Boyarsky.
ARCHITECTS' JOURNAL 1990 Mar.14,
v.191, no.11, p.14-15, port.

SCHOOLS OF ARCHITECTURE--ENGLAND--
PLYMOUTH--PLYMOUTH POLYTECHNIC
Changing plans for education / Mungo
Park.
"Vision and Vocation" symposium on
architecture education in Britain,
held at Plymouth Polytechnic.
ARCHITECTS' JOURNAL 1990 July 18,
v.192, no.3, p.15, ill.

SCHOOLS OF ARCHITECTURE--FRANCE--
RENNES--ECOLE D'ARCHITECTURE DE
BRETAGNE
Une annee d'architecture 1990.
Survey of French architecture in
1990 arranged by building type,
with focus on three award winning
buildings: Hotel industriel, Paris
XIIIe; architect: Dominique
Perrault --L'ecole d'architecture
de Rennes; architect: Patrick
Berger --Unites de soins
palliatifs, Villejuif; architects:
Avant-Travaux. Includes essays by
Wolfgang Pehnt, Jacques Lucan,
Bruno Fortier and Marc Bedarida.
LE MONITEUR ARCHITECTURE AMC 1990
Dec., no.17, p.15-206, axonometric
views, dets., elevs., models,
photos., plans, secns., site
plans.

SCHOOLS OF ARCHITECTURE--GERMANY
(EAST)--DESSAU--BAUHAUS
Interdisziplinar, international,
kommunikativ: das 1987
neugegrundete "Bauhaus Dessau".
On the "re-established Bauhaus" in
Dessau. English summary, p.152.
DEUTSCHE BAUZEITUNG 1990 June,
v.124, no.6, p.144-154,
axonometric views, dwgs., models,
photos., plans.

SCHOOLS OF ARCHITECTURE--HUNGARY--
BUDAPEST--BUDAPESTI MUSZAKI EGYETEM
Hungary learns with the West /
Robert Kronenburg.
Short profile of Hungary's only
school of architecture, the
Technical University of Budapest
(TUB).
ARCHITECTS' JOURNAL 1990 July 4,
v.192, no.1, p.14, sketches.

SCHOOLS OF ARCHITECTURE--INDIA--
PANAJI--COLEGIO E SEMINARIO DE
RACHOL
Colegio e seminario de Rachol: Goa
College of Architecture, Panaji,
Goa.
ARCHITECTURE + DESIGN 1990
Jan.-Feb., v.7, no.1, p.112-115,
dets., elevs., map, plans, secns.,
site plan.

SCHOOLS OF ARCHITECTURE--ITALY--
GENOA--FACOLTA DI ARCHITETTURA
Ignazio Gardella: Sede della Facolta
di Architettura, Genova / Eduardo
Benvenuto.
In Italian and English.
DOMUS 1990 June, no.717,
p.[40-49],XXIII, dets., elevs.,
photos., plans, secns., site
plans, sketch.

SCHOOLS OF ARCHITECTURE--ITALY--
MILAN--POLITECNICO DI MILANO--
FACOLTA DI ARCHITETTURA
Piero Bottoni: gli anni della
formazione tra modernita e
tradizione / Graziella Tonon.
On the architect and teacher and
his years at the Scuola degli
Architetti Civili del Politecnico
di Milano (1921-26).
URBANISTICA 1989 June, no.95,
p.45-56, dwgs., elevs., plans,
sketches, refs.

SCHOOLS OF ARCHITECTURE--ROMANIA--
BUCHAREST--INSTITUTUL DE ARHITECTURA
"ION MINCU"
Testing times [Romanian student
competition] / Louise Rogers.
Design competition held at the
"Ion Mincu" Architecture Institute
in Bucharest. Student winners
will spend 3 weeks in British
practices sponsored by the RIBA.
ARCHITECTS' JOURNAL 1990 May 23,
v.191, no.21, p.24-29, dwgs.,
elevs., plans, secns., sketches.

SCHOOLS OF ARCHITECTURE--SOUTH AFRICA
Speaking up for South Africa / Jane
Drew.
The author criticizes RIBA's
attitude to South African schools
of architecture.
ARCHITECTS' JOURNAL 1990 Apr.18,
v.191, no.16, p.14-15, port.

SCHOOLS OF ARCHITECTURE--UNITED
STATES--CORAL GABLES (FLORIDA)--
UNIVERSITY OF MIAMI--SCHOOL OF
ARCHITECTURE
Nueva escuela de arquitectura en la
Universidad de Miami Coral Gables
Florida = New school of
architecture at the University of
Miami Coral Gables Florida / Aldo
Rossi, Morris Adjumi.
Architect: Aldo Rossi.
COMPOSICION ARQUITECTONICA, ART &
ARCHITECTURE 1990 Feb., no.5,
p.[25]-34, elevs., model, plan,
secns., site plan, sketches.

SCHOOLS OF ARCHITECTURE--UNITED
STATES--TEMPE (ARIZONA)--ARIZONA
STATE UNIVERSITY--COLLEGE OF
ARCHITECTURE AND ENVIRONMENTAL
DESIGN
Arizona State University College of
Architecture and Environmental
Design, Tempe / Thomas Fisher.
Architects: Hillier Group with
Architecture One, Ltd.
PROGRESSIVE ARCHITECTURE 1990
Apr., v.71, no.4, p.82-91, dets.,
photos., plans, secn.

SCHOOLS OF ARCHITECTURE--UNITED
STATES--WARREN (VERMONT)--
YESTERMORROW DESIGN / BUILD SCHOOL
Travel: a home-building vacation in
Vermont / Jane Margolies.
Yestermorrow Design / Build
School.
HOUSE BEAUTIFUL 1986 May, v.128,
no.5, p.41-42,46, photo.

SCHOOLS OF NURSING
See NURSING SCHOOLS

SCHOOLS--SECONDARY--ALTERATIONS AND
ADDITIONS--COMPETITIONS--GERMANY
(WEST)--MARKT INDERSDORF
Erste Preise: Schulen.
Four projects: Kaufmannische
Berufsschule, Ohringen (winner:
Architekten Behnisch & Partner);
addition to Realschule, Markt
Indersdorf (winner: Peter Kaup,
Helmut M. Scholz & Partner);
addition and double gymnasium,
Gesamtschule, Rodingshausen
(winner: Gunter Schmidt +
Friedrich Schmersahl); new
gymnasium and sports building, Bad
Neuenahr-Ahrweiler (winner: Georg
A. Schutz).
DEUTSCHES ARCHITEKTENBLATT 1990
Jan.1, v.22, no.1, p.55-58, dwgs.,
models, plan, secns., site plans.

SCHOOLS--SECONDARY--ALTERATIONS AND
ADDITIONS--FRANCE--PARIS--LYCEE
DORIAN
Extension du Lycee Dorian, Paris.
Architects: Gilles Barre, Loeiz
Caradec, Francoise Risterucci.
English summary, p.119; Spanish
summary, p.173.
TECHNIQUES ET ARCHITECTURE 1990
Oct.-Nov., no.392, p.118-119,
elevs., plan, secn., site plan.

SCHOOLS--SECONDARY--ALTERATIONS AND
ADDITIONS--SCOTLAND--ALLOA--ALLOA
ACADEMY
Alloa Academy.
Renovation to secondary school,
Alloa, Scotland. Architect:
Central Regional Council. Project
architect for design: John
Davison.
BUILDING 1990 Apr.27, v.255,
no.17, p.55-62, photos., plans,
secn., site plan, tables.

SCHOOLS--SECONDARY--AUSTRALIA--
LAKELAND--LAKELAND HIGH SCHOOL
The Western edge / Geoffrey London,
Simon Anderson.
Work by 3 young architects in
Western Australia: Robert Moore,
Donaldson + Warn, and Paul Jones.
ARCHITECTURE AUSTRALIA 1990 May,
v.79, no.4, p.48-55, axonometric
view, models, photos., plans.

SCHOOLS--SECONDARY--BRICK--AUSTRALIA--
MANDURAH--COODANUP HIGH SCHOOL
1990 Clay Brick Award.
Awarded to Coodanup High School,
Mandurah.
THE ARCHITECT, W.A.: THE OFFICIAL
JOURNAL OF THE ROYAL AUSTRALIAN
INSTITUTE OF ARCHITECTS, W.A.
CHAPTER 1990, v.30, no.4,
p.12-[13], photos.

SCHOOLS--SECONDARY--COMPETITIONS--
GERMANY (WEST)--KOBLENZ
Fachhochschule Koblenz.
Report on competition. First
prize: Karl Eichler. Second
prize: Joseph Schmitz.
BAUWELT 1990 Mar.2, v.81, no.9,
p.366, models.

SCHOOLS--SECONDARY--ENGLAND--LONDON--
FINCHLEY CATHOLIC HIGH SCHOOL--CDT
BUILDING
School report: CDT Building,
Finchley [Catholic High School].
Martin Goalen Architects.
Contents: Appraisal, by David
Jenkins; Economic appraisal, by
Roger Barbrook; Cost analysis;
External walls and roof, school,
Martin Goalen Architects.
ARCHITECTS' JOURNAL 1990 Mar.7,
v.191, no.10 p.39-45,50-53,55,
61-63, dets., elev., model,
photos., plans, secns., site
plans, table, isometric dwg.,
refs.

SCHOOLS--SECONDARY--FINLAND--TUUSULA--
TUUSULAN SOSIIALIALAN OPPILAITOS
Tuusulan sosiaalialan oppilaitos,
Tuusula = Tuusula School of Social
Studies.
Architects: Arkkitehtitoimisto NVO
KY. Includes essay by Anna-Maija
Ylimaula and an English
translation.
ARKKITEHTI 1989, v.86, no.8,
p.58-63, elevs., photos., plans,
site plan.

SCHOOLS--SECONDARY--FRANCE--BOBIGNY--
COLLEGE PIERRE SEMARD
College Pierre Semard, Bobigny.
Architect: Iwona Buczkowska.
English summary, p.124; Spanish
summary, p.173.
TECHNIQUES ET ARCHITECTURE 1990
Oct.-Nov., no.392, p.122-124,
dwgs., models, plan, secns.

SCHOOLS--SECONDARY--FRANCE--ORVAULT
Equipements scolaires.
Focus on four school buildings:
high school, Paris 15e,
architects: Olivier Brenac and
Xavier-Jose Gonzalez; middle
school, Mas-d'Azil, architects:
Joseph Almudever and Christian
Lefebvre; elementary school, Evry,
architects: Bernard Dufournet,
Alain Rihn and high school,
Orvault, architects: Gaelle and
Dominique Peneau.
TECHNIQUES ET ARCHITECTURE 1990
Mar., no.388, p.32-44, photos.,
plans, site plans, sketch.

SCHOOLS--SECONDARY--FRANCE--PARIS--ZAC
CITROEN-CEVENNES
Equipements scolaires.
Focus on four school buildings:
high school, Paris 15e,
architects: Olivier Brenac and
Xavier-Jose Gonzalez; middle
school, Mas-d'Azil, architects:
Joseph Almudever and Christian
Lefebvre; elementary school, Evry,
architects: Bernard Dufournet,
Alain Rihn and high school,
Orvault, architects: Gaelle and
Dominique Peneau.
TECHNIQUES ET ARCHITECTURE 1990
(Continued next column)

SCHOOLS--SECONDARY--FRANCE--PARIS--ZAC
CITROEN-CEVENNES (CONTINUED)
Equipements scolaires. (CONTINUED)
Mar., no.388, p.32-44, photos.,
plans, site plans, sketch.

SCHOOLS--SECONDARY--FRANCE--
SAINT-DENIS--COLLEGE ELSA TRIOLET
Porro, rue Paul Eluard a Saint-Denis
/ Marie-Jeanne Dumont.
College Elsa Triolet is shaped
like a dove. Architects: Ricardo
Porro, Renaud de La Noue. English
summary, p.85.
ARCHITECTURE D'AUJOURD'HUI 1990
Sept., no.270, p.82-85, model,
photos., plans, site plans.

SCHOOLS--SECONDARY--GERMANY (WEST)--
ALZEY--GUSTAV-HEINEMANN REALSCHULE
Alzey: Haupt-und Schulzentrum
Gustav-Heinemann-Realschule /
Hans=Joachim Aminde.
Architects: Landkreis Alzey-Worms,
Stadt Alzey, Rudolf Frangel.
Landscape architect: Peter Wirth,
Luz + Partner.
BAUWELT 1990 Apr.27, v.81, no.16,
p.799-803, photos., plans, secns.,
site plan.

SCHOOLS--SECONDARY--GERMANY (WEST)--
BERLIN--ALBERT-EINSTEIN-SCHULE
Erweiterung der
Albert-Einstein-Schule in
Berlin-Neukolln.
Architect: Stefan Scholz, of
Bangert, Jansen, Scholz, Schultes.
BAUWELT 1990 Sept.28, v.81, no.36,
p.1752-1753, dwg., photos.

SCHOOLS--SECONDARY--GERMANY (WEST)--
INGOLSTADT--FACHOBERSCHULE
Eine neue Schule in einer alter
Kaserne: Samierung der
Flandernkaserne fur die
Fachoberschule Ingolstadt.
Architect for the conversion:
Erhard Fischer.
BAUWELT 1990 July 13, v.81, no.26,
p.1338-1342, photos., plans, secn.

SCHOOLS--SECONDARY--GERMANY (WEST)--
LORCH
Special feature: Guenter Behnisch.
Contents: Seven works: Hysolar
Institute building, Stuttgart
University.-- New facility for
Leybold AG.-- Library building of
the Catholic University.--
Administration building of the
charitable services of Lutheran
church.-- Secondary school,
Schafersfeld.-- German Postal
Museum.-- Station Square,
Stuttgart. Twelve projects: German
national bank.-- Central
administration building for the
LTG.-- Garage in the Olympic
park.-- School and sports hall.--
Restaurant in the Olympic swimming
pool.-- Kindergarten.-- Olympic
stadium.== Exhibition center.--
Exhibition and conference
center.-- Central area of the
German Federal Parliament.--
German National Library. Essay:
Guenter Behnisch and Partners: a
continuing contribution to the
organic tradition in German
Modernism / Peter Blundell Jones.
ARCHITECTURE AND URBANISM 1990
(Continued next page)

SCHOOLS--SECONDARY--GERMANY (WEST)--
LORCH (CONTINUED)
Special feature:...(CONTINUED)
May, no.5(236), p.34-138, elevs.,
models, photos., plans, secns.,
site plans.

SCHOOLS--SECONDARY--GERMANY (WEST)--
REUTLINGEN--VOLKSHOCHSCHULE
Neubau Volkshochschule / Amber
Sayah.
Located on the Spendhausstrasse on
the outskirts of Reutlingen.
Architect: Rossmann + Partner.
Interior designers: Herta Maria
Witzemann, Robert Haussmann.
BAUWELT 1990 Jan.19, v.81, no.2-3,
p.103-107, elevs., photos., plans,
secns., site plan.

SCHOOLS--SECONDARY--GERMANY (WEST)--
SULZBACH
Lesen und Lernen: Volkshochschule
und Bucherei in Sulzbach.
Architects: Miroslav Volf,
Katarina Hrankovicova.
DEUTSCHE BAUZEITUNG 1990 Mar.,
v.124, no.3, p.60-61, elev.,
photos., plan, secn.

SCHOOLS--SECONDARY--ITALY--DOLO--
MASSIMA SCUOLA SECONDARIA
Centro scolastico distrettuale di
Dolo.
School designed and built
1978-1987. Architect: Valeriano
Pastor, with Silvio Paolini,
Renato Rizzi and Patrizia Valle.
Text in Italian and English.
ANFIONE ZETO 1989, v.1, no.1,
p.16-211, axonometric views,
port., elevs., photos., plans,
secns., site plans.

SCHOOLS--SECONDARY--ITALY--SAMBRUSON--
SCUOLA MEDIA
Silvio Paolini e Patrizia Valle:
Scuola media a Sambruson-Dolo
(VE), Ing. Luigi Muffato
(strutture) / Valeriano Pastor.
Text in Italian and English.
ANFIONE ZETO 1989, v.1, no.2-3,
p.256-277, axonometric view,
elevs., model, photos., plans,
secns., site plans.

SCHOOLS--SECONDARY--JAPAN--
TOKOROZAWA--WASEDA SEMINAR
Waseda Seminar in Tokorozawa /
Yuzuru Tominaga.
Secondary school. Architects:
Yuzuru Tominaga, Form System
Institute.
JAPAN ARCHITECT 1990 July, v.65,
no.7(399), p.20-25, axonometric
view, elevs., photos., plans,
secn., site plan.

SCHOOLS--SECONDARY--RESEARCH--NEW
ZEALAND--CHRISTCHURCH
Improving secondary school grounds:
do we have it all wrong? / David
Richardson.
Study of 14 State schools in
Christchurch area.
THE LANDSCAPE 1989 Winter-Spring,
no.42/43, p.13-17, photos.,
tables, biblio.

SCHOOLS--SECONDARY--SPAIN--BADALONA--
SALAVADOR ESPRIU
Escuela en Badalona: J.I. de
Llorens, J. Ma. Massot y A.
Soldevila, arquitectos.
Spanish, English text.
ON DISENO 1990, no.113, p.114-121,
elevs., photos., plans.

SCHOOLS--SECONDARY--SPAIN--BARCELONA--
INSTITUTO HUGUE
Public facilities.
Part of a special feature on
Spanish contemporary architecture.
Contents: Museo de Navarra, by
Jordi Garces, Enric Soria.--
Biblioteca Publica, by Victor
Lopez Cotelo, Carlos Puente.--
Molinos del Rio Segura, by Juan
Navarro Baldeweg.-- Puerta de
Toledo, by Nuan Navarro
Baldeweg.-- Escuela de artes y
oficios artisticos, by Jose
Antonio Corrales.-- Instituto
Hugue, by Luis Bravo Farre, Albert
Blanch Rubio.-- Brief Histories.
Text in Japanese.
SPACE DESIGN 1990 May, no.308,
p.11-54, ports., elevs., photos.,
plans, secns., site plans.

SCHOOLS--SECONDARY--SPAIN--BARCELONA--
LA LLUANA
Inclined planes, calibrated with
care / Philip Arcidi.
La Lluana high school, Barcelona,
which was converted from a
factory. Architects: Ehric
Miralles, Carme Pinos.
PROGRESSIVE ARCHITECTURE 1990
Aug., v.71, no.8, p.108-109,
photos., plans, secns.

SCHOOLS--SECONDARY--SPAIN--CALDES DE
MONTBUI
Liceo intorno a un fulcro presso
Barcellona.
Architects: Lluis Bravo, Albert
Blanch.
ARCHITETTURA; CRONACHE E STORIA
1990 May, v.36, no.5(415),
p.368-369, photos., plans, secn.

SCHOOLS--SECONDARY--SWEDEN--
OSTERFARNEBO--KYRKSKOLAN
Teori och praktik / Lis Hogdahl.
Features two elementary schools,
in Vastervik and Taby (architects:
ATRIO Arkitekter; Dranger och
Kvant Arkitektkontor); a parish
secondary school in Osterfarnebo
(architect: Carlson Fernberg
Arkitektkontor); and a crafts
school in Stockholm (architect:
Asmussens arkitektkontor).
ARKITEKTUR: THE SWEDISH REVIEW OF
ARCHITECTURE 1990 Dec., v.90,
no.10, p.10-21,cover, photos.,
plans, site plans.

SCHOOLS--SECONDARY--UNITED STATES--
SIMSBURY (CONNECTICUT)--WESTMINSTER
SCHOOL
Building Types Study 682: Campus
buildings: Extracurricular
education / Grace Anderson.
Four recently-completed buildings:
Salomon Center for Teaching, Brown
Univ. (Goody, Clancy & Assoc.);
Psychology Building, Vanderbilt
Univ. (Stubbins Assoc.);
Centennial Performing Arts Center,
(Continued next column)

SCHOOLS--SECONDARY--UNITED STATES--
SIMSBURY (CONNECTICUT)--WESTMINSTER
SCHOOL (CONTINUED)
Building Types Study...(CONTINUED)
Westminster School, Simsbury Conn.
(Graham Gund Architects); and
Price Center, Univ. of Calif. at
San Diego (Kaplan/McLaughlin/Diaz
Architects).
ARCHITECTURAL RECORD 1990 Aug.,
v.178, no.9, p.83-[95], elevs.,
photos., plans, secns., site
plans.

SCHOOLS--SECONDARY--UNITED STATES--
SUNLAND PARK (NEW MEXICO)--CAPITAL
HIGH SCHOOL
Una scuola nel deserto del Nuovo
Messico = Riverside School in
Sunland Park, New Mexico / Silvano
Stucchi.
Architects: Perkins & Will.
Includes English translation;
French, German, and Spanish
summaries, p.4.
L'INDUSTRIA DELLE COSTRUZIONI 1990
Jan., v.24, no.219, p.32-37,cover,
axonometric views, dwgs., elev.,
photos., plans, site plan.

SCHOOLS--SPAIN--BARCELONA--BIG BEN
SCHOOL
Acondicionamiento de una escuela:
Daniel Navas y Neus Sole,
arquitectos.
Spanish, English text.
ON DISENO 1989, no.104, p.140-145,
photos., plans, sketches.

SCHOOLS--SPAIN--MASQUEFA
Civic monuments.
Three projects by Esteve Bonell:
School, Masquefa, with Josep Maria
Gil; law courts, Gerona, with
Josep Maria Gil and the sports
arena, Badalona, with Francesc
Rius.
ARCHITECTURAL REVIEW 1990 July,
v.188, no.1121, p.69-73, elevs.,
models, photos., plans, secns.,
site plan.

SCHOOLS--SPAIN--PORT DE SAGUNT
La arquitectura de Vetges Tu:
Mediterrania = The architecture of
Vetges Tu: Mediterrania.
Most of issue devoted to works by
this Spanish firm. Contents:
Jardin del Turia, Valencia;
Televisio Valenciana; cementerio
de Tavernes de la Valldigna;
Centro escolar publico en Port de
Sagunt; viviendas en quart de
Poblet; estudio de detalle y
viviendas en La Flota, Murcia; dos
viviendas rehabilitadas en la
huerta murciana; vestuarios en
tavernes de la Valldigna,
Valencia. Text in Italian and
English.
ON DISENO 1990, no.112(suppl.),
p.113-191, axonometric views,
ill., dwgs., elevs., models,
photos., plans, site plans, aerial
photos.

SCHOOLS - SPECIAL
See also MILITARY ACADEMIES
See also SCHOOLS - VOCATIONAL
See also SCHOOLS FOR THE HANDICAPPED

SCHOOLS--SPECIAL--ALTERATIONS AND
ADDITIONS--GERMANY (WEST)--BERLIN--
EVANGELISCHE SCHULE CHARLOTTENBURG
Berlin: Evangelische Schule
Charlottenburg.
School built 1969-1972
(Architects: Gerd Neumann, Dietmar
Grotzebach, Gunter Plessow, NGP).
Facade modernized 1988-1989
(architects: Gerd Neumann, Gunter
Plessow).
BAUWELT 1990 Apr.27, v.81, no.16,
p.808-813, photos., plans, secn.,
site plan.
Cemento come pelle e/o come volume =
Cement like skin and/or like
volume [Evangelical school,
Berlin-Charlottenburg].
Architects: G. Neumann, G.
Plessow; D. Grotzebach.
ARCHITETTURA: CRONACHE E STORIA
1990 Oct., v.36, no.10(420),
p.722-723, photos., plan, secn.,
site plans.

SCHOOLS--SPECIAL--ALTERATIONS AND
ADDITIONS--SWITZERLAND--THUN--
SEMINAR THUN
Kunstvoll eingestreut: Umbau und
Erweiterung Staatliches
Lehrerseminar in Thun.
Architects: Atelier 5.
DEUTSCHE BAUZEITUNG 1990 Apr.,
v.124, no.4, p.20-25, photos.,
plans, site plan.

SCHOOLS--SPECIAL--AUSTRALIA--RYDE--
AUSTRALIAN FILM, TELEVISION AND
RADIO SCHOOL
Daryl Jackson: four projects / Daryl
Jackson.
The Australian Film, Television
and Radio School, North Ryde, NSW;
Bond University, Queensland;
Penguin Parade, Phillip Island,
Victoria; and Australian Chancery,
Riyadh, Saudi Arabia.
ARCHITECTURE AUSTRALIA 1990 Mar.,
v.79, no.2, p.27-42, dets., dwgs.,
photos., plans, secns., site
plans, aerial photo.

SCHOOLS--SPECIAL--BELGIUM--LIEGE--
MAISON HEUREUSE
Een kunst van weinig woorden: vier
ontwerpen van Bruno Albert,
Charles Vandenhove en John Berhaut
/ Arthur Wortmann.
Four Liege projects: design for
the Hogere Handelsschool (1989),
with Camille Ghysen; Le Balloir
(1988-1991); La Maison Heureuse,
Ans (1986-1989); Woning Sutoor,
Embourg (1988-1989).
ARCHIS 1990 July, no.7, p.15-24,
elevs., photos., plans, secn.,
refs.

SCHOOLS--SPECIAL--CANADA--CHILCOTIN
(BRITISH COLUMBIA)--STONE BAND
SCHOOL
The Canadian Architect 1990 22nd
Annual Awards of Excellence.
Eight awards. Architects: Steven
Fong, A.J. Diamond, Donald Schmitt
& Co. with Kolker Kolker Epstein
Architects, Meltzer Igra
(Continued next column)

SCHOOLS--SPECIAL--CANADA--CHILCOTIN
(BRITISH COLUMBIA)--STONE BAND
SCHOOL (CONTINUED)
The Canadian...(CONTINUED)
Architects, Bugod Figueiredo
Krendel Architects, Peter Cardew
Architects, Richard Henriquez
Architect, Laszlo Nemeth Assoc.,
Kearns Mancini Architects, Patkan
Architects, Saucier + Perrotte,
and Kuwabara Payne McKenna
Blumberg.
CANADIAN ARCHITECT 1990 Dec.,
v.35, no.12, p.9-24,29, dwgs.,
elevs., models, plans, secns.,
site plans.

SCHOOLS--SPECIAL--DENMARK--HERNING--
EKSPORTSKOLEN
Eksportskolen i Herning / Erik
Nygaard.
Located at Uldjydevej, in Birk,
northern Jutland. Architect: C.F.
Mollers Tegnestue. Includes
English and German summaries.
ARKITEKTUR DK 1990, v.34, no.7,
p.337-343, photos., plans, secns.,
site plan.

SCHOOLS--SPECIAL--FRANCE--AMBOISE--
LYCEE VITICOLE
Fins de chantier.
Contents: Public library, Avrille,
France; architects: Martine
Weissmann & Jean Leonard-- Nursery
school, 1-3 square Alban-Satragne,
Paris; architect: Emmanuelle
Colboc-- Nursery school,
Marseille, France; architects: CCD
Architecture-- Viticulture school,
Amboise, France; architects:
Pierre Caillot & Philippe Alluin.
LE MONITEUR ARCHITECTURE AMC 1990
Oct., no.15, p.17-23, elevs.,
photos., plans, secn.

SCHOOLS--SPECIAL--GERMANY (EAST)--
HELLERAU--INSTITUT DALCROZE
Hellerau: ein neuer Anfang.
The Festspielhaus of 1911-1912 was
used by troops during World War II
and in May 1990 by art students.
Architect: Heinrich Tessenow.
BAUWELT 1990 Dec.7, v.81, no.46,
p.2286, photos.
Modernity and reform, Heinrich
Tessenow and the Institut Dalcroze
at Hellerau / Marco De Michelis.
Built ca. 1911-1912, and visited
by Le Corbusier. Appendix includes
biographical data on five key
participants in the institute.
PERSPECTA 1990, no.26, p.143-170,
dwgs., elevs., photos., plans,
refs.

SCHOOLS--SPECIAL--GERMANY (WEST)--
ROMMELSBACH
Per aspera ad astra, oder: die
Umkehrung der Quadratur des
Kreises: Zwei Schulen von Peter
Hubner.
Grundschul-Pavillon in
Stuttgart-Stammheim, and
Christian-Morgenstern-Schule in
Reutlingen.
DEUTSCHE BAUZEITUNG 1990 Feb.,
v.124, no.2, p.28-33, models,
photos., plans, secns., site plan,
sketches, isometric dwg.

SCHOOLS--SPECIAL--SWEDEN--STOCKHOLM--
KRISTOFFERSKOLAN
Teori och praktik / Lis Hogdahl.
Features two elementary schools,
in Vastervik and Taby (architects:
ATRIO Arkitekter; Dranger och
Kvant Arkitektkontor); a parish
secondary school in Osterfarnebo
(architect: Carlson Fernberg
Arkitektkontor); and a crafts
school in Stockholm (architect:
Asmussens arkitektkontor).
ARKITEKTUR: THE SWEDISH REVIEW OF
ARCHITECTURE 1990 Dec., v.90,
no.10, p.10-21,cover, photos.,
plans, site plans.

SCHOOLS--SPECIAL--UNITED STATES--
FINLAND (MINNESOTA)--WOLF RIDGE
ENVIRONMENTAL LEARNING CENTER
Rooms with a view: Setter Leach &
Lindstrom gives young people a
front-row seat in nature's
classroom.
Wolf Ridge Environmental Learning
Center, Finland, Minnesota.
ARCHITECTURE MINNESOTA 1990
Sept.-Oct., v.16, no.5, p.26-29,
photos., site plan.

SCHOOLS--SWEDEN
Diskussion pagar / Gunnar
Lowenhielm.
On the General Study Plan for
Swedish Schools, with
illustrations of works by FFNS,
Studio 4, A-TRE Arkitekter,
Dranger & Kvant Arkitektkontor,
and Fritzell Carlsen
Arkitektkontor. Includes English
summary.
ARKITEKTUR: THE SWEDISH REVIEW OF
ARCHITECTURE 1990 Dec., v.90,
no.10, p.4-9,59-60, photos.,
plans, secns.
En Skola for livet?
Introduction to issue featuring
schools. Individual articles are
indexed separately. Includes
English summary.
ARKITEKTUR: THE SWEDISH REVIEW OF
ARCHITECTURE 1990 Dec., v.90,
no.10, p.2-3,59, photo.

SCHOOLS--SWEDEN--JARNA--RUDOLF STEINER
SEMINARIET
Bewegt ruhende Form: die Architektur
von Erik Asmussen / Gary Coates,
Susanne Siepl-Coates.
Seven buildings at the
Rudolf-Steiner-Seminariet, Jarna,
Sweden, built 1973-1991.
ARCHITHESE 1990 Sept.-Oct., v.20,
no.5, p.19-27, elevs., photos.,
plans, secns., site plans.

SCHOOLS--SWITZERLAND--ARZIER
Monumentalitat und Demokratie:
Schulhauser in Nyon, Arzier und
Tannay / Paolo Fumagalli.
Architect: Vincent Mangeat. French
text, p.67.
WERK, BAUEN + WOHNEN 1989 Oct.,
no.10, p.4-11, axonometric views,
elev., photos., plans, secns.,
site plan, isometric dwg., aerial
photo.

SCHOOLS--SWITZERLAND--NYON
    Gymnasium und Hohere Handelsschule
      in Nyon.
      Architect: Vincent Mangeat.
      DEUTSCHE BAUZEITSCHRIFT 1990 Dec.,
      v.38, no.12, p.1767-1774,
      axonometric views, elevs.,
      photos., plans, secns., site
      plans.
    Monumentalitat und Demokratie:
      Schulhauser in Nyon, Arzier und
      Tannay / Paolo Fumagalli.
      Architect: Vincent Mangeat. French
      text, p.67.
      WERK, BAUEN + WOHNEN 1989 Oct.,
      no.10, p.4-11, axonometric views,
      elev., photos., plans, secns.,
      site plan, isometric dwg., aerial
      photo.

SCHOOLS--SWITZERLAND--RIVA SAN VITALE
    Intorno al grande atrio: scuola a
      Riva San Vitale di Giancarlo
      Durisch = Around the great
      entrance: school at Riva San
      Vitale by Giancarlo Durisch / Luca
      Ortelli.
      LOTUS INTERNATIONAL 1989, no.63,
      p.90-95, elevs., photos., plans,
      secn., site plans.

SCHOOLS--SWITZERLAND--ROTKREUZ
    Oberstufenschulhaus Rotkreuz.
      Architects: Ammann & Baumann.
      WERK, BAUEN + WOHNEN 1990
      July-Aug., no.7-8, p.1-6 (folded,
      at back), photos., plans, secns.,
      site plan, table.

SCHOOLS - THEOLOGICAL
    See THEOLOGICAL SEMINARIES

SCHOOLS - VOCATIONAL
    See also JOB TRAINING CENTERS

SCHOOLS--VOCATIONAL--ALTERATIONS AND
    ADDITIONS--GERMANY (WEST)--
    INGOLSTADT--FLANDERNKASERNE
    Umbau der Flandernkaserne Ingolstadt
      (BRD).
      Built 1985-88. Architect: Erhard
      Fischer.
      WERK, BAUEN + WOHNEN 1990 Dec.,
      no.12, p.1-4, photos., plans,
      secn., site plans, aerial photo.

SCHOOLS--VOCATIONAL--AUSTRIA--
    SALZBURG--LEHRBAUHOF
    Lehrbauhof - Bauhutte Salzburg:
      Ausbildungszentrum fur das
      Baugewerbe, 1989.
      Architects: Michael Alder,
      Hanspeter Muller.
      WERK, BAUEN + WOHNEN 1990 May,
      no.5, p.4-11, det., photos.,
      plans, secns., site plan.

SCHOOLS--VOCATIONAL--BANGLADESH--
    DHAKA--ISLAMIC CENTRE FOR TECHNICAL
    AND VOCATIONAL TRAINING AND RESEARCH
    Islamic Centre for Technical and
      Vocational Training and Research,
      Dhaka / Abu H. Imamuddin.
      Founded in 1985, as an organ of
      the Organization of the Islamic
      Conference (OIC); building
      completed in 1987. Architects:
      Mehmet Doruk Pamir, Ercument
      Gumruk Associates.
      MIMAR: ARCHITECTURE IN DEVELOPMENT
      1990 Dec., v.10, no.4(37),
      p.34-[39], axonometric views,
      elevs., photos., site plan.

SCHOOLS--VOCATIONAL--BELGIUM--LIEGE--
    HOGERE HANDELSSCHOOL
    Een kunst van weinig woorden: vier
      ontwerpen van Bruno Albert,
      Charles Vandenhove en John Berhaut
      / Arthur Wortmann.
      Four Liege projects: design for
      the Hogere Handelsschool (1989),
      with Camille Ghysen; Le Balloir
      (1988-1991); La Maison Heureuse,
      Ans (1986-1989); Woning Sutoor,
      Embourg (1988-1989).
      ARCHIS 1990 July, no.7, p.15-24,
      elevs., photos., plans, secn.,
      refs.

SCHOOLS--VOCATIONAL--COMPETITIONS--
    GERMANY (WEST)--OHRINGEN--
    KAUFMANNISCHE BERUFSSCHULE
    Erste Preise: Schulen.
      Four projects: Kaufmannische
      Berufsschule, Ohringen (winner:
      Architekten Behnisch & Partner);
      addition to Realschule, Markt
      Indersdorf (winner: Peter Kaup,
      Helmut M. Scholz & Partner);
      addition and double gymnasium,
      Gesamtschule, Rodingshausen
      (winner: Gunter Schmidt +
      Friedrich Schmersahl); new
      gymnasium and sports building, Bad
      Neuenahr-Ahrweiler (winner: Georg
      A. Schutz).
      DEUTSCHES ARCHITEKTENBLATT 1990
      Jan.1, v.22, no.1, p.55-58, dwgs.,
      models, plan, secns., site plans.

SCHOOLS--VOCATIONAL--ENGLAND--DORSET--
    PARNHAM TRUST
    Forestry commission / Peter Davey.
      Parnham Trust woodworking school
      and research center in Dorset,
      built with forest thinnings.
      Architects: Richard Burton and
      Buro Happold.
      ARCHITECTURAL REVIEW 1990 Sept.,
      v.188, no.1123, p.[44]-48, dets.,
      photos., plans, secns., site
      plans.

SCHOOLS--VOCATIONAL--ENGLAND--HOOKE
    PARK--NEW WOODLAND INDUSTRIES SCHOOL
    Fruits of the forest / Richard
      Burton, William Moorwood, Anne
      Wilder.
      Two buildings in Hooke Park using
      untreated wood jointing structural
      technology. Architects: Frei Otto,
      Buro Happold, ABK.
      BUILDING DESIGN 1990 June, suppl.,
      p.12-13, dets., photos., secn.

SCHOOLS--VOCATIONAL--ENGLAND--
    LOUGHBOROUGH--ROYAL NATIONAL
    INSTITUTE FOR THE BLIND VOCATIONAL
    COLLEGE
    Touch has a memory / Julian Holder.
      Features the Royal National
      Institute for the Blind Vocational
      College, Loughborough.
      Architects: MacNeish Design
      Partnership.
      BUILDING DESIGN 1990 Apr.20,
      no.982, p.28-29, photos.

SCHOOLS--VOCATIONAL--FRANCE--
    MARSEILLE--LYCEE DIDEROT
    Lycee technique du batiment,
      Marseille.
      Lycee Diderot. Architects: Bui
      Kien Quoc with Pascal Urbain,
      Bernard Desmoulin, Jean-Marc
      Chancel. English summary, p.97;
      Spanish summary, p.172.
      TECHNIQUES ET ARCHITECTURE 1990
      Oct.-Nov., no.392, p.94-97,
      axonometric view, photos., plan,
      site plan.

SCHOOLS--VOCATIONAL--FRANCE--PARIS--
    LYCEE TECHNIQUE DIDEROT
    Lycee Technique Diderot, Paris.
      Architect: Jean-Francois Laurent.
      English summary, p.85. Spanish
      summary, p.172.
      TECHNIQUES ET ARCHITECTURE 1990
      Oct.-Nov., no.392, p.84-85,
      elevs., model, plan.

SCHOOLS--VOCATIONAL--GERMANY (WEST)--
    BERNAU--BUNDESSCHULE DES ALLGEMEINEN
    DEUTSCHEN GEWERKSCHAFTSBUNDES
    Dokumente der Architektur des 20.
      Jahrhunderts: Die Bundesschule des
      ADGB in Bernau / Roland Schneider.
      Built late 1920s. Architects:
      Hannes Meyer, Hans Wittwer.
      DER ARCHITEKT 1990 July-Aug.,
      no.7-8, p.330, photos.

SCHOOLS--VOCATIONAL--GERMANY (WEST)--
    GRUB--BAYERISCHE LANDESANSTALT FUR
    TIERZUCHT
    Unterrichts- und Internatsgebaude in
      Grub bei Munchen, D = Seminar and
      boarding school building in Grub
      near Munich, G.
      New building for an agricultural
      training school. Architects:
      Helmut Gebhard, Bernhard
      Landbrecht, Gunter Wagmann.
      DETAIL 1990 Feb.-Mar., v.30, no.1,
      p.39-46, dets., photos., plans,
      secns.

SCHOOLS--VOCATIONAL--GERMANY (WEST)--
    INGOLSTADT
    Berufsschulzentrum Ingolstadt =
      Vocational school centre
      Ingolstadt.
      Architect: Erhard Fischer.
      DETAIL 1990 Oct.-Nov., v.30, no.5,
      p.BI-BIV, dets., photos., plans,
      secns., site plans.
    Fachoberschule in Ingolstadt:
      Sanierte "Flandernkaserne".
      Architect: Erhard Fischer.
      Includes English summary.
      BAUMEISTER 1990 Feb., v.87, no.2,
      p.57-59, dets., elevs., dwgs.,
      photos., plans, secns.

SCHOOLS--VOCATIONAL--ITALY--LUCCA--
    ISTITUTO TECNICO INDUSTRIALE
    Istituto Tecnico Industriale a S.
      Filippo, Lucca.
      Architects: Lamberto Molteni with
      Rinaldo Evangelisti. Summaries in
      English, French, German, and
      Spanish.
      ARCHITETTURA; CRONACHE E STORIA
      1990 Jan., v.36, no.1(411),
      p.[6-15], elevs., model, photos.,
      plans, secns., site plan.

SCHOOLS--VOCATIONAL--ITALY--MORTISE--
ISTITUTO INDUSTRIALE TECNICO STATALE
FRANCESCO SEVERI
Un istituto tecnico a Padova.
On the Istituto Industriale
Tecnico Statale Francesco Severi,
Mortise. Architects: Domenico
Bagliani, Virgilio Corsico, Erinna
Roncarolo. Summaries in English,
French and Spanish.
ABACUS 1990 July-Sept., v.6,
no.23, p.46-55, dets., photos.,
plans, site plans.

SCHOOLS--VOCATIONAL--SPAIN--CAMBRILS--
ESCUELA DE HOSTELARIA
Escuela de hosteleria = Professional
training centre: Cambrils,
Tarragona, 1986/1988.
Architect: Victor Rahola.
EL CROQUIS 1990 Apr.-June, v.9,
no.43, p.124-131, dets., elevs.
photos., plans, secns.

SCHOOLS--VOCATIONAL--SPAIN--ESPIEL--
MERCE ROSELL
Meister der sensuellen Form: neue
Arbeiten von Bach und Mora.
Three projects: Kindertagesstatte
"Torre Baldovina" in Santa Coloma
de Gramenet; Weinbausschule "Merce
Rosell" in Espiells; Weinkellerei
"Cavas Raventos Blanc" in Sant
Sadurni d'Anoia. One of four
articles on the theme "Barcelona
bauen".
BAUWELT 1990 Mar.2, v.81, no.9,
p.386-387, axonometric view,
plans, photos.

SCHOOLS--VOCATIONAL--SPAIN--SAN
SADURNI DE NOYA--CAVAS RAVENTOS
BLANC
Archaic in Arcadia.
Features two wine-related projects
in Sant-Sadurni d'Anoia by Jaume
Bach and Gabriel Mora: Raventos
Blanc winery, and the school of
viticulture and enology.
ARCHITECTURAL REVIEW 1990 July,
v.188, no.1121, p.60-67, elevs.,
photos., plans, secns., site
plans, aerial photos.
Archaische Anklange an Arkadien:
Weinkellerei und Schule fur
Weinbau in Sant Sadurni d'Anota
[sic], 1986-1988.
Architects: Jaume Bach & Gabriel
Mora.
WERK, BAUEN + WOHNEN 1990 Nov.,
no.11, p.2-11, elevs., photos.,
plans, secns., site plans, aerial
photo.
Meister der sensuellen Form: neue
Arbeiten von Bach und Mora.
Three projects: Kindertagesstatte
"Torre Baldovina" in Santa Coloma
de Gramenet; Weinbausschule "Merce
Rosell" in Espiells; Weinkellerei
"Cavas Raventos Blanc" in Sant
Sadurni d'Anoia. One of four
articles on the theme "Barcelona
bauen".
BAUWELT 1990 Mar.2, v.81, no.9,
p.386-387, axonometric view,
plans, photos.
Spagna, Alto Penedes: le Cantine
Raventos i Blanc = Spain, Alto
Penedes: the Raventos i Blanc
Winery / Tamara Holihari.
Architects: Jaume Bach, Gabriel
Mora.

(Continued next column)

SCHOOLS--VOCATIONAL--SPAIN--SAN
SADURNI DE NOYA--CAVAS RAVENTOS
BLANC (CONTINUED)
Spagna, Alto Penedes:...(CONTINUED)
ABITARE 1990 June, no.286,
p.134-[141], photos, plans,
secns., site plan, aerial photo.

SCHOONERS--19TH CENTURY--CONSERVATION
AND RESTORATION--UNITED STATES--
CAMDEN (MAINE)--GRACE BAILEY
(MATTIE)
Restoring Grace Bailey / James P.
Delgado.
A two-masted schooner built in
1882, renamed Mattie in 1906, and
since 1986 being restored in
Camden, Maine.
CRM BULLETIN: A NATIONAL PARK
SERVICE TECHNICAL BULLETIN 1990,
v.13, no.4, p.33, photos.

SCHOOR, HENK VAN DER
De Papaverhof in ere hersteld:
renovatie in de geest van
oorspronkelijk ontwerp / Henk van
der Schoor.
On the 1920 design for the garden
apartment complex, the De Stijl
movement, F.L. Wright's influence,
and the recent restoration of the
buildings. Original architect: Jan
Wils. Renovation architect: J.
Franso.
DE ARCHITECT 1989 Dec., v.20,
no.12, p.92-99, dwg., photos.,
plans, secns., site plan.

SCHOPENHAUER, ARTHUR, 1788-1860
Ethics and architecture / John
Capelli, Paul Naprstek, Bruce
Prescott, editors.
Theme of issue. Seven articles
are indexed separately. The
others are: Art and ethics in
Kant, Hegel, and Schopenhauer, by
Lucian Krukowski -- Inmediasres,
by David Bell -- The act of music,
by Robert Fripp.
VIA 1990, no.10, p.[5]-165, ill.,
photos.

SCHRAGER, IAN
For Ian Schrager, design is
paramount / Fred A. Bernstein.
Renovation and interior design of
Paramount Hotel, at Eight Ave. and
46th St., New York by Schrager and
Philippe Starck.
METROPOLITAN HOME 1990 Nov., v.22,
no.11, p.63-[70],164, port.,
photos.
Hall of Fame: celebrations and
memories [1990].
Profiles of twelve new inductees
into the Interior Design Hall of
Fame and the winners of three
special citations.
INTERIOR DESIGN 1990 Dec., v.61,
no.16, p.105-[125], ports.,
photos.

SCHRAMM, VON BASSEWITZ UND HUPERTZ
Grossburger lich: das Cafe im
Literaturhaus Hamburg.
Architects: Schramm, von
Bassewitz, Hupertz & Partner.
DEUTSCHE BAUZEITUNG 1990 Oct.,
v.124, no.10, p.76-81, photos.,
plan, secn.

SCHRAMMEL, HANS
Einrichtung des Staatsarchivs
Schwaben in Augsburg.
On several types of metal shelving
used in the archive in Augsburg.
Architect: Hans Schrammel.
DEUTSCHES ARCHITEKTENBLATT 1990
Apr.1, v.22, no.4, p.616-617,
photos.

SCHREGENBERGER, THOMAS
Das Detail als Kommentar / Gunter
Bock.
An addition to a studio by Harry
Roos and Thomas Schregenberger,
Zurich, 1987.
ARCHITHESE 1990 Nov.-Dec., v.20,
no.6, p.54-[55], photos., models,
sketches.

SCHREIBER, DETLEF
Lagerhalle Gundelfingen und
Montagehalle Stonehouse.
Two buildings with flat roofs.
Architect: Detlef Schreiber.
Includes English summary.
BAUMEISTER 1990 Oct., v.87, no.10,
p.15-27, dets., dwg., photos.,
plans, secns., site plan, aerial
photos.

SCHREIBER, PHILIP A.
Restoration at the Hill house /
Philip A. Schreiber.
CHARLES RENNIE MACKINTOSH SOCIETY.
NEWSLETTER 1990 Spring, no.53,
p.7, elev.

SCHREIBER, STEPHEN D.
Architecture on the edge / Stephen
D. Schreiber.
On the landscape in South Florida
and the boundaries (barrier
islands, coastal ridge and
landfill) that have influenced the
constructed ewnvironment.
CRIT 1990 Spring, no.24, p.16-20,
refs.

SCHREIBER, WALTER
Berlin: Dreilinden Grundschule in
Nikolassee / Jan C. Bassenge.
Architect: Architektengemeinschaft
Jan C. Bassenge, Kay Puhan-Schulz,
Johannes Heinrich, Walter
Schreiber. Planner: Walter
Schreiber.
BAUWELT 1990 Apr.27, v.81, no.16,
p.794-798, elevs., photos., plans,
secns., site plans.

SCHREYER, MICHAELE, 1951-
Der Verfall der Stadte in der DDR.
Issue features East German
architecture. Contents: Wovon
spricht die Architektur der DDR?,
by Walter Kruger-- Blindes
Fortschrittsdenken und boses
Erwachen, by Bruno Flierl--
Stadterhaltung in der DDR: Stand
April 1990, by Peter Goralczyk--
Stadtzerstorung in... [10
cities] - Schlicht und einfach
nach GRW? [interview with Jan C.
Bassenge, Joachim Ganz, Hans
Kollhoff, Wolfgang Nagel, Michaele
Schreyer, Eberhard Weinbrenner.
BAUWELT 1990 May 18, v.81, no.19,
p.938-961, maps, photos.

SCHROCKER, RUDOLF
"Licht im Raum" / Rudolf Schricker.
Report on the Ludwigsburger
Forums-Dialog sponsored by the
BDIA Landesverband
Baden-Wurttemberg, including
comments by Harald Hoffrann, Hans
T. von Malotki, and Karl-Fritz
Roll.
DEUTSCHES ARCHITEKTENBLATT 1990
Mar.1, v.22, no.1, p.385-388,
photos.

SCHRODER, HERMANN, 1928-
An der Mauer: "Wohn- und Gewerbehof
am Park" in der Sudlichen
Friedrichstadt, Berlin / Falk
Jaeger.
Torhaus Kochstrasse, architects:
Bohigas Martorell Mackay; Wohn-und
Gewerbehaus Kochstrasse,
architects: Peter Faller, C.
Muschalek, H. Schroder.
DEUTSCHE BAUZEITUNG 1990 Aug.,
v.124, no.8, p.38-43, photos.,
plans, secns., site plan.
Architektur unterwegs.
Four projects: Austellungshalle
"Alter Bahnhof", Rosenheim
(architect: Joseph Karg); Rathaus
Husum am Binnenhafen, Husum
(architect: Patschan - Werner -
Winking); Schulpark
Gottingen-Weende, Gottingen
(landscape architect: Gunther
Quentin); Bayerische
Demonstrativbaum-assnahme,
Passau-Neustift (architect: Herman
Schroder & Sampo Widmann).
DEUTSCHES ARCHITEKTENBLATT 1990
May 1, v.22, no.5, p.727-730,
elevs., photos., plans, secn.,
site plans.
Wohnungspolitische Konzepte:
Wohnungsbauprojekte / Rudi Kujath.
Section on many new housing
projects in Germany. Contents:
Berlin, by Rudi Kujath.--Koln, by
Uwe Kessler.--Bayern, by Dieter
Gutekunst.--Frankfurt, by Martin
Wentz.--Hannover, by Hanns
Adrian.--Der LEG
Nordrhein-Westfalen, by Roswitha
Sinz.--Anmerkungen..., by Hartmut
Grosshans. Among the architects
represented are Otto Steidle +
Partner; Andreas Brandt & Rudolf
Bottcher; Joachim Ganz, Walter
Rolfes; Axel Schultes; Wolfgang
Scharlach und Rainer Wischhusen;
Rebecca Chestnutt et al; Hubertus
Hoffmann; Paul Petry; Hermann
Schroder, Sampo Widmann; Gerhart
Laage; Freed Ahrens.
BAUWELT 1990 Mar.30, v.81, no.12,
p.572-598, elevs., plans, secns.,
site plans, tables.

SCHRODER, ULRICH
Worstward Ho - Aufs schlimmste zu?
Hannover auf dem Weg zur Expo 2000
/ Ulrich Schroder.
BAUWELT 1990 Sept.28, v.81, no.36,
p.1829-1831, dwgs., refs.

SCHROEDER MURCHIE LAYA ASSOCIATES
Spaces for a spiritual existence /
Karen E. Klages.
Renovation of a "two-flat" house
in Chicago. Architect: Schroeder
Murchie Laya Associates.
INLAND ARCHITECT 1990 Mar.-Apr.,
(Continued next column)

SCHROEDER MURCHIE LAYA ASSOCIATES
(CONTINUED)
Spaces for a...(CONTINUED)
v.34, no.2, p.4-5, photos., secn.

SCHROTH, STEFAN
A place in Berlin / Stefan Schroth.
IBA-commissioned apartment house,
Lutzowplatz, Berlin. Architects:
Cook & Hawley.
ARCHITECTURAL REVIEW 1990 Dec.,
v.188, no.1126, p.44-49, elev.,
photos., plans, secn., site plan.

SCHROWE, NORBERT
Kostbar: Juweliergeschaft Breede in
Munchen.
Architect: Norbert Schrowe.
DEUTSCHE BAUZEITUNG 1990 Oct.,
v.124, no.10, p.36-37, axonometric
view, photos., plan.

SCHUBERT, PETER
Theatralische Entausserung eines
Interieurs = Theatrical
renunciation of the interior.
Auditorium ceiling painting by
Peter Schubert. Architect: Paul
Baumgarten.
DAIDALOS 1990 June 15, no.36,
p.122-125, photos.

SCHUBIGER, BENNO
Zwei unbekannte Federzeichnungen von
Urs Graf mit den fruhesten
Ansichten der Stadt Solothurn /
Christiane Andersson, Benno
Schubiger.
ZEITSCHRIFT FUR SCHWEIZERISCHE
ARCHAOLOGIE UND KUNSTGESCHICHTE
1990, v.47, no.1, p.8-20, dwgs.,
maps, engrs., refs.

SCHUHMACHER, KLAUS
Erste Preise: Wohnbauten.
Four projects: "Schlossmarkt"
Rechberghausen (architect: Dieter
Beyer et al.);
Muhlenstrasse/Rosengarten, Neuss
(architect: Robert Ingenhoven);
garden apartments, Forchheim
(architect: Walter Prokop);
Bewohnerzentrum, Konstanz
(architects: Klaus Schumacher,
Michael Hoffmann).
DEUTSCHES ARCHITEKTENBLATT 1990
Mar.1, v.22, no.1, p.345-348,
elevs., models, plans, secns.,
site plans.

SCHUITEN, FRANCOIS. ARCHIVARIS
De Archivaris [by] Francois
Schuiten, Benoit Peeters [book
review] / Arthur Wortmann.
ARCHIS 1990 Feb., no.2, p.54-55,
dwg.

SCHULITZ, HELMUT C.
Architektur des Machens / Norman
Foster.
Includes a discussion on
architecture and technology by Otl
Aicher, Gunter Behnisch, Fritz
Haller, Helmut Schulitz, Peter von
Seidlein, and others.
ARCH PLUS 1990 Jan., no.102,
p.29-36, dets., ill., model,
photos.

SCHULITZ, HELMUT C. (CONTINUED)
Konstruktive Intelligenz / Peter
Rice.
Includes a discussion by
architects G. Behnisch, C.
Vasconi, O. Aicher, J. Nouvel, H.
Schulitz & R. Rogers and engineers
S. Polonyi, P. Rice, and H.
Malotki.
ARCH PLUS 1990 Jan., no.102,
p.42-52, dets., photos.
Technik und Poesie: Haus Vasa in
West-Los Angeles (1984-1985).
Architects: Jurg Lang, Helmut C.
Schulitz.
ARCHITEKTUR, INNENARCHITEKTUR,
TECHNISCHER AUSBAU 1990 Jan.-Feb.,
v.98, no.1-2, p.18-21, dets.,
photos., plans, secns.

SCHULT, CHRISTA
Aufbau eines Gartenamtes / Christa
Schult.
On the formation of a parks dept.
in Stralsund, East Germany.
English summary and captions.
GARTEN UND LANDSCHAFT 1990, v.100,
no.11, p.44-46, photo., aerial
photo.

SCHULTE, A. G.
Le chateau de Mheer - interaction
entre demeure et ferme / A.G.
Schulte.
MAISONS D'HIER ET D'AUJOURD'HUI =
DE WOONSTEDE DOOR DE EEUWEN HEEN
1990 Sept., no.87, p.21-32,
photos., plans.

SCHULTES, AXEL, 1943-
Absichten = Intentions / Axel
Schultes.
Alexandria Library competition
project; architect: Axel Schultes.
Text in German and English.
DAIDALOS 1990 June 15, no.36,
p.22-29, model, plans, secn.
Weltausstellungsarchitektur: der
Wettbewerb fur den deutschen
Pavillon fur die EXPO'92 Sevilla
und Fragen zur Architektur.
Projects by: Auer + Weber (1st
prize); Frei Otto; Joachim
Schurmann. Axel Schultes; Helmut
Striffler; Heinz Mihl; Storch +
Ehlers; Kurt Ackermann und Peter
Jaeger; Gottfried Bohm und
Friedrich Steinigeweg; Heinz
Hilmer & Christoph Sattler; PAS;
Kiessler + Partner.
BAUMEISTER 1990 June, v.87, no.6,
p.15-29, ill., dwgs., elevs.,
models, photo., plans, secns.,
site plans, aerial photos.
Wohnungsbau mit Neubau einer
Kegelhalle und einer
Kindertagestatte "an der
Hasenheide" in Berlin-Kreuzberg =
Housing with new bowling hall and
children's day home "An der
Hasenheide" in Berlin-Kreuzberg.
Competition. Winning architect:
Axel Schultes. Text in German.
ARCHITEKTUR + WETTBEWERBE 1990
June, no.142, p.33-37, axonometric
view, elevs., models, plans,
secns., site plans.
Wohnungspolitische Konzepte:
Wohnungsbauprojekte / Rudi Kujath.
Section on many new housing
projects in Germany. Contents:
Berlin, by Rudi Kujath.--Koln, by
(Continued next page)

SCHULTES, AXEL, 1943- (CONTINUED)
Wohnungspolitische...(CONTINUED)
Uwe Kessler.--Bayern, by Dieter
Gutekunst.--Frankfurt, by Martin
Wentz.--Hannover, by Hanns
Adrian.--Der LEG
Nordrhein-Westfalen, by Roswitha
Sinz.--Anmerkungen..., by Hartmut
Grosshans. Among the architects
represented are Otto Steidle +
Partner; Andreas Brandt & Rudolf
Bottcher; Joachim Ganz, Walter
Rolfes; Axel Schultes; Wolfgang
Scharlach und Rainer Wischhusen;
Rebecca Chestnutt et al; Hubertus
Hoffmann; Paul Petry; Hermann
Schroder; Sampo Widmann; Gerhart
Laage; Freed Ahrens.
BAUWELT 1990 Mar.30, v.81, no.12,
p.572-598, elevs., plans, secns.,
site plans, tables.

SCHULTZ, GUNTER
Parkproblem in den Zentrum von
Klein-und Mittelstadten / Gunter
Shultz.
German, Russian, English and
French summaries, p.55-56.
ARCHITEKTUR DER DDR 1990 Jan.,
v.38, no.1, p.32-35, graphs, site
plans, tables, refs.

SCHULTZ, MATT
Architectural salvage to the rescue
/ J. Randall Cotton, Matt Schultz.
Includes list of sources.
OLD-HOUSE JOURNAL 1990 Mar.-Apr.,
v.18, no.2, p.28-39, photos.

SCHULTZ, PATRICIA
Building with bamboo / Patricia
Schultz.
GARDEN DESIGN 1990 summer, v.9,
no.2, p.17-[20], photos.
Gardens of a fairy-tale Danish
castle / Patricia Schultz.
1554 Egeskov Castle on the island
of Funen.
GARDEN DESIGN 1990 autumn, v.9,
no.3, p.24-26, photos.
The Imperial Palace Gardens of Tokyo
/ Patricia Schultz.
GARDEN DESIGN 1990 Spring, v.9,
no.1, p.22-23, photos.

SCHULTZE AND WEAVER
Southern traditions: preservation
efforts in today's South show new
interest in 20th-century
landmarks, as well as earlier ones
/ Clifford A. Pearson.
A portfolio of Southeast projects:
Epping Forest Yacht Club,
Jacksonville, Fla. (Pappas
Associates); Freedom Tower, Miami
(Heisenbottle Architects);
Venetian Pool, Coral Gables, Fla.
(H. Carlton Decker & Assoc.);
Howard Memorial Library, New
Orleans (E. Barron, M. Toups); and
Linden Row Inn, Richmond, Va.
(Glave Newman Anderson).
ARCHITECTURAL RECORD 1990 Mar.,
v.178, no.3, p.66-75, photos.,
plans, site plans.

SCHULZ-COULON, WOLFGANG
Kindertagesheim Zeiseweg,
Hamburg-Altona.
Architects: Conrad Holthey,
Wolfgang Schulz-Coulon.
BAUWELT 1990 June 15, v.81, no.23,
p.1126-1127, photos., isometric
dwg.

SCHULZ, KARIN
Zeichenhaftes Bild ein Beispiel der
Architekten Armin Gasser und
Hans-Dieter Nielander / Karin
Schulz.
ARCHITEKTUR, INNENARCHITEKTUR,
TECHNISCHER AUSBAU 1990 Apr.,
v.98, no.4, p.68-73, det.,
photos., plan, secns.

SCHULZ, PETER
A systematic approach to historic
structures reports / Thomas
Winter, Peter Schulz.
ASSOCIATION FOR PRESERVATION
TECHNOLOGY. BULLETIN 1990, v.22,
no.1-2, p.142-148, ill., photos.,
tables, refs.

SCHULZE, FRANZ
American architects [book review].
Review of books on Louis Sullivan,
Philip Trammell Shutze, Louis
Kahn, and Gordon Bunshaft, by
Lauren S. Weingarden, Keith
Morgan, David B. Brownlee, and
Franz Schulze.
SOCIETY OF ARCHITECTURAL
HISTORIANS. JOURNAL 1990 June,
v.49, no.2, p.222-229.

SCHULZE, JORG
Moglichkeiten und Grenzen der
Denkmalpflege: Teil I / Jorg
Schulze.
DEUTSCHES ARCHITEKTENBLATT 1990
Oct.1, v.22, no.10, p.1523-1527,
dets., photos., refs.
Moglichkeiten und Grenzen der
Denkmalpflege: Teil II / Jorg
Schulze.
Part I appeared in the previous
issue (no.10, p.1523-1527).
DEUTSCHES ARCHITEKTENBLATT 1990
Nov.1, v.22, no.11, p.1717-1720,
photos.
Vernichtung einer Kulturlandschaft:
Braunkohlenabbau und Denkmalpflege
im rheinschen Revier / Jorg
Schulze.
DEUTSCHES ARCHITEKTENBLATT 1990
Apr.1, v.22, no.4, p.597-599,602,
map, photos., aerial photos.,
refs.

SCHUMAN LICHTENSTEIN CLAMAN EFRON
Wild, riled West / Tom McGhee.
Manhattan West, a mixed-use
development, was approved in Feb.
by the NYC Board of Estimate.
Architects: Buck/Cane, with
Schuman Lichtenstein Claman &
Efron.
METROPOLIS 1990 Sept., v.10, no.2,
p.22-25.

SCHUMAN, TONY
La rehabilitation de la Z U P de
Perseigne a Alencon: participation
prise de pouvoir et urbanism /
Tony Schuman.
Z U P = Zones d'Urbanisation
Prioritaire, or, urban planning
priority zones. Project designed
by Lucien Kroll. French, English,
Spanish and German summaries,
p.246-252.
LES ANNALES DE LA RECHERCHE
URBAINE 1989 Dec., no.44-45,
p.40-48, [246], 248-249, 251,
axonometric view, elev., secns.,
sketch, refs.

SCHUMANN, WERNER
Von den Athenern lernen: der
Architekt, das geplagte Wesen /
Werner Schumann.
DER ARCHITEKT 1990 Feb., no.2,
p.91-94, dwgs., photos.

SCHUNCK, EBERHARD
Das geneigte Dach: Interview mit
Professor Eberhard Schunck.
Schunck is the author of the
manual on sloping roofs. Includes
English summary.
DETAIL 1990 Feb.-Mar., v.30, no.1,
p.10-11, photos.
Neubau eines Rathauses und
Gestaltung des Rathausplatzes in
Oberammergau = Building a new city
hall and designing the city hall
square in Oberammergau.
Competition. First prize winners:
Eberhard Schunck, Dieter Ulrich,
Norbert Krausen. Text in German.
ARCHITEKTUR + WETTBEWERBE 1990
Dec., no.144, p.59-63, elevs.,
models, plans, secn.
Seite an Seite: Okumenisches
Kirchenzentrum in
Nurnberg-Langwasser / Sabibe
Schneider.
Architects: Eberhard Schunck,
Dieter Ullrich.
DEUTSCHE BAUZEITUNG 1990 Apr.,
v.124, no.4, p.[30]-35, photos.,
secn., site plans.

SCHUPP, FRITZ, 1896-1974
Industriearchitektur und
Landschaftsgestalt: die Bauten des
Architekten Fritz Schupp in und
bei Goslar / Reinhard Roseneck.
Practiced with Martin Kremmer.
DEUTSCHE BAUZEITUNG 1990 Apr.,
v.124, no.4, p.128-136, photos.,
secns.

SCHUPP, MANUEL
Foreign affairs / Denys Hinton,
David Turnbull, Manuel Schupp.
Second in series on British
architectural education.
ARCHITECTS' JOURNAL 1990 Nov.21,
v.192, no.20, p.36-39, ill.

SCHURK, GUNTHER F.
Burgerhaus in Unterhaching: Kultur-
und Bildungszentrum.
Architects: Christian Raupach,
Gunther F. Schurk, Bernhard
Steiner. Includes English summary.
BAUMEISTER 1990 Sept., v.87, no.9,
p.50-55, photos., plans, secns.,
site plans, isometric dwgs.

SCHURMANN, JOACHIM
Architektur unterwegs.
Three projects: Gastehaus der DDR,
Petersberg, Bonn (architect: Plan
ngsgemeinshaft Bundesgastehaus
Petersburg; Horst Linde); Rathaus,
5340 Bad Honnef (architect:
Joachim Schurmann); "ostlich
Musiktheater", Gelsenkirchen
(architect: Wittig, Eising,
Glasmeier und Drengwitz).
DEUTSCHES ARCHITEKTENBLATT 1990
Nov.1, v.22, no.11, p.1703-1706,
photos., elevs., plans, site
plans, aerial photo.
Burgerhaus in Rheda-Wiedenbruck =
Civic centre in Rheda-Wiedenbruck.
Architects: Joachim and Margot
Schurmann.
DETAIL 1990 Feb.-Mar., v.30, no.1,
p.47-50, dets., photos., plans,
site plans.
Postverteilamt 3 und Erweiterung
Postgiroamt in Koln / Ulf Brychcy.
Architects: Joachim Schurmann,
Margot Schurmann.
BAUWELT 1990 Dec.28, v.81, no.48,
p.2386-2387, photos., plans,
secn., site plan.
Weltausstellungsarchitektur: der
Wettbewerb fur den deutschen
Pavillon fur die EXPO'92 Sevilla
und Fragen zur Architektur.
Projects by: Auer + Weber (1st
prize); Frei Otto; Joachim
Schurmann. Axel Schultes; Helmut
Striffler; Heinz Mihl; Storch +
Ehlers; Kurt Ackermann und Peter
Jaeger; Gottfried Bohm und
Friedrich Steinigeweg; Heinz
Hilmer & Christoph Sattler; PAS;
Kiessler + Partner.
BAUMEISTER 1990 June, v.87, no.6,
p.15-29, ill., dwgs., elevs.,
models, photo., plans, secns.,
site plans, aerial photos.

SCHURMANN, MARGOT
Burgerhaus in Rheda-Wiedenbruck =
Civic centre in Rheda-Wiedenbruck.
Architects: Joachim and Margot
Schurmann.
DETAIL 1990 Feb.-Mar., v.30, no.1,
p.47-50, dets., photos., plans,
site plans.
Postverteilamt 3 und Erweiterung
Postgiroamt in Koln / Ulf Brychcy.
Architects: Joachim Schurmann,
Margot Schurmann.
BAUWELT 1990 Dec.28, v.81, no.48,
p.2386-2387, photos., plans,
secn., site plan.

SCHURMANN, PETER
Museo delle Poste sullo Schaumainkai
a Francoforte / Luigi Biscogli.
Architects: Studio Behnisch &
Partner, with Peter Schurmann,
Felix Hessmert, Gotthard
Geiselmann. Summaries in English,
French, German, and Spanish,
p.112.
ARCHITETTURA; CRONACHE E STORIA
1990 Feb., v.36, no.2(412),
p.[110-122], det., models,
photos., plans, secns., site plan.

SCHURMANN, RAINER
Das Silberwerk: Kraftwerk
Bremen-Hastedt, Block 15.
Architects: Manfred Schomers,
Rainer Schurmann, Walter Stridde.
BAUWELT 1990 Oct.5, v.81, no.37,
p.1874-1881 cover, dets., elev.,
photos., site plan.

SCHUSTER, FRANZ
Plan furniture 1932-1938: the German
connection / Barbara Tilson.
A modernist experiment in the
manufacture and retail of
contemporary furnishings, founded
by Serge Chermayeff and involving
Franz Schuster and Walter Knoll &
Co.
JOURNAL OF DESIGN HISTORY 1990,
v.3, no.2-3, p.1435-155, photos.,
refs.

SCHUSTER, GERHARD
Facades decorees des fermes saxonnes
en Transylvanie / Gerhard
Schuster.
Survey of facade decorations on
16th-20th cent. saxon farmhouses
in Transylvania, Romania.
MONUMENTS HISTORIQUES 1990
June-July, no.169, p.47-[51],
photos., refs.

SCHUSTER, J. MARK DAVIDSON
Growth and the loss of regional
character / J. Mark Davidson
Schuster.
Includes inset article on village
centers in New England.
PLACES 1990 Spring, v.6, no.3,
p.78-87, photos., plans, refs.

SCHUSTER, ROLF
Blendstatt-Halle in Schwabisch Hall.
Architects: Klaus Mahler, Rainer
Gumpp, Rolf Schuster.
DEUTSCHE BAUZEITSCHRIFT 1990 Apr.,
v.38, no.4, p.[521]-528, dets.,
elevs., photos., plans, site
plans.
Ziegeldacher in der Architektur /
Ingeborg Flagge.
Brief history of tile roofs and
announcement on 30 Nov.1989 of
winners of the
Leon-Battista-Alberti-Plakette
1989-90. First prize:
Blendstatthalle, Schwabisch Hall
(architects:
Mahler-Gumpp-Schuster).
DEUTSCHES ARCHITEKTENBLATT 1990
Feb.1, v.22, no.2, p.231-236,
photos.

SCHUTTE, THOMAS, 1954-
Thomas Schutte / Lars Morell.
In Danish and English.
SKALA 1990, no.21, p.10, photo.

SCHUTTE, THOMAS, 1954---EXHIBITIONS
Architectuur als "levensontwerp":
Het werk van Thomas Schutte /
Marieke van Giersbergen.
In conjunction with an exhibition
opening in Oct. at the Van
Abbermuseum in Eindhoven and ones
in Bern and Paris.
ARCHIS 1990 Oct., no.10, p.42-45,
dwg., models, photos., plans.

SCHUTTE, ULRICH. ORDNUNG UND
VERZIERUNG
Ordnung und Verzierung... [by]
Ulrich Schutte [book review] /
Herman van Bergelijk.
Also reviews Deutsche
Architekturtheorie zwischen Gotik
und Renaissance, by Hubertus
Gunther.
ARCHIS 1989 Oct., no.10, p.57-58,
ill.

SCHUTZ, GEORG A.
Erste Preise: Schulen.
Four projects: Kaufmannische
Berufsschule, Ohringen (winner:
Architekten Behnisch & Partner);
addition to Realschule, Markt
Indersdorf (winner: Peter Kaup,
Helmut M. Scholz & Partner);
addition and double gymnasium,
Gesamtschule, Rodingshausen
(winner: Gunter Schmidt +
Friedrich Schmersahl); new
gymnasium and sports building, Bad
Neuenahr-Ahrweiler (winner: Georg
A. Schutz).
DEUTSCHES ARCHITEKTENBLATT 1990
Jan.1, v.22, no.1, p.55-58, dwgs.,
models, plan, secns., site plans.

SCHUURMAN, MARTINUS
The Strand Inter-Continental,
Helsinki / Juliana Balint.
Architect: Martinus Schuurman.
Text in Italian and English.
L'ARCA 1990 Mar., no.36, p.36-47,
elev., photos., plans, secns.,
site plan.

SCHWAB, JIM
Alaska's Northwest Area plan / Jim
Schwab.
Winner of 1990 APA Paul Davidoff
Award for advocacy planning for
resource and land management of
Native American tribes in Alaska.
PLANNING 1990 Mar., v.56, no.3,
p.11, photo.
Along the soft path [Amory Lovins] /
Jim Schwab.
On the environmentalist.
PLANNING 1990 Sept., v.56, no.9,
p.26-27, port., photo.
Hanging together [small town
clusters for rural development] /
Jim Schwab.
Examples in Iowa and Canada.
PLANNING 1990 Jan., v.56, no.1,
p.24-25, photos., aerial photo.
In the wake of the quake [northern
California] / John King.
Includes inset article: "Waiting
for the big one", by Jim Schwab;
on natural disasters around the
country.
PLANNING 1989 Dec., v.55, no.12,
p.12-17, ports., model, maps,
photos.

SCHWAB, WILLIAM A.
Divergent perspectives on the future
of Cleveland's neighborhoods:
economic, planning, and
sociological approaches to the
study of neighborhood change /
William A. Schwab.
JOURNAL OF URBAN STUDIES 1989,
v.11, no.2, p.[141]-154, tables,
refs.

SCHWANER, KURT
Verbindungen im Holzbau / Kurt
Schwaner.
DER ARCHITEKT 1990 May, no.5,
p.256-260, dets., photos.

SCHWARTING, JON MICHAEL
Morality and reality: in search of
the better argument / Jon Michael
Schwarting.
On non-tangible aspects of
architectural discourse over
several centuries. Examples
include various villas and four
recent projects in New York by the
author.
VIA 1990, no.10, p.[62]-79,
diagrs., dwgs., models, photos.,
plans, sketches, refs.

SCHWARTZ, FREDERIC
Extending the architectural impulse
into interior design.
Features comments by Billie Tsien,
Michael Graves, Arthur Erickson,
Tod Williams, Fred Schwartz, Roger
Ferri, Allan Greenberg, Frank
Israel, and Christopher Rudolph.
ARCHITECTURAL DIGEST 1990 Dec.,
v.47, no.13, p.58,62,68,72,76,78,
photos.

SCHWARTZ, GLENN M.
Excavations at Tell al-Raqa'i: a
small rural site of early urban
northern Mesopotamia / Hans H.
Curvers, Glenn M. Schwartz.
AMERICAN JOURNAL OF ARCHAEOLOGY
1990 Jan., v.94, no.1, p.3-23,
figs., maps, photos, plans, refs.

SCHWARTZ, JERRY
Will it work? Ask Hammer, Siler,
George / Jerry Schwartz.
PLANNING 1989 Aug., v.55, no.8,
p.16-18, aerial photo.

SCHWARTZ, MARTHA
Garten der Zukunft? / Elke von
Radziewsky, Vera Graaf.
Features work by the following
American landscape architects:
Peter Walker, Martha Schwartz,
George Hargreaves, and Michael Van
Valkenburgh. english summary,
p.2-3.
ARCHITEKTUR & WOHNEN 1990
Oct.-Nov., no.5, p.90-[98],100,
ports., photos.

SCHWARTZ, MICHAEL
Chambre d'amis oder der Ruckzug der
Kunst = Chambre d'amis or the
retreat of art / Michael Schwartz.
Text in German and English.
DAIDALOS 1990 June 15, no.36,
p.72-79, photos., refs.

SCHWARTZ SILVER ARCHITECTS
Campus beacon: Wheeler School
Library, Schwartz/Silver
Architects, Providence, Rhode
Island / Michael J. Crosbie.
ARCHITECTURE: THE MAGAZINE OF THE
AMERICAN INSTITUTE OF ARCHITECTS
1990 July, v.79, no.7, p.78-81,
photos., plans.
Spa at the Heritage / Edie Lee
Cohen.
Interiors of health club and salon
in Boston's mixed-use building,
Heritage on the Garden.
(Continued next column)

SCHWARTZ SILVER ARCHITECTS
(CONTINUED)
Spa at the Heritage /...(CONTINUED)
Architects/ Interior designers:
Schwartz Silver Architects.
INTERIOR DESIGN 1990 Nov., v.61,
no.15, p.172-[175], photos., plan.

SCHWARTZ, THOMAS A.
Against the wall: cladding systems /
Raymond W. LaTona, Thomas A.
Schwartz.
ARCHITECTURE: THE MAGAZINE OF THE
AMERICAN INSTITUTE OF ARCHITECTS
1990 May, v.79, no.5, p.129-131,
dets., ill.

SCHWARTZMAN, ALLAN
Fruit of the boom / Allan
Schwartzman.
Fountain designed by Claes
Oldenburg and Coosje van Bruggen
for a Miami plaza.
HOUSE & GARDEN 1990 Nov., v.162,
no.11, p.[202]-203, photos.

SCHWARZ, HANS-PETER
Hauptverwaltung der Deutschen
Leasing AG in Bad-Homburg /
Hans-Peter Schwarz.
Architect: Ulrich Heiken.
Designers: Borek Sipek, David
Palterer.
BAUWELT 1990 Oct.26, v.81, no.40,
p.2018-2019, det., photos., plans.
Jochem Jourdan, Bernhard Muller:
hoch hinaus / Hans-Peter Schwarz.
Profile of the architects' recent
work.
ARCHITEKTUR & WOHNEN 1990
Mar.-Apr., no.2,dp.132-138, ill.,
dwgs., port., models, photos.,
sketch, isometric dwgs.
"Ohne einen Glaspalast ist das Leben
eine Last": Die Architektur als
Schicksal des Glases / Hans-Peter
Schwarz.
KUNST UND KIRCHE 1990, no.3,
p.128-133, dwg., photos., secns.,
engr.

SCHWARZ, HANS-PETER. ARCHITEKTUR DER
SYNAGOGUE
Die Architektur der Synagogue...
[exhibition review] / Friedhelm
Grundmann.
Reviews exhibit at the Deutsches
Architekturmuseum, Franfurt a.M.,
Nov.11, 1988-Feb.12, 1989, and the
catalog by Hans-Peter Schwarz.
KUNST UND KIRCHE 1990, no.1,
p.48-49, dwgs., photo.

SCHWARZ, JURGEN
Erste Preise: Kirchen.
Three projects: plans for chapel,
Stiftung Kloster Frenswegen,
Nordhorn (architect: Hans Busso
von Busse); Catholic church and
parish hall, Mossingen (architect:
Wolfgang Liese-Grasser); Catholic
church and regional offices,
Ravensburg-Sonnenbuchel
(architects: Bert Perlia,
Hans-Werner Schliebitz, Jurgen
Schwarz).
DEUTSCHES ARCHITEKTENBLATT 1990
Dec.1, v.22, no.12, p.1831-1834,
elevs., models, plans, secn., site
plans.

SCHWARZ, MARIO
Ein neuentdecktes Tympanon-Relief in
der Wiener Michaelerkirche / Mario
Schwarz.
OSTERREICHISCHE ZEITSCHRIFT FUR
KUNST UND DENKMALPFLEGE 1990,
v.44, no.1-2, p.67-69, photos.,
refs.

SCHWARZ, POUL, 1935-
Arkitektureksport [interview] / Leer
Sorensen.
Interviews with Danish architects
about their projects elsewhere:
PLH Arkitekter, Dissing + Wetling,
Kjaer & Richter, Poul Schwarz'
Tegnestue A/S, Hvidt & Molgaard,
Nils Madsen, Skaarup & Jespersen,
Arkitekfirmaet KHR A/S.
ARKITEKTEN 1990 Oct., v.92, no.15,
p.500-508, elev., models, photos.,
plan, secns., site plans.

SCHWARZ, RUDOLF, 1897-1961
Mit neuem Inhalt: Museum fur
angewandte Kunst jetzt im fruheren
Wallraf-Richartz-Museum / Klaus J.
Jurgenson.
Architects: Rudolf Schwarz, Walter
von Lom.
DEUTSCHE BAUZEITUNG 1990 Feb.,
v.124, no.2, p.108-109, photos.,
plans.
Object lessons: four new design
museums are exhibiting everything
from trendy chairs to Zippo
lighters / Jonathan Turner.
ART NEWS 1990 Apr., v.89, no.4,
p.134-139, photos.

SCHWARZ, ULLRICH
Amburgo: politiche urbane per la
citta portuale / Egbert Kossak,
Ullrich Schwarz.
The fourth annual Bauforum, an
open design seminar held in
Hamburg, Sept. 1989, focussing on
the Speicherstadt warehouse
district near the port. Includes
English summary; Captions in
Italian and English.
CASABELLA 1990 Jan., v.54, no.564,
p.44-51,61, models, maps, photos.,
secn., sketches, aerial photos.

SCHWARZ-ZANETTI, WERNER
Planning for retail change in West
Germany / Joachim Zentes, Werner
Schwarz-Zanetti.
BUILT ENVIRONMENT 1988, v.14,
no.1, p.38-46, charts, photos.,
refs.

SCHWEGER & PARTNER
TK-Hauptverwaltung, Hamburg = Health
insurance HQ, Hamburg.
Architects: Schweger & Partner.
DETAIL 1990 Aug.-Sept., v.30,
no.4, p.378-383, dets., photos.,
plans, secn., site plan.

SCHWEGER + PARTNER
Auf die 60er: Aufstockund eines
Geschaftschauses in Hamburg /
Cornelia Krause.
Architects: Schweger und Partner.
DEUTSCHE BAUZEITUNG 1990 May,
v.124, no.5, p.25-27, photos.,
plans, site plan.

SCHWEGER + PARTNER (CONTINUED)
Denkmal mit Kuhkopf: das neue
Domizil des Hamburgischen
Architekturarchivs / Karin von
Behr.
Reuse of 1926 factory. Original
architects: Grell & Pruter;
renovation architects: Schweger +
Partner.
DEUTSCHE BAUZEITUNG 1990 Oct.,
v.124, no.10, p.194-195, photos.
In zweiter Reihe: Umbau und
Erweiterung Rathaus Bad Pyrmont /
Klaus-Dieter Weiss.
Architect: Schweger + Partner.
BAUWELT 1990 May 4, v.81, no.4,
p.844-847, photos., plans, secn.

SCHWEGER, PETER, 1935-
Arbeitsamt Bremerhaven / Monika
Daldrop.
Competition for addition to 1942
shipbuilding facility (original
architect: Egon Eiermann). First
prize: Buro Peter Schweger.
BAUWELT 1990 Feb.2, v.81, no.5,
p.190, models.

SCHWEIG, KARL-HEINZ
Pedestrian-related goals and
innovations, step by step /
Karl-Heinz Schweig.
Pedestrian safety and traffic
restrictions in West Germany.
TRANSPORTATION QUARTERLY 1990
Oct., v.44, no.4, p.595-606,
graphs, ill., photos., plans,
tables.

SCHWEIGHOFER, ANTON
Criticism: Anton Schweighofer /
Masato Kawamukai.
Text in Japanese.
ARCHITECTURE AND URBANISM 1990
June, no.6(237), p.3-6, photos.

SCHWEITZER BIM
Desert Bloom: The Monument, Joshua
Tree, California / Aaron Betsky.
The Architect's weekend house.
Architects: Schweitzer BIM.
ARCHITECTURAL RECORD 1990
Mid-Apr., v.178, no.5, p.[64-69],
axonometric view, photos., plan.
Schweitzer BIM: Mark Hanauer Studio,
Los Angeles, California, 1988-89.
Text in Japanese and English.
GA HOUSES 1990 Dec., no.30,
p.134-135, axonometric view,
photos., plan.
Schweitzer BIM: the Monument, Joshua
Tree, California, 1987-90.
Desert retreat. Text in Japanese
and English.
GA HOUSES 1990 Dec., no.30,
p.126-133, axonometric views,
photos., plan.
Valley of the lost house / Michael
Webb.
The Monument (Schweitzer) house;
architects: Schweitzer BIM.
BLUEPRINT (LONDON, ENGLAND) 1990
July-Aug., no.69, p.24-25, photos.

SCHWEITZER, JOSH
Josh Schweitzer.
Features desert home, the
Monument, Joshua Tree, Calif.
English summary.
ARCHITECTURE D'AUJOURD'HUI 1990
Oct., no.271, p.164-[167],
axonometric view, photos., plan.

SCHWEITZER, JOSH (CONTINUED)
Kitchens that cook: hot news, cool
choices / Julie V. Iovine.
Five projects, including an
expansion of the Sprecher house,
Los Angeles (architect: Michele
Saee); a Connecticut kitchen
renovation (architect: Louis
Mackall); Reichel-Singer house
conversion, Los Angeles (designer:
Josh Schweitzer); Sagalyn kitchen
(architect: Scott Simons); Laurie
and Maurie Williams' kitchen
renovation, Ore.
METROPOLITAN HOME 1990 May, v.22,
no.5, p.[123-136], det., photos.
The new frontier [house, Joshua
Tree, Calif.] / Charles Gandee.
Architect: Josh Schweitzer.
HOUSE & GARDEN 1990 June, v.162,
no.6, p.[120-125], port., photos.

SCHWEITZER, MARC
Healing revolution / Michael Wagner.
Interiors of the 25-bed Planetree
Model Hospital Unit at the San
Jose Medical Center, Calif.
Architects: John Liu and Marc
Schweitzer, Interior designers:
Victoria Fay & Associates.
INTERIORS 1990 Dec., v.150, no.5,
p.96-97, photos., plan.

SCHWEITZER, OTTO ERNST, 1890-1965
Otto Ernst Schweizer (1890-1865),
ein Sportstattenbauer der Moderne.
WERK, BAUEN + WOHNEN 1990 May,
no.5, p.76,78, photos.
Otto Ernst Schweizer zum 100.
Geburtstag / Immo Boyken.
BAUWELT 1990 May 4, v.81, no.4,
p.868-871, photos., site plan.

SCHWENKE, MELANIE
An african perspective / Melanie
Schwenke.
In Kenya.
LANDSCAPE DESIGN 1989 Dec.-1990
Jan., no.186, p.40-42, photos.

SCHWEYER, ANNE-VALERIE
Observations sur une tombe sculptee
de Limyra / Anne-Valerie Schweyer.
Description of the relief
sculpture on the architrave,
dating from the 4th cent.
REVUE ARCHEOLOGIQUE 1990, no.2,
p.[367]-386, dwgs., photos., site
plan.

SCHWIEGER, HANS JOCHEN
Kindergarten weende in Gottingen.
Architect: Hans Jochen Schwieger.
DEUTSCHE BAUZEITSCHRIFT 1989 Dec.,
v.37, no.12, p.1617-1620,
axonometric views, dets., photos.,
plan, secn., site plan.

SCHYMA, ANGELIKA
Dokumente der Architektur des 20.
Jahrhunderts: Amerikanisches
Generalkonsulat Dusseldorf,
Architekten: Skidmore, Owings &
Merrill mit Otto Apel, Bauzeit
1954-1955 / Angelika Schyma.
DER ARCHITEKT 1990 Apr., no.4,
p.170, photo., refs.

SCIANDA, MIRELLA, 1945-
M. Scianda, V.A. Sorgentone: la
bocciofila di ospedaletti.
In Italian and English.
DOMUS 1990 June, no.717, p.8-9,
elevs., photos., plans, refs.

SCIENCE AND ARCHITECTURE
See ARCHITECTURE AND SCIENCE

**SCIENCE MUSEUM (GREAT BRITAIN)--
EXHIBITIONS**
Designer toys: The art and science
of Lego [exhibition review] /
Penny Wright.
Exhibition at the Science Museum,
London, through 30 April 1990.
ARCHITECTS' JOURNAL 1990 Apr.18,
v.191, no.16, p.85, photos.
The Italian example: Forma &
funzione [exhibition review] /
Murray Fraser.
Exhibition of Italian office
design at the Science Museum,
London, through 2 Sept. 1990.
ARCHITECTS' JOURNAL 1990 June 6,
v.191, no.23, p.77, photos.

SCIENCE MUSEUMS
See MUSEUMS - SCIENCE

SCIENCES
See SCIENCE

SCILLO, MARK
MFP and VFT: our future in an
acronym [book review] / Mark
Scillo.
On proposals for the Multifunction
Polis (MFP) and the Very Fast
Train (VFT) in Australia, as
discussed in "Technocratic
Dreaming," ed. by Paul James.
TRANSITION 1990, no.33, p.82-83,

SCIORTINO, GASPARI
Le forme del paesaggio / Angela di
Noto, Gaspari Sciortino.
URBANISTICA 1989 Dec., no.97,
p.118-120, axonometric views,
dwgs., plans.

**SCKELL, FRIEDRICH LUDWIG VON,
1750-1823**
Verborgene Achsen. Geometrie im
englischen Landschaftsgarten =
Hidden axes. Geometry in English
landscape gardens / Christoph
Valentien, Peter Weyman.
Design of Oppenweiler Castle
grounds, Wurttemberg, 1790-98;
landscape architect: Friedrich
Ludwig von Sckell.
DAIDALOS 1989 Dec.15, no.34,
p.72-79, photos., site plans,
refs.

SCOGIN, ELAM & BRAY ARCHITECTS
Buckhead Branch Public Library,
Atlanta, Georgia.
Architects: Scogin, Elam & Bray
Architects. Spanish, English text.
QUADERNS D'ARQUITECTURA I
URBANISME 1990 Jan.-Feb.-Mar.,
no.184, p.56-61, axonometric view,
photos., plans, secn.
Building on the big idea / John
Welsh.
Features the Buckhead Branch
Library, Atlanta. Architects:
Scogin, Elam & Bray Architects.
BUILDING DESIGN 1990 Nov.23,
(Continued next page)

SCOGIN, ELAM & BRAY ARCHITECTS
(CONTINUED)
Building on the big... (CONTINUED)
no.1013, p.10, elevs., photos.,
plans, secns.
Clayton County Headquarters Library,
Jonesboro, Georgia.
Architects: Scogin, Elam & Bray
Architects. Spanish, English text.
QUADERNS D'ARQUITECTURA I
URBANISME 1990 Jan.-Feb.-Mar.,
no.184, p.52-55, photos., plans,
secns., site plan.
Due punti in una piazza piena
d'acqua: ponte ad Atlanta [Ga.].
Architects: Scogin, Elam & Bray.
ARCHITETTURA; CRONACHE E STORIA
1990 May, v.36, no.5(415),
p.363-365, elevs., photo., secns.,
site plan.
Embracing the vernacular: Atlanta's
Scogin Elam and Bray elevate the
ordinary to art / Catherine Fox.
SOUTHERN ACCENTS 1990 Sept., v.13,
no.7, p.48-54, port., photos.
Focal point: [D. Abbott Turner
Center, Emory University] / Jim
Murphy.
On the community center of the
Candler School of Theology.
Includes small chapel and the
renovated Turner Village Housing.
Architects: Scogin, Elam & Bray,
Architects.
PROGRESSIVE ARCHITECTURE 1990
Dec., v.71, no.13, p.66-73, dets.,
photos., plan, site plan.
The High Museum at Georgia-Pacific
Centre, Atlanta, Georgia, 1986.
Architects: Scogin, Elam & Bray
Architects.
9H 1989, no.8, p.98-103,
axonometric views, photos., plans,
secns., site plan.
Meaning from chaos: [Buchhead Branch
Library, Atlanta] / Jim Murphy.
Architects: Scogin, Elam & Bray
Architects.
PROGRESSIVE ARCHITECTURE 1990
Dec., v.71, no.13, p.60-[65],
elev., photos., plan, site plan.
Ponte pedonale ad Atlanta = A bridge
at Concourse in Atlanta, Ga. /
Silvano Stucchi.
Across an artificial lake at the
Perimeter Center, north of
Atlanta. Architect: Scogin Elam
and Bray. Includes English
translation; French, German, and
Spanish summaries, p.4.
L'INDUSTRIA DELLE COSTRUZIONI 1990
Jan., v.24, no.219, p.38-41,
elevs., photos., plan, secns.,
sketches.
Scogin Elam and Bray.
Features four projects in Georgia:
Clayton County Library, Jonesboro;
Buckhead Branch Library, Atlanta;
Chmar house, Atlanta; and Turner
Village, Candler School of
Theology, Emory Univ., Atlanta.
English summaries.
ARCHITECTURE D'AUJOURD'HUI 1990
Oct., no.271, p.134-144, elevs.,
models, photos., plans, secns.,
site plans.
Scogin Elam and Bray Architects:
House Chmar, Atlanta, Georgia,
1989-90.
Text in Japanese and English.
GA HOUSES 1990 Dec., no.30,
p.32-45, elevs., photos., plans,
site plan.

SCOGIN, ELAM & BRAY ARCHITECTS
(CONTINUED)
Scogin, Elam, Bray: Clayton County
Library, Jonesboro, Georgia, 1988.
Architects: Scogin, Elam & Bray,
Architects.
9H 1989, no.8, p.94-98, elevs.,
photos., plan, secns., site plan.
Lo spazio che rimalza: Showroom ad
Atlanta.
Architects: Scogin Elam & Bray.
ARCHITETTURA; CRONACHE E STORIA
1990 Mar., v.36, no.3(413),
p.204-205, photos, plan.

SCOGIN, MACK, 1943-
Big Mack / John Welsh.
On the appointment of Mack Scogin
as chairman of the Harvard
Graduate School of Design.
BUILDING DESIGN 1990 Oct.5,
no.1006, p.24-25, port., elev.,
plans.
Scogin appointed chairman of the
Department of Architecture.
GSD NEWS / HARVARD UNIVERSITY.
GRADUATE SCHOOL OF DESIGN 1990
Spring, v.18, no.4, p.1-2, port.,
model, photos.

SCOTLAND--ALLOA--SCHOOLS--SECONDARY--
ALTERATIONS AND ADDITIONS--ALLOA
ACADEMY
Alloa Academy.
Renovation to secondary school,
Alloa, Scotland. Architect:
Central Regional Council. Project
architect for design: John
Davison.
BUILDING 1990 Apr.27, v.255,
no.17, p.55-62, photos., plans,
secn., site plan, tables.

SCOTLAND--ALMSHOUSES--HISTORY
"Every district should have one":
pioneer hospitals in the Scottish
Highlands / Fiona Watson.
Includes asylums and poorhouses.
THE JOURNAL AND ANNUAL REPORT /
THE SCOTTISH GEORGIAN SOCIETY FOR
THE STUDY AND PROTECTION OF
SCOTTISH ARCHITECTURE 1989, no.16,
p.43-54, photos., plan, engr.,
refs.

SCOTLAND--ARCHITECTURE
Guiding lights of Scotland / Simon
Berry.
Review of the latest RIAS guide to
Scottish architecture, Banff and
Buchan, edited by Charles McKean.
Includes a review of its
precursors.
RIBA JOURNAL 1990 July, v.97,
no.7, p.50-52, ill., photo.
Scots habitat [book review] / John
Frew.
Reviews four books: The Hebrides:
a natural history, by J.M. and
I.L. Boyd; Central Glasgow: an
illustrated architectural guide,
by Charles McKean...et al.; The
District of Moray: an illustrated
architectural guide, by Charles
McKean; and Banff and Buchan: an
illustrated architectural guide,
by Charles McKean.
ROYAL SOCIETY OF ARTS, LONDON. RSA
JOURNAL 1990 Dec., v.139, no.5413,
p.952-953.

SCOTLAND--ARCHITECTURE--19TH CENTURY--
EXHIBITIONS
A wee celebration: For a wee
country: architectural
contributions to Scottish society
since 1840 [exhibition review] /
David Walker.
Exhibition to celebrate the 150th
anniversary of the founding of the
Royal Incorporation of Architects
in Scotland's (RIAS) predecessor
body, the Institute of Architects
of Scotland. The exhibition is
drawn from RIAS' drawings
collection. Held in Parish Halls,
Glasgow, through 18 Apr.1990, then
on tour.
ARCHITECTS' JOURNAL 1990 Apr.4,
v.191, no.14, p.88-90, dwgs.,
photo.

SCOTLAND--ARCHITECTURE--20TH CENTURY
Glasgow reconsidered / Brian
Edwards.
Recent architecture.
BLUEPRINT (LONDON, ENGLAND) 1990
Mar., no.65, p.26-29, photos.

SCOTLAND--ARCHITECTURE--20TH CENTURY--
EXHIBITIONS
A wee celebration: For a wee
country: architectural
contributions to Scottish society
since 1840 [exhibition review] /
David Walker.
Exhibition to celebrate the 150th
anniversary of the founding of the
Royal Incorporation of Architects
in Scotland's (RIAS) predecessor
body, the Institute of Architects
of Scotland. The exhibition is
drawn from RIAS' drawings
collection. Held in Parish Halls,
Glasgow, through 18 Apr.1990, then
on tour.
ARCHITECTS' JOURNAL 1990 Apr.4,
v.191, no.14, p.88-90, dwgs.,
photo.

SCOTLAND--ARCHITECTURE--CONSERVATION
AND RESTORATION
The Society's casework 1988-89.
The Architectural Heritage Society
of Scotland, formerly the Scottish
Georgian Society.
THE JOURNAL AND ANNUAL REPORT /
THE SCOTTISH GEORGIAN SOCIETY FOR
THE STUDY AND PROTECTION OF
SCOTTISH ARCHITECTURE 1989, no.16,
p.59-64, elevs., photos., secn.

SCOTLAND--ARCHITECTURE--EXHIBITIONS
Distilling Scots design [exhibition
review] / Martin Spring.
A travelling exhibit (For a Wee
Country: Architectural
Contributions to the Development
of Scotland) opens on 13 Mar.1990
in Glasgow, marking the 150th
Jubilee of the RIAS.
BUILDING 1990 Mar.9, v.255, no.10,
p.22-23, ill.

SCOTLAND--ARCHITECTURE--HISTORY
Scots style revival / Charles
McKean.
History of Scottish architecture.
RIBA JOURNAL 1990 Sept., v.97,
no.9, p.42-45,48-50, ill., photos.

SCOTLAND--ARCHITECTURE--RENAISSANCE
Ornamentally Scottish / John
Cornforth.
Distinctive Renaissance
architecture in Scotland, in
conjunction with an exhibition at
the Royal Incorporation of
Architects in Scotland, Edinburgh,
13 Aug.-20 Sept. 1990.
COUNTRY LIFE 1990 Aug.9, v.184,
no.32, p.58-61, ill., elev.,
photos., plan.

SCOTLAND--ARCHITECTURE--RENAISSANCE--
EXHIBITIONS
The work of kings: The architecture
of the Scottish renaissance
1500-1600 [exhibition review] /
David M. Walker.
Exhibition at the RIAS Gallery,
Edinburgh, through 19 Sept. 1990.
ARCHITECTS' JOURNAL 1990 Sept.5,
v.192, no.10, p.86-87, dwgs.,
elevs.

SCOTLAND--ARGYLL--POWDER MILLS--19TH
CENTURY
The powder mills of Argyll / John
Robertson.
Includes a summary, and a note on
the Melfort Gunpowder site, by
Alan Crocker.
INDUSTRIAL ARCHAEOLOGY REVIEW 1990
Spring, v.12, no.2, p.205-215,
dwgs., maps, photos.

SCOTLAND--ASYLUMS--HISTORY
"Every district should have one":
pioneer hospitals in the Scottish
Highlands / Fiona Watson.
Includes asylums and poorhouses.
THE JOURNAL AND ANNUAL REPORT /
THE SCOTTISH GEORGIAN SOCIETY FOR
THE STUDY AND PROTECTION OF
SCOTTISH ARCHITECTURE 1989, no.16,
p.43-54, photos., plan, engr.,
refs.

SCOTLAND--BANKS--ALTERATIONS AND
ADDITIONS--SAINT ANDREWS--TSB BANK
Buildings update banks 2: case
studies.
Changes in bank design, part 2.
Contents: TSB Bank, St. Andrews,
Scotland architect: Nicoll Russell
Studio; Midland Bank, Surrey
Quays, London, architect: Midland
Bank Premises Dept.; Halifax Bldg.
Soc. Bank, Kensington, London,
architect: McColl; and Lloyds
Bank, Basingstoke, architects:
Tilney Lumsden Shane.
ARCHITECTS' JOURNAL 1990 June 27,
v.191, no.26, p.57-63, photos.,
plans, site plans.

SCOTLAND--BROCHS--IRON AGE
Broch building in northern Scotland:
the context of innovation / Ian
Armit.
WORLD ARCHAEOLOGY 1990 Feb., v.21,
no.3, p.[435]-445, map, photos.,
plans, reconst. dwgs., refs.

SCOTLAND--CARDIFF--VISITORS' CENTERS
Star roll / John Welsh.
On the Cardiff Bay Visitors'
Center. Architects: Alsop &
Lyall.
BUILDING DESIGN 1990 Nov.2,
no.1010, p.16,33, dets., photos.,
secns., sketches.

SCOTLAND--CARDIFF--VISITORS' CENTERS
(CONTINUED)
[Three projects by Will Alsop] /
Jonathan Adams.
Contents: Visitors' center,
Cardiff, Scotland --Apartment
house, Hafenstrasse, Hamburg --
Hotel du Department, Marseilles,
France. Architect: William Alsop
of Alsop & Lyall.
AA FILES 1990 Autumn, no.20,
p.22-30, dwgs., elev., photos.,
secn.

SCOTLAND--CASTLES--17TH CENTURY--
CRAIGIEVAR CASTLE
Craigievar Castle, Scotland.
17th-cent. castle in Aberdeenshire
is now a museum.
COLONIAL HOMES 1990 June, v.16,
no.3, p.[104-109],150, photos.

SCOTLAND--CASTLES--19TH CENTURY--
INTERIOR DESIGN--LANCASTER HOUSE
Laird of the tower / Marc Lancaster.
19th-cent. castle in Scotland,
home of artist Mark Lancaster.
HOUSE & GARDEN 1990 Dec., v.162,
no.12, p.[172-177],188, port.,
photos.

SCOTLAND--CASTLES--INTERIOR DESIGN--
BRAEMER
Braemer Castle / Ros Byam Shaw.
Features interiors of castle built
in 1628 as a fortress and hunting
lodge. Restored by John Adam in
the 18th cent. Now owned by Capt.
and Mrs. Alwyne Farquharson.
THE WORLD OF INTERIORS 1990 Dec.,
p.94-105, port., photos.

SCOTLAND--CASTLES--INTERIOR DESIGN--
BRODIE CASTLE
Celebrating the epochs of Scotland's
Brodie Castle / John Julius
Norwich.
Features various rooms in Brodie
Castle, which date from the
17th-19th centuries.
ARCHITECTURAL DIGEST 1990 Sept.,
v.47, no.10, p.[156-163],288,
port., photos.

SCOTLAND--CENTRAL LOWLANDS--HOUSES--
STONE
Heart of stone: the unique character
of vernacular architecture in
Scotland's Central Lowlands /
Geoffrey Stell.
TRADITIONAL HOMES 1990 Feb., v.6,
no.5, p.35-39, photos., biblio.

SCOTLAND--CENTRAL LOWLANDS--TENEMENT
HOUSES--STONE
Heart of stone: the unique character
of vernacular architecture in
Scotland's Central Lowlands /
Geoffrey Stell.
TRADITIONAL HOMES 1990 Feb., v.6,
no.5, p.35-39, photos., biblio.

SCOTLAND--CENTRAL LOWLANDS--VERNACULAR
ARCHITECTURE
Heart of stone: the unique character
of vernacular architecture in
Scotland's Central Lowlands /
Geoffrey Stell.
TRADITIONAL HOMES 1990 Feb., v.6,
no.5, p.35-39, photos., biblio.

SCOTLAND--CITIES AND TOWNS--HISTORY
North of the border: The story of
Scotland's towns, by R. J.
Naismith [book review] / Jan
Magnus Fladmark.
ARCHITECTS' JOURNAL 1990 Sept.26,
v.192, no.13, p.79.

SCOTLAND--CITY PLANNING
Aspects of planning in Scotland: an
introductory paper / Ross
Henderson.
PLANNING OUTLOOK 1989, v.32, no.2,
p.73-76, table, refs.
An assessment of Scottish
development planning / A. G. Coon.
PLANNING OUTLOOK 1989, v.32, no.2,
p.77-85, table, refs.

SCOTLAND--CITY PLANNING--STUDY AND
TEACHING
Planning education in Scotland /
Hugh Begg.
THE PLANNER 1990 Apr.13, v.76,
no.14, p.15,17,19,21, tables,
refs.

SCOTLAND--COUNTRY HOUSES--GEORGIAN--
AIRLIE
The bonnie house of Airlie: a family
saga of Scottish country living
David Ogilvy.
History of Airlie castle, which
was burned down in 1640 and
replaced by a Georgian country
house ca.1792.
ARCHITECTURAL DIGEST 1990 June,
v.47, no.6, p.96,100,102, port.,
photos.

SCOTLAND--COUNTRY HOUSES--INTERIOR
DESIGN--TRAQUAIR
Traquair in Scotland / John Julius
Norwich.
Interiors of Scotland's oldest
continuously inhabited house which
incorporates castle walls dating
from 1107.
ARCHITECTURAL DIGEST 1990 June,
v.47, no.6, p.144-149, photos.

SCOTLAND--COUNTRY HOUSES--KELBURN
CASTLE
Kelburn Castle, Ayrshire - I: the
home of the Earl and Countess of
Glasgow / Gervase Jackson-Stops.
COUNTRY LIFE 1990 Sept.13, v.184,
no.37, p.198-201, ill., elev.,
photos., plans, engr.
Kelburn Castle, Ayrshire - II: the
home of the Earl and Countess of
Glasgow / Gervase Jackson-Stops.
COUNTRY LIFE 1990 Sept.20, v.184
no.38, p.136-139, photos.

SCOTLAND--DOLLAR--HOUSES--
ARCHITECTS'--WHALLEY HOUSE
Warmender Kristall: Haus Whalley,
Kellyburn Bridge, Dollar,
Schottland.
Architects: Andrew Whalley, Fiona
Galbraith.
ARCH PLUS 1990 July, no.104, p.36,
dwgs., photos., plan, secn.

SCOTLAND--GLASGOW--BUILDINGS--19TH
CENTURY
First architect of the second city /
Brian Edwards.
On the career of John Carrick
(1819-1890) and his contribution
to Glasgow.
RIBA JOURNAL 1990 May, v.97, no.5,
p.52-56, ill., photos., site plan,
engrs.

SCOTLAND--GLASGOW--CANALS--
CONSERVATION AND RESTORATION--FORTH
AND CLYDE CANAL
Infrastructure restoration as a tool
for stimulating urban renewal: the
Glasgow Canal / Kenneth J. Button,
David W. Pearce.
URBAN STUDIES 1989 Dec., v.26,
no.6, p.559-571, map., tables,
refs.

SCOTLAND--GLASGOW--CITIES AND TOWNS
A city in search of an identity
[Glasgow] / Malcolm Fraser.
Discussion on Glasgow as the 1990
European City of Culture.
ARCHITECTS' JOURNAL 1990 July 11,
v.192, no.2, p.15, photos.
Fighting for funds / Ruth Owens.
Glasgow as "City of Culture 1990"
continues its regeneration
schemes.
ARCHITECTS' JOURNAL 1990 May 30,
v.191, no.22, p.26-27, 29,
sketches.
Glasgow: how the energy of the city
reflects in its architecture /
Charles McKean.
ROYAL SOCIETY OF ARTS, LONDON. RSA
JOURNAL 1990 Dec., v.139, no.5413,
p.914-925, ill., elevs., photos.,
plans, engrs.
Gough goes to Glasgow / Piers Gough.
ARCHITECTS' JOURNAL 1990 May 30,
v.191, no.22, p.40-43, sketches.

SCOTLAND--GLASGOW--CITIES AND TOWNS--
EXHIBITIONS
Cultural collision [exhibition
review] / Brian Hatton.
Review of the exhibition,
Glasgow's Glasgow, located beneath
Glasgow's Central Station.
BUILDING DESIGN 1990 June 1,
no.988, p.26,28-29, dwgs., photos.
Glasgow's Glasgow [exhibition
review] / Mark Dudek, Michael
Stiff.
On the temporary exhibition which
features the centerpiece of "The
Year of Culture" in Glasgow,
created by architect Doug
Clelland.
BUILDING DESIGN 1990 June 1,
no.988, p.24-25, photo., plans.

SCOTLAND--GLASGOW--CITIES AND TOWNS--
GROWTH
Elementi della trasformazione urbana
di Glasgow / Andrew Gibb.
In Italian.
URBANISTICA 1989 Oct., no.96,
p.105-108, ill., maps, plans,
aerial photos.
Glasgow: dopo il declino = Glasgow:
after the decline / Raffaele
Paloscia.
Introduces four articles on the
regeneration of Glasgow,
separately indexed. English
summary, p.128.
(Continued next column)

SCOTLAND--GLASGOW--CITIES AND TOWNS--
GROWTH (CONTINUED)
Glasgow: dopo il...(CONTINUED)
URBANISTICA 1989 Oct., no.96,
p.103-104,128, plans, site plans,
maps, refs.

SCOTLAND--GLASGOW--CITY PLANNING
A city in search of an identity
[Glasgow] / Malcolm Fraser.
Discussion on Glasgow as the 1990
European City of Culture.
ARCHITECTS' JOURNAL 1990 July 11,
v.192, no.2, p.15, photos.
Creating the context [Glasgow] /
George Mulvagh, Brian Evans.
City planning proposals for
Glasgow by Gillespie's.
ARCHITECTS' JOURNAL 1990 May 30,
v.191, no.22, p.44-49, axonometric
view, maps, photos., sketches,
aerial photo.

SCOTLAND--GLASGOW--CITY PLANNING--
GORBALS
Reviving the Gorbals / Clare
Melhuish.
Redevelopment of the Gorbals area
of Glasgow. Architects: Campbell,
Zogolovitch, Wilkinson and Gough.
BUILDING DESIGN 1990 Sept.21,
no.1004, p.16, dwgs., maps.

SCOTLAND--GLASGOW--CITY PLANNING--
PRACTICE
Zoom me in Scottie / Denise Chevin.
On a computer model of Glasgow
used by town planners.
BUILDING 1990 Jan.12, v.255, no.2,
p.70-71, ill.

SCOTLAND--GLASGOW--COMMUNITY
DEVELOPMENT--URBAN
Force et faiblesse des initiatives
economiques communautaires: les
exemples de Glasgow et de
l'Irlande du Nord / Andrew
MacArthur, Alan MacGregor.
French, English, German and
Spanish summaries, p.[125]-127.
LES ANNALES DE LA RECHERCHE
URBAINE 1990 Oct., no.48,
p.[63]-73, ports., photos., refs.

SCOTLAND--GLASGOW--CONSERVATORIES OF
MUSIC--ROYAL SCOTTISH ACADEMY OF
MUSIC AND DRAMA
Parkyn's progress: Glasgow.
A tour of 8 new projects: Forum
Hotel (architects: Cobban and
Lironie); Scottish Exhibition and
Conference Centre (architects:
Parr Partnership); Britoil
Headquarters (architects: Hugh
Martin Partnership); Council Hall
(architects: Leslie Martin, RMJM);
Royal Scottish Academy of Music
and Drama (architect: Leslie
Martin); 58 W. Regent St.
(architects: Comprehensive Design
Group); Princes Square, Buchanan
St. (architect: Hugh Martin
Partnership); Ingram-Wilson St.
housing (Elder and Cannon); St.
Enoch Sheriff Court (architects:
Keppie Henderson and Partners).
BUILDING 1989 Sept.29, v.254,
no.39, p.54-58, map, photos.

SCOTLAND--GLASGOW--CORPORATE OFFICE
BUILDINGS--BRITOIL
Parkyn's progress: Glasgow.
A tour of 8 new projects: Forum
Hotel (architects: Cobban and
Lironie); Scottish Exhibition and
Conference Centre (architects:
Parr Partnership); Britoil
Headquarters (architects: Hugh
Martin Partnership); Council Hall
(architects: Leslie Martin, RMJM);
Royal Scottish Academy of Music
and Drama (architect: Leslie
Martin); 58 W. Regent St.
(architects: Comprehensive Design
Group); Princes Square, Buchanan
St. (architect: Hugh Martin
Partnership); Ingram-Wilson St.
housing (Elder and Cannon); St.
Enoch Sheriff Court (architects:
Keppie Henderson and Partners).
BUILDING 1989 Sept.29, v.254,
no.39, p.54-58, map, photos.

SCOTLAND--GLASGOW--DEPARTMENT STORES--
INTERIOR DESIGN--LIBERTY
Free range / David Redhead.
Interiors of Liberty department
store, Glasgow. Architects: Harper
MacKay.
DESIGNERS' JOURNAL 1990 Oct.,
no.61, p.60-63, photos., secns.

SCOTLAND--GLASGOW--EXHIBITION
BUILDINGS--SCOTTISH EXHIBITION AND
CONFERENCE CENTRE
Parkyn's progress: Glasgow.
A tour of 8 new projects: Forum
Hotel (architects: Cobban and
Lironie); Scottish Exhibition and
Conference Centre (architects:
Parr Partnership); Britoil
Headquarters (architects: Hugh
Martin Partnership); Council Hall
(architects: Leslie Martin, RMJM);
Royal Scottish Academy of Music
and Drama (architect: Leslie
Martin); 58 W. Regent St.
(architects: Comprehensive Design
Group); Princes Square, Buchanan
St. (architect: Hugh Martin
Partnership); Ingram-Wilson St.
housing (Elder and Cannon); St.
Enoch Sheriff Court (architects:
Keppie Henderson and Partners).
BUILDING 1989 Sept.29, v.254,
no.39, p.54-58, map, photos.

SCOTLAND--GLASGOW--EXHIBITION
BUILDINGS--TEMPORARY--EURODROME
Glasgow, citta della cultura =
Glasgow, city of culture / Luigi
Moiraghi.
Project for exhibition building;
architects: Benson & Forsyth;
engineer: Mark Whitby.
L'ARCA 1990 Nov., no.43, p.60-67,
axonometric view, elevs., model,
plan, secn.

SCOTLAND--GLASGOW--GREENBELTS
Development pressure in the
metropolitan fringe / Michael
Pacione.
Principally in Glasgow, Scotland.
LAND DEVELOPMENT STUDIES 1990 May,
v.7, no.2, p.69-82, maps, tables,
refs.

SCOTLAND--GLASGOW--OFFICE BUILDINGS--
TAY HOUSE (CONTINUED)
Office overhead [Tay...(CONTINUED)
p.50-54, diagrs., photos., secn.,
isometric dwg., aerial photo.

SCOTLAND--GLASGOW--OFFICES--
ARCHITECTS'--SBT KEPPIE
Religious conversion / Heather Rose.
1929 John Ross Memorial Church,
Glasgow, converted into offices
for the architectural firm, SBT
Keppie. Original architect: Norman
A. Dick.
BUILDING DESIGN 1990 Aug., suppl.,
p.V, photos.

SCOTLAND--GLASGOW--PLAYGROUNDS
Greener Glasgow is child's play /
Ruth Owens.
West German environmental artist
Dieter Magnus has designed a park
and playground space in Glasgow
that is both urban park and water
garden.
ARCHITECTS' JOURNAL 1990 Feb.28,
v.191, no.9, p.17, port., model,
photos.

SCOTLAND--GLASGOW--REAL ESTATE
DEVELOPMENT
Development pressure in the
metropolitan fringe / Michael
Pacione.
Principally in Glasgow, Scotland.
LAND DEVELOPMENT STUDIES 1990 May,
v.7, no.2, p.69-82, maps, tables,
refs.

SCOTLAND--GLASGOW--SHOPPING CENTERS--
PRINCES SQUARE
Parkyn's progress: Glasgow.
A tour of 8 new projects: Forum
Hotel (architects: Cobban and
Lironie); Scottish Exhibition and
Conference Centre (architects:
Parr Partnership); Britoil
Headquarters (architects: Hugh
Martin Partnership); Council Hall
(architects: Leslie Martin, RMJM);
Royal Scottish Academy of Music
and Drama (architect: Leslie
Martin); 58 W. Regent St.
(architects: Comprehensive Design
Group); Princes Square, Buchanan
St. (architect: Hugh Martin
Partnership); Ingram-Wilson St.
housing (Elder and Cannon); St.
Enoch Sheriff Court (architects:
Keppie Henderson and Partners).
BUILDING 1989 Sept.29, v.254,
no.39, p.54-58, map, photos.

SCOTLAND--GLASGOW--SHOPPING CENTERS--
SAINT ENOCH CENTRE
Parkyn's progress: Glasgow.
A tour of 8 new projects: Forum
Hotel (architects: Cobban and
Lironie); Scottish Exhibition and
Conference Centre (architects:
Parr Partnership); Britoil
Headquarters (architects: Hugh
Martin Partnership); Council Hall
(architects: Leslie Martin, RMJM);
Royal Scottish Academy of Music
and Drama (architect: Leslie
Martin); 58 W. Regent St.
(architects: Comprehensive Design
Group); Princes Square, Buchanan
St. (architect: Hugh Martin
Partnership); Ingram-Wilson St.
housing (Elder and Cannon); St.
(Continued next column)

SCOTLAND--GLASGOW--SHOPPING CENTERS--
SAINT ENOCH CENTRE (CONTINUED)
Parkyn's progress:...(CONTINUED)
Enoch Sheriff Court (architects:
Keppie Henderson and Partners).
BUILDING 1989 Sept.29, v.254,
no.39, p.54-58, map, photos.

SCOTLAND--GLASGOW--STORES--CLOTHING--
KATHARINE HAMNETT
Guaridas de la moda: Katharine
Hamnett, de Foster a Coates /
Adrian Dannatt.
Clothing stores in London and
Glasgow.
ARQUITECTURA VIVA 1990 Jan.-Feb.,
no.10, p.58-61, elev., photos.,
plan.

SCOTLAND--GLASGOW--STUDENT HOUSING--
UNIVERSITY OF STRATHCLYDE--FORBES
HALL
Halls of residence 2: case studies.
Student accomodation in Glasgow,
Edinburgh, and east London.
Architects: MacCormac Jamieson
Prichard for Queen Mary and
Westfield College, University of
London; The Kennedy Partership for
Forbes Hall, University of
Strathclyde, Glasgow; and Davis
Duncan Partnership for Robertson's
Close, University of Edinburgh.
ARCHITECTS' JOURNAL 1990 Aug.1,
v.192, no.5, p.49-53, axonometric
view, photos., plans, secn., site
plans.

SCOTLAND--GLASGOW--STUDENT PROJECTS--
AWARDS AND PRIZES
East wind / Brian Edwards.
On the winners of the Newman
Levinson Award for architecture
student work in Glasgow.
BUILDING DESIGN 1990 Sept.7,
no.1002, p.28-29, axonometric
view, elev., model, plan, secn.,
site plan, sketch.

SCOTLAND--GLASGOW--TEA ROOMS--19TH
CENTURY--ALTERATIONS AND ADDITIONS--
ARGYLE STREET TEA ROOMS
The redevelopment of the Argyle
Street Tea Rooms / Jonathan
Kinghorn.
Refurbishment of exterior and
alteration of interior of
Mackintosh building in Glasgeow,
built in 1897.
CHARLES RENNIE MACKINTOSH SOCIETY.
NEWSLETTER 1990 Autumn, no.54,
p.10-13, photo.

SCOTLAND--GLASGOW--TENEMENT HOUSES--
19TH CENTURY--145 BUCCLEUCH STREET
(TENEMENT HOUSE)
A hoard of history: the rich legacy
of a middle-class Glaswegian /
Margaret Henderson.
Interiors of a tenement flat of
1892 in the Garnethill area.
TRADITIONAL HOMES 1990 Oct., v.7,
no.1, p.39-42, photos.

SCOTLAND--GLASGOW--TENEMENT HOUSES--
WEST END PARK STREET
Tenement tradition [Glasgow] / Mark
Cousins.
New version of Glasgow's 19th
cent. tenements by Assist
Architects.
ARCHITECTS' JOURNAL 1990 May 30,
v.191, no.22, p.36-37, photos.,
plans.

SCOTLAND--GLASGOW--THEATERS--19TH
CENTURY--CONSERVATION AND
RESTORATION--OLD ATHENAEUM (SCOTTISH
YOUTH THEATRE)
Upstaging a concert hall [Old
Athenaeum, Glasgow] / Callum
Murray.
Restoration of late 19th cent. Old
Athenaeum, now the headquarters
for the Scottish Youth Theatre.
Original architect: Sir J.J.
Burnet; restoration architects:
Campbell and Arnott.
ARCHITECTS' JOURNAL 1990 Jan.31,
v.191, no.5, p.15, photos.

SCOTLAND--GLASGOW--THEATERS--
VICTORIAN--ALTERATIONS AND
ADDITIONS--CITIZENS THEATRE
Cultural beacon in the Gorbals /
Brian Edwards.
On the new atrium and facade
addition to the 1878 Citizens
Theatre, Glasgow. Original
architect: Campbell Douglas.
Renovation architects: Building
Design Partnership.
RIBA JOURNAL 1990 May, v.97, no.5,
p.48-50, photos.

SCOTLAND--GLASGOW--TRANSPORTATION
PLANNING
Creating the context [Glasgow] /
George Mulvagh, Brian Evans.
City planning proposals for
Glasgow by Gillespie's.
ARCHITECTS' JOURNAL 1990 May 30,
v.191, no.22, p.44-49, axonometric
view, maps, photos., sketches,
aerial photo.

SCOTLAND--GLASGOW--UNIVERSITIES AND
COLLEGES--BUILDINGS--UNIVERSITY OF
STRATHCLYDE--FORBES HALL
Halls of residence 2: case studies.
Student accomodation in Glasgow,
Edinburgh, and east London.
Architects: MacCormac Jamieson
Prichard for Queen Mary and
Westfield College, University of
London; The Kennedy Partership for
Forbes Hall, University of
Strathclyde, Glasgow; and Davis
Duncan Partnership for Robertson's
Close, University of Edinburgh.
ARCHITECTS' JOURNAL 1990 Aug.1,
v.192, no.5, p.49-53, axonometric
view, photos., plans, secn., site
plans.

SCOTLAND--GLASGOW--URBAN FRINGES
Development pressure in the
metropolitan fringe / Michael
Pacione.
Principally in Glasgow, Scotland.
LAND DEVELOPMENT STUDIES 1990 May,
v.7, no.2, p.69-82, maps, tables,
refs.

SCOTLAND--GLASGOW--URBAN PARKS
Greener Glasgow is child's play /
Ruth Owens.
West German environmental artist
Dieter Magnus has designed a park
and playground space in Glasgow
that is both urban park and water
garden.
ARCHITECTS' JOURNAL 1990 Feb.28,
v.191, no.9, p.17, port., model,
photos.

SCOTLAND--GLASGOW--URBAN RENEWAL
Fighting for funds / Ruth Owens.
Glasgow as "City of Culture 1990"
continues its regeneration
schemes.
ARCHITECTS' JOURNAL 1990 May 30,
v.191, no.22, p.26-27, 29,
sketches.
GEAR: la gestion des partenaires
publics de la renovation / Urlan
Wannop.
Urban renewal in Scotland's
Glasgow Eastern Area Renewal
(GEAR) project. French, English,
German and Spanish summaries,
p.[125]-127.
LES ANNALES DE LA RECHERCHE
URBAINE 1990 Oct., no.48,
p.[74]-85, port., photos., tables.
La genesi della citta
post-industriale [Glasgow] / W. F.
Lever.
In Italian.
URBANISTICA 1989 Oct., no.96,
p.109-112, photos., biblio.
IFHP study visit 'Glasgow (S)miles
Better' / Harry Bentham.
PROSPECT 1989, no.3, p.2-4,
photos.
Infrastructure restoration as a tool
for stimulating urban renewal: the
Glasgow Canal / Kenneth J. Button,
David W. Pearce.
URBAN STUDIES 1989 Dec., v.26,
no.6, p.559-571, map., tables,
refs.
Revival urbano ovvero la riscoperta
della citta [Glasgow] / A. G.
Vogt.
In Italian; Italian and English
captions.
URBANISTICA 1989 Oct., no.96,
p.112-115, photos., aerial photo.,
refs.
La riqualificazione dell'east end:
il gear project / Raffaele
Paloscia.
The Glasgow Eastern Area Renewal
project (GEAR), an inner-city
urban renewal project. In Italian,
with Italian and English captions.
URBANISTICA 1989 Oct., no.96,
p.115-119, maps, photos., refs.

SCOTLAND--GLASGOW--WAR MEMORIALS--19TH
CENTURY--DUKE OF WELLINGTON
Carlo Marochetti and the Glasgow
Wellington memorial / Philip
Ward-Jackson.
BURLINGTON MAGAZINE 1990 Dec.,
v.132, no.1053, p.851-862,
photos., engr., refs.

SCOTLAND--GLASGOW--WATER GARDENS
Greener Glasgow is child's play /
Ruth Owens.
West German environmental artist
Dieter Magnus has designed a park
and playground space in Glasgow
that is both urban park and water
garden.
ARCHITECTS' JOURNAL 1990 Feb.28,
v.191, no.9, p.17, port., model,
photos.

SCOTLAND--GLASGOW--WATERFRONT
BUILDINGS--CARRICK QUAY
Quay features / Brian Edwards.
On the new riverside housing
development Carrick Quay, Glasgow.
Architect: Davis Duncan
Partnership.
BUILDING DESIGN 1990 Oct.26,
no.1009, p.26, axonometric views,
photos., plans, secns.

SCOTLAND--GLASGOW--WINDOWS--MARYHILL
Tenement for the twenty-first
century / Ken Macrae.
Analysis of the windows in the new
housing project in Maryhill,
Glasgow for the Maryhill Housing
Association.
RIBA JOURNAL 1990 Dec., v.97,
no.12, p.57,61, photo, serial
photo.

SCOTLAND--GREEN DESIGN--STUDENT
PROJECTS--COMPETITIONS
Room to move / Brian Edwards.
Report on a green design
competition held at Edinburgh
University's dept. of
architecture. Sponsor: the
Association of Scottish Schools of
Architecture.
BUILDING DESIGN 1990 Mar.16,
no.977, p.26-27, models, sketches.

SCOTLAND--GREENBELTS--CONGRESSES
A future for Scotland's greenbelts /
Aileen Grant.
Green Belt Forum, a conference
held in Edinburgh 27 Jan. 1990.
THE PLANNER 1990 Mar.2, v.76,
no.8, p.14, aerial photo.

SCOTLAND--GUIDEBOOKS
Scots habitat [book review] / John
Frew.
Reviews four books: The Hebrides:
a natural history, by J.M. and
I.L. Boyd; Central Glasgow: an
illustrated architectural guide,
by Charles McKean...et al.; The
District of Moray: an illustrated
architectural guide, by Charles
McKean; and Banff and Buchan: an
illustrated architectural guide,
by Charles McKean.
ROYAL SOCIETY OF ARTS, LONDON. RSA
JOURNAL 1990 Dec., v.139, no.5413,
p.952-953.

SCOTLAND--HEBRIDES--SAINT KILDA--
ARCHITECTURE
Buildings of St. Kilda, by Geoffrey
P. Stell and Mary Harman [book
review] / Eurwyn Wiliam.
POST-MEDIEVAL ARCHAEOLOGY 1989,
v.23, p.84-85.

SCOTLAND--HELENSBURGH--HOUSES--
CONSERVATION AND RESTORATION--HILL
HOUSE
Restoration at the Hill house /
Philip A. Schreiber.
CHARLES RENNIE MACKINTOSH SOCIETY.
NEWSLETTER 1990 Spring, no.53,
p.7, elev.

SCOTLAND--HISTORIC HOUSE MUSEUMS--
CRAIGIEVAR CASTLE
Craigievar Castle, Scotland.
17th-cent. castle in Aberdeenshire
is now a museum.
COLONIAL HOMES 1990 June, v.16,
no.3, p.[104-109],150, photos.

SCOTLAND--HISTORIC PRESERVATION
The Society's casework 1988-89.
The Architectural Heritage Society
of Scotland, formerly the Scottish
Georgian Society.
THE JOURNAL AND ANNUAL REPORT /
THE SCOTTISH GEORGIAN SOCIETY FOR
THE STUDY AND PROTECTION OF
SCOTTISH ARCHITECTURE 1989, no.16,
p.59-64, elevs., photos., secn.

SCOTLAND--HOSPITALS--18TH CENTURY
Incessant construction beyond our
reach: two centuries of hospital
architecture in Scotland / Derek
A. Dow.
From the 1720's to the early 20th
century.
THE JOURNAL AND ANNUAL REPORT /
THE SCOTTISH GEORGIAN SOCIETY FOR
THE STUDY AND PROTECTION OF
SCOTTISH ARCHITECTURE 1989, no.16,
p.34-42, axonometric view, engr.,
refs.

SCOTLAND--HOSPITALS--19TH CENTURY
Incessant construction beyond our
reach: two centuries of hospital
architecture in Scotland / Derek
A. Dow.
From the 1720's to the early 20th
century.
THE JOURNAL AND ANNUAL REPORT /
THE SCOTTISH GEORGIAN SOCIETY FOR
THE STUDY AND PROTECTION OF
SCOTTISH ARCHITECTURE 1989, no.16,
p.34-42, axonometric view, engr.,
refs.

SCOTLAND--HOSPITALS--TYPOLOGY--HISTORY
"Every district should have one":
pioneer hospitals in the Scottish
Highlands / Fiona Watson.
Includes asylums and poorhouses.
THE JOURNAL AND ANNUAL REPORT /
THE SCOTTISH GEORGIAN SOCIETY FOR
THE STUDY AND PROTECTION OF
SCOTTISH ARCHITECTURE 1989, no.16,
p.43-54, photos., plan, engr.,
refs.

SCOTLAND--HOUSES--ALTERATIONS AND
ADDITIONS
A new direction / Brian Edwards.
Addition to Scottish croft north
of Glasgow. Architects: McGurn
Logan Duncan & Opfer.
BUILDING DESIGN 1990 June 8,
no.989, p.20-23, elevs., photos.,
plans.

SCOTLAND--HOUSING FOR ELDERLY
  The development of private sheltered
  housing in Scotland: a changing
  market / W. M. Edgar, D. Bochel.
  PLANNING OUTLOOK 1989, v.32, no.2,
  p.95-100, tables, refs.

SCOTLAND--HOUSING POLICY
  The development of private sheltered
  housing in Scotland: a changing
  market / W. M. Edgar, D. Bochel.
  PLANNING OUTLOOK 1989, v.32, no.2,
  p.95-100, tables, refs.

SCOTLAND--HOY (ISLAND)--COUNTRY
HOUSES--MELSETTER HOUSE
  Melsetter House / Peter Blundell
  Jones.
    1898 house by William Lethaby on
    the island of Hoy in the Orkneys.
    ARCHITECTS' JOURNAL 1990 Oct.10,
    v.192, no.15, p.36-45,48-57,
    dets., elevs., map, photos.,
    plans, secns., refs.

SCOTLAND--HUNTING LODGES--19TH CENTURY
  Tales from Crummie-Toddie / Giles
  Worsley.
    COUNTRY LIFE 1990 Aug.2, v.184,
    no.31, p.78-82, photos.

SCOTLAND--INVERNESS--STORES--STUDENT
PROJECTS
  Brief encounter for Andy and Isi /
  Charles Rattray.
    RIAs masterclass in Cromarty with
    Scottish architects Andy MacMillan
    and Isi Metzstein; design brief
    for a retail development in
    Inverness.
    ARCHITECTS' JOURNAL 1990 Feb.21,
    v.191, no.8, p.17, ports.,
    sketches.
  Cullinan masterclass / Charles
  Rattray.
    Report on Ted Cullinan's RIAS CPD
    masterclass held in Cromary.
    Project: retail development in
    Inverness.
    RIBA JOURNAL 1990 June, v.97,
    no.6, p.40-41,[44-45], ports.,
    plan, sketches.

SCOTLAND--IONA--MONASTERIES--EARLY
CHRISTIAN
  On the origin of the form of the
  Irish high cross / Martin Werner.
    Suggests Coptic influences, via a
    textile fragment, on composition
    of Celtic crosses at Iona and
    elsewhere. Includes abstract.
    GESTA 1990, v.29, no.1, p.98-110,
    dwgs., photos., refs.

SCOTLAND--IONA--RELIGIOUS
COMMUNITIES--MACLEOD CENTER
  Island retreat [Iona] / Charles
  Rattray.
    Religious hostel on the island of
    Iona. Architects: Feilden Clegg
    Design.
    ARCHITECTS' JOURNAL 1990 June 27,
    v.191, no.26, p.34-37,39, photos.,
    plans, secn.

SCOTLAND--KILBARCHAN--HISTORIC HOUSE
MUSEUMS--WEAVER'S COTTAGE
  The Weaver's Cottage, [Kilbarchan]
  Scotland.
    1723 stone house, now a museum.
    COLONIAL HOMES 1990 June, v.16,
    no.3, p.[88-91],150, photos.

SCOTLAND--KILBARCHAN--HOUSES--18TH
CENTURY--STONE
  The Weaver's Cottage, [Kilbarchan]
  Scotland.
    1723 stone house, now a museum.
    COLONIAL HOMES 1990 June, v.16,
    no.3, p.[88-91],150, photos.

SCOTLAND--KILCONQUHAR--COUNTRY
HOUSES--CHARLETON
  Charleton, Fife: The home of Baron
  and Baroness St. Clair Bonde /
  William Kay.
    Architects: William Burn, Robert
    S. Lorimer.
    COUNTRY LIFE 1990 Feb.22, v.184,
    no.8, p.94-101, photos.

SCOTLAND--LIVINGSTON--CITY PLANNING--
HUMAN FACTORS
  Heart and soul [Livingston,
  Scotland] / Robert Cowan.
    New town in central Scotland
    poorly planned, with consequences
    for its continued growth.
    ARCHITECTS' JOURNAL 1990 Jan.3-10,
    v.191, no.1-2, p.26-29, ports.,
    elevs., photos., plan.

SCOTLAND--LIVINGSTON--GROWTH CENTERS
  Heart and soul [Livingston,
  Scotland] / Robert Cowan.
    New town in central Scotland
    poorly planned, with consequences
    for its continued growth.
    ARCHITECTS' JOURNAL 1990 Jan.3-10,
    v.191, no.1-2, p.26-29, ports.,
    elevs., photos., plan.

SCOTLAND--LIVINGSTON--NEW TOWNS
  Heart and soul [Livingston,
  Scotland] / Robert Cowan.
    New town in central Scotland
    poorly planned, with consequences
    for its continued growth.
    ARCHITECTS' JOURNAL 1990 Jan.3-10,
    v.191, no.1-2, p.26-29, ports.,
    elevs., photos., plan.

SCOTLAND--LOCKERBIE--DAMAGE TO
BUILDINGS
  Rebuilding Lockerbie / Sandra
  MacPherson.
    BUILDING 1990 Oct.12, v.255,
    no.40, p.22-23, port., photos.

SCOTLAND--NEW TOWNS--POLITICAL ASPECTS
  Winding up of the new town
  development corporations in
  Scotland / Anthony Ramsay.
    PLANNING OUTLOOK 1989, v.32, no.2,
    p.87-94, tables, biblio.

SCOTLAND--QUEENSFERRY--BRIDGES--19TH
CENTURY--RAILROAD--FORTH BRIDGE
  The Forth Bridge centenary.
    A brief history and discussion of
    publications about the bridge.
    INDUSTRIAL ARCHAEOLOGY REVIEW 1990
    Spring, v.12, no.2, p.125-126,
    photos.

SCOTLAND--QUEENSFERRY--BRIDGES--
CANTILEVER--FORTH BRIDGE
  Forth Bridge at one hundred / Chris
  Norman.
    Engineers: Sir John Fowler, Sir
    Benjamin Baker.
    THE PLANNER 1990 Mar.16, v.76,
    no.10, p.17, photos.
  A labour for Hercules: the building
  of the Forth Bridge / Ivor
  Smullen.
    Engineers: Sir John Fowler and Sir
    Benjamin Baker.
    COUNTRY LIFE 1990 Mar.22, v.184,
    no.12, p.174, photo.

SCOTLAND--REGIONAL PLANNING
  Aspects of planning in Scotland: an
  introductory paper / Ross
  Henderson.
    PLANNING OUTLOOK 1989, v.32, no.2,
    p.73-76, table, refs.
  An assessment of Scottish
  development planning / A. G. Coon.
    PLANNING OUTLOOK 1989, v.32, no.2,
    p.77-85, table, refs.

SCOTLAND--RHUM--CASTLES--EDWARDIAN--
KINLOCH CASTLE
  The Laird's folly: a castle on the
  Isle of Rhum is Scotland's most
  eccentric hotel / Charles Maclean.
    Kinloch Castle, built in 1901 by
    Sir George Bullough.
    HOUSE & GARDEN 1990 Jan., v.162,
    no.1, p.[42],48, ill., photos.

SCOTLAND--RHUM--HOTELS--KINLOCH CASTLE
  The Laird's folly: a castle on the
  Isle of Rhum is Scotland's most
  eccentric hotel / Charles Maclean.
    Kinloch Castle, built in 1901 by
    Sir George Bullough.
    HOUSE & GARDEN 1990 Jan., v.162,
    no.1, p.[42],48, ill., photos.

SCOTLAND--ROXBOROUGH--RAILROAD
STATIONS--CONSERVATION AND
RESTORATION--SAUGHTREE
  Geoffrey Mann / Alastair Stewart.
    Rebuilding of the Saughtree
    railroad station near Roxborough
    in the Scottish Borders, by a
    partner in RHWL Partnership.
    BUILDING 1990 Sept.28, v.255,
    no.38, p.46-47, port., photo.

SCOTLAND--SAINT ANDREWS--BANKS--
ALTERATIONS AND ADDITIONS--TSB BANK
  TSB Bank, St. Andrews.
    Housed in a Victorian building,
    originally remodelled in the
    1970s, located at 12 Church St.
    Architects: Nicoll Russell Studio.
    BUILDING 1990 Jan.12, v.255, no.2,
    p.43-50, dets., elevs., photos.,
    plans, secns., tables.

SCOTLAND--SAINT ANDREWS--HOTELS--
ALTERATIONS AND ADDITIONS--OLD
COURSE HOTEL
  Links with the past / Richard Carr.
    Radical renovation of 1969 Old
    Course Hotel, Saint Andrews,
    Scotland. Renovation architects:
    Hurd Rolland Partnership.
    BUILDING DESIGN 1990 Aug., suppl.,
    p.XIV, photos.

SCOTLAND--SAINT ANDREWS--OFFICE
BUILDINGS--VICTORIAN--ALTERATIONS
AND ADDITIONS--TSB BANK
TSB Bank, St. Andrews.
Housed in a Victorian building,
originally remodelled in the
1970s, located at 12 Church St.
Architects: Nicoll Russell Studio.
BUILDING 1990 Jan.12, v.255, no.2,
p.43-50, dets., elevs., photos.,
plans, secns., tables.

SCOTLAND--SANATORIUMS--HISTORY
"Declined into a profitable
consumption": the tuberculosis
sanatorium in Scotland / Harriet
Richardson.
THE JOURNAL AND ANNUAL REPORT /
THE SCOTTISH GEORGIAN SOCIETY FOR
THE STUDY AND PROTECTION OF
SCOTTISH ARCHITECTURE 1989, no.16,
p.55-58, photo., refs.

SCOTLAND--SELF-BUILD ARCHITECTURE--
FINDHORN FOUNDATION--ENVIRONMENTAL
ASPECTS
Breathing life into housing /
Michael Schimmelschmidt.
On the ecological, self-build,
timber-frame houses designed by
Keystone Architects & Designers
Co-operative for the Findhorn
Foundation, Scotland.
RIBA JOURNAL 1990 Nov., v.97,
no.11, p.56-58, photo., plan,
secn.

SCOTLAND--STIRLING--CHURCHES--19TH
CENTURY--ALTERATIONS AND ADDITIONS--
SOUTH CHURCH
Religious convert / Richard Carr.
Renovation of 1851 South Church,
Stirling, Scotland. Renovation
architects: Inglis & Carr.
BUILDING DESIGN 1990 Feb.16,
no.973, p.18-19, photos.

SCOTLAND--STONYPATH (LITTLE SPARTA)--
GARDENS
Ut hortus poesis. Die Gartenkunst
des Ian Finlay = Ut hortus poesis.
The garden art of Ian Hamilton
Finlay / Karl Schawelka.
Stonypath (Little Sparta) garden,
Lanarkshire, Scotland.
DAIDALOS 1990 Dec.15, no.38,
p.80-89, photos.

SCOTLAND--URBANIZATION--HISTORY
North of the border: The story of
Scotland's towns, by R. J.
Naismith [book review] / Jan
Magnus Fladmark.
ARCHITECTS' JOURNAL 1990 Sept.26,
v.192, no.13, p.79,

SCOTLAND--VERNACULAR ARCHITECTURE
Crofts to castles: the classic
dwelling types of the Highlands
and Islands / Geoffrey Stell.
TRADITIONAL HOMES 1990 Mar., v.6,
no.6, p.14-18, photos., biblio.
Scottish ancestral homes.
COLONIAL HOMES 1990 June, v.16,
no.3, p.[86-87],150, photos.
Vernacular architecture: Scottish
division: the homes of the border
/ Geoffrey Stell.
TRADITIONAL HOMES 1990 Jan., v.6,
no.4, p.16-20, photos., biblios.

SCOTLAND--VERNACULAR ARCHITECTURE--
INFLUENCE
James MacLaren / Alan Calder.
Townhouses in Bayswater, London,
and cottages in Glenlyon,
Scotland, by Arts and Crafts
architect James MacLaren.
Exhibition of the architect's
works at the Heinz Gallery,
London, beginning Jan.1990.
ARCHITECTS' JOURNAL 1990 Jan.17,
v.191, no.3, p.34-53, dets.,
dwgs., ports., photos., plans,
sketches, refs.
Modern history [Scandic Crown Hotel,
Edinburgh] / Malcolm Fraser.
250 bedroom hotel on Edinburgh's
Royal Mile. Architect: Ian Begg.
ARCHITECTS' JOURNAL 1990 Apr.25,
v.191, no.17, p.26-29, dwg.,
photos., plan, secns., site plan.
A new direction / Brian Edwards.
Addition to Scottish croft north
of Glasgow. Architects: McGurn
Logan Duncan & Opfer.
BUILDING DESIGN 1990 June 8,
no.989, p.20-23, elevs., photos.,
plans.

SCOTT, BARBARA
Henri IV and the Chateau of Pau /
Barbara Scott.
APOLLO 1990 Mar., v.131, no.337,
p.201-203,215, ill., photos.,
refs.
The renovation of the Musee des
Beaux-Arts in Lyon / Barbara
Scott.
On repairs and expansion of
exhibition space, begun in 1989
and to be completed in 1995.
APOLLO 1990 May, v.131, no.339,
p.334-336, photos., refs.

SCOTT BROWN, DENISE, 1931-
Architecture: a place for women.
Contents: Room at the top? Sexism
and the star system in
architecture, by Denise Scott
Brown.--Educating for the future,
by Matilda McQuaid.--The studio
experience: differences for women
students, by Anne Vytlacil.
ARCHITECTURAL DESIGN 1990, v.60,
no.1-2, p.[X]-[XIV],
La contraddizione decorata = The
decorated gap / Mark Wigley.
On Denise Scott-Brown and Robert
Venturi's work, including
"Complexity and contradiction in
architecture" and "Learning from
Las Vegas."
OTTAGONO 1990 Mar., no.94,
p.36-55, dwgs., elevs., models,
photos., plans, secns., sketches,
refs.
HB architecture today: Robert
Venturi and Denise Scott Brown
[interview] / Barbaralee
Diamonstein.
HOUSE BEAUTIFUL 1986 May, v.128,
no.5, p.172, port., photo.
Hennepin Avenue, Minneapolis.
One of six urban design reports
included in special issue, Urban
Concepts. Extracted from a 1981
plan by Denise Scott Brown, in
collaboration with
Bennett-Ringrose-Wolsfeld-Jarvis-G
ardner and Williams/O'Brien
Associates.
ARCHITECTURAL DESIGN 1990, v.60,
(Continued next column)

SCOTT BROWN, DENISE, 1931-
(CONTINUED)
Hennepin Avenue,...(CONTINUED)
no.1-2, p.62-69, dwgs., elev.,
photos., site plans, sketches.
JA interview: Robert Venturi and
Denise Scott Brown / Toshio
Nakamura.
JAPAN ARCHITECT 1990 May, v.65,
no.5(397), p.6-8, ports.
Robert Venturi and Denise Scott
Brown speak out on issues of urban
contextualism, postmodernism and
"willful disharmony" [interview] /
Kurt Andersen.
ARCHITECTURAL DIGEST 1990 Feb.,
v.47, no.2, p.68,72,74,78,82,
ports., elevs., model, photo.
Urban concepts [Architectural design
profile 83] / Denise Scott Brown.
Contents: Paralipomena in urban
design.-- Between three stools.--
Public realm, public sector and
the public interest in urban
design.-- Rise and fall of
community architecture.-- Urban
design reports [six, indexed
separately]. Includes a discussion
with Martin Pawley, Simon Jenkins,
Robert Thorne, Jake Brown, Ken
Powell, Charles Jencks, and John
Thompson.
ARCHITECTURAL DESIGN 1990, v.60,
no.1-2, p.[1]-96, dwgs., elevs.,
photos., site plans, aerial
photos., biblio., refs.

SCOTT BROWN, DENISE, 1931---ADDRESSES,
ESSAYS, LECTURES
Urban concepts [Architectural design
profile 83] / Denise Scott Brown.
Contents: Paralipomena in urban
design.-- Between three stools.--
Public realm, public sector and
the public interest in urban
design.-- Rise and fall of
community architecture.-- Urban
design reports [six, indexed
separately]. Includes a discussion
with Martin Pawley, Simon Jenkins,
Robert Thorne, Jake Brown, Ken
Powell, Charles Jencks, and John
Thompson.
ARCHITECTURAL DESIGN 1990, v.60,
no.1-2, p.[1]-96, dwgs., elevs.,
photos., site plans, aerial
photos., biblio., refs.

SCOTT, BROWNRIGG AND TURNER
Mixed media [new BBC headquarters,
London] / Robert Cowan.
White City site for BBC corporate
headquarters. Architects for first
phase: Scott Brownrigg and Turner;
architects for phases two and
three: RHWL in competition with
RMJM and BDP.
ARCHITECTS' JOURNAL 1990 Jan.24,
v.191, no.4, p.30-31, elevs., site
plan, sketches.

SCOTT, DIANA
A new idea in New Haven [Yale
Psychiatric Institute] / Diana
Scott.
Residential treatment center for
mentally ill young adults and
adolescents. Architects: Frank O.
Gehry and Allan Dehar.
METROPOLIS 1990 Apr., v.9, no.8,
p.18-19, photo.

SCOTT, GEORGE GILBERT, 1839-1897
Currants and cornelians / Michael Hall.
Choir design by George Gilbert Scott.
COUNTRY LIFE 1990 Mar.29, v.184, nc.13, p.72-75, photos.

SCOTT, GEORGE GILBERT, SIR, 1811-1878
English 18th and 19th century architecture [book review] / John Newman, Michael Brooks.
Review of James Paine, by Peter Leach, and The Foreign Office: an architectural history, by Ian Toplis.
SOCIETY OF ARCHITECTURAL HISTORIANS. JOURNAL 1990 Mar., v.49, no.1, p.109-110.
Sudeley Castle, Gloucestershire: the home of Lord and Lady Ashcombe / Michael Hall.
Architects for renovations to the medieval fortified house: Harvey Eginton, Sir George Gilbert Scott, John Drayton Wyatt. Decorators: Colefax & Fowler.
COUNTRY LIFE 1990 Apr.19, v.184, no.16, p.154-159, photos.
Victorian varieties - church tiles at Lichfield and Ashbourne / Philip Brown, Dorothy Brown.
Tiles for Victorian church restorations of Lichfield Cathedral and St. Oswald's Church, Ashbourne by Sir George Gilbert Scott.
GLAZED EXPRESSIONS / TILES & ARCHITECTURAL CERAMICS SOCIETY 1989 Spring, no.18, p.2, photos., refs.

SCOTT, GILES GILBERT, SIR, 1880-1960
390 Chasewood Park.
Located on Sudbury Hill, Harrow, at the site of the former Calvary nursing home, on which the chapel still stands (architect: Giles Gilbert Scott). Architect: Phippen Randall and Parks.
BUILDING 1990 Apr.13, v.255, no.15, p.51-58, charts, photos., plans, secn., site plan.
Britain's phone kiosks / Howard Mansfield.
Campaign to save Britain's red telephone booths from replacement by modern designs. Designer of the original boxes: Sir Giles Gilbert Scott.
PLACES 1990 Winter, v.6, no.2, p.7-9, photos.

SCOTT, JOHN, 17TH CENT.
Rococo survival [Dalton Hall gardens] / Giles Worsley.
Gardens laid out in 1730s. Gardeners: Richard North, Richard Davies, John Scott.
COUNTRY LIFE 1990 May 17, v.184, no.20, p.198-200, elevs., photos., site plans, engrs.

SCOTT, KEITH
Designing in historic cities / Keith Scott.
Example of Carlisle, in the north of England. Architects: BDP.
THE PLANNER 1990 Feb.23, v.76, no.7, p.23-24, port., photos.

SCOTT, KEITH (CONTINUED)
Old Mill cottages.
Conversion of an 18th-cent. corn mill in Witherslack, Cumbria, into apartments. Architect: Keith Scott.
BUILDING 1990 May 25, v.255, no.21, p.49-54, dets., photos., plans, site plan, tables.

SCOTT, N. KEITH. SHOPPING CENTRE DESIGN
Shopping centre design, by N. Keith Scott [book review] / Henry Herzberg.
ARCHITECTS' JOURNAL 1990 Apr.4, v.191, no.14, p.91, photo.

SCOTT, PATRICIA KAY
A fort called Niagara / Stuart D. Scott, Patricia Kay Scott.
Originally estab. in 1688 and recently excavated.
ARCHAEOLOGY 1990 Jan.-Feb., v.43, no.1, p.64-66,84, ill., site plans, aerial photo.

SCOTT, PHILIPPA
The Raj in repose: India's hill stations rise above it all / Philippa Scott.
British bungalows built in the late 19th cent. as high-altitude retreats from the heat.
ELLE DECOR 1990 May, v.1, no.4, p.46-48, photos.

SCOTT, STUART D.
A fort called Niagara / Stuart D. Scott, Patricia Kay Scott.
Originally estab. in 1688 and recently excavated.
ARCHAEOLOGY 1990 Jan.-Feb., v.43, no.1, p.64-66,84, ill., site plans, aerial photo.

SCOTTISH GEORGIAN SOCIETY
The Society's casework 1988-89.
The Architectural Heritage Society of Scotland, formerly the Scottish Georgian Society.
THE JOURNAL AND ANNUAL REPORT / THE SCOTTISH GEORGIAN SOCIETY FOR THE STUDY AND PROTECTION OF SCOTTISH ARCHITECTURE 1989, no.16, p.59-64, elevs., photos., secn.

SCREEN WALLS
See PIERCED WALLS

SCREENING ROOMS
A Roxy in your basement / Ed Sikov.
Features several private movie theaters, "home theaters," designed by Theo Kalomirakis.
CONNOISSEUR 1990 Apr., v.220, no.939, p.112-119,155, port., photos.

SCREENS
See also SCREENS (CHURCH DECORATION)
See also MESHREBEEYEHS

SCREENS (CHURCH DECORATION)
See also ALTARPIECES
See also CHOIR SCREENS
See also ICONOSTASES
See also ROOD SCREENS

SCRUTON, ROGER
Principios arquitectonicos en una edad de nihilismo = Architectural principles in an age of nihihilism / Roger Scruton.
COMPOSICION ARQUITECTONICA, ART & ARCHITECTURE 1990 Feb., no.5, p.93-120, dwgs., photos., refs.

SCULLY, DANIEL V.
Scully house, Dublin, New Hampshire, 1981-.
Architect & owner: Daniel V. Scully. Text in Japanese and English.
GA HOUSES 1990 July, no.29, p.144-147, elevs., photos., plans, secns., site plan.

SCULLY, VINCENT JOSEPH, 1920-
Animal spirits / Vincent Scully.
Focus on the Walt Disney World Swan Hotel by Michael Graves.
PROGRESSIVE ARCHITECTURE 1990 Oct., v.71, no.10, p.90-91, photos.
Golden anniversary for the Merritt Parkway / Catherine Lynn.
Includes a short piece by Vincent Scully, "The automobile is a destroyer."
CONNECTICUT PRESERVATION NEWS 1990 Sept.-Oct., v.13, no.5, p.[1]-5, photos.
Das Meyer May House in seiner Umgebung: exzellente Restaurierung eines "prairie house" von F.L. Wright in Grand Rapids, Michigan / Vincent Scully.
Funded by The Steelcase Co.
ARCHITEKTUR, INNENARCHITEKTUR, TECHNISCHER AUSBAU 1990 Jan.-Feb., v.98, no.1-2, p.44-50, photos., plans.
Shingle-minded pursuits: a Massachusetts town is rediscovering its legacy of master builders / Vincent Scully.
On the work of preservation architect Stephen Roberts Holt in Manchester-by-the-Sea.
HOUSE & GARDEN 1990 Nov., v.162, no.11, p.[57]-66, dwgs., port., photos.
Teoria y deleite: las abstracciones de Eisenman / Vincent Scully.
The Wexner Center for the Visual Arts, Ohio State University.
ARQUITECTURA VIVA 1990 Mar.-Apr., no.11, p.27-31, photos, plans.

SCULLY, VINCENT JOSEPH, 1920-.
ARCHITECTURE OF THE AMERICAN SUMMER: THE FLOWERING OF THE SHINGLE STYLE
The architecture of the American summer: the flowering of the shingle style [by] Vincent Scully [and] Modern classicism [by] Robert A. M. Stern, Raymond W. Gastil [book review]/ Leland M. Roth.
SOCIETY OF ARCHITECTURAL HISTORIANS. JOURNAL 1990 Dec., v.49, no.4, p.453-455,

SCULPTORS--GERMANY (WEST)--POSENENSKE,
CHARLOTTE
Charlotte Posenenske / Hans Ulrich
Reck.
On the work of this German
sculptor.
ARCHITHESE 1990 July-Aug., v.20,
no.4, p.62-66, photos.

SCULPTURE
See also SCULPTURE GARDENS
See also EARTHWORKS (SCULPTURE)
See also INSTALLATION WORKS
See also MONUMENTS AND MEMORIALS
See also OUTDOOR SCULPTURE
See also RELIEF (SCULPTURE)
Adolfo Natalini a Francoforte /
Paolo Riani.
Project: Casa d'Angolo in
Saalgasse n.4, modeled in bronze.
VILLE GIARDINI 1990 Sept., no.251,
p.34-37, dwgs., models.
Art work: Robert and Marion Einbeck
transform a corporate lobby / Edie
Lee Cohen.
Lobby transformed with 3-D
sculpture for the Rhone-Poulenc
Sante co., Antony, France.
INTERIOR DESIGN 1990 Mar., v.61,
no.5, p.[186-189], photos., plan.
Hejduk houses at Georgia Tech /
Claire Downey.
Features the "House of the
Suicide" and "House of the Mother
of the Suicide" designed by John
Hejduk and built by students at
the Georgia Tech School of
Architecture.
PROGRESSIVE ARCHITECTURE 1990
June, v.71, no.6, p.24, photos.
History and verse: Indoor
Memorials, Atlanta, Georgia, John
Hejduk, Architect / Michael J.
Crosbie.
Two sculptural projects designed
by Hejduk and built by students at
Georgia Institute of Technology.
ARCHITECTURE: THE MAGAZINE OF THE
AMERICAN INSTITUTE OF ARCHITECTS
1990 June, v.79, no.6, p.70-73,
photos.
Le temple de la Melancolie,
sculptures pour une architecture
imaginaire d'Auguste de
Niederhausern, dit Rodo / Claude
Lapaire.
ZEITSCHRIFT FUR SCHWEIZERISCHE
ARCHAOLOGIE UND KUNSTGESCHICHTE
1990, v.47, no.1, p.75-82, port.,
photos., refs.

SCULPTURE--20TH CENTURY
Place defined by time and light /
Dale Eldred.
The author is an artist whose
sculptures are placed in open
spaces where the passage of light
across the surfaces parallels the
passing of time. Examples from
Denmark, Finland, Turkey, and the
U.S.
PLACES 1990 Summer, v.6, no.4,
p.34-[41], photos.

SCULPTURE--20TH CENTURY--ESTONIA
Hahmoja leijailevassa tilassa:
omaelamakerrallisia merkintoja /
Vilen Kunnapu.
"Figures in a floating
space/biographical signs":
sculptures by the Estonian
architect.
(Continued next column)

SCULPTURE--20TH CENTURY--ESTONIA
(CONTINUED)
Hahmoja leijailevassa...(CONTINUED)
ARKKITEHTI 1989, v.86, no.7,
p.38-40, ill.

SCULPTURE--20TH CENTURY--GERMANY
(WEST)--BERLIN
Stadt, Architektur, Bildende Kunst /
Hans-Michael Herzog.
Several works since 1972 by Berlin
sculptor Georg Seibert.
BAUWELT 1990 Dec.28, v.81, no.48,
p.2402-2403, dwg., models.

SCULPTURE--20TH CENTURY--SCANDINAVIA
Nordisk rumkunst.
Installation works at the Volvo
Personvagnar AB office in
Torslanda, outside of Gothenburg,
Sweden. In Danish and English.
SKALA 1990, no.22, p.10, photos.

SCULPTURE--ANCIENT
Two statues of Hercules in the Forum
Boarium in Rome / Olga Palagia.
OXFORD JOURNAL OF ARCHAEOLOGY 1990
Mar., v.9, no.1, p.51-70, photos.,
site plan, biblio., refs.

SCULPTURE--ANCIENT--COLLECTIONS--
ENGLAND--LONDON--BRITISH MUSEUM
Five ways to conquer a city / Erika
Bleibtreu.
On 19th-cent. excavations of
Nimrud, Nineveh and related sites,
and the Assyrian reliefs now in
the British Museum.
BIBLICAL ARCHAEOLOGY REVIEW 1990
May-June, v.16, no.3, p.36-44,
diagr., photo., table, engrs.

SCULPTURE--ANCIENT--INFLUENCE
Toward a new language of form: Karl
Bitter and the beginnings of
archaism in American sculpture /
Susan Rather.
Examples include reliefs and
memorials from the 1900-1915
period.
WINTERTHUR PORTFOLIO 1990 Spring,
v.25, no.1, p.[1]-19, photos.,
refs.

SCULPTURE - ARCHITECTURAL
See also BACINI
See also GARGOYLES
Oldenburg/Van Bruggen: il coltello
affetta muro.
The Margo Leavin Gallery, Los
Angeles, a converted post office,
features a work by artists Claes
Oldenburg and Coosje van Bruggen.
In Italian and English.
DOMUS 1990 May, no.716, p.[14-15],
dwgs., photos.

SCULPTURE--ARCHITECTURAL--10TH
CENTURY--INDIA--NARAYANAPURAM
Narayanapuram: a tenth century site
in Kalinga / Mary F. Linda.
On the four 10th cent. temples
which were part of the medieval
principality of Kalinga.
ARTIBUS ASIAE 1990, v.50, no.3-4,
p.232-262, map, photos., plans,
refs.

SCULPTURE--ARCHITECTURAL--12TH
CENTURY--CORNICE DI SANT'APOLLINARE
La "cornice di Sant'Apollinare"
custodia nelle Grotte Vaticane /
Francesca Bottari.
On the original position of the
six fragments, dating back to the
early 12th cent., now in one of
the halls of the Vatican grottoes.
Summaries in English, French,
German and Spanish.
PALLADIO 1988 Dec., v.1, no.2,
p.5-14, ill., photos., refs.

SCULPTURE--ARCHITECTURAL--16TH
CENTURY--FRANCE--PARIS--LOUVRE
Les sculptures de l'attique du
Louvre par l'atelier de Jean
Goujon / Genevieve Bresc-Bautier.
On the history of the Piety and
Justice reliefs, now on the
mezzanine rotunda of the Hall
Napoleon.
REVUE DU LOUVRE ET DES MUSEES DE
FRANCE 1989, no.2, p.97-111,
dwgs., photos., plan, engrs.,
refs.

SCULPTURE--ARCHITECTURAL--18TH
CENTURY--ITALY--SICILY--BAGHERIA--
VILLA PALAGONIA
Petrified in Palagonia / Martin
Gayford.
Focus on the Baroque sculptural
decoration added to the early 18th
cent. Villa Palagonia at Bagheria,
near Palermo. Architect: Maria
Tommaso Napoli.
THE WORLD OF INTERIORS 1990 Oct.,
p.[164-171], photos.

SCULPTURE--ARCHITECTURAL--20TH
CENTURY--AUSTRIA
Architettura e statua tra Wiener
Secession e Jugendstil /
Alessandra Muntoni.
Including works by O. Wagner, J.
M. Olbrich, J. Hoffmann. English,
French, German, Spanish summaries,
p.138.
STORIA DELLA CITTA 1988 Oct.-Dec.,
v.13, no.48, p.69-82, dwgs.,
photos., refs.

SCULPTURE--ARCHITECTURAL--20TH
CENTURY--GERMANY (WEST)
Charlotte Posenenske / Hans Ulrich
Reck.
On the work of this German
sculptor.
ARCHITHESE 1990 July-Aug., v.20,
no.4, p.62-66, photos.

SCULPTURE--ARCHITECTURAL--ALTERATIONS
AND ADDITIONS--SPAIN--BARCELONA--
SAGRADA FAMILIA
Continuation of Sagrada Familia in
dispute / C.C. Sullivan.
On the new sculpture by Jose Maria
Subirachs installed on the
"Passion" facade of the Church of
the Sagrada Familia, Barcelona.
Original architect: Antoni Gaudi.
PROGRESSIVE ARCHITECTURE 1990
Nov., v.71, no.12, p.26, photos.

SCULPTURE--ARCHITECTURAL--BAROQUE--
ITALY--ROME--CHIESA DELLE STIMMATE--
SAN FRANCESCO D'ASSISI
La fabbrica della chiesa delle
Stimmate in Roma e la statua di
San Francesco di Bernardino
Cametti / Paola Ferraris.
Ca.1717. Architects: Giovanni
Battista Contini, Antonio
Carnevari. Sculptor: Bernardino
Cametti.
STORIA DELL'ARTE 1989, no.65,
p.[69]-86, dwgs., photos., plans,
site plans, refs.

SCULPTURE--ARCHITECTURAL--CAMBODIA--
ANGKOR
Restoring the Angkor Temples: a
struggle against nature and man /
Bonnie Burnham.
ART INTERNATIONAL 1990 Winter, new
ser., no.13, p.79-[83], photos.

SCULPTURE--ARCHITECTURAL--FRANCE--
AULNAY-DE-SAINTONGE--
SAINT-PIERRE-DE-LA-TOUR
Aulnay-de-Saintonge and high
romanesque figure sculpture in
Aquitane / Anat Tcherikover.
BRITISH ARCHAEOLOGICAL
ASSOCIATION. JOURNAL 1990, v.143,
p.[77]-94, pl.12-17, map, photos.,
refs.

SCULPTURE--ARCHITECTURAL--FRANCE--
PARIS--LOUVRE
Le decor exterieur du Louvre sur la
cour Carree et la rue de Rivoli
(1851-1936) / Anne Pingeot.
REVUE DU LOUVRE ET DES MUSEES DE
FRANCE 1989, no.2, p.112-125,
elevs., photos., tables.

SCULPTURE--ARCHITECTURAL--GOTHIC--
FRANCE--REIMS--NOTRE DAME
La facade de la cathedrale de Reims:
Architecture et sculpture des
portails. Etude archeologique et
stylistique [by] Peter Kurmann
[book review] / Carina Jacobsson.
KONSTHISTORISK TIDSKRIFT 1989,
v.58, no.4, p.176-178,

SCULPTURE--ARCHITECTURAL--GOTHIC--
FRANCE--SAINT-DENIS--ABBAYE DE
SAINT-DENIS
Medieval architecture [book review]
/ Roger Stalley.
A joint review of The Royal Abbey
of Saint-Denis..., by Sumner
McKnight Crosby, ed. by Pamela Z.
Blum, and Abbot Suger and Saint
Denis: a symposium, ed. by Paula
Lieber Gerson.
SOCIETY OF ARCHITECTURAL
HISTORIANS. JOURNAL 1990 Dec.,
v.49, no.4, p.440-441,

SCULPTURE--ARCHITECTURAL--GOTHIC--
ITALY--ABRUZZI E MOLISE
"Magistri" e cantieri nel "Regnum
Siciliae": l'Abruzzo e la cerchia
federiciana / Francesco Aceto.
Analysis of architectural
sculpture from the 13th cent. in
the Abruzzi e Molise region of
southern Italy.
BOLLETTINO D'ARTE 1990, v.75,
no.59, p.15-96, dwgs., photos.,
refs.

SCULPTURE--ARCHITECTURAL--GOTHIC--
ITALY--MILAN--DUOMO DI MILANO
I Giganti e le vicende della prima
scultura del Duomo di Milano /
Francesca Tasso.
Probable designer: Giovannino de'
Grassi. English summary p.186.
ARTE LOMBARDA 1990, no.92-93,
p.55-62, dwgs., photos., refs.

SCULPTURE--ARCHITECTURAL--GREEK--
ITALY--LOCRI--LOCRI EPIZEFIRI
Gronde in calcare a testa leonina da
Locri Epizefiri / Marcella Barra
Bagnasco.
Analysis of Greek lion head
sculptures dating from the 5th
cent.
BOLLETTINO D'ARTE 1990 Mar.-Apr.,
v.76, no.60, p.[i]-24, dwgs.,
photos., plan, tables, refs.

SCULPTURE--ARCHITECTURAL--HINDU--
INFLUENCE
Baron Palace, Cairo , Egypt / Veena
Wig, Siddhartha Wig.
Built in the late 1920s and
influenced by Hindu temples and
sculpture. Architects included
Alexander Marcel.
ARCHITECTURE + DESIGN 1990
July-Aug., v.7, no.4, p.16-17,
photos.

SCULPTURE--ARCHITECTURAL--INDIA--
TANJORE
Art forms of Tanjore / Marcello
Tranchini.
Sculpture, and architectural
sculpture of Tanjore in the state
of Tamil Nadv.
ARTS OF ASIA 1989 Nov.-Dec., v.19,
no.6, p.130-141, photos.

SCULPTURE--ARCHITECTURAL--MEDIEVAL--
FRANCE--NORMANDY
La sculpture preromane en Normandie
et ses prolongements jusqu'au
debut du XI siecle / Maylis Bayle.
CAHIERS ARCHEOLOGIQUES; FIN DE
L'ANTIQUITE ET MOYEN AGE 1990,
v.38, p.37-62, dwgs., photos.,
refs.

SCULPTURE--ARCHITECTURAL--MEDIEVAL--
ITALY--BENEVENTO--CHIOSTRO DI SANTA
SOFIA
Ritorno al chiostro di Santa Sofia a
Benevento / Riccardo Naldi.
Cloister dates from the
mid-to-late 12th century.
BOLLETTINO D'ARTE 1990 Mar.-Apr.,
v.76, no.60, p.25-66, photos.,
plan, refs.

SCULPTURE--ARCHITECTURAL--
RENAISSANCE--ITALY--NAPLES--SAN
GIOVANNI A CARBONARA--CAPPELLA
CARACCIOLO
Ancora sulla cappella Caracciolo di
Vico in San Giovanni a Carbonara a
Napoli / Francesco Abbate.
Attribution of some portal
sculpture to Diego de Siloe.
PROSPETTIVA 1988 Apr.-1989 Jan.,
no.53-56, p.362-366, photos.,
refs.

SCULPTURE--ARCHITECTURAL--ROMAN--
ITALY--ROME--FORUM OF TRAJAN
Foro Traiano.
Eleven articles on the Forum of
Trajan including historical and
architectural reconstructions.
Authors: L. Messa, L. Ungaro, M.
Milella, P. Pensabene, G.
Piazzesi, B.M. Tummarello, S.
Stucchi.
ARCHAEOLOGIA CLASSICA 1989, v.41,
no.2, p.[27]-292, dets., dwgs.,
models, maps, plans, site plans,
recont. dwgs., refs.

SCULPTURE--ARCHITECTURAL--ROMANESQUE--
FRANCE
Concerning Angouleme, riders and the
art of the Gregorian reform / Anat
Tcherikover.
ART HISTORY 1990 Dec., v.13, no.4,
p.[425]-457, dets., photos., refs.

SCULPTURE--ARCHITECTURAL--ROMANESQUE--
FRANCE--ANGOULEME--ANGOULEME
CATHEDRAL
Concerning Angouleme, riders and the
art of the Gregorian reform / Anat
Tcherikover.
ART HISTORY 1990 Dec., v.13, no.4,
p.[425]-457, dets., photos., refs.

SCULPTURE--ARCHITECTURAL--ROMANESQUE--
FRANCE--DIE
Souvenirs antiques et creations
romanes: les sculptures de
l'ancienne cathedrale de Die /
Jacques Thirion.
English summary, p.162.
GAZETTE DES BEAUX-ARTS 1990 Apr.,
ser.6,v.115, no.1455, p.[141]-162,
photos., refs.

SCULPTURE--ARCHITECTURAL--ROMANESQUE--
FRANCE--ROUSSILLON
Quelques sculptures romanes du
Roussillon dans les collections
americaines / Eda Diskant.
LES CAHIERS DE SAINT-MICHEL DE
CUXA 1990 July, no.21,
p.199-[218], photos., refs.

SCULPTURE--ARCHITECTURAL--ROMANESQUE--
ITALY--CIVATE--SAN PIETRO AL MONTE
Arte e liturgia nel complesso
monastico di Civate / Vincenzo
Gatti.
Paper presented at the Qualita
ecclesiale nell'arte conference in
1989, on liturgical aspects of the
decorations at the late 11th cent.
church.
ARTE CRISTIANA 1990 Mar.-July,
v.78, no.737-738, p.91-102, dets.,
photos., refs.

SCULPTURE--ARCHITECTURAL--ROMANESQUE--
SPAIN--ATIENZA--SANTA MARIA DEL REY
El programa teologico de la portada
romanica de Santa Maria del Rey en
Atienza / Antonio Herrera Casado.
Porch dates between 1260-1270.
English summary.
ARCHIVO ESPANOL DE ARTE 1990
Oct.-Dec., v.63, no.252,
p.[593]-607, dwgs., refs.

SCULPTURE--ARCHITECTURAL--ROMANESQUE--
SWITZERLAND--LANGENBRUCK--KLOSTER
SCHONTAL
Lowe, Drache, Ritter und Madonna /
Carola Jaggi, Hans-Rudolf Meier.
An examination of the 12th-cent.
sculpture on the west portal of
Kloster Schontal, in Langenbruck,
Switzerland. Summaries in French
and Italian.
UNSERE KUNSTDENKMALER 1989, v.40,
no.4, p.412-419, dets., elevs.,
photos., refs.

SCULPTURE--ARCHITECTURAL--ROMANESQUE--
SWITZERLAND--LOCARNO--SAN VITTORE DI
MURALTO
La sirena nel San Vittore di Muralto
/ Rossana Cardani.
A study of three Romanesque
sculptures in a church near
Locarno, Switzerland. Summaries
in French and German.
UNSERE KUNSTDENKMALER 1989, v.40,
no.4, p.393-401, dets., photos.,
plan, sketches, refs.

SCULPTURE--ARCHITECTURAL--UNITED
STATES--WALT DISNEY WORLD
(FLORIDA)--SWAN HOTEL
Swan statues, Swan Hotel, Walt
Disney World Lake Buena Vista,
Florida.
Architects: Michael Graves
Architect.
PROGRESSIVE ARCHITECTURE 1990
Mar., v.71, no.3, p.119, det.,
dwgs., photo., secn.

SCULPTURE--BAROQUE--ITALY--NAPLES--
CAPPELLA SANSEVERO
Sansevero: the power of marble /
Marina Causa Picone.
Photographs of the recently
restored Sansevero Chapel, the
funerary sacellum of the
Neapolitan Sangro family. Built
in 1608, the chapel contains many
sculptures from the Baroque and
Neoclassical periods.
FMR 1990 Dec., v.9, no.47,
p.21-52, port., photos.

SCULPTURE--BRICK
Sculpted brick / Daniel
Winterbottom.
Features work by artists Ken
Williams and Walter Ritchie.
LANDSCAPE ARCHITECTURE 1990 Nov.,
v.80, no.11, p.76-77, photos.
Sculpted brick II / Daniel
Winterbottom.
Second article in two-part series
on the reemergence of sculpted
brick in landscape architectural
design.
LANDSCAPE ARCHITECTURE 1990 Dec.,
v.80, no.12, p.62-64, port.,
photos.

SCULPTURE--BRONZE--ROMAN--ITALY--
ROME--MARCUS AURELIUS
Il gruppo equestre di Marco Aurelio
e il Laterano: ricerche per una
storia della fortuna del monumento
dall'eta medievale sino al 1538 /
Lucilla de Lachenal.
BOLLETTINO D'ARTE 1990 May-June,
v.74 [76], no.61, p.1-52, photos.,
engrs., refs.

SCULPTURE GARDENS--17TH CENTURY--
AUSTRIA--SALZBURG--PARK MIRABELL--
ZWERGLGARTEN
Il disegno del luogo = Designing the
site / Tamara Molinari.
Features 3 parks: The Garden of
Dwarfs, Salzburg; Campo del Sole,
Italy; and Lancy, Geneva (George
Descombes).
ABITARE 1990 June, no.286,
p.156-175, axonometric views, map,
photos., secns., site plans,
sketches.

SCULPTURE GARDENS--20TH CENTURY--
FRANCE--VANNES--KERGUEHENNEC
In nature's shadow [Kerguehennec] /
Klaus Kertess.
Sculpture garden in Brittany.
ART IN AMERICA 1987 Sept., v.75,
no.9, p.57-59, photos.

SCULPTURE GARDENS--20TH CENTURY--
ITALY--PUNTA NAVACCIA--CAMPO DEL
SOLE
Il disegno del luogo = Designing the
site / Tamara Molinari.
Features 3 parks: The Garden of
Dwarfs, Salzburg; Campo del Sole,
Italy; and Lancy, Geneva (George
Descombes).
ABITARE 1990 June, no.286,
p.156-175, axonometric views, map,
photos., secns., site plans,
sketches.

SCULPTURE GARDENS--BELGIUM
Toefjes cultuur in het landschap:
Beeldenparken en -tuinen in
Nederland en Belgie / Brigitte van
der Sande.
ARCHIS 1990 Sept., no.9, p.8-10,
photos.

SCULPTURE GARDENS--CANADA--MONTREAL
(QUEBEC)--CANADIAN CENTRE FOR
ARCHITECTURE
Garden allegory [Canadian Center for
Architecture] / Heidi Landecker.
On Phyllis Lambert; the director
and creator of the CCA, Montreal.
Architect: Lambert and Peter Rose.
A new sculpture garden was
designed by Melvin Charney.
ARCHITECTURE: THE AIA JOURNAL 1990
Dec., v.79, no.12, p.[60-65],
dwg., port., photo., site plan.
Melvin Charney: giardino-scultura
del CCA a Montreal / Pierre
Restany.
In Italian and English.
DOMUS 1990 Jan., no.712, p.6-[7],
axonometric view, models, site
plans.

SCULPTURE GARDENS--FRANCE
French sculpture gardens / Barbara
Abbs.
LANDSCAPE DESIGN 1989 Dec.-1990
Jan., no.186, p.15-17, photos.

SCULPTURE GARDENS--ITALY--SICILY--
FIUMARA D'ARTE
La fiumara d'arte / Giusetta Cavolo,
Giuseppe Parisi.
Sculpture garden in Sicily near
Santo Stefano di Camastra.
SPAZIO E SOCIETA 1990 July-Sept.,
v.13, no.51, p.112-115, map,
photos.

SCULPTURE GARDENS--NETHERLANDS
Toefjes cultuur in het landschap:
Beeldenparken en -tuinen in
Nederland en Belgie / Brigitte van
der Sande.
ARCHIS 1990 Sept., no.9, p.8-10,
photos.

SCULPTURE GARDENS--SOUTH AFRICA--NEW
BETHESDA--A CAMEL YARD
The Owl House / James Graham.
Features sculpture garden and
interiors of the late artist Helen
Martins' house in New Bethesda,
South Africa.
THE WORLD OF INTERIORS 1990 Apr.,
p.140-[149], photos.

SCULPTURE GARDENS--SWEDEN--LIDINGO--
MILLESGARDEN
Abgehoben .... / Hermann Orth.
On the sculpture garden of Carl
Milles, Millesgarden, on the
Swedish island of Lindingo.
ARCHITEKTUR & WOHNEN 1990
Feb.-Mar., no.1, p.72-76, photos.

SCULPTURE GARDENS--UNITED STATES--
HOUSTON (TEXAS)--MUSEUM OF FINE
ARTS--LILLIE AND HUGH ROY CULLEN
SCULPTURE GARDEN
Lillie and Hugh Roy Cullen Sculpture
Garden.
Whole issue. Created by Isamu
Noguchi.
MUSEUM OF FINE ARTS, HOUSTON.
BULLETIN - THE MUSEUM OF FINE
ARTS, HOUSTON 1986 Summer, v.9,
no.3, p.[2]-32, photos.

SCULPTURE GARDENS--UNITED STATES--NEW
YORK (NEW YORK)--MUSEUM OF MODERN
ART
Der Skulpturengarten des "Museum of
Modern Art" in New York: ein
Garten als Museumsmitte / Norbert
Schindler.
GARTEN UND LANDSCHAFT 1990, v.100,
no.10, p.5-6, photo., plan.

SCULPTURE--GLASS--DENMARK--EXHIBITIONS
Randmonumenter [exhibition review] /
Morten Daugaard.
An exhibit of Danish glass
designs, marking the 25th
anniversary of the Statens
Kunstfond, at the
Rosenkjaerhallen, Christianshaven,
Oct.28-Nov.1, 1989.
ARKITEKTEN 1990 Apr., v.92, no.4,
p.134-136, dwgs., photos.

SCULPTURE--LIMESTONE--3RD MILLENIUM
B.C.--ENVIRONMENTAL ASPECTS--EGYPT
Conservation research proposal for
the Great Sphinx presented in
Cairo.
THE GETTY CONSERVATION INSTITUTE
NEWSLETTER 1990 Winter, v.5, no.1,
p.1-3, photos.

SCULPTURE--MEDIEVAL--COLLECTIONS--
UNITED STATES--NEW YORK (NEW YORK)--
METROPOLITAN MUSEUM OF ART
The temptations of Christ: the
iconography of a twelfth-century
capital in the Metropolitan Museum
of Art / Lucy A. Adams.
Attribution is uncertain (possibly
Champagne). Includes abstract.
GESTA 1989, v.28, no.2, p.130-135,
dets., photos., refs.

SCULPTURE--MEDIEVAL--ENGLAND
Early medieval wall painting and
painted sculpture in England / ed.
by Sharon Cather, David Park, Paul
Williamson.
Based on the proceedings of a
symposium at the Courtauld
Institute of Art, Feb. 1985.
BAR BRITISH SERIES 1990, no.216,
p.[1]-262, dwgs., photos., plans,
site plans, reconst. dwgs., refs.

SCULPTURE, SOUND
See SOUND SCULPTURE

SCULPTURE--STONE--UNITED STATES--
MILWAUKEE (WISCONSIN)--TOWER OF
BABEL
The house with a heart of stone /
Victor M. Cassidy.
Home near Milwaukee, Wisc., which
was constructed around massive
stone sculpture, Tower of Babel.
Architect: Charles Moore. Artist:
Dan Yarbrough.
CONNOISSEUR 1990 May, v.220,
no.940, p.104-107,148, axonometric
view, port., photos.

SCULPTURE--STUCCO--17TH CENTURY--
ITALY--ROME--CHIESA DI SANTA MARTA
Gli stucchi di Santa Marta al
Collegio Romano nell'attività di
Leonardo Retti / Maria Barbara
Guerrieri Borsoi.
Sculpture dates from the late 17th
cent.
BOLLETTINO D'ARTE 1990 May-June,
v.74 [76], no.61, p.99-112,
photos., engrs., refs.

SCURI, PIERA
Reviving the senses / Michael
Wagner.
Redesigned control room of factory
belonging to Himont Srl Italia,
Ferrara. Architects/Interior
designers: Piera Scuri, Douglas
Skene.
INTERIORS 1990 Dec., v.150, no.5,
p.98-99, photos., plan.

SCYTHIAN
See "SCYTHIAN" AS A SUBHEADING AFTER
SPECIFIC BUILDING TYPES OR OTHER
MAIN HEADINGS.

SEA-LOCKS
See LOCKS (HYDRAULIC ENGINEERING)

SEALANTS
See SEALING COMPOUNDS

SEALE, WILLIAM
The Leonardo of historic
architecture [William Seale] /
Clem Labine.
CLEM LABINE'S TRADITIONAL BUILDING
1990 Sept.-Oct., v.3, no.5, p.5,
44, photos., port.
Photo finish: vintage photos aid
restoration of Eastman House
[George Eastman House, Rochester,
N.Y.] / Sebby Wilson Jacobson.
McKim Mead and White designed the
public rooms, built 1904-05.
William Seale supervised its
recent restoration.
PRESERVATION NEWS 1990 Apr., v.30,
no.4, p.7, port., photos.

SEALING COMPOUNDS
See also CALKING
See also PUTTY
How to increase the life of your
sealant / John L. Margeson.
CANADIAN ARCHITECT 1990 Mar.,
v.35, no.3, p.49,53.
Sealant configurations and
performance / James C. Myers,
James S. Russell.
Fillet joints.
ARCHITECTURAL RECORD 1990 Jan.,
v.178, no.1, p.150-153, dets.,
ill., photo., table, biblio.
Update on structural sealant glazing
/ Mark S. Brook.
CANADIAN ARCHITECT 1990 June,
v.35, no.6, p.31,33, photos., ref.
The Wright way: restoring a pair of
landmark structures / Amy Gray
Light.
Repairs using the latest
developments in roofing and
sealant technologies, for the
Grady-Gammage Auditorium at Ariz.
State Univ. and for the Affleck
House in Bloomfield Hills, Mich.
ARCHITECTURE: THE AIA JOURNAL 1990
Nov., v.79, no.11, p.153, photos.

SEAMON, DAVID. DWELLING PLACE AND
ENVIRONMENT
Fascinating mystery: Dwelling place
and environment, edited by David
Seamon and Robert Mugerauer [book
review] / Martin Symes.
Pub. in 1989 by Columbia Univ.
Pr., reprint of 1985 Nijhoff ed.
ARCHITECTS' JOURNAL 1990 Mar.28,
v.191, no.13, p.91.

SEAR-BROWN GROUP
Spray pools: no wading / Richard A.
Arenella.
Spotlights a facility in Great
Neck, L.I. Project designers:
Sear-Brown Group.
PARKS & RECREATION 1990 Nov.,
v.25, no.11, p.30-33,71, ports.,
photos.

SEARING, HELEN
CAA as Museum of Architecture /
Helen Searing.
RACAR: REVUE D'ART CANADIENNE.
CANADIAN ART REVIEW 1989, v.16,
no.2, p.181-192,308-335, dets.,
elevs., photos., plans, aerial
photos., refs.
In the shadow of Mies: Ludwig
Hilberseimer, architect, educator
and urban planner / Helen Searing.
Review of the 1988 book that
includes reminiscences by George
E. Danforth; critical essays by
Richard Pommer, David Spaeth, and
Kevin Harrington.
SOCIETY OF ARCHITECTURAL
HISTORIANS. JOURNAL 1990 Mar.,
v.49, no.1, p.113-114.

SEARL DESIGN
Murphy & Durieu: the New York
brokerage firm's spaces by Searl
Design Inc. / Monica Geran.
INTERIOR DESIGN 1990 May, v.61,
no.7, p.256-[259], photos., plan.

SEASIDE BUILDINGS--19TH CENTURY--
ALTERATIONS AND ADDITIONS--ENGLAND--
BLACKPOOL--WINTER GARDENS
New wave [Blackpool] / Louise
Rogers.
Renovation of Blackpool Winter
Gardens. Architects: David Quigley
Architects.
ARCHITECTS' JOURNAL 1990 Feb.14,
v.191, no.7, p.24-27, axonometric
view, dets., dwg., photos., plan.
The sense of sea-change.
On the refurbishment of the 19th
cent. seaside complex, Winter
Gardens, Blackpool. Architects:
David Quigley Architects.
DESIGNERS' JOURNAL 1990 June,
no.58, p.8, photos.
Winter Gardens blossom / Richard
Wilcock.
On the refurbishment of the
seaside 19th cent. complex in
Blackpool. Architects for the
renovation: David Quigley
Architects.
RIBA JOURNAL 1990 Apr., v.97,
no.4, p.90-93, photos., plan.

SEASIDE BUILDINGS--19TH CENTURY--
EUROPE
Sulla architettura della citta
balneare ottocentesca.
Published in conjunction with a
1989 book and exhibition on
19th-cent. bathing and seaside
buildings.
L'INDUSTRIA DELLE COSTRUZIONI 1990
Jan., v.24, no.219, p.66-67,
elevs., plan, secns., site plans.

SEASIDE BUILDINGS--DENMARK--JUTLAND
Nordjyske Billeder / Erik Iversen.
Recent work by Aldo Rossi,
Arkitektfirmaet Dommergaarden, and
Malthas Tegnestue, and vernacular
buildings in north Jutland.
ARKITEKTEN 1990 Dec., v.92, no.18,
p.572-573, photos.

SEASIDE BUILDINGS--ENGLAND--BEXHILL--
DE LA WARR PAVILION
Earl De La Warr and the competition
for the Bexhill Pavilion, 1933-34
/ Russell Stevens, Peter Willis.
Includes discussion of the
controversy. Winners Erich
Mendelsohn and Serge Chermayeff.
ARCHITECTURAL HISTORY 1990, v.33,
p.[135-166], dwgs., ports.,
elevs., photos., plans, aerial
photos., refs.

SEASIDE BUILDINGS--NETHERLANDS--ALMERE
Bauausstellung Almere
"Meerfasewoningen".
Architect: Teun Koolhaas.
BAUWELT 1990 Oct.5, v.81, no.37,
p.1858-1859, photos.

SEASIDE TOWNS
Ontwerpen tussen droom en daad: vier
voorstellen voor de boulevard van
Domburg / D'Laine Camp.
Projects by Wiel Arets, Ben van
Berkel, Chris Kempe, Stephane
Beel.
DE ARCHITECT 1990 Nov., v.21,
no.11, p.44-47, dwgs., elevs.,
models.

SECTILE OPUS
See PAVEMENTS - TILE

SECURITY MEASURES
See "SECURITY MEASURES" AS A
SUBHEADING AFTER SPECIFIC BUILDING
TYPES OR OTHER MAIN HEADINGS.
See also SECURITY SYSTEMS

SECURITY SYSTEMS
See also BURGLAR ALARMS
See also ELECTRONIC SECURITY SYSTEMS
Building high tech security systems
/ Craig Willcut, Martin Mancini.
In corporate and research
facilities.
DEVELOPMENT 1990 May-June, v.21,
no.3, p.26-27, photos.
Fire and security.
Ten articles on prevention,
building regulations, halon,
security in houses, standards,
associations for information, card
access systems, barriers,
ductwork, and case studies.
BUILDING 1990 Oct.5, v.255, no.39,
Suppl., p.[1]-32, diagrs., photos.
Locked in danger / Jonathan Stearn.
Describes situations whereby
highly efficient security devices
prevent fire brigades from
reaching victims.
HOUSING 1989 Feb., v.25, no.1,
p.20-23, photos.

SEDDON, CHRISTOPHER RICHARD
How to foster Japanese ties / Chris
Seddon.
Foster Associates' commission for
the Century Tower in Tokyo
required setting up a new office
there.
ARCHITECTS' JOURNAL 1990 Sept.19,
v.192, no.12, p.68-71, photos.

SEDGWICK, LINSAY
The Russian experience / Siobhan
O'Dea, Linsay Sedgwick.
Tour of the U.S.S.R. by Irish
architects and planners; report on
the differences they observed
between the roles of Irish and
Soviet architects.
PLAN: ARCHITECTURE AND BUILDING
DESIGN IN IRELAND 1990 Nov., v.36,
no.11, p.[36]-38, port., photos.

SEDLER, ANDREAS
Eine neue Bibliothek in einem
ehemaligen Tabakspeicher / Ulrich
Hamann.
Conversion of stone tobacco
storage houses in Viernheim into a
public library. Architects:
Rittmannsperger, Kleebank und
Partner. Project architect:
Andreas Sedler.
BAUWELT 1990 July 13, v.81, no.26,
p.1343-1348, photos., plans,
secn., site plan.

SEEBACHER, OSWALD
Erzbischofliches Bauamt Heidelberg,
Aussenstelle Karlsruhe.
3 new churches.
DAS MUNSTER 1990, v.43, no.2,
p.104-112, photos., plans.

SEEBOHM, CAROLINE
Maine tradition / Caroline Seebohm.
Interior decorator: Nancy
Pierrepont.
HOUSE & GARDEN 1990 Aug., v.162,
no.8, p.[128-133], port., photos.

SEELIG, LORENZ
Tableaux des neo-classicismes
francais et belge de la Residence
de Coblence / Lorenz Seelig.
REVUE DE L'ART 1990, no.87,
p.52-58, dwgs., photos., plan,
engr., refs.

SEELS
See CANOPIES

SEEST, KNUD, 1879-
Togenese katedral: Norrebro Station.
Photographs of the 1933 elevated
railway station over Norrebrogade,
Copenhagen (chief architect: K. T.
Seest). In Danish and English.
SKALA 1990, no.21, p.40-41,
photos.

SEGAL, JOEL
AA diploma honours 1989-90 / Raoul
Bunschoten, Wiel Arets, Stefano de
Martino, Peter Salter, Ron Herron,
Andrew Holmes and John Frazer.
Diploma prizes to Joel Segal, Voon
Yee Wong, Simon Hart, Toru Ogata,
Bobby Desai, Shin Egashira and
Matthew Waltman.
AA FILES 1990 Autumn, no.20,
p.95-101, dwgs., models, photo.

SEGALEN, MARTINE
S'installer dans une ville, Nanterre
1900-1980 / Martine Segalen,
Francoise Bekus.
French, English, German and
Spanish summaries, p.[123]-126.
LES ANNALES DE LA RECHERCHE
URBAINE 1989 Mar.-Apr., no.41,
p.51-58,[123]-126, chart., ports.,
photos., refs.

SEGAWA, HUGO
Arquitetura do comercio ou
arquitetura comercial?:
Supermercados: voce ja pensou? /
Hugo Segawa.
PROJETO 1990 [June]., no.132,
p.42-48, dwg., ports., photos.,
plan, aerial photo.
A camara de Brasilia: a fenix
abrindo as asas / Hugo Segawa.
Second and 3rd Place entries for a
legislative chamber. Architects:
R. Rondino and C. Correa, and P.
Neves and N. Godoy.
PROJETO 1990 Apr.-May, no.131,
p.41-44, dwg., models, secn.,
sketch.
Contextos y limites: entre la
modernidad y la tradicion / Hugo
Segawa.
ARQUITECTURA VIVA 1990 May-June,
no.12, p.44-45, dwg., photos.
Os dez mais significativos livros de
arquitetura dos anos 80:
biblioteca / Hugo Segawa, ed.
Five architects and critics submit
their lists of the 10 best books
on Brazilian architecture
published in the 80s.
PROJETO 1990 Jan.-Feb., no.129,
p.46-53, biblios.

SEGAWA, HUGO (CONTINUED)
Dilemas da modernidade e da tradicao
na arquitetura brasileira / Hugo
Segawa.
PROJETO 1990 Apr.-May, no.131,
p.49-50, refs.
Dossie interior / Hugo Segawa.
Architecture in Brazil's interior
provinces.
PROJETO 1990 Oct., no.135,
p.[49]-77, photos.
Helio Duarte (1906-1989): moderno e
peregrino [obituary] / Hugo
Segawa, Jose Silveira.
PROJETO 1990 Apr.-May, no.131,
p.51-52, photo.
Memoravel Memorial.
A series of texts on the Memorial
da America Latina, in Sao Paulo.
Architect: Oscar Niemeyer.
Articles by Joaquim Guedes, Carlos
Lemos, and Hugo Segawa.
PROJETO 1990 Nov., no.136,
p.99-[106], port., photo.

SEGELKEN, SABINE
Arbeitsgerichte Buroraume / Ottomar
Gottschalk, Sabine Segelken.
DEUTSCHE BAUZEITSCHRIFT 1990 Dec.,
v.38, no.12, p.1795-1798, graphs,
ill., plans.

SEGERSON, ANNE MULLIN
Playing with tradition / Glenn
Harrell.
Interiors of designer Anne Mullin
Segerson's Connecticut house.
HOUSE BEAUTIFUL 1990 Dec., v.132,
no.12, p.56-[61], photos.

SEGRE, CARLO
Sotto il pergolato di pietra
/cDaniela Invernizzi.
House near Monte Rosa, Italy.
Architects: Carlo Segre, Antonino
Piattone.
VILLE GIARDINI 1990 Jan., no.244,
p.[10]-17, photos., plans.

SEGRE, ROBERTO
La chispa de Ginzburg: entrevista
con Khan-Magomedou [interview] /
Roberto Segre.
ARQUITECTURA VIVA 1990 Mar.-Apr.,
no.11, p.10-13, ill., dwgs.,
port., photos.
Dialogo com Salinas, Segre, Tosca e
Calventi, em Havana / Nildo Carlos
Oliveira.
PROJETO 1989 Apr., no.120,
p.127-129, port.

SEGREGATION IN HOUSING
See DISCRIMINATION IN HOUSING

SEGUNDO ARANA, LUIS, 1956-
Ristorante Gala, Madrid: Javier
Garcia Garcia, Luis Segundo Arana
/ Duccio Malagamba.
In Italian and English.
DOMUS 1990 July-Aug., no.718,
p.[52]-56, axonometric view,
photos., plan.

SEIBERT, GEORG, 1938-
Stadt, Architektur, Bildende Kunst /
Hans-Michael Herzog.
Several works since 1972 by Berlin
sculptor Georg Seibert.
BAUWELT 1990 Dec.28, v.81, no.48,
p.2402-2403, dwg., models.

SEIBOLD, LLEWELLYN
The representation of making in
urban form / Murali Ramaswami,
Llewellyn Seibold.
OZ / COLLEGE OF ARCHITECTURE AND
DESIGN, KANSAS STATE UNIVERSITY
1989, v.11, p.28-29, photo.,
sketches.

SEIDEL, GUNTER
Borsentreff: Informationszentrum fur
Wertpapiere der Volksbank in
Wiesbaden.
Architect: Gunter Seidel.
ARCHITEKTUR, INNENARCHITEKTUR,
TECHNISCHER AUSBAU 1990 Dec.,
v.98, no.12, p.50-51, photos.,
plan, secn.

SEIDEL, HAUSMANN UND PARTNER
Post, Mahlzeit! FTZ-Kantine in
Darmstadt.
Architects: Seidel, Hausmann +
Partner, Klaus Bonnet.
DEUTSCHE BAUZEITUNG 1990 Dec.,
v.124, no.12, p.48-51, elevs.,
photos., plans, secns., site
plans.

SEIDEL, MAX, 1904-. KIRCHEN VON SIENA
"Progetti Siena": storia e regesto
delle chiese [book review] /
Riccardo Pacciani.
Review of vol.1 of Die Kirchen von
Siena, ed. by P.A. Riedl and M.
Seidel (1985): Abbadia dell'Arco -
S. Biagio.
CASABELLA 1990 Dec., v.54, no.574,
p.23-24, axonometric view, secn.

SEIDEL, UWE
Ein freundliches Entree: Postamt 13
in Saarbrucken.
Architects: OPD Saarbrucken, under
the direction of Uwe Seidel.
DEUTSCHE BAUZEITUNG 1990 Dec.,
v.124, no.12, p.14-17, photos.,
plan, secn.

SEIDEL, WILFRIED
Datenbankmitzung durch Architekten
bei Kostenermittlungen, Teil 3 /
Wilfried Seidel.
"Neue Form der
Informationsvermittlung aus der
Baukostendatenbank der
Bauwirtschaft und Erweiterung auf
Bundesebene...". On the use of the
BKB database, developed in
Stuttgart and disseminated through
several other countries in
Germany.
DEUTSCHES ARCHITEKTENBLATT 1990
Aug.1, v.22, no.8, p.1205-1206,
diagr., map.
Datenbanknutzung durch Architekten
bei Kostenermiltlungen, Teil? /
Wilfried Seidel.
"Beispiel einer Kostenberechnung
auf der Grundlage einer
Datenbankrecherche". Explains the
use of the BKB database for cost
estimates, using a hypothetical
gymnasium in southern Germany.
DEUTSCHES ARCHITEKTENBLATT 1990
July 1, v.22, no.7, p.1127-1128,
plan, table.
Datenbanknutzung durch Architekten
bei Kostenermittlungen, Teil 1 /
Wilfried Seidel.
"Datenbankrecherche - eine neue
Dienstleistung fur Architekten bei
(Continued next column)

SEIDEL, WILFRIED (CONTINUED)
Datenbanknutzung...(CONTINUED)
Kostenschatzungen und
Kostenberechnungen". Explanation
of Gebaudekatalog '88-'89, a
database for estimating building
costs.
DEUTSCHES ARCHITEKTENBLATT 1990
June 1, v.22, no.6, p.987-990,
elevs., plan, secn., tables, refs.

SEIDL, GABRIEL VON, 1848-1913
The Alpine retreat of a musical
legend / Nicholas Shrady.
Features the interiors of Richard
Strauss' villa in
Garmisch-Partenkirchen, built in
the early 1900s. Architect:
Gabriel von Seidl.
ARCHITECTURAL DIGEST 1990 Mar.,
v.47, no.3, p.262,264,268,[270],
photos.

SEIDL, ROBERT
Alias "im Wunderland" / Robert
Seidl.
ARCHITHESE 1990 May-June, v.20,
no.3, p.54-58, ill., photos.

SEIDLEIN, PETER C. VON
Bayern, Westufer des Orientalischen
/ Christoph Hackelsberger, Peter
C. von Seidlein.
Theme of issue.
DER ARCHITEKT 1990 June, no.6,
p.293-298, photos.

SEIDLEIN, PETER C. VON, 1925-
Architektur des Machens / Norman
Foster.
Includes a discussion on
architecture and technology by Otl
Aicher, Gunter Behnisch, Fritz
Haller, Helmut Schulitz, Peter von
Seidlein, and others.
ARCH PLUS 1990 Jan., no.102,
p.29-36, dets., ill., model,
photos.
Bauen fur die Industrie: zur
Eroffnung der Peter Behrens
Ausstellung im Hoechst
Verwaltungsbau / Peter C. von
Seidlein.
DER ARCHITEKT 1990 May, no.5,
p.251-255, photos.

SEIDLER, HARRY, 1923-
Harry Seidler e a modernidade
[interview] / Jorge Glusberg.
PROJETO 1990 Apr.-May, no.131,
p.18, port., photo.

SEIFERT ARCHITECTS
A hard stare at Paddington.
Seven separate proposals for
development of the area
surrounding Paddington Station,
London. Architects involved in the
various schemes include: Building
Design Partnership; Seifert;
Llewelyn-Davies Weeks; YRM;
Halpern Partnership; HOK
International; and Heery.
ARCHITECTS' JOURNAL 1990 Apr.4,
v.191, no.14, p.26-31, axonometric
views, dwgs., elevs., model,
plans, secn., site plan, sketches.

SEIFERT (FIRM)
Summer deadline for Moscow trio.
Three British competition entries
for Moscow's Chamber Theatre Arts
Centre in the Hermitage Gardens:
Peter Baynes and David Whitehead;
John Seifert; and Mills Beaumont
Leavy (MBL).
ARCHITECTS' JOURNAL 1990 Sept.26,
v.192, no.13, p.12-13, axonometric
view, elev., model, secns.,
sketches.

SEIFERT, PETER
Sport- und Freizeitanlage in
Eichenau, BRD.
Architect: Peter Seifert.
WERK, BAUEN + WOHNEN 1990 May,
no.5, p.1-6 (folded, at back),
dets., photos., plans, secns.,
tables.

SEIGNEUR, FRANCOIS, 1942-
Actualites: ciel de France a
Seville.
Project for French pavilion at
Exposicion Universal 1992;
architects: Jean-Paul Viguier,
Jean-Francois Jodry, Francois
Seigneur.
LE MONITEUR ARCHITECTURE AMC 1990
Apr., no.10, p.5, model, secn.
Pavillon francais de Seville: cinq
projets pour l'exposition
universelle de 1992.
Winning architects: Jean-Paul
Viguier, Jean-Francois Jodry,
Francois Seigneur. English
summary, p.68. Spanish summary,
p.148.
TECHNIQUES ET ARCHITECTURE 1990
Mar., no.388, p.64-69, axonometric
view, dets., ill., dwgs., models,
plans, site plans..
Ein Quadrat im Himmel Spaniens:
Wettbewerb: Franzosischer Pavillon
fur die Expo 92 in Sevilla.
First prize: J.-P. Viguier, J.-F.
Jodry, F. Seigneur.
ARCH PLUS 1990 July, no.104,
p.34-35, dwg., models, plans,
secns.
Seville, enfin / M.H. Contal.
Project for French pavilion for
the Exposicion Universal 1992.
Architects: Francois Seigneur,
Jean-Paul Viguier and
Jean-Francois Jodry.
ARCHITECTURE INTERIEURE CREE 1990
Mar., no.235, p.17, model, plan,
secn.
Seville, tragi-comedie d'un concours
/ Frederique de Gravelaine.
On the competition for the French
pavilion for the 1992 Expo in
Seville. Winning architects:
Jean-Paul Viguier, Jean-Francois
Jodry and Francois Seigneur.
ARCHITECTURE D'AUJOURD'HUI 1990
June, no.269, p.16-20, ill.,
models, plans.

SEIJIMA, KAZUYO
The "Transfiguration" exhibition in
Europalia Japan.
Special feature. Works by Kazuyo
Seijima + Noriyuki Tanaka, Toyo
Ito, Keiichi Irie, Hiromi Fujii,
Shin Takamatsu, and Yutaka Saito.
Essays by Riichi Miyake; Toyo Ito,
Alvin Boyarsky, and Nigel Coates;
Keiichi Irie and Kobun ito; Hiromi
(Continued next page)

SEIJIMA, KAZUYO (CONTINUED)
The "Transfiguration"...(CONTINUED)
Fujii and Shusaku Arakawa; Shin
Takamatsu and Daniel Libeskind;
Yutaka Saito and Issei Miyake.
Text in Japanese.
SPACE DESIGN 1990 Feb., no.305,
p.13-44, dets., dwgs., models,
photos., sketches.

SEILER, JOSEF
Beton + Stahl = Verbund: Zwei
Beispiele der Verbundbauweise in
Karlsruhe / Klaus Stiglat,
Bernhard Hockelmann, Josef Seiler.
The BGV, Karlsruhe, and the
Institut fur Meteorologie und
Klimatologie, Karlsruhe.
DEUTSCHE BAUZEITUNG 1990 Apr.,
v.124, no.4, p.91-98, dets.,
dwgs., elevs., photos., plans.

SEILER, P.
The survival of Roman antiquities in
the Middle Ages [by] Michael
Greenhalgh [book review] / P.
Seiler.
BURLINGTON MAGAZINE 1990 July,
v.132, no.1048, p.496-497,

SEJIMA, KAZUYO, 1956-
Kazuyo Sejima & Associates: Platform
II. Kitakoma-gun, Yamanashi,
Japan, 1988-90 / Kazuyo Sejima.
Text in Japanese and English.
GA HOUSES 1990 Dec., no.30,
p.[80]-89, photos., plans.
Platform II / Kazuyo Seijima.
House in Kitakoma-Gun, Yamanashi
Prefecture. Architects: Kazuyo
Sejima, Architect & Associates.
JAPAN ARCHITECT 1990 Nov.-Dec.,
v.65, no.11-12(403-404),
p.[60]-66, axonometric views,
elev., model, photos., plans,
secn.
Residence Platform a Yamanashi.
Architect: Kazuyo Sejima.
Includes statement by architect.
English summary.
TECHNIQUES ET ARCHITECTURE 1990
June-July, no.390, p.140-141,
photos., plan, secn.
Sejima platforms.
Features Platform I house,
Katsura, Japan. Architect: Kazuyo
Sejima. Includes photos and model
of Platform II.
ARCHITECTURAL REVIEW 1990 Apr.,
v.187, no.1118, p.61-[66],
axonometric view, elev., models,
photos., plans, secn., site plan.

SEJIMA, KOZUYO, 1956-
Yokohama city creation Bay '90:
exhibition of waterfront
redevelopment.
Five temporary towers, called
Yokohama Towers, which are part of
the Bay 90 exhibition. Architects:
Hirofumi Sugimoto, Noriaki Furuya,
Katsuhiro Kobayashi, Kiyoshi
Takeyama and Kazuyo Sejima.
JAPAN ARCHITECT 1990 June, v.65,
no.6(398), p.4, photos.

SEKINE, TAKESHI
A modified wind tunnel experiment
for blockage effects and air flow
around buildings / Yasuo Kurotani,
Takeshi Sekine.
Txt in Japanese. Includes English
summary.
NIHON KENCHIKU GAKKAI KEIKAKUKEI
RONBUN HOKOKU SHU = JOURNAL OF
ARCHITECTURE, PLANNING AND
ENVIRONMENTAL ENGINEERING 1990
Sept., no.9(415), p.1-8, graphs,
tables, refs.

SELBERT, CLIFFORD
Residential sculpture: It's in the
Mail / Kirk Von Blunck.
Mailboxes designed by Graves,
Venturi, and Selbert.
IOWA ARCHITECT 1990 Winter., v.39,
no.4, p.5, photos.

SELBMANN, BERND
Noch ist alles offen - Raum als
Instrument: katholische Kirche St.
Judas Thaddaus in Karlsruhe -
Neureut / Ottokar Uhl, Bernd
Selbmann.
Architects: Ottokar Uhl, and
Schmitt, Kasimir und Partner.
KUNST UND KIRCHE 1990, no.1,
p.20-25, models, photos., plans.

SELDMAN, RICHARD
Interior design and space planning:
planning your space / Richard
Seldman.
ARCHITECTURE AUSTRALIA 1990 Mar.,
v.79, no.2, p.99-100, photos.

SELEUCID
See "SELEUCID" AS A SUBHEADING AFTER
SPECIFIC BUILDING TYPES OR OTHER
MAIN HEADINGS.

SELF-BUILD ARCHITECTURE
See also OWNER-BUILT HOUSES
See also SELF-HELP HOUSING

SELF-BUILD ARCHITECTURE--IRAN
Design and change: the case of rural
settlements in Iran / Ali R.
Madani Pour.
OPEN HOUSE INTERNATIONAL 1988,
v.13, no.4, p.29-35, axonometric
views, diagrs., elevs., photos.,
plans, biblios.

SELF-BUILD ARCHITECTURE--LATIN AMERICA
Habitat populaire en Amerique Latin
= Low-income housing in Latin
America.
Theme issue. Includes articles in
French and/or English.
ARCHITECTURE & COMPORTEMENT =
ARCHITECTURE & BEHAVIOUR 1990,
v.6, no.2, p.107-199, maps,
photos., plans, biblios., refs.

**SELF-BUILD ARCHITECTURE--SCOTLAND--
FINDHORN FOUNDATION--ENVIRONMENTAL
ASPECTS**
Breathing life into housing /
Michael Schimmelschmidt.
On the ecological, self-build,
timber-frame houses designed by
Keystone Architects & Designers
Co-operative for the Findhorn
Foundation, Scotland.
RIBA JOURNAL 1990 Nov., v.97,
no.11, p.56-58, photo., plan,
secn.

SELF-BUILD ARCHITECTURE--SOUTH AMERICA
An analysis of Latin American
auto-construction: a plural and
mass phenomenon / Julian Salas.
OPEN HOUSE INTERNATIONAL 1988,
v.13, no.4, p.2-11, axonometric
view, graphs, dwgs., photos.,
refs.

SELF-BUILT ARCHITECTURE
See SELF-BUILD ARCHITECTURE

SELF-HELP ARCHITECTURE
See SELF-BUILD ARCHITECTURE

SELF-HELP HOUSING--AFGHANISTAN
Afghan refugee housing / Olivier
Scherrer.
The author, a French architect,
went to Afgan refugee camps in
northern Pakistan to assess a
program begun in 1987 by
ACROTERRE.
MIMAR: ARCHITECTURE IN DEVELOPMENT
1990 Mar., v.10, no.1(34),
p.[42]-49, axonometric views, map,
photos., plans, secns.

SELF-HELP HOUSING--CHINA
Self-help and "step-by-step housing"
in China / Florian Steinberg.
BUILDING IN CHINA 1989 June, v.2,
no.2, p.30-35, photos.

**SELF-HELP HOUSING--ENGLAND--LONDON--
TOWER HAMLETS**
Self-build: homeless young people /
Gill Haigh.
Self-build project in Tower
Hamlets, London.
HOUSING AND PLANNING REVIEW 1990
Dec.-1991 Jan., v.45, no.6,
p.10-11, ports.

SELF-HELP HOUSING--GERMANY (WEST)
Wege zur Bescheidenheit.
Contents: Das Behelfsheim des
Deutschen Wohnungshilfswerks, by
Leopold Sautter (excerpt reprinted
from Bauwelt, 1943, no.27-28); Das
Einpersonenreihenhaus im
Schwabisch Gmund.
BAUWELT 1990 July 20, v.81, no.27,
p.1372-1373, plan, secn.

**SELF-HELP HOUSING--GERMANY (WEST)--
HAMBURG--DRACHENBAU**
"Drachenbau": Alternatives Wohnen in
Hamburg-St. Georg / Cornelia
Krause.
Architects: Planerkollektiv.
DEUTSCHE BAUZEITUNG 1990 Sept.,
v.124, no.9, p.34-35, photos.,
plan.

**SELF-HELP HOUSING--GERMANY (WEST)--
HERZOGENRATH--ALTE WINDKUNST**
"Alte Windkunst": Reihenhausgruppe
in Herzogenrath-Kohlscheid /
Ingrid Leifgen.
Built 1987-88. Architects:
Planungsgruppe Alte Windkunst:
Buro fur humanes und okologisches
Bauen.
DEUTSCHE BAUZEITUNG 1990 Sept.,
v.124, no.9, p.[12]-16, port.,
photos., plan, secn.

SELF-HELP HOUSING--LIBERIA
Self-help shelter and related
programs in Liberia / Linda Lacey,
Stephen E. Owusu.
AMERICAN PLANNING ASSOCIATION.
JOURNAL 1987 Spring, v.53, no.2,
p.206-212, map, photos., tables,
biblio.

SELF-HELP HOUSING--PAKISTAN--HYDERABAD
Step by step: enabling Pakistan's
urban poor to build / Brian Brace
Taylor.
A pilot project (Khuda-Ki-Basti)
of the Hyderabad Development
Authority.
MIMAR: ARCHITECTURE IN DEVELOPMENT
1990 June, v.10, no.2(35),
p.47-52, elevs., photos., plans.

SELF-HELP HOUSING--RESEARCH--JAPAN
Study on the improvement of the
residential environment from the
acutual [sic] condition of
self-help housing improvement
action by owner-occupant in small
site detached and row houses
congested area / Masanori Koh.
Survey defines self-help housing
actions and proposes a policy.
Text in Japanese. Includes English
summary.
NIHON KENCHIKU GAKKAI KEIKAKUKEI
RONBUN HOKOKU SHU = JOURNAL OF
ARCHITECTURE, PLANNING AND
ENVIRONMENTAL ENGINEERING 1990
June [July], no.7(413), p.95-105,
maps, tables, refs.

SELF-HELP HOUSING--SOUTH AMERICA
An analysis of Latin American
auto-construction: a plural and
mass phenomenon / Julian Salas.
OPEN HOUSE INTERNATIONAL 1988,
v.13, no.4, p.2-11, axonometric
view, graphs, dwgs., photos.,
refs.

SELF, PETER
The challenge of regional
development / Peter Self.
Paper presented at the
International Conference on Local
Planning, Sydney, Australia, March
1990, "From Images to
Achievements."
AUSTRALIAN PLANNER: JOURNAL OF THE
ROYAL AUSTRALIAN PLANNING
INSTITUTE 1990 June, v.28, no.2,
p.18-22, refs.
The challenge of regional
development / Peter Self.
Paper presented at the
International Conference on Local
Planning, Sydney, Australia, March
1990, "From Images to
Achievements."
AUSTRALIAN PLANNER: JOURNAL OF THE
ROYAL AUSTRALIAN PLANNING
INSTITUTE 1990 June, v.28, no.2,
p.18-22, refs.

SELF SERVICE LAUNDRIES
See COIN-OPERATED LAUNDRIES

SELF-SERVICE RESTAURANTS
See CAFETERIAS

SELIER, HERMAN
Berlage Instituut in Burgerweeshuis:
Topopleiding geleid door
Hertzberger [interview] / Herman
Selier.
Interview with the dean of the
Berlage Instituut, on the
restoration of an orphanage (built
in 1959) on the Amstelveensweg,
south Amsterdam. Original
architect: Aldo van Eyck.
DE ARCHITECT 1989 Oct., v.20,
no.10, p.46-49, port., photos.,
aerial photos.
Hannes Meyer in een nieuw licht:
tragisch utopist zonder vaderland
/ Herman Selier.
DE ARCHITECT 1990 May, v.21, no.5,
p.63-69, dwgs., ports., photos.,
aerial photos.
Supervisoren, stadsbouwmeesters en
welstandstoezicht / Herman Selier.
One of several articles in
Themanummer 41: "Thema:
architectuur en macht." Covers the
role of public architects in
Amsterdam (Tjeerd Dijkstra),
Maastricht (Jo Coenen), Groningen
(J.P. Kleihues), and Haarlem
(Thijs Asselbergs).
DE ARCHITECT THEMA 1990 Nov.,
v.21, no.11 suppl., p.33-39,
photos.
Vendex - driehoek Amsterdam:
uithuilen en opnieuw beginnen /
Herman Selier.
Alterations proposed for
triangular area between Singel,
Kalverstraat, and Heiligeweg. Plan
by ZZOP.
DE ARCHITECT 1990 May, v.21, no.4,
p.37-43, ill., models, photos.,
secns., site plans.

SELJUK
See "SELJUK" AS A SUBHEADING AFER
SPECIFIC BUILDING TYPES OR OTHER
MAIN HEADINGS.

SELKIRK, PETER, 1928-1990
Peter Selkirk [obituary] / Gerald
Beale.
RIBA JOURNAL 1990 Dec., v.97,
no.12, p.85,

SELLARS, PETER
Peter Sellar's: on the LA Festival
[interview].
L. A. ARCHITECT 1990 Jan., p.5,11,
photos.

SELLARS, RICHARD WEST
Why take a trip to Bountiful--won't
America do? Perception and
manipulation of the historic past
/ Richard West Sellars.
LANDSCAPE 1990, v.30, no.3,
p.14-19, dwg., photos, biblio.

SELLERI, RAFFAELE
Aperto alla citta: il municipio di
Agrate Brianza, Milan= Open to the
city: town hall at Agrate,
Brianza, Milan / Pierluigi
Bulgheroni, Raffaele Selleri.
Architects: Pierluigi Bulgheroni,
Raffaele Selleri.
SPAZIO E SOCIETA 1990 July-Sept.,
v.13, no.51, p.50-57, ports.,
photos., plans, secns.

SELLERI, RAFFAELE (CONTINUED)

SELLERS, VANESSA
Sources and ideas for the
seventeenth-century Dutch garden /
Vanessa Sellers.
Text of paper presented at CAA,
1989.
THE RUTGERS ART REVIEW 1988-1989,
v.9-10, p.135-149, dwgs., site
plans, engrs.

SELMER, JENS 1911-
Exempel Selmer [book review] /
Lennart Holm.
Review of Sosial boligbygging i
Norge 1945-1980: en studie av
arkitekt Jens Selmbers arbeider,
by Mette Sjolie.
ARKITEKTUR: THE SWEDISH REVIEW OF
ARCHITECTURE 1990 Aug., v.90,
no.6, p.48-49, photos., plan, site
plan.

SELSE, ELISABETH
Delight fantastic / Elisabeth Selse.
On the Rococo designs of Claude
III Audran.
THE WORLD OF INTERIORS 1990 Apr.,
p.[112]-119, photos.
Regnaholm / Elisabeth Selse.
Interiors of 18th cent. country
house outside Stockholm, owned by
Lars and Ursula Sjoberg.
THE WORLD OF INTERIORS 1990 June,
p.[96-105], photos.
When Jorgen met Gaga / Elisabeth
Selse.
Features interiors of Gaga Bonnier
and Jorgen Alfort's renovated
attic apartment in Stockholm.
Interior designer: Gaga Bonnier.
THE WORLD OF INTERIORS 1990 June,
p.156-163, photos.

SELVAFOLTA, ORNELLA
Alle radici del mutamento [book
review] / Ornella Selvafolta.
Review of Alle radici
dell'architettura contemporanea,
by Roberto Gabetti and Carlo Olmo.
Includes English captions.
CASABELLA 1990 Mar., v.54, no.566,
p.34-35, ill.
Carlo Cattaneo and the "Beautiful
Regained": the argument for
ornamentation / Cornella
Selvafolta.
RASSEGNA 1990 Mar., v.12, no.41/1,
p.30-39, ill., engrs., refs.

SELWYN, JUDITH
Technics: cleaning the Carnegie /
John Dender, Judith Selwyn.
Built 1895 and later expanded.
Original architects: Longfellow,
Alden and Harlow. Restoration
architects: Williams Trebilcock
Whitehead. Preservation
consultants: Preservation
Technology Associates.
PROGRESSIVE ARCHITECTURE 1990
Oct., v.71, no.10, p.38-41,
photos., aerial photo.

SEM PARTNERS
Sound education / Michael Wagner.
On the conversion of a high school
gymnasium into a community and
high school theater, Dublin, Ohio.
Architects: SEM Partners with
Jaffe Acoustics.
(Continued next page)

SEM PARTNERS (CONTINUED)
Sound education /...(CONTINUED)
INTERIORS 1990 Jan., v.149, no.6,
p.56, photo., plan, secn.

SEMBACH, KLAUS-JURGEN. HENRY VAN DE
VELDE
Henry van de Velde [by] Klaus-Jurgen
Sembach [book review] / Luc
Verpoest.
ARCHIS 1990 May, no.5, p.52-53,
port., photos., refs.

SEMERANI, LUCIANO
Concorso per la riqualificazione
dell' area di Via Veneto [Trento].
Presents 10 entries, including 1st
prize entry by Oswald Zoeggeler.
PARAMETRO 1990, Nov.-Dec., no.181,
p.52-69, axonometric views, ill.,
dwgs., elevs., photos., plans,
secns., aerial photo.
Terminal automobilistico a Trieste =
Terminal conversion in Trieste /
Stefania Mornati.
Conversion of a 19th-cent.
terminal warehouse into a bus
terminal and car park.
Architects: Luciano Semerani,
Gigetta Tamaro. Includes English
translation. French, German, and
Spanish summaries, p.3.
L'INDUSTRIA DELLE COSTRUZIONI 1990
Sept., v.24, no.227, p.20-27,3,
elevs., photos., plans, secns.,
aerial photo.

SEMIDETACHED HOUSES
See DOUBLE HOUSES

SEMINARIES, THEOLOGICAL
See THEOLOGICAL SEMINARIES
See THEOLOGICAL SEMINARIES

SEMIOTICS IN ARCHITECTURE
See SIGNS AND SYMBOLS IN
ARCHITECTURE

SEMPER, GOTTFRIED, 1803-1879
Anthological excerpts from Gottfried
Semper to Henri Focillon.
Excerpts from eight writers' works
on decoration and ornament.
RASSEGNA 1990 Mar., v.12, no.41/1,
p.77-88, ill.
Gottfried und Mannfred Sempers
Projekt eines Hoftheaters fur
Darmstadt (MV199) / Valentin
Hammerschmidt.
ARCHITECTURA 1990, v.20, no.2,
p.142-159, ill., dwgs., elevs.,
photos., plans, secn., site plan,
sketch, refs.
The Munich Festival Theater letters
/ Sophie Gobran.
Never built, but functional as a
prototype for opera houses in
Central Europe. Article includes
excerpts from correspondence
between architect Gottfried Semper
and Richard Wagner.
PERSPECTA 1990, no.26, p.47-68,
ports., elev., models, map,
photos., plans, site plans, refs.
Semper ubique / Jeremy Melvin.
On Gottfried Semper's concepts of
walling.
BUILDING DESIGN 1990 Mar., suppl.,
p.20-23, dwg., port., photos.

SEMPER, GOTTFRIED, 1803-1879. FOUR
ELEMENTS OF ARCHITECTURE AND OTHER
WRITINGS
The four elements of architecture
and other writings [by] Gottfried
Semper [book review] / Ian Gow.
Work of 19th cent. German
architect; English trans. pub.
1989.
THE JOURNAL AND ANNUAL REPORT /
THE SCOTTISH GEORGIAN SOCIETY FOR
THE STUDY AND PROTECTION OF
SCOTTISH ARCHITECTURE 1989, no.16,
p.66,

SEMPER, GOTTFRIED, 1803-1879 STIL
Gottfried Semper: il governo dello
stile = Gottfried Semper: the
government of style / Marco
Pogacnik.
OTTAGONO 1990 Mar., no.94,
p.7-[15], dets., ill., dwgs.,
engrs.
Semper's "morphology" / Joseph
Rykwert.
On Semper's book, Der Stil in den
technischen und tektonischen
Kunsten oder Praktische Asthetik.
Ein Handbuch fur Techniker,
Kunstler und Kuntfreunde von
Gottfried Semper, Munich, 1878.
RASSEGNA 1990 Mar., v.12, no.41/1,
p.40-47, ill., dwgs., elev., plan,
refs.

SEMPER, MANNFRED, B. 1837
Gottfried und Mannfred Sempers
Projekt eines Hoftheaters fur
Darmstadt (MV199) / Valentin
Hammerschmidt.
ARCHITECTURA 1990, v.20, no.2,
p.142-159, ill., dwgs., elevs.,
photos., plans, secn., site plan,
sketch, refs.

SEMPRINI, ANDREA
L'oggetto muro / Andrea Semprini, G.
Avezzu.
2 articles on the destruction of
the Berlin Wall.
PARAMETRO 1990 Jan.-Feb., no.176,
p.[54]-63, photos.

SEMPRINI, ROBERTO
La citta balneare: una proposta di
Emilio Ambasz per una architettura
marina a Rimini / Roberto
Semprini.
MODO 1990 Oct., v.13, no.126,
p.52-53, elev., model, site plan.

SENEGAL--CAP SKIRRING--RESORTS--
SEASIDE--VILLAGE CLUB AQUARIUS
Village Club Aquarius, Senegal /
Serge Santelli.
A coastal resort in the Casamance
region, for developer Aquarius
International. Expected completion
date: Sept.1991. Architect: Serge
Santelli.
MIMAR: ARCHITECTURE IN DEVELOPMENT
1990 Sept., v.10, no.3(36),
p.60-62, ill., elevs., map, plan,
site plan, sketch.

SENFT, BRET
Trump redux / Bret Senft.
A discussion of the present status
of Donald Trump's proposed
development on Manhattan's west
side.
METROPOLIS 1990 Nov., v.10, no.4,
p.17-18, aerial photo.

SENIOR CENTERS
See also ADULT DAY CARE CENTERS

SENKEVITCH, ANATOLE
Dropping the curtain: rediscoveries
in Eastern Europe and the Soviet
Union.
Letters from Prague, Poland, and
Moscow, by Scott Nathan, Wojciech
Lesnikowski, and Anatole
Senkevitch, including description
of events celebrating Melnikov.
INLAND ARCHITECT 1990 Nov.-Dec.,
v.34, no.6, p.48-55, photos.
Trends in Soviet avant-garde
architecture of the twenties and
their current Deconstructive
echoes / Anatole Senkevitch.
Also, Rationalism.
INLAND ARCHITECT 1990 May-June,
v.34, no.3, p.73-79, ill., dwgs.,
models, photos.

SEO, FUMIAKI
Toward time space of "Kankyo" /
Fumiaki Seo.
KENCHIKU BUNKA 1990 Aug., v.45,
no.526, p.25-34, diagrs., ill.

SEP (FIRM)
Integriertes Wohnen: Wohnanlage in
Munchen-Nymphenburg.
Architects: Steidle + Partner and
SEP.
DEUTSCHE BAUZEITUNG 1990 Feb.,
v.124, no.2, p.48-51, photos.,
plans, secn., site plans,
sketches, isometric dwgs.

SEPULCHRAL CHAPELS
See also MARTYRIA

SEPULCHRAL CHAPELS--ITALY--TURIN
Il cimitero come museo.
Project for memorial chapel at
Turin Cemetery. Architect: Alberto
Galardi.
L'ARCA 1990 Dec., no.44 suppl.
l'Arca 2, p.103, elev., model,
plan.

SEPULCHRAL MONUMENTS
See also BRASSES
See also CENOTAPHS
See also CROSSES
See also PYRAMIDS
See also SARCOPHAGI
See also TOMBS
See also URNS
See also LANTERNS OF THE DEAD
"Denn alle Lust will Ewigkeit..." =
'...For all desire strives for
eternity / Gerrit Confurius.
Death represented as a beautiful
and sensual sleep on funerary
monuments.
DAIDALOS 1990 Dec.15, no.38,
p.26-31, photos., refs.

SERLIO, SEBASTIANO, 1475-1554
  On the method of composing facade of
  Palazzo in Serlio's fourth book on
  architecture / Yasusuke Ishikawa.
  Text in Japanese; English summary,
  p.165.
  NIHON KENCHIKU GAKKAI KEIKAKUKEI
  RONBUN HOKOKU SHU = JOURNAL OF
  ARCHITECTURE, PLANNING AND
  ENVIRONMENTAL ENGINEERING 1990
  June, no.6(412), p.165-172,
  elevs., refs.
  On the method of constructing a
  porta in Serlio's first book on
  architecture / Yasusuke Ishikawa.
  English summary, p.171.
  NIHON KENCHIKU GAKKAI KEIKAKUKEI
  RONBUN HOKOKU SHU = JOURNAL OF
  ARCHITECTURE, PLANNING AND
  ENVIRONMENTAL ENGINEERING 1990
  Jan., no.1(407), p.163-171,
  diagrs., dwggs., refs.

SERNINI, MICHELE
  Il pennacchio etnico
  dell'architettura / Michele
  Sernini.
  "The urban ethnic problem":
  English translation, p.9.
  MODO 1990 June-July, v.13, no.124,
  p.66-68, ill., plans, aerial
  photo.
  Politiche per Venezia / Cristina
  Bianchetti, Chiara Merlini.
  Introduces eight articles on city
  planning in Venice. English
  summaries, p.124-126. Contents:
  Osservare le politiche per
  Venezia: perche?; Marittima e
  Arsenale nel contesto delle
  trasformazioni urbane a Venezia;
  Vedute della laguna; Il consorzio
  Venezia nuova, concessionario
  dello stato per le opere di
  salvaguardia di Venezia; La casa a
  Venezia; Infrastrutture per la
  mobilita (e l'uranistica) nella
  nuova dimensione di Venezia;
  Appunti sulla questione della
  metropolitana a Venezia; Alcuni
  limiti alla delegittimazione
  sociale delle istituzioni
  pubbliche di governo urbano.
  URBANISTICA 1990 Mar., no.98,
  p.33-86,124-126, graphs, maps,
  photos., plans, secn., site plan,
  tables, refs.

SERODINE, GIOVANNI BATTISTA,
  CA.1587-CA.1626
  La facciata della casa dei Serodine
  ad Axona / Vera Segre Rutz.
  Restored and expanded in 1620 by
  sculptor-stuccoist Giovanni
  Battista Serodine.
  ZEITSCHRIFT FUR SCHWEIZERISCHE
  ARCHAOLOGIE UND KUNSTGESCHICHTE
  1989, v.46, no.1, p.39-48, dwgs.,
  photos., refs.

SEROTA, NICHOLAS
  The art of space [Tate Gallery] /
  Stephen Greenberg.
  Reorganization of exhibits at
  London's Tate Gallery. Rehang
  supervised by new director
  Nicholas Serota.
  ARCHITECTS' JOURNAL 1990 Apr.11,
  v.191, no.15, p.26-29,31,33,
  photos., plans, isometric dwg.,
  refs.

SERPA, HUMBERTO
  Casa em Belo Horizonte / Humberto
  Serpa.
  Casa Van Damme. Architect: H.
  Serpa.
  PROJETO 1990 Aug., no.134,
  p.59-61, dwg., photos., plans.

SERPENTINE GALLERY--EXHIBITIONS
  Briefing: Return of the
  constructors: Family workshop,
  Rodchenko & Stepanova, Serpentine
  Gallery, London [exhibition
  review] / Brian Hatton.
  BLUEPRINT (LONDON, ENGLAND) 1990
  Feb., no.64, p.49-50, ill.

SERRA, GERALDO G.
  Centro Civico-Cultural de
  Piracicaba.
  Architects: Geraldo and Vera
  Serra.
  PROJETO 1990 Apr.-May, no.131,
  p.38-40, photos., plan, secns.,
  site plan.

SERRA GRAU, ENRIC
  Fins de chantier / Joan Pascuale
  Argente ... [et al.].
  Contents: Former tannery converted
  to association building,
  Chatillon-sur-Indre, France;
  architect: Thierry Van de
  Wingaert.--Hospital Paul-Brousse,
  Villejuif, France; architects:
  Avant-Travaux.--Housing complex,
  Barcelona, Spain; architects: Joan
  Pascual Argente, Ramon Ausio
  Mateu, Lluis Badenas Oradanos,
  Joan Forgas Coll, Teresa Gimeno
  Marin, Enric Serra Grau.
  LE MONITEUR ARCHITECTURE AMC 1990
  May, no.11, p.11-16, photos.,
  plans.

SERRA, VEVA CATUNDA
  Centro Civico-Cultural de
  Piracicaba.
  Architects: Geraldo and Vera
  Serra.
  PROJETO 1990 Apr.-May, no.131,
  p.38-40, photos., plan, secns.,
  site plan.

SERRES, MICHEL
  La boite / Michel Serres.
  Theoretical article on the house.
  Includes English and Spanish
  summaries.
  TECHNIQUES ET ARCHITECTURE 1990
  June-July, no.390, p.56-57,179,
  axonometric view, photos.

SERT, JOSE LUIS, 1902-1983
  Archivo en blanco y negro: cronica
  grafica de tres generaciones/
  Francese Catala-Roca.
  Six projects from 1951-1988, by
  architects Antoni Gaudi, Barba
  Corsini, Antoni de Moragas, Jose
  Antonio Coderch, Josep Lluis Sert,
  Helio Pinon y Albert Viaplana.
  ARQUITECTURA VIVA 1990 May-June,
  no.12, p.33-35, photos.
  Museumserweiterung -- Imitation als
  Architektursprache.
  Kimbell Art Museum, Ft. Worth,
  Tex.; Fundacio Miro, Barcelona;
  and the Jewish Museum, New York.
  Includes English summary.
  BAUMEISTER 1990 Nov., v.87, no.11,
  p.44-47, dwgs., models, photos.,
  plans.

SERVANDONI, GIOVANNI NICCOLO,
  1695-1766
  Servandoni, Oudry, Watteau et ses
  eleves au chateau de Conde-en-Brie
  / Marc Gaillard.
  Focus on the history of the
  chateau and the work undertaken by
  Servandoni in the 1720-30s.
  L'OEIL 1990 Apr., no.417,
  p.[44]-49, dets., ill., photos.

SERVANTS ROOMS--FRANCE--PARIS
  Les chambres de bonne a Paris /
  Corinne Riche.
  Maids' rooms in Paris. French,
  English and Spanish summaries,
  p.4, English translation, p.98.
  CAHIERS DE L'INSTITUT
  D'AMENAGEMENT ET D'URBANISME DE LA
  REGION D'ILE-DE-FRANCE 1990 June,
  no.93, p.91-98, graph, photos.,
  plans, refs.

SERVICE GARAGES--GERMANY (WEST)--
  REUTLINGEN
  Reifenservice-Zentrum, Reutlingen =
  Tyre service center, Reutlingen.
  Architects: Planungsgruppe
  Caspari.
  DETAIL 1990 June-July, v.30, no.3,
  p.SI-SIV, dets., photos., plan.

SERVICE GARAGES--PREFABRICATED--
  DENMARK--BP
  Benzinstationer ved danske motorveje
  / Bent Moudt.
  The author's comments on the
  design of service stations, 12
  July 1990.
  ARKITEKTEN 1990 Aug. v.92, no.12,
  p.405, axonometric views.

SERVIN, JAMES
  A diversified portfolio: from show
  windows to show houses, multimedia
  designer Robert Currie displays
  his flair for versatility / James
  Servin.
  HOUSE & GARDEN 1990 May, v.162,
  no.5, p.[166-171], port., photo.
  A tale of two cities: YSL's Joy
  Henderiks is just as much at home
  in New York as in Paris / James
  Servin.
  HOUSE & GARDEN 1990 Dec., v.162,
  no.12, p.[40],42, port., photos.

SESSA, CESARE DE
  Architetto Franco Minissi: sei
  interventi museali = Six museum
  projects / a cura di Cesare de
  Sessa.
  Museo archeologico, Syracuse;
  Palazzo Venezia, Rome; Palazzo
  Varisano, Enna; museum, Aidone;
  museum extension, Gela; and
  archaeological park, Himera.
  ARCHITETTURA; CRONACHE E STORIA
  1990 July-Aug., v.36,
  no.7-8(417-418), p.[502]-537,
  dets., photos., plans, secns.,
  aerial photos.
  Parma: edifizio servizi di una casa
  farmaceutica = Service building
  for a pharmaceutical plant /
  Cesare de Sessa.
  Architects: Dante Benini & Ingex.
  ARCHITETTURA: CRONACHE E STORIA
  1990 Nov., v.36, no.11(421),
  p.[758]-769, elevs., photos.,
  plans.

SESTO, CRISTINA DEL
Computers: electronic code information / Cristina Del Sesto.
On various building code-related databases. Includes addresses of five electronic building code services.
PROGRESSIVE ARCHITECTURE 1990 July, v.71, no.7, p.52,

SESTOFT, JORGEN
Barcelona / Peder Boas Jensen ... [et al.].
Theme of issue. Contents: By eller OL, by Peder Boas Jensen and Elith Juul Moller.-- Idraettens arenaer, by Ebbe Melgaard.-- Kataloniens hovedstad, by Jorgen Sestoft.-- Gensyn med Gaudi, by Nils-Ole Lund.-- Parkerne i Barcelona, by Jorgen Peder Hansen and Anna Maria Indrio.-- Den nordiske inspiration, by Nils-Ole Lund.-- Ny katalansk arkitektur, by Jan Christiansen and Gosta Knudsen.-- Miralles og Pinos, by Thomas Wiesner.
ARKITEKTEN 1990 May, v.92, no.7, p.[212]-249,cover, axonometric views, diagrs., maps, photos., secns., aerial photos., biblios.
Bevar Rosenkjaerhallen / Jorgen Sestoft.
On an exhibition marking the 25th anniversary of the Christianshavn building, sponsored by the Statens Kunstfond. Original architect: Niels Rosenkjaer.
ARKITEKTEN 1989 Nov.28, v.91, no.21, p.509-514, dwg., elev., models, photos.
Van Doesburg [book review] / Jorgen Sestoft.
Review of the translation of the original Dutch edition of On European architecture: complete essays from Het Bouwbedrijf 1924-1931.
ARKITEKTEN 1990 Sept., v.92, no.13, p.441, photos.

SETA, CESARE DE
Architecture in miniature: Vanvitelli / Cesare de Seta.
Wooden scale models of Caserta, the palace of Charles of Bourbon. Architect: Luigi Vanvitelli; made by Antonio Rosz between 1756-1761.
FMR 1990 Feb., v.9, no.42, p.81-96, ill., models.
See Naples: views of Naples / Cesare de Seta.
European views of Naples from 1500 to 1900.
FMR 1990 June, v.9, no.44, p.89-112, ill., site plans, engrs., biblio.

SETA, CESARE DE. CITTA E LE MURA
Ieri e oggi la mura = The city and the walls [book review] / Maurizio Vitta.
Review of La citta e le mura, ed. by Cesare De Seta. Text in Italian and English.
L'ARCA 1990 Jan., no.34 suppl. press, p.109,

SETTER LEACH AND LINDSTROM
Rooms with a view: Setter Leach & Lindstrom gives young people a front-row seat in nature's classroom.
Wolf Ridge Environmental Learning Center, Finland, Minnesota.
ARCHITECTURE MINNESOTA 1990 Sept.-Oct., v.16, no.5, p.26-29, photos., site plan.

SETTIMI, EMANUELA
Notizie d'archivio sull'opera di Francesco de Sanctis architetto del primo settecento romano / Emanuela Settimi.
English, French, German and Spanish summaries, p.158.
PALLADIO 1989 July-Dec., v.2, no.4, p.113-126, photos., plans, engrs., refs.

SETTLEMENT HOUSES--19TH CENTURY-- ENGLAND--LONDON--TOYNBEE HALL
The architecture of Victorian philanthropy: the settlement house as manorial residence / Deborah E. B. Weiner.
Toynbee Hall, London. Architect: Elijah Hoole.
ART HISTORY 1990 June, v.13, no.2, p.212-227, ill., photo., engrs., refs.

SETTLEMENTS
See also BOOMTOWNS
See also COLLECTIVE SETTLEMENTS
See also LAND SETTLEMENT
See also SQUATTER SETTLEMENTS
See also TEMPORARY SETTLEMENTS

SETTLEMENTS--1ST CENTURY--DENMARK-- GUDME
Beyond the Roman Empire: archaeological discoveries in Gudme on Funen, Denmark / Klavs Randsborg.
Report on excavations of a royal settlement dating from 200-600. Includes abstract.
OXFORD JOURNAL OF ARCHAEOLOGY 1990 Nov., v.9, no.3, p.355-366, ill., maps, photo., site plan, table, biblio.

SETTLEMENTS--16TH CENTURY--CANADA--RED BAY (LABRADOR)
A sixteenth century Basque whaling port in southern Labrador [Red Bay] / Judith A. Logan, James A. Tuck.
ASSOCIATION FOR PRESERVATION TECHNOLOGY. BULLETIN 1990, v.22, no.3, p.65-72, photos., refs., site plan.

SETTLEMENTS--ANCIENT--IRAN--HASANLU SITE
Constructing the chronology and historical implications of Hasanlu IV / Robert H. Dyson, Oscar White Muscarella.
IRAN 1989, v.27, p.1-27, charts., plans, tables, biblio., refs.

SETTLEMENTS--ANCIENT--ISRAEL--NEGEV DESERT
How ancient man first utilized the rivers in the desert / Thomas E. Levy.
On the author's site survey of the northwestern Negev for identification of Pottery Neolithic, Chalcolithic, and Early Bronze Age settlement locations.
BIBLICAL ARCHAEOLOGY REVIEW 1990 Nov.-Dec., v.16, no.6, p.20-31, maps, photos., aerial photos., refs.

SETTLEMENTS--ANCIENT--ISRAEL--REPHAIM VALLEY--EIN YAEL
What's a Roman villa doing outside Jerusalem? / Gershon Edelstein.
Ein Yael, the site of an ancient agricultural settlement in the Rephaim Valley, five miles west of Jerusalem.
BIBLICAL ARCHAEOLOGY REVIEW 1990 Nov.-Dec., v.16, no.6, p.32-42, photos., plans, secn., refs.

SETTLEMENTS--ANCIENT--SYRIA--TELL AL-RAQA'I
Excavations at Tell al-Raqa'i: a small rural site of early urban northern Mesopotamia / Hans H. Curvers, Glenn M. Schwartz.
AMERICAN JOURNAL OF ARCHAEOLOGY 1990 Jan., v.94, no.1, p.3-23, figs., maps, photos, plans, refs.

SETTLEMENTS--ANGLO-SAXON--ENGLAND-- WEST STOW
Sheep, horses, swine and kine: a zooarchaeological perspective on the Anglo-Saxon settlement of England / Pam J. Crabtree.
Excavations at West Stow on the River Lark, of a 5th-7th cent. B.C. site.
JOURNAL OF FIELD ARCHAEOLOGY 1989 Summer, v.16, no.2, p.205-213, graphs, map, site plan, tables, biblio.

SETTLEMENTS--BRAZIL--JAGUARARI-- CARAIBA
Projetos e seus caminhos na caatinga baiana: Caraiba, Jaguarari / Maria Ines Camargo.
Architect: J. Guedes e Associados.
PROJETO 1989 Oct., no.126, p.103-[108], elevs., photos., plans, site plans, aerial photos.

SETTLEMENTS--BRONZE AGE--GREECE--NAXOS (ISLAND)--MIKRE VIGLA
Mikre Vigla: a Bronze Age settlement on Naxos / R.L.N. Barber, O. Hadjianastasiou.
THE ANNUAL OF THE BRITISH SCHOOL AT ATHENS 1989, no.84, p.[63]-162, pl.13-34, dwgs., maps, photos, tables, refs.

SETTLEMENTS--BRONZE AGE--WALES--WEST GLAMORGAN--GOWER--CEFN BRYN
Cairns and "cairn fields": evidence of early agriculture on Cefn Bryn, Gower, West Glamorgan / Anthony H. Ward.
Discusses "the nature of early agriculture and its relationship to ritual and settlement in the local landscape."
LANDSCAPE HISTORY 1989, v.11,

(Continued next page)

SETTLEMENTS--BRONZE AGE--WALES--WEST
GLAMORGAN--GOWER--CEFN BRYN
(CONTINUED)
Cairns and "cairn...(CONTINUED)
p.[5]-18, diagrs., graphs, maps,
tables, biblio.

SETTLEMENTS--INCA--PERU
[Peruvian settlements--book review]
/ Izumi Shimada.
An assessment of five recent books
on Andean archaeology.
JOURNAL OF FIELD ARCHAEOLOGY 1990
summer, v.17, no.2, p.221-229,
biblio.

SETTLEMENTS--IRAN
Design and change: the case of rural
settlements in Iran / Ali R.
Madani Pour.
OPEN HOUSE INTERNATIONAL 1988,
v.13, no.4, p.29-35, axonometric
views, diagrs., elevs., photos.,
plans, biblios.

SETTLEMENTS--IRON AGE--ISRAEL
Ekron of the Philistines / Trude
Dothan, Seymour Gitin.
"How they lived, worked and
worshipped for five hundred years"
and "Part I: Where they came from,
how they settled down and the
place they worshipped in".
BIBLICAL ARCHAEOLOGY REVIEW 1990
Jan.-Feb., v.16, no.1, p.[20]-36,
maps, photos.

SETTLEMENTS--ISLAMIC--HISTORY
Khatta and the territorial structure
of early Muslim towns / Jamel
Akbar.
Focus on the military garrison
towns of Kufa and Basra in Iraq,
Fusat, Egypt and Qairawan,
Tunisia.
MUQARNAS 1990, v.6, p.[22]-32,
fig., refs.

SETTLEMENTS--JAPAN--OCHIAI DISTRICT
The concept of spatial composition
and organization of Shuraku
(Settlements) viewed through the
spatial language / Yukio Terakado.
Based on research at Karakida in
Ochiai-district, Tama City, Tokyo.
Text in Japanese; includes English
summary.
NIHON KENCHIKU GAKKAI KEIKAKUKEI
RONBUN HOKOKU SHU = JOURNAL OF
ARCHITECTURE, PLANNING AND
ENVIRONMENTAL ENGINEERING 1990
Oct., no.10(416), p.55-65, maps,
tables, refs.

SETTLEMENTS--MAYAN--BELIZE--AMBERGRIS
CAY
Excavations at the Marco Gonzalez
site, Ambergris Cay, Belize, 1986
/ Elizabeth Graham, David M.
Pendergast.
JOURNAL OF FIELD ARCHAEOLOGY 1989
Spring, v.16, no.1, p.1-16, dets.,
dwgs., maps, photos., site plan,
biblios.

SETTLEMENTS--MAYAN--BELIZE--CAYO--
PACBITUN
Excavations at Pacbitun, Belize:
preliminary report on the 1986 and
1987 investigations / Paul F.
Healy.
A medium-size Maya center in the
Cayo district, settled c.900 B.C.
Includes abstract.
JOURNAL OF FIELD ARCHAEOLOGY 1990
Fall, v.17, no.3, p.247-262, maps,
photos., site plans, tables,
biblio.

SETTLEMENTS--MEDIEVAL--ENGLAND--
BEDFORDSHIRE
The origins of dispersed settlement:
some results from fieldwork in
Bedfordshire / Anthony E. Brown,
Christopher C. Taylor.
Analysis of Scald End, Thurleigh;
Hobbs Green Odell; Thrupp End,
Lidlington; and North End,
Bletsoe.
LANDSCAPE HISTORY 1989, v.11,
p.[61]-81, maps, site plans,
tables, biblio., refs.

SETTLEMENTS--MEDIEVAL--ENGLAND--
CONGRESSES
Lordship and settlement in the
Medieval period / Carenza Lewis.
Report on papers presented at the
third annual conference on the
Medieval Settlement Research Group
(MSRG), 1-2 Apr.1989.
LANDSCAPE HISTORY 1989, v.11,
p.106-107,

SETTLEMENTS--MESOLITHIC--FIRE DAMAGE--
ENGLAND
The Later Mesolithic Period
(6000-5000bp) on Glaisdale Moor,
North Yorkshire / I. G. Simmons,
J. B. Innes.
Includes abstract.
ARCHAEOLOGICAL JOURNAL 1988,
v.145, p.1-12, graphs, maps,
tables, biblios.

SETTLEMENTS--NEOLITHIC--IRAQ--NEMRIK
Architecture of the pre-pottery
neolithic settlement in Nemrik,
Iraq / Stefan K. Kozlowski,
Andrzej Kempisty.
WORLD ARCHAEOLOGY 1990 Feb., v.21,
no.3, p.[348]-362, dwgs., photo.,
plans, site plans, refs.

SETTLEMENTS--PREHISTORIC--NEPAL--DANG
VALLEY
Archaeological remains of the Dang
Valley / Dilli Raj Sharma.
In the inner region of West Nepal.
PR-AC-INA NEP-ALA 1988 June-July,
no.106, p.8-12, photos., refs.

SETTLEMENTS--PREHISTORIC--PERU--
HUAYNUNA
Huaynuna, a late cotton perceramic
site on the north coast of Peru /
Thomas Pozorski, Sheila Pozorski.
On excavations at two distinct
prehistoric Andean religious
traditions north of the Casma
Valley and conclusions from
radiocarbon evidence.
JOURNAL OF FIELD ARCHAEOLOGY 1990
summer, v.17, no.2, p.17-26, map,
photos, plans, tables, biblio.

SETTLEMENTS--ROMAN--ITALY
La colonizzazione romana tra la
guerra latina e la guerra
annibalica / Filippo Cassola ...
[et al.].
Entire volume (12 essays).
DIALOGHI DI ARCHEOLOGIA 1988,
ser.3, no.2, p.5-133, axonometric
views, dwgs., maps, photos.,
plans, secns., site plans, aerial
photos., refs.

SETTLEMENTS--ROMAN--NETHERLANDS--
NIJMEGEN--ULPIA NOVIOMAGUS
Neues aus Noviomagus / Jan Kees
Haalebos.
Excavations of a Roman settlement
located in the modern-day eity of
Nijmegen, Netherlands.
ARCHAOLOGISCHES KORRESPONDENZBLATT
1990, v.20, no.2, p.193-200, maps,
photo., secn., refs.

SETTLEMENTS--ROMAN--WALES--PRESTATYN
Prestatyn 1984-5: an Iron-age
farmstead and Romano-British
industrial settlement in North
Wales / Kevin Blockley.
BAR BRITISH SERIES 1989, no.210,
p.iii-231, graphs, dwgs., photos.,
plans, secns., site plans, tables,
reconst. dwgs., biblio.

SETTLEMENTS - SQUATTER
See SQUATTER SETTLEMENTS

SETTLEMENTS--TANZANIA--BIBLIOGRAPHY
Human settlements in Tanzania: an
interdisciplinary bibliography /
Carolyn Hannan-Andersson.
Cites 832 general references on
Tanzania, 185 government
publications, and 66 references on
East Africa.
SWEDISH COUNCIL FOR BUILDING
RESEARCH. DOCUMENT 1990, D15,
[i-viii],[1]-407,

SETTLEMENTS - TEMPORARY
See TEMPORARY SETTLEMENTS

SETTLEMENTS--URARTIAN--IRAN--HASANLU
SITE
Constructing the chronology and
historical implications of Hasanlu
IV / Robert H. Dyson, Oscar White
Muscarella.
IRAN 1989, v.27, p.1-27, charts.,
plans, tables, biblio., refs.

SETTLEMENTS--YORUBA--NIGERIA
Oyo ruins of NW Yorubaland, Nigeria
/ Babatundo Agbaje-Williams.
Identifies two Oyo-related sites:
Koso and Ipapo Ile.
JOURNAL OF FIELD ARCHAEOLOGY 1990
Fall, v.17, no.3, p.367-373, maps,
photos., site plans, refs.

SEULLIET, PHILIPPE
Mikhail Baryshnikov on St.
Barthelemy / Philippe Seulliet.
Features the interiors of
neighboring Mexican vernacular
style vacation houses owned by the
dancer. Architect: Rob Miles
Reincke. Interior designer: Bille
du Mesnil.
ARCHITECTURAL DIGEST 1990 Aug.,
v.47, no.8, p.132-137, photos.

SEX ROLE IN ARCHITECTURE
See also ARCHITECTURE AND WOMEN
Gender and the meaning of home /
Ruth Madigan, Moira Munro, Susan
J. Smith.
English and French summaries.
INTERNATIONAL JOURNAL OF URBAN AND
REGIONAL RESEARCH 1990 Dec., v.14,
no.4, p.[625]-647, refs.
Gold's Gym in Venice, Ca. / Ann
Bergren.
Includes portions of interviews
with Ed Connors (owner), Jeffrey
Kipnis, Langston Hardaway, Michael
Rotondi.
ASSEMBLAGE 1990 Dec., no.13,
p.[6]-33, photos., refs.
Planning theory and women's role in
the city / Helen Meller.
URBAN HISTORY YEARBOOK 1990, v.17,
p.[85]-98, diagrs., refs.
Sexuality and space: interview with
Beatriz Colomina.
A reflection on the issues raised
at a symposium of the same name,
held on March 10-11, 1990 at
Princeton University and organized
by Colomina. Includes a paper
presented by Jennifer Bloomer,
"D'Or".
COLUMBIA UNIVERSITY. GRADUATE
SCHOOL OF ARCHITECTURE, PLANNING
AND PRESERVATION. NEWSLINE 1990
Apr., v.2, no.7, p.6-7, photos.,
refs.

SEX ROLE IN ARCHITECTURE--UNITED
STATES
Room at the Top? Sexism and the Star
System in Architecture / Denise
Scott Brown.
One of four sections in a special
feature on "Women in American
Architecture". English
translation, p.73-75.
SPACE DESIGN 1990 June, no.309,
p.54-71,73-75, dwgs., ports.,
elevs., photos., plans, secns.,
site plams, refs.

SEYFERT, WERNER
Das Geschehen gestalten: adaquate
Form in der Architektur der
Waldorfschule / Peter Ferger.
Built 1974. Architect: Werner
Seyfert.
ARCHITHESE 1990 Sept.-Oct., v.20,
no.5, p.56-59, photos., plans.

SEYLER, ODILE
Amenagement interieur / Elisabeth
Allain-Dupre and Odile Seyler.
Survey of recent interior design
in France. Includes interview
with Patrick Rubin. Several works
indexed seperately.
LE MONITEUR ARCHITECTURE AMC 1990
July-Aug., no.13, p.27-74,
axonometric views, photos. plans.

SEZESSION
See SECESSION MOVEMENT

SGARAVATTI, PAOLO
Nel parco, un capanno / Franca
Rinaldi.
"La Pergola", a small, thatched
cottage in the garden of Villa la
Cipressina, in Rocca di Asolo.
Architects: Manlio Brusatin, Paolo
Sgaravatti.
VILLE GIARDINI 1990 July-Aug.,
(Continued next column)

SGARAVATTI, PAOLO (CONTINUED)
Nel parco, un capanno...(CONTINUED)
no.250, p.20-25, photos.

SGPA PLANNING AND ARCHITECTURE
Uptown District, San Diego: looking
at the future of mixed-use
development in American cities /
Janice Fillip.
Residential and commercial project
in the Hillcrest section.
Architects: SGPA Planning and
Architecture and Lorimer-Case;
landscape architects Karen
Scarborough, with Roger Deweese,
Inc.
URBAN LAND 1990 June, v.49, no.6,
p.2-7, photos., site plan, aerial
photo.
Urban delight: a 14-acre "new town"
has been sensitively inserted into
one of San Diego's most
distinctive neighborhoods / Donald
J. Canty.
Uptown District, in the Hillcrest
neighborhood. Architects: SGPA.
ARCHITECTURAL RECORD 1990 Oct.,
v.178, no.11, p.62-[67], map,
photos.

SHACKELFORD, JOHN P.
Maison du Cygne: metamorphosis on
the Georgia Coast / Helen C.
Griffith.
Rosemary Anderson house, Sea
Island. Architect for renovations:
John Shackelford of William Frank
McCall Architects and Interior
Designer: Elizabeth Tucker.
SOUTHERN ACCENTS 1990 July-Aug.,
v.13, no.6, p.76-83, photos.

SHACKS--RESEARCH--UNITED STATES--CAPE
COD (MASSACHUSETTS)
Using GIS in cultural resources /
Betsy Chittenden.
Within the National Park System,
including a project to study dune
shacks in an historic area of Cape
Cod, Mass.
CRM BULLETIN: A NATIONAL PARK
SERVICE TECHNICAL BULLETIN 1989,
v.12, no.6, p.21-22, ill.

SHADES
See also WINDOW SHADES

SHADES AND SHADOWS
See SHADOWS

SHADOWS
"An act protecting open spaces."
On a proposal in the Massachusetts
Senate, to bar approval by local
authorities of new buidings tall
enough to shadow historic open
spaces.
BOSTON PRESERVATION ALLIANCE
LETTER 1990 May, v.11, no.3, p.1,
ill.
Architectural projection / Robin
Evans.
VIA 1990, no.11, p.134-139, dwgs.,
elevs., plans, refs.
Chiaroscuro and non-finito in
Piranesi's Prisons / Malcolm
Campbell.
The stylistic development of the
Prisons etchings in context of
18th century Roman political
developments.
VIA 1990, no.11, p.90-101, engrs.,
refs.

SHADOWS (CONTINUED)
Corbusiers Schatten / Peter Farber.
DER ARCHITEKT 1990 Sept., no.9,
p.388-390, dwgs., photos.,
sketches.
De Chirico / Joseph Rykwert.
VIA 1990, no.11, p.112-115,
photos.
Let the sun shine in: how zoning to
preserve light is significantly
affecting cities across the U.S. /
Terry Jill Lassar.
ARCHITECTURE: THE MAGAZINE OF THE
AMERICAN INSTITUTE OF ARCHITECTS
1990 May, v.79, no.5, p.102-105,
155-156,159, ill., map, diagr.
Licht und Schatten in der
Architektur der Renaissance /
Wolfgang Liebenwein.
DER ARCHITEKT 1990 Sept., no.9,
p.384-388, photos., engrs., refs.
Light, shadow and form: the koshino
house / Tadao Ando.
Tadao Ando's use of light and
shadow.
VIA 1990, no.11, p.52-61, photos.
A secret semiotic skiagraphy: the
corporal theatre of meanings in
Vincenzo Scamozzi's idea of
architecture / Marco Frascari.
On the symbolic use of shadows in
Scamozzi's treatise.
VIA 1990, no.11, p.32-51, elevs.,
photos., plans, secns., refs.
The shadow does not know:
disconnected power / Frances
Butler.
The symbolism of shadows in the
works of Giorgio De Chirico.
VIA 1990, no.11, p.116-123,
photos.
Shadows, symbiosis, and a culture of
wood / Kisho Kurokawa.
Shadows in traditional Japanese
wooden buildings.
VIA 1990, no.11, p.26-31, photos.
Signifying shadows / Arden Reed.
VIA 1990, no.11, p.12-25, photos.
"The simple day and the light of the
sun": lights and shadows in the
museum / Georges Teyssot.
ASSEMBLAGE 1990 Aug., no.12,
p.[58]-83, ill., photos., refs.
Skiagraphy and the ipsum of
architecture / Donald Kunze.
The "architecture" of shadows.
VIA 1990, no.11, p.62-75, ill.,
refs.
Suite: luna de miel / Karen Hillier
and Thomas Woodfin.
VIA 1990, no.11, p.124-133,
photos.
Tadao Ando und das Ratsel des
Schattens / Gerhard G. Feldmeyer.
DER ARCHITEKT 1990 Sept., no.9,
p.397-399, photos.
Vom Umgang mit Licht und Schatten /
Max Bacher.
Theme of issue. 10 articles
indexed separately.
DER ARCHITEKT 1990 Sept., no.9,
p.383, photo.
Working with shadow: Damascus Gate,
Jerusalem / Alison and Peter
Smithson.
Project: Damascus Gate Site
Complex; architects: Alison and
Peter Smithson.
VIA 1990, no.11, p.76-83, dwgs.,
photos., site plans.

SHAFER, HARRY J.
A Mimbres burial with associated colon remains from the NAN ranch ruin, New Mexico / Harry J. Shafer, Marianne Marek, Karl J, Reinhard.
A find dating from the 11th cent., in Grant County.
JOURNAL OF FIELD ARCHAEOLOGY 1989 Spring, v.16, no.1, p.17-30, map, photos., site plan, tables, biblio.

SHAFI, SAYED S.
The Golden Temple [by] Patwant Singh [book review] / Sayed S. Shafi.
In Amristar, India.
ARCHITECTURE + DESIGN 1989 May-June, v.5, no.4, p.118-119, photo., dwg.

SHAFT GRAVES
See also TOMBS

SHAKER
See "SHAKER" AS A SUBHEADING AFTER SPECIFIC BUILDING TYPES OR OTHER MAIN HEADINGS.

SHALOM BARANES ASSOCIATES
Escaping the box: ... Washington's 12 Best office buildings / James Goode.
1718 Connecticut Ave., NW (David M. Schwarz); 1250 24th St., NW (Don Hisaka & Assoc.); Republic Place (Keyes, Condon, Florance); Potomac Tower (Pei Cobb Freed & Partners); 317 Massachusetts Ave., NE (Weinstein Assoc.); 816 Connnecticut Ave., NW (Shalom Baranes Assoc.); Franklin Square (Phillip Johnson & John Burgee); 500 E St., SW (Kohn Pedersen Fox Assoc.); Jefferson Court (SOM); 1001 Pennsylvania Ave., NW (Hartman-Cox); 2631 Connecticut Ave., NW (Martin & Jones).
MUSEUM & ARTS WASHINGTON 1990 Mar.-Apr., v.6, no.2, p.[58-65], 140, photos.

SHANE, GRAHAM
Exhibition review: Street performance; The Homeless Vehicle Project / Graham Shane.
A rollable cart designed by Krzystof Wodiczko and Rudolph Luria.
JOURNAL OF ARCHITECTURAL EDUCATION 1990 summer, v.43, no.4, p.37-42, elevs., models, photos., plans.

SHANE, GRAHAME
Abstraktion und Einfuhlung: zu der Praxis Margaret Helfand Architekten, New York / Grahame Shane.
ARCHITHESE 1990 May-June, v.20, no.3, p.80-82, photos.
Die Russen Kommen! New Yorker Ausstellungen zur russischen Architektur des 20. Jahrhunderts [exhibition review] / Grahame Shane.
On a number of recent exhibits in New York City featuring Russian architecture and architects.
ARCHITHESE 1990 Nov.-Dec., v.20, no.6, p.74-79, ill., dwgs., models, photos., refs.

SHANE, GRAHAME (CONTINUED)
Strassenleben: ein Wohnmobil fur Obdachlose / Grahame Shane.
ARCHITHESE 1990 Jan.-Feb., v.20, no.1, p.31-[37], dwgs., elevs., models, photos., plan.
Teatro di strada: progetto di veicolo per senzatetto = street performance: the homeless vehicle project / Grahame Shane.
Text in English and Italian.
SPAZIO E SOCIETA 1990 Oct.-Dec., v.13, no.52, p.46-53, dwgs., models, photos.

SHANG
See "SHANG" AS A SUBHEADING AFTER SPECIFIC BUILDING TYPES OR OTHER MAIN HEADINGS.

SHANG-YIN
See SHANG

SHANGHAI--QUARTERS (DISTRICTS)-- CHINA--QIANJIATANG
L'isolato di Shanghai / Pierre Clement....[et al.].
On a cooperative planning project for the Qianjiatang district in Shanghai, with the Institut Francais d'Architecture.
CASABELLA 1990 May, v.54, no.568, p.28-32, axonometric views, elevs., models, maps, photos., plans, refs.

SHANI, RAYA
On the stylistic idiosyncrasies of a Saljuq stucco workshop from the region of Kashan / Raya Shani.
IRAN 1989 v.27, p.67-74, plates, dets., map, photos., refs.

SHANKAR, SUJATHA
Trustees of tradition / Sujatha Shankar.
Excerpts from a conversation with Ganapathi Sthapathi, head of the Mahaballipuram College of Architecture and Sculpture.
ARCHITECTURE + DESIGN 1990 Jan.-Feb., v.7, no.1, p.101-104, port.

SHANNON, ROBERT FOOTE
Shannon house, Windham, Vermont, design: 1986; completion: 1990 (est.).
Architect & owner: Robert Foote Shannon. Text in Japanese and English.
GA HOUSES 1990 Mar., no.28, p.134-135, elev., plans, secns.

SHANTIES
See SHACKS

SHANTY TOWNS
See SHANTYTOWNS

SHANTYTOWNS
See also SQUATTER SETTLEMENTS

SHANTYTOWNS--MEXICO--MEXICO CITY-- SANTA ANITA
The glories of Santa Anita: a Mexican horror story / Sigismund Engelkind Kesling.
Small town absorbed by Mexico City, now a shantytown.
PROSPECT 1989, no.3, p.5-8, map, photos.

SHANTYTOWNS--SRI LANKA--COLOMBO-- KIRILLAPONE
The Kirillapone shanty settlement: learning through experience. Physical improvements to six-acre settlement in Colombo, Sri Lanka.
HABITAT NEWS 1989 Aug., v.11, no.2, p.38-41, ports., photos.

SHAO, ZHOUMIN
On safety design of building structures in China / Shao Zhoumin.
BUILDING IN CHINA 1989 June, v.2, no.2, p.4-8, tables.

SHAPE
See FORM

SHAPIRO, BARBARA E.
"Tout ca est foutaise, foutaise et demi!": Le Corbusier and UNESCO / Barbara E. Shapiro.
RACAR: REVUE D'ART CANADIENNE. CANADIAN ART REVIEW 1989, v.16, no.2, p.171-179,298-307, dwgs., elev., site plans, refs.

SHAPLAND AND PETTER
Doors and windows.
Features articles on new products, specifications changes, insulation, Shapland and Petter door designers, replacement doors, biometric access control systems, BSI and BSA references, testing facilities, ironmongery, and Nathalie Bagnoud's use of steel windows.
BUILDING 1990 Sept.28, v.255, no.38, p.[1]-67, photos.

SHARMA, DILLI RAJ
Archaeological remains of the Dang Valley / Dilli Raj Sharma.
In the inner region of West Nepal.
PR-AC-INA NEP-ALA 1988 June-July, no.106, p.8-12, photos., refs.

SHARMA, UDAY R.
An overview of park-people interactions in Royal Chitwan National Park, Nepal / Uday R. Sharma.
LANDSCAPE AND URBAN PLANNING 1990 May, v.19, no.2, p.133-144, map, tables, refs.

SHARP, DENNIS
British modern architecture of the 30s: the work of Connell, Ward and Lucas / Dennis Sharp.
Text in Japanese and English. Includes a chronology of buildings and projects, 1927-39.
ARCHITECTURE AND URBANISM 1990 Sept., no.9(240), p.37-50, ports., photos., refs.
Bruce Goff: toward absolute architecture by David G. de Long [book review] / Dennis Sharp.
AA FILES 1990 Spring, no.19, p.110, dwg.
Cardinal virtues / Dennis Sharp.
On the National Museum of Civilization, Hull, Quebec. Architect: Douglas Cardinal.
BUILDING DESIGN 1990 Aug.24, no.1000, p.12-13, photos., site plans.

SHARP, DENNIS (CONTINUED)

Croix purpose / Dennis Sharp.
On the endangered Villa Cavroix
(1931-1932), Croix, France.
Architect: Robert Mallet-Stevens.
BUILDING DESIGN 1990 Oct.19,
no.1008, p.20-21, elevs., photos.,
secn., site plan.

Entwurfe: zum Werk von Walter Burley
Griffin / Dennis Sharp.
ARCHITHESE 1990 Sept.-Oct., v.20,
no.5, p.50-55, dwgs., elevs.,
maps, plans, refs.

The fourth international conference
of the British "Planning History
Group" / Dennis Sharp.
The "Garden city tradition
re-examined" conference held at
Bournville, U.K.
ARCHITECTURE AND URBANISM 1989
Dec., no.12(231), p.3-4, photo.,
site plan.

The National Gallery of Canada,
Ottawa, Ontario, Canada, 1982-1988
/ Moshe Safdie.
Architects: Moshe Safdie and
Associates. Text in Japanese and
English. Includes essay:
Fortuitous triangular amalgam /
Dennis Sharp.
ARCHITECTURE AND URBANISM 1990
Sept., no.9(240), p.[3]-[36],
axonometric view, photos., plans,
secns., site plan.

Nordic light / Dennis Sharp.
On the work of Sven Markelius
(1889-1972).
BUILDING DESIGN 1990 Apr.6,
no.980, p.22-24, photos., port.

Out of East Africa / Dennis Sharp.
On the work of the Kenya-based
practice, Dalgliesh Marshall
Johnson.
RIBA JOURNAL 1990 Aug., v.97,
no.8, p.30-33, photos.

Report: a neglected Scandinavian
modernist: an exhibition of the
work of architect and planner Sven
Markelius (1889-1972) [exhibition
review] / Dennis Sharp.
Traveling exhibition organized by
Swedish Museum of Architecture.
Text in Japanese and English.
ARCHITECTURE AND URBANISM 1990
Aug., no.8(239), p.4-6,

Die teurste Verkehrsinsel der Welt:
zum neuen Parlamentsgebaude in
Canberra, Australien / Dennis
Sharp.
Architects: Mitchell, Giurgola &
Thorp.
ARCHITHESE 1990 Sept.-Oct., v.20,
no.5, p.70-73, elevs., photos.,
plans, aerial photos.

Wright and wrong / Dennis Sharp.
Report on Edgar A. Tafel's lecture
at the Architectural Association,
London.
BUILDING DESIGN 1990 Apr.20,
no.982, p.46-47, port., photos.

SHAVIV, E.

Implementation of solid modeling in
high hierarchy architectural
language / E. Shaviv, O. Gavish,
U. Amir.
Solid modeling software for
computer-aided design called
CHURCH.
ENVIRONMENT AND PLANNING B 1990
Apr., v.17, no.2, p.205-220,
axonometric views, chart, diagrs.,
figs., dwgs., elevs., refs.

SHAW, BARRY

From theory into practice 8: case
studies / Robert Cowan.
Last in series on urban design.
Contents: Greenland Dock, by Barry
Shaw; Charterhouse Estates,
Liverpool, by Ian Hogan and Gail
Hallyburton; and Port Greenwich,
by Jon Rowland.
ARCHITECTS' JOURNAL 1990 Nov.14,
v.192, no.20, p.35-45, dwgs.,
elevs., map, photos., plans, site
plans, sketches.

SHAW, DENNIS

Welcome to the backyard California /
Erica Goebel.
Gardens in San Francisco, Los
Angeles and Santa Barbara.
Landscape architects: Peder Jens
Pedersen, Calvin Abe & Assoc. with
Ron McCoy, Isabelle Greene, Ron
Lutsko, and Dennis Shaw.
GARDEN DESIGN 1990 autumn, v.9,
no.3, p.[38-45], photos.

SHAW, EDWARD

Living with art: Jorge and Marion
Helft international relations /
Edward Shaw.
International contemporary art
collection in home of Helfts, in
Buenos Aires, Argentina.
ART NEWS 1990 Apr., v.89, no.4,
p.117-118,120, photos.

SHAW, HOWARD VAN DOREN, 1869-1926

History in the making / Justin
Henderson.
Interiors of the renovated 1911
Lake Shore Country Club, Glencoe
Ill. Original architect: Howard
van Doren Shaw. Renovation
architect: John Vinci.
INTERIORS 1990 June, v.149, no.11,
p.100-103, photos., plan.

Ragdale, an architect's dream home /
Cynthia A. Fuener.
Architect Howard Van Doren Shaw's
home, Lake Forest, Ill., built
1896.
HISTORIC ILLINOIS 1990 Dec., v.13,
no.4, p.10-12,

SHAW, J. MARTIN

Environmental government: the
example of the Broads / J. Martin
Shaw.
THE PLANNER 1990 Feb.23, v.76,
no.7, p.11-14, port., photo.,
aerial photo.

SHAW, PATRICK

Second Roche building proposed for
Chicago [One North Wacker] /
Barbara K. Hower.
Plans for a 1,275-foot-high
building at the corner of Wacker
Drive and Madison St. Architects:
Kevin Roche, with Patrick Shaw.
INLAND ARCHITECT 1990 May-June,
v.34, no.3, p.81-82, model.

SHAW, PEGGY

Classic Beaux Arts: architectural
drawings from the French School /
Peggy Shaw.
SOUTHERN ACCENTS 1990 May, v.13,
no.4, p.42-48, ill., dwgs.

SHAW, PHYLLIDA

Estate of the art / Phyllida Shaw.
Artists are increasingly being
used by local authorities and
housing associations in Britain to
work with tenants to transform run
down housing estates and give
individuality to new developments.
HOUSING 1990 Dec.-1991 Jan., v.26,
no.10, p.20-21,23,25, ports.,
photos.

SHAW, ROS BYAM

Braemer Castle / Ros Byam Shaw.
Features interiors of castle built
in 1628 as a fortress and hunting
lodge. Restored by John Adam in
the 18th cent. Now owned by Capt.
and Mrs. Alwyne Farquharson.
THE WORLD OF INTERIORS 1990 Dec.,
p.94-105, port., photos.

SHAW, TIM

A way forward for planning education
/ Tim Shaw.
THE PLANNER 1990 Apr.13, v.76,
no.14, p.23,25,

SHAYLOR, GRAHAM

Planning in the West Midlands /
Graham Shaylor.
THE PLANNER 1990 Dec.14, v.76,
no.49, p.41-43, port., photo.,
aerial photo.

SHEA ARCHITECTS

Busing it: Shea Architects gives MTC
a lift.
The MTC Transit Store,
Minneapolis.
ARCHITECTURE MINNESOTA 1990
Sept.-Oct., v.16, no.5, p.46-47,
photos.

SHEA, GREGORY

Management: Redirecting a firm /
Gregory Shea, Peter Piven.
"Case study of how a firm regained
its purpose."
PROGRESSIVE ARCHITECTURE 1990
July, v.71, no.7, p.51,

SHEA, LISEANN

Office renovation in midtown
Manhattan: lessons learned /
Jacques N. Gordon, Liseann Shea.
In the late 1980s.
URBAN LAND 1990 Jan., v.49, no.1,
p.6-10, graph, map, photos.,
tables.

SHEAR WALLS--PLYWOOD

Plywood shear walls: a new report
offers updated guidelines for
designing quake-resistant
structures / Timothy B. McDonald.
ARCHITECTURE: THE MAGAZINE OF THE
AMERICAN INSTITUTE OF ARCHITECTS
1990 July, v.79, no.7, p.112-118,
dets., photos.

SHEATHING--GLASS

Made in Japan: glass: cladding
innovations / Nancy B. Solomon.
A new exterior sheathing made of
crystallized glass.
ARCHITECTURE: THE MAGAZINE OF THE
AMERICAN INSTITUTE OF ARCHITECTS
1990 Aug., v.79, no.8, p.101-104,
dets., photo., tables.

SHECHTER, M.
Physical and environmental
determinants of urban
deterioration and rehabilitation:
a conceptual framework and a case
study / H. Law Yone, M. Shechter.
Case study of Haifa, Israel.
ENVIRONMENT AND PLANNING A 1990
June, v.22, no.6, p.763-777,
charts, map, tables, refs.

SHEDS
See also HELMS

SHEED, WILFRID
Sag Harbor, an American beauty /
Wilfrid Sheed.
ARCHITECTURAL DIGEST 1990 May,
v.47, no.5, p.29-40, photos.

SHEEHAN, MICHAEL
Air-conditioning takes off / Michael
Sheehan.
Individually controlled internal
environment and air-conditioning
systems are now forming an
integral part of building design.
PLAN: ARCHITECTURE + BUILDING
DESIGN IN IRELAND 1990 May, v.25,
no.5, p.67, photo.

SHEEHY, SANDY
Bermuda's colorful heritage / Sandy
Sheehy.
Describes the characteristic
architecture and gardens of
Bermuda.
HOUSE BEAUTIFUL 1990 Feb., v.132,
no.2, p.34,38,43,103-104, photos.

SHEEPCOTES
See SHEEPFOLDS

SHEEPFOLDS--17TH CENTURY--ALTERATIONS
AND ADDITIONS--FRANCE--GRASSE
In a shepherd's house: transforming
a 17th-century sheepfield in
France / Daniel H. Minassian.
Interiors of renovated and rebuilt
stone sheep house in Grasse.
ARCHITECTURAL DIGEST 1990 June,
v.47, no.6, p.[178-181], photos.

SHEETROCK
See WALLBOARD

SHEFER, DANIEL
Evaluation methods in urban and
regional planning theory and
practice / Daniel Shefer, Lisa
Kaess.
TOWN PLANNING REVIEW 1990 Jan.,
v.61, no.1, p.75-88, table, refs.
Tribute: plan evaluation method: an
essay in memory of Morris (Moshe)
Hill / Daniel Shefer, Vera
Tsubari.
Includes complete bibliography of
the works of Morris Hill.
JOURNAL OF PLANNING EDUCATION AND
RESEARCH 1990 Fall, v.10, no.1,
p.5-14, biblio., refs.

SHEINE, JUDITH
Moderne Wohnbauarchitektur =
L'architecture d'habitat moderne =
Modern domestic architecture /
Judith Sheine.
A selection of Los Angeles houses
dating from 1913-1959. Text in
German; summaries in German,
French, and English.
(Continued next column)

SHEINE, JUDITH (CONTINUED)
Moderne...(CONTINUED)
WERK, BAUEN + WOHNEN 1990
July-Aug., no.7-8, p.46-53, dwg.,
photos., plan, refs.

SHELBURNE, FIONA
England's Bowood House / Elizabeth
Lambert.
Features refurbished interiors of
18th cent. residence in Wiltshire
designed by Fionn Shelburne.
Architect for Diocletion Wing:
Robert Adam. Landscape architect:
Capability Brown.
ARCHITECTURAL DIGEST 1990 May,
v.47, no.5, p.162-171,[264],
photos.

SHELDON, TOBY
Children's play and recreation /
Toby Sheldon.
THE PLANNER 1990 Apr.6, v.76,
no.13, p.20-21, photo.

SHELL ROOFS
La modernita della stazione Brin =
The modernity of Brin station.
Elliptical metal and glass train
station enclosure; architects:
Building Workshop.
L'ARCA 1990 Oct., no.42 suppl.
l'Arca 2, p.99, photos., secns.

SHELL ROOFS--ALUMINUM
Tecnologio sofisticate per opere in
alluminio.
Curved roof at Stazione Brin, of
Progetto Metrogenova.
L'INDUSTRIA DELLE COSTRUZIONI 1990
Nov., v.24, no.229, p.79, det.,
photos.

SHELL ROOFS--SWITZERLAND
Elegante Modelle: die moderne Form
des Schalenbaus / Heinz Isler.
DEUTSCHE BAUZEITUNG 1990 July,
v.124, no.7, p.62-65, photos.,
aerial photos.

SHELL STRUCTURES
See also DOMES
See also GEODESIC DOMES
See also VAULTS (ARCHITECTURE)

SHELL STRUCTURES--STAINLESS STEEL
Piano a Bercy / Jean-Pierre Menard.
Focus on the shell structure of
the Bercy 2 shopping mall,
Charenton. Architects: Renzo
Piano, Building Workshop. English
summary, p.166.
ARCHITECTURE D'AUJOURD'HUI 1990
June, no.269, p.[162]-166, dets.,
models, photos., secn.

SHELLS (STRUCTURAL ENGINEERING)
See SHELL STRUCTURES

SHELTER
See HOUSING

SHELTERS
See also AIR RAID SHELTERS
See also ATOMIC BOMB SHELTERS
See also BLINDS (SHELTERS)
See also BUS SHELTERS
See also PUBLIC SHELTERS

SHELTERS (CONTINUED)
Noli me tangere: project 165 "the
Drop" / Giorgio Fonio.
Project for short-stay living
capsule; architects: Future
Systems. Text in Italian and
English.
L'ARCA 1990 Jan., no.34, p.58-65,
axonomtric view, ill., elev.,
model, plans, secns.
Un ombrello per rifugio = An
umbrella shelter / Maurizio Vitta.
Transportable emergency shelter
design; architects: Future
Systems.
L'ARCA 1990 Oct., no.42 suppl.
l'Arca 2, p.97-98, dwgs., elevs.,
photo.
Shelter that spun off from space /
John Welsh.
On the Universal Shelter, designed
with heat-retaining fabric and
collapsible ribs. Future Systems
Consultants.
BUILDING DESIGN 1990 Jan.19,
no.969, p.12, dwgs., elev.,
photo., isometric dwg.

SHELTERS - AIR RAID
See AIR RAID SHELTERS

SHELTERS - ATOMIC BOMB
See ATOMIC BOMB SHELTERS

SHELTERS, CRISIS
See CRISIS SHELTERS

SHELTERS, PUBLIC
See PUBLIC SHELTERS

SHELTON, BARRIE
A centennium of Sitte / Barrie
Shelton.
Celebrates the anniversary of the
publication of Der Stadtebau by
Camillo Sitte: City planning
according to artistic principles.
AUSTRALIAN PLANNER: JOURNAL OF THE
ROYAL AUSTRALIAN PLANNING
INSTITUTE 1989 Dec., v.27, no.4,
p.29-32, plans, refs.

SHELTON, MINDEL ASSOCIATES
The big picture / Monica Geran.
Interiors of New York apartment
for contemporary art collectors
designed by Shelton, Mindel
Associates.
INTERIOR DESIGN 1990 Jan., v.61,
no.1, p.156-[165], photos., plans.
Breaking away / Monica Geran.
Home in Princeton, NJ. Architects:
Shelton, Mindel Associates.
INTERIOR DESIGN 1990 June, v.61,
no.9, p.236-[243], axonometric
view, photos., plan.
Central Park East: architects Peter
Shelton and Lee Mindel bring the
park indoors in their decoration
of an Upper Fifth Avenue apartment
/ Joan Kron.
HOUSE & GARDEN 1990 Oct., v.162,
no.10, p.[230-235], port., photos.
Words and music: Lee Mindel, Peter
Shelton attune furnishings to
architecture / Veronica McNiff.
ELLE DECOR 1990 Apr., v.1, no.3,
p.114-121, photos., ill., ports.

SHELTON, MINDEL ASSOCIATES
                    (CONTINUED)
Yankee hospitality: a Connecticut house decorated by Peter Shelton and Lee Mindel / Amy Fine Collins.
HOUSE & GARDEN 1990 July, v.162, no.7, p.[104]-109,134, photos.

SHELVES, BOOK
See BOOKSHELVES

SHENG, YAP KIOE
The incremental development scheme in Hyderabad: an innovative approach to low income housing / Adnan Hameed Aliani, Yap Kioe Sheng.
CITIES 1990 May, v.7, no.2, p.133-148, chart, maps, plan, tables, refs.

SHENYANG MUNICIPAL COMMITTEE FOR THE COORDINATION OF URBAN AND RURAL PLANNING AND CONSTRUCTION
Comprehensive urban renewal of old urban districts in Shenyang.
CHINA CITY PLANNING REVIEW 1988 Mar., v.4, no.1, p.15-32, maps, plans, tables.

SHEPARD, PAUL
Selections from "Colstrip, Montana" / David Hansen, Paul Shepard. Photos and essay on a mining landscape. Photographer listed variously as David Hansen and David T. Hanson.
PLACES 1990 Summer, v.6, no.4, p.[68]-81, photos., aerial photos., refs.

SHEPERD, KEVIN L.
Indoor radon rouses the commercial real estate industry / Kevin L. Sheperd.
THE JOURNAL OF REAL ESTATE DEVELOPMENT 1989 Summer, v.5, no.1, p.45-50,

SHEPHEARD, EPSTEIN AND HUNTER
Council crack down / Martin Spring. Defective precast reinforced concrete houses in Bristol, England are being rebuilt, including the Sea Mills and Upper Horfield projects. Architects: Levitt Bernstein Associates; Shepheard Epstein & Hunter.
BUILDING 1990 July 27, v.255, no.30, p.38-42, dwg., elevs., maps, photos., plans.

SHEPHEARD, PETER FAULKNER, SIR, 1913-
Reflections on landscape: the lives and work of six British landscape architects [edited by] S. Harvey [book review] / David Singleton. Oral histories from G. Jellicoe, S. Crowe, P. Shepheard, B. Hackett, P. Youngman, and B. Colvin.
ANCIENT MONUMENTS SOCIETY. TRANSACTIONS 1990, new ser.,v.34, p.199,

SHEPLEY, CHRIS
Planning and football league grounds: an RTPI survey / Chris Shepley.
THE PLANNER 1990 Sept.28, v.76, no.38, p.15-17, photos.

SHEPLEY, RUTAN AND COOLIDGE
Cheering restoration of Boston's South Station / Jane Holtz Kay. Refurbishment of 1890 railroad station. Original architects: Shepley, Rutan and Coolidge. Restoration architects: Stubbins Associates and others.
PROGRESSIVE ARCHITECTURE 1990 Aug., v.71, no.8, p.30-31, photos.

SHEPPARD-FIDLER, ALWYN, 1909-1990
Alwyn Sheppard-Fidler [obituary].
BUILDING DESIGN 1990 Feb.23, no.974, p.5,
Alwyn Sheppard-Fidler [obituary]. British architect and city planner of Birmingham, Eng., died at 80.
ARCHITECTS' JOURNAL 1990 Feb.21, v.191, no.8, p.13,
Alwyn Sheppard-Fidler [obituary] / M.M.E. Jeffries.
RIBA JOURNAL 1990 June, v.97, no.6, p.91,
Birmingham pioneer [obituary]. Obit. of John Alwyn Sheppard-Fidler.
BUILDING DESIGN 1990 Jan.19, no.969, p.7,

SHEPPARD, NORMAN JAMES
New challenge on King's Cross / Robert Cowan. Alternative to Norman Foster's plan proposed by Ian Haywood and Norman Sheppard of the King's Cross Team (KXT).
ARCHITECTS' JOURNAL 1990 Sept.26, v.192, no.13, p.14-15, ports., photo., plans, sketch.

SHEPPARD ROBSON
To integrate or not to integrate / Jonathon Greig. British firm Sheppard Robson is managing the change from computer specialists to general use of CAD throughout the firm.
ARCHITECTS' JOURNAL 1990 Aug.22-29, v.192, no.7-8, p.44-45, port.

SHERFY, MARCELLA
Guidelines for evaluating and nominating properties that have achieved significance within the last fifty years / Marcella Sherfy, W. Ray Luce.
NATIONAL REGISTER BULLETIN [1989], no.22, p.[1]-11, photos. Interpretation.
Nine articles on historic site methods. Authors: Sandra S. Weber, F.A. Ketterson, Marcella Sherfy, Edward Tabor Linenthal, Raymond H. Thompson, Michael E. Whatley, Marie T. Myers, Karen Sweeny-Justice, Kathleen Hunter.
CRM BULLETIN: A NATIONAL PARK SERVICE TECHNICAL BULLETIN 1990, v.13, no.3, p.1-21, photos.

SHERIDAN, DAVID
Sulle colline del Colorado. Gardens of a house in Castle Pines, Colo. Landscape architect: David Sheridan.
VILLE GIARDINI 1990 Apr., no.247, p.60-65, photos.

SHERIDAN, ROBERT
Turning old factories into new-style industrial buildings / Robert Sheridan.
URBAN LAND 1990 Feb., v.49, no.2, p.2-5, photo., plan, aerial photo.

SHERMAN, DANIEL J.
Art history and art politics: the museum according to Orsay / Daniel J. Sherman. Criticism of the Musee d'Orsay, Paris. Architect: Gae Aulenti.
OXFORD ART JOURNAL 1990, v.13, no.2, p.55-67, photos., refs.

SHERMAN, M. H.
Tracer-gas techniques for measuring ventilation in a single zone / M. H. Sherman.
BUILDING AND ENVIRONMENT 1990, v.25, no.4, p.365-374, table, refs.

SHERMYEN, ANNE H.
Ideal urban form and visions of the good life: Florida's growth management dilemma / Ivonne Audirac, Anne H. Shermyen, Marc T. Smith.
AMERICAN PLANNING ASSOCIATION. JOURNAL 1990 Autumn, v.56, no.4, p.470-482, photos., tables, aerial photos., refs.

SHERRATT, ANDREW
The genesis of megaliths: monumentality, ethnicity and social complexity in Neolithic north-west Europe / Andrew Sherratt.
WORLD ARCHAEOLOGY 1990 Oct., v.22, no.2, p.147-167, chart, maps, biblio.

SHERRILL, BETTY
Georgian grace in Atlanta: renewing southern traditions for Charlotte and Rankin Smith / Jeffrey Simpson. Interiors of Georgian-style home in northwestern Atlanta. Architect: William Frank McCall. Interior designers: Betty Sherrill and Ethel Smith of McMillen.
ARCHITECTURAL DIGEST 1990 May, v.47, no.5, p.220-225, photos.

SHERWOOD, TOPPER
Restoration and transition: preservation amidst a changing East Germany [Erfurt] / Topper Sherwood.
PRESERVATION NEWS 1990 Mar., v.30, no.3, p.8, ports., photo.

SHETTLEWORTH, EARLE G. JOHN CALVIN STEVENS
John Calvin Stevens: domestic architecture, 1890-1930 [by] John Calvin Stevens II, Earle G. Shettleworth, Jr. [book review] / William David Barry.
LANDMARKS OBSERVER 1990 Fall,
(Continued next page)

SHINOHARA, KAZUO, 1925- (CONTINUED)
Kazuo Shinohara / Kazuo Shinohara.
Contents: K2 Building,
Miyakojima-ku, Osaka, design:
1987-88; under construction --
Kumamoto-kita Police Station,
design: 1988-90; under
construction. With Taikoh
Architectural Office. Text in
Japanese and English.
GA DOCUMENT 1990 Apr., no.25,
p.161-165, elevs., model, photos.,
plans, secns.
Tokyo, die Schonheit des Chaos /
Kazuo Shinohara.
Centennial Hall, an art building
for the Tokyo Institute of
Technology. Architect: K.
Shinohara.
ARCH PLUS 1990 Oct., no.105-106,
p.48-50, elevs., photos., plans,
secns., site plans.

SHINOHARA, SATOKO, 1958-
Kiyosato-kaku / Satoko Shinohara.
Mountain vacation house.
Architects: Satoko Shinohara,
Kengo Kuma.
JAPAN ARCHITECT 1990 Apr., v.65,
no.4 (396), p.58-62, elevs.,
photos., site plan.

SHINTO
See "SHINTO" AS A SUBHEADING AFTER
SPECIFIC BUILDING TYPES OR OTHER
MAIN HEADINGS.

SHINZO TERUI ARCHITECT & ASSOCIATES
Special edition III: scene of frame
and membrane / Shinzo Terui.
Features three projects by Shinzo
Terui: sail of Obama (Office
building), Roof of Iida
(restaurant), and Tower of
Katsuradai (dental clinic).
Includes dialogue, System and
locality of architecture by
Toshiaki Ishida and Terui. English
summary, p.23.
KENCHIKU BUNKA 1990 Sept., v.45,
no.527, p.93-113, ports., elevs.,
models, photos., plans.

SHIODA, JUNICHI
Urasoe Art Museum.
Located in Okinawa. Architects:
Shozo Uchii, Architect and
Associates; Kamimori Architect &
Associates. English summary, p.19.
Includes tripartite talk, Art
Museum for its staff, by M. Ono,
J. Shioda, and R. Kuroda.
KENCHIKU BUNKA 1990 July, v.45,
no.525, p.[73]-88, elevs.,
photos., plans, secns.

SHIOTSUKI, YOSHITAKE
Combined effect of earth cooling and
ventilation on passive cooling of
dwellings (continued report) /
Tadahisa Katayama et al.
English summary, p.83.
NIHON KENCHIKU GAKKAI KEIKAKUKEI
RONBUN HOKOKU SHU = JOURNAL OF
ARCHITECTURE, PLANNING AND
ENVIRONMENTAL ENGINEERING 1990
Jan., no.1(407), p.75-83, figs.,
graphs, tables, refs.

SHIP TERMINALS
See MARINE TERMINALS

SHIPBUILDING WORKS
See SHIPYARDS

SHIPMAN, ELLEN BIDDLE, 1869-
Bayou Bend: the plan and history of
the gardens / David B. Warren.
Houston estate of the Hogg family.
Landscape designer: Ellen Shipman.
MUSEUM OF FINE ARTS, HOUSTON.
BULLETIN - THE MUSEUM OF FINE
ARTS, HOUSTON 1989 Winter-Spring,
v.12, no.2, p.66-93, ports.,
photos., plan.

SHIPS
See also OCEAN LINERS
See also SAILING SHIPS

SHIPS--CONSERVATION AND RESTORATION
Documentation of historic museum
vessels: Bureaucratic paperwork or
vital working tool? / David A.
Walker.
ASSOCIATION FOR PRESERVATION
TECHNOLOGY BULLETIN 1990, v.22,
no.1-2, p.104-108, photos.,
tables.

SHIPS--DOCUMENTATION
Documentation of historic museum
vessels: Bureaucratic paperwork or
vital working tool? / David A.
Walker.
ASSOCIATION FOR PRESERVATION
TECHNOLOGY BULLETIN 1990, v.22,
no.1-2, p.104-108, photos.,
tables.

SHIPS--HISTORY--EXHIBITIONS
Schip en schoonheid: Tentoonstelling
scheepsarchitectuur [exhibition
review] / Arjen Oosterman.
Exhibit at the Maritiem Museum
Prins Hendrik, Rotterdam, until
Mar.25,1990, with a catalogue by
Paul Groenendijk.
ARCHIS 1990 Feb., no.2, p.5-6,
photo.

SHIPS--INFLUENCE
Ti'lil: villa of the dunes / Claire
Touchard.
A ship-inspired house at
Finistere, Brittany. Architects:
Caroline Bapst, Bruno Pantz.
ELLE DECOR 1990 Mar., v.1, no.2,
p.[18]-24, axonometric view,
photos., plans.

SHIPS--INVENTORIES--UNITED STATES
The National Register and historic
ships / James P. Delgado.
On the National Maritime
Initiative, an inventory of 50-yr.
or older U.S. vessels.
CRM BULLETIN: A NATIONAL PARK
SERVICE TECHNICAL BULLETIN 1990,
v.13, no.6, p.26,

SHIPS--JADERA
Tavoli di rilievo per il piroscafo
Jadera (1928) / Sergio Coradeschi.
Illustrations of a 1928 steamship.
Text in Italian and English.
DOMUS 1990 Dec., no.722,
p.[56-59],XXIV, ill., secns.

SHIPS--JADERA (CONTINUED)

SHIPS--WOODEN--17TH CENTURY--
CONSERVATION AND RESTORATION--VASA
Vasamuseet: Ett Masterverk.
Introduction to issue featuring
the Stockholm museum built for the
17th-cent. Dutch ship. Architect:
Mansson Dahlback Arkitektkontor.
Includes essay by Marianne
Dahlback and Goran Mansson, and
commentary by Bengt O.H.
Johansson, Brita
Koefoed-Jespersen, and Wilfried
Wang. English translations,
p.61-62.
ARKITEKTUR: THE SWEDISH REVIEW OF
ARCHITECTURE 1990 Oct., v.90,
no.8, p.2-35,cover, dets., elevs.,
photos., plans, secns., site
plans.

SHIPYARDS--GERMANY (WEST)--BREMERHAVEN
Zum Wert oder Unwert einer
Industriehalle von Egon Eiermann /
Immo Boyken.
A 1939-1941 shipbuilding hall in
Bremerhaven.
BAUWELT 1990 Mar.16, v.81, no.11,
p.472-474, ill., elev., photos.,
plan.

SHIRAI, HIDEKAZU
The notion of beauty in architecture
/ Hidekazu Shirai.
The theories of Quatremere de
Quincy. Text in Japanese; includes
English summary.
NIHON KENCHIKU GAKKAI KEIKAKUKEI
RONBUN HOKOKU SHU = JOURNAL OF
ARCHITECTURE, PLANNING AND
ENVIRONMENTAL ENGINEERING 1990
Aug., no.8(414), p.109-116,
ports., refs.
On Jacques-Francois Blondel
(1705-1774) / Hidekazu Shirai.
Text in Japanese; English summary,
p.143.
NIHON KENCHIKU GAKKAI KEIKAKUKEI
RONBUN HOKOKU SHU = JOURNAL OF
ARCHITECTURE, PLANNING AND
ENVIRONMENTAL ENGINEERING 1990
June, no.6(412), p.143-152, port.,
plans, secn., site plans, refs.
Three faculties of "Ame (Soul)"
concerning architectural beauty /
Hidekazu Shirai.
"On the architectural beauty in
Quatremere de Quincy's Treatise
II. Text in Japanese; includes
English summary.
NIHON KENCHIKU GAKKAI KEIKAKUKEI
RONBUN HOKOKU SHU = JOURNAL OF
ARCHITECTURE, PLANNING AND
ENVIRONMENTAL ENGINEERING 1990
Nov., no.11(417), p.109-116,

SHIRAI, HIROYASU
On the aspect of successive
diminution in a five-storied stupa
/ Hiroyasu Shirai.
English summary, p.131.
NIHON KENCHIKU GAKKAI KEIKAKUKEI
RONBUN HOKOKU SHU = JOURNAL OF
ARCHITECTURE, PLANNING AND
ENVIRONMENTAL ENGINEERING 1990
Feb., no.2(408), p.123-131,
graphs, secns., tables, refs.

SHIRAKAWA, NAOYUKI
Traces of architects early in this century: Kikuji Ishimoto / Naoyuki Shirakawa.
KENCHIKU BUNKA 1990 Oct., v.45, no.528, p.165-172, axonometric views, port., elevs., photos., aerial photos.

SHIRDEL, BAHRAM
Four projects of Aks Runo.
Contents: "Metapolis" Los Angeles project, 1987 -- Olympic West office towers, Los Angeles, 1988 -- Tokyo International Forum, Tokyo, 1989 -- Alexandria Library project, Egypt, 1989. Architects: Aks Runo, Bahram Shirdel and Andrew Zago. Text in Japanese and English.
ARCHITECTURE AND URBANISM 1990 June, no.6(237), p.[7]-28, elevs., models, plans, site plan.
Projekt Olympic-West-Burohauser, 1988.
Architects: Bahram Shirdel, Andrew Zago.
WERK, BAUEN + WOHNEN 1990 July-Aug., no.7-8, p.56-57, models, plans.

SHIRVANI, HAMID
San Diego's environmental planning process ten years later / Hamid Shirvani, Michael Stepner.
AMERICAN PLANNING ASSOCIATION. JOURNAL 1986 Spring, v.52, no.2, p.212-219, dwgs., maps, biblio.

SHLAY, ANNE B.
Financing community: methods for assessing residential credit disparites, market barriers, and institutional reinvestment performance in the metropolis / Anne B. Shlay.
JOURNAL OF URBAN AFFAIRS 1988, v.11, no.3, p.[201]-223, charts, tables, refs.

SHNIER, JOHN, 1955-
New rules for Prix de Rome / Val Rynnimeri.
A history of the Canadian prize and a look at the work of the first winner, John Shnier.
CANADIAN ARCHITECT 1990 Jan., v.35, no.1, p.16-20, dwgs., port., models, map, site plans.

SHOE SHOWROOMS
See SHOWROOMS - SHOE

SHOE STORES
See STORES - SHOE

SHOEMAKE, CARRIE GLASSMAN
Architecture for the '90s.
Holt Hinshaw Pfau Jones, Astronaut Memorial; San Francisco Henry Myerberg, house in Vieques, P.R.-- Walter Chatham, house in Seaside, Fla.--Carrie Glassman Shoemake, house near Austin, Tex.--Mark Domiteaux, house in Tex.--Frank Lupo, Daniel Rowan, loft in NYC-- Michael Codwell, 4 projects in New England.
METROPOLITAN HOME 1990 Jan., v.22, no.1, p.[72]-96, ports., photos.

SHOP FRONTS
See STORE FRONTS

SHOPE, RENO, WHARTON ASSOCIATES
Across the grain: a university building offers lessons in detailing wood / Douglas E. Gordon, M. Stephanie Stubbs.
Alumni house, Univ. of Conn. Architects: Shope Reno Wharton Associates.
ARCHITECTURE: THE AIA JOURNAL 1990 Apr., v.79, no.4, p.95-97, dets., photos., secn.
Intimate grandeur on the water: Shope Reno Wharton gives new life to a Connecticut mansion / Paul Goldberger.
Interiors of renovated 1880 waterfront home in Greenwich. Landmarked pedestrian bridge designed by John Augustus Roebling also on the site linking shore to nearby dock.
ARCHITECTURAL DIGEST 1990 Dec., v.47, no.13, p.[152-159], port., photos., plan.
Shope Reno Wharton: a shingled cottage / Suzanne Stephens.
Vacation home on Conn. island.
ARCHITECTURAL DIGEST 1990 Sept., v.47, no.10, p.[94-97],108, photos., plans.

SHOPPING ARCADES
Il concetto di Galleria tra "disegno" & "costruzione" = The concept of the gallery, between "design" and "construction" / Brunetto de Batte.
ANFIONE ZETO 1990, .v.2, no.4-5, p.205-217, dwgs., photo.
Spaces for business by day and parties by night / Herb McLaughlin.
The use of gallerias, atriums and arcades in shoping centers, office towers, etc. for after-hours uses.
URBAN LAND 1990 May, v.49, no.5, p.30-31, photos.

SHOPPING ARCADES--GERMANY (WEST)-- HAMBURG--BLEICHENHOF
Hamburgs Neunte: der Bleichenhof in Hamburg / Dirk Meyhofer.
Architects: Nietz Prasch Sigl.
DEUTSCHE BAUZEITUNG 1990 Oct., v.124, no.10, p.26-31, maps, photos., plans, secns.

SHOPPING ARCADES--GERMANY (WEST)-- REUTLINGEN
Eine Ladenpassage in Reutlingen. Located on Metzgerstrasse.
Architect: Werkatelier Rolf Malessa.
BAUWELT 1990 Mar.9, v.81, no.10, p.446-447, photos., plan, secn., site plan.

SHOPPING ARCADES--GERMANY (WEST)-- SIEGBURG
Architektur unterwegs.
Four projects: Brauerei, Munchen-Riem (architect: Gabor Benedek); Alten-und Pflegeheim, Salzgitter-Lebenstedt (architects: Brutt-Matthies + Partner P. Gorres, W. Kraatz); Geschaftszentrum Siegburg (architect: Atelier fur Architektur und Design Ortwin
(Continued next column)

SHOPPING ARCADES--GERMANY (WEST)-- SIEGBURG (CONTINUED)
Architektur unterwegs. (CONTINUED) Hillnhutter plus Team); Kulturzentrum Waldkraiburg, Kreis Muhldorf/Inn (architects: Kaup, Scholz, Wortmann).
DEUTSCHES ARCHITEKTENBLATT 1990 Sept.1, v.22, no.9, p.1305-1308, elevs., photos., plans, secns.

SHOPPING ARCADES--SWEDEN--STOCKHOLM-- GALLERIA DI LADUGARDS-BRON
Stoccolma, nel centro storico: l'intarsio = Stockholm, the historic centre: inlaying. Five examples of new buildings coexisting with old buildings. Architects: AOS; Studio Coordinator; Studio Alf Oreberg; Studio Hans Murman; Studio Arndt Malmquist; Studio Nyren.
ABITARE 1990 July-Aug., no.287, p.108-[119], axonometric view, photos., plans, secns., site plan, aerial photo.

SHOPPING ARCADES--SWEDEN--STOCKHOLM-- STURE GALLERIAN
Stoccolma, nel centro storico: l'intarsio = Stockholm, the historic centre: inlaying. Five examples of new buildings coexisting with old buildings. Architects: AOS; Studio Coordinator; Studio Alf Oreberg; Studio Hans Murman; Studio Arndt Malmquist; Studio Nyren.
ABITARE 1990 July-Aug., no.287, p.108-[119], axonometric view, photos., plans, secns., site plan, aerial photo.

SHOPPING ARCADES--UNITED STATES-- MINNEAPOLIS (MINNESOTA)--GAVIIDAE COMMON
Nicollet's new neighbor: Gaviidae Common establishes uncommon standards for retail design / Kira Obolensky.
Minneapolis shopping center. Architects: Cesar Pelli & Associates.
ARCHITECTURE MINNESOTA 1990 Jan.-Feb., v.16, no.1, p.32-33, photos.

SHOPPING CENTERS
See also SHOPPING ARCADES
See also SHOPPING MALLS
See also STRIP RETAIL CENTERS
See also SUPERMARKETS
The emerging super community center / Dennis Burr.
"A new category of shopping centers..." examined by ULI.
URBAN LAND 1990 Dec., v.49, no.12, p.30-31, graphs, tables.
Retail architecture / Bill Hames.
THE ARCHITECT, W.A.. THE OFFICIAL JOURNAL OF THE ROYAL AUSTRALIAN INSTITUTE OF ARCHITECTS, W.A. CHAPTER 1990, v.30, no.4, p.15-16, photos.
Shopping centre design, by N. Keith Scott [book review] / Henry Herzberg.
ARCHITECTS' JOURNAL 1990 Apr.4, v.191, no.14, p.91, photo.

SHOPPING CENTERS (CONTINUED)
Shopping for trends / Dan Martin.
Stores, shopping centers, malls,
and strip centers in the 1990s.
PLANNING 1990 Dec., v.56, no.12,
p.14-18, graph, dwgs., photos.,
secn.
Special report: shopping centres.
Theme issue on shopping centers
and shopping malls, including
Bercy 2, Charenton-le-Pont,
architect: Renzo Piano and
Zaailand, Leeuwarden, Netherlands,
architects: Architektenbureau
Lucas en Ellerman.
BUILDING DESIGN 1990 Apr., suppl.,
p.2-21, axonometric views, dets.,
models, dwgs., photos., plans,
secns., site plans, aerial photos.

SHOPPING CENTERS--ALTERATIONS AND
ADDITIONS
Shopping center renovations / David
A. Mulvihill.
Renovation and expansion of
shopping centers in place of new
development.
URBAN LAND 1990 Dec., v.49, no.12,
p.38, biblio.

SHOPPING CENTERS--ALTERATIONS AND
ADDITIONS--DENMARK--HVIDORE--
HVIDOVRE STATIONSCENTER
Overdaekning og udbygning af
Hvidovre Stationscenter / Jorgen
Hegner Christiansen.
Renovation of a late 1970s
shopping center, with new roofing
and additional facilities.
Architect: Marianne Ingvartsen.
Includes English and German
summaries.
ARKITEKTUR DK 1990, v.34, no.6,
p.300-305, photos., plan, secn.,
sketch.

SHOPPING CENTERS--ARGENTINA--BUENOS
AIRES--ALTO PALERMO SHOPPING
Alto Palermo Shopping, Buenos Aires,
Argentina.
Architects: Juan Carlos Lopez y
Asociados.
PROJETO 1990 Dec.-1991 Jan.,
no.137, p.60-61, photos., plan.

SHOPPING CENTERS--BRAZIL
Arquitetura brasiliera de shoppings
chega ao exterior.
PROJETO 1990 Dec.-1991 Jan.,
no.137, p.[49]-55, model, photos.,
table, refs.
Criatividade tenta ir alem do modelo
imposto / Nildo Carlos Oliveira.
On shopping centers.
PROJETO 1990 Mar., no.130,
p.65-68, dwgs., ports., photos.

SHOPPING CENTERS--BRAZIL--BELO
HORIZONTE--SHOPPING SUL
Ceramico e vidro na composicao da
fachada.
Shopping Sul, Belo Horizonte.
Architects: Oscar Ferreira, et al.
PROJETO 1990 Mar., no.130,
p.76-77, dwg., photo., plans,
secn.

SHOPPING CENTERS--BRAZIL--LONDRINA--
CATUAI SHOPPING CENTER
Catuai Shopping Center, Londrina.
Architects: C. Dominguez, F.
Larrea, L. Capelas.
PROJETO 1990 Dec.-1991 Jan.,
no.137, p.58-59, photos., plans,
site plan.

SHOPPING CENTERS--BRAZIL--RIO DE
JANEIRO--SHOPPING CULTURAL FUNDICAO
PROGRESSO
Progresso: de fundicao a shopping
center cultural.
In Rio de Janeiro. Architect: M.
G. Moura.
PROJETO 1989 Apr., no.120,
p.88-94, elevs., model, photos.,
secns., site plans.

SHOPPING CENTERS--BRAZIL--SAO PAULO--
PARQUE DO POVO
Bases para ocupacao do Parque do
Povo / Carlos Bratke.
Parque do Povo, Sao Paulo.
Architect: Carlos Bratke.
PROJETO 1990 Mar., no.130,
p.78-81, dwgs., site plan.

SHOPPING CENTERS--BRAZIL--SAO PAULO--
SHOPPING INTERLAGOS
Espaco publico em ambiente fechado.
Shopping. Interlagos, Sao Paulo.
Architect: Juan Cabeza Sastre.
PROJETO 1990 Mar., no.130,
p.72-73, photos., plans.

SHOPPING CENTERS--BRAZIL--SAO PAULO--
SHOPPING JARDIM SUL
Vocacao de area muda plano e gera
Jardim Sul.
Shopping center, Sao Paulo.
Architects: E.R. Carvalho Mange,
Ariaki Kato.
PROJETO 1990 Mar., no.130,
p.69-71, ill., dwgs., model,
photo., plans, site plan.

SHOPPING CENTERS--COLOMBIA--
BUCARAMANGA
Cuatro proyectos de Andres Rueda.
All unbuilt.
PROA 1988 Nov., no.377, p.48-56,
axonometric views, ill., elevs.,
models, photos., plans, secns.,
site plans.

SHOPPING CENTERS--CONSERVATION AND
RESTORATION--ARGENTINA--BUENOS
AIRES--MERCADO NORTE
Mercado Norte, Buenos Aires,
Argentina / Jorge Glusberg.
Renovation of 1900 market.
Architects: Raul Lier, Alberto
Tonconogy.
PROJETO 1990 Dec.-1991 Jan.,
no.137, p.56-57, elev., photos.

SHOPPING CENTERS--ENGLAND--BROMLEY--
GLADES SHOPPING CENTRE
Playing by access [Glades shopping
centre] / Graham Ridout.
On logistical and spatial aspects
of construction for a project in
the center of Bromley, England.
Architects: Chapman Taylor
Partners.
BUILDING 1990 Mar.2, v.255, no.9,
p.44-47, elev., photos.

SHOPPING CENTERS--ENGLAND--GATESHEAD--
METROCENTRE
Gateshead Metrocentre: an
environment of belonging / John
Smith.
DESIGN FOR SPECIAL NEEDS 1989
Dec., no.50, p.15-17, photos.

SHOPPING CENTERS--ENGLAND--LEEDS--CORN
EXCHANGE
With the grain / Leslie
Geddes-Brown.
1861 Leeds Corn Exchange to be
converted into a shopping center.
Original architect: Cuthbert
Brodrick. Architect for the
conversion: John Lyall.
THE WORLD OF INTERIORS 1990 Oct.,
p.216-221, photos.

SHOPPING CENTERS--ENGLAND--LONDON--
TOBACCO DOCK
Special feature: Terry Farrell &
Company.
Contents: Editor's introduction.--
Statement for this special
feature, by Terry Farrell.--Essay:
On Terry Farrell, by Rowan
Moore.--Works: Tobacco Dock,
Shopping village, London.--Comyn
Ching Triangle, urban project.--
Henley Royal Regatta
headquarters.--TV-am
headquarters.--Midland Bank &
offices.--Embankment Place, urban
project.--Alban Gate, offices &
housing.--Vauxhall Cross,
government offices.--The South
Bank.--Hungerford Bridge walkway
project.--Brief history. Text in
Japanese and English.
ARCHITECTURE AND URBANISM 1989
Dec., no.12(231), p.[37]-132,
port., elevs., models, photos.,
plans, secns., site plans.
Tobacco Dock in London.
Warehouse converted into shopping
center. Original architect: Daniel
Asher Alexander. Conversion
architects: Terry Farrell &
Company.
DEUTSCHE BAUZEITSCHRIFT 1990 Apr.,
v.38, no.4, p.499-508, dets.,
photos., plan, site plan.
Tobacco Dock, London.
Conversion of a warehouse into a
commercial development.
Architects: Terry Farrell & Co.
DETAIL 1990 Oct.-Nov., v.30, no.5,
p.494-497, dets., elevs., photos.,
plans, secns., site plan.

SHOPPING CENTERS--ENGLAND--SAINT
ALBANS--SAINSBURY'S SAVACENTRE
Savacentre, London Colney.
A "hypermarket" for one-stop
shopping, at Barnet Road.
Architect: Percy Thomas
Partnership.
BUILDING 1990 June 22, v.255,
no.25, p.43-48, diagrs., photos.,
plan, secns., site plan.

SHOPPING CENTERS--ENGLAND--
WINCHESTER--BROOKS
Winchester pump action / Graham
Ridout.
PRoblems with groundwater level
control and nearby buildings
during construction of the Brooks
shopping centre. Architect:
Building Design Partnership.
(Continued next page)

SHOPPING CENTERS--ENGLAND--
WINCHESTER--BROOKS (CONTINUED)
Winchester pump...(CONTINUED)
BUILDING 1990 Apr.20, v.255,
no.16, p.61-65, photos., secns.

SHOPPING CENTERS--EUROPE
Waren-Welt, oder: die Lust,
Passanten zu verfuhren /
Klaus-Dieter Weiss.
Features several European shopping
centers and malls.
DEUTSCHE BAUZEITSCHRIFT 1990 Oct.,
v.38, no.10, p.1403-1410,1413,
photos., refs.

SHOPPING CENTERS--FRANCE
Shedlands / F.A. Pater.
Critical analysis of contemporary
retail/commercial building which
lines the routes into many
provincial French towns.
ARCHITECTURAL REVIEW 1990 May,
v.187, no.1119, p.102, photos.

SHOPPING CENTERS--FRANCE--DIJON
Fins de chantiers.
Contents: Shopping center, Parc de
la Toison-d'Or, Les Quartiers de
Pouilly, Dijon; architects:
Jean-Marie Charpentier, Francois
Ceria and Alain Coupel -- Public
library, Veyras; architects:
Olivier Arene and Christine
Edeikins.
LE MONITEUR ARCHITECTURE AMC 1990
June, no.12, p.9-10,14-17,
photos., plans, secn.

SHOPPING CENTERS--FRANCE--
FRANCONVILLE--CIRCUIT ET COURT
Flatterndes Gewand: Einkaufszentrum
Circuit et Court in Franconville,
Frankreich.
Architects: Cuno Brullmann and
Fougeras Lavergnolle, with Stefan
Nil and Jean-Jacques Cachau.
WERK, BAUEN + WOHNEN 1990 Nov.,
no.11, p.14-15, photos., plan,
site plan.

SHOPPING CENTERS--FRANCE--
SAINT-NAZAIRE--CENTRE REPUBLIQUE
Urban Mun / Frances Anderton.
On the Centre Republique,
Saint-Nazaire. Architect: Claude
Vasconi.
ARCHITECTURAL REVIEW 1990 Jan.,
v.187, no.1115, p.70-74, det.,
dwg., photos., plans, secns., site
plan.

SHOPPING CENTERS--GERMANY (WEST)
Planning for retail change in West
Germany / Joachim Zentes, Werner
Schwarz-Zanetti.
BUILT ENVIRONMENT 1988, v.14,
no.1, p.38-46, charts, photos,
refs.

SHOPPING CENTERS--GERMANY (WEST)--
COLOGNE--HEUMARKT
Special feature: Gottfried Bohm.
Contents: Essay:
"Ja...was...mochten wir nicht
alles!" (Yes...what...isn't all we
want!) / Manfred Speidel-- Works:
Renovation of Saarbrucken Palace--
Assembly hall at the Folkwang
School-- University library and
auditorium in Mannheim-- Der
Heumarkt in Koln-- Project for
(Continued next column)

SHOPPING CENTERS--GERMANY (WEST)--
COLOGNE--HEUMARKT (CONTINUED)
Special feature:...(CONTINUED)
German Pavilion at Expo in
Seville-- Project for museum
extension in Hamburg-- Project for
International Tribunal for the Law
of the Sea in Hamburg. Text in
Japanese and English.
ARCHITECTURE AND URBANISM 1990
Sept., no.9(240), p.[51]-[128],
axonometric views, elevs.,
photos., plans, secns., site
plans, sketches.

SHOPPING CENTERS--GERMANY (WEST)--
FRIEDRICHSHAFEN--FAUF- UND PARKHAUS
Kaufhaus ahoi! Kauf-und Parkhaus in
Friedrichshafen.
Architektengruppe F 70 Manfred
Sass und Partner.
DEUTSCHE BAUZEITUNG 1990 Oct.,
v.124, no.10, p.62-66, photos.,
plans, secns., site plan.

SHOPPING CENTERS--GERMANY (WEST)--
FRIEDRICHSHAFEN--KAUF- UND PARKHAUS
Kauf- und Parkhaus Friedrichshafen.
Architects: Architektengruppe F70,
Manfred Sass + Partner.
BAUWELT 1990 Aug.17, v.81, no.31,
p.1514, photos., plan.

SHOPPING CENTERS--GERMANY (WEST)--
HAMBURG--BLEICHENHOF
Hamburgs Neunte: der Bleichenhof in
Hamburg / Dirk Meyhofer.
Architects: Nietz Prasch Sigl.
DEUTSCHE BAUZEITUNG 1990 Oct.,
v.124, no.10, p.26-31, maps,
photos., plans, secns.

SHOPPING CENTERS--IRELAND--CORK--
DOUGLAS COURT
Douglas Court, Cork.
Shopping center, Cork, Ireland.
Architects: Kelly and Barry &
Associates.
PLAN: ARCHITECTURE + BUILDING
DESIGN IN IRELAND 1990 Apr., v.29,
no.4, p.2-10, photos., plan.

SHOPPING CENTERS--IRELAND--DUBLIN--
MERRION CENTRE
Merrion Centre, phase 2, Dublin.
Additional shopping areas and new
office space for mixed-use
complex. Architects: Clinton
Associates.
PLAN: ARCHITECTURE AND BUILDING
DESIGN IN IRELAND 1990 July, v.32,
no.7, p.3-8, dwgs., photos., plan,
secn.

SHOPPING CENTERS--ITALY--PARMA--CENTRO
TORRI
Centro commerciale a Parma =
Shopping centre in Parma /
Giancarlo Priori.
In the San Leonardo district;
completed in Sept.1988.
Architects: Aldo Rossi, Gianni
Braghieri. Includes English
translation. French, German, and
Spanish summaries, p.3.
L'INDUSTRIA DELLE COSTRUZIONI 1990
Mar., v.24, no.221, p.16-23,
dwgs., elev., photos., plan.

SHOPPING CENTERS--ITALY--PARMA--CENTRO
TORRI (CONTINUED)
Raume des Alltags: Einkaufszentrum
in Parma und Interieurs in
Barcelona.
Torri center (1989), architect:
Aldo Rossi, Gianni Braghieri; and
Ekseption interiors (1989);
architect: Eduard Samso. Text in
German; summaries in German,
French, and English.
WERK, BAUEN + WOHNEN 1990 June,
no.6, p.54-65, axonometric views,
elevs., photos., plans, site
plans, sketches.

SHOPPING CENTERS--ITALY--VALMADRERA
Complesso residenziale e commerciale
a Valmadrera, Como.
Architect: Giovanni Rigoli.
English, French, German, and
Spanish summaries.
ARCHITETTURA; CRONACHE E STORIA
1990 June, v.36, no.6(416),
p.[418]-425, photos., elevs.,
plans, secns., site plans.

SHOPPING CENTERS--JAPAN--KYOTO--SYNTAX
Rapport de forces: Syntax a Kyoto.
Syntax, four-story shopping
center. Architects: Shin
Takamatsu, Architect and
Associates.
ARCHITECTURE INTERIEURE CREE 1990
Oct.-Nov., no.239, p.115-117,
photos., plan, secn.
Syntax / Shin Takamatsu.
Feature four-story shopping
center, Sakyo Ward, Kyoto.
Architects: Shin Takamatsu,
Architect and Associates.
JAPAN ARCHITECT 1990 June, v.65,
no.6(398), p.[56]-66, elev.,
models, photos., secns.

SHOPPING CENTERS--JAPAN--OSAKA--
GALLERIA AKKA
Osaka Akka.
On the Galleria Akka Shopping
Center and art gallery, Osaka.
Architect: Tadao Ando.
ARCHITECTURAL REVIEW 1990 Jan.,
v.187, no.1115, p.[47]-51,
photos., plans, secns., isometric
dwgs.

SHOPPING CENTERS--NETHERLANDS
Planning for retail change in the
Netherlands / Johan G. Borchert.
BUILT ENVIRONMENT 1988, v.14,
no.1, p.22-37, graph, photo,
tables, aerial photo, refs.

SHOPPING CENTERS--NEW ZEALAND
Retailing: a peep into the future /
Gordon Davies.
In New Zealand.
PLANNING QUARTERLY 1989 Sept.,
no.95, p.5-10, photos., tables

SHOPPING CENTERS--NEW ZEALAND--
WANGANUI--TRAFALGAR SQUARE
Wanganui welcomes the big guys / Jan
Wotton, Usman Ali.
Real estate development in the
form of large retail stores in the
New Zealand provincial city of
Wanganui.
PLANNING QUARTERLY 1989 Sept.,
no.95, p.21-23, photos., plans.

SHOPPING MALLS--ENGLAND--HATFIELD--A1
GALLERIAS
Top shop / Bruce Meechan.
On the A1 Gallerias shopping mall,
Hatfield. Mall spans motorway
tunnel. Architects: Aukett
Associates.
BUILDING DESIGN 1990 June, suppl.,
p.10-11, model, photo., secns.

SHOPPING MALLS--ENGLAND--SHEFFIELD--
MEADOWHALL
Inside fortress shopping / Carl
Gardner.
On the Meadowhall shopping mall,
Sheffield. Architects: Chapman
Taylor Partners.
RIBA JOURNAL 1990 Nov., v.97,
no.11, p.70-74, photos., plan.
Spending on a grand scale / Joe
Holyoak.
On Meadowhall Centre, a shopping
center and mall in the English
Midlands near Sheffield.
Architects: Chapman Taylor
Partners. Includes second article
on "Mall details", p.49-51.
ARCHITECTS' JOURNAL 1990 Nov.21,
v.192, no.20, p.32-43,49-51,
dets., map, photos., plans,
secns., site plan, refs.

SHOPPING MALLS--EUROPE
Waren-Welt, oder: die Lust,
Passanten zu verfuhren /
Klaus-Dieter Weiss.
Features several European shopping
centers and malls.
DEUTSCHE BAUZEITSCHRIFT 1990 Oct.,
v.38, no.10, p.1403-1410,1413,
photos., refs.

SHOPPING MALLS--FRANCE--
CHARENTON-LE-PONT--BERCY 2
Centro commerciale a Parigi di Renzo
Piano - Building Workshop.
At the intersection of the Seine
and Boulevard Peripherique.
English translation, p.59.
CASABELLA 1990 Sept., v.54,
no.571, p.4-9, photos., plans,
secn., site plan, aerial photo.
Un futur si procke: centre
commercial de Bercy 2 a Charenton
de Pont.
Architects: Building Workshop,
Renzo Piano.
ARCHITECTURE INTERIEURE CREE 1990
Oct.-Nov., no.239, p.118-119,
photos.
Piano a Bercy / Jean-Pierre Menard.
Focus on the shell structure of
the Bercy 2 shopping mall,
Charenton. Architects: Renzo
Piano, Building Workshop. English
summary, p.166.
ARCHITECTURE D'AUJOURD'HUI 1990
June, no.269, p.[162]-166, dets.,
models, photos., secn.
Special report: shopping centres
Theme issue on shopping centers
and shopping malls, including
Bercy 2, Charenton-le-Pont,
architect: Renzo Piano and
Zaailand, Leeuwarden, Netherlands,
architects: Architektenbureau
Lucas en Ellerman.
BUILDING DESIGN 1990 Apr., suppl.,
p.2-21, axonometric views, dets.,
models, dwgs., photos., plans,
secns., site plans, aerial photos.

SHOPPING MALLS--GERMANY (WEST)--
FRANKFURT AM MAIN--NORDWEST-ZENTRUM
FRANKFURT
Erst ode, jetzt edel:
Revitalisierung des
Nordwest-Zentrums Frankfurt.
Architects: Architekten RKW.
ARCHITEKTUR, INNENARCHITEKTUR,
TECHNISCHER AUSBAU 1989 Sept.,
v.97, no.9, p.12-16, photos.,
secn., site plan, aerial photos.

SHOPPING MALLS--NETHERLANDS--
LEEUWARDEN--ZAAILAND
Special report: shopping centres.
Theme issue on shopping centers
and shopping malls, including
Bercy 2, Charenton-le-Pont,
architect: Renzo Piano and
Zaailand, Leeuwarden, Netherlands,
architects: Architektenbureau
Lucas en Ellerman.
BUILDING DESIGN 1990 Apr., suppl.,
p.2-21, axonometric views, dets.,
models, dwgs., photos., plans,
secns., site plans, aerial photos.

SHOPPING MALLS--TEMPORARY--UNITED
STATES--SANTA CRUZ (CALIFORNIA)--
PHOENIX PAVILIONS
Post-earthquake placemaking in
downtown Santa Cruz / James E.
Pepper.
Destruction of the Pacific Garden
Mall in Santa Cruz by a
seven-tent, 34,000 sq. ft.
temporary complex known as the
Phoenix Pavilions.
PLACES 1990 Spring, v.6, no.3,
p.92-93, photos., plans.

SHOPPING MALLS--UNITED STATES--CHICAGO
(ILLINOIS)--1800 CLYBOURN
Spirited rebirths / Karen E. Klages.
Two Chicago projects by
Pappageorge Haymes: adaptive reuse
of the Turtle Wax factory at 1800
Clybourn, Chicago into a shopping
mall, and renovation of the 1910
warehouse at 750 North Orleans St.
for BMT Design.
INLAND ARCHITECT 1990 Nov.-Dec.,
v.34, no.6, p.6-7, photos., plans.

SHOPPING MALLS--UNITED STATES--DALLAS
(TEXAS)--GALLERIA
Dallas Galleria, Dallas, Texas, USA,
1983.
Architects: Hellmuth, Obata &
Kassabaum, with Kendall Heaton
Associates. Text in Japanese and
English.
ARCHITECTURE AND URBANISM 1990
Dec., no.12 extra edition,
p.58-[65], photos., plans, secns.,
site plan.

SHOPPING MALLS--UNITED STATES--NEW
YORK (NEW YORK)
Stadt als "Interieur": Malls in New
York.
Text in German; summaries in
German, French and English.
WERK, BAUEN + WOHNEN 1990 June,
no.6, p.46-53, map, photos.

SHOPPING MALLS--UNITED STATES--NEW
YORK (NEW YORK)--A & S PLAZA
Reshuffling the deck: Building Types
Study 677: Retail facilities /
Clifford A. Pearson.
Fashion Island, Newport Beach,
Calif. (Jerde Partnership), North
Pier, Chicago (Booth Hansen &
Assoc., The Austin Co.); Napa Town
Center, Napa Calif. (Field Paoli
Architects); and A & S Plaza, New
York City (RTKL Assoc.).
ARCHITECTURAL RECORD 1990 Apr.,
v.178, no.4, p.97-111, photos.,
plans, secns., site plans.

SHOPPING MALLS--UNITED STATES--NEWPORT
BEACH (CALIFORNIA)--FASHION ISLAND
Reshuffling the deck: Building Types
Study 677: Retail facilities /
Clifford A. Pearson.
Fashion Island, Newport Beach,
Calif. (Jerde Partnership), North
Pier, Chicago (Booth Hansen &
Assoc., The Austin Co.); Napa Town
Center, Napa Calif. (Field Paoli
Architects); and A & S Plaza, New
York City (RTKL Assoc.).
ARCHITECTURAL RECORD 1990 Apr.,
v.178, no.4, p.97-111, photos.,
plans, secns., site plans.

SHOPPING MALLS--UNITED STATES--SANTA
CRUZ (CALIFORNIA)--PACIFIC GARDEN
MALL
Post-earthquake placemaking in
downtown Santa Cruz / James E.
Pepper.
Destruction of the Pacific Garden
Mall in Santa Cruz by a
seven-tent, 34,000 sq. ft.
temporary complex known as the
Phoenix Pavilions.
PLACES 1990 Spring, v.6, no.3,
p.92-93, photos., plans.

SHOPS
See STORES

SHOPS--INTERIOR DESIGN--DENMARK--
COPENHAGEN--C7 DESIGN
C7 Design, Kobenhavn.
A small exhibition space for
designer products, on Grabrodre
Torv square. Architect: Charlotte
Weile. Includes English caption.
ARKITEKTUR DK 1990, v.34, no.3,
p.132, photos., plan.

SHORE, LISA
A community takes charge / Lisa
Shore.
Creation of a playground in Lake
Waterford Park, Pasadena, Md.
PARKS & RECREATION 1990 Aug.,
v.25, no.8, p.30-35,71, photos.

SHORE TILBE HENSCHEL IRWIN PETERS
Police hospitality: Metropolitan
Toronto Police Headquarters /
Clifford A. Pearson.
Architect: Shore Tilbe Henschel
Irwin Peters. Architects and
Engineers; Mathers & Haldenby.
ARCHITECTURAL RECORD 1990 Nov.,
v.178, no.12, p.84-[89], elev.,
photos., plans, secn., site plan,

SHORT AND FORD ARCHITECTS
Design awards [New Jersey Society of
Architects 1989 Design Awards
Competition].
Excellence in architecture awards
to The Hillier Group; Frederick
Schmitt; Michael Graves; Short and
Ford; Venturi, Rauch and Scott
Brown. Other awards also included.
ARCHITECTURE NEW JERSEY 1990,
v.26, no.1, p.9-24, axonometric
view, dwgs., elevs., models,
photos., plans, secns.

SHORTELL, ELLEN
An image of the Abbey Church of
Premontre under construction /
Ellen Shortell.
Stained glass made in 1643 by Jean
de Caumont for the cloister of the
Premonstratension abbey of Parc,
Louvain. Includes abstract.
GESTA 1990, v.29, no.2, p.234-238,
photos., refs.

SHORTT, BARBARA
Coordination design effort for new
French trains / Barbara Shortt.
On the French train system, Train
a Grande Vitesse (TGV) Atlantique.
PROGRESSIVE ARCHITECTURE 1990
Sept., v.71, no.9, p.28,30,
photos.
Kudos for an American museum in
France / Barbara Shortt.
The Musee national de la
cooperation franco-americaine,
Blerancourt, wins the 1989 Equerre
d'Argent prize. Architects: Yves
Lion and Alan Levitt. Original
chateau architect: Saloman de
Brosse.
PROGRESSIVE ARCHITECTURE 1990
Aug., v.71, no.8, p.31-32, photos.

SHOTGUN HOUSES--UNITED STATES--NEW
MEXICO
Oil patch shacks: boom town housing
in New Mexico's little Texas /
Boyd C. Pratt.
TRIGLYPH 1989-1990 Winter, no.9,
p.34-47, maps, photos., refs.

SHOUP, CHARLES
Staging a Greek revival: Charles
Shoup's villa on the Peloponnese /
Malise Ruthven.
Features interiors of
artist/architect's neoclassical
style home in Greece.
ARCHITECTURAL DIGEST 1990 June,
v.47, no.6, p.[128-137], port.,
photos.

SHOW HOUSES
See DECORATORS' SHOW HOUSES

SHOW-WINDOWS--UNITED STATES--NEW YORK
(NEW YORK)--SAKS FIFTH AVENUE
Through the fourth wall / Kristen
Richards.
Window designs at Saks Fifth
Avenue, New York, feature
architectural conference scenarios
with models from Kohn Pederson Fox
and Robert A.M. Stern tables.
INTERIORS 1990 July, v.149, no.12,
p.68-69, photos.

SHOWA
See "SHOWA" AS A SUBHEADING AFTER
SPECIFIC BUILDING TYPES OR OTHER
MAIN HEADINGS.

SHOWROOMS
See also DESIGN CENTERS

SHOWROOMS--AUTOMOBILE--GERMANY
(WEST)--AURICH--MERCEDES-BENZ
Autoschauhauser - Glasvitrinen fur
Ulumschtraume / Klaus Idelberger.
Features three automobile
showrooms in W. Germany with glass
facades.
DEUTSCHE BAUZEITSCHRIFT 1989 Dec.,
v.37, no.12, p.1629-1634, photos.,
plans, secns.

SHOWROOMS--AUTOMOBILE--GERMANY
(WEST)--ESSEN-LEUG
Autoschauhauser - Glasvitrinen fur
Ulumschtraume / Klaus Idelberger.
Features three automobile
showrooms in W. Germany with glass
facades.
DEUTSCHE BAUZEITSCHRIFT 1989 Dec.,
v.37, no.12, p.1629-1634, photos.,
plans, secns.

SHOWROOMS--AUTOMOBILE--GERMANY
(WEST)--KRONBERG--JAGUAR DEUTSCHLAND
Autoschauhauser - Glasvitrinen fur
Ulumschtraume / Klaus Idelberger.
Features three automobile
showrooms in W. Germany with glass
facades.
DEUTSCHE BAUZEITSCHRIFT 1989 Dec.,
v.37, no.12, p.1629-1634, photos.,
plans, secns.

SHOWROOMS--AUTOMOBILE--GERMANY
(WEST)--STUTTGART--MERCEDES-BENZ
Erlebenswertes Buro-Ambiente: mit
"Gesika Nova," ein Autohaus zeigt
Flagge / Petra Lasar.
Mercedes dealership, Stuttgart.
Architects: W. Held, G. Varga.
ARCHITEKTUR, INNENARCHITEKTUR,
TECHNISCHER AUSBAU 1990 Apr.,
v.98, no.4, p.100-102, photos.

SHOWROOMS--AUTOMOBILE--JAPAN--TOKYO--
TOWER OF SILENCE
Ranalli's tower [of silence].
Project for the center of Tokyo,
by American architect George
Ranalli. In Danish and English.
SKALA 1990, no.22, p.10-11, model.
Special feature: George Ranalli.
Contents: Essays: George Ranalli
statement: elements of
architecture/ George Ranalli--
Autonomous structures/ Ross
Miller--Interview: George Ranalli/
Ross Miller--Works 1979-1989:
Callender school renovation,
Newport, R.I.--Ranalli studio
apartment, New York City,
1982-83--Peak competition project,
Hong Kong, 1982--Paris Opera
competition project, 1983--Chicago
Tribune competition project,
1980--Times Tower competition
project, 1984--New York loft,
1985-86--Valentine chair--House
addition for "G" family,
Westchester, New York, 1987-88--
Conversion of barn to residence,
Red Hook, N.Y., 1988-89--K project
"Tower of Silence," Tokyo, Japan,
1989. Text in Japanese and
(Continued next column)

SHOWROOMS--AUTOMOBILE--JAPAN--TOKYO--
TOWER OF SILENCE (CONTINUED)
Special feature:... (CONTINUED)
English.
ARCHITECTURE AND URBANISM 1990
Aug., no.8(239), p.[71-136],
axonometric views, port., elevs.,
models, photos., plans, secns.,
site plans.

SHOWROOMS--AUTOMOBILE--UNITED STATES--
ENGLEWOOD (NEW JERSEY)--MERCEDES
BENZ
Emilio Ambasz: recent works.
Includes Nichii Obihiro Department
Store, various products, and
Mercedes Benz Showroom, New
Jersey. In Japanese and English.
SPACE DESIGN 1990 Feb., no.305,
p.102-106, models, photos., secns.

SHOWROOMS--CLOTHING--ENGLAND--LONDON--
CENTRAL LONDON FASHION SHOWROOMS
Current concerns / Clare Melhuish.
Features two London projects by
Bernhard Blauel: Central London
Fashion Showrooms and East Bank
Studio.
BUILDING DESIGN 1990 Apr.20,
no.982, p.24-26, axonometric
views, elevs., model, photos.,
plan.

SHOWROOMS--CLOTHING--INTERIOR DESIGN--
ENGLAND--LONDON--NICOLE FARHI
Cafe couture / Leslie Geddes-Brown.
Features interiors of Nicole Farhi
couture showroom, Soho, London.
Interior designers: Din
Associates.
THE WORLD OF INTERIORS 1990 Feb.,
p.116-121, port., photos.

SHOWROOMS--CLOTHING--JAPAN--TOKYO--
COLLECTIONE
"Collectione"-Italian fashion in
Tokyo / G. G. Feldmeyer.
Features two showrooms in the
Collectione building, Tokyo.
Architect: Tadao Ando.
DEUTSCHE BAUZEITSCHRIFT 1990 Nov.,
v.38, no.11, p.[1579]-1582,
photos.

SHOWROOMS--CLOTHING--JAPAN--TOKYO--
POINT UP
Point Up showroom.
Clothing showroom, Kita-Aoyama
3-5-6, Tokyo, 1986. Architect:
Tashiro Otsuka.
ARCHITECTURE D'AUJOURD'HUI 1990
Oct., no.271, p.244-245,
axonometric view, photos.

SHOWROOMS--CLOTHING--SPAIN--MADRID--
JESUS DEL POZO
Showroom Jesus del Pozo, Madrid;
Alberto Campo Baeza, Antonio
Romero Fernandez / Duccio
Malagamba.
In Italian and English.
DOMUS 1990 July-Aug., no.718,
p.[57-59], axonometric views,
photos.

SHOWROOMS--CLOTHING--UNITED STATES--
LOS ANGELES (CALIFORNIA)--LEON MAX
Show-room in L.A.: Leon Max
show-room, 127, East Ninth Street,
Los Angeles / Birgit C. Dietsch.
Architect: Morphosis.
BAUWELT 1990 Sept.7, v.81, no.34,
p.1690-1691, photos., plans.

SHOWROOMS--COMPUTER--INTERIOR DESIGN--
FRANCE--PARIS--APPLE
[Amenagement interieur]: commerces.
Contents: Boutique Koshino, Paris
VIIe; architect: Jean-Michel
Wilmotte-- Apple showroom, ave. de
la Grande Armee, Paris; architect:
Berbesson Racine et Associes--
Castelli showroom, Paris;
designer: Ronald Cecil Sportes--
Unifor furniture showroom, Milan,
Italy; architects: Afra & Tobia
Scarpa-- Boutique Jean-Louis
Imbert, Marseille, France;
architect: Rudy Ricciotti--
Recorded music store, Nantes,
France; architect: Studio Naco.
LE MONITEUR ARCHITECTURE AMC 1990
July-Aug., no.13, p.36-45,
axonometric views, photos., plans.

SHOWROOMS--COMPUTER--UNITED STATES--
DALLAS (TEXAS)--INFOMART--APPLE
COMPUTER MARKET CENTER
Interiors [five Dallas showrooms].
Apple Computer Market Center
(Gensler & Associates); W. Joe
Sanders, (Gensler & Associates);
Gunlocke (Hermanovski Lauck);
DesignTex Fabrics (Hermanovski
Lauck): and Haworth Interiors
(HOK).
TEXAS ARCHITECT 1990 May-June,
v.40, no.3, p.40-47, photos,
plans.

SHOWROOMS--DESIGN--INTERIOR DESIGN--
UNITED STATES --CHICAGO (ILLINOIS)--
ICF
ICF, Chicago / Edie Lee Cohen.
Interiors of showroom in the
Chicago Merchandise Mart designed
by Janine James.
INTERIOR DESIGN 1990 Jan., v.61,
no.1, p.180-[183], photos. plan.

SHOWROOMS--DESIGN--SPAIN--BARCELONA--
GAYA
Comercio de Ceramicas Gaya.
Showroom for ceramic products,
Barcelona. Designers: Magi
Boronat, Josep Maria Magem.
English text, p.191-192.
ON DISENO 1990, "Ceramica" suppl.,
p.141-146, photos., plan.

SHOWROOMS--DESIGN--SPAIN--MADRID--PAZ
Y CIA
Paz y Cia, Madrid.
Showroom for ceramic products.
Architects: Javier and Carlos
Climent.
ON DISENO 1990, "ceramica" suppl.,
p.156-159, photos.

SHOWROOMS--DESIGN--SPAIN--TAU CERAMICA
Taugres: estructura arquitectonica
de A. Bofill.
Showroom for ceramic products.
Architects: Taller de
Arquitectura.
ON DISENO 1990, "ceramica" suppl.,
p.160-161, photos.

SHOWROOMS--DESIGN--UNITED STATES--
KOHLER (WISCONSIN)--KOHLER DESIGN
CENTER
Fresh ideas from Kohler / Karen
Maserjian.
Features showrooms at the Kohler
Design Center, Kohler, Wisc.
INTERIOR DESIGN 1990 Apr., v.61,
no.6, p.210-[211], photos.

SHOWROOMS--ENGLAND--BLACKBURN--LEO
DESIGN CENTRE
Floor coverings: products survey /
Penny McGuire.
Survey of samples on view at the
Leo Design Centre, Blackburn, a
floor coverings showroom.
ARCHITECTURAL REVIEW 1990 Jan.,
v.187, no.1115, p.83-91, photos.

SHOWROOMS--ENGLAND--LONDON--ELEMENTER
Space makers.
Features two projects by Armstrong
Associates: Elementer Showroom,
London; artists' studios, Maida
Vale.
BUILDING DESIGN 1989 Oct., suppl.,
p.45, axonometric views, dwgs.,
model, plans, isometric dwg.

SHOWROOMS--ENGLAND--ROCHESTER--JCB
Fantasy factor / Jan Burney.
JCB heavy machinery showroom,
Rochester, Staffordshire.
Architects: Fitch-RS.
BUILDING DESIGN 1989 Oct., suppl.,
p.42-43, photos.

SHOWROOMS--FRANCE--TOULOUSE--ESPACE
TECHNAL
L'alu s'expose.
On the Espace Technal showroom,
Toulouse. Architect: Jean-Michel
Wilmotte.
TECHNIQUES ET ARCHITECTURE 1990
June-July, no.390, p.169, photos.

SHOWROOMS--FURNITURE--ALTERATIONS AND
ADDITIONS--ENGLAND--LONDON--PROJECT
Adding finesse: Project showroom
Euston / Matthew Coomber.
Refurbishment of a 1960s showroom
for office furniture in London.
Architect: ORMS.
BUILDING 1990 Sept.7, v.255,
no.35, p.74-75, photos.

SHOWROOMS--FURNITURE--BELGIUM--
ANTWERP--INSOLITO
Insolito Showroom.
A showroom for displaying lighting
and furniture located in an
Antwerp town house. Architect: Jan
van Lierde. In Italian and
English.
ABITARE 1990 Mar., no.283,
p.130-[133], photos., plans.

SHOWROOMS--FURNITURE--DENMARK--
COPENHAGEN--PAUSTIAN
La "foresta" di Utzon a Copenhagen /
Christian Norberg-Schultz.
The Paustian furniture showroom.
Includes English captions.
CASABELLA 1990 Dec., v.54, no.574,
p.38-39, photos., plan, secns.,
sketch.
Paustians hus / Christian
Norberg-Schulz.
A furniture showroom and
restaurant at Kalkbroenderilobskaj
2, Copenhagen. Architect: Utzon
(Continued next column)

SHOWROOMS--FURNITURE--DENMARK--
COPENHAGEN--PAUSTIAN (CONTINUED)
Paustians hus /...(CONTINUED)
Associates. Includes commentary
by Boje Lundgaard. Includes
English and German captions and
summaries.
ARKITEKTUR DK 1989, v.33, no.8,
p.353-369, photos., plans, secns.,
site plans, sketches.

SHOWROOMS--FURNITURE--FRANCE--PARIS--
CASTELLI
Docks Castelli, quai 25.
Furniture showroom, Paris.
Architect: Roland Cecil Sportes.
Includes interview with Claude
Gozlan, general manager of
Castelli France.
ARCHITECTURE INTERIEURE CREE 1990
Aug.-Sept., no.238, p.180-185,
dets., ports., photos., secn.
Partition marine: l'espace Castelli
a Paris.
Furniture showroom. Architect:
Ronald Cecil Sportes.
TECHNIQUES ET ARCHITECTURE 1990
Aug.-Sept., no.391, p.156-157,
axonometric views, dets., photos.

SHOWROOMS--FURNITURE--FRANCE--PARIS--
SOCIETE IMMOBILIERE DE PRESTIGE
En rupture / Christine Colin.
Features interiors of Paris
furniture showroom, Societe
Immobiliere de Prestige.
ARCHITECTURE INTERIEURE CREE 1990
Apr.-May, no.236, p.[118-119],
photos.

SHOWROOMS--FURNITURE--INTERIOR
DESIGN--FRANCE--PARIS--CASTELLI
[Amenagement interieur]: commerces.
Contents: Boutique Koshino, Paris
VIIe; architect: Jean-Michel
Wilmotte-- Apple showroom, ave. de
la Grande Armee, Paris; architect:
Berbesson Racine et Associes--
Castelli showroom, Paris;
designer: Ronald Cecil Sportes--
Unifor furniture showroom, Milan,
Italy; architects: Afra & Tobia
Scarpa-- Boutique Jean-Louis
Imbert, Marseille, France;
architect: Rudy Ricciotti--
Recorded music store, Nantes,
France; architect: Studio Naco.
LE MONITEUR ARCHITECTURE AMC 1990
July-Aug., no.13, p.36-45,
axonometric views, photos., plans.

SHOWROOMS--FURNITURE--INTERIOR
DESIGN--FRANCE--PARIS--ERGAM RONEO
Le showroom Ergam Roneo.
Furniture showroom, Paris.
Architects: B. Grenot, C. Kubicki.
TECHNIQUES ET ARCHITECTURE 1990
Dec.-1991 Jan., no.393, p.148,
photos., plan, secn.

SHOWROOMS--FURNITURE--INTERIOR
DESIGN--UNITED STATES--CHICAGO
(ILLINOIS)--BERNHARDT FURNITURE
Bernhardt Furniture / Judith
Davidsen.
Interiors of redesigned Chicago
Merchandise Mart showroom.
Interior designers: Vanderbyl
Design.
INTERIOR DESIGN 1990 Oct., v.61,
no.14, p.248-[251], photos.,
isometric dwg.

SHOWROOMS--FURNITURE--INTERIOR
DESIGN--UNITED STATES--CHICAGO
(ILLINOIS)--STEELCASE
Steelcase, Inc. / Monica Geran.
Interiors of Chicago showroom
designed by the firm's in-house
design team.
INTERIOR DESIGN 1990 Oct., v.61,
no.14, p.246-[247], photos.

SHOWROOMS--FURNITURE--INTERIOR
DESIGN--UNITED STATES--LOS ANGELES
(CALIFORNIA)--ATELIER INTERNATIONAL
Atelier International / Judith
Nasatir.
Interiors of furniture showroom in
the Pacific Design Center, Los
Angeles. Interior designers:
Richard Penney Group.
INTERIOR DESIGN 1990 Feb., v.61,
no.3, p.[220-223], photos., plan.

SHOWROOMS--FURNITURE--INTERIOR
DESIGN--UNITED STATES--QUEENS (NEW
YORK)--BRIGHT CHAIR CO.
Bright Chair Co.: ISD Incorporated
revitalizes the firm's existing
showroom / Monica Geran.
Located in the IDCNY.
INTERIOR DESIGN 1990 Sept., v.61,
no.12, p.236-[237], dwg., photos.

SHOWROOMS--FURNITURE--ITALY--MILAN--B
& B
Etat, prospectives et
representations de l'industrie
europeenne du bureau.
On the office furniture industry.
Features four showrooms and a
factory by the following
architects: Frank Gehry, Afra and
Tobia Scarpa, Pierluigi Cerri and
Paolo Ferrari. English summary,
p.182-183.
ARCHITECTURE INTERIEURE CREE 1990
Apr.-May, no.236, p.[138-157],153,
ports., elev., photos., plans,
site plan.

SHOWROOMS--FURNITURE--ITALY--MILAN--
UNIFOR
[Amenagement interieur]: commerces.
Contents: Boutique Koshino, Paris
Ville; architect: Jean-Michel
Wilmotte-- Apple showroom, ave. de
la Grande Armee, Paris; architect:
Berbesson Racine et Associes--
Castelli showroom, Paris;
designer: Ronald Cecil Sportes--
Unifor furniture showroom, Milan,
Italy; architects: Afra & Tobia
Scarpa-- Boutique Jean-Louis
Imbert, Marseille, France;
architect: Rudy Ricciotti--
Recorded music store, Nantes,
France; architect: Studio Naco.
LE MONITEUR ARCHITECTURE AMC 1990
July-Aug., no.13, p.36-45,
axonometric views, photos., plans.
Etat, prospectives et
representations de l'industrie
europeenne du bureau.
On the office furniture industry.
Features four showrooms and a
factory by the following
architects: Frank Gehry, Afra and
Tobia Scarpa, Pierluigi Cerri and
Paolo Ferrari. English summary,
p.182-183.
ARCHITECTURE INTERIEURE CREE 1990
Apr.-May, no.236, p.[138-157],153,
ports., elev., photos., plans,
site plan.

SHOWROOMS--FURNITURE--ITALY--MILAN--
UNIFOR (CONTINUED)
Showroom Unifor, Milan.
Furniture showroom. Architects:
Afra and Tobia Scarpa.
TECHNIQUES ET ARCHITECTURE 1990
Mar., no.388, p.126-129, photos.,
plans.

SHOWROOMS--FURNITURE--JAPAN--TOKYO--
CASSINA JAPAN
"Collectione"-Italian fashion in
Tokyo / G. G. Feldmeyer.
Features two showrooms in the
Collectione building, Tokyo.
Architect: Tadao Ando.
DEUTSCHE BAUZEITSCHRIFT 1990 Nov.,
v.38, no.11, p.[1579]-1582,
photos.
East meets west at Cassina.
Cassina Japan showroom, Tokyo,
designed by Mario Bellini is
located in Tadao Ando's collezione
building.
RIBA JOURNAL 1990 Mar., v.97,
no.3, p.64-65, photos., secn.
Etat, prospectives et
representations de l'industrie
europeenne du bureau.
On the office furniture industry.
Features four showrooms and a
factory by the following
architects: Frank Gehry, Afra and
Tobia Scarpa, Pierluigi Cerri and
Paolo Ferrari. English summary,
p.182-183.
ARCHITECTURE INTERIEURE CREE 1990
Apr.-May, no.236, p.[138-157],153,
ports., elev., photos., plans,
site plan.

SHOWROOMS--FURNITURE--JAPAN--TOKYO--
INTERDECOR
Showroom a Tokyo.
Interdecor furniture showroom,
Tokyo. Architects: King-Miranda
Associates.
ARCHITECTURE D'AUJOURD'HUI 1990
Oct., no.271, p.257, photos.

SHOWROOMS--FURNITURE--TEMPORARY--
UNITED STATES--LOS ANGELES
(CALIFORNIA)--VECTA
Stuhle am laufende Baud / Birgit C.
Dietsch.
Two furniture showrooms for Vecta:
New York and Los Angeles.
Architect: Morphosis.
BAUWELT 1990 Sept.7, v.81, no.34,
p.1687-1689, photos., plan.

SHOWROOMS--FURNITURE--TEMPORARY--
UNITED STATES--NEW YORK (NEW YORK)--
STEELCASE DESIGN PARTNERSHIP
Sinuous scenarios / Justin
Henderson.
Stellcse Design Partnership's
temporary showroom design for
Eastweek. Interior designers: FTL
Associates.
INTERIORS 1990 July, v.149, no.12,
p.64-[65], photos., plan.

SHOWROOMS--FURNITURE--TEMPORARY--
UNITED STATES--QUEENS (NEW YORK)--
VECTA
Breaking down the wall: Morphosis
creates a mystifying temporary
exhibition for Vecta at the IDCNY
in New York / Michael Wagner.
INTERIORS 1990 Jan., v.149, no.6,
p.146-147, photos., plan.
Stuhle am laufende Baud / Birgit C.
Dietsch.
Two furniture showrooms for Vecta:
New York and Los Angeles.
Architect: Morphosis.
BAUWELT 1990 Sept.7, v.81, no.34,
p.1687-1689, photos., plan.

SHOWROOMS--FURNITURE--UNITED STATES--
ALLENTOWN (PENNSYLVANIA)--VITRA
SEATING
High-tech in high style / Kristen
Richards.
Focus on Vitra Seating
office/showroom, Allentown, Pa.
Architects: Haigh Space.
INTERIORS 1990 Sept., v.149,
no.14, p.122-125, axonometric
view, photos.

SHOWROOMS--FURNITURE--UNITED STATES--
ATLANTA (GEORGIA)--HERMAN MILLER
Lo spazio che rimalza: Showroom ad
Atlanta.
Architects: Scogin Elam & Bray.
ARCHITETTURA; CRONACHE E STORIA
1990 Mar., v.36, no.3(413),
p.204-205, photos, plan.

SHOWROOMS--FURNITURE--UNITED STATES--
CHICAGO (ILLINOIS)--HAWORTH
Haworth, Inc. / Monica Geran.
Interiors of furniture showroom in
Chicago's Merchandise Mart.
Architects: Tigerman McCurry.
INTERIOR DESIGN 1990 Oct., v.61,
no.14, p.240-243, photos.,
isometric dwg.

SHOWROOMS--FURNITURE--UNITED STATES--
DALLAS (TEXAS)--GUNLOCKE
Gunlocke / Monica Geran.
Interiors of furniture showroom,
Dallas. Interior designers:
Hermanovski Lauck Design.
INTERIOR DESIGN 1990 June, v.61,
no.9, p.248-[249], photos., plan.
Interiors [five Dallas showrooms].
Apple Computer Market Center
(Gensler & Associates); W. Joe
Sanders, (Gensler & Associates);
Gunlocke (Hermanovski Lauck);
DesignTex Fabrics (Hermanovski
Lauck); and Haworth Interiors
(HOK).
TEXAS ARCHITECT 1990 May-June,
v.40, no.3, p.40-47, photos,
plans.

SHOWROOMS--FURNITURE--UNITED STATES--
DALLAS (TEXAS)--HAWORTH
Interiors [five Dallas showrooms].
Apple Computer Market Center
(Gensler & Associates); W. Joe
Sanders, (Gensler & Associates);
Gunlocke (Hermanovski Lauck);
DesignTex Fabrics (Hermanovski
Lauck); and Haworth Interiors
(HOK).
TEXAS ARCHITECT 1990 May-June,
v.40, no.3, p.40-47, photos,
plans.

SHOWROOMS--FURNITURE--UNITED STATES--
DALLAS (TEXAS)--W. JOE SANDERS
Interiors [five Dallas showrooms].
Apple Computer Market Center
(Gensler & Associates); W. Joe
Sanders, (Gensler & Associates);
Gunlocke (Hermanovski Lauck);
DesignTex Fabrics (Hermanovski
Lauck): and Haworth Interiors
(HOK).
TEXAS ARCHITECT 1990 May-June,
v.40, no.3, p.40-47, photos,
plans.

SHOWROOMS--FURNITURE--UNITED STATES--
LOS ANGELES (CALIFORNIA)--BERNHARDT
FURNITURE
Bernhardt, Los Angeles / Judith
Nasatir.
Interiors of furniture showroom in
the Pacific Design Center, Los
Angeles. Interior designers:
Vanderbyl Design.
INTERIOR DESIGN 1990 Feb., v.61,
no.3, p.230-[233], axonometric
view, photos.
Shoebox drama on a shoestring budget
/ Kristen Richards.
Features Bernhardt Furniture
Showroom, Pacific Design Center,
Los Angeles. Designers: Vanderbyl
Design.
INTERIORS 1990 Jan., v.149, no.6,
p.164-165, photos., plan.

SHOWROOMS--FURNITURE--UNITED STATES--
LOS ANGELES (CALIFORNIA)--JAZZ
FURNITURE
Jazz Furniture's PDC showroom by Ron
Rezek.
Located in the Pacific Design
Center, Los Angeles.
INTERIOR DESIGN 1990 May, v.61,
no.7, p.70, photos.

SHOWROOMS--FURNITURE--UNITED STATES--
NEW YORK (NEW YORK)--CHARTWELL GROUP
Chartwell Group in New York / Monica
Geran.
Furniture showroom in the New York
Design Center, better known as 200
Lex. Designers: Salsano
Associates.
INTERIOR DESIGN 1990 Jan., v.61,
no.1, p.188-[191], axonometric
view, photos., plans.

SHOWROOMS--FURNITURE--UNITED STATES--
WASHINGTON (DISTRICT OF COLUMBIA)--
HERMAN MILLER OFFICE PAVILION
Wheeling and dealing / Michael
Wagner.
On the Herman Miller office
Pavilion, Washington, D.C.
Architects: STUDIOS.
INTERIORS 1990 Apr., v.149, no.9,
p.74-[77], photos., plan.

SHOWROOMS--GERMANY (WEST)--
MARKTHEIDENFELD--WAREMA
Sonnenschutz am Glashaus:
Ausstellungspavillon der Firma
Warema in Marktheidenfeld.
Architect: M. Geisendorfer.
ARCHITEKTUR, INNENARCHITEKTUR,
TECHNISCHER AUSBAU 1989 Sept.,
v.97, no.9, p.122-123, photos.

SHOWROOMS--INTERIOR DESIGN
30 years of full-service interior
planning: Milo Kleinberg Design
Associates, Inc. / John L. Wolz.
Interior designers for corporate
office space.
REAL ESTATE FORUM 1989 Dec., v.44,
no.12, p.74-82, ports., photos.

SHOWROOMS--INTERIOR DESIGN--
COMPETITIONS--UNITED STATES--CHICAGO
(ILLINOIS)--NEOCON
8th annual AIA Neocon product
display competition / Paula Rice
Jackson.
Includes 14 winning showrooms in
the Merchandise Mart, Chicago.
INTERIORS 1990 Aug., v.149, no.13,
p.81-87, port., photos.

SHOWROOMS--INTERIOR DESIGN--FRANCE--
PARIS--BERNARD PICTET
Showroom d'un graveur sur verre,
Paris.
Bernard Pictet showroom.
Architects: Francois Fauconnet,
Karin Leopold, Jean-Claude
Marechaux.
ARCHITECTURE D'AUJOURD'HUI 1990
Sept., no.270, p.183, photos.

SHOWROOMS--INTERIOR DESIGN--FRANCE--
TOULOUSE--TECHNAL
Interieurs: Toulouse: un espace du
profile.
Technal 3, rue des Arts.
Architects: Jean-Michel Wilmotte,
Massimo Quendolo.
LE MONITEUR ARCHITECTURE AMC 1990
May, no.11, p.18-20, axonometric
views, photos.
Objets bruts.
Technal showroom, Toulouse.
Interior architect: Jean-Michel
Wilmotte.
ARCHITECTURE INTERIEURE CREE 1990
Oct.-Nov., no.239, p.140-143,
photos.

SHOWROOMS--INTERIOR DESIGN--JAPAN--
TOKYO--CABIN
Lignes de fuite: Eric Raffy, en
piste au Japon.
Interiors of Cabin Showroom,
Tokyo. Architect: Eric Raffy.
TECHNIQUES ET ARCHITECTURE 1990
Mar., no.388, p.124-125, photos.,
plan.

SHOWROOMS--INTERIOR DESIGN--
NETHERLANDS--AMSTERDAM--HULST
SHOWROOM
Le design tel qu'on le vit / Sonia
Rachline.
Features loft/showroom of interior
designer Yvonne Hulst in
Amsterdam. English summary, p.III.
MAISON FRANCAISE 1990 Nov.,
no.441, p.82-[89], photos.

SHOWROOMS--INTERIOR DESIGN--UNITED
STATES--CHICAGO (ILLINOIS)--ALLIED
FIBERS
Allied Fibers / Monica Geran.
Interiors of textile showroom in
Chicago's Merchandise Mart.
Interior designer: Sally O'Malley.
INTERIOR DESIGN 1990 Oct., v.61,
no.14, p.244-[245], photos., plan.

SHOWROOMS--INTERIOR DESIGN--UNITED
STATES--CHICAGO (ILLINOIS)--DEEPA
Timeless textures / Kristen
Richards.
Interiors of Deepa textile
showroom, Chicago. Interior
designers: Loebl, Schlossman and
Hackl.
INTERIORS 1990 July, v.149, no.12,
p.70-[71], photos.

SHOWROOMS--INTERIOR DESIGN--UNITED
STATES--CHICAGO (ILLINOIS)--
INTERFACE FLOORING SYSTEMS
Planned evolution / Jean Gorman.
Interiors of remodeled Interface
Flooring Systems showroom,
Chicago.
INTERIORS 1990 Dec., v.150, no.5,
p.26, photos.

SHOWROOMS--INTERIOR DESIGN--UNITED
STATES--CHICAGO (ILLINOIS)--
LACKAWANNA LEATHER.
Leather pirouettes: Lackawanna
Leather in Chicago / Justin
Henderson.
Showroom designed by Andrew
Belscher Joseph Vincent Design
Partnership.
INTERIORS 1990 Jan., v.149, no.6,
p.184-149, photos., plan.

SHOWROOMS--INTERIOR DESIGN--UNITED
STATES--CHICAGO (ILLINOIS)--VECTA
SHOWROOM
Vecta's Chicago showroom / Gregory
Littleton.
Interior designer: Lee Stout.
INTERIORS 1989 Feb., v.148, no.7,
p.98, photos., plan.

SHOWROOMS--INTERIOR DESIGN--UNITED
STATES--DALLAS (TEXAS)--DESIGNTEX
FABRICS
Interiors [five Dallas showrooms].
Apple Computer Market Center
(Gensler & Associates); W. Joe
Sanders, (Gensler & Associates);
Gunlocke (Hermanovski Lauck);
DesignTex Fabrics (Hermanovski
Lauck): and Haworth Interiors
(HOK).
TEXAS ARCHITECT 1990 May-June,
v.40, no.3, p.40-47, photos,
plans.

SHOWROOMS--INTERIOR DESIGN--UNITED
STATES--DANIA (FLORIDA)--JERRY PAIR
Jerry pair / Mayer Rus.
Showroom interiors in the Design
Center of the Americas (DCOTA) in
Dania, Fl. Interior designers:
Richard Plumer Design.
INTERIOR DESIGN 1990 Jan., v.61,
no.1, p.202-205, photos., plan.

SHOWROOMS--INTERIOR DESIGN--UNITED
STATES--LOS ANGELES (CALIFORNIA)--
HARPERS
Harpers / Edie Lee Cohen.
Interiors of showroom in the
Pacific Design Center, Los
Angeles. Architects: Lomax Rock
Associates Architects. Interior
designer: George Kaneko.
INTERIOR DESIGN 1990 Feb., v.61,
no.3, p.226-[229], axonometric
view, photos.

SHOWROOMS--INTERIOR DESIGN--UNITED
STATES--QUEENS (NEW YORK)--AMERICAN
STANDARD
American Standard / Monica Geran.
Interiors of IDCNY showroom
designed by Tigerman McCurry.
INTERIOR DESIGN 1990 Sept., v.61,
no.12, p.238-[241], dwgs., photos.

SHOWROOMS--ITALY--TOLENTINO--POLTRONA
FRAU
Purely Italian / Alice S. Feiring.
Poltrona Fran Showroom, Tolentino,
Italy. Interior designers:
Vignelli Associates.
INTERIORS 1990 Aug., v.149, no.13,
p.92-95, photos., plan.

SHOWROOMS--JAPAN--TOKYO--KOIZUMI
SANGYO BUILDING
Peter Eisenman.
Most of the issue devoted to this
architect. Nine projects featured.
Includes interview with David
Cohn. Text in Spanish and English.
EL CROQUIS 1989 Dec., v.8, no.41,
p.4-126,cover, axonometric views,
ill., dwgs., ports., elevs.,
models, photos., plans, secns.,
refs.

SHOWROOMS--JAPAN--TOKYO--TEPIA
Fins de chantier.
Contents: Apartment house:
20-28, rue Ramponneau, Paris;
architect: Fernando Montes --
Showroom building, Kita-Aoyama,
Tokyo, Japan; architect: Fumihiko
Maki -- College du Mas-d'Azil,
Ariege, France; architects:
Joseph Almudever and Christian
Lefebvre.
LE MONITEUR ARCHITECTURE AMC 1990
Apr., no.10, p.15-21, axonometric
view, photos., plans, secn.

SHOWROOMS--LIGHTING--FRANCE--PHILIPS
ECLAIRAGE
L'espace cercle lumiere.
Features the Philips Eclairage
showroom. Interior designers:
Philippe Noir, Christine de
Vichet.
TECHNIQUES ET ARCHITECTURE 1990
June-July, no.390, p.48, photos.

SHOWROOMS--LIGHTING--UNITED STATES--
DANIA (FLORIDA)--KOCH & LOWY / PAF
SHOWROOM
Koch & Lowy PAF Florida showroom /
Justin Henderson.
Interiors of lighting showroom in
the Design Center of the Americas,
Dania, Florida. Designer: Piotr
Sierakowski.
INTERIORS 1990 Oct., v.150, no.3,
p.24, photos.

SHOWROOMS--LIGHTING--UNITED STATES--
NEW YORK (NEW YORK)--REGGIANI LIGHT
GALLERY
Seeiing the light / Justin
Henderson.
On the Reggiani Light Gallery, New
York. Architect: Toni Zuccheri.
INTERIORS 1990 July, v.149, no.12,
p.72-[73], photos.

SHOWROOMS--TEMPORARY--UNITED STATES--
QUEENS (NEW YORK)--AMERICAN STANDARD
Shower of angels / Michael Wagner.
Temporary bathroom fixtures
showroom for American Standard,
IDCNY. Architects: Tigerman
McCurry.
INTERIORS 1990 July, v.149, no.12,
p.76-[77], photos.

SHOWROOMS--TEMPORARY--UNITED STATES--
QUEENS (NEW YORK)--LACKAWANNA
LEATHER
Lackawanna Leather: a temporary
exhibit adjunct designed by Andrew
Belschner Joseph Vincent / Monica
Geran.
Designed on the occasion of the
1989 Designers' Saturday.
INTERIOR DESIGN 1990 Sept., v.61,
no.12, p.232-235, photos., plan.

SHOWROOMS--TEXTILE--INTERIOR DESIGN--
UNITED STATES--CHICAGO (ILLINOIS)--
ARCHITEX INTERNATIONAL
Paying homage [Architex showroom] /
Alice Feiring.
Interiors of Chicago showroom.
Designer: Ben Kramer of Fotoys.
INTERIORS 1990 Oct., v.150, no.3,
p.42, photo.

SHOWROOMS--UNITED STATES--DU PONT
RESOURCE CENTER
Du Pont Resource Center / Monica
Geran.
Multi-media showroom,
"communications complex." Interior
designers: Eva Maddox Associates.
INTERIOR DESIGN 1990 Nov., v.61,
no.15, p.144-[147], photos., plan.

SHOWROOMS--UNITED STATES--LONG ISLAND
CITY (NEW YORK)--AMERICAN STANDARD
SHOWROOM
Anything but standard: American
Standard Showroom, Long Island
City, New York, Tigerman McCurry
Architects / Paul M. Sachner.
ARCHITECTURAL RECORD 1990 Sept.,
v.178, no.10, p.[94-97], photos.,
plan.

SHOWROOMS--UNITED STATES--NEW YORK
(NEW YORK)--KRAVET FABRICS
Kravet Fabrics / Monica Geran.
Interiors of New York showroom in
the New York Design Center.
Interior designers: Salsano
Associates.
INTERIOR DESIGN 1990 June, v.61,
no.9, p.254-[257], diagr., photos.

SHOWROOMS--UNITED STATES--SAN
FRANCISCO (CALIFORNIA)--DIAMOND AND
JEWELRY MART
Building with blocks / Sally B.
Woodbridge.
Diamond and Jewelry Mart, San
Francisco, features glass block
walls. Architects: Tanner Leddy
Maytum Stacy, Architects.
PROGRESSIVE ARCHITECTURE 1990
Dec., v.71, no.13, p.74-75,
photos., plan.

SHOZO UCHII, ARCHITECT AND ASSOCIATES
Urasoe Art Museum.
Located in Okinawa. Architects:
Shozo Uchii, Architect and
Associates; Kamimori Architect &
Associates. English summary, p.19.
Includes tripartite talk, Art
Museum for its staff, by M. Ono,
J. Shioda, and R. Kuroda.
KENCHIKU BUNKA 1990 July, v.45,
no.525, p.[73]-88, elevs.,
photos., plans, secns.

SHRADY, NICHOLAS
The Alpine retreat of a musical
legend / Nicholas Shrady.
Features the interiors of Richard
Strauss' villa in
Garmisch-Partenkirchen, built in
the early 1900s. Architect:
Gabriel von Seidl.
ARCHITECTURAL DIGEST 1990 Mar.,
v.47, no.3, p.262,264,268,[270],
photos.
Gardens: a landscape in Segovia /
Nicholas Shrady.
On landscape architect Leandro
Silva Delgado's garden outside the
old walls.
ARCHITECTURAL DIGEST 1990 Oct.,
v.47, no.11, p.[238]-243, 286,
288, photos.
A progressive heritage in Bavaria:
Count and Countess Anton-Wolfgang
von Faber-Castell's lodge and
palace near Nuremberg / Nicholas
Shrady.
On the interiors of the 1955
addition to the 350-year-old
Faber-Castell home in
Durrenhembach, architect: Eduard
von Lippe, and the interiors of
the Schloss Stein built in the
1840s and expanded in 1906 by
Theodor von Kramer.
ARCHITECTURAL DIGEST 1990 Feb.,
v.47, no.2, p.180-187, port.,
photos.
Spanish acquisitions: a Madrid
couple celebrate their country's
art / Nicholas Shrady.
Home interior. Architect: Luis
Gutierrez Soto. Interior designer:
Jaime Parlade.
ARCHITECTURAL DIGEST 1990 Mar.,
v.47, no.3, p.166-171,240, photos.

SHRESTHA, SUKRA SAGAR
Baghbhairav Temple / Sukra Sagar
Shrestha.
The oldest shrine in Kirtipur, in
the Kathmandu valley.
PR-AC-INA NEP-ALA 1988 Oct.-Nov.,
no.108, p.[1]-11, elev., photo.,
plans, refs.

SHREWSBURY, ELIZABETH HARDWICK TALBOT,
COUNTESS OF, 1520-1608
Plaster puzzle decoded / David
Bostick.
Tudor plasterwork decoration of
New Hall at Hardwick Hall,
executed for Bess of Hardwick.
COUNTRY LIFE 1990 July 26, v.184,
no.30, p.76-79, photos.
Plaster to puzzle over / David
Bostick.
Plasterwork commissioned by Bess
of Hardwick at Sheffield Manor,
Yorkshire and Hardwick Hall,
Derbyshire.
COUNTRY LIFE 1990 July 12, v.184,
(Continued next page)

SHREWSBURY, ELIZABETH HARDWICK TALBOT, COUNTESS OF, 1520-1608 (CONTINUED)
Plaster to puzzle...(CONTINUED)
no.28, p.90-93, photos.

SHRINES
See also MARTYRIA
See also NAISKOS
See also RELICS AND RELIQUARIES
See also SACRED SITES
See also TOMBS

SHRINES--13TH CENTURY--ENGLAND--LONDON--WESTMINSTER ABBEY--SHRINE OF SAINT EDWARD
The Cosmati at Westminster and the English court style / Paul Binski.
A study of the historical and archaeological evidence on the commission of the Roman Cosmati mosaics in the late 13th-cent. at Westminster Abbey and specifics of the shrine of St. Edward, the tomb of Henry III, and the sanctuary pavement.
ART BULLETIN 1990 Mar., v.72, no.1, p.[6]-34, photos., site plans, biblio., refs.

SHRINES--18TH CENTURY--CONSERVATION AND RESTORATION--ITALY--ROME--SANTUARIO DEL MADONNA DEL DIVINO AMORE
La rivincita della belleza: il nuovo santuario di colle a Roma / Glauco Gresleri.
Project for renovation of the 18th-cent. sanctuary of the Madonna del Divino Amore. Architects: Costantino Ruggeri, Luigi Leoni. Text in Italian; captions in Italian and English.
PARAMETRO 1989 Sept.-Oct., v.20, no.174, p.88-91, ill., elevs., model, photo., plan, secn., site plan.

SHRINES--BUDDHIST--INDIA--HARWAN
The enigma of Harwan / Robert E. Fisher.
MARG [1989?], v.40, no.2, p.1-16, photos., refs.

SHRINES--EGYPTIAN--EGYPT
Notes on the exterior construction signs from Tutankhamun's shrines / Martha R. Bell.
On the four shrines found in tomb.
JOURNAL OF EGYPTIAN ARCHAEOLOGY 1990, v.76, p.107-124, charts, refs.

SHRINES--GREEK--CONSERVATION AND RESTORATION--GREECE--DELOS--MONUMENT AUX HEXAGONES
Les monuments aux hexagones du sanctuaire delien / Paul Courbin.
Un the restitution of a block to the south oikos. This is a follow up on block 109 as discussed in the Exploration archeologique de Delos, XXXII, 1979. English summary, p.445.
REVUE ARCHEOLOGIQUE 1990, no.2, p.[361]-366, dwgs., photos., reconst. dwgs., refs.

SHRINES--GREEK--GREECE--APHYSSOU--TSAKONA--SANCTUARY OF ZEUS MESSAPEUS
A sanctuary of Zeus Messapeus: excavations at Aphyssou, Tsakona, 1989 / H. W. Catling.
THE ANNUAL OF THE BRITISH SCHOOL AT ATHENS 1990, no.85, p.[15]-35, pl.3-6, photos., maps, site plans, reconst. dwgs.

SHRINES--HINDU--INDIA--GAYA
Gaya: monuments of the pilgrimage town / Frederick M. Asher.
MARG [1989?], v.40, no.1, p.45-60, ill., photos., refs.

SHRINES--ISLAMIC--14TH CENTURY--ALGERIA--UBBAD--SHRINE OF ABU MADYAN SHUAYB
Sufi saints and shrine architecture in the early fourteenth century / Sheila S. Blair.
Discussion of three 14th cent. Sufi shrine complexes: Shrine of Abu Madyan Shuayb, Ubbad, Algeria; Shrine of Zayn al-Din Yusuf, Cairo; and Shrine of Abd al-Samad, Natanz, Iran.
MUQARNAS 1990, v.7, p.[35]-49, photos., plan, refs.

SHRINES--ISLAMIC--14TH CENTURY--EGYPT--CAIRO--SHRINE OF ZAYN AL-DIN YUSUF
Sufi saints and shrine architecture in the early fourteenth century / Sheila S. Blair.
Discussion of three 14th cent. Sufi shrine complexes: Shrine of Abu Madyan Shuayb, Ubbad, Algeria; Shrine of Zayn al-Din Yusuf, Cairo; and Shrine of Abd al-Samad, Natanz, Iran.
MUQARNAS 1990, v.7, p.[35]-49, photos., plan, refs.

SHRINES--ISLAMIC--14TH CENTURY--IRAN--NATANZ--SHRINE OF ABD AL-SAMAD
Sufi saints and shrine architecture in the early fourteenth century / Sheila S. Blair.
Discussion of three 14th cent. Sufi shrine complexes: Shrine of Abu Madyan Shuayb, Ubbad, Algeria; Shrine of Zayn al-Din Yusuf, Cairo; and Shrine of Abd al-Samad, Natanz, Iran.
MUQARNAS 1990, v.7, p.[35]-49, photos., plan, refs.

SHRINES--ITALY--LORENTO--SANTA MARIA DI LORETO--SANTUARIO DELLA SANTA CASA
La Santa Casa di Loreto: l'edificio sacro e le sue copie = The holy house of Loreto: the sacred building and its copies / Massimo Bulgarelli.
LOTUS INTERNATIONAL 1990, no.65, p.78-89, dwgs., elevs., photos., plans.

SHRINES--JAPAN--USHIMADO--KISHIMA (ISLAND)
The Kishima shrine / Akira Kuryu.
Shrine with seashell-shaped roof, on Kishima, an islet in the Seto Inland Sea. Architects: Akira Kuryu Architect & Associates.
JAPAN ARCHITECT 1990 Feb., v.65, no.2(394), p.61-66, dwg., photos., plans.

SHRINES--JAPAN--USHIMADO--KISHIMA (ISLAND) (CONTINUED)
Shinjisyumeikai the Kishima shrine. Shrine en Kishima island features shell-shaped roof. Architects: Akira Kuryu Architect & Associates. English summary, p.17.
KENCHIKU BUNKA 1990 Jan., v.45, no.519, p.36-46, elevs., models, photos., plans, secns., aerial photo.

SHRINES--MEDIEVAL--JAPAN
"Higan-sho" of Hie-sha shrine / Ryuji Kuroda.
Attempts to clarify their function and character. In Japanese; English summary, p.115.
NIHON KENCHIKU GAKKAI KEIKAKUKEI RONBUN HOKOKU SHU = JOURNAL OF ARCHITECTURE, PLANNING AND ENVIRONMENTAL ENGINEERING 1990 May, no.5(411), p.115-122, refs.

SHRINES--MINOAN--GREECE--CRETE--CHRISTOS
Minoan sanctuaries at Christos and Koumasa, Crete: new field research / Bogdan Rutkowski.
Includes German summary.
ARCHAOLOGISCHES KORRESPONDENZBLATT 1989, v.19, no.1, p.47-51,pl.4-9, photos., plan, refs.

SHRINES--MINOAN--GREECE--CRETE--KOUMASA
Minoan sanctuaries at Christos and Koumasa, Crete: new field research / Bogdan Rutkowski.
Includes German summary.
ARCHAOLOGISCHES KORRESPONDENZBLATT 1989, v.19, no.1, p.47-51,pl.4-9, photos., plan, refs.

SHRINES--MINOAN--GREECE--CRETE--SYME SANCTUARY
Aspects of Minoan cult: Sacred enclosures: the evidence from the Syme Sanctuary (Crete) / Angeliki Lebessi, Polymnia Muhly.
Report on investigations since 1970 at the site on the slopes of Mt. Dikte.
ARCHAOLOGISCHER ANZEIGER 1990, no.3, p.[315]-336, dwgs., photos., plan, secns., refs.

SHRINES--SHINTO--JAPAN
A study of partitive points-analysis and physical-analysis in approach spaces of Shinto shrines [part 1] / Tohru Funakoshi, Hiroshi Tsumita, Misako Shimizu.
Text in Japanese. English summary, p.62.
NIHON KENCHIKU GAKKAI KEIKAKUKEI RONBUN HOKOKU SHU = JOURNAL OF ARCHITECTURE, PLANNING AND ENVIRONMENTAL ENGINEERING 1988 Feb., no.2(384), p.53-62, site plans, charts, tables, graphs, dwgs.

SHUBERT, HOWARD
Lloyd Wright and the Lehigh Airport competition / Howard Shubert.
RACAR: REVUE D'ART CANADIENNE. CANADIAN ART REVIEW 1989, v.16, no.2, p.165-170,288-297, dets., elevs., plans, site plans, refs.

SHULMAN, JULIUS
[Architectural photography: interview].
Interviews with the photographers: Julius Shulman, Tom Bonner, Grant Mudford, Marvin Rand, Wayne Thom, and Tim Street-Porter.
L. A. ARCHITECT 1990 Apr., p.4-7, photos.

SHUTTERS
Chiusure esterne verticali per l'edilizia residenziale - Analisi tecnologica qualitativa ed economica / Antonio De Vecchi, Mario Lucentini.
L'INDUSTRIA DELLE COSTRUZIONI 1990 June, v.24, no.224, p.58-68, dets., tables, refs.
Dynamic effects of thermal shutters / M. Zaheer-Uddin.
BUILDING AND ENVIRONMENT 1990, v.25, no.1, p.33-35, graphs, refs.

SHUTTERS--HISTORY
Putting up the shutters / George Jaffa.
TRADITIONAL HOMES 1990 Oct., v.7, no.1, p.97-99, photos., refs.

SHUTZE, PHILIP TRAMMELL, 1890-1982
American architects [book review].
Review of books on Louis Sullivan, Philip Trammell Shutze, Louis Kahn, and Gordon Bunshaft, by Lauren S. Weingarden, Keith Morgan, David B. Brownlee, and Franz Schulze.
SOCIETY OF ARCHITECTURAL HISTORIANS. JOURNAL 1990 June, v.49, no.2, p.222-229,
Tracing the Rome-Atlanta axis [book review] / John Blatteau.
Review of: "American classicist: the architecture of Philip Trammell Shutze," by Elizabeth Meredith Dowling.
PROGRESSIVE ARCHITECTURE 1990 June, v.71, no.6, p.127,206,209, photos.

SIARKIEVICZ, BARBARA
Mini-golf: maxi profits / Barbara Siarkievicz.
Describes various types of miniature golf courses.
PARKS & RECREATION 1990 Dec., v.25, no.12, p.32-35, photos.

SICA, PAOLO, 1935-1985--EXHIBITIONS
Paolo Sica: progetti per Firenze [exhibition review].
Exhibition at the Palazzo dei Congresso, Florence.
L'INDUSTRIA DELLE COSTRUZIONI 1990 Mar., v.24, no.221, p.69, dwg., model, photo.

SICCA, CINZA MARIA
Giulio Romano in Mantua and Vienna [exhibition review] / Cinzia Maria Sicca.
"Princely courts of the Renaissance. Giulio Romano and the classical tradition", at the Palazzo Te and the Ducal Palace, Mantua, 2 Sept.-12 Nov.1989, and later at the Kunsthistorisches Museum, Vienna.
APOLLO 1990 Mar., v.131, no.337, p.189-191,

SICCA, CINZIA
The architecture of the wall: Astylism in the architecture of Lord Burlington / Cinzia Sicca.
ARCHITECTURAL HISTORY 1990, v.33, p.83-101, elevs., photos., plans, refs.

SICILY--RUINS--VIEWS
Landscapes of light: an artist's itinerary / Madeleine Pinault.
Gouache paintings by Jean-Pierre-Laurent Houel, who visited Sicily between 1776 and 1780.
FMR 1990 Apr., v.9, no.43, p.129-144, ill., refs.

SICK BUILDING SYNDROME
Buildings and health [book review] / Denise Chevin.
On the "green guide" to be published by Rosehaugh, entitled Buildings and health: the Rosehaugh guide to design, construction, use and management of buildings.
BUILDING 1990 Nov.2, v.255, no.43, p.55-59, ill.
Indoor air quality problem complicated by the variety of possible contaminants / Harold Kelman.
REAL ESTATE FORUM 1990 June, v.45, no.6, p.[82]-85, ports., photos.
Indoor air quality: the architects role / James S. Russell.
ARCHITECTURAL RECORD 1990 Nov., v.178, no.12, p.105-106, tables, refs.
Indoor ecology: air pollution in offices and homes forces architects to design safety into interiors / Douglas Gantenbein.
ARCHITECTURE: THE MAGAZINE OF THE AMERICAN INSTITUTE OF ARCHITECTS 1990 June, v.79, no.6, p.107-109, ill., photo.
Is your house making you sick? / Stephen Fenichell.
METROPOLITAN HOME 1990 Nov., v.22, no.11, p.73-74,81,165, dwg.
Sick building syndrome / Terry Jill Lassar.
Includes approaches to the problem of SBS by architects William McDonough and Randolph Croxton.
URBAN LAND 1990 June, v.49, no.6, p.34-35, photo.
Tight building syndrome / David Kichula.
ARCHITECTURE NEW JERSEY 1990, v.26, no.6, p.24-25,31,

SIDDIG, MOHAMMAD YUSUF
An epigraphical journey to an eastern Islamic land / Mohammad Yusuf Siddig.
Study of Islamic period inscriptions from Bengal.
MUQARNAS 1990, v.7, p.[83]-108, dwgs., photos., refs.

SIDDIGI, SALLY
Czech conference targets consumption / Sally Siddigi.
Report on the International Prague Assembly of Architects, Planners, and Designers conference held in Prague, Nov.6-11, 1989.
Co-sponsors: International Architects / Designers / Planners
(Continued next column)

SIDDIGI, SALLY (CONTINUED)
Czech conference...(CONTINUED)
for the Prevention of Nuclear War and the Union of Czechoslovak Architects.
PROGRESSIVE ARCHITECTURE 1990 Feb., v.71, no.2, p.24,

SIDERAKIS, KRITI
Back in the public domain / Kriti Siderakis.
New York City lobbies.
METROPOLIS 1990 Oct., v.10, no.3, p.[68-73],87, dwg., photos.
A brave new world / Kriti Siderakis.
On Paul Nelson's design for a Suspended House (1936-38), which was on exhibit at Columbia University's Ross Gallery in the Spring.
METROPOLIS 1990 Sept., v.10, no.2, p.27, models.

SIDEWALKS
See also BOARDWALKS

SIDEWALKS--MAINTENANCE AND REPAIR-- RESEARCH
Does the left hand know where the right one digs? / David Smith.
Principles and guidelines on pavement cuts and the improvement of street and sidewalk appearance; research conducted by the American Public Works Association.
AMERICAN CITY & COUNTY 1990 Sept., v.105, no.9, p.32,34, photo.

SIDFORD, HENRY J.
Key Bank: an architectural achievement renewed.
Greek revival building at 60 State St., downtown Albany. Original architects: York & Sawyer. Architect for restoration: H.J. Sidford, Jr.
ALBANY PRESERVATION REPORT 1990 Summer, v.9, no.2, p.3, photo.

SIDHU, JASMEET
Getting serious about CADD / Jasmeet Sidhu.
ARCHITECTURE AUSTRALIA 1990 June, v.79, no.5, p.77-78, ill.

SIDING
See also BEVEL SIDING
Against the wall: cladding systems / Raymond W. LaTona, Thomas A. Schwartz.
ARCHITECTURE: THE MAGAZINE OF THE AMERICAN INSTITUTE OF ARCHITECTS 1990 May, v.79, no.5, p.129-131, dets., ill.
Befestigung von Fassadenplatten / Konrad Probsthain.
DEUTSCHE BAUZEITSCHRIFT 1990 Apr., v.38, no.4, p.549-[550],553-555, dets., tables, refs.
Cladding & curtain walling.
Thirteen articles, on subjects such as standards, energy efficiency, fire-resistance, and insulation.
BUILDING 1990 Apr.27, v.255, no.17 suppl., p.3-66, photos.
Cladding: an integral part of architectural design / Ron McWilliam.
Irish examples.
PLAN: ARCHITECTURE + BUILDING DESIGN IN IRELAND 1990 Mar., v.28,
(Continued next page)

SIDING--STAINLESS STEEL
An office building with a stainless reputation / Carol Poh Miller. Landerbrook Place in Lyndhurst, outside of Cleveland, Ohio. Exterior cladding is of corrugated stainless steel panels. Architect: Gerald J. Payto.
INLAND ARCHITECT 1990 Nov.-Dec., v.34, no.6, p.9,12, photos., plan.
William B. Gleckman: stainless-steel siding for a cedar-lined country house in Sagaponack / Suzanne Stephens.
ARCHITECTURAL DIGEST 1990 Feb., v.47, no.2, p.98-[103], port., photos.

SIDING--STANDARDS--EUROPE
Cold bridge war / Matthew Coomber. Thermal Measurement, a testing house located in Rugby, England uses a profiling analysis technique based on the W. German DIN standards.
BUILDING 1990 Mar.9, v.255, no.10, p.52-53, chart, port.

SIDING--STEEL
Bomassa med stalhus / Zacharias Toivio. Tall apartment building with steel exterior, in Tammerfors. Architect: 8 Studio, and Mikko Kaira.
ARKITEKTUR: THE SWEDISH REVIEW OF ARCHITECTURE 1990 Dec., v.90, no.10, p.53-54, axonometric view, photos., plan.

SIDING--STONE
A thin-stone veneer primer / Ian R. Chin, John P. Stecich, Bernard Erlin.
ARCHITECTURAL RECORD 1990 June, v.178, no.7, p.108-113, dets., photos, tables.

SIDING--STONE--MAINTENANCE AND REPAIR
Schaden an Belagen und Bekleidungen aus Naturstein / Gunter Zimmermann.
DEUTSCHES ARCHITEKTENBLATT 1990 Nov.1, v.22, no.11, p.1737-1742, photos., det., refs.

SIDING--TILE
Technics focus: ceramic tile. Includes four articles: Prefabricated exterior ceramic tile cladding; Ceramic tile floors; Tile in wet environments and Manufacturers' directory.
PROGRESSIVE ARCHITECTURE 1990 Apr., v.71, no.4, p.131-161, dets., photos., secns.

SIDING--TIMBER
A wood finish: how to clad walls with timber matchboarding / Richard Wiles.
TRADITIONAL HOMES 1990 Mar., v.6, no.6, p.119-122, photos.

SIDOR, NEVEN
Floating voters / Amanda Baillieu. On the floating city project, Millenium City. Architect: Neven Sidor.
BUILDING DESIGN 1990 Mar.30, no.979, p.12, secns., sketches.

SIEBER, HEINZ G., 1944-
Energie gespart: Haus mit Arztpraxis in Russelsheim-Konigstadten. Architect: Heinz G. Sieber.
DEUTSCHE BAUZEITUNG 1990 Sept., v.124, no.9, p.17-21, elevs., models, photos., plans, table.
Haus Einsiedel in Russelsheim. Passive solar house. Architect: Heinz G. Seiber.
DEUTSCHE BAUZEITSCHRIFT 1990 Aug., v.38, no.8, p.1111-1116, dets., elevs., models, photos., secn., table.

SIEBURTH, RICHARD
Benjamin the scrivener / Richard Sieburth. Historical, thematic and methodological aspects of "Das Passagen-Werk" (Arcades Project), conceived in 1927 and publ. in 1982 as vol. 5 of the Suhrkamp "Gesammelte Schriften," ed. by Rolf Tiedemann.
ASSEMBLAGE 1988 June, no.6, p.[6]-23, ill., photos., site plans, refs.

SIEDLER, WOLF JOBST
Hauptstadt gesucht: Berlin als Metropole eines geeinten Deutschland? / Wolf Jobst Siedler. On Berlin becoming the capital of Germany once again. English summary, p.251.
DEUTSCHE BAUZEITUNG 1990 June, v.124, no.6, p.14-16, photo.

SIEDLUNGEN
See HOUSING DEVELOPMENTS

SIEFERT, PETER
Gebaudebeispiel: Vorabdruck aus dem neuen Dachatlas Geneigte Dacher. Roof details from 4 projects: swimming center, Albstadt, W.G. (P.Siefert et al); housing development, Gebensdorf, Switzerland (C. Tognola, C. Stahel, D. Zulauf); student housing, Wales (D. Lea); and housing for handicapped, Eastleigh, England (D. White).
DETAIL 1990 Feb.-Mar., v.30, no.1, p.[16-23], dets., elev., photos., plans, secns., site plans.

SIEGEL, ALAN M.
Compromising positions: Part I / Jerrold M. Sonet, Alan M. Siegel. Design business feature: focus on negotiating skills in the context of the negotiation of a residential design contract.
INTERIOR DESIGN 1990 Feb., v.61, no.3, p.92,96,
Compromising positions, part II / Jerrold M. Sonet, Alan M. Siegel. Continuation of article on contract negotiation in the interior design business.
INTERIOR DESIGN 1990 June, v.61, no.9, p.86,90,
Compromising positions, part III / Jerrold M. Sonet, Alan M. Siegel. On interior designer/client relations.
INTERIOR DESIGN 1990 Oct., v.61, no.14, p.100,

SIEGEL DIAMOND ARCHITECTS
Utopia revised: at the University of California at Irvine, the struggle to adapt the unyielding geometry of the campus continues / John Parman. On William Pereira's 1963 master plan, and subsequent buildings by other architects.
ARCHITECTURE: THE AIA JOURNAL 1990 Jan., v.79, no.1, p.66-77, dwg., elev., photos., plans, site plans.

SIEGEL, JOYCE
Mixing incomes at Timberlawn Crescent / Tom Doerr, Joyce Siegel. 83-unit housing development in Montgomery Co., Md., outside Washington, D.C. Architects: Larry Kester of Architects Collective.
URBAN LAND 1990 Apr., v.49, no.4, p.8-11, photos., table, site plan.

SIEGEL, STEPHEN
From broker to developer: a dream come true [Chubb Realty, Inc.]. Former chairman of Cushman & Wakefield, Stephen Siegel, establishes new firm.
REAL ESTATE FORUM 1990 Mar., v.45, no.3, p.74-75, dwgs., ports., model.

SIEGRIST, PETER
Ranch-house add-up / April Tome, Peter Siegrist. Addition designed by the architect authors for their house in Greenwich, Conn.
FINE HOMEBUILDING 1989 Aug., no.55, p.69, dets., photo.

SIENKIEWICZ, HENRYK
Christmas in Cracow / Karol Lowicz; with a text by Henryk Sienkiewicz. Miniature nativity scenes featuring spires and towers were folk creations of the 19th century to the present. The examples shown are from the Milanese collection of Alina Kalczynska Scheiwiller.
FMR 1990 Dec., v.9, no.47, p.131-144, photos.

SIEPL-COATES, SUSAN
Bewegt ruhende Form: die Architektur von Erik Asmussen / Gary Coates, Susanne Siepl-Coates. Seven buildings at the Rudolf-Steiner-Seminariet, Jarna, Sweden, built 1973-1991.
ARCHITHESE 1990 Sept.-Oct., v.20, no.5, p.19-27, elevs., photos., plans, secns., site plans.

SIERAKOWSKI, PIOTR
Koch & Lowy PAF Florida showroom / Justin Henderson. Interiors of lighting showroom in the Design Center of the Americas, Dania, Florida. Designer: Piotr Sierakowski.
INTERIORS 1990 Oct., v.150, no.3, p.24, photos.

SIERRA ALVAREZ, JOSE
Cantilever piers for shipping iron ore on the Cantabrian coast of Spain, 1888-1889 / Jose Sierra Alvarez.
On the evolution of Belgian designs by a Spanish construction company, at six sites in Santander. Includes abstract.
INDUSTRIAL ARCHAEOLOGY REVIEW 1990 Autumn, v.13, no.1, p.59-68, maps, photos., secns., refs.

SIEVERDING, CLAUS
Letzte Rettung?:
Altbaumodernisierung in der DDR / Heinz Schmitz, Claus Sieverding.
DEUTSCHE BAUZEITUNG 1990 June, v.124, no.6, p.110-126, elev., photos., plan, secns., tables.

SIEVERTS, ERNST
Aktueller Stand der Planung von Buroarbeitsplatzon / Ernst Sieverts.
DEUTSCHES ARCHITEKTENBLATT 1990 Sept.1, v.22, no.9, p.1353-1356, dets., graph, ill., model, photos., plans.
Sonnenschutz / Ernst Sieverts.
Various uses of window shades for sun protection in large office buildings.
DEUTSCHES ARCHITEKTENBLATT 1990 June 1, v.22, no.6, p.981-985, graphs, photos., tables.

SIGBRAND, LONE
En baeredygtig fremtid / Lone Sigbrand.
Report on an energy conference held in June 1989 by the Teknologisk Institut.
ARKITEKTEN 1989 Dec.22, v.91, no.23, p.617-619, ill.

SIGHISOARA--CITIES AND TOWNS--
ROMANIA--HISTORY
Sighisoara / Francois Blanc.
History of Romanian town in the Transylvania.
MONUMENTS HISTORIQUES 1990 June-July, no.169, p.89-[92], photos.

SIGMAN, DONALD A.
Build-to-suit automated distribution centers spell opportunity for developers / Donald A. Sigman.
Modern, large-scale, automated regional distribution centers.
DEVELOPMENT 1990 Nov.-Dec., v.21, no.6, p.34-36, port., photos., table.

SIGNORINI, BRUNO
Il Monte dei Paschi di Siena a Perugia = The Monte dei Paschi di Siena bank in Perugia / Giorgio Operelli.
Architect: Bruno Signorini.
L'ARCA 1990 Feb., no.35,suppl. l'Arca 2, p.68-73, photos, plan, secns.

SIGNS AND SIGN-BOARDS
See also BILLBOARDS
See also BUILDING DIRECTORIES
See also POSTERS

SIGNS AND SIGN-BOARDS (CONTINUED)
Du commerce des signes [interview] / Florence Michel.
Interview with Joseph Abram on the occasion of the exhibition, Art et Publicite, on view at the Pompidou Center until Feb.25, 1991.
English summary, p.214.
ARCHITECTURE INTERIEURE CREE 1990 Oct.-Nov., no.239, p.124-129, ill., photos.
The effect of sign complexity and coherence on the perceived quality of retail scenes / Jack L. Nasar.
AMERICAN PLANNING ASSOCIATION. JOURNAL 1987 Autumn, v.53, no.4, p.499-509, graphs, photos., tables, biblio., refs.
Fur gute Orientierung.
Signage for the Fachhochschule in Langen. Architects: Parade und Partner.
ARCHITEKTUR, INNENARCHITEKTUR, TECHNISCHER AUSBAU 1990 May, v.98, no.5, p.60-66, photos., plans, site plans.
Urban legibility and signs / Lance Wyman.
THE WHEEL EXTENDED 1990, v.19, no.4, p.8-15, axonometric views, ill., maps, photos.

SIGNS AND SIGN-BOARDS--JAPAN
An investigation into the state of improvement plans for public signs: proposals for and themes in public signs in Setagaya wark, Tokyo / Hyunsuk Kim et al.
Text in Japanese. Includes English summary.
NIHON KENCHIKU GAKKAI KEIKAKUKEI RONBUN HOKOKU SHU = JOURNAL OF ARCHITECTURE, PLANNING AND ENVIRONMENTAL ENGINEERING 1990 Sept., no.9(415), p.67-78, photo., maps, tables, refs.

SIGNS AND SIGN-BOARDS--JAPAN--TOKYO
Signs and the total landscape / Shoji Ekuan.
Locational clues within cities, principally Tokyo.
THE WHEEL EXTENDED 1990, v.19, no.4, p.2-7, photos., aerial photo.

SIGNS AND SIGN-BOARDS--NEON--UNITED STATES--LAS VEGAS (NEVADA)
Neon high noon: Viva Las Vegas / Guilllermo Cabrera Infante.
FMR 1990 Apr., v.9, no.43, p.21-40, photos.

SIGNS AND SIGN-BOARDS--PSYCHOLOGICAL ASPECTS
Developments: not getting older....just better / Jon Lorenc.
"Re-imaging" commercial properties, particularly dated office and industrial space, with new signage, artwork and landscaping.
DEVELOPMENT 1990 Mar.-Apr., v.21, no.2, p.24-26, port., photos.
Forming an image for a revitalized city / Jim Kettner.
Creating a positive visual image with limited funds.
AMERICAN CITY & COUNTY 1990 Apr., v.105, no.4, p.45-46,48, photo.

SIGNS AND SIGN-BOARDS--UNITED STATES--
LAS VEGAS (NEVADA)
Commercial vernacular in Las Vegas / Steve Izenour, David A. Dashiell III.
Update on the state of the Las Vegas Strip.
RASSEGNA 1990 Sept., v.12, no.43/3, p.80-88, photos.

SIGNS AND SIGN-BOARDS--UNITED STATES--
NEW YORK (NEW YORK)--WORLD FINANCIAL CENTER
Building directories go futuristic / Alan Levinsohn.
Three-dimensional and video-interactive displays featured at the World Financial Center in New York.
REAL ESTATE FORUM 1990 July, v.45, no.7, p.22, photos.

SIGNS AND SIGN-BOARDS--UNITED STATES--
PENNSYLVANIA
Hex-sign designs.
Examples of Pennsylvania Dutch hex signs.
COLONIAL HOMES 1990 Oct., v.16, no.5, p.44-48, ill., photos.

SIGNS AND SIGNBOARDS--UNITED STATES--
MEMPHIS (TENNESSEE)--RIDGEWAY CENTER--REGALIA
Signs: the difference between night and day.
Example at Ridgeway Center office park in Memphis, Tenn. Signage and lighting designers: Lorenc Design.
URBAN LAND 1990 Apr., v.49, no.4, p.26-27, photos., site plan.

SIGNS AND SYMBOLS IN ARCHITECTURE
Architectureproduction: papers on architectural theory and criticism [book review] / Hilde Heynen.
Review of the 1988 volume of essays edited by Beatriz Colomina.
ARCHIS 1990 Dec., no.12, p.52-53, axonometric view, ref.
De l'emprise des signes / Marie Helene Contal.
Interview with Paul Virilio, Jean Pierre Le Dantac and Patrice Goulet about the new "architecture of signs." English summary, p.214.
ARCHITECTURE INTERIEURE CREE 1990 Oct.-Nov., no.239, p.[108]-114, dwgs., ports., sketches.
Du commerce des signes [interview] / Florence Michel.
Interview with Joseph Abram on the occasion of the exhibition, Art et Publicite, on view at the Pompidou Center until Feb.25, 1991.
English summary, p.214.
ARCHITECTURE INTERIEURE CREE 1990 Oct.-Nov., no.239, p.124-129, ill., photos.
Irish vernacular architecture: an illustration of semiotic analysis / Ann C. Ziebarth.
Studies "the interaction of culture and design."
HOUSING AND SOCIETY 1990, v.17, no.1, p.27-34, plans, refs.
A secret semiotic skiagraphy: the corporal theatre of meanings in Vincenzo Scamozzi's idea of architecture / Marco Frascari.
On the symbolic use of shadows in Scamozzi's treatise.

(Continued next page)

SIGNS AND SYMBOLS IN ARCHITECTURE
                    (CONTINUED)
   A secret semiotic...(CONTINUED)
   VIA 1990, no.11, p.32-51, elevs.,
   photos., plans, secns., refs.
   Skiagraphy and the ipsum of
   architecture / Donald Kunze.
   The "architecture" of shadows.
   VIA 1990, no.11, p.62-75, ill.,
   refs.

SIGRIST, MARKUS
   Von der Klostertaverne uber den
   Landgasthof zum Palasthotel und
   Punkthochhaus / Markus Sigrist.
   19th cent. grand hotels in
   Interlaken. Discusses influence of
   architects Horace Edouard Daviner
   and Robert II Roller. French and
   Italian summaries.
   UNSERE KUNSTDENKMALER 1989, v.40,
   no.2, p.144-153, ill., engrs.,
   refs.

SIIM, ANDRES
   Kilpailut: monumentin dekonstruointi
   = Deconstruction of a monument /
   Juhani Pallasmaa.
   On the 1988 international
   competition for a monument in Los
   Angeles. Winners: Hani Rashid
   Studio Asymptote. Second prize:
   Kunnapu, Padrik and Siim.
   Includes English translation.
   ARKKITEHTI 1989, v.86, no.7,
   p.79-85, cover, axonometric view,
   dwgs., models, plan, secns.

SIK, MIROSLAV, 1953-
   Peripherie und Techniklandschaft /
   Miroslav Sik.
   ARCHITHESE 1990 Jan.-Feb., v.20,
   no.1, p.50-[53], dwgs., elevs.,
   plans, secns., site plans.
   Projekt Uberbauung Stafa, 1989.
   Architect: Miroslav Sik.
   WERK, BAUEN + WOHNEN 1989 Dec.,
   no.12, p.46, dwgs., model, plans,
   site plan.

SIKH
   See "SIKH" AS A SUBHEADING AFTER
   SPECIFIC BUILDING TYPES OR OTHER
   MAIN HEADINGS.

SIKOV, ED
   A Roxy in your basement / Ed Sikov.
   Features several private movie
   theaters, "home theaters,"
   designed by Theo Kalomirakis.
   CONNOISSEUR 1990 Apr., v.220,
   no.939, p.112-119,155, port.,
   photos.

SILBERMAN, NEIL ASHER
   Lure of the Holy Land / Neil Asher
   Silberman.
   Reviews the results and effects of
   a century of excavations.
   ARCHAEOLOGY 1990 Nov.-Dec., v.43,
   no.6, p.28-34, photos.

SILDING, GRETHE
   Byens rum, historien og buggelysten
   / Allan de Waal, Grethe Silding.
   Presents Danish methods of town
   planning and preservation, using
   Roskilde and Nakskov as examples.
   ARKITEKTEN 1990 Apr., v.92, no.5,
   p.152-157, photos., site plans,
   sketches.

SILK, STUART
   The ranch sees red / Barbara
   Flanagan.
   House on Bainbridge Island, Wash.
   Architect: Stuart Silk.
   METROPOLITAN HOME 1990 July, v.22,
   no.7, p.52-57, photos.

SILLS
   Window sill flashings: the why and
   how / James C. Myers.
   PROGRESSIVE ARCHITECTURE 1990
   June, v.71, no.6, p.41,43,
   photos., biblio.

SILLS, STEPHEN
   Country's new light ... a
   Southampton house decorated by
   Stephen Sills / Charles Gandee.
   House of Nan Swid.
   HOUSE & GARDEN 1990 June, v.162,
   no.6, p.[90-99],172, port.,
   photos.

SILOE, DIEGO DE, CA. 1495-1563
   Ancora sulla cappella Caracciolo di
   Vico in San Giovanni a Carbonara a
   Napoli / Francesco Abbate.
   Attribution of some portal
   sculpture to Diego de Siloe.
   PROSPETTIVA 1988 Apr.-1989 Jan.,
   no.53-56, p.362-366, photos.,
   refs.

SILOS
   Une thebaide a Lukasod / Eberhard
   Stauss.
   Silo house. Architect: Eberhard
   Stauss. English summary, p.52.
   ARCHITECTURE INTERIEURE CREE 1990
   Feb., no.234, p.[128-131],
   photos., plans, secn.

SILOS--UNITED STATES
   Turning grain elevators into
   prisons?
   Proposal by The Eggers Group (TEG)
   for additional prison space in New
   York State, with applications
   elsewhere.
   URBAN LAND 1990 Jan., v.49, no.1,
   p.28, secn.

SILVA DELGADO, LEANDRO
   Gardens: a landscape in Segovia /
   Nicholas Shrady.
   On landscape architect Leandro
   Silva Delgado's garden outside the
   old walls.
   ARCHITECTURAL DIGEST 1990 Oct.,
   v.47, no.11, p.[238]-243, 286,
   288, photos.

SILVA, N. MATOS
   Palazzo delle esposizioni e degli
   sport di Braga = Exhibition and
   sports hall in Braga, [Portugal].
   Architects: Goncalo Byrne with E.
   Trigo de Sousa, N. Matos Silva and
   M. Mateus.
   LOTUS INTERNATIONAL 1989, no.63,
   p.62-73, det., elevs., photos.,
   plans, secns.

SILVAN, PIERLUIGI
   I cicli pittorici delle Grotte
   Vaticane: alcuni aspetti poco noti
   dell'opera di Giovan Battista
   Ricci da Novara e di Carlo
   Pellegrini / Pierluigi Silvan.
   English summary, p.242.
   ARTE LOMBARDA 1989, no.90-91,
              (Continued next column)

SILVAN, PIERLUIGI (CONTINUED)
   I cicli pittorici...(CONTINUED)
   p.104-121, dwgs., photos., plans,
   refs.

SILVEIRA, JOSE
   Helio Duarte (1906-1989): moderno e
   peregrino [obituary] / Hugo
   Segawa, Jose Silveira.
   PROJETO 1990 Apr.-May, no.131,
   p.51-52, photo.

SILVEIRA, ROBERTO PY GOMES DA
   O ensino de tecnologia no curso de
   arquitetura da UFRGS / Roberto Py
   Gomes da Silveira.
   PROJETO 1989 Oct., no.126,
   p.133-134,

SILVESTRIN, CLAUDIO
   Claudio-Silvestrin: a sensibility of
   space / Clare Farrow.
   Alterations to existing buildings,
   by a young Milanese architect in
   London.
   ARCHITECTURAL DESIGN 1990, v.60,
   no.3-4, p.90-93, photos.
   Casa a Hampstead in apparenza,
   tipica = A house in Hampstead
   apparently stereotypical.
   Interior renovations to 1864
   house. Architects: John Pawson,
   Claudio Silvestrin.
   ABITARE 1990 Jan., no.281,
   p.76-[81], photos., plans, site
   plan.
   Much ado about nothing / John Welsh.
   Victoria Miro gallery, Florence.
   Architect: Claudio Silvestrin.
   BUILDING DESIGN 1990 Aug.10-17,
   no.998-999, p.13, axonometric
   view, photos., plan.
   Silvestrin's spartan house / Jeremy
   Myerson.
   Features minimalist interiors of
   1864 Victorian Hampstead home,
   London. Architect: Claudio
   Silvestrin.
   RIBA JOURNAL 1990 May, v.97, no.5,
   p.66-69, photos., plan.
   Wohnskulptur / Gesa Engelschall.
   Features Hans Neuendorf's vacation
   house in Majorca. Architect:
   Claudio Silvestrin.
   ARCHITEKTUR & WOHNEN 1990
   Dec.-1991 Jan., no.6, p.36-43,
   port., photos., isometric dwg.

SILVETTI, JORGE, 1942-
   Genova: concorso di idee per la
   nuova Piazza Dante.
   First prize to Jorge Silvetti.
   Illustrates nine other entries as
   well. Text in Italian and English.
   DOMUS 1990 Sept., no.719,
   p.[50]-57, dwgs., maps, photos.
   Silvetti named Nelson Robinson, Jr.
   professor of Architecture.
   A native of Argentina, on the
   faculty of the GSD at Harvard
   since 1975.
   GSD NEWS / HARVARD UNIVERSITY.
   GRADUATE SCHOOL OF DESIGN 1990
   Summer-Fall, v.19, no.1, p.3,
   port.
   Special feature: Machado and
   Silvetti.
   Contents: Brief history.--
   Statement / R. Machado, J.
   Silvetti.-- The material force of
   the architectural imagination / K.
   Michael Hays.-- Works: Portantina,
              (Continued next page)

SILVETTI, JORGE, 1942- (CONTINUED)
Special feature:... (CONTINUED)
New York, N.Y., 1986.-- Steps of
Providence, Rhode Island School of
Design, Providence, R.I., 1975.--
Municipal cemetery,
Polizzi-Generosa, Sicily, 1986.--
Sesquicentennial Park, Houston,
Tex., 1986.-- Central
transportation facility "la Porta
Meridionale," Palermo, Sicily,
1987.-- Four public squares,
Leonforte, Sicily, 1983. Text in
Japanese and English.
ARCHITECTURE AND URBANISM 1990
Apr., no.4(235), p.65-138,
axonometric views, elevs., models,
photos., plans, secns., site
plans.

SIM, ANDREW
Cultivating a quinta: the vernacular
traditions of the Algarve were
observed in the restoration and
extension of an abandoned
farmhouse / Andrew Sim.
Renovation Case History no.70:
Chestnut Farm, built early
19th-cent., restored by architect
Michael Brown.
TRADITIONAL HOMES 1990 July, v.6,
no.10, p.22-27, photos.
Domesticating the dovecote / Andrew
Sim.
TRADITIONAL HOMES 1990 Apr., v.6,
no.7, p.15-17, photos., ref.
The Folly Fellowship: a society
dedicated to pointless buildings!
/ Andrew Sim.
Society estab. in 1986, "dedicated
to the protection and preservation
of all follies, grottoes and
garden buildings".
TRADITIONAL HOMES 1990 Mar., v.6,
no.6, p.125, photo.
Kept alive: Keeper's Cottage, an
unrecorded timber-framed building,
was saved from the bulldozers:
Renovation case history no.67 /
Andrew Sim.
17th-cent. farmworker's cottage at
Chittern Hills, S. Oxfordshire was
renovated into a home for
architect Michael Brown.
TRADITIONAL HOMES 1990 Apr., v.6,
no.7, p.20-25, photos., plan.
National & Provincial Building
Society Restoration Case History
Awards / Andrew Sim.
First prize awarded to the
restoration of Rampside Hall,
Barrow-in-Furness, by its owners.
TRADITIONAL HOMES 1990 Aug., v.6,
no.11, p.22-29, photos.
Pattern book restoration / Andrew
Sim.
Renovation of Beckside, a
"Gothicised Georgian" house, by
architectural historian John
Martin Robinson, original
architect: Attrib. to John Hird.
TRADITIONAL HOMES 1990 Mar., v.6,
no.6, p.28-32, photos.
Renovation case history no.66:
providing a new use / Andrew Sim.
Conversion of a 19th-cent. tape
mill at Wirksworth into a house
and business for owners Ralph
Selby and Lu Jeffery. Architect:
Keith Hamilton.
TRADITIONAL HOMES 1990 Mar., v.6,
no.6, p.20-26, photos., plans,
secn.

SIM, ANDREW (CONTINUED)
Renovation case history no.68: back
from the dead: a dilapidated house
turned cottage hospital was
restored to its original Jacobean
elegance / Andrew Sim.
Babington House, Wirksworth,
Derbyshire, now home of Mollie
McKinley. Architects for
restoration: Ritchie & Rennie.
TRADITIONAL HOMES 1990 May, v.6,
no.8, p.22-27, dets., photos.,
plans.
Renovation case history no.69:
hidden treasures / Andrew Sim.
"Behind the Victorianised facade
of a terraced house in Frome lay a
well-preserved 17th cent.
interior." 4 Selwood Rd., home of
Andrew and Charlotte Rathbone.
TRADITIONAL HOMES 1990 June, v.6,
no.9, p.20-24, photos.
Renovation case history no.71: model
restoration / Andrew Sim.
Renovation of Model Farm, Skeyton,
North Norfolk, built in the 1830s.
TRADITIONAL HOMES 1990 Sept., v.6,
no.12, p.16-20, photos., plans.
Restored to life: how a subdivided
and worn-out early Georgian house
was restored and revitalised with
skill and panache / Andrew Sim.
Renovation Case History no. 65.
Sion Row, a row of Georgian houses
in Twickenham. No. 4 was restored
by Roger Howe. Architects:
Renaissance.
TRADITIONAL HOMES 1990 Feb., v.6,
no.5, p.20-26, elevs., photos.,
plans.
Vernacular architecture: feudal and
far between / Andrew Sim.
A trip to the "landowner's
landscape" of the far Northeast
England, mostly featuring
fortified sandstone houses of the
upper classes.
TRADITIONAL HOMES 1990 Sept., v.6,
no.12, p.89-92, photos.
Vernacular architecture: home
assortment: the varied buildings
of the Western Home Counties /
Andrew Sim.
The counties surrounding London.
TRADITIONAL HOMES 1990 June, v.6,
no.9, p.33-36, photos., ref.
Vernacular architecture: limestone
country / Andrew Sim.
Houses along the "Cotswold
limestone belt" of England.
TRADITIONAL HOMES 1990 Aug., v.6,
no.11, p.15-20, photos.

SIM, SANGUG
A study on the structure of land use
distribution at great area in
Japan / Hiroshi Aizawa, Sangug
Sim.
Text in Japanese; includes English
summary
NIHON KENCHIKU GAKKAI KEIKAKUKEI
RONBUN HOKOKU SHU = JOURNAL OF
ARCHITECTURE, PLANNING AND
ENVIRONMENTAL ENGINEERING 1990
Nov., no.11(417), p.75-85, graphs,
tables, refs.

SIMAN, B. BERNARD
Discussion: application of woonerf
and other traffic-restraint
concepts / Kozo Amano, B. Bernard
Siman, Tham Kok-Seng.
Applying European concepts in
Japan.
THE WHEEL EXTENDED 1990, no.73,
p.[18]-23, ports., photo.

SIMCH, FRANCISCO PEDRO, 1934-
Em bairro nobre, com passareles para
o lazer: Edifício Villa Pablo
Picasso, Porto Alegre.
Architects: Pedro Simch, Carlos
Flesch.
PROJETO 1989 June, no.122,
p.76-77, photos, plans, secn.

SIMMEL, GEORG, 1858-1918--INFLUENCE
Form as the object of experience:
Georg Simmel's influence on Mies
van der Rohe / W. Gordon Brown.
JOURNAL OF ARCHITECTURAL EDUCATION
1990 Winter, v.43, no.2, p.42-46,
dwgs., refs.

SIMMIE, JAMES
Participation in planning: theory
and practice in Yugoslavia / James
Simmie.
THE PLANNER 1989 July, v.75,
no.11, p.19-22, photos, refs.
Self-management and town planning in
Yugoslavia / James Simmie.
TOWN PLANNING REVIEW 1989 July,
v.60, no.3, p.271-286, charts,
photos., plans, refs.

SIMMONS, I. G.
The Later Mesolithic Period
(6000-5000bp) on Glaisdale Moor,
North Yorkshire / I. G. Simmons,
J. B. Innes.
Includes abstract.
ARCHAEOLOGICAL JOURNAL 1988,
v.145, p.1-12, graphs, maps,
tables, biblios.

SIMMONS, MARTIN
Land use and transportation in East
London / Martin Simmons.
THE PLANNER 1990 Nov.16, v.76,
no.45, p.9-11, maps, photo., refs.
London through the eyes of LPAC /
Martin Simmons.
The London Planning Advisory
Committee (LPAC) was formed in
1985 upon the dissolution of the
Greater London Council.
THE PLANNER 1990 Dec.14, v.76,
no.49, p.36-40, chart, diagr.,
port., map, refs.

SIMO, MELANIE LOUISE, 1949-. LOUDON
AND THE LANDSCAPE
The British Isles [book review].
Reviews of recent books on Inigo
Jones, Wren's design of St
Paul's, John Claudius Loudon, six
vernacular topics. Reviewers: John
Bold, A. A. Tait, Anthony Quiney.
SOCIETY OF ARCHITECTURAL
HISTORIANS. JOURNAL 1990 June,
v.49, no.2, p.217-221,
Loudon and the landscape [book
review] / Gerrie Andela.
Reviews a 1988 monograph by
Melanie Louise Simo.
ARCHIS 1990 July, no.7, p.52-53,
elev., maps, plan, secn.

SIMO, TRINIDAD
La ciudad de Miguel Navarro = The
city of Miguel Navarro / Trinidad
Simo.
QUADERNS D'ARQUITECTURA I
URBANISME 1989 Oct.-Dec., no.183,
p.151-155, models.

SIMON ESPAR, MIGUEL
La arquitectura residencial de la
Villa Olimpica / Justo Isasi.
Includes 13 projects. English
summary, p.86.
A & V 1990, no.22, p.26-54, dets.,
ill., elevs., models, plans,
secns., site plans, sketches.

SIMON, LOUIS, 1901-1965
Royon 1950 / Gilles Ragot.
Analysis of town rebuilt in 1950s
by architects Claude Ferret, Louis
Simon and Andre Morisseau.
LE MONITEUR ARCHITECTURE AMC 1990
Sept., no.14, p.50-54, photos.,
site plan, refs.

SIMON, MARK
Haunted house [McKim house, Fishers
Island, NY] / Thomas Fisher.
Vacation house. Architects: Mark
Simon and Leonard Wyeth of
Centerbrook Architects.
PROGRESSIVE ARCHITECTURE 1990
Nov., v.71, no.12, p.70-73,
photos., plans, secn., site plan.

SIMON MARTIN-VEGUE WINKELSTEIN MORIS
Apple computer / Edie Lee Cohen.
Interiors of western operations
headquarters, San Jose, Calif.
Architects: Simon Martin-Vegue
Winkelstein Moris.
INTERIOR DESIGN 1990 Apr., v.61,
no.6, p.[190-195], photos., plan.
Lessons in civility: two schools in
San Francisco exemplify the
multiple challenges of melding new
construction and existing
buildings into a single entity /
Donald J. Canty.
The Waldorf School, by Tanner
Leddy Maytum Stacy Architects; and
the San Francisco Day School, by
Simon Martin-Vegue Winkelstein
Moris.
ARCHITECTURAL RECORD 1990 Mar.,
v.178, no.3, p.84-91, elevs.,
photos., plans, secn., site plans.
Site-sensitive technology: Simon
Martin Vegue Winkelstein Moris of
San Francisco.
Three designs for projects that
meld high technology and sensitive
design: Oceanside Control
Facility, Contra Costa Water
Treatment complex, and addition to
Lawrence Hall.
ARCHITECTURE: THE MAGAZINE OF THE
AMERICAN INSTITUTE OF ARCHITECTS
1990 May, v.79, no.5, p.48, elev.,
models, secn.
Telling details / Lisa S. Cohen.
The teller's station Raychem
Corp's credit union faciclity,
Menlo Park, CA. Architects: Simon
Martin-Vegue Winkelstein Moris.
INTERIORS 1990 May, v.149, no.10,
p.38-39, dets., photo., plan,
secn., elev.

SIMON MARTIN-VEGUE WINKELSTEIN MORIS
(CONTINUED)
Upping the profile / Michael Wagner.
On the award-winning Raychem
headquarters worldwide. Architects
for Menlo Park headquarters: Cabak
Randall Jasper Griffiths
Associates. Interior designers:
Simon Martin-Vegue Winkelstein
Moris.
INTERIORS 1990 May, v.149, no.10,
p.178-191, dwgs., models, photos.,
plans, site plan.

SIMON, MELANIE LOUISE. LOUDON AND THE
LANDSCAPE
London and the landscape: from
country seat to metropolis [by]
Melanie Louise Simon [book review]
/ Judith K. Major.
Review of 1988 book.
JOURNAL OF GARDEN HISTORY 1990
Oct.-Dec., v.10, no.4, p.251-252,

SIMON, PHILIPPE
La Metropole imaginaire [exhibition
review] / Pascale Joffroy.
Exhibition held at L'Institut
francais d'architecture until Feb.
17, 1990. Designer: Bruno Fortier,
with Herve Chapon, Francois
Dardel, Fernando Garcia-Vega, Jean
Hue, Philippe Prost, Philippe
Simon, ntoine Grumbach, Italo
Rota.
LE MONITEUR ARCHITECTURE AMC 1990
Feb., no.8, p.20-21, models,
photos.
I piani pre-haussmanniani di Parigi.
Contents: Fra la rivoluzione dei
lumi e i lumi della rivoluzione,
by Juan Luis Pinon Pallares.--Dal
1790 al 1830: l'utilizzazione dei
"bei nazionali", urbanistica e
lottizzazioni a Parigi, by Bernard
Rouleau.--Rue Laffitte: dal
palazzo Thelusson alla chiesa di
Notre Dame de Lorette, by Bruno
Fortier, Philippe Simon.--I
progetti di ingrandimento e di
ristrutturazione di Parigi prima
del secolo XIX, by Maurice
Halbwachs.--La grande planimetria
di Parigi di Edme Verniquet,
1774-1791, by Jeanne Pronteau.
STORIA URBANA 1989 July-Dec.,
v.13, no.48-49, p.3-126,
axonometric views, maps, site
plans, table, refs.

SIMON, PIUS B.
Mixed land-use patterns and the
development of spatial structure
of Nigerian cities / Pius B.
Simon.
PLANNING OUTLOOK 1989, v.32, no.1,
p.43-53, chart, diagrs., map, site
plans, tables, refs.

SIMONCISCS, EMMERICH
Special edition V: education of
architectural designing, applied
aesthetics / Emmerich Simmoncsics.
English summary, p.23.
KENCHIKU BUNKA 1990 Sept., v.45,
no.527, p.159-168, dwgs., models,
photos.

SIMONE, ROSARIO DE. CH. E. JEANNERET -
LE CORBUSIER
Sull'apprendistato di Le Corbusier
[book review] / Giuliano Gresleri.
Review of Ch. E. Jeanneret-Le
Corbusier, viaggio in Germania
1910-11.
CASABELLA 1990 June, v.54, no.569,
p.25, photo., sketches.

SIMONETTI, PAOLO
Neuer italienischer Pavillon an der
Biennale in Venedig.
Architects: Francesco Cellini with
Paolo Simonetti, Nicoletta
Cosentino.
DEUTSCHE BAUZEITSCHRIFT 1990
Sept., v.38, no.9, p.1184, dwgs.

SIMONINI, GIAN LUCA
Il Giardina Majorelle di Marrakesh /
Gian Luca Simonini.
Public gardens created in the
1930s by painter Jacques
Majorelle.
VILLE GIARDINI 1990 May, no.248,
p.70-75, photos.

SIMONNE, KATE
Pueblo for two / Kate Simonne.
Sonoma, Calif., house resembles
adobe village. Architect: Don
Sandy of Sandy & Babcock;
landscape architects: Garden
Design.
HOUSE BEAUTIFUL 1990 May, v.132,
no.5, p.70-[77], dets., ports.,
photos., plan.

SIMONS DESIGN CONSULTANTS
Made to measure / David Redhead.
Interiors of three London clothing
stores: Issey Miyake, Michiko
Koshino and Karl Lagerfeld.
DESIGNERS' JOURNAL 1990 July-Aug.,
no.59, p.[28]-33, photos.

SIMONS, SCOTT
Kitchens that cook: hot news, cool
choices / Julie V. Iovine.
Five projects, including an
expansion of the Sprecher house,
Los Angeles (architect: Michele
Saee); a Connecticut kitchen
renovation (architect: Louis
Mackall); Reichel-Singer house
conversion, Los Angeles (designer:
Josh Schweitzer); Sagalyn kitchen
(architect: Scott Simons); Laurie
and Maurie Williams' kitchen
renovation, Ore.
METROPOLITAN HOME 1990 May, v.22,
no.5, p.[123-136], det., photos.

SIMOUNET, ROLAND, 1927-
Housing, rue de Strasbourg,
Saint-Denis (quartier Basilique),
1976-1986.
Architects: Roland Simounet, Emile
Duhart. Text in Japanese and
English.
ARCHITECTURE AND URBANISM 1990
Sept., no.9 Extra edition,
p.164-173,263, photos.

SIMPSON, ALAN
Britain's Fair Towns: a national
competition proposal for
environmental and economic
regeneration of the smaller town /
Alan Simpson, Gerry Kemp.
URBAN FUTURES 1989 Spring, v.2,
(Continued next page)

SIMPSON, ALAN (CONTINUED)
Britain's Fair Towns:...(CONTINUED)
no.1, p.5-12, axonometric view,
plans, sketches.

SIMPSON, ELIZABETH
"Midas' bed" and a royal Phrygian
funeral / Elizabeth Simpson.
A reexamination of the furniture
at Tumulus MM at Gordion, Turkey.
JOURNAL OF FIELD ARCHAEOLOGY 1990
spring, v.17, no.1, p.69-87,
axonometric view, figs., dwgs.,
map, photos., reconst. dwgs.,
biblio.

SIMPSON, HARRY, 1917-1988
Tribute: Housing's devoted and
distinguished servant / Mary
Smith.
HOUSING REVIEW 1988 Nov.-Dec.,
v.37, no.6, p.192, port.

SIMPSON, JEFFREY
Classical grace in Palm Beach /
Jeffrey Simpson.
Apartment interiors designed by
William Hodgins.
ARCHITECTURAL DIGEST 1990 Oct,
v.47, no.11, p.[188-195], photos.
Georgian grace in Atlanta: renewing
southern traditions for Charlotte
and Rankin Smith / Jeffrey
Simpson.
Interiors of Georgian-style home
in northwestern Atlanta.
Architect: William Frank McCall.
Interior designers: Betty Sherrill
and Ethel Smith of McMillen.
ARCHITECTURAL DIGEST 1990 May,
v.47, no.5, p.220-225, photos.
Grand illusion by the Bay:
recreating a Genoese Palazzo in
San Francisco / Jeffrey Simpson.
Interiors of Doan apartment.
Interior designers: Valerian
Rybar, Jean-Francois Daigre.
ARCHITECTURAL DIGEST 1990 Feb.,
v.47, no.2, p.170-[179], photos.
Melvyn Douglas: a hilltop house for
the Best Supporting Actor in Hud
and Being There / Jeffrey Simpson.
Features 1938 ranch-style home in
the Hollywood Hills designed by
Roland E. Coate.
ARCHITECTURAL DIGEST 1990 Apr.,
v.47, no.4, p.212-213,296, port.,
photos.
Pittsburgh folk: designing to suit a
spirited collection / Jeffrey
Simpson.
Interiors of Pittsburgh home
feature owners' collection of folk
art. Interior designer: Charles E.
Bolton.
ARCHITECTURAL DIGEST 1990 June,
v.47, no.6, p.[118]-127,218,
port., photos.
Reflected glories in Palm Beach /
Jeffrey Simpson.
Features interiors of Rose Sach's
Palm Beach apartment. Interior
designers: Robert Metzger, Michael
Christiano.
ARCHITECTURAL DIGEST 1990 Mar.,
v.47, no.3, p.[172]-179, photos.
A spirited lecture series with the
nation's leading designers /
Jeffrey Simpson.
On the series, Architectural
Digest at the Smithsonian, held in
April and May in Washington, D. C.
(Continued next column)

SIMPSON, JEFFREY (CONTINUED)
A spirited lecture...(CONTINUED)
ARCHITECTURAL DIGEST 1990 Oct,
v.47, no.11, p.146-162, ports.

SIMPSON, JOHN ANTHONY, 1955-
Code of conduct / Dan Cruickshank.
Examines the potential of codes to
improve general standards of
design. Example of Stoke Gifford
designed by John Simpson.
ARCHITECTS' JOURNAL 1990 July 18,
v.192, no.3, p.26-27, dwg., elev.
Controversy: Paternoster Square /
Ziva Freiman.
PROGRESSIVE ARCHITECTURE 1990
Mar., v.71, no.3, p.115-116, ill.

SIMPSON, NAN BOOTH
Ancient meets avant-garde: in
Houston, an extraordinary
collection begged an extraordinary
setting / Nan Booth Simpson.
Levy house interiors.
Architectural designer: Larry S.
Davis.
SOUTHERN ACCENTS 1989 May-June,
v.12, no.3, p.[164]-173, photos.
Playful formality: a Houston home
packed with personal treasures /
Nan Booth Simpson.
Home of Cristina Zilkha. Interior
design: Letelier-Rock Design.
SOUTHERN ACCENTS 1990 Sept., v.13,
no.7, p.[68]-79, port., photos.
Poolside paradise: glorious outdoor
entertaining complex graces a
Dallas garden / Nan Booth Simpson.
Architects: Loyd-Paxton; Landscape
architects: Boyd & Heiderich.
SOUTHERN ACCENTS 1990 July-Aug.,
v.13, no.6, p.[96]-100, photos.
Sociable structure: a Houston home
designed for entertaining / Nan
Booth Simpson.
Anderson house. Architect: Joe
Carroll Williams.
SOUTHERN ACCENTS 1990 Oct., v.13,
no.8, p.[98]-105, ports., photos.
Spirited approach: a bright and
lively penthouse overlooks the
Dallas skyline / Nan Booth
Simpson.
Apartment of Carol Young. Interior
architect: Chris Carson.
SOUTHERN ACCENTS 1990 Nov., v.13,
no.9, p.[86]-91, photos.
Structural evolution / Nan Booth
Simpson.
Focus on the playgrounds
influenced by the work of Paul
Friedburg.
LANDSCAPE ARCHITECTURE 1990 Sept.,
v.80, no.9, p.72-75, photos.
Thrice blessed: Santa Fe's museums
weave a multicultural tapestry /
Nan Booth Simpson.
SOUTHERN ACCENTS 1989 May-June,
v.12, no.3, p.200-A-200-T, ill.,
photos.
Tranquility base: serene livability
in a Houston high rise / Nan Booth
Simpson.
Interior designer: Kelly Gale
Amen.
SOUTHERN ACCENTS 1990 May, v.13,
no.4, p.[128]-134, port., photos.

SIMULATION GAMES
See also MATHEMATICAL MODELS

SINAN, MIMAR, 1489 OR 90-1588
Istamboul au XVIe siecle: l'oeuvre
de Sinan / Jale Erzen.
French, English, Spanish and
German summaries, p.[122]-124.
(Some summaries incorrectly show
XIXe s.).
LES ANNALES DE LA RECHERCHE
URBAINE 1989 [Mar.-Apr.], no.42,
p.[11]-18,[122]-124, photos.,
engrs., refs.
A note on the dating of the mosque
of Rustem Pasa in Istanbul /
Leslie Meral Schick.
Argues that the mosque was
constructed in 1561 under Sinan
and may have been completed in or
after 1562.
ARTIBUS ASIAE 1990, v.50, no.3-4,
p.285-288, refs.

SINCLAIR, LONNIE
Tailored to suit: Johnston residence
/ J. Mark Schmidt.
West Des Moines, Iowa. Architect:
Lon Sinclair.
IOWA ARCHITECT 1990 Summer, v.39,
no.2, p.18-[19], photos., plan.

SINCLAIR, M. THEA
Tourism and accommodation in London:
alternative policies and the
Docklands experience / Stephen
Page, M. Thea Sinclair.
Planning for tourism accommodation
in London's Docklands.
BUILT ENVIRONMENT 1989, v.15,
no.2, p.125-137, maps, photo,
refs.

SINCLAIR, NICK
Dame Jennifer's empire / Nick
Sinclair.
Dame Jennifer Jenkins, Chairman of
National Trust.
BLUEPRINT (LONDON, ENGLAND) 1990
Apr., no.66, p.38-40, port.

SINGAPORE--ARCHITECTURE--HUMAN FACTORS
The supportive environment: a
strategy for creating quality in
the built environment in the
Singapore context / Richard Hyde.
OPEN HOUSE INTERNATIONAL 1989,
v.14, no.3, p.36-43, graphs,
plans, table, refs.

SINGAPORE--ARCHITECTURE--SOCIOLOGICAL
ASPECTS
The supportive environment: a
strategy for creating quality in
the built environment in the
Singapore context / Richard Hyde.
OPEN HOUSE INTERNATIONAL 1989,
v.14, no.3, p.36-43, graphs,
plans, table, refs.

SINGAPORE--CITY PLANNING--19TH CENTURY
Historical study on the colonial
cities of Southeast Asia and their
architecture / Hideo Izumida.
Part 1: Singapore's town planning
and shophouse. Text in Japanese.
Includes English summary.
NIHON KENCHIKU GAKKAI KEIKAKUKEI
RONBUN HOKOKU SHU = JOURNAL OF
ARCHITECTURE, PLANNING AND
ENVIRONMENTAL ENGINEERING 1990
June [July], no.7(413), p.161-172,
ill., site plans, refs.

SINGAPORE--HISTORIC BUILDINGS--
CONSERVATION AND RESTORATION
Reclaiming old Singapore / Thomas W.
Sweeney.
HISTORIC PRESERVATION 1990
May-June, v.42, no.3, p.[42]-49,
ports., models, photos.

SINGAPORE--HISTORIC PRESERVATION
Reclaiming old Singapore / Thomas W.
Sweeney.
HISTORIC PRESERVATION 1990
May-June, v.42, no.3, p.[42]-49,
ports., models, photos.

SINGAPORE--HOUSES--19TH CENTURY
Historical study on the colonial
cities of Southeast Asia and their
architecture / Hideo Izumida.
Part 1: Singapore's town planning
and shophouse. Text in Japanese.
Includes English summary.
NIHON KENCHIKU GAKKAI KEIKAKUKEI
RONBUN HOKOKU SHU = JOURNAL OF
ARCHITECTURE, PLANNING AND
ENVIRONMENTAL ENGINEERING 1990
June [July], no.7(413), p.161-172,
ill., site plans, refs.

SINGAPORE--HOUSING--PUBLIC
The supportive environment: a
strategy for creating quality in
the built environment in the
Singapore context / Richard Hyde.
OPEN HOUSE INTERNATIONAL 1989,
v.14, no.3, p.36-43, graphs,
plans, table, refs.

SINGELL, LARRY D.
An empirical examination of the
effect of impact fees on the
housing market / Larry D. Singell,
Jane H. Lillydahl.
LAND ECONOMICS 1990 Feb., v.66,
no.1, p.[82]-92, graphs, tables,
refs.

SINGER MUSEUM (LARENS, NETHERLANDS)--
EXHIBITIONS
Villaparken in het Gooi [exhibition
review] / Gerrie Andela.
Exhibition at the Singer Museum in
Laren until May 14, 1990.
ARCHIS 1990 May, no.5, p.6-7,
photo.

SINGLE ROOM OCCUPANCY HOTELS--UNITED
STATES--NEW YORK (NEW YORK)
Making a house a home / Jeffrey
Hoff.
Projects by architects to provide
"real homes" for the homeless in
NYC.
METROPOLIS 1990 Sept., v.10, no.2,
p.46-[51],79-81, elev., model,
photos., plans.

SINGLE ROOM OCCUPANCY HOTELS--UNITED
STATES--SAN DIEGO (CALIFORNIA)
SRO revival: a hybrid building type
profitably solves San Diego's
housing problem / Karin Tetlow.
Five single room occupancy hotels.
Architects: Rob Wellington
Quigley, Jackson and Associates.
ARCHITECTURE: THE MAGAZINE OF THE
AMERICAN INSTITUTE OF ARCHITECTS
1990 July, v.79, no.7, p.60-63,
ill., photos., plans.

SINGLETON, BARRIE
Koln-Deutz and romanesque
architecture / Barrie Singleton.
Discusses churches at Aachen,
Cologne, Mettlach, Trier, Speyer,
Mainz.
BRITISH ARCHAEOLOGICAL
ASSOCIATION. JOURNAL 1990, v.143,
p.[49]-76,pl.7-11, photos., plans,
secns., refs.

SINGLETON, DAVID
Reflections on landscape: the lives
and work of six British landscape
architects [edited by] S. Harvey
[book review] / David Singleton.
Oral histories from G. Jellicoe,
S. Crowe, P. Shepheard, B.
Hackett, P. Youngman, and B.
Colvin.
ANCIENT MONUMENTS SOCIETY.
TRANSACTIONS 1990, new ser.,v.34,
p.199,

SINGLETON, JOHN
Building evaluations: risky business
/ John Singleton.
CANADIAN ARCHITECT 1990 Jan.,
v.35, no.1, p.21,34,
A dangerous precedent from Down
Under / John Singleton.
Report of a case where an
Australian couple successfully
sued building professionals for
damages to their "health and
well-being."
CANADIAN ARCHITECT 1990 May, v.35,
no.5, p.36,75,
"I only work here" doesn't always
work / John Singleton.
On the personal liability of
employees.
CANADIAN ARCHITECT 1990 Sept.,
v.35, no.9, p.47,55,
Liability to builders: some good
news / John Singleton.
CANADIAN ARCHITECT 1990 Feb.,
v.35, no.2, p.33,56,
Misjudgement, not negligence / John
Singleton.
Legal distinctions.
CANADIAN ARCHITECT 1990 Apr.,
v.35, no.4, p.51,70, refs.
No contract, no duty / John
Singleton.
CANADIAN ARCHITECT 1990 Nov.,
v.35, no.11, p.37,43,
Tender information and the client /
John Singleton, Derek Brindle.
CANADIAN ARCHITECT 1990 July,
v.35, no.7, p.27,35, refs.
Tender information and the
contractor / John Singleton, Derek
Brindle.
CANADIAN ARCHITECT 1990 Aug.,
v.35, no.8, p.37,43, refs.

SINKS--ROUND
Boffi: Eroica soluzione = Heroic
achievement.
A round kitchen unit (island).
Designers: R. Didaglio, A. Rizzi.
In Italian and English.
OTTOGANO 1990 Sept., no.96,
p.160-163, elevs., photos.

SINZ, ROSWITHA
Wohnungspolitische Konzepte:
Wohnungsbauprojekte / Rudi Kujath.
Section on many new housing
projects in Germany. Contents:
Berlin, by Rudi Kujath.--Koln, by
Uwe Kessler.--Bayern, by Dieter
Gutekunst.--Frankfurt, by Martin
Wentz.--Hannover, by Hanns
Adrian.--Der LEG
Nordrhein-Westfalen, by Roswitha
Sinz.--Anmerkungen..., by Hartmut
Grosshans. Among the architects
represented are Otto Steidle +
Partner; Andreas Brandt & Rudolf
Bottcher; Joachim Ganz, Walter
Rolfes; Axel Schultes; Wolfgang
Scharlach und Rainer Wischhusen;
Rebecca Chestnutt et al; Hubertus
Hoffmann; Paul Petry; Hermann
Schroder; Sampo Widmann; Gerhart
Laage; Freed Ahrens.
BAUWELT 1990 Mar.30, v.81, no.12,
p.572-598, elevs., plans, secns.,
site plans, tables.

SIOLA, UBERTO
Napoli, architettura e citta:
secondoi seminario di
progettazione / Uberto Siola.
On the 1990 International Seminar
on Architectural Design, "Naples,
Architecture and City." Presents
student projects for the
revitalization of 4 areas of
Naples. Text in Italian and
English.
DOMUS 1990 Dec., no.722,
p.[11]-[16], dwgs., elevs., model,
site plans.
Progetto urbano I = Urban Project I
/ Stefano Boeri, Francesco
Infussi, Ugo Ischia.
City planning in Italian cities.
Contributions by: Augusto
Cagnardi, Giuseppe Campos Venuti,
Bruno Gabrielli, Cesare Macchi
Cassia, Luigi Mazza, Alberto Mioni
and Uberto Siola. In Italian;
Italian and English captions;
English summary, p.121.
URBANISTICA 1989 June, no.95,
p.57-72, 121, plans, ref.

SIPEK, BOREK
Hauptverwaltung der Deutschen
Leasing AG in Bad-Homburg /
Hans-Peter Schwarz.
Architect: Ulrich Heiken.
Designers: Borek Sipek, David
Palterer.
BAUWELT 1990 Oct.26, v.81, no.40,
p.2018-2019, det., photos., plans.
Master of riddles [Borek Sipek] /
Hugh Pearman.
Profile of the Czech
architect/designer.
DESIGNERS' JOURNAL 1990 Sept.,
no.60, p.[62]-63,65-66, port.,
photos.
Ontwerp en emotie: architectonisch
werk van Borek Sipek / Egbert
Koster.
Covers Sipek's glass designs,
walls, fences, Beddlington's
restaurant in Amsterdam, and Day
Break coffee shop on Prinsenstraat
in Amsterdam.
DE ARCHITECT 1990 June., v.21,
no.6, p.69-77, axonometric view,
photos., plans.

SIPINEN, ARTO, 1936-
Espoo Cultural Center.
Completed in Jan. 1989. Architect:
Arto Sipinen.
LIVING ARCHITECTURE 1990, no.9,
p.144-[153], photos., plans.
Kulturzentrum in Espoo, Finnland =
Espoo Cultural Centre, Finland.
Architect: Arto Sipinen.
ARCHITEKTUR + WETTBEWERBE 1990
Sept., no.143, p.23-24, photos.,
site plans.
Tapiola culture / Peter Davey.
Cultural center, Tapiola, Finland.
Architect: Arto Sipinen.
ARCHITECTURAL REVIEW 1990 Mar.,
v.187, no.1117, p.51-[57], photos,
plans, secns., site plans.

SIREN, JOHAN SIGFRID, 1889-1961--
EXHIBITIONS
J.S. Sirenin elamantyo nayttelyna:
J. S. Siren arkkitehti-architect
1889-1961 [exhibition review] /
Mona Schalin.
Exhibition at Helsingen
Jugendsalissa, Mar.31-Apr.28,
1989.
ARKKITEHTI 1989, v.86, no.4, p.20,
elevs.

SIRONI, GRAZIOSO
Un nuovo documento per la cascina
Pozzobonelli / Giovanni Battista
Sannazzaro, Grazioso Sironi.
15th cent. chapel and portico,
Milan.
ARTE CRISTIANA 1990 July-Aug.,
v.78, no.739, p.280, plan.

SIRVIN BADUEL MONMARSON
Adolescences: salle de sport, Douai.
Textile-covered, metal-framed
building. Architects: Sirvin
Baduel Monmarson. English summary,
p.85.
TECHNIQUES ET ARCHITECTURE 1990
Dec.-1991 Jan., no.393, p.84-85,
det., dwg., elev., plan, secns.,
site plan.

SIRVIN, PAUL, 1871-1977
The Butte Rouge Garden suburb,
Chateney-Malabry, [France],
1929-1934.
Architects: Joseph Bassompierre,
Paul de Rutte and Paul Sirvin.
Text in Japanese and English.
ARCHITECTURE AND URBANISM 1990
Sept., no.9 Extra edition,
p.114-125,263, photos.

SIRY, JOSEPH
Louis Sullivan's building for John
D. Van Allen and Son / Joseph
Siry.
A hisoty of the Clinton, Iowa
building (1913-1915), with
discussion o f design development,
ornamental motifs, and the
influences of mercantile interests
and regional agriculture upon the
clients. Includes abstract.
SOCIETY OF ARCHITECTURAL
HISTORIANS. JOURNAL 1990 Mar.,
v.49, no.1, p.67-89, dets., ill.,
dwgs., photos., plans, refs.

SIRY, JOSEPH. CARSON PIRIE SCOTT;
LOUIS SULLIVAN ADN THE CHICAGO
DEPARTMENT STORE
Caroon, Pirie, Scott: Louis Sullivan
and the Chicago department store
[by] Joseph Siry [book review] /
Mark S. Foster.
1990 Winter, v.25, no.4,
p.303-305,

SIRY, JOSEPH. CARSON PIRIE SCOTT;
LOUIS SULLIVAN AND THE CHICAGO
DEPARTMENT STORE
American architects [book review].
Review of books on Louis Sullivan,
Philip Trammell Shutze, Louis
Kahn, and Gordon Bunshaft, by
Lauren S. Weingarden, Keith
Morgan, David B. Brownlee, and
Franz Schulze.
SOCIETY OF ARCHITECTURAL
HISTORIANS. JOURNAL 1990 June,
v.49, no.2, p.222-229,

SIRY, JOSEPH.[TCARSON PIRIE SCOTT;
LOUIS SULLIVAN AND THE CHICAGO
DEPARTMENT STORE
Caroon, Pirie, Scott: Louis Sullivan
and the Chicago department store
[by] Joseph Siry [book review] /
Mark S. Foster.
1990 Winter, v.25, no.4,
p.303-305,

SISA, JOZSEF
Joseph Hoffer and the study of
ancient architecture / Jozsef
Sisa.
The Hungarian architect worked in
Greece 1833-1838.
SOCIETY OF ARCHITECTURAL
HISTORIANS. JOURNAL 1990 Dec.,
v.49, no.4, p.430-439, dets.,
elevs., plans, refs.

SISCHY, INGRID
The Samaras spectrum: high above
Manhattan, artist Lucas Samaras
puts a spin on his own color wheel
/ Ingrid Sischy.
HOUSE & GARDEN 1990 Dec., v.162,
no.12, p.[122-129],191, port.,
photos.

SITE, INC.
Green architecture...The role of
architecture in the built
environment: a recent SITE
project... / James Wines.
The Four Continents Bridge,
Hiroshima, Japan. Principal
architect: Joshua Weinstein.
ARCHITECTURAL RECORD 1990 Apr.,
v.178, no.4, p.78-83,163, ill.,
photos., plan, secn.
Interview: James Wines, Joshua
Weinstein, SITE / Thomas Fisher.
On "their method of working and
the meaning of their
architecture."
PROGRESSIVE ARCHITECTURE 1990
Aug., v.71, no.8, p.116-117,
dwgs., port.
Urbanist without Portfolio: Notes on
a career / by Jane Thompson.
One of four sections in a special
feature on "Women in American
Architecture". Contents: Marion G.
Weiss. -- Inea Elskop/1100
Architect. Billie Tsien.--
Patricia Sapinsley.--Alison
Sky+Michelle Stone/SITE Projects,
(Continued next column)

SITE, INC. (CONTINUED)
Urbanist without...(CONTINUED)
Inc.--Karen Bausman+Leslie Gill.--
Deborah Berke.--Amy Weinstein.--
Adele Naude Santos. English
translation, p.73.
SPACE DESIGN 1990 June, no.309,
p.36-53,73, axonometric views,
dwgs., ports., elevs., models,
photos., plans, secns.

SITE PLANNING
See BUILDING SITES

SITES - SLOPING
See SLOPING SITES

SITING
See ORIENTATION (ARCHITECTURE)

SITTE, CAMILLO, 1843-1903. STADTE-BAU
NACH SEINEN KUNSTLERISCHEN
GRUNDSATZEN
A centennium of Sitte / Barrie
Shelton.
Celebrates the anniversary of the
publication of Der Stadtebau by
Camillo Sitte: City planning
according to artistic principles.
AUSTRALIAN PLANNER: JOURNAL OF THE
ROYAL AUSTRALIAN PLANNING
INSTITUTE 1989 Dec., v.27, no.4,
p.29-32, plans, refs.

SITTEL-CZYPIONKA, WOLFGANG
Stadtplanung im Zeichen des
Baumarktes / Wolfgang
Sittel-Czypionka.
ALTE STADT 1989, v.16 no.4,
p.[582]-591, charts, map, photos.,
refs.

SITTING ROOMS
See LIVING ROOMS

SIVE, ANDRE, 1899-1958
Metallic housing development, Route
des Gardes, Meudon, [France],
1951.
Architects: Jean Prouve, Andre
Sive. Text in Japanese and
English.
ARCHITECTURE AND URBANISM 1990
Sept., no.9 Extra edition,
p.134-[139],263, photos., plan.

SIZA, ALVARO, 1933-
106 habitatges a La Haia.
Housing project,
Schilderswijkward, the Hague.
Architect: Alvaro Siza. English
summary, p.14.
QUADERNS D'ARQUITECTURA I
URBANISME 1988 July-Sept., no.178,
p.10-[15], axonometric views,
elevs., photos., plans.
Alvaro Siza.
Theme, with articles on 14
projects dating from 1960-1988,
including the Beires House, Povoa
de Varzim; swimming pool, Leca da
Palmeira; Pinto & Sotto Maior
bank, Oliveira de Azemeis; Quinta
da Malagueira housing, Evora; and
Van der Venne-Park, the Hague.
BAUWELT 1990 Aug.10, v.81,
no.29-30, p.1462-1498,cover,1449,
dwgs., port., models, photos.,
plans, secns., site plans,
isometric dwgs., aerial photos.

SIZA, ALVARO, 1933- (CONTINUED)
Alvaro Siza ou la passion patiente /
Dominique Machabert.
Profile of Alvaro Siza on the
occasion of the exhibition of his
work at the CCI, Centre Georges
Pompidou, Paris, May 30-Sept.3,
1990.
TECHNIQUES ET ARCHITECTURE 1990
Apr.-May, no.389, p.28, port.,
photo.
Alvaro Siza Vieira: Premi Europeu
D'arquitectura Mies Van De Rohe,
1988 [interview].
Text in Catalan and English.
QUADERNS D'ARQUITECTURA I
URBANISME 1988 July-Sept., no.178,
p.16-19,
Casa Cardoso, Oporto.
Architect: Edouardo Souto de
Moura. Text in Italian and
English.
LOTUS INTERNATIONAL 1989, no.63,
p.118-121, axonometric view,
elevs., photos.
El cilindro atrapado: Centro
Cultural de la Defensa, Madrid.
Architect: Alvaro Siza. English
summary, p.92.
A & V 1990, no.26, p.70-74,
axonometric views, dwgs., elevs.,
models, maps, plans, site plans,
sketches.
Il concorso per il centro culturale
della Difesa a Madrid / Antonio
Velez Catrain.
Publishes the entries by Juan
Navarro Baldeweg, Lluis Clotet
Ballus and Ignacio Paricio,
Francisco Javier Saenz de Oiza,
and Alvaro Siza, and contains an
interview with Eduardo Mangada.
Includes English summary,
captions, and translation.
CASABELLA 1990 May, v.54, no.568,
p.40-51, 61-63, axonometric view,
models, map, plans, secns.,
sketches, aerial photos.
Dos habitatges unifamiliars.
2 single-family houses
(1987-1988), Van der
Vennepark-Schilderswijk, the
Hague. Architect: Alvaro Siza.
QUADERNS D'ARQUITECTURA I
URBANISME 1988 July-Sept., no.178,
p.20-[31], elevs., photos., plans,
site plan.
Due interventi residenziali a L'Aja
= Two housing developments in the
Hague / Salvatore Polito.
Area 5 in the Schilderswijk
Centrum (105 units) and two houses
in the Van der Vennepark.
Architect: Alvaro Siza Vieira.
Includes english translation.
French, German, and Spanish
summaries, p.3.
L'INDUSTRIA DELLE COSTRUZIONI 1990
Mar., v.24, no.221, p.24-33,
elevs., photos., plans, secns.,
site plans.
Full-Stop and Comma / Peter
Buchanan.
On two housing projects, Full-Stop
and Comma in the Schilderswijk
section of the Hague. Architects:
Alvaro Siza, Carlos Castanheira
with Architectengemeenschap Van
den Broek en Bakema.
ARCHITECTURAL REVIEW 1990 Oct.,
v.188, no.1124, p.[49]-53,
axonometric views, elevs.,
photos., plans.

SIZA, ALVARO, 1933- (CONTINUED)
Geometrias talladas: centro
meteorologico = carved geometries.
Project for the meterological
center for the Olympic Village,
Barcelona. Architect: Alvaro Siza.
English text, p.88.
A & V 1990, no.22, p.70-73,
axonometric view, plans, secns.,
site plan, sketches.
Lisbona: una citta vulnerabile: il
Chiado di Alvaro Siza = Lisbon: a
vulnerable city: Alvaro Siza's
Chiado / Goncalo Byrne.
Proposed rebuilding of the Baixa
Pombalina quarter, Lisbon, after
fire Aug.25, 1988. Architect:
Alvaro Siza.
LOTUS INTERNATIONAL 1989, no.64,
p.32-37, elevs., site plan.
Nuovi progetti alla Giudecca: tipi
di edificazione e morfologia
dell'isola = new projects at the
Giudecca: building types and
morphology of the island / Marco
De Michelis.
Includes projects by Gregotti
Associati; Studio STNR; Iginio
Cappai, Pietro Mainardis,
Valeriano Pastor; Giuseppe
Gambirasio, Bruno Minardi; Giorgio
Bellavitis, F. Nani Valle; Alvaro
Siza.
LOTUS INTERNATIONAL 1986, no.51,
p.78-107, axonometric views,
dwgs., elevs., maps, photos.,
plans, secns., site plans, engrs.,
aerial photo.
Un paso al frente: el Centro
Cultural de la Defensa / Juan
Miguel Hernandez Leon.
Four entries in the competition
for Madrid cultural center.
ARQUITECTURA VIVA 1990 Mar.-Apr.,
no.11, p.34-36, axonometric view,
dwgs., models, plans, secns.,
sketches.
Piscina a Leca de Palmeira, 1961-66
= The swimming pool at Leca de
Palmeira, 1961-66 / Maria Bottero.
Architect: Alvaro Siza.
ABITARE 1990 June, no.286,
p.122-123, photos, site plan.
Portogallo: Ovar, 1981-85, Casa
Duarte = Portugal: the Duarte
house / Maria Bottero.
Architect: Alvaro Siza.
ABITARE 1990 June, no.286,
p.114-120, photos, elevs., plans,
secns., sketches.
Progetto di recupero per l'area del
Chiado, Lisboa: Alvaro Siza.
Text in Italian and English.
DOMUS 1990 Mar., no.714,
p.[48-55], axonometric view,
elevs., model, maps, photos.,
plans, secns., site plans,
sketches, aerial photo.
Proposta per il recupero della zona
sinistrata del Chiado = Proposal
for the recovery of the Chiado
damaged zone.
Architects: Alvaro Siza, with C.
Castanheira, L. Mendes, A.
Angelillo and A. Braga.
LOTUS INTERNATIONAL 1989, no.64,
p.40-53, elevs., models, photos.,
plans, secns., site plans.

SIZA, ALVARO, 1933- (CONTINUED)
Quello che e = What it is / Alvaro
Siza.
Commentary of Siza after Chiado,
Lisbon fire, 1988.
LOTUS INTERNATIONAL 1989, no.64,
p.38-39, dwg., photo.
Il ristorante Boa Nova a Leca de
Palmeira, 1958-63 = The Boa Nova
restarurant at Leca de Palmeira,
1958-63 / Maria Bottero.
Architect: Alvaro Siza.
ABITARE 1990 June, no.286, p.121,
photos.
Viagem / Alvaro Siza Vieira.
Travel sketches reproduced from
book: Alvaro Siza: esquissos de
viagem/travel sketches; 1988.
Catalan, English text.
QUADERNS D'ARQUITECTURA I
URBANISME 1989 Apr.-Sept.,
no.181-182, p.[82]-85, sketches.

SIZA, ALVARO, 1933---EXHIBITIONS
Hommage: Alvaro Siza: Werkschau im
Centre Pompidou, Paris, bis
3.9.1990 [exhibition review] /
Holger Fischer.
DEUTSCHE BAUZEITUNG 1990 Aug.,
v.124, no.8, p.121, port., photo.

SJOBERG, URSULA
Vibyholm och Safstaholm:
moderniseringen av tra
sormlandsslott / Ursula Sjoberg.
On the modernization of two
Swedish manor houses in the 1790s
and early 1800s for Gustaf and
Carl Bonde. Architect: Carl
Christoffer Gjorwell. Includes
English summary.
BEBYGGELSEHISTORISK TIDSKRIFT
1989, no.17-18, p.125-140, dwgs.,
elevs., photos., plans, site plan,
engrs., biblio., refs.

SJOLIE, METTE. SOSIAL BOLIGBYGGING I
NORGE 1945-1980
Exempel Selmer [book review] /
Lennart Holm.
Review of Sosial boligbygging i
Norge 1945-1980: en studie av
arkitekt Jens Selmbers arbeider,
by Mette Sjolie.
ARKITEKTUR: THE SWEDISH REVIEW OF
ARCHITECTURE 1990 Aug., v.90,
no.6, p.48-49, photos., plan, site
plan.

SJOSTROM, INGRID
Stone, style and truth: The vogue
for natural stone in Nordic
architecture 1880-1910 [by] Sixten
Ringbom [book review] / Ingrid
Sjostrom.
KONSTHISTORISK TIDSKRIFT 1989,
v.58, no.4, p.181-182,

SJOSTROM, JOHN
Bygglada for bostader [book review]
/ John Sjostrom.
Review of Bostadsstyrelsen
Bostadsbygglada, by Hakan Persson.
ARKITEKTUR: THE SWEDISH REVIEW OF
ARCHITECTURE 1990 Mar., v.90,
no.2, p.61-62, dwgs., elevs.,
plans.

SKIDMORE, OWINGS & MERRILL
(CONTINUED)
Tight line / John...(CONTINUED)
BUILDING DESIGN 1990 May 4,
no.984, p.32-33, dwgs., elevs.,
site plans.
Urban civility: Worldwide Plaza, New
York City, New York / Andrea
Oppenheimer Dean.
Architects: SOM/New York; Frank
Williams & Associates.
ARCHITECTURE: THE AIA JOURNAL 1990
Apr., v.79, no.4, p.[84-89],
photos., site plans, aerial photo.
Urban issues: Mission Bay / Sally
B. Woodbridge.
On the four plans proposed during
the 1980s for San Francisco's
Mission Bay. Includes plans by
John Carl Warnecke (1980), I.M.
Pei/Wallace Roberts & Todd (1985),
EDAW et al. (Mission Bay Planning
Team, 1987) and SOM (1989).
PROGRESSIVE ARCHITECTURE 1990 May,
v.71, no.5, p.121-122, figs.,
plans, site plans.
Het verhaal van een tweeling: SOM in
Brussel / Marc Dubois.
Plans for an addition to the BBL
(Bank Brussel Lambert) office
building, based on the 1974 design
by Gordon Bunshaft.
ARCHIS 1989 Sept., no.9, p.3-4,
dwg., models, site plan.
Yankees at the court of Lord St.
John / Stephen Trombley.
Focus on the reaction of Bruce
Graham of Som's London office to
Lord St. John of Fawsley's speech
at the Building Design 20th
anniversary dinner, condemning the
U.S. architectural practices'
invasion.
BUILDING DESIGN 1990 Mar.16,
no.977, p.12, ports.

SKILL TRAINING CENTERS
See TRAINING CENTERS

SKILLING WARD MAGNUSSON BARKSHIRE
Double strength [composite
structure] / Denise Chevin.
Benefits from combining steel
frames with high-strength concrete
in columns of tall buildings.
Examples are engineered by SWMB, a
Seattle firm.
BUILDING 1990 July 20, v.255,
no.29, p.62-65, photos., plans.

SKINNER, DAVID NEAVE, 1928-1989
Professor David Skinner: a personal
appreciation [obituary] / Mark
Trumbull.
LANDSCAPE DESIGN 1989 Apr.,
no.179, p.57.

SKJOLD SAEGROV TORPE
Fornyelse av boligstrok og bygulv i
Bergen / Ola Bettum.
Rehabilitation of granite
cobblestone streets since 1980.
Landscape architects:
Aall-Lokeland-Ragde
Arkitektkontor;
Skjold-Saegrov-Torpe; Cubus.
Includes English translation.
LANDSKAB 1990 Sept., v.71, no.6,
p.N-14-N-15, photos., site plan.

SKJOLD, SVEINUNG
Statoil-Verwaltung in Stavanger /
Sveinung Skjold.
English captions.
GARTEN UND LANDSCHAFT 1990, v.100,
no.8, p.30-33, dwg., photos., site
plan.

SKJONNEMAND, BJARNE, 1945-1990
Bjarne Skjonnemand [obituary].
INTERIOR DESIGN 1990 Oct., v.61,
no.14, p.60.

SKLAREK, NORMA MERRICK, 1928-
Conversations with Women Architects
/ Toshira Sato.
One of four sections in a special
feature on "Women in American
Architecture". Contents: Julie
Eizenberg.--Norma Sklarek/The
Jerda Partnership.--Deborah
Sussman.--Diane M. Caughey.--
Pamela Burton+Katherine Spitz.--
Dolores Hayden.--Sheila Levrant de
Bretteville.
SPACE DESIGN 1990 June, no.309,
p.06-22, dwgs., ports., elev.,
models, phgotos., plans, secn.

SKM ARCHITECTS & PLANNERS
Daita housing project / Yasumitsu
Matsunaga.
5-unit apartment house, Tokyo.
Architects: Yasumitsu Matsunaga,
SKM Architects & Planners.
JAPAN ARCHITECT 1990 Jan., v.65,
no.1(393), p.[48]-53, photos.,
plans, secn., site plan, isometric
dwg.
Mure housing project.
Apartment complex in Tokyo suburb.
Architects: SKM Architects &
Planners; Yasumitsu Matsunaga.
English summary, p.27.
KENCHIKU BUNKA 1990 June, v.45,
no.524, p.165-175, axonometric
views, photos., plans, secns.,
site plans.

SKORUPA, RAYMOND V.
A classical solution / Elizabeth H.
Hunter.
Screened porch replaced by room
addition with many French doors;
architect; Raymond Skorupa;
owner/interior designer: Leah
Lenney.
HOUSE BEAUTIFUL 1990 Aug., v.132,
no.8, p.41,76, port., photos.

SKOUGAARD, METTE
Reform og tradition: byggeskik pa
landet i Danmark i tiden omkring
de store landboreformer / Mette
Skougaard.
Ways of building in rural Denmark
at the time of the land-parcelling
legislation reforms. Includes
English summary.
BEBYGGELSESHISTORISK TIDSKRIFT
1989, no.17-18, p.31-42, elev.,
map, photos., plans, refs.

SKOUSBOLL, KARIN
"Concetto" / Karin Skousboll.
Organic designs by Danish artists,
including Niels Guttormsen and
Knud Haastrup, such as the
Egebjerggard II projects and
"Vingehuset" in Ballerup.
ARKITEKTEN 1990 Dec., v.92, no.18,
p.574-577,cover, photos.,
sketches.

SKOUSBOLL, KARIN (CONTINUED)
Paris, Paris.
Introduction to issue on Paris,
with articles by Jacques Berg,
Thomas Thiis-Evensen, and Karin
Skousboll. Seven other articles
are indexed separately.
ARKITEKTEN 1989 Dec.22, v.91,
no.23, p.573-607, axonometric
views, ill., ports., elevs.,
models, photos., plans, secns.,
site plans.
Problemstillinger i det abne land
Danmark... / Karin Skousboll.
Reports on a visit by members of
the Royal Academy to Jutland June
1-3 1989 to review open space
problems and propose development
strategies to meet future needs.
LANDSKAB 1990 Sept., v.71, no.6,
p.91-100, dwgs., photos.

SKOV, KAREN
Stojafskraermning i Landskabet /
Hans Bendtsen, Karen Skov.
On a recent report of the Danish
Road Institute on noise abatement,
with ideas for the use of noise
shields and baffle walls.
LANDSKAB 1990 Mar., v.71, no.2,
p.43-47,48, photos.

SKOVGAARD, N.C.
Hojhus i Horsens midtby.
Located on Raedersgade. Architect:
Kurt Birch. Engineer: N.C.
Skovgaard.
ARKITEKTEN 1990 Sept., v.92,
no.13, p.438, elev., model, site
plan.

SKRIVER, POUL ERIK
Ap Pension, Osterbrogade / Poul Erik
Skriver.
Renovation of a 1963 store and
office building in Copenhagen,
adding anodized aluminum panels on
the facade. Architect: Hvidt &
Molgaard. Includes English and
German summaries.
ARKITEKTUR DK 1990, v.34, no.6,
p.288-292, dwg., photos., plans,
site plan.
Cite de science et de l'industrie /
Poul Erik Skriver.
Architect: Adrien Fainsilber.
ARKITEKTEN 1989 Dec.22, v.91,
no.23, p.590-591, photos., secn.
Danisco pa Christianshavn / Poul
Erik Skriver.
Conversion of a 1912 sugar factory
at Langebrogade 1 in Copenhagen
into a company headquarters.
Architect: Hvidt & Molgaard.
Includes English and German
summaries.
ARKITEKTUR DK 1990, v.34, no.6,
p.277-281, photos., plan, site
plan.
Digital Danmark / Poul Erik Skriver.
New office building in Horsholm
for the Danish division of DEC.
Architect: Hvidt & Molgaard.
Includes English and German
summaries.
ARKITEKTUR DK 1990, v.34, no.6,
p.282-287, photos., plan, site
plan, isometric dwg.

SKRIVER, POUL ERIK (CONTINUED)

Droit morale [Aalborg] / Poul Erik Skriver.
Controversy over mural paintings and interior decoration of Aalborghallen. Painter: Knud Erik Faergemann.
ARKITEKTEN 1989 Dec.22, v.91, no.23, p.617, photos.

Formdannende studier / Poul Erik Skriver.
Projects by second-year students of Cort Ross Dinesen and Erik Werner Petersen at the Kunstakademiets Arkitektskole.
ARKITEKTEN 1990 Nov. v.92, no.16, p.528-531, elevs., models, plans.

Institut du monde arabe / Poul Erik Skriver.
Architect: Jean Nouvel.
ARKITEKTEN 1989 Dec.22, v.91, no.23, p.592-595, axonometric view, det., photos., plans.

Jaegersborg alle midtpunkt / Poul Erik Skriver.
Construction of a new shopping, office, and apartment complex on the site of an old dairy.
Architect: KHR A/S Arkitekter.
Includes English and German summaries.
ARKITEKTUR DK 1990, v.34, no.6, p.293-299, photos., plans, site plans.

Lund & Slaatto / Poul Erik Skriver.
Projects include Det Norske Veritas, Veritas II, Norges Bank, Kreditkassen, Kulturhus i Stavanger, Hotel Skagen Brygge, Eidsvag Kirke, St. Magnus Kirke, Sentrumplan. Includes English and German summaries.
ARKITEKTUR DK 1990, v.34, no.5, p.221-257,cover, dets., dwgs., elev., models, photos., plans, secns., site plans, isometric dwg., aerial photos.

SKRIVER, SOREN

Leprahospitalet i Lasur, Indien / Soren Skriver.
Architects: Per Christian Brynildsen, Jan Olav Jensen.
ARKITEKTUR DK 1990, v.34, no.6, p.A90,A92,A94, photo., plans, secns.

SKUDE, FLEMMING, 1944-

Arkitonisk autenticitet - om to arbejder af John Hejduk / Flemming Skude.
A double house in Tegel, W. Berlin and apartment house on Friedrichstadt, W. Berlin.
ARKITEKTUR DK 1989, v.33, no.8, p.A170-A172, det., photos., plan, secn.

Erindringens eufori - om J. P. Kleihues' forhistoriske museum i Frankfurt / Flemming Skude.
ARKITEKTUR DK 1989, v.33, no.8, p.A174-A180, det., photos., plan.

Fantasiens frie flugt [exhibition review] / Flemming Skude.
Exhibit in Rundetarn, Jan.25-Feb.18,1990.
ARKITEKTEN 1990 Apr., v.92, no.4, p.137, dwgs., port.

SKUDE, FLEMMING, 1944- (CONTINUED)

Kritiske konstruktioner - om Gordon Matta-Clark / Flemming Skude.
ARKITEKTUR DK 1989, v.33, no.7, p.A160-A162, photos.

Musikstue, Vaserne.
A music rehearsal room added to a 20-yr. old, one story house.
Architect: Flemming Skude.
Includes English and German summaries.
ARKITEKTUR DK 1990, v.34, no.7, p.355-356, photos., plan, secn., sketch.

Overens med universet [Christopher Alexander] / Flemming Skude.
ARKITEKTEN 1990 July, v.92, no.9, p.288-295, dets., elevs., photos., plans, secns., site plans.

Romersk resonans - om Spaniens nye nationalmuseum for romersk kunst / Flemming Skude.
Located in Merida, Spain.
Architect: Rafael Moneo.
ARKITEKTUR DK 1989, v.33, no.7, p.A150-A159, elev., photos., plans, secns., isometric dwg.

Strukturalistiske spidsfindigheder-- om Wexner-centret for visuel kunst / Fleming Skude.
Architect: Peter Eisenman.
Reprinted from Progressive architecture, 1989, no.10.
ARKITEKTUR DK 1990, v.34, no.1-2, p.A2-A12, dwgs., photo., plan, site plan.

Vitra / Flemming Skude.
Design Museum, Weil am Rhein.
Architect: Frank Gehry.
ARKITEKTEN 1990 May, v.92, no.6, p.198-201, dets., model, photos., plan, secn., sketch.

SKULJ, IGOR, 1946-

Igor Skulj: biblioteca a Ljubljana.
Text in Italian and English.
DOMUS 1990 Nov., no.721, p.6-7, axonometric view, elev., photos., plans.

SKURKA, NORMA

Tuxedo Park [New York] / Norma Skurka.
Original planner: Pierre Lorillard.
HOUSE BEAUTIFUL 1986 May, v.128, no.5, p.68-77, photos.

SKY, ALISON

Urbanist without Portfolio: Notes on a career / by Jane Thompson.
One of four sections in a special feature on "Women in American Architecture". Contents: Marion G. Weiss.-- Inea Elskop/1100 Architect. Billie Tsien.-- Patricia Sapinsley.--Alison Sky+Michelle Stone/SITE Projects, Inc.--Karen Bausman+Leslie Gill.-- Deborah Berke.--Amy Weinstein.-- Adele Naude Santos. English translation, p.73.
SPACE DESIGN 1990 June, no.309, p.36-53,73, axonometric views, dwgs., ports., elevs., models, photos., plans, secns.

SKYLIGHTS

See also OCULI

New technologies in glass: a round up of six new installations.
ARCHITECTURE: THE AIA JOURNAL 1990 Jan., v.79, no.1, p.136, dwgs., photos.

Roofing.
Ten articles, on materials, decorative and aesthetic aspects, corrosion, standards and references, weathering, skylights, and products.
BUILDING 1990 July 27, v.255, no.30 suppl., p.3-68, diagrs., photos.

Il tema del lucernario / Walter Bianchi, Mauro Colombo.
Examples of glass atriums in buildings by Mario Botta.
VILLE GIARDINI 1990 June, no.249, p.46-47, dets., dwgs., photos., secn.

SKYLINES--CANADA--TORONTO (ONTARIO)

Driving us crazy: stoplights in Downtown Toronto / [Mark Franklin].
"The changing roles of government, business and the architect in shaping the skyline."
CANADIAN ARCHITECT 1990 Feb., v.35, no.2, p.16-22, graphs, ill., models, photos., aerial photos.

SKYLINES--ENGLAND--LONDON

Planning for tall buildings in London / Gregory Wilson, Roger Norton.
THE PLANNER 1990 Oct.19, v.76, no.41, p.9-11, photo., sketch, refs.

SKYLINES--RESEARCH

On visual complexity on the urban skyline / Toshinobu Oku.
Text in Japanese; English summary, p.61.
NIHON KENCHIKU GAKKAI KEIKAKUKEI RONBUN HOKOKU SHU = JOURNAL OF ARCHITECTURE, PLANNING AND ENVIRONMENTAL ENGINEERING 1990 June, no.6(412), p.61-71, graphs, tables, refs.

SKYSCRAPERS

See TALL BUILDINGS

SKYWALKS

See RAISED PEDESTRIAN WALKWAYS

SLAATO, NILS, 1923-

Veritasparken, Baerum / Ola Bettum.
A two-phase conversion of old industrial area into an office park. Landscape architects: Hindhamar-Sundt-Thomassen.
Architects: Kjell Lund and Nils Slaatto. Includes English translation.
LANDSKAB 1990 May, v.71, no.3-4, p.N-7-N-11, photos., secns., site plans.

SLACK, WILLIAM J.

Technics: curtain walls - options and issues / Gordon H. Smith, William J. Slack.
A review of systems and considerations for cladding high-rise buildings.
PROGRESSIVE ARCHITECTURE 1990
(Continued next page)

SLACK, WILLIAM J. (CONTINUED)
Technics: curtain...(CONTINUED)
Apr., v.71, no.4, p.[53-57],
photos., biblio.

SLAPETA, VLADIMIR
Architektur, Gesundheit Politik: zum
Werk von Bedrich Rozehnal /
Vladimir Slapeta.
ARCHITHESE 1990 July-Aug., v.20,
no.4, p.46-53, dwgs., elevs.,
photos., plans, refs.
Bata architecture / Vladimir
Slapeta.
On the projects and architects
sponsored by the Bata firm,
particularly in Zlin.
RASSEGNA 1990 Sept., v.12,
no.43/3, p.70-79, dwgs., photos.
Die "Bata"-Architektur oder die
Architektur eines Unternehmens /
Vladimir Slapeta.
On the projects and architects
sponsored by the firm Bat'a,
especially in Czechoslovakia.
BAUFORUM 1990, v.23, no.136,
p.19-48,cover, dwgs., ports.,
elevs., photos., plans, secns.,
site plans, sketches, biblio.
Introduction to the city [Breslau] /
Vladimir Slapeta.
Introduction to theme issue on
Breslau, Poland. Articles indexed
separately.
RASSEGNA 1989 Dec., v.11, no.40/4,
p.7-13, photos.
Luxury country houses / Vladimir
Slapeta.
Features four houses: Dr. Rabe's
house, Zwenkau, Leipzig, 1928-30,
architect: Adolf Rading; Hasek
house, Jablonec, Czechoslovakia,
1930-31 and the Schmelowsky house,
Jablonec, 1931-32, architect:
Heinrich Lauterbach and Schminke
house, Lobau, E. Germany, 1930-33,
architect: Hans Scharoun.
RASSEGNA 1989 Dec., v.11, no.40/4,
p.78-88, dwg., photos., plans,
refs.
Neues Bauen in Breslau / Vladimir
Slapeta.
On the work of Ernst May, Hans
Poelzig, Max Berg and Adolf
Rading, Erich Mendelsohn, and
others in Breslau during the early
part of the 20th cent.
RASSEGNA 1989 Dec., v.11, no.40/4,
p.14-62, ill., dwgs., ports.,
elevs., models, photos, plans,
site plans, aerial photo., refs.
Pupils of the Academy / Vladimir
Slapeta.
On the work of five former
architecture students at the
Breslau Academy of Arts and
Artistic Crafts: Emil Lange, Karl
Joseph Erbs, Moritz Hadda,
Heinrich Tischler and Heinrich
Lauterbach.
RASSEGNA 1989 Dec., v.11, no.4014,
p.73-77, dwgs., photos., plans,
refs.

SLATE
See "SLATE" AS A SUBHEADING AFTER
SPECIFIC BUILDING TYPES OR OTHER
MAIN HEADINGS.

SLATER & MOBERLY
Sloane leader.
On the Peter Jones store in Sloane
Square, London, completed in
stages from 1935-1939. Architects:
William Crabtree, Slater &
Moberly. Includes interview with
Crabtree.
ARCHITECTURAL REVIEW 1990 Jan.,
v.187, no.1115, p.75-79, dwgs.,
photos., plans.

SLATER, MARTIN JOHNS, 1892-1990
Martin Johns Slater [obituary] /
John L. Harding.
RIBA JOURNAL 1990 Mar., v.97,
no.3, p.106,

SLATIN, PETER
A housing enterprise / Peter Slatin.
The Enterprise Foundation and
LESCH, a community group, have
renovated 3 tenement buildings at
250-254 East 4th St. on the Lower
East Side of Manhattan.
METROPOLIS 1990 July-Aug., v.10,
no.1, p.18-20, photo.

**SLAUGHTERHOUSES--19TH CENTURY--UNITED
STATES--CINCINNATI (OHIO)**
From slaughterhouse to soap-boiler:
Cincinnati's meat packing
industry, changing technologies,
and the rise of mass production,
1825-1870 / Steve C. Gordon.
SOCIETY FOR INDUSTRIAL ARCHEOLOGY.
JOURNAL 1990, v.16, no.1, p.55-67,
ill., dwgs., secns., refs.

SLAV
See "SLAV" AS A SUBHEADING AFTER
SPECIFIC BUILDING TYPES OR OTHER
MAIN HEADINGS.

SLAVIC
See SLAV

SLAVONIC
See SLAV

SLAWIK, HAN
Het Burgerweeshuis: Aldo van Eycks
Waisenhaus in Amsterdam / Han
Slawik.
DEUTSCHE BAUZEITUNG 1990 Feb.,
v.124, no.2, p.84-88, photos.,
plans, secn., aerial photo.
Haus der Zukunft: Geballte
Haustechnik im "Huis van de
Toekomst", Rosmalen / Han Slawik.
House of the Future, in the
Netherlands. Architect: Cees Dam.
DEUTSCHE BAUZEITUNG 1990 Aug.,
v.124, no.8, p.78-82, dwgs.,
photos.
"Schiphol 2000": der Ausbau der
Amsterdamer Flughafens Schiphol
(Benthem, Crouwel mit Netherlands
Airport Consults) / Han Slawik.
DEUTSCHE BAUZEITUNG 1990 Nov.,
v.124, no.11, p.128-132, dwgs.,
elevs., models, secns., site
plans.

SLESIN, SUZANNE
Artist in wonderland [Izhar Patkin]
/ Suzanne Slesin.
Loft of the Israeli-born artist,
located on the Lower East Side of
Manhattan.
METROPOLITAN HOME 1990 Aug., v.22,
no.8, p.142-145, photos.

SLESIN, SUZANNE (CONTINUED)
Hamptons style: Slesin/Steinberg
house, Bridgehampton, New York.
Alteration of a small 1930s
cottage. Architect: Lee H.
Skolnick Architecture and Design.
ARCHITECTURAL RECORD 1990
Mid-Apr., v.178, no.5, p.34-[41],
axonometric views, photos., plans.

SLESIN, SUZANNE. INDIA STYLE
India style.
Excerpted from: India style, by
Suzanne Slesin, pub.1990.
HOUSE BEAUTIFUL 1990 Sept., v.132,
no.9, p.34-36,108, photos.

SLESSOR, CATHERINE
Building biology: green labelling /
Catherine Slessor.
Issues concerning
environmentally-safe products and
their labelling.
ARCHITECTS' JOURNAL 1990 Feb.7,
v.191, no.6, p.61-63, ill.,
photos., refs.
Buildings update: halls of
residence 1: policy and practice
/ Catherine Slessor.
Educational residence halls in
Britain.
ARCHITECTS' JOURNAL 1990 July 25,
v.192, no.4, p.51-54, photos.,
table, refs., elevs.
Buildings update: swimming pools 1:
a bigger splash / Catherine
Slessor.
In Britain.
ARCHITECTS' JOURNAL 1990 Oct.10,
v.192, no.15, p.67-71, photos.,
plan.
Current account [Shad Thames,
London] / Catherine Slessor.
Current planning and projects in
Shad Thames in London's Docklands.
ARCHITECTS' JOURNAL 1990 May 16,
v.191, no.20, p.[38]-43,46-51,
53-54, axonometric views, elevs.,
photos., plans, secns., site
plans, table, ref.
Irish identity: New directions in
Irish architecture / Catherine
Slessor.
Report of a lecture delivered at
the RIBA 20 Mar. 1990.
ARCHITECTS' JOURNAL 1990 Apr.4,
v.191, no.14, p.90-91, photo.,
secn.
Office politics / Catherine Slessor.
New Thamesside offices for Foster
Associates, with additional
residential and commercial space.
ARCHITECTS' JOURNAL 1990 Oct.3,
v.192, no.14, p.34-47, axonometric
views, diagrs., elev., photos.,
plans, secn., site plan, refs.
Pleasure palace: The Dome,
Doncaster.
Architects: Faulkner Browns
Contents: Appraisal, by Catherine
Slessor; Architect's account, by
Neil Taylor; Economic appraisal,
energy comment by Derek Poole;
Cost comment, by Roger Barbrook;
Cost analysis; Atrium roof,
leisure centre.
ARCHITECTS' JOURNAL 1990 Mar.21,
v.191, no.12, p.39-69, axonometric
views, dets., dwg., elevs., maps,
photos., plans, secns., site
plans, sketches, table, isometric
dwg.

SLESSOR, CATHERINE (CONTINUED)
Prize writer.
A short notice on the
Architectural Journalist of the
Year award to Catherine Slessor.
ARCHITECTS' JOURNAL 1990 Nov.21,
v.192, no.20, p.9, port.
Tropical hardwoods: fruits of the
forest / Catherine Slessor, Mary
Halnan.
Alternatives for architects.
ARCHITECTS' JOURNAL 1990 Aug.8,
v.192, no.6, p.45-52, graph, maps,
photos., tables, aerial photo.,
biblio., refs.

SLOAN, DENIS
L'atelier de Guy-Rachel Grataloup /
Marc Gaillard.
Interiors of artist's studio/home
in Paris. Architect: Denis Sloan.
L'OEIL 1990 Oct., no.423,
p.[64]-69, photos.
Institut Europeen des Normes de
Telecommunications Sophia
Antipolis / Denis Sloan.
Architect: D. Sloan.
LE MUR VIVANT 1990, no.96,
p.52-57, axonometric view, elevs.,
photos., site plan.

SLOANE, JOHN
Regeneration in action / John
Sloane.
In Wigan.
HOUSING AND PLANNING REVIEW 1990
Aug.-Sept., v.45, no.4, p.10-11,
photo.

SLOCOVICH, GIOVANNA
Il futuro ha un cuore antico: civic
stadium of Florence / Loris G.
Macci.
Renovation and expansion of
stadium built in 1930s. Original
architect: Pier Luigi Nervi;
architects for renovation: Italo
Gamberini, Loris G. Macci, Enrico
Novelli, Giovanna Slocovich. Text
in Italian and English.
L'ARCA 1990 May, no.38, p.74-79,
elevs., photos., plans, secns.

SLOPING SITES
See "SLOPING SITES" AS A SUBDIVISION
AFTER SPECIFIC BUILDINGS TYPES OR
OTHER MAIN HEADINGS.

SLUM CLEARANCE
See CITY PLANNING

SLUMS
See also SHANTYTOWNS
See also SQUATTER SETTLEMENTS
See also TENEMENT HOUSES

SLUMS--BRAZIL--SAO PAULO
A convivencia com a contradicao
metropolitana.
PROJETO 1990 Dec.-1991 Jan.,
no.137, p.A1-A24, elevs., maps,
photos., plans, secns., site
plans, tables, aerial photo.

SLUMS--INDIA
The stark reality of India's slums /
Arun Misra.
VOLUNTARY HOUSING 1990 June,
p.36-37, port.

SLUMS--THAILAND--BANGKOK
Slumforbedring i Bangkok / Asger
Mollerup.
ARKITEKTEN 1990 Apr., v.92, no.4,
p.A80-A83, photos.

SLUYMER, JOHANNES MARIA
Europan '89: abitare (e progettare)
in Europa.
Projects by Miriam Dubois,
Wilfried Kneffel, J.M. Sluymer, C.
Liebermann and A. Daniel, J.-P.
Calori, P. Costanzo and A. Cesari,
Jaap Udema, A. Muller, and Chiche
Carola Guerrier Guffroy Locicero.
PARAMETRO 1990 Jan.-Feb., no.176,
p.82-91, axonometric views, ill.,
dwgs., plans, secns., site plans.

SMALL
See "SMALL" AS A SUBHEADING AFTER
SPECIFIC BUILDING TYPES OR OTHER
MAIN HEADINGS.

SMALL, JIM
A visual recording / Jim Small.
On an audio-visual recording in
1988 with former president Jimmy
Carter, in conjunction with the
future development of the Jimmy
Carter National Historic Site,
Plains, Ga.
CRM BULLETIN: A NATIONAL PARK
SERVICE TECHNICAL BULLETIN 1990,
v.13, no.2, p.[1],4-5, photo.

SMALL, MICHAEL
Portrait of a home / Michael Small.
Four American photographers' views
of the interior of their homes:
Erica Lennard, Barbara Kasten,
Jean Pagliuso, and Bonnie
Schiffman. Three are in New York,
one is in West Hollywood, Calif.
METROPOLITAN HOME 1990 May, v.22,
no.5, p.[111-121], dets., ports.,
photos.

SMALLBONE, CHARLES
The flavor of southern France.
Charles Smallbone's family kitchen
in St. Tropez; founder of
Smallbone Kitchens.
HOUSE BEAUTIFUL 1990 Apr., v.132,
no.4, p.80-83, photos., plan.

SMALLBONE KITCHENS
The flavor of southern France.
Charles Smallbone's family kitchen
in St. Tropez; founder of
Smallbone Kitchens.
HOUSE BEAUTIFUL 1990 Apr., v.132,
no.4, p.80-83, photos., plan.

SMAN, GERT VAN DER
L'Eoila di Villa Trento: arte e
umanesimo letterario nel Vicentino
/ Gert Van der Sman.
On the function of the 1560 Eolia
of the Villa Trento, Vicenza and
1570 mural painting by Giovanni
Antonio Fasolo.
ARTE VENETA 1988, v.42, p.58-67,
photos., refs.

SMARGIASSI, MICHELE
Genesi del piccone demolitore: Un
secolo e mezzo di trasformazioni
urbane a Modena (1760-1915) /
Michele Smargiassi.
STORIA URBANA 1989 Apr.-June,
v.13, no.47, p.[129]-173, maps,
refs.

SMART, A.
Forgotten obstacles, neglected
forces: explaining the origins of
Hong Kong public housing / A.
Smart.
ENVIRONMENT AND PLANNING D.
SOCIETY & SPACE 1989 June, v.7,
no.2, p.179-196, refs.

SMART BUILDINGS
See INTELLIGENT BUILDINGS

SMART, C.M. MUSCULAR CHURCHES:
ECCLESIASTICAL ARCHITECTURE OF THE
HIGH VICTORIAN PERIOD
High falutin': Muscular churches:
ecclesiastical architecture of the
High Victorian period, by C.M.
Smart, Jr. / Gavin Stamp.
ARCHITECTS' JOURNAL 1990 Mar.14,
v.191, no.11, p.95, sketch.
Monuments to the other world [book
review] / Tyrrell Burgess.
Review of: Muscular churches:
ecclesiastical architecture of the
High Victorian period, by C. M.
Smart.
ROYAL SOCIETY OF ARTS, LONDON. RSA
JOURNAL 1990 July, v.138, no.5408,
p.566-567.

SMART, ERIC
Orlando's City Commons: a model
public/private venture / Lewis
Oliver, Eric Smart.
Major 7-acre development,
including a new city hall, public
park and plaza, commercial office
and retail space, and parking in
Orlando's Southern Gateway area.
Planners: Project for Public
Spaces (PPS, Inc.), and Heller &
Leake; architects for the city
hall: HKS and CRS Sirrine.
URBAN LAND 1990 Jan., v.49, no.1,
p.21-25, dwg., site plan, aerial
photo.

SMEDBERG, JOHAN, 1851-1913
Moderne kunst i tidligere el-vaerk /
Lasse Freisleben.
Renovation of a 90-year old
gasworks on Gasverksgatan/Stora
Nygatan, Malmo, Sweden for use as
an exhibition hall for modern art.
Original architect: John Smedberg.
Restoration architect: White
Arkitekter.
ARKITEKTEN 1989 Dec.12, v.91,
no.22, p.A544-A546, photos., plan.

SMEDSVIG, ARNE
Stadterneuerung in Bergen / Arne
Smedsrig.
English summary and captions.
GARTEN UND LANDSCHAFT 1990, v.100,
no.8, p.56-60, photos., site
plans.

SMELLS
See ODORS

SMET, ANTOINE DE
Le chateau Grenier / Antoine De
Smet.
History of 19th cent. house in
Gavere, Belgium, built by the
Grenier family. The neoclassical
renovation in 1837-1839 was
designed by Bruno Renard.
MAISONS D'HIER ET D'AUJOURD'HUI =
DE WOONSTEDE DOOR DE EEUWEN HEEN
(Continued next page)

SMET, ANTOINE DE (CONTINUED)
Le chateau Grenier /...(CONTINUED)
1990 Sept., no.87, p.2-13, ports.,
photos., biblio.

SMETS, MARCEL
Hoog-Kortrijk: het structureren van
de hedendaagse stadsontwikkeling /
Marcel Smets.
Proposals by four architects and
planners for development of the
Dutch city: Stephane Beel, Rem
Koolhaas, Bob van Reeth, and
Bernardo Secchi).
ARCHIS 1990 Dec., no.12, p.45-51,
dwgs., models, maps, photos., site
plans.

SMITH, ADRIAN
Energy and the urban environment /
Adrian Smith.
THE PLANNER 1990 May 18, v.76,
no.19, p.12-13, photos., aerial
photo.

SMITH, ADRIAN D.
Heightened profiles / Cynthia Chapin
Davidson.
Two Chicago projects: NBC Tower at
Cityfront Center and AT&T
Corporate Center at corner of
Franklin and Monroe streets, which
reflect influences from 1930's
skyscrapers. Architect: Adrian
Smith and SOM.
INLAND ARCHITECT 1990 Jan.-Feb.,
v.34, no.1, p.28-35, elev.,
photos., plan.
"Modern Classicism, un esempio = an
example: NBC Tower, Chicago,
Cityfront Center.
Architect: Adrian Smith of SOM.
ARCHITETTURA: CRONACHE E STORIA
1990 Nov., v.36, no.11(421),
p.795-797, photos., secn., site
plan.
Rich as Rockefeller: the NBC Tower
in Chicago's Cityfront Center... /
Paul M. Sachner.
Architect: Adrian Smith of SOM.
ARCHITECTURAL RECORD 1990 Apr.,
v.178, no.4, p.68-[73], photos.,
plans, secn., site plan.

SMITH, ASHLEY
Arthur Dayson: architect of the
American spirit / Ashley Smith.
Architect: Arthur Dayson. Text in
Japanese and English.
ARCHITECTURE AND URBANISM 1990
July, no.7(238), p.40-49, photos.

SMITH, AUGUSTUS, 1804-1872
Un giardino tropicale in Cornovaglio
/ Gilberto Oneto.
Gardens on the island of Scilly,
England begun in 1834. architect:
Augustus Smith.
VILLE GIARDINI 1990 June, no.249,
p.82-87, photos.

SMITH, BRIAN
Conservation in a historic city:
Norwich / Brian Smith.
THE PLANNER 1990 Feb.23, v.76,
no.7, p.65-68, port., photos.

SMITH, BRUCE
The formation of urban
infrastructure through
nongovernmental planning: the
private places of St. Louis,
1869-1920 / David T. Beito, Bruce
Smith.
Examples drawn from the work of
architect Julius Pitzman.
JOURNAL OF URBAN HISTORY 1990 May,
v.16, no.3, p.263-303, photos.,
site plans, refs.

SMITH, CHARLES SAUMAREZ
English neo-classical architecture,
by Damie Stillman [book review] /
Charles Saumarez Smith.
2-volume work pub. in 1988.
BURLINGTON MAGAZINE 1990 Mar.,
v.132, no.1044, p.217-218,

SMITH, COLIN STANSFIELD, 1932-
Acid house / Robert Cowan.
Report on a debate organized by
the Cambridge Forum for the
Construction Industry, held at the
Cambridge Union. Participants
included: Leon Krier, Colin
Stansfield Smith, Peter Clegg,
Quinlan Terry, and Richard
Biscoe-Taylor.
ARCHITECTS' JOURNAL 1990 Feb.7,
v.191, no.6, p.24-25, ports.
Gebaudebeispiel: Vorabdruck aus dem
neuen Dachatlas Geneigte Dacher.
Roof details from 4 projects:
swimming center, Albstadt, W.G.
(P.Siefert et al); housing
development, Gebensdorf,
Switzerland (C. Tognola, C.
Stahel, D. Zulauf); student
housing, Wales (D. Lea); and
housing for handicapped,
Eastleigh, England (D. White).
DETAIL 1990 Feb.-Mar., v.30, no.1,
p.[16-23], dets., elev., photos.,
plans, secns., site plans.
Gold Medal for county class.
1991 RIBA Gold Medal awarded to
Colin Stansfield Smith.
BUILDING DESIGN 1990 Nov.9,
no.1011, p.[1]-2, dwgs., port.
Public sector wins royal Gold Medal.
Colin Stansfield Smith awarded the
1991 RIBA Gold Medal.
RIBA JOURNAL 1990 Dec., v.97,
no.12, p.11, port., photo.
Smith grabs gold for public sector /
Colin Davies.
Colin Stansfield Smith is the
first public sector architect to
win the Royal Gold Medal for 17
years.
ARCHITECTS' JOURNAL 1990 Nov.14,
v.192, no.20, p.13, port., photos.

SMITH, DAVE
Towards a public policy for
floodplain management; a case
study of the experience in Moose
Jaw, Saskatchewan / Dave Smith.
PLAN CANADA 1989 Jan., v.29, no.1,
p.52-62, maps, photos., table,
biblios. refs.

SMITH, DAVID
Does the left hand know where the
right one digs? / David Smith.
Principles and guidelines on
pavement cuts and the improvement
of street and sidewalk appearance;
research conducted by the American
(Continued next column)

SMITH, DAVID (CONTINUED)
Does the left hand... (CONTINUED)
Public Works Association.
AMERICAN CITY & COUNTY 1990 Sept.,
v.105, no.9, p.32,34, photo.
The representation of industry on
large-scale county maps of England
and Wales 1700-c.1840 / David
Smith.
Includes summary.
INDUSTRIAL ARCHAEOLOGY REVIEW 1990
Spring, v.12, no.2, p.153-177,
maps, photos., tables, refs.

SMITH, DESMOND
Local area conservation: how one
suburban municipality utilizes
environmental planning to conserve
its natural heritage / Desmond
Smith.
The "Alpine Area Official
Community Plan" of the District of
North Vancouver; winner of the
1988 CIP Award for Planning
Excellence.
PLAN CANADA 1989 Sept., v.29,
no.5, p.39-42, model, photos.

SMITH, ELIZABETH A. T. 1958-.
BLUEPRINTS FOR MODERN LIVING:
HISTORY AND LEGACY OF THE CASE STUDY
HOUSES
California case study: Blueprints
for modern living: history and
legacy of the Case Study Houses,
edited by Elizabeth A. T. Smith
[book review] / Ivor Richards.
Accompanies exhibition at the
Museum of Contemporary art, Los
Angeles 17 Oct.1989 - 18 Feb.1990.
ARCHITECTS' JOURNAL 1990 Oct.3,
v.192, no.14, p.71, photo.

SMITH, ETHEL
Georgian grace in Atlanta: renewing
southern traditions for Charlotte
and Rankin Smith / Jeffrey
Simpson.
Interiors of Georgian-style home
in northwestern Atlanta.
Architect: William Frank McCall.
Interior designers: Betty Sherrill
and Ethel Smith of McMillen.
ARCHITECTURAL DIGEST 1990 May,
v.47, no.5, p.220-225, photos.

SMITH, FAUSE & ASSOCIATES
Acoustics: [Winter Garden] / Michael
Wagner.
On the acoustics in the Winter
Garden atrium, New York City.
Architects: Cesar Pelli &
Associates. Acoustics: Smith,
Fause & Associates.
INTERIORS 1990 Dec., v.150, no.5,
p.33, photo., plan.

SMITH, FRANCIS, 1672-1738
Nosely Hall, Leicestershire: the
seat of Lord Hazlerigg / John
Martin Robinson.
Here attributed to Francis and
William Smith of Warwick.
COUNTRY LIFE 1990 Mar.29, v.184,
no.13, p.86-91, photos.

SMITH, G. WENTWORTH
Carpet's life cycle cost is not
clear cut / G. Wentworth Smith.
FACILITIES DESIGN & MANAGEMENT
1989 Aug., v.8, no.7, p.68-69,
photos.

SMITH, GORDON
A machine for growing: climate
control / Robert A. Ivy.
The Dorthy Chapman Fuqua
Conservatory, Atlanta Botanical
Garden, Atlanta, Ga. Architects:
Heery Architects & Engineers
(Gregory Peirce, principal
designer; Gordon Smith, project
architect); landscape architects:
Edward L. Dougherty & Associates.
ARCHITECTURE: THE MAGAZINE OF THE
AMERICAN INSTITUTE OF ARCHITECTS
1990 May, v.79, no.5, p.[66-73],
dets., photos., secn., site plan.

SMITH, GORDON H.
Technics: curtain walls - options
and issues / Gordon H. Smith,
William J. Slack.
A review of systems and
considerations for cladding
high-rise buildings.
PROGRESSIVE ARCHITECTURE 1990
Apr., v.71, no.4, p.[53-57],
photos., biblio.

SMITH, HAYDN W.
George Greaves [obituary] / Haydn W.
Smith, C. Stuart Ellis.
RIBA JOURNAL 1990 Dec., v.97,
no.12, p.85.

SMITH, IAN
Fire regs consultation: B3 fire
spread: structure / Ian Smith.
Third in series on British fire
regulations.
ARCHITECTS' JOURNAL 1990 Apr.25,
v.191, no.17, p.63-67, photos.,
tables.

SMITH, JANE WEBB
Streamlining with friction: an
exhibition review / Jane Webb
Smith.
"Streamlining America", at the
Henry Ford Museum, Dearborn,
Mich., Sept.1986-Dec.1989,
attempted to show how a concept
"became a system of social values
as well as a marketing tool...in
the 1930s".
WINTERTHUR PORTFOLIO 1990 Spring,
v.25, no.1, p.[55]-66, photos.,
refs.

SMITH, JANET CHARLOTTE
Form and function of the side
chambers of Fifth- and
Sixth-Century churches in Ravenna
/ Janet Charlotte Smith.
Examines typology, chronology,
Byzantine influences, liturgical
functions and iconography, and
compares the chambers with
"pastophoria." Based on the
author's dissertation, 1987;
includes abstract.
SOCIETY OF ARCHITECTUAL
HISTORIANS. JOURNAL 1990 June,
v.49, no.2, p.181-204, dwgs.,
photos., plans, refs.

SMITH, JANET CHARLOTTE (CONTINUED)
The side chambers of San Giovanni
Evangelista in Ravenna: church
libraries of the fifth century /
Janet Charlotte Smith.
Based on a section of the author's
dissertation (1987). Includes
abstract.
GESTA 1990, v.29, no.1, p.86-97,
dwg., photos., plans, sketches,
refs.

SMITH, JANET MARIE
Playing the field: Janet Marie Smith
/ David Masello.
Profile of the V.P. for new
stadium planning and development
for the Baltimore Orioles.
ARCHITECTURAL RECORD 1990 Oct.,
v.178, no.11, p.45-46, port.

SMITH, JENIFER
Clear minded: Jan Abrams meets a
very precise pair / Jan[et]
Abrams.
Report on work of Kenneth
Armstrong and his partner Jenifer
Smith.
BLUEPRINT (LONDON, ENGLAND) 1990
July-Aug., no.69, p.12, port.,
model.
Seine perspective: Japanese House of
Culture, Paris: exhibition of
competition entries [exhibition
review] / Peter Wislocki.
Held at the Pavillon de l'Arsenal
through 11 Nov. 1990. Exhibition
documented all 453 entries.
Winners: Masayuki Yamanaka,
Kenneth Armstrong, and Jennifer
Smith.
ARCHITECTS' JOURNAL 1990 Oct.24,
v.192, no.17, p.81-82, elev.,
model.
Winners in the competition for
Maison de la Culture du Japon a
Paris.
First prize: Masayuki Yamanaka,
Kenneth Armstrong, Jenifer Smith.
JAPAN ARCHITECT 1990 June, v.65,
no.6(398), p.33-55, dwgs., elevs.,
models, plans, secns., site plans.

SMITH, JOHN
Gateshead Metrocentre: an
environment of belonging / John
Smith.
DESIGN FOR SPECIAL NEEDS 1989
Dec., no.50, p.15-17, photos.

SMITH, JULIA ABEL
Decorating a revival / Julia Abel
Smith.
Revived interest in decorative
qualities of terra-cotta.
COUNTRY LIFE 1990 Nov.1, v.184,
no.44, p.94-96, photos.

SMITH, KENDRA SCHANK
Architectural sketches and the power
of caricature / Kendra Schank
Smith.
Includes abstract.
JOURNAL OF ARCHITECTURAL EDUCATION
1990 Nov., v.44, no.1, p.49-58,
dwgs., sketches, refs.

SMITH, KENNETH
Landscapes for the 21st century
[competition].
Features 15 winning projects,
which include descriptions in the
designers' own words. Competition
sponsored by "Landscape
Architecture". Includes articles
by the judges, Jory Johnson, M.
Paul Friedburg and James Wines.
LANDSCAPE ARCHITECTURE 1990 Dec.,
v.80, no.12, p.[32-54], ill.,
ports., site plans, aerial photo.

SMITH, MARC T.
Ideal urban form and visions of the
good life: Florida's growth
management dilemma / Ivonne
Audirac, Anne H. Shermyen, Marc T.
Smith.
AMERICAN PLANNING ASSOCIATION.
JOURNAL 1990 Autumn, v.56, no.4,
p.470-482, photos., tables, aerial
photos., refs.

SMITH, MARY
Sense of community.
Hanover Court, housing for elderly
in Dulverton, Somerset, cited as
an example of good design by
housing advocate Mary Smith.
VOLUNTARY HOUSING 1990 July, v.23,
no.6, p.[12], port., photo.
Tribute: Housing's devoted and
distinguished servant / Mary
Smith.
HOUSING REVIEW 1988 Nov.-Dec.,
v.37, no.6, p.192, port.

SMITH, MICHAEL E.
Architectural patterns at three
Aztec-period sites in Morelos,
Mexico / Michael E. Smith.
JOURNAL OF FIELD ARCHAEOLOGY 1989
Summer, v.16, no.2, p.185-203,
map, photos., plans, secn., site
plans, tables, biblio.

SMITH, MICHAEL J. P.
Buildup: Chicago booms with
high-rise construction and
proposals for more / Michael J. P.
Smith.
Includes commentary on 30 tall
office and apartment buildings
scheduled for completion in the
early 1990s.
INLAND ARCHITECT 1990 Jan.-Feb.,
v.34, no.1, p.49-57, axonometric
views, elevs., elevs., models.
The firm in its maturity / Michael
J. P. Smith.
A humorous statement about a
fictitious firm CPF and
"metroplexes" in the year 2028.
INLAND ARCHITECT 1990 Jan.-Feb.,
v.34, no.1, p.[58]-59, model.
Formgiving frontiers [fractals] /
Michael J.P. Smith.
Essay on the use of fractal
geometry in architectural
formgiving.
INLAND ARCHITECT 1990 May-June,
v.34, no.3, p.[58]-59, ill.
Goes around, comes around / Michael
J.P. Smith.
Restoration of 1910s clock on
tower of the City's Central Office
Building, Chicago.
INLAND ARCHITECT 1990 July-Aug.,
v.34, no.4, p.72-73, photos.

SMITH, ROGER C.
   Establishing an underwater
   archaeological preserve in the
   Florida Keys: a case study, [San
   Pedro Wreck site] / Roger C.
   Smith, Robert Finegold, Eric
   Stephens.
   The New Spain Fleet was wrecked
   along the Florida Keys in 1733.
   ASSOCIATION FOR PRESERVATION
   TECHNOLOGY. BULLETIN 1990, v.22,
   no.3, p.11-18, photo., site plan,
   refs.

SMITH, RON
   Culs-de-sac: A. V. Jennings'
   contribution / Ron Smith.
   Australian "private home order
   builder" and pioneer in the use of
   culs-de sac in Melbourne housing
   estates, from 1934 to present.
   AUSTRALIAN PLANNER: JOURNAL OF THE
   ROYAL AUSTRALIAN PLANNING
   INSTITUTE 1989 Sept., v.27, no.3,
   p.12-16, ill., elevs., model,
   photos., plans, refs.

SMITH, SHELLEY L.
   The stuff of parking / Shelley L.
   Smith.
   URBAN LAND 1990 Feb, v.49, no.2,
   p.36-39, ill., table, biblio.

SMITH, SUSAN J.
   Gender and the meaning of home /
   Ruth Madigan, Moira Munro, Susan
   J. Smith.
   English and French summaries.
   INTERNATIONAL JOURNAL OF URBAN AND
   REGIONAL RESEARCH 1990 Dec., v.14,
   no.4, p.[625]-647, refs.

SMITH, THOMAS P.
   Saying yes to group homes / Thomas
   P. Smith.
   Assessing local planning and
   zoning compliance.
   PLANNING 1989 Dec., v.55, no.12,
   p.24-26, ports.

SMITH, WILLIAM, 1705-1747
   Nosely Hall, Leicestershire: the
   seat of Lord Hazlerigg / John
   Martin Robinson.
   Here attributed to Francis and
   William Smith of Warwick.
   COUNTRY LIFE 1990 Mar.29, v.184,
   no.13, p.86-91, photos.

SMITHIES
   See IRON WORKS

SMITHSON, ALISON
   Wild-Wege = Wild ways / Alison
   Smithson, Peter Smithson.
   Proposed green open areas along
   disused railway tracks in Berlin;
   architects: Alison and Peter
   Smithson.
   DAIDALOS 1989 Dec.15, no.34,
   p.58-61, photos., site plans.
   Working with shadow: Damascus Gate,
   Jerusalem / Alison and Peter
   Smithson.
   Project: Damascus Gate Site
   Complex; architects: Alison and
   Peter Smithson.
   VIA 1990, no.11, p.76-83, dwgs.,
   photos., site plans.

SMITHSON, ALISON MARGARET, 1928-
   Bakema e il complesso Siemens a
   Perlach, Monaco = Bakema and the
   Siemens complex in Perlach, Munich
   / Alison Smithson, Peter Smithson.
   On a visit in 1985 to the Siemens
   complex by the authors as part of
   their work as guest professors at
   the Lehrstuhl fur Entwerfen und
   Industrielles Bauen, Technische
   Universitat, Munich. Text in
   Italian and English.
   SPAZIO E SOCIETA 1990 July-Sept.,
   v.13, no.51, p.68-81, ill.,
   ports., models, photos., plans,
   site plans, sketches.

SMITHSON, PETER
   Wild-Wege = Wild ways / Alison
   Smithson, Peter Smithson.
   Proposed green open areas along
   disused railway tracks in Berlin;
   architects: Alison and Peter
   Smithson.
   DAIDALOS 1989 Dec.15, no.34,
   p.58-61, photos., site plans.
   Working with shadow: Damascus Gate,
   Jerusalem / Alison and Peter
   Smithson.
   Project: Damascus Gate Site
   Complex; architects: Alison and
   Peter Smithson.
   VIA 1990, no.11, p.76-83, dwgs.,
   photos., site plans.

SMITHSON, PETER, 1923-
   Bakema e il complesso Siemens a
   Perlach, Monaco = Bakema and the
   Siemens complex in Perlach, Munich
   / Alison Smithson, Peter Smithson.
   On a visit in 1985 to the Siemens
   complex by the authors as part of
   their work as guest professors at
   the Lehrstuhl fur Entwerfen und
   Industrielles Bauen, Technische
   Universitat, Munich. Text in
   Italian and English.
   SPAZIO E SOCIETA 1990 July-Sept.,
   v.13, no.51, p.68-81, ill.,
   ports., models, photos., plans,
   site plans, sketches.

SMOKE DETECTORS
   See FIRE DETECTORS

SMOLKA, JOSE LUIS RAMOS
   Preocupacao com a forma, o conforto
   e o ambiente: Edificio Le Coin,
   Curitiba.
   Architects: Julio Pechman, Jose
   Smolka.
   PROJETO 1989 June, no.122,
   p.94-95, photos., plan.

SMULLEN, IVOR
   A labour for Hercules: the building
   of the Forth Bridge / Ivor
   Smullen.
   Engineers: Sir John Fowler and Sir
   Benjamin Baker.
   COUNTRY LIFE 1990 Mar.22, v.184,
   no.12, p.174, photo.

SNAPE, PETER
   Rate collector [Peter Snape] /
   Denise Chevin.
   Partner and chairman of quantity
   sureying at BDP.
   BUILDING 1990 Nov.9, v.255, no.44,
   p.71, port.

SNEDDON, TOM
   Three-piece retreat [Sinderins
   housing, Dundee] / Tom Sneddon.
   Sheltered housing in three units.
   Architects: Page and Park.
   Includes second article: External
   walls, housing, Page & Park
   Architects, p.57-59.
   ARCHITECTS' JOURNAL 1990 May 2,
   v.191, no.18, p.[46]-51,57-59,
   dets., photos., plans, secns.,
   site plan.

SNELL, GEOFFREY P. BUILDINGS OF SAINT
KILDA
   Buildings of St. Kilda, by Geoffrey
   P. Stell and Mary Harman [book
   review] / Eurwyn Wiliam.
   POST-MEDIEVAL ARCHAEOLOGY 1989,
   v.23, p.84-85.

SNELL, JAMES
   Renovation case history no. 72:
   Britannia rules, a Worcester
   townhouse made worthy of its
   historic setting once again / Kit
   Wedd.
   1845 terraced house in Britannia
   Square, Worcester, England.
   Architect for restoration: James
   Snell.
   TRADITIONAL HOMES 1990 Oct., v.7,
   no.1, p.16-21, photos., plans.

SNIBBE, RICHARD W.
   Una.tensostruttura cinetica =
   Kinetic tensile structure /
   Richard W. Snibbe.
   Competition design for Opera de la
   Bastille, Paris. Architect:
   Richard W. Snibbe.
   L'ARCA 1990 July-Aug., no.40,
   p.30-35, elev., model, plans,
   secns., site plan.

SNOHETTA ARKITEKTUR LANDSKAP
   Alexandria analogue.
   National library, Alexandria,
   Egypt. Architects: Snohetta.
   ARCHITECTURAL REVIEW 1990 June,
   v.187, no.1120, p.60-63, ill.,
   elevs., models, plans, secns.
   Alexandria Library competition.
   Winner: Snohetta Arkitektur
   Landscap [sic].
   MIMAR: ARCHITECTURE IN DEVELOPMENT
   1990 Mar., v.10, no.1(34), p.9-10,
   elev., plan, secn.
   Bibliotheca Alexandrina.
   Competition projects by Snohetta;
   Dall & Lindhardtsen; Knud Munk
   Tegnestue; and others.
   ARKITEKTEN 1990 Feb., v.92, no.2,
   p.60-63, dwg., elevs., model,
   secns.
   Bibliothek von Alexandria, Agypten =
   Library of Alexandria, Egypt.
   Competition. Winning architects:
   Snohetta Arkitektur Landskap.
   Includes three other entries.
   Text in German.
   ARCHITEKTUR + WETTBEWERBE 1990
   Sept., no.143, p.41-46, plans,
   secns., site plans, models, dets.,
   elevs., dwgs.
   Egyptian revival: the Alexandria
   Library / Murray Fraser.
   A presentation given by Snohetta
   at Oxford Polytechnic School of
   Architecture, 8 Mar. 1990.
   ARCHITECTS' JOURNAL 1990 Mar.21,
   v.191, no.12, p.92-93, model, site
   plan.

SNOHETTA ARKITEKTUR LANDSKAP
(CONTINUED)
Noors bureau wint prijsvraag
Bibliotheek Alexandrie.
Winner: Snohetta Arkitektur
Landskap & Associates.
ARCHIS 1989 Nov., no.11, p.3,
axonometric view, plan, site plan.

SNOOK, KEITH
BSI in Europe: raising standards /
Keith Snook.
The British Standards Institution
is involved in the production of
European standards as well. BSI
director general: Dr. Ivan
Dunstan.
ARCHITECTS' JOURNAL 1990 July 18,
v.192, no.3, p.61-63, port.

SNOW FENCES
Danger: falling snow / Don Taylor.
CANADIAN ARCHITECT 1990 Jan.,
v.35, no.1, p.33, dets.

SNOZZI, LUIGI, 1932-
Architetture di Luigi Snozzi /
Pierre-Alain Croset.
Four recent projects: new
Liechtenstein Parliament, Vaduz;
Netherlands Institute of
Architecture, Rotterdam; Casa
Diener, Ronco; and Casa
Bernasconi, Carona. Includes an
interview by Claudio Negrini and
English captions and summary.
CASABELLA 1990 Apr., v.54, no.567,
p.4-22,59-60, axonometric view,
diagr., elev., models, photos.,
plans, secns., site plans,
sketches, aerial photos.
Luigi Snozzi 11/89 [letter] / Ernst
E. Boesch.
Response to recent issue featuring
the Swiss architect.
DU 1990 Feb., no.588, p.6-7.
Neugestaltung des Zentrums von Monte
Carasso, Schweiz = Redesigning the
center of Monte Carasso,
Switzerland.
Features various projects by Luigi
Snozzi including the Raiffeisen
Bank, Sports Hall and the Baidottl
house.
ARCHITEKTUR + WETTBEWERBE 1990
Dec., no.144, p.13, photos., site
plan.
Neuordnung des Bereichs "Piazza
Grande-Largo Zorzi-Giardini
Pubblici" in Locarno, Schweiz =
Reorganization of the area "Piazza
grande-Largo Zorzi-Giardini
Pubblici" in Locarno, Switzerland.
Idea competition. Winning
architect: Luigi Snozzi. Text in
German.
ARCHITEKTUR + WETTBEWERBE 1990
Dec., no.144, p.79-83, dwgs.,
elevs., site plans.
Projet pour un musee de
l'architecture, Rotterdam, 1988.
Architect: Luigi Snozzi.
WERK, BAUEN + WOHNEN 1989 Dec.,
no.12, p.68, elev., model, plans,
secn.
Svizzera anni '90: tre culture, tre
architetture = Switzerland 1990:
three cultures, three
architectures / Paolo Fumagalli.
Features projects by Jacques
Herzog and Pierre de Meuron; Livio
Vacchini; Atelier 5; Willi Egli;
(Continued next column)

SNOZZI, LUIGI, 1932- (CONTINUED)
Svizzera anni '90:...(CONTINUED)
Mario Botta; Jean-Jacques Oberson;
Giancarlo Durisch; Aurelio
Galfetti; Luigi Snozzi; Roger
Diener; Atelier Cube; Matti,
Burgi, Ragaz; Schnebli, Ammann &
Partner; R. Luscher; V. Mangeat;
S. Calatrava, A. Amsler, and W.
Rueger; Mario Campi and Franco
Pessina; and Peter Zumthor.
Includes an article by Werner
Jehle, "The mountain: painters,
engineers, and architects." Text
in Italian and English.
ABITARE 1990 Nov., no.290,
p.150-191, axonometric views,
dets., ill., elevs., maps,
photos., plans, secns., site
plans, sketch, aerial photo.
Uber den "Vorsatz zur Vitalitat" und
dessen Folgen fur die Architektur
/ Norbert Weickenmeier.
DER ARCHITEKT 1990 July-Aug.,
no.7-8, p.356-359, photos., plans,
site plans, isometric dwg.

SOANE, JOHN, SIR, 1753-1837
La Bank Stock Office revivida = The
Bank Stock Office revived / John
Keyworth.
London bank built in 1792 by Sir
John Soane. Rebuilt by Sir Howard
Baker 1925-1939, it is now part of
the Bank of England Museum. Text
in Spanish and English.
COMPOSICION ARQUITECTONICA, ART &
ARCHITECTURE 1989 Feb., no.2,
p.[103]-114, photos.
Dulwich competition winners / Clive
Aslet.
Country Life competition for new
Dulwich Picture Gallery addition;
architects: Christopher J. Grasby,
Brendan T. O'Neill and Tom Zetek
(winners); Allies and Morrison
(second prize); Peter Clash (third
prize). Original architect Sir
John Soane.
COUNTRY LIFE 1990 Sept.13, v.184,
no.37, p.178-179,202-203,
axonometric views, models, plans,
secns., site plans.
Dulwich revisited / Clare Melhuish.
Features twelve entries in the
Dulwich Picture Gallery extension
competition.
BUILDING DESIGN 1990 Nov.9,
no.1011, p.22-33, axonometric
views, dwgs., model, plans, secns.
Mending monuments / Michael Hall.
Rescue and restoration efforts by
the Soane Monuments Trust.
COUNTRY LIFE 1990 June 14, v.184,
no.24, p.302-303, ill., photos.
Modernism and Soane / Dan
Cruickshank.
Competition winners for extension
to Dulwich Picture Gallery,
designed by Sir John Soane. First
prize: Christopher Grasby, Brendan
O'Neill and Tom Zetek. Two
additional entries by Allies and
Morrison, and Peter Clash.
ARCHITECTS' JOURNAL 1990 Sept.19,
v.192, no.12, p.26-33, elevs.,
models, photos., plans, secns.,
sketches.

SOANE, JOHN, SIR, 1753-1837
(CONTINUED)
Sir John Soane's Museum.
Editorial and five articles.
Contents: Sir John Soane's Museum:
A Conversation Piece without a
Family, by Arata Isozaki.--The
Soane as It Was, by Peter
Thornton.--Soane's Use of
Drawings, by Margaret
Richardson.--Sir John Soane's
Library: 'O, Books! Ye Monuments
of Mind', by Eileen Harris.--The
Papers of Sir John Soane, by Susan
Palmer.
APOLLO 1990 Apr., v.131, no.338,
p.224-251, ill., dwgs., port.,
elevs., photos., plans, engrs.,
refs.
Soane, el hombre y el estilo =
Soane, the man the style / John
Summerson.
Text in Spanish and English.
COMPOSICION ARQUITECTONICA, ART &
ARCHITECTURE 1989 Feb., no.2,
p.[67]-102, dwgs., elevs.,
photos., plans, sketches, refs.
Soane success / Clare Melhuish.
Features three winning entries and
one highly commended entry in the
competition for the addition to
the Dulwich Picture Gallery,
designed by Sir John Soane. First
prize: Christopher J. Grasby,
Brendan T. O'Neill and Tom Zetek.
BUILDING DESIGN 1990 Sept.14,
no.1003, p.13-16, axonometric
view, dwgs., elevs., model, plans,
secns., site plans.
Soane success [Dulwich Picture
Gallery].
Features eight highly commended
entries in Dulwich Picture Gallery
competition. Original architect:
Sir John Soane.
BUILDING DESIGN 1990 Sept.21,
no.1004, p.36-43, axonometric
views, elevs., plans, secns., site
plans, sketches.
Working for Soane / Margaret
Richardson.
The office of Sir John Soane was
organized for the education of the
assistants who worked on his
commissions. Fifth article in
feature "How architects design".
ARCHITECTS' JOURNAL 1990
Dec.19-26, v.192, no.25-26,
p.48-53, dets., dwgs., elevs.,
photos., plan, sketches, ref.

SOANE MONUMENTS TRUST
Mending monuments / Michael Hall.
Rescue and restoration efforts by
the Soane Monuments Trust.
COUNTRY LIFE 1990 June 14, v.184,
no.24, p.302-303, ill., photos.

SOBEJANO, ENRIQUE
Entrevista. Alejandro de la Sota
[interview] / Sara de la Mata,
Enrique Sobejano.
Text in Spanish and English.
ARQUITECTURA 1990 Mar.-June, v.72,
no.283-284, p.152-161, port.,
models, photos., secns., sketches.
Proyeto del parque Cuna Verde, La
Latina, Madrid.
Architects: F. Nieto E. Sobejano.
ARQUITECTURA 1990 July-Aug., v.72,
no.285, p.32-35, elevs., models,
plans, secns., site plans.

SOBEK, WERNER
Pneu und Schale: Betonschalen und
pneumatish vorgespannte Membranen
/ Werner Sobek.
DEUTSCHE BAUZEITUNG 1990 July,
v.124, no.7, p.66-71, dwgs.,
photos.

SOBERANIS, PAT
After the quake: how H/CD officials
responded to the San Francisco
disaster / Pat Soberanis.
JOURNAL OF HOUSING 1990
Sept.-Oct., v.47, no.5, p.276-277,
279, port., photo.

SOCIAL CENTERS
See COMMUNITY CENTERS

SOCIAL ECOLOGY
See HUMAN ECOLOGY

SOCIAL REFORMERS--GREAT BRITAIN--HILL,
OCTAVIA
Housing matters: Octavia Hill by
Gillian Darley [book review] /
Colin Ward.
Biography of social reformer and
housing advocate. Co-founder of
the National Trust.
ARCHITECTS' JOURNAL 1990 Jan.31,
v.191, no.5, p.74, port.

SOCIETY AND ASSOCIATION BUIDINGS--
ROUND--FRANCE--LE HAILLAN--SOCIETE
D'ETUDES DE PROPULSION (SEP)
Societe d'Etudes de Propulsion, Le
Haillan.
Two round buildings. Architects:
Jean Ferrando, Alain Loisier, Jean
de Giacinto. English summary,
p.137; Spanish summary, p.173.
TECHNIQUES ET ARCHITECTURE 1990
Oct.-Nov., no.392, p.136-137,
dwg., photos., plan, secn.

SOCIETY AND ASSOCIATION BUILDINGS
See also CHAMBER OF COMMERCE
BUILDINGS
See also LABOR UNION BUILDINGS
See also MASONIC BUILDINGS
See also OFFICE BUILDINGS

SOCIETY AND ASSOCIATION BUILDINGS--
19TH CENTURY--ALTERATIONS AND
ADDITIONS--SPAIN--BARCELONA--
FONDAZIONE TAPIES
La Fondazione Tapies a Barcellona /
Roser Amado, Lluis Domenech.
Alterations to roof and facade of
building on Calle Aragon,
including a sculpture by Antoni
Tapies. Original architect: Lluis
Domenech i Montaner. Includes
English captions.
CASABELLA 1990 Dec., v.54, no.574,
p.34-35, photos., plans, secn.

SOCIETY AND ASSOCIATION BUILDINGS--
19TH CENTURY--ALTERATIONS AND
ADDITIONS--SPAIN--CANARY ISLANDS--
LAS PALMAS
Biblioteca insular de Las Palmas de
Gran Canaria: Jose Luis Gago,
arquitecto.
Spanish, English text.
ON DISENO 1990, no.111, p.138-151,
photos., plans, secns., sketch.

SOCIETY AND ASSOCIATION BUILDINGS--
ALTERATIONS AND ADDITIONS--ENGLAND--
LONDON--ROYAL SOCIETY OF ARTS
Converting the vaults and developing
the Society's house, 1977-1990 /
Sam Lloyd.
Conversion of 18th cent. vaults
for additional space for the Royal
Society of Arts, London.
Architects: Green Lloyd.
ROYAL SOCIETY OF ARTS, LONDON. RSA
JOURNAL 1990 Oct., v.138, no.5411,
p.734-737, photos., secn.
Putting art in the vaults / Kenneth
Powell.
On two London projects: the
conversion of Somerset House,
designed by Sir William Chambers,
into space for the Courtauld
Institute and Galleries and the
expansion and restoration of the
underground vaults of the Royal
Society of Arts.
RIBA JOURNAL 1990 Aug., v.97,
no.8, p.48-51,54-56, photos.,
secns.
Underworld society makes good.
Features renovated vault area
under the Royal Society of Arts
building, London. Architects:
Green Lloyd.
DESIGNERS' JOURNAL 1990 Sept.,
no.60, p.11, photos.
Vaults.
Opening of the RSA vaults by HRH
Prince Philip; expansion and
restoration of underground vaults
at headquarters of the Royal
Society of Arts, London.
Architects: Green Lloyd Adams.
ROYAL SOCIETY OF ARTS, LONDON. RSA
JOURNAL 1990 July, v.138, no.5408,
p.512-514, ports., photos.

SOCIETY AND ASSOCIATION BUILDINGS--
ALTERATIONS AND ADDITIONS--
NETHERLANDS--AMSTERDAM--
INTERNATIONAAL INSTITUUT VOOR
SOCIALE GESCHIEDENIS
Internationales Institut fur
Sozialgeschichte in Amsterdam.
Alterations to the IIHS by Atelier
Pro.
BAUWELT 1990 Feb.9, v.81, no.6,
p.242, photos., plan.
Massiviteit doorbroken: Atelier Pro
verbouwt pakhuis / Liesbeth Melis.
New headquarters for the
Internationaal Instituut voor
Sociale Geschiedenis (IISG) in the
harbor area of Amsterdam.
DE ARCHITECT 1989 Nov., v.20,
no.11, p.68-73, photos., plans,
secns., site plan.

SOCIETY AND ASSOCIATION BUILDINGS--
CHILE--CHILLAN--COOPERATIVA
ELECTRICA CHILLAN
Cooperativa Electrica Chillan:
lectura critica / Rodrigo de la
Cruz.
On architects Juan Borchers, Jesus
Bermejo, and Isidro Suarez.
ARQ 1989 Aug., no.13, p.25-31,
ports., photos., plans, secns.,
sketches.

SOCIETY AND ASSOCIATION BUILDINGS--
COMPETITIONS--CANADA--NORTH YORK
(ONTARIO)--ONTARIO ARCHITECTURAL
ASSOCIATION HEADQUARTERS
The elegant revival of drive-in
architecture / Larry Richards.
New headquarters of the OAA, to be
built in suburban North York in
1991. Architects: Ruth Cawker and
Michael McColl.
CANADIAN ARCHITECT 1990 Feb.,
v.35, no.2, p.24-29, ill., ports.,
elevs., models, maps, photos.,
plans, secns., site plans.

SOCIETY AND ASSOCIATION BUILDINGS--
COMPETITIONS--GERMANY (WEST)--
HEILBRONN--KUNSTVEREIN
Kunsthalle Heilbronn.
First prize (shared): G.A. Sahner;
Buro Heckmann, Christel + Jung.
BAUWELT 1990 July 13, v.81, no.26,
p.1324-1325, models.

SOCIETY AND ASSOCIATION BUILDINGS--
COMPETITIONS--GERMANY (WEST)--
STUTTGART--HAUS DER GESCHICHTE
BADEN-WURTTEMBERG
Erste Preise: Kulturbauten.
Four projects: Haus der Geschichte
Baden-Wurttenberg, Stuttgart
(architect: Behnisch und Partner);
Regierungsprasidium und
Staatstheater, Kassel (architect:
Bieling und Bieling); Musik- und
Kongresshalle, Wallhalbinsel in
Lubeck (architect: Meinhard von
Gerkan); Gutenberg-Museum Mainz
(architects: Eric Rossmann, Karl
Platte).
DEUTSCHES ARCHITEKTENBLATT 1990
Sept.1, v.22, no.9, p.1301-1304,
elevs., models, plans, secns.

SOCIETY AND ASSOCIATION BUILDINGS--
CONSERVATION AND RESTORATION--
BRAZIL--MANGUINHOS--CASTELO DE
MANGUINHOS
O processo de recuperacao do Castelo
de Manguinhos / Benedito Tadeu de
Oliveira.
Restoration of 1904 building.
Original architect: Luis de Moraes
Junior. Restoration architects:
Benedito T. Oliveira, M.C.F. de
Mello.
PROJETO 1989 Apr., no.120,
p.154-155, photos.

SOCIETY AND ASSOCIATION BUILDINGS--
FRANCE--BRY-SUR-MARNE--L'INSTITUT
NATIONAL DE L'AUDIOVISUEL
La Societe Francaise de Production,
l'Institut National de
l'Audiovisuel, Bry-sur-Marne.
A combined site for new studios
and offices. Architects: J.-F.
Jambry, D. Milojevic.
LE MUR VIVANT 1990, no.95,
p.37-44, dwgs., elevs., photos.,
plans, secn., site plan, isometric
dwgs., aerial photo.

SOCIETY AND ASSOCIATION BUILDINGS--
FRANCE--CHATILLON-SUR-INDRE
Fins de chantier / Joan Pascuale
Argente ... [et al.].
Contents: Former tannery converted
to association building,
Chatillon-sur-Indre, France;
architect: Thierry Van de
Wingaert.--Hospital Paul-Brousse,
Villejuif, France; architects:
Avant-Travaux.--Housing complex,
Barcelona, Spain; architects: Joan
Pascual Argente, Ramon Ausio
Mateu, Lluis Badenas Oradanos,
Joan Forgas Coll, Teresa Gimeno
Marin, Enric Serra Grau.
LE MONITEUR ARCHITECTURE AMC 1990
May, no.11, p.11-16, photos.,
plans.

SOCIETY AND ASSOCIATION BUILDINGS--
FRANCE--INSTITUT EUROPEEN DES NORMES
DE TELECOMMUNICATIONS
Institut Europeen des Normes de
Telecommunications Sophia
Antipolis / Denis Sloan.
Architect: D. Sloan.
LE MUR VIVANT 1990, no.96,
p.52-57, axonometric view, elevs.,
photos., site plan.

SOCIETY AND ASSOCIATION BUILDINGS--
FRANCE--PARIS--FONDATION AVICENNE
Avicenne Foundation (formerly Maison
de l'Iran), Cite Universitaire,
Boulevard Jourdan, Paris, 1968.
Architects: Claude Parent and
Mohsen Foroughi. Text in Japanese
and English.
ARCHITECTURE AND URBANISM 1990
Sept., no.9 Extra edition,
p.146-151,263, photos.

SOCIETY AND ASSOCIATION BUILDINGS--
FRANCE--PARIS--INSTITUT DU MONDE
ARABE
Institut du monde arabe / Poul Erik
Skriver.
Architect: Jean Nouvel.
ARKITEKTEN 1989 Dec.22, v.91,
no.23, p.592-595, axonmetric view,
det., photos., plans.
Institut du Monde Arabe, Quai
Saint-Bernard, Paris, 1988.
Architects: Jean Nouvel, Pierre
Soria, Gilbert Lezenes and
Architecture Studio. Text in
Japanese and English.
ARCHITECTURE AND URBANISM 1990
Sept., no.9 Extra edition,
p.216-237,263, photos., plan.

SOCIETY AND ASSOCIATION BUILDINGS--
GERMANY (WEST)--HILDEN--INSTITUT FUR
OFFENTLICHE VERWALTUNG
NORDRHEIN-WESTFALEN
Architektur unterwegs.
Three projects: Commerzbank
Bochum-Wattenscheid, Bochum
(architect: Bernd Fuldner);
Sotronic Kabelsysteme GmbH,
Baunach (architect: Michael
Juckers); Institut fur offentliche
verwaltung Nordrhein-Westfalen,
Hilden (architect: Wachenfeld &
Endert).
DEUTSCHES ARCHITEKTENBLATT 1990
Mar 1, v.22, no.1, p.349-352,
elevs., photos., plans.

SOCIETY AND ASSOCIATION BUILDINGS--
INDIA--AHMADABAD--CENTRE FOR
ENVIRONMENT EDUCATION
Centre for Environment Education,
Ahmedabad / Neelkanth Chhaya.
Client: Nehru Foundation for
Development. To be completed in
June 1990. Architects: Neelkanth
Chhaya, Kallol Joshi.
ARCHITECTURE + DESIGN 1990
May-June, v.7, no.3, p.54-61,
dets., photos., plans, secns.,
site plans, sketches.

SOCIETY AND ASSOCIATION BUILDINGS--
INTERIOR DESIGN--SWEDEN--STOCKHOLM--
SVENSKA AKADEMIEN
Bonnierrummet, Handelshogskolan &
Gyldene Freden, Stockholm.
Renovation and interior design of
the Handelshogskolan (1988) and
the Svenska Akademien (1990).
Architect: Ake Axelsson
Arkitektkontor.
ARKITEKTUR: THE SWEDISH REVIEW OF
ARCHITECTURE 1990 Sept., v.90,
no.7, p.14-15, photos.

SOCIETY AND ASSOCIATION BUILDINGS--
ITALY--CARRARA--INTERNAZIONALE MARMI
E MACCHINE
Il linguaggio della materia = The
language of materials / Andrea
Campioli.
Stone designs: Cono-cielo
monument, Los Angeles, 1988 --
Project for headquarters of
Internazionale Marmi e Macchine,
Carrara, Italy. Architect: Angelo
Mangiarotti.
L'ARCA 1990 Dec., no.44,
p.68-[75], dwgs., model, photos.,
plans.

SOCIETY AND ASSOCIATION BUILDINGS--
ITALY--VENICE--FONDAZIONE CINI
Il patrimonio storico: Venezia, la
Fondazione Cini = Historical
heritage: Venice, the Cini
Foundation / Renzo Zorzi.
The buildings on the island of San
Giorgio Maggiore, owned and
restored by the Cini Foundation.
ABITARE 1990 Nov., no.290,
p.192-[205].256, photos., aerial
photo.

SOCIETY AND ASSOCIATION BUILDINGS--
JAPAN--KAWABE--KENTOUSHIKAN
"Kentoushikan".
Cooking school in Kawabe, in the
mountains of Kagoshima prefecture,
Japan. Architects: Hiromichi
Matsui.
ARKITEKTUR DK 1990, v.34, no.6,
p.A100,A102, photos., plans, secn.

SOCIETY AND ASSOCIATION BUILDINGS--
JAPAN--TOKYO--YWCA
Tokyo YWCA building.
Architects: Kohyama Atelier.
English summary, p.27.
KENCHIKU BUNKA 1990 June, v.45,
no.524, p.127-138, elev., photos.,
plans, secn., sketches.

SOCIETY AND ASSOCIATION BUILDINGS--
NORWAY--HOVIK--VERITAS
Lund & Slaatto / Poul Erik Skriver.
Projects include Det Norske
Veritas, Veritas II, Norges Bank,
Kreditkassen, Kulturhus i
Stavanger, Hotel Skagen Brygge,
Eidsvag Kirke, St. Magnus Kirke,
Sentrumplan. Includes English and
German summaries.
ARKITEKTUR DK 1990, v.34, no.5,
p.221-257,cover, dets., dwgs.,
elev., models, photos., plans,
secns., site plans, isometric
dwg., aerial photos.

SOCIETY AND ASSOCIATION BUILDINGS--
SPAIN--MAJORCA--FUNDACION JOAN Y
PILAR MIRO
Atlantic cries - Mediterranean
whispers / Luis Fernandez-Galiano.
On the Centro Atlantico de Arte
Moderno, Las Palmas, Canary
Islands, architect: Francisco
Javier Saenz de Oiza and the Juan
and Pilar Miro Foundation, Son
Abrines, Majorca, architect: Jose
Rafael Moneo.
ARCHITECTURAL REVIEW 1990 July,
v.188, no.1121, p.44-[51], models,
photos., plans, secn., site plan.
El jardin de la estrella: Fundacion
Joan y Pilar Miro, Palma de
Mallorca.
Architect: Jose Rafael Moneo.
English summary, p.91-92.
A & V 1990, no.24, p.54-57,
elevs., models, plans, secn.

SOCIETY AND ASSOCIATION BUILDINGS--
SWITZERLAND
Neue Angemessenheit: Velountestand
in Schaffhausen, 1989, und Projekt
Vereinsgebaude (Ausfuhrung 1991).
Architects: Markus Friedli,
Gerhard Wittwer. Text in German;
summaries in German, French, and
English.
WERK, BAUEN + WOHNEN 1990 Nov.,
no.11, p.54-61, dets., models,
photos., plans, site plans.

SOCIETY AND ASSOCIATION BUILDINGS--
TYPOLOGY--INDIA
The centre and the periphery
[interview] / Rajeev Kathpalia.
Balkrisha V. Doshi provides the
introduction to a section which
features five institutions as
examples of this building type.
Articles are indexed separately.
ARCHITECTURE + DESIGN 1990
May-June, v.7, no.3, p.22-23.

SOCIETY AND ASSOCIATION BUILDINGS--
UNITED STATES--CHICAGO (ILLINOIS)--
AMERICAN MEDICAL ASSOCIATION
HEADQUARTERS
Chicago on the rise: a wave of
speculative office towers... /
Howard Decker.
NBC Tower (SOM); 225 W. Wacker Dr.
(Kohn Pedersen Fox); 900 N.
Michigan Ave. (Kohn Pedersen Fox);
AT&T Center (SOM); Burnett
Headquarters (Roche Dinkeloo); AMA
Headquarters (Kenzo Tange); 181 W.
Madison St. (Cesar Pelli); Chicago
Skyneedle (Cesar Pelli).
ARCHITECTURE: THE AIA JOURNAL 1990
Feb., v.79, no.2, p.78-83, photos,
model, aerial photo.

SOLA MORALES, MANUEL DE
  Un'altra tradizione moderna: dalla
    rottura dell'anno trenta al
    progetto urbano moderno = Another
    modern tradition: from the break
    of 1930 to the modern urban
    project / Manuel de Sola Morales.
    Principal themes in urban planning
    since the 1920s.
    LOTUS INTERNATIONAL 1989, no.64,
    p.6-31, ill., models, photos.,
    site plans.
  Barcelona Diagonal / Mirko Zardini.
    Competition projects for new
    buildings along the planned
    extension of the Diagonal.
    Architects: Rafael Moneo and
    Manuel de Sola Morales (winners);
    Richard Plunz and Roberto Collova.
    Text in Italian and English.
    LOTUS INTERNATIONAL 1989, no.64,
    p.86-107, axonometric views,
    elevs., models, plans, secns.,
    site plans.
  La citta e il suo fiume = The city
    and its river / Jef Vanreusel.
    Stad aan de stroom project designs
    from international competition for
    urban renewal of three areas of
    Antwerp; Quay, Islet and South;
    architects: Yves Lion, Manuel de
    Sola-Morales, Bob van Reeth, Beth
    Gali, Rem Koolhaas, Toyo Ito, Van
    Berkel & Bos, Van Veen & Van Meer,
    Bureau of Urban Design. Overall
    site plan: Spea - Ingegneria
    Europa (Gruppo-Italstat).
    L'ARCA 1990 Dec., no.44, p.32-43,
    models, map, photos., plans, site
    plans.
  Las largas respuestas de Ludovico
    Quaroni= Ludovico Quaroni, answers
    at length [interview] / Manuel de
    Sola-Morales.
    In Spanish and English.
    URBANISMO REVISTA 1989, no.7,
    p.2-17, dets., ill., ports.,
    models, photos., plans, secns.,
    sketches, aerial photos.
  Quaroni: la distante lucidez =
    Quaroni, a distant lucidity /
    Manuel de Sola-Morales.
    Review of the city planning
    projects of Ludovico Quaroni. In
    Spanish and English.
    URBANISMO REVISTA 1989, no.7,
    p.37-[46], det., dwgs., elevs.,
    models, photos., plans, sketch.
  Regisseurs van het moderne
    stadsleven: Joan Busquets en
    Manuel de Sola-Morales [interview]
    / Han Meyer.
    The second of two articles in an
    issue featuring Barcelona.
    DE ARCHITECT 1989 Oct., v.20,
    no.10, p.56-61,cover, photos.,
    secns., site plans.
  La riforma della Barceloneta:
    tracciati e regolamenti = the
    Barceloneta reform: urban grids
    and regulations / Manuel de Sola
    Morales.
    Fishing quarter plannned in 1749.
    LOTUS INTERNATIONAL 1986, no.51
    p.30-45, elevs., models, plans,
    secns., site plans, engr.
  Sleutelen aan het Antwerpse trauma:
    Stad aan de stroom;
    stedebouwkundige prijsvraag voor
    Antwerps havengebied / Paul
    Vermeulen.
    Competition entries by Manuel de
        (Continued next column)

SOLA MORALES, MANUEL DE (CONTINUED)
  Sleutelen aan het...(CONTINUED)
    Sola-Morales, OMA, Toyo Ito, Beth
    Gali, Ben van Berkel, Yves Lion,
    Bob van Reeth.
    ARCHIS 1990 Sept., no.9, p.46-51,
    dwgs., models, maps, site plans,
    refs.
  Spazio, tempo e citta = space, time
    and the city / Manuel de Sola
    Morales.
    LOTUS INTERNATIONAL 1986, no.51,
    p.25-29,
  Stenen Stad: Inrichtingsvoorstellen
    voor Rotterdam Avenue / Matthijs
    de Boer.
    On projects from a workshop held
    29 Sept.-1 Oct.1989 at the
    Academie van Bouwkunst, Rotterdam,
    for redesign of Rotterdam Avenue.
    Leaders: Manuel de Sola-Morales,
    Antonio Monestiroli, and Willem
    Jan Neutelings.
    ARCHIS 1989 Nov., no.11, p.5,
    models, sketch.

SOLA-MORALES RUBIO, IGNASI, 1942-
  La construccio de l'historia de
    l'arquitectura: utillatge mental
    en la obra de Sigfried Gideon
    [sic] / Ignasi de Sola-Morales.
    Catalan, English text.
    QUADERNS D'ARQUITECTURA I
    URBANISME 1989 Apr.-Sept.,
    no.181-182, p.[192]-207, photos.,
    refs.
  De las plazas a los juegos: diez
    anos de intervenciones urbanas /
    Ignasi de Sola-Morales.
    On Barcelona, English summary,
    p.81-82, and city planning
    projects in preparation for the
    1992 Olympics.
    A & V 1990, no.22, p.10-15, dwgs.,
    elevs., photos., site plans,
    aerial photos.
  Democratie on Olympische dromen:
    tien jaar stedelijke interventies
    in Barcelona, 1979-1989 / Ignasi
    de Sola-Morales.
    ARCHIS 1989 Nov., no.11, p.13-19,
    ill., maps, photos., secns.
  Que caigan esos dioses! / Jordi
    Ambros.
    Commentary on an article in the
    newspaper "El Pais" by Ignasi de
    Sola Morales on the current status
    of Spanish architects. Spanish,
    English text.
    ON DISENO 1990, no.107, p.88-93,
    dwgs.
  Special feature: recent works of
    Peter Eisenman.
    Contents: Editor's introduction.--
    Essays: Peter Eisenman: releasing
    time imprisoned in space / Tadao
    Ando.-- A framework for the future
    / Kurt W. Forster.-- Four notes on
    the recent architecture of Peter
    Eisenman / Ignasi de
    Sola-Morales.-- A matter of
    respect.-- Works: Wexner Center
    for the Visual Arts, Ohio State
    University.-- Columbus Convention
    Center.-- Banyoles Olympic Hotel
    competition.-- College of Design,
    Architecture, Art and Planning,
    University of Cincinnati.
    Interview: Peter Eisenman / Jeff
    Kipnis. Text in Japanese and
    English.
    ARCHITECTURE AND URBANISM 1990
        (Continued next column)

SOLA-MORALES RUBIO, IGNASI, 1942-
        (CONTINUED)
  Special feature:... (CONTINUED)
    Jan., no.1(232), p.[7]-182,
    axonometric views, elevs., models,
    photos., plans, secns., sketches.

SOLA-MORALES RUBIO, IGNASI DE, 1942-
  Murallas que no separan: Amado y
    Domenech en Lerida / Ignasi de
    Sola-Morales.
    Urban renewal project in the El
    Canyeret de Lerida. Includes an
    elevator-tower which links the old
    town to the urban centers and a
    retaining wall.
    ARQUITECTURA VIVA 1990 Nov.-Dec.,
    no.15, p.16-20, elevs., models,
    hotos., plans, secns., site plans.

SOLAGUREN-BEASCOA, FELIX
  El muro blanco = The white wall /
    Felix Solaguren-Beascoa.
    Introductory article to theme
    issue of the work of the Danish
    architect Arne Jacobsen. 12
    articles indexed separately.
    ARQUITECTURA 1990 Mar.-June, v.72,
    no.283-284, p.50-59, dwgs.,
    elevs., photos., plans, aerial
    photo., refs.

SOLANES, ANTONI
  La biblioteca Joan Miro a Barcellona
    / Beth Gali et al.
    Architects: Beth Gali, Marius
    Quintana, Antoni Solanas [sic].
    Captions in Italian and English.
    CASABELLA 1990 Nov., v.54, no.573,
    p.36-37, elev., photos., plans,
    secns., site plan.

SOLAR
  See "SOLAR" AS A SUBHEADING AFTER
    SPECIFIC BUILDING TYPES OR OTHER
    MAIN HEADINGS.
  See also SOLAR ACCESS RIGHTS
  See also SOLAR COLLECTORS
  See also SOLAR HEATING
  See also SOLAR ORIENTATION

SOLAR ACCESS RIGHTS
  See also ORIENTATION (ARCHITECTURE)
  See also ZONING LAW
  Let the sun shine in: how zoning to
    preserve light is significantly
    affecting cities across the U.S. /
    Terry Jill Lassar.
    ARCHITECTURE: THE MAGAZINE OF THE
    AMERICAN INSTITUTE OF ARCHITECTS
    1990 May, v.79, no.5, p.102-105,
    155-156,159, ill., map, diagr.

SOLAR BUILDINGS
  See BUILDINGS - SOLAR

SOLAR COLLECTORS
  See also PHOTOVOLTAICS

SOLAR ENVELOPES
  See SOLAR ORIENTATION

SOLAR GREENHOUSES
  See GREENHOUSES - SOLAR

SOLAR HEATED GREENHOUSES
  See GREENHOUSES - SOLAR

SOLAR HEATING
Light duty: building systems:
alternative energies / Alex
Wilson.
Solar water heating and
photovoltaics.
ARCHITECTURE: THE AIA JOURNAL 1990
Dec., v.79, no.12, p.[81]-86,
graph, dwgs., photos.
Zwei Wege, die Sonne zu nutzen:
Photovoltaik und Solarthermik.
ARCH PLUS 1990 July, no.104,
p.71-73, dets., graphs, elevs.,
photos., secns., aerial photos.

SOLAR HEATING--RESEARCH
Neues Energiemanagement in der
Fassade / Helmut Koster.
Methods of controlling daylight
and solar heating, including a
USD-System (uplightsupported
daylightsystem).
DEUTSCHES ARCHITEKTENBLATT 1990
Mar.1, v.22, no.1, p.399-402,
secns.

SOLAR HOUSES
See HOUSES - SOLAR

SOLAR ORIENTATION
"Declined into a profitable
consumption": the tuberculosis
sanatorium in Scotland / Harriet
Richardson.
THE JOURNAL AND ANNUAL REPORT /
THE SCOTTISH GEORGIAN SOCIETY FOR
THE STUDY AND PROTECTION OF
SCOTTISH ARCHITECTURE 1989, no.16,
p.55-58, photo., refs.
Reflected sun in urban spaces /
Vladimir Matus.
CANADIAN ARCHITECT 1990 May, v.35,
no.5, p.46-48, figs., elev., plan,
tables.
Sonnenschutz / Ernst Sieverts.
Various uses of window shades for
sun protection in large office
buildings.
DEUTSCHES ARCHITEKTENBLATT 1990
June 1, v.22, no.6, p.981-985,
graphs, photos., tables.

SOLARIUMS--COMPETITIONS--DENMARK
Byggesystemer til glastilbygninger /
Esben Larsen.
Report on an Oct.1989 idea
competition for modular glass sun
rooms for an apartment house.
First prize: Tegnestuen Plan 1.
Second prize: KHR A/S.
ARKITEKTEN 1990 Apr., v.92, no.4,
p.A74-A76, axonometric views,
dets., secn.

SOLBERG & LOWE ARCHITECTS
Flying sculpture: designers Solberg
& Lowe Architects creates DC-3 /
Michael Wagner.
Interiors of Santa Monica
restaurant DC-3. Collaborating
artist/designer: Charles Arnoldi.
INTERIORS 1990 Jan., v.149, no.6,
p.156-157, photos., plan.

SOLDAVILA I BARBOSA, ALFONS
Pasarela peatonal en Sant Adria del
Besos: Josep I. de Llorens y A.
Soldevila, arquitectos.
Pedestrian walkway. Spanish,
English text.
ON DISENO 1990, no.113, p.138-145,
elevs., photos.

SOLDEVILA I BARBOSA, ALFONS
Escuela en Badalona: J.I. de
Llorens, J. Ma. Massot y A.
Soldevila, arquitectos.
Spanish, English text.
ON DISENO 1990, no.113, p.114-121,
elevs., photos., plans.
Rehabilitacion de una masia como
restaurante en Badalona: J.I. de
Llorens y A. Soldevila,
arquitectos.
Spanish, English text.
ON DISENO 1990, no.113, p.130-137,
elev., photos., plan.
Vivienda unifamiliar en Alella,
Barcelona: Josep I. de Llorens y
A. Soldevila, arquitectos.
Spanish, English text.
ON DISENO 1990, no.113, p.122-129,
elevs., photos., plans.

SOLE, J.
Rotterdam: dopo il tunnel
ferroviario: tre proposte =
Rotterdam: after the railway
tunnel: three concepts / Pierluigi
Nicolin.
Competition projects for tunnel
beneath the Maas river and the
planning for an adjacent district.
Architects: Joan Busquets, with J.
A. Tajadura, J. Sole, M. M.
Busquets, P. Ortega; Andreas
Brandt, with R. Bottcher;
Pierluigi Nicolin, with G.
Marinoni, M. Pugliese, E.
Cavedini.
LOTUS INTERNATIONAL 1989, no.64,
p.54-71, models, photos., site
plans.

SOLE, NEUS
Acondicionamiento de una escuela:
Daniel Navas y Neus Sole,
arquitectos.
Spanish, English text.
ON DISENO 1989, no.104, p.140-145,
photos., plans, sketches.
"Arees de nova centralitat" in
Barcelona / Niclas Dunnebacke.
New public square in Barcelona:
Placa de Navas; architects: Daniel
Navas, Neus Sole, Imma Jansana --
Parc del Clot; architects: Dani
Freixes, Vicente Miranda --Parc de
l'espanya Industrial; architects:
Luis Pena Ganchegui, Francesc
Rius. Text in German and English.
DAIDALOS 1989Dec.15, no.34,
p.48-57, map, photos., plan,
aerial photos.
Pabellon de informacion en una
estacion de ferrocarril: Daniel
Navas y Neus Sole, arquitectos.
Spanish, English text.
ON DISENO 1989, no.104, p.126-139,
ill., elev., photos., plans.

SOLER, ANNA
Hangar para dos aviones: S. Farriol
y A. Soler, arquitectas.
Barcelona. Spanish, English text.
ON DISENO 1990, no.115, p.138-143,
elev., photos.

SOLER, FRANCIS
Centro internazionale Congressi a
Parigi.
Winner: Francesco Soleri [i.e.,
Francis Soler]: Projects by Jean
Nouvel and Emmanuel Cattani.
Claude Vasconi, and others.
(Continued next column)

SOLER, FRANCIS (CONTINUED)
Centro internazionale... (CONTINUED)
L'INDUSTRIA DELLE COSTRUZIONI 1990
Dec. v.24, no.230, p.70-72,
models, secns.
Discipline and anarchy / Ziva
Freiman.
Nursery school, rue Peileport,
Paris, features a facade of
layered transparent and opaque
planes. Architect: Francis Soler.
PROGRESSIVE ARCHITECTURE 1990
Aug., v.71, no.8, p.106-107,
dwgs., photos., plan.
Un double pour Soler / M.H. Contal.
Focus on Francis Soler's project
for the Centre de Conferences
Internationales du Quai Branly,
Paris. Includes models of four
other proposals.
ARCHITECTURE INTERIEURE CREE 1990
Apr.-May, no.236, p.17,20, models.
I fantasmi allo specchio [Centre de
Conferences Internationales] /
Paul Chemetov.
Report on the Quai Branly Centre,
Paris, competition. Winner:
Atelier d'Architecture Francis
Soler.
CASABELLA 1990 July-Aug., v.54,
no.570, p.38-39,61, models, secn.
Francis Soler - bureaux en ville /
M.H. Contal.
On the headquarters for the
Federation nationale des artisans
du taxi, Paris.
ARCHITECTURE INTERIEURE CREE 1990
Apr.-May, no.236, p.84-[89],
axonometric view, dwgs., port.,
photos.
Grands prix nationaux 1990.
Focus on Francis Soler, winner of
the prize for Architecture.
Includes winners in three other
related categories.
TECHNIQUES ET ARCHITECTURE 1990
Mar., no.388, p.12, port.
Grands travaux: suite et ... fin?
[interview] / Philip Jodidio.
Interview with Emile Biasini, the
French Secretary of State on the
Grands Travaux with the focus on
Dominique Perrault's Bibliotheque
de France and Francis Soler's
Centre de conferences
international.
CONNAISSANCE DES ARTS 1990
July-Aug., no.461-462, p.96-99,
ports., models.
Quai Branly / Jean-Paul Robert.
Entries by 7 French firms in the
competition to design an
international conference center in
Paris near the Eiffel Tower.
Winning architect: Francois Soler.
Includes English summaries.
ARCHITECTURE D'AUJOURD'HUI 1990
Apr., no.268, p.[20]-38,
axonometric views, dwgs., ports.,
elev., models, photos., plans,
secns., aerial photo.
Sept projets pour le Quai Branly:
Centre de conferences
internationales.
Includes seven entries in the
competition for an international
conference center near the Quai
Branly, Paris. Winning architect:
Francis Soler.
TECHNIQUES ET ARCHITECTURE 1990
Apr.-May, no.389, p.17-26, dwgs.,
models, plans, secns., site plans,
aerial photo.

SOLER, FRANCIS (CONTINUED)
Territoires d'exploration
[interview] / Jean-Francois
Pousse.
Interview with Francis Soler on
his design for the CIC, Centre
International de Conferences,
Paris. English summary, p.75.
Spanish summary, p.168.
TECHNIQUES ET ARCHITECTURE 1990
Aug.-Sept., no.391, p.74-75.

SOLERI, PAOLO, 1919-
Il mondo di Soleri = The world of
Soleri / Michele Bazan Giordano.
Includes interview with Paolo
Soleri.
L'ARCA 1990 Apr., no.37 suppl.
l'Arca, p.100-101, photo.
La ricerca di Paolo Soleri = Paolo
Soleri's research / Luca Zevi.
Includes an interview.
ARCHITETTURA: CRONACHE E STORIA
1990 Dec., v.36, no.12(422),
p.[838]-874, ill., dwgs., photos.,
plans, secns., site plans,
sketches, aerial photos., biblio.

SOLERI, PAOLO, 1919---EXHIBITIONS
The urban spaceman [exhibition
review] / Julian Holder.
On the exhibitions, Paolo Soleri.
Habitats: Exologic Minutiae, on
view at the New York Academy of
Sciences.
BUILDING DESIGN 1990 June 22,
no.991, p.16, port., elev.

SOLFISBURG, ROY J.
A Sanikel cameleon / Beth Dunlop.
Architects' vacation house, Casa
Cameleon on Sanibel Island, Fla.
Architects: Roy J. Solfisburg.
ARCHITECTURAL DIGEST 1990 Aug.,
v.47, no.8, p.138-[143], photos.

SOLID WASTE MANAGEMENT
See REFUSE AND REFUSE DISPOSAL

SOLINAS, MARIO
Juwelierladen in Perugia = Jewellery
shop in Perugia.
Architects: Mario Solinas, Marco
Morettini.
DETAIL 1990 Oct.-Nov., v.30, no.5,
p.478-479, dets., elevs., photos.,
plans, site plans.

SOLOMON, ANDREW
Escape to the Campagna / Andrew
Solomon.
The room of a palace near
Filacciano, called La Fontanella;
Now the residence of Gian Enzo
Sperone.
HOUSE & GARDEN 1990 Apr., v.162,
no.4, p.196-201, port., photos.
Gotham romance: in her grand Fifth
Avenue apartment, decorator Hethea
Nye indulges her taste for luxury
/ Andrew Solomon.
HOUSE & GARDEN 1990 Oct., v.162,
no.10, p.[164-171], photos., port.
Remaking history / Andrew Solomon.
London apartment of antiques
dealer Christopher Hodsoll.
HOUSE & GARDEN 1990 Sept., v.162,
no.9, p.174-[179],212, port.,
photos.

SOLOMON, ANDREW (CONTINUED)
Sensuous Modernism: Jeffrey Bilhuber
distills the luxurious simplicity
of the twenties in a house for the
nineties / Andrew Solomon.
Frova house, eastern Penn.
HOUSE & GARDEN 1990 May, v.162,
no.5, p.[128]-135,212, port.,
photos.
Showing his colors: the bold designs
of Patrick Frey break the greige
barrier of conventional French
taste / Andrew Solomon.
Paris apartment of the fabric
designer.
HOUSE & GARDEN 1990 Nov., v.162,
no.11, p.[168]-171, ports.,
photos.

SOLOMON CORDWELL BUENZ
Shop and shine / Karin Tetlow.
On award-winning design of Crate &
Barrel's corporate headquarters in
Northbrook, Ill. Architects:
Solomon Cordwell Buenz.
INTERIORS 1990 May, v.149, no.10,
p.206-[219], dwgs., photos., plan.

SOLOMON, DANIEL
American housing 1980-1990 / James
Tice.
Features: Castro Common, San
Francisco (Daniel Solomon, Paulett
Taggart); Sun-Tech Housing, Santa
Monica (Steve Andre, David Van
Hoy); Pacific Townhouses, Santa
Monica (Rebecca Binder, James
Stafford); Hoyt Square
Condominiums, Portland, OR (Robert
S. Leeb). Text in Italian and
English.
METAMORFOSI 1989, no.12, p.38-51,
axonometric views, models,
photos., plans, secns.
Cities to walk in: Laguna West
Project / Todd W. Bressi.
The concept of "pedestrian
pockets" in urban centers, as
developed by Peter Calthorpe and
Dan Solomon.
METROPOLIS 1990 Mar., v.9, no.7,
p.54-58, dwgs., site plans.
Emerald City [Pasadena, Calif.] /
Daniel Solomon, Susan Haviland.
OZ / COLLEGE OF ARCHITECTURE AND
DESIGN, KANSAS STATE UNIVERSITY
1989, v.11, p.42-45, dwgs.,
photos., plans, site plans.

SOLOMON, NANCY B.
Drawing from logic: practice:
working drawings / Nancy B.
Solomon.
ConDoc, a computer software
package for the production of
working drawings.
ARCHITECTURE: THE AIA JOURNAL 1990
Dec., v.79, no.12, p.107-112,
dets., dwgs.
Layers of meaning: computers: CAD
guidelines / Nancy B. Solomon.
How to maximize communication and
efficiency of working drawings.
ARCHITECTURE: THE AIA JOURNAL 1990
Oct., v.79, no.10, p.109-112,
port., tables.
Up in the air: preservation:
asbestos removal / Nancy B.
Solomon.
ARCHITECTURE: THE AIA JOURNAL 1990
Nov., v.79, no.11, p.127-130,
photos., tables.

SOLOMON R. GUGGENHEIM MUSEUM--
EXHIBITIONS
Merz al Guggenheim: lo spazio
infinito della spirale costruttiva
[exhibition review] / Bruno Cora.
Exhibition at the Guggenheim
Museum, New York, 28 Sept.-26
Nov.1989.
CASABELLA 1990 Feb., v.54, no.565,
p.27-28, photos.

SOLOMON, SHOSHANNA
Making the most of a technicality
[salaries] / Shoshanna Solomon.
Status and salary of architectural
technicians in relation to
practicing architects with
degrees. The group is represented
in Britain by the British
Institute of Architectural
Technicians (BIAT).
ARCHITECTS' JOURNAL 1990 Feb.14,
v.191, no.7, p.15, dwg.

SOLTAN, JERZY, 1913-
Interview: Jerzy Soltan / Philip
Arcidi.
Reflections on Modernism.
PROGRESSIVE ARCHITECTURE 1990
Feb., v.71, no.2, p.120, dwg.,
port., photos.

SOLTASS, ELTORE, 1917-
Interview: Ettore Sottsass.
On his plans for a "vacation
village" in Log Hill Mesa,
Colorado.
PROGRESSIVE ARCHITECTURE 1990
Nov., v.71, no.12, p.96-97, dwgs.,
photo., sketches.

SOMBIGO DE SALCEDO, BARTOLOME,
1620-1682
La coleccion de pinturas del
arquitecto toledano Bartolome
Zumbigo y Salcedo (1620-1682) /
Diego Suarez Quevedo.
ARCHIVO ESPANOL DE ARTE 1989
Jan.-Mar., v.62, no.245, p.91-98,
refs.

SOMMER, DEGENHARD
Holztragwerke im Industriebau /
Degenhard Sommer.
DEUTSCHE BAUZEITSCHRIFT 1990 Dec.,
v.38, no.12, p.1802-1804,
1807-1808,1810, dets., graph,
photo., table, ref.

SOMMERFIELD, FRANK
Learning from history [New York City
public schools] / Frank
Sommerfield.
METROPOLIS 1990 Dec., v.10, no.5,
p.[56]-61, photos.

SOMOL, R. E.
No place like home: domesticating
assemblages / R. E. Somol.
Essays discusses Preston Scott
Cohen, Jesse Reiser and Nanako
Umemoto, and Ben Nicholson.
ASSEMBLAGE 1990 Dec., no.13,
p.[59]-71, refs.
Peter Eisenman: Wexner Center for
the Visual Arts, Columbus, Ohio /
R.E. Somol.
In Italian and English.
DOMUS 1990 Jan., no.712,
p.[38-47], dets., elevs., photos.,
plans, secns., site plans,
sketches.

SOMOL, R. E. (CONTINUED)
Wexner Center for the Visual Arts
[Architectural Design Profile 82].
Feature of issue. Includes "A
personal note," by Philip Johnson;
"Eisenman's White holes," by
Charles Jencks; "Between the
sphere and the labyrinth," by R.
E. Somol; "A framework for the
future," by Kurt W. Forster.
ARCHITECTURAL DESIGN 1989, v.59,
no.11-12, p.[1]-80, back cover,
axonometric views, port., photos.,
plans, secns., site plans,
sketches, aerial photos., refs.

SONCK, LARS ELIEL, 1870-1956--
EXHIBITIONS
Lars Sonck in mostra a Venezia
[exhibition review].
The work of the Finnish architect
(1870-1956), at the Fondazione
Masieri.
L'INDUSTRIA DELLE COSTRUZIONI 1990
Nov., v.24, no.229, p.68-69,
photos., plans.

SONE, YOKO
On relations between changing type
of entrances and a degree of
renewal works in the facility
conversion / Yoko Sone.
"Study on functional change of
public building, part 2". Text in
Japanese. Includes English
summary.
NIHON KENCHIKU GAKKAI KEIKAKUKEI
RONBUN HOKOKU SHU = JOURNAL OF
ARCHITECTURE, PLANNING AND
ENVIRONMENTAL ENGINEERING 1990
June [July], no.7(413), p.39-48,
photos., plans, tables, refs.

SONET, JERROLD M.
Compromising positions: Part I /
Jerrold M. Sonet, Alan M. Siegel.
Design business feature: focus on
negotiating skills in the context
of the negotiation of a
residential design contract.
INTERIOR DESIGN 1990 Feb., v.61,
no.3, p.92,96,
Compromising positions, part II /
Jerrold M. Sonet, Alan M. Siegel.
Continuation of article on
contract negotiation in the
interior design business.
INTERIOR DESIGN 1990 June, v.61,
no.9, p.86,90,
Compromising positions, part III /
Jerrold M. Sonet, Alan M. Siegel.
On interior designer/client
relations.
INTERIOR DESIGN 1990 Oct., v.61,
no.14, p.100,

SONG, SUN, 1493-1583
Dwelling between mountain and river:
Myonangjong Songsun / Yasuhiko
Nishigahi.
An ideal pavilion described by the
Japanese poet (1493-1582). Text in
Japanese; English summary, p.149.
NIHON KENCHIKU GAKKAI KEIKAKUKEI
RONBUN HOKOKU SHU = JOURNAL OF
ARCHITECTURE, PLANNING AND
ENVIRONMENTAL ENGINEERING 1990
Mar., no.3(409), p.143-149, refs.

SONNAY, JEAN-FRANCOIS
Paix et bon gouvernement a propos
d'un monument funeraire du
trecento / Jean-Francois Sonnay.
On the relief sculpture on the
Lombard funerary monument, the
Arca of Berardo Maggi, dating from
the early 1300s, in Brescia.
Summaries in English and Italian,
p.192-193.
ARTE MEDIEVALE 1990, v.4, no.2,
p.179-193, ill., photos., refs.

SONNTAG, SABINE
Alterspflegeheim auf der Sonnmatt,
Nideruzwil, SG = Hospice de
vieillards a la Sonnmatt,
Niederuzwil, SG = Nursing home for
the aged on Sonnmatt, Nideruzwil,
SG / Tobias Pauli.
Landscape architect: T. Pauli,
with Daniel Ernst and Sabine
Sonntag.
ANTHOS 1989, v.28, no.4, p.35-38,
photos., site plan.

SOPELSA, BUCI
La villa degli archi / Giulia Conto.
Single-family house, Colli Berici,
Italy. Architects: Gigi Lanaro and
Buci Sopelsa.
VILLE GIARDINI 1990 July-Aug.,
no.250, p.[10]-19, photos., plans.

SOPPER, HEINZ LUDWIG
Neubau fur den Post- und
Fernmeldedienst, Rosenheim.
Architects: Oberpostdirektion
Munchen, Heinz Ludwig Sopper,
Heinrich Winkler.
BAUWELT 1990 Mar.16, v.81, no.11,
p.466, photos.
Post- und Fernmeldeamt in Rosenheim.
Architects: Oberpostdirektion
Munchen, H.L. Sopper, H. Winkler,
W. Weinberg, F. Bauer.
DEUTSCHE BAUZEITSCHRIFT 1990 Oct.,
v.38, no.10, p.1369-1377, dets.,
photos., plan, secn., site plans.

SORAGNI, UGO
Rovigo e le sue difese: indagini
stratigrafiche sulla porta di San
Bartolomeo (secc.XV-XIX) / Ugo
Soragni, Stefania Ferrari,
Annalisa Venturini.
Restoration of a city gate.
English, French, German, Spanish
summaries, p.125.
STORIA DELLA CITTA 1989 Apr.-June,
v.14, no.50, p.51-76, maps,
photos., plans, tables, reconst.
dwgs.

SORDO, STEPHEN DEL
Bathtubs: an architectural history /
Stephen Del Sordo.
OLD-HOUSE JOURNAL 1990 Sept.-Oct.,
v.18, no.5, p.[38-42], ill.

SORENSEN, C. TH. (CARL THEODOR),
1893-1979
Funktionalismen.
In a survey of Danish gardens;
features round designs by C. Th.
Sorensen and others and the Borge
Mogensen garden by Morten Klint.
In Danish and English.
ARKITEKTUR DK 1990, v.34, no.4,
p.172-175, dwgs., elev., photos.,
plans.

SORENSEN, C. TH. (CARL THEODOR),
1893-1979 (CONTINUED)
Gronne strukturer.
Several Danish landscape projects
since the 1950s by Aksel Andersen,
J. P. Schmidt, C.Th. Sorensen,
Michael Bellham, and Norgard,
Harboe, Ginman and others.
ARKITEKTUR DK 1990, v.34, no.4,
p.199-205, dwgs., photos., plans,
site plans.
Neoklassicismen.
In a survey on Danish gardens;
features designs by G. N. Brandt
and C. Th. Sorensen, and refers to
Lutyens' influence. In Danish and
English.
ARKITEKTUR DK 1990, v.34, no.4,
p.166-169, photos., plans.
Vitus Beringsparken i Horsens.
Park designed in 1945 in Jutland
by C.Th Sorensen in honor of Vitus
Bering. In Danish and English.
ARKITEKTUR DK 1990, v.34, no.4,
p.176-177, dwg., photos., site
plan.

SORENSEN, C. TH. (CARL THEODOR),
1893-1979--EXHIBITIONS
Havekunstneren: Udstilling om C.Th.
Sorensen og hans tradition
[exhibition review].
Exhibit at the Arkitektskolen,
Aarhus, 20 Apr.-9 May 1990.
ARKITEKTEN 1990 Aug., v.92, no.10,
p.345, dwg., models.

SORENSEN, HENRIK MEHLSEN
Gellerupparken, Friarealrenovering /
Henrik Mehlsen Sorensen.
The grounds for a division of
Braband Housing Association,
Arhus, built between 1967 and
1970. Includes English captions
and summary (p.76).
LANDSKAB 1990 Aug., v.71, no.5,
p.53-58,76, photos., site plans.

SORENSEN, JONNY
Pragmatisk revolution: om
moobelarkitekterne Rud Thygesen og
Jonny Soorensen / Mike Romer/
Includes English and German
summaries.
ARKITEKTUR DK 1990, v.34, no.3,
p.116-125, photos., secns.,
sketches.

SORENSEN, LEE
Arkitektureksport [interview] / Leer
Sorensen.
Interviews with Danish architects
about their projects elsewhere:
PLH Arkitekter, Dissing + Wetling,
Kjaer & Richter, Poul Schwarz'
Tegnestue A/S, Hvidt & Molgaard,
Nils Madsen, Skaarup & Jespersen,
Arkitekfirmaet KHR A/S.
ARKITEKTEN 1990 Oct., v.92, no.15,
p.500-508, elev., models, photos.,
plan, secns., site plans.

SORENSEN, LEIF LEER
Bydels-eksperiment / Leif Leer
Sorensen.
Initial concept for an
experimental building district in
Skejby, Denmark, planned for 1994.
ARKITEKTEN 1990 June, v.92, no.8,
p.268-269, dwg., site plans.

SORENSEN, LEIF LEER (CONTINUED)
Danmark gar i hojden / Leif Leer
Sorensen.
ARKITEKTEN 1990 June, v.92, no.8,
p.272-273, plans, secns.
G1. Vindinge konference center /
Leif Leer Sorensen.
In Nyborg; completed in 1990,
after a competition by the Danish
Enployers' Association. Architect:
C.F. Mollers Tegnestue. Includes
English and German summaries.
ARKITEKTUR DK 1990, v.34, no.8,
p.368-373, photos., plans, secns.,
site plan, aerial photos.
Hotel Koldingfjord / Leif Leer
Sorensen.
Conversion of a 1909 sanatorium
with a 1940s annex into a hotel
and conference center. Architects:
Vilhelm Lauritzen, with Chr.Holm
and Arkitektfirmaet Jorgen
Staermose. Landscape architect:
Jeppe Aagaard Andersen. Includes
English and German summaries.
ARKITEKTUR DK 1990, v.34, no.8,
p.357-367,cover, elevs., photos.,
plans, secns., site plan.
Pensions kasseboliger kontra
almennyttige boliger / Leif Leer
Sorensen.
ARKITEKTEN 1990 Aug., v.92, no.10,
p.318-321, elevs., photos., plans,
secn., site plan.
Tegnestuen Mejeriet / Leif Leer
Sorensen.
Projects by the Kolding firm,
chiefly renovation along Slotsgade
and including the A.L.Passagen,
Sydbank, Loveapoteket pharmacy,
and Town Hall council hall.
Includes English and German
summaries.
ARKITEKTUR DK 1990, v.34, no.8,
p.394-404, elevs., models,
photos., plans, site plan,
isometric dwg.
Tendernser i estisk arkitektur /
Leif Leer Sorensen.
Recent works in Estonia, by Adu
Eigi, Tonu Laigu and others.
ARKITEKTEN 1989 Nov.28, v.91,
no.21, p.515-521, axonometric
views, elevs., models, photos.,
plans, secn., site plans.

SORENSON, ERIK VERNER, 1942-
Um den Globus...Flughafen in Japan,
den USA, Danemark und Deutschland
/ Ursula Baus.
Kansai Airport, Osaka (Renzo
Piano, Paul Andreu); O'Hare
Airport, Chicago (Helmut Jahn with
Epstein & Sons); Copenhagen
Airport, Kastrup (Holscher,
Axelsson, Sorensen); Flughafen
Hamburg, Fuhlsbuttel (Von Gerkan,
Marg und Partner); and Terminal
Ost, Frankfurt (Buro J. S. K).
DEUTSCHE BAUZEITUNG 1990 Nov.,
v.124, no.11, p.54-63, dwgs.,
elevs., models, photos., plans,
secns., site plans.

SORGENTONE, VANNI ANTONIO, 1950-
M. Scianda, V.A. Sorgentone: la
bocciofila di ospedaletti.
In Italian and English.
DOMUS 1990 June, no.717, p.8-9,
elevs., photos., plans, refs.

SORGENTONE, VANNI ANTONIO, 1950-
(CONTINUED)
Sale di registrazione Metropolis,
Londra / Vanni A. Sorgentone.
Renovation of 19th-century power
station into a recording studio on
Chiswick High Rd. Original
architect: W.C. Green.
DOMUS 1990 Apr., no.715,
p.[63]-67,xxiv, axonometric view,
dwg., photos, plans.

SORIA, ENRIC, 1937-
Casa Salgot en Sant Feliu de
Guixols: J. Garces y E. Soria,
arquitectos.
Spanish, English text.
ON DISENO 1990, no.115, p.160-167,
photos., plans.
Casa Salgot = Single-family house:
Sant Feliu de Guixols, Gerona,
1989.
Architects: Jordi Garces, Enric
Soria.
EL CROQUIS 1990 Apr.-June, v.9,
no.43, p.60-67, photos., plans,
site plan.
Escola d'Arts i Oficis = Arts and
Crafts School.
1884 unfinished hospital converted
to art school, San Saturnino de
Noya, Spain. Original architect:
Ubaldo Iranzo. Conversion
architects: Enric Soria, Jordi
Garces. Text in Catalan and
English.
QUADERNS D'ARQUITECTURA I
URBANISME 1988 July-Sept., no.178,
p.[81-85], photos., plan.
Museo de Navarra = Museum
remodelling: Pamplona, 1986/1990.
Architects: Jordi Garces, Enric
Soria.
EL CROQUIS 1990 Apr.-June, v.9,
no.43, p.68-91, elev., photos.,
plans, secns., site plans.
Public facilities.
Part of a special feature on
Spanish contemporary architecture.
Contents: Museo de Navarra, by
Jordi Garces, Enric Soria.--
Biblioteca Publica, by Victor
Lopez Cotelo, Carlos Puente.--
Molinos del Rio Segura, by Juan
Navarro Baldeweg.-- Puerta de
Toledo, by Nuan Navarro
Baldeweg.-- Escuela de artes y
oficios artisticos, by Jose
Antonio Corrales.-- Instituto
Hugue, by Luis Bravo Farre, Albert
Blanch Rubio.-- Brief Histories.
Text in Japanese.
SPACE DESIGN 1990 May, no.308,
p.11-54, ports., elevs., photos.,
plans, secns., site plans.
El seno anadido: Museo de Navarra,
Pamplona.
Museum remodelling. Architects:
Jordi Garces, Enric Soria. English
text; p.90-91.
A & V 1990, no.26, p.42-46, dwgs.,
photos., plans, secns., site plan.
Spagna: Sant Feliu de Guixols, 1989,
Casa Salgot = Spain: the Salgot
house.
On the Costa Brava. Architects:
Jordi Garces, Enric Soria.
ABITARE 1990 June, no.286,
p.106-111, photos., plans, site
plan.

SORIA, ENRIC, 1937- (CONTINUED)
La ventana y el cristal: comentarios
a la obra de Garces y Soria = The
window and the glass: commentaries
on the work of Garces and Soria /
Jose Luis Gonzalez Cobelo.
EL CROQUIS 1990 Apr.-June, v.9,
no.43, p.52-59, elevs., models,
photos., plans.

SORIA, PIERRE
Institut du Monde Arabe, Quai
Saint-Bernard, Paris, 1988.
Architects: Jean Nouvel, Pierre
Soria, Gilbert Lezenes and
Architecture Studio. Text in
Japanese and English.
ARCHITECTURE AND URBANISM 1990
Sept., no.9 Extra edition,
p.216-237,263, photos., plan.

SORIANO, FEDERICO
Arquitectos en la M-30 / Alejandro
Zaera, Manuel Gausa.
Roundtable with Inaki Abalos, Juan
Herreros, Rafael Terrelo, Federico
Soriano, Fernando Porras, Mateo
Corrales. Includes 8 projects.
Spanish, English text.
QUADERNS D'ARQUITECTURA I
URBANISME 1989 Apr.-Sept.,
nos.181-182, p.[48-81], elevs.,
models, photos., plans, secns.,
site plans.

SORIANO, RAPHAEL SIMON, 1907-1988
Metal-frame houses of the Modern
Movement in Los Angeles, Part 2 /
Neil Jackson.
"The style that nearly...".
Appendix lists 44 works by
architect's name, including
several Case Study Houses, by
Craig Ellwood, Pierre Koenig,
Raphael Soriano, and others.
ARCHITECTURAL HISTORY 1990, v.33,
p.[167-187], dwgs., photos.,
plans, site plans, refs.

SORKIN, MICHAEL, 1948-
The Aga Khan balancing act: the
latest set of Aga Khan Award
winners / Michael Sorkin.
ARCHITECTURAL RECORD 1990 Apr.,
v.178, no.4, p.57-61, photos.
Architektur erhebt sich. Lebbeus
Wood's Projekt Aerial Paris =
Architecture rising. Lebbeus
Wood's Aerial Paris project /
Michael Sorkin.
Aerial Paris project, 1989;
architect: Lebbeus Woods.
DAIDALOS 1990 Sept.15, no.37,
p.118-121, dwgs.
Lebbeus Woods: architecture rising /
Michael Sorkin.
COLUMBIA UNIVERSITY. GRADUATE
SCHOOL OF ARCHITECTURE, PLANNING
AND PRESERVATION. NEWSLINE 1990
Nov., v.3, no.3, p.4, dwgs.,
model.

SORO, FRANCESCO
Progetti oggetti architetture:
Francesco Soro.
His furniture, objects and
architecture.
ARCHITETTURA: CRONACHE E STORIA
1987 Jan., v.33, no.1(375),
p.65-77, dwgs., port., elevs.,
photos., plans.

SORRELL, JOHN
Anarchists in the post office:
Design in the public service: the
Dutch PTT, 1920-1990 [exhibition
review] / John Sorrell.
Exhibition held at Design Museum,
London.
BLUEPRINT (LONDON, ENGLAND) 1990
Dec.-1991 Jan., no.73, p.46,
photo.

SOTA MARTINEZ, ALEJANDRO DE LA, 1913-
Alejandro de la Sota: un maestro
spagnoto [book review] / Lluis
Domenech Girbau.
Reviews a 1989 monograph on the
Spanish architect and prints an
accompanying essay by him.
Captions in Italian and English.
CASABELLA 1990 Oct., v.54, no.572,
p.31-33, photos., secn.
El amacen transparente: Museo
Provincial, Leon.
Architect: Alejandro de la Sota
Martinez. English summary, p.92.
A & V 1990, no.26, p.78-80,
axonometric view, dwgs., plans,
secns.
Naturaleza de la arquitectura -
Nature of architecture / Jose
Manuel Lopez-Pelaez.
On a 1989 book about Alejandro de
la Sota.
EL CROQUIS 1990 Apr.-June, v.9,
no.43, p.163-165, refs.
La realidad y el proyecto (a partir
de unas conversaciones con Jose
Manuel Lopez Pelaez) / Alejandro
Zaera.
Includes discussion on Alejandro
de la Sota and various younger
architects covered in depth later
in volume. Spanish, English text.
QUADERNS D'ARQUITECTURA I
URBANISME 1989 Apr.-Sept.,
no.181-182, p.8-17, photos.
Das Schweigen der Formen: zum
Gimnasio Maravillas von Alejandro
de la Sota / Luis
Fernandez-Galiano.
Built 1962, in Madrid.
ARCHITHESE 1990 Jan.-Feb., v.20,
no.1, p.54, photos., sketch.

SOTA MARTINEZ, ALEJANDRO DE LA, 1913--
-EXHIBITIONS
Alejandro de la Sota [exhibition
review] / U.P.W. Nagel.
On a traveling exhibition on three
Spanish architect's work, at
Lausaunne, Zurich, Biel, and
London.
BAUWELT 1990 May 18, v.81, no.19,
p.933, photo.

SOTH, DIETER
Erzbischofliches Bauamt Heidelberg,
Aussenstelle Karlsruhe.
3 new churches.
DAS MUNSTER 1990, v.43, no.2,
p.104-112, photos., plans.

SOTTSASS ASSOCIATI
Multiple talents / Edie Lee Cohen.
On the hotel, Il Palazzo, Fukuoka,
Japan. Architects: Aldo Rossi,
Morris Adjmi. Interior designers:
Sottsass Associati, Gaetano Pesce,
Sigeru Uchida and Shiro Kuramata.
INTERIOR DESIGN 1990 May, v.61,
no.7, p.[202-209], photos., plans,
secn.

SOTTSASS ASSOCIATI (CONTINUED)
New frontier: Wolf house, Ridgway,
Colorado, Sottsass Associati,
architect / Karen D. Stein.
ARCHITECTURAL RECORD 1990 Oct.,
v.178, no.11, p.78-83, elev.,
photos., plans.

SOTTSASS, ETTORE, 1917-
Architecture prete a porter.
Jewelry designed by architects,
available through Palazzetti: A
book, Jewelry by Architects, is
available.
ARCHITECTURAL RECORD 1990 Nov.,
v.178, no.12, p.[135], photos.
Bravo Ettore! Sottsass builds an
American dream house / Richard
Lacayo.
Vacation house for Daniel Wolf
near Telluride, Colo.
METROPOLITAN HOME 1990 Nov., v.22,
no.11, p.115-125, dwg., port.,
photos.
Esprit butiksindretning, Kobenhaun.
Shop located on "Stroget."
Architect: Ettore Sottsass.
Includes English caption.
ARKITEKTUR DK 1990, v.34, no.3,
p.132, photos.
Ein Haus wie ein Dorf / Barbara
Friedrich.
On the Alessi house, Lago d'Orta,
Italy, designed by Alessandro
Mindini. Contributing architects:
Ricardo Dalisi, Ettore Sottsass,
Robert Venturi, Achille
Castiglioni, Frank O. Gehry, Aldo
Rossi and Milton Glaser.
ARCHITEKTUR & WOHNEN 1990
Feb.-Mar., no.1, p.30-38, ports.,
photos., plans.
Memphis, the avant-garde designs at
a new turning point / Paula Rice
Jackson.
HOUSE BEAUTIFUL 1986 June, v.128,
no.6, p.13,157, photos.
Il Palazzo / Sylvie Chirat.
Hotel, Fukuoka, Japan. Architect:
Aldo Rossi. Interior designers:
Ettore Sottsass, Gaetano Pesce,
Uchida Shigeru, Shiro Kuramata,
and Alfredo Arribas. English
summary, p.162.
ARCHITECTURE INTERIEURE CREE 1990
Mar., no.235, p.[94]-103, photos.,
plans, secn.
Sottsass times two: two shops for
Marisa in Milan / Edie Lee Cohen.
Features shop interiors on Via
della Spiga and Porta Ticinese.
Architect: Ettore Sottsass.
INTERIOR DESIGN 1990 Aug., v.61,
no.11, p.[136]-139, photos.
Tower of power: Hotel Il Palazzo,
Fukuoka, Japan / Karen D. Stein.
Architect: Aldo Rossi, Studio di
Architettura/New York; associate
architects: Studio 80; interior
designers: Shigeru Uchida, Ikuyo
Mitsuhashi, Aldo Rossi, Morris
Adjmi, Ettore Sottsass, Gaetano
Pesce, Shiro Kuramata, Alfredo
Arribas.
ARCHITECTURAL RECORD 1990 May,
v.178, no.6, p.70-[77], dets.,
photos., plans, secn.

SOUFFLOT, JACQUES-GERMAIN, 1713-1780
Une source fondamentale pour l'etude
des jardins anterieurs a la
revolution: l'"atlas de rente
noble" / Marie-Helene Benetiere.
English summary, p.133.
HISTOIRE DE L'ART 1990 Dec.,
no.12, p.49-58, maps, site plans,
refs.

SOUFFLOT, JACQUES GERMAIN, 1713-1780--
EXHIBITIONS
Le Pantheon symbole des revolutions:
de l'eglise de la nation au temple
des grandes hommes [book review] /
Fabienne Cirio.
Catalog of exhibition on the
Pantheon of Paris (formerly
Sainte-Genevieve); co-produced by
the Caisse Nationale des Monuments
Historiques et des Sites and the
Canadian Centre for Architecture.
Held at the Hotel de Sully, Paris
through July 31, 1989, and at the
Canadian Centre for Architecture,
Montreal, 12 Sept. to 15 Oct.1989.
BULLETIN MONUMENTAL 1990, v.148,
no.3, p.336-337.

SOUILEE, DANIEL
Esquisse d'une typologie des villes
fortifiees de l'Egypte pharaonique
/ Daniel Soulie.
HISTOIRE DE L'ART 1990 May,
no.9-10, p.3-8, site plans, refs.

SOULARD, THIERRY
Une tour-porche du XI siecle a
l'abbaye de
Saint-Augustin-les-Limoges /
Thierry Soulard.
French, English, German summaries,
p.[467-469].
BULLETIN MONUMENTAL 1990, v.148,
no.4, p.[423]-426, plan, engr.,
refs.

SOULE, MARGARET W.
A village copes with growth
[Yarmouth, Maine] / Margaret W.
Soule.
LANDMARKS OBSERVER 1990 Spring,
v.16, no.3, p.3-5,1, ports.,
photos.

SOUND INSULATION
See SOUNDPROOFING

SOUND SCULPTURE
Larm.
Issue features ten articles on
aspects of sound, including
standards, psychological factors,
insulation, sound sculpture
(including one 45 rpm record, "Mut
zur Fuge"), noise in housing
units, and noise pollution.
Authors: Joachim-Ernst Berendt,
Dorothea Baumann, Gerd Jansen,
August Schick, Jurgen Becker,
Gustav Kilian Ringel, Wolfgang
Moll, Ralf Kurer, and Martin
Kirchner.
BAUWELT 1990 May 25, v.81, no.20,
p.980-1014, graphs, map, photos.,
tables, refs.

SOUND STUDIOS
See also RECORDING STUDIOS
See also SOUND STAGES
See also TELEVISION STUDIOS

SOUND STUDIOS--AUSTRIA--SALZBURG--
SOUND SPACE FOR MEREDITH MONK
Projects by Dagmar Richter / Ulrich
Hinrichsmeyer.
Contents: "The Vessel" Los Angeles
Gateway competition [3rd prize]--
Berlin III, Germany, 1988 --
Advertising agency Grey,
Dusseldorf, Germany, 1988 --
Gallery UND, Dusseldorf, W.
Germany, 1987 -- Artists' housing
in Boston, Mass., 1987 -- Town
Hall for Kassel, W. Germany, 1986
-- Museum for the Brothers Grimm,
Kassel, W. Germany, 1986 -- A gate
for an ancient city, Paestum,
Italy, 1985 -- Sound space for
Meredith Monk, music by Meredith
Monk "Dolmen music," Salzburg,
Austria, 1985. Architects: Dagmar
Richter, Ulrich Hinrichsmeyer, MAX
1, MAX 2. Text in Japanese and
English.
ARCHITECTURE AND URBANISM 1990
Feb., no.2(233), p.34-58,
axonometric views, elevs., models,
photos., plans, secns.

SOUNDPROOFING
Concrete products.
Supplement has eight articles,
including ones on blocking sound,
interior wall specifications,
color in cladding, bricks, block
paving, and foundation walls.
Includes a guide to essential
standards, approvals, contacts,
and associations.
BUILDING 1990 June 29, v.255,
no.26 suppl., p.3-23, photos.,
secn., table.
Larm.
Issue features ten articles on
aspects of sound, including
standards, psychological factors,
insulation, sound sculpture
(including one 45 rpm record, "Mut
zur Fuge"), noise in housing
units, and noise pollution.
Authors: Joachim-Ernst Berendt,
Dorothea Baumann, Gerd Jansen,
August Schick, Jurgen Becker,
Gustav Kilian Ringel, Wolfgang
Moll, Ralf Kurer, and Martin
Kirchner.
BAUWELT 1990 May 25, v.81, no.20,
p.980-1014, graphs, map, photos.,
tables, refs.
The right side of the track.
On the soundproofing solutions for
the conversion of a 1920s British
Rail staff hostel in Euston, Iron
Bridge House, into 11
office-suites. Architects for the
conversion: Hirials Wybrow Wood,
RIBA JOURNAL 1990 Dec., v.97,
no.12, p.69, photo.
Sound perfect / Michael Wagner.
On the acoustical and
soundproofing work undertaken at
the Wexner Center for the Visual
Arts, Columbus, Ohio. Architects:
Peter Eisenman, Richard Trott with
Jaffe Acoustics
INTERIORS 1990 May, v.149, no.10,
p.78, photo., plan.

SOUNDPROOFING--RESEARCH
Neufassung von DIN 4109: richtige
Anwendung bei Planung und
Ausfuhrung des Schallschutzes von
Fenstern und Turen / Hans
Froehlich.
DEUTSCHES ARCHITEKTENBLATT 1990
June 1, v.22, no.6, p.969-975,
978, dets., graphs, tables.

SOUNDPROOFING--STANDARDS
Schalldammung von Turen am Bau /
Fritz Holtz.
On the new code (DIN 4109) for
soundproofing of doors.
DEUTSCHES ARCHITEKTENBLATT 1990
Apr.1, v.22, no.4, p.611-612,614,

SOUSA, E. TRIGO DE
Palazzo delle esposizioni e degli
sport di Braga = Exhibition and
sports hall in Braga, [Portugal].
Architects: Goncalo Byrne with E.
Trigo de Sousa, N. Matos Silva and
M. Mateus.
LOTUS INTERNATIONAL 1989, no.63,
p.62-73, det., elevs., photos.,
plans, secns.

SOUTERRAINS
See also HYPOGEA
Welten-Wurfel = Cosmic cubes /
Manfred Speidel.
Cubic designs of
sculptor/architect Bukichi Inoue.
Text in German and English.
DAIDALOS 1990 Mar.15, no.35,
p.100-109, axonometric views,
elevs., photos., plans, secns.

SOUTH AFRICA--ARCHITECTURE--
CONSERVATION AND RESTORATION
Conserving South Africa's heritage.
The Cape Environmental Trust was
estab. in 1978 with interest in
both the natural and built
environment.
HERITAGE OUTLOOK 1987 July-Aug.,
v.7, no.4, p.83-86, photos.

SOUTH AFRICA--ARCHITECTURE--DUTCH
COLONIAL
Oor die bronne van ons volksbarok /
Barrie Biermann.
ARCHITECTURE SA = ARGITEKTUUR SA
1989 July-Aug., no.7-8, p.25-28,
site plans, engrs.

SOUTH AFRICA--ARCHITECTURE--POLITICAL
ASPECTS
No end yet for anti-apartheid.
UK Architects Against Apartheid
(UKAAA), Peter Ahrends, Finna
Ayres, and Glen Robinson strongly
object to opinions put forward by
architect Jane Drew in a previous
issue of AJ (Apr.18, 1990, p.14).
ARCHITECTS' JOURNAL 1990 May 30,
v.191, no.22, p.14-15, ports,
Speaking up for South Africa / Jane
Drew.
The author criticizes RIBA's
attitude to South African schools
of architecture.
ARCHITECTS' JOURNAL 1990 Apr.18,
v.191, no.16, p.14-15, port.

SOUTH AFRICA--ARCHITECTURE--STUDY AND
TEACHING
Speaking up for South Africa / Jane
Drew.
The author criticizes RIBA's
attitude to South African schools
of architecture.
ARCHITECTS' JOURNAL 1990 Apr.18.
v.191, no.16, p.14-15, port.

SOUTH AFRICA--ARCHITECTURE--STUDY AND
TEACHING--POLITICAL ASPECTS
No end yet for anti-apartheid.
UK Architects Against Apartheid
(UKAAA), Peter Ahrends, Finna
Ayres, and Glen Robinson strongly
object to opinions put forward by
architect Jane Drew in a previous
issue of AJ (Apr.18, 1990, p.14).
ARCHITECTS' JOURNAL 1990 May 30,
v.191, no.22, p.14-15, ports.

SOUTH AFRICA--BLOEMFONTEIN--CIVIC
CENTERS
The proposed Bloemfontein Civic
Centre / David W. B. Yuill.
ARCHITECTURE SA = ARGITEKTUUR SA
1989 Nov.-Dec., no.11-12, p.43-45,
model.

SOUTH AFRICA--CAPE TOWN--CITY
PLANNING--GREEN AND SEA POINT
Green and Sea Point draft policy /
Fabio Todeschini.
City planning for Cape Town areas,
by Todeschini and Japha.
ARCHITECTURE SA = ARGITEKTUUR SA
1989 May-June, no.5-6, p.42-[43],
graphs, elev., photos., secn.,
site plan, aerial photos.

SOUTH AFRICA--CAPE TOWN--RESTAURANTS--
INTERIOR DESIGN--FLORIS SMIT HUIJS
Paint magic / Penny Swift.
In conjunction with the author's
book, Plascon paint techniques,
discusses the use of paint in
interior design. Feature three
projects: Salvago boutique, Camp's
Bay, Cape Town (architect: Roger
Martin); "Herculaneum", home of
designer Jacqueline Cole; Floris
Smit Huijs restaurant, Cape Town
(interior decorator: Francois du
Plessis).
ADA: ARCHITECTURE, DESIGN, ART
1989, no.7, p.27-33, ports.,
photos.

SOUTH AFRICA--CAPE TOWN--STORES--
CLOTHING--SALVAGO
Paint magic / Penny Swift.
In conjunction with the author's
book, Plascon paint techniques,
discusses the use of paint in
interior design. Feature three
projects: Salvago boutique, Camp's
Bay, Cape Town (architect: Roger
Martin); "Herculaneum", home of
designer Jacqueline Cole; Floris
Smit Huijs restaurant, Cape Town
(interior decorator: François du
Plessis).
ADA: ARCHITECTURE, DESIGN, ART
1989, no.7, p.27-33, ports.,
photos.

SOUTH AFRICA--PRETORIA--PUBLIC
BUILDINGS--NEOCLASSICAL--UNION
BUILDINGS
Visions of greatness: Herbert
Baker's imperial idealism and the
Union Buildings / Michael Keath.
In English, with Africans summary.
ARCHITECTURE SA = ARGITEKTUUR SA
1989 May-June, no.5-6, p.35-36,
photos., site plans, refs.

SOUTH AFRICA--SCHOOLS OF ARCHITECTURE
Speaking up for South Africa / Jane
Drew.
The author criticizes RIBA's
attitude to South African schools
of architecture.
ARCHITECTS' JOURNAL 1990 Apr.18,
v.191, no.16, p.14-15, port.

SOUTH AFRICA--VERNACULAR
ARCHITECTURE--HISTORY
Origins and diffusion of vernacular
architecture in Southern Africa /
Dennis Radford.
ARCHITECTURE SA = ARGITEKTUUR SA
1989 July-Aug., no.7-8, p.19-24,
elev., maps, photos, refs.

SOUTH AFRICA--VILLAS--INTERIOR
DESIGN--HOUSE COLE (HERCULANEUM)
Paint magic / Penny Swift.
In conjunction with the author's
book, Plascon paint techniques,
discusses the use of paint in
interior design. Feature three
projects: Salvago boutique, Camp's
Bay, Cape Town (architect: Roger
Martin); "Herculaneum", home of
designer Jacqueline Cole; Floris
Smit Huijs restaurant, Cape Town
(interior decorator: Francois du
Plessis).
ADA: ARCHITECTURE, DESIGN, ART
1989, no.7, p.27-33, ports.,
photos.

SOUTH AMERICA--ARCHITECTURE--INCA
Special issue on Andean archaeology.
Nine articles.
EXPEDITION 1988, v.30, no.3,
p.2-64, dwgs., maps, photos.,
plans.

SOUTH AMERICA--ARCHITECTURE--
PRE-COLUMBIAN
Special issue on Andean archaeology.
Nine articles.
EXPEDITION 1988, v.30, no.3,
p.2-64, dwgs., maps, photos.,
plans.

SOUTH AMERICA--HACIENDAS
Les haciendas des Andes
equatoriennes / Andre Stevens.
NOUVELLES DU PATRIMOINE 1989 Oct.,
no.29, p.25-27.

SOUTH AMERICA--SELF-BUILD ARCHITECTURE
An analysis of Latin American
auto-construction: a plural and
mass phenomenon / Julian Salas.
OPEN HOUSE INTERNATIONAL 1900,
v.13, no.4, p.2-11, axonometric
view, graphs, dwgs., photos.,
refs.

SOUTH AMERICA--SELF-HELP HOUSING
An analysis of Latin American
auto-construction: a plural and
mass phenomenon / Julian Salas.
OPEN HOUSE INTERNATIONAL 1988,
v.13, no.4, p.2-11, axonometric
view, graphs, dwgs., photos.,
refs.

SOUTH ASIA--PUBLIC SERVICES
New approaches in urban services
delivery: a comparison of emerging
experience in selected Asian
countries / Emiel A. Wegelin.
CITIES 1990 Aug., v.7. no.3,
p.244-258, refs.

SOUTH ASIA--URBANIZATION
New approaches in urban services
delivery: a comparison of emerging
experience in selected Asian
countries / Emiel A. Wegelin.
CITIES 1990 Aug., v.7, no.3,
p.244-258, refs.

SOUTH KOREA--SEOUL--CITIES AND TOWNS--
GROWTH
Urban redevelopment of green belt
villages: a case study of Seoul /
Joochul Kim.
CITIES 1990 Nov., v.7, no.4,
p.323-332, diagr., photos., refs.

SOUTH KOREA--SEOUL--GREENBELTS
Urban redevelopment of green belt
villages: a case study of Seoul /
Joochul Kim.
CITIES 1990 Nov., v.7, no.4,
p.323-332, diagr., photos., refs.

SOUTHEASTERN ASIA--CITIES AND TOWNS--
GROWTH
The South-East Asian city: a review
of the seminar workshop in Jakarta
/ Akhtar Badshah.
Held 20-25 Jan.1990. Sponsors:
Aga Khan Programme for Islamic
Architecture, and Indonesian
Institute of Architecture.
MIMAR: ARCHITECTURE IN DEVELOPMENT
1990 June, v.10, no.2(35), p.9,

SOUTHERN CALIFORNIA INSTITUTE OF
ARCHITECTURE
Recent student work (and a few
comments) from SCI-ARC.
Includes discussion of the
architecture program at the
Southern California Institute of
Architecture.
L. A. ARCHITECT 1990 July-Aug.,
p.6-7, dwgs., models, sketch.

SOUTHWORTH, MICHAEL
Theory and practice of contemporary
urban design: a review of urban
design plans in the United States
/ Michael Southworth.
TOWN PLANNING REVIEW 1989 Oct.,
v.60, no.4, p.369-402, axonometric
view, charts, graph, maps, plans,
secns., sketches, tables, refs.

SOUTO DE MOURA, EDUARDO
Amenagement interieur / Elisabeth
Allain-Dupre and Odile Seyler.
Survey of recent interior design
in France. Includes interview
with Patrick Rubin. Several works
indexed seperately.
LE MONITEUR ARCHITECTURE AMC 1990
July-Aug., no.13, p.27-74,
axonometric views, photos. plans.

SOUTO DE MOURA, EDUARDO (CONTINUED)
Ampliacio d'una casa a Porto, una
casa a l'Algarve / Wilfried Wang.
Architect: Eduardo Souto de Moura.
Portuguese, English text.
QUADERNS D'ARQUITECTURA I
URBANISME 1989 Apr.-Sept.,
no.181-182, p.[120]-137, elevs.,
photos., plans, secns.
Centro culturale per la Segreteria
di stato della cultura, Oporto =
Cultural centre for the Secretary
of State of Culture, Oporto.
Architect: Edouardo Souto de
Moura.
LOTUS INTERNATIONAL 1989, no.63,
p.126-128, elevs., photos., plans,
secns.
Eduardo Souto de Moura: House annexe
and landscaping, Porto, 1988.
Client: Manuel de Oliviera.
Original architect: Jose Porto.
Architect of alterations: Eduardo
Souto de Moura.
9H 1989, no.8, p.82-87, photos.,
plans, secns., site plan.
Giovane generazione portoghese:
Eduardo Souto de Moura / Alexandre
Alves Costa.
Four projects from the mid-1980s:
vacation house, Quinto do Lago,
Algarve; exterior renovations,
Casa Manuel Oliveira, Porto;
renovation of houses, Geres;
cultural center, Porto. Includes
English summary; captions in
Italian and English.
CASABELLA 1990 Jan., v.54, no.564,
p.4-15,59, axonometric views,
port., elevs., photos., plans,
secn., sketches, refs.
Sistemazione degli esterni di casa
de Oliveira (Oporto) =
Organization of the surroundings
of Casa de Oliveira (Oporto).
Original architect (1938): Jose
Porto; architect for additions:
Edourdo Souto de Moura.
LOTUS INTERNATIONAL 1989, no.63,
p.122-125, graphs, plans, secns.,
site plan.

SOVIET UNION--ARCHITECTURAL DRAWINGS--
20TH CENTURY
Architecture on paper: the evolution
of dreams / Irina V.Kokkinaki.
In the Soviet Union since the 1917
Revolution, by Konstantin Melnikov
and others.
APOLLO 1990 Jan., v.131, no.335,
p.14-17, dwgs.

SOVIET UNION--ARCHITECTURAL DRAWINGS--
20TH CENTURY--EXHIBITIONS
Iakov Chernikhov: educator / Lynne
Breslin.
In conjunction with an exhibition
at the Arthur Ross Gallery,
Columbia University, Dec 7, 1990
Mar.9, 1991, entitled The Drawings
of Iakov Chernikhov.
COLUMBIA UNIVERSITY. GRADUATE
SCHOOL OF ARCHITECTURE PLANNING
AND PRESERVATION. NEWSLINE 1990
Dec.-1991 Jan., v.3, no.4, p.3,
dwg., model.

SOVIET UNION--HISTORIC HOUSE MUSEUMS--
ABRAMTSEVO
A Russian Bloomsbury: visiting the
prerevolutionary idyll of
Abramtsevo / Dale Harris.
Features interiors of 19th cent.
country estate of Sergey Aksakov
which is now a museum. Architect:
I. P. Ropet-Petroff.
ARCHITECTURAL DIGEST 1990 Mar.,
v.47, no.3, p.[86]-93, maps,
photos.

SOVIET UNION--HOUSING--SOCIOLOGICAL
ASPECTS
Gibt es einen Wohnungsmart in der
UdSSR? / Axel Busch, Leonid
Lavrov.
BAUWELT 1990 Mar.30, v.81, no.12,
p.610-613, graphs, photos., refs.

SOVIET UNION--KALININ--HOUSING--20TH
CENTURY--HOUSE OF THE YOUNG PIONEERS
Das Haus der jungen Pioniere in
Kalinin: zur Wiederentdeckung
eines Gebaudes von Iwan Leonidow /
Dietrich Schmidt.
Built 1937-39, in Estonia.
ARCHITHESE 1990 July-Aug., v.20,
no.4, p.37-39, elev., photos.,
plans, biblio.

SOVIET UNION--KARELIA--CHURCHES--
WOODEN--CONSERVATION AND RESTORATION
Les eglises en bois de Karelie =
Wooden churches in Karelia / Hakon
Christie.
Includes article in French on the
same topic by Boris Gousev.
Summaries in French, Italian and
Spanish.
ICOMOS INFORMATION 1990 Jan.-Mar.,
no.1, p.3-10, photos., plan, secn.

SOVIET UNION--KIGI--CHURCHES--WOODEN--
CONSERVATION AND RESTORATION--CHURCH
OF THE TRANSFIGURATION
Les eglises en bois de Karelie =
Wooden churches in Karelia / Hakon
Christie.
Includes article in French on the
same topic by Boris Gousev.
Summaries in French, Italian and
Spanish.
ICOMOS INFORMATION 1990 Jan.-Mar.,
no.1, p.3-10, photos., plan, secn.

SOVIET UNION--KIZHI--ARCHITECTURE
The rustic charm of old Russia /
Elizabeth Gaynor.
HOUSE BEAUTIFUL 1990 Mar., v.132,
no.3, p.[60-63], photos.

SOVIET UNION--LENINGRAD--
ARCHITECTURE--NEOCLASSICAL--
EXHIBITIONS
A Russian celebration: St.
Petersburg 1703-1914 [exhibition
review] / Gavin Stamp.
Exhibit at the City Art Gallery,
Manchester, through 22 July 1990.
ARCHITECTS' JOURNAL 1990 July 18,
v.192, no.3, p.72-73, ill., map.

SOVIET UNION--LENINGRAD--CITIES AND
TOWNS--18TH CENTURY--VIEWS--
EXHIBITIONS
A Russian celebration: St.
Petersburg 1703-1914 [exhibition
review] / Gavin Stamp.
Exhibit at the City Art Gallery,
Manchester, through 22 July 1990.
ARCHITECTS' JOURNAL 1990 July 18,
v.192, no.3, p.72-73, ill., map.

SOVIET UNION--LENINGRAD--CITIES AND
TOWNS--19TH CENTURY--VIEWS--
EXHIBITIONS
A Russian celebration: St.
Petersburg 1703-1914 [exhibition
review] / Gavin Stamp.
Exhibit at the City Art Gallery,
Manchester, through 22 July 1990.
ARCHITECTS' JOURNAL 1990 July 18,
v.192, no.3, p.72-73, ill., map.

SOVIET UNION--LENINGRAD--PALACES--
NEOCLASSICAL--CONSERVATION AND
RESTORATION--PALACE OF PAVLOVSK
Royal home: Why the Reds restored
Pavlovsk so lovingly / Peter
Dragadze.
Completed in 1824. Architects:
Charles Cameron, Vincenzo Brenna.
CONNOISSEUR 1990 Jan., v.220,
no.936, p.51-57, ports., photos.

SOVIET UNION--LENINGRAD--PALACES--
NEOCLASSICAL--INTERIOR DESIGN--
YUSUPOV PALACE
Inside Yusupov Palace / Dale Harris.
Features interiors of neoclassical
palace in Leningrad.
ARCHITECTURAL DIGEST 1990 Oct,
v.47, no.11, p.[120-126], port.,
maps, photos.

SOVIET UNION--LENINGRAD--ROOMS--19TH
CENTURY--INTERIOR DESIGN--WINTER
PALACE--MALACHITE ROOM
Der grune Stein der Zaren / Ursula
Bode.
Interiors of the 1839 Malachite
Hall in the Winter Palace,
Leningrad. Architect: Alexander
Bruloff.
ARCHITEKTUR & WOHNEN 1990
June-July, no.3, p.164-168,170,
photos.

SOVIET UNION--MAZAR-I SHARIF--
MAUSOLEA--ISLAMIC--MAUSOLEUM OF
MUHAMMAD BOSHARO
The mausoleum of Muhammad Bosharo /
Sergei Chmelnizkij.
Located in Mazar-i Sharif, Soviet
Union. Tomb construction history
has been dated from the 11-14th
centuries.
MUQARNAS 1990, v.7, p.[23]-34,
det., photos., plans, secns.,
refs.

SOVIET UNION--MONUMENTS AND
MEMORIALS--20TH CENTURY--POLITICAL
ASPECTS
Program art in the Soviet Union /
Vieri Quilici.
RASSEGNA 1990 Sept., v.12,
no.43/3, p.30-37, ill., photos.,
refs.

SOVIET UNION--MOSCOW--AMUSEMENT PARKS
Un parc d'attractions sur la Moscova
/ Anne de Goriainoff, Slava
Danicic, Denise Ragu.
Plans for an amusement or theme
park in Moscow. French, English
and Spanish summaries, p.3,
English translation, p.34-35.
CAHIERS DE L'INSTITUT
D'AMENAGEMENT ET D'URBANISME DE LA
REGION D'ILE-DE-FRANCE. 1990 June,
no.93, p.25-35, ill., model,
photo., plans, refs.

SOVIET UNION--MOSCOW--APARTMENT
COMPLEXES--NAGATINO
Il complesso residenziale di
nagatino (Mosca) = Presentation of
the Nagatino residential complex
in Moscow / L. Kozaeva.
Architects: R. Aldominaia, P.
Zapasov, P. Zamiatin. In Italian,
with English summary.
METAMORFOSI 1988, no.11, p.40-41,
photos., elev.

SOVIET UNION--MOSCOW--APARTMENT
HOUSES--GORKI STREET
Il complesso residenziale di via
Gorkij (Mosca) = Presentation of
the residential project in Gorki
street in Moscow / S. Svatin.
Built 1985-88. Architects: A.
Meerson, E. Podol'skaia, O. Palei,
L. Visnicenko.
METAMORFOSI 1988, no.11, p.53-56,
photos., site plans.

SOVIET UNION--MOSCOW--APARTMENTS--
INTERIOR DESIGN--GLAZUNOV APARTMENT
Conversations with Russia's most
famous artist / Malise Ruthven.
Interiors of Ilya Glazunov's
apartment in Moscow.
ARCHITECTURAL DIGEST 1990 Feb.,
v.47, no.2, p.38,40,44,46, port.,
photos.

SOVIET UNION--MOSCOW--ARCHITECTURE--
STUDY AND TEACHING--MOSCOW INSTITUTE
OF ARCHITECTURE
Il seminario sovietico-americano
"Marchi-Columbia"-Mosca 1988 =
Columbia GSAPP and MARKHI joint
summer workshop.
A pilot program leading to
exchange between Columbia Univ.
and Moscow Institute of
Architecture. In Italian, with
English summary..
METAMORFOSI 1988, no.11, p.67-74,
port., elevs., models, photos.,
secn., site plan, sketches.

SOVIET UNION--MOSCOW--ART--20TH
CENTURY
Dropping the curtain: rediscoveries
in Eastern Europe and the Soviet
Union.
Letters from Prague, Poland, and
Moscow, by Scott Nathan, Wojciech
Lesnikowski, and Anatole
Senkevitch, including description
of events celebrating Melnikov.
INLAND ARCHITECT 1990 Nov.-Dec.,
v.34, no.6, p.48-55, photos.

SOVIET UNION--MOSCOW--BUILDINGS--
  TYPOLOGY
  Le tipologie formali nelle
  costruzioni moscovite = The formal
  typologies in muscovite buildings
  / L. Kozaeva.
  In Italian, with English summary.
  METAMORFOSI 1988, no.11, p.24-29,
  ill., photos.

SOVIET UNION--MOSCOW--CITIES AND TOWNS
  Il paesaggio urbano di Mosca = The
  urban landscape of Moscow / S.
  Lobachev.
  In Italian, with English summary.
  METAMORFOSI 1988, no.11, p.21-23,
  map, photo., secns.
  Some thoughts on the historical fate
  of twentieth century Moscow /
  Natalya Dushkina.
  On the demolition of Russian
  architecture as promoted by
  "modernists" such as Malevich,
  Corbusier, and Ladovsky.
  Translated from Russian.
  TRANSITION 1990, no.33, p.40-57,
  ill., photos., refs.

SOVIET UNION--MOSCOW--CITY PLANNING--
  20TH CENTURY--HISTORY
  Some thoughts on the historical fate
  of twentieth century Moscow /
  Natalya Dushkina.
  On the demolition of Russian
  architecture as promoted by
  "modernists" such as Malevich,
  Corbusier, and Ladovsky.
  Translated from Russian.
  TRANSITION 1990, no.33, p.40-57,
  ill., photos., refs.

SOVIET UNION--MOSCOW--DESIGN--20TH
  CENTURY
  Note sui nuovi indirizzi progettuali
  a Mosca = Notes on Moscow's new
  design tendencies / Alessandra
  Latour.
  In Italian, with English summary.
  METAMORFOSI 1988, no.11, p.8-9,
  ill.

SOVIET UNION--MOSCOW--FAST-FOOD
  RESTAURANTS--PIZZA HUT (GORKY
  STREET)
  On site, in Moscow / Peter Cooper.
  Two construction projects in
  Moscow: Pizza Huts, Gorky Street
  and Kutovoski Prospect (architect:
  Fairington [sic] Dennys & Fisher);
  Fyodorov Clinic Hotel (architect:
  Glavmosarchitectura).
  BUILDING 1990 June 15, v.255,
  no.24, p.53-58, ports., photos.

SOVIET UNION--MOSCOW--FAST-FOOD
  RESTAURANTS--PIZZA HUT (KUTOVOSKI
  PROSPECT)
  On site, in Moscow / Peter Cooper.
  Two construction projects in
  Moscow: Pizza Huts, Gorky Street
  and Kutovoski Prospect (architect:
  Fairington [sic] Dennys & Fisher);
  Fyodorov Clinic Hotel (architect:
  Glavmosarchitectura).
  BUILDING 1990 June 15, v.255,
  no.24, p.53-58, ports., photos.

SOVIET UNION--MOSCOW--HISTORIC HOUSE
  MUSEUMS--MAIAKOVSKI MUSEUM
  Progetto per il museo Majakovskija
  Mosca = Presentation of the
  project Maiakovski Museum in
  Moscow / Olga Kabanova.
  Architects: A. Bokov, E. Budni; B.
  Chernov. In Italian, with English
  summary.
  METAMORFOSI 1988, no.11, p.57-61,
  axonometric view, dwgs., plans,
  engr.

SOVIET UNION--MOSCOW--HISTORIC
  PRESERVATION--20TH CENTURY--HISTORY
  Some thoughts on the historical fate
  of twentieth century Moscow /
  Natalya Dushkina.
  On the demolition of Russian
  architecture as promoted by
  "modernists" such as Malevich,
  Corbusier, and Ladovsky.
  Translated from Russian.
  TRANSITION 1990, no.33, p.40-57,
  ill., photos., refs.

SOVIET UNION--MOSCOW--PLAZAS--
  KUZHMINKI
  L'isola pedonale "Kuz'minki" a Mosca
  = The "Kushminki" pedestrian plaza
  in Moscow / V. Judincev.
  Architect: V. Judincev, et al. In
  Italian, with English summary.
  METAMORFOSI 1988, no.11, p.38-39,
  models.

SOVIET UNION--MOSCOW--ROADSIDE REST
  AREAS--GOLDEN RING AREA
  Aree attrezzate per il turismo lungo
  l'"Anello d'oro della Russia"
  [interview].
  Interview with Michele Reginaldi
  and description of an Italian
  contractor's work for the Ministry
  of Transport in the Soviet Union,
  for design of rest areas along the
  "Golden Ring" northeast of Moscow.
  Includes English summary,
  captions, and translation.
  CASABELLA 1990 June, v.54, no.569,
  p.12-18,59-60, dwgs., elevs., map,
  plans, secns., site plans.

SOVIET UNION--MOSCOW--STREETS
  Il centro di Mosca e le attivita
  urbane = Urban acitivites and the
  centre of Moscow / V. Judincev.
  In Italian, with English summary.
  METAMORFOSI 1988, no.11, p.16-20,
  photos., maps, refs.

SOVIET UNION--MOSCOW--SUBWAYS
  Il fenomeno della metropolitana di
  Mosca = The phenomenon of the
  Moscow underground / Natalia
  Dushkina.
  In Italian, with English summary.
  METAMORFOSI 1988, no.11, p.10-15,
  dwg., photos., sketches, refs.

SOVIET UNION--MOSCOW--TALL BUILDINGS
  El Lissitzkys Wolkentraum: ein
  Hochhaus auf drei Beinen / J.
  Christoph Burkle.
  DEUTSCHE BAUZEITUNG 1990 Jan.,
  v.124, no.1, p.114-115, port.,
  models, photo., sketches.

SOVIET UNION--MOSCOW--THEATERS--
  COMPETITIONS--CHAMBER THEATRE ARTS
  CENTRE
  Summer deadline for Moscow trio.
  Three British competition entries
  for Moscow's Chamber Theatre Arts
  Centre in the Hermitage Gardens:
  Peter Baynes and David Whitehead;
  John Seifert; and Mills Beaumont
  Leavy (MBL).
  ARCHITECTS' JOURNAL 1990 Sept.26,
  v.192, no.13, p.12-13, axonometric
  view, elev., model, secns.,
  sketches.

SOVIET UNION--MOSCOW--THEATERS--
  CONSERVATION AND RESTORATION--V.
  MAIAKOVSKI THEATRE
  La ristrutturazione globale del
  teatro "V. Majakovskij" a Mosca =
  The renovation of the "V.
  Maiakovski" theatre in Moscow /
  Andrei Nekrasov.
  Architects: A. Nekrasov, D.
  Velickin, A. Gnezdilov, A.
  Cel'cov. In Italian, with English
  summary.
  METAMORFOSI 1988, no.11, p.30-34,
  models.

SOVIET UNION--MOSCOW--THEME PARKS
  Un parc d'attractions sur la Moscova
  / Anne de Goriainoff, Slava
  Danicic, Denise Ragu.
  Plans for an amusement or theme
  park in Moscow. French, English
  and Spanish summaries, p.3,
  English translation, p.34-35.
  CAHIERS DE L'INSTITUT
  D'AMENAGEMENT ET D'URBANISME DE LA
  REGION D'ILE-DE-FRANCE. 1990 June,
  no.93, p.25-35, ill., model,
  photo., plans, refs.

SOVIET UNION--NEW TOWNS
  Soviet new towns, planning and
  national urban policy / Jack A.
  Underhill.
  TOWN PLANNING REVIEW 1990 July,
  v.61, no.3, p.263-285, chart,
  model, maps, photos., plans, refs.

SOVIET UNION--PERIODICALS
  Avant-gardes et revues
  d'architecture en Russie,
  1917-1941 / Jean-Louis Cohen.
  REVUE DE L'ART 1990, no.89,
  p.29-38, dwgs., elevs., photos.,
  plans, refs.

SOVIET UNION--PROPERTY
  First steppes / Peter Cooper.
  On changes expected July 1, 1990
  in laws affecting Soviet
  construction and housing
  ownership.
  BUILDING 1990 May 18, v.255,
  no.20, p.24-26, ports., photos.

SOVIET UNION--SAMARKAND--MADRASAHS
  Images of Samarkand / Klaus Herdeg.
  On changes in Uzbek since the
  author's visit in 1975.
  MIMAR: ARCHITECTURE IN DEVELOPMENT
  1990 Dec., v.10, no.4(37),
  p.12-[19], axonometric view, map,
  photos.

SOVIET UNION--SAMARKAND--VERNACULAR
  ARCHITECTURE
  Images of Samarkand / Klaus Herdeg.
  On changes in Uzbek since the
  author's visit in 1975.
  MIMAR: ARCHITECTURE IN DEVELOPMENT
  1990 Dec., v.10, no.4(37),
  p.12-[19], axonometric view, map,
  photos.

SOVIET UNION--SPAS
  A curtain up on wellness / Karin
  Tetlow.
  U.S. delegation visits several
  Soviet balneological spas.
  INTERIORS 1990 Dec., v.150, no.5,
  p.74-77, photos.

SOVIET UNION--TASHKENT--HOUSING POLICY
  Basic factors determining housing
  standards in Tashkent / Oskhan
  Sattorovich Djabbar.
  INTERNATIONAL JOURNAL FOR HOUSING
  SCIENCE AND ITS APPLICATIONS 1990,
  v.14, no.4, p.233-243, diagrs.,
  graphs, plan, tables, biblio.

SOVIET UNION--TASHKENT--HOUSING--
  PUBLIC--STANDARDS
  Basic factors determining housing
  standards in Tashkent / Oskhan
  Sattorovich Djabbar.
  INTERNATIONAL JOURNAL FOR HOUSING
  SCIENCE AND ITS APPLICATIONS 1990,
  v.14, no.4, p.233-243, diagrs.,
  graphs, plan, tables, biblio.

SOVIET UNION--TOWERS--RED TOWER
  La torre rossa / Constantin Boym.
  On the work of Yuri Avvakumov, a
  member of the Paper Architecture
  group. The Red Tower is a homage
  to Letatlin, a famous glider of
  the 1930s. English text on p.9.
  MODO 1990 Oct., v.13, no.126,
  p.42-43, models.

SOVIET UNION--UKRAINE--BUILDINGS--
  WOODEN
  Masterpieces in wood: houses of
  worship in Ukraine [by] Titus D.
  Hewryk [and] the wooden
  architecture of Russia; houses,
  fortifications, churches [by]
  Alexander Opolovnikov, Yelena
  Opolovnikova [book review] /
  Albert J. Schmidt.
  SOCIETY OF ARCHITECTURAL
  HISTORIANS. JOURNAL 1990 Dec.,
  v.49, no.4, p.460-462,

SOVIET UNION--UKRAINE--CHURCHES--
  INFLUENCE
  Byzantium on the prairies: the
  eccentric heritage of Father
  Philip Ruh / Robert Hunter.
  The French priest was responsible
  for the building of numerous
  Ukrainian-style churches in Canada
  from 1913 through 1960.
  CANADIAN HERITAGE 1990 spring,
  v.15, no.4, p.14-18,37,41,43,
  port., photos.

SOVIET UNION--ULUGH BEK--MINARETS--
  CONSERVATION AND RESTORATION
  Eine Baumassen-Wanderung, Prinzip
  Suchov: Aufrichtung eines Minarets
  in Samarkand = A wandering of
  masses, principle Sukhov: The
  realignment of a minaret in
  Samarkand / Rainer Graefe.
            (Continued next column)

SOVIET UNION--ULUGH BEK--MINARETS--
  CONSERVATION AND RESTORATION
            (CONTINUED)
  Eine...(CONTINUED)
  Realignment of minaret of Nadrash
  of Ulugh Bek, Samarkand, in 1930s
  by Russian engineer Vladimir
  Grigor'evic Sukhov.
  DAIDALOS 1990 Sept.15, no.37,
  p.40-43, dwgs., photos.

SOVIET UNION--URBANIZATION
  The cities of the USSR and China:
  streets apart? / John Cole.
  CITIES 1990 May, v.7, no.2,
  p.159-168, graphs, map, photos.,
  tables, refs.

SOVIET UNION--VERNACULAR
  ARCHITECTURE--INFLUENCE
  Russian reverie: Yves Saint Laurent
  retreats to a dacha on his Norman
  estate / Edmund White.
  Russian-style dacha near his
  chateau at Deauville.
  HOUSE & GARDEN 1990 Jan., v.162,
  no.1, p.[118-123],146, port.,
  photos.

SPACE AND ARCHITECTURAL MASS
  See SPACE (ARCHITECTURE)

SPACE (ARCHITECTURE)
  See also OPEN SPACES
  See also PERSONAL SPACE
  See also STORAGE
  Analysis of space in Turkish folk
  houses / Tatsuya Yamamoto.
  Text in Japanese.
  SPACE DESIGN 1990 Feb., no.305,
  p.45-68, dets., map, photos.,
  plans, table.
  Architecture, space, figure and
  narrative / Nicholas Penny.
  AA FILES 1990 Autumn, no.20,
  p.34-41, photos.
  Architektur als Pornographie.
  Uberlegungen zu einer Architektur
  des "Innen" = Architecture as
  pornography. Reflections on an
  architecture of the inside / Franz
  Xaver Baier.
  Text in German and English.
  DAIDALOS 1990 June 15, no.36,
  p.42-51, ill., isometric dwg.,
  refs.
  Architektur im Raum - Raum in der
  Architektur / Jurgen Pahl.
  DEUTSCHES ARCHITEKTENBLATT 1990
  May 1, v.22, no.5, p.733-736,
  refs.
  La arquitectura del espacio-luz: la
  visualizacion del absoluto = The
  architecture of space-light:
  visualization of the absolute /
  Jose L. Gonzalez Cobelo.
  On Eugenio Trias' work titled "Los
  limites del mundo", which deals
  with space and light.
  EL CROQUIS 1990 Apr.-June, v.9,
  no.43, p.172-178, photo.
  Behavior, performance, and
  performance space: an interview
  with Richard Schechner.
  Conducted by the editors of
  Perspecta in New York, Spring
  1988.
  PERSPECTA 1990, no.26, p.97-102,

SPACE (ARCHITECTURE) (CONTINUED)
  The burdens of linearity / Catharine
  Ingraham.
  COLUMBIA UNIVERSITY. GRADUATE
  SCHOOL OF ARCHITECTURE, PLANNING
  AND PRESERVATION. NEWSLINE 1990
  Dec.-1991 Jan., v.3, no.4, p.3,
  photo.
  De forma, de espacio: la idea de
  superficie en la obra de Luigi
  Moretti / Pedro Feduchi Canosa.
  In English and Spanish.
  ARQUITECTURA 1990 Jan.-Feb., v.72,
  no.282, p.28-42, ill., dwgs.,
  photos., refs.
  La distribution de l'espace
  monastique, prefiguration de la
  distribution domestique moderne /
  Albert Levy.
  Example of the plan of St. Gall.
  French, English and Spanish
  summaries.
  ESPACES ET SOCIETES 1990, no.56,
  p.107-123, refs.
  L'eapace des sens / Maurice Sauzet.
  On the work of Sauzet and the
  influence of Buddhist temple
  architecture. Includes English and
  Spanish summaries.
  TECHNIQUES ET ARCHITECTURE 1990
  June-July, no.390, p.96-100,180,
  photos., plans.
  Entwurfsprozesse: 4. Kapitel, Uber
  den Umgang mit dem Raum, Teil 5 /
  Berthold Mallmann.
  DEUTSCHE BAUZEITSCHRIFT 1990 Feb.,
  v.38, no.2, p.243-246,248-250,
  dwgs., plans, secns., refs.
  Especes d'espaces / Georges Perec.
  Excerpt from Perec's 1985 book
  eith the same title. Summaries in
  English and Spanish.
  TECHNIQUES ET ARCHITECTURE 1990
  June-July, no.390, p.64-65,179,
  photos.
  Die Gewichtsempfindung als
  bildnerisches Element = The
  sensation of weight as a visual
  element / Paul Klee.
  DAIDALOS 1990 Sept.15, no.37,
  p.78-89, diagrs., ill., dwgs.
  Human behavior and spatial design /
  Keijin Kamino.
  THE WHEEL EXTENDED 1990, v.19,
  no.3, p.2-7,
  Das Innen im Aussen im Innen = The
  interior in the outside of inner
  worlds / Frauke Tomczak.
  Text in German and English.
  DAIDALOS 1990 June 15, no.36,
  p.80-87, ill., photos., plan,
  refs.
  Innen Welt = Inner world / Gert
  Kahler.
  Commentary on the unreal utopian
  environments within large urban
  complexes. Text in German and
  English.
  DAIDALOS 1990 June 15, no.36,
  p.30-41, ill., elev., photos.,
  plans, refs.
  Das innere als Exil und Abgrund:
  Bilder zur Geschichte der
  Abgeschiedenheit = The inside as
  exil[e] and abyss: images from the
  history of seclusion / Ulrike
  Brunotte.
  Expressions of inwardness in
  spatial treatments of 19th-cent.
  German artists Caspar D. Friedrich
  and Johann E. Hummel.
  DAIDALOS 1990 June 15, no.36,
            (Continued next page)

SPACE FRAME STRUCTURES--JAPAN--MITO--
ART TOWER MITO
An exegesis of the Art Tower Mito /
Arata Isozaki.
Includes text from 1986 New York
exhibition catalog, Architecture
with or without irony.
JAPAN ARCHITECT 1990 Oct., v.65,
no.10(402), p.8-14, photos.

SPACE IN ARCHITECTURE
See SPACE (ARCHITECTURE)

SPACE PERCEPTION
See also ANAMORPHOSIS
Density perception on residential
streets / James R. Bergdoll, Rick
W. Williams.
Study to examine which physical
characteristics influence people's
perception of density on urban
residential streets; examples
taken from San Francisco, Ca.
BERKELEY PLANNING JOURNAL 1990,
v.5, p.15-38, ill., elevs., map,
photos., plans, tables, biblio.
Espaco, arquitetura e inconsciente /
Emanuel Dimas de Melo Pimenta.
PROJETO 1989 Oct., no.126,
p.127-128,
Fluktuation der Formen. Flugzeug und
Raumerfahrung = Fluctuation of
forms. The airplane and spatial
experience / Christoph Asendorf.
DAIDALOS 1990 Sept.15, no.37,
p.24-39, ill., photos., refs.
Die Gewichtsempfindung als
bildnerisches Element = The
sensation of weight as a visual
element / Paul Klee.
DAIDALOS 1990 Sept.15, no.37,
p.78-89, diagrs., ill., dwgs.
Human behavior and spatial design /
Keijin Kamino.
THE WHEEL EXTENDED 1990, v.19,
no.3, p.2-7,
Representation de l'espace paysan
[Romania] / Ernest Bernea.
MONUMENTS HISTORIQUES 1990
June-July, no.169, p.31-[35],
photos.
Run it down the field again, fellows
/ Grady Clay.
The football field as a standard
measurement, as illustrated in a
wide variety of quotes.
PLACES 1990 Summer, v.6, no.4,
p.4-8, photo., plan, aerial
photos.
Straffe Rhythmen: Labile
Konstruktionen im russischen
Konstruktivismus = Tight rhythms:
Unstable constructions in Russian
constructivism / Hubertus Gassner.
DAIDALOS 1990 Sept.15, no.37,
p.64-71, ill.
Time, speed, and design / Hiroyuki
Suzuki.
THE WHEEL EXTENDED 1990, v.19,
no.3, p.16-23, ill., photos.

SPACE PERCEPTION--RESEARCH
Environmental cognition: the
prediction of preference in rural
Indiana / H. Randy Gimblett.
Research on the perception of
landscape, using a rural site in
Henry County, Ind. Includes
abstract.
JOURNAL OF ARCHITECTURAL AND
PLANNING RESEARCH 1990 Autumn,
v.7, no.3, p.222-234, photos.,
biblio.

SPACE PERCEPTION--RESEARCH
(CONTINUED)
Understanding buildings: the
ecoanalysis of places / Arie
Peled.
"Ecoanalysis is a method of
exploring the individual
experience of places in a way
relevant to design decisions,
relevant to making the core
identity of places explicit."
ARCHITECTS' JOURNAL 1990 Aug.15,
v.192, no.7, p.49-55, diagrs.,
photos., plans.

SPACE SHUTTLES
See REUSABLE SPACE VEHICLES

SPACE STATIONS
See also REUSABLE SPACE VEHICLES
See also SPACE VEHICLES
Design goes to space: NASA and a
program at the University of
Houston are developing innovative
structures for living in space /
Karin Tetlow.
The Sasakawa International Center
for Space Architecture is working
on NASA's latest program, Space
Station Freedom.
ARCHITECTURE: THE MAGAZINE OF THE
AMERICAN INSTITUTE OF ARCHITECTS
1990 May, v.79, no.5, p.[98]-101,
ill., model.
Home, sweet space station / Joel
Warren Barna.
Students at the Sasakawa
International Center for Space
Architecture at the Univ. of
Houston face the problems of
long-term habitation elsewhere in
the solar system.
TEXAS ARCHITECT 1990 May-June,
v.40, no.3, p.26-29, ill., dwgs.,
models.

SPADA, CHARLES
AIDS hospice / Judith Davidsen.
On the collaborative project to
design a hospice in Mission Hill,
Boston. Interior designers:
Charles Spada, William Hodgins.
INTERIOR DESIGN 1990 Mar., v.61,
no.5, p.204-[205], photos.
Design as healer: Boston AIDS
hospice / Linda Hayes Tischler.
The Hospice at Mission Hill, in a
converted rowhouse and dating from
c.1987. Organizer: designer
Charles Spada.
METROPOLITAN HOME 1990 Sept.,
v.22, no.9, p.62, photo.

SPADA, PAOLO
L'ultima colonna = The last column /
Paolo Spada.
On the Capo Colonna archaeological
park and visitor center, Crotone,
Italy. Architects: Paolo Spada
Italo Insolera, Tommaso Tedesco.
SPAZIO E SOCIETA 1990 Apr.-June,
v.13, no.50, p.112-119, maps,
photos., aerial photo.

SPADE, ROBERT L.
Historic mining resources conference
/ Robert L. Spade.
Report on conference held Jan.1989
at Death Valley National Monument.
CRM BULLETIN: A NATIONAL PARK
SERVICE TECHNICAL BULLETIN 1990,
v.13, no.4, p.16-18,

SPAETH, DAVID
Mies and the Baukunst: an oriental
connection? / David Spaeth.
Discussion of the 1929 German
Pavilion at the International
Exposition, Barcelona.
REFLECTIONS: THE JOURNAL OF THE
SCHOOL OF ARCHITECTURE UNIVERSITY
OF ILLINOIS AT URBANA-CHAMPAIGN
1990 Spring, no.7, p.18-22, refs.

SPAETH, DAVID. IN THE SHADOW OF MIES:
LUDWIG HILBERSEIMER, ARCHITECT,
EDUCATOR AND URBAN PLANNER
In the shadow of Mies: Ludwig
Hilberseimer, architect, educator
and urban planner / Helen Searing.
Review of the 1988 book that
includes reminiscences by George
E. Danforth; critical essays by
Richard Pommer, David Spaeth, and
Kevin Harrington.
SOCIETY OF ARCHITECTURAL
HISTORIANS. JOURNAL 1990 Mar.,
v.49, no.1, p.113-114,
Vit de shaduw van Mies [book review]
/ Helene Damen.
Review of a 1988 monograph on
Ludwig Hilberseimer by Richard
Pommer, David Spaeth, and Kevin
Harrington.
DE ARCHITECT 1989 Nov., v.20,
no.11, p.103, dwg.

SPAGNESI, GIANFRANCO
ICOMOS: 25 anni di vita, bilancio e
avvenire / ed. by Rosa Anna
Genovese.
In conjunction with an
international colloquim held in
Lausanne, 6-11 Oct.1990, entitled
ICOMOS: un quart de siecle
d'existence, bilan et avenir.
Articles by Roberto di Stefano,
Mario F. Roggero, Gianfranco
Spagnesi, Franco Borsi, Gaetano
Miarelli Mariani, Marco Dezzi
Bardeschi, and Angelo Calvani.
RESTAURO 1990 May-June, v.19,
no.109, p.[3]-90, refs.

SPAIN--ACALA DE HENARES--BOULEVARDS--
ALTERATIONS AND ADDITIONS--AVENIDA
COMPLUTENSE
Rehabilitacion de la Avenida
Complutense, Acala de Henares,
1990.
Architects: Jose Luis Iniguez,
Fernando Pardo.
ARQUITECTURA 1990 July-Aug., v.72,
no.285, p.106-111, photos., plans,
site plans.

SPAIN--AGUILAS--HOSTELS
Albergue para jovenes = Youth
hostel.
On the Cala Reona beach, Aguilas,
Spain. Architects: Jose M. Torres
Nadal. Text in Spanish and
English.
QUADERNS D'ARQUITECTURA I
URBANISME 1988 July-Sept., no.178,
p.86-89, elevs., photos., plans,
secns., site plan.

SPAIN--ALAMEDA--LANDSCAPE GARDENS--
CONSERVATION AND RESTORATION--EL
CAPRICHO
A caprice well named / Tony Venison.
El Capricho landscape gardens,
outside Madrid.
COUNTRY LIFE 1990 Dec.20, v.184,
no.51, p.46-49, photos.

SPAIN--ALBAYCIN--HEALTH CARE
BUILDINGS--CENTRO DE SALUD
Tres arquitectos en Granada.
Four projects by E. Martin Martin,
L.J. Martin Martin and R. Ruiz
Fuentes: house in Granada, Centro
Provincial de Documentation e
Informacion Juvenil de Granada,
health center in Guadix, and
health center in Granada. Text in
Spanish and English.
ON DISENO 1990, no.116,
p.[176]-212, axonometric view,
det., ill., dwgs., elevs.,
photos., plans, secn., site plan.

SPAIN--ALCANTARILLA--APARTMENT HOUSES
Carbonell, Gadea, Alvarez, Moreno:
abitazioni ad Alcantarilla, Murcia
/ Duccio Malagamba.
Text in Italian and English.
DOMUS 1990 Mar., no.714, p.[1]-3,
elevs., photos, plans.

SPAIN--ALCOY--QUARTERS (DISTRICTS)--
CONSERVATION AND RESTORATION--BUIDA
OLI
Progetti recenti di Francesco
Venezia / Vittorio Savi, Giordano
Tironi.
Includes restoration of Buida Oli
waterfront, Alcoy, Spain;
renovation to Palazzo Faina
museum, Orvieto; competition entry
for gardens, Park de la Fontaine,
Nimes; and urban center
alterations, San Pietro a
Patierno, Naples. Includes
English captions and summary.
CASABELLA 1990 Mar., v.54, no.566,
p.4-17,59-60, axonometric view,
models, photos., plans, secns.,
site plans, sketches.

SPAIN--ALELLA--HOUSES
Vivienda unifamiliar en Alella:
Jordi Salvat y Joan Carles Vert,
arquitectos.
Spanish and English text.
ON DISENO 1989, no.106, p.110-117,
photos., plans, secns.

SPAIN--ALELLA--HOUSES--CASA RIERA
Vivienda unifamiliar en Alella,
Barcelona: Josep I. de Llorens y
A. Soldevila, arquitectos.
Spanish, English text.
ON DISENO 1990, no.113, p.122-129,
elevs., photos., plans.

SPAIN--ALELLA--PARKS
Sul fiume e nel giardino = Across
the river and into the garden /
Enric Battle, Joan Roig.
Features two projects by Enric
Battle and Joan Roig: bridge, Sani
Adria del Besos, Barcelona and a
park in a rectory orchard, Alella.
SPAZIO E SOCIETA 1990 Apr.-June,
v.13, no.50, p.102-107., figs.,
photos., plans, site plans, aerial
photos.

SPAIN--ALMAZAN--CHURCHES--CONCRETE
Gebaude der Gotter / Oswin M.
Muller.
Concrete church complex, Almazan,
Spain. Architects: Javier
Bellosillo Amunategui, Barbara W.
Baluffi.
DEUTSCHE BAUZEITSCHRIFT 1990 Jan.,
v.38, no.1, p.106-109, photos.

SPAIN--ALMAZAN--RELIGIOUS BUILDINGS--
20TH CENTURY
Gebaude der Gotter / Oswin M.
Muller.
Concrete church complex, Almazan,
Spain. Architects: Javier
Bellosillo Amunategui, Barbara W.
Baluffi.
DEUTSCHE BAUZEITSCHRIFT 1990 Jan.,
v.38, no.1, p.106-109, photos.

SPAIN--ALTO PENEDES--WINERIES--
CODORNIU
Spagna, Alto Penedes: le Cantine
Codorniu = Spain, Alto Penedes:
the Codoriu Winery / Tamara
Molinari.
Architect: Josep Puig i Cadafalch.
ABITARE 1990 June, no.286,
p.142-147, dwgs., photos.

SPAIN--AMETLLA DEL VALLES--SPORTS
FACILITIES
Pabellon Polideportivo en L'Ametlla
del Valles: J. Ll. Canosa y C.
Ferrater, arquitectos.
Spanish, English text.
ON DISENO 1990, no.114, p.124-133,
photos., plans.

SPAIN--ANDALUSIA--APARTMENT HOUSES--
COMPETITIONS
En spansk massa / Mona Jonsson.
Several projects from a housing
competition in Andalusia.
ARKITEKTUR: THE SWEDISH REVIEW OF
ARCHITECTURE 1990 Jan.-Feb., v.90,
no.1, p.48-49, ill., photos.,
plans, secn.

SPAIN--ANDALUSIA--ARCHITECTURE--
VISIGOTH
Las influencias visigoticas en
al-Andalus / Juan Zozaya.
Seminario Internazionale di Studi
su "Archeologia e arte nella
Spagna tardoromana, visigota e
mozarabica"; Ravenna, 4-11 April
1987.
CORSO DI CULTURA SULL'ARTE
RAVENNATE E BIZANTINA 1987, v.34,
p.395-425, photos., biblio.

SPAIN--ANDALUSIA--ART--VISIGOTH
Las influencias visigoticas en
al-Andalus / Juan Zozaya.
Seminario Internazionale di Studi
su "Archeologia e arte nella
Spagna tardoromana, visigota e
mozarabica"; Ravenna, 4-11 April
1987.
CORSO DI CULTURA SULL'ARTE
RAVENNATE E BIZANTINA 1987, v.34,
p.395-425, photos., biblio.

SPAIN--ANDALUSIA--LANDSCAPE PROTECTION
Raumordnung und Landschaftsplanung
in Spanien / Andrea Hessel.
Landscape planning in Andalusia.
Includes English summary.
GARTEN UND LANDSCHAFT 1990, v.100,
no.3, p.23-28, photos., refs.

SPAIN--ANDALUSIA--REGIONAL PLANNING
Raumordnung und Landschaftsplanung
in Spanien / Andrea Hessel.
Landscape planning in Andalusia.
Includes English summary.
GARTEN UND LANDSCHAFT 1990, v.100,
no.3, p.23-28, photos., refs.

SPAIN--ANTEQUERA--CITY PLANNING
Plan especial de conservacion y
reforma interior de Antequera /
Luis Machuca, Carlos Verdu.
URBANISMO / COAM 1990 Jan., no.9,
p.57-64, photo., plans, dwgs.,
elevs., chart, axonometric views.

SPAIN--ANTEQUERA--COMPREHENSIVE PLANS
Plan especial de conservacion y
reforma interior de Antequera /
Luis Machuca, Carlos Verdu.
URBANISMO / COAM 1990 Jan., no.9,
p.57-64, photo., plans, dwgs.,
elevs., chart, axonometric views.

SPAIN--ANTEQUERA--HISTORIC DISTRICTS--
CONSERVATION AND RESTORATION
Plan especial de conservacion y
reforma interior de Antequera /
Luis Machuca, Carlos Verdu.
URBANISMO / COAM 1990 Jan., no.9,
p.57-64, photo., plans, dwgs.,
elevs., chart, axonometric views.

SPAIN--ARANJUEZ--INDUSTRIAL PARKS--EL
REGAJAL
Actuacion industrial de Aranjuez
(Madrid).
URBANISMO / COAM 1990 Sept.,
no.11, p.99-100, map, plan, table.

SPAIN--ARCHITECTURAL LITERATURE
Les revues d'architecture en Espagne
au XIXe siecle (de 1846 aux
environs de 1928) / Esteban
Castaner Munoz.
REVUE DE L'ART 1990, no.89,
p.57-64, dwgs., elevs., engrs.,
refs.

SPAIN--ARCHITECTURE
Un material que se identifica con la
arquitectura mediterranea / Jose
Luis Porcar.
The use of ceramics in
architecture in Spain. Text in
English, p.176-179.
ON DISENO 1990, "ceramica suppl.,
p.57-71, ill., photos.

SPAIN--ARCHITECTURE--16TH CENTURY--
BIBLIOGRAPHY
L'architecture espagnole au XVI
siecle: ouvrages recents /
Veronique Gerard Powell.
Bibliography.
BULLETIN MONUMENTAL 1990, v.148,
no.4, p.[417]-422, engrs., refs.

SPAIN--ARCHITECTURE--19TH CENTURY
Les revues d'architecture en Espagne au XIXe siecle (de 1846 aux environs de 1928) / Esteban Castaner Munoz.
REVUE DE L'ART 1990, no.89, p.57-64, dwgs., elevs., engrs., refs.

SPAIN--ARCHITECTURE--20TH CENTURY
Antologia come storia [book review] / Juan Miguel Hernandez Leon. Review of Spagna, architettura 1965-1988, by Gabriel Ruiz Cabrero.
CASABELLA 1990 Sept., v.54, no.571, p.29-30, photos.
Arquitectos en la M-30 / Alejandro Zaera, Manuel Gausa.
Roundtable with Inaki Abalos, Juan Herreros, Rafael Terrelo, Federico Soriano, Fernando Porras, Mateo Corrales. Includes 8 projects. Spanish, English text.
QUADERNS D'ARQUITECTURA I URBANISME 1989 Apr.-Sept., nos.181-182, p.[48-81], elevs., models, photos., plans, secns., site plans.
Contemporaneidad, contexto y posiciones en la arquitectura espanola reciente = Contemporaneity, context and positions in recent Spanish architecture / Josep Maria Montaner.
Discusses 18 recent projects by 21 Spanish architects. In English and Spanish.
EL CROQUIS 1989 Dec., v.8, no.41, p.128-154, photos.
Critica y regionalista / Alexander Tzonis, Liane Lefaivre.
On contemporary Spanish "critical regionalist" architecture. English summary, p.87.
A & V 1990, no.24, p.22-24, axonometric views, ill., dwgs., elevs., refs.
Jacobsen 4 - Espana 4 / Alfonso Valdes.
Text in Spanish and English.
ARQUITECTURA 1990 Mar.-June, v.72, no.283-284, p.140-151, elevs., model, photos., plans.
Una perspectiva historica: Espana durante los ochenta = A historical perspective: Spain during the eighties / William Curtis.
On Spanish architecture of the 1980s. English text, p.81-82.
A & V 1990, no.24, p.4-9, elev., photos., plans, sketch.
Spain fetes modernism / David Cohn.
A new generation of architects design in the Modernist tradition.
ARCHITECTURAL RECORD 1990 June, v.178, no.7, p.47-48, axonometric view, elevs., photo, plans.
Special feature: Spanish contemporary architecture.
Consists of four sections, separately indexed, and introductory essay "An approach to Spanish contemporary architecture", by Richard Levene and Fernando Marquez Cecilia. Text in Japanese.
SPACE DESIGN 1990 May, no.308, p.05-132, dets., ports., elevs., model, photos., plans, secns., site plans, sketches, isometric dwgs.

SPAIN--ARCHITECTURE--20TH CENTURY (CONTINUED)
Tras la decada dovada: el desafio de los noventa = After the golden decade: the challenge of the nineties / Peter Buchanan. English text, p.83-86.
A & V 1990, no.24, p.10-21, elevs., models, photos., secns.

SPAIN--ARCHITECTURE--20TH CENTURY--CRITICISM--BIBLIOGRAPHY
Figuras canonicas: la imagen dela Espana reciente = Canonical figures: the image of recent Spain / Thomas Reese.
Review of the literature on Spanish architects and architecture since Franco's death. English text, p.88-90.
A & V 1990, no.24, p.25-32, ports., refs.

SPAIN--ARCHITECTURE--20TH CENTURY--THEORY
Que caigan esos dioses! / Jordi Ambros.
Commentary on an article in the newspaper "El Pais" by Ignasi de Sola Morales on the current status of Spanish architects. Spanish, English text.
ON DISENO 1990, no.107, p.88-93, dwgs.

SPAIN--ARCHITECTURE--AWARDS AND PRIZES
Premisos FAD de arquitectura e interiorismo (y 3).
Presents 10 projects, each indexed seperately. Text in Spanish and English.
ON DISENO 1990, no.116, p.102-175, dwgs., elevs., photos., plans, secns., site plans, serial photos.

SPAIN--ARCHITECTURE--CONSERVATION AND RESTORATION
Rehabilitacion de la arquitectura / Carme Ferrer, Carme Llopis.
Introduction to nine articles indexed separately on conservation in Spain. Spanish, English text.
ON DISENO 1990, no.109, p.102-105, photo.

SPAIN--AREVALO--INDUSTRIAL PARKS
Actuacion industrial de Arevalo (Avila).
URBANISMO / COAM 1990 Sept., no.11, p.95-96, map, plan, table.

SPAIN--ARNEDO--INDUSTRIAL PARKS--EL RAPOSAL
Actuacion industrial de Arnedo (La Rioja).
URBANISMO / COAM 1990 Sept., no.11, p.97-98, map, plan, table, aerial photo.

SPAIN--ARUSA--ARTISTS' STUDIOS
Dos habitatges: mercat, museu.
Features four projects by Manuel Gallego. Text in Spanish and English.
QUADERNS D'ARQUITECTURA I URBANISME 1988 July-Sept., no.178, p.32-[57], dets., elevs., photos., plans, secns.

SPAIN--ASTURIAS--REGIONAL PLANNING
La ordenacion territorial en el principado de Asturias = Land planning in the principality of Asturias / Fernando Arrojo Martinez.
English summary, p.35.
URBANISMO / COAM 1989 Sept., no.8, p.28-35, graphs, maps, photos.

SPAIN--ATIENZA--PORTALS--ROMANESQUE--SANTA MARIA DEL REY
El programa teologico de la portada romanica de Santa Maria del Rey en Atienza / Antonio Herrera Casado. Porch dates between 1260-1270. English summary.
ARCHIVO ESPANOL DE ARTE 1990 Oct.-Dec., v.63, no.252, p.[593]-607, dwgs., refs.

SPAIN--ATIENZA--SCULPTURE--ARCHITECTURAL--ROMANESQUE--SANTA MARIA DEL REY
El programa teologico de la portada romanica de Santa Maria del Rey en Atienza / Antonio Herrera Casado. Porch dates between 1260-1270. English summary.
ARCHIVO ESPANOL DE ARTE 1990 Oct.-Dec., v.63, no.252, p.[593]-607, dwgs., refs.

SPAIN--AUDITORIUMS, CONCERT HALLS--20TH CENTURY
Arquitecturas orquestadas: los auditorios espanoles de los noventa / Miguel Verdu.
Projects by Jose Maria Garcia de Paredes, and others.
ARQUITECTURA VIVA 1990 Jan.-Feb., no.10, p.6-10, model, photo., secn., table.

SPAIN--BADAJOZ--BRIDGES--COMPETITIONS--PUENTE SOBRE EL RIO GUADIANA
Concurso internacional europeo de puente sobre el Rio Guadiana, Badajoz 1990.
First prize project by Francisco Sanchez de Leon, architect, and Ramon Alfonso Sanchez de Leon, engineer.
ARQUITECTURA 1990 July-Aug., v.72, no.285, p.26-27, elevs., models, secns.

SPAIN--BADALONA--ARENAS
Civic monuments.
Three projects by Esteve Bonell: School, Masquefa, with Josep Maria Gil; law courts, Gerona, with Josep Maria Gil and the sports arena, Badalona, with Francesc Rius.
ARCHITECTURAL REVIEW 1990 July, v.188, no.1121, p.69-73, elevs., models, photos., plans, secns, site plan.

SPAIN--BADALONA--BOARDWALKS--PASEO MARITIMO
Las arquitectural publicas de Mario Luis Corea, Francisco Gallardo y Edgardo Manino.
Six articles. Includes the boardwalk and beach at Badalona; Public Health center, Badalona; Plaza, Badalona; San Roc community center and residence for the elderly handicapped, Badalona;
(Continued next page)

SPAIN--BADALONA--BOARDWALKS--PASEO
MARITIMO (CONTINUED)
Las arquitectural...(CONTINUED)
Primary school Santa Rosa,
Cerdanyola. Spanish and English
text.
ON DISENO 1990, no.107,
p.[100]-141, elevs., photos.,
plans, secns., site plan,
sketches.

SPAIN--BADALONA--HEALTH CARE
BUILDINGS--CENTRO DE ASISTENCIA
PRIMARIA
Las arquitectural publicas de Mario
Luis Corea, Francisco Gallardo y
Edgardo Manino.
Six articles. Includes the
Boardwalk and beach at Badalona;
Public Health center, Badalona;
Plaza, Badalona; San Roc community
center and residence for the
elderly handicapped, Badalona;
Primary school Santa Rosa,
Cerdanyola. Spanish and English
text.
ON DISENO 1990, no.107,
p.[100]-141, elevs., photos.,
plans, secns., site plan,
sketches.

SPAIN--BADALONA--HOUSING FOR ELDERLY--
CASAL-RESIDENCIA EN SANT-ROC
Las arquitectural publicas de Mario
Luis Corea, Francisco Gallardo y
Edgardo Manino.
Six articles. Includes the
Boardwalk and beach at Badalona;
Public Health center, Badalona;
Plaza, Badalona; San Roc community
center and residence for the
elderly handicapped, Badalona;
Primary school Santa Rosa,
Cerdanyola. Spanish and English
text.
ON DISENO 1990, no.107,
p.[100]-141, elevs., photos.,
plans, secns., site plan,
sketches.

SPAIN--BADALONA--HOUSING FOR
HANDICAPPED--CASAL-RESIDENCIA EN
SANT-ROC
Las arquitectural publicas de Mario
Luis Corea, Francisco Gallardo y
Edgardo Manino.
Six articles. Includes the
Boardwalk and beach at Badalona;
Public Health center, Badalona;
Plaza, Badalona; San Roc community
center and residence for the
elderly handicapped, Badalona;
Primary school Santa Rosa,
Cerdanyola. Spanish and English
text.
ON DISENO 1990, no.107,
p.[100]-141, elevs., photos.,
plans, secns., site plan,
sketches.

SPAIN--BADALONA--PLAZAS
Las arquitectural publicas de Mario
Luis Corea, Francisco Gallardo y
Edgardo Manino.
Six articles. Includes the
Boardwalk and beach at Badalona;
Public Health center, Badalona;
Plaza, Badalona; San Roc community
center and residence for the
elderly handicapped, Badalona;
Primary school Santa Rosa,
Cerdanyola. Spanish and English
(Continued next column)

SPAIN--BADALONA--PLAZAS (CONTINUED)
Las arquitectural...(CONTINUED)
text.
ON DISENO 1990, no.107,
p.[100]-141, elevs., photos.,
plans, secns., site plan,
sketches.

SPAIN--BADALONA--RESTAURANTS
Rehabilitacion de una masia como
restaurante en Badalona: J.I. de
Llorens y A. Soldevila,
arquitectos.
Spanish, English text.
ON DISENO 1990, no.113, p.130-137,
elev., photos., plan.

SPAIN--BADALONA--SCHOOLS--SECONDARY--
SALAVADOR ESPRIU
Escuela en Badalona: J.I. de
Llorens, J. Ma. Massot y A.
Soldevila, arquitectos.
Spanish, English text.
ON DISENO 1990, no.113, p.114-121,
elevs., photos., plans.

SPAIN--BAEZA--CITY PLANNING
Plan especial de proteccion y
reforma interior de Baeza / Berta
L. Brusilovsky, Piedad Martinez.
URBANISMO / COAM 1990 Jan., no.9,
p.65-71, photos., plans, dwgs.,
site plans, elevs., sketches.

SPAIN--BAEZA--COMPREHENSIVE PLANS
Plan especial de proteccion y
reforma interior de Baeza / Berta
L. Brusilovsky, Piedad Martinez.
URBANISMO / COAM 1990 Jan., no.9,
p.65-71, photos., plans, dwgs.,
site plans, elevs., sketches.

SPAIN--BAEZA--HISTORIC DISTRICTS--
CONSERVATION AND RESTORATION
Plan especial de proteccion y
reforma interior de Baeza / Berta
L. Brusilovsky, Piedad Martinez.
URBANISMO / COAM 1990 Jan., no.9,
p.65-71, photos., plans, dwgs.,
site plans, elevs., sketches.

SPAIN--BAEZA--OLD TOWNS--CONSERVATION
AND RESTORATION
Plan especial de proteccion y
reforma interior de Baeza / Berta
L. Brusilovsky, Piedad Martinez.
URBANISMO / COAM 1990 Jan., no.9,
p.65-71, photos., plans, dwgs.,
site plans, elevs., sketches.

SPAIN--BANOLAS--FARMHOUSES--
ALTERATIONS AND ADDITIONS
Reforma de una antigua masoveria en
Banyoles: C. Bosch y J. Ll.
Frigola, arquitectos.
Farmhouse alterations. Spanish,
English text.
ON DISENO 1990, no.114, p.120-123,
photos., plans.

SPAIN--BANOLAS--HOTELS--BANYOLES
OLYMPIC HOTEL
Banyoles Hotel.
Banyoles Olympic Hotel, Banyoles,
Spain. Architects: Eisenman
Architects.
PROGRESSIVE ARCHITECTURE 1990
Jan., v.71, no.2, p.86-88,
diagrs., dwgs., elevs., models,
plans, secns.

SPAIN--BANOLAS--HOTELS--BANYOLES
OLYMPIC HOTEL (CONTINUED)
Peter Eisenman.
Most of the issue devoted to this
architect. Nine projects featured.
Includes interview with David
Cohn. Text in Spanish and English.
EL CROQUIS 1989 Dec., v.8, no.41,
p.4-126,cover, axonometric views,
ill., dwgs., ports., elevs.,
models, photos., plans, secns.,
refs.
Special feature: recent works of
Peter Eisenman.
Contents: Editor's introduction.--
Essays: Peter Eisenman: releasing
time imprisoned in space / Tadao
Ando.-- A framework for the future
/ Kurt W. Forster.-- Four notes on
the recent architecture of Peter
Eisenman / Ignasi de
Sola-Morales.-- A matter of
respect.-- Works: Wexner Center
for the Visual Arts, Ohio State
University.-- Columbus Convention
Center.-- Banyoles Olympic Hotel
competition.-- College of Design,
Architecture, Art and Planning,
University of Cincinnati.--
Interview: Peter Eisenman / Jeff
Kipnis. Text in Japanese and
English.
ARCHITECTURE AND URBANISM 1990
Jan., no.1(232), p.[7]-182,
axonometric views, elevs., models,
photos., plans, secns., sketches.

SPAIN--BARCELONA--APARTMENT
COMPLEXES--MAQUINISTA
Auf den Spuren der Katalanischen
Moderne: neue Arbeiten von
Martorell, Bohigas, Mackay.
Three projects: Burobau der
"Sociedad Nestle" in Espluegues de
Llobregat in Barcelona; Wohnanlage
"La Maquinista" in Barceloneta in
Barcelona; Wohnanlage Mollet in
Gallecs in Mollet. One of four
issues on the theme "Barcelona
bauen".
BAUWELT 1990 Mar.2, v.81, no.9,
p.378-385, axonometric views,
photos., plans, secns., site
plans.

SPAIN--BARCELONA--APARTMENT
COMPLEXES--TEIA
Fins de chantier / Joan Pascuale
Argente ... [et al.].
Contents: Former tannery converted
to association building,
Chatillon-sur-Indre, France;
architect: Thierry Van de
Wingaert.--Hospital Paul-Brousse,
Villejuif, France; architects:
Avant-Travaux.--Housing complex,
Barcelona, Spain; architects: Joan
Pascual Argente, Ramon Ausio
Mateu, Lluis Badenas Oradanos,
Joan Forgas Coll, Teresa Gimeno
Marin, Enric Serra Grau.
LE MONITEUR ARCHITECTURE AMC 1990
May, no.11, p.11-16, photos.,
plans.

SPAIN--BARCELONA--APARTMENT HOUSES--
BARCELONETA
Archivo en blanco y negro: cronica
grafica de tres generaciones/
Francese Catala-Roca.
Six projects from 1951-1988, by
architects Antoni Gaudi, Barba
Corsini, Antoni de Moragas, Jose
Antonio Coderch, Josep Lluis Sert,
Helio Pinon y Albert Viaplana.
ARQUITECTURA VIVA 1990 May-June,
no.12, p.33-35, photos.

SPAIN--BARCELONA--APARTMENT HOUSES--
CASA MILA (LA PEDRERA)
Archivo en blanco y negro: cronica
grafica de tres generaciones/
Francese Catala-Roca.
Six projects from 1951-1988, by
architects Antoni Gaudi, Barba
Corsini, Antoni de Moragas, Jose
Antonio Coderch, Josep Lluis Sert,
Helio Pinon y Albert Viaplana.
ARQUITECTURA VIVA 1990 May-June,
no.12, p.33-35, photos.

SPAIN--BARCELONA--APARTMENT HOUSES--
COMPETITIONS
Wohnung und Stadt - Barcelona,
Spanien = Housing and city -
Barcelona, Spain.
Competition for apartment house
along the Diagonal Avenue,
Barcelona. Three joint
first-prize-winning teams. Text in
German.
ARCHITEKTUR + WETTBEWERBE 1990
June, no.142, p.70-73, elevs.,
plans, secns., site plans.

SPAIN--BARCELONA--APARTMENT HOUSES--
CONSERVATION AND RESTORATION--CASA
MILA (LA PEDRERA)
Il restauro della facciata di Casa
Mila "La Pedrera" = The
restoration of the facade of Casa
Mila / Rafael Villa [sic]
Rodriguez.
Restoration of 1906-1910 apartment
building at 92 Paseo de Gracia,
Barcelona. Original architect:
Antoni Gaudi Jornet. Architects
for restorations: Josef Emilio
Hernandez-Cros, Rafael Vila
Rodriguez.
FRAMES, PORTE & FINESTRE 1990
July-Sept., no.28, p.52-57,
photos.

SPAIN--BARCELONA--ARCHITECTURE
Barcelona / Peder Boas Jensen ...
[et al.].
Theme of issue. Contents: By
eller OL, by Peder Boas Jensen and
Elith Juul Moller.-- Idraettens
arenaer, by Ebbe Melgaard.--
Kataloniens hovedstad, by Jorgen
Sestoft.-- Gensyn med Gaudi, by
Nils-Ole Lund.-- Parkerne i
Barcelona, by Jorgen Peder Hansen
and Anna Maria Indrio.-- Den
nordiske inspiration, by Nils-Ole
Lund.-- Ny katalansk arkitektur,
by Jan Christiansen and Gosta
Knudsen.-- Miralles og Pinos, by
Thomas Wiesner.
ARKITEKTEN 1990 May, v.92, no.7,
p.[212]-249, cover, axonometric
views, diagrs., maps, photos.,
secns., aerial photos., biblios.

SPAIN--BARCELONA--ARCHITECTURE--19TH
CENTURY
Moderne architectuur in Barcelona
[book review] / Stans Henneman.
Review of 1989 monograph by David
Mackay.
DE ARCHITECT 1989 Dec., v.20,
no.12, p.64-65, photo.

SPAIN--BARCELONA--ARCHITECTURE--20TH
CENTURY
Arquitetura catala contemporanea /
Josep-Maria Montaner.
A panorama of Catalan architecture
between 1951 and 1987.
PROJETO 1988 Nov., no.116,
p.139-146, dwgs., photos., site
plan.
Barcelona.
Introduces special section on
Barcelona. Contents: Modernism is
alive and well (interview with
Oriol Bohigas); Rebuilding a
public realm; and Incidents in the
city grain. Three additional
articles separately indexed.
ARCHITECTS' JOURNAL 1990 July 11,
v.192, no.2, p.[22]-39, dwg.,
port., elevs., models, photos.,
plans, secns., sketches, site
plans.
Barcelona.
Theme issue (17 articles) on
Barcelona. Includes an interview
with Oriol Bohigas.
RASSEGNA 1989 Mar., v.11, no.37/1,
p.1-88, dwgs., elevs., models,
maps, photos., plans, secns., site
plans.
Headstart / Patrick Kelly.
On the work of David Mackay and
Peter Hodgkinson in Barcelona.
BUILDING DESIGN 1990 Mar.2,
no.975, p.30-31, port., photo.
Moderne architectuur in Barcelona
[book review] / Stans Henneman.
Review of 1989 monograph by David
Mackay.
DE ARCHITECT 1989 Dec., v.20,
no.12, p.64-65, photo.

SPAIN--BARCELONA--ART CENTERS--
FUNDACION JOAN MIRO
Archivo en blanco y negro: cronica
grafica de tres generaciones/
Francese Catala-Roca.
Six projects from 1951-1988, by
architects Antoni Gaudi, Barba
Corsini, Antoni de Moragas, Jose
Antonio Coderch, Josep Lluis Sert,
Helio Pinon y Albert Viaplana.
ARQUITECTURA VIVA 1990 May-June,
no.12, p.33-35, photos.

SPAIN--BARCELONA--ART GALLERIES
Galeria de arte en Barcelona: M.
Meyetta y R. Diez, arquitectos.
Spanish, English text.
ON DISENO 1990, no.113, p.100-113,
photos., plans, secns.

SPAIN--BARCELONA--ART GALLERIES--
ALTERATIONS AND ADDITIONS--PALAU
FINESTRES
Provocative and participatory
places.
Features seven projects in the
Barcelona area by Enric Miralles
and Carme Pinos.
ARCHITECTURAL REVIEW 1990 July,
v.188, no.1121, p.74-89, dets.,
ill., elevs., plans, secns., site
plans, sketches.

SPAIN--BARCELONA--ARTISTS' STUDIOS--
MARISCAL STUDIO
Nuovi usi per la citta dismessa:
Barcellona, il Poble Nou = New
uses for run-down city areas:
Barcelona, the Poble Nou.
A feature on changes in this
outlying suburb. Includes an essay
by Octavio Mestre.
ABITARE 1990 May, no.285,
p.186-207, ill., dwg., elev.,
maps, photos., plans, secns.

SPAIN--BARCELONA--ATHLETIC CLUBS
Complejo deportivo Arsenal Augusta:
L. Alonso y S. Balaguer,
arquitectos.
Spanish, English text.
ON DISENO 1990, no.108, p.162-169,
photos., plans.
Complejo deportivo Arsenal: L.
Alonso y S. Balaguer, arquitectos.
Spanish, English text.
ON DISENO 1990, no.108, p.154-161,
elevs., photos., plans.

SPAIN--BARCELONA--AUDITORIUMS, CONCERT
HALLS--ART NOUVEAU--ALTERATIONS AND
ADDITIONS--PALAU DE LA MUSICA
CATALANA
Ampliacion, remodelacion y
restauracion del Palau de la
Musica Catalana: Tusquets, Diaz &
Associats, arquitectos.
Original architect (1905): Lluis
D. i Montaner. Text in Spanish and
English.
ON DISENO 1990, no.116, p.109-117,
photos., plans.
Gathering establishments.
Part of a special feature on
Spanish contemporary architecture.
Contents: Palau de la Musica
Catalana, by Oscar Tusquets
Blanca, Carlos M. Diaz, Lluis
Clotet, Ignacio Paricio --
Television Andaluza, by Gonzalo
Diaz-Y. Recasens --Banco de
Espana, Jaen, by Rafael Moneo --
Almacenes Simon, by Lluis Clotet,
Ignacio Paricio --Mercado
Vilaseca-Salou, by Carlos Ferrater
Lambarri, Jose Luis Canosa --
Pabellon Rius i Taulet, by Pep
Bonet --Velodromo de Horta, by
Esteban Bonell, Francesc Rius --
Brief histories --Views through
the Camera's Finder, by Hisao
Suzuki. Text in Japanese.
SPACE DESIGN 1990 May, no.308,
p.93-131, dets., ports., elevs.,
model, photos., plans, secns.,
site plan, sketch, isometric dwg.
Modernismo modernized / Magda Saura.
On the remodeling of 1905-1908
Palau de la Musica Catalana,
Barcelona. Original architect:
Lluis Domenechi Montaner.
Renovation architects: Tusquets,
Diaz & Associates. Includes
interview with Tusquets.
PROGRESSIVE ARCHITECTURE 1990
June, v.71, no.6, p.84-[91],
elevs., photos., plans, secns.,
site plan.
Palau de la Musica Catalana = Music
palace, Barcelona, 1981-1989.
On the remodeling of 1905-1908
Palau de al Musica Catalana,
Barcelona. Original architect:
Lluis Domenech Montaner.
Renovation architects: O.Tusquets,
(Continued next page)

SPAIN--BARCELONA--AUDITORIUMS, CONCERT
HALLS--ART NOUVEAU--ALTERATIONS AND
ADDITIONS--PALAU DE LA MUSICA
CATALANA (CONTINUED)
Palau de la Musica...(CONTINUED)
Ll. Clotet y C. Diaz.
EL CROQUIS 1990 Mar., v.9, no.42,
p.80-107, dets., elevs., photos.,
plans, secns., site plans,
sketches.
Proyectar para una arquitectura
dada: analogia y diversidad = To
design for a given architecture:
analogy and diversity / Anton
Capitel.
Discusses 4 recent projects in
Spain.
EL CROQUIS 1990 Mar., v.9, no.42,
p.64-79, photos.
La vitrine du palais: extension du
Palais de la musique catalane,
Espagne / Marc Bedarida.
Addition to 1905-08 building in
Barcelona. Original architect:
Lluis Domenech i Montaner.
Renovation arhcitects: Tusquets,
Diaz & Associates. English
summary, p.120. Spanish summary,
p.169.
TECHNIQUES ET ARCHITECTURE 1990
Aug.-Sept., no.391, p.120-121,
photos., secn., site plan.

SPAIN--BARCELONA--BANKS--CAIXA PENEDES
Dos oficinas bancarias en Barcelona:
J.J. Mestre y Josep Ma. Rovira,
arquitectos.
Spanish, English text.
ON DISENO 1990, no.113, p.147-157,
photos., plans.

SPAIN--BARCELONA--BARS (EATING AND
DRINKING ESTABLISHMENTS)
Figuras de interior: Hacia el
"existenzmaximun. / Juli Capella,
Quim Larrea.
Interior projects of the 1980's in
Barcelona.
ARQUITECTURA VIVA 1990 Nov.-Dec.,
no.15, p.6-11, photos., plans,
secn.

SPAIN--BARCELONA--BARS (EATING AND
DRINKING ESTABLISHMENTS)--INTERIOR
DESIGN--ZSA ZSA
Puppet master / David Redhead.
On the Barcelona bar, Zsa Zsa.
Interior designer: Daniel Freixes.
DESIGNERS' JOURNAL 1990 Jan.,
no.53, p.38-[43], port., photos.,
plan, secn.

SPAIN--BARCELONA--BARS (EATING AND
DRINKING ESTABLISHMENTS)--TERRAZA
TIBIDABO
Eduardo Samso.
Includes criticism by Josep Maria
Montaner and four projects by the
architect. Text in Spanish and
English.
EL CROQUIS 1990 Nov., v.9, no.45,
p.125-162, axonometric views,
dets., port., elevs., models,
photos., plans, secns., site
plans.

SPAIN--BARCELONA--BICYCLE RACING
TRACKS--VELODROMO DE HORTA
Gathering establishments.
Part of a special feature on
Spanish contemporary architecture.
Contents: Palau de la Musica
Catalana. by Oscar Tusquets
Blanca, Carlos M. Diaz, Lluis
Clotet, Ignacio Paricio --
Television Andaluza, by Gonzalo
Diaz-Y. Recasens --Banco de
Espana, Jaen, by Rafael Moneo --
Almacenes Simon, by Lluis Clotet,
Ignacio Paricio --Mercado
Vilaseca-Salou, by Carlos Ferrater
Lambarri, Jose Luis Canosa --
Pabellon Rius i Taulet, by Pep
Bonet --Velodromo de Horta, by
Esteban Bonell, Francesc Rius --
Brief histories --Views through
the Camera's Finder, by Hisao
Suzuki. Text in Japanese.
SPACE DESIGN 1990 May, no.308,
p.93-131, dets., ports., elevs.,
model, photos., plans, secns.,
site plan, sketch, isometric dwg.
Salonatmosphare: Stadien in
Barcelona, Sportanlagen in
Eichstatt, Kricketstadion bei
London, Amphitheater in Nimes.
Architects: Esteve Bonell and
Francesc Rius, Karljosef Schattner
with Wilhelm Huber, Michael
Hopkins and Partner, Finn Geipel
and Nicolas Michelin. Text in
German, French and English.
WERK, BAUEN + WOHNEN 1990 Sept.,
no.9, p.46-65, dets., elevs.,
models, photos., plans, secns.,
site plans.

SPAIN--BARCELONA--BOULEVARDS--
ALTERATIONS AND ADDITIONS--VIA JULIA
Stadtebauliche Neuordnung der Via
Julia in Barcelona, Spanien =
Replanning of the Via Julia in
Barcelona, Spain.
Architects: Josep Maria Julia i
Capdevila, Bernardo de Sola, Pedro
Barragan.
ARCHITEKTUR + WETTBEWERBE 1990
Dec., no.144, p.10-[11], photos.,
secns., site plans.

SPAIN--BARCELONA--BRIDGES--PUENTA BACH
DE RODA
Urban space [Barcelona].
Part of a special feature on
Spanish contemporary architecture.
Contents: Plaza Granollers, by
Albert Viaplana, Helio Pinon.--
Parc de L'Espanya Industrial, by
Luis Pena Ganchegui.--Funicular de
Vallvidrera, by Josep Llinas.--
Puente Bach de Roda, by Santiago
Calatrava.--Brief Histories. Text
in Japanese.
SPACE DESIGN 1990 May, no.308,
p.75-92, dets., ports., elevs.,
photos., plans, secns., sketch,
isometric dwg.

SPAIN--BARCELONA--BRIDGES--SANI ADRIA
DEL BESOS
Sul fiume e nel giardino = Across
the river and into the garden /
Enric Battle, Joan Roig.
Features two projects by Enric
Battle and Joan Roig: bridge, Sani
Adria del Besos, Barcelona and a
park in a rectory orchard, Alella.
SPAZIO E SOCIETA 1990 Apr.-June,
(Continued next column)

SPAIN--BARCELONA--BRIDGES--SANI ADRIA
DEL BESOS (CONTINUED)
Sul fiume e nel...(CONTINUED)
v.13, no.50, p.102-107., figs.,
photos., plans, site plans, aerial
photos.

SPAIN--BARCELONA--BUILDINGS--20TH
CENTURY
As castanholas de Aalto / Anita
Regina di Marco.
PROJETO 1989 Oct., no.126,
p.[54]-55, elevs., photos., plans,
secn., aerial photos.
Spanische Impressionen: Anstiftung
zur Architektur / Wilfried Dechau.
Recent buildings and restoration
projects in anticipation of the
1992 Olympics.
DEUTSCHE BAUZEITUNG 1990 Dec.,
v.124, no.12, p.92-98, photos.

SPAIN--BARCELONA--BUILDINGS--20TH
CENTURY--CASA DE LOS TOROS
Archivo en blanco y negro: cronica
grafica de tres generaciones/
Francese Catala-Roca.
Six projects from 1951-1988, by
architects Antoni Gaudi, Barba
Corsini, Antoni de Moragas, Jose
Antonio Coderch, Josep Lluis Sert,
Helio Pinon y Albert Viaplana.
ARQUITECTURA VIVA 1990 May-June,
no.12, p.33-35, photos.

SPAIN--BARCELONA--BUILDINGS--
CONSERVATION AND RESTORATION
Spanische Impressionen: Anstiftung
zur Architektur / Wilfried Dechau.
Recent buildings and restoration
projects in anticipation of the
1992 Olympics.
DEUTSCHE BAUZEITUNG 1990 Dec.,
v.124, no.12, p.92-98, photos.

SPAIN--BARCELONA--CAFES
Figuras de interior: Hacia el
"existenzmaximun. / Juli Capella,
Quim Larrea.
Interior projects of the 1980's in
Barcelona.
ARQUITECTURA VIVA 1990 Nov.-Dec.,
no.15, p.6-11, photos., plans,
secn.

SPAIN--BARCELONA--CEMETERIES--IGUALADA
Provocative and participatory
places.
Features seven projects in the
Barcelona area by Enric Miralles
and Carme Pinos.
ARCHITECTURAL REVIEW 1990 July,
v.188, no.1121, p.74-89, dets.,
ill., elevs., plans, secns., site
plans, sketches.

SPAIN--BARCELONA--CHURCHES--
ROMANESQUE--CONSERVATION AND
RESTORATION--IGLESIA PARROQUIAL DE
SANT CRISTOFOR DE LA CASTANYA
Restauracion de la iglesia de Sant
Cristofor de la Castanya: Josep
Rovira, arquitecto.
Spanish, English text.
ON DISENO 1990, no.110, p.157-163,
photos., plan.

SPAIN--BARCELONA--CITIES AND TOWNS--
20TH CENTURY--GROWTH
Democratie on Olympische dromen:
tien jaar stedelijke interventies
in Barcelona, 1979-1989 / Ignasi
de Sola-Morales.
ARCHIS 1989 Nov., no.11, p.13-19,
ill., maps, photos., secns.

SPAIN--BARCELONA--CITIES AND TOWNS--
GROWTH
Barcelona / Peder Boas Jensen ...
[et al.].
Theme of issue. Contents: By
eller OL, by Peder Boas Jensen and
Elith Juul Moller.-- Idraettens
arenaer, by Ebbe Melgaard.--
Kataloniens hovedstad, by Jorgen
Sestoft.-- Gensyn med Gaudi, by
Nils-Ole Lund.-- Parkerne i
Barcelona, by Jorgen Peder Hansen
and Anna Maria Indrio.-- Den
nordiske inspiration, by Nils-Ole
Lund.-- Ny katalansk arkitektur,
by Jan Christiansen and Gosta
Knudsen.-- Miralles og Pinos, by
Thomas Wiesner.
ARKITEKTEN 1990 May, v.92, no.7,
p.[212]-249,cover, axonometric
views, diagrs., maps, photos.,
secns., aerial photos., biblios.

SPAIN--BARCELONA--CITY PLANNING
Barcelona.
Introduces special section on
Barcelona. Contents: Modernism is
alive and well (interview with
Oriol Bohigas); Rebuilding a
public realm; and Incidents in the
city grain. Three additional
articles separately indexed.
ARCHITECTS' JOURNAL 1990 July 11,
v.192, no.2, p.[22]-39, dwg.,
port., elevs., models, photos.,
plans, secns., site plans,
sketches.
Barcelona: una renovacion de la
forma urbana / Octavio Mestre.
Text in Spanish and English.
ARQUITECTURA 1990 July-Aug., v.72,
no.285, p.74-81, photos.
Breathing hope into the city / Mary
Halnan.
Urban design in Barcelona and
Glasgow.
ARCHITECTS' JOURNAL 1990 Apr.25,
v.191, no.17, p.15, photo.
L'Idea del villaggio olimpico di
Barcellona: tipi e morfologie =
The idea of the Olympic Village in
Barcelona: types and morphologies
/ Josep Maria Montaner.
Architects: Masterplan: Martorell,
Bohigas, Mackay, Puigdomenech.
Includes 16 projects by various
architects.
LOTUS INTERNATIONAL 1990, no.67,
p.18-53, dwgs., elevs., model,
photos., plans, secns., site
plans, aerial photos.
Is het Barcelonese experiment
herhaalbaar? [editorial] / Hans
van Dijk.
On the influence of Oriol Botigas.
Introd. to an issue on recent
projects in Barcelona; articles
are indexed separately.
ARCHIS 1989 Nov., no.11, p.7.

SPAIN--BARCELONA--CITY PLANNING
(CONTINUED)
Regisseurs van het moderne
stadsleven: Joan Busquets en
Manuel de Sola-Morales [interview]
/ Han Meyer.
The second of two articles in an
issue featuring Barcelona.
DE ARCHITECT 1989 Oct., v.20,
no.10, p.56-61,cover, photos.,
secns., site plans.
La strada, elemento unificante nella
costruzione della citta: l'esempio
di Barcelona = The Street,
unifying element in the
construction of cities / Lilia
Pagano.
Planning of Barcelona streets.
LOTUS INTERNATIONAL 1989, no.64,
p.72-85, maps, photos., plans,
secns., site plans.

SPAIN--BARCELONA--CITY PLANNING--20TH
CENTURY
Barcelona.
Theme issue (17 articles) on
Barcelona. Includes an interview
with Oriol Bohigas.
RASSEGNA 1989 Mar., v.11, no.37/1,
p.1-88, dwgs., elevs., models,
maps, photos., plans, secns., site
plans.
Barcelone, l'olympiade des prodigies
/ Marie-Christine Loriers.
English summary, p.108. spanish
summary, p.155.
TECHNIQUES ET ARCHITECTURE 1990
Dec.-1991 Jan., no.393, p.100-109,
dwgs., photos., plans, secns.,
site plans, aerial photo.
La ciudad de la tolerancia: sobre la
construccion del presente /
Vittorio Magnago Lampugnani.
On the city planning projects
underway in Barcelona in
preparation for the 1992 Olympics.
A & V 1990, no.22, p.4-9, ill.,
maps.
El ensanche litoral: la Villa
Olimpica, historia de una idea /
Josep Maria Montaner.
English summary, p.83-85.
A & V 1990, no.22, p.16-24, dwgs.,
elevs., models, maps, plans,
aerial photos.
Il futuro delle periferie urbane:
Barcellona = The future of urban
peripheries: Barcelona / Per Erik
Bjornson, Marco Ceccaroni.
Discussion of six projects: Parc
del Clot, Placa Salvador Allende,
Parc de la Creuta del Coll, Placa
d'Angel Pestanta, Placa de
Francesc Layret and Avinguda Rio
de Janeiro.
SPAZIO E SOCIETA 1990 Jan.-Mar.,
v.13, no.49, p.80-93, dets.,
elevs., model, maps, photos., site
plans, aerial photos.
Labyrintisch landschap, laboratorium
van stadsontwerp: de olympische
lokatie Vall d'Hebron / Rein
Geursten.
ARCHIS 1989 Nov., no.11, p.33-40,
maps. photos., secns., site plans,
refs.
"Onze gesprekken met aannemers gaan
bijna nooit over vierkante meters.
Ze gaan over kwaliteit."
[interview] / Hans van Dijk, Rob
de Graaf.
Joan Busquets answers questions
(Continued next column)

SPAIN--BARCELONA--CITY PLANNING--20TH
CENTURY (CONTINUED)
"Onze gesprekken met...(CONTINUED)
about recent planning projects in
Barcelona.
ARCHIS 1989 Nov., no.11, p.20-23,
model, site plan.
Public spaces and the reconstruction
of the city: learning from
Barcelona and Berlin / Beatrice
Sokoloff.
French summary.
ARCHITECTURE & COMPORTEMENT =
ARCHITECTURE & BEHAVIOR 1990, v.6,
no.4, p.[339]-356, axonometric
view, photos., site plan, aerial
photo., biblio.

SPAIN--BARCELONA--CITY PLANNING--20TH
CENTURY--POLITICAL ASPECTS
De las plazas a los juegos: diez
anos de intervenciones urbanas /
Ignasi de Sola-Morales.
On Barcelona, English summary,
p.81-82, and city planning
projects in preparation for the
1992 Olympics.
A & V 1990, no.22, p.10-15, dwgs.,
elevs., photos., site plans,
aerial photos.

SPAIN--BARCELONA--CITY PLANNING--
COMPETITIONS--AVENIDA DIAGONAL
Barcelona Diagonal / Mirko Zardini.
Competition projects for new
buildings along the planned
extension of the Diagonal.
Architects: Rafael Moneo and
Manuel de Sola Morales (winners);
Richard Plunz and Roberto Collova.
Text in Italian and English.
LOTUS INTERNATIONAL 1989, no.64,
p.86-107, axonometric views,
elevs., models, plans, secns.,
site plans.
Barcelone: prolonger la diagonal
jusqu'a la mer / Octavio Mestre.
Report on proposal for extension
of Avenida Diagonal, Barcelona.
LE MONITEUR ARCHITECTURE AMC 1990
Sept., no.14, p.24-25, photo.,
plan, map, isometric dwg.
Droom, daad en Diagonaal:
prijsvraagontwerpen voor
Barcelona's langste straat /
Manuel Gausa.
ARCHIS 1989 Nov., no.11, p.41-46,
dwgs., photos., plans, site plans,
refs.

SPAIN--BARCELONA--CITY PLANNING--
HISTORY
La riforma della Barceloneta:
tracciati e regolamenti = the
Barceloneta reform: urban grids
and regulations / Manuel de Sola
Morales.
Fishing quarter plannned in 1749.
LOTUS INTERNATIONAL 1988, no.51
p.30-45, elevs., models, plans,
secns., site plans, engr.

SPAIN--BARCELONA--CITY PLANNING--
INFLUENCE
The sum of the parks.
Can the urban design initiatives
being undertaken in Barcelona be
applied in the U.K.?
ARCHITECTS' JOURNAL 1990 July 11,
v.192, no.2, p.54, photo.

SPAIN--BARCELONA--CITY PLANNING--LA
  NOVA ICARIA
  Redesigning urban design / David
  Mackay, Barrie Evans.
  Nova Icaria and the Olympic
  Village, Barcelona. Architects:
  Martorell-Bohigas-Mackay-Puigdomen
  ech.
  ARCHITECTS' JOURNAL 1990 July 11,
  v.192, no.2, p.42-49, dwg.,
  elevs., models, plan, secns., site
  plan, sketches.

SPAIN--BARCELONA--CITY PLANNING--PORT
  VELL
  Proyecto de remodelacion de los
  Almacenes Generales de Comercio
  [interview]: Lawrence Halprin.
  The urban planner discusses his
  project to remodel the Port Vell
  area of Barcelona. In "On
  oficina", 1990 supplement issue.
  English text, p.180-181.
  ON DISENO 1990, suppl., p.60-63,
  ports.

SPAIN--BARCELONA--CLINICS
  Centro de asistencia primaria en
  Barcelona: Carlos Ferrater,
  arquitecto.
  Spanish, English text.
  ON DISENO 1990, no.108, p.112-119,
  photos., plans, secn., isometric
  dwgs.

SPAIN--BARCELONA--COMMUNITY CENTERS--
  PISTA
  Das Barcelona Experiment: soziales
  Begegnungszentrum "La Pista".
  Architects: Miralles/Pinos. One
  of four articles on the theme
  "Barcelona bauen".
  BAUWELT 1990 Mar.2, v.81, no.9,
  p.376-377, photos.

SPAIN--BARCELONA--CONVENTION
  FACILITIES
  Architectural landmarks.
  Features three buildings by Elias
  Torres Tur and Jose Antonio
  Martinez Lapena: hospital, Mora de
  Ebro; congress center, Barcelona,
  and sports hall, Granollers.
  ARCHITECTURAL REVIEW 1990 July,
  v.188, no.1121, p.52-59, elevs.,
  models, photos., plans, secns.,
  site plan.
  Crestas de perfil: palacio de
  congresos y convenciones.
  Convention facility for
  Barcelona's Olympic village.
  Architects: Jose Antonio Martinez
  Lapena, Elias Torres Tur, Miguel
  Maria Usandizaga Calparsoro.
  English summary, p.88.
  A & V 1990, no.22, p.78-80, dwgs.,
  elevs., models, plans, secns.,
  site plans.

SPAIN--BARCELONA--CORPORATE OFFICE
  BUILDINGS--INTERIOR DESIGN
  Nueva imagen de una antigua nave:
  proyecto de interiorismo: Pilar
  Libano.
  Warehouse converted to office
  building, in Sabadell, Barcelona.
  English text, p.181-182. In "On
  oficina," 1990 supplement issue.
  ON DISENO 1990, suppl., p.142-147,
  photos.

SPAIN--BARCELONA--CULTURAL CENTERS--
  ALTERATIONS AND ADDITIONS--CENTRE
  CULTURAL DE LA CAIXA
  Remodelacion del Centre Cultural de
  la Caixa de Pensions, Barcelona:
  J. Bach y G. Mora, arquitectos.
  Original architect: Josep Puig i
  Cadafalch; 1901. Spanish, English
  text.
  ON DISENO 1990, no.114, p.140-143,
  dwg., photos., secn.

SPAIN--BARCELONA--DETENTION CENTERS--
  CENTRO DE MENORES DIFICILES
  Centre for problem children in Palau
  de Plegamans, Barcelona, Spain,
  1986.
  Architect: Eduard Bru.
  9H 1989, no.8, p.114-119, elevs.,
  photos., site plan.

SPAIN--BARCELONA--EXHIBITION
  BUILDINGS--GERMAN PAVILION
  Deutscher, Pavillon, Weltausstellung
  Barcelona 1929 / Markus Meyer.
  Architect: Mies van der Rohe.
  DER ARCHITEKT 1990 Dec., no.12,
  p.580, photo., plan, refs.

SPAIN--BARCELONA--EXHIBITION
  BUILDINGS--GERMAN PAVILION AND
  INDUSTRIAL EXHIBITS
  The Barcelona Pavilion as landscape
  garden: modernity and the
  picturesque / Caroline Constant.
  AA FILES 1990 Autumn, no.20,
  p.47-54.
  Mies and the Baukunst: an oriental
  connection? / David Spaeth.
  Discussion of the 1929 German
  Pavilion at the International
  Exposition, Barcelona.
  REFLECTIONS: THE JOURNAL OF THE
  SCHOOL OF ARCHITECTURE UNIVERSITY
  OF ILLINOIS AT URBANA-CHAMPAIGN
  1990 Spring, no.7, p.18-22, refs.
  Mies van der Rohe's paradoxial
  symmetries / Robin Evans.
  Architect: Ludwig Mies van der
  Rohe.
  AA FILES 1990 Spring, no.19,
  p.56-68, photos., elevs., plans,
  sketches, aerial photo.

SPAIN--BARCELONA--EXHIBITION
  BUILDINGS--PABELLON RIUS I TAULET
  Gathering establishments.
  Part of a special feature on
  Spanish contemporary architecture.
  Contents: Palau de la Musica
  Catalana, by Oscar Tusquets
  Blanca, Carlos M. Diaz, Lluis
  Clotet, Ignacio Paricio --
  Television Andaluza, by Gonzalo
  Diaz-Y. Recasens --Banco de
  Espana, by Rafael Moneo --
  Almacenes Simon, by Lluis Clotet,
  Ignacio Paricio --Mercado
  Vilaseca-Salou, by Carlos Ferrater
  Lambarri, Jose Luis Canosa --
  Pabellon Rius i Taulet, by Pep
  Bonet --Velodromo de Horta, by
  Esteban Bonell, Francesc Rius --
  Brief histories --Views through
  the Camera's Finder, by Hisao
  Suzuki. Text in Japanese.
  SPACE DESIGN 1990 May, no.308,
  p.93-131, dets., ports., elevs.,
  model, photos., plans, secns.,
  site plan, sketch, isometric dwg.

SPAIN--BARCELONA--FACADES--ART
  NOUVEAU--CONSERVATION AND
  RESTORATION--CASA MILA (LA PEDRERA)
  Il restauro della facciata di Casa
  Mila "La Pedrera" = The
  restoration of the facade of Casa
  Mila / Rafael Villa [sic]
  Rodriguez.
  Restoration of 1906-1910 apartment
  building at 92 Paseo de Gracia,
  Barcelona. Original architect:
  Antoni Gaudi Jornet. Architects
  for restorations: Josef Emilio
  Hernandez-Cros, Rafael Vila
  Rodriguez.
  FRAMES, PORTE & FINESTRE 1990
  July-Sept., no.28, p.52-57,
  photos.

SPAIN--BARCELONA--FACADES--TEMPORARY--
  PALAU ROBERT
  Els Tallers de Miro: Luis Pera y
  Ramon Robert (R&B Associates).
  On the designs for the Palau
  Robert, Barcelona, for an
  exhibition on Miro. Text in
  Spanish and English.
  ON DISENO 1990, no.116, p.118-123,
  photos.

SPAIN--BARCELONA--FACTORIES--19TH
  CENTURY--ALTERATIONS AND ADDITIONS--
  EDIFICIO DEL RELOJ
  Remodelacion del Edificio del Reloj
  de Barcelona: Carles Buxade y Joan
  Margarit, arquitectos.
  The "Clock Building", built
  1869-1875, now offices of the
  Provencial Authority. Original
  architect: R. Guastavino. Text in
  Spanish and English.
  ON DISENO 1990, no.116, p.134-137,
  photos.

SPAIN--BARCELONA--FOUNTAINS--
  COMPETITIONS--OLYMPIC VILLAGE
  Magic fountain: competition for the
  design of a monumental fountain,
  Olympic Village, Barcelona /
  Xavier Costa.
  First prize architects: Yago Conde
  and Bea Goller.
  AA FILES 1990 Spring, no.19,
  p.53-55, dwgs., model, plans, site
  plan.

SPAIN--BARCELONA--GATEWAYS--EUROCITY 1
  La puerta del cielo: edificio de
  oficinas Eurocity 1.
  Gateway/office building, Calle
  Juan de Austria, Barcelona.
  Architects: Luis Domenech, Roser
  Amado. English summary, p.87.
  A & V 1990, no.22, p.56-59, dets.,
  models, plans, site plan, sketch.

SPAIN--BARCELONA--GATEWAYS--EUROCITY
  2, 3 Y 4
  Fugas escalonadas: edificios de
  oficinas Eurocity 2, 3 y 4 =
  Vanishing steps.
  Located along the calle Zamora,
  Barcelona.
  A & V 1990, no.22, p.60-61,
  elevs., models, plans, site plan,
  sketches.

SPAIN--BARCELONA--HANGARS--AEREOPUERTO
DE BARCELONA
Hangar para dos aviones: S. Farriol
y A. Soler, arquitectas.
Barcelona. Spanish, English text.
ON DISENO 1990, no.115, p.138-143,
elev., photos.

SPAIN--BARCELONA--HOSPITALS--OPTHALMIC
AND AURAL--CLINICA BARRAQUER
La clinica Barraquer a Barcellona =
The Barraquer clinic in Barcelona.
Architect: Joaquim Lloret.
OTTAGONO 1990 Sept., no.96,
p.[136]-150, port., photos.,
models, plans, secns.
Vedere l'invisibile = Seeing the
invisible / Paolo Legrenzi.
On the design of the Barraquer
Clinic, Barcelona, which opened in
1941. Architect: Joaquim Lloret.
OTTAGONO 1990 Sept., no.96,
p.130-135, photos., refs.

SPAIN--BARCELONA--HOUSES
Vivienda unifamiliar en Barcelona:
Tonet Sunyer, arquitecto.
Spanish, English text.
ON DISENO 1990, no.115, p.176-183,
photos., plans, secn.

SPAIN--BARCELONA--HOUSES--CONSERVATION
AND RESTORATION--CASA LLEO MORERA
Oficinas en Barcelona: Carles M.
Ferruz (Atri).
Offices installed in the Casa Lleo
Morera originality built 1903-1905
by Lluis Domenech i Montaner.
Spanish, English text.
ON DISENO 1989, no.104, p.154-159,
photos.

SPAIN--BARCELONA--HOUSING
La arquitectura residencial de la
Villa Olimpica / Justo Isasi.
Includes 13 projects. English
summary, p.86.
A & V 1990, no.22, p.26-54, dets.,
ill., elevs., models, plans,
secns., site plans, sketches.

SPAIN--BARCELONA--HOUSING--
COMPETITIONS
Barcelona Diagonal / Mirko Zardini.
Competition projects for new
buildings along the planned
extension of the Diagonal.
Architects: Rafael Moneo and
Manuel de Sola Morales (winners);
Richard Plunz and Roberto Collova.
Text in Italian and English.
LOTUS INTERNATIONAL 1989, no.64,
p.86-107, axonometric views,
elevs., models, plans, secns.,
site plans.

SPAIN--BARCELONA--HOUSING--STUDENT
PROJECTS--NOSTRA SENYORA DEL PORT
Wohnungsbau "Nostra Senyora del
Port" in Barcelona, Spanien =
Housing "Nostra Senyora del Port"
in Barcelona, Spain.
Student project from the
Technische Universitat Delft. Text
in German.
ARCHITEKTUR + WETTBEWERBE 1990
June, no.142, p.89, models, plan,
site plan.

SPAIN--BARCELONA--INDUSTRIAL
BUILDINGS--ALTERATIONS AND
ADDITIONS--HISPANO OLIVETTI
Barcelona Activa = Industrial
building rehabilitation,
Barcelona, 1987-1988.
Renovation of the 1950's Hispano
Olivetti complex for use as a
company work center and offices.
Architects for renovation: J.A.
Martinez Lapena and Elias Torres.
EL CROQUIS 1990 Mar., v.9, no.42,
p.108-123, dets., elevs., photos.,
plans, secns.

SPAIN--BARCELONA--INDUSTRIAL
BUILDINGS--BARCELONA ACTIVA
Proyectar para una arquitectura
dada: analogia y diversidad = To
design for a given architecture:
analogy and diversity / Anton
Capitel.
Discusses 4 recent projects in
Spain.
EL CROQUIS 1990 Mar., v.9, no.42,
p.64-79, photos.

SPAIN--BARCELONA--INSTALLATION WORKS--
TEMPORARY--FESTIVAL DE LA INFANCIA Y
LA JUVENTUD
Barcelona sona: D. Freixes, P.
Angli, E. Gonzalez y V. Miranda.
Installation at the Festival of
Childhood and Youth combing light,
shape and sound. Spanish, English
text.
ON DISENO 1990, no.115, p.150-153,
photos., plan.

SPAIN--BARCELONA--INTERIOR DESIGN
Special feature: Commercial
interiors in Barcelona.
Contents: Between minimalism and
Movid, by Naoki Inagawa -- Alfredo
Arribas -- Josep Val and Xavier
Vendrell -- Dani Freixes and
Vicente Miranda -- Tonet Sunyer
and Jordi Badia -- Eduard Samso --
Ventura Valcarce and Carlos Valls.
Includes interviews and
biographical information and
features 13 individual commercial
projects. Text in Japanese.
SPACE DESIGN 1990 Nov.,
no.11(314), p.005-072, dets.,
ports., photos., plans, secns.,
refs.

SPAIN--BARCELONA--KITCHENS
Josep Luis Mateo: Bathroom and
kitchen, Barcelona, 1985.
9H 1989, no.8, p.80-81, elevs.,
photos., plans.

SPAIN--BARCELONA--LIBRARIES--PUBLIC--
BIBLIOTECA JOAN MIRO
La biblioteca Joan Miro a Barcellona
/ Beth Gali et al.
Architects: Beth Gali, Marius
Quintana, Antoni Solanas [etc]
Captions in Italian and English.
CASABELLA 1990 Nov., v.54, no.573,
p.36-37, elev., photos., plans,
secns., site plan.

SPAIN--BARCELONA--LIBRARIES--
UNIVERSITY AND COLLEGE--UNIVERSIDAD
POLITECNICA BARCELONA
Biblioteca y departamentos; U.
Politecnica Barcelona, 1989-90.
Architect: Jose Llinas.
ARQUITECTURA 1990 Jan.-Feb., v.72,
no.282, p.122-129, elevs.,
photos., plans, secns.
Bibliotek og Kontorer, Polyteknisk
Universitet, Barcelona.
Architect: Jose Llinas.
ARKITEKTUR DK 1990, v.34, no.7,
p.A114-A115, photos., plans,
secns.

SPAIN--BARCELONA--MEDIAN STRIPS--
ALTERATIONS AND ADDITIONS--VIA JULIA
Stadtebauliche Neuordnung der Via
Julia in Barcelona, Spanien =
Replanning of the Via Julia in
Barcelona, Spain.
Architects: Josep Maria Julia i
Capdevila, Bernardo de Sola, Pedro
Barragan.
ARCHITEKTUR + WETTBEWERBE 1990
Dec., no.144, p.10-[11], photos.,
secns., site plans.

SPAIN--BARCELONA--MEDIAN STRIPS--
AVENIDA RIO DE JANEIRO
Urbanizacion de la avenida Rio de
Janeiro de Barcelona: P. Bardaji y
C. Teixidor, arquitectos.
Text in Spanish and English.
ON DISENO 1990, no.116, p.124-133,
photos., site plan.

SPAIN--BARCELONA--METEOROLOGICAL
STATIONS
Geometrias talladas: centro
meteorologico = carved geometries.
Project for the meterological
center for the Olympic Village,
Barcelona. Architect: Alvaro Siza.
English text, p.88.
A & V 1990, no.22, p.70-73,
axonometric view, plans, secns.,
site plan, sketches.

SPAIN--BARCELONA--METROPOLITAN AREAS
Infraestructuras logisticas en la
Region Metropolitana de Barcelona
= Logistic infrastructures in the
metropolitan region of Barcelona
(M.R.B.) / J. Audicana...et al.
English summary, p.37.
URBANISMO / COAM 1990 May, no.10,
p.29-37, maps, photos., site
plans, table, aerial photos.

SPAIN--BARCELONA--MIDDLE SCHOOLS
Mittelschule in Barcelona, Spanien =
Secondary school in Barcelona,
Spain.
Conversion of 19th cent. factory
into middle school for boys.
Architects: Enric Miralles, Carme
Pinos.
ARCHITEKTUR + WETTBEWERBE 1989
Dec., no.140, p.18-19, elev.,
photos., plans.

SPAIN--BARCELONA--MONUMENTS AND
MEMORIALS--20TH CENTURY--FOSSAR DE
LAS MORERES
Fossar de les Moreres, Barcelona
1989.
Outdoor sculpture memorial.
Architect: Carmen Fiol.
ARQUITECTURA 1990 July-Aug., v.72,
no.285, p.88-91, photos., plan,
secns., elev.

SPAIN--BARCELONA--OLYMPIC BUILDINGS
(CONTINUED)
Provocative and participatory
places.
Features seven projects in the
Barcelona area by Enric Miralles
and Carme Pinos.
ARCHITECTURAL REVIEW 1990 July,
v.188, no.1121, p.74-89, dets.,
ill., elevs., plans, secns., site
plans, sketches.
Salonatmosphare: Stadien in
Barcelona, Sportanlagen in
Eichstatt, Kricketstadion bei
London, Amphitheater in Nimes.
Architects: Esteve Bonell and
Francesc Rius, Karljosef Schattner
with Wilhelm Huber, Michael
Hopkins and Partner, Finn Geipel
and Nicolas Michelin. Text in
German, French and English.
WERK, BAUEN + WOHNEN 1990 Sept.,
no.9, p.46-65, dets., elevs.,
models, photos., plans, secns.,
site plans.
Scenari per i giochi olimpici del
'91 = Setting for the 1992 Olympic
games / Agnoldomenico Pica.
New stadium built within exterior
of stadium built by architect
Domenech y Montaner Jr. in 1929;
architects: Arata Isozaki &
Associates.
L'ARCA 1990 May, no.38, p.34-47,
photos., secns.
Villa Olympica 1992: Bohigas
regisseert varianten op het
bouwblok / Sebastiaan Gribling.
Proposals by several architects
for a building in Olympic village
in Barcelona.
DE ARCHITECT 1989 Nov., v.20,
no.11, p.58-65, elevs., models,
map, plans, site plans.

SPAIN--BARCELONA--OLYMPIC BUILDINGS--
MONTJUIC OLYMPIC STADIUM
Remodelacion del Estadio de Montjuic
en Barcelona: Vittorio Gregotti,
Federico Correa, Alfonso Mila,
Carles Buxade y Joan Margarit,
arquitectos.
Text in Spanish and English.
ON DISENO 1990, no.116, p.155-169,
photos., plans, secn., site plan,
aerial photos.

SPAIN--BARCELONA--OLYMPIC BUILDINGS--
PALAU SANT JORDI
El Palau Sant Jordi, Barcelona:
Arata Isozaki & Associates.
Includes statement by Isozaki.
Text in Spanish and English.
ON DISENO 1990, no.118, p.106-171,
cover, ill., elevs., photos.,
plans, secns., sketches.

SPAIN--BARCELONA--OLYMPIC VILLAGES
La arquitectura residencial de la
Villa Olimpica / Justo Isasi.
Includes 13 projects. English
summary, p.86.
A & V 1990, no.22, p.26-54, dets.,
ill., elevs., models, plans,
secns., site plans, sketches.
La ciudad de la tolerancia: sobre la
construccion del presente /
Vittorio Magnago Lampugnani.
On the city planning projects
underway in Barcelona in
preparation for the 1992 Olympics.
A & V 1990, no.22, p.4-9, ill.,
maps.

SPAIN--BARCELONA--OLYMPIC VILLAGES
(CONTINUED)
El ensanche litoral: la Villa
Olimpica, historia de una idea /
Josep Maria Montaner.
English summary, p.83-85.
A & V 1990, no.22, p.16-24, dwgs.,
elevs., models, maps, plans,
aerial photos.
L'Idea del villaggio olimpico di
Barcellona: tipi e morfologie =
The idea of the Olympic Village in
Barcelona: types and morphologies
/ Josep Maria Montaner.
Architects: Masterplan: Martorell,
Bohigas, Mackay, Puigdomenech.
Includes 16 projects by various
architects.
LOTUS INTERNATIONAL 1990, no.67,
p.18-53, dwgs., elevs., model,
photos., plans, secns., site
plans, aerial photos.
Redesigning urban design / David
Mackay, Barrie Evans.
Nova Icaria and the Olympic
Village, Barcelona. Architects:
Martorell-Bohigas-Mackay-Puigdomen
ech.
ARCHITECTS' JOURNAL 1990 July 11,
v.192, no.2, p.42-49, dwg.,
elevs., models, plan, secns., site
plan, sketches.
La trasformazione urbana come
progetto urbanistico: la Villa
Olimpica de Barcelona = Urban
transformation as urban project:
la Villa Olimpica de Barcelona /
Joan Busquets.
Master plan architects: Martorell,
Bohigas, Mackay, Puigdomenech.
LOTUS INTERNATIONAL 1990, no.67,
p.6-17, model, photos., site
plans, aerial photos., refs.

SPAIN--BARCELONA--OLYMPIC VILLAGES--
VALL D'HEBRON SITE
The wasteland and the park / Iona
Foster.
Planning of the Vall d'Hebron
Olympic site in Barcelona.
Architect: Eduard Bru.
ARCHITECTS' JOURNAL 1990 Nov.28,
v.192, no.22, p.14-15, elev.,
plan.

SPAIN--BARCELONA--OPEN SPACES
Urban space [Barcelona].
Part of a special feature on
Spanish contemporary architecture.
Contents: Plaza Granollers, by
Albert Viaplana, Helio Pinon.--
Parc de L'Espanya Industrial, by
Luis Pena Ganchegui.--Funicular de
Vallvidrera, by Josep Llinas.--
Puente Bach de Roda, by Santiago
Calatrava.--Brief Histories. Text
in Japanese.
SPACE DESIGN 1990 May, no.308,
p.75-92, dets., ports., elevs.,
photos., plans, secns., sketch,
isometric dwg.

SPAIN--BARCELONA--OUTDOOR SCULPTURE
Stedelijke theaters: de continuiteit
van het Barcelonese experiment /
Hans van Dijk.
Six plazas and parks in Barcelona
completed since 1986. Designers:
Pedro Barragan and Bernardo de
Sola, Andreu Arriola and Carme
Fiol, Beth Gali, Dani Freixes,
Vicente Miranda, Josep Martorell
(Continued next column)

SPAIN--BARCELONA--OUTDOOR SCULPTURE
(CONTINUED)
Stedelijke theaters:... (CONTINUED)
and David Mackay, Enric Pericas.
ARCHIS 1989 Nov., no.11, p.24-32,
photos., site plans.

SPAIN--BARCELONA--OUTDOOR SCULPTURE--
FOSSAR DE LES MORERES
Fossar de les Moreres, Barcelona
1989.
Outdoor sculpture memorial.
Architect: Carmen Fiol.
ARQUITECTURA 1990 July-Aug., v.72,
no.285, p.88-91, photos., plan,
secns., elev.
Fossar de les Moreres, Barcelona:
Carme Fiol, arquitecta.
Outdoor sculpture memorial.
Spanish, English text.
ON DISENO 1990, no.114, p.134-139,
photos.

SPAIN--BARCELONA--PALO ALTO--STUDIOS
Nuovi usi per la citta dismessa:
Barcellona, il Poble Nou = New
uses for run-down city areas:
Barcelona, the Poble Nou.
A feature on changes in this
outlying suburb. Includes an essay
by Octavio Mestre.
ABITARE 1990 May, no.285,
p.186-207, ill., dwg., elev.,
maps, photos., plans, secns.

SPAIN--BARCELONA--PARKS
Barcelona 1992--die olympische
Landschaft / Miquel Vidal Pla.
Includes English summary.
GARTEN UND LANDSCHAFT 1990, v.100,
no.3, p.41-44, ill., dwgs.,
models, maps, photos., site
plans, aerial photo.
Barcelona / Peder Boas Jensen ...
[et al.].
Theme of issue. Contents: By
eller OL, by Peder Boas Jensen and
Elith Juul Moller.-- Idraettens
arenaer, by Ebbe Melgaard.--
Kataloniens hovedstad, by Jorgen
Sestoft.-- Gensyn med Gaudi, by
Nils-Ole Lund.-- Parkerne i
Barcelona, by Jorgen Peder Hansen
and Anna Maria Indrio.-- Den
nordiske inspiration, by Nils-Ole
Lund.-- Ny katalansk arkitektur,
by Jan Christiansen and Gosta
Knudsen.-- Miralles og Pinos, by
Thomas Wiesner.
ARKITEKTEN 1990 May, v.92, no.7,
p.[212]-249,cover, axonometric
views, diagrs., maps, photos.,
secns., aerial photos., biblios.
Die Mobilisierung des Aussenraumes:
neue Platze und Parks in Barcelona
/ Gerhard Ullmann.
WERK, BAUEN + WOHNEN 1990 June,
no.6, p.2-7, photos., site plans,
aerial photos.
Moderne stedelijke complexiteit in
Barcelona / Han Meyer.
The first of two articles in an
issue featuring Barcelona.
DE ARCHITECT 1989 Oct., v.20,
no.10, p.51-55, photo., biblio.
Het stadslandschap van Barcelona:
plannen voor herstel van een
bijzondere relatie / Sebastiaan
Gribling.
DE ARCHITECT THEMA 1990 Sept.,
v.21, no.9 suppl., p.45-49, dwgs.,
photos., plans, secn.

SPAIN--BARCELONA--PARKS--20TH CENTURY
Stedelijke theaters: de continuiteit
van het Barcelonese experiment /
Hans van Dijk.
Six plazas and parks in Barcelona
completed since 1986. Designers:
Pedro Barragan and Bernardo de
Sola, Andreu Arriola and Carme
Fiol, Beth Gali, Dani Freixes,
Vicente Miranda, Josep Martorell
and David Mackay, Enric Pericas.
ARCHIS 1989 Nov., no.11, p.24-32,
photos., site plans.

SPAIN--BARCELONA--PARKS--ART NOUVEAU--
CONSERVATION AND RESTORATION--PARCO
GUELL
Reconstruir los suenos de una
artista: restauracion del Park
Guell.
Original architect: Antonio Gaudi.
Architects for restoration: J.
Antonio Martinez Lapena, Elias
Torres Tur. English text,
p.190-191.
ON DISENO 1990, "ceramica" suppl.,
p.130-134, photos.

SPAIN--BARCELONA--PARKS--CREUETA DEL
COLL
Creueta Del Coll Park in Barcelona,
Spanien = Creueta Del Coll Park in
Barcelona, Spain.
Architects: Martorell, Bohigas,
Mackay.
ARCHITEKTUR + WETTBEWERBE 1990
Mar., no.141, p.15, photo., site
plan.

SPAIN--BARCELONA--PARKS--FUNICULAR DE
VALLVIDRERA
Urban space [Barcelona].
Part of a special feature on
Spanish contemporary architecture.
Contents: Plaza Granollers, by
Albert Viaplana, Helio Pinon.--
Parc de L'Espanya Industrial, by
Luis Pena Ganchegui.--Funicular de
Vallvidrera, by Josep Llinas.--
Puente Bach de Roda, by Santiago
Calatrava.--Brief Histories. Text
in Japanese.
SPACE DESIGN 1990 May, no.308,
p.75-92, dets., ports., elevs.,
photos., plans, secns., sketch,
isometric dwg.

SPAIN--BARCELONA--PARKS--PARC DE
L'ESPANYA
"Arees de nova centralitat" in
Barcelona / Niclas Dunnebacke.
New public square in Barcelona:
Placa de Navas; architects: Daniel
Navas, Neus Sole, Imma Jansana --
Parc del Clot; architects: Dani
Freixes, Vicente Miranda --Parc de
l'espanya Industrial; architects:
Luis Pena Ganchegui, Francesc
Rius. Text in German and English.
DAIDALOS 1989Dec.15, no.34,
p.48-57, map, photos., plan,
aerial photos.

SPAIN--BARCELONA--PARKS--PARC DE
L'ESPANYA INDUSTRIAL
Urban space [Barcelona].
Part of a special feature on
Spanish contemporary architecture.
Contents: Plaza Granollers, by
Albert Viaplana, Helio Pinon.--
Parc de L'Espanya Industrial, by
Luis Pena Ganchegui.--Funicular de
(Continued next column)

SPAIN--BARCELONA--PARKS--PARC DE
L'ESPANYA INDUSTRIAL (CONTINUED)
Urban space...(CONTINUED)
Vallvidrera, by Josep Llinas.--
Puente Bach de Roda, by Santiago
Calatrava.--Brief Histories. Text
in Japanese.
SPACE DESIGN 1990 May, no.308,
p.75-92, dets., ports., elevs.,
photos., plans, secns., sketch,
isometric dwg.

SPAIN--BARCELONA--PARKS--PARC DEL CLOT
"Arees de nova centralitat" in
Barcelona / Niclas Dunnebacke.
New public square in Barcelona:
Placa de Navas; architects: Daniel
Navas, Neus Sole, Imma Jansana --
Parc del Clot; architects: Dani
Freixes, Vicente Miranda --Parc de
l'espanya Industrial; architects:
Luis Pena Ganchegui, Francesc
Rius. Text in German and English.
DAIDALOS 1989Dec.15, no.34,
p.48-57, map, photos., plan,
aerial photos.

SPAIN--BARCELONA--PARKS--PARQUE DEL
MOLINET
Parque del Molinet, Area
Metropolitana de Barcelona
1983-1987.
Architects: Andreu Arriola, Carme
Fiol, with Marius Quintana.
ARQUITECTURA 1990 July-Aug., v.72,
no.285, p.92-97, dets., photos.,
elevs., site plans.

SPAIN--BARCELONA--PARKS--VALLE DE
HEBRON
El vacio urbano = The urban void /
Eduard Bru.
Includes project for a park in
Barcelona.
QUADERNS D'ARQUITECTURA I
URBANISME 1989 Oct.-Dec., no.183,
p.50-[57], dwgs., models, maps,
plans, site plans.

SPAIN--BARCELONA--PEDESTRIAN STREETS--
VIA JULIA
Stadtebaulische Neuordnung der Via
Julia in Barcelona, Spanien =
Replanning of the Via Julia in
Barcelona, Spain.
Architects: Josep Maria Julia i
Capdevila, Bernardo de Sola, Pedro
Barragan.
ARCHITEKTUR + WETTBEWERBE 1990
Dec., no.144, p.10-[11], photos.,
secns., site plans.

SPAIN--BARCELONA--PLAZAS
Barcelona: una renovacion de la
forma urbana / Octavio Mestre.
Text in Spanish and English.
ARQUITECTURA 1990 July-Aug., v.72,
no.285, p.74-81, photos.
Die Mobilisierung des Aussenraumes:
neue Platze und Parks in Barcelona
/ Gerhard Ullmann.
WERK, BAUEN + WOHNEN 1990 June,
no.6, p.2-7, photos., site plans,
aerial photos.

SPAIN--BARCELONA--PLAZAS--20TH CENTURY
Stedelijke theaters: de continuiteit
van het Barcelonese experiment /
Hans van Dijk.
Six plazas and parks in Barcelona
completed since 1986. Designers:
Pedro Barragan and Bernardo de
(Continued next column)

SPAIN--BARCELONA--PLAZAS--20TH CENTURY
(CONTINUED)
Stedelijke theaters:...(CONTINUED)
Sola, Andreu Arriola and Carme
Fiol, Beth Gali, Dani Freixes,
Vicente Miranda, Josep Martorell
and David Mackay, Enric Pericas.
ARCHIS 1989 Nov., no.11, p.24-32,
photos., site plans.

SPAIN--BARCELONA--PLAZAS--PLACA
BARANGE
Archivo en blanco y negro: cronica
grafica de tres generaciones/
Francese Catala-Roca.
Six projects from 1951-1988, by
architects Antoni Gaudi, Barba
Corsini, Antoni de Moragas, Jose
Antonio Coderch, Josep Lluis Sert,
Helio Pinon y Albert Viaplana.
ARQUITECTURA VIVA 1990 May-June,
no.12, p.33-35, photos.

SPAIN--BARCELONA--PLAZAS--PLACA DE
NAVAS
"Arees de nova centralitat" in
Barcelona / Niclas Dunnebacke.
New public square in Barcelona:
Placa de Navas; architects: Daniel
Navas, Neus Sole, Imma Jansana --
Parc del Clot; architects: Dani
Freixes, Vicente Miranda --Parc de
l'espanya Industrial; architects:
Luis Pena Ganchegui, Francesc
Rius. Text in German and English.
DAIDALOS 1989Dec.15, no.34,
p.48-57, map, photos., plan,
aerial photos.

SPAIN--BARCELONA--PLAZAS--PLAZA
GRANOLLERS
Urban space [Barcelona].
Part of a special feature on
Spanish contemporary architecture.
Contents: Plaza Granollers, by
Albert Viaplana, Helio Pinon.--
Parc de L'Espanya Industrial, by
Luis Pena Ganchegui.--Funicular de
Vallvidrera, by Josep Llinas.--
Puente Bach de Roda, by Santiago
Calatrava.--Brief Histories. Text
in Japanese.
SPACE DESIGN 1990 May, no.308,
p.75-92, dets., ports., elevs.,
photos., plans, secns., sketch,
isometric dwg.

SPAIN--BARCELONA--PUBLIC BUILDINGS
Barcelona.
Introduces special section on
Barcelona. Contents: Modernism is
alive and well (interview with
Oriol Bohigas); Rebuilding a
public realm; and Incidents in the
city grain. Three additional
articles separately indexed.
ARCHITECTS' JOURNAL 1990 July 11,
v.192, no.2, p.[22]-39, dwg.,
port., elevs., models, photos.,
plans, secns., site plans,
sketches.

SPAIN--BARCELONA--PUBLIC BUILDINGS--
20TH CENTURY
Making places in Spain: public
buildings by Madrid and Barcelona
architects / Peter Buchanan.
Essay for theme issue on new
public buildings in Madrid and
Barcelona. Eight articles indexed
separately.
ARCHITECTURAL REVIEW 1990 July,
(Continued next page)

SPAIN--BARCELONA--STADIUMS--BADALONA
STADIUM (CONTINUED)
  Salonatmosphare:...(CONTINUED)
  German, French and English.
  WERK, BAUEN + WOHNEN 1990 Sept.,
  no.9, p.46-65, dets., elevs.,
  models, photos., plans, secns.,
  site plans.

SPAIN--BARCELONA--STADIUMS--MONTJUIC
OLYMPIC STADIUM
  Remodelacion del Estadio de Montjuic
  en Barcelona: Vittorio Gregotti,
  Federico Correa, Alfonso Mila,
  Carles Buxade y Joan Margarit,
  arquitectos.
  Text in Spanish and English.
  ON DISENO 1990, no.116, p.155-169,
  photos., plans, secn., site plan,
  aerial photos.

SPAIN--BARCELONA--STADIUMS--SPORTS
PALACE
  Scenari per i giochi olimpici del
  '91 = Setting for the 1992 Olympic
  games / Agnoldomenico Pica.
  New stadium built within exterior
  of stadium built by architect
  Domenech y Montaner Jr. in 1929;
  architects: Arata Isozaki &
  Associates.
  L'ARCA 1990 May, no.38, p.34-47,
  photos., secns.

SPAIN--BARCELONA--STADIUMS--VALL
D'HEBRON
  Labyrintisch landschap, laboratorium
  van stadsontwerp: de olympische
  lokatie Vall d'Hebron / Rein
  Geursten.
  ARCHIS 1989 Nov., no.11, p.33-40,
  maps. photos., secns., site plans,
  refs.

SPAIN--BARCELONA--STAIRWAYS--SPIRAL
  Wendeltreppe in einem Schuhgeschaft
  in Barcelona, E = Spiral stair
  case in a shop in Barcelona,
  Spain.
  Interior architects: M.
  Ybarguengoitia, M. del Mar Nogues.
  DETAIL 1990 Apr.-May, v.30, no.2,
  p.146-147, det., photos., plan,
  secn., elevs.

SPAIN--BARCELONA--STORES
  Figuras de interior: Hacia el
  "existenzmaximun. / Juli Capella,
  Quim Larrea.
  Interior projects of the 1980's in
  Barcelona.
  ARQUITECTURA VIVA 1990 Nov.-Dec.,
  no.15, p.6-11, photos., plans,
  secn.

SPAIN--BARCELONA--STORES--ACCESORIS DE
MODA
  Tienda de complementos en Barcelona:
  M. Ybarguengoitia y Ma. del Mar
  Nogues.
  Spanish, English text.
  ON DISENO 1990, no.113, p.158-165,
  photos., plans, secn.

SPAIN--BARCELONA--STORES--CLOTHING--A2
  Tienda de modas A2 = Fashion shop,
  Manresa, Barcelona, 1988.
  Interior designer: Pepe Cortes.
  EL CROQUIS 1990 Mar., v.9, no.42,
  p.162-168, dets., photos., plans,
  secns.

SPAIN--BARCELONA--STORES--CLOTHING--
EKSEPTION
  Raume des Alltags: Einkaufszentrum
  in Parma und Interieurs in
  Barcelona.
  Torri center (1989), architect:
  Aldo Rossi, Gianni Braghieri; and
  Ekseption interiors (1989);
  architect: Eduard Samso. Text in
  German; summaries in German,
  French, and English.
  WERK, BAUEN + WOHNEN 1990 June,
  no.6, p.54-65, axonometric views,
  elevs., photos., plans, site
  plans, sketches.

SPAIN--BARCELONA--STORES--CLOTHING--
FOCHE MAINA
  Tienda de confeccion para caballeros
  en Barcelona: M. Ybarguengoitia y
  Ma. del Mar Nogues.
  Spanish, English text.
  ON DISENO 1990, no.113, p.166-173,
  elevs., photos., plans.

SPAIN--BARCELONA--STORES--CLOTHING--
LURDES BERGADA
  Eduardo Samso.
  Includes criticism by Josep Maria
  Montaner and four projects by the
  architect. Text in Spanish and
  English.
  EL CROQUIS 1990 Nov., v.9, no.45,
  p.125-162, axonometric views,
  dets., port., elevs., models,
  photos., plans, secns., site
  plans.

SPAIN--BARCELONA--STORES--INTERIOR
DESIGN
  Special feature: Commercial
  interiors in Barcelona.
  Contents: Between minimalism and
  Movid, by Naoki Inagawa -- Alfredo
  Arribas -- Josep Val and Xavier
  Vendrell -- Dani Freixes and
  Vicente Miranda -- Tonet Sunyer
  and Jordi Badia -- Eduard Samso --
  Ventura Valcarce and Carlos Valls.
  Includes interviews and
  biographical information and
  features 13 individual commercial
  projects. Text in Japanese.
  SPACE DESIGN 1990 Nov.,
  no.11(314), p.005-072, dets.,
  ports., photos., plans, secns.,
  refs.

SPAIN--BARCELONA--STORES--SHOE
  Wendeltreppe in einem Schuhgeschaft
  in Barcelona, E = Spiral stair
  case in a shop in Barcelona,
  Spain.
  Interior architects: M.
  Ybarguengoitia, M. del Mar Nogues.
  DETAIL 1990 Apr.-May, v.30, no.2,
  p.146-147, det., photos., plan,
  secn., elevs.

SPAIN--BARCELONA--STREETS
  La strada, elemento unificante nella
  costruzione della citta: l'esempio
  di Barcellona = The Street,
  unifying element in the
  construction of cities / Lilia
  Pagano.
  Planning of Barcelona streets.
  LOTUS INTERNATIONAL 1989, no.64,
  p.72-85, maps, photos., plans,
  secns., site plans.

SPAIN--BARCELONA--STREETS--ALTERATIONS
AND ADDITIONS--AVENIDA RIO DE
JANEIRO
  Urbanizacion de la avenida Rio de
  Janeiro de Barcelona: P. Bardaji y
  C. Teixidor, arquitectos.
  Text in Spanish and English.
  ON DISENO 1990, no.116, p.124-133,
  photos., site plan.

SPAIN--BARCELONA--SUBURBS--POBLE NOU
  Nuovi usi per la citta dismessa:
  Barcellona, il Poble Nou = New
  uses for run-down city areas:
  Barcelona, the Poble Nou.
  A feature on changes in this
  outlying suburb. Includes an essay
  by Octavio Mestre.
  ABITARE 1990 May, no.285,
  p.186-207, ill., dwg., elev.,
  maps, photos., plans, secns.

SPAIN--BARCELONA--SUBWAYS--STATIONS
  Dos interiores para el metro de
  Barcelona: Javier San Jose,
  arquitecto.
  Spanish, English text.
  ON DISENO 1990, no.110, p.85-99,
  dets., photos., plans, secns.

SPAIN--BARCELONA--SUBWAYS--STATIONS--
URGELL
  Estacion de metro Urgell, Linea 1:
  Javier San Jose, arquitecto.
  In Barcelona.
  ON DISENO 1990, no.116, p.174-175,
  photos.

SPAIN--BARCELONA--TELEPHONE BUILDINGS
  Cuerpos enfrentados: edificio para
  oficinas y central telefonica =
  Bodies in confrontation.
  Located in Barcelona, near the
  Calle Juan de Austria, the
  buildings are connected by a
  "bridge." Architects: Jaume Bach,
  Gabriel Mora. English text, p.87.
  A & V 1990, no.22, p.62-64,
  elevs., models, plans, secns.,
  site plans.

SPAIN--BARCELONA--TRANSPORTATION
PLANNING
  Infraestructuras logisticas en la
  Region Metropolitana de Barcelona
  = Logistic infrastructures in the
  metropolitan region of Barcelona
  (M.R.B.) / J. Audicana...et al.
  English summary, p.37.
  URBANISMO / COAM 1990 May, no.10,
  p.29-37, maps, photos., site
  plans, table, aerial photos.

SPAIN--BARCELONA--UNIVERSITIES AND
COLLEGES--BUILDINGS--UNIVERSIDAD
POLITECNICA BARCELONA
  Biblioteca y departamentos; U.
  Politecnica Barcelona, 1989-90.
  Architect: Jose Llinas.
  ARQUITECTURA 1990 Jan.-Feb., v.72,
  no.282, p.122-129, elevs.,
  photos., plans, secns.

SPAIN--BARCELONA--VETERINARY COLLEGES
  Jordi Fabre e Merce Torras: Facolta
  di veterinaria di Bellaterra
  (Barcellona) / Duccio Malagamba.
  Text in Italian and English.
  DOMUS 1990 Apr., no.715, p.10-11,
  xxii, axonometric view, elevs.,
  photos., plan, site plan.

SPAIN--BARCELONA--VILLAS--19TH
CENTURY--ALTERATIONS AND ADDITIONS--
TORRE D'ALTURES (CASA DE LAS AIGUES)
Rehabilitacion de la Torre d'Altures
de Barcelona : Victor Argenti,
arquitecto.
Spanish, English text.
ON DISENO 1990, no.109, p.172-177,
photos., plans.

SPAIN--BARCELONA--VISITORS' CENTERS--
ALTERATIONS AND ADDITIONS--OFICINA
DE TURISMO
La redistribucion de una espacio
para una mayor funcionalidad:
David Gallego, Xavier de Pablo.
Remodeling of tourism information
office, Barcelona. English text,
p.184-185. In "On oficina," 1990
supplement issue.
ON DISENO 1990, suppl., p.94-97,
photos.

SPAIN--BARCELONA--WAR MEMORIALS--
FOSSAR DE LA PEDRERA
Barcellona, il Fossar de la Pedrera:
il recupero della memoria =
Barcelona, the Fossar de la
Pedrera: a reawareness of
memories.
A monument to the dead of the
Civil War, located in an abandoned
quarry. Architect: Beth Gali.
ABITARE 1990 Oct., no.289,
p.256-261, photos., site plan,
aerial photo.

SPAIN--BARCELONA--WAREHOUSES--SIMON
Gathering establishments.
Part of a special feature on
Spanish contemporary architecture.
Contents: Palau de la Musica
Catalana, by Oscar Tusquets
Blanca, Carlos M. Diaz, Lluis
Clotet, Ignacio Paricio --
Television Andaluza, by Gonzalo
Diaz-Y. Recasens --Banco de
Espana, Jaen, by Rafael Moneo --
Almacenes Simon, by Lluis Clotet,
Ignacio Paricio --Mercado
Vilaseca-Salou, by Carlos Ferrater
Lambarri, Jose Luis Canosa --
Pabellon Rius i Taulet, by Pep
Bonet --Velodromo de Horta, by
Esteban Bonell, Francesc Rius --
Brief histories --Views through
the Camera's Finder, by Hisao
Suzuki. Text in Japanese.
SPACE DESIGN 1990 May, no.308,
p.93-131, dets., ports., elevs.,
model, photos., plans, secns.,
site plan, sketch, isometric dwg.
Muros perifericos: un almacen de
Clotet y Paricio / Jaime Cervera.
Warehouse for Simon in Barcelona.
ARQUITECTURA VIVA 1990 Jan.-Feb.,
no.10, p.50-52, axonometric views,
elev., photos., plan.

SPAIN--BARCELONA--WATERFRONT BUILDINGS
Pabellones de cubierta: el puerto
olimpico = Deck pavilions.
On the Barcelona waterfront
buildings. Projects by Martorell,
Bohigas, Mackay, Puigdomenech,
including a sailing school,
reception building and athlete
housing. English text, p.88.
A & V 1990, no.22, p.66-69, dwg.,
elevs., models, plans, secns.,
site plans.

SPAIN--BARCELONA--WATERFRONTS
El ensanche litoral: la Villa
Olimpica, historia de una idea /
Josep Maria Montaner.
English summary, p.83-85.
A & V 1990, no.22, p.16-24, dwgs.,
elevs., models, maps, plans,
aerial photos.
Pabellones de cubierta: el puerto
olimpico = Deck pavilions.
On the Barcelona waterfront
buildings. Projects by Martorell,
Bohigas, Mackay, Puigdomenech,
including a sailing school,
reception building and athlete
housing. English text, p.88.
A & V 1990, no.22, p.66-69, dwg.,
elevs., models, plans, secns.,
site plans.
Regisseurs van het moderne
stadsleven: Joan Busquets en
Manuel de Sola-Morales [interview]
/ Han Meyer.
The second of two articles in an
issue featuring Barcelona.
DE ARCHITECT 1989 Oct., v.20,
no.10, p.56-61,cover, photos.,
secns., site plans.

SPAIN--BARCELONA--WORKSHOPS--BARCELONA
ACTIVA
Barcelona Activa = Industrial
building rehabilitation,
Barcelona, 1987-1988.
Renovation of the 1950's Hispano
Olivetti complex for use as a
company work center and offices.
Architects for renovation: J.A.
Martinez Lapena and Elias Torres.
EL CROQUIS 1990 Mar., v.9, no.42,
p.108-123, dets., elevs., photos.,
plans, secns.

SPAIN--BARCELONA--WORLD FAIRS--19TH
CENTURY--EXPOSICION UNIVERSAL 1888
Barcelona.
Theme issue (17 articles) on
Barcelona. Includes an interview
with Oriol Bohigas.
RASSEGNA 1989 Mar., v.11, no.37/1,
p.1-88, dwgs., elevs., models,
maps, photos., plans, secns., site
plans.

SPAIN--BARCELONA--WORLD FAIRS--20TH
CENTURY--EXPOSICION UNIVERSAL 1929
Barcelona.
Theme issue (17 articles) on
Barcelona. Includes an interview
with Oriol Bohigas.
RASSEGNA 1989 Mar., v.11, no.37/1,
p.1-88, dwgs., elevs., models,
maps, photos., plans, secns., site
plans.

SPAIN--BARCELONA--ZOOLOGICAL MUSEUMS--
ALTERATIONS AND ADDITIONS--MUSEO DE
ZOOLOGIA
Edificio de servicios para el Museo
de Zoologia de Barcelona: C. Basso
y C. Cirici, arquitectos.
Laboratory addition. Original
architect: Lluis Domenech i
Montaner. Spanish, English text.
ON DISENO 1990, no.114, p.94-103,
elev., photos., plans, site plan.

SPAIN--BARCELONA--ZOOS
Arquitecturas zoologicas: F. Javier
Aguilar, arquitecto.
Spanish, English text.
ON DISENO 1989, no.104, p.161-166,
dwgs., photos.

SPAIN--BEACHES--CONSERVATION AND
RESTORATION
Actuaciones del MOPU en la costa
espanola / Juan Carlos
Fernandez-Ranada.
URBANISMO / COAM 1988 May, no.4,
p.22-29, graphs, map, photos.,
secns., aerial photos.

SPAIN--BILBAO--CITY PLANNING
Avance del plan general de Bilbao /
Ibon Areso.
URBANISMO / COAM 1989 Sept., no.8,
p.83-90, plans, site plans.

SPAIN--BILBAO--COMPREHENSIVE PLANS
Avance del plan general de Bilbao /
Ibon Areso.
URBANISMO / COAM 1989 Sept., no.8,
p.83-90, plans, site plans.

SPAIN--BILBAO--SUBWAYS--STATIONS
Stations chics pour metros de choc.
Features subway stations in Milan,
Lyon and Bilbao designed by the
following architects: Ignazio
Gardella, Aldo Rossi, Foster
Associates, Jourda et Perraudin.
ARCHITECTURE D'AUJOURD'HUI 1990
Feb., no.267, p.52-53, ill.,
models, photos.

SPAIN--BILBAO--THEATERS--19TH
CENTURY--CONSERVATION AND
RESTORATION--TEATRO ARRIAGA
Rehabilitacion del Teatro Arriaga de
Bilbao: Francisco Hurtado,
arquitecto.
Original architect: Joaquin
Rucoba. Alterations 1915 by
Federico Ugalde. Spanish, English
text.
ON DISENO 1990, no.109, p.178-186,
photos., plans.

SPAIN--BURGOS--CHURCHES--MEDIEVAL--
IGLESIA DEL MONASTERIO DE SANTA
MARIA LA REAL DE LAS HUELGAS
Significacion de la Iglesia en el
panorama de la arquitectura de la
orden del Cister / Jose Carlos
Valle Perez.
Article in issue devoted to the
Iglesia del Monasterio de Santa
Maria la Real de Huelgas, in
Burgos, Spain.
REALES SITIOS 1990, v.27, no.105,
49-56.[1] folded leaf, photos.,
refs.

SPAIN--CADIZ--CITIES AND TOWNS--VIEWS
I Cadiz Ropar Ljuset ut Sig / Rolf
Wohlin.
ARKITEKTUR: THE SWEDISH REVIEW OF
ARCHITECTURE 1990 Apr., v.90,
no.3, p.46-49, photos.

SPAIN--CADIZ--CONVENTION FACILITIES--
PALACIO DE CONGRESOS DE CADIZ
Citadels and communion.
Features the designs for the
Salamanca and Cadiz conference
centers. Architect: Juan Navarro
Baldeweg.
ARCHITECTURAL REVIEW 1990 July,
(Continued next page)

SPAIN--CADIZ--CONVENTION FACILITIES--
PALACIO DE CONGRESOS DE CADIZ
(CONTINUED)
Citadels and communion. (CONTINUED)
v.188, no.1121, p.32-37, ill.,
elevs., models, photos., plans,
secns., site plan.

SPAIN--CADIZ--HOUSING PROJECTS--ROTA
Espagne: du silence au mouvement.
Features 60-unit housing project,
Rota, Cadiz. Architect: Antonio
Gonzalez Cordon. English summary,
p.180-181.
ARCHITECTURE INTERIEURE CREE 1990
June-July, no.237, p.128-131,
dwg., photos., plans, site plan.
Housing and residence.
Part of a special feature on
Spanish contemporary architecture.
Contents: Rota, by Antonio
Gonzalez Cordon.-- Viviendas Ramon
y Cajal, by Guillermo Vazquez
Consuegra.-- Castillo de Maqueda,
by Luis Burnillo Lafarga, Jaime L.
Lorenzo.-- Casa Turegano, by
Alberto Campo Baeza.-- Brief
histories. Text in Japanese.
SPACE DESIGN 1990 May, no.308,
p.55-74, ports., elevs., photos.,
plans, secns., isometric dwgs.

SPAIN--CADIZ--MUSEUMS--ART--MUSEO DE
CADIZ
Patios de cristal: Museo de Cadiz.
Convent converted into museums.
Architect: Javier Feduchi
Benlliure. English text, p.91.
A & V 1990, no.26, p.52-55, dets.,
photos., plans, secns.

SPAIN--CADIZ--MUSEUMS--MARITIME--
BALUARTE DE CANDELARIA
Adattamento a Museo del Mare del
"Baluarte de la Candelaria", Cadiz
/ Duccio Malagamba.
Old military fortress incorporated
in new maritime museum.
DOMUS 1990 Mar., no.714,
p.[56-63], dets., model, photos.,
plans.
Cadice, il Museo del Mare =
Museumtime: the Maritime Museum,
Cadiz.
Architects: Antonio Cruz, Antonio
Ortiz.
ABITARE 1990 Sept., no.288,
p.256-261, photos., plans.
Museo del Mar en el Baluarte de la
Candelaria: Antonio Cruz y Antonio
Ortiz, arquitectos.
Spanish, English text.
ON DISENO 1990, no.111, p.111-121,
models, photos., plan.

SPAIN--CAMBRILS--HOTELS
Para ir con dos proyectos de Victor
Rahola / Josep Quetglas.
2 hotels. Catalan, English text.
QUADERNS D'ARQUITECTURA I
URBANISME 1989 Apr.-Sept.,
no.181-182, p.138-151, photos.,
plans, secns, site plans.

SPAIN--CAMBRILS--SCHOOLS--VOCATIONAL--
ESCUELA DE HOSTELARIA
Escuela de hosteleria = Professional
training centre: Cambrils,
Tarragona, 1986/1988.
Architect: Victor Rahola.
EL CROQUIS 1990 Apr.-June, v.9,
no.43, p.124-131, dets., elevs.
photos., plans, secns.

SPAIN--CANARY ISLANDS--LAS PALMAS--ART
CENTERS--CENTRO ATLANTICO DE ARTE
MODERNO
Atlantic cries - Mediterranean
whispers / Luis Fernandez-Galiano.
On the Centro Atlantico de Arte
Moderno, Las Palmas, Canary
Islands, architect: Francisco
Javier Saenz de Oiza and the Juan
and Pilar Miro Foundation, Son
Abrines, Majorca, architect: Jose
Rafael Moneo.
ARCHITECTURAL REVIEW 1990 July,
v.188, no.1121, p.44-[51], models,
photos., plans, secn., site plan.
Centro Atlantico de Arte Moderno =
Modern art centre, Las Palmas de
Gran Canaria, 1958-1989.
Architect: F. Javier Saenz de
Oiza.
EL CROQUIS 1990 Mar., v.9, no.42,
p.124-137, dets., photos., plans,
secns.
Proyectar para una arquitectura
dada: analogia y diversidad = To
design for a given architecture:
analogy and diversity / Anton
Capitel.
Discusses 4 recent projects in
Spain.
EL CROQUIS 1990 Mar., v.9, no.42,
p.64-79, photos.

SPAIN--CANARY ISLANDS--LAS PALMAS--
BANKS--CAJA DEL COLEGIO OFICIAL DE
ARQUITECTOS DE CANARIAS
Oficina bancaria del Colegio Oficial
de Arquitectos de Canarias: Maria
Luisa Gonzalez, Antonio Bucar.
Interiors of Canary Islands Law
Society Bank. English text, p.185.
In "On oficina," 1990 supplement
issue.
ON DISENO 1990, suppl., p.114-119,
photos.

SPAIN--CANARY ISLANDS--LAS PALMAS--
LIBRARIES
Biblioteca insular de Las Palmas de
Gran Canaria: Jose Luis Gago,
arquitecto.
Spanish, English text.
ON DISENO 1990, no.111, p.138-151,
photos., plans, secns., sketch.

SPAIN--CANARY ISLANDS--LAS PALMAS--
SOCIETY AND ASSOCIATION BUILDINGS--
19TH CENTURY--ALTERATIONS AND
ADDITIONS
Biblioteca insular de Las Palmas de
Gran Canaria: Jose Luis Gago,
arquitecto.
Spanish, English text.
ON DISENO 1990, no.111, p.138-151,
photos., plans, secns., sketch.

SPAIN--CANARY ISLANDS--LIGHTHOUSES--
COMPETITIONS--FARO PUNTA ALDEA
Concorsi: Faro Punta Aldea (Gran
Canaria) = Competitions: the Punta
Aldea Lighthouse (Gran Canaria).
The 1st prize awarded nationally
by the M.O.P.U. Archiects: Rafael
Aranda, Carmen Pigem and Ramon
Vilalta.
ANFIONE ZETO 1989, v.1, no.2-3,
p.298-303, ill., ports., elev.,
model, plans, site plan.

SPAIN--CANARY ISLANDS--SANTA CRUZ DE
TENERIFE--OFFICES--CAJA CANARIAS
Tratamiento innovador para un
material tradicional: Francisco
Artengo, Jose Angel Domingues,
Antonio Bucar.
Head office of the savings bank
Caja Canaria, Canary Islands,
Spain. English text, p.185. In "On
oficina," 1990 supplement issue.
ON DISENO 1990, suppl., p.120-121,
photos.
Tratamiento innovador para un
material tradicional: Francisco
Artengo, Jose Angel Domingues,
Antonio Bucar.
Head office of the savings bank
Caja Canarias, Canary Islands,
Spain. English text, p.185. In "On
oficina," 1990 supplement issue.
ON DISENO 1990, suppl., p.120-121,
photos.

SPAIN--CANTABRIAN MOUNTAINS--IRON
WORKS--19TH CENTURY
Cantilever piers for shipping iron
ore on the Cantabrian coast of
Spain, 1888-1889 / Jose Sierra
Alvarez.
On the evolution of Belgian
designs by a Spanish construction
company, at six sites in
Santander. Includes abstract.
INDUSTRIAL ARCHAEOLOGY REVIEW 1990
Autumn, v.13, no.1, p.59-68, maps,
photos., secns., refs.

SPAIN--CASARRUBIOS--INDUSTRIAL PARKS--
MONTE BOYAL
Actuacion urbanistica "Monte Boyal",
Casarrubios del Monte (Toledo).
URBANISMO / COAM 1990 Sept.,
no.11, p.105-106, map, plan,
table.

SPAIN--CASTILE--CANALS--18TH CENTURY
Corso storico di un canale: il
canale di Castiglia = Historic
course of a canal: the canal of
Castile / Carlos Sambricio.
LOTUS INTERNATIONAL 1986, no.52,
p.[6]-12, photos., secn.
Lungo il canale di Castiglia: un
percorso attraverso i manufatti =
Along the canal of Castile: a trip
back to manufacturing / Juan
Navarro Baldeweg.
LOTUS INTERNATIONAL 1986, no.52,
p.13-25, axonometric views, maps,
photos., secns., site plans.

SPAIN--CATALONIA--ARCHITECTURE
Barcelona / Peder Boas Jensen ...
[et al.].
Theme of issue. Contents: By
eller OL, by Peder Boas Jensen and
Elith Juul Moller.-- Idraettens
arenaer, by Ebbe Melgaard.--
Katalensans havedstad, by Jorgen
Sestoft.-- Gensyn med Gaudi, by
Nils-Ole Lund.-- Parkerne i
Barcelona, by Jorgen Peder Hansen
and Anna Maria Indrio.-- Den
nordiske inspiration, by Nils-Ole
Lund.-- Ny katalansk arkitektur,
by Jan Christiansen and Gosta
Knudsen.-- Miralles og Pinos, by
Thomas Wiesner.
ARKITEKTEN 1990 May, v.92, no.7,
p.[212]-249, cover, axonometric
views, diagrs., maps, photos.,
secns., aerial photos., biblios.

SPAIN--CATALONIA--ARCHITECTURE--20TH
CENTURY
Architecture of J.A. Martinez Lapena
+ Elias Torres Tur.
Special feature. Contents:
Careers.--Catalonian
architecture...., by Naoki
Inagawa.--Works [13 projects
1981-1989]. Text in Japanese.
SPACE DESIGN 1990 Apr., no.307,
p.05-44, axonometric view, ports.,
models, map, photos., plans,
secns., site plans.
Arquitetura catala contemporanea /
Josep-Maria Montaner.
A panorama of Catalan architecture
between 1951 and 1987.
PROJETO 1988 Nov., no.116,
p.139-146, dwgs., photos., site
plan.

SPAIN--CATALONIA--ARCHITECTURE--EARLY
MEDIEVAL
Continuite et rupture dans le
paysage monumental entre
l'antiquite tardive et le moyen
age en Catalogne / Xavier Barral I
Altet.
Seminario Internazionale di Studi
su "Archeologia e arte nella
Spagna tardoromana, visigota e
mozarabica"; Ravenna, 4-11 April
1987.
CORSO DI CULTURA SULL'ARTE
RAVENNATE E BIZANTINA 1987, v.34,
p.19-26, biblio.

SPAIN--CATALONIA--ARCHITECTURE--LATE
ANTIQUE
Continuite et rupture dans le
paysage monumental entre
l'antiquite tardive et le moyen
age en Catalogne / Xavier Barral I
Altet.
Seminario Internazionale di Studi
su "Archeologia e arte nella
Spagna tardoromana, visigota e
mozarabica"; Ravenna, 4-11 April
1987.
CORSO DI CULTURA SULL'ARTE
RAVENNATE E BIZANTINA 1987, v.34,
p.19-26, biblio.

SPAIN--CATALONIA--REGIONAL PLANNING
El plan territorial general de
Cataluna = The land plan for
Catalonia / Xavier Subias.
English summary, p.72.
URBANISMO / COAM 1989 Sept., no.8,
p.63-72, ill., maps, table.

SPAIN--CATALUNYA--HOUSING--
COMPETITIONS--HABITATGE I CIUTAT
Sobre el concurso "vivienda y
ciudad" = on the competition
"housing and the city" / Kenneth
Frampton.
Competition sponsored by the
Colegio de Arquitectos de
Catalunya. Project presented by
Helmut Christen.
QUADERNS D'ARQUITECTURA I
URBANISME 1989 Oct.-Dec., no.183,
p.[144-149], dwg., site plans.

SPAIN--CATHEDRALS
Entrevista: Pedro Navascues del
Palacio: monasterios y catedrales
[interview] / Juan Hernandez.
REALES SITIOS 1990, v.27, no.106,
p.[11]-16, ports.

SPAIN--CERDANYOLA--BRIDGES--20TH
CENTURY--PUENTE SOBRE LA RIERA DELS
GORCHS
Puente sobre la Riera dels Gorchs:
Cerdanyola, Barcelona 1987-89.
Architects: Enric Battle, Juan
Roig. No text.
ARQUITECTURA 1990 July-Aug., v.72,
no.285, p.118-121, dets., elevs.,
photos., plans, secns.

SPAIN--CERDANYOLA--SCHOOLS--
ELEMENTARY--COLEGIO PUBLICO SANTA
ROSA
Las arquitectural publicas de Mario
Luis Corea, Francisco Gallardo y
Edgardo Manino.
Six articles. Includes the
Boardwalk and beach at Badalona;
Public Health center, Badalona;
Plaza, Badalona; San Roc community
center and residence for the
elderly handicapped, Badalona;
Primary school Santa Rosa,
Cerdanyola. Spanish and English
text.
ON DISENO 1990, no.107,
p.[100]-141, elevs., photos.,
plans, secns., site plan,
sketches.

SPAIN--CHURCHES--EARLY CHRISTIAN
Las iglesias paleocristianas y
visigodas hispanicas a traves de
las fuentes literarias / Rafael
Puertas Tricas.
Seminario Internazionale di Studi
su "Archeologia e arte nella
Spagna tardoromana, visigota e
mozarabica"; Ravenna, 4-11 April
1987.
CORSO DI CULTURA SULL'ARTE
RAVENNATE E BIZANTINA 1987, v.34,
p.327-337, iblio.

SPAIN--CHURCHES--VISIGOTH
Arquitectura de culto cristiano y
epoca visigoda en la peninsula
iberica / Luis Caballero Zoreda.
Seminario Internazionale di Studi
su "Archeologia e arte nella
Spagna tardoroma, visigota e
mozarabica"; Ravenna, 4-11 April
1987.
CORSO DI CULTURA SULL'ARTE
RAVENNATE E BIZANTINA 1987, v.34,
p.31-84, charts, plans, table,
biblio.
Las iglesias paleocristianas y
visigodas hispanicas a traves de
las fuentes literarias / Rafael
Puertas Tricas.
Seminario Internazionale di Studi
su "Archeologia e arte nella
Spagna tardoromana, visigota e
mozarabica"; Ravenna, 4-11 April
1987.
CORSO DI CULTURA SULL'ARTE
RAVENNATE E BIZANTINA 1987, v.34,
p.327-337, iblio.

SPAIN--CITIES AND TOWNS--19TH
CENTURY--GROWTH
Le citta e l'urbanistica in Spagna
durante l'Ottocento / Luis Alonso
de Armino Perez, Juan Luis Pinon
Pallares.
STORIA URBANA 1989 Jan.-Mar.,
v.13, no.46, p.3-58, graphs,
elevs., maps, plans, tables,
engrs., refs.

SPAIN--CITY PLANNING
Piani e politiche urbane in Spagna =
Plans and policies in Spain /
Maurizio Marcelloni, Oriol Nel lo.
Introduces 6 articles, separately
indexed. In Italian, with English
captions and summaries.
URBANISTICA 1989 Mar., no.94,
p.31,
La stagione dell'urbanistica
spagnola = New urban project in
Spain / Maurizio Marcelloni.
In Italian; English summary,
p.123.
URBANISTICA 1989 Mar., no.94,
p.32-34,123, plans.
Territorio struttura urbana e
pianificazione: gli antecedenti /
Oriol Nel lo.
Regional and urban planning in
Spain from 1959 to the present. In
Italian.
URBANISTICA 1989 Mar., no.94,
p.72-74,

SPAIN--CITY PLANNING--LAW AND
LEGISLATION
Los centro historicos espanoles
entre la realidad y la legalidad =
Historical city centers in Spain
between reality and current
legislation / Juan Lopez Jaen.
English summary, p.24.
URBANISMO / COAM 1990 Jan., no.9,
p.14-24, table, refs., plans,
aerial photos., dwgs., maps.

SPAIN--CITY PLANNING--POLITICAL
ASPECTS
I piani degli anni Ottanta = Spanish
planning through the 1980s /
Eduardo Leira, Damian Quero.
In Italian; English summary,
p.123.
URBANISTICA 1989 Mar., no.94,
p.34-43,123, dwgs., models, plans,
aerial photo.

SPAIN--COMPREHENSIVE PLANS
I piani degli anni Ottanta = Spanish
planning through the 1980s /
Eduardo Leira, Damian Quero.
In Italian; English summary,
p.123.
URBANISTICA 1989 Mar., no.94,
p.34-43,123, dwgs., models, plans,
aerial photo.

SPAIN--CONSTRUCTION INDUSTRY--17TH
CENTURY
El Superintendente de Obras Reales
en el siglo XVII / Maria Victoria
Garcia Morales.
REALES SITIOS 1990, v.27, no.104,
p.65-74, ill., ports., elev.,
engrs., refs.

SPAIN--CONSTRUCTION MANAGEMENT--17TH
CENTURY
El Superintendente de Obras Reales
en el siglo XVII / Maria Victoria
Garcia Morales.
REALES SITIOS 1990, v.27, no.104,
p.65-74, ill., ports., elev.,
engrs., refs.

SPAIN--COSTA BRAVA--CITY PLANNING--
POLITICAL ASPECTS
Urban development, land use planning
and political change: the case of
Costa Brava, Spain / Phillip C.
Emmi, Maria Angels Santigosa.
LAND USE POLICY 1989 Apr., v.6,
no.2, p.103-120, graphs, maps,
refs.

SPAIN--COSTA BRAVA--LAND USE--
POLITICAL ASPECTS
Urban development, land use planning
and political change: the case of
Costa Brava, Spain / Phillip C.
Emmi, Maria Angels Santigosa.
LAND USE POLICY 1989 Apr., v.6,
no.2, p.103-120, graphs, maps,
refs.

SPAIN, DAPHNE
Why higher income households move to
central cities / Daphne Spain.
JOURNAL OF URBAN AFFAIRS 1989,
v.11, no.3, p.[283]-299, tables,
refs.

SPAIN--EL PARDO--COUNTRY HOUSES--
CASITA DEL PRINCIPE
La Casita del Principe, El Pardo: a
property of the Patrimonio
Nacional / Giles Worsley.
Built in 1784 for the future King
Carlos IV; architect: Juan de
Villanueva.
COUNTRY LIFE 1990 Dec.20, v.184,
no.51, p.56-61, photos.

SPAIN--EL SARDINERO--CITY PLANNING--
19TH CENTURY
Sematica de la Ciudad-Balneario: el
Caso del Sardinero en Santander
(1840-1900) / Luis Sazatornil
Ruiz.
ARCHIVO ESPANOL DE ARTE 1989
Oct.-Dec., v.62, no.248,
p.[421]-434. On the history of El
Sardinero, Spain. English summary,
p.434.

SPAIN--EL SARDINERO--RESORTS--19TH
CENTURY--SEASIDE
Sematica de la Ciudad-Balneario: el
Caso del Sardinero en Santander
(1840-1900) / Luis Sazatornil
Ruiz.
ARCHIVO ESPANOL DE ARTE 1989
Oct.-Dec., v.62, no.248,
p.[421]-434. On the history of El
Sardinero, Spain. English summary,
p.434.

SPAIN--EL SARDINERO--SEASIDE TOWNS--
HISTORY
Sematica de la Ciudad-Balneario: el
Caso del Sardinero en Santander
(1840-1900) / Luis Sazatornil
Ruiz.
ARCHIVO ESPANOL DE ARTE 1989
Oct.-Dec., v.62, no.248,
p.[421]-434. On the history of El
Sardinero, Spain. English summary,
p.434.

SPAIN--ELDA--HOUSING DEVELOPMENTS
Actuacion industrial y residencial
de Elda (Alicante).
URBANISMO / COAM 1990 Sept.,
no.11, p.103-104, map, plan.

SPAIN--ELDA--INDUSTRIAL PARKS
Actuacion industrial y residencial
de Elda (Alicante).
URBANISMO / COAM 1990 Sept.,
no.11, p.103-104, map, plan.

SPAIN--ENVIRONMENTAL PROTECTION
Landscape planning in Spain / Miguel
Aguilo, Santiago Gonzalez Alonso,
Angel Ramos.
BUILT ENVIRONMENT 1990, v.16,
no.2, p.98-110, map, photos.,
tables, refs.

SPAIN--ESPIEL--SCHOOLS--VOCATIONAL--
MERCE ROSELL
Meister der sensuellen Form: neue
Arbeiten von Bach und Mora.
Three projects: Kindertagesstatte
"Torre Baldovina" in Santa Coloma
de Gramenet; Weinbausschule "Merce
Rosell" in Espiells; Weinkellerei
"Cavas Raventos Blanc" in Sant
Sadurni d'Anoia. One of four
articles on the theme "Barcelona
bauen".
BAUWELT 1990 Mar.2, v.81, no.9,
p.386-387, axonometric view,
plans, photos.

SPAIN--ESPLUGAS--CORPORATE OFFICE
BUILDINGS--ALTERATIONS AND
ADDITIONS--NESTLE
Auf den Spuren der Katalanischen
Moderne: neue Arbeiten von
Martorell, Bohigas, Mackay.
Three projects: Burobau der
"Sociedad Nestle" in Espluegues de
Llobregat in Barcelona; Wohnanlage
"La Maquinista" in Barceloneta in
Barcelona; Wohnanlage Mollet in
Gallecs in Mollet. One of four
issues on the theme "Barcelona
bauen".
BAUWELT 1990 Mar.2, v.81, no.9,
p.378-385, axonometric views,
photos., plans, secns., site
plans.

SPAIN--ESTELLA--PLAZAS--PLAZA DE LA
CORONACION
Plaza de la Coronacion Estella 1987.
Architect: Francisco Javier
Biurrun.
ARQUITECTURA 1990 July-Aug., v.72,
no.285, p.96-105, photos., site
plans.

SPAIN--FORMAL GARDENS--PAZO DE OCA
Green voyage: a centuries-old
Spanish garden encloses a watery
dominion / John Dobkin.
The Pazo de Oca, near Santiago de
Compostela, begun in the 17th
cent.
HOUSE & GARDEN 1990 Jan., v.162,
no.1, p.[102]-109, photos.

SPAIN--GALICIA--CITY PLANNING--STUDENT
PROJECTS
Propuestas de desarrollo residencial
en periferias urbanas gallegas /
Jose Gonzalez-Cebrian.
Student project planning for urban
fringe and suburban housing in
Galicia in the Escuela de
(Continued next column)

SPAIN--GALICIA--CITY PLANNING--STUDENT
PROJECTS (CONTINUED)
Propuestas de...(CONTINUED)
Arquitectura de la Coruna, Spain.
URBANISMO / COAM 1990 Jan., no.9,
p.91-94, plans, elevs., site
plans, ref.

SPAIN--GALICIA--HOUSING--STUDENT
PROJECTS
Propuestas de desarrollo residencial
en periferias urbanas gallegas /
Jose Gonzalez-Cebrian.
Student project planning for urban
fringe and suburban housing in
Galicia in the Escuela de
Arquitectura de la Coruna, Spain.
URBANISMO / COAM 1990 Jan., no.9,
p.91-94, plans, elevs., site
plans, ref.

SPAIN--GARDENS--20TH CENTURY
Nicolau Maria Rubio i Tuduri /
Andrew Zerwas.
On the late Spansih architect,
planner, and garden designer.
Includes English summary.
GARTEN UND LANDSCHAFT 1990, v.100,
no.3, p.37-40, port., photos.,
aerial photo.

SPAIN--GARDENS--MOORISH--INFLUENCE
Gardens: a landscape in Segovia /
Nicholas Shrady.
On landscape architect Leandro
Silva Delgado's garden outside the
old walls.
ARCHITECTURAL DIGEST 1990 Oct.,
v.47, no.11, p.[238]-243, 286,
288, photos.

SPAIN--GARDENS--TROPICAL
Die tropischen Garten an der
Mittelmeerkste / Jochen R.
Klicker.
Tropical gardens along Spain's
Mediterranean coast. Includes
English summary.
GARTEN UND LANDSCHAFT 1990, v.100,
no.3, p.33-37, photos., site
plans.

SPAIN--GARRAF--WINE CELLARS--CASTILLO
DE GARRAF (BODEGAS GUELL)
Bodegas Guell in Garraf (1895-1901)
/ Manfred Speidel.
Former wine cellars built for Don
Eusebio Gell y Bacigalupa;
architect: Antoni Gaudi. Text in
Japanese and English.
ARCHITECTURE AND URBANISM 1990
July, no.7(238), p.50-[63],
elevs., photos., plans, secns.,
site plans, refs.

SPAIN--GERONA--BANKS--BANCO DE ESPANA
Banco de Espana en Girona: L. Clotet
e I. Paricio, arquitectos.
Spanish, English text.
ON DISENO 1990, no.115, p.104-113,
photos., plans, secns.
Una rotula monumental. sede del
Banco de Espana, Gerona.
Architects: Lluis Clotet, Ignacio
Paricio. English summary, p.91.
A & V 1990, no.24, p.40-47,
elevs., photos., plans, secns.,
site plan

SPAIN--GERONA--BUILDINGS
Leyes comprometidas: Bonell y Gil en
Gerona / Angel Luis Fernandez.
ARQUITECTURA VIVA 1990 Nov.-Dec.,
no.15, p.21-23, models, plans,
secns., site plans.

SPAIN--GERONA--COURTHOUSES
Civic monuments.
Three projects by Esteve Bonell:
School, Masquefa, with Josep Maria
Gil; law courts, Gerona, with
Josep Maria Gil and the sports
arena, Badalona, with Francesc
Rius.
ARCHITECTURAL REVIEW 1990 July,
v.188, no.1121, p.69-73, elevs.,
models, photos., plans, secns.,
site plan.

SPAIN--GRANADA--CITY PLANNING--
COMPETITIONS--ALHAMBRA AREA
Neuorganisation des Zugangsbereichs
zur Alhambra, Granada, Spanien =
Reorganization of the areas
surrounding the new access to the
Alhambra, Granada, Spain.
International idea competition.
Features winning designs by Peter
Nigst, Erich Hubmann, Andreas
Vass, for the overall plan, and
the design for the Parque de los
Alijares and cemetery by Daniele
Vitale. Text in German.
ARCHITEKTUR + WETTBEWERBE 1990
Dec., no.144, p.56-58, dwgs.,
models, secns., site plans.
Niew entreigebied voor het Alhambra:
Bureau Maatwerk in tweede ronde
van prijsvraag / Helene Damen.
DE ARCHITECT 1989 Dec., v.20,
no.12, p.32-33, site plan.
Prijsvraag Alhambra, Granada:
Nederlands bureau uitgenodigd voor
meervoudige opdracht.
The Dutch firm, Maatwerk, was one
of seven winners.
ARCHIS 1989 Nov., no.11, p.6, site
plan.

SPAIN--GRANADA--CUPOLAS--14TH
CENTURY--ISLAMIC--ALHAMBRA
Methods of constructing geometric
ornamental systems in the cupola
of the Alhambra / Sergei
Chmelnizkij.
Wooden cupola is preserved in the
Museum of Islamic Art, West
Berlin.
MUQARNAS 1990, v.6, p.[43]-49,
diagrs., dwgs.

SPAIN--GRANADA--PALACES--ISLAMIC--
ALHAMBRA
From dome of heaven to pleasure dome
/ Oleg Grabar.
Text of a paper delivered at the
1989 annual meeting of the SAH,
discussing Suetonius, domes at the
Alhambra, Orientalism, and
questions of ethics, aesthetics,
and praxis.
SOCIETY OF ARCHITECTURAL
HISTORIANS. JOURNAL 1990 Mar.,
v.49, no.1, p.15-21, photos.,
plan, refs.

SPAIN--GRANADA--PLAZAS--LA CHANA
Circunvalacion de La Chana: Y. Brasa
y E. Jimenez, arquitectos.
Plaza with fountain and seating.
Spanish, English text.
ON DISENO 1990, no.111, p.100-109,
axonometric view, photos.

SPAIN--GRANADA--PUBLIC BUILDINGS--
CENTRO PROVINCIAL DE DOCUMENTACION E
INFORMACION JUVENIL
Tres arquitectos en Granada.
Four projects by E. Martin Martin,
L.J. Martin Martin and R. Ruiz
Fuentes: house in Granada, Centro
Provincial de Documentation e
Informacion Juvenil de Granada,
health center in Guadix, and
health center in Granada. Text in
Spanish and English.
ON DISENO 1990, no.116,
p.[176]-212, axonometric view,
det., ill., dwgs., elevs.,
photos., plans, secn., site plan.

SPAIN--GRANADA--YOUTH CENTERS--CENTRO
PROVINCIAL DE DOCUMENTACION E
INFORMACION JUVENIL
Tres arquitectos en Granada.
Four projects by E. Martin Martin,
L.J. Martin Martin and R. Ruiz
Fuentes: house in Granada, Centro
Provincial de Documentation e
Informacion Juvenil de Granada,
health center in Guadix, and
health center in Granada. Text in
Spanish and English.
ON DISENO 1990, no.116,
p.[176]-212, axonometric view,
det., ill., dwgs., elevs.,
photos., plans, secn., site plan.

SPAIN--GRANOLLERS--SPORTS FACILITIES
Architectural landmarks.
Features three buildings by Elias
Torres Tur and Jose Antonio
Martinez Lapena: hospital, Mora de
Ebro; congress center, Barcelona,
and sports hall, Granollers.
ARCHITECTURAL REVIEW 1990 July,
v.188, no.1121, p.52-59, elevs.,
models, photos., plans, secns.,
site plan.

SPAIN--GRENADA--HOUSES--20TH CENTURY--
LA VEGA DE GRANADA
Tres arquitectos en Granada.
Four projects by E. Martin Martin,
L.J. Martin Martin and R. Ruiz
Fuentes: house in Granada, Centro
Provincial de Documentation e
Informacion Juvenil de Granada,
health center in Guadix, and
health center in Granada. Text in
Spanish and English.
ON DISENO 1990, no.116,
p.[176]-212, axonometric view,
det., ill., dwgs., elevs.,
photos., plans, secn., site plan.

SPAIN--GUADALAJARA--RELIGIOUS
BUILDINGS--RENAISSANCE
El mecenazgo de los Mendoza en
Guadalajara / Maria Teresa
Fernandez Madrid.
GOYA 1989 Mar.-Apr., no.209,
p.274-281, ill., photos.

SPAIN--GUADARRAMA--WATER TREATMENT
PLANTS
Tres estaciones depuradoras de aguas
residuales = Three water
purification plants.
In Majadahonda, Guadarrama and
Villalba. Architects: Juan
Herreros, Inaki Abalos. Text in
Spanish and English.
QUADERNS D'ARQUITECTURA I
URBANISME 1988 July-Sept., no.178,
p.102-119, photos., plans, secn.,
site plan.

SPAIN--GUADIX--HEALTH CARE BUILDINGS--
CENTRO DE SALUD
Tres arquitectos en Granada.
Four projects by E. Martin Martin,
L.J. Martin Martin and R. Ruiz
Fuentes: house in Granada, Centro
Provincial de Documentation e
Informacion Juvenil de Granada,
health center in Guadix, and
health center in Granada. Text in
Spanish and English.
ON DISENO 1990, no.116,
p.[176]-212, axonometric view,
det., ill., dwgs., elevs.,
photos., plans, secn., site plan.

SPAIN--HISTORIC DISTRICTS--
CONSERVATION AND RESTORATION
Un programa de planeamiento de
centros historicos / Rufina
Fernandez.
URBANISMO / COAM 1990 Jan., no.9,
p.54-56, photo.

SPAIN--HISTORIC PRESERVATION--LAW AND
LEGISLATION
Los centro historicos espanoles
entre la realidad y la legalidad =
Historical city centers in Spain
between reality and current
legislation / Juan Lopez Jaen.
English summary, p.24.
URBANISMO / COAM 1990 Jan., no.9,
p.14-24, table, refs., plans,
aerial photos., dwgs., maps.

SPAIN--HOSTALETS--COMMUNITY CENTERS
Aristas oblicuas: Centro social de
Hostalets, Barcelona.
Community center. Architects:
Miralles y Pinos. English summary,
p.91.
A & V 1990, no.24, p.48-53, dets.,
elevs., models, plans, site plan.
Nun ist es nicht mehr Gebaude, es
ist Ort: das Gemeinschaftszentrum
in Hostalets de Balenya bei
Barcelona/ Enric Miralles, Carme
Pinos.
ARCHITHESE 1990 Jan.-Feb., v.20,
no.1, p.55-57, elevs., photos.,
plans, secns., site plans,
sketches.

SPAIN--HOSTALETS--COMMUNITY CENTERS--
PISTA
Konstruktivistische Ansatze aus
Katalanien: neue Arbeiten von
Miralles und Pinos.
Three projects: Platzgestaltung
"Placa Mayor" in Parets del
Valles; Friedhofsanlage mit
Kapelle in Igualada; Soziales
Begegnungszentrum "La Pista" in
Hostalets. One of four articles
on the theme "Barcelona bauen".
BAUWELT 1990 Mar.2, v.81, no.9,
p.392-395, photos., plans, secns.,
site plans.

SPAIN--HOUSING DEVELOPMENTS
Abstractos y modernos: fotogramas de los cincuenta / Luis Fernandez-Galiano.
On the architecture of Jose Luis Fernandez del Amo, from 1947-67.
ARQUITECTURA VIVA 1990 May-June, no.12, p.40-42, photos.

SPAIN--HUELVA--BUS STATIONS
Epilogo ondulante: Cruz y Ortiz en Huelva / Vicente Paton.
Project for bus stations.
ARQUITECTURA VIVA 1990 May-June, no.12, p.50-51, elevs., models, plan.

SPAIN--HUESCA--GYMNASIUMS
Provocative and participatory places.
Features seven projects in the Barcelona area by Enric Miralles and Carme Pinos.
ARCHITECTURAL REVIEW 1990 July, v.188, no.1121, p.74-89, dets., ill., elevs., plans, secns., site plans, sketches.

SPAIN--IBIZA--APARTMENTS--INTERIOR DESIGN
Un peu diabolique: appartement a Ibiza.
Interiors of 3-floor apartment.
Architects: Elias Torres Tur and Jose Antonio Martinez Lapana.
English summary, p.52.
ARCHITECTURE INTERIEURE CREE 1990 Feb., no.234, p.[152]-153, photos., plans, secn.

SPAIN--IBIZA--CAP MARTINET--VACATION HOUSES
Angles on Ibiza / Peter Buchanan.
Vacation house, Cap Martinet, Ibiza, Spain. Architects: Jose Antonio Martinez Lapena and Elias Torres Tur.
ARCHITECTURAL REVIEW 1990 Apr., v.187, no.1118, p.56-[60], photos., plans, secns.
Pour l'horizon: maison du Cap Martinet, Ibiza, Baleares.
Architect: Elias Torres Tur, Jose Antonio Martinez Lapena. Includes English and Spanish summaries.
TECHNIQUES ET ARCHITECTURE 1990 June-July, no.390, p.90-[95],180, elev., photos., plans, secns.

SPAIN--IBIZA--HOTELS
Hotel en Ibiza = Hotel design: San Jose, Ibiza, 1988/1990.
Architect: Victor Rahola, Bartolome Mestre.
EL CROQUIS 1990 Apr.-June, v.9, no.43, p.114-123, dets., elevs., photos., plans, site plans.

SPAIN--IBIZA--SAN MATEO--HOUSES--CONSERVATION AND RESTORATION
Come scolpita nella pietra [restoration of a villa, Ibiza, Spain] / Giulia Conte.
Architect: Nicolas Besset.
VILLE GIARDINI 1990 Apr., no.247, p.[22]-29, photos, plan.

SPAIN--IBIZA--STORES--CLOTHING--NYC
Local comercial en Eivissa: Francisco Jose Mangado, arquitecto.
Spanish, English text.
ON DISENO 1990, no.111, p.172-179, det., photos., plans.

SPAIN--IBIZA--STORES--CLOTHING--THE END
Eduardo Samso.
Includes criticism by Josep Maria Montaner and four projects by the architect. Text in Spanish and English.
EL CROQUIS 1990 Nov., v.9, no.45, p.125-162, axonometric views, dets., port., elevs., models, photos., plans, secns., site plans.

SPAIN--IGUALADA--CHAPELS
Konstruktivistische Ansatze aus Katalanien: neue Arbeiten von Miralles und Pinos.
Three projects: Platzgestaltung "Placa Mayor" in Parets del Valles; Friedhofsanlage mit Kapelle in Igualada; Soziales Begegnungszentrum "La Pista" in Hostalets. One of four articles on the theme "Barcelona bauen".
BAUWELT 1990 Mar.2, v.81, no.9, p.392-395, photos., plans, secns., site plans.

SPAIN--IGUALADA--CHURCHYARDS
Konstruktivistische Ansatze aus Katalanien: neue Arbeiten von Miralles und Pinos.
Three projects: Platzgestaltung "Placa Mayor" in Parets del Valles; Friedhofsanlage mit Kapelle in Igualada; Soziales Begegnungszentrum "La Pista" in Hostalets. One of four articles on the theme "Barcelona bauen".
BAUWELT 1990 Mar.2, v.81, no.9, p.392-395, photos., plans, secns., site plans.

SPAIN--IGUALADA--FACTORIES
Nave para almacen y oficinas en Igualada: Mario Corea y Francisco Gallardo, arquitectos.
Spanish, English text.
ON DISENO 1990, no.108, p.134-139, dwgs., photos., plan, site plan.

SPAIN--INDUSTRIAL PARKS
Poligonos industriales, hoy areas de actividad economica / Gonzalo Navarro.
Industrial estates, now areas of economic activity. In Spanish; English summary p.45.
URBANISMO / COAM 1990 Sept., no.11, p.30-45, plans, aerial photos.

SPAIN--INDUSTRIES, LOCATION OF
Poligonos industriales, hoy areas de actividad economica / Gonzalo Navarro.
Industrial estates, now areas of economic activity. In Spanish; English summary p.45.
URBANISMO / COAM 1990 Sept., no.11, p.30-45, plans, aerial photos.

SPAIN--INTERIOR DESIGN--AWARDS AND PRIZES
Premisos FAD de arquitectura e interiorismo (y 3).
Presents 10 projects, each indexed seperately. Text in Spanish and English.
ON DISENO 1990, no.116, p.102-175, dwgs., elevs., photos., plans, secns., site plans, serial photos.

SPAIN--INTERIOR DESIGN--HISTORY
Contradecoradores: del confort y los espacios / Gines Sanchez Hevia.
ARQUITECTURA VIVA 1990 Nov.-Dec., no.15, p.12-13, dwgs., photos.

SPAIN--JAEN--BANKS--BANCO DE ESPANA
Edificio del Banco de Espana a Jaen, Andalusia: Jose Rafael Moneo.
In Italian and English.
DOMUS 1990 July-Aug., no.718, p.[44-51], det., dwgs., elevs., photos., plans, site plan.
Gathering establishments.
Part of a special feature on Spanish contemporary architecture. Contents: Palau de la Musica Catalana, by Oscar Tusquets Blanca, Carlos M. Diaz, Lluis Clotet, Ignacio Paricio -- Television Andaluza, by Gonzalo Diaz-Y. Recasens --Banco de Espana, Jaen, by Rafael Moneo -- Almacenes Simon, by Lluis Clotet, Ignacio Paricio --Mercado Vilaseca-Salou, by Carlos Ferrater Lambarri, Jose Luis Canosa -- Pabellon Rius i Taulet, by Pep Bonet --Velodromo de Horta, by Esteban Bonell, Francesc Rius -- Brief histories --Views through the Camera's Finder, by Hisao Suzuki. Text in Japanese.
SPACE DESIGN 1990 May, no.308, p.93-131, dets., ports., elevs., model, photos., plans, secns., site plan, sketch, isometric dwg.

SPAIN--JAEN--BATHS--ISLAMIC--BANOS ARABES
Restauracion de los Banos Arabes de Jaen.
Restaurant of 16th-cent. Arab baths. Architect: Luis Berges Roldan. Includes English summary.
ON DISENO 1990, no.112, p.193-206, axonometric views, photos., plans.

SPAIN--LA CORUNA--ART SCHOOLS--ESCUELA DE ARTES Y OFICIOS ARTISTICOS
Public facilities.
Part of a special feature on Spanish contemporary architecture. Contents: Museo de Navarra, by Jordi Garces, Enric Soria.-- Biblioteca Publica, by Victor Lopez Cotelo, Carlos Puente.-- Molinos del Rio Segura, by Juan Navarro Baldeweg.-- Puerta de Toledo, by Nuan Navarro Baldeweg.-- Escuela de artes y oficios artisticos, by Jose Antonio Corrales.-- Instituto Hugue, by Luis Bravo Farre, Albert Blanch Rubio.-- Brief Histories. Text in Japanese.
SPACE DESIGN 1990 May, no.308, p.11-54, ports., elevs., photos., plans, secns., site plans.

SPAIN--LA CORUNA--HOUSES
Dos habitatges: mercat, museu.
Features four projects by Manuel
Gallego. Text in Spanish and
English.
QUADERNS D'ARQUITECTURA I
URBANISME 1988 July-Sept., no.178,
p.32-[57], dets., elevs., photos.,
plans, secns.

SPAIN--LA CORUNA--MARKETS--MERCADO DE
SANTA LUCIA
Dos habitatges: mercat, museu.
Features four projects by Manuel
Gallego. Text in Spanish and
English.
QUADERNS D'ARQUITECTURA I
URBANISME 1988 July-Sept., no.178,
p.32-[57], dets., elevs., photos.,
plans, secns.

SPAIN--LA CORUNA--MUSEUMS--ART--MUSEO
DE BELLAS ARTES
Al borde del casco antiguo: Museo de
Bellas Artes, La Coruna.
Architect: Jose Manuel Gallego.
English summary, p.92.
A & V 1990, no.26, p.75-77, elev.,
mdoels, plans, secns., site plan.

SPAIN--LA CORUNA--MUSEUMS--COLEGIATA
DE SANTA MARIA
Dos habitatges: mercat, museu.
Features four projects by Manuel
Gallego. Text in Spanish and
English.
QUADERNS D'ARQUITECTURA I
URBANISME 1988 July-Sept., no.178,
p.32-[57], dets., elevs., photos.,
plans, secns.

SPAIN--LA RUA--INDUSTRIAL PARKS--AS
PEDREIRAS
Actuacion industrial de la Rua
(Orense).
URBANISMO / COAM 1990 Sept.,
no.11, p.101-102, map, plan,
table.

SPAIN--LAND USE
Landschaftsplanung an Spaniens
Mittelmeerkuste / Christian
Nitsche.
Includes English summary.
GARTEN UND LANDSCHAFT 1990, v.100,
no.3, p.29-32, photos., site plan.

SPAIN--LANDSCAPE--EVALUATION
Landscape planning in Spain / Miguel
Aguilo, Santiago Gonzalez Alonso,
Angel Ramos.
BUILT ENVIRONMENT 1990, v.16,
no.2, p.98-110, map, photos.,
tables, refs.

SPAIN--LANDSCAPE PROTECTION
Landschaftsplanung an Spaniens
Mittelmeerkuste / Christian
Nitsche.
Includes English summary.
GARTEN UND LANDSCHAFT 1990, v.100,
no.3, p.29-32, photos., site plan.

SPAIN--LEGANES--CAMPUS PLANNING--
STUDENT PROJECTS
Developing a new urban university.
Student projects for a new
university campus in Leganes,
outside Madrid, Spain. The urban
design course was taught by
Antonio Diaz and Gabriel Feld.
GSD NEWS / HARVARD UNIVERSITY.
(Continued next column)

SPAIN--LEGANES--CAMPUS PLANNING--
STUDENT PROJECTS (CONTINUED)
Developing a new...(CONTINUED)
GRADUATE SCHOOL OF DESIGN 1990
Spring, v.18, no.4, p.16, dwg.,
model, site plan.

SPAIN--LEON--CATHEDRALS--16TH CENTURY
Diseno de la planta de la catedral
de Leon realizado en 1514 / M.
Dolores Campos Sanchez-Bordona.
ARCHIVO ESPANOL DE ARTE 1990
Oct.-Dec., v.63, no.252,
p.640-646, plans, sketch, table,
refs.

SPAIN--LEON--MUSEUMS--MUSEO PROVINCIAL
El amacen transparente: Museo
Provincial, Leon.
Architect: Alejandro de la Sota
Martinez. English summary, p.92.
A & V 1990, no.26, p.78-80,
axonometric view, dwgs., plans,
secns.

SPAIN--LEON--PLANS--16TH CENTURY--
CATEDRAL DE LEON
Diseno de la planta de la catedral
de Leon realizado en 1514 / M.
Dolores Campos Sanchez-Bordona.
ARCHIVO ESPANOL DE ARTE 1990
Oct.-Dec., v.63, no.252,
p.640-646, plans, sketch, table,
refs.

SPAIN--LERIDA--BARS (EATING AND
DRINKING ESTABLISHMENTS)--BIG BEN
Bar y fast food para el Big Ben =
Bar and fast-food, Mollerusa,
Lerida, 1989.
Interior designer: Pepe Cortes.
EL CROQUIS 1990 Mar., v.9, no.42,
p.152-161, dets., photos., plans,
secns., elevs.

SPAIN--LERIDA--FAST-FOOD RESTAURANTS--
BIG BEN
Bar y fast food para el Big Ben =
Bar and fast-food, Mollerusa,
Lerida, 1989.
Interior designer: Pepe Cortes.
EL CROQUIS 1990 Mar., v.9, no.42,
p.152-161, dets., photos., plans,
secns., elevs.

SPAIN--LERIDA--RETAINING WALLS
Murallas que no separan: Amado y
Domenech en Lerida / Ignasi de
Sola-Morales.
Urban renewal project in the El
Canyeret de Lerida. Includes an
elevator-tower which links the old
town to the urban centers and a
retaining wall.
ARQUITECTURA VIVA 1990 Nov.-Dec.,
no.15, p.16-20, elevs., models,
hotos., plans, secns., site plans.

SPAIN--LERIDA--SCHOOLS OF
ARCHITECTURE--COMPETITIONS--COLEGIO
DE ARQUITECTOS DE CATALUNA
Concurso de ideas para la nueva sede
colegial de C.O.A. de Cataluna en
Lerida.
First prize: Francisco Burgos,
Luis de Pereda. Also shows 2nd &
3rd prize entries.
ARQUITECTURA 1990 Mar.-June, v.72,
no.283-284, p.16-19, axonometric
view, elevs., plans, secns.

SPAIN--LERIDA--TOWERS
Murallas que no separan: Amado y
Domenech en Lerida / Ignasi de
Sola-Morales.
Urban renewal project in the El
Canyeret de Lerida. Includes an
elevator-tower which links the old
town to the urban centers and a
retaining wall.
ARQUITECTURA VIVA 1990 Nov.-Dec.,
no.15, p.16-20, elevs., models,
hotos., plans, secns., site plans.

SPAIN--LESACA--CITY HALLS--18TH
CENTURY--CONSERVATION AND
RESTORATION
Caja de piedra, corazon de madera:
Ayuntamiento de Lesaka, Navarra.
Restoration of 18th century City
Hall, Lesaca, Spain. Architects:
Alberto Ustarroz, Manuel Iniguez.
English summary, p.87.
A & V 1990, no.21, p.50-53,
photos., plans, secns.

SPAIN--L'ESTARTIT--HOUSES
Vivienda unifamiliar en L'Estartit:
Carlos Ferrater, arquitecto.
Spanish, English text.
ON DISENO 1990, no.108, p.104-111,
photos., plans, secn., site plans.

SPAIN--L'ESTARTIT--HOUSES--20TH
CENTURY
Vivienda unifamiliar en L'Estartit:
Carlos Ferrater, arquitecto.
ON DISENO 1990, no.116, p.170-171,
photos.

SPAIN--LLEIDA--EXHIBITION BOOTHS--
PALACIO DE CRISTAL--COAC
Stand del COAC en Lleida: Salvador
Gine, arquitecto.
Spanish, English summary.
ON DISENO 1990, no.111, p.162-171,
photos., plan, secn.

SPAIN--LLEIDA--RESEARCH FACILITIES --
UNIDAD DOCENTE Y CENTRO DE
INVESTIGACION MEDICA
Unidad Docente y Centro de
Investigacion Medica en Lleida: H.
Costas y M. Gomez, arquitectos.
Spanish, English text.
ON DISENO 1990, no.115, p.120-127,
elev., photos., plans.

SPAIN--LLICA DE VALL--CORPORATE OFFICE
BUILDINGS--EPIDOR
Sede central de Epidor S.A. en Llica
de Vall: J. Henrich y P. Marieges,
arquitectos.
Spanish, English text.
ON DISENO 1990, no.115, p.114-119,
photos., plans.

SPAIN--LOGRONO--COURTHOUSES
Edificio de juzgados en Logrono:
Juan Montes, arquitecto.
Spanish, English text.
ON DISENO 1990, no.110, p.132-139,
elev., photos., plans.

SPAIN--LONGARES--CHURCHES--16TH
CENTURY--IGLESIA PARROQUIAL
La Inglesia Parroquial de Longares
(Zaragoza) / Jose Luis Pano
Gracia.
SEMINARIO DE ARTE ARAGONES
1988-1989, v.42-43, p.115-204,
photos., plan, secn., biblio.,
refs.

SPAIN--MADINAT AL-ZAHRA--GARDENS--
UMAYYAD
The mirador in Abbasid and
Hispano-Umayyad garden typology /
D. Fairchild Ruggles.
Argues that Madinat al-Zahra,
outside Cordoba, was influenced by
Abbasid palace typology, including
the use of the mirador, or view.
MUQARNAS 1990, v.7, p.[73]-82,
photos., plans, sketch, refs.

SPAIN--MADINAT AL-ZAHRA--PALACES--
UMAYYAD
The mirador in Abbasid and
Hispano-Umayyad garden typology /
D. Fairchild Ruggles.
Argues that Madinat al-Zahra,
outside Cordoba, was influenced by
Abbasid palace typology, including
the use of the mirador, or view.
MUQARNAS 1990, v.7, p.[73]-82,
photos., plans, sketch, refs.

SPAIN--MADRID--APARTMENT COMPLEXES--
CARABANCHEL
Viviendas en Carabanchel = Multiple
dwellings, Madrid, 1986/1989.
Architects: Antonio Cruz, Antonio
Ortiz.
EL CROQUIS 1990 Apr.-June, v.9,
no.43, p.148-155, elevs., photos.,
plans, secns., sketches.

SPAIN--MADRID--APARTMENT HOUSES
Edificio de viviendas en la plaza de
San Francisco de Madrid: I. de Las
Casas y J. L. Lorenzo,
arquitectos.
Spanish, English text.
ON DISENO 1989, no.104, p.118-125,
photos., plan.

SPAIN--MADRID--APARTMENT HOUSES--PAZ Y
CIA
Edificio Paz y Cia = Three
apartments showroom buildings,
Torrelodones, Madrid, 1986/1989.
Architects: Carlo y Javier Climent
Ortiz.
EL CROQUIS 1990 Apr.-June, v.9,
no.43, p.156-162, photos., plans,
secns.

SPAIN--MADRID--APARTMENT HOUSES--PLAZA
DE CASCORRO
Plaza de Cascorro in Madrid, Spanien
= Plaza de Cascorro in Madrid,
Spain.
25-unit apt. house with central
plaza. Architect: Mariano Bayon
Alvarez.
ARCHITEKTUR + WETTBEWERBE 1990
Dec., no.144, p.6-[7], photos.,
plan.

SPAIN--MADRID--APARTMENT HOUSES--
ROUND--MORATALAZ
346 Sozialwohnungen in Moratalaz,
Madrid
Architect: Fransisco Javier Saenz
de Oiza.
BAUWELT 1990 July 6, v.81, no.25,
p.1302-1303, photos., plan, site
plan.

SPAIN--MADRID--APARTMENT HOUSES--TRES
CANTOS
Edificio de viviendas, Tres Cantos,
Madrid, 1987-89.
Architects: E. Alvarez-Sala
Walther, C. Rubio Carvajal, and C.
Ruiz-Larrea Cangas.
ARQUITECTURA 1990 Jan.-Feb., v.72,
no.282, p.114-121, dets., elevs.,
photos., plans, secns.
Premios COAM-89.
Prizes awarded to 3 Madrid
projects by the Colegio Oficial de
Arquitectos: apartment building,
street design, and Multihispano
store.
ARQUITECTURA 1990 July-Aug., v.72,
no.285, p.15-23, dets., dwgs.,
photos., plans, site plans.

SPAIN--MADRID--APARTMENTS--INTERIOR
DESIGN--LIZCANO APARTMENT
[Municipal stadium and private
apartment, Madrid].
Contents: Sports stadium project,
Aluche, 1985 -- Lizcano apartment,
La Moraleja, 1984-85. Architects:
Mateo Corrales Lantero and Esteban
Becerril Heredero.
9H 1989, no.8, p.110-113, elevs.,
photos., plans, secns., site plan.

SPAIN--MADRID--AVENIDA DE LOS
POBLADOS-ALUCHE--CITY PLANNING
Plan especial de reforma interior
Avda. de los Poblados-Aluche,
Madrid / Javier Botella, Victoria
E. Flores.
URBANISMO / COAM 1990 Jan., no.9,
p.50-53, aerial photo.,
axonometric view, plans, secn.,
site plan, map.

SPAIN--MADRID--BALCONIES--ROCOCO--
PLAZA MAYOR
Disenos para las "luminarias"
realizadas en la Plaza Mayor de
Madrid para festejar el matrimonio
de una infanta de Espana /
Virginia Tovar Martin.
On the 1750 Rococo decoration and
ornament on the balconies of the
buildings surrounding the Plaza
Mayor.
ARCHIVO ESPANOL DE ARTE 1990
Apr.-June, v.63, no.250,
p.[283]-288, dwgs.

SPAIN--MADRID--BANKS--BANCO
HISPANO-AMERICANO
Oficina bancaria en Madrid: Enrique
Colomes, Estudio BAU, arquitecto.
Spanish, English text.
ON DISENO 1990, no.111, p.180-186,
axonometric view, photos., plan.

SPAIN--MADRID--CITY PLANNING
Las estrategias territoriales de
ambito sub-regional = Territorial
guidelines for Madrid and its
region / Felix Arias, Vicente
Gago.
English summary, p.62.
URBANISMO / COAM 1989 Sept., no.8,
p.45-62, axonometric view, maps,
plans, refs.

SPAIN--MADRID--CITY PLANNING--20TH
CENTURY
Making the most of Madrid / Seamus
Filor.
Discussion of civic improvements
currently in progress in Madrid.
LANDSCAPE DESIGN 1990 June,
no.191, p.30-31, photos., refs.
Los nuevos ministerios de Madrid,
una propuesta arquitectonica de
Secundino Zuazo = The new
ministeries in Madrid, and
architectural proposal by
Secundino Zuazo / Lilia Maure
Rubio.
COMPOSICION ARQUITECTONICA, ART &
ARCHITECTURE 1989 June, no.3,
p.[103]-136, dwgs., elevs., maps,
photos., plans, refs.

SPAIN--MADRID--CITY PLANNING--RANCHO
DEL CORDOBES
Plan especial reforma interior
"Ranco del Cordobes," Madrid /
Javier Botella, Victoria E.
Flores.
URBANISMO / COAM 1990 Jan., no.9,
p.46-49, table, aerial photo.,
site plans, map, elev.

SPAIN--MADRID--COMMUNITY CENTERS
Die Kunst der Ecke: Juan Navarro
Baldewegs "Centro Social" in
Madrid / Kaye Geipel.
DEUTSCHE BAUZEITUNG 1990 May,
v.124, no.5, p.20-24, photos.,
plans, secns., site plan.

SPAIN--MADRID--COMMUNITY CENTERS--
PUERTA DE TOLEDO--CENTRO DE
SERVICIOS
Centro de servicios sociales / Juan
Navarro Baldeweg.
Madrid, 1986. Spanish, English
text.
QUADERNS D'ARQUITECTURA I
URBANISME 1989 Apr.-Sept.,
no.181-182, p.[30]-35, photos.,
plans, secns.
Palazzo & Acropolis / Peter
Buchanan.
Features new Spanish projects:
Prevision Espanola headquarters,
Seville, architect: Rafael Moneo;
Porta de Toledo social center,
Madrid, architect: Juan Navarro
Baldeweg.
ARCHITECTURAL REVIEW 1990 Jan.,
v.187, no.1115, p.24-39, dets.,
elevs., photos., plans, secns.,
site plan.
Public facilities.
Part of a special feature on
Spanish contemporary architecture.
Contents: Museo de Navarra, by
Jordi Garces, Enric Soria.--
Biblioteca Publica, by Victor
Lopez Cotelo, Carlos Puente.--
Molinos del Rio Segura, by Juan
Navarro Baldeweg.-- Puerta de
Toledo, by Nuan Navarro
Baldeweg.-- Escuela de artes y
oficios artisticos, by Jose
Antonio Corrales.-- Instituto
Hugue, by Luis Bravo Farre, Albert
Blanch Rubio.-- Brief Histories.
Text in Japanese.
SPACE DESIGN 1990 May, no.308,
p.11-54, ports., elevs., photos.,
plans, secns., site plans.

SPAIN--MADRID--COMPREHENSIVE PLANS
L'elaborazione del Piano di Madrid e il su metodo: uno squardo retrospettivo = The Madrid Master Plan: drafting and method, a retrospective / Jesus Gago Davila. In Italian; English summary, p.123-4.
URBANISTICA 1989 Mar., no.94, p.44-52,123-4, axonometric views, charts, ill., dwgs., photos., plans, refs.

SPAIN--MADRID--CORPORATE OFFICE BUILDINGS--IBM ESPANA
Un edificio "intelligent" per la IBM Espana. In Madrid. Architects: S. Gayarre, T. Dominguez, J. Martin. L'INDUSTRIA DELLE COSTRUZIONI 1990 Oct., v.24, no.228, p.68-69, dwg., photos.

SPAIN--MADRID--CULTURAL CENTERS--COMPETITIONS--CENTRO CULTURAL DE LA DEFENSA
El cilindro atrapado: Centro Cultural de la Defensa, Madrid. Architect: Alvaro Siza. English summary, p.92.
A & V 1990, no.26, p.70-74, axonometric views, dwgs., elevs., models, maps, plans, site plans, sketches.
Il concorso per il centro culturale della Difesa a Madrid / Antonio Velez Catrain. Publishes the entries by Juan Navarro Baldeweg, Lluis Clotet Ballus and Ignacio Paricio, Francisco Javier Saenz de Oiza, and Alvaro Siza, and contains an interview with Eduardo Mangada. Includes English summary, captions, and translation.
CASABELLA 1990 May, v.54, no.568, p.40-51, 61-63, axonometric view, models, map, plans, secns., sketches, aerial photos.
Un paso al frente: el Centro Cultural de la Defensa / Juan Miguel Hernandez Leon. Four entries in the competition for Madrid cultural center. ARQUITECTURA VIVA 1990 Mar.-Apr., no.11, p.34-36, axonometric view, dwgs., models, plans, secns., sketches.

SPAIN--MADRID--DECORATION AND ORNAMENT--18TH CENTURY--STUCCO--PALACIO DE EL PARDO
Los estucos de Roberto Michel para el Palacio de El Pardo / Maria Luisa Tarraga. English summary, p.329.
ARCHIVO ESPANOL DE ARTE 1989 July-Sept., v.62, no.247, p.[315]-329, photos., refs.

SPAIN--MADRID--DECORATION AND ORNAMENT--ROCOCO--PLAZA MAYOR
Disenos para las "luminarias" realizadas en la Plaza Mayor de Madrid para festejar el matrimonio de una infanta de Espana / Virginia Tovar Martin. On the 1750 Rococo decoration and ornament on the balconies of the buildings surrounding the Plaza Mayor.
ARCHIVO ESPANOL DE ARTE 1990
(Continued next column)

SPAIN--MADRID--DECORATION AND ORNAMENT--ROCOCO--PLAZA MAYOR (CONTINUED)
Disenos para las... (CONTINUED) Apr.-June, v.63, no.250, p.[283]-288, dwgs.

SPAIN--MADRID--DESIGN CENTERS
Edificio comercial en Madrid: Mariano Bayon, arquitecto. Spanish, English text.
ON DISENO 1990, no.108, p.94-103, axonometric view, photos., plans, secns.

SPAIN--MADRID--FACADES--ALTERATIONS AND ADDITIONS--ALCAZAR
La estatua ecuestre de Felipe IV de Pietro Tacca y la fachada del Alcazar de Madrid / Karin Hellwig-Konkerth. English summary, p.233.
ARCHIVO ESPANOL DE ARTE 1990 Apr.-June, v.63, no.250, p.[233]-241, photo., plan, engrs., refs.

SPAIN--MADRID--FACADES--NEOCLASSICAL--ALTERATIONS AND ADDITIONS
Parlamentariergebaude der spanischen Abgeordnetenkammer in Madrid / U.P.W. Nagel. Conversion of a 1918 apartment building for use by the Spanish Parliament. Original architect: Cesareo Iradier. Renovation architect: Mariano Bayon Alvarez.
BAUWELT 1990 Nov.2, v.81, no.41, p.2066-2067, elev., photo., plan, secn.

SPAIN--MADRID--GALLERIES (ROOMS AND SPACES)--ESCORIAL--SALAS CAPITULARES
Las Salas Capitulares del Monasterio de San Lorenzo: actual ordenacion de sus colecciones pictoricas / Juan Martinez Cuesta.
REALES SITIOS 1990, v.27, no.103, p.37-44, ill., photos.

SPAIN--MADRID--GARDEN STRUCTURES--STUDENTS PROJECTS--BUEN RETIRO
Parque y pabellon en el retiro = Park and pavilion. Student project by Asuncion Agullo, 1989, for a park in Madrid.
EL CROQUIS 1990 Mar., v.9, no.42, p.169-174, elevs., plans, secns.

SPAIN--MADRID--GYMNASIUMS--GIMNASIO MARAVILLAS
Das Schweigen der Formen: zum Gimnasio Maravillas von Alejandro de la Sota / Luis Fernandez-Galiano. Built 1962, in Madrid.
ARCHITHESE 1990 Jan.-Feb., v.20, no.1, p.54, photos., sketch.

SPAIN--MADRID--HOSPITALS--18TH CENTURY--MILITARY--ALTERATIONS AND ADDITIONS
Un pulso con la mole: Centro de Arte Reina Sofia, Madrid. Renovation of 18th cent. military hospital into an art museum. Architects: Antonio Vazquez de Castro, Jose Luis Iniguez de Onzono. English text, p.90.
A & V 1990, no.26, p.26-31, elevs., photos., plans, site plans.

SPAIN--MADRID--HOUSES
Infraestructuras / Paco Alonso. Theories on architecture and the city. Includes discussion on a one-family house in Madrid, 1986. Architect: Francisco Alonso de Santos. Spanish, English text.
QUADERNS D'ARQUITECTURA I URBANISME 1989 Apr.-Sept., nos.181-182, p.18-29, photos.

SPAIN--MADRID--HOUSES--20TH CENTURY--CASA ENTRECANALES
Archivo en blanco y negro: cronica grafica de tres generaciones/ Francese Catala-Roca. Six projects from 1951-1988, by architects Antoni Gaudi, Barba Corsini, Antoni de Moragas, Jose Antonio Coderch, Josep Lluis Sert, Helio Pinon y Albert Viaplana.
ARQUITECTURA VIVA 1990 May-June, no.12, p.33-35, photos.

SPAIN--MADRID--HOUSES--CASA TUREGANO
Housing and residence. Part of a special feature on Spanish contemporary architecture. Contents: Rota, by Antonio Gonzalez Cordon.-- Viviendas Ramon y Cajal, by Guillermo Vazquez Consuegra.-- Castillo de Maqueda, by Luis Burnillo Lafarga, Jaime L. Lorenzo.-- Casa Turegano, by Alberto Campo Baeza.-- Brief histories. Text in Japanese.
SPACE DESIGN 1990 May, no.308, p.55-74, ports., elevs., photos., plans, secns., isometric dwgs.

SPAIN--MADRID--HOUSES--INTERIOR DESIGN--ABELLO HOUSE
Spanish acquisitions: a Madrid couple celebrate their country's art / Nicholas Shrady. Home interior. Architect: Luis Gutierrez Soto. Interior designer: Jaime Parlade.
ARCHITECTURAL DIGEST 1990 Mar., v.47, no.3, p.166-171,240, photos.

SPAIN--MADRID--HOUSING--ALEJANDRO RODRIGUEZ 37
Edificio de viviendas en Madrid: Enrique Colomes/Estudio Bau, arquitecto. Spanish, English text.
ON DISENO 1990, no.110, p.111-119, axonometric views, photos., plan.

SPAIN--MADRID--HOUSING PROJECTS--LA ELIPA
48 viviendas en La Elipa = 48 dwellings in La Elipa, Madrid. Housing project. Architects: Victor Lopez Cotelo, Carlos Puente.
QUADERNS D'ARQUITECTURA I URBANISME 1988 July-Sept., no.178, p.64-65, elevs., plan.

SPAIN--MADRID--HOUSING PROJECTS--MORATALAZ
346 Sozialwohnungen in Moratalaz, Madrid. Architect: Fransisco Javier Saenz de Oiza.
BAUWELT 1990 July 6, v.81, no.25, p.1302-1303, photos., plan, site plan.

SPAIN--MADRID--HOUSING--PUBLIC--
PALOMERAS
50 Sozialwohnungen in Palomeras,
Madrid.
Architect: Mariano Bayon Alvarez.
BAUWELT 1990 July 6, v.81, no.25,
p.1301, elev., photo., plan.

SPAIN--MADRID--INDUSTRIES, LOCATION OF
El cambio industrial en la Comunidad
de Madrid: tendencias y
perspectivas / Ricardo Mendez.
The evolution of industrial sites
in the Madrid Autonomous
Community. In Spanish; English
summary, p.29.
URBANISMO / COAM 1990 Sept.,
no.11, p.18-29, chart, maps,
photos., tables, aerial photos.,
biblio., refs.

SPAIN--MADRID--INTELLIGENT BUILDINGS--
IBM ESPANA
Un edificio "intelligent" per la IBM
Espana.
In Madrid. Architects: S. Gayarre,
T. Dominguez, J. Martin.
L'INDUSTRIA DELLE COSTRUZIONI 1990
Oct., v.24, no.228, p.68-69, dwg.,
photos.

SPAIN--MADRID-LAS ROZAS--INDUSTRIAL
PARKS
Parque empresarial Madrid-Las Rozas
/ Bernardo Ynzenga.
URBANISMO / COAM 1990 Sept.,
no.11, p.60-67, dwgs., models,
map, photo., plans.

SPAIN--MADRID--MANSIONS--19TH
CENTURY--ALTERATIONS AND ADDITIONS
Rehabilitacion de edificio en Madrid
Ignacio Gonzalez Perez,
arquitecto.
Spanish, English text.
ON DISENO 1990, no.109, p.148-155,
axonometric views, photos., plans.

SPAIN--MADRID--MONASTERIES--17TH
CENTURY--MONASTERIO DES LAS
TRINITRIAS DECALZAS DE SAN
ILDEFONSO--HISTORY
El monasterio de las religiosas
Trinitarias Descalzas de San
Ildefonso de Madrid / Virginia
Tovar Martin.
History of the building from its
initial use as a convent in the
early 1600s to its redesign in the
early 1700s.
ARCHIVO ESPANOL DE ARTE 1990
July-Sept., v.63, no.251,
p.[401]-418, map, photos., plan,
refs.

SPAIN--MADRID--MONASTERIES--
CONSERVATION AND RESTORATION--
ESCORIAL
Reconstruccion del Monasterio de El
Escorial despues del incendio de
1671 / Jose Luis Sancho, Maria
Teresa Fernandez Talaya.
REALES SITIOS 1990, v.27, no.103,
p.57-64, elevs., secns.

SPAIN--MADRID--MONASTERIES--ESCORIAL
Las Salas Capitulares del Monasterio
de San Lorenzo: actual ordenacion
de sus colecciones pictoricas /
Juan Martinez Cuesta.
REALES SITIOS 1990, v.27, no.103,
p.37-44, ill., photos.

SPAIN--MADRID--MONUMENTS AND
MEMORIALS--17TH CENTURY--FELIPE IV
La estatua ecuestre de Felipe IV de
Pietro Tacca y la fachada del
Alcazar de Madrid / Karin
Hellwig-Konkerth.
English summary, p.233.
ARCHIVO ESPANOL DE ARTE 1990
Apr.-June, v.63, no.250,
p.[233]-241, photo., plan, engrs.,
refs.

SPAIN--MADRID--MULTI-USE BUILDINGS--
PLAZA DE LA CEBADA
Wohn- und Geschaftsgebaude Plaza de
la Cebada in Madrid, Spanien =
Residential and commercial
building Plaza de la Cebada in
Madrid, Spain.
Architects: Pedro Casariego
Hernandez-Vaquero, Antonio Velez
Catrain.
ARCHITEKTUR + WETTBEWERBE 1990
June, no.142, p.20, photos., plan.

SPAIN--MADRID--MUSEUMS--ART--CENTRO DE
ARTE REINA SOFIA
Un pulso con la mole: Centro de Arte
Reina Sofia, Madrid.
Renovation of 18th cent. military
hospital into an art museum.
Architects: Antonio Vazquez de
Castro, Jose Luis Iniguez de
Onzono. English text, p.90.
A & V 1990, no.26, p.26-31,
elevs., photos., plans, site
plans.

SPAIN--MADRID--MUSEUMS--COMPETITIONS--
MUSEO DEL ESPACIO
Concurso de anteproyectos museo del
espacio en Madrid.
First prize: Manuel J. Fernandez
Iglesias and Adolfo Sanchez de la
Blanca.
ARQUITECTURA 1990 Jan.-Feb., v.72,
no.282, p.12-15, axonometric
views, elevs., plans, secns.

SPAIN--MADRID--MUSEUMS--SCIENCE--
ALTERATIONS AND ADDITIONS--MUSEO
NACIONAL DE CIENCIAS NATURALES
La colina olvidada: Museo Nacional
de Ciencias Naturales.
Museum renovation. Architects:
Javier Alau Massa, Antonio Lopera.
English summary, p.90.
A & V 1990, no.26, p.56-59,
elevs., photos., plans, secns.

SPAIN--MADRID--NURSERY SCHOOLS
Guarderia infantil en Palomeras,
Madrid: J. Frechilla, C. Herrero,
J. M. Lopez-Pelaez, E. Rodriguez,
y E. Sanchez, arquitectos.
Nursery school. Spanish, English
text.
ON DISENO 1989, no.104, p.111-117,
photos., plan.

SPAIN--MADRID--OFFICE BUILDINGS--
SOCIEDAD ESTATAL DE GESTION PARA LA
REHABILITACION Y CONSTRUCCION DE LA
VIVIENDA
Rehabilitacion de edificio en Madrid
Ignacio Gonzalez Perez,
arquitecto.
Spanish, English text.
ON DISENO 1990, no.109, p.148-155,
axonometric views, photos., plans.

SPAIN--MADRID--PARKS--20TH CENTURY--
PARCO ENRIQUE TIERNO GALVAN
Der Park Enrique Tierno Galvan in
Madrid / Iris Huber-Werthwcin.
Includes English summary.
GARTEN UND LANDSCHAFT 1990, v.100,
no.3, p.49-51, photos.

SPAIN--MADRID--PARKS--CUNA VERDE
Proyeto del parque Cuna Verde, La
Latina, Madrid.
Architects: F. Nieto E. Sobejano.
ARQUITECTURA 1990 July-Aug., v.72,
no.285, p.32-35, elevs., models,
plans, secns., site plans.

SPAIN--MADRID--PARKS--PARQUE CAMPO DE
LAS NACIONES
Proyecto Parque Campo de las
Naciones, Ayuntamiento de Madrid.
Architects: E. Esteras Martin,
J.L. Esteban Penelas.
ARQUITECTURA 1990 July-Aug., v.72,
no.285, p.36-39, models, secns.,
site plans.

SPAIN--MADRID--PEDESTRIAN STREETS--
PRECIADOS
Premios COAM-89.
Prizes awarded to 3 Madrid
projects by the Colegio Oficial de
Arquitectos: apartment building,
street design, and Multihispano
store.
ARQUITECTURA 1990 July-Aug., v.72,
no.285, p.15-23, dets., dwgs.,
photos., plans, site plans.

SPAIN--MADRID--PLASTERWORK,
DECORATIVE--18TH CENTURY--PALACIO DE
EL PARDO
Los estucos de Roberto Michel para
el Palacio de El Pardo / Maria
Luisa Tarraga.
English summary, p.329.
ARCHIVO ESPANOL DE ARTE 1989
July-Sept., v.62, no.247,
p.[315]-329, photos., refs.

SPAIN--MADRID--PLAZAS--ALTERATIONS AND
ADDITIONS--PLAZA PICASSO
Plaza Picasso.
Projects for the modifications to
the Madrid plaza. Architect: Juan
Daniel Fullaondo. Text in Spanish
and English.
ARQUITECTURA 1990 July-Aug., v.72,
no.285, p.40-51, dwg., elevs.,
models, plans, site plans.

SPAIN--MADRID--PLAZAS--PLAZA DE
CASCORRO
Plaza de Cascorro in Madrid, Spanien
= Plaza de Cascorro in Madrid,
Spain.
25-unit apt. house with central
plaza. Architect: Mariano Bayon
Alvarez.
ARCHITEKTUR + WETTBEWERBE 1990
Dec., no.144, p.6-[7], photos.,
plan.

SPAIN--MADRID--PUBLIC BUILDINGS--20TH
CENTURY
Making places in Spain: public
buildings by Madrid and Barcelona
architects / Peter Buchanan.
Essay for theme issue on new
public buildings in Madrid and
Barcelona. Eight articles indexed
separately.
ARCHITECTURAL REVIEW 1990 July,
v.188, no.1121, p.[28]-31, elev.,
photos., plan.

SPAIN--MADRID--PUBLIC BUILDINGS--20TH
CENTURY--NUEVOS MINISTERIOS
Los nuevos ministerios de Madrid,
una propuesta arquitectonica de
Secundino Zuazo = The new
ministeries in Madrid, and
architectural proposal by
Secundino Zuazo / Lilia Maure
Rubio.
COMPOSICION ARQUITECTONICA, ART &
ARCHITECTURE 1989 June, no.3,
p.[103]-136, dwgs., elevs., maps,
photos., plans, refs.

SPAIN--MADRID--PUBLIC BUILDINGS--
ENRESA
Sede social de ENRESA: calle Emilio
Vargas, Madrid, 1987-89.
Architects: J. Junquera, E.
Perez-Pita.
ARQUITECTURA 1990 Jan.-Feb., v.72,
no.282, p.104-113, elevs.,
photos., plans.

SPAIN--MADRID--PUBLIC BUILDINGS--
PARLIAMENT OFFICES
Parlamentariergebaude der spanischen
Abgeordnetenkammer in Madrid /
U.P.W. Nagel.
Conversion of a 1918 apartment
building for use by the Spanish
Parliament. Original architect:
Cesareo Iradier. Renovation
architect: Mariano Bayon Alvarez.
BAUWELT 1990 Nov.2, v.81, no.41,
p.2066-2067, elev., photo., plan,
secn.

SPAIN--MADRID--PUBLISHING OFFICES--
EDITORIAL ARANZADI
Proyecto de interiorismo de una
editorial: Allende Arquitectos.
Offices of Aranzadi publishers,
Madrid. English text, p.183. In
"On oficina", 1990 supplement
issue.
ON DISENO 1990, suppl., p.122-127,
dwg., photos., plan.

SPAIN--MADRID--RAILROAD STATIONS--
ATOCHA
Das Tor zur Innenstadt: der neue
Atocha Bahnhof in Madrid /
Patricia Catalano.
Architects: Rafael Moneo with
Emilio Tunon, Javier Revillo.
ARCHITEKTUR, INNENARCHITEKTUR,
TECHNISCHER AUSBAU 1990 July-Aug.,
v.98, no.7-8, p.54-55, photos.

SPAIN--MADRID--RAILROAD TERMINALS--
ATOCHA
J.R. Moneo: progetto per la Stazione
di Atocha a Madrid.
In conjunction with an exhibition
at the Fondazione Angelo Masieri.
L'INDUSTRIA DELLE COSTRUZIONI 1990
Jan., v.24, no.219, p.64-65,
photos., plan, secn., aerial
photo.

SPAIN--MADRID--REGIONAL PLANNING
Las estrategias territoriales de
ambito sub-regional = Territorial
guidelines for Madrid and its
region / Felix Arias, Vicente
Gago.
English summary, p.62.
URBANISMO / COAM 1989 Sept., no.8,
p.45-62, axonometric view, maps,
plans, refs.

SPAIN--MADRID--REGIONAL PLANNING--
ECONOMIC ASPECTS
Economic and social restructuring in
the Metropolitan Area of Madrid
(1970-85) / Constanza Tobio.
INTERNATIONAL JOURNAL OF URBAN AND
REGIONAL RESEARCH 1989 June, v.13,
no.2, p.[324]-338, fig., map,
refs.

SPAIN--MADRID--RESTAURANTS--GALA
Restaurante en Madrid: F. J. Garcia
Garcia y L. Segundo Arana,
arquitectos.
Spanish, English text.
ON DISENO 1990, no.108, p.127-133,
axonometric view, photos., plan.
Ristorante Gala, Madrid: Javier
Garcia Garcia, Luis Segundo Arana
/ Duccio Malagamba.
In Italian and English.
DOMUS 1990 July-Aug., no.718,
p.[52]-56, axonometric view,
photos., plan.

SPAIN--MADRID--RESTAURANTS--INTERIOR
DESIGN--TEATRIZ
[Amenagement]: hotellerie.
Contents: Bar la Funambule,
Strasbourg, France; architects:
Georges Heintz and Philippe Lacaze
-- L'Oreal restaurant, Clichy,
France; architect: Alain Bailly --
Cafereria de la Comedie Francaise,
Paris; architect: Marie-Christine
Dorner -- Teatriz restaurant,
Madrid, Spain; designer: Philippe
Starck.
LE MONITEUR ARCHITECTURE AMC 1990
July-Aug., no.13, p.58-67,
axonometric views, photos., plans.
Armchair theatre: Starck in Madrid /
Rick Poynor.
Teatriz restaurant; designer:
Philippe Starck.
BLUEPRINT (LONDON, ENGLAND) 1990
June, no.68, p.46-48, photos.
Dream sequence / David Redhead.
Interiors of Madrid restaurant,
Teatriz. Interior designer:
Philippe Starck.
DESIGNERS' JOURNAL 1990 July-Aug.,
no.59, p.72-76, photos., plan.
Perversion didactica: el Teatriz de
Starck / Vicente Paton.
Conversion of a Madrid theater
into a complex of bars,
restaurant, and discotheque.
ARQUITECTURA VIVA 1990 Nov.-Dec.,
no.15, p.49-53, elevs., photos.,
plan.
Teatriz ole! / Christine Colin.
Interiors of Teatriz restaurant,
Madrid. Interior designer:
Philippe Starck. English summary,
p.163.
ARCHITECTURE INTERIEURE CREE 1990
Mar., no.235, p.114-121, photos.,
plan.

SPAIN--MADRID--RURAL-URBAN MIGRATION
The Madrid neighborhood remodelling
programme: a case study / Robert
Chubb.
LAND DEVELOPMENT STUDIES 1989
Jan., v.6, no.1, p.[3]-11, biblio.

SPAIN--MADRID--SHOWROOMS--CLOTHING--
JESUS DEL POZO
Showroom Jesus del Pozo, Madrid;
Alberto Campo Baeza, Antonio
Romero Fernandez / Duccio
Malagamba.
In Italian and English.
DOMUS 1990 July-Aug., no.718,
p.[57-59], axonometric views,
photos.

SPAIN--MADRID--SHOWROOMS--DESIGN--PAZ
Y CIA
Paz y Cia, Madrid.
Showroom for ceramic products.
Architects: Javier and Carlos
Climent.
ON DISENO 1990, "ceramica" suppl.,
p.156-159, photos.

SPAIN--MADRID--SQUATTER SETTLEMENTS
The Madrid neighborhood remodelling
programme: a case study / Robert
Chubb.
LAND DEVELOPMENT STUDIES 1989
Jan., v.6, no.1, p.[3]-11, biblio.

SPAIN--MADRID--STADIUMS
[Municipal stadium and private
apartment, Madrid].
Contents: Sports stadium project,
Aluche, 1985 -- Lizcano apartment,
La Moraleja, 1984-85. Architects:
Mateo Corrales Lantero and Esteban
Becerril Heredero.
9H 1989, no.8, p.110-113, elevs.,
photos., plans, secns., site plan.

SPAIN--MADRID--STORES--CLOTHING--
EKSEPTION
Eduardo Samso.
Includes criticism by Josep Maria
Montaner and four projects by the
architect. Text in Spanish and
English.
EL CROQUIS 1990 Nov., v.9, no.45,
p.125-162, axonometric views,
dets., port., elevs., models,
photos., plans, secns., site
plans.

SPAIN--MADRID--STORES--MULTIHISPANO
Premios COAM-89.
Prizes awarded to 3 Madrid
projects by the Colegio Oficial de
Arquitectos: apartment building,
street design, and Multihispano
store.
ARQUITECTURA 1990 July-Aug., v.72,
no.285, p.15-23, dets., dwgs.,
photos., plans, site plans.

SPAIN--MADRID--TRANSIT SYSTEMS
The growth of metro systems in
Madrid, Rome and Athens / Frank J.
Costa, Allen G. Noble.
CITIES 1990 Aug., v.7, no.3,
p.224-229, plans, tables, refs.

SPAIN--MADRID--URBAN DESIGN--20TH
CENTURY
Making the most of Madrid / Seamus
Filor.
Discussion of civic improvements
currently in progress in Madrid.
LANDSCAPE DESIGN 1990 June,
no.191, p.30-31, photos., refs.

SPAIN--MADRID--URBAN PARKS--
ALTERATIONS AND ADDITIONS--STUDENT
PROJECTS--BUEN RETIRO
Parque y pabellon en el retiro =
Park and pavilion.
Student project by Asuncion
Agullo, 1989, for a park in
Madrid.
EL CROQUIS 1990 Mar., v.9, no.42,
p.169-174, elevs., plans, secns.

SPAIN--MADRID--URBAN RENEWAL
The Madrid neighborhood remodelling
programme: a case study / Robert
Chubb.
LAND DEVELOPMENT STUDIES 1989
Jan., v.6, no.1, p.[3]-11, biblio.

SPAIN--MAIRENA DEL ALJARAFE--HOUSES--
CASA ROLANDO
Casa Rolando, Mairena del Aljarafe.
Architect: Giullermo Vasquez
Consuegra. Text in Italian and
English.
LOTUS INTERNATIONAL 1989, no.63,
p.34-41, axonometric views,
elevs., photos., plans, secn.

SPAIN--MAJADAHONDA--WATER TREATMENT
PLANTS
Tres estaciones depuradoras de aguas
residuales = Three water
purification plants.
In Majadahonda, Guadarrama and
Villalba. Architects: Juan
Herreros, Inaki Abalos. Text in
Spanish and English.
QUADERNS D'ARQUITECTURA I
URBANISME 1988 July-Sept., no.178,
p.102-119, photos., plans, secn.,
site plan.

SPAIN--MAJORCA--ALCUDIA--LIBRARIES--
PUBLIC
Bibliothek als Kulturzentrum auf
Mallorca / Siegfried Linke.
Library located in part of 14th
cent. Palacio Con Torro, in
Alcudia. Architects: Massanet,
Palma y Pedreroll.
DEUTSCHE BAUZEITSCHRIFT 1990
Sept., v.38, no.9, p.1186, photos.

SPAIN--MAJORCA--CASTLES--CONSERVATION
AND RESTORATION--ALMUDAINA
Obras de rehabilitacion en La
Almudaina / Manuel del Rio.
Renovations to the Castell Reial
in Mallorca, Spain.
REALES SITIOS 1990, v.27, no.104,
p.29-34, photos.

SPAIN--MAJORCA--CATHEDRALS--
ALTERATIONS AND ADDITIONS--MAJORCA
CATHEDRAL
La cattedrale di Mallorca
restaurata: la maniera di Gaudi =
The renovation of the Majorca
cathedral: in the manner of Gaudi
/ Juan Jose Lahuerta.
Interior renovations of 1903-1904;
architect: Antoni Gaudi.
LOTUS INTERNATIONAL 1990, no.65,
(Continued next column)

SPAIN--MAJORCA--CATHEDRALS--
ALTERATIONS AND ADDITIONS--MAJORCA
CATHEDRAL (CONTINUED)
La cattedrale di...(CONTINUED)
p.105-117, dwgs., photos.

SPAIN--MAJORCA--COUNTRY HOUSES
Das andere Mallorca / Justin Thyme,
Pedro de Montaner.
Includes various famous country
houses on Majorca including Son
Marroig, Son Bergen, Can Vivot,
Sarria, Alfabia and the Raixa
gardens.
ARCHITEKTUR & WOHNEN 1990
June-July, no.3, p.104-[116],
port., photos.

SPAIN--MAJORCA--HOUSES--ARCHITECTS'
Nella metropoli Balneare / Marinetta
Nunziante.
House with architectural offices
on the 1st floor, in Majorca,
Spain. Architects: A. Morado
Vila, E. Nadal De Olives, P.
Nicolau Bover.
VILLE GIARDINI 1990 Sept., no.251,
p.18-23, photos., plans, secn.

SPAIN--MAJORCA--HOUSES--VU - JAKOBER
HOUSE
A hispano-moresque legacy on Majorca
/ G.Y. Dryansky.
Features Yannick Vu and Ben
Jakober's home. Architect: Hassan
Fathy.
ARCHITECTURAL DIGEST 1990 Aug.,
v.47, no.8, p.94-[99],181, photos.

SPAIN--MAJORCA--OFFICES--ARCHITECTS'
Nella metropoli Balneare / Marinetta
Nunziante.
House with architectural offices
on the 1st floor, in Majorca,
Spain. Architects: A. Morado
Vila, E. Nadal De Olives, P.
Nicolau Bover.
VILLE GIARDINI 1990 Sept., no.251,
p.18-23, photos., plans, secn.

SPAIN--MAJORCA--SOCIETY AND
ASSOCIATION BUILDINGS--FUNDACION
JOAN Y PILAR MIRO
Atlantic cries - Mediterranean
whispers / Luis Fernandez-Galiano.
On the Centro Atlantico de Arte
Moderno, Las Palmas, Canary
Islands, architect: Francisco
Javier Saenz de Oiza and the Juan
and Pilar Miro Foundation, Son
Abrines, Majorca, architect: Jose
Rafael Moneo.
ARCHITECTURAL REVIEW 1990 July,
v.188, no.1121, p.44-[51], models,
photos., plans, secn., site plan.
El jardin de la estrella: Fundacion
Joan y Pilar Miro, Palma de
Mallorca.
Architect: Jose Rafael Moneo.
English summary, p.91-92.
A & V 1990, no.24, p.54-57,
elevs., models, plans, secn.

SPAIN--MAJORCA--VACATION HOUSES--
NEUENDORF HOUSE
Wohnskulptur / Gesa Engelschall.
Features Hans Neuendorf's vacation
house in Majorca. Architect:
Claudio Silvestrin.
ARCHITEKTUR & WOHNEN 1990
Dec.-1991 Jan., no.6, p.36-43,
port., photos., isometric dwg.

SPAIN--MARBELLA--CULTURAL CENTERS--
COMPETITIONS
Concurso de ideas para complejo
cultural en Marbella, Malaga,
1989.
First prize: Angel F. Perez Mora.
ARQUITECTURA 1990 Jan.-Feb., v.72,
no.282, p.16-17, dwgs., elevs.,
plans.

SPAIN--MASQUEFA--SCHOOLS
Civic monuments.
Three projects by Esteve Bonell:
School, Masquefa, with Josep Maria
Gil; law courts, Gerona, with
Josep Maria Gil and the sports
arena, Badalona, with Francesc
Rius.
ARCHITECTURAL REVIEW 1990 July,
v.188, no.1121, p.69-73, elevs.,
models, photos., plans, secns.,
site plan.

SPAIN--MELILLA--HOSPITALS--HOSPITAL
COMARCAL
Hospital Comarcal de Melilla:
Alfonso Casares y Reinaldo Ruiz,
arquitectos.
Spanish, English text.
ON DISENO 1990, no.110, p.120-131,
axonometric view, photos., plans.

SPAIN--MERIDA--MUSEUMS--
ARCHAEOLOGICAL--MUSEO NACIONAL DE
ARTE ROMANO
Romersk resonans - om Spaniens nye
nationalmuseum for romersk kunst /
Flemming Skude.
Located in Merida, Spain.
Architect: Rafael Moneo.
ARKITEKTUR DK 1989, v.33, no.7,
p.A150-A159, elev., photos.,
plans, secns., isometric dwg.

SPAIN--METROPOLITAN AREAS--POLITICAL
ASPECTS
Politiche urbane e realta
metropolitane = Urban policy and
the metropolis / Jordi Borja.
In Italian; English summary,
p.124.
URBANISTICA 1989 Mar., no.94,
p.64-71,124, maps.

SPAIN. MINISTERIO DE OBRAS PUBLICAS Y
URBANISMO
Actuaciones del MOPU en la costa
espanola / Juan Carlos
Fernandez-Ranada.
URBANISMO / COAM 1988 May, no.4,
p.22-29, graphs, map, photos,
secns., aerial photos.

SPAIN--MOLLERUSA--NIGHTCLUBS--INTERIOR
DESIGN--BIG BEN
Club Class / David Redhead, Helen
Elias.
Review of five nightclubs: two in
Norway, one in the United States,
and two in Spain.
DESIGNERS' JOURNAL 1990 Jan.,
no.53, p.[24]-32, axonometric
view, dets., photos., plans.

SPAIN--MOLLET--APARTMENT COMPLEXES
Casa a corte pressa Barcellona =
Courtyard housing near Barcelona /
Silvano Stucchi.
Located in Mollet, 20km from
Barcelona. Architects: Josep
Martorell, Oriol Bohigas, David
Mackay. Includes English
(Continued next page)

SPAIN--MOLLET--APARTMENT COMPLEXES
(CONTINUED)
Casa a corte pressa...(CONTINUED)
translation. French, German, and
Spanish summaries, p.4.
L'INDUSTRIA DELLE COSTRUZIONI 1990
Mar., v.24, no.221, p.34-45,
axonometric view, dets., elevs.,
photos., plans, sketch.

SPAIN--MOLLET--APARTMENT COMPLEXES--
GALLECS
Auf den Spuren der Katalanischen
Moderne: neue Arbeiten von
Martorell, Bohigas, Mackay.
Three projects: Burobau der
"Sociedad Nestle" in Espluegues de
Llobregat in Barcelona; Wohnanlage
"La Maquinista" in Barceloneta in
Barcelona; Wohnanlage Mollet in
Gallecs in Mollet. One of four
issues on the theme "Barcelona
bauen".
BAUWELT 1990 Mar.2, v.81, no.9,
p.378-385, axonometric views,
photos., plans, secns., site
plans.

SPAIN--MONASTERIES
Entrevista: Pedro Navascues del
Palacio: monasterios y catedrales
[interview] / Juan Hernandez.
REALES SITIOS 1990, v.27, no.106,
p.[11]-16, ports.

SPAIN--MORA DE EBRO--HOSPITALS
Architectural landmarks.
Features three buildings by Elias
Torres Tur and Jose Antonio
Martinez Lapena: hospital, Mora de
Ebro; congress center, Barcelona,
and sports hall, Granollers.
ARCHITECTURAL REVIEW 1990 July,
v.188, no.1121, p.52-59, elevs.,
models, photos., plans, secns.,
site plan.

SPAIN--MORELLA--SCHOOLS--BOARDING
Provocative and participatory
places.
Features seven projects in the
Barcelona area by Enric Miralles
and Carme Pinos.
ARCHITECTURAL REVIEW 1990 July,
v.188, no.1121, p.74-89, dets.,
ill., elevs., plans, secns., site
plans, sketches.

SPAIN--MOSTOLES--CLINICS
Contexual construction.
Features the Zaragoza library and
health center in Mostoles.
Architects: Victor Lopez Cotelo
and Carlos Puente.
ARCHITECTURAL REVIEW 1990 July,
v.188, no.1121, p.38-43, elevs.,
photos., plans, secn., site plans.

SPAIN--MURCIA--CULTURAL CENTERS
Progetto per la ristrutturazione dei
Mulini Vecchi di Murcia = Project
for the reconversion of the old
watermills of Murcia / Juan
Navarro Baldeweg.
Architects: Juan Navarro Baldeweg
with Jose Maria Merce.
LOTUS INTERNATIONAL 1986, no.52,
p.26-29, elevs., model, photo.,
plans, secns., site plans.

SPAIN--MURCIA--HOUSES--ALTERATIONS AND
ADDITIONS
La arquitectura de Vetges Tu:
Mediterrania = The architecture of
Vetges Tu: Mediterrania.
Most of issue devoted to works by
this Spanish firm. Contents:
Jardin del Turia, Valencia;
Televisio Valenciana; cementerio
de Tavernes de la Valldigna;
Centro escolar publico en Port de
Sagunt; viviendas en quart de
Poblet; estudio de detalle y
viviendas en La Flota, Murcia; dos
viviendas rehabilitadas en la
huerta murciana; vestuarios en
tavernes de la Valldigna,
Valencia. Text in Italian and
English.
ON DISENO 1990, no.112(suppl.),
p.113-191, axonometric views,
ill., dwgs., elevs., models,
photos., plans, site plans, aerial
photos.

SPAIN--MURCIA--HOUSING--PUBLIC--LA
FLOTA
La arquitectura de Vetges Tu:
Mediterrania = The architecture of
Vetges Tu: Mediterrania.
Most of issue devoted to works by
this Spanish firm. Contents:
Jardin del Turia, Valencia;
Televisio Valenciana; cementerio
de Tavernes de la Valldigna;
Centro escolar publico en Port de
Sagunt; viviendas en quart de
Poblet; estudio de detalle y
viviendas en La Flota, Murcia; dos
viviendas rehabilitadas en la
huerta murciana; vestuarios en
tavernes de la Valldigna,
Valencia. Text in Italian and
English.
ON DISENO 1990, no.112(suppl.),
p.113-191, axonometric views,
ill., dwgs., elevs., models,
photos., plans, site plans, aerial
photos.

SPAIN--MURCIA--MUSEUMS--ART
Rehabilitacion de Colegio de San
Esteban de Murcia: J. Plaza, E.
Sancho, V. Perez, M. de la Villa,
P. Sanmartin y S. Moreno.
Spanish, English text.
ON DISENO 1990, no.109, p.128-135,
photos., plans.

SPAIN--MURCIA--MUSEUMS--INDUSTRIAL--
CENTRO CULTURAL Y MUSEO HIDRAULICO
Guided by the river's current /
Philip Arcidi.
On the Hydraulics Museum, (Centro
Cultural y Museo Hidraulico),
Murcia, Spain. Architect: Juan
Navarro Baldeweg. Museum
incorporates old mill building.
PROGRESSIVE ARCHITECTURE 1990 May,
v.71, no.5, p.106-107, elevs.,
photos., secn., plans.
Kulturzentrum und Museum fur
Hydraulik in Murcia, Spanien.
Architect: Juan Navarro Baldeweg.
BAUWELT 1990 Nov.16, v.81,
no.42-43, p.2140-2144, photos.,
plans, secn.
Murcia metaphors / Peter Buchanan.
The Centro Culturel y Museo
Hidraulico, Murcia, Spain which
incorporates an historic mill.
Architect: Juan Navarro Baldeweg.
(Continued next column)

SPAIN--MURCIA--MUSEUMS--INDUSTRIAL--
CENTRO CULTURAL Y MUSEO HIDRAULICO
(CONTINUED)
Murcia metaphors /...(CONTINUED)
ARCHITECTURAL REVIEW 1990 June,
v.187, no.1120, p.48-[56], elev.,
photos., plans, secns., site plan.
Public facilities.
Part of a special feature on
Spanish contemporary architecture.
Contents: Museo de Navarra, by
Jordi Garces, Enric Soria.--
Biblioteca Publica, by Victor
Lopez Cotelo, Carlos Puente.--
Molinos del Rio Segura, by Juan
Navarro Baldeweg.-- Puerta de
Toledo, by Nuan Navarro
Baldeweg.-- Escuela de artes y
oficios artisticos, by Jose
Antonio Corrales.-- Instituto
Hugue, by Luis Bravo Farre, Albert
Blanch Rubio.-- Brief Histories.
Text in Japanese.
SPACE DESIGN 1990 May, no.308,
p.11-54, ports., elevs., photos.,
plans, secns., site plans.

SPAIN--MURCIA--SCHOOLS--ALTERATIONS
AND ADDITIONS--COLEGIO DE SAN
ESTEBAN
Rehabilitacion de Colegio de San
Esteban de Murcia: J. Plaza, E.
Sancho, V. Perez, M. de la Villa,
P. Sanmartin y S. Moreno.
Spanish, English text.
ON DISENO 1990, no.109, p.128-135,
photos., plans.

SPAIN--MURCIA--WATER MILLS--
ALTERATIONS AND ADDITIONS
Progetto per la ristrutturazione dei
Mulini Vecchi di Murcia = Project
for the reconversion of the old
watermills of Murcia / Juan
Navarro Baldeweg.
Architects: Juan Navarro Baldeweg
with Jose Maria Merce.
LOTUS INTERNATIONAL 1986, no.52,
p.26-29, elevs., model, photo.,
plans, secns., site plans.

SPAIN--MUSEUMS--20TH CENTURY
Museos a media luz: noticias desde
el ano noventa / Carlos Baztan.
English text, p.83-86.
A & V 1990, no.26, p.8-17, dets.,
dwgs., models, photos., plans.
El protagonismo del contenedor:
espacios para el arte y la cultura
/ Josep Maria Montaner.
On new Spanish museums. English
text, p.87-89.
A & V 1990, no.26, p.18-24, dwgs.,
elev., models, photos., plans,
secns., sketches.

SPAIN--MUSEUMS--20TH CENTURY--ART
El protagonismo del contenedor:
espacios para el arte y la cultura
/ Josep Maria Montaner.
On new Spanish museums. English
text, p.87-89.
A & V 1990, no.26, p.18-24, dwgs.,
elev., models, photos., plans,
secns., sketches.

AVERY INDEX TO ARCHITECTURAL PERIODICALS

SPAIN--MUSEUMS--ART
Eslabones de una tradicion ausente:
breve historia de los museos
espanoles / Alfonso Munoz.
English text, p.81-82.
A & V 1990, no.26, p.4-7, elevs.,
photos., plans, refs.

SPAIN--MUSEUMS--ART--CONSERVATION AND
RESTORATION--BARCELONA--PALACIO
NACIONAL
Iniziato il restauro del "Palau
Nacional" di Barcellana.
Built in 1929 (architects:
Domenech, Cendoya e Cata).
L'INDUSTRIA DELLE COSTRUZIONI 1990
Oct., v.24, no.228, p.79, model,
photo.

SPAIN--MUSEUMS--HISTORY
Eslabones de una tradicion ausente:
breve historia de los museos
espanoles / Alfonso Munoz.
English text, p.81-82.
A & V 1990, no.26, p.4-7, elevs.,
photos., plans, refs.

SPAIN--NARON--INDUSTRIAL PARKS--RIO DO
POZO
Actuacion urbanistica industrial
"Rio do Pozo", en Naron (La
Coruna).
URBANISMO / COAM 1990 Sept.,
no.11, p.107-108, map, plan,
table.

SPAIN--OFFICES--INTERIOR DESIGN
ON oficina 1990.
Special supplement issue featuring
office interiors in Spain. 13
projects indexed separately. Text
in Spanish, with English
translations, p.172-190.
ON DISENO 1990, suppl., p.entire
issue (190 p.), dwg., photos.,
plans, secns.

SPAIN--OLD TOWNS--CONSERVATION AND
RESTORATION
Un programa de planeamiento de
centros historicos / Rufina
Fernandez.
URBANISMO / COAM 1990 Jan., no.9,
p.54-56, photo.

SPAIN--OLITE--INSTALLATION WORKS
Plaza en Olite: Francisco Mangado
Beloqui, arquitecto.
Spanish, English text.
ON DISENO 1990, no.111, p.85-99,
dets., photos., site plans.

SPAIN--OLITE--PLAZAS
Plaza en Olite: Francisco Mangado
Beloqui, arquitecto.
Spanish, English text.
ON DISENO 1990, no.111, p.85-99,
dets., photos., site plans.

SPAIN OLITE PLAZAS ALTERATIONS AND
ADDITIONS--PLAZA DE OLITE
Plaza de Olite, Spanien = Plaza de
Olite, Spain.
Plaza in historic center
redesigned to link the modern town
and center. Architect: Francisco
Mangado Beloqui.
ARCHITEKTUR + WETTBEWERBE 1990
Dec., no.144, p.8-9, photos., site
plan.

SPAIN--OROPESA--CHURCHES--17TH
CENTURY--IGLESIA DE SAN BERNARDO
La iglesia de San Bernardo en
Oropesa (Toledo), disenada por
Francisco de Mora / Luis Cervera
Vera.
Early 17th cent. church had
previously been attributed to Juan
de Herrera.
ARCHIVO ESPANOL DE ARTE 1990
Apr.-June, v.63, no.250,
p.[199]-218, dets., dwgs., elevs.,
plans, secns., biblio., refs.

SPAIN--PALOMERAS--HOUSING--UNIDAD 24
Edificio de viviendas en Palomeras:
Pablo Carvajal y Juan Montes,
arquitectos.
Spanish, English summary.
ON DISENO 1990, no.110, p.140-149,
photos., plan.

SPAIN--PAMPLONA--MUSEUMS--ART--
ALTERATIONS AND ADDITIONS--MUSEO DE
NAVARRA
Museo de Navarra = Museum
remodelling: Pamplona, 1986/1990.
Architects: Jordi Garces, Enric
Soria.
EL CROQUIS 1990 Apr.-June, v.9,
no.43, p.68-91, elev., photos.,
plans, secns., site plans.
Public facilities.
Part of a special feature on
Spanish contemporary architecture.
Contents: Museo de Navarra, by
Jordi Garces, Enric Soria.--
Biblioteca Publica, by Victor
Lopez Cotelo, Carlos Puente.--
Molinos del Rio Segura, by Juan
Navarro Baldeweg.-- Puerta de
Toledo, by Nuan Navarro
Baldeweg.-- Escuela de artes y
oficios artisticos, by Jose
Antonio Corrales.-- Instituto
Hugue, by Luis Bravo Farre, Albert
Blanch Rubio.-- Brief Histories.
Text in Japanese.
SPACE DESIGN 1990 May, no.308,
p.11-54, ports., elevs., photos.,
plans, secns., site plans.
El seno anadido: Museo de Navarra,
Pamplona.
Museum remodelling. Architects:
Jordi Garces, Enric Soria. English
text, p.90-91.
A & V 1990, no.26, p.42-46, dwgs.,
photos., plans, secns., site plan.

SPAIN--PARETS DEL VALLES--PLAZAS--
PLACA MAYOR
Konstruktivistische Ansatze aus
Katalonien: neue Arbeiten von
Miralles und Pinos.
Three projects: Platzgestaltung
"Placa Mayor" in Parets del
Valles; Friedhofsanlage mit
Kapelle in Igualada; Soziales
Begegnungszentrum "La Pista" in
Hostalets. One of four articles
on the theme "Barcelona bauen".
BAUWELT 1990 Mar.2, v.81, no.9,
p.392-395, photos., plans, secns.,
site plans.

SPAIN--PATERNA--INDUSTRIAL PARKS
Parque technologico de Paterna
(Valencia).
URBANISMO / COAM 1990 Sept.,
no.11, p.90-92, model, map, plan,
table.

SPAIN--PLAZAS
Platze und Freiraume in Spanien -
auf der Suche nach einer
kulturellen Tradition / U.P.W.
Nagel.
ARCHITEKTUR + WETTBEWERBE 1990
Dec., no.144, p.4-5, port.,
photos., aerial photo.

SPAIN--POLIGON CAN PARELLADA--
FACTORIES--BESSIUS, S.A.
Fabrica textil = Textile factory.
Located in Poligon Can Parellada,
Spain. Architects: Yago Conde,
Jose Manuel Mir. Text in Catalan
and English.
QUADERNS D'ARQUITECTURA I
URBANISME 1988 July-Sept., no.178,
p.90-93, photos., plans, secns.

SPAIN--PORT DE SAGUNT--SCHOOLS
La arquitectura de Vetges Tu:
Mediterrania = The architecture of
Vetges Tu: Mediterrania.
Most of issue devoted to works by
this Spanish firm. Contents:
Jardin del Turia, Valencia;
Televisio Valenciana; cementerio
de Tavernes de la Valldigna;
Centro escolar publico en Port de
Sagunt; viviendas en quart de
Poblet; estudio de detalle y
vivendas en La Flota, Murcia; dos
viviendas rehabilitadas en la
huerta murciana; vestuarios en
tavernes de la Valldigna,
Valencia. Text in Italian and
English.
ON DISENO 1990, no.112(suppl.),
p.113-191, axonometric views,
ill., dwgs., elevs., models,
photos., plans, site plans, aerial
photos.

SPAIN--POTES--CITY PLANNING
Plan especial de proteccion in
reform interior de Pores / J.
Aguilera, J. de la Dehesa, D.
Pe'rez-Medina.
URBANISMO / COAM 1990 Jan., no.9,
p.72-79, photos., plans, site
plans, aerial photos.

SPAIN--POTES--COMPREHENSIVE PLANS
Plan especial de proteccion in
reform interior de Pores / J.
Aguilera, J. de la Dehesa, D.
Pe'rez-Medina.
URBANISMO / COAM 1990 Jan., no.9,
p.72-79, photos., plans, site
plans, aerial photos.

SPAIN--PUBLIC BUILDINGS--20TH CENTURY
Public facilities.
Part of a special feature on
Spanish contemporary architecture.
Contents: Museo de Navarra, by
Jordi Garces, Enric Soria.--
Biblioteca Publica, by Victor
Lopez Cotelo, Carlos Puente.--
Molinos del Rio Segura, by Juan
Navarro Baldeweg.-- Puerta de
Toledo, by Nuan Navarro
Baldeweg.-- Escuela de artes y
oficios artisticos, by Jose
(Continued next page)

Page 2445

SPAIN--PUBLIC BUILDINGS--20TH CENTURY
(CONTINUED)
Public facilities. (CONTINUED)
Antonio Corrales.-- Instituto
Hugue, by Luis Bravo Farre, Albert
Blanch Rubio.-- Brief Histories.
Text in Japanese.
SPACE DESIGN 1990 May, no.308,
p.11-54, ports., elevs., photos.,
plans, secns., site plans.

SPAIN--PUERTO DE SANTA MARIA--WEEKEND
HOUSES--SLOPING SITES--GUARDIOLA
HOUSE
Eisenman Architects [houses].
Contents: Guardiola house, Puerto
de Santa Maria, Cadiz, Spain, 1988
-- Social housing for 200,000th
home housing fesival at
Dedemsvaartweg, the Hague,
Netherlands, 1989. Architects:
Eisenman Architects. Text in
Japanese and English.
GA HOUSES 1990 Mar., no.28,
p.20-26, axonometric views, dwgs.,
models, photos., plans., secns.
Peter Eisenman.
Most of the issue devoted to this
architect. Nine projects featured.
Includes interview with David
Cohn. Text in Spanish and English.
EL CROQUIS 1989 Dec., v.8, no.41,
p.4-126,cover, axonometric views,
ill., dwgs., ports., elevs.,
models, photos., plans, secns.,
refs.

SPAIN--RAILROADS
La insercion de la red ferroviaria
espanola en la malla europea de
alta velocidad = The inclusion of
the Spanish railway network in the
European hig [sic]-speed system /
A. Lopez Pita.
English summary, p.57.
URBANISMO / COAM 1990 May, no.10,
p.48-57, graphs, maps, tables.

SPAIN--RECOPOLIS--BASILICAS--VISIGOTH
Arquitectura religiosa y
organizacion liturgica en epoca
visigoda: la basilica de Recopolis
/ Lauro Olmo Enciso.
Spanish and English summaries.
ARCHIVO ESPANOL DE ARQUEOLOGIA
1988, v.61, nos.157-158,
p.[157]-178, maps, plans, refs.

SPAIN--REGIONAL PLANNING
Landscape planning in Spain / Miguel
Aguilo, Santiago Gonzalez Alonso,
Angel Ramos.
BUILT ENVIRONMENT 1990, v.16,
no.2, p.98-110, map, photos.,
tables, refs.
Territorio struttura urbana e
pianificazione: gli antecedenti /
Oriol Nel lo.
Regional and urban planning in
Spain from 1959 to the present. In
Italian.
URBANISTICA 1989 Mar., no.94,
p.72-74,

SPAIN--REUS--HOUSES--ART NOUVEAU--
INTERIOR DESIGN--CASA NAVAS
Homage to Catalonia [Casa Navas] /
Maria Font de Rubinat.
House in Reus, built 1902-1907 for
Joaquim Navas. Architect: Lluis
Domenech i Montaner.
ART & ANTIQUES 1990 Nov., v.7,
(Continued next column)

SPAIN--REUS--HOUSES--ART NOUVEAU--
INTERIOR DESIGN--CASA NAVAS
(CONTINUED)
Homage to Catalonia...(CONTINUED)
no.9, p.[78]-[83], photos.

SPAIN--ROADS
Un nuevo plan de carreteras urbanas
y interurbanas (1992-2000) = A new
plan for urban and intercity roads
(1992/2000) / Justo Borrajo, Jesus
Rubio.
English summary, p.19.
URBANISMO / COAM 1990 May, no.10,
p.6-19, maps, photos., tables,
aerial photos.

SPAIN--RURAL DEVELOPMENT--20TH
CENTURY--HISTORY
Actuaciones del Instituto Nacional
de Colonization 1939-1970 / Jose
Tames Alarcon.
Whole issue devoted to planning in
rural environments. English
summary on p.12.
URBANISMO / COAM 1988 Jan., no.3,
p.4-12, dwgs., maps, plans, site
plans, aerial photos.

SPAIN--RURAL LAND USE--20TH CENTURY--
HISTORY
Actuaciones del Instituto Nacional
de Colonization 1939-1970 / Jose
Tames Alarcon.
Whole issue devoted to planning in
rural environments. English
summary on p.12.
URBANISMO / COAM 1988 Jan., no.3,
p.4-12, dwgs., maps, plans, site
plans, aerial photos.

SPAIN--SAGUNTO--THEATERS--OPEN-AIR--
TEATRO ROMANO
Due progetti di Giorgio Grassi a
Venezia [exhibition review].
Exhibition at the Fondazione A.
Masieri, on the Teatro romano.
L'INDUSTRIA DELLE COSTRUZIONI 1990
May, v.24, no.223, p.68-69,
axonometric view, elev., models,
secns., site plan.

SPAIN--SAGUNTO--THEATERS--ROMAN--
ALTERATIONS AND ADDITIONS
Due progetti di Giorgio Grassi a
Venezia [exhibition review].
Exhibition at the Fondazione A.
Masieri, on the Teatro romano.
L'INDUSTRIA DELLE COSTRUZIONI 1990
May, v.24, no.223, p.68-69,
axonometric view, elev., models,
secns., site plan.

SPAIN--SALAMANCA--CONVENTION
FACILITIES
Citadels and communion.
Features the designs for the
Salamanca and Cadiz conference
centers. Architect: Juan Navarro
Baldeweg.
ARCHITECTURAL REVIEW 1990 July,
v.188, no.1121, p.32-37, ill.,
elevs., models, photos., plans,
secns., site plan.
La cupula ingravida: Palacio de
Congresos, Salamanca = The
weightless dome.
Architect: Juan Navarro Baldeweg.
English text, p.92.
A & V 1990, no.24, p.58-63,
elevs., photos., plans, sketch.

SPAIN--SALAMANCA--UNIVERSITIES AND
COLLEGES--BUILDINGS--COMPETITIONS--
UNIVERSIDAD SALAMANCA
Concurso de anteproyectos para el
campus de ciencas
juridicas-sociales y empresiales,
Univ. Salamanca, Nov. 1989.
First prize to Luis Garcia Gil, et
al..
ARQUITECTURA 1990 Jan.-Feb., v.72,
no.282, p.18-19, elevs., plans,
site plan.

SPAIN--SAN MARTI VELL--HOUSES--
INTERIOR DESIGN--PERETTI HOUSE
Le beau, le brut et le brilliant /
Sonia Rachline.
Features interiors of one of Elsa
Peretti's houses in San Marti
Vell, Spain. English summary,
p.III.
MAISON FRANCAISE 1990 Nov.,
no.441, p.74-[81], photos.

SPAIN--SAN MARTI VELL--HOUSES--STONE--
INTERIOR DESIGN--PERETTI HOUSE
Elsa Peretti in Spain / Regan
Charles.
House in the village of San Marti
Vell.
ELLE DECOR 1990 Apr., v.1, no.3,
p.84-93, photos.

SPAIN--SAN SADURNI DE NOYA--ART
SCHOOLS--ESCOLA D'ARTS I OFICIS
Escola d'Arts i Oficis = Arts and
Crafts School.
1884 unfinished hospital converted
to art school, San Saturnino de
Noya, Spain. Original architect:
Ubaldo Iranzo. Conversion
architects: Enric Soria, Jordi
Garces. Text in Catalan and
English.
QUADERNS D'ARQUITECTURA I
URBANISME 1988 July-Sept., no.178,
p.[81-85], photos., plan.

SPAIN--SAN SADURNI DE NOYA--SCHOOLS--
VOCATIONAL--CAVAS RAVENTOS BLANC
Archaic in Arcadia.
Features two wine-related projects
in Sant-Sadurni d'Anoia by Jaume
Bach and Gabriel Mora: Raventos
Blanc winery, and the school of
viticulture and enology.
ARCHITECTURAL REVIEW 1990 July,
v.188, no.1121, p.60-67, elevs.,
photos., plans, secns., site
plans, aerial photos.
Archaische Anklange an Arkadien:
Weinkellerei und Schule fur
Weinbau in Sant Sadurni d'Anota
[sic], 1986-1988.
Architects: Jaume Bach & Gabriel
Mora.
WERK, BAUEN + WOHNEN 1990 Nov.,
no.11, p.2-11, elevs., photos.,
plans, secns., site plans, aerial
photo.
Meister der sensuellen Form: neue
Arbeiten von Bach und Mora.
Three projects: Kindertagesstatte
"Torre Baldovina" in Santa Coloma
de Gramenet; Weinbausschule "Merce
Rosell" in Espiells; Weinkellerei
"Cavas Raventos Blanc" in Sant
Sadurni d'Anoia. One of four
articles on the theme "Barcelona
bauen".
BAUWELT 1990 Mar.2, v.81, no.9,
p.386-387, axonometric view,
plans, photos.

SPAIN--SAN SADURNI DE NOYA--SCHOOLS--
VOCATIONAL--CAVAS RAVENTOS BLANC
(CONTINUED)
Spagna, Alto Penedes: le Cantine
Raventos i Blanc = Spain, Alto
Penedes: the Raventos i Blanc
Winery / Tamara Molinari.
Architects: Jaume Bach, Gabriel
Mora.
ABITARE 1990 June, no.286,
p.134-[141], photos, plans,
secns., site plan, aerial photo.

SPAIN--SAN SADURNI DE NOYA--WINE
CELLARS--CAVAS RAVENTOS BLANC
Archaic in Arcadia.
Features two wine-related projects
in Sant-Sadurni d'Anoia by Jaume
Bach and Gabriel Mora: Raventos
Blanc winery, and the school of
viticulture and enology.
ARCHITECTURAL REVIEW 1990 July,
v.188, no.1121, p.60-67, elevs.,
photos., plans, secns., site
plans, aerial photos.
Archaische Anklange an Arkadien:
Weinkellerei und Schule fur
Weinbau in Sant Sadurni d'Anota
[sic], 1986-1988.
Architects: Jaume Bach & Gabriel
Mora.
WERK, BAUEN + WOHNEN 1990 Nov.,
no.11, p.2-11, elevs., photos.,
plans, secns., site plans, aerial
photo.
Meister der sensuellen Form: neue
Arbeiten von Bach und Mora.
Three projects: Kindertagesstatte
"Torre Baldovina" in Santa Coloma
de Gramenet; Weinbausschule "Merce
Rosell" in Espiells; Weinkellerei
"Cavas Raventos Blanc" in Sant
Sadurni d'Anoia. One of four
articles on the theme "Barcelona
bauen".
BAUWELT 1990 Mar.2, v.81, no.9,
p.386-387, axonometric view,
plans, photos.
Spagna, Alto Penedes: le Cantine
Raventos i Blanc = Spain, Alto
Penedes: the Raventos i Blanc
Winery / Tamara Molinari.
Architects: Jaume Bach, Gabriel
Mora.
ABITARE 1990 June, no.286,
p.134-[141], photos, plans,
secns., site plan, aerial photo.

SPAIN--SAN SADURNI DE NOYA--WINERIES--
CAVAS RAVENTOS BLANC
Archaische Anklange an Arkadien:
Weinkellerei und Schule fur
Weinbau in Sant Sadurni d'Anota
[sic], 1986-1988.
Architects: Jaume Bach & Gabriel
Mora.
WERK, BAUEN + WOHNEN 1990 Nov.,
no.11, p.2-11, elevs., photos.,
plans, secns., site plans, aerial
photo.
Meister der sensuellen Form: neue
Arbeiten von Bach und Mora.
Three projects: Kindertagesstatte
"Torre Baldovina" in Santa Coloma
de Gramenet; Weinbausschule "Merce
Rosell" in Espiells; Weinkellerei
"Cavas Raventos Blanc" in Sant
Sadurni d'Anoia. One of four
articles on the theme "Barcelona
bauen".
BAUWELT 1990 Mar.2, v.81, no.9,
p.386-387, axonometric view,
plans, photos.

SPAIN--SAN SADURNI DE NOYA--WINERIES--
CAVAS RAVENTOS BLANC (CONTINUED)
Spagna, Alto Penedes: le Cantine
Raventos i Blanc = Spain, Alto
Penedes: the Raventos i Blanc
Winery / Tamara Molinari.
Architects: Jaume Bach, Gabriel
Mora.
ABITARE 1990 June, no.286,
p.134-[141], photos, plans,
secns., site plan, aerial photo.

SPAIN--SAN SEBASTIAN--AUDITORIUMS,
CONCERT HALLS--COMPETITIONS
Seis propuestas para el solar k de
San Sebastian: concurso
internacional = Six proposals for
site K in San Sebastian:
international competition.
Proposals for a conference center
and auditorium and exhibition
hall. Architects: Rafael Moneo,
Juan Navarro Baldeweg, Pena
Ganchegui/Corrales, Mario Botta,
Foster Associates, and Arata
Isozaki & Associates. Includes
critical commentary by Richard
Levene and Fernando Marquez
Cecilia. In English and Spanish.
EL CROQUIS 1990 Apr.-June, v.9,
no.43, p.[4]-40, ill., elevs.,
photos., plans, secns., site
plans, aerial photos.

SPAIN--SAN SEBASTIAN--CONVENTION
FACILITIES--COMPETITIONS
Seis propuestas para el solar k de
San Sebastian: concurso
internacional = Six proposals for
site K in San Sebastian:
international competition.
Proposals for a conference center
and auditorium and exhibition
hall. Architects: Rafael Moneo,
Juan Navarro Baldeweg, Pena
Ganchegui/Corrales, Mario Botta,
Foster Associates, and Arata
Isozaki & Associates. Includes
critical commentary by Richard
Levene and Fernando Marquez
Cecilia. In English and Spanish.
EL CROQUIS 1990 Apr.-June, v.9,
no.43, p.[4]-40, ill., elevs.,
photos., plans, secns., site
plans, aerial photos.

SPAIN--SAN SEBASTIAN--CULTURAL
CENTERS--COMPETITIONS
San Sebastian, concorso per un
centro culturale / Alberto
Ustarroz.
Projects by Juan N. Baldeweg,
Mario Botta, Norman Foster, Arata
Isozaki, Luis Pena, and Rafael
Moneo (winner). Text in Italian
and English.
DOMUS 1990 Dec., no.722,
p.[48-55],XXIV, dwgs., elevs.,
models, plans, secns., site plans,
aerial photos.

SPAIN--SAN SEBASTIAN--EXHIBITION
BUILDINGS--COMPETITIONS
Seis propuestas para el solar k de
San Sebastian: concurso
internacional = Six proposals for
site K in San Sebastian:
international competition.
Proposals for a conference center
and auditorium and exhibition
hall. Architects: Rafael Moneo,
Juan Navarro Baldeweg, Pena
(Continued next column)

SPAIN--SAN SEBASTIAN--EXHIBITION
BUILDINGS--COMPETITIONS
(CONTINUED)
Seis propuestas para... (CONTINUED)
Ganchegui/Corrales, Mario Botta,
Foster Associates, and Arata
Isozaki & Associates. Includes
critical commentary by Richard
Levene and Fernando Marquez
Cecilia. In English and Spanish.
EL CROQUIS 1990 Apr.-June, v.9,
no.43, p.[4]-40, ill., elevs.,
photos., plans, secns., site
plans, aerial photos.

SPAIN--SAN SEBASTIAN--GAMBLING
CASINOS--ALTERATIONS AND ADDITIONS--
COMPETITIONS--KURSAAL
Centro Kursaal, San Sebastian, Abril
1990.
Competition projects by: Rafael
Moneo (first prize), Mario Botta,
Foster & Associates, Arata Isozaki
& Assoc., Juan Navarro Baldeweg.
Includes a history of the
competition by Miguel A. Alonso de
Val.
ARQUITECTURA 1990 Mar.-June, v.72,
no.283-284, p.25-49, dwgs.,
elevs., models, plans, secns.,
site plans.

SPAIN--SANT ADRIA DEL BESOS--
PEDESTRIAN BRIDGES--CALLE ALARCON
Pasarela peatonal en Sant Adria del
Besos: Josep I. de Llorens y A.
Soldevila, arquitectos.
Pedestrian walkway. Spanish,
English text.
ON DISENO 1990, no.113, p.138-145,
elevs., photos.

SPAIN--SANT BOI DE LLUCANES--BELL
TOWERS--18TH CENTURY
Restauracion del campanario de la
iglesia de Sant Boi de Llucanes:
Josep Rovira, arquitecto.
Spanish, English text.
ON DISENO 1990, no.110, p.164-169,
elevs., photos., secn.

SPAIN--SANT FELIU DE GUIXOLS--HOUSES--
20TH CENTURY--CASA SALGOT
Casa Salgot = Single-family house:
Sant Feliu de Guixols, Gerona,
1989.
Architects: Jordi Garces, Enric
Soria.
EL CROQUIS 1990 Apr.-June, v.9,
no.43, p.60-67, photos., plans,
site plan.
Spagna: Sant Feliu de Guixols, 1989,
Casa Salgot = Spain: the Salgot
house.
On the Costa Brava. Architects:
Jordi Garces, Enric Soria.
ABITARE 1990 June, no.286,
p.106-111, photos., plans, site
plan.

SPAIN--SANT JOAN DESPI--BRIDGES--20TH
CENTURY--PUENTE FONTSANTA
Puente sobre el Barranco de la
Fontsanta, Sant Joan Despi,
Barcelona, 1987-89.
Architects: Enric Battle, Joan
Roig.
ARQUITECTURA 1990 July-Aug., v.72,
no.285, p.122-125, elevs.,
photos., plans.

SPAIN--SANTA COLOMA DE GRAMENET--DAY
CARE CENTERS--TORRE BALDOVINA
Meister der sensuellen Form: neue
Arbeiten von Bach und Mora.
Three projects: Kindertagesstatte
"Torre Baldovina" in Santa Coloma
de Gramenet; Weinbausschule "Merce
Rosell" in Espiells; Weinkellerei
"Cavas Raventos Blanc" in Sant
Sadurni d'Anoia. One of four
articles on the theme "Barcelona
bauen".
BAUWELT 1990 Mar.2, v.81, no.9,
p.386-387, axonometric view,
plans, photos.

SPAIN--SANTA COLOMA DE QUERALT--PLAZAS
Plaza del Castillo de Santa Coloma
de Queralt: Josep Maria Rovira i
Gimeno, arquitecto.
Spanish, English text.
ON DISENO 1990, no.115, p.154-159,
photos., plan.

SPAIN--SANTA COLOMA DEL QUERALT--
PLAZAS
Plaza y edificio de servicios, Santa
Coloma del Queralt, Tarragona,
1986-89: Jose Maria Rovira Gimeno.
ARQUITECTURA 1990 July-Aug., v.72,
no.285, p.82-87, elev., photos.,
plans, site plans.

SPAIN--SANTA COLOMA DEL QUERALT--
PUBLIC BUILDINGS
Plaza del Castillo de Santa Coloma
de Queralt: Josep Maria Rovira i
Gimeno, arquitecto.
Spanish, English text.
ON DISENO 1990, no.115, p.154-159,
photos., plan.
Plaza y edificio de servicios, Santa
Coloma del Queralt, Tarragona,
1986-89: Jose Maria Rovira Gimeno.
ARQUITECTURA 1990 July-Aug., v.72,
no.285, p.82-87, elev., photos.,
plans, site plans.

SPAIN--SANTANDER--AUDITORIUMS, CONCERT
HALLS--PALACIO DE FESTIVALES
El odeon varado: Teatro de
Festivales, Santander = The
beached odeon.
Architect: Francisco Javier Saenz
de Oiza. English text, p.92.
A & V 1990, no.24, p.68-75,
elevs., photos., plans, secns.,
sketches.

SPAIN--SANTANDER--CAPITOLS--SEDE DE LA
ASEMBLEA REGIONAL DE CANTABRIA
Rehabilitacion del antiguo Hospital
de San Rafael en Santander: Juan
Manuel Sanz y Juan Lopez-Rioboo,
arquitectos.
Spanish, English text.
ON DISENO 1990, no.109, p.136-147,
photos., plans, secn.

SPAIN--SANTANDER--EXHIBITION
BUILDINGS--PALACETE-EMBARCADERO
Rehabilitacion del
Palacete-Embarcadero de Santander:
J. Junquera, E. Perez Pita y M.
Fenwick, arquitectos.
Spanish, English text.
ON DISENO 1990, no.109, p.118-127,
elev., photos., plans, secn.

SPAIN--SANTANDER--HOSPITALS--18TH
CENTURY--ALTERATIONS AND ADDITIONS--
HOSPITAL DE SAN RAFAEL
Rehabilitacion del antiguo Hospital
de San Rafael en Santander: Juan
Manuel Sanz y Juan Lopez-Rioboo,
arquitectos.
Spanish, English text.
ON DISENO 1990, no.109, p.136-147,
photos., plans, secn.

SPAIN--SANTANDER--PIERS--19TH
CENTURY--RUINED, EXTINCT, ETC.
Cantilever piers for shipping iron
ore on the Cantabrian coast of
Spain, 1888-1889 / Jose Sierra
Alvarez.
On the evolution of Belgian
designs by a Spanish construction
company, at six sites in
Santander. Includes abstract.
INDUSTRIAL ARCHAEOLOGY REVIEW 1990
Autumn, v.13, no.1, p.59-68, maps,
photos., secns., refs.

SPAIN--SANTANDER--PIERS--ALTERATIONS
AND ADDITIONS--PALACETE-EMBARCADERO
Rehabilitacion del
Palacete-Embarcadero de Santander:
J. Junquera, E. Perez Pita y M.
Fenwick, arquitectos.
Spanish, English text.
ON DISENO 1990, no.109, p.118-127,
elev., photos., plans, secn.

SPAIN--SANTIAGO DE COMPOSTELA--
AUDITORIUMS, CONCERT HALLS--
AUDITORIO DE GALICIA
Palacio de Congresos, musica y
teatro = convention centre,
Santiago de Compestela, La Coruna,
1986-1989.
Architects: Julio Cano Lasso and
Diego Cano Pintos.
EL CROQUIS 1990 Apr.-June, v.9,
no.43, p.42-51, dets., dwg.,
elevs., photos., plans, secns.

SPAIN--SANTIAGO DE COMPOSTELA--
BARRACKS
Rehabilitacion del edificio de San
Caetano de Santiago de Compostela:
A. Baltar, J. Diaz, M. Gallego y
J. E. Perez-Arda, arquitectos.
Spanish, English text.
ON DISENO 1990, no.109, p.156-163,
elev., photos.

SPAIN--SANTIAGO DE COMPOSTELA--
BARRACKS--ALTERATIONS AND
ADDITIONS--CUARTEL DEL HORREO
Rehabilitacion del Cuartel del
Horreo de Santiago de Compostela:
Manuel-Andres Reboredo,
arquitecto.
Original architects: Antonio
Bermejo y Arteaga and Arturo
Calvo. Spanish, English text.
ON DISENO 1990, no.109, p.106-117,
elevs., photos., plans.

SPAIN--SANTIAGO DE COMPOSTELA--
CAPITOLS
Rehabilitacion del Cuartel del
Horreo de Santiago de Compostela:
Manuel-Andres Reboredo,
arquitecto.
Original architects: Antonio
Bermejo y Arteaga and Arturo
Calvo. Spanish, English text.
ON DISENO 1990. no.109, p.106-117,
elevs., photos., plans.

SPAIN--SANTIAGO DE COMPOSTELA--
CAPITOLS--SEDE DE LAS CONSELLERIAS
DE LA XUNTA DE GALICIA
Rehabilitacion del edificio de San
Caetano de Santiago de Compostela:
A. Baltar, J. Diaz, M. Gallego y
J. E. Perez-Arda, arquitectos.
Spanish, English text.
ON DISENO 1990, no.109, p.156-163,
elev., photos.

SPAIN--SANTIAGO DE COMPOSTELA--
CONVENTION FACILITIES--PALACIO DE
CONGRESOS
Palacio de Congresos, musica y
teatro = convention centre,
Santiago de Compestela, La Coruna,
1986-1989.
Architects: Julio Cano Lasso and
Diego Cano Pintos.
EL CROQUIS 1990 Apr.-June, v.9,
no.43, p.42-51, dets., dwg.,
elevs., photos., plans, secns.

SPAIN--SANTO DOMINGO DE SILOS--RELIEF
(SCULPTURE)--ROMANESQUE
Triumphal visions and monastic
devotion: the annunciation relief
of Santo Domingo de Silos /
Elizabeth Valdez del Alamo.
Located in the lower cloister of
the Benedictine monastery.
Includes abstract.
GESTA 1990, v.29, no.2, p.167-188,
photos., refs.

SPAIN--SCHOOLS--SECONDARY--CALDES DE
MONTBUI
Liceo intorno a un fulcro presso
Barcellona.
Architects: Lluis Bravo, Albert
Blanch.
ARCHITETTURA; CRONACHE E STORIA
1990 May, v.36, no.5(415),
p.368-369, photos., plans, secn.

SPAIN--SEGOVIA--GARDENS
Gardens: a landscape in Segovia /
Nicholas Shrady.
On landscape architect Leandro
Silva Delgado's garden outside the
old walls.
ARCHITECTURAL DIGEST 1990 Oct.,
v.47, no.11, p.[238]-243, 286,
288, photos.

SPAIN--SERRA--HOTELS--PRAIA SOL
Hotel Praia Sol, Serra, ES.
Architects: P. Vargas, G.
Apolinario.
PROJETO 1990 Nov., no.136,
p.45-47, photos., plans, secns.

SPAIN--SEVILLE--APARTMENT HOUSES--
CONSERVATION AND RESTORATION
Sanierung eines Wohngebaudes in
Sevilla = Refurbishment of a
residential building in Seville.
At Plaza del Pan and Calle Huelva.
Architect: G. Vazquez Consuegra.
DETAIL 1990 Oct.-Nov., v.30, no.5,
p.484-485, axonometric view, det.,
photos., plan, secn., site plan.

SPAIN--SEVILLE--APARTMENT HOUSES--
VIVIENDAS RAMON Y CAJAL
  Edificio di abitazioni Ramon y
  Cajal, Siviglia = Ramon y Cajal
  building, Seville.
  38-unit four-storey apartment
  house; architect: Guillermo
  Vasquez Consuegra.
  LOTUS INTERNATIONAL 1989, no.63,
  p.42-49, axonometric views,
  elevs., photos., plans, secns.,
  site plans.
  Housing and residence.
  Part of a special feature on
  Spanish contemporary architecture.
  Contents: Rota, by Antonio
  Gonzalez Cordon.-- Viviendas Ramon
  y Cajal, by Guillermo Vazquez
  Consuegra.-- Castillo de Maqueda,
  by Luis Burnillo Lafarga, Jaime L.
  Lorenzo.-- Casa Turegano, by
  Alberto Campo Baeza.-- Brief
  histories. Text in Japanese.
  SPACE DESIGN 1990 May, no.308,
  p.55-74, ports., elevs., photos.,
  plans, secns., isometric dwgs.
  Spanish context / Peter Buchanan.
  Ramon y Cajal housing project,
  Seville, Spain. Architect:
  Guillermo Vazquez Consuegra.
  ARCHITECTURAL REVIEW 1990 Oct.,
  v.188, no.1124, p.70-75,
  axonometric view, photos., plans,
  secns., site plan.

SPAIN--SEVILLE--ARCHITECTURAL
CENTERS--INSTITUTO DE ARQUITECTURA
  Istituto di architettura di Siviglia
  = Institute of architecture at
  Seville.
  Site: Patio de Banderas.
  Architect: Guillermo Vasquez
  Consuegra.
  LOTUS INTERNATIONAL 1989, no.63,
  p.50-55, photos., plans, secns.

SPAIN--SEVILLE--ARCHIVE BUILDINGS--
ARCHIVO GENERAL DE INDIAS
  La Lonja de Mercaderes de Sevilla:
  de los proyectos a la ejecucion /
  Alfonso Plequezuelo Hernandez.
  History of the 16th cent.
  Sevillian Merchants exchange
  designed by Juan de Herrera. It
  was renovated in the 18th cent. to
  house the Archivo General de
  Indias. English summary, p.15.
  ARCHIVO ESPANOL DE ARTE 1990
  Jan.-Mar., v.63, no.249,
  p.[15]-40, elev., photos., plans,
  secn., refs.

SPAIN--SEVILLE--BRIDGES
  Puentes para un expo = Bridges for
  an Expo / Jose L. Gomez-Ordonez.
  Bridges for Seville, Spain. In
  Spanish and English.
  URBANISMO REVISTA 1989, no.7,
  p.47-48, models, photos., site
  plan.

SPAIN--SEVILLE--BROADCASTING STUDIOS
  Alhambra meets Zonnestraal / Peter
  Buchanan.
  Television studios, Seville.
  Architect: Gonzalo Diaz Recasens.
  ARCHITECTURAL REVIEW 1990 Nov.,
  v.188, no.1125, p.58-63, photos.,
  plans, secns.

SPAIN--SEVILLE--CITY TRAFFIC
  El trafico y el transporte en la
  ciudad de Sevilla = Traffic and
  transport in the city of Seville /
  Miguel Durban.
  English summary, p.47.
  URBANISMO / COAM 1990 May, no.10,
  p.38-47, maps, photos., plans,
  aerial photos.

SPAIN--SEVILLE--CORPORATE OFFICE
BUILDINGS--PREVISION ESPANOLA, S.A.
  Palazzo & Acropolis / Peter
  Buchanan.
  Features new Spanish projects;
  Prevision Espanola headquarters,
  Seville, architect: Rafael Moneo;
  Porta de Toledo social center,
  Madrid, architect: Juan Navarro
  Baldeweg.
  ARCHITECTURAL REVIEW 1990 Jan.,
  v.187, no.1115, p.24-39, dets.,
  elevs., photos., plans, secns.,
  site plan.

SPAIN--SEVILLE--EXHIBITION BUILDINGS--
COMPETITIONS--EXPOSICION UNIVERSAL
1992--AUSTRIAN PAVILION
  Landschaft in der Landschaft.
  Competition project for the
  Austrian pavilion at Expo '92,
  Seville. Architect: Volker
  Giencke.
  BAUFORUM 1990, v.23, no.136,
  p.15-18, dets., dwgs., models,
  plans, secns.

SPAIN--SEVILLE--EXHIBITION BUILDINGS--
COMPETITIONS--EXPOSICION UNIVERSAL
1992--BRITISH PAVILION
  Im Einklang mit den Elementen:
  Wettbewerb: Britischer Pavillen
  fur die Expo 92 in Sevilla.
  First prize: Nicholas Grimshaw and
  Partners.
  ARCH PLUS 1990 July, no.104,
  p.32-33, models, secns.
  Licht, Klang und Temperatur:
  Wettbewerb: Britischer Pavillen
  fur die Expo 92 in Sevilla.
  Entry by Spence & Webster.
  ARCH PLUS 1990 July, no.104,
  p.38-39, dwg., photos., secns.

SPAIN--SEVILLE--EXHIBITION BUILDINGS--
COMPETITIONS--EXPOSICION UNIVERSAL
1992--DANISH PAVILION
  Den danske pavillon i Sevilla.
  Competition entries by KHR; Tage
  Lyneborg; Henning Larsens
  Tegnestue; Tegnestuen Vandkunsten;
  Arkitektfirmaet Kjaer & Richter.
  ARKITEKTEN 1990 Jan., v.92, no.1,
  p.20-28, axonometric views, dwgs.,
  elevs., models, plans, secns.,
  sketches.
  Pavillon du Danemark pour Seville.
  For 1992 World's Fair, Seville.
  Architects: Krohn & Hartvig
  Rasmussen. English summary, p.61.
  ARCHITECTURE D'AUJOURD'HUI 1990
  Feb., no.267, p.60-61, models,
  plans, secn.
  Sevilla - Pavillon til EXPO '92.
  On Danish competition entries for
  the exhibition building in
  Seville. First prize: Krohn &
  Hartvig Rasmussen.
  ARKITEKTEN 1989 Dec.12, v.91,
  no.22, p.572, model.

SPAIN--SEVILLE--EXHIBITION BUILDINGS--
COMPETITIONS--EXPOSICION UNIVERSAL
1992--EUROPEAN COMMUNITY PAVILION
  Gebaude mit variabler Haut / Robin
  Spence.
  Entry for the European Pavilion
  for Expo 92 in Seville.
  Architects: Spence & Webster.
  ARCH PLUS 1990 July, no.104, p.37,
  ill., secns.
  Una immagine per l'Europa: Samyn in
  Seville / Fabrizio Bonomo.
  Competition project by Samyn et
  Associes architects. Text in
  Italian and English.
  L'ARCA 1990 June, no.39
  suppl.l'Arca 2, p.99, dwg., plans,
  secn.
  Six for Seville / John Welsh.
  Features six UK entries for the
  Seville Expo European Community
  Pavilion competition.
  BUILDING DESIGN 1990 Jan.26,
  no.970, p.18-21, ill., elevs.,
  models, plan, secn.

SPAIN--SEVILLE--EXHIBITION BUILDINGS--
COMPETITIONS--EXPOSICION UNIVERSAL
1992--FRENCH PAVILION
  Franzosischer Biennale-Pavillon in
  Venedig.
  First-prize competition entry by
  Jean Nouvel and Emmanuel Cattani.
  Includes English summary.
  BAUMEISTER 1990 Sept., v.87, no.9,
  p.28-29, models, plans, isometric
  dwgs.
  Pavillon francais de Seville: cinq
  projets pour l'exposition
  universelle de 1992.
  Winning architects: Jean-Paul
  Viquier, Jean-Francois Jodry,
  Francois Seigneur. English
  summary, p.68. Spanish summary,
  p.148.
  TECHNIQUES ET ARCHITECTURE 1990
  Mar., no.388, p.64-69, axonometric
  view, dets., ill., dwgs., models,
  plans, site plans..
  Ein Quadrat im Himmel Spaniens:
  Wettbewerb: Franzosischer Pavillon
  fur die Expo 92 in Sevilla.
  First prize: J.-P. Viguier, J.-F.
  Jodry, F. Seigneur.
  ARCH PLUS 1990 July, no.104,
  p.34-35, dwg., models, plans,
  secns.
  Seville, tragi-comedie d'un concours
  / Frederique de Gravelaine.
  On the competition for the French
  pavilion for the 1992 Expo in
  Seville. Winning architects:
  Jean-Paul Viguier, Jean-Francois
  Jodry and Francois Seigneur.
  ARCHITECTURE D'AUJOURD'HUI 1990
  June, no.269, p.16-20, ill.,
  models, plans.

SPAIN--SEVILLE--EXHIBITION BUILDINGS--
COMPETITIONS--EXPOSICION UNIVERSAL
1992--GERMAN PAVILION
  Der deutsche Pavillon auf der EXPO
  '92.
  Report on design of German
  pavillon, "Deutschlandscaft".
  Competition winner: Auer + Weber.
  BAUWELT 1990 Apr.20, v.81, no.15,
  p.741, model.

SPAIN--SEVILLE--URBAN TRANSPORTATION
El trafico y el transporte en la
ciudad de Sevilla = Traffic and
transport in the city of Seville /
Miguel Durban.
English summary, p.47.
URBANISMO / COAM 1990 May, no.10,
p.38-47, maps, photos., plans,
aerial photos.

SPAIN--SEVILLE--WORLD FAIRS--
EXPOSICION UNIVERSAL 1992
How to get your roads repaired /
Callum Murray.
Infrastructure improvements in and
around Seville in preparation for
Expo '92.
ARCHITECTS' JOURNAL 1990 Dec.12,
v.192, no.24, p.14-15, models,
photos, secn.
Parkgestaltung auf dem Gelande der
Weltausstellung / Jose A. Mejias,
M. Cristina Andres.
Park design for Expo '92 on the
Isla de la Cartuja, Seville,
Spain. Includes English summary.
GARTEN UND LANDSCHAFT 1990, v.100,
no.3, p.55-66, map, photos, site
plan.
El recinto apresurado: Sevilla: la
cuenta atras de la Expo / Adela
Garcia-Herrera.
ARQUITECTURA VIVA 1990 Sept.-Oct.,
no.14, p.6-11, elevs., models,
secns.
Verdensudstillingen 1992: the Big
Bang i Sevilla / Martin Keiding.
ARKITEKTEN 1990 Jan., v.92, no.1,
p.18-19, photos.
Een verleden voor de toekomst: de
wereldtentoostelling in Sevilla
1992 / Arjen Oosterman.
ARCHIS 1990 Oct., no.10, p.13-21,
ill., dwgs., models, secns., site
plans, aerial photos.

SPAIN--SHOWROOMS--DESIGN--TAU CERAMICA
Taugres: estructura arquitectonica
de A. Bofill.
Showroom for ceramic products.
Architects: Taller de
Arquitectura.
ON DISENO 1990, "ceramica" suppl.,
p.160-161, photos.

SPAIN--TARAZONA--CHURCHES--17TH
CENTURY--IGLESIA DE OLVES
Estudio documental sobre la Iglesia
de Olves / Maria Sancho Menjon
Ruiz.
SEMINARIO DE ARTE ARAGONES
1988-1989, v.42-43, p.47-65,
photos., biblio., refs.

SPAIN--TARRAGONA--AMPHITHEATERS--
ROMAN--CONSERVATION AND
RESTORATION--CIRCO E DELL'ANFITEATRO
Tarragona: recupero del Circo e
dell'Anfiteatro romano.
Restoration architect: Andrea
Bruno.
L'INDUSTRIA DELLE COSTRUZIONI 1990
Dec., v.24, no.230, p.62-63,
model, photos., secn.

SPAIN--TARRAGONA--BUS STATIONS
Estacion de autobuses en Tarragona:
Lluis Nadal y Enric Beltran,
arquitectos.
Spanish, English text.
ON DISENO 1990, no.110, p.100-109,
photos., plans, secn.

SPAIN--TARRAGONA--MARKETS--MERCADO
VILASECA-SALOU
Gathering establishments.
Part of a special feature on
Spanish contemporary architecture.
Contents: Palau de la Musica
Catalana, by Oscar Tusquets
Blanca, Carlos M. Diaz, Lluis
Clotet, Ignacio Paricio --
Television Andaluza, by Gonzalo
Diaz-Y. Recasens --Banco de
Espana, Jaen, by Rafael Moneo --
Almacenes Simon, by Lluis Clotet,
Ignacio Paricio --Mercado
Vilaseca-Salou, by Carlos Ferrater
Lambarri, Jose Luis Canosa --
Pabellon Rius i Taulet, by Pep
Bonet --Velodromo de Horta, by
Esteban Bonell, Francesc Rius --
Brief histories --Views through
the Camera's Finder, by Hisao
Suzuki. Text in Japanese.
SPACE DESIGN 1990 May, no.308,
p.93-131, dets., ports., elevs.,
model, photos., plans, secns.,
site plan, sketch, isometric dwg.

SPAIN--TENERIFE--INDUSTRIAL PARKS--
GRANADILLA
Parque technologico de Granadilla
(Tenerife) / Juan M.
Alonso-Velasco.
URBANISMO / COAM 1990 Sept.,
no.11, p.87-89, map, plan, table.

SPAIN--TENERIFE--RESEARCH PARKS--
GRANADILLA
Parque technologico de Granadilla
(Tenerife) / Juan M.
Alonso-Velasco.
URBANISMO / COAM 1990 Sept.,
no.11, p.87-89, map, plan, table.

SPAIN--TERUEL--CITY PLANNING
Plan especial del centro historico
de Teruel / J. M. Alonso Velasco,
M. A. Troitino, I. Gonzalez
Adalid.
URBANISMO / COAM 1990 Jan., no.9,
p.80-90, photos., site plan, map.

SPAIN--TERUEL--COMPREHENSIVE PLANS
Plan especial del centro historico
de Teruel / J. M. Alonso Velasco,
M. A. Troitino, I. Gonzalez
Adalid.
URBANISMO / COAM 1990 Jan., no.9,
p.80-90, photos., site plan, map.

SPAIN--TERUEL--HISTORIC DISTRICTS--
CONSERVATION AND RESTORATION
Plan especial del centro historico
de Teruel / J. M. Alonso Velasco,
M. A. Troitino, I. Gonzalez
Adalid.
URBANISMO / COAM 1990 Jan., no.9,
p.80-90, photos., site plan, map.

SPAIN--TILES
Diseno ceramico arquitectura /
Ferran Renau.
Ceramic tile design and
architecture. English text,
p.186-190.
ON DISENO 1990, "ceramica" suppl.,
p.117-129, photos.
Un material que se identifica con la
arquitectura mediterranea / Jose
Luis Porcar.
The use of ceramics in
architecture in Spain. Text in
English, p.176-179.
ON DISENO 1990, "ceramica suppl.,
p.57-71, ill., photos.

SPAIN--TOBED--CEILINGS--MUDEJAR--
IGLESIA DE LA VIRGEN
Un alfarje mudejar en la Iglesia de
la Virgen de Tobed / Celia Uson
Sardana, Ines Ducar Esteban.
Decorated ceiling.
SEMINARIO DE ARTE ARAGONES
1988-1989, v.42-43, p.5-46, dwgs.,
photos., refs.

SPAIN--TOLEDO--ALTARPIECES--BAROQUE--
CAPILLA DE SAN ILDEFONSO
Proyectos para el retablo de la
capilla de San Ildefonso en la
Catedral de Toledo / Jose Maria
Prados.
Features three Baroque designs by
Narciso Tome for the chapel and
the executed altarpiece by Ventura
Rodriguez.
ARCHIVO ESPANOL DE ARTE 1990
Apr.-June, v.63, no.250,
p.288-294, dwgs., photo., plan,
refs.

SPAIN--TOLEDO--BARRACKS--15TH
CENTURY--ALTERATIONS AND ADDITIONS--
CASTILLO DE MAQUEDA
Housing and residence.
Part of a special feature on
Spanish contemporary architecture.
Contents: Rota, by Antonio
Gonzalez Cordon.-- Viviendas Ramon
y Cajal, by Guillermo Vazquez
Consuegra.-- Castillo de Maqueda,
by Luis Burnillo Lafarga, Jaime L.
Lorenzo.-- Casa Turegano, by
Alberto Campo Baeza.-- Brief
histories. Text in Japanese.
SPACE DESIGN 1990 May, no.308,
p.55-74, ports., elevs., photos.,
plans, secns., isometric dwgs.
Umbau des Castillo de Maqueda in
Andalusien.
Architects: L. Burillo Lafarga,
J.L. Lorenzo Saiz-Calleja.
Includes English summary.
BAUMEISTER 1990 May, v.87, no.5,
p.62-63, photos., plan, secns.,
isometric dwg.

SPAIN--TOLEDO--FACADES--MUDEJAR--
AYUNTAMIENTO DE TOLEDO
La fachada mudejar del ayuntamiento
de Toledo: antigua portada del
hospital de nuestra Senora de la
Paz / Clara Delgado Valero,
Ricardo Izquierdo Benito.
English summary, p.289.
ARCHIVO ESPANOL DE ARTE 1989
July-Sept., v.62, no.247,
p.[275]-289, elevs., photos.,
plans, refs.

SPAIN--TOLEDO--HOSPITALS--18TH
CENTURY--HOSPITAL DE NUESTRA SENORA
DE LA VISITACION (HOSPITAL DEL
NUNCIO)
Rehabilitacion del edificio del
Nuncio de Toledo: G. Cabeza, J. M.
Gentil y J. M. Marsa, arquitectos.
Spanish, English text.
ON DISENO 1990, no.109, p.164-171,
axonometric views, photos., plans.

SPAIN--TOLEDO--MURAL PAINTING AND
DECORATION--18TH CENTURY--CATEDRAL
DE TOLEDO--CAPILLA DE SAN ILDEFONSO
Proyectos para el retablo de la
capilla de San Ildefonso en la
Catedral de Toledo / Jose Maria
Prados.
Features three Baroque designs by
Narciso Tome for the chapel and
the executed altarpiece by Ventura
Rodriguez.
ARCHIVO ESPANOL DE ARTE 1990
Apr.-June, v.63, no.250,
p.288-294, dwgs., photo., plan,
refs.

SPAIN--TOLEDO--PUBLIC BUILDINGS--SEDE
DE LOS SERVICIOS CENTRALES
Rehabilitacion del edificio del
Nuncio de Toledo: G. Cabeza, J. M.
Gentil y J. M. Marsa, arquitectos.
Spanish, English text.
ON DISENO 1990, no.109, p.164-171,
axonometric views, photos., plans.

SPAIN--TOLEDO--STORES--CLOTHING
Ilusion color cafe: una tienda de
modas de Mario Bernedo / Yago
Bonnet.
In Toledo.
ARQUITECTURA VIVA 1990 Nov.-Dec.,
no.15, p.60-61, elevs., photos.,
plan.

SPAIN--TOLEDO--STORES--FURNITURE--
PROVISORIA
La Provisoria, Toledo: Benjamin Juan
y J. Gomez-Escalonilla,
arquitectos.
Spanish, English text.
ON DISENO 1989, no.104, p.146-151,
photos., plan.

SPAIN--TOLEDO--STORES--JEWELRY--
ANTONIO IBANEZ
El hueco blanco: una joyeria de Yago
Bonet / Mario Bernedo.
Jewelry store in Toledo.
ARQUITECTURA VIVA 1990 Nov.-Dec.,
no.15, p.58-59, axonometric view,
photos.

SPAIN--TOLOSA--PORTICOES--18TH
CENTURY--SANTA MARIA DE TOLOSA
El portico y el cancel de Santa
Maria de Tolosa: Tomas de Jaurequi
y Jose Ignacio de Lavi / Maria
Isabel Astiazarain Achabal.
Portico and tympanum date from the
1750s-1760s.
ARCHIVO ESPANOL DE ARTE 1990
Oct.-Dec., v.63, no.252,
p.[633]-640, dwg., photos., refs.

SPAIN--TOLOSA--TYMPANA
(ARCHITECTURE)--18TH CENTURY--SANTA
MARIA DE TOLOSA
El portico y el cancel de Santa
Maria de Tolosa: Tomas de Jaurequi
y Jose Ignacio de Lavi / Maria
Isabel Astiazarain Achabal.
Portico and tympanum date from the
1750s-1760s.
ARCHIVO ESPANOL DE ARTE 1990
Oct.-Dec., v.63, no.252,
p.[633]-640, dwg., photos., refs.

SPAIN--TOMELLOSO--MUSEUMS--ART--MUSEO
LOPEZ TORRES
Licht-Kuppel das Lopez Torres Museum
Tomelloso, Spanien / Wilfried
Dechau.
Built 1982-84. Architects: F.
Higueras Diaz, J. Benito Roman.
DEUTSCHE BAUZEITUNG 1990 July,
v.124, no.7, p.76-79, photos.,
plans, secn.

SPAIN--TORDESILLAS--CONVENTS AND
NUNNERIES--CONVENTO DE SANTA CLARA
El regimen juridico de los Reales
Patronatos y el del Convento de
Santa Clara de Tordesillas /
Fernando Diez Moreno.
REALES SITIOS 1990, v.27, no.106,
p.37-44, dwg., photos., refs.

SPAIN--TORDESILLAS--MONASTERIES--
CONSERVATION AND RESTORATION--REAL
MONASTERIO DE SANTA CLARA
Compana general de restauracion en
el Real Monasterio de Tordesillas
/ A. Lobo.
Begun in the 14th cent.
REALES SITIOS 1990, v.27, no.106,
p.21-[28], photos.

SPAIN--TORDESILLAS--MONASTERIES--
MUDEJAR--REAL MONASTERIO DE SANTA
CLARA
Antecedentes historicos del Real
Monasterio de Santa Clara de
Tordesillas / Paloma
Gonzalez-Valcarel Sanchez-Puelles.
REALES SITIOS 1990, v.27, no.106,
p.73-76, dwgs., plans, secns.,
sketch, biblios.
El palacio mudejar de Tordesillas /
Maria Luisa Bujarrabal, Jose Luis
Sancho.
REALES SITIOS 1990, v.27, no.106,
p.29-36, elev., photos., plans.

SPAIN--TORDESILLAS--MURAL PAINTING AND
DECORATION--CONSERVATION AND
RESTORATION--REAL MONASTERIO DE
SANTA CLARA
Compana general de restauracion en
el Real Monasterio de Tordesillas
/ A. Lobo.
Begun in the 14th cent.
REALES SITIOS 1990, v.27, no.106,
p.21-[28], photos.

SPAIN--TORDESILLAS--MURAL PAINTING AND
DECORATION--MUDEJAR--CONSERVATION
AND RESTORATION--REAL MONASTERIO DE
SANTA CLARA--BANOS ARABES
Restauracion de los banos arabes en
el Monasterio de Santa Clara /
Angel Balao Gonzalez.
REALES SITIOS 1990, v.27, no.106,
p.49-54, photos., biblios.

SPAIN--TORDESILLAS--PALACES--MUDEJAR--
CONSERVATION AND RESTORATION--REAL
MONASTERIO DE SANTA CLARA
Restauracion de los banos arabes en
el Monasterio de Santa Clara /
Angel Balao Gonzalez.
REALES SITIOS 1990, v.27, no.106,
p.49-54, photos., biblios.

SPAIN--TORDESILLAS--PALACES--MUDEJAR--
REAL MONASTERIO DE SANTA CLARA
El palacio mudejar de Tordesillas /
Maria Luisa Bujarrabal, Jose Luis
Sancho.
REALES SITIOS 1990, v.27, no.106,
p.29-36, elev., photos., plans.

SPAIN--TOURISM
Landschaftsplanung an Spaniens
Mittelmeerkuste / Christian
Nitsche.
Includes English summary.
GARTEN UND LANDSCHAFT 1990, v.100,
no.3, p.29-32, photos., site plan.

SPAIN--TOURIST TOWNS
Historia del urbanismo contemporaneo
espanol: Emilio Larrodera Lopez /
Luis Rodriguez-Avial ... [et al.].
Entire issue devoted to urban
planning in tourist areas.
URBANISMO / COAM 1988 May, no.4,
p.101-107, ill., ports., plans,
refs.

SPAIN--TRANSPORTATION PLANNING
Un nuevo plan de carreteras urbanas
y interurbanas (1992-2000) = A new
plan for urban and intercity roads
(1992/2000) / Justo Borrajo, Jesus
Rubio.
English summary, p.19.
URBANISMO / COAM 1990 May, no.10,
p.6-19, maps, photos., tables,
aerial photos.

SPAIN--URBAN RENEWAL
Le politiche di recupero dei centri
storici nella Spagna degli anni
Ottanta = Spain's inner-city
rehabilitation policy for the
1980s / Francisco Pol.
In Italian; English captions;
English summary, p.124.
URBANISTICA 1989 Mar., no.94,
p.53-63, axonometric views, dwgs.,
elevs., model, photos., plans,
secns., aerial photos.

SPAIN--VALENCIA--BATHHOUSES--TAVERNES
DE LA VALLDIGNA
La arquitectura de Vetges Tu:
Mediterrania = The architecture of
Vetges Tu: Mediterrania.
Most of issue devoted to works by
this Spanish firm. Contents:
Jardin del Turia, Valencia;
Televisio Valenciana; cementerio
de Tavernes de la Valldigna;
Centro escolar publico en Port de
Sagunt; viviendas en quart de
Poblet; estudio de detalle y
vivendas en La Flota, Murcia; dos
viviendas rehabilitadas en la
huerta murciana; vestuarios en
tavernes de la Valldigna,
Valencia. Text in Italian and
English.
ON DISENO 1990, no.112(suppl.),
p.113-191, axonometric views,
ill., dwgs., elevs., models,
photos., plans, site plans, aerial
photos.

SPAIN--VALENCIA--BRIDGES--PUENTE NEUVE
DE OCTUBRE
Movimento inmovil: Puente 'Neuve de
Octubre', Valencia = Motionless
movement.
Ninth of October bridge, Valencia.
Architect: Santiago Calatrava.
English text, p.91.
A & V 1990, no.24, p.34-39, dets.,
models, secns., sketches.

SPAIN--VALENCIA--CEMETERIES--TAVERNES
DE LA VALLDIGNA
La arquitectura de Vetges Tu:
Mediterrania = The architecture of
Vetges Tu: Mediterrania.
Most of issue devoted to works by
this Spanish firm. Contents:
Jardin del Turia, Valencia;
Televisio Valenciana; cementerio
de Tavernes de la Valldigna;
Centro escolar publico en Port de
Sagunt; viviendas en quart de
Poblet; estudio de detalle y
vivendas en La Flota, Murcia; dos
viviendas rehabilitadas en la
huerta murciana; vestuarios en
tavernes de la Valldigna,
Valencia. Text in Italian and
English.
ON DISENO 1990, no.112(suppl.),
p.113-191, axonometric views,
ill., dwgs., elevs., models,
photos., plans, site plans, aerial
photos.

SPAIN--VALENCIA--CITY PLANNING--
STUDENT PROJECTS
Observaciones sobre la ensenanza de
la urbanistica / Juan Luis Pinon.
Five student redevelopment
projects for Valencia, Spain.
URBANISMO / COAM 1990 Sept.,
no.11, p.109-117, axonometric
views, models, plans, secn., site
plans.

SPAIN--VALENCIA--GARDENS--JARDIN DEL
TURIA
La arquitectura de Vetges Tu:
Mediterrania = The architecture of
Vetges Tu: Mediterrania.
Most of issue devoted to works by
this Spanish firm. Contents:
Jardin del Turia, Valencia;
Televisio Valenciana; cementerio
de Tavernes de la Valldigna;
Centro escolar publico en Port de
Sagunt; viviendas en quart de
Poblet; estudio de detalle y
vivendas en La Flota, Murcia; dos
viviendas rehabilitadas en la
huerta murciana; vestuarios en
tavernes de la Valldigna,
Valencia. Text in Italian and
English.
ON DISENO 1990, no.112(suppl.),
p.113-191, axonometric views,
ill., dwgs., elevs., models,
photos., plans, site plans, aerial
photos.

SPAIN--VALENCIA--HOUSING--PUBLIC--
QUART DE POBLET
La arquitectura de Vetges Tu:
Mediterrania = The architecture of
Vetges Tu: Mediterrania.
Most of issue devoted to works by
this Spanish firm. Contents:
Jardin del Turia, Valencia;
Televisio Valenciana; cementerio
de Tavernes de la Valldigna;
(Continued next column)

SPAIN--VALENCIA--HOUSING--PUBLIC--
QUART DE POBLET (CONTINUED)
La arquitectura de...(CONTINUED)
Centro escolar publico en Port de
Sagunt; viviendas en quart de
Poblet; estudio de detalle y
vivendas en La Flota, Murcia; dos
viviendas rehabilitadas en la
huerta murciana; vestuarios en
tavernes de la Valldigna,
Valencia. Text in Italian and
English.
ON DISENO 1990, no.112(suppl.),
p.113-191, axonometric views,
ill., dwgs., elevs., models,
photos., plans, site plans, aerial
photos.

SPAIN--VALENCIA--MUSEUMS--ART
Restauracion y rehabilitacion del
Palacio del Marques de Campo de
Valencia: Manuel Portaceli,
arquitecto.
Adapted into an art museum.
Spanish, English text.
ON DISENO 1990, no.111, p.122-137,
photos., plans, secn.

SPAIN--VALENCIA--MUSEUMS--ART--
INSTITUTO VALENCIANO DE ARTE MODERNO
Caja Juerte: Instituto Valenciano de
Arte Moderno, Valencia.
Architects: Emilio Gimenez Julian,
Vicent Garcia, Jose Francisco
Murcia Vidal, Carlos Salvadores
Navarro, Joaquin Vicente Sanchis
Serrano. English summary, p.90.
A & V 1990, no.26, p.32-34,
elevs., photos., plans, secns.
Institut Valencia d'Art Modern:
Emilio Gimenez Julian, arquitecto.
Spanish and English text.
ON DISENO 1989, no.106, p.89-101,
photos., plans.

SPAIN--VALENCIA--PALACES--18TH
CENTURY--ALTERATIONS AND ADDITIONS--
PALACIO DEL MARQUES DE CAMPO
Restauracion y rehabilitacion del
Palacio del Marques de Campo de
Valencia: Manuel Portaceli,
arquitecto.
Adapted into an art museum.
Spanish, English text.
ON DISENO 1990, no.111, p.122-137,
photos., plans, secn.

SPAIN--VERGARA--APARTMENT HOUSES
Esencial y desnudo: edificio de
viviendas en Vergara, Guipuzcoa.
Apartment house. Architect: Jose
Ignacio Linazasoro. English
summary, p.87.
A & V 1990, no.21, p.58-59, det.,
dwgs., elev., photos.

SPAIN--VICH--FACADES--ROMANESQUE--SANT
PERE
The Last Supper of the Vic Cathedral
facade rediscovered / Xavier
Barral I Altat.
On now dispersed 12th cent.
reliefs from Sant Pere. Includes
abstract.
GESTA 1989, v.28, no.2, p.121-126,
dets., photos., plan, refs.

SPAIN--VICH--RELIEF (SCULPTURE)--12TH
CENTURY--SANT PERE
The Last Supper of the Vic Cathedral
facade rediscovered / Xavier
Barral I Altat.
On now dispersed 12th cent.
reliefs from Sant Pere. Includes
abstract.
GESTA 1989, v.28, no.2, p.121-126,
dets., photos., plan, refs.

SPAIN--VICH--STORES--CLOTHING
Local comercial en Vic: Cristobal
Julian Ramirez, arquitecto.
Spanish, English text.
ON DISENO 1990, no.110, p.150-155,
photos., secns., sketches.

SPAIN--VIGO--INDUSTRIAL PARKS--COTO
GRANDE
Actuacion urbanistica de "Coto
Grande", Vigo (Pontevedra).
URBANISMO / COAM 1990 Sept.,
no.11, p.93-94, map, plan, table.

SPAIN--VILANOVA DEL CAMI--SPORTS
FACILITIES
Pabellon polideportivo en Vilanova
del Cami, Barcelona: Pere Puig,
arquitecto.
Spanish, English text.
ON DISENO 1990, no.113, p.174-181,
elev., photos., plans.

SPAIN--VILLAGARCIA--MARINE AQUARIUMS
Horreos del mar: Acuario en
Villagarcia de Arosa, Pontevedra.
Marine aquarium. Architect: Cesar
Portela. English summary, p.92.
A & V 1990, no.24, p.64-67,
axonometric view., dwg., elevs.,
photos., plans.

SPAIN--VILLALBA--WATER TREATMENT
PLANTS
Tres estaciones depuradoras de aguas
residuales = Three water
purification plants.
In Majadahonda, Guadarrama and
Villalba. Architects: Juan
Herreros, Inaki Abalos. Text in
Spanish and English.
QUADERNS D'ARQUITECTURA I
URBANISME 1988 July-Sept., no.178,
p.102-119, photos., plans, secns.,
site plan.

SPAIN--ZAMUDIO--INDUSTRIAL PARKS
El parque technologico de Zamudio:
una experiencia de diseno urbano
flexible / Miguel Aguirre...et al.
URBANISMO / COAM 1990 Sept.,
no.11, p.68-73, plans, secns.,
aerial photos.

SPAIN--ZARAGOZA--LIBRARIES--PUBLIC--
BIBLIOTECA PUBLICA DE ARAGON
Biblioteca pubblica dello Stato,
Zaragoza.
Architects: Carlos Puente
Fernandez, Victor Lopez Cotelo,
Javier Garcia Delgado. Text in
Italian and English.
DOMUS 1990 Sept., no.719,
p.[58-65], elevs., photos., plans,
secns., site plan.
Contexual construction.
Features the Zaragoza library and
health center in Mostoles.
Architects: Victor Lopez Cotelo
and Carlos Puente.
ARCHITECTURAL REVIEW 1990 July,
(Continued next page)

SPAIN--ZARAGOZA--LIBRARIES--PUBLIC--
  BIBLIOTECA PUBLICA DE ARAGON
                    (CONTINUED)
  Contexual construction. (CONTINUED)
    v.188, no.1121, p.38-43, elevs.,
    photos., plans, secn., site plans.
  Public facilities.
    Part of a special feature on
    Spanish contemporary architecture.
    Contents: Museo de Navarra, by
    Jordi Garces, Enric Soria.--
    Biblioteca Publica, by Victor
    Lopez Cotelo, Carlos Puente.--
    Molinos del Rio Segura, by Juan
    Navarro Baldeweg.-- Puerta de
    Toledo, by Nuan Navarro
    Baldeweg.-- Escuela de artes y
    oficios artisticos, by Jose
    Antonio Corrales.-- Instituto
    Hugue, by Luis Bravo Farre, Albert
    Blanch Rubio.-- Brief Histories.
    Text in Japanese.
    SPACE DESIGN 1990 May, no.308,
    p.11-54, ports., elevs., photos.,
    plans, secns., site plans.
  Victor Lopez Cotelo, Carlos Puente
    [interview] / Manuel Gausa.
    Madrid, Feb. 1989. Includes public
    library, Zaragoza, Spain. Spanish,
    English text.
    QUADERNS D'ARQUITECTURA I
    URBANISME 1989 Apr.-Sept.,
    no.181-182, p.36-47, photos.,
    plans, secns., site plans.

SPANDRILS
  See SPANDRELS

SPANGLER, SEMIER & SCHLENKER
  Matteson Library winner announced /
    Annemarie Mannion.
    INLAND ARCHITECT 1990 July-Aug.,
    v.34, no.4, p.74-76, axonometric
    view, plans.

SPANISH COLONIAL
  See "SPANISH COLONIAL" AS A
    SUBHEADING AFTER SPECIFIC BUILDING
    TYPES OR OTHER MAIN HEADINGS.
  See also TERRITORIAL STYLE

SPANISH COLONIAL REVIVAL
  See "SPANISH COLONIAL REVIVAL" AS A
    SUBHEADING AFTER SPECIFIC BUILDING
    TYPES OR OTHER MAIN HEADINGS.
  See also MISSION REVIVAL
  See also SANTA FE STYLE

SPANISH GUINEA--FERNANDO PO--
  EMBASSIES--MALABO--AMBASSADE DE
  FRANCE
  Ambassade de France a Malabo, Guinee
    Equatoriale.
    Architect: G. Autran.
    LE MUR VIVANT 1990, no.96,
    p.43-46, elevs., model, photos.,
    secn.

SPANISH MEDITERRANEAN REVIVAL
  See "SPANISH MEDITERRANEAN REVIVAL"
    AS A SUBHEADING AFTER SPECIFIC
    BUILDING TYPES OR OTHER MAIN
    HEADINGS.
  See also MISSION REVIVAL
  See also SPANISH COLONIAL REVIVAL

SPANU, MARCELLO
  Considerazioni sull'architettura di
    Efeso in eta augustea / Marcello
    Spanu.
    PROSPETTIVA 1988 Jan., no.52,
    p.41-49, photos., plans, secns.,
    reconst. dwgs., refs.

SPAS
  See also BATHS

SPAS--COMPETITIONS--FRANCE--VICHY--
  CENTRE SANTE BEAUTE
  Gesundheits und Schonheitszentrum in
    Vichy, Frankreich = Health and
    beauty centre in Vichy, France.
    Competition for spa incorporating
    hotel facilities. Winning
    architects: Jean Nouvel et
    associes. Text in German.
    ARCHITEKTUR + WETTBEWERBE 1990
    Mar., no.141, p.42-45, dwgs.,
    elevs., models, plans, site plans.
  Kurhotel mit Thermalbad, Vichy 1988.
    Project architects: Jean Nouvel,
    Emmanuel Cattani et Associes.
    WERK, BAUEN + WOHNEN 1990 Mar.,
    no.3, p.52-53, dwgs., models, site
    plans.

SPAS--COMPETITIONS--GERMANY (WEST)--
  BONEN
  Erste Preise: Bauten fur Freizeit
    und Sport.
    Four competitions: "Wildenstein"
    leisure center, Messtetten
    (architect: Heinz Becsei); outdoor
    pool, Bad Rappenau (architects:
    Rudolf und Ingeborg Geier, Jorg
    Stotzer); leisure and health club,
    Bonen (architect: Isermann &
    Jensen); gymnasium, Passau
    (architect: Willi Mortl).
    DEUTSCHES ARCHITEKTENBLATT 1990
    Oct.1, v.22, no.10, p.1511-1514,
    models, plans, secns., site plans.

SPAS--CONSERVATION AND RESTORATION--
  ITALY--MERANO
  Merano restaurata = Urban
    realizations: Meran restored.
    Restoration of a health spa in
    Italy. Kurhaus architect:
    Friedrich Ohmann; theater
    architect: Martin Dulfer.
    Restoration architect: Vincenzo
    Pavan.
    ABITARE 1990 Apr., no.284,
    p.188-[203],242, photos., plan,
    secn., site plans.

SPAS--FINLAND--OULU--EDEN
  Baden am Polarkreis:
    Erholungsparadies mit tropischem
    Klima in Oulu, Finnland.
    Architects: Arktes Oy.
    ARCHITEKTUR, INNENARCHITEKTUR,
    TECHNISCHER AUSBAU 1990 July-Aug.,
    v.98, no.7-8, p.18-19, photos.,
    plan, aerial photos.

SPAS--INTERIOR DESIGN--UNITED STATES--
  BOSTON (MASSACHUSETTS)--SPA AT THE
  HERITAGE
  Spa at the Heritage / Edie Lee
    Cohen.
    Interiors of health club and salon
    in Boston's mixed-use building,
    Heritage on the Garden.
    Architects/ Interior designers:
    Schwartz Silver Architects.
    INTERIOR DESIGN 1990 Nov., v.61,
                  (Continued next column)

SPAS--INTERIOR DESIGN--UNITED STATES--
  BOSTON (MASSACHUSETTS)--SPA AT THE
  HERITAGE (CONTINUED)
  Spa at the Heritage /...(CONTINUED)
    no.15, p.172-[175], photos., plan.

SPAS--JAPAN--ATAMI REFRESH CENTER
  Atami Refresh Center.
    Spa for members of an
    architectural consulting and
    engineering union. Architects:
    Toshihito Yokouchi, Kunio
    Mayekawa, Architect and
    Associates. English summary, p.23.
    KENCHIKU BUNKA 1990 Mar., v.45,
    no.521, p.77-86, dets., photos.,
    plans, secns., site plan.

SPAS--SOVIET UNION
  A curtain up on wellness / Karin
    Tetlow.
    U.S. delegation visits several
    Soviet balneological spas.
    INTERIORS 1990 Dec., v.150, no.5,
    p.74-77, photos.

SPATH, FRIEDRICH
  Deutscher Architekturpreis 1989
    verlichen.
    Presents the ten winners and
    includes commentary by Friedrich
    Spath.
    DEUTSCHES ARCHITEKTENBLATT 1990
    Feb.1, v.22, no.2, p.223-226,
    photos., aerial photo.

SPATH, LOTHAR
  "Science-City": das Konzept fur eine
    Wissenschaft Ulm / Lothar Spath.
    The Ministry president's
    discussion of ideas and goals for
    planning university and research
    facilities in Ulm. Includes a
    project by Richard Meier.
    BAUWELT 1990 Sept.28, v.81, no.36,
    p.1816-1818, dwg., port.

SPEA (GRUPPO IRI-ITALSTAT)
  La citta e il suo fiume = The city
    and its river / Jef Vanreusel.
    Stad aan de stroom project designs
    from international competition for
    urban renewal of three areas of
    Antwerp; Quay, Islet and South;
    architects: Yves Lion, Manuel de
    Sola-Morales, Bob van Reeth, Beth
    Gali, Rem Koolhaas, Toyo Ito, Van
    Berkel & Bos, Van Veen & Van Meer,
    Bureau of Urban Design. Overall
    site plan: Spea - Ingegneria
    Europa (Gruppo-Italstat).
    L'ARCA 1990 Dec., no.44, p.32-43,
    models, map, photos., plans, site
    plans.
  Fiumicino 2005: la nuova citta
    dell'aria = Fiumicino 2005: the
    new city of the air / Furio
    Giovannoni.
    Project for extension and
    renovation of Leonardo da Vinci
    airport, Rome. Architects:
    Bonifica (Gruppa IRI-Italstat),
    SPEA (Gruppo IRI-Italstat), Austin
    Italia. Associate architects:
    Reynolds, Smith and Hills,
    Architects, Engineers, Planners.
    L'ARCA 1990 June, no.39, p.40-47,
    dwgs., plans, site plans.

SPEAIGHT, ANTHONY
 Direct opinions: advice from
  barristers / Anthony Speaight, Kim
  Franklin.
  Architects in Britain now have the
  right of direct access to
  barristers.
  ARCHITECTS' JOURNAL 1990 Sept.26,
  v.192, no.13, p.71-73, ill., refs.
 Murphy v Brentwood: implications /
  Anthony Speaight.
  British legal case concerning
  architects' liability.
  ARCHITECTS' JOURNAL 1990 Oct.17,
  v.192, no.16, p.81-84, ill.

SPEAR, ALISON
 Uptown downtown: Alison Spear
  redesigned a Greenwich Village
  town house to accomodate the
  unusual domestic needs of modeling
  mogul Katie Ford and entrepeneur
  Andre Balazs / Brad Gooch.
  HOUSE & GARDEN 1990 Oct., v.162,
  no.10, p.214-219, ports., photos.

SPEAR, LAURINDA, 1950-
 Arquitectonica at home: Laurinda
  Spear and Bernardo Fort-Brescia's
  Miami residence / Beth Dunlop.
  Located in Coconut Grove.
  ARCHITECTURAL DIGEST 1990 Dec.,
  v.47, no.13, p.42,46,50,54, port.,
  photos.
 Miami architect Laurinda Spear is
  not what you'd expect / Charles
  Gandee.
  HOUSE & GARDEN 1990 July, v.162,
  no.7, p.140, port.
 Room at the Top? Sexism and the Star
  System in Architecture / Denise
  Scott Brown.
  One of four sections in a special
  feature on "Women in American
  Architecture". English
  translation, p.73-75.
  SPACE DESIGN 1990 June, no.309,
  p.54-71,73-75, dwgs., ports.,
  elevs., photos., plans, secns.,
  site plans, refs.

SPEARS, BEVERLY
 Santa Fe's Westside/Guadalupe
  Historic District: Hispanic
  vernacular versus Pueblo revival /
  Beverly Spears.
  NEW MEXICO ARCHITECTURE 1990
  Sept.-Dec., v.31, no.5-6, p.9-13,
  cover, photos.

SPEARS, LYNN
 Caretakers of time-proven beliefs:
  The Central States Regional Awards
  [1989] / Lynn Spears.
  15 premiated projects in Iowa,
  Nebr., Mo., and Okla.
  IOWA ARCHITECT 1990 Spring, v.39,
  no.1, p.26-35, photos.
 Collected fortunes: Penthouse
  renovation, Des Moines, Iowa /
  Lynn Spears.
  Architects: Herbert Lewis Kruse
  Blunck.
  IOWA ARCHITECT 1990 Summer, v.39,
  no.2, p.14-[17], photos., plans.
 The value (s) of the small town.
  Shenandoah, Iowa / Lynn Spears.
  IOWA ARCHITECT 1990 Winter, v.39,
  no.4, p.26-27, photos.

SPECIAL EDUCATION FACILITIES
 See also SCHOOLS FOR THE HANDICAPPED

SPECIFICATION WRITING
 Making your specifications stick /
  William Dyer.
  ARCHITECTURAL RECORD 1990 Dec.,
  v.178, no.13, p.37-38,
 Software for specifications / Oliver
  Witte.
  ARCHITECTURE: THE AIA JOURNAL 1990
  Jan., v.79, no.1, p.118-123, ill.,
  tables.
 Specifications: getting physical /
  Walter Rosenfeld.
  On the functional considerations
  of the project manual.
  PROGRESSIVE ARCHITECTURE 1990
  Feb., v.71, no.2, p.59,
 Specifications: the document river /
  William Lohmann.
  Description of the three stages in
  specifications writing:
  preliminary description, outline
  specification and project manual.
  PROGRESSIVE ARCHITECTURE 1990
  Dec., v.71, no.13, p.55,

SPECIFICATIONS
 See also BUILDING - ESTIMATES
 See also SPECIFICATION WRITING
 See also "CONTRACTS AND
  SPECIFICATIONS" AS A SUBHEADING
  AFTER GENERAL TOPICS AND SPECIFIC
  BUILDING TYPES, E.G., BUILDINGS -
  CONTRACTS AND SPECIFICATIONS.
 Getting what you want from
  specifications / Timothy Kirby.
  A guide to choosing the right
  specification methods for your
  firm.
  ARCHITECTURAL RECORD 1990 Nov.,
  v.178, no.12, p.45-46, diagrs.
 Making your specifications stick /
  William Dyer.
  ARCHITECTURAL RECORD 1990 Dec.,
  v.178, no.13, p.37-38,
 Specifications: rules of the game /
  Walter Rosenfeld.
  PROGRESSIVE ARCHITECTURE 1990
  Oct., v.71, no.10, p.53,

SPECIFICATIONS--GREAT BRITAIN
 Flat roofing.
  Nine articles, including ones on
  the use of roofs by helicopters,
  standards and references, and
  products.
  BUILDING 1990 Apr.20, v.255,
  no.16, suppl., p.3-50, photos.
 Roofing.
  Ten articles, on materials,
  decorative and aesthetic aspects,
  corrosion, standards and
  references, weathering, skylights,
  and products.
  BUILDING 1990 July 27, v.255,
  no.30 suppl., p.3-68, diagrs.,
  photos.
 Specification 90 [book review] /
  Alastair Stewart.
  On the 1990 version of the British
  specifier's handbook.
  BUILDING 1990 Feb.2, v.255, no.5,
  p.74-75, photos.
 Specification 90: two reviews [book
  review] / Patrick Landucci, Alan
  Blanc.
  ARCHITECTS' JOURNAL 1990 Feb.7,
  v.191, no.6, p.75-77, photo., ref.

SPECK, LAWRENCE W.
 Lawrence W. Speck: reshaping the
  Texas ranch house.
  Home near Austin features 2
  barrel-vaulted bedroom suites with
  galvanized-metal roofs.
  ARCHITECTURAL DIGEST 1990 Sept.,
  v.47, no.10, p.98-99, photo.,
  plans.
 Wohnhaus in Austin.
  Architect: Lawrence W. Speck.
  Includes English summary.
  BAUMEISTER 1990 Nov., v.87, no.11,
  p.58-61, photos., plans, site
  plan.

SPECTRE, JAY
 Restrained glamour for the city /
  Peter Carlsen.
  Interiors of New York apartment
  overlooking Central Park.
  Interior designers: Jay Spectre,
  Geoffrey N. Bradfield.
  ARCHITECTURAL DIGEST 1990 Nov.,
  v.47, no.12, p.264-[271], 312,
  photos.

SPEER, ALBERT, 1905-1981
 Herrscher Tod. Kreig, Zerstorung,
  Opfer- und Todeskult in der
  NS-Architektur = Sovereign death.
  War, destruction, sacrifice and
  death cult in Nazi architecture /
  Wolfgang Schache.
  DAIDALOS 1990 Dec.15, no.38,
  p.52-59, ill., models, photos.,
  refs.
 Over rook zonder vuur en vuur zonder
  rook: architectuur als uitdrukking
  van macht / Bart Lootsma.
  One of several articles in
  Themanummer 41: "Thema:
  architectuur en macht." Discusses
  symbolic aspects of buildings,
  including work by Albert Speer and
  Le Corbusier.
  DE ARCHITECT THEMA 1990 Nov.,
  v.21, no.11 suppl., p.7-13, dwgs.,
  maps, photos., refs.

SPEER, ALBERT, 1924-
 Rahmenplanung "Olympische Spiele in
  Frankfurt am Main" / Albert Speer.
  ARCHITEKTUR + WETTBEWERBE 1990
  Mar., no.141, p.94, map.

SPEER, ALBERT, 1934-
 Zur Person: Gesprach mit dem
  Stadtplaner Albert Speer
  [interview] / Oliver G. Hamm.
  DEUTSCHE BAUZEITUNG 1990 Aug.,
  v.124, no.8, p.122-124, ports.

SPEIDEL, MANFRED
 Bodegas Guell in Garraf (1895-1901)
  / Manfred Speidel.
  Former wine cellars built for Don
  Eusebio Gell y Bacigalupa;
  architect: Antoni Gaudi. Text in
  Japanese and English.
  ARCHITECTURE AND URBANISM 1990
  July, no.7(238), p.50-[63],
  elevs., photos., plans, secns.,
  site plans, refs.
 Special feature: Gottfried Bohm.
  Contents: Essay:
  "Ja...was...mochten wir nicht
  alles!" (Yes...what...isn't all we
  want!) / Manfred Speidel-- Works:
  Renovation of Saarbrucken Palace--
  Assembly hall at the Folkwang
  School-- University library and
  (Continued next page)

SPEIDEL, MANFRED (CONTINUED)
Special feature:... (CONTINUED)
auditorium in Mannheim-- Der
Heumarkt in Koln-- Project for
German Pavilion at Expo in
Seville-- Project for museum
extension in Hamburg-- Project for
International Tribunal for the Law
of the Sea in Hamburg. Text in
Japanese and English.
ARCHITECTURE AND URBANISM 1990
Sept., no.9(240), p.[51]-[128],
axonometric views, elevs.,
photos., plans, secns., site
plans, sketches.
Welten-Wurfel = Cosmic cubes /
Manfred Speidel.
Cubic designs of
sculptor/architect Bukichi Inoue.
Text in German and English.
DAIDALOS 1990 Mar.15, no.35,
p.100-109, axonometric views,
elevs., photos., plans, secns.

SPEIDEL UND PARTNER
Kantine Lechstahlwerke in
Herbertshofen.
Architects: Speidel und Partner.
DEUTSCHE BAUZEITSCHRIFT 1990 Mar.,
v.38, no.3, p.345-350, dets.,
photos., plans.

SPEIRANI, F.
Ponti mobili per la citta = Moving
bridges for the city / Fabrizio
Bonomo.
Project for pedestrian bridge with
moving stairs and sidewalk;
architects: R. Guantieri, R.
Morisi, F. Speirani. Text in
English and Italian.
L'ARCA 1990 Feb., no.35,suppl.
l'Arca 2, p.102-103, dwg., model,
secns.

SPENCE & WEBSTER
Energiehaus Milton Keynes:
Wettbewerb, Milton Keynes
Energiehaus, 1988.
Architects: Spence & Webster.
ARCH PLUS 1990 July, no.104,
p.40-41, dets., dwgs., models,
plans, secns.
Gebaude mit variabler Haut / Robin
Spence.
Entry for the European Pavilion
for Expo 92 in Seville.
Architects: Spence & Webster.
ARCH PLUS 1990 July, no.104, p.37,
ill., secns.
Licht, Klang und Temperatur:
Wettbewerb: Britischer Pavillen
fur die Expo 92 in Sevilla.
Entry by Spence & Webster.
ARCH PLUS 1990 July, no.104,
p.38-39, dwg., photos., secns.

SPENCE, ALAN
New town Russia / Alan Spence.
Proposal for a series of
English-style garden cities to be
built on poor-quality agricultural
land in Russia.
ARCHITECTS' JOURNAL 1990 Oct.10,
v.192, no.15, p.26-29, ill.,
photos., plan.

SPENCE, ROBIN
Gebaude mit variabler Haut / Robin
Spence.
Entry for the European Pavilion
for Expo 92 in Seville.
Architects: Spence & Webster.
ARCH PLUS 1990 July, no.104, p.37,
ill., secns.
Pompidou coup [exhibition review] /
Robin Spence.
Review of the exhibition, Jean
Prouve Constructeur, on view in
the CCI Gallery, Centre Georges
Pompidou, Paris, Oct. 24,
1990-Jan. 28, 1991.
ARCHITECTURAL REVIEW 1990 Dec.,
v.188, no.1126, p.12, photos.

SPENCE, RORY
Tasmanian trio / Rory Spence.
Features three projects in Hobart:
garden room, South Hobart,
architect: Jim Jones; house
addition, West Hobart, architect:
Leigh Woolley and studio house,
West Hobart, architect: Peter
Willmott.
ARCHITECTURAL REVIEW 1990 Apr.,
v.187, no.1118, p.87-[93],
photos., plans, secns., site
plans.

SPENCE, Y.
Was there a guarded southern
entrance way to the first palace
at Mallia? / Y. Spence.
THE ANNUAL OF THE BRITISH SCHOOL
AT ATHENS 1990, no.85,
p.[369]-374, map, site plans,
refs.

SPENCER, JAYME
Mashrabeya: an architectural
language / Jayme Spencer.
History of this turned woodwork
used throughout the Middle East
for centuries.
ARTS & THE ISLAMIC WORLD 1990
Summer, v.5, no.2(18), p.49-52,
photos.

SPENCER, LINDA
The Preservation Tax Incentives
Program in Connecticut: an
overview and update / Linda
Spencer.
CONNECTICUT PRESERVATION NEWS 1990
Jan.-Feb., v.13, no.1, p.10-11,

SPENDER, NATASHA
Shades of Provence / Natasha
Spender.
Gardens surrounding the home of
Anne Cox Chambers, called Le Petit
Fontanille. Garden designer: Peter
Coats.
HOUSE & GARDEN 1990 Sept., v.162,
no.9, p.[168-173],212-213, port.,
photos.

SPENGLER, TILMAN
Hamburg comes into its own.
Includes three articles on
Hamburg: Some wry reflections on a
city of water, by Tilman Spengler;
An art lover's tour, by Thomas
Hoving; An insider's guide to the
best tours, restaurants, theater,
and nightlife, by Adele Riepe.
CONNOISSEUR 1990 Sept., v.220,
no.944, p.113-124, ill., maps,
photos.

SPENS, MICHAEL
The nineteenth hole / Michael Spens.
Golf clubhouse, Schloss
Ebreichsdorf, Austria. Architect:
Hans Hollein.
ARCHITECTURAL REVIEW 1990 Aug.,
v.188, no.1122, p.40-43, ill.,
photos., plans, secns., site
plans.

SPERANZA, GAETANO
The African museum / Gaetano
Speranza.
On role, image, infrastructure,
and techniques, using the National
Museum of Mali, Bamako, as an
example.
MIMAR: ARCHITECTURE IN DEVELOPMENT
1990 June, v.10, no.2(35),
p.21-23, photos.

SPERELLI, GIORGIO
Il Monte dei Paschi di Siena a
Perugia = The Monte dei Paschi di
Siena bank in Perugia / Giorgio
Sperelli.
Architect: Bruno Signorini.
L'ARCA 1990 Feb., no.35,suppl.
l'Arca 2, p.68-73, photos, plan,
secns.
Lo Stadio Olimpico di Roma = The
Olympic stadium in Rome / Giorgio
Sperelli.
New roof for 1930s stadium.
Architects: Studio Zucker: Josef
N. Zucker and Patrizia Zucker.
L'ARCA 1990 May, no.38, p.60-65,
elevs., photos., plans, secns.

SPERLING, CHRISTINE M.
Leon Battista Alberti's inscriptions
on the Holy Sepulchre in the
Cappella Rucellai, San Pancrazio,
Florence / Christine M. Sperling.
JOURNAL OF THE WARBURG AND
COURTAULD INSTITUTES 1989, v.52,
p.221-228,pl.42-47, dwgs.,
photos., refs.

SPETS, CHARLES E.
Marseilles Hydro Power Station
powered early transportation
system / Charles E. Spets.
Opened in 1911 and operated until
1988. Now on the National Register
of Historic Places. Designed in
Classical Revival style by
engineer C.W. Humphrey.
HISTORIC ILLINOIS 1990 Feb., v.12,
no.5, p.[1]-3,12-14, map, aerial
photo.

**SPHERICAL BUILDINGS--SWEDEN--
STOCKHOLM--GLOBE**
L'attraction du Globe: stade
omnisports, Stockholm.
Architects: Berg Arkitektkontor.
English summary, p.99. Spanish
summary, p.155.
TECHNIQUES ET ARCHITECTURE 1990
Dec.-1991 Jan., no.393, p.96-99,
photos., plans, secn., site plan.
Globen city, Stockholm / Sture
Koinberg, Lasse Vretblad.
Architects: Berg Arkitektkontor.
ARKITEKTUR: THE SWEDISH REVIEW OF
ARCHITECTURE 1990 Jan.-Feb., v.90,
no.1, p.22-29, photos., plans.

SPORTES, RONALD CECIL (CONTINUED)
[Amenagement interieur]: commerces.
Contents: Boutique Koshino, Paris
Ville; architect: Jean-Michel
Wilmotte-- Apple showroom, ave. de
la Grande Armee, Paris; architect:
Berbesson Racine et Associes--
Castelli showroom, Paris;
designer: Ronald Cecil Sportes--
Unifor furniture showroom, Milan,
Italy; architects: Afra & Tobia
Scarpa-- Boutique Jean-Louis
Imbert, Marseille, France;
architect: Rudy Ricciotti--
Recorded music store, Nantes,
France; architect: Studio Naco.
LE MONITEUR ARCHITECTURE AMC 1990
July-Aug., no.13, p.36-45,
axonometric views, photos., plans.
Docks Castelli, quai 25.
Furniture showroom, Paris.
Architect: Roland Cecil Sportes.
Includes interview with Claude
Gozlan, general manager of
Castelli France.
ARCHITECTURE INTERIEURE CREE 1990
Aug.-Sept., no.238, p.180-185,
dets., ports., photos., secn.
Espace Castelli, Paris / Brigitte
Fitoussi.
Furniture store, features spiral
stairway. Architect: Ronald Cecil
Sportes.
ARCHITECTURE D'AUJOURD'HUI 1990
Sept., no.270, p.193-196, dwgs.,
photos.
L'hotellerie en mouvement.
On the hotel industry. Includes
eight recent hotel projects.
English summary, p.162.
ARCHITECTURE INTERIEURE CREE 1990
Mar., no.235, p.48-83, dwgs.,
ports., photos., plans, isometric
dwgs.
Partition marine: l'espace Castelli
a Paris.
Furniture showroom. Architect:
Ronald Cecil Sportes.
TECHNIQUES ET ARCHITECTURE 1990
Aug.-Sept., no.391, p.156-157,
axonometric views, dets., photos.

SPORTING GOODS STORES
See STORES - SPORTING GOODS

SPORTS BUILDINGS
See SPORTS FACILITIES

SPORTS CLUBS
See ATHLETIC CLUBS

SPORTS FACILITIES
See also AQUATIC SPORTS BUILDINGS
See also ARENAS
See also ATHLETIC CLUBS
See also ATHLETIC FIELDS
See also BICYCLE RACING TRACKS
See also BOWLING ALLEYS
See also CRICKET GROUNDS
See also CROQUET COURTS
See also FIELD HOUSES
See also GOLF COURSES
See also GYMNASIUMS
See also PALASTRAE
See also PHYSICAL EDUCATION
   FACILITIES
See also PLAYGROUNDS
See also RACETRACKS
See also RECREATION AREAS
See also RECREATION CENTERS
See also RIDING HALLS
See also RUNNING TRACKS
      (Continued next column)

SPORTS FACILITIES (CONTINUED)
See also AQUATIC... (CONTINUED)
See also SKATEBOARDING PARKS
See also SKATING RINKS
See also SKI LIFTS
See also STADIUMS
See also SWIMMING POOLS
See also TENNIS CLUBS
See also TENNIS COURTS
See also WINTER SPORTS FACILITIES
Architect projects by Reginald
Malcolmson.
A sports and cultural center
(1953-1973); a convention hall
(1954-1984).
OFFRAMP 1988 Spring, v.1, no.1,
p.[29-32], ill., dwgs., elevs.
Architettura e sport = Architecture
and sport / Mario A. Arnaboldi.
L'ARCA 1990 May, no.38, p.1-4,
photo.
Bedarfsgerechte Sportbauten, Teil 2
/ F. Roskam.
DEUTSCHE BAUZEITSCHRIFT 1990 July,
v.38, no.7, p.1001-1004, dwgs.,
photos.
Gedanken zu der Entwicklung von
Sport- und Freizeitzentren /
Christoph Parade.
ARCHITEKTUR + WETTBEWERBE 1990
Mar., no.141, p.3-4, port., elev.,
maps, photos., aerial photo.
Les lieux du sport.
Theme issue on sports facilities.
Articles indexed separately.
TECHNIQUES ET ARCHITECTURE 1990
Dec.-1991 Jan., no.393,
p.[29]-123, axonometric views,
dets., dwgs., elevs., models,
maps, photos., plans, secns., site
plans, sketches, aerial photos.
Uber den "Vorsatz zur Vitalitat" und
dessen Folgen fur die Architektur
/ Norbert Weickenmeier.
DER ARCHITEKT 1990 July-Aug.,
no.7-8, p.356-359, photos., plans,
site plans, isometric dwg.

SPORTS FACILITIES--AUSTRIA--LINZ
Sporthalle in Linz.
Architect: Franz Riepl. Includes
English summary.
BAUMEISTER 1990 Mar., v.87, no.3,
p.40-47, dets., photos., plans,
secns., site plans.

SPORTS FACILITIES--BRAZIL--CANOAS--
ASSOCIACAO ATLETICA SULPETRO
Em Canoas, um centro de vivencia
incorprado a refinaria.
Associacao Atletica Sulpetro.
Architect: C. Luiz Araujo, C.M.
Fayet.
PROJETO 1989 Apr., no.120,
p.98-[101], dets., photos., plans,
elevs.

SPORTS FACILITIES--BRAZIL--CURITIBA--
CLUBE CULTURAL DE CURITIBA
Parque nactico: atracao popular em
Curitiba.
Clube Cultural de Curitiba.
Architects: J.R. Junior, R.L.
Reinert, L. Ribeiro.
PROJETO 1989 Apr., no.120,
p.102-105, elevs., photos., plans.

SPORTS FACILITIES--BRAZIL--SAO PAULO--
FABRICA POMPEIA
Lina Bo Bardi: centro sociale e
sportivo "Fabrica Pompeia," San
Paolo / Vittorio Magnago
Lampugnani.
Reuse of a 1930s factory. In
Italian and English.
DOMUS 1990 June, no.717,
p.[56]-57, elevs., photos.,
secns., site plans.

SPORTS FACILITIES--CHINA--PEKING
XI Asian Games - 1990 Beijing / Liu
Kaiji.
BUILDING IN CHINA 1990 June, v.3,
no.2 p.2-8,12, photos., plans,
aerial photo.

SPORTS FACILITIES--COMPETITIONS--
FRANCE--LEVALLOIS-PERRET
Sportkomplex in Levallois-Perret,
Frankreich = Sports hall in
Levallois-Perret, France.
Competition. Winning architects:
ARCHI-TECTURE. Text in German.
ARCHITEKTUR + WETTBEWERBE 1990
Mar., no.141, p.32-36, dwgs.,
models, plans, secns., site plans.

SPORTS FACILITIES--COMPETITIONS--
GERMANY (WEST)--BERLIN--SPORTHALLE
SCHARNWEBERSTRASSE
Sporthalle Scharnweberstrasse in
Berlin = Sports hall
Scharnweberstrasse in Berlin.
Competition. Winning architects:
Walter A. Noebel, Michele
Reginaldi. Text in German.
ARCHITEKTUR + WETTBEWERBE 1990
Mar., no.141, p.46-51, elevs.,
models, plans, secns., site plans.

SPORTS FACILITIES--COMPETITIONS--
GERMANY (WEST)--BERLIN--SPORTHALLE
STADION NEUKOLLN
Sporthalle Stadion Neukolln in
Berlin = Sports hall stadium
Neukolln in Berlin.
Competition. Winning architects:
Pysall und Stahrenberg
Architekten. Text in German.
ARCHITEKTUR + WETTBEWERBE 1990
Mar., no.141, p.52-57, axonometric
views, elevs., models, plans,
secns.

SPORTS FACILITIES--COMPETITIONS--
GERMANY (WEST)--STARNBERG--
BRUNNANGERHALLE
Architektur unterwegs.
Three projects: Horsaal und
Bibliotheksgebaude A3, Universitat
Mannheim (architect: Gottfr.
Bohm); Colonia-Victoire
Versicherung, Cologne (architects:
Architekten Dansard, Kalenborn &
Partner, and BHLM Architekten
Stadtplaner); Brunnangerhalle
Starnberg (architects: Moritz
Hauschild, Rudiger Fritsch).
DEUTSCHES ARCHITEKTENBLATT 1990
Dec.1, v.22, no.12, p.1835-1838,
photos., plans.
Brunnangerhalle in Starnberg.
Gymnasium. Architect for
competition entry: Moritz
Hauschild. Project architect:
Architekengemeinschaft Starnberg.
BAUWELT 1990 Jan.26, v.81, no.4,
p.159-163, photos., plans, secn.,
site plan.

SPORTS FACILITIES--GERMANY (WEST)--
STARNBERG--BRUNNANGERHALLE
    Gammes de lumiere: complexe sportif
    polyvalent, Starnberg, Allemagne.
    Architects: P. Moritz Hauschild,
    Leo Fritsch. English summary,
    p.72. Spanish summary, p.154.
    TECHNIQUES ET ARCHITECTURE 1990
    Dec.-1991 Jan., no.393, p.70-74,
    axonometric view, photos., plans,
    secns., site plan.

SPORTS FACILITIES--GERMANY (WEST)--
WERNAU--SPORTHALLE NECKARTAL
    Sporthalle Neckartal, [Wernau].
    Architect: Gerber + Gabeler.
    Planner: Gerber + Partner.
    BAUWELT 1990 Jan.26, v.81, no.4,
    p.164-167, photos., plans, secn.
    Sporthalle Neckartal, Wernau =
    Sports Hall Nekartal, Wernau.
    Architects: Wergemeinschaft Gerber
    + Gabeler.
    DETAIL 1990 June-July, v.30, no.3,
    p.279-283, dets., elevs., secns.,
    site plans.

SPORTS FACILITIES--GREAT BRITAIN
    Planning and football league
    grounds: an RTPI survey / Chris
    Shepley.
    THE PLANNER 1990 Sept.28, v.76,
    no.38, p.15-17, photos.

SPORTS FACILITIES--IRELAND--DUBLIN--
ALSAA COMPLEX
    Cityscapes / Barry Mason.
    Photos of three modern Dublin
    buildings: EBS building, by
    Turlough O'Donnell; ALSAA leisure
    and sports complex, by Desmond
    O'Dwyer; and the Central Bank,
    Dame Street., by Sean Stephenson.
    PLAN: ARCHITECTURE + BUILDING
    DESIGN IN IRELAND 1990 May, v.25,
    no.5, p.62-63, photos.

SPORTS FACILITIES--ITALY--MOZZATE
    Centro sportivo polivalente a
    Mozzate (Como).
    Swimming pool-bocci green complex.
    Architects: Antonio and Amedeo
    Petrilli. English, French, and
    Spanish summaries.
    ABACUS 1990 Apr.-June, v.6, no.22,
    p.44-57, dets., dwgs., elevs.,
    photos., plans, secns., site plan.

SPORTS FACILITIES--ITALY--SICILY--
RAGUSA
    Centro sportivo a Ragusa.
    Architect: Salvo Giliberto.
    Summaries in English, German,
    French, and Spanish.
    ARCHITETTURA; CRONACHE E STORIA
    1990 June, v.36, no.6(416),
    p.[430]-432, elevs., photos., site
    plans.

SPORTS FACILITIES--ITALY--TRENTO--
PALAZZO DELLO SPORT
    Per un razionalismo dello spirito
    (del luogo) le ragioni di un
    naturale artificio / Giannantonio
    Avezzu.
    Project for a new "palazzo dello
    sport" in Trent. Architects:
    Renato Rizzi, Franco Allocca.
    PARAMETRO 1990 Mar.-Apr., no.177,
    p.83-87, axonometric views, dwgs.,
    elev., models.

SPORTS FACILITIES--JAPAN--KAWABE--
AKITA SKY DOME
    Akita Sky Dome / Masaru Ozaki.
    Sports facility with giant
    translucent tent structure roof,
    Kawabe-gun. Architects: Kajima
    Kensetsu Kabushiki Kaisha.
    JAPAN ARCHITECT 1990 July, v.65,
    no.7(399), p.40-43, dets., dwgs.,
    photos., plan, secn.
    Herald city / Yukio Sano.
    Four "domed" tent structure
    buildings by Kajima Kensetsu
    Kabushiki Kaisha. English summary,
    p.19.
    KENCHIKU BUNKA 1990 Oct., v.45,
    no.528, p.91-102, dwgs., models,
    maps, photos., plans, aerial
    photos.

SPORTS FACILITIES--JAPAN--TOKYO
    Douce armure: complexe sportif de
    Sendagaya, Tokyo, Japan / Manuel
    Tardits.
    Architects: Maki and Associates.
    TECHNIQUES ET ARCHITECTURE 1990
    Dec.-1991 Jan., no.393, p.110-115,
    elev., photos., plan, secns.,
    aerial photo.

SPORTS FACILITIES--JAPAN--TOKYO--TOKYO
BUDOKAN
    Le marziali (e leggere) losanghe
    entro il parco = The martial (and
    lightweight) lozenges in the park.
    Tokyo Budokan. Architects: Kijo
    Rokkaku & Associates.
    ARCHITETTURA: CRONACHE E STORIA
    1990 Nov., v.36, no.11(421),
    p.802-803, axonometric view,
    elevs., photos.
    Special contribution: Tokyo Budokan
    is not dynamism / Toyokazu
    Watanabe.
    Text in Japanese.
    KENCHIKU BUNKA 1990 Sept., v.45,
    no.527, p.181-184, photos.
    Tokyo Budokan.
    Martial arts center. Architects:
    Kijo Rokkaku, Architect and
    Associates. Includes essay,
    sparkling spirit, by Iwao
    Matsuyama and a "dialogue",
    wonderful devices of Tokyo
    Budokan, by Syuji Funo nad Kijo
    Rokkaku. English summary, p.19.
    KENCHIKU BUNKA 1990 Apr., v.45,
    no.522, p.21-56, axonometric view,
    dets., ports., elevs., photos.,
    plans, secns.
    Tokyo Budokan.
    Martial arts Center. Architects:
    Kijo Rokkaku, Architect and
    Associates. Includes an essay by
    Rokkaku on the martial arts of
    Japan.
    JAPAN ARCHITECT 1990 May, v.65,
    no.5(397), p.[10]-26, dets.,
    elevs., photos., plans, secns.

SPORTS FACILITIES--JAPAN--TOKYO--TOKYO
METROPOLITAN GYMNASIUM
    Lightness / David B. Stewart.
    On the Tokyo Metropolitan
    Gymnasium. Architects: Maki and
    Associates.
    JAPAN ARCHITECT 1990 Aug.-Sept.,
    v.65, no.8-9(400-401), p.26-33,
    sketch, secns.

SPORTS FACILITIES--JAPAN--TOKYO--TOKYO
METROPOLITAN GYMNASIUM (CONTINUED)
    Special edition: city and collective
    forms.
    Features nine projects including
    competition entries and works in
    progress by Maki and Associates,
    1989-1992. Includes dialogue:
    Architecture, city, public spirit,
    by Riichi Miyake and Fumihiko
    Maki. English summary, p.27.
    KENCHIKU BUNKA 1990 June, v.45,
    no.524, p.31-112, dwgs., ports.,
    elevs., models, photos., plans,
    secns., site plans, sketches.
    Tokyo Metropolitan Gymnasium,
    Shibuya Ward, Tokyo, 1990 /
    Fumihiko Maki.
    Architects: Maki and Associates.
    JAPAN ARCHITECT 1990 Aug.-Sept.,
    v.65, no.8-9(400-401), p.[10]-25,
    dets., elevs., model, photos.,
    plans, secns., site plans, aerial
    photos.
    Two landmarks for Tokyo / Hiroshi
    Watanabe, John Morris Dixon.
    Two projects by Fumihiko Maki and
    Maki and Associates: Makuhari
    Messe, or Nippon Convention
    Center, and the Tokyo Metropolitan
    Gymnasium.
    PROGRESSIVE ARCHITECTURE 1990
    Aug., v.71, no.8, p.74-87,
    axonometric views, port., model,
    photos., plans, secns., site plan,
    aerial photos.

SPORTS FACILITIES--PORTUGAL--BRAGA
    Palazzo delle esposizioni e degli
    sport di Braga = Exhibition and
    sports hall in Braga, [Portugal].
    Architects: Goncalo Byrne with E.
    Trigo de Sousa, N. Matos Silva and
    M. Mateus.
    LOTUS INTERNATIONAL 1989, no.63,
    p.62-73, det., elevs., photos.,
    plans, secns.

SPORTS FACILITIES--SAUDI ARABIA--
RIYADH--KHASHM ALAAN NATIONAL GUARD
SPORTS CENTER
    National Guard Sports Center. Khashm
    Alaan / Maurizio Vitta.
    Architect: Claudio Salocchi. Text
    in Italian and English.
    L'ARCA 1990 May, no.38, p.26-33,
    photos., plans, secns., site
    plans.

SPORTS FACILITIES--SLOPING SITES--
GERMANY--BERLIN--HORST KORBER SPORTS
COMPLEX
    Force subtile: complexe sportif,
    Berlin Allemagne.
    Horst Korber Sports Complex.
    Architects: Christoph Langhof
    Architekten. Consultants: Ove
    Arup & Partner. English summary,
    68. Spanish summary, p.154.
    TECHNIQUES ET ARCHITECTURE 1990
    Dec.-1991 Jan., no.393, p.64-[69],
    photos., plans, secns., site
    plans, sketches.

SPORTS FACILITIES--SOCIOLOGICAL
ASPECTS--FRANCE
    Le sport comme generateur de
    mobilite et structurant de
    l'espace / Nuria Puig...et al.
    The role of sporting events in
    contemporary life, with reference
    to the siting of sports
    facilities. French, English, and
    Spanish summaries.
    ESPACES ET SOCIETES 1988,
    no.54-55, p.[119]-133, maps, refs.

SPORTS FACILITIES--SPAIN--AMETLLA DEL
VALLES
    Pabellon Polideportivo en L'Ametlla
    del Valles: J. Ll. Canosa y C.
    Ferrater, arquitectos.
    Spanish, English text.
    ON DISENO 1990, no.114, p.124-133,
    photos., plans.

SPORTS FACILITIES--SPAIN--BARCELONA--
COMPLEJO CATEX
    Complejo CATEX = Public facilities,
    Poble Nou, Barcelona, 1984-1989.
    Reuse of former factory as public
    sports facilities. Architect:
    Josep Lluis Mateo.
    EL CROQUIS 1990 Mar., v.9, no.42,
    p.138-149, axonometric view,
    dets., photos., plans, secns.
    Proyectar para una arquitectura
    dada: analogia y diversidad = To
    design for a given architecture:
    analogy and diversity / Anton
    Capitel.
    Discusses 4 recent projects in
    Spain.
    EL CROQUIS 1990 Mar., v.9, no.42,
    p.64-79, photos.

SPORTS FACILITIES--SPAIN--BARCELONA--
GRACIAS
    Pabellon polideportivo en Gracia,
    Barcelona: J. Bach, G. Mora y R.
    Brufau, arquitectos.
    Spanish, English text.
    ON DISENO 1990, no.114, p.104-113,
    photos., plans, secns., site
    plans.
    Respuesta urbana: polideportivo en
    Gracia / Josep Muntanola.
    Architects: Jaume Bach, Gabriel
    Mora.
    ARQUITECTURA VIVA 1990 July-Aug.,
    no.13, p.54-57, elevs., photos.,
    plans, secns.

SPORTS FACILITIES--SPAIN--BARCELONA--
PALAU SANT JORDI
    El Palau Sant Jordi, Barcelona:
    Arata Isozaki & Associates.
    Includes statement by Isozaki.
    Text in Spanish and English.
    ON DISENO 1990, no.118, p.106-171,
    cover, ill., elevs., photos.,
    plans, secns., sketches.

SPORTS FACILITIES--SPAIN--GRANOLLERS
    Architectural landmarks.
    Features three buildings by Elias
    Torres Tur and Jose Antonio
    Martinez Lapena: hospital, Mora de
    Ebro; congress center, Barcelona,
    and sports hall, Granollers.
    ARCHITECTURAL REVIEW 1990 July,
    v.188, no.1121, p.52-59, elevs.,
    models, photos., plans, secns.,
    site plan.

SPORTS FACILITIES--SPAIN--VILANOVA DEL
CAMI
    Pabellon polideportivo en Vilanova
    del Cami, Barcelona: Pere Puig,
    arquitecto.
    Spanish, English text.
    ON DISENO 1990, no.113, p.174-181,
    elev., photos., plans.

SPORTS FACILITIES--SWITZERLAND--MONTE
CARASSO
    Uber den "Vorsatz zur Vitalitat" und
    dessen Folgen fur die Architektur
    / Norbert Weickenmeier.
    DER ARCHITEKT 1990 July-Aug.,
    no.7-8, p.356-359, photos., plans,
    site plans, isometric dwg.

SPORTS FACILITIES--SWITZERLAND--
THAYNGEN--SPORTHALLE STOCKWIESEN
    Sporthalle Stockwiesen, Thayngen.
    Architects: Fritz Tissi + Peter
    Gotz.
    WERK, BAUEN + WOHNEN 1990
    Jan.-Feb., no.1-2, p.1-4 (folded
    at back), photos., plans, secns.,
    tables.

SPORTS FACILITIES--UNITED STATES--ANN
ARBOR (MICHIGAN)--MONAGHAN
SETTLEMENT POOL HOUSE
    Domino's effect / Michael J.
    Crosbie.
    On buildings designed for Thomas
    Monaghan, president of Domino's
    Pizza. Architects: Gunnar
    Birkerts, Mockbee Coker
    Architects, Hardy Holzman Pfeiffer
    Associates, Fay Jones + Maurice
    Jennings Architects, and Charles
    W. Moore.
    ARCHITECTURE: THE AIA JOURNAL 1990
    Dec., v.79, no.12, p.[48-55],127,
    dwgs., port., models, photos.,
    secn., site plans.

SPORTS FACILITIES--UNITED STATES--
BOSTON (MASSACHUSETTS)--HARVARD
UNIVERSITY--SHAD HALL
    Academic fitness: Shad Hall, Harvard
    University, Boston, Massachusetts
    / Robert Campbell.
    Athletic center for the Graduate
    School of Business Administration.
    Architects: Kallmann, McKinnell &
    Wood.
    ARCHITECTURE: THE AIA JOURNAL 1990
    Mar., v.79, no.3, p.128-133,
    elevs., photos., secns., site
    plan.

SPORTS FACILITIES--UNITED STATES--
MISSOULA (MONTANA)--WESTERN MONTANA
SPORTS MEDICINE AND FITNESS CENTER
    George Oommen Cambridge,
    Massachusetts.
    Four projects: Briggs Athletic
    Centre, Malkin Athletic Centre,
    and McCurdy Track, at Harvard
    University; Western Montana Sports
    Medicine and Fitness Centre,
    Missoula.
    ARCHITECTURE + DESIGN 1990
    Jan.-Feb., v.7, no.1, p.32-37,
    photos., plans, aerial photos.

SPORTS FACILITIES--UNITED STATES--
NASHVILLE (TENNESSEE)--CENTENNIAL
SPORTSPLEX
    Centennial Sportsplex: a win-win
    scenario / Julie C. Pursell.
    Centennial Sportsplex, Nashville,
    Tenn. Architects: Thomas, Miller &
    Partners.
    PARKS & RECREATION 1990 Dec.,
    v.25, no.12, p.22-27,56, photos.
    Water and ice: Centennial
    Sportsplex, Nashville Tennessee,
    Thomas, Miller & Partners,
    Architects / Robert A. Ivy.
    ARCHITECTURE: THE MAGAZINE OF THE
    AMERICAN INSTITUTE OF ARCHITECTS
    1990 Aug., v.79, no.8, p.[76]-79,
    photos., plans, site plan.

SPRACHMAN, MANDEL
    Restoring dreams / Mark Alden
    Branch, Abby Bussel.
    On the restoration of six 1920-30s
    American movie palaces.
    PROGRESSIVE ARCHITECTURE 1990
    June, v.71, no.6, p.92-99,
    photos., plans, secns.

SPRECKELSEN, JOHAN OTTO VON
    Blessures de l'arche [film review].
    On the film about Johan Otto Von
    Spreckelsen, Hommage a l'humanite,
    shown at the Fifarc Festival.
    Producer: Dan Tschernia.
    ARCHITECTURE D'AUJOURD'HUI 1990
    Sept., no.270, p.50, ports.
    The Grande Arche, La Defense,
    [Paris], 1989.
    Johan Otto von Spreckelsen and
    Paul Andreu. Text in Japanese and
    English.
    ARCHITECTURE AND URBANISM 1990
    Sept., no.9 Extra edition,
    p.216-225,263, photos.
    La Grande Arche [Paris].
    Architects: Johan Otto von
    Spreckelsen, Paul Andreu.
    LE MUR VIVANT 1989, no.93,
    p.60-[84], dets., models, photos.,
    plans, secns., sketches, aerial
    photos.
    Johan Otto von Spreckelsen: L'Arche
    de la Defense.
    Issue consists of ten articles on
    La Defense, including the 1973
    competition and landscape design;
    and of articles on Danish churches
    in Hvidovre, Aarhus, Forum, and
    Esbjerg, and the Carlsberg
    planetarium in Copenhagen.
    Includes English and German
    captions and summaries.
    ARKITEKTUR DK 1990, v.34, no.1-2,
    p.1-88, axonometric views, dets.,
    dwgs., elevs., models, photos.,
    plans, secns., site plans.
    Le nozze di cubo e piramide /
    Elizabeth Frolet.
    The Pyramide du Grand Louvre,
    Grande Arche de la Defense, Opera
    de la Bastille.
    ART E DOSSIER 1989 July-Aug.,
    no.37, p.10-14, photos.
    Ontledigde tekens: de piramide van
    Pei en de boog van Von Spreckelson
    / Paul Vermeulen.
    ARCHIS 1989 Oct., no.10, p.14-21,
    dwgs., models, photos., secns.,
    site plans, engrs., refs.

SPRECKELSEN, JOHAN OTTO VON
(CONTINUED)
Spreckelsens Ark / Francois Chaslin.
La Grande Arche, Paris.
ARKITEKTEN 1989 Dec.22, v.91,
no.23, p.596-601, ill., dwgs.,
elevs., photos., plans, secns.,
site plans.
Stavnsholtkirkens arkitektoniske
sigte / Svend Jacobsen.
Analysis of the plan and elevation
of the Copenhagen church, with
reference to musical compositions
of Johan Sebastian Bach.
Architect: J.O. Van Spreckelsen.
ARKITEKTEN 1990 May, v.92, no.6,
p.194-197, ill., photos., plans.

SPRENG, DANIEL
Acciaio come misura del distacco /
Lucia Bisi.
House with a studio addition on
the roof, Bern, Switzerland.
Architect: Daniel Spreng.
VILLE GIARDINI 1990 Oct., no.252,
p.2-9, axonometric view, photos.,
plans, secn.

SPRING, MARTIN
Architects apocalypse / Martin
Spring.
BUILDING 1990 Dec.14, v.255,
no.49, p.20-21, dwgs.
Bowers between towers [Canary Wharf]
/ Martin Spring.
On plans for open spaces, street
furniture, and landscape design,
recently revealed by Olympia &
York.
BUILDING 1990 May 18, v.255,
no.20, p.51-53, ill., photos.
Civic Trust awards 1990 / Martin
Spring.
Presents the 22 winning projects.
BUILDING 1990 Dec.7, v.255, no.48,
p.43-50, photos.
Classical revival / Martin Pawley,
Martin Spring.
Includes a review of Classical
architecture: a complete handbook,
by Robert Adam, in conjunction
with an exhibit at the Heinz
Gallery entitled Classical design
in the late 20th century.
BUILDING 1990 Nov.9, v.255, no.44,
p.61-65.
Council crack down / Martin Spring.
Defective precast reinforced
concrete houses in Bristol,
England are being rebuilt,
including the Sea Mills and Upper
Horfield projects. Architects:
Levitt Bernstein Associates;
Shepheard Epstein & Hunter.
BUILDING 1990 July 27, v.255,
no.30, p.38-42, dwg., elevs.,
maps, photos., plans.
Criticism: Nippon Convention Center
/ Martin Spring.
Architects: Maki and Associates.
This article is reprinted from
Jan. 26, 1990 issue of Building
magazine, London.
JAPAN ARCHITECT 1990 Aug.-Sept.,
v.65, no.8-9(400-401), p.49-50,
elev.
Distilling Scots design [exhibition
review] / Martin Spring
A travelling exhibit (For a Wee
Country: Architectural
Contributions to the Development
of Scotland) opens on 13 Mar.1990
(Continued next column)

SPRING, MARTIN (CONTINUED)
Distilling Scots...(CONTINUED)
in Glasgow, marking the 150th
jubilee of the RIAS.
BUILDING 1990 Mar.9, v.255, no.10,
p.22-23, ill.
Epic volumes [British Library] /
Martin Spring.
On the Library construction,
during the installation of its
extensive services. Architects:
Colin St. John Wilson & Partners.
BUILDING 1990 Apr.20, v.255,
no.16, p.50-55, axonometric view,
dwg., photos.
Fjord fiesta [Aker Brygge, Oslo] /
Martin Spring.
Waterfront complex with shops,
restaurants, housing, offices, and
theaters. Architect: Niels Torp.
BUILDING 1990 July 13, v.255,
no.28, p.42-46, photos., aerial
photo.
Glasgow's hall of fame / Martin
Spring.
The Royal Concert Hall.
Architects: Sir Leslie Martin with
RMJM.
BUILDING 1990 Oct.19, v.255,
no.41, p.63-67, ill., photos.,
plan, secn.
Home from the office [Middlesex
House] / Martin Spring.
Conversion of a 15-story office
building on Northwick Rd. in
Greenford, west of London, into 78
flats for homeless families.
Architect: Brock Carmichael
Associates.
BUILDING 1990 Feb.16, v.255, no.7,
p.38-41, photos, plan.
Japanese Roman-Tec / Martin Spring.
Two works by Fumihiko Maki: Nippon
Convention Centre, Tokyo Bay, and
Tepia Pavilion.
BUILDING 1990 Jan.26, v.255, no.4,
p.49-58, axonometric views,
photos.
Matching Matcham / Martin Spring.
The County Arcade, completed in
1904 (architect: Frank Matcham) in
the Victoria Quarter, Leeds
(restoration architect: Derek
Latham & Company).
BUILDING 1990 Sept.14, v.255,
no.36, p.61-66, photos.
Modernists honoured in RIBA National
Architecture Awards / Martin
Spring.
The 16 National Awards for 1989.
BUILDING 1990 Jan.5, v.255, no.1,
p.8, photos.
News knight [ITN headquarters] /
Martin Spring.
The Independent Television News
offices, 200 Grays Inn Rd., London
WC1. Architect: Foster Associates.
Engineers: Ove Arup & Partners.
BUILDING 1990 July 13, v.255,
no.28, p.22-23, photos.
On site in Tokyo: opening up the
Japanese honey pot / Martin
Spring.
Two projects: Century Tower
(architects: Foster Associates)
and Gotoh Private Museum
(architects: David Chipperfield &
Partners).
BUILDING 1990 Jan.19, v.255, no.3,
p.49-57, dwgs., ports., model,
photos., secn.

SPRING, MARTIN (CONTINUED)
Parking at the crossroads [office
parks, West London] / Martin
Spring.
Plans for two new projects:
Chiswick Park (developer, Stanhope
Trafalgar; architect, Terry
Farrell; landscape architect,
Laurie Olin) and Bedfont Lakes
(developers, MEPC and IBM;
architect, Michael Hopkins).
BUILDING 1990 June 1, v.255,
no.22, p.40-45, diagrs., ill.,
model, photos., site plan.
Pillars of society / Martin Spring.
Mothers' Square, Hackney, London,
with housing for low-income
families and mental patients.
Architect: Hunt Thompson
Associates.
BUILDING 1990 June 15, v.255,
no.24, p.47-49, axonometric view,
photos.
Pre-flight services [Stansted
Airport Terminal] / Martin Spring.
Architect: Foster Associates. An
article in the Sept.11, 1987 issue
featured structural erection and
project management of this site.
BUILDING 1990 Mar.16, v.255,
no.11, p.52-58, photos., secn.
Royal abdication [Royal Docks] /
Martin Spring.
Strategy and economic setbacks for
the LDDC's development of the
Docklands.
BUILDING 1990 May 25, v.255.
no.21, p.24-25, map, photo.
Royal ripple effect / Martin Spring.
On the influence of Prince
Charles' opinions on architecture
and a report on a recent debate at
the Cambridge Union.
BUILDING 1990 Feb.2, v.255, no.5,
p.26-28, ports., models, photos.
Spec-built cosmos [Ludgate Hill] /
Martin Spring.
Located at 200 Queen Victoria St.,
London. Architect: John Outram
Associates.
BUILDING 1989 Dec.8, v.254, no.49,
p.26-30, dwgs., ports., elevs.,
models, secns., site plans,
sketches.
World Cup winner [Meazza Stadium;
Milan] / Martin Spring.
Architects and engineers: Edilnord
Progetti.
BUILDING 1990 Jan.5, v.255, no.1,
p.39-43, photos., plan, secn.

SPROATS, KEVIN
Bathurst-Orange: lessons from an
over-ambitious initiative in
selective decentralization / Kevin
Sproats.
AUSTRALIAN PLANNER: JOURNAL OF THE
ROYAL AUSTRALIAN PLANNING
INSTITUTE 1990 Sept., v.28, no.3,
p.20-24, tables, refs.

SPROSON, ROBERT HENRY
Designing for life and death [AIDS
hospice] / Robert Cowan.
London Lighthouse. Architect:
Robert Sproson and First
Architecture.
ARCHITECTS' JOURNAL 1990 Aug.15,
v.192, no.7, p.14, ports., photos.

SPUHLER, MARTIN
Projekt Bahnhof Uster, 1989.
Architect: Martin Spuhler.
WERK, BAUEN + WOHNEN 1989 Dec.,
no.12, p.50, axonometric view,
photo., plan, secns.

SPUR (ORGANIZATION)
Cities build coalitions with clout.
Citizen participation and
political activism in New York,
Birmingham, Ala., and San
Francisco.
ARCHITECTS' JOURNAL 1990 Mar.14,
v.191, no.11, p.50-57, elev.,
photos., aerial photos.

SPYCHER, DAVID
Suisse: le credo de l'habitat
groupe.
Feature four projects: Castel
Schmitten, Fribourg, architects:
Martin Wagner, David and Samuel
Spycher; Merzenacker project,
Bern, architects: ARB
Arbeitsgruppe; Habitat industriel,
Givisiez, architect: Rodolphe
Luscher and a multi-use building,
Geneva, architect: Rodolpke
Luscher and a multi-use building,
Geneva, architect: Chantal Scaler.
English summary, p.180.
ARCHITECTURE INTERIEURE CREE 1990
June-July, no.237, p.[108]-119,
dwgs., photos., secns.

SPYCHER, SAMUEL
Suisse: le credo de l'habitat
groupe.
Feature four projects: Castel
Schmitten, Fribourg, architects:
Martin Wagner, David and Samuel
Spycher; Merzenacker project,
Bern, architects: ARB
Arbeitsgruppe; Habitat industriel,
Givisiez, architect: Rodolphe
Luscher and a multi-use building,
Geneva, architect: Rodolpke
Luscher and a multi-use building,
Geneva, architect: Chantal Scaler.
English summary, p.180.
ARCHITECTURE INTERIEURE CREE 1990
June-July, no.237, p.[108]-119,
dwgs., photos., secns.

SQARBI, CLAUDIO
"Sinds jaren denken architecten met
niet meer aan een tastbaar
fenomeen ... een gesprek met
Joseph Rykwert" [interview] /
Herman van Bergeijk, Claudio
Sqarbi.
ARCHIS 1990 Mar., no.3, p.42-45,
dwgs., ports.

SQUARES (CITIES)
See PLAZAS

SQUARES - PUBLIC
See PLAZAS

SQUASH RACQUET COURTS--GERMANY
(WEST)--NEUSS--CITY-SQUASH
City-Squash in Neuss.
Features cafe in squash facility
in Neuss. Architect: Burkhard
Moosdorf. Interior architect:
Michael Reder.
DEUTSCHE BAUZEITSCHRIFT 1990 Dec.,
v.38, no.12, p.1743-1746, photos.,
plans, secns., site plan,
isometric dwg.

SQUASH RACQUET COURTS--GERMANY
(WEST)--OSTFILDERN--SQUASHZENTRUM
TRICK
Squashzentrum Trick in Ostfildern.
Squash facilitiy. Architects: Drei
Architekten.
DEUTSCHE BAUZEITSCHRIFT 1990 Dec.,
v.38, no.12, p.1747-[1754],
axonometric view, elevs., photos.,
plan, secns., site plans.

SQUATTER SETTLEMENTS
See also SHANTYTOWNS
The TOADS: a new American urban
epidemic / Michael R. Greenberg,
Frank J. Popper, Bernadette M.
West.
"Temporarily obsolete abandoned
derelict sites": deserted
industrial sites and housing that
become makeshift housing for the
homeless, fire safety hazards and
toxic waste sites.
URBAN AFFAIRS QUARTERLY 1990 Mar.,
v.25, no.3, p.435-454, tables,
refs.

SQUATTER SETTLEMENTS--BRAZIL--SAO
PAULO
A convivencia com a contradicao
metropolitana.
PROJETO 1990 Dec.-1991 Jan.,
no.137, p.A1-A24, maps,
photos., plans, secns., site
plans, tables, aerial photo.

SQUATTER SETTLEMENTS--DEVELOPING
COUNTRIES
Smabyerne i den 3. verden - en
overset storrelse? / Peder Boas
Jensen.
Report on a seminar held Nov.1,
1989 at the Kunstakademiets
Arkitektskole.
ARKITEKTEN 1990 Mar., v.92, no.3,
p.100-101, photos.

SQUATTER SETTLEMENTS--LATIN AMERICA
Planning in squatter settlements: an
interview with a community leader
/ Donald T. Lauria, Dale
Whittington.
In Latin America.
JOURNAL OF PLANNING EDUCATION AND
RESEARCH 1990 summer, v.9, no.3,
p.207-212,

SQUATTER SETTLEMENTS--PAKISTAN--
HYDERABAD--KHUDA-KI-BASTI
Step by step: enabling Pakistan's
urban poor to build / Brian Brace
Taylor.
A pilot project (Khuda-Ki-Basti)
of the Hyderabad Development
Authority.
MIMAR: ARCHITECTURE IN DEVELOPMENT
1990 June, v.10, no.2(35),
p.47-52, elevs., photos., plans.

SQUATTER SETTLEMENTS--SPAIN--MADRID
The Madrid neighborhood remodelling
programme: a case study / Robert
Chubb.
LAND DEVELOPMENT STUDIES 1989
Jan., v.6, no.1, p.[3]-11, biblio.

SQUATTER SETTLEMENTS--TYPOLOGY
The analysis of layout patterns in
squatter settlements / Gulsun
Saglamer, Halil Dincel.
INTERNATIONAL JOURNAL FOR HOUSING
SCIENCE AND ITS APPLICATIONS 1990,
v.14, no.2, p.107-113, graphs,
plans, tables, refs.

SQUATTERS--UNITED STATES--NEW YORK
(NEW YORK)
Rebels with a cause? / Doug
Turetsky.
Squatters in vacant New York City
buildings.
CITY LIMITS 1990 Apr., v.15, no.4,
p.12-15, ports., photos.

SQUIER, PRUDENCE
Pamela Harriman's Willow Oaks: an
English garden in the Virigina
countryside / Prudence Squier.
SOUTHERN ACCENTS 1990 May, v.13,
no.4, p.[120]-127, port., photos.

SRI LANKA--AHUNGALLA--RESORTS--TRITON
HOTEL
The architecture of Geoffrey Bawa,
an intimacy of experience and
expression.
Features four projects: Madura
Club, Madura, ladia; Triton Hotel,
Ahungalla, Sri Lanka; New
Parliamentary complex, Sri
Jayawardenepura, Kotte; Ruhuna
University, Matara.
ARCHITECTURE + DESIGN 1990
Mar.-Apr., v.7, no.2, p.57-71,
dwg., photos., plans, secns., site
plans, sketches.

SRI LANKA--ARCHITECTURE
Architecture Sri Lanka.
Feature of issue. Includes two
articles separately indexed;
Foreword by Ashok B. Lall; Trends
and transitions, by Anjalendran C.
and Rajiv Wanasundara; The Sri
Lankan vernacular; The eighties.
ARCHITECTURE + DESIGN 1990
Mar.-Apr., v.7, no.2, p.23-113,
dwgs., photos., plans, secns.,
site plans.

SRI LANKA--BERUWELA - BENTOTA--
GARDENS--BRIEF
A garden called "Brief" : a patch of
paradise created by Bevis Bawa.
On the west coast of Sri Lanka, in
Alutgama, between Beruwela and
Bentota.
ARCHITECTURE + DESIGN 1990
Mar.-Apr., v.7, no.2, p.109-113,
dwgs., photos.
A Sri Lankan garden / Michelle
Fonseka, Dilshan Ferdinando,
Romesh Fonseka.
Brief, a garden on the west coast
between Beruwela and Bentota,
designed by Bevis Bawa in 1929.
MIMAR: ARCHITECTURE IN DEVELOPMENT
1990 June, v.10, no.2(35),
p.66-69, dwg., photos., site plan.

SRI LANKA--COLOMBO--COMMUNITY
DEVELOPMENT--KIRILLAPONE
The Kirillapone shanty settlement:
learning through experience.
Physical improvements to six-acre
settlement in Colombo, Sri Lanka.
HABITAT NEWS 1989 Aug., v.11,
no.2, p.38-41, ports., photos.

SRI LANKA--COLOMBO--SHANTYTOWNS--
KIRILLAPONE
The Kirillapone shanty settlement:
learning through experience.
Physical improvements to six-acre
settlement in Colombo, Sri Lanka.
HABITAT NEWS 1989 Aug., v.11,
no.2, p.38-41, ports., photos.

SRI LANKA--HOUSING
Services by a support approach:
infrastructure for urban housing
in Sri Lanka / Richard Franceys,
Andrew Cotton.
OPEN HOUSE INTERNATIONAL 1988,
v.13, no.4, p.43-48, photos,
tables, refs.

SRI LANKA--KOTTE--CAPITOLS
The architecture of Geoffrey Bawa,
an intimacy of experience and
expression.
Features four projects: Madura
Club, Madura, India; Triton Hotel,
Ahungalla, Sri Lanka; New
Parliamentary complex, Sri
Jayawardenepura, Kotte; Ruhuna
University, Matara.
ARCHITECTURE + DESIGN 1990
Mar.-Apr., v.7, no.2, p.57-71,
dwg., photos., plans, secns., site
plans, sketches.

SRI LANKA--NARAHENPITA--OFFICE
BUILDINGS--MILK INDUSTRIES OF LANKA
CO.
Offices for Milco, Narahenpita.
On the west coast of Sri Lanka;
completed in Oct.1987. Architect:
C. Anjalendran.
MIMAR: ARCHITECTURE IN DEVELOPMENT
1990 June, v.10, no.2(35),
p.60-64, elevs., map, photos.,
site plan.

SRI LANKA--VERNACULAR ARCHITECTURE
Architecture Sri Lanka.
Feature of issue. Includes two
articles separately indexed;
Foreword by Ashok B. Lall; Trends
and transitions, by Anjalendran C.
and Rajiv Wanasundara; The Sri
Lankan vernacular; The eighties.
ARCHITECTURE + DESIGN 1990
Mar.-Apr., v.7, no.2, p.23-113,
dwgs., photos., plans, secns.,
site plans.

SRI LANKA--WEST DINAJPUR--CLINICS--
JAMUNA
Rural health development centre
Jamuna Village, West Dinajpur
District, 1989 / Ranjit Mitra.
Architect: Samaresh Mukherjee.
ARCHITECTURE + DESIGN 1990
Mar.-Apr., v.7, no.2, p.13,
photos.

SRO HOTELS
SEE SINGLE ROOM OCCUPANCY HOTELS

ST. GEORGE, ROBERT BLAIR
Dawns and beliefs: architecture,
commerce, and conversion in early
New England / Robert Blair St.
George.
Appendix is an excerpt from a 17th
century document, "The building
and enclosing of our countrie
farm".
WINTERTHUR PORTFOLIO 1990 Winter,
v.25, no.4, p.[241]-287, dwgs.,
photos., plans, engrs., refs.

ST. JOHN-STEVAS, NORMAN, 1929-
Yankees at the court of Lord St.
John / Stephen Trombley.
Focus on the reaction of Bruce
Graham of Som's London office to
Lord St. John of Fawsley's speech
at the Building Design 20th
anniversary dinner, condemning the
U.S. architectural practices'
invasion.
BUILDING DESIGN 1990 Mar.16,
no.977, p.12, ports.

ST. JOHN WILSON, COLIN
No.1 Poultry, City of London, 1986-.
Office building project.
Architects: James Stirling,
Michael Wilford and Associates.
Includes essay: No.1 Poultry, a
great building for the 90s /Colin
St. John Wilson. Text in Japanese
and English.
ARCHITECTURE AND URBANISM 1990
May, no.5 extra edition,
p.136-159, axonometric views,
elevs., models, photos., plans,
site plan.
Recent work of James Stirling
Michael Wilford and Associates /
edited by Toshio Nakamura.
Contents: Editor's introduction /
Toshio Nakamura-- Essays by
Francesco Dal Co, Brendan Gill,
Geoffrey Baker and Colin St. John
Wilson-- Opening speech: James
Stirling: opening day of
Performing Arts Centre, Cornell
University-- Works (indexed
separately)-- Credit list of
project[s] since Cornell,
p.260-61-- Biography of James
Stirling & Michael Wilford,
p.261-65-- Chronological list of
buildings and projects, 1950-1989.
Text in Japanese and English.
ARCHITECTURE AND URBANISM 1990
May, no.5 extra edition,
p.[1]-267, axonometric views,
dwgs., ports., elevs., models,
photos., plans, secns., site
plans.

STABENOW, JORG
Im Kontext der modernen Stadt /
Thomas Will, Jorg Stabenow.
ARCH PLUS 1990 Oct., no.105-106,
p.88-94, dwgs., models, photos.,
plans, aerial photos., refs.
Der Ort der Stadt: eine
Wanderausstellung zur
Wechselwirkung von Topographie und
urbaner Form / Jorg Stabenow.
Student projects at TU Munchen
entitled "Stadt und Topographie,"
directed by Tomas Valena, use
Ljubljana as their basis.
ARCH PLUS 1990 Apr., no.103,
p.32-33, maps.
Rudolf Vorhoelzer und Lois
Welzenbacher, zwei Ausstellungen
uber alternative Wege des Neuen
Bauens [exhibition review] / Jorg
Stabenow.
Exhibitions in Munich and
Innsbruck.
ARCH PLUS 1990 July, no.104,
p.14-15, models, photos., plans.

STABILITY OF STRUCTURES
See STRUCTURAL STABILITY

STABLER, MIKE
Timeshare: a new dimension in
tourism / Mike Stabler, Brian
Goodall.
Timeshare ownership of tourism
accomodation by U.K. residents;
includes illustrated examples of
different types of timeshare
property.
BUILT ENVIRONMENT 1989, v.15,
no.2, p.101-124, graphs, ill.,
table, refs.

STABLES
See also MEWS

STABLES--ALTERATIONS AND ADDITIONS--
GERMANY (WEST)--LASBEK
Weiterbau: zu Arbeiten von Helmut
Riemann.
Five restoration projects in West
Germany. Includes English
summaries.
BAUMEISTER 1990 Apr., v.87, no.4,
p.13-31, axonometric views, dets.,
elevs., photos., plans, secns.,
site plans.

STABLES--ENGLAND--NORFOLK--HOUGHTON
HALL
Riding on status: the stables at
Houghton / Giles Worsley.
COUNTRY LIFE 1990 Sept.27, v.184,
no.39, p.108-111, photos.

STABLES--FRANCE
Architecture equestre.
Theme issue on equestrian
architecture in France including
horse farms, racetracks and
stables.
MONUMENTS HISTORIQUES 1990
Jan.-Feb., no.167, p.[2]-127,
dets., diagrs., dwgs., clevs.,
maps, photos., plans, aerial
photos.

STABLES--UNITED STATES--DUTCHESS
COUNTY (NEW YORK)
New twist to the farmhouse
vernacular in New York / Paul
Goldberger.
On the stable and coach house
addition to a Dutchess Co. horse
farm. Architects:: Tigerman
McCurry. Architects of older main
house: Albert Kahn Associates.
ARCHITECTURAL DIGEST 1990 June,
v.47, no.6, p.86,90,94, dwg.,
elevs., model, photos., plans.

STADIA
See STADIUMS

STADIUMS
See also BASEBALL STADIUMS
See also ENCLOSED STADIUMS
Run it down the field again, fellows
/ Grady Clay.
The football field as a standard
measurement, as illustrated in a
wide variety of quotes.
PLACES 1990 Summer, v.6, no.4,
p.4-8, photo., plan, aerial
photos.

STADIUMS (CONTINUED)
Stadien = stades = stadiums.
Introduction to special section on new stadiums. Three articles indexed separately.
WERK, BAUEN + WOHNEN 1990 Sept., no.9, p.20-21, photo.

STADIUMS--ALTERATIONS AND ADDITIONS--ENGLAND--LONDON--TWICKENHAM RUGBY FOOTBALL GROUND
La nuova tribuna dello stadio di Twickenham = New North Stand at Twickenham / Luigi Moiraghi.
North grandstand addition to Twickenham Rugby Football Ground, London; architects: Husband & Company.
L'ARCA 1990 May, no.38, p.20-25, dwgs., elevs., plans, secns.

STADIUMS--ALTERATIONS AND ADDITIONS--FRANCE--LYON
Ristrutturazione dello Stadio di Garnier a Lione.
On the grandstand covering of the 1920 Gerland stadium, Lyon. Original architect: Tony Garnier. Renovation architects: Rene Gages, Michel Relave. Summaries in English, French and Spanish.
ABACUS 1990 July-Sept., v.6, no.23, p.78-79, dwgs., photos., secns.

STADIUMS--ALTERATIONS AND ADDITIONS--ITALY--FLORENCE--STADIO COMUNALE
Il futuro ha un cuore antico: civic stadium of Florence / Loris G. Macci.
Renovation and expansion of stadium built in 1930s. Original architect: Pier Luigi Nervi; architects for renovation: Italo Gamberini, Loris G. Macci, Enrico Novelli, Giovanna Slocovich. Text in Italian and English.
L'ARCA 1990 May, no.38, p.74-79, elevs., photos., plans, secns.

STADIUMS--ALTERATIONS AND ADDITIONS--ITALY--GENOA--STADIO LUIGI FERRARIS
A identidade dos estadios / Vittorio Gregotti.
Four stadiums designed by Gregotti Associados.
PROJETO 1990 [June]., no.132, p.26-34, elevs., models, photos., plans, secns., site plans.
Ort und Stadion: neue Fussballstadien in Italien.
New football stadiums in Bari and Genoa. Architects: Renzo Piano Building Workshop, Gregotti Associati. Text in German, French and English.
WERK, BAUEN + WOHNEN 1990 Sept., no.9, p.22-35, dets., elevs., map, photos., plans, secns., site plans, aerial photos.
Puissance d'integration: restructuration du stade Luigi Ferraris, Genes, Italie. Renovation architects: Gregotti Associati. English summary, p.41. Spanish summary, p.153.
TECHNIQUES ET ARCHITECTURE 1990 Dec.-1991 Jan., no.393, p.40-41, photos., plan, secns.

STADIUMS--ALTERATIONS AND ADDITIONS--ITALY--MILAN--SAN SIRO
Hoch hinaus: die Erweiterung des San Siro Stadions in Mailand / Silvia Pizzocaro.
Architects: G. Ragazzi, E. Hoffer.
ARCHITEKTUR, INNENARCHITEKTUR, TECHNISCHER AUSBAU 1990 July-Aug., v.98, no.7-8, p.20-23, ill., elevs., photos., plans.

STADIUMS--ALTERATIONS AND ADDITIONS--ITALY--ROME--STADIO OLIMPICO
Il nuovo Stadio Olimpico a Roma = The renovated Olympic Stadium in Rome / Giuseppe Nannerini.
Project head: Annibale Vitellozzi et al. Project architect: Studio Zucker. Includes English translation; French, German and Spanish summaries p.[3].
L'INDUSTRIA DELLE COSTRUZIONI 1990 Oct., v.24, no.228, p.6-17, dets., models, photos., plans, secns.

STADIUMS--COMPETITIONS--DENMARK--BRONDBY--DANMARK
Stadion "Danmark" in Brondby, Danemark = Stadium "Danmark" in Brondby, Denmark.
Competition. First prize: Krohn & Hartvig Rasmussen. Text in German.
ARCHITEKTUR + WETTBEWERBE 1990 Mar., no.141, p.58-63, ill., models, plans, secns., site plans.

STADIUMS--COMPETITIONS--FRANCE--ILE-DE-FRANCE
Pour un grand stade / Jean-Francois Pousse.
On the nine proposals for the World Cup stadium to be located near Paris. English summary, p.51. Spanish summary, p.153.
TECHNIQUES ET ARCHITECTURE 1990 Dec.-1991 Jan., no.393, p.50-51, dwgs., model, map.

STADIUMS--CONSERVATION AND RESTORATION--ENGLAND--LONDON--WEMBLEY STADIUM
Leisure.
Nine articles, including ones on Wembley Stadium, the Leeds and Liverpool canal, tourism, and hotel design.
BUILDING 1990 Apr.13, v.255, no.15 suppl., p.3-, photos.

STADIUMS--ENGLAND
Gazza plays a classical game / Simon Inglis.
New football (i.e., soccer) stadiums in Dorchester, Yeovil and Walsall, Eng.
ARCHITECTS' JOURNAL 1990 Sept.12, v.192, no.11, p.14-15, photos.

STADIUMS--ENGLAND--LONDON--LORD'S CRICKET GROUND
Salonatmosphare: Stadien in Barcelona, Sportanlagen in Eichstatt, Kricketstadion bei London, Amphitheater in Nimes. Architects: Esteve Bonell and Francesc Rius, Karljosef Schattner with Wilhelm Huber, Michael Hopkins and Partner, Finn Geipel and Nicolas Michelin. Text in German, French and English.
WERK, BAUEN + WOHNEN 1990 Sept., no.9, p.46-65, dets., elevs.,
(Continued next column)

STADIUMS--ENGLAND--LONDON--LORD'S CRICKET GROUND (CONTINUED)
Salonatmosphare:...(CONTINUED)
models, photos., plans, secns., site plans.

STADIUMS--ENGLAND--YEOVIL
Yeovil football stadium.
Architect: Peter Smith & Partners. Landscape architect: Tony Male Associates.
BUILDING 1990 Nov.30, v.255, no.47, p.45-52, photos., plans, secns., site plan, tables.

STADIUMS--EUROPE
Ahead of the game [stadiums] / Simon Inglis.
Three European sports stadiums: Galgenwaard Stadium, Utrecht; New Comunale Stadium, Bari, by Renzo Piano; and Arnhem's Eurodrome by Joseph Wund. Includes second article: External walls and roof, football stadium; Renzo Piano, p.50-53.
ARCHITECTS' JOURNAL 1990 June 6, v.191, no.23, p.[36]-41,[44]-47, 50-53, dets., models, photos., plans, secns., aerial photo.
Materiali sintetici per impianti sportivi.
Synthetic materials used in stadium roofs over seating in European stadiums.
L'INDUSTRIA DELLE COSTRUZIONI 1990 Oct., v.24, no.228, p.83, photos.

STADIUMS--FRANCE--NIMES
A identidade dos estadios / Vittorio Gregotti.
Four stadiums designed by Gregotti Associados.
PROJETO 1990 [June]., no.132, p.26-34, elevs., models, photos., plans, secns., site plans.

STADIUMS--FRANCE--PARIS--STADE CHARLETY
Stade Charlety [Paris] / Marie-Jeanne Dumont.
Architects: Henri and Bruno Gaudin. English summary, p.130.
ARCHITECTURE D'AUJOURD'HUI 1990 June, no.269, p.124-131, dets., ill., elevs., models, secns., site plans, sketches.

STADIUMS--GERMANY (WEST)
Big is beautiful: Hallenfieber an Rhein und Ruhr / Roland Stimpel.
Includes sections on EuroPalast Koln, by Rainer Wallmann (architects: Ellerbe Becket; Lister, Drew, Haines, Barrow; Petry & Partner, Mronz/Kottmair) and Grosshalle FORUM Gelsenkirchen (architect: Josef Wund).
BAUWELT 1990 June 29, v.81, no.24, p.1249-1255, ill., elev., models, photos., plan, secns., aerial photo.

STADIUMS--GREAT BRITAIN
An impasse for the nineties / Simon Inglis.
Sports stadium guidelines in Britain.
ARCHITECTS' JOURNAL 1990 Nov.21, v.192, no.20, p.15, axonometric views.

STADIUMS--GREAT BRITAIN (CONTINUED)
New Goals for stadiums.
Section has four articles: on
design quality, European stadiums,
greenbelts, and alternate uses for
stadiums.
BUILDING 1990 Mar.23, v.255,
no.12, p.47-52, dwgs., ports.,
models, photos.

STADIUMS--HISTORY
Histoires de stades / Jean-Francois
Pousse.
English summary, p.39. Spanish
summary, p.53.
TECHNIQUES ET ARCHITECTURE 1990
Dec.-1991 Jan., no.393, p.36-39,
photos., secns., elevs.

STADIUMS--INTERIOR DESIGN--ENGLAND--
WALTHAMSTOW STADIUM--ASCOT SUITE
A dogs' diner / Sarah Kitchen.
The new Ascot Suite, a private
enclosure at Walthamstow Stadium,
designed by architect Timothy
French.
BUILDING 1990 Sept.28, v.255,
no.38, p.68-69, photos.

STADIUMS--ITALY
Groszstadien 1990.
Issue features stadiums. In
addition to several articles
indexed separately, includes
essays by Felix Zwoch,
Heinz-Joachim Fischer, Karl
Valentin, Mara Pinardi, Marco
Degl'Innocenti, and Ermanno
Ranzani, and features the stadiums
at Bari, Florence, Genoa, Milan,
Palermo, Rome, Turin, and Udine.
BAUWELT 1990 June 29, v.81, no.24,
p.1202-1246, ill., elevs., models,
photos., plans, secns., site
plans, aerial photos.
Schmuckstuche und Skandale: du
Stadien der
Fussball-Weltmeisterschaft in
Italien / Oliver G. Hamm.
DEUTSCHE BAUZEITUNG 1990 May,
v.124, no.5, p.163-164, dwgs.,
elev., photo., secn.
A sporting advantage: 1990 stadiums
in Italy, edited by Silvio San
Pietro [book review] / Simon
Inglis.
ARCHITECTS' JOURNAL 1990 Oct.24,
v.192, no.17, p.82, photos.
La trastienda del Mundial: estadios
para Italia 90 / Richard
Ingersoll.
In Mian, Genoa and Bari.
ARQUITECTURA VIVA 1990 July-Aug.,
no.13, p.50-53, elev., photos.,
secn.

STADIUMS--ITALY--BARI
Ahead of the game [stadiums] / Simon
Inglis.
Three European sports stadiums:
Galgenwaard Stadium, Utrecht; New
Comunale Stadium, Bari, by Renzo
Piano; and Arnhem's Eurodrome by
Joseph Wund. Includes second
article: External walls and roof,
football stadium; Renzo Piano,
p.50-53.
ARCHITECTS' JOURNAL 1990 June 6,
v.191, no.23, p.[36]-41,[44]-47,
50-53, dets., models, photos.,
plans, secns., aerial photo.

STADIUMS--ITALY--BARI (CONTINUED)
Ort und Stadion: neue
Fussballstadien in Italien.
New football stadiums in Bari and
Genoa. Architects: Renzo Piano
Building Workshop, Gregotti
Associati. Text in German, French
and English.
WERK, BAUEN + WOHNEN 1990 Sept.,
no.9, p.22-35, dets., elevs., map,
photos., plans, secns., site
plans, aerial photos.
Renzo Piano: stadio di calcio e
atletica leggera, Bari / Ermanno
Ranzani.
Architects: Renzo Piano/Building
Workshop; associated architect:
Shinji Ishida. In Italian and
English.
DOMUS 1990 May, no.716, p.[33-39],
dets., elev., map, photos., plans,
secns., site plans, aerial photos.
Le stade de Bari / Anne Demerle.
Architects: Renzo Piano and
Building Workshop.
LE MONITEUR ARCHITECTURE AMC 1990
June, no.12, p.32-39, elev.,
photos., plan, secn.

STADIUMS--ITALY--BARI--STADIO DE
CARBONARA
Le grand souffle: stade de
Carbonara, Bari, Italie.
Architects: Renzo Piano, Building
Workshop with Ishida & Associates.
English summary, p.48. Spanish
summary, p.153.
TECHNIQUES ET ARCHITECTURE 1990
Dec.-1991 Jan., no.393, p.44-49,
elevs., photos., plans, secns.,
site plan.

STADIUMS--ITALY--ROME
A identidade dos estadios / Vittorio
Gregotti.
Four stadiums designed by Gregotti
Associados.
PROJETO 1990 [June]., no.132,
p.26-34, elevs., models, photos.,
plans, secns., site plans.

STADIUMS--ITALY--TURIN--STADIO
COMMUNALE
Uno stadio nel parco = A stadium in
the park / Philippe Vernier.
Architects: Sergio Hutter, Toni
Cordero, Francesco Ossola.
L'ARCA 1990 May, no.38, p.66-73,
1folded leaf, axonometric views,
dets., dwgs., photos., plans,
secns.

STADIUMS--NETHERLANDS--ARNHEM--
EURODOME
Ahead of the game [stadiums] / Simon
Inglis.
Three European sports stadiums:
Galgenwaard Stadium, Utrecht; New
Comunale Stadium, Bari, by Renzo
Piano; and Arnhem's Eurodrome by
Joseph Wund. Includes second
article: External walls and roof,
football stadium; Renzo Piano,
p.50-53.
ARCHITECTS' JOURNAL 1990 June 6,
v.191, no.23, p.[36]-41,[44]-47,
50-53, dets., models, photos.,
plans, secns., aerial photo.

STADIUMS--NETHERLANDS--UTRECHT--
GALGENWAARD STADIUM
Ahead of the game [stadiums] / Simon
Inglis.
Three European sports stadiums:
Galgenwaard Stadium, Utrecht; New
Comunale Stadium, Bari, by Renzo
Piano; and Arnhem's Eurodrome by
Joseph Wund. Includes second
article: External walls and roof,
football stadium; Renzo Piano,
p.50-53.
ARCHITECTS' JOURNAL 1990 June 6,
v.191, no.23, p.[36]-41,[44]-47,
50-53, dets., models, photos.,
plans, secns., aerial photo.

STADIUMS--SPAIN--BARCELONA
A identidade dos estadios / Vittorio
Gregotti.
Four stadiums designed by Gregotti
Associados.
PROJETO 1990 [June]., no.132,
p.26-34, elevs., models, photos.,
plans, secns., site plans.

STADIUMS--SPAIN--BARCELONA--BADALONA
STADIUM
Salonatmosphare: Stadien in
Barcelona, Sportanlagen in
Eichstatt, Kricketstadion bei
London, Amphitheater in Nimes.
Architects: Esteve Bonell and
Francesc Rius, Karljosef Schattner
with Wilhelm Huber, Michael
Hopkins and Partner, Finn Geipel
and Nicolas Michelin. Text in
German, French and English.
WERK, BAUEN + WOHNEN 1990 Sept.,
no.9, p.46-65, dets., elevs.,
models, photos., plans, secns.,
site plans.

STADIUMS--SPAIN--BARCELONA--MONTJUIC
OLYMPIC STADIUM
Remodelacion del Estadio de Montjuic
en Barcelona: Vittorio Gregotti,
Federico Correa, Alfonso Mila,
Carles Buxade y Joan Margarit,
arquitectos.
Text in Spanish and English.
ON DISENO 1990, no.116, p.155-169,
photos., plans, secn., site plan,
aerial photos.

STADIUMS--SPAIN--BARCELONA--SPORTS
PALACE
Scenari per i giochi olimpici del
'91 = Setting for the 1992 Olympic
games / Agnoldomenico Pica.
New stadium built within exterior
of stadium built by architect
Domenech y Montaner Jr. in 1929;
architects: Arata Isozaki &
Associates.
L'ARCA 1990 May, no.38, p.34-47,
photos., secns.

STADIUMS--SPAIN--BARCELONA--VALL
D'HEBRON
Labyrintisch landschap, laboratorium
van stadsontwerp: de olympische
lokatie Vall d'Hebron / Rein
Geursten.
ARCHIS 1989 Nov., no.11, p.33-40,
maps. photos., secns., site plans,
refs.

STADIUMS--SPAIN--MADRID
[Municipal stadium and private apartment, Madrid].
Contents: Sports stadium project, Aluche, 1985 -- Lizcano apartment, La Moraleja, 1984-85. Architects: Mateo Corrales Lantero and Esteban Becerril Heredero.
9H 1989, no.8, p.110-113, elevs., photos., plans, secns., site plan.

STADIUMS--STUDENT PROJECTS
Olympiastadion fur Gelsenkirchen = Olympic stadium for Gelsenkirchen. Student projects from the Universitat Dortmund. Text in German.
ARCHITEKTUR + WETTBEWERBE 1990 Mar., no.141, p.92-93, dets., elevs., models, plans, site plans.

STADIUMS--SWITZERLAND--BADEN
Sportanlage Esp der Gemeinden Baden und Fislisbach = Le centre sportif Esp des communes de Baden et de Fislisbach = The Esp sports ground jointly owned by the municipalities of Baden and Fislisbach / M. Lang.
Sportsground: A. Zulauf + Partner, M. Lang Building construction: Tognola + Stahel + Zulauf, Meier + Kern.
ANTHOS 1989, v.28, no.4, p.18-21, photos., site plan.

STADIUMS--SWITZERLAND--ZURICH--HALLENSTADION
"Auch will es leer nicht gesehen sein...." das Zurcher Hallenstadion, 1938/39; Architekt: Karl Egender (1897-1969) / Werner Jehle.
Text in German, French and English.
WERK, BAUEN + WOHNEN 1990 Sept., no.9, p.36-45, photos., plans, secns.

STADIUMS--TURKEY--ISTANBUL--OLYMPIC STADIUM
Special feature: Guenter Behnisch. Contents: Seven works: Hysolar Institute building, Stuttgart University.-- New facility for Leybold AG.-- Library building of the Catholic University.-- Administration building of the charitable services of Lutheran church.-- Secondary school, Schafersfeld.-- German Postal Museum.-- Station Square, Stuttgart. Twelve projects: German national bank.-- Central administration building for the LTG.-- Garage in the Olympic park.-- School and sports hall.-- Restaurant in the Olympic swimming pool.-- Kindergarten.-- Olympic stadium.-- Exhibition center.-- Exhibition and conference center.-- Central area of the German Federal Parliament.-- German National Library. Essay: Guenter Behnisch and Partners: a continuing contribution to the organic tradition in German Modernism / Peter Blundell Jones.
ARCHITECTURE AND URBANISM 1990 May, no.5(236), p.34-138, elevs., models, photos., plans, secns., site plans.

STADIUMS--TYPOLOGY
Grundtypen und Elemente der Olympia-Stadien: eine chronologische Ubersicht / Thomas Schmidt.
BAUWELT 1990 June 29, v.81, no.24, p.1208-1214, photos., secns., aerial photos.

STADIUMS--UNITED STATES--DADE COUNTY (FLORIDA)--JOE ROBBIE STADIUM
Joe Robbie Stadium, Dade County, Florida, USA, 1987.
Architects: Hellmuth, Obata & Kassabaum. Text in Japanese and English.
ARCHITECTURE AND URBANISM 1990 Dec., no.12 extra edition, p.120-125, photos., plan, site plan.

STADIUMS--UNITED STATES--LOS ANGELES (CALIFORNIA)--LOS ANGELES MEMORIAL COLISEUM
L.A. stadium threatened [Los Angeles Memorial Coliseum] / Rachel S. Cox.
Designed by John Parkinson and Donald B. Parkinson, and completed in 1923.
PRESERVATION NEWS 1990 Mar., v.30, no.3, p.1,11, dwg., photo.

STADLINGER, M.
Schnell, aber schon: Gestaltung eines fast-food-Restaurants in Munchen.
McDonald's Restaurant. Architects: STM-Plan; Interior architects: M. Stadlinger, N. Breitfuss.
ARCHITEKTUR, INNENARCHITEKTUR, TECHNISCHER AUSBAU 1990 June, v.98, no.6, p.52-53, photos., plan.

STADTBAUPLAN
Es ist angerichetet: Landesbehordenhaus in Darmstadt / Oliver G. Hamm.
Architecs: Stadt Bau Plan.
DEUTSCHE BAUZEITUNG 1990 Apr., v.124, no.7, p.14-19, ill., photos., plans, secn., site plan.
Es ist angerichtet: Landesbehordenhaus in Darmstadt / Olivier G. Hamm.
Architects: StadtBauPlan.
DEUTSCHE BAUZEITUNG 1990 Apr., v.124, no.4, p.14-19, ill., photos., plans, secn., site plan.

STAEHLI, ALFRED M.
Restoring leather-covered doors / Alred M. Staehli.
ASSOCIATION FOR PRESERVATION TECHNOLOGY. BULLETIN 1989, v.21, no.3-4, p.94-95, photos.

STAERMOSE, JORGEN, 1920-
Hotel Koldingfjord / Leif Leer Sorensen.
Conversion of a 1909 sanatorium with a 1940s annex into a hotel and conference center. Architects: Vilhelm Lauritzen, with Chr.Holm and Arkitektfirmaet Jorgen Staermose. Landscape architect: Jeppe Aagaard Andersen. Includes English and German summaries.
ARKITEKTUR DK 1990. v.34, no.8, p.357-367,cover, elevs., photos., plans, secns., site plan.

STAFFA, ANDREA R.
Teramo: nuovi dati per la ricostruzione dell'assetto antico della citta / Andrea R. Staffa.
XENIA 1990, v.19, p.[19]-30, maps, photos., refs.

STAFFORD, FREDERICK
Planning policy 1: guidance for councils Frederick Stafford. Explains nos. 1-7 of the British Planning Policy Guidance (PPG) notes. First of a two-part series.
ARCHITECTS' JOURNAL 1990 Sept.5, v.192, no.10, p.77-80, ill.
Planning policy 2: guidance for councils / Frederick Stafford. Second of two-part article examines notes 8-15 of the British Planning Policy Guidance (PPG) notes.
ARCHITECTS' JOURNAL 1990 Sept.12, v.192, no.11, p.75-77, ill.

STAFFORD, JAMES
American housing 1980-1990 / James Tice.
Features: Castro Common, San Francisco (Daniel Solomon, Paulett Taggart); Sun-Tech Housing, Santa Monica (Steve Andre, David Van Hoy); Pacific Townhouses, Santa Monica (Rebecca Binder, James Stafford); Hoyt Square Condominiums, Portland, OR (Robert S. Leeb). Text in Italian and English.
METAMORFOSI 1989, no.12, p.38-51, axonometric views, models, photos., plans, secns.
Zimmerman/Stafford, Hamburger Hamlet, Hollywood / Francesca Garcia-marquez.
Text in Italian and English.
DOMUS 1990 Mar., no.714, p.[6-7], axonometric view, dets., photos., plan, secn.

STAGE LIGHTING
Rolling Stones / Mark Fisher, Jonathan Park.
High-tech stage sets for the 1989 U.S. tour. Section includes "It's only rock'n'roll" and "Jagger: in response to questions", by Andreas Papadakis.
ARCHITECTURAL DESIGN 1990, v.60, no.3-4, p.44-61, ill., photos.

STAGE-SETTING
See THEATERS - STAGE-SETTING AND SCENERY

STAGEBERG, JAMES E.
Crayon-colored dream house / Susan Allen Toth.
Wisconsin weekend house designed by James Stageberg.
HOUSE BEAUTIFUL 1990 Apr., v.132, no.4, p.[94]-95,121, photos., secn.
A place of one's own / Adelheid Fischer.
Pavilion and porch at a farmhouse in Minnesota. Architect: James Stageberg.
ARCHITECTURE MINNESOTA 1990 Mar.-Apr., v.16, no.2, p.19, port., photos.

STAGEBERG PARTNERS
Quiet spirit: Prairie Pavilion, Lac Qui Parle County, Minnesota / Bruce N. Wright.
The Stageberg Partners, Architects.
ARCHITECTURE: THE AIA JOURNAL 1990 Mar., v.79, no.3, p.154-[157], photos., site plan.
Regional portfolio: The Midwest: a tale of two cities / Clifford A. Pearson.
Minneapolis and Milwaukee have become two of the most livable cities in the U.S. Contents: 100 E. Wisconsin Ave., Milwaukee (Clark Tribble Harris & Li Architects); Milwaukee Repertory Theater (Beckley/Myers Architects); 5th St. Parking Facility, Minneapolis (Stageberg Partners); Valspar Varnish Factory renovation, Minneapolis (Meyer, Scherer & Rockcastle); and the Ceresota, Minneapolis (Ellerbe Becket).
ARCHITECTURAL RECORD 1990 Aug., v.178, no.9, p.62-71, axonometric view, photos., plans, secns., site plans.

STAGER, CLAUDETTE
Vernacular houses: Middle Tennessee I-house / Claudette Stager, Elizabeth Straw.
A regional interpretation of the central-passage house, frequently embellished with Greek revival details, built from the 1820s to 1880s.
OLD-HOUSE JOURNAL 1990 Sept.-Oct., v.18, no.5, p.[4] of cover, photos., plan.

STAGES--OUTDOOR--JAPAN--NAGANO--PLAYHOUSES
A survey of the actual conditions, preservation and utilization of outdoor stage "playhouse" in Nagano prefecture / Yasuhiro Yamashita, Naoji Matsumoto, Hirokuni Taniguchi.
"A systematic study of the outdoor stage playhouse, 1". Text in Japanese. Includes English summary.
NIHON KENCHIKU GAKKAI KEIKAKUKEI RONBUN HOKOKU SHU = JOURNAL OF ARCHITECTURE, PLANNING AND ENVIRONMENTAL ENGINEERING 1990 Sept., no.9(415), p.39-47, graphs, elevs., maps, photos., plans, secn., tables.

STAGING
See SCAFFOLDS

STAHL, FRIEDEMANN
Wintergarten: Grundlagen, Bauphysik und Nutzung / Friedemann Stahl.
DEUTSCHE BAUZEITUNG 1990 May, v.124, no.5, p.102-110, photo., tables, refs.

STAHL, PAUL-HENRI
L'architecture de bois [Romania] / Paul-Henri Stahl.
MONUMENTS HISTORIQUES 1990 June-July, no.169, p.[36]-42, photos.

STAHN, GUNTER
Zur gebauten Zukunft eines Gesamtberlins / Gunter Stahn.
BAUMEISTER 1990 May, v.87, no.5, p.53-55, photos., site plan.

STAHR, GERRIT
Friedhof Neuried bei Munchen / Eike Schmidt, Gerrit Stahr.
Competition for a chapel and landscaped cemetery. Winners: Christoph Brandt and Schmidt and Stahr. Includes English summary.
GARTEN UND LANDSCHAFT 1989, v.99, no.12, p.40-43, dwgs., photos., site plan.

STAINED GLASS
See also GLASS PAINTING AND STAINING
See also "STAINED GLASS" AS A SUBHEADING AFTER SPECIFIC BUILDING TYPES OR OTHER MAIN HEADINGS.
Tiffany's treasures.
Windows, vases and lamps of Louis Comfort Tiffany.
COLONIAL HOMES 1990 Feb., v.16, no.1, p.[70]-75,140-141, port., photos.

STAINED GLASS--CANADA--MONTREAL (QUEBEC)--MCGILL UNIVERSITY--HOSMER COLLECTION
Retour aux traditions -- signe de reussite sociale: les rondels de la Collection Hosmer (Universite McGill, Montreal) / Ariane Isler-de Jongh.
Collection of domestic stained glass and glass painting set up in new building at McGill School of Architecture. Formerly decoration of Charles Hosmer's house built by Montreal architect Edward Maxwell ca. 1900. English summary.
RACAR: REVUE D'ART CANADIENNE. CANADIAN ART REVIEW 1989, v.16, no.1, p.29-112, dwgs., photos., engrs., refs.

STAINED GLASS--CONSERVATION AND RESTORATION
Revivals, revivalists, and architectural stained glass / Virginia Chieffo Raguin.
Addresses "the implications of the revival of stained glass for an understanding of the medieval past, the 19th century, and the ethics of restoration." Includes abstract.
SOCIETY OF ARCHITECTURAL HISTORIANS. JOURNAL 1990 Sept., v.49, no.3, p.310-329, dwg., photos., refs.

STAINED GLASS--CONSERVATION AND RESTORATION--GERMANY (EAST)--BERLIN--WEDERSCHE KIRCHE
Farbfassung und Raumerlebnis / Gottfried Grafe.
Restoration of interior and glass of Schinkel's Wedersche Kirche, Berlin. German, Russian, English and French summaries, p.55-56.
ARCHITEKTUR DER DDR 1990 Jan., v.38, no.1, p.17-20, photos., dwg., elev., refs.

STAINED GLASS--GOTHIC--CONSERVATION AND RESTORATION--FRANCE--TROYES--SAINT-PIERRE
Restoring the stained glass of Troyes Cathedral: the ambiguous legacy of Viollet-le-Duc / Elizabeth Carson Pastan.
Includes abstract.
GESTA 1990, v.29, no.2, p.155-166, axonometric view, photos., engr., refs.

STAINED GLASS--IRELAND
Through multi-coloured glasses / Padraig Ferry.
On-going tradition of stained glass in Ireland.
PLAN: ARCHITECTURE AND BUILDING DESIGN IN IRELAND 1990 Aug., v.33, no.8, p.35-40, photos.

STAINED GLASS--REPRODUCTIONS
A place of one's own [Century Studios, Minneapolis].
Stained glass showroom and studio, specializing in reproduction of Tiffany lampshades.
ARCHITECTURE MINNESOTA 1990 May-June, v.16, no.3, p.31, port.

STAINED GLASS--UNITED STATES--HINSDALE (ILLINOIS)
The Zook look: a suburban fantasy / Michael J.P. Smith.
Houses and stained glass windows by Hinsdale, Ill. architect: Roscoe Harold Zook (d.1949).
INLAND ARCHITECT 1990 Mar.-Apr., v.34, no.2, p.26, photos.

STAINED GLASS WINDOWS
See WINDOWS - STAINED GLASS

STAINER, GIOVANNI
Concorso per la riqualificazione dell' area di Via Veneto [Trento].
Presents 10 entries, including 1st prize entry by Oswald Zoeggeler.
PARAMETRO 1990, Nov.-Dec., no.181, p.52-69, axonometric views, ill., dwgs., elevs., photos., plans, secns., aerial photo.

STAINLESS STEEL
See also "STAINLESS STEEL" AS A SUBHEADING AFTER SPECIFIC BUILDING TYPES OR OTHER MAIN HEADINGS.

STAINS
See PAINT

STAIR BUILDING
See also HAND-RAILING
See also STAIRWAYS
Flights of fancy.
Recreation of original early 18th cent. timber staircase in No.15 Queen Sq., Bath, designed by John Wood the Elder. Woodwork for new staircase by Donal Channer & Co.
ARCHITECTS' JOURNAL 1990 Sept.26, v.192, no.13, p.46 [47],49, axonometric view, elev., photos., secn.
The many ways to climb to the top: staircases & parts / Clem Labine.
Contains two directories of sources for staircases and their parts.
CLEM LABINE'S TRADITIONAL BUILDING 1990 July-Aug., v.3, no.4, p.27-36, cover, ill., photos., tables.

STAIR BUILDING (CONTINUED)
Revealing masons' mystery / Russell Taylor.
Open wall stone staircase construction, and a discussion of its 17th cent. origins in British buildings.
ARCHITECTS' JOURNAL 1990 Sept.26, v.192, no.13, p.34-43, dets., diagrs., elevs., photos., plans, secns., refs.

STAIRCASES
See STAIRWAYS

STAIRHALLS
See HALLS

STAIRS
See also FIRE ESCAPES
See also STAIR BUILDING
See also STAIRWAYS
On the case.
Features three staircases by engineers Dewhurst Macfarlane & Partners.
BUILDING DESIGN 1990 June, suppl., p.6-7, dets., photos.
Upwardly mobile / Adrian Danatt.
On the "cult of the staircase."
BUILDING DESIGN 1989 Oct., suppl., p.30-32, dwgs., photos.

STAIRS--CONCRETE--ITALY--CARBONATE--
CASA GRIMOLDI-CAGNIN
Come un albero di pietra / Walter Bianchi, Mauro Colombo.
Details of a cast concrete stairway at the Casa Grimoldi-Cagnin, Carbonate, Italy.
Architect: Walter Bianchi.
VILLE GIARDINI 1990 Oct., no.252, p.54-55, dets., photos.

STAIRS--DIRECTORIES
The many ways to climb to the top: staircases & parts / Clem Labine.
Contains two directories of sources for staircases and their parts.
CLEM LABINE'S TRADITIONAL BUILDING 1990 July-Aug., v.3, no.4, p.27-36, cover, ill., photos., tables.

STAIRS--MAINTENANCE AND REPAIR
Treppen und Treppenhauser / Ingo Grun.
DETAIL 1990 Apr.-May, v.30, no.2, p.183-186, photos.

STAIRS--PLEXIGLAS
Transparente Treppenelemente / Helga Muller, Dieter Muller.
DEUTSCHE BAUZEITSCHRIFT 1990 Aug., v.38, no.8, p.1133-1134, dets., photos.

STAIRS--STONE
Revealing masons' mystery / Russell Taylor.
Open wall stone staircase construction, and a discussion of its 17th cent. origins in British buildings.
ARCHITECTS' JOURNAL 1990 Sept.26, v.192, no.13, p.34-43, dets., diagrs., elevs., photos., plans, secns., refs.

STAIRWAYS
See also ESCALATORS
See also STOOPS
Der Anonymitat entgegnet: Treppenhausgestaltung im Kinderheim Aachen/Evangelischer Frauenverein.
Architects: Duo-Design.
ARCHITEKTUR, INNENARCHITEKTUR, TECHNISCHER AUSBAU 1990 Nov., v.98, no.11, p.52-53, elev., photos., plans.
Gebaute Bewegung: Schwelle, Stufe, Treppe = Built movement: sill, step, stair / Michael Gaenssler.
Introduction to theme issue on stairs and stairways. 21 articles indexed separately.
DETAIL 1990 Apr.-May, v.30, no.2, p.114-122, photos.
On the case.
Features three staircases by engineers Dewhurst Macfarlane & Partners.
BUILDING DESIGN 1990 June, suppl., p.6-7, dets., photos.
Stairs for stars / Martin Pawley.
By Eva Jiricna Architects.
Includes English captions.
CASABELLA 1990 Dec., v.54, no.574, p.36, dets., photo.
Step by step / Jose Manser.
On the work of architect/engineer Matthew Wells.
DESIGNERS' JOURNAL 1990 Feb., no.54, p.52-55, dwgs., port.
Upwardly mobile / Adrian Danatt.
On the "cult of the staircase."
BUILDING DESIGN 1989 Oct., suppl., p.30-32, dwgs., photos.

STAIRWAYS--20TH CENTURY
Tread loudly / James Dunnett.
"On the rise of the modern staircase."
BUILDING DESIGN 1989 Oct., suppl., p.27-29, photos.

STAIRWAYS--DIRECTORIES
The many ways to climb to the top: staircases & parts / Clem Labine.
Contains two directories of sources for staircases and their parts.
CLEM LABINE'S TRADITIONAL BUILDING 1990 July-Aug., v.3, no.4, p.27-36, cover, ill., photos., tables.

STAIRWAYS--ENGLAND--LONDON--JOSEPH
Flights of fancy: details elevate staircases to new artistic heights / Michael J. Crosbie.
LaFrak Stair, Alexandria, Va., designed by Tom Luckey, and Joseph Shop stairs, London, Jiricna Associates, Architects.
ARCHITECTURE: THE MAGAZINE OF THE AMERICAN INSTITUTE OF ARCHITECTS 1990 June, v.79, no.6, p.101-103, dets., photos., secn.
Historia de una escalera: Eva Jiricna para Joseph / Gines Sanchez Hevia.
Store in London.
ARQUITECTURA VIVA 1990 Jan.-Feb., no.10, p.62-63, photos., plan.
Stahl-glas-Treppe in einem Modegeschaft = Stairway in a fashion shop in London.
Joseph Ltd. on Sloane Street.
Architect: Eva Jiricna Architects.
(Continued next column)

STAIRWAYS--ENGLAND--LONDON--JOSEPH
(CONTINUED)
Stahl-glas-Treppe in...(CONTINUED)
DETAIL 1990 Apr.-May, v.30, no.2, p.156-158, dets., dwg., photos., plan.

STAIRWAYS--ENGLAND--LONDON--ROGERS HOUSE
Wohnen als Manifest = Richard Rogers' home-theatre on Royal Avenue in London.
Details of stairways. Architect: Richard Rogers.
DETAIL 1990 Apr.-May, v.30, no.2, p.159-163, axonometric views, dets., photos., plans, secns.

STAIRWAYS--ENGLAND--LONDON--STOCKLEY PARK--ARENA
Centre point [Arena, Stockley Park] / Patrick Hannay.
Examines a "new building type" which provides shops, sport and social facilities. Architects: Arup Associates; Michael Sumner Associates; the Milner Group; Fletcher Priest, and Brian Beardsmore.
ARCHITECTS' JOURNAL 1990 Aug.1, v.192, no.5, p.[30]-41,45-47, dets., elevs., photos., plans, secns., site plan.

STAIRWAYS--GERMANY (WEST)--EDLING
Treppe in einem Wohnhaus in Edling bei Wasserburg am Inn = Staircase in a home near Wasserburg, Upper Bavaria.
Architect: Herbert Kriegisch.
DETAIL 1990 Apr.-May, v.30, no.2, p.130-131, dets., photos., plan, secn.

STAIRWAYS--GERMANY (WEST)--EICHSTATT
Treppenhaus in ehemaligen Waisenhaus in Eichstatt = Staircase in a former orphanage in Eichstatt, Bavaria.
Architect: K. Schattner.
DETAIL 1990 Apr.-May, v.30, no.2, p.162-164, axonometric views, det., photos., plans, secn.

STAIRWAYS--GERMANY (WEST)--GROBENZELL
Ateliertreppe in einem Wohnhaus in Grobenzell bei Munchen = Studio staircase in a dwelling house in a suburb of Munich.
Architect: Werner Wirsing.
DETAIL 1990 Apr.-May, v.30, no.2, p.134-135, dets., photos., plan, secn.

STAIRWAYS--GERMANY (WEST)--
HEILIGKREUZTAL
Treppenanlage in Stegenhaus der Klosteranlage Heiligkreuztal = Staircase in the former cloister of Heiligkreuztal.
Architect: Johannes Mandersheid.
DETAIL 1990 Apr.-May, v.30, no.2, p.140-141, det., photos., plan.

STAIRWAYS--GERMANY (WEST)--PULLACH--
JAKOBUSKIRCHE
Fichtenholztreppe in der Jakobuskirche in Pullach = Transformation of a church interior in Pullach near Munich.
Architects: Georg and Ingrid Kuttinger.
(Continued next page)

STAIRWAYS--GERMANY (WEST)--PULLACH--
JAKOBUSKIRCHE (CONTINUED)
Fichtenholztreppe in...(CONTINUED)
DETAIL 1990 Apr.-May, v.30, no.2,
p.HII-HIII, dets., elev., photos.,
plan.

STAIRWAYS--HISTORY
Stepping back: the history of the
staircase / Michael Thornton.
TRADITIONAL HOMES 1990 June, v.6,
no.9, p.123-126, photo, plans,
secns.

STAIRWAYS--IRON--ITALY--CESANA
Scala in ferro nel centro storico di
Cesena.
Features staircase in a retirement
home. Architects: Delio Corbara,
Giordano Conti. English, French,
and Spanish summaries.
ABACUS 1990 Apr.-June, v.6, no.22,
p.74-77, dets., photos., secns.

STAIRWAYS--JAPAN--OSAKA--AKKA
Akka Kunstgalerie in Osaka, Japan =
Akka Art Gallery in Osaka, Japan.
Details of the stairways.
Architect: Tadao Ando.
DETAIL 1990 Apr.-May, v.30, no.2,
p.bi-biv, axonometric views,
dets., photos., plans, secns.,
site plans.

STAIRWAYS--JAPAN--TOKYO
Hundegedenkstatte in Tokio, Japan =
Burial chamber for dogs in Tokyo,
Japan.
Architects: Hideo Yasui, Makoto
Araki.
DETAIL 1990 Apr.-May, v.30, no.2,
p.144-145, axonometric view, det.,
photos., plans.
Treppenlabyrinth in einer Wohnanlage
in Tokio, Japan = Labyrinthine
stair system of a residential
development in Tokyo.
Architects: Kunihiko Haykawa &
Partner.
DETAIL 1990 Apr.-May, v.30, no.2,
p.142-143, axonometric view, det.,
photos., plans.

STAIRWAYS--MAINTENANCE AND REPAIR
Flight problems: remedies for some
common staircase defects / Michael
Thornton.
TRADITIONAL HOMES 1990 July, v.6,
no.10, p.87-90, det., ill.,
photos.
Treppen und Treppenhauser / Ingo
Grun.
DETAIL 1990 Apr.-May, v.30, no.2,
p.183-186, photos.

STAIRWAYS--PLEXIGLAS
Transparente Treppenelemente / Helga
Muller, Dieter Muller.
DEUTSCHE BAUZEITSCHRIFT 1990 Aug.,
v.38, no.8, p.1133-1134, dets.,
photos.

STAIRWAYS--RESEARCH
Foot accommodation on various stair
tread sizes / Ian M. Lockwood,
John P. Braaksma.
Includes abstract.
JOURNAL OF ARCHITECTURAL AND
PLANNING RESEARCH 1990 Spring,
v.7, no.1, p.1-12, charts,
diagrs., photos., biblio.

STAIRWAYS--ROUND
Leonard de Vinci et les astuces de
la construction solognote / Jean
Martin-Demezil.
REVUE DE L'ART 1990, no.87,
p.84-86, fig., dwg., photo., refs.

STAIRWAYS--ROUND--UNITED STATES--
ALEXANDRIA (VIRGINIA)--LAFRAK STAIR
Flights of fancy: details elevate
staircases to new artistic heights
/ Michael J. Crosbie.
LaFrak Stair, Alexandria, Va.,
designed by Tom Luckey, and Joseph
Shop stairs, London, Jiricna
Associates, Architects.
ARCHITECTURE: THE MAGAZINE OF THE
AMERICAN INSTITUTE OF ARCHITECTS
1990 June, v.79, no.6, p.101-103,
dets., photos., secn.

STAIRWAYS--SCOTLAND--EDINBURGH--35
SAINT ANDREW SQUARE
Fit for an empress: imperial
staircase in Edinburgh / Ian Gow.
Staircase within no.35 St. Andrew
Square, built in 1769; architects:
James Craig and Archibald Elliott.
COUNTRY LIFE 1990 Sept.13, v.184,
no.37, p.216,218, ill., photos.

STAIRWAYS--SPAIN--SEVILLE--INSTITUTO
DE ARQUITECTURA
Institut fur Architektur in Sevilla,
E = Institute for Architecture in
Sevilla, E.
Details of the stairway.
Architect: G. Vasquez Consuegra.
DETAIL 1990 Apr.-May, v.30, no.2,
p.152-155, axonometric view,
dets., photos., secn.

STAIRWAYS--SPIRAL
City spiral / Marcus Field.
Features the renovated Jardine
Insurance Brokers office building,
London. Renovation architects: Eva
Jiricna, Michael Hopkins.
DESIGNERS' JOURNAL 1990 Apr.,
no.56, p.8, photos.
Espace Castelli, Paris / Brigitte
Fitoussi.
Furniture store, features spiral
stairway. Architect: Ronald Cecil
Sportes.
ARCHITECTURE D'AUJOURD'HUI 1990
Sept., no.270, p.193-196, dwgs.,
photos.

STAIRWAYS--SPIRAL--GERMANY (WEST)--
MUNICH--HEIDEMANNSTRASSE
Gartenstadt Heidemannstrasse,
Munchen = Garden town
"Heidemannstrasse" in Munich.
Features the central spiral
staircase of the housing
department. Architects: Steidle +
Partner.
DETAIL 1990 Apr.-May, v.30, no.2,
p.138-139, det., photos., plan,
secn.

STAIRWAYS--SPIRAL--GERMANY (WEST)--
RODENKIRCHEN
Wendeltreppe in einem Wohnhaus in
Koln-Rodenkirchen = Spiral
staircase in a home in
Koln-Rodenkirchen.
Architect: Heinz Bienefeld.
DETAIL 1990 Apr.-May, v.30, no.2,
p.150-151, dets., elev., photos.,
plan.

STAIRWAYS--SPIRAL--GERMANY (WEST)--
STEINHAUSEN
Neue Zeitungsdruckerei in Munchen -
Steinhausen = Spiral staircase in
a printing works.
Architektengemeinschaft P. von
Seidlein.
DETAIL 1990 Apr.-May, v.30, no.2,
p.SI,SIV, elev., photo., plan.

STAIRWAYS--SPIRAL--NETHERLANDS--
ZEEWOLDE
Spiral staircase, library: Koen van
Velsen.
In the new municipal library of
Zeewolde, Netherlands.
ARCHITECTS' JOURNAL 1990 July 4,
v.192, no.1, p.57-59, dets.,
photos., plans, secns.

STAIRWAYS--SPIRAL--SPAIN--BARCELONA
Wendeltreppe in einem Schuhgeschaft
in Barcelona, E = Spiral stair
case in a shop in Barcelona,
Spain.
Interior architects: M.
Ybarguengoitia, M. del Mar Nogues.
DETAIL 1990 Apr.-May, v.30, no.2,
p.146-147, det., photos., plan,
secn., elevs.

STAIRWAYS--SPIRAL--STONE
Revealing masons' mystery / Russell
Taylor.
Open wall stone staircase
construction, and a discussion of
its 17th cent. origins in British
buildings.
ARCHITECTS' JOURNAL 1990 Sept.26,
v.192, no.13, p.34-43, dets.,
diagrs., elevs., photos., plans,
secns., refs.

STAIRWAYS--STEEL
In the mind's eye / Ziva Freiman.
Former Kress dept. store in
Riverside, Calif. converted into
the California Museum of
Photography. Architect: Stanley
Saitowitz. Includes Selected
Detail article on the steel
staircase in the museum.
PROGRESSIVE ARCHITECTURE 1990
Sept., v.71, no.9, p.130-136,
dets., ill., dwgs., photos.,
plans.

STAIRWAYS--STEEL--GERMANY (WEST)--
REUTLINGEN
Stahltreppe am Parkhaus in
Reutlingen = Steel staircase for a
car park in Reutlingen,
Baden-Wurttemberg.
Architect: Dieter Herrmann.
DETAIL 1990 Apr.-May, v.30, no.2,
p.SII-SIII, dets., elev., photos.

STAIRWAYS--STONE
Revealing masons' mystery / Russell
Taylor.
Open wall stone staircase
construction, and a discussion of
its 17th cent. origins in British
buildings.
ARCHITECTS' JOURNAL 1990 Sept.26,
v.192, no.13, p.34-43, dets.,
diagrs., elevs., photos., plans,
secns., refs.

STAIRWAYS--SYMBOLIC ASPECTS
Stairs and graces / Jeremy Melvin.
On the history of the staircase as allegory.
BUILDING DESIGN 1989 Oct., suppl., p.24-26, photos., plan, secn., engr., refs.

STAIRWAYS--UNITED STATES--PHILADELPHIA (PENNSYLVANIA)--COMCAST
Elegant stairway / Lisa S. Cohen.
Features stairway designed by Karen Daroff for the Comcast Corporation offices in Philadelphia.
INTERIORS 1990 Jan., v.149, no.6, p.40-41, dets., photo.

STAIRWAYS--UNITED STATES--SAN FRANCISCO (CALIFORNIA)--SBG PARTNERS
Umbau eines Getreidespeichers in San Francisco, USA = Converted grain warehouse in San Francisco, USA.
Details of the stairway.
Architects: Richard Fernau, Laura Hartman & Partner.
DETAIL 1990 Apr.-May, v.30, no.2, p.148-149, axonometric view, dets., photos.

STAIRWAYS--WOODEN--19TH CENTURY-- CONSERVATION AND RESTORATION-- ENGLAND--BATH--NO.15 QUEEN SQUARE
Flights of fancy.
Recreation of original early 18th cent. timber staircase in No.15 Queen Sq., Bath, designed by John Wood the Elder. Woodwork for new staircase by Donal Channer & Co.
ARCHITECTS' JOURNAL 1990 Sept.26, v.192, no.13, p.46-[47],49, axonometric view, elev., photos., secn.

STAIRWAYS--WOODEN--GERMANY (WEST)-- MURNAU--CHRISTUSKIRCHE
Holztreppe in der Christuskirche in Murnau, Oberbayern = Sprucewood stairway in a church in Murnau, Upper Bavaria.
Architects: Georg and Ingrid Kuttinger.
DETAIL 1990 Apr.-May, v.30, no.2, p.HI, HIV, dets., plan.

STAIRWELLS
See STAIRWAYS

STALLEY, ROGER
Medieval architecture [book review] / Roger Stalley.
A joint review of The Royal Abbey of Saint-Denis..., by Sumner McKnight Crosby, ed. by Pamela Z. Blum, and Abbot Suger and Saint Denis: a symposium, ed. by Paula Lieber Gerson.
SOCIETY OF ARCHITECTURAL HISTORIANS. JOURNAL 1990 Dec., v.49, no.4, p.440-441.
Medieval naturalism and the botanical carvings at Corcomroe Abbey (County Clare) / E. Charles Nelson, Roger A. Stalley.
Identification of models of living plants depicted in capitals from ca.1205-1210. Includes abstract.
GESTA 1989, v.28, no.2, p.165-174, dets., dwgs., photos., plans, refs.

STALLEY, ROGER. CISTERCIAN MONASTERIES OF IRELAND
Cistercian monasteries of Ireland: an account of the history, art and architecture of the White Monks in Ireland from 1142 to 1540 [book review].
Book written by Roger Stalley.
ARTE MEDIEVALE 1990, v.4, no.2, p.233-234,

STALLS - CHOIR
See CHOIR STALLS

STAM, MARTINUS ADRIANUS, 1899-1986
Avant-garde design and the law: litigation over the cantilever chair / Otakar Macel.
Involves designs by Mart Stam, Anton Lorenz, Marcel Breuer, Mies van der Rohe and others. Includes documents, p.166-174.
JOURNAL OF DESIGN HISTORY 1990, v.3, no.2-3, p.125-143,166-174, dwg., diagrs., photos., refs.

STAMP, GAVIN
Enlightened shots: Travels in modern architecture 1927-30 [exhibition review] / Gavin Stamp.
Exhibition of architectural photography at the Architectural Association, London, through 17 Feb.1990.
ARCHITECTS' JOURNAL 1990 Jan.24, v.191, no.4, p.74, photos.
The Greek tragedies / Gavin Stamp.
On the neoclassical architecture of Glasgow architect Alexander 'Greek' Thomson.
ARCHITECTS' JOURNAL 1990 May 30, v.191, no.22, p.50-57, dwgs., photos., sketches.
High falutin': Muscular churches: ecclesiastical architecture of the High Victorian period, by C.M. Smart, Jr. / Gavin Stamp.
ARCHITECTS' JOURNAL 1990 Mar.14, v.191, no.11, p.95, sketch.
Robert Atkinson 1883-1952: AA Members' Room & Bar, 4-28 October 1989 [exhibition review] / Gavin Stamp.
AA FILES 1990 Autumn, no.20, p.69-76, dwgs., elev., photos., refs.
A Russian celebration: St. Petersburg 1703-1914 [exhibition review] / Gavin Stamp.
Exhibit at the City Art Gallery, Manchester, through 22 July 1990.
ARCHITECTS' JOURNAL 1990 July 18, v.192, no.3, p.72-73, ill., map.
Tale of two cities: New places for work: the Berlin model [exhibition review] / Gavin Stamp.
Exhibition of recent industrial architecture designed for Berlin. Held at Cumbrae House, Glasgow, through 14 Oct.1990.
ARCHITECTS' JOURNAL 1990 Oct.3, v.192, no.14, p.68-69, dwgs.,

STANDARDS
See "STANDARDS" AS A SUBHEADING AFTER SPECIFIC BUILDING TYPES OR OTHER MAIN HEADINGS.

STANDS (MERCANTILE STRUCTURES)
See also FOOD STANDS
See also NEWSSTANDS

STANDS--SOUTH AFRICA--KHAYELITSHA
Spazas of Khayelitsha / Martin Duys.
On the informal and improvisatory nature of shops, called spazas in Xhosa.
ADA: ARCHITECTURE, DESIGN, ART 1989, no.7, p.48-49, photos.

STANHOPE TRAFALGAR
Parking at the crossroads [office parks, West London] / Martin Spring.
Plans for two new projects: Chiswick Park (developer, Stanhope Trafalgar; architect, Terry Farrell; landscape architect, Laurie Olin) and Bedfont Lakes (developers, MEPC and IBM; architect, Michael Hopkins).
BUILDING 1990 June 1, v.255, no.22, p.40-45, diagrs., ill., model, photos., site plan.

STANIC, JACQUELINE
Erik Gunnar Asplund [exhibition review] / Jacqueline Stanic.
Exhibition held Feb.15-Apr.17, 1989 at the Centre de Creation Industrielle, Paris.
CNAC MAGAZINE 1989 Jan.15-Mar.15, no.49, p.15-16, photos.

STANNEK, NORBERT
Anpassung von vorhandenen Bauteilen an das Baurecht / Heinz Schmitz, Norbert Stannek.
DEUTSCHES ARCHITEKTENBLATT 1990 Mar.1, v.22, no.1, p.389-392, photos., refs.
Recycling von Abbruchmassen bei Modernisierung / Heinz Schmitz, Norbert Stannek.
On the disposal and recycling of building materials removed during renovations.
DEUTSCHES ARCHITEKTENBLATT 1990 July 1, v.22, no.7, p.1123-1126, photos., tables, refs.
Schutz von Bauteilen bei Modernisierungsmassnahmen / Heinz Schmitz, Norbert Stannek.
Ways to protect building details and parts during renovations.
DEUTSCHES ARCHITEKTENBLATT 1990 Apr.1, v.22, no.4, p.567-570, photos.
Weiterverwendung von elektrischen Installationen / Heinz Schmitz, Norbert Stannek.
DEUTSCHES ARCHITEKTENBLATT 1990 Nov.1, v.22, no.11, p.1725-1726, photos.
Weiterverwendung von Heizungsanlagen und Schornsteinen / Heinz Schmitz, Norbert Stannek.
DEUTSCHES ARCHITEKTENBLATT 1990 Oct.1, v.22, no.10, p.1573-1574, photos.
Weiterverwendung von sanitaren Installationen / Heinz Schmitz, Norbert Stannek.
DEUTSCHES ARCHITEKTENBLATT 1990 Sept.1, v.22, no.9, p.1337-1338, photos.

STANSFIELD, KATHY
Gateshead Garden Festival strategy /
Kathy Stansfield.
Britain's fourth garden festival,
running May-Sept.,1990.
THE PLANNER 1990 June 1, v.76,
nc.21, p.12-13, photos.

STANTON & WILLIAMS
Holy orders / Liz Hoggard.
On Winchester Cathedral's
Triforium Gallery. Architects:
Stanton & Williams.
DESIGNERS' JOURNAL 1990 Sept.,
no.60, p.88-[89], photos.
Made to measure / David Redhead.
Interiors of three London clothing
stores: Issey Miyake, Michiko
Koshino and Karl Lagerfeld.
DESIGNERS' JOURNAL 1990 July-Aug.,
no.59, p.[28]-33, photos.
Sloane neighbour / John Welsh.
On the Clearings III speculative
office building, London.
Architects: Stanton & Williams,
YRM Partnership.
BUILDING DESIGN 1990 Oct.26,
no.1009, p.12, photos., plans,
site plans.

STANTON, MICHAEL
Small town revitalization: lessons
from Watsonville, California /
Michael Stanton.
Small town devastated by the
Oct.17, 1989 California earthquake
is replanned.
URBAN LAND 1990 Nov., v.49, no.11,
p.20-24, photo., plan, sketches.

STARA, MARIO
La nuova Pretura di Altamura, Bari =
A new magistrate's court near Bari
/ Stefania Mornati.
Architect: Mario Stara. In Italian
and English.
L'INDUSTRIA DELLE COSTRUZIONI 1990
July-Aug., v.24, no.225-226,
p.42-47, elevs., photos., plans,
secns.

STARBUCK, DAVID R.
Those ingenious Shakers / David R.
Starbuck.
The Canterbury, New Hampshire,
Museum village.
ARCHAEOLOGY 1990 July-Aug., v.43,
no.4, p.[40]-47, ports., photos.

STARCK, PHILIPPE, 1949-
[Amenagement]: hotellerie.
Contents: Bar la Funambule,
Strasbourg, France; architects:
Georges Heintz and Philippe Lacaze
-- L'Oreal restaurant, Clichy,
France; architect: Alain Bailly --
Cafereria de la Comedie Francaise,
Paris; architect: Marie-Christine
Dorner -- Teatriz restaurant,
Madrid, Spain; designer; Philippe
Starck.
LE MONITEUR ARCHITECTURE AMC 1990
July-Aug., no.13, p.58-67,
axonometric views, photos., plans.
Armchair theatre: Starck in Madrid /
Rick Poynor.
Teatriz restaurant; designer:
Philippe Starck.
BLUEPRINT (LONDON, ENGLAND) 1990
June, no.68, p.46-48, photos.

STARCK, PHILIPPE, 1949- (CONTINUED)
Arte versus architettura = Art
versus architecture / Pier Luigi
Tazzi.
Subtitle: Three projects for the
French pavilion at the Venice
Biennale. Architects: Jean Nouvel,
Christian de Portzamparc, and
Philippe Starck.
OTTAGONO 1990 Sept., no.96,
p.7-18, elevs., models, photos.,
plans.
Asahi Beer Azumabashi Hall (Super
Dry Hall) / Philippe Terrien.
Located in Tokyo. Architect:
Philippe Starck.
JAPAN ARCHITECT 1990 Apr., v.65,
no.4 (396), p.8-21, dwgs.,
photos., plans, secns.
Asahi Super Dry Hall.
Architects: Philippe Starck,
Makoto Nozawa and Gett.
KENCHIKU BUNKA 1990 Jan., v.45,
no.519, p.[72]-75, photos., plans.
Biennale de Venise / Francois
Chaslin.
On the installation projects by
Christian de Portzamparc, Philippe
Starck and Jean Nouvel. English
summary, p.12.
ARCHITECTURE D'AUJOURD'HUI 1990
Sept., no.270, p.10-13, dwgs.,
elevs., models, plans, site plans.
Brasserie Asahi Beer, Tokyo /
Brigitte Fitoussi.
Architect: Philippe Starck.
ARCHITECTURE D'AUJOURD'HUI 1990
Sept., no.270, p.188-192, photos.
Divine fire.
Features interiors of Philippe
Starck's Asahi Beer Hall, Tokyo.
BUILDING DESIGN 1990 Apr.20,
no.982, p.12, photos.
Dream sequence / David Redhead.
Interiors of Madrid restaurant,
Teatriz. Interior designer:
Philippe Starck.
DESIGNERS' JOURNAL 1990 July-Aug.,
no.59, p.72-76, photos., plan.
Drie ontwerpen voor een nieuw Frans
paviljoen in Venetie.
Models by Jean Nouvel (two
versions), Christian de
Portzamparc, and Philippe Starck,
for the Pavillon Francais des
Giardini, Biennale, 1990.
ARCHIS 1990 July, no.7, p.7,
models.
Far-out inns / Regina S. Baraban.
Ian Schrager's new Manhattan
hotels for hip travellers.
METROPOLIS 1990 Nov., v.10, no.4,
p.48-[53], photos., model.
For Ian Schrager, design is
paramount / Fred A. Bernstein.
Renovation and interior design of
Paramount Hotel, at Eight Ave. and
46th St., New York by Schrager and
Philippe Starck.
METROPOLITAN HOME 1990 Nov., v.22,
no.11, p.63-[70],164, port.,
photos.
French leave / Adrian Dannat.
On the controversy surrounding the
French pavillion for the 1990
Biennale di Venezia. Architects:
Philippe Starck, Christian de
Portzamparc and Jean Nouvel.
BUILDING DESIGN 1990 July
27-Aug.3, no.996-997, p.16,
models, photos.

STARCK, PHILIPPE, 1949- (CONTINUED)
Green imagery.
On the Nani Nani office building,
Tokyo. Architect: Philippe Starck.
BUILDING DESIGN 1990 May 18,
no.986, p.16, photos., plans,
secn.
Hall of Fame: celebrations and
memories [1990].
Profiles of twelve new inductees
into the Interior Design Hall of
Fame and the winners of three
special citations.
INTERIOR DESIGN 1990 Dec., v.61,
no.16, p.105-[125], ports.,
photos.
Le Nani-nani de Starck.
Office building, Tokyo. Architect:
Philippe Starck. English summary,
p.80.
ARCHITECTURE D'AUJOURD'HUI 1990
Sept., no.270, p.78-80, photos.,
plans, secns.
Paperweight architecture: Starck in
Toyko / Peter Popham.
Contents: Asahi Beer company
building--Nani Nani building.
Architect: Philippe Starck.
BLUEPRINT (LONDON, ENGLAND) 1990
June, no.68, p.40-44, photos.
Paramount / Edie Lee Cohen.
Interiors of the New York hotel
designed by Philippe Starck.
INTERIOR DESIGN 1990 Dec., v.61,
no.16, p.142-[147], photos.,
plans.
Paramount Hotel.
Features interiors of New York
hotel designed by Philippe Starck.
Includes interview with hotel
owner, Ian Schrager. English
summary, p.215.
ARCHITECTURE INTERIEURE CREE 1990
Oct.-Nov., no.239, p.146-151,
photos.
Perversion didactica: el Teatriz de
Starck / Vicente Paton.
Conversion of a Madrid theater
into a complex of bars,
restaurant, and discotheque.
ARQUITECTURA VIVA 1990 Nov.-Dec.,
no.15, p.49-53, elevs., photos.,
plan.
Philippe Starck: architetture a
Tokyo tra il 1987 e il 1990 /
Marco Romanelli.
NaniNani Buildings; Asahi
Building. Text in Italian and
English.
DOMUS 1990 Nov., no.721,
p.[46-55], ill., elevs., photos.,
plans, secns.
Royalton Hotel, New York / Birgit
Dietsch.
Renovations to hotel on West 44th
St. Architect: Philippe Starck.
BAUWELT 1990 Mar.30, v.81, no.12,
p.530-531, photos., plans.
Starck struck / Andrea Truppin.
Profile of the work of Philippe
Starck.
INTERIORS 1989 Feb., v.148, no.7,
p.121-129,156, photos.
Super-Starck in Tokyo / Barbara
Friedrich.
Features two Tokyo multi-use
buildings designed by Philippe
Starck: La Flamme and Nani Nani.
English summary, p.5.
ARCHITEKTUR & WOHNEN 1990
Aug.-Sept., no.4, p.116-121, ill.,
port., photos.

STARCK, PHILIPPE, 1949- (CONTINUED)
Teatriz ole! / Christine Colin.
Interiors of Teatriz restaurant,
Madrid. Interior designer:
Philippe Starck. English summary,
p.163.
ARCHITECTURE INTERIEURE CREE 1990
Mar., no.235, p.114-121, photos.,
plan.
Unhex Nani Nani / Philippe Terrien.
Office building, Tokyo. Architect:
Philippe Starck.
JAPAN ARCHITECT 1990 Apr., v.65,
no.4 (396), p.22-25, photos.,
plans, secn.

STARKE, GERDA
Vorschuleinrichtungen fur
innerstadtische Wohngebiete /
Gerda Starke.
Examples in Dresden of preschool
facilities located on the ground
floor of apartment buildings.
German, Russian, English and
French summaries, p.55-56.
ARCHITEKTUR DER DDR 1990 Jan.,
v.38, no.1, p.27-31, dwgs.,
elevs., plans, secns., site plan,
isometric dwgs., refs.

STASIOWSKI, FRANK
Management: reducing liability /
Frank Stasiowski.
"Describes five ways to reduce
lawsuits through project
management."
PROGRESSIVE ARCHITECTURE 1990 May,
v.71, no.5, p.65-66,
Marketing: when the economy turns
down / Frank Stasiowski.
PROGRESSIVE ARCHITECTURE 1990
Mar., v.71, no.3, p.55,

STATE AND ARCHITECTURE
See ARCHITECTURE AND STATE

STATE AND ART
See ART AND STATE

STATE AND ENVIRONMENT
See ENVIRONMENTAL POLICY

STATE AND HOUSING
See HOUSING POLICY

STATEHOUSES
See CAPITOLS

STATENS KUNSTFOND (DENMARK)
Randmonumenter [exhibition review] /
Morten Daugaard.
An exhibit of Danish glass
designs, marking the 25th
anniversary of the Statens
Kunstfond, at the
Rosenkjaerhallen, Christianshaven,
Oct.28-Nov.1, 1989.
ARKITEKTEN 1990 Apr., v.92, no.4,
p.134-136, dwgs., photos.

STATENS KUNSTFOND (DENMARK)--
EXHIBITIONS
Bevar Rosenkjaerhallen / Jorgen
Sestoft.
On an exhibition marking the 25th
anniversary of the Christianshavn
building, sponsored by the Statens
Kunstfond. Original architect:
Niels Rosenkjaer.
ARKITEKTEN 1989 Nov.28, v.91,
no.21, p.509-514, dwg., elev.,
models, photos.

STATES - IDEAL
See UTOPIAS

STATIONS - ELECTRIC (SUBSTATIONS)
See ELECTRIC SUBSTATIONS

STATIONS - TELEVISION
See TELEVISION STATIONS

STATUES
See SCULPTURE

STAUB, ALEXANDRA
Grossrachen: ein Dorf stirbt fur den
Tagebau / Alexandra Staub.
BAUWELT 1990 July 20, v.81, no.27,
p.1396-1397, photos.

STAUCH VORSTER + PARTNERS
Rand Water Board headquarters.
Located in the Klipriviersberg
range, south of Johannesburg.
Architects: Stauch Vorster +
Partners.
ARCHITECT & BUILDER 1989 July,
p.6-9, dwg., elevs., photos.,
plans.

STAUD, ERNST, 1929-
Ernst Staud - 60 Jahre.
Garden and landscape architect
(b.29.Dec.1929) in Trier.
DEUTSCHES ARCHITEKTENBLATT 1990
Jan.1, v.22, no.1, p.20-21, port.

STAUFENBIEL, FRED
Stadtsoziologische Forschung und
intensive Stadtreproduktion / Fred
Staufenbiel.
German, Russian, English and
French summaries, p.55-56.
ARCHITEKTUR DER DDR 1990 Feb.,
v.38, no.2, p.11-12, refs.

STAUSS, EBERHARD
Une thebaide a Lukasod / Eberhard
Stauss.
Silo house. Architect: Eberhard
Stauss. English summary, p.52.
ARCHITECTURE INTERIEURE CREE 1990
Feb., no.234, p.[128-131],
photos., plans, secn.

STAVE CHURCHES--NORWAY--BERGEN--
FANTOFT CHURCH
Linked with the landscape: Norway's
delicately decorative buildings
have survived a tough history and
a harsh climate.
Fantoft Church; Bryggen Hansa
merchant's buildings; and the home
of Edvard Grieg.
TRADITIONAL HOMES 1990 Feb., v.6,
no.5, p.107-109, photos.

STAVE CHURCHES--WOODEN--SOVIET UNION--
UKRAINE
Masterpieces in wood: houses of
worship in Ukraine [by] Titus D.
Hewryk [and] the wooden
architecture of Russia; houses,
fortifications, churches [by]
Alexander Opolovnikov, Yelena
Opolovnikova [book review] /
Albert J. Schmidt.
SOCIETY OF ARCHITECTURAL
HISTORIANS. JOURNAL 1990 Dec.,
v.49, no.4, p.460-462,

STAVROS, DAVID
Aida's / David Lasker.
Interiors of Lebanese fast-food
restaurant, on Yonge Street,
Toronto. Interior designers:
David Stavros, Tarek El-Khatib.
INTERIOR DESIGN 1990 Mar., v.61,
no.5, p.[212-213], photos.

STEADMAN, PHILIP. NUCLEAR DISASTERS
AND THE BUILT ENVIRONMENT
Accident or design? [book review] /
James Lewis.
Review of the RIBA report, Nuclear
Disasters and the Built
Environment by Philip Steadman and
Simon Hodgkinson.
RIBA JOURNAL 1990 July, v.97,
no.7, p.34-35, ill.

STEARN, JONATHAN
East Berlin: at home behind the
crumbling wall / Jonathan Stearn.
HOUSING 1989 Dec.-1990 Jan., v.26,
no.10, p.20-22, photos., aerial
photo.
Let the buyer beware / Jonathan
Stearn.
Financial failure of a recent
British housing scheme.
HOUSING 1990 Dec.-1991 Jan., v.26,
no.10, p.9-12, ports., photo.
Locked in danger / Jonathan Stearn.
Describes situations whereby
highly efficient security devices
prevent fire brigades from
reaching victims.
HOUSING 1989 Feb., v.25, no.1,
p.20-23, photos.
Low cost homes: the share option /
Jonathan Stearn.
Shared home ownership in Britain.
HOUSING 1990 Dec.-1991 Jan., v.26,
no.10, p.27,29,31, photos.
Practising what you preach /
Jonathan Stearn.
The author responds to a recent
Church of England publication,
"Living faith in the city", which
criticizes the housing situation
in England by suggesting that the
church contribute some of its vast
real estate holdings for use by
the homeless.
HOUSING 1990 Mar., v.26, no.2,
p.13-17, photos.

STECICH, JOHN P.
A thin-stone veneer primer / Ian R.
Chin, John P. Stecich, Bernard
Erlin.
ARCHITECTURAL RECORD 1990 June,
v.178, no.7, p.108-113, dets.,
photos, tables.

STEDELIJK VAN ABBEMUSEUM--EXHIBITIONS
Architectuur als "levensontwerp":
Het werk van Thomas Schutte /
Marieke van Giersbergen.
In conjunction with an exhibition
opening in Oct. at the Van
Abbermuseum in Eindhoven and ones
in Bern and Paris.
ARCHIS 1990 Oct., no.10, p.42-45,
dwg., models, photos., plans.
Bewoners maken vuist tegen
kunststoframen: Dudoks Witte Dorp
in Eindhoven [exhibition review] /
Jeroen Schilt.
Exhibition in the Van Abbemuseum,
until 6 Nov.1989; sponsored by
Witte Dorp De Burgh. Architect:
(Continued next page)

STEDELIJK VAN ABBEMUSEUM--EXHIBITIONS
(CONTINUED)
  Bewoners maken vuist...(CONTINUED)
    W.M. Dudok.
    ARCHIS 1989 Oct., no.10, p.4,
    dwg., photo.

STEDEN, BERT
  Spotlight im Siegerkranz: das
    Brandenburger tor im neuen Licht /
    Hans-Joachin Dombrowski, Bert
    Steden.
    Architect (1789): Carl Gotthard
    Langhans.
    DEUTSCHE BAUZEITUNG 1990 June,
    v.124, no.6, p.128-129, photos.,
    plans.

STEDMAN, JOHN, 1920-1990
  John Stedman [obituary] / Denis
    Harper.
    RIBA JOURNAL 1990 Aug., v.97,
    no.8, p.75,

STEEDMAN, NEIL
  Christchurch Square, Dublin / Neil
    Steedman.
    Commercial development in Dublin's
    historic city center. Architects:
    Horan Cotter Associates.
    PLAN: ARCHITECTURE & INTERIOR
    DESIGN IN IRELAND 1989 June, v.22,
    no.6, p.3-12, model, photos,
    plans.
  Terminal building, Rosslare / Neil
    Steedman.
    Major passenger terminal on
    reclaimed land in Rosslare Harbour
    Ireland, integrates movement
    between ferries, trains, buses and
    cars. Architects: John Clancey.
    PLAN: ARCHITECTURE + INTERIOR
    DESIGN IN IRELAND 1989 June, v.22,
    no.6, p.29-36, photos.

STEEG, EDOUARD
  Containers a quaix aux Pays-Bas.
    Waterfront housing block,
    Rotterdam. Architects: Herve
    Daridan, Isabelle Manescau,
    Jean-Marie Dancy, Francois
    Marzelle, Edouard Steeg. English
    summary, p.93; Spanish summary,
    p.172.
    TECHNIQUES ET ARCHITECTURE 1990
    Oct.-Nov., no.392, p.92-93, dwg.,
    elev., models.
  Profils: les elus 1989: Albums de
    la jeune architecture.
    Contents: Epinard Bleu, Pascal
    Marchant, Philtre Avant-Travaux,
    Patricia Leboucq, Shinobu Akahori,
    Pascal Quintard Hofstein, and
    Herve Daridan.
    LE MONITEUR ARCHITECTURE AMC 1990
    Mar., no.9, p.55, ports.

STEEL
  See also STAINLESS STEEL
  See also STEEL AS A SUBHEADING
  AFTER SPECIFIC BUILDING TYPES OR
  OTHER MAIN HEADINGS.
  Architekturmaschinen aus Stahl.
    Theme of issue emphasizing steel
    construction in Germany. The
    individual articles are indexed
    separately.
    BAUWELT 1990 Dec.1, v.81, no.45,
    p.2233,cover, dwgs., photo.,
    model.

STEEL (CONTINUED)
  Steel construction.
    A "technology special" section,
    with articles on the reduction in
    British Standard fire protection
    requirements, steel works in the
    U.K., prioritieis of the British
    Constructional Steelwork
    Association and a Swedish on site
    steel building system.
    BUILDING 1990 June 22. v.255,
    no.25, p.53-66, port., photos.,
    secns.

STEEL MILLS--UNITED STATES--LACKAWANNA
(NEW YORK)--BETHLEHEM STEEL
  The work of rolling rails in the 32"
    mill at Bethlehem Steel's
    Lackawanna Plant: industrial
    archeology and labor history /
    Thomas E. Leary.
    SOCIETY FOR INDUSTRIAL ARCHEOLOGY.
    JOURNAL 1990, v.16, no.1, p.39-54,
    dwgs., photos., plans, refs.

STEEL - PRESTRESSED
  See PRESTRESSED STEEL

STEEL - STAINLESS
  See STAINLESS STEEL

STEELCASE DESIGN PARTNERSHIP--
EXHIBITIONS
  Sugar and spice: designs for DIFFA
    [exhibition review] / Abby Bussel.
    Review of Edible architecture:
    delicious designs, on view in the
    Steelcase gallery, New York in the
    fall of 1989. The sale proceeds
    went to the Design Industries'
    Foundation for AIDS.
    PROGRESSIVE ARCHITECTURE 1990
    Jan., v.71, no.1, p.28-29, models.

STEELE, FLETCHER, 1885-1971
  Family heirloom: a romantic garden
    by Fletcher Steele flourishes at
    Mill Pond Farm / Ellen Count.
    At the Country home of Francis J.
    Kellogg, Bedford, N.Y.
    ELLE DECOR 1990 May, v.1, no.4,
    p.[84-91], photos.
  Fletcher Steele, landscape
    architect: an account of the
    gardenmaker's life: 1885-1971 [by]
    Robin Karson [book review] /
    Leslie Rose Close.
    SOCIETY OF ARCHITECTURAL
    HISTORIANS. JOURNAL 1990 Dec.,
    v.49, no.4, p.452-453,

STEELE, FLETCHER, 1885-1971--
EXHIBITIONS
  Modernist landscapes: the
    adventurous gardens of Fletcher
    Steele stretched the aesthetic
    boundaries of early twentieth
    century design [exhibition review]
    / Mac Griswold.
    Exhibition through Mar. 30 at the
    Paine Webber Art Gallery, New
    York.
    HOUSE & GARDEN 1990 Mar., v.162,
    no.3, p.116-[118], photos., port.,
    secn.

STEELE, JAMES
  The Aga Khan Award for architecture
    / James Steele.
    On the fourth awards ceremony,
    held Oct.15, 1989 in Cairo, and
    the winners.
    ARCHITECTURAL DESIGN 1990, v.60,
    no.1-2, p.iv-vii, dwg., photos.
  Hassan Fathy: the new
    traditionalists / James Steele.
    ARCHITECTURAL DESIGN 1989, v.59.
    no.11-12, p.ii-vii, dwg., elevs.,
    plan, secns., site plans.
  Obituary: Hassan Fathy / James
    Steele.
    ARCHITECTURAL REVIEW 1990 Jan.,
    v.187, no.1115, p.9, port., photo.

STEELE, JOHN
  Classicism's light new touch /
    Carolyn Ulrich.
    Small residential backyard gardens
    in Chicago, New Haven, Houston,
    and Washington, D.C. Landscape
    architects: Timothy Lally, Ralph
    Synnestvedt, Jr., Paul Bailey,
    Douglas Kycia, McDugald-Steele,
    Lanson Jones, and Jane Macleish.
    GARDEN DESIGN 1990 autumn, v.9,
    no.3, p.[30-37], photos.

STEELWORKS
  See STEEL MILLS

STEEMERS, KOEM
  Domestic low energy, 4: beyond the
    regs / David Turrent, Koen
    Steemers.
    Fourth and last in series on
    energy efficient housing.
    ARCHITECTS' JOURNAL 1990 Apr.11,
    v.191, no.15, p.61-65,67, diagrs.,
    graph, photos., secns.

STEEMERS, THEO
  Vitstalkast van het nieuwe wonen:
    Buitenexpositie NWR Bouw RAI /
    Theo Steemens.
    ARCHIS 1990 May, no.5, p.25-30,
    photos., plans, secn., site plans.

STEEN, ANTHONY
  Bucking the planning system /
    Anthony Steen.
    What happens when a building
    starts without planning
    permission.
    HOUSING AND PLANNING REVIEW 1990
    Apr.-May, v.45, no.2, p.13-14,
    photos.

STEENHUIS, ROB M. J. A., 1949-
  Vierbaans over de gouwe / Arjen
    Oosterman.
    Drawbridge in Gouda, engineered by
    the Nederlandse Spoorwegen. Built
    1987-1989. Architect: Rob
    Steenhuis.
    ARCHIS 1990 Apr., no.4, p.20-22,
    photos.

STEENHUIS, ROELF, 1956-
  Thema: nieuwbouwwijken.
    "Themanummer 39", with seven
    articles on housing projects in
    the Netherlands, at Prinsenland,
    Amsterdam and elsewhere, by Ashok
    Bhalotra, Roelf Steenhuis and
    others. Authors: Evelien Brandes,
    Frits Palmboom, Maurits de Hoog,
    Egbert Koster, Janny Rodermond,
    Wijnand Looise.
    (Continued next page)

STEENHUIS, ROELF, 1956- (CONTINUED)
Thema: nieuwbouwwijken. (CONTINUED)
DE ARCHITECT THEMA 1990 May, v.21,
no.5 suppl., p.3-65, axonometric
views, dwgs., elevs., maps,
photos., plans, site plans.
Tussen dorp en stad: woningbouw van
Roelf Steenhuis in Groningen /
Janny Rodermond.
Corpus den Hoorn Zuid, deelplan
oost 1, a 350-unit housing
complex. Architects: Mecanoo.
DE ARCHITECT 1990 Jan., v.21,
no.1, p.22-31, elevs., photos.,
plans, site plans.

STEEPLES
See SPIRES

STEFANELLI, PIERCARLO
Sotto la montagna sopra la citta /
Lucia Bisi.
Two-family home, Sondrio, Italy.
Architect: Piercarlo Stefanelli.
VILLE GIARDINI 1990 Sept., no.251,
p.2-9, photos., plans, secn., site
plan.

STEFANIDIS, JOHN
Light supremacy / Stephen Long.
Interiors of Belgravia terrace
house, London. Interior designer:
John Stefanidis.
THE WORLD OF INTERIORS 1990
July-Aug., p.[104-115], dets.,
photos.
Orderliness is next to wilderness /
Patrick Taylor.
On interior designer John
Stefanidis' garden, Cock Crow
Farm.
THE WORLD OF INTERIORS 1990 Apr.,
p.[128-139], photos.
Past perfect on Patmos:
reinterpreting island idioms for a
house in the Aegean / Peter
Dragadze.
Features interiors of 19th cent.
home. Interior designer: John
Stefanidis.
ARCHITECTURAL DIGEST 1990 Aug.,
v.47, no.8, p.116-[123], photos.

STEFANO, ROBERTO DI
Casi di restauro di monumenti allo
stato di rovina / Roberto di
Stefano.
Case studies on the restoration
and structural reinforcment of
five building in Naples, including
several Renaissance churches.
RESTAURO 1989 May-June, v.18,
no.103, entire issue (95 p.),
dets., photos., plans, secns.,
site plans, isometric dwgs.,
biblios.
ICOMOS: 25 anni di vita, bilancio e
avvenire / ed. by Rosa Anna
Genovese.
In conjunction with an
international colloquim held in
Lausanne, 6-11 Oct.1990, entitled
ICOMOS: un quart de siecle
d'existence, bilan et avenir.
Articles by Roberto di Stefano,
Mario F. Roggero, Gianfranco
Spagnesi, Franco Borsi, Gaetano
Miarelli Mariani, Marco Dezzi
Bardeschi, and Angelo Calvani.
RESTAURO 1990 May-June, v.19,
no.109, p.[3]-90, refs.

STEFANO, ROBERTO DI (CONTINUED)
Le vicende del restauro del palazzo
carafa di Roccella in Napoli
(1964-87) / Roberto di Stefano,
Alberto Defez.
RESTAURO 1987 Sept.-Oct., v.16,
no.93, p.69-86, elevs., maps,
photos., plans.

STEFFIAN & BRADLEY ASSOCIATES
A developer responds to corporate
day care needs in Massachusetts /
Theodore R. Tye.
Architects: SBA, Steffian Bradley
Associates; Developer: National
Development Associates, Inc.
THE JOURNAL OF REAL ESTATE
DEVELOPMENT 1989 Summer, v.5,
no.1, p.38-44, plan, refs.

STEFFY, GARY
Shedding light on the law / Justin
Henderson, Peter Barna.
Lighting for Philadelphia law
offices. Interior designers:
Daroff Design. Lighting Designer:
Gary Steffy.
INTERIORS 1990 Jan., v.149, no.6,
p.52, dets., photos., plan.

STEGERS, RUDOLF
Platzkampfe, Platzangste: wie das
vereint Berlin seine Mitte plant /
Rudolf Stegers.
ARCHITHESE 1990 Nov.-Dec., v.20,
no.6, p.69-72, dwgs., models,
photos., site plan, aerial photos.
Saulenordnung contra Mikrochips:
Prince Charles und die Zukunft der
Architektur / Rudolf Stegers.
ARCH PLUS 1990 July, no.104,
p.62-65, dets., ports., photos.,
plans, refs.

STEGGELL, CARMEN D.
Kitchen design: a twenty-year
comparison 1968:1988 / Carmen D.
Steggell, Joan R. McFadden.
HOUSING AND SOCIETY 1990, v.17,
no.1, p.43-52, graph, tables,
refs.

STEIB, KATHARINA
Haus zum Wendelin, Alters-und
Plegeheim, Riehen BS, 1986-1988.
Architects: Wilfrid und Katharina
Steib.
WERK, BAUEN + WOHNEN 1989 Dec.,
no.12, p.55, photos.
Schweizerisches Paraplegiker-Zentrum
Nottwil, Wettbewerb 1985, in
Ausfuhrung.
Architects: Wilfrid and Katharina
Steib.
WERK, BAUEN + WOHNEN 1990 May,
no.5, p.43-45, model, photos.,
plan, site plan.
Umbauen, erganzen, neu
interpretieren: drei Projekte fur
eine Erweiterung des Zurcher
Kunsthauses, 1989.
Competition entries by Mario Campi
& Franco Pessina, Willi Egli, and
Wilfrid & Katharina Steib.
WERK, BAUEN + WOHNEN 1990 May,
no.5, p.14-18, models, plans,
secns., site plans.

STEIB, WILFRID
Haus zum Wendelin, Alters-und
Plegeheim, Riehen BS, 1986-1988.
Architects: Wilfrid und Katharina
Steib.
WERK, BAUEN + WOHNEN 1989 Dec.,
no.12, p.55, photos.
Schweizerisches Paraplegiker-Zentrum
Nottwil, Wettbewerb 1985, in
Ausfuhrung.
Architects: Wilfrid and Katharina
Steib.
WERK, BAUEN + WOHNEN 1990 May,
no.5, p.43-45, model, photos.,
plan, site plan.
Umbauen, erganzen, neu
interpretieren: drei Projekte fur
eine Erweiterung des Zurcher
Kunsthauses, 1989.
Competition entries by Mario Campi
& Franco Pessina, Willi Egli, and
Wilfrid & Katharina Steib.
WERK, BAUEN + WOHNEN 1990 May,
no.5, p.14-18, models, plans,
secns., site plans.

STEIDLE, OTTO, 1943-
Planungsgeschichte der Universitat
Ulm / Herbert Fecher.
First prize plan by Otto Steidle.
BAUWELT 1990 Sept.28, v.81, no.36,
p.1819-1821, site plans, aerial
photos.

STEIDLE UND PARTNER
Gartenstadt Heidemannstrasse,
Munchen = Garden town
"Heidemannstrasse" in Munich.
Features the central spiral
staircase of the housing
department. Architects: Steidle +
Partner.
DETAIL 1990 Apr.-May, v.30, no.2,
p.138-139, det., photos., plan,
secn.
Integriertes Wohnen: Wohnanlage in
Munchen-Nymphenburg.
Architects: Steidle + Partner and
SEP.
DEUTSCHE BAUZEITUNG 1990 Feb.,
v.124, no.2, p.48-51, photos.,
plans, secn., site plans,
sketches, isometric dwgs.
Ulm Universitat 2.
Winner of 1988 competition for a
campus plan: Steidle + Partner.
BAUWELT 1990 Sept.28, v.81, no.36,
p.1826-1827, plans, models, site
plan.
Wohnungspolitische Konzepte:
Wohnungsbauprojekte / Rudi Kujath.
Section on many new housing
projects in Germany. Contents:
Berlin, by Rudi Kujath.--Koln, by
Uwe Kessler.--Bayern, by Dieter
Gutekunst.--Frankfurt, by Martin
Wentz.--Hannover, by Hanns
Adrian.--Der LEG
Nordrhein-Westfalen, by Roswitha
Sinz.--Anmerkungen..., by Hartmut
Grosshans. Among the architects
represented are Otto Steidle +
Partner; Andreas Brandt & Rudolf
Bottcher; Joachim Ganz, Walter
Rolfes; Axel Schultes; Wolfgang
Scharlach und Rainer Wischhusen;
Rebecca Chestnutt et al; Hubertus
Hoffmann; Paul Petry; Hermann
Schroder, Sampo Widmann; Gerhart
Laage; Freed Ahrens.
BAUWELT 1990 Mar.30, v.81, no.12,
p.572-598, elevs., plans, secns.,
site plans, tables.

STEIGENGA, MADELEINE
Architectuur met meubilair:
Kinderdagverblijven van Madeleine
Steigenga / Helene Damen.
The Creche Express day care center
in The Hague.
DE ARCHITECT 1990 June., v.21,
no.6, p.57-61, axonometric views,
photos., plans, refs.

STEIGENGA SMIT ARCHITECTEN
Niet aangepast inpassen: meervoudige
opdracht Victorieplein Amsterdam /
Hans Stoutjesdijk.
Apartment buildings by Alberts &
van Huut, Steigenga Smit
Architecten, Holvast en van
Woerden, Roelf Steenhuis
Architecten, Kees Christiaanse
Architects & Planners, Claus en
Kaan, Kingma en Roorda
Architecten, and DKV.
DE ARCHITECT 1990 Nov., v.21,
no.11, p.50-55, axonometric views,
dwgs., elevs., plans, secns., site
plans, aerial photo.

STEIGENHOFER, BOHUMIL, 1905-1989
K architektonickemu dilu Bohumila
Steigenhofera / Rostislav Svacha.
On the work of Czech architect B.
Steigenhofer (1905-1989).
Includes English summary.
UMENI 1990, v.38, no.3, p.274-278,
dwgs., photos., refs.

STEIGER, LUDWIG
Reihenhausumbau in Munchen.
Architects: H. Fischer, L.
Stieger, A. Tschaidse. Includes
English summary.
BAUMEISTER 1990 May, v.87, no.5,
p.56-58, elevs., photos., plans,
secns.
Umbau eines Wohnhauses in Gastag.
Architects: Heinz Fischer, Ludwig
Steiger. Includes English
summary..
BAUMEISTER 1990 Jan., v.87, no.1,
p.52-55, elev., photos., plans,
secns.

STEIN & ASSOCIATES
Setting the stage / Jean Gorman.
Features renovated interiors of
Boston video company, Envision.
Architects: Stein & Associates.
INTERIORS 1990 Nov., v.150, no.4,
p.16, photos.

STEIN, CLARENCE S., 1882-1975
Clarence Stein and the greenbelt
towns: settling for less / K. C.
Parsons.
Architect and planner Clarence S.
Stein's role in the formation of
greenbelt towns during the New
Deal.
AMERICAN PLANNING ASSOCIATION,
JOURNAL 1990 Spring, v.56, no.2,
p.161-183, dwg., ports., photo.,
plans, refs.

STEIN, KAREN D.
Building types study 683: Record
interiors 1990 / Karen D. Stein.
Eight interiors by architects,
each project indexed separately.
ARCHITECTURAL RECORD 1990 Sept.,
v.178, no.10, p.69-[117], ill.,
photos., secn.

STEIN, KAREN D. (CONTINUED)
City on a hill...Herman Miller's new
factory / Karen D. Stein.
The Western Region Manufacturing
and Distribution Facility,
Rocklin, Calif. Architect: Frank
O. Gehry & Associates; consulting
architect: Tigerman McCurry
Architects; assoc. architect:
Dreyfuss and Blackford; landscape
architects: Peter Walker / Martha
Schwartz.
ARCHITECTURAL RECORD 1990 Jan.,
v.178, no.1, p.108-115, elev.,
photos., plan, secns., site plan.
Down the strip: Las Vegas
Library/Discovery Museum / Karen
D. Stein.
Antoine Predock, Architect.
ARCHITECTURAL RECORD 1990 Oct.,
v.178, no.11, p.68-[75],
axonometric view, photos., plans.
Dressing for the office: Building
Types Study 679: commercial
interiors / Karen D. Stein.
Three projects: Vogue conference
room (Tod Williams, Billie Tsien);
Spy offices (Chan and Mohney); and
Deloitte & Touche Headquarters
(Peter Pran and Carlos Zapata for
Ellerbe Becket).
ARCHITECTURAL RECORD 1990 May,
v.178, no.6, p.103-115, photos.,
plans, secn.
Gravesian images: for the Johnstown,
Pennsylvania headquarters of Crown
American Corporation, Michael
Graves used classical forms /
Karen D. Stein.
ARCHITECTURAL RECORD 1990 Feb.,
v.178, no.2, p.76-83, photos.,
plans, secn.
New frontier: Wolf house, Ridgway,
Colorado, Sottsass Associati,
architect / Karen D. Stein.
ARCHITECTURAL RECORD 1990 Oct.,
v.178, no.11, p.78-83, elev.,
photos., plans.
Penthouse suite: Manhattan Triplex
Apartment, New York City, Steven
Forman, architect / Karen D.
Stein.
ARCHITECTURAL RECORD 1990 Sept.,
v.178, no.10, p.110-[117],
axonometric views, photos.
A plane solution: a run-down men's
club in downtown Toronto is reborn
as a finely crafted mixed-use
structure housing a graphic design
studio and retail / Karen D.
Stern.
At 284 King St. Architects:
Kuwabara Payne McKenna Blumberg.
ARCHITECTURAL RECORD 1990 July,
v.178, no.8, p.[60]-63, photos.,
plans, secns., site plan.
Portrait of an artist ...
transformation of a South of
Market warehouse into the loft of
a graphic artist, San Francisco /
Karen Stein.
Architects: John Randolph, Bruce
Tomb, of the Interim Office of
Architecture.
ARCHITECTURAL RECORD 1990 Apr.,
v.178, no.4, p.74-[77], photos.,
plans.
Raising Arizona: Zuber house,
Paradise Valley, Arizona / Karen
D. Stein.
Architect: Antoine Predock.
ARCHITECTURAL RECORD 1990
(Continued next column)

STEIN, KAREN D. (CONTINUED)
Raising Arizona:...(CONTINUED)
Mid-Apr., v.178, no.5, p.[88]-95,
axonometric views, photos., plans.
Shadow box: house in Kumamoto,
Japan / Karen D. Stein.
A house to promote the Japanese
lumber industry. Architect:
Studio Citterio/Dwan.
ARCHITECTURAL RECORD 1990
Mid-Apr., v.178, no.5, p.[78]-83,
axonometric view, photos., plans.
Throwing a curve / Karen D. Stein.
Furniture designed by Arthur
Cotton Moore.
ARCHITECTURAL RECORD 1990 Sept.,
v.178, no.10, p.78-[79], dwgs.,
photos.
Tower of power: Hotel Il Palazzo,
Fukuoka, Japan / Karen D. Stein.
Architect: Aldo Rossi, Studio di
Architettura/New York; associate
architects: Studio 80; interior
designers: Shigeru Uchida, Ikuyo
Mitsuhashi, Aldo Rossi, Morris
Adjmi, Ettore Sottsass, Gaetano
Pesce, Shiro Kuramata, Alfredo
Arribas.
ARCHITECTURAL RECORD 1990 May,
v.178, no.6, p.70-[77], dets.,
photos., plans, secn.

STEIN, MARTIN
Dessau--im Zeitenwechsel / Martin
Stein, Harald Kegler, Iris
Reuther.
ARCH PLUS 1990 Apr., no.103,
p.84-87, ill., maps, photos., site
plans.

STEIN, PAT
Three perspectives on preservation
planning / Bruce J. Noble, Jr.
Summarizes three presentations
about improving state and Federal
management of cultural resources
at the Preservation Challenges for
the 1990s conference, held in
Washington, June 5-7, 1990.
Speakers were Pat Stein, Judy
Propper, and Brit Storey.
CRM BULLETIN: A NATIONAL PARK
SERVICE TECHNICAL BULLETIN 1990,
v.13, no.5, p.5-6, 17,

STEIN, RICHARD G., 1917-1990
Richard Stein [obituary].
PROGRESSIVE ARCHITECTURE 1990
Nov., v.71, no.12, p.26,

STEINBERG, FLORIAN
Self-help and "step-by-step housing"
in China / Florian Steinberg.
BUILDING IN CHINA 1989 June, v.2,
no.2, p.30-35, photos.
Transformations of formal housing:
unintended evolutionary
developments as inspiration for
innovative design / Otto Koenigsberger,
Florian Steinberg.
OPEN HOUSE INTERNATIONAL 1988,
v.13, no.2, p.23-35, axonometric
views, photos., plans, secns.,
refs.

STEINBERG, MICHAEL
Hamptons style: Slesin/Steinberg
house, Bridgehampton, New York.
Alteration of a small 1930s
cottage. Architect: Lee H.
Skolnick Architecture and Design.
ARCHITECTURAL RECORD 1990
(Continued next page)

STEINBERG, MICHAEL (CONTINUED)
Hamptons style:...(CONTINUED)
Mid-Apr., v.178, no.5, p.34-[41],
axonometric views, photos., plans.

STEINBRUCK, WOLFGANG, 1949-
Strasse der Befreiung: Neugestaltung
des Platzes der Einheit in
Prestlen.
Public housing project.
Architects: Wolfgang Steinbruck,
Klausjurgen Scholer.
DEUTSCHE BAUZEITUNG 1990 June,
v.124, no.6, p.17-21, photos.,
plans, site plan.

STEINEM, GLORIA
Ms. Steinem on the home front /
Gloria Steinem.
The writer's recently decorated
NYC brownstone. Interior designer
Filippa Naess.
HOUSE & GARDEN 1990 Oct., v.162,
no.10, p.[180]-185, port., photos.

STEINER, BERNHARD
Burgerhaus in Unterhaching: Kultur-
und Bildungszentrum.
Architects: Christian Raupach,
Gunther F. Schurk, Bernhard
Steiner. Includes English summary.
BAUMEISTER 1990 Sept., v.87, no.9,
p.50-55, photos., plans, secns.,
site plans, isometric dwgs.

STEINER, DIETMAR
Coop Himmelblau: das Projekt
Melun-Senart / Dietmar Steiner.
Competition for a satellite town
on the outskirts of Paris.
BAUWELT 1990 Sept.28, v.81, no.36,
p.1832-1835, site plans.
Die frohliche Normalitat: Wohnanlage
"Wienerberger-Grunde" in Graz /
Dietmar Steiner.
Architects: Ralph Erskine, Hubert
Riess.
BAUWELT 1990 Mar.30, v.81, no.12,
p.604-607, axonometric views,
elevs., photos., plans, site
plans.
L'Hans-Sachs-Hof a Salisburgo di
Diener & Diener / Dietmar Steiner.
An apartment complex on the edge
of the historic center of
Salzburg, built 1986-1989.
Buildings A, B, and C relate to
existing houses. Includes English
summary, captions and translation.
CASABELLA 1990 June, v.54, no.569,
p.4-11,59, axonometric views,
photos., plans, secns., site
plans.
Un museo a Salisburgo di Hans
Hollein / Dietmar Steiner.
Includes English captions and
summary.
CASABELLA 1990 Mar., v.54, no.566,
p.18-22,60, axonometric view,
models, plans, secn., site plan,
sketch.
Museumsquartier Wien / Dietmar
Steiner.
Architects: Laurids Ortner &
Manfred Ortner.
BAUWELT 1990 June 1, v.81, no.21,
p.1030-1031, model.
Der Salzburger Forellenweg: ein
Kommunalpolitischer Kriminalroman
/ Dietmar Steiner.
A housing project in Salzburg,
with several architects
(Continued next column)

STEINER, DIETMAR (CONTINUED)
Der Salzburger...(CONTINUED)
participating.
BAUWELT 1990 Mar.30, v.81, no.12,
p.601-603, dwgs., models, photos.,
plans.
Scheiding der machten als
architectonische strategie: het
ontwerp voor het museumkwartier in
Wenen van Ortner Architekten /
Dietmar Steiner.
ARCHIS 1990 Nov., no.11, p.15-17,
models, plans, secns., site plans.
El sueno americano = The American
dream / Dietmar Steiner.
QUADERNS D'ARQUITECTURA I
URBANISME 1990 Jan.-Feb.-Mar.,
no.184, p.5-12, sketches.
A Vienna: il nuovo quartiere dei
musei / Dietmar Steiner.
Includes English captions.
CASABELLA 1990 Dec., v.54, no.574,
p.30-31, model, plans, secn.

STEINER, HANS
Interview: Dr. Arcot Ramachandran /
Hans Steiner, Andre Dzikus.
The Executive Director, United
Nations Centre for Human
Settlements (UNCHS/Habitat)
discusses the Global Shelter
Strategy for the Year 2000.
THIRD WORLD PLANNING REVIEW 1990
May, v.12, no.2, p.[99]-108,
port., refs.

STEINER, RON, 1952-
Incursione suprematista nel
Mediterraneo: Therma Hotel, baia
di Gera, Lesbo = Suprematist
incursion in the Mediterranean:
Therma Hotel, Bay of Gera, Lesvos.
Architects: Elia Zenghelis, Ron
Steiner, Elias Veneris, Zoe
Zenghelis.
LOTUS INTERNATIONAL 1986, no.52,
p.30-39, axonometric views,
elevs., models, plans, secns.,
site plans.
Karlsruhe: Centre des Arts et des
Technologies / Dominique Boudet.
Architects: Rem Koolhaas, with
Xaveer de Geyter, Heike Lohmann,
Rients Dijtestra, Alex Wall,
Christophe Cornubert, Georges
Heintz, Mark Schendel, Ron
Steiner.
LE MONITEUR ARCHITECTURE AMC 1990
Feb., no.8, p.12-13, dwgs., plans,
secns.

STEINGUT, ILENE
Vallifuoco e Steingut: progetti e
opere recenti = The work of
Vallifuoco and Steingut /
Francesco Garofalo.
In English and Italian; summaries
in French, German, and Spanish,
p.3.
L'INDUSTRIA DELLE COSTRUZIONI 1990
Nov., v.24, no.229, p.6-21,
axonometric views, elevs., models,
photos., plans, secns., site
plans.

STEINHAUSER, MONIKA
Im Bild des Erhabenen / Monika
Steinhauser.
WERK, BAUEN + WOHNEN 1990 June,
no.6, p.16-21, ill., photo.

STEINHAUSER, THEO
Ev. Gemeindehaus Kempten im Allgau.
Architect: Theo Steinhauser.
KUNST UND KIRCHE 1990, no.1,
p.38-39, photos., plans, secns.,
site plan.

STEINIGEWEG, FRIEDRICH
Weltausstellungsarchitektur: der
Wettbewerb fur den deutschen
Pavillon fur die EXPO'92 Sevilla
und Fragen zur Architektur.
Projects by: Auer + Weber (1st
prize); Frei Otto; Joachim
Schurmann. Axel Schultes; Helmut
Striffler; Heinz Mihl; Storch +
Ehlers; Kurt Ackermann und Peter
Jaeger; Gottfried Bohm und
Friedrich Steinigeweg; Heinz
Hilmer & Christoph Sattler; PAS;
Kiessler + Partner.
BAUMEISTER 1990 June, v.87, no.6,
p.15-29, ill., dwgs., elevs.,
models, photo., plans, secns.,
site plans, aerial photos.

STEINITZ, BERNARD
A roman renaissance: noted antiques
dealer Bernard Steinitz takes on
the 16th-century Palazzo alle
Colonne / Charlotte Aillaud.
Restoration of 1533 Palazzo
Massimo alle Colonne, Rome.
Original architect: Baldassare
Peruzzi.
ARCHITECTURAL DIGEST 1990 Jan.,
v.47, no.1, p.148-156, port.,
photos.

STEINITZ, CARL
Academic assemblage.
Profile of six educators among
various landscape architecture
faculties.
LANDSCAPE ARCHITECTURE 1990 Sept.,
v.80, no.9, p.58-63, ports.,
photos., site plan.
A framework for theory applicable to
the education of landscape
architects (and other
environmental design
professionals) / Carl Steinitz.
LANDSCAPE JOURNAL 1990 Fall, v.9,
no.2, p.136-143, tables, refs.
Toward a sustainable landscape with
high visual preference and high
ecological integrity: the Loop
Road in Acadia National Park,
U.S.A. / Carl Steinitz.
LANDSCAPE AND URBAN PLANNING 1990
June, v.19, no.3, p.213-250, maps,
graphs, photos., tables, refs.

STEINITZ, DAVID
Razzle-Dazzle on the beach:
high-tech highlights the abstract
forms of a Malibu beach house /
Aaron Betsky.
Irmus house. Architect: Warren
Gray; lighting designer: David
Steinitz.
ARCHITECTURAL RECORD 1990 Aug.,
v.178, no.9 suppl., p.[16-19],
photos.

STEINMANN, MARTIN
Warehouse, Ricola, Switzerland,
1986-87 / Martin Steinmann.
Architects: Jacques Herzog and
Pierre de Meuron.
9H 1989, no.8, p.74-75, photos.,
secn.

STELE (ARCHAEOLOGY)
See also MENHIRS

STELE (ARCHAEOLOGY)--ITALY--SARDINIA--
GALLURA
Stazzo in Gallura.
A shepherd's shelter in Gallura,
Sardinia, has been restored as a
house by Alessandra Bocchetti.
Text in Italian and English.
ABITARE 1990 Mar., no.283,
p.118-123, dwg., photos., plan.

STELL, GEOFFREY
Crofts to castles: the classic
dwelling types of the Highlands
and Islands / Geoffrey Stell.
TRADITIONAL HOMES 1990 Mar., v.6,
no.6, p.14-18, photos., biblio.
Heart of stone: the unique character
of vernacular architecture in
Scotland's Central Lowlands /
Geoffrey Stell.
TRADITIONAL HOMES 1990 Feb., v.6,
no.5, p.35-39, photos., biblio.
Vernacular architecture: Scottish
division: the homes of the border
/ Geoffrey Stell.
TRADITIONAL HOMES 1990 Jan., v.6,
no.4, p.16-20, photos., biblios.

STELLA, DOMINIQUE
Palestra comunale a Mouans Sartoux /
Dominique Stella.
Architects: Christian Mace,
Jean-Paul Gomis. Summaries in
English, French and Spanish.
ABACUS 1990 Jan.-Mar., v.6, no.21,
p.52-61, axonometric views, dets.,
elevs., photos., secns., site
plans.

STELLINO, ANNA MARIA
Segreta, come in un'oasi / Anna
Maria Stellino.
House and garden at San Gregorio,
Italy. Architect: Marcello
D'Olivo.
VILLE GIARDINI 1990 May, no.248,
p.24-29, photos.

STELLWAG, PETER
Hair-Styling:
Einrichtungsgegenstande im
Frisiersalon Klinger, Stuttgart.
Designers: Heinz Legler, Peter
Stellwag.
DEUTSCHE BAUZEITUNG 1990 Oct.,
v.124, no.10, p.172-173, photos.,
plan, secn.
Illusion: das Cafe Stella in
Stuttgart.
Designer: Peter Stellwag.
DEUTSCHE BAUZEITUNG 1990 Oct.,
v.124, no.10, p.52-53, photos.,
plans.

STELZER, GIULIANO
Concorso per la riqualificazione
dell' area di Via Veneto [Trento].
Presents 10 entries, including 1st
prize entry by Oswald Zoeggeler.
PARAMETRO 1990, Nov.-Dec., no.181,
p.52-69, axonometric views, ill.,
dwgs., elevs., photos., plans,
secns., aerial photo.

STEMSHORN, AXEL
Anpassbares Bauen in den
Niederlanden / Axel Stemshorn.
Plans and key dimensions for small
apartments.
DEUTSCHES ARCHITEKTENBLATT 1990
Apr.1, v.22, no.4, p.557-559,
plans.

STENCIL WORK
See also STENCILS AND STENCIL
CUTTING
Brush on the charm [stencilling] /
Dara Caponigro.
Stencilling for walls and fabrics.
HOUSE BEAUTIFUL 1990 July, v.132,
no.7, p.[62]-65, dets., photos.
A stencil artist paints a fantasy
world / Sally Clark.
Old Customs House interiors,
Penzance, Cornwall, home of
stencil artist Lyn Le Grice.
HOUSE BEAUTIFUL 1990 Oct., v.132,
no.10, p.104-111, port., photos.

STENCIL WORK--19TH CENTURY--GREAT
BRITAIN
Brushing through the tulips: a
Victorian stencilled wallcovering
comes to life once more /
Christine Woods.
Reproduction of "Tulip Garden", an
1890s design originally used in
the billard room of a country
house near Bushey Heath.
TRADITIONAL HOMES 1990 Oct., v.7,
no.1, p.51-54, photos.

STENCIL WORK--CONSERVATION AND
RESTORATION
"Proud of what I've done": Romanian
emigre blossoms in new world /
Thomas W. Sweeney.
Aurelian Ilie, a specialist in
marbleizing, scagliola and
stenciling, has restored the
painted interior finish of Union
Station, Wahington, D.C., and the
Riggs Bank (formerly Farmers and
Mechanics Bank), Georgetown, D.C.
PRESERVATION NEWS 1990 Feb., v.30,
no.2, p.14-15, ports., photos.

STENCIL WORK--DIRECTORIES
The decorative painting revival /
Eve Kahn.
Contains two directories of
decorative painting companies.
CLEM LABINE'S TRADITIONAL BUILDING
1990 Mar.-Apr., v.3, no.2, cover,
p.7-15, ill., photos.

STENCIL WORK--UNITED STATES
Stencil deigns for a room with
personality [Decorating a teen's
room, Part II].
VICTORIAN HOMES 1990 Summer, v.9,
no.3, p.58-63,78-79, diagrs.,
photos.

STENCILS AND STENCIL CUTTING
Brushing through the tulips: a
Victorian stencilled wallcovering
comes to life once more /
Christine Woods.
Reproduction of "Tulip Garden", an
1890s design originally used in
the billard room of a country
house near Bushey Heath.
TRADITIONAL HOMES 1990 Oct., v.7,
no.1, p.51-54, photos.

STENTI, SERGIO
Boston Back Bay: Atene d'America /
Sergio Stenti.
English, French, German, Spanish
summaries p.126-127.
STORIA DELLA CITTA 1989 Jan.-Mar.,
v.14, no.49, p.7-42, elevs., maps,
photos., plans, engrs., aerial
photos., biblio., refs.
Citta americane / Sergio Stenti.
Theme issue on American cities.
Six articles indexed separately.
STORIA DELLA CITTA 1989 Jan.-Mar.,
v.14, no.49, entire issue, ill.,
refs.
Manhattan manners, architecture and
style 1850-1900 [by] M. Christine
Boyer [book review] / Sergio
Stenti.
Published 1985.
STORIA DELLA CITTA 1989 Jan.-Mar.,
v.14, no.49, p.83-85, map, photos.

STEP-BY-STEP HOUSING
See INCREMENTAL HOUSING

STEPANOVA, VARVARA FEDOROVNA,
1894-1958
Varvara Stepanova: the complete work
[book review] / Harriet Edquist.
Review of 1988 book by Alexander
Lavrentiev.
TRANSITION 1990, no.33, p.84-87,
port., photo.

STEPANOVA, VARVARA FEDOROVNA,
1894-1958--EXHIBITIONS
Briefing: Return of the
constructors: Family workshop,
Rodchenko & Stepanova, Serpentine
Gallery, London [exhibition
review] / Brian Hatton.
BLUEPRINT (LONDON, ENGLAND) 1990
Feb., no.64, p.49-50, ill.

STEPHANI, MANFRED K.
Moderne Photogrammetrie, ein
Werkzeug des Architekten = Modern
photogrammetry, a tool for
architects / Manfred K. Stephani.
DETAIL 1990 Oct.-Nov., v.30, no.5,
p.457-460, elevs., photos., plans,
tables.

STEPHEN B. JACOBS AND ASSOCIATES
Affordable housing in Brooklyn.
Stuyvesant Mews, factory-built
rowhouses for the
Bedford-Stuyvesant neighborhood.
Architects: Stephen B. Jacobs.
ARCHITECTURAL RECORD 1990 Sept.,
v.178, no.10, p.27, model.

STEPHEN R. TEEPLE, ARCHITECT
Eight young firms / Bronwen Ledger.
Saucier & Perrotte; Stephen R.
Teeple; Jenkins & Sturgess; Brian
Allsopp; Natale Scott Browne; Ruth
Cawker Architect; Busby Bridger;
and Brian MacKay-Lyons
Architecture and Urban Design.
CANADIAN ARCHITECT 1990 Sept.,
v.35, no.9, p.19-35, axonometric
views, dwgs., ports., elevs.,
models, photos., plans.

STERN, ROBERT A. M., 1939-
                        (CONTINUED)
Gandee at large: Bob Stern has a
  dream / Charles Gandee.
  On his latest design venture:
  Martex sheets.
  HOUSE & GARDEN 1990 Jan., v.162,
  no.1, p.150, port.
An indigenous thing: the story of
  William Wurster and the Gregory
  farmhouse / Daniel P. Gregory.
  Includes contributions by Joseph
  P. Esherick, Morley Baer, Lawrence
  B. Anderson, and Robert A. M.
  Stern.
  PLACES 1990 Fall, v.7, no.1,
  p.78-93, ill., elev., photos.,
  plans, refs.
Remaking the Mediterranean style /
  Robert Campbell.
  Italianate-style home near the New
  Jersey shore. Architects: Robert
  A. M. Stern with Thomas A.
  Kligerman.
  ARCHITECTURAL DIGEST 1990 Dec.,
  v.47, no.13, p.[102]-111,218,
  axonometric view, port., photos.
A touch of magic: Robert A.M.
  Stern's fantasy world for the Walt
  Disney World Casting Center in
  Orlando, Florida / Nayana
  Currimbhoy.
  INTERIORS 1990 Jan., v.149, no.6,
  p.130-[133], photos., plan.
Why (and how) does Disney do it? /
  Mark Alden Branch.
  Focus on work of Robert A. M.
  Stern and Michael Graves at Disney
  World, Orlando, Florida.
  PROGRESSIVE ARCHITECTURE 1990
  Oct., v.71, no.10, p.78-81,
  photos., models.

STERN, ROBERT A. M., 1939-. MODERN
  CLASSICISM
The architecture of the American
  summer: the flowering of the
  shingle style [by] Vincent Scully
  [and] Modern classicism [by]
  Robert A. M. Stern, Raymond W.
  Gastil [book review]/ Leland M.
  Roth.
  SOCIETY OF ARCHITECTURAL
  HISTORIANS. JOURNAL 1990 Dec.,
  v.49, no.4, p.453-455.

STERN, ROBERT A. M., 1939-. NEW YORK
  1930
New York 1930: Architecture and
  urbanism between the two world
  wars [book review] / Auke van der
  Woud.
  Authors are Robert A.M. Stern,
  Gregory Gilmartin, Thomas Mellins.
  ARCHIS 1990 Jan., no.1, p.56,
  photo.

STERNBERG, MARY ANN
Historic Baton Rouge / Mary Ann
  Sternberg.
  HISTORIC PRESERVATION 1990
  May-June, v.42, no.3, p.16-19,
  photo.

STEUBER, HANS-JURGEN
Altenwohnungen in Aschaffenburg.
  Architect: Hans-Jurgen Steuber.
  DEUTSCHE BAUZEITSCHRIFT 1989 Dec.,
  v.37, no.12, p.1613-1616,
  axonometric views, photos., plans,
  secns.

STEVEN HOLL ARCHITECTS
American Memorial Library.
  Addition to existing library in
  West Berlin. Architects: Steven
  Holl Architects.
  PROGRESSIVE ARCHITECTURE 1990
  Jan., v.71, no.1, p.80-82, dwgs.,
  models, plans, secn., site plan.
American Memorial Library, Berlin,
  West Germany, design: 1988-89;
  construction: 1993-95 (est.).
  Competition design for addition to
  library built in 1954; architects:
  Steven Holl Architects. Text in
  Japanese and English.
  GA DOCUMENT 1990 May, no.26,
  p.114-119, diagrs., dwgs., elevs.,
  model, plans, secns., site plan.
Kashii District Housing, Fukuoka,
  Japan, design: 1988-89;
  construction: 1989-90.
  28-unit apartment house project.
  Architects: Steven Holl
  Architects. Text in Japanese and
  English.
  GA HOUSES 1990 Mar., no.28,
  p.50-53, axonometric views, model,
  plans, secns., site plan.
Milan project: Porta Vittoria area,
  Milan, Italy, 1986-1987.
  Steven Holl Architects proposal
  for a new use for the Porta
  Vittoria Railroad Yard.
  OFFRAMP 1988 Spring, v.1, no.1,
  p.[9-25], ill., dwgs., site plan.
School of Architecture.
  Addition and renovation of the
  School of Architecture and
  Landscape Architecture, University
  of Minnesota, Minneapolis. Design
  architects: Steven Holl
  Architects. Project architects:
  Ellerbe Becket.
  PROGRESSIVE ARCHITECTURE 1990
  Jan., v.71, no.1, p.83-85,
  axonometric view, models, plans,
  secn., site plan.

STEVEN WINTER ASSOCIATES
Earthquake glass damage.
  On the report: Glass damage from
  the 1985 Mexico City earthquake,
  prepared by Steven Winter
  Associates, Nanita-Kennett
  Associates.
  PROGRESSIVE ARCHITECTURE 1990
  Jan., v.71, no.1, p.123, ill.

STEVENS, ALBERT
Dal micro al macro: il graphics
  design system = From micro to
  macro: the graphic design system /
  Albert Stevens.
  Text in Italian and English.
  L'ARCA 1990 June, no.39, p.70-77,
  dwgs.
Il parco tecnologico di Trieste =
  Trieste technology park / Albert
  Stevens.
  Site: Karst Plateau. Architects:
  Giovanni Caproglio, Roberto
  Dambrosi, Giovanni Cervesi.
  L'ARCA 1990 Jan., no.34, p.66-73,
  elevs., models, plans, secns.,
  site plans.
Tecnologie semplici a Madras =
  Madras Museum of Simple Technology
  / Albert Stevens.
  Architects: Yona Friedman, Eda
  Schaur.
  L'ARCA 1990 Feb., no.35, p.44-51,
  axonometric view, elevs., photos,
  plans, secns.

STEVENS, ANDRE
Les "casas de haciendas" des Andes
  equatoriennes / Andre Stevens.
  Summaries in English, Italian and
  Spanish.
  ICOMOS INFORMATION 1989 Jan.-Mar.,
  no.1, p.10-17, photos., plan,
  biblio., refs.
Les haciendas des Andes
  equatoriennes / Andre Stevens.
  NOUVELLES DU PATRIMOINE 1989 Oct.,
  no.29, p.25-27.

STEVENS, HANS
Vermaning aan Antwerpen: Hou 'n stuk
  haven in de staad / Hans Stevens.
  Waterfront development, "Stad aan
  de Stroom."
  BOUW 1990 Oct.5, v.45, no.20,
  p.22-24, photo., models, engr.

STEVENS, JOHN CALVIN, 1855-1940
John Calvin Stevens: domestic
  architecture, 1890-1930 [by] John
  Calvin Stevens II, Earle G.
  Shettleworth, Jr. [book review] /
  William David Barry.
  LANDMARKS OBSERVER 1990 Fall,
  v.16, no.4, p.10, photo.

STEVENS, JOHN CALVIN, 1908-1990
A tribute: John Calvin Stevens II
  [obituary] / Neal W. Allen.
  Architect, founding member of
  Greater Portland Landmarks, died
  Sept. 11, 1990.
  LANDMARKS OBSERVER 1990 Fall,
  v.16, no.4, p.11, port.

STEVENS, JOHN CALVIN, 1908-1990. JOHN
CALVIN STEVENS
John Calvin Stevens: domestic
  architecture, 1890-1930 [by] John
  Calvin Stevens II, Earle G.
  Shettleworth, Jr. [book review] /
  William David Barry.
  LANDMARKS OBSERVER 1990 Fall,
  v.16, no.4, p.10, photo.

STEVENS, PATRICIA M.
Willingdon village pump, Willingdon,
  near Eastbourne, East Sussex /
  Patricia M. Stevens.
  Remarkable for its animal bone
  panels; well built early 18th c.;
  pump-house built 1880.
  SUSSEX ARCHAEOLOGICAL COLLECTIONS
  1988, v.126, p.253-255, det.,
  graph, photos., refs.

STEVENS, RUSSELL
Earl De La Warr and the competition
  for the Bexhill Pavilion, 1933-34
  / Russell Stevens, Peter Willis.
  Includes discussion of the
  controversy. Winners Erich
  Mendelsohn and Serge Chermayeff.
  ARCHITECTURAL HISTORY 1990, v.33,
  p.[135-166], dwgs., ports.,
  elevs., photos., plans, aerial
  photos., refs.

STEVENSON, CHRISTINE
Fra Nyklassicisme til Historicisme:
  arkitekten G. F. Hetsch, by Kjeld
  von Folsach [book review] /
  Christine Stevenson.
  BURLINGTON MAGAZINE 1990 Mar.,
  v.132, no.1044, p.218.

AVERY INDEX TO ARCHITECTURAL PERIODICALS

STEVINSTICHTING, SIMON
Duitse bunkers aan de belgische Kust / Didier Tempere, Simon Stevinstichting.
German bunkers from both world wars. English summary, p.75.
MONUMENTEN EN LANDSCHAPPEN 1990 July-Aug., v.9, no.4, p.8-20, maps, photos., plans, biblios.

STEWARD, JOYCE NAZZITTO
Main Street revitalization: a success story / Joyce Nazzitto Steward.
PLANNING NEWS 1990 July-Aug., v.54, no.4, p.3-4,

STEWART, ALASTAIR
'allo 'allo: BDP's Cheriton Terminal / Alastair Stewart.
Located outside Folkestone.
BUILDING 1990 Nov.9, v.255, no.44, p.22-26, port., models, photo., plan, secns., table.
British Gypsum marketing hq / Alastair Stewart.
In East Leake, south Nottingham. Architect: Faulks Perry Culley & Rech.
BUILDING 1990 Jan.19, v.255, no.3, p.66-67, photos.
Design trends in the 1990s / Alastair Stewart.
Report on a one-day Design-Interiors-Trends seminar held at RIBA in Feb. 1990.
BUILDING 1990 Feb.16, v.255, no.7, p.78-79, graphs, photos.
Fifteen months to take-off: Harlequin Hotel Stansted / Alastair Stewart.
Architect: Michael Hyde & Associates.
BUILDING 1990 July 27, v.255, no.30, p.60-61, photos.
Fires and fireplaces / Alastair Stewart.
Reproductions in Britain, including wooden mantels, by Marble Hill and Real Flame.
BUILDING 1990 Mar.9, v.255, no.10, p.58-59, photos.
Geoffrey Mann / Alastair Stewart.
Rebuilding of the Saughtree railroad station near Roxborough in the Scottish Borders, by a partner in RHWL Partnership.
BUILDING 1990 Sept.28, v.255, no.38, p.46-47, port., photo.
Marks & Spencer: Fosse Park / Alastair Stewart.
In Leicester. Architect: Norman Jones Sons & Rigby.
BUILDING 1990 Feb.9, v.255, no.6, p.86-87, photos.
Neil Way; starting over / Alastair Stewart.
British architect, formerly with Peter Taylor Associates, in Uckfield, Sussex.
BUILDING 1990 Nov.9, v.255, no.44, p.44-45, port.
Over-built, over-stretched and over there / Peter Cooper, Alastair Stewart.
On British construction work in the U.S.
BUILDING 1990 Oct.19, v.255, no.41, p.22-23, graphs, map, table.

STEWART, ALASTAIR (CONTINUED)
Pole position / Alastair Stewart.
Construction industry in Poland and opportunities for Western firms.
BUILDING 1990 June 15, v.255, no.24, p.24-25, ports., photo.
Profits in the red / Alastair Stewart.
On opportunities for trade and investment in construction in Central Europe.
BUILDING 1990 Jan.5, v.255, no.1, p.14-15, ports., photos.
Specification 90 [book review] / Alastair Stewart.
On the 1990 version of the British specifier's handbook.
BUILDING 1990 Feb.2, v.255, no.5, p.74-75, photos.
Spotlight: [ironmongery] / Alastair Stewart.
BUILDING 1990 Jan.26, v.255, no.4, p.86-87, photos.
We're off! Building Industry Half Marathon.
In conjunction with the 7 Oct. 1990 charity event, provides a profile of architect Richard Rogers ("Champion hurdler", by Alastair Stewart) and on housing near Warrington for persons with cerebral palsy ("Drawing together", by Sarah Kitchen).
BUILDING 1990 June 8, v.255, no.23, p.[43]-47, ports., photos.

STEWART, DAVID B.
Lightness / David B. Stewart.
On the Tokyo Metropolitan Gymnasium. Architects: Maki and Associates.
JAPAN ARCHITECT 1990 Aug.-Sept., v.65, no.8-9(400-401), p.26-33, sketch, secns.

STEWART, MURRAY
Les politiques urbaines dans une ville prospere: Bristol / Murray Stewart.
French, English, German and Spanish summaries, p.[125]-127.
LES ANNALES DE LA RECHERCHE URBAINE 1990 Oct., no.48, p.[50]-61, maps, photos., refs.

STEWEN, HOLGER
Deutschland wird dekoriert / Barbara Friedrich.
Profiles of seven German interior designers. English summary, p.4.
ARCHITEKTUR & WOHNEN 1990 Dec.-1991 Jan., no.6, p.108-125, ports., photos.

STEZAKER, JOHN
Responding to the operatic / Brian Hatton.
Focus on the floor and ceiling designs by John Stezaker for John Outram's entry in the Compton Verney Opera House competition.
BUILDING DESIGN 1989 Oct., suppl., p.12-15, ill., dwgs.

STHAPATHI, GANAPATHI
Trustees of tradition / Sujatha Shankar.
Excerpts from a conversation with Ganapathi Sthapathi, head of the Mahaballipuram College of Architecture and Sculpture.
(Continued next column)

STHAPATHI, GANAPATHI (CONTINUED)
Trustees of tradition...(CONTINUED)
ARCHITECTURE + DESIGN 1990 Jan.-Feb., v.7, no.1, p.101-104, port.

STICHTING DE BEURS VAN BERLAGE-- EXHIBITIONS
Milano, Atene, Amsterdam [exhibition review] / Aldo van Eyck.
Features Aldo Van Eyck's exhibition at the Stock Exchange, Amsterdam, held from Nov. 10, 1989-Jan.3,1990. Text in Italian and English.
SPAZIO E SOCIETA 1990 Oct.-Dec., v.13, no.52, p.6-17, dwgs., photos., plans, secns.
Theater voor het voetlicht [review] / Robde Graaf.
Exhibition (De verbeelding vooruit) until Apr.23 and symposium ("Ruimte als theatraal middel") on Mar.12-13, 1990, both at the Beurs, Amsterdam. Also reviews a book by Lia Gieling, Toneelbeeld vanat 1945 in Nederland.
ARCHIS 1990 Apr., no.4, p.8-11, photos.
Van Eyck retrospective [exhibition review] / Peter Buchanan.
Review of retrospective show held at the Stichting de Beurs Van Berlage, Amsterdam, Nov.1989-Jan.1990.
ARCHITECTURAL REVIEW 1990 Feb., v.187, no.1116, p.4, elevs., plans.

STICHTING WERKGROEP 5X5
Oproepen tot bevlogenheid: Week van de volkshuisvesting / Ton Verstegen.
On a manifesto ("Women in de jaren '90), by Werkgroep 5x5 and events held Nov.22-24, 1989 at the Kunsthal in Rotterdam about housing.
ARCHIS 1990 Jan., no.1, p.12-13, photo., aerial photo., ref.

STICHTING WESTERS--CONGRESSES
De moderne stad en het virus van de tijd: status stadsconcept problematisch.
Report on a conference (The Modern City) held 22 June 1989 in Rotterdam. Sponsor: Stichting Westers. Participants included Italo Campofiorito, Riek Bakker, Len de Klerk, and Rem Koolhaas.
DE ARCHITECT 1989 Nov., v.20, no.11, p.78-87, cover, dwgs., maps, photos., plans, refs.

STICK STYLE
See "STICK STYLE" AS A SUBHEADING AFTER SPECIFIC BUILDING TYPES OR OTHER MAIN HEADINGS.

STICKLAND, JONATHAN
A nursery storey / Joe Kerr, Jonathan Stickland.
Day care center and nursery in south London, Canterbury House Day Nursery. Architects: Greenhill Jenner.
ARCHITECTS' JOURNAL 1990 May 2, v.191, no.18, p.38-43,45, axonometric view, elevs., photos., plan, site plan.

Page 2482

STICKLEY (ARCHITECTURAL STYLE)
See CRAFTSMAN

STICKLEY, GUSTAV, 1858-1942
Celebrating the arts and crafts
ethos in Manhattan / Thomas Hines.
Focus on the Stickley furniture in
the interiors of Vivien Bonink and
Arthur S. Cobin's New York loft.
ARCHITECTURAL DIGEST 1990 Mar.,
v.47, no.3, p.130,134,138,142,
photos.
Craftsman Farms set to open,
meanwhile, the hunt for Stickley
pieces goes on [Parsippany, N.J.]
/ Patricia Herold.
PRESERVATION NEWS 1990 Apr., v.30,
no.4, p.6,23, photos.
Preservation: Stickley's Craftsman
Farms / Abby Bussel.
1907 home and five other original
craftsman buildings in
Parsippany-Troy Hills, N.J. to be
restored.
PROGRESSIVE ARCHITECTURE 1990
June, v.71, no.6, p.26, photo.
Stout-hearted sticks: craftsman
furniture and decoration / John
Crosby Freeman.
VICTORIAN HOMES 1990 Winter, v.9,
no.1, p.44-45, dwgs., refs.

STICKNEY, JOHN
Searching for quality of life / John
Stickney.
A linen business headquarters in
farm buildings, Tunbridge, Vt.
METROPOLITAN HOME 1990 Dec., v.22,
no.12, p.101-111, port., photos.

STIEBER, NANCY
Das Buch von Groningen: Daniel
Libeskinds "sechzehn Arten, die
Amsel zu betrachten" / Nancy
Stieber.
ARCHITHESE 1990 Nov.-Dec., v.20,
no.6, p.56-66, dwgs., models,
maps, photos., engrs., refs.

STIEGLITZ, ALFRED, 1864-1946
Lessons from history: four early
architectural photographs / Donna
Kempner.
On the work of Eugene Atget,
Frederick Evans, Alfred Stieglitz
and Walker Evans.
L. A. ARCHITECT 1990 Apr., p.9.13,
photos.

STIEGLITZ, MARIA
Saving "marvelous monuments":
Desmond Guinness boosts Irish
preservation / Maria Stieglitz.
"The president and prime mover of
the Irish Georgian Society
throughout its 32-year history."
PRESERVATION NEWS 1990 May, v.30,
no.5, p.17,19, port., photo.

STIFF, MICHAEL
Glasgow's Glasgow [exhibition
review] / Mark Dudek, Michael
Stiff.
On the temporary exhibition which
features the centerpiece of "The
Year of Culture" in Glasgow,
created by architect Doug
Clelland.
BUILDING DESIGN 1990 June 1,
no.988, p.24-25, photo., plans.

STIFTEL, BRUCE
Perspectives on identity.
Two articles on planning practice:
Caring for ourselves as a
community of planners by Howell S.
Baum; and On retaining our best
and brightest, by Bruce Stiftel.
AMERICAN PLANNING ASSOCIATION.
JOURNAL 1990 Winter, v.56, no.1,
p.64-68, refs.

STIGLAT, KLAUS
Beton + Stahl = Verbund: Zwei
Beispiele der Verbundbauweise in
Karlsruhe / Klaus Stiglat,
Bernhard Hockelmann, Josef Seiler.
The BGV, Karlsruhe, and the
Institut fur Meteorologie und
Klimatologie, Karlsruhe.
DEUTSCHE BAUZEITUNG 1990 Apr.,
v.124, no.4, p.91-98, dets.,
dwgs., elevs., photos., plans.

STIJL
See DE STIJL

STIJNEN, LEON--EXHIBITIONS
Retrospectief Leon Stijnen:
Eerbewijs aan ambivalent architect
[exhibition review] / Jan Thomaes.
At the deSingel, Antwerp, Dec.20,
1990-Feb.3,1991.
DE ARCHITECT 1990 Dec., v.21,
no.12, p.72-73, photos.

STILE LIBERTY
See ART NOUVEAU - ITALY

STILE MOBILI MODERNI
ICF: destinazione Banca = Banking on
success.
Interiors of the Brescia branch of
the Banca di Trento e Bolzano.
Architect: Studio Boffoli
Marpicati Associati. Interior
designer: Stile Mobili Moderni. In
Italian and English.
OTTOGANO 1990 Sept., no.96,
p.172-[175], dets., photos.

STILES DOWELL, SUSAN
Bounds Lott: livable authenticity in
one of Maryland's oldest homes /
Susan Stiles Dowell.
Restored 17th-cent. house on
Maryland's Eastern Shore, home of
Robert Withey.
SOUTHERN ACCENTS 1990 Nov., v.13,
no.9, p.[70-79], photos.
Quinn-tessential favorite: the
Georgetown living room of Sally
Quinn and Ben Bradlee / Susan
Stiles Dowell.
SOUTHERN ACCENTS 1990 Sept., v.13,
no.7, p.86-[88], port., photos.

STILLMAN, DAMIE. ENGLISH NEO-CLASSICAL
ARCHITECTURE
English neo-classical architecture
[by] Damie Stillman [book review]
/ David Cast
ART BULLETIN 1990 Dec., v.72,
no.4, p.664-667, refs.
English neo-classical architecture,
by Damie Stillman [book review] /
Charles Saumarez Smith.
2-volume work pub. in 1988.
BURLINGTON MAGAZINE 1990 Mar.,
v.132, no.1044, p.217-218,

STIMPEL, ROLAND
Big is beautiful: Hallenfieber an
Rhein und Ruhr / Roland Stimpel.
Includes sections on EuroPalast
Koln, by Rainer Wallmann
(architects: Ellerbe Becket;
Lister, Drew, Haines, Barrow;
Petry & Partner, Mronz/Kottmair)
and Grosshalle FORUM Gelsenkirchen
(architect: Josef Wund).
BAUWELT 1990 June 29, v.81, no.24,
p.1249-1255, ill., elev., models,
photos., plan, secns., aerial
photo.

STINY, G.
What is a design? / G. Stiny.
ENVIRONMENT AND PLANNING B 1990
Jan. v.17, no.1, p.97-103, refs.

STIPELEN, PETER VAN
Trier: neue Nutzung fur St. Maximin
/ Alois Peitz.
History of the monastery and
several proposals for restoration,
by Dieter G. Baumewerd; Gottfried
Bohm; Ulrich Craemer and Gunter
Kleinjohann; Herbert Herrmann and
Peter van Stipelen; Bernhard
Kramatschek et al. Includes "Der
Totentanz" by Goethe.
BAUWELT 1990 Mar.16, v.81, no.11,
p.503-511, photos., plans, secns.,
sketches, engrs.

STIRLING, JAMES FRAZER, 1926-
The future in ruins / Brian Hatton.
Demolition of architect James
Stirling's Southgate estate,
Runcorn, England.
BLUEPRINT (LONDON, ENGLAND) 1990
Sept., no.70, p.46-50, photos.
James Stirling: circumstances
against style / Sarah Ksiazek.
COLUMBIA UNIVERSITY. GRADUATE
SCHOOL OF ARCHITECTURE, PLANNING
AND PRESERVATION. NEWSLINE 1990
Nov., v.3, no.3, p.2, dwgs.,
elevs., models, secns., site
plans.
Nueva galeria para la coleccion
Thyssen-Bornemisza Villa Favorita
Lugano = A new gallery for the
Thyssen-Bornemisza Collection
Villa Favorita Lugano / James
Stirling, Michael Wilford.
Architects: James Stirling,
Michael Wilford and Associates.
Text in Spanish and English.
COMPOSICION ARQUITECTONICA, ART &
ARCHITECTURE 1989 Feb., no.2,
p.[45]-66, axonometric views,
dwgs., models, photos., plans,
secns., site plans.
La nuova Biblioteca di Francia / D.
Mandolesi.
Competition entries by Dominique
Perrault, Mario Botta, Bernard
Huet, Henri Ciriani, Richard
Meier, James Stirling, Jan
Kaplicky, D. Chaix andJ.-P. Morel,
and Nicholas Grimshaw.
L'INDUSTRIA DELLE COSTRUZIONI 1990
Jan., v.24, no.219, p.76-81,
axonometric view, dwgs., models,
plan, secns.
Recent work of James Stirling
Michael Wilford and Associates /
edited by Toshio Nakamura.
Contents: Editor's introduction /
Toshio Nakamura-- Essays by
Francesco Dal Co, Brendan Gill,
(Continued next page)

STIRLING, JAMES FRAZER, 1926-
                              (CONTINUED)
  Recent work of James...(CONTINUED)
    Geoffrey Baker and Colin St. John
    Wilson-- Opening speech: James
    Stirling: opening day of
    Performing Arts Centre, Cornell
    University-- Works (indexed
    separately)-- Credit list of
    project[s] since Cornell,
    p.260-61-- Biography of James
    Stirling & Michael Wilford,
    p.261-65-- Chronological list of
    buildings and projects, 1950-1989.
    Text in Japanese and English.
    ARCHITECTURE AND URBANISM 1990
    May, no.5 extra edition,
    p.[1]-267, axonometric views,
    dwgs., ports., elevs., models,
    photos., plans, secns., site
    plans.
  Shelf life / John Welsh.
    On the design for the Venice
    Biennale bookstore. Architect:
    James Stirling.
    BUILDING DESIGN 1990 June 29,
    no.992, p.24-25, axonometric
    views, dwgs., elevs., models,
    secns., site plans, sketches.
  Stirling exchange / John Welsh.
    On the work of James Stirling on
    the occasion of the exhibition of
    his designs at the Galleria
    Communale d'Arte Moderna, Bologna.
    BUILDING DESIGN 1990 Oct.5,
    no.1006, p.2, port.

STIRLING, LEE
  Volunteer profile: Susan C. Ruch /
    Lee Stirling.
    Newly-elected president of Greater
    Portland Landmarks.
    LANDMARKS OBSERVER 1990 Spring,
    v.16, no.3, p.12, port.

STM-PLAN
  Schnell, aber schon: Gestaltung
    eines fast-food-Restaurants in
    Munchen.
    McDonald's Restaurant. Architects:
    STM-Plan; Interior architects: M.
    Stadlinger, N. Breitfuss.
    ARCHITEKTUR, INNENARCHITEKTUR,
    TECHNISCHER AUSBAU 1990 June,
    v.98, no.6, p.52-53, photos.,
    plan.

STOAE
  See STOAS

STOCK EXCHANGES
  See also COMMODITY EXCHANGES
  See also MARKETS

STOCK EXCHANGES--19TH CENTURY--
  CONSERVATION AND RESTORATION--
  ENGLAND--LONDON--STOCK EXCHANGE
  LIFFE must go on / Denise Chevin.
    Refurbishment of the Royal
    Exchange, London. Built 1841-1844
    (architect: Sir William Tite); new
    roof added in 1884 (architect:
    Charles Barry). Architect:
    Fitzroy Robinson Partnership.
    BUILDING 1990 Nov.2, v.255, no.43,
    p.46-50, axonometric view, elevs.,
    photos., secns.

STOCK EXCHANGES--ALTERATIONS AND
  ADDITIONS--GERMANY (WEST)--FRANKFURT
  AM MAIN--FRANKFURTER BORSE
  Geldanlage: Umbau und Sanierung des
    Gebaudes der IHK Frankfurt und der
    Frankfurter Wertpapierborse.
    Architect: Wilfried Hilger.
    ARCHITEKTUR, INNENARCHITEKTUR,
    TECHNISCHER AUSBAU 1990 Dec.,
    v.98, no.12, p.26-33, elev.,
    photos., secns.

STOCK EXCHANGES--ENGLAND--LONDON--
  EXCHANGE HOUSE
  London Bridge: engineering:
    structural steel / Marc S.
    Harriman.
    Exchange House, London, is
    suspended by a structural steel
    framework over a plaza concealing
    train tracks. Architects: SOM.
    ARCHITECTURE: THE AIA JOURNAL 1990
    Sept., v.79, no.9, p.109-112,
    det., dwgs., photos., plans,
    secns.

STOCK EXCHANGES--INTERIOR DESIGN--
  UNITED STATES--NEW YORK (NEW YORK)--
  WELLS FARGO BANK INTERNATIONAL
  Wells Fargo Bank's New York trading
    room / Karin Tetlow.
    Architects: Alan Gaynor & Co.
    INTERIORS 1989 Feb., v.148, no.7,
    p.5, det., photo.

STOCK, WOLFGANG JEAN
  Eine Fleissarbeit ohne Biss: zur
    Wanderausstellung "Stadt und
    Topographie der Munchner TU"
    [exhibition review] / Wolfgang
    Jean Stock.
    Exhibition organized by Haus der
    Bayerischen Geschichte and shown
    in Munich, Coburg and 14 other
    cities.
    BAUWELT 1990 July 6, v.81, no.25,
    p.1273-1274, photo., engrs.
  Landeszentralbank in Bayern -- ein
    Wettbewerb fur Munchen / Wolfgang
    Jean Stock.
    Report on competition for the LZB
    and project by Behnisch & Partner.
    BAUWELT 1990 Mar.9, v.81, no.10,
    p.417, model.

STOCK YARDS
  See STOCKYARDS

STOCKBRIDGE, JERRY G.
  Learning from experience: cladding
    systems / Jerry G. Stockbridge.
    PROGRESSIVE ARCHITECTURE 1990
    Apr., v.71, no.4, p.45, photo.

STOCKEL, GEORGIANA
  Great beginnings [1990 showhouse
    winners].
    Winners from a variety of
    decorators' showhouses in 1990:
    Frank Babb Randolph; Barbara
    Ostrom; Noel Jeffrey; Taylor
    Johnson; Manijeh Emery; Winnie
    Levin; C. Smith Grubbs; Thomas
    Bartlett; Arnold Copper; Richard
    E. Eustice; Carolyn Bronson and
    Georgiana Stockel.
    HOUSE BEAUTIFUL 1990 Oct., v.132,
    no.10, p.73-85, photos.

STOCKER, D. A.
  Minsters and parish churches: the
    local church in transition
    950-1200 [ed. by] John Blair [book
    review] / D.A. Stocker.
    BRITISH ARCHAEOLOGICAL
    ASSOCIATION. JOURNAL 1990, v.143,
    p.140-143,

STOCKINGER, HERB
  Fox hunting in Oakland: hunters are
    stalking the rare Oakland Fox [Fox
    Oakland Theatre] / Herb
    Stockinger.
    The Fox Oakland Theatre was
    completed in 1928, Weeks and Day,
    architects.
    MARQUEE 1990, v.22, no.3, p.3-6,
    photos., secn.

STOCKMAN, HOLGER
  Psykiatri og boligformer [book
    review] / Niels Peter Agger.
    An ideas project by affiliates of
    the Arkitektskolen i Aarhus, for
    design of psychiatric hospitals.
    The review considers two
    publications: Den intensive
    behandlingsenhed for
    langtidspsykotiske patienter, by
    Kirsten Spliid Pedersen and Holger
    Stockman; Psykiatrisk
    indaeggelseshyppighed fra nyere
    drabantbe byggelser, by Jan Uwe
    Klahn and Soren Haastrup.
    ARKITEKTEN 1990 Nov. v.92, no.16,
    p.532-533, dwgs., plans.

STOCKSIEFEN, WILL
  Bodenbelag aus
    Carrara-Marmorplatten:
    Fleckenbildung durch Umwandlung
    von Pyrit / Karl-Hans Emmermann.
    One of two articles on damage to
    buildings. The second is on marble
    cladding for facades, by Will
    Stocksiefen.
    DEUTSCHES ARCHITEKTENBLATT 1990
    Apr.1, v.22, no.4, p.619-620,
    photos., ref.
  Hinterluftete Fassadenbekleidung mit
    Marmorplatten: Konkave Verformung,
    Rissbildung Ausbruche / Will
    Stocksiefen.
    DEUTSCHES ARCHITEKTENBLATT 1990
    July 1, v.22, no.7, p.1137,
    photos.

STOCKTON, EVE
  Downtown split-level / Julie V.
    Iovine.
    Conversion of a former beer
    warehouse in Brooklyn into a home.
    Architects and owners: Frank Lupo
    and Eve Stockton.
    METROPOLITAN HOME 1990 Oct., v.22,
    no.10, p.130-134, port., photos.

STOELTIE, BARBARA
  Just like in the movies / Barbara
    Stoeltie.
    Parisian apartment interiors
    resemble 1940s Hollywood movie
    set. Located on the Avenue Foch.
    Interior design: Fredric Mechiche.
    THE WORLD OF INTERIORS 1990 Mar.,
    p.96-103, photos.
  Other voices other lives / Barbara
    Stoeltie.
    Interiors of decorator
    Pierre-Herve Walbaum's apartment
    near the Tuileries in Paris.
                    (Continued next page)

STOELTIE, BARBARA (CONTINUED)
Other voices other... (CONTINUED)
THE WORLD OF INTERIORS 1990 Nov.,
p.106-[115], port., photos.

STOHLMANN, BRIGITTE
Deutschland wird dekoriert / Barbara
Friedrich.
Profiles of seven German interior
designers. English summary, p.4.
ARCHITEKTUR & WOHNEN 1990
Dec.-1991 Jan., no.6, p.108-125,
ports., photos.

STOKDYK, JOHN
BAS-relief / John Stokdyk.
Integration of building automation
systems at Lloyd's of London, by a
project team.
BUILDING 1990 Nov.2, v.255, no.43,
p.63, photo.
Battle to defend the home front /
John Stokdyk.
"Computers in the slump, Part
two"--the second of three articles
on the British construction
industry.
BUILDING 1990 Sept.7, v.255,
no.35, p.70-71, ill.
Expert on the line [BREXBAS] / John
Stokdyk.
Support for research on a building
automation system developed by the
Building Research Establishment.
BUILDING 1990 Aug.3, v.255, no.31,
p.37, ill.
Open sesame [OSI] / John Stokdyk.
Open Systems Interconnection, an
initiative begun in the early
1980s to facilitate broader
communications through networks.
BUILDING 1990 Oct.12, v.255,
no.40, p.71-72, ill.
Revealing the plot / John Stokdyk.
On plotters used with CAD systems.
BUILDING 1990 Nov.16, v.255,
no.45, p.92-93, photos.
Time to go with the flow / John
Stokdyk.
"Computers in the slump, part 3",
on the need to standardize
information in the building
industry, including the use of
electronic data interchange (EDI)
and the Co-ordinated Project
Initiative (CPI).
BUILDING 1990 Sept.14, v.255,
no.36, p.90-91, ill.
When the chips are down / John
Stokdyk.
Computers in the slump, Part One--
the first of three articles on the
British construction industry.
BUILDING 1990 Aug.31, v.255,
no.34, p.48-49, ill.

STOKES, ADRIAN DURHAM, 1902-1972
Aesthete in the city / David
Carrier.
ARTS MAGAZINE 1990 Apr., v.64,
no.8, p.67-73, refs.

STOLLARD, PAUL
Building safer neighbourhoods / Paul
Stollard.
Outline of the research carried
out at the Institute of Advanced
Architectural Studies on crime
prevention and housing estate
design.
RIBA JOURNAL 1990 May, v.97, no.5,
p.81,84, ill.

STOLLER, EZRA
Paisajes arquitectonicos: seis
maestros, seis imagenes / Ezra
Stoller.
Six landmark buildings by
Corbusier, Alvar Aalto, F.L.
Wright, Mies, Gordon Bunshaft, and
Richard Meier.
ARQUITECTURA VIVA 1990 May-June,
no.12, p.36-39, photos.

STOLZL, CHRISTOPH
Nachdenken uber Deutsches
Historisches Museum / Christoph
Stolzl ... [et al.].
Presents the revised design by
Aldo Rossi, and commentaries on
the museum.
BAUWELT 1990 Jan.5, v.81, no.1,
p.22-27, photos.

STOMMER, RAINER
Der Traum von den fliegenden
Stadten. Zu El Lissitzkys
Wolkenbugel = The dream of the
flying cities. On El Lissitzky's
sky hook / Rainer Stommer.
Extract of lecture delivered at
opening of exhibition 'El
Lissitsky. the dream of the
Skyhook' on 17 May, 1990 at the
Institut fur Geschichte und
Theorie der Architektur of the
ETH, Zurich.
DAIDALOS 1990 Sept.15, no.37,
p.60-63, dwgs., model.
Vom Traumpalast zum Warencontainer:
die Warenhaus-Architektur der
zwanziger Jahre / Rainer Stommer.
DEUTSCHE BAUZEITUNG 1990 Oct.,
v.124, no.10, p.132-151, dwgs.,
models, photos., secn., refs.

STONE
See also ALABASTER
See also COBBLESTONE
See also GRANITE
See also LIMESTONE
See also MARBLE
See also SANDSTONE
See also SLATE
See also STONEWORK
See also "STONE" AS A SUBHEADING
AFTER SPECIFIC BUILDING TYPES OR
OTHER MAIN HEADINGS.
Over de oudste gesteenten van de
Nederlanden / Bart Fobe.
The Brabant massif, which was used
for building blocks. English
summary, p.63.
MONUMENTEN EN LANDSCHAPPEN 1990
Jan.-Feb., v.9, no.1, p.57-62,
maps, photos., biblio.
Romanced by the stone: postmodernism
has sparked a second honeymoon in
the ancient marriage between
architects and stone / Adelheid
Fischer.
ARCHITECTURE MINNESOTA 1990
Mar.-Apr., v.16, no.2, p.11,62-65,
photos.

STONE - ARTIFICIAL
See also COADE STONE
See also STONE - CAST

STONE--ARTIFICIAL--RESEARCH--SCOTLAND
Set in their ways / Richard Carr.
On current research into
architectural cast stone in
Scotland.
BUILDING DESIGN 1990 Oct.26,
no.1009, p.32-33, photos.

STONE--CAST--RESEARCH--SCOTLAND
Set in their ways / Richard Carr.
On current research into
architectural cast stone in
Scotland.
BUILDING DESIGN 1990 Oct.26,
no.1009, p.32-33, photos.

STONE--CONSERVATION AND RESTORATION
La pierre: symbole du materiau
indestructible? / Jean Kerisel.
ARCHEOLOGIA 1989 Sept., no.249,
p.[44]-55, graph, photos., secn.,
biblio.

STONE-CUTTERS' MARKS
See BANKER-MARKS

STONE-CUTTING
See also BANKER-MARKS

STONE-CUTTING--MEDIEVAL
Werkzeuge der Steinmetzen im
Mittelalter: Ausgangspunkte zur
Forschung / Dankwart Leistikow.
ARCHITECTURA 1989, v.20, no.1,
p.65-72, ill., photos., refs.

STONE, ELIZABETH C.
The Tell Abu Duwari Project, Iraq,
1987 / Elizabeth C. Stone.
Report on mapping and surface
survey of an ancient Mesopotamian
city dating from the 2nd millenium
B.C.
JOURNAL OF FIELD ARCHAEOLOGY 1990
summer, v.17, no.2, p.141-162,
ill., maps, plan, tables, biblio.,
refs.

STONE--MAINTENANCE AND REPAIR--ITALY
La manutenzioine dei materiali
lapidei / Paolo Rota Rossi Doria.
RESTAURO 1989 Nov.-Dec., v.18,
no.106, p.[3]-58, photos., biblio.

STONE-MASONS
See STONEMASONS

STONE, MICHELLE
Urbanist without Portfolio: Notes on
a career / by Jane Thompson.
One of four sections in a special
feature on "Women in American
Architecture". Contents: Marion G.
Weiss.-- Inea Elskop/1100
Architect. Billie Tsien.--
Patricia Sapinsley.--Alison
Sky+Michelle Stone/SITE Projects,
Inc.--Karen Bausman+Leslie Gill.--
Deborah Berke.--Amy Weinstein--
Adele Naude Santos. English
translation, p.73.
SPACE DESIGN 1990 June, no.309,
p.36-53,73, axonometric views,
dwgs., ports., elevs., models,
photos., plans, secns.

STONE, NIGEL
Moving spirit / David Redhead.
Profile of Carlos Virgile and
Nigel Stone of Imagination.
DESIGNERS' JOURNAL 1990 Sept.,
no.60, p.90-91, port.

STONE, ROBERT A.
[Distinguished Leadership Awards
1990].
Winners of 1990 APA Awards: Norman
Krumhoiz, Gov. Joe Frank Harris
(Georgia), and Robert A Stone. The
Diana Donald Award, for planning
service on behalf of women, was
awarded to Marsha Ritzdorf.
PLANNING 1990 Mar., v.56, no.3,
p.[12]-14, ports.

STONEMASONS
See also BRICKLAYERS

STONEMASONS--GREAT BRITAIN
Master masons of the diocese of
Lichfield: a study in 14th-century
architecture at the time of the
Black Death / J.M. Maddison.
Covering the western portion of
the Midlands.
LANCASHIRE AND CHESHIRE
ANTIQUARIAN SOCIETY. TRANSACTIONS
1988, v.85, p.107-172, dets.,
diagrs., photos., refs.

STONEMASONS--GREAT BRITAIN--REID, DICK
Chisel me timbers / Pat Garratt.
Profile of the firm Dick Reid,
Stone and Wood Carver, York.
THE WORLD OF INTERIORS 1990
July-Aug., p.23,25-26, dets.,
port., photos.

STONEMASONS--MEDIEVAL
Werkzeuge der Steinmetzen im
Mittelalter: Ausgangspunkte zur
Forschung / Dankwart Leistikow.
ARCHITECTURA 1989, v.20, no.1,
p.65-72, ill., photos., refs.

STONER, BRIAN
Shifting focus: design partners
Brian Stoner and John Hutton take
a new perspective on classic forms
in a downtown apartment / Victoria
Geibel.
HOUSE & GARDEN 1990 Oct., v.162,
no.10, p.192-[197], port., photos.

STONEWORK
See also COBBLESTONE
See also STONE
The house with a heart of stone /
Victor M. Cassidy.
Home near Milwaukee, Wisc., which
was constructed around massive
stone sculpture, Tower of Babel.
Architect: Charles Moore. Artist:
Dan Yarbrough.
CONNOISSEUR 1990 May, v.220,
no.940, p.104-107,148, axonometric
view, port., photos.

STONEWORK--ENGLAND--SOUTH PENNINES
Vernacular architecture: industrial
legacy: the traditional stonework
of the South Pennines / Bill Laws.
TRADITIONAL HOMES 1990 May, v.6,
no.8, p.37-40, dets., photos.,
biblio.

STONEWORK--MEDIEVAL
Werkzeuge der Steinmetzen im
Mittelalter: Ausgangspunkte zur
Forschung / Dankwart Leistikow.
ARCHITECTURA 1989, v.20, no.1,
p.65-72, ill., photos., refs.

STOOPS--LAW AND LEGISLATION--UNITED
STATES--NEW YORK (NEW YORK)
A Stoop-id story.
The New York City Dept. of
Transportation has recently levied
a "stoop rent" which affects
brownstone owners.
BROWNSTONER 1990 fall, p.[1].

STOPPING HOUSES
See POSTHOUSES

STORAGE
See also CLOSETS
Estimating the volume in the system
/ Kahoru Kitaura, Hiroko Ichimune,
Yoko Fukuda.
"Development of a new system on
estimating the volume of storage
space in a house, part 2". Text
in Japanese. Includes English
summary.
NIHON KENCHIKU GAKKAI KEIKAKUKEI
RONBUN HOKOKU SHU = JOURNAL OF
ARCHITECTURE, PLANNING AND
ENVIRONMENTAL ENGINEERING 1990
June [July], no.7(413), p.61-77,
graphs, tables.
Storage with style / Elaine Martin
Petrowski.
Built-in storage planning.
HOUSE BEAUTIFUL 1990 Mar., v.132,
no.3, p.46,48-49, photo.

STORAGE FACILITIES
See also HELMS
See also SHEDS
See also WAREHOUSES

STORAGE FACILITIES--GERMANY (WEST)--
MUNICH
Grosser Bahnhof: Paketumschlaghalle
der Post in Munchen / Wilfried
Dechau.
Architects: R. Rosenfeld, H.
Zettel.
DEUTSCHE BAUZEITUNG 1990 Dec.,
v.124, no.12, p.78-85, dets.,
elev., photos., secn.

STORAGE FACILITIES--UNITED STATES--
LANHAM (MARYLAND)--MUSEUM AND
ARCHAEOLOGICAL REGIONAL STORAGE
FACILITY
A trip to MARS / Pam West.
The new Museum and Archaeological
Regional Storage Facility, in
Lanham, Md. serves the parks and
institutions within the National
Capital Region (NCR).
CRM BULLETIN: A NATIONAL PARK
SERVICE TECHNICAL BULLETIN 1990,
v.13, no.5, p.9,17.

STORAGE TANKS--UNDERGROUND--
ENVIRONMENTAL ASPECTS--UNITED STATES
Underground storage tanks: Subtitle
1 responsibilities / Edward
Cichon.
AMERICAN CITY & COUNTY 1990 June,
v.105, no.6, p.46,48,50, photo.

STORAGE TANKS--UNDERGROUND--LAW AND
LEGISLATION--UNITED STATES
Beware of underground storage tanks
/ Joseph B. Pereles.
DEVELOPMENT 1990 May-June, v.21,
no.3, p.10-12, port., photos.
Underground storage tanks: Subtitle
1 responsibilities / Edward
Cichon.
AMERICAN CITY & COUNTY 1990 June,
v.105, no.6, p.46,48,50, photo.

STORCH + EHLERS
Architektur unterwegs.
Three projects:
Werner-Heisenberg-Haus
Internationales Begegnungszentrum,
Garching (architects: Jurgen Adam
and Marita Adam); Tagungs-Centrum
Messe Hannover (architects:
Hinrich Storch and Walter Ehlers);
Wasser und Schiffahrtsamt,
Cuxhaven (architect: Volker
Kersten et al).
DEUTSCHES ARCHITEKTENBLATT 1990
June 1, v.22, no.6, p.935-938,
elevs., photos., plans, secns.
Hanger in Hanover / Layla Dawson.
On the Tagungszentrum Messe,
Hannover. Architects: Storch &
Ehlers.
BUILDING DESIGN 1990 Mar.16,
no.977, p.20-21, photos., elev.,
site plan.
Stadtbucherei in Ludencheid.
Architects: Storch + Ehlers.
DEUTSCHE BAUZEITSCHRIFT 1990 July,
v.38, no.7, p.957-964, det.,
photos., elevs., plans site plans.
Tagungszentrum Hannover Messe.
Architects: Storch + Ehlers.
DEUTSCHE BAUZEITSCHRIFT 1990 Mar.,
v.38, no.3, p.329-338, dets.,
photos., plans, secns., sketches.
Tagungszentrum Messe Hannover = New
conference centre trade fair
Hanover.
Architects: Hinrich Storch, Walter
Ehlers.
DETAIL 1990 June-July, v.30, no.3,
p.275-278, dets., elev., photos.,
secn., site plans.
Weltausstellungsarchitektur: der
Wettbewerb fur den deutschen
Pavillon fur die EXPO'92 Sevilla
und Fragen zur Architektur.
Projects by: Auer + Weber (1st
prize); Frei Otto; Joachim
Schurmann. Axel Schultes; Helmut
Striffler; Heinz Mihl; Storch +
Ehlers; Kurt Ackermann und Peter
Jaeger; Gottfried Bohm und
Friedrich Steinigeweg; Heinz
Hilmer & Christoph Sattler; PAS;
Kiessler + Partner.
BAUMEISTER 1990 June, v.87, no.6,
p.15-29, ill., dwgs., elevs.,
models, photo., plans, secns.,
site plans, aerial photos.

STORCH, HINRICH
Umbau eines Wohnhauses in Hannover.
Architects: Hinrich Storch, Walter
Ehlers. Includes English summary.
BAUMEISTER 1990 Jan., v.87, no.1,
p.48-51, photos., plans.

STORCHI, CERES MAGGI
Forma em leque assegura a melhor
risao para a cidade: Edificio
Firenze, Porto Alegre.
Architects: Ceres Storchi, Luiz
Rocha.
PROJETC 1989 June, no.122,
p.66-67, photos, plans.
Uma imagem forte, marcando o local:
Condominio Edificio Amelia Telles,
Porto Alegre.
Architects: Luis Rocha, Sergio
Marques, Ceres Storchi.
PROJETO 1989 June, no.122,
p.74-75, photos, plans, secns.

STORE FRONTS--ENGLAND--BATH
Shop soiled / F. A. Pater.
"The character of many historic
town centres is being eroded by an
increase of shops offering
non-essential services and which
present insensitive and
stereotyped facades to the
street." Compares Bath and Nimes.
ARCHITECTS' JOURNAL 1990 Oct.31,
v.192, no.18, p.26-29, photos.

STORE FRONTS--FRANCE--NIMES
Shop soiled / F. A. Pater.
"The character of many historic
town centres is being eroded by an
increase of shops offering
non-essential services and which
present insensitive and
stereotyped facades to the
street." Compares Bath and Nimes.
ARCHITECTS' JOURNAL 1990 Oct.31,
v.192, no.18, p.26-29, photos.

STORE FRONTS--UNITED STATES--
MINNEAPOLIS (MINNESOTA)--MTC TRANSIT
STORE
Busing it: Shea Architects gives MTC
a lift.
The MTC Transit Store,
Minneapolis.
ARCHITECTURE MINNESOTA 1990
Sept.-Oct., v.16, no.5, p.46-47,
photos.

STOREFRONTS
See STORE FRONTS

STOREFRONTS--ENGLAND--CHESTER--ROWS
The Rows of Chester: some thoughts
on the results of recent research
/ Jane Grenville.
WORLD ARCHAEOLOGY 1990 Feb., v.21,
no.3, p.[446]-460, map, plans,
secns., reconst. dwgs., refs.

STOREHOUSES--JAPAN--FISHERMAN MUSEUM
The Fisherman Museum store-center.
Museum storage facility.
Architects: Hiroshi Naito,
Architect and Associates. English
summary, p.19.
KENCHIKU BUNKA 1990 July, v.45,
no.525, p.89-98, dels., elevs.,
models, photos., site plans.

STORELLI, FRANCO
La biblioteca della Facolta di
Ingegneria dell'Universita di Roma
=The faculty of engineering's
library, University of Rome /
Franco Storelli.
Architect: Enrico Mandolesi. In
Italian and English.
L'INDUSTRIA DELLE COSTRUZIONI 1990
July-Aug., v.24, no.225-226,
(Continued next column)

STORELLI, FRANCO (CONTINUED)
La biblioteca della...(CONTINUED)
p.34-41, photos., plans, secns.,
refs.

STORES
See also ANTIQUE SHOPS
See also ART SUPPLY STORES
See also BEAUTY SHOPS
See also BOOKSTORES
See also CONVENIENCE STORES
See also COUNTRY STORES
See also DEPARTMENT STORES
See also DRUGSTORES
See also DRY GOODS STORES
See also FLORIST SHOPS
See also GROCERY STORES
See also POST EXCHANGES
See also SHOPHOUSES
See also SHOPPING CENTERS
See also SHOPPING MALLS
See also SOUVENIR SHOPS
See also STORE FRONTS
See also STRIP RETAIL CENTERS
The effect of sign complexity and
coherence on the perceived quality
of retail scenes / Jack L. Nasar.
AMERICAN PLANNING ASSOCIATION.
JOURNAL 1987 Autumn, v.53, no.4,
p.499-509, graphs, photos.,
tables, biblio., refs.
Erlebnisorientiertes Einkaufen /
Harald Bergfeld.
ARCHITEKTUR, INNENARCHITEKTUR,
TECHNISCHER AUSBAU 1989 Sept.,
v.97, no.9, p.22-23, photos.
Making connections / Keith W.
Strandberg.
Relationship between mass transit
and retail development.
MASS TRANSIT 1990 Nov.-Dec., v.17,
no.11, p.21-23, photos.
Shopping for trends / Dan Martin.
Stores, shopping centers, malls,
and strip centers in the 1990s.
PLANNING 1990 Dec., v.56, no.12,
p.14-18, graph, dwgs., photos.,
secn.

STORES--ALTERATIONS AND ADDITIONS--
GERMANY (WEST)--BONN--MAGAZIN
Low-Budget: Ladenumbau und
Fassadenrenovierung der Firma
Magazin, Bonn.
Architects: Riemann + Roy.
DEUTSCHE BAUZEITUNG 1990 Oct.,
v.124, no.10, p.71-72, dwg.,
photos., plan, secn.

STORES--ALTERATIONS AND ADDITIONS--
GERMANY (WEST)--MONCHENGLADBACH--
PILLEN
Aufgestockt: Erweiterung und Umbau
eines Wohn- und Geschaftshauses in
Monchengladbach-Rheydt.
Architect: dt8.
ARCHITEKTUR, INNENARCHITEKTUR,
TECHNISCHER AUSBAU 1990 Sept.,
v.98, no.9, p.18-19, photos.,
plans.

STORES - ANTIQUES
See ANTIQUE SHOPS

STORES--ART NOUVEAU--BELGIUM--
BRUSSELS--WARENHUIS WAUCQUEZ
Restoration of Magasins Waucquez;
Brussels architect of the former
building: Victor Horta.
Restoration architects: P. Van
Asche and others. Text in
Japanese.
(Continued next column)

STORES--ART NOUVEAU--BELGIUM--
BRUSSELS--WARENHUIS WAUCQUEZ
(CONTINUED)
Restoration of...(CONTINUED)
SPACE DESIGN 1990 Feb., no.305,
p.[05-12], elev., photos., plan,
secn.

STORES - BOOKS
See BOOKSTORES

STORES--CANADA--TORONTO (ONTARIO)--
HIVI ELECTRONICS
Mad Max meets Star Wars: renovation:
HiVi Electronics, Toronto.
Baldwin & Franklin Architects.
CANADIAN ARCHITECT 1990 Oct.,
v.35, no.10, p.28-30, axonometric
view, elev., plans.

STORES--CLOTHING--ART DECO--INTERIOR
DESIGN--FRANCE--PARIS--MAISON DE
COUTURE MADELEINE VIONNET
Georges de Feure et la Maison de
Couture Madeleine Vionnet / Ian
Millman.
Features Parisian store interiors
designed ca.1923.
SOCIETE DE L'HISTOIRE DE L'ART
FRANCAIS. BULLETIN 1990,
p.[309]-320, photos., plan, secn.

STORES--CLOTHING--AUSTRALIA--MELBOURNE
Interiors: image is everything in
the retail trade: three retail
fitouts by Geyer Design.
ARCHITECTURE AUSTRALIA 1990 Apr.,
v.79, no.3, p.58-59, photos.

STORES--CLOTHING--CANADA--MONTREAL
(QUEBEC)--FOOD
Montreal, Jacques Rousseau.
Features three recent Montreal
projects by Rousseau: Boutique
Food, Maison Coloniale (Rousseau
house), and bar, Business.
English summaries.
ARCHITECTURE D'AUJOURD'HUI 1990
Sept., no.270, p.133-139, port.,
photos., plans, sketches.

STORES--CLOTHING--CANADA--TORONTO
(ONTARIO)--MARC LAURENT
Bruce Kuwabara, Thomas Payne:
negozio di abbligliamento,
Toronto.
Marc Laurent clothing store. In
Italian and English.
DOMUS 1990 July-Aug., no.718,
p.[6]-8, photos., plans, sketches.

STORES--CLOTHING--DENMARK--
COPENHAGEN--ESPRIT
Esprit butiksindretning, Kobenhaun.
Shop located on "Stroget."
Architect: Ettore Sottsass.
Includes English caption.
ARKITEKTUR DK 1990, v.34, no.3,
p.132, photos.

STORES--CLOTHING--ENGLAND--LONDON--
KATHARINE HAMNETT
Guaridas de la moda: Katharine
Hamnett, de Foster a Coates /
Adrian Dannatt.
Clothing stores in London and
Glasgow.
ARQUITECTURA VIVA 1990 Jan.-Feb.,
no.10, p.58-61, elev., photos.,
plan.

STORES--CLOTHING--ENGLAND--LONDON--
ROBOT
Minima y artesanal: la "opera prima"
de AO / Janet Lamacraft.
Robot, a London store.
ARQUITECTURA VIVA 1990 July-Aug.,
no.13, p.58-59, photos., secn.

STORES--CLOTHING--FRANCE--PARIS--
JEAN-PAUL GAULTIER
Segreto e menzogna negli spazi di
vendita di Gaultier e Gigli a
Parigi [1] / Giulia Ceriani.
PARAMETRO 1990 Nov.-Dec., no.181,
p.80-83, photos., plans.

STORES--CLOTHING--FRANCE--PARIS--ROMEO
GIGLI
Segreto e menzogna negli spazi di
vendita di Gaultier e Gigli a
Parigi [1] / Giulia Ceriani.
PARAMETRO 1990 Nov.-Dec., no.181,
p.80-83, photos., plans.

STORES--CLOTHING--GERMANY (WEST)--
COLOGNE--GUGU ERNESTO
Gugus Haus: der Laden von Gugu
Ernesto in Koln.
Architects: Dahlbender Gatermann
Schossig.
ARCHITEKTUR, INNENARCHITEKTUR,
TECHNISCHER AUSBAU 1989 Sept.,
v.97, no.9, p.36-41, dets.,
photos., plans.
Schone Strenge Geschafts-und
Atelierraume in Koln.
Architects: Dahlbender Gatermann
Schossig.
DEUTSCHE BAUZEITUNG 1990 Oct.,
v.124, no.10, p.14-17, photos.,
plans, secn.

STORES--CLOTHING--GERMANY (WEST)--
DARMSTADT--LISBETH XXX
Archaiser Reiz: "lisbeth XXX," ein
Modegeschaft in Darmstadt,
Elisabethenstrasse 30.
Designers: Klaus Phl, Willi
Bucher.
ARCHITEKTUR, INNENARCHITEKTUR,
TECHNISCHER AUSBAU 1989 Sept.,
v.97, no.9, p.48-49, dets.,
photos.

STORES--CLOTHING--GERMANY (WEST)--
DUSSELDORF
Mode- und Schmuck-Boutique in
Dusseldorf.
Architects: H + H (Angelika and
Ingo Hulser).
DEUTSCHE BAUZEITSCHRIFT 1990 Oct.,
v.38, no.10, p.[1395]-1398, dets.,
photos., plans, sketch.

STORES--CLOTHING--GERMANY (WEST)--
DUSSELDORF--C. WIRSCHKE
Einladend: Umbau eines
Konfektionsladens in der
Dusseldorfer Steinstrasse.
Architects: H+H (Angelika and Ingo
Hulser).
ARCHITEKTUR, INNENARCHITEKTUR,
TECHNISCHER AUSBAU 1990 Mar.,
v.98, no.3, p.36-39, dets.,
photos., secn.

STORES--CLOTHING--GERMANY (WEST)--
KARLSRUHE--CALLA MODE FEMININ
Mit System: die Boutique "Calla Mode
Feminin" in Karlsruhe.
Architect: Andreas Winkler with
Barbara Grosse-Rhode.
ARCHITEKTUR, INNENARCHITEKTUR,
TECHNISCHER AUSBAU 1989 Sept.,
v.97, no.9, p.42-45, axonometric
view, dets., photos.

STORES--CLOTHING--GERMANY (WEST)--
NEUWIED--IM RAHMEN
Im Rahmen: Mode-Laden in Neuwied.
Architect: Wolfgang Grub.
ARCHITEKTUR, INNENARCHITEKTUR,
TECHNISCHER AUSBAU 1989 Sept.,
v.97, no.9, p.62, photos.

STORES--CLOTHING--GERMANY (WEST)--
NURNBERG
Ruhe und Spannung: Umbau der dritten
Etage eines Bekleidungshauses in
Nurnberg.
Architect: Manfred Knappe.
ARCHITEKTUR, INNENARCHITEKTUR,
TECHNISCHER AUSBAU 1989 Sept.,
v.97, no.9, p.60-61, photos.

STORES--CLOTHING--INTERIOR DESIGN--
ENGLAND--LONDON--ING
Next store neighbour / Fay Sweet.
On London clothing store, ing.
Architects: Harper MacKay.
DESIGNERS' JOURNAL 1990 Jan.,
no.53, p.64-[67], dets., photos.,
plans.

STORES--CLOTHING--INTERIOR DESIGN--
ENGLAND--LONDON--ISSEY MIYAKE
Made to measure / David Redhead.
Interiors of three London clothing
stores: Issey Miyake, Michiko
Koshino and Karl Lagerfeld.
DESIGNERS' JOURNAL 1990 July-Aug.,
no.59, p.[28]-33, photos.

STORES--CLOTHING--INTERIOR DESIGN--
ENGLAND--LONDON--KARL LAGERFELD
Made to measure / David Redhead.
Interiors of three London clothing
stores: Issey Miyake, Michiko
Koshino and Karl Lagerfeld.
DESIGNERS' JOURNAL 1990 July-Aug.,
no.59, p.[28]-33, photos.

STORES--CLOTHING--INTERIOR DESIGN--
ENGLAND--LONDON--MICHIKO KOSHINO
Made to measure / David Redhead.
Interiors of three London clothing
stores: Issey Miyake, Michiko
Koshino and Karl Lagerfeld.
DESIGNERS' JOURNAL 1990 July-Aug.,
no.59, p.[28]-33, photos.

STORES--CLOTHING--INTERIOR DESIGN--
FINLAND--TAMPERE--KINO
Finn detail / Helen Elias.
Interiors of Kino clothing store,
Tampere, Finland. Interior
designers: 20/20 Ltd.
DESIGNERS' JOURNAL 1990 Mar.,
no.55, p.76-78, photos., plan.

STORES--CLOTHING--INTERIOR DESIGN--
FRANCE--PARIS--BOUTIQUE UNGARO
Sharp chic shop / Helen Elias.
Interiors of Boutique Ungaro,
Paris. Architect: Christian de
Portzamparc.
DESIGNERS' JOURNAL 1990 Apr.,
no.56, p.90-92, photos., plan.

STORES--CLOTHING--INTERIOR DESIGN--
FRANCE--PARIS--COMME DES GARCONS
Du blanc...et du sens.
Three "white wall" projects in
Paris: Galerie Crousel- Robelin,
architect: Patrick Mellet; Galerie
Anne de Villepoix, architect:
Kazutoshi Morita; Comme des
Garcons, architect: Takao
Kawasaki.
ARCHITECTURE INTERIEURE CREE 1990
Oct.-Nov., no.239, 154-161,
photos.

STORES--CLOTHING--INTERIOR DESIGN--
FRANCE--PARIS--JUNKO KOSHINO
[Amenagement interieur]: commerces.
Contents: Boutique Koshino, Paris
VIIIe; architect: Jean-Michel
Wilmotte-- Apple showroom, ave. de
la Grande Armee, Paris; architect:
Berbesson Racine et Associes--
Castelli showroom, Paris;
designer: Ronald Cecil Sportes--
Unifor furniture showroom, Milan,
Italy; architects: Afra & Tobia
Scarpa-- Boutique Jean-Louis
Imbert, Marseille, France;
architect: Rudy Ricciotti--
Recorded music store, Nantes,
France; architect: Studio Naco.
LE MONITEUR ARCHITECTURE AMC 1990
July-Aug., no.13, p.36-45,
axonometric views, photos., plans.
Sur le mode de la fugue.
Interiors of the Junko Koshino
boutique, Paris. Architect:
Jean-Michel Wilmotte.
ARCHITECTURE INTERIEURE CREE 1990
Oct.-Nov., no.239, p.132-133,
photos.

STORES--CLOTHING--INTERIOR DESIGN--
FRANCE--PARIS--TEHEN
Theme et divagations.
Tehen boutique, Paris. Interior
architect: Denis Colomb.
ARCHITECTURE INTERIEURE CREE 1990
Oct.-Nov., no.239, p.152-153,
phoots.

STORES--CLOTHING--INTERIOR DESIGN--
GERMANY (WEST)--DUSSELDORF
Lebendige Gegensatze: showroom fur
Ledertaschen und Accessoires in
Dusseldorf.
Architect: Klaus Burger.
ARCHITEKTUR, INNENARCHITEKTUR,
TECHNISCHER AUSBAU 1990 Sept.,
v.98, no.9, p.33, photos.

STORES--CLOTHING--INTERIOR DESIGN--
GERMANY (WEST)--ESSEN--PRO FASHION
Spannungsreich: Modeladen in Essen,
1. Preis beim Deutschen
Innenarchitekturpreis 1990.
Architect: Klaus Burger.
ARCHITEKTUR, INNENARCHITEKTUR,
TECHNISCHER AUSBAU 1990 Sept.,
v.98, no.9, p.31-32, photos.

STORES--CLOTHING--INTERIOR DESIGN--
GERMANY (WEST)--ESSEN--VOGUE ALLEY
En Vogue: Modeladen in Essen.
Interior architect: Klaus Burger.
DEUTSCHE BAUZEITUNG 1990 Oct.,
v.124, no.10, p.54-56, dwgs.,
photos.

STORES--CLOTHING--INTERIOR DESIGN--
GERMANY (WEST)--ESSEN--VOGUE ALLEY
(CONTINUED)
Modeladen "Vogue Alley" in Essen /
K. Burger.
Interior designer: Klaus Burger.
DEUTSCHE BAUZEITSCHRIFT 1990 Oct.,
v.38, no.10, p.1391-1394,
axonometric view, dets., dwgs.,
photos.

STORES--CLOTHING--INTERIOR DESIGN--
GERMANY (WEST)--HAMBURG--BOUTIQUE
OLLY-POP
Jung und bunt: Boutique Olly-Pop,
Hamburg.
Architect: Klaus Huwendiek.
ARCHITEKTUR, INNENARCHITEKTUR,
TECHNISCHER AUSBAU 1990 Sept.,
v.98, no.9, p.34-35, photos.

STORES--CLOTHING--INTERIOR DESIGN--
ITALY--MILAN--GIANNI VERSACE
Gianfranco Cavaglia, Eraldo
Comoglio: Negozio Versace, Milano.
In Italian and English.
DOMUS 1990 Jan., no.712, p.59-63,
dets., elevs., photos, plans,
secns.

STORES--CLOTHING--INTERIOR DESIGN--
ITALY--MILAN--MARISA (PORTA
TICINESE)
Sottsass times two: two shops for
Marisa in Milan / Edie Lee Cohen.
Features shop interiors on Via
della Spiga and Porta Ticinese.
Architect: Ettore Sottsass.
INTERIOR DESIGN 1990 Aug., v.61,
no.11, p.[136]-139, photos.

STORES--CLOTHING--INTERIOR DESIGN--
ITALY--MILAN--MARISA (VIA DELLA
SPIGA)
Sottsass times two: two shops for
Marisa in Milan / Edie Lee Cohen.
Features shop interiors on Via
della Spiga and Porta Ticinese.
Architect: Ettore Sottsass.
INTERIOR DESIGN 1990 Aug., v.61,
no.11, p.[136]-139, photos.

STORES--CLOTHING--INTERIOR DESIGN--
JAPAN--OSAKA--SHINJUKU TAKANO
Yasuo Kondoh / Sylvie Chirat.
Three projects: La Costa D
restaurant, Tokyo, beauty shop,
Hakata, Fukuoka, and clothing
store, Shinjuku Takano, Osaka.
ARCHITECTURE D'AUJOURD'HUI 1990
Oct., no.271, p.246-253, port.,
elevs., model, photos.

STORES--CLOTHING--INTERIOR DESIGN--
UNITED STATES--BOSTON
(MASSACHUSETTS)--BARNEYS NEW YORK
Shop right / Karin Tetlow.
The interiors of four Barneys New
York stores located in suburban
malls. Architects: Rosenblum Harb
Architects.
INTERIORS 1990 July, v.149, no.12,
p.82-89, photos., plans.

STORES--CLOTHING--INTERIOR DESIGN--
UNITED STATES--MANHASSET (NEW
YORK)--BARNEYS NEW YORK
Shop right / Karin Tetlow.
The interiors of four Barneys New
York stores located in suburban
malls. Architects: Rosenblum Harb
Architects.
INTERIORS 1990 July, v.149, no.12,
p.82-89, photos., plans.

STORES--CLOTHING--INTERIOR DESIGN--
UNITED STATES--NEW JERSEY--LAST CALL
Interiors studio / Jean Gorman.
Interiors of Neiman Marcus
clearance center, Last Call, in
New Jersey shopping mall. Interior
designers: Hermanovski Lauck.
INTERIORS 1990 Sept., v.149,
no.14, p.24, photos.

STORES--CLOTHING--INTERIOR DESIGN--
UNITED STATES--NEW YORK (NEW YORK)--
KYOTO ARTS AND FASHIONS
Kyoto Arts and Fashions / Edie Lee
Cohen.
Interiors of Manhattan retail
interior on Madison Avenue
designed by Toshiko Mori.
INTERIOR DESIGN 1990 Jan., v.61,
no.1, p.[184-187], dwg., photos.
Traditional twist: architect Toshiko
Mori's elegant and minimal design
for Kyoto Arts and Fashions'
Madison Avenue shop / Amy Dana.
Located in New York, New York.
INTERIORS 1990 Jan., v.149, no.6,
p.142-143, photos., plan.

STORES--CLOTHING--INTERIOR DESIGN--
UNITED STATES--NEW YORK (NEW YORK)--
MATSUDA
Matsuda / Edie Lee Cohen.
Interiors of Manhattan clothing
store, located in the Flatiron
district. Interior designer:
Ryoichi Yokota.
INTERIOR DESIGN 1990 Sept., v.61,
no.12, p.[190-193], axonometric
view, photos.

STORES--CLOTHING--INTERIOR DESIGN--
UNITED STATES--NEW YORK (NEW YORK)--
REPORTER
Reporter: a Madison Avenue men's
shop by Clea Rocco / Edie Lee
Cohen.
INTERIOR DESIGN 1990 Sept., v.61,
no.12, p.196-199, photos.,
isometric dwg.

STORES--CLOTHING--INTERIOR DESIGN--
UNITED STATES--NEW YORK (NEW YORK)--
SEDONA
Sedona / Karen Maserjian.
Interiors of New York clothing
store located on Park Ave.S.
Architects: Andaloro Associates.
INTERIOR DESIGN 1990 Sept., v.61,
no.12, p.194-[145], photos., plan.

STORES--CLOTHING--INTERIOR DESIGN--
UNITED STATES--NEW YORK (NEW YORK)--
SOHO SURPLUS
Forms and function / Amy Dana.
Interiors of SoHo Surplus clothing
store, New York. Architects:
Deborah Weintraub and Townsend
Moore.
INTERIORS 1990 July, v.149, no.12,
p.92-[93], photos.

STORES--CLOTHING--INTERIOR DESIGN--
UNITED STATES--NEW YORK (NEW YORK)--
ZARA INTERNATIONAL
Zara International / Edie Lee Cohen.
Interiors of two-level clothing
store in Manhattan. Interior
designers: ISD Inc.
INTERIOR DESIGN 1990 Nov., v.61,
no.15, p.168-171, photos., plans.

STORES--CLOTHING--INTERIOR DESIGN--
UNITED STATES--SAN FRANCISCO
(CALIFORNIA)--JASMIN BY APPOINTMENT
Jasmin by Appointment / Lois Wagner
Green.
Interiors of San Francisco fashion
boutique. Interior designer:
Bradley Rytz.
INTERIOR DESIGN 1990 Apr., v.61,
no.6, p.[182-185], photos., plans.

STORES--CLOTHING--INTERIOR DESIGN--
UNITED STATES--SHORT HILLS (NEW
JERSEY)--BARNEYS NEW YORK
Shop right / Karin Tetlow.
The interiors of four Barneys New
York stores located in suburban
malls. Architects: Rosenblum Harb
Architects.
INTERIORS 1990 July, v.149, no.12,
p.82-89, photos., plans.

STORES--CLOTHING--ITALY--ALBA--CARAVAN
Michela formia, Walter Vallini:
negozio Caravan ad Alba.
Text in Italian and English.
DOMUS 1990 Apr., no.715, p.[1-3],
photos, plans, secn.

STORES--CLOTHING--ITALY--LIGNANO
SABBIADORO--SBAIZ
Claudio Nardi: negozio Sbaiz a
Lignano Sabbiadoro / Luca Forno.
Refurbishment of a 1960's building
for a clothing store. In Italian
and English.
DOMUS 1990 May, no.716, p.[64-69],
axonometric view, photos., plans,
sketches.
Palais mythique.
1960s building in Lignano
Sabbiadoro, Italy, renovated for
the Sbaiz clothing store.
Architect: Claudio Nardi.
ARCHITECTURE INTERIEURE CREE 1990
Oct.-Nov., no.239, p.[130]-131,
photos.

STORES--CLOTHING--ITALY--MILAN--STRENG
Streng: Showroom Marisa in Mailand /
Patrizia Catalano.
Architects: Studio Vittorio
Gregotti.
ARCHITEKTUR, INNENARCHITEKTUR,
TECHNISCHER AUSBAU 1989 Sept.,
v.97, no.9, p.58, photos.

STORES--CLOTHING--ITALY--OMEGNA
Una finestra per la moda = A window
for fashion / Gian Carlo
Primatesta.
Clothing store in a historic
building in Omegna, Italy.
Architect: Fabrizio Bianchetti.
FRAMES, PORTE & FINESTRE 1990
July-Sept., no.28, p.58-63, dets.,
dwgs., photos.

STORES--CLOTHING--JAPAN--KYOTO
  Spazi per la moda: la palazzina
    d'Angolo = Spaces for fashion: the
    corner building.
  Fashion boutique in Kyoto;
    architect: Roberto Querci. Jil
    Sander store; architects: Martin &
    Elisabeth Boesch.
  ABITARE 1990 Mar., no.283,
    p.164-[167], photos., plans, secn.

STORES--CLOTHING--JAPAN--TOKYO--
INTRIGUE SALON
  Special feature 2: Recent works of
    Naoki Iijima.
  Six projects, including the
    Yokohama Gakuin chapel and the
    Intrigue salon boutique. Includes
    essays by Toshikazu Ishida and
    Naoki Iijima. Text in Japanese.
  SPACE DESIGN 1990 July, no.310,
    p.33-48, axonometric views, dets.,
    photos., plans.

STORES--CLOTHING--LIGHTING--GERMANY
(WEST)--DUSSELDORF--DOLF SELBACH
  Verkaufsambiente nach Mass:
    Inszenierung mit Licht und edlen
    Materialen.
  Architects: Ernsting & Partner.
  ARCHITEKTUR, INNENARCHITEKTUR,
    TECHNISCHER AUSBAU 1990 Sept.,
    v.98, no.9, p.74-75, photos.

STORES--CLOTHING--SCOTLAND--GLASGOW--
KATHARINE HAMNETT
  Guaridas de la moda: Katharine
    Hamnett, de Foster a Coates /
    Adrian Dannatt.
  Clothing stores in London and
    Glasgow.
  ARQUITECTURA VIVA 1990 Jan.-Feb.,
    no.10, p.58-61, elev., photos.,
    plan.

STORES--CLOTHING--SOUTH AFRICA--CAPE
TOWN--SALVAGO
  Paint magic / Penny Swift.
  In conjunction with the author's
    book, Plascon paint techniques,
    discusses the use of paint in
    interior design. Feature three
    projects: Salvago boutique, Camp's
    Bay, Cape Town (architect: Roger
    Martin); "Herculaneum", home of
    designer Jacqueline Cole; Floris
    Smit Huijs restaurant, Cape Town
    (interior decorator: Francois du
    Plessis).
  ADA: ARCHITECTURE, DESIGN, ART
    1989, no.7, p.27-33, ports.,
    photos.

STORES--CLOTHING--SPAIN--BARCELONA--A2
  Tienda de modas A2 = Fashion shop,
    Manresa, Barcelona, 1988.
  Interior designer: Pepe Cortes.
  EL CROQUIS 1990 Mar., v.9, no.42,
    p.162-168, dets., photos., plans,
    secns.

STORES--CLOTHING--SPAIN--BARCELONA--
EKSEPTION
  Raume des Alltags: Einkaufszentrum
    in Parma und Interieurs in
    Barcelona.
  Torri center (1989), architect:
    Aldo Rossi, Gianni Braghieri; and
    Ekseption interiors (1989);
    architect: Eduard Samso. Text in
    German; summaries in German,
    French, and English.
              (Continued next column)

STORES--CLOTHING--SPAIN--BARCELONA--
EKSEPTION (CONTINUED)
  Raume des Alltags:...(CONTINUED)
  WERK, BAUEN + WOHNEN 1990 June,
    no.6, p.54-65, axonometric views,
    elevs., photos., plans, site
    plans, sketches.

STORES--CLOTHING--SPAIN--BARCELONA--
FOCHE MAINA
  Tienda de confeccion para caballeros
    en Barcelona: M. Ybarguengoitia y
    Ma. del Mar Nogues.
  Spanish, English text.
  ON DISENO 1990, no.113, p.166-173,
    elevs., photos., plans.

STORES--CLOTHING--SPAIN--BARCELONA--
LURDES BERGADA
  Eduardo Samso.
  Includes criticism by Josep Maria
    Montaner and four projects by the
    architect. Text in Spanish and
    English.
  EL CROQUIS 1990 Nov., v.9, no.45,
    p.125-162, axonometric views,
    dets., port., elevs., models,
    photos., plans, secns., site
    plans.

STORES--CLOTHING--SPAIN--IBIZA--NYC
  Local comercial en Eivissa:
    Francisco Jose Mangado,
    arquitecto.
  Spanish, English text.
  ON DISENO 1990, no.111, p.172-179,
    det., photos., plans.

STORES--CLOTHING--SPAIN--IBIZA--THE
END
  Eduardo Samso.
  Includes criticism by Josep Maria
    Montaner and four projects by the
    architect. Text in Spanish and
    English.
  EL CROQUIS 1990 Nov., v.9, no.45,
    p.125-162, axonometric views,
    dets., port., elevs., models,
    photos., plans, secns., site
    plans.

STORES--CLOTHING--SPAIN--MADRID--
EKSEPTION
  Eduardo Samso.
  Includes criticism by Josep Maria
    Montaner and four projects by the
    architect. Text in Spanish and
    English.
  EL CROQUIS 1990 Nov., v.9, no.45,
    p.125-162, axonometric views,
    dets., port., elevs., models,
    photos., plans, secns., site
    plans.

STORES--CLOTHING--SPAIN--TOLEDO
  Ilusion color cafe: una tienda de
    modas de Mario Bernedo / Yago
    Bonnet.
  In Toledo.
  ARQUITECTURA VIVA 1990 Nov.-Dec.,
    no.15, p.60-61, elevs., photos.,
    plan.

STORES--CLOTHING--SPAIN--VICH
  Local comercial en Vic: Cristobal
    Julian Ramirez, arquitecto.
  Spanish, English text.
  ON DISENO 1990, no.110, p.150-155,
    photos., secns., sketches.

STORES--CLOTHING--STUDENT PROJECTS--
GERMANY (WEST)--KARLSRUHE--KLEIBER
  Ungestaltung eines Modehauses.
    Student project, FH Darmstadt.
  ARCHITEKTUR, INNENARCHITEKTUR,
    TECHNISCHER AUSBAU 1990 Sept.,
    v.98, no.9, p.46-51, axonometric
    views, dwgs., elev., plans.

STORES--CLOTHING--SWEDEN--VARNAMO--
FRIBERGS
  Fribergs, Varnamo & JC, Boras.
  Interiors of clothing shop at
    Storgatsbacken 21 in Varnamo and
    of offices at Katrinedalsgaten 14
    in Boras. Architect: Rupert
    Gardner Design.
  ARKITEKTUR: THE SWEDISH REVIEW OF
    ARCHITECTURE 1990 Sept., v.90,
    no.7, p.26-27, elev., photos.

STORES--CLOTHING--SWITZERLAND--JIL
SANDER
  Spazi per la moda: la palazzina
    d'Angolo = Spaces for fashion: the
    corner building.
  Fashion boutique in Kyoto;
    architect: Roberto Querci. Jil
    Sander store; architects: Martin &
    Elisabeth Boesch.
  ABITARE 1990 Mar., no.283,
    p.164-[167], photos., plans, secn.

STORES--CLOTHING--UNITED STATES--
MARINA DEL REY (CALIFORNIA)--ECRU
  Le corps en morceaux d'architecture.
  Features Ecru Clothing store,
    Marina del Rey, Calif. Architect:
    Michele Saee.
  ARCHITECTURE INTERIEURE CREE 1990
    Oct.-Nov., no.239, p.138-[139],
    photos.
  Out on a limb / Ziva Freiman.
  Focus on two Marina del Rey
    projects by Michele Saee of
    Building: Ecru clothing store,
    and Angeli Mare restaurant.
    Includes selected detail article
    on the ceiling structure of the
    restaurant.
  PROGRESSIVE ARCHITECTURE 1990
    Apr., v.71, no.4, p.108-116,
    dets., photos., plans, secns.

STORES--CLOTHING--UNITED STATES--
MINNEAPOLIS (MINNESOTA)--AVALANCHE
  When less is more: Avalanche's
    minimalism sets the stage for the
    fine art of retailing.
  Clothing store, Minneapolis.
    Designer: Steve Andersen.
  ARCHITECTURE MINNESOTA 1990
    Jan.-Feb., v.16, no.1, p.34-35,
    photos.

STORES--CLOTHING--UNITED STATES--
MINNEAPOLIS (MINNESOTA)--INTOTO
  Gauging good design: InToto takes a
    fresh angle on retail.
  Minneapolis clothing store in
    renovated house. Architect:
    Daniel Larson; designer: Timothy
    Huff.
  ARCHITECTURE MINNESOTA 1990
    Jan.-Feb., v.16, no.1, p.36-37,
    photos.

STORES--CONCRETE BLOCK--UNITED
STATES--NORFOLK (MICHIGAN)--
SCHNEIDER STORE
The apartment over the store / Tom
H. Gerhardt.
The home of Ken and Ruth Cooper,
in a 1910 concrete block store,
Norwalk, Mich., built by Pete
Schneider.
VICTORIAN HOMES 1990 Fall, v.9,
no.4, p.39-45, photos.

STORES - DEPARTMENT
See DEPARTMENT STORES

STORES--ENGLAND--BRENTFORD--KEEP ABLE
CENTRE
How to keep able.
The new Keep Able Centre shop in
Brentford, Middlesex and its
products for the elderly and the
handicapped.
DESIGN FOR SPECIAL NEEDS 1989
Dec., no.50, p.21-22, photos.

STORES--ENGLAND--LONDON--PETER JONES
Sloane leader.
On the Peter Jones store in Sloane
Square, London, completed in
stages from 1935-1939. Architects:
William Crabtree, Slater &
Moberly. Includes interview with
Crabtree.
ARCHITECTURAL REVIEW 1990 Jan.,
v.187, no.1115, p.75-79, dwgs.,
photos., plans.

STORES FOOD
See GROCERY STORES

STORES--FRANCE--NANTES--TACOMA
Studio Naco: architecture and
design.
Four projects by Alain Renk and
Marcelo Joulia-Lagares.
Belfort-Council, Belfort, France
(1989); Music store "Tacoma",
Nantes, France (1989); model for
design center, Paris (1993);
Jipo-Jopo lighting fixture (1990).
Text in Japanese. Includes English
summaries.
SPACE DESIGN 1990 Sept., no.312,
p.089-100, dwgs., elevs., models,
photos., plans, photos.
Tacoma: un vasisseau musical.
Record store, Nantes. Architects:
Naco.
TECHNIQUES ET ARCHITECTURE 1990
Apr.-May, no.389, p.167-169, det.,
photos., plan, secn.

STORES--FRANCE--PARIS--VIRGIN
El gesto atormillado: Virgin se
instala en Paris / Mercedes Reig.
Music store. Architects: Peter
Leonard Associates.
ARQUITECTURA VIVA 1990 July-Aug.,
no.13, p.60-61, photos., plan.

STORES--FURNITURE--FRANCE--PARIS--
ESPACE CASTELLI
Espace Castelli, Paris / Brigitte
Fitoussi.
Furniture store, features spiral
stairway. Architect: Ronald Cecil
Sportes.
ARCHITECTURE D'AUJOURD'HUI 1990
Sept., no.270, p.193-196, dwgs.,
photos.

STORES--FURNITURE--GERMANY (WEST)--
BERLIN--KONTOR
Das Ding mit Eigenwert:
Mobelgeschaft und Designgalerie
Kontor in Berlin-Tiergarten / Falk
Jaeger.
Planners: Christoph Meyer, Karl
Reuther.
ARCHITEKTUR, INNENARCHITEKTUR,
TECHNISCHER AUSBAU 1990 Mar.,
v.98, no.3, p.12-15, dets.,
photos., plan, secn., isometric
dwgs.

STORES--FURNITURE--GERMANY (WEST)--
ERTINGEN--ERPO
"Stressless" Konzept fur ein
Shop-in-Shop-System.
Furniture store, Ertingen.
Architects: Kurth + Partner.
ARCHITEKTUR, INNENARCHITEKTUR,
TECHNISCHER AUSBAU 1990 Sept.,
v.98, no.9, p.86-87, axonometric
view, photos., plan.

STORES--FURNITURE--GERMANY (WEST)--
HANNOVER--RB WOHNEN
Prasentation furs Wohnen: das
Einrichtungshaus RB Wohnen in der
Berliner Allee, Hannover.
Architects: V. Kersten, E.
Martinoff.
ARCHITEKTUR, INNENARCHITEKTUR,
TECHNISCHER AUSBAU 1990 Mar.,
v.98, no.3, p.58-62, dets.,
elevs., photos., plans, secns.

STORES--FURNITURE--GERMANY (WEST)--
HANNOVER--STEINHOFF
Klassiker mit Zylinder:
Einrichtungshaus Steinhoff in
Hannover.
Architects: Bahlo Kohnke Stosberg
+ Partner.
DEUTSCHE BAUZEITUNG 1990 Oct.,
v.124, no.10, p.18-21, photos.,
plans, secn., site plan.

STORES--FURNITURE--SPAIN--TOLEDO--
PROVISORIA
La Provisoria, Toledo: Benjamin Juan
y J. Gomez-Escalonilla,
arquitectos.
Spanish, English text.
ON DISENO 1989, no.104, p.146-151,
photos., plan.

STORES--FURNITURE--UNITED STATES--
CHICAGO (ILLINOIS)--CRATE & BARREL
Crate & Barrel brings Modernism to
Michigan Avenue / Paul Glassman.
Store at 646 N. Michigan, Chicago,
designed by John Buenz of Solomon
Cordwell Buenz & Associates with
Raymond Arenson of the store's
design team.
INLAND ARCHITECT 1990 Nov.-Dec.,
v.34, no.6, p.16,19, axonometric
view, photos.

STORES--FURNITURE--UNITED STATES--
EDINA (MINNESOTA)--ROOM & BOARD
Contemporary tempo: a new Room &
Board steps to the beat of the
'90s with light, energy and color.
Edina home furnishings store.
Architect: Martha Yunker.
ARCHITECTURE MINNESOTA 1990
Jan.-Feb., v.16, no.1, p.38-39,
photos.

STORES--GERMANY (WEST)
Architekt contra Ladeneinrichter:
Cornelia Krause im Gesprach mit
Andreas Winkler [interview].
DEUTSCHE BAUZEITUNG 1990 Oct.,
v.124, no.10, p.46-51, axonometric
views, dets., port., photos.,
plans, secns.
Planning for retail change in West
Germany / Joachim Zentes, Werner
Schwarz-Zanetti.
BUILT ENVIRONMENT 1988, v.14,
no.1, p.38-46, charts, photos,
refs.

STORES--GERMANY (WEST)--BREMEN--OPTIK
CREATIV
Optikfachgeschaft fur jungere
Kunden.
Planungsburo elfers.
ARCHITEKTUR, INNENARCHITEKTUR,
TECHNISCHER AUSBAU 1990 Nov.,
v.98, no.11, p.62-64, photos.,
plan.

STORES--GERMANY (WEST)--DORTMUND
Horen und Sehen: Individuelle
Verkaufsraume fur eine Ladenkette,
die Horgerate verkauft.
Audio-visual store in Dortmund.
Engineers: G. Bickenbach, B.
Grashorn.
ARCHITEKTUR, INNENARCHITEKTUR,
TECHNISCHER AUSBAU 1990 Mar.,
v.98, no.3, p.26-29, photos.,
plans, secns., isometric dwgs.
Laden fur Horgerate in Dortmund.
Architects: G. Bickenbach, G.
Grashorn.
DEUTSCHE BAUZEITSCHRIFT 1990 Oct.,
v.38, no.10, p.1379-1382, dets.,
photos., plans, secns., sketches.

STORES--GERMANY (WEST)--FULDA--ARS
VIVENDI
Ars Vivendi: ein Laden fur
Handtaschen und Reisegepack in der
Altstadt von Fulda.
Architects: Reith + Wehner.
ARCHITEKTUR, INNENARCHITEKTUR,
TECHNISCHER AUSBAU 1989 Sept.,
v.97, no.9, p.54-55, photos.,
plan, secns.

STORES--GERMANY (WEST)--STADTBERGEN
Geschaftshaus fur Hifi-und
audiovisuelle Gerate, Stadtbergen
(BRD).
Architects: S. Ottl, N. Helfert,
W. Tanzer.
WERK, BAUEN + WOHNEN 1990 Apr.,
no.4, p.68, photos., plans,
secns., site plan.

STORES--GERMANY (WEST)--WESEL--ISERLOH
Vom "Optiker-Laden" zum Augenoptiker
- Fachgeschaft: Zeitgemasse
Modernisierung in Wesel.
Architects: Ullrich Schmidt, Roland
Viehl.
ARCHITEKTUR, INNENARCHITEKTUR,
TECHNISCHER AUSBAU 1989 Sept.,
v.97, no.9, p.74-76, photos.,
plan.

STORES--INTERIOR DESIGN
Shop 2000: "der Konsument wird
Lebensqualitat forden": "Visual
Merchandising" - nicht nur ein
Schlagwort / Heinz Heiner.
ARCHITEKTUR, INNENARCHITEKTUR,
TECHNISCHER AUSBAU 1989 Sept.,
v.97, no.9, p.68-72, photos.
Shopping around / Helen Elias,
Pamela Buxton.
Features merchandising systems by
six British architecture firms.
DESIGNER'S JOURNAL 1990 Mar.,
no.55, p.38-40, diagrs., dwgs.

STORES--INTERIOR DESIGN--FRANCE--
NANTES
[Amenagement interieur]: commerces.
Contents: Boutique Koshino, Paris
VIIIe; architect: Jean-Michel
Wilmotte-- Apple showroom, ave. de
la Grande Armee, Paris; architect:
Berbesson Racine et Associes--
Castelli showroom, Paris;
designer: Ronald Cecil Sportes--
Unifor furniture showroom, Milan,
Italy; architects: Afra & Tobia
Scarpa-- Boutique Jean-Louis
Imbert, Marseille, France;
architect: Rudy Ricciotti--
Recorded music store, Nantes,
France; architect: Studio Naco.
LE MONITEUR ARCHITECTURE AMC 1990
July-Aug., no.13, p.36-45,
axonometric views, photos., plans.

STORES--INTERIOR DESIGN--FRANCE--
PARIS--IMBERT
[Amenagement interieur]: commerces.
Contents: Boutique Koshino, Paris
VIIIe; architect: Jean-Michel
Wilmotte-- Apple showroom, ave. de
la Grande Armee, Paris; architect:
Berbesson Racine et Associes--
Castelli showroom, Paris;
designer: Ronald Cecil Sportes--
Unifor furniture showroom, Milan,
Italy; architects: Afra & Tobia
Scarpa-- Boutique Jean-Louis
Imbert, Marseille, France;
architect: Rudy Ricciotti--
Recorded music store, Nantes,
France; architect: Studio Naco.
LE MONITEUR ARCHITECTURE AMC 1990
July-Aug., no.13, p.36-45,
axonometric views, photos., plans.

STORES--INTERIOR DESIGN--FRANCE--
PARIS--L'ECLAIREUR
L'espace collectionneur.
Interiors of L'Eclaireur boutique,
Paris, located in 19th cent.
industrial building. Interior
architects: Maurice Marty, Patrick
Le Huerou.
ARCHITECTURE INTERIEURE CREE 1990
Oct.-Nov., no.239, p.144-[145],
photos.

STORES--INTERIOR DESIGN--GERMANY
(WEST)--GIESSEN
Visual merchandising: zwei
Konfektionshauser im neuen Outfit.
Planner: Elke Peper.
ARCHITEKTUR, INNENARCHITEKTUR,
TECHNISCHER AUSBAU 1990 Sept.,
v.98, no.9, p.56-57, photos.

STORES--INTERIOR DESIGN--GERMANY
(WEST)--STEINHEIM
Individuell gestaltet: ein
Optik-Uhren-Schmuck-Fachgeschaft
vor und nach dem Umbau.
Architects: Kurth + Partner.
ARCHITEKTUR, INNENARCHITEKTUR,
TECHNISCHER AUSBAU 1990 Sept.,
v.98, no.9, p.64-65, photos.,
plan.

STORES--INTERIOR DESIGN--NETHERLANDS--
UTRECHT--STAND 222
Stand 222 - Beatrixgebouw in
Utrecht.
Architect: Otto van Dijk.
DEUTSCHE BAUZEITSCHRIFT 1990 Oct.,
v.38, no.10, p.[1383]-1386, elev.,
photos., plans., secn., isometric
dwg.

STORES--INTERIOR DESIGN--SCOTLAND--
EDINBURGH--VIRGIN MEGASTORE
Rock and roll-out / Liz Hoggard.
Features interiors of Virgin
Megastore, an Edinburgh record
store. Interior designers: 20/20
Ltd.
DESIGNERS' JOURNAL 1990 Sept.,
no.60, p.84-[87], photos., plans.

STORES--INTERIOR DESIGN--SPAIN--
BARCELONA
Special feature: Commercial
interiors in Barcelona.
Contents: Between minimalism and
Movid, by Naoki Inagawa -- Alfredo
Arribas -- Josep Val and Xavier
Vendrell -- Dani Freixes and
Vicente Miranda -- Tonet Sunyer
and Jordi Badia -- Eduard Samso --
Ventura Valcarce and Carlos Valls.
Includes interviews and
biographical information and
features 13 individual commercial
projects. Text in Japanese.
SPACE DESIGN 1990 Nov.,
no.11(314), p.005-072, dets.,
ports., photos., plans, secns.,
refs.

STORES--INTERIOR DESIGN--SWEDEN--
STOCKHOLM--SVENSKT PAPPER
Butik Svenskt Papper, Stockholm.
Shop at Birger Jarlsgatan 23.
Architect: Tommy Martensson.
ARKITEKTUR: THE SWEDISH REVIEW OF
ARCHITECTURE 1990 Sept., v.90,
no.7, p.24-25, photos., plan.

STORES--INTERIOR DESIGN--UNITED
STATES--HOUSTON (TEXAS)--HERMES
Hermes / Karen Maserjian.
Houston boutique in the Pavillon
Shopping Galleria. Architects:
Rena Dumas Architecture
Interieure, Whisler-Patri
Architects.
INTERIOR DESIGN 1990 June, v.61,
no.9, p.250-[251], photos.

STORES--INTERIOR DESIGN--UNITED
STATES--NEW YORK (NEW YORK)--
PORTANTINA
Special feature: Machado and
Silvetti.
Contents: Brief history.--
Statement / R. Machado, J.
Silvetti.-- The material force of
the architectural imagination / K.
Michael Hays.-- Works: Portantina,
New York, N.Y., 1986.-- Steps of
(Continued next column)

STORES--INTERIOR DESIGN--UNITED
STATES--NEW YORK (NEW YORK)--
PORTANTINA (CONTINUED)
Special feature:...(CONTINUED)
Providence, Rhode Island School of
Design, Providence, R.I., 1975.--
Municipal cemetery,
Polizzi-Generosa, Sicily, 1986.--
Sesquicentennial Park, Houston,
Tex., 1986.-- Central
transportation facility "la Porta
Meridionale," Palermo, Sicily,
1987.-- Four public squares,
Leonforte, Sicily, 1983. Text in
Japanese and English.
ARCHITECTURE AND URBANISM 1990
Apr., no.4(235), p.65-138,
axonometric views, elevs., models,
photos., plans, secns., site
plans.

STORES--INTERIOR DESIGN--UNITED
STATES--NEW YORK (NEW YORK)--SOHO
For galleriet / Anja Hubener, Bror
Karlsson.
Interiors of four SoHo boutiques:
Knoll International, Parachute,
Comme des Garcons, Yohji Yamamoto.
ARKITEKTUR: THE SWEDISH REVIEW OF
ARCHITECTURE 1990 May, v.90, no.4,
p.42-47, photos., plan.

STORES--INTERIOR DESIGN--UNITED
STATES--PHILADELPHIA
(PENNSYLVANIA)--WINE RESERVE
The Wine Reserve, Philadelphia,
Pennsylvania.
Store and display area for the
Pennsylvania State Liquor Board.
Interiors by Boyd & Associates.
ARCHITECTURE NEW JERSEY 1990 v.26,
no.6, p.10, photos.

STORES--INTERIOR DESIGN--UNITED
STATES--SEATTLE (WASHINGTON)--IL
VECCHIO
Functional art / Justin Henderson.
Il Vecchio, Seattle, a custom
bicycle shop includes repair
workshop. Architects: Edward
Weinstein Associates Architects.
INTERIORS 1990 Feb., v.149, no.7,
p.116-[117], axonometric view,
photos.

STORES--ITALY--MILAN--MANDARINA-DUCK
Taschenbuhne: der Showroom von
Mandarina-Duck in Mailand /
Patrizia Catalano.
Architect: Michele De Lucchi.
ARCHITEKTUR, INNENARCHITEKTUR,
TECHNISCHER AUSBAU 1989 Sept.,
v.97, no.9, p.56-57, photos.,
plan, isometric dwg.

STORES--JAPAN--TOKYO--HARAJUKU
ILLUMINACION
Projects: Adele Naude Santos in
Tokyo / Philip Arcidi.
Features three projects: Fantasia
office building, Harajuku
Illuminacion and a duplex house.
PROGRESSIVE ARCHITECTURE 1990
Nov., v.71, no.12, p.102-104,
elevs., models, plans, secns.,
site plan.

STORES--JEWELRY--ALTERATIONS AND
ADDITIONS--GERMANY (WEST)--
MANNHEIM--BRAUN
Juwel: Umbau eines
Juweliergeschaftes in Mannheim.
Architect: R.M. Kresing.
ARCHITEKTUR, INNENARCHITEKTUR,
TECHNISCHER AUSBAU 1990 Mar.,
v.98, no.3, p.22-23, photos.,
plan.

STORES--JEWELRY--ALTERATIONS AND
ADDITIONS--GERMANY (WEST)--
STRAUBING--HILZ
Ohne Vorbild: Umbau des Schmuck-und
Juwelenateliers Hilz in Straubing.
Architect: Friedrich Herr.
ARCHITEKTUR, INNENARCHITEKTUR,
TECHNISCHER AUSBAU 1990 Mar.,
v.98, no.3, p.24-25, elevs.,
photos., plan.
Schmuck- und Juwelenatelier "Hilz"
in Straubing.
Focus on exterior corner
renovation project. Architect: F.
Herr.
DEUTSCHE BAUZEITSCHRIFT 1990 Oct.,
v.38, no.10, p.1387-1390, elevs.,
photos., plan, sketches.

STORES--JEWELRY--CANADA--TORONTO
(ONTARIO)--COCO LOCO
Going Loco: Susan Speigel's designs
for two Toronto jewelry stores.
Coco Loco jewelry stores,
completed in 1989.
CANADIAN ARCHITECT 1990 Sept.,
v.35, no.9, p.42-45, axonometric
view, photos., plans.

STORES--JEWELRY--FRANCE--PARIS--MARINA
B.
Marina B., avenue Montaigne: un
espace concu par Gae Aulenti /
Marc Gaillard.
Paris jewelry store.
L'OEIL 1990 Nov., no.424, p.78-79,
port., photos.

STORES--JEWELRY--GERMANY (WEST)--
DUSSELDORF--GALERIE FU
Ambiente fur Schmuck und Kunst:
Gestaltung der Galerie FU in der
Trinkaus-Galerie an der
Konigsallee in Dusseldorf.
Designer: Inga FU.
ARCHITEKTUR, INNENARCHITEKTUR,
TECHNISCHER AUSBAU 1990 Mar.,
v.98, no.3, p.16-18, port.,
photos.

STORES--JEWELRY--GERMANY (WEST)--
ESSLINGEN--BODEN
Prasentationsmobel: Umbau des
Uhrmacher- und Juweliergeschaftes
Boden in Esslingen.
Architects: Mayer-Schneck-Mayer.
ARCHITEKTUR, INNENARCHITEKTUR,
TECHNISCHER AUSBAU 1989 Sept.,
v.97, no.9, p.50-53, dets.,
photos., plans, sech., sketches.

STORES--JEWELRY--GERMANY (WEST)--
GAILDORF--KUHN
Moderne Ladengestaltung in
historischer Bausubstanz: ein
Juweliergeschaft in Gaildorf nach
dem Umbau.
Architect: Daniela Kuhn.
ARCHITEKTUR, INNENARCHITEKTUR,
TECHNISCHER AUSBAU 1989 Sept.,
v.97, no.9, p.64-65, dwg.,
photos., plans.

STORES--JEWELRY--GERMANY (WEST)--
MUNICH--BREEDE
Kostbar: Juweliergeschaft Breede in
Munchen.
Architect: Norbert Schrowe.
DEUTSCHE BAUZEITUNG 1990 Oct.,
v.124, no.10, p.36-37, axonometric
view, photos., plan.

STORES--JEWELRY--INTERIOR DESIGN--
GERMANY (WEST)--HERFORD--JUWELIER
HEINO BACKES
Dezente Eleganz: Juweliergeschaft in
Herford: Eine Anerkennung beim
Deutschen Innenarchitekturpreis
1990.
Architect: Richard Pawlowski.
ARCHITEKTUR, INNENARCHITEKTUR,
TECHNISCHER AUSBAU 1990 Sept.,
v.98, no.9, p.70, photos.

STORES--JEWELRY--INTERIOR DESIGN--
GERMANY (WEST)--KREFELD--GIESSMANN
Schmuckstuck: Uhrenfachgeschaft in
Krefeld, 1. Preis beim Deutschen
Innenarchitekturpreis 1990.
Architect: Klaus Burger.
ARCHITEKTUR, INNENARCHITEKTUR,
TECHNISCHER AUSBAU 1990 Sept.,
v.98, no.9, p.28-30, photos.,
plan.

STORES--JEWELRY--INTERIOR DESIGN--
UNITED STATES--NEW YORK (NEW YORK)--
NIESSING
Niessing / Edie Lee Cohen.
Interiors of jewelry store on
Madison Ave., New York.
Architect: Toshiko Mori.
INTERIOR DESIGN 1990 Sept., v.61,
no.12, p.186-189, dwg., photos.

STORES--JEWELRY--ITALY--PERUGIA
Juwelierladen in Perugia = Jewellery
shop in Perugia.
Architects: Mario Solinas, Marco
Morettini.
DETAIL 1990 Oct.-Nov., v.30, no.5,
p.478-479, dets., elevs., photos.,
plans, site plans.

STORES--JEWELRY--JAPAN--TOKYO--VASARA
Atsushi Kitagawara / Atsushi
Kitagawara.
Contents: Vasara, Minato-ku,
Tokyo, design: 1989; construction:
1989 -- Kashiwara Town Center,
Minami-ku, Fukuoka, design: 1989;
completion: Sept. 1991. Text in
Japanese and English.
GA DOCUMENT 1990 Apr., no.25,
p.112-117, model, photos., plan.

STORES--JEWELRY--LIGHTING--UNITED
STATES--SEATTLE (WASHINGTON)--MONROE
JEWELERS
Jewel box: Monroe Jewelers, Seattle,
Washington / Donald J. Canty.
Interior lighting. Architect:
Olson/Sundberg.
ARCHITECTURAL RECORD 1990 Aug.,
v.178, no.9 suppl., p.14-[15],
photos., plan.

STORES--JEWELRY--SPAIN--TOLEDO--
ANTONIO IBANEZ
El hueco blanco: una joyeria de Yago
Bonet / Mario Bernedo.
Jewelry store in Toledo.
ARQUITECTURA VIVA 1990 Nov.-Dec.,
no.15, p.58-59, axonometric view,
photos.

STORES--JEWELRY--UNITED STATES--KANSAS
CITY (MISSOURI)--MEASE JEWELERS
Mease mystique / Robert Tibbetts.
Mease jewelry store, Kansas City,
Mo. Architects: Herbert Lewis
Kruse Blunck Architecture.
IOWA ARCHITECT 1990 Spring, v.39,
no.1, p.12-[13], photos., plan.

STORES--JEWELRY--UNITED STATES--
MINNEAPOLIS (MINNESOTA)--S-VINCENT
Lean elegance: a jeweler's studio
functions as both showroom and
gallery.
S-Vincent, Minneapolis store.
Architect: Gary Johnson.
ARCHITECTURE MINNESOTA 1990
Jan.-Feb., v.16, no.1, p.30-31,
photos.

STORES--JEWELRY--UNITED STATES--NEW
YORK (NEW YORK)--BULGARI
730 Fifth Avenue, New York = Il
nuovo negozio Bulgari / Paul
Goldberger.
Architects: Piero Sartogo
Architetti Associati: Piero
Sartogo and Nathalie Grenon.
L'ARCA 1990 Apr., no.37, p.72-79,
elevs., photos, plans, secn.
730 Fifth Avenue, New York / Paul
Goldberger and Richard Reid.
Bulgari shop, Crown Building.
Architect: Piero Sartogo.
L'ARCA 1990 June, no.39 suppl.,
p.[1]-61, dets., elevs., photos.

STORES--JEWELRY--UNITED STATES--NEW
YORK (NEW YORK)--EBEL
Ebel, here.
On the Manhattan shop and
headquarters. Architect: Andree
Putman.
INTERIOR DESIGN 1990 Mar., v.61,
no.5, p.154-[157], photos.

STORES--LIGHTING--MEXICO--MEXICO
CITY--CENTRO DE ILUMINACION
Bringing light: Centro de
Iluminacion, Mexico City /
Maragaret Gaskie.
Reuse of a 1940's apt. house into
a store. Architect: T.E.N., Taller
de Enrique Norten y Asociados.
ARCHITECTURAL RECORD 1990 Feb.,
v.178, no.2, p.84-87, elev.,
photos., plans.
Nitide luci in un fodero grezzo =
clear lights within a rough lining
[Light Center, Mexico City],
Architect: Enrique Norten.
ARCHITETTURA: CRONACHE E STORIA
1990 Oct., v.36, no.10(420),
p.72-71, elev., photos., plan.

STORES--UNITED STATES--NEW YORK (NEW YORK)--MOMA DESIGN STORE
MoMA store / Edie Lee Cohen.
Museum of Modern Art Design Store, New York. Architects: Hambrecht Terrell International.
INTERIOR DESIGN 1990 June, v.61, no.9, p.258-[261], photos., plan.

STORES--UNITED STATES--SAINT LOUIS (MISSOURI)--GREETING GALLERY
The Greeting Gallery, Missouri: Mario Corea y D. Gray, arquitectos.
Spanish, English text.
ON DISENO 1990, no.108, p.140-145, dwg., photos., plan.

STOREY, BRIT ALLAN
Federal Preservation Forum / Brit Allan Storey.
Report on a meeting held in Denver, December (?) 1989, for the purpose of organizing the FPF, with objectives "To enhance the quality, efficiency, and economy in ...Federal historic preservation programs."
CRM BULLETIN: A NATIONAL PARK SERVICE TECHNICAL BULLETIN 1990, v.13, no.5, p.7,
Three perspectives on preservation planning / Bruce J. Noble, Jr.
Summarizes three presentations about improving state and Federal management of cultural resources at the Preservation Challenges for the 1990s conference, held in Washington, June 5-7, 1990.
Speakers were Pat Stein, Judy Propper, and Brit Storey.
CRM BULLETIN: A NATIONAL PARK SERVICE TECHNICAL BULLETIN 1990, v.13, no.5, p.5-6, 17,

STORM WATER RETENTION BASINS
Stormwater management for the 1990s / Larry Roesner, Robert Matthews.
AMERICAN CITY & COUNTY 1990 Feb., v.105, no.2, p.44,46,48,50,52-54, photos.

STORM WATER RETENTION BASINS--UNITED STATES--FAIR OAKS (VIRGINIA)--HIGH RIDGE OFFICE PARK
A stormwater pond is wetlands mitigation amenity.
Stormwater management results in expanded and protected wetlands environment at High Ridge Office Park, Fair Oaks, Va. Engineers and designers: Greenhorne & O'Mara.
URBAN LAND 1990 Dec., v.49, no.12, p.28-29, plan, secns.

STORM WINDOWS
Interior storms for steel casement windows: the Drake Hotel (Drake Tower) Philadelphia Pennsylvania / Charles F. Fisher, Christina Henry.
PRESERVATION TECH NOTES 1986 Nov., no.20, p.1-6, diagr., photos.

STORMWATER RETENTION BASINS
See STORM WATER RETENTION BASINS

STORSLETTEN, OLA
Architectural photogrammetry: should the results be presented graphically or photographically? / Ola Storsletten.
Summaries in French, Italian and Spanish.
ICOMOS INFORMATION 1989 Oct.-Dec., no.4, p.26-32, dwgs., photos.

STOTZER, JORG
Erste Preise: Bauten fur Freizeit und Sport.
Four competitions: "Wildenstein" leisure center, Messtetten (architect: Heinz Becsei); outdoor pool, Bad Rappenau (architects: Rudolf und Ingeborg Geier, Jorg Stotzer); leisure and health club, Bonen (architect: Isermann & Jensen); gymnasium, Passau (architect: Willi Mortl).
DEUTSCHES ARCHITEKTENBLATT 1990 Oct.1, v.22, no.10, p.1511-1514, models, plans, secns., site plans.

STOUFFER & SMITH ARCHITECTS
Flying colors: Olmsted Center renovation, Drake University / Linda Mason Hunter.
Stouffer and Smith Architects.
IOWA ARCHITECT 1990 Fall, v.39, no.3, p.12-[15], photos., plan.
Stilwell Junior High School: School daze / Linda Mason Hunter.
Remodeling of principal's office.
Architects: Stouffer and Smith.
IOWA ARCHITECT 1990 Spring, v.39, no.1, p.18-[19], photos., plan.

STOUT, LEE
Vecta's Chicago showroom / Gregory Littleton.
Interior designer: Lee Stout.
INTERIORS 1989 Feb., v.148, no.7, p.98, photos., plan.

STOUT, WILLIAM, 1941-
Case con vista: San Francisco, un osservatorio attraverso i tetti = Houses with a view: San Francisco, an observatory through the rooftops.
Renovation of a Victorian cottage in North Beach, now the home of the architects, Bill Stout and Paulett Taggart.
ABITARE 1990 Oct., no.289, p.214-[221], axonometric view, photos., plans.
Per una brillante e cosciente modernita / Lucia Bisi.
House in San Francisco suburbs.
Architect: Bill Stout.
VILLE GIARDINI 1990 Jan., no.244, p.2-9, photos., plans, secns.

STOUTJESDIJK, HANS
Atrium als extraatje en als noodzaak: twee kantoorgebouwen van Lucas & Ellerman / Hans Stoutjesdijk.
The Tiel-Utrecht Verzekeringen, Utrecht, and the NMB-hoofdkantoor, Amsterdam, both completed late in 1989.
DE ARCHITECT 1990 Mar., v.21, no.3, p.79-89, axonometric view, elev., photos., plans, secns., site plan.

STOUTJESDIJK, HANS (CONTINUED)
Gezondheidscentrum Zoetermeer: rationaliteit niet identiek aan kwaliteit / Hans Stoutjesdijk.
Architect: Frits van Dongen, of de Architekten Cie.
DE ARCHITECT 1989 Oct., v.20, no.10, p.101-105, elevs., photos., plans.
Niet aangepast inpassen: meervoudige opdracht Victorieplein Amsterdam / Hans Stoutjesdijk.
Apartment buildings by Alberts & van Huut, Steigenga Smit Architecten, Holvast en van Woerden, Roelf Steenhuis Architecten, Kees Christiaanse Architects & Planners, Claus en Kaan, Kingma en Roorda Architecten, and DKV.
DE ARCHITECT 1990 Nov., v.21, no.11, p.50-55, axonometric views, dwgs., elevs., plans, secns., site plans, aerial photo.
Palazzo's in de Csaar Peter Buurt : Uytenhaak introduceert nieuw verkavelingstype / Hans Stoutjesdijk.
A 141-unit apartment complex located on Conradstraat, Amsterdam. Completed in July 1990.
Architect: Rudy Uytenhaak.
DE ARCHITECT 1990 Sept., v.21, no.9, p.100-105, elev., photos., plans, site plan.
Passage herstelt vitale schakel: Waagoverbouwing Dordrecht van Post Ter Avest Van Remundt / Hans Stoutjesdijk.
DE ARCHITECT 1990 Oct., v.21, no.10, p.121-125, photos., plans, secn., site plan.
Roze woonlint als groot gebaar: Van Herk & De Kleijn in Zuiderpolder Haarlem / Hans Stoutjesdijk.
Housing project, completed in Dec.1989.
DE ARCHITECT 1990 Apr., v.21, no.4, p.45-49, photos., plans, site plan.

STOVEL, HERB
Heritage recording: growth of a profession / Herb Stovel.
ASSOCIATION FOR PRESERVATION TECHNOLOGY. BULLETIN 1990, v.22, no.1-2, p.5-8, port.

STOVES--19TH CENTURY--UNITED STATES
"We have got a very good cooking stove"; advertising, design, and consumer response to the cookstove, 1815-1880 / Priscilla J. Brewer.
In the U.S.
WINTERTHUR PORTFOLIO 1990 Spring, v.25, no.1, p.[35]-54, ill., photos., engrs., refs.

STOVEWOOD MASONRY
See LOG-END HOUSES

STOYANOV, DAMIAN
Altered States / John Welsh.
On the work of Bulgarian architect Damian Stoyanov.
BUILDING DESIGN 1990 Mar.16, no.977, p.22-23, axonometric view, elevs., model, plan.

STOYE, WILFRIED
   Stadtebau und archaologische
      Stadtkernforschung: Ergebnisse -
      Erfahrungen - Probleme / Wilfred
      Stoye.
   Excavation report on the
      12th-cent. structures in
      Nicolaiplatz (now Regerplatz),
      Zwickau.
   ARCHITEKTUR DER DDR 1989 Dec.,
      v.38, no.12. p.30-33, elev.,
      photos., site plans, refs.

STRAESSER POLI LITTLE & ASSOCIATES
   Refurbishing an architectural
      landmark: 261 George Street,
      Sydney / Guy Allenby.
   One of Sydney's first "moderne"
      buildings, built 1939. Original
      architect: Adam Wright & Apperly.
      Architects: for restoration:
      Straesser Poli Little &
      Associates. Interior design: EGO
      Design.
   ARCHITECTURE AUSTRALIA 1990 Feb.,
      v.79, no.1, p.70-[71], photos.

STRAETEN, CHARLES VANDER, 1771-1834
   Le sculpteur Francois Rude
      (1784-1855) et les architectes
      Charles Vander Straeten
      (1771-1834) et Tilman-Francois
      Suys (1783-1861) au Palais royal
      de Bruxelles / Anne van Ypersele
      de Strihou.
   To be continued.
   MAISONS D'HIER ET D'AUJOURD'HUI =
      DE WOONSTEDE DOOR DE EEUWEN HEEN
      1989, no.81, p.4-[17], dwg.,
      elevs., photos., refs.

STRAIGHT TRACKS
   See LEYS

STRALEN, MARIETTE VAN
   Architectuur contra stedebouw:
      Ideeen en werk van Hans Kollhoff /
      Bart Lootsma, Mariette van
      Stralen.
   Projects by the Berlin architect,
      including a Berlin Museum design
      and Luisenplatz, housing, and
      KNSM-eiland in Amsterdam.
   DE ARCHITECT 1990 Oct., v.21,
      no.10, p.[60]-73, axonometric
      views, ill., elevs., models,
      photos., plans, secn., site plans,
      refs.
   Het atelier als manifest: woningen
      van kunstenaars en architekten /
      Mariette Van Stralen.
   Published in conjunction with a
      Fall 1989 exhibition at the DAM in
      Frankfurt, "Kunstlerhauser, eine
      Architekturgeschichte des
      Privaten".
   DE ARCHITECT 1989 Nov., v.20,
      no.11, p.105-109, photos., plan,
      refs.
   De opdrachtgever als visionair:
      Koolhaas blaast de Klassieke rol
      van de architect nieuw leven in /
      Bart Lootsma, Mariette van
      Stralen.
   Three recent projects: Sea Trade
      Center, Zeebrugge; Zentrum fur
      Kunst und Medientechnologie,
      Karlsruhe; Bibliotheque de France,
      Paris.
   ARCHIS 1990 May, no.5, p.36-45,
      ill., models, plans, secns.

STRALEN, MARIETTE VAN (CONTINUED)
   Prix de Rome als meeuwenkolonie:
      spektakel verdringt inhoudelijke
      aspecten / Bart Lootsma, Mariette
      van Stralen.
   Winners announced on 31 Aug.1990.
      Projects by Bert Dirrix, Roberto
      Meyer, Erik Knippers, and Rik
      Lagerwaard.
   DE ARCHITECT 1990 Oct., v.21,
      no.10, p.41-51, models, plans,
      secns., site plans, aerial photo.
   Retauratie atelierwoningen
      Zomerdijkstraat / Mariette van
      Stralen.
   Renovation of an apartment house
      in Amsterdam (built 1932-1934;
      architects: Zanstra, Giesen en
      Sijmons). Current architect:
      Bertus Mulder.
   DE ARCHITECT 1990 May, v.21, no.5,
      p.30-31, photos., plan, secn.,
      refs.
   Retoriek en pragmatische poezie:
      twee recente villa-ontwerpen van
      Jo Coenen en Rein Van Wylich /
      Bart Lootsma, Mariette van
      Stralen.
   Projects are a house with dental
      office, Berg aan de Maas, Limburg
      province (1989) and Villa Haans,
      Oisterwijk, Brabant (1987-1989),
      both in the Netherlands.
   ARCHIS 1990 Apr., no.4, p.44-50,
      axonometric views, models,
      photos., plans, secns., site
      plans, refs.

STRAND, MARK
   Nature study: the Maine woods
      provide a fertile landscape for
      painter Neil Welliver / Mark
      Strand.
   Studio and house.
   HOUSE & GARDEN 1990 June, v.162,
      no.6, p.108-[115],172, port.,
      photos.

STRANDBERG, KEITH W.
   Making connections / Keith W.
      Strandberg.
   Relationship between mass transit
      and retail development.
   MASS TRANSIT 1990 Nov.-Dec., v.17,
      no.11, p.21-23, photos.

STRAPPA, GIUSEPPE
   La biblioteca di Alessandria
      "ritrovata" / G. Strappa.
   L'INDUSTRIA DELLE COSTRUZIONI 1990
      May, v.24, no.223, p.70-71, dwgs.,
      elev., secn., site plan.
   Il nuovo cimitero di Terni.
   Competition. First place: Giuseppe
      Strappa and others. Second place:
      Luigi Caruso and others.
   L'INDUSTRIA DELLE COSTRUZIONI 1990
      May, v.24, no.223, p.76-77, dwgs.,
      elevs., site plans.

STRASBOURG (FRANCE). MUSEE D'ART
MODERNE--EXHIBITIONS
   Les batisseurs de cathedrales
      [exhibition review].
   Exhibition at the Musee de
      l'Ancienne douane, Strasbourg,
      through 26 Nov. 1989, on the
      achievement of the gothic
      cathedral.
   ARCHEOLOGIA 1989 Nov., no.251,
      p.17-18, ill., dwg., photo.

STRASKY, JIRI
   Fritz-Schumacher-Preise und
      Heinrich-Tessenow-Medaillen in
      Gold 1990.
   DEUTSCHE BAUZEITSCHRIFT 1990 Dec.,
      v.38, no.12, p.1727,

STRATA, MAURO
   Abitazioni a Lentale sul Seveso =
      Housing in Lentate sul Seveso,
      Milan / Roberto Gamba.
   Architects: Enrico B. Bona, Mauro
      Strata. Includes English
      translation; French, German, and
      Spanish summaries, p.3.
   L'INDUSTRIA DELLE COSTRUZIONI 1990
      Feb., v.24, no.220, p.12-17,
      axonometric views, photos., plans,
      sketches.
   Corti d'abitazione a Lentate sul
      Seveso / Roberto Gamba.
   Apartment complex. Architects:
      Enrico D. Bona, Mauro Strata.
      English, French, and Spanish
      summaries.
   ABACUS 1990 Apr.-June, v.6, no.22,
      p.66-73, dets., photos., plans,
      site plans.

STRATTON, MICHAEL
   Industrial monuments: a protection
      programme / Michael Stratton.
   On a 1986 program initiated by
      English Heritage. Includes
      abstract.
   INDUSTRIAL ARCHAEOLOGY REVIEW 1990
      Autumn, v.13, no.1, p.35-49,
      photos., refs.

STRAUVEN, FRANCIS
   Bakema = Bakema.
   Contents: Editorial, by Dick Apon.
      The big scale, by Arjen Oosterman.
      't Hool, twenty years of modern
      living, by Tom Dubbelman. A
      baker's cart in Buikslotermeer, by
      Inge Timmermans. Bakema, by
      Francis Strauven. Space for the
      pedestrian and the Friendships
      Model, by Wilma Visser. From the
      Euromast to the Dutch pavilion for
      Osaka, by Rob Dettingmeijer. And
      Bakema..., by Rob Dettingmeijer &
      Frans Hooijkaas. Biography. In
      Dutch and English.
   FORUM 1990 Sept., v.34, no.3,
      p.[1]-[49], dwgs., models,
      photos., secns., refs.
   Een functionele geest in een vreemd
      lichaam: De opera van de Bastille
      / Francis Strauven.
   ARCHIS 1990 Apr., no.4, p.12-19,
      axonometric views, models,
      photos., plans, secns., site plan,
      aeriel photo.

STRAW, ELIZABETH
   Vernacular houses: Middle Tennessee
      I-house / Claudette Stager,
      Elizabeth Straw.
   A regional interpretation of the
      central-passage house, frequently
      embellished with Greek revival
      details, built from the 1820s to
      1880s.
   OLD-HOUSE JOURNAL 1990 Sept.-Oct.,
      v.18, no.5, p.[4] of cover,
      photos., plan.

STREAMS--ENGLAND
  Some evidence for 12th- and
    13th-century linen and woolen
    textile processing / Mary C.
    Higham.
    Evidence of flax-retting pools, in
    northwestern England. Includes
    abstract.
    MEDIEVAL ARCHAEOLOGY 1989, v.33,
    p.38-52, maps, site plans, refs.

STREAMS--ENVIRONMENTAL ASPECTS--UNITED
STATES--FAIR OAKS (VIRGINIA)--HIGH
RIDGE OFFICE PARK
  A stormwater pond is wetlands
    mitigation amenity.
    Stormwater management results in
    expanded and protected wetlands
    environment at High Ridge Office
    Park, Fair Oaks, Va. Engineers and
    designers: Greenhorne & O'Mara.
    URBAN LAND 1990 Dec., v.49, no.12,
    p.28-29, plan, secns.

STREBEL, ERNST
  Stahlkonstruktion und Metallbau: Le
    Corbusiers & Pierre Jeannerets
    "moderne" architektonische
    Interpretation [book review] /
    Ernst Strebel.
    On "Immeuble Clarte Genf von Le
    Corbusier & Pierre Jeanneret," by
    Christian Sumi (1989).
    WERK, BAUEN + WOHNEN 1990 Oct.,
    no.10, p.16-19, photos., plans,
    secns.

STREET CORNERS
  Denkspiele im Quadrat: ein Exkurs
    uber Ecken / Gerhard Ullmann.
    DEUTSCHE BAUZEITUNG 1990 May,
    v.124, no.5, p.36-41, photos.
  Eckgeschichte: die Ecke in der
    Architektur / Horst Thomas.
    DEUTSCHE BAUZEITUNG 1990 May,
    v.124, no.5, p.115-124, photos.,
    table, refs.
  Lauter Ecken.
    Introduction to theme issue on
    "corners." 22 articles indexed
    separately.
    DEUTSCHE BAUZEITUNG 1990 May,
    v.124, no.5, p.12-13, photos.

STREET CORNERS--ALTERATIONS AND
ADDITIONS--GERMANY (WEST)--
SAARBRUCKEN
  Kecke Ecke: Umbau eines Eckegebaudes
    in Saarbrucken.
    Architect: B. Focht.
    DEUTSCHE BAUZEITUNG 1990 Mar.,
    v.124, no.3, p.34-35, photos.,
    plans, secn.

STREET DECORATION--TEMPORARY
  Incidental architecture / Stuart
    Pertz.
    Forms within cities of casual
    objects, such as stacked cardboard
    boxes, steam vents, signs, garbage
    cans, etc.
    PLACES 1990 Fall, v.7, no.1,
    p.4-7, photos.

STREET FURNITURE
  See also MAILBOXES
  Le design urbain au FIFARC /
    Beatrice Loyer.
    On the exhibition of street
    furniture organized by FIFARC.
    Includes interview with Ugo la
    Pietra.
                    (Continued next column)

STREET FURNITURE (CONTINUED)
  Le design urbain au...(CONTINUED)
    TECHNIQUES ET ARCHITECTURE 1990
    Mar., no.388, p.130-133, det.,
    dwgs., photos.
  I piani di urban design = Planning
    urban design / Claudio Germak.
    Urban furniture plan projects for
    public spaces. Architects: Studio
    De Ferrari, Jacomussi, Germak,
    Laurini Architetti.
    L'ARCA 1990 July-Aug., no.40,
    p.82-87, photos., plans, secns.,
    site plans.
  La qualita dell'ambiente urbano = A
    quality approach to the urban
    environment / Bruno Gandino,
    Pierluigi Molinari.
    Street lighting and fixtures
    designed by Bruno Gandino and
    Pierluigi Molinari.
    L'ARCA 1990 July-Aug., no.40,
    p.74-81, charts, elevs., map,
    photos.
  Street furniture / Stephen Cluer.
    "A special Planner feature."
    THE PLANNER 1990 May 11, v.76,
    no.18, p.13-16, ill., port.,
    photos.

STREET FURNITURE--ENGLAND--LONDON--
GREENLAND DOCK
  Hard landscaping, Greenland Dock,
    Conran Roche Architects.
    ARCHITECTS' JOURNAL 1990 Nov.14,
    v.192, no.20, p.51-53, dets.,
    photos., plans, secns.

STREET FURNITURE--TEMPORARY
  Incidental architecture / Stuart
    Pertz.
    Forms within cities of casual
    objects, such as stacked cardboard
    boxes, steam vents, signs, garbage
    cans, etc.
    PLACES 1990 Fall, v.7, no.1,
    p.4-7, photos.

STREET, GEORGE EDMUND, 1824-1881
  Arley Hall, Cheshire: the property
    of the Hon. Michael and Mrs.
    Flower / Michael Hall.
    Site: 5 mi. north of Northwich;
    architect: George Latham; chapel
    architects: Anthony Salvin, George
    E. Street.
    COUNTRY LIFE 1990 June 7, v.184,
    no.23, p.140-145, elevs., photos.

STREET-LIGHTING
  See STREET LIGHTING
  La qualita dell'ambiente urbano = A
    quality approach to the urban
    environment / Bruno Gandino,
    Pierluigi Molinari.
    Street lighting and fixtures
    designed by Bruno Gandino and
    Pierluigi Molinari.
    L'ARCA 1990 July-Aug., no.40,
    p.74-81, charts, elevs., map,
    photos.

STREET LIGHTING--ALTERATIONS AND
ADDITIONS--UNITED STATES--CHICAGO
(ILLINOIS)--SOUTH LASALLE STREET
  What light breaks yonder window? /
    Michael J. P. Smith.
    Renovation of street lampposts on
    South LaSalle Street, Chicago.
    INLAND ARCHITECT 1990 Sept.-Oct.,
    v.34, no.5, p.23,24, photo.

STREET LIGHTING--GERMANY (WEST)
  Hennef: Komfortabler gehen,
    langsamer fahren / Reinhold Baier,
    Christof Peter.
    Redesign of Frankfurter Strasse in
    Hennef, Germany.
    BAUWELT 1990 Feb.23, v.81, no.7-8,
    p.338-339, photos., site plan.

STREET LIGHTING--SWEDEN--STOCKHOLM
  Lys over Stockholm / Sophus
    Frandsen.
    ARKITEKTEN 1990 Mar., v.92, no.3,
    p.86-89, dwgs., elevs., photos.

STREET-PORTER, TIM
  [Architectural photography:
    interview].
    Interviews with the photographers:
    Julius Shulman, Tom Bonner, Grant
    Mudford, Marvin Rand, Wayne Thom,
    and Tim Street-Porter.
    L. A. ARCHITECT 1990 Apr., p.4-7,
    photos.

STREET-RAILROADS--UNITED STATES
  On the rails / John Ellis.
    On the new light rail routes in
    the western U.S.
    ARCHITECTURAL REVIEW 1990 Sept.,
    v.188, no.1123, p.77-79, photos.

STREETCAR LINES
  See STREETCAR SYSTEMS

STREETCAR SYSTEMS--CONSERVATION AND
RESTORATION--UNITED STATES--NEW
ORLEANS (LOUISIANA)
  Transit transformation; New Orleans
    revives street lines / Thomas W.
    Sweeney.
    PRESERVATION NEWS 1990 Jan., v.30,
    no.1, p.1,3,20, photos.

STREETCAR SYSTEMS--UNITED STATES
  On the rails / John Ellis.
    On the new light rail routes in
    the western U.S.
    ARCHITECTURAL REVIEW 1990 Sept.,
    v.188, no.1123, p.77-79, photos.

STREETS
  See also ALLEYS
  See also BOULEVARDS
  See also CITY TRAFFIC
  See also CYCLING PATHS
  See also DEAD-END STREETS
  See also DRIVEWAYS
  See also MAIN STREETS
  See also PARKWAYS
  See also PAVEMENTS
  See also PEDESTRIAN STREETS
  See also PROCESSIONAL WAYS
  See also ROADS
  See also SHOPPING MALLS
  See also SIDEWALKS
  Discussion: streets as dramatic
    space / Osamu Hirao, Motoko Ishii,
    Manabu Saito.
    THE WHEEL EXTENDED 1990, v.19,
    no.4, p.16-23, ports., photos.
  Fractal analysis of street forms /
    Setsuko Mizuno, Hidekazu Kakei.
    Uses case studies of medieval
    German and Islamic cities. Text in
    Japanese; includes English
    summary.
    NIHON KENCHIKU GAKKAI KEIKAKUKEI
    RONBUN HOKOKU SHU = JOURNAL OF
    ARCHITECTURE, PLANNING AND
    ENVIRONMENTAL ENGINEERING 1990
    Aug., no.8(414), p.103-108,
    graphs, maps, tables, refs.

STREETS (CONTINUED)
  Never mind the width - feel the
    quality! / Ray Brindle.
    Design quality of urban local
    roads.
    AUSTRALIAN PLANNER: JOURNAL OF THE
    ROYAL AUSTRALIAN PLANNING
    INSTITUTE 1989 Dec., v.27, no.4,
    p.19-28, refs.
  Strassenzeichen / Nigel Coates.
    ARCHITHESE 1990 Jan.-Feb., v.20,
    no.1, p.58-65,72, photos., refs.
  Traffic safety, usability and
    streetscape effects of new design
    principles for major urban roads /
    Hartmut H. Topp.
    TRANSPORTATION 1989-1990, v.16,
    no.4, p.297-310, diagr., photos.,
    plans, sketches, refs.

STREETS--14TH CENTURY--ITALY--BOLOGNA
  Il controllo della citta: l'ufficio
    dei fanghi e strade a Bologna nel
    XIII secolo / Roberto Greci.
    In Italian; English, French,
    German and Spanish summaries,
    p.128.
    STORIA DELLA CITTA 1988
    July-Sept., v.13, no.47,
    p.119-124, 128, refs.

STREETS--19TH CENTURY--ENGLAND--LONDON
  James Pennethorne and London street
    improvements, 1838-1855 / Geoffrey
    Tyack.
    LONDON JOURNAL 1990, v.15, no.1,
    p.[38]-56, ill., elev., photos.,
    plans, refs.

STREETS--ALTERATIONS AND ADDITIONS--
COMPETITIONS--GERMANY (WEST)--
STUTTGART--NECKARSTRASSE
  Erste Preise: Stadt- und Ortskerne.
    Three projects: Innenstadt
    Grevenbroich (architects: Ruth
    Paffrath-Baureis, Heinrich
    Schneider); Neckarstrasse
    Stuttgart (architect: Gunter H.
    Telian); Innenstadt Puttlingen
    (architect: Hubertus Wandel).
    DEUTSCHES ARCHITEKTENBLATT 1990
    Nov.1, v.22, no.11, p.1699-1702,
    dwgs., models, site plans.
  Neckarstrase in Stuttgart =
    Neckarstrasse in Stuttgart.
    Competition. Winning architect:
    Gunter H. Telian. Includes four
    other entries. Text in German.
    ARCHITEKTUR + WETTBEWERBE 1990
    Sept., no.143, p.47-53, models,
    maps, secns., site plans,
    sketches.
  Stadtebaulicher Ideenwettbewerb
    Neckarstrasse Stuttgart.
    First prize: Gunter H. Telian.
    Second prize: Kammerer, Belz,
    Kucher.
    BAUWELT 1990 Feb.9, v.81, no.6,
    p.245-248, models, site plans.

STREETS--ALTERATIONS AND ADDITIONS--
GERMANY (WEST)--HENNEF--FRANKFURTER
STRASSE
  Hennef: Komfortabler gehen,
    langsamer fahren / Reinhold Baier,
    Christof Peter.
    Redesign of Frankfurter Strasse in
    Hennef, Germany.
    BAUWELT 1990 Feb.23, v.81, no.7-8,
    p.338-339, photos., site plan.

STREETS--ALTERATIONS AND ADDITIONS--
ITALY--ROME--VIA DEI FORI IMPERIALI
  Proposta di sistemazione della
    testata di via dei Fori Imperiali
    su piazza del Colosseo: proposal
    for settlement of the Via dei Fori
    Imperiali head facing Piazza del
    Colosseo / Sergio Rotondi.
    L'INDUSTRIA DELLE COSTRUZIONI 1990
    June, v.24, no.224, p.50-57,
    axonometric views, dwgs., photos.,
    site plans, refs.

STREETS--ALTERATIONS AND ADDITIONS--
SPAIN--BARCELONA--AVENIDA RIO DE
JANEIRO
  Urbanizacion de la avenida Rio de
    Janeiro de Barcelona: P. Bardaji y
    C. Teixidor, arquitectos.
    Text in Spanish and English.
    ON DISENO 1990, no.116, p.124-133,
    photos., site plan.

STREETS--ALTERATIONS AND ADDITIONS--
UNITED STATES--MEMPHIS (TENNESSEE)--
BEALE STREET
  Peabody Place & Beale Street,
    downtown Memphis.
    One of six urban design reports
    included in special issue, Urban
    Concepts. Extracted from a 1987
    Center City Development Plan for
    Downtown Memphis.
    ARCHITECTURAL DESIGN 1990, v.60,
    no.1-2, p.76-87, dwgs., maps,
    photos., sketches, aerial photos.

STREETS--ALTERATIONS AND ADDITIONS--
UNITED STATES--MEMPHIS (TENNESSEE)--
PEABODY PLACE
  Peabody Place & Beale Street,
    downtown Memphis.
    One of six urban design reports
    included in special issue, Urban
    Concepts. Extracted from a 1987
    Center City Development Plan for
    Downtown Memphis.
    ARCHITECTURAL DESIGN 1990, v.60,
    no.1-2, p.76-87, dwgs., maps,
    photos., sketches, aerial photos.

STREETS--ALTERATIONS AND ADDITIONS--
UNITED STATES--MIAMI BEACH
(FLORIDA)--WASHINGTON AVENUE
  Washington Avenue, Miami Beach.
    One of six urban design reports
    included in special issue, Urban
    Concepts. Extracted from a 1979
    plan for the revitalisation of the
    neighborhood. Architects: Venturi
    and Rauch.
    ARCHITECTURAL DESIGN 1990, v.60,
    no.1-2, p.70-75, dwgs., elevs.,
    photos., site plans.

STREETS--ALTERATIONS AND ADDITIONS--
UNITED STATES--MINNEAPOLIS
(MINNESOTA)--HENNEPIN AVENUE
  Hennepin Avenue, Minneapolis.
    One of six urban design reports
    included in special issue, Urban
    Concepts. Extracted from a 1981
    plan by Denise Scott Brown, in
    collaboration with
    Bennett-Ringrose-Wolsfeld-Jarvis-G
    ardner and Williams/O'Brien
    Associates.
    ARCHITECTURAL DESIGN 1990, v.60,
    no.1-2. p.62-69, dwgs., elev.,
    photos., site plans, sketches.

STREETS--ALTERATIONS AND ADDITIONS--
UNITED STATES--MINNEAPOLIS
(MINNESOTA)--HENNEPIN AVENUE
                    (CONTINUED)
  Unbuilt Minnesota: Venturi, Rauch &
    Scott Brown's 1981 redesign
    proposal for Hennepin Avenue /
    Robert Gerloff.
    ARCHITECTURE MINNESOTA 1990
    July-Aug., v.16, no.4, p.49, ill.

STREETS--AUSTRALIA
  Residential road planning in western
    Australia: from policy to practice
    / Michael Pearson.
    "Underwidth" roads in residential
    neighborhoods.
    AUSTRALIAN PLANNER: JOURNAL OF THE
    ROYAL AUSTRALIAN PLANNING
    INSTITUTE 1989 Sept., v.27, no.3,
    p.21-23, photos.
  The S. A. [South Australian]
    residential street management
    (RSM) guidelines: motivations and
    some key practical outcomes / Sam
    Amamoo.
    AUSTRALIAN PLANNER: JOURNAL OF THE
    ROYAL AUSTRALIAN PLANNING
    INSTITUTE 1989 Sept., v.27, no.3,
    p.24-25, biblio., ref.

STREETS--AUSTRALIA--ADELAIDE
  Then, before, and after: a suburban
    triology: a case study of a
    hundred years of urban
    consolidation ina suburban street
    / Brian Y. Harper.
    AUSTRALIAN PLANNER: JOURNAL OF THE
    ROYAL AUSTRALIAN PLANNING
    INSTITUTE 1990 Sept., v.28, no.3,
    p.48-52, ill., plans.

STREETS--AUSTRALIA--RESEARCH
  JVMAH findings on residential
    streets / Barry E. Howe, George
    Alexiou.
    Studies sponsored by the Joint
    Venture for More Affordable
    Housing.
    AUSTRALIAN PLANNER: JOURNAL OF THE
    ROYAL AUSTRALIAN PLANNING
    INSTITUTE 1989 Sept., v.27, no.3,
    p.6-11, plans, secns., tables,
    refs.

STREETS--BELGIUM--BRUGES
  Flanderns popler / John Jedbo.
    Four examples of the use of rows
    of poplars, in Flanders, along
    streets and canals.
    LANDSKAB 1990 Feb., v.71, no.1,
    p.18-21, photos.

STREETS--CLEANING--UNITED STATES--NEW
YORK (NEW YORK)
  Scorecard: New York recherche
    proprete desesperement: evaluation
    et conscience civique / Michel
    Conan.
    Keeping New York's streets clean
    despite fiscal cutbacks. In
    French; summaries in French,
    English, Spanish and German
    pp.[123]-125.
    LES ANNALES DE LA RECHERCHE
    URBAINE 1990 June-July, no.47,
    p.34-44, photos., refs.

STREETS--COBBLESTONE--NORWAY--BERGEN
Fornyelse av boligstrok og bygulv i Bergen / Ola Bettum.
Rehabilitation of granite cobblestone streets since 1980. Landscape architects: Aall-Lokeland-Ragde Arkitektkontor; Skjold-Saegrov-Torpe; Cubus. Includes English translation.
LANDSKAB 1990 Sept., v.71, no.6, p.N-14-N-15, photos., site plan.

STREETS--ECONOMIC ASPECTS
Congestion: market pricing for parking /David Banister.
BUILT ENVIRONMENT 1989, v.15, no.3-4, p.251-256, photos., tables, refs.

STREETS--ENGLAND--LONDON--SHAD THAMES
Street wise [Shad Thames, London] / Dan Cruickshank.
In the London Docklands development area.
ARCHITECTS' JOURNAL 1990 May 16, v.191, no.20, p.26-29, map, photos.

STREETS--ENVIRONMENTAL ASPECTS--RESEARCH--JAPAN
Three dimensional analysis of turbulent flowfield around street blocks by means of large eddy simulation / Shuzo Murakami.
"Large eddy simulation 1". Text in Japanese; English summary, p.1.
NIHON KENCHIKU GAKKAI KEIKAKUKEI RONBUN HOKOKU SHU = JOURNAL OF ARCHITECTURE, PLANNING AND ENVIRONMENTAL ENGINEERING 1990 June, no.6(412), p.1-10, graphs, ill., tables.

STREETS--EUROPE
Die Dimension der Lange und der Reihung: das Probleme der Monotonie in stadtischen Strassenraumen / Franz Fischl.
SCHWEIZER BAUMARKT 1990 July 2, v.25, no.8, p.VI-VIII, plans, refs.

STREETS--FRANCE--PARIS--CHAMPS ELYSEES
Les diables et le bon pain / Claude Parent.
Criticism of the development and commercialization of the Champs-Elysees, Paris.
ARCHITECTURE D'AUJOURD'HUI 1990 Sept., no.270, p.36, ill.

STREETS--FRANCE--PARIS--RUE LAFFITTE
I piani pre-haussmanniani di Parigi.
Contents: Fra la rivoluzione dei lumi e i lumi della rivoluzione, by Juan Luis Pinon Pallares.--Dal 1790 al 1830: l'utilizzazione dei "bei nazionali", urbanistica e lottizzazioni a Parigi, by Bernard Rouleau.--Rue Laffitte: dal palazzo Thelusson alla chiesa di Notre Dame de Lorette, by Bruno Fortier, Philippe Simon.--I progetti di ingrandimento e di ristrutturazione di Parigi prima del secolo XIX, by Maurice Halbwachs.--La grande planimetria di Parigi di Edme Verniquet, 1774-1791, by Jeanne Pronteau.
STORIA URBANA 1989 July-Dec., v.13, no.48-49, p.3-126,
(Continued next column)

STREETS--FRANCE--PARIS--RUE LAFFITTE (CONTINUED)
I piani...(CONTINUED)
axonometric views, maps, site plans, table, refs.

STREETS--GERMANY (EAST)
3-D-Simulationsmodell zur Bewertung von Strassentrassen / Andreas Thierbach, Dietz Kohlhoff.
ARCHITEKTUR DER DDR 1990 Jan., v.38, no.1, p.36-37, dwgs.

STREETS--GERMANY (WEST)--BERLIN--FRIEDRICHSTRASSE - ECKE KOCHSTRASSE
Keine Kreuzung wie jede andere: Friedrichstrasse, Ecke Kochstrasse.
Written in 1984 for "Leitfaden", in conjunction with the IBA in Berlin. The first of three articles, indexed separately, in issue entitled "Zwischen West und Ost".
BAUWELT 1990 Apr.20, v.81, no.15, p.752-753, photos.

STREETS--GERMANY (WEST)--BONN
Tempo-30-Zonen: mehr Lebensqualitat in innerortlichen Wohngebieten? / Klaus Borchard, Theo Kotter.
On speed limit and street planning done in Bonn.
DEUTSCHE BAUZEITSCHRIFT 1990 Mar., v.38, no.3, p.389-392,395-397, dwgs., photos., tables, refs.

STREETS--GERMANY (WEST)--SPEYER--MAXIMILIANSTRASSE
Stadt und Verkehr.
Special issue on towns and traffic. 22 projects illustrated. English summary, p.53.
BAUMEISTER 1990 Aug., v.87, no.8, p.13-53, dwgs., models, photos., plans, secns., site plans, aerial photos.

STREETS--HUMAN FACTORS
Center stage for human drama: streets as common space / Yasuhiro Hamano.
THE WHEEL EXTENDED 1990, no.74, p.[10-16], axonometric view, dwgs., elev., photos.

STREETS--ITALY--BOLOGNA
Piano della mobilita per la citta di Bologna / Bernhard Winkler.
Article forms most of this issue. Presents the traffic scheme for Bologna proposed by Prof. Winkler. Summaries in French, English, German, and Spanish, p.1. Captions in Italian and English. Includes commentary by Claudio Sassi, and German text on p.88-89.
PARAMETRO 1990 Mar.-Apr., no.177, p.19-67,cover, dwgs., port., maps, photos., site plans, tables, engrs., aerial photos.

STREETS--ITALY--ROME--VIA DEL CORSO
Alexander VII and the private builder: two case studies in the development of Via del Corso in Rome / Dorothy Metzger Habel.
A study of construction history of the Piazza del Collegio Romano and the Palazzo D'Aste, during the late 1650s and 1660s. Includes abstract.
(Continued next column)

STREETS--ITALY--ROME--VIA DEL CORSO (CONTINUED)
Alexander VII and the...(CONTINUED)
SOCIETY OF ARCHITECTURAL HISTORIANS. JOURNAL 1990 Sept., v.49, no.3, p.293-309, elevs., maps, photos., plans, engrs., refs.

STREETS--ITALY--ROME--VIA NAZIONALE
Roma, via Nazionale: una strada per la citta (1859-1876) / Ivana Palermo.
English, French, German, Spanish summaries, p.125.
STORIA DELLA CITTA 1989 Apr.-June, v.14, no.50, p.11-50, dwgs., elevs., maps, plans, site plans, refs.

STREETS--ITALY--ROME--VIA TIBURTINA
Un intervento "modello" per Roma.
The Via Tiburtina viaduct, between the Via dei Monti Tiburtini and the Via F. Fiorentini.
L'INDUSTRIA DELLE COSTRUZIONI 1990 Oct., v.24, no.228, p.76-77, photos., secn.

STREETS--MAINTENANCE AND REPAIR
New streetscapes can revitalize cities / Fred Correale.
AMERICAN CITY & COUNTY 1990 Sept., v.105, no.9, p.36,38,40,42, det., photos.

STREETS--MAINTENANCE AND REPAIR--GERMANY (WEST)
Betonverbundstein-Pflasterdecke auf Umkehrdach: Verformungen des Pflasters.
DEUTSCHES ARCHITEKTENBLATT 1990 Feb.1, v.22, no.2, p.254-260, photos., refs.

STREETS--MAINTENANCE AND REPAIR--RESEARCH
Does the left hand know where the right one digs? / David Smith.
Principles and guidelines on pavement cuts and the improvement of street and sidewalk appearance; research conducted by the American Public Works Association.
AMERICAN CITY & COUNTY 1990 Sept., v.105, no.9, p.32,34, photo.

STREETS--NETHERLANDS--ROTTERDAM--ROTTERDAM AVENUE
Stenen Stad: Inrichtingsvoorstellen voor Rotterdam Avenue / Matthijs de Boer.
On projects from a workshop held 29 Sept.-1 Oct.1989 at the Academie van Bouwkunst, Rotterdam, for redesign of Rotterdam Avenue. Leaders: Manuel de Sola-Morales, Antonio Monestiroli, and Willem Jan Neutelings.
ARCHIS 1989 Nov., no.11, p.5, models, sketch.

STREETS--PSYCHOLOGICAL ASPECTS
Streets as landmarks / Giancarlo De Carlo.
Design of roads at urban peripheries.
PLACES 1990 Winter, v.6, no.2, p.80-83, photo., plan, aerial photo.

STREETS--RESEARCH--UNITED STATES
Patterns of behavior in urban public
spaces / Jack L. Nasas, A. Rengin
Yurdakul.
Includes abstract.
JOURNAL OF ARCHITECTURAL AND
PLANNING RESEARCH 1990 Spring,
v.7, no.1, p.71-85, charts,
diagrs., photos, biblio.

STREETS--SOCIOLOGICAL ASPECTS
Center stage for human drama:
streets as common space / Yasuhiro
Hamano.
THE WHEEL EXTENDED 1990, no.74,
p.[10-16], axonometric view,
dwgs., elev., photos.

STREETS--SOCIOLOGICAL ASPECTS--UNITED
STATES
Taking it to the streets: expert
prescriptions for healthy urban
arteries / Jane Jacobs.
Includes "The sensory street", an
excerpt from City: Rediscovering
the Center, by William Whyte.
CARTOUCHE 1990 Winter, v.19,
p.14-16,

STREETS--SOVIET UNION--MOSCOW
Il centro di Mosca e le attivita
urbane = Urban acitivites and the
centre of Moscow / V. Judincev.
In Italian, with English summary.
METAMORFOSI 1988, no.11, p.16-20,
photos., maps, refs.

STREETS--SPAIN--BARCELONA
La strada, elemento unificante nella
costruzione della citta: l'esempio
di Barcellona = The Street,
unifying element in the
construction of cities / Lilia
Pagano.
Planning of Barcelona streets.
LOTUS INTERNATIONAL 1989, no.64,
p.72-85, maps, photos., plans,
secns., site plans.

STREETS--UNITED STATES--LAS VEGAS
(NEVADA)--LAS VEGAS STRIP
Commercial vernacular in Las Vegas /
Steve Izenour, David A. Dashiell
III.
Update on the state of the Las
Vegas Strip.
RASSEGNA 1990 Sept., v.12,
no.43/3, p.80-88, photos.

STREETS--UNITED STATES--PHILADELPHIA
(PENNSYLVANIA)--BROAD STREET
A broad perspective: Philadelphia's
Broad Street claims a rich
architectural diversity / Thomas
Hine.
HISTORIC PRESERVATION 1990
July-Aug., v.42, no.4, p.16-19,
photo.

STREETS--UNITED STATES--SAN DIEGO
(CALIFORNIA)--BROADWAY CIRCLE
Reclaiming the streets: Horton Plaza
versus the need for a new retail
vision / Frank Wolden.
On various design concepts
presented for a pocket of retail
development in San Diego.
CARTOUCHE 1990 Winter, v.19,
p.8-9, dwgs., photos.

STREETS--UNITED STATES--SAN FRANCISCO
(CALIFORNIA)--BROADWAY
Broadway and Columbus / Larrisa
Bilaniuk...et al.
Intersection in San Francisco.
PLACES 1990 Winter, v.6, no.2,
p.72-79, photos., plan, sketches.

STREETS--UNITED STATES--SAN FRANCISCO
(CALIFORNIA)--COLUMBUS AVENUE
Broadway and Columbus / Larrisa
Bilaniuk...et al.
Intersection in San Francisco.
PLACES 1990 Winter, v.6, no.2,
p.72-79, photos., plan, sketches.

STREETS--UNITED STATES--WASHINGTON
(DISTRICT OF COLUMBIA)--CONSTITUTION
AVENUE
Un plan para la mejora ambiental de
las avenidas Constitution e
Independence de Washington / Abel
Enguita.
URBANISMO / COAM 1990 May, no.10,
p.118-127, charts, dwgs., photos.,
plans, secns., aerial photo.

STREETS--UNITED STATES--WASHINGTON
(DISTRICT OF COLUMBIA)--INDEPENDENCE
AVENUE
Un plan para la mejora ambiental de
las avenidas Constitution e
Independence de Washington / Abel
Enguita.
URBANISMO / COAM 1990 May, no.10,
p.118-127, charts, dwgs., photos.,
plans, secns., aerial photo.

STREHLE, UTZ PETER
Eine Schule zum Entspannen / Gerrit
Confurius.
School complex for hearing and
speech-disabled children, in
Johanneskirchen, Munich.
Architect: Utz-Peter Strehle.
BAUWELT 1990 June 15, v.81, no.23,
p.1136-1143, photos., plans,
secns., site plans.
Zum Wohl-Fuhlen und Lernen: Neubau
der Schwerhorigen- und
Sprachheilschule in
Munchen-Johanneskirchen.
Architect: Utz-Peter Strehle.
ARCHITEKTUR, INNENARCHITEKTUR,
TECHNISCHER AUSBAU 1990 May, v.98,
no.5, p.36-41, photos., plans,
secns., site plans.
Zwischen-Chaos und Zwischen-Ordnung,
in ubler Lage? / Utz-Peter
Strehle.
DER ARCHITEKT 1990 Jan., no.1,
p.30-31, models, photos.

STREK, BLA
Tourist tanks / Ulf Gronvold.
Marine aquarium, Lofoten, Norway.
Architect: Bla Strek.
ARCHITECTURAL REVIEW 1990 Aug.,
v.188, no.1122, p.49-[51], dwg.,
photos., plans.

STREY, BERND
Wohngebiet Benderstrasse / Bergische
Landstrasse, Dusseldorf-Gerresheim
= Residential area Benderstrasse /
Bergische Landstrasse,
Dusseldorf-Gerresheim.
Competition in Dusseldorf suburb.
Winning architect: Bernd Strey.
Text in German.
ARCHITEKTUR + WETTBEWERBE 1990
June, no.142, p.66-69, dwgs.,
models, secns., site plans.

STRIDDE, WALTER
Das Silberwerk: Kraftwerk
Bremen-Hastedt, Block 15.
Architects: Manfred Schomers,
Rainer Schurmann, Walter Stridde.
BAUWELT 1990 Oct.5, v.81, no.37,
p.1874-1881 cover, dets., elev.,
photos., site plan.

STRIFFLER, HELMUT
Der Fall Sevilla: Architektur ist
Botschaft / Helmut Striffler.
On exhibition buildings, followed
by 2 articles on the competition
for the German Pavilion at Expo
'92, Seville.
DER ARCHITEKT 1990 Dec., no.12,
p.569-573, models, photos., plans.
Money, Money .... Neubau der
Landeszentralbank in Saarlouis.
Architect: Helmut Striffler with
K. Kruger and L. Rieger.
DEUTSCHE BAUZEITUNG 1990 Mar.,
v.124, no.3, p.54-59, photos.,
plans.
Weltausstellungsarchitektur: der
Wettbewerb fur den deutschen
Pavillon fur die EXPO'92 Sevilla
und Fragen zur Architektur.
Projects by: Auer + Weber (1st
prize); Frei Otto; Joachim
Schurmann. Axel Schultes; Helmut
Striffler; Heinz Mihl; Storch +
Ehlers; Kurt Ackermann und Peter
Jaeger; Gottfried Bohm und
Friedrich Steinigeweg; Heinz
Hilmer & Christoph Sattler; PAS;
Kiessler + Partner.
BAUMEISTER 1990 June, v.87, no.6,
p.15-29, ill., dwgs., elevs.,
models, photo., plans, secns.,
site plans, aerial photos.

STRIKER, CECIL L.
Dendrochronology and the
architectural history of the
Church of the Holy Apostles in
Thessaloniki / Peter Ian Kuniholm,
Cecil L. Striker.
ARCHITECTURA 1989, v.20, no.1,
p.1-26, graphs., ill., elevs.,
photos., plans, secns., tables,
refs.

STRINER, RICHARD
Art deco: polemics and synthesis /
Richard Striner.
WINTERTHUR PORTFOLIO 1990 Spring,
v.25, no.1, p.[21]-34, photos.,
refs.

STRIP RETAIL CENTERS
Shopping for trends / Dan Martin.
Stores, shopping centers, malls,
and strip centers in the 1990s.
PLANNING 1990 Dec., v.56, no.12,
p.14-18, graph, dwgs., photos.,
secn.

STRIP RETAIL CENTERS--FRANCE
Shedlands / F.A. Pater.
Critical analysis of contemporary
retail/commercial building which
lines the routes into many
provincial French towns.
ARCHITECTURAL REVIEW 1990 May,
v.187, no.1119, p.102, photos.

STRIP RETAIL CENTERS--UNITED STATES--
LAS VEGAS (NEVADA)
Relearning from Las Vegas / Steven
Izenour, David A. Dashiell.
A return to Las Vegas to evaluate
how the strip has changed.
ARCHITECTURE: THE AIA JOURNAL 1990
Oct., v.79, no.10, p.[46-51],
photos.

STROBEL, ELISABETTA DE
Corte Amata: una cascina bergamasca
ritornata alle origini /
Elisabetta De Strobel.
Home of artist/poet Alfredo Pizzo
Greco. Architect for renovation:
Rosmary Pirotta.
AREA 1989 July-Aug., v.9, no.47,
p.40-[47], photos., port.

STROBEL, FRANK
Zwei zeitgenossische
Bestattungsprojekte = Two
contemporary burial projects.
Contents: Funeral island
mausoleum, Cologne, West Germany,
1989; architect: Frank Strobel --
Columbaria, Berlin, West Germany,
1988; architect: Michael Mussoter.
DAIDALOS 1990 Dec.15, no.38,
p.96-99, axonometric view, models,
photo., plans, secns., site plans.

STRODTHOFF, WERNER
Eine Ausstellung:
Revolutionsarchitektur [exhibition
review] / Werner Strodthoff.
DER ARCHITEKT 1990 Mar., no.3,
p.117-118, elevs.
Die Kirche als Bauherr-- ein
Beispiel: die Neugestaltung der
Benediktinerabtei Konigsmunster in
Meschede / Peter Kulka, Werner
Strodthoff.
Architect: Peter Kulka.
KUNST UND KIRCHE 1989, no.2,
p.82-83, axonometric view,
photos., site plan.
Redaktions- und Verlagsgebaude M.
DuMont Schauberg in Koln-Niehl /
Werner Strodthoff.
1st prize: Jean Nouvel. 2nd prize:
Behnisch & Partner. 3rd prize:
Hentrich/Petschnigg & Partner.
BAUWELT 1990 Sept.1, v.81, no.33,
p.1600, models.

STROHL, WERNER
Auszeichnung vorbildlicher Bauten im
Lande Hessen 1985-1989:
Vorstellung der Einzelergebnisse.
The 10th and 11th winning projects
in this competition: Grosser
Sendesaal, Funkhaus am Dornbusch,
Frankfurt (architects: Eugen
Soder, Werner Strohl) and
Diakoniezentrum der
Kathinkaplatzhoff-Stiftung, Hanau
(architects: Wilhelm Zuschlag,
Benita von Perbandt).
DEUTSCHES ARCHITEKTENBLATT 1990
Dec.1, v.22, no.12, p.316-317,
photos., plans.

STROLL, IRWIN N.
Melrose Bar & Grill / Mayer Rus.
Interiors of revamped restaurant
in the Pacific Design Center, Los
Angeles. Interior designer: Irwin
N. Stroll.
INTERIOR DESIGN 1990 Feb., v.61,
no.3, p.224-[225], photos.

STROM, MARIANNE
Under jorgens valv / Marianne Strom.
On design and materials of
ceilings in subway tunnels.
ARKITEKTUR: THE SWEDISH REVIEW OF
ARCHITECTURE 1990 Nov., v.90,
no.9, p.24-27, photos.

STROMBERG, KYRA
Von der Museumsinsel bis zum
Kulturforum: ein Zwischenbericht
zur neuen Berliner
Museumssituation / Kyra Stromberg.
KUNST & ANTIQUITATEN 1990, no.7-8,
p.8-12, photos.

STROOBANTS, JOS
De Onze-Lieve-Vrouw-Geboorte en
Heilige Philippuskerk te
Vivenkapelle: een Kroniek van
verwarming en verlichting / Jos
Stroobants.
A history of the heating and
lighting of this neo-gothic church
in Flanders. English summary,
p.75.
MONUMENTEN EN LANDSCHAPPEN 1990
Sept.-Oct., v.9, no.5, p.52-55,
photos., refs.

STROUD, RON
From images to achievement [Seaview
Marina, Wellington, N. Z.] / Ron
Stroud.
Inadequate facilities stimulate
studies for new recreational
access to Wellington Harbour, N.
Z.
PLANNING QUARTERLY 1989 Dec,
no.96, p.25-27, dwg., plan, aerial
photo.

STRUBIN, JOHANNA
Die Berner Werkmeister des spaten
16. bis zum Ende des 18.
Jahrhunderts / Andreas Kellerhals,
Johanna Strubin.
Summaries in German, French,
Italian and English.
ZEITSCHRIFT FUR SCHWEIZERISCHE
ARCHAOLOGIE UND KUNSTGESCHICHTE
1990, v.47, no.2, p.113-121,
chart, ill., refs.

STRUCTURAL FAILURES
See BUILDING FAILURES

STRUCTURAL FRAMES
See also HEADERS
Det konstruktive grundlag er
arkitekturen [book review]/ Karl
Christiansen, Per Dombernowsky.
Review of Arkitekturens
konstruktive grunnlag, by Bjorn
Normann Sandaker and Arne Eggen.
ARKITEKTEN 1990 Aug., v.92, no.10,
p.346-347, diagr., model, sketch.
Inspecting structural systems.
Based on an article by Thomas
Riggs.
COMMON BOND 1990 Winter-Spring,
v.6, no.1-2, p.5-7, diagrs.,
isometric dwg.
Structure design of architecture.
Theme issue on "structural
design." Includes six articles:
The future of structural design
with Fumihiko Maki and Terunobu
Fujimori; Circumstance and
periphery of structural design;
the past of structural design
1960-1990; Between structural
(Continued next column)

STRUCTURAL FRAMES (CONTINUED)
Structure design of...(CONTINUED)
engineering and architecture;
technology supporting structural
design and an interview with ten
architects entitled, Talking on
structural design. English
summary, p.31.
KENCHIKU BUNKA 1990 Nov., v.45,
no.529, p.entire issue, ill.

STRUCTURAL FRAMES--19TH CENTURY--GREAT
BRITAIN
Chi dimensionava le travi? / Andrew
Saint.
CASABELLA 1990 Dec., v.54, no.574,
p.25-26, dets., secn.

STRUCTURAL FRAMES--CHINA
Current structural features of
highrise buildings / Hu Shide.
BUILDING IN CHINA 1989 June, v.2,
no.2, p.9-14,35, ill., photos.

STRUCTURAL FRAMES--CONCRETE
High-strength concrete keeps going
up / Patrick J. Quinn.
For use in structural frames of
tall buildings.
CANADIAN ARCHITECT 1990 Aug.,
v.35, no.8, p.39, photo.

STRUCTURAL FRAMES--CONCRETE--GREAT
BRITAIN
Concrete.
"Technology special", with
articles on foam concrete, the
Concrete Advisory Service,
Broadwalk House in London
(architects: SOM), economy of
steel vs. concrete, and reinforced
concrete in recent projects.
BUILDING 1990 Apr.6, v.255, no.14,
p.51-74, port., photos., tables.

STRUCTURAL FRAMES--MAINTENANCE AND
REPAIR
Casi di restauro di monumenti allo
stato di rovina / Roberto di
Stefano.
Case studies on the restoration
and structural reinforcement of
five building in Naples, including
several Renaissance churches.
RESTAURO 1989 May-June, v.18,
no.103, entire issue (95 p.),
dets., photos., plans, secns.,
site plans, isometric dwgs.,
biblios.

STRUCTURAL FRAMES--STANDARDS
Structural glazing.
In Danish.
ARKITEKTEN 1990 June, v.92, no.8,
p.A198,A200, dets., photos.

STRUCTURAL FRAMES--STEEL
Beton + Stahl = Verbund: Zwei
Beispiele der Verbundbauweise in
Karlsruhe / Klaus Stiglat,
Bernhard Hockelmann, Josef Seiler.
The BGV, Karlsruhe, and the
Institut fur Meteorologie und
Klimatologie, Karlsruhe.
DEUTSCHE BAUZEITUNG 1990 Apr.,
v.124, no.4, p.91-98, dets.,
dwgs., elevs., photos., plans,
Double strength [composite
structure] / Denise Chevin.
Benefits from combining steel
frames with high-strength concrete
in columns of tall buildings.
(Continued next page)

STRUCTURAL FRAMES--STEEL (CONTINUED)
Double strength...(CONTINUED)
Examples are engineered by SWMB, a
Seattle firm.
BUILDING 1990 July 20, v.255,
no.29, p.62-65, photos., plans.
London Bridge: engineering:
structural steel / Marc S.
Harriman.
Exchange House, London, is
suspended by a structural steel
framework concealing a plaza
train tracks. Architects: SOM.
ARCHITECTURE: THE AIA JOURNAL 1990
Sept., v.79, no.9, p.109-112,
det., dwgs., photos., plans,
secns.
Metal-frame houses of the Modern
Movement in Los Angeles, Part 2 /
Neil Jackson.
"The style that nearly...".
Appendix lists 44 works by
architect's name, including
several Case Study Houses, by
Craig Ellwood, Pierre Koenig,
Raphael Soriano, and others.
ARCHITECTURAL HISTORY 1990, v.33,
p.[167-187], dwgs., photos.,
plans, site plans, refs.
Open bouwen met stalen dragers: ISB
woningbouwsysteem begint
proeffase / Joop Niesten.
New uses for metal in house
framings in the Netherlands,
including the Innovatief Systeem
van Bouwen.
DE ARCHITECT 1990 June, v.21,
no.6, p.86-89, axonometric views,
dets., photos., ref.
Polder als uitgangspunt: lichtvoetig
ontwerp van Teun Koolhaas /
Liesbeth Melis.
"Polderblik", house on stilts near
water in Almere.
DE ARCHITECT 1990 June, v.21,
no.6, p.81-85, elevs., photos.,
plans, secns.

STRUCTURAL FRAMES--STEEL--ENGLAND--
LONDON--BROADGATE--EXCHANGE HOUSE
(PHASE II)
External wall: offices: Skidmore,
Owings & Merrill.
Exchange House, phase II of the
Broadgate development, London.
ARCHITECTS' JOURNAL 1990 Oct. 24,
v.192, no.17, p.57-59, dets.,
elev.,photos., plan, secns.

STRUCTURAL FRAMES--STEEL--FRANCE
Details: logements: ossature acier /
Jean-Pierre Menard.
Contents: structural framework for
residential projects at Dijon,
Boulogne, and Givors; architects:
Eric Dubosc. Marc Landowski--
Artists' residence, Cachan,
France; architects: J.B.
Cremnitzer, A. Heinz-- Apartment
house, Troyes, France; architects:
C. Puaux, S. Maillard-- Office,
Paris; architect: Georges Maurios.
LE MONITEUR ARCHITECTURE AMC 1990
Sept.1, no.14, p.57-62, dets.,
photos.

STRUCTURAL FRAMES--STEEL--
NETHERLANDS--ARNHEM--BURGERS BUSH
Tropische Urwaldhalle "Burgers Bush"
in Arnheim, Niederlande = Tropical
forest hall "Burgers Bush" in
Arnheim, Netherlands.
Large greenhouse. Architects: Buro
Wiegerinck Architekten.
ARCHITEKTUR + WETTBEWERBE 1990
Mar., no.141, p.20, model, photos.

STRUCTURAL FRAMES--STEEL--SWEDEN
Steel construction.
A "technology special" section,
with articles on the reduction in
British Standard fire protection
requirements, steel works in the
U.K., prioritieis of the British
Constructional Steelwork
Association and a Swedish on site
steel building system.
BUILDING 1990 June 22, v.255,
no.25, p.53-66, port., photos.,
secns.

STRUCTURAL FRAMES - WOODEN
See also HAMMER-BEAM ROOFS
Lamelle-Colle: le bois en beaute /
Pascale Blin.
On the uses of glue-laminated
structural components.
TECHNIQUES ET ARCHITECTURE 1990
Dec.-1991 Jan., no.393, p.116-123,
dets., dwgs., photos.
Seaside story / Julie V. Iovine.
House in Seaside, Fla. Architect:
Victoria Casasco.
METROPOLITAN HOME 1990 July, v.22,
no.7, p.70-[75], photos.

STRUCTURAL FRAMES--WOODEN--
CONSERVATION AND RESTORATION
Altwohnbauten der Grunderzeit in
Sachsen - Geschichtspunkte der
Tragwerksplanung bei ihrer
Sanierung / Eberhard Berndt, Peter
Liebau, Udo Richter.
Technical information about
alterations to Mansard roofs.
DEUTSCHES ARCHITEKTENBLATT 1990
Dec.1, v.22, no.12, p.1859-1862,
1865, dets., graphs, photos.

STRUCTURAL FRAMES--WOODEN--ENGLAND--
DORSET--PARNHAM TRUST
Forestry commission / Peter Davey.
Parnham Trust woodworking school
and research center in Dorset,
built with forest thinnings.
Architects: Richard Burton and
Buro Happold.
ARCHITECTURAL REVIEW 1990 Sept.,
v.188, no.1123, p.[44]-48, dets.,
photos., plans, secns., site
plans.

STRUCTURAL FRAMES--WOODEN--GERMANY
(WEST)
Historische Holzkonstruktionen:
Gefuge und Statik von
Fachwerkhausern / Karl Hofmann.
DEUTSCHES ARCHITEKTENBLATT 1990
May 1, v.22, no.5, p.782-788,
elevs., secns., sketches, refs.

STRUCTURAL FRAMES--WOODEN--JAPAN
Size and layout of structural
members about Japanese wooden
building systems / Takashi Oono.
"A research survey on carpenter's
or builder's knowledges [sic] and
skills to work about wooden
building systems in Tokyo and
Kanagawa (Part 2)". In Japanese;
English summary, p.17.
NIHON KENCHIKU GAKKAI KEIKAKUKEI
RONBUN HOKOKU SHU = JOURNAL OF
ARCHITECTURE, PLANNING AND
ENVIRONMENTAL ENGINEERING 1990
May, no.5(411), p.17-23, graphs,
plans, tables, refs.

STRUCTURAL FRAMES--WOODEN--MAINTENANCE
AND REPAIR
Modernisierung eines Fachwerkhauses
in Velbert / Jorg Bohning.
The Haus Am Offers, built in the
late 17th cent. Architect for
restoration: J. Bohning.
DEUTSCHES ARCHITEKTENBLATT 1990
Jan.1, v.22, no.1, p.87-91, elev.,
photos., plans.

STRUCTURAL FRAMES--WOODEN--RESEARCH--
JAPAN
Plan and capacity of a house with
airtightness, thermal insulation
from the outside of the wooden
frame / Masashi Iida, Hiroaki
Kikuchi.
"A fundamental research on a
wooden construction method with
airtightness and thermal
insulation from the outside of the
wooden frame (part 2)". Text in
Japanese. Includes English
summary.
NIHON KENCHIKU GAKKAI KEIKAKUKEI
RONBUN HOKOKU SHU = JOURNAL OF
ARCHITECTURE, PLANNING AND
ENVIRONMENTAL ENGINEERING 1990
Sept., no.9(415), p.29-38, dets.,
graphs, photos., secns., tables,
refs.

STRUCTURAL SHELLS
See SHELL STRUCTURES

STRUCTURAL STABILITY
See also BRIDGE FAILURES
Det konstruktive grundlag er
arkitekturen [book review]/ Karl
Christiansen, Per Dombernowsky.
Review of Arkitekturens
konstruktive grunnlag, by Bjorn
Normann Sandaker and Arne Eggen.
ARKITEKTEN 1990 Aug., v.92, no.10,
p.346-347, diagr., model, sketch.
Et stalbaseret byggesystem / Frits
Gravesen.
ARKITEKTEN 1990 Apr., v.92, no.5,
p.170-173, axonometric views,
dets., dwgs., plans.
Statische Zwischenzustande beim
Umbau der Sanierung von
Mauerwerksbauten / Helmut
Bruckner.
DEUTSCHES ARCHITEKTENBLATT 1990
Nov.1, v.22, no.11, p.1727-1729,
1732, dets., secns., tables.
Vermeidung von Baufehlern und
Bauschaden bei
Stahlbeton-Schwimmbecken /
Cristoph Saunus.
DEUTSCHES ARCHITEKTENBLATT 1990
Nov.1, v.22, no.11, p.1745-1749,
dets., photos., refs.

STUBBS, M. STEPHANIE (CONTINUED)
EIFS get respect: manufacturers
discuss improvements in synthetic
stucco-based products / Douglas E.
Gordon, M. Stephanie Stubbs.
Exterior insulation finish
systems.
ARCHITECTURE: THE AIA JOURNAL 1990
Apr., v.79, no.4, p.119-122,
dets., diagrs., photos.
Federal building code: why still a
no-go / M. Stephanie Stubbs,
Douglas E. Gordon.
On the proposed new Fire
Prevention Code.
ARCHITECTURAL RECORD 1990 July,
v.178, no.8, p.31-32.
Light-filled heavy metal ...
professional services building
near Newark, New Jersey / M.
Stephanie Stubbs.
Arrchitects: Ronald Schmidt &
Associates.
ARCHITECTURE: THE AIA JOURNAL 1990
Jan., v.79, no.1, p.128-129,
dets., photos., secn.
Tent revival: Knott Athletic
Recreation/Convocation Complex /
M. Stephanie Stubbs.
In Md. Architects: Bohlin Powell
Larkin Cywinski. Structured
engineers: Horst Berger Partners.
ARCHITECTURE: THE AIA JOURNAL 1990
Jan., v.79, no.1, p.105-109,
dets., dwg., elev., photos.,
plans, secn.
The triumph of Union Station /
Stephanie Stubbs, Douglas E.
Gordon.
In Washington; completed in 1907.
Original architect: Daniel
Burnham. Restoration architect:
Harry Weese & Associates.
INLAND ARCHITECT 1990 Sept.-Oct.,
v.34, no.5, p.[43]-47, photos.,
aerial photos.

STUCCHI, SANDRO
Foro Traiano.
Eleven articles on the Forum of
Trajan including historical and
architectural reconstructions.
Authors: L. Messa, L. Ungaro, M.
Milella, P. Pensabene, G.
Piazzesi, B.M. Tummarello, S.
Stucchi.
ARCHAEOLOGIA CLASSICA 1989, v.41,
no.2, p.[27]-292, dets., dwgs.,
models, maps, plans, site plans,
recont. dwgs., refs.

STUCCHI, SILVANO
Alloggi universitari a Princeton =
Class of 1927 - Clapp Hall,
Princeton University, New Jersey /
Silvano Stucchi.
Architect: Koetter, Kim &
Associates. in Italian and
English; French, German and
Spanish summaries, p.3-4.
L'INDUSTRIA DELLE COSTRUZIONI 1990
June, v.24, no.224, p.26-31,3-4,
dwgs., elevs., photos., plans,
site plan.
L'ampliamento del Pacific Design
Center a Hollywood = Pacific
Design Center, Phase II, West
Hollywood, Calif. / Silvano
Stucchi.
Architects: Cesar Pelli &
Associates, Gruen Associates. In
Italian and English; French,
(Continued next column)

STUCCHI, SILVANO (CONTINUED)
L'ampliamento del... (CONTINUED)
German and Spanish summaries, p.4.
L'INDUSTRIA DELLE COSTRUZIONI 1990
June, v.24, no.224, p.32-37,4,
elev., photos., plans, secns.,
site plans.
L'ampliamento dello Stadio San Siro
di Milano = Extension of San Siro
Stadium, Milan / Silvano Stucchi.
Architects: Giancarlo Ragazzi,
Enrico Hoffer.
L'INDUSTRIA DELLE COSTRUZIONI 1990
May, v.24, no.223, p.36-53,3,
dets., elevs., photos., plans,
secns.
Ampliamento di uno stabilimento
industriale ad Aylesbury, G.B. = A
new headquarter extension for
Schwarzkopf Ltd., Great Britain /
Silvano Stucchi.
A hairdressing products firm.
Architect: Denton Scott
Associates.
L'INDUSTRIA DELLE COSTRUZIONI 1990
Feb., v.24, no.220, p.28-37,cover,
dets., elev., photos., plans,
secns.
Casa a corte pressa Barcellona =
Courtyard housing near Barcelona /
Silvano Stucchi.
Located in Mollet, 20km from
Barcelona. Architects: Josep
Martorell, Oriol Bohigas, David
Mackay. Includes English
translation. French, German, and
Spanish summaries, p.4.
L'INDUSTRIA DELLE COSTRUZIONI 1990
Mar., v.24, no.221, p.34-45,
axonometric view, dets., elevs.,
photos., plans, sketch.
Collegamento metropolitano di
superficie per l'area di Portland
= Banfield Freeway: a light rail
project, Portland, Or. / Silvano
Stucchi.
Architects: Zimmer Gunsul Frasca
Partnership. Includes English
translation. French, German and
Spanish summaries, p.3.
L'INDUSTRIA DELLE COSTRUZIONI 1989
June, v.23, no.212, p.26-33,
elevs., photos., site plans.
Complesso polifunzionale "Galileo" a
Firenze = "Galileo" multipurpose
complex in Florence / Silvano
Stucchi.
Architects: Marco Mattei, Alberto
Primi. Includes English
translation; French, German, and
Spanish summaries, p.3.
L'INDUSTRIA DELLE COSTRUZIONI 1990
Jan., v.24, no.219, p.14-21,
dwgs., elevs., model, photos.,
plans, secns.
Intervento residenziale nell'area
ex-Saffa a Venezia = Housing
development in the former Saffa
area in Venice / Silvano Stucchi.
Architect: Gregotti Associati.
Includes English translation.
French, German, and Spanish
summaries, p.3.
L'INDUSTRIA DELLE COSTRUZIONI 1990
Mar., v.24, no.221, p.6-15, cover,
dwgs., elevs., photos., plans,
secns., site plan.
Museo della storia dell'Industria a
Youngstown = Youngstown's Museum
of Industry, Ohio / Silvano
Stucchi.
Architect: Michael Graves. In
(Continued next column)

STUCCHI, SILVANO (CONTINUED)
Museo della storia... (CONTINUED)
English and Italian; summaries in
French, German and Spanish, p.4.
L'INDUSTRIA DELLE COSTRUZIONI 1990
Nov., v.24, no.229, p.38-43,
elev., photos., plans, secn.
Museo per l'architettura a Montreal
= Museum of architecture / Silvano
Stucchi.
The CCA. Architect: Peter Rose.
Includes English translation;
French, German and Spanish
summaries, p.[4].
L'INDUSTRIA DELLE COSTRUZIONI 1990
Oct., v.24, no.228, p.38-43,
elevs., photos., plans, secns.,
site plans.
Il Norwest Center a Minneapolis =
Norwest Center tower, Minneapolis,
Minn. / Silvano Stucchi.
Architect: Cesar Pelli &
Associates. Includes English
translation; French, German and
Spanish summaries, p.[3-4].
L'INDUSTRIA DELLE COSTRUZIONI 1990
Oct., v.24, no.228, p.32-37,
elev., photos., plans, site plan.
Nuove aule per l'Universita del
Colorado = North Classroom
Building, Denver, Colorado /
Silvano Stucchi.
At the Auraria Higher Education
Center. Architect: Hoover Berg
Desmond. Includes English
translation; French, German and
Spanish summaries, p.[4].
L'INDUSTRIA DELLE COSTRUZIONI 1990
Oct., v.24, no.228, p.28-31,
photos., plans, site plans.
Un nuovo edificio per la Liverpool
School of Architecture = New
addition to the Liverpool School
of Architecture / Silvano Stucchi.
Architects: Dave King, Rod
McAllister. Includes English
translation; French, German, and
Spanish summaries, p.3-4.
L'INDUSTRIA DELLE COSTRUZIONI 1990
Jan., v.24, no.219, p.22-31,
axonometric view, dets., photos.,
plans, secns., site plan.
Un nuovo edificio per l'Universita
della Pennsylvania = A new
building for the Pennsylvania /
Silvano Stucchi.
An information center and office
building between 34th St. and
Walnut St., completed 1985.
Architects: Geddes, Brecher,
Qualls, Cunningham.
L'INDUSTRIA DELLE COSTRUZIONI 1990
Feb., v.24, no.220, p.22-27,
photos., plans, secn., site plan.
Ponte pedonale ad Atlanta = A bridge
at Concourse in Atlanta, Ga. /
Silvano Stucchi.
Across an artificial lake at the
Perimeter Center, north of
Atlanta. Architect: Scogin Elam
and Bray. Includes English
translation; French, German, and
Spanish summaries, p.4.
L'INDUSTRIA DELLE COSTRUZIONI 1990
Jan., v.24, no.219, p.38-41,
elevs., photos., plan, secns.,
sketches.
Quartiere residenziale Rovezzano a
Firenze = Rovezzano housing
district in Florence / Silvano
Stucchi.
Architect: Gianfranco Di Pietro.
(Continued next page)

STUDENT HOUSING--ITALY--PISA--VIA
DELL'OCCHIO
Studentenwohnungen: Umbau in der Via
dell'Occhio.
Renovation to 18th-20th cent.
townhouses for student housing at
the University of Pisa, completed
in 1982. Architect: Massimo
Carmassi, with Gabriele Berti.
BAUWELT 1990 Feb.2, v.81, no.5,
p.219-221, photos., isometric
dwgs.

STUDENT HOUSING--JAPAN--TOKYO--OHTA
MEMORIAL HALL
Tokyo Metropolitan Ohta Memorial
Hall.
Built as student housing for
students from Beijing.
Architects: Masako Hayashi;
Hayashi--Yamada--Nakahara,
Architects. English summary,
p.27.
KENCHIKU BUNKA 1990 June, v.45,
no.524, p.139-148, photos., plans,
secns., site plan.

STUDENT HOUSING--SCOTLAND--EDINBURGH--
UNIVERSITY OF EDINBURGH--ROBERTSON'S
CLOSE
Halls of residence 2: case studies.
Student accomodation in Glasgow,
Edinburgh, and east London.
Architects: MacCormac Jamieson
Prichard for Queen Mary and
Westfield College, University of
London; The Kennedy Partership for
Forbes Hall, University of
Strathclyde, Glasgow; and Davis
Duncan Partnership for Robertson's
Close, University of Edinburgh.
ARCHITECTS' JOURNAL 1990 Aug.1,
v.192, no.5, p.49-53, axonometric
view, photos., plans, secn., site
plans.

STUDENT HOUSING--SCOTLAND--GLASGOW--
UNIVERSITY OF STRATHCLYDE--FORBES
HALL
Halls of residence 2: case studies.
Student accomodation in Glasgow,
Edinburgh, and east London.
Architects: MacCormac Jamieson
Prichard for Queen Mary and
Westfield College, University of
London; The Kennedy Partership for
Forbes Hall, University of
Strathclyde, Glasgow; and Davis
Duncan Partnership for Robertson's
Close, University of Edinburgh.
ARCHITECTS' JOURNAL 1990 Aug.1,
v.192, no.5, p.49-53, axonometric
view, photos., plans, secn., site
plans.

STUDENT HOUSING--STUDENT PROJECTS
Centro de Exposiciones = Exhibition
center.
Graduate student project by
Asuncion Rodriguez Montejano,
1989. Also a project for a
postgraduate residency. Text in
Spanish and English.
EL CROQUIS 1989 Dec., v.8, no.41,
p.170-179, dets., dwgs., elevs.,
model, secns., site plan.

STUDENT HOUSING--STUDENT PROJECTS--
MEXICO--MEXICO CITY--UNIVERSIDAD
IBEROAMERICANA--PLAYAS DE TIJUANA
Universidad Iberoamericana / Ralph
Roesling.
On Jorge A. Ozorno, dean of the
architecture school in Mexico
City, and the student projects
from there and from the New School
of Architecture (Chula Vista,
Calif.) for student housing at
Playas de Tijuana in Mexico City.
CARTOUCHE 1990 Summer, v.21,
p.8-9, 12-14, axonometric view,
diagrs., plan, elevs.

STUDENT HOUSING--UNITED STATES--NEW
YORK (NEW YORK)--COOPER UNION FOR
THE ADVANCEMENT OF SCIENCE AND ART
Bones and skin: competition for
student housing, Cooper Union, New
York, 1989 / Diane Lewis.
Architect: Diane Lewis.
AA FILES 1990 Autumn, no.20,
p.42-45, elevs., plans, secn.,
aerial photo.

STUDENT HOUSING--UNITED STATES--NEW
YORK (NEW YORK)--NEW YORK
UNIVERSITY--FILOMEN D'AGOSTINO HALL
Places to learn: New York University
Law School, Washington Square,
West Third Street, New York, New
York.
Contents: Mercer Residence Hall --
D'Agostino Hall -- Law Library.
Architects: Benjamin Thompson &
Associates. Text in Japanese and
English.
PROCESS: ARCHITECTURE 1990 June,
no.89, p.80-83, photos., secn.,
site plan.

STUDENT HOUSING--WALES--CIRENCESTER--
ROYAL AGRICULTURAL COLLEGE
Gebaudebeispiel: Vorabdruck aus dem
neuen Dachatlas Geneigte Dacher.
Roof details from 4 projects:
swimming center, Albstadt, W.G.
(P.Siefert et al); housing
development, Gebensdorf,
Switzerland (C. Tognola, C.
Stahel, D. Zulauf); student
housing, Wales (D. Lea); and
housing for handicapped,
Eastleigh, England (D. White).
DETAIL 1990 Feb.-Mar., v.30, no.1,
p.[16-23], dets., elev., photos.,
plans, secns., site plans.

STUDENT PROJECTS
See also "STUDENT PROJECTS" AS A
SUBHEADING AFTER SPECIFIC BUILDING
TYPES OR OTHER MAIN HEADINGS.
Assoziativer Raum: Diplomarbeit zu
einer raumlichen Analogie.
Student project by Silvia Sauer,
FH Mainz.
ARCHITEKTUR, INNENARCHITEKTUR,
TECHNISCHER AUSBAU 1990 Nov.,
v.98, no.11, p.76-79, dwgs.,
plans, secns., isometric dwgs.
History and verse: Indoor
Memorials, Atlanta, Georgia, John
Hejduk, Architect / Michael J.
Crosbie.
Two sculptural projects designed
by Hejduk and built by students at
Georgia Institute of Technology.
ARCHITECTURE: THE MAGAZINE OF THE
AMERICAN INSTITUTE OF ARCHITECTS
1990 June, v.79, no.6, p.70-73,
photos.

STUDENT PROJECTS (CONTINUED)
Islamic world architects at
Mackintosh School of Architecture
/ A.G. Vogt.
ARTS & THE ISLAMIC WORLD 1990
Autumn-Winter, no.19, p.105-107,
111, axonometric view, dwgs.,
maps, photos.
Movable feast / Justin Henderson.
Student Ken Jacobsen designs a
temporary restaurant at the
Pacific Design Center, Los
Angeles, for Westweek 1990.
INTERIORS 1990 July, v.149, no.12,
p.62-[63], photos.
Sei citta "ideali": ragione, storia,
arte / a cura di Enrico Guidoni.
Six student projects from the
Dept. of Architecture, Rome.
English, French, German, Spanish
summaries, p.127.
STORIA DELLA CITTA 1989 Apr.-June,
v.14, no.50, p.87-121, dwgs.,
models, maps, plans, biblio.
[Student projects 1988-1989].
YALE UNIVERSITY. SCHOOL OF
ARCHITECTURE. RETROSPECTA
1988-1989, p.[1-27], dwgs.,
ports., elevs., models, photos.,
secns.
[Student projects 1989-1990].
YALE UNIVERSITY. SCHOOL OF
ARCHITECTURE. RETROSPECTA
1989-1990, p.[1-27], ports.,
elevs., models, photos., plans,
secns., site plans.
[Student studio work].
Studio work from 1st-5th yrs.
MONTANA STATE ARCHITECTURAL REVIEW
1990 Spring, v.7, p.18-25, dwgs.,
elevs., models, plans, secns.,
site plans.
Washington University, Journal of
Student Work, School of
Architecture.
Entire issue devoted to studio
projects.
APPROACH 1989, no.6, p.[1]-[95],
axonometric views, dwgs., elevs.,
models, photos., plans, secn.,
site plans.

STUDENT PROJECTS--AWARDS AND PRIZES
'Poetic' design wins Moscow prize
for UCD graduate / Emer Hughes.
University College, Dublin student
Sam Gaine is first prize winner of
the First International
Competition for Graduate Projects,
held in Moscow. Winning project
was awarded for his design for the
School of Music, Iveagh Gardens,
Dublin.
PLAN: ARCHITECTURE AND BUILDING
DESIGN IN IRELAND 1990 July, v.32,
no.7, p.18-19, port., secn., elev.

STUDENT PROJECTS--COMPETITIONS
Arbeiten in der Stadt: ein
europaweiter Ideenwettbewerb fur
Architekten und
Architekturstudenten / Alex Lohr.
A competition design
energy-efficient work spaces
(schools, libraries, offices,
etc.).
ARCHITEKTUR, INNENARCHITEKTUR,
TECHNISCHER AUSBAU 1990 May, v.98,
no.5, p.76-80, dwgs., plans,
secns.

STUDENT PROJECTS--COMPETITIONS
(CONTINUED)
Concurso Internacinal de
Arquitectura para Estudiantes,
mayo 1990: American Institute of
Architecture Students.
2nd prize illustrated, for a
gallery in Helsinki, by 3 students
from the Madrid School of
Architecture.
ARQUITECTURA 1990 July-Aug., v.72,
no.285, p.24-25, dwgs., plans,
secn., site plan, aerial photo.
GE Superabrasives Student Design
Competition continues to grow with
worldwide participation.
On the 1989 award winners.
CRIT 1989 Fall, no.23, p.6-7,
ports.
'Poetic' design wins Moscow prize
for UCD graduate / Emer Hughes.
University College, Dublin student
Sam Gaine is first prize winner of
the First International
Competition for Graduate Projects,
held in Moscow. Winning project
was awarded for his design for the
School of Music, Iveagh Gardens,
Dublin.
PLAN: ARCHITECTURE AND BUILDING
DESIGN IN IRELAND 1990 July, v.32,
no.7, p.18-19, port., secn., elev.

STUDENT PROJECTS--COMPETITIONS--BRAZIL
Concurso Opera Prima: Premiacao 88.
Prize-winning student projects.
PROJETO 1989 June, no.122,
p.[101]-165, axonometric views,
ports., elevs., models., photos.,
plans, secns., site plans,
sketches., isometric dwgs.

STUDENT PROJECTS--COMPETITIONS--
ROMANIA--BUCHAREST
Testing times [Romanian student
competition] / Louise Rogers.
Design competition held at the
"Ion Mincu" Architecture Institute
in Bucharest. Student winners
will spend 3 weeks in British
practices sponsored by the RIBA.
ARCHITECTS' JOURNAL 1990 May 23,
v.191, no.21, p.24-29, dwgs.,
elevs., plans, secns., sketches.

STUDENT PROJECTS--COMPETITIONS--
THEATRE A PLACE FOR ALL
Theatre a place for all: eighth RIBA
international student competition
1990.
Presentation of winning schemes.
First prizes won by Yen Ming Huang
(Grad. School of Arch. Taiwan).
ARCHITECTURAL REVIEW 1990 Aug.,
v.188, no.1122, p.63-82, dets.,
ill., elevs., models, plans,
secns., site plans, isometric
dwgs.

STUDENT PROJECTS--DENMARK--
COPENHAGEN--KUNSTAKADEMIETS
ARKITEKSKOLEN
Det bevidste brud / Jens Bertelsen.
Projects by four students in Cort
Ross Dinesen's studio at the
Kunstakademiets Arkitektskolen.
ARKITEKTEN 1990 Nov., v.92, no.17,
p.546-551, axonometric views,
elevs., models, plans, secns.

STUDENT PROJECTS--ENGLAND--LONDON
AA diploma honours 1989-90 / Raoul
Bunschoten, Wiel Arets, Stefano de
Martino, Peter Salter, Ron Herron,
Andrew Holmes and John Frazer.
Diploma prizes to Joel Segal, Voon
Yee Wong, Simon Hart, Toru Ogata,
Bobby Desai, Shin Egashira and
Matthew Waltman.
AA FILES 1990 Autumn, no.20,
p.95-101, dwgs., models, photo.

STUDENT PROJECTS--ENGLAND--LONDON--
BARTLETT SCHOOL OF ARCHITECTURE &
PLANNING
From the site to the metropolis /
Robert Cowan.
Innovative student project in
planning and architecture for
London at the Bartlett School.
ARCHITECTS' JOURNAL 1990 Nov.7,
v.192, no.19, p.13, axonometric
view, sketch.

STUDENT PROJECTS--EXHIBITIONS
Lernen durch lehren [exhibition
review] / Paulgerd Jesberg.
Review of student projects from
the Stadelschule Frankfurt on view
at the Deutscher Werkbund,
Frankfurt am Main.
DEUTSCHE BAUZEITSCHRIFT 1990 Dec.,
v.38, no.12, p.1722-1723, dwgs.,
elev.

STUDENT PROJECTS--EXHIBITIONS--GREAT
BRITAIN
Exhibitionism / Patrick Hannay.
Features projects from eight
degree shows in the U.K.
DESIGNERS' JOURNAL 1990 Sept.,
no.60, p.38-44, models, photos.,
plan, secns., sketches.

STUDENT PROJECTS--GERMANY (WEST)--
KAISERSLAUTERN--ZWISCHEN RATHAUS UND
BLECHHAMMER
Zwischen Rathaus und Blechhammer /
Peter Arnke.
Features projects from the
architecture student workshop held
in Kaiserslautern, Nov.27-Dec.2,
1989.
DEUTSCHE BAUZEITSCHRIFT 1990 Oct.,
v.38, no.10, p.1360-1365, models,
sketches.

STUDENT PROJECTS--GERMANY (WEST)--
LUBECK--FACHHOCHSCHULE LUBECK
Deutsch-deutsche
Stegreifarchitektur.
Student project from
Fachhochschule Lubeck.
DEUTSCHE BAUZEITSCHRIFT 1990 Jan.,
v.38, no.1, p.14-15, elev. plans,
sketches.

STUDENT PROJECTS--GREAT BRITAIN
Hello campus.
Features projects from summer
shows from several British
architecture schools.
BUILDING DESIGN 1990 Oct.5,
no.1006, p.26-33, axonometric
views, det., ill., dwgs., elevs.,
models, secns.

STUDENT PROJECTS--GREAT BRITAIN--
AWARDS AND PRIZES
Winning essays.
Presentation of the 1990 winning
projects in the RIBA President's
Medals for Architecture in
Education.
BUILDING DESIGN 1990 Dec.7,
no.1015, p.18-23, axonometric
views., dwgs., models, plans,
secns.

STUDENT PROJECTS--GREAT BRITAIN--
EXHIBITIONS
Express yourself / Mark Dudek.
Features student projects from
eight British architecture
schools. Discussion of diploma
shows at the Architectural
Association, Polytechnic of
Central London and the Brighton
School.
BUILDING DESIGN 1990 Oct.12,
no.1007, p.22,24,26-32, dwgs.,
ports., elevs., models, plans,
secns.

STUDENT PROJECTS--IRELAND--AWARDS AND
PRIZES
Creating a landmark for Derry City /
Emer Hughes.
Proposed waterfront development
for Derry by graduate student in
design at the Univ. of Ulster,
Belfast, wins the 1989 Graduate
Designer Award.
PLAN: ARCHITECTURE + INTERIOR
DESIGN IN IRELAND 1989 Nov., v.25,
no.11, p.17, ports., site plan.

STUDENT PROJECTS--ITALY--MILAN--DOMUS
ACADEMY
Scuola e design: la ricerca di Domus
Academy.
Student projects. Text in Italian
and English.
DOMUS 1990 Jan., no.712,
p.[70]-75, ill., models.

STUDENT PROJECTS--ITALY--SIENA--ILAUD
Mit Studenten arbeiten: ain
Werkstattbericht aus Siena.
Report an ILAUD.
BAUWELT 1990 Sept.28, v.81, no.36,
p.1760, photo.

STUDENT PROJECTS--SCOTLAND--GLASGOW--
AWARDS AND PRIZES
East wind / Brian Edwards.
On the winners of the Newman
Levinson Award for architecture
student work in Glasgow.
BUILDING DESIGN 1990 Sept.7,
no.1002, p.28-29, axonometric
view, elev., model, plan, secn.,
site plan, sketch.

STUDENT PROJECTS--SWEDEN--GOTEBORG--
CHALMERS TEKNISKA HOGSKOLA
Tema: utbildningen.
Introduction to section on
architectural education.
Contents: En skola for livet...,
by Jens Arnfred.--Mot en ny
helhet, by Thomas Thiis-Evensen.--
Elevprojekt. Includes student
projects from three Swedish
schools: LTH, CTH, and KTH.
English translations, p.57-58.
ARKITEKTUR: THE SWEDISH REVIEW OF
ARCHITECTURE 1990 Apr., v.90,
no.3, p.2-25,57-58,cover, dwgs.,
(Continued next page)

STUDENT PROJECTS--SWEDEN--GOTEBORG--
CHALMERS TEKNISKA HOGSKOLA
                    (CONTINUED)
Tema: utbildningen. (CONTINUED)
elevs., models, photos., plans,
secns., site plans.

STUDENT PROJECTS--SWEDEN--LUND--LUNDS
TEKNISKA HOGSKOLA
Tema: utbildningen.
Introduction to section on
architectural education.
Contents: En skola for livet...,
by Jens Arnfred.--Mot en ny
helhet, by Thomas Thiis-Evensen.--
Elevprojekt. Includes student
projects from three Swedish
schools: LTH, CTH, and KTH.
English translations, p.57-58.
ARKITEKTUR: THE SWEDISH REVIEW OF
ARCHITECTURE 1990 Apr., v.90,
no.3, p.2-25,57-58,cover, dwgs.,
elevs., models, photos., plans,
secns., site plans.

STUDENT PROJECTS--SWEDEN--STOCKHOLM--
KUNGL. TEKNISKA HOGSKOLAN
Tema: utbildningen.
Introduction to section on
architectural education.
Contents: En skola for livet...,
by Jens Arnfred.--Mot en ny
helhet, by Thomas Thiis-Evensen.--
Elevprojekt. Includes student
projects from three Swedish
schools: LTH, CTH, and KTH.
English translations, p.57-58.
ARKITEKTUR: THE SWEDISH REVIEW OF
ARCHITECTURE 1990 Apr., v.90,
no.3, p.2-25,57-58,cover, dwgs.,
elevs., models, photos., plans,
secns., site plans.

STUDENT PROJECTS--UNITED STATES--
CAMBRIDGE (MASSACHUSETTS)--HARVARD
UNIVERSITY--GRADUATE SCHOOL OF
DESIGN
A public rowing facility on the
Charles River.
Studio project at GSD, for site on
north bank of the Charles River
between the Mass. Ave. and Boston
Univ. bridges.
GSD NEWS / HARVARD UNIVERSITY.
GRADUATE SCHOOL OF DESIGN 1990
Winter, v.18, no.3, p.6-7, dwg.,
models, secn.
Transforming a strategic urban site
/ Joseph Ryan.
Student projects for the area
surrounding the Forest Hills MBTA
Station, Boston, in the urban
design studio led by M. David Lee.
GSD NEWS / HARVARD UNIVERSITY.
GRADUATE SCHOOL OF DESIGN 1990
Winter, v.18, no.3, p.9, site
plans.
Using landscape architecture to
address a civic space / Beth
McKinney.
Student projects for a 4.5-acre
civic complex in Burnaby, B. C.,
in a studio led by visiting
critics William Callaway and John
Wong.
GSD NEWS / HARVARD UNIVERSITY.
GRADUATE SCHOOL OF DESIGN 1990
Winter, v.18, no.3, p.8, models,
site plan.

STUDENT PROJECTS--UNITED STATES--NEW
YORK (NEW YORK)--PRATT INSTITUTE--
SCHOOL OF ARCHITECTURE
Form; being; absence -- Architecture
and philosophy.
Issue includes an editorial by
Stephen Perrella (p.84-87), and
sections entitled Language:
phenomenology and hermeneutics.--
Deconstruction: theory, practice,
and criticism.--Pratt faculty
projects.--Pratt student projects.
27 articles or projects are
indexed separately.
PRATT JOURNAL OF ARCHITECTURE
1988, v.2, p.1-228, ports.,
elevs., models, photos., plans,
secns., biblio., refs.

STUDENT PROJECTS--UNITED STATES--SANTA
MONICA (CALIFORNIA)--SOUTHERN
CALIFORNIA INSTITUTE OF ARCHITECTURE
Recent student work (and a few
comments) from SCI-ARC.
Includes discussion of the
architecture program at the
Southern California Institute of
Architecture.
L. A. ARCHITECT 1990 July-Aug.,
p.6-7, dwgs., models, sketch.

STUDENT PROJECTS--VENEZUELA--CARACAS--
SIMON BOLIVAR UNIVERSITY--SCHOOL OF
ARCHITECTURE
Cross-cultural explorations in a
company town: Judibana, Venezuela.
Exchange during spring and summer
1990 with the School of
Architecture at Simon Bolivar
University, Caracas, Venezuela.
Leaders: Alex Krieger, David
Gouverneur, Jose Miguel Roig.
Projects were for urban design of
the Lagover oil company town.
GSD NEWS / HARVARD UNIVERSITY.
GRADUATE SCHOOL OF DESIGN 1990
Summer-Fall, v.19, no.1, p.11,
photo., site plans.

STUDENT UNIONS--ALTERATIONS AND
ADDITIONS--UNITED STATES--DES MOINES
(IOWA)--DRAKE UNIVERSITY--OLMSTED
CENTER
Flying colors: Olmsted Center
renovation, Drake University /
Linda Mason Hunter.
Stouffer and Smith Architects.
IOWA ARCHITECT 1990 Fall, v.39,
no.3, p.12-[15], photos., plan.

STUDENT UNIONS--ALTERATIONS AND
ADDITIONS--UNITED STATES--HOUSTON
(TEXAS)--RICE UNIVERSITY--LEY
STUDENT CENTER
Special feature: recent works of
Cesar Pelli.
Contents: Editor's introduction--
Architects' statement / Cesar
Pelli-- Essay: Urban iconography
and the medium of architecture /
Gavin Macrae-Gibson, p.130-137--
Works: World Financial Center--
Norwest Tower-- Pacific Design
Center expansion-- Mattatuck
Museum-- Ley Student Center
expansion, Rice University-- Yale
Center for Molecular Medicine,
Yale University-- Carnegie Hall
tower-- Sunarhauserman
headquarters-- Fan Pier master
plan. Architects: Cesar Pelli &
Associates. Text in Japanese and
            (Continued next column)

STUDENT UNIONS--ALTERATIONS AND
ADDITIONS--UNITED STATES--HOUSTON
(TEXAS)--RICE UNIVERSITY--LEY
STUDENT CENTER (CONTINUED)
Special feature:...(CONTINUED)
English.
ARCHITECTURE AND URBANISM 1990
Feb., no.2(233), p.[59]-148,
dwgs., elevs., photos., plans,
secns., site plans.

STUDENT UNIONS--INTERIOR DESIGN--
UNITED STATES--DALLAS (TEXAS)--EL
CENTRO COLLEGE
Interiors.
Contents: Berg & Androphy Law
Offices, Houston (William F. Stern
and Associates); Majestic Diner,
Austin (STUDIO Texas); and, El
Centro College Student Center,
Dallas (Oglesby Group).
TEXAS ARCHITECT 1990 Sept.-Oct.,
v.40, no.5, p.40-43, photos.,
plans.

STUDENT UNIONS--UNITED STATES--MILTON
(MASSACHUSETTS)--MILTON ACADEMY
Low budget, high power / Justin
Henderson.
On the student center at Milton
Academy, Milton, Mass. Architect:
Cameron Roberts.
INTERIORS 1990 June, v.149, no.11,
p.134-[135], photos., plan.

STUDENT UNIONS--UNITED STATES--NORTON
(MASSACHUSETTS)--WHEATON COLLEGE--
BALFOUR-HOOD CAMPUS CENTER
A mending wall: Balfour-Hood Campus
Center, Wheaton College, Norton
Massachusetts / Michael J.
Crosbie.
Amsler Hagenah MacLean Architects
with Robert Neiley Architects.
ARCHITECTURE: THE AIA JOURNAL 1990
Jan., v.79, no.1, p.82-83, photos.

STUDENT UNIONS--UNITED STATES--SAN
DIEGO (CALIFORNIA)--UNIVERSITY OF
CALIFORNIA AT SAN DIEGO--PRICE
CENTER
Building Types Study 682: Campus
buildings: Extracurricular
education / Grace Anderson.
Four recently-completed buildings:
Salomon Center for Teaching, Brown
Univ. (Goody, Clancy & Assoc.);
Psychology Building, Vanderbilt
Univ. (Stubbins Assoc.);
Centennial Performing Arts Center,
Westminster School, Simsbury Conn.
(Graham Gund Architects); and
Price Center, Univ. of Calif. at
San Diego (Kaplan/McLaughlin/Diaz
Architects).
ARCHITECTURAL RECORD 1990 Aug.,
v.178, no.9, p.83-[95], elevs.,
photos., plans, secns., site
plans.

STUDENT UNIONS--UNITED STATES--SANTA
CRUZ (CALIFORNIA)--UNIVERSITY OF
CALIFORNIA, SANTA CRUZ
Centre of gravitas / John Ellis.
Student Center, U.C. Santa Cruz.
Architects: Fernau and Hartman.
ARCHITECTURAL REVIEW 1990 Nov.,
v.188, no.1125, p.64-67, map,
photos., plans, secns., site plan.

STUDENT UNIONS--UNITED STATES--SANTA CRUZ (CALIFORNIA)--UNIVERSITY OF CALIFORNIA, SANTA CRUZ (CONTINUED)
A regionalist union / Sally Woodbridge.
Student Center, U.C. Santa Cruz. Architects: Fernau and Hartman.
PROGRESSIVE ARCHITECTURE 1990 June, v.71, no.6, p.106-113, photo., plans, site plan.

STUDENT UNIONS--UNITED STATES-- SWARTHMORE (PENNSYLVANIA)-- SWARTHMORE COLLEGE--TARBLE STUDENT CENTER
Special feature: Venturi Scott Brown and Associates.
Contents: Brief history-- Works: Primate Center, Philadelphia Zoological Garden.-- Lewis Thomas Laboratory for Molecular Biology, Princeton University, 1986.-- Malcolm S. Forbes Jr. College, Princeton University, 1984.-- Gordon Wu Hall, Princeton University, 1983.-- Venturi house, Philadelphia, 1974-present.-- Izenour house, Stony Creek, Conn., 1984.-- House in New Castle County, Delaware, 1983.-- Coxe-Hayden house, Block Island, R.I., 1981.-- Tarble Student Center, Swarthmore College, 1985.-- Tree House, Philadelphia Zoo, 1985.-- Welcome Park, Philadelphia, 1982.-- Decorative designs.-- Essay: "Body language" and artifice: on some recent designs by Venturi Scott Brown and Associates. Text in Japanese and English.
ARCHITECTURE AND URBANISM 1990 June, no.6(237), p.[39]-150, ports., elevs., photos., plans, secns., site plans.

STUDENTS - HOUSING
See STUDENT HOUSING

STUDER, RAYMOND G.
The scientification of design: alternative platforms / Raymond G. Studer.
TRIGLYPH 1990 Summer, no.10, p.16-21, refs.

STUDIO 4
Diskussion pagar / Gunnar Lowenhielm.
On the General Study Plan for Swedish Schools, with illustrations of works by FFNS, Studio 4, A-TRE Arkitekter, Dranger & Kvant Arkitektkontor, and Fritzell Carlsen Arkitektkontor. Includes English summary.
ARKITEKTUR: THE SWEDISH REVIEW OF ARCHITECTURE 1990 Dec., v.90, no.10, p.[9,59,60], photos., plans, secns.

STUDIO 02 SIAL
Stavoprojekt Liberec Atelier 02: edifici per il centro culturale di Teplice / Sebastiano Brandolini, Silvia Milesi.
English translation.
CASABELLA 1987, v.51, no.541, p.4-13, elevs., photos., plans, secns., site plans.

STUDIO 80 (JAPAN)
Tower of power: Hotel Il Palazzo, Fukuoka, Japan / Karen D. Stein.
Architect: Aldo Rossi, Studio di Architettura/New York; associate architects: Studio 80; interior designers: Shigeru Uchida, Ikuyo Mitsuhashi, Aldo Rossi, Morris Adjmi, Ettore Sottsass, Gaetano Pesce, Shiro Kuramata, Alfredo Arribas.
ARCHITECTURAL RECORD 1990 May, v.178, no.6, p.70-[77], dets., photos., plans, secn.

STUDIO A
Yaokichi.
Two-family home with green grocery shop on first floor. Architects: Studio A, Kei Morozumi, Takeshi Matsumoto. English summary, p.19.
KENCHIKU BUNKA 1990 Apr., v.45, no.522, p.[75]-82, diagrs., photos., plans, secns., site plan.

STUDIO ACQUAMARINA
Linee contro curve / Marinetta Nunziate.
Porto Massimo, a cliffside resort village complex on the island of La Maddalena. Architects: Studio Acquamarina.
VILLE GIARDINI 1990 Feb., no.245, p.22-29, photos., plans, secn., site plan.

STUDIO ALCHIMIA
La casa delle Tartarughe: Centro Carapax per la cura delle tartarughe, Massa Marittima (GR) / Paolo Corrado.
Architects: Studio Alchimia.
PARAMETRO 1990 Nov.-Dec., no.181, p.6-7, ill., dwgs., elevs., photos.

STUDIO ALPHA ARCHITECTURAL DESIGN OFFICE
The cylinder house.
House in Todoroki Keikoku, 3-story cyclindrical element in the rear. Architects: Studio Alpha. English summary, p.23.
KENCHIKU BUNKA 1990 Aug., v.45, no.526, p.[85]-92, dwg., elevs., photos., plans, secn.

STUDIO APARTMENTS
See APARTMENTS

STUDIO ASYMPTOTE
Kilpailut: monumentin dekonstruointi = Deconstruction of a monument / Juhani Pallasmaa.
On the 1988 international competition for a monument in Los Angeles. Winners: Hani Rashid Studio Asymptote. Second prize: Kunnapu, Padrik and Siim. Includes English translation.
ARKKITEHTI 1989, v.86, no.7, p.79-85, cover, axonometric view, dwgs., models, plan, secns.
Three projects by Studio Asymptote: Hani Rashid, Lise Anne Couture.
Contents: Architects' statement, by Hani Rashid & Lise Anne Couture.--Project 1: Concorso do Comune di Lunciano, Italy, 1987.--Project 2: Los Angeles West Coast Gateway, Los Angeles, CA.-- Project 3: The Alexandria Library, (Continued next column)

STUDIO ASYMPTOTE (CONTINUED)
Three projects by...(CONTINUED)
Alexandria, Egypt.--Brief history. Text in Japanese and English.
ARCHITECTURE AND URBANISM 1989 Dec., no.12(231), p.[5]-28, dwgs., elevs., model, plans, secns., site plans.

STUDIO BOFFOLI MARPICATI ASSOCIATI
ICF: destinazione Banca = Banking on success.
Interiors of the Brescia branch of the Banca di Trento e Bolzano. Architect: Studio Boffoli Marpicati Associati. Interior designer: Stile Mobili Moderni. In Italian and English.
OTTOGANO 1990 Sept., no.96, p.172-[175], dets., photos.

STUDIO CITTERIO DWAN
Antonio Citterio / Brigitte Fitoussi.
Profile of the work of Citterio and Terry Dwan and their firm, Studio Citterio Dwan. Includes seven projects.
ARCHITECTURE D'AUJOURD'HUI 1990 June, no.269, p.[202]-222, axonometric views, ports., models, photos., plans, secns.
Antonio Citterio, Terry Dwan: casa sperimentale, Kumamoto.
An experimental house commissioned by the local government to demonstrate the use of timber for building. Text in Italian and English.
DOMUS 1990 Feb., no.713, p.8-9, axonometric view, photos., plans.
Shadow box: house in Kumamoto, Japan / Karen D. Stein.
A house to promote the Japanese lumber industry. Architect: Studio Citterio/Dwan.
ARCHITECTURAL RECORD 1990 Mid-Apr., v.178, no.5, p.[78]-83, axonometric view, photos., plans.

STUDIO DE FERRARI, JACOMUSSI, GERMAK, LAURINI ARCHITETTI
I piani di urban design = Planning urban design / Claudio Germak.
Urban furniture plan projects for public spaces. Architects: Studio De Ferrari, Jacomussi, Germak, Laurini Architetti.
L'ARCA 1990 July-Aug., no.40, p.82-87, photos., plans, secns., site plans.

STUDIO DINI E CAPELLI
La terza linea della metropolitana di Milano = Line 3 of the Milan underground / Michele Bazan Giordano.
Architects: Studio Dini e Capelli.
L'ARCA 1990 July-Aug., no.40, p.60-65, map, photos., secns.

STUDIO GPI
L'aeroporto su tre livelli = The airport on three levels / Lucia Bisi.
Project for enlargement of Bologna airport; architects: Studio GPI and PI4.
L'ARCA 1990 Apr., no.37 suppl. l'Arca 2, p.99, dwgs.

STUDIO GPI (CONTINUED)
La scuola dell''IBM = The IBM
education center / Anty Pansera.
IBM education center in Milan;
architect: Angelo Cortesi of
Studio GPI.
L'ARCA 1990 June, no.39, p.80-83,
photos., plans.

STUDIO GRANTA
Building on an awkward plot / John
Welsh.
On the Koenig house competition,
Wiesbaden. Winning architects:
Studio Granta. Includes second and
third prize designs by Beevor Mull
& Associates and Tom Heneghan.
BUILDING DESIGN 1990 Jan.26,
no.970, p.24-27, elevs., plans,
secns., site plans.
Drommenes hus i Wiesbaden / Esben
Larsen.
Competition entries by Danish
architects. First prize: Studio
Granta [sic]. Other prizes: Helle
Juul and Flemming Frost; Poul
Ingemann.
ARKITEKTEN 1990 Jan., v.92, no.1,
p.12-17, dwgs., models, photos.,
plans, secns., sketches.
Fit for the gods: Forty two dreams
for a house [exhibition review] /
Diana Periton.
Exhibition of competition
submissions for a house for the
Koenig family outside Wwiesbaden;
held at the RIBA, London, until 12
June 1990. Winning entry by
Studio Granta.
ARCHITECTS' JOURNAL 1990 June 6,
v.191, no.23, p.75, elev., model.

STUDIO HOF
Proposta per una piazza a Umbertide.
In Perugia. Architect: Studio HOF.
L'INDUSTRIA DELLE COSTRUZIONI 1990
July-Aug., v.24, no.225-226,
p.70-71, elevs., plan, site plans.

STUDIO METAMORPH
Case per la "Cooperativa desposito
locomotive Roma San Lorenzo",
Roma.
Architects: Studio Metamorph.
English summary, p.52.
METAMORFOSI 1989, no.12, p.52-63,
axonometric views, elevs., plans,
secns.

STUDIO NACO
[Amenagement interieur]: commerces.
Contents: Boutique Koshino, Paris
Ville; architect: Jean-Michel
Wilmotte-- Apple showroom, ave. de
la Grande Armee, Paris; architect:
Berbesson Racine et Associes--
Castelli showroom, Paris;
designer: Ronald Cecil Sportes--
Unifor furniture showroom, Milan,
Italy; architects: Afra & Tobia
Scarpa-- Boutique Jean-Louis
Imbert, Marseille, France;
architect: Rudy Ricciotti--
Recorded music store, Nantes,
France; architect: Studio Naco.
LE MONITEUR ARCHITECTURE AMC 1990
July-Aug., no.13, p.36-45,
axonometric views, photos., plans.

STUDIO NIZZOLI
Edificio per uffici a Milano.
Agricoltura Assicurazioni
building. Architects: Studio
Nizzoli. Summaries in English,
French and Spanish.
ABACUS 1990 Jan.-Mar., v.6, no.21,
p.34-41, elevs., photos., plan,
secn., site plan.
Lignano Sabbiadoro, il giardino dei
labirinti = The garden of the
labyrinths.
Open-air theater and walkway in an
Italian "tourist village."
Architects: Studio Nizzoli (G.M.
Oliveri, P. Viola).
ARCHITETTURA: CRONACHE E STORIA
1990 Nov., v.36, no.11(421),
p.770-777, elevs., photos., plans,
secns.

STUDIO STNR
Nuovi progetti alla Giudecca: tipi
di edificazione e morfologia
dell'isola = new projects at the
Giudecca: building types and
morphology of the island / Marco
De Michelis.
Includes projects by Gregotti
Associati; Studio STNR; Iginio
Cappai, Pietro Mainardis,
Valeriano Pastor; Giuseppe
Gambirasio, Bruno Minardi; Giorgio
Bellavitis, F. Nani Valle; Alvaro
Siza.
LOTUS INTERNATIONAL 1986, no.51,
p.78-107, axonometric views,
dwgs., elevs., maps, photos.,
plans, secns., site plans, engrs.,
aerial photo.

STUDIO TEXAS
Interiors.
Contents: Berg & Androphy Law
Offices, Houston (William F. Stern
and Associates); Majestic Diner,
Austin (STUDIO Texas); and, El
Centro College Student Center,
Dallas (Oglesby Group).
TEXAS ARCHITECT 1990 Sept.-Oct.,
v.40, no.5, p.40-43, photos.,
plans.

STUDIO ZOEVOX
L'hotellerie en mouvement.
On the hotel industry. Includes
eight recent hotel projects.
English summary, p.162.
ARCHITECTURE INTERIEURE CREE 1990
Mar., no.235, p.48-83, dwgs.,
ports., photos., plans, isometric
dwgs.

STUDIO ZUCKER
Il nuovo Stadio Olimpico a Roma =
The renovated Olympic Stadium in
Rome / Giuseppe Nannerini.
Project head: Annibale Vitellozzi
et al. Project architect: Studio
Zucker. Includes English
translation; French, German and
Spanish summaries p.[3].
L'INDUSTRIA DELLE COSTRUZIONI 1990
Oct., v.24, no.228, p.6-17, dets.,
models, photos., plans, secns.
Lo Stadio Olimpico di Roma = The
Olympic stadium in Rome / Giorgio
Sperelli.
New roof for 1930s stadium.
Architects: Studio Zucker: Josef
N. Zucker and Patrizia Zucker.
L'ARCA 1990 May, no.38, p.60-65,
elevs., photos., plans, secns.

STUDIOS
See also FILMMAKERS' STUDIOS
See also PHOTOGRAPHERS' STUDIOS

STUDIOS--ALTERATIONS AND ADDITIONS--
SWITZERLAND--ZURICH
Das Detail als Kommentar / Gunter
Bock.
An addition to a studio by Harry
Roos and Thomas Schregenberger,
Zurich, 1987.
ARCHITHESE 1990 Nov.-Dec., v.20,
no.6, p.54-[55], photos., models,
sketches.

STUDIOS - ARTISTS'
See ARTISTS' STUDIOS

STUDIOS (FIRM)
Apple Corps / Michael Wagner.
Feature interiors of Apple
Computer's office in Washington,
D.C. Architects: STUDIOS.
INTERIORS 1990 Apr., v.149, no.9,
p.78-[81], photos., plan.
Collaborative art / Amy Dana.
Interiors of Norwest Corp.
corporate offices, Minneapolis,
Minn. Interior designers: STUDIOS.
Architect: Cesar Pelli.
INTERIORS 1990 June, v.149, no.11,
p.108-119, ports., photos., plans,
models.
Legal maneuvers / Michael Wagner.
On the law offices of Rogovin,
Huge & Schiller, Washington, D.C.
Architects: STUDIOS.
INTERIORS 1990 Apr., v.149, no.9,
p.70-[73], axonometric view,
photos.
On the move, new AIA chapter
headquarters in San Francisco /
Justin Henderson.
Open plan offices located in the
1917 Hallidie Building.
Architects: STUDIOS.
INTERIORS 1989 Feb., v.148, no.7,
p.135, photos., plan.
Silicon Graphics / Edie Lee Cohen.
On the new corporate headquarters
for Silicon Graphics Computer
Systems, Moutain View, Calif.
Architects: STUDIOS.
INTERIOR DESIGN 1990 Apr., v.61,
no.6, p.166-[171], dwg., photos.,
plan.
Wheeling and dealing / Michael
Wagner.
On the Herman Miller office
Pavilion, Washington, D.C.
Architects: STUDIOS.
INTERIORS 1990 Apr., v.149, no.9,
p.74-[77], photos., plan.

STUDIOS - PHOTOGRAPHERS'
See PHOTOGRAPHERS' STUDIOS

STUDIOS - SOUND
See SOUND STUDIOS

STUDIOS--SPAIN--BARCELONA--PALO ALTO
Nuovi usi per la citta dismessa:
Barcellona, il Poble Nou = New
uses for run-down city areas:
Barcelona, the Poble Nou.
A feature on changes in this
outlying suburb. Includes an essay
by Octavio Mestre.
ABITARE 1990 May, no.285,
p.186-207, ill., dwg., elev.,
maps, photos., plans, secns.

STUDIOS - TELEVISION
See BROADCASTING STUDIOS

STUDIOS--UNITED STATES--SHELTER ISLAND
(NEW YORK)--PEDERSEN HOUSE
Formal axis in weekend clcthes /
Mark Alden Branch.
Features architect William
Pedersen's renovated 80-year-old
weekend home and studio on Shelter
Island, NY.
PROGRESSIVE ARCHITECTURE 1990
Nov., v.71, no.12, p.86-89,
photos., plans, secn., site plan.

STUDY AND TEACHING
See "STUDY AND TEACHING" AS A
SUBHEADING AFTER MAIN HEADINGS.

STUMPF, BILL
Memories at play: can design recover
the spirit of play and put
imagination to work? / Bill
Stumpf, Susan Packard.
ARCHITECTURE MINNESOTA 1990
Sept.-Oct., v.16, no.5, p.48-51,
photos.
To market, to market....a local
designer inventories the sights,
smells and civilities of the
grocery store of his dreams / Bill
Stumpf, Susan Packard.
ARCHITECTURE MINNESOTA 1990
Jan.-Feb., v.16, no.1, p.40-41,
photos.

STUPAS--CONSERVATION AND RESTORATION--
TIBET--SVAYAMBHUNATH
A renovation of Svayambhunath-stupa
in the 18th century and its
history (according to Tibetan
sources) / Franz-Karl Ehrhard.
PRAACINA NEPALA 1989 Oct.-Nov.,
no.114, p.[1]-8,1 plate, photo.,
refs.

STUPAS--INDIA--LAMPHUN--PHRA MAHA THAT
Inscriptions and images on the Phra
Maha That in Lamphun / Hans Penth.
ARTIBUS ASIAE 1988-1989, v.49,
no.3-4, p.351-369, ill., photos.,
aerial photo., biblio., refs.

STUPAS--JAPAN
On the aspect of successive
diminution in a five-storied stupa
/ Hiroyasu Shirai.
English summary, p.131.
NIHON KENCHIKU GAKKAI KEIKAKUKEI
RONBUN HOKOKU SHU = JOURNAL OF
ARCHITECTURE, PLANNING AND
ENVIRONMENTAL ENGINEERING 1990
Feb., no.2(408), p.123-131,
graphs, secns., tables, refs.

STURKENBOOM, FRANZ, 1960-
EUROPAN-Wettbewerbsergebnisse.
Five entries by young architects
for a European housing
competition.
ARCH PLUS 1990 Jan., no.102,
p.13-18, axonometric view, dwgs.,
models, photos., plans, secns.

STURM, ISA
Locker angedichtet: Anmerkung zum
offentlichen Wettbewerb auf den
Rontgenareal im Zurcher
Industriequartier.
1st prize to Isa Sturm & Urs Wolf.
WERK, BAUEN + WOHNEN 1990 Dec.,
no.12, p.12, models, site plans.

STURM, ISA (CONTINUED)
Rontgenareal Zurich:
Projektwettbewerb.
Projects in a competition for a
mixed use complex in the area
around the Rontgenstrasse train
station. First prize to the
"Khan" project by Isa Sturm and
Urs Wolf.
SCHWEIZER BAUMARKT 1990 Oct.29,
v.25, no.13, p.[I]-IV, models.

STURZEBECHER, PETER
Ausgetuftelt prazise: Wochenendhaus
im Pfalzer Wald / Klaus-Dieter
Weiss.
Architect: Peter Sturzebecher.
BAUWELT 1990 Oct.12, v.81, no.38,
p.1930-1933, axonometric view,
elev., photos., plans, secn.
Wohnhaus im Haardtgebirge.
Architect: Peter Sturzebecher.
Includes English summary.
BAUMEISTER 1990 Nov., v.87, no.11,
p.48-51, photos., plans, secns.,
isometric dwg.

STUTTGART (GERMANY). HOCHBAUAMT
Schulturnhalle: Erweiterung der
Prag-Turnhalle in Stuttgart.
Architects: Hochbauamt der Stadt
Stuttgart.
DEUTSCHE BAUZEITUNG 1990 Feb.,
v.124, no.2, p.34-36, elevs.,
models, photos., plans, secns.

STYLE (ARCHITECTURE)
Den "glemte" boligfunktion / Axel
Jurgensen.
Reviews several designs by Danish
architects for single-family
houses over the past two decades.
ARKITEKTEN 1990 June, v.92, no.8,
p.256-257, dwgs., plans, secn.
On the western style design of the
public facilities of Mie
prefecture in the Meiji era /
Yoichi Sugawara.
Subtitile: The buildings of Mie
2nd, 3rd, and 4th Middle School.
English summary, p.177.
NIHON KENCHIKU GAKKAI KEIKAKUKEI
RONBUN HOKOKU SHU = JOURNAL OF
ARCHITECTURE, PLANNING AND
ENVIRONMENTAL ENGINEERING 1990
Feb., no.2(408), p.165-177,
charts., photos., site plans,
tables, refs.
Revivals, revivalists, and
architectural stained glass /
Virginia Chieffo Raguin.
Addresses "the implications of the
revival of stained glass for an
understanding of the medieval
past, the 19th century, and the
ethics of restoration." Includes
abstract.
SOCIETY OF ARCHITECTURAL
HISTORIANS. JOURNAL 1990 Sept.,
v.49, no.3, p.310-329, dwg.,
photos., refs.
Urban design 5: regional identity /
Hildebrand Frey.
Maintaining city identity during
the process of urbanization and
growth. Fifth in series on urban
design.
ARCHITECTS' JOURNAL 1990 Oct.31,
v.192, no.18, p.63-65, photos.,
plans.

STYLE (ARCHITECTURE)--18TH CENTURY--
GREAT BRITAIN
The architecture of the wall:
Astylism in the architecture of
Lord Burlington / Cinzia Sicca.
ARCHITECTURAL HISTORY 1990, v.33,
p.83-101, elevs., photos., plans,
refs.

STYLE (ARCHITECTURE)--19TH CENTURY--
THEORY--EUROPE
Gottfried Semper: il governo dello
stile = Gottfried Semper: the
government of style / Marco
Pogacnik.
OTTAGONO 1990 Mar., no.94,
p.7-[15], dets., ill., dwgs.,
engrs.

STYLE (ARCHITECTURE)--20TH CENTURY
Art deco: polemics and synthesis /
Richard Striner.
WINTERTHUR PORTFOLIO 1990 Spring,
v.25, no.1, p.[21]-34, photos.,
refs.

STYLE (ARCHITECTURE)--20TH CENTURY--
ENGLAND
Classical revival / Martin Pawley,
Martin Spring.
Includes a review of Classical
architecture: a complete handbook,
by Robert Adam, in conjunction
with an exhibit at the Heinz
Gallery entitled Classical design
in the late 20th century.
BUILDING 1990 Nov.9, v.255, no.44,
p.61-65.

STYLE (ARCHITECTURE)--20TH CENTURY--
EUROPE
Strategie met stijl: over de rol van
de architectuur in het machtsspel
/ Hans Krop.
One of several articles in
Themanummer 41: "Thema:
architectuur en macht". Uses
examples from Groninger and
incorporates a chart that
classifies aspects of modern
architecture (from Charles Jencks'
The new moderns).
DE ARCHITECT THEMA 1990 Nov.,
v.21, no.11 suppl., p.15-19, ill.,
elevs., models, photos., site
plans, table.

STYLE (ARCHITECTURE)--20TH CENTURY--
GERMANY
Hannes Meyer in een nieuw licht:
tragisch utopist zonder vaderland
/ Herman Selier.
DE ARCHITECT 1990 May, v.21, no.5,
p.63-69, dwgs., ports., photos.,
aerial photos.

STYLE (ARCHITECTURE)--20TH CENTURY--
UNITED STATES
Coming home to America.
A selection of six recent American
houses that reflect various
styles; articles are indexed
separately.
METROPOLITAN HOME 1990 July, v.22,
no.7, p.45-[75].
Reflections on the need for an
avant-garde / Wojciech
Lesnikowski.
In the U.S.
INLAND ARCHITECT 1990 May-June,
v.34, no.3, p.[68]-72, photos.

STYLE (ARCHITECTURE)--JAPAN
A methodological study on the classification of the type of housing-design intention / Tomoko Okada, Satoshi Togashi. "Study on the classification of the type of dwelling-culture no.1". Text in Japanese. Includes English summary.
NIHON KENCHIKU GAKKAI KEIKAKUKEI RONBUN HOKOKU SHU = JOURNAL OF ARCHITECTURE, PLANNING AND ENVIRONMENTAL ENGINEERING 1990 Sept., no.9(415), p.49-56, photos., tables, refs.

STYLE (ARCHITECTURE)--ROMANESQUE--FRANCE--POITOU
The chevet of Saint-Jouin-de-Marnes / Anat Tcherikover. A stylistic analysis that places this chevet within the context of early 12th-cent. sculpture and architecture in Poitou.
GESTA 1989, v.28, no.2, p.147-164, dets., map, photos, plans, refs.

STYLE (ARCHITECTURE)--SOCIOLOGICAL ASPECTS--GREAT BRITAIN
Leeds: the smotherer of invention / Sarah Kitchen. On the role of planners and architects in new developments in Leeds felt to be unimaginative in design.
BUILDING 1990 Feb.23, v.255, no.8, p.24-25, ports., photos.

STYLES (ARCHITECTURE)--19TH CENTURY--THEORY
Naissance d'une anthropologie du style en architecture au XIX siecle / Chantal Lecas, Jean-Pierre Martinon. On the history of architectural styles in the 19th century. Includes English summary.
ARCHITECTURE & COMPORTEMENT = ARCHITECTURE & BEHAVIOUR 1990, v.6, no.1, p.63-79, diagrs., figs., dwgs., biblio.

STYLES-MCLEOD, CATHERINE
Historic houses: Voltaire at Ferney / Catherine Styles-McLeod. Features 18th-cent. interiors of Voltaire's home in Ferney-Voltaire, France.
ARCHITECTURAL DIGEST 1990 Mar., v.47, no.3, p.[180-185],244, photos.

STYLES OF ARCHITECTURE
See STYLE (ARCHITECTURE)

STYLIANOPOULOS, LEONIDAS C.
Value engineering on projects in Asia / Leonidas C. Stylianopoulos.
EKISTICS 1989 May-Aug., v.56, no.336-337, p.202-210, charts, diagrs., map, plans, table, biblio.

STYNEN, LEON, 1899-1990
Architect Leon Stynen 1899-1990 [obituary] / Marc Dubois.
ARCHIS 1990 June, no.6, p.6, photos.

STYNEN, LEON, 1899-1990 (CONTINUED)
Architect Leon Stynen 1899-1990 [obituary] / Marc Dubois.
ARCHIS 1990 June, no.6, p.6, photos.

SUAGEE, DEAN B.
Reconfiguring the cultural mission: tribal historic preservation programs / Dean B. Suagee, Karen J. Funk.
CRM BULLETIN: A NATIONAL PARK SERVICE TECHNICAL BULLETIN 1990, v.13, no.4, p.21-24, refs.

SUARES, J. C.
Ultimate panoramas / J.C. Suares. On the panorama wallpapers produced by Zuber & Cie of Rixheim, France.
CONNOISSEUR 1990 July, v.220, no.942, p.60-[65],106-107, ill., photos.

SUAREZ, ISIDRO
Cooperativa Electrica Chillan: lectura critica / Rodrigo de la Cruz. On architects Juan Borchers, Jesus Bermejo, and Isidro Suarez.
ARQ 1989 Aug., no.13, p.25-31, ports., photos., plans, secns., sketches.

SUAREZ QUEVEDO, DIEGO
La coleccion de pinturas del arquitecto toledano Bartolome Zumbigo y Salcedo (1620-1682) / Diego Suarez Quevedo.
ARCHIVO ESPANOL DE ARTE 1989 Jan.-Mar., v.62, no.245, p.91-98, refs.

SUBDIVISION OF LAND
See LAND SUBDIVISION

SUBES-PICOT, MARIE-PASQUINE
Mayenne: Eglise de Cosse-en-Champagne: decouverte de peintures murales / Marie-Pasquine Subes-Picot. A Romanesque church, located east of Laval, with murals from the second quarter of the 15th cent. in the Sainte Anne Chapel.
BULLETIN MONUMENTAL 1990, v.148, no.1, p.91-95, elev., photos., refs.
Vienne: Decouverte de peintures murales dans la cathedrale Saint-Pierre de Poitiers / Marie-Pasquine Subes-Picot.
BULLETIN MONUMENTAL 1990, v.148, no.2, p.200-203, dwgs., elevs., photo., refs.

SUBIAS I FAGES, XAVIER
El plan territorial general de Cataluna = The land plan for Catalonia / Xavier Subias. English summary, p.72.
URBANISMO / COAM 1989 Sept., no.8, p.63-72, ill., maps, table.

SUBIRACHS, JOSE MARIA, 1927-
Continuation of Sagrada Familia in dispute / C.C. Sullivan. On the new sculpture by Jose Maria Subirachs installed on the "Passion" facade of the Church of the Sagrada Familia, Barcelona. Original architect: Antoni Gaudi.
(Continued next column)

SUBIRACHS, JOSE MARIA, 1927- (CONTINUED)
Continuation of...(CONTINUED)
PROGRESSIVE ARCHITECTURE 1990 Nov., v.71, no.12, p.26, photos.

SUBLIME, THE
The Beautiful and the Sublime: two neoclassical houses compared / Gervase Jackson-Stops. Castle Coole, near Enniskillen, Northern Ireland, begun in 1790 (architects: Richard Johnston, James Wyatt), and Ickworth, near Bury St. Edmunds, ca. 1796 (architect: Francis Sandys).
ANTIQUES 1990 June, v.137, no.6, p.[1356]-1367, dets., ill., dwg., elevs., model, photos., secns., engr., refs.
Notes on the sublime: from Neoclassicism to Postmodernism / Anthony Vidler. With reference to Longinus, Burke, Hegel and others.
THE PRINCETON JOURNAL 1988, v.3, p.165-190, dwgs., elevs.

SUBMARINE ARCHAEOLOGY
See UNDERWATER ARCHAEOLOGY

SUBMERGED BUILDINGS
See UNDERWATER BUILDINGS

SUBSIDENCE OF BUILDINGS
See EARTH MOVEMENTS AND BUILDING

SUBSIDENCES (EARTH MOVEMENTS)
See also EARTH MOVEMENTS AND BUILDING
See also EARTHQUAKES AND BUILDING

SUBSIDIES - RENT
See RENT SUBSIDIES

SUBSIDIZED HOUSING
See HOUSING - PUBLIC

SUBSTATIONS - ELECTRIC
See ELECTRIC SUBSTATIONS

SUBSTITUTE BUILDING MATERIALS
See SYNTHETIC MATERIALS

SUBTERRANEAN CONSTRUCTION
See UNDERGROUND CONSTRUCTION

SUBURBS
See also GARDEN SUBURBS
Cities to walk in: Laguna West Project / Todd W. Bressi. The concept of "pedestrian pockets" in urban centers, as developed by Peter Calthorpe and Dan Solomon.
METROPOLIS 1990 Mar., v.9, no.7, p.54-58, dwgs., site plans.
The evolution of new community planning concepts / Reid Ewing. Describes types of new community planning concepts from the 1920s to the 1990s.
URBAN LAND 1990 June, v.49, no.6, p.13-17, ill., photos., tables, aerial photo.
Il monumento mobile: la circolazione e l'arte della memoria = The mobile monument: circulation and the suburban art of memory / Deirdre Gilfedder.
PARAMETRO 1990 Jan.-Feb., no.176, p.64-67, photos., refs.

SUBURBS (CONTINUED)
Suburban sketchbook / Richard
Hedman.
Suburban design.
PLANNING 1989 Dec., v.55, no.12,
p.18-19, diagrs., sketches.

SUBURBS--ALTERATIONS AND ADDITIONS--
UNITED STATES--CHESAPEAKE
(VIRGINIA)--RIVER WALK
River Walk civic places.
On the series of gateways and
public spaces among a 484-acre
suburban community on the
Elizabeth River in Chesapeake, Va.
Architects: Eric R. Kuhne and
Associates.
PROGRESSIVE ARCHITECTURE 1990
Jan., v.71, no.1, p.113-115,
dwgs., elevs., photo., site plans.

SUBURBS--CANADA--VANCOUVER (BRITISH
COLUMBIA)--SURREY
Suburbs in transition: the
urbanization and greening of
Surrey / Barton Reid.
CITY MAGAZINE 1990 Summer, v.11,
no.4, p.38-41, map, plan, sketch.

SUBURBS--ENGLAND--LIVERPOOL
Municipal suburbia in Liverpool,
1919-1939 / Madeline McKenna.
TOWN PLANNING REVIEW 1989 July,
v.60, no.3, p.287-318, photos.,
plans, aerial photo., refs.

SUBURBS--ENVIRONMENTAL ASPECTS--UNITED
STATES--CHICAGO (ILLINOIS)
I think that I shall never see ....
/ Riva Feshbach.
Environmental and landscape
preservation issues in the Chicago
suburbs.
INLAND ARCHITECT 1990 Sept.-Oct.,
v.34, no.5, p.86, 89-90, photo.

SUBURBS--FRANCE
French lessons down to earth / Judi
Loach.
Banlieues 89 is a project
established in 1983 to "analyse
the social, economic and political
problems of [French] housing
estates", particularly the
Parisian suburbs. Director: Roland
Castro.
ARCHITECTS' JOURNAL 1990 Oct.17,
v.192, no.16, p.14, port., model.

SUBURBS--FRANCE--PARIS
Riflessioni intorno alle villes
nouvelles della regione Parigina
alle soglie degli anni novanta /
Carlos Jullian de La Fuente.
PARAMETRO 1990 Jan.-Feb., no.176,
p.33-39, dwgs., models, maps,
photos.

SUBURBS--GROWTH--AUSTRALIA
The case for urban consolidation /
Michael J. S. Collie.
Paper presented at the
International Conference on local
Planning, Sydney, Australia, March
1990, "From Images to
Achievements."
AUSTRALIAN PLANNER: JOURNAL OF THE
ROYAL AUSTRALIAN PLANNING
INSTITUTE 1990 June, v.28, no.2,
p.26-33, biblio.

SUBURBS--GROWTH--CANADA
Planes, trains and automobiles: how
new transportation schemes are
Americanizing our suburbs / Barton
Reid.
In Canada, principally Vancouver,
Toronto and Montreal.
CITY MAGAZINE 1989 Summer-Fall,
v.11, no.1, p.4-6, maps.

SUBURBS--GROWTH--ENGLAND
Development pressure, development
control and suburban townscape
change: case studies in south-east
England / J. W. R. Whitehand.
TOWN PLANNING REVIEW 1989 Oct.,
v.60, no.4, p.403-420, map,
photos., site plans, tables, refs.

SUBURBS--GROWTH--ENGLAND--HARROW
An environmental assessment of the
residential areas of Harrow / Bill
Munro, Rob Lane.
Pressures of new housing
development on the London suburb.
THE PLANNER 1990 Jan.12, v.76,
no.1, p.15-18, plans, table.

SUBURBS--GROWTH--ENGLAND--LONDON--
BARNET
Suburban redevelopment: an appraisal
of recent pressures and policy
responses in an outer London
borough / Douglas Crockett.
Example of Barnet.
THE PLANNER 1990 Aug.10, v.76,
no.31, p.11-14, photo., table.

SUBURBS--GROWTH--UNITED STATES
Beyond gridlock: looking for the new
suburban city / Joseph. E. Brown,
Michael E. Hickok.
Problems of definition for
"suburban urbanization", and the
transportation issues involved.
DEVELOPMENT 1990 July-Aug., v.21,
no.4, p.17-20, ill., dwgs.,
photos.
Pumping up suburban downtowns /
Philip Langdon.
Examples in Reston, Va., Miami
Lakes, Fla., and Buffalo Grove,
Ill.
PLANNING 1990 July, v.56, no.7,
p.22-28, dwg., model, map,
photos., plans, aerial photo.

SUBURBS--GROWTH--UNITED STATES--
BALTIMORE (MARYLAND)
Vernacular form and early suburban
housing: the case of the Lockard
house, Baltimore / Michael A.
Grimes.
Near Frederick Avenue; built
ca.1899.
MATERIAL CULTURE 1990 Spring,
v.22, no.1, p.33-48, maps,
photos., plans, biblio.

SUBURBS--GROWTH--UNITED STATES--
LINCOLN (MASSACHUSETTS)
Evolutionary growth management in
Lincoln, Massachusetts / Bob
Narus.
Rural suburb 13 miles west of
Boston.
URBAN LAND 1990 Jan., v.49, no.1,
p.18-19, photos.

SUBURBS--GROWTH--UNITED STATES--MORENO
VALLEY (CALIFORNIA)
The long commute / William Fulton.
Affordable housing in the suburbs
of Moreno Valley, Ca. requires
long commuting time and distance
to work.
PLANNING 1990 July, v.56, no.7,
p.4-10, map, photos., aerial
photo.

SUBURBS--HISTORY
Bourgeois utopias: the rise and fall
of suburbia [by] Robert Fishman
[book review] / Peter O. Miller.
JOURNAL OF URBAN STUDIES 1989,
v.11, no.2, p.190-192.

SUBURBS--JAPAN--TOKYO--KARAKIDA
The concept of spatial composition
and organization of Shuraku
(Settlements) viewed through the
spatial language / Yukio Terakado.
Based on research at Karakida in
Ochiai-district, Tama City, Tokyo.
Text in Japanese; includes English
summary.
NIHON KENCHIKU GAKKAI KEIKAKUKEI
RONBUN HOKOKU SHU = JOURNAL OF
ARCHITECTURE, PLANNING AND
ENVIRONMENTAL ENGINEERING 1990
Oct., no.10(416), p.55-65, maps,
tables, refs.

SUBURBS--SOCIOLOGICAL ASPECTS--GERMANY
(EAST)
Innerstadtische Wohnmobilitat und
demographische Wellen / Dieter
Bock.
German, Russian, English and
French summaries, p.55-56.
ARCHITEKTUR DER DDR 1990 Feb.,
v.38, no.2, p.13-14, graphs, map,
tables, refs.

SUBURBS--SPAIN--BARCELONA--POBLE NOU
Nuovi usi per la citta dismessa:
Barcellona, il Poble Nou = New
uses for run-down city areas:
Barcelona, the Poble Nou.
A feature on changes in this
outlying suburb. Includes an essay
by Octavio Mestre.
ABITARE 1990 May, no.285,
p.186-207, ill., dwg., elev.,
maps, photos., plans, secns.

SUBURBS--SWEDEN--STOCKHOLM
La grande Stoccolma = Greater
Stockholm / Marina Botta.
New towns: Vallingby, Skarpnack,
Enskede. Master planner: Sven
Markelius. Architects: Arken;
Brunnberggruppen; FFNS; Malmquist
& Skoogh; Per Olof Hallman.
ABITARE 1990 July-Aug., no.287,
p.156-163,224, axonometric views,
dets., elevs., map, photos.,
aerial photos.

SUBURBS--SWITZERLAND
Mitten im Land = Au milieu du pays =
In the middle of the country.
Suburban developments in
Switzerland is the topic of this
issue.
WERK, BAUEN + WOHNEN 1990 May,
no.5, p.24-41, ill., maps, photos.

SUBURBS--UNITED STATES
Breaking the code: urban design
portfolio / Beth Dunlop.
Small-town alternatives to
suburban sprawl, as offered by
Andres Duany and Elizabeth
Plater-Zyberk.
ARCHITECTURE: THE AIA JOURNAL 1990
Apr., v.79, no.4, p.80-83, ill.,
elev., plans, site plans.
Repent, ye sinners, repent / Ruth
Eckdish Knack.
PLANNING 1989 Aug., v.55, no.8,
p.4-8, diagr., port., photos.,
plans.

SUBURBS--UNITED STATES--WEST LAGUNA
(CALIFORNIA)
The first pedestrian pocket / Gary
Delsohn.
Designing the suburbs for
pedestrians in West Laguna, Ca.
Architect: Peter Calthorpe.
PLANNING 1989 Dec., v.55, no.12,
p.20-22, plans, sketches.

SUBWAY TUNNELS
Under jorgens valv / Marianne Strom.
On design and materials of
ceilings in subway tunnels.
ARKITEKTUR: THE SWEDISH REVIEW OF
ARCHITECTURE 1990 Nov., v.90,
no.9, p.24-27, photos.

SUBWAYS--ALTERATIONS AND ADDITIONS--
ENGLAND--LONDON--JUBILEE LINE
Jubilee options / Amanda Baillieu.
On the latest proposals for the
Jubilee Tube line, London.
BUILDING DESIGN 1990 Mar.2,
no.975, p.10-11, plans, secns.,
aerial photos.

SUBWAYS--BRAZIL--SAO PAULO
A cidade e a arquitetura im vinte
anos de metro.
A series of articles on Sao
Paulo's metro system.
PROJETO 1988 Nov., no.116,
p.108-138, photos., plans, secns.,
site plans, aerial photo.

SUBWAYS--ENGLAND--LONDON--EXHIBITIONS
Tube centenary: 100 years of
underground electric railways
exhibition at the London Transport
Museum, 18 May 1990 to 6 October
1991 [exhibition review] / Theo
Barker.
LONDON JOURNAL 1990, v.15, no.2,
p.[160]-163,

SUBWAYS--ENGLAND--LONDON--UNDERGROUND
Out of the ashes / Bill Godwin.
London's Underground rebuilds with
a new emphasis on safety after
fatal fire in 1987.
MASS TRANSIT 1990 May, v.17, no.5,
p.22-26, photos.

SUBWAYS--ITALY--MILAN--METROPOLITAN
MILANESE
La terza linea della metropolitana
di Milano = Line 3 of the Milan
underground / Michele Bazan
Giordano.
Architects: Studio Dini e Capelli.
L'ARCA 1990 July-Aug. no.40,
p.60-65, map, photos., secns.

SUBWAYS--LATVIA--RIGA
The planned metro of Riga: is it
necessary or even desirable? /
Sigurd Grava.
TRANSPORTATION QUARTERLY 1989
July, v.43, no.3, p.451-472, refs.

SUBWAYS--MAINTENANCE AND REPAIR--
UNITED STATES--NEW YORK (NEW YORK)
Is New York's transit off track? /
Margaret Mittelbach.
Maintenance and repair of New
York's subways and stations is a
continuing problem.
CITY LIMITS 1990 Dec., v.15,
no.10, p.8-11, ports., photos.

SUBWAYS--POLITICAL ASPECTS--LATVIA--
RIGA
The planned metro of Riga: is it
necessary or even desirable? /
Sigurd Grava.
TRANSPORTATION QUARTERLY 1989
July, v.43, no.3, p.451-472, refs.

SUBWAYS--SOVIET UNION--MOSCOW
Il fenomeno della metropolitana di
Mosca = The phenomenon of the
Moscow underground / Natalia
Dushkina.
In Italian, with English summary.
METAMORFOSI 1988, no.11, p.10-15,
dwg., photos., sketches, refs.

SUBWAYS--STATIONS--BRAZIL--SAO PAULO--
MARECHAL DEODORO
O tratamento especial nas estacoes
subterraneas / Olair de Camillo.
PROJETO 1988 Nov., no.116,
p.136-137, photos., plans, secns.

SUBWAYS--STATIONS--FRANCE--LYON
Stations chics pour metros de choc.
Features subway stations in Milan,
Lyon and Bilbao designed by the
following architects: Ignazio
Gardella, Aldo Rossi, Foster
Associates, Jourda et Perraudin.
ARCHITECTURE D'AUJOURD'HUI 1990
Feb., no.267, p.52-53, ill.,
models, photos.

SUBWAYS--STATIONS--FRANCE--LYON--
PARILLY STATION
Tre progetti per la metropolitana di
Lione = Three projects for the
Lyon Metro.
Architects: Jourda et Perraudin.
L'ARCA 1990 Dec., no.44 suppl.
l'arca 2, p.100, dwg., plan,
secns.

SUBWAYS--STATIONS--GERMANY (WEST)--
MUNICH--BAHNHOF
RICHARD-STRAUSS-STRASSE
Architektur unterwegs.
Three projects: U-Bahn=Bahnhof
Richard-Strauss-Strasse, Munchen
(architect: Erhard Fischer);
Arbeitsamt Augsburg (architect:
Koch + Partner); renovation and
expansion of Kunsthalle, Kiel
(architect: Jungjohann + Hoffmann
+ Krug).
DEUTSCHES ARCHITEKTENBLATT 1990
Apr.1, v.22, no.4, p.535-538,
plans, secns., site plans.

SUBWAYS--STATIONS--GERMANY (WEST)--
NURNBERG--HOHE MARTER
La Torre di Babele di Peter
Angermann.
Mosaic in the Hohe Marter subway
station, Nuremberg. Text in
Italian and English.
DOMUS 1990 Feb., no.713, p.10-11,
ill.

SUBWAYS--STATIONS--ITALY--MILAN
Stations chics pour metros de choc.
Features subway stations in Milan,
Lyon and Bilbao designed by the
following architects: Ignazio
Gardella, Aldo Rossi, Foster
Associates, Jourda et Perraudin.
ARCHITECTURE D'AUJOURD'HUI 1990
Feb., no.267, p.52-53, ill.,
models, photos.

SUBWAYS--STATIONS--MAINTENANCE AND
REPAIR--ENGLAND--LONDON--UNDERGROUND
Out of the ashes / Bill Godwin.
London's Underground rebuilds with
a new emphasis on safety after
fatal fire in 1987.
MASS TRANSIT 1990 May, v.17, no.5,
p.22-26, photos.

SUBWAYS--STATIONS--MAINTENANCE AND
REPAIR--UNITED STATES--NEW YORK (NEW
YORK)
Is New York's transit off track? /
Margaret Mittelbach.
Maintenance and repair of New
York's subways and stations is a
continuing problem.
CITY LIMITS 1990 Dec., v.15,
no.10, p.8-11, ports., photos.

SUBWAYS--STATIONS--SECURITY MEASURES--
CANADA--TORONTO (ONTARIO)
Moving forward on public transit.
The safety of women on Toronto's
public transit system.
WOMEN AND ENVIRONMENTS 1989
Fall-1990 Winter, v.12, no.1,
p.10-11, photos.

SUBWAYS--STATIONS--SPAIN--BARCELONA
Dos interiores para el metro de
Barcelona: Javier San Jose,
arquitecto.
Spanish, English text.
ON DISENO 1990, no.110, p.85-99,
dets., photos., plans, secns.

SUBWAYS--STATIONS--SPAIN--BARCELONA--
URGELL
Estacion de metro Urgell, Linea 1:
Javier San Jose, arquitecto.
In Barcelona.
ON DISENO 1990, no.116, p.174-175,
photos.

SUBWAYS--STATIONS--SPAIN--BILBAO
Stations chics pour metros de choc.
Features subway stations in Milan,
Lyon and Bilbao designed by the
following architects: Ignazio
Gardella, Aldo Rossi, Foster
Associates, Jourda et Perraudin.
ARCHITECTURE D'AUJOURD'HUI 1990
Feb., no.267, p.52-53, ill.,
models, photos.

SUBWAYS--STATIONS--UNITED STATES--NEW YORK (NEW YORK)--INTERVALE AVENUE
Transportation blues / Alexander Farnsworth.
The Intervale Ave. subway stop, in the South Bronx, closed due to vandalism, will be rebuilt and opened in 2 1/2 years.
METROPOLIS 1990 July-Aug., v.10, no.1, p.17-18, photos.

SUCHMAN, DIANE R.
An action plan for revitalizing south central Fort Wayne / Diane R. Suchman.
URBAN LAND 1990 Sept., v.49, no.9, p.20-25, photos., plans.

SUCHOV, VLADIMIR GRIGOREVIC, 1853-1939
Eine Baumassen-Wanderung, Prinzip Suchov: Aufrichtung eines Minarets in Samarkand = A wandering of masses, principle Sukhov: The realignment of a minaret in Samarkand / Rainer Graefe.
Realignment of minaret of Nadrash of Ulugh Bek, Samarkand, in 1930s by Russian engineer Vladimir Grigor'evic Sukhov.
DAIDALOS 1990 Sept.15, no.37, p.40-43, dwgs., photos.
Un ingegnere rivoluzionario: Vladimir Grigor'evic Suchov 1853-1939 / Rainer Graefe, Ottmar Pertschi.
Essays extracted from a book on the Soviet engineer, by the authors and Murat Gappoev, subtitled "Die Kunst der sparsamen Konstruktion". In Italian and English.
CASABELLA 1990 Nov., v.54, no.573, p.38-58,61-63, dets., ill., elevs., maps, photos.
De network-architectuur van Suchov: Inventiere constructies met een organische vorm / Jos Tomlow.
The Work of the Russian engineer (1853-1939).
DE ARCHITECT 1990 July-Aug., v.21, no.7-8, p.66-71, dwgs., photos., secns., biblio., ref.
Virtuose Sparsamkeit?: Dachkonstruktionen des russishen Ingenieurs Vladimir G. Suchov / Rainer Graefe.
DEUTSCHE BAUZEITUNG 1990 July, v.124, no.7, p.24-31, elevs., photos., plans.

SUCHTING, ANTJE
Gut versteckt.... / Antje Suchting.
Features home on the Costa Smeralda of Sardinia owned by a family from Hamburg.
ARCHITEKTUR & WOHNEN 1990 June-July, no.3, p.[52]-57, port., photos.

SUCKALE, ROBERT
Aspetti della simbologia architettonica del dodicesimo secolo in Francia: Il santuario / Robert Suckale.
Paper presented at the Qualita ecclesiale nell'arte conference in 1989, on methodological and theoretical foundations. Includes abstract in English.
ARTE CRISTIANA 1990 Mar.-July, v.78, no.737-738, p.111-122, photos., refs.

SUCKALE, ROBERT (CONTINUED)
Neue Literatur uber die Abteikirche von Saint-Denis [book review] / Robert Suckale.
Reviews five recent books.
KUNSTCHRONIK 1990 Feb., v.43, no.2, p.62-80, refs.

SUDJIC, DEYAN
Carta desde Fukuoka: la "mini-IBA" de Isozaki / Deyan Sudjic.
ARQUITECTURA VIVA 1990 Mar.-Apr., no.11, p.50-52, dwg., models, secns., sketches.
Instant City / Deyan Sudjic.
Concert set used by the Rolling Stones in 1989, designed by Jonathan Park and others. First published in English in Blueprint, 9/89.
BAUWELT 1990 Dec.1, v.81, no.45, p.2268-2271, dwgs., photos.
The lost art of the pub / Deyan Sudjic.
Site: Holloway Road building; architect: Florian Beigel of the Polytechnic of North London's Architecture Research Unit.
BLUEPRINT (LONDON, ENGLAND) 1990 Apr., no.66, p.42-45, photos.
The man who shaped Milan: Gio Ponti: the complete work 1923-1978 [book review] / Deyan Sudjic.
BLUEPRINT (LONDON, ENGLAND) 1990 Sept., no.70, p.60,62,
Rediscovering the public realm: an exhibition at the Heinz Gallery [exhibition review] / Deyan Sudjic.
Exhibition held from March 29 to May 26, 1990.
BLUEPRINT (LONDON, ENGLAND) 1990 Apr., no.66, p.51-54, photos.

SUDJIC, DEYAN. RON ARAD: RESTLESS FURNITURE
Ron Arad: restless furniture [and] Nigel Coates: the city in motion [book review] / Robert Mull.
AA FILES 1990 Spring, no.19, p.108-109, photos.

SUETONIUS, CA. 69-CA. 122
From dome of heaven to pleasure dome / Oleg Grabar.
Text of a paper delivered at the 1989 annual meeting of the SAH, discussing Suetonius, domes at the Alhambra, Orientalism, and questions of ethics, aesthetics, and praxis.
SOCIETY OF ARCHITECTURAL HISTORIANS. JOURNAL 1990 Mar., v.49, no.1, p.15-21, photos., plan, refs.

SUGAWARA, YOICHI
On the western style design of the public facilities of Mie prefecture in the Meiji era / Yoichi Sugawara.
Subtitle: The buildings of Mie 2nd, 3rd, and 4th Middle School. English summary, p.177.
NIHON KENCHIKU GAKKAI KEIKAKUKEI RONBUN HOKOKU SHU = JOURNAL OF ARCHITECTURE, PLANNING AND ENVIRONMENTAL ENGINEERING 1990 Feb., no.2(408), p.165-177, charts., photos., site plans, tables, refs.

SUGDEN, DEREK
Housing the airship: AA Exhibition Gallery, Members' Room & Bar 26 April-27 May 1989 [exhibition review] / Derek Sugden.
AA FILES 1990 Spring, no.19, p.101-107, photos., elevs., secn.

SUGER, ABBOT OF SAINT-DENIS, 1081-1151
Medieval architecture [book review] / Roger Stalley.
A joint review of The Royal Abbey of Saint-Denis..., by Sumner McKnight Crosby, ed. by Pamela Z. Blum, and Abbot Suger and Saint Denis: a symposium, ed. by Paula Lieber Gerson.
SOCIETY OF ARCHITECTURAL HISTORIANS. JOURNAL 1990 Dec., v.49, no.4, p.440-441,

SUGIMOTO, HIROFUMI
Yokohama city creation Bay '90: exhibition of waterfront redevelopment.
Five temporary towers, called Yokohama Towers, which are part of the Bay 90 exhibition. Architects: Hirofumi Sugimoto, Noriaki Furuya, Katsuhiro Kobayashi, Kiyoshi Takeyama and Kazuyo Sejima.
JAPAN ARCHITECT 1990 June, v.65, no.6(398), p.4, photos.

SUGINO, NOBORU
Distribution of the types of plans and development of the main hall of Buddhist temples of the Sodo Zen sect in the Middle Edo Period - mainly in Tokai and Koshin districts / Noboru Sugino.
Text in Japanese; includes English summary.
NIHON KENCHIKU GAKKAI KEIKAKUKEI RONBUN HOKOKU SHU = JOURNAL OF ARCHITECTURE, PLANNING AND ENVIRONMENTAL ENGINEERING 1990 Aug., no.8(414), p.141-154, photos., plans, maps, refs.
Plans and development of the main hall of Buddhist temples of the Sodo zen sect in the early Edo period / Noboru Sugino.
English summary, p.187.
NIHON KENCHIKU GAKKAI KEIKAKUKEI RONBUN HOKOKU SHU = JOURNAL OF ARCHITECTURE, PLANNING AND ENVIRONMENTAL ENGINEERING 1990 Jan., no.1(407), p.173-187, charts, photos., plans, refs.

SUHONEN, PEKKA
Il funzionalismo in Finlandia / Pekka Suhonen.
Illustrated with examples of drawings and photographs from the Finnish Museum of Architecture, Helsinki. Architects include: Alvar Aalto, Hilding Ekelund, Erik Bryggman, Ekki Huttunen, Pauli Ernesti Blomstedt, and Yrjo Lindegren. Includes English summary and captions.
CASABELLA 1990 Mar., v.54, no.566, p.40-47,61-63, ill., dwgs., photos.

SUISMAN, DOUGLAS R.
Utopia in the Suburbs [exhibition review] / Douglas R. Suisman.
Exhibition "Blueprints for Modern Living," MOCA, Los Angeles, Oct. 17, 1989-Feb. 17, 1990.
ART IN AMERICA 1990 Mar., v.78, no.3, p.184-193, models, photos.

SUKIYA
See "SUKIYA" AS A SUBHEADING AFTER SPECIFIC BUILDING TYPES OR OTHER MAIN HEADINGS.

SUKKAH
See SUKKOTH

SULLIVAN, ARTHUR
Is nature good? / Arthur Sullivan.
The author "interject[s] an argument based on floral and faunal rights into the discussion of place quality, and ... discuss[es] who should be responsible for assuring those rights."
PLACES 1990 Summer, v.6, no.4, p.82-87, refs.

SULLIVAN, C. C.
Continuation of Sagrada Familia in dispute / C.C. Sullivan.
On the new sculpture by Jose Maria Subirachs installed on the "Passion" facade of the Church of the Sagrada Familia, Barcelona. Original architect: Antoni Gaudi.
PROGRESSIVE ARCHITECTURE 1990 Nov., v.71, no.12, p.26, photos.

SULLIVAN, CHIP
Academic assemblage.
Profile of six educators among various landscape architecture faculties.
LANDSCAPE ARCHITECTURE 1990 Sept., v.80, no.9, p.58-63, ports., photos., site plan.
Landscapes for the 21st century [competition].
Features 15 winning projects, which include descriptions in the designers' own words. Competition sponsored by "Landscape Architecture". Includes articles by the judges, Jory Johnson, M. Paul Friedburg and James Wines.
LANDSCAPE ARCHITECTURE 1990 Dec., v.80, no.12, p.[32-54], ill., ports., site plans, aerial photo.

SULLIVAN, DONALD G., 1942 OR 3-1989
Deceased: Donald G. Sullivan [obituary].
Director of the Urban Planning Dept. at Hunter College, N.Y., and architectural historian.
PLANNING 1990 Feb., v.56, no.2, p.41,

SULLIVAN, LOUIS H., 1856-1924
American architects [book review].
Review of books on Louis Sullivan, Philip Trammell Shutze, Louis Kahn, and Gordon Bunshaft, by Lauren S. Weingarden, Keith Morgan, David B. Brownlee, and Franz Schulze.
SOCIETY OF ARCHITECTURAL HISTORIANS. JOURNAL 1990 June, v.49, no.2, p.222-229,

SULLIVAN, LOUIS H., 1856-1924
(CONTINUED)
Caroon, Pirie, Scott: Louis Sullivan and the Chicago department store [by] Joseph Siry [book review] / Mark S. Foster.
1990 Winter, v.25, no.4, p.303-305,
Eat it! A dead fragment on how Louis Sullivan dies / John Whileman.
INLAND ARCHITECT 1990 May-June, v.34, no.3, p.111, photo.
Essay: finding Sullivan's thread / Thomas Kubala.
"Argues that Louis Sullivan's unitary impulse in architecture is a precursor to premises of chaos theory."
PROGRESSIVE ARCHITECTURE 1990 Oct., v.71, no.10, p.102-104, dwgs., refs.
Louis Sullivan's building for John D. Van Allen and Son / Joseph Siry.
A hisoty of the Clinton, Iowa building (1913-1915), with discussion o f design development, ornamental motifs, and the influences of mercantile interests and regional agriculture upon the clients. Includes abstract.
SOCIETY OF ARCHITECTURAL HISTORIANS. JOURNAL 1990 Mar., v.49, no.1, p.67-89, dets., ill., dwgs., photos., plans, refs.

SULLIVAN, LOUIS H., 1865-1924
Caroon, Pirie, Scott: Louis Sullivan and the Chicago department store [by] Joseph Siry [book review] / Mark S. Foster.
1990 Winter, v.25, no.4, p.303-305,

SULLIVAN, ORIEL
Housing tenure as a consumption sector divide: a critical perspective / Oriel Sullivan.
INTERNATIONAL JOURNAL OF URBAN AND REGIONAL RESEARCH 1989 June, v.13, no.2, p.[183]-200, refs.

SULPHUR
See SULFUR

SULTAN, GHAZI
Kuwait City waterfront development / Brian Brace Taylor.
Completed in 1988. Consultants: Ghazi Sultan, architect, Kuwait Engineers Office; Sasaki Associates, Boston.
MIMAR: ARCHITECTURE IN DEVELOPMENT 1990 Mar., v.10, no.1(34), p.[12]-20,cover, map, photos., plans, secns., site plans.

SULTANATE
See "SULTANATE" AS A SUBHEADING AFTER SPECIFIC BUILDING TYPES OR OTHER MAIN HEADINGS, E.G., PALACES - SULTANATE.

SULZBERGER - ROLFE, INC.
Sulzberger-Rolfe manages its management function.
BETTER BUILDINGS 1989 Aug., v.8, no.8, p.19-22, ports., photos.

SULZER, PETER
Alternatives Kulturzentrum: "Haus am Westbahnhof" in Landau (Pfalz).
Architect: Peter Sulzer.
DEUTSCHE BAUZEITUNG 1990 Feb., v.124, no.2, p.37-39, photos., plans, secn., site plan.
Die "Ecke" in der Architektur: Essay in 18 Bildern / Peter Sulzer.
DEUTSCHES ARCHITEKTENBLATT 1989 Apr.1, v.21, no.4, p.517-519, photos., refs.
Laudatio fur Renzo Piano / Peter Sulzer.
At the Universitat Stuttgart.
BAUWELT 1990 July 20, v.81, no.27, p.1363-1364, port., photo.
Proven powers / Kester Rattenbury.
Report on Peter Sulzer's lecture on Jean Prouve.
BUILDING DESIGN 1990 Dec.7, no.1015, p.2, port.

SUMI, CHRISTIAN
Eine prekare Konstruktion: Strasseninstallation in Biel, 1986 / Christian Sumi.
Student project of the ETH Zurich.
WERK, BAUEN + WOHNEN 1990 Nov., no.11, p.18-21, det., elev., photos., plan.

SUMI, CHRISTIAN. IMMEUBLE CLARTE GENF VON LE CORBUSIER & PIERRE JEANNERET
Stahlkonstruktion und Metallbau: Le Corbusiers & Pierre Jeannerets "moderne" architektonische Interpretation [book review] / Ernst Strebel.
On "Immeuble Clarte Genf von Le Corbusier & Pierre Jeanneret," by Christian Sumi (1989).
WERK, BAUEN + WOHNEN 1990 Oct., no.10, p.16-19, photos., plans, secns.

SUMKA, HOWARD J.
Shelter policy and planning in developing countries / Howard J. Sumka.
Introduction to seven articles indexed separately.
AMERICAN PLANNING ASSOCIATION. JOURNAL 1987 Spring, v.53, no.2, p.171-175, iblio.

SUMMER CAMPS--RUSTIC--INTERIOR DESIGN--UNITED STATES--ADIRONDACKS (NEW YORK)
Rustic interiors of the Adirondack camps / Harvey H. Kaiser.
The style of private resorts built in this N.Y. area from 1870-1930.
OLD-HOUSE JOURNAL 1990 Jan.-Feb., v.18, no.1, p.45-48, photos.

SUMMER HOMES
See SUMMER HOUSES

SUMMER HOUSES
See also SUMMER PALACES

SUMMER HOUSES--20TH CENTURY--SWEDEN--VASTERAS--VILLA BARKARO
Villa Barkaro bei Vasteras, S = Villa Barkaro near Vasteras, S.
Architects: Sodergruppen Arkitektkontor AB.
DETAIL 1990 Feb.-Mar., v.30, no.1, p.57-60, dets., elevs., photos., plans, secns.

SUMMER HOUSES--ALTERATIONS AND
ADDITIONS--UNITED STATES--NORFOLK
(CONNECTICUT)--GILL HOUSE
Wright and wrong in a Connecticut
country house / Brendan Gill.
Author's recollections of his
repeated alterations to his summer
house in Norfolk, Ct., including
his remodeling efforts after Frank
Lloyd Wright's Usonian houses.
ARCHITECTURAL DIGEST 1990 June,
v.47, no.6, p.34,[40-41],44, ill.,
port.

SUMMER HOUSES--ENVIRONMENTAL ASPECTS--
TURKEY
Problems and potentials of second
homes / Cemal Arkon.
On the Aegean coasts. (principally
Turkey).
INTERNATIONAL JOURNAL FOR HOUSING
SCIENCE AND ITS APPLICATIONS 1990,
v.14, no.1, p.065-070, map.

SUMMER HOUSES--INTERIOR DESIGN--
SWITZERLAND--LA SAPINIERE (GAGNEBIN
HOUSE)
Wie in seinen besten Tagen / Ursula
Bode.
Interiors of mid-19th cent.
French-style summer home outside
Geneva owned by Nicholas and
Mariejeanne Gagnebin. Interior
designer: Mariejeanne Gagnebin.
English summary, p.1.
ARCHITEKTUR & WOHNEN 1990
Dec.-1991 Jan., no.6, p.24-32,
port., photos.

SUMMER HOUSES--INTERIOR DESIGN--UNITED
STATES--SOUTHAMPTON (NEW YORK)--
SALOMON HOUSE
Beachside fantasy / Glenn Harrell.
Summer house of New York decorator
David Salomon in Southampton, N.Y.
HOUSE BEAUTIFUL 1990 July, v.132,
no.7, p.[44]-49, port., photos.

SUMMER HOUSES--RUSTIC--INTERIOR
DESIGN--UNITED STATES--ADIRONDACKS
(NEW YORK)
Rustic interiors of the Adirondack
camps / Harvey H. Kaiser.
The style of private resorts built
in this N.Y. area from 1870-1930.
OLD-HOUSE JOURNAL 1990 Jan.-Feb.,
v.18, no.1, p.45-48, photos.

SUMMER HOUSES--UNITED STATES--LONG
ISLAND (NEW YORK)
House in Long Island, New York,
design: 1985-87; completion: 1990
(est.).
A shingle style summer house.
Architects: Venturi, Rauch and
Scott Brown. Text in Japanese and
English.
GA HOUSES 1990 Mar., no.28,
p.102-103, elevs., model, plans,
secns., site plan.

SUMMER HOUSES--UNITED STATES--
WASHINGTON ISLAND (WISCONSIN)--
BENNETT HOUSE
Town and country [two houses by
Frederick Phillips & Associates] /
Clifford A. Pearson.
Phillips Townhouse, Chicago; and
Bennett house, Washington Island,
Wisc.
ARCHITECTURAL RECORD 1990
Mid-Apr., v.178, no.5, p.68-63,
photos., plans, secns.

SUMMER HOUSES--VICTORIAN--INDIA
The Raj in repose: India's hill
stations rise above it all /
Philippa Scott.
British bungalows built in the
late 19th cent. as high-altitude
retreats from the heat.
ELLE DECOR 1990 May, v.1, no.4,
p.46-48, photos.

SUMMER PALACES--BAROQUE--INTERIOR
DESIGN--GERMANY (WEST)--FULDA--
FASANERIE
Fasanerie: a German castle preserves
the rich history of an ancient
dynasty / Marton Radkai.
Baroque castle near Fulda.
Interiors redesigned in 1821 by
Johann Conrad Bromeis.
HOUSE & GARDEN 1990 Jan., v.162,
no.1, p.78-87,147, photos.

SUMMER PALACES--ITALY--ROME--CASTEL
GANDOLFO
Castel Gandolfo tra Medioevo e
Barocco / Renato Lefevre.
L'URBE: RIVISTA ROMANA DI STORIA,
ARTE, LETTERE, COSTUMANZE 1988
Mar.-Apr., v.51, no.2, p.24-37,
photos., engrs., refs.

SUMMER PALACES--SWEDEN--DROTTNINGHOLM
Drottningholm.
An island on Lake Malaren, west of
Stockholm. Features the 17th-cent.
summer palace of Queen Eleonora
(architects: Nikodemus Tessin The
Elder and Younger); the house of
architect Ralph Erskine; and the
Ekero quarter. Text in Italian and
English.
ABITARE 1990 July-Aug., no.287,
p.172-179, dwg., port., elev.,
photos., plans, secns., site plan.

SUMMERHAYES WAY & ASSOCIATES
The Norfolk Hotel.
Restaurant renovated to resemble
English public house, Fremantle.
Architects: Martin Grounds;
Summerhayes Way & Associates.
THE ARCHITECT, W.A.: THE OFFICIAL
JOURNAL OF THE ROYAL AUSTRALIAN
INSTITUTE OF ARCHITECTS, W.A.
CHAPTER 1989, v.30, no.1, p.21-23,
dets., photos., plans.

SUMMERS, GENE R.
Toward the education of architect /
Gene R. Summers.
Seven tenets established in
1989-1990 as principles for the
College of Architecture at
Illinois Institute of Technology.
INLAND ARCHITECT 1990 Sept.-Oct.,
v.34, no.5, p.66-69,

SUMMERSON, JOHN NEWENHAM, SIR, 1904-
AJ Christmas books [book review].
Eight reviewers highlight their
choices for the best architecture
books of 1990.
ARCHITECTS' JOURNAL 1990 Dec.5,
v.192, no.23, p.66-69, ill.,
port., model, photos, plans, engr.
The Dane with a vision of London
[obituary] / Sir John Summerson.
Steen Eiler Rasmussen's
observations on London, as
remembered by Sir John Summerson.
ARCHITECTS' JOURNAL 1990 July 25,
v.192, no.4, p.15, ill., port.

SUMMERSON, JOHN NEWENHAM, SIR, 1904-
(CONTINUED)
J. H. Mansart, Sir Christopher Wren
and the dome of St. Paul's
Cathedral [book review] / John
Summerson.
Review of Sir Christopher Wren:
the designs of St. Paul's
Cathedral, by Kerry Downes, pub.
1989.
BURLINGTON MAGAZINE 1990 Jan.,
v.132, no.1042, p.32-36, dets.,
elevs., secns., refs.
Model restoration / John Summerson.
Restoration of the model for Edwin
Lutyens' unexecuted Liverpool
Cathedral.
ARCHITECTS' JOURNAL 1990 Nov.7,
v.192, no.19, p.30, models.
Soane, el hombre y el estilo =
Soane, the man the style / John
Summerson.
Text in Spanish and English.
COMPOSICION ARQUITECTONICA, ART &
ARCHITECTURE 1989 Feb., no.2,
p.[67]-102, dwgs., elevs.,
photos., plans, sketches, refs.
A square in the round: Bedford
Square: an architectural study by
Andrew Byrne [book review] / John
Summerson.
ARCHITECTS' JOURNAL 1990 Aug.8,
v.192, no.6, p.59-60, elev.,
photos.

SUMMERSON, JOHN NEWENHAM, SIR, 1904-.
UNROMANTIC CASTLE AND OTHER ESSAYS
Castles in the air: The unromantic
castle and other essays, by John
Summerson [book review] / James
Stevens Curl.
Review of The unromantic castle
and other essays by Sir John
Summerson, a companion volume to
his earlier: Heavenly mansions and
other essays on architecture.
ARCHITECTS' JOURNAL 1990 July 25,
v.192, no.4, p.63, port.
The Unromantic castle by John
Summerson [book review] / Andrew
Saint.
AA FILES 1990 Autumn, no.20,
p.109-110,

SUMNER, ANNE MARIE
Duas casas en Campos do Jordao /
Anne Marie Sumner.
House Orsi and House Sumner.
Architect: A. Sumner.
PROJETO 1990 Aug., no.134,
p.62-64, axonometric views,
photos., plans.

SUN-BREAKS
Produits: les protections solitaires
/ Laurence Madani.
LE MONITEUR ARCHITECTURE AMC 1990
May, no.11, p.64-66,68-69, dwgs.,
photos.

SUN DECKS (ARCHITECTURE)
See DECKS

SUN LOUVERS
See SUN-BREAKS

SUN ROOMS
See SOLARIUMS

SUNBURST LIGHTS
See FANLIGHTS

SUNDBERG, BO
Kapellkrematorium, Linkoping / Ove
Hidemark.
Located at Lilla Aska Griftegard.
Architect: Ove Hidemark
Arkitektkontor. Includes
commentary by Bo Sundberg; English
translation, p.63-64.
ARKITEKTUR: THE SWEDISH REVIEW OF
ARCHITECTURE 1990 Mar., v.90,
no.2, p.38-47,63-64, axonometric
view, elev., photos., plans,
secns., site plan.

SUNER, BRUNO
Christian de Portzamparc: Cite de la
Musique / Bruno Suner.
Located in Paris. Includes
commentary by Bruno Fortier.
English summary, p.106.
ARCHITECTURE D'AUJOURD'HUI 1990
Sept., no.270, p.[98-113],
photos., plans, secns., site plan.
Contrapunto barroco: I.M. Pei en
Dallas / Bruno Suner.
The new Dallas Auditorium.
ARQUITECTURA VIVA 1990 Jan.-Feb.,
no.10, p.18-20, photos., plans.
Details: l'acoustique a la Villette
/ Bruno Suner.
The Cite de la Musique, Paris 19e.
Architect: Christian de
Portzamparc.
LE MONITEUR ARCHITECTURE AMC 1990
Mar., no.9, p.47-53, axonometric
views, dets., elevs., photos.,
plan.
Ecritures musicales de l'espace
[interview] / Bruno Suner,
Jean-Pascal Jullien.
Interview with composer/conductor
Pierre Boulez. English summary,
p.117.
ARCHITECTURE D'AUJOURD'HUI 1990
Apr., no.268, p.[114-117], port.
Les murs ont des oreilles / Bruno
Suner.
Esssay for theme issue on music,
opera houses and concert halls.
English summary, p.113.
ARCHITECTURE D'AUJOURD'HUI 1990
Feb., no.267, p.[112]-113, dwgs.,
photo.
Ott a l'opera Bastille / Bruno
Suner.
Focus on the acoustics at the
Opera de la Bastille, Paris.
Architect: Carlos Ott. English
summary, p.134.
ARCHITECTURE D'AUJOURD'HUI 1990
Apr., no.268, p.[126]-134, ill.,
photos., plans, secns.
Pei: Banque de Chine a Hong Kong /
Bruno Suner.
ARCHITECTURE D'AUJOURD'HUI 1990
Sept., no.270, p.[120]-126,
photos., map, plans, secns., site
plans.
La salle modulable de la Cite de la
musique a La Villette / Bruno
Suner.
Located in Paris. Architect:
Christian de Portzamparc. English
summary, p.120.
ARCHITECTURE D'AUJOURD'HUI 1990
Apr., no.268, p.118-120,
(Continued next column)

SUNER, BRUNO (CONTINUED)
La salle modulable de...(CONTINUED)
axonometric view, dwgs., photos.,
plans, secns., site plan,
isometric dwg.
Une salle qui chante / Bruno Suner.
On the architectural acoustics of
the renovated 1910-1913 Theatre
des Champs-Elysees, Paris.
Original architect: Auguste
Perret. English summary.
ARCHITECTURE D'AUJOURD'HUI 1990
Oct., no.271, p.206-207, secn.,
sketch, biblio.
Tsiomis a Villecroze / Brumo Suner.
On the Academie musicale de
Villecroze, including the student
housing. Architect: Yannis
Tsiomis. English summary, p.185.
ARCHITECTURE D'AUJOURD'HUI 1990
Feb., no.267, p.[182]-189, dets.,
photos., elevs., plans, secns.,
site plans.
Venturi et Scott Brown a
Philadelphie / Bruno Suner.
On the Philadelphia Orchestra
Hall. English summary, p.176-177.
ARCHITECTURE D'AUJOURD'HUI 1990
Apr., no.268, p.175-177, dwgs.,
model., plans, secn., site plan.

SUNG, DOUGLAS
Real Problems result / Steven
Geoffrion, Robert Leach.
Winners of the 1990 Real Problems
competitions, which focused on the
adaptive reuse of the Pan Pacific
Auditorium. Winners: Douglas Sung,
Anthony Cheung.
L. A. ARCHITECT 1990 Mar., p.1,
elev., plan, secn.

SUNKEN CITIES
See CITIES AND TOWNS - RUINED,
EXTINCT, ETC.

SUNKEN FENCES
See HA-HAS

SUNKEN-FLOOR HUTS
See SUNKEN HUTS

SUNYER, TONET
Cocinas y banos 1990.
Special suppl. issue featuring
kitchen and bath designs by Tonet
Sunyer, Carlos Ferrater, C.M.
Ferrus, J. Montoya, Alfredo
Arribas, Alberto Esquerdo, Camilla
Hamm. English translations,
p.178-192.
ON DISENO 1990, no.112(suppl.),
entire issue(192p.),
Nuevas oficinas de Tiempo/BBDO: T.
Sunyer y J. Badia, arquitectos.
In Barcelona. Text in Spanish and
English.
ON DISENO 1990, no.116, p.148-153,
photos., plan.
Special feature: Commercial
interiors in Barcelona.
Contents: Between minimalism and
Movid, by Naoki Inagawa -- Alfredo
Arribas -- Josep Val and Xavier
Vendrell -- Dani Freixes and
Vicente Miranda -- Tonet Sunyer
and Jordi Badia -- Eduard Samso --
Ventura Valcarce and Carlos Valls.
Includes interviews and
biographical information and
features 13 individual commercial
projects. Text in Japanese.
(Continued next column)

SUNYER, TONET (CONTINUED)
Special feature:...(CONTINUED)
SPACE DESIGN 1990 Nov.,
no.11(314), p.005-072, dets.,
ports., photos., plans, secns.,
refs.
Vivienda unifamiliar en Barcelona:
Tonet Sunyer, arquitecto.
Spanish, English text.
ON DISENO 1990, no.115, p.176-183,
photos., plans, secn.

SUOMEN ARKKITEHTILIITTO
Desperately seeking synthesis / Iris
Helkama.
Report on a conference held on
Sept.4-6,1989 in Tapiola, Espoo,
entitled Architecture,
Craftsmanship and Design.
Sponsors: SAFA, AIA, ORNAMO, and
ACSA.
ARKKITEHTI 1989, v.86, no.8,
p.22-23, photos.

SUOMEN KORISTETAITEILIJAIN LIITTO
ORNAMO
Desperately seeking synthesis / Iris
Helkama.
Report on a conference held on
Sept.4-6,1989 in Tapiola, Espoo,
entitled Architecture,
Craftsmanship and Design.
Sponsors: SAFA, AIA, ORNAMO, and
ACSA.
ARKKITEHTI 1989, v.86, no.8,
p.22-23, photos.

SUOMEN RAKENNUSTAITEEN MUSEO
Il funzionalismo in Finlandia /
Pekka Suhonen.
Illustrated with examples of
drawings and photographs from the
Finnish Museum of Architecture,
Helsinki. Architects include:
Alvar Aalto, Hilding Ekelund, Erik
Bryggman, Ekki Huttunen, Pauli
Ernesti Blomstedt, and Yrjo
Lindegren. Includes English
summary and captions.
CASABELLA 1990 Mar., v.54, no.566,
p.40-47,61-63, ill., dwgs.,
photos.

SUOMEN RAKENNUSTAITEEN MUSEO--
EXHIBITIONS
Il cemento nell'architettura
finlandese [exhibition review] /
Georg Grotenfeld.
"Tehdaan betonista", a late 1989
exhibition at the Finnish Museum
of Architecture.
CASABELLA 1990 May, v.54, no.568,
p.23-24, elev., photos.
Finnish modernism: An architectural
present: seven approaches
[exhibition review] / Richard
Weston.
Exhibition at the Museum of
Finnish Architecture, Helsinki,
through 14 Sept. 1990, then
touring to Stockholm.
ARCHITECTS' JOURNAL 1990 Sept.12,
v.192, no.11, p.82-84, dwg.,
models, photos.
Nordisk klassicisme og Italien [book
review] / Fredrik Fogh.
Review of Classicismo nordico:
architettura nel paesi scandinavi
1910-1930, published in
conjunction with a 1982
exhibition.
ARKITEKTEN 1990 Feb., v.92, no.2,
(Continued next page)

SUOMEN RAKENNUSTAITEEN MUSEO--
EXHIBITIONS (CONTINUED)
Nordisk klassicisme...(CONTINUED)
p.72, dwgs., elevs., photos.,
refs.

SUPER MARKETS
See SUPERMARKETS

SUPERMARKETS
See also GROCERY STORES

SUPERMARKETS--BRAZIL
Arquitetura do comercio ou
arquitetura comercial?:
Supermercados: voce ja pensou? /
Hugo Segawa.
PROJETO 1990 [June]., no.132,
p.42-48, dwg., ports., photos.,
plan, aerial photo.

SUPERMARKETS--ENGLAND--LONDON--CAMDEN
TOWN--SAINSBURY SUPERSTORE
Camden Town / Jacopo Della Fontana.
Contents: Sainsbury Supermarket,
Camden, London --Row houses along
Grand Union Canal, London.
Architects: Nicholas Grimshaw &
Partners. Text in Italian and
English.
L'ARCA 1990 Dec., no.44,
p.10-[17], axonometric views,
photos., plans, site plan.
Graue Fregatte, silberner Rumpf:
Supermarkt und Wohnungen in
London, Camden Town / Peter Davey.
Architects: Nicholas Grimshaw &
Partners. Article is a shorter
version of one published in
Architectural Review, Oct.1989.
BAUWELT 1990 Oct.5, v.81, no.37,
p.1882,1887-1893, axonometric
views, dets., photos., plans,
secn., site plan.
Grimshaw and Partners.
Focus on two projects: Financial
Times printing plant, London and
the Sainsbury Complex, Camden
Town, London. English text, p.
130, 132-133,135.
ARCHITECTURE D'AUJOURD'HUI 1990
Feb., no.267, p.130-135,
axomonetric views, elev., map,
photos., plans, secn., site plans.
Tecnologia del molteplice: complesso
rionale a Camden Town, Londra.
Complex containing a supermarket,
housing, and artists' studies.
Architects: Nicholas Grimshaw &
Partners.
ARCHITETTURA; CRONACHE E STORIA
1990 May, v.36. no.5(415),
p.372-374, axonometric views,
dets., photos.
Wohnbebauung und Einkaufszentrum in
Camden Town, London = Housing and
supermarket in Camden Town,
London.
Architects: Nicholas Grimshaw &
Partners.
DETAIL 1990 Aug.-Sept., v.30,
no.4, p.384-388, dets., photos.,
plans, site plan, isometric dwg.

SUPERMARKETS--NEW ZEALAND
Retailing: a peep into the future /
Gordon Davies.
In New Zealand.
PLANNING QUARTERLY 1989 Sept.,
no.95, p.5-10, photos., tables.

SUPERMARKETS--UNITED STATES--BELLEVUE
(WASHINGTON)--THE SHOPS AT LARRY'S
MARKET
Food chain: the Shops at Larry's
market, Bellevue, Washington,
Carlson/Ferrin Architects / Heidi
Landecker.
ARCHITECTURE: THE AIA JOURNAL 1990
Oct., v.79, no.10, p.[60]-63,
photos., plan, secns.

SUPERMARKETS--UNITED STATES--KIRKLAND
(WASHINGTON)--LARRY'S MARKET
Northwest passage: regional
portfolio: the Pacific Northwest.
Six recent projects: Two Union
Sq., Seattle (NBBJ Group);
Washington Mutual Tower, Seattle
(Kohn Pedersen Fox, McKinley
Architects); Pacific First Centre,
Seattle (Callison Partnership);
Evergreen State College Studio
addition, Olympia (Miller/Hull
Partnership); Larry's Market,
Kirkland, Wash. (Carlson/Ferrin);
and Andover Park, Beaverton, Ore.
(Fisher-Friedman Associates).
ARCHITECTURAL RECORD 1990 May,
v.178, no.6, p.84-93, dwg.,
photos., plans, secns., site
plans.

SUPERMARKETS--UNITED STATES--NEW YORK
(NEW YORK)
Starving for supermarkets / Eve
Heyn.
Shortage of supermarkets in some
New York City neighborhoods. Inset
article by Erika Mallin.
CITY LIMITS 1990 Aug.-Sept., v.15,
no.7, p.22-25, photo., table.

SUPREMATISM
Some thoughts on the historical fate
of twentieth century Moscow /
Natalya Dushkina.
On the demolition of Russian
architecture as promoted by
"modernists" such as Malevich,
Corbusier, and Ladovsky.
Translated from Russian.
TRANSITION 1990, no.33, p.40-57,
ill., photos., refs.

SURREALISM
Surrealist Paris / Alexander C.
Irwin.
PLACES 1990 Winter, v.6, no.2,
p.56-67, photos., refs.

SURVEYING
See also ARCHAEOLOGICAL SURVEYING
See also SURVEYORS

SURVEYING, ARCHAEOLOGICAL
See ARCHAEOLOGICAL SURVEYING

SURVEYORS, QUANTITY
See QUANTITY SURVEYORS

SURVEYS, ARCHAEOLOGICAL
See ARCHAEOLOGICAL INVENTORIES

SURVEYS - ARCHITECTURAL
See BUILDINGS - INVENTORIES

SURVEYS - CADRASTRAL
See CADASTRAL SURVEYS

SUSAN MAXMAN ARCHITECTS
Winter quarters: a year-round cabin
complex makes camping an event for
all seasons / Margaret Gaskie.
Girl Scout cabin complex, Camp
Tweedale, Lower Oxford township,
Penn. Susan Maxman Architects.
ARCHITECTURAL RECORD 1990 July,
v.178, no.8, p.64-67, photos.,
plans, secns., site plan.

SUSANKA, SARAH
Designing from the heart: an essay /
Sarah Susanka.
ARCHITECTURE MINNESOTA 1990
May-June, v.16, no.3, p.28-29,
112-115, dwgs.

SUSPENSION STRUCTURES
See also SUSPENSION BRIDGES
See also "SUSPENDED" AS A SUBHEADING
AFTER OTHER MAIN HEADINGS.

SUSPENSION STRUCTURES--ENGLAND--
LONDON--BRIDGE BUILDING
Composite: projet d'immeuble de
bureaux, Londres, G-B. / Francois
Magendie.
Bridge Building, an office block
which forms a bridge over the
Grand Union Canal at Battlebridge
Basin. Architects: David Marks,
Julia Barfield. English summary,
p.107. Spanish summary, p.169.
TECHNIQUES ET ARCHITECTURE 1990
Aug.-Sept., no.391, p.106-107,
det., dwgs., models.

SUSSMAN, DEBORAH
Conversations with Women Architects
/ Toshira Sato.
One of four sections in a special
feature on "Women in American
Architecture". Contents: Julie
Eizenberg.--Norma Sklarek/The
Jerda Partnership.--Deborah
Sussman.--Diane M. Caughey.--
Pamela Burton+Katherine Spitz.--
Dolores Hayden.--Sheila Levrant de
Bretteville.
SPACE DESIGN 1990 June, no.309,
p.06-22, dwgs., ports., elev.,
models, phgotos., plans, secn.

SUSTAINABLE DEVELOPMENT
Congres '89 atelier thematique: les
boises urbains- conservation ou
developpement / Marcel Piuze.
Report on a 1989 conference held
in Quebec City.
LANDSCAPE ARCHITECTURAL REVIEW
1990 Mar., v.11, no.1, p.27-28,
The Federal agenda: conservation
strategies and sustainability / E.
W. Manning.
LANDSCAPE ARCHITECTURAL REVIEW
1989 Mar., v.10, no.1, p.21-25,
biblio.
Formed by natural process: defining
the sustainable city / Michael
Hough.
Based on a paper presented in
Feb.1989 at the annual congress of
(Continued next page)

SUSTAINABLE DEVELOPMENT (CONTINUED)
Formed by natural...(CONTINUED)
the CSLA. Includes French summary.
LANDSCAPE ARCHITECTURAL REVIEW
1990 Oct., v.11, no.4, p.8-11,
map, photos.
Sustainable development in
professional planning: a potential
contribution of the EIA and UET
concepts / J.M. Kozlowski.
Application of environmental
impact assessments (EIA) and the
determination of ultimate
environmental thresholds (UET) on
sustainable development.
LANDSCAPE AND URBAN PLANNING 1990
Dec., v.19, no.4, p.307-332,
charts, maps, refs.
Sustainable development in the rural
landscape: an Ontario case study /
James R. Taylor.
Includes French summary.
LANDSCAPE ARCHITECTURAL REVIEW
1989 Mar., v.10, no.1, p.13-15,
ill., biblios.

SUSTAINABLE DEVELOPMENT--ARID REGIONS
Building in the Air and Tenere
Region, Niger / John Norton.
On building associated with a
conservation program for the
sub-Saharan strip.
MIMAR: ARCHITECTURE IN DEVELOPMENT
1990 Mar., v.10, no.1(34),
p.[50]-57, photos.

SUSTAINABLE DEVELOPMENT--CANADA
Sustainable development and private
stewardship: the landowner's role
in resource conservation / Stewart
Hilts.
Based on a paper presented in Feb.
1989 at a congress in Quebec.
Includes French summary.
LANDSCAPE ARCHITECTURAL REVIEW
1990 May, v.11, no.2, p.10-13,
ports., biblio.

SUSTAINABLE DEVELOPMENT--INDIA
Leh, Ladakh / Anuradha Chaturvedi.
Report on an INTACH-initiated
study of the socio-economic,
cultural, political, and
developmental issues involved in
preservation and sustainable
development of this area of India.
ARCHITECTURE + DESIGN 1989
Nov.-Dec., v.6, no.1, p.[82]-89,
graphs, elev., photos, site plans.

SUTCLIFFE, ANTHONY
From town-country to town planning:
changing priorities in the British
Garden city movement, 1899-1914 /
Anthony Sutcliffe.
PLANNING PERSPECTIVES: PP 1990
Sept., v.5, no.3, p.257-269, refs.
Metropolis: the world's great cities
[by] E. Jones [book review] /
Anthony Sutcliffe.
LONDON JOURNAL 1990, v.15, no.2,
p.[176]-177,
Post-industrial cities: politics and
planning in New York, Paris and
London [by] H.V. Savitch [book
review] / Anthony Sutcliffe.
LONDON JOURNAL 1990, v.15, no.1,
p.74-77,

SUTER UND SUTER
Haupstelle der Wurttembergischen
Handelsbank in Stuttgart / Falk
Jaeger.
Architects: Suter + Suter.
BAUWELT 1990 July 20, v.81, no.27,
p.1362, photos.
Konstruktion als Struktur und Form:
Textilfabrik Beldona, Widnan SG,
1987 / Erich Offermann.
Architects: Suter + Suter.
WERK, BAUEN + WOHNEN 1989 Oct.,
no.10, p.15-17, folded p. at end,
axonometric view, dets., dwgs.,
photos., plans, secn.
Ein neuer Impuls fur die Stadt: die
Hauptstelle der WHB in Stuttgart /
Peter Lorenz.
Architects: Suter + Suter.
ARCHITEKTUR, INNENARCHITEKTUR,
TECHNISCHER AUSBAU 1990 Dec.,
v.98, no.12, p.46-48, photos.,
plan.
Portfolio: technology and humanity /
Jim Murphy.
On two industrial buildings:
Beldona Fabrikations AG, Widnau,
Switzerland, architects: Suter und
Suter and ERCO Leuchten GmbH,
Ludenscheid, Germany, architects:
Kiessler und Partner.
PROGRESSIVE ARCHITECTURE 1990
Oct., v.71, no.10, p.96-[99],
photos., plans.

SUTER, URSULA
"Das Werk dieses Kommunisten lohnt
sich nicht zu erhalten / Ursula
Suter.
On the renovation of the 1928 Haus
"zum Neuen Singer," in Basel.
Original architects: Artaria &
Schmidt.
ARCHITHESE 1990 July-Aug., v.20,
no.4, p.73-74, photos.

SUTERS ARCHITECTS & PLANNERS
Newcastles Regional Museum: Suters
Architects & Planners.
Adaptive reuse of old brewery
buildings.
ARCHITECTURE AUSTRALIA 1989 Dec.,
v.78, no.11, p.44, photos., plan.

SUTRO, DIRK
The Linear Park: will it salvage
pedestrian dignity on Harbor
Drive? [interview] / Dirk Sutro.
In San Diego. Landscape
architects: Peter Walker and
Martha Schwartz with the Austin
Hansen Group.
CARTOUCHE 1990 Winter, v.19,
p.10-11, maps, photos.
Regional transit: Rob Quigley's
Escondido Transit Center / Dirk
Sutro.
In Escondido, Calif.
ARCHITECTURAL RECORD 1990 Sept.,
v.178, no.10, p.[128-131], dwg.,
photos., site plan.

SUTTON, GERTRUD KOBKE
Kunst i rummet, er alt pa sin rette
plads? [book review] / Gertrud
Kobke Sutton.
Review of "Kunst i rummet":
monumentaludsmykning i Danmark
1964-1988, by Leila Krogh.
LANDSKAB 1990 Feb., v.71, no.1,
p.22-23, photos.

SUTTON, GERTRUD KOBKE (CONTINUED)
Land art: Vildmarken, hegnet, kunst
og kult - i Danmark,
Storbritannien og USA / Gertrud
Kobke Sutton.
Review of two decades of land art,
in Denmark, Britain and the U.S.
Includes English summaries and
caption.
LANDSKAB 1989 Dec., v.70, no.8,
p.176-189,192, dwg., photos.,
biblio.

SUYS, TILMAN-FRANCOIS, 1783-1861
Le sculpteur Francois Rude
(1784-1855) et les architectes
Charles Vander Straeten
(1771-1834) et Tilman-Francois
Suys (1783-1861) au Palais royal
de Bruxelles / Anne van Ypersele
de Strihou.
To be continued.
MAISONS D'HIER ET D'AUJOURD'HUI =
DE WOONSTEDE DOOR DE EEUWEN HEEN
1989, no.81, p.4-[17], dwg.,
elevs., photos., refs.

SUZUKI, EDWARD, 1947-
Maison Serpente a Karuizawa.
Built for family and employees of
family business. Architect:
Edward Suzuki. English summary.
TECHNIQUES ET ARCHITECTURE 1990
June-July, no.390, p.136-137,
photos., plan.

SUZUKI, EIKI
Study on the introduction of
"kenchikusikichi-zousei
tochikukau-seiri" or excess
condemnation to the town planning
act of 1919 / Eiki Suzuki.
A "land readjustment system".
English summary, p.79.
NIHON KENCHIKU GAKKAI KEIKAKUKEI
RONBUN HOKOKU SHU = JOURNAL OF
ARCHITECTURE, PLANNING AND
ENVIRONMENTAL ENGINEERING 1990
Feb., no.2(408), p.71-79, refs.

SUZUKI, GUEN BERTHEAU
Watari-Um.
Multi-use building, Tokyo.
Architects: Mario Botta with
Takenaka Komuten Company. Includes
interview with Botta, entitled
Swiss architecture on Tokyo.
English summary, p.23.
KENCHIKU BUNKA 1990 Sept., v.45,
no.527, p.[154]-158, port.,
photos., plans.

SUZUKI, HIROYUKI
Time, speed, and design / Hiroyuki
Suzuki.
THE WHEEL EXTENDED 1990, v.19,
no.3, p.16-23, ill., photos.

SUZUKI, HISAO
Gathering establishments.
Part of a special feature on
Spanish contemporary architecture.
Contents: Palau de la Musica
Catalana, by Oscar Tusquets
Blanca, Carlos M. Diaz, Lluis
Clotet, Ignacio Paricio --
Television Andaluza, by Gonzalo
Diaz-Y. Recasens --Banco de
Espana, Jaen, by Rafael Moneo --
Almacenes Simon, by Lluis Clotet,
Ignacio Paricio --Mercado
Vilaseca-Salou, by Carlos Ferrater
(Continued next page)

SUZUKI, HISAO (CONTINUED)
Gathering...(CONTINUED)
Lambarri, Jose Luis Canosa --
Pabellon Rius i Taulet, by Pep
Bonet --Velodromo de Horta, by
Esteban Bonell, Francesc Rius --
Brief histories --Views through
the Camera's Finder, by Hisao
Suzuki. Text in Japanese.
SPACE DESIGN 1990 May, no.308,
p.93-131, dets., ports., elevs.,
model, photos., plans, secns.,
site plan, sketch, isometric dwg.

SUZUKI, KENJI
The housing-style limitation act of
tempo 14 (1843) and its effects on
"Chonin" houses / Kenji Suzuki.
Text in Japanese. Includes English
summary.
NIHON KENCHIKU GAKKAI KEIKAKUKEI
RONBUN HOKOKU SHU = JOURNAL OF
ARCHITECTURE, PLANNING AND
ENVIRONMENTAL ENGINEERING 1990
Sept., no.9(415), p.129-137,
graphs, ill.

SUZUKI, MARCELO
Paco municipal de Cambui.
Architects: Ferraz, Suzuki, Filho,
Roman.
PROJETO 1990 Apr.-May, no.131,
p.36-37, elev., photos., plns,
secn.

SUZUKI, RYOJI, 1944-
Folly 13(3), Expo '90.
Contents: Folly 13 story, by
Hajime Yatsuka.--Martinez Lapena +
Elias Torres, Ryoji Suzuki, Peter
Wilson, Morphosis. Text in
Japanese.
SPACE DESIGN 1990 Apr., no.307,
p.45-53, axonometric views, dwgs.,
elevs., models, plan.
Recent works: Daniel Libeskind
[interview] / Hajime Yatsuka,
Ryoji Suzuki.
Extension of the Berlin Museum
with the Jewish Museum, and Urban
Villa Lutzowplatz. Text in
Japanese.
SPACE DESIGN 1990 Feb., no.305,
p.73-84, dwgs., port., models.
Recent works: Peter Wilson.
Projects: Munster City Library,
and ZKM, Karlsruhe. Includes
interviews conducted by Koji Taki,
Hajime Yatsuka, and Ryogi Suzuki.
Text in Japanese.
SPACE DESIGN 1990 Apr., no.307,
p.54-68, dwg., elevs., models,
plans, secns., site plan.

SUZUKI, SHIGEFUMI
Kobe Institute of Art Technology.
Established in 1989. Architects:
Yasumi Yoshitake, Shigefumi
Suzuki. English summary, p.23.
KENCHIKU BUNKA 1990 Mar., v.45
no.521, p.111-122, diagr.,
photos., plans, elevs., site
plans, sketches.

SUZUKI, TAKAYUKI
Architecture critique II / Takayuki
Suzuki.
Features the Art Tower Mito
complex with the Tsukuba Center
Building auditorium. Architect:
Takayuki Suzuki. English summary,
p.19.

(Continued next column)

SUZUKI, TAKAYUKI (CONTINUED)
Architecture critique...(CONTINUED)
KENCHIKU BUNKA 1990 July, v.45,
no.525, p.[21]-34, dwgs., elev.,
photos., plans, secns.
SD Review, 1990.
Special feature: The 9th
exhibition of winning
architectural models + drawings.
Contents: Winning projects (Dai
Nagasaka + Mega; Shinichi Ogawa;
Kazuyo Sejima Architect
Associates; Gin Johannes; Hisaya
Noritomi) -- 16 projects -- Essays
by Hiroshi Hara, Kunihiko
Hayakawa, Kijo Rokkaku, Riichi
Miyake, and Takayuki Suzuki. Text
in Japanese.
SPACE DESIGN 1990 Dec.,
no.12(315), p.05-52, elevs.,
models, photos., plans, secns.,
site plans, isometric dwgs.

SVACHA, ROSTISLAV
K architektonickemu dilu Bohumila
Steigenhofera / Rostislav Svacha.
On the work of Czech architect B.
Steigenhofer (1905-1989).
Includes English summary.
UMENI 1990, v.38, no.3, p.274-278,
dwgs., photos., refs.
Krystof Dientzenhofer a cesky
dejepis umeni / Rostislav Svacha.
On the Prague builder and
architect and his place in Czech
art history. Includes English
summary.
UMENI 1989, v.37, no.6, p.506-519,
photos., refs.

SVANBERG, LENA. CENTRALBADET: ETT
VATTENHAL I STENSTADEN
Stympat centralbad [book review] /
Lars-Eric Jonsson.
Review of volume of essays on the
public baths in Stockholm, edited
by Lena Svanberg.
ARKITEKTUR: THE SWEDISH REVIEW OF
ARCHITECTURE 1990 Nov., v.90,
no.9, p.57-58, photo., secn.

SVATIN, S.
Il complesso residenziale di via
Gorkij (Mosca) = Presentation of
the residential project in Gorki
street in Moscow / S. Svatin.
Built 1985-88. Architects: A.
Meerson, E. Podol'skaia, O. Palei,
L. Visnicenko.
METAMORFOSI 1988, no.11, p.53-56,
photos., site plans.

SVAZ ARCHITEKTU CSSR--CONGRESSES
Czech conference targets consumption
/ Sally Siddigi.
Report on the International Prague
Assembly of Architects, Planners,
and Designers conference held in
Prague, Nov.6-11, 1989.
Co-sponsored: International
Architects / Designers / Planners
for the Prevention of Nuclear War
and the Union of Czechoslovak
Architects.
PROGRESSIVE ARCHITECTURE 1990
Feb., v.71, no.2, p.24,

SVEDBERG, OLLE
Dansk gigant [book review] / Olle
Svedberg.
Review of Arkitekten Mogens
Lassen, by Lisbet Balslev
Jorgensen.
ARKITEKTUR: THE SWEDISH REVIEW OF
ARCHITECTURE 1990 June-July, v.90,
no.5, p.46-47, photos., secns.,
site plan.

SVEDBERG, OLLE. VARLDEN DEN LILLA DEN
STORA
Egna Ogon & Andras [book review] /
Rasmus Waern.
Review of Varlden den lilla den
stora: Lustvandringar i
Klassicismens arkitektur och
tradgardar, by Anna-Maria Blenow
and Olle Svedberg, and Stader,
byggnader..., byNils Erik
Wickberg.
ARKITEKTUR: THE SWEDISH REVIEW OF
ARCHITECTURE 1990 Nov., v.90,
no.9, p.55-57, dwg., photos.

SVEDBURG, OLLE. ARKITEKTERNAS
ARHUNDRADE
Den moderne arkitektur - historie pa
svensk [book review] / Nils-Ole
Lund.
Review two 1988 surveys of
European architecture by Olle
Svedburg, on the 19th and 20th
centuries.
ARKITEKTEN 1990 Apr., v.92, no.5,
p.180, ill.

SVEDBURG, OLLE. PLANERARNAS ARHUNDRADE
Den moderne arkitektur - historie pa
svensk [book review] / Nils-Ole
Lund.
Review two 1988 surveys of
European architecture by Olle
Svedburg, on the 19th and 20th
centuries.
ARKITEKTEN 1990 Apr., v.92, no.5,
p.180, ill.

SVETCHINE, LUC
Deux chambres et des cloisons.
Features interiors of architect
Luc Svetchine's renovated
apartment in Nice.
MAISON FRANCAISE 1990 Mar.,
no.434, p.66-[71], photos.

SVOBODA, JAN
Josef Zasche / Zdenek Lukes, Jan
Svoboda.
On the work of Czech architect
Zasche (1871-1957). Includes
German summary.
UMENI 1990, v.38, no.6, p.534-543,
dwg., photos., refs.

SWA GROUP
Breaking new ground in the desert:
Hyatt Regency, Scottsdale,
Arizona, Hornberger Worstell &
Associates, architects.
Landscape architects; SWA Group.
ARCHITECTURAL RECORD 1990 Feb.,
v.178, no.2, p.122-125, photos.,
plan, site plan.
Utopia revised: at the University of
California at Irvine, the struggle
to adapt the unyielding geometry
of the campus continues / John
Parman.
On William Pereira's 1963 master
plan, and subsequent buildings by
(Continued next page)

SWA GROUP (CONTINUED)
  Utopia revised: at...(CONTINUED)
    other architects.
    ARCHITECTURE: THE AIA JOURNAL 1990
    Jan., v.79, no.1, p.66-77, dwg.,
    elev., photos., plans, site plans.
  Williams Square: where public space
    becomes public art / David Dillon.
    Public plaza in Dallas' Las
    Colinas development. Architect:
    James Reeves of the SWA Group.
    Sculptor: Robert Glen.
    SOUTHERN ACCENTS 1989 Nov.-Dec.,
    v.12, no.6, p.176B-176J, photos.

SWAHILI
  See "SWAHILI" AS A SUBHEADING AFTER
    SPECIFIC BUILDING TYPES OR OTHER
    MAIN HEADINGS.

SWAINE, RICHARD CARTER
  Friary Courts, Beverley.
    81 housing units built for the
    Beverley Borough Council, at
    Eastgate, Beverley. Architect: LNS
    Partnership in association with
    Richard Swaine.
    BUILDING 1990 July 13, v.255,
    no.28, p.49-54, dets., map,
    photos., plans, site plans.

SWAN, JOHN SYDNEY
  St. Gerard's Monastery, Wellington /
    Wayne Nelson.
    Earliest portion dates from 1910,
    architect: John Sydney Swan.
    Monastery portion dates from 1932,
    architect: Frederick de Jersey
    Clere. It is now for sale.
    HISTORIC PLACES IN NEW ZEALAND
    1989 June, no.25, p.19-20, photo.

SWANKE HAYDEN CONNELL ARCHITECTS
  Americans in London / Deborah K.
    Dietsch.
    On developments by American firms
    in Canary Wharf, Bishopsgate,
    Broadgate, and Spitalfields.
    ARCHITECTURE: THE AIA JOURNAL 1990
    Sept., v.79, no.9, p.[64-71],
    dwgs., models, photos., site
    plans, aerial photos.
  The color of money / Nayana
    Currimbhoy.
    Interiors of Central Federal
    Savings Bank, Mineola, NY.
    Architects: Swanke Hayden Connell.
    INTERIORS 1990 Apr., v.149, no.9,
    p.96-[99], photos., plan.
  Highway revisited.
    On five designs for the redesign
    of Birmingham's "Spaghetti
    Junction", sponsored by a British
    television show.
    BUILDING DESIGN 1990 June 15,
    no.990, p.14-16, sketches.
  Lighter legal touch / Nick Jones.
    Interiors of four London law
    offices.
    BUILDING DESIGN 1989 Oct., suppl.,
    p.36-39, photos., plans.
  McBride Baker & Coles / Edie Lee
    Cohen.
    Interiors of Chicago law offices
    located in the Northwest Atrium
    Center. Interior designers: Swanke
    Hayden Connell Architects.
    INTERIOR DESIGN 1990 May, v.61,
    no.7, p.234-[237], photos., plans.

SWANKE HAYDEN CONNELL ARCHITECTS
    (CONTINUED)
  Minimalist message / Karin Tetlow.
    Interiors of Swanke Hayden Connell
    Architects offices, Chicago.
    INTERIORS 1990 June, v.149, no.11,
    p.106-[107], photos., plan.
  Spitalfields inspiration / Francis
    Tibbalds.
    Comparison of Swanke Hayden
    Connell's masterplan for the
    Spitalfields area of London with
    Richard MacCormac's masterplan.
    BUILDING DESIGN 1990 Jan.12,
    no.968, p.14-17, dets., ill.,
    elevs., plans, site plans.
  Swanke avoids the poison pill /
    Michael J.P. Smith.
    Renovation of 18-year old office
    building at 55 East Monroe, by
    Swanke Hayden Connell Architects.
    Original architect: Alfred Shaw &
    Associates.
    INLAND ARCHITECT 1990 Sept.-Oct.,
    v.34, no.5, p.74-81, dwg., photo.
  Swanke Hayden Connell: the firm
    builds a building for its New York
    headquarters / Edie Lee Cohen.
    Office interiors.
    INTERIOR DESIGN 1990 July, v.61,
    no.10, p.[148-153], photos.,
    plans.

SWEDEN--ALMUNDSRYD--CHURCHES--19TH
CENTURY
  Landsorten Kontra centralstyret /
    Birgitta Sandstrom.
    Attitudes of rural parishes in
    Smaland, Sweden (Urshult and
    Almundsryd) toward the Swedish
    Board of Public Works, 1794-1917.
    Includes English summary.
    BEBYGGELSEHISTORISK TIDSKRIFT
    1989, no.17-18, p.114-124, elevs.,
    photos., plans, secns., biblio.

SWEDEN--APARTMENT COMPLEXES
  Bostader som bast / Karin Lidmar.
    Essay on the planning, siting and
    design of individual flat-type
    buildings, illustrated with work
    of Coordinator Arkitekter, Bengt
    Lindroos Arkitektkontor
    Sodergruppen Arkitektkontor, White
    Arkitekter, Ahlgren-Edblom
    Arkitekter, and Riksbyggen
    Konsult. English translation,
    p.55-56.
    ARKITEKTUR: THE SWEDISH REVIEW OF
    ARCHITECTURE 1990 Aug., v.90,
    no.6, p.4-9, dwgs., photos.,
    plans, site plan.

SWEDEN--ARCHITECTURAL DESIGN--THEORY
  Ritandets ritualer [Lennart Holm] /
    Soren Thurell.
    ARKITEKTUR: THE SWEDISH REVIEW OF
    ARCHITECTURE 1990 Sept., v.90,
    no.7, p.58-60, ports., site plan,
    refs.

SWEDEN--ARCHITECTURE
  Egna Ogon & Andras [book review] /
    Rasmus Waern.
    Review of Varlden den lilla den
    stora: Lustvandringar i
    Klassicismens arkitektur och
    tradgardar, by Anna-Maria Blenow
    and Olle Svedberg, and Stader,
    byggnader..., byNils Erik
    Wickberg.
    ARKITEKTUR: THE SWEDISH REVIEW OF
    (Continued next column)

SWEDEN--ARCHITECTURE (CONTINUED)
  Egna Ogon & Andras...(CONTINUED)
    ARCHITECTURE 1990 Nov., v.90,
    no.9, p.55-57, dwg., photos.

SWEDEN--ARCHITECTURE--18TH CENTURY
  Fredrik Henrik af Chapman och Carl
    August Ehrensvard som arkitekter
    [book review] / Urve Lepasoon.
    Review of Lantstallet Skarva, by
    Kerstin Barup and Mats Edstrom.
    BEBYGGELSEHISTORISK TIDSKRIFT
    1989, no.17-18, p.177-185, elevs.,
    photos., plans.

SWEDEN--ARCHITECTURE--19TH CENTURY
  Den parisiska lanken: Axel Nystrom
    vid Ecole des Beaux-Arts 1819-21 /
    Johan Martelius.
    Includes English summary.
    BEBYGGELSEHISTORISK TIDSKRIFT
    1989, no.17-18, p.161-176, elevs.,
    photo., plans, secns., refs.

SWEDEN--ARCHITECTURE--20TH CENTURY
  Svezia.
    Theme issue devoted to
    architecture in Sweden. 13
    articles indexed separately. Text
    in Italian and English.
    ABITARE 1990 July-Aug., no.287,
    p.87-224, ill.

SWEDEN--ARCHITECTURE--HUMAN FACTORS
  Fran bord till jord / Monika Jonson.
    ARKITEKTUR: THE SWEDISH REVIEW OF
    ARCHITECTURE 1990 Sept., v.90,
    no.7, p.52-53, dwgs., photos.

SWEDEN--ARCHITECTURE--THEORY
  Om tid eller plats.
    Introduction to issue entitled
    "Fasad", on the concept of
    facades. Includes three articles
    indexed separately and one
    entitled "Vad ar en fasad?" by
    Fredrik Wulz.
    ARKITEKTUR: THE SWEDISH REVIEW OF
    ARCHITECTURE 1990 June-July, v.90,
    no.5, p.2-3,24-27, cover, photos.,
    sketch.
  Skrivandets svarigheter [review] /
    Jahani Pallasmaa.
    Review of the shadow of thought:
    the James concept in architecture,
    by Soren Thurell, which first
    appeared in 1989 Swedish journal.
    ARKITEKTUR: THE SWEDISH REVIEW OF
    ARCHITECTURE 1990 Oct., v.90,
    no.8, p.58-60, dwgs.

SWEDEN--BORAS--OFFICES--INTERIOR
DESIGN--JC INKOPS
  Fribergs, Varnamo & JC, Boras.
    Interiors of clothing shop at
    Storgatsbacken 21 in Varnamo and
    of offices at Katrinedalsgaten 14
    in Boras. Architect: Rupert
    Gardner Design.
    ARKITEKTUR: THE SWEDISH REVIEW OF
    ARCHITECTURE 1990 Sept., v.90,
    no.7, p.26-27, elev., photos.

SWEDEN--BRIDGES--ENVIRONMENTAL ASPECTS
  Influence of pollution on mortar and
    concrete / Satish Chandra.
    Analysis of effects of, and
    remedies for, atmospheric gases,
    using several bridges and tunnels
    in Sweden as examples. Includes
    Swedish summary.
    SWEDISH COUNCIL FOR BUILDING
    (Continued next page)

SWEDEN--LINKOPING--FUNERARY CHAPELS--
LILLA ASKA KAPELLKREMATORIUM
Life in death / Henry Miles.
Crematorium, Lilla Aska (near
Linkoping), Sweden. Architect: Ove
Hidemark Arkitektkontor.
ARCHITECTURAL REVIEW 1990 Nov.,
v.188, no.1125, p.36-42, photos.,
plans, secns., site plan.

SWEDEN--LULEA--THEATERS
Le case di legno non sono solo rosse
= Wooden houses are not just red.
A 1648 farmhouse in Skraeddatorp;
18th-cent. houses in Stockholm;
house of architect Jan Gezelius,
Stockholm; the Anthropological
Museum at Eketorp; and the theater
workshop in Lulea (architects:
FFNS).
ABITARE 1990 July-Aug., no.287,
p.190-201, dwg., port., photos.,
plans, secns., site plan.

SWEDEN--LUND--CITIES AND TOWNS--
CONSERVATION AND RESTORATION
Growth and renewal: the Swedish
model / John Miller.
Example of city planning and
conservation in Lund.
EKISTICS 1989 Jan.-Apr., v.56,
no.334-335, p.56-64, maps,
photos., plans, refs.

SWEDEN--LUND--CITY PLANNING
Growth and renewal: the Swedish
model / John Miller.
Example of city planning and
conservation in Lund.
EKISTICS 1989 Jan.-Apr., v.56,
no.334-335, p.56-64, maps,
photos., plans, refs.

SWEDEN--LUND--OLD TOWNS--CONSERVATION
AND RESTORATION
Growth and renewal: the Swedish
model / John Miller.
Example of city planning and
conservation in Lund.
EKISTICS 1989 Jan.-Apr., v.56,
no.334-335, p.56-64, maps,
photos., plans, refs.

SWEDEN--LUND--RESTAURANTS--KULTURENS
RESTAURANG
Kulturens restaurang, Lund / Marten
Duner, Ivo Waldhor.
Restaurant pavilion at
Tegnersplatsen 1 (1988-1989).
Architect: A-Plan Arkitektkontor
AB. Includes commentary by
Madeleine Brechensbauer Brandin.
ARKITEKTUR: THE SWEDISH REVIEW OF
ARCHITECTURE 1990 Nov., v.90,
no.9, p.48-53, photos., plans,
site plan.

SWEDEN--LUND--STUDENT PROJECTS--LUNDS
TEKNISKA HOGSKOLA
Tema: utbildningen.
Introduction to section on
architectural education.
Contents: En skola for livet...,
by Jens Arnfred.--Mot en ny
helhet, by Thomas Thiis-Evensen.--
Elevprojekt. Includes student
projects from three Swedish
schools: LTH, CTH, and KTH.
English translations, p.57-58.
ARKITEKTUR: THE SWEDISH REVIEW OF
ARCHITECTURE 1990 Apr., v.90,
no.3, p.2-25,57-58,cover, dwgs.,
(Continued next column)

SWEDEN--LUND--STUDENT PROJECTS--LUNDS
TEKNISKA HOGSKOLA (CONTINUED)
Tema: utbildningen. (CONTINUED)
elevs., models, photos., plans,
secns., site plans.

SWEDEN--MALMO--EXHIBITION BUILDINGS--
STORA NYGATAN
Moderne kunst i tidligere el-vaerk /
Lasse Freisleben.
Renovation of a 90-year old
gasworks on Gasverksgatan/Stora
Nygatan, Malmo, Sweden for use as
an exhibition hall for modern art.
Original architect: John Smedberg.
Restoration architect: White
Arkitekter.
ARKITEKTEN 1989 Dec.12, v.91,
no.22, p.A544-A546, photos., plan.

SWEDEN--MALMO--FACTORIES--AUTOMOBILE--
SAAB
SAAB, Malmo / Mats Olsson.
Automobile factory located at
Vastra Varvsgatan 10. Architects:
LCA Arkitekter AB. Commentary,
p.46-47.
ARKITEKTUR: THE SWEDISH REVIEW OF
ARCHITECTURE 1990 Jan.-Feb., v.90,
no.1, p.32-37,46-47, photos.,
plan, secn., site plan.

SWEDEN--MALMO--GAS MANUFACTURE AND
WORKS--CONSERVATION AND RESTORATION
Moderne kunst i tidligere el-vaerk /
Lasse Freisleben.
Renovation of a 90-year old
gasworks on Gasverksgatan/Stora
Nygatan, Malmo, Sweden for use as
an exhibition hall for modern art.
Original architect: John Smedberg.
Restoration architect: White
Arkitekter.
ARKITEKTEN 1989 Dec.12, v.91,
no.22, p.A544-A546, photos., plan.

SWEDEN--MALMO--PARKING LOTS--MALMO
ENERGI
En anderledes parkeringsplads /
Kerstin Johanssen.
Landscape and parking area
designed in 1989 by Monika Gora
for Malmo Engergi AB's five-story
office building. Includes English
captions and summary.
LANDSKAB 1990 Feb., v.71, no.1,
p.14-17,24, ill., plan.

SWEDEN--MALMO--PARKS--COMPETITIONS--
MALMOHUS
Ein "Park der 90er Jahre" in Malmo,
Schweden = A "Park of the 90's" in
Malmo, Sweden.
Competition for park on the site
of the Castle, Malmohus. Winning
landscape architects: Jonna
Malgaard-Krarup, Frode Birk
Nielsen. Text in German.
ARKITEKTUR + WETTBEWERBE 1990
Dec., no.144, p.32-34, dwgs., site
plans.

SWEDEN--MODEL HOUSES--ENVIRONMENTAL
ASPECTS
Ventilation and airtightness in
low-rise residential buildings:
analyses and full-scale
measurements / Ake Blomsterberg.
Includes testing of six
experimental houses in Sweden, by
the National Swedish Testing
Institute.
(Continued next column)

SWEDEN--MODEL HOUSES--ENVIRONMENTAL
ASPECTS (CONTINUED)
Ventilation and...(CONTINUED)
SWEDISH COUNCIL FOR BUILDING
RESEARCH. DOCUMENT 1990, D10,
p.[1]-223, graphs, photos., plans,
tables, biblio.

SWEDEN--NACKA--CHURCHES--19TH
CENTURY--ALTERATIONS AND ADDITIONS
Le chiese, luoghi di aggregazione =
Churches, places of cohesion /
Carl Goran Bergman.
Markuskyran, Skarpnack, 1960 (S.
Lewerentz); church at Nacka (G.
Wickman; additions by Carl Nyren);
Gammelstad church.
ABITARE 1990 July-Aug., no.287,
p.184-189, elev., photos., plans,
site plan.

SWEDEN--NACKA--MULTI-USE BUILDINGS--
FORUM NACKA
Forum Nacka: FFNS Arkitekter / Ulf
Gillberg, Kjell Lundberg.
Shopping mall and community center
located on
Varmdovagen-Vikdalsvagan.
ARKITEKTUR: THE SWEDISH REVIEW OF
ARCHITECTURE 1990 Jan.-Feb., v.90,
no.1, p.16-21, photos., plans,
secns., site plan.

SWEDEN--NORRKOPING--CULTURAL CENTERS--
HOLMENOMRADET AHLGREN OLSSON SILOW
ARKITEKTKONTOR
Holmenomradet, Norrkoping / Kai
Wartiainen.
ARKITEKTUR: THE SWEDISH REVIEW OF
ARCHITECTURE 1990 June-July, v.90,
no.5, p.28-31, dwgs., elev.,
model, site plan, aerial photos.

SWEDEN--NORRKOPING--INDUSTRIAL
BUILDINGS--HOLMENTORGET
Holmens bruk: Joto Ulf Celander.
Photographic views of factories in
the Holmentorget area of
Norrkoping.
ARKITEKTUR: THE SWEDISH REVIEW OF
ARCHITECTURE 1990 June-July, v.90,
no.5, p.32-37, photos.

SWEDEN--NORRKOPING--WATERFRONT
BUILDINGS--ALTERATIONS AND
ADDITIONS--HOLMENOMRADET
Holmenomradet, Norrkoping / Kai
Wartiainen.
ARKITEKTUR: THE SWEDISH REVIEW OF
ARCHITECTURE 1990 June-July, v.90,
no.5, p.28-31, dwgs., elev.,
model, site plan, aerial photos.

SWEDEN--NYKOPING--CULTURAL CENTERS
Culturum, Nykoping: Nyrens
Arkitektkontor / Lars Gauffin.
Includes new library and concert
hall. Located on Hospitalsgatan
4. Commentary by Johan Martelius.
ARKITEKTUR: THE SWEDISH REVIEW OF
ARCHITECTURE 1990 Apr., v.90,
no.3, p.36-45, photos., plan,
secn., site plan.

SWEDEN--OIJARED--COUNTRY CLUBS--
OIJARED EXECUTIVE COUNTRY CLUB
Oijared Executive Country Club,
Oijared, Sweden, 1988.
Architects: Wingardh & Wingardh.
Includes essay: Arising out of the
ground / Claes Dreijer. Text in
Japanese and English.
(Continued next page)

SWEDEN--OIJARED--COUNTRY CLUBS--
OIJARED EXECUTIVE COUNTRY CLUB
(CONTINUED)
Oijared Executive...(CONTINUED)
ARCHITECTURE AND URBANISM 1990
July, no.7(238), p.[68]-81,
photos., plan, secn., site plan.

SWEDEN--OPEN SPACES
La progettazione degli spazi aperti
nell'edilizia residenziale svedese
/ Eivor Bucht.
URBANISTICA 1989 Dec., no.97,
p.76-78, axonometric view, photos.

SWEDEN--ORESUND--HOUSES--ITALIANATE--
ALTERATIONS AND ADDITIONS
To haver ved Sundet / Jeppe Aagaard
Andersen.
Two new gardens by the author for
a 1906 Italianate villa "by the
sound". Includes English
translation.
LANDSKAB 1990 Sept., v.71, no.6,
p.DK1-DK4, photos., site plans.

SWEDEN--ORESUND--RESIDENTIAL GARDENS
To haver ved Sundet / Jeppe Aagaard
Andersen.
Two new gardens by the author for
a 1906 Italianate villa "by the
sound". Includes English
translation.
LANDSKAB 1990 Sept., v.71, no.6,
p.DK1-DK4, photos., site plans.

SWEDEN--OSTERFARNEBO--SCHOOLS--
SECONDARY--KYRKSKOLAN
Teori och praktik / Lis Hogdahl.
Features two elementary schools,
in Vastervik and Taby (architects:
ATRIO Arkitekter; Dranger och
Kvant Arkitektkontor); a parish
secondary school in Osterfarnebo
(architect: Carlson Fernberg
Arkitektkontor); and a crafts
school in Stockholm (architect:
Asmussens arkitektkontor).
ARKITEKTUR: THE SWEDISH REVIEW OF
ARCHITECTURE 1990 Dec., v.90,
no.10, p.10-21,cover, photos.,
plans, site plans.

SWEDEN--PALACES--RENAISSANCE
Forlorad fasadutsmyckning pa
Ulriksdal och Venngarn / Ingrid
Rosell.
On the 17th-cent. facade
decorations on the palaces of
Ulriksdal (Jakobsdal) and
Venngarn, Sweden, particularly the
role of architects Jean de la
Vallee and Matthias Holl.
Includes English summary.
KONSTHISTORISK TIDSKRIFT 1989,
v.58, no.4, p.[151]-156, engrs.,
refs.

SWEDEN--PHOTOGRAPHY--ARCHITECTURAL
Gatt f till om / Rolf Wohlin.
Essay on form in architecture,
illustrated with five photographs
of European structures.
ARKITEKTUR: THE SWEDISH REVIEW OF
ARCHITECTURE 1990 Dec., v.90,
no.10, p.26-31, photos.

SWEDEN--PUBLIC BUILDINGS--18TH CENTURY
Overintendentsambetels organisation
och arbetsuppgifter / Barbro
Edling.
The organization and tasks of the
Swedish Board of Public Works in
the 18th cent., with discussion of
the role of the first
Superintendent, Nicodemus Tessin
the younger. Includes English
summary.
BEBYGGELSEHISTORISK TIDSKRIFT
1989, no.17-18, p.103-118,
photos., plans, secns., biblio.,
refs.

SWEDEN--ROBACK--GARDEN APARTMENTS--
KRAVATTEN
KV Kravaten, Umea / Thorsten Asbjer.
A garden apartment complex at
Roback. Includes commentary by
Monika Jonson and English summary,
p.56.
ARKITEKTUR: THE SWEDISH REVIEW OF
ARCHITECTURE 1990 Aug., v.90,
no.6, p.18-23, photos., plans,
site plan.

SWEDEN--RONNEBY--GARDENS--RONNEBY
BRUNN
Friskt vatten - Ronneby Brunn /
Elisabeth Norrby.
Restoration of an historically
significant former mineral spring
resort in Sweden with several
special gardens (scent; Japanese;
rose) and an animal farm. Project
conceived by Sven-Ingvar
Andersson. Includes English
translation and captions.
LANDSKAB 1990 May, v.71, no.3-4,
p.S1-S5, photos., site plans.

SWEDEN--RONNEBY--PARKS--RONNEBY BRUNN
Friskt vatten - Ronneby Brunn /
Elisabeth Norrby.
Restoration of an historically
significant former mineral spring
resort in Sweden with several
special gardens (scent; Japanese;
rose) and an animal farm. Project
conceived by Sven-Ingvar
Andersson. Includes English
translation and captions.
LANDSKAB 1990 May, v.71, no.3-4,
p.S1-S5, photos., site plans.

SWEDEN--SCHOOLS
Diskussion pagar / Gunnar
Lowenhielm.
On the General Study Plan for
Swedish Schools, with
illustrations of works by FFNS,
Studio 4, A-TRE Arkitekter,
Dranger & Kvant Arkitektkontor,
and Fritzell Carlsen
Arkitektkontor. Includes English
summary.
ARKITEKTUR: THE SWEDISH REVIEW OF
ARCHITECTURE 1990 Dec., v.90,
no.10, p.4-9,59-60, photos.,
plans, secns.
En Skola for livet?
Introduction to issue featuring
schools. Individual articles are
indexed separately. Includes
English summary.
ARKITEKTUR: THE SWEDISH REVIEW OF
ARCHITECTURE 1990 Dec., v.90,
no.10, p.2-3,59, photo.

SWEDEN--SHOPPING CENTERS
Drama i trestad / Lennart Karlsson.
On the location of shopping
centers in the vicinity of
Lysekil, Uddevalla, and Overby,
Sweden.
ARKITEKTUR: THE SWEDISH REVIEW OF
ARCHITECTURE 1990 Jan.-Feb., v.90,
no.1, p.30-31, photo., site plan.

SWEDEN--SIGTUNA--CHURCHES--13TH
CENTURY--MARIAKYRKAN
Franciscus och Dominicus i en
vaggmalning i Mariakyrkan i
Sigtuna / Rudolf Zeitler.
15th-cent. wall paintings in
13th-cent. Swedish church.
Includes commentary by Jarl Galler
and a German summary.
KONSTHISTORISK TIDSKRIFT 1990,
v.59, no.1-2, p.[144]-150,
photos., ref.

SWEDEN--SKANE--ESTATES (AGRICULTURAL
COMPLEXES)--19TH CENTURY--
SOCIOLOGICAL ASPECTS
Godsorganisation i forandring:
statsystemets uppkomst i Skane /
Jens Moller.
Changes in work organization on
large estates in the province of
Skane, Sweden, in the 19th cent.
Uses the Araslov farm near
Kristianstad as an example.
Includes English summary.
BEBYGGELSEHISTORISK TIDSKRIFT
1989, no.17-18, p.43-58, graphs,
maps, photos., table, biblio.,
refs.

SWEDEN--SKARPNACK--CHURCHES--20TH
CENTURY--MARKUSKYRAN
Le chiese, luoghi di aggregazione =
Churches, places of cohesion /
Carl Goran Bergman.
Markuskyran, Skarpnack, 1960 (S.
Lewerentz); church at Nacka (G.
Wickman; additions by Carl Nyren);
Gammelstad church.
ABITARE 1990 July-Aug., no.287,
p.184-189, elev., photos., plans,
site plan.

SWEDEN--SKARPNACK--GROUNDS
Landschaftsgestaltung in Skarpnack /
Par Gustafsson.
Landsaping at the new town of
Skarpnack, Sweden. Includes
English summary and captions.
GARTEN UND LANDSCHAFT 1990, v.100,
no.4, p.34-38, ill., photos.,
plans, secns., site plans, aerial
photos.

SWEDEN--SKARPNACK--NEW TOWNS
La grande Stoccolma = Greater
Stockholm / Marina Botta.
New towns: Vallingby, Skarpnack,
Enskede. Master planner: Sven
Markelius. Architects: Arken;
Brunnberggruppen; FFNS; Malmquist
& Skoogh; Per Olof Hallman.
ABITARE 1990 July-Aug., no.287,
p.156-163,224, axonometric views,
dets., elevs., map, photos.,
aerial photos.
Landschaftsgestaltung in Skarpnack /
Par Gustafsson.
Landsaping at the new town of
Skarpnack, Sweden. Includes
English summary and captions.
GARTEN UND LANDSCHAFT 1990, v.100,
(Continued next page)

SWEDEN--SKARPNACK--NEW TOWNS
                    (CONTINUED)
    Landschaftsgestaltung...(CONTINUED)
    no.4, p.34-38, ill., photos.,
    plans, secns., site plans, aerial
    photos.

SWEDEN--SKARPNACK--OPEN SPACES
    Landschaftsgestaltung in Skarpnack /
    Par Gustafsson.
    Landsaping at the new town of
    Skarpnack, Sweden. Includes
    English summary and captions.
    GARTEN UND LANDSCHAFT 1990, v.100,
    no.4, p.34-38, ill., photos.,
    plans, secns., site plans, aerial
    photos.

SWEDEN--SKRAEDDATORP--FARMHOUSES--17TH
    CENTURY
    Le case di legno non sono solo rosse
    = Wooden houses are not just red.
    A 1648 farmhouse in Skraeddatorp;
    18th-cent. houses in Stockholm;
    house of architect Jan Gezelius,
    Stockholm; the Anthropological
    Museum at Eketorp; and the theater
    workshop in Lulea (architects:
    FFNS).
    ABITARE 1990 July-Aug., no.287,
    p.190-201, dwg., port., photos.,
    plans, secns., site plan.

SWEDEN--SMALAND--PUBLIC BUILDINGS--
    SOCIOLOGICAL ASPECTS
    Landsorten Kontra centralstyret /
    Birgitta Sandstrom.
    Attitudes of rural parishes in
    Smaland, Sweden (Urshult and
    Almundsryd) toward the Swedish
    Board of Public Works, 1794-1917.
    Includes English summary.
    BEBYGGELSEHISTORISK TIDSKRIFT
    1989, no.17-18, p.114-124, elevs.,
    photos., plans, secns., biblio.

SWEDEN--SORMLAND--MANOR HOUSES--19TH
    CENTURY--ALTERATIONS AND ADDITIONS--
    SAFSTAHOLM
    Vibyholm och Safstaholm:
    moderniseringen av tra
    sormlandsslott / Ursula Sjoberg.
    On the modernization of two
    Swedish manor houses in the 1790s
    and early 1800s for Gustaf and
    Carl Bonde. Architect: Carl
    Christoffer Gjorwell. Includes
    English summary.
    BEBYGGELSEHISTORISK TIDSKRIFT
    1989, no.17-18, p.125-140, dwgs.,
    elevs., photos., plans, site plan,
    engrs., biblio., refs.

SWEDEN--SORMLAND--MANOR HOUSES--19TH
    CENTURY--ALTERATIONS AND ADDITIONS--
    VIBYHOLM
    Vibyholm och Safstaholm:
    moderniseringen av tra
    sormlandsslott / Ursula Sjoberg.
    On the modernization of two
    Swedish manor houses in the 1790s
    and early 1800s for Gustaf and
    Carl Bonde. Architect: Carl
    Christoffer Gjorwell. Includes
    English summary.
    BEBYGGELSEHISTORISK TIDSKRIFT
    1989, no.17-18, p.125-140, dwgs.,
    elevs., photos., plans, site plan,
    engrs., biblio., refs.

SWEDEN--STOCKHOLM--APARTMENT
    COMPLEXES--SLOPING SITES--SPJUTET
    Spjutet, Stockholm / Allan
    Pettersson.
    A 320-unit apartment complex at
    Hornstall in central Stockholm.
    Includes commentary by Eva
    Bjorklund and English summary,
    p.56.
    ARKITEKTUR: THE SWEDISH REVIEW OF
    ARCHITECTURE 1990 Aug., v.90,
    no.6, p.24-31, photos., plans,
    secn., site plan.

SWEDEN--STOCKHOLM--APARTMENTS--
    INTERIOR DESIGN--BONNIER - ALFORT
    APARTMENT
    When Jorgen met Gaga / Elisabeth
    Selse.
    Features interiors of Gaga Bonnier
    and Jorgen Alfort's renovated
    attic apartment in Stockholm.
    Interior designer: Gaga Bonnier.
    THE WORLD OF INTERIORS 1990 June,
    p.156-163, photos.

SWEDEN--STOCKHOLM--ARCHITECTURE--20TH
    CENTURY
    Stockholm panorerat [book review] /
    Fredric Bedoire.
    Review of Stockholmsperspektiv, by
    Barbara Noren-Brunback et al.
    ARKITEKTUR: THE SWEDISH REVIEW OF
    ARCHITECTURE 1990 Aug., v.90,
    no.6, p.51-52, site plan.

SWEDEN--STOCKHOLM--ARCHITECTURE--
    NEOCLASSICAL
    Classicismo iperboreo = Hyperborean
    classicism / Henrik O. Andersson.
    Swedish classicist architecture in
    Stockholm. Features the Rodabergen
    Quarter.
    ABITARE 1990 July-Aug., no.287,
    p.138-147, photos., secn.

SWEDEN--STOCKHOLM--BATHHOUSES--19TH
    CENTURY--ALTERATIONS AND ADDITIONS--
    STUREBADET
    Stoccolma, nel centro storico:
    l'intarsio = Stockholm, the
    historic centre: inlaying.
    Five examples of new buildings
    coexisting with old buildings.
    Architects: AOS; Studio
    Coordinator; Studio Alf Oreberg;
    Studio Hans Murman; Studio Arndt
    Malmquist; Studio Nyren.
    ABITARE 1990 July-Aug., no.287,
    p.108-[119], axonometric view,
    photos., plans, secns., site plan,
    aerial photo.

SWEDEN--STOCKHOLM--BATHS--CENTRALBAD
    Stympat centralbad [book review] /
    Lars-Eric Jonsson.
    Review of volume of essays on the
    public baths in Stockholm, edited
    by Lena Svanberg.
    ARKITEKTUR: THE SWEDISH REVIEW OF
    ARCHITECTURE 1990 Nov., v.90,
    no.9, p.57-58, photo., secn.

SWEDEN--STOCKHOLM--BUS STATIONS--
    STOCKHOLM CITY BUS TERMINAL
    Erskine & C.: stazione in piena
    luce.
    Bus station, Stockholm.
    ARCHITETTURA; CRONACHE E STORIA
    1990 June, v.36, no.6(416),
    p.446-447, plans, site plans.

SWEDEN--STOCKHOLM--CAPITOLS--
    ALTERATIONS AND ADDITIONS--
    PARLIAMENT
    Stoccolma, nel centro storico:
    l'intarsio = Stockholm, the
    historic centre: inlaying.
    Five examples of new buildings
    coexisting with old buildings.
    Architects: AOS; Studio
    Coordinator; Studio Alf Oreberg;
    Studio Hans Murman; Studio Arndt
    Malmquist; Studio Nyren.
    ABITARE 1990 July-Aug., no.287,
    p.108-[119], axonometric view,
    photos., plans, secns., site plan,
    aerial photo.

SWEDEN--STOCKHOLM--CEMETERIES--
    SKOGSKYRKOGARDEN
    Il parco della meditazione = The
    meditation park [Skogskyrkogarden,
    Stockholm] / Carlo Santi.
    Woodland Cemetery. Architects of
    landscape and of buildings: Gunnar
    Asplund and Sigurd Lewerentz.
    ABITARE 1990 July-Aug., no.287,
    p.164-171, photos., secn., site
    plans.

SWEDEN--STOCKHOLM--CENTRAL BUSINESS
    DISTRICTS
    Stoccolma, nel centro storico: la
    svolta razionalista = Stockholm,
    the historic centre: the
    rationalist turning point / Marina
    Botta.
    Architecture of the 1950s in
    Stockholm's business center.
    Architect and chief planner: Sven
    Markelius.
    ABITARE 1990 July-Aug., no.287,
    p.120-[123], photos., port.,
    aerial photo.

SWEDEN--STOCKHOLM--CITIES AND TOWNS--
    19TH CENTURY
    Staden i tornrosens bok / Bjorner
    Torsson.
    Images of Sweden in literature,
    including the work of C.J.L.
    Almqvist.
    ARKITEKTUR: THE SWEDISH REVIEW OF
    ARCHITECTURE 1990 Mar., v.90,
    no.2, p.10-14, ill., secn.

SWEDEN--STOCKHOLM--CITY HALLS
    Il Premio Nobel = The Nobel Prize
    [Stockholm City Hall].
    Built 1923.
    ABITARE 1990 July-Aug., no.287,
    p.152-[155], ports., photos.

SWEDEN--STOCKHOLM--CITY PLANNING
    Planning in Stockholm: RTPI study
    tour 1990 / Lynn Haslam.
    THE PLANNER 1990 Sept.14, v.76,
    no.36, p.17, photos.
    Uber oder neben den Geleisen? Der
    neue City-Terminal in Stockholm,
    1989 / Ernst Zietzschmann.
    Architects: Anders Tengbom, Ralph
    Erskine.
    WERK, BAUEN + WOHNEN 1989 Dec.,
    no.12, p.12-13, model, photos.,
    plans.

SWEDEN--STOCKHOLM--CLUBHOUSES--
INTERIOR DESIGN--HANDELSHOGSKOLAN
Bonnierrummet, Handelshogskolan &
Gyldene Freden, Stockholm.
Renovation and interior design of
the Handelshogskolan (1988) and
the Svenska Akademien (1990).
Architect: Ake Axelsson
Arkitektkontor.
ARKITEKTUR: THE SWEDISH REVIEW OF
ARCHITECTURE 1990 Sept., v.90,
no.7, p.14-15, photos.

SWEDEN--STOCKHOLM--DEPARTMENT STORES--
ART NOUVEAU--ALTERATIONS AND
ADDITIONS--NK
Stoccolma, nel centro storico:
l'intarsio = Stockholm, the
historic centre: inlaying.
Five examples of new buildings
coexisting with old buildings.
Architects: AOS; Studio
Coordinator; Studio Alf Oreberg;
Studio Hans Murman; Studio Arndt
Malmquist; Studio Nyren.
ABITARE 1990 July-Aug., no.287,
p.108-[119], axonometric view,
photos., plans, secns., site plan,
aerial photo.

SWEDEN--STOCKHOLM--ENCLOSED STADIUMS--
GLOBE
L'attraction du Globe: stade
omnisports, Stockholm.
Architects: Berg Arkitektkontor.
English summary, p.99. Spanish
summary, p.155.
TECHNIQUES ET ARCHITECTURE 1990
Dec.-1991 Jan., no.393, p.96-99,
photos., plans, secn., site plan.
Globen city, Stockholm / Sture
Koinberg, Lasse Vretblad.
Architects: Berg Arkitektkontor.
ARKITEKTUR: THE SWEDISH REVIEW OF
ARCHITECTURE 1990 Jan.-Feb., v.90,
no.1, p.22-29, photos., plans.
Globushalle in Stockholm, Schweden =
Globe Arena in Stockholm, Sweden.
Globen, multi-use sports and
cultural building. Architects:
Berg Arkitektkontor.
ARCHITEKTUR + WETTBEWERBE 1990
Mar., no.141, p.6-7, photos.,
plan.
Stoccolma: le megastrutture =
Stockholm: mega-buildings.
The World Trade Center (Arken,
Erskine & Tengbom); The Globe
(Berg Arkitektkontor).
ABITARE 1990 July-Aug., no.287,
p.124-129, dwg., photos., plans,
secns., site plan, aerial photo.

SWEDEN--STOCKHOLM--FARMHOUSES--18TH
CENTURY--INTERIOR DESIGN--LARS
SJOBERG HOUSE
Simply Swedish [farmhouse] / Marion
Fox.
18th century farmhouse near
Stockholm.
HOUSE BEAUTIFUL 1990 Mar., v.132,
no.3, p.72-79, photos.

SWEDEN--STOCKHOLM--FUNERARY CHAPELS--
SKOGSKYRKOGARDEN
Il parco della meditazione = The
meditation park [Skogskyrkogarden,
Stockholm] / Carlo Santi.
Woodland Cemetery. Architects of
landscape and of buildings: Gunnar
Asplund and Sigurd Lewerentz.
ABITARE 1990 July-Aug., no.287,
(Continued next column)

SWEDEN--STOCKHOLM--FUNERARY CHAPELS--
SKOGSKYRKOGARDEN (CONTINUED)
Il parco della...(CONTINUED)
p.164-171, photos., secn., site
plans.

SWEDEN--STOCKHOLM--HISTORIC
BUILDINGS--CONSERVATION AND
RESTORATION--GAMLA STAN
L'origine della citta = The Origins
of the city: Gamla Stan.
Many historic buildings have been
restored on this island in the
center of Stockholm. Features the
studios of Carl Nyren and Bengt
Lindroos.
ABITARE 1990 July-Aug., no.287,
p.[96-107], ports., photos.,
secns., site plan.

SWEDEN--STOCKHOLM--HISTORIC
DISTRICTS--GAMLA STAN
L'origine della citta = The Origins
of the city: Gamla Stan.
Many historic buildings have been
restored on this island in the
center of Stockholm. Features the
studios of Carl Nyren and Bengt
Lindroos.
ABITARE 1990 July-Aug., no.287,
p.[96-107], ports., photos.,
secns., site plan.

SWEDEN--STOCKHOLM--HOTELS--INTERIOR
DESIGN--SCANDIC CROWN HOTEL
White noise / David Redhead.
Interiors of the Scandic Crown
Hotel, Stockholm. Interior
designers: Wingardh och Wingardh
och Wilhelmsson.
DESIGNERS' JOURNAL 1990 June,
no.58, p.84-[87], photos., plan.

SWEDEN--STOCKHOLM--HOUSES--18TH
CENTURY--WOODEN
Le case di legno non sono solo rosse
= Wooden houses are not just red.
A 1648 farmhouse in Skraeddatorp;
18th-cent. houses in Stockholm;
house of architect Jan Gezelius,
Stockholm; the Anthropological
Museum at Eketorp; and the theater
workshop in Lulea (architects:
FFNS).
ABITARE 1990 July-Aug., no.287,
p.190-201, dwg., port., photos.,
plans, secns., site plan.

SWEDEN--STOCKHOLM--HOUSES--
ARCHITECTS'--GEZELIUS HOUSE
Le case di legno non sono solo rosse
= Wooden houses are not just red.
A 1648 farmhouse in Skraeddatorp;
18th-cent. houses in Stockholm;
house of architect Jan Gezelius,
Stockholm; the Anthropological
Museum at Eketorp; and the theater
workshop in Lulea (architects:
FFNS).
ABITARE 1990 July-Aug., no.287,
p.190-201, dwg., port., photos.,
plans, secns., site plan.

SWEDEN--STOCKHOLM--HOUSES--INTERIOR
DESIGN--WALLENIUSREDERIERNA
Atlantic Song, Walleniusrederierna,
Stockholm.
A combined office and residence
for a Swedish shipping firm, at
Fatbursgatan 1, built 1988-1989.
Architect for house: L. Bergstrom
Arkitektkontor. Interior
(Continued next column)

SWEDEN--STOCKHOLM--HOUSES--INTERIOR
DESIGN--WALLENIUSREDERIERNA
(CONTINUED)
Atlantic Song,...(CONTINUED)
architects: Brygghuset Arkitekter.
ARKITEKTUR: THE SWEDISH REVIEW OF
ARCHITECTURE 1990 Sept., v.90,
no.7, p.22-23, photos., plans,
secn.

SWEDEN--STOCKHOLM--HOUSING--
HAMMARBYHOJDEN
Den vita staden [book review] / Eva
Rudberg.
Review of Den vita staden -
Hammarbyhojden under femtio ar, by
Ulrika Sax.
ARKITEKTUR: THE SWEDISH REVIEW OF
ARCHITECTURE 1990 Aug., v.90,
no.6, p.50-51, photo., aerial
photo.

SWEDEN--STOCKHOLM--INNS--KALLHAGEN
Kallhagen, Stockholm / Kristen
Bjurstrom.
Inn at Djurgardsbrunnsvagen 10-14.
Architect: Bjurstrom & Brodin
Arkitekter. Includes commentary by
Caroline Constant.
ARKITEKTUR: THE SWEDISH REVIEW OF
ARCHITECTURE 1990 Nov., v.90,
no.9, p.34-43, elev., photos.,
plans, secns., site plan.

SWEDEN--STOCKHOLM--LANDSCAPE
ARCHITECTURE--SKOGSKYKOGARDEN
Skogskykogarden / Fredric Bedoire.
In Stockholm. Architect: Sigurd
Lewerentz.
ARKITEKTUR: THE SWEDISH REVIEW OF
ARCHITECTURE 1990 May, v.90, no.4,
p.34-41, dets., ill., dwgs.,
elevs., photos., aerial photos.,
refs.

SWEDEN--STOCKHOLM--LAW OFFICES--
INTERIOR DESIGN--
JUSTITIEKANSLERAMBETET
Justitiekanslerambetet, Stockholm.
Redesign (1988-1989) of the
attorney general's office in the
18th-cent. Ryningska palatset at
Stora Nygatan 2b. Architect:
Carita Kull.
ARKITEKTUR: THE SWEDISH REVIEW OF
ARCHITECTURE 1990 Sept., v.90,
no.7, p.16-17, photos., plan.

SWEDEN--STOCKHOLM--LIBRARIES--PUBLIC--
STADSBIBLIOTEK
Emile Gummar Asplund:
Stadsbiblioteketi Stockholm
1918-1927.
Photographs.
SKALA 1990, no.21, p.22-25, elev.,
photos., plan, secn.

SWEDEN--STOCKHOLM--LIBRARIES (ROOMS
AND SPACES)--18TH CENTURY
CONSERVATION AND RESTORATION--
BERNADOTTEBIBLIOTHEK
Einer literarischer Ort / Hermann
Orth.
On the restored 18th cent.
Bernadottebibliothek; Stockholm.
Original architect: Johann Carl
Cronstedt.
ARCHITEKTUR & WOHNEN 1990
Oct.-Nov., no.5, p.[196]-200,
port., photos.

(Continued next page)

SWEDEN--STRUCTURAL FRAMES--STEEL
Steel construction.
A "technology special" section,
with articles on the reduction in
British Standard fire protection
requirements, steel works in the
U.K., prioritieis of the British
Constructional Steelwork
Association and a Swedish on site
steel building system.
BUILDING 1990 June 22, v.255,
no.25, p.53-66, port., photos.,
secns.

SWEDEN--SUNDBORN--HISTORIC HOUSE
MUSEUMS--LARSSON HOUSE
A homemade house [Lilla Hyttnas] /
Witold Rybczynski.
The home of artist Carl Larsson
and his wife Karin, a traditional
log cabin in Sundborn, over 100
miles from Stockholm.
ART & ANTIQUES 1990 Dec., v.7,
no.10, p.[74]-81,120, ports.,
photos.

SWEDEN--SUNDBORN--HOUSES--LILLA
HYTTNAS
A homemade house [Lilla Hyttnas] /
Witold Rybczynski.
The home of artist Carl Larsson
and his wife Karin, a traditional
log cabin in Sundborn, over 100
miles from Stockholm.
ART & ANTIQUES 1990 Dec., v.7,
no.10, p.[74]-81,120, ports.,
photos.

SWEDEN--TABY--SCHOOLS--ELEMENTARY--
MYRANGEN
Teori och praktik / Lis Hogdahl.
Features two elementary schools,
in Vastervik and Taby (architects:
ATRIO Arkitekter; Dranger och
Kvant Arkitektkontor); a parish
secondary school in Osterfarnebo
(architect: Carlson Fernberg
Arkitektkontor); and a crafts
school in Stockholm (architect:
Asmussens arkitektkontor).
ARKITEKTUR: THE SWEDISH REVIEW OF
ARCHITECTURE 1990 Dec., v.90,
no.10, p.10-21,cover, photos.,
plans, site plans.

SWEDEN--TALL BUILDINGS--SOCIOLOGICAL
ASPECTS
Nej till hoghus! [editorial].
Introduction to section on
multi-storey buildings in Sweden.
The three articles are indexed
separately. Includes English
translation.
ARKITEKTUR: THE SWEDISH REVIEW OF
ARCHITECTURE 1990 May, v.90, no.4,
p.2,57.

SWEDEN--TRANSPORTATION PLANNING
Langs vagen.
Introduction to issue featuring
transportation topics. Articles
are indexed separately.
ARKITEKTUR: THE SWEDISH REVIEW OF
ARCHITECTURE 1990 Nov., v.90,
no.9, p.2-3, photo.

SWEDEN--TUNNELS--ENVIRONMENTAL ASPECTS
Influence of pollution on mortar and
concrete / Satish Chandra.
Analysis of effects of, and
remedies for, atmospheric gases,
using several bridges and tunnels
in Sweden as examples. Includes
Swedish summary.
SWEDISH COUNCIL FOR BUILDING
RESEARCH. DOCUMENT 1990, D6,
p.1-83, diagrs., graphs, photos.,
secn., table, biblio.

SWEDEN--UDDEVALLA--FACTORIES--
AUTOMOBILE--VOLVO
Volvo Uddevalla / Gunnar Werner.
Automobile factory located at F d
Uddevallavarvet. Architects: White
arkitekter, Mitchell Giurgola
Architects, AKOS arkitektkontor.
Includes commentary by Anders
Tornqvist and Peter Ullmark.
ARKITEKTUR: THE SWEDISH REVIEW OF
ARCHITECTURE 1990 Jan.-Feb., v.90,
no.1, p.38-47, photos., plans,
site plans, sketches.

SWEDEN--ULRIKSDAL--FACADES--17TH
CENTURY
Forlorad fasadutsmyckning pa
Ulriksdal och Venngarn / Ingrid
Rosell.
On the 17th-cent. facade
decorations on the palaces of
Ulriksda! (Jakobsdal) and
Venngarn, Sweden, particularly the
role of architects Jean de la
Vallee and Matthias Holl.
Includes English summary.
KONSTHISTORISK TIDSKRIFT 1989,
v.58, no.4, p.[151]-156, engrs.,
refs.

SWEDEN--UPPSALA--CATHEDRALS--GOTHIC--
UPPSALA DOMKYRKAS
Fragor rorande Uppsala domkyrkas
aldsta byggnadshistoria / Rudolf
Zeitler.
Includes German summary.
KONSTHISTORISK TIDSKRIFT 1990,
v.59, no.3, p.[159]-168, dets.,
photos., plans, refs.

SWEDEN--UPPSALA--COUNTRY HOUSES--18TH
CENTURY--HAMMARBY (LINNAEUS HOUSE)
A naturalist's roots: an
eighteenth-century Swedish house
and garden preserve the habitat
of botanist Carolus Linnaeus /
Christopher Petkanas.
Hammarby, 18th. estate and gardens
near the University of Uppsala.
HOUSE & GARDEN 1990 July, v.162,
no.7, p.[96-103],134, ill., port.,
photos., engr.

SWEDEN--UPPSALA--GARDENS--18TH
CENTURY--CONSERVATION AND
RESTORATION--HAMMARBY (LINNAEUS
GARDENS)
A naturalist's roots: an
eighteenth-century Swedish house
and garden preserve the habitat
of botanist Carolus Linnaeus /
Christopher Petkanas.
Hammarby, 18th. estate and gardens
near the University of Uppsala.
HOUSE & GARDEN 1990 July, v.162,
no.7, p.[96-103],134, ill., port.,
photos., engr.

SWEDEN--UPPSALA--SCHOOLS--ELEMENTARY--
VAKSALASKOLAN
Skolhusets betydelse / Ann Skantze.
Theoretical aspects of school
design, with reference to the 1925
Vaksalaskolan in Uppsala
(architect: Gunnar Leche).
ARKITEKTUR: THE SWEDISH REVIEW OF
ARCHITECTURE 1990 Dec., v.90,
no.10, p.22-25, photos., biblio.

SWEDEN--URBAN FRINGES
Tema: externt.
Introduction to issue on "external
centers". Articles are indexed
separately. Commentary by Olof
Hultin, p.28. English
translation, p.55.
ARKITEKTUR: THE SWEDISH REVIEW OF
ARCHITECTURE 1990 Jan.-Feb., v.90,
no.1, p.2-3, cover, photo.

SWEDEN--URBAN PARKS
La progettazione degli spazi aperti
nell'edilizia residenziale svedese
/ Eivor Bucht.
URBANISTICA 1989 Dec., no.97,
p.76-78, axonometric view, photos.

SWEDEN--URSHULT--CHURCHES--19TH
CENTURY
Landsorten Kontra centralstyret /
Birgitta Sandstrom.
Attitudes of rural parishes in
Smaland, Sweden (Urshult and
Almundsryd) toward the Swedish
Board of Public Works, 1794-1917.
Includes English summary.
BEBYGGELSEHISTORISK TIDSKRIFT
1989, no.17-18, p.114-124, elevs.,
photos., plans, secns., biblio.

SWEDEN--VACATION HOUSES--ARCHITECTS'
Arcaica e moderna [vacation house,
Sweden] / Elisa Dal Canto.
Architect: Karin Mattson-Nordin.
VILLE GIARDINI 1990 Apr., no.247,
p.18-21, photos, plan.

SWEDEN--VADERSTAD--CHURCHES--19TH
CENTURY
Utsikt fran Vaderstads kyrka / Axel
Unnerback.
Analysis of church building in
Sweden 1760-1860, using Vaderstad
as an example and discussing
architects Carl Harleman, C.F.
Adelcrantz, and Axel Nystrom.
Includes English summary.
BEBYGGELSEHISTORISK TIDSKRIFT
1989, no.17-18, p.141-160, elevs.,
photos., plans, secns., biblio.,
refs.

SWEDEN--VALLINGBY--NEW TOWNS
La grande Stoccolma = Greater
Stockholm / Marina Botta.
New towns: Vallingby, Skarpnack,
Enskede. Master planner: Sven
Markelius. Architects: Arken;
Brunnberggruppen; FFNS; Malmquist
& Skoogh; Per Olof Hallman.
ABITARE 1990 July-Aug., no.287,
p.156-163,224, axonometric views,
dets., elevs., map, photos.,
aerial photos.

SWEDEN--VARNAMO--STORES--CLOTHING--
FRIBERGS
Fribergs, Varnamo & JC, Boras.
Interiors of clothing shop at
Storgatsbacken 21 in Varnamo and
of offices at Katrinedalsgaten 14
in Boras. Architect: Rupert
Gardner Design.
ARKITEKTUR: THE SWEDISH REVIEW OF
ARCHITECTURE 1990 Sept., v.90,
no.7, p.26-27, elev., photos.

SWEDEN--VASTERAS--APARTMENT
COMPLEXES--ALTERATIONS AND
ADDITIONS--JULIUS & JORGEN
KV Julius & Jorgen, Vasteras / Lars
Dahlskog, Hans Broberg.
Housing project on Ostermalmsgatan
with renovation of three buildings
and construction of 102 new units.
Architect: K-Konsult. Includes
commentary by Olof Hultin and
English summary, p.56.
ARKITEKTUR: THE SWEDISH REVIEW OF
ARCHITECTURE 1990 Aug., v.90,
no.6, p.10-17,cover, elev.,
photos., plans, site plans, aerial
photo.

SWEDEN--VASTERAS--MULTI-USE
BUILDINGS--KVARTERET LORENS
KV Lorens, Vasteras / Boris Culjat.
Located at ArosCenter and
completed in 1990. Architect:
Ahlqvist & Culjat Arkitekter.
Includes commentary by Bosse
Bergman.
ARKITEKTUR: THE SWEDISH REVIEW OF
ARCHITECTURE 1990 May, v.90, no.4,
p.22-29, photos., plans, secn.,
site plans, isometric dwg.

SWEDEN--VASTERAS--SUMMER HOUSES--20TH
CENTURY--VILLA BARKARO
Villa Barkaro bei Vasteras, S =
Villa Barkaro near Vasteras, S.
Architects: Sodergruppen
Arkitektkontor AB.
DETAIL 1990 Feb.-Mar., v.30, no.1,
p.57-60, dets., elevs., photos.,
plans, secns.

SWEDEN--VASTERVIK--SCHOOLS--
ELEMENTARY--KVANNAREN
Teori och praktik / Lis Hogdahl.
Features two elementary schools,
in Vastervik and Taby (architects:
ATRIO Arkitekter; Dranger och
Kvant Arkitektkontor); a parish
secondary school in Osterfarnebo
(architect: Carlson Fernberg
Arkitektkontor); and a crafts
school in Stockholm (architect:
Asmussens arkitektkontor).
ARKITEKTUR: THE SWEDISH REVIEW OF
ARCHITECTURE 1990 Dec., v.90,
no.10, p.10-21,cover, photos.,
plans, site plans.

SWEDEN--VENNGARN--FACADES--17TH
CENTURY
Forlorad fasadutsmyckning pa
Ulriksdal och Venngarn / Ingrid
Rosell.
On the 17th-cent. facade
decorations on the palaces of
Ulriksdal (Jakobsdal) and
Venngarn, Sweden, particularly the
role of architects Jean de la
Vallee and Matthias Holl.
Includes English summary.
KONSTHISTORISK TIDSKRIFT 1989,
(Continued next column)

SWEDEN--VENNGARN--FACADES--17TH
CENTURY (CONTINUED)
Forlorad...(CONTINUED)
v.58, no.4, p.[151]-156, engrs.,
refs.

SWEDEN--VERNACULAR ARCHITECTURE
A homemade house [Lilla Hyttnas] /
Witold Rybczynski.
The home of artist Carl Larsson
and his wife Karin, a traditional
log cabin in Sundborn, over 100
miles from Stockholm.
ART & ANTIQUES 1990 Dec., v.7,
no.10, p.[74]-81,120, ports.,
photos.

SWEDEN--VISBY--ARCHITECTURE--
CONSERVATION AND RESTORATION--
KVARTERET TRIANGELN
KV triangeln, Visby / Annalena
Mosseen.
Renovation to shops and residences
on the Hastgatan, Sodra
Kyrkogatan, Smittens block.
Architect: Visby Arkitektgrupp.
Completed in 1988. Includes
commentary by Kristian Berg.
ARKITEKTUR: THE SWEDISH REVIEW OF
ARCHITECTURE 1990 Sept., v.90,
no.7, p.40-47, photos., plan, site
plans.

SWEDEN--VISBY--CENTRAL BUSINESS
DISTRICTS--CONSERVATION AND
RESTORATION--KVARTERET TRIANGELN
KV triangeln, Visby / Annalena
Mosseen.
Renovation to shops and residences
on the Hastgatan, Sodra
Kyrkogatan, Smittens block.
Architect: Visby Arkitektgrupp.
Completed in 1988. Includes
commentary by Kristian Berg.
ARKITEKTUR: THE SWEDISH REVIEW OF
ARCHITECTURE 1990 Sept., v.90,
no.7, p.40-47, photos., plan, site
plans.

SWEENEY, THOMAS W.
City may save Nevada rail landmark
[Virginia and Truckee Railroad
Engine House, Carson City] /
Thomas W. Sweeney.
1873 limestone structure.
PRESERVATION NEWS 1990 May, v.30,
no.5, p.1,19, photo.
Crowning history with metalsmith
Hank Hart / Thomas W. Sweeney.
Restoration of the copper dome of
the Foellinger Auditorium,
University of Ill.
PRESERVATION NEWS 1990 June, v.30,
no.6, p.8-9, ports., photos.
Enhancing a legacy: Trust guides
historic Maryland house into the
future [Batchelor's Hope, St.
Mary's County] / Thomas W.
Sweeney.
"One of southern Maryland's most
unusual, and charming, small
18th-century houses has been given
by Walter and Elizabeth Simpson to
the National Trust..."
PRESERVATION NEWS 1990 June, v.30,
no.6, p.3,15, photos.
Finding the unvarnished truth about
wood floors / Thomas W. Sweeney.
Michael Purser, Atlanta, a
specialist who restores and
refinishes wooden floors.
PRESERVATION NEWS 1990 Jan., v.30,
(Continued next column)

SWEENEY, THOMAS W. (CONTINUED)
Finding the...(CONTINUED)
no.1, p.12-13, ports., photos.
History on the mend: Hugo, quake
victims work to save and rebuild /
Arnold Berke, Thomas W. Sweeney.
Reports on preservation efforts
following Hurricane Hugo and
northern California's earthquake.
PRESERVATION NEWS 1990 May, v.30,
no.5, p.1,18, photos.
Making Bell House sound: U.S. WEST
restores Georgetown landmark /
Thomas W. Sweeney.
The 1853 house, bought in 1881 by
Alexander Graham Bell as a
residence for his father, has been
acquired by U.S. WEST, the
telephone company, and restored
under the supervision of Bette
Anderson.
PRESERVATION NEWS 1990 Feb., v.30,
no.2, p.7,16, photos.
Plastics: new crop at landmark
plantation? [Whitney Plantation,
St. John the Baptist Parish,
Wallace, La.] / Thomas W. Sweeney.
"One of Louisiana's most important
early plantation houses may be
purchased by a Taiwanese plastics
company for the site of proposed
rayon fiber plant..."
PRESERVATION NEWS 1990 Apr., v.30,
no.4, p.1,23, photos.
"Proud of what I've done": Romanian
emigre blossoms in new world /
Thomas W. Sweeney.
Aurelian Ilie, a specialist in
marbleizing, scagliola and
stenciling, has restored the
painted interior finish of Union
Station, Wahington, D.C., and the
Riggs Bank (formerly Farmers and
Mechanics Bank), Georgetown, D.C.
PRESERVATION NEWS 1990 Feb., v.30,
no.2, p.14-15, ports., photos.
Reclaiming old Singapore / Thomas W.
Sweeney.
HISTORIC PRESERVATION 1990
May-June, v.42, no.3, p.[42]-49,
ports., models, photos.
Sand castles / Thomas W. Sweeney.
McMillan Reservoir site and park,
Washington, D.C., threatened by
development. Landscape architect:
Frederick Law Olmstead, Jr.
HISTORIC PRESERVATION 1990
July-Aug., v.42, no.4, p.38-[43],
72, photos.
Shoe house: a perfect fit? [Haines
Shoe House, York County, Pa.] /
Thomas W. Sweeney.
Mahlon Haines built his Shoe House
in 1948 to advertise his shoe
business.
PRESERVATION NEWS 1989 Dec., v.29,
no.12, p.1,17, port., photo.
Transit transformation; New Orleans
revives street lines / Thomas W.
Sweeney.
PRESERVATION NEWS 1990 Jan., v.30,
no.1, p.1,3,20, photos.
A wide embrace: Todd Dickenson
masters many crafts / Thomas
Sweeney.
Restoration craftsman,
Hillsborough, N.C.
PRESERVATION NEWS 1990 May, v.30,
no.5, p.8-9, ports., photos.

SWEENY-JUSTICE, KAREN
Interpretation.
Nine articles on historic site
methods. Authors: Sandra S. Weber,
F.A. Ketterson, Marcella Sherfy,
Edward Tabor Linenthal, Raymond H.
Thompson, Michael E. Whatley,
Marie T. Myers, Karen
Sweeny-Justice, Kathleen Hunter.
CRM BULLETIN: A NATIONAL PARK
SERVICE TECHNICAL BULLETIN 1990,
v.13, no.3, p.1-21, photos.

SWEET, FAY
Commercial properties / Fay Sweet,
David Redhead.
Features interiors of five
advertising agencies.
DESIGNER'S JOURNAL 1990 Mar.,
no.55, p.30-37, photos., plans.
Flexible friends: The plastics age:
from modernity to post-modernity
[exhibition review] / Fay Sweet.
Exhibition of plastic as a
building industrial and decorative
material at the Victoria and
Albert Museum, London, through 29
Apr. 1990.
ARCHITECTS' JOURNAL 1990 Feb.28,
v.191, no.9, p.78-79, photos.
Next store neighbour / Fay Sweet.
On London clothing store, ing.
Architects: Harper MacKay.
DESIGNERS' JOURNAL 1990 Jan.,
no.53, p.64-[67], dets., photos.,
plans.
Restoring glory / Fay Sweet, Helen
Elias.
On the refurbished interiors of
four department stores, three in
London and one in Helsinki.
DESIGNERS' JOURNAL 1990 Feb.,
no.54, p.28-33, photos.
Tales of the riverbank / Fay Sweet.
Features the new offices of Foster
Associates, London, along the
south bank of the Thames.
DESIGNERS' JOURNAL 1990 Sept.,
no.60, p.80-[83], photos., plan.

SWEITZER, JOSH
Non sono "tesseracts" pero... = They
aren't "tesseracts" but...
[weekend house, Joshua Tree,
Calif.].
Architect: Josh Sweitzer.
ARCHITETTURA: CRONACHE E STORIA
1990 Nov., v.36, no.11(421),
p.800-801, axonometric view,
photos., plan.

SWENARTON, MARK. ARTISANS AND
ARCHITECTS: THE RUSKINIAN TRADITION
IN ARCHITECTURAL THOUGHT
Arts and crafts as an ideological
myth [book review] / Margaret
Crawford.
Review of 2 books on the Arts and
Crafts movement, by Mark Swenarton
and Eileen Boris.
JOURNAL OF ARCHITECTURAL EDUCATION
1990 Nov., v.44, no.1, p.59-61,

SWENTZELL, RINA
Conflicting landscape values: the
Santa Clara Pueblo and day school
/ Rina Swentzell.
PLACES 1990 Fall, v.7, no.1,
p.[18]-27, photos., plans, refs.
Seeing beyond the dominant culture /
Wilbur Zelinsky.
Discussion with three authors in
this issue on "cultural
landscapes."
PLACES 1990 Fall, v.7, no.1,
p.[32]-37, photo.

SWERDLOFF, LUCIEN
Process and knowledge in design
computation / Yehuda Kalay, Lucien
Swerdhoff, Bruce Majkowski.
JOURNAL OF ARCHITECTURAL EDUCATION
1990 Winter, v.43, no.2, p.47-53,
refs.

SWERZ, CHARLES
NYU Medical Center / Monica Geran.
Features one of the twenty luxury
suites designed by Charles P.
Swerz Interior Design.
INTERIOR DESIGN 1990 Nov., v.61,
no.15, p.188-[189], photos., plan.

SWICZINSKY, HELMUT, 1944-
Projects by Coop Himmelblau: AA
exhibition Gallery & Bedford
Square, 11 November-10 December
1988 [exhibition review].
Wolf Prix and Helmut Swiczinsky in
conversation with Alvin Boyarsky.
AA FILES 1990 Spring, no.19,
p.70-77, photos., model, sketches.

SWIFT, PENNY
Paint magic / Penny Swift.
In conjunction with the author's
book, Plascon paint techniques,
discusses the use of paint in
interior design. Feature three
projects: Salvago boutique, Camp's
Bay, Cape Town (architect: Roger
Martin); "Herculaneum", home of
designer Jacqueline Cole; Floris
Smit Huijs restaurant, Cape Town
(interior decorator: Francois du
Plessis).
ADA: ARCHITECTURE, DESIGN, ART
1989, no.7, p.27-33, ports.,
photos.

SWIFT, PENNY. PLASCON PAINT TECHNIQUES
Paint magic / Penny Swift.
In conjunction with the author's
book, Plascon paint techniques,
discusses the use of paint in
interior design. Feature three
projects: Salvago boutique, Camp's
Bay, Cape Town (architect: Roger
Martin); "Herculaneum", home of
designer Jacqueline Cole; Floris
Smit Huijs restaurant, Cape Town
(interior decorator: Francois du
Plessis).
ADA: ARCHITECTURE, DESIGN, ART
1989, no.7, p.27-33, ports.,
photos.

SWIFT, PETER
Contrasts in processing coastal
marina applications in South
Australia / Nick Harvey, Peter
Swift.
AUSTRALIAN PLANNER: JOURNAL OF THE
ROYAL AUSTRALIAN PLANNING
INSTITUTE 1990 Sept., v.28, no.3,
(Continued next column)

SWIFT, PETER (CONTINUED)
Contrasts in... (CONTINUED)
p.44-47, maps, refs.

SWIMMING POOLS
See also WATER PARKS
The complete aquatic guide / Alison
Osinsky.
New building materials, equipment,
and design features for swimming
pools, water parks, etc.
PARKS & RECREATION 1990 Feb.,
v.25, no.2, p.36-43,83.
Fun for everyone: the aquatic
formula / Alan Heuss.
Aquatic recreation centers,
including swimming pools, water
slides, and other aquatic
features.
PARKS & RECREATION 1990 Nov.,
v.25, no.11, p.34-38, photos.
Piscine / Gilberto Oneto.
VILLE GIARDINI 1990 Feb., no.245,
p.75-79, diagrs., photos., plans,
tables.
Repertorio 1991: materiali,
componenti, impianti, tecnologie
per progettare, costruire,
ristrutturare la casa.
Special suppl. to Ville giardini
on building materials. Includes
indexes.
VILLE GIARDINI 1990 Oct.,
no.252(suppl.), entire issue (328
p.), dets., ill., photos.
A waterpark planner / Joshua L.
Brener.
PARKS & RECREATION 1990 Nov.,
v.25, no.11, p.42-[44],71, photos.

SWIMMING POOLS--19TH CENTURY--
ALTERATIONS AND ADDITIONS--GERMANY
(WEST)
Alte Bader neu genutzt: Beispiele
fur die Umgestaltung von
Hallenbadern der Jahrhundertwende.
Five examples of bath halls
converted to other uses.
BAUMEISTER 1990 Mar., v.87, no.3,
p.52-57, photos., plans, secns.

SWIMMING POOLS--ALTERATIONS AND
ADDITIONS--FRANCE--PARIS--MOLITOR
Molitor, la future memoire.
Renovation of 1920s-30s swimming
complex in Paris, Molitor.
Renovation architects: Reichen et
Robert.
TECHNIQUES ET ARCHITECTURE 1990
Aug.-Sept., no.391, p.44-45,
elev., models, photo., secn.

SWIMMING POOLS--ALTERATIONS AND
ADDITIONS--UNITED STATES--CAMBRIDGE
(MASSACHUSETTS)--HARVARD
UNIVERSITY--MALKIN ATHLETIC CENTER
George Oommen Cambridge,
Massachusetts.
Four projects: Briggs Athletic
Centre, Malkin Athletic Centre,
and McCurdy Track, at Harvard
University; Western Montana Sports
Medicine and Fitness Centre,
Missoula.
ARCHITECTURE + DESIGN 1990
Jan.-Feb., v.7, no.1, p.32-37,
photos., plans, aerial photos.

SWIMMING POOLS--AUSTRIA--SERFAUS
  Hotelhallenbad STIGLGRYZGTE in
    Serfaus/Tirol Osterreich = Indoor
    hotel swimming pool STIGLGRYZGTE
    in Serfaus/Tyrol, Austria.
    Architects: Reinhardt Honold,
    Wolfgang Poschl.
    ARCHITEKTUR + WETTBEWERBE 1990
    Mar., no.141, p.12, photos.
  Serfaus seasons.
    Swimming pool addition to Serfaus
    hotel, Austria. Architects:
    Wolfgang Poschl, Reinhardt Honold.
    ARCHITECTURAL REVIEW 1990 Aug.,
    v.188, no.1122, p.36-39, photos.,
    secns.

SWIMMING POOLS--COMPETITIONS--GERMANY
  (WEST)--BAD RAPPENAU
  Erste Preise: Bauten fur Freizeit
    und Sport.
    Four competitions: "Wildenstein"
    leisure center, Messtetten
    (architect: Heinz Becsei); outdoor
    pool, Bad Rappenau (architects:
    Rudolf und Ingeborg Geier, Jorg
    Stotzer); leisure and health club,
    Bonen (architect: Isermann &
    Jensen); gymnasium, Passau
    (architect: Willi Mortl).
    DEUTSCHES ARCHITEKTENBLATT 1990
    Oct.1, v.22, no.10, p.1511-1514,
    models, plans, secns., site plans.

SWIMMING POOLS--COMPETITIONS--GERMANY
  (WEST)--BIBERACH AN DER RISS
  Freibad Biberach an der Riss =
    Swimming pool Biberach an der
    Riss.
    Competition. Winning architect:
    Kurt Knecht. Text in German.
    ARCHITEKTUR + WETTBEWERBE 1990
    Mar., no.141, p.64-69, elevs.,
    models, secns., site plans.

SWIMMING POOLS--CONSERVATION AND
  RESTORATION--UNITED STATES--CORAL
  GABLES (FLORIDA)--VENETIAN POOL
  Southern traditions: preservation
    efforts in today's South show new
    interest in 20th-century
    landmarks, as well as earlier ones
    / Clifford A. Pearson.
    A portfolio of Southeast projects:
    Epping Forest Yacht Club,
    Jacksonville, Fla. (Pappas
    Associates); Freedom Tower, Miami
    (Heisenbottle Architects);
    Venetian Pool, Coral Gables, Fla.
    (H. Carlton Decker & Assoc.);
    Howard Memorial Library, New
    Orleans (E. Barron, M. Toups); and
    Linden Row Inn, Richmond, Va.
    (Glave Newman Anderson).
    ARCHITECTURAL RECORD 1990 Mar.,
    v.178, no.3, p.66-75, photos.,
    plans, site plans.

SWIMMING POOLS--FRANCE--
  VILLAINES-LA-JUHEL
  Paysage avec eau: piscine,
    Villaines-la-Juhel.
    Architects: Francois Fauconnet,
    Phillppe Rousseau. Landscape
    architect: Andre Peter. English
    summary, p.87.
    TECHNIQUES ET ARCHITECTURE 1990
    Dec.-1991 Jan., no.393, p.86-87,
    photos., secns., site plan.

SWIMMING POOLS--GERMANY (WEST)--
  BERLIN--KREUZBERG--GORLITZER BAD
  Gorlitzer Bad in Berlin-Kreuzberg =
    The Gorlitz baths in
    Berlin-Kreuzberg.
    Architects: Christoph Langhof
    Architekten.
    ARCHITEKTUR + WETTBEWERBE 1990
    Mar., no.141, p.13-14, photos.,
    site plan.

SWIMMING POOLS--GERMANY (WEST)--ESSEN
  Ein anderer Kreisrunder
    Ellipsenzglinderschmitt:
    Schwimmhalle fur ein Wohnhaus in
    Essen-Bredeney.
    Architect: Peter Rudolph.
    WERK, BAUEN + WOHNEN 1990 Nov.,
    no.11, p.16, photos.

SWIMMING POOLS--GERMANY (WEST)--
  WERNE--NATURSOLEBAD WERNE
  Natursolebad Werne.
    Built 1987-89. Landscape
    Architect: Buro Menke.
    GARTEN UND LANDSCHAFT 1990, v.100,
    no.1, p.64, det., photos., site
    plan.

SWIMMING POOLS--GREAT BRITAIN
  Buildings update: swimming pools 1:
    a bigger splash / Catherine
    Slessor.
    In Britain.
    ARCHITECTS' JOURNAL 1990 Oct.10,
    v.192, no.15, p.67-71, photos.,
    plan.
  Buildings update: swimming pools 2:
    case studies.
    Second in series on British
    swimming pools. Case studies of
    The Rapids, Romsey, architects:
    Sargent & Potiriadis; Ainslie
    Park, architects: Faulkner Browns;
    and Coral Reef, Bracknell,
    architects: Sargent & Potiriadis.
    ARCHITECTS' JOURNAL 1990 Oct.17,
    v.192, no.16, p.69-75, photos.,
    plans, site plans.

SWIMMING POOLS--ITALY--FLORENCE
  Sulle colline di Firenze.
    Hillside swimming pool. Landscape
    architect: Marco Pozzoli.
    VILLE GIARDINI 1990 Apr., no.247,
    p.54-59, photos.

SWIMMING POOLS--PORTUGAL--LECA DA
  PALMEIRA
  Alvaro Siza.
    Theme, with articles on 14
    projects dating from 1969-1988,
    including the Beires house, Povoa
    de Varzim; swimming pool, Leca da
    Palmeira; Pinto & Sotto Maior
    bank, Oliveira de Azemeis; Quinta
    da Malagueira housing, Evora; and
    Van der Venne-Park, the Hague.
    BAUWELT 1990 Aug.10, v.81,
    no.29-30, p. 1463-1499, axnar,1443,
    dwgs., port., models, photos.,
    plans, secns., site plans,
    isometric dwgs., aerial photos.

SWIMMING POOLS--PORTUGAL--LECA DE
  PALMEIRA
  Piscina a Leca de Palmeira, 1961-66
    = The swimming pool at Leca de
    Palmeira, 1961-66 / Maria Bottero.
    Architect: Alvaro Siza.
    ABITARE 1990 June, no.286,
    p.122-123, photos, site plan.

SWIMMING POOLS--ROUND--FINLAND--
  HELSINKI--PARTEK
  The Partek Group Helsinki office.
    Includes a round swimming pool and
    sauna. Architect: Mauri Tommila.
    LIVING ARCHITECTURE 1990, no.9,
    p.140-143, photos., plans.

SWIMMING POOLS--SLOPING SITES--ITALY--
  SONDRIO
  Sotto la montagna sopra la citta /
    Lucia Bisi.
    Two-family home, Sondrio, Italy.
    Architect: Piercarlo Stefanelli.
    VILLE GIARDINI 1990 Sept., no.251,
    p.2-9, photos., plans, secn., site
    plan.

SWIMMING POOLS--STANDARDS
  Vermeidung von Baufehlern und
    Bauschaden bei
    Stahlbeton-Schwimmbecken /
    Cristoph Saunus.
    DEUTSCHES ARCHITEKTENBLATT 1990
    Nov.1, v.22, no.11, p.1745-1749,
    dets., photos., refs.

SWIMMING POOLS--UNDERGROUND--ENGLAND--
  LONDON
  These poolish things / Leslie
    Geddes-Brown.
    On the underground faux Roman
    temple and pool built for a London
    businessman. Architects: Child
    Wilson Associates.
    THE WORLD OF INTERIORS 1990
    July-Aug., p.[84-87], photos.

SWIMMING POOLS--UNITED STATES--DALLAS
  (TEXAS)
  Poolside paradise: glorious outdoor
    entertaining complex graces a
    Dallas garden / Nan Booth Simpson.
    Architects: Loyd-Paxton; Landscape
    architects: Boyd & Heiderich.
    SOUTHERN ACCENTS 1990 July-Aug.,
    v.13, no.6, p.[96]-100, photos.

SWIMMING POOLS--UNITED STATES--
  MICHIGAN
  Acquattato nel paesaggio: nel fianco
    di una collina del Michigan /
    Gilberto Oneto.
    Gardens of a house in the Huron
    Valley. Landscape architect:
    Charles Cares.
    VILLE GIARDINI 1990 Feb., no.245,
    p.[64]-67, photos.

SWIMMING POOLS--UNITED STATES--NEW
  HAMPSHIRE
  New England natatorium: rustic
    poolhouse addition to a New
    Hampshire farmhouse / Suzanne
    Stephens.
    Addition to 1770's Cape-style
    farmhouse. Architect: Jon Evans.
    ARCHITECTURAL DIGEST 1990 June,
    v.47, no.6, p.[204-207],226,
    photos.

SWITZERLAND--AARAU--MULTI-USE
  COMPLEXES--BEHMEN II
  Projekt Behmen II, Aarau, 1989.
    Architects: Fierz & Baader.
    WERK, BAUEN + WOHNEN 1989 Dec.,
    no.12, p.51, model, plans, secn.

SWITZERLAND--BADEN--APARTMENT HOUSES--
COMPETITIONS
Wohn- und Geschaftshaus in Baden,
Wettbewerbsprojekt, 1988 (in
Ausfuhrung) / Willi Voney.
Architects: Burkhard & Mueller.
WERK, BAUEN + WOHNEN 1990 Apr.,
no.4, p.38-41, dwg., elevs.,
plans, secns., site plan.

SWITZERLAND--BADEN--ATHLETIC FIELDS
Sportanlage Esp der Gemeinden Baden
und Fislisbach = Le centre sportif
Esp des communes de Baden et de
Fislisbach = The Esp sports ground
jointly owned by the
municipalities of Baden and
Fislisbach / M. Lang.
Sportsground: A. Zulauf + Partner,
M. Lang Building construction:
Tognola + Stahel + Zulauf, Meier +
Kern.
ANTHOS 1989, v.28, no.4, p.18-21,
photos., site plan.

SWITZERLAND--BADEN--CITY HALLS--
ALTERATIONS AND ADDITIONS
Neuer Kern in alter Schale: Umbau
des Amtshauses Baden, Schweiz /
Matthias Saxer.
Architects: H. Eppler, L. Maraini.
DEUTSCHE BAUZEITUNG 1990 Apr.,
v.124, no.4, p.58-60, axonometric
views, photos., plan, site plan.

SWITZERLAND--BADEN--GAMBLING CASINOS--
ALTERATIONS AND ADDITIONS--
STADTCASINO BADEN
Stadtcasino Baden.
Architects: Werner Egli + Hans
Rohr. Includes English summary.
BAUMEISTER 1990 Mar., v.87, no.3,
p.32-39, det., photos., plans,
secns., site plans.

SWITZERLAND--BADEN--HOUSING--STUDENT
PROJECTS--BAHNHOF OBERSTADT
Planung und Gestaltung der Areale
Klosterli und Bahnhof Oberstadt in
Baden, Schweiz = Planning and
design of the areas "Kloesterli"
and "Bahnhof Oberstadt" in Baden,
Switzerland.
Student project from ETH Zurich.
ARCHITEKTUR + WETTBEWERBE 1990
June, no.142, p.90, elev., model,
plan, site plan.

SWITZERLAND--BADEN--HOUSING--STUDENT
PROJECTS--KLOESTERLI
Planung und Gestaltung der Areale
Klosterli und Bahnhof Oberstadt in
Baden, Schweiz = Planning and
design of the areas "Kloesterli"
and "Bahnhof Oberstadt" in Baden,
Switzerland.
Student project from ETH Zurich.
ARCHITEKTUR + WETTBEWERBE 1990
June, no.142, p.90, elev., model,
plan, site plan.

SWITZERLAND--BADEN--INFILL BUILDINGS--
COMPETITIONS
Wohn- und Geschaftshaus in Baden,
Wettbewerbsprojekt, 1988 (in
Ausfuhrung) / Willi Voney.
Architects: Burkhard & Mueller.
WERK, BAUEN + WOHNEN 1990 Apr.,
no.4, p.38-41, dwg., elevs.,
plans, secns., site plan.

SWITZERLAND--BADEN--MULTI-USE
BUILDINGS--ZURCHERSTRASSE 13
Svizzera anni '90: tre culture, tre
architetture = Switzerland 1990:
three cultures, three
architectures / Paolo Fumagalli.
Features projects by Jacques
Herzog and Pierre de Meuron; Livio
Vacchini; Atelier 5; Willi Egli;
Mario Botta; Jean-Jacques Oberson;
Giancarlo Durisch; Aurelio
Galfetti; Luigi Snozzi; Roger
Diener; Atelier Cube; Matti,
Burgi, Ragaz; Schnebli, Ammann &
Partner; R. Luscher; V. Mangeat;
S. Calatrava, A. Amsler, and W.
Rueger; Mario Campi and Franco
Pessina; and Peter Zumthor.
Includes an article by Werner
Jehle, "The mountain: painters,
engineers, and architects." Text
in Italian and English.
ABITARE 1990 Nov., no.290,
p.150-191, axonometric views,
dets., ill., elevs., maps,
photos., plans, secns., site
plans, sketch, aerial photo.

SWITZERLAND--BADEN--OFFICE BUILDINGS
Dolf Schnebli.
Most of issue devoted to the work
of this Swiss architect.
Introduction by Paolo Fumagalli.
Text in German, French and
English.
WERK, BAUEN + WOHNEN 1990 Dec.,
no.12, p.20-69, axonometric views,
dets., dwgs., port., elevs.,
models, photos., plans, secns.,
site plans, sketches, aerial
photo.

SWITZERLAND--BADEN--STADIUMS
Sportanlage Esp der Gemeinden Baden
und Fislisbach = Le centre sportif
Esp des communes de Baden et de
Fislisbach = The Esp sports ground
jointly owned by the
municipalities of Baden and
Fislisbach / M. Lang.
Sportsground: A. Zulauf + Partner,
M. Lang Building construction:
Tognola + Stahel + Zulauf, Meier +
Kern.
ANTHOS 1989, v.28, no.4, p.18-21,
photos., site plan.

SWITZERLAND--BALERNA--OFFICE
BUILDINGS--SAIMA
Centro di spedizioni a Balerna
(Canton Ticino).
SAIMA offices and shopping center.
Architects: Franco and Paolo Moro.
English, French, and Spanish
summaries.
ABACUS 1990 Apr.-June, v.6, no.22,
p.58-65, dets., elevs., photos.,
plans, secns.

SWITZERLAND--BASEL--APARTMENT HOUSES--
CONSERVATION AND RESTORATION--ZUM
NEUEN SINGER
"Das Werk dieses Kommunisten lohnt
sich nicht zu erhalten / Ursula
Suter.
On the renovation of the 1928 Haus
"zum Neuen Singer," in Basel.
Original architects: Artaria &
Schmidt.
ARCHITHESE 1990 July-Aug., v.20,
no.4, p.73-74, photos.

SWITZERLAND--BASEL--APARTMENT HOUSES--
HEBELSTRASSE 11
Herzog et de Meuron / Elisabeth
Allain-Dupre.
Contents: Apartment houses,
Basel--Project for Greek Orthodox
church, Zurich--Project for
railway depot, Basel--Interview
with Jacques Herzog.
LE MONITEUR ARCHITECTURE AMC 1990
Mar., no.9, p.28-39, dets.,
models, photos., plans, secns.,
site plan.
Svizzera anni '90: tre culture, tre
architetture = Switzerland 1990:
three cultures, three
architectures / Paolo Fumagalli.
Features projects by Jacques
Herzog and Pierre de Meuron; Livio
Vacchini; Atelier 5; Willi Egli;
Mario Botta; Jean-Jacques Oberson;
Giancarlo Durisch; Aurelio
Galfetti; Luigi Snozzi; Roger
Diener; Atelier Cube; Matti,
Burgi, Ragaz; Schnebli, Ammann &
Partner; R. Luscher; V. Mangeat;
S. Calatrava, A. Amsler, and W.
Rueger; Mario Campi and Franco
Pessina; and Peter Zumthor.
Includes an article by Werner
Jehle, "The mountain: painters,
engineers, and architects." Text
in Italian and English.
ABITARE 1990 Nov., no.290,
p.150-191, axonometric views,
dets., ill., elevs., maps,
photos., plans, secns., site
plans, sketch, aerial photo.
Swiss authenticity / Peter Blundell
Jones.
Features two apartment buildings
in Basel: Schwitter Building and
building on Hebelstrasse.
Architects: Herzog & de Meuron.
ARCHITECTURAL REVIEW 1990 Oct.,
v.188, no.1124, p.36-43, photos.,
plans, site plan.

SWITZERLAND--BASEL--APARTMENT HOUSES--
SCHWITTER BUILDING
Herzog et de Meuron / Elisabeth
Allain-Dupre.
Contents: Apartment houses,
Basel--Project for Greek Orthodox
church, Zurich--Project for
railway depot, Basel--Interview
with Jacques Herzog.
LE MONITEUR ARCHITECTURE AMC 1990
Mar., no.9, p.28-39, dets.,
models, photos., plans, secns.,
site plan.
Swiss authenticity / Peter Blundell
Jones.
Features two apartment buildings
in Basel: Schwitter Building and
building on Hebelstrasse.
Architects: Herzog & de Meuron.
ARCHITECTURAL REVIEW 1990 Oct.,
v.188, no.1124, p.36-43, photos.,
plans, site plan.

SWITZERLAND--BASEL--CHAPELS--
ALTERATIONS AND ADDITIONS--
DEUTSCHRITTERKAPELLE
Architektenburo in Basel: Umbau der
Deutschritterkapelle.
Architects: Dorenbach AG. Includes
English summary.
BAUMEISTER 1990 Feb., v.87, no.2,
p.40-45, dets., elev., photos.,
plans, secns.

SWITZERLAND--BASEL--RAILROADS--
BUILDINGS AND STRUCTURES--DEPOT
CENTRAL SCHWEIZERISCHES BUNDES BAHN
(SBB)
Herzog et de Meuron / Elisabeth
Allain-Dupre.
Contents: Apartment houses,
Basel--Project for Greek Orthodox
church, Zurich--Project for
railway depot, Basel--Interview
with Jacques Herzog.
LE MONITEUR ARCHITECTURE AMC 1990
Mar., no.9, p.28-39, dets.,
models, photos., plans, secns.,
site plan.

SWITZERLAND--BASEL--STORES--SHOE--
ARODE
Schuhladen Arode, Basel, Lausanne.
Architects: Martin & Elisabeth
Boesch.
WERK, BAUEN + WOHNEN 1990 Oct.,
no.10, p.69-72, photos., plans,
secns.

SWITZERLAND--BASEL--WAREHOUSES--RICOLA
Svizzera anni '90: tre culture, tre
architetture = Switzerland 1990:
three cultures, three
architectures / Paolo Fumagalli.
Features projects by Jacques
Herzog and Pierre de Meuron; Livio
Vacchini; Atelier 5; Willi Egli;
Mario Botta; Jean-Jacques Oberson;
Giancarlo Durisch; Aurelio
Galfetti; Luigi Snozzi; Roger
Diener; Atelier Cube; Matti,
Burgi, Ragaz; Schnebli, Ammann &
Partner; R. Luscher; V. Mangeat;
S. Calatrava, A. Amsler, and W.
Rueger; Mario Campi and Franco
Pessina; and Peter Zumthor.
Includes an article by Werner
Jehle, "The mountain: painters,
engineers, and architects." Text
in Italian and English.
ABITARE 1990 Nov., no.290,
p.150-191, axonometric views,
dets., ill., elevs., maps,
photos., plans, secns., site
plans, sketch, aerial photo.

SWITZERLAND--BATHROOMS
Bagni di villa.
Special publication as suppl. to
Ville giardini, on bathrooms.
VILLE GIARDINI 1990 Sept.,
no.251(suppl.) entire issue (48
p.), dets., photos., plans.

SWITZERLAND--BELLINZONA--APARTMENT
HOUSES--BIANCO
Appartement-Hauser "Bianco e Nero"
in Bellinzona, Schweiz = Apartment
buildings "Bianco e Nero" in
Bellinzona, Switzerland.
Architect: Aurelio Galfetti.
ARCHITEKTUR + WETTBEWERBE 1990
June, no.142, p.18-19, elevs.,
photos., plans.
Immeubles d'habitations "blanc et
noir," Bellinzone, 1988.
Architect: Aurdio Galfetti.
WERK, BAUEN + WOHNEN 1989 Dec.,
no.12, p.69, photos.

SWITZERLAND--BELLINZONA--APARTMENT
HOUSES--NERO
Appartement-Hauser "Bianco e Nero"
in Bellinzona, Schweiz = Apartment
buildings "Bianco e Nero" in
Bellinzona, Switzerland.
Architect: Aurelio Galfetti.
ARCHITEKTUR + WETTBEWERBE 1990
June, no.142, p.18-19, elevs.,
photos., plans.
Immeubles d'habitations "blanc et
noir," Bellinzone, 1988.
Architect: Aurdio Galfetti.
WERK, BAUEN + WOHNEN 1989 Dec.,
no.12, p.69, photos.

SWITZERLAND--BELLINZONA--CASTLES--
CONSERVATION AND RESTORATION--
CASTELGRANDE
Felsenfest: Restaurierung des
Castelgrande in Bellinzona / Paolo
Fumagalli.
Architect: Aurelio Galfetti.
DEUTSCHE BAUZEITUNG 1990 Apr.,
v.124, no.4, p.50-55, elevs.,
photos., plans, secns.

SWITZERLAND--BELLINZONA--HOTELS--
ALBERGO MOVENPICK
Bruno Reichlin, Fabio Reinhart:
Albergo Movenpick, Bellinzona /
Ermanno Ranzani.
Text in Italian and English.
DOMUS 1990 Nov., no.721,
p.[29]-37, elevs., photos., plans,
site plans, sketches.

SWITZERLAND--BELLINZONA--HOUSES--20TH
CENTURY--VILLA CARENINI
La tradizione del moderno / Ruggero
Borghi.
Villa Carenini, near Bellinzona,
Switzerland. Architect: Claudio F.
Pellegrini.
VILLE GIARDINI 1990 Dec., no.254,
p.16-21, photos., plans.

SWITZERLAND--BELLINZONA--MUNICIPAL
BUILDINGS
Svizzera anni '90: tre culture, tre
architetture = Switzerland 1990:
three cultures, three
architectures / Paolo Fumagalli.
Features projects by Jacques
Herzog and Pierre de Meuron; Livio
Vacchini; Atelier 5; Willi Egli;
Mario Botta; Jean-Jacques Oberson;
Giancarlo Durisch; Aurelio
Galfetti; Luigi Snozzi; Roger
Diener; Atelier Cube; Matti,
Burgi, Ragaz; Schnebli, Ammann &
Partner; R. Luscher; V. Mangeat;
S. Calatrava, A. Amsler, and W.
Rueger; Mario Campi and Franco
Pessina; and Peter Zumthor.
Includes an article by Werner
Jehle, "The mountain: painters,
engineers, and architects." Text
in Italian and English.
ABITARE 1990 Nov., no.290,
p.150-191, axonometric views,
dets., ill., elevs., maps,
photos., plans, secns., site
plans, sketch, aerial photo.

SWITZERLAND--BELLINZONA--TOWNHOUSES
Trittico dell'amicizia / Giulia
Conte.
3-family housing unit, Bellinzona,
Switzerland. Architect: Aldo
Guscetti.
VILLE GIARDINI 1990 June, no.249,
p.[10]-15, photos., plans, secn.

SWITZERLAND--BERN--ANIMAL HOUSING--
TIERPARK DAHLHOLZLI
Tierisch gut, od'r?: Erweiterung des
Vivariums im Tierpark Dahlholzli,
Bern.
Architect: Andreas Furrer.
DEUTSCHE BAUZEITUNG 1990 Apr.,
v.124, no.4, p.36-41, elevs.,
photos., plan, site plan.

SWITZERLAND--BERN--ARTISANS--HISTORY
Die Berner Werkmeister des spaten
16. bis zum Ende des 18.
Jahrhunderts / Andreas Kellerhals,
Johanna Strubin.
Summaries in German, French,
Italian and English.
ZEITSCHRIFT FUR SCHWEIZERISCHE
ARCHAOLOGIE UND KUNSTGESCHICHTE
1990, v.47, no.2, p.113-121,
chart, ill., refs.

SWITZERLAND--BERN--CHURCHES--20TH
CENTURY--SANKT MAURITIUS
Kirche St. Mauritius,
Bern-Bethlehem.
Architect: Willi Egli.
WERK, BAUEN + WOHNEN 1989 Dec.,
no.12, p.34-35, photos., plans,
secns.

SWITZERLAND--BERN--CHURCHES--20TH
CENTURY--SANKT MORITZ
Svizzera anni '90: tre culture, tre
architetture = Switzerland 1990:
three cultures, three
architectures / Paolo Fumagalli.
Features projects by Jacques
Herzog and Pierre de Meuron; Livio
Vacchini; Atelier 5; Willi Egli;
Mario Botta; Jean-Jacques Oberson;
Giancarlo Durisch; Aurelio
Galfetti; Luigi Snozzi; Roger
Diener; Atelier Cube; Matti,
Burgi, Ragaz; Schnebli, Ammann &
Partner; R. Luscher; V. Mangeat;
S. Calatrava, A. Amsler, and W.
Rueger; Mario Campi and Franco
Pessina; and Peter Zumthor.
Includes an article by Werner
Jehle, "The mountain: painters,
engineers, and architects." Text
in Italian and English.
ABITARE 1990 Nov., no.290,
p.150-191, axonometric views,
dets., ill., elevs., maps,
photos., plans, secns., site
plans, sketch, aerial photo.

SWITZERLAND--BERN--CLASSROOMS--
MIGROS-KLUBSCHULE
Migros-Klubschule Bern.
Architects: Anton Hermann,
Chi-Chain Hermann-Chong.
ARCHITHESE 1990 Nov.-Dec., v.20,
no.6, p.82-83, photos.

SWITZERLAND--BERN--CONSTRUCTION
MANAGEMENT--HISTORY
Die Berner Werkmeister des spaten
16. bis zum Ende des 18.
Jahrhunderts / Andreas Kellerhals,
Johanna Strubin.
Summaries in German, French,
Italian and English.
ZEITSCHRIFT FUR SCHWEIZERISCHE
ARCHAOLOGIE UND KUNSTGESCHICHTE
1990, v.47, no.2, p.113-121,
chart, ill., refs.

SWITZERLAND--BERN--CONSTRUCTION
WORKERS--HISTORY
Die Berner Werkmeister des spaten
16. bis zum Ende des 18.
Jahrhunderts / Andreas Kellerhals,
Johanna Strubin.
Summaries in German, French,
Italian and English.
ZEITSCHRIFT FUR SCHWEIZERISCHE
ARCHAOLOGIE UND KUNSTGESCHICHTE
1990, v.47, no.2, p.113-121,
chart, ill., refs.

SWITZERLAND--BERN--COUNTRY HOUSES--
17TH CENTURY--INTERIOR DESIGN
Die Inszenierung des "Adeligen
Landlebens": Private Auftraggeber
und bildkunstlerische Produktion
im Bern der 2. Halfte des 17.
Jahrhunderts / Georges Herzog,
Elisabeth Ryter.
Includes summaries in German,
French, Italian and English.
ZEITSCHRIFT FUR SCHWEIZERISCHE
ARCHAOLOGIE UND KUNSTGESCHICHTE
1990, v.47, no.2, p.122-129, ill.,
photos., refs.

SWITZERLAND--BERN--EXHIBITION BOOTHS--
SCHWEIZERISCHE MOBELMESSE 1989
Messestand "Forum Kreativer
Fabrikanten der Schweiz", Bern '89
/ Alfred Hablutzel.
Architect: Stefan Zwicky.
WERK, BAUEN + WOHNEN 1990
July-Aug., no.7-8, p.79-82, dets.,
dwgs., photos., plan.

SWITZERLAND--BERN--HOSPITALS--
KRANKENHEIM WITTIGKOFEN
Sichtbar Konstruiert: Krankenheim
Bern- Wittigkofen, 1988/89, und
neues Betriebsgebaude
psychiatrische Klinik Munsingen,
1986/87.
Architects: Atelier 5. Text in
German, summaries in German,
French and English.
WERK, BAUEN + WOHNEN 1990 Nov.,
no.11, p.36-47, axonometric views,
dets., photos., plans, secns.,
site plans.

SWITZERLAND--BERN--HOUSES--20TH
CENTURY
Acciaio come misura del distacco /
Lucia Bisi.
House with a studio addition on
the roof, Bern, Switzerland.
Architect: Daniel Spreng.
VILLE GIARDINI 1990 Oct., no.252,
p.2-9, axonometric view, photos.,
plans, secn.

SWITZERLAND--BERN--HOUSING
DEVELOPMENTS--BAUMGARTEN
Wohnsiedlung Baumgarten, Bern.
Architect: Jurg Althaus.
WERK, BAUEN + WOHNEN 1990 Apr.,
no.4, p.1-4 (folded at back),
axonometric views, det., photos.,
plans, secn., site plan.
Wohnsiedlung in Bern.
In the Baumgarten district.
Archtitect: Jurg Althaus.
BAUWELT 1990 July 20, v.81, no.27,
p.1374-1377, photos., plans,
aerial photos.

SWITZERLAND--BERN--HOUSING PROJECTS--
MERZENACKER
Diversita coordinate: quartiero
presso Berna [Switzerland].
Architects: Studio ARB.
ARCHITETTURA; CRONACHE E STORIA
1990 May, v.36, no.5(415),
p.370-371, axonometric view,
photos., plan.
Suisse: le credo de l'habitat
groupe.
Feature four projects: Castel
Schmitten, Fribourg, architects:
Martin Wagner, David and Samuel
Spycher; Merzenacker project,
Bern, architects: ARB
Arbeitsgruppe; Habitat industriel,
Givisiez, architect: Rodolphe
Luscher and a multi-use building,
Geneva, architect: Rodolpke
Luscher and a multi-use building,
Geneva, architect: Chantal Scaler.
English summary, p.180.
ARCHITECTURE INTERIEURE CREE 1990
June-July, no.237, p.[108]-119,
dwgs., photos., secns.

SWITZERLAND--BERN--MUSEUMS--ART--
ALTERATIONS AND ADDITIONS--
KUNSTMUSEUM
Licht von Oben: Erweiterung und
Umbau des bestehenden Kunstmuseums
in Bern.
Architects: Atelier 5.
DEUTSCHE BAUZEITUNG 1990 Jan.,
v.124, no.1, p.62-67, photos.,
plans, secn., isometric dwg.

SWITZERLAND--BERN--PAINTING--17TH
CENTURY--SOCIOLOGICAL ASPECTS
Die Inszenierung des "Adeligen
Landlebens": Private Auftraggeber
und bildkunstlerische Produktion
im Bern der 2. Halfte des 17.
Jahrhunderts / Georges Herzog,
Elisabeth Ryter.
Includes summaries in German,
French, Italian and English.
ZEITSCHRIFT FUR SCHWEIZERISCHE
ARCHAOLOGIE UND KUNSTGESCHICHTE
1990, v.47, no.2, p.122-129, ill.,
photos., refs.

SWITZERLAND--BERN--PARKS--INVENTORIES
Inventar der offentlichen Anlagen in
der Statd Bern = Inventaire des
espaces verts de la ville de Berne
= Inventory of green areas in the
City of Berne / Kurt Huber,
Susanne Bollinger-Kobelt.
ANTHOS 1989, v.28, no.4, p.2-7,
fig., photos.

SWITZERLAND--BERN--PUBLIC BUILDINGS--
REITERSTRASSE
Svizzera anni '90: tre culture, tre
architetture = Switzerland 1990:
three cultures, three
architectures / Paolo Fumagalli.
Features projects by Jacques
Herzog and Pierre de Meuron; Livio
Vacchini; Atelier 5; Willi Egli;
Mario Botta; Jean-Jacques Oberson;
Giancarlo Durisch; Aurelio
Galfetti; Luigi Snozzi; Roger
Diener; Atelier Cube; Matti,
Burgi, Ragaz; Schnebli, Ammann &
Partner; R. Luscher; V. Mangeat;
S. Calatrava, A. Amsler, and W.
Rueger; Mario Campi and Franco
Pessina; and Peter Zumthor.
Includes an article by Werner
Jehle, "The mountain: painters,
engineers, and architects." Text
in Italian and English.
ABITARE 1990 Nov., no.290,
p.150-191, axonometric views,
dets., ill., elevs., maps,
photos., plans, secns., site
plans, sketch, aerial photo.

SWITZERLAND--BERN--PUBLIC GARDENS--
INVENTORIES
Inventar der offentlichen Anlagen in
der Statd Bern = Inventaire des
espaces verts de la ville de Berne
= Inventory of green areas in the
City of Berne / Kurt Huber,
Susanne Bollinger-Kobelt.
ANTHOS 1989, v.28, no.4, p.2-7,
fig., photos.

SWITZERLAND--BERN--ROOFTOP
ARCHITECTURE--METAL
Acciaio come misura del distacco /
Lucia Bisi.
House with a studio addition on
the roof, Bern, Switzerland.
Architect: Daniel Spreng.
VILLE GIARDINI 1990 Oct., no.252,
p.2-9, axonometric view, photos.,
plans, secn.

SWITZERLAND--BERN--TRAFFIC
Ein Preis fur "stadtgerechten
Verkehr" [interview] / Richard
Pfister.
Interview with Bern traffic
planner Kurt Hoppe.
SCHWEIZER BAUMARKT 1990 Oct.8,
v.25, no.12, p.I-III, port.,
photos.

SWITZERLAND--BERN--TRANSPORTATION
PLANNING
Ein Preis fur "stadtgerechten
Verkehr" [interview] / Richard
Pfister.
Interview with Bern traffic
planner Kurt Hoppe.
SCHWEIZER BAUMARKT 1990 Oct.8,
v.25, no.12, p.I-III, port.,
photos.

SWITZERLAND--BERN--UNIVERSITIES AND
COLLEGES--BUILDINGS--LEHRGEBAUDE DER
VET.-MED.
Lehrgebaude der Vet.-Med. Fakultat
Universitat Bern, 1989/90.
Architect: Franz Oswald.
WERK, BAUEN + WOHNEN 1989 Dec.,
no.12, p.53, dwgs., elev., plan,
secn., site plan.

SWITZERLAND--BERN--ZOOS--TIERPARK
DAHLHOLZLI
    Tierisch gut, od'r?: Erweiterung des
    Vivariums im Tierpark Dahlholzli,
    Bern.
    Architect: Andreas Furrer.
    DEUTSCHE BAUZEITUNG 1990 Apr.,
    v.124, no.4, p.36-41, elevs.,
    photos., plan, site plan.

SWITZERLAND--BEX--PLAZAS--ALTERATIONS
AND ADDITIONS--COMPETITIONS--PLACE
DU MARCHE
    Place du Marche in Bex, Schweiz =
    Place du Marche in Bex,
    Switzerland.
    Competition. First prize winners:
    Pierre Plancherel, Andreas Schmid.
    Text in German.
    ARCHITEKTUR + WETTBEWERBE 1990
    Dec., no.144, p.88-89, dwg.,
    elev., model, site plans.

SWITZERLAND--BIASCA--CENTRAL BUSINESS
DISTRICTS
    Centre commercial, Biasca, en
    construction.
    Architect: Ivano Gianola.
    WERK, BAUEN + WOHNEN 1989 Dec.,
    no.12, p.70, elev., model.

SWITZERLAND--BIASCA--COMMERCIAL
BUILDINGS
    Centre commercial, Biasca, en
    construction.
    Architect: Ivano Gianola.
    WERK, BAUEN + WOHNEN 1989 Dec.,
    no.12, p.70, elev., model.

SWITZERLAND--BIEL--GARDENS--ENGLER
KERN GARDEN
    Der Garten von Rosmarie Engler-Kern
    in Biel-Benken / Nicole Newmark.
    MITTEILUNGEN DER GESELLSCHAFT FUR
    GARTENKULTUR 1989, v.7, no.1,
    p.7-10, photo.

SWITZERLAND--BIEL--INSTALLATION
WORKS--STUDENT PROJECTS
    Eine prekare Konstruktion:
    Strasseninstallation in Biel, 1986
    / Christian Sumi.
    Student project of the ETH Zurich.
    WERK, BAUEN + WOHNEN 1990 Nov.,
    no.11, p.18-21, det., elev.,
    photos., plan.

SWITZERLAND--BIEL--OUTDOOR SCULPTURE--
STUDENT PROJECTS
    Eine prekare Konstruktion:
    Strasseninstallation in Biel, 1986
    / Christian Sumi.
    Student project of the ETH Zurich.
    WERK, BAUEN + WOHNEN 1990 Nov.,
    no.11, p.18-21, det., elev.,
    photos., plan.

SWITZERLAND--BOTTSTEIN--CHAPELS--17TH
CENTURY--INTERIOR DESIGN--
SCHLOSSKAPELLE
    Die von Roll als Auftraggeber: Die
    Dekoration der Schlosskapelle
    Bottstein im Vergleich mit
    Tessiner Vorbildern / Romana
    Anselmetti.
    Early 17th cent. Focus on stucco
    decoration, 1615-17.
    ZEITSCHRIFT FUR SCHWEIZERISCHE
    ARCHAOLOGIE UND KUNSTGESCHICHTE
    1989, v.46, no.1, p.30-38,
    photos., refs.

SWITZERLAND--BOTTSTEIN--DECORATION AND
ORNAMENT--17TH CENTURY--STUCCO--
SCHLOSSKAPELLE
    Die von Roll als Auftraggeber: Die
    Dekoration der Schlosskapelle
    Bottstein im Vergleich mit
    Tessiner Vorbildern / Romana
    Anselmetti.
    Early 17th cent. Focus on stucco
    decoration, 1615-17.
    ZEITSCHRIFT FUR SCHWEIZERISCHE
    ARCHAOLOGIE UND KUNSTGESCHICHTE
    1989, v.46, no.1, p.30-38,
    photos., refs.

SWITZERLAND--BREGANZONA--HOUSES
    Tessitura e tecnologia di mattoni e
    blocchi / Walter Bianchi, Mauro
    Colombo.
    Features a house in Breganzona,
    Switzerland. Architect: Mario
    Botta.
    VILLE GIARDINI 1990 Feb., no.245,
    p.48-51, ill., dwgs., photos.

SWITZERLAND--BUREN--SCHOOLS--
ALTERATIONS AND ADDITIONS--
COMPETITIONS
    Mimikry: zum ersten Preis im
    Wettbewerb "Schulhauserweiterung
    Buren" / Bruno Salzmann.
    Architects: Marques & Zurkirchen.
    ARCHITHESE 1990 July-Aug., v.20,
    no.4, p.78-80, elevs., models,
    plans, site plan.

SWITZERLAND--BURGDORF--CITY PLANNING--
COMPETITIONS--STEINHOF
    Steinhof, Burgdorf.
    Competition project. First prize:
    Jurg Althaus.
    SCHWEIZER BAUMARKT 1989 Oct.2,
    no.13, p.v-viii, elev., models,
    secn., site plans.

SWITZERLAND--BURGDORF--MULTI-USE
COMPLEXES--COMPETITIONS--TURMALIN
    Steinhof, Burgdorf.
    Competition project. First prize:
    Jurg Althaus.
    SCHWEIZER BAUMARKT 1989 Oct.2,
    no.13, p.v-viii, elev., models,
    secn., site plans.

SWITZERLAND--BURIER--VILLAS--20TH
CENTURY--CONSERVATION AND
RESTORATION--VILLA KENWIN
    Ein Restaurationsversuch: die Villa
    Kenwin in Burier/La Tour-de-Peilz
    / Gilles Barbey.
    Architects: Hermann Henselmann
    (1931), Giovanni Pezzoli (1987).
    WERK, BAUEN + WOHNEN 1990 Oct.,
    no.10, p.2-8, elevs., photos.,
    plans, sketch., refs.

SWITZERLAND--CASTELLETTO TICINO--
FARMHOUSES--ALTERATIONS AND
ADDITIONS--CASCINO PINEROLA
    Insieme, dissonanti / Vittoria
    Bocconi.
    Restoration of farmhouse into an
    office building, in Castelletto
    Ticino. Architect: Teodoro Pasini.
    VILLE GIARDINI 1990 June, no.249,
    p.16-21, photos., plans, secn.

SWITZERLAND--CHALETS--INTERIOR
DESIGN--COUR DE FERME (YOUMANS
HOUSE)
    Switzerland's La Cour de Ferme:
    restoring a 17th-century chalet
    near Gstaad / William Weaver.
    Focus on the interiors of 1695
    chalet owned by Scott and Valerie
    Youmans.
    ARCHITECTURAL DIGEST 1990 Oct,
    v.47, no.11, p.[256]-263,294,
    port., photos.

SWITZERLAND--CHESEREX--COMMUNITY
CENTERS
    Centre communal, Cheserex VD.
    Architect: Fonso Boschetti.
    WERK, BAUEN + WOHNEN 1990 June,
    no.6, p.1-4 (folded, at end),
    photos., plan, secns., site plan.
    Centre communal de Cheserex, 1989.
    Architect: Fonso Boschetti.
    WERK, BAUEN + WOHNEN 1989 Dec.,
    no.12, p.56-57, elev., photos.,
    plans, secn., site plan.

SWITZERLAND--CHUR--RAILROAD STATIONS
    Umschlagplatze: neue Bahnhofhalle in
    Luzern und Projekt Neugestaltung
    Bahnhof Chur.
    Projects by Ammann and Baumann
    with S. Calatrava and Richard
    Brosi + Obrist und Partner. Text
    in German; summaries in German,
    French and English.
    WERK, BAUEN + WOHNEN 1990 June,
    no.6, p.36-45, models, photos.,
    plans, secns., site plans.

SWITZERLAND--CHURCHES--20TH CENTURY
    Schweizer Kirchenbau der 80er Jahre
    / Fabrizio Brentini.
    Features seven churches.
    Architects: Rene Antoniel and Kurt
    Huber, Herbert Oberholzer,
    Hansjorg Ruch und Husler, Mario
    Campi and Franco Pessina, Peter
    Zumthor, Egon Dachtler and Erwin
    P. Nigg, Jakob Montalta.
    KUNST UND KIRCHE 1990, no.1,
    p.3-17, axonometric views,
    photos., plans, secns., site
    plans, refs.

SWITZERLAND--CLARO--APARTMENT HOUSES--
CONCRETE
    Casa d'appartamenti a Claro (Canton
    Ticino).
    Architect: Ivan Fontana. Summaries
    in English, French and Spanish.
    ABACUS 1990 Oct.-Dec., v.6, no.24,
    p.38-47, axonometric view, dets.,
    elevs., photos., plans, secns.,
    site plan.

SWITZERLAND--COLOMBIER--AUDITORIUMS,
CONCERT HALLS--COMPETITIONS
    Veranstaltungs-/Theatersaal in
    Colombier, NE, Schweiz =
    Performance / Theater Hall in
    Clombier, NE, Switzerland.
    Competition. Winning architect:
    Claude Rollier. Includes two other
    entries. Text in German.
    ARCHITEKTUR + WETTBEWERBE 1990
    Sept., no.143, p.84-87, elevs.,
    models, plans, site plans.

SWITZERLAND--COMOLOGNO--RELIGIOUS
BUILDINGS--VIA CRUCIS
Mecenatismo a Comologno / Bixio
Candolfi.
1952 renovation of 18th-cent. Via
Crucis with stations of the cross.
Italian, with French and German
summaries.
UNSERE KUNSTDENKMALER 1989, v.40,
no.3, p.277-282, port., photos.

SWITZERLAND--DANIKEN--HOUSES--20TH
CENTURY
Trocken gebaut: Einfamilienhaus in
Daniken SO, 1988/89.
Architect: Ueli Zbinden. Text in
German; summaries in German,
French and English.
WERK, BAUEN + WOHNEN 1990 Nov.,
no.11, p.28-35, axonometric views,
dets., photos., plans, secns.,
site plans.

SWITZERLAND--EMMENBRUCKE--CENTRAL
BUSINESS DISTRICTS--COMPETITIONS
Klare Sprache im Zentrum:
Projektwettbewerb im Zentrum von
Emmenbrucke.
First place entry by Bucher, Hotz
und Burkhart; second place entry
by Ammann + Baumann.
SCHWEIZER BAUMARKT 1990 June 11,
v.25, no.7, p.[I]-III, models.

SWITZERLAND--EMMENBRUCKE--MULTI-USE
BUILDINGS--EMMENBAUM
Wohn-und Geschaftshaus "Emmenbaum",
Emmenbrucke LU.
Architects: A. Scheitlin + M.
Syfrig.
WERK, BAUEN + WOHNEN 1990 May,
no.5, p.1-4, photos., plans,
secn., table, aerial photo.

SWITZERLAND--ENGADINE--HOUSES--17TH
CENTURY--CONSERVATION AND
RESTORATION
"Chesa" engadinese = An Engadin
"chesa".
Restoration of 17th-cent. Swiss
house. Architect: Hans-Jorg Ruch
of Ruch & Husler.
ABITARE 1990 Mar., no.283,
p.134-139, photos., plans, secn.

SWITZERLAND--ENGADINE--VERNACULAR
ARCHITECTURE
"Chesa" engadinese = An Engadin
"chesa".
Restoration of 17th-cent. Swiss
house. Architect: Hans-Jorg Ruch
of Ruch & Husler.
ABITARE 1990 Mar., no.283,
p.134-139, photos., plans, secn.

SWITZERLAND--EVRY--CHURCHES--ROUND
Projet pour la cathedrale d'Evry,
1988.
Architect: Mario Botta.
WERK, BAUEN +WOHNEN 1989 Dec.,
no.12, p.64-65, dwg., elev.,
plans, secns.

SWITZERLAND--FREIBURG--FARMHOUSES
Jean-Pierre Anderegg: Die
Bauernhauser des Kantons Freiburg
[book review] / Peter F. Kopp.
ZEITSCHRIFT FUR SCHWEIZERISCHE
ARCHAOLOGIE UND KUNSTGESCHICHTE
1989, v.46, no.4, p.323-325, plan.

SWITZERLAND--FREIBURG--VERNACULAR
ARCHITECTURE
Jean-Pierre Anderegg: Die
Bauernhauser des Kantons Freiburg
[book review] / Peter F. Kopp.
ZEITSCHRIFT FUR SCHWEIZERISCHE
ARCHAOLOGIE UND KUNSTGESCHICHTE
1989, v.46, no.4, p.323-325, plan.

SWITZERLAND--FRIBOURG--APARTMENT
HOUSES--CASTEL SCHMITTEN
Suisse: le credo de l'habitat
groupe.
Feature four projects: Castel
Schmitten, Fribourg, architects:
Martin Wagner, David and Samuel
Spycher; Merzenacker project,
Bern, architects: ARB
Arbeitsgruppe; Habitat industriel,
Givisiez, architect: Rodolphe
Luscher and a multi-use building,
Geneva, architect: Rodolpke
Luscher and a multi-use building,
Geneva, architect: Chantal Scaler.
English summary, p.180.
ARCHITECTURE INTERIEURE CREE 1990
June-July, no.237, p.[108]-119,
dwgs., photos., secns.

SWITZERLAND--FRIBOURG--CORPORATE
OFFICE BUILDINGS--CARTIER
Mit Charme und Kleinen Fehlern:
statement / Jean Nouvel.
Offices and warehouse of Cartier
Co., Fribourg, Switzerland, 1990.
Architects: Jean Nouvel, Emmanuel
Cattani et associes.
ARCHITHESE 1990 Nov.-Dec., v.20,
no.6, p.[52-53], det., photos.

SWITZERLAND--GARDEN APARTMENTS
Freiraumplanning in
Reihenhaussiedlungen / Thomas
Ryffel.
Open space planning in two
terraced housing developments in
Switzerland. Includes English
summary and captions.
GARTEN UND LANDSCHAFT 1990, v.100,
no.4, p.30-33, axonometric view,
photos., site plans.

SWITZERLAND--GEBENSDORF--HOUSING
DEVELOPMENTS--RUSSDORFLI
Gebaudebeispiel: Vorabdruck aus dem
neuen Dachatlas Geneigte Dacher.
Roof details from 4 projects:
swimming center, Albstadt, W.G.
(P.Siefert et al); housing
development, Gebensdorf,
Switzerland (C. Tognola, C.
Stahel, D. Zulauf); student
housing, Wales (D. Lea); and
housing for handicapped,
Eastleigh, England (D. White).
DETAIL 1990 Feb.-Mar., v.30, no.1,
p.[16-23], dets., elev., photos.,
plans, secns., site plans.
Siedlung "Russdorfli", Gebenstorf
AG, 1984.
Architects: Carlo Tognola,
Christian Stahel, Dieter Zulauf.
WERK, BAUEN + WOHNEN 1990 May,
no.5, p.54-57, photos., plan,
secn., site plan.

SWITZERLAND--GELNHAUSEN--ROOFS--20TH
CENTURY--SCHUTZDACHER KAISERPFALZ
Schutzdacher Kaiserpfalz,
Gelnhausen, Projekt 1989.
Project for a new roof to cover a
medieval fort. Architect:
Karljosef Schattner with Jorg
Homeier.
WERK, BAUEN + WOHNEN 1990 Apr.,
no.4, p.44-45, elevs., model.

SWITZERLAND--GENEVA--APARTMENT
HOUSES--IMMEUBLE CLARTE
Stahlkonstruktion und Metallbau: Le
Corbusiers & Pierre Jeannerets
"moderne" architektonische
Interpretation [book review] /
Ernst Strebel.
On "Immeuble Clarte Genf von Le
Corbusier & Pierre Jeanneret," by
Christian Sumi (1989).
WERK, BAUEN + WOHNEN 1990 Oct.,
no.10, p.16-19, photos., plans,
secns.

SWITZERLAND--GENEVA--ATRIUMS--
INTERNATIONAL MUSEUM OF THE RED
CROSS
Geheimnisse der Lichtpyramide /
Pierre Zoelly.
On a project by Zoelly: Atrium
Rotkreuzmuseum, Geneva.
DER ARCHITEKT 1990 Sept., no.9,
p.401-402, dwgs., photos.

SWITZERLAND--GENEVA--CONVENTION
FACILITIES
Nouvelle salle de conference du
GATT, Geneve, projet, 1988.
Architect: Ugo Brunoni.
WERK, BAUEN + WOHNEN 1989 Dec.,
no.12, p.59, plans, secns.

SWITZERLAND--GENEVA--MULTI-USE
BUILDINGS
Suisse: le credo de l'habitat
groupe.
Feature four projects: Castel
Schmitten, Fribourg, architects:
Martin Wagner, David and Samuel
Spycher; Merzenacker project,
Bern, architects: ARB
Arbeitsgruppe; Habitat industriel,
Givisiez, architect: Rodolphe
Luscher and a multi-use building,
Geneva, architect: Rodolpke
Luscher and a multi-use building,
Geneva, architect: Chantal Scaler.
English summary, p.180.
ARCHITECTURE INTERIEURE CREE 1990
June-July, no.237, p.[108]-119,
dwgs., photos., secns.

SWITZERLAND--GENEVA--MUSEUMS--18TH
CENTURY--ART
Les collections d'art a Geneve de la
Revolution a Waterloo [1789-1815]
/ Armand Brulhart.
German and Italian summaries.
UNSERE KUNSTDENKMALER 1989, v.40,
no.3, p.257-267, ill., dwgs.,
refs.

SWITZERLAND--GENEVA--MUSEUMS--19TH
CENTURY--ART
Les collections d'art a Geneve de la
Revolution a Waterloo [1789-1815]
/ Armand Brulhart.
German and Italian summaries.
UNSERE KUNSTDENKMALER 1989, v.40,
no.3, p.257-267, ill., dwgs.,
refs.

SWITZERLAND--GENEVA--PARC LANCY--
PARKS--20TH CENTURY
Il disegno del luogo = Designing the
site / Tamara Molinari.
Features 3 parks: The Garden of
Dwarfs, Salzburg; Campo del Sole,
Italy; and Lancy, Geneva (George
Descombes).
ABITARE 1990 June, no.286,
p.156-175, axonometric views, map,
photos., secns., site plans,
sketches.

SWITZERLAND--GENEVA--VILLAS--19TH
CENTURY--VILLA LA GORDANNE
Classical romance: a
nineteenth-century rotunda
encompasses a small but stately
realm / Christopher Simon Sykes.
Villa La Gordanne, overlooking
Lake Geneva was commissioned ca.
1800 as a copy of Belle Isle, an
18th-cent. house in the English
Lake District. Interior designer:
Tom Parr, of Colefax & Fowler.
HOUSE & GARDEN 1990 Mar., v.162,
no.3, p.188-195,211, port.,
photos.

SWITZERLAND--GENEVA--VISITORS'
CENTERS--EUROPEAN ORGANIZATION FOR
NUCLEAR RESEARCH (CERN)--MICROCOSM
Gaia, habitat interplanetario =
Gaia, an interplanetary habitat /
Michele Caldarelli.
Project for "Microcosm" visitors'
center; architect: Filippo Avalle.
L'ARCA 1990 Jan., no.34, p.92-96,
axonometric view, dwgs., model.

SWITZERLAND--GENOLIER--VACATION HOUSES
Colonie de vacances a Genolier
(Vaud).
Built 1987-89. Architect:
Pierre-Alain Renaud.
WERK, BAUEN + WOHNEN 1990 Dec.,
no.12, p.1-4(folded, at back),
dets., photos., plans, secns.,
site plan, isometric dwgs., aerial
photo.

SWITZERLAND--GIORNICO--CHURCH
DECORATION AND ORNAMENT--15TH
CENTURY--SAN NICOLAO
Der Kreuznimbus im Christusbild /
Joachim Schmidt.
Includes the 15th cent. wall
paintings in San Nicolao in
Giornico, Switzerland.
DAS MUNSTER 1990, v.43, no.1,
p.20-28, photos.

SWITZERLAND--GIOVA--CHURCHES--20TH
CENTURY--NOSTRA SIGNORA DI FATIMA
Svizzera anni '90: tre culture, tre
architetture = Switzerland 1990:
three cultures, three
architectures / Paolo Fumagalli.
Features projects by Jacques
Herzog and Pierre de Meuron; Livio
Vacchini; Atelier 5; Willi Egli;
Mario Botta; Jean-Jacques Oberson;
Giancarlo Durisch; Aurelio
Galfetti; Luigi Snozzi; Roger
Diener; Atelier Cube; Matti,
Burgi, Ragaz; Schnebli, Ammann &
Partner; R. Luscher; V. Mangeat;
S. Calatrava, A. Amsler, and W.
Rueger; Mario Campi and Franco
Pessina; and Peter Zumthor.
Includes an article by Werner
Jehle, "The mountain: painters,
(Continued next column)

SWITZERLAND--GIOVA--CHURCHES--20TH
CENTURY--NOSTRA SIGNORA DI FATIMA
(CONTINUED)
Svizzera anni '90:...(CONTINUED)
engineers, and architects." Text
in Italian and English.
ABITARE 1990 Nov., no.290,
p.150-191, axonometric views,
dets., ill., elevs., maps,
photos., plans, secns., site
plans, sketch, aerial photo.

SWITZERLAND--GIVISIEZ--INDUSTRIAL
HOUSING--HABITAT INDUSTRIEL
Suisse: le credo de l'habitat
groupe.
Feature four projects: Castel
Schmitten, Fribourg, architects:
Martin Wagner, David and Samuel
Spycher; Merzenacker project,
Bern, architects: ARB
Arbeitsgruppe; Habitat industriel,
Givisiez, architect: Rodolphe
Luscher and a multi-use building,
Geneva, architect: Rodolpke
Luscher and a multi-use building,
Geneva, architect: Chantal Scaler.
English summary, p.180.
ARCHITECTURE INTERIEURE CREE 1990
June-July, no.237, p.[108]-119,
dwgs., photos., secns.

SWITZERLAND--GOSSAU--CHAPELS--20TH
CENTURY--STUDENTENKAPELLE
Studentenkapelle, Gossau SG.
Architects: R. Antoniol + K.
Huber.
WERK, BAUEN + WOHNEN 1990 Mar.,
no.3, p.1-4(folded, at back),
axonometric views, plans, secns.,
tables.

SWITZERLAND--GREIFSWALD--CATHEDRALS--
CONSERVATION AND RESTORATION--SANKT
NIKOLAI
Renovierung des Domes St. Nikolai in
Greifswald.
Architect: Friedhelm Grundmann.
Artist: Hans Kock.
KUNST UND KIRCHE 1990, no.1,
p.26-29, photos., plans, secn.

SWITZERLAND--GROSSHOCHSTETTEN--
HOSPITALS--BEZIRKSSPITAL
GROSSHOCHSTETTEN
Bezirksspital Grosshochstetten.
Built 1987-1989. Architects: Marc
and Yvonne Hausammann.
WERK, BAUEN + WOHNEN 1990 Nov.,
no.11, 4 folded p. at end,
photos., plans, secn., site plans.

SWITZERLAND--HALDENSTEIN--OFFICES--
ARCHITECTS'--ATELIER ZUMTHOR
Un 'architettura di silenziose
articolazioni: sull'opera di Peter
Zumthor = An architecture of
silent articulations on the work
of Peter Zumthor / Wilfried Wang.
Works include Atelier Zumthor,
Haldenstein, Switzerland (1987).
In Italian and English.
OTTAGONO 1990 Dec., no.97,
p.[48-80], dets., dwgs., elevs.,
photos., plans, secns.

SWITZERLAND--HISTORIC BUILDINGS--
CONSERVATION AND RESTORATION
Denmalschutz in der Praxis: eine
Pressefahrt der Zurcher Kantonalen
Denkmalpflege.
SCHWEIZER BAUMARKT 1990 Aug.27,
v.25, no.10, p.I-IV, photos.

SWITZERLAND--HOBEWEG INTERLAKEN--
HOTELS--19TH CENTURY
Von der Klostertaverne uber den
Landgasthof zum Palasthotel und
Punkthochhaus / Markus Sigrist.
19th cent. grand hotels in
Interlaken. Discusses influence of
architects Horace Edouard Daviner
and Robert II Roller. French and
Italian summaries.
UNSERE KUNSTDENKMALER 1989, v.40,
no.2, p.144-153, ill., engrs.,
refs.

SWITZERLAND--INTERLAKEN--ALPINE
BUILDINGS--BERGHAUS JUNGFRAUJOCH
Berghaus Jungfraujoch.
In Interlaken, Switzerland. Built
1983-87. Architect: Ernst E.
Anderegg.
WERK, BAUEN + WOHNEN 1990 Sept.,
no.9, p.1-4, dets., photos.,
plans, secns.

SWITZERLAND--INTERLAKEN--GAMBLING
CASINOS--KURSAAL INTERLAKEN
Kursale: in Interlaken und anderswo
/ Martin Frohlich.
Includes discussion of Paul
Bouvier's Kursaal Interlaken, ca.
1902.
UNSERE KUNSTDENKMALER 1989, v.40.
no.2, p.154-169, elev., photos.,
refs.

SWITZERLAND--INTERLAKEN--MULTI-USE
BUILDINGS--BERGHAUS JUNGFRAUJOCH
Berghaus Jungfraujoch.
In Interlaken, Switzerland. Built
1983-87. Architect: Ernst E.
Anderegg.
WERK, BAUEN + WOHNEN 1990 Sept.,
no.9, p.1-4, dets., photos.,
plans, secns.

SWITZERLAND--KITCHENS--COMPETITIONS
Architektenwettbewerb um "Kuche des
Jahres."
Competition projects for "Die gute
Kuche 1990." First prize to Kurt
Erni.
SCHWEIZER BAUMARKT 1990 Sept.17,
v.25, no.11, p.I-IV, photos.,
plans.

SWITZERLAND--KLOTEN--SPORTS
FACILITIES--COMPETITIONS
Sportanlage Trottacher in Kloten,
Schweiz = Sports grounds
Trottacher in Kloten, Switzerland.
Competition. First prize winners:
Hertig, Hertig und Schoch. Text in
German.
ARCHITEKTUR + WETTBEWERBE 1990
Mar., no.141, p.79-83, elevs.,
models, secns., site plans.

SWITZERLAND--LA CHAUX-DE-FONDS--
VILLAS--INTERIOR DESIGN--VILLA
SCHWOB
    Ebel, abroad.
        Features two projects by Andree
        Putman: Ebel exhibition stand for
        the 1985 Basel fair and the
        restoration of Le Corbusier's
        Villa Schwob in La Chaux-de-Fonds,
        which serves as Ebel's main
        headquarters. Includes photo of
        billboard-facade of Ebel Paris
        shop, now under construction.
        INTERIOR DESIGN 1990 Mar., v.61,
        no.5, p.158-[163], photos.

SWITZERLAND--LAND SETTLEMENT
    Mitten im Land = Au milieu du pays =
    In the middle of the country.
        Suburban developments in
        Switzerland is the topic of this
        issue.
        WERK, BAUEN + WOHNEN 1990 May,
        no.5, p.24-41, ill., maps, photos.

SWITZERLAND--LAND USE
    Mitte des Mittellandes--Vakuum der
    Schweiz?
        Urbanization of midlands lying
        between cities. Text in German;
        summaries in German, French and
        English.
        WERK, BAUEN + WOHNEN 1990 May,
        no.5, p.58-63, maps, photos.,
        aerial photos., refs.

SWITZERLAND--LANGENBRUCK--PORTALS--
ROMANESQUE--KLOSTER SCHONTAL
    Lowe, Drache, Ritter und Madonna /
    Carola Jaggi, Hans-Rudolf Meier.
        An examination of the 12th-cent.
        sculpture on the west portal of
        Kloster Schontal, in Langenbruck,
        Switzerland. Summaries in French
        and Italian.
        UNSERE KUNSTDENKMALER 1989, v.40,
        no.4, p.412-419, dets., elevs.,
        photos., refs.

SWITZERLAND--LANGENBRUCK--SCULPTURE--
ARCHITECTURAL--ROMANESQUE--KLOSTER
SCHONTAL
    Lowe, Drache, Ritter und Madonna /
    Carola Jaggi, Hans-Rudolf Meier.
        An examination of the 12th-cent.
        sculpture on the west portal of
        Kloster Schontal, in Langenbruck,
        Switzerland. Summaries in French
        and Italian.
        UNSERE KUNSTDENKMALER 1989, v.40,
        no.4, p.412-419, dets., elevs.,
        photos., refs.

SWITZERLAND--LANGENTHAL--BANKS--
COMPETITIONS--ERSPARNISKASSE
    Wettbewerb Fordert Dialog.
        New bank building, Langenthal.
        Architect: Ernst und Nyffeler.
        SCHWEIZER BAUMARKT 1990 Jan.29,
        v.25, no.2,].[I]-III, photos.

SWITZERLAND--LAUFEN--WAREHOUSES--
SOCIETE RICOLA
    Warehouse, Ricola, Switzerland,
    1986-87 / Martin Steinmann.
        Architects: Jacques Herzog and
        Pierre de Meuron.
        9H 1989, no.8, p.74-75, photos.,
        secn.

SWITZERLAND--LAUSANNE--APARTMENT
COMPLEXES--LA GRANGETTE
    Logements subventionnes "la
    Grangette", Lausanne.
        Architect: Fonso Boschetti.
        WERK, BAUEN + WOHNEN 1990
        July-Aug., no.7-8, p.1-4 (folded,
        at back), photos., plans, site
        plans, tables.

SWITZERLAND--LAUSANNE--APARTMENT
HOUSES
    Immeuble de logements et de
    commerces, Lausanne, 1988.
        Architects: Atelier Cube.
        WERK, BAUEN + WOHNEN 1989 Dec.,
        no.12, p.58, axonometric view,
        photos., plan.

SWITZERLAND--LAUSANNE--CATHEDRALS--
ALTERATIONS AND ADDITIONS--
CATHEDRALE DE LAUSANNE
    Ein Turmmuseum: Projekt des Museums
    der Kathedrale von Lausanne, 1989
    Architekt: Fonso Boschetti.
        French text, p.65.
        WERK, BAUEN + WOHNEN 1990
        Jan.-Feb., no.1-2, p.12, model,
        photos., plans, secns.

SWITZERLAND--LAUSANNE--DAY CARE
CENTERS--CENTRE DE VIE ENFANTINE DE
VALENCY
    Centre de vie enfantine de Valency a
    Lausanne.
        Architect: Rodolphe Luscher.
        WERK, BAUEN + WOHNEN 1990 Oct.,
        no.10, p.4 folded p. at end, det.,
        photos., plans, secns., site plan.
    Le Centre de vie enfantine de
    Valency, Lausanne, 1989.
        Architect: Rodolphe Luscher.
        WERK, BAUEN + WOHNEN 1989 Dec.,
        no.12, p.61, photos., plans, secn.
    Construire a l'echelle de l'enfant /
    Rodolphe Luscher.
        Centre de vie enfantine de
        Valency, Lausanne. Architect:
        Rodolphe Luscher.
        TECHNIQUES ET ARCHITECTURE 1990
        June-July, no.390, p.26-29,
        photos., plans, secns., aerial
        photo.
    Kindertagesstatte Valency, Lausanne
    = Day Nursery Valency, Lausanne.
        Architect: Rodolphe Luscher.
        DETAIL 1990 Dec.,-1991 Jan., v.30,
        no.6, p.620-624, axonometric view,
        dets., photos., plan, secn., site
        plans.
    Svizzera anni '90: tre culture, tre
    architetture = Switzerland 1990:
    three cultures, three
    architectures / Paolo Fumagalli.
        Features projects by Jacques
        Herzog and Pierre de Meuron; Livio
        Vacchini; Atelier 5; Willi Egli;
        Mario Botta; Jean-Jacques Oberson;
        Giancarlo Durisch; Aurelio
        Galfetti; Luigi Snozzi; Roger
        Diener; Atelier Cube; Matti,
        Burgi, Ragaz; Schnebli, Ammann &
        Partner; R. Luscher; V. Mangeat;
        S. Calatrava, A. Amsler, and W.
        Rueger; Mario Campi and Franco
        Pessina; and Peter Zumthor.
        Includes an article by Werner
        Jehle, "The mountain: painters,
        engineers, and architects." Text
        in Italian and English.
        ABITARE 1990 Nov., no.290,
        p.150-191, axonometric views,
        (Continued next column)

SWITZERLAND--LAUSANNE--DAY CARE
CENTERS--CENTRE DE VIE ENFANTINE DE
VALENCY (CONTINUED)
    Svizzera anni '90:...(CONTINUED)
        dets., ill., elevs., maps,
        photos., plans, secns., site
        plans, sketch, aerial photo.
    Wohnmaschine wortlich genommen: der
    Kinderhort in Valency-Lausanne,
    1989 / Christoph Luchsinger.
        Architect: Rodolphe Luscher. Text
        in German; summaries in German,
        French and English.
        WERK, BAUEN + WOHNEN 1990 Oct.,
        no.10, p.56-63, axonometric views,
        photos., plans, secns., site
        plans.

SWITZERLAND--LAUSANNE--LOW INCOME
HOUSING--CHEMIN DE BOISSENET
    Svizzera anni '90: tre culture, tre
    architetture = Switzerland 1990:
    three cultures, three
    architectures / Paolo Fumagalli.
        Features projects by Jacques
        Herzog and Pierre de Meuron; Livio
        Vacchini; Atelier 5; Willi Egli;
        Mario Botta; Jean-Jacques Oberson;
        Giancarlo Durisch; Aurelio
        Galfetti; Luigi Snozzi; Roger
        Diener; Atelier Cube; Matti,
        Burgi, Ragaz; Schnebli, Ammann &
        Partner; R. Luscher; V. Mangeat;
        S. Calatrava, A. Amsler, and W.
        Rueger; Mario Campi and Franco
        Pessina; and Peter Zumthor.
        Includes an article by Werner
        Jehle, "The mountain: painters,
        engineers, and architects." Text
        in Italian and English.
        ABITARE 1990 Nov., no.290,
        p.150-191, axonometric views,
        dets., ill., elevs., maps,
        photos., plans, secns., site
        plans, sketch, aerial photo.

SWITZERLAND--LAUSANNE--MULTI-USE
BUILDINGS
    Immeuble de logements et de
    commerces, Lausanne, 1988.
        Architects: Atelier Cube.
        WERK, BAUEN + WOHNEN 1989 Dec.,
        no.12, p.58, axonometric view,
        photos., plan.

SWITZERLAND--LAUSANNE--MULTI-USE
BUILDINGS--MONTCHOISI-CENTRE
    Nuove superfici di vetro a Losanna =
    Montchoisi-Centre in Lausanne /
    Lucia Bisi.
        Residential-shopping complex.
        Architects: Wurlod Architectes.
        L'ARCA 1990 Jan., no.34, p.38-47,
        elev., map, photos., plans, secns,
        sote plans.

SWITZERLAND--LAUSANNE--RELIGIOUS
MUSEUMS--MUSEE DE LA CATHEDRALE DE
LAUSANNE
    Ein Turmmuseum: Projekt des Museums
    der Kathedrale von Lausanne, 1989
    Architekt: Fonso Boschetti.
        French text, p.65.
        WERK, BAUEN + WOHNEN 1990
        Jan.-Feb., no.1-2, p.12, model,
        photos., plans, secns.

SWITZERLAND--LAUSANNE--STORES--SHOE--
ARODE
Schuhladen Arode, Basel, Lausanne.
Architects: Martin & Elisabeth
Boesch.
WERK, BAUEN + WOHNEN 1990 Oct.,
no.10, p.69-72, photos., plans,
secns.

SWITZERLAND--LAUTERHOFEN--HOUSES--20TH
CENTURY
Wohnhaus mit Arztpraxis in
Lauterhofen, 1989 / Joachim
Andreas Joedicke.
Architects: Werner Brandl, Gerhard
Wolfrum.
WERK, BAUEN + WOHNEN 1990 June,
no.6, p.74-76, photos., plans,
secn.

SWITZERLAND--LEMGO--CHURCHES--
COMPETITIONS--STIFTUNG EBEN-EZER
Wettbewerb Evang. Kirche Eben-Ezer
in Lemgo.
First prize: Kallmeyer und Herbst.
Second prizes: Fritz Brand, Regina
Dohle.
KUNST UND KIRCHE 1990, no.1,
p.32-35, elevs., models, plans,
secns., site plans.

SWITZERLAND--LIESTAL--HOUSES--20TH
CENTURY
Einfamilienhaus in Liestal, 1989.
Architects: Fierz & Baader.
WERK, BAUEN + WOHNEN 1990 Apr.,
no.4, p.34-37, det., photos.,
plans, secns.

SWITZERLAND--LITTAU--HOUSING
DEVELOPMENTS--RUOPIGEN
Dolf Schnebli.
Most of issue devoted to the work
of this Swiss architect.
Introduction by Paolo Fumagalli.
Text in German, French and
English.
WERK, BAUEN + WOHNEN 1990 Dec.,
no.12, p.20-69, axonometric views,
dets., dwgs., port., elevs.,
models, photos., plans, secns.,
site plans, sketches, aerial
photo.

SWITZERLAND--LOCARNO--CHURCHES--
ROMANESQUE--SAN VITTORE DI MURALTO
La sirena nel San Vittore di Muralto
/ Rossana Cardani.
A study of three Romanesque
sculptures in a church near
Locarno, Switzerland. Summaries
in French and German.
UNSERE KUNSTDENKMALER 1989, v.40,
no.4, p.393-401, dets., photos.,
plan, sketches, refs.

SWITZERLAND--LOCARNO--CITY PLANNING--
COMPETITIONS
Neuordnung des Bereichs "Piazza
Grande-Largo Zorzi Giardini
Pubblici" in Locarno, Schweiz =
Reorganization of the area "Piazza
grande-Largo Zorzi-Giardini
Pubblici" in Locarno, Switzerland.
Idea competition. Winning
architect: Luigi Snozzi. Text in
German.
ARCHITEKTUR + WETTBEWERBE 1990
Dec., no.144, p.79-83, dwgs.,
elevs., site plans.

SWITZERLAND--LOCARNO--HOUSING FOR
ELDERLY
Residenzia per la terza eta a
Locarno.
Old age home. Architect: Guido
Tallone. Summaries in English,
French and Spanish.
ABACUS 1990 July-Sept., v.6,
no.23, p.56-63, dets., dwgs.,
elevs., photos., plans.

SWITZERLAND--LOCARNO--OLD AGE HOMES
Residenzia per la terza eta a
Locarno.
Old age home. Architect: Guido
Tallone. Summaries in English,
French and Spanish.
ABACUS 1990 July-Sept., v.6,
no.23, p.56-63, dets., dwgs.,
elevs., photos., plans.

SWITZERLAND--LOCARNO--POST OFFICES
Projet pour un batiment des Postes,
Locarno, 1989.
Architect: Livio Vacchini.
WERK, BAUEN + WOHNEN 1989 Dec.,
no.12, p.67, elevs., plan, site
plan.

SWITZERLAND--LOCARNO--SCULPTURE--
ARCHITECTURAL--ROMANESQUE--SAN
VITTORE DI MURALTO
La sirena nel San Vittore di Muralto
/ Rossana Cardani.
A study of three Romanesque
sculptures in a church near
Locarno, Switzerland. Summaries
in French and German.
UNSERE KUNSTDENKMALER 1989, v.40,
no.4, p.393-401, dets., photos.,
plan, sketches, refs.

SWITZERLAND--LOTZWIL--OLD AGE HOMES--
ALTERSHEIM AM DORFPLATZ
Altersheim "am Dorfplatz", Lotzwil
BE.
Architects: Urs & Sonja Grandjean.
WERK, BAUEN + WOHNEN 1990
Jan.-Feb., no.1-2, p.1-4 (folded,
at back), photos., plans, secns.,
tables.

SWITZERLAND--LOURTIER--CHAPELS--
CHAPELLE DE LOURTIER
Quand la tradition permet la
modernite, l'Abbaye de
Saint-Maurice et la chapelle de
Lourtier / Bernard Wyder.
Chapel built 1932. Architect:
Alberto Sartoris. German and
Italian summaries.
UNSERE KUNSTDENKMALER 1989, v.40,
no.3, p.268-276, axonometric view,
dwg., photos., refs.

SWITZERLAND--LUCERNE--APARTMENT
HOUSES--ALTERATIONS AND ADDITIONS--
HIRSCHENGRABEN 15
Lichtspiele auf engem Raum: Umbau
und Renovation eines Wohn - und
Geschaftshauses in Luzern, 1990.
Architect: Peter Erni.
WERK, BAUEN + WOHNEN 1990 Dec.,
no.12, p.10-11, photos., plans,
secns.

SWITZERLAND--LUCERNE--BUS SHELTERS
Bushaltestelle in Luzern.
Architect: Hannes Ineichen.
WERK, BAUEN + WOHNEN 1989 Dec.,
no.12, p.1-4 (folded, at back),
dets., elevs., photos., plans,
secns., tables, aerial photo.

SWITZERLAND--LUCERNE--CULTURAL
CENTERS--COMPETITIONS--LUZERNER
KULTURZENTRUM
Luzerner Kulturzentrum: Wettbewerb.
1st prize to Jean Nouvel, Emmanuel
Cattani et Associes.
SCHWEIZER BAUMARKT 1990 July 2,
v.25, no.8, p.[I]-III, ill.

SWITZERLAND--LUCERNE--MULTI-USE
BUILDINGS
Projekt Wohn- und Geschaftshaus,
Luzern, 1987.
Architects: Daniele Marques, Bruno
Zurkirchen.
WERK, BAUEN + WOHNEN 1989 Dec.,
no.12, p.38, dwg., plans.

SWITZERLAND--LUCERNE--RAILROAD
STATIONS
Umschlagplatze: neue Bahnhofhalle in
Luzern und Projekt Neugestaltung
Bahnhof Chur.
Projects by Ammann and Baumann
with S. Calatrava and Richard
Brosi + Obrist und Partner. Text
in German; summaries in German,
French and English.
WERK, BAUEN + WOHNEN 1990 June,
no.6, p.36-45, models, photos.,
plans, secns., site plans.

SWITZERLAND--LUGANO--APARTMENT
HOUSES--LOW-RISE
Speculari lungo la strada / Daniela
Invernizzi.
Apartment house near Lugano,
Switzerland. Architects: Balestra
& Mazzi.
VILLE GIARDINI 1990 Feb., no.245,
p.8-13, elev., photos, plans,
secn.

SWITZERLAND--LUGANO--HOUSES
Rationalism revisited in Switzerland
/ Joseph Rykwert.
Geometric house near Lugano,
Switzerland. Architects: Mario
Campi, Franco Pessina.
ARCHITECTURAL DIGEST 1990 Dec.,
v.47, no.13, p.130-[133], 220,
ports., photos., plan.

SWITZERLAND--LUGANO--HOUSES--20TH
CENTURY--CONCRETE
Cemeto, la forza della superficie /
Vittoria Bocconi.
House on Lake Lugano. Architect:
Claudio F. Pellegrini.
VILLE GIARDINI 1990 Oct., no.252,
p.10-17, photos., plans.

SWITZERLAND--LUGANO--MULTI-USE
BUILDINGS--VIA CIANI
Svizzera anni '90: tre culture, tre
architetture = Switzerland 1990:
three cultures, three
architectures / Paolo Fumagalli.
Features projects by Jacques
Herzog and Pierre de Meuron; Livio
Vacchini; Atelier 5; Willi Egli;
Mario Botta; Jean-Jacques Oberson;
Giancarlo Durisch; Aurelio
Galfetti; Luigi Snozzi; Roger
(Continued next page)

SWITZERLAND--LUGANO--MULTI-USE
  BUILDINGS--VIA CIANI (CONTINUED)
  Svizzera anni '90:...(CONTINUED)
    Diener; Atelier Cube; Matti,
    Burgi, Ragaz; Schnebli, Ammann &
    Partner; R. Luscher; V. Mangeat;
    S. Calatrava, A. Amsler, and W.
    Rueger; Mario Campi and Franco
    Pessina; and Peter Zumthor.
    Includes an article by Werner
    Jehle, "The mountain: painters,
    engineers, and architects." Text
    in Italian and English.
    ABITARE 1990 Nov., no.290,
    p.150-191, axonometric views,
    dets., ill., elevs., maps,
    photos., plans, secns., site
    plans, sketch, aerial photo.

SWITZERLAND--LUGANO--MUSEUMS--ART--
  ALTERATIONS AND ADDITIONS--SAMMLUNG
  THYSSEN-BORNEMISZA
  Nueva galeria para la coleccion
    Thyssen-Bornemisza Villa Favorita
    Lugano = A new gallery for the
    Thyssen-Bornemisza Collection
    Villa Favorita Lugano / James
    Stirling, Michael Wilford.
    Architects: James Stirling,
    Michael Wilford and Associates.
    Text in Spanish and English.
    COMPOSICION ARQUITECTONICA, ART &
    ARCHITECTURE 1989 Feb., no.2,
    p.[45]-66, axonometric views,
    dwgs., models, photos., plans,
    secns., site plans.
  Thyssen Art Gallery, Lugano,
    Switzerland, 1986.
    Architects: James Stirling,
    Michael Wilford and Associates.
    Text in Japanese and English.
    ARCHITECTURE AND URBANISM 1990
    May, no.5 extra edition,
    p.160-171, axonometric views,
    elevs., models, photos., plans,
    secns., site plan.

SWITZERLAND--LUGANO--OFFICE
  BUILDINGS--COLOMBO
  Svizzera anni '90: tre culture, tre
    architetture = Switzerland 1990:
    three cultures, three
    architectures / Paolo Fumagalli.
    Features projects by Jacques
    Herzog and Pierre de Meuron; Livio
    Vacchini; Atelier 5; Willi Egli;
    Mario Botta; Jean-Jacques Oberson;
    Giancarlo Durisch; Aurelio
    Galfetti; Luigi Snozzi; Roger
    Diener; Atelier Cube; Matti,
    Burgi, Ragaz; Schnebli, Ammann &
    Partner; R. Luscher; V. Mangeat;
    S. Calatrava, A. Amsler, and W.
    Rueger; Mario Campi and Franco
    Pessina; and Peter Zumthor.
    Includes an article by Werner
    Jehle, "The mountain: painters,
    engineers, and architects." Text
    in Italian and English.
    ABITARE 1990 Nov., no.290,
    p.150-191, axonometric views,
    dets., ill., elevs., maps,
    photos., plans, secns., site
    plans, sketch, aerial photo.

SWITZERLAND--LUGANO--RESIDENTIAL
  GARDENS
  In vista del Lago di Lugano /
    Gilberto Oneto.
    Residential landscaping by Paolo
    Burgi.
    VILLE GIARDINI 1990 June, no.249,
    p.68-73, photos.

SWITZERLAND--LUGANO--ROW HOUSES --20TH
  CENTURY
  Una ripetizione differente /
    Marinetta Nunziante.
    A rowhouse of 9 units, near
    Lugano, Switzerland. Architects:
    Mario Campi, Franco Pessina.
    VILLE GIARDINI 1990 June, no.249,
    p.22-29, photos., plans, secn.

SWITZERLAND--MANNO--HOUSES
  Mario Botta: Single family house in
    Manno, Switzerland, 1974-90.
    Text in Japanese and English.
    GA HOUSES 1990 Dec., no.30,
    p.46-55, photos., plans, site
    plan, sketches.

SWITZERLAND--MARTIGNY-VILLE--CITY
  PLANNING--COMPETITIONS--PLACE DE
  ROME
  Place de Rome in Martigny, Schweiz =
    Place de Rome in Martigny,
    Switzerland.
    Competition. First prize winners:
    Sandro Cabrini, Bruno Keller,
    Gianmaria Verda. Text in German.
    ARCHITEKTUR + WETTBEWERBE 1990
    Dec., no.144, p.84-87, elevs.,
    models, site plans.

SWITZERLAND--MARTIGNY-VILLE--PLAZAS--
  COMPETITIONS--PLACE DE ROME
  Place de Rome in Martigny, Schweiz =
    Place de Rome in Martigny,
    Switzerland.
    Competition. First prize winners:
    Sandro Cabrini, Bruno Keller,
    Gianmaria Verda. Text in German.
    ARCHITEKTUR + WETTBEWERBE 1990
    Dec., no.144, p.84-87, elevs.,
    models, site plans.

SWITZERLAND--MEYRIN-SATIGNY--CORPORATE
  OFFICE BUILDINGS--FIRMENICH
  Svizzera anni '90: tre culture, tre
    architetture = Switzerland 1990:
    three cultures, three
    architectures / Paolo Fumagalli.
    Features projects by Jacques
    Herzog and Pierre de Meuron; Livio
    Vacchini; Atelier 5; Willi Egli;
    Mario Botta; Jean-Jacques Oberson;
    Giancarlo Durisch; Aurelio
    Galfetti; Luigi Snozzi; Roger
    Diener; Atelier Cube; Matti,
    Burgi, Ragaz; Schnebli, Ammann &
    Partner; R. Luscher; V. Mangeat;
    S. Calatrava, A. Amsler, and W.
    Rueger; Mario Campi and Franco
    Pessina; and Peter Zumthor.
    Includes an article by Werner
    Jehle, "The mountain: painters,
    engineers, and architects." Text
    in Italian and English.
    ABITARE 1990 Nov., no.290,
    p.150-191, axonometric views,
    dets., ill., elevs., maps,
    photos., plans, secns., site
    plans, sketch, aerial photo.

SWITZERLAND--MEYRIN-SATIGNY--CORPORATE
  OFFICE BUILDINGS--FIRMENICH
  (CONTINUED)
  Transpararenz des Glases -- Leere
    des Raumes: Verwaltungsgebaude der
    Firmenich SA in Meyrin - Satigny,
    1989.
    Architekturburo Jean-Jacques
    Oberson. French text on p.74.
    WERK, BAUEN + WOHNEN 1989 Dec.,
    no.12, p.4-7,63, model, photos.,
    plans.

SWITZERLAND--MONTAGNOLA--APARTMENT
  HOUSES
  Habitations a Montagnola, 1989.
    Architects: Mario Campi, Franco
    Pessina.
    WERK, BAUEN + WOHNEN 1989 Dec.,
    no.12, p.71, axonometric view,
    photo., plans.

SWITZERLAND--MONTAGNOLA--HOUSES--
  SLOPING SITES
  Case monofamiliari a Monatagnola
    (Svizzera) / Ermanno Ranzani.
    Architects: Mario Campi, Franco
    Pessina. Text in Italian and
    English.
    DOMUS 1990 Apr., no.715,
    p.[46-51], axonometric view, dwg.,
    elevs., photos, plans, secns.,
    site plans.

SWITZERLAND--MONTAGNOLA--SCHOOLS--
  ELEMENTARY
  Escola primaria cria a praca
    principal da cidade.
    In Montagnola, Switzerland.
    Architect: Civio Vacchini.
    PROJETO 1989 June, no.122,
    p.44-50, elev, photos, plans,
    secns., site plan.

SWITZERLAND--MONTE CARASSO--
  ARCHITECTURE--20TH CENTURY
  Neugestaltung des Zentrums von Monte
    Carasso, Schweiz = Redesigning the
    center of Monte Carasso,
    Switzerland.
    Features various projects by Luigi
    Snozzi including the Raiffeisen
    Bank, Sports Hall and the Baidotti
    house.
    ARCHITEKTUR + WETTBEWERBE 1990
    Dec., no.144, p.13, photos., site
    plan.

SWITZERLAND--MONTE CARASSO--CENTRAL
  BUSINESS DISTRICTS--ALTERATIONS AND
  ADDITIONS
  Neugestaltung des Zentrums von Monte
    Carasso, Schweiz = Redesigning the
    center of Monte Carasso,
    Switzerland.
    Features various projects by Luigi
    Snozzi including the Raiffeisen
    Bank, Sports Hall and the Baidotti
    house.
    ARCHITEKTUR + WETTBEWERBE 1990
    Dec., no.144, p.13, photos., site
    plan.

SWITZERLAND--MONTE CARASSO--MUNICIPAL
  BUILDINGS
  Svizzera anni '90: tre culture, tre
    architetture = Switzerland 1990:
    three cultures, three
    architectures / Paolo Fumagalli.
    Features projects by Jacques
    Herzog and Pierre de Meuron; Livio
    Vacchini; Atelier 5; Willi Egli;
    (Continued next page)

SWITZERLAND--MONTE CARASSO--MUNICIPAL
BUILDINGS (CONTINUED)
Svizzera anni '90:...(CONTINUED)
Mario Botta; Jean-Jacques Oberson;
Giancarlo Durisch; Aurelio
Galfetti; Luigi Snozzi; Roger
Diener; Atelier Cube; Matti,
Burgi, Ragaz; Schnebli, Ammann &
Partner; R. Luscher; V. Mangeat;
S. Calatrava, A. Amsler, and W.
Rueger; Mario Campi and Franco
Pessina; and Peter Zumthor.
Includes an article by Werner
Jehle, "The mountain: painters,
engineers, and architects." Text
in Italian and English.
ABITARE 1990 Nov., no.290,
p.150-191, axonometric views,
dets., ill., elevs., maps,
photos., plans, secns., site
plans, sketch, aerial photo.

SWITZERLAND--MONTE CARASSO--SPORTS
FACILITIES
Uber den "Vorsatz zur Vitalitat" und
dessen Folgen fur die Architektur
/ Norbert Weickenmeier.
DER ARCHITEKT 1990 July-Aug.,
no.7-8, p.356-359, photos., plans,
site plans, isometric dwg.

SWITZERLAND--MORBIO INFERIORE--
HOUSES--20TH CENTURY--CASA PESSINA
Facciata continua per un desiderio
di luce / Walter Bianchi, Mauro
Colombo.
Casa Pessina, in Morbio Inferiore,
Switzerland. Architect: Alberto
Caldelari.
VILLE GIARDINI 1990 July-Aug.,
no.250, p.58-[59], det., dwg.,
elev., photos.

SWITZERLAND--MOUDON--MURAL PAINTING
AND DECORATION--17TH CENTURY
L'iconographie animale sur les
plafonds polychromes apres la
Reforme: iconographie specifique
ou iconographie d'emprunt? /
Brigitte Pradervand.
16th and 17th cent. ceiling
paintings found in the Vaud Region
of Switzerland. Summaries in
German and Italian.
UNSERE KUNSTDENKMALER 1989, v.40,
no.4, p.402-411, dets., ill.,
photos., engr., refs.

SWITZERLAND--MULLIGEN--HOUSING
DEVELOPMENTS--LOH
Freiraumplanning in
Reihenhaussiedlungen / Thomas
Ryffel.
Open space planning in two
terraced housing developments in
Switzerland. Includes English
summary and captions.
GARTEN UND LANDSCHAFT 1990, v.100,
no.4, p.30-33, axonometric view,
photos., site plans.

SWITZERLAND--MUNSINGEN--HOSPITALS--
PSYCHIATRIC--KLINIK MUNSINGEN
Sichtbar Konstruiert: Krankenheim
Bern- Wittigkofen, 1988/89, und
neues Betriebsgebaude
psychiatrische Klinik Munsingen,
1986/87.
Architects: Atelier 5. Text in
German, summaries in German,
French and English.
WERK, BAUEN + WOHNEN 1990 Nov.,
(Continued next column)

SWITZERLAND--MUNSINGEN--HOSPITALS--
PSYCHIATRIC--KLINIK MUNSINGEN
(CONTINUED)
Sichtbar Konstruiert:...(CONTINUED)
no.11, p.36-47, axonometric views,
dets., photos., plans, secns.,
site plans.

SWITZERLAND--MURAL PAINTING AND
DECORATION--16TH CENTURY
L'iconographie animale sur les
plafonds polychromes apres la
Reforme: iconographie specifique
ou iconographie d'emprunt? /
Brigitte Pradervand.
16th and 17th cent. ceiling
paintings found in the Vaud Region
of Switzerland. Summaries in
German and Italian.
UNSERE KUNSTDENKMALER 1989, v.40,
no.4, p.402-411, dets., ill.,
photos., engr., refs.

SWITZERLAND--MURAL PAINTING AND
DECORATION--GOTHIC
Profane Wandmalerei der Gotik und
Renaissance: Aspekte der fruhen
Wohnkultur am Beispiel von
Konstanz und Zurich / Elisabeth
von Gleichenstein.
KUNST & ANTIQUITATEN 1989, no.4,
p.39-45, photos., refs.

SWITZERLAND--MURAL PAINTING AND
DECORATION--RENAISSANCE
Profane Wandmalerei der Gotik und
Renaissance: Aspekte der fruhen
Wohnkultur am Beispiel von
Konstanz und Zurich / Elisabeth
von Gleichenstein.
KUNST & ANTIQUITATEN 1989, no.4,
p.39-45, photos., refs.

SWITZERLAND--MUZZANO--APARTMENT HOUSES
Edifice d'habitations, Muzzano, en
construction.
Architects: Emilio Bernegger,
Bruno Keller, Edy Quaglia.
WERK, BAUEN + WOHNEN 1989 Dec.,
no.12, p.73, elevs., plans, secn.

SWITZERLAND--NOTTWIL--HEALTH CARE
BUILDINGS--SCHWEIZERISCHES
PARAPLEGIKER-ZENTRUM
Schweizerisches Paraplegiker-Zentrum
Nottwil, Wettbewerb 1985, in
Ausfuhrung.
Architects: Wilfrid and Katharina
Steib.
WERK, BAUEN + WOHNEN 1990 May,
no.5, p.43-45, model, photos.,
plan, site plan.

SWITZERLAND--NOTTWIL--REHABILITATION
CENTERS--SCHWEIZERISCHES
PARAPLEGIKER-ZENTRUM
Schweizerisches Paraplegiker-Zentrum
Nottwil, Wettbewerb 1985, in
Ausfuhrung.
Architects: Wilfrid and Katharina
Steib.
WERK, BAUEN + WOHNEN 1990 May,
no.5, p.43-45, model, photos.,
plan, site plan.

SWITZERLAND--NOTTWIL--TRAINING
CENTERS--SCHWEIZERISCHE ROTEN KREUZ
(SRK)
Ausbildungszentrum des
Schweizerischen Roten Kreuzes,
Unterkunftspavillons, Nottwill
1986-1990.
Fischer Architekten.
WERK, BAUEN + WOHNEN 1990 May,
no.5, p.46-49, photos., plan,
secns.

SWITZERLAND--NYON--GYMNASIUMS
Gymnasium und Hohere Handelsschule
in Nyon.
Architect: Vincent Mangeat.
DEUTSCHE BAUZEITSCHRIFT 1990 Dec.,
v.38, no.12, p.1767-1774,
axonometric views, elevs.,
photos., plans, secns., site
plans.
Svizzera anni '90: tre culture, tre
architetture = Switzerland 1990:
three cultures, three
architectures / Paolo Fumagalli.
Features projects by Jacques
Herzog and Pierre de Meuron; Livio
Vacchini; Atelier 5; Willi Egli;
Mario Botta; Jean-Jacques Oberson;
Giancarlo Durisch; Aurelio
Galfetti; Luigi Snozzi; Roger
Diener; Atelier Cube; Matti,
Burgi, Ragaz; Schnebli, Ammann &
Partner; R. Luscher; V. Mangeat;
S. Calatrava, A. Amsler, and W.
Rueger; Mario Campi and Franco
Pessina; and Peter Zumthor.
Includes an article by Werner
Jehle, "The mountain: painters,
engineers, and architects." Text
in Italian and English.
ABITARE 1990 Nov., no.290,
p.150-191, axonometric views,
dets., ill., elevs., maps,
photos., plans, secns., site
plans, sketch, aerial photo.

SWITZERLAND--NYON--SCHOOLS
Gymnasium und Hohere Handelsschule
in Nyon.
Architect: Vincent Mangeat.
DEUTSCHE BAUZEITSCHRIFT 1990 Dec.,
v.38, no.12, p.1767-1774,
axonometric views, elevs.,
photos., plans, secns., site
plans.
Monumentalitat und Demokratie:
Schulhauser in Nyon, Arzier und
Tannay / Paolo Fumagalli.
Architect: Vincent Mangeat. French
text, p.67.
WERK, BAUEN + WOHNEN 1989 Oct.,
no.10, p.4-11, axonometric views,
elev., photos., plans, secns.,
site plan, isometric dwg., aerial
photo.

SWITZERLAND--OBERBURG BEI BURGDORF--
HOUSES--SOLAR
100% Sonnenenergie: : Forschungs-und
Demonstrationshaus in oferburg bei
Burgotorf (Schweiz) / Josef Jenni.
Built 1989. Designer: J. Jenni.
DEUTSCHE BAUZEITUNG 1990 Sept.,
v.124, no.4, p.72-74, photos.

SWITZERLAND--OBERBURG BEI BURGDORF--
MODEL HOUSES
100% Sonnenenergie: : Forschungs-und
Demonstrationshaus in oferburg bei
Burgotorf (Schweiz) / Josef Jenni.
Built 1989. Designer: J. Jenni.
DEUTSCHE BAUZEITUNG 1990 Sept.,
v.124, no.4, p.72-74, photos.

SWITZERLAND--OBWALDEN--TOWERS--
CONSERVATION AND RESTORATION--
HEXENTURM SARNEN
Hexenturm Sarnen, Obwalden.
Built 1985-86. Architect: Bruno
Scheuner.
WERK, BAUEN + WOHNEN 1990 Dec.,
no.12, p.1-4, axonometric view,
photos., plans, secn.

SWITZERLAND--OPEN SPACES
Freiraumplanning in
Reihenhaussiedlungen / Thomas
Ryffel.
Open space planning in two
terraced housing developments in
Switzerland. Includes English
summary and captions.
GARTEN UND LANDSCHAFT 1990, v.100,
no.4, p.30-33, axonometric view,
photos., site plans.

SWITZERLAND--OSTERMUNDIGEN--HEALTH
CLUBS
Silber in der Grube: Einkaufs- und
Fitnesszentrum in Ostermundigen,
Kanton Bern.
Architect: Justus Dahinden.
BAUWELT 1990 Oct.5, v.81, no.37,
p.1894-1898, axonometric views,
photos.

SWITZERLAND--PFAFFIKON--WATERFRONTS--
COMPETITIONS
Projektwettbewerb Seeuferanlage
Pfaffikon SZ = Concours de projets
pour l'amenagement du bord du lac
a Pfaffikon SZ = Project
competition for lakeside
facilities at Pfaffikon SZ /
Christian Stern.
Winning project by Walter Vetsch.
ANTHOS 1989, v.28, no.4, p.39-42,
site plans, sketches.

SWITZERLAND--PORZA--HOUSES--20TH
CENTURY
Geometrie sul lago / Lucia Bisi.
House on Lago Maggiore, near
Porza, Switzerland. Architects:
Franco and Paolo Moro.
VILLE GIARDINI 1990 May, no.248,
p.16-23, axonometric view,
photos., plans.

SWITZERLAND--PULLACH--DUPLEX HOUSES
Dopplewohnhaus in Pullach,
1986-1989.
Architects: Thomas Herzog, Michael
Volz.
WERK, BAUEN + WOHNEN 1990 June,
no.6, p.8-11, axonometric view,
photos., plans, secn.

SWITZERLAND--REGENSBURG--COLLECTIVE
GARDENS
Naturnahe Kleingarten: ein Modell
vorhaben in Regensburg = Jardins
familiaux en harmonie avec la
nature: un projet modele a
Regensburg = Natural family
gardens: a model project in
Regensburg / Gunther Bartholmai.
(Continued next column)

SWITZERLAND--REGENSBURG--COLLECTIVE
GARDENS (CONTINUED)
Naturnahe...(CONTINUED)
ANTHOS 1989, v.28, no.4, p.8-13,

SWITZERLAND--REGENSBURG--RESIDENTIAL
GARDENS
Naturnahe Kleingarten: ein Modell
vorhaben in Regensburg = Jardins
familiaux en harmonie avec la
nature: un projet modele a
Regensburg = Natural family
gardens: a model project in
Regensburg / Gunther Bartholmai.
ANTHOS 1989, v.28, no.4, p.8-13,

SWITZERLAND--REGIONALISM
Ein paar Bauten, viele Plane /
Marcel Meili.
Regionalism in recent Swiss-German
architecture. Summaries in German,
French and English. French text,
p.75-77.
WERK, BAUEN + WOHNEN 1989 Dec.,
no.12, p.26-31, dwgs., models,
photos.

SWITZERLAND--RIEHEN--OLD AGE HOMES--
HAUS ZUM WENDELIN
Haus zum Wendelin, Alters-und
Plegeheim, Riehen BS, 1986-1988.
Architects: Wilfrid und Katharina
Steib.
WERK, BAUEN + WOHNEN 1989 Dec.,
no.12, p.55, photos.

SWITZERLAND--RIVA SAN VITALE--MIDDLE
SCHOOLS
Ecole Moyenne, Riva S. Vitale, 1982.
Architect: Giancarlo Durisch.
WERK, BAUEN + WOHNEN 1989 Dec.,
no.12, p.66, photo., plans, site
plan.

SWITZERLAND--RIVA SAN VITALE--SCHOOLS
Intorno al grande atrio: scuola a
Riva San Vitale di Giancarlo
Durisch = Around the great
entrance: school at Riva San
Vitale by Giancarlo Durisch / Luca
Ortelli.
LOTUS INTERNATIONAL 1989, no.63,
p.90-95, elevs., photos., plans,
secn., site plans.

SWITZERLAND--RONCO--HOUSES--CASA
DIENER
Architetture di Luigi Snozzi /
Pierre-Alain Croset.
Four recent projects: new
Liechtenstein Parliament, Vaduz;
Netherlands Institute of
Architecture, Rotterdam; Casa
Diener, Ronco; and Casa
Bernasconi, Carona. Includes an
interview by Claudio Negrini and
English captions and summary.
CASABELLA 1990 Apr., v.54, no.567,
p.4-22,59-60, axonometric view,
diagr., elev., models, photos.,
plans, secns., site plans,
sketches, aerial photos.

SWITZERLAND--RORSCHACHERBERG--HOUSING
DEVELOPMENTS--COMPETITIONS--ROSENEGG
Uberbauung Rosenegg,
Rorschacherberg, Schweiz =
Development Rosenegg,
Rorschacherberg, Switzerland.
Competition. Winning architect:
Alex Buob. Text in German.
ARCHITEKTUR + WETTBEWERBE 1990
(Continued next column)

SWITZERLAND--RORSCHACHERBERG--HOUSING
DEVELOPMENTS--COMPETITIONS--ROSENEGG
(CONTINUED)
Uberbauung Rosenegg (CONTINUED)
June, no.142, p.79-83, elevs.,
models, plans, site plans.

SWITZERLAND--ROTKREUZ--SCHOOLS
Oberstufenschulhaus Rotkreuz.
Architects: Ammann & Baumann.
WERK, BAUEN + WOHNEN 1990
July-Aug., no.7-8, p.1-6 (folded,
at back), photos., plans, secns.,
site plan, table.

SWITZERLAND--RUSSO--APARTMENT HOUSES
Maison de retraite, Russo, 1988.
Architects: Franco and Paolo Moro.
WERK, BAUEN + WOHNEN 1989 Dec.,
no.12, p.72, photos., plans.

SWITZERLAND--SAINT GALL--GARDENS
Des Ratsels Losung / Eeva Ruoff.
On a garden in Sankt Gallen,
described in the 19th cent. by
Englishman L. Simon.
MITTEILUNGEN DER GESELLSCHAFT FUR
GARTENKULTUR 1989, v.7, no.1,
p.4-6, dwg., ref.

SWITZERLAND--SAINT GALL--MONASTERIES--
CAROLINGIAN--ALTERATIONS AND
ADDITIONS--KLOSTER SANKT GALLEN
Der spanische Konig als Stifter von
Pontifikalornaten fur den Abt von
St. Gallen im 17. und 18.
Jahrhundert / Werner Vogler.
French and Italian summaries.
UNSERE KUNSTDENKMALER 1989, v.40,
no.3, p.247, plan, engrs., refs.

SWITZERLAND--SAINT GALL--MONASTERIES--
CAROLINGIAN--KLOSTER SANKT GALLEN
La distribution de l'espace
monastique, prefiguration de la
distribution domestique moderne /
Albert Levy.
Example of the plan of St. Gall.
French, English and Spanish
summaries.
ESPACES ET SOCIETES 1990, no.56,
p.107-123, refs.

SWITZERLAND--SAINT GALL--NEW TOWNS--
COMPETITIONS--WITTENBACH--OEDENHOF
"Kleine Stadt": Ideenwettbewerb
Oedenhof, Wittenbach bei St.
Gallen.
Competition entry by Karl Dudler.
BAUWELT 1990 Mar.30, v.81, no.12,
p.608-609, axonometric views,
dwg., site plans.

SWITZERLAND--SAINT GALL--OFFICE
COMPLEXES--COMPETITIONS--
GIRTANNERSBERG
Komposition im Park.
Competition entries in the
Girtannersberg area of Sankt
Gallen, Switzerland. Architects:
Jacques Herzog and Pierre de
Meuron, Marcel Meili and Markus
Peter, and Ruedi Dietiker and Beat
Klaus.
WERK, BAUEN + WOHNEN 1990 Mar.,
no.3, p.10-12, elevs., models,
plans, site plan.

SWITZERLAND--SUHR--AUDITORIUMS,
CONCERT HALLS
Les ailes blanches: salle de concert
et de conference, Suhr, Suisse.
Concert and conference hall, Suhr,
Switzerland. Architect: Santiago
Calatrava. English summary, p.124.
Spanish summary, p.198-199.
TECHNIQUES ET ARCHITECTURE 1990
Apr.-May, no.389, p.120-125,
dets., photos., plans, secn.

SWITZERLAND--SUHR--AUDITORIUMS,
CONCERT HALLS--ZENTRUM BARENMATTE
Zentrum Barenmatte, Suhr.
Architects: Hertig + Partners,
Atelier fur Architektur.
WERK, BAUEN + WOHNEN 1989 Dec.,
no.12, p.1-4(folded, at back),
axonometric view, photos., plans,
secn., site plans, tables.

SWITZERLAND--SUMMER HOUSES--INTERIOR
DESIGN--LA SAPINIERE (GAGNEBIN
HOUSE)
Wie in seinen besten Tagen / Ursula
Bode.
Interiors of mid-19th cent.
French-style summer home outside
Geneva owned by Nicholas and
Mariejeanne Gagnebin. Interior
designer: Mariejeanne Gagnebin.
English summary, p.1.
ARCHITEKTUR & WOHNEN 1990
Dec.-1991 Jan., no.6, p.24-32,
port., photos.

SWITZERLAND--TEGNA--HOUSES--20TH
CENTURY--HAUS SZEEMANN - LUSCHER
Innen-Aussen-Haus: Wohn- und
Atelierhaus Harold
Szeemann-Ingeborg Luscher in Tegna
TI, 1990.
Architect: Christoph Zurcher.
WERK, BAUEN + WOHNEN 1990 Nov.,
no.11, p.12-13, photos., plans,
secn.

SWITZERLAND--TELEPHONE BOOTHS--TOBTEL
90
"Dank dra-- lut a!" neue
Telefonkabinen in der Schweiz.
Designer: Wolfram Elwert.
DEUTSCHE BAUZEITUNG 1990 Dec.,
v.124, no.12, p.88-89, det., dwg.,
photos.

SWITZERLAND--THAYNGEN--SPORTS
FACILITIES--SPORTHALLE STOCKWIESEN
Sporthalle Stockwiesen, Thayngen.
Architects: Fritz Tissi + Peter
Gotz.
WERK, BAUEN + WOHNEN 1990
Jan.-Feb., no.1-2, p.1-4 (folded
at back), photos., plans, secns.,
tables.

SWITZERLAND--THUN--SCHOOLS--SPECIAL--
ALTERATIONS AND ADDITIONS--SEMINAR
THUN
Kunstvoll eingestreut: Umbau und
Erweiterung Staatliches
Lehrerseminar in Thun.
Architects: Atelier 5.
DEUTSCHE BAUZEITUNG 1990 Apr.,
v.124, no.4, p.20-25, photos.,
plans, site plan.

SWITZERLAND--THUN--TRAINING CENTERS--
LEHRERSEMINAR
Svizzera anni '90: tre culture, tre
architetture = Switzerland 1990:
three cultures, three
architectures / Paolo Fumagalli.
Features projects by Jacques
Herzog and Pierre de Meuron; Livio
Vacchini; Atelier 5; Willi Egli;
Mario Botta; Jean-Jacques Oberson;
Giancarlo Durisch; Aurelio
Galfetti; Luigi Snozzi; Roger
Diener; Atelier Cube; Matti,
Burgi, Ragaz; Schnebli, Ammann &
Partner; R. Luscher; V. Mangeat;
S. Calatrava, A. Amsler, and W.
Rueger; Mario Campi and Franco
Pessina; and Peter Zumthor.
Includes an article by Werner
Jehle, "The mountain: painters,
engineers, and architects." Text
in Italian and English.
ABITARE 1990 Nov., no.290,
p.150-191, axonometric views,
dets., ill., elevs., maps,
photos., plans, secns., site
plans, sketch, aerial photo.

SWITZERLAND--TRUBBACH--APARTMENT
HOUSES
Haus mit drei Geschosswohnungen in
Trubbach SG, 1989.
Architect: Peter Markli.
WERK, BAUEN + WOHNEN 1990 May,
no.5, p.50-53, elev., photos.,
plan, secn., site plan.

SWITZERLAND--URBANIZATION
Mitte des Mittellandes--Vakuum der
Schweiz?
Urbanization of midlands lying
between cities. Text in German;
summaries in German, French and
English.
WERK, BAUEN + WOHNEN 1990 May,
no.5, p.58-63, maps, photos.,
aerial photos., refs.

SWITZERLAND--USTER--RAILROAD STATIONS
Projekt Bahnhof Uster, 1989.
Architect: Martin Spuhler.
WERK, BAUEN + WOHNEN 1989 Dec.,
no.12, p.50, axonometric view,
photo., plan, secns.

SWITZERLAND--VACALLO--HOUSES
Mario Botta: Single family house in
Vacallo, Morbio Inferiore,
Switzerland, 1986-89.
Text in Japanese and English.
GA HOUSES 1990 Dec., no.30,
p.56-67, elevs., photos., plans,
site plan.

SWITZERLAND--VADUZ--OFFICES--
ARCHITECTS'--ARCHITEKTURBURO
BARGETZE UND PARTNER
Architekturburo Bargetze, Vaduz.
Architects: Toni Bargetze und
Partner.
WERK, BAUEN + WOHNEN 1990 Dec.,
no.12, p.75-78, photos., isometric
dwg.

SWITZERLAND--VICO MORCOTE--SCHOOLS OF
ARCHITECTURE--ALTERATIONS AND
ADDITIONS--VILLA RUGGIA (SCI-ARC)
Ristrutturazione a Vico Morcote
(Canton Ticino) / Renzo
Salmoiraghi.
On the renovation of Villa Ruggia,
the seat of the Southern
California Institute of
Architecture (SCI-ARC) school.
Architect: Martin Wagner.
English, French and Spanish
summaries.
ABACUS 1990 Apr.-June, v.6, no.22,
p.34-43, axonometric views, dets.,
photos., plans, secns.

SWITZERLAND--VIERWALDSTATTERSEE--
EXHIBITION BUILDINGS
Form als treibende Kraft: drei
Projekte von Santiago Calatrava /
Andreas Moser.
FSB exhibition pavillion; floating
pavilion; and Bauschanzli
restaurant in Zurich.
ARCHITHESE 1990 Nov.-Dec., v.20,
no.6, p.34-[48], dets., models,
photos., plans, secns., sketches,
refs.

SWITZERLAND--VIERWALDSTATTERSEE--
FLOATING BUILDINGS
Form als treibende Kraft: drei
Projekte von Santiago Calatrava /
Andreas Moser.
FSB exhibition pavillion; floating
pavilion; and Bauschanzli
restaurant in Zurich.
ARCHITHESE 1990 Nov.-Dec., v.20,
no.6, p.34-[48], dets., models,
photos., plans, secns., sketches,
refs.

SWITZERLAND--VIRA--HOUSES--20TH
CENTURY
Severa, al limite del bosco / Elisa
Dal Canto.
House in Vira, in the Ticino
region of Switzerland. Architect:
Elio Valeggia.
VILLE GIARDINI 1990 May, no.248,
p.30-35, photos., plans, secn.

SWITZERLAND--VOGORNO--HOUSES
Einfamilienhaus in Vogorno, 1985 /
Paulo Fumagalli.
Architect: Livio Vacchini.
WERK, BAUEN + WOHNEN 1990 Apr.,
no.4, p.29-33, elev., photos.,
plans.
Enfamiliehus i Vogorno.
Stone house on sloping site in
Switzerland. Architect: Livio
Vacchini.
ARKITEKTUR DK 1990, v.34, no.6,
p.A98-A99, photos., plans, elev.

SWITZERLAND--WERMELSKIRCHEN--
FACTORIES--ALBERT SCHULTE SOHNE
Produktionsgebaude in
Wermelskirchen.
Architect: Herbert Heuser.
WERK, BAUEN + WOHNEN 1990 Nov.,
no.11, p.4 folded p. at end,
dets., photos., plans, secns.

SWITZERLAND--WETTINGEN--HOUSING
DEVELOPMENTS--KLOSERBRUHL
Quartierbebauung "Klosterbruhl" beim
Bahnhof Wettingen, 1989-90.
Architects: Burkard Meyer Steiger
und Partner.
WERK, BAUEN + WOHNEN 1989 Dec.,
no.12, p.52, elev., plan, secn.,
site plan.

SWITZERLAND--WETTINGEN--OFFICE
BUILDINGS
Projekt fur kleines Gewerbe- und
Burohaus in Wettingen, 1989.
Architect: Peter Zumthor.
WERK, BAUEN + WOHNEN 1989 Dec.,
no.12, p.33, elevs.

SWITZERLAND--WIDNAU--TEXTILE MILLS--
BELDONA FABRIKATIONS AG
Konstruktion als Struktur und Form:
Textilfabrik Beldona, Widnan SG,
1987 / Erich Offermann.
Architects: Suter + Suter.
WERK, BAUEN + WOHNEN 1989 Oct.,
no.10, p.15-17, folded p. at end,
axonometric view, dets., dwgs.,
photos., plans, secn.
Portfolio: technology and humanity /
Jim Murphy.
On two industrial buildings:
Beldona Fabrikations AG, Widnau,
Switzerland, architects: Suter und
Suter and ERCO Leuchten GmbH,
Ludenscheid, Germany, architects:
Kiessler und Partner.
PROGRESSIVE ARCHITECTURE 1990
Oct., v.71, no.10, p.96-[99],
photos., plans.

SWITZERLAND--WILEN--HOUSES--
ARCHITECTS'--SCHAFER HOUSE
Ohne Unterbruch: ausgewahlte Bauten
aus dem Werk von Peter Schafer.
Text in German; summaries in
German, French and English.
WERK, BAUEN + WOHNEN 1990 Oct.,
no.10, p.34-47, axonometric views,
elevs., photos., plans, secns.,
aerial photos.

SWITZERLAND--WINTERTHUR--CITY PLANNING
"Die Neustadt aus der Werkstadt" /
Irma Noseda.
On a city planning scheme for
Winterthur, Switzerland.
WERK, BAUEN + WOHNEN 1990 Apr.,
no.4, p.19, map.

SWITZERLAND--WINTERTHUR--INDUSTRIAL
BUILDINGS
Aus der Werkstatt die Neustadt?
Winterthur eine Industriestadt im
Umbruch / Hans Peter Bartschi.
Text in German; summaries in
German, French and English.
WERK, BAUEN + WOHNEN 1990 Oct.,
no.10, p.22-33, dwgs., maps,
photos.

SWITZERLAND--WINTERTHUR--INDUSTRIAL
TOWNS
Aus der Werkstatt die Neustadt?
Winterthur eine Industriestadt im
Umbruch / Hans Peter Bartschi.
Text in German; summaries in
German, French and English.
WERK, BAUEN + WOHNEN 1990 Oct.,
no.10, p.22-33, dwgs., maps,
photos.

SWITZERLAND--WINTERTHUR--INDUSTRIES,
LOCATION OF
"Die Neustadt aus der Werkstadt" /
Irma Noseda.
On a city planning scheme for
Winterthur, Switzerland.
WERK, BAUEN + WOHNEN 1990 Apr.,
no.4, p.19, map.

SWITZERLAND--WINTERTHUR--SCHOOLS--
ALTERATIONS AND ADDITIONS--
KANTONSSCHULE BUELRAIN
Erweiterung Kantonsschule Buelrain,
Winterthur, 1987.
Architect: Arnold Amsler.
WERK, BAUEN + WOHNEN 1989 Dec.,
no.12, p.49, plan, elev., secns.

SWITZERLAND--WITTIGKOFEN--ASYLUMS--
ASYL GOTTESGNAD
Neubau Asyl Gottesgnad, Wittigkofen,
1989.
Architects: Atelier 5.
WERK, BAUEN + WOHNEN 1989 Dec.,
no.12, p.39, photos., plan, site
plan.

SWITZERLAND--WOHLEN--APARTMENT HOUSES
Unita di forma, diversita di
funzione / Lucia Bisi.
Three-unit apartment house in
Wohlen, Switzerland. Architects:
Furter & Eppler.
VILLE GIARDINI 1990 Feb., no.245,
p.[14]-21, photos., plans, secns.,
site plan.

SWITZERLAND--WURENLINGEN--HOUSING
DEVELOPMENTS--UNTER DER HALDE
Dolf Schnebli.
Most of issue devoted to the work
of this Swiss architect.
Introduction by Paolo Fumagalli.
Text in German, French and
English.
WERK, BAUEN + WOHNEN 1990 Dec.,
no.12, p.20-69, axonometric views,
dets., dwgs., port., elevs.,
models, photos., plans, secns.,
site plans, sketches, aerial
photo.
Wohnuberbauung "Unter der Halde",
Wurenlingen, 1988.
Architects: Schnebli und Ammann.
WERK, BAUEN + WOHNEN 1989 Dec.,
no.12, p.48, photo., plans, secn.,
site plan.

SWITZERLAND--ZIEGELRIED--HOUSES--
ARCHITECTS'--ZALOTAY HOUSE
Elmer Zalotay: experimental house.
Text in Japanese.
ARCHITECTURE AND URBANISM 1990
July, no.7(238), p.64-[67],
photos.

SWITZERLAND--ZUG--CITY PLANNING
Zug: Planung in einer
Wohlstandsregion / Fritz Wagner,
SCHWEIZER BAUMARKT 1989 Oct.2,
no.13, p.ii-iv, photos.

SWITZERLAND--ZUG--DUPLEX HOUSES--
DOPPELHAUS MOSER-SCHERER
Deppelhaus Moser-Scherer, Zug,
1983-1986.
Architects: Ueli Marbach, Arthur
Ruegg.
WERK, BAUEN + WOHNEN 1989 Dec.,
no.12, p.54, photos., plan, site
plan.

SWITZERLAND--ZUG--HOUSES--20TH CENTURY
Blocchi e doghe, il linguaggio delle
differenze / Marinetta Nunziante.
House in Zug, Switzerland.
Architect: Bany Maier.
VILLE GIARDINI 1990 Oct., no.252,
p.24-31, photos., plans, secn.
"Complessita e contraddizioni" per
un rivestimento in legno / Walter
Bianchi, Mauro Colombo.
Corner details of a house in Zug,
Switzerland. Architect: Bany
Meier.
VILLE GIARDINI 1990 May, no.248,
p.52-[53], dets., photos., plan,
secn.

SWITZERLAND--ZUG--HOUSING FOR
HANDICAPPED
Dauerwohnheim fur Schwerbehinderte,
Maihof, Zug.
Architects: H.P. Amman, P.
Baumann.
WERK, BAUEN + WOHNEN 1990 Nov.,
no.11, p.4, folded p. at end,
photos., plans, secns.

SWITZERLAND--ZUG--HOUSING FOR
HANDICAPPED--SCHWERBEHINDERTENHEIM
MAIHOF
Dauerwohnheim fur Schwerbehinderte,
Maihof, Zug, 1989.
Architects: Ammann + Baumann.
WERK, BAUEN + WOHNEN 1989 Dec.,
no.12, p.44, photo., plan, site
plan.

SWITZERLAND--ZUG--REGIONAL PLANNING
Zug: Planung in einer
Wohlstandsregion / Fritz Wagner.
SCHWEIZER BAUMARKT 1989 Oct.2,
no.13, p.ii-iv, photos.

SWITZERLAND--ZURICH--APARTMENT
HOUSES--IM WALDER
Projekt Uberbauung Genossenschaft
"Im Walder," Zurich, 1989.
Architects: Carlo Tognola,
Christian Stahel.
WERK, BAUEN + WOHNEN 1989 Dec.,
no.12, p.40, plans, elevs., secn.,
site plan, model.

SWITZERLAND--ZURICH--APARTMENTS--
INTERIOR DESIGN--DOVAT APARTMENT
Meister der Nuancen / Ursula Bode.
The interiors of designer
Jean-Pierre Dovat's apartment in
Zurich.
ARCHITEKTUR & WOHNEN 1990
Feb.-Mar., no.1, p.20-27, port.,
photos.

SWITZERLAND--ZURICH--ATHLETIC FIELDS
Allwetterplatze der Stadt Zurich =
Les terrains toutes intemperies de
la ville de Zurich = All-weather
sports grounds in the City of
Zurich / Werner Klabar.
Sand and artificial turf surface.
ANTHOS 1989, v.28, no.4, p.22-25,
det., photos., plan, secn.

SWITZERLAND--ZURICH--BANKS
Zeichenhaftes Bild ein Beispiel der
Architekten Armin Gasser und
Hans-Dieter Nielander / Karin
Schulz.
ARCHITEKTUR, INNENARCHITEKTUR,
TECHNISCHER AUSBAU 1990 Apr.,
v.98, no.4, p.68-73, det.,
photos., plan, secns.

SWITZERLAND--ZURICH--BARRACKS--KASERNE
ZURICH REPPISCHTAL
Kaserne Zurich Reppischtal.
Architects: Dorer + Stegar +
Dieterle.
WERK, BAUEN + WOHNEN 1990 June,
no.6, p.1-4 (folded, at back),
model, photos., plans, secns.,
site plans.

SWITZERLAND--ZURICH--CAMPUSES--
WORBIGER
Die Schulanlage Worbiger in Rumland:
"Revitalisierung" der
Aussenanlagen = Lecole de Worbiger
a Rumlang: revitalisation des
installations exterieures =
Worbiger school grounds in
Rumlang: "Revitalisation" of the
outside grounds / Heinz Ruedi,
Klaus Holzhausen.
Landscape architects: H. Ruedi and
K. Holzhausen, of Atelier Stern +
Partners.
ANTHOS 1989, v.28, no.4, p.30-34,
photos., site plan.

SWITZERLAND--ZURICH--CHURCHES
Herzog et de Meuron / Elisabeth
Allain-Dupre.
Contents: Apartment houses,
Basel--Project for Greek Orthodox
church, Zurich--Project for
railway depot, Basel--Interview
with Jacques Herzog.
LE MONITEUR ARCHITECTURE AMC 1990
Mar., no.9, p.28-39, dets.,
models, photos., plans, secns.,
site plan.

SWITZERLAND--ZURICH--CITIES AND
TOWNS--HISTORY
Zurichs Rindermarkt und Neumarkt:
Entstehung und Entwicklung eines
Quartiers / Jurg E. Schneider.
Monograph.
MITTEILUNGEN DER ANTIQUARISCHEN
GESELLSCHAFT IN ZURICH 1989, v.56,
p.5-171, dets., dwgs., elevs.,
maps, photos., site plans, biblio.

SWITZERLAND--ZURICH--CITY PLANNING
Arnold Burkli: Stadt- und
Quai-Ingenieur.
He was recently the subject of a
poster exhibit in the Zurich
Stadelhofer Passage.
SCHWEIZER BAUMARKT 1990 Oct.29,
v.25, no.13, p.VIII,

SWITZERLAND--ZURICH--CITY PLANNING--
COMPETITIONS--RONTGENAREAL
Locker angedichtet: Anmerkung zum
offentlichen Wettbewerb auf den
Rontgenareal im Zurcher
Industriequartier.
1st prize to Isa Sturm & Urs Wolf.
WERK, BAUEN + WOHNEN 1990 Dec.,
no.12, p.12, models, site plans.

SWITZERLAND--ZURICH--CITY PLANNING--
HISTORY
Zurichs Rindermarkt und Neumarkt:
Entstehung und Entwicklung eines
Quartiers / Jurg E. Schneider.
Monograph.
MITTEILUNGEN DER ANTIQUARISCHEN
GESELLSCHAFT IN ZURICH 1989, v.56,
p.5-171, dets., dwgs., elevs.,
maps, photos., site plans, biblio.

SWITZERLAND--ZURICH--CITY PLANNING--
HISTORY--HAUPTBAHNHOF
Zurcher Hauptbahnhofprojekte
1846-1990 / Pietro Maggi.
SCHWEIZER BAUMARKT 1990 June 11,
v.25, no.7, p.IV,VI-VII, photos.

SWITZERLAND--ZURICH--CITY PLANNING--
RONTGENAREAL
Rontgenareal Zurich:
Projektwettbewerb.
Projects in a competition for a
mixed use complex in the area
around the Rontgenstrasse train
station. First prize to the
"Khan" project by Isa Sturm and
Urs Wolf.
SCHWEIZER BAUMARKT 1990 Oct.29,
v.25, no.13, p.[I]-IV, models.

SWITZERLAND--ZURICH--CLINICS--
ALTERATIONS AND ADDITIONS--KLINIK
HIRSLANDEN
Dolf Schnebli.
Most of issue devoted to the work
of this Swiss architect.
Introduction by Paolo Fumagalli.
Text in German, French and
English.
WERK, BAUEN + WOHNEN 1990 Dec.,
no.12, p.20-69, axonometric views,
dets., dwgs., port., elevs.,
models, photos., plans, secns.,
site plans, sketches, aerial
photo.

SWITZERLAND--ZURICH--COMMUNICATIONS
TOWERS--STAINLESS STEEL--
UETLIBERGTURM
Der neue Uetlibergturm: Form,
Konstruktion, Baustelle / Rudolf
Wolfensberger.
Built 1990.
SCHWEIZER BAUMARKT 1990 Dec.10,
v.25, no.15, p.IV-VI, port.,
photos.

SWITZERLAND--ZURICH--COMMUNITY GARDENS
Siedlungsgarten in der Stadt Zurich:
ein Pilotprojekt = Jardins dans
les lotissements residentiels de
Zurich: un projet pilote = Housing
estate gardens in the city of
Zurich: a pilot project / Felix
Guhl, Jorg Villiger.
ANTHOS 1989, v.28, no.4, p.14-17,

SWITZERLAND--ZURICH--DEPARTMENT
STORES--LIGHTING--JELMOLI
Boutiquen-Ambiente: Intensiveres
Einkaufserlebnis im Warenhaus
Jelmoli, Zurich, durch
inszeniertes Licht.
ARCHITEKTUR, INNENARCHITEKTUR,
TECHNISCHER AUSBAU 1990 Sept.,
v.98, no.9, p.52-54, photos.

SWITZERLAND--ZURICH--INDUSTRIAL
PARKS--COMPETITIONS--RONTGENAREAL
Locker angedichtet: Anmerkung zum
offentlichen Wettbewerb auf den
Rontgenareal im Zurcher
Industriequartier.
1st prize to Isa Sturm & Urs Wolf.
WERK, BAUEN + WOHNEN 1990 Dec.,
no.12, p.12, models, site plans.

SWITZERLAND--ZURICH--MULTI-USE
COMPLEXES--COMPETITIONS--
RONTGENAREAL--KHAN
Rontgenareal Zurich:
Projektwettbewerb.
Projects in a competition for a
mixed use complex in the area
around the Rontgenstrasse train
station. First prize to the
"Khan" project by Isa Sturm and
Urs Wolf.
SCHWEIZER BAUMARKT 1990 Oct.29,
v.25, no.13, p.[I]-IV, models.

SWITZERLAND--ZURICH--MULTI-USE
COMPLEXES--MUHLE TIEFENBRUNNEN
Um- und Ausbau Muhle Tiefenbrunnen
in Zurich, Schweiz = Conversion
and extension of Tiefenbrunnen
Mill in Zurich, Switzerland.
19th cent. mill buildings now used
for housing restaurants,
galleries, offices, etc.
Architect: Pierre Zoelly.
ARCHITEKTUR + WETTBEWERBE 1989
Dec., no.140, p.15, dwg., photos.

SWITZERLAND--ZURICH--MUSEUMS--ART--
ALTERATIONS AND ADDITIONS--KUNSTHAUS
Umbauen, erganzen, neu
interpretieren: drei Projekte fur
eine Erweiterung des Zurcher
Kunsthauses, 1989.
Competition entries by Mario Campi
& Franco Pessina, Willi Egli, and
Wilfrid & Katharina Steib.
WERK, BAUEN + WOHNEN 1990 May,
no.5, p.14-18, models, plans,
secns., site plans.

SWITZERLAND--ZURICH--NEWSPAPER
BUILDINGS--TAGES ANZEIGER
Dolf Schnebli.
Most of issue devoted to the work
of this Swiss architect.
Introduction by Paolo Fumagalli.
Text in German, French and
English.
WERK, BAUEN + WOHNEN 1990 Dec.,
no.12, p.20-69, axonometric views,
dets., dwgs., port., elevs.,
models, photos., plans, secns.,
site plans, sketches, aerial
photo.

SWITZERLAND--ZURICH--OLD AGE HOMES--
ALTERSHEIM STAMPFENBACH
Altersheim Stampfenbach Zurich.
Architect: Ernst Gisel.
WERK, BAUEN + WOHNEN 1990 Apr.,
no.4, p.1-4 (folded, at back),
photos., plans, secn., site plans.

SWITZERLAND--ZURICH--OPEN-AIR
RESTAURANTS--BAUSCHANZLI
Form als treibende Kraft: drei
Projekte von Santiago Calatrava /
Andreas Moser.
FSB exhibition pavillion; floating
pavilion; and Bauschanzli
restaurant in Zurich.
ARCHITHESE 1990 Nov.-Dec., v.20,
no.6, p.34-[48], dets., models,
photos., plans, secns., sketches,
refs.

SWYNGEDOUW, ERIK
A thematic cartography software package for personal computers / Luc Desager, Erik Swyngedouw. EKISTICS 1989 Sept.-Dec., v.56, no.338-339, p.267-271, maps, biblio.

SYDNOR, DOUGLAS B.
House in Paradise Valley, Arizona / Douglas B. Sydnor. House V. Architect: Douglas B. Sydnor of Sydnor Architects. TRIGLYPH 1990 Summer, no.10, p.28-32, photos., secns., site plan.

SYKES, CHRISTOPHER SIMON
Classical romance: a nineteenth-century rotunda encompasses a small but stately realm / Christopher Simon Sykes. Villa La Gordanne, overlooking Lake Geneva was commissioned ca. 1800 as a copy of Belle Isle, an 18th-cent. house in the English Lake District. Interior designer: Tom Parr, of Colefax & Fowler. HOUSE & GARDEN 1990 Mar., v.162, no.3, p.188-195,211, port., photos.

SYKES O'CONNOR SALERNO HAZAVEH
Additions and alterations / Regan Young, Robert Cerutti. On the architect's job of adding to existing structures. Examples of 12 projects in and near New Jersey by New Jersey architects: Katz Novoa Architects and Planners; John DeFazio; Michael Burns; Frederick Schmitt; Michael Ryan Architects; Sykes O'Connor Salerno Hazaveh; Parette and Associates; Nadaskay Kopelson; Michael Graves; Carla Bonacci; Robert N. Auld; and Albert F. Zaccone. ARCHITECTURE NEW JERSEY 1990, v.26, no.5, p.9-22, axonometric view, ill., elevs., models, photos., plans, secn.

SYLBERT, RICHARD
The unreal McCoy: Hollywood sends up the pretensions of New York society on the set of Bonfire of the Vanities / Donald Albrecht. Warner Brothers stage set, designed by Richard Sylbert. HOUSE & GARDEN 1990 Nov., v.162, no.11, p.[172-177], photos.

SYLVESTER, ADAM, 1943-
Special feature: Contemporary Hungarian architecture / edited by Botond Bognar. Works illustrated by architects: Imre Makovecz, Gabor Mezei, Andras Erdei, Sandor Devenyi, Attila Kovacs, Laszlo Saros, Tamas Nagy, Gyorgy Csete, Peter Oltai, Istvan Kistelegdi, Tibor Jankovics, Csasa Bodonyi, Istvan Ferencz, Tamas Noll, Beno Taba, Janos Golda, Agnes Thoma, Jozsef Kerenyi, Gyorgy Vadasz, Gyorgy Keves, Adam Sylvester and Gabor Turanyi. Text in Japanese and English. ARCHITECTURE AND URBANISM 1990 Mar., no.3(234), p.7-126, axonometric views, dwgs., elevs., photos., plans, secns.

SYMBOLIC ASPECTS
See "SYMBOLIC ASPECTS" AS A SUBHEADING AFTER SPECIFIC BUILDING TYPES OR OTHER MAIN HEADINGS EXCLUDING THE HEADING "ARCHITECTURE". FOR GENERAL ARTICLES ON ARCHITECTURAL SYMBOLISM USE "SYMBOLISM IN ARCHITECTURE".

SYMBOLISM IN ARCHITECTURE
See also ANTHROPOMORPHISM
See also BUILDINGS - SYMBOLIC ASPECTS
See also EMBLEMS
See also GARDENS - SYMBOLIC ASPECTS
See also SIGNS AND SYMBOLS IN ARCHITECTURE
Industribyggandets metaforer / Anders Tornqvist, Peter Ullmark. In conjunction with an international congress in Stockholm and a related publication entitled "When people matter". ARKITEKTUR: THE SWEDISH REVIEW OF ARCHITECTURE 1990 Sept., v.90, no.7, p.28-35, model, photo., secns., site plan.
Ornamento e simbolo: La decorazinne pittorica nei conventi dell'osservanza agostiniana: esempi lombardi / Maria Luisa Gatti Perer. Paper presented at the Qualita ecclesiale nell'arte conference in 1989, on the decoration of the Milanese convent of S. Maria Incoronata. Includes abstract in English. ARTE CRISTIANA 1990 Mar.-July, v.78, no.737-738, p.143-160, dets., photos., plan, engrs., reconst. dwgs., refs.
Over rook zonder vuur en vuur zonder rook: architectuur als uitdrukking van macht / Bart Lootsma. One of several articles in Themanummer 41: "Thema: architectuur en macht." Discusses symbolic aspects of buildings, including work by Albert Speer and Le Corbusier. DE ARCHITECT THEMA 1990 Nov., v.21, no.11 suppl., p.7-13, dwgs., maps, photos., refs.
Shoe house: a perfect fit? [Haines Shoe House, York County, Pa.] / Thomas W. Sweeney. Mahlon Haines built his Shoe House in 1948 to advertise his shoe business. PRESERVATION NEWS 1989 Dec., v.29, no.12, p.1,17, port., photo.

SYMBOLISM IN ARCHITECTURE--12TH CENTURY--FRANCE
Aspetti della simbologia architettonica del dodicesimo secolo in Francia: il santuario / Robert Suckale. Paper presented at the Qualita ecclesiale nell'arte conference in 1989, on methodological and theoretical foundations. Includes abstract in English. ARTE CRISTIANA 1990 Mar.-July, v.78, no.737-738, p.111-122, photos., refs.

SYMES, MARTIN
Fascinating mystery: Dwelling place and environment, edited by David Seamon and Robert Mugerauer [book review] / Martin Symes. Pub. in 1989 by Columbia Univ. Pr., reprint of 1985 Nijhoff ed. ARCHITECTS' JOURNAL 1990 Mar.28, v.191, no.13, p.91.
Research on the human problems of architectural education: an introduction / Martin Symes. JOURNAL OF ARCHITECTURAL AND PLANNING RESEARCH 1989 Autumn, v.6, no.3, p.181-185, refs.
The value of architecture as a university discipline / Martin Symes. In Britain. JOURNAL OF ARCHITECTURAL AND PLANNING RESEARCH 1989 Autumn, v.6, no.3, p.251-257, refs.

SYMES, MICHAEL
Westonbirt Gardens: a Victorian Elysium / Michael Symes. Designer: Robert Stayner Holford. GARDEN HISTORY 1990 autumn, v.18, no.2, p.[155]-173, photos., map, plans, secns., site plans, engrs., refs.

SYMMES MAINI & MCKEE ARCHITECTS
I luoghi del lavoro: un esempio contemporeano nel Massachusetts = Talbots Distribution Center, Lakeville, Mass. / Stefania Mornati. Architects: Symmes Maini & McKee Associates. Includes English translation. French, German, and Spanish summaries, p.4. L'INDUSTRIA DELLE COSTRUZIONI 1990 Apr., v.24, no.222, p.37-[43], dwgs., photos., site plan.

SYMMETRY
See also SYMMETRICAL BUILDINGS
Design procedure of the Parthenon / Rihee Goshima. Analysis by means of "the grid method". In Japanese; English summaries, p.147, 164. NIHON KENCHIKU GAKKAI KEIKAKUKEI RONBUN HOKOKU SHU = JOURNAL OF ARCHITECTURE, PLANNING AND ENVIRONMENTAL ENGINEERING 1990 May, no.5(411), p.147-164, diagrs., figs., plans, refs.

SYNAGOGUES--18TH CENTURY--FRANCE--CARPENTRAS
Synagogues en Vaucluse / Martine Audibert. Discussion of Jewish history in Avignon and Comtat Venaissin, and the synagogues in Cavaillon, Carpentras and Avignon. MONUMENTS HISTORIQUES 1990 Sept.-Oct., no.170, p.53-58, ill., photos., plan, biblio.

SYNAGOGUES--18TH CENTURY--FRANCE--CAVAILLON
Synagogues en Vaucluse / Martine Audibert. Discussion of Jewish history in Avignon and Comtat Venaissin, and the synagogues in Cavaillon, Carpentras and Avignon. MONUMENTS HISTORIQUES 1990 Sept.-Oct., no.170, p.53-58, ill., photos., plan, biblio.

SYNTHETIC MATERIALS--RESEARCH
Isolerend maar doorschijnend:
transparante isolatiematerialen /
Tjerk Reijenga.
Report on various translucent
materials and their insulation
value, based on results of an
international workshop held in
Mar.1988 in Freiburg.
DE ARCHITECT 1990 May, v.21, no.5,
p.108-111, photos., table, refs.

SYNTHRONON
See SYNTHRONI

SYRIA--DAMASCUS--MINARETS
Minarets of Damascus / John H.
Harvey.
ANCIENT MONUMENTS SOCIETY.
TRANSACTIONS 1990, new ser.,v.34,
p.[151]-170, map, photos., plan,
biblio., refs.

SYRIA--EUPHRATES BASIN--LAND
SETTLEMENT
Land settlement in the Euphrates
basin of Syria / Hans Meliczek.
EKISTICS 1986 May-Aug., v.53,
no.318-319, p.202-212, maps,
tables, refs.

SYRIA--TELL AL-RAQA'I--EXCAVATIONS
(ARCHAEOLOGY)
Excavations at Tell al-Raqa'i: a
small rural site of early urban
northern Mesopotamia / Hans H.
Curvers, Glenn M. Schwartz.
AMERICAN JOURNAL OF ARCHAEOLOGY
1990 Jan., v.94, no.1, p.3-23,
figs., maps, photos, plans, refs.

SYRIA--TELL AL-RAQA'I--SETTLEMENTS--
ANCIENT
Excavations at Tell al-Raqa'i: a
small rural site of early urban
northern Mesopotamia / Hans H.
Curvers, Glenn M. Schwartz.
AMERICAN JOURNAL OF ARCHAEOLOGY
1990 Jan., v.94, no.1, p.3-23,
figs., maps, photos, plans, refs.

SYRIA--TELL LEILAN--EXCAVATIONS
(ARCHAEOLOGY)
1985 excavations at Tell Leilan,
Syria / Harvey Weiss ...et al.
Excavation report.
AMERICAN JOURNAL OF ARCHAEOLOGY
1990 Oct., v.94, no.4, p.529-581,
figs., photos., map, plans, secn.,
site plan, tables, isometric dwg.,
refs.

SYRIA--URBANIZATION
A decentralized approach to
urbanization: the case of Syria /
Riad G. Mahayni.
JOURNAL OF PLANNING EDUCATION AND
RESEARCH 1990 Winter, v.9, no.2,
p.117-125, map, tables, refs.

SYROP, ARNOLD
Best dressed restaurants: La Cite /
Regina S. Baraban.
Restaurant and grill at 120 W.
51st St., Manhattan. Architect:
Arnold Syrop. Interior designer:
Joanne Syrop.
METROPOLIS 1990 Apr., v.9, no.8,
p.29, photo.

SYROP, JOANNE
Best dressed restaurants: La Cite /
Regina S. Baraban.
Restaurant and grill at 120 W.
51st St., Manhattan. Architect:
Arnold Syrop. Interior designer:
Joanne Syrop.
METROPOLIS 1990 Apr., v.9, no.8,
p.29, photo.

SYSTEMS BUILDING
See BUILDINGS - PREFABRICATED

SZAFRANSKA, MALGORZATA
The philosophy of nature and the
grotto in the Renaissance garden /
Malgorzala Szafranska.
JOURNAL OF GARDEN HISTORY 1989
Apr.-June, v.9, no.2, p.[76]-85,
ill., refs.
Polish bibliography of garden
history (1981-1986) / Malgorzata
Szafranska.
JOURNAL OF GARDEN HISTORY 1989
Jan.-Mar., v.9, no.1, p.[48]-51,
biblios.

SZAMBIEN, WERNER
L'inventaire apres dices de
Jean-Jacques Lequeu / Werner
Szambien.
Author of l'Architecture civile;
died in Paris, 1826. The inventory
is MS M.C., XXX, 693 at the
Archives nationales and includes
books, engravings, and drawings.
REVUE DE L'ART 1990, no.90,
p.104-107, plan.
Revolutions-Architektur [exhibition
review] / Werner Szambien.
Review of exhibition in Frankfurt,
19Jan.-25 March 1990.
CASABELLA 1990 June, v.54, no.569,
p.30-31, dwgs., elevs., refs.
Die Standardisierung der
architektonischen
Kompositionsverfahren bei J.N.L.
Durand = The standardization of
the architectural mode of
composition by J.N.L. Durand /
Werner Szambien.
DAIDALOS 1990 Mar.15, no.35,
p.42-45, elevs., plans, secn.

SZEEMANN, HARALD
L'eco del triangolo: Botta a Tokio /
Harald Szeemann.
The Watari-um building
(1985-1990), executed with the
Takenaka Corp. Includes English
captions.
CASABELLA 1990 Dec., v.54, no.574,
p.32-33, photos., plans.

SZEGEDY-MASZAK, ANDREW
A perfect ruin / Andrew
Szegedy-Maszak.
The Colosseum in Rome.
ARCHAEOLOGY 1990 Jan.-Feb., v.43,
no.1, p.74-79, photo.

SZENASY, SUSAN S.
Mixing poetry with electricity ...
Lighting designers using evolving
techniques and technics / Susan S.
Szenasy.
METROPOLIS 1990 Apr., v.9, no.8,
p.[66]-77, photos.

SZVITEK, ERZSEBET
A bucsuszentlaszloi barokk templom
es Kegykapolnaja / Szvitek
Erzsebet.
The baroque church and chapel of
Bucsuszentlaszlo.
MUVESZET 1989 Apr., v.30, no.4,
p.50-53, photos.

SZYMANOWSKI, JANEK
Paint magic / Penny Swift.
In conjunction with the author's
book, Plascon paint techniques,
discusses the use of paint in
interior design. Feature three
projects: Salvago boutique, Camp's
Bay, Cape Town (architect: Roger
Martin); "Herculaneum", home of
designer Jacqueline Cole; Floris
Smit Huijs restaurant, Cape Town
(interior decorator: Francois du
Plessis).
ADA: ARCHITECTURE, DESIGN, ART
1989, no.7, p.27-33, ports.,
photos.

SZYSZKOWITZ-KOWALSKI (FIRM)
Autriche: cooperatives et concours.
Features two projects: cluster
housing project, Eisbach-Rein,
architects: Szyszkowitz-Kowalski;
Project Casa Nostra, Graz,
architects: Roger Riewe, Florian
Riegler. English summary, p.180.
ARCHITECTURE INTERIEURE CREE 1990
June-July, no.237, p.120-123,
Il caos si ferma al dettaglio:
Istituto di Biochimica e
Biotecnologia a Graz.
Architects: Michael and Karla
Szyszkowitz.
ARCHITETTURA; CRONACHE E STORIA
1990 Apr., v.36, no.4(414),
p.286-287, axonometric view,
elev., photos., plan, sketch.
Dinamicita placata in forma =
Dynamism placated by form.
Church, Ragnitz, Austria.
Architects: Michael Szyskowitz,
Karla Kowalski.
ARCHITETTURA: CRONACHE E STORIA
1990 Dec., v.36, no.12(422),
p.875-877, photos., plans, secns.,
aerial photos.
Qualche fiaba disegnata = Some
designed fairy tale [houses,
Austria].
Architects: Szyszkowitz &
Kowalski.
ARCHITETTURA: CRONACHE E STORIA
1990 Oct., v.36, no.10(420),
p.718-719, photos., plans, secn.
Special feature: Michael Szyszkowitz
& Karla Kowalski.
Contents: Essay: Clear unclarity:
personal notes on the work of
Szyszkowitz and Kowalski, an
Austrian team of architects based
in Graz / Frank Werner.--Works:
Church complex at Graz-Ragnitz,
Austria, 1987.--House in Harmisch,
Austria, 1988.--Berlin project.
Text in Japanese and English.
ARCHITECTURE AND URBANISM 1990
July, no.7(238), p.[101]-140,
models, photos., plans, secns.,
aerial photo.

SZYSZKOWITZ-KOWALSKI, KARLA, 1941-
  Graz.
    One of three sections in special
    feature on "Contemporary Austrian
    architecture". Architects
    included: Klaus Kada, Michael
    Szyszkowitz, Karla
    Szyskowitz-Kowalski, Manfred
    Zernig, Hermann Eisenkock, Ernst
    Giselbrecht, Volker Giencke.
    SPACE DESIGN 1990 Mar., no.306,
    p.[47]-84, axonometric views,
    dets., ports., elevs., models.
    photos., plans, secns., site
    plans, isometric dwgs.

SZYSZKOWITZ, MICHAEL, 1944-
  Graz.
    One of three sections in special
    feature on "Contemporary Austrian
    architecture". Architects
    included: Klaus Kada, Michael
    Szyszkowitz, Karla
    Szyskowitz-Kowalski, Manfred
    Zernig, Hermann Eisenkock, Ernst
    Giselbrecht, Volker Giencke.
    SPACE DESIGN 1990 Mar., no.306,
    p.[47]-84, axonometric views,
    dets., ports., elevs., models,
    photos., plans, secns., site
    plans, isometric dwgs.

T & T DESIGN
Water als typerend element:
Inzendingen Nederlands pavilion
Expo '92 / Joop Niesten.
Several proposals for the Dutch
pavillion in Seville. Features one
by Bureau voor Architectuur en
Produktontwikkeling (M. Zwarts
and R. Jansma) and T & T Design
(F. Temme and P. Trimp).
DE ARCHITECT 1989 Dec., v.20,
no.12, p.34-39, elevs., models,
plans, secns., site plans.

**T.A.U. (THEORY - ARCHITECTURE -
URBANISM)**
Una gabbia nel bosco = A cage in the
woods [Jack in the Box house,
Japan].
Architects: Studio Tau.
ARCHITETTURA: CRONACHE E STORIA
1990 Sept., v.36, no.9(419),
p.638-639, photos., plan.

**T.E.N., TALLER DE ENRIQUE NORTEN Y
ASOCIADOS**
Bringing light: Centro de
Iluminacion, Mexico City /
Maragaret Gaskie.
Reuse of a 1940's apt. house into
a store. Architect: T.E.N., Taller
de Enrique Norten y Asociados.
ARCHITECTURAL RECORD 1990 Feb.,
v.178, no.2, p.84-87, elev.,
photos., plans.
Mexican architecture: new directions
/ John V. Mutlow.
Profiles works by: Agustin
Hernandez, David Munoz Suarez,
Enrique Norten and Associates S.C.
Workshop (T.E.N.), Gutierrez
Cortina, Sanchez Arquitectos Y
Asociados, Legorreta Arquitectos,
and Teodoro Gonzalez de Leon.
L. A. ARCHITECT 1990 Jan., p.7-11,

TABA, BENO, 1954-
Special feature: Contemporary
Hungarian architecture / edited by
Botond Bognar.
Works illustrated by architects:
Imre Makovecz, Gabor Mezei, Andras
Erdei, Sandor Devenyi, Attila
Kovacs, Laszlo Saros, Tamas Nagy,
Gyorgy Csete, Peter Oltai, Istvan
Kistelegdi, Tibor Jankovics, Csasa
Bodonyi, Istvan Ferencz, Tamas
Noll, Beno Taba, Janos Golda,
Agnes Thoma, Jozsef Kerenyi,
Gyorgy Vadasz, Gyorgy Keves, Adam
Sylvester and Gabor Turanyi. Text
in Japanese and English.
ARCHITECTURE AND URBANISM 1990
Mar., no.3(234), p.7-126,
axonometric views, dwgs., elevs.,
photos., plans, secns.

**TABERNACLES (ALTAR COMPONENTS)--
MEDIEVAL--FRANCE**
Les tabernacles eucharistiques dans
la France du Moyen Age / Jacques
Foucart-Borville.
Shaped like buildings. French,
English, German summaries.
p.[467-469].
BULLETIN MONUMENTAL 1990, v.148,
no.4, p.[251]-381, ill., photos.,
engrs., refs.

**TABERNACLES (ALTAR COMPONENTS)--
RENAISSANCE--ITALY**
Saint Antonin de Florence et l'art:
theologie pastorale,
administration et commande
d'oeuvres / Creighton Gilbert.
Includes discussion of the
tabernacle at the Duomo in
Florence, with reference to
sculpture by Donatello, Benedetto
da Maiano, Francesco di Giorgio
and others.
REVUE DE L'ART 1990, no.90,
p.9-20, ill., photos., plan, refs.

TABERY, LOTHAR
Friedhofskapelle in
Bremervorde-Hesedorf.
Architect: Lothar Tabery.
DEUTSCHE BAUZEITSCHRIFT 1990 July,
v.38, no.7, p.979-984, dets.,
photos., plan.

TABOR, JAN
Contemporary Austrian architecture.
Special feature. Contents: Between
harmony and revolt..., by Jan
Tabor.--Wein.--Graz.--Linz,.
Innsbrook, Bregenz. Three sections
are indexed separately. Text in
Japanese.
SPACE DESIGN 1990 Mar., no.306,
p.5-112, axonometric views, dwgs.,
ports.,elevs., models, map,
photos., plans, secns., site
plans.
Loos a Vienna / Jan Tabor.
On the restoration of the ground
floor of the Looshaus on the
Michaelerplatz and an exhibition
at the Albertina, Vienna, 2
Dec.1989-25 Feb.1990. Captions in
Italian and English.
CASABELLA 1990 Feb., v.54, no.565,
p.24,23, sketch.

TACCA, PIETRO, 1577-1640
La estatua ecuestre de Felipe IV de
Pietro Tacca y la fachada del
Alcazar de Madrid / Karin
Hellwig-Konkerth.
English summary, p.233.
ARCHIVO ESPANOL DE ARTE 1990
Apr.-June, v.63, no.250,
p.[233]-241, photo., plan, engrs.,
refs.

TACCHINI, RUGGERO, 1929-
Quattro interpretazioni della
residenza in chiave organica.
Four houses by Ugo Bartorelli and
Ruggero Tacchini: at S. Maurizio
d'Opaglio, Gozzano, and
Borgomanero. Summaries in English,
French, German, and Spanish.
ARCHITETTURA; CRONACHE E STORIA
1990 Apr., v.36, no.4(414),
p.[262]-269, photos., plans,
secns., site plans, aerial photo.
Il tiglio "ispiratore" / Roberto
Apostolo.
Multi-family house on Lago d'Orta,
Italy. Architects: Ugo Bartorelli,
Ruggero Tacchini.
VILLE GIARDINI 1990 June, no.249,
p.2-9, dets., photos., plans,
secns.

TACTILE ORIENTATION MODELS
See BRAILLE MAPS

TADAO ANDO, ARCHITECT AND ASSOCIATES
Children's Museum, Hyogo.
Architects: Tadao Ando Architect
and Associates. English summary,
p.23.
KENCHIKU BUNKA 1990 Aug., v.45,
no.526, p.149-[164], photos.,
plans, secns., site plan, sketch.
Collezione building a Tokio di Tadao
Ando & Associates.
In Italian and English.
CASABELLA 1990 Nov., v.54, no.573,
p.4-11,59, dwgs., photos., plans,
secn., aerial photos.
Collezione / Tadao Ando.
Multi-use Tokyo building contains
commercial space, parking garage,
athletic club and owner's living
quarters. Architects: Tadao Ando,
Architect and Associates.
JAPAN ARCHITECT 1990 Mar., v.65,
no.3(395), p.51-60, axonometric
view, photos., plans, secn., site
plan, sketches.
Raika headquarters building.
Architects: Tadao Ando, Architect
and Associates. English summary,
p.19.
KENCHIKU BUNKA 1990 July, v.45,
no.525, p.[113-131], elevs.,
photos., plans, site plans,
sketches.
Tadao Ando and Associates: Hyogo
Children's Museum, Himeji, Hyogo,
Japan, design: 1987-88;
construction: 1988-89 / Tadao
Ando.
Text in Japanese and English.
GA DOCUMENT 1990 Sept., no.27,
p.[106]-119, photos., plans,
secns.
Tadao Ando and the contemporary ruin
/ Jackie Kestenbaum.
On two recent projects: the Raika
Headquarters Bldg., Osaka and
Children's Museum, Hyogo. Text in
Japanese and English.
KENCHIKU BUNKA 1990 July, v.45,
no.525, p.[132], dwgs., port.,
model, photos., site plan, refs.
Tadao Ando / Tadao Ando.
Contents: RAIKA headquarters
building, Osaka, design: 1986-87;
construction: 1987-89 -- Temple
with Lotus (Hompukuji; a Shingon
sect Buddhist temple), Hyogo,
design: 1989-90; completion: Nov.
1991. Text in Japanese and
English.
GA DOCUMENT 1990 Apr., no.25,
p.[18]-31, elevs., model, photos.,
plans, secns., site plan.

TADAO ANDO, ARCHITECTS AND ASSOCIATES
Casa e bottega; + la mano di Tadao
Ando = Home and business, plus the
land of Tadao Ando.
"Collezione," building with a
house, gallery, and athletic club
in Japan.
ARCHITETTURA: CRONACHE E STORIA
1990 Nov., v.36, no.11(421),
p.804-805, axonometric view,
photos.

TADASHI SAITO AND ATELIER R
Fascinating moulded concrete block
structure / Tadashi Saito.
Two concrete block structures by
Tadashi Saito and Atelier R:
Aoyama Cemetery office, Tokyo and
Villa Shiomisaki. English summary,
p.19.
KENCHIKU BUNKA 1990 Oct., v.45,
no.528, p.73-90, axonometric view,
dwgs., ports., photos., plans,
site plan.

**TADGELL, CHRISTOPHER, 1939-. HISTORY
OF ARCHITECTURE IN INDIA**
Fertile melting pot: The history of
architecture in India, by
Christopher Tadgell [book review]
/ Philip Davies.
ARCHITECTS' JOURNAL 1990 Aug.1,
v.192, no.5, p.58-59, photos.

**TAFEL, EDGAR A.--ADDRESSES, ESSAYS,
LECTURES**
Wright and wrong / Dennis Sharp.
Report on Edgar A. Tafel's lecture
at the Architectural Association,
London.
BUILDING DESIGN 1990 Apr.20,
no.982, p.46-47, port., photos.

TAFT ARCHITECTS
Rothwell House, Houston, Texas,
design: 1988-89; construction:
1990.
Architects: Taft Architects. Text
in Japanese and English.
GA HOUSES 1990 Mar., no.28,
p.114-115, model, plans, secns.

TAFURI, MANFREDO, 1935-
Die Krise der Linearitat / Manfredo
Tafuri.
ARCH PLUS 1990 Oct., no.105-106,
p.98-106, dwgs., models, maps,
photos., site plans, engrs.

**TAFURI, MANFREDO, 1935-. HISTORY OF
ITALIAN ARCHITECTURE 1944-1985**
Italian dreams retold [book review]
/ David Dunster.
Review of the book, History of
Italian architecture, 1944-1985,
by Manfredo Tafuri.
BUILDING DESIGN 1990 Feb.2,
no.971, p.23, photos., site plan.

TAGGART, PAULETT
American housing 1980-1990 / James
Tice.
Features: Castro Common, San
Francisco (Daniel Solomon, Paulett
Taggart); Sun-Tech Housing, Santa
Monica (Steve Andre, David Van
Hoy); Pacific Townhouses, Santa
Monica (Rebecca Binder, James
Stafford); Hoyt Square
Condominiums, Portland, OR (Robert
S. Leeb). Text in Italian and
English.
METAMORFOSI 1989, no.12, p.38-51,
axonometric views, models,
photos., plans, secns.
Case con vista: San Francisco, un
osservatorio attraverso i tetti =
Houses with a view: San Francisco,
an observatory through the
rooftops.
Renovation of a Victorian cottage
in North Beach, now the home of
the architects, Bill Stout and
Paulett Taggart.
(Continued next column)

TAGGART, PAULETT (CONTINUED)
Case con vista: San...(CONTINUED)
ABITARE 1990 Oct., no.289,
p.214-[221], axonometric view,
photos., plans.
Press up: San Francisco architect
Paulett Taggart moves a printer
into a new space / Paula Rice
Jackson.
On the Holocomb Print Shop located
in a newly renovated "printer's
building" south of Market Street.
INTERIORS 1989 Feb., v.148, no.7,
p.138-139, photos., plan.

TAGLIABUE, ANNA
Un ciclo bergamasco di primo
Duecento: gli affreschi dell'Aula
della Curia / Laura Polo
D'Ambrosio, Anna Tagliabue.
On early 13th-cent. mural
paintings at the Basilica di S.
Maria Maggiore, Bergamo. Includes
English summary.
ARTE CRISTIANA 1989 July-Aug.,
v.77, no.733, p.269-282, photos.,
plans, refs.

TAGTOW, RICK
The need for urban forests / Rick
Tagtow.
AMERICAN CITY & COUNTY 1990 Mar.,
v.105, no.3, p.74,76, photo.

TAI SOO KIM ASSOCIATES, ARCHITECTS
Positive space: Tai Soo Kim's
multifaceted new complex presents
the University of Hartford with a
lively hub for cultural activities
/ Margaret Gaskie.
ARCHITECTURAL RECORD 1990 Feb.,
v.178, no.2, p.104-109, elevs.,
photos., plans, secns., site plan.

TAIKOH ARCHITECTURAL OFFICE
Kazuo Shinohara / Kazuo Shinohara.
Contents: K2 Building,
Miyakojima-ku, Osaka, design:
1987-88; under construction --
Kumamoto-kita Police Station,
design: 1988-90; under
construction. With Taikoh
Architectural Office. Text in
Japanese and English.
GA DOCUMENT 1990 Apr., no.25,
p.161-165, elevs., model, photos.,
plans, secns.

TAILORED FABRIC REINFORCEMENT
See WELDED WIRE FABRIC

TAINER, DARIO
Cafe bravissimo / Justin Henderson.
Interiors of Pinuccio, cafe,
Highland Park, Ill. Architect:
Dario Tainer.
INTERIORS 1990 June, v.149, no.11,
p.104-[105], photos., plan.

TAIPALE, KAARIN
Kultuurikeskus Poleeni, Pieksamaki =
Poleeni, the Pieksamaki Cultural
Centre / Kristian Gullichsen.
Architects:
Gullichsen-Kairamo-Vormala
Arkkitehdit. Includes an essay by
Kaarin Taipale and an English
translation.
ARKKITEHTI 1989, v.86, no.8,
p.44-51, cover, photos., plans,
secns., site plan.

TAIPALE, KAARIN (CONTINUED)
Politiikka ja byrokratia: Kysymyksia
Helsingin kaupungin
ylipormestarille Raimo Ilaskivelle
[interview] / Kaarin Taipale.
Interview with the mayor of
Helsinki, about politics and
bureaucracy.
ARKKITEHTI 1989, v.86, no.8,
p.70-71, port.

TAISEI CORPORATION
Ampi spazi per una citta sotto e
sopra = Large spaces for a city
above and below / Fabrizio Bonomo.
Architects: Taisei Corporation.
L'ARCA 1990 Mar., no.36 suppl.
l'Arca 2, p.97-98, dwg., secns.

TAISNE, CATHERINE
Le 1% et le logement social /
Catherine Taisne.
Employer-subsidized rental housing
in the Ile-de-France. English
summaries, p.4, 75-76; French and
Spanish summaries, p.4.
CAHIERS DE L'INSTITUT
D'AMENAGEMENT ET D'URBANISME DE LA
REGION D'ILE-DE-FRANCE 1990 Sept.,
no.94, p.65-76, graphs, photos.,
tables, refs.

TAIT, A. A.
The British Isles [book review].
Reviews of recent books on Inigo
Jones, Wren's design of St.
Paul's, John Claudius Loudon, six
vernacular topics. Reviewers: John
Bold, A. A. Tait, Anthony Quiney.
SOCIETY OF ARCHITECTURAL
HISTORIANS. JOURNAL 1990 June,
v.49, no.2, p.217-221.

TAIT, JOYCE
Farmers' attitudes to conservation /
Susan Carr, Joyce Tait.
BUILT ENVIRONMENT 1990, v.16,
no.3, p.218-231, photos., tables,
refs.

**TAIWAN--TAIPEI--RESTAURANTS--INTERIOR
DESIGN--M**
Bridge party / David Redhead.
Features interiors of M, Taipei
restaurant. Architects:
Powell-Tuck Connor and Orefelt.
DESIGNERS' JOURNAL 1990 Jan.,
no.53, p.72-[75], dets., photos.,
plans.

TAJADURA, J. A.
Rotterdam: dopo il tunnel
ferroviario: tre proposte =
Rotterdam: after the railway
tunnel: three concepts / Pierluigi
Nicolin.
Competition projects for tunnel
beneath the Maas river and the
planning for an adjacent district.
Architects: Joan Busquets, with J.
A. Tajadura, J. Sole, M. M.
Busquets, P. Ortega; Andreas
Brandt, with R. Bottcher;
Pierluigi Nicolin, with G.
Marinoni, M. Pugliese, E.
Cavedini.
LOTUS INTERNATIONAL 1989, no.64,
p.54-71, models, photos., site
plans.

TAK ASSOCIATED ARCHITECTS
Kasumaza Nakagawa Art Museum, Manazuru.
Architects: TAK Associated Architects. English summary, p.19.
KENCHIKU BUNKA 1990 July, v.45, no.525, p.[65]-72, photos., plans, secn.

TAKABU, MOTOJUKI
Survey of renewal works of buildings / Yoshihisa Takebayashi, Motoyuki Takabu.
In commercial buildings, focusing on the renovation of mechanical systems. Text in Japanese; English summary, p.122.
NIHON KENCHIKU GAKKAI KEIKAKUKEI RONBUN HOKOKU SHU = JOURNAL OF ARCHITECTURE, PLANNING AND ENVIRONMENTAL ENGINEERING 1990 Mar., no.3(409), p.115-122, graphs, tables, refs.

TAKAHAMA, KAZUHIDE
Villa at Yunomoto / Kazuhide Takahama.
Designer: Kazuhide Takahama. Text in Japanese.
SPACE DESIGN 1990 Aug., no.311 p.61-68, dets., elevs., photos., plans, secns.

TAKAHASHI, KUNIAKI
Winners in the Central Glass International Architectural Design Competition 1989.
Theme: a terminal for the linear motor car. Winners: Sotaro Yamamoto and Kuniaki Takahashi (1st place). Includes twelve other winning designs.
JAPAN ARCHITECT 1990 Jan., v.65, no.1(393), p.61-66, dwgs.

TAKAHASHI, MAKOTO, 1926-
Daikanyama house.
Apartment house. Architect: Makoto Takahashi. English summary, p.17.
KENCHIKU BUNKA 1990 Jan., v.45, no.519, p.127-136, dets., photos., elevs., plans, secn.

TAKAMATSU, SHIN, 1948-
Attitudes toward technology: Shin Takamatsu / Mark Alden Branch.
First of an occasional series of essays on attitudes toward technology.
PROGRESSIVE ARCHITECTURE 1990 Aug., v.71, no.8, p.115, photos.
Japan: monastic to fantastic / Hiroshi Watanabe.
Works by various architects.
ART IN AMERICA 1990 Apr., v.78, no.4, p.220-[227], photos.
Kisho Kurokawa and Shin Takamatsu design redevelopment projects exhibition of architecture in Nimes.
Features two projects in Nimes: Noa, office complex, architect: Shin Takamatsu and Corrize, housing/office complex, architect: Kisho Kurokawa.
JAPAN ARCHITECT 1990 July, v.65, no.7(399), p.4, dwg., elevs.
Shin Takamatsu / Shin Takamatsu.
Contents: Syntax, Sakyo-ku, Kyoto, design: 1988; construction: 1988-90 -- Solaris, Amagasaki, Hyogo, design: 1988-89;
(Continued next column)

TAKAMATSU, SHIN, 1948- (CONTINUED)
Shin Takamatsu / Shin...(CONTINUED) completion: Nov.1990. Text in Japanese and English.
GA DOCUMENT 1990 Apr., no.25, p.[166]-[173], axonometric views, elevs., photos., plans, secns.
Syntax / Shin Takamatsu.
Feature four-story shopping center, Sakyo Ward, Kyoto.
Architects: Shin Takamatsu, Architect and Associates.
JAPAN ARCHITECT 1990 June, v.65, no.6(398), p.[56]-66, elev., models, photos., secns.
Temples devoted to earthly power / Neal Morris.
On Shin Takamatsu.
ARCHITECTS' JOURNAL 1990 Sept.19, v.192, no.12, p.48-49,51-53, dwgs., port., photos.
The "Transfiguration" exhibition in Europalia Japan.
Special feature. Works by Kazuyo Seijima + Noriyuki Tanaka, Toyo Ito, Keiichi Irie, Hiromi Fujii, Shin Takamatsu, and Yutaka Saito.
Essays by Riichi Miyake; Toyo Ito, Alvin Boyarsky, and Nigel Coates; Keiichi Irie and Kobun ito; Hiromi Fujii and Shusaku Arakawa; Shin Takamatsu and Daniel Libeskind; Yutaka Saito and Issei Miyake.
Text in Japanese.
SPACE DESIGN 1990 Feb., no.305, p.13-44, dets., dwgs., models, photos., sketches.

TAKAMI, TAKASHI
The planning techniques used on the plotting of residential area in the post towns on the Nagasaki Highway and its influence upon present city area / Takashi Takami.
English summary, p.97.
NIHON KENCHIKU GAKKAI KEIKAKUKEI RONBUN HOKOKU SHU = JOURNAL OF ARCHITECTURE, PLANNING AND ENVIRONMENTAL ENGINEERING 1988 Sept., no.9(391), p.86-97, charts., graphs, maps, refs.

TAKANAKA KOMUTEN COMPANY
L'eco del triangolo: Botta a Tokio / Harald Szeemann.
The Watari-um building (1985-1990), executed with the Takenaka Corp. Includes English captions.
CASABELLA 1990 Dec., v.54, no.574, p.32-33, photos., plans.

TAKASAKI, MASAHARU, 1953-
Villa Energie de la Terre a Nagoya.
Earth Energy Villa. Architect: Masaharu Takasaki. Includes statement by Takasaki. Text in French and English.
TECHNIQUES ET ARCHITECTURE 1990 June-July, no.390, p.132-133, photos., plan, secn.

TAKASAKI, MASAHARU, 1953---EXHIBITIONS
"Energy void" installation by Masaharu Takasaki [exhibition review].
Exhibition held at the Azabu Arts and Crafts Museum.
JAPAN ARCHITECT 1990 Feb., v.65, no.2(394), p.5, photos., sketch.

TAKEBAYASHI, YOSHIHISA
Survey of renewal works of buildings / Yoshihisa Takebayashi, Motoyuki Takabu.
In commercial buildings, focusing on the renovation of mechanical systems. Text in Japanese; English summary, p.122.
NIHON KENCHIKU GAKKAI KEIKAKUKEI RONBUN HOKOKU SHU = JOURNAL OF ARCHITECTURE, PLANNING AND ENVIRONMENTAL ENGINEERING 1990 Mar., no.3(409), p.115-122, graphs, tables, refs.

TAKEHARA, AKIKO
Editorial design in action: the world of Tsutomu Toda, 10: Ecology of designers and books / Akiko Takehara.
Text in Japanese.
SPACE DESIGN 1990 Nov., no.11(314), p.[082]-[087], ill.
Editorial design in action: the world of Tsutomu Toda, 11 / Akiko Takehara.
"Books for the memory of touch: editorial design for the 21th century." Text in Japanese.
SPACE DESIGN 1990 Dec., no.12(315), p.74-79, ill.

TAKENAKA KOMUTEN COMPANY
Le projet Sky City.
Project for 1000m tower containing offices and housing for 35,000 people. Architects: Takenaka Komuten Company, Shizuo Harada.
English summary, p. 64.
ARCHITECTURE D'AUJOURD'HUI 1990 Feb., no.267, p.62-64, ill., dwg., model, secns.
Takenaka: multinational in "turn key"-architectuur / Egbert Koster.
Workl by the Japanese firm during the past decade.
DE ARCHITECT 1990 Apr., v.21, no.4, p.67-71, photos., plans, secn.
Watari-Um.
Multi-use building, Tokyo.
Architects: Mario Botta with Takenaka Komuten Company. Includes interview with Botta, entitled Swiss architecture on Tokyo. English summary, p.23.
KENCHIKU BUNKA 1990 Sept., v.45, no.527, p.[154]-158, port., photos., plans.

TAKEYAMA, KIYOSHI SEY, 1954-
Al di la della facciata = Beyond the facade / Philippe Vernier.
Contents: OXY building and D-Hotel, Tokyo, Japan; architects: Kiyoshi Sey Takeyama and Amphore Architects and Associates.
Includes essay: From trans-territory to another world: OXY building and D-Hotel / Kiyoshi Sey Takeyama. Text in Italian and English.
L'ARCA 1990 Feb., no.35, p.12-23, axonometric view, elevs., photos., plans, secns.
Retreat in Midorigaoka / Kiyoshi Sey Takeyama, Hiroyuki Enomoto.
Reinforced concrete house on very small triangular site by railway line in Tokyo. Architects: Amorphe Architects Studio.
JAPAN ARCHITECT 1990 Apr., v.65,
(Continued next page)

TAKEYAMA, KIYOSHI SEY, 1954-
(CONTINUED)
Retreat in...(CONTINUED)
no.4 (396), p.[63]-67, elev.,
photos., plans.
Yokohama city creation Bay '90:
exhibition of waterfront
redevelopment.
Five temporary towers, called
Yokohama Towers, which are part of
the Bay 90 exhibition. Architects:
Hirofumi Sugimoto, Noriaki Furuya,
Katsuhiro Kobayashi, Kiyoshi
Takeyama and Kazuyo Sejima.
JAPAN ARCHITECT 1990 June, v.65,
no.6(398), p.4, photos.

TAKI, KOJI
Recent works: Elia Zenghelis, Eleni
Gigantes.
Four projects, 1986-1989,
including the Chalkiades villa,
Mytilene. Includes an interview by
Koji Taki and Hajime Yatsuka.
SPACE DESIGN 1990 Mar., no.306,
p.121-128, elevs., photos., plans,
secns., site plans, isometric
dwgs.
Recent works: Peter Wilson.
Projects: Munster City Library,
and ZKM, Karlsruhe. Includes
interviews conducted by Koji Taki,
Hajime Yatsuka, and Ryogi Suzuki.
Text in Japanese.
SPACE DESIGN 1990 Apr., no.307,
p.54-68, dwg., elevs., models,
plans, secns., site plan.

TAKIGUCHI, NORIHIKO
Directions in urban housing, part
II: Messages from Fukuoka.
Contents: International Housing
Exhibition in Kashii.--Steven
Holl.--Rem Koolhaas.--Mark Mack.--
Osamu Ishiyama.--Christian de
Portzamparc.--Oscar Tusguets.--
Arata Isozaki.--Nexus Momochi,
Michael Graves, Stanley
Tigerman.--Fukouka International
Architects' Conference '89.--
Experation and Defiance in the
Debate over the City as "Chaos",
by Noriko Takiguchi. Includes
English summary and biographical
information on participants.
SPACE DESIGN 1990 Jan., no.304,
p.53-84, axonometric views, dwgs.,
ports., elevs., models, map,
photos., plans, secns., site
plans.

TALIA, MICHELE
El campo de la produccion entre el
declive industrial y los procesos
innovadores: el caso italiano /
Michele Talia.
The field of production between
industrial decline and innovatory
processes: the Italian case. In
Spanish. English summary, p.17.
URBANISMO / COAM 1990 Sept.,
no.11, p.6-17, maps, photo., site
plans, table, aerial photos.

TALIESIN ASSOCIATED ARCHITECTS OF THE
FRANK LLOYD WRIGHT FOUNDATION
Apple grows at Taliesin West /
Steven S. Ross.
Testing Mac software.
ARCHITECTURAL RECORD 1990 Jan.,
v.178, no.1, p.171-178, ports.

TALIESIN ASSOCIATED ARCHITECTS OF THE
FRANK LLOYD WRIGHT FOUNDATION
(CONTINUED)
Legacy of F.L.Wright: unfinished
plans realized.
Boulder House, Beverly Hills,
Calif.(1951) and Pottery House,
Santa Fe(1939-1942). Text in
Japanese. Architects of record:
Taliesin Associated Architects of
the Frank Lloyd Wright Foundation.
SPACE DESIGN 1990 Aug., no.311,
p.69-76, dwgs., map, photos., site
plans.

TALL BUILDINGS
Le architetture verticali (seconda
parte) = vertical architectures
(part two) / Roberto Apostolo.
Tall buildings, from Mies' Lake
Shore Drive complex to the
present.
FRAMES, PORTE & FINESTRE 1990
Apr.-June, no.27, p.34-39, elev.,
photos.
Designing the super-thin new
buildings / James S. Russell.
Features 6 projects for tall
buildings in New York City,
Chicago and Paris.
ARCHITECTURAL RECORD 1990 Oct.,
v.178, no.11, p.105-109,
axonometric views, elev., models,
photos., plans.
Double strength [composite
structure] / Denise Chevin.
Benefits from combining steel
frames with high-strength concrete
in columns of tall buildings.
Examples are engineered by SWMB, a
Seattle firm.
BUILDING 1990 July 20, v.255,
no.29, p.62-65, photos., plans.
High rise go faster stripes: Chicago
skyscrapers: a selection of
drawings from the permanent
collection [exhibition review] /
David Dunster.
Exhibition held at Art Institute,
Chicago, Oct.-Dec.,1990.
BLUEPRINT (LONDON, ENGLAND) 1990
Oct., no.71, p.58.
High-risk high rises: Building Types
Study 685: high-rise office
buildings / Paul M. Sachner.
Presents 3 recent speculative
office buildings, each indexed
separately.
ARCHITECTURAL RECORD 1990 Oct.,
v.178, no.11, p.87-[101], dwg.,
photos.
In search of the city / Helen J.
Maib.
OZ / COLLEGE OF ARCHITECTURE AND
DESIGN, KANSAS STATE UNIVERSITY
1989, v.11, p.18-21, photos.,
refs.
Selecting glass for tall buildings /
Joseph E. Minor.
ARCHITECTURAL RECORD 1990 June,
v.178, no.7, p.105-107, graphs,
elevs., photos, tables.
Technics: high profiles / Andrea E.
Monfried.
On decorative building crowns.
Includes six case studies which
address a variety of design and
construction issues, and a
discussion of exterior maintenance
equipment by Lee B. Herzog.
PROGRESSIVE ARCHITECTURE 1990
Feb., v.71, no.2, p.49-54,
photos., secns.

TALL BUILDINGS (CONTINUED)
Der Traum von den fliegenden
Stadten. Zu El Lissitzkys
Wolkenbugel = The dream of the
flying cities. On El Lissitzky's
sky hook / Rainer Stommer.
Extract of lecture delivered at
opening of exhibition 'El
Lissitsky. the dream of the
Skyhook' on 17 May, 1990 at the
Institut fur Geschichte und
Theorie der Architektur of the
ETH, Zurich.
DAIDALOS 1990 Sept.15, no.37,
p.60-63, dwgs., model.
Utopie der Moderne als postmoderne
Utopie? / J. Christoph Burkle.
On 1924 plans for a skyscraper by
El Lissitzky and Emil Roth.
DEUTSCHE BAUZEITUNG 1990 Oct.,
v.124, no.10, p.174-178, dwgs.,
models, plans, secns.

TALL BUILDINGS--AUSTRALIA--PERTH--ST.
GEORGE'S SQUARE TOWER 1
St. George's Square [Tower 1,
Perth].
Tall office building. Architects:
Oldham Boas Ednie-Brown.
THE ARCHITECT, W.A.: THE OFFICIAL
JOURNAL OF THE ROYAL AUSTRALIAN
INSTITUTE OF ARCHITECTS, W.A.
CHAPTER 1990, v.30, no.4, p.17-19,
photos., site plan.

TALL BUILDINGS--CHINA
Current structural features of
highrise buildings / Hu Shide.
BUILDING IN CHINA 1989 June, v.2,
no.2, p.9-14,35, ill., photos.

TALL BUILDINGS--CHINA--PEKING--CAPITAL
MANSION
Capital Mansion - high-rise steel
structure in Beijing / Qiu Guohua.
A commercial-residential complex
located on the Liangma River in
eastern Beijing, with a 180-story
main building. Construction began
in Aug.1989. Planners: China
International Trust & Investment
Corporation. Architects: Shimizu
Construction Co. of Japan.
BUILDING IN CHINA 1990 Mar., v.3,
no.1, p.30-33,45, dets., photo.,
plan, secn., tables.

TALL BUILDINGS--CHINA--SHENZHEN
China's first super-highrise steel
structure [SDCM] / Jian Junyu.
Shenzhen Development Center
Mansion, a multi-purpose
commercial building, near the
railroad station in Shenzhen.
BUILDING IN CHINA 1989 June, v.2,
no.2, p.15-17, photos., plan.

TALL BUILDINGS--CHINA--SHENZHEN--
ENVIRONMENTAL ASPECTS
Validation of computer modelling of
vehicular exhaust dispersion near
a tower block / Y. Qin, S.C. Kot.
Study undertaken in Shenzhen,
China by the Institute of
Environmental Science, Zhongshan
University.
BUILDING AND ENVIRONMENT 1990,
v.25, no.2, p.125-131, graphs,
refs., dets., diagrs.

TALL BUILDINGS--COMPETITIONS--GERMANY
(WEST)--BERLIN--HOCHHAUS AM BAHNHOF
FRIEDRICHSTRASSE
Der Schrei nach dem Turmhouse: Der
Ideenwettbewerb Hochhaus am
Bahnhof Friedrichstrasse Berlin
1921-22 [ed. by Florian
Zimmermann] [book review] /
Dietrich Neumann.
KUNSTCHRONIK 1989 Oct., v.42,
no.10, p.593.

TALL BUILDINGS--CONCRETE
High-strength concrete keeps going
up / Patrick J. Quinn.
For use in structural frames of
tall buildings.
CANADIAN ARCHITECT 1990 Aug.,
v.35, no.8, p.39, photo.
High strength: high-strength
concrete in high-rise construction
/ Marc S. Harriman.
Contents: Two Prudential Plaza,
Chicago (Loebl Schlossman and
Hackl); 311 S. Wacker, Chicago
(Kohn Pedersen Fox); and Two Union
Sq., Seattle (NBBJ Group).
ARCHITECTURE: THE AIA JOURNAL 1990
Oct., v.79, no.10, p.85-92,
photos., plans, secns.

TALL BUILDINGS--DENMARK
Danmark gar i hojden / Leif Leer
Sorensen.
ARKITEKTEN 1990 June, v.92, no.8,
p.272-273, plans, secns.

TALL BUILDINGS--DENMARK--AARHUS--SHELL
Tarnenes by-endnu et tarn-projekt i
Arhus.
Office Tower on Silkeborgveg and
Viborgvej. Architects: Friis &
Moltke.
ARKITEKTEN 1990 Aug., v.92, no.10,
p.342, ill., model, plans.

TALL BUILDINGS--DENMARK--HORSENS
Hojhus i Horsens midtby.
Located on Raedersgade. Architect:
Kurt Birch. Engineer: N.C.
Skovgaard.
ARKITEKTEN 1990 Sept., v.92,
no.13, p.438, elev., model, site
plan.

TALL BUILDINGS--ENGLAND--LONDON
Planning for tall buildings in
London / Gregory Wilson, Roger
Norton.
THE PLANNER 1990 Oct.19, v.76,
no.41, p.9-11, photo., sketch,
refs.

TALL BUILDINGS--ENGLAND--LONDON--
CANARY WHARF
Canary Wharf / Drummund Robson.
Report from the RTPI.
THE PLANNER 1990 Oct.12, v.76,
no.40, p.8-10, dwg., photo.
La gran canaria / Martin Pawley.
Plan for new tower by Cesar Pelli
Associates.
CASABELLA 1990 July-Aug., v.54,
no.570, p.28, photo.

TALL BUILDINGS--ENGLAND--LONDON--
KING'S CROSS SITE
No funny hats at King's Cross /
Robert Cowan.
Revision of Norman Foster design.
ARCHITECTS' JOURNAL 1990 Aug.8,
v.192, no.6, p.14-15, dwg., model,
sketches.

TALL BUILDINGS--ENVIRONMENTAL
ASPECTS--JAPAN
A study on modelling of turbulent
flows within plant and urban
canopies / Hisashi Hiraoka ... [et
al.].
"Verification of the turbulence
model (Part 2)". Text in Japanese;
includes English summary.
NIHON KENCHIKU GAKKAI KEIKAKUKEI
RONBUN HOKOKU SHU = JOURNAL OF
ARCHITECTURE, PLANNING AND
ENVIRONMENTAL ENGINEERING 1990
Oct., no.10(416), p.1-8, graphs,
refs.

TALL BUILDINGS--ENVIRONMENTAL
ASPECTS--JAPAN--TOKYO
Research and investigation on space
attribute and space use on each
floor of buildings in Tokyo /
Shih-yeh Wang....[et al.].
Analysis of three categories of
space: public and private, over
and under, inner and outer. Text
in Japanese; English summary,
p.105.
NIHON KENCHIKU GAKKAI KEIKAKUKEI
RONBUN HOKOKU SHU = JOURNAL OF
ARCHITECTURE, PLANNING AND
ENVIRONMENTAL ENGINEERING 1990
Apr., no.4(410), p.105-112,
graphs, ill., maps, tables, refs.

TALL BUILDINGS--ENVIRONMENTAL
ASPECTS--UNITED STATES--BOSTON
(MASSACHUSETTS)
"An act protecting open spaces."
On a proposal in the Massachusetts
Senate, to bar approval by local
authorities of new buidings tall
enough to shadow historic open
spaces.
BOSTON PRESERVATION ALLIANCE
LETTER 1990 May, v.11, no.3, p.1,
ill.

TALL BUILDINGS--FINLAND--TAMPERE
Bomassa med stalhus / Zacharias
Toivio.
Tall apartment building with steel
exterior, in Tammerfors.
Architect: 8 Studio, and Mikko
Kaira.
ARKITEKTUR: THE SWEDISH REVIEW OF
ARCHITECTURE 1990 Dec., v.90,
no.10, p.53-54, axonometric view,
photos., plan.

TALL BUILDINGS--FRANCE--PARIS--TOUR DE
LA DEFENSE
Entretien avec l'architecte, Jean
Nouvel [interview] / F. de
Graveleine, E. Doutriaux.
On the Tour de la Defense, Paris.
English summary, p.154.
ARCHITECTURE D'AUJOURD'HUI 1990
June, no.269, p.152-[155], port.,
plans.

TALL BUILDINGS--FRANCE--PARIS--TOUR DE
LA DEFENSE (CONTINUED)
Entretien avec l'ingenieur, Tony
Fitzpatrick [interview] / Jacques
Ferrier, Emmanuel Doutriaux.
Focus on the Tour de la Defense,
Paris. English summary,
p.159-160.
ARCHITECTURE D'AUJOURD'HUI 1990
June, no.269, p.156-[161], ill.,
ports., models, sketches.
La tour sans fins: comment evolue un
projet / Emmanuel Doutriaux.
On the Tour de la Defense, Paris.
Architects: Jean Nouvel, Jean-Marc
Ibos. Engineer: Tony Fitzpatrick.
English summary, p.[147].
ARCHITECTURE D'AUJOURD'HUI 1990
June, no.269, p.[146]-152, models,
plans, secns., site plans.

TALL BUILDINGS--FRANCE--PARIS--TOUR
SANS FINS
Designing the super-thin new
buildings / James S. Russell.
Features 6 projects for tall
buildings in New York City,
Chicago and Paris.
ARCHITECTURAL RECORD 1990 Oct.,
v.178, no.11, p.105-109,
axonometric views, elev., models,
photos., plans.

TALL BUILDINGS--GERMANY (WEST)
Hochhauser.
On projects for tall buildings in
German cities. Includes commentary
by architects and city planners.
BAUMEISTER 1990 Feb., v.87, no.2,
p.15-28, ill., elevs., models,
plans, secns., site plans.

TALL BUILDINGS--GERMANY (WEST)--
FRANKFURT AM MAIN--MESSE TURM
Building Europe's tallest tower
[Messe Turm building, Frankfurt].
Architect: Helmut Jahn;
developers: Tishman Speyer.
REAL ESTATE FORUM 1990 July, v.45,
no.7, p.108-110,114-115,120,
model.

TALL BUILDINGS--GERMANY (WEST)--
STUTTGART--BERLINER PLATZ
Schatten uber Stuttgart.
Projects for tall buildings on
Berliner Platz by Helmut Jahn and
Behnisch & Partner.
DEUTSCHE BAUZEITUNG 1990 Mar.,
v.124, no.3, p.8-9, ill., photo.

TALL BUILDINGS--HISTORY
Architettura verticale (parte prima)
= Vertical architecture (part one)
/ Roberto Apostolo.
History of skyscrapers, especially
in Chicago.
FRAMES, PORTE & FINESTRE 1990
Jan.-Mar., no.26, p.34-39, dwgs.,
photos., aerial photos., biblio.

TALL BUILDINGS--HISTORY--UNITED
STATES--CHICAGO (ILLINOIS)
Architettura verticale (parte prima)
= Vertical architecture (part one)
/ Roberto Apostolo.
History of skyscrapers, especially
in Chicago.
FRAMES, PORTE & FINESTRE 1990
Jan.-Mar., no.26, p.34-39, dwgs.,
photos., aerial photos., biblio.

TALL BUILDINGS--UNITED STATES
  Skyscrapers the late imperial mob /
    Max Kozloff.
    Brief review of skyscrapers in the
    United States.
    ARTFORUM 1990 Dec., v.28, no.4,
    p.96-101, ill., photos., dwg.,
    refs.

TALL BUILDINGS--UNITED STATES--CHICAGO
  (ILLINOIS)
  Buildup: Chicago booms with
    high-rise construction and
    proposals for more / Michael J. P.
    Smith.
    Includes commentary on 30 tall
    office and apartment buildings
    scheduled for completion in the
    early 1990s.
    INLAND ARCHITECT 1990 Jan.-Feb.,
    v.34, no.1, p.49-57, axonometric
    views, elevs., elevs., models.
  Chicago on the rise: a wave of
    speculative office towers... /
    Howard Decker.
    NBC Tower (SOM); 225 W. Wacker Dr.
    (Kohn Pedersen Fox); 900 N.
    Michigan Ave. (Kohn Pedersen Fox);
    AT&T Center (SOM); Burnett
    Headquarters (Roche Dinkeloo); AMA
    Headquarters (Kenzo Tange); 181 W.
    Madison St. (Cesar Pelli); Chicago
    Skyneedle (Cesar Pelli).
    ARCHITECTURE: THE AIA JOURNAL 1990
    Feb., v.79, no.2, p.78-83, photos,
    model, aerial photo.

TALL BUILDINGS--UNITED STATES--CHICAGO
  (ILLINOIS)--INFLUENCE
  Heightened profiles / Cynthia Chapin
    Davidson.
    Two Chicago projects: NBC Tower at
    Cityfront Center and AT&T
    Corporate Center at corner of
    Franklin and Monroe streets, which
    reflect influences from 1930's
    skyscrapers. Architect: Adrian
    Smith and SOM.
    INLAND ARCHITECT 1990 Jan.-Feb.,
    v.34, no.1, p.28-35, elev.,
    photos., plan.

TALL BUILDINGS--UNITED STATES--CHICAGO
  (ILLINOIS)--LOOP
  Jahn in the Loop / Amy Gray Light.
    Recent projects for Chicago
    towers.
    ARCHITECTURE: THE AIA JOURNAL 1990
    Feb., v.79, no.2, p.34, ill.,
    dwgs., model.

TALL BUILDINGS--UNITED STATES--CHICAGO
  (ILLINOIS)--MAGLIN-BEITLER TOWER
  Designing the super-thin new
    buildings / James S. Russell.
    Features 6 projects for tall
    buildings in New York City,
    Chicago and Paris.
    ARCHITECTURAL RECORD 1990 Oct.,
    v.178, no.11, p.105-109,
    axonometric views, elev., models,
    photos., plans.

TALL BUILDINGS--UNITED STATES--CHICAGO
  (ILLINOIS)--ONE NORTH WACKER
  Second Roche building proposed for
    Chicago [One North Wacker] /
    Barbara K. Hower.
    Plans for a 1,275-foot-high
    building at the corner of Wacker
    Drive and Madison St. Architects:
    Kevin Roche, with Patrick Shaw.
                (Continued next column)

TALL BUILDINGS--UNITED STATES--CHICAGO
  (ILLINOIS)--ONE NORTH WACKER
                (CONTINUED)
  Second Roche building...(CONTINUED)
    INLAND ARCHITECT 1990 May-June,
    v.34, no.3, p.81-82, model.

TALL BUILDINGS--UNITED STATES--
  CINCINNATI (OHIO)--FOUNTAIN SQUARE
  WEST
  Deja vu: Helmut Jahn in Cincinnati /
    Jayne Merkel.
    Proposal for Fountain Square West,
    successor to an earlier plan
    (Fountain Place, by KPF). Plans
    are for 48 stories on a
    half-block, with offices, hotel, a
    shopping mall, and garage.
    INLAND ARCHITECT 1990 Sept.-Oct.,
    v.34, no.5, p.9, model, photo.

TALL BUILDINGS--UNITED STATES--
  CLEVELAND (OHIO)
  Cleveland grows up and up / Wilma
    Salisbury.
    Recent projects by Cesar Pelli,
    Kohn Pedersen Fox, Frank Gehry,
    I.M. Pei, and others.
    INLAND ARCHITECT 1990 Jan.-Feb.,
    v.34, no.1, p.22-25, aerial photo.

TALL BUILDINGS--UNITED STATES--LOS
  ANGELES (CALIFORNIA)--FIRST
  INTERSTATE WORLD TOWER
  Design for the big one: an L.A.
    tower resists quakes with a dual
    structure / Douglas E. Gordon.
    First Interstate World Tower.
    Architect: Henry Cobb of Pei Cobb
    Freed & Partners, and Ellerbe
    Becket.
    ARCHITECTURE: THE AIA JOURNAL 1990
    Feb., v.79, no.2, p.103-104,
    photos.

TALL BUILDINGS--UNITED STATES--
  MINNEAPOLIS (MINNESOTA)
  Four new skyscrapers in Minneapolis
    / Larry Millett.
    Architects: I. M. Pei,
    Ellerbe-Becket, Lohan Associates,
    and Walsh-Bishop Associates.
    INLAND ARCHITECT 1990 Jan.-Feb.,
    v.34, no.1, p.[19]-22, ill., dwg.,
    elev., model.

TALL BUILDINGS--UNITED STATES--NEW
  YORK (NEW YORK)
  Brute force and ignorance:
    Skyscraper [by] Karl Sabbagh [book
    review] / Hugh Aldersey-Williams.
    BLUEPRINT (LONDON, ENGLAND) 1990
    Feb., no.64, p.51, port.
  Delirious New York / Rem Koolhaas.
    ARCH PLUS 1990 Oct., no.105-106,
    p.58-67, ill., dwgs., photos.,
    plans, site plans, aerial photos.

TALL BUILDINGS--UNITED STATES--NEW
  YORK (NEW YORK)--CARNEGIE TOWER
  Designing the super-thin new
    buildings / James S. Russell.
    Features 6 projects for tall
    buildings in New York City,
    Chicago and Paris.
    ARCHITECTURAL RECORD 1990 Oct.,
    v.178, no.11, p.105-109,
    axonometric views, elev., models,
    photos., plans.

TALL BUILDINGS--UNITED STATES--NEW
  YORK (NEW YORK)--EQUITABLE BUILDING
  A reconsideration of the Equitable
    Building in New York / Sally Kitt
    Chappell.
    On ideologies surrounding the 1916
    zoning movement, elevator
    engineering, and management
    techniques used in the 1912-1915
    building, located at 120 S.
    Broadway (architect: E.R. Graham).
    Includes abstract.
    SOCIETY OF ARCHITECTURAL
    HISTORIANS. JOURNAL 1990 Mar.,
    v.49, no.1, p.90-95, dwg.,
    photos., refs.

TALL BUILDINGS--UNITED STATES--NEW
  YORK (NEW YORK)--INFLUENCE
  Monument 22 / Claes Caldenby.
    Develops 11 arguments for or
    against multi-storey buildings and
    uses Ralph Erskine's building
    Lilla Bommen in Gothenburg as an
    example.
    ARKITEKTUR: THE SWEDISH REVIEW OF
    ARCHITECTURE 1990 May, v.90, no.4,
    p.3-11, dwgs., elevs., models,
    photos., plans, site plans,
    isometric dwg., aerial photo.

TALL BUILDINGS--UNITED STATES--NEW
  YORK (NEW YORK)--TIMES SQUARE TOWER
  Public places for American cities:
    three projects / Rodolfo Machado.
    Includes Times Square Tower, New
    York (1984); Pershing Square, Los
    Angeles (1986); and
    Sesquicentennial Park, Houston
    (1986).
    ASSEMBLAGE 1988 June, no.6,
    p.[98]-113, axonometric views,
    dets., dwgs., elevs., model,
    photos., plans, secns., site
    plans.

TALL BUILDINGS--UNITED STATES--RACINE
  (WISCONSIN)--S.C. JOHNSON & SON
  ADMINISTRATION BUILDING
  Le gratte-ciel en verre / Frank
    Lloyd Wright.
    Excerpt from Mon autobiographie,
    by Frank Lloyd Wright, Editions
    Plon, 1955, on the Johnson Wax
    Laboratory Tower in Racine Wisc.
    English summary, p.65. Spanish
    summary, p.168.
    TECHNIQUES ET ARCHITECTURE 1990
    Aug.-Sept., no.391, p.64-65, dwg.,
    photo., plan, secn.

TALLENT, ELIZABETH
  A collector's Santa Fe / Elizabeth
    Tallent.
    Profile of 13 art galleries in
    Santa Fe specializing in Native
    American arts.
    ARCHITECTURAL DIGEST 1990 May,
    v.47, no.5, p.102-110, photos.

TALLER DE ARQUITECTURA
  L'amenagement du Vieux-port: un
    dossier [Montreal].
    Eight entries in the competition
    for the Vieux-Port area.
    Architects: Bernard Tschumi
    Architects, Berridge Lewinberg
    Greenberg, JFP & associes, Peter
    Rose, Ricardo Bofill, Taller de
    Arquitectura, Daniel Arbour &
    associes, Atelier de recherches
    urbaines appliquees, Cardinal &
                (Continued next page)

TANGE, KENZO, 1913- (CONTINUED)
Un nouveau centre culturel dans le
port de Yokohama / Francois
Daulte.
Yokohama Museum of Fine Arts.
Architect: Kenzo Tange.
L'OEIL 1990 Jan.-Feb., no.414-415,
p.36-41, dwgs., ports., photos.
Surrealistic night scene
illuminating Tokyo's new city
hall.
Building is illuminated while
under construction. Architect:
Kenzo Tange.
JAPAN ARCHITECT 1990 Mar., v.65,
no.3(395), p.4, photo.
Tange em Paris: Place d'Italie.
PROJETO 1990 Nov., no.136,
p.31-33, photos., models.

TANI, NAOKI
On the organization of the
carpenters who were under the
control of the Nakai family in the
Kan'ei Era / Naoki Tani.
Text in Japanese. Includes English
summary.
NIHON KENCHIKU GAKKAI KEIKAKUKEI
RONBUN HOKOKU SHU = JOURNAL OF
ARCHITECTURE, PLANNING AND
ENVIRONMENTAL ENGINEERING 1990
Sept., no.9(415), p.101-109,
tables, refs.

TANIGUCHI AND ASSOCIATES
Nagano Prefectural Shinano Art
Museum Higashiyama Kaii Gallery /
Yoshio Taniguchi.
Architects: Taniguchi and
Associates.
JAPAN ARCHITECT 1990 Nov.-Dec.,
v.65, no.11-12(403-404), p.67-77,
elevs., photos., plans, secns.,
site plans.
Nagano prefectural Shinano Art
Museum, Higashiyama Kaii Gallery.
Architects: Taniguchi and
Associates. English summary, p.19.
KENCHIKU BUNKA 1990 July, v.45,
no.525, p.47-56, elevs., photos.,
plans, secn., site plan.
Tokyo Sea Life Park / Yoshio
Taniguchi.
Architects: Taniguchi and
Associates.
JAPAN ARCHITECT 1990 Feb., v.65,
no.2(394), p.13-25, elev.,
photos., plans, secn., site plan,
aerial photo.
Yoshio Taniguchi / Yoshio Taniguchi.
Contents: Tokyo Sea Life Park,
design: 1985-87; construction:
1987-89 -- Genichiro Inokuma
Marugame City Modern Art Museum,
design: 1988-89; completion:
Spring 1991. Text in Japanese and
English.
GA DOCUMENT 1990 Apr., no.25,
p.[174]-183, axonometric views,
elevs., model, photos., plans,
secns.

TANIGUCHI, HIROKUNI
A study on the ways of using
furniture and household goods in
urban apartment houses in Korea /
Jae-soon Choi, Hirokuni Taniguchi.
Text in Japanese; includes English
summary.
NIHON KENCHIKU GAKKAI KEIKAKUKEI
RONBUN HOKOKU SHU = JOURNAL OF
ARCHITECTURE, PLANNING AND
(Continued next column)

TANIGUCHI, HIROKUNI (CONTINUED)
A study on the ways...(CONTINUED)
ENVIRONMENTAL ENGINEERING 1990
Nov., no.11(417), p.61-74, elevs.,
plans, tables, refs.
A survey of the actual conditions,
preservation and utilization of
outdoor stage "playhouse" in
Nagano prefecture / Yasuhiro
Yamashita, Naoji Matsumoto,
Hirokuni Taniguchi.
"A systematic study of the outdoor
stage playhouse, 1". Text in
Japanese. Includes English
summary.
NIHON KENCHIKU GAKKAI KEIKAKUKEI
RONBUN HOKOKU SHU = JOURNAL OF
ARCHITECTURE, PLANNING AND
ENVIRONMENTAL ENGINEERING 1990
Sept., no.9(415), p.39-47, graphs,
elevs., maps, photos., plans,
secn., tables.

TANIGUCHI, YOSHIO, 1937-
Nagano Prefectural Shinano Art
Museum Higashiyama Kaii Gallery /
Yoshio Taniguchi.
Architects: Taniguchi and
Associates.
JAPAN ARCHITECT 1990 Nov.-Dec.,
v.65, no.11-12(403-404), p.67-77,
elevs., photos., plans, secns.,
site plans.
Tokyo Sea Life Park / Yoshio
Taniguchi.
Architects: Taniguchi and
Associates.
JAPAN ARCHITECT 1990 Feb., v.65,
no.2(394), p.13-25, elev.,
photos., plans, secn., site plan,
aerial photo.
Yoshio Taniguchi won the 31st
Mainichi Art Prize.
Won for his latest project, Tokyo
Sea Life Park.
JAPAN ARCHITECT 1990 Mar., v.65,
no.3(395), p.4, port., photos.
Yoshio Taniguchi / Yoshio Taniguchi.
Contents: Tokyo Sea Life Park,
design: 1985-87; construction:
1987-89 -- Genichiro Inokuma
Marugame City Modern Art Museum,
design: 1988-89; completion:
Spring 1991. Text in Japanese and
English.
GA DOCUMENT 1990 Apr., no.25,
p.[174]-183, axonometric views,
elevs., model, photos., plans,
secns.

TANIMIZU, JUN
Turkey: pilgrimage to cities /
edited by Hidenobu Jinnai, Jun
Tanimizu and Cengiz Eruzun.
Survey of Turkish cities and their
architecture. Includes articles by
Hidenobu Jinnai, Jun Tanimizu and
Cengiz Eruzun. Text in Japanese
and English.
PROCESS: ARCHITECTURE 1990 Dec.,
no.93, p.[1]-168, maps, photos.,
plans.

TANKS
See also STORAGE TANKS

TANKS, WATER
See WATER TANKS

TANNER LEDDY MAYTUM STACY, ARCHITECTS
Building with blocks / Sally B.
Woodbridge.
Diamond and Jewelry Mart, San
Francisco, features glass block
walls. Architects: Tanner Leddy
Maytum Stacy, Architects.
PROGRESSIVE ARCHITECTURE 1990
Dec., v.71, no.13, p.74-75,
photos., plan.
Lessons in civility: two schools in
San Francisco exemplify the
multiple challenges of melding new
construction and existing
buildings into a single entity /
Donald J. Canty.
The Waldorf School, by Tanner
Leddy Maytum Stacy Architects; and
the San Francisco Day School, by
Simon Martin-Vegue Winkelstein
Moris.
ARCHITECTURAL RECORD 1990 Mar.,
v.178, no.3, p.84-91, elevs.,
photos., plans, secn., site plans.
Sleek house / Mayer Rus.
Industrial building converted into
a house in San Francisco's North
Beach. Archiects: Tanner Leddy
Maytum Stacy, Architects.
INTERIOR DESIGN 1990 Apr., v.61,
no.6, p.212-[217], photos., plans,
secns.

TANTRIC
See "TANTRIC" AS A SUBHEADING AFTER
SPECIFIC BUILDING TYPES OR OTHER
MAIN HEADINGS.

TANZANIA--DAR-ES-SALAAM--CITY
PLANNING--CITIZEN PARTICIPATION--
KARIAKOO
Low cost urban renewal in Tanzania:
community participation in
Dar-Es-Salaam / Sababu Kaitilla.
In the Kariakoo neighborhood.
CITIES 1990 Aug., v.7, no.3,
p.211-223, plans, tables, refs.

TANZANIA--DAR-ES-SALAAM--COMMUNITY
DEVELOPMENT--URBAN--KARIAKOO
Low cost urban renewal in Tanzania:
community participation in
Dar-Es-Salaam / Sababu Kaitilla.
In the Kariakoo neighborhood.
CITIES 1990 Aug., v.7, no.3,
p.211-223, plans, tables, refs.

TANZANIA--DAR-ES-SALAAM--URBAN
RENEWAL--KARIKOO
Low cost urban renewal in Tanzania:
community participation in
Dar-Es-Salaam / Sababu Kaitilla.
In the Kariakoo neighborhood.
CITIES 1990 Aug., v.7, no.3,
p.211-223, plans, tables, refs.

TANZANIA--DODOMA--CAPITALS (CITIES)--
ENVIRONMENTAL ASPECTS
Dodoma, new capital of Tanzania: a
case of non-sustainable
development / Nick van Vliet.
LANDSCAPE ARCHITECTURAL REVIEW
1990 Oct., v.11, no.4, p.13-18,
maps, photos., biblios.

TANZANIA--HOUSING--BIBLIOGRAPHY
Human settlements in Tanzania: an interdisciplinary bibliography / Carolyn Hannan-Andersson.
Cites 832 general references on Tanzania, 185 government publications, and 66 references on East Africa.
SWEDISH COUNCIL FOR BUILDING RESEARCH. DOCUMENT 1990, D15, [i-viii],[1]-407,

TANZANIA--NATIONAL PARKS AND RESERVES
The game of wildlife conservation: conflicts in the Serengeti / Nick van Vliet.
An ecological entity of open and wooded grasslands in northern Tanzania and southwestern Kenya. Includes French summary.
LANDSCAPE ARCHITECTURAL REVIEW 1990 Mar., v.11, no.1, p.6-12, map, photos., biblios.

TANZANIA--RURAL DEVELOPMENT--ENVIRONMENTAL ASPECTS
The game of wildlife conservation: conflicts in the Serengeti / Nick van Vliet.
An ecological entity of open and wooded grasslands in northern Tanzania and southwestern Kenya. Includes French summary.
LANDSCAPE ARCHITECTURAL REVIEW 1990 Mar., v.11, no.1, p.6-12, map, photos., biblios.

TANZANIA--SETTLEMENTS--BIBLIOGRAPHY
Human settlements in Tanzania: an interdisciplinary bibliography / Carolyn Hannan-Andersson.
Cites 832 general references on Tanzania, 185 government publications, and 66 references on East Africa.
SWEDISH COUNCIL FOR BUILDING RESEARCH. DOCUMENT 1990, D15, [i-viii],[1]-407,

TANZER, WOLFGANG
Geschaftshaus fur Hifi-und audiovisuelle Gerate, Stadtbergen (BRD).
Architects: S. Ottl, N. Helfert, W. Tanzer.
WERK, BAUEN + WOHNEN 1990 Apr., no.4, p.68, photos., plans, secns., site plan.

TAPIA, RODRIGO
Vivienda social / Rodrigo Tapia.
Several projects for the outskirts of Santiago.
ARQ 1990 Mar., no.14, p.16-31, models, maps, photos., plans, aerial photo.

TAPIES, ANTONI, 1923-
La Fondazione Tapies a Barcellona / Roser Amado, Lluis Domenech Alterations to roof and facade of building on Calle Aragon, including a sculpture by Antoni Tapies. Original architect: Lluis Domenech i Montaner. Includes English captions.
CASABELLA 1990 Dec., v.54, no.574, p.34-35, photos., plans, secn.

TARANTINO ARCHITECT
Current work.
Fourteen projects recently completed or currently on the boards by N.J. architects.
ARCHITECTURE NEW JERSEY 1990, v.26, no.2, p.9-20, axonometric views, dets., dwgs., elevs., models, photos., plans, site plans.

TARANTOLA, MARINA
Piani e progetti per Siena: una storia ragionata / Patrizia Gabellini.
Three articles on master plans for Siena. In Italian; English summaries, p.127-128.
URBANISTICA 1990 June, no.99, p.97-122, axonometric view, dwgs., elev., maps, plans, secns., site plans, refs.

TARCHYS, REBECKA
Gotland - an island in the Baltic Sea / Rebecka Tarchys.
Views of traditional buildings and related arts.
LIVING ARCHITECTURE 1990, no.9, p.110-139, photos.

TARDIEU, J.
Loire: le chevet du XIe siecle du prieure d'Ambierle / B. Carcel, J. Tardieu.
BULLETIN MONUMENTAL 1990, v.148, no.2, p.196-199, photos., plan, site plan, refs.

TARDITS, MANUEL
Douce armure: complexe sportif de Sendagaya, Tokyo, Japan / Manuel Tardits.
Architects: Maki and Associates.
TECHNIQUES ET ARCHITECTURE 1990 Dec.-1991 Jan., no.393, p.110-115, elev., photos., plan, secns., aerial photo.

TARDITS, PHILIPPE
Fins de chantier.
Contents: ZAC du Nouvelet housing complex, Orly, France; architects: Jean and Maria Deroche-- Sports clinic, Paris Ve: architects: Yves Collet, Dominique Burger-- School, Blois, France; architects: Gilbert Autret, Francois Dupleix, Reynald Eugene, Philippe Tardits.
LE MONITEUR ARCHITECTURE AMC 1990 Nov., no.16, p.13-18, elevs., photos., plans, secns.

TARR, JOEL A. TECHNOLOGY AND THE RISE OF THE NETWORKED CITY IN EUROPE AND AMERICA
The networked city: a Euro-American review [book review] / Eugene P. Moehring.
Review of: Technology and the rise of the networked city in Europe and America, ed. by Joel A. Tarr and Gabriel Dupuy, 1988.
JOURNAL OF URBAN HISTORY 1990 Nov., v.17, no.1, p.88-97, refs.

TARRAGA, MARIA LUISA
Los estucos de Roberto Michel para el Palacio de El Pardo / Maria Luisa Tarraga.
English summary, p.329.
ARCHIVO ESPANOL DE ARTE 1989 July-Sept., v.62, no.247, p.[315]-329, photos., refs.

TARRIUS, ALAIN
London Docklands: ouvriers, dockers et yuppies: une nouvelle ville internationale / Genevieve Marotel, Alain Tarrius.
French, English, German, and Spanish summaries, p.[123]-126.
LES ANNALES DE LA RECHERCHE URBAINE 1990 Mar.-Apr., no.46, p.[75]-86, map, photos., tables.

TASA, JYRKI, 1944-
Eclectic extravaganza / Richard Weston.
BePOP complex in Pori, Finland, includes hotel, shops, banks and offices. Architect: Jyrki Tasa.
ARCHITECTS' JOURNAL 1990 Nov.28, v.192, no.22, p.32-37, dets., photos., plans, secn., aerial photo.

TASKER, GEORGIA
Habitats go home: replanting "wild" areas on residential sites / Georgia Tasker.
GARDEN DESIGN 1990 Spring, v.9, no.1, p.[36-45], photos., secns., site plan.

TASKER, SID
William (Bill) White [obituary] / Sid Tasker.
RIBA JOURNAL 1990 Dec., v.97, no.12, p.85,

TASSINI, SONIA
Faustino Rodi: un architetto neoclassico nella Cremona del XVIII-XIX secolo: saggio di esplorazione / Sonia Tassini, Mariella Morandi.
English summary, p.243.
ARTE LOMBARDA 1989, no.90-91, p.162-177, elevs., photos., plans, refs.

TASSO, FRANCESCA
I Giganti e le vicende della prima scultura del Duomo di Milano / Francesca Tasso.
Probable designer: Giovannino de' Grassi. English summary p.186.
ARTE LOMBARDA 1990, no.92-93, p.55-62, dwgs., photos., refs.

TATE GALLERY--EXHIBITIONS
Rewarding walks: Richard Long revisited [exhibition review] / Giles Auty.
Three installations at the Tate Gallery until Jan.1991.
APOLLO 1990 Dec., v.132, no.346, p.399-, photos.

TATLIN, VLADIMIR EVGRAFOVICH, 1885-1953--CONGRESSES
Vladimir Tatlin: een internationaal symposium in Dusseldorf / Antje van Graevenitz.
In conjunction with an exhibition at the Kunsthalle.
ARCHIS 1990 Jan., no.1, p.4, photos.

TATSUMI LABORATORY

Special edition III: today's aspects of three public apartment houses. Features Inokodani Project, architects: Tatsumi Laboratory. Heiwacho Apartment, architects: Atsushi Ueda Atelier and Public housing, Kokubunji, architects: Gendai Keikaku Architecture & Planning Office. English summary, p.19.
KENCHIKU BUNKA 1990 Apr., v.45, no.522, p.137-164, axonometric views, charts, graphs, dwgs., elevs., models, photos., plans, secns., site plans.

TAUBER, CORNELIUS

Eine Nekropole fur Kunstler = A necropolis for artists / Cornelius Tauber.
Proposed cemetery for artists in Habichtswald, near Kassel, Germany; architect: Harry Kramer.
DAIDALOS 1990 Dec.15, no.38, p.90-93, ill., model, refs.

TAUCH, MAX

Biedermeier am Niederrhein / Max Tauch.
The Haus Rottels, in Neuss, now a part of the Clemens-Sels-Museum.
KUNST & ANTIQUITATEN 1990, no.3, p.43-47, ports., photos., refs.

TAUT, BRUNO, 1880-1938

Architetture di luce = Architectures of light / Marino Ferrari.
On glass architecture. Includes text of a letter from Paul Scheerbart to Bruno Taut on the "house of glass", dated 1914.
FRAMES, PORTE & FINESTRE 1990 July-Sept., no.28, p.68-73, photos.
Introduzione alla dissoluzione delle citta di Bruno Taut: reprint / Giovanni Klaus Koenig.
Reprint of 1920 article.
PARAMETRO 1989 Nov.-Dec., v.20, no.175, p.80-91, ill., dwgs.
Reinventing Jefim Golyscheff: lives of a minor modernist / Joan Ockman.
On the career of the Ukrainian-born artist, active in Berlin in the 1920's and the early 1930's, including contact with Gropius, Behne and Taut.
ASSEMBLAGE 1990 Apr., no.11, p.[70]-106, ill., dwgs., ports., photos., refs.

TAVANI, GIUSEPPE

L'edilizia residenziale sovvenzionata ad Ancona (1900-1940) / Renzo Petrelli, Giuseppe Tavani, Maurizio Perinetti Casoni.
STORIA URBANA 1989 Apr.-June, v.13, no.47, p.[175-197], elevs., maps, plans., secns., table, refs.

TAVERNE, ED

De bevrijding van de architectuur: wie doorbreekt de wooncocon? / Ed Taverne.
A theoretical essay on houses, with references to the work of Rietveld, Rossi, and Eisenman.
DE ARCHITECT 1990 Jan., v.21, no.1, p.18-21, ill., photos.

TAVERNE, ED (CONTINUED)

De periferie van Florence.
Feature section. Contents: La Firenze brutta, by Ed Taverne.-- Beeld en werkelijkheid van een stad en haar periferie, by Charles van den Heuvel.--De verplaatsing van een volksprobleem, by Francis Prins.
ARCHIS 1989 Sept., no.9, p.27-53, axonometric views, ill., elevs., maps, photos., plans, secns., site plans, aerial photos., refs.
La progettazione come forma di ricerca / Ed Taverne.
In Italian; English summary, p.124-125.
URBANISTICA 1990 June, no.99, p.7-14, map, photos., plan, biblio., ref.

TAVERNE, ED. CAREL WEEBER:ARCHITECT

Carel Weeber [by] Ed Taverne [book review] / Johann Van de Beek.
DE ARCHITECT 1990 June, v.21, no.6, p.65-67, dwg., photos.

TAVERNOR, ROBERT

The alternative path of modernism / Robert Tavernor.
On the one-day discussion at the University of Bath, A case for Aalto.
BUILDING DESIGN 1990 June 1, no.988, p.16, port., photo.
Palladio parade: Palladio's villas: life in the Renaissance countryside, by Paul Holberton [book review] / Robert Tavernor.
ARCHITECTS' JOURNAL 1990 Sept.19, v.192, no.12, p.87.
Rogers' new age: the Walter Nevrath Memorial Lecture: Architecture - a modern view / Robert Tavernor.
Report of a lecture given by Richard Rogers at the University of London, 6 Mar. 1990.
ARCHITECTS' JOURNAL 1990 Mar.21, v.191, no.12, p.93, port.

TAVERNS

See also BARS (EATING AND DRINKING ESTABLISHMENTS)
See also BEER CELLARS
See also BEER HALLS
See also NIGHTCLUBS
See also PUBS
See also SALOONS

TAVERNS--18TH CENTURY--CONSERVATION AND RESTORATION--UNITED STATES-- CHARLOTTESVILLE (VIRGINIA)-- WOODSTOCK HALL

Woodstock Hall B & B.
An 18th cent. tavern near Charlottesville, Va.; now a bed-and-breakfast inn.
COLONIAL HOMES 1990 Oct., v.16, no.5, p.134-[139],147,149,153, ports., photos.

TAVERNS--COLONIAL--CONSERVATION AND RESTORATION--UNITED STATES--TAPPAN (NEW YORK)--OLD '76 HOUSE

In the spirit of '76: Tappan, New York's Old '76 House is once again a quiet country tavern / Betsy Dance.
HISTORIC PRESERVATION 1990 May-June, v.42, no.3, p.52-55, photos.

TAX INCENTIVES--UNITED STATES-- CONNECTICUT

The Preservation Tax Incentives Program in Connecticut: an overview and update / Linda Spencer.
CONNECTICUT PRESERVATION NEWS 1990 Jan.-Feb., v.13, no.1, p.10-11,

TAYEB, S.

Japan Tower, Paris La Defense / S. Tayeb.
Architects: K. Kurokawa, M. Mussche.
LE MUR VIVANT 1990, no.95, p.51-55, elev., models, plans, isometric dwgs.

TAYLOR, ANDREW

Hitting a highnote / Dan Cruickshank.
Patel and Taylor's scheme for a choral center in the Rhondda Valley, Wales.
ARCHITECTS' JOURNAL 1990 Oct.24, v.192, no.17, p.26-27, axonometric view, elevs., plan, secn.
Scarpa and the mothers of invention / John Welsh.
Barn in North Wales converted into house for architect's parents. Architects: Andrew Taylor, Pankaj Patel.
BUILDING DESIGN 1990 Mar.2, no.975, p.12, axonometric view, det., elevs., plans, site plan.
Under sail.
Goodge Place offices of the engineering firm, Atelier One, London. Architects: Pankaj Patel, Andrew Taylor.
DESIGNERS' JOURNAL 1990 Sept., no.60, p.6, photos.

TAYLOR, ANNE

KB topics: architecture and children / Anne Taylor ...et al.
KENCHIKU BUNKA 1990 Aug., v.45, no.526, p.139-148, ill., ports., photos.

TAYLOR, BRIAN BRACE

Hotels [editorial] / Brian Brace Taylor.
Introduction to theme of issue. Includes "Misplaced values", by Jimmy Lin and "Lead us not", by Romi Khosla. Eight articles indexed separately.
MIMAR: ARCHITECTURE IN DEVELOPMENT 1990 Sept., v.10, no.3(36), p.7, ill., photos.
Kuwait City waterfront development / Brian Brace Taylor.
Completed in 1988. Consultants: Ghazi Sultan, architect, Kuwait Engineers Office; Sasaki Associates, Boston.
MIMAR: ARCHITECTURE IN DEVELOPMENT 1990 Mar., v.10, no.1(34), p.[12]-20,cover, map, photos., plans, secns., site plans.
Ramses Wissa Wassef Museum / Brian Brace Taylor.
On the outskirts of Cairo. Addition completed in 1989 (architect: Badie Habib Gorgy). Original architect: Ramses Wissa Wassef.
MIMAR: ARCHITECTURE IN DEVELOPMENT 1990 June, v.10, no.2(35), p.34-39, photos., plan, secns.

TAYLOR, ROBERT, SIR, 1714-1788
Lord Shelburne's 'costly fabrick': Scheemakers, Roubiliac and Taylor as rivals / Malcolm Baker.
"The monument by Peter Scheemakers to Henry Petty, 1st Earl of Shelburne at High Wycombe is among the largest and most costly monuments to have been erected in an English parish church in the 18th century."
BURLINGTON MAGAZINE 1990 Dec., v.132, no.1053, p.841-848, ill., dwg., photos., refs.

TAYLOR, RON
Building evaluations: checking it out / Ron Taylor.
CANADIAN ARCHITECT 1990 Oct., v.35, no.10, p.43-44, table.

TAYLOR, RUSSELL
Revealing masons' mystery / Russell Taylor.
Open wall stone staircase construction, and a discussion of its 17th cent. origins in British buildings.
ARCHITECTS' JOURNAL 1990 Sept.26, v.192, no.13, p.34-43, dets., diagrs., elevs., photos., plans, secns., refs.

TAYLOR, S. WATTS
Moving history: the struggle over Virginia must not end in "backsliding" / S. Watts Taylor.
Lockwood, Robert E. Lee's headquarters, has been sold to Media General which wants to move the house and this is being opposed.
PRESERVATION NEWS 1990 June, v.30, no.6, p.5, port., photo.

TAZZI, PIER LUIGI
Arte versus architettura = Art versus architecture / Pier Luigi Tazzi.
Subtitle: Three projects for the French pavilion at the Venice Biennale. Architects: Jean Nouvel, Christian de Portzamparc, and Philippe Starck.
OTTAGONO 1990 Sept., no.96, p.7-18, elevs., models, photos., plans.

TCHERIKOVER, ANAT
Aulnay-de-Saintonge and high romanesque figure sculpture in Aquitane / Anat Tcherikover.
BRITISH ARCHAEOLOGICAL ASSOCIATION. JOURNAL 1990, v.143, p.[77]-94, pl.12-17, map, photos., refs.
The chevet of Saint-Jouin-de-Marnes / Anat Tcherikover.
A stylistic analysis that places this chevet within the context of early 12th-cent. sculpture and architecture in Poitou.
GESTA 1989, v.28, no.2, p.147-164, dets., map, photos., plans, refs.
Concerning Angouleme, riders and the art of the Gregorian reform / Anat Tcherikover.
ART HISTORY 1990 Dec., v.13, no.4, p.[425]-457, dets., photos., refs.

TEA GARDENS--JAPAN--NAGOYA--SHIROTORI TEA HOUSE
Motoo Yoshimura: creation of contemporary Japanese gardens / edited by Motoo Yoshimura and Dina Yando Yoshimura.
Contents: Essay: Construction of Japanese landscape gardens in the age of urbanization / Motoo Yoshimura --Works: Shirotori Park --Shirotori Tea House garden --Fukuda house garden, Kyoto --Yoshida Steak House garden --Kyoto Historical Museum garden --Yamamoto Tea Shop & garden, Shigaraki --World Orchid Exhibition grounds, Tokyo --Katsurazaka pedestrian footpath, Kyoto --Osaka International Exposition Memorial Park. Landscape architect: Motto Yoshimura. Text in Japanese and English.
PROCESS: ARCHITECTURE 1990 Sept., no.91, p.[1]-154, dwgs., port., photos., plans, secns., site plans, aerial photos.

TEA GARDENS--JAPAN--SHIGARAKI--YAMAMOTO TEA SHOP GARDEN
Motoo Yoshimura: creation of contemporary Japanese gardens / edited by Motoo Yoshimura and Dina Yando Yoshimura.
Contents: Essay: Construction of Japanese landscape gardens in the age of urbanization / Motoo Yoshimura --Works: Shirotori Park --Shirotori Tea House garden --Fukuda house garden, Kyoto --Yoshida Steak House garden --Kyoto Historical Museum garden --Yamamoto Tea Shop & garden, Shigaraki --World Orchid Exhibition grounds, Tokyo --Katsurazaka pedestrian footpath, Kyoto --Osaka International Exposition Memorial Park. Landscape architect: Motto Yoshimura. Text in Japanese and English.
PROCESS: ARCHITECTURE 1990 Sept., no.91, p.[1]-154, dwgs., port., photos., plans, secns., site plans, aerial photos.

TEA HOUSES
See also CHASHITSU
See also TEA ROOMS

TEA HOUSES--JAPAN--AMAMI OSHIMA--SHIGEMURA TEA HOUSE
A Japanese tea house from silent beginnings / Ray Don Tilley.
Project to be built on a Japanese island. Architect: Gerlinde Leiding.
TEXAS ARCHITECT 1990 July-Aug., v.40, no.4, p.58, models, site plan.

TEA HOUSES--JAPAN--YAMANASHI--CHATEI SOSHIN-AN
Yamanashi Prefectural Museum of Literature + Chatei Soshin-an of Yamanashi Arts Park.
Museum includes library and lecture hall. Chatei Soshin-an, tea ceremony house named by Ryuta Iida, haiku poet. Architects: Ohune / Ehira Architects & Associates. English summary, p.17.
(Continued next column)

TEA HOUSES--JAPAN--YAMANASHI--CHATEI SOSHIN-AN (CONTINUED)
Yamanashi Prefectural...(CONTINUED)
KENCHIKU BUNKA 1990 Jan., v.45, no.519, p.87-96, dets., elevs., photos., plans, secns., site plan, aerial photo.

TEA ROOMS
See also CHASHITSU
See also TEA HOUSES

TEA ROOMS--19TH CENTURY--ALTERATIONS AND ADDITIONS--SCOTLAND--GLASGOW--ARGYLE STREET TEA ROOMS
The redevelopment of the Argyle Street Tea Rooms / Jonathan Kinghorn.
Refurbishment of exterior and alteration of interior of Mackintosh building in Glasgeow, built in 1897.
CHARLES RENNIE MACKINTOSH SOCIETY. NEWSLETTER 1990 Autumn, no.54, p.10-13, photo.

TEACHING
See "STUDY AND TEACHING" AS A SUBHEADING AFTER MAIN HEADINGS.

TEAM (FIRM)
New wing of the National Gallery of Modern Art, New Delhi.
To be completed in 1996. Architects: TEAM, New Delhi.
MIMAR: ARCHITECTURE IN DEVELOPMENT 1990 June, v.10, no.2(35), p.30-33, models, photos., plans, secn., site plan.

TEAM FOUR
Scrap value / Martin Pawley.
Examples of minimal architecture from the 1960s and 1970s by Norman Foster and Richard Rogers; principally the Reliance Controls factory at Swindon (1965), when both were part of the firm Team Four.
ARCHITECTS' JOURNAL 1990 Mar.21, v.191, no.12, p.26-31, axonometric views, dets., dwgs., photos., secn., sketch.

TEAM HOU
Houston design portfolio: slow recovery.
Sesquicentennial Park (Team HOU); Caldwell house (Natalye Appel); Court at Museums Gate (Josiah Baker); Gilliland house (Peter Jay Zweig Architects); Finnell house (Wittenberg Partnership); and St. Mary's Episcopal Church (Gerald Moorhead).
ARCHITECTURE: THE AIA JOURNAL 1990 Apr., v.79, no.4, p.54-73, axonometric views, ill., elev., photos., plans, secns., site plans.
Houston Park phased into reality / Peter Papademetriou.
Phase I of Sesquicentennial Park completed. Architects: Team HOU.
PROGRESSIVE ARCHITECTURE 1990 Feb., v.71, no.2, p.24, photo.

TECHNICIANS, ARCHITECTURAL
See ARCHITECTURAL TECHNICIANS

TECHNISCHE HOGESCHOOL DELFT
Staalprijs voor afstudeeontwerp
dansopleiding: resultaten
twee-fasenopleiding van hoog
niveau / Joop Niesten.
Student projects at the TU-Delft
for the Dansacademie Amsterdam.
DE ARCHITECT 1989 Nov., v.20,
no.11, p.143-147, axonometric
view, dets., elev., model, plans,
secn.

TECHNISCHE HOGESCHOOL DELFT. AFDELING
BOUKUNDE
Automatisierung der
Architekturausbildung durch
Computerisierung der Architektur:
Architectural Basics in
Computerized Design Education
(ABCDE) at the Faculty of
Architecture, Delft University of
Technology / A. Tzonis, A.
Koutamanis.
ARCHITHESE 1990 May-June, v.20,
no.3, p.70-72, refs.

TECHNISCHE HOGESCHOOL DELFT. AFDELING
BOUWKUNDE--CONGRESSES
Parenthese zum "Kritischen
Regionalismus": zum
internationalen Seminar "Context
and Modernity" and der
Architekturschule der TU Delft
12.-15. Juni, 1990 / Richard
Ingersoll.
ARCHITHESE 1990 July-Aug., v.20,
no.4, p.71-73,

TECHNISCHE HOOGESCHOOL DELFT--
CONGRESSES
Afscheid Koolhaas in teken van moed
en wanhoop: symposium in Delft /
Arthur Wortmann.
Report on conference held by the
Technische Universiteit Delft, 27
Apr.1990, entitled "Hoe modern is
de Nederlandse architectuur?"
Issue includes one article
(separately indexed) from the
symposium.
ARCHIS 1990 June, no.6, p.6-7,
Het banier "Kritisch regionalisme"
gestreken: Symposium context and
modernity in Delft.
Report on symposium held 12-15
June 1990 at the Faculteit der
Bouwkunde, TU.
ARCHIS 1990 July, no.7, p.3-4,
ports.

TECHNISCHE UNIVERSITAT DRESDEN.
WISSENSCHAFTSBEREICH
LANDSCHAFTSARCHITEKTUR UND STADTEBAU
Wie studieren Landschaftsarchitekten
in der DDR? / Harald Linke.
Landscape architecture studies in
Dresden. Includes English summary.
GARTEN UND LANDSCHAFT 1990, v.100,
no.2, p.41-42,

TECHNISCHE UNIVERSITAT GRAZ. INSTITUT
FUR LANDWIRTSCHAFTLICHES BAUWESEN
UND LANDLICHES SIEDLUNGSWESEN
Siedlung bei Graz.
Housing from an old factory.
Architects: Institut fur
Landwirtschaftliches Bauwesen und
Siedlungswesen der TU Graz.
Includes English summary.
BAUMEISTER 1990 July, v.87, no.7,
p.36-39, photos., plans, secns.,
site plans.

TECHNISCHE UNIVERSITAT MUNCHEN--
EXHIBITIONS
Eine Fleissarbeit ohne Biss: zur
Wanderausstellung "Stadt und
Topographie der Munchner TU"
[exhibition review] / Wolfgang
Jean Stock.
Exhibition organized by Haus der
Bayerischen Geschichte and shown
in Munich, Coburg and 14 other
cities.
BAUWELT 1990 July 6, v.81, no.25,
p.1273-1274, photo., engrs.

TECHNISHCE HOGESCHOOL DELFT--
CONGRESSES
Op de vleugels van VINEX:
Ontwerpdagen en Symposium van
55-jarige BNS.
Report on a Nov. symposium: Tussen
stad en stedebouw: ontwerpen og
weg naar 2015. Cosponsors: Bond
van Nederlandse Stedebouwkundigen
(BNS) and Faculteit Bouwkunde van
de TU Delft.
ARCHIS 1990 Dec., no.12, p.6-7,
ref.

TECHNOLOGY AND ARCHITECTURE
See ARCHITECTURE AND TECHNOLOGY

TECHNOLOGY AND CITY PLANNING
See CITY PLANNING AND TECHNOLOGY

TECHNOLOGY AND INTERIOR DESIGN
See INTERIOR DESIGN AND TECHNOLOGY

TECHNOLOGY AND LANDSCAPE ARCHITECTURE
See LANDSCAPE ARCHITECTURE AND
TECHNOLOGY

TECTON
Arquitecto: Berthold Lubetkin.
Seven projects in England, built
1932-1938.
ARQUITECTURA 1990 Jan.-Feb., v.72,
no.282, p.[79]-103, axonometric
view, photos., plans, secns., site
plan.
La espiral y la cariatide: Berthold
Lubetkin = The spiral and the
caryatid: Berthold Lubetkin / Juan
M. Otxotorena.
ARQUITECTURA 1990 Jan.-Feb., v.72,
no.282, p.64-78, dwgs., ports.,
plans, secns., biblios.

TECTONICS
Rappel a l'ordre: the case for the
tectonic / Kenneth Frampton.
Form is discussed with respect to
"the current tendency to reduce
architecture to scenography".
ARCHITECTURAL DESIGN 1990, v.60,
no.3-4, p.19-25, axonometric
views, dwgs., sketches, refs.

TECTUS (FIRM)
A break with tradition / Richard
Wilcock.
Two London museum restaurants
designed by Tectus.
RIBA JOURNAL 1990 June, v.97,
no.6, p.57-58,60-61, photos.,
plans.

TED CULLINAN ARCHITECTS
Special report: business parks.
Theme issue on British office
parks including Chiswick Park,
Gunnersbury, Stockley Park,
London, and Bedfont Lakes,
Brentford and Chiswick.
BUILDING DESIGN 1990 July, suppl.,
p.2-22, axonometric views, dwgs.,
elevs., models, photos., plans,
secns., site plans.

TEDESCO, TOMMASO
L'ultima colonna = The last column /
Paolo Spada.
On the Capo Colonna archaeological
park and visitor center, Crotone,
Italy. Architects: Paolo Spada,
Italo Insolera, Tommaso Tedesco.
SPAZIO E SOCIETA 1990 Apr.-June,
v.13, no.50, p.112-119, maps,
photos., aerial photo.

TEGETHOFF, WOLF
Le musee imaginaire: la Neue
Sammlungen di Monaco, ovvero il
design invisibile = Le musee
imaginaire: the Munich Neue
Sammlungen or invisible design /
Wolf Tegethoff.
OTTAGONO 1990 June, no.95,
p.64-77, photos., refs.

TEGNESTUEN KVISTEN
Nykredits arkitekturpris.
On the Danish award given on
Sept.27, 1989, and commentary on
works by Poul Ingemann and
Tegnestuen Kvisten.
ARKITEKTEN 1989 Nov.28, v.91,
no.21, p.538-539, dwg., photos.

TEGNESTUEN MEJERIET
Tegnestuen Mejeriet / Leif Leer
Sorensen.
Projects by the Kolding firm,
chiefly renovation along Slotsgade
and including the A.L.Passagen,
Sydbank, Loveapoteket pharmacy,
and Town Hall council hall.
Includes English and German
summaries.
ARKITEKTUR DK 1990, v.34, no.8,
p.394-404, elevs., models,
photos., plans, site plan,
isometric dwg.

TEGNESTUEN PLAN 1
Byggesystemer til glastilbygninger /
Esben Larsen.
Report on an Oct.1989 idea
competition for modular glass sun
rooms for an apartment house.
First prize: Tegnestuen Plan 1.
Second prize: KHR A/S.
ARKITEKTEN 1990 Apr., v.92, no.4,
p.A74-A76, axonometric views,
dets., secn.

TEGNESTUEN THURE NIELSEN & RUBOW
Boliger og institutioner:
konkurrence i gladsaxe.
Report on a Nov.1989 housing
competition for 90 units. The
invited architects included
Tegnestuen Thure Nielsen & Rubow.
Cosponsor: Danske Arkitekters
Landsforbund.
ARKITEKTEN 1990 June, v.92, no.8,
p.258-263, axonometric views,
dwgs., elevs., model, photos.,
plans, secns., site plans.

TEGNESTUEN VANDKUNSTEN
Arkitektur pa NordForm / Kim
Dirckinck-Holmfeld, Lard Nevald.
Model town houses for the summer
1990 exhibit in Malmo, by
Tegnestuen Vandkunsten, Gudrun
Molden and Per Hojgaard, Ori Merom
and Peter Hesselgren, Kari Kousma
and Esko Valkama, and Gudmundur
Jonsson.
ARKITEKTEN 1990 Nov., v.92, no.17,
p.540-545, photos., model, plans,
secns.
Boligbyggeri i vandret og lodret
bevaegelse / Lasse Freisleben.
The Garvergarden apartment complex
in Copenhagen. Architect:
Tognestuen Vandkunsten.
ARKITEKTEN 1989 Dec.12, v.91,
no.22, p.A530-A533, photos.,
aerial photos.
Den danske pavillon i Sevilla.
Competition entries by KHR; Tage
Lyneborg; Henning Larsens
Tegnestue; Tegnestuen Vandkunsten;
Arkitektfirmaet Kjaer & Richter.
ARKITEKTEN 1990 Jan., v.92, no.1,
p.20-28, axonometric views, dwgs.,
elevs., models, plans, secns.,
sketches.
Pays Scandinaves: une qualite
d'echanges.
Features Tinggarden 2, Herfolge.
Architects: Tegnestuen
Vandkunsten. English summary,
p.180.
ARCHITECTURE INTERIEURE CREE 1990
June-July, no.237, p.124-127,
photos.
Tegnestuen Vandkunsten:
Wohnungsbauten des danischen Buros
1985-1990 / Oliver G. Hamm.
DEUTSCHE BAUZEITUNG 1990 Aug.,
v.124, no.8, p.111-114, dwgs.,
elevs., photos., plans.

TEGNESTUEN VOLDEN
Torsted vest - en ny og anderledes
bydel / Ebbe Nielsen, Torben Gade.
Plans for a large housing
development in Horsens, Denmark,
including proposals by Holsting og
Engelund, Tegnestuen Volden, and
Anna Maria Indrio & Ass.
ARKITEKTEN 1990 June, v.92, no.8,
p.264-267, dwgs., elevs., plans,
secns., site plans.

TEICHOLZ, ERIC
CAFM: It's poised for take-off /
Eric Teicholz.
Computer-aided facilities
management. Includes results of
CAFM user survey.
FACILITIES DESIGN & MANAGEMENT
1989 Aug., v.8, no.7, p.62-67,
graphs, tables.

TEICHOLZ, ERIC (CONTINUED)
Computers: animation and rendering /
Eric Teicholz.
PROGRESSIVE ARCHITECTURE 1990
Feb., v.71, no.2, p.61.
Computers: approaches to integration
/ Eric Teicholz.
Focus on approaches by two major
architectural vendors, Autodesk
and Intergraph.
PROGRESSIVE ARCHITECTURE 1990 May,
v.71, no.5, p.61.
Computers: the architect of the
Capitol / Eric Teicholz.
On the use of CAD and the
automation of facility management
at the AOC.
PROGRESSIVE ARCHITECTURE 1990
Aug., v.71, no.8, p.62.

TEIXIDOR FELIP, CARLOS
Urbanizacion de la avenida Rio de
Janeiro de Barcelona: P. Bardaji y
C. Teixidor, arquitectos.
Text in Spanish and English.
ON DISENO 1990, no.116, p.124-133,
photos., site plan.

TEJA BACH, FRIEDRICH
Brancusi el estudio como modelo y
metafora de la ciudad = Brancusi:
the studio as model and metaphor
of the city / Friedrich Teja Bach.
QUADERNS D'ARQUITECTURA I
URBANISME 1989 Oct.-Dec., no.183,
p.[33]-49, photos.

TEJEDA, CARLOS
The International City Design
Competition / Jeffrey E. Ollswang.
Sponsored by the University of
Wisconsin, Milwaukee. Contents:
Incremental utopias, by Allan B.
Jacobs; Cities of culture, cities
of places, by Carlos Tejeda; let
Milwaukee be Milwaukee, by Cynthia
Weese; Solutions in search of a
problem, by Amos Rapoport; and
Places are not impositions, by
William Turnbull, Jr.
PLACES 1990 Winter, v.6, no.2,
p.32-47, axonometric views, dwgs.,
map, photos., plans, site plans,
aerial photo., refs.

TEKNOLOGISK INSTITUT (DENMARK)--
CONGRESSES
En baeredygtig fremtid / Lone
Sigbrand.
Report on an energy conference
held in June 1989 by the
Teknologisk Institut.
ARKITEKTEN 1989 Dec.22, v.91,
no.23, p.617-619, ill.

TELAMONES
See CARYATIDS

TELBANY, M. M. M. EL
Transfer rates in single-sided
ventilation / M.R.
Mokhtarzadeh-Dehghan, M.M.M. El
Telbany, A.J. Reynolds.
BUILDING AND ENVIRONMENT 1990,
v.25, no.2, p.155-161, diagrs.,
tables, refs.

TELECOMMUNICATION SYSTEMS
Access floors: a way to handle the
cabling mess.
ARCHITECTURAL RECORD 1990 Sept.,
v.178, no.10, p.157-159,203,
dwgs., photos.
Down to the wire:
telecommunications: AT&T Software
Lab, Menlo Park, California /
Karin Tetlow.
Architect: George W. Famous.
ARCHITECTURE: THE MAGAZINE OF THE
AMERICAN INSTITUTE OF ARCHITECTS
1990 May, v.79, no.5, p.119-122,
photos., plans.
La pianificazione invisibile = The
invisible planning / Giorgio
Trebbi.
Telecommunication planning,
particularly in Milan.
PARAMETRO 1990 Jan.-Feb., no.176,
p.12-13, maps.
Picture perfect / Paula Rice
Jackson.
Features video-conference
conference room designed by
representatives from the Houston
offices of Gensler and Associates,
Architects.
INTERIORS 1990 Nov., v.150, no.4,
p.38-43, photos.

TELECOMMUNICATIONS BUILDINGS
See also COMMUNICATIONS TOWERS
See also RADIO STATIONS
See also RELAY STATIONS
See also SATELLITE TRACKING STATIONS
See also TELEPHONE BUILDINGS
See also TELEVISION STATIONS

TELECOMMUNICATIONS BUILDINGS--
ENGLAND--LONDON--BBC HEADQUARTERS
Mixed media [new BBC headquarters,
London] / Robert Cowan.
White City site for BBC corporate
headquarters. Architects for first
phase: Scott Brownrigg and Turner;
architects for phases two and
three: RHWL in competition with
RMJM and BDP.
ARCHITECTS' JOURNAL 1990 Jan.24,
v.191, no.4, p.30-31, elevs., site
plan, sketches.

TELECOMMUNICATIONS BUILDINGS--FRANCE--
PARIS--DIRECTION GENERALE DES
TELECOMMUNICATIONS
Direction Generale des
Telecommunications Paris.
Located at 6, place d'Alleray, in
the 15th arr. Architect: P.
Vigneron.
LE MUR VIVANT 1990, no.95,
p.66-69, photos., plans, secn.

TELECOMMUNICATIONS BUILDINGS--FRANCE--
VILLEPRINTE--FRANCE TELECOM
Autocommutateur pour France Telecom.
Telecommunications building,
Villepinte. Architects: Pierre
Bolze, Simon Rodriguez-Pages,
Herve Bleton. English summary,
p.101; Spanish summary, p.172.
TECHNIQUES ET ARCHITECTURE 1990
Oct.-Nov., no.392, p.101, dwg.,
plan, secn., site plan.

TELECOMMUNICATIONS BUILDINGS--GERMANY
(WEST)--ROSENHEIM
Neubau fur den Post- und
Fernmeldedienst, Rosenheim.
Architects: Oberpostdirektion
Munchen, Heinz Ludwig Sopper,
Heinrich Winkler.
BAUWELT 1990 Mar.16, v.81, no.11,
p.466, photos.
Post- und Fernmeldeamt in Rosenheim.
Architects: Oberpostdirektion
Munchen, H.L. Sopper, H. Winkler,
W. Weinberg, F. Bauer.
DEUTSCHE BAUZEITSCHRIFT 1990 Oct.,
v.38, no.10, p.1369-1377, dets.,
photos., plan, secn., site plans.

TELEPHONE BOOTHS--GREAT BRITAIN
Britain's phone kiosks / Howard
Mansfield.
Campaign to save Britain's red
telephone booths from replacement
by modern designs. Designer of the
original boxes: Sir Giles Gilbert
Scott.
PLACES 1990 Winter, v.6, no.2,
p.7-9, photos.

TELEPHONE BOOTHS--SWITZERLAND--TOBTEL
90
"Dank dra-- lut a!" neue
Telefonkabinen in der Schweiz.
Designer: Wolfram Elwert.
DEUTSCHE BAUZEITUNG 1990 Dec.,
v.124, no.12, p.88-89, det., dwg.,
photos.

TELEPHONE BOXES
See TELEPHONE BOOTHS

TELEPHONE BUILDINGS--ALTERATIONS AND
ADDITIONS--PORTUGAL--MAIA
Ampliacio d'una central telefonica =
Addition to a telephone exchange.
Located in Maia, Portugal.
Architect: Joao Alvaro Rocha.
QUADERNS D'ARQUITECTURA I
URBANISME 1988 July-Sept., no.178,
p.70-75, elev., photos., plan.

TELEPHONE BUILDINGS--ALTERATIONS AND
ADDITIONS--UNITED STATES--OKLAHOMA
CITY (OKLAHOMA)--SOUTHWESTERN BELL
Communications tone / Karin Tetlow.
Features interiors of renovated
Southwestern Bell's Communications
Center, Oklahoma City, OK.
Architects: HTB.
INTERIORS 1990 Nov., v.150, no.4,
p.52-[55], photos., plan.

TELEPHONE BUILDINGS--GERMANY (WEST)--
STUTTGART--OVST
Anbau an eine OVST in Stuttgart.
Architects: Arno Lederer, Jorunn
Ragnarsdottir. Includes English
summary.
BAUMEISTER 1990 May, v.87, no.5,
p.46-49, elevs., photos., plans,
site plans

TELEPHONE BUILDINGS--SPAIN--BARCELONA
Cuerpos enfrentados: edificio para
oficinas y central telefonica =
Bodies in confrontation.
Located in Barcelona, near the
Calle Juan de Austria, the
buildings are connected by a
"bridge." Architects: Jaume Bach,
Gabriel Mora. English text, p.87.
A & V 1990, no.22, p.62-64,
elevs., models, plans, secns.,
site plans.

TELEPHONE BUILDINGS--UNITED STATES--
ILLINOIS--ILLINOIS BELL TELEPHONE
Switching & changing / Michael J. P.
Smith.
Survey of buildings for Illinois
Bell Telephone (IBT) over 70
years, including several by
Holabird & Root and Holabird and
Roche.
INLAND ARCHITECT 1990 Nov.-Dec.,
v.34, no.6, p.42-47, dwg., photos.

TELEPHONE BUILDINGS--UNITED STATES--
LINCOLNSHIRE (ILLINOIS)--ILLINOIS
BELL TELEPHONE REMOTE SWITCHING UNIT
P/A Portfolio: the Chicago School:
today's curriculum / Philip
Arcidi.
Features two projects: Municipal
Fueling Facility, Glenview, Ill.,
architects: Lubotsky Metter
Worthington & Law; Illinois Bell
Telephone Remote Switching Unit,
Lincolnshire, Ill., architects:
Holabird and Root.
PROGRESSIVE ARCHITECTURE 1990
Feb., v.71, no.2, p.112-115,
photos., plan, site plan.

TELEVISION BROADCASTING
Catering for charity [review] / Tom
Woolley.
"Raising the roof", television
program aired on the BBC showed
volunteers constructing two
timber-framed houses in three days
in York, Pa.
ARCHITECTS' JOURNAL 1990
Aug.22-29, v.192, no.7-8, p.71,
ports.
Down to earth: Omnibus: Building for
a new age: a Romanian story
[review] / Sherban Cantacuzino.
Television program aired on the
BBC on 12 Oct. 1990.
ARCHITECTS' JOURNAL 1990 Oct.24,
v.192, no.17, p.83, port., photo.
Paternoster pranks: Signals: let the
people choose [review] / Martin
Pawley.
Review of television program
broadcast on Channel Four (U.K.)
28 Mar. 1990.
ARCHITECTS' JOURNAL 1990 Apr.11,
v.191, no.15, p.79-80, ill.,
ports.
Renaissance man: Designs on Europe
[review] / David Jenkins.
Review of a BBC series of six
profiles of British and European
architects, beginning 4 Aug. 1990.
First program on Michael Hopkins.
ARCHITECTS' JOURNAL 1990 Aug.15,
v.192, no.7, p.64, photo.
Satellite signal receiving dishes /
Tony Michael.
Planning policies for placement of
satellite dishes.
THE PLANNER 1990 Feb.2, v.76,
no.4, p.13-17, diagrs., photo.,
secn., tables.
Spaghetti brainstorm: Spaghetti
Junction Project [review] / Robert
Cowan.
Review of television broadcast on
"The Late Show" 13 June 1990 on
scheme commissioned by the BBC for
ideas on improving "the urban
wasteland under, over, and around
Spaghetti Junction in the West
Midlands".
ARCHITECTS' JOURNAL 1990 June 27,
(Continued next column)

TELEVISION BROADCASTING (CONTINUED)
Spaghetti brainstorm:...(CONTINUED)
v.191, no.26, p.71,73, dwg.,
sketch.
Spoiled by impatience: The Late
Show: Terminal [review] / Martin
Pawley.
The Late Show, a BBC arts program,
aired "Terminal", about Foster
Associates' Stansted Airport
building, on 5 Sept.1990.
ARCHITECTS' JOURNAL 1990 Sept.19,
v.192, no.12, p.86,

TELEVISION BROADCASTING STUDIOS
See BROADCASTING STUDIOS

TELEVISION RELAY SYSTEMS
See RELAY STATIONS

TELEVISION STATIONS--ENGLAND--LONDON--
INDEPENDENT TELEVISION NEWS
Foster is taking to the airwaves.
Norman Foster's ITN building,
London.
ARCHITECTS' JOURNAL 1990 June 27,
v.191, no.26, p.15, dwg., photos.,
plan, secn.
News knight [ITN headquarters] /
Martin Spring.
The Independent Television News
offices, 200 Grays Inn Rd., London
WC1. Architect: Foster Associates.
Engineers: Ove Arup & Partners.
BUILDING 1990 July 13, v.255,
no.28, p.22-23, photos.

TELEVISION STATIONS--ENGLAND--LONDON--
TV-AM
Special feature: Terry Farrell &
Company.
Contents: Editor's introduction.--
Statement for this special
feature, by Terry Farrell.--Essay:
On Terry Farrell, by Rowan
Moore.--Works: Tobacco Dock,
Shopping village, London.--Comyn
Ching Triangle, urban project.--
Henley Royal Regatta
headquarters.--TV-am
headquarters.--Midland Bank &
offices.--Embankment Place, urban
project.--Alban Gate, offices &
housing.--Vauxhall Cross,
government offices.--The South
Bank.--Hungerford Bridge walkway
project.--Brief history. Text in
Japanese and English.
ARCHITECTURE AND URBANISM 1989
Dec., no.12(231), p.[37]-132,
port., elevs., models, photos.,
plans, secns., site plans.

TELEVISION STATIONS--FRANCE--
CLERMONT-FERRAND--MAISON DU CABLE
Maison du cable, Clermont-Ferrand.
Cable television station.
Architect: Bernard Desmoulin.
English summary, p.111 Spanish
summary, p.173.
TECHNIQUES ET ARCHITECTURE 1990
Oct.-Nov., no.392, p.110-111,
dwg., photos., plan.

TELEVISION STATIONS--FRANCE--PARIS--
CANAL + HEADQUARTERS
Canal + Headquarters.
Administrative offices and
audio-visual production facilities
for Paris television station.
Architects: Richard Meier and
Partners.
PROGRESSIVE ARCHITECTURE 1990
Jan., v.71, no.1, p.92-93, models,
plans, secn., site plan.

TELEVISION STATIONS--SPAIN--SEVILLE
Alhambra meets Zonnestraal / Peter
Buchanan.
Television studios, Seville.
Architect: Gonzalo Diaz Recasens.
ARCHITECTURAL REVIEW 1990 Nov.,
v.188, no.1125, p.58-63, photos.,
plans, secns.

TELEVISION STATIONS--SPAIN--SEVILLE--
TELEVISION ANDALUZA
Gathering establishments.
Part of a special feature on
Spanish contemporary architecture.
Contents: Palau de la Musica
Catalana, by Oscar Tusquets
Blanca, Carlos M. Diaz, Lluis
Clotet, Ignacio Paricio --
Television Andaluza, by Gonzalo
Diaz-Y. Recasens --Banco de
Espana, Jaen, by Rafael Moneo --
Almacenes Simon, by Lluis Clotet,
Ignacio Paricio --Mercado
Vilaseca-Salou, by Carlos Ferrater
Lambarri, Jose Luis Canosa --
Pabellon Rius i Taulet, by Pep
Bonet --Velodromo de Horta, by
Esteban Bonell, Francesc Rius --
Brief histories --Views through
the Camera's Finder, by Hisao
Suzuki. Text in Japanese.
SPACE DESIGN 1990 May, no.308,
p.93-131, dets., ports., elevs.,
model, photos., plans, secns.,
site plan, sketch, isometric dwg.

TELEVISION STATIONS--UNITED STATES--
NEW YORK (NEW YORK)--ABC
ABC phase II, office, studio
building, New York, New York,
1984-86.
Architects: Kohn Pedersen Fox
Associates; partner in charge:
Sheldon Fox.
PROCESS: ARCHITECTURE 1989 Nov.,
no.86, p.44-45, axonometric view,
elev., photos.
Television romance / Victoria
Geibel.
New York Buildings for American
Broadcasting Co. designed by Kohn
Pedersen Fox Associates.
ARCHITECTURE: THE AIA JOURNAL 1990
Dec., v.79, no.12, p.56-[59],
models, photos., plans, site
plans.

TELEVISION STATIONS--VALENCIA--
TELEVISIO VALENCIANA
La arquitectura de Vetges Tu:
Mediterrania = The architecture of
Vetges Tu: Mediterrania.
Most of issue devoted to works by
this Spanish firm. Contents:
Jardin del Turia, Valencia;
Televisio Valenciana; cementerio
de Tavernes de la Valldigna;
Centro escolar publico en Port de
Sagunt; viviendas en quart de
Poblet; estudio de detalle y
(Continued next column)

TELEVISION STATIONS--VALENCIA--
TELEVISIO VALENCIANA (CONTINUED)
La arquitectura de...(CONTINUED)
vivendas en La Flota, Murcia; dos
viviendas rehabilitadas en la
huerta murciana; vestuarios en
tavernes de la Valldigna,
Valencia. Text in Italian and
English.
ON DISENO 1990, no.112(suppl.),
p.113-191, axonometric views,
ill., dwgs., elevs., models,
photos., plans, site plans, aerial
photos.

TELEVISION STUDIOS
See BROADCASTING STUDIOS

TELIAN, GUNTER H.
Erste Preise: Stadt- und Ortskerne.
Three projects: Innenstadt
Grevenbroich (architects: Ruth
Paffrath-Baureis, Heinrich
Schneider); Neckarstrasse
Stuttgart (architect: Gunter H.
Telian); Innenstadt Puttlingen
(architect: Hubertus Wandel).
DEUTSCHES ARCHITEKTENBLATT 1990
Nov.1, v.22, no.11, p.1699-1702,
dwgs., models, site plans.
Neckarstrase in Stuttgart =
Neckarstrasse in Stuttgart.
Competition. Winning architect:
Gunter H. Telian. Includes four
other entries. Text in German.
ARCHITEKTUR + WETTBEWERBE 1990
Sept., no.143, p.47-53, models,
maps, secns., site plans,
sketches.
Stadtebaulicher Ideenwettbewerb
Neckarstrasse Stuttgart.
First prize: Gunter H. Telian.
Second prize: Kammerer, Belz,
Kucher.
BAUWELT 1990 Feb.9, v.81, no.6,
p.245-248, models, site plans.

TELL, RICHARD
Fighting crime: an architectural
approach / Richard Tell.
Rehabilitation of 577 units at
Glenarden Apartments, a government
subsidized housing complex in
Prince George's Co., Md., for
crime prevention. Rehabilitation
architects: CHK Architects.
JOURNAL OF HOUSING 1990 July-Aug.,
v.47, no.4, p.207-212, dwg.,
photos.

TELLES, AUGUSTO C. DA SILVA
Paulo F. Santos, um mestre da
historia da arquitetura [obituary]
/ Augusto C. da Silva Telles.
PROJETO 1988 Nov., no.116, p.152,

TELOW, KARIN
Down to the wire:
telecommunications: AT&T Software
Lab, Menlo Park, California /
Karin Tetlow.
Architect: George W. Famous.
ARCHITECTURE: THE MAGAZINE OF THE
AMERICAN INSTITUTE OF ARCHITECTS
1990 May, v.79, no.5, p.119-122,
photos., plans.

TEMMERMAN, CLEMY
Le SLOT, dit aussi Chateau de
HINNISDAEL a Woluwe-Saint-Lambert
/ Clemy Temmerman.
MAISONS D'HIER ET D'AUJOURD'HUI =
DE WOONSTEDE DOOR DE EEUWEN HEEN
1990 Mar, no.85, p.28-41, dets.,
ill., photos., plans.

TEMPE (ARIZONA)--ART CENTERS--
UNIVERSITY OF ARIZONA--FINE ARTS
CENTER
El desierto edificado: Predock,
centro de arte en Arizona / Sylvia
Lavin.
Fine Arts Center of the Univ. of
Ariz., Tempe.
ARQUITECTURA VIVA 1990 Nov.-Dec.,
no.15, p.24-28, dwgs., photos.,
plans.

TEMPEL, EGON G.
Galavorstellung mit Fehlbesetzung:
Auftritt des BDIA in der
ehemaligen DDR mit
BRD-Rumpfmannschaft / Egon G.
Tempel.
ARCHITEKTUR, INNENARCHITEKTUR,
TECHNISCHER AUSBAU 1990 Nov.,
v.98, no.11, p.88-91, map, photos.

TEMPELMAN, OLAF, 1745-1816
Historic houses: Haga Pavilion /
Philip Mansel.
The interiors of the 1792 country
house of Gustav III, King of
Sweden, in Haga Park outside
Stockholm. Architect: Olaf
Tempelman. Interior designer:
Louis Adrien Masreliez.
ARCHITECTURAL DIGEST 1990 Oct.,
v.47, no.11, p.[270]-278, photos.

TEMPERE, DIDIER
Duitse bunkers aan de belgische Kust
/ Didier Tempere, Simon
Stevinstichting.
German bunkers from both world
wars. English summary, p.75.
MONUMENTEN EN LANDSCHAPPEN 1990
July-Aug., v.9, no.4, p.8-20,
maps, photos., plans, biblios.

TEMPIETTI--RENAISSANCE--ITALY--ROME--
SAN PIETRO IN MONTORIO
The Tempietto and the roots of
coincidence / Mark Wilson Jones.
Analysis of the dimensions of
Bramante's design for the
tempietto at San Pietro in
Montorio, Rome (1502-1514?).
ARCHITECTURAL HISTORY 1990, v.33,
p.1-28, photos., plans, secns.,
tables, refs.

TEMPIETTO
See TEMPIETTI

TEMPLER, JOHN
Pons Asinorum / John Templer.
"This fable is a meditation on the
nature and existence of
architectural research
that-is-not-just-building-science.
"
JOURNAL OF ARCHITECTURAL EDUCATION
1990 Nov., v.44, no.1, p.4-10,
dwgs., refs.

TEMPLES
See also CAVE TEMPLES
See also ROCK-CUT TEMPLES
See also TEMPIETTI

TEMPLES--18TH CENTURY--ITALY--
POSSAGNO--TEMPIO CANOVA
In a classical mold: a majestic
temple and museum in the Veneto
enshrine the timeless ideal of
sculptor Antonio Canova / Arthur
C. Danto.
Tempio and Gipsoteca Canova,
Possagno.
HOUSE & GARDEN 1990 Apr., v.162,
no.4, p.176-181,220, photos.

TEMPLES--ANCIENT--ISRAEL--JERUSALEM--
TEMPLE MOUNT
The Temple, the Sepulchre, and the
Martyrion of the Savior / Robert
Ousterhout.
Examines the ideological
relationship between the Holy
Sepulchre and the Temple of
Jerusalem. Includes abstract.
GESTA 1990, v.29, no.1, p.44-53,
dwgs., models, photos., plans,
secns., aerial photo., refs.

TEMPLES--ASSYRIAN--SYRIA--TELL LEILAN
1985 excavations at Tell Leilan,
Syria / Harvey Weiss ...et al.
Excavation report.
AMERICAN JOURNAL OF ARCHAEOLOGY
1990 Oct., v.94, no.4, p.529-581,
figs., photos., map, plans, secn.,
site plan, tables, isometric dwg.,
refs.

TEMPLES--ASSYRO-BABYLONIAN--IRAQ--TELL
AL RIMAH--GREAT TEMPLE
Innovations in mud-brick: decorative
and structural techniques in
ancient Mesopotamia/ David Oates.
Focus on the Great Temple, Tell al
Rimah, ca. 1800 B.C.
WORLD ARCHAEOLOGY 1990 Feb., v.21,
no.3, p.[388]-406, axonometric
view, dets., map, photos., plans,
secns., reconst. dwgs., refs.

TEMPLES--BUDDHIST
Plans and development of the main
hall of Buddhist temples of the
Sodo zen sect in the early Edo
period / Noboru Sugino.
English summary, p.187.
NIHON KENCHIKU GAKKAI KEIKAKUKEI
RONBUN HOKOKU SHU = JOURNAL OF
ARCHITECTURE, PLANNING AND
ENVIRONMENTAL ENGINEERING 1990
Jan., no.1(407), p.173-187,
charts, photos., plans, refs.

TEMPLES--BUDDHIST--INDIA--BODHGAYA--
MAHABODHI TEMPLE
Bodhgaya and south-east Asia /
Robert L. Brown.
MARG [1989?], v.40, no.1, p.61-84,
dwgs., photos., refs.
The Mahabodhi Temple / Geri H.
Malandra.
MARG [1989?], v.40, no.1, p.9-28,
photos., plans, engr., refs.

TEMPLES--BUDDHIST--JAPAN
Distribution of the types of plans
and development of the main hall
of Buddhist temples of the Sodo
Zen sect in the Middle Edo Period
- mainly in Tokai and Koshin
districts / Noboru Sugino.
Text in Japanese; includes English
summary.
NIHON KENCHIKU GAKKAI KEIKAKUKEI
RONBUN HOKOKU SHU = JOURNAL OF
ARCHITECTURE, PLANNING AND
ENVIRONMENTAL ENGINEERING 1990
Aug., no.8(414), p.141-154,
photos., plans, maps, refs.

TEMPLES--BUDDHIST--JAPAN--HIGASHIURA--
TEMPLE WITH LOTUS
Tadao Ando / Tadao Ando.
Contents: RAIKA headquarters
building, Osaka, design: 1986-87;
construction: 1987-89 -- Temple
with Lotus (Hompukuji; a Shingon
sect Buddhist temple), Hyogo,
design: 1989-90; completion: Nov.
1991. Text in Japanese and
English.
GA DOCUMENT 1990 Apr., no.25,
p.[18]-31, elevs., model, photos.,
plans, secns., site plan.

TEMPLES--BUDDHIST--JAPAN--KAMAKURA--
ZUISEN TEMPLE
The garden in Zuisen Temple,
Kamakura, Japan: design form and
phylogenetic meaning / Norris
Brock Johnson.
JOURNAL OF GARDEN HISTORY 1990
Oct.-Dec., v.10, no.4, p.214-236,
ill., dwgs., port., photos.,
secn., refs.

TEMPLES--BUDDHIST--JAPAN--KYOTO--
INFLUENCE
L'eapace des sens / Maurice Sauzet.
On the work of Sauzet and the
influence of Buddhist temple
architecture. Includes English and
Spanish summaries.
TECHNIQUES ET ARCHITECTURE 1990
June-July, no.390, p.96-100,180,
photos., plans.

TEMPLES--BUDDHIST--JAPAN--KYUSHU
On the types of gates and the
direction and disposition Tennoden
in Obakushu Buddhist temples in
Kyushu district / Teruo Yamamoto.
Four types, from the late 17th
cent. through the 19th cent. Text
in Japanese. Includes English
summary.
NIHON KENCHIKU GAKKAI KEIKAKUKEI
RONBUN HOKOKU SHU = JOURNAL OF
ARCHITECTURE, PLANNING AND
ENVIRONMENTAL ENGINEERING 1990
Sept., no.9(415), p.139-151,
dets., ill., elevs., plans.

TEMPLES--BUDDHIST--JAPAN--UJI--BYODOIN
Heian and Ming temples in Uji,
Japan: part 1: Byodoin, part 2:
Manpukuji / Victor Dove.
ARTS OF ASIA 1990 Jan.-Feb., v.20,
no.1, p.102-110, dwgs., maps,
photos.

TEMPLES--CHINESE--CONSERVATION AND
RESTORATION--CHINA--QUFU--CONFUCIUS
TEMPLE COMPLEX
Heritage conservation: east and west
/ Chen Wei and Andreas Aass.
Comparison of the approaches to
heritage conservation in the West
and in China, as exemplified in
the Acropolis in Athens and the
Confucius Temple Complex in Qufu.
Summaries in French, Italian and
Spanish.
ICOMOS INFORMATION 1989 July-Aug.,
no.3, p.3-8, photos., plans,
biblio.

TEMPLES--CONSERVATION AND
RESTORATION--INDIA
The Archaeological Survey of India /
M.C. Joshi, B.M. Pande.
The ASI was established in 1861,
and Joshi is its Joint Director
General.
ARCHITECTURE + DESIGN 1989
Nov.-Dec., v.6, no.1, p.29-31,
photo.

TEMPLES--EDO--JAPAN
On the genealogy of the Izumis as
master-carvers in the
architectural professions under
the Shogunate during the Edo era /
Ryuichi Ito, Kiyoshi Hirai.
English summary, p.121.
NIHON KENCHIKU GAKKAI KEIKAKUKEI
RONBUN HOKOKU SHU = JOURNAL OF
ARCHITECTURE, PLANNING AND
ENVIRONMENTAL ENGINEERING 1990
Feb., no.2(408), p.111-121,
tables, refs.

TEMPLES--EGYPTIAN--EGYPT--ELEPHANTINE
(ISLAND)
Stadt und Tempel von Elephantine:
15.-16. Grabungsbericht / Werner
Kaiser....[et. al.].
DEUTSCHES ARCHAOLOGISCHES
INSTITUT. ABTEILUNG, KAIRO
MITTEILUNGEN 1988, v.44,
p.[135]-182, dwgs., elevs., maps,
plans, secns., refs.

TEMPLES--EGYPTIAN--EGYPT--KHARGA
OASIS--HIBIS TEMPLE
Oasis of the spirit [Hibis
sanctuary, Khargha Oasis, Egypt] /
Eugene Cruz-Uribe.
New Kingdom (1500-1100 B.C.)
Egyptian temple dedicated to
Amun-Re. Bibliography, p.80.
ARCHAEOLOGY 1989 Sept.-Oct., v.42,
no.5, p.48-53,80, ports., photos.,
plan.

TEMPLES--EGYPTIAN--EGYPT--MEMPHIS--
TEMPLE OF APIS
The Temple of Apis in Memphis /
Michael Jones.
JOURNAL OF EGYPTIAN ARCHAEOLOGY
1990, v.76, p.141-147,pl.VI-VII,
photos., refs.

TEMPLES--GREEK--CONSERVATION AND
RESTORATION--GREECE--ATHENS--
ACROPOLIS
Heritage conservation: east and west
/ Chen Wei and Andreas Aass.
Comparison of the approaches to
heritage conservation in the West
and in China, as exemplified in
the Acropolis in Athens and the
Confucius Temple Complex in Qufu.
(Continued next page)

TEMPLES--GREEK--CONSERVATION AND
  RESTORATION--GREECE--ATHENS--
  ACROPOLIS (CONTINUED)
  Heritage...(CONTINUED)
    Summaries in French, Italian and
    Spanish.
    ICOMOS INFORMATION 1989 July-Aug.,
    no.3, p.3-8, photos., plans,
    biblio.

TEMPLES--GREEK--GREECE--ATHENS--
  ACROPOLIS--ERECHTHEUM
  Ionisches und Atlisches am
    sogenannten Erechtheion in Athen /
    Ulrich Schadler.
    ARCHAOLOGISCHER ANZEIGER 1990,
    no.3, p.[361]-378, dwg., photos.,
    plans, refs.

TEMPLES--GREEK--GREECE--ATHENS--
  ACROPOLIS--PARTHENON
  Design procedure of the Parthenon /
    Rihee Goshima.
    Analysis by means of "the grid
    method". In Japanese; English
    summaries, p.147, 164.
    NIHON KENCHIKU GAKKAI KEIKAKUKEI
    RONBUN HOKOKU SHU = JOURNAL OF
    ARCHITECTURE, PLANNING AND
    ENVIRONMENTAL ENGINEERING 1990
    May, no.5(411), p.147-164,
    diagrs., figs., plans, refs.
  A visual perceptive analysis of
    Greek refinement / Masami Kuroda.
    Curvature, at the Parthenon and
    elsewhere. Text in Japanese;
    includes English summaries.
    NIHON KENCHIKU GAKKAI KEIKAKUKEI
    RONBUN HOKOKU SHU = JOURNAL OF
    ARCHITECTURE, PLANNING AND
    ENVIRONMENTAL ENGINEERING 1990
    Oct., no.10(416), p.135-143,
    elevs., photos., tables, refs.

TEMPLES--GREEK--INFLUENCE
  El Walhalla = The Walhalla / David
    J. Watkin.
    Monument to the German nation,
    1832-1842. Architect: Leo von
    Klenze. Includes designs
    submitted in the 1814-16
    competition for the monument by
    Karl Haller von Hallerstein, Karl
    von Fischer and Daniel Ohlmuller.
    COMPOSICION ARQUITECTONICA, ART &
    ARCHITECTURE 1990 Feb., no.5,
    p.[63]-92, ill., dwgs., elevs.,
    photos., plans, secns., refs.

TEMPLES--GREEK--REPRODUCTIONS--
  GREECE--ATHENS--ACROPOLIS--PARTHENON
  C.R. Cockerell's designs for the
    northern Athenian Parthenon / Ian
    Gow.
    Lost designs for a proposed
    National Monument on Edinburgh's
    Calton Hill.
    THE JOURNAL AND ANNUAL REPORT /
    THE SCOTTISH GEORGIAN SOCIETY FOR
    THE STUDY AND PROTECTION OF
    SCOTTISH ARCHITECTURE 1989, no.16,
    p.20-25, dwgs., secns., refs.

TEMPLES--GREEK--TURKEY--KASTABOS--
  TEMPLE OF HEMITHEA
  The Temple of Athena-Polias at
    Priene and the Temple of Hemithea
    at Kastabos / J. J. de Jong.
    Building began ca. 335 B. C. and
    330 B. C. respectively.
    BABESCH. BULLETIN ANTIEKE
    BESCHAVING 1988, no.63, p.129-137,
    (Continued next column)

TEMPLES--GREEK--TURKEY--KASTABOS--
  TEMPLE OF HEMITHEA (CONTINUED)
  The Temple of...(CONTINUED)
    diagrs., photos., plans, biblio.,
    refs.

TEMPLES--GREEK--TURKEY--PRIENE--TEMPLE
  OF ATHENA POLIAS
  The Temple of Athena-Polias at
    Priene and the Temple of Hemithea
    at Kastabos / J. J. de Jong.
    Building began ca. 335 B. C. and
    330 B. C. respectively.
    BABESCH. BULLETIN ANTIEKE
    BESCHAVING 1988, no.63, p.129-137,
    diagrs., photos., plans, biblio.,
    refs.

TEMPLES--HEIAN--JAPAN--UJI--BYODOIN
  Heian and Ming temples in Uji,
    Japan: part 1: Byodoin, part 2:
    Manpukuji / Victor Dove.
    ARTS OF ASIA 1990 Jan.-Feb., v.20,
    no.1, p.102-110, dwgs., maps,
    photos.

TEMPLES--HINDU--11TH CENTURY--INDIA--
  KHAJURAHO--LAKSMANA TEMPLE
  The Laksmana temple, Khajuraho, and
    its meanings / Hiram W. Woodward.
    11th cent. temple. Focus on
    iconographic analysis of temple
    sculpture in light of certain
    texts.
    ARS ORIENTALIS 1989, v.19,
    p.[27]-48, diagr., dwg., photos.,
    plan, refs.

TEMPLES--HINDU--INDIA
  Prasada as palace: Kutina origins of
    the Nagara Temple / Michael W.
    Meister.
    ARTIBUS ASIAE 1988-1989, v.49,
    no.3-4, p.254-280, axonometric
    views, elevs., photos., refs.

TEMPLES--HINDU--INDIA--GAYA
  Gaya: monuments of the pilgrimage
    town / Frederick M. Asher.
    MARG [1989?], v.40, no.1, p.45-60,
    ill., photos., refs.

TEMPLES--HINDU--INDIA--HIMACHAL
  PRADESH
  Application of vastupurasamandala in
    the Indian temple architecture /
    Laxman S. Thakur.
    Analysis of the Nagara temple
    plans of Himachal Pradesh.
    ARTIBUS ASIAE 1990, v.50, no.3-4,
    p.263-284, dwgs., plans, refs.

TEMPLES--HINDU--INDIA--NARAYANAPURAM
  Narayanapuram: a tenth century site
    in Kalinga / Mary F. Linda.
    On the four 10th cent. temples
    which were part of the medieval
    principality of Kalinga.
    ARTIBUS ASIAE 1990, v.50, no.3-4,
    p.232-262, map, photos., plans,
    refs.

TEMPLES--HINDU--INFLUENCE
  Baron Palace, Cairo, Egypt / Veena
    Wig, Siddhartha Wig.
    Built in the late 1920s and
    influenced by Hindu temples and
    sculpture. Architects included
    Alexander Marcel.
    ARCHITECTURE + DESIGN 1990
    July-Aug., v.7, no.4, p.16-17,
    photos.

TEMPLES--HINDU--INFLUENCE
      (CONTINUED)
  Le palais hindou du Baron Empain se
    meurt a Heliopolis / Antoine
    Gerard.
    On the exotic 1905 villa outside
    Cairo which is now in peril.
    Architect: Alexandre Marcel.
    English summary, p.192.
    ARCHITECTURE D'AUJOURD'HUI 1990
    June, no.269, p.191-193, photos.

TEMPLES--HITTITE--TURKEY--BOGAZKOY
  Die Ausgrabungen in Bogazkoy-Hattusa
    1988 / Peter Neve.
    Excavation report for Temple 30
    area at the Hittite site in north
    central Turkey, with a
    contribution on hieroglyphics by
    Heinrich Otten.
    ARCHAOLOGISCHER ANZEIGER 1989,
    no.3, p.[271]-337, dwgs., port.,
    photos., plans, secns., site
    plans, aerial photo., refs.

TEMPLES--ITALY--ROME--TEMPLE FORGETFUL
  Ins Gewicht fallend. Zwei
    Balanceakte von Douglas Darden =
    Tipping scales. Two balancing acts
    by Douglas Darden.
    Contents: Project for saloon,
    Great Salt Lake, Utah --Project
    for Temple Forgetful, at Romun
    Romanum, Rome. Architect: Douglas
    Darden.
    DAIDALOS 1990 Sept.15, no.37,
    p.102-105, dwg., elevs., model,
    plans, secn.

TEMPLES--JAPAN--SHINJISYMEIKAI
  Conchiglia approdata [temple,
    Shinjisymeikai, Japan].
    Architect: Akira Kuryu.
    ARCHITETTURA; CRONACHE E STORIA
    1990 June, v.36, no.6(416),
    p.450-451, photos., plans, site
    plans, aerial photos.

TEMPLES--JAPANESE--JAPAN--KYOTO--
  TENRYU-JI
  Geomancy, sacred geometry, and the
    idea of a garden: Tenryu-ji
    temple, Kyoto, Japan / Norris
    Brock Johnson.
    JOURNAL OF GARDEN HISTORY 1989
    Jan.-Mar., v.9, no.1, p.[1]-19,
    dwgs., site plans, refs.

TEMPLES, JEWISH
  See SYNAGOGUES

TEMPLES--KHMER--CONSERVATION AND
  RESTORATION--CAMBODIA--ANGKOR
  Restoring the Angkor Temples: a
    struggle against nature and man /
    Bonnie Burnham.
    ART INTERNATIONAL 1990 Winter, new
    ser., no.13, p.79-[83], photos.

TEMPLES--MING--JAPAN--UJI--MANPUKUJI
  Heian and Ming temples in Uji,
    Japan: part 1: Byodoin, part 2:
    Manpukuji / Victor Dove.
    ARTS OF ASIA 1990 Jan.-Feb., v.20,
    no.1, p.102-110, dwgs., maps,
    photos.

TEMPLES--NEPAL
Report on the monuments of Northern
Nepal (continued) / Corneille
Jest.
In the Dolakha district, including
Temple of Dharpa (Dharka Gyang),
Monastery of Bigu, village temple
of Bigr, and Temple of Puri.
PRACINA NEPALA 1986 Feb.-1987
Jan., no.92-97 p.[6]-13, refs.

TEMPLES--NEPAL--KIRTIPUR--BAGHBHAIROV
TEMPLE
Baghbhairav Temple / Sukra Sagar
Shrestha.
The oldest shrine in Kirtipur, in
the Kathmandu valley.
PR-AC-INA NEP-ALA 1988 Oct.-Nov.,
no.108, p.[1]-11, elev., photo.,
plans, refs.

TEMPLES--ROMAN--GREECE--CORINTH--
TEMPLE E
Pausanias, Octavia and Temple E at
Corinth / Mary E. Hoskins Walbank.
THE ANNUAL OF THE BRITISH SCHOOL
AT ATHENS 1989, no.84,
p.[361]-394, photos., plans, refs.

TEMPLES--ROMAN--ITALY--ROME--PANTHEON
Bemerkungen zu Reliefs am Pantheon
und aus der Villa Hadriana / Helga
Herdejurgen.
ARCHAOLOGISCHER ANZEIGER 1990,
no.1, p.[123]-131, photos., engr.,
refs.
A rereading of the interior
elevation of Hadrian's Rotunda /
William C. Loerke.
Presents history of criticism of
the Rotunda and interprets its
Hadrianic state as a projection of
the Roman idea of the "templum
mundi". Includes abstract.
SOCIETY OF ARCHITECTURAL
HISTORIANS. JOURNAL 1990 Mar.,
v.49, no.1, p.22-43, ill., dwgs.,
photos., plans, secns., reconst.
dwg., refs.

TEMPLES--ROMAN--ITALY--ROME--TEMPLE OF
FORTUNA VIRILIS
A note on the medieval name of the
so-called 'Temple of Fortuna
Virilis' at Rome / John Osborne.
Italian summary, p.[x].
BRITISH SCHOOL AT ROME PAPERS OF
THE BRITISH SCHOOL AT ROME 1988,
v.56, p.[210]-212, refs.

TEMPLES--ROMAN--REPRODUCTIONS--
ENGLAND--LONDON
These poolish things / Leslie
Geddes-Brown.
On the underground faux Roman
temple and pool built for a London
businessman. Architects: Child
Wilson Associates.
THE WORLD OF INTERIORS 1990
July-Aug., p.[84-87] photos.

TEMPLES--SIKH--INDIA--AMRISTAR--GOLDEN
TEMPLE
The Golden Temple [by] Patwant Singh
[book review] / Sayed S. Shafi.
In Amristar, India.
ARCHITECTURE + DESIGN 1989
May-June, v.5, no.4, p.118-119,
photo., dwg.

TEMPLES--STONE--INDIA--KASHMIR
Stone temples / Robert E. Fisher.
MARG [1989?], v.40, no.2, p.29-40,
photos., refs.

TEMPORARY BUILDINGS
See BUILDINGS - TEMPORARY

TENANTS
See LANDLORD AND TENANT

TENCA, ANGELO
Trasformazioni urbanistiche di una
citta: Mantova in periodo fascista
/ Angelo Tenca.
One of four case studies on cities
in northeastern Italy.
STORIA URBANA 1990 Apr.-June,
v.14, no.51, p.[223]-251, maps,
photos., plans, refs.

TENEGGI, TIZIANO
Concorso per la riqualificazione
dell' area di Via Veneto [Trento].
Presents 10 entries, including 1st
prize entry by Oswald Zoeggeler.
PARAMETRO 1990, Nov.-Dec., no.181,
p.52-69, axonometric views, ill.,
dwgs., elevs., photos., plans,
secns., aerial photo.

TENEMENT-HOUSES
See TENEMENT HOUSES

TENEMENT HOUSES--17TH CENTURY--
CONSERVATION AND RESTORATION--
SCOTLAND--EDINBURGH--GLADSTONE'S
LAND
The merchant's house, Scotland.
Gladstone's land, ca. 1600
tenement house in Edinburgh's Old
Town, is now a museum. Architect
for restoration: Robert Hurd.
COLONIAL HOMES 1990 June, v.16,
no.3, p.[92-97],150,168, photos.,
engr.

TENEMENT HOUSES--19TH CENTURY--
SCOTLAND--GLASGOW--145 BUCCLEUCH
STREET (TENEMENT HOUSE)
A hoard of history: the rich legacy
of a middle-class Glaswegian /
Margaret Henderson.
Interiors of a tenement flat of
1892 in the Garnethill area.
TRADITIONAL HOMES 1990 Oct., v.7,
no.1, p.39-42, photos.

TENEMENT HOUSES--ALTERATIONS AND
ADDITIONS--GERMANY (WEST)--MUNICH--
HAIDHAUSEN
Okologische Modellsanierung, Munchen
= Model ecological refurbishment.
Restoration of a tenement building
in the Haidhausen section.
Architects: Per Krusche, Rudolf
Meissner.
DETAIL 1990 Oct.-Nov., v.30, no.5,
p.474-477, dets., elev., photos.,
plans, secns., site plan.

TENEMENT HOUSES--CONSERVATION AND
RESTORATION--UNITED STATES--NEW YORK
(NEW YORK)--250-254 EAST 4TH STREET
A housing enterprise / Peter Slatin.
The Enterprise Foundation and
LESCH, a community group, have
renovated 3 tenement buildings at
250-254 East 4th St. on the Lower
East Side of Manhattan.
METROPOLIS 1990 July-Aug., v.10,
no.1, p.18-20, photo.

TENEMENT HOUSES--SCOTLAND--GLASGOW--
WEST END PARK STREET
Tenement tradition [Glasgow] / Mark
Cousins.
New version of Glasgow's 19th
cent. tenements by Assist
Architects.
ARCHITECTS' JOURNAL 1990 May 30,
v.191, no.22, p.36-37, photos.,
plans.

TENEMENT HOUSES--STONE--SCOTLAND--
CENTRAL LOWLANDS
Heart of stone: the unique character
of vernacular architecture in
Scotland's Central Lowlands /
Geoffrey Stell.
TRADITIONAL HOMES 1990 Feb., v.6,
no.5, p.35-39, photos., biblio.

TENGBOMS ARKITEKTKONTOR
Terminal solution / Brian Walters.
On the Stockholm downtown airline
terminal. Architects: Arken
Arkitekter, Ralph Erskine
Architect and Planner, Ahlquist &
Culjat and Tengboms
Arkitektkontor.
BUILDING DESIGN 1990 Apr.20,
no.982, p.42-43, photos.
Uber oder neben den Geleisen? Der
neue City-Terminal in Stockholm,
1989 / Ernst Zietzschmann.
Architects: Anders Tengbom, Ralph
Erskine.
WERK, BAUEN + WOHNEN 1989 Dec.,
no.12, p.12-13, model, photos.,
plans.
"Vasaterminalen" -- World Trade
Center in Stockholm.
Architects: Arken Arkitekter,
Ralph Erskine Architect and
Planner, Alquist & Culjat,
Architektkontoren AET, and
Tengboms Arkitektkontor.
DEUTSCHE BAUZEITSCHRIFT 1990 Aug.,
v.38, no.8, p.1077-1084, det.,
photos., plans, secn., site plan.

TENNENBAUM, ROBERT
Hail, Columbia [Md.] / Robert
Tennenbaum.
New town built in the early 1960s.
Chief architect and planner:
Robert Tennenbaum.
PLANNING 1990 May, v.56, no.5,
p.16-17, photos., plan.

TENNESSEE VALLEY AUTHORITY
Benton MacKaye: the TVA years /
Daniel Schaffer.
Regional planner and sometime
associate of Lewis Mumford.
PLANNING PERSPECTIVES: PP 1990
Jan., v.5, no.1, p.5-21, refs.

TENNIS CLUBS
See also TENNIS COURTS

TENNIS COURTS
See also TENNIS CLUBS

TENNIS COURTS--MAINTENANCE AND
REPAIR--UNITED STATES--OCEAN CITY
(NEW JERSEY)
Building a home-court advantage /
John Kutch.
Tennis courts and recreational
areas in Ocean City, N.J.
PARKS & RECREATION 1990 July,
v.25, no.7, p.38-41, photos.

TENSILE ARCHITECTURE
See TENT STRUCTURES

TENSILE STRUCTURES
Una tensostruttura cinetica =
Kinetic tensile structure /
Richard W. Snibbe.
Competition design for Opera de la
Bastille, Paris. Architect:
Richard W. Snibbe.
L'ARCA 1990 July-Aug., no.40,
p.30-35, elev., model, plans,
secns., site plan.

TENSILE STRUCTURES--FRANCE--
SAINT-LOUIS BALE
Poste de douane Saint-Louis Bale.
Architect: Paul Andreu.
LE MUR VIVANT 1990, no.97,
p.20-27, photos.

TENSILE STRUCTURES--ITALY--ROME--
STADIO OLIMPICO
Il nuovo Stadio Olimpico a Roma =
The renovated Olympic Stadium in
Rome / Giuseppe Nannerini.
Project head: Annibale Vitellozzi
et al. Project architect: Studio
Zucker. Includes English
translation; French, German and
Spanish summaries p.[3].
L'INDUSTRIA DELLE COSTRUZIONI 1990
Oct., v.24, no.228, p.6-17, dets.,
models, photos., plans, secns.

TENSILE STRUCTURES--JAPAN--OHNOJO--
WAKITA HI-TECS
Wakita-Hi-Tecs-Hauptverwaltung / W.
Nedderhut-Heeschen.
Tensile structure office building,
Ohnojo. Architects: Yoh Design
Office.
DEUTSCHE BAUZEITSCHRIFT 1990 Nov.,
v.38, no.11, p.1595-1598, dets.,
dwgs., photos., plan, secn.
Wakita Hi-Tecs / Shoei Yoh.
Tensile structure office building,
Ohnojo. Architect: Shoei Yoh.
JAPAN ARCHITECT 1990 July, v.65,
no.7(399), p.[36]-39, dets.,
elev., photos., plan.

TENSILE STRUCTURES--TEMPORARY--UNITED
STATES--NEW YORK (NEW YORK)--BATTERY
PARK CITY--WINTER GARDEN
Dramatic tension: temporary
performance structures in the
Winter Garden, Battery Park City /
Justin Henderson.
Architect: FTL Associates.
INTERIORS 1990 Jan., v.149, no.6,
p.154-[155], photos., plan.

TENSINI, FRANCESCO
Francesco Tensini and the defences
of Modena / Herman van Bergeijk.
Italian Renaissance engineer.
FORT 1990, v.18, p.29-42, port.,
plans, engrs., refs.

TENSION STRUCTURES
See TENT STRUCTURES

TENT STRUCTURES
Architetture sotto la tenda = Tent
architecture / Lucia Bisi.
Lightweight metal arch and cable
tensile structure for Sinco
research center, Venafro, Italy;
architects: Samyn et Associes.
L'ARCA 1990 Oct., no.42,
p.48-[55], elevs., models, plans,
secns.

TENT STRUCTURES (CONTINUED)
Groupe Arcora.
Focus on two textile roof
structure projects: Batiment
d'Ordonnancement des Palette
(BOP), Roissy; TGV railroad
station, Nantes. English summary,
p.86.
ARCHITECTURE D'AUJOURD'HUI 1990
Feb., no.267, p.84-87, photos.,
plans, secns.
Herald city / Yukio Sano.
Four "domed" tent structure
buildings by Kajima Kensetsu
Kabushiki Kaisha. English summary,
p.19.
KENCHIKU BUNKA 1990 Oct., v.45,
no.528, p.91-102, dwgs., models,
maps, photos., plans, aerial
photos.
Shelter that spun off from space /
John Welsh.
On the Universal Shelter, designed
with heat-retaining fabric and
collapsible ribs. Future Systems
Consultants.
BUILDING DESIGN 1990 Jan.19,
no.969, p.12, dwgs., elev.,
photo., isometric dwg.
Zeltstrukturen.
Suppliers of systems.
ARCH PLUS 1990 Apr., no.103,
p.90-93, dets., dwgs., photos.

TENT STRUCTURES--FINLAND--KAUSTINAN--
KANSANMUSIIKKIJUHLIEN KATOS
Kansanmusiikkijuhlien katos,
Kaustinan.
A seasonal tent-canopy for an
outdoor folk music theater,
completed in 1988. Architect: Roy
Manttari. Includes English
captions and summaries.
ARKKITEHTI 1989, v.86, no.4,
p.62-64, dets., elevs., photos.,
site plans.

TENT STRUCTURES--GERMANY (WEST)--BAD
MUNDER--WILKHAHN
Frei Otto: Pavillons des ateliers
Wilkhahn.
Workshops for Wilkhahn furniture
factory, Bad Munder. English
text, p. 58.
ARCHITECTURE D'AUJOURD'HUI 1990
Feb., no.267, p.58-[59], photos.,
secns., site plan.

TENT STRUCTURES--JAPAN--KAWABE--AKITA
SKY DOME
Akita Sky Dome / Masaru Ozaki.
Sports facility with giant
translucent tent structure roof,
Kawabe-gun. Architects: Kajima
Kensetsu Kabushiki Kaisha.
JAPAN ARCHITECT 1990 July, v.65,
no.7(399), p.40-43, dets., dwgs.,
photos., plan, secn.

TENT STRUCTURES--UNITED STATES--SANTA
CRUZ (CALIFORNIA)--PHOENIX PAVILIONS
Post-earthquake placemaking in
downtown Santa Cruz / James E.
Pepper.
Destruction of the Pacific Garden
Mall in Santa Cruz by a
seven-tent, 34,000 sq. ft.
temporary complex known as the
Phoenix Pavilions.
PLACES 1990 Spring, v.6, no.3,
p.92-93, photos., plans.

TENTS
See also ROOFS - FABRIC
See also TENT STRUCTURES

TENTS--AUSTRALIA
Building and construction materials:
hi-tech tents / Bob Barrow.
ARCHITECTURE AUSTRALIA 1990 Apr.,
v.79, no.3, p.71-72, photos.

TENTS--KENYA--BEARD CAMP
Into Africa / Liza Campbell Athill.
Photographer Peter Beard's
compound in the Kenyan bush.
HOUSE & GARDEN 1990 Nov., v.162,
no.11, p.[140]-147,232, ports.,
photos.

TENTS--MAURITANIA--NOUAKCHOTT
Una tenda per la rete d'acqua di
Nouakchott = a tent for the
Nouakchott water system / Fabrizio
Bonomo.
Architects: Samyn et Associes.
Text in Italian and English.
L'ARCA 1990 Sept., no.41 suppl.
l'Arca 2, p.97-98.

TEODORO, FRANCESCO P. DI
Francesco di Giorgio e le
proporzioni del tiburio del Duomo
di Milano / Francesco P. di
Teodoro.
Discussion of the lantern and the
"perfect" number 28. English
summary,p.240.
ARTE LOMBARDA 1989, no.90-91,
p.42-46, dwgs., plans, refs.

TEPPERT, HORST
Stahlhaus in Harlaching bei Munchen,
D = Steelhouse in Harlaching,
Munich, G.
Architect: Horst Teppert.
DETAIL 1990 Feb.-Mar., v.30, no.1,
p.SI-SIV, dets., elev., photos.,
plan.

TERADA, HIDEO
On the method to find the
rectangular mosaic patterns
defined by given room adjacencies
/ Hideo Terada.
"A study of the method of analysis
and synthesis for space layout
planning (1)". Text in Japanese;
includes English summary.
NIHON KENCHIKU GAKKAI KEIKAKUKEI
RONBUN HOKOKU SHU = JOURNAL OF
ARCHITECTURE, PLANNING AND
ENVIRONMENTAL ENGINEERING 1990
Aug., no.8(414), p.69-80, graphs,
tables, refs.

TERAKADO, YUKIO
The concept of spatial composition
and organization of Shuraku
(Settlements) viewed through the
spatial language / Yukio Terakado.
Based on research at Karakida in
Ochiai-district, Tama City, Tokyo.
Text in Japanese; includes English
summary.
NIHON KENCHIKU GAKKAI KEIKAKUKEI
RONBUN HOKOKU SHU = JOURNAL OF
ARCHITECTURE, PLANNING AND
ENVIRONMENTAL ENGINEERING 1990
Oct., no.10(416), p.55-65, maps,
tables, refs.

TERMINALS, MARINE
See MARINE TERMINALS

TERMINALS, SHIP
See MARINE TERMINALS

TERMINOLOGY
See "TERMINOLOGY" AS A SUBHEADING
AFTER SPECIFIC BUILDING TYPES OR
OTHER MAIN HEADINGS.

TERRA-COTTA
See also "TERRA-COTTA" AS A
SUBHEADING AFTER SPECIFIC BUILDING
TYPES OR OTHER MAIN HEADINGS.
Decorating a revival / Julia Abel
Smith.
Revived interest in decorative
qualities of terra-cotta.
COUNTRY LIFE 1990 Nov.1, v.184,
no.44, p.94-96, photos.
Produits: brique et terre cuite /
Patrick Cheruette.
LE MONITEUR ARCHITECTURE AMC 1990
Oct., no.15, p.65,67-68, diagrs.,
photos.

TERRACE HOUSES
See ROW HOUSES

TERRACES
See also ROOF TERRACES
Tra porticato e terrazza / Walter
Bianchi, Mauro Colombo.
VILLE GIARDINI 1990 Apr., no.247,
p.44-[45], diagrs., dwg., elev.,
photos.

TERRACES--ANCIENT--TURKEY--BURGAZ
Ein Heiligtum bei Alt-Knidos /
Dietrich Berges, Numan Tuna.
Report on excavations of terraces,
Burgaz, Turkey.
ARCHAOLOGISCHER ANZEIGER 1990,
no.1, p.[19]-35, maps, photos.,
refs.

TERRAGNI, GIUSEPPE, 1904-1943
Giuseppe Terragni: ein autonomer
Architekt im Dienst eines
politischen Regimes / Vittorio
Magnago Lampugnani.
DER ARCHITEKT 1990 Mar., no.3,
p.133-137, dwgs., site plans,
refs.
Giuseppe Terragni und sein
Kindergarten in Como / Achim
Preiss, Stefan Germer.
Completed in 1937.
BAUWELT 1990 Feb.9, v.81, no.6,
p.262-270, photos., site plan,
isometric dwgs., biblio.
Other place(s): an examination of
"place" in the work of Aalto and
Terragni / Brian L. McLaren.
REFLECTIONS: THE JOURNAL OF THE
SCHOOL OF ARCHITECTURE UNIVERSITY
OF ILLINOIS AT URBANA-CHAMPAIGN
1990 Spring, no.7, p.44-49,
photos, refs.
La progettazione dell'E42: la prima
fase = The planning of the E42:
the first phase / Riccardo
Mariani.
The planning of the E42:
Esposizione Universale in Roma
1941-1942; architects: Giuseppe
Pagano, Marcello Piacentini, Luigi
Piccinato, Ettore Rossi, Luigi
Vietti, Adalberto Libera, Giuseppe
Terragni, Pietro Lingeri, Cesare
Cattaneo, Giovanni Guerrini,
(Continued next column)

TERRAGNI, GIUSEPPE, 1904-1943
(CONTINUED)
La progettazione...(CONTINUED)
Ernesto La Padula, Mario Romano,
Gian Luigi Banfi, Ludovico B. di
Belgioso, Gaetano Ciocca, Enrico
Peressutti, Ernesto N. Rogers,
Franco Albini, Ignazio Gardella,
Giancarlo Palanti, Giovanna
Romano, Luciano Baldessari,
Ernesto Saliva, Luigi Moretti,
Gino Pollini, Luigi Figini, and
Giuseppe Vaccaro.
LOTUS INTERNATIONAL 1990, no.67,
p.90-125, elevs., models, photos.,
plans, secns., site plans,
sketches, aerial photos.

TERRANOVA, ANTONIO
El diseno de la ciudad= The design
of the city / Antonio Terranova.
The urban design work of Italian
architect and city planner
Ludovico Quaroni. In Spanish and
English.
URBANISMO REVISTA 1989, no.7,
p.18-[33], dwgs., models, plans,
secns., sketches, aerial photo.

TERRAZZO
See also "TERRAZZO" AS A SUBHEADING
AFTER SPECIFIC BUILDING TYPES OR
OTHER MAIN HEADINGS.

TERRELO, RAFAEL
Arquitectos en la M-30 / Alejandro
Zaera, Manuel Gausa.
Roundtable with Inaki Abalos, Juan
Herreros, Rafael Terrelo, Federico
Soriano, Fernando Porras, Mateo
Corrales. Includes 8 projects.
Spanish, English text.
QUADERNS D'ARQUITECTURA I
URBANISME 1989 Apr.-Sept.,
nos.181-182, p.[48-81], elevs.,
models, photos., plans, secns.,
site plans.

TERRIEN, PHILIPPE
Asahi Beer Azumabashi Hall (Super
Dry Hall) / Philippe Terrien.
Located in Tokyo. Architect:
Philippe Starck.
JAPAN ARCHITECT 1990 Apr., v.65,
no.4 (396), p.8-21, dwgs.,
photos., plans, secns.
Unhex Nani Nani / Philippe Terrien.
Office building, Tokyo. Architect:
Philippe Starck.
JAPAN ARCHITECT 1990 Apr., v.65,
no.4 (396), p.22-25, photos.,
plans, secn.

TERRITORIAL STYLE
See "TERRITORIAL STYLE" AS A
SUBHEADING AFTER SPECIFIC BUILDING
TYPES OR OTHER MAIN HEADINGS.

TERRY FARRELL & COMPANY
Parking at the crossroads [office
parks, West London] / Martin
Spring.
Plans for two new projects:
Chiswick Park (developer, Stanhope
Trafalgar; architect, Terry
Farrell; landscape architect,
Laurie Olin) and Bedfont Lakes
(developers, MEPC and IBM;
architect, Michael Hopkins).
BUILDING 1990 June 1, v.255,
no.22, p.40-45, diagrs., ill.,
model, photos., site plan.

TERRY FARRELL & COMPANY (CONTINUED)
Round the corner: die Midland Bank
in der City von London.
Architects: Terry Farrell & Co.
DEUTSCHE BAUZEITUNG 1990 May,
v.124, no.5, p.52-54, dwg.,
photos., plans, secn., site plan.
Special feature: Terry Farrell &
Company.
Contents: Editor's introduction.--
Statement for this special
feature, by Terry Farrell.--Essay:
On Terry Farrell, by Rowan
Moore.--Works: Tobacco Dock,
Shopping village, London.--Comyn
Ching Triangle, urban project.--
Henley Royal Regatta
headquarters.--TV-am
headquarters.--Midland Bank &
offices.--Embankment Place, urban
project.--Alban Gate, offices &
housing.--Vauxhall Cross,
government offices.--The South
Bank.--Hungerford Bridge walkway
project.--Brief history. Text in
Japanese and English.
ARCHITECTURE AND URBANISM 1989
Dec., no.12(231), p.[37]-132,
port., elevs., models, photos.,
plans, secns., site plans.
Tobacco Dock in London.
Warehouse converted into shopping
center. Original architect: Daniel
Asher Alexander. Conversion
architects: Terry Farrell &
Company.
DEUTSCHE BAUZEITSCHRIFT 1990 Apr.,
v.38, no.4, p.499-508, dets.,
photos., plan, site plan.
Tobacco Dock, London.
Conversion of a warehouse into a
commercial development.
Architects: Terry Farrell & Co.
DETAIL 1990 Oct.-Nov., v.30, no.5,
p.494-497, dets., elevs., photos.,
plans, secns., site plan.

TERRY FARRELL PARTNERSHIP
Demountable structure: Garden
Centre: Terry Farrell Partnership.
Demountable greenhouse, now 10
years old.
ARCHITECTS' JOURNAL 1990 Jan.17,
v.191, no.3, p.57-59, diagrs.,
photos., plan, secn., isometric
dwg.
Farrell's final plan for centre.
Masterplan for Edinburgh's
Financial and Conference Centre by
Terry Farrell.
ARCHITECTS' JOURNAL 1990
Aug.22-29, v.192, no.7-8, p.13,
model, site plan, sketch.

TERRY, QUINLAN, 1937-
Acid house / Robert Cowan.
Report on a debate organized by
the Cambridge Forum for the
Construction Industry, held at the
Cambridge Union. Participants
included: Leon Krier, Colin
Stansfield Smith, Peter Clegg,
Quinlan Terry, and Richard
Biscoe-Taylor.
ARCHITECTS' JOURNAL 1990 Feb.7,
v.191, no.6, p.24-25, ports.
La batalla del posmoderno: pugna pro
un estilo de fin de siglo / Hugh
Honour.
Focus on the Sainsbury Wing
extension to the National Gallery,
London. Architects: Venturi, Rauch
(Continued next page)

TERRY, QUINLAN, 1937- (CONTINUED)
La batalla del...(CONTINUED)
and Scott Brown. English summary,
p.84-85.
A & V 1990, no.21, p.12-19, dets.,
dwgs., models, photos.
Classical quartet: new country
houses / John Martin Robinson.
Contents: Crooked Pightle House,
Hampshire; architect: Robet Adam
-- Pie Corner, Hertfordshire;
architect: James Gorst -- Green
Manor, Hertfordshire; architect:
Piers Gough -- Fawley House,
Hampshire; architect: Quinlan
Terry.
COUNTRY LIFE 1990 Aug.30, v.184,
no.35, p.74-77, photos.

TERUI, SHINZU
Special edition III: scene of frame
and membrane / Shinzo Terui.
Features three projects by Shinzo
Terui: sail of Obama (Office
building), Roof of Iida
(restaurant), and Tower of
Katsuradai (dental clinic).
Includes dialogue, System and
locality of architecture by
Toshiaki Ishida and Terui. English
summary, p.23.
KENCHIKU BUNKA 1990 Sept., v.45,
no.527, p.93-113, ports., elevs.,
models, photos., plans.

TESAR, HEINZ, 1939-
Pfarrkirche Edelsbach, Steiermark.
Architect: Heinz Tesar.
KUNST UND KIRCHE 1990, no.1,
p.42-43, axonometric view, elev.,
photos., plans, site plan.
Wien.
One of three sections in special
feature on "Contemporary Austrian
architecture". Architects: Heinz
Tesar, Luigi Blau, Franco Fonatti
+ Helmut Hempel, Sylvia Fritz,
Ernst Hoffmann, Gert Mayr-keber,
Rudiger Lainer + Gertraud Auer,
Ernst Beneder, Georg Reinberg, and
Martin Treberspurg.
SPACE DESIGN 1990 Mar., no.306,
p.9-46, axonometric views, dwgs.,
ports., elevs., models, photos.,
plans, secn.

TESSENOW, HEINRICH, 1876-1950
Architecture as craft / Giorgio
Grassi.
Essay first published as an
introduction to the Italian
translation of Heinrich Tessenow's
"Hasbau und dergleichen" in
"Osservazioni elementari sul
costruire," Milan, 1974.
9H 1989, no.8, p.34-53, elev.,
photos., plans.
Hellerau: ein neuer Anfang.
The Festspielhaus of 1911-1912 was
used by troops during World War II
and in May 1990 by art students.
Architect: Heinrich Tessenow.
BAUWELT 1990 Dec.7, v.81, no.46,
p.2286, photo.
Housebuilding and such things /
Heinrich Tessenow.
9H 1989, no.8, p.9-33, ill.,
elevs., photos., plans, secns.

TESSENOW, HEINRICH, 1876-1950
(CONTINUED)
Introduction to Heinrich Tessenow's
"House-building and such things" /
Walter Jessen.
9H 1989, no.8, p.6-8,
Modernity and reform, Heinrich
Tessenow and the Institut Dalcroze
at Hellerau / Marco De Michelis.
Built ca. 1911-1912, and visited
by Le Corbusier. Appendix includes
biographical data on five key
participants in the institute.
PERSPECTA 1990, no.26, p.143-170,
dwgs., elevs., photos., plans,
refs.
Tessenow a St. Moritz: requiem for
Villa Bohler / Heinz Adamek.
Demolition of villa built in
1916-17 for Friedrich Bohler,:
architect: Heinrich von Tessenow.
Text in Italian and English.
L'ARCA 1990 Mar., no.36, p.4-7,
ill., photos, plan.
Tessenow riformatore: Siedlung e
piccola citta / Marco de Michelis.
On Am Schankenberg, Hellerau; and
Am Gruneberg, Am Gries, and
Bahnhofstrasse, Possneck. Includes
English summary; captions in
Italian and English.
CASABELLA 1990 Feb., v.54, no.565,
p.44-58,61-63, dwgs., elevs.,
photos., plans, refs.
Tessenow wiederentdeckt / Roland
Ostertag.
House in Steinhorst, built c.1908.
BAUWELT 1990 Sept.7, v.81, no.34,
p.1650-1651, elev., photos., plan.
Tessenow's architecture as national
allegory: critique of capitalism
or protofascism? / Michael Hays.
9H 1989, no.8, p.54-71, photos.,
plans, site plans, refs.
Weggeklotzt [Villa Bohler] / Rene
Furer.
In Oberalpina, St. Moritz, built
1916. Architect: Heinrich
Tessenow.
ARCHITHESE 1990 Sept.-Oct., v.20,
no.5, p.75-76, elev., photos.

TESSENOW, HEINRICH, 1876-1950. HAUSBAU
UND DERGLEICHEN
Architecture as craft / Giorgio
Grassi.
Essay first published as an
introduction to the Italian
translation of Heinrich Tessenow's
"Hasbau und dergleichen" in
"Osservazioni elementari sul
costruire," Milan, 1974.
9H 1989, no.8, p.34-53, elev.,
photos., plans.
Introduction to Heinrich Tessenow's
"House-building and such things" /
Walter Jessen.
9H 1989, no.8, p.6-8,

TESSIN, NICODEMUS, 1615-1681
Drottningholm.
An island on Lake Malaren, west of
Stockholm. Features the 17th-cent.
summer palace of Queen Eleonora
(architects: Nikodemus Tessin The
Elder and Younger); the house of
architect Ralph Erskine; and the
Ekero quarter. Text in Italian and
English.
ABITARE 1990 July-Aug., no.287,
p.172-179, dwg., port., elev.,
photos., plans, secns., site plan.

TESSIN, NICODEMUS, 1659-1728
Drottningholm.
An island on Lake Malaren, west of
Stockholm. Features the 17th-cent.
summer palace of Queen Eleonora
(architects: Nikodemus Tessin The
Elder and Younger); the nouse of
architect Ralph Erskine; and the
Ekero quarter. Text in Italian and
English.
ABITARE 1990 July-Aug., no.287,
p.172-179, dwg., port., elev.,
photos., plans, secns., site plan.
I maktens alleer: Riksplan,
Stockholm / Gunilla Lundahl.
Park on Norrbro, with historical
references to earlier landmarks
including Tessin's plan and design
by Aron Johansson. Landscape
architects: Walter Bauer, Jurek
Karon. Includes English
translation and captions.
LANDSKAB 1990 May, v.71, no.3-4,
p.[S15-S17], photos., site plan,
sketch.
Overintendentsambetels organisation
och arbetsuppgifter / Barbro
Edling.
The organization and tasks of the
Swedish Board of Public Works in
the 18th cent., with discussion of
the role of the first
Superintendent, Nicodemus Tessin
the younger. Includes English
summary.
BEBYGGELSEHISTORISK TIDSKRIFT
1989, no.17-18, p.103-118,
photos., plans, secns., biblio.,
refs.

TESTA, CHICCO
Politiche per l'ambiente / Chicco
Testa.
English summary, p.123.
URBANISTICA 1989 Dec., no.97,
p.29-31, photos.

TESTA, ENZO--CORRESPONDENCE AND
RECORDS
Il granchio e la farfalla:
riflessioni sull'architettura in
una lettura a Anthony Halasz /
Enzo Testa.
Letter dated Aug.22, 1988.
PARAMETRO 1990 July-Aug., v.21,
no.179, p.64-73, dwgs., elev.,
photos., plans.

TESTA, GIUSI
Orvieto, le fil interrompu / Giusi
Testa, Keith Christiansen.
Focus on the conservation and
restoration of the cathedral of
Orvieto, begun in the 13th cent.
Includes essay entitled, Gentile
et l'ange, by Keith Christiansen,
on the conservation of the mural
painting in the cathedral by
Gentile da Fabriano.
CONNAISSANCE DES ARTS 1990 Apr.,
no.458, p.114-128, dets., photos.

TESTA, LAURA
Gli affreschi absidali della chiesa
di Sant'Onofrio al Gianicolo:
committenza, interpretazione ed
attribuzione / Laura Testa.
STORIA DELL'ARTE 1989, no.66,
p.[171]-186,pl.1-26, photos.,
refs.

TESTA, LUCIANO
  Edificio municipale di
  Reze-le-Nantes = Reze-le-Nantes
  Town Hall.
  Contents: Alessandro Anselmi
  biography -- A history [of
  project] -- "Limit" of the project
  /Alessandro Anselmi -- Alessandro
  Anselmi: arhcaeology of the future
  / Francesco Moschini -- Synthesis
  between classical and modern /
  Francesco Moschini -- Materials of
  the work: skin and soul / Luciano
  Testa. Architect: Alessandro
  Anselmi.
  ANFIONE ZETO 1990, v.2, no.4-5,
  p.16-132, port, elevs., photos.,
  plans, secns., site plan.

TESTING
  See also QUALITY CONTROL
  See also STANDARDS

TESTING--GREAT BRITAIN
  Block busting / Denise Chevin.
  Onplans for use of full-scale
  buildings as laboratories for
  testing and research on how
  buildings perform in conditions
  such as fire, strong wind, or
  explosion.
  BUILDING 1990 Jan.5, v.255, no.1,
  p.53, photos.
  Cold bridge war / Matthew Coomber.
  Thermal Measurement, a testing
  house located in Rugby, England
  uses a profiling analysis
  technique based on the W. German
  DIN standards.
  BUILDING 1990 Mar.9, v.255, no.10,
  p.52-53, chart, port.
  Utopia goes on trial / Penny Guest.
  Plans by geographer Alice Coleman
  to test ways that bad design
  causes or encourages crime, in a
  program called DICE (Design
  Improvement Controlled
  Experiment).
  BUILDING 1990 Nov.23, v.255,
  no.46, p.20-22, port., elevs.,
  photos., plan.

TESTING--JAPAN
  Heat and mass transfer at outside
  surface of buildings / Akihito
  Ozaki, et al.
  Subtitle: Wind tunnel tests of
  heat and mass transfer on
  horizontal surfaces. English
  summary, p.25.
  NIHON KENCHIKU GAKKAI KEIKAKUKEI
  RONBUN HOKOKU SHU = JOURNAL OF
  ARCHITECTURE, PLANNING AND
  ENVIRONMENTAL ENGINEERING 1990
  Jan., no.1(407), p.11-25, charts,
  diagrs., graphs, tables, refs.

TESTING--NETHERLANDS--DELFT--
TECHNISCHE HOGESCHOOL DELFT
  Met minder energie een beter
  klimaat: regelsysteem passieve
  zonne-energie en raamvenhilatie /
  Joop Niesten.
  Research at the TU-Delft.
  DE ARCHITECT 1990 Oct., v.21,
  no.10, p.132-135, diagrs., graphs,
  dwgs., photos.

TESTING--POLITICAL ASPECTS
  Arguing over the monopoly board /
  Graham Ridout.
  Controversy over the British Board
  of Agrement's role in product
  testing certification in the
  European market.
  BUILDING 1990 Aug.3, v.255, no.31,
  p.34-35, photos.

TETLOW, KARIN
  Banking by waterfall / Karin Tetlow.
  On the atrium in the corporate
  headquarters of Home Savings of
  America, Irwindale, Calif.
  Interior designers: PHH
  Environments.
  INTERIORS 1990 Apr., v.149, no.9,
  p.94-[95], photos.
  Business tactics [interior design
  title registration] / Karin
  Tetlow.
  INTERIORS 1990 Dec., v.150, no.5,
  p.39, table.
  Communications tone / Karin Tetlow.
  Features interiors of renovated
  Southwestern Bell's Communications
  Center, Oklahoma City, OK.
  Architects: HTB.
  INTERIORS 1990 Nov., v.150, no.4,
  p.52-[55], photos., plan.
  Conference comfort / Karin Tetlow.
  On the Conference Express
  teleconferencing center, Toronto,
  Ontario. Architects: Marshall
  Cummings Mufson & Associates.
  INTERIORS 1990 May, v.149, no.10,
  p.74, photo., plan.
  A curtain up on wellness / Karin
  Tetlow.
  U.S. delegation visits several
  Soviet balneological spas.
  INTERIORS 1990 Dec., v.150, no.5,
  p.74-77, photos.
  Design goes to space: NASA and a
  program at the University of
  Houston are developing innovative
  structures for living in space /
  Karin Tetlow.
  The Sasakawa International Center
  for Space Architecture is working
  on NASA's latest program, Space
  Station Freedom.
  ARCHITECTURE: THE MAGAZINE OF THE
  AMERICAN INSTITUTE OF ARCHITECTS
  1990 May, v.79, no.5, p.[98]-101,
  ill., model.
  Design heals / Karin Tetlow.
  On the interior design of an
  intensive care unit, which was
  presented at the Third Symposium
  on Health Care Interior Design at
  San Francisco's Contract Design
  Center. Interior designer:
  Orlando Diaz-Azcuy.
  INTERIORS 1990 Dec., v.150, no.5,
  p.[60]-65, photos., plans.
  Discriminatory taxation / Karin
  Tetlow.
  NYC law imposes 4% sales tax on
  charges for interior design
  services.
  INTERIORS 1990 May, v.149, no.10,
  p.46, port.
  Easy cruising / Karin Tetlow.
  On the wheelchair-accessible
  features of Celebrity Cruise's M/V
  Horizon cruise ship.
  INTERIORS 1990 Oct., v.150, no.3,
  p.82-83, photos.

TETLOW, KARIN (CONTINUED)
  Foreign exchange: Practice: working
  abroad / Karin Tetlow.
  British and American architects
  discuss working overseas.
  ARCHITECTURE: THE AIA JOURNAL 1990
  Sept., v.79, no.9, p.101-105,
  ports., photos.
  Low budget marketing / Karin Tetlow.
  INTERIORS 1990 Mar., v.149, no.8,
  p.26, port.
  Marketing Macintoshes / Karin
  Tetlow.
  Interiors of Apple Computer's
  Computer Market Center in the
  Dallas Infomart. Architects:
  Gensler and Associates,
  Architects.
  INTERIORS 1990 Apr., v.149, no.9,
  p.44, photo., plan.
  Marketing with art / Karin Tetlow.
  On the Cooper Carry Studio
  offices, Atlanta.
  INTERIORS 1990 June, v.149, no.11,
  p.36, port., photo.
  Minimalist message / Karin Tetlow.
  Interiors of Swanke Hayden Connell
  Architects offices, Chicago.
  INTERIORS 1990 June, v.149, no.11,
  p.106-[107], photos., plan.
  Pepsi's new generation / Karin
  Tetlow.
  Interiors of Pepsi-Cola Worldwide
  Beverages headquarters, Somers,
  N.Y. Interior designers: Rosen
  Perry Preston.
  INTERIORS 1990 Mar., v.149, no.8,
  p.102-[109], photos., plan.
  Pursuit of success: Designer of the
  year Karen Daroff / Karin Tetlow.
  Profile of work of her firm,
  Daroff Design.
  INTERIORS 1990 Jan., v.149, no.6,
  p.96-126, photos., plans.
  Qualifying performance / Karin
  Tetlow.
  On the National Council for
  Interior Design Qualification
  exam.
  INTERIORS 1990 May, v.149, no.10,
  p.50, diagr.
  Red hot / Karin Tetlow.
  Interiors of the Tomato Bank,
  Okayama, Japan. Interior
  designer: Masanori Umeda.
  INTERIORS 1990 Apr., v.149, no.9,
  p.100-[101], photos., plan.
  Remote area ambiance / Karin Tetlow.
  On the design of the AT&T Remote
  Work Center, Oakland, Calif.
  Architect: George W. Famous.
  INTERIORS 1990 Mar., v.149, no.8,
  p.36, photo., isometric dwg.
  Shop and shine / Karin Tetlow.
  On award-winning design of Crate &
  Barrel's corporate headquarters in
  Northbrook, Ill. Architects:
  Solomon Cordwell Buenz.
  INTERIORS 1990 May, v.149, no.10,
  p.206-[219], dwgs., photos., plan.
  Shop right / Karin Tetlow.
  The interiors of four Barneys New
  York stores located in suburban
  malls. Architects: Rosenblum Harb
  Architects.
  INTERIORS 1990 July, v.149, no.12,
  p.82-89, photos., plans.
  Soft-tash / Karin Tetlow.
  On the Manulife Leasing Center
  located in the new Los Angeles
  office tower at 865 South
  Figueroa. Architects: Albert C.
(Continued next page)

TEXTILE MILLS--19TH CENTURY--ENGLAND--
WIRKSWORTH--JOHN BOWMER & SONS
Renovation case history no.66:
providing a new use / Andrew Sim.
Conversion of a 19th-cent. tape
mill at Wirksworth into a house
and business for owners Ralph
Selby and Lu Jeffery. Architect:
Keith Hamilton.
TRADITIONAL HOMES 1990 Mar., v.6,
no.6, p.20-26, photos., plans,
secn.

TEXTILE MILLS--19TH CENTURY--UNITED
STATES--NORTH PROVIDENCE (RHODE
ISLAND)--ALLENDALE MILL
The 1822 Allendale mill and
slow-burning construction: a case
study in the transmission of an
architectural technology / Richard
M. Candee.
On the framing technique used in
Zachariah Allen's textile mill in
North Providence, RI.
SOCIETY FOR INDUSTRIAL ARCHEOLOGY.
JOURNAL 1989, v.15, no.1, p.21-34,
dets., elevs., photos., plans,
secns., engrs., refs.

TEXTILE MILLS--GERMANY (WEST)--
AUGSBURG--TEXTILVIERTEL
Schutzwurdige Industrie-landschaft:
Vorgaben fur die Planung im
Augsburger Textilviertel / Astrid
Debold-Kritter.
BAUWELT 1989 Dec.22, v.80, no.48,
p.2310-2315, photos., engrs.,
aerial photos.

TEXTILE MILLS--ITALY--PONZANO VENETO--
BENETTON
Paesaggi attorno al lavoro: Ponzano
Veneto, Italia: Benetton =
Landscapes of labour: Benetton, at
Ponzano Veneto, Italy.
Corporate headquarters and
factory. Architects: Afra and
Tobia Scarpa.
ABITARE 1990 Oct., no.289,
p.230-243, model, photos., site
plan, sketches.

TEXTILE MILLS--SWITZERLAND--WIDNAU--
BELDONA FABRIKATIONS AG
Konstruktion als Struktur und Form:
Textilfabrik Beldona, Widnan SG,
1987 / Erich Offermann.
Architects: Suter + Suter.
WERK, BAUEN + WOHNEN 1989 Oct.,
no.10, p.15-17, folded p. at end,
axonometric view, dets., dwgs.,
photos., plans, secn.
Portfolio: technology and humanity /
Jim Murphy.
On two industrial buildings:
Beldona Fabrikations AG, Widnau,
Switzerland, architects: Suter und
Suter and ERCO Leuchten GmbH,
Ludenscheid, Germany, architects:
Kiessler und Partner.
PROGRESSIVE ARCHITECTURE 1990
Oct., v.71, no.10, p.96-[99],
photos., plans.

TEXTILES
See TEXTILE FABRICS

TEYSSOT, GEORGES, 1946-
Cancellazione e scorporamento:
dialoghi con Diller + Scofidio =
Erasure and disembodiment:
dialogues with Diller + Scofidio /
Georges Teyssot.
OTTAGONO 1990 Sept., no.96,
p.[56]-88, photos., refs.
The disease of the domicile /
Georges Teyssot.
Attempts "to form a provisional
view of the genealogy of
residential building types as seen
in France from 1850 to 1914."
Originally publ. in Italian in
1981; translated by Alan Jones and
Janet Abrams.
ASSEMBLAGE 1988 June, no.6,
p.[72]-97, ill., dwgs., photos.,
plans, secn., site plans, refs.
"The simple day and the light of the
sun": lights and shadows in the
museum / Georges Teyssot.
ASSEMBLAGE 1990 Aug., no.12,
p.[58]-83, ill., photos., refs.
Symposium: architecture on exhibit.
Seven architectural curators
respond to questions about
exhibiting architecture at their
institutions; Mildred Friedman,
Walker Art Center; Georges
Teyssot, Milan Triennale; John
Zukowsky, Art Insitute of Chicago;
Paolo Polledri, San Francisco
Museum of Modern Art; Stuart
Wrede, Museum of Modern Art, New
York; Ulriche Jehle-Schulte
Strathaus, Architekturmuseum,
Basel; Francois Burkhardt, Centre
Creation Industrielle, Centre
Pompidou, Paris.
DESIGN BOOK REVIEW 1989 summer,
no.16, p.23-32, photos.

THACKARA, JOHN
Profile: Italy's new dialectical
materialist / John Thackara.
Architect Ezio Manzini as design
critic.
BLUEPRINT (LONDON, ENGLAND) 1990
Sept., no.70, p.[20], port.
Stars and bars [Hotel Il Palazzo,
Fukuoka, Japan] / John Thackara.
Architect: Aldo Rossi.
BLUEPRINT (LONDON, ENGLAND) 1990
Mar., no.65, p.32-39, photos.

THAILAND--BAN WART NAM TON--VACATION
HOUSES--BOEHM-BEZING HOUSE
Mystik auf Stelzen / Erdtrud
Muhlens.
Features Suhid and Diether von
Boehm-Bezing's vacation home in
Ban Wart Nam Ton, Thailand.
English summary, p.2.
ARCHITEKTUR & WOHNEN 1990
Aug.-Sept., no.4, p.40-43,
photos., plan.

THAILAND--BANGKOK--AFFORDABLE HOUSING
The down-market trend in housing
production in Bangkok, 1980-87 /
Shlomo Angel, Sureeporn Chuated.
THIRD WORLD PLANNING REVIEW 1990
Feb., v.12, no.1, p.[1]-20,
graphs. dwgs., map, plans, tables,
refs.

THAILAND--BANGKOK--CITY TRAFFIC--
PSYCHOLOGICAL ASPECTS
Congestion or enlightenment /
Stephen Tyler.
Differences in philosophical
approaches to city traffic
congestion between Westerners and
travelers in Bangkok, Thailand.
BERKELEY PLANNING JOURNAL 1990,
v.5, p.114-116, ref.

THAILAND--BANGKOK--CITY TRAFFIC--
SOCIOLOGICAL ASPECTS
Congestion or enlightenment /
Stephen Tyler.
Differences in philosophical
approaches to city traffic
congestion between Westerners and
travelers in Bangkok, Thailand.
BERKELEY PLANNING JOURNAL 1990,
v.5, p.114-116, ref.

THAILAND--BANGKOK--HOUSING--ECONOMIC
ASPECTS
Bangkok: a profile of an efficiently
performing housing market / David
E. Dowall.
URBAN STUDIES 1989 June, v.26,
no.3, p.327-339, figs., tables,
refs.

THAILAND--BANGKOK--LAND VALUES--
ECONOMIC ASPECTS
Bangkok: a profile of an efficiently
performing housing market / David
E. Dowall.
URBAN STUDIES 1989 June, v.26,
no.3, p.327-339, figs., tables,
refs.

THAILAND--BANGKOK--LOW INCOME HOUSING
The down-market trend in housing
production in Bangkok, 1980-87 /
Shlomo Angel, Sureeporn Chuated.
THIRD WORLD PLANNING REVIEW 1990
Feb., v.12, no.1, p.[1]-20,
graphs, dwgs., map, plans, tables,
refs.

THAILAND--BANGKOK--LOW INCOME
HOUSING--SOCIOLOGICAL ASPECTS
Cultural housing preferences in
low-income resettlement
communities in Bangkok, Thailand /
Vimolsiddhi Horayangkura.
HOUSING AND SOCIETY 1988, v.15,
no.2, p.145-157, photos, plan,
tables, refs.

THAILAND--BANGKOK--SLUMS
Slumforbedring i Bangkok / Asger
Mollerup.
ARKITEKTEN 1990 Apr., v.92, no.4,
p.A80-A83, photos.

THAILAND--HUA-HIN--HOTELS--ALTERATIONS
AND ADDITIONS--HOTEL SOFITEL CENTRAL
Hotel Sofitel Central, Hua-Hin /
Bundit Chulasai.
Alterations to the Hotel Hua Hin
(opened in 1923), on the West
coast of Thailand. Architect:
Chulasai Co.
MIMAR: ARCHITECTURE IN DEVELOPMENT
1990 Sept., v.10, no.3(36),
p.34-39, map, photos., plans.

THAILAND--PHUKET--RESORTS--SEASIDE--
AMANPURI
Amanpuri, Phuket Island.
Resort hotel on the site of a
coconut plantation, western
Thailand. Architect: Ed Tuttle.
MIMAR: ARCHITECTURE IN DEVELOPMENT
1990 Sept., v.10, no.3(36),
p.40-45, map, photos., site plan.

THAILAND--SACRED SITES--BUDDHIST--
CONSERVATION AND RESTORATION--
SUKKHOTHAI HISTORICAL PARK
Reflections on a "golden age":
restorer's of Thailand's ancient
city of Sukhothai appear to have
sacrificed historical accuracy for
an idealized version of the past /
Betty Gosling.
Sukhothai Historical Park.
ARCHAEOLOGY 1990 July-Aug., v.43,
no.4, p.24-31, ill., map, photos.

THAILAND--SUKHOTHAI--CITIES AND
TOWNS--BUDDHIST--CONSERVATION AND
RESTORATION
Reflections on a "golden age":
restorer's of Thailand's ancient
city of Sukhothai appear to have
sacrificed historical accuracy for
an idealized version of the past /
Betty Gosling.
Sukhothai Historical Park.
ARCHAEOLOGY 1990 July-Aug., v.43,
no.4, p.24-31, ill., map, photos.

THAILAND--VERNACULAR ARCHITECTURE--
INFLUENCE
Mystik auf Stelzen / Erdtrud
Muhlens.
Features Suhid and Diether von
Boehm-Bezing's vacation home in
Ban Wart Nam Ton, Thailand.
English summary, p.2.
ARCHITEKTUR & WOHNEN 1990
Aug.-Sept., no.4, p.48-53,
photos., plan.

THAKUR, LAXMAN S.
Application of vastupurasamandala in
the Indian temple architecture /
Laxman S. Thakur.
Analysis of the Nagara temple
plans of Himachal Pradesh.
ARTIBUS ASIAE 1990, v.50, no.3-4,
p.263-284, dwgs., plans, refs.

THAKUR, NALINI
Mehrauli, Delhi / Nalini Thakur.
On the "heritage zone" of the
Mahrauli historic settlement of
the metropolitan region of New
Delhi.
ARCHITECTURE + DESIGN 1989
Nov.-Dec., v.6, no.1, p.[95]-104,
axonometric view, maps, photos,
plan, site plans.

THARALDSEN, ESPEN
Spieltrieb / Espen Tharaldsen.
Work by the Arbeidsgruppen HUS in
Bergen and Stavanger, Norway.
ARCHITHESE 1990 Sept.-Oct., v.20,
no.5, p.28-33,66, elevs., photos.,
plans, secns., refs.

THATCHED ROOFS
See ROOFS - THATCHED

THATCHER, CARROLL
CAD, part 3 / Carroll Thatcher, Guy
Thatcher.
Detailed analysis of CAD's costs
and benefits for interior
designers.
INTERIOR DESIGN 1990 Oct., v.61,
no.14, p.214-217, tables.
CAD: selection and management, part
2 / Carroll Thatcher.
On the principles of CAD
operations.
INTERIOR DESIGN 1990 Aug., v.61,
no.11, p.56,61,

THATCHER, GUY
CAD, part 3 / Carroll Thatcher, Guy
Thatcher.
Detailed analysis of CAD's costs
and benefits for interior
designers.
INTERIOR DESIGN 1990 Oct., v.61,
no.14, p.214-217, tables.

THAU, CARSTEN
AAA 25 aar.
Issue on the 25th anniversary of
the Arkitektskolen, Aarhus.
Contents: Dengang i 1960'erne, by
Knud Friis -- En skoles
indflydelse, by Nils-Ole Lund --
Ideologier og miljoer, by Carsten
Thau -- Den harde virkelighed, by
Gosta Knudsen -- Det svundne er en
drom, by Mogens Brandt Poulsen --
En betaenkelig
professorbetaenkning, by Jonas
Moller.
ARKITEKTEN 1990 Oct., v.92, no.14,
p.[444]-473,cover, axonometric
views, dwgs., ports., elevs.,
models, maps, photos., plans.
Berlin / Carsten Thau.
ARKITEKTEN 1990 Feb., v.92, no.2,
p.38-45, axonometric views,
models, map, photos., aerial
photos.
I tegningens laboratorium / Carsten
Thau.
Chernikhov's work in Moscow in the
1920s and early 1930s.
ARKITEKTEN 1990 July, v.92, no.9,
p.296-301, dwgs., photos.,
sketches, ref.
I tegningens laboratorium / Carsten
Thau.
Chernikhov's work in Moscow in the
1920s and early 1930s.
ARKITEKTEN 1990 July, v.92, no.9,
p.296-301, dwgs., photos.,
sketches, ref.
Storbyen i biografens morke: Our
filmen, arkitekturen og byens
poetik = The metropolis in the
darkness of the cinema - on film,
architecture and the poetics of
the urban / Carsten Thau.
In Danish and English.
SKALA 1990, no.22, p.28-35, dwgs.,
photos.

THAW, JACQUELINE
Teaching Times Square a lesson /
Andrew Mandel, Jacqueline Thaw.
While Times Square awaits
redevelopment, the theater group
En-Garde Arts performs "Crowbar"
in one of the area's saved
theaters, the Victory.
(Continued next column)

THAW, JACQUELINE (CONTINUED)
Teaching Times Square...(CONTINUED)
PLACES 1990 Summer, v.6, no.4,
p.[91-92], det., photos.

THAYER, ISAAC
New Orleans elan: the restoration of
this nineteenth-century residence
marked a unique new beginning for
its owners / Anne Elizabeth
Powell.
The Gleason-Ewin house in the
Garden district, now the
Christovich home. Original
architect (1853): Isaac Thayer.
HISTORIC PRESERVATION 1990
Jan.-Feb., v.42, no.1, p.24-[29],
photos.

THAYER, ROBERT L.
Pragmatism in paradise: technology
and the American landscape /
Robert L . Thayer, Jr.
LANDSCAPE 1990, v.30, no.3,
p.1-11, diagr., photos., table,
biblio.

THEATER
Behavior, performance, and
performance space: an interview
with Richard Schechner.
Conducted by the editors of
Perspecta in New York, Spring
1988.
PERSPECTA 1990, no.26, p.97-102,
Theater, theatricality, and
architecture / edited by Hans
Baldauf, Baker Goodwin, Amy
Reichert.
Issue consists of 19 articles; 16
are indexed separately. The other
three are "Erinnerung an eine
Revolution: an installation" by
Robert Wilson -- Meditations on
the Frame, by Jose Ortega y Gasset
-- Chairs, by Robert Wilson.
PERSPECTA 1990, no.26, p.1-[290],
ill., photos., refs.

THEATER BOXES
See BOXES (THEATER SPACES)

THEATER CURTAINS
See also THEATERS - STAGE-SETTING
AND SCENERY

THEATER--INDIA
Theatre in India / Girish Karnad.
A personal and theoretical essay
by a playwright.
ARCHITECTURE + DESIGN 1990
July-Aug., v.7, no.4, p.87-99,
refs.

THEATER - STAGE LIGHTING
See STAGE LIGHTING

THEATER--THEORY
Theatricality and re-presentation /
Karsten Harries.
PERSPECTA 1990, no.26, p.21-40,
dwgs., elev., photos., secn.,
aerial photo., refs.

THEATER--THEORY--GERMANY
Peter Behrens's highest Kultur
symbol, the theater / Stanford
Anderson.
A slightly revised version of
chapter 3 of the author's Ph.D.
dissertation, 1968, on inventive
theater ideas during the first
(Continued next page)

THEATER--THEORY--GERMANY (CONTINUED)
Peter Behrens's...(CONTINUED)
decade of the 20th century.
PERSPECTA 1990, no.26, p.103-134,
dwgs., maps, photos., plans, refs.

THEATERS
See also AMPHITHEATERS
See also DRIVE-IN THEATERS
See also MINIATURE THEATERS
See also MOVIE THEATERS
See also OPERA HOUSES

THEATERS--16TH CENTURY--ENGLAND--
LONDON--BOAR'S HEAD PLAYHOUSE
The human stage: English theatre
design, 1567-1640 [by] John Orrell
[book review] / S.J. Wiseman.
Reviewed with: The Boar's Head
Playhouse, by Herbert Berry.
LONDON JOURNAL 1990, v.15, no.1,
p.84-86.

THEATERS--18TH CENTURY--FRANCE--PARIS
Parigi: i teatri negli anni della
Rivoluzione / Giuseppe Radicchio,
Michele Sajous D'Oria.
In Italian; English, French,
German and Spanish summaries,
p.127. Also includes index of
theaters.
STORIA DELLA CITTA 1988
Jul.-Sept., v.13, no.47, p.7-118,
127, axonometric views, dwgs.,
elevs., plans, secns., sketches,
engrs., biblio., refs.

THEATERS--18TH CENTURY--ITALY--GENOA--
TEATRO CARLO FELICE--HISTORY
Per un profilo dell' architettura
dei teatri liguri: il Carlo Felice
e le sale ottocentesche / Nicolo
De Mari.
Summaries in English, French,
German and Spanish, p.157.
PALLADIO 1990 Jan.-June, v.3,
no.5, p.91-112, elevs., photos.,
plans., refs.

THEATERS--19TH CENTURY--CONSERVATION
AND RESTORATION--ITALY--PISA--TEATRO
VERDI
Conservazione e restauro = A
conserving restoration / Massimo
Carmassi.
Restoration of 1867 Teatro Verdi,
Pisa. Original architect: Andrea
Scala. Restoration architect:
Massimo Carmassi.
SPAZIO E SOCIETA 1990 Apr.-June,
v.13, no.50, p.66-79, ports.,
maps, photos., plans, secns.

THEATERS--19TH CENTURY--CONSERVATION
AND RESTORATION--NETHERLANDS--
HAGUE--KONINKLIJKE SCHOUWBURG
Vandenhove Verbouwt Haage
Schouwburg.
Renovation of the 1804 Koninklijke
Schouwburg. Architect for
renovation: Charles Vandenhove.
DE ARCHITECT 1990 Mar., v.21,
no.3, p.19, model.

THEATERS--19TH CENTURY--CONSERVATION
AND RESTORATION--SCOTLAND--GLASGOW--
OLD ATHENAEUM (SCOTTISH YOUTH
THEATRE)
Upstaging a concert hall [Old
Athenaeum, Glasgow] / Callum
Murray.
Restoration of late 19th cent. Old
Athenaeum, now the headquarters
for the Scottish Youth Theatre.
Original architect: Sir J.J.
Burnet; restoration architects:
Campbell and Arnott.
ARCHITECTS' JOURNAL 1990 Jan.31,
v.191, no.5, p.15, photos.

THEATERS--19TH CENTURY--CONSERVATION
AND RESTORATION--SPAIN--BILBAO--
TEATRO ARRIAGA
Rehabilitacion del Teatro Arriaga de
Bilbao: Francisco Hurtado,
arquitecto.
Original architect: Joaquin
Rucoba. Alterations 1915 by
Federico Ugalde. Spanish, English
text.
ON DISENO 1990, no.109, p.178-186,
photos., plans.

THEATERS--19TH CENTURY--ITALY--LIGURIA
Per un profilo dell' architettura
dei teatri liguri: il Carlo Felice
e le sale ottocentesche / Nicolo
De Mari.
Summaries in English, French,
German and Spanish, p.157.
PALLADIO 1990 Jan.-June, v.3,
no.5, p.91-112, elevs., photos.,
plans., refs.

THEATERS--20TH CENTURY--CONSERVATION
AND RESTORATION--BRAZIL--SAO PAULO--
TEATRO JOSE DE ALENCAR
Teatro Jose de Alencar resgata sua
historia.
Restoration of an eclectic 1910
theater in Sao Paulo.
PROJETO 1990 Dec.-1991 Jan.,
no.137, p.99-[100], photos.

THEATERS--20TH CENTURY--EUROPE
Peter Behrens's highest Kultur
symbol, the theater / Stanford
Anderson.
A slightly revised version of
chapter 3 of the author's Ph.D.
dissertation, 1968, on inventive
theater ideas during the first
decade of the 20th century.
PERSPECTA 1990, no.26, p.103-134,
dwgs., maps, photos., plans, refs.

THEATERS--20TH CENTURY--ITALY
The theaters of the architect /
Alberto Ferlenga.
Projects by Aldo Rossi.
PERSPECTA 1990, no.26, p.191-202,
axonometric view, dwgs., maps,
photos., plans, secns., aerial
photos.

THEATERS--ALTERATIONS AND ADDITIONS--
COMPETITIONS--GERMANY (WEST)--
KASSEL--STAATSTHEATER
Erste Preise: Kulturbauten.
Four projects: Haus der Geschichte
Baden-Wurttemberg, Stuttgart
(architect: Behnisch und Partner);
Regierungsprasidium und
Staatstheater, Kassel (architect:
Bieling und Bieling); Musik- und
Kongresshalle, Wallhalbinsel in
(Continued next column)

THEATERS--ALTERATIONS AND ADDITIONS--
COMPETITIONS--GERMANY (WEST)--
KASSEL--STAATSTHEATER (CONTINUED)
Erste Preise:...(CONTINUED)
Lubeck (architect: Meinhard von
Gerkan); Gutenberg-Museum Mainz
(architects: Eric Rossmann, Karl
Platte).
DEUTSCHES ARCHITEKTENBLATT 1990
Sept.1, v.22, no.9, p.1301-1304,
elevs., models, plans, secns.
Regierungsprasidium und
Staatstheater Kassel / Jurgen
Noll.
Results of competition, for
addition to a public building,
announced in Dec.1989. First
prize: Bieling und Bieling.
Second prize: Gerber und Partner.
Third prize: Peter Scheele.
BAUWELT 1990 Jan.19, v.81, no.2-3,
p.63, models.

THEATERS--ALTERATIONS AND ADDITIONS--
FRANCE--PARIS--THEATRE DES
CHAMPS-ELYSEES
Cote cour, cote journaux / Michele
Champenois.
On the controversy surrounding the
renovation of the Theatre des
Champs-Elysees, Paris and the
addition of a rooftop restaurant.
Original architect: Auguste
Perret. English summary.
ARCHITECTURE D'AUJOURD'HUI 1990
Oct., no.271, p.208-[211], dwg.,
photos., sketches.
Renouvellement ou ecrasement? Le
Theatre des Champs-Elysees /
Bernard Marrey.
Original architect: Auguste
Perret.
SITES ET MONUMENTS 1990, no.128,
p.15-18, photo.
Le restaurant sur le toit, ouvrage
d'art a la hauteur / Frederique de
Gravelaine.
On the restaurant recently added
to the rooftop of the Theatre des
Champs-Elysees, Paris. Architects:
Brigit de Kosmi, eSpace. English
summary.
ARCHITECTURE D'AUJOURD'HUI 1990
Oct., no.271, p.212-215, photos.,
secn.
Une salle qui chante / Bruno Suner.
On the architectural acoustics of
the renovated 1910-1913 Theatre
des Champs-Elysees, Paris.
Original architect: Auguste
Perret. English summary.
ARCHITECTURE D'AUJOURD'HUI 1990
Oct., no.271, p.206-207, secn.,
sketch, biblio.
Theatre des Champs-Elysees / Francis
Lacloche, Youssef Baccouche.
Renovation of 1913 theater in
Paris. Original architect: Auguste
Perret. English summary.
ARCHITECTURE D'AUJOURD'HUI 1990
Oct., no.271, p.[188-189], photos,

THEATERS--ALTERATIONS AND ADDITIONS--
GERMANY (WEST)--SAARBRUCKEN--
STAATSTHEATER
Gastspiel: vier Bauten von Gottfried
Bohm in Saarbrucken / Susanne
Ehrlinger, Kaye Geipel.
DEUTSCHE BAUZEITUNG 1990 Mar.,
v.124, no.3, p.46-53, elevs.,
photos., plans, site plan, sketch.

THEATERS--ALTERATIONS AND ADDITIONS--
IRELAND--DUBLIN--ABBEY THEATRE
The Abbey portico.
    Portico addition to the front
    elevation of the Abbey Theatre,
    Dublin. Architects: Niall
    McCullough and Valerie Mulvin.
    PLAN: ARCHITECTURE AND BUILDING
    DESIGN IN IRELAND 1990 July, v.32,
    no.7, p.[29]-31, dwg., elev.,
    photos., plans.

THEATERS--ALTERATIONS AND ADDITIONS--
UNITED STATES--OKLAHOMA CITY
(OKLAHOMA)--MUMMERS THEATER
A mummers' tale: a true life story /
    Barbara Koerble.
    Functional improvements planned
    for the Mummers Theater (1971),
    Oklahaoma City. Original
    architect: John Johansen.
    Renovation architect: Elliott &
    Associates.
    CITE: THE ARCHITECTURE AND DESIGN
    REVIEW OF HOUSTON 1990 Fall,
    no.25, p.14-17, model, photos.,
    plan, secn., refs.

THEATERS--ALTERATIONS AND ADDITIONS--
UNITED STATES--OKLAHOMA CITY
(OKLAHOMA)--STAGE CENTER
Renewing our modern legacy / Andrea
    Oppenheimer Dean.
    Four additions to buildings of the
    1950s and 1960s.
    ARCHITECTURE: THE AIA JOURNAL 1990
    Nov., v.79, no.11, p.66-69, ill.,
    elevs., models, photos.

THEATERS--ART NOUVEAU--SWEDEN--
STOCKHOLM--KUNGLIGA DRAMATISKA
TEATERN
Il Dramatiska Teatern = The Royal
    Dramatic Theatre [Stockholm].
    Art nouveau building, built
    1901-1908. Architect: Fredrik
    Lilljekvist.
    ABITARE 1990 July-Aug., no.287,
    p.148-[151], port., photos.

THEATERS--CANADA--MONTREAL (QUEBEC)--
CENTRE DU THEATRE D'AUJOURD'HUI
The Canadian Architect 1990 22nd
    Annual Awards of Excellence.
    Eight awards. Architects: Steven
    Fong, A.J. Diamond, Donald Schmitt
    & Co. with Kolker Kolker Epstein
    Architects, Meltzer Igra
    Architects, Bugod Figueiredo
    Krendel Architects, Peter Cardew
    Architects, Richard Henriquez
    Architect, Laszlo Nemeth Assoc.,
    Kearns Mancini Architects, Patkan
    Architects, Saucier + Perrotte,
    and Kuwabara Payne McKenna
    Blumberg.
    CANADIAN ARCHITECT 1990 Dec.,
    v.35, no.12, p.9-24,29, dwgs.,
    elevs., models, plans, secns.,
    site plans.

THEATERS--COMPETITIONS--ITALY--
RIMINI--TEATRO AMINTORE GALLI
Tra progetto e didattica: Vicenzo
    Giuseppe Berti, 1980-90 / Glauco
    Gresleri.
    Four projects: Cassa di Risparmio,
    San Marino -- Railroad station,
    Bologna -- City walls, Florence --
    Teatro Amintore Galli, Rimini.
    PARAMETRO 1990 Jan.-Feb., no.176,
    p.70-81, axonometric views.,
                (Continued next column)

THEATERS--COMPETITIONS--ITALY--
RIMINI--TEATRO AMINTORE GALLI
                        (CONTINUED)
Tra progetto e...(CONTINUED)
    elevs., photos., plans, secns.,
    site plans.

THEATERS--COMPETITIONS--SOVIET UNION--
MOSCOW--CHAMBER THEATRE ARTS CENTRE
Summer deadline for Moscow trio.
    Three British competition entries
    for Moscow's Chamber Theatre Arts
    Centre in the Hermitage Gardens:
    Peter Baynes and David Whitehead;
    John Seifert; and Mills Beaumont
    Leavy (MBL).
    ARCHITECTS' JOURNAL 1990 Sept.26,
    v.192, no.13, p.12-13, axonometric
    view, elev., model, secns.,
    sketches.

THEATERS--CONSERVATION AND
RESTORATION--ITALY--GENOA--TEATRO
CARLO FELICE
Aldo Rossi a Genes / Emmanuel
    Doutriaux.
    Reconstruction of the Teatro Carlo
    Felice, Genoa. Original architect:
    Carlo Barabino. Reconstruction
    architects: Aldo Rossi, Fabio
    Reinhart, Ignazio Gardella.
    English summary, p.154.
    ARCHITECTURE D'AUJOURD'HUI 1990
    Apr., no.268, p.152-[155], dwgs.,
    models, photos., plan, secn., site
    plan.
Aldo Rossi Opera buffa: Wiederaufbau
    des Teatro Carlo Felice in Genua /
    Sebastian Redecke.
    Alterations at the Teatro Carlo
    Felice. Architects: Ignazio
    Gardella, Fabio Reinhart, Aldo
    Rossi. Original architect: Carlo
    Barabino.
    BAUWELT 1990 July 27, v.81, no.28,
    p.1418-1427, dwg., map, photos.,
    plans, secns.
Completata la ricostruzione del
    teatro Carlo Felice a Genova.
    Engineer: Mario Valle Engineering.
    Architect: Aldo Rossi.
    CASABELLA 1990 July-Aug., v.54,
    no.570, p.33, plans., secn.
Das neue Teatro Carlo Felice in
    Genua / Vittorio Savi.
    Architects: Aldo Rossi, Ignazio
    Gardella, Fabio Reinhart.
    WERK, BAUEN + WOHNEN 1990 Dec.,
    no.12, p.2-9, dwgs., maps,
    photos., plans, secns., aerial
    photos.
Nuovo Teatro Carlo Felice , Genova:
    Ignazio Gardella, Aldo Rossi /
    Vittorio Savi.
    Text in Italian and English.
    DOMUS 1990 Sept., no.719,
    p.[33-49], dets., dwgs., elevs.,
    models, maps, photos., plans,
    secns., site plans, sketches,
    aerial photos.
Een ventiel voor de stad: Aldo
    Rossi's Teatro Carlo Felice in
    Genua / Arthur Wortmann.
    ARCHIS 1990 Oct., no.10, p.36-41,
    dwgs., elevs., model, photos.,
    plans, secns., site plans, aerial
    photos.

THEATERS--CONSERVATION AND
RESTORATION--SOVIET UNION--MOSCOW--
V. MAIAKOVSKI THEATRE
La ristrutturazione globale del
    teatro "V. Majakovskij" a Mosca =
    The renovation of the "V.
    Maiakovski" theatre in Moscow /
    Andrei Nekrasov.
    Architects: A. Nekrasov, D.
    Velickin, A. Gnezdilov, A.
    Cel'cov. In Italian, with English
    summary.
    METAMORFOSI 1988, no.11, p.30-34,
    models.

THEATERS--ENGLAND--LEEDS--WEST
YORKSHIRE PLAYHOUSE
External walls and roof, theatre,
    the Appleton Partnership.
    The West Yorkshire Playhouse,
    Leeds. See also p.44-45.
    ARCHITECTS' JOURNAL 1990 Apr.25,
    v.191, no.17, p.59, dets., elev.,
    photos., secns., isometric dwg.

THEATERS--FINLAND--JYVASKYLA--
TYOVAENTALO
Alberti evocado por Alvar Aalto =
    Alberti evoked by Alvar Aalto /
    Carmen Jorda.
    On the work of Alvar Aalto, Text
    in Spanish and English. In
    particular the Tyovaentalo,
    Jyvaskyla.
    COMPOSICION ARQUITECTONICA, ART &
    ARCHITECTURE 1990 June, no.6,
    p.[103], dwgs., elev., photos.,
    plans, secns.

THEATERS--FRANCE--PARIS--THEATRE DE LA
COLLINE
Fabre, Perrottet, Cattani et les
    autres: du Theatre de la Ville au
    Theatre de la Colline.
    Theatre de la Colline, national
    theater, Paris. Architects:
    Valentin Fabre, Jean Perrottet,
    Alberto Cattani. English summary,
    p.128. Spanish summary, p.199.
    TECHNIQUES ET ARCHITECTURE 1990
    Apr.-May, no.389, p.126-129,
    photos., secns.

THEATERS--FRANCE--PARIS--THEATRE DES
CHAMPS-ELYSEES
Champs Elysees Theatre, Avenue
    Montaigne, Paris, 1913.
    Architects: Auguste and Gustave
    Perret, with Roger Bouvard, Henry
    van de Velde and Antoine
    Bourdelle. Text in Japanese and
    English.
    ARCHITECTURE AND URBANISM 1990
    Sept., no.9 Extra edition,
    p.58-65,262, photos., plan, secn.
Le theatre de l'ossature /
    Jean-Louis Cohen.
    On the controversy concerning the
    architects of the 1910-1913
    Theatre des Champs-Elysees, Paris.
    English summary.
    ARCHITECTURE D'AUJOURD'HUI 1990
    Oct., no.271, p.200-205, elev.,
    photos., plans, secn., sketches,
    biblio.

THEATERS--GERMANY (EAST)--HELLERAU--
FESTSPIELHAUS
Hellerau: ein neuer Anfang.
The Festspielhaus of 1911-1912 was
used by troops during World War II
and in May 1990 by art students.
Architect: Heinrich Tessenow.
BAUWELT 1990 Dec.7, v.81, no.46,
p.2286, photos.

THEATERS--GERMANY (EAST)--POTSDAM
Der Theaterneubau in Potsdam, Ende
oder Neubeginn? / Christian
Wendland.
BAUWELT 1990 Aug.10, v.81,
no.29-30, p.1451-1453, ill., maps,
photo., aerial photo.

THEATERS--GERMANY (EAST)--POTSDAM--
POTSDAMER THEATER
Theaterbau in Potsdam: Postdamer
Bautheater? / Christian Wendland.
DER ARCHITEKT 1990 May, no.5,
p.221-222, ill.

THEATERS--GERMANY (WEST)--DARMSTADT--
HOF THEATER
Gottfried und Mannfred Sempers
Projekt eines Hoftheaters fur
Darmstadt (MV199) / Valentin
Hammerschmidt.
ARCHITECTURA 1990, v.20, no.2,
p.142-159, ill., dwgs., elevs.,
photos., plans, secn., site plan,
sketch, refs.

THEATERS--GERMANY (WEST)--FRANKFURT AM
MAIN--SCHAUSPIEL FRANKFURT
Bockenheimer Depot in Frankfurt =
Bockenheimer tram depot in
Frankfurt.
Conversion of railroad station
into a theater. Architects for
the conversion: Klaus Peter
Heinrici, Karl-Georg Geiger.
ARCHITEKTUR + WETTBEWERBE 1989
Dec., no.140, p.20-21, photos.,
plan, secn.

THEATERS--GERMANY (WEST)--HAMBURG--
FLORA-THEATER AM HOLSTENBAHNHOF
Das Raumschiff lost den Dampfer ab:
das Flora-Theater am
Holstenbahnhof in Hamburg / Karin
von Behr.
Architects: Kleffel + Kohnholdt.
DEUTSCHE BAUZEITUNG 1990 Oct.,
v.124, no.10, p.191-192, elev.,
photos.

THEATERS--GERMANY (WEST)--HAMBURG--
NEUE FLORA
"Neue Flora" in Hamburg: Theater und
fremdgenutzte Randbebauung.
Architect: Kleffel & Kohnholdt.
Includes English summary.
BAUMEISTER 1990 Nov., v.87, no.11,
p.15-21, photos., plans, secn.,
site plan.

THEATERS--GREEK--GREECE--ATHENS
Representing the body politic: the
theater of manhood in classical
Athens / John Winkler.
PERSPECTA 1990, no.26, p.215-228,
photos., plans, tables, aerial
photos., refs.

THEATERS--GREEK REVIVAL--UNITED
STATES--COLLINSVILLE (ILLINOIS)--
MINER'S INSTITUTE THEATER
The theater that miners built:
Collinsville's Miner's Institute
Theater / David Newton.
Built in 1916, at 204 W. Main St.
Architect: Robert G. Kirsch.
HISTORIC ILLINOIS 1990 June, v.13,
no.1, p.6-7,12-13, photos.

THEATERS--HELLENISTIC--CONSERVATION
AND RESTORATION--ITALY--SARNO
Il teatro tardo-ellenistico di Foce
Sarno: note sull'intervento di
restauro / Raffaele D'Andria.
L'URBE: RIVISTA ROMANA DI STORIA,
ARTE, LETTERE, COSTUMANZE 1989
May-Aug., v.52, nos.3-4, p.32-36,
plan, ref.

THEATERS--INDIA
Theatre in India / Girish Karnad.
A personal and theoretical essay
by a playwright.
ARCHITECTURE + DESIGN 1990
July-Aug., v.7, no.4, p.87-99,
refs.

THEATERS--INTERIOR DESIGN--FRANCE--
DAX--ATRIUM-CASINO
Interieurs: l'Atrium-Casino de Dax,
[France].
Interior renovation. Site: cours
marechal Foch. Original architect:
Andre Granet. Architects for
renovation: J. de Giacinto, A.
Loisier and B. Nivelle.
LE MONITEUR ARCHITECTURE AMC 1990
Sept., no.14, p.65-67, photos.,
plans, secn.

THEATERS--INTERIOR DESIGN--GERMANY
(WEST)--SAARBRUCKEN--
GRENZLANDTHEATER
Theatralische Entausserung eines
Interieurs = Theatrical
renunciation of the interior.
Auditorium ceiling painting by
Peter Schubert. Architect: Paul
Baumgarten.
DAIDALOS 1990 June 15, no.36,
p.122-125, photos.

THEATERS--INTERIOR LIGHTING
MACK Architects exercises the
state-of-the-art lighting
simulation for the design of a
theater / David Lord.
Use of Radiance simulation
software.
PROGRESSIVE ARCHITECTURE 1990
Nov., v.71, no.12, p.130, photos.

THEATERS--ITALY--FLORENCE--TEATRO
DELLA COMPAGNIA
"Teatro della Compagnia" in Florenz.
Site: Via Cavour. Architects:
Adolfo Natalini with Fabrizio
Natalini.
DEUTSCHE BAUZEITSCHRIFT 1990 Aug.,
v.38, no.8, p.1089-1096, dets.,
photos., plans, secns., site
plans, sketches, isometric dwg.

THEATERS--ITALY--GENOA--TEATRO CARLO
FELICE
L'acoustique des salles d'opera a
l'heure du compact disc / Jose
Bernhart.
Focus on the acoustics in the
Teatro Carlo Felice, Genoa.
ARCHITECTURE D'AUJOURD'HUI 1990
Apr., no.268, p.156-[157], det.,
fig., photo.

THEATERS--NEOCLASSICAL--CONSERVATION
AND RESTORATION--ITALY--MERANO
Merano restaurata = Urban
realizations: Meran restored.
Restoration of a health spa in
Italy. Kurhaus architect:
Friedrich Ohmann; theater
architect: Martin Dulfer.
Restoration architect: Vincenzo
Pavan.
ABITARE 1990 Apr., no.284,
p.188-[203],242, photos., plan,
secn., site plans.

THEATERS--NETHERLANDS--BERGEN OP
ZOOM--MAAGD
Theatrale kerk: Theater De Maagd in
Bergen op Zoom.
Alterations to a neo-Baroque
church (Heilige Maagdkerk, 1829)
in Bergen op Zoom. Original
architects: Onno Greiner, Bart
Mispelblom Beyer.
ARCHIS 1990 Sept., no.9, p.3,
photo., plans.
Van kerk tot theater: Onno Greiner
verbouult kerk in Bergen op Zoom /
Joop Niesten.
Renovation of the 1829
Waterstaatskerk for use as a
theater, De Maagd. Original
architect: Josephus-Emmanuel
Franssen.
DE ARCHITECT 1990 Nov., v.21,
no.11, p.108-111, photos., plan,
secn.

THEATERS--NETHERLANDS--HAGUE--
NEDERLANDS DANS THEATER
Tanztheater in Den Haag, 1987.
Architect: Rem Koolhaas, Office
for Metropolitan Architecture.
WERK, BAUEN + WOHNEN 1990 Mar.,
no.3, p.32-37, photos., plans,
secns., site plan.

THEATERS--NETHERLANDS--LEEUWARDEN--
HARMONIE
Frits van Dongen ontwerpt theater /
Peter Huygen.
The De Harmonie, in Leeuwarden.
DE ARCHITECT 1990 Dec., v.21,
no.12, p.28-29, model, photo.,
secn.

THEATERS--OPEN-AIR--ITALY
Italy's green theatres / Gordon
Taylor, Guy Cooper.
The garden theaters of Italian
villas.
COUNTRY LIFE 1990 Sept.20, v.184
no.38, p.162-163, photos.

THEATERS--OPEN-AIR--ITALY--LIGNANO
SABBIADORO
Lignano Sabbiadoro, Il giardino dei
labirinti = The garden of the
labyrinths.
Open-air theater and walkway in an
Italian "tourist village."
Architects: Studio Nizzoli (G.M.
(Continued next page)

THEATERS--OPEN-AIR--ITALY--LIGNANO
SABBIADORO (CONTINUED)
Lignano Sabbiadoro,...(CONTINUED)
Oliveri, P. Viola).
ARCHITETTURA: CRONACHE E STORIA
1990 Nov., v.36, no.11(421),
p.770-777, elevs., photos., plans,
secns.

THEATERS--OPEN-AIR--ITALY--
PORTOROTONDO
Classicita a Portorotondo =
Classicism at Portorotondo.
Project for open-air theater;
architect: Gianfranco Fini.
L'ARCA 1990 Sept., no.41 suppl.
l'Arca 2, p.104, dwgs., plan.

THEATERS--OPEN-AIR--SPAIN--SAGUNTO--
TEATRO ROMANO
Due progetti di Giorgio Grassi a
Venezia [exhibition review].
Exhibition at the Fondazione A.
Masieri, on the Teatro romano.
L'INDUSTRIA DELLE COSTRUZIONI 1990
May, v.24, no.223, p.68-69,
axonometric view, elev., models,
secns., site plan.

THEATERS--OPEN-AIR--UNITED STATES--SAN
DIEGO (CALIFORNIA)--MUNK GARDEN
THEATER
Dramatically designed: in San Diego,
a very theatrical garden / Carolyn
Hufbauer.
Small garden theatre designed by
Judith Munk.
GARDEN DESIGN 1990 Spring, v.9,
no.1, p.77-80, site plan, photos.

THEATERS--RECONSTRUCTION--ENGLAND--
LONDON--GLOBE THEATRE
Jonson joins a global war / Callum
Murray.
Reconstruction of Shakespeare's
Globe Theatre on London's
Bankside. Architects: Pentagram.
ARCHITECTS' JOURNAL 1990 Feb.14,
v.191, no.7, p.17, model, secn.

THEATERS--RENAISSANCE--ENGLAND
The human stage: English theatre
design, 1567-1640 [by] John Orrell
[book review] / S.J. Wiseman.
Reviewed with: The Boar's Head
Playhouse, by Herbert Berry.
LONDON JOURNAL 1990, v.15, no.1,
p.84-86.

THEATERS--ROMAN
The ancient Roman roofed theater /
George Izenour.
Proposes a reinterpretation of
theater design, based on
increasing archaeological
evidence.
PERSPECTA 1990, no.26, p.69-82,
photos., plans, secns., aerial
photos.
Vitruvius and Roman theater design /
Frank B. Sear.
AMERICAN JOURNAL OF ARCHAEOLOGY
1990 Apr., v.94, no.2, p.249-258,
diagrs., plans, refs.

THEATERS--ROMAN--ALTERATIONS AND
ADDITIONS--SPAIN--SAGUNTO
Due progetti di Giorgio Grassi a
Venezia [exhibition review].
Exhibition at the Fondazione A.
Masieri, on the Teatro romano.
L'INDUSTRIA DELLE COSTRUZIONI 1990
May, v.24, no.223, p.68-69,
axonometric view, elev., models,
secns., site plan.

THEATERS--ROUND--ENGLAND--LONDON--
GLOBE THEATRE
Jonson joins a global war / Callum
Murray.
Reconstruction of Shakespeare's
Globe Theatre on London's
Bankside. Architects: Pentagram.
ARCHITECTS' JOURNAL 1990 Feb.14,
v.191, no.7, p.17, model, secn.

THEATERS--ROUND--JAPAN--TOKYO--KARAZA
THEATER
Kara-za, a movable theater: an
interview with Tadao Ando.
An outdoor theater, designed for
the Asakusa district of Tokyo.
PERSPECTA 1990, no.26, p.171-184,
dets., elevs., maps, photos.,
plans, secn., sketches.

THEATERS - STAGE-SETTING AND SCENERY
See also FILM SETS
Architekturzitat als szenische Macht
/ Hermann Wiesler.
BAUWELT 1990 July 27, v.81, no.28,
p.1428-1433, dwg., photo., site
plans.
Lenguajes escenograficos: entrevista
con Ezio Frigerio [interview] /
Mario Bernedo.
ARQUITECTURA VIVA 1990 July-Aug.,
no.13, p.33-35, photos.
No stone unturned: Unplanned
entertainment / Penny Wright.
Report of talk given 19 Oct. 1990
at the Architectural Association,
London, by Mark Fisher of Fisher
Park, designers of demountable
stage sets for performers such as
the Rolling Stones.
ARCHITECTS' JOURNAL 1990 Oct.31,
v.192, no.18, p.73,75, elev.,
photo.
Gli oggetti impenetrabili / Paolo
Zani.
On the theater designs of Robert
Wilson. English summary, p.[8]
MODO 1990 Apr., v.13, no.122,
p.46-49, ill., photos.
On art for the stage / Peter
Behrens.
Translated from the German article
"Uber die Kunst auf der Buhne",
published in Frankfurter Zeitung,
LIV, 78 (Mar. 20, 1910). Introd.
by Stanford Anderson.
PERSPECTA 1990, no.26, p.135-142,
refs.
Opera round the clock / Denise
Chevin.
Renovations to stage and backstage
technical and mechanical systems
at the Royal Opera House, London.
BUILDING 1990 Feb.16, v.255, no.7,
p.74-75, isometric dwg.
Rappel a l'ordre: the case for the
tectonic / Kenneth Frampton.
Form is discussed with respect to
"the current tendency to reduce
architecture to scenography".
ARCHITECTURAL DESIGN 1990, v.60,
(Continued next column)

THEATERS - STAGE-SETTING AND SCENERY
(CONTINUED)
Rappel a l'ordre: the... (CONTINUED)
no.3-4, p.19-25, axonometric
views, dwgs., sketches, refs.
Stage names / David Redhead.
Profiles four stage set designers:
Bob Crowley, David Fielding,
William Dudley, and Maria
Bjornson.
DESIGNERS' JOURNAL 1990 Apr.,
no.56, p.35-[43], dwgs., ports.
Theater, theatricality, and
architecture / edited by Hans
Baldauf, Baker Goodwin, Amy
Reichert.
Issue consists of 19 articles; 16
are indexed separately. The other
three are "Erinnerung an eine
Revolution: an installation" by
Robert Wilson -- Meditations on
the Frame, by Jose Ortega y Gasset
-- Chairs, by Robert Wilson.
PERSPECTA 1990, no.26, p.1-[290],
ill., photos., refs.
Theater voor het voetlicht [review]
/ Robde Graaf.
Exhibition (De verbeelding
vooruit) until Apr.23 and
symposium ("Ruimte als theatraal
middel") on Mar.12-13, 1990, both
at the Beurs, Amsterdam. Also
reviews a book by Lia Gieling,
Toneelbeeld vanat 1945 in
Nederland.
ARCHIS 1990 Apr., no.4, p.8-11,
photos.

THEATERS--STAGE-SETTING AND SCENERY--
17TH CENTURY--ENGLAND--LONDON--
MASQUE OF QUEENS
Il Filarete and Inigo Jones: the
House of Fame in Ben Jonson's "The
Masque of Queens" / John F.
Moffitt.
Stage set possibly influenced by
Filarete. Italian summary,p.241.
ARTE LOMBARDA 1989, no.90-91,
p.61-66, dwgs., elev., plan, refs.

THEATERS--STAGE-SETTING AND SCENERY--
20TH CENTURY--UNITED STATES--ROLLING
STONES CONCERTS
Rolling Stones / Mark Fisher,
Jonathan Park.
High-tech stage sets for the 1989
U.S. tour. Section includes "It's
only rock'n'roll" and "Jagger: in
response to questions", by Andreas
Papadakis.
ARCHITECTURAL DESIGN 1990, v.60,
no.3-4, p.44-61, ill., photos.

THEATERS--STAGE-SETTING AND SCENERY--
ENGLAND--LONDON--ROYAL OPERA HOUSE
Blood, sweat and cheers [dance
review] / Peter Dormer.
Review of "Bloodlines", a new work
for the Royal Ballet. Sets by
Deanna Petherbridge. Performed at
Covent Garden, London 13 and 20
Dec. 1990.
ARCHITECTS' JOURNAL 1990 Dec.12,
v.192, no.24, p.56, ill., photo.

THEATERS--STAGE-SETTING AND SCENERY--
GREAT BRITAIN
Designing for theatre: British
theatre design: the Modern age,
edited by John Goodwin [book
review] / Marina Vaizey.
Scenery design and states sets.
ROYAL SOCIETY OF ARTS, LONDON. RSA
JOURNAL 1990 Apr., v.138, no.5405,
p.375-376.

THEATERS--STAGE-SETTING AND SCENERY--
ITALY--VENICE
"I cieli e le ombre, e la facciata
del tempio": il Festival
Internazionale del Teatro di
Venezia nel secondo dopoguerra
(1947-1950) / Carmelo Alberti.
Held outdoors in various theaters
as part of the Biennale di
Venezia.
VENEZIA ARTI 1990, v.4, p.114-126,
photos., refs.

THEATERS--STAGE-SETTING AND SCENERY--
TEMPORARY--UNITED STATES--WASHINGTON
(DISTRICT OF COLUMBIA)--CITADEL
SOUNDSTAGE
Setting a marriage / Justin
Henderson.
Stage sets for a wedding held in
the Citadel Soundstage,
Washington, D.C. Architects: David
M. Schwarz Architectural Services.
INTERIORS 1990 Apr., v.149, no.9,
p.90-[93], photos., plans.

THEATERS--STAGE-SETTING AND SCENERY--
UNITED STATES
De rol van het meuble: Robert Wilson
als ontwerper / Janny Donker.
Stage sets for "Einstein on the
Beach" and 1980s productions.
ARCHIS 1989 Sept., no.9, p.7-9,
photos.

THEATERS--STAGE-SETTING AND SCENERY--
UNITED STATES--INSTANT CITY
Instant City / Deyan Sudjic.
Concert set used by the Rolling
Stones in 1989, designed by
Jonathan Park and others. First
published in English in Blueprint,
9/89.
BAUWELT 1990 Dec.1, v.81, no.45,
p.2268-2271, dwgs., photos.

THEATERS--SWEDEN--LULEA
Le case di legno non sono solo rosse
= Wooden houses are not just red.
A 1648 farmhouse in Skraeddatorp;
18th-cent. houses in Stockholm;
house of architect Jan Gezelius,
Stockholm; the Anthropological
Museum at Eketorp; and the theater
workshop in Lulea (architects:
FFNS).
ABITARE 1990 July-Aug., no.287,
p.190-201, dwg., port., photos.,
plans, seems., site plan.

THEATERS--TEMPORARY--COMPETITIONS
Un teatro di provincia per le
compagnie in tournee = A
provincial theatre for companies
on tour / Andrei Nekrasov.
Architects: A. Nekrasov, S.
Romanov, N. Novikov, N. Golanov.
In Italian, with English summary.
METAMORFOSI 1988, no.11, p.35-37,
ill., plans, secns.

THEATERS--TEMPORARY--JAPAN--KARAKUWA
Karakuwa story '88-'90.
On the festival of Karakuwa.
Includes work by Osamu Ishiyama.
English summary, p.23.
KENCHIKU BUNKA 1990 Dec., v.45,
no.530, p.37-48,61-72,105-108,
dwgs., photos., site plans.

THEATERS--UNITED STATES--BARABOO
(WISCONSIN)--AL. RINGLING THEATRE
The Al. Ringling Theatre, Baraboo,
Wisconsin, 1915-1990 [Historic
American Building Survey, HABS
No.WIS-261].
Rapp and Rapp, architects.
THEATRE HISTORICAL SOCIETY. ANNUAL
1990, v.17, cover, p.1-24, ill.,
dwgs., port., photos., plans.

THEATERS--UNITED STATES--CEDAR CITY
(UTAH)--RANDALL L. JONES MEMORIAL
THEATER
Act one: Randal L. Jones Memorial
Theater Cedar City, Utah, FFKR
Architects / Lynn Nesmith.
ARCHITECTURE: THE MAGAZINE OF THE
AMERICAN INSTITUTE OF ARCHITECTS
1990 Aug., v.79, no.8, p.80-83,
ill., photos., plans, secns.

THEATERS--UNITED STATES--DUBLIN (OHIO)
Sound education / Michael Wagner.
On the conversion of a high school
gymnasium into a community and
high school theater, Dublin, Ohio.
Architects: SEM Partners with
Jaffe Acoustics.
INTERIORS 1990 Jan., v.149, no.6,
p.56, photo., plan, secn.

THEATERS--UNITED STATES--MILWAUKEE
(WISCONSIN)--MILWAUKEE REPERTORY
THEATER
Regional portfolio: The Midwest: a
tale of two cities / Clifford A.
Pearson.
Minneapolis and Milwaukee have
become two of the most livable
cities in the U.S. Contents: 100
E. Wisconsin Ave., Milwaukee
(Clark Tribble Harris & Li
Architects); Milwaukee Repertory
Theater (Beckley/Myers
Architects);5th St. Parking
Facility, Minneapolis (Stageberg
Partners); Valspar Varnish Factory
renovation, Minneapolis (Meyer,
Scherer & Rockcastle); and the
Ceresota, Minneapolis (Ellerbe
Becket).
ARCHITECTURAL RECORD 1990 Aug.,
v.178, no.9, p.62-71, axonometric
view, photos., plans, secns., site
plans.

THEATERS--UNITED STATES--NEW YORK (NEW
YORK)
The theaters of Herts and Tallant /
Bill Morrison.
MARQUEE 1990, v.22, no.4, cover,
p.3-22, ill., dwg., ports.,
photos., plan.

THEATERS--UNITED STATES--NEW YORK (NEW
YORK)--VICTORY
Teaching Times Square a lesson /
Andrew Mandel, Jacqueline Thaw.
While Times Square awaits
redevelopment, the theater group
En-Garde Arts performs "Crowbar"
in one of the area's saved
(Continued next column)

THEATERS--UNITED STATES--NEW YORK (NEW
YORK)--VICTORY (CONTINUED)
Teaching Times Square...(CONTINUED)
theaters, the Victory.
PLACES 1990 Summer, v.6, no.4,
p.[91-92], det., photos.

THEATERS--UNITED STATES--SAINT PAUL
(MINNESOTA)--ORDWAY MUSIC THEATER
Places for performance: Ordway Music
Theatre, St. Paul, Minnesota.
Architects: Benjamin Thompson &
Associates. Text in Japanese and
English.
PROCESS: ARCHITECTURE 1990 June
no.89, p.124-127, photos., plans.

THEATERS--UNITED STATES--SAN FRANCISCO
(CALIFORNIA)--YERBA BUENA THEATER
Special feature: James Polshek.
Contents: Introduction / Toshio
Nakamura --Architects' statement /
James S. Polshek and James G.
Garrison: --Works & projects:
United States Embassy, Muscat,
Oman --Centennial Hall, Barnard
College, New York, N.Y. --Alumni
houses, Bard College, Annandale,
N.Y. --Hastings Hall, Union
Theological Seminary, New York,
N.Y. --IBM-ISG North Central
Marketing Division headquarters,
White Plains, N.Y. --Seaman's
Church Institute, New York, N.Y.
--Yerba Buena Gardens Theater, San
Francisco, Calif. --National
Inventors Hall of Fame, Akron,
Ohio --New York University Medical
Center Biomolecular Research
building, New York, N.Y. --
Biographies of James S. Polshek,
Joseph L. Fleischer, Timothy P.
Hartung, and James G. Garrison,
p.126. Architects: James Stewart
Polshek & Partners. Text in
Japanese and English.
ARCHITECTURE AND URBANISM 1990
Nov., no.11(242), p.62-126,
axonometric views, models,
photos., plans, secns., site
plans.

THEATERS--UNITED STATES--SPOKANE
(WASHINGTON)
The Spokane spectacle [theaters
constructed in Spokane,
Washington, 1883-1983] / George L.
Lufkin.
MARQUEE 1990, v.22, no.1, cover,
p.3-16, photos.

THEATERS--VICTORIAN--ALTERATIONS AND
ADDITIONS--SCOTLAND--GLASGOW--
CITIZENS THEATRE
Cultural beacon in the Gorbals /
Brian Edwards.
On the new atrium and facade
addition to the 1878 Citizens
Theatre, Glasgow. Original
Architect: Campbell Douglas
Renovation architects: Building
Design Partnership.
RIBA JOURNAL 1990 May, v.97, no.5,
p.48-50, photos.

THEORY
See "THEORY" AS A SUBHEADING AFTER
MAIN HEADINGS.

THEORY--GERMANY (WEST)--RUHR
DISTRICT--CITY PLANNING
Zur Innenentwicklung in den Stadten
des Ruhrgebietes / Hans - Dieter
Krupinski.
DEUTSCHES ARCHITEKTENBLATT 1990
Sept.1, v.22, no.9, p.1371-1372,

THERET, SERGE
Profils: les elus 1989: Albums de
la jeune architecture.
Contents: Epinard Bleu, Pascal
Marchant, Philtre Avant-Travaux,
Patricia Leboucq, Shinobu Akahori,
Pascal Quintard Hofstein, and
Herve Daridan.
LE MONITEUR ARCHITECTURE AMC 1990
Mar., no.9, p.55, ports.

THERIVEL, R. B.
Airport developments and EIA: Kansai
International Airport, Japan / R.
B. Therivel, B. F. D. Barrett.
LAND USE POLICY 1990 Jan., v.7,
no.1, p.80-86, chart, maps, table,
refs.

THERMAE
See BATHS

THERMAL BRIDGES
Geometrische Warmebrrucken,
Schwitzwasser und Schimmel und
Massnahmen zur Schadensbehebung.
DEUTSCHES ARCHITEKTENBLATT 1990
Mar.1, v.22, no.1, p.432, dwg.,
photos.

THERMAL BRIDGES--MATHEMATICAL MODELS
Gravity driven counterflow through
an open door in a sealed room / D.
J. Wilson, D. E. Kiel.
BUILDING AND ENVIRONMENT 1990,
v.25, no.4, p.379-388, diagrs.,
graphs, plan, refs.
An idealized model for room radiant
exchange / M. G. Davies.
BUILDING AND ENVIRONMENT 1990,
v.25, no.4, p.375-378, refs.
Thermal bridges across multilayer
walls: an integral approach /
Samuel Hassid.
BUILDING AND ENVIRONMENT 1990,
v.25, no.2, p.143-150, graphs,
refs.
Transfer rates in single-sided
ventilation / M.R.
Mokhtarzadeh-Dehghan, M.M.M. El
Telbany, A.J. Reynolds.
BUILDING AND ENVIRONMENT 1990,
v.25, no.2, p.155-161, diagrs.,
tables, refs.

THERMAL BRIDGES--RESEARCH
A comparison between measured and
calculated heat losses through a
slab-on-ground floor / A.E.
Delsante.
BUILDING AND ENVIRONMENT 1990,
v.25, no.1, p.25-31, graphs, refs.
Dynamic effects of thermal shutters
/ M. Zaheer-Uddin.
BUILDING AND ENVIRONMENT 1990,
v.25, no.1, p.33-35, graphs, refs

THERMAL BRIDGES--RESEARCH
(CONTINUED)
Estimating thermal parameters of
outdoor test cells / U. Norlen.
BUILDING AND ENVIRONMENT 1990,
v.25, no.1, p.17-24, photo.,
tables, refs.
Gravity driven counterflow through
an open door in a sealed room / D.
J. Wilson, D. E. Kiel.
BUILDING AND ENVIRONMENT 1990,
v.25, no.4, p.379-388, diagrs.,
graphs, plan, refs.
An idealized model for room radiant
exchange / M. G. Davies.
BUILDING AND ENVIRONMENT 1990,
v.25, no.4, p.375-378, refs.

THERMAL INSULATION
See INSULATION (HEAT)

THERMES, LAURA, 1943-
Latin lessons / Clare Melhuish.
Features recent work by six
Italian architects.
BUILDING DESIGN 1990 Mar.9,
no.976, p.20-22,24-27, axonometric
views, dwgs., models, photos.,
plans, secns.

THERMOSETTING POWDERS
See POWDER COATINGS

THEROUX, ALEXANDER
Edward Hopper's Cape Cod / Alexander
Theroux.
Paintings from 1930-c.1942, when
Hopper spent summers in Truro.
ART & ANTIQUES 1990 Jan., v.7,
no.1, p.[56-67],97, dwgs., ports.

THEVENIN, JACQUES-JEAN
Laiteries royales, laiteries
imperiales: Trianon et Rambouillet
/ Annick Heitzmann.
HISTOIRE DE LART 1990 Oct., no.11,
p.37-45, dwgs., dets., elevs.,
photos., plans, secn., refs.
The Queen's Dairy, Rambouillet /
Pierre de la Ruffiniere du Prey.
Architect: Jacques-Jean Thevenin.
COUNTRY LIFE 1990 Jan.25, v.184,
no.4, p.88-91, photos., secn.

THIAGARAJAN, DEBORAH
Udaipur, Jaiselmer, Pondicherry,
Fountainhas.
Four examples that reflect the
diversity of conservation issues
in India, including the
consequences of tourism and of
cultural plurality. Authors: Parul
Zaveri, Nimish Patel; Kulbhushan
and Minakshi Jain; Deborah
Thiagarajan, Pierre Richard; Asesh
K. Maitra.
ARCHITECTURE + DESIGN 1989
Nov.-Dec., v.6, no.1, p.45-57,
ill., elevs., maps, photos, plan,
secns.

THIBERG, SVEN
Housing research and design in
Sweden / edited by Sven Thiberg.
A collection of 12 articles on
aspects including renovation,
access for disabled residents, and
technological changes.
SWEDISH COUNCIL FOR BUILDING
RESEARCH DOCUMENT 1990, D13,
p.[3]-281, diagrs.. graphs,
photos. plans, tables, biblios.

THIEBAUT, BRUNO
Bibliotheque centrale de pret,
Rennes.
Bibliotheque centrale de pret
d'Ille-et-Vilaine. Architects:
Jean-Philippe Pargade, with Gilles
Cohen and Bruno Thiebaut. English
summary, p.89; Spanish summary,
p.172.
TECHNIQUES ET ARCHITECTURE 1990
Oct.-Nov., no.392, p.88-89, dwg.,
photo., plan.

THIEL, HEINZ
EXPO 2000 in Hannover? ein
Ideenworkshop fur Architekten
Kunstler und Landschaftsplaner /
Heinz Thiel.
Observations about one of three
cities under consideration and the
planning process.
BAUWELT 1990 June 15, v.81, no.23,
p.1160-1161, sketches.

THIEMANN-POHL, ISABEL
Messestand fur eine
Beleuchtungsfirma.
Student project by I.
Thiemann-Pohl.
ARCHITEKTUR, INNENARCHITEKTUR,
TECHNISCHER AUSBAU 1989 Sept.,
v.97, no.9, p.104-105, dets.,
model, photos., plans, secns.,
isometric dwgs.

THIERBACH, ANDREAS
3-D-Simulationsmodell zur Bewertung
von Strassentrassen / Andreas
Thierbach, Dietz Kohlhoff.
ARCHITEKTUR DER DDR 1990 Jan.,
v.38, no.1, p.36-37, dwgs.

THIERIG, JORG
Neu in Alt: Modernisierung der
Raiffeisenbank Bamberg.
Architect: Jorg Thierig.
ARCHITEKTUR, INNENARCHITEKTUR,
TECHNISCHER AUSBAU 1990 Oct.,
v.98, no.10, p.88-89, photos.,
plan.

THIERRY, SOLANGE
Le salon Cheret / Solange Thierry.
On the restored 1903 mural
decoration in this room in the
Hotel de Ville, Paris. Artist:
Jules Cheret.
L'OEIL 1990 July-Aug., no.420-421,
p.40-[45], photos.

THIES, FRANZ
Brautladen: Diplomarbeit FH
Hannover.
Student project by Franz Thies.
ARCHITEKTUR, INNENARCHITEKTUR,
TECHNISCHER AUSBAU 1989 Sept.,
v.97, no.9, p.110, plan, secns.,
isometric dwg.

THIES, KLEMENS
Datenaustausch Leistungsverzeichnis
neu geregelt / Klemens Thies.
DEUTSCHES ARCHITEKTENBLATT 1990
Nov.1, v.22, no.11, p.1751-1752,
dwgs.

THIESS, BARBARA
Bahnhof Oberkassel in Dusseldorf.
1st prize: Barbara and Walter
Thiess.
BAUWELT 1990 Sept.7, v.81, no.34,
p.1652-1653, models.

THIESS, WALTER
Bahnhof Oberkassel in Dusseldorf.
1st prize: Barbara and Walter
Thiess.
BAUWELT 1990 Sept.7, v.81, no.34,
p.1652-1653, models.

THIIS-EVENSEN, THOMAS
Howdee, Charlie! / Thomas
Thiis-Evensen.
On Prince Charles opinions on
architecture, Paternoster Square
proposals, and buildings in
Seaside, Fla.
ARKITEKTEN 1990 Mar., v.92, no.3,
p.80-85, dwgs., elevs., models,
photos., secns.
Paris, Paris.
Introduction to issue on Paris,
with articles by Jacques Berg,
Thomas Thiis-Evensen, and Karin
Skousboll. Seven other articles
are indexed separately.
ARKITEKTEN 1989 Dec.22, v.91,
no.23, p.573-607, axonometric
views, ill., ports., elevs.,
models, photos., plans, secns.,
site plans.
En postmoderne kliche [Opera de la
Bastille] / Thomas Thiis-Evensen.
Architect: Carlos Ott.
ARKITEKTEN 1989 Dec.22, v.91,
no.23, p.587-589, axonometric
views, model, photos., site plan.
Tema: utbildningen.
Introduction to section on
architectural education.
Contents: En skola for livet...,
by Jens Arnfred.--Mot en ny
helhet, by Thomas Thiis-Evensen.--
Elevprojekt. Includes student
projects from three Swedish
schools: LTH, CTH, and KTH.
English translations, p.57-58.
ARKITEKTUR: THE SWEDISH REVIEW OF
ARCHITECTURE 1990 Apr., v.90,
no.3, p.2-25,57-58,cover, dwgs.,
elevs., models, photos., plans,
secns., site plans.
Den urbane pyramide / Thomas
Thiis-Evensen.
Architect: I. M. Pei.
ARKITEKTEN 1989 Dec.22, v.91,
no.23, p.584-586, axonometric
view, photo.

THILLART, CASPAR VAN DEN
Theoreticus of practicus, ethicus of
idealist... : Architecten over de
dilemmas van het restaureren /
Joris Molenaar.
Theories on renovation, with
reference to the ideas of
Hubert-Jan Henket, Wytze Patijn,
Van Velsen, Van den Thillart,
Meindert Booy, Jaap Franso, Bertus
Mulder.
ARCHIS 1990 Sept., no.9, p.24-37,
models, photos., plan, refs.

THINIUS-HUSER, KLAUS
Raum und Konstruktion / Klaus
Thinius-Huser.
DEUTSCHE BAUZEITSCHRIFT 1990 Dec.,
v.38, no.12, p.1777-1782, photos.,
biblio.

THIRD GOTHIC
See FLAMBOYANT

THIRD WORLD
See DEVELOPING COUNTRIES

THIRIEZ, REGINE
Les palais europeens du Yuanmingyuan
a travers la photographie:
1860-1940 / Regine Thiriez.
Photos of palaces built between
1747 and 1759 by the Jesuits who
worked at the court of emperor
Qianlong.
ARTS ASIATIQUES 1990, v.45,
p.90-96, photos., site plan, refs.

THIRION, JACQUES
Remarques sur la crypte el les
structures recemment degagees de
leglise de Saint-Dalmas-Valdeblore
/ Jacques Thirion.
CAHIERS ARCHEOLOGIQUES; FIN DE
L'ANTIQUITE ET MOYEN AGE 1990,
v.38, p.63-79, photos., plans,
secns., refs.
Souvenirs antiques et creations
romanes: les sculptures de
l'ancienne cathedrale de Die /
Jacques Thirion.
English summary, p.162.
GAZETTE DES BEAUX-ARTS 1990 Apr.,
ser.6,v.115, no.1455, p.[141]-162,
photos., refs.

THIRIOT, JACQUES
Fouilles en devenir au Petit Palais
d'Avignon / Jacques Thiriot.
Discussion of excavation work
undertaken between 1977-1981 in
and around the area of the Petit
Palace.
MONUMENTS HISTORIQUES 1990
Sept.-Oct., no.170, p.16-20,
photos., secns., site plans,
engrs.

THOM, BING
Going to the fair: Vancouver
architect Bing Thom has been given
the task of portraying Canada to
the world at Expo '92 in Seville,
Spain.
CANADIAN ARCHITECT 1990 Oct.,
v.35, no.10, p.37-39, models,
plans, secns.

THOM, WAYNE
[Architectural photography:
interview].
Interviews with the photographers:
Julius Shulman, Tom Bonner, Grant
Mudford, Marvin Rand, Wayne Thom,
and Tim Street-Porter.
L. A. ARCHITECT 1990 Apr., p.4-7,
photos.

THOMA, AGNES, 1955-
Special feature: Contemporary
Hungarian architecture / edited by
Botond Bognar.
Works illustrated by architects:
Imre Makovecz, Gabor Mezei, Andras
Erdei, Sandor Devenyi, Attila
Kovacs, Laszlo Saros, Tamas Nagy,
(Continued next column)

THOMA, AGNES, 1955- (CONTINUED)
Special feature: ...(CONTINUED)
Gyorgy Csete, Peter Oltai, Istvan
Kistelegdi, Tibor Jankovics, Csasa
Bodonyi, Istvan Ferencz, Tamas
Noll, Benc Taba, Janos Golda,
Agnes Thoma, Jozsef Kerenyi,
Gyorgy Vadasz, Gyorgy Keves, Adam
Sylvester and Gabor Turanyi. Text
in Japanese and English.
ARCHITECTURE AND URBANISM 1990
Mar., no.3(234), p.7-126,
axonometric views, dwgs., elevs.,
photos., plans, secns.

THOMA, PETER
Bilderhauerateliers der Staatlichen
Akademie der Bildenden Kunste in
Karlsruhe.
Planners: Staatliches Hochbauamt
I, Karlsruhe. Designers: Nikolaus
Kranzle, Helmut Knecht, Peter
Thoma and others.
BAUWELT 1990 May 11, v.81, no.18,
p.883, photos.
Bildhauerateliers der Staatlichen
Akademie der Bildenden Kunste in
Karlsruhe.
Planners: Staatliche Hochbauamt I.
Designers: Nikolaus Kranzle,
Helmut Knecht, Peter Thoma and
others.
DEUTSCHE BAUZEITSCHRIFT 1990 Dec.,
v.38, no.12, p.1763-1766, dets.,
photos., plans, secns.

THOMA, STREET
Fingertip directionals / Alice
Feiring.
On the tactile orientation model
presented and designed by Kurt
Milam and Street Thoma to the
Maryland Rehabilitation Center.
INTERIORS 1990 Nov., v.150, no.4,
p.68, photos.

THOMAES, JAN
Retrospectief Leon Stijnen:
Eerbewijs aan ambivalent architect
[exhibition review] / Jan Thomaes.
At the deSingel, Antwerp, Dec.20,
1990-Feb.3,1991.
DE ARCHITECT 1990 Dec., v.21,
no.12, p.72-73, photos.

THOMANN, KLAUS
Eine Stadt im Wandel: Gesprach mit
dem Erfurter Stadtplaner Klaus
Thomann [interview] / Holger
Fischer.
DEUTSCHE BAUZEITUNG 1990 June,
v.124, no.6, p.86,88, ill.,
photos.

THOMAS & BOOZIOTIS ARCHITECTS
Best laid plans: Goldsmith Hall,
University of Texas, Austin,
Thomas & Booziotis Architects and
Chartier Newton & Associates,
Architects / David Dillon.
Addition to 1933 building designed
by Paul Cret.
ARCHITECTURE: THE AIA JOURNAL 1990
Nov., v.79, no.11, p.[84]-89,
photos., plans, secn., site plan.
Goldsmith Hall.
Addition to UT Austin building.
Architects: Thomas & Booziotis.
TEXAS ARCHITECT 1990 Jan.-Feb.,
v.40, no.1, p.32, photos., plan.

THOMAS, BURTON W.
Calculated risk: practice: liability insurance / Burton W. Thomas.
ARCHITECTURE: THE MAGAZINE OF THE AMERICAN INSTITUTE OF ARCHITECTS 1990 Aug., v.79, no.8, p.109-111,

THOMAS, CHARLES
Christians, chapels, churches and charters--or, "Proto-parochial provisions for the pious in a peninsula" (Land's End) / Charles Thomas.
During the early 2nd millennium A.D., in West Penwith, Cornwall, England.
LANDSCAPE HISTORY 1989, v.11, p.[19]-26, map, biblio.

THOMAS FORD & PARTNERS
Execution of an ideal / John Martin Robinson.
Controversial and costly restoration of the Queen's House, Greenwich, by Inigo Jones. Consultant architects for the restoration: Thomas Ford & Partners.
ARCHITECTS' JOURNAL 1990 July 4, v.192, no.1, p.32-39,41, dwgs., photos., plans, secn., sketches.
A house fit for a queen / Richard Wilcock.
On the restoration of the 1660s interiors of the Queen's House, Greenwich. Original architects: Inigo Jones, later enlarged by John Webb. Restoration architects: Thomas Ford and Partners.
RIBA JOURNAL 1990 June, v.97, no.6, p.71,73-74, photos.

THOMAS, HORST
Eckgeschichte: die Ecke in der Architektur / Horst Thomas.
DEUTSCHE BAUZEITUNG 1990 May, v.124, no.5, p.115-124, photos., table, refs.

THOMAS, JANIE
Ian Charles Laurie [obituary] / Janie Thomas.
LANDSCAPE DESIGN 1989 Dec.-1990 Jan., no.186, p.59,

THOMAS, JEROEN
Hofhaus in Kralingen.
Architects: Rem Koolhaas, et al. Includes English summary.
BAUMEISTER 1990 Nov., v.87, no.11, p.56-57, photos., plans.

THOMAS, JULIAN
Monuments from the inside: the case of the Irish megalithic tombs / Julian Thomas.
WORLD ARCHAEOLOGY 1990 Oct., v.22, no.2, p.168-178, chart, plans, biblio.

THOMAS, KEITH
Planning students and careers / Keith Thomas.
"... the enrollment of planning students and career destinations of new planning graduates 1977 to 1989." In Britain.
THE PLANNER 1990 Sept.14, v.76, no.35, p.13-16, graphs, tables, biblio., refs.

THOMAS, MILLER & PARTNER
Centennial Sportsplex: a win-win scenario / Julie C. Pursell.
Centennial Sportsplex, Nashville, Tenn. Architects: Thomas, Miller & Partners.
PARKS & RECREATION 1990 Dec., v.25, no.12, p.22-27,56, photos.

THOMAS, MILLER & PARTNERS
Water and ice: Centennial Sportsplex, Nashville Tennessee, Thomas, Miller & Partners, Architects / Robert A. Ivy.
ARCHITECTURE: THE MAGAZINE OF THE AMERICAN INSTITUTE OF ARCHITECTS 1990 Aug., v.79, no.8, p.[76]-79, photos., plans, site plan.

THOMAS, PERCIVAL R.
Water supply and wastewater treatment for low income housing projects / Percival R. Thomas.
INTERNATIONAL JOURNAL FOR HOUSING SCIENCE AND ITS APPLICATIONS 1990, v.14, no.1, p.057-063, chart, secn., refs.

THOMAS SANDELL ARKITEKTKONTOR
FGH annonsbyra, Stockholm.
Renovation of buildup at Sturegatan 4, for a design office. Completed in 1990. Architect: Thomas Sandell Arkitektkontor.
ARKITEKTUR: THE SWEDISH REVIEW OF ARCHITECTURE 1990 Sept., v.90, no.7, p.12-13,cover, photos., plan.

THOMAS SAUNDERS PARTNERSHIP
Lighter legal touch / Nick Jones.
Interiors of four London law offices.
BUILDING DESIGN 1989 Oct., suppl., p.36-39, photos., plans.

THOMAS, TORI WINKLER
Garten der Zukunft? / Elke von Radziewsky, Vera Graaf.
Features work by the following American landscape architects: Peter Walker, Martha Schwartz, George Hargreaves, and Michael Van Valkenburgh. english summary, p.2-3.
ARCHITEKTUR & WOHNEN 1990 Oct.-Nov., no.5, p.90-[98],100, ports., photos.

THOMASSEN, OLE
Om Steen Eiler / Ole Thomassen.
Features the architects' design for Runde Hus, Helsinge, Denmark, a 1917 student project.
ARKITEKTEN 1990 Aug., v.92, no.11, p.354-359,cover, dets., dwgs., ports., elevs., photos., plans, site plans.

THOMASSEN, WILLY
Veritas-Park / Willy Thomassen.
In Oslofjord, Norway: Landscape architects: Hindhamar, Sundt, Thomassen; architects: Kjell Lund, Nils Slaatto with Ostbye, Kleven, Almaas. Built 1972-1989. English captions.
GARTEN UND LANDSCHAFT 1990, v.100, no.8, p.34-36, photos., site plan.

THOME, VALTER, 1874-1918
Erottajankatu 9-11: Peruskorjaus ja uudisrakennus, Helsinki.
Renovation and extension of two Helsinki buildings owned by the Sanoma Corp. No.9, by Valter Thome, was completed in 1911; no.11, by Essen, Kallio, Ikalainen, was completed in 1910. Architect: Jan Soderlund Oy. In Finnish and English.
ARKKITEHTI 1989, v.86, no.5-6, p.62-67, map, photos., plans, secn.

THOMLEY, TOM
Subtle evolution: the ever-changing town house of two Memphis designers / Susannah M. Wilson.
Interior designers and owners: Steven Hickman and Tom Thomley. Architect for the remodeling: Oscar E. Menzer.
SOUTHERN ACCENTS 1990 Oct., v.13, no.8, p.[124]-130, photos.

THOMMES, CORNELIA
Rettung eines Rauchhauses: ein Gesprach der Architektin Cornelia Thommes, Braunschweig, mit einer Kreisarchitektin aus dem Bezirk Schwerin [interview].
DEUTSCHE BAUZEITUNG 1990 June, v.124, no.6, p.101-108, elevs., photos., plans, secns.

THOMPSON, BENJAMIN
Benjamin Thompson & Associates / edited by Dennis J. de Witt.
Survey of the firms buildings and urban projects (several indexed separately). Includes essays by Dennis J. De Witt, Benjamin Thompson, Jane Thompson, a list of partners, p.158-159, and list of buildings projects and awards, 1946-1990, p.160-164. Text in Japanese and English.
PROCESS: ARCHITECTURE 1990 June, no.89, p.[1]-164, ports., elevs., models, photos., plans, secns., site plans, sketches.

THOMPSON, BENJAMIN, 1918-
Mall wonder / Michelle Huneven.
Features renovated Century City Shopping Center, Los Angeles. Architect: Benjamin Thompson.
CONNOISSEUR 1990 Feb., v.220, no.937, p.90-93, photos.
Urban alchemist: Benjamin Thompson turns downtown decay into gold / Andrea Oppenheimer Dean.
HISTORIC PRESERVATION 1990 July-Aug., v.42, no.4, p.12-15, port.

THOMPSON, BERWICK, PRATT AND PARTNERS
Bowen Island orientation: a Shinto-influenced house spans rain forest and ocean bluff in British Columbia / Jon Krakauer.
Home owned by James and Martine Thom. Architects: Brian Hemingway and Fook-Weng Chan of Thompson, Berwick, Pratt, & Partners.
ARCHITECTURAL DIGEST 1990 Aug., v.47, no.8, p.[150-159], photos.

THOMPSON, VENTULETT, STAINBACK &
ASSOCIATES
A pause that refreshes [The World of
Coca-Cola] / Lynn Nesmith.
A museum of the soft drink
company, in Atlanta, Ga.
Architects: Thompson, Ventulett,
Stainback & Associates and Turner
Associates.
ARCHITECTURE: THE AIA JOURNAL 1990
Dec., v.79, no.12, p.[74-79],
photos., plans, site plan.
Taming the Behemoth: Building Types
Study 676: convention centers /
Margaret Gaskie.
San Jose, Calif., Convention
Center (MGA Partners); Sydney,
Australia, Convention Center (John
Andrews International); Adelaide,
Australia, Convention Center (John
Andrews International); and Miami
Beach Convention Center expansion
(Thompson, Ventulett, Stainback &
Associates).
ARCHITECTURAL RECORD 1990 Mar.,
v.178, no.3, p.99-113, photo.,
plans, secns., site plans.

THOMSEN, CHRISTIAN W.
Lebbeus Woods, RIEA, and its Berlin
exhibition of experimental
architecture [exhibition review] /
Christian W. Thomsen.
Report on exhibition held at Aedes
Gallery. Text in Japanese and
English.
ARCHITECTURE AND URBANISM 1990
Oct., no.10(241), p.30-[43],
dwgs., photos.
Der Walkman-Effekt. Neue Konzepte
fur mobile Raume und
Klanfarchitekturen = The Walkman
effect. New concepts for mobile
spaces and sound architectures /
Christian W. Thomsen, Angela
Krewani, Hartmut Winkler.
Text in German and English.
DAIDALOS 1990 June 15, no.36,
p.52-61, ill., photos., refs.

THOMSEN, OLE RAMSGAARD, 1937-
Gentofte-Vangede Idraetsforening /
Henry Voss.
Clubhouse for an athletic
association in a Copenhagen
suburb, completed in 1989.
Architect: Ole Ramsgaard Thomsen.
Includes English and German
summaries.
ARKITEKTUR DK 1990, v.34, no.7,
p.351-354, photos., plan, site
plan.

THOMSON, ALEXANDER, 1817-1875
The Greek tragedies / Gavin Stamp.
On the neoclassical architecture
of Glasgow architect Alexander
'Greek' Thomson.
ARCHITECTS' JOURNAL 1990 May 30,
v.191, no.11, p.30-9, dwgs.,
photos., sketches.

THOMSON, DAVID
Baptiste Androuet du Cerceau,
architecte de la cour de Henri III
/ David Thomson.
Publishes two documents from the
Archives nationales pertaining to
the Chateau de Fresnes.
BULLETIN MONUMENTAL 1990, v.148,
no.1, p.[47]-81, dets., dwgs.,
elevs., maps, photos., plans,
secns., site plans, engrs., refs.

THORBURN, ANDREW
Leisure at the waterfront / Andrew
Thorburn.
THE PLANNER 1990 Apr.6, v.76,
no.13, p.18-19, photo.

THORNE, ROBERT
George Godwin, ou la revue
d'architecture comme croisade
sociale / Ruth Richardson, Robert
Thorne.
Editor-in-chief of The Builder.
REVUE DE L'ART 1990, no.89,
p.72-76, dwgs., port., engrs.,
refs.
An iron constitution: The Iron
Revolution: architects, engineers
and structural innovation
1780-1880 [exhibition review] /
Robert Thorne.
Exhibition opening at the Heinz
Gallery, London on 14 June 1990.
ARCHITECTS' JOURNAL 1990 June 13,
v.191, no.24, p.74-75,77, dwgs.
Urban concepts [Architectural design
profile 83] / Denise Scott Brown.
Contents: Paralipomena in urban
design.-- Between three stools.--
Public realm, public sector and
the public interest in urban
design.-- Rise and fall of
community architecture.-- Urban
design reports [six, indexed
separately]. Includes a discussion
with Martin Pawley, Simon Jenkins,
Robert Thorne, Jake Brown, Ken
Powell, Charles Jencks, and John
Thompson.
ARCHITECTURAL DESIGN 1990, v.60,
no.1-2, p.[1]-96, dwgs., elevs.,
photos., site plans, aerial
photos., biblio., refs.

THORNTON, CLIVE
Geordie pride.
Affordable housing at St. Thomas,
Newcastle, is choice of Clive
Thornton for commendation.
VOLUNTARY HOUSING 1990 Apr., v.23,
no.3, p.35, port., photo.

THORNTON, HARTNELL, CHARTERED
ARCHITECTS
Bristol: Parkyn's progress.
Higlights eight recent commercial
and office projects. Architects
include Thornton Hartnell, MWT,
BGP Group, Leslie Jones
Architects, Alec Freneh
Partnership, John Wells-Thorpe,
and Richard Hemingway.
BUILDING 1990 Aug.31, v.255,
no.34, p.28-33, port., map,
photos.

THORNTON, M. K. JULIO-CLAUDIAN
BUILDING PROGRAMS
Julio-Claudian building programs: a
quantitative study in political
management, by M. K. Thornton and
R. L. Thornton [book review] /
James C. Anderson.
AMERICAN JOURNAL OF ARCHAEOLOGY
1990 July, v.94, no.3, p.515.

THORNTON, MICHAEL
Appropriately dressed: applying
plaster / Michael Thornton.
TRADITIONAL HOMES 1990 Jan., v.6,
no.4, p.86, dets., photo.,
sketches.
Bricky situations / Michael
Thornton.
Includes list of "useful
addresses".
TRADITIONAL HOMES 1990 Sept., v.6,
no.12, p.94-97, photos.
Bricky situations / Michael
Thornton.
One of a series: how to match old
brick when making an addition.
TRADITIONAL HOMES 1990 Oct., v.7,
no.1, p.104-106,
Door keeping: the perils of
"freezing history" and the
characteristics of period front
doors / Michael Thornton.
TRADITIONAL HOMES 1990 Apr., v.6,
no.7, p.107-110, diagr., dwgs.,
photos.
Door matters / Michael Thornton.
Glazing in front doors, and common
historical alterations to internal
doors.
TRADITIONAL HOMES 1990 May, v.6,
no.8, p.107,109,110, dwgs.,
photos., plan, secns.
Flight problems: remedies for some
common staircase defects / Michael
Thornton.
TRADITIONAL HOMES 1990 July, v.6,
no.10, p.87-90, det., ill.,
photos.
Keeping the character: five golden
rules for you to follow when
restoring a period property /
Michael Thornton.
TRADITIONAL HOMES 1990 Aug., v.6,
no.11, p.87-89, photos.
The mix for the bricks / Michael
Thornton.
On mortar.
TRADITIONAL HOMES 1990 Nov., v.7,
no.2, p.103-104, photos.
Stepping back: the history of the
staircase / Michael Thornton.
TRADITIONAL HOMES 1990 June, v.6,
no.9, p.123-126, photo, plans,
secns.
Woodwork examination: how original
joinery survives changing fashion
/ Michael Thornton.
TRADITIONAL HOMES 1990 Mar., v.6,
no.6, p.89-93, dwgs., photos.

THORNTON, PETER
Sir John Soane's Museum.
Editorial and five articles.
Contents: Sir John Soane's Museum:
A Conversation Piece without a
Family, by Arata Isozaki.--The
Soane as It Was, by Peter
Thornton.--Soane's Use of
Drawings, by Margaret
Richardson.--Sir John Soane's
Library: 'O. Books! Ye Monuments
of Mind', by Eileen Harris.--The
Papers of Sir John Soane, by Susan
Palmer.
APOLLO 1990 Apr., v.131, no.338,
p.224-251, ill., dwgs., port.,
elevs., photos., plans, engrs.,
refs.

THORNTON, R. L. JULIO-CLAUDIAN
BUILDING PROGRAMS
Julio-Claudian building programs: a
quantitative study in political
management, by M. K. Thornton and
R. L. Thornton [book review] /
James C. Anderson.
AMERICAN JOURNAL OF ARCHAEOLOGY
1990 July, v.94, no.3, p.515,

THORNTON, WILLIAM, 1759-1828
Anatomy of a restoration: the
meticulous preservation of The
Octagon, one of America's most
remarkable homes / Alice L.
Powers.
Designed in 1798 by William
Thornton, the architect of the
U.S. Capitol, it is now an
architectural museum.
HISTORIC PRESERVATION 1990
Mar.-Apr., v.42, no.2, p.[38-43],
74, photos.

THORP, ALFRED H. (ALFRED HUIDEKOPER),
1863-1919
Il Coogan Building: un edificio a
rischio / Tom Killian.
In New York; built 1875-1876.
Architect: Alfred H. Thorp.
CASABELLA 1990 May, v.54, no.568,
p.32, photo.

THORP, JOHN BROWN
Lutyens' Roman Catholic Cathedral in
Liverpool: the restoration of a
"great model" / Edward Morris.
Designed in the early 1930s and
not executed. Model by John Brown
Thorp.
APOLLO 1990 Dec., v.132, no.346,
p.414-415, models.

THORPE, PATRICIA
Planting between the lines: Gus and
Judith Lieber's garden / Patricia
Thorpe.
In Springs, Long Island, N.Y.
HOUSE & GARDEN 1990 Aug., v.162,
no.8, p.122-[127],151, ports.,
photos.

THORPE, STEPHEN
The Design Museum, London Docklands
/ Stephen Thorpe, Barry
Fitzgerald.
Architects: Conran Roche.
DESIGN FOR SPECIAL NEEDS 1989
Dec., no.50, p.8-12, photos.,
secn.

THORVALDSSON, THORVALDUR S.
Anlaeg ved Det islandski
Nationalbibliotek / Reynir
Vilhjalmsson.
Landscaping by the author of
grounds in Reykjavik, for national
library begun in 1978 and not yet
complete. Architects: Manfred
Vilhjalmsson, Thorvaldur S.
Thorvaldsson. Includes English
trnaslation and captions.
LANDSKAB 1990 May, v.71, no.3-4,
p.1S1-1S4, photos., plan, site
plan.

THOURET, NICOLAUS FRIEDRICH, 1767-1845
A German Baroque villa devoted to
the pursuit of pleasure / Nicholas
Fox Weber.
On the 1732 Schloss Favorite,
Ludwigsburg. Architect: Donato
Giuseppe Frisoni. Interiors
remodeled between 1799 and 1801 by
Nicolaus Friedrich Thouret.
ARCHITECTURAL DIGEST 1990 May,
v.47, no.5, p.134-146, photos.

THROGMORTON, J. A.
Power, planning and conflict /
Charles Hoch, guest editor.
Special issue. Contents: Power,
planning and conflict, by C. Hoch
-- Planners in conflict:
experience and perceptions in
California, by Linda C. Dalton --
Neighborhood redevelopment: the
planner's role in conflict
management, by Sanda Kaufman --
Environmental movement politics,
mandates to plan, and professional
planners..., by Sy Adler --
Passion, reason and power: the
rhetorics of electric power
planning in Chicago, by J.A.
Throgmorton.
JOURNAL OF ARCHITECTURAL AND
PLANNING RESEARCH 1990 Winter, v.7
no.4, p.271-350, graph, tables,
biblios., refs.

THROGMORTON, JAMES A.
Community energy planning: winds of
change from the San Gorgonio Pass
/ James A. Throgmorton.
AMERICAN PLANNING ASSOCIATION.
JOURNAL 1987 Summer, v.53, no.3,
p.358-367, maps, photo., biblio.,
refs.

THRONES
See also CHAIRS (CATHEDRA)

THROSSELL, ERIC
Hartwell House, Bucks / Gervase
Jackson-Stops.
Former house, built ca. 1600 and
later altered by architects James
Gibbs, Henry Keene and James
Wyatt, now converted to hotel;
architect of conversion: Eric
Throssell.
COUNTRY LIFE 1990 Nov.22, v.184,
no.47, p.68-73, ill., photos.,
plan.

THUN, MATTEO
Different Thuns / Jan Burney.
Milan penthouse of designer Matteo
Thun.
HOUSE & GARDEN 1990 Apr., v.162,
no.4, p.[182-187]222, port.,
photos.
The Heavy Dress: der Architekt als
Visagist der Metropolen / Volker
Fischer.
On Matteo Thun's latest project,
Heavy Dress.
DEUTSCHE BAUZEITSCHRIFT 1989 Dec.,
v.37, no.12, p.1590-1593, models.

THUPAS
See STUPAS

THURE NIELSEN & RUBOW
Faaborg havn.
Results of a 1989 ideas
competition for alterations to the
Danish harbor. First prize: Bo
Lautrup, Peter Dalsgaard, Lars
Juel Thiis Knudsen, Ib V. Nielsen.
Second prize: Jorn Boldsen. Third
prize: Thure Nielsen & Rubow.
ARKITEKTEN 1990 Apr., v.92, no.4,
p.120-130, dwgs., maps, photos.,
site plans.

THURELL, SOREN, 1933-
Hus som sprak [book review] / Soren
Thurell.
Review of Husens sprak - Den
byggda tingsligheten och de
arkitektoniska intentionernas
dialeklik, by Kaj Nyman.
ARKITEKTUR: THE SWEDISH REVIEW OF
ARCHITECTURE 1990 Aug., v.90,
no.6, p.52-54, ill.
PS: Jorn Utzon: Utzon pa nytt /
Soren Thurell.
ARKITEKTUR: THE SWEDISH REVIEW OF
ARCHITECTURE 1990 May, v.90, no.4,
p.48-51, models, photos., plans,
secns., biblio.
Ritandets ritualer [Lennart Holm] /
Soren Thurell.
ARKITEKTUR: THE SWEDISH REVIEW OF
ARCHITECTURE 1990 Sept., v.90,
no.7, p.58-60, ports., site plan,
refs.

THURELL, SOREN, 1933-. SHADOW OF A
THOUGHT: THE JANUS CONCEPT IN
ARCHITECTURE
Skrivandets svarigheter [review] /
Jahani Pallasmaa.
Review of the shadow of thought:
the James concept in architecture,
by Soren Thurell, which first
appeared in 1989 Swedish journal.
ARKITEKTUR: THE SWEDISH REVIEW OF
ARCHITECTURE 1990 Oct., v.90,
no.8, p.58-60, dwgs.

THURLEY, SIMON
The sixteenth-century kitchens at
Hampton Court / Simon Thurley.
BRITISH ARCHAEOLOGICAL
ASSOCIATION. JOURNAL 1990, v.143,
p.[1]-28,pl.1-2, photos., plans,
secns., site plans, engr., refs.

THURMAN, JUDITH
Architectural digest visits: Bobby
Short / Judith Thurman.
Interiors of New York apartment.
ARCHITECTURAL DIGEST 1990 Nov.,
v.47, no.12, p.238-[243], ports.,
photos.
Denmark's Louisiana Museum / Judith
Thurman.
Modern art museum, Humlebaek.
ARCHITECTURAL DIGEST 1990 Oct.,
v.47, no.11, p.92,94,[97],-98,
port., photos.
Park Avenue thoroughbred / Judith
Thurman.
1929 New York apartment interiors
designed by Robert Bray and
Michael Schaible.
ARCHITECTURAL DIGEST 1990 Mar.,
v.47, no.3, p.[158]-165, photos.
Villa Santo Guglielmo: Grace
Mirabella and Dr. William Cahan's
New York State residence / Judith
Thurman.
Architect: Alexander Gorlin.
(Continued next page)

(Continued next page)

TIBBETTS, ROBERT (CONTINUED)
 Old times, only...(CONTINUED)
    no.3, p.16-[19], photos., plans,
    secns.
  State of Iowa Historical Building:
    modern history / Robert Tibbetts.
    Architect: Brown Healey Bock.
    IOWA ARCHITECT 1989 Winter, v.38,
    no.5, p.26-29, photos., plans.
  Stepping ahead: the John W. Eckstein
    Medical Research Building, the
    University of Iowa College of
    Medicine / Robert Tibbetts.
    Architects/engineers: Hansen Lind
    Meyer.
    IOWA ARCHITECT 1990 Fall, v.39,
    no.3, p.20-21, plan.
  UNI Communications Art Building:
    Campus collage / Robert Tibbetts.
    At the University of Northern
    Iowa, Cedar Rapids. Architects:
    RDG Bussard Dikis Associates.
    IOWA ARCHITECT 1990 Spring, v.39,
    no.1, p.20-21, photos., site plan.
  Veterans Auditorium and Allied Group
    Skywalk Connections: Reaching new
    heights / Robert Tibbetts.
    Herbert Lewis Kruse Blunck
    Architecture.
    IOWA ARCHITECT 1990 Spring, v.39,
    no.1, p.16-[17], photos., plan.

TIBET--STUPAS--CONSERVATION AND
RESTORATION--SVAYAMBHUNATH
  A renovation of Svayambhunath-stupa
    in the 18th century and its
    history (according to Tibetan
    sources) / Franz-Karl Ehrhard.
    PRAACINA NEPALA 1989 Oct.-Nov.,
    no.114, p.[1]-8,1 plate, photo.,
    refs.

TICKET OFFICES
  See also TRAVEL AGENCIES

TICKET OFFICES--TEMPORARY--ENGLAND--
LONDON--EAST CROYDON
  Screens and counter: ticket office:
    Alan Brookes Associates.
    Temporary ticket office in East
    Croydon, London.
    ARCHITECTS' JOURNAL 1990 Aug.15,
    v.192, no.7, p.45-47, axonometric
    view, dets., elev., photos, plans,
    secn.

TIEDEMANN, ROLF. GESAMMELTE SCHRIFTEN
  Benjamin the scrivener / Richard
    Sieburth.
    Historical, thematic and
    methodological aspects of "Das
    Passagen-Werk" (Arcades Project),
    conceived in 1927 and publ. in
    1982 as vol. 5 of the Suhrkamp
    "Gesammelte Schriften," ed. by
    Rolf Tiedemann.
    ASSEMBLAGE 1988 June, no.6,
    p.[6]-23, ill., photos., site
    plans, refs.

TIEPOLO, GIOVANNI BATTISTA,
1696-1770,--EXHIBITIONS
  Pittura, scultura e architettura
    nella Vicenza settecentesca
    [exhibition review] / Valeria
    Farinati.
    "Il Tiepolo e il settecento
    vicentino", in Vicenza, 26 May-20
    Sept.1990. Captions in Italian and
    English.
    CASABELLA 1990 Nov., v.54, no.573,
    p.27, elev.

TIEPOLO, MAURIZIO
  La cartografia di Brazzaville nel
    periodo coloniale (1885-1957) /
    Maurizio Tiepolo.
    STORIA URBANA 1989 Jan.-Mar.,
    v.13, no.46, p.121-160, maps, site
    plans, refs.
  Fonti per la ricerca urbana sul
    Congo-Brazzaville in alcuni
    archivi e biblioteche francesi /
    Maurizio Tiepolo.
    STORIA URBANA 1989 Apr.-June,
    v.13, no.47, p.[229-246], refs.

TIETZ, KARL, 1832-1874
  Ein feudales Erbe / Jutta Kohout.
    On the 1875 Villa Lanna in the
    Salzkammergut, Austria, owned by
    the Trauttenberg family.
    Architect: Karl Tietz.
    ARCHITEKTUR & WOHNEN 1990
    Feb.-Mar., no.1, p.40-49, ports.,
    photos., plans.

TIETZE, BARBARA
  Menschen ohne Unterleib: Kritik an
    ergonomischen Planungen fur das
    moderne Buro / Barbara Tietze.
    BAUWELT 1990 Feb.23, v.81, no.7-8,
    p.340-341, ill., ref.

TIFFANY, J.B.
  Wilderstein: a loved and lived-in
    family home in Rhinebeck, New York
    / Anne Needham.
    Queen Anne style house completed
    in the 1880s. Interior by J.B.
    Tiffany; grounds by Calvert Vaux;
    architect for exterior, Arnout
    Cannon. Current owner: Wilderstein
    Foundation.
    VICTORIAN HOMES 1990 summer, v.9,
    no.3, p.54-57, ill., photos.

TIFFANY, LOUIS COMFORT, 1848-1933
  Divine light ... Louis Comfort
    Tiffany / Steven Saltzman.
    Tiffany windows in New York City.
    METROPOLIS 1990 May, v.9, no.9,
    p.92-95,119-123, photos.
  Tiffany's treasures.
    Windows, vases and lamps of Louis
    Comfort Tiffany.
    COLONIAL HOMES 1990 Feb., v.16,
    no.1, p.[70]-75,140-141, port.,
    photos.

TIFFANY, LOUIS COMFORT, 1848-1933--
INFLUENCE
  A place of one's own [Century
    Studios, Minneapolis].
    Stained glass showroom and studio,
    specializing in reproduction of
    Tiffany lampshades.
    ARCHITECTURE MINNESOTA 1990
    May-June, v.16, no.3, p.31, port.

TIGERMAN, FUGMAN MCCURRY
  Paesaggi attorno al lavoro:
    Sacramento, California: Herman
    Miller = Landscapes of labour:
    Herman Miller, in Sacramento,
    California.
    Furniture factory in Rocklin.
    Architects: Frank O. Gehry &
    Associates; Tigerman, Fugman &
    McCurry. Landscape architects:
    Peter Walker and Martha Schwartz.
    ABITARE 1990 Oct., no.289,
    p.244-255, elev., photos., plans,
    secns., site plan.

TIGERMAN MCCURRY
  American Standard / Monica Geran.
    Interiors of IDCNY showroom
    designed by Tigerman McCurry.
    INTERIOR DESIGN 1990 Sept., v.61,
    no.12, p.238-[241], dwgs., photos.
  Anything but standard: American
    Standard Showroom, Long Island
    City, New York, Tigerman McCurry
    Architects / Paul M. Sachner.
    ARCHITECTURAL RECORD 1990 Sept.,
    v.178, no.10, p.[94-97], photos.,
    plan.
  City on a hill...Herman Miller's new
    factory / Karen D. Stein.
    The Western Region Manufacturing
    and Distribution Facility,
    Rocklin, Calif. Architect: Frank
    O. Gehry & Associates; consulting
    architect: Tigerman McCurry
    Architects; assoc. architect:
    Dreyfuss and Blackford; landscape
    architects: Peter Walker / Martha
    Schwartz.
    ARCHITECTURAL RECORD 1990 Jan.,
    v.178, no.1, p.108-115, elev.,
    photos., plan, secns., site plan.
  Design 100: the people, products,
    ideas that shape our lives.
    "Special issue." Architects
    mentioned include Venturi and
    Scott Brown, Robert A. M. Stern,
    Frank Gehry, Richard Meier,
    Morphosis, Coop Himmelblau, Andres
    Duany + Elizabeth Plater-Zyberk,
    Stanley Tigerman and Margaret
    McCurry, Eric Owen Moss, Charles
    Warren, Michael Graves, Peter
    Eisenman, and Lake/Flato
    Architects.
    METROPOLITAN HOME 1990 Apr., v.22,
    no.4, p.[67-199], ports., photos.
  Hall of Fame: celebrations and
    memories [1990].
    Profiles of twelve new inductees
    into the Interior Design Hall of
    Fame and the winners of three
    special citations.
    INTERIOR DESIGN 1990 Dec., v.61,
    no.16, p.105-[125], ports.,
    photos.
  Haworth, Inc. / Monica Geran.
    Interiors of furniture showroom in
    Chicago's Merchandise Mart.
    Architects: Tigerman McCurry.
    INTERIOR DESIGN 1990 Oct., v.61,
    no.14, p.240-243, photos.,
    isometric dwg.
  Model homes / Lynn Nesmith.
    Housing projects in Fukuoka,
    Japan, by Tigerman McCurry and
    Michael Graves.
    ARCHITECTURE: THE AIA JOURNAL 1990
    Sept., v.79, no.9, p.[90]-97,
    elev., models, photos., plans,
    site plans.
  New twist to the farmhouse
    vernacular in New York / Paul
    Goldberger.
    On the stable and coach house
    addition to a Dutchess Co. horse
    farm. Architects:: Tigerman
    McCurry. Architects of older main
    house: Albert Kahn Associates.
    ARCHITECTURAL DIGEST 1990 June,
    v.47, no.6, p.86,90,94, dwg.,
    elevs., model, photos., plans.
  Shower of angels / Michael Wagner.
    Temporary bathroom fixtures
    showroom for American Standard,
    IDCNY. Architects: Tigerman
    McCurry.

(Continued next page)

TIGERMAN MCCURRY (CONTINUED)
Shower of angels /...(CONTINUED)
INTERIORS 1990 July, v.149, no.12,
p.76-[77], photos.

T'GERMAN, STANLEY, 1930-
Directions in urban housing, part
II: Messages from Fukuoka.
Contents: International Housing
Exhibition in Kashii.--Steven
Holl.--Rem Koolhaas.--Mark Mack.--
Osamu Ishiyama.--Christian de
Portzamparc.--Oscar Tusguets.--
Arata Isozaki.--Nexus Momochi,
Michael Graves, Stanley
Tigerman.--Fukuoka International
Architects' Conference '89.--
Experation and Defiance in the
Debate over the City as "Chaos",
by Noriko Takiguchi. Includes
English summary and biographical
information on participants.
SPACE DESIGN 1990 Jan., no.304,
p.53-84, axonometric views, dwgs.,
ports., elevs., models, map,
photos., plans, secns., site
plans.
The elliptical architecture of
Stanley Tigerman / David A.
Greenspan.
INLAND ARCHITECT 1990 Mar.-Apr.,
v.34, no.2, p.12,15-16, ill.,
photo.
Exhibition: Chicago categorized
[exhibition review] / Stanley
Tigerman.
On the exhibit "Chicago
architecture-the new Zeitgeist: in
search of closure", organized by
Stanley Tigerman, on view in 1989
at the Fundacao Calouste
Gulbenkian, Lisbon. Focus on
Tigerman's organization of the
work of 99 architects into six
categories.
PROGRESSIVE ARCHITECTURE 1990
Sept., v.71, no.9, p.140-141,
dets., photos., secns.
Den nye tigerman = The new Tigerman
[interview].
An interview conducted in
Copenhagen about religious and
theoretical factors in
architecture. Includes
illustrations of a "house block"
in Kiushu, Japan. In Danish and
English.
SKALA 1990, no.20, p.10-11,
photos.
The sacred garden versus the city of
man: Fukuoka City mixed-use
apartment building Kiushi, Japan,
1988-89: Stanley Tigerman.
OZ / COLLEGE OF ARCHITECTURE AND
DESIGN, KANSAS STATE UNIVERSITY
1989, v.11, p.22-23, axonometric
view, elevs., model, plans,
sketches.
Stanley Tigerman: a suburban Chicago
kitchen with a classical frame of
reference.
ARCHITECTURAL DIGEST 1990 Feb.,
v.47, no.2, p.110, photo., plan.
Unconventional wit near Chicago:
Stanley Tigerman infuses a
suburban house with playful
complexities / Kurt Andersen.
ARCHITECTURAL DIGEST 1990 Dec.,
v.47, no.13, p.[124-129], 220,
port., photos., plan.

TIGERMAN, STANLEY, 1930---EXHIBITIONS
Master visions / Malcolm Fraser,
Roddy Langmuir.
Installations by the following
architects at the Glasgow School
of Art to illustrate the influence
of Charles Rennie Mackintosh: Aldo
van Eyck, Stanley Tigerman, Leon
Krier, Hans Hollein, Ted Cullinan,
Arata Isozaki, and Filippo Alison.
ARCHITECTS' JOURNAL 1990
Aug.22-29, v.192, no.7-8, p.26-29,
photos.

TIHANY, ADAM
Baci for Bice / Justin Henderson.
Interiors of Bice restaurant, Los
Angeles, which features an
"updated version of Italian Art
Deco of the 1920s and 1930s."
Designer: Adam Tihany.
INTERIORS 1990 Nov., v.150, no.4,
p.64-[65], photos., plan.
Best dressed restaurants: Remi /
Regina S. Baraban.
At 145 W. 53rd St., New York.
Designer: Adam Tihany.
METROPOLIS 1990 Dec., v.10, no.5,
p.31, photos.
Biba / Edie Lee Cohen.
Boston restaurant interiors.
Interior designer: Adam Tihany.
INTERIOR DESIGN 1990 Oct., v.61,
no.14, p.204-207, photos., plans.
Pomodoro / Edie Lee Cohen.
On the Italian trattoria in
Beverly Hills designed by Adam
Tihany.
INTERIOR DESIGN 1990 Apr., v.61,
no.6, p.186-[189], photos., plan.
Remi redux / Edie Lee Cohen.
Interiors of relocated New York
restaurant, Remi. Interior
designer: Adam Tihany.
INTERIOR DESIGN 1990 Sept., v.61,
no.12, p.182-[185], photos., plan.

TILE PAVEMENTS
See PAVEMENTS - TILE

TILES
See also MATHEMATICAL TILES
See also PANTILES
See also "TILE" AS A SUBHEADING
AFTER SPECIFIC BUILDING TYPES OR
OTHER MAIN HEADINGS.
The bathroom get a glamourous look
from tiles by a star designer /
Angi Bates.
Features the Edition Number One
collection by Villeroy & Boch.
Designer: Paloma Picasso.
INTERIORS 1989 Feb., v.148, no.7,
p.102, port., photos.
Fabel-haft dekoriert / Justin Thyme.
On the 1905 Arts and crafts
movement tile and mosaic
decoration designed by William de
Morgan in Sir Ernest Debenham's
home in London.
ARCHITEKTUR & WOHNEN 1990
Aug.-Sept., no.4, p.140-145,
port., photos.
Marazzi mondiale.
The National Science and
Technology Center, Canberra,
Australia, features tiles made by
Marazzi Tecnica. Architect:
Lawrence Nield and Partners.
ARCHITETTURA; CRONACHE E STORIA
1990 June, v.36, no.6(416),
p.[478-480], photos., plan.

TILES (CONTINUED)
Modern mosaic: the rebirth of
Pewabic Pottery / Daniel Cohen.
1907 ceramics studio in Detroit is
once again producing quality
objects.
HISTORIC PRESERVATION 1990
Mar.-Apr., v.42, no.2, p.30-35,78,
port., photos.
Technics focus: ceramic tile.
Includes four articles:
Prefabricated exterior ceramic
tile cladding; Ceramic tile
floors; Tile in wet environments
and Manufacturers' directory.
PROGRESSIVE ARCHITECTURE 1990
Apr., v.71, no.4, p.131-161,
dets., photos., secns.
Tile news.
New tile designs and techniques.
HOUSE BEAUTIFUL 1990 Oct., v.132,
no.10, p.92-92, photos.

TILES--19TH CENTURY
New life for your brownstone: the
rediscovery of encaustic tile.
This type of tile was a common
feature of 19th-cent. houses.
BROWNSTONER 1990 summer, p.4-5,
ill.

TILES--CLAY--STANDARDS--GREAT BRITAIN
Tile Council / Robin Mackley.
On the new British standard, BS
402, for plain clay roofing tiles.
RIBA JOURNAL 1990 Oct., v.97,
no.10, p.81,84, photos.

TILES--DIRECTORIES
Reviving the tile tradition / Eve M.
Kahn.
Coontains directory titles:
Fireplace tiles sourcelist.
CLEM LABINE'S TRADITIONAL BUILDING
1990 Sept.-Oct., v.3, no.5,
p.31-34, photos., table, ill.

TILES--EXHIBITIONS
Fliesenmekka Bologna.
On the annual tile manufacturers
exhibition in Bologna.
DEUTSCHE BAUZEITSCHRIFT 1989 Dec.,
v.37, no.12, p.1582-1585, photos.

TILES--INDIA--HISTORY
Tiles in India / Aman Nath.
Brief history and development of
tilemaking in India. Excerpt from
a chapter on the blue pottery of
Jaipur from, The Arts and Crafts
of Rajasthan, by Aman Nath and
Francis Wacziarg.
GLAZED EXPRESSIONS / TILES &
ARCHITECTURAL CERAMICS SOCIETY
1989 Spring, no.18, p.6-7, photos.

TILES--ISLAMIC--16TH CENTURY
From international Timurid to
Ottoman: a change of taste in
sixteenth-century ceramic tiles /
Gulru Necipoglu.
MUQARNAS 1990, v.7, p.[136]-170,
ill., dwg., photos., plan, refs.

TILES--MAINTENANCE AND REPAIR
Gneisplatten als Terrassenbelag:
Braunfarbung durch eisenhaltige
Kleskorner / Gunter Zimmermann.
DEUTSCHES ARCHITEKTENBLATT 1990
Oct.1, v.22, no.10, p.1583,
photos.

TILES--MAINTENANCE AND REPAIR
                    (CONTINUED)
  Reconstruir los suenos de una
    artista: restauracion del Park
    Guell.
    Original architect: Antonio Gaudi.
    Architects for restoration: J.
    Antonio Martinez Lapena, Elias
    Torres Tur. English text,
    p.190-191.
    ON DISENO 1990, "ceramica" suppl.,
    p.130-134, photos.

TILES--MEDIEVAL--REPRODUCTIONS
  Stamp of authenticity: Diana Hall,
    creator of modern tiles in the
    medieval idiom / Nick Roe.
    TRADITIONAL HOMES 1990 Feb., v.6,
    no.5, p.71-73, ports., photos.

TILES--OTTOMAN--HISTORY
  From international Timurid to
    Ottoman: a change of taste in
    sixteenth-century ceramic tiles /
    Gulru Necipoglu.
    MUQARNAS 1990, v.7, p.[136]-170,
    ill., dwg., photos., plan, refs.

TILES--SPAIN
  Diseno ceramico arquitectura /
    Ferran Renau.
    Ceramic tile design and
    architecture. English text,
    p.186-190.
    ON DISENO 1990, "ceramica" suppl.,
    p.117-129, photos.
  Un material que se identifica con la
    arquitectura mediterranea / Jose
    Luis Porcar.
    The use of ceramics in
    architecture in Spain. Text in
    English, p.176-179.
    ON DISENO 1990, "ceramica suppl.,
    p.57-71, ill., photos.

TILES--TIMURID
  From international Timurid to
    Ottoman: a change of taste in
    sixteenth-century ceramic tiles /
    Gulru Necipoglu.
    MUQARNAS 1990, v.7, p.[136]-170,
    ill., dwg., photos., plan, refs.

TILES--VICTORIAN--ENGLAND--ASHBOURNE--
SAINT OSWALD'S CHURCH
  Victorian varieties - church tiles
    at Lichfield and Ashbourne /
    Philip Brown, Dorothy Brown.
    Tiles for Victorian church
    restorations of Lichfield
    Cathedral and St. Oswald's Church,
    Ashbourne by Sir George Gilbert
    Scott.
    GLAZED EXPRESSIONS / TILES &
    ARCHITECTURAL CERAMICS SOCIETY
    1989 Spring, no.18, p.2, photos.,
    refs.

TILES--VICTORIAN--ENGLAND--LICHFIELD--
LICHFIELD CATHEDRAL
  Victorian varieties - church tiles
    at Lichfield and Ashbourne /
    Philip Brown, Dorothy Brown.
    Tiles for Victorian church
    restorations of Lichfield
    Cathedral and St. Oswald's Church,
    Ashbourne by Sir George Gilbert
    Scott.
    GLAZED EXPRESSIONS / TILES &
    ARCHITECTURAL CERAMICS SOCIETY
    1989 Spring, no.18, p.2, photos.,
    refs.

TILES--VICTORIAN--REPRODUCTIONS
  Ceramic comeback: the wall tile
    revival / Tony Herbert.
    TRADITIONAL HOMES 1990 June, v.6,
    no.9, p.61-66, dwgs., photos.
  Relearning geometry: the Victorian
    fashion for geometric floor tiles
    is taking shape once again / Tony
    Herbert.
    Includes a list of suppliers.
    TRADITIONAL HOMES 1990 May, v.6,
    no.8, p.89-90,93,94, dets., dwgs.,
    photos.

TILL, BARRY
  The tomb of Yuan Shih-K'ai: the man
    who would be emperor / Barry Till.
    Tomb of ambitious commoner Yuan
    Shih-K'ai, modelled after Ming
    (1368-1644) and Ching (1644-1911)
    dynasties, constructed near Anyang
    in Hunan province.
    ARTS OF ASIA 1989 Nov.-Dec., v.19,
    no.6, p.104-105,108-111, photos.,
    site plan.

TILLEY, RAY DON
  2nd Annual Graphics Competition /
    Ray Don Tilley.
    24 winning entries in a
    competition sponsored by the
    magazine.
    TEXAS ARCHITECT 1990 Sept.-Oct.,
    v.40, no.5, p.34-39, ill., dwgs.,
    models, photos., sketches.
  Alumni center adds more and Moore /
    Ray Don Tilley.
    The UT Austin Alumni Center
    addition. Architects: Charles
    Moore, Richard Dodge, and Jessen
    Inc.
    TEXAS ARCHITECT 1990 July-Aug.,
    v.40, no.4, p.59, dwgs., site
    plan.
  A Japanese tea house from silent
    beginnings / Ray Don Tilley.
    Project to be built on a Japanese
    island. Architect: Gerlinde
    Leiding.
    TEXAS ARCHITECT 1990 July-Aug.,
    v.40, no.4, p.58, models, site
    plan.
  A myth for Texas architecture / Ray
    Don Tilley.
    Photographs of Mexican towns by
    Hal Box.
    TEXAS ARCHITECT 1990 Mar.-Apr.,
    v.40, no.2, p.[36]-39, photos.
  Reclaimed resources: building
    systems: recycling wastewater /
    Ray Don Tilley.
    Plumbing systems that conserve and
    reuse water.
    ARCHITECTURE: THE AIA JOURNAL 1990
    Dec., v.79, no.12, p.97-99,102,
    dwgs., photos.

TILLOTSON, G. H. R. CONTINUITY,
CONTROVERSY AND CHANGE SINCE 1850:
THE TRADITION OF INDIAN ARCHITECTURE
  An imperial vision: Indian
    architecture and Britain's Raj, by
    Thomas R. Metcalf [book review] /
    Jeremy Melvin.
    Reviewed with: The Indian
    metropolis; a view toward the
    West, by Norma Evenson, and
    Continuity, controversy and change
    since 1850: the tradition of
    Indian architecture, by G. H. R.
    Tillotson, all pub. 1989.
    BURLINGTON MAGAZINE 1990 Aug.,
    v.132, no.1049, p.585-586,

TILLOTSON, G. H. R. RAJPUT PALACES:
THE DEVELOPMENT OF AN ARCHITECTURAL
STYLE, 1450-1750
  The Rajput palaces [book review] /
    George T. Scanlon.
    Review of a 1987 book by G.H.R.
    Tillotson.
    APOLLO 1990 Feb., v.131, no.336,
    p.132,

TILLOTSON, G. H. R. TRADITION OF
INDIAN ARCHITECTURE
  An imperial vision: Indian
    architecture and Britain's Raj, by
    Thomas R. Metcalf [book review] /
    Jeremy Melvin.
    Reviewed with: The Indian
    metropolis; a view toward the
    West, by Norma Evenson, and
    Continuity, controversy and change
    since 1850: the tradition of
    Indian architecture, by G. H. R.
    Tillotson, all pub. 1989.
    BURLINGTON MAGAZINE 1990 Aug.,
    v.132, no.1049, p.585-586,
  Revealing India [book review] / Dan
    Cruickshank.
    Three reviews: The Penguin guide
    to the monuments of India, v.1:
    Buddhist, Jain, Hindu, by George
    Michell; v.2: Islamic, Rajput,
    European, by Philip Davis; and The
    tradition of Indian architecture,
    by G.H.R. Tillotson, all pub.
    1989.
    ARCHITECTS' JOURNAL 1990 Feb.7,
    v.191, no.6, p.80-82, photos.

TILNEY LUMSDEN SHANE
  Buildings update banks 2: case
    studies.
    Changes in bank design, part 2.
    Contents: TSB Bank, St. Andrews,
    Scotland architect: Nicoll Russell
    Studio; Midland Bank, Surrey
    Quays, London, architect: Midland
    Bank Premises Dept.; Halifax Bldg.
    Soc. Bank, Kensington, London,
    architect: McColl; and Lloyds
    Bank, Basingstoke, architects:
    Tilney Lumsden Shane.
    ARCHITECTS' JOURNAL 1990 June 27,
    v.191, no.26, p.57-63, photos.,
    plans, site plans.
  Facelift for IBM / Jane Payne.
    Features refurbished interiors of
    IBM UK Customer Centre, London.
    Architects: Tilney Lumsden Shane.
    RIBA JOURNAL 1990 Feb., v.97,
    no.2, p.70-72, photos.

TILSON, BARBARA
  Plan furniture 1932-1938: the German
    connection / Barbara Tilson.
    A modernist experiment in the
    manufacture and retail of
    contemporary furnishings, founded
    by Serge Chermayeff and involving
    Franz Schuster and Walter Knoll &
    Co.
    JOURNAL OF DESIGN HISTORY 1990,
    v.3, no.2-3, p.1435-155, photos.,
    refs.

TILTON & LEWIS ASSOCIATES
  The Wright way: restoration of the
    Meyer May house / Amy Dana.
    1909 house in Grand Rapids, Mich.,
    now owned by Steelcase, Inc.
    Original architect: Frank Lloyd
    Wright. Restoration architects:
    Tilton & Lewis Associates.
                (Continued next page)

TILTON & LEWIS ASSOCIATES
                    (CONTINUED)
   The Wright way:...(CONTINUED)
   INTERIORS 1990 Jan., v.149, no.6,
   p.160-[163], photos., plan.

TIM BRENNAN ARCHITECTS
   A touch of glass / Carl Gardner.
   On the new seminar / interview
   room in the ceramics and glass
   dept. of the Royal College of Art,
   London. Room features new glass
   product by Solaglas Marksman.
   Architects: Tim Brennan
   Architects.
   RIBA JOURNAL 1990 Dec., v.97,
   no.12, p.49-50, photos.

TIM RONALDS ARCHITECTS
   Highgate haven / David Jenkins.
   Multi-purpose garden building
   serves as tool shed, changing
   room, offices, and storage for the
   training of handicapped gardeners
   in Highgate, London. Architect:
   Tim Ronalds Architects. Includes
   second article: Roof, gardeners'
   centre, Tim Ronalds Architects,
   p.59-61.
   ARCHITECTS' JOURNAL 1990 Sept.12,
   v.192, no.11, p.[46]-51,59-61,
   det., elev., photos., plans,
   secns., isometric dwg.

TIM RONALDS ARCHITECTS--EXHIBITIONS
   Mixed quartet: Reality and project:
   four British architects
   [exhibition review] / David
   Jenkins.
   Exhibition at the 9H Gallery,
   London, showing the work of
   Armstrong Associates, Pierre
   d'Avoine, Tony Fretton, and Tim
   Ronalds. Through 22 July 1990.
   ARCHITECTS' JOURNAL 1990 July 4,
   v.192, no.1, p.70-72, axonometric
   view, models.

TIMBER
   See WOOD

TIMBER-FRAMED BUILDINGS
   See also HALF-TIMBERED BUILDINGS
   Fruits of the forest / Richard
   Burton, William Moorwood, Anne
   Wilder.
   Two buildings in Hooke Park using
   untreated wood jointing structural
   technology. Architects: Frei Otto,
   Buro Happold, ABK.
   BUILDING DESIGN 1990 June, suppl.,
   p.12-13, dets., photos., secn.
   Holztragwerke im Industriebau /
   Degenhard Sommer.
   DEUTSCHE BAUZEITSCHRIFT 1990 Dec.,
   v.38, no.12, p.1802-1804,
   1807-1808.1810, dets., graph,
   photo., table, ref.

TIMBER-FRAMED BUILDINGS--ALTERATIONS
AND ADDITIONS--GERMANY (WEST)
   Anpassung von vorhandenen Bauteilen
   an das Baurecht / Heinz Schmitz,
   Norbert Stannek.
   DEUTSCHES ARCHITEKTENBLATT 1990
   Mar.1, v.22, no.1, p.389-392,
   photos., refs.

TIMBER-FRAMED BUILDINGS--
COMPETITIONS--WALES--SWANSEA--
PENPLAS
   Verdichteter Wohnungsbau in
   Holzkonstruktion Penplas/Swansea,
   Grossbritannien = Urbanbuild
   timberframe housing,
   Penplas/Swansea, Great Britain.
   Competition. Winning architects:
   PCKO Partnership. Text in German.
   ARCHITEKTUR + WETTBEWERBE 1990
   June, no.142, p.52-55, dwgs.,
   elevs., maps, plans, site plans.

TIMBER-FRAMED BUILDINGS--CONSERVATION
AND RESTORATION--GREAT BRITAIN
   Into the wood / Pat Garratt.
   Profile of Peter McCurdy, an
   architect and craftsman, whose
   company, McCurdy & Co.,
   specializes in the conservation of
   timber-framed buildings in
   Britain.
   THE WORLD OF INTERIORS 1990 Nov.,
   p.41,43-44,46,48, photos.

TIMBER-FRAMED BUILDINGS--ENGLAND
   Diamonds and dragons: the medieval
   tradition of decorative timber
   framing / Dick and Jean Randall.
   TRADITIONAL HOMES 1990 Aug., v.6,
   no.11, p.95-99, photos., biblio.

TIMBER-FRAMED BUILDINGS--ENGLAND--
LONDON--LEWISHAM
   Roof and external walls: housing:
   Lewisham Architects' Dept.
   First timber-framed housing to be
   built for an inner London borough
   (late 1970s).
   ARCHITECTS' JOURNAL 1990 Oct.10,
   v.192, no.15, p.63-65, dets.,
   photos., plans, secns.

TIMBER-FRAMED BUILDINGS--ENVIRONMENTAL
ASPECTS--GREAT BRITAIN
   Plying for trade / Denise Chevin.
   On recent promotion of timber
   frame construction in Great
   Britain.
   BUILDING 1990 July 27, v.255,
   no.30, p.52-53, dets., photos.

TIMBER-FRAMED BUILDINGS--JAPAN--
SHIMODA--ARAKAWA
   Arakawa-Sommerschule in Shimoda.
   Architects: Sakakura Associates,
   Architects and Engineers.
   DEUTSCHE BAUZEITSCHRIFT 1990 Nov.,
   v.38, no.11, p.1587-1590, photos.,
   isometric dwgs.

TIMBER-FRAMED BUILDINGS--MEDIEVAL
   Clues written in wood / David
   Pearce.
   The Medieval Harmondsworth
   timber-framed barn.
   COUNTRY LIFE 1990 Dec.27, v.184,
   no.52, p.40-42, photos.

TIMBER-FRAMED BUILDINGS--STUDENT
PROJECTS
   Timber frame Hauser: drei Entwurfe
   der FH Wiesbaden, SS 89.
   DEUTSCHE BAUZEITSCHRIFT 1990
   Sept., v.38, no.9, p.1194-1199,
   dets., models, plans, secn.

TIMBER-FRAMED BUILDINGS--UNITED
STATES--YORK (PENNSYLVANIA)
   Catering for charity [review] / Tom
   Woolley.
   "Raising the roof", television
   program aired on the BBC showed
   volunteers constructing two
   timber-framed houses in three days
   in York, Pa.
   ARCHITECTS' JOURNAL 1990
   Aug.22-29, v.192, no.7-8, p.71,
   ports.

TIMBER - PRESERVATION
   See WOOD - PRESERVATION

TIME
   Ornamento e tempo = Ornament and
   time / Yehuda Safran.
   Refers to A. Loos' 1908 essay
   "Ornament and crime". In Italian
   and English.
   OTTAGONO 1990 Dec., no.97, p.3-10,
   dwgs., ports., photos., sketches,
   refs.
   Place defined by time and light /
   Dale Eldred.
   The author is an artist whose
   sculptures are placed in open
   spaces where the passage of light
   across the surfaces parallels the
   passing of time. Examples from
   Denmark, Finland, Turkey, and the
   U.S.
   PLACES 1990 Summer, v.6, no.4,
   p.34-[41], photos.
   Rumlige eksempler.
   "Spatial examples" -- gardens
   conveying form, time, diversity,
   and related concepts. In Danish
   and English.
   ARKITEKTUR DK 1990, v.34, no.4,
   p.183-187, ill., dwgs., photos.,
   site plans.
   Time, speed, and design / Hiroyuki
   Suzuki.
   THE WHEEL EXTENDED 1990, v.19,
   no.3, p.16-23, ill., photos.
   Toward time space of "Kankyo" /
   Fumiaki Seo.
   KENCHIKU BUNKA 1990 Aug., v.45,
   no.526, p.25-34, diagrs., ill.

TIMESHARING (REAL ESTATE)--GREAT
BRITAIN
   Timeshare: a new dimension in
   tourism / Mike Stabler, Brian
   Goodall.
   Timeshare ownership of tourism
   accomodation by U.K. residents;
   includes illustrated examples of
   different types of timeshare
   property.
   BUILT ENVIRONMENT 1989, v.15,
   no.2, p.101-124, graphs, ill.,
   table, refs.

TIMMERMANS, INGE
   Bakema = Bakema
   Contents: Editorial, by Dick Apon.
   The big scale, by Arjen Oosterman.
   't Hool, twenty years of modern
   living, by Tom Dubbelman. A
   baker's cart in Buikslotermeer, by
   Inge Timmermans. Bakema, by
   Francis Strauven. Space for the
   pedestrian and the Friendships
   model, by Wilma Visser. From the
   Euromast to the Dutch pavilion for
   Osaka, by Rob Dettingmeijer. And
   Bakema..., by Rob Dettingmeijer &
   Frans Hooijkaas. Biography. In
                    (Continued next page)

TIMMERMANS, INGE (CONTINUED)
Bakema = Bakema. (CONTINUED)
Dutch and English.
FORUM 1990 Sept., v.34, no.3,
p.[1]-[49], dwgs., models,
photos., secns., refs.

TIMON, KALMAN
Zum 5. Mal "Wohnhaus des Jahres" in
Ungarn / Kalman Timon.
Six projects. Architects: Gabor
Farkas, Gyorgy Radvanyi, Ferenc
Lorincz, Jozsef Pinczei, Arpad
Vonnak, and Gyorgy Ruisz. German,
Russian, English and French
summaries.p.55-56.
ARCHITEKTUR DER DDR 1990 Feb.,
v.38, no.2, p.43-48, photos.,
plans.

TIMURID
See "TIMURID" AS A SUBHEADING AFTER
SPECIFIC BUILDING TYPES OR OTHER
MAIN HEADINGS.

TINDALE, PAT
Housing project design awards / Pat
Tindale.
Review of the seven winners of the
1990 RIBA/DOE/NHBC awards.
RIBA JOURNAL 1990 Aug., v.97,
no.8, p.42-45, dwgs., elevs.,
plans, site plans.

TINKER, ANTHEA
Housing associations and very
sheltered housing / Anthea Tinker.
VOLUNTARY HOUSING 1990 Mar., v.23,
no.2, p.21,

TIPPETTS-ABBETT-MCCARTHY-STRATTON
A lesson in tectonics / Thomas
Fisher.
On the gymnasium and classroom
additions to the 1920s Mount
Pleasant Elementary School,
Nashua, N.H. Architects: TAMS
Consultants. Includes Selected
Detail article on a wall section
of the addition.
PROGRESSIVE ARCHITECTURE 1990
Aug., v.71, no.8, p.110-112, det.,
photos., plans.

TIRONI, GIORDANO
Progetti recenti di Francesco
Venezia / Vittorio Savi, Giordano
Tironi.
Includes restoration of Buida Oli
waterfront, Alcoy, Spain;
renovation to Palazzo Faina
museum, Orvieto; competition entry
for gardens, Park de la Fontaine,
Nimes; and urban center
alterations, San Pietro a
Patierno, Naples. Includes
English captions and summary.
CASABELLA 1990 Mar., v.54, no.566,
p.4-17,59-60, axonometric view,
models, photos., plans, secns.,
site plans, sketches.

TISCHLER, HEINRICH
Pupils of the Academy / Vladimir
Slapeta.
On the work of five former
architecture students at the
Breslau Academy of Arts and
Artistic Crafts: Emil Lange, Karl
Joseph Erbs, Moritz Hadda,
Heinrich Tischler and Heinrich
Lauterbach.
(Continued next column)

TISCHLER, HEINRICH (CONTINUED)
Pupils of the Academy...(CONTINUED)
RASSEGNA 1989 Dec., v.11, no.4014,
p.73-77, dwgs., photos., plans,
refs.

TISCHLER, LINDA HAYES
Design as healer: Boston AIDS
hospice / Linda Hayes Tischler.
The Hospice at Mission Hill, in a
converted rowhouse and dating from
c.1987. Organizer: designer
Charles Spada.
METROPOLITAN HOME 1990 Sept.,
v.22, no.9, p.62, photo.

TISE, SUZANNE
Une demeure 1930 / Suzanne Tise.
Villa Cavrois, Croix, France,
built in 1932; architect: Robert
Mallet-Stevens.
LE MONITEUR ARCHITECTURE AMC 1990
July-Aug., no.13, p.84-89,
photos., plans.

TISHLER, WILLIAM H.
At the beginning, looking back /
Michael Leccese.
Four American landscape architects
discuss the state of the
profession. Participants: Ian
McHarg, M. Paul Friedberg, Ray
Freeman and William Tishler.
LANDSCAPE ARCHITECTURE 1990 Oct.,
v.80, no.10, p.92-97, dwgs.,
ports., photos.

TISHMAN SPEYER
Building Europe's tallest tower
[Messe Turm building, Frankfurt].
Architect: Helmut Jahn;
developers: Tishman Speyer.
REAL ESTATE FORUM 1990 July, v.45,
no.7, p.108-110,114-115,120,
model.
The global approach: Tishman Speyer
Properties / Patric Dolan.
REAL ESTATE FORUM 1990 July, v.45,
no.7, p.72-93,98,102-103,107,
ports., photos., plans.

TISSI, FRITZ
Sechsfamilienhaus in Schaffhausen.
Architects: Fritz Tissi + Peter
Gotz.
WERK, BAUEN + WOHNEN 1990 Mar.,
no.3, p.1-4(folded, at back),
plans, secn., site plan, tables.
Sporthalle Stockwiesen, Thayngen.
Architects: Fritz Tissi + Peter
Gotz.
WERK, BAUEN + WOHNEN 1990
Jan.-Feb., no.1-2, p.1-4 (folded
at back), photos., plans, secns.,
tables.

TISSIER, YVES
Emboitements: maison a Bagnolet.
Group of 19th cent. cottages
converted to art collector's home.
Architects: Yves Tissier, Bernard
Wauthier-Wurmser. Summaries in
English and Spanish.
TECHNIQUES ET ARCHITECTURE 1990
June-July, no.390, p.72-73,179,
photos., plan, secn.
La maison reconsideree / Yves
Tissier, Bernard Wauthier-Wurmser.
Includes English and Spanish
summaries.
TECHNIQUES ET ARCHITECTURE 1990
June-July, no.390, p.104-105,180,
photos., refs.

TITE, WILLIAM, SIR, 1798-1873
LIFFE must go on / Denise Chevin.
Refurbishment of the Royal
Exchange, London. Built 1841-1844
(architect: Sir William Tite); new
roof added in 1884 (architect:
Charles Barry). Architect:
Fitzroy Robinson Partnership.
BUILDING 1990 Nov.2, v.255, no.43,
p.46-50, axonometric view, elevs.,
photos., secns.

TITHE BARNS--18TH CENTURY--GERMANY
(WEST)--KUSEL--BURG LICHTENBERG
Wiederaufbau der Zehntscheune Burg
Lichtenberg, Kusel =
Reconstruction of Tithe Barn, Burg
Lichtenberg, Kusel.
The barn was built in 1738 and
destroyed by fire in 1799. The
reconstructed barn is now a museum
and public hall. Architects: Heinz
Gaiser, Bruno Feigenbutz.
DETAIL 1990 Oct.-Nov., v.30, no.5,
p.487-489, dets., photos., plans,
secns.

TITTLE LUTHER LOVING ARCHITECTS
Tittle Luther Loving of Abilene:
firm profile.
TEXAS ARCHITECT 1990 Mar.-Apr.,
v.40, no.2, p.58,61, photos.

TITTMANN, JOHN BARCLAY
John Barclay Tittmann: classical
canons in New England / Robert
Campbell.
Greek revival-inspired home in
Concord, Mass.
ARCHITECTURAL DIGEST 1990 Sept.,
v.47, no.10, p.[100]-104, port.,
photos., plan.

TITUS, RICHARD M.
Security works: shopping enclaves
bring hope, investment to blighted
inner-city neighborhoods / Richard
M. Titus.
High security retail centers in
the Watts section of Los Angeles,
and elsewhere.
URBAN LAND 1990 Feb., v.49, no.1,
p.2-5, photos.

TOBIN, RICHARD
Introducing geographic information
systems to a small municipality /
Richard Tobin.
Example of Limerick, Ireland.
EKISTICS 1989 Sept.-Dec., v.56,
no.338-339, p.296-299, tables.
Knowledge-based stystems in
development planning and control /
Richard Tobin.
Example of Limerick, Ireland.
EKISTICS 1989 Sept.-Dec., v.56,
no.338-339, p.331-335, table,
refs.

TOD WILLIAMS, BILLIE TSIEN &
ASSOCIATES
Dressing for the office: Building
Types Study 679: commercial
interiors / Karen D. Stein.
Three projects: Vogue conference
room (Tod Williams, Billie Tsien);
Spy offices (Chan and Mohney); and
Deloitte & Touche Headquarters
(Peter Pran and Carlos Zapata for
Ellerbe Becket).
ARCHITECTURAL RECORD 1990 May,
v.178, no.6, p.103-115, photos.,
plans, secn.

TOD WILLIAMS, BILLIE TSIEN &
ASSOCIATES (CONTINUED)
Eisenberg residence, Hampton Bays,
Long Island.
Architects: Tod Williams, Billie
Tsien & Associates. Spanish,
English text.
QUADERNS D'ARQUITECTURA I
URBANISME 1990 Jan.-Feb.-Mar.,
no.184, p.66-[67], photos., plan,
secn.
Hall of Fame: celebrations and
memories [1990].
Profiles of twelve new inductees
into the Interior Design Hall of
Fame and the winners of three
special citations.
INTERIOR DESIGN 1990 Dec., v.61,
no.16, p.105-[125], ports.,
photos.
The Los Angeles Arts Park / Philip
Arcidi.
Features five projects by the
following architects: Tod
Williams, Billie Tsien &
Associates, Mark Mack, Hodgetts
and Fung Design Associates, Adele
Naude Santos and Morphosis.
PROGRESSIVE ARCHITECTURE 1990
Sept., v.71, no.9, p.143-146.,
axonometric views, ill., models,
plans, secns., site plan.
Manhattan merger / Edie Lee Cohen.
Fusion of three apartments into
one within the Metropolitan Tower,
New York. Architects: Tod
Williams. Billie Tsien &
Associates.
INTERIOR DESIGN 1990 Sept., v.61,
no.12, p.216-[221], photos.,
plans.
Serene pursuits: Tod Williams and
Billie Tsien: "Our work is getting
quieter and stronger" / Christine
Pittel.
ELLE DECOR 1990 Mar., v.1, no.2,
p.128-[133], port., model, photos.
Sophistications haute couture.
Interiors of Vogue Magazine
conference room, New York.
Architects: Tod Williams, Billie
Tsien & Associates.
ARCHITECTURE INTERIEURE CREE 1990
Aug.-Sept., no.238, p.166-167,
photos., plan.
Tod Williams - Billie Tsien
[interview] / Kate Nesbitt.
Illustrates three projects: Arts
Park Center, Los Angeles; Feinberg
Hall, Princeton University; Tarlo
House, Sagaponack, N.Y. In Danish
and English.
SKALA 1990, no.20, p.34-39,
models, photos., refs.
Tod Williams et Billie Tsien /
Philippe Barriere.
Features four recent projects:
Battery Park pavilion, NYC; Vacant
Lots competition entry, NYC;
Arts-Park Center competition
entry, Los Angeles; and the
Domestic Arrangements traveling
exhibition. English summaries.
ARCHITECTURE D'AUJOURD'HUI 1990
Oct., no.271, p.127-131, models.
Vacant lots proposal: site #7, 511
West 133rd Street, Harlem,
Manhattan: Tod Williams and Billie
Tsien.
OZ / COLLEGE OF ARCHITECTURE AND
DESIGN, KANSAS STATE UNIVERSITY
1989, v.11, p.36-37, ill., models,
plan.

TOD WILLIAMS, BILLIE TSIEN &
ASSOCIATES--EXHIBITIONS
Domestic arrangements at the Walker
[exhibition review] / Linda Mack.
Review of the installation by Tod
Williams, Billie Tsien and
Associates, part of the
Architecture Tomorrow series at
the Walker Art Center in
Minneapolis.
ARCHITECTURE: THE AIA JOURNAL 1990
Feb., v.79, no.2, p.20, photos,
plan.
Experiments in Domestic Arrangements
[exhibition review] / Larry
Millett.
Reviews the third of six exhibits
in the "Architecture Tomorrow"
series at the Walker Art Center,
Minneapolis. Presents a model
house, experimenting with
materials and elements.
Architects: Tod Williams, Billie
Tsien.
INLAND ARCHITECT 1990 Mar.-Apr.,
v.34, no.2, p.9,12, plan.
An interim report on the possible
future: Tod Williams and Billie
Tsien present an ambitious but
compromised vision of domestic
life at the Walker Art Center
[exhibition review].
ARCHITECTURAL RECORD 1990 Mar.,
v.178, no.3, p.49, photos., plan.
Interview: Tod Williams and Billie
Tsien.
Discussion of their touring
exhibition, Domestic Arrangements,
and museums.
PROGRESSIVE ARCHITECTURE 1990 May,
v.71, no.5, p.119-120, ports.,
photos.
Sistemazioni domestiche = domestic
arrangements / Patricia Phillips.
On the second installation by Tod
Williams and Billie Tsien, at the
Whitney Museum of American Art
branch at Federal Plaza. In
Italian and English.
OTTAGONO 1990 Dec., no.97,
p.17-[23], models, photos.
Tod Williams and Billie Tsien
uncover new aesthetic and
functional possibilities with
"Architecture Tomorrow".
On the traveling exhibition,
Domestic Arrangements.
INTERIOR DESIGN 1990 Mar., v.61,
no.5, p.48, photos.
Tod Williams, Billie Tsien: Domestic
Arrangements.
The architects discuss their house
on exhibit at the Walker Art
Center and the Whitney Museum. In
Italian and English.
DOMUS 1990 June, no.717,
p.[58-65], photos., plan.
What is a house? ... architects Tod
Williams and Billie Tsien build an
experimental house out if ordinary
industrial materials / Marisa
Bartolucci.
A house created for their exhibit
"Domestic Arrangements.
METROPOLIS 1990 Sept., v.10, no.2,
p.52-55, photos.
Williams & Tsien's Walker
experiments [exhibition review] /
Bruce Wright.
On the exhibition, Domestic
Arrangements on view at the
Whitney Museum Downtown at Federal
(Continued next column)

TOD WILLIAMS, BILLIE TSIEN &
ASSOCIATES--EXHIBITIONS
(CONTINUED)
Williams & Tsien's...(CONTINUED)
Reserve Plaza, New York, Mar.
14-May 18, 1990.
PROGRESSIVE ARCHITECTURE 1990
Feb., v.71, no.2, p.24, photo.

TODA, TSUTOMU
Editorial design in action: the
world of Tsutomu Toda, 10: Ecology
of designers and books / Akiko
Takehara.
Text in Japanese.
SPACE DESIGN 1990 Nov.,
no.11(314), p.[082]-[087], ill.
Editorial design in action: the
world of Tsutomu Toda, 11 / Akiko
Takehara.
"Books for the memory of touch:
editorial design for the 21th
century." Text in Japanese.
SPACE DESIGN 1990 Dec.,
no.12(315), p.74-79, ill.

TODD, JAMES W.
A developers [sic] challenge to meet
tenant needs: mixed-use parts /
James W. Todd.
DEVELOPMENT 1990 Jan.-Feb., v.21,
no.1, p.33-35, port., photo.

TODESCHINI AND JAPHA, ASSOCIATED
ARCHITECTS AND PLANNERS
Green and Sea Point draft policy /
Fabio Todeschini.
City planning for Cape Town areas,
by Todeschini and Japha.
ARCHITECTURE SA = ARGITEKTUUR SA
1989 May-June, no.5-6, p.42-[43],
graphs, elev., photos., secn.,
site plan, aerial photos.

TODESCHINI, FABIO
Green and Sea Point draft policy /
Fabio Todeschini.
City planning for Cape Town areas,
by Todeschini and Japha.
ARCHITECTURE SA = ARGITEKTUUR SA
1989 May-June, no.5-6, p.42-[43],
graphs, elev., photos., secn.,
site plan, aerial photos.

TOFFOLON, GIUSEPPE
Concorso per la riqualificazione
dell' area di Via Veneto [Trento].
Presents 10 entries, including 1st
prize entry by Oswald Zoeggeler.
PARAMETRO 1990, Nov.-Dec., no.181,
p.52-69, axonometric views, ill.,
dwgs., elevs., photos., plans,
secns., aerial photo.

TOGARI, SATOSHI
Air tightness of main doors and
exterior walls / Shin Hayakawa,
Satoshi Togari.
"Study on the stack effect of tall
office buildings (Part 2)." In
Japanese. Includes English
summary.
NIHON KENCHIKU GAKKAI KEIKAKUKEI
RONBUN HOKOKU SHU = JOURNAL OF
ARCHITECTURE, PLANNING AND
ENVIRONMENTAL ENGINEERING
(TRANSACTIONS OF AIJ) 1989 Aug.,
no.8(402), p.9-18, dets., graphs,
photos., tables, refs.

TOGARI, SATOSHI (CONTINUED)
The evaluation of infiltration air
rates caused by stack effect and
wind for tall buildings / Shin
Hayakawa, Satoshi Togari.
"Study on the stack effect of tall
office buildings (Part 3)."
English summary, p.56.
NIHON KENCHIKU GAKKAI KEIKAKUKEI
RONBUN HOKOKU SHU = JOURNAL OF
ARCHITECTURE, PLANNING AND
ENVIRONMENTAL ENGINEERING 1990
Jan., no.1(407), p.47-56, charts,
graphs, plans, tables, refs.

TOGASHI, SATOSHI
A methodological study on the
classification of the type of
housing-design intention / Tomoko
Okada, Satoshi Togashi.
"Study on the classification of
the type of dwelling-culture
no.1". Text in Japanese. Includes
English summary.
NIHON KENCHIKU GAKKAI KEIKAKUKEI
RONBUN HOKOKU SHU = JOURNAL OF
ARCHITECTURE, PLANNING AND
ENVIRONMENTAL ENGINEERING 1990
Sept., no.9(415), p.49-56,
photos., tables, refs.

TOHARZ, BERNHARD
Wie Tag und Nacht: Weitgespannte
Dachen mit Tagesbelichtung /
Bernhard Toharz.
DEUTSCHE BAUZEITUNG 1990 July,
v.124, no.7, p.46-55, models,
secns., refs.

TOIT, ANTON E. DU
Robert Schmikl I.A. L.I.A. argitek /
Anton E. du Toit.
Viennse architect who worked in
Pretoria, 1940-80. In Africaans,
with English summary.
ARCHITECTURE SA = ARGITEKTUUR SA
1989 May-June, no.5-6, p.37-38,
port., photos., biblio., refs.

TOIVIO, ZACHARIAS
Bomassa med stalhus / Zacharias
Toivio.
Tall apartment building with steel
exterior, in Tammerfors.
Architect: 8 Studio, and Mikko
Kaira.
ARKITEKTUR: THE SWEDISH REVIEW OF
ARCHITECTURE 1990 Dec., v.90,
no.10, p.53-54, axonometric view,
photos., plan.

TOJNER, PAUL ERIK
Hjorring Bymidte.
The P. Nordjaers Plads in
Hjorring, Denmark. Architect:
Kjeld Bjerg. Fountain by sculptor
Bjorn Norgaard. Includes captions
and summaries in English and
German and commentaries by Olaf
Lind and Poul Erik Tojner.
ARKITEKTUR DK 1989, v.33, no.7,
p.320-329, dwgs., elevs., models,
photos., plans, site plan,
sketches.

TOJNER, POUL ERIK
Hussene er ikke pa ver side = The
houses are not on our side / Poul
Erik Tojner.
Subtitle: On the mental and the
monumental in the work of Palle
Nielsen. In Danish and English.
(Continued next column)

TOJNER, POUL ERIK (CONTINUED)
Hussene er ikke pa...(CONTINUED)
SKALA 1990, no.21, p.12-19, dwgs.,
refs.

TOKUGAWA
See EDO

TOKYO DESIGNER'S SPACE--EXHIBITIONS
Exhibition: tropical heights at
Tokyo Designer's Space [exhibition
review] / P.G. Raman.
Exhibition, Jan.8-20, 1990.
Architect: Kenneth Yeang.
ARCHITECTURE AND URBANISM 1990
Apr., no.4(235), p.6-7,
axonometric view, photos.

TOLCHINSKY & GOODZ
Quelques projets en cours de
realisation [Montreal].
Includes seven projects.
Architects: LeMoyne Lapointe
Magne, Werleman Guy McMahon,
Tolchinsky & Goodz, Kohn Pedersen
Fox Associates, Dan S. Hanganu,
Arcop Associates, Roy Provencher,
L'Atelier, JLP & Associes and
Blouin et associes.
ARQ: ARCHITECTURE/QUEBEC 1990
Apr., no.54, p.42-48, elevs.,
models, photos., plans, secns.,
site plans, refs.

TOLL BOOTHS
See also TOLL PLAZAS

TOLL PLAZAS
See also TOLL BOOTHS

TOLL ROADS
See TURNPIKES

TOLLBOOTHS
See TOLL BOOTHS

TOLLESON, KATRIN
'80s glamour for a '50s ranch
[Houston] / Katrin Tolleson.
House of interior designer Stephen
Farish.
HOUSE BEAUTIFUL 1986 May, v.128,
no.5, p.84-[87], photos.

TOM HATCH ARCHITECTS
Robert Shaw ECHO Village.
Housing for elderly, Austin. Tom
Hatch Architects.
TEXAS ARCHITECT 1990 Jan.-Feb.,
v.40, no.1, p.24, photo., plan,
site plan.
Small is suitable: small-scale
community-based low-rent houses /
Tom Hatch.
Robert Shaw ECHO Village (Elderly
Cottage Housing Opportunity)
project of detached rental houses
for low-income elderly tenants in
Austin, Texas. Architects: Tom
Hatch Architects.
URBAN LAND 1990 July, v.49, no.7,
p.24-25, photos., plans.

TOM KANE AND ASSOCIATES
Scanticon, Denver, USA.
Convention center located at
Inverness Business Park,
Englewood, Colo. Architects: Friis
og Moltke, with RNL Architects.
Landscape architects: Tom Kane and
Associates, with Denton Harper
Marshall. Includes English and
(Continued next column)

TOM KANE AND ASSOCIATES (CONTINUED)
Scanticon, Denver, USA. (CONTINUED)
German captions and summaries.
ARKITEKTUR DK 1989, v.33, no.8,
p.377-387, photos., plans, secns.,
site plan.

TOMB, BRUCE
Portrait of an artist ...
transformation of a South of
Market warehouse into the loft of
a graphic artist, San Francisco /
Karen Stein.
Architects: John Randolph, Bruce
Tomb, of the Interim Office of
Architecture.
ARCHITECTURAL RECORD 1990 Apr.,
v.178, no.4, p.74-[77], photos.,
plans.

TOMBESI, PAOLO
Architetture per gli aborigeni = The
dark side architectures for
aborigines / Paolo Tombesi.
Features two projects: Mutitjulu
Community Housing near Ayers Rock,
architect: Paul Pholeros and the
Aboriginal Alcoholic
Rehabilitation Centre, Kinchela
Creek, architect: Glenn Murcutt.
SPAZIO E SOCIETA 1990 Jan.-Mar.,
v.13, no.49, p.94-105, dwgs.,
elevs., models, photos., plans,
secns., site plans.

TOMBS
See also BURIAL CHAMBERS
See also BURIAL TOWERS
See also CENOTAPHS
See also COLUMBARIA
See also MARTYRIA
See also ROCK-CUT TOMBS

TOMBS--13TH CENTURY--ENGLAND--LONDON--
WESTMINSTER ABBEY--TOMB OF HENRY III
The Cosmati at Westminster and the
English court style / Paul Binski.
A study of the historical and
archaeological evidence on the
commission of the Roman Cosmati
mosaics in the late 13th-cent. at
Westminster Abbey and specifics of
the shrine of St. Edward, the tomb
of Henry III, and the sanctuary
pavement.
ART BULLETIN 1990 Mar., v.72,
no.1, p.[6]-34, photos., site
plans, biblio., refs.

TOMBS--16TH CENTURY--HUNGARY--
BUDAPEST--TURBE OF GUL BABA
Back to Budapest / Geza Fehervari.
On the new center for Islamic
culture, Islamic Religious and
Cultural Centre in Budapest.
Architect: Basil Al-Bayati.
BUILDING DESIGN 1990 May 11,
no.985, p.34-35, elev., photo.,
plans.
A centre for Islamic culture in
Hungary / Geza Fehervari.
Describes project for the Islamic
Religious and Cultural Centre,
Budapest. Architect: Basil
Al-Bayati. The complex includes
the restored 16th cent. tomb or
turbe of Gul Baba.
ARTS & THE ISLAMIC WORLD 1990
Summer, v.5, no.2(18), p.46-48,
elev., photos.

TOMBS--19TH CENTURY--CHINA--ANYANG--
YUAN SHIH-K'AIS TOMB
The tomb of Yuan Shih-K'ai: the man
who would be emperor / Barry Till.
Tomb of ambitious commoner Yuan
Shih-K'ai, modelled after Ming
(1368-1644) and Ching (1644-1911)
dynasties, constructed near Anyang
in Hunan province.
ARTS OF ASIA 1989 Nov.-Dec., v.19,
no.6, p.104-105,108-111, photos.,
site plan.

TOMBS--ANCIENT--ISRAEL--JERUSALEM--
TOMB OF DAVID
Church of the Apostles found on Mt.
Zion / Bargil Pixner.
Discusses the location of the tomb
of David in the Roman-period
synagogue and argues that this was
a Judeo-Christian synagogue.
Current monastery dates from the
14th cent.
BIBLICAL ARCHAEOLOGY REVIEW 1990
May-June, v.16, no.3, p.16-[35],
60, elevs., photos., plans, site
plan.

TOMBS--FRANCE--PARIS--SAINT-DENIS
Royal dreams: the final cortege /
Alain Erlande-Brandenburg, with a
text by Jules Maze.
The tombs of the kings of France,
now in the abbey of St-Denis in
Paris.
FMR 1990 Apr., v.9, no.43,
p.65-96, ill., photos.

TOMBS--HELLENISTIC--TURKEY--NEMRUD
DAG--TOMB OF ANTIOCHOS I OF
COMMAGENE
Das Grabmal von Konig Antiochos 1.
von Kommagene duf dem Nemrud Dag /
Spencer Sahin, Jorg Wagner.
ANTIKE WELT 1989, v.20, no.1,
p.55-58, dwg., photos, refs.

TOMBS--ISLAMIC--SOVIET UNION--
BUKHARA--TOMB OF THE SAMANIDS
Ein Wurfel in der Wuste = A cube in
the desert / Ursula Daus.
Tomb of the Samanids, Bukhara,
Uzbekistan. Text in German and
English.
DAIDALOS 1990 Mar.15, no.35,
p.76-79, photos., plan, secn.

TOMBS--ITALY--TURIN--CIMITERO DI
GRUGLIASCO--TOMBA GALASSO
Quattro opere di Giorgio Raineri.
Four tombs in Turin. Text in
Italian and English.
DOMUS 1990 July-Aug., no.718,
p.10-11, photos., secns.

TOMBS--ITALY--TURIN--CIMITERO DI
TORINO SASSI--TOMBA BOCCA
Quattro opere di Giorgio Raineri.
Four tombs in Turin. Text in
Italian and English.
DOMUS 1990 July-Aug., no.718,
p.10-11, photos., secns.

TOMBS--ITALY--TURIN--CIMITERO DI
TORINO SUD--TOMBA MILANESE
Quattro opere di Giorgio Raineri.
Four tombs in Turin. Text in
Italian and English.
DOMUS 1990 July-Aug., no.718,
p.10-11, photos., secns.

TOMBS--ITALY--TURIN--CIMITERO
GENERALE--TOMBA ROSSI
Quattro opere di Giorgio Raineri.
Four tombs in Turin. Text in
Italian and English.
DOMUS 1990 July-Aug., no.718,
p.10-11, photos., secns.

TOMBS - MEGALITHIC
See also MEGALITHIC MONUMENTS

TOMBS--MOGHUL--INDIA--
VIJAYAMANDIRGARH--TOMB OF SHAIKH
PHUL
New light on the history of two
early Mughal monuments of Bayana /
Iqtidar Alam Khan.
On the manzil and tomb of Shaikh
Phul, Vijayamandirgarh.
MUQARNAS 1990, v.6, p.[75]-82,
photos., plans, refs.

TOMBS--MYCENAEAN--GREECE
The spatial distribution of
Mycenaean tombs / C.B. Mee, W.G.
Cavanagh.
THE ANNUAL OF THE BRITISH SCHOOL
AT ATHENS 1990, no.85,
p.[225]-243, graphs, maps, site
plans, refs.

TOMBS--NEOLITHIC--FRANCE
Vaulted construction in French
Megalithic tombs / W.G. Cavanagh,
R.R. Laxton.
An analysis of vaults in passage
graves at Barnenez and Ile Carn,
in northwestern France. Includes
abstract.
OXFORD JOURNAL OF ARCHAEOLOGY 1990
July, v.9, no.2, p.141-167, maps,
photos., plans, secns., tables,
biblio.

TOMBS--NEOLITHIC--IRELAND
Monuments from the inside: the case
of the Irish megalithic tombs /
Julian Thomas.
WORLD ARCHAEOLOGY 1990 Oct., v.22,
no.2, p.168-178, chart, plans,
biblio.

TOMBS--RENAISSANCE--ITALY--FLORENCE--
SAN PANCRAZIO--CAPPELLA RUCELLAI--
HOLY SEPULCHRE
Leon Battista Alberti's inscriptions
on the Holy Sepulchre in the
Cappella Rucellai, San Pancrazio,
Florence / Christine M. Sperling.
JOURNAL OF THE WARBURG AND
COURTAULD INSTITUTES 1989, v.52,
p.221-228,pl.42-47, dwgs.,
photos., refs.

TOMBS--RENAISSANCE--ITALY--FLORENCE--
TOMB OF LEONARDO BONAFEDE
Francesco da Sangallo's tomb of
Leonardo Bonafede in the Certosa
del Galluzzo / Rona Roisman.
THE RUTGERS ART REVIEW 1988-1989,
v.9-10, p.17-41, dwgs., photos.,
plans, refs.

TOMBS--SYMBOLIC ASPECTS
L'autre maison / Didier Laroque.
On the tomb-like installation work
of Pascal Convert in the gardens
of the Villa Medici, Rome.
ARCHITECTURE D'AUJOURD'HUI 1990
Sept., no.270, p.62,[64], dwg.,
photo.

TOMBSTONES
See SEPULCHRAL MONUMENTS

TOMCZAK, FRAUKE
Das Innen im Aussen im Innen = The
interior in the outside of inner
worlds / Frauke Tomczak.
Text in German and English.
DAIDALOS 1990 June 15, no.36,
p.80-87, ill., photos., plan,
refs.

TOME, APRIL
Ranch-house add-up / April Tome,
Peter Siegrist.
Addition designed by the architect
authors for their house in
Greenwich, Conn.
FINE HOMEBUILDING 1989 Aug.,
no.55, p.69, dets., photo.

TOME, NARCISO, D.1724
Proyectos para el retablo de la
capilla de San Ildefonso en la
Catedral de Toledo / Jose Maria
Prados.
Features three Baroque designs by
Narciso Tome for the chapel and
the executed altarpiece by Ventura
Rodriguez.
ARCHIVO ESPANOL DE ARTE 1990
Apr.-June, v.63, no.250,
p.288-294, dwgs., photo., plan,
refs.

TOMINAGA, YUZURU, 1943-
Special feature: Yuzuru Tominaga.
Contents: Houses(13) --
Projects(6) -- Urban architecture
-- Notes about Architecture and
Time, by Yuzuru Tominaga --
Pioneer of a Timeless
Architecture, by Kiyonori Kikutake
-- Architecture Viewed from within
the City, by Fumihiko Maki --
Discussion: Toward Communicative
Architecture, by Tadao Ando &
Yuzuru Tominaga -- The Maturation
of Design, by Kenichi Echigojima
-- Data of Works -- A
Chronological List. In Japanese
and English.
SPACE DESIGN 1990 Oct.,
no.10(313), p.003-152,cover,
dwgs., ports., elevs., models,
photos., plans, secns., site
plans, isometric dwgs., aerial
photos., refs.
Waseda Seminar in Tokorozawa /
Yuzuru Tominaga.
Secondary school. Architects:
Yuzuru Tominaga, Form System
Institute.
JAPAN ARCHITECT 1990 July, v.65,
no.7(399), p.20-25, axonometric
view, elevs., photos., plans,
secn., site plan.

TOMLAN, MICHAEL A.
Who will care in the 1990s?: ethnic
diversity will play a greater role
in the preservation movement,
particularly in urban
neighborhoods / Michael A. Tomlan.
PRESERVATION FORUM 1990 Winter,
v.3, no.4, p.20-21, ill.

TOMLINSON, R. A.
The sequence of construction of Mnesikles' Propylaia / R.A. Tomlinson.
THE ANNUAL OF THE BRITISH SCHOOL AT ATHENS 1990, no.85, p.[405]-413, dwg., refs.

TOMLOW, JOS
De network-architectuur van Suchov: Inventiere constructies met een organische vorm / Jos Tomlow.
The Work of the Russian engineer (1853-1939).
DE ARCHITECT 1990 July-Aug., v.21, no.7-8, p.66-71, dwgs., photos., secns., biblio., ref.

TOMMILA, MAURI
The Partek Group Helsinki office. Includes a round swimming pool and sauna. Architect: Mauri Tommila.
LIVING ARCHITECTURE 1990, no.9, p.140-143, photos., plans.
Physische Trennung, raumliche Kontinuitat: Burogebaude der Partek Group, Helsinki, 1988. Architects: K. Lofstrom, M. Makinen, M. Tommila. Summaries in German, French and English.
WERK, BAUEN + WOHNEN 1989 Oct., no.10, p.50-54, axonometric view, dets., photos., plans, secns.

TONCONOGY, ALBERTO
Mercado Norte, Buenos Aires, Argentina / Jorge Glusberg. Renovation of 1900 market. Architects: Raul Lier, Alberto Tonconogy.
PROJETO 1990 Dec.-1991 Jan., no.137, p.56-57, elev., photos.
Mercato in Argentine. Renovation of ca.1900 market. Architects: Raul Lier, Alberto Tonconogy. English, French, and Spanish summaries.
ABACUS 1990 Apr.-June, v.6, no.22, p.78-81, elev., photos., plans, secns., sketch.

TONG, SUSANNA T. Y.
The hydrologic effects of urban land use: a case study of the Little Miami River Basin / Susanna T.Y. Tong.
LANDSCAPE AND URBAN PLANNING 1990 Apr., v.19, no.1, p.99-105, graphs, tables, refs.

TONN, BRUCE E.
500-year planning: a speculative provocation / Bruce E. Tonn.
AMERICAN PLANNING ASSOCIATION. JOURNAL 1986 Spring, v.52, no.2, p.185-193, biblio., refs.

TONNA, JO
The poetics of Arab-Islamic architecture / Jo Tonna.
MUQARNAS 1990, v.7, p.[182]-197, dwgs., elevs., plans, refs.

TONON, GRAZIELLA
Piero Bottoni: gli anni della formazione tra modernita e tradizione / Graziella Tonon. On the architect and teacher and his years at the Scuola degli Architetti Civili del Politecnico di Milano (1921-26).
URBANISTICA 1989 June, no.95,
(Continued next column)

TONON, GRAZIELLA (CONTINUED)
Piero Bottoni: gli...(CONTINUED) p.45-56, dwgs., elevs., plans, sketches, refs.

TONUMA, KOUICHI
Study on typology of transformation of population and urban construction projects at local small scale towns / Yoshiaki Horikoshi, Kouichi Tonuma. Subtitle: A research on municipalities with densely inhabited districts. Treats 18 small towns in the Touhoku region, northern Japan. Text in Japanese. Includes English summary.
NIHON KENCHIKU GAKKAI KEIKAKUKEI RONBUN HOKOKU SHU = JOURNAL OF ARCHITECTURE, PLANNING AND ENVIRONMENTAL ENGINEERING 1990 Sept., no.9(415), p.57-65, tables.

TONY MALE ASSOCIATES
Yeovil football stadium. Architect: Peter Smith & Partners. Landscape architect: Tony Male Associates.
BUILDING 1990 Nov.30, v.255, no.47, p.45-52, photos., plans, secns., site plan, tables.

TOOLE, ROBERT M.
Springside: A. J. Downing's only extant garden / Robert M. Toole. Located in Poughkeepsie, N.Y.
JOURNAL OF GARDEN HISTORY 1989 Jan.-Mar., v.9, no.1, p.[20]-39, dwgs., ports., elevs., photos., plans, site plans, refs.

TOOLS
See TOOLS AND EQUIPMENT

TOOLS AND EQUIPMENT
See also DRAWING INSTRUMENTS
See also MILLSTONES
See also PLOTTERS
See also PNEUMATIC TOOLS
Bautechnische Untersuchungen mit dem Endoskop - Anwendungsmoglickkeiten und -grenzen / Ulli Meisel, Peter Braunmuller.
DEUTSCHES ARCHITEKTENBLATT 1990 Apr.1, v.22, no.4, p.573-579, dets., graph, ill., photos.
Bauvorbereitung und Bauleitungsempfehlungen / Heinz Schmitz.
Advice on ways to prepare and tools to use in renovation of older buildings, from an architect in Aachen.
DEUTSCHES ARCHITEKTENBLATT 1990 June 1, v.22, no.6, p.961-964, 966-967, photos., tables.

TOOLS AND EQUIPMENT--GREAT BRITAIN
Keeping cool / Denise Chevin.
BUILDING 1990 Nov.9, v.255, no.44, p.68-69, photo.

TOOLS AND EQUIPMENT--MEDIEVAL
Werkzeuge der Steinmetzen im Mittelalter: Ausgangspunkte zur Forschung / Dankwart Leistikow.
ARCHITECTURA 1989, v.20, no.1, p.65-72, ill., photos., refs.

TOON, JOHN
Raise high the roof beam -- planner!: the Denis Winston Memorial lecture 1990 / John Toon. Presented at the International Conference on Local Planning, Sydney Australia.
AUSTRALIAN PLANNER: JOURNAL OF THE ROYAL AUSTRALIAN PLANNING INSTITUTE 1990 June, v.28, no.2, p.45-48,
Urban planning and urban design / John Toon.
EKISTICS 1988 Jan.-June, v.55, no.328-330, p.95-105, refs.

TOPALOV, CHRISTIAN
Le origini dell'urbanistica moderna: Francia e Stati Uniti. Contents: Ragione e visione: la mentalita pianificatoria negli Stati Uniti e l'indagine urbana, 1890-1930, by Christine Boyer.-- L'urbanistica come movimento sociale: militanti e professionisti del City Planning negli Stati Uniti, 1909-1917, by Christian Topalov.-- "Reconstituir la cite": dalla concezione organicistica della citta alla riforma del quartiere popolare in Francia nel primo quarto del secolo, by Susanna Magri.-- La genesi dell'urbanistica di piano e la questione della modernizzazione politica, 1900-1930, by Jean Pierre Gaudin.
STORIA URBANA 1989 July-Dec., v.13, no.48-49, p.127-245, tables, refs.
Scientific urban planning and the ordering of daily life: the first "war housing" experiment in the United States, 1917-1919 / Christian Topalov.
JOURNAL OF URBAN HISTORY 1990 Nov., v.17, no.1, p.14-45, maps, photos., aerial photo., refs.
L'urbanisme comme mouvement social: militants et professionnels du city planning aux Etats-Unis (1909-1917) / Christian Topalov. French, English, Spanish and German summaries, p.247-252.
LES ANNALES DE LA RECHERCHE URBAINE 1989 Dec., no.44-45, p.139-154, 247-248, 250, 252, ill., dwgs., photo., plans, refs.

TOPES (MONUMENTS)
See STUPAS

TOPIARY
A new leaf: Abbie Zabar's art and writing branch out beyond the topiary in her Fifth Avenue penthouse / Celia McGee.
HOUSE & GARDEN 1990 May, v.162, no.5, p.118,[120], port., photos.

TOPIARY GARDENS
See also TOPIARY WORK

TOPIARY WORK
Gli elementi di arredo delle arec Verdi / Gilberto Oneto. Second part.
VILLE GIARDINI 1990 Nov., no.253, p.76-79, dets., photos.

TOPIARY WORK (CONTINUED)
A place for whimsy / Tony Venison.
COUNTRY LIFE 1990 Feb.2, v.184,
no.5, p.62-64, photos.
Topiary I: design / Anthony du Gard
Pasley.
COUNTRY LIFE 1990 Jan.11, v.184,
no.2, p.48-52, photos.
Topiary II: history / Arthur
Hellyer.
COUNTRY LIFE 1990 Jan.18, v.184,
no.3, p.52-55, photos.
Topiary III: Clipsham Hall / Tony
Venison.
COUNTRY LIFE 1990 Jan.25, v.184,
no.4, p.96-97, photos.
Topiary V: gazetteer: British
gardens with outstanding topiary /
Tony Venison.
Includes list of houses with
locations and hours.
COUNTRY LIFE 1990 Feb.8, v.184,
no.6, p.72-75, photos.
Topiary VI: practicalities / A. M.
Clevely.
COUNTRY LIFE 1990 Feb.15, v.184,
no.7, p.46-49, photos.

TOPLIS, IAN. FOREIGN OFFICE: AN
ARCHITECTURAL HISTORY
English 18th and 19th century
architecture [book review] / John
Newman, Michael Brooks.
Review of James Paine, by Peter
Leach, and The Foreign Office: an
architectural history, by Ian
Toplis.
SOCIETY OF ARCHITECTURAL
HISTORIANS. JOURNAL 1990 Mar.,
v.49, no.1, p.109-110,

TOPOGRAPHY
Der Ort der Stadt: eine
Wanderausstellung zur
Wechselwirkung von Topographie und
urbaner Form / Jorg Stabenow.
Student projects at TU Munchen
entitled "Stadt und Topographie,"
directed by Tomas Valena, use
Ljubljana as their basis.
ARCH PLUS 1990 Apr., no.103,
p.32-33, maps.
Die Topo-Graphie und die Aneignung
des Stadtraumes / Tomas Valena.
DER ARCHITEKT 1990 Nov., no.11,
p.502-508, photos., site plans,
aerial photo.

TOPOGRAPHY--EXHIBITIONS
Eine Fleissarbeit ohne Biss: zur
Wanderausstellung "Stadt und
Topographie der Munchner TU"
[exhibition review] / Wolfgang
Jean Stock.
Exhibition organized by Haus der
Bayerischen Geschichte and shown
in Munich, Coburg and 14 other
cities.
BAUWELT 1990 July 6, v.81, no.25,
p.1273-1274, photo., engrs
Der Stadt auf den Grund gehen
[exhibition review] / Thomas Will.
Review of "Stadt und Topographie,"
at the Bayerische Akademie der
Schonen Kunste, Munich, May
27-July 1, 1990.
ARCHITHESE 1990 May-June, v.20,
no.3, p.78-80, maps, engr., aerial
photo., refs.

TOPOGRAPHY--ITALY--SICILY--AGRIGENTO
Eclettismo dell'oggetto, Unita del
contesto / Nicola Giuliano Leone.
In Italian; some English captions.
URBANISTICA 1989 Dec., no.97,
p.106-111, axonometric views,
dets., maps, plans, secns.,
sketches.

TOPOGRAPHY--UNITED STATES--FLORIDA
Architecture on the edge / Stephen
D. Schreiber.
On the landscape in South Florida
and the boundaries (barrier
islands, coastal ridge and
landfill) that have influenced the
constructed ewnvironment.
CRIT 1990 Spring, no.24, p.16-20,
refs.

TOPP, HARTMUT H.
Traffic safety, usability and
streetscape effects of new design
principles for major urban roads /
Hartmut H. Topp.
TRANSPORTATION 1989-1990, v.16,
no.4, p.297-310, diagr., photos.,
plans, sketches, refs.

TOPPING, TINKA
Weekends in Wainscott / Bob Felner.
Interior renovations of a Long
Island farmhouse by owner Bryan
Bantry. Interior decorator: Tinka
Topping.
HOUSE & GARDEN 1990 Aug. v.162,
no.8, p.[112-117], photos.

TORBARINA, SNJEZANA
Urban faith / Snjezana Torbarina,
Bruce Macpherson.
Two winning designs in the Italian
competition, three churches for
2000. Architects: Giangiacomo
d'Arcia and Ariella Zattera for
San Romano in Gallaretese, Milan;
Mauro Galantino for San Ireneo,
Cesaro Boscone.
BUILDING DESIGN 1990 Sept.7,
no.1002, p.20-21, dwgs., elevs.,
plans, secns., site plan.

TORNKVIST, ENAR
Weatherproofing membranes on roofs:
felt and nonwoven fabric of rubber
and plastics / Enar Tornkvist.
SWEDISH COUNCIL FOR BUILDING
RESEARCH. DOCUMENT 1990, D22,
p.[1]-109, diagrs., photos.,
secns.

TORNQVIST, ANDERS
Industribyggandets metaforer /
Anders Tornqvist, Peter Ullmark.
In conjunction with an
international congress in
Stockholm and a related
publication entitled "When people
matter".
ARKITEKTUR: THE SWEDISH REVIEW OF
ARCHITECTURE 1990 Sept., v.90,
no.7, p.28-35, model, photo.,
secns., site plan.
Volvo Uddevalla / Gunnar Werner.
Automobile factory located at F d
Uddevallavarvet. Architects: White
arkitekter, Mitchell Giurgola
Architects, AKOS arkitektkontor,
includes commentary by Anders
Tornqvist and Peter Ullmark.
ARKITEKTUR: THE SWEDISH REVIEW OF
ARCHITECTURE 1990 Jan.-Feb., v.90,
(Continued next column)

TORNQVIST, ANDERS (CONTINUED)
Volvo Uddevalla /...(CONTINUED)
no.1, p.38-47, photos., plans,
site plans, sketches.

TORP, FREDRIK A. S., 1937-
Til forsvar for Aker Brygge
[letter]/ Fredrik A.S. Torp, Kim
Dirckinck-Holmfeld.
Correspondence relating to an
article in the May 1990 issue of
this journal.
ARKITEKTEN 1990 July, v.92, no.9,
p.304, photos., aerial photo.

TORP, NIELS
Aker Brygge / Francis Duffy.
Waterfront multi-use development,
Oslo. Architect: Niels Torp.
ARCHITECTURAL REVIEW 1990 Aug.,
v.188, no.1122, p.[55]-62,
photos., plans, secn., site plan.
Fjord fiesta [Aker Brygge, Oslo] /
Martin Spring.
Waterfront complex with shops,
restaurants, housing, offices, and
theaters. Architect: Niels Torp.
BUILDING 1990 July 13, v.255,
no.28, p.42-46, photos., aerial
photo.
Masters of change / Frank Duffy.
Competition for new British
Airways headquarters at Heathrow
Airport. Winning scheme by Niels
Torp, plus five runners-up.
ARCHITECTS' JOURNAL 1990 June 13,
v.191, no.24, p.26-31, det.,
elevs., plan, secn., site plans,
sketch.
Vetrati aggetti e ponti di Niels
Torp: "Aker Brygge" ad Oslo.
ARCHITETTURA; CRONACHE E STORIA
1990 Apr., v.36, no.4(414),
p.292-294, photos., site plan.

TORP, NIELS--ADDRESSES, ESSAYS,
LECTURES
Internal affairs: Neils [sic] Torp /
Murray Fraser.
Report of a lecture by Norwegian
architect Niels Torp at the Oxford
Polytechnic 3 May 1990.
ARCHITECTS' JOURNAL 1990 May 23,
v.191, no.21, p.72-73, photo.,
plan.

TORRAS, MERCE
Jordi Fabre e Merce Torras: Facolta
di veterinaria di Bellaterra
(Barcellona) / Duccio Malagamba.
Text in Italian and English.
DOMUS 1990 Apr., no.715, p.10-11,
xxii, axonometric view, elevs.,
photos, plan, site plan.

TORREGROSSA, TERESA
La cosiddetta sala araba nel
complesso di S. Giovanni degli
Eremiti a Palermo / Adele Daidone.
Also includes the article "Il
Chiostro di S. Giovanni degli
Eremiti a Palermo" by Teresa
Torregrossa.
STORIA ARCHITETTURA 1987
Jan.-Dec., v.10, no.1-2, p.25-54,
dets., elevs., photos, plans,
secns., site plans, reconst. dwgs.

TORRES NADAL, JOSE M.
Albergue para jovenes = Youth
hostel.
On the Cala Reona beach, Aguilas,
Spain. Architects: Jose M. Torres
Nadal. Text in Spanish and
English.
QUADERNS D'ARQUITECTURA I
URBANISME 1988 July-Sept., no.178,
p.86-89, elevs., photos., plans,
secns., site plan.

TORRES TUR, ELIAS
Angles on Ibiza / Peter Buchanan.
Vacation house, Cap Martinet,
Ibiza, Spain. Architects: Jose
Antonio Martinez Lapena and Elias
Torres Tur.
ARCHITECTURAL REVIEW 1990 Apr.,
v.187, no.1118, p.56-[60],
photos., plans, secns.
Architectural landmarks.
Features three buildings by Elias
Torres Tur and Jose Antonio
Martinez Lapena: hospital, Mora de
Ebro; congress center, Barcelona,
and sports hall, Granollers.
ARCHITECTURAL REVIEW 1990 July,
v.188, no.1121, p.52-59, elevs.,
models, photos., plans, secns.,
site plan.
Architecture of J.A. Martinez Lapena
+ Elias Torres Tur.
Special feature. Contents:
Careers.--Catalonian
architecture..., by Naoki
Inagawa.--Works [13 projects
1981-1989]. Text in Japanese.
SPACE DESIGN 1990 Apr., no.307,
p.05-44, axonometric view, ports.,
models, map, photos., plans,
secns., site plans.
La arquitectura residencial de la
Villa Olimpica / Justo Isasi.
Includes 13 projects. English
summary, p.86.
A & V 1990, no.22, p.26-54, dets.,
ill., elevs., models, plans,
secns., site plans, sketches.
Barcelona Activa = Industrial
building rehabilitation,
Barcelona, 1987-1988.
Renovation of the 1950's Hispano
Olivetti complex for use as a
company work center and offices.
Architects for renovation: J.A.
Martinez Lapena and Elias Torres.
EL CROQUIS 1990 Mar., v.9, no.42,
p.108-123, dets., elevs., photos.,
plans, secns.
Crestas de perfil: palacio de
congresos y convenciones.
Convention facility for
Barcelona's Olympic village.
Architects: Jose Antonio Martinez
Lapena, Elias Torres Tur, Miguel
Maria Usandizaga Calparsoro.
English summary, p.88.
A & V 1990, no.22, p.78-80, dwgs.,
elevs., models, plans, secns.,
site plans.
Folly 13(3). Expo '90.
Contents: Folly 13 story, by
Hajime Yatsuka.--Martinez Lapena +
Elias Torres, Ryoji Suzuki, Peter
Wilson, Morphosis. Text in
Japanese.
SPACE DESIGN 1990 Apr., no.307,
p.45-53, axonometric views, dwgs.,
elevs., models, plan.

TORRES TUR, ELIAS (CONTINUED)
Un peu diabolique: appartement a
Ibiza.
Interiors of 3-floor apartment.
Architects: Elias Torres Tur and
Jose Antonio Martinez Lapena.
English summary, p.52.
ARCHITECTURE INTERIEURE CREE 1990
Feb., no.234, p.[152]-153,
photos., plans, secn.
Pour l'horizon: maison du Cap
Martinet, Ibiza, Baleares.
Architect: Elias Torres Tur, Jose
Antonio Martinez Lapena. Includes
English and Spanish summaries.
TECHNIQUES ET ARCHITECTURE 1990
June-July, no.390, p.90-[95],180,
elev., photos., plans, secns.
Proyectar para una arquitectura
dada: analogia y diversidad = To
design for a given architecture:
analogy and diversity / Anton
Capitel.
Discusses 4 recent projects in
Spain.
EL CROQUIS 1990 Mar., v.9, no.42,
p.64-79, photos.
Reconstruir los suenos de una
artista: restauracion del Park
Guell.
Original architect: Antonio Gaudi.
Architects for restoration: J.
Antonio Martinez Lapena, Elias
Torres Tur. English text,
p.190-191.
ON DISENO 1990, "ceramica" suppl.,
p.130-134, photos.

TORRICE, ANTONIO F., 1951-
Antonio Torrice, ASID, receives IFDA
award.
International Furnishings and
Design Association's 1990
Trailblazer award.
INTERIOR DESIGN 1990 Apr., v.61,
no.6, p.[55], port.

TORRICELLA, AGATA
Le stanze di servizio = The utility
rooms.
Milan apartment in former
servants' quarters. Architect:
Agata Torricella.
ABITARE 1990 Mar., no.283,
p.152-[157], photos., plans, secn.

TORSELLO, B. PAOLO
Le geometrie del paesaggio / B.
Paolo Torsello.
Captions in Italian and English.
CASABELLA 1990 Sept., v.54,
no.571, p.31-33, ill., maps, refs.

TORSSON, BJORNER
Staden i tornrosens bok / Bjorner
Torsson.
Images of Sweden in literature,
including the work of C.J.L.
Almqvist.
ARKITEKTUR: THE SWEDISH REVIEW OF
ARCHITECTURE 1990 Mar., v.90,
no.2, p.10-14, ill., secn.

TORTEBAT, FRANCOIS, 1616-1690
Les artistes de l'entree de Louis
XIV en 1660 / Christoph Frank.
On the architects and artists of
the temporary structures erected
for Louis XIV's celebrated
procession through Paris on August
26, 1660, as recorded in archival
documents in the Archives
(Continued next column)

TORTEBAT, FRANCOIS, 1616-1690
(CONTINUED)
Les artistes de...(CONTINUED)
Nationals.
SOCIETE DE L'HISTOIRE DE L'ART
FRANCAIS. BULLETIN 1990,
p.[53]-74, dwgs., engrs., refs.

TORU MURAKAMI, ARCHITECT AND
ASSOCIATES
Toru Murakami & Associates: House at
Ajina, Hatsukaichi, Hiroshima,
Japan, 1988-90 / Toru Murakami.
Text in Japanese and English.
GA HOUSES 1990 Dec., no.30,
p.100-108, elevs., photos., plans,
secns., site plan.

TOSCA, JUAN
Dialogo com Salinas, Segre, Tosca e
Calventi, em Havana / Nildo Carlos
Oliveira.
PROJETO 1989 Apr., no.120,
p.127-129, port.

TOSI, ANTONIO
Il trattamento delle differenze e le
teorie urbane = Dealing with
difference and urban theories /
Antonio Tosi.
Italian; English summary,
p.124-125.
URBANISTICA 1989 Oct., no.96,
p.39-44, 124-125, diagr., map,
biblio.

TOTAL CONCEPT, NEW YORK
First Boston / Edie Lee Cohen.
Interiors of Houston offices.
Interior designers: Total Concept
Inc.
INTERIOR DESIGN 1990 June, v.61,
no.9, p.252-[253], photos.

TOTANI, HIDEYO
The comparative study of building
codes in Japan, the USA and Canada
[part 2] / Hideyo Totani.
Subtitle: Japanese wood products
trading practice named under SUPER
301 and the problems of Japanese
domestic codes and standards.
Text in Japanese; English summary,
p.45.
NIHON KENCHIKU GAKKAI KEIKAKUKEI
RONBUN HOKOKU SHU = JOURNAL OF
ARCHITECTURE, PLANNING AND
ENVIRONMENTAL ENGINEERING 1990
Apr., no.4(410), p.45-52, table,
refs.
The comparative study of the
building codes in Japan, the USA
and Canada [part 1] / Hideyo
Totani.
Subtitle: Discussion on the
practical use of building codes.
Text in Japanese; English summary,
p.37.
NIHON KENCHIKU GAKKAI KEIKAKUKEI
RONBUN HOKOKU SHU = JOURNAL OF
ARCHITECTURE, PLANNING AND
ENVIRONMENTAL ENGINEERING 1990
Apr., no.4(410), p.37-44, refs.
The comparative study of the
building codes in Japan, USA and
Canada / Hideyo Totani.
Subtitle: The amendment for the
inovation [sic] of the building
technology. Text in Japanese;
includes English summary.
NIHON KENCHIKU GAKKAI KEIKAKUKEI
RONBUN HOKOKU SHU = JOURNAL OF
(Continued next page)

TOURIST CAMPS
See also HOSTELS
See also MOTELS
See also TRAILER CAMPS

TOURIST CAMPS--ALTERATIONS AND
ADDITIONS--FINLAND--ROVANIEMI
Arctic arrak.
Extension to tourist center in
Rovaniemi, Finnish Lapland.
Architects: Arkkitehtiryhmma
ARRAK.
ARCHITECTURAL REVIEW 1990 Mar.,
v.187, no.1117, p.[62]-66,
photos., plans, secns., site plan.

TOURIST COURTS
See TOURIST CAMPS

TOURIST HOMES
See TOURIST CAMPS

TOURIST INFORMATION CENTERS
See VISITORS' CENTERS

TOURIST TOWNS--AUSTRALIA--GOLD COAST
Tourist cities as new cities:
Australia's Gold Coast and
Sunshine Coast / Patrick Mullins.
AUSTRALIAN PLANNER: JOURNAL OF THE
ROYAL AUSTRALIAN PLANNING
INSTITUTE 1990 Sept., v.28, no.3,
p.37-41, tables, refs.

TOURIST TOWNS--AUSTRALIA--SUNSHINE
COAST
Tourist cities as new cities:
Australia's Gold Coast and
Sunshine Coast / Patrick Mullins.
AUSTRALIAN PLANNER: JOURNAL OF THE
ROYAL AUSTRALIAN PLANNING
INSTITUTE 1990 Sept., v.28, no.3,
p.37-41, tables, refs.

TOURIST TOWNS--ENVIRONMENTAL ASPECTS--
TURKEY--SELIMIYE
Ancient and modern / Gary Holliday.
On the impact of tourism on the
historic site of Side, in
Selimiye, Turkey.
LANDSCAPE DESIGN 1989 Nov.,
no.185, p.16-17, photos.

TOURIST TOWNS--INDIA--SARNATH
Development directions for a sacred
site in India / Brian Orland,
Vincent J. Bellafiore.
Buddhist pilgrimage site in
Sarnath, India.
LANDSCAPE AND URBAN PLANNING 1990
May, v.19, no.2, p.181-196,
photos., plan, refs.

TOURIST TOWNS--MEXICO--TIJUANA
Tijuana: an urban perspective /
Lesley Henegar.
CARTOUCHE 1990 Summer, v.21,
p.4-5, maps, photos., refs.

TOURIST TOWNS--SPAIN
Historia del urbanismo contemporaneo
espanol: Emilio Larrodera Lopez /
Luis Rodriguez-Avial ... [et al.].
Entire issue devoted to urban
planning in tourist areas.
URBANISMO / COAM 1988 May, no.4,
p.101-107, ill., ports., plans,
refs.

TOURIST TOWNS--STUDENT PROJECTS--
ITALY--LUCIGNANO
Planen in der Toskana: Lucignano.
Student projects.
DEUTSCHE BAUZEITUNG 1990 May,
v.124, no.5, p.158-159, dwgs.
plans.

TOURIST TOWNS--WALES--PORTMEIRION
Village of dreams: the holiday
village of Portmeirion in North
Wales / Vivien Bellamy.
TRADITIONAL HOMES 1990 Mar., v.6,
no.6, p.11-13, photos.

TOURIST TRADE
See TOURISM

TOURNANT, JACQUES
La reconstruction et la negociation
du plan avec proprietaires et
architectes: Jacques Tournant, un
urbaniste du Havre / Regis
Bertrand.
French urban planner, associated
with the firm of Auguste Perret
for the reconstruction of Le
Havre. French, English, Spanish
and German summaries, p.217-252.
LES ANNALES DE LA RECHERCHE
URBAINE 1989 Dec., no.44-45,
p.155-162,247-252, axonometric
view, chart, ports., photos.,
plan, aerial photos.

TOURNIER, FRANCOISE
Armani plays prospero: castaway
elegance on a Mediterranean isle /
Francoise Tournier.
The designer's house on
Pantelleria. Architect: Gabriella
Giuntoli.
ELLE DECOR 1990 Mar., v.1, no.2,
p.[82]-93, photos.

TOURNIER, LAURENT
Profils: les elus 1989: Albums de
la jeune architecture.
Contents: Epinard Bleu, Pascal
Marchant, Philtre Avant-Travaux,
Patricia Leboucq, Shinobu Akahori,
Pascal Quintard Hofstein, and
Herve Daridan.
LE MONITEUR ARCHITECTURE AMC 1990
Mar., no.9, p.55, ports.

TOURNON-BRANLY, MARION
Brasilia in hartje Berlijn:
prijsvraag "Hauptstadte Berlin"
1957-1958 / Wolfgang Voigt.
Winners included Alison and Peter
Smithson, Marion Tournon-Branly.
ARCHIS 1990 Dec., no.12, p.4-5,
dwg., plan, site plan.

TOURS--AUSTRIA--VIENNA
Loos e Vienna: itinerario n.55 /
Francesca Ale.
A guide to buildings by Adolf Loos
in Vienna. Text in Italian and
English.
DOMUS 1990 Mar., no.714,
p.xiii-xviii, axonometric view,
elevs., map, photos, plans,
secns., site plans.

TOURS--BELGIUM--FLANDERS
Itineraire touristique de Zottegem a
Brakel / Danny de Mulder.
MAISONS D'HIER ET D'AUJOURD'HUI =
DE WOONSTEDE DOOR DE EEUWEN HEEN
1990 Mar., no.85, p.66-73, ill.,
dwgs., map, aerial photo.

TOURS--ENGLAND
The English Garden Tour [by] Mavis
Batey and David Lambert [and] The
National Trust Book of the English
Garden [by] Richard Bisgrove [book
review] / David Jacques.
Reviews of 2 1990 books.
GARDEN HISTORY 1990 Autumn, v.18,
no.2, p.[192]-195.

TOURS--ENGLAND--LONDON--ENGLAND/HIGH
TECH
Fachstudienreise der
Architektenkammer Rheinland-Pfalz
nach London vom 24. bis 27. August
1989: Bericht und Resumee / Peter
Weller.
Report on German architects' tour:
England/High Tech.
DEUTSCHES ARCHITEKTENBLATT 1990
Jan.1, v.22, no.1, p.18-20,
photos.

TOURS--FINLAND
Domus itinerario no.63: Aalto /
Marsio e il Classicismo Nordico /
Paolo Angeletti, Gaia Remiddi.
14 buildings in Finland dating
from the 1930s. Introduction in
Italian and English.
DOMUS 1990 Dec., no.722, p.[4]
folded at end., elevs., maps,
photos., plans, secns., site
plans, biblio.

TOURS--FRANCE--LYON
Garnier e Lione: Domus Itinerario n.
58 / Antonella Quaglia.
A guide to buildings designed by
Tony Garnier in Lyon, France.
DOMUS 1990 June, no.717 n.p.,
dets., maps, photos., plans, site
plans.

TOURS--GERMANY (WEST)--FRANKFURT AM
MAIN
Nuovi musei a Francoforte: Domus
Itinerario n. 61 / Vittorio
Magnago Lampugnani.
A guided tour of 13 new museums in
Frankfurt. Text in Italian and
English.
DOMUS 1990 Oct., no.720,
p.[xiii-xvi], axonometric views,
dwgs., maps, photos., plans,
secns.

TOURS--ITALY--GENOA
Daneri e Genova: Domus Itinerario
n.59 / Marco Brandolisio, Marco
Vido.
A guide to buildings in Genoa
designed by Luigi Carlo Daneri. In
Italian and English.
DOMUS 1990 July-Aug., no.718,
p.[4] folded p. at end of issue,
maps, photos., plans, secns.
Domus itinerario n 60: Barabino e
Genova / Mirco Grassi.
A guide to 17 projects by Carlo
Barabino in Genoa. Text in Italian
and English.
DOMUS 1990 Sept., no.719,
p.[xiii-xvi], elevs., maps,
(Continued next page)

TOURS--ITALY--GENOA (CONTINUED)
Domus itinerario n...(CONTINUED)
photos., plans, secns., engr.,
biblio.

TOURS--ITALY--MILAN
Bottoni e Milano: Domus itinerio
n.62.
Guide to 15 buildings designed by
Piero Bottoni. Introduction in
Italian and English.
DOMUS 1990 Nov., no.721, p.[6]
folded p. at end, dwgs., elevs.,
model, map, photos., plans, site
plans.

TOURS--ITALY--PAVIA
Pollach e Pavia: itierario n. 56 /
Vittorio Prina.
A guide to buildings by Leopold
Pollack in Pavia, Italy.
Introduction in Italian and
English.
DOMUS 1990 Apr., no.715, p.[6]
folded p. at end, dwgs., elevs.,
photos, plans, site plans, refs.

TOURS--ITALY--ROME
Roma design guide = A guide to Rome
/ Renato Nicolini, Marina
Fiorentino.
Special Abitare supplement listing
architectural tours, hotels and
restaurants, shops, galleries,
design offices, etc.
ABITARE 1990 June, no.286(suppl.),
1 booklet(96 p.),

TOURS--ITALY--TRIESTE
Zaninovich e Trieste: Domus
Itinerario n. 57 / Coop Alea, Eva
Monai.
A guide to building by Giorgio
Zaninovich in Trieste, 1902-1914.
In Italian and English.
DOMUS 1990 May, no.716, p.[4]
folded p. at end of issue.,
elevs., maps, photos., plans,
secns.

TOURS--ITALY--TUSCANY
A walk in Tuscany / Frank Welch.
TEXAS ARCHITECT 1990 July-Aug.,
v.40, no.4, p.42-45, photos.

TOURS--SWEDEN--STOCKHOLM
Planning in Stockholm: RTPI study
tour 1990 / Lynn Haslam.
THE PLANNER 1990 Sept.14, v.76,
no.36, p.17, photos.

TOURS--UNITED STATES--MISSISSIPPI
RIVER VALLEY--EXPEDITION OF THE
FOURTH COAST
Along the lazy river / David Dillon.
"Expedition of the Fourth Coast"
summer study tour of cities and
towns along the Mississippi River
by Univ. of Minnesota planning
students.
PLANNING 1990 Nov., v.56, no.11,
p.20-23, ports., photos.,
sketches, aerial photo.
Expedition of the Fourth Coast /
Mary Henderson Gass.
Report on a six-week trip on the
Mississippi River run by the Univ.
of Minnesota Design Center for
American Urban Landscape.
INLAND ARCHITECT 1990 Nov.-Dec.,
v.34, no.6, p.63-66, dwgs.

TOURS--UNITED STATES--NEWCOMB (NEW
YORK)
Summer hike to Adirondack Great
Camp.
Held in July 1990 at Camp
Santanoni, Newcomb, NY. Built
1888-1890. Architect: Robert H.
Robertson.
PRESERVATION LEAGUE OF NEW YORK
STATE. NEWSLETTER 1990 Fall, v.16,
no.2, p.3, photos.

TOUSSAINT, PATRICK
Le chateau de Gisors aux XIIe et
XIIIe siecles / Jean Mesqui,
Patrick Toussaint.
ARCHEOLOGIE MEDIEVALE 1990, v.20,
p.[253]-317, axonometric views,
dwgs., photos., plans, refs.

TOVAR MARTIN, VIRGINIA
Disenos para las "luminarias"
realizadas en la Plaza Mayor de
Madrid para festejar el matrimonio
de una infanta de Espana /
Virginia Tovar Martin.
On the 1750 Rococo decoration and
ornament on the balconies of the
buildings surrounding the Plaza
Mayor.
ARCHIVO ESPANOL DE ARTE 1990
Apr.-June, v.63, no.250,
p.[283]-288, dwgs.
El monasterio de las religiosas
Trinitarias Descalzas de San
Ildefonso de Madrid / Virginia
Tovar Martin.
History of the building from its
initial use as a convent in the
early 1600s to its redesign in the
early 1700s.
ARCHIVO ESPANOL DE ARTE 1990
July-Sept., v.63, no.251,
p.[401]-418, map, photos., plan,
refs.

TOWERS
See also AIRPORTS - CONTROL TOWERS
See also BROCHS
See also BURIAL TOWERS
See also CLOCK TOWERS
See also COMMUNICATIONS TOWERS
See also CROSSING TOWERS
See also LAUNCH TOWERS
See also MARTELLO TOWERS
See also MINARETS
See also NURAGHI
See also PAGODAS
See also SPIRES
See also TALL BUILDINGS
See also WATER TOWERS
See also ZIGGURATS
Alchemistische Spekulationen in
Pratolino: Wiederentdeckung einer
Wiederentdeckung = Alchemical
speculations in Pratolino:
Rediscovery of a rediscovery /
Gerd Neumann.
Hypothetical and symbolic
interpretation of former towers at
ducal villa, Pratolino by
architect: Gerd Neumann.
DAIDALUS 1989 Dec.15, no.34,
p.22-29, ill., dwgs., photos.,
plans.
De network-architectuur van Suchov:
Inventiere constructies met een
organische varm / Jos Tomlow.
The Work of the Russian engineer
(1853-1939).
DE ARCHITECT 1990 July-Aug., v.21,
no.7-8, p.66-71, dwgs., photos.,
secns., biblio., ref.

TOWERS--11TH CENTURY--FRANCE--
LIMOGES--ABBAYE DE SAINT-AUGUSTIN
Une tour-porche du XI siecle a
l'abbaye de
Saint-Augustin-les-Limoges /
Thierry Soulard.
French, English, German summaries,
p.[467-469].
BULLETIN MONUMENTAL 1990, v.148,
no.4, p.[423]-426, plan, engr.,
refs.

TOWERS--19TH CENTURY--CONSERVATION AND
RESTORATION--FRANCE--PARIS--TOUR
EIFFEL
Remodelacion de la Torre Eiffel,
Paris, Francia.
Architect: Emilio Duhart
Harosteguy.
CA: REVISTA OFICIAL DEL COLEGIO DE
ARQUITECTOS DE CHILE 1989
Apr.-June, no.56, p.[34-37],
dets., dwgs., port., secn., site
plans, aerial photos.

TOWERS--19TH CENTURY--FRANCE--PARIS--
TOUR EIFFEL
Fontane e guglie per il primo
centenario: le celebrazioni del
1889 / Riccardo Florio.
Projects connected to the first
centenary of the French
revolution. Includes the Eiffel
Tower.
ART E DOSSIER 1989 July-Aug.,
no.37, p.6-9, dwg., photo, engr.,
refs.

TOWERS--CONSERVATION AND RESTORATION--
SWITZERLAND--OBWALDEN--HEXENTURM
SARNEN
Hexenturm Sarnen, Obwalden.
Built 1985-86. Architect: Bruno
Scheuner.
WERK, BAUEN + WOHNEN 1990 Dec.,
no.12, p.1-4, axonometric view,
photos., plans, secn.

TOWERS--ENGLAND--LONDON--TOWER OF
LONDON
A lighthouse for Roman London? /
Nicholas Fuentes.
General description of the Roman
pharos, or lighthouse, and
conjecture on its possible
representation as a graffito on a
Roman London brick in the British
Museum.
LONDON ARCHAEOLOGIST 1990 Autumn,
v.6 no.8, p.208-215, dets., figs.,
ill., elevs., photos., plan,
reconst. dwg., refs.

TOWERS--EXHIBITIONS
Il mondo delle torri: da Babilonia a
Manhattan [exhibition review] / R.
Gamba.
Exhibition sponsor: Comune di
Milano, Settore Cultura e
Spettacolo. Held at the Palazzo
Reale.
L'INDUSTRIA DELLE COSTRUZIONI 1990
Oct., v.24, no.228, p.72-73,
elevs., photos.
Reach for the sky [exhibition
review] / Adrian Dannatt.
On the exhibition on view in the
Palazzo Reale, Milan, Il mondo
delle torri da Babilonia a
Manhattan.
BUILDING DESIGN 1990 Oct.19,
no.1008, p.28-29, dwgs.

TOWERS--GEOMETRIC--JAPAN--MITO--ART
TOWER MITO
An exegesis of the Art Tower Mito /
Arata Isozaki.
Includes text from 1986 New York
exhibition catalog, Architecture
with or without irony.
JAPAN ARCHITECT 1990 Oct., v.65,
no.10(402), p.8-14, photos.

TOWERS--GERMANY (WEST)--BREMEN--
TECHNOLOGIEPARK UNIVERSITAT BREMEN--
ZENTRUM FUR ANGEWANDTE
RAUMFAHRTTECHNOLOGIE UND
MIKROGRAVITATION
Technologiepark Universitat Bremen.
Architects: Gert Schulze and
Heinrich Campe; Hochbauamt Bremen;
Wolfram Dahms; Haslob Hartlich
Schutz; Oswald M. Ungers;
Rosengart + Partner; Kurt Schmidt.
Includes English summary.
BAUMEISTER 1990 Dec., v.87, no.12,
p.32-41, photos., plans, secns.,
site plans, aerial photos.

TOWERS--GLASS--ENGLAND--MANCHESTER--1
CITY ROAD
Cladding and curtain walling.
Ten articles on topics such as
aluminum products, Belgian blue
limestone, design variation for
shape and pitch, the five towers
at 1 City Road in Manchester
(architects: Architects Group
Practice), vinyl cladding used for
housing refurbishments, and new
standards and references for
cladding.
BUILDING 1990 Oct.26, v.255,
no.42,Suppl., p.[1]-54, photos.,
port.

TOWERS--GREEK--GREECE--ANDROS
Towers from North-West Andros /
Anthi Koutsoukou, Chrysanthos
Kanellopoulos.
THE ANNUAL OF THE BRITISH SCHOOL
AT ATHENS 1990, no.85,
p.[155]-174,pl.21-23, maps,
photos., plans, reconst. dwgs.,
refs.

TOWERS--ITALY--ROME--URBAN AXIS
L'idea di citta = The idea of the
city / Carlo Moretti and Daniele
Geltrudi.
Project for twelve cylindrical
towers aligned with an urban axis,
Rome. Architects: Carlo Moretti
and Daniele Geltrudi.
L'ARCA 1990 July-Aug., no.40,
p.48-55, dwgs., models, site
plans.

TOWERS--MEDIEVAL--ALTERATIONS AND
ADDITIONS--ITALY--MESTRE
La torre della memoria: il recupero
della torre civica di Mestre = a
tower in search of its past: the
Mestre's public tower renewal /
Guido Zordan.
Architect: Guido Zordan. English
summary.
SPAZIO E SOCIETA 1990 Jan.-Mar.,
v.13, no.49, p.48-57, ill., dwgs.,
port., elevs., models, maps,
secns., site plans.

TOWERS--MEDIEVAL--FRANCE--LA
ROCHELLE--TOUR SAINT-NICOLAS
Une double revolution a La Rochelle:
la Tour Saint-Nicolas / Jean
Mesqui.
BULLETIN MONUMENTAL 1990, v.148,
no.2, p.[155]-190, diagrs., dwgs.,
elevs., map, photos., plans,
secns., engrs., refs.

TOWERS--MEDIEVAL--FRANCE--PERIGORD
Un dispositif de protection
territoriale et de defense des
populations rurales en Perigord au
XIIIe siecle / Bernard Fournioux.
ARCHEOLOGIE MEDIEVALE 1990, v.20,
p.[335-349], elevs., maps,
photos., plans, refs.

TOWERS--ROMAN--ENVIRONMENTAL ASPECTS
Wind towers in Roman wall paintings?
/ Elfried R. Knauer.
METROPOLITAN MUSEUM OF ART.
METROPOLITAN MUSEUM JOURNAL 1990,
v.25, p.5-20, dets., dwgs.,
elevs., photos., sketches,
biblio., refs.

TOWERS--SOVIET UNION--RED TOWER
La torre rossa / Constantin Boym.
On the work of Yuri Avvakumov, a
member of the Paper Architecture
group. The Red Tower is a homage
to Letatlin, a famous glider of
the 1930s. English text on p.9.
MODO 1990 Oct., v.13, no.126,
p.42-43, models.

TOWERS--SPAIN--LERIDA
Murallas que no separan: Amado y
Domenech en Lerida / Ignasi de
Sola-Morales.
Urban renewal project in the El
Canyeret de Lerida. Includes an
elevator-tower which links the old
town to the urban centers and a
retaining wall.
ARQUITECTURA VIVA 1990 Nov.-Dec.,
no.15, p.16-20, elevs., models,
hotos., plans, secns., site plans.

TOWERS--STEEL--CHINA
Design and construction of steel
towers and masts in China / Li
Ruihua, Cai Yiyan.
BUILDING IN CHINA 1990 Mar., v.3,
no.1, p.16-26, photos., ports.

TOWERS--STONE--ENGLAND--NORTHUMBERLAND
Vernacular architecture: feudal and
far between / Andrew Sim.
A trip to the "landowner's
landscape" of the far Northeast
England, mostly featuring
fortified sandstone houses of the
upper classes.
TRADITIONAL HOMES 1990 Sept., v.6,
no.12, p.89-92, photos.

TOWERS--STONE--MEDIEVAL--ALTERATIONS
AND ADDITIONS--ITALY--VAL D'OSSOLA
Il presente e il passato / Lucia
Bisi.
Conversion of a medieval stone
tower into a house in the Val
d'Ossola, Italy. Architects:
Mauro Bisattini, Alessandra Cane.
VILLE GIARDINI 1990 Dec., no.254,
p.28-33, photos., plans, secn.

TOWERS--TEMPORARY--JAPAN--YOKOHAMA--
EXHIBITIONS
Yokohama city creation Bay '90:
exhibition of waterfront
redevelopment.
Five temporary towers, called
Yokohama Towers, which are part of
the Bay 90 exhibition. Architects:
Hirofumi Sugimoto, Noriaki Furuya,
Katsuhiro Kobayashi, Kiyoshi
Takeyama and Kazuyo Sejima.
JAPAN ARCHITECT 1990 June, v.65,
no.6(398), p.4, photos.

TOWERS--UNITED STATES--MINNEAPOLIS
(MINNESOTA)--WONDERLAND BEACON TOWER
Lost Minnesota: Wonderland's Beacon
Tower, Minneapolis, 1905-1911 /
Jack El-Hai.
Amusement park tower, built 1905;
razed in 1911.
ARCHITECTURE MINNESOTA 1990
Sept.-Oct., v.16, no.5, p.72,
photo.

TOWERS--UNITED STATES--SEASIDE
(FLORIDA)
"Belvederes' en el golfo: casa y
torre en Seaside, Florida =
Belvederes by the Gulf.
On Leon Krier's summer house.
English text, p.87.
A & V 1990, no.21, p.54-57, dwgs.,
elevs., photos., plans.

TOWN HALLS
See CITY HALLS

TOWN HOUSES
See TOWNHOUSES

TOWN PLANNERS
See CITY PLANNERS

TOWN PLANNING
See CITY PLANNING

TOWNDROW, JENNIFER
Making waves in the New World /
Jennifer Towndrow.
On the work of Melbourne
architect, Daryl Jackson.
RIBA JOURNAL 1990 July, v.97,
no.7, p.36-40, ill., port.,
photos.

TOWNHOUSES
See also ROW HOUSES

TOWNHOUSES--18TH CENTURY--ALTERATIONS
AND ADDITIONS--ENGLAND--LONDON--
KENYAN HIGH COMMISSSION
Adam revival / Phil Bangs.
On the refurbishment of the 1774
London townhouse designed by James
Adam which is now the Kenyan High
Commission. Restoration
architects: John Assael and
Partners.
RIBA JOURNAL 1990 Mar., v.97,
no.3, p.75,77,80, dets., photos.,
secn., elev.

TOWNHOUSES--18TH CENTURY--
DOCUMENTATION--ENGLAND--BRISTOL
The design of a house for a
merchant, 1724 [Bristol] / John
Bold.
Makes available a document
relating to an article by Kerry
Downes in v.10(1967) of this
journal. Appendix gives text of
the manuscript from "Sir John
Vanburgh's designs for Kings
Weston".
ARCHITECTURAL HISTORY 1990, v.33,
p.75-82, elev., plans, refs.

TOWNHOUSES--18TH CENTURY--UNITED
STATES--CHARLESTON (SOUTH
CAROLINA)--RUTLEDGE HOUSE (116 BROAD
STREET)
John Rutledge B&B [Charleston,
S.C.].
1763 townhouse, now an inn.
Architects for restoration: Evans
and Schmidt. Interior designers:
Pulliam Morris Interiors.
COLONIAL HOMES 1990 June, v.16,
no.3, p.[82-85],146, photos.,
port.

TOWNHOUSES--19TH CENTURY--TRINIDAD
Home and colonial: flamboyance and
nostalgia among Trinidad's
townhouses / Len Mitchell.
TRADITIONAL HOMES 1990 Mar., v.6,
no.6, p.127-130, photos.

TOWNHOUSES--19TH CENTURY--UNITED
STATES--NEW ORLEANS (LOUISIANA)--
KAVANAUGH HOUSE
Latitudes of the sun: a
nineteenth-century town house in
the Marigny / Susannah M. Wilson.
Architectural renovation by Frank
W. Masson. Interior designer:
Decorations-Lucullus.
SOUTHERN ACCENTS 1990 June, v.13,
no.5, p.[70-81], photos.

TOWNHOUSES--ENGLAND--LONDON--ELLIS
HOUSE
Exploding the box / Stephen
Greenburg.
Mews house in Twickenham, London,
by Eldred Evans and David Shalev.
ARCHITECTS' JOURNAL 1990 Feb.28,
v.191, no.9, p.28-31, dets.,
elevs., photos., plan, secns.

TOWNHOUSES--FEDERAL--ALTERATIONS AND
ADDITIONS--UNITED STATES--
PHILADELPHIA (PENNSYLVANIA)
Sculpturing space / Judith Nasatir.
Renovation of 1860 Federal-style
townhouse near Rittenhouse Square,
Philadelphia. Architects: Kieran
Timberlake Harris.
INTERIOR DESIGN 1990 Mar., v.61,
no.5, p.164-[167], model, photos.,
plans.

TOWNHOUSES--GEORGIAN--CONSERVATION AND
RESTORATION--ENGLAND--BATH--CHILCOTT
HOUSE
Townhouse treasures: Georgian house
full of curios in the city of Bath
/ Iola Brenard.
Built 1791-1793. Architect: John
Palmer.
TRADITIONAL HOMES 1990 Sept., v.6,
no.12, p.23-28, photos.

TOWNHOUSES--GEORGIAN--CONSERVATION AND
RESTORATION--ENGLAND--LONDON--57
MANSELL STREET
Elementary connection [57 Mansell
St., London] / Peter Weatherhead.
Refurbishment of a Georgian
townhouse, and of a Victorian
warehouse behind it, and
conversion into offices for an
insurance company. Architect:
Trehearne & Norman.
BUILDING 1990 Apr.13, v.255,
no.15, p.46-48, photos.

TOWNHOUSES--GREEK REVIVAL--
CONSERVATION AND RESTORATION--UNITED
STATES--RICHMOND (VIRGINIA)--
FRANKLIN STREET
Southern traditions: preservation
efforts in today's South show new
interest in 20th-century
landmarks, as well as earlier ones
/ Clifford A. Pearson.
A portfolio of Southeast projects:
Epping Forest Yacht Club,
Jacksonville, Fla. (Pappas
Associates); Freedom Tower, Miami
(Heisenbottle Architects);
Venetian Pool, Coral Gables, Fla.
(H. Carlton Decker & Assoc.);
Howard Memorial Library, New
Orleans (E. Barron, M. Toups); and
Linden Row Inn, Richmond, Va.
(Glave Newman Anderson).
ARCHITECTURAL RECORD 1990 Mar.,
v.178, no.3, p.66-75, photos.,
plans, site plans.

TOWNHOUSES--GREEK REVIVAL--UNITED
STATES--CHARLESTON (SOUTH
CAROLINA)--ROPER HOUSE
The Robert William Roper House,
Charleston, South Carolina /
Kenneth and Martha Severens.
Address: 9 East Battery. Built
1838-c.1840. Architect: Charles F.
Reichardt.
ANTIQUES 1990 May, v.137, no.5,
p.1154-[1165], ill., ports.,
photos.

TOWNHOUSES--INTERIOR DESIGN--UNITED
STATES--ATLANTA (GEORGIA)
A little collaboration: amity and
art in Atlanta.
Townhouse interiors by T. Gordon
Little.
SOUTHERN ACCENTS 1989 Mar.-Apr.,
v.12, no.2, p.134-139, photos.

TOWNHOUSES--INTERIOR DESIGN--UNITED
STATES--MEMPHIS (TENNESSEE)--HICKMAN
THOMLEY HOUSE
Subtle evolution: the ever-changing
town house of two Memphis
designers / Susannah M. Wilson.
Interior designers and owners:
Steven Hickman and Tom Thomley.
Architect for the remodeling:
Oscar E. Menzer.
SOUTHERN ACCENTS 1990 Oct., v.13,
no.8, p.[124]-130, photos.

TOWNHOUSES--INTERIOR DESIGN--UNITED
STATES--NEW YORK (NEW YORK)
In Greenwich Village: amiable
sophistication defines an 1840s
town house / John Taylor.
Interior designer: Thomas Fleming
of Irvine & Fleming.
ARCHITECTURAL DIGEST 1990 Nov.,
v.47, no.12, p.286-291,316,

TOWNHOUSES--INTERIOR DESIGN--UNITED
STATES--NEW YORK (NEW YORK)--HEPBURN
HOUSE
Katharine Hepburn: four-time Best
Actress in New York, Connecticut
and California / A. Scott Berg.
ARCHITECTURAL DIGEST 1990 Apr.,
v.47, no.4, p.192-[197],292,294,
ports., photos.

TOWNHOUSES--INTERIOR DESIGN--UNITED
STATES--NEW YORK (NEW YORK)--
NUNNERLEY HOUSE
Manhattan moderne: where glamour
gets gutsy [Nunnerley townhouse] /
Julie V. Iovine.
Interior design of Upper East Side
home. Interior designer and owner:
Sandra Nunnerley./
METROPOLITAN HOME 1990 Aug., v.22,
no.8, p.124-[125], port., photos.

TOWNHOUSES--INTERIOR DESIGN--UNITED
STATES--PALM BEACH (FLORIDA)--HORN
HOUSE
Tropical trompe l'oeil: Steve and
Linda Horn's town house in Palm
Beach / Steven M. L. Aronson.
ARCHITECTURAL DIGEST 1990 Feb.,
v.47, no.2, p.704-709, port.,
photos.

TOWNHOUSES--INTERIOR DESIGN--UNITED
STATES--WASHINGTON (DISTRICT OF
COLUMBIA)--POLING HOUSE
Textural context: Marilyn Poling's
subtle new direction in design /
Susan Stiles Dowell.
House in the Kalorama district of
Washington, D.C.
SOUTHERN ACCENTS 1990 June, v.13,
no.5, p.[90]-96, dets., photos.

TOWNHOUSES--NEOCLASSICAL--ENGLAND--
LONDON--20 SAINT JAMES'S SQUARE
20 St. James's Square, part 1 / John
Olley.
First of two-part article on an
18th cent. London terrace house
designed by Robert Adam.
ARCHITECTS' JOURNAL 1990 Feb.21,
v.191, no.8, p.34-47,52-[55],57,
dets., dwg., elevs., map, photos.,
plans, engrs., refs.

TOWNHOUSES--NEOCLASSICAL--INTERIOR
DESIGN--ENGLAND--LONDON--20 SAINT
JAMES'S SQUARE
20 St. James's Square, part 2 / John
Olley.
Second and last of two-part
article on 18th cent. London
terrace house designed by Robert
Adam; features interior decoration
and ornament.
ARCHITECTS' JOURNAL 1990 Feb.28,
v.191, no.9, p.34-43,48-53, dets.,
ill., dwgs., elevs., photos.,
plan, engrs., refs.

TOWNHOUSES--QUEEN ANNE--CONSERVATION
AND RESTORATION--ENGLAND--
CHICHESTER--PALLANT HOUSE
An artistic restoration: Pallant
House in Chichester, a restored
Queen Anne townhouse / Maureen
Connett.
Built 1713.
TRADITIONAL HOMES 1990 Dec., v.7,
no.3, p.29-31, photos.

TOWNHOUSES--QUEEN ANNE--ENGLAND--
CHICHESTER--PALLANT HOUSE
  Pallant House, Chichester: a tale of
  restoration and benefaction / Sue
  Warren.
  Queen Anne town house, built in
  1713; now housing the 20th-cent.
  art collections of Walter Hussey
  and Charles Kearley.
  APOLLO 1990 Nov., v.132, no.345,
  p.342-343, port., photo.

TOWNHOUSES--SWITZERLAND--BELLINZONA
  Trittico dell'amicizia / Giulia
  Conte.
  3-family housing unit, Bellinzona,
  Switzerland. Architect: Aldo
  Guscetti.
  VILLE GIARDINI 1990 June, no.249,
  p.[10]-15, photos., plans, secn.

TOWNHOUSES--UNITED STATES--CAMBRIDGE
(MASSACHUSETTS)--HARVARD UNIVERSITY
FACULTY HOUSING
  Uncommon dwellings: Harvard faculty
  housing, Cambridge, Massachusetts,
  Woo + Williams, Architects /
  Robert Campbell.
  Townhouses.
  ARCHITECTURE: THE AIA JOURNAL 1990
  Jan., v.79, no.1, p.78-81,
  photos., plan, secns., site plan.

TOWNHOUSES--UNITED STATES--SAN MATEO
(CALIFORNIA)--MEADOW COURT
  The coastal condition: regional
  portfolio: California housing /
  Paul M. Sachner.
  The first of a series of regional
  portfolios, on 5 multifamily
  projects: Armacost Duplex, Los
  Angeles [Rebecca Binder]; 14-16
  Leroy Pl., San Francisco (Hood
  Miller); 1150 Lombard St., San
  Francisco (Hood Miller); Meadow
  Court, San Mateo (David Baker
  Assoc.); and Seacliff, Malibu
  (Kanner Associates).
  ARCHITECTURAL RECORD 1990 Jan.,
  v.178, no.1, p.90-99, elevs.,
  photos., plans, secns., site
  plans.

TOWNHOUSES--UNITED STATES--SANTA
MONICA (CALIFORNIA)--PACIFIC
TOWNHOUSES
  American housing 1980-1990 / James
  Tice.
  Features: Castro Common, San
  Francisco (Daniel Solomon, Paulett
  Taggart); Sun-Tech Housing, Santa
  Monica (Steve Andre, David Van
  Hoy); Pacific Townhouses, Santa
  Monica (Rebecca Binder, James
  Stafford); Hoyt Square
  Condominiums, Portland, OR (Robert
  S. Leeb). Text in Italian and
  English.
  METAMORFOSI 1989, no.12, p.38-51,
  axonometric views, models,
  photos., plans, secns.

TOWNHOUSES--UNITED STATES--SANTA
MONICA (CALIFORNIA)--SUN-TECH
TOWNHOUSES
  American housing 1980-1990 / James
  Tice.
  Features: Castro Common, San
  Francisco (Daniel Solomon, Paulett
  Taggart); Sun-Tech Housing, Santa
  Monica (Steve Andre, David Van
  Hoy); Pacific Townhouses, Santa
  (Continued next column)

TOWNHOUSES--UNITED STATES--SANTA
MONICA (CALIFORNIA)--SUN-TECH
TOWNHOUSES (CONTINUED)
  American housing...(CONTINUED)
  Monica (Rebecca Binder, James
  Stafford); Hoyt Square
  Condominiums, Portland, OR (Robert
  S. Leeb). Text in Italian and
  English.
  METAMORFOSI 1989, no.12, p.38-51,
  axonometric views, models,
  photos., plans, secns.

TOWNHOUSES--VICTORIAN--ALTERATIONS AND
ADDITIONS--UNITED STATES--CHICAGO
(ILLINOIS)--CARRIGAN HOUSE
  Stuart Cohen and Anders Nerein: the
  visual expansion of a 19th century
  Chicago town house.
  Townhouse owned by Richard H.
  Carrigan.
  ARCHITECTURAL DIGEST 1990 Feb.,
  v.47, no.2, p.108-109, photos.,
  plans.

TOWNS
  See CITIES AND TOWNS

TOWNS - SEASIDE
  See SEASIDE TOWNS

TOWNSCAPES
  See also SKYLINES
  Stadt - Teil der Landschaft.
  Okologischer stadtumbau fur die
  Zukunft / Adolf Schmitt.
  Introductory remarks given early
  in 1990 by the president of the
  BDLA at the Landestag NW.
  DEUTSCHES ARCHITEKTENBLATT 1990
  Oct.1, v.22, no.10, p.1547,

TOWNSCAPES--18TH CENTURY
  Il fiume e le citta / Renzo Dubbini.
  Captions in Italian and English.
  CASABELLA 1990 Oct., v.54, no.572,
  p.26-29, ill., site plans, biblio.

TOWNSCAPES--19TH CENTURY--CANADA--
HAMILTON (ONTARIO)
  Landscapes of Victorian Hamilton:
  the use of visual materials in
  recreating and interpreting the
  past / Walter G. Peace.
  URBAN HISTORY REVIEW. REVUE
  D'HISTOIRE URBAINE 1989 June,
  v.18, no.1, p.75-85, axonometric
  views, photos, tables, aerial
  photo, refs.

TOWNSCAPES--20TH CENTURY--CRITICISM
  Bauen fur wen? Die Verunsicherung
  der gemeinnutzigen
  Wohnungswirtschaft / Reinhart C.
  Bartholomai.
  One of several articles in issue
  entitled "Konzepte und Projekte
  fur den Wohnungsbau".
  BAUWELT 1990 Mar.30, v.81, no.12,
  p.566-571, photos.
  Panik Poing / Gerrit Confurius.
  Commentary on the built landscape
  20km east of Munich. One of
  several articles in issue entitled
  "Konzepte und Projekte fur den
  Wohnungsbau".
  BAUWELT 1990 Mar.30, v.81, no.12,
  p.564-565, ill., photo.

TOWNSCAPES--CONSERVATION AND
RESTORATION--GERMANY (EAST)--MURITZ
AREA
  Stadtbildsanierung durch Eigenheime
  in Waren-Murits / Harald Korthals.
  Examples of new houses and infill
  homes that blend with existing
  traditional structures in this
  area of E. Germany. Architects:
  Wolfgang Hermann (design), Harald
  Korthals (project).
  ARCHITEKTUR DER DDR 1989 Nov.,
  v.38, no.11, p.26-28, elevs.,
  photos., plan, secn.

TOWNSCAPES--EARLY CHRISTIAN--CYPRUS
  Maison et paysage urbain dans les
  villes du Proche-Orient (IIe-Ve
  siecles ap. J.-C.) / Catherine
  Saliou.
  HISTOIRE DE L'ART 1990 May,
  no.9-10, p.9-20, photos., site
  plans, refs.

TOWNSCAPES--ENGLAND
  Development pressure, development
  control and suburban townscape
  change: case studies in south-east
  England / J. W. R. Whitehand.
  TOWN PLANNING REVIEW 1989 Oct.,
  v.60, no.4, p.403-420, map,
  photos., site plans, tables, refs.

TOWNSCAPES--EVALUATION--UNITED
STATES--CHATTANOOGA (TENNESSEE)
  The evaluative image of the city /
  Jack L. Nasar.
  Methods for determining how the
  public evaluates the cityscape,
  providing the basis for a visual
  plan. Examples from Knoxville and
  Chattanooga, Tenn.
  AMERICAN PLANNING ASSOCIATION
  JOURNAL 1990 Winter, v.56, no.1,
  p.41-53, maps, tables, aerial
  photos., refs.

TOWNSCAPES--EVALUATION--UNITED
STATES--KNOXVILLE (TENNESSEE)
  The evaluative image of the city /
  Jack L. Nasar.
  Methods for determining how the
  public evaluates the cityscape,
  providing the basis for a visual
  plan. Examples from Knoxville and
  Chattanooga, Tenn.
  AMERICAN PLANNING ASSOCIATION
  JOURNAL 1990 Winter, v.56, no.1,
  p.41-53, maps, tables, aerial
  photos., refs.

TOWNSCAPES--GERMANY (EAST)--ZWICKAU
  Grunflachen zwischen Wohnbauten /
  Susanne Kosmale.
  Vegetation and plantings in
  Zwickau, E. Germany.
  ARCHITEKTUR DER DDR 1989 Dec.,
  v.38, no.12, p.28-29, photos.

TOWNSCAPES--GERMANY (WEST)--WURZBURG
  Ein gigantischer Sendeturm uber
  Wurzburg? / Stefan Kummer.
  KUNSTCHRONIK 1990 June, v.43,
  no.6, p.248-250, [1 p. of plates],
  photo.

TOWNSCAPES--ITALY--LUCCA
  Sede del Banco di Napoli a Lucca =
    New offices for a bank in Lucca /
    Pier Carlo Santini.
    On the outskirts of the old town
    and influenced by the city view.
    Architects: Raffaello Lotti,
    Angela Chiantelli. Includes
    English translation; French,
    German, and Spanish summaries,
    p.3.
    L'INDUSTRIA DELLE COSTRUZIONI 1990
    Feb., v.24, no.220, p.6-11,
    photos., plans, secsn., site plan,
    aerial photo.

TOWNSCAPES--ITALY--PIENZA
  Where Gaia and Duranos make love /
    Bruno Queysanne.
    The author experiences the
    "richness of...spatiality" in the
    meeting of Earth and Sky in his
    views of Pienza and San Francisco.
    PLACES 1990 Winter, v.6, no.2,
    p.4-6, photos., refs.

TOWNSCAPES--MIDDLE EAST
  Maison et paysage urbain dans les
    villes du Proche-Orient (IIe-Ve
    siecles ap. J.-C.) / Catherine
    Saliou.
    HISTOIRE DE L'ART 1990 May,
    no.9-10, p.9-20, photos., site
    plans, refs.

TOWNSCAPES--POLAND--WARSAW
  Warschau, Phantom einer schonen
    Stadt / Peter Lachmann.
    In an issue entitled "Warschau,
    Der Anfang einer Geschichte".
    Includes English summary, p.[ii].
    DU 1990 Feb., no.588, p.84-89,

TOWNSCAPES--UNITED STATES--BOULDER
(COLORADO)
  Streetscapes in an American city
    [Boulder, CO] / Louis Sauer.
    ARCHITECTURE & COMPORTEMENT =
    ARCHITECTURE & BEHAVIOR 1990, v.6,
    no.4, p.[357]-371, photos., map,
    site plan, biblio.

TOWNSCAPES--UNITED STATES--SAN
FRANCISCO (CALIFORNIA)
  Where Gaia and Duranos make love /
    Bruno Queysanne.
    The author experiences the
    "richness of...spatiality" in the
    meeting of Earth and Sky in his
    views of Pienza and San Francisco.
    PLACES 1990 Winter, v.6, no.2,
    p.4-6, photos., refs.

TOWNSCAPES (VIEWS)
  See CITIES AND TOWNS - VIEWS

TOY STORES
  See STORES - TOY

TOYKA, ROLF
  Auszeichnung vorbildlicher Bauten im
    Lande Hessen 1985 bis 1989:
    Ergebnisse des Wettbewerbs / Rolf
    Toyka.
    Competition winners, including
    several projects in Frankfurt and
    Darmstadt.
    DEUTSCHES ARCHITEKTENBLATT 1990
    Mar.1, v.22, no.1, p.353-356,
    photos., plans, sketch.

TOYKA, ROLF (CONTINUED)
  Zusammenarbeit mit
    DDR-Architekten/-innen / R.Toyka,
    S.Burghardt.
    Report on a meeting between
    members of the Akademie der
    Architektenkammer Hessen and the
    Architektenkammer Thuringen, 30
    Apr.1990.
    DEUTSCHES ARCHITEKTENBLATT 1990
    May 1, v.22, no.5, p.117-119,
    photos.

TOYO ITO & ASSOCIATES
  Surface of glass / Toyo Ito.
    Two office buildings and one
    project by Toyo Ito & Associates:
    T Building at Nakameguro, I
    Building at Asakusabashi and
    "Media-ships floating on the
    Seine," project for the Maison de
    la culture du Japon, Paris.
    English summary, p.19.
    KENCHIKU BUNKA 1990 Oct., v.45,
    no.528, p.[21]-41, elevs., models,
    photos., plans.
  Toyo Ito / Toyo Ito.
    Contents: Guest house for Sapporo
    Breweries, Eniwa, Hokkaido,
    design: 1987-88; construction:
    1988-89 -- Project N, Tama, Tokyo,
    design: 1988-89; completion: Mar.
    1992. Text in Japanese and
    English.
    GA DOCUMENT 1990 Apr., no.25,
    p.[92]-97, elev., model, photos.,
    plans, site plan.

TOYOKAZU WATANABE, ARCHITECT AND
ASSOCIATES
  Yogo Forestry Culture Center.
    Architects: Toyokazu Watanabe,
    Architect and Associates. English
    summary, p.19.
    KENCHIKU BUNKA 1990 Oct., v.45,
    no.528, p.[103]-112, photos.,
    plans, secns.

TRA (FIRM)
  Sparkling station: brightly colored
    neon and glass "marquees" and a
    varied and artful approach to
    lighting help make this a bright
    stop in Seattle's new downtown
    transit systems.
    Convention Place Station, Downtown
    Seattle Transit Project.
    Architects: Parsons Brinckerhoff
    Quade & Douglas; TRA; lighting
    consultant: Lighthouse, Inc.
    ARCHITECTURAL RECORD 1990 Aug.,
    v.178, no.9 suppl., p.28-31,
    dets., photos., plan.
  Stadt und Verkehr.
    Special issue on towns and
    traffic. 22 projects illustrated.
    English summary, p.53.
    BAUMEISTER 1990 Aug., v.87, no.8,
    p.13-53, dwgs., models, photos.,
    plans, secns., site plans, aerial
    photos.

TRACKS, RUNNING
  See RUNNING TRACKS

TRADARDI, MARIA GIUSEPPINA
  Nuova edilizia residenziale publica
    al Tiburtino, Roma = A new public
    housing development in Rome /
    Giovanna Latour.
    Architects: Giorgio Blanco, Maria
    Giuseppina Tradardi. In Italian
              (Continued next column)

TRADARDI, MARIA GIUSEPPINA
              (CONTINUED)
  Nuova edilizia...(CONTINUED)
    and English; French, German, and
    Spanish summaries, p.3.
    L'INDUSTRIA DELLE COSTRUZIONI 1990
    Dec. v.24, no.230, p12-17, dets.,
    photos., plans, secns., site plan.

TRADE CATALOGS
  See COMMERCIAL CATALOGS

TRADE MARTS
  See also SHOWROOMS

TRADE SCHOOLS
  See SCHOOLS - VOCATIONAL

TRADE UNION BUILDINGS
  See LABOR UNION BUILDINGS

TRAFFIC
  See also CITY TRAFFIC
  See also ROADS
  Discussion: cars, people, and
    shopping districts / Namiki Oka,
    Kozo Amano.
    THE WHEEL EXTENDED 1990, no.74,
    p.17-23, ports., photos.
  Il monumento mobile: la circolazione
    e l'arte della memoria = The
    mobile monument: circulation and
    the suburban art of memory /
    Deirdre Gilfedder.
    PARAMETRO 1990 Jan.-Feb., no.176,
    p.64-67, photos., refs.
  Non-residential road environments: a
    progress report / Hans Westerman.
    Describes areas of friction
    between road traffic and land use
    frontages along roads.
    AUSTRALIAN PLANNER: JOURNAL OF THE
    ROYAL AUSTRALIAN PLANNING
    INSTITUTE 1989 Sept., v.27, no.3,
    p.17-18, graphs, plans, refs.
  Traffic safety, usability and
    streetscape effects of new design
    principles for major urban roads /
    Hartmut H. Topp.
    TRANSPORTATION 1989-1990, v.16,
    no.4, p.297-310, diagr., photos.,
    plans, sketches, refs.
  Vackrare vagar / Ib Moller.
    Commentary on traffic and
    roadsides, with examples from
    Denmark.
    ARKITEKTUR: THE SWEDISH REVIEW OF
    ARCHITECTURE 1990 Nov., v.90,
    no.9, p.20-23, photos., biblio.

TRAFFIC--18TH CENTURY--ENGLAND--LONDON
  Walking the city streets: the urban
    odyssey in eighteenth-century
    England / Penelope J. Corfield.
    JOURNAL OF URBAN HISTORY 1990
    Feb., v.16, no.2, p.132-174, ill.,
    refs.

TRAFFIC--CHINA--PEKING
  Studies on Beijing's development
    strategies / Zhao Dongri.
    Covers population structure;
    sub-centers, satellite towns,
    urban region; water shortage;
    traffic.
    BUILDING IN CHINA 1989 Mar., v.2,
    no.1, p.18-22, table.

TRAFFIC--FRANCE--ILE-DE-FRANCE
Las politicas de desplazamientos en
Ile-de-France = Transport policies
in the Ile-de-France / Pascale
Pecheur.
English summary, p.28.
URBANISMO / COAM 1990 May, no.10,
p.20-28, graph, ill., maps,
photos., plans, table.

TRAFFIC--GERMANY (EAST)
Parkproblem in den Zentrum von
Klein-und Mittelstadten / Gunter
Shultz.
German, Russian, English and
French summaries, p.55-56.
ARCHITEKTUR DER DDR 1990 Jan.,
v.38, no.1, p.32-35, graphs, site
plans, tables, refs.

TRAFFIC--GERMANY (WEST)
Pedestrian-related goals and
innovations, step by step /
Karl-Heinz Schweig.
Pedestrian safety and traffic
restrictions in West Germany.
TRANSPORTATION QUARTERLY 1990
Oct., v.44, no.4, p.595-606,
graphs, ill., photos., plans,
tables.

TRAFFIC--GREAT BRITAIN
"No particular place": a meditation
on mobility / Graham A. D. King.
THE PLANNER 1990 Feb.23, v.76,
no.7, p.43-46, port., photos.,
refs.

TRAFFIC ISLANDS
See also MEDIAN STRIPS

TRAFFIC--NETHERLANDS
Tempo 160: Transkription eines
Dia-Vortrags zur "Plankton City" /
Rem Koolhaas.
ARCHITHESE 1990 Jan.-Feb., v.20,
no.1, p.39-43, models, photos.

TRAFFIC--SWITZERLAND--BERN
Ein Preis fur "stadtgerechten
Verkehr" [interview] / Richard
Pfister.
Interview with Bern traffic
planner Kurt Hoppe.
SCHWEIZER BAUMARKT 1990 Oct.8,
v.25, no.12, p.I-III, port.,
photos.

TRAFFIC--UNITED STATES
Containing traffic congestion in
America / Robert Cervero, Peter
Hall.
BUILT ENVIRONMENT 1989, v.15,
no.3-4, p.176-184, table, refs.

TRAGARDH, JAN--EXHIBITIONS
Fra formgirning til industriel
design: arbejder af Jan Tragardh
[exhibition review].
Exhibit at the
kunstindustrimuseet, closing
Oct.22, 1989.
ARKITEKTEN 1989 Sept.19, v.91,
no.16, p.403, dwgs.

TRAGESER, DIETER J.
Clean: Grossklaranlage in
Saarbrucken-Burbach.
Architects: D. Trageser, H.
Wagner.
DEUTSCHE BAUZEITUNG 1990 Mar.,
v.124, no.3, p.36-39, axonometric
view, photos., plan, secn.

TRAILER CAMPS
See also MOBILE HOME PARKS

TRAILS
See also HERITAGE TRAILS
See also NATURE TRAILS

TRAILS--UNITED STATES--CONNECTICUT--
FARMINGTON CANAL GREENWAY
Farmington Canal Greenway.
A biking and hiking trail which
follows the old 19th cent. canal.
Architects: Cesar Pelli and
Associates.
CONNECTICUT PRESERVATION: NEWS
1989 May-June, v.12, no.3, p.6,
dwg.

TRAIN STATIONS
See RAILROAD STATIONS

TRAIN TERMINALS
See RAILROAD TERMINALS

TRAINING CENTERS--AUSTRIA--SALZBURG
Lehrbauhof, Bauhutte Salzburg, 1989.
Architect: Michael Alder with H.P.
Muller.
WERK, BAUEN + WOHNEN 1989 Dec.,
no.12, p.43, photos., plan.
Lehrbauhof Salzburg.
Architect: Michael Alder,
Hanspeter Muller. Includes English
summary.
BAUMEISTER 1990 Mar., v.87, no.3,
p.15-23, dets., model, photos.,
plans, secns., site plan.

TRAINING CENTERS--COMPETITIONS--
AUSTRIA--SALZBURG
Semplice e perfetto, Il Lehrbauhof a
Salisburgo di Michael Alder / Otto
Kapfinger.
A professional building school,
built 1986-1989.
CASABELLA 1990 June, v.54, no.569,
p.26-29, det., photos., plan,
secn.

TRAINING CENTERS--GERMANY (WEST)--
DARMSTADT--FTZ
FTZ-Bildungszentrum in Darmstadt =
Telecommunications training centre
in Darmstadt.
Architects: H. Pfeiffer + C.
Ellermann.
DETAIL 1990 June-July, v.30, no.3,
p.266-270, dets., elevs., photos.,
plans, isometric dwg.
Ein Hauch von Stijl:
FTZ-Bildungszentrum in Darmstadt.
Architects: Pfeiffer & Ellermann.
DEUTSCHE BAUZEITUNG 1990 Dec.,
v.124, no.12, p.52-55, elev.,
photos., plans, secn.

TRAINING CENTERS--INDIA--BOMBAY--
MARITIME TRAINING INSTITUTE
Maritime Training Institute, Powai,
Bombay / CP Kukreja.
Located on the site of an
abandoned quarry and built
partially with red sandstone.
Completed in 1990. Architect:
C.P. Kukreja Associates.
ARCHITECTURE + DESIGN 1990
May-June, v.7, no.3, p.38-45,
axonometric views, dets., photos.,
plans, site plan.

TRAINING CENTERS--INDIA--PUNE--
HINDUSTAN PETROLEUM CORPORATION--
MANAGEMENT DEVELOPMENT INSTITUTE
Management Development Institute,
Pune / Vasant Kamath.
For the Hindustan Petroleum
Corporation Ltd. (HPCL).
Architects: Revathi and Vasant
Kamath.
ARCHITECTURE + DESIGN 1990
May-June, v.7, no.3, p.24-31,
dets., photos., plans, secns.

TRAINING CENTERS--IRELAND--CASTLEBAR--
CASTLEBAR CENTRE REHABILITATION
WORKSHOP
New rehab centre, Castlebar.
Castlebar Centre ReHabilitation
Workshop, a building housing
training units for catering,
confectionery, headware, weaving,
retail and general employment,
Castlebar, Ireland. Architects:
Hamilton Young & Associates.
PLAN: ARCHITECTURE & BUILDING
DESIGN IN IRELAND 1990 Jan., v.27,
no.1, p.18-21, photo., plan.

TRAINING CENTERS--ITALY--MILAN--IBM
La scuola dell'IBM = The IBM
education center / Anty Pansera.
IBM education center in Milan;
architect: Angelo Cortesi of
Studio GPI.
L'ARCA 1990 June, no.39, p.80-83,
photos., plans.

TRAINING CENTERS--JAPAN--MOCCON KWANN
Architecture of earth.
Four projects by Hideaki Katsura:
Kuma-mura F.O.A. Computer Center,
Kuma-mura Promotion Center, Moccon
Kwann training center and
Kuma-mura F.O.A. lumber factory.
English summary, p.23.
KENCHIKU BUNKA 1990 Aug., v.45,
no.526, p.119-138, dets., photos.,
plans, secns., site plan.

TRAINING CENTERS--NEPAL--DHANKUTA--
AUXILIARY HEALTH TRAINING CENTRE
Dhankuta Community Medicine Training
Centre, Nepal.
The CMA project, located on
terraces west of Dhankuta.
Project designers: David
Dobereiner, Alexander Leviksky.
ARCHITECTURE + DESIGN 1990
July-Aug., v.7, no.4, p.86-91,
elevs., photos., plans, site plan.

TRANSIT SYSTEMS--SPAIN--MADRID
   The growth of metro systems in
   Madrid, Rome and Athens / Frank J.
   Costa, Allen G. Noble.
   CITIES 1990 Aug., v.7, no.3,
   p.224-229, plans, tables, refs.

TRANSIT SYSTEMS--UNITED STATES--DALLAS
(TEXAS)--DART
   Trains, planes, and automobiles /
   Joel Warren Barna.
   Mass transit rail lines in Dallas
   and Houston.
   TEXAS ARCHITECT 1990 Mar.-Apr.,
   v.40, no.2, p.22-29, dwgs.,
   models, maps, photos., site plans.

TRANSIT SYSTEMS--UNITED STATES--
HOUSTON (TEXAS)--METRO
   Metro's park-and-rides: busing up to
   rail / Bruce C. Webb.
   CITE: THE ARCHITECTURE AND DESIGN
   REVIEW OF HOUSTON 1990 Fall,
   no.25, p.12-13, photos.
   Trains, planes, and automobiles /
   Joel Warren Barna.
   Mass transit rail lines in Dallas
   and Houston.
   TEXAS ARCHITECT 1990 Mar.-Apr.,
   v.40, no.2, p.22-29, dwgs.,
   models, maps, photos., site plans.

TRANSIT SYSTEMS--UNITED STATES--LAS
COLINAS (TEXAS)--AREA PERSONAL
TRANSIT (APT)
   The power of the people mover: Las
   Colinas and the Area Personal
   Transit System / John W. Kapala.
   Transportation system devised for
   Texas new town Las Colinas.
   DEVELOPMENT 1990 July-Aug., v.21,
   no.4, p.14-16, port., photos.

TRANSIT SYSTEMS--UNITED STATES--SAN
FRANCISCO BAY AREA (CALIFORNIA)--BAY
AREA RAPID TRANSIT (BART)
   Land use around suburban transit
   stations / Henry Moon.
   Land uses around 20 stations in
   suburban Washington, D.C. and San
   Francisco/Oakland.
   TRANSPORTATION 1990, v.17, no.1,
   p.67-88, diagrs., graphs, maps,
   tables, aerial photos., refs.
   Transit system meets crisis / John
   McCloud.
   Effect of 1989 earthquake on BART,
   the Bay Area Rapid Transit system
   serving San Francisco and
   surrounding area.
   AMERICAN CITY & COUNTY 1989 Dec.,
   v.104, no.12, p.28, 30, 32,

TRANSIT SYSTEMS--UNITED STATES--
WASHINGTON (DISTRICT OF COLUMBIA)--
METRO
   Land use around suburban transit
   stations / Henry Moon.
   Land uses around 20 stations in
   suburban Washington, D.C. and San
   Francisco/Oakland.
   TRANSPORTATION 1990, v.17, no.1,
   p.67-88, diagrs., graphs, maps,
   tables, aerial photos., refs.

TRANSMISSION TOWERS
   See COMMUNICATIONS TOWERS

TRANSPORTATION BUILDINGS
   See also AIRPORTS
   See also BUS GARAGES
   See also BUS SHELTERS
   See also BUS STATIONS
   See also CABLEWAY STATIONS
   See also GARAGES
   See also HANGARS
   See also RAILROAD STATIONS
   See also RAILROAD TERMINALS
   See also RAILROADS - BUILDINGS AND
      STRUCTURES
   See also SUBWAYS - STATIONS
   See also STREETCAR GARAGES
   See also TRAM DEPOTS

TRANSPORTATION BUILDINGS--IRELAND--
ROSSLARE--ROSSLARE TERMINAL
   Award for Rosslare Terminal.
      The National Rehabilitation Board
      of Ireland has awarded the Liam
      Maguire Award to Rosslare Terminal
      for its design for the physically
      disabled. Architect: John Clancey.
   PLAN: ARCHITECTURE AND BUILDING
   DESIGN IN IRELAND 1990 June, v.31,
   no.6, p.11, photo.
   Terminal building, Rosslare / Neil
   Steedman.
      Major passenger terminal on
      reclaimed land in Rosslare Harbour
      Ireland, integrates movement
      between ferries, trains, buses and
      cars. Architects: John Clancey.
   PLAN: ARCHITECTURE + INTERIOR
   DESIGN IN IRELAND 1989 June, v.22,
   no.6, p.29-36, photos.

TRANSPORTATION BUILDINGS--ITALY--
SICILY--PALERMO--PORTA MERIDIONALE
   Special feature: Machado and
   Silvetti.
      Contents: Brief history.--
      Statement / R. Machado, J.
      Silvetti.-- The material force of
      the architectural imagination / K.
      Michael Hays.-- Works: Portantina,
      New York, N.Y., 1986.-- Steps of
      Providence, Rhode Island School of
      Design, Providence, R.I., 1975.--
      Municipal cemetery,
      Polizzi-Generosa, Sicily, 1986.--
      Sesquicentennial Park, Houston,
      Tex., 1986.-- Central
      transportation facility "la Porta
      Meridionale," Palermo, Sicily,
      1987.-- Four public squares,
      Leonforte, Sicily, 1983. Text in
      Japanese and English.
   ARCHITECTURE AND URBANISM 1990
   Apr., no.4(235), p.65-138,
   axonometric views, elevs., models,
   photos., plans, secns., site
   plans.

TRANSPORTATION BUILDINGS--UNITED
STATES--SECAUCUS (NEW JERSEY)--
ALLIED JUNCTION
   All aboard at Allied Junction: a
   public-private partnership spurs
   the planning of the New Jersey
   transit link / Bruce Ross.
   New transportation hub planned for
   northern New Jersey. Commercial
   complex and transfer station
   architects: Brennan Beer Gorman
   Architects.
   MASS TRANSIT 1990 Apr., v.17,
   no.4, p.22-23, dwg.

TRANSPORTATION MUSEUMS
   See also MUSEUMS - AUTOMOBILE
   See also MUSEUMS - MARITIME
   See also MUSEUMS - RAILROAD

TRANSPORTATION PLANNING
   See also TRAFFIC
   Discussion: cars, people, and
   shopping districts / Namiki Oka,
   Kozo Amano.
   THE WHEEL EXTENDED 1990, no.74,
   p.17-23, ports., photos.
   Discussion: mobility and urban space
   design / Keijin Kamino, Nobuyuki
   Hata, Tadahiko Higuchi.
   THE WHEEL EXTENDED 1990, v.19,
   no.3, p.8-15, dets., ill., ports.,
   model, photos.
   Measures for traffic calming in
   residential areas / Hideo
   Yamanaka, Michiyasu Odani.
   THE WHEEL EXTENDED 1990, no.73,
   p.24-32, axonometric views, chart,
   photos., table, refs.
   Rail plans for Houston, Dallas /
   Joel Warren Barna.
   PROGRESSIVE ARCHITECTURE 1990
   Aug., v.71, no.8, p.32,37, plan.
   Traditional neighborhood
   development: will the traffic
   work? / Walter Kulash, Joe Anglin,
   David Marks.
   DEVELOPMENT 1990 July-Aug., v.21,
   no.4, p.21-24, ill., plans.
   Transportation and urban form.
   Theme issue. 8 articles indexed
   separately.
   TEXAS ARCHITECT 1990 Mar.-Apr.,
   v.40, no.2, entire issue (65 p.),
   ill.

TRANSPORTATION PLANNING--19TH
CENTURY--ITALY--LOMBARDY
   Un servizio privato di trasporto su
   diligenza in Lombardia: l'impresas
   franchetti, 1813-1870 / Carla
   Savare.
   STORIA URBANA 1990 July-Sept.,
   v.14, no.52, p.[49]-73, refs.

TRANSPORTATION PLANNING--AUSTRALIA
   MFP and VFT: our future in an
   acronym [book review] / Mark
   Scillo.
   On proposals for the Multifunction
   Polis (MFP) and the Very Fast
   Train (VFT) in Australia, as
   discussed in "Technocratic
   Dreaming," ed. by Paul James.
   TRANSITION 1990, no.33, p.82-83,

TRANSPORTATION PLANNING--CANADA
   Planes, trains and automobiles: how
   new transportation schemes are
   Americanizing our suburbs / Barton
   Reid.
   In Canada, principally Vancouver,
   Toronto and Montreal.
   CITY MAGAZINE 1989 Summer-Fall,
   v.11, no.1, p.4-6, maps.

TRANSPORTATION PLANNING--CANADA--
NIAGARA FALLS (ONTARIO)
   Ontario's Niagara parks.
   On the plan to improve the
   transportation and riverfront
   development along the Canadian
   shore of the Niagara River.
   Architects: Moriyama and Teshima.
   PROGRESSIVE ARCHITECTURE 1990
   Jan., v.71, no.1, p.116-117, maps.

TRANSPORTATION PLANNING--
--COMPETITIONS--GERMANY (WEST)
"Die Stadt von morgen - planen fur den Menschen" - Stadtvertragliche Hauptverkehrstrasse = "The city of tomorrow - planning for people" - main thouroughfares that are acceptable to a city.
Idea competition. Three joint first prize winners: Hans-Rainer Rung, Karsten Winkels; Albert Moritz; Jochen Dittus, Siegfried Volmer. Text in German.
ARCHITEKTUR + WETTBEWERBE 1990 Dec., no.144, p.75-78, photos., plans, secns., site plans.

TRANSPORTATION PLANNING--DENMARK--
COPENHAGEN
Bedre bytrafik i Kobenhavn / Lasse Freiesleben.
Planning for the new M-bane.
ARKITEKTEN 1989 Dec.22, v.91, no.23, p.A562-A563, map, photo.

TRANSPORTATION PLANNING--DEVELOPING
COUNTRIES
Non-routine travel in urban transportation planning: the case of developing countries / Krys Ochia.
CITIES 1990 Aug., v.7, no.3, p.230-235, table, refs.

TRANSPORTATION PLANNING--ECONOMIC
ASPECTS--ENGLAND
Road-oriented policy offers developers a joy-ride / Nigel Moor.
On strategic planning and infrastructure in England and the growth in office parks along transportation routes.
BUILDING 1990 July 13, v.255, no.28, p.38, map.

TRANSPORTATION PLANNING--ECONOMIC
ASPECTS--ITALY--MILAN
Building Milan: alternative machines of growth / Serena Vicari, Harvey Molotch.
Transportation planning for underground rapid transit in Milan and the various forces which influence decision-making.
English and French summaries.
INTERNATIONAL JOURNAL OF URBAN AND REGIONAL RESEARCH 1990 Dec., v.14, no.4, p.[602]-624, axonometric view, plans, refs.

TRANSPORTATION PLANNING--ENGLAND--
BIRMINGHAM
Integrating transport planning: the Birmingham experience / Alan Wenban-Smith, Tony May, Doug Jones.
THE PLANNER 1990 June 22, v.76, no.24, p.11-15, dwg., photos., skethces, refs.

TRANSPORTATION PLANNING--ENGLAND--BURY
SAINT EDMUNDS
Conservation and traffic in the historic town of Bury St. Edmunds / Denvil Coombe...et al.
THE PLANNER 1990 May 4, v.76, no.17, p.11-16, axonometric view, charts, dwg., maps, photos., plans, tables.

TRANSPORTATION PLANNING--ENGLAND--
CHANNEL TUNNEL RAIL LINK
The Channel Tunnel Rail link / Jiggy Lloyd.
Presents landscape practices working on the Link and the history of the project up to Nov.1989.
LANDSCAPE DESIGN 1990 May, no.190, p.14-16, diagr., model, map, site plan, table.

TRANSPORTATION PLANNING--ENGLAND--
LONDON
Land use and transportation in East London / Martin Simmons.
THE PLANNER 1990 Nov.16, v.76, no.45, p.9-11, maps, photo., refs.

TRANSPORTATION PLANNING--ENGLAND--
LONDON--DOCKLANDS
Transport and urban regeneration in London Docklands: a victim of success or a failure to plan? / Andrew Church.
CITIES 1990 Nov., v.7, no.4, p.289-303, maps, photo., refs.

TRANSPORTATION PLANNING--ENGLAND--
LONDON--JUBILEE LINE
Jubilee options / Amanda Baillieu.
On the latest proposals for the Jubilee Tube line, London.
BUILDING DESIGN 1990 Mar.2, no.975, p.10-11, plans, secns., aerial photos.

TRANSPORTATION PLANNING--ENGLAND--
OXFORD
Oxford: an evolving transport policy / Peter Jones.
BUILT ENVIRONMENT 1989, v.15, no.3-4, p.231-243, photos., plans, refs.

TRANSPORTATION PLANNING--ENVIRONMENTAL
ASPECTS
Green urban transport / Jeff Lowe.
CITY MAGAZINE 1989 Summer-Fall, v.11, no.1, p.28-30,

TRANSPORTATION PLANNING--ENVIRONMENTAL
ASPECTS--BIBLIOGRAPHY
Transport bibliography / Sheila Harvey.
Topics include: airports, canals, Channel Tunnel, railways, roads, and traffic restraint.
LANDSCAPE DESIGN 1990 May, no.190, p.47,

TRANSPORTATION PLANNING--ENVIRONMENTAL
ASPECTS--EUROPE
European transit and the environment / Francois Batisse.
MASS TRANSIT 1990 Sept-Oct., v.17, no.9-10, p.43-45, 48, aerial photo, ill.
Sowing the caraway seed ["green" transportation] / John Roberts.
European transport alternatives to the automobile.
BUILT ENVIRONMENT 1989, v.15, no.3-4, p.215-230, photos., plans, refs.

TRANSPORTATION PLANNING--ENVIRONMENTAL
ASPECTS--GREAT BRITAIN
The route of the problem / Chris Blandford, Philip Masters.
On the environmental factors to be considered in route selection.
LANDSCAPE DESIGN 1990 May, no.190, p.41-43, ill., map, sketch.

TRANSPORTATION PLANNING--EUROPE
Die Dimension der Lange und der Reihung: das Probleme der Monotonie in stadtischen Strassenraumen / Franz Fischl.
SCHWEIZER BAUMARKT 1990 July 2, v.25, no.8, p.VI-VIII, plans, refs.
Public transport and integrated transport policies in large metropolitan areas of Europe / Carmen Hass-Klau.
Includes case studies of Zurich and Munich.
THE PLANNER 1990 May 25, v.76, no.20, p.13-20, photos., tables, aerial photos., refs.

TRANSPORTATION PLANNING--EUROPE--
HISTORY
The networked city: a Euro-American review [book review] / Eugene P. Moehring.
Review of: Technology and the rise of the networked city in Europe and America, ed. by Joel A. Tarr and Gabriel Dupuy, 1988.
JOURNAL OF URBAN HISTORY 1990 Nov., v.17, no.1, p.88-97, refs.

TRANSPORTATION PLANNING--EUROPE--
INFLUENCE
Discussion: application of woonerf and other traffic-restraint concepts / Kozo Amano, B. Bernard Siman, Tham Kok-Seng.
Applying European concepts in Japan.
THE WHEEL EXTENDED 1990, no.73, p.[18]-23, ports., photo.

TRANSPORTATION PLANNING--FRANCE--
ILE-DE-FRANCE
Las politicas de desplazamientos en Ile-de-France = Transport policies in the Ile-de-France / Pascale Pecheur.
English summary, p.28.
URBANISMO / COAM 1990 May, no.10, p.20-28, graph, ill., maps, photos., plans, table.

TRANSPORTATION PLANNING--GAMBIA--
GREATER BANJUL
Land use and transportation policy in a small African city: the example of Greater Banjul. / Brendan McGrath.
THIRD WORLD PLANNING REVIEW 1990 Feb., v.12, no.1, p.[41]-57, maps, tables, refs.

TRANSPORTATION PLANNING--GERMANY
(EAST)
Parkproblem in den Zentrum von Klein-und Mittelstadten / Gunter Shultz.
German, Russian, English and French summaries, p.55-56.
ARCHITEKTUR DER DDR 1990 Jan., v.38, no.1, p.32-35, graphs, site plans, tables, refs.

TRANSPORTATION PLANNING--GERMANY
(WEST)
Stadt und Verkehr.
Special issue on towns and
traffic. 22 projects illustrated.
English summary, p.53.
BAUMEISTER 1990 Aug., v.87, no.8,
p.13-53, dwgs., models, photos.,
plans, secns., site plans, aerial
photos.

TRANSPORTATION PLANNING--GERMANY
(WEST)--FOHR--WYK
Tourismus und Verkehr: das Beispiel
Fohr /cHeinz Masur.
Traffic and tourism in the town of
Wyk on the island of Fohr,
Germany. English summary p.27.
GARTEN UND LANDSCHAFT 1990, v.100,
no.7, p.23-27, figs., photos.,
maps.

TRANSPORTATION PLANNING--GERMANY
(WEST)--MUNICH
Public transport and integrated
transport policies in large
metropolitan areas of Europe /
Carmen Hass-Klau.
Includes case studies of Zurich
and Munich.
THE PLANNER 1990 May 25, v.76,
no.20, p.13-20, photos., tables,
aerial photos., refs.

TRANSPORTATION PLANNING--GREAT BRITAIN
"No particular place": a meditation
on mobility / Graham A. D. King.
THE PLANNER 1990 Feb.23, v.76,
no.7, p.43-46, port., photos.,
refs.
The open road / Ken Fieldhouse.
On the role of landscape
architects in transportation
planning in the UK.
LANDSCAPE DESIGN 1990 May, no.190,
p.10-13, photos., refs.
Urban congestion and gridlock in
Britain / David Banister.
BUILT ENVIRONMENT 1989, v.15,
no.3-4, p.166-175, photos.,
tables, refs.
Viewpoint: traffic calming and town
planning / John Russell.
Defines "traffic calming" and the
reasons for its currency in
Britain.
TOWN PLANNING REVIEW 1990 Apr.,
v.61, no.2, p.iii-vi, refs.

TRANSPORTATION PLANNING--HONG KONG
Road pricing in Hong Kong: a viable
proposal / Timothy D. Hau.
BUILT ENVIRONMENT 1989, v.15,
no.3-4, p.195-214, diagr., map,
photo., table, refs.

TRANSPORTATION PLANNING--ITALY--
BOLOGNA
Piano della mobilita per la citta di
Bologna / Bernhard Winkler.
Article forms most of this issue.
Presents the traffic scheme for
Bologna proposed by Prof. Winkler.
Summaries in French, English,
German, and Spanish, p.1. Captions
in Italian and English. Includes
commentary by Claudio Sassi, and
German text on p.88-89.
PARAMETRO 1990 Mar.-Apr., no.177,
p.19-67,cover, dwgs., port., maps,
photos., site plans, tables,
engrs., aerial photos.

TRANSPORTATION PLANNING--ITALY--
BRESCIA
La citta intelligente = The
intelligent city / Giulio De
Carli, Antonio Nuzzo.
On computerization and technical
change affecting services in
cities, with Minitel in France
(for access to services) and Start
in Italy (a traffic regulation
system).
OTTAGONO 1989 Dec., no.93,
p.19-25, diagrs.

TRANSPORTATION PLANNING--ITALY--LUCCA
Una citta col guscio: Lucca:
interventi per la citta = A city
with its shell: Lucca: projects
for the city / Simone Micheli,
Leonardo Benevolo.
On the problems of the city walls,
traffic and parking areas.
Includes article by Leonardo
Benevolo entitled, Per Lucca, con
discrezione. Text in Italian and
English.
SPAZIO E SOCIETA 1990 July-Sept.,
v.13, no.51, p.26-33, port., maps,
photos., aerial photo.

TRANSPORTATION PLANNING--ITALY--VENICE
Politiche per Venezia / Cristina
Bianchetti, Chiara Merlini.
Introduces eight articles on city
planning in Venice. English
summaries, p.124-126. Contents:
Osservare le politiche per
Venezia: perche?; Marittima e
Arsenale nel contesto delle
trasformazioni urbane a Venezia;
Vedute della laguna; Il consorzio
Venezia nuova, concessionario
dello stato per le opere di
salvaguardia di Venezia; La casa a
Venezia; Infrastrutture per la
mobilita (e l'uranistica) nella
nuova dimensione di Venezia;
Appunti sulla questione della
metropolitana a Venezia; Alcuni
limiti alla delegittimazione
sociale delle istituzioni
pubbliche di governo urbano.
URBANISTICA 1990 Mar., no.98,
p.33-86,124-126, graphs, maps,
photos., plans, secn., site plan,
tables, refs.

TRANSPORTATION PLANNING--JAPAN--TAMA
NEW TOWN
Urban development and road building:
a brief history of Tama New Town/
Hiroshi Konno.
In Japan.
THE WHEEL EXTENDED 1990, no.73,
p.9-17, axonometric views, maps,
photos., aerial photos.

TRANSPORTATION PLANNING--JAPAN--TOKYO
Advanced traffic information systems
in Tokyo / Shigeru Kashima.
BUILT ENVIRONMENT 1989, v.15,
no.3-4, p.244-250, diagrs., table,
refs.

TRANSPORTATION PLANNING--MALAYSIA--
KUALA LUMPUR
Urban transport in Kuala Lumpur /
Ibrahim Bin Wahab.
CITIES 1990 Aug., v.7, no.3,
p.236-243, graph, maps, tables,
refs.

TRANSPORTATION PLANNING--POLITICAL
ASPECTS--ITALY--MILAN
Building Milan: alternative machines
of growth / Serena Vicari, Harvey
Molotch.
Transportation planning for
underground rapid transit in Milan
and the various forces which
influence decision-making.
English and French summaries.
INTERNATIONAL JOURNAL OF URBAN AND
REGIONAL RESEARCH 1990 Dec., v.14,
no.4, p.[602]-624, axonometric
view, plans, refs.

TRANSPORTATION PLANNING--SCOTLAND--
GLASGOW
Creating the context [Glasgow] /
George Mulvagh, Brian Evans.
City planning proposals for
Glasgow by Gillespie's.
ARCHITECTS' JOURNAL 1990 May 30,
v.191, no.22, p.44-49, axonometric
view, maps, photos., sketches,
aerial photo.

TRANSPORTATION PLANNING--SOCIOLOGICAL
ASPECTS--EUROPE
Kommunionsmiljon och samhallet /
Bjorn Linn.
Essay on efficiency in society and
the role of communication.
Includes English summary.
ARKITEKTUR: THE SWEDISH REVIEW OF
ARCHITECTURE 1990 Nov., v.90,
no.9, p.4-11,61-62, ill., dwgs.,
photos., aerial photos., biblio.,
refs.

TRANSPORTATION PLANNING--SPAIN
Un nuevo plan de carreteras urbanas
y interurbanas (1992-2000) = A new
plan for urban and intercity roads
(1992/2000) / Justo Borrajo, Jesus
Rubio.
English summary, p.19.
URBANISMO / COAM 1990 May, no.10,
p.6-19, maps, photos., tables,
aerial photos.

TRANSPORTATION PLANNING--SPAIN--
BARCELONA
Infraestructuras logisticas en la
Region Metropolitana de Barcelona
= Logistic infrastructures in the
metropolitan region of Barcelona
(M.R.B.) / J. Audicana...et al.
English summary, p.37.
URBANISMO / COAM 1990 May, no.10,
p.29-37, maps, photos., site
plans, table, aerial photos.

TRANSPORTATION PLANNING--SPAIN--
SEVILLE
El trafico y el transporte en la
ciudad de Sevilla = Traffic and
transport in the city of Seville /
Miguel Durban.
English summary, p.47.
URBANISMO / COAM 1990 May, no.10,
p.38-47, maps, photos., plans,
aerial photos.

TRANSPORTATION PLANNING--SWEDEN
Langs vagen.
Introduction to issue featuring
transportation topics. Articles
are indexed separately.
ARKITEKTUR: THE SWEDISH REVIEW OF
ARCHITECTURE 1990 Nov., v.90,
no.9, p.2-3, photo.

TRANSPORTATION PLANNING--SWITZERLAND--
BERN
Ein Preis fur "stadtgerechten
Verkehr" [interview] / Richard
Pfister.
Interview with Bern traffic
planner Kurt Hoppe.
SCHWEIZER BAUMARKT 1990 Oct.8,
v.25, no.12, p.I-III, port.,
photos.

TRANSPORTATION PLANNING--SWITZERLAND--
ZURICH
Public transport and integrated
transport policies in large
metropolitan areas of Europe /
Carmen Hass-Klau.
Includes case studies of Zurich
and Munich.
THE PLANNER 1990 May 25, v.76,
no.20, p.13-20, photos., tables,
aerial photos., refs.

TRANSPORTATION PLANNING--UNITED STATES
Beyond gridlock: looking for the new
suburban city / Joseph. E. Brown,
Michael E. Hickok.
Problems of definition for
"suburban urbanization", and the
transportation issues involved.
DEVELOPMENT 1990 July-Aug., v.21,
no.4, p.17-20, ill., dwgs.,
photos.
Containing traffic congestion in
America / Robert Cervero, Peter
Hall.
BUILT ENVIRONMENT 1989, v.15,
no.3-4, p.176-184, table, refs.

TRANSPORTATION PLANNING--UNITED
STATES--CHICAGO (ILLINOIS)
The Chicago Area Transportation
Study: a case study of rational
planning / Alan Black.
JOURNAL OF PLANNING EDUCATION AND
RESEARCH 1990 Fall, v.10, no.1,
p.27-37, refs.

TRANSPORTATION PLANNING--UNITED
STATES--HISTORY
The networked city: a Euro-American
review [book review] / Eugene P.
Moehring.
Review of: Technology and the rise
of the networked city in Europe
and America, ed. by Joel A. Tarr
and Gabriel Dupuy, 1988.
JOURNAL OF URBAN HISTORY 1990
Nov., v.17, no.1, p.88-97, refs.

TRANSPORTATION PLANNING--UNITED
STATES--MINNEAPOLIS (MINNESOTA)
Hennepin Avenue, Minneapolis.
One of six urban design reports
included in special issue, Urban
Concepts. Extracted from a 1981
plan by Denise Scott Brown, in
collaboration with
Bennett-Ringrose-Wolsfeld-Jarvis-G
ardner and Williams/O'Brien
Associates.
ARCHITECTURAL DESIGN 1990, v.60,
no.1-2, p.62-69, dwgs., elev.,
photos., site plans, sketches.

TRANSPORTATION PLANNING--UNITED
STATES--SEATTLE (WASHINGTON)
Seattle Metro Tunnel:
state-of-the-art maintenance /
Richard Locke.
Underground transportation tunnel
for downtown Seattle will
accomodate buses and light rail,
and be serviced by five passenger
stations. Designers and engineers:
Parsons, Brinckerhoff, Quade &
Douglas.
MASS TRANSIT 1990 Sept.-Oct.,
v.17, no.9-10, p.24,26, photo.

TRAPHAGEN, OLIVER B., FL. 1897-1905
A new moon over Moana / Paula Rice
Jackson.
Features the restored interiors of
the 1901 Sheraton Moana Surfrider,
Honolulu. Original architect:
Oliver P. Traphagen. Restoration
architect: Virginia D. Murison.
INTERIORS 1990 Oct., v.150, no.3,
p.68-[71], photos.

TRASH - DISPOSAL OF
See REFUSE AND REFUSE DISPOSAL

TRAUZETTEL, H.
Das Poetische in der Entwurfsarbeit
des Architekten / H. Trauzettel.
English, French, German, and
Russian summaries, p.55-56.
ARCHITEKTUR DER DDR 1989 Dec.,
v.38, no.12, p.34-37, plans,
secn., sketches, biblio.

TRAVEL AGENCIES
See also TICKET OFFICES

TRAVEL BUREAUS
See TRAVEL AGENCIES

TRAVEL DIARIES
Hejduk's Vladivostok [book review] /
Lois E. Nesbitt.
Review of Riga, Vladivostok, Lake
Baikal, in which the author
mingles travel experiences with
graphic and theoretical
exploration.
COLUMBIA UNIVERSITY. GRADUATE
SCHOOL OF ARCHITECTURE, PLANNING
AND PRESERVATION. NEWSLINE 1990
Mar., v.2, no.6, p.8, dwgs.
Viagem / Alvaro Siza Vieira.
Travel sketches reproduced from
book: Alvaro Siza: esquissos de
viagem/travel sketches; 1988.
Catalan, English text.
QUADERNS D'ARQUITECTURA I
URBANISME 1989 Apr.-Sept.,
no.181-182, p.[82]-85, sketches.

TRAVEL DIARIES--18TH CENTURY
William Hodges and the Daniells at
Agra / Pauline Rohatgi.
18th and 19th cent. travellers to
India who published sketches and
diaries.
M-ARG [1989?], v.40, no.4,
p.37-52, plan., engrs., refs.

TRAVEL DIARIES--19TH CENTURY
The travels of Henry Salt and Lord
Valentia in India / Pheroza
Godrej
Published journals include
illustrations by Salt.
MARG [1989?], v.40, no.4, p.71-88,
engrs., biblio.

TRAVEL DIARIES--19TH CENTURY
(CONTINUED)
William Hodges and the Daniells at
Agra / Pauline Rohatgi.
18th and 19th cent. travellers to
India who published sketches and
diaries.
M-ARG [1989?], v.40, no.4,
p.37-52, plan., engrs., refs.

TRAVEL DIARIES--20TH CENTURY
Le Corbusier's epiphany on Mount
Athos / Ivan Zaknic.
On the journey that Corbusier made
to Greece in 1911.
JOURNAL OF ARCHITECTURAL EDUCATION
1990 Summer, v.43, no.4, p.27-36,
ports., photos., plan, sketches,
refs.
Odilon Redon e Venezia / Giuseppina
Dal Canton.
Sketches from his visits in 1900,
1908.
VENEZIA ARTI 1990, v.4, p.107-113,
dwgs., sketches, refs.

TRAVERS MORGAN LANDSCAPE LTD.
Student talent: Travers Morgan
design competition.
Lists winners of design
competition for landscape
architecture students for the
Oxford Science Park. Masterplan
prepared by Travers Morgan.
LANDSCAPE DESIGN 1990 July-Aug.,
no.192, p.27, site plans.

TRAVERS, SHAUN
Returning to a "greener" built
enviromnent / Shaun Travers.
1990 TCPSS prize paper.
THE PLANNER 1990 Dec.14, v.76,
no.49, p.49-55, graphs, ill.,
secns., refs.

TREADAWAY, DAN
Profile of a leader: Trenton's Art
Holland: a leader of mayors / Dan
Treadaway.
AMERICAN CITY & COUNTY 1989 June,
v.104, no.6, p.58-60, port.
Putting the squeeze on America's
land fills / Dan Treadaway.
AMERICAN CITY & COUNTY 1989 Aug.,
v.104, no.8, p.42-50, ill., port.

TREATISES - ARCHITECTURAL
See ARCHITECTURAL LITERATURE

TREBBI, GIORGIO
La pianificazione invisibile = The
invisible planning / Giorgio
Trebbi.
Telecommunication planning,
particularly in Milan.
PARAMETRO 1990 Jan.-Feb., no.176,
p.12-13, maps.
Piano regolatore del Comune di
Trento: relazione generale.
City planning policies for the
expansion of Trent. Coordinators:
Marcello Vittorini, Giorgio
Trebbi. Summaries in French,
English, German, and Spanish, p.1.
Captions in Italian and English.
PARAMETRO 1990 Nov.-Dec., no.181,
p.16-51, maps, photos., plans,
site plans, tables, aerial photos.

TREBBI, GIORGIO (CONTINUED)
Rinnovo urbano: due episodi olandesi = Urban renewal: two Dutch episodes / Giorgio Trebbi.
Bijlmermeer area, Amsterdam, and Witte Dorp housing estate by J. J. P. Oud, in Rotterdam.
PARAMETRO 1989 Sept.-Oct., v.20, no.174, p.10-11, model, photo., site plans.
Tavola rotonda: razionalismo oggi, eredita e tranzione.
A round-table discussion held in conjunction with the exhibition "Enea Manfredini: Architettura 1939-1989," at the Sala Convegni Hotel Posta, Reggio Emilia, Nov.22, 1989. Participants: Giancarlo De Carlo, Enrico Mantero, Riccardo Mariani, and Giorgio Trebbi.
PARAMETRO 1989 Nov.-Dec., v.20, no.175, p.68-79, dets., elevs., models, photos, plans, secns., site plan.

TREBERSPURG, MARTIN, 1953-
Wien.
One of three sections in special feature on "Contemporary Austrian architecture". Architects: Heinz Tesar, Luigi Blau, Franco Fonatti + Helmut Hempel, Sylvia Fritz, Ernst Hoffmann, Gert Mayr-keber, Rudiger Lainer + Gertraud Auer, Ernst Beneder, Georg Reinberg, and Martin Treberspurg.
SPACE DESIGN 1990 Mar., no.306, p.9-46, axonometric views, dwgs., ports., elevs., models, photos., plans, secn.

TREE, CHRISTINA
Windjammer days / Christina Tree.
The preservation of Maine's windjammer fleets.
HISTORIC PRESERVATION 1990 July-Aug., v.42, no.4, p.[22-29], photos.

TREE-RING DATING
See DENDROCHRONOLOGY

TREEHOUSES
See TREE HOUSES

TREES
See also LUMBER
See also TIMBER
Flanderns popler / John Jedbo.
Four examples of the use of rows of poplars, in Flanders, along streets and canals.
LANDSKAB 1990 Feb., v.71, no.1, p.18-21, photos.
Housing planning method attaching importance to conservation and utilization of natural environment [part 1] / Kazuhisa Iki...[et al.].
"Description of environmental impact by construction with an indicatior of tree vitality." Text in Japanese; English summary, p.52.
NIHON KENCHIKU GAKKAI KEIKAKUKEI RONBUN HOKOKU SHU = JOURNAL OF ARCHITECTURE, PLANNING AND ENVIRONMENTAL ENGINEERING 1990 Mar., no.3(409), p.45-52, map, tables, refs.

TREES (CONTINUED)
In defense of street trees / Allan B. Jacobs.
PLACES 1990 Winter, v.6, no.2, p.84-87, elevs., photos., plans, ref.
Il materiale vegetale (Terza parte) / Gilberto Oneto.
VILLE GIARDINI 1990 July-Aug., no.250, p.74-79, dwgs., elevs., photos., plans, site plans.
The old North European "meadow copse" and the English landscape park / Asger Orum-Larsen.
GARDEN HISTORY 1990 Autumn, v.18, no.2, p.[174]-179, photos., plan, sketch, refs.
Temperate and boreal forests: design opportunities with red maple / Jon Bryan Burley.
A review of the uses of plants in interior landscapes (interiorscapes). Includes French summary.
LANDSCAPE ARCHITECTURAL REVIEW 1990 Oct., v.11, no.4, p.20-22, photo., biblio.
Trained tree form / Maggie Roe.
On the use of trained trees in urban spaces.
LANDSCAPE DESIGN 1990 Feb., no.187, p.17-20, dwgs., photos., biblio.
Trees in period gardens / Janet Marinelli.
OLD-HOUSE JOURNAL 1990 Mar.-Apr., v.18, no.2, p.26-27, engrs.

TREES--ENGLAND--LONDON
Trees in London.
Reprinted from the Dec.19, 1890 issue of the journal.
ROYAL SOCIETY OF ARTS, LONDON. RSA JOURNAL 1990 Dec., v.139, no.5413, p.955.

TREES--ICONOGRAPHY
The migration of the palm: a case-study of architectural ornament as a vehicle of meaning / David Watkin.
An examination of this motif, its changing significance, and revivals.
APOLLO 1990 Feb., v.131, no.336, p.78-84, photos., engrs., refs.

TREES IN CITIES
See URBAN FORESTRY

TREES--SYMBOLIC ASPECTS
Zur kulturgeschichtlichen Rolle des Baumes im sakralen Ambiente / Paul Werner.
ARS BAVARICA 1989, v.55-56, p.115-130, ill., photos., engrs., refs.

TREHEARNE & NORMAN
Elementary connection [57 Mansell St., London] / Peter Weatherhead.
Refurbishment of a Georgian townhouse, and of a Victorian warehouse behind it, and conversion into offices for an insurance company. Architect: Trehearne & Norman.
BUILDING 1990 Apr.13, v.255, no.15, p.46-48, photos.

TREIB, MARC, 1943-
Helsinki Jugendstil architecture, 1895-1915 and Armas Lindgren, 1874-1929 [book review] / Marc Treib.
Review of 1987 book by Jonathan Moorhouse et al. and of 1988 book by Riita Nikula.
SOCIETY OF ARCHITECTURAL HISTORIANS. JOURNAL 1990 Sept., v.49, no.3, p.341-343.
Landscape on the edge / Marc Treib.
An essay on landscape architecture in Scandinavia, from a global perspective.
LANDSKAB 1990 May, v.71, no.3-4, p.I-VIII, port., photos., plan, refs.
Osaka Expo misses the park / Marc Treib.
On the follies at the International Garden and Greenery Exposition.
PROGRESSIVE ARCHITECTURE 1990 July, v.71, no.7, p.21-22, photos.
Reduction, elaboration and Yugen: The Garden of Saiho-ji / Marc Trein.
Located in Kyoto.
JOURNAL OF GARDEN HISTORY 1989 Apr.-June, v.9, no.2, p.[95]-101, photos., site plans, refs.

TREISTER, KENNETH
Kenneth Treister: architecture as sculptural environment.
Entire issue on Treister. Discussion of five projects.
FRIENDS OF KEBYAR 1990 Oct.-Dec., v.8.4, no.48, p.3-20, photos., site plan.

TRELLISES
See also ESPALIERS
The timeless appeal of treillage / Glenn Harrell.
Trelliswork.
HOUSE BEAUTIFUL 1990 June, v.132, no.6, p.90-95, photos.

TRESCOTT, JERRY
Restoring a period porch / Jerry Trescott.
OLD-HOUSE JOURNAL 1990 July-Aug, v.18, no.4, p.[41-44], photos.

TRESSERA, JAIME
Eldorado Petit / Regina S. Baraban.
New York restaurant. Architects: Jaime Tressera, Roberto Paulee.
METROPOLIS 1990 Oct., v.10, no.3, p.35, photos.

TRETIACK, PHILIPPE
Portrait de groupe / Philippe Tretiack.
On the group of young French architects featured in the exhibition catalog, 40 architects de moins de 40 ans, sponsored by the Institut Francais d' Architecture. Spanish summary, p.172.
TECHNIQUES ET ARCHITECTURE 1990 Oct.-Nov., no.392, p.72-77, dwgs., elevs., model., photo., plan.

TREVOR SALEEBA & ASSOCIATES
 Earl of Spencer Inn, Albany: Trevor
 Saleeba & Associates.
 Renovation of an 1870 inn.
 ARCHITECTURE AUSTRALIA 1989 Dec.,
 v.78, no.11, p.45, photos., plan.

TRIAD ARCHITECTS PLANNERS
 Healthy in Chelsea / Carl Gardner.
 On the health club in the Conrad
 hotel, London. Architects: TRIAD
 Architects Planners.
 RIBA JOURNAL 1990 Sept., v.97
 no.9, p.70-72,74, photos., secn.

TRIANGLES (FIRM)
 Banking on childcare / Jennifer
 Havinden.
 Woodville Lodge, a workplace
 nursery for Midland Bank in
 Sheffield, which is in a Victorian
 sea captain's house. Architects:
 Triangle.
 RIBA JOURNAL 1990 Mar., v.97,
 no.3, p.58-60, photos.

TRIAS, EUGENIO, 1942- . LIMITES DEL
MUNDO
 La arquitectura del espacio-luz: la
 visualizacion del absoluto = The
 architecture of space-light:
 visualization of the absolute /
 Jose L. Gonzalez Cobelo.
 On Eugenio Trias' work titled "Los
 limites del mundo", which deals
 with space and light.
 EL CROQUIS 1990 Apr.-June, v.9,
 no.43, p.172-176, photo.

TRIBOLO, NICCOLO, 1500-1550
 Niccolo Tribolo nel giardino di
 Castello / Alessandro Conti.
 ANTICHITA VIVA 1989, v.28, no.5-6,
 p.51-61, dets., ill., photos.,
 sketches, refs.

TRICKETT ASSOCIATES
 Standing orders / Mary Powell.
 On exhibition design. Includes
 discussion with three interior
 design firms with exhibition
 design experience: Trickett
 Associates, Din Associates and
 Platform Design.
 DESIGNERS' JOURNAL 1990 Apr.,
 no.56, p.44-47, photos.

TRIFORIUMS--GOTHIC--ENGLAND--
CANTERBURY--CANTERBURY CATHEDRAL
 Some observations on the early
 flying buttress and choir
 triforium of Canterbury Cathedral
 / Yoshio Kusaba.
 Dates from the late 1170s.
 Builder: William of Sens. Includes
 abstract.
 GESTA 1989, v.28, no.2, p.175-189,
 fig., photos., plans, secns.,
 refs.

TRIGGER, BRUCE G.
 Monumental architecture: a
 thermodynamic explanation of
 symbolic behaviour / Bruce G.
 Trigger.
 WORLD ARCHAEOLOGY 1990 Oct., v.22,
 no.2, p.119-132, biblio.

TRINIDAD--TOWNHOUSES--19TH CENTURY
 Home and colonial: flamboyance and
 nostalgia among Trinidad's
 townhouses / Len Mitchell.
 TRADITIONAL HOMES 1990 Mar., v.6,
 no.6, p.127-130, photos.

TRINIDAD--VERNACULAR ARCHITECTURE--
19TH CENTURY
 Home and colonial: flamboyance and
 nostalgia among Trinidad's
 townhouses / Len Mitchell.
 TRADITIONAL HOMES 1990 Mar., v.6,
 no.6, p.127-130, photos.

TRIPE, LINNAEUS
 Linnaeus Tripe: documenting South
 Indian architecture / Janet Dewan.
 HISTORY OF PHOTOGRAPHY 1989
 Apr.-June, v.13, no.2, p.145-156,
 photos., engrs., refs.

TRIPLE-DECKER HOUSES--19TH CENTURY--
CANADA--MONTREAL (QUEBEC)
 Architecture et forme urbaine:
 L'example du triplex a Montreal de
 1870 a 1914 / Rejean Legault.
 URBAN HISTORY REVIEW. / REVUE
 D'HISTOIRE URBAINE 1989 June,
 v.18, no.1, p.1-10, axonometric
 views, maps, plans, refs.

TRIPLE-DECKER HOUSES--20TH CENTURY--
CANADA--MONTREAL (QUEBEC)
 Architecture et forme urbaine:
 L'example du triplex a Montreal de
 1870 a 1914 / Rejean Legault.
 URBAN HISTORY REVIEW. / REVUE
 D'HISTOIRE URBAINE 1989 June,
 v.18, no.1, p.1-10, axonometric
 views, maps, plans, refs.

TRIPLE-DECKER HOUSES--UNITED STATES
 Rediscovering the three decker house
 / Howard Husock.
 Potential of "the common New
 England three family houses or
 'three deckers'" in the search for
 more private low- and
 moderate-income housing.
 THE PUBLIC INTEREST 1990 Winter,
 no.98, p.49-60, tables, refs.

TRIPLE-DECKER HOUSES--UNITED STATES--
PORTLAND (MAINE)--PARKSIDE
 Parkside / Arthur Gerrier.
 Survey of houses and history of
 the area of Portland, Maine,
 between Deering St. and Deering
 Oaks Park. Written prior to the
 author's death on Oct.15,1990.
 LANDMARKS OBSERVER 1990 Fall,
 v.16, no.4, p.5-9, photos.

TRIPLE-DECKERS
 See TRIPLE-DECKER HOUSES

TRIPPLE, PATRICIA
 The need to internationalize housing
 programs / Carole J. Makela,
 Patricia Tripple.
 HOUSING AND SOCIETY 1989, v.16,
 no.3, p.57-61, refs.

TRIPPLE, PATRICIA A.
 Elder-cottage housing: a housing
 alternative for the older
 population / Patricia A.
 Tripple...et al.
 Small, free-standing removable
 housing units designed for one or
 two elderly occupants, usually
 (Continued next column)

TRIPPLE, PATRICIA A. (CONTINUED)
 Elder-cottage...(CONTINUED)
 located near an existing
 single-family detached house.
 Known in some places as "granny
 flats".
 HOUSING AND SOCIETY 1990, v.17,
 no.2, p.17-31, tables, refs.

TRIVEDI, AMRITBHAI
 A master builder: Amritbhai Sompura
 [interview] / A. G. Krishna Menon.
 The ca. 80-year old architect of
 temples, also known by the surname
 Trivedi.
 ARCHITECTURE + DESIGN 1989
 Nov.-Dec., v.6, no.1, p.121,123,
 port., secn.

TROGER, PAUL
 Darum Sichtinstallation:
 medizinische Fakultat der
 Technischen Hochschule Aachen.
 Architects: Jurgen Kunz with Paul
 Troger and Wolfgang Weber.
 Includes English summary.
 DETAIL 1990 Dec.-1991 Jan., v.30,
 no.6, p.581-584, dwgs., photos.,
 secns., isometric dwgs.

TROIS, CHARLES
 Modern Mayan in Texas: an artist's
 design for a stone house outside
 Austin / Michael Ennis.
 Charles Trois' home/studio.
 ARCHITECTURAL DIGEST 1990 Sept.,
 v.47, no.10, p.[218-224], port.,
 photos.

TROITINO, MIGUEL ANGEL
 Plan especial del centro historico
 de Teruel / J. M. Alonso Velasco,
 M. A. Troitino, I. Gonzalez
 Adalid.
 URBANISMO / COAM 1990 Jan., no.9,
 p.80-90, photos., site plan, map.

TROJAN, KLAUS
 Gestaltung der Ortsmitte und
 Rathauserweiterung in Elz = Design
 of the town center and city hall
 extension in Elz.
 Competition. Winning architects:
 Klaus and Verena Trojan. Text in
 German.
 ARCHITEKTUR + WETTBEWERBE 1990
 Dec., no.144, p.68-71, elevs.,
 models, photo., plans, site plans.

TROJAN, VERENA
 Gestaltung der Ortsmitte und
 Rathauserweiterung in Elz = Design
 of the town center and city hall
 extension in Elz.
 Competition. Winning architects:
 Klaus and Verena Trojan. Text in
 German.
 ARCHITEKTUR + WETTBEWERBE 1990
 Dec., no.144, p.68-71, elevs.,
 models, photo., plans, site plans.

TROLDNER, JORG D.
 Zuganglich: Neubau der
 Hauptverwaltung der Volksbank
 Baden-Baden EG.
 Architects: Kurt E. Walker, Jorg
 D. Troldner.
 ARCHITEKTUR, INNENARCHITEKTUR,
 TECHNISCHER AUSBAU 1990 Dec.,
 v.98, no.12, p.52-53, photos.,
 plans.

TROTT, RICHARD (CONTINUED)
Special feature:...(CONTINUED)
Eisenman / Ignasi de
Sola-Morales.-- A matter of
respect.-- Works: Wexner Center
for the Visual Arts, Ohio State
University.-- Columbus Convention
Center.-- Banyoles Olympic Hotel
competition.-- College of Design,
Architecture, Art and Planning,
University of Cincinnati.--
Interview: Peter Eisenman / Jeff
Kipnis. Text in Japanese and
English.
ARCHITECTURE AND URBANISM 1990
Jan., no.1(232), p.[7]-182,
axonometric views, elevs., models,
photos., plans, secns., sketches.
Wexner-Zentrum der visuellen Kunste
und Bibliothek in Columbus/Ohio,
USA = Wexner Centre for the Visual
Arts and Fine Arts Library in
Columbus/Ohio, USA.
Architects: Peter Eisenman,
Richard Trott.
ARCHITEKTUR + WETTBEWERBE 1990
Sept., no.143, p.6-7, photos.,
plan.

TROTTER, ROBERT T.
Cultural resource work at Wupatki
National Monument / Steve
Cinnamon.
In north central Arizona. Includes
essays by Muriel Crespi and Robert
T. Trotter, II.
CRM BULLETIN: A NATIONAL PARK
SERVICE TECHNICAL BULLETIN 1989,
v.12, no.6, p.5-8, photo.

TROUGHTON MCASLAN ARCHITECTS
Alternative show at the station.
Redevelopment of Edinburgh's
Waverley station. Architects:
Troughton McAslan; masterplan by
BDP. Based on previous
competition: "Waverley Challenge".
ARCHITECTS' JOURNAL 1990
Aug.22-29, v.192, no.7-8, p.12,
dwg., aerial photo.
Cornering the market / John Welsh.
Features the winning design of a
small office block for the
Lipstick site in the London
Docklands. Architects: Troughton
McAslan.
BUILDING DESIGN 1990 July 13,
no.994, p.12,14-15, axonometric
view, dwg., model, plans.
Ecologia arquitectonica: oficinas y
almacen proyectados por
Troughton-McAslan.
Offices and warehouse of Alexander
House, London. English text,
p.176. In "On oficina", 1990
supplement issue.
ON DISENO 1990, suppl., p.98-101,
photos., plan, secn.
Industrial appeal: nel magazzino
vittoriano = industrial appeal: in
a Victorian warehouse.
Warehouse at 3 St. Peters St.,
Islington, converted to the
offices of an ad agency.
Architects: Jamie troughton and
John McAslan, with Mark Wilson.
ABITARE 1990 Dec., no.291,
p.82-87, axonometric view, elevs.,
photos., plans.

TROUGHTON MCASLAN ARCHITECTS
(CONTINUED)
Of mice and men / Callum Murray,
Karen Salman, Charlotte Ellis.
Profiles of British firms John
Winter and Associates, YRM
Partnership, Eric Parry: EP
Associates, Troughton McAslan, Eva
Jiricna, Richard Rogers, and Jean
Nouvel and their approaches to
architectural design for the
series "How architects design."
ARCHITECTS' JOURNAL 1990
Dec.19-26, v.192, no.25-26,
p.24-37, axonometric views, dets.,
dwgs., ports., model, photos.,
secn.
Poets of pragmatism [Troughton
McAslan Architects] / Rowan Moore.
BLUEPRINT (LONDON, ENGLAND) 1990
June, no.68, p.32-35, photos.
Portfolio: recent work of Troughton
McAslan / Thomas Fisher.
Includes three London projects: 3
Saint Peters Street, 18 Pond Place
and 155 Merton Road.
PROGRESSIVE ARCHITECTURE 1990
Apr., v.71, no.4, p.94-99,
axonometric views, photos., plans,
secns.
St. Catherine's at Kobe / Dan
Cruickshank.
First Oxford University building
constructed outside of the city is
St. Catherine's College in Kobe,
Japan. Troughton McAslan
Architects.
ARCHITECTS' JOURNAL 1990 Nov.7,
v.192, no.19, p.26-29, axonometric
view, dwgs., elev., models, secn.

TROUSSEL, JEAN-FRANCOIS
L'art domestique a Rennes autour de
1910 / Jean-Francois Troussel.
HISTOIRE DE L'ART 1990 May,
no.9-10, p.89-98, photos.

TROVATO, CARMELO NINO
Piano e amministrazione: ie piano
regolatore generale di Trieste,
1934 / Giovanni Delise, Carmelo
Nino Trovato.
One of four case studies in
northeastern Italy.
STORIA URBANA 1990 Apr.-June,
v.14, no.51, p.[155]-187, dwgs.,
models, photos., site plans, refs.

TROY, PATRICK N.
The greenhouse effect and the city /
Patrick N. Troy.
AUSTRALIAN PLANNER: JOURNAL OF THE
ROYAL AUSTRALIAN PLANNING
INSTITUTE 1990 Mar., v.28, no.1,
p.17-22, biblio.

TRUDNAK, STEVE
Regional style: eco-logic at work.
A brief survey of six
"environmental" gardens in the
U.S. Landscape architects: Steven
K. Domigan, Edith Eddleman, Ron
Lutsco, Steve Trudnak, James Weht,
and David Cropp.
GARDEN DESIGN 1990 spring, v.9,
no.1, p.46-59, photos., site
plans, sketch.

TRUJILLO JARMILLO, SERGIO
Edificio em Bogota quer manter
tradicao local: Edificio Lina
Paola, 1984, Bogota, Colombia.
Architects: Juan Gutierrez A., G.
Rodriquez Amayo, S. Jaramillo.
PROJETO 1989 June, no.122,
p.98-100, axonometric view,
elevs., photos, plans, secns.,
elevs., site plans.

TRUMBULL ARCHITECTS
Best Small House 1990 / Susan Zevon,
Katie Ridder.
Competition sponsored by HB and
the American Wood Council. Winning
house in Amenia, N.Y. by Jonathan
Lanman and Debra Wassman of
Trumbull Architects, N.Y.C.
Interior designer: Paul Leonard.
HOUSE BEAUTIFUL 1990 Nov., v.132,
no.11, p.81-91, photos., plans.

TRUMBULL, JEFF
RAIA Gold Medal 1990: Peter
McIntyre.
Most of issue devoted to this
architect. Contents: Struggle for
Meaning, 1990 speech by McIntyre
-- Optimism and experiment / by
Philip Goad--works 1950-1990 --
Dinner Plain /by Jeff Trumbull.
ARCHITECTURE AUSTRALIA 1990 June,
v.79, no.5, p.29-62, ill., dwgs.,
ports., elevs., models, photos.,
plans, secns., site plans, refs.

TRUMBULL, MARK
Professor David Skinner: a personal
appreciation [obituary] / Mark
Trumbull.
LANDSCAPE DESIGN 1989 Apr.,
no.179, p.57.

TRUMP, DONALD
Trump Taj Mahal: the new jewel of
Atlantic City / Patric Dolan.
Project architect: Francis Xavier
Dumont. Developer: Donald J.
Trump.
REAL ESTATE FORUM 1990 Mar., v.45,
no.3, p.44-50, ports., photos.

TRUMPLER, STEFAN. NEUE FORSCHUNGEN ZU
MOISSAC
Stefan Trumpler: Neue Forschungen zu
Moissac.
Review of a 1987 Ph.D. thesis from
Bern.
DAS MUNSTER 1990, v.43, no.2,
p.166-167, engr.

TRUPPIN, ANDREA
Starck struck / Andrea Truppin.
Profile of the work of Philippe
Starck.
INTERIORS 1989 Feb., v.148, no.7,
p.121-129,156, photos.

TRUSCOTT, JAMES S.
Inspiration for an artist / James
Truscott.
COUNTRY LIFE 1990 Mar.1, v.184,
no.9, p.86-91, photos., site plan.
No resting on laurels / James
Truscott.
Site: Friockheim, By Forfar,
Angus.
COUNTRY LIFE 1990 July 12, v.184,
no.28, p.74-79, site plan.

TRUSCOTT, JAMES S. (CONTINUED)
Tableau of the gardener's art
[Halecat House] / James Truscott.
Site: 10 mi. s.w. of Kendal,
Cumbria.
COUNTRY LIFE 1990 June 14, v.184,
no.24, p.268-271, photos.
Within the garden walls / James S.
Truscott.
Gardens at Biddick Hall, Durham.
COUNTRY LIFE 1990 June 7, v.184,
no.23, p.134-137, photos.

TRUSS BRIDGES
See BRIDGES - TRUSS

TRUSSED RAFTER ROOFS
Un tunnel sulla stazione = The
Waterloo enclosure / Maurizio
Vogliazzo.
New international train terminal
of Waterloo Station, London.
Architects: Nicholas Grimshaw &
Partners. Structural engineers:
YRM, Anthony Hunt Associates. Text
in Italian and English.
L'ARCA 1990 Sept., no.41, p.26-39,
dwgs., models, photos., plans,
secns., site plan.

TRUSSES
See also HAMMER-BEAM ROOFS
See also OPEN TRUSS BEAMS
See also TRUSSED RAFTER ROOFS
Ampliamento di uno stabilimento
industriale ad Aylesbury, G.B. = A
new headquarter extension for
Schwarzkopf Ltd., Great Britain /
Silvano Stucchi.
A hairdressing products firm.
Architect: Denton Scott
Associates.
L'INDUSTRIA DELLE COSTRUZIONI 1990
Feb., v.24, no.220, p.28-37,cover,
dets., elev., photos., plans,
secns.
Ranch-house add-up / April Tome,
Peter Siegrist.
Addition designed by the architect
authors for their house in
Greenwich, Conn.
FINE HOMEBUILDING 1989 Aug.,
no.55, p.69, dets., photo.
Una trave "reattiva" = Responsive
trusses / Christopher McCarthy,
Andrew Whalley.
Experimental "responsive truss"
design; architects: Fiona
Galbraith, Christopher McCarthy,
Andrew Whalley.
L'ARCA 1990 Oct., no.42, p.56-61,
diagrs., dwgs, model.

TRUSSES--STEEL
Steel trusses, pre- and early-
history museum, Frankfurt, West
Germany.
Steel trusses in museum roof
replace the original stone vaults
which were destroyed by fire
during WWII. Architect: Josef Paul
Kleihues.
PROGRESSIVE ARCHITECTURE 1990 May,
v.71, no.5, p.93, dets., photo.,
secn.

TRUSSES--WOODEN
Verbindungen im Holzbau / Kurt
Schwaner.
DER ARCHITEKT 1990 May, no.5,
p.256-260, dets., photos.

TRUSSES--WOODEN--MEDIEVAL--ENGLAND--
LONDON--WESTMINSTER HALL
The Westminster Hall roof: a new
archaeological source / Lynn T.
Courtenay.
Includes discussion of a
restoration done 1913-22 by Sir
Frank Baines. Original architect:
Hugh Herland.
BRITISH ARCHAEOLOGICAL
ASSOCIATION. JOURNAL 1990, v.143,
p.[95]-111,pl.18, dets., photos.,
secns., refs.

TSAKIRGIS, BARBARA
The decorated pavements of
Morgantina II: the Opus Signinum /
Barbara Tsakirgis.
AMERICAN JOURNAL OF ARCHAEOLOGY
1990 July, v.94, no.3, p.425-443,
photos., plans, refs.

TSALIKIDIS, IOANNIS A.
Gardens of eclectic villas in
Thessaloniki: a concept of
landscaping in the Southern
Balkans in the Late 19th Century /
Ioannis A. Tsalikidis.
LANDSCAPE JOURNAL 1990 Spring,
v.9, no.1, p.28-41, maps, photos.,
site plan, refs.

TSCHAIDSE, ASLAN
Reihenhausumbau in Munchen.
Architects: H. Fischer, L.
Stieger, A. Tschaidse. Includes
English summary.
BAUMEISTER 1990 May, v.87, no.5,
p.56-58, elevs., photos., plans,
secns.

TSCHERNIA, DAN. HOMMAGE A L'HUMANITE
Blessures de l'arche [film review].
On the film about Johan Otto Von
Spreckelsen, Hommage a l'humanite,
shown at the Fifarc Festival.
Producer: Dan Tschernia.
ARCHITECTURE D'AUJOURD'HUI 1990
Sept., no.270, p.50, ports.

TSCHOLL, WERNER
Giovani architetti di montagna =
Young mountain architects.
Examples of work by South Tyrolean
architects, Josef Kostner, Werner
Tscholl, C. Mayr-Fingerle, and
Walter Dietl.
ABITARE 1990 Dec., no.291,
p.116-133, photos., plans, secns.,
elevs.

TSCHUMI, BERNARD, 1944-
"Es hora de cambiar" = It's time for
change: Bernard Tschumi
[interview] / Marta Cervello.
QUADERNS D'ARQUITECTURA I
URBANISME 1990 Jan.-Feb.-Mar.,
no.184, p.13-22, site plans.
Gekooid: clips in pavilijoens /
Camiel van Winkel.
Five projects for "video clips"
(kiosks or pavilions) in
Groningen. Co-sponsor: Groninger
Museum. Architects: Zaha Hadid,
Peter Eisenman, Bernard Tschumi,
Rem Koolhaas, and Coop Himmelblau.
(Continued next column)

TSCHUMI, BERNARD, 1944- (CONTINUED)
Gekooid: clips in...(CONTINUED)
ARCHIS 1990 Oct., no.10, p.4-5,
photos.
Passepartout: mellem den tekniske og
den kunsteriske tegning = In
between the technical and the
artistic drawing / Lars Morell.
Refers to the article in no.20 of
Skala, and to the work of D.
Libeskind, B. Tschumi, and P.
Eisenman. In Danish and English.
SKALA 1990, no.21, p.36-39, dwgs.
La terminal de la isla: concurso del
aeropuerto de Kansai / Vittorio
Magnago Lampugnani.
Entries by Renzo Piano, O.M.
Ungers, Henry Cobb, Bernard
Tschumi, Cesar Pelli, Jean Nouvel,
and Norman Foster.
ARQUITECTURA VIVA 1990 May-June,
no.12, p.14-18, axonometric views,
elevs., models, plans, secns.
Theory and practice [interview].
Oculus interviews 6 "theoretical
practitioners," asking whether
theory and practice can be
integrated in architectural work.
Architects: Peter Eisenman,
Bernard Tschumi, Diana Agrest,
Mario Gandelsonas, Marwan
Al-Sayed, and Thomas Leeser.
OCULUS 1990 Nov., v.53, no.3,
p.6-10, axonometric view, dwgs.,
ports., model, site plan.
Transpositions: on the intellectual
origins of Tschumi's architectural
theory / Louis Martin.
On French activists, Roland
Barthes, Jacques Derrida and
others influencing Tschumi in the
1970's.
ASSEMBLAGE 1990 Apr., no.11,
p.[22]-35, refs.
Urban architectural theory and the
contemporary city: Tschumi and
Koolhaas at the Parc de la
Villette / Richard Dagenhart.
EKISTICS 1989 Jan.-Apr., v.56,
no.334-335, p.84-92, axonometric
view, diagrs., plans, site plans,
refs.
What a wonderful world / Elke von
Radziewsky.
Features the five Video pavilions
in Groningen designed by the
following architects: Peter
Eisenman, Bernard Tschumi, Zaha
Hadid, Coop Himmelblau and Rem
Koolhaas. English summary, p.5.
ARCHITEKTUR & WOHNEN 1990
Dec.-1991 Jan., no.6, p.144-148,
photos.
What a wonderful world:
Videopaviljoens in Groningen / Jos
Roodbol.
Small pavilions at five sites.
Architects: Coop Himmelblau, Peter
Eisenman, Bernard Tschumi, Zaha
Hadid, and Rem Koolhaas.
DE ARCHITECT 1990 Oct., v.21,
no.10, p.54-59, photos., site
plan.
Zentrum fur Kunst und
Medientechnologie, Karlsruhe /
Heinrich Klotz.
Results of the 1989 ZKM
competition. Winner: Rem Koolhaas.
Entries by Julia Bolles-Wilson,
Bernard Tschumi, Coop Himmelblau,
Rossmann und Partner,
Haus-Rucker-Co, and Albert Speer +
(Continued next page)

TSCHUMI, BERNARD, 1944- (CONTINUED)
Zentrum fur Kunst und (CONTINUED)
Partner.
BAUWELT 1989 Dec.22, v.80, no.48,
p.2264-2275, ill., elevs., models,
plans, site plans, isometric dwg.

TSCHUMI, JEAN, 1904-1962
Reklame & architektur / Jacques
Gubler.
The architectural image as a relay
of economic and political power.
RASSEGNA 1990 Sept., v.12,
no.43/3, p.6-11, dwgs., engrs.

TSIEN, BILLIE
Extending the architectural impulse
into interior design.
Features comments by Billie Tsien,
Michael Graves, Arthur Erickson,
Tod Williams, Fred Schwartz, Roger
Ferri, Allan Greenberg, Frank
Israel, and Christopher Rudolph.
ARCHITECTURAL DIGEST 1990 Dec.,
v.47, no.13, p.58,62,68,72,76,78,
photos.
Tod Williams, Billie Tsien: Domestic
Arrangements.
The architects discuss their house
on exhibit at the Walker Art
Center and the Whitney Museum. In
Italian and English.
DOMUS 1990 June, no.717,
p.[58-65], photos., plan.
Tod Williams - Billie Tsien
[interview] / Kate Nesbitt.
Illustrates three projects: Arts
Park Center, Los Angeles; Feinberg
Hall, Princeton University; Tarlo
House, Sagaponack, N.Y. In Danish
and English.
SKALA 1990, no.20, p.34-39,
models, photos., refs.
Urbanist without Portfolio: Notes on
a career / by Jane Thompson.
One of four sections in a special
feature on "Women in American
Architecture". Contents: Marion G.
Weiss.-- Inea Elskop/1100
Architect. Billie Tsien.--
Patricia Sapinsley.--Alison
Sky+Michelle Stone/SITE Projects,
Inc.--Karen Bausman+Leslie Gill.--
Deborah Berke.--Amy Weinstein.--
Adele Naude Santos. English
translation, p.73.
SPACE DESIGN 1990 June, no.309,
p.36-53,73, axonometric views,
dwgs., ports., elevs., models,
photos., plans, secns.

TSINGHUA UNIVERSITY. ARCHITECTURE
COLLEGE
Boxing-match hall for 1990 Asian
Games / Lin Amei.
A multi-functional gymnasium of
the Beijing Institute of Physical
Education completed late in 1988.
Architects: Architecture College
of Tsinghua University and
Architectural Design Institute of
the Chinese Academy of Sciences.
BUILDING IN CHINA 1990 Sept., v.3,
no.3, p.42-44,[1 p. insert],
photos., plan.

TSIOMIS, YANNIS
Tsiomis a Villecroze / Brumo Suner.
On the Academie musicale de
Villecroze, including the student
housing. Architect: Yannis
Tsiomis. English summary, p.185.
ARCHITECTURE D'AUJOURD'HUI 1990
Feb., no.267, p.[182]-189, dets.,
photos., elevs., plans, secns.,
site plans.

TSUBARI, VERA
Tribute: plan evaluation method: an
essay in memory of Morris (Moshe)
Hill / Daniel Shefer, Vera
Tsubari.
Includes complete bibliography of
the works of Morris Hill.
JOURNAL OF PLANNING EDUCATION AND
RESEARCH 1990 Fall, v.10, no.1,
p.5-14, biblio., refs.

TSUCHIDA, MITSUYOSHI
On the character of the early
churches centered in Nagasaki
prefecture / Hideto Kawakami,
Mitsuyoshi Tsuchida, Michio
Maekawa.
Characteristics of six churches
"built in about the 10's of the
Meiji era". English summary,
p.164.
NIHON KENCHIKU GAKKAI KEIKAKUKEI
RONBUN HOKOKU SHU = JOURNAL OF
ARCHITECTURE, PLANNING AND
ENVIRONMENTAL ENGINEERING 1990
Feb., no.2(408), p.157-164,
elevs., plans, secns., tables,
refs.

TSUDA, MICHIKO
Prospects of residential movement of
the wooden apartment inhabitants /
Michiko Tsuda, Haruo Nagamine.
"A report on the household
characteristics of the wooden
apartments compared with the
renewed houses, part 3." Text in
Japanese; includes English
summary.
NIHON KENCHIKU GAKKAI KEIKAKUKEI
RONBUN HOKOKU SHU = JOURNAL OF
ARCHITECTURE, PLANNING AND
ENVIRONMENTAL ENGINEERING 1990
June [July], no.7(413), p.129-138,
tables.

TSUDA, YOSHIKI
The planning form and the scale of
the farm houses in the Edo period
from the historical materials of
Nikkou Shasan / Yoshiki Tsuda,
Kiyoshi Hirai.
Text in Japanese. Includes English
summary.
NIHON KENCHIKU GAKKAI KEIKAKUKEI
RONBUN HOKOKU SHU = JOURNAL OF
ARCHITECTURE, PLANNING AND
ENVIRONMENTAL ENGINEERING 1990
June [July], no.7(413), p.175-188,
graphs, map, tables.
Prosperity and decline of the Buntou
style of the farm house from the
historicals of Nikkou Shasan /
Yoshiki Tsuda.
In the Utsunomia district at the
beginning of the 18th century.
Text in Japanese; includes English
summary.
NIHON KENCHIKU GAKKAI KEIKAKUKEI
RONBUN HOKOKU SHU = JOURNAL OF
ARCHITECTURE, PLANNING AND
(Continued next column)

TSUDA, YOSHIKI (CONTINUED)
Prosperity and...(CONTINUED)
ENVIRONMENTAL ENGINEERING 1990
Oct., no.10(416), p.93-99, graphs,
plans, refs.

TSUKIDATE, TOSHIEI
A study on the transform-process of
the eaves-style of traditional
farmhouses from a point of view of
wind and snow damage at Kuroishi
Clan, Aomori prefecture / Toshiei
Tsukidate.
Text in Japanese. Includes English
summary.
NIHON KENCHIKU GAKKAI KEIKAKUKEI
RONBUN HOKOKU SHU = JOURNAL OF
ARCHITECTURE, PLANNING AND
ENVIRONMENTAL ENGINEERING 1990
Sept., no.9(415), p.153-160,
dets., map, photos., tables, refs.

TSUMITA, HIROSHI
A study of partitive points-analysis
and physical-analysis in approach
spaces of Shinto shrines [part 1]
/ Tohru Funakoshi, Hiroshi
Tsumita, Misako Shimizu.
Text in Japanese. English summary,
p.62.
NIHON KENCHIKU GAKKAI KEIKAKUKEI
RONBUN HOKOKU SHU = JOURNAL OF
ARCHITECTURE, PLANNING AND
ENVIRONMENTAL ENGINEERING 1988
Feb., no.2(384), p.53-62, site
plans, charts, tables, graphs,
dwgs.

TSUTSUMI, JUN-ICHIRO
Combined effect of earth cooling and
ventilation on passive cooling of
dwellings (continued report) /
Tadahisa Katayama et al.
English summary, p.83.
NIHON KENCHIKU GAKKAI KEIKAKUKEI
RONBUN HOKOKU SHU = JOURNAL OF
ARCHITECTURE, PLANNING AND
ENVIRONMENTAL ENGINEERING 1990
Jan., no.1(407), p.75-83, figs.,
graphs, tables, refs.

TUBELLO, LUCIANO
Il restauro dell'altare di
Sant'Ignazio al Gesu / Luciano
Tubello.
Artist and architect: Andrea
Pozzo.
L'URBE: RIVISTA ROMANA DI STORIA,
ARTE, LETTERE, COSTUMANZE 1989
Sept.-Dec., v.52, nos.5-6, p.5-10,
photos., engr.

TUBS
See BATHTUBS

TUBY, JEAN BAPPTISTE, I, 1635-1700
Les artistes de l'entree de Louis
XIV en 1660 / Christoph Frank.
On the architects and artists of
the temporary structures erected
for Louis XIV's celebrated
procession through Paris on August
26, 1660, as recorded in archival
documents in the Archives
Nationals.
SOCIETE DE L'HISTOIRE DE L'ART
FRANCAIS. BULLETIN 1990,
p.[53]-74, dwgs., engrs., refs.

TUCK HINTON EVERTON ARCHITECTS
All'ombra dei grattacieli fra i
reperti del produrre / Nicola
Anguilano.
148-unit housing development in a
former industrial area of
Nashville, Tenn. Architects: Tuck
Hinton Everton.
VILLE GIARDINI 1990 Sept., no.251,
p.10-17, axonometric views, dwgs.,
photos., plans, secns., site
plans.
Riverfront Apartments, Nashville.
Architects: Tuck Hinton Everton
Architects. Text in Italian and
English.
LOTUS INTERNATIONAL 1990, no.66,
p.58-65, axonometric views,
elevs., photos., plans, site plan.

TUCK, JAMES A.
A sixteenth century Basque whaling
port in southern Labrador [Red
Bay] / Judith A. Logan, James A.
Tuck.
ASSOCIATION FOR PRESERVATION
TECHNOLOGY. BULLETIN 1990, v.22,
no.3, p.65-72, photos., refs.,
site plan.

TUCKER, BARBARA
Personnel: finding professionals /
Barbara Tucker.
PROGRESSIVE ARCHITECTURE 1990
Jan., v.71, no.1, p.53-54,56,

TUCKER, ELIZABETH
Maison du Cygne: metamorphosis on
the Georgia Coast / Helen C.
Griffith.
Rosemary Anderson house, Sea
Island. Architect for renovations:
John Shackelford of William Frank
McCall Architects and Interior
Designer: Elizabeth Tucker.
SOUTHERN ACCENTS 1990 July-Aug.,
v.13, no.6, p.76-83, photos.

TUDOR
See "TUDOR" AS A SUBHEADING AFTER
SPECIFIC BUILDING TYPES OR OTHER
MAIN HEADINGS.

TUDOR REVIVAL
See "TUDOR REVIVAL" AS A SUBHEADING
AFTER SPECIFIC BUILDING TYPES OR
OTHER MAIN HEADINGS.

TUGHLAK
See TUGHLAQ

TUGHLAQ
See "TUGHLAQ" AS A SUBHEADING AFTER
SPECIFIC BUILDING TYPES OR OTHER
MAIN HEADINGS.

TUGNUTT, TONY
The American invasion / Andrew
Rabeneck.
Urban developments in Britain,
particularly London, are
increasingly commissioned to
American architectural firms.
Responses by Richard MacCormac,
Tony Tugnutt and Leon Krier.
ARCHITECTS' JOURNAL 1990 Mar.28,
v.191, no.13, p.[36]-57, dets.,
dwgs., models, photos., plans,
sketches, tables, refs.

TUMMARELLO, BIANCA MARIA
Foro Traiano.
Eleven articles on the Forum of
Trajan including historical and
architectural reconstructions.
Authors: L. Messa, L. Ungaro, M.
Milella, P. Pensabene, G.
Piazzesi, B.M. Tummarello, S.
Stucchi.
ARCHAEOLOGIA CLASSICA 1989, v.41,
no.2, p.[27]-292, dets., dwgs.,
models, maps, plans, site plans,
recont. dwgs., refs.

TUMULI
See also TELLS

TUMULI--PHRYGIAN--TURKEY--GORDION--
TUMULUS MM
"Midas' bed" and a royal Phrygian
funeral / Elizabeth Simpson.
A reexamination of the furniture
at Tumulus MM at Gordion, Turkey.
JOURNAL OF FIELD ARCHAEOLOGY 1990
spring, v.17, no.1, p.69-87,
axonometric view, figs., dwgs.,
map, photos., reconst. dwgs.,
biblio.

TUMULUS
See TUMULI

TUMULUS TOMBS
See TUMULI

TUNA, NUMAN
Ein Heiligtum bei Alt-Knidos /
Dietrich Berges, Numan Tuna.
Report on excavations of terraces,
Burgaz, Turkey.
ARCHAOLOGISCHER ANZEIGER 1990,
no.1, p.[19]-35, maps, photos.,
refs.

TUNG, ANTHONY MAX
The Historic City Report: ignoring
the lessons of history / Anthony
Max Tung.
Includes text of the report "New
York: The Historic City", prepared
by The NYC Landmarks Preservation
Commission, Feb.6,1989.
VILLAGE VIEWS 1989, v.5, no.4,
p.2-55, chart., graphs, port.

TUNISIA--FORTIFICATION--BYZANTINE
Byzantinische Befootigungen in
Algerien und Tunesien / Erwin M
Ruprechtsberger.
ANTIKE WELT 1989, v.20, no.1,
p.3-21, photos, refs.

TUNISIA--KERKOUANE--CITIES AND TOWNS--
ANCIENT
Kerkouane cite punique / M'hamed
Fantar.
ARCHEOLOGIA 1989 Sept., no.249,
p.[26]-37, photos., map.

TUNISIA--KERKOUANE--EXCAVATIONS
(ARCHAEOLOGY)
Kerkouane cite punique / M'hamed
Fantar.
ARCHEOLOGIA 1989 Sept., no.249,
p.[26]-37, photos., map.

TUNISIA--MAHDIYA--RESORTS--SEASIDE--
MOEZ HOTEL
El Moez Hotel, Mahdiya.
Located on the coast in Tunisia.
Completed in Dec.1984. Architects:
Tarek Ben Miled, Wassim Ben
Mahmoud.
MIMAR: ARCHITECTURE IN DEVELOPMENT
1990 Sept., v.10, no.3(36),
p.55-59, map, photos., plan.

TUNISIA--TUNIS--HOUSING POLICY
Housing needs and policies in Tunis
/ Richard Lawless.
EKISTICS 1986 May-Aug., v.53,
no.318-319, p.157-161, map,
photos, refs.

TUNISIA--TUNIS--HOUSING--SOCIOLOGICAL
ASPECTS
Housing needs and policies in Tunis
/ Richard Lawless.
EKISTICS 1986 May-Aug., v.53,
no.318-319, p.157-161, map,
photos, refs.

TUNNARD, CHRISTOPHER GARDENS IN THE
MODERN LANDSCAPE LANDSCAPE
Strident modernism/ambivalent
reconsiderations: Christopher
Tunnard's Gardens in the modern
landscape / Lance M. Neckar.
On a 1938 book published in
Britain.
JOURNAL OF GARDEN HISTORY 1990
Oct.-Dec., v.10, no.4, p.237-246,
photos., aerial photo., refs.

TUNNELS
See also PEDESTRIAN TUNNELS
See also RAILROAD TUNNELS
See also SUBWAY TUNNELS
See also TUNNELING
See also UNDERPASSES
See also WATER TUNNELS
See also WIND TUNNELS

TUNNELS--ECONOMIC ASPECTS--ENGLAND--
ENGLISH CHANNEL TUNNEL
The plight at the end of the tunnel
/ Michael Nutley.
On above-ground projects in Dover
and Folkestone associated with
economic changes expected after
the Channel Tunnel opens.
BUILDING 1990 Jan.19, v.255, no.3,
p.26-27, dwgs., port., model.

TUNNELS--ENGLAND--ENGLISH CHANNEL
TUNNEL
Risk analysis for the Channel Tunnel
/ Douglas Parkes, Charles Milloy.
THE ARUP JOURNAL 1989 Spring,
v.24, no.1, p.21-23, ill., secns.

TUNNELS--ENVIRONMENTAL ASPECTS--SWEDEN
Influence of pollution on mortar and
concrete / Satish Chandra.
Analysis of effects of, and
remedies for, atmospheric gases,
using several bridges and tunnels
in Sweden as examples. Includes
Swedish summary.
SWEDISH COUNCIL FOR BUILDING
RESEARCH. DOCUMENT 1990, D6,
p.1-83, diagrs., graphs, photos.,
secn., table, biblio.

TUNNELS--FRANCE--LA MANCHE
Risk analysis for the Channel Tunnel / Douglas Parkes, Charles Milloy. THE ARUP JOURNAL 1989 Spring, v.24, no.1, p.21-23, ill., secns.

TUNNELS--GERMANY (WEST)--MUNICH--BRUDERMUHLSTRASSE
Stadt und Verkehr.
Special issue on towns and traffic. 22 projects illustrated. English summary, p.53.
BAUMEISTER 1990 Aug., v.87, no.8, p.13-53, dwgs., models, photos., plans, secns., site plans, aerial photos.

TUNNELS--HONG KONG--EASTERN HARBOUR TUNNEL
Start your engines: the Eastern Harbour Tunnel / Edward Donoghue. ASIAN ARCHITECT AND CONTRACTOR 1989 Aug., v.19, no.8, p.12-20, cover, diagr., dwg., port., model, photos, secn.

TUNNELS--ITALY--TRENTO
Giancarlo De Carlo: Pizza della Mostra a Trento.
In Italian and English.
DOMUS 1990 May, no.716, p.[40]-45, dets., models, secns., site plans, aerial photo.

TUNNELS--UNITED STATES--SEATTLE (WASHINGTON)--METRO TUNNEL
Seattle Metro Tunnel: state-of-the-art maintenance / Richard Locke.
Underground transportation tunnel for downtown Seattle will accomodate buses and light rail, and be serviced by five passenger stations. Designers and engineers: Parsons, Brinckerhoff, Quade & Douglas.
MASS TRANSIT 1990 Sept.-Oct., v.17, no.9-10, p.24,26, photo.

TUNON ALVAREZ, EMILIO
Das Tor zur Innenstadt: der neue Atocha Bahnhof in Madrid / Patricia Catalano.
Architects: Rafael Moneo with Emilio Tunon, Javier Revillo. ARCHITEKTUR, INNENARCHITEKTUR, TECHNISCHER AUSBAU 1990 July-Aug., v.98, no.7-8, p.54-55, photos.

TUOHY, THOMAS
Lost architectural splendour of Georgian India / Thomas Tuohy.
In conjunction with an exhibition (Calcutta, city of palaces) at the British Library through Sept.30, 1990.
APOLLO 1990 Sept., v.132, no.343, p.178-180, photos.

TUPA
See HOUSES

TUPKER, HANS
Autonoom element in straatwand: Hans Tupker ontwerpt arbeidsbureau Almere / Liesbeth Melis.
Office building for the Rijksbouwendienst directie Noord-West Haarlem, located on a corner behind the Grote Markt.
DE ARCHITECT 1990 Apr., v.21, no.4, p.109-113, dwgs., photos., plans, secns., site plan.

TUPKER, HANS (CONTINUED)
Prentieloosheid versus banaliteit: Tupkers arbeidsbureau in Almere. ARCHIS 1990 May, no.5, p.4-5, photos., plan, secn., site plan.

TURANYI, GABOR, 1948-
Special feature: Contemporary Hungarian architecture / edited by Botond Bognar.
Works illustrated by architects: Imre Makovecz, Gabor Mezei, Andras Erdei, Sandor Devenyi, Attila Kovacs, Laszlo Saros, Tamas Nagy, Gyorgy Csete, Peter Oltai, Istvan Kistelegdi, Tibor Jankovics, Csasa Bodonyi, Istvan Ferencz, Tamas Noll, Beno Taba, Janos Golda, Agnes Thoma, Jozsef Kerenyi, Gyorgy Vadasz, Gyorgy Keves, Adam Sylvester and Gabor Turanyi. Text in Japanese and English.
ARCHITECTURE AND URBANISM 1990 Mar., no.3(234), p.7-126, axonometric views, dwgs., elevs., photos., plans, secns.

TURBINI, GASPARE ANTONIO, B. 1728
Gaspare Antonio Turbini "restauratore" / Pierluigi Panza. Particularly his views on the restoration of the cupola of the civic loggia in Brescia. English summary p.187.
ARTE LOMBARDA 1990, no.92-93, p.122-125, elev., plans, secns., refs.

TURETSKY, DOUG
Is bigger still better? / Doug Turetsky.
Large developments at the Hunters Point waterfront in Queens and in Times Square are about to begin construction despite slack in real estate market.
CITY LIMITS 1990 Aug.-Sept., v.15, no.7, p.12-15, port., photo.
Rebels with a cause? / Doug Turetsky.
Squatters in vacant New York City buildings.
CITY LIMITS 1990 Apr., v.15, no.4, p.12-15, ports., photos.
Shame of the city: New York City's new generation of bad landlords / Lisa Glazer, Doug Turetsky.
Profiles eight negligent New York City landlords and conditions in the buildings they own.
CITY LIMITS 1990 Jan., v.15, no.1, p.10-18, ports., photos.

TURF ROOFS
See ROOFS - GRASS COVERED

TURKEY--ANKARA--CITY PLANNING
Urban planning in Ankara / O. Altaban, M. Guvenc.
CITIES 1990 May, v.7, no.2, p.149-158, diagrs., maps, table, ref.

TURKEY--ANKARA--COMPREHENSIVE PLANS
Urban planning in Ankara / O. Altaban, M. Guvenc.
CITIES 1990 May, v.7, no.2, p.149-158, diagrs., maps, table, ref.

TURKEY--APHRODISIAS--CITIES AND TOWNS--GRECO-ROMAN
Master of Aphrodisias: Kenan T. Erim / Sharon Nelton.
On the archaeologist responsible for 30 yrs. of excavations of this Greco-Roman city in Turkey. ARCHAEOLOGY 1990 Jan.-Feb., v.43, no.1, p.50-57, ports., map, photos., site plan.

TURKEY--ARCHITECTURE--ISLAMIC
Turkey: pilgrimage to cities / edited by Hidenobu Jinnai, Jun Tanimizu and Cengiz Eruzun. Survey of Turkish cities and their architecture. Includes articles by Hidenobu Jinnai, Jun Tanimizu and Cengiz Eruzun. Text in Japanese and English.
PROCESS: ARCHITECTURE 1990 Dec., no.93, p.[1]-168, maps, photos., plans.

TURKEY--AYDER--HOUSES--WOODEN--TYPOLOGY
Ayder Mezra: thematic variation in middle meadow houses / Bill Boehm. A typological study of seasonal mountain houses in Turkey.
MIMAR: ARCHITECTURE IN DEVELOPMENT 1990 Sept., v.10, no.3(36), p.13-17, photos., sketches.

TURKEY--BERGAMA--CITIES AND TOWNS--GREEK--PERGAMON
Pergamon: Vorbericht uber die Kampagne 1989 / Wolfgang Radt. ARCHAOLOGISCHER ANZEIGER 1990, no.3, p.[397]-424, photos., secn., site plans, reconst. dwgs., isometric dwgs., aerial photos., refs.
Pergamon / Wolfgang Radt.
Preliminary report on 1987 excavations.
ARCHAOLOGISCHER ANZEIGER 1988, no.3, p.[461]-485, photos, site plans, aerial photo.

TURKEY--BERGAMA--EXCAVATIONS (ARCHAEOLOGY)--PERGAMON
Pergamon / Wolfgang Radt.
Preliminary report on 1987 excavations.
ARCHAOLOGISCHER ANZEIGER 1988, no.3, p.[461]-485, photos, site plans, aerial photo.

TURKEY--BESIK-TEPE--EXCAVATIONS (ARCHAEOLOGY)
Besik-Tepe / Manfred Korfmann. Preliminary report on 1985-86 excavations.
ARCHAOLOGISCHER ANZEIGER 1988, no.3, p.[390]-398, photos, site plan.

TURKEY--BOGAZKOY--TEMPLES--HITTITE
Die Ausgrabungen in Bogazkoy-Hattusa 1988 / Peter Neve.
Excavation report for Temple 30 area at the Hittite site in north central Turkey, with a contribution on hieroglyphics by Heinrich Otten.
ARCHAOLOGISCHER ANZEIGER 1989, no.3, p.[271]-337, dwgs., port., photos., plans, secns., site plans, aerial photo., refs.

TURKEY--BURGAZ--TERRACES--ANCIENT
Ein Heiligtum bei Alt-Knidos /
Dietrich Berges, Numan Tuna.
Report on excavations of terraces,
Burgaz, Turkey.
ARCHAOLOGISCHER ANZEIGER 1990,
no.1, p.[19]-35, maps, photos.,
refs.

TURKEY--CAYONU TEPESI--EXCAVATIONS
(ARCHAEOLOGY)
Some aspects of building at the
'aceramic-neolithic' settlement of
Cayonu Tepesi [Turkey] / Wulf
Schirmer.
WORLD ARCHAEOLOGY 1990 Feb., v.21,
no.3, p.[363]-387, axonometric
view, dets., figs., photos.,
plans, site plans, reconst. dwgs.,
isometric dwgs., aerial photos.,
refs.

TURKEY--CITIES AND TOWNS--GROWTH
Urbane metamorfoser / Lars
Marcussen.
Analysis of growth patterns for
housing in Third World Locations,
including a case study of urban
expansion in Turkey.
ARKITEKTEN 1990 Aug., v.92, no.10,
p.330-333, photos., site plans.

TURKEY--EPHESUS--ARCHITECTURE--ROMAN
Considerazioni sull'architettura di
Efeso in eta augustea / Marcello
Spanu.
PROSPETTIVA 1988 Jan., no.52,
p.41-49, photos., plans, secns.,
reconst. dwgs., refs.

TURKEY--ERYTHRAI--DECORATION AND
ORNAMENT--STUCCO--HELLENISTIC
Der erste Wanddekorations-Stil in
Erythrai / Orhan Bingol.
Based on fragments discovered
1977-78.
ARCHAOLOGISCHER ANZEIGER 1988,
no.3, p.[501]-522, dets., dwgs.,
photos, refs.

TURKEY--EXCAVATIONS (ARCHAEOLOGY)
Archaeology in Anatolia / Machteld
J. Mellink.
Excavation report for 1988.
AMERICAN JOURNAL OF ARCHAEOLOGY
1990 Jan., v.94, no.1, p.125-151,
figs., graph, map, photos, plans,
secns., biblio.

TURKEY--GORDION--TUMULI--PHRYGIAN--
TUMULUS MM
"Midas' bed" and a royal Phrygian
funeral / Elizabeth Simpson.
A reexamination of the furniture
at Tumulus MM at Gordion, Turkey.
JOURNAL OF FIELD ARCHAEOLOGY 1990
spring, v.17, no.1, p.69-87,
axonometric view, figs., dwgs.,
map, photos., reconst. dwgs.,
biblio.

TURKEY--HOUSES
Turkey: pilgrimage to cities /
edited by Hidenobu Jinnai, Jun
Tanimizu and Cengiz Eruzun.
Survey of Turkish cities and their
architecture. Includes articles by
Hidenobu Jinnai, Jun Tanimizu and
Cengiz Eruzun. Text in Japanese
and English.
PROCESS: ARCHITECTURE 1990 Dec.,
no.93, p.[1]-168, maps, photos.,
plans.

TURKEY--HOUSES--TYPOLOGY
Analysis of space in Turkish folk
houses / Tatsuya Yamamoto.
Text in Japanese.
SPACE DESIGN 1990 Feb., no.305,
p.45-68, dets., map, photos.,
plans, table.

TURKEY--INCREMENTAL HOUSING
An evolutionary housing supply mode
towards design of the quality
environments for low-income groups
in Turkey / Demet Irkli, Nilgun
Gorer.
OPEN HOUSE INTERNATIONAL 1989,
v.14, no.3, p.44-48, diagrs.,
plans, secns., refs.

TURKEY--ISTANBUL--ARCHITECTURE--
OTTOMAN
Istamboul au XVIe siecle: l'oeuvre
de Sinan / Jale Erzen.
French, English, Spanish and
German summaries, p.[122]-124.
(Some summaries incorrectly show
XIXe s.).
LES ANNALES DE LA RECHERCHE
URBAINE 1989 [Mar.-Apr.], no.42,
p.[11]-18,[122]-124, photos.,
engrs., refs.

TURKEY--ISTANBUL--BAKIRKOY--BANKS
Bankgebaude in Bakirkoy, Istanbul/T.
Architect: Cengiz Bektas.
DEUTSCHE BAUZEITSCHRIFT 1990 Aug.,
v.38, no.8, p.1085-1088, det.,
photos., plans, secns.

TURKEY--ISTANBUL--CHURCHES--
BYZANTINE--SEYH MURAD MESCIDI
The Seyh Murad Mescidi at
Constantinople / E.A. Ivison.
Byzantine church later a mosque.
THE ANNUAL OF THE BRITISH SCHOOL
AT ATHENS 1990, no.85, p.[79]-87,
dwg., map, photos., plan, engr.,
refs.

TURKEY--ISTANBUL--GARDENS--BYZANTINE--
ARETAI PALACE GARDEN
A description of the Aretai palace
and its garden / Henry Maguire.
A Byzantine garden in the vicinity
of Constantinople.
JOURNAL OF GARDEN HISTORY 1990
Oct.-Dec., v.10, no.4, p.209-213,
refs.

TURKEY--ISTANBUL--HISTORIC DISTRICTS--
BEYAZIT SQUARE
The design criteria of public spaces
in historical environment: Beyazit
Square as a case study / Semra
Aydinli, Hale Ciraci, Ayse Kubat.
Example of Beyazit Square,
Istanbul.
INTERNATIONAL JOURNAL FOR HOUSING
SCIENCE AND ITS APPLICATIONS 1990,
v.14, no.3, p.197-208, models,
plans, site plans, refs.

TURKEY--ISTANBUL--HOUSING--17TH
CENTURY
Communal living in Ottoman Istanbul:
searching for the foundations of
an urban tradition / Rhoads
Murphey.
JOURNAL OF URBAN HISTORY 1990
Feb., v.16, no.2, p.115-131, refs.

TURKEY--ISTANBUL--HOUSING--18TH
CENTURY
Communal living in Ottoman Istanbul:
searching for the foundations of
an urban tradition / Rhoads
Murphey.
JOURNAL OF URBAN HISTORY 1990
Feb., v.16, no.2, p.115-131, refs.

TURKEY--ISTANBUL--LAND USE
Informal land and housing markets:
the case of Istanbul, Turkey /
Ayse Yonder.
AMERICAN PLANNING ASSOCIATION.
JOURNAL 1987 Spring, v.53, no.2,
p.213-219, photos.

TURKEY--ISTANBUL--LOW INCOME HOUSING
Informal land and housing markets:
the case of Istanbul, Turkey /
Ayse Yonder.
AMERICAN PLANNING ASSOCIATION.
JOURNAL 1987 Spring, v.53, no.2,
p.213-219, photos.

TURKEY--ISTANBUL--MONASTERIES--
BYZANTINE--CHORA
The Saviour in Chora: the monastery
of the Grand Logothete / Maria
Vittoria Marini-Clarelli.
Byzantine frescoes and mosaics in
a Constantinople monastery.
FMR 1990 Aug., v.9, no.45,
p.21-52, photos., biblio.

TURKEY--ISTANBUL--MOSAICS--BYZANTINE--
CHORA
The Saviour in Chora: the monastery
of the Grand Logothete / Maria
Vittoria Marini-Clarelli.
Byzantine frescoes and mosaics in
a Constantinople monastery.
FMR 1990 Aug., v.9, no.45,
p.21-52, photos., biblio.

TURKEY--ISTANBUL--MOSQUES--OTTOMAN--
MOSQUE OF RUSTEM PASA
A note on the dating of the mosque
of Rustem Pasa in Istanbul /
Leslie Meral Schick.
Argues that the mosque was
constructed in 1561 under Sinan
and may have been completed in or
after 1562.
ARTIBUS ASIAE 1990, v.50, no.3-4,
p.285-288, refs.

TURKEY--ISTANBUL--MURAL PAINTING AND
DECORATION--BYZANTINE--CHORA
The Saviour in Chora: the monastery
of the Grand Logothete / Maria
Vittoria Marini-Clarelli.
Byzantine frescoes and mosaics in
a Constantinople monastery.
FMR 1990 Aug., v.9, no.45,
p.21-52, photos., biblio.

TURKEY--ISTANBUL--OPEN SPACES--BEYAZIT
SQUARE
The design criteria of public spaces
in historical environment: Beyazit
Square as a case study / Semra
Aydinli, Hale Ciraci, Ayse Kubat.
Example of Beyazit Square,
Istanbul.
INTERNATIONAL JOURNAL FOR HOUSING
SCIENCE AND ITS APPLICATIONS 1990,
v.14, no.3, p.197-208, models,
plans, site plans, refs.

TURNBULL, WILLIAM (CONTINUED)
The International...(CONTINUED)
William Turnbull, Jr.
PLACES 1990 Winter, v.6, no.2,
p.32-47, axonometric views, dwgs.,
map, photos., plans, site plans,
aerial photo., refs.

TURNER ASSOCIATES
A pause that refreshes [The World of
Coca-Cola] / Lynn Nesmith.
A museum of the soft drink
company, in Atlanta, Ga.
Architects: Thompson, Ventulett,
Stainback & Associates and Turner
Associates.
ARCHITECTURE: THE AIA JOURNAL 1990
Dec., v.79, no.12, p.[74-79],
photos., plans, site plan.

TURNER, J. M. W. (JOSEPH MALLORD
WILLIAM), 1775-1851
J.M.W. Turner at Petworth House,
West Sussex / Ian Warrell.
Sketches done at and depicting
scenes of the "House of Art".
ANTIQUES 1990 Apr., v.137, no.4,
p.914-927,cover, photos.

TURNER, JOHN
Cause for celebration / John Turner.
Discussion of the after-use of
five festival sites of the
National Garden Festival at
Gateshead.
LANDSCAPE DESIGN 1990 July-Aug.,
no.192, p.38-39, photos.
National garden festival:
regeneration or degeneration? /
John Turner.
URBAN FUTURES 1989 Spring, v.2,
no.1, p.41-44, photos.

TURNER, JONATHAN
Object lessons: four new design
museums are exhibiting everything
from trendy chairs to Zippo
lighters / Jonathan Turner.
ART NEWS 1990 Apr., v.89, no.4,
p.134-139, photos.

TURNER, SUZANNE
Academic assemblage.
Profile of six educators among
various landscape architecture
faculties.
LANDSCAPE ARCHITECTURE 1990 Sept.,
v.80, no.9, p.58-63, ports.,
photos., site plan.

TURNER, TOM
Parks in peril / Robert Holden, Tom
Turner.
On the state of London's parks.
BUILDING DESIGN 1990 May 4,
no.984, p.41-43, photos.
Was 'landscape architecture' a good
idea? / Tom Turner.
On the choice of the name of the
profession.
LANDSCAPE DESIGN 1990 June,
no.191, p.28-29, ill., refs.

TURNER, WELDON
Quattrocento clarity / Michael
Ennis.
Interiors of Fort Worth home of
Nelda and Gray Mills. Architect:
Weldon Turner. Interior designer:
Joseph Minton.
ARCHITECTURAL DIGEST 1990 Oct.,
v.47, no.11, p.[180]-187, photos.

TURNOCK, DAVID
City profile: Bucharest / David
Turnock.
CITIES 1990 May, v.7, no.2,
p.107-118, maps, photos., tables,
refs.

TUROK, I.
Public investment and privatisation
in the new towns: a financial
assessment of Bracknell / I.
Turok.
ENVIRONMENT AND PLANNING A 1990
Oct., v.22, no.10, p.1323-1336,
graph, tables, refs.

TURQUENITCH, BENATO
Mais para residencia do que para
espigao: Edificio Baia de Quatro
Ilhas, Porte Alegre.
Architect: Renato Turquenitch.
PROJETO 1989 June, no.122,
p.78-79, ill., photos, plans,
secns.

TURRENT, DAVID
Domestic low energy, 4: beyond the
regs / David Turrent, Koen
Steemers.
Fourth and last in series on
energy efficient housing.
ARCHITECTS' JOURNAL 1990 Apr.11,
v.191, no.15, p.61-65,67, diagrs.,
graph, photos., secns.
Saving energy on the rates / David
Turrent, Jes Mainwaring.
On the new National House Energy
Rating scheme and the solar
housing designed in the Energy
Park, Milton Keynes. Architects:
ECD Partnership.
RIBA JOURNAL 1990 Sept., v.97,
no.9, p.85-86, dwgs., elevs.,
plans.

TUSA, M. SERENA
La Chiesa di S. Teresa alla Kalsa in
Palermo di Giacomo Amato: disegni
autografi e "apoche" delle
fabbriche / M. Serena Tusa,
Guiseppe Liuzzo.
STORIA ARCHITETTURA 1987
Jan.-Dec., v.10, no.1-2, p.55-68,
dets., elevs., plans.

TUSQUETS, DIAZ & ASSOCIATES
Ampliacion, remodelacion y
restauracion del Palau de la
Musica Catalana: Tusquets, Diaz &
Associats, arquitectos.
Original architect (1905): Lluis
D. i Montaner. Text in Spanish and
English.
ON DISENO 1990, no.116, p.109-117,
photos., plans.
La arquitectura residencial de la
Villa Olimpica / Justo Isasi.
Includes 13 projects. English
summary, p.86.
A & V 1990, no.22, p.26-54, dets.,
ill., elevs., models, plans,
secns., site plans, sketches.
Modernismo modernized / Magda Saura.
On the remodeling of 1905-1908
Palau de la Musica Catalana,
Barcelona. Original architect:
Lluis Domenechi Montaner.
Renovation archicects: Tusquets,
Diaz & Associates. Includes
interview with Tusquets.
PROGRESSIVE ARCHITECTURE 1990
June, v.71, no.6, p.84-[91],
(Continued next column)

TUSQUETS, DIAZ & ASSOCIATES
(CONTINUED)
Modernismo modernized...(CONTINUED)
elevs., photos., plans, secns.,
site plan.
Palau de la Musica Catalana = Music
palace, Barcelona, 1981-1989.
On the remodeling of 1905-1908
Palau de al Musica Catalana,
Barcelona. Original architect:
Lluis Domenech Montaner.
Renovation architects: O.Tusquets,
Ll. Clotet y C. Diaz.
EL CROQUIS 1990 Mar., v.9, no.42,
p.80-107, dets., elevs., photos.,
plans, secns., site plans,
sketches.
Proyectar para una arquitectura
dada: analogia y diversidad = To
design for a given architecture:
analogy and diversity / Anton
Capitel.
Discusses 4 recent projects in
Spain.
EL CROQUIS 1990 Mar., v.9, no.42,
p.64-79, photos.
La vitrine du palais: extension du
Palais de la musique catalane,
Espagne / Marc Bedarida.
Addition to 1905-08 building in
Barcelona. Original architect:
Lluis Domenech i Montaner.
Renovation arhcitects: Tusquets,
Diaz & Associates. English
summary, p.120. Spanish summary,
p.169.
TECHNIQUES ET ARCHITECTURE 1990
Aug.-Sept., no.391, p.120-121,
photos., secn., site plan.

TUSQUETS, OSCAR, 1941-
Directions in urban housing, part
II: Messages from Fukuoka.
Contents: International Housing
Exhibition in Kashii.--Steven
Holl.--Rem Koolhaas.--Mark Mack.--
Osamu Ishiyama.--Christian de
Portzamparc.--Oscar Tusguets.--
Arata Isozaki.--Nexus Momochi,
Michael Graves, Stanley
Tigerman.--Fukouka International
Architects' Conference '89.--
Experation and Defiance in the
Debate over the City as "Chaos",
by Noriko Takiguchi. Includes
English summary and biographical
information on participants.
SPACE DESIGN 1990 Jan., no.304,
p.53-84, axonometric views, dwgs.,
ports., elevs., models, map,
photos., plans, secns., site
plans.
Gathering establishments.
Part of a special feature on
Spanish contemporary architecture.
Contents: Palau de la Musica
Catalana, by Oscar Tusquets
Blanca, Carlos M. Diaz, Lluis
Clotet, Ignacio Paricio --
Television Andaluza, by Gonzalo
Diaz-Y. Recasens --Banco de
Espana, Jaen, by Rafael Moneo --
Almacenes Simon, by Lluis Clotet,
Ignacio Paricio --Mercado
Vilaseca-Salou, by Carlos Ferrater
Lambarri, Jose Luis Canosa --
Pabellon Rius i Taulet, by Pep
Bonet --Velodromo de Horta, by
Esteban Bonell, Francesc Rius --
Brief histories --Views through
the Camera's Finder, by Hisao
Suzuki. Text in Japanese.
(Continued next page)

TUSQUETS, OSCAR, 1941- (CONTINUED)
Gathering...(CONTINUED)
SPACE DESIGN 1990 May, no.308,
p.93-131, dets., ports., elevs.,
model, photos., plans, secns.,
site plan, sketch, isometric dwg.
Modernismo modernized / Magda Saura.
On the remodeling of 1905-1908
Palau de la Musica Catalana,
Barcelona. Original architect:
Lluis Domenechi Montaner.
Renovation architects: Tusquets,
Diaz & Associates. Includes
interview with Tusquets.
PROGRESSIVE ARCHITECTURE 1990
June, v.71, no.6, p.84-[91],
elevs., photos., plans, secns.,
site plan.
Palau de la Musica Catalana = Music
palace, Barcelona, 1981-1989.
On the remodeling of 1905-1908
Palau de al Musica Catalana,
Barcelona. Original architect:
Lluis Domenech Montaner.
Renovation architects: O.Tusquets,
Ll. Clotet y C. Diaz.
EL CROQUIS 1990 Mar., v.9, no.42,
p.80-107, dets., elevs., photos.,
plans, secns., site plans,
sketches.

TUTANKHAMEN, KING OF EGYPT
Notes on the exterior construction
signs from Tutankhamun's shrines /
Martha R. Bell.
On the four shrines found in tomb.
JOURNAL OF EGYPTIAN ARCHAEOLOGY
1990, v.76, p.107-124, charts,
refs.

TUTTLE, EDWARD
Amanpuri, Phuket Island.
Resort hotel on the site of a
coconut plantation, western
Thailand. Architect: Ed Tuttle.
MIMAR: ARCHITECTURE IN DEVELOPMENT
1990 Sept., v.10, no.3(36),
p.40-45, map, photos., site plan.
Housekeeping on Hydra / Adrian Cook.
Interiors of John and Elinor
McGuire's home on Hydra.
Architect: Edward Tuttle.
Interior renovation designer:
Andrew Delfino.
ARCHITECTURAL DIGEST 1990 Aug.,
v.47, no.8, p.[144-149], photos.

TUTTLE, PAUL
Suave furniture that blends fantasy
and technology / Hunter
Drohojowska.
Profile of furniture designer Paul
Tuttle.
ARCHITECTURAL DIGEST 1990 Feb.,
v.47, no.2, p.122,126,130, port.,
photos.

TWAIN, MARK
Un americano a Villa Viviani = an
American in Villa Viviani / Mark
Twain.
Excerpt from the Autobiography of
Mark Twain, Harper & Brothers, NY,
1959. Includes article on the
history of the villa. Twain
rented this villa in 1892. Text
in Italian and English.
SPAZIO E SOCIETA 1990 July-Sept.,
v.13, no.51, p.116-121, port.,
photos.

TWINCH, RICHARD
Design and building innovations at
the Point [exhibition review] /
Richard Twinch.
Review of PLAN EXPO '90, held at
Point Depot, Dublin, Ireland.
PLAN: ARCHITECTURE AND BUILDING
DESIGN IN IRELAND 1990 Oct., v.35,
no.10, p.13, ports.
Generation games / Richard Twinch.
On the work of Unit 14 at the
Architectural Association which is
investigating the use of machine
intelligence in architecture.
BUILDING DESIGN 1990 Aug.24,
no.1000, p.16, photos.
Player with promise / Richard
Twinch.
Discussion of the GDS cad software
system.
BUILDING DESIGN 1990 June 8,
no.989, p.24-26, dets.
Screen test [book review] / Richard
Twinch.
On the report, Microcad Software
Evaluated, by Paul Richens,
Commissioned by the Construction
Industry Computing Association.
BUILDING DESIGN 1990 Mar.16,
no.977, p.36-37, dwgs.
YRM thrives on glasnost policy /
Richard Twinch.
On the use of the Intergraph CAD
system at YRM Partnership.
BUILDING DESIGN 1989 Sept.,
suppl., p.3-4, diagr., dwgs.,
photos.

TWO-FAMILY HOUSES
See DUPLEX HOUSES

TWOMBLY, ROBERT, ED. LOUIS SULLIVAN:
THE PUBLIC PAPERS
American architects [book review].
Review of books on Louis Sullivan,
Philip Trammell Shutze, Louis
Kahn, and Gordon Bunshaft, by
Lauren S. Weingarden, Keith
Morgan, David B. Brownlee, and
Franz Schulze.
SOCIETY OF ARCHITECTURAL
HISTORIANS. JOURNAL 1990 June,
v.49, no.2, p.222-229,

TYACK, GEOFFREY
"A gallery worthy of the British
people": James Pennethorne's
designs for the National Gallery,
1845-1867 / Geoffrey Tyack.
Plans for new galleries. Original
architect: William Wilkins.
ARCHITECTURAL HISTORY 1990, v.33,
p.120-134, dwgs., plans, secns.,
site plans, refs.
James Pennethorne and London street
improvements, 1838-1855 / Geoffrey
Tyack.
LONDON JOURNAL 1990, v.15, no.1,
p.[38]-56, ill., elev., photos.,
plans, refs.

TYE, ALAN
Open and shut case / Alan Tye.
On contemporary hardware. Includes
list of manufacturers and
designers.
DESIGNERS' JOURNAL 1990 May,
no.57, p.72-75, photos.

TYE, THEODORE R.
A developer responds to corporate
day care needs in Massachusetts /
Theodore R. Tye.
Architects: SBA, Steffian Bradley
Associates; Developer: National
Development Associates, Inc.
THE JOURNAL OF REAL ESTATE
DEVELOPMENT 1989 Summer, v.5,
no.1, p.38-44, plan, refs.

TYGHEM, FRIEDA VAN
Het kasteel van Moregem bij
Oudenaarde (1792-1798): een
merkwaardig ensemble uit de
'Directoire'-tijd / Frieda Van
Tyghem, Jean Van Cleven.
GENTSE BIJDRAGEN TOT DE
KUNSTGESCHIEDENIS EN OUDHEIDKUNDE
1988, v.27, p.[39]-78, dwg.,
ports., elevs., plans, site plan,
refs.

TYLER, STEPHEN
Congestion or enlightenment /
Stephen Tyler.
Differences in philosophical
approaches to city traffic
congestion between Westerners and
travelers in Bangkok, Thailand.
BERKELEY PLANNING JOURNAL 1990,
v.5, p.114-116, ref.

TYMPANA (ARCHITECTURE)--18TH CENTURY--
SPAIN--TOLOSA--SANTA MARIA DE TOLOSA
El portico y el cancel de Santa
Maria de Tolosa: Tomas de Jaurequi
y Jose Ignacio de Lavi / Maria
Isabel Astiazarain Achabal.
Portico and tympanum date from the
1750s-1760s.
ARCHIVO ESPANOL DE ARTE 1990
Oct.-Dec., v.63, no.252,
p.[633]-640, dwg., photos., refs.

TYMPANA (ARCHITECTURE)--CONSERVATION
AND RESTORATION--AUSTRIA--VIENNA--
MICHAELERKIRCHE
Ein neuentdecktes Tympanon-Relief in
der Wiener Michaelerkirche / Mario
Schwarz.
OSTERREICHISCHE ZEITSCHRIFT FUR
KUNST UND DENKMALPFLEGE 1990,
v.44, no.1-2, p.67-69, photos.,
refs.

TYMPANA (ARCHITECTURE)--ROMAN--
FRANCE--ALISE-SAINTE-REINE
Corniches et couronnements
gallo-romains a Alesia
(Alise-Saint-Reine, Cote-d'Or) /
Alberic Olivier.
GALLIA 1989, v.46, p.[43]-69,
dets., dwgs., photos., site plans,
reconst. dwgs., refs.

TYMPANUMS (ARCHITECTURE)
See TYMPANA (ARCHITECTURE)

TYPOLOGY
See also "TYPOLOGY" AS A SUBHEADING
AFTER SPECIFIC BUILDING TYPES OR
OTHER MAIN HEADINGS.
Tipologie atopiche [editorial] /
Vittorio Gregotti.
Essay on "placeless typologies".
Includes English translation.
CASABELLA 1990 May, v.54, no.568,
p.2-3,63.

TYSON, BLAKE
  Some nineteenth-century inscriptions
    at Kirkby-in-Furness, Cumbria /
    Blake Tyson.
    ANCIENT MONUMENTS SOCIETY.
    TRANSACTIONS 1990, new ser.,v.34,
    p.[133]-150, figs., elevs., maps,
    plans, refs.

TZAMIR, YIGAL
  An ethical perspective on knowledge
    in architectural education / Yigal
    Tzamir, Arza Churchman.
    JOURNAL OF ARCHITECTURAL AND
    PLANNING RESEARCH 1989 Autumn,
    v.6, no.3, p.227-239, graphs,
    refs.

TZANNES, ALEX
  House at Pittwater: Alexander
    Tzannes.
    Located on Mackerel Beach.
    ARCHITECTURE AUSTRALIA 1989 Dec.,
    v.78, no.11, p.46, photos., secn.
  Quatre maisons a Sydney / Francoise
    Fromonot.
    Holmes house, Paddington,
    architect: Alex Tzannes; Kinsella
    house, Mackerel Beach, architect:
    Alex Tzannes; house, Kilminster
    Lane, Woollahra, architect: Glenn
    Murcutt; Harrison house, Waverley,
    architects: Glenn Murcutt, Alex
    Tzannes. English summary, p.47.
    ARCHITECTURE INTERIEURE CREE 1990
    Feb., no.234, p.110-123, dets.,
    map, photos., plans, secn., site
    plans, isometric dwg.

TZONIS, ALEXANDER
  Automatisierung der
    Architekturausbildung durch
    Computerisierung der Architektur:
    Architectural Basics in
    Computerized Design Education
    (ABCDE) at the Faculty of
    Architecture, Delft University of
    Technology / A. Tzonis, A.
    Koutamanis.
    ARCHITHESE 1990 May-June, v.20,
    no.3, p.70-72, refs.
  Critica y regionalista / Alexander
    Tzonis, Liane Lefaivre.
    On contemporary Spanish "critical
    regionalist" architecture. English
    summary, p.87.
    A & V 1990, no.24, p.22-24,
    axonometric views, ill., dwgs.,
    elevs., refs.
  Un dragon en las dunas: Van Eyck
    amplia el ESTEC / Alexander
    Tzonis, Liane Lefaivre.
    In Noordwijk, Holland.
    ARQUITECTURA VIVA 1990 Sept.-Oct.,
    no.14, p.42-44, axonometric view,
    port., photos., plans, aerial
    photo.
  Hutten, Schiffe und
    Flaschengestelle: analogischer
    Entwurf fur Architekten und/oder
    Maschinen / Alexander Tzonis.
    ARCHITHESE 1990 May-June, v.20,
    no.3, p.16-27, dwgs., elevs.,
    sketches.
  Why critical regionalism today? /
    Alexander Tzonis, Liane Lefaivre.
    Text in Japanese and English.
    ARCHITECTURE AND URBANISM 1990
    May, no.5(236), p.23-33, ill.,
    photos., refs.

TZONIS, ALEXANDER (CONTINUED)
  Zettelwerk / Alexander Tzonis.
    ARCHITHESE 1990 Nov.-Dec., v.20,
    no.6, p.14-[17], dets., photos.

UBALDI, ROBERTO
Linee flessibili per i trasporti
urbani = Flexible public transport
routes / Roberto Ubaldi.
Contents: Elevated light transit
station project, Milan, Italy;
architects: G14 Progettazione --
AEG Westinghouse "People Mover"
transit system -- Advanced Light
Railway System (ALRT) transit
system -- the M-Bahn magnetic
suspension transport system --
EM403 monorail transport system --
Von Roll monorail transport
system. Text in Italian and
English.
L'ARCA 1990 Sept., no.41, p.54-65,
dwgs., elevs., photos., plans,
secns., site plans.
Portali d'interscambio = Commuter
stations north of Milan / Michele
Bazan Giordano.
New railway stations of the
Ferrovie Nord Milano. Architects:
G14 Progettazione. Text in Italian
and English.
L'ARCA 1990 Sept., no.41, p.48-53,
dwg., photos., site plans.

UBER, PAOLA
Esercito e citta: piacenza nella
seconda meta dell'Ottocento /
Paola Uber.
STORIA URBANA 1989 Jan.-Mar.,
v.13, no.46, p.[81]-102, maps,
refs.

UCHIDA, SHIGERU
Multiple talents / Edie Lee Cohen.
On the hotel, Il Palazzo, Fukuoka,
Japan. Architects: Aldo Rossi,
Morris Adjmi. Interior designers:
Sottsass Associati, Gaetano Pesce,
Sigeru Uchida and Shiro Kuramata.
INTERIOR DESIGN 1990 May, v.61,
no.7, p.[202-209], photos., plans,
secn.
Tower of power: Hotel Il Palazzo,
Fukuoka, Japan / Karen D. Stein.
Architect: Aldo Rossi, Studio di
Architettura/New York; associate
architects: Studio 80; interior
designers: Shigeru Uchida, Ikuyo
Mitsuhashi, Aldo Rossi, Morris
Adjmi, Ettore Sottsass, Gaetano
Pesce, Shiro Kuramata, Alfredo
Arribas.
ARCHITECTURAL RECORD 1990 May,
v.178, no.6, p.70-[77], dets.,
photos., plans, secn.

UCHIDA, YOSHIO
Traces of architects early in this
century: Toshiro Yamashita /
Yoshio Uchida.
KENCHIKU BUNKA 1990 July, v.45,
no.525, p.137-144, port., photos.,
table.

UDA ARCHITECTS/URBAN DESIGN ASSOCIATES
Taming the city edge: urban design
portfolio / Andrea Oppenheimer
Dean.
The latest frontier--"outcities."
Mission Bay, San Francisco;
Downtown Norfolk, Va; Carr Norfolk
Southern Project, Alexandria, Va.;
and Arverne, New York City
ARCHITECTURE: THE AIA JOURNAL 1990
Apr., v.79, no.4, p.[74]-79,147,
ill., model, plans, sketches,
aerial photos.

UDEMA, JAAP
Europan '89: abitare (e progettare)
in Europa.
Projects by Miriam Dubois,
Wilfried Kneffel, J.M. Sluymer, C.
Liebermann and A. Daniel, J.-P.
Calori, P. Costanzo and A. Cesari,
Jaap Udema, A. Muller, and Chiche
Carola Guerrier Guffroy Locicero.
PARAMETRO 1990 Jan.-Feb., no.176,
p.82-91, axonometric views, ill.,
dwgs., plans, secns., site plans.

UEDA, MAKOTO
"Cosmos" urban house 1990.
4-story home, Tokyo. Architect:
Ken Yokogawa, Architect and
Associates. Includes essay, From
tunnel house to Cosmos, by Makoto
Ueda. English summary, p.106.
KENCHIKU BUNKA 1990 Mar., v.45,
no.521, p.101-110, axonometric
views, photos., plans, secn.,
sketch.
Directions in urban housing, part I:
Housing complexes--a topical
study.
Contents: Discussion (Kunihiko
Hayakawa, Makoto Motokura, Makoto
Ueda).--Works (Hoichiro Itai +
Section R Architects; Makoto
Watanabe + Yoko Kinoshita + A. D.
H.; Kunihiko Hayakawa; HEXA;
Hiroshi Nishioka; Makoto Motokura
+ KENCHIKU Design Studio, Tokyo;
Tadasu Ohe). Text in Japanese.
SPACE DESIGN 1990 Jan., no.304,
p.05-52, axonometric views, elev.,
models, photos., plans, secns.,
site plans.
Special edition II: producing of
architecture / Mitsuru Kiryu.
Includes dialogue: The third
dimension of plan, by Makoto Ueda,
Mitsuru Kiryu. English summary,
p.19.
KENCHIKU BUNKA 1990 Feb, v.45,
no.520, p.59-66, dwgs., ports.,
photos., plans.

UEDA, SATOSHI
Cities and villages of the Yemen
Arab Republic / Satoshi Ueda.
Includes "The contemporary
significance of the Islamic city",
by Nobuhide Jinnai. Text in
Japanese.
SPACE DESIGN 1990 Sept., no.312,
p.077-088, maps, photos., plans,
secns., refs.

UEMATU, NAMI
An experimental study on visual
effects of colours in living rooms
/ Hiroko Tanaka, Nami Uematu, and
Takuko Yanase.
English summary, p.41.
NIHON KENCHIKU GAKKAI KEIKAKUKEI
RONBUN HOKOKU SHU = JOURNAL OF
ARCHITECTURE, PLANNING AND
ENVIRONMENTAL ENGINEERING 1990
Feb., no.2(408), p.33-41, diagrs.,
graphs, photos., tables, refs.

UENO, YUN
Psychological simulation experiment
about the appropriate interval
dimension of beds in the hospital
ward / Jun Ueno ... [et al.].
Text in Japanese; English summary,
p.65.
NIHON KENCHIKU GAKKAI KEIKAKUKEI
(Continued next column)

UENO, YUN (CONTINUED)
Psychological...(CONTINUED)
RONBUN HOKOKU SHU = JOURNAL OF
ARCHITECTURE, PLANNING AND
ENVIRONMENTAL ENGINEERING 1990
Apr., no.4(410), p.65-76, graphs,
photos., plans, tables.

UGALDE, FEDERICO
Rehabilitacion del Teatro Arriaga de
Bilbao: Francisco Hurtado,
arquitecto.
Original architect: Joaquin
Rucoba. Alterations 1915 by
Federico Ugalde. Spanish, English
text.
ON DISENO 1990, no.109, p.178-186,
photos., plans.

UGOLINI, ROBERTO
Stadtischer Park auf dem Gelande
einer ehemaligen Tabakfabrik in
Bologna, Italien = Urban park on
the area of a former tobacco
factory in Bologna, Italy.
Architects: Alessandro Anselmi,
Francesco Cellini, Andrea
Salvioni, Roberto Ugolini.
ARCHITEKTUR + WETTBEWERBE 1990
Dec., no.144, p.17, dwgs.

UHL, OTTOKAR
Noch ist alles offen - Raum als
Instrument: katholische Kirche St.
Judas Thaddaus in Karlsruhe -
Neureut / Ottokar Uhl, Bernd
Selbmann.
Architects: Ottokar Uhl, and
Schmitt, Kasimir und Partner.
KUNST UND KIRCHE 1990, no.1,
p.20-25, models, photos., plans.

UHLMANN, KAREN
Savvy spending: where to invest your
remodeling dollars / Barbara B.
Buchholz, Karen Uhlmann.
Remodeling for resale in a
sluggish real estate market.
HOUSE BEAUTIFUL 1990 Sept., v.132,
no.9, p.120-122-124,

UIDE, A.
A bridge for Europe / A. Uide.
On Gaetano Pesce's proposal for a
gigantic, symbolic bridge that
will unite France and Germany
south of Strasbourg.
ARCHITECTURAL REVIEW 1990 May,
v.187, no.1119, p.93, models.

UK ARCHITECTS AGAINST APARTHEID
No end yet for anti-apartheid.
UK Architects Against Apartheid
(UKAAA), Peter Ahrends, Finna
Ayres, and Glen Robinson strongly
object to opinions put forward by
architect Jane Drew in a previous
issue of AJ (Apr.18, 1990, p.14).
ARCHITECTS' JOURNAL 1990 May 30,
v.191, no.22, p.14-15, ports.

ULLI G. HASSIG + PARTNER
Erste Preise: Sozialbauten.
Four projects: Altenpflegeheim
Sachsenheim (architect: Ulli G.
Hassig + Partner); Pflegeheim der
Barmherzigen Bruder, Algasing
Dorfen (architect: Jurgen Krug +
Partner); Kinderzentrum
Ludwigshafen am Rhein (architect:
Erwin Morlock et al); conversion
of Mullerwohnhaus to a meeting
(Continued next page)

ULLI G. HASSIG + PARTNER (CONTINUED)
   Erste Preise:...(CONTINUED)
      house, Ortschaft Sudhemmern
      (architect: Jorg Weber).
      DEUTSCHES ARCHITEKTENBLATT 1990
      June 1, v.22, no.6, p.931-934,
      elevs., models, plans, secns.,
      site plans.

ULLMANN, GERHARD
   Grenzverlaufe in gegenlaufiger
      Blickrichtung / Gerhard Ullmann.
      DER ARCHITEKT 1990 Feb., no.2,
      p.100-102, photos.

ULLMANN, GERHARD, 1935-
   Denkspiele im Quadrat: ein Exkurs
      uber Ecken / Gerhard Ullmann.
      DEUTSCHE BAUZEITUNG 1990 May,
      v.124, no.5, p.36-41, photos.
   Drei Amerikaner in Berlin:
      Zeichnende Poeten und bauunlustige
      Architekten / Gerhard Ullmann.
      IBA buildings by Peter Eisenmann,
      John Hejduk and Raimund Abraham.
      DEUTSCHE BAUZEITUNG 1990 Aug.,
      v.124, no.8, p.106-108, dwg.,
      photos., plans, secn., sketches.
   Energiesparend-- und behaglich:
      Anmerkungen zu einem Solarhaus in
      Berlin / Gerhard Ullmann.
      Architects: Institut fur Bau-,
      Umwelt- und Solarforschung (IBUS).
      DEUTSCHE BAUZEITUNG 1990 Sept.,
      v.124, no.9, p.40-44, photos.,
      plans, secn.
   Der Fliegende Hollander: Versuch
      einer Bestandsaufnahme zur
      Stadtgeschichte Potsdams / Gerhard
      Ullmann.
      Restoration of housing built
      1737-42. English summary, p.251.
      DEUTSCHE BAUZEITUNG 1990 June,
      v.124, no.6, p.38-42, photos.
   Fotografie am Bauhaus oder die
      Entdeckung eines Mediums: eine
      Ausstellung am Berliner
      Bauhaus-Archiv vom 4. Februar bis
      27. April 1990 [exhibition review]
      / Gerhard Ullmann.
      WERK, BAUEN + WOHNEN 1990 Apr.,
      no.4, p.16-18, ill., photos.
   Der gelbe Riese: die Post als
      Bauherr, oder: Das schwankende
      Outfit des gelben Riesen / Gerhard
      Ullmann.
      DEUTSCHE BAUZEITUNG 1990 Dec.,
      v.124, no.12, p.30-33, photos.,
      plans.
   Kunstlerhauser und der Kult des
      Privaten [exhibition review] /
      Gerhard Ullmann.
      On the exhibition
      "Kunstlerhauser-- eine
      Architektur-geschichte des
      Privaten", at the Deutsches
      Architekturmuseum, Frankfurt.
      WERK, BAUEN + WOHNEN 1990
      Jan.-Feb., no.1-2, p.10-11, model,
      photos.
   Die Mobilisierung des Aussenraumes:
      neue Platze und Parks in Barcelona
      / Gerhard Ullmann.
      WERK, BAUEN + WOHNEN 1990 June,
      no.6, p.2-7, photos., site plans,
      aerial photos.
   Patchwork-Hauser: Anmerkungen zu
      Frei Ottos Oko-Hausern im Berliner
      Tiergarten / Gerhard Ullmann.
      DEUTSCHE BAUZEITUNG 1990 Sept.,
      v.124, no.9, p.45-51, photos.,
      plans, secns., site plans.

ULLMANN, GERHARD, 1935- (CONTINUED)
   El rayo del entendimiento:
      Libeskind, Museo Judio en Berlin /
      Gerhard Ullmann.
      ARQUITECTURA VIVA 1990 Mar.-Apr.,
      no.11, p.14-19, dwgs., models,
      plans.
   Sperrige Orte, verquere Objekte:
      Ruckblick auf die Ausstellung "Die
      Endlichkeit der Freiheit" in
      Berlin Ost und West... [exhibition
      review] / Gerhard Ullmann.
      WERK, BAUEN + WOHNEN 1990 Dec.,
      no.12, p.14-19, photos.
   Sudliches Licht: Kykladenarchitektur
      auf der griechischen Insel
      Santorin / Gerhard Ullmann.
      DER ARCHITEKT 1990 Sept., no.9,
      p.403-404, photos.
   Vorarlberger Raum: Terrassensiedlung
      in Bregenz / Gerhard Ullman[n].
      Architects: Dietmar Eberle, Carlo
      Baumschlager.
      DEUTSCHE BAUZEITUNG 1990 Aug.,
      v.124, no.8, p.26-[33], elev.,
      photos., plans.
   Zeichnende Poeten und bauunlustige
      Architekten: Neue IBA-Bauten von
      Peter Eisenman, John Heyduk [sic]
      und Raimund Abraham / Gerhard
      Ullman.
      WERK, BAUEN + WOHNEN 1990 Sept.,
      no.9, p.12-15, elev., photos.,
      secns., sketches.

ULLMARK, PETER
   Industribyggandets metaforer /
      Anders Tornqvist, Peter Ullmark.
      In conjunction with an
      international congress in
      Stockholm and a related
      publication entitled "When people
      matter".
      ARKITEKTUR: THE SWEDISH REVIEW OF
      ARCHITECTURE 1990 Sept., v.90,
      no.7, p.28-35, model, photo.,
      secns., site plan.
   Volvo Uddevalla / Gunnar Werner.
      Automobile factory located at F d
      Uddevallavarvet. Architects: White
      arkitekter, Mitchell Giurgola
      Architects, AKOS arkitektkontor.
      Includes commentary by Anders
      Tornqvist and Peter Ullmark.
      ARKITEKTUR: THE SWEDISH REVIEW OF
      ARCHITECTURE 1990 Jan.-Feb., v.90,
      no.1, p.38-47, photos., plans,
      site plans, sketches.

ULLRICH, DIETER
   Seite an Seite: Okumenisches
      Kirchenzentrum in
      Nurnberg-Langwasser / Sabibe
      Schneider.
      Architects: Eberhard Schunck,
      Dieter Ullrich.
      DEUTSCHE BAUZEITUNG 1990 Apr.,
      v.124, no.4, p.[30]-35, photos.,
      secn., site plans.

ULMER, GREGORY L.
   Anchor -A(electronic) architecture/
      Gregory L. Ulmer.
      Essay on the media and questions
      raised by Aug. 1990 events in the
      Middle East, from the perspective
      of the Florida Research Ensemble
      (FRE) and its interest in
      electronic culture.
      COLUMBIA UNIVERSITY. GRADUATE
      SCHOOL OF ARCHITECTURE, PLANNING
      AND PRESERVATION. NEWSLINE 1990
      (Continued next column)

ULMER, GREGORY L. (CONTINUED)
   Anchor -A(electronic)...(CONTINUED)
      Nov., v.3, no.3, p.6, ports.

ULRICH, BARBARA
   Barrington's Catlow Theatre: the
      poor man's ticket to England /
      Barbara Ulrich.
      1927 Tudor revival movie and
      vaudeville theater. Architects:
      Betts & Holcomb. Interior
      designer: Alfonso Iannelli.
      HISTORIC ILLINOIS 1990 Oct., v.13,
      no.3, p.12-13, photos.
   Jackson County Landmark: Grange Hall
      / Barbara Ulrich.
      Built in 1912.
      HISTORIC ILLINOIS 1990 Oct., v.13,
      no.3, p.6-7, photos.

ULRICH, CAROLYN
   Childish gardens / Carolyn Ulrich.
      GARDEN DESIGN 1990 Spring, v.9,
      no.1, p.82-[85], photos.
   Classicism's light new touch /
      Carolyn Ulrich.
      Small residential backyard gardens
      in Chicago, New Haven, Houston,
      and Washington, D.C. Landscape
      architects: Timothy Lally, Ralph
      Synnestvedt, Jr., Paul Bailey,
      Douglas Kycia, McDugald-Steele,
      Lanson Jones, and Jane Macleish.
      GARDEN DESIGN 1990 autumn, v.9,
      no.3, p.[30-37], photos.

ULRICH, DIETER
   Neubau eines Rathauses und
      Gestaltung des Rathausplatzes in
      Oberammergau = Building a new city
      hall and designing the city hall
      square in Oberammergau.
      Competition. First prize winners:
      Eberhard Schunck, Dieter Ulrich,
      Norbert Krausen. Text in German.
      ARCHITEKTUR + WETTBEWERBE 1990
      Dec., no.144, p.59-63, elevs.,
      models, plans, secn.

UMAYYAD
   See "UMAYYAD" AS A SUBHEADING AFTER
      SPECIFIC BUILDING TYPES OR OTHER
      MAIN HEADINGS.

UMEDA, MASANORI
   Red hot / Karin Tetlow.
      Interiors of the Tomato Bank,
      Okayama, Japan. Interior
      designer: Masanori Umeda.
      INTERIORS 1990 Apr., v.149, no.9,
      p.100-[101], photos., plan.

UMEMOTO, NANAKO
   Aktion Poliphile: Hypnerotomachia >
      Ero/machia/hypniahouse / Jesse
      Reiser, Nanako Umemoto.
      A competition project by the
      authors for a home that
      incorporates "the mazes of
      Renaissance allegory" with a site
      "on the banks of a lately
      suburbanized Rhine".
      ASSEMBLAGE 1990 Dec., no.13,
      p.[88]-105, elevs., models, plans.
   No place like home: domesticating
      assemblages / R. E. Somol.
      Essays discusses Preston Scott
      Cohen, Jesse Reiser and Nanako
      Umemoto, and Ben Nicholson.
      ASSEMBLAGE 1990 Dec., no.13,
      p.[59]-71, refs.

UMENOTO, NANAKO
Jesse Reiser - Nanako Umenoto.
Contents: A secret conversation
with Jesse Reiser, himself,
conducted by Daniel Libeskind --
Globe Theater project --
Hypnerotomachia house. Architects:
Jesse Reiser and Nanako Umenoto.
Text in Japanese and English.
ARCHITECTURE AND URBANISM 1990
Nov., no.11(242), p.38-61, ill.,
photos., plans.

UMINOWICZ, GLENN
Portland's monuments / Glenn
Uminowicz.
LANDMARKS OBSERVER 1990 Fall,
v.16, no.4, p.1,3-4, photos.,
aerial photo.

UMLANDVERBAND FRANKFURT
Electronic data processing in
planning at the Umlandverband
Frankfurt / Lorenz Rautenstrauch.
EKISTICS 1989 Sept.-Dec., v.56,
no.338-339, p.254-258, charts,
maps.

UNDERDEVELOPED AREAS
See DEVELOPING COUNTRIES

UNDERGROUND
See "UNDERGROUND" AS A SUBHEADING
AFTER SPECIFIC BUILDING TYPES OR
OTHER MAIN HEADINGS.

UNDERGROUND BUILDINGS
See BUILDINGS - UNDERGROUND

UNDERGROUND CONSTRUCTION
See CONSTRUCTION - UNDERGROUND

UNDERGROUND RAILROADS
See SUBWAYS

UNDERGROUND STRUCTURES
See BUILDINGS - UNDERGROUND

UNDERHILL, JACK A.
Soviet new towns, planning and
national urban policy / Jack A.
Underhill.
TOWN PLANNING REVIEW 1990 July,
v.61, no.3, p.263-285, chart,
model, maps, photos., plans, refs.

UNDERPASSES
See also PEDESTRIAN TUNNELS

UNDERPINNINGS
See also FOUNDATIONS
Settling claims / Matthew Coomber.
Evaluation of a BRE report on
costs and needs for underpinning
of houses.
BUILDING 1990 June 29, v.255,
no.26, p.52-53, graph, ill.,
photo.

UNDERWATER ARCHAEOLOGY--BULGARIA--NESEBAR
Nesebar: trent'anni di ricerche di
terra e subacquee / Ljuba Ognenova
Marinova.
BOLLETTINO D'ARTE 1990, v.75,
no.59, p.125-129, maps, photos.,
refs.

**UNDERWATER ARCHAEOLOGY--UNITED
STATES--FLORIDA KEYS (FLORIDA)--SAN
PEDRO WRECK SITE**
Establishing an underwater
archaeological preserve in the
Florida Keys: a case study, [San
Pedro Wreck site] / Roger C.
Smith, Robert Finegold, Eric
Stephens.
The New Spain Fleet was wrecked
along the Florida Keys in 1733.
ASSOCIATION FOR PRESERVATION
TECHNOLOGY. BULLETIN 1990, v.22,
no.3, p.11-18, photo., site plan,
refs.

UNDERWATER CONSTRUCTION
See also UNDERWATER BUILDINGS

**UNDERWATER CONSTRUCTION--NORTH SEA--
RAVENSPURN NORTH**
Ravenspurn North concrete gravity
substructure / John Roberts.
Underwater substructure for North
Sea oil platform, known as
"concrete gravity substructure"
(CGS). Architects/engineers: Ove
Arup & Partners.
THE ARUP JOURNAL 1989 Autumn,
v.24, no.3, p.cover-11,
axonometric views, dwgs., maps,
photos., secns., aerial photo.

UNEXECUTED DESIGNS
Architect projects by Reginald
Malcolmson.
A sports and cultural center
(1953-1973); a convention hall
(1954-1984).
OFFRAMP 1988 Spring, v.1, no.1,
p.[29-32], ill., dwgs., elevs.
Ausdruck einer neuen Einheit der
Kunste zu Oskar Kokoschkas
Entwurfen fur ein Krematorium in
Breslau (Worclaw) / Manfred
Scholze.
Date: 1914.
JAHRBUCH DER STAATLICHEN
KUNSTSAMMLUNGEN DRESDEN 1986,
v.18, p.123-131, dwgs., sketch,
refs.
Bericht uber eine Akademie / Ingrid
Krau.
Designs from the summer academy
for architecture in the Ruhr
region, done in July and Aug.
1989, featuring a research
facility. Includes proposals for
two sites by Gruppe Dudler, Gruppe
Kelp, Gruppe Van Lengen, and
Gruppe Reginaldi.
BAUWELT 1989 Dec.22, v.80, no.48,
p.2298-2309, dwgs., elevs.,
models, maps, secns.
La ciudad de Miguel Navarro = The
city of Miguel Navarro / Trinidad
Simo.
QUADERNS D'ARQUITECTURA I
URBANISME 1989 Oct.-Dec., no.183,
p.151-155, models.
Courtney Place: cemetery or car park
/ Daryl Cockburn.
Answers criticism to proposed
design of Wakefield Centre in
Wellington, New Zealand. The
multi-purpose complex was never
built. Architects: Cockburn
Architects & Planners, Ltd.
PLANNING QUARTERLY 1989 Sept.,
no.95, p.34, secn., site plan,
sketches.

UNEXECUTED DESIGNS (CONTINUED)
Documenti sul bozzetto per il
monumento a Francesco Pesaro di
Antonio Canova / Maria Giovanna
Miggiani.
VENEZIA ARTI 1990, v.4, p.176-185,
refs.
El Lissitzkys Wolkentraum: ein
Hochhaus auf drei Beinen / J.
Christoph Burkle.
DEUTSCHE BAUZEITUNG 1990 Jan.,
v.124, no.1, p.114-115, port.,
models, photo., sketches.
Estudio del palacio dibujado por
Leonardo en el folio 16 recto del
Codice B / Sebastian di Girolamo
Armanet.
ACHADEMIA LEONARDI VINCI 1990,
v.3, p.140-[144],pl.1-5, elevs.,
models, plan, secns., sketches.
The leaves and the flowers / N. John
Habraken.
The author describes the rationale
behind his design exercise ten
years earlier for a new Amsterdam
town hall.
URBAN FUTURES 1989 Winter, v.2,
no.4, p.5-16, elev., maps, photo.,
plans, secns., sketches, aerial
photo.
Liberta di progettare = Freedom to
design.
Two unexecuted designs by
self-taught architect Renato
Criscuolo. Text in Italian and
English.
SPAZIO E SOCIETA 1990 July-Sept.,
v.13, no.51, p.82-83, plans.
Lutyens' Roman Catholic Cathedral in
Liverpool: the restoration of a
"great model" / Edward Morris.
Designed in the early 1930s and
not executed. Model by John Brown
Thorp.
APOLLO 1990 Dec., v.132, no.346,
p.414-415, models.
Model restoration / John Summerson.
Restoration of the model for Edwin
Lutyens' unexecuted Liverpool
Cathedral.
ARCHITECTS' JOURNAL 1990 Nov.7,
v.192, no.19, p.30, models.
Plans for the original Hollywood
dream palace / Charles Lockwood.
On the unexecuted designs for Mike
Sennett's Hollywood Hills estate.
Architect: John De Lario.
ARCHITECTURAL DIGEST 1990 Apr.,
v.47, no.4, p.90,94, dwg., port.
Proyecto de club de golf: Carlos
Ferrater, Agusti Borrell y Carles
Borrell, arquitectos.
Spanish, English text.
ON DISENO 1990, no.108, p.120-126,
axonometric view, models, plans,
secns., site plans.
Scene di un museo italiano del
design = Scenes from an Italian
museum of design / Pierluigi
Nicolin.
Images illustrate ideas for a
museum to include prototypes and
unrealized projects.
OTTAGONO 1990 June, no.95, p.9-21,
dwgs., photos.

UNEXECUTED DESIGNS--19TH CENTURY--
GERMANY
The Munich Festival Theater letters
/ Sophie Gobran.
Never built, but functional as a
prototype for opera houses in
Central Europe. Article includes
excerpts from correspondence
between architect Gottfried Semper
and Richard Wagner.
PERSPECTA 1990, no.26, p.47-68,
ports., elev., models, map,
photos., plans, site plans, refs.

UNEXECUTED DESIGNS--20TH CENTURY--
GREAT BRITAIN
Geddes and Mackintosh / James S.
McGrath.
Supplements the author's article
in no.50 of this journal,
concerning plans dating from 1915
to 1918 in association with town
planning surveysin India.
CHARLES RENNIE MACKINTOSH SOCIETY.
NEWSLETTER 1990 Spring, no.53,
p.5, dwg.

UNEXECUTED DESIGNS--20TH CENTURY--
UNITED STATES--CHICAGO (ILLINOIS)
Sketches for the 1992 Chicago
World's Fair: John Hejduk and
Thomas Beeby.
PERSPECTA 1990, no.26, p.229-230,
sketches.

UNEXECUTED DESIGNS--ENGLAND--SPAGHETTI
JUNCTION PROJECT
Spaghetti brainstorm: Spaghetti
Junction Project [review] / Robert
Cowan.
Review of television broadcast on
"The Late Show" 13 June 1990 on
scheme commissioned by the BBC for
ideas on improving "the urban
wasteland under, over, and around
Spaghetti Junction in the West
Midlands".
ARCHITECTS' JOURNAL 1990 June 27,
v.191, no.26, p.71,73, dwg.,
sketch.

UNEXECUTED DESIGNS--EXHIBITIONS
LHdeK e le opere postume progettate
in vita [exhibition review] /
Jacques Gubler.
On projects from ca. 1922, in
conjunction with an exhibition at
the Fondation pour l'architecture
in Brussels, 5 Dec.1989-25
Feb.1990. Captions in Italian and
English.
CASABELLA 1990 Jan., v.54, no.564,
p.26,25, ill., sketch.

UNEXECUTED DESIGNS--FRANCE--NANTES
Un manifesto irritante ["Atlanpole"]
/ Hans Kollhoff.
The author's 1988 project for the
waterfront in Nantes--a single
large complex housing a hotel,
research, university, and
technology facilities. Includes
English summary; captions in
Italian and English.
CASABELLA 1990 Jan., v.54, no.564,
p.33-35,61, photo., plans, secn.

UNEXECUTED DESIGNS--FRANCE--PARIS--
TERRA INCOGNITA II
Terra incognita II / Lars Morell.
Entry in the 1989 exhibition
Paris: architecture et utopie,
which is an adaptation of the Gare
d'Austrelitz area of Paris.
Architects: Helle Juul and
Flemming Frost.
SKALA 1990, no.21, p.34-35, dwg.,
model.

UNEXECUTED DESIGNS--HOUSE FOR PIRANESI
AT HADRIAN'S VILLA
New rules for Prix de Rome / Val
Rynnimeri.
A history of the Canadian prize
and a look at the work of the
first winner, John Shnier.
CANADIAN ARCHITECT 1990 Jan.,
v.35, no.1, p.16-20, dwgs., port.,
models, map, site plans.

UNEXECUTED DESIGNS--SOVIET UNION
Russian revolution / Clare Melhuish.
Discussion of "paper architecture"
in the Soviet Union by a leading
exponent. Michael Belov.
BUILDING DESIGN 1990 Mar.9,
no.976, p.18, dwgs.

UNEXECUTED DESIGNS--UNITED STATES--
MINNESOTA
Unbuilt Minnesota: a glimpse of what
might have been / Robert Gorloff.
Unbuilt projects for Minn. sites,
1891-1989.
ARCHITECTURE MINNESOTA 1990
Mar.-Apr., v.16, no.2, p.[42]-47,
dwgs., elev., models.

UNGARO, LUCREZIA
Foro Traiano.
Eleven articles on the Forum of
Trajan including historical and
architectural reconstructions.
Authors: L. Messa, L. Ungaro, M.
Milella, P. Pensabene, G.
Piazzesi, B.M. Tummarello, S.
Stucchi.
ARCHAEOLOGIA CLASSICA 1989, v.41,
no.2, p.[27]-292, dets., dwgs.,
models, maps, plans, site plans,
recont. dwgs., refs.

UNGER, SUSANNE
Fussbodenheizung am Beispiel der
Raststatte Bruchsal / Susanne
Unger.
DEUTSCHE BAUZEITSCHRIFT 1990 June,
v.38, no.6, p.867-868, 870, dets.,
diagrs., photos.

UNGERICHT, HANSMARTIN
Geometrie und Politik. Zur
Raumplanung im Karolingerreich =
Geometry and politics. Regional
planning within the Carolingian
empire / Hansmartin Ungericht.
DAIDALOS 1989 Dec.15, no.34,
p.116-120, diagrs., maps, refs.

UNGERS, OSWALD MATHIAS, 1926-
Concurso de ideas en la zona
industrial de Hohenacker,
Pforzheim, Republica Federal
Alemana, marzo 1990.
Projects by E. Bardaji Alvarez and
A. Herrera (first prize);
Herkommer und Schmidt; Oswald
Mathias Ungers.
ARQUITECTURA 1990 July-Aug., v.72,
(Continued next column)

UNGERS, OSWALD MATHIAS, 1926-
(CONTINUED)
Concurso de ideas en... (CONTINUED)
no.285, p.28-31, dwgs., plans,
site plans.
Der "Forellenweg" in Salzburg.
Housing development. Architects:
Rob Krier; Adolf Krischanitz;
Franz Fonatsch, Heinz Wondra;
Reiner Kaschl, Heide Muhlfellner;
Aldo Rossi; Franz Demblin; Erwin
Pontiller; and O.M. Ungers.
Includes English summary.
BAUMEISTER 1990 June, v.87, no.6,
p.56-62, photos., plans, site
plan, aerial photos.
Museum fur Volkerkunde in Frankfurt.
Competition projects by Richard
Meier (winner); O.M. Ungers; and
Voigt & Herzig; Becker, Grossman,
Meiler.
BAUMEISTER 1990 June, v.87, no.6,
p.40-45, axonometric views,
models, site plans.
Neugestaltung Domplatz in Speyer =
Redesigning the Domplatz in
Speyer.
Architect: Oswald Mathias Ungers.
ARCHITEKTUR + WETTBEWERBE 1990
Dec., no.144, p.20-21, photos.,
site plan.
Piazza Matteotti und Piazza Gramsci
in Siena, Italien = Piazza
Matteotti and Piazza Gramsci in
Siena, Italy.
Competition. Features winning
designs by Martorell, Bohigas,
Mackay and runner-up, O.M. Ungers,
Walter Arno Noebel. Text in
German.
ARCHITEKTUR + WETTBEWERBE 1990
Dec., no.144, p.44-48, axonometric
view, dwg., model, maps, site
plans.
Progetti di aeroporti di Oswald
Mathias Ungers.
The 1989 plans for Hurum airport,
Oslo (with Arkitektgruppen K4) and
the 1988-89 plans for new East
Terminal, Frankfurt. Includes
English summary; captions in
Italian and English.
CASABELLA 1990 Feb., v.54, no.565,
p.10-22,59-60, axonometric view,
ill., elev., models, plans,
secns., site plans.
Technologiepark Universitat Bremen.
Architects: Gert Schulze and
Heinrich Campe; Hochbauamt Bremen;
Wolfram Dahms; Haslob Hartlich
Schutz; Oswald M. Ungers;
Rosengart + Partner; Kurt Schmidt.
Includes English summary.
BAUMEISTER 1990 Dec., v.87, no.12,
p.32-41, photos., plans, secns.,
site plans, aerial photos.
La terminal de la isla: concurso del
aeropuerto de Kansai / Vittorio
Magnago Lampugnani.
Entries by Renzo Piano, O.M.
Ungers, Henry Cobb, Bernard
Tschumi, Cesar Pelli, Jean Nouvel,
and Norman Foster.
ARQUITECTURA VIVA 1990 May-June,
no.12, p.14-18, axonometric views,
elevs., models, plans, secns.
Verpackung fur die Phantasie:
Wurfelgedanken = Wrapping for
imagination: cubic thoughts.
Cubical designs by architects
Oswald M. Ungers, Hans Peter
Reuter, Ganz & Rolfes.
(Continued next page)

UNITED STATES--AIRPORTS (CONTINUED)
From military surplus to municipal gold mine / John P. Kennedy.
Municipal uses for closed United States military air bases.
AMERICAN CITY & COUNTY 1990 June, v.105, no.6, p.28-30, photo.
Regional airports needed to solve capacity problems / J. Donald Reilly.
AMERICAN CITY & COUNTY 1990 June, v.105, no.6, p.32,34-35.

UNITED STATES--AKRON (OHIO)--HALLS OF FAME--NATIONAL INVENTORS HALL OF FAME
Special feature: James Polshek. Contents: Introduction / Toshio Nakamura --Architects' statement / James S. Polshek and James G. Garrison; --Works & projects: United States Embassy, Muscat, Oman --Centennial Hall, Barnard College, New York, N.Y. --Alumni houses, Bard College, Annandale, N.Y. --Hastings Hall, Union Theological Seminary, New York, N.Y. --IBM-ISG North Central Marketing Division headquarters, White Plains, N.Y. --Seaman's Church Institute, New York, N.Y. --Yerba Buena Gardens Theater, San Francisco, Calif. --National Inventors Hall of Fame, Akron, Ohio --New York University Medical Center Biomolecular Research building, New York, N.Y. -- Biographies of James S. Polshek, Joseph L. Fleischer, Timothy P. Hartung, and James G. Garrison, p.126. Architects: James Stewart Polshek & Partners. Text in Japanese and English.
ARCHITECTURE AND URBANISM 1990 Nov., no.11(242), p.62-126, axonometric views, models, photos., plans, secns., site plans.
The spirit of invention in Akron / Wilma Salisbury.
The National Inventors Hall of Fame. Architect: James Stewart Polshek & Partners.
INLAND ARCHITECT 1990 Sept.-Oct., v.34, no.5, p.10, dwg., models.

UNITED STATES--ALACHUA COUNTY (FLORIDA)--HOUSING--EVALUATION--METHODOLOGY
Searching for substandard housing in Alachua County: a case study / Paul D. Zwick, Richard H. Schneider.
Computer automated methodology for the inventory and identification of substandard housing.
COMPUTERS, ENVIRONMENT AND URBAN SYSTEMS 1990, v.14, no.4, p.273-282, chart, plans, refs.

UNITED STATES--ALACHUA COUNTY (FLORIDA)--HOUSING--INVENTORIES--METHODOLOGY
Searching for substandard housing in Alachua County: a case study / Paul D. Zwick, Richard H. Schneider.
Computer automated methodology for the inventory and identification of substandard housing.
COMPUTERS, ENVIRONMENT AND URBAN SYSTEMS 1990, v.14, no.4,
(Continued next column)

UNITED STATES--ALACHUA COUNTY (FLORIDA)--HOUSING--INVENTORIES--METHODOLOGY (CONTINUED)
Searching for...(CONTINUED)
p.273-282, chart, plans, refs.

UNITED STATES--ALASKA--CONSERVATION OF NATURAL RESOURCES
Alaska's Northwest Area plan / Jim Schwab.
Winner of 1990 APA Paul Davidoff Award for advocacy planning for resource and land management of Native American tribes in Alaska.
PLANNING 1990 Mar., v.56, no.3, p.11, photo.

UNITED STATES--ALASKA--REGIONAL PLANNING--AWARDS AND PRIZES
Alaska's Northwest Area plan / Jim Schwab.
Winner of 1990 APA Paul Davidoff Award for advocacy planning for resource and land management of Native American tribes in Alaska.
PLANNING 1990 Mar., v.56, no.3, p.11, photo.

UNITED STATES--ALBANY (NEW YORK)--AFFORDABLE HOUSING
Preservation providing housing / Nancy A. Kupiec.
Albany projects that are converting historic buildings into affordable housing and services in low-income neighborhoods.
ALBANY PRESERVATION REPORT 1990 Feb., v.9, no.1, p.[1],7, photos.

UNITED STATES--ALBANY (NEW YORK)--BANKS--GREEK REVIVAL--CONSERVATION AND RESTORATION--KEY BANK
Key Bank: an architectural achievement renewed.
Greek revival building at 60 State St., downtown Albany. Original architects: York & Sawyer. Architect for restoration: H.J. Sidford, Jr.
ALBANY PRESERVATION REPORT 1990 Summer, v.9, no.2, p.3, photo.

UNITED STATES--ALBANY (NEW YORK)--HISTORIC BUILDINGS--ALTERATIONS AND ADDITIONS
Preservation providing housing / Nancy A. Kupiec.
Albany projects that are converting historic buildings into affordable housing and services in low-income neighborhoods.
ALBANY PRESERVATION REPORT 1990 Feb., v.9, no.1, p.[1],7, photos.

UNITED STATES--ALBANY (NEW YORK)--IRONWORK--ARCHITECTURAL
Ornamental ironwork in Albany and Troy / Diana S. Waite.
Excerpt from Ornamental ironwork: two centuries of craftsmanship in Albany and Troy, New York.
PRESERVATION LEAGUE OF NEW YORK STATE. NEWSLETTER 1990 Spring, v.16, no.1 p.4-5, photos.

UNITED STATES--ALBUQUERQUE (NEW MEXICO)--AIRPORTS--ALTERATIONS AND ADDITIONS--ALBUQUERQUE INTERNATIONAL AIRPORT
International Airport, Albuquerque, New Mexico / Ronald L. Peters.
Renovation architects: BPLW Architects & Engineers.
TRIGLYPH 1990 Summer, no.10, p.22-27, photos., plans.

UNITED STATES--ALBUQUERQUE (NEW MEXICO)--CITY PLANNING--STUDY AND TEACHING--UNIVERSITY OF NEW MEXICO
Teaching students to become effective planners through communication: a planning communications studio / Paul Lusk, Min Kantrowitz.
At the University of New Mexico.
JOURNAL OF PLANNING EDUCATION AND RESEARCH 1990 Fall, v.10, no.1, p.55-59, table, refs.

UNITED STATES--ALBUQUERQUE (NEW MEXICO)--CLINICS--NEW MEXICO HEART CLINIC
New Mexico Heart Clinic, Albuquerque, New Mexico.
Architect: Antoine Predock. Spanish, English text.
QUADERNS D'ARQUITECTURA I URBANISME 1990 Jan.-Feb.-Mar., no.184, p.50, photos., plan.

UNITED STATES--ALBUQUERQUE (NEW MEXICO)--HOUSES--PRINCE HOUSE
Bart Prince.
Features home of architect's parents, Brad and June Prince in Albuquerque. Text in French and English.
ARCHITECTURE D'AUJOURD'HUI 1990 Oct., no.271, p.[171]-176, photos., plan, secns.

UNITED STATES--ALBUQUERQUE (NEW MEXICO)--HOUSES--ROBINSON - BURNEY HOUSE
D'adobe et de stuc: hacienda a Albuquerque / Claudine Mulard.
The Robinson-Burney house. Architects: Antoine Predock Architect. English summary, p.47.
ARCHITECTURE INTERIEURE CREE 1990 Feb., no.234, p.[100]-103, photos., plan, site plan.

UNITED STATES--ALEXANDRIA (VIRGINIA)--MULTI-USE COMPLEXES--CARR NORFOLK SOUTHERN PROJECT
Taming the city edge: urban design portfolio / Andrea Oppenheimer Dean.
The latest frontier--"outcities." Mission Bay, San Francisco; Downtown Norfolk, Va; Carr Norfolk Southern Project, Alexandria, Va.; and Arverne, New York City.
ARCHITECTURE: THE AIA JOURNAL 1990 Apr., v.79, no.4, p.[74]-79,147, ill., model, plans, sketches, aerial photos.

UNITED STATES--ALEXANDRIA (VIRGINIA)--
STAIRWAYS--ROUND--LAFRAK STAIR
Flights of fancy: details elevate
staircases to new artistic heights
/ Michael J. Crosbie.
LaFrak Stair, Alexandria, Va.,
designed by Tom Luckey, and Joseph
Shop stairs, London, Jiricna
Associates, Architects.
ARCHITECTURE: THE MAGAZINE OF THE
AMERICAN INSTITUTE OF ARCHITECTS
1990 June, v.79, no.6, p.101-103,
dets., photos., secn.

UNITED STATES--ALLENTOWN
(PENNSYLVANIA)--AIRPORT TERMINALS--
COMPETITIONS--LEHIGH AIRPORT
Lloyd Wright and the Lehigh Airport
competition / Howard Shubert.
RACAR: REVUE D'ART CANADIENNE.
CANADIAN ART REVIEW 1989, v.16,
no.2, p.165-170,288-297, dets.,
elevs., plans, site plans, refs.

UNITED STATES--ALLENTOWN
(PENNSYLVANIA)--OFFICES--INTERIOR
DESIGN--VITRA SEATING
High-tech in high style / Kristen
Richards.
Focus on Vitra Seating
office/showroom, Allentown, Pa.
Architects: Haigh Space.
INTERIORS 1990 Sept., v.149,
no.14, p.122-125, axonometric
view, photos.

UNITED STATES--ALLENTOWN
(PENNSYLVANIA)--SHOWROOMS--
FURNITURE--VITRA SEATING
High-tech in high style / Kristen
Richards.
Focus on Vitra Seating
office/showroom, Allentown, Pa.
Architects: Haigh Space.
INTERIORS 1990 Sept., v.149,
no.14, p.122-125, axonometric
view, photos.

UNITED STATES--AMAGANSETT (NEW YORK)--
HOUSES--COLONIAL REVIVAL
Williamsburg cottage.
Modern house in a Colonial style,
built by Vira Goldman of
Hladun/Goldman.
COLONIAL HOMES 1990 Aug., v.16,
no.4, p.[40-43], photos.

UNITED STATES--AMENIA (NEW YORK)--
HOUSES--WOODEN
Best Small House 1990 / Susan Zevon,
Katie Ridder.
Competition sponsored by HB and
the American Wood Council. Winning
house in Amenia, N.Y. by Jonathan
Lanman and Debra Wassman of
Trumbull Architects, N.Y.C.
Interior designer: Paul Leonard.
HOUSE BEAUTIFUL 1990 Nov., v.132,
no.11, p.81-91, photos., plans.

UNITED STATES--AMES (IOWA)--CITY
PLANNING--CITIZEN PARTICIPATION
The Ames plan: insights in action /
Martha Huntington.
On a community planning effort
assisted by Alan Fujimori of
Sasaki Associates.
IOWA ARCHITECT 1990 Winter, v.39,
no.4, p.24-25, site plans.

UNITED STATES--AMES (IOWA)--COMMUNITY
DEVELOPMENT
The Ames plan: insights in action /
Martha Huntington.
On a community planning effort
assisted by Alan Fujimori of
Sasaki Associates.
IOWA ARCHITECT 1990 Winter, v.39,
no.4, p.24-25, site plans.

UNITED STATES--AMES (IOWA)--
LABORATORIES--BIOLOGICAL--IOWA STATE
UNIVERSITY--MOLECULAR BIOLOGY
BUILDING
Decoding nature in Ames / Barbara K.
Hower.
The Molecular Biology Building at
Iowa State University. Architects:
Hansen Lind Meyer.
INLAND ARCHITECT 1990 Sept.-Oct.,
v.34, no.5, p.12, dwgs.

UNITED STATES--AMES (IOWA)--
UNIVERSITIES AND COLLEGES--
BUILDINGS--ALTERATIONS AND
ADDITIONS--IOWA STATE UNIVERSITY--
ALUMNI HALL
Old times, only better: Alumni Hall,
Iowa State University / Robert
Tibbetts.
In Ames. Architects: Herbert Lewis
Kruse Blunck.
IOWA ARCHITECT 1990 Fall, v.39,
no.3, p.16-[19], photos., plans,
secns.

UNITED STATES--AMES (IOWA)--
UNIVERSITIES AND COLLEGES--
BUILDINGS--IOWA STATE UNIVERSITY--
AGRONOMY HALL
A future with a past: Agronomy Hall,
Iowa State University / Martha
Huntington.
In Ames. Architects: RDG
Bussard/Dikis.
IOWA ARCHITECT 1990 Fall, v.39,
no.3, p.22-[25], photos., plans,
site plan.

UNITED STATES--AMES (IOWA)--
UNIVERSITIES AND COLLEGES--
BUILDINGS--IOWA STATE UNIVERSITY--
MOLECULAR BIOLOGY BUILDING
Decoding nature in Ames / Barbara K.
Hower.
The Molecular Biology Building at
Iowa State University. Architects:
Hansen Lind Meyer.
INLAND ARCHITECT 1990 Sept.-Oct.,
v.34, no.5, p.12, dwgs.

UNITED STATES--AMHERST
(MASSACHUSETTS)--UNIVERSITIES AND
COLLEGES--BUILDINGS--AMHERST
COLLEGE--CONVOCATION CENTER
Breaking ground / Michael Wagner.
Three projects: Kitchener, Ontario
city hall, architects: Kuwabara
Payne Mckenna Blumberg Architects;
Convocation Center, Amherst
College, Amherst, Mass.,
architects: Cambridge Seven
Associates; model home, part of
Living Environments program by GE
Plastics.
INTERIORS 1990 Feb., v.149, no.7,
p.128, dwgs.

UNITED STATES--AMPHITHEATERS--
ALTERATIONS AND ADDITIONS--TEMPORARY
Rolling Stones / Mark Fisher,
Jonathan Park.
High-tech stage sets for the 1989
U.S. tour. Section includes "It's
only rock'n'roll" and "Jagger: in
response to questions", by Andreas
Papadakis.
ARCHITECTURAL DESIGN 1990, v.60,
no.3-4, p.44-61, ill., photos.

UNITED STATES--ANDERSON (INDIANA)--
HOUSES--20TH CENTURY--BIXLER HOUSE
Bixler residence, Anderson, Indiana,
1988.
Architect: Charles Griffith. Text
in Japanese and English.
ARCHITECTURE AND URBANISM 1990
Dec., no.12(243), p.48-[55],
dwgs., photos., plans.

UNITED STATES--ANDERSON (INDIANA)--
MOVIE THEATERS--PARAMOUNT
Of Paramount concern: Indiana town
works to restore movie palace
[Paramount, Anderson, Ind.] / Ray
Begovich.
Opened in 1929, John Eberson,
architect.
PRESERVATION NEWS 1990 Mar., v.30,
no.3, p.6, photo.

UNITED STATES--ANDERSONVILLE
(GEORGIA)--WALLS--19TH CENTURY--
BRICK--NATIONAL CEMETERY
Restoring a historic brick wall /
Mark Ragan.
A five-foot wall built in
1878-1879 around the National
Cemetery in Andersonville, Ga.
CRM BULLETIN: A NATIONAL PARK
SERVICE TECHNICAL BULLETIN 1990,
v.13, no.5, p.8, port.

UNITED STATES--ANDOVER
(MASSACHUSETTS)--CITY HALLS--19TH
CENTURY--CONSERVATION AND
RESTORATION--ANDOVER TOWN HALL
To gather together: Andover Town
Hall restoration / Paul M.
Sachner.
In Andover, Mass. Architects: Ann
Beha Associates. Original
architect (1855): Theodore
Voelker.
ARCHITECTURAL RECORD 1990 Nov.,
v.178, no.12, p.62-65, photos.,
plans, secn.

UNITED STATES--ANDOVER
(MASSACHUSETTS)--DAY CARE CENTERS--
NEW ENGLAND BUSINESS CENTER--BRIGHT
HORIZONS CHILDREN'S CENTER
A developer responds to corporate
day care needs in Massachusetts /
Theodore R. Tye.
Architects: SBA, Steffian Bradley
Associates; Developer: National
Development Associates, Inc.
THE JOURNAL OF REAL ESTATE
DEVELOPMENT 1989 Summer, v.5,
no.1, p.38-44, plan, refs.

UNITED STATES--ANN ARBOR (MICHIGAN)--
CITY PLANNING--STUDY AND TEACHING--
UNIVERSITY OF MICHIGAN
Integrative planning workshops: the
Michigan experience / Anna Vakil,
Robert W. Marans, Allan Feldt.
JOURNAL OF PLANNING EDUCATION AND
RESEARCH 1990 Fall, v.10, no.1,
p.61-69, refs.

UNITED STATES--ANN ARBOR (MICHIGAN)--
CORPORATE OFFICE BUILDINGS--DOMINO'S
FARMS
Domino's effect / Michael J.
Crosbie.
On buildings designed for Thomas
Monaghan, president of Domino's
Pizza. Architects: Gunnar
Birkerts, Mockbee Coker
Architects, Hardy Holzman Pfeiffer
Associates, Fay Jones + Maurice
Jennings Architects, and Charles
W. Moore.
ARCHITECTURE: THE AIA JOURNAL 1990
Dec., v.79, no.12, p.[48-55],127,
dwgs., port., models, photos.,
secn., site plans.

UNITED STATES--ANN ARBOR (MICHIGAN)--
HOUSES--20TH CENTURY
Domino's effect / Michael J.
Crosbie.
On buildings designed for Thomas
Monaghan, president of Domino's
Pizza. Architects: Gunnar
Birkerts, Mockbee Coker
Architects, Hardy Holzman Pfeiffer
Associates, Fay Jones + Maurice
Jennings Architects, and Charles
W. Moore.
ARCHITECTURE: THE AIA JOURNAL 1990
Dec., v.79, no.12, p.[48-55],127,
dwgs., port., models, photos.,
secn., site plans.

UNITED STATES--ANN ARBOR (MICHIGAN)--
HOUSES--MONAGHAN HOUSE
Domino's effect / Michael J.
Crosbie.
On buildings designed for Thomas
Monaghan, president of Domino's
Pizza. Architects: Gunnar
Birkerts, Mockbee Coker
Architects, Hardy Holzman Pfeiffer
Associates, Fay Jones + Maurice
Jennings Architects, and Charles
W. Moore.
ARCHITECTURE: THE AIA JOURNAL 1990
Dec., v.79, no.12, p.[48-55],127,
dwgs., port., models, photos.,
secn., site plans.

UNITED STATES--ANN ARBOR (MICHIGAN)--
MOVIE THEATERS--MOORISH REVIVAL--
CONSERVATION AND RESTORATION--
MICHIGAN THEATER
Restoring dreams / Mark Alden
Branch, Abby Bussel.
On the restoration of six 1920-30s
American movie palaces.
PROGRESSIVE ARCHITECTURE 1990
June, v.71, no.6, p.92-99,
photos., plans, secns.

UNITED STATES--ANN ARBOR (MICHIGAN)--
RESEARCH FACILITIES--INDUSTRIAL
TECHNOLOGY INSTITUTE
Due recenti opere di William Kessler
= The Industrial Technology
Institute in Ann-Arbor, and The
State Library and Historical
Museum in Lansing, Mich. /
Stefania Mornati.
The buildings opened in 1987 and
1989.
L'INDUSTRIA DELLE COSTRUZIONI 1990
May, v.24, no.223, p.54-59,4,
elevs., photos., plans.

UNITED STATES--ANN ARBOR (MICHIGAN)--
SPORTS FACILITIES--MONAGHAN
SETTLEMENT POOL HOUSE
Domino's effect / Michael J.
Crosbie.
On buildings designed for Thomas
Monaghan, president of Domino's
Pizza. Architects: Gunnar
Birkerts, Mockbee Coker
Architects, Hardy Holzman Pfeiffer
Associates, Fay Jones + Maurice
Jennings Architects, and Charles
W. Moore.
ARCHITECTURE: THE AIA JOURNAL 1990
Dec., v.79, no.12, p.[48-55],127,
dwgs., port., models, photos.,
secn., site plans.

UNITED STATES--ANNANDALE (NEW YORK)--
DORMITORIES--BARD COLLEGE
Special feature: James Polshek.
Contents: Introduction / Toshio
Nakamura --Architects' statement /
James S. Polshek and James G.
Garrison: --Works & projects:
United States Embassy, Muscat,
Oman --Centennial Hall, Barnard
College, New York, N.Y. --Alumni
houses, Bard College, Annandale,
N.Y. --Hastings Hall, Union
Theological Seminary, New York,
N.Y. --IBM-ISG North Central
Marketing Division headquarters,
White Plains, N.Y. --Seaman's
Church Institute, New York, N.Y.
--Yerba Buena Gardens Theater, San
Francisco, Calif. --National
Inventors Hall of Fame, Akron,
Ohio --New York University Medical
Center Biomolecular Research
building, New York, N.Y. --
Biographies of James S. Polshek,
Joseph L. Fleischer, Timothy P.
Hartung, and James G. Garrison,
p.126. Architects: James Stewart
Polshek & Partners. Text in
Japanese and English.
ARCHITECTURE AND URBANISM 1990
Nov., no.11(242), p.62-126,
axonometric views, models,
photos., plans, secns., site
plans.

UNITED STATES--ANNAPOLIS (MARYLAND)--
HOUSES--20TH CENTURY
Wohnhaus bei Annapolis, Maryland.
Architects: Bohlin Powell Larkin
Cywinski. Includes English
summary.
BAUMEISTER 1990 Jan., v.87, no.1,
p.62-63, photos., plans.

UNITED STATES--APPLETON (WISCONSIN)--
ART CENTERS--LAWRENCE UNIVERSITY--
WRISTON ART CENTER
For art's sake: Wriston Art Center,
Lawrence University, Appleton,
Wisconsin, Centerbrook Architects
/ Lynn Nesmith.
ARCHITECTURE: THE AIA JOURNAL 1990
Jan., v.79, no.1, p.[84]-89,
photos., plans, site plan.

UNITED STATES--APPLETON (WISCONSIN)--
UNIVERSITIES AND COLLEGES--
BUILDINGS--LAWRENCE UNIVERSITY--
WRISTON ART CENTER
For art's sake: Wriston Art Center,
Lawrence University, Appleton,
Wisconsin, Centerbrook Architects
/ Lynn Nesmith.
ARCHITECTURE: THE AIA JOURNAL 1990
Jan., v.79, no.1, p.[84]-89,
photos., plans, site plan.

UNITED STATES--ARCATA (CALIFORNIA)--
ARCHITECTURE--VICTORIAN
Victoriana West: California's
Humboldt County claims some of the
finest Victorian architecture in
the country / Suzie Boss.
HISTORIC PRESERVATION 1990
Jan.-Feb., v.42, no.1, p.60-63,
photos.

UNITED STATES--ARCHITECT-DESIGNED
MERCHANDISE
Graves just wants to have fun /
Arlene Hirst.
Features the resort and convention
center at Walt Disney World,
including the Swan Hotel, as well
as furniture.
METROPOLITAN HOME 1990 Mar., v.22,
no.3, p.28,30, photos.

UNITED STATES. ARCHITECT OF THE
CAPITOL
Computers: the architect of the
Capitol / Eric Teicholz.
On the use of CAD and the
automation of facility management
at the AOC.
PROGRESSIVE ARCHITECTURE 1990
Aug., v.71, no.8, p.62,

UNITED STATES--ARCHITECTURAL DESIGN
The large firm artistically
considered / Edward R. Frenette.
"An investigation of excellence
and mediocrity in America's design
establishment", based on a study
conducted from 1986 to 1989.
INLAND ARCHITECT 1990 July-Aug.,
v.34, no.4, p.58-63, ill.

UNITED STATES--ARCHITECTURAL DESIGN--
SOCIOLOGICAL ASPECTS
Regulation: a realization of social
ethics / Francis T. Ventre.
Ethics relating to design, in the
U.S.
VIA 1990, no.10, p.[50]-61, dets.,
photos., sketches, tables, refs.

UNITED STATES--ARCHITECTURAL DESIGN--
STUDY AND TEACHING
Formgiving frontiers [fractals] /
Michael J.P. Smith.
Essay on the use of fractal
geometry in architectural
formgiving.
INLAND ARCHITECT 1990 May-June,
v.34, no.3, p.[58]-59, ill.

UNITED STATES--ARCHITECTURAL DESIGN--
THEORY--ADDRESSES, ESSAYS, LECTURES
Rafael Moneo: today's American
architecture.
Report on the Gropius Lecture,
given Apr.25, 1990, in which Moneo
examined two projects: Symphony
Hall, Philadelphia (Venturi Scott
Brown and Associates) and Disney
Concert Hall, Los Angeles (Frank
Gehry and Associates).
GSD NEWS / HARVARD UNIVERSITY.
GRADUATE SCHOOL OF DESIGN 1990
Summer-Fall, v.19, no.1, p.13-14,

UNITED STATES--ARCHITECTURAL
DRAWINGS--20TH CENTURY--EXHIBITIONS
Drawing the Wright way [exhibition
review] / Stanley Allan.
Review of exhibit at the Phoenix
Art Museum early in 1990, of 300
drawings from the Taliesin West
archives.
INLAND ARCHITECT 1990 May-June,
v.34, no.3, p.90-96, elev., secns.

UNITED STATES--ARCHITECTURAL
DRAWINGS--COLLECTIONS
HABS/HAER: a user's guide / Robert
J. Kapsch.
ASSOCIATION FOR PRESERVATION
TECHNOLOGY. BULLETIN 1990, v.22,
no.1-2, p.21-34, axonometric
views, dets., elev., secns.,
tables, isometric dwg., refs.

UNITED STATES--ARCHITECTURAL
LITERATURE--19TH CENTURY
La presse architecturale aux
Etats-Unis, 1870-1910 / David Van
Zanten, Mary Woods.
REVUE DE L'ART 1990, no.89,
p.19-28, photos., plans, engrs.

UNITED STATES--ARCHITECTURAL
LITERATURE--20TH CENTURY
La contraddizione decorata = The
decorated gap / Mark Wigley.
On Denise Scott-Brown and Robert
Venturi's work, including
"Complexity and contradiction in
architecture" and "Learning from
Las Vegas."
OTTAGONO 1990 Mar., no.94,
p.36-55, dwgs., elevs., models,
photos., plans, secns., sketches,
refs.

UNITED STATES--ARCHITECTURE
LA to NY.
Spanish, English text.
QUADERNS D'ARQUITECTURA I
URBANISME 1990 Jan.-Feb.-Mar.,
no.184, p.II-III, [38-41],[78-79],
photo.
USA 1990: topografia de un
territorio artificial = USA 1990:
Topography of an artificial
territory / Alejandro Zaera.
QUADERNS D'ARQUITECTURA I
URBANISME 1990 Jan.-Feb.-Mar.,
no.184, p.29-37. models, photos.,
site plan,

UNITED STATES--ARCHITECTURE--19TH
CENTURY--CONGRESSES
American architecture and the German
connection / Richard Pommer, Barry
Bergdoll.
KUNSTCHRONIK 1989 Oct., v.42,
no.10, p.570-574,

UNITED STATES--ARCHITECTURE--19TH
CENTURY--THEORY
Medievalism: an annotated
bibliography of recent research in
the architecture and art of
Britain and North America [book
review] / Kathleen Curran.
Review of the 1988 publication by
Edward Kaufman and Sharon Irish.
SOCIETY OF ARCHITECTURAL
HISTORIANS. JOURNAL 1990 Mar.,
v.49, no.1, p.112-113,

UNITED STATES--ARCHITECTURE--20TH
CENTURY
Voix distantes / Olivier Boissiere.
English summary, p.113.
ARCHITECTURE D'AUJOURD'HUI 1990
Oct., no.271, p.111-113,

UNITED STATES--ARCHITECTURE--20TH
CENTURY--AWARDS AND PRIZES
1990 AIA Componenet Awards / Amy
Gray Light.
A sampling of distinctive
buildings that have been honored
by the AIA's state, local, and
regional component organizations.
ARCHITECTURE: THE AIA JOURNAL 1990
Mar., v.79, no.3, p.44-64,
axononmetric view, photos., aerial
photo.
AIA Honor Awards 1990.
ARCHITECTURE: THE AIA JOURNAL 1990
Mar., v.79, no.3, p.82-113,
axonometric views, dwgs., port.,
elevs.,photos., plans, site plans.
AIA Honor Awards for 1990.
19 awards.
ARCHITECTURAL RECORD 1990 Mar.,
v.178, no.3, p.26-29, photos.

UNITED STATES--ARCHITECTURE--20TH
CENTURY--CONGRESSES
American architecture and the German
connection / Richard Pommer, Barry
Bergdoll.
KUNSTCHRONIK 1989 Oct., v.42,
no.10, p.570-574,

UNITED STATES--ARCHITECTURE--20TH
CENTURY--CRITICISM
Reflections on the need for an
avant-garde / Wojciech
Lesnikowski.
In the U.S.
INLAND ARCHITECT 1990 May-June,
v.34, no.3, p.[68]-72, photos.

UNITED STATES--ARCHITECTURE--20TH
CENTURY--SOCIOLOGICAL ASPECTS
These are a few of my favorite
things / David A. Greenspan.
Essay by the Chicago architect and
editor, on the culture of the
1980s, particularly music.
INLAND ARCHITECT 1990 May-June,
v.34, no.3, p.56-57,

UNITED STATES--ARCHITECTURE--20TH
CENTURY--THEORY
In search of the avant-garde
[editorial].
Introduction to eight articles
(indexed separately) on Eisenman
and Netsch.
INLAND ARCHITECT 1990 May-June,
v.34, no.3, p.[33], ill

UNITED STATES--ARCHITECTURE--21ST
CENTURY--ANECDOTES, FACETIAE,
SATIRE, ETC.
The firm in its maturity / Michael
J. P. Smith.
A humorous statement about a
fictitious firm CPF and
"metroplexes" in the year 2028.
INLAND ARCHITECT 1990 Jan.-Feb.,
v.34, no.1, p.[58]-59, model.

UNITED STATES--ARCHITECTURE--
COLLECTIONS
Quelques sculptures romanes du
Roussillon dans les collections
americaines / Eda Diskant.
LES CAHIERS DE SAINT-MICHEL DE
CUXA 1990 July, no.21,
p.199-[218], photos., refs.

UNITED STATES--ARCHITECTURE--
CONSERVATION AND RESTORATION
Who will care in the 1990s?: ethnic
diversity will play a greater role
in the preservation movement,
particularly in urban
neighborhoods / Michael A. Tomlan.
PRESERVATION FORUM 1990 Winter,
v.3, no.4, p.20-21, ill.

UNITED STATES--ARCHITECTURE--
CONSERVATION AND RESTORATION--
ECONOMIC ASPECTS
The business of preservation is
bullish and diverse / Sally
Oldham.
"Preservation's popular success
has resulted in dramatic benefits
for an ever-broadening industry."
PRESERVATION FORUM 1990 Winter,
v.3, no.4, p.14-19, graph, ill.,
photos., refs.

UNITED STATES--ARCHITECTURE--
CONSERVATION AND RESTORATION--
HISTORY
100 years of historic battles
[A.I.A.'s Committee on Historic
Resources] / Clem Labine.
"This year the AIA celebrates the
100th anniversary of its formal
committment to historic
preservation. The evolution of
AIA's role reflects America's
changing attitudes toward
preservation."
CLEM LABINE'S TRADITIONAL BUILDING
1990 Jan-Feb., v.3, no.1, p.3,28,
photo., ports.

UNITED STATES--ARCHITECTURE--
CONSERVATION AND RESTORATION--STUDY
AND TEACHING
A directory of training
opportunities in cultural
resources management October
1990-December 1991 / Amy Federman,
Emogene Bevitt, compilers.
Covers Federal agencies, state
agencies, and university and
college programs in the U.S. and
includes indexes by topic and
state.
CRM BULLETIN: A NATIONAL PARK
SERVICE TECHNICAL BULLETIN 1990
Sept., special issue p.[1-39],

UNITED STATES--ARCHITECTURE--FEDERAL
Yankee Federalist: Samuel McIntire
laid a firm foundation for
architecture in early America /
Martin Filler.
HOUSE & GARDEN 1990 Mar., v.162,
no.3, p.64,69, port., photos.

UNITED STATES--ARCHITECTURE--GREEK
REVIVAL
Behind Antebellum [book review] /
Jill Miller.
Greek Revival America by Roger G.
Kennedy.
MUSEUM & ARTS WASHINGTON 1990
Mar.-Apr., v.6, no.2, p.[36],
port.
Disorderly orders: Greek revival
America, by Roger C. [sic] Kennedy
[book review] / James Stevens
Curl.
ARCHITECTS' JOURNAL 1990 Sept.5,
v.192, no.10, p.89, photos.

UNITED STATES--ARCHITECTURE--HISTORY--
AWARDS AND PRIZES
From 1947: the Society of
Architectural Historians / Osmund
Overby.
Appendix includes lists of
Presidents, Editors, and award
winners.
SOCIETY OF ARCHITECTURAL
HISTORIANS. JOURNAL 1990 Mar.,
v.49, no.1, p.9-14, table.

UNITED STATES--ARCHITECTURE--NATIVE
AMERICAN--CONSERVATION AND
RESTORATION
Reconfiguring the cultural mission:
tribal historic preservation
programs / Dean B. Suagee, Karen
J. Funk.
CRM BULLETIN: A NATIONAL PARK
SERVICE TECHNICAL BULLETIN 1990,
v.13, no.4, p.21-24, refs.

UNITED STATES--ARCHITECTURE--
NEOCLASSICAL
The apostle of Classicism [Donald
Rattner] / Eve M. Kahn.
CLEM LABINE'S TRADITIONAL BUILDING
1990 Nov.-Dec., v.3, no.6, p.5,45,
dwgs., port., table.

UNITED STATES--ARCHITECTURE--SHINGLE
STYLE
The architecture of the American
summer: the flowering of the
shingle style [by] Vincent Scully
[and] Modern classicism [by]
Robert A. M. Stern, Raymond W.
Gastil [book review]/ Leland M.
Roth.
SOCIETY OF ARCHITECTURAL
HISTORIANS. JOURNAL 1990 Dec.,
v.49, no.4, p.453-455.

UNITED STATES--ARCHITECTURE--STUDY AND
TEACHING
Architecture: a place for women.
Contents: Room at the top? Sexism
and the star system in
architecture, by Denise Scott
Brown.--Educating for the future,
by Matilda McQuaid.--The studio
experience: differences for women
students, by Anne Vytlacil.
ARCHITECTURAL DESIGN 1990, v.60,
no.1-2, p.[X]-[XIV],

UNITED STATES--ARCHITECTURE--STUDY AND
TEACHING (CONTINUED)
Rafael Moneo: contemporary
curriculum [interview].
On differences between Europe and
the United States and the
relationship between architecture
schools and the profession.
COLUMBIA UNIVERSITY. GRADUATE
SCHOOL OF ARCHITECTURE, PLANNING
AND PRESERVATION. NEWSLINE 1990
Mar., v.2, no.6, p.5.

UNITED STATES--ARCOSANTI (ARIZONA)--
UTOPIAN COMMUNITIES
Il mondo di Soleri = The world of
Soleri / Michele Bazan Giordano.
Includes interview with Paolo
Soleri.
L'ARCA 1990 Apr., no.37 suppl.
l'Arca, p.100-101, photo.
La ricerca di Paolo Soleri = Paolo
Soleri's research / Luca Zevi.
Includes an interview.
ARCHITETTURA: CRONACHE E STORIA
1990 Dec., v.36, no.12(422),
p.[838]-874, ill., dwgs., photos.,
plans, secns., site plans,
sketches, aerial photos., biblio.

UNITED STATES--ARIZONA--ARCHITECTURE--
ARID REGIONS
Kamal Amin: dal Cairo all'Arizona,
sette opere organiche = from Cairo
to Arizona, seven organic works.
Houses in Va. and Ariz. and
medical centers in Tempe and
Scottsdale, Ariz.
ARCHITETTURA: CRONACHE E STORIA
1990 Sept., v.36, no.9(419),
p.[612-634], dets., photos.,
plans, secns., site plans.

UNITED STATES--ARIZONA--GREENHOUSES--
RESEARCH--BIOSPHERE II
Building a new biosphere / Walter
Scott Perry.
On Biosphere II, north of Tucson,
a sealed self-sustaining research
lab. Architect: Pearce Structures.
L. A. ARCHITECT 1990 Feb., p.5,
photos.

UNITED STATES--ARIZONA--HISTORIC
SITES--NATIVE AMERICAN--WUPATKI
NATIONAL MONUMENT
Cultural resource work at Wupatki
National Monument / Steve
Cinnamon.
In north central Arizona. Includes
essays by Muriel Crespi and Robert
T. Trotter, II.
CRM BULLETIN: A NATIONAL PARK
SERVICE TECHNICAL BULLETIN 1989,
v.12, no.6, p.5-8, photo.

UNITED STATES--ARIZONA--LABORATORIES--
ENVIRONMENTAL--BIOSPHERE II
Building a new biosphere / Walter
Scott Perry.
On Biosphere II, north of Tucson,
a sealed self-sustaining research
lab. Architect: Pearce Structures.
L. A. ARCHITECT 1990 Feb., p.5,
photos.

UNITED STATES--ARKANSAS--AFFORDABLE
HOUSING
Country living: a Mississippi
architect designs dignified
dwellings for the rural poor /
Robert A. Ivy.
Affordable housing in Arkansas
designed by Billy Wenzil: Lakeview
Estates; Prototype FHA Housing;
Keystone Apts.; and DeQueen
Villas.
ARCHITECTURE: THE MAGAZINE OF THE
AMERICAN INSTITUTE OF ARCHITECTS
1990 July, v.79, no.7, p.[68]-73,
elevs., photos., site plans.

UNITED STATES--ARKANSAS--HISTORIC
DISTRICTS--BIG BUFFALO VALLEY
HISTORIC DISTRICT
Boxley Valley, Buffalo National
River NPS historic district in
private hands / Jim Liles.
Adapted from a presentation made
Nov.17, 1988 at a conference in
Tucson.
CRM BULLETIN: A NATIONAL PARK
SERVICE TECHNICAL BULLETIN 1990,
v.13, no.4, p.14-15, photos.

UNITED STATES--ARKANSAS--HOUSING
DEVELOPMENTS--DEQUEEN VILLAS
Country living: a Mississippi
architect designs dignified
dwellings for the rural poor /
Robert A. Ivy.
Affordable housing in Arkansas
designed by Billy Wenzil: Lakeview
Estates; Prototype FHA Housing;
Keystone Apts.; and DeQueen
Villas.
ARCHITECTURE: THE MAGAZINE OF THE
AMERICAN INSTITUTE OF ARCHITECTS
1990 July, v.79, no.7, p.[68]-73,
elevs., photos., site plans.

UNITED STATES--ARKANSAS--HOUSING--
PUBLIC
Country living: a Mississippi
architect designs dignified
dwellings for the rural poor /
Robert A. Ivy.
Affordable housing in Arkansas
designed by Billy Wenzil: Lakeview
Estates; Prototype FHA Housing;
Keystone Apts.; and DeQueen
Villas.
ARCHITECTURE: THE MAGAZINE OF THE
AMERICAN INSTITUTE OF ARCHITECTS
1990 July, v.79, no.7, p.[68]-73,
elevs., photos., site plans.

UNITED STATES--ARKANSAS--HOUSING--
PUBLIC--PROTOTYPE FMHA HOUSING
Country living: a Mississippi
architect designs dignified
dwellings for the rural poor /
Robert A. Ivy.
Affordable housing in Arkansas
designed by Billy Wenzil: Lakeview
Estates; Prototype FHA Housing;
Keystone Apts.; and DeQueen
Villas.
ARCHITECTURE: THE MAGAZINE OF THE
AMERICAN INSTITUTE OF ARCHITECTS
1990 July, v.79, no.7, p.[68]-73,
elevs., photos., site plans.

UNITED STATES--ARKANSAS--NATIONAL
PARKS AND RESERVES--BUFFALO NATIONAL
RIVER
Boxley Valley, Buffalo National
River NPS historic district in
private hands / Jim Liles.
Adapted from a presentation made
Nov.17, 1988 at a conference in
Tucson.
CRM BULLETIN: A NATIONAL PARK
SERVICE TECHNICAL BULLETIN 1990,
v.13, no.4, p.14-15, photos.

UNITED STATES--ARKANSAS--PROTOTYPE
BUILDINGS--PROTOTYPE FMHA HOUSING
Country living: a Mississippi
architect designs dignified
dwellings for the rural poor /
Robert A. Ivy.
Affordable housing in Arkansas
designed by Billy Wenzil: Lakeview
Estates; Prototype FHA Housing;
Keystone Apts.; and DeQueen
Villas.
ARCHITECTURE: THE MAGAZINE OF THE
AMERICAN INSTITUTE OF ARCHITECTS
1990 July, v.79, no.7, p.[68]-73,
elevs., photos., site plans.

UNITED STATES--ARLINGTON (TEXAS)--
MERRY-GO-ROUNDS--SILVER STAR
CAROUSEL
When the parade passes by: a
dazzling Texas carousel goes
around again / Derro Evans.
A vintage 1920s carousel from the
Dentzel workshop has been restored
and is in use at Six Flags over
Texas, Arlington.
SOUTHERN ACCENTS 1989 July-Aug.,
v.12, no.4, p.82-87, photos.

UNITED STATES--ARLINGTON (VIRGINIA)--
WAR MEMORIALS--COMPETITIONS--
ARLINGTON NATIONAL CEMETERY--WOMEN
IN MILITARY SERVICE FOR AMERICA
MEMORIAL
In memoriam / Victoria Geibel.
On the design for a memorial to
honor American women who served in
the military, to be placed at
Arlington Cemetery. Architects:
Marion Gail Weiss and Michael A.
Manfredi.
METROPOLIS 1990 Jan.-Feb., v.9,
no.6, p.32, models.
Military Women's Memorial winner
announced / Douglas E. Gordon.
Winning design by Manfredi/Weiss.
ARCHITECTURE: THE AIA JOURNAL 1990
Jan., v.79, no.1, p.28, models.
Woman's memorial design chosen /
Thomas Vonier.
Winning design for the entrance of
Arlington National Cemetary
incorporates glass prisms atop
existing Beaux-Arts hemicycle
designed by McKim, Mead and White.
Architects: Marion Gail Weiss,
Michael A. Manfredi; Associate
Winners: Teresa Norton, Cleveland
Harp.
PROGRESSIVE ARCHITECTURE 1990
Jan., v.71, no.1, p.30, models.

UNITED STATES--ART CENTERS--COLUMBUS
(OHIO)--OHIO STATE UNIVERSITY--
WEXNER CENTER FOR THE VISUAL ARTS
Strukturalistiske spidsfindigheder--
om Wexner-centret for visuel kunst
/ Fleming Skude.
Architect: Peter Eisenman.
Reprinted from Progressive
architecture, 1989, no.10.
ARKITEKTUR DK 1990, v.34, no.1-2,
p.A2-A12, dwgs., photo., plan,
site plan.

UNITED STATES--ASHFORD (CONNECTICUT)--
FARMS--19TH CENTURY--CONSERVATION
AND RESTORATION--CHURCH FARM
Ashford: farmland easement /
Christopher Wigren.
30 acres of open farmland
surrounding 19th-cent. buildings
will be preserved.
CONNECTICUT PRESERVATION NEWS 1990
Jan.-Feb., v.13, no.1, p.4-5,
photo.

UNITED STATES--ASPEN (COLORADO)--
HOUSES--BENTON GRADOW HOUSE
Bart Prince Architect [houses].
Contents: Vacation house, Sun
Valley, Ida., design: 1988-89 --
Barbi Benton George Gradow family
residence, Aspen, Colo., design:
1989. Text in Japanese and
English.
GA HOUSES 1990 Mar., no.28,
p.128-133, elevs., models, plans,
secns.

UNITED STATES--ASPEN (COLORADO)--
HOUSES--TURNER HOUSE
Sette conferme di John Lautner delle
sette invarianti dell'architettura
moderna.
7 projects: Turner house, Aspen,
CO; Walstrom house, Los Angeles,
CA; Reiner house Los Angeles;
Arango house, Acapulco, Mexico;
house, Malibu, CA; children's
rehab center, Woodland Hills, CA;
house at Lechuza Point, Malibu.
English, French, German, Spanish
summaries.
ARCHITETTURA: CRONACHE E STORIA
1987 Jan., v.33, no.1(375),
p.[22]-40, photos., plans, secns.,
site plans.

UNITED STATES--ASPEN (COLORADO)--RANCH
HOUSES--INTERIOR DESIGN--GRUBER
HOUSE
Aspen on location: hotshot producer
Peter Guber creates the ultimate
Western movie set / Kent Black.
Interior designer: Dayna Van
Kleeck.
HOUSE & GARDEN 1990 Feb., v.162,
no.2, p.126-131,162, ports.,
photos.

UNITED STATES--ASTRONOMICAL
OBSERVATORIES--CONSERVATION AND
RESTORATION
Making technological facilities NHLs
[part 1] / Harry Butowsky.
Includes "The designation of
technological facilities as
National Historic Landmarks: a
report", covering the application
of the Historic Preservation Act
of 1966 to NASA properties and
observatories, such as those in
Pasadena, San Diego County, and
(Continued next column)

UNITED STATES--ASTRONOMICAL
OBSERVATORIES--CONSERVATION AND
RESTORATION (CONTINUED)
Making technological...(CONTINUED)
Cleveland.
CRM BULLETIN: A NATIONAL PARK
SERVICE TECHNICAL BULLETIN 1989,
v.12, no.6, p.1-4, dwg., photos.

UNITED STATES--ATLANTA (GEORGIA)--ART
GALLERIES--INTERIOR DESIGN--SANDLER
HUDSON GALLERY
Sandler Hudson / Karen Maserjian.
Interiors of Atlanta art gallery.
Architects: Associated Space
Design.
INTERIOR DESIGN 1990 Nov., v.61,
no.15, p.[166]-167, photos., plan.

UNITED STATES--ATLANTA (GEORGIA)--
CHAPELS--EMORY UNIVERSITY
Focal point: [D. Abbott Turner
Center, Emory University] / Jim
Murphy.
On the community center of the
Candler School of Theology.
Includes small chapel and the
renovated Turner Village Housing.
Architects: Scogin, Elam & Bray,
Architects.
PROGRESSIVE ARCHITECTURE 1990
Dec., v.71, no.13, p.66-73, dets.,
photos., plan, site plan.

UNITED STATES--ATLANTA (GEORGIA)--
CITIES AND TOWNS
Atlanta / Rem Koolhaas.
From a lecture given in 1988.
Spanish, English text.
QUADERNS D'ARQUITECTURA I
URBANISME 1990 Jan.-Feb.-Mar.,
no.184, p.105-113, map.

UNITED STATES--ATLANTA (GEORGIA)--
CITIES AND TOWNS--GROWTH
City profile: Atlanta / Ebenezer
Aka.
CITIES 1990 Aug., v.7, no.3,
p.186-193, maps, photos., tables,
refs.

UNITED STATES--ATLANTA (GEORGIA)--CITY
PLANNING
Das Atlanta-Experiment / Rem
Koolhaas.
ARCH PLUS 1990 Oct., no.105-106,
p.73-75, photos., site plans.
City profile: Atlanta / Ebenezer
Aka.
CITIES 1990 Aug., v.7, no.3,
p.186-193, maps, photos., tables,
refs.

UNITED STATES--ATLANTA (GEORGIA)--
COMMUNITY CENTERS--EMORY
UNIVERSITY--D. ABBOTT TURNER CENTER
Focal point: [D. Abbott Turner
Center, Emory University] / Jim
Murphy.
On the community center of the
Candler School of Theology.
Includes small chapel and the
renovated Turner Village Housing.
Architects: Scogin, Elam & Bray,
Architects.
PROGRESSIVE ARCHITECTURE 1990
Dec., v.71, no.13, p.66-73, dets.,
photos., plan, site plan.

UNITED STATES--ATLANTA (GEORGIA)--
PEDESTRIAN BRIDGES--BRIDGE AT
CONCOURSE (CONTINUED)
Ponte pedonale ad Atlanta = A bridge
at Concourse in Atlanta, Ga. /
Silvano Stucchi.
Across an artificial lake at the
Perimeter Center, north of
Atlanta. Architect: Scogin Elam
and Bray. Includes English
translation; French, German, and
Spanish summaries, p.4.
L'INDUSTRIA DELLE COSTRUZIONI 1990
Jan., v.24, no.219, p.38-41,
elevs., photos., plan, secns.,
sketches.

UNITED STATES--ATLANTA (GEORGIA)--
RANCH HOUSES--ALTERATIONS AND
ADDITIONS
Getting a second wind: contemporary
revitalization for an Atlanta
ranch house / Laura C. Lieberman.
Post-modern transformation.
Architect: Kemp Mooney. Interior
designers: Gandy/Peace.
SOUTHERN ACCENTS 1989 May-June,
v.12, no.3, p.138-143, photos.

UNITED STATES--ATLANTA (GEORGIA)--
SHOWROOMS--FURNITURE--HERMAN MILLER
Lo spazio che rimalza: Showroom ad
Atlanta.
Architects: Scogin Elam & Bray.
ARCHITETTURA; CRONACHE E STORIA
1990 Mar., v.36, no.3(413),
p.204-205, photos, plan.

UNITED STATES--ATLANTA (GEORGIA)--
STUDENT HOUSING--ALTERATIONS AND
ADDITIONS--EMORY UNIVERSITY--TURNER
VILLAGE HOUSING
Focal point: [D. Abbott Turner
Center, Emory University] / Jim
Murphy.
On the community center of the
Candler School of Theology.
Includes small chapel and the
renovated Turner Village Housing.
Architects: Scogin, Elam & Bray,
Architects.
PROGRESSIVE ARCHITECTURE 1990
Dec., v.71, no.13, p.66-73, dets.,
photos., plan, site plan.

UNITED STATES--ATLANTA (GEORGIA)--
TOWNHOUSES--INTERIOR DESIGN
A little collaboration: amity and
art in Atlanta.
Townhouse interiors by T. Gordon
Little.
SOUTHERN ACCENTS 1989 Mar.-Apr.,
v.12, no.2, p.134-139, photos.

UNITED STATES--ATLANTA (GEORGIA)--
UNIVERSITIES AND COLLEGES--
BUILDINGS--EMORY UNIVERSITY--D.
ABBOTT TURNER CENTER
Focal point: [D. Abbott Turner
Center, Emory University] / Jim
Murphy.
On the community center of the
Candler School of Theology.
Includes small chapel and the
renovated Turner Village Housing.
Architects: Scogin, Elam & Bray,
Architects.
PROGRESSIVE ARCHITECTURE 1990
Dec., v.71, no.13, p.66-73, dets.,
photos., plan, site plan.

UNITED STATES--ATLANTA (GEORGIA)--
UNIVERSITIES AND COLLEGES--
BUILDINGS--EMORY UNIVERSITY--TURNER
VILLAGE
Scogin Elam and Bray.
Features four projects in Georgia:
Clayton County Library, Jonesboro;
Buckhead Branch Library, Atlanta;
Chmar house, Atlanta; and Turner
Village, Candler School of
Theology, Emory Univ., Atlanta.
English summaries.
ARCHITECTURE D'AUJOURD'HUI 1990
Oct., no.271, p.134-144, elevs.,
models, photos., plans, secns.,
site plans.

UNITED STATES--ATLANTA (GEORGIA)--
UNIVERSITY MUSEUMS--EMORY
UNIVERSITY--MUSEUM OF ART AND
ARCHAEOLOGY
Museum of Art and Archeology, Emory
University, Atlanta, Georgia.
Michael Graves, architect.
ARCHITECTURE NEW JERSEY 1990,
v.26, no.6, p.11, photos.

UNITED STATES--ATLANTIC CITY (NEW
JERSEY)--GAMBLING CASINOS
Urban issues: Atlantic City / Donald
Prowler.
On the "architectural consequences
of casino gambling on Atlantic
City's Boardwalk," with mention of
Donald Trump's Taj Mahal.
Architect: Alan Lapidus.
PROGRESSIVE ARCHITECTURE 1990
Mar., v.71, no.3, p.117, ill.,
photo.

UNITED STATES--ATLANTIC CITY (NEW
JERSEY)--GAMBLING CASINOS--TAJ MAHAL
Trump Taj Mahal: the new jewel of
Atlantic City / Patric Dolan.
Project architect: Francis Xavier
Dumont. Developer: Donald J.
Trump.
REAL ESTATE FORUM 1990 Mar., v.45,
no.3, p.44-50, ports., photos.

UNITED STATES--ATLANTIC CITY (NEW
JERSEY)--HOTELS--TAJ MAHAL
Trump Taj Mahal: the new jewel of
Atlantic City / Patric Dolan.
Project architect: Francis Xavier
Dumont. Developer: Donald J.
Trump.
REAL ESTATE FORUM 1990 Mar., v.45,
no.3, p.44-50, ports., photos.
Urban issues: Atlantic City / Donald
Prowler.
On the "architectural consequences
of casino gambling on Atlantic
City's Boardwalk," with mention of
Donald Trump's Taj Mahal.
Architect: Alan Lapidus.
PROGRESSIVE ARCHITECTURE 1990
Mar., v.71, no.3, p.117, ill.,
photo.

UNITED STATES--AUBURN HILLS
(MICHIGAN)--FACTORIES--AUTOMOBILE
CHRYSLER TECHNOLOGY CENTER
Hi-lo gloss: automotive architecture
[Technology Center] / Catherine T.
Ingraham.
Research and development building
for Chrysler Corporation, located
in Auburn Hills, Mich. Architects
and engineers: CRSS.
INLAND ARCHITECT 1990 Nov.-Dec.,
v.34, no.6, p.[27-33], cover, dwg.,
photos., plan, secns.

UNITED STATES--AUBURN HILLS
(MICHIGAN)--RESEARCH FACILITIES--
CHRYSLER TECHNOLOGY CENTER
Hi-lo gloss: automotive architecture
[Technology Center] / Catherine T.
Ingraham.
Research and development building
for Chrysler Corporation, located
in Auburn Hills, Mich. Architects
and engineers: CRSS.
INLAND ARCHITECT 1990 Nov.-Dec.,
v.34, no.6, p.[27-33], cover, dwg.,
photos., plan, secns.

UNITED STATES--AUBURN (NEW YORK)--
CHAPELS--ROMANESQUE REVIVAL--WILLARD
MEMORIAL CHAPEL
Extraordinary efforts save Willard
Chapel.
A Romanesque revival chapel and
the adjoining Welch Memorial
Building, built 1892-1894 are the
only remaining buildings from
Auburn Theological Seminary and
have been purchased by the Cayuga
County Community Preservation
Committee. Architects: Andrew
Jackson Warner.
PRESERVATION LEAGUE OF NEW YORK
STATE. NEWSLETTER 1990 Spring,
v.16, no.1, p.1-2, photos.

UNITED STATES--AUBURN (NEW YORK)--
THEOLOGICAL SEMINARIES--19TH
CENTURY--AUBURN THEOLOGICAL SEMINARY
Extraordinary efforts save Willard
Chapel.
A Romanesque revival chapel and
the adjoining Welch Memorial
Building, built 1892-1894 are the
only remaining buildings from
Auburn Theological Seminary and
have been purchased by the Cayuga
County Community Preservation
Committee. Architects: Andrew
Jackson Warner.
PRESERVATION LEAGUE OF NEW YORK
STATE. NEWSLETTER 1990 Spring,
v.16, no.1, p.1-2, photos.

UNITED STATES--AURORA (COLORADO)--
COURTHOUSES--AURORA MUNICIPAL
JUSTICE CENTER
Justice served: Aurora Municipal
Justice Center, Aurora, Colorado.
Architects: SOM.
ARCHITECTURAL RECORD 1990 Nov.,
v.178, no.12, p.96-[101], photos.,
plans, secns., site plans.

UNITED STATES--AURORA (ILLINOIS)--
FACTORIES--19TH CENTURY--FIRE
DAMAGE--AURORA WATCH COMPANY
History up in smoke [Aurora Watch
Co.] / Barbara K. Hower.
On Dec. 19, 1989, the former watch
factory (later the Aurora Corset
Co., Formfit; and Mikulik
Manufacturing Co, burned. Designed
in 1883. Architects: Adler and
Sullivan.
INLAND ARCHITECT 1990 Mar.-Apr.,
v.34, no.2, p.16, photos.

UNITED STATES--AURORA (NEW YORK)--
FARMHOUSES--19TH CENTURY--
MACKENZIE-CHILDS HOUSE
Fanciful farm: Richard and Victoria
MacKenzie-Childs apply wit and
whimsy to design / Stephanie
Vaughn.
1810 farmhouse of designers, in
western N.Y. State.
HOUSE & GARDEN 1990 July, v.162,
no.7, p.[36,38], photos.

UNITED STATES--AUSTIN (TEXAS)--ALUMNI
CENTERS--ALTERATIONS AND ADDITIONS--
UNIVERSITY OF TEXAS AT AUSTIN--
ALUMNI CENTER
Alumni center adds more and Moore /
Ray Don Tilley.
The UT Austin Alumni Center
addition. Architects: Charles
Moore, Richard Dodge, and Jessen
Inc.
TEXAS ARCHITECT 1990 July-Aug.,
v.40, no.4, p.59, dwgs., site
plan.

UNITED STATES--AUSTIN (TEXAS)--
ARTISTS' STUDIOS--TROIS HOUSE
Modern Mayan in Texas: an artist's
design for a stone house outside
Austin / Michael Ennis.
Charles Trois' home/studio.
ARCHITECTURAL DIGEST 1990 Sept.,
v.47, no.10, p.[218-224], port.,
photos.

UNITED STATES--AUSTIN (TEXAS)--
DETENTION CENTERS--GARDNER/BETTS
JUVENILE JUSTICE CENTER
Juveniles' separate shelter / Julius
M. Gribou.
Three Texas juvenile justice
centers: Gardner/Betts Juvenile
Justice Center, Austin (Cox
Croslin Associates); Enrique M.
Pena Juvenile Justice Center, El
Paso (Mervin Moore Associates);
and Bexar Co. Juvenile Center
(Golemon & Rolfe and L.K. Travis
and Assoc.).
TEXAS ARCHITECT 1990 July-Aug.,
v.40, no.4, p.34-37, dwg.,
photos., site plan.
Kids behind bars: Gardner/Betts
Juvenile Justice Center, Austin,
Texas.
Architects: Cox/Croslin and
Associates.
ARCHITECTURAL RECORD 1990 Sept.,
v.178, no.10, p.152-[153],
photos., plans, site plan.

UNITED STATES--AUSTIN (TEXAS)--DINERS
(RESTAURANTS)--MAJESTIC DINER
Interiors.
Contents: Berg & Androphy Law
Offices, Houston (William F. Stern
and Associates); Majestic Diner,
Austin (STUDIO Texas); and, El
Centro College Student Center,
Dallas (Oglesby Group).
TEXAS ARCHITECT 1990 Sept.-Oct.,
v.40, no.5, p.40-43, photos.,
plans.

UNITED STATES--AUSTIN (TEXAS)--
DISTRICTS--ALTERATIONS AND
ADDITIONS--REPUBLIC SQUARE DISTRICT
The Republic Square District,
Austin.
One of six urban design reports
included in special issue, Urban
Concepts. Extracted from a 1984
plan. Designers: Venturi, Rauch
and Scott Brown.
ARCHITECTURAL DESIGN 1990, v.60,
no.1-2, p.88-95, dwgs., elevs.,
maps, photos., sketches, aerial
photo.

UNITED STATES--AUSTIN (TEXAS)--HOUSES
Lawrence W. Speck: reshaping the
Texas ranch house.
Home near Austin features 2
barrel-vaulted bedroom suites with
galvanized-metal roofs.
ARCHITECTURAL DIGEST 1990 Sept.,
v.47, no.10, p.98-99, photo.,
plans.

UNITED STATES--AUSTIN (TEXAS)--
HOUSES--20TH CENTURY--SUNNY SLOPE
HOUSE
House on Sunny Slope.
In Austin. Architects: Lawrence W.
Speck Associates.
TEXAS ARCHITECT 1990 Jan.-Feb.,
v.40, no.1, p.27, photos., plans.

UNITED STATES--AUSTIN (TEXAS)--
HOUSES--ARCHITECTS'--SPECK HOUSE
Wohnhaus in Austin.
Architect: Lawrence W. Speck.
Includes English summary.
BAUMEISTER 1990 Nov., v.87, no.11,
p.58-61, photos., plans, site
plan.

UNITED STATES--AUSTIN (TEXAS)--
HOUSES--MCCURDY LODGE
Architecture for the '90s.
Holt Hinshaw Pfau Jones, Astronaut
Memorial, San Francisco--Henry
Myerberg, house in Vieques, P.R.--
Walter Chatham, house in Seaside,
Fla.--Carrie Glassman Shoemake,
house near Austin, Tex.--Mark
Domiteaux, house in Tex.--Frank
Lupo, Daniel Rowan, loft in NYC--
Michael Codwell, 4 projects in New
England.
METROPOLITAN HOME 1990 Jan., v.22,
no.1, p.[72]-96, ports., photos.

UNITED STATES--AUSTIN (TEXAS)--
HOUSES--STONE--TROIS HOUSE
Modern Mayan in Texas: an artist's
design for a stone house outside
Austin / Michael Ennis.
Charles Trois' home/studio.
ARCHITECTURAL DIGEST 1990 Sept.,
v.47, no.10, p.[218-224], port.,
photos.

UNITED STATES--AUSTIN (TEXAS)--HOUSING
FOR ELDERLY--ROBERT SHAW ECHO
VILLAGE
Robert Shaw ECHO Village.
Housing for elderly, Austin. Tom
Hatch Architects.
TEXAS ARCHITECT 1990 Jan.-Feb.,
v.40, no.1, p.24, photo., plan,
site plan.

UNITED STATES--AUSTIN (TEXAS)--HOUSING
FOR ELDERLY--ROBERT SHAW ECHO
VILLAGE (CONTINUED)
Small is suitable: small-scale
community-based low-rent houses /
Tom Hatch.
Robert Shaw ECHO Village (Elderly
Cottage Housing Opportunity)
project of detached rental houses
for low-income elderly tenants in
Austin, Texas. Architects: Tom
Hatch Architects.
URBAN LAND 1990 July, v.49, no.7,
p.24-25, photos., plans.

UNITED STATES--AUSTIN (TEXAS)--ICE
CREAM PARLORS--INTERIOR DESIGN--
AMY'S ICE CREAMS
Amy's Ice Creams / Judith Nasatir.
Interiors of shop in Austin, Tx.
Interior designers: Laurie Smith
Design Associates.
INTERIOR DESIGN 1990 Nov., v.61,
no.15, p.[152]-155, photos., plan.

UNITED STATES--AUSTIN (TEXAS)--LOW
INCOME HOUSING--ROBERT SHAW ECHO
VILLAGE
Small is suitable: small-scale
community-based low-rent houses /
Tom Hatch.
Robert Shaw ECHO Village (Elderly
Cottage Housing Opportunity)
project of detached rental houses
for low-income elderly tenants in
Austin, Texas. Architects: Tom
Hatch Architects.
URBAN LAND 1990 July, v.49, no.7,
p.24-25, photos., plans.

UNITED STATES--AUSTIN (TEXAS)--
MUSEUMS--ART--LAGUNA GLORIA ART
MUSEUM
Laguna Gloria Art Museum en Austin
Texas = Laguna Gloria Art Museum
in Austin Texas.
Architects: Venturi, Rauch and
Scott Brown. Text in Spanish and
English.
COMPOSICION ARQUITECTONICA, ART &
ARCHITECTURE 1989 Oct., no.4,
p.[85]-96, dwgs., ports., elevs.,
plans, secns., site plans,
sketches.

UNITED STATES--AUSTIN (TEXAS)--PUBLIC
BUILDINGS--BROWN - HEATLY STATE
OFFICE BUILDING
Supplanting the state-office
stereotype / Joel Warren Barna.
Brown-Heatly State Office
Building, Austin. Architects:
White Budd Van Ness Partnership.
TEXAS ARCHITECT 1990 July-Aug.,
v.40, no.4, p.49, photos., plan.

UNITED STATES--AUSTIN (TEXAS)--RENTAL
HOUSING--ROBERT SHAW ECHO VILLAGE
Small is suitable: small-scale
community-based low-rent houses /
Tom Hatch.
Robert Shaw ECHO Village (Elderly
Cottage Housing Opportunity)
project of detached rental houses
for low-income elderly tenants in
Austin, Texas. Architects: Tom
Hatch Architects.
URBAN LAND 1990 July, v.49, no.7,
p.24-25, photos., plans.

UNITED STATES--AUSTIN (TEXAS)--
UNIVERSITIES AND COLLEGES--
BUILDINGS--ALTERATIONS AND
ADDITIONS--UNIVERSITY OF TEXAS AT
AUSTIN--GOLDSMITH HALL
Best laid plans: Goldsmith Hall,
University of Texas, Austin,
Thomas & Booziotis Architects and
Chartier Newton & Associates,
Architects / David Dillon.
Addition to 1933 building designed
by Paul Cret.
ARCHITECTURE: THE AIA JOURNAL 1990
Nov., v.79, no.11, p.[84]-89,
photos., plans, secn., site plan.
Goldsmith Hall.
Addition to UT Austin building.
Architects: Thomas & Booziotis.
TEXAS ARCHITECT 1990 Jan.-Feb.,
v.40, no.1, p.32, photos., plan.

UNITED STATES--AUSTIN (TEXAS)--
UNIVERSITIES AND COLLEGES--
BUILDINGS--UNIVERSITY OF TEXAS AT
AUSTIN--ALUMNI CENTER
Alumni center adds more and Moore /
Ray Don Tilley.
The UT Austin Alumni Center
addition. Architects: Charles
Moore, Richard Dodge, and Jessen
Inc.
TEXAS ARCHITECT 1990 July-Aug.,
v.40, no.4, p.59, dwgs., site
plan.

UNITED STATES--AVERY COUNTY (NORTH
CAROLINA)--LAND USE
Avery County growth management
program: the evolution of planning
in a western North Carolina county
/ David H. Quinn.
CAROLINA PLANNING 1990 Fall, v.16,
no.2, p.9-13, map, photos., ref.

UNITED STATES--AVERY COUNTY (NORTH
CAROLINA)--REGIONAL PLANNING
Avery County growth management
program: the evolution of planning
in a western North Carolina county
/ David H. Quinn.
CAROLINA PLANNING 1990 Fall, v.16,
no.2, p.9-13, map, photos., ref.

UNITED STATES--BAC (ARIZONA)--
CHURCHES--SPANISH COLONIAL--
CONSERVATION AND RESTORATION--SAN
XAVIER DEL BAC
The restoration of San Xavier del
Bac: Phase I / Robert Vint.
Restoration of 1797 Spanish
Colonial church, Bac, Ariz.
Restoration architect: Eleazar
Herreras. Architect of record:
Robert Vint. Article focuses on
the refinishing of the building's
exterior.
TRIGLYPH 1990 Summer, no.10,
p.33-43, photos., secn., refs.

UNITED STATES--BAINBRIDGE ISLAND
(WASHINGTON)--HOUSES
The ranch sees red / Barbara
Flanagan.
House on Bainbridge Island, Wash.
Architect: Stuart Silk.
METROPOLITAN HOME 1990 July, v.22,
no.7, p.52-57, photos.

UNITED STATES--BALTIMORE (MARYLAND)--
ARTISTS' STUDIOS--TEMPORARY--
MARYLAND INSTITUTE COLLEGE OF ART
Artistic activity / Amy Dana.
On temporary sculpture studio for
visiting Japanese artists erected
at the Maryland Institute College
of Art, Baltimore. Architects:
RTKL Associates.
INTERIORS 1990 July, v.149, no.12,
p.80-81, models, plan, sketches.

UNITED STATES--BALTIMORE (MARYLAND)--
BASEBALL STADIUMS
Playing the field: Janet Marie Smith
/ David Masello.
Profile of the V.P. for new
stadium planning and development
for the Baltimore Orioles.
ARCHITECTURAL RECORD 1990 Oct.,
v.178, no.11, p.45-46, port.

UNITED STATES--BALTIMORE (MARYLAND)--
CORPORATE OFFICE BUILDINGS--19TH
CENTURY--CONSERVATION AND
RESTORATION--BALTIMORE GAS &
ELECTRIC
Delineating waterproofing / James S.
Russell.
Drawings of flashing details for
two restoration projects by
Ehrenkrantz, Eckstut & Whitelaw.
ARCHITECTURAL RECORD 1990 Aug.,
v.178, no.9, p.100-103, photo.

UNITED STATES--BALTIMORE (MARYLAND)--
CORPORATE OFFICE BUILDINGS--FIDELITY
& GUARANTY LIFE INSURANCE COMPANY
Essential baroque: Fidelity &
Guaranty Life Insurance Company
Headquarters, Baltimore, Maryland
/ Edward Gunts.
Architects: Peterson and
Brickbauer; Emery Roth & Sons.
ARCHITECTURE: THE AIA JOURNAL 1990
Oct., v.79, no.10, p.[64-71],
dets., photos., plans, secn.

UNITED STATES--BALTIMORE (MARYLAND)--
HISTORIC HOUSE MUSEUMS--HOMEWOOD
Homewood: Federal jewel of Baltimore
/ Susan Stiles Dowell.
Built 1801-06 by Charles Carroll,
Jr., and is now a museum.
Architects for the renovation:
Mendel, Mesick, Cohen, Waite and
Hall.
SOUTHERN ACCENTS 1989 May-June,
v.12, no.3, p.144-153, photos.

UNITED STATES--BALTIMORE (MARYLAND)--
HOUSES--19TH CENTURY--ALTERATIONS
AND ADDITIONS--LOCKARD HOUSE
Vernacular form and early suburban
housing: the case of the Lockard
house, Baltimore / Michael A.
Grimes.
Near Frederick Avenue; built
ca.1899.
MATERIAL CULTURE 1990 Spring,
v.22, no.1, p.33-48, maps,
photos., plans, biblio.

UNITED STATES--BALTIMORE (MARYLAND)--
MANSIONS--FEDERAL--INTERIOR DESIGN--
HOMEWOOD
Homewood: Federal jewel of Baltimore
/ Susan Stiles Dowell.
Built 1801-06 by Charles Carroll,
Jr., and is now a museum.
Architects for the renovation:
Mendel, Mesick, Cohen, Waite and
Hall.
SOUTHERN ACCENTS 1989 May-June,
v.12, no.3, p.144-153, photos.

UNITED STATES--BALTIMORE (MARYLAND)--
PENTHOUSES--INTERIOR DESIGN--JUDD
PENTHOUSE
For the love of art: an
antique-filled penthouse
overlooking Baltimore's Inner
Harbor / Susan Stiles Dowell.
Home of James Judd. Architect
Robert Berman; interior designer:
Henry Johnson.
SOUTHERN ACCENTS 1990 Oct., v.13,
no.8, p.[82]-91, ports., photos.

UNITED STATES--BALTIMORE (MARYLAND)--
RESIDENTIAL GARDENS--SMALL--DUNHAM
GARDEN
Simple solutions / Cheryl Weber.
Tiny backyard garden of Michael
Dunham in Baltimore. Landscape
designer: Michael McWilliams.
GARDEN DESIGN 1990 autumn, v.9,
no.3, p.46-49, photos., plan.

UNITED STATES--BALTIMORE (MARYLAND)--
SUBURBS--GROWTH
Vernacular form and early suburban
housing: the case of the Lockard
house, Baltimore / Michael A.
Grimes.
Near Frederick Avenue; built
ca.1899.
MATERIAL CULTURE 1990 Spring,
v.22, no.1, p.33-48, maps,
photos., plans, biblio.

UNITED STATES--BARABOO (WISCONSIN)--
THEATERS--AL. RINGLING THEATRE
The Al. Ringling Theatre, Baraboo,
Wisconsin, 1915-1990 [Historic
American Building Survey, HABS
No.WIS-261].
Rapp and Rapp, architects.
THEATRE HISTORICAL SOCIETY. ANNUAL
1990, v.17, cover, p.1-24, ill.,
dwgs., port., photos., plans.

UNITED STATES--BARRINGTON (ILLINOIS)--
MOVIE THEATERS--TUDOR REVIVAL--
CATLOW THEATRE
Barrington's Catlow Theatre: the
poor man's ticket to England /
Barbara Ulrich.
1927 Tudor revival movie and
vaudeville theater. Architects:
Betts & Holcomb. Interior
designer: Alfonso Iannelli.
HISTORIC ILLINOIS 1990 Oct., v.13,
no.3, p.12-13, photos.

UNITED STATES--BATH (MAINE)--MUSEUMS--
MARITIME--MAINE MARITIME MUSEUM
Harboring tradition: for a new
marine museum on the coast of
Maine, architect Winton Scott was
inspired by the powerful
industrial vernacular of a local
19th-century foundry / Nancy
Levinson.
The Maine Maritime Museum, Bath.
(Continued next page)

UNITED STATES--BATH (MAINE)--MUSEUMS--
MARITIME--MAINE MARITIME MUSEUM
(CONTINUED)
Harboring tradition:...(CONTINUED)
ARCHITECTURAL RECORD 1990 June,
v.178, no.7, p.72-[75], photos,
plans, secn.

UNITED STATES--BATON ROUGE
(LOUISIANA)--CAPITALS (CITIES)
Historic Baton Rouge / Mary Ann
Sternberg.
HISTORIC PRESERVATION 1990
May-June, v.42, no.3, p.16-19,
photo.

UNITED STATES--BATON ROUGE
(LOUISIANA)--CITIES AND TOWNS
Historic Baton Rouge / Mary Ann
Sternberg.
HISTORIC PRESERVATION 1990
May-June, v.42, no.3, p.16-19,
photo.

UNITED STATES--BATON ROUGE
(LOUISIANA)--HOUSES--18TH CENTURY--
CONSERVATION AND RESTORATION--JOSEPH
KLEINPETER HOUSE
Winning big: the fourteen winners of
the Trust's 1989 Great American
Home Awards / Jane Gillette.
Grand prize to Robert Hodges for
the renovation of the French
Creole Joseph Kleinpeter House in
Baton Rouge, La.
HISTORIC PRESERVATION 1990
Jan.-Feb., v.42, no.1, p.42-51,
photos.

UNITED STATES--BATTLE CREEK
(MICHIGAN)--CORPORATE OFFICE
BUILDINGS--KELLOGG COMPANY
Kellogg Company corporate
headquarters, Battle Creek,
Michigan, USA, 1986.
Architects: Gyo Obata of Hellmuth,
Obata & Kassabaum. Text in
Japanese and English.
ARCHITECTURE AND URBANISM 1990
Dec., no.12 extra edition,
p.84-[91], photos., plans, secn.,
site plan.

UNITED STATES--BAY OAKS (TEXAS)--
HOUSES--WETCHER HOUSE
Peter Waldman Architects [houses].
Contents: Wetcher house: a fable
of the Stegosaurus and the Trojan
horse, Bay Oaks, Texas, desgin:
1989 -- Fen house: a text for
nomads, surveyors and lunatics,
Princeton, N.J., design: 1988-89.
Architects: Peter Waldman
Architects. Text in Japanese and
English.
GA HOUSES 1990 Mar., no.28,
p.120-127, elevs., models, plans,
secns.

UNITED STATES--BEAR RUN
(PENNSYLVANIA)--HOUSES--CONSERVATION
AND RESTORATION--FALLINGWATER
Linking preservation to
architectural design [Wank Adams
Slavin Associates] / Clem Labine.
Their Preservation Department's
projects include Fallingwater and
the New York Municipal Building.
CLEM LABINE'S TRADITIONAL BUILDING
1990 Mar.-Apr., v.3, no.2,
p.5.24-25, ports., photos.

UNITED STATES--BEAR RUN
(PENNSYLVANIA)--HOUSES--FALLINGWATER
Edgar Kaufmann, Jr.-Secrets of
Wright and Fallingwater [obituary]
/ Brendan Gill.
ARCHITECTURAL DIGEST 1990 Mar.,
v.47. no.3, p.50-64, dwgs.,
ports., photos.

UNITED STATES--BEATRICE (NEBRASKA)--
CITY PLANNING
Assessing readiness for economic
development strategic planning: a
community case study / Christine
M. Reed, B. J. Reed, Jeffrey S.
Luke.
Beatrice, Neb.
AMERICAN PLANNING ASSOCIATION.
JOURNAL 1987 Autumn, v.53, no.4,
p.521-530, charts, photos.,
tables, biblio., refs.

UNITED STATES--BEAUTY SHOPS
Luoghi di bellezza fotografati /
Bruce J. Archer.
Photographs of American roadside
beauty salons by John Margolies.
Text in Italian and English.
DOMUS 1990 Jan., no.712, p.8-9,
photos.

UNITED STATES--BEAVERTON (OREGON)--
HOUSING DEVELOPMENTS--ANDOVER PARK
Northwest passage: regional
portfolio: the Pacific Northwest.
Six recent projects: Two Union
Sq., Seattle (NBBJ Group);
Washington Mutual Tower, Seattle
(Kohn Pedersen Fox, McKinley
Architects); Pacific First Centre,
Seattle (Callison Partnership);
Evergreen State College Studio
addition, Olympia (Miller/Hull
Partnership); Larry's Market,
Kirkland, Wash. (Carlson/Ferrin);
and Andover Park, Beaverton, Ore.
(Fisher-Friedman Associates).
ARCHITECTURAL RECORD 1990 May,
v.178, no.6, p.84-93, dwg.,
photos., plans, secns., site
plans.

UNITED STATES--BEDFORD (NEW YORK)--
RESIDENTIAL GARDENS--MILL POND FARM
Family heirloom: a romantic garden
by Fletcher Steele flourishes at
Mill Pond Farm / Ellen Count.
At the Country home of Francis J.
Kellogg, Bedford, N.Y.
ELLE DECOR 1990 May, v.1, no.4,
p.[84-91], photos.

UNITED STATES--BEDROOMS--CHILDREN'S
Met kids: living with style -- and
children, too.
A triennial section "on family
style", with profiles of three
interior designs of children's
bedrooms including one in southern
Calif. by architect Melinda Gray.
METROPOLITAN HOME 1990 Dec., v.22,
no.12, p.65-87, photos.

UNITED STATES--BEDROOMS--HISTORY
Sleeping aroung: a history of
American beds and bedrooms /
Elizabeth Collins Cromley.
"The second Banham Memorial
Lecture", delivered at the
Victoria and Albert Museum on 10
Jan.1990. Examples date through
1909.

(Continued next column)

UNITED STATES--BEDROOMS--HISTORY
(CONTINUED)
Sleeping aroung: a...(CONTINUED)
JOURNAL OF DESIGN HISTORY 1990,
v.3, no.1, p.[1]-17, dwgs., elev.,
photos., plans, refs.

UNITED STATES--BEL AIR (CALIFORNIA)--
HOUSES--INTERIOR DESIGN--LUBITSCH
HOUSE
Ernst Lubitsch: deft director of
Ninotchka and Heaven can wait /
Michael Frank.
Features interiors of 1934 home in
Bel Air designed by set designer
Harold Grieve.
ARCHITECTURAL DIGEST 1990 Apr.,
v.47, no.4, p.150-151,285, port.,
photos.

UNITED STATES--BEL AIR (CALIFORNIA)--
HOUSES--INTERIOR DESIGN--OBERON
HOUSE
Merle Oberon: Bel-Air estate of the
Best Actress nominee for The dark
angel / A. Scott Berg.
ARCHITECTURAL DIGEST 1990 Apr.,
v.47, no.4, p.[208-211], ports.,
photos.

UNITED STATES--BEL AIR (CALIFORNIA)--
MANSIONS--TUDOR REVIVAL--BAXTER
HOUSE
Warner Baxter: Bel-Air mansion of
enigmatic best actor for In old
Arizona / Richard Schickel.
Tudor revival home built in 1933.
ARCHITECTURAL DIGEST 1990 Apr.,
v.47, no.4, p.170-172, port.,
photos.

UNITED STATES--BELLEVUE (WASHINGTON)--
OFFICE BUILDINGS--FIRST INTERSTATE
PLAZA
First Interstate Plaza, Bellevue,
Washington, 1991.
Proposed office tower; architects:
Kohn Pedersen Fox Associates;
associate architects: Callison
Partnership. Text in Japanese and
English.
PROCESS: ARCHITECTURE 1989 Nov.,
no.86, p.78-81, elevs., model,
plans.

UNITED STATES--BELLEVUE (WASHINGTON)--
SUPERMARKETS--THE SHOPS AT LARRY'S
MARKET
Food chain: the Shops at Larry's
market, Bellevue, Washington,
Carlson/Ferrin Architects / Heidi
Landecker.
ARCHITECTURE: THE AIA JOURNAL 1990
Oct., v.79, no.10, p.[60]-63,
photos., plan, secns.

UNITED STATES--BERKELEY (CALIFORNIA)--
HOUSES--BARBEE HOUSE
Nella natura a viso aperto: opere
californiane di Robert K.
Overstreet.
Barbee House, Berkeley;
architect's house, Corte Madera;
Cottage Champion, Madison, Miss.;
house over water, Sausalito;
mausoleum, Colma; restaurant.
Summaries in English, French,
German, and Spanish.
ARCHITETTURA; CRONACHE E STORIA
1990 Jan., v.36, no.1(411),
p.[32]-42, dwgs., photos., plans,
secns.

UNITED STATES--BERKELEY (CALIFORNIA)--
HOUSES--BAUM HOUSE
California: Berkeley, 1988, Casa
Baum = California: the Baum house.
Architect: Mark Mack.
ABITARE 1990 June, no.286,
p.[124-133], photos, elevs.,
plans.
Mark Mack.
Most of issue devoted to the work
of this California-based
architect. Includes an interview
with David Cohn. Text in Spanish
and English.
EL CROQUIS 1990 Mar., v.9, no.42,
p.4-62, axonometric views, ill.,
dwgs., port., elevs., models,
photos., plans, secns., site
plans, refs.
Relectures: maisons a Los Angeles et
San Francisco, USA.
On two houses by Mark Mack: Baum
house, Berkeley and Whitney house,
Santa Monica. Summaries in English
and Spanish.
TECHNIQUES ET ARCHITECTURE 1990
June-July, no.390, p.112-118,181,
axonometric view, photos., plans,
elevs.

UNITED STATES--BERKELEY (CALIFORNIA)--
LIBRARIES--UNIVERSITY AND COLLEGE--
GRADUATE THEOLOGICAL UNION--FLORA
LAMSON HEWLETT LIBRARY
1990 AIA Component Awards: San
Francisco Chapter.
Three awards, one photo each.
ARCHITECTURE: THE MAGAZINE OF THE
AMERICAN INSTITUTE OF ARCHITECTS
1990 May, v.79, no.5, p.52,
photos.
Flora-Lamson-Hewlett-Bibliothek in
Berkeley/ Kalifornien, USA = Flora
Lamson Hewlett Library of the
Graduate Theological Union in
Berkeley/California USA.
Based on a 1974 Louis I. Kahn
design. Architects: Esherick
Homsey Dodge and Davis.
ARCHITEKTUR + WETTBEWERBE 1990
Sept., no.143, p.19-20, photos.,
plans.

UNITED STATES--BERKELEY (CALIFORNIA)--
OFFICES--LIGHTING--PEERLESS LIGHTING
CROPORATION
In the clouds / Justin Henderson,
Peter Barna.
Focus on the interior lighting in
the Peerless Lighting Corp.
headquarters, Berkeley, Calif.
Architects: MBT Associates.
INTERIORS 1990 Feb., v.149, no.7,
p.56, photos.

UNITED STATES--BERKELEY (CALIFORNIA)--
PARISH HALLS--SAINT MARK'S CHURCH--
HODGKIN HALL
Compound complex: Hodgkin Hall, St.
Mark's Church, Berkeley,
California / Donald J. Canty.
Architects: David Baker
Architects.
ARCHITECTURAL RECORD 1990 Apr.,
v.178, no.4, p.90-93, dwg.,
photos., plan, site plan.

UNITED STATES--BERKELEY (CALIFORNIA)--
UNIVERSITIES AND COLLEGES--
BUILDINGS--ALTERATIONS AND
ADDITIONS--UNIVERSITY OF CALIFORNIA,
BERKELEY--UNIVERSITY HALL
Seismic upgrade, structurally
expressed / Jeff Cohen ... [et
al.].
On the retrofit of the 1957
University Hall at UC Berkeley.
Original architects: Welton Becket
Associates. Renovation architects:
Hansen Murakami Eshima, Architects
and Planners. Engineers: H.J.
Degenkolb Associates.
PROGRESSIVE ARCHITECTURE 1990
Dec., v.71, no.13, p.41-42, dets.,
model, photo.

UNITED STATES--BERKELEY HEIGHTS (NEW
JERSEY)--REAL ESTATE DEVELOPMENT
Development of Berkeley Heights
property, Berkeley Heights, New
Jersey.
Architect: Michael Burns.
ARCHITECTURE NEW JERSEY 1989,
v.25, no.3, p.8, sketch.

UNITED STATES--BERKS COUNTY
(PENNSYLVANIA)--HOUSES--19TH CENTURY
Vernacular Houses: two-door houses /
Michelle Nicholl.
One of the mast common house types
in western Berks Co., Penn.,
evolved from the traditional
Pennsylvania Deutsch farmhouse.
OLD-HOUSE JOURNAL 1990 May-June,
v.18, no.3, p.[4] of cover,
photos., plan.

UNITED STATES--BERKS COUNTY
(PENNSYLVANIA)--VERNACULAR
ARCHITECTURE--19TH CENTURY
Vernacular Houses: two-door houses /
Michelle Nicholl.
One of the mast common house types
in western Berks Co., Penn.,
evolved from the traditional
Pennsylvania Deutsch farmhouse.
OLD-HOUSE JOURNAL 1990 May-June,
v.18, no.3, p.[4] of cover,
photos., plan.

UNITED STATES--BETHESDA (MARYLAND)--
HOUSES
Cesar Pelli & Associates: Maryland
residence, Bethesda, Maryland,
1985-89.
Text in Japanese and English.
GA HOUSES 1990 Dec., no.30,
p.152-159, axonometric view,
elev., photos., plans, site plan.

UNITED STATES--BEVERLY HILLS
(CALIFORNIA)--BANKS--COLUMBIA
SAVINGS & LOAN
Special feature: Richard Keating:
years at SOM 1976-1990.
Essays: Editor's introduction /
Toshio Nakamura --Architect's
statement --Richard Keating and
the varieties of Modernism / John
Pastier --Works: Columbia Savings
& Loan, Beverly Hills, CA --Grand
Avenue Plaza, Los Angeles, CA,
1992 --Latham Watkins law offices,
Los Angeles, CA, 1989 --Gas Tower,
Los Angeles, CA, 1992 --Ocean
Boulevard Condominiums, Long
Beach, CA, 1989 --lower City
Center competition, Cleveland,
Ohio, 1989 --Canon Building,
(Continued next column)

UNITED STATES--BEVERLY HILLS
(CALIFORNIA)--BANKS--COLUMBIA
SAVINGS & LOAN (CONTINUED)
Special feature:... (CONTINUED)
Beverly Hills, CA --Tokyo
International Forum honorable
mention project, Tokyo, Japan,
1989 --Katsuura Condominiums,
Katsuura, Japan, 1992. Architects:
Richard Keating of Skidmore,
Owings & Merrill and Keating Mann
Jernigan Rottet Architecture and
Interiors. Text in Japanese and
English.
ARCHITECTURE AND URBANISM 1990
Oct., no.10(241), p.58-128,
axonometric views, elevs.,
photos., plans.

UNITED STATES--BEVERLY HILLS
(CALIFORNIA)--CORPORATE OFFICE
BUILDINGS--CREATIVE ARTISTS AGENCY
Invidiabili dettagli Creative
Artists Agency a Beverly Hills di
I.M. Pei.
CASABELLA 1990 June, v.54, no.569,
p.22-24, dets., photos., plans,
secns., site plan.
Star quality: I. M. Pei & Partners'
concisely elegant Creative Artists
Agency in Beverly Hills... /
Martin Filler.
ARCHITECTURAL RECORD 1990 Jan.,
v.178, no.1, p.82-[89], photos.,
plans, secns., site plan.

UNITED STATES--BEVERLY HILLS
(CALIFORNIA)--HOTELS--INTERIOR
DESIGN--REGENT BEVERLY WILSHIRE
The Regent Beverly Wilshire /
Stanley Abercrombie.
Features remodeled interiors of
Beverley Hills hotel. Interior
designers: Glenn Texeira.
INTERIOR DESIGN 1990 June, v.61,
no.9, p.192-[201], photos., plan.

UNITED STATES--BEVERLY HILLS
(CALIFORNIA)--HOUSES--ALTERATIONS
AND ADDITIONS--ARANGO - BERRY HOUSE
Angeleno abstraction: Arango/Berry
House, Los Angeles, California /
Leon Whiteson.
Architect: Franklin D. Israel
Design Associates.
ARCHITECTURE: THE AIA JOURNAL 1990
Mar., v.79, no.3, p.[150]-153,
axonometric view, photos.
Due case unifamiliari a Los Angeles:
Franklin D. Israel.
Arango-Berry house and Lamy-Newton
house. Text in Italian and
English.
DOMUS 1990 Sept., no.719,
p.[74-81], axonometric view,
elevs., photos., plans.
Franklin D. Israel.
Features the Keith Bright and
Associates office building,
Venice, Calif. and the
Berry-Arango house, Beverly Hills.
English summary.
ARCHITECTURE D'AUJOURD'HUI 1990
Oct., no.271, p.159-163,
axonometric views, elev., photos.,
plans, secn.
Franklin D. Israel Design Assciates:
Arango-Berry residence, Beverly
Hills, California, 1989.
Clients: Marisa Arango. William
Berry. Text in Japanese and
English.
(Continued next page)

UNITED STATES--BEVERLY HILLS
(CALIFORNIA)--OFFICE BUILDINGS--
CANON BUILDING
Special feature: Richard Keating:
years at SOM 1976-1990.
Essays: Editor's introduction /
Toshio Nakamura --Architect's
statement --Richard Keating and
the varieties of Modernism / John
Pastier --Works: Columbia Savings
& Loan, Beverly Hills, CA --Grand
Avenue Plaza, Los Angeles, CA,
1992 --Latham Watkins law offices,
Los Angeles, CA, 1989 --Gas Tower,
Los Angeles, CA, 1992 --Ocean
Boulevard Condominiums, Long
Beach, CA, 1989 --Tower City
Center competition, Cleveland,
Ohio, 1989 --Canon Building,
Beverly Hills, CA --Tokyo
International Forum honorable
mention project, Tokyo, Japan,
1989 --Katsuura Condominiums,
Katsuura, Japan, 1992. Architects:
Richard Keating of Skidmore,
Owings & Merrill and Keating Mann
Jernigan Rottet Architecture and
Interiors. Text in Japanese and
English.
ARCHITECTURE AND URBANISM 1990
Oct., no.10(241), p.58-128,
axonometric views, elevs.,
photos., plans.

UNITED STATES--BEVERLY HILLS
(CALIFORNIA)--RESTAURANTS--INTERIOR
DESIGN--MAPLE DRIVE
Cool set [Maple Drive restaurant,
Beverly Hills] / Justin Henderson.
Architect: L. Anthony Greenberg.
INTERIORS 1990 Oct., v.150, no.3,
p.62-[63], photos.
A feast for the eyes / Leon
Whiteson.
On the Maple Drive Restaurant,
Beverly Hills, Calif. Architects:
L. Anthony Greenberg, Widom Wein
Cohen.
PROGRESSIVE ARCHITECTURE 1990
Sept., v.71, no.9, p.116-[119],
photos., plan.

UNITED STATES--BEVERLY HILLS
(CALIFORNIA)--RESTAURANTS--INTERIOR
DESIGN--POMODORO
Pomodoro / Edie Lee Cohen.
On the Italian trattoria in
Beverly Hills designed by Adam
Tihany.
INTERIOR DESIGN 1990 Apr., v.61,
no.6, p.186-[189], photos., plan.

UNITED STATES--BEXAR COUNTY (TEXAS)--
DETENTION CENTERS--BEXAR COUNTY
JUVENILE CENTER
Juveniles' separate shelter / Julius
M. Gribou.
Three Texas juvenile justice
centers: Gardner/Betts Juvenile
Justice Center, Austin (Cox
Graeber Associates); Enrique M.
Pena Juvenile Justice Center, El
Paso (Marvin Moore Associates);
and Bexar Co. Juvenile Center
(Golemon & Rolfe and L.K. Travis
and Assoc.).
TEXAS ARCHITECT 1990 July-Aug.,
v.40, no.4, p.34-37, dwg.,
photos., site plan.

UNITED STATES--BIG SUR (CALIFORNIA)--
INNS--VENTANA INN
Splendido isolamento = Splendid
isolation.
Ventana Inn, Calif. Architect:
Kipp Stuart.
ARCHITETTURA: CRONACHE E STORIA
1990 Dec., v.36, no.12(422),
p.878-879, photos.

UNITED STATES--BIRMINGHAM (ALABAMA)--
CITY PLANNING--CITIZEN PARTICIPATION
Cities build coalitions with clout.
Citizen participation and
political activism in New York,
Birmingham, Ala., and San
Francisco.
ARCHITECTS' JOURNAL 1990 Mar.14,
v.191, no.11, p.50-57, elev.,
photos., aerial photos.

UNITED STATES--BIRMINGHAM (ALABAMA)--
CORPORATE OFFICE BUILDINGS--SOUTHERN
PROGRESS CORPORATION
Into the woods: Southern Progress
Corporation Birmingham, Alabama /
Lynn Nesmith.
Architects: Jova Daniels Busby;
Kidd Plosser Sprague Architects.
ARCHITECTURE: THE AIA JOURNAL 1990
Oct., v.79, no.10, p.72-75,
axonometric view, photos., plan.

UNITED STATES--BIRMINGHAM (ALABAMA)--
HOUSES--INTERIOR DESIGN--ATCHISON
HOUSE
View from Red Mountain: a dazzling
cityscape in Birmingham / Susannah
M. Wilson.
Atchison house. Architect for
renovations: Bob Barnett.
SOUTHERN ACCENTS 1989 May-June
v.12, no.3 p.180-186, port.,
photos.

UNITED STATES--BIRMINGHAM (ALABAMA)--
HOUSES--ITALIANATE--VILLA COMACINA
Italian inspiration: formal but warm
decor for an Alabama residence /
Susannah M. Wilson.
In Birmingham. Architect: Randolph
Marks. Interior designer: Anna H.
Donald.
SOUTHERN ACCENTS 1990 May, v.13,
no.4, p.106-115, photos.

UNITED STATES--BIRMINGHAM (ALABAMA)--
OFFICE BUILDINGS--AMSOUTH HARBERT
PLAZA
AmSouth Harbert Plaza mixed use
center, Birmingham, Alabama, USA,
1989.
Architects: Hellmuth, Obata &
Kassabaum, with Gresham, Smith and
Partners. Text in Japanese and
English.
ARCHITECTURE AND URBANISM 1990
Dec., no.12 extra edition,
p.162-167, elev., photos., plans.

UNITED STATES--BLOCK ISLAND (RHODE
ISLAND)--BEACH HOUSES--COXE HAYDEN
HOUSE
Special feature: Venturi Scott Brown
and Associates.
Contents: Brief history-- Works:
Primate Center, Philadelphia
Zoological Garden.-- Lewis Thomas
Laboratory for Molecular Biology,
Princeton University, 1986.--
Malcolm S. Forbes Jr. College,
Princeton University, 1984.--
(Continued next column)

UNITED STATES--BLOCK ISLAND (RHODE
ISLAND)--BEACH HOUSES--COXE HAYDEN
HOUSE (CONTINUED)
Special feature:...(CONTINUED)
Gordon Wu Hall, Princeton
University, 1983.-- Venturi house,
Philadelphia, 1974-present.--
Izenour house, Stony Creek, Conn.,
1984.-- House in New Castle
County, Delaware, 1983.--
Coxe-Hayden house, Block Island,
R.I., 1981.-- Tarble Student
Center, Swarthmore College,
1985.-- Tree House, Philadelphia
Zoo, 1985.-- Welcome Park,
Philadelphia, 1982.-- Decorative
designs.-- Essay: "Body language"
and artifice: on some recent
designs by Venturi Scott Brown and
Associates. Text in Japanese and
English.
ARCHITECTURE AND URBANISM 1990
June, no.6(237), p.[39]-150,
ports., elevs., photos., plans,
secns., site plans.

UNITED STATES--BLOOMFIELD HILLS
(MICHIGAN)--ART SCHOOLS--CRANBROOK
ACADEMY OF ART
L'accademia Cranbrook = The academy:
Cranbrook / Juliana Balint.
A visit to the American design
school near Detroit, including the
house of Eliel Saarinen, recently
restored.
ABITARE 1990 Jan., no.281,
p.108-[115], ill., photos., aerial
photo.
Cranbrook foto Hans Cogne / Janne
Ahlin.
Photographs taken by Cogne during
a 1983 visit to Cranbrook Academy.
ARKITEKTUR: THE SWEDISH REVIEW OF
ARCHITECTURE 1990 Aug., v.90,
no.6, p.36-41, photos.

UNITED STATES--BLOOMFIELD HILLS
(MICHIGAN)--HOUSES--ARCHITECTS'--
INTERIOR DESIGN--YOUNGREN HOUSE
Timeless appeal: Ralph and Ann
Youngren show the virtues of
modern furnishings in their
Bloomfield Hills, Michigan,
residence / Edie Lee Cohen.
Interiors of architects' home.
INTERIOR DESIGN 1990 May, v.61,
no.7, p.278-[285], photos., plan.

UNITED STATES--BLOOMFIELD HILLS
(MICHIGAN)--HOUSES--ARCHITECTS'--
SAARINEN HOUSE
L'accademia Cranbrook = The academy:
Cranbrook / Juliana Balint.
A visit to the American design
school near Detroit, including the
house of Eliel Saarinen, recently
restored.
ABITARE 1990 Jan., no.281,
p.108-[115], ill., photos., aerial
photo.

UNITED STATES--BLOOMFIELD HILLS
(MICHIGAN)--HOUSES--MAINTENANCE AND
REPAIR--AFFLECK HOUSE
The Wright way: restoring a pair of
landmark structures / Amy Gray
Light.
Repairs using the latest
developments in roofing and
sealant technologies, for the
Grady-Gammage Auditorium at Ariz.
State Univ. and for the Affleck
(Continued next page)

UNITED STATES--BOSTON
(MASSACHUSETTS)--CHAPELS--SAINT
MARGARET'S CHAPEL
St. Margaret's Convent Chapel /
Kimberly A. Shilland.
Situated at Louisburg Square and
Pickney St., Boston. Designed in
1882 and completed in 1921.
Architect: Henry Vaughan.
BOSTON PRESERVATION ALLIANCE
LETTER 1990 Jan., v.11, no.1, p.3,
photo.

UNITED STATES--BOSTON
(MASSACHUSETTS)--CITY HALLS--
COMPETITIONS--BOSTON CITY HALL
Anbuilt Minnesota: Progressive
Design Associates, Boston City
Hall Competition, 1961 / Robert
Gerloff.
ARCHITECTURE MINNESOTA 1990
Nov.-Dec., v.16, no.6 p.55, dwg.

UNITED STATES--BOSTON
(MASSACHUSETTS)--CITY PLANNING
Boston Visions / Antonio DiMambro.
Plan for Boston 2088.
PLACES 1990 Winter, v.6, no.2,
p.48-55, axonometric views,
diagr., dwgs., plans, site plans,
aerial photo.
City Visions put life in good ideas.
"City Visions" competitions
sponsored by Philadelphia's
Foundation for Architecture
inspire similar projects in civic
excellence in Boston.
ARCHITECTS' JOURNAL 1990 Mar.14,
v.191, no.11, p.38-39,41,43-45,
dwgs., port., photos., plans,
secn., sketch.
How the BRA got some respect / John
King.
Boston Redevelopment Authority.
PLANNING 1990 May, v.56, no.5,
p.4-9, ports., photos., plan,
aerial photo.
Linking downtown development to
broader community goals: an
analysis of linkage policy in
three cities / W. Dennis Keating.
San Francisco, Santa Monica and
Boston.
AMERICAN PLANNING ASSOCIATION.
JOURNAL 1986 Spring, v.52, no.2,
p.133-141, biblio., refs.

UNITED STATES--BOSTON
(MASSACHUSETTS)--CITY PLANNING--BACK
BAY
Boston Back Bay: Atene d'America /
Sergio Stenti.
English, French, German, Spanish
summaries p.126-127.
STORIA DELLA CITTA 1989 Jan.-Mar.,
v.14, no.49, p.7-42, elevs., maps,
photos., plans, engrs., aerial
photos., biblio., refs.

UNITED STATES--BOSTON
(MASSACHUSETTS)--CITY PLANNING--
SOCIOLOGICAL ASPECTS
Design review and development in
Boston: not at odds / Peter Smith.
THE JOURNAL OF REAL ESTATE
DEVELOPMENT 1989 Spring, v.4,
no.4, p.45-50, dwgs., aerial
photos.

UNITED STATES--BOSTON
(MASSACHUSETTS)--CITY PLANNING--
STUDENT PROJECTS--FOREST HILLS MBTA
STATION AREA
Transforming a strategic urban site
/ Joseph Ryan.
Student projects for the area
surrounding the Forest Hills MBTA
Station, Boston, in the urban
design studio led by M. David Lee.
GSD NEWS / HARVARD UNIVERSITY.
GRADUATE SCHOOL OF DESIGN 1990
Winter, v.18, no.3, p.9, site
plans.

UNITED STATES--BOSTON
(MASSACHUSETTS)--COMMONS--BOSTON
COMMON
Probing the Boston Common / Steven
R. Pendery.
Archaeological finds.
ARCHAEOLOGY 1990 Mar.-Apr., v.43,
no.2, p.[42]-47, map, photos.,
engrs.

UNITED STATES--BOSTON
(MASSACHUSETTS)--CONGRESSES AND
CONVENTIONS--SACRED TRUSTS III
Boston to host Sacred Trusts III.
On meeting June 13-16, 1990.
PRESERVATION NEWS 1990 Feb., v.30,
no.2, p.4.

UNITED STATES--BOSTON
(MASSACHUSETTS)--CONVENTION
FACILITIES--JOHN B. HYNES VETERANS
MEMORIAL CONVENTION CENTER
Conventional difference: Boston's
new convention center / Amy Dana.
John B. Hynes Veterans Memorial
Convention Center. Architects:
Kallmann McKinnell & Wood,
Architects. Interior designer:
Stephanie Mallis.
INTERIORS 1990 Jan., v.149, no.6,
p.150-153, photos., plan.

UNITED STATES--BOSTON
(MASSACHUSETTS)--CORPORATE OFFICE
BUILDINGS--THE LIMITED
Unlimited vision [Leslie Wexner] /
Lynn Nesmith.
Buildings designed under the
patronage of Wexner. Architects:
Beyer Blinder Belle and Graham
Gund Architects; Jaquelin
Robertson, Hanna / Olin.
ARCHITECTURE: THE AIA JOURNAL 1990
Dec., v.79, no.12, p.[66]-73,
elevs., photos., plans, site
plans.

UNITED STATES--BOSTON
(MASSACHUSETTS)--COTTAGES--GOTHIC
REVIVAL--LLOYD HOUSE
Treasuring the past/ Elizabeth H.
Hunter.
Gothic revival cottage built in
1826. Attributed to A. J. Downing;
interior designer William Hodgins.
HOUSE BEAUTIFUL 1990 Jan., v.132,
no.1, p.48-55, ports., photos.

UNITED STATES--BOSTON
(MASSACHUSETTS)--DAY CARE CENTERS--
GOODWIN, PROCTOR AND HOAR--
CHILD-CARE CENTER
New kid on the block / Alice
Feiring.
On the Child-Care Center at Boston
law firm, Goodwin, Proctor and
Hoar. Architects; Jung Brannen
Associates.
INTERIORS 1990 Sept., v.149,
no.14, p.132-133, photos., plans.

UNITED STATES--BOSTON
(MASSACHUSETTS)--DESIGN REVIEW
Design review and development in
Boston: not at odds / Peter Smith.
THE JOURNAL OF REAL ESTATE
DEVELOPMENT 1989 Spring, v.4,
no.4, p.45-50, dwgs., aerial
photos.

UNITED STATES--BOSTON
(MASSACHUSETTS)--ENTRANCES--METAL--
101 FEDERAL STREET
An affinity for ornament: the work
of Kohn Pedersen Fox... / Donald
London.
Decorative uses of metal on 4
recent projects: 225 W. Wacker
Dr., Chicago; 101 Federal St.,
Boston; 1 O'Hare Center,
Rosemount, III., and 900 N.
Michigan Ave., Chicago.
ARCHITECTURAL RECORD 1990 May,
v.178, no.6, p.121-125,
axonometric view, dets., elevs.,
photos., secns.

UNITED STATES--BOSTON
(MASSACHUSETTS)--FACADES--19TH
CENTURY--CONSERVATION AND
RESTORATION--SUMMER STREET
Good manners: 125 Summer Street,
Boston, Massachusetts, Kohn
Pederson Fox Associates,
Architects.
300' tall tower incorporating the
elevations of four 19th-cent.
buildings.
ARCHITECTURAL RECORD 1990 Oct.,
v.178, no.11, p.[98-101], photos.,
plans, secn.

UNITED STATES--BOSTON
(MASSACHUSETTS)--FIRE STATIONS--
BOSTON FIRE DEPARTMENT DIVISION 1
HEADQUARTERS
Yankee ingenuity: Division 1
Headquarters, Boston Fire
Department.
Architects: Jung/Brannen
Associates.
ARCHITECTURAL RECORD 1990 Nov.,
v.178, no.12, p.72-75, photos.,
plans, secn., site plan.

UNITED STATES--BOSTON
(MASSACHUSETTS)--HOSPICES--INTERIOR
DESIGN--HOSPICE AT MISSION HILL
AIDS hospice / Judith Davidsen
On the collaborative project to
design a hospice in Mission Hill,
Boston. Interior designers:
Charles Spada, William Hodgins.
INTERIOR DESIGN 1990 Mar., v.61,
no.5, p.204-[205], photos.
Design as healer: Boston AIDS
hospice / Linda Hayes Tischler.
The Hospice at Mission Hill, in a
converted rowhouse and dating from
c.1987. Organizer: designer
(Continued next page)

UNITED STATES--BOSTON
(MASSACHUSETTS)--HOSPICES--INTERIOR
DESIGN--HOSPICE AT MISSION HILL
(CONTINUED)
Design as healer:...(CONTINUED)
Charles Spada.
METROPOLITAN HOME 1990 Sept.,
v.22, no.9, p.62, photo.

UNITED STATES--BOSTON
(MASSACHUSETTS)--HOUSING PROJECTS--
HARBOR POINT
On the waterfront: Harbor Point,
Boston, Massachusetts / Michael
Leccese.
Mixed-income housing project.
Architects: Goody, Clancy &
Associates, Mintz Associates.
ARCHITECTURE: THE MAGAZINE OF THE
AMERICAN INSTITUTE OF ARCHITECTS
1990 July, v.79, no.7, p.64-67,
ill., elev., photos., plans, site
plans.

UNITED STATES--BOSTON
(MASSACHUSETTS)--INDUSTRIES,
LOCATION OF
Silicon Valley y Route 128: i
prototipos regionales o
excepciones historicas? / Annalee
Saxenian.
Concentrations of technology-based
industries in northern California
and suburban Boston. In Spanish;
English summary p.57.
URBANISMO / COAM 1990 Sept.,
no.11, p.46-57, maps, photos.,
aerial photos.

UNITED STATES--BOSTON
(MASSACHUSETTS)--LAW OFFICES--
ALTERATIONS AND ADDITIONS--GOODWIN,
PROCTOR AND HOAR
New kid on the block / Alice
Feiring.
On the Child-Care Center at Boston
law firm, Goodwin, Proctor and
Hoar. Architects; Jung Brannen
Associates.
INTERIORS 1990 Sept., v.149,
no.14, p.132-133, photos., plans.

UNITED STATES--BOSTON
(MASSACHUSETTS)--MARKETS--QUINCY
MARKET
Urban marketplaces: Faneuil Hall
Marketplace, Boston,
Massachusetts.
Architects: Benjamin Thompson &
Associates. Text in Japanese and
English.
PROCESS: ARCHITECTURE 1990 June,
no.89, p.94-97, photos.

UNITED STATES--BOSTON
(MASSACHUSETTS)--MASS TRANSIT
STATIONS--BACK BAY STATION
Una stazione della Metropolitana di
Boston = Back Bay Station, Boston,
Mass. / Silvano Stucchi.
Architect: Kallmann, McKinnell &
Wood Architects. Includes English
translation. French, German, and
Spanish summaries p.4.
L'INDUSTRIA DELLE COSTRUZIONI 1990
Sept., v.24, no.227, p.42-47,
cover,4, elevs., photos., plans,
secns.

UNITED STATES--BOSTON
(MASSACHUSETTS)--MULTI-USE
BUILDINGS--360 NEWBURY STREET
Frank O. Gehry.
Entire issue devoted to the work
of this American architect.
Criticism by A. Zaera Polo and
David Cohn. 15 projects and
buildings from 1987-1990 featured.
Text in Spanish and English.
EL CROQUIS 1990 Nov., v.9, no.45,
p.1-124, ports., elevs., models,
photos., plans, secns., site
plans., refs.

UNITED STATES--BOSTON
(MASSACHUSETTS)--MULTI-USE
COMPLEXES--FAN PIER MASTER PLAN
Special feature: recent works of
Cesar Pelli.
Contents: Editor's introduction--
Architects' statement / Cesar
Pelli-- Essay: Urban iconography
and the medium of architecture /
Gavin Macrae-Gibson, p.130-137--
Works: World Financial Center--
Norwest Tower-- Pacific Design
Center expansion-- Mattatuck
Museum-- Ley Student Center
expansion, Rice University-- Yale
Center for Molecular Medicine,
Yale University-- Carnegie Hall
tower-- Sunarhauserman
headquarters-- Fan Pier master
plan. Architects: Cesar Pelli &
Associates. Text in Japanese and
English.
ARCHITECTURE AND URBANISM 1990
Feb., no.2(233), p.[59]-148,
dwgs., elevs., photos., plans,
secns., site plans.

UNITED STATES--BOSTON
(MASSACHUSETTS)--NEIGHBORHOODS--BACK
BAY
Boston Back Bay: Atene d'America /
Sergio Stenti.
English, French, German, Spanish
summaries p.126-127.
STORIA DELLA CITTA 1989 Jan.-Mar.,
v.14, no.49, p.7-42, elevs., maps,
photos., plans, engrs., aerial
photos., biblio., refs.

UNITED STATES--BOSTON
(MASSACHUSETTS)--OFFICE BUILDINGS--
75-101 FEDERAL STREET
101 Federal Street office building,
Boston, Massachusetts, 1984-88.
26-storey office building;
architects: Kohn Pedersen Fox
Associates; partner in charge: A.
Eugene Kohn.
PROCESS: ARCHITECTURE 1989 Nov.,
no.86, p.52-55, elevs., photos,
plan, secn.

UNITED STATES--BOSTON
(MASSACHUSETTS)--OFFICE BUILDINGS--
125 SUMMER STREET
Good manners: 125 Summer Street,
Boston, Massachusetts, Kohn
Pederson Fox Associates,
Architects.
300' tall tower incorporating the
elevations of four 19th-cent.
buildings.
ARCHITECTURAL RECORD 1990 Oct.,
v.178, no.11, p.[98-101], photos.,
plans, secn.

UNITED STATES--BOSTON
(MASSACHUSETTS)--OFFICE BUILDINGS--
ALTERATIONS AND ADDITIONS--73
TREMONT STREET
New tops for old buildings / Richard
Bertman, Dan Pinck.
Zoning restrictions limiting
building heights result in the
addition of new "tops" to old
buildings that are only a few
stories below maximum height
limits. Two examples in Boston: 73
Tremont St. and the Grant-Hoffman
Building at 745 Boylston St.
Architects: CBT/Childs Bertman
Tseckares & Casendino.
THE JOURNAL OF REAL ESTATE
DEVELOPMENT 1989 Summer, v.5,
no.1, p.78-80, photo.

UNITED STATES--BOSTON
(MASSACHUSETTS)--OFFICE BUILDINGS--
ALTERATIONS AND ADDITIONS--360
NEWBURY STREET
Presa de lo oblicuo: reforma del
edificio 360 Newbury Street,
Boston, Massachusetts, 1985-1988.
Architects: Frank O. Gehry and
Associates. English text, p.86.
A & V 1990, no.25, p.24-29, det.,
elevs., photos., plans, secn.,
site plan.

UNITED STATES--BOSTON
(MASSACHUSETTS)--OFFICE BUILDINGS--
ALTERATIONS AND ADDITIONS--
GRANT-HOFFMAN BUILDING (745 BOYLSTON
STREET)
New tops for old buildings / Richard
Bertman, Dan Pinck.
Zoning restrictions limiting
building heights result in the
addition of new "tops" to old
buildings that are only a few
stories below maximum height
limits. Two examples in Boston: 73
Tremont St. and the Grant-Hoffman
Building at 745 Boylston St.
Architects: CBT/Childs Bertman
Tseckares & Casendino.
THE JOURNAL OF REAL ESTATE
DEVELOPMENT 1989 Summer, v.5,
no.1, p.78-80, photo.

UNITED STATES--BOSTON
(MASSACHUSETTS)--OFFICE COMPLEXES--
20 AND 21 CUSTOM HOUSE STREET
The developer as peacemaker / Leland
Cott.
Development process for 20 and 21
Custom House Street, and office
project in Boston's historic
financial district. Architects:
Bruner/Cott Associates.
URBAN LAND 1990 June, v.49, no.6,
p.28-29, model, photos.

UNITED STATES--BOSTON
(MASSACHUSETTS)--OFFICES--INTERIOR
DESIGN--ENVISON
Setting the stage / Jean Gorman.
Features renovated interiors of
Boston video company, Envision.
Architects: Stein & Associates.
INTERIORS 1990 Nov., v.150, no.4,
p.16, photos.

UNITED STATES--BOSTON
(MASSACHUSETTS)--PARKS--19TH
CENTURY--MAINTENANCE AND REPAIR
Keeping the necklace bright / Nick
Burton, Russel Matthews.
On the establishment of a
landscape management plan for the
parks, the "Emerald Necklace"
designed by Frederick law Olmsted
in the Boston area.
LANDSCAPE DESIGN 1989 Nov.,
no.185, p.11-13, dwgs., tables,
ref.

UNITED STATES--BOSTON
(MASSACHUSETTS)--PARKS--BOSTON
COMMON
Probing the Boston Common / Steven
R. Pendery.
Archaeological finds.
ARCHAEOLOGY 1990 Mar.-Apr., v.43,
no.2, p.[42]-47, map, photos.,
engrs.

UNITED STATES--BOSTON
(MASSACHUSETTS)--PRISONS--SUFFOLK
COUNTY JAIL
Rooms with a view of the Charles:
Suffolk County Jail, Boston,
Massachusetts.
Architects: Stubbins Associates.
ARCHITECTURAL RECORD 1990 Sept.,
v.178, no.10, p.148-151,
axonometric view, photos., plans,
secn., site plan.

UNITED STATES--BOSTON
(MASSACHUSETTS)--RAILROAD STATIONS--
19TH CENTURY--CONSERVATION AND
RESTORATION--SOUTH STATION
Cheering restoration of Boston's
South Station / Jane Holtz Kay.
Refurbishment of 1890 railroad
station. Original architects:
Shepley, Rutan and Coolidge.
Restoration architects: Stubbins
Associates and others.
PROGRESSIVE ARCHITECTURE 1990
Aug., v.71, no.8, p.30-31, photos.

UNITED STATES--BOSTON
(MASSACHUSETTS)--RESTAURANTS--
INTERIOR DESIGN--BIBA
Biba / Edie Lee Cohen.
Boston restaurant interiors.
Interior designer: Adam Tihany.
INTERIOR DESIGN 1990 Oct., v.61,
no.14, p.204-207, photos., plans.

UNITED STATES--BOSTON
(MASSACHUSETTS)--RESTAURANTS--
INTERIOR DESIGN--ROCCO'S
Rocco's in Boston / Monica Geran.
Interiors of Boston restaurant.
Architects: Ahearn-Schopfer
Associates.
INTERIOR DESIGN 1990 June, v.61,
no.9, p.204-[207], photos., plan.

UNITED STATES--BOSTON
(MASSACHUSETTS)--ROW HOUSES--BACK OF
THE HILL ROWHOUSES
The search continues. Building types
study 681, multifamily housing /
Donald J. Canty.
Four low-rise condominium
projects: The Waterworks, New
Hope, Penn, (Cecil Baker &
Associates, Architects); Back of
the Hill Rowhouses, Boston
(William Rawn Associates,
Architects); Samoset Resort and
(Continued next column)

UNITED STATES--BOSTON
(MASSACHUSETTS)--ROW HOUSES--BACK OF
THE HILL ROWHOUSES (CONTINUED)
The search continues:...(CONTINUED)
Village, Rockport, Me. (Sasaki
Associates, Architects); and
Parkview Commons, San Francisco
(David Baker Architects).
ARCHITECTURAL RECORD 1990 July,
v.178, no.8, p.15-87, axonometric
views, elev., photos., plans, site
plans.

UNITED STATES--BOSTON
(MASSACHUSETTS)--ROW HOUSES--GREEK
REVIVAL--12-20 LAGRANGE STREET
(DISTILLHOUSE LOT)
LaGrange Street [Boston] / Nicholas
J. Greene.
Building nos.12-20, adjacent to
Richardson's 1875 Hayden Building
(681 Washington St.); also known
as "distillhouse lot."
BOSTON PRESERVATION ALLIANCE
LETTER 1990 Feb., v.11, no.2,
p.7-8, photo.

UNITED STATES--BOSTON
(MASSACHUSETTS)--SPAS--INTERIOR
DESIGN--SPA AT THE HERITAGE
Spa at the Heritage / Edie Lee
Cohen.
Interiors of health club and salon
in Boston's mixed-use building,
Heritage on the Garden.
Architects/ Interior designers:
Schwartz Silver Architects.
INTERIOR DESIGN 1990 Nov., v.61,
no.15, p.172-[175], photos., plan.

UNITED STATES--BOSTON
(MASSACHUSETTS)--STORES--CLOTHING--
INTERIOR DESIGN--BARNEYS NEW YORK
Shop right / Karin Tetlow.
The interiors of four Barneys New
York stores located in suburban
malls. Architects: Rosenblum Harb
Architects.
INTERIORS 1990 July, v.149, no.12,
p.82-89, photos., plans.

UNITED STATES--BOSTON
(MASSACHUSETTS)--SYNAGOGUES--
CONSERVATION AND RESTORATION--VILNA
SHUL
Synagogue survival: Bostonians
wrestle over future of Vilna Shul
/ Arnold Berke.
Built in 1919, at 14-18 Phillips
St., Boston. Architect: Max M.
Kalman. Interior architect: Sam
Katz.
PRESERVATION NEWS 1990 Feb., v.30,
no.2, p.1,9, ports., photos.
Vilna Shul update.
A report on the status of the
Boston building, first described
in the May 1989 issue of this
newsletter.
BOSTON PRESERVATION ALLIANCE
LETTER 1990 Feb., v.11, no.2, p.5,
photos.

UNITED STATES--BOSTON
(MASSACHUSETTS)--TALL BUILDINGS--
ENVIRONMENTAL ASPECTS
"An act protecting open spaces."
On a proposal in the Massachusetts
Senate, to bar approval by local
authorities of new buidings tall
enough to shadow historic open
spaces.
BOSTON PRESERVATION ALLIANCE
LETTER 1990 May, v.11, no.3, p.1,
ill.

UNITED STATES--BOSTON
(MASSACHUSETTS)--UNIVERSITIES AND
COLLEGES--BUILDINGS--HARVARD
UNIVERSITY--SHAD HALL
Academic fitness: Shad Hall, Harvard
University, Boston, Massachusetts
/ Robert Campbell.
Athletic center for the Graduate
School of Business Administration.
Architects: Kallmann, McKinnell &
Wood.
ARCHITECTURE: THE AIA JOURNAL 1990
Mar., v.79, no.3, p.128-133,
elevs., photos., secns., site
plan.

UNITED STATES--BOSTON
(MASSACHUSETTS)--UNIVERSITIES AND
COLLEGES--BUILDINGS--NORTHEASTERN
UNIVERSITY BOATHOUSE
Team spirit: Northeastern University
Boathouse, Boston, Massachusetts,
Graham Gund Architects / Michael
J. Crosbie.
ARCHITECTURE: THE MAGAZINE OF THE
AMERICAN INSTITUTE OF ARCHITECTS
1990 Aug., v.79, no.8, p.72-75,
photos., plans, site plan.

UNITED STATES--BOSTON
(MASSACHUSETTS)--URBAN DESIGN--
STUDENT PROJECTS
Exploring the elements of urban
design.
Student projects for two sites in
greater Boston, for Elements of
Urban Design course taught by
Peter G. Rowe and Ellen
Whittemore.
GSD NEWS / HARVARD UNIVERSITY.
GRADUATE SCHOOL OF DESIGN 1990
Spring, v.18, no.4, p.15, dwg.,
models, site plan.

UNITED STATES--BOULDER (COLORADO)--
AFFORDABLE HOUSING
Must growth restrictions eliminate
moderate-priced housing? / Thomas
I. Miller.
Cases cited: Boulder, CO;
Petaluma, CA.
AMERICAN PLANNING ASSOCIATION.
JOURNAL 1986 Summer, v.52, no.3,
p.319-325, maps, photo., tables,
biblio., refs.

UNITED STATES--BOULDER (COLORADO)--
CITIES AND TOWNS
Streetscapes in an American city
[Boulder, CO] / Louis Sauer.
ARCHITECTURE & COMPORTEMENT =
ARCHITECTURE & BEHAVIOR 1990, v.6,
no.4, p.[357]-371, photos., map,
site plan, biblio.

UNITED STATES--BOULDER (COLORADO)--
CITIES AND TOWNS--GROWTH
The town that said no to sprawl /
Sylvia Lewis.
Boulder, Colo.
PLANNING 1990 Apr., v.56, no.4,
p.[14]-19, ports., map, photos.

UNITED STATES--BOULDER (COLORADO)--
CITY PLANNING
The town that said no to sprawl /
Sylvia Lewis.
Boulder, Colo.
PLANNING 1990 Apr., v.56, no.4,
p.[14]-19, ports., map, photos.

UNITED STATES--BOULDER (COLORADO)--
TOWNSCAPES
Streetscapes in an American city
[Boulder, CO] / Louis Sauer.
ARCHITECTURE & COMPORTEMENT =
ARCHITECTURE & BEHAVIOR 1990, v.6,
no.4, p.[357]-371, photos., map,
site plan, biblio.

UNITED STATES--BOXLEY (ARKANSAS)--
FARMS--19TH CENTURY
Boxley Valley, Buffalo National
River NPS historic district in
private hands / Jim Liles.
Adapted from a presentation made
Nov.17, 1988 at a conference in
Tucson.
CRM BULLETIN: A NATIONAL PARK
SERVICE TECHNICAL BULLETIN 1990,
v.13, no.4, p.14-15, photos.

UNITED STATES--BRAMBLETON (VIRGINIA)--
NEW TOWNS
Brambleton.
On the new town to be located in a
375-acre core of a 1200-acre rural
site in Loudoun County, Va.
Architects: Sasaki Associates.
PROGRESSIVE ARCHITECTURE 1990
Jan., v.71, no.1, p.118-119,
plans, site plans.

UNITED STATES--BRANDY STATION
(VIRGINIA)--BATTLEFIELDS--19TH
CENTURY--RESEARCH
GIs technology used in American
battlefield protection program /
Betsy Chittenden.
On a project to analyze the Brandy
Station, Va. battlefield.
CRM BULLETIN: A NATIONAL PARK
SERVICE TECHNICAL BULLETIN 1990,
v.13, no.5, p.4, photo.

UNITED STATES--BRENTWOOD
(CALIFORNIA)--HOUSES
Les variations Gehry: maison a
Brentwood (Los Angeles) / Olivier
Boissiere.
Architect: Frank O. Gehry.
ARCHITECTURE INTERIEURE CREE 1990
Feb., no.234, p.[104-109], elev.,
photos., site plan.

UNITED STATES--BRENTWOOD
(CALIFORNIA)--HOUSES--SCHNABEL HOUSE
Frank O. Gehry.
Entire issue devoted to the work
of this American architect.
Criticism by A. Zaera Polo and
David Cohn. 15 projects and
buildings from 1987-1990 featured.
Text in Spanish and English.
EL CROQUIS 1990 Nov., v.9, no.45,
p.1-124, ports., elevs., models,
photos., plans, secns., site
plans, refs.

UNITED STATES--BRENTWOOD
(CALIFORNIA)--HOUSES--SCHNABEL HOUSE
(CONTINUED)
Schnabel residence, Brentwood,
California, 1986-89.
Architects: Frank O. Gehry &
Associates. Text in Japanese and
English.
GA HOUSES 1990 July, no.29,
p.82-[93], photos., plans, secn.,
site plan.
Schnabel residence, Brentwood,
California, design: 1986-87;
construction: 1987-89.
Architects: Frank O. Gehry &
Associates. Text in Japanese and
English.
GA HOUSES 1990 Mar., no.28,
p.30-33, models.

UNITED STATES--BRENTWOOD
(CALIFORNIA)--RANCH HOUSES--INTERIOR
DESIGN
A civilized rustic: redefining a
ranch house in Brentwood,
California / Michael Frank.
Home interiors. Interior designer:
Val Arnold.
ARCHITECTURAL DIGEST 1990 July,
v.47, no.7, p.[144]-149, photos.

UNITED STATES--BRENTWOOD
(CALIFORNIA)--RESTAURANTS--INTERIOR
DESIGN--NEW YORK BAGEL COMPANY
N.Y. Bagel: Frank O. Gehry's
bi-coastal eatery / Mayer Rus.
Located in Brentwood, Ca.
INTERIOR DESIGN 1990 Sept., v.61,
no.12, p.[246-247], photos.

UNITED STATES--BREWERIES--19TH CENTURY
Artificial refrigeration and the
architecture of 19th-century
American breweries / Susan K.
Appel.
SOCIETY FOR INDUSTRIAL ARCHEOLOGY.
JOURNAL 1990, v.16, no.1, p.21-38,
ill., dwgs., photo., secns., refs.

UNITED STATES--BRIDGEHAMPTON (NEW
YORK)--HOUSES--ALTERATIONS AND
ADDITIONS--SLESIN STEINBERG HOUSE
Hamptons style: Slesin/Steinberg
house, Bridgehampton, New York.
Alteration of a small 1930s
cottage. Architect: Lee H.
Skolnick Architecture and Design.
ARCHITECTURAL RECORD 1990
Mid-Apr., v.178, no.5, p.34-[41],
axonometric views, photos., plans.

UNITED STATES--BRIDGEPORT
(CONNECTICUT)--CORPORATE OFFICE
BUILDINGS--BRIDGEPORT CENTER
Bridgeport Center, Bridgeport,
Connecticut, 1984-1989.
Architects: Richard Meier and
Partners. Text in Japanese and
English.
ARCHITECTURE AND URBANISM 1990
Apr., no.4(235), p.[8-25],
photos., plans, site plan.
Bridgeport Center: re-minding
Richard Meier / Gevork Hartoonian.
JOURNAL OF ARCHITECTURAL EDUCATION
1990 Nov., v.44, no.1, p.33-36,
photos., plan, site plan.

UNITED STATES--BRIDGES--HISTORY
[Theme issue: bridges].
Includes four articles.
INDUSTRIAL ARCHAEOLOGY 1989, v.15,
no.2, p.3-71, dwgs., photos.,
biblio, refs.

UNITED STATES--BRIDGES--INVENTORIES--
BIBLIOGRAPHY
Bibliography of state historic
bridge inventories / Eric DeLony.
SOCIETY FOR INDUSTRIAL ARCHEOLOGY.
JOURNAL 1990, v.16, no.1, p.68,
biblio.

UNITED STATES--BRONX (NEW YORK)--
AFFORDABLE HOUSING--SHOREHAVEN
Housing America / Andrea Oppenheimer
Dean.
Introductory article in theme
issue discusses the reasons for
the rise in homelessness in the
U.S. Cites 4 specific projects:
Shorehaven, Bronx, N.Y. (Liebman
Melting Partnership); Spring
Creek, Brooklyn, N.Y. (Liebman
Melting Partnership and Costas
Kondylis Architects); Turning
Point, San Mateo, Calif. (David
Baker Architects); and Bennett
Place Housing for the Elderly,
Pittsburgh, Pa. (Arthur Lubetz
Assoc.).
ARCHITECTURE: THE MAGAZINE OF THE
AMERICAN INSTITUTE OF ARCHITECTS
1990 July, v.79, no.7, p.51-55,
photos., plans, site plans.

UNITED STATES--BRONX (NEW YORK)--
HOUSING FOR HOMELESS
POTS and PANS are cooking up in the
Bronx / Cory Johnson.
"Part Of The Solution" (POTS) and
"People Are Not Satisfied" (PANS)
provide homeless shelter and
counseling in the Bronx.
CITY LIMITS 1990 Oct., v.15, no.8,
p.6-7, ports.

UNITED STATES--BROOKLINE
(MASSACHUSETTS)--PARKS--19TH
CENTURY--MAINTENANCE AND REPAIR
Keeping the necklace bright / Nick
Burton, Russel Matthews.
On the establishment of a
landscape management plan for the
parks, the "Emerald Necklace"
designed by Frederick law Olmsted
in the Boston area.
LANDSCAPE DESIGN 1989 Nov.,
no.185, p.11-13, dwgs., tables,
ref.

UNITED STATES--BROOKLYN (NEW YORK)--
AFFORDABLE HOUSING--STUYVESANT MEWS
Affordable housing in Brooklyn.
Stuyvesant Mews, factory-built
rowhouses for the
Bedford-Stuyvesant neighborhood.
Architects: Stephen B. Jacobs.
ARCHITECTURAL RECORD 1990 Sept.,
v.178, no.10, p.27, model.

UNITED STATES--BROOKLYN (NEW YORK)--
COMMUNITY DEVELOPMENT--URBAN--
BEDFORD-STUYVESANT
Pride and poverty in
Bedford-Stuyvesant / Lisa Glazer.
CITY LIMITS 1990 May, v.15, no.5,
p.12-16, ports., photos.

UNITED STATES--BROOKLYN (NEW YORK)--
FARMHOUSES--DUTCH COLONIAL--
CHRISTIAN DURYEA FARMHOUSE
The Christian Duryea farmhouse / Ira
Kaplan.
  The 18th cent. Dutch farmhouse at
  562 Jerome St. in Brooklyn was
  destroyed by arson in Nov. 1989.
  METROPOLIS 1990 Apr., v.9, no.8,
  p.17-18, photos.

UNITED STATES--BROOKLYN (NEW YORK)--
HAND-RAILINGS--CAST-IRON--
CONSERVATION AND RESTORATION--235
BERKELEY PLACE
How to install a railing the
nineteenth-century way / E.H.
Ortner.
  At the 235 Berkeley Place, Park
  Slope, Brooklyn.
  BROWNSTONER 1990 fall, p.[1]-4,
  photos.

UNITED STATES--BROOKLYN (NEW YORK)--
HOSPITALS--ALTERATIONS AND
ADDITIONS--KINGS COUNTY HOSPITAL
CENTER
Kings County Hospital Center,
Brooklyn, New York, USA, 1997.
Proposed addition and renovations;
architects: Hellmuth, Obata &
Kassabaum, with Ellerbe Becket.
Text in Japanese and English.
ARCHITECTURE AND URBANISM 1990
Dec., no.12 extra edition,
p.200-[203],

UNITED STATES--BROOKLYN (NEW YORK)--
HOUSES--ZAFARANI HOUSE
Zafarani Residence, Mill Basin,
Brooklyn, New York.
Architects: Arquitectonica
International Corporation. Text in
Japanese and English.
GA HOUSES 1990 Mar., no.28,
p.48-49, axonometric views,
elevs., plans, secn., site plan.

UNITED STATES--BROOKLYN (NEW YORK)--
LOW INCOME HOUSING--SPRING CREEK
Housing America / Andrea Oppenheimer
Dean.
  Introductory article in theme
  issue discusses the reasons for
  the rise in homelessness in the
  U.S. Cites 4 specific projects:
  Shorehaven, Bronx, N.Y. (Liebman
  Melting Partnership); Spring
  Creek, Brooklyn, N.Y. (Liebman
  Melting Partnership and Costas
  Kondylis Architects); Turning
  Point, San Mateo, Calif. (David
  Baker Architects); and Bennett
  Place Housing for the Elderly,
  Pittsburgh, Pa. (Arthur Lubetz
  Assoc.).
  ARCHITECTURE: THE MAGAZINE OF THE
  AMERICAN INSTITUTE OF ARCHITECTS
  1990 July, v.79, no.7, p.51-55,
  photos., plans, site plans.

UNITED STATES--BROOKLYN (NEW YORK)--
MERRY-GO ROUNDS
Roundabout [New York City carousels]
/ Lisa English.
  METROPOLIS 1990 July-Aug., v.10,
  no.1, p.[56-61],69, photos.

UNITED STATES--BROOKLYN (NEW YORK)--
MULTI-USE COMPLEXES--ALTANTIC CENTER
Terminal gets a new start / Tom
McGhee.
  Atlantic City, a 3 million-sq. ft.
  mixed use development on the site
  of the old Atlantic Terminal in
  downtown Brooklyn. Developer: Rose
  Associates.
  METROPOLIS 1990 June, v.9, no.10,
  p.17-18, photos.

UNITED STATES--BROOKLYN (NEW YORK)--
NEIGHBORHOODS--BEDFORD-STUYVESANT
Pride and poverty in
Bedford-Stuyvesant / Lisa Glazer.
  CITY LIMITS 1990 May, v.15, no.5,
  p.12-16, ports., photos.

UNITED STATES--BROOKLYN (NEW YORK)--
NEIGHBORHOODS--BRIGHTON BEACH
Dwelling on the beach ... Brighton
Beach / Ronda Wist.
  METROPOLIS 1990 Apr., v.9, no.8,
  p.80-[84],95-97, photos.

UNITED STATES--BROOKLYN (NEW YORK)--
ROW HOUSES--PREFABRICATED--
STUYVESANT MEWS
Affordable housing in Brooklyn.
  Stuyvesant Mews, factory-built
  rowhouses for the
  Bedford-Stuyvesant neighborhood.
  Architects: Stephen B. Jacobs.
  ARCHITECTURAL RECORD 1990 Sept.,
  v.178, no.10, p.27, model.

UNITED STATES--BROWNSVILLE (TEXAS)--
BORDER STATIONS--B & M BRIDGE
STATION
A bullet-proof welcome [border
stations] / Natalye Appel.
  B & M Bridge Station, Brownsville
  (RioGroup Architects & Planners,
  Joneskell Architects); and Border
  Patrol Station, Eagle Pass
  (O'Neill & Perez).
  TEXAS ARCHITECT 1990 July-Aug.,
  v.40, no.4, p.38-41, elev.,
  photos., plan, secn., site plan.

UNITED STATES--BRUNSWICK (MAINE)--
CAMPUSES--BOWDOIN COLLEGE
The architecture of Bowdoin College
[by] Patricia McGraw Anderson
[book review] / Margaret Henderson
Floyd.
  SOCIETY OF ARCHITECTURAL
  HISTORIANS. JOURNAL 1990 Sept.,
  v.49, no.3, p.346-347,

UNITED STATES--BRUNSWICK (MAINE)--
UNIVERSITIES AND COLLEGES--
BUILDINGS--BOWDOIN COLLEGE
The architecture of Bowdoin College
[by] Patricia McGraw Anderson
[book review] / Margaret Henderson
Floyd.
  SOCIETY OF ARCHITECTURAL
  HISTORIANS. JOURNAL 1990 Sept.,
  v.49, no.3, p.346-347.

UNITED STATES--BRUNSWICK (NEW
JERSEY)--MULTI-USE COMPLEXES--GOLDEN
TRIANGLE PLAZA
Golden Triangle Plaza, New
Brunswick, New Jersey.
  Office complex. Architects:
  Rothe-Johnson Associates.
  ARCHITECTURE NEW JERSEY 1989,
  v.25, no.3, p.10-11, photos., site
  plan, aerial photo.

UNITED STATES--BUCKS COUNTY
(PENNSYLVANIA)--FARMHOUSES--18TH
CENTURY--CONSERVATION AND
RESTORATION--BOHN FIORE HOUSE
Country's new colors / Heather Smith
MacIsaac.
  Renovation of an 18th-cent.
  farmhouse in Penn. Designers:
  Lembo Bohn.
  HOUSE & GARDEN 1990 Dec., v.162,
  no.12, p.[108-115],191, photos.

UNITED STATES--BUDA (TEXAS)--
FACTORIES--ALTERATIONS AND
ADDITIONS--CARRARO HOUSE
Cement plant reused as house / Joel
Warren Barna.
  The Carraro house, near Buda,
  built out of portions of an
  abandoned cement plant in 1990.
  Architect: Lake/Flato Architects.
  CITE: THE ARCHITECTURE AND DESIGN
  REVIEW OF HOUSTON 1990 Fall,
  no.25, p.26, photos.

UNITED STATES--BUDA (TEXAS)--HOUSES--
CARRARO HOUSE
Cement plant reused as house / Joel
Warren Barna.
  The Carraro house, near Buda,
  built out of portions of an
  abandoned cement plant in 1990.
  Architect: Lake/Flato Architects.
  CITE: THE ARCHITECTURE AND DESIGN
  REVIEW OF HOUSTON 1990 Fall,
  no.25, p.26, photos.

UNITED STATES--BUFFALO GROVE
(ILLINOIS)--NEW TOWNS
Pumping up suburban downtowns /
Philip Langdon.
  Examples in Reston, Va., Miami
  Lakes, Fla., and Buffalo Grove,
  Ill.
  PLANNING 1990 July, v.56, no.7,
  p.22-28, dwg., model, map,
  photos., plans, aerial photo.

UNITED STATES--BUFFALO (NEW YORK)--
AUDITORIUMS, CONCERT HALLS--
CONSERVATION AND RESTORATION--
KLEINHANS MUSIC HALL
Preservation: the Saarinens in
Buffalo [exhibition review] /
Mathew Ginal.
  On the exhibition and symposium,
  Kleinhans Music Hall: the
  Saarinens in Buffalo, 1940- a
  streamline vision, at Buffalo
  State College's Burchfield Center.
  PROGRESSIVE ARCHITECTURE 1990
  June, v.71, no.6, p.28, photo.

UNITED STATES--BUFFALO (NEW YORK)--
BASEBALL STADIUMS--PILOT FIELD
Pilot Field, Buffalo, New York, USA,
1988.
  Architects: Hellmuth, Obata &
  Kassabaum. Text in Japanese and
  English.
  ARCHITECTURE AND URBANISM 1990
  Dec., no.12 extra edition,
  p.[132]-137, photos., plans,
  aerial photo.

UNITED STATES--BUFFALO (NEW YORK)--
OFFICE BUILDINGS--CONSERVATION AND
RESTORATION--GUARANTY BUILDING
Replicating historic elevator
enclosures: Guaranty Building,
Buffalo, New York / Marilyn E.
Kaplan.
PRESERVATION TECH NOTES 1989 June,
no.24, p.1-6, diagrs., photos.,
plans.

UNITED STATES--BUILDING LAWS
Regulation: a realization of social
ethics / Francis T. Ventre.
Ethics relating to design, in the
U.S.
VIA 1990, no.10, p.[50]-61, dets.,
photos., sketches, tables, refs.

UNITED STATES--BUILDINGS--
DOCUMENTATION
HABS/HAER: a user's guide / Robert
J. Kapsch.
ASSOCIATION FOR PRESERVATION
TECHNOLOGY. BULLETIN 1990, v.22,
no.1-2, p.21-34, axonometric
views, dets., elev., secns.,
tables, isometric dwg., refs.

UNITED STATES--BUILDINGS--HEIGHT
RESTRICTIONS
Urban space man / Sarah Kitchen.
BUILDING 1990 Nov.30, v.255,
no.47, p.22-24, dwgs.

UNITED STATES--BUILDINGS--WOODEN--
AWARDS AND PRIZES
Awards for wood buildings.
4 First Awards and 9 Merit Awards,
sponsored by the Cedar Shake &
Shingle Bureau and the AIA.
ARCHITECTURAL RECORD 1990 Feb.,
v.178, no.2, p.24-25, photos.

UNITED STATES--BUNGALOWS
Builder style: America's little
houses / James C. Massey, Shirley
Maxwell.
Homestead, Foursquare, Cottage,
and Bungalow styles.
OLD-HOUSE JOURNAL 1990 Sept.-Oct.,
v.18, no.5, p.45-49, ill., photos.

UNITED STATES--BUNGALOWS--
PREFABRICATED
Pre-cut houses: "catalog homes" /
James C. Massey & Shirley Maxwell.
Mail-order kit houses flourished
from 1900 to 1940.
OLD-HOUSE JOURNAL 1990 Nov.-Dec.,
v.18, no.6, p.36-41, ill., photos.

UNITED STATES--BURLINGTON (VERMONT)--
BANKS--VERMONT NATIONAL BANK
Vt. defends good old modern [Vermont
National Bank, Burlington] / Amy
Worden.
Built 1958, Freeman, French and
Freeman, architects. Threatened
with having its original glass
curtain wall replaced by a brick
facade.
PRESERVATION NEWS 1990 Jan., v.30,
no.1, p.1,6, photo.

UNITED STATES--BURLINGTON (VERMONT)--
ENDANGERED PLACES--VERMONT NATIONAL
BANK
Vt. defends good old modern [Vermont
National Bank, Burlington] / Amy
Worden.
Built 1958, Freeman, French and
Freeman, architects. Threatened
with having its original glass
curtain wall replaced by a brick
facade.
PRESERVATION NEWS 1990 Jan., v.30,
no.1, p.1,6, photo.

UNITED STATES--CALIFORNIA--
ARCHITECTURE--20TH CENTURY
An American saga ... Esther McCoy's
writings / Michael McDonough.
METROPOLIS 1990 Mar., v.9, no.7,
p.38-43,60-61, port., models,
photos.

UNITED STATES--CALIFORNIA--
ARCHITECTURE--20TH CENTURY--AWARDS
AND PRIZES
1990 Design Awards, California
Council, AIA.
17 premiated projects.
ARCHITECTURAL RECORD 1990 June,
v.178, no.7, p.28-29, photos.

UNITED STATES--CALIFORNIA--BEACH
HOUSES--INTERIOR DESIGN--BALDWIN
HOUSE
A shoreline composition / Irene
Borger.
Interiors of ocean-front home of
Jim and Nancy Baldwin in southern
California. Architect: Fred M.
Briggs. Interior designer: Steve
Chase.
ARCHITECTURAL DIGEST 1990 Mar.,
v.47, no.3, p.[198-205],248,
photos.

UNITED STATES--CALIFORNIA--BEACH
HOUSES--INTERIOR DESIGN--HOCKNEY
HOUSE
Color makes a splash / Timothy J.
Ward.
Two interiors by designer Gregory
Evans: Dagny Corcoran house, Los
Angeles, and David Hockney beach
house, Calif.
METROPOLITAN HOME 1990 June, v.22,
no.6, p.73-[81], port., photos.

UNITED STATES--CALIFORNIA--BUNGALOWS
Who they were: Greene & Greene /
Jeff Wilkinson.
OLD-HOUSE JOURNAL 1990 July-Aug,
v.18, no.4, p.26,28, port.,
photos.

UNITED STATES--CALIFORNIA--BUNGALOWS--
INTERIOR DESIGN
California Arts & Crafts unveiled /
William L. Hamilton.
Events and houses open to the
public, and the work of Greene and
Greene.
ART & ANTIQUES 1990 Sept., v.7,
no.7, p.82-87, photos.

UNITED STATES--CALIFORNIA--CITY
PLANNING
Computer adoption and use in
California planning agencies:
implications for education /
Steven P. French, Lyna L. Wiggins.
JOURNAL OF PLANNING EDUCATION AND
RESEARCH 1989 Winter, v.8, no.2,
(Continued next column)

UNITED STATES--CALIFORNIA--CITY
PLANNING (CONTINUED)
Computer adoption and...(CONTINUED)
p.97-108, charts, graphs, refs.

UNITED STATES--CALIFORNIA--CITY
PLANNING--METHODOLOGY
California planning agency
experiences with automated mapping
and geographic information systems
/ S.P. French, L.L. Wiggins.
ENVIRONMENT AND PLANNING B 1990
Oct., v.17, no.4, p.441-450,
tables, refs.

UNITED STATES--CALIFORNIA--EARTHQUAKES
AND BUILDING
Loma Prieta, October 17, 1989:
comments on the earthquake.
Architects' and engineers'
comments on the earthquake.
PROGRESSIVE ARCHITECTURE 1990
Mar., v.71, no.3, p.39,41, photos.

UNITED STATES--CALIFORNIA--HISTORIC
HOUSE MUSEUMS
Celebrating the holidays in Gold
Mine Country / Maureen Gilmer.
Features two northern California
buildings: Empire Mine Cottage,
Grass Valley (architect: Willis
Polk) and Red Castle Inn, Nevada
City (a brick Gothic revival house
on "Prospect Hill" built in 1857
for John Williams).
VICTORIAN HOMES 1990 Holidays,
v.9, no.5, p.38-[45], photos.

UNITED STATES--CALIFORNIA--HOUSES--
ALTERATIONS AND ADDITIONS
Enclosed entity: Michael Wu's
addition to a suburban residence /
Edie Lee Cohen.
INTERIOR DESIGN 1990 May, v.61,
no.7, p.286-[287], axonometric
view, photos.

UNITED STATES--CALIFORNIA--HOUSES--
ARCHITECTS'--INTERIOR DESIGN--GRAY
HOUSE
Met kids: living with style -- and
children, too.
A triennial section "on family
style", with profiles of three
interior designs of children's
bedrooms including one in southern
Calif. by architect Melinda Gray.
METROPOLITAN HOME 1990 Dec., v.22,
no.12, p.65-87, photos.

UNITED STATES--CALIFORNIA--HOUSES--
MISSION REVIVAL
Realizing aromantic vision: a wave
of Spanish Revival architecture
swept across Southern California
during the 1920s, and Architect
Palmer Sabin rode it to success /
Christopher Weeks.
METROPOLIS 1990 Mar., v.9, no.7,
p.[44]-49,77,79,81, photos., ill.,
dwgs.

UNITED STATES--CALIFORNIA--HOUSES--
PRICE HOUSE
Of a visionary nature: Bart Prince's
sculptural design for Joe and
Etsuko Price in California /
Michael Webb.
Beach-front residence in southern
California.
ARCHITECTURAL DIGEST 1990 Dec.,
v.47, no.13, p.[182]-189, 228,
ports., photos., plan.

UNITED STATES--CALIFORNIA--HOUSES--
SPANISH COLONIAL REVIVAL
   Realizing aromantic vision: a wave
      of Spanish Revival architecture
      swept across Southern California
      during the 1920s, and Architect
      Palmer Sabin rode it to success /
      Christopher Weeks.
   METROPOLIS 1990 Mar., v.9, no.7,
      p.[44]-49,77,79,81, photos., ill.,
      dwgs.

UNITED STATES--CALIFORNIA--HOUSES--
WING WALK (DOOLITTLE HOUSE)
   Kendrick Bangs Kellogg [houses].
      Contents: Doolittle house "Wing
      Walk," Sin Barnyards County, [sic]
      CA, 1988 --Bailey house, San Diego
      County, CA, 1985 --Wing Sweep
      house, Riverside County, CA, 1986.
      Text in Japanese and English.
   GA HOUSES 1990 Mar., no.28,
      p.136-139, models, plans, site
      plans.

UNITED STATES--CALIFORNIA--HOUSING
   The coastal condition: regional
      portfolio: California housing /
      Paul M. Sachner.
   The first of a series of regional
      portfolios, on 5 multifamily
      projects: Armacost Duplex, Los
      Angeles [Rebecca Binder]; 14-16
      Leroy Pl., San Francisco (Hood
      Miller); 1150 Lombard St., San
      Francisco (Hood Miller); Meadow
      Court, San Mateo (David Baker
      Assoc.); and Seacliff, Malibu
      (Kanner Associates).
   ARCHITECTURAL RECORD 1990 Jan.,
      v.178, no.1, p.90-99, elevs.,
      photos., plans, secns., site
      plans.

UNITED STATES--CALIFORNIA--INTERIOR
DESIGN
   California style.
      Four articles, indexed separately.
   HOUSE BEAUTIFUL 1990 May, v.132,
      no.5, p.55, photo.

UNITED STATES--CALIFORNIA--NATIONAL
PARKS AND RESERVES--YOSEMITE
NATIONAL PARK
   Frederick Law Olmsted, Yosemite
      pioneer / Victoria Post Ranney.
   PLACES 1990 Spring, v.6, no.3,
      p.61, ports.
   Olmsted's Yosemite, a vision
      betrayed / Joseph L. Sax.
   PLACES 1990 Spring, v.6, no.3,
      p.60.
   Yosemite: perceptions and prospects
      / Randolph T. Hester.
      Special feature on Yosemite
      National Park. Some articles
      separately indexed.
   PLACES 1990 Spring, v.6, no.3,
      p.[18]-77, ill., maps, photos.,
      secns., sections.

UNITED STATES--CALIFORNIA--OPEN SPACES
   Integrated open space planning /
      Paul M. Rookwood.
      Citing Southern Calif.
   LANDSCAPE DESIGN 1990 Mar.,
      no.188, p.25-29, photos., site
      plan, refs.

UNITED STATES--CALIFORNIA--PLAZAS
   Reinventing the square: everyone
      knows that corporate plazas are
      all wrong ... / Michael Webb.
      Examples of corporate plazas as
      civic spaces in Calif., especially
      Horton Plaza, San Diego, and
      Levi's Plaza, San Fransisco.
   METROPOLIS 1990 Mar., v.9, no.7,
      p.[50]-53,62-63, ill., photos.,
      aerial photo.

UNITED STATES--CALIFORNIA--VACATION
HOUSES--SEA RANCH
   Sea Ranch e i mari d'argento / Paolo
      Riani.
      Landscaping: Lawrence Halprin.
      Architect: Charles Moore.
   VILLE GIARDINI 1990 Apr., no.247,
      p.32-35, ill., dwgs., photos.

UNITED STATES--CALIFORNIA--YOSEMITE
VALLEY--ARCHITECTURE
   Towards an architecture of the
      valley / Hugh Hardy.
      Architecture in the Yosemite
      Valley.
   PLACES 1990 Spring, v.6, no.3,
      p.28-31, photos.

UNITED STATES--CALISTOGA
(CALIFORNIA)--HOUSES--INTERIOR
DESIGN--CA'TOGA
   Palladio of the Napa Valley /
      Alexandria Edwards.
      On the interiors of Ca'Toga,
      artist Carlo Marchiori's home
      outside Calistoga.
   THE WORLD OF INTERIORS 1990 June,
      p.[136]-145, photos.

UNITED STATES--CALISTOGA
(CALIFORNIA)--WINERIES--CLOS PEGASE
   Mitologia de colores: Bodegas Clos
      Pegase en Napa Valley, California
      = Colored mythologies.
      Architect: Michael Graves. English
      text, p.86.
   A & V 1990, no.21, p.38-41, dwg.,
      photos., secn., site plan.

UNITED STATES--CALUMET (MICHIGAN)--
HOUSES
   A comparative study of the miners'
      homes in Cornwall, England and the
      miners' homes of the Cornish in
      Michigan / Mary Jo Rowell Brown,
      Evelyn M. Franklin.
   HOUSING AND SOCIETY 1988, v.15,
      no.2, p.108-125, charts, maps,
      photos, plans, refs.

UNITED STATES--CALUMET (MICHIGAN)--
MINING TOWNS
   A comparative study of the miners'
      homes in Cornwall, England and the
      miners' homes of the Cornish in
      Michigan / Mary Jo Rowell Brown,
      Evelyn M. Franklin.
   HOUSING AND SOCIETY 1988, v.15,
      no.2, p.108-125, charts, maps,
      photos, plans, refs.

UNITED STATES--CAMBRIA (CALIFORNIA)--
HOUSES--GREEK REVIVAL--INTERIOR
DESIGN--OLALLIEBERRY INN
   Victorian summer travel.
      Features buildings in Ferndale,
      Calif. (Including Linden Hall),
      the Olallieberry Inn, Cambria,
      Calif., and Patton House Inn,
      Wooster, Ark.
(Continued next column)

UNITED STATES--CAMBRIA (CALIFORNIA)--
HOUSES--GREEK REVIVAL--INTERIOR
DESIGN--OLALLIEBERRY INN
                     (CONTINUED)
   Victorian summer...(CONTINUED) ·
   VICTORIAN HOMES 1990 Summer, v.9,
      no.3, p.[65]-70,72,74, photos.

UNITED STATES--CAMBRIDGE
(MASSACHUSETTS)--BOATHOUSES--STUDENT
PROJECTS--CHARLES RIVER
   A public rowing facility on the
      Charles River.
      Studio project at GSD, for site on
      north bank of the Charles River
      between the Mass. Ave. and Boston
      Univ. bridges.
   GSD NEWS / HARVARD UNIVERSITY.
      GRADUATE SCHOOL OF DESIGN 1990
      Winter, v.18, no.3, p.6-7, dwg.,
      models, secn.

UNITED STATES--CAMBRIDGE
(MASSACHUSETTS)--CITY PLANNING--
UNIVERSITY PARK
   La citta a strati, piazze e isolati
      = MIT University Park.
      Project for multi-use urban
      center; architects: Koetter, Kim &
      Associates.
   L'ARCA 1990 July-Aug., no.40,
      suppl.l'Arca 2, p.100, dwgs.,
      model, site plan.

UNITED STATES--CAMBRIDGE
(MASSACHUSETTS)--CORPORATE OFFICE
BUILDINGS--ALTERATIONS AND
ADDITIONS--HASTINGS-TAPLEY INSURANCE
AGENCY
   Double Indemnity: Hastings-Tapley
      Insurance Agency, Cambridge,
      Massachusetts, Koetter, Kim &
      Associates / Michael J. Crosbie.
   ARCHITECTURE: THE AIA JOURNAL 1990
      Nov., v.79, no.11, p.[80]-83,
      axonometric view, elevs., photos.,
      sketches.

UNITED STATES--CAMBRIDGE
(MASSACHUSETTS)--FACULTY HOUSING--
HARVARD UNIVERSITY
   Uncommon dwellings: Harvard faculty
      housing, Cambridge, Massachusetts,
      Woo + Williams, Architects /
      Robert Campbell.
      Townhouses.
   ARCHITECTURE: THE AIA JOURNAL 1990
      Jan., v.79, no.1, p.78-81,
      photos., plan, secns., site plan.

UNITED STATES--CAMBRIDGE
(MASSACHUSETTS)--GATES--
COMPETITIONS--HARVARD UNIVERSITY--
HARVARD GATE
   Merzbau U.S.A.,1983-1989.
      Competition entry for Harvard
      Gate. Architect: David Sabatello.
      English summary, p.90.
   METAMORFOSI 1990, no.18, p.89,90,
      axonometric views, dwgs., elevs.,
      plans, secns.

UNITED STATES--CAMBRIDGE
(MASSACHUSETTS)--GYMNASIUMS--
ALTERATIONS AND ADDITIONS--HARVARD
UNIVERSITY--BRIGGS ATHLETIC CENTER
   George Oommen Cambridge,
      Massachusetts.
      Four projects: Briggs Athletic
      Centre, Malkin Athletic Centre,
      and McCurdy Track, at Harvard
      University; Western Montana Sports
(Continued next page)

UNITED STATES--CAMBRIDGE
(MASSACHUSETTS)--GYMNASIUMS--
ALTERATIONS AND ADDITIONS--HARVARD
UNIVERSITY--BRIGGS ATHLETIC CENTER
(CONTINUED)
George Oommen...(CONTINUED)
    Medicine and Fitness Centre,
    Missoula.
    ARCHITECTURE + DESIGN 1990
    Jan.-Feb., v.7, no.1, p.32-37,
    photos., plans, aerial photos.

UNITED STATES--CAMBRIDGE
(MASSACHUSETTS)--GYMNASIUMS--HARVARD
UNIVERSITY--SHAD HALL
A gym shapes up: Shad Hall, Boston,
    Massachusetts, Harvard University
    / James S. Russell.
    Architects: Kallmann, McKinnell &
    Wood.
    ARCHITECTURAL RECORD 1990 May,
    v.178, no.6, p.78-[83], det.,
    photos., plans, secns., site plan.

UNITED STATES--CAMBRIDGE
(MASSACHUSETTS)--MULTI-USE
COMPLEXES--UNIVERSITY PARK
La citta a strati, piazze e isolati
    = MIT University Park.
    Project for multi-use urban
    center; architects: Koetter, Kim &
    Associates.
    L'ARCA 1990 July-Aug., no.40,
    suppl.1'Arca 2, p.100, dwgs.,
    model, site plan.

UNITED STATES--CAMBRIDGE
(MASSACHUSETTS)--RUNNING TRACKS--
HARVARD UNIVERSITY--MCCURDY TRACK
George Oommen Cambridge,
    Massachusetts.
    Four projects: Briggs Athletic
    Centre, Malkin Athletic Centre,
    and McCurdy Track, at Harvard
    University; Western Montana Sports
    Medicine and Fitness Centre,
    Missoula.
    ARCHITECTURE + DESIGN 1990
    Jan.-Feb., v.7, no.1, p.32-37,
    photos., plans, aerial photos.

UNITED STATES--CAMBRIDGE
(MASSACHUSETTS)--SWIMMING POOLS--
ALTERATIONS AND ADDITIONS--HARVARD
UNIVERSITY--MALKIN ATHLETIC CENTER
George Oommen Cambridge,
    Massachusetts.
    Four projects: Briggs Athletic
    Centre, Malkin Athletic Centre,
    and McCurdy Track, at Harvard
    University; Western Montana Sports
    Medicine and Fitness Centre,
    Missoula.
    ARCHITECTURE + DESIGN 1990
    Jan.-Feb., v.7, no.1, p.32-37,
    photos., plans, aerial photos.

UNITED STATES--CAMBRIDGE
(MASSACHUSETTS)--TOWNHOUSES--HARVARD
UNIVERSITY FACULTY HOUSING
Uncommon dwellings: Harvard faculty
    housing, Cambridge, Massachusetts,
    Woo + Williams, Architects /
    Robert Campbell.
    Townhouses.
    ARCHITECTURE: THE AIA JOURNAL 1990
    Jan., v.79, no.1, p.78-81,
    photos., plan, secns., site plan.

UNITED STATES--CAMBRIDGE
(MASSACHUSETTS)--UNIVERSITIES AND
COLLEGES--17TH CENTURY--BUILDINGS--
HARVARD UNIVERSITY--STOUGHTON HALL
Thomas Brattle,
    mathematician-architect in the
    transition of the New England
    mind, 1690-1700 / Rick Kennedy.
    A study of the transition from
    Puritanism to the Enlightenment in
    Boston, the building of Stoughton
    Hall at Harvard and its
    Renaissance style, and the
    influence of Brattle's
    mathematical idealism.
    WINTERTHUR PORTFOLIO 1989 Winter,
    v.24, no.4, p.[231]-245, elev.,
    engrs., refs.

UNITED STATES--CAMBRIDGE
(MASSACHUSETTS)--UNIVERSITIES AND
COLLEGES--BUILDINGS--ALTERATIONS AND
ADDITIONS--HARVARD UNIVERSITY--FOGG
MUSEUM
Renewing our modern legacy / Andrea
    Oppenheimer Dean.
    Four additions to buildings of the
    1950s and 1960s.
    ARCHITECTURE: THE AIA JOURNAL 1990
    Nov., v.79, no.11, p.66-69, ill.,
    elevs., models, photos.

UNITED STATES--CAMBRIDGE
(MASSACHUSETTS)--UNIVERSITIES AND
COLLEGES--BUILDINGS--HARVARD
UNIVERSITY
George Oommen Cambridge,
    Massachusetts.
    Four projects: Briggs Athletic
    Centre, Malkin Athletic Centre,
    and McCurdy Track, at Harvard
    University; Western Montana Sports
    Medicine and Fitness Centre,
    Missoula.
    ARCHITECTURE + DESIGN 1990
    Jan.-Feb., v.7, no.1, p.32-37,
    photos., plans, aerial photos.

UNITED STATES--CAMBRIDGE
(MASSACHUSETTS)--UNIVERSITIES AND
COLLEGES--BUILDINGS--HARVARD
UNIVERSITY--SHAD HALL
A gym shapes up: Shad Hall, Boston,
    Massachusetts, Harvard University
    / James S. Russell.
    Architects: Kallmann, McKinnell &
    Wood.
    ARCHITECTURAL RECORD 1990 May,
    v.178, no.6, p.78-[83], det.,
    photos., plans, secns., site plan.

UNITED STATES--CAMDEN (MAINE)--
SCHOONERS--19TH CENTURY--
CONSERVATION AND RESTORATION--GRACE
BAILEY (MATTIE)
Restoring Grace Bailey / James P.
    Delgado.
    A two-masted schooner built in
    1882, renamed Mattie in 1906, and
    since 1986 being restored in
    Camden, Maine.
    CRM BULLETIN: A NATIONAL PARK
    SERVICE TECHNICAL BULLETIN 1990,
    v.13, no.4, p.33, photos.

UNITED STATES--CAMDEN (NEW JERSEY)--
AQUARIUMS--NEW JERSEY STATE AQUARIUM
Fish or fowl? [Camden, N.J.
    aquarium] / Robert Guskind.
    New Jersey State Aquarium planned
    for Camden, N.J., and other new
    aquariums in American cities.
    PLANNING 1990 May, v.56, no.5,
    p.10-14, dwgs., model, photos.,
    plan, aerial photo.

UNITED STATES--CAMDEN (NEW JERSEY)--
CIVIC CENTERS--ALTERATIONS AND
ADDITIONS--ROOSEVELT PLAZA
Roosevelt Plaza redevelopment,
    Camden, New Jersey.
    Architects: Lammey & Giorgio.
    ARCHITECTURE NEW JERSEY 1989,
    v.25, no.3, p.12, axonometric
    view.

UNITED STATES--CAMDEN (NEW JERSEY)--
MARINE AQUARIUMS
Sharks and seals to Camden's rescue
    / Martin McNamara.
    Projected waterfront development
    for Camden, N.J.
    METROPOLIS 1990 Oct., v.10, no.3,
    p.25-26, model.

UNITED STATES--CAMDEN (NEW JERSEY)--
OPEN SPACES--ROOSEVELT PLAZA
Roosevelt Plaza redevelopment,
    Camden, New Jersey.
    Architects: Lammey & Giorgio.
    ARCHITECTURE NEW JERSEY 1989,
    v.25, no.3, p.12, axonometric
    view.

UNITED STATES--CAMDEN (NEW JERSEY)--
PLAZAS--ALTERATIONS AND ADDITIONS--
ROOSEVELT PLAZA
Roosevelt Plaza redevelopment,
    Camden, New Jersey.
    Architects: Lammey & Giorgio.
    ARCHITECTURE NEW JERSEY 1989,
    v.25, no.3, p.12, axonometric
    view.

UNITED STATES--CAMDEN (NEW JERSEY)--
REAL ESTATE DEVELOPMENT
Sharks and seals to Camden's rescue
    / Martin McNamara.
    Projected waterfront development
    for Camden, N.J.
    METROPOLIS 1990 Oct., v.10, no.3,
    p.25-26, model.

UNITED STATES--CAMDEN (NEW JERSEY)--
WATERFRONT BUILDINGS
Sharks and seals to Camden's rescue
    / Martin McNamara.
    Projected waterfront development
    for Camden, N.J.
    METROPOLIS 1990 Oct., v.10, no.3,
    p.25-26, model.

UNITED STATES--CAMELBACK (ARIZONA)--
HOUSES
Kamal Amin: dal Cairo all'Arizona,
    sette opere organiche = from Cairo
    to Arizona, seven organic works.
    Houses in Va. and Ariz. and
    medical centers in Tempe and
    Scottsdale, Ariz.
    ARCHITETTURA: CRONACHE E STORIA
    1990 Sept., v.36, no.9(419),
    p.[612-634], dets., photos.,
    plans, secns., site plans.

UNITED STATES--CAMP HILL
(PENNSYLVANIA)--OFFICE BUILDINGS--
IBM U.S. MARKETING AND SERVICE
DIVISION
IBM U.S. Marketing and Services
Division, Camp Hill, Pennsylvania.
Architects: Grad Partnership.
ARCHITECTURE NEW JERSEY 1990,
v.26, no.6, p.15, photos.

UNITED STATES--CAMPBELL HALL (NEW
YORK)--FARMHOUSES--GEORGIAN--
HILL-HOLD FARM
Hudson Valley scenes: Hill-Hold
Farm.
A working farm museum, with a
stone Georgian farmhouse.
COLONIAL HOMES 1990 June, v.16,
no.3, p.[118-127],142,144, photos.

UNITED STATES--CAMPBELL HALL (NEW
YORK)--FARMS--19TH CENTURY--
HILL-HOLD FARM
Hudson Valley scenes: Hill-Hold
Farm.
A working farm museum, with a
stone Georgian farmhouse.
COLONIAL HOMES 1990 June, v.16,
no.3, p.[118-127],142,144, photos.

UNITED STATES--CAMPBELL HALL (NEW
YORK)--HISTORIC HOUSE MUSEUMS--
HILL-HOLD FARM
Hudson Valley scenes: Hill-Hold
Farm.
A working farm museum, with a
stone Georgian farmhouse.
COLONIAL HOMES 1990 June, v.16,
no.3, p.[118-127],142,144, photos.

UNITED STATES--CANANDAIGUA (NEW
YORK)--FORMAL GARDENS--CONSERVATION
AND RESTORATION--SONNENBERG
Sonnenberg gardens / Gail Greco.
At the 19th cent. estate
overlooking Lake Canandaigua, N.Y.
Original owners: Frederick and
Mary Thompson.
VICTORIAN HOMES 1990 Summer, v.9,
no.3, p.[38]-43, photos.

UNITED STATES--CANANDAIGUA (NEW
YORK)--MANSIONS--19TH CENTURY--
SONNENBERG
Sonnenberg gardens / Gail Greco.
At the 19th cent. estate
overlooking Lake Canandaigua, N.Y.
Original owners: Frederick and
Mary Thompson.
VICTORIAN HOMES 1990 Summer, v.9,
no.3, p.[38]-43, photos.

UNITED STATES--CANON CITY (COLORADO)--
OUTDOOR SCULPTURE--COMPETITIONS--
COLORADO TERRITORIAL CORRECTIONAL
FACILITIES ("OLD MAX")
Ethics in Paradise / Garth
Rockcastle.
On the 1985 competition and
winning project funded by Art in
Public Places for a
maximum-security prison in Canon
City, Colo. Winner: Andrew
Leicester.
VIA 1990, no.10, p.[38]-49,
photos., plans, sketches, refs.

UNITED STATES--CANON CITY (COLORADO)--
PRISONS--COLORADO TERRITORIAL
CORRECTIONAL FACILITIES ("OLD MAX")
Ethics in Paradise / Garth
Rockcastle.
On the 1985 competition and
winning project funded by Art in
Public Places for a
maximum-security prison in Canon
City, Colo. Winner: Andrew
Leicester.
VIA 1990, no.10, p.[38]-49,
photos., plans, sketches, refs.

UNITED STATES--CANTERBURY (NEW
HAMPSHIRE)--MUSEUM VILLAGES--SHAKER
Those ingenious Shakers / David R.
Starbuck.
The Canterbury, New Hampshire,
Museum village.
ARCHAEOLOGY 1990 July-Aug., v.43,
no.4, p.[40]-47, ports., photos.

UNITED STATES--CANTERBURY (NEW
HAMPSHIRE)--RELIGIOUS COMMUNITIES--
SHAKER
Those ingenious Shakers / David R.
Starbuck.
The Canterbury, New Hampshire,
Museum village.
ARCHAEOLOGY 1990 July-Aug., v.43,
no.4, p.[40]-47, ports., photos.

UNITED STATES--CANYON LAKE (TEXAS)--
WEEKEND HOUSES--SALGE HOUSE
Texas breeze [Salgo Lakehouse,
Canyon Lake, Texas] / Joel Warren
Barna.
Weekend house. Architects: Lake
Flato Architects.
PROGRESSIVE ARCHITECTURE 1990
Nov., v.71, no.12, p.78-79,
photos., plans.

UNITED STATES--CAPE COD
(MASSACHUSETTS)--CITIES AND TOWNS--
VIEWS
Edward Hopper's Cape Cod / Alexander
Theroux.
Paintings from 1930-c.1942, when
Hopper spent summers in Truro.
ART & ANTIQUES 1990 Jan., v.7,
no.1, p.[56-67],97, dwgs., ports.

UNITED STATES--CAPE COD
(MASSACHUSETTS)--SHACKS--RESEARCH
Using GIS in cultural resources /
Betsy Chittenden.
Within the National Park System,
including a project to study dune
shacks in an historic area of Cape
Cod, Mass.
CRM BULLETIN: A NATIONAL PARK
SERVICE TECHNICAL BULLETIN 1989,
v.12, no.6, p.21-22, ill.

UNITED STATES--CAPE ELIZABETH
(MAINE)--HOUSES--WITCH WAY (DAVIS
HOUSE)
Bette Davis' best address for
Jezebel and Dangerous at Witch Way
/ A. Scott Berg.
Features interiors of home in Cape
Elizabeth, Maine.
ARCHITECTURAL DIGEST 1990 Apr.,
v.47, no.4, p.248-249,310, port.,
photos.

UNITED STATES--CAPE HATTERAS (NORTH
CAROLINA)--LIGHTHOUSES--CONSERVATION
AND RESTORATION--CAPE HATTERAS
LIGHTHOUSE
Hatteras Light to be moved [Cape
Hatteras Lighthouse, North
Carolina] / Eddie Nickens.
The National Park Service wants to
move the Cape Hatteras Lighthouse
500 feet from its present
location.
PRESERVATION NEWS 1990 Feb., v.30,
no.2, p.1,19, diagr., dwgs., map,
photo.

UNITED STATES--CAPE HATTERAS (NORTH
CAROLINA)--MOVING OF BUILDINGS,
BRIDGES, ETC.--CAPE HATTERAS
LIGHTHOUSE
Hatteras Light to be moved [Cape
Hatteras Lighthouse, North
Carolina] / Eddie Nickens.
The National Park Service wants to
move the Cape Hatteras Lighthouse
500 feet from its present
location.
PRESERVATION NEWS 1990 Feb., v.30,
no.2, p.1,19, diagr., dwgs., map,
photo.

UNITED STATES--CAPISTRANO BEACH
(CALIFORNIA)--BEACH HOUSES
Capistrano Beach Glass House,
Capistrano Beach, California,
design: 1989.
Architect: Rob Wellington Quigley.
Text in Japanese and English.
GA HOUSES 1990 Mar., no.28,
p.64-66, dwgs., model, plans.

UNITED STATES--CARMEL (CALIFORNIA)--
COTTAGES--ALTERATIONS AND
ADDITIONS--PROPSTRA - LANE HOUSE
Cottage karma / Jody
Thompson-Kennedy, Kirsten Harwood.
Remodelled Carmel, Calif. cottage.
Renovation architect: Stephen
Wilmoth.
HOUSE BEAUTIFUL 1990 June, v.132,
no.6, p.72-75, photos.

UNITED STATES--CARMEL (CALIFORNIA)--
COTTAGES--INTERIOR DESIGN--PROPSTRA
- LANE HOUSE
Cottage karma / Jody
Thompson-Kennedy, Kirsten Harwood.
Remodelled Carmel, Calif. cottage.
Renovation architect: Stephen
Wilmoth.
HOUSE BEAUTIFUL 1990 June, v.132,
no.6, p.72-75, photos.

UNITED STATES--CARMEL MOUNTAIN RANCH
(CALIFORNIA)--CLINICS--SCRIPPS
CLINIC
Centro Medico in California =
Scripps Medical Chic, Carmel
Mountain Ranch, Cal. / Stefania
Mornati.
Architect: Austin Hansen Fehlman
Group. Includes English
translation; French, German, and
Spanish summmaries, p.3.
L'INDUSTRIA DELLE COSTRUZIONI 1990
Feb., v.24, no.220, p.18-21,
photos., plans, site plan.

UNITED STATES--CARMICHAEL
(CALIFORNIA)--LIFE CARE
COMMUNITIES--ESKATON VILLAGE.
Eskaton Village: a lifecare project
that made neighbors part of the
development team / Deborah S.
Brittan.
Architects: Vitiello and
Associates.
URBAN LAND 1990 Feb, v.49, no.2,
p.21-23, diagrs., plans, elevs.,
site plans.

UNITED STATES--CAROL STREAM
(ILLINOIS)--RECOVERY PLANTS--DU PAGE
COUNTY INTERMEDIATE PROCESSING
FACILITY
What sort of place is this? /
Barbara K. Hower.
The Du Page County Intermediate
Processing Facility, Carol Stream,
Ill. Construction begins in late
1990. Engineers and planners: Camp
Dresser & McKee Inc.
INLAND ARCHITECT 1990 May-June,
v.34, no.3, p.13, diagr.

UNITED STATES--CARRIAGE HOUSES--
INTERIOR DESIGN
Where opposites attract / Dylan
Landis.
Interiors of 1920s carriage house
by Peter Wheeler.
HOUSE BEAUTIFUL 1990 Sept., v.132,
no.9, p.72-75, photos.

UNITED STATES--CARSON CITY (NEVADA)--
RAILROADS--BUILDINGS AND
STRUCTURES--VIRGINIA AND TRUCKEE
RAILROAD ENGINE HOUSE AND SHOPS
City may save Nevada rail landmark
[Virginia and Truckee Railroad
Engine House, Carson City] /
Thomas W. Sweeney.
1873 limestone structure.
PRESERVATION NEWS 1990 May, v.30,
no.5, p.1,19, photo.

UNITED STATES--CASTLE PINES
(COLORADO)--RESIDENTIAL GARDENS--
SLOPING SITES
Sulle colline del Colorado.
Gardens of a house in Castle
Pines, Colo. Landscape architect:
David Sheridan.
VILLE GIARDINI 1990 Apr., no.247,
p.60-65, photos.

UNITED STATES--CATSKILL MOUNTAINS (NEW
YORK)--COTTAGES
Victorian cottage [Catskill
Mountains]
Architect: Lester Walker.
HOUSE BEAUTIFUL 1986 May, v.128,
no.5, p.49-[61], photos., plans.

UNITED STATES--CAVE CREEK (ARIZONA)--
OWNER-BUILT HOUSES--FOSTER HOUSE
Desert Mansion / Barbara Yost.
A three story "Victorian" house
built 30 miles north of Phoenix in
Cave Creek area. Owner and
builder: Norman Foster.
VICTORIAN HOMES 1990 Fall, v.9,
no.4, p.[33]-38, photos.

UNITED STATES--CEDAR CITY (UTAH)--
THEATERS--RANDALL L. JONES MEMORIAL
THEATER
Act one: Randal L. Jones Memorial
Theater Cedar City, Utah, FFKR
Architects / Lynn Nesmith.
ARCHITECTURE: THE MAGAZINE OF THE
AMERICAN INSTITUTE OF ARCHITECTS
1990 Aug., v.79, no.8, p.80-83,
ill., photos., plans, secns.

UNITED STATES--CEDAR RAPIDS (IOWA)--
MUSEUMS--ART--CEDAR RAPIDS MUSEUM OF
ART
Cedar Rapids Museum of Art / Kirk
Von Blunck.
Architects: Charles W. Moore and
Centerbrook.
IOWA ARCHITECT 1990 Fall, v.39,
no.3, p.5-7.
Iowa Museum opens / Kirk Blunck.
The Cedar Rapids Museum of Art.
Arhcitects: Centerbrook Architects
with Charles Moore.
ARCHITECTURE: THE AIA JOURNAL 1990
Feb., v.79, no.2, p.24, photos,
plan.

UNITED STATES--CEDAR RAPIDS (IOWA)--
UNIVERSITIES AND COLLEGES--
BUILDINGS--UNIVERSITY OF NORTHERN
IOWA--COMMUNICATIONS ART CENTER
UNI Communications Art Building:
Campus collage / Robert Tibbetts.
At the University of Northern
Iowa, Cedar Rapids. Architects:
RDG Bussard Dikis Associates.
IOWA ARCHITECT 1990 Spring, v.39,
no.1, p.20-21, photos., site plan.

UNITED STATES--CEMETERIES
The ultimate open space [cemeteries]
/ Ruth Eckdish Knack.
Cemeteries and development.
PLANNING 1990 Feb., v.56, no.2,
p.13-15, det., photos., site plan.

UNITED STATES--CENTRAL BUSINESS
DISTRICTS
Urban renewal: Downtown inc.: how
America rebuilds cities, by
Bernard J. Frieden and Lynne B.
Sagalyn [book review] / Francis
Tibbalds.
ROYAL SOCIETY OF ARTS, LONDON. RSA
JOURNAL 1990 Dec., v.139, no.5413,
p.947.

UNITED STATES--CENTRAL BUSINESS
DISTRICTS--ENVIRONMENTAL ASPECTS
Patterns of behavior in urban public
spaces / Jack L. Nasas, A. Rengin
Yurdakul.
Includes abstract.
JOURNAL OF ARCHITECTURAL AND
PLANNING RESEARCH 1990 Spring,
v.7, no.1, p.71-85, charts,
diagrs., photos, biblio.

UNITED STATES--CENTRAL BUSINESS
DISTRICTS--HISTORY
American downtowns: past and present
attempts at revitalization /
Robert J. Carey.
BUILT ENVIRONMENT 1988, v.14,
no.1, p.47-59, graphs, photos,
tables, refs.

UNITED STATES--CENTRAL ISLIP (NEW
YORK)--ABANDONED BUILDINGS
Toward the suburb of the 1990s:
planning a center for Long
Island's Central Islip / Nancy
Gould.
Abandoned psychiatric hospital
buildings form the basis of master
plan for Central Islip, including
a research park and campus for the
New York Institute of Technology
(NYIT). Architects for master
plan: Haines Lundberg Waehler.
URBAN LAND 1990 Oct., v.49, no.10,
p.23-26, photos., plan.

UNITED STATES--CENTRAL ISLIP (NEW
YORK)--CAMPUS PLANNING--NEW YORK
INSTITUTE OF TECHNOLOGY
Toward the suburb of the 1990s:
planning a center for Long
Island's Central Islip / Nancy
Gould.
Abandoned psychiatric hospital
buildings form the basis of master
plan for Central Islip, including
a research park and campus for the
New York Institute of Technology
(NYIT). Architects for master
plan: Haines Lundberg Waehler.
URBAN LAND 1990 Oct., v.49, no.10,
p.23-26, photos., plan.

UNITED STATES--CENTRAL ISLIP (NEW
YORK)--COMPREHENSIVE PLANS
Toward the suburb of the 1990s:
planning a center for Long
Island's Central Islip / Nancy
Gould.
Abandoned psychiatric hospital
buildings form the basis of master
plan for Central Islip, including
a research park and campus for the
New York Institute of Technology
(NYIT). Architects for master
plan: Haines Lundberg Waehler.
URBAN LAND 1990 Oct., v.49, no.10,
p.23-26, photos., plan.

UNITED STATES--CENTRAL ISLIP (NEW
YORK)--RESEARCH PARKS
Toward the suburb of the 1990s:
planning a center for Long
Island's Central Islip / Nancy
Gould.
Abandoned psychiatric hospital
buildings form the basis of master
plan for Central Islip, including
a research park and campus for the
New York Institute of Technology
(NYIT). Architects for master
plan: Haines Lundberg Waehler.
URBAN LAND 1990 Oct., v.49, no.10,
p.23-26, photos., plan.

UNITED STATES--CENTRAL VALLEY
(CALIFORNIA)--REGIONAL PLANNING
Valley talk [Central Valley, Ca.] /
Gary Delsohn.
Growth debate in the towns of
Central Valley, Ca.
PLANNING 1990 Oct., v.56, no.10,
p.12-16, ports., maps, photos.,
aerial photo.

UNITED STATES--CENTRAL VALLEY
(CALIFORNIA)--RURAL DEVELOPMENT
Valley talk [Central Valley, Ca.] /
Gary Delsohn.
Growth debate in the towns of
Central Valley, Ca.
PLANNING 1990 Oct., v.56, no.10,
p.12-16, ports., maps, photos.,
aerial photo.

UNITED STATES--CHAPEL HILL (NORTH
CAROLINA)--CITY PLANNING--STUDY AND
TEACHING--UNIVERSITY OF NORTH
CAROLINA--DEPT. OF CITY AND REGIONAL
PLANNING
An interview with John A. Parker /
Carolina Planning Staff.
Founder of the Dept. of City and
Regional Planning, University of
North Carolina at Chapel Hill.
CAROLINA PLANNING 1990 Fall,
v.16, no.2, p.2-3, port.

UNITED STATES--CHARLESTON (SOUTH
CAROLINA)--ARCHITECTURE--19TH
CENTURY
Architectural history and urban
history: a difficult marriage
[book review] / Joseph L. Arnold.
Review essay of Charleston:
antebellum architecture and civic
destiny, by Kenneth Severens; and
Public sculpture and the civic
ideal in New York City, 1890-1930,
by Michele Bogart.
JOURNAL OF URBAN HISTORY 1990
Nov., v.17, no.1, p.70-78, refs.
Architecture in the United States
[book review] / Rhodri Windsor
Liscombe, John Vincent Boyer,
William G. Farrar, IV, Robert
Winter.
Review of Charleston antebellum
architecture and civic destiny, by
Kenneth Severens; Structures and
styles: guided tours of Hartford
architecture, by Gregory E.
Andrews and David F. Ransom;
Vernacular architecture in
southern Illinois, by John M.
Coggeshall and Jo Anne Nast; and
Bruce Goff: toward aboslute
architccture, by David Delong.
SOCIETY OF ARCHITECTURAL
HISTORIANS. JOURNAL 1990 Mar.,
v.49, no.1, p.115-120,

UNITED STATES--CHARLESTON (SOUTH
CAROLINA)--BUILDINGS--MAINTENANCE
AND REPAIR
NPS helps Charleston after Hugo.
CRM BULLETIN: A NATIONAL PARK
SERVICE TECHNICAL BULLETIN 1989,
v.12, no.6, p.11-14,cover, photos.

UNITED STATES--CHARLESTON (SOUTH
CAROLINA)--COUNTRY CLUBS--CHARLESTON
NATIONAL COUNTRY CLUB
Winds of change: Charleston National
Country Club after Hurricane Hugo
/ Joel Werblow.
Golf club and community
development which sustained heavy
damage from Hurricane Hugo.
URBAN LAND 1990 Aug., v.49, no.8,
p.16-19, photos., table.

UNITED STATES--CHARLESTON (SOUTH
CAROLINA)--DAMAGE TO BUILDINGS--
INVENTORIES
NPS surveys yield data on the
effects of Hurricane Hugo / Thomas
A. Vitanza.
CRM BULLETIN: A NATIONAL PARK
SERVICE TECHNICAL BULLETIN 1990,
v.13, no.1, p.12-14, photos.,
aerial photos.

UNITED STATES--CHARLESTON (SOUTH
CAROLINA)--GOLF COURSE COMMUNITIES--
CHARLESTON NATIONAL COUNTRY CLUB
Winds of change: Charleston National
Country Club after Hurricane Hugo
/ Joel Werblow.
Golf club and community
development which sustained heavy
damage from Hurricane Hugo.
URBAN LAND 1990 Aug., v.49, no.8,
p.16-19, photos., table.

UNITED STATES--CHARLESTON (SOUTH
CAROLINA)--HISTORIC BUILDINGS--
MAINTENANCE AND REPAIR
Bi-coastal disaster assistance /
Michael Adlerstein.
Report on assistance efforts made
by the NPS in Charleston, S.C.
after the Sept. 22, 1989 hurricane
and in San Francisco after the
Oct. 1989 Loma Prieta earthquake.
CRM BULLETIN: A NATIONAL PARK
SERVICE TECHNICAL BULLETIN 1990,
v.13, no.1, p.10-12,

UNITED STATES--CHARLESTON (SOUTH
CAROLINA)--HOUSES--19TH CENTURY--
CONSERVATION AND RESTORATION--
SIMMONS-EDWARDS HOUSE (BENNETT
HOUSE)
Low Country classic: preeminent
among Charleston's historic homes.
1800 Adam-style house of Mr. &
Mrs. Thomas Bennett.
SOUTHERN ACCENTS 1989 Mar.-Apr.,
v.12, no.2, p.[140]-147, photos.

UNITED STATES--CHARLESTON (SOUTH
CAROLINA)--HOUSES--20TH CENTURY--
CROFFEAD HOUSE
Villa Carolina: Croffead House,
Charleston, North Carolina / Paul
M. Sachner.
Architect: Clark & Menefee
Architects.
ARCHITECTURAL RECORD 1990
Mid-Apr., v.178, no.5, p.42-[47],
photos., plans, secn., site plan.

UNITED STATES--CHARLESTON (SOUTH
CAROLINA)--HOUSES--CONCRETE
Chip off the old block / Julie V.
Iovine.
A concrete, 32-foot cube house
located near the confluence of two
rivers in Charleston, S.C.
Architect: W. G. Clark & Menefee.
METROPOLITAN HOME 1990 July, v.22,
no.7, p.[62-65], photos.

UNITED STATES--CHARLESTON (SOUTH
CAROLINA)--HOUSES--GEORGIAN--
INTERIOR DESIGN--CONSERVATION AND
RESTORATION--BLAKE HOUSE (HANAHAN
HOUSE)
Local colors: a venerable Charleston
house is restored with an
eighteenth-century palette / Nancy
Lemann.
Georgian-style house built in the
1790s by John Blake. Interior
decorator: Arnold Copper.
HOUSE & GARDEN 1990 Jan., v.162,
no.1, p.124-[129], photos.

UNITED STATES--CHARLESTON (SOUTH
CAROLINA)--INNS--JOHN RUTLEDGE HOUSE
INN
John Rutledge B&B [Charleston,
S.C.].
1763 townhouse, now an inn.
Architects for restoration: Evans
and Schmidt. Interior designers:
Pulliam Morris Interiors.
COLONIAL HOMES 1990 June, v.16,
no.3, p.[82-85],146, photos.,
port.

UNITED STATES--CHARLESTON (SOUTH
CAROLINA)--INNS--MIDDLETON INN
[Reid house and Waterside Inn, South
Carolina].
Contents: Reid house, John Island,
South Carolina -- Middleton Inn,
Charleston, South Carolina.
Architects: Clark & Menefee.
9H 1989, no.8, p.104-109, photos.,
plans, secns., site plan.
Rigorst [Middleton Inn, S.C.] /
Claes Caldenby.
In Charleston. Architect: Clark &
Menefee [sic].
ARKITEKTUR: THE SWEDISH REVIEW OF
ARCHITECTURE 1990 Oct., v.90,
no.8, p.56, photo., secn., site
plan.

UNITED STATES--CHARLESTON (SOUTH
CAROLINA)--NATURAL DISASTERS
NPS helps Charleston after Hugo.
CRM BULLETIN: A NATIONAL PARK
SERVICE TECHNICAL BULLETIN 1989,
v.12, no.6, p.11-14,cover, photos.

UNITED STATES--CHARLESTON (SOUTH
CAROLINA)--PARTERRES--19TH CENTURY--
CONSERVATION AND RESTORATION--58
SOUTH BATTERY
Parterre redux: an award-winning
restoration is re-created
following Hugo's devastation /
Allen Freeman.
Restoration of private, ca.1880,
garden at 58 South Battery,
Charleston, S.C. Landscape
architects: Hugh Dargan
Associates.
HISTORIC PRESERVATION 1990
May-June, v.42, no.3, p.60-61,
photo.

UNITED STATES--CHARLESTON (SOUTH
CAROLINA)--RESIDENTIAL GARDENS--
WHALEY GARDEN
My mother's garden: in Charleston /
Marty Whaley Adams.
The Emily Whaley garden. Landscape
designer: Loutriel Briggs.
SOUTHERN ACCENTS 1989 July-Aug.,
v.12, no.4, p.[94-103], photos.

UNITED STATES--CHARLESTON (SOUTH
CAROLINA)--TOWNHOUSES--18TH
CENTURY--RUTLEDGE HOUSE (116 BROAD
STREET)
   John Rutledge B&B [Charleston,
   S.C.].
      1763 townhouse, now an inn.
      Architects for restoration: Evans
      and Schmidt. Interior designers:
      Pulliam Morris Interiors.
      COLONIAL HOMES 1990 June, v.16,
      no.3, p.[82-85],146, photos.,
      port.

UNITED STATES--CHARLESTON (WEST
VIRGINIA)--HOUSES--OFFICIAL
RESIDENCES--INTERIOR DESIGN--
GOVERNOR'S MANSION
   West Virginia governor's mansion /
   Monica Geran.
      Interiors of renovated
      Georgian-style mansion in
      Charleston. Original architect:
      Walker Martens. Interior
      designers: Carleton Varney of
      Dorothy Draper & Co.
      INTERIOR DESIGN 1990 Mar., v.61,
      no.5, p.176-[183], photos., plan.

UNITED STATES--CHARLOTTE (NORTH
CAROLINA)--GREENWAYS
   Greenway use and users: an
   examination of Raleigh and
   Charlotte greenways / Owen J.
   Furuseth, Robert E. Altman.
      CAROLINA PLANNING 1990 Fall, v.16,
      no.2, p.37-43, maps, photo.,
      tables, refs.

UNITED STATES--CHARLOTTE (NORTH
CAROLINA)--LIBRARIES--PUBLIC--
ALTERATIONS AND ADDITIONS--PUBLIC
LIBRARY OF CHARLOTTE AND MECKLENBURG
COUNTY
   Latest edition: Public Library of
   Charlotte and Mecklenburg County,
   Charlotte, North Carolina, Morris
   Architects and Middleton,
   McMillan, Architects, Inc. / Lynn
   Nesmith.
      ARCHITECTURE: THE MAGAZINE OF THE
      AMERICAN INSTITUTE OF ARCHITECTS
      1990 July, v.79, no.7, p.[82]-85,

UNITED STATES--CHARLOTTE (VERMONT)--
HOUSES--COLONIAL REVIVAL--MOSSMAN
HOUSE
   Lakeside Noel [Mossman house,
   Charlotte, Vt.]
      A new Colonial-style home.
      COLONIAL HOMES 1990 Dec., v.16,
      no.6, p.[59-69], photos.

UNITED STATES--CHARLOTTESVILLE
(VIRGINIA)--BED-AND-BREAKFAST GUEST
HOUSES--WOODSTOCK HALL B & B
   Woodstock Hall B & B.
      An 18th cent. tavern near
      Charlottesville, Va.; now a
      bed-and-breakfast inn.
      COLONIAL HOMES 1990 Oct., v.16,
      no.5, p.134-[139],147,149,153,
      ports., photos.

UNITED STATES--CHARLOTTESVILLE
(VIRGINIA)--HISTORIC SITES--
UNIVERSITY OF VIRGINIA--ACADEMICAL
VILLAGE
   "The Academical Village of Thomas
   Jefferson" / James Murray Howard.
      On the restoration of these
      buildings which are part of the
      Univ. of Virginia, Charlottesville
      campus. Summaries in French,
      Italian and Spanish.
      ICOMOS INFORMATION 1989 Oct.-Dec.,
      no.4, p.19-25, dwg., port.,
      photos., site plan, refs.

UNITED STATES--CHARLOTTESVILLE
(VIRGINIA)--TAVERNS--18TH CENTURY--
CONSERVATION AND RESTORATION--
WOODSTOCK HALL
   Woodstock Hall B & B.
      An 18th cent. tavern near
      Charlottesville, Va.; now a
      bed-and-breakfast inn.
      COLONIAL HOMES 1990 Oct., v.16,
      no.5, p.134-[139],147,149,153,
      ports., photos.

UNITED STATES--CHARLOTTESVILLE
(VIRGINIA)--UNIVERSITIES AND
COLLEGES--BUILDINGS--CONSERVATION
AND RESTORATION--UNIVERSITY OF
VIRGINIA--ACADEMICAL VILLAGE
   "The Academical Village of Thomas
   Jefferson" / James Murray Howard.
      On the restoration of these
      buildings which are part of the
      Univ. of Virginia, Charlottesville
      campus. Summaries in French,
      Italian and Spanish.
      ICOMOS INFORMATION 1989 Oct.-Dec.,
      no.4, p.19-25, dwg., port.,
      photos., site plan, refs.

UNITED STATES--CHATTANOOGA
(TENNESSEE)--HOTELS--INTERIOR
DESIGN--RADISSON READ HOUSE
   Radisson Read Home: architectural
   triumph in vibrant Chattanooga.
      The 1926 hotel designed by
      Holabird and Roche has been
      recently refurbished.
      SOUTHERN ACCENTS 1989 Mar.-Apr.,
      v.12, no.2, p.218-276, photos.

UNITED STATES--CHATTANOOGA
(TENNESSEE)--TOWNSCAPES--EVALUATION
   The evaluative image of the city /
   Jack L. Nasar.
      Methods for determining how the
      public evaluates the cityscape,
      providing the basis for a visual
      plan. Examples from Knoxville and
      Chattanooga, Tenn.
      AMERICAN PLANNING ASSOCIATION
      JOURNAL 1990 Winter, v.56, no.1,
      p.41-53, maps, tables, aerial
      photos., refs.

UNITED STATES--CHESAPEAKE (VIRGINIA)--
SUBURBS--ALTERATIONS AND ADDITIONS--
RIVER WALK
   River Walk civic places.
      On the series of gateways and
      public spaces among a 484-acre
      suburban community on the
      Elizabeth River in Chesapeake, Va.
      Architects: Eric R. Kuhne and
      Associates.
      PROGRESSIVE ARCHITECTURE 1990
      Jan., v.71, no.1, p.113-115,
      dwgs., elevs., photo., site plans.

UNITED STATES--CHESAPEAKE (VIRGINIA)--
WATERFRONTS--RIVER WALK
   River Walk civic places.
      On the series of gateways and
      public spaces among a 484-acre
      suburban community on the
      Elizabeth River in Chesapeake, Va.
      Architects: Eric R. Kuhne and
      Associates.
      PROGRESSIVE ARCHITECTURE 1990
      Jan., v.71, no.1, p.113-115,
      dwgs., elevs., photo., site plans.

UNITED STATES--CHESTERTOWN
(MARYLAND)--HOUSES--ARCHITECTS'--
ARENA HOU
   Great stories.
      Feature section on ca.15 recent
      American houses, including ones by
      architects Andy Dean, in S.
      Dartmouth, Mass.; Peter Anders, in
      Jersey City, N.J.; Chip Arena, in
      Chestertown, Md.; Cory Buckner and
      Nicholas Roberts, in Malibu,
      Calif.; Robby Reid, in Tempe,
      Ariz.
      METROPOLITAN HOME 1990 Feb., v.22,
      no.2, p.125-166, photos., ports.

UNITED STATES--CHICAGO (ILLINOIS)--
AIRPORT TERMINALS--CHICAGO O'HARE
INTERNATIONAL AIRPORT--INTERNATIONAL
TERMINAL
   A new terminal taking off / Cheryl
   Kent.
      On the new International Terminal
      at Chicago's O'Hare Airport.
      Architect: Ralph Johnson.
      PROGRESSIVE ARCHITECTURE 1990
      Feb., v.71, no.2, p.22-23, dwgs.

UNITED STATES--CHICAGO (ILLINOIS)--
AIRPORT TERMINALS--CHICAGO O'HARE
INTERNATIONAL AIRPORT--INTERNATIONAL
TERMINAL FIVE
   O'Hare's International Terminal /
   Michael J. P. Smith.
      Plans for Terminal Five (T-5), to
      be begun in Oct.1990 on a 100-acre
      site southeast of the O'Hare
      domestic terminals. Architects:
      Perkins & Will.
      INLAND ARCHITECT 1990 Jan.-Feb.,
      v.34, no.1, p.26, dwgs.

UNITED STATES--CHICAGO (ILLINOIS)--
AIRPORT TERMINALS--CHICAGO O'HARE
INTERNATIONAL AIRPORT--UNITED
TERMINAL
   Um den Globus...Flughafen in Japan,
   den USA, Danemark und Deutschland
   / Ursula Baus.
      Kansai Airport, Osaka (Renzo
      Piano, Paul Andreu); O'Hare
      Airport, Chicago (Helmut Jahn with
      Epstein & Sons); Copenhagen
      Airport, Kastrup (Holscher,
      Axelsson, Sorensen); Flughafen
      Hamburg, Fuhlsbuttel (Von Gerkan,
      Marg und Partner); and Terminal
      Ost, Frankfurt (Buro J. S. K).
      DEUTSCHE BAUZEITUNG 1990 Nov.,
      v.124, no.11, p.54-63, dwgs.,
      elevs., models, photos., plans,
      secns., site plans.

UNITED STATES--CHICAGO (ILLINOIS)--
APARTMENTS
Chicago Modern / Pilar Viladas.
Apartment renovation by Krueck &
Olsen.
HOUSE & GARDEN 1990 Nov., v.162,
no.11, p.[154-159], photos.

UNITED STATES--CHICAGO (ILLINOIS)--
APARTMENTS--ALTERATIONS AND
ADDITIONS--860 LAKE SHORE DRIVE
Restorative powers: Architects
Powell/Kleinschmidt revive the
Miesian spirit / Judith Neisser.
Renovation of an apartment in
Mies' 860 Lake Shore Dr. building,
Chicago, based on the architects'
original floor plan.
ELLE DECOR 1990 May, v.1, no.4,
p.116-123, photos.

UNITED STATES--CHICAGO (ILLINOIS)--
APARTMENTS--ARCHITECTS'--INTERIOR
DESIGN--KLEINSCHMIDT APARTMENT
At home at 880 Lake Shore Drive. /
Stanley Abercrombie.
Features Robert Kleinschmidt's
newly expanded apartment in a Mies
van der Rohe-designed building in
Chicago. Architects: Powell
Kleinschmidt.
INTERIOR DESIGN 1990 Aug., v.61,
no.11, p.154-[163], photos., plan,
site plan.

UNITED STATES--CHICAGO (ILLINOIS)--
APARTMENTS--INTERIOR DESIGN
Untitled no. 5 [duplex apartment],
Chicago, Illinois, design:1989;
completion: 1991 (est.).
Architects: Krueck & Olsen
Architects. Text in Japanese and
English.
GA HOUSES 1990 Mar., no.28,
p.58-59, dwgs., elev., plans,
secns.

UNITED STATES--CHICAGO (ILLINOIS)--
ARCHITECTURE--20TH CENTURY
"The six lamps of architecture
[sic]".
On contemporary architecture in
Chicago.
DEUTSCHE BAUZEITSCHRIFT 1990 May,
v.38, no.5, p.649, axonometric
views, photo.

UNITED STATES--CHICAGO (ILLINOIS)--
ARCHITECTURE--20TH CENTURY--HISTORY
"Schule von Chicago": ein
architekturgeschichtlicher Essay /
Wolf Nedderhut-Heeschen.
DEUTSCHE BAUZEITSCHRIFT 1990 May,
v.38, no.5, p.685-686,691-692,
dwgs., plans, refs.

UNITED STATES--CHICAGO (ILLINOIS)--
ARCHITECTURE--20TH CENTURY--
HISTORY--EXHIBITIONS
Architektonische Gesichtspunkte zur
Chicago [exhibition review].
On the exhibition, 100 years of
architecture in Chicago:
continuity of structure and form,
on view at the Museum of
Contemporary Art, Chicago.
DEUTSCHE BAUZEITSCHRIFT 1990 May,
v.38, no.5, p.648, photos.

UNITED STATES--CHICAGO (ILLINOIS)--
ARCHITECTURE--EXHIBITIONS
Exhibition: Chicago categorized
[exhibition review] / Stanley
Tigerman.
On the exhibit "Chicago
architecture-the new Zeitgeist: in
search of closure", organized by
Stanley Tigerman, on view in 1989
at the Fundacao Calouste
Gulbenkian, Lisbon. Focus on
Tigerman's organization of the
work of 99 architects into six
categories.
PROGRESSIVE ARCHITECTURE 1990
Sept., v.71, no.9, p.140-141,
dets., photos., secns.

UNITED STATES--CHICAGO (ILLINOIS)--
ARCHITECTURE--STUDY AND TEACHING--
ILLINOIS INSTITUTE OF TECHNOLOGY
Toward the education of architect /
Gene R. Summers.
Seven tenets established in
1989-1990 as principles for the
College of Architecture at
Illinois Institute of Technology.
INLAND ARCHITECT 1990 Sept.-Oct.,
v.34, no.5, p.66-69,

UNITED STATES--CHICAGO (ILLINOIS)--
ARCHIVES--ART INSTITUTE OF CHICAGO
Goff archives come to Art Institute
/ Barbara K. Hower.
Donated by Shin'enKan, Ind.
INLAND ARCHITECT 1990 July-Aug.,
v.34, no.4, p.71,

UNITED STATES--CHICAGO (ILLINOIS)--
BANKS--ALTERATIONS AND ADDITIONS--
FEDERAL RESERVE BANK OF CHICAGO
Federal Reserve Bank of Chicago /
Monica Geran.
Expansion and renovation of 1921
building by Holabird and Root.
INTERIOR DESIGN 1990 July, v.61,
no.10, p.162-[169], photos.,
plans, secn.

UNITED STATES--CHICAGO (ILLINOIS)--
CHINATOWNS--CHINATOWN
New life for Chicago's Chinatown /
Annie Morse.
A 32-acre commercial residential
project by the Chinese American
Development Corporation (CADC) and
Link Programs (a division of the
Himmel Group). Phases I-III will
be completed 1991-c1997.
Architect: Harry Weese.
INLAND ARCHITECT 1990 Nov.-Dec.,
v.34, no.6, p.22, dwg.

UNITED STATES--CHICAGO (ILLINOIS)--
CHURCHES--CONSERVATION AND
RESTORATION
Struggle continues to save Detroit,
Chicago churches / Bonnie
DeSimone.
PRESERVATION NEWS 1990 Mar., v.31,
no.3, p.7,19,

UNITED STATES--CHICAGO (ILLINOIS)--
CHURCHES--OLD SAINT MARY'S CHURCH
Precast rock of ages / Barbara K.
Hower.
Plans to replace Old St. Mary's
Church, located at Van Buren and
Wabash in Chicago, with a
two-story parking garage. Original
architect (Isabella Building
section): William Le Baron Jenney.
(Continued next column)

UNITED STATES--CHICAGO (ILLINOIS)--
CHURCHES--OLD SAINT MARY'S CHURCH
(CONTINUED)
Precast rock of ages... (CONTINUED)
Current architects: McBride and
Kelley.
INLAND ARCHITECT 1990 Mar.-Apr.,
v.34, no.2, p.80-82, ill.

UNITED STATES--CHICAGO (ILLINOIS)--
CITY PLANNING
Urbs in horto: boulevard restoration
in Chicago / Riva Feshbach.
INLAND ARCHITECT 1990 May-June,
v.34, no.3, p.20,22, map, photo.

UNITED STATES--CHICAGO (ILLINOIS)--
CITY PLANNING--BURNHAM PLAN
Big plans, divine details: the
Burnham plan and citywide
development in modern Chicago /
Philip Bess.
INLAND ARCHITECT 1990 Mar.-Apr.,
v.34, no.2, p.56-63, ill., refs.

UNITED STATES--CHICAGO (ILLINOIS)--
CITY PLANNING--CENTRAL STATION AREA
Central Station: opening up
Chicago's near south side / Gerald
Fogelson.
Master plan by Ehrenkrantz,
Eckstut Whitelaw.
URBAN LAND 1990 Oct., v.49, no.10,
p.2-4, dwg., site plan, aerial
photo.
Next stop, Central Station / Nevin
Noel Hedlund.
On plans for the 38-acre site of
Central Station (demolished in
1974). Developer: Fogelson
Properties.
INLAND ARCHITECT 1990 Jan.-Feb.,
v.34, no.1, p.65,67,[69-70],
photo., site plan.

UNITED STATES--CHICAGO (ILLINOIS)--
CLOCK TOWERS--CONSERVATION AND
RESTORATION--CENTRAL OFFICE BUILDING
Goes around, comes around / Michael
J.P. Smith.
Restoration of 1910s clock on
tower of the City's Central Office
Building, Chicago.
INLAND ARCHITECT 1990 July-Aug.,
v.34, no.4, p.72-73, photos.

UNITED STATES--CHICAGO (ILLINOIS)--
CONFERENCE ROOMS--INTERIOR DESIGN--
SIDLEY AND AUSTIN
A glowing conference / Nayana
Currimbhoy.
On the entire floor of conference
rooms in the law firm Sidley and
Austin's Chicago offices.
Designers: ISD Inc.
INTERIORS 1990 Jan., v.149, no.6,
p.134-135, photos., plan.

UNITED STATES--CHICAGO (ILLINOIS)--
CORPORATE OFFICE BUILDINGS AT&T
CORPORATE CENTER
Chicago on the rise: a wave of
speculative office towers... /
Howard Decker.
NBC Tower (SOM); 225 W. Wacker Dr.
(Kohn Pedersen Fox); 900 N.
Michigan Ave. (Kohn Pedersen Fox);
AT&T Center (SOM); Burnett
Headquarters (Roche Dinkeloo); AMA
Headquarters (Kenzo Tange); 181 W.
Madison St. (Cesar Pelli); Chicago
Skyneedle (Cesar Pelli).
(Continued next page)

UNITED STATES--CHICAGO (ILLINOIS)--
CORPORATE OFFICE BUILDINGS--AT&T
CORPORATE CENTER (CONTINUED)
  Chicago on the rise:...(CONTINUED)
    ARCHITECTURE: THE AIA JOURNAL 1990
    Feb., v.79, no.2, p.78-83, photos,
    model, aerial photo.
  Good connections: AT&T Corporate
    Center, Chicago, Illinois,
    Skidmore, Owings & Merrill,
    Architects.
    ARCHITECTURAL RECORD 1990 Oct.,
    v.178, no.11, p.94-97, dwg.,
    elev., photos., plans.
  Heightened profiles / Cynthia Chapin
    Davidson.
    Two Chicago projects: NBC Tower at
    Cityfront Center and AT&T
    Corporate Center at corner of
    Franklin and Monroe streets, which
    reflect influences from 1930's
    skyscrapers. Architect: Adrian
    Smith and SOM.
    INLAND ARCHITECT 1990 Jan.-Feb.,
    v.34, no.1, p.28-35, elev.,
    photos., plan.

UNITED STATES--CHICAGO (ILLINOIS)--
CORPORATE OFFICE BUILDINGS--INTERIOR
DESIGN--LEO BURNETT BUILDING
  Inside out from the ground up at Leo
    Burnett / Karen E. Klages.
    Located at 35 West Wacker Dr.,
    Chicago, and housing the
    advertising agency. Architect:
    Kevin Roche. Interior designer:
    ISD.
    INLAND ARCHITECT 1990 Jan.-Feb.,
    v.34, no.1, p.4-5, photos., plan.

UNITED STATES--CHICAGO (ILLINOIS)--
CORPORATE OFFICE BUILDINGS--INTERIOR
DESIGN--PLAYBOY ENTERPRISES
  Lighting up Playboy / Michael
    Wagner.
    Interiors of Playboy Enterprises,
    Chicago. Architects: Himmel Bonner
    Architects.
    INTERIORS 1990 June, v.149, no.11,
    p.92-[99], photos., plans.

UNITED STATES--CHICAGO (ILLINOIS)--
CORPORATE OFFICE BUILDINGS--LEO
BURNETT BUILDING
  Chicago on the rise: a wave of
    speculative office towers... /
    Howard Decker.
    NBC Tower (SOM); 225 W. Wacker Dr.
    (Kohn Pedersen Fox); 900 N.
    Michigan Ave. (Kohn Pedersen Fox);
    AT&T Center (SOM); Burnett
    Headquarters (Roche Dinkeloo); AMA
    Headquarters (Kenzo Tange); 181 W.
    Madison St. (Cesar Pelli); Chicago
    Skyneedle (Cesar Pelli).
    ARCHITECTURE: THE AIA JOURNAL 1990
    Feb., v.79, no.2, p.78-83, photos,
    model, aerial photo.
  Illusions in fin de siecle Chicago:
    900 North Michigan and the Leo
    Burnett Building / Edward Keegan.
    Architects: KPF; Roche Dinkeloo
    and Associates.
    INLAND ARCHITECT 1990 Jan.-Feb.,
    v.34, no.1, p.[36]-43, photos.,
    plans, secn.

UNITED STATES--CHICAGO (ILLINOIS)--
CORPORATE OFFICE BUILDINGS--NBC
TOWER
  Heightened profiles / Cynthia Chapin
    Davidson.
    Two Chicago projects: NBC Tower at
    Cityfront Center and AT&T
    Corporate Center at corner of
    Franklin and Monroe streets, which
    reflect influences from 1930's
    skyscrapers. Architect: Adrian
    Smith and SOM.
    INLAND ARCHITECT 1990 Jan.-Feb.,
    v.34, no.1, p.28-35, elev.,
    photos., plan.

UNITED STATES--CHICAGO (ILLINOIS)--
DECORATION AND ORNAMENT--RUINED,
EXTINCT, ETC.
  Eat it! A dead fragment on how Louis
    Sullivan dies / John Whileman.
    INLAND ARCHITECT 1990 May-June,
    v.34, no.3, p.111, photo.

UNITED STATES--CHICAGO (ILLINOIS)--
DEPARTMENT STORES--CARSON PIRIE
SCOTT
  Caroon, Pirie, Scott: Louis Sullivan
    and the Chicago department store
    [by] Joseph Siry [book review] /
    Mark S. Foster.
    1990 Winter, v.25, no.4,
    p.303-305,

UNITED STATES--CHICAGO (ILLINOIS)--
ENDANGERED PLACES--CHICAGO BUILDING
  "Chicago's Chicago Building is
    threatened."
    Citicorps Savings of Illinois is
    considering demolishing the 1905
    Chicago Building. Holabird and
    Roche, architects.
    PRESERVATION NEWS 1990 Mar., v.30,
    no.3, p.10, photo.

UNITED STATES--CHICAGO (ILLINOIS)--
FOUNTAINS--CENTENNIAL FOUNTAIN
  Liquid symbol: Centennial Fountain
    is Lohan Associates' symbolic
    salute to the 1889 reversal of the
    Chicago River.
    Water arch spanning the River.
    ARCHITECTURAL RECORD 1990 Mar.,
    v.178, no.3, p.92-[95], photos.,
    secn., site plan, aerial photos.

UNITED STATES--CHICAGO (ILLINOIS)--
GREENWAYS
  Urbs in horto: boulevard restoration
    in Chicago / Riva Feshbach.
    INLAND ARCHITECT 1990 May-June,
    v.34, no.3, p.20,22, map, photo.

UNITED STATES--CHICAGO (ILLINOIS)--
HOTELS--FAIRMONT HOTEL
  Fairmont Hotel, Chicago, Illinois,
    USA, 1988.
    Architects: Hellmuth, Obata &
    Kassabaum, with Fujikawa Johnson
    and Associates. Text in Japanese
    and English.
    ARCHITECTURE AND URBANISM 1990
    Dec., no.12 extra edition,
    p.98-103, photos., plans, site
    plan.

UNITED STATES--CHICAGO (ILLINOIS)--
HOTELS--HOTEL INTER-CONTINENTAL
  Regilding Ahlschlager's Golden Dome
    / Jane H. Clarke.
    Restoration and conversion of the
    Medinah Athletic Club, 505 N.
    Michigan, Chicago, into the Hotel
    Inter-Continental. Original
    architect: Walter W. Ahlschlager.
    Restoration architect: Harry Weese
    & Associates.
    INLAND ARCHITECT 1990 Mar.-Apr.,
    v.34, no.2, p.71-78, ill., photo.

UNITED STATES--CHICAGO (ILLINOIS)--
HOUSES--ALTERATIONS AND ADDITIONS
  Arbeiter Cottage in Chicago.
    Renovation of house in the Old
    Town section. Architect: Ast &
    Dagdelen.
    DEUTSCHE BAUZEITSCHRIFT 1990 May,
    v.38, no.5, p.661-664, ill.,
    photos., isometric dwgs.

UNITED STATES--CHICAGO (ILLINOIS)--
HOUSES--ARCHITECTS'--PHILLIPS HOUSE
  Chicago three-flat 1990s style /
    Cynthia Chapin Davidson.
    House on Mohawk St. Chicago. Owner
    and architect: Frederick Phillips.
    INLAND ARCHITECT 1990 Mar.-Apr.,
    v.34, no.2, p.53-55, photos.,
    plans, secn.
  Town and country [two houses by
    Frederick Phillips & Associates] /
    Clifford A. Pearson.
    Phillips Townhouse, Chicago; and
    Bennett house, Washington Island,
    Wisc.
    ARCHITECTURAL RECORD 1990
    Mid-Apr., v.178, no.5, p.68-63,
    photos., plans, secns.

UNITED STATES--CHICAGO (ILLINOIS)--
HOUSES--INTERIOR DESIGN
  Spaces for a spiritual existence /
    Karen E. Klages.
    Renovation of a "two-flat" house
    in Chicago. Architect: Schroeder
    Murchie Laya Associates.
    INLAND ARCHITECT 1990 Mar.-Apr.,
    v.34, no.2, p.4-5, photos., secn.

UNITED STATES--CHICAGO (ILLINOIS)--
HOUSES--ROBIE HOUSE
  Cassina: vivere con un genio =
    Living with genius.
    Furniture modelled on F.L.
    Wright's designs for the Robie
    House and others.
    OTTAGONO 1990 Sept., no.96,
    p.164-[167], dwgs., photos.

UNITED STATES--CHICAGO (ILLINOIS)--
HOUSES--ROMANESQUE REVIVAL--GLESSNER
HOUSE
  H. H. Richardson's Glessner House: a
    garden in the machine / Thomas C.
    Hubka.
    On the evolution of, and
    influences upon, the plan and
    exterior of the Chicago house;
    completed in 1887.
    WINTERTHUR PORTFOLIO 1989 Winter,
    v.24, no.4, p.[209]-229, dwgs.,
    photos., plans, site plan, refs.
  Kitchens and bathrooms with a
    Victorian flair.
    Discusses the gallery kitchen of
    Allison Kyle Leopold in a
    19th-cent. duplex, N.Y.C.; the
    kitchen of Nancy Graham in an 1894
    (Continued next page)

UNITED STATES--CHICAGO (ILLINOIS)--
OFFICE BUILDINGS--CONSERVATION AND
RESTORATION--ECONOMIC ASPECTS--
CHICAGO BUILDING
Citicorp no city saver / Vincent L.
Michael.
On an offer to buy and demolish
the 1904 Chicago Building, at
corner of State and Madison
streets. Architects: Holabird &
Roche.
INLAND ARCHITECT 1990 Jan.-Feb.,
v.34, no.1, p.88, photos.

UNITED STATES--CHICAGO (ILLINOIS)--
OFFICE BUILDINGS--HIGH-RISE--WRIGLEY
BUILDING
The Wrigley Building and Tribune
Tower: gateposts of Michigan
Avenue / David Newton.
Two Chicago skyscrapers of the
1920s: The Wrigley Building
(architects: Graham, Anderson,
Probst, and White), and the
Tribune Tower (architects: Raymond
Hood and John Mead Howells).
HISTORIC ILLINOIS 1989 Aug., v.12,
no.2, p.[1]-3,10-14, port.,
photos., aerial photo.

UNITED STATES--CHICAGO (ILLINOIS)--
OFFICE BUILDINGS--LOOP
Jahn in the Loop / Amy Gray Light.
Recent projects for Chicago
towers.
ARCHITECTURE: THE AIA JOURNAL 1990
Feb., v.79, no.2, p.34, ill.,
dwgs,. model.

UNITED STATES--CHICAGO (ILLINOIS)--
OFFICE BUILDINGS--NBC TOWER
Chicago on the rise: a wave of
speculative office towers... /
Howard Decker.
NBC Tower (SOM); 225 W. Wacker Dr.
(Kohn Pedersen Fox); 900 N.
Michigan Ave. (Kohn Pedersen Fox);
AT&T Center (SOM); Burnett
Headquarters (Roche Dinkeloo); AMA
Headquarters (Kenzo Tange); 181 W.
Madison St. (Cesar Pelli); Chicago
Skyneedle (Cesar Pelli).
ARCHITECTURE: THE AIA JOURNAL 1990
Feb., v.79, no.2, p.78-83, photos,
model, aerial photo.
"Modern Classicism, un esempio = an
example: NBC Tower, Chicago,
Cityfront Center.
Architect: Adrian Smith of SOM.
ARCHITETTURA: CRONACHE E STORIA
1990 Nov., v.36, no.11(421),
p.795-797, photos., secn., site
plan.
Rich as Rockefeller: the NBC Tower
in Chicago's Cityfront Center... /
Paul M. Sachner.
Architect: Adrian Smith of SOM.
ARCHITECTURAL RECORD 1990 Apr.,
v.178, no.4, p.68-[73], photos.,
plans, secn, site plan.

UNITED STATES--CHICAGO (ILLINOIS)--
OFFICE BUILDINGS--STATE OF ILLINOIS
CENTER
An examination of architectural
interpretation: architects versus
non-architects / Kimberly Devlin.
Compares interpretations of two
Chicago office buildings: The
State of Illinois Center (Helmut
Jahn) and 333 Wacker Drive (Kohn
Pederson [sic] Fox). Includes
(Continued next column)

UNITED STATES--CHICAGO (ILLINOIS)--
OFFICE BUILDINGS--STATE OF ILLINOIS
CENTER (CONTINUED)
An examination of...(CONTINUED)
abstract.
JOURNAL OF ARCHITECTURAL AND
PLANNING RESEARCH 1990 Autumn,
v.7, no.3, p.235-244, table, refs.

UNITED STATES--CHICAGO (ILLINOIS)--
OFFICE PARKS
The new main street / Robert
Bruegmann.
New office developments along
expressways west and north of
Chicago.
INLAND ARCHITECT 1990 Nov.-Dec.,
v.34, no.6, p.34-41, dwgs., map,
photos., site plans, aerial photo.

UNITED STATES--CHICAGO (ILLINOIS)--
OFFICES--ARCHITECTS'--INTERIOR
DESIGN--SWANKE HAYDEN CONNELL
Minimalist message / Karin Tetlow.
Interiors of Swanke Hayden Connell
Architects offices, Chicago.
INTERIORS 1990 June, v.149, no.11,
p.106-[107], photos., plan.

UNITED STATES--CHICAGO (ILLINOIS)--
OFFICES--DESIGNERS'--BMT DESIGN
Spirited rebirths / Karen E. Klages.
Two Chicago projects by
Pappageorge Haymes: adaptive reuse
of the Turtle Wax factory at 1800
Clybourn, Chicago into a shopping
mall, and renovation of the 1910
warehouse at 750 North Orleans St.
for BMT Design.
INLAND ARCHITECT 1990 Nov.-Dec.,
v.34, no.6, p.6-7, photos., plans.

UNITED STATES--CHICAGO (ILLINOIS)--
OFFICES--INTERIOR DESIGN--AMERICAN
NATIONAL CAN
Can do / Kristen Richards.
Interiors of American National Can
offices in triangular Chicago
office building. Interior
designers: ISD Inc.
INTERIORS 1990 Mar., v.149, no.8,
p.128-131, photos., plan.

UNITED STATES--CHICAGO (ILLINOIS)--
OFFICES--INTERIOR DESIGN--
MCCONNAUGHY BAROCCI BROWN
Commercial properties / Fay Sweet,
David Redhead.
Features interiors of five
advertising agencies.
DESIGNER'S JOURNAL 1990 Mar.,
no.55, p.30-37, photos., plans.
McConnaughy Barocci Brown / Edie Lee
Cohen.
Interiors of Chicago ad agency.
Architects: Krueck & Olsen
Architects.
INTERIOR DESIGN 1990 May, v.61,
no.7, p.228-[233], axonometric
view, photos., plan.

UNITED STATES--CHICAGO (ILLINOIS)--
OFFICES--INTERIOR DESIGN--NORTH
AMERICAN TAISEI CORPORATION
North American Taisei / Karen
Maserjian.
Interiors of branch office in
Chicago. Interior designers:
Perkins & Will.
INTERIOR DESIGN 1990 Nov., v.61,
no.15, p.148-[151], axonometric
view, photo., plan.

UNITED STATES--CHICAGO (ILLINOIS)--
PARKING GARAGES--VAN BUREN AND
WABASH CORNER
Precast rock of ages / Barbara K.
Hower.
Plans to replace Old St. Mary's
Church, located at Van Buren and
Wabash in Chicago, with a
two-story parking garage. Original
architect (Isabella Building
section): William Le Baron Jenney.
Current architects: McBride and
Kelley.
INLAND ARCHITECT 1990 Mar.-Apr.,
v.34, no.2, p.80-82, ill.

UNITED STATES--CHICAGO (ILLINOIS)--
PARKS--19TH CENTURY--CONSERVATION
AND RESTORATION--LINCOLN PARK
Lincoln Park to get face-lifting /
Riva Feshbach.
Founded in 1861 and known as Lake
Park; renamed in 1864. Plans by
Sven (Swain) Nelson and later by
Alfred Caldwell.
INLAND ARCHITECT 1990 July-Aug.,
v.34, no.4, p.28,64,67, photo.,
site plan, aerial photo.

UNITED STATES--CHICAGO (ILLINOIS)--
POWER PLANTS--POLITICAL ASPECTS
Power, planning and conflict /
Charles Hoch, guest editor.
Special issue. Contents: Power,
planning and conflict, by C. Hoch
-- Planners in conflict:
experience and perceptions in
California, by Linda C. Dalton --
Neighborhood redevelopment: the
planner's role in conflict
management, by Sanda Kaufman --
Environmental movement politics,
mandates to plan, and professional
planners..., by Sy Adler --
Passion, reason and power: the
rhetorics of electric power
planning in Chicago, by J.A.
Throgmorton.
JOURNAL OF ARCHITECTURAL AND
PLANNING RESEARCH 1990 Winter, v.7
no.4, p.271-350, graph, tables,
biblios., refs.

UNITED STATES--CHICAGO (ILLINOIS)--
PUBLIC BUILDINGS--ALTERATIONS AND
ADDITIONS--STATE JUDICIAL AND OFFICE
COMPLEX
The state of the State building /
Barbara K. Hower.
Plans for rehabilitation of
67-year old building at corner of
LaSalle and Randolph streets,
Chicago, for offices. Original
architects: Burnham Brothers.
Renovation architects: Holabird
and Root.
INLAND ARCHITECT 1990 Sept.-Oct.,
v.34, no.5, p.20, dwg.

UNITED STATES--CHICAGO (ILLINOIS)--
RAILROAD STATIONS--RUINED, EXTINCT,
ETC.--CENTRAL STATION
Central Station: opening up
Chicago's near south side / Gerald
Fogelson.
Master plan by Ehrenkrantz,
Eckstut Whitelaw.
URBAN LAND 1990 Oct., v.49, no.10,
p.2-4, dwg., site plan, aerial
photo.

UNITED STATES--CHICAGO (ILLINOIS)--
RAILROAD STATIONS--RUINED, EXTINCT,
ETC.--CENTRAL STATION (CONTINUED)
Next stop, Central Station / Nevin
Noel Hedlund.
On plans for the 38-acre site of
Central Station (demolished in
1974). Developer: Fogelson
Properties.
INLAND ARCHITECT 1990 Jan.-Feb.,
v.34, no.1, p.65,67,[69-70],
photo., site plan.

UNITED STATES--CHICAGO (ILLINOIS)--
REAL ESTATE DEVELOPMENT
Chicago's steady-state real estate
markets / Deborah L. Brett.
Includes inset articles on North
Pier; Grand Boulevard Plaza by
Sarah W. Mulliken; and Chicago's
plans for the 21st century, by
David R. Mosena.
URBAN LAND 1990 Oct., v.49, no.10,
p.10-17, dwg., map, photos.,
table, aerial photos.

UNITED STATES--CHICAGO (ILLINOIS)--
REAL ESTATE DEVELOPMENT--CHINATOWN
SQUARE
New life for Chicago's Chinatown /
Annie Morse.
A 32-acre commercial residential
project by the Chinese American
Development Corporation (CADC) and
Link Programs (a division of the
Himmel Group). Phases I-III will
be completed 1991-c1997.
Architect: Harry Weese.
INLAND ARCHITECT 1990 Nov.-Dec.,
v.34, no.6, p.22, dwg.

UNITED STATES--CHICAGO (ILLINOIS)--
REAL ESTATE DEVELOPMENT--CITYFRONT
CENTER
Establishing a long-range framework
for development.
Cityfront Center, in Chicago.
Master plan proposed by Lohan
Associates.
URBAN LAND 1990 Oct., v.49, no.10,
p.32-33, models, photos.
Urban critique: Cityfront Center /
Cheryl Kent.
On the design guidelines for
Chicago development located on the
banks of the Chicago River.
Masterplanners: Alexander Cooper
& Partners.
PROGRESSIVE ARCHITECTURE 1990
Feb., v.71, no.2, p.121-122,
dwgs., photos., site plans.

UNITED STATES--CHICAGO (ILLINOIS)--
REAL ESTATE INVESTMENT
Chicago's steady-state real estate
markets / Deborah L. Brett.
Includes inset articles on North
Pier; Grand Boulevard Plaza by
Sarah W. Mulliken; and Chicago's
plans for the 21st century, by
David R. Mosena.
URBAN LAND 1990 Oct., v.49, no.10,
p.10-17, dwg., map, photos.,
table, aerial photos.

UNITED STATES--CHICAGO (ILLINOIS)--
REFECTORIES--CONSERVATION AND
RESTORATION--CAFE BRAUER
Perkins in the park / Jane H.
Clarke.
Restoration and landmarking of the
1907-1908 derelict South Pond
Refectory and boat house (Cafe
Brauer) in the Lincoln Park
district. Original architect:
Dwight Heald Perkins. Restoration
architects: Meisel and Associates,
and others.
INLAND ARCHITECT 1990 Sept.-Oct.,
v.34, no.5, p.40-42, photos.,
plans.

UNITED STATES--CHICAGO (ILLINOIS)--
RESIDENTIAL GARDENS--SMALL
Classicism's light new touch /
Carolyn Ulrich.
Small residential backyard gardens
in Chicago, New Haven, Houston,
and Washington, D.C. Landscape
architects: Timothy Lally, Ralph
Synnestvedt, Jr., Paul Bailey,
Douglas Kycia, McDugald-Steele,
Lanson Jones, and Jane Macleish.
GARDEN DESIGN 1990 autumn, v.9,
no.3, p.[30-37], photos.

UNITED STATES--CHICAGO (ILLINOIS)--
RESTAURANTS--INTERIOR DESIGN--UDO'S
BISTRO
20,000 leagues beneath Chicago /
Justin Henderson.
Interiors of Chicago seafood
restaurant, Udo's Bistro.
Architect: Jordan Mozer.
INTERIORS 1990 Mar., v.149, no.8,
p.132-[133], photos., plan.

UNITED STATES--CHICAGO (ILLINOIS)--
RESTAURANTS--INTERIOR DESIGN--VIVERE
A new mood / Justin Henderson.
Features illus. of neo-Baroque
interiors of Vivere restaurant, in
the Italian Village restaurant
complex, Chicago.
Architects/Interior designers:
Jordan Mozer and Associates.
INTERIORS 1990 Aug., v.149, no.13,
p.22, dwgs.

UNITED STATES--CHICAGO (ILLINOIS)--
RIVERS--CHICAGO RIVER
Liquid symbol: Centennial Fountain
is Lohan Associates' symbolic
salute to the 1889 reversal of the
Chicago River.
Water arch spanning the River.
ARCHITECTURAL RECORD 1990 Mar.,
v.178, no.3, p.92-[95], photos.,
secn., site plan, aerial photos.

UNITED STATES--CHICAGO (ILLINOIS)--
ROADS
The new main street / Robert
Bruegmann.
New office developments along
expressways west and north of
Chicago.
INLAND ARCHITECT 1990 Nov.-Dec.,
v.34, no.6, p.34-41, dwgs., map,
photos., site plans, aerial photo.

UNITED STATES--CHICAGO (ILLINOIS)--
SHOPPING MALLS--1800 CLYBOURN
Spirited rebirths / Karen E. Klages.
Two Chicago projects by
Pappageorge Haymes: adaptive reuse
of the Turtle Wax factory at 1800
Clybourn, Chicago into a shopping
mall, and renovation of the 1910
warehouse at 750 North Orleans St.
for BMT Design.
INLAND ARCHITECT 1990 Nov.-Dec.,
v.34, no.6, p.6-7, photos., plans.

UNITED STATES--CHICAGO (ILLINOIS)--
SHOWROOMS--DESIGN--INTERIOR DESIGN--
ICF
ICF, Chicago / Edie Lee Cohen.
Interiors of showroom in the
Chicago Merchandise Mart designed
by Janine James.
INTERIOR DESIGN 1990 Jan., v.61,
no.1, p.180-[183], photos. plan.

UNITED STATES--CHICAGO (ILLINOIS)--
SHOWROOMS--FURNITURE--HAWORTH
Haworth, Inc. / Monica Geran.
Interiors of furniture showroom in
Chicago's Merchandise Mart.
Architects: Tigerman McCurry.
INTERIOR DESIGN 1990 Oct., v.61,
no.14, p.240-243, photos.,
isometric dwg.

UNITED STATES--CHICAGO (ILLINOIS)--
SHOWROOMS--FURNITURE--INTERIOR
DESIGN--BERNHARDT FURNITURE
Bernhardt Furniture / Judith
Davidsen.
Interiors of redesigned Chicago
Merchandise Mart showroom.
Interior designers: Vanderbyl
Design.
INTERIOR DESIGN 1990 Oct., v.61,
no.14, p.248-[251], photos.,
isometric dwg.

UNITED STATES--CHICAGO (ILLINOIS)--
SHOWROOMS--FURNITURE--INTERIOR
DESIGN--STEELCASE
Steelcase, Inc. / Monica Geran.
Interiors of Chicago showroom
designed by the firm's in-house
design team.
INTERIOR DESIGN 1990 Oct., v.61,
no.14, p.246-[247], photos.

UNITED STATES--CHICAGO (ILLINOIS)--
SHOWROOMS--INTERIOR DESIGN--ALLIED
FIBERS
Allied Fibers / Monica Geran.
Interiors of textile showroom in
Chicago's Merchandise Mart.
Interior designer: Sally O'Malley.
INTERIOR DESIGN 1990 Oct., v.61,
no.14, p.244-[245], photos., plan.

UNITED STATES--CHICAGO (ILLINOIS)--
SHOWROOMS--INTERIOR DESIGN--
COMPETITIONS--NEOCON
8th annual AIA Neocon product
display competition / Paula Rice
Jackson.
Includes 14 winning showrooms in
the Merchandise Mart, Chicago.
INTERIORS 1990 Aug., v.149, no.13,
p.81-87, port., photos.

UNITED STATES--CHICAGO (ILLINOIS)--
SHOWROOMS--INTERIOR DESIGN--DEEPA
Timeless textures / Kristen
    Richards.
    Interiors of Deepa textile
    showroom, Chicago. Interior
    designers: Loebl, Schlossman and
    Hackl.
    INTERIORS 1990 July, v.149, no.12,
    p.70-[71], photos.

UNITED STATES--CHICAGO (ILLINOIS)--
SHOWROOMS--INTERIOR DESIGN--
INTERFACE FLOORING SYSTEMS
Planned evolution / Jean Gorman.
    Interiors of remodeled Interface
    Flooring Systems showroom,
    Chicago.
    INTERIORS 1990 Dec., v.150, no.5,
    p.26, photos.

UNITED STATES--CHICAGO (ILLINOIS)--
SHOWROOMS--INTERIOR DESIGN--
LACKAWANNA LEATHER.
Leather pirouettes: Lackawanna
    Leather in Chicago / Justin
    Henderson.
    Showroom designed by Andrew
    Belscher Joseph Vincent Design
    Partnership.
    INTERIORS 1990 Jan., v.149, no.6,
    p.184-149, photos., plan.

UNITED STATES--CHICAGO (ILLINOIS)--
SHOWROOMS--INTERIOR DESIGN--VECTA
SHOWROOM
Vecta's Chicago showroom / Gregory
    Littleton.
    Interior designer: Lee Stout.
    INTERIORS 1989 Feb., v.148, no.7,
    p.98, photos., plan.

UNITED STATES--CHICAGO (ILLINOIS)--
SHOWROOMS--TEXTILE--INTERIOR
DESIGN--ARCHITEX INTERNATIONAL
Paying homage [Architex showroom] /
    Alice Feiring.
    Interiors of Chicago showroom.
    Designer: Ben Kramer of Fotoys.
    INTERIORS 1990 Oct., v.150, no.3,
    p.42, photo.

UNITED STATES--CHICAGO (ILLINOIS)--
SOCIETY AND ASSOCIATION BUILDINGS--
AMERICAN MEDICAL ASSOCIATION
HEADQUARTERS
Chicago on the rise: a wave of
    speculative office towers... /
    Howard Decker.
    NBC Tower (SOM); 225 W. Wacker Dr.
    (Kohn Pedersen Fox); 900 N.
    Michigan Ave. (Kohn Pedersen Fox);
    AT&T Center (SOM); Burnett
    Headquarters (Roche Dinkeloo); AMA
    Headquarters (Kenzo Tange); 181 W.
    Madison St. (Cesar Pelli); Chicago
    Skyneedle (Cesar Pelli).
    ARCHITECTURE: THE AIA JOURNAL 1990
    Feb., v.79, no.2, p.78-83, photos,
    model, aerial photo.

UNITED STATES--CHICAGO (ILLINOIS)--
SPIRES--METAL--225 WEST WACKER DRIVE
An affinity for ornament: the work
    of Kohn Pedersen Fox... / Donald
    London.
    Decorative uses of metal on 4
    recent projects: 225 W. Wacker
    Dr., Chicago; 101 Federal St.,
    Boston; 1 O'Hare Center,
    Rosemount, Ill., and 900 N.
    Michigan Ave., Chicago.
            (Continued next column)

UNITED STATES--CHICAGO (ILLINOIS)--
SPIRES--METAL--225 WEST WACKER DRIVE
                    (CONTINUED)
An affinity for...(CONTINUED)
    ARCHITECTURAL RECORD 1990 May,
    v.178, no.6, p.121-125,
    axonometric view, dets., elevs.,
    photos., secns.

UNITED STATES--CHICAGO (ILLINOIS)--
STORES--FURNITURE--CRATE & BARREL
Crate & Barrel brings Modernism to
    Michigan Avenue / Paul Glassman.
    Store at 646 N. Michigan, Chicago,
    designed by John Buenz of Solomon
    Cordwell Buenz & Associates with
    Raymond Arenson of the store's
    design team.
    INLAND ARCHITECT 1990 Nov.-Dec.,
    v.34, no.6, p.16,19, axonometric
    view, photos.

UNITED STATES--CHICAGO (ILLINOIS)--
STREET LIGHTING--ALTERATIONS AND
ADDITIONS--SOUTH LASALLE STREET
What light breaks yonder window? /
    Michael J. P. Smith.
    Renovation of street lampposts on
    South LaSalle Street, Chicago.
    INLAND ARCHITECT 1990 Sept.-Oct.,
    v.34, no.5, p.23,24, photo.

UNITED STATES--CHICAGO (ILLINOIS)--
SUBURBS--ENVIRONMENTAL ASPECTS
I think that I shall never see ....
    / Riva Feshbach.
    Environmental and landscape
    preservation issues in the Chicago
    suburbs.
    INLAND ARCHITECT 1990 Sept.-Oct.,
    v.34, no.5, p.86, 89-90, photo.

UNITED STATES--CHICAGO (ILLINOIS)--
TALL BUILDINGS
Buildup: Chicago booms with
    high-rise construction and
    proposals for more / Michael J. P.
    Smith.
    Includes commentary on 30 tall
    office and apartment buildings
    scheduled for completion in the
    early 1990s.
    INLAND ARCHITECT 1990 Jan.-Feb.,
    v.34, no.1, p.49-57, axonometric
    views, elevs., elevs., models.
Chicago on the rise: a wave of
    speculative office towers... /
    Howard Decker.
    NBC Tower (SOM); 225 W. Wacker Dr.
    (Kohn Pedersen Fox); 900 N.
    Michigan Ave. (Kohn Pedersen Fox);
    AT&T Center (SOM); Burnett
    Headquarters (Roche Dinkeloo); AMA
    Headquarters (Kenzo Tange); 181 W.
    Madison St. (Cesar Pelli); Chicago
    Skyneedle (Cesar Pelli).
    ARCHITECTURE: THE AIA JOURNAL 1990
    Feb., v.79, no.2, p.78-83, photos,
    model, aerial photo.

UNITED STATES--CHICAGO (ILLINOIS)--
TALL BUILDINGS--HISTORY
Architettura verticale (parte prima)
    = Vertical architecture (part one)
    / Roberto Apostolo.
    History of skyscrapers, especially
    in Chicago.
    FRAMES, PORTE & FINESTRE 1990
    Jan.-Mar., no.26, p.34-39, dwgs.,
    photos., aerial photos., biblio.

UNITED STATES--CHICAGO (ILLINOIS)--
TALL BUILDINGS--LOOP
Jahn in the Loop / Amy Gray Light.
    Recent projects for Chicago
    towers.
    ARCHITECTURE: THE AIA JOURNAL 1990
    Feb., v.79, no.2, p.34, ill.,
    dwgs,. model.

UNITED STATES--CHICAGO (ILLINOIS)--
TALL BUILDINGS--MAGLIN-BEITLER TOWER
Designing the super-thin new
    buildings / James S. Russell.
    Features 6 projects for tall
    buildings in New York City,
    Chicago and Paris.
    ARCHITECTURAL RECORD 1990 Oct.,
    v.178, no.11, p.105-109,
    axonometric views, elev., models,
    photos., plans.

UNITED STATES--CHICAGO (ILLINOIS)--
TALL BUILDINGS--ONE NORTH WACKER
Second Roche building proposed for
    Chicago [One North Wacker] /
    Barbara K. Hower.
    Plans for a 1,275-foot-high
    building at the corner of Wacker
    Drive and Madison St. Architects:
    Kevin Roche, with Patrick Shaw.
    INLAND ARCHITECT 1990 May-June,
    v.34, no.3, p.81-82, model.

UNITED STATES--CHICAGO (ILLINOIS)--
TALL BUILDINGS--SOCIOLOGICAL ASPECTS
Why the skyscraper? Towards a
    theoretical framework for analysis
    / J. Bonshek.
    ENVIRONMENT AND PLANNING B 1990
    Apr., v.17, no.2, p.[131]-148,
    refs.

UNITED STATES--CHICAGO (ILLINOIS)--
TOWNHOUSES--VICTORIAN--ALTERATIONS
AND ADDITIONS--CARRIGAN HOUSE
Stuart Cohen and Anders Nerein: the
    visual expansion of a 19th century
    Chicago town house.
    Townhouse owned by Richard H.
    Carrigan.
    ARCHITECTURAL DIGEST 1990 Feb.,
    v.47, no.2, p.108-109. photos.,
    plans.

UNITED STATES--CHICAGO (ILLINOIS)--
TRANSPORTATION PLANNING
The Chicago Area Transportation
    Study: a case study of rational
    planning / Alan Black.
    JOURNAL OF PLANNING EDUCATION AND
    RESEARCH 1990 Fall, v.10, no.1,
    p.27-37, refs.

UNITED STATES--CHICAGO (ILLINOIS)--
URBAN FRINGES
The new main street / Robert
    Bruegmann.
    New office developments along
    expressways west and north of
    Chicago.
    INLAND ARCHITECT 1990 Nov.-Dec.,
    v.34, no.6, p.34-41, dwgs., map.
    photos., site plans, aerial photo.

UNITED STATES--CHICAGO (ILLINOIS)--
WAREHOUSES--ALTERATIONS AND
ADDITIONS--NORTH PIER
Reuse + retail = Razzmatazz / Paul
Glassman.
Adaptive reuse of North Pier, one
of the Pugh Warehouses along Ogden
Slip in Chicago, into a retail and
office complex. Completed in 1920.
Original architect: Christian
Albert Eckstrom. Architect:
Laurence Booth. Interior designer:
David Peterhans.
INLAND ARCHITECT 1990 Sept.-Oct.,
v.34, no.5, p.[48]-51, photos.,
plan.

UNITED STATES--CHICAGO (ILLINOIS)--
WATERFRONT BUILDINGS--BURNHAM HARBOR
STATION
Snug harbor: Burnham Harbor Station,
Chicago, Illinois.
Public harbor station on the
lakefront. Architects: Chicago
Park District; William Latoza,
senior designer.
ARCHITECTURAL RECORD 1990 Nov.,
v.178, no.12, p.[82]-83, photos.,
plan.

UNITED STATES--CHICAGO (ILLINOIS)--
WATERFRONTS--ALTERATIONS AND
ADDITIONS--CHICAGO RIVER
Making big plans for the Chicago
River / Howard S. Decker.
INLAND ARCHITECT 1990 July-Aug.,
v.34, no.4, p.9-10, photos., site
plan.

UNITED STATES--CHICAGO (ILLINOIS)--
WATERFRONTS--CITYFRONT CENTER
Establishing a long-range framework
for development.
Cityfront Center, in Chicago.
Master plan proposed by Lohan
Associates.
URBAN LAND 1990 Oct., v.49, no.10,
p.32-33, models, photos.
Urban critique: Cityfront Center /
Cheryl Kent.
On the design guidelines for
Chicago development located on the
banks of the Chicago River.
Masterplanners: Alexander Cooper
& Partners.
PROGRESSIVE ARCHITECTURE 1990
Feb., v.71, no.2, p.121-122,
dwgs., photos., site plans.

UNITED STATES--CHICAGO (ILLINOIS)--
WORLD FAIRS
Sketches for the 1992 Chicago
World's Fair: John Hejduk and
Thomas Beeby.
PERSPECTA 1990, no.26, p.229-230,
sketches.

UNITED STATES--CHULA VISTA
(CALIFORNIA)--ARCHITECTURE--STUDY
AND TEACHING--NEW SCHOOL OF
ARCHITECTURE
Universidad Iberoamericana / Ralph
Roesling.
On Jorge A. Ozorno, dean of the
architecture school in Mexico
City, and the student projects
from there and from the New School
of Architecture (Chula Vista,
Calif.) for student housing at
Playas de Tijuana in Mexico City.
CARTOUCHE 1990 Summer, v.21,
p.8-9, 12-14, axonometric view,
diagrs., plan, elevs.

UNITED STATES--CINCINNATI (OHIO)--
ENTRANCES--CINCINNATI GATEWAY
SCULPTURE
From sow's ear to silk purse: an
unusual architect-client
relationship transforms an
abandoned waterfront in the
nation's Porkopolis into an
award-winning design.
The Cincinnati Gateway Sculpture,
at the entrance to the
Bicentennial Commons Park.
Sculptor: Andrew Leicester;
architects: Meyer, Scherer &
Rockcastle.
ARCHITECTURE MINNESOTA 1990
Nov.-Dec., v.16, no.6, p.38-41,
photos.

UNITED STATES--CINCINNATI (OHIO)--
FACTORIES--19TH CENTURY
From slaughterhouse to soap-boiler:
Cincinnati's meat packing
industry, changing technologies,
and the rise of mass production,
1825-1870 / Steve C. Gordon.
SOCIETY FOR INDUSTRIAL ARCHEOLOGY.
JOURNAL 1990, v.16, no.1, p.55-67,
ill., dwgs., secns., refs.

UNITED STATES--CINCINNATI (OHIO)--
MULTI-USE BUILDINGS--ONE FOUNTAIN
PLACE
One Fountain Place, Cincinnati,
Ohio.
Project for mixed-use (retail,
hotel, offices) high-rise;
architects: Kohn Pedersen Fox
Associates and PC/RTKL Associates,
Inc.
PROCESS: ARCHITECTURE 1989 Nov.,
no.86, p.[82]-85, elevs., model,
plans, secn.

UNITED STATES--CINCINNATI (OHIO)--
OUTDOOR SCULPTURE--CINCINNATI
GATEWAY SCULPTURE
From sow's ear to silk purse: an
unusual architect-client
relationship transforms an
abandoned waterfront in the
nation's Porkopolis into an
award-winning design.
The Cincinnati Gateway Sculpture,
at the entrance to the
Bicentennial Commons Park.
Sculptor: Andrew Leicester;
architects: Meyer, Scherer &
Rockcastle.
ARCHITECTURE MINNESOTA 1990
Nov.-Dec., v.16, no.6, p.38-41,
photos.

UNITED STATES--CINCINNATI (OHIO)--
SLAUGHTERHOUSES--19TH CENTURY
From slaughterhouse to soap-boiler:
Cincinnati's meat packing
industry, changing technologies,
and the rise of mass production,
1825-1870 / Steve C. Gordon.
SOCIETY FOR INDUSTRIAL ARCHEOLOGY.
JOURNAL 1990, v.16, no.1, p.55-67,
ill., dwgs., secns., refs.

UNITED STATES--CINCINNATI (OHIO)--TALL
BUILDINGS--FOUNTAIN SQUARE WEST
Deja vu: Helmut Jahn in Cincinnati /
Jayne Merkel.
Proposal for Fountain Square West,
successor to an earlier plan
(Fountain Place, by KPF). Plans
are for 48 stories on a
half-block, with offices, hotel, a
shopping mall, and garage.
INLAND ARCHITECT 1990 Sept.-Oct.,
v.34, no.5, p.9, model, photo.

UNITED STATES--CINCINNATI (OHIO)--
UNIVERSITIES AND COLLEGES--
BUILDINGS--UNIVERSITY OF
CINCINNATI--COLLEGE OF DESIGN,
ARCHITECTURE, ART AND PLANNING
Special feature: recent works of
Peter Eisenman.
Contents: Editor's introduction.--
Essays: Peter Eisenman: releasing
time imprisoned in space / Tadao
Ando.-- A framework for the future
/ Kurt W. Forster.-- Four notes on
the recent architecture of Peter
Eisenman / Ignasi de
Sola-Morales.-- A matter of
respect.-- Works: Wexner Center
for the Visual Arts, Ohio State
University.-- Columbus Convention
Center.-- Banyoles Olympic Hotel
competition.-- College of Design,
Architecture, Art and Planning,
University of Cincinnati.--
Interview: Peter Eisenman / Jeff
Kipnis. Text in Japanese and
English.
ARCHITECTURE AND URBANISM 1990
Jan., no.1(232), p.[7]-182,
axonometric views, elevs., models,
photos., plans, secns., sketches.

UNITED STATES--CINCINNATI (OHIO)--
WATERFRONTS--ALTERATIONS AND
ADDITIONS
From sow's ear to silk purse: an
unusual architect-client
relationship transforms an
abandoned waterfront in the
nation's Porkopolis into an
award-winning design.
The Cincinnati Gateway Sculpture,
at the entrance to the
Bicentennial Commons Park.
Sculptor: Andrew Leicester;
architects: Meyer, Scherer &
Rockcastle.
ARCHITECTURE MINNESOTA 1990
Nov.-Dec., v.16, no.6, p.38-41,
photos.

UNITED STATES--CINCINNATTI (OHIO)--
UNIVERSITIES AND COLLEGES--
BUILDINGS--UNIVERSITY OF
CINCINNATTI--COLLEGE OF DESIGN,
ARCHITECTURE, ART AND PLANNING
Taking risks: Eisenman in Ohio /
Cynthia Chapin Davidson.
On form and the depiction of
movement in the Columbus
Convention Center; the College of
Design, Architecture, Art &
Planning (DAAP) at the University
of Cincinnati; and the Wexner
Center at Ohio State University.
INLAND ARCHITECT 1990 May-June,
v.34, no.3, p.[44]-51, dwgs.,
elevs., models, plans, secns.,
site plans.

UNITED STATES--CITIES AND TOWNS
Citta americane / Sergio Stenti.
Theme issue on American cities.
Six articles indexed separately.
STORIA DELLA CITTA 1989 Jan.-Mar.,
v.14, no.49, entire issue, ill.,
refs.
The city maelstrom / Rafael
Argullol.
As seen in motion pictures.
Spanish, English text.
QUADERNS D'ARQUITECTURA I
URBANISME 1990 Jan.-Feb.-Mar.,
no.184, p.89-97, photos.
The impact of the car on American
urban form / Richard W. Pohlman.
OZ / COLLEGE OF ARCHITECTURE AND
DESIGN, KANSAS STATE UNIVERSITY
1989, v.11, p.12-17, maps,
photos., aerial photos., refs.
An interview with Mario Gandelsonas:
"The American City; an
architectural continuum / Patricia
Zingsheim, Gregory Quick.
Gandelsonas is heading a 3-year
study of Des Moines, to culminate
in a new master plan.
IOWA ARCHITECT 1989 Winter, v.38,
no.5, p.30-33, ill., ports.,
sketch.

UNITED STATES--CITIES AND TOWNS--20TH
CENTURY
Flexible accumulation through
urbanization: reflections on
"Post-Modernism" in the American
City / David Harvey.
PERSPECTA 1990, no.26, p.251-272,
table, refs.
Urban concepts [Architectural design
profile 83] / Denise Scott Brown.
Contents: Paralipomena in urban
design.-- Between three stools.--
Public realm, public sector and
the public interest in urban
design.-- Rise and fall of
community architecture.-- Urban
design reports [six, indexed
separately]. Includes a discussion
with Martin Pawley, Simon Jenkins,
Robert Thorne, Jake Brown, Ken
Powell, Charles Jencks, and John
Thompson.
ARCHITECTURAL DESIGN 1990, v.60,
no.1-2, p.[1]-96, dwgs., elevs.,
photos., site plans, aerial
photos., biblio., refs.

UNITED STATES--CITIES AND TOWNS--
GROWTH
Jobs and housing: the search for
balance / Lloyd W. Bookout.
Studies the locational
relationship between jobs and
housing to determine whether
public policies can or should be
implemented to encourage closer
proximity between the two.
URBAN LAND 1990 Oct., v.49, no.10,
p.4-9, photo.
Urban cores: development trends and
real estate opportunities in the
1990s / Christopher B. Leinberger.
URBAN LAND 1990 Dec., v.49, no.12,
p.4-9, photo., table, aerial
photos.

UNITED STATES--CITIES AND TOWNS--
HISTORY
Rediscovering the active city [book
review] / Terrence J. McDonald.
Review of: America becomes urban,
the development of U.S. cities and
towns, 1780-1980, by Eric H.
Monkkonen, Berkeley, 1988.
JOURNAL OF URBAN HISTORY 1990 May,
v.16, no.3, p.304-311, refs.

UNITED STATES--CITIES AND TOWNS--
PSYCHOLOGICAL ASPECTS
Women and downtown open spaces /
Louise Mozingo.
"Focus on issues designers should
consider in order to make downtown
open spaces more acceptable to
women users."
PLACES 1989 Fall, v.6, no.1,
p.38-47, maps, photos., site
plans, refs.

UNITED STATES--CITIES AND TOWNS--VIEWS
The American city / Fritz Neumeyer.
Photos of various cities with
short text. Spanish, English text.
QUADERNS D'ARQUITECTURA I
URBANISME 1990 Jan.-Feb.-Mar.,
no.184, p.80-87, photos.

UNITED STATES--CITY PLANNERS--EDAW,
INC.
The niche business: EDAW spreads its
wings / John McCloud.
PLANNING 1989 Aug., v.55, no.8,
p.14-15, site plans.

UNITED STATES--CITY PLANNERS--HAMMER,
SILER, GEORGE ASSOCIATES
Will it work? Ask Hammer, Siler,
George / Jerry Schwartz.
PLANNING 1989 Aug., v.55, no.8,
p.16-18, aerial photo.

UNITED STATES--CITY PLANNING
Citta americane / Sergio Stenti.
Theme issue on American cities.
Six articles indexed separately.
STORIA DELLA CITTA 1989 Jan.-Mar.,
v.14, no.49, entire issue, ill.,
refs.
The evolution of spatial modeling in
the USA / Richard K. Brail.
EKISTICS 1989 Sept.-Dec., v.56,
no.338-339, p.249-253, refs.
Le origini dell'urbanistica moderna:
Francia e Stati Uniti.
Contents: Ragione e visione: la
mentalita pianificatoria negli
Stati Uniti e l'indagine urbana,
1890-1930, by Christine Boyer.--
L'urbanistica come movimento
sociale: militanti e
professionisti del City Planning
negli Stati Uniti, 1909-1917, by
Christian Topalov.-- "Reconstituir
la cite": dalla concezione
organicistica della citta alla
riforma del quartiere popolare in
Francia nel primo quarto del
secolo, by Susanna Magri.-- La
genesi dell'urbanistica di piano e
la questione della modernizzazione
politica, 1900-1930, by Jean
Pierre Gaudin.
STORIA URBANA 1989 July-Dec.,
v.13, no.48-49, p.127-245, tables,
refs.

UNITED STATES--CITY PLANNING
(CONTINUED)
Pumping up suburban downtowns /
Philip Langdon.
Examples in Reston, Va., Miami
Lakes, Fla., and Buffalo Grove,
Ill.
PLANNING 1990 July, v.56, no.7,
p.22-28, dwg., model, map,
photos., plans, aerial photo.
Repent, ye sinners, repent / Ruth
Eckdish Knack.
PLANNING 1989 Aug., v.55, no.8,
p.4-8, diagr., port., photos.,
plans.

UNITED STATES--CITY PLANNING--20TH
CENTURY
Developing and financing the 'garden
metropolis': urban planning and
housing policy in
twentieth-century America / Marc
A. Weiss.
"Examines the evolution of garden
city ideas in the U.S. during the
20th cent.", with emphasis on "the
central role of Thomas Adams, the
British planner who served as a
leading proponent of the garden
metropolis in the U.S.".
PLANNING PERSPECTIVES: PP 1990
Sept., v.5, no.3, p.307-319, refs.

UNITED STATES--CITY PLANNING--
ADDRESSES, ESSAYS, LECTURES
From high-minded reformism to
hard-boiled pragmatism: American
city planning faces the next
century / Stuart Meck.
Lecture delivered at the Bartlett
School of Architecture and
Planning, University College,
London, by the president of the
American Planning Assn.
THE PLANNER 1990 Feb.16, v.76,
no.6, p.11-15, ports., refs.

UNITED STATES--CITY PLANNING--CITIZEN
PARTICIPATION
Planting the seeds of change
[RUDATs].
The application of AIA's RUDATs
(Regional/Urban Design Assistance
Teams) in over 100 American
cities, most notably Pittsburgh.
ARCHITECTS' JOURNAL 1990 Mar.14,
v.191, no.11, p.48-49, ports.,
photos.

UNITED STATES--CITY PLANNING--
CONGRESSES
Designing mayors / Ruth Eckdish
Knack.
First regional Mayors Institute
for Civic Design, held in
Minneapolis, Nov.1989.
PLANNING 1990 Aug., v.56, no.8,
p.20-25, dwg., ports., sketches.
Learning a new kind of language;
U.S. mayors discuss architecture
at the Mayors Institute of Civic
Design at the University of
Virginia (i.e., Mayors Institute
on City Design).
ARCHITECTS' JOURNAL 1990 Mar.14,
v.191, no.11, p.46-47, ports.,
photos.
Shaping the city: international
names to be featured at UCSD
symposium.
On the five speakers scheduled for
a May 5, 1990 conference and plans
(Continued next page)

UNITED STATES--CITY PLANNING--
CONGRESSES (CONTINUED)
Shaping the city:...(CONTINUED)
for the Fall 1992 opening of the
San Diego architecture school.
CARTOUCHE 1990 Spring, v.20, p.5,
photo.

UNITED STATES--CITY PLANNING--
ENVIRONMENTAL ASPECTS
Ecology and aesthetics / Michael
Laurie.
On the design of open space.
PLACES 1989 Fall, v.6, no.1,
p.48-51, photos.

UNITED STATES--CITY PLANNING--
ENVIRONMENTAL ASPECTS--CONGRESSES
Eco echoes / John King.
First International Ecocity
Conference convened in March 1990
in Berkeley, Calif.
PLANNING 1990 June, v.56, no.6,
p.27, model, photo.

UNITED STATES--CITY PLANNING--HISTORY
L'urbanisme comme mouvement social:
militants et professionnels du
city planning aux Etats-Unis
(1909-1917) / Christian Topalov.
French, English, Spanish and
German summaries, p.247-252.
LES ANNALES DE LA RECHERCHE
URBAINE 1989 Dec., no.44-45,
p.139-154, 247-248, 250, 252,
ill., dwgs., photo., plans, refs.

UNITED STATES--CITY PLANNING--
POLITICAL ASPECTS
Scientific urban planning and the
ordering of daily life: the first
"war housing" experiment in the
United States, 1917-1919 /
Christian Topalov.
JOURNAL OF URBAN HISTORY 1990
Nov., v.17, no.1, p.14-45, maps,
photos., aerial photo., refs.

UNITED STATES--CITY PLANNING--PRACTICE
Faire ou ne pas faire: l'ethique des
amenageurs / Jerome L. Kaufman.
In the U.S. French, English,
Spanish and German summaries,
p.246-252.
LES ANNALES DE LA RECHERCHE
URBAINE 1989 Dec., no.44-45,
p.26-32, [246]-247, 249, 251,
photos., biblio.
Les theories americaines de
l'amenagement urbain: la question
des professions / Gilles Verpraet.
French, English, Spanish and
German summaries, p.246-252.
LES ANNALES DE LA RECHERCHE
URBAINE 1989 Dec., no.44-45,
p.15-25, [246]-247, 249, 251,
photos., biblio., refs.
Les urbanistes aux U.S.A. et le sens
de leur travail / Howell S. Baum.
French, English, Spanish and
German summaries, p.246-257.
LES ANNALES DE LA RECHERCHE
URBAINE 1989 Dec., no.44-45,
p.81-87, [246], 248, 250-251,
photos., refs.

UNITED STATES--CITY PLANNING--
PROFESSIONAL ETHICS
Faire ou ne pas faire: l'ethique des
amenageurs / Jerome L. Kaufman.
In the U.S. French, English,
Spanish and German summaries,
p.246-252.
LES ANNALES DE LA RECHERCHE
URBAINE 1989 Dec., no.44-45,
p.26-32, [246]-247, 249, 251,
photos., biblio.

UNITED STATES--CITY PLANNING--RESEARCH
Theory and practice of contemporary
urban design: a review of urban
design plans in the United States
/ Michael Southworth.
TOWN PLANNING REVIEW 1989 Oct.,
v.60, no.4, p.369-402, axonometric
view, charts, graph, maps, plans,
secns., sketches, tables, refs.

UNITED STATES--CITY PLANNING--STUDY
AND TEACHING
Creating the future for
undergraduate education in
planning / ACSP Commission on
Undergraduate Education.
JOURNAL OF PLANNING EDUCATION AND
RESEARCH 1990 Fall, v.10, no.1,
p.15-26, charts, table, refs.
Specialized land use curricula in
urban planning graduate programs /
Donald Miller, Frank Westerlund.
In North America.
JOURNAL OF PLANNING EDUCATION AND
RESEARCH 1990 summer, v.9, no.3,
p.203-206, tables, refs.

UNITED STATES--CITY PLANNING--STUDY
AND TEACHING--HISTORY
Physical planning thought:
retrospect and prospect / Gary
Pivo ... [et al.].
Includes abstract.
JOURNAL OF ARCHITECTURAL AND
PLANNING RESEARCH 1990 Spring,
v.7, no.1, p.53-70, biblio.

UNITED STATES--CITY PLANNING--THEORY
Les theories americaines de
l'amenagement urbain: la question
des professions / Gilles Verpraet.
French, English, Spanish and
German summaries, p.246-252.
LES ANNALES DE LA RECHERCHE
URBAINE 1989 Dec., no.44-45,
p.15-25, [246]-247, 249, 251,
photos., biblio., refs.

UNITED STATES--CITY TRAFFIC
Containing traffic congestion in
America / Robert Cervero, Peter
Hall.
BUILT ENVIRONMENT 1989, v.15,
no.3-4, p.176-184, table, refs.

UNITED STATES--CLARKDALE (ARIZONA)--
COMPANY TOWNS--HISTORY
Clarkdale: Million dollar town /
Janet Ball.
History of Arizona company town,
founded in 1912, by the United
Verde Copper Company. Company
president: W. A. Clark. Clarkdale
is now listed in the National
Register of Historic Places.
TRIGLYPH 1990 Summer, no.10,
p.45-53, dwgs., photos., plans,
site plan, refs.

UNITED STATES--CLARKDALE (ARIZONA)--
HISTORIC SITES
Clarkdale: Million dollar town /
Janet Ball.
History of Arizona company town,
founded in 1912, by the United
Verde Copper Company. Company
president: W. A. Clark. Clarkdale
is now listed in the National
Register of Historic Places.
TRIGLYPH 1990 Summer, no.10,
p.45-53, dwgs., photos., plans,
site plan, refs.

UNITED STATES--CLARKDALE (ARIZONA)--
MINING TOWNS
Clarkdale: Million dollar town /
Janet Ball.
History of Arizona company town,
founded in 1912, by the United
Verde Copper Company. Company
president: W. A. Clark. Clarkdale
is now listed in the National
Register of Historic Places.
TRIGLYPH 1990 Summer, no.10,
p.45-53, dwgs., photos., plans,
site plan, refs.

UNITED STATES--CLARKSDALE
(MISSISSIPPI)--PLANTATION HOUSES--
CONSERVATION AND RESTORATION--
BELMONT PLANTATION
Family structure: one couple revives
a Delta plantation house / Estil
Curtis Pennington.
Belmont Plantation, near
Clarksdale, Miss., home of the
Stovall family. Restoration
architect: Lewis Graeber III.
SOUTHERN ACCENTS 1989 Nov.-Dec.,
v.12, no.6, p.150-154, photos.

UNITED STATES--CLASSICISM
Please pass the Civitas [editorial]
/ Clem Labine.
CLEM LABINE'S TRADITIONAL BUILDING
1990 Nov.-Dec., v.3, no.6, p.4,6,
port., photo.

UNITED STATES--CLEVELAND (OHIO)--
ARCHITECTURE
A Cleveland ostinato by Cervin
Robinson [book review] / Geraldine
Wojno Kiefer.
Review of "Cleveland, Ohio", by
Cervin Robinson.
INLAND ARCHITECT 1990 May-June,
v.34, no.3, p.25,28,81, photos.

UNITED STATES--CLEVELAND (OHIO)--
CORPORATE OFFICE BUILDINGS--BP
AMERICA
BP America, Inc., Corporate
Headquarters, Cleveland, Ohio,
USA, 1986.
Architects: Hellmuth, Obata &
Kassabaum. Text in Japanese and
English.
ARCHITECTURE AND URBANISM 1990
Dec., no.12 extra edition,
p.78-83, photos., plans.

UNITED STATES--CLEVELAND (OHIO)--
CORPORATE OFFICE BUILDINGS--
SUNARHAUSERMAN
Special feature: recent works of
Cesar Pelli.
Contents: Editor's introduction--
Architects' statement / Cesar
Pelli-- Essay: Urban iconography
and the medium of architecture /
Gavin Macrae-Gibson, p.130-137--
(Continued next page)

UNITED STATES--CLEVELAND (OHIO)--
CORPORATE OFFICE BUILDINGS--
SUNARHAUSERMAN (CONTINUED)
Special feature:...(CONTINUED)
Works: World Financial Center--
Norwest Tower-- Pacific Design
Center expansion-- Mattatuck
Museum-- Ley Student Center
expansion, Rice University-- Yale
Center for Molecular Medicine,
Yale University-- Carnegie Hall
tower-- Sunarhauserman
headquarters-- Fan Pier master
plan. Architects: Cesar Pelli &
Associates. Text in Japanese and
English.
ARCHITECTURE AND URBANISM 1990
Feb., no.2(233), p.[59]-148,
dwgs., elevs., photos., plans,
secns., site plans.

UNITED STATES--CLEVELAND (OHIO)--
MULTI-USE COMPLEXES--COMPETITIONS--
TOWER CITY CENTER
Special feature: Richard Keating:
years at SOM 1976-1990.
Essays: Editor's introduction /
Toshio Nakamura --Architect's
statement --Richard Keating and
the varieties of Modernism / John
Pastier --Works: Columbia Savings
& Loan, Beverly Hills, CA --Grand
Avenue Plaza, Los Angeles, CA,
1992 --Latham Watkins law offices,
Los Angeles, CA, 1989 --Gas Tower,
Los Angeles, CA, 1992 --Ocean
Boulevard Condominiums, Long
Beach, CA, 1989 --Tower City
Center competition, Cleveland,
Ohio, 1989 --Canon Building,
Beverly Hills, CA --Tokyo
International Forum honorable
mention project, Tokyo, Japan,
1989 --Katsuura Condominiums,
Katsuura, Japan, 1992. Architects:
Richard Keating of Skidmore,
Owings & Merrill and Keating Mann
Jernigan Rottet Architecture and
Interiors. Text in Japanese and
English.
ARCHITECTURE AND URBANISM 1990
Oct., no.10(241), p.58-128,
axonometric views, elevs.,
photos., plans.

UNITED STATES--CLEVELAND (OHIO)--
NEIGHBORHOODS--ECONOMIC ASPECTS
Divergent perspectives on the future
of Cleveland's neighborhoods:
economic, planning, and
sociological approaches to the
study of neighborhood change /
William A. Schwab.
JOURNAL OF URBAN STUDIES 1989,
v.11, no.2, p.[141]-154, tables,
refs.

UNITED STATES--CLEVELAND (OHIO)--
NEIGHBORHOODS--SOCIOLOGICAL ASPECTS
Divergent perspectives on the future
of Cleveland's neighborhoods:
economic, planning, and
sociological approaches to the
study of neighborhood change /
William A. Schwab.
JOURNAL OF URBAN STUDIES 1989,
v.11, no.2, p.[141]-154, tables,
refs.

UNITED STATES--CLEVELAND (OHIO)--TALL
BUILDINGS
Cleveland grows up and up / Wilma
Salisbury.
Recent projects by Cesar Pelli,
Kohn Pedersen Fox, Frank Gehry,
I.M. Pei, and others.
INLAND ARCHITECT 1990 Jan.-Feb.,
v.34, no.1, p.22-25, aerial photo.

UNITED STATES--CLINTON (IOWA)--
DEPARTMENT STORES--VAN ALLEN AND SON
Louis Sullivan's building for John
D. Van Allen and Son / Joseph
Siry.
A hisoty of the Clinton, Iowa
building (1913-1915), with
discussion o f design development,
ornamental motifs, and the
influences of mercantile interests
and regional agriculture upon the
clients. Includes abstract.
SOCIETY OF ARCHITECTURAL
HISTORIANS. JOURNAL 1990 Mar.,
v.49, no.1, p.67-89, dets., ill.,
dwgs., photos., plans, refs.

UNITED STATES--CLINTON (NEW YORK)--
AQUATIC SPORTS BUILDINGS--HAMILTON
COLLEGE--WILLIAM M. BRISTOL JR.
NATATORIUM
Aquatic art: William M. Bristol Jr.
Natatorium, Hamilton College,
Clinton, New York / Margaret
Gaskie.
Architects: Perry Dean Rogers &
Partners.
ARCHITECTURAL RECORD 1990 Apr.,
v.178, no.4, p.84-[89], elev.,
photos., plan, secns., site plans.

UNITED STATES--CLINTON (NEW YORK)--
UNIVERSITIES AND COLLEGES--
BUILDINGS--HAMILTON COLLEGE--WILLIAM
M. BRISTOL JR. NATATORIUM
Aquatic art: William M. Bristol Jr.
Natatorium, Hamilton College,
Clinton, New York / Margaret
Gaskie.
Architects: Perry Dean Rogers &
Partners.
ARCHITECTURAL RECORD 1990 Apr.,
v.178, no.4, p.84-[89], elev.,
photos., plan, secns., site plans.

UNITED STATES--CLOVIS (CALIFORNIA)--
HOSPITALS--CLOVIS COMMUNITY HOSPITAL
Imported ingenuity: engineering...
Ove Arup & Partners / Andrea
Oppenheimer Dean.
On six recent U.S. projects.
ARCHITECTURE: THE MAGAZINE OF THE
AMERICAN INSTITUTE OF ARCHITECTS
1990 May, v.79, no.5, p.90-97,
ill., dwgs., models, photos.

UNITED STATES--COCONUT GROVE
(FLORIDA)--HOUSES--INTERIOR DESIGN--
VILLA MALAGA
Colorful syntax: Dennis Jenkins'
personal design language / Mary
Kay Culpepper.
Villa Malaga, in Coconut Grove,
Fla., home of Dennis Jenkins and
Sunny McLean.
SOUTHERN ACCENTS 1990 Sept., v.13,
no.7, p.96-103, port., photos.

UNITED STATES--COCONUT GROVE
(FLORIDA)--VILLAS--ITALIANATE--
INTERIOR DESIGN--VIZCAYA
Coconut Grove rococo [Vizcaya,
Miami] / William L. Hamilton.
On the interiors of the 1914
villa. Designer: Paul Chalfin.
ART & ANTIQUES 1990 Oct., v.7,
no.7, p.116-120,139, photos.

UNITED STATES--COLCHESTER
(CONNECTICUT)--ANTIQUE SHOPS--TROIS
PROVINCES
Les Trois Provinces [antique shop,
Colchester, Conn.].
House built in 1792 by Henry
Champion.
COLONIAL HOMES 1990 Oct., v.16,
no.5, p.88-[93],154, photos.,
port.

UNITED STATES--COLCHESTER
(CONNECTICUT)--HOUSES--COLONIAL--
CHAMPION HOUSE
Les Trois Provinces [antique shop,
Colchester, Conn.].
House built in 1792 by Henry
Champion.
COLONIAL HOMES 1990 Oct., v.16,
no.5, p.88-[93],154, photos.,
port.

UNITED STATES--COLEBROOK
(CONNECTICUT)--HISTORIC DISTRICTS
Colebrook Historic District
Commission / Nancy Phelps Blum.
CONNECTICUT PRESERVATION NEWS 1989
July-Aug., v.12, no.4, p.10, engr.

UNITED STATES--COLLEGE STATION
(TEXAS)--HOUSES--ARCHITECTS'--
MASHBURN-MAFFEI HOUSE
Mashburn house, College Station,
Texas.
Architects: Joseph Mashburn.
Spanish, English text.
QUADERNS D'ARQUITECTURA I
URBANISME 1990 Jan.-Feb.-Mar.,
no.184, p.51, photos., plan.

UNITED STATES--COLLINSVILLE
(CONNECTICUT)--HISTORIC DISTRICTS--
COLLINSVILLE HISTORIC DISTRICT
Collinsville Historic District /
Roger Clarke.
CONNECTICUT PRESERVATION: NEWS
1989 May-June, v.12, no.3, p.9,
12, photos.

UNITED STATES--COLLINSVILLE
(ILLINOIS)--THEATERS--GREEK
REVIVAL--MINER'S INSTITUTE THEATER
The theater that miners built:
Collinsville's Miner's Institute
Theater / David Newton.
Built in 1916, at 204 W. Main St.
Architect: Robert G. Kirsch.
HISTORIC ILLINOIS 1990 June, v.13,
no.1, p.6-7,12-13, photos.

UNITED STATES--COLMA (CALIFORNIA)--
MAUSOLEA
Nella natura a viso aperto: opere
californiane di Robert K.
Overstreet.
Barbee House, Berkeley;
architect's house, Corte Madera;
Cottage Champion, Madison, Miss.;
house over water, Sausalito;
mausoleum, Colma; restaurant.
Summaries in English, French,
German, and Spanish.
(Continued next page)

UNITED STATES--COLMA (CALIFORNIA)--
MAUSOLEA (CONTINUED)
Nella natura a viso...(CONTINUED)
ARCHITETTURA; CRONACHE E STORIA
1990 Jan., v.36, no.1(411),
p.[32]-42, dwgs., photos., plans,
secns.

UNITED STATES--COLORADO--HISTORIC
DISTRICTS--GEORGETOWN - SILVER PLUME
Looking for the mother lode: hard
lessons learned by the NPS /
Ronald W. Johnson, John C. Paige.
Describes controversy over a
National Park Service study for a
new National Historic Landmark in
Georgetown and Silver Plume,
Colo., 50 miles west of Denver.
CRM BULLETIN: A NATIONAL PARK
SERVICE TECHNICAL BULLETIN 1990,
v.13, no.4, p.18-20,

UNITED STATES--COLORADO--VACATION
HOUSES--INTERIOR DESIGN
Colorado spirit: infusing a
southwestern-style vacation house
with bold sophistication / Suzanne
Stephens.
Interior designer: Thomas Britt.
ARCHITECTURAL DIGEST 1990 May,
v.47, no.5, p.[172]-177, photos.

UNITED STATES--COLSTRIP (MONTANA)--
MINES
Selections from "Colstrip, Montana"
/ David Hansen, Paul Shepard.
Photos and essay on a mining
landscape. Photographer listed
variously as David Hansen and
David T. Hanson.
PLACES 1990 Summer, v.6, no.4,
p.[68]-81, photos., aerial
photos., refs.

UNITED STATES--COLSTRIP (MONTANA)--
MINING TOWNS
Selections from "Colstrip, Montana"
/ David Hansen, Paul Shepard.
Photos and essay on a mining
landscape. Photographer listed
variously as David Hansen and
David T. Hanson.
PLACES 1990 Summer, v.6, no.4,
p.[68]-81, photos., aerial
photos., refs.

UNITED STATES--COLUMBIA BASIN
(WASHINGTON)--RECLAIMED LAND--
COLUMBIA BASIN PROJECT
Planning new landscapes: a
comparison of the Columbia Basin
Project and the IJsselmeerpolders
/ Donna Hall ... et al.
Regional planning and land
reclamation projects in the U.S.
and the Netherlands.
LANDSCAPE AND URBAN PLANNING 1989
Dec., v.18, no.2, p.97-116, maps,
plans, tables, refs.

UNITED STATES--COLUMBIA BASIN
(WASHINGTON)--REGIONAL PLANNING
Planning new landscapes: a
comparison of the Columbia Basin
Project and the IJsselmeerpolders
/ Donna Hall ... et al.
Regional planning and land
reclamation projects in the U.S.
and the Netherlands.
LANDSCAPE AND URBAN PLANNING 1989
Dec., v.18, no.2, p.97-116, maps,
plans, tables, refs.

UNITED STATES--COLUMBIA COUNTY (NEW
YORK)--HOUSES--DUTCH COLONIAL--VAN
ALEN FARM
Dutch treat [Dutch Colonial manor,
Columbia Co., N.Y.].
Architectural consultant: Roderic
Blackburn. Interior designer:
Renee Nelson.
COLONIAL HOMES 1990 Aug., v.16,
no.4, p.[74]-79, photos.

UNITED STATES--COLUMBIA (MARYLAND)--
NEW TOWNS
Ciudades de promocion privada:
Columbia (Maryland) / Abel
Enguita.
URBANISMO / COAM 1990 May, no.10,
p.58-67, map, photos., plan,
aerial photos.
Hail, Columbia [Md.] / Robert
Tennenbaum.
New town built in the early 1960s.
Chief architect and planner:
Robert Tennenbaum.
PLANNING 1990 May, v.56, no.5,
p.16-17, photos., plan.

UNITED STATES--COLUMBIA (MISSOURI)--
UNIVERSITIES AND COLLEGES--
BUILDINGS--UNIVERSITY OF MISSOURI--
STUDENT RECREATION CENTER
Body buildings: designing multi-use
campus recreational facilities /
Martha Huntington.
Univ. of Mo. Recreation Facility
and Univ. of Iowa Fieldhouse.
IOWA ARCHITECT 1990 Fall, v.39,
no.3, p.26-31, dwg., photos.,
plan, isometric dwg.

UNITED STATES--COLUMBIA RIVER VALLEY
(WASHINGTON)--VACATION HOUSES
In the family way [vacation home,
Washington state] / Julie V.
Iovine.
A family compound, on the Columbia
River. Architect: Tiger Warren.
METROPOLITAN HOME 1990 June, v.22,
no.6, p.88-94, photo.

UNITED STATES--COLUMBUS (INDIANA)--
ARCHITECTURE--20TH CENTURY
Revving up to quality: Cummins
Engine Company / Amy Dam.
Focus primarily on the
architecture program funded by the
Cummins Engine Foundation, which
provides financial support for
public architecture in Columbus,
Ind. Includes Cummins Engine Co.
Corporate headquarters.
INTERIORS 1990 May, v.149, no.10,
p.192-[205], dwg., ports.,
photos., plan.

UNITED STATES--COLUMBUS (INDIANA)--
CHURCHES--20TH CENTURY--SAINT
PETER'S LUTHERAN CHURCH
Il Gotico moderno di Gunnar Birkerts
= Gunnar Birkerts' modern Gothic /
Maurizio Vitta.
On St. Peter's Lutheran Church,
Columbus, Ind., designed in 1980
and recently completed.
L'ARCA 1990 Feb., no.35, p.24-33,
elev., photos, plans, secns., site
plans, sketch.

UNITED STATES--COLUMBUS (INDIANA)--
CORPORATE OFFICE BUILDINGS--CUMMINS
ENGINE COMPANY
Revving up to quality: Cummins
Engine Company / Amy Dam.
Focus primarily on the
architecture program funded by the
Cummins Engine Foundation, which
provides financial support for
public architecture in Columbus,
Ind. Includes Cummins Engine Co.
Corporate headquarters.
INTERIORS 1990 May, v.149, no.10,
p.192-[205], dwg., ports.,
photos., plan.

UNITED STATES--COLUMBUS (INDIANA)--
HOSPITALS--ALTERATIONS AND
ADDITIONS--BARTHOLOMEW COUNTY
HOSPITAL
Robert A. M. Stern.
Addition to the Bartholomew County
Hospital, Columbus, Ind., in
association with Falick / Klein
Partnership.
COLUMBIA UNIVERSITY. GRADUATE
SCHOOL OF ARCHITECTURE PLANNING
AND PRESERVATION. NEWSLINE 1990
Dec.-1991 Jan., v.3, no.4, p.6,
axonometric view, model, site
plan.

UNITED STATES--COLUMBUS (INDIANA)--
HOSPITALS--BARTHOLOMEW COUNTY
HOSPITAL
Hoosier patron: Cummins Engine
Foundation continues to foster
design in Columbus, Indiana.
Two projects under development:
Northside Middle School (Leers,
Weinzapfel Associates) and
Bartholomew Co. Hospital (Robert
A. M. Stern Architects and
Falick/Klein Partnership).
ARCHITECTURE: THE AIA JOURNAL 1990
Dec., v.79, no.12, p.41, elevs.,
secn.

UNITED STATES--COLUMBUS (INDIANA)--
PRISONS--BARTHOLOMEW COUNTY JAIL
Double identity: Bartholomew County
Jail, Columbus, Indiana, Hisaka &
Associates, Architects.
ARCHITECTURAL RECORD 1990 Nov.,
v.178, no.12, p.66-[71], photos.,
plans, secn., site plan.

UNITED STATES--COLUMBUS (INDIANA)--
SCHOOLS--ALTERATIONS AND ADDITIONS--
NORTHSIDE MIDDLE SCHOOL
Hoosier patron: Cummins Engine
Foundation continues to foster
design in Columbus, Indiana.
Two projects under development:
Northside Middle School (Leers,
Weinzapfel Associates) and
Bartholomew Co. Hospital (Robert
A. M. Stern Architects and
Falick/Klein Partnership).
ARCHITECTURE: THE AIA JOURNAL 1990
Dec., v.79, no.12, p.41, elevs.,
secn.

UNITED STATES--COLUMBUS (OHIO)--PUBLIC
BUILDINGS--VERN RIFFE CENTER
Sound government / Michael Wagner.
On the new state office building
in Columbus, Ohio, the Vern Riffe
Center, which includes three
performing arts theaters.
Architects: Bohm-NBBJ Architects,
Jaffe Acoustics.
INTERIORS 1990 Apr., v.149, no.9,
p.98, photo., secn.

UNITED STATES--COLUMBUS (OHIO)--
UNIVERSITIES AND COLLEGES--
BUILDINGS--COMPETITIONS--OHIO STATE
UNIVERSITY--WEXNER CENTER FOR THE
VISUAL ARTS
Conflicto de intereses: el concurso
para el Wexner Center / Alan
Colquhoun.
ARQUITECTURA VIVA 1990 Mar.-Apr.,
no.11, p.24-26, axonometric view,
dwgs., elevs., models.

UNITED STATES--COLUMBUS (OHIO)--
UNIVERSITIES AND COLLEGES--
BUILDINGS--OHIO STATE UNIVERSITY--
WEXNER CENTER FOR THE VISUAL ARTS
Gebouw als gebeurtenis: Peter
Eisenmans Wexner Center for the
Visual Arts / Marian van der
Waals.
In Columbus, Ohio.
DE ARCHITECT 1990 May, v.21, no.5,
p.51-55, axonometric views,
photos., plans, site plans.
The grid and the grain / Diane
Ghirardo.
Wexner Center for the Visual Arts.
Ohio State Univ., Columbus.
Architects: Peter Eisenman,
Richard Trott.
ARCHITECTURAL REVIEW 1990 June,
v.187, no.1120, p.79-86, map,
photos, plans, secn., aerial
photo.
Un manifesto decostruttivista = A
deconstructivist manifesto [Wexner
Center for the Visual Arts, Ohio
State University].
Architects: Peter Eisenman, with
Richard Trott and Arthur Baker.
ARCHITETTURA; CRONACHE E STORIA
1990 July-Aug., v.36,
no.7-8(417-418), p.553-555,
photos., plans, aerial photo.
Peter Eisenman.
Most of the issue devoted to this
architect. Nine projects featured.
Includes interview with David
Cohn. Text in Spanish and English.
EL CROQUIS 1989 Dec., v.8, no.41,
p.4-126,cover, axonometric views,
ill., dwgs., ports., elevs.,
models, photos., plans, secns.,
refs.
Peter Eisenman: Wexner Center for
the Visual Arts, Columbus, Ohio /
R.E. Somol.
In Italian and English.
DOMUS 1990 Jan., no.712,
p.[38-47], dets., elevs., photos,
plans, secns., site plans,
sketches.
Special feature: recent works of
Peter Eisenman.
Contents: Editor's introduction.--
Essays: Peter Eisenman: releasing
time imprisoned in space / Tadao
Ando.-- A framework for the future
/ Kurt W. Forster.-- Four notes on
the recent architecture of Peter
(Continued next column)

UNITED STATES--COLUMBUS (OHIO)--
UNIVERSITIES AND COLLEGES--
BUILDINGS--OHIO STATE UNIVERSITY--
WEXNER CENTER FOR THE VISUAL ARTS
(CONTINUED)
Special feature:...(CONTINUED)
Eisenman / Ignasi de
Sola-Morales.-- A matter of
respect.-- Works: Wexner Center
for the Visual Arts, Ohio State
University.-- Columbus Convention
Center.-- Banyoles Olympic Hotel
competition.-- College of Design,
Architecture, Art and Planning,
University of Cincinnati.--
Interview: Peter Eisenman / Jeff
Kipnis. Text in Japanese and
English.
ARCHITECTURE AND URBANISM 1990
Jan., no.1(232), p.[7]-182,
axonometric views, elevs., models,
photos., plans, secns., sketches.
Strukturalistiske spidsfindigheder--
om Wexner-centret for visuel kunst
/ Fleming Skude.
Architect: Peter Eisenman.
Reprinted from Progressive
architecture, 1989, no.10.
ARKITEKTUR DK 1990, v.34, no.1-2,
p.A2-A12, dwgs., photo., plan,
site plan.
Taking risks: Eisenman in Ohio /
Cynthia Chapin Davidson.
On form and the depiction of
movement in the Columbus
Convention Center; the College of
Design, Architecture, Art &
Planning (DAAP) at the University
of Cincinnati; and the Wexner
Center at Ohio State University.
INLAND ARCHITECT 1990 May-June,
v.34, no.3, p.[44]-51, dwgs.,
elevs., models, plans, secns.,
site plans.
Teoria y deleite: las abstracciones
de Eisenman / Vincent Scully.
The Wexner Center for the Visual
Arts, Ohio State University.
ARQUITECTURA VIVA 1990 Mar.-Apr.,
no.11, p.27-31, photos, plans.
Wexing eloquent in Columbus / Robert
Benson.
The Wexner Center for the Visual
Arts, Ohio State University.
Architect: Peter Eisenman.
INLAND ARCHITECT 1990 May-June,
v.34, no.3, p.34-43, photos.,
plans, aerial photo.
Wexner Center for the Visual Arts
[Architectural Design Profile 82].
Feature of issue. Includes "A
personal note," by Philip Johnson;
"Eisenman's White holes," by
Charles Jencks; "Between the
sphere and the labyrinth," by R.
E. Somol; "A framework for the
future," by Kurt W. Forster.
ARCHITECTURAL DESIGN 1989, v.59,
no.11-12, p.[1]-80, back cover,
axonometric views, port., photos.,
plans, secns., site plans,
sketches, aerial photos., refs.
The Wexner fragments for the visual
arts / Kay Bea Jones.
Criticism of the Wexner Center for
the Visual Arts at Ohio State
Univ. Architect: Peter Eisenman.
JOURNAL OF ARCHITECTURAL EDUCATION
1990 Spring, v.43, no.3, p.34-38,
photos., refs.

UNITED STATES--COLUMBUS (OHIO)--
UNIVERSITIES AND COLLEGES--
BUILDINGS--OHIO STATE UNIVERSITY--
WEXNER CENTER FOR THE VISUAL ARTS
(CONTINUED)
Wexner-Zentrum der visuellen Kunste
und Bibliothek in Columbus/Ohio,
USA = Wexner Centre for the Visual
Arts and Fine Arts Library in
Columbus/Ohio, USA.
Architects: Peter Eisenman,
Richard Trott.
ARCHITEKTUR + WETTBEWERBE 1990
Sept., no.143, p.6-7, photos.,
plan.

UNITED STATES--COMMERCIAL BUILDINGS
On the road / Kristian Berg,
Lars-Eric Jonsson.
Roadside architecture in the U.S.
ARKITEKTUR: THE SWEDISH REVIEW OF
ARCHITECTURE 1990 Nov., v.90,
no.9, p.12-19, dwg., photos.,
aerial photos., biblio.

UNITED STATES--COMMUNITY DEVELOPMENT--
AWARDS AND PRIZES
The NAHRO H/CD Excellence Awards.
National Association of Housing
and Redevelopment Officials.
Eleven awards given in 1989.
JOURNAL OF HOUSING 1990 Jan.-Feb.,
v.47, no.1, p.30-44, photos.

UNITED STATES--COMMUNITY DEVELOPMENT--
SOCIOLOGICAL ASPECTS
Seeing beyond the dominant culture /
Wilbur Zelinsky.
Discussion with three authors in
this issue on "cultural
landscapes."
PLACES 1990 Fall, v.7, no.1,
p.[32]-37, photo.

UNITED STATES--COMMUNITY DEVELOPMENT--
URBAN--SAINT LOUIS (MISSOURI)
The formation of urban
infrastructure through
nongovernmental planning: the
private places of St. Louis,
1869-1920 / David T. Beito, Bruce
Smith.
Examples drawn from the work of
architect Julius Pitzman.
JOURNAL OF URBAN HISTORY 1990 May,
v.16, no.3, p.263-303, photos.,
site plans, refs.

UNITED STATES--COMMUNITY GARDENS
The urban garden as public space /
Mark Francis.
PLACES 1989 Fall, v.6, no.1,
p.52-59, photos., plan, aerial
photo., refs.

UNITED STATES--CONCERT PAVILIONS--
TEMPORARY
Instant City / Deyan Sudjic.
Concert set used by the Rolling
Stones in 1989, designed by
Jonathan Park and others. First
published in English in Blueprint,
9/89.
BAUWELT 1990 Dec.1, v.81, no.45,
p.2268-2271, dwgs., photos.

UNITED STATES--CONNECTICUT--HOUSES--
INTERIOR DESIGN--SEGERSON HOUSE
Playing with tradition / Glenn
Harrell.
Interiors of designer Anne Mullin
Segerson's Connecticut house.
HOUSE BEAUTIFUL 1990 Dec., v.132,
no.12, p.56-[61], photos.

UNITED STATES--CONNECTICUT--KITCHENS--
INTERIOR DESIGN--SCOTT HOUSE
Country kitchen, household hub /
Elizabeth Gaynor.
In Connecticut. Designer: Everett
Brown.
HOUSE BEAUTIFUL 1990 Apr., v.132,
no.4, p.74-77, ports., photos.,
plans.

UNITED STATES--CONNECTICUT--LANDMARK
BUILDINGS
New listings on the National
Register / Leland Burnham.
Lists 8 new sites.
CONNECTICUT PRESERVATION NEWS 1990
Sept.-Oct., v.13, no.5, p.13,
photo.

UNITED STATES--CONNECTICUT--LOG
CABINS--INTERIOR DESIGN--SIEGEL
CABIN
Critic's choice: off the air, Joel
Siegel shifts his focus to a log
cabin filled with pop Americana /
Jennet Conant.
HOUSE & GARDEN 1990 June, v.162,
no.6, p.60,[62], port., photos.

UNITED STATES--CONNECTICUT--MANSIONS
Colonial y 'palladinano': casa de
campo en Connecticut.
Mansion in Conn. contains
references to Mount Vernon and
Palladian Villas. Architect: Allan
Greenberg. English summary, p.88.
A & V 1990, no.21, p.72-75,
photos.

UNITED STATES--CONNECTICUT--OFFICES--
INTERIOR DESIGN
Espaces en mouvance.
Interiors of offices for company
in Connecticut. Architects: Peter
Pran and Carlos Zapata of Ellerbe
Becket.
ARCHITECTURE INTERIEURE CREE 1990
Aug.-Sept., no.238, p.176-177,
photos., plan.

UNITED STATES--CONNECTICUT--PARKWAYS--
MERRITT PARKWAY
Fifty years on the Merritt / Jim
Appenzeller.
On Connecticut's Merritt Parkway.
METROPOLIS 1990 Nov., v.10, no.4,
p.[58]-67, photos.
Golden anniversary for the Merritt
Parkway / Catherine Lynn.
Includes a short piece by Vincent
Scully, "The automobile is a
destroyer."
CONNECTICUT PRESERVATION NEWS 1990
Sept.-Oct., v.13, no.5, p.[1]-5,
photos.

UNITED STATES--CONNECTICUT--SALTBOX
HOUSES--18TH CENTURY
East Hampton, N. Y.: Connecticut
transplant.
Goldman house, a 1787 saltbox
moved from Conn.
COLONIAL HOMES 1990 Apr., v.16,
no.2, p.[80]-89,136, photo.

UNITED STATES--CONNECTICUT--TAX
INCENTIVES
The Preservation Tax Incentives
Program in Connecticut: an
overview and update / Linda
Spencer.
CONNECTICUT PRESERVATION NEWS 1990
Jan.-Feb., v.13, no.1, p.10-11,

UNITED STATES--CONNECTICUT--TRAILS--
FARMINGTON CANAL GREENWAY
Farmington Canal Greenway.
A biking and hiking trail which
follows the old 19th cent. canal.
Architects: Cesar Pelli and
Associates.
CONNECTICUT PRESERVATION: NEWS
1989 May-June, v.12, no.3, p.6,
dwg.

UNITED STATES--CONNECTICUT--VACATION
HOUSES
Shope Reno Wharton: a shingled
cottage / Suzanne Stephens.
Vacation home on Conn. island.
ARCHITECTURAL DIGEST 1990 Sept.,
v.47, no.10, p.[94-97],108,
photos., plans.

UNITED STATES--CONTRA COSTA
(CALIFORNIA)--WATER TREATMENT
PLANTS--CONTRA COSTA WATER TREATMENT
COMPLEX
Site-sensitive technology: Simon
Martin Vegue Winkelstein Moris of
San Francisco.
Three designs for projects that
meld high technology and sensitive
design: Oceanside Control
Facility, Contra Costa Water
Treatment complex, and addition to
Lawrence Hall.
ARCHITECTURE: THE MAGAZINE OF THE
AMERICAN INSTITUTE OF ARCHITECTS
1990 May, v.79, no.5, p.48, elev.,
models, secn.

UNITED STATES--CONWAY (ARKANSAS)--
OFFICES--ARCHITECTS'--GEORG ANDERSEN
ASSOCIATES
Georg Andersen Associates / Monica
Geran.
Interiors of the Conway, Ark.,
architecture firm's new office
building designed by the firm.
INTERIOR DESIGN 1990 July, v.61,
no.10, p.154-[157], photos., plan.

UNITED STATES--COOPERATIVE HOUSING
Options to conventional public
management / William Peterman.
JOURNAL OF URBAN AFFAIRS 1989,
v.11, no.1, p.[53]-68, charts,
refs.

UNITED STATES--COOPERSTOWN (NEW
YORK)--CIDER MILLS--19TH CENTURY--
CONSERVATION AND RESTORATION--FLY
CREEK CIDER MILL
Fly Creek Cider Mill, Otsego County,
New York.
Built in 1856, three miles from
Cooperstown, N.Y.
OLD MILL NEWS 1989 Summer, v.17,
no.3(68), p.8, photos.

UNITED STATES--CORAL GABLES
(FLORIDA)--CAMPUSES--ALTERATIONS AND
ADDITIONS--COMPETITIONS--UNIVERSITY
OF MIAMI CAMPUS MASTER PLAN
An urban design proposal for the
University of Miami Campus Master
Plan Competition / Marleen Davis,
Thomas K. Davis.
JOURNAL OF ARCHITECTURAL EDUCATION
1990 Summer, v.43, no.4, p.8-15,
axonometric views, ill., photo.,
site plans, aerial photo, biblio.

UNITED STATES--CORAL GABLES
(FLORIDA)--SCHOOLS OF ARCHITECTURE--
UNIVERSITY OF MIAMI--SCHOOL OF
ARCHITECTURE
Nueva escuela de arquitectura en la
Universidad de Miami Coral Gables
Florida = New school of
architecture at the University of
Miami Coral Gables Florida / Aldo
Rossi, Morris Adjumi.
Architect: Aldo Rossi.
COMPOSICION ARQUITECTONICA, ART &
ARCHITECTURE 1990 Feb., no.5,
p.[25]-34, elevs., model, plan,
secns., site plan, sketches.

UNITED STATES--CORAL GABLES
(FLORIDA)--SWIMMING POOLS--
CONSERVATION AND RESTORATION--
VENETIAN POOL
Southern traditions: preservation
efforts in today's South show new
interest in 20th-century
landmarks, as well as earlier ones
/ Clifford A. Pearson.
A portfolio of Southeast projects:
Epping Forest Yacht Club,
Jacksonville, Fla. (Pappas
Associates); Freedom Tower, Miami
(Heisenbottle Architects);
Venetian Pool, Coral Gables, Fla.
(H. Carlton Decker & Assoc.);
Howard Memorial Library, New
Orleans (E. Barron, M. Toups); and
Linden Row Inn, Richmond, Va.
(Glave Newman Anderson).
ARCHITECTURAL RECORD 1990 Mar.,
v.178, no.3, p.66-75, photos.,
plans, site plans.

UNITED STATES--CORNISH (NEW
HAMPSHIRE)--HOUSES--AUGUSTUS
SAINT-GAUDENS HOUSE
Life-size canvases / Eleanor Berman.
Houses of painters and sculptors:
Daniel Chester French (designed
with architect Henry Bacon);
Augustus Saint-Gaudens; Frida
Kahlo; Evelyn and Frederic
Bartlett.
HOUSE BEAUTIFUL 1990 July, v.132,
no.7, p.30,32, photos.

UNITED STATES--CORPORATE OFFICE
BUILDINGS--IBM--EXHIBITIONS
IBM's architecture at Building
Museum [exhibition review] /
Thomas Vonier.
Part of the National Building
Museum's fourth annual design
award program. On view through
Sept. 1990.
PROGRESSIVE ARCHITECTURE 1990 May,
v.71, no.5, p.26, photos.

UNITED STATES--CORPUS CHRISTI
(TEXAS)--ART CENTERS--DEL MAR
COLLEGE--FINE ARTS CENTER
A vaulted spine at Del Mar College /
Joel Warren Barna.
Del Mar College Fine Arts Center,
Corpus Christi. Architects: Kipp,
Richter & Associates.
TEXAS ARCHITECT 1990 July-Aug.,
v.40, no.4, p.48, photos., plan,
site plan.

UNITED STATES--CORPUS CHRISTI
(TEXAS)--CHAPELS--INTERIOR DESIGN--
CORPUS CHRISTI CATHEDRAL--EMMANUEL
CHAPEL
Interiors: two Corpus Christi
churches; A backdrop for industry.
St. Mark's Episcopal Church
(architects: Kipp, Richter &
Associates); Emmanuel Chapel at
the Corpus Christi Cathedral
(architect: James G. Rome); and
offices for Hixo, Inc., Austin
(Barbee Pardo Architects).
TEXAS ARCHITECT 1990 Mar.-Apr.,
v.40, no.2, p.40-42, photos.,
plans.

UNITED STATES--CORPUS CHRISTI
(TEXAS)--CHURCHES--20TH CENTURY--
SAINT MARK'S EPISCOPAL CHURCH
Interiors: two Corpus Christi
churches; A backdrop for industry.
St. Mark's Episcopal Church
(architects: Kipp, Richter &
Associates); Emmanuel Chapel at
the Corpus Christi Cathedral
(architect: James G. Rome); and
offices for Hixo, Inc., Austin
(Barbee Pardo Architects).
TEXAS ARCHITECT 1990 Mar.-Apr.,
v.40, no.2, p.40-42, photos.,
plans.

UNITED STATES--CORPUS CHRISTI
(TEXAS)--OFFICES--HIXO, INC.
Interiors: two Corpus Christi
churches; A backdrop for industry.
St. Mark's Episcopal Church
(architects: Kipp, Richter &
Associates); Emmanuel Chapel at
the Corpus Christi Cathedral
(architect: James G. Rome); and
offices for Hixo, Inc., Austin
(Barbee Pardo Architects).
TEXAS ARCHITECT 1990 Mar.-Apr.,
v.40, no.2, p.40-42, photos.,
plans.

UNITED STATES--CORPUS CHRISTI
(TEXAS)--UNIVERSITIES AND COLLEGES--
BUILDINGS--DEL MAR COLLEGE--FINE
ARTS CENTER
A vaulted spine at Del Mar College /
Joel Warren Barna
Del Mar College Fine Arts Center,
Corpus Christi. Architects: Kipp,
Richter & Associates.
TEXAS ARCHITECT 1990 July-Aug.,
(Continued next column)

UNITED STATES--CORPUS CHRISTI
(TEXAS)--UNIVERSITIES AND COLLEGES--
BUILDINGS--DEL MAR COLLEGE--FINE
ARTS CENTER (CONTINUED)
A vaulted spine at...(CONTINUED)
v.40, no.4, p.48, photos., plan,
site plan.

UNITED STATES--CORTE MADERA
(CALIFORNIA)--HOUSES--ARCHITECTS'--
OVERSTREET HOUSE
Nella natura a viso aperto: opere
californiane di Robert K.
Overstreet.
Barbee House, Berkeley;
architect's house, Corte Madera;
Cottage Champion, Madison, Miss.;
house over water, Sausalito;
mausoleum, Colma; restaurant.
Summaries in English, French,
German, and Spanish.
ARCHITETTURA; CRONACHE E STORIA
1990 Jan., v.36, no.1(411),
p.[32]-42, dwgs., photos., plans,
secns.

UNITED STATES--COSTA MESA
(CALIFORNIA)--AUDITORIUMS, CONCERT
HALLS--ORANGE COUNTY PERFORMING ARTS
CENTER
An amazing new performing arts
center in California / Michael
Wagner, Dennis Paoletti.
Orange County Performing Arts
Center, Costa Mesa, Calif.
Architects: Caudill Rowlett Scott,
Blue Rock Partnership.
INTERIORS 1989 Feb., v.148, no.7,
p.58, dwg., photo.

UNITED STATES--COTTAGES
Builder style: America's little
houses / James C. Massey, Shirley
Maxwell.
Homestead, Foursquare, Cottage,
and Bungalow styles.
OLD-HOUSE JOURNAL 1990 Sept.-Oct.,
v.18, no.5, p.45-49, ill., photos.

UNITED STATES--COTTAGES--PREFABRICATED
Pre-cut houses: "catalog homes" /
James C. Massey & Shirley Maxwell.
Mail-order kit houses flourished
from 1900 to 1940.
OLD-HOUSE JOURNAL 1990 Nov.-Dec.,
v.18, no.6, p.36-41, ill., photos.

UNITED STATES--COUNTRY HOUSES
American translation / Clive Aslet.
COUNTRY LIFE 1990 July 12, v.184,
no.28, p.80-81, photos.

UNITED STATES--CRAVEN COUNTY (NORTH
CAROLINA)--ARCHITECTURE
The historic architecture of New
Bern and Craven County, North
Carolina [by] Peter B. Sandbeck
[book review] / Carl Lounsbury.
SOCIETY OF ARCHITECTURAL
HISTORIANS. JOURNAL 1990 Sept.,
v.49, no.3, p.344-345,

UNITED STATES--CRESTED BUTTE
(COLORADO)--VACATION HOUSES--
SOUCHERAY HOUSE
Home away from home: a Colorado
vacation house with a heart of
glass.
Soucheray house, Crested Butte.
Architect: Kelly Davis.
ARCHITECTURE MINNESOTA 1990
Nov.-Dec., v.16, no.6, p.34-35,
photos.

UNITED STATES--CRISIS SHELTERS--
PSYCHOLOGICAL ASPECTS
Dimensions of person-environment
relationships in shelters for
victims of domestic violence / Ben
J. Refuerzo, Stephen Verderber.
A study of shelters for battered
women and children, conducted in
Los Angeles and New Orleans.
Includes abstract.
JOURNAL OF ARCHITECTURAL AND
PLANNING RESEARCH 1990 Spring,
v.7, no.1, p.33-52, charts,
diagrs., photos., biblio.

UNITED STATES--CRYSTAL CITY
(VIRGINIA)--CASCADES--CRYSTAL CITY
WATER PARK
Waterscapes: a creative evolution /
Martin L. Epps.
First of five articles on the use
of water in development projects;
some separately indexed.
DEVELOPMENT 1990 Sept.-Oct., v.21,
no.5, p.10-12, photos., aerial
photo.

UNITED STATES--CULVER CITY
(CALIFORNIA)--OFFICE BUILDINGS--8522
NATIONAL BOULEVARD
Burogebaude 8522 National Boulevard
in Culver City, USA = Office
building 8522 National Boulevard
in Culver City, USA.
Five adjoining warehouses
[1920-1940] converted into an
office building. Architect: Eric
Owen Moss.
ARCHITEKTUR + WETTBEWERBE 1989
Dec., no.140, p.10-11, dets.,
photos., plans.

UNITED STATES--CULVER CITY
(CALIFORNIA)--OFFICE BUILDINGS--GARY
GROUP
Eric Owen Moss.
Focus on two office buildings in
Culver City, Calif.: Gary Group
and the warehouse conversion
project on National Blvd.,
National Warehouse. English
summary.
ARCHITECTURE D'AUJOURD'HUI 1990
Oct., no.271, p.153-158,
axonometric views, photos., plans,
models.

UNITED STATES--CULVER CITY
(CALIFORNIA)--OFFICE BUILDINGS--
INTERIOR DESIGN--QUALITATIVE
RESEARCH CENTER
Pentagone variable / Claudine
Mulard.
Interiors of renovated warehouse
containing the offices of
Qualitative Research Center,
Culver City, Calif. Renovation
architect: Eric Moss.
ARCHITECTURE INTERIEURE CREE 1990
Aug.-Sept., no.238, p.178-[179],
photos.

UNITED STATES--CULVER CITY
(CALIFORNIA)--OFFICE BUILDINGS--
NATIONAL WAREHOUSE
Eric Owen Moss.
Focus on two office buildings in
Culver City, Calif.: Gary Group
and the warehouse conversion
project on National Blvd.,
National Warehouse. English
summary.

(Continued next page)

UNITED STATES--CULVER CITY
(CALIFORNIA)--OFFICE BUILDINGS--
NATIONAL WAREHOUSE (CONTINUED)
Eric Owen Moss. (CONTINUED)
ARCHITECTURE D'AUJOURD'HUI 1990
Oct., no.271, p.153-158,
axonometric views, photos., plans,
models.

UNITED STATES--CULVER CITY
(CALIFORNIA)--OFFICES--HYBRID ARTS
Circumstantial evidence: Hybrid
Arts, Qualitative Research Centre,
Culver City, California, Eric Owen
Moss Architect / Deborah K.
Dietsch.
ARCHITECTURE: THE MAGAZINE OF THE
AMERICAN INSTITUTE OF ARCHITECTS
1990 June, v.79, no.6, p.90-95,
axonometric views, dwgs., photos.,
plans.

UNITED STATES--CULVER CITY
(CALIFORNIA)--OFFICES--QUALITATIVE
RESEARCH CENTRE
Circumstantial evidence: Hybrid
Arts, Qualitative Research Centre,
Culver City, California, Eric Owen
Moss Architect / Deborah K.
Dietsch.
ARCHITECTURE: THE MAGAZINE OF THE
AMERICAN INSTITUTE OF ARCHITECTS
1990 June, v.79, no.6, p.90-95,
axonometric views, dwgs., photos.,
plans.

UNITED STATES--CUSTOMHOUSES--19TH
CENTURY
Civic and aesthetic reserve: Ammi
Burnham Young's 1850s Federal
Customhouse designs / Daniel
Bluestone.
For Boston, Cincinnati, Norfolk,
Mobile, Providence, Chicago and
other cities, and dating from the
1830s to 1860.
WINTERTHUR PORTFOLIO 1990 Autumn,
v.25, no.2-3, p.[131]-156, dets.,
elevs., maps, photos., plans,
refs.

UNITED STATES--CYPRESS (TEXAS)--
CHURCHES--20TH CENTURY--SAINT MARY'S
EPISCOPAL CHURCH
A church's complex anchor [St.
Mary's Episcopal Church, Cypress,
Tex.].
Phase I. Architects: Gregory
Harper Associates with Gerald
Moorhead.
TEXAS ARCHITECT 1990 Mar.-Apr.,
v.40, no.2, p.56-57, photos.,
plan, site plan.
Houston design portfolio: slow
recovery.
Sesquicentennial Park (Team HOU);
Caldwell house (Natalye Appel);
Court at Museums Gate (Josiah
Baker); Gilliland house (Peter Jay
Zweig Architects); Finnell house
(Wittenberg Partnership); and St.
Mary's Episcopal Church (Gerald
Moorhead).
ARCHITECTURE: THE AIA JOURNAL 1990
Apr., v.79, no.4, p.54-73,
axonometric views, ill., elev.,
photos., plans, secns., site
plans.

UNITED STATES--DADE COUNTY (FLORIDA)--
STADIUMS--JOE ROBBIE STADIUM
Joe Robbie Stadium, Dade County,
Florida, USA, 1987.
Architects: Hellmuth, Obata &
Kassabaum. Text in Japanese and
English.
ARCHITECTURE AND URBANISM 1990
Dec., no.12 extra edition,
p.120-125, photos., plan, site
plan.

UNITED STATES--DALLAS COUNTY (IOWA)--
WEEKEND HOUSES
Clear retreat / Mark E. Blunck.
Weekend house, Dallas Co., Iowa.
Architects: Wells Woodburn O'Neil.
IOWA ARCHITECT 1990 Spring, v.39,
no.1, p.10-[11], photos., plans.

UNITED STATES--DALLAS (TEXAS)--
APARTMENT HOUSES--TRAVIS STREET
CONDOMINIUMS
Travis Street Condominiums, Dallas.
Architect: Lionel
Morrison/OMNIPLAN.
TEXAS ARCHITECT 1990 Jan.-Feb.,
v.40, no.1, p.30, axonometric
view, photos.

UNITED STATES--DALLAS (TEXAS)--
ARBORETUMS--DALLAS ARBORETUM AND
BOTANICAL GARDEN
A kaleidoscope of Texas blossoms:
the Dallas Arboretum and Botanical
Garden ushers in spring / Derro
Evans.
SOUTHERN ACCENTS 1989 Mar.-Apr.,
v.12, no.2, p.196B-196H, photos.

UNITED STATES--DALLAS (TEXAS)--
AUDITORIUMS, CONCERT HALLS--MORTON
H. MEYERSON SYMPHONY CENTER
Contrapunto barroco: I.M. Pei en
Dallas / Bruno Suner.
The new Dallas Auditorium.
ARQUITECTURA VIVA 1990 Jan.-Feb.,
no.10, p.18-20, photos., plans.
Dallas palace / Jeremy Melvin.
On the Morton H. Meyerson Symphony
Center, Dallas. Architects: I. M.
Pei & Partners.
BUILDING DESIGN 1989 Oct., suppl.,
p.16-17, elevs., model, photos.,
plans, secn., site plan.
Geometries imbriquees: centre
symphonique Morton H. Meyerson,
Dallas, U.S.A. / I. M. Pei,
Russell Johnson.
Morton H. Meyerson Symphony
Center, Dallas. Architects: I. M.
Pei & Partners. Acoustics: Artec
Consultants. English summary,
p.106. Spanish summary, p.198.
TECHNIQUES ET ARCHITECTURE 1990
Apr.-May, no.389, p.100-[107],
diagr., photos., plans, secns.
The Morton H. Meyerson Symphony
Center, Dallas, Texas.
Architects: Pei Cobb Freed &
Partners. Includes essay: Concerto
for building: the Morton H.
Meyerson Symphony Center / Sandy
Heck. Text in Japanese and
English.
ARCHITECTURE AND URBANISM 1990
Nov., no.11(242), p.[7]-37,
photos., plans, site plan.

UNITED STATES--DALLAS (TEXAS)--
AUDITORIUMS, CONCERT HALLS--MORTON
H. MEYERSON SYMPHONY CENTER
(CONTINUED)
Pei avvolge im parallelepipedo in
una conchiglia = Pei wraps a
parallelepiped in a shell.
Concert hall, Dallas Art Center.
ARCHITETTURA: CRONACHE E STORIA
1990 Nov., v.36, no.11(421),
p.798-799, photos., plan, site
plan.
Pei, l'auditorium de Dallas.
On the Morton H. Meyerson Symphony
Center, Dallas. Architects: I.M.
Pei & Partners. English summary,
167, 170. Acoustics: Artec
Consultants.
ARCHITECTURE D'AUJOURD'HUI 1990
Apr., no.268, p.162-[171], dets.,
photos., plans, secns., site
plans.

UNITED STATES--DALLAS (TEXAS)--
AUDITORIUMS, CONCERT HALLS--MORTON
H. MEYERSON SYMPHONY CENTER--EUGENE
MCDERMOTT CONCERT HALL
An acoustic jewel: a symphony center
in Dallas boasts old world sound /
Douglas E. Gordon.
The Eugene McDermott Concert Hall,
within the Morton H. Meyerson
Symphony Center, designed by Pei
Cobb Freed & Partners. Acoustic
consultants: Artec Consultants
Inc.
ARCHITECTURE: THE AIA JOURNAL 1990
Feb., v.79, no.2, p.99-100, dwg.,
photos.

UNITED STATES--DALLAS (TEXAS)--
BOTANICAL GARDENS--DALLAS ARBORETUM
AND BOTANICAL GARDEN
A kaleidoscope of Texas blossoms:
the Dallas Arboretum and Botanical
Garden ushers in spring / Derro
Evans.
SOUTHERN ACCENTS 1989 Mar.-Apr.,
v.12, no.2, p.196B-196H, photos.

UNITED STATES--DALLAS (TEXAS)--
FOUNTAINS
In the capital of white noise: the
fountains of Dallas / Richard
Ingersoll.
TEXAS ARCHITECT 1990 Jan.-Feb.,
v.40, no.1, p.[36]-41, photos.,
map.

UNITED STATES--DALLAS (TEXAS)--
HOUSES--20TH CENTURY--HOUSE BEHIND A
WALL
A house behind a wall.
In Dallas. Architect: Max Levy.
TEXAS ARCHITECT 1990 Jan.-Feb.,
v.40, no.1, p.28, photos., plan.

UNITED STATES--DALLAS (TEXAS)--
HOUSES--20TH CENTURY--POWER HOUSE
The ghost of Reddy Kilowatt: living
the good life in a Dallas power
station / Stephen Ross.
1923 electrical substation
converted to a house. Architects:
Gary Cunningham and Sharon Odom.
ELLE DECOR 1990 June-July, v.1,
no.5, p.100-[105], photos.
Power house, Dallas.
Conversion of 1929 electrical
switching station in Oak Lawn into
a house. Cunningham Architects.
TEXAS ARCHITECT 1990 Jan.-Feb.,
(Continued next page)

UNITED STATES--DALLAS (TEXAS)--
HOUSES--20TH CENTURY--POWER HOUSE
(CONTINUED)
Power house, Dallas. (CONTINUED)
v.40, no.1, p.29, photos., plans.

UNITED STATES--DALLAS (TEXAS)--
HOUSES--ARCHITECTS'--DOMITEAUX HOUSE
Architecture for the '90s.
Holt Hinshaw Pfau Jones, Astronaut
Memorial, San Francisco--Henry
Myerberg, house in Vieques, P.R.--
Walter Chatham, house in Seaside,
Fla.--Carrie Glassman Shoemake,
house near Austin, Tex.--Mark
Domiteaux, house in Tex.--Frank
Lupo, Daniel Rowan, loft in NYC--
Michael Codwell, 4 projects in New
England.
METROPOLITAN HOME 1990 Jan., v.22,
no.1, p.[72]-96, ports., photos.

UNITED STATES--DALLAS (TEXAS)--
HOUSES--EAGLE HOUSE
Eagle Residence, Dallas, Texas,
design: 1986-87.
Architects: Himmel Bonner
Architects. Text in Japanese and
English.
GA HOUSES 1990 Mar., no.28,
p.90-91, dwgs., elevs., plans,
site plan.

UNITED STATES--DALLAS (TEXAS)--
HOUSES--P HOUSE
Steven Holl.
Features four projects: P House,
Dallas; apartment house, Fukuoka,
Japan; American Memorial Library
extension competition entry,
Berlin; and the addition to the
School of Architecture, Univ. of
Minn., Minneapolis. English
summaries.
ARCHITECTURE D'AUJOURD'HUI 1990
Oct., no.271, p.122-126, dwgs.,
models, plan, secns., site plan.

UNITED STATES--DALLAS (TEXAS)--
HOUSES--POWER HOUSE
Centrale elettrica, Dallas =
Electric center, Dallas.
Electrical substation converted to
house; architects: Gary Cunningham
and Sharon Odom.
LOTUS INTERNATIONAL 1990, no.66,
p.84-91, photos., plans.

UNITED STATES--DALLAS (TEXAS)--LAS
COLINAS--OUTDOOR SCULPTURE--WILLIAMS
SQUARE
Williams Square: where public space
becomes public art / David Dillon.
Public plaza in Dallas' Las
Colinas development. Architect:
James Reeves of the SWA Group.
Sculptor: Robert Glen.
SOUTHERN ACCENTS 1989 Nov.-Dec.,
v.12, no.6, p.176B-176J, photos.

UNITED STATES--DALLAS (TEXAS)--LAW
OFFICES--INTERIOR DESIGN--BAKER &
BOTTS
Baker & Botts: the law firm's Dallas
offices designed by Gensler and
Associates Architects/Houston /
Monica Geran.
INTERIOR DESIGN 1990 May, v.61,
no.7, p.266-[269], photos., plans.

UNITED STATES--DALLAS (TEXAS)--LOFTS--
INTERIOR DESIGN--CARPENTER LOFT
Artistic revival in Deep Ellum: a
striking collection of
contemporary art for Laura
Carpenter's Dallas loft / Michael
Ennis.
Interior designer: James Foy.
ARCHITECTURAL DIGEST 1990 May,
v.47, no.5, p.238-[243], port.,
photos.

UNITED STATES--DALLAS (TEXAS)--
MULTI-USE COMPLEXES--TURTLE CREEK
DEVELOPMENT
Frank O. Gehry.
Entire issue devoted to the work
of this American architect.
Criticism by A. Zaera Polo and
David Cohn. 15 projects and
buildings from 1987-1990 featured.
Text in Spanish and English.
EL CROQUIS 1990 Nov., v.9, no.45,
p.1-124, ports., elevs., models,
photos., plans, secns., site
plans, refs.
Variaciones sobre un tema americano:
conjunto Turtle Creek, Dallas,
Tejas, 1985-1986.
Architects: Frank O. Gehry and
Associates. English summary, p.87.
A & V 1990, no.25, p.66-67,
models, site plan, sketches.

UNITED STATES--DALLAS (TEXAS)--
OFFICES--INTERIOR DESIGN--APPLE
COMPUTER MARKET CENTER
Marketing Macintoshes / Karin
Tetlow.
Interiors of Apple Computer's
Computer Market Center in the
Dallas Infomart. Architects:
Gensler and Associates,
Architects.
INTERIORS 1990 Apr., v.149, no.9,
p.44, photo., plan.

UNITED STATES--DALLAS (TEXAS)--
OFFICES--INTERIOR DESIGN--NASHER
Nasher / Judith Davidsen.
Interiors of Raymond D. Nasher's
real estate development office in
Dallas, which incorporates
Nasher's art collection. Interior
designers: Hermanovski Lauck
Design.
INTERIOR DESIGN 1990 Nov., v.61,
no.15, p.[156-159], photos., plan.

UNITED STATES--DALLAS (TEXAS)--
PAVILIONS
Poolside paradise: glorious outdoor
entertaining complex graces a
Dallas garden / Nan Booth Simpson.
Architects: Loyd-Paxton; Landscape
architects: Boyd & Heiderich.
SOUTHERN ACCENTS 1990 July-Aug.,
v.13, no.6, p.[96]-100, photos.

UNITED STATES--DALLAS (TEXAS)--
PEDESTRIAN MALLS--DALLAS MAIN CENTER
MALL
Downtown Mall developer chosen,
Dallas / Joel Warren Barna.
To be called Dallas Main Center
Mall. Developer: Bramalea Texas.
Architects: Urban Design Group.
TEXAS ARCHITECT 1990 Jan.-Feb.,
v.40, no.1, p.11, dwgs., site
plan.

UNITED STATES--DALLAS (TEXAS)--
PENTHOUSES--INTERIOR DESIGN--YOUNG
PENTHOUSE
Spirited approach: a bright and
lively penthouse overlooks the
Dallas skyline / Nan Booth
Simpson.
Apartment of Carol Young. Interior
architect: Chris Carson.
SOUTHERN ACCENTS 1990 Nov., v.13,
no.9, p.[86]-91, photos.

UNITED STATES--DALLAS (TEXAS)--
PLAZAS--LAS COLINAS--WILLIAMS SQUARE
Williams Square: where public space
becomes public art / David Dillon.
Public plaza in Dallas' Las
Colinas development. Architect:
James Reeves of the SWA Group.
Sculptor: Robert Glen.
SOUTHERN ACCENTS 1989 Nov.-Dec.,
v.12, no.6, p.176B-176J, photos.

UNITED STATES--DALLAS (TEXAS)--RAPID
RAIL TRANSIT SYSTEMS--DALLAS AREA
RAPID TRANSIT
Rail plans for Houston, Dallas /
Joel Warren Barna.
PROGRESSIVE ARCHITECTURE 1990
Aug., v.71, no.8, p.32,37, plan.

UNITED STATES--DALLAS (TEXAS)--
SHOPPING MALLS--GALLERIA
Dallas Galleria, Dallas, Texas, USA,
1983.
Architects: Hellmuth, Obata &
Kassabaum, with Kendall Heaton
Associates. Text in Japanese and
English.
ARCHITECTURE AND URBANISM 1990
Dec., no.12 extra edition,
p.58-[65], photos., plans, secns.,
site plan.

UNITED STATES--DALLAS (TEXAS)--
SHOWROOMS--COMPUTER--INFOMART--APPLE
COMPUTER MARKET CENTER
Interiors [five Dallas showrooms].
Apple Computer Market Center
(Gensler & Associates); W. Joe
Sanders, (Gensler & Associates);
Gunlocke (Hermanovski Lauck);
DesignTex Fabrics (Hermanovski
Lauck): and Haworth Interiors
(HOK).
TEXAS ARCHITECT 1990 May-June,
v.40, no.3, p.40-47, photos,
plans.

UNITED STATES--DALLAS (TEXAS)--
SHOWROOMS--FURNITURE--GUNLOCKE
Gunlocke / Monica Geran.
Interiors of furniture showroom,
Dallas. Interior designers:
Hermanovski Lauck Design.
INTERIOR DESIGN 1990 June, v.61,
no.9, p.248-[249], photos., plan.
Interiors [five Dallas showrooms].
Apple Computer Market Center
(Gensler & Associates); W. Joe
Sanders, (Gensler & Associates);
Gunlocke (Hermanovski Lauck);
DesignTex Fabrics (Hermanovski
Lauck): and Haworth Interiors
(HOK).
TEXAS ARCHITECT 1990 May-June,
v.40, no.3, p.40-47, photos,
plans.

UNITED STATES--DALLAS (TEXAS)--
SHOWROOMS--FURNITURE--W. JOE SANDERS
  Interiors [five Dallas showrooms].
    Apple Computer Market Center
    (Gensler & Associates); W. Joe
    Sanders, (Gensler & Associates);
    Gunlocke (Hermanovski Lauck);
    DesignTex Fabrics (Hermanovski
    Lauck): and Haworth Interiors
    (HOK).
    TEXAS ARCHITECT 1990 May-June,
    v.40, no.3, p.40-47, photos,
    plans.

UNITED STATES--DALLAS (TEXAS)--
SHOWROOMS--INTERIOR DESIGN--
DESIGNTEX FABRICS
  Interiors [five Dallas showrooms].
    Apple Computer Market Center
    (Gensler & Associates); W. Joe
    Sanders, (Gensler & Associates);
    Gunlocke (Hermanovski Lauck);
    DesignTex Fabrics (Hermanovski
    Lauck): and Haworth Interiors
    (HOK).
    TEXAS ARCHITECT 1990 May-June,
    v.40, no.3, p.40-47, photos,
    plans.

UNITED STATES--DALLAS (TEXAS)--STUDENT
UNIONS--INTERIOR DESIGN--EL CENTRO
COLLEGE
  Interiors.
    Contents: Berg & Androphy Law
    Offices, Houston (William F. Stern
    and Associates); Majestic Diner,
    Austin (STUDIO Texas); and, El
    Centro College Student Center,
    Dallas (Oglesby Group).
    TEXAS ARCHITECT 1990 Sept.-Oct.,
    v.40, no.5, p.40-43, photos.,
    plans.

UNITED STATES--DALLAS (TEXAS)--
SWIMMING POOLS
  Poolside paradise: glorious outdoor
    entertaining complex graces a
    Dallas garden / Nan Booth Simpson.
    Architects: Loyd-Paxton; Landscape
    architects: Boyd & Heiderich.
    SOUTHERN ACCENTS 1990 July-Aug.,
    v.13, no.6, p.[96]-100, photos.

UNITED STATES--DALLAS (TEXAS)--TRANSIT
SYSTEMS--DART
  Trains, planes, and automobiles /
    Joel Warren Barna.
    Mass transit rail lines in Dallas
    and Houston.
    TEXAS ARCHITECT 1990 Mar.-Apr.,
    v.40, no.2, p.22-29, dwgs.,
    models, maps, photos., site plans.

UNITED STATES--DANBURY (CONNECTICUT)--
PAVILIONS--CHARLES IVES CENTER
PAVILION
  Indoor sound outdoors / Michael
    Wagner.
    Music pavilion, called the Charles
    Ives Center Pavilion, Danbury
    Conn. Architects: Kosinki
    Associates with Jaffe Acoustics.
    INTERIORS 1990 Feb., v.149, no.7,
    p.58, photos., plan, secn.

UNITED STATES--DANIA (FLORIDA)--
SHOWROOMS--INTERIOR DESIGN--JERRY
PAIR
  Jerry pair / Mayer Rus.
    Showroom interiors in the Design
    Center of the Americas (DCOTA) in
    Dania, Fl. Interior designers:
    Richard Plumer Design.
    INTERIOR DESIGN 1990 Jan., v.61,
    no.1, p.202-205, photos., plan.

UNITED STATES--DANIA (FLORIDA)--
SHOWROOMS--LIGHTING--KOCH & LOWY /
PAF SHOWROOM
  Koch & Lowy PAF Florida showroom /
    Justin Henderson.
    Interiors of lighting showroom in
    the Design Center of the Americas,
    Dania, Florida. Designer: Piotr
    Sierakowski.
    INTERIORS 1990 Oct., v.150, no.3,
    p.24, photos.

UNITED STATES--DAYTON (OHIO)--HISTORIC
HOUSE MUSEUMS--DUNBAR HOUSE
  The Paul Laurence Dunbar House,
    America's first publicly owned
    Afro-American historic site / W.
    Ray Luce.
    In Dayton, Ohio, purchased by the
    state in 1936.
    CRM BULLETIN: A NATIONAL PARK
    SERVICE TECHNICAL BULLETIN 1990,
    v.13, no.1, p.15-18, port., photo.

UNITED STATES--DECORATION AND
ORNAMENT--20TH CENTURY
  The "pique" of perfection / Donna
    Sapolin.
    On the revival of a folk art
    technique (pique assiette) using
    pottery and glass fragments. Work
    shown includes that of Robert
    Bellamy, a Dallas landscape
    designer.
    METROPOLITAN HOME 1990 July, v.21,
    no.7, p.76-80,106, port., photos.

UNITED STATES--DECORATORS' SHOW HOUSES
  Great beginnings [1990 showhouse
    winners].
    Winners from a variety of
    decorators' showhouses in 1990:
    Frank Babb Randolph; Barbara
    Ostrom; Noel Jeffrey; Taylor
    Johnson; Manijeh Emery; Winnie
    Levin; C. Smith Grubbs; Thomas
    Bartlett; Arnold Copper; Richard
    E. Eustice; Carolyn Bronson and
    Georgiana Stockel.
    HOUSE BEAUTIFUL 1990 Oct., v.132,
    no.10, p.73-85, photos.

UNITED STATES--DEKALB (ILLINOIS)--
MOVIE THEATERS--EGYPTIAN REVIVAL--
CONSERVATION AND RESTORATION--
EGYPTIAN THEATER
  Restoring dreams / Mark Alden
    Branch, Abby Bussel.
    On the restoration of six 1920-30s
    American movie palaces.
    PROGRESSIVE ARCHITECTURE 1990
    June, v.71, no.6, p.92-99,
    photos., plans, secns.

UNITED STATES--DELAND (FLORIDA)--
PUBLIC BUILDINGS--VOLUSIA COUNTY
ADMINISTRATIVE CENTER
  On axis with the past: a new
    administration center by Spillis
    Candela & Partners / Clifford A.
    Pearson.
    Volusia Co. Administrative Center,
    DeLand, Fla.
    ARCHITECTURAL RECORD 1990 June,
    v.178, no.7, p.[61-77], photos,
    plans.

UNITED STATES--DENTON (TEXAS)--
COURTHOUSES--19TH CENTURY--
ALTERATIONS AND ADDITIONS--DENTON
COUNTY COURTHOUSE
  Denton County Courthouse.
    Restoration of 1895 courthouse in
    Denton. Original architect: W.
    C. Dodson. Restoration architect:
    Ward Bogard & Associates.
    TEXAS ARCHITECT 1990 Jan.-Feb.,
    v.40, no.1, p.33, photos.

UNITED STATES--DENVER (COLORADO)--
AFFORDABLE HOUSING--PARIS HOTEL
BUILDING
  Recipe for reuse: disparate tenants
    strike harmony in an enterprising
    Denver rehab / Kim Keister.
    The 1891 Paris Hotel Building now
    houses a restaurant and affordable
    apartments. Original architect:
    Richard Phillips. Architect for
    renovation: Bill Adams.
    HISTORIC PRESERVATION 1990
    July-Aug., v.42, no.4, p.56-[57],
    photo.

UNITED STATES--DENVER (COLORADO)--
AIRPORTS--DENVER INTERNATIONAL
AIRPORT
  El aeropuerto internacional de
    Denver.
    URBANISMO / COAM 1990 May, no.10,
    p.96-103, graphs, dwgs., map,
    photo., plans, site plan, tables,
    aerial photo.
  Denver: taxiing for takeoff /
    Douglas R. Porter.
    Development proposals for Denver
    sparked by planning for the new
    international airport.
    URBAN LAND 1990 Sept., v.49, no.9,
    p.32-34, plans.
  Way out yonder, a new airport is
    taking shape [Denver] / Ruth
    Eckdish Knack.
    On the new Denver International
    Airport, planned for 1993, and the
    existing Stapleton Airport.
    PLANNING 1990 Apr., v.56, no.4,
    p.20-25, axonometric views, dwgs.,
    ports., photo., plans.

UNITED STATES--DENVER (COLORADO)--
AIRPORTS--STAPLETON AIRPORT
  Way out yonder, a new airport is
    taking shape [Denver] / Ruth
    Eckdish Knack.
    On the new Denver International
    Airport, planned for 1993, and the
    existing Stapleton Airport.
    PLANNING 1990 Apr., v.56, no.4,
    p.20-25, axonometric views, dwgs.,
    ports., photo., plans.

UNITED STATES--DENVER (COLORADO)--
ARCHITECTURE
Denver: the city beautiful and its
architects, 1893-1941 [by] Thomas
J. Noel, Barbara S. Norgren [book
review] / Gail Fenske.
SOCIETY OF ARCHITECTURAL
HISTORIANS. JOURNAL 1990 Sept.,
v.49, no.3, p.347-349,

UNITED STATES--DENVER (COLORADO)--
CAMPUS PLANNING--AURARIA HIGHER
EDUCATION CENTER
The Auraria campus: an example of
American landscape design / Hermke
Helsper...et al.
The characteristics of
contemporary American campus
design are explored in a case
study of the Auraria campus,
Denver, Colo.
LANDSCAPE AND URBAN PLANNING 1990
Apr., v.19, no.1, p.1-16, photo.,
plans, secns., site plans, refs.

UNITED STATES--DENVER (COLORADO)--
CAMPUSES--AURARIA HIGHER EDUCATION
CENTER
The Auraria campus: an example of
American landscape design / Hermke
Helsper...et al.
The characteristics of
contemporary American campus
design are explored in a case
study of the Auraria campus,
Denver, Colo.
LANDSCAPE AND URBAN PLANNING 1990
Apr., v.19, no.1, p.1-16, photo.,
plans, secns., site plans, refs.

UNITED STATES--DENVER (COLORADO)--
CITIES AND TOWNS
Denver nuggets / Suzanne Weiss.
PLANNING 1990 Apr., v.56, no.4,
p.[6-12], map, photo.
Denver: the city beautiful and its
architects, 1893-1941 [by] Thomas
J. Noel, Barbara S. Norgren [book
review] / Gail Fenske.
SOCIETY OF ARCHITECTURAL
HISTORIANS. JOURNAL 1990 Sept.,
v.49, no.3, p.347-349,

UNITED STATES--DENVER (COLORADO)--
COMPREHENSIVE PLANS
Denver: taxiing for takeoff /
Douglas R. Porter.
Development proposals for Denver
sparked by planning for the new
international airport.
URBAN LAND 1990 Sept., v.49, no.9,
p.32-34, plans.

UNITED STATES--DENVER (COLORADO)--
HISTORIC PRESERVATION
Exploring Denver: the preservation
movement in the Mile High City is
gaining newfound vitality / Tim
McGovern.
HISTORIC PRESERVATION 1990
Jan.-Feb., v.42, no.1, p.14-18,
photo.

UNITED STATES--DENVER (COLORADO)--
HOTELS--VICTORIAN--ALTERATIONS AND
ADDITIONS--PARIS HOTEL
Recipe for reuse: disparate tenants
strike harmony in an enterprising
Denver rehab / Kim Keister.
The 1891 Paris Hotel Building now
houses a restaurant and affordable
apartments. Original architect:
(Continued next column)

UNITED STATES--DENVER (COLORADO)--
HOTELS--VICTORIAN--ALTERATIONS AND
ADDITIONS--PARIS HOTEL (CONTINUED)
Recipe for reuse:...(CONTINUED)
Richard Phillips. Architect for
renovation: Bill Adams.
HISTORIC PRESERVATION 1990
July-Aug., v.42, no.4, p.56-[57],
photo.

UNITED STATES--DENVER (COLORADO)--
MUNICIPAL BUILDINGS--PERMITTING
CENTER
Civic facelift: synthetic stucco
uplifts a permit center / M.
Stephanie Stubbs.
New face and use for the former
Univ. of Denver Law Library.
Architects: C.W. Fentress &
Associates.
ARCHITECTURE: THE AIA JOURNAL 1990
Mar., v.79, no.3, p.173-175,
dets., photos., plan.

UNITED STATES--DENVER (COLORADO)--REAL
ESTATE DEVELOPMENT
Denver: taxiing for takeoff /
Douglas R. Porter.
Development proposals for Denver
sparked by planning for the new
international airport.
URBAN LAND 1990 Sept., v.49, no.9,
p.32-34, plans.

UNITED STATES--DENVER (COLORADO)--
UNIVERSITIES AND COLLEGES--
BUILDINGS--UNIVERSITY OF COLORADO,
DENVER--AURARIA HIGHER EDUCATION
CENTER--NORTH CLASSROOM BUILDING
Nuove aule per l'Universita del
Colorado = North Classroom
Building, Denver, Colorado /
Silvano Stucchi.
At the Auraria Higher Education
Center. Architect: Hoover Berg
Desmond. Includes English
translation; French, German and
Spanish summaries, p.[4].
L'INDUSTRIA DELLE COSTRUZIONI 1990
Oct., v.24, no.228, p.28-31,
photos., plans, site plans.
Una parete che invece si apre:
Blocco di aule per L'universita di
Denver, Colorado.
Architects: Studio Hoover Berg
Desmond.
ARCHITETTURA; CRONACHE E STORIA
1990 Apr., v.36, no.4(414),
p.284-285, axonometric view,
photos., site plan.

UNITED STATES DEPARTMENT OF STATE
FOREIGN BUILDINGS OPERATIONS
Safe diplomacy: security: new
safeguards established by the U.S.
State Department / Lynn Nesmith.
On 5 new U.S. embassy projects to
be built with security
requirements of the U.S. State
Dept. Foreign Buildings
Operations.
ARCHITECTURE: THE MAGAZINE OF THE
AMERICAN INSTITUTE OF ARCHITECTS
1990 May, v.79, no.5, p.78-83,
ill., elevs., models, secn., site
plans.

UNITED STATES--DES MOINES (IOWA)--CITY
PLANNING--COMPETITIONS
International Winter Cities 1990,
urban examples competition
enhancing the public realm of
Central Des Moines / Robert A.
Findlay.
An urban design collaboration by
Iowa State Univ. faculty and
students and P. Zingsheim won a
first place award.
IOWA ARCHITECT 1990 Winter, v.39,
no.4, p.16-19, ill., aerial photo.

UNITED STATES--DES MOINES (IOWA)--CITY
PLANNING--DES MOINES VISION PLAN
The Des Moines Vision Plan Project:
the American City: an
architectural continuum / Patricia
Zingsheim.
Plans by Agrest and Gandelsonas.
IOWA ARCHITECT 1990 Winter, v.39,
no.4, p.10-15, ill., ports.,
photos., site plans.

UNITED STATES--DES MOINES (IOWA)--
COMPREHENSIVE PLANS
An interview with Mario Gandelsonas:
"The American City; an
architectural continuum / Patricia
Zingsheim, Gregory Quick.
Gandelsonas is heading a 3-year
study of Des Moines, to culminate
in a new master plan.
IOWA ARCHITECT 1989 Winter, v.38,
no.5, p.30-33, ill., ports.,
sketch.

UNITED STATES--DES MOINES (IOWA)--
CORPORATE OFFICE BUILDINGS--GENEX
Industrial redux: GenEx / Mark E.
Blunck.
Corporate headquarters created in
an old warehouse. (Phase II).
Architects: Herbert Lewis Kruse
Blunck Architecture.
IOWA ARCHITECT 1990 Spring, v.39,
no.1, p.14-[15], photos., plan.

UNITED STATES--DES MOINES (IOWA)--
HOUSES--20TH CENTURY--COPPOLA HOUSE
Coppola residence: the right stuff /
Linda Mason Hunter.
"Neo-modern" house, Des Moines.
Architectures Wells Woodburn
O'Neil.
IOWA ARCHITECT 1990 Spring, v.39,
no.1, p.23, photo.

UNITED STATES--DES MOINES (IOWA)--
HOUSES--ART DECO--CONSERVATION AND
RESTORATION--BUTLER HOUSE
The Butler House: due respect / Mark
E. Blunck.
Renovations and addition to a
50-yr. old "house of tomorrow."
Architects: Wells Woodburn O'Neil.
IOWA ARCHITECT 1990 Spring, v.39,
no.1, p.22, photo.
Deco Moderne adapted: Des Moines's
famed Butler Mansion finds new
life as an advertising firm /
Jonathan Walters.
Original architect (1937): George
Kraetsch. Architects for
renovation: Wells, Woodburn, and
O'Neil.
HISTORIC PRESERVATION 1990
Jan.-Feb., v.42, no.1, p.64-65,
photo.

UNITED STATES--DES MOINES (IOWA)--
HOUSES--ART DECO--CONSERVATION AND
RESTORATION--BUTLER HOUSE
                (CONTINUED)
Streamlined reborn in Des Moines /
   Mark E. Blunck.
   Restoration and addition to Butler
   House, built in the 1930s at Fleur
   Drive and Bell Ave., for use by
   Kragie/Newell Advertising.
   Restoration architects: Douglas A.
   Wells and Michael J. Kastner.
   INLAND ARCHITECT 1990 Mar.-Apr.,
   v.34, no.2, p.65-[68], photos.

UNITED STATES--DES MOINES (IOWA)--
HOUSES--CRAFTSMAN--ALTERATIONS AND
ADDITIONS--HUNTER HOUSE
A Midwestern homestead house: living
   the simple life / Linda Mason
   Hunter.
   Back porch addition to a 1910
   house in Des Moines, Iowa.
   Architect for addition: William J.
   Wagner.
   IOWA ARCHITECT 1990 Summer, v.39,
   no.2, p.32-33, ill., photos.,
   biblio.

UNITED STATES--DES MOINES (IOWA)--
LOBBIES--ALTERATIONS AND ADDITIONS--
HUBBELL BUILDING
Hubbell Building lobby: A timely
   entrance / Linda Mason Hunter.
   In Des Moines. Brooks Borg and
   Skiles Architects-Engineers.
   IOWA ARCHITECT 1990 Spring, v.39,
   no.1, p.25, photos.

UNITED STATES--DES MOINES (IOWA)--
MUNICIPAL BUILDINGS--DES MOINES
WATER WORKS PUBLIC UTILITIES
HEADQUARTERS
Des Moines Water Works Public
   Utilities Headquarters: A
   thoughtful reflection / Robert
   Tibbetts.
   Shiffler Frey Baldwin Architects.
   IOWA ARCHITECT 1990 Spring, v.39,
   no.1, p.24, photo.

UNITED STATES--DES MOINES (IOWA)--
OFFICE BUILDINGS--801 GRAND AVENUE
801 Grand Avenue, Des Moines, Iowa,
   USA, 1990.
   44 story office building;
   architects: Hellmuth, Obata &
   Kassabaum, with Brook, Borg &
   Skiles. Text in Japanese and
   English.
   ARCHITECTURE AND URBANISM 1990
   Dec., no.12 extra edition
   p.168-[171], photos., plans.

UNITED STATES--DES MOINES (IOWA)--
OFFICES--KRAGIE NEWELL ADVERTISING
Streamlined reborn in Des Moines /
   Mark E. Blunck.
   Restoration and addition to Butler
   House, built in the 1930s at Fleur
   Drive and Bell Ave., for use by
   Kragie/Newell Advertising.
   Restoration architects: Douglas A.
   Wells and Michael J. Kastner.
   INLAND ARCHITECT 1990 Mar.-Apr.,
   v.34, no.2, p.65-[68], photos.

UNITED STATES--DES MOINES (IOWA)--
PEDESTRIAN TUNNELS
Principal Park: a park with
   principles / Debra Kurtz.
   Urban park in downtown Des Moines.
   Architects: Brooks Borg and
   Skiles.
   IOWA ARCHITECT 1989 Winter, v.38,
   no.5, p.22-25, photos, site plan.

UNITED STATES--DES MOINES (IOWA)--
PENTHOUSES--CONSERVATION AND
RESTORATION
Collected fortunes: Penthouse
   renovation, Des Moines, Iowa /
   Lynn Spears.
   Architects: Herbert Lewis Kruse
   Blunck.
   IOWA ARCHITECT 1990 Summer, v.39,
   no.2, p.14-[17], photos., plans.

UNITED STATES--DES MOINES (IOWA)--
PUBLIC BUILDINGS--STATE OF IOWA
HISTORICAL BUILDING
State of Iowa Historical Building:
   modern history / Robert Tibbetts.
   Architect: Brown Healey Bock.
   IOWA ARCHITECT 1989 Winter, v.38,
   no.5, p.26-29, photos, plans.

UNITED STATES--DES MOINES (IOWA)--
RAISED PEDESTRIAN WALKWAYS--VETERANS
AUDITORIUM AND ALLIED GROUP SKYWALK
CONNECTIONS
Lofty expectations / Robert
   Tibbetts.
   Veterans Auditorium and Allied
   Group Skywalk Connections, Des
   Moines, Iowa. Architects: Herbert
   Lewis Kruse Blunck Architecture.
   IOWA ARCHITECT 1989 Winter, v.38,
   no.5, p.18-[21], photos.
Veterans Auditorium and Allied Group
   Skywalk Connections: Reaching new
   heights / Robert Tibbetts.
   Herbert Lewis Kruse Blunck
   Architecture.
   IOWA ARCHITECT 1990 Spring, v.39,
   no.1, p.16-[17], photos., plan.

UNITED STATES--DES MOINES (IOWA)--
RETIREMENT HOMES--WESLEY GRAND
Grand design: Wesley Grand / Dennis
   Rodkin.
   Retirement apartment housing, Des
   Moines. Architects: Wells Woodburn
   O'Neil.
   IOWA ARCHITECT 1990 Summer, v.39,
   no.2, p.20-23, photos., plans,
   secn.

UNITED STATES--DES MOINES (IOWA)--
STUDENT UNIONS--ALTERATIONS AND
ADDITIONS--DRAKE UNIVERSITY--OLMSTED
CENTER
Flying colors: Olmsted Center
   renovation, Drake University /
   Linda Mason Hunter.
   Stouffer and Smith Architects.
   IOWA ARCHITECT 1990 Fall, v.39,
   no.3, p.12-[15], photos., plan.

UNITED STATES--DES MOINES (IOWA)--TALL
BUILDINGS--HISTORY
Iowa tallest buildings: tallest in
   town / John Zeller.
   IOWA ARCHITECT 1990 Winter, v.39,
   no.4, p.20-23, dwgs., elevs.,
   photos.

UNITED STATES--DES MOINES (IOWA)--
UNIVERSITIES AND COLLEGES--
BUILDINGS--DRAKE UNIVERSITY--LAW
SCHOOL LEGAL CLINIC
Legal precedence: Law School Legal
   Clinic, Drake University, Des
   Moines, Iowa / Robert Tibbetts.
   Architects: Herbert Lewis Kruse
   Blunck Architecture.
   ARCHITECTURE: THE AIA JOURNAL 1990
   Feb., v.79, no.2, p.84-85, photos,
   plans.

UNITED STATES--DES MOINES (IOWA)--
URBAN PARKS--PRINCIPAL PARK
Principal Park: a park with
   principles / Debra Kurtz.
   Urban park in downtown Des Moines.
   Architects: Brooks Borg and
   Skiles.
   IOWA ARCHITECT 1989 Winter, v.38,
   no.5, p.22-25, photos, site plan.

UNITED STATES--DESERT HIGHLANDS
(ARIZONA)--COURTYARD HOUSES--WINANDY
HOUSE
Antoine Predock architect [houses].
   Contents: Winandy house, Desert
   Highlands, Arizona, 1988-89 --
   Rose house, Desert Highlands,
   Arizona, 1987-89. Architect:
   Antoine Predock. Text in Japanese
   and English.
   GA HOUSES 1990 Mar., no.28,
   p.67-71, axonometric views,
   elevs., models, plans, secns.

UNITED STATES--DESERT HIGHLANDS
(ARIZONA)--HOUSES--ROSE HOUSE
Antoine Predock architect [houses].
   Contents: Winandy house, Desert
   Highlands, Arizona, 1988-89 --
   Rose house, Desert Highlands,
   Arizona, 1987-89. Architect:
   Antoine Predock. Text in Japanese
   and English.
   GA HOUSES 1990 Mar., no.28,
   p.67-71, axonometric views,
   elevs., models, plans, secns.

UNITED STATES--DESIGN
Design 100: the people, products,
   ideas that shape our lives.
   "Special issue." Architects
   mentioned include Venturi and
   Scott Brown, Robert A. M. Stern,
   Frank Gehry, Richard Meier,
   Morphosis, Coop Himmelblau, Andres
   Duany + Elizabeth Plater-Zyberk,
   Stanley Tigerman and Margaret
   McCurry, Eric Owen Moss, Charles
   Warren, Michael Graves, Peter
   Eisenman, and Lake/Flato
   Architects.
   METROPOLITAN HOME 1990 Apr., v.22,
   no.4, p.[67-199], ports., photos.

UNITED STATES--DESIGN--20TH CENTURY--
HISTORY
The complete Eames [book review] /
   Ray Leigh.
   Review of: Eames design, by John
   and Marilyn Neuhart and Ray Eames,
   pub. 1989.
   ROYAL SOCIETY OF ARTS, LONDON. RSA
   JOURNAL 1990 May, v.138, no.5406,
   p.438-439, photos.
Eames design: the work of the office
   of Charles and Ray Eames by James
   Neuhart, Marilyn Neuhart and Ray
   Eames [book review] / Craig
   Hodgetts.

(Continued next page)

UNITED STATES--DESIGN--20TH CENTURY--
HISTORY (CONTINUED)
Eames design: the...(CONTINUED)
AA FILES 1990 Autumn, no.20,
p.108-109.

UNITED STATES--DETACHED HOUSES
The flexible house: designing for
changing needs / Deborah A. Howe.
AMERICAN PLANNING ASSOCIATION.
JOURNAL 1990 Winter, v.56, no.1,
p.69-76, dwg., plans, site plan,
refs.

UNITED STATES--DETROIT (MICHIGAN)--
AIRPORT TERMINALS--WAYNE COUNTY
AIRPORT--NORTHWEST AIRLINES
Northwest Airlines World Travel
Center, Wayne County Airport,
Detroit, Michigan, USA, 1990.
Competition design; architects:
Hellmuth, Obata & Kassabaum. Text
in Japanese and English.
ARCHITECTURE AND URBANISM 1990
Dec., no.12 extra edition,
p.214-217, dwgs., model, plans,
site plans.

UNITED STATES--DETROIT (MICHIGAN)--
ARTS AND CRAFTS MOVEMENT
Modern mosaic: the rebirth of
Pewabic Pottery / Daniel Cohen.
1907 ceramics studio in Detroit is
once again producing quality
objects.
HISTORIC PRESERVATION 1990
Mar.-Apr., v.42, no.2, p.30-35,78,
port., photos.

UNITED STATES--DETROIT (MICHIGAN)--
AUDITORIUMS, CONCERT HALLS--
CONSERVATION AND RESTORATION--
ORCHESTRA HALL
Orchestra Hall, Detroit: C. Howard
Crane, architect / A. Craig
Morrison, Lucy Pope Wheeler.
Built 1919.
MARQUEE 1989, v.21, no.4, cover,
p.2-10, ill., dwg., elev.,
photos., plans, secns.

UNITED STATES--DETROIT (MICHIGAN)--
CHURCHES--CONSERVATION AND
RESTORATION
Struggle continues to save Detroit,
Chicago churches / Bonnie
DeSimone.
PRESERVATION NEWS 1990 Mar., v.30,
no.3, p.7,19.

UNITED STATES--DETROIT (MICHIGAN)--
MOVIE THEATERS--CONSERVATION AND
RESTORATION--FOX THEATER
Restoring dreams / Mark Alden
Branch, Abby Bussel.
On the restoration of six 1920-30s
American movie palaces.
PROGRESSIVE ARCHITECTURE 1990
June, v.71, no.6, p.92-99,
photos., plans, secns.

UNITED STATES--DOWNERS GROVE
(ILLINOIS)--RESIDENTIAL GARDENS--
NOWICKI GARDEN
Solarized surroundings / Peggy
Rector.
A low-maintenance garden replaced
the lawn of the Nowicki house,
Downers Grove, Ill. Landscape
architect: Ron Nowicki.
GARDEN DESIGN 1990 summer, v.9,
no.2, p.76-79, port., photo.,
plan.

UNITED STATES--DRUMMOND ISLAND
(MICHIGAN)--BOWLING ALLEYS--DRUMMOND
ISLAND BOWLING CENTER
Domino's effect / Michael J.
Crosbie.
On buildings designed for Thomas
Monaghan, president of Domino's
Pizza. Architects: Gunnar
Birkerts, Mockbee Coker
Architects, Hardy Holzman Pfeiffer
Associates, Fay Jones + Maurice
Jennings Architects, and Charles
W. Moore.
ARCHITECTURE: THE AIA JOURNAL 1990
Dec., v.79, no.12, p.[48-55],127,
dwgs., port., models, photos.,
secn., site plans.

UNITED STATES--DRUMMOND ISLAND
(MICHIGAN)--CHAPELS--20TH CENTURY--
OUTDOOR CHAPEL
Domino's effect / Michael J.
Crosbie.
On buildings designed for Thomas
Monaghan, president of Domino's
Pizza. Architects: Gunnar
Birkerts, Mockbee Coker
Architects, Hardy Holzman Pfeiffer
Associates, Fay Jones + Maurice
Jennings Architects, and Charles
W. Moore.
ARCHITECTURE: THE AIA JOURNAL 1990
Dec., v.79, no.12, p.[48-55],127,
dwgs., port., models, photos.,
secn., site plans.

UNITED STATES--DRUMMOND ISLAND
(MICHIGAN)--HOTELS
Domino's effect / Michael J.
Crosbie.
On buildings designed for Thomas
Monaghan, president of Domino's
Pizza. Architects: Gunnar
Birkerts, Mockbee Coker
Architects, Hardy Holzman Pfeiffer
Associates, Fay Jones + Maurice
Jennings Architects, and Charles
W. Moore.
ARCHITECTURE: THE AIA JOURNAL 1990
Dec., v.79, no.12, p.[48-55],127,
dwgs., port., models, photos.,
secn., site plans.

UNITED STATES--DRUMMOND ISLAND
(MICHIGAN)--HOUSES--MONAGHAN HOUSE
Una scultura per abitare = Sculpture
for living / Michele Bazan
Giordano.
Marge Monaghan house, Drummond
Island, Mich. Architect: Gunnar
Birkerts.
L'ARCA 1990 Mar., no.36, p.60-63,
axonometric views, elevs., model,
plans, secns., site plan.

UNITED STATES--DUBLIN (NEW
HAMPSHIRE)--HOUSES--ARCHITECTS'--
SCULLY HOUSE
Scully house, Dublin, New Hampshire,
1981.
Architect & owner: Daniel V.
Scully. Text in Japanese and
English.
GA HOUSES 1990 July, no.29,
p.144-147, elevs., photos., plans,
secns., site plan.

UNITED STATES--DUBLIN (OHIO)--THEATERS
Sound education / Michael Wagner.
On the conversion of a high school
gymnasium into a community and
high school theater, Dublin, Ohio.
Architects: SEM Partners with
Jaffe Acoustics.
INTERIORS 1990 Jan., v.149, no.6,
p.56, photo., plan, secn.

UNITED STATES--DURHAM (NORTH
CAROLINA)--AFFORDABLE HOUSING
A simple formula for producing
affordable detached housing /
James W. Wentling.
Examples in Crystal Meadows and
Breckenridge, both in Durham,
North Carolina. Architects: James
Wentling Architects.
URBAN LAND 1990 May, v.49, no.5,
p.2-5, dwg., photo., plans,
tables.

UNITED STATES--DURHAM (NORTH
CAROLINA)--DETACHED HOUSES
A simple formula for producing
affordable detached housing /
James W. Wentling.
Examples in Crystal Meadows and
Breckenridge, both in Durham,
North Carolina. Architects: James
Wentling Architects.
URBAN LAND 1990 May, v.49, no.5,
p.2-5, dwg., photo., plans,
tables.

UNITED STATES--DURHAM (NORTH
CAROLINA)--HOUSING DEVELOPMENTS
A simple formula for producing
affordable detached housing /
James W. Wentling.
Examples in Crystal Meadows and
Breckenridge, both in Durham,
North Carolina. Architects: James
Wentling Architects.
URBAN LAND 1990 May, v.49, no.5,
p.2-5, dwg., photo., plans,
tables.

UNITED STATES--DUTCHESS COUNTY (NEW
YORK)--CARRIAGE HOUSES
New twist to the farmhouse
vernacular in New York / Paul
Goldberger.
On the stable and coach house
addition to a Dutchess Co. horse
farm. Architects:: Tigerman
McCurry. Architects of older main
house: Albert Kahn Associates.
ARCHITECTURAL DIGEST 1990 June,
v.47, no.6, p.86,90,94, dwg.,
elevs., model, photos., plans.

UNITED STATES--DUTCHESS COUNTY (NEW
YORK)--HORSE FARMS--ALTERATIONS AND
ADDITIONS
New twist to the farmhouse
vernacular in New York / Paul
Goldberger.
On the stable and coach house
addition to a Dutchess Co. horse
farm. Architects:: Tigerman
McCurry. Architects of older main
house: Albert Kahn Associates.
ARCHITECTURAL DIGEST 1990 June,
v.47, no.6, p.86,90,94, dwg.,
elevs., model, photos., plans.

UNITED STATES--DUTCHESS COUNTY (NEW
  YORK)--STABLES
  New twist to the farmhouse
    vernacular in New York / Paul
    Goldberger.
  On the stable and coach house
    addition to a Dutchess Co. horse
    farm. Architects:: Tigerman
    McCurry. Architects of older main
    house: Albert Kahn Associates.
  ARCHITECTURAL DIGEST 1990 June,
    v.47, no.6, p.86,90,94, dwg.,
    elevs., model, photos., plans.

UNITED STATES--EAGLE PASS (TEXAS)--
  BORDER STATIONS--BORDER PATROL
  STATION
  A bullet-proof welcome [border
    stations] / Natalye Appel.
  B & M Bridge Station, Brownsville
    (RioGroup Architects & Planners,
    Joneskell Architects); and Border
    Patrol Station, Eagle Pass
    (O'Neill & Perez).
  TEXAS ARCHITECT 1990 July-Aug.,
    v.40, no.4, p.38-41, elev.,
    photos., plan, secn., site plan.

UNITED STATES--EAST AURORA (NEW
  YORK)--ARTIST COLONIES--ROYCROFT
  CAMPUS
  Outlook brightens for saving
    Roycroft Inn and Roycroft Campus,
    East Aurora, N.Y. / Edward J.
    Healy.
  PRESERVATION NEWS 1990 May, v.30,
    no.5, p.6, photo.

UNITED STATES--EAST AURORA (NEW
  YORK)--INNS--ROYCROFT INN
  Outlook brightens for saving
    Roycroft Inn and Roycroft Campus,
    East Aurora, N.Y. / Edward J.
    Healy.
  PRESERVATION NEWS 1990 May, v.30,
    no.5, p.6, photo.

UNITED STATES--EAST HAMPTON (NEW
  YORK)--AIRPORT TERMINALS--EAST
  HAMPTON AIRPORT
  Tra terra e cielo = High terminal.
    Project for East Hampton Airport
    terminal; architect: Lester
    Korzilius. Text in Italian and
    English.
  L'ARCA 1990 June, no.39 suppl.
    l'Arca 2, p.102, elevs., model,
    plans, secns.

UNITED STATES--EAST HAMPTON (NEW
  YORK)--AIRPORTS--COMPETITIONS--EAST
  HAMPTON AIRPORT
  Fear of flying in East Hampton /
    Peter Papademetriou.
  On the controversy surrounding the
    competition and ultimate defeat of
    the appropriation for the East
    Hampton, N. Y. airport.
  PROGRESSIVE ARCHITECTURE 1990
    Jan., v.71, no.1, p.27,34, model.

UNITED STATES--EAST HAMPTON (NEW
  YORK)--COUNTRY HOUSES--DANIELSON
  HOUSE
  East Hampton, N. Y.: English
    enclave.
  Sven Danielson house, built 1810.
  COLONIAL HOMES 1990 Apr., v.16,
    no.2, p.[68-73], photos.

UNITED STATES--EAST HAMPTON (NEW
  YORK)--COUNTRY HOUSES--INTERIOR
  DESIGN--WENNER HOUSE
  Jann Wenner's retreat / Steven M. L.
    Aronson.
  Interiors of renovated country
    house in East Hampton. Architects
    for the renovation: Pietro
    Cicognani, Ann Kalla.
  ARCHITECTURAL DIGEST 1990 July,
    v.47, no.7, p.168-[174],186,
    port., photos.

UNITED STATES--EAST HAMPTON (NEW
  YORK)--HISTORIC HOUSE MUSEUMS--HOME
  SWEET HOME MUSEUM
  Home Sweet Home [Payne house, East
    Hampton, N.Y.].
  Saltbox house, built ca. 1715, now
    a museum.
  COLONIAL HOMES 1990 June, v.16,
    no.3, p.76-[81], port., photos.

UNITED STATES--EAST HAMPTON (NEW
  YORK)--HOUSES--19TH CENTURY
  East Hampton, N.Y.: meetinghouse
    revived.
  1860 Quaker meetinghouse now a
    private home.
  COLONIAL HOMES 1990 Apr., v.16,
    no.2, p.[90-95], photos.

UNITED STATES--EAST HAMPTON (NEW
  YORK)--HOUSES--COLONIAL REVIVAL--
  PASCUCCI-PURCELL HOUSE
  East Hampton, N. Y.: shingled
    showpiece.
  Pascucci-Purcell house, built in a
    Colonial style.
  COLONIAL HOMES 1990 Apr., v.16,
    no.2, p.[74]-79,136, photos.

UNITED STATES--EAST HAMPTON (NEW
  YORK)--SALTBOX HOUSES--18TH
  CENTURY--GOLDMAN HOUSE
  East Hampton, N. Y.: Connecticut
    transplant.
  Goldman house, a 1787 saltbox
    moved from Conn.
  COLONIAL HOMES 1990 Apr., v.16,
    no.2, p.[80]-89,136, photo.

UNITED STATES--EAST HAMPTON (NEW
  YORK)--SALTBOX HOUSES--COLONIAL--
  PAYNE HOUSE
  Home Sweet Home [Payne house, East
    Hampton, N.Y.].
  Saltbox house, built ca. 1715, now
    a museum.
  COLONIAL HOMES 1990 June, v.16,
    no.3, p.76-[81], port., photos.

UNITED STATES--EAST HAMPTON (NEW
  YORK)--SYNAGOGUES--20TH CENTURY--
  GATES OF THE GROVE SYNAGOGUE
  Schlicht ergreifend / Vera Graaf.
    Features East Hampton, N.Y.
    synagogue, Gates of the Grove
    (1988). Architect: Norman Jaffe.
  ARCHITEKTUR & WOHNEN 1990
    June-July, no.3, p.126-131,
    photos., elev., plans.
  La serittura e la luce = The written
    word and the light [Grove
    Synagogue, East Hampton, N.Y.].
    Architect: Norman Jaffe.
  ARCHITETTURA; CRONACHE E STORIA
    1990 July-Aug., v.36,
    no.7-8(417-418), p.556-557,
    photos., plan, secn., site plan.

UNITED STATES--EAST HAMPTON (NEW
  YORK)--SYNAGOGUES--20TH CENTURY--
  GATES OF THE GROVE SYNAGOGUE
  (CONTINUED)
  To gather together: Building types
    study 674: religious buildings /
    Margaret Gaskie.
  Four projects: Gates of the Grove
    Synagogue, East Hampton, N.Y.
    (Norman Jaffe); Beach United
    Methodist Church, Jacksonville
    Beach, Fla. (William Morgan
    Architects); Blackhawk Bapist
    Church, Fort Wayne, Ind.(Harding
    Assoc.); and St. Peter's Catholic
    Church, Olney, Md. (Hugh N.
    Jacobsen).
  ARCHITECTURAL RECORD 1990 Jan.,
    v.178, no.1, 123-135, elevs.,
    photos., plans, secns., site
    plans.

UNITED STATES--EAST HAMPTON (NEW
  YORK)--VILLAGES
  East Hampton, N. Y.: village by the
    dunes.
  COLONIAL HOMES 1990 Apr., v.16,
    no.2, p.64-[67],136, map, photo.

UNITED STATES--EAST HAMPTON (NEW
  YORK)--WEEKEND HOUSES
  Architecture: Gwathmey Siegel &
    Associates / Kurt Andersen.
  East Hampton weekend house,
    including guesthouse on 4-acre
    beachfront site. Architect:
    Charles Gwathmey.
  ARCHITECTURAL DIGEST 1990 May,
    v.47, no.5, p.[206-213],276,
    photos., site plan.

UNITED STATES--EAU CLAIRE
  (WISCONSIN)--HOUSES--RESEARCH
  The character of place: building
    materials and architectural
    characteristics in Eau Claire,
    Wisconsin / Ingolf Vogeler.
  Analysis of house styles
    (1860's-1970's) using field
    observations and data obtained
    from the assessor's office.
  MATERIAL CULTURE 1990 Spring,
    v.22, no.1, p.1-21, graphs, maps,
    biblio.

UNITED STATES--EDINA (MINNESOTA)--
  HOUSES--20TH CENTURY--ALTERATIONS
  AND ADDITIONS--FRENCH HOUSE
  Living on borrowed light: a family
    discovers its roots through
    architecture.
  Redesign of a 1970 split-level for
    the French family, Edina.
    Architect: Cheryl Fosdick.
  ARCHITECTURE MINNESOTA 1990
    May-June, v.16, no.3, p.38-41,
    photos.

UNITED STATES--EDINA (MINNESOTA)--
  STORES--FURNITURE--ROOM & BOARD
  Contemporary tempo: a new Room &
    Board steps to the beat of the
    '90s with light, energy and color.
    Edina home furnishings store.
    Architect: Martha Yunker.
  ARCHITECTURE MINNESOTA 1990
    Jan.-Feb., v.16, no.1, p.38-39,
    photos.

UNITED STATES--EVERGREEN (COLORADO)--
HOUSES--20TH CENTURY--DAVENPORT
HOUSE
  Art and Craft: Davenport house,
    Evergreen, Colorado / Donald J.
    Canty.
    Architects: Fay Jones & Maurice
    Jennings Architects.
    ARCHITECTURAL RECORD 1990
    Mid-Apr., v.178, no.5, p.70-[77],
    dets., elevs., photos., plans.

UNITED STATES--EVERGREEN
(WASHINGTON)--UNIVERSITIES AND
COLLEGES--BUILDINGS--ALTERATIONS AND
ADDITIONS--EVERGREEN STATE COLLEGE--
ART STUDIO AD
  Northwest passage: regional
    portfolio: the Pacific Northwest.
    Six recent projects: Two Union
    Sq., Seattle (NBBJ Group);
    Washington Mutual Tower, Seattle
    (Kohn Pedersen Fox, McKinley
    Architects); Pacific First Centre,
    Seattle (Callison Partnership);
    Evergreen State College Studio
    addition, Olympia (Miller/Hull
    Partnership); Larry's Market,
    Kirkland, Wash. (Carlson/Ferrin);
    and Andover Park, Beaverton, Ore.
    (Fisher-Friedman Associates).
    ARCHITECTURAL RECORD 1990 May,
    v.178, no.6, p.84-93, dwg.,
    photos., plans, secns., site
    plans.

UNITED STATES--EXCELSIOR SPRINGS
(MISSOURI)--POLICE STATIONS
  Peaceful coexistence: a municipal
    building complements the historic
    character of a former resort /
    Lawrence Goldblatt.
    Excelsior Springs, Mo., Police
    Station. Architect: Gastinger
    Rees Walker Architects.
    ARCHITECTURE: THE AIA JOURNAL 1990
    Feb., v.79, no.2, p.76-[77],
    photos., plan.

UNITED STATES--EXETER (NEW
HAMPSHIRE)--LIBRARIES--PHILLIPS
EXETER ACADEMY--LIBRARY
  Louis I. Kahn and the library:
    genesis and expression of "form" /
    Peter Kohane.
    Three projects, one unbuilt and
    one altered, all for schools:
    Washington University, St. Louis;
    Phillips Exeter Academy, Exeter
    N.H.; Graduate Theological Union,
    Berkeley.
    VIA 1990, no.10, p.[98]-131,
    models, photos., plans, secns.,
    sketches, refs.

UNITED STATES--FAIR OAKS (VIRGINIA)--
STORM WATER RETENTION BASINS--HIGH
RIDGE OFFICE PARK
  A stormwater pond is wetlands
    mitigation amenity.
    Stormwater management results in
    expanded and protected wetlands
    environment at High Ridge Office
    Park, Fair Oaks, Va. Engineers and
    designers: Greenhorne & O'Mara.
    URBAN LAND 1990 Dec., v.49, no.12,
    p.28-29, plan, secns.

UNITED STATES--FAIR OAKS (VIRGINIA)--
STREAMS--ENVIRONMENTAL ASPECTS--HIGH
RIDGE OFFICE PARK
  A stormwater pond is wetlands
    mitigation amenity.
    Stormwater management results in
    expanded and protected wetlands
    environment at High Ridge Office
    Park, Fair Oaks, Va. Engineers and
    designers: Greenhorne & O'Mara.
    URBAN LAND 1990 Dec., v.49, no.12,
    p.28-29, plan, secns.

UNITED STATES--FAIR OAKS (VIRGINIA)--
WETLANDS--CONSERVATION AND
RESTORATION--HIGH RIDGE OFFICE PARK
  A stormwater pond is wetlands
    mitigation amenity.
    Stormwater management results in
    expanded and protected wetlands
    environment at High Ridge Office
    Park, Fair Oaks, Va. Engineers and
    designers: Greenhorne & O'Mara.
    URBAN LAND 1990 Dec., v.49, no.12,
    p.28-29, plan, secns.

UNITED STATES--FAIRFAX COUNTY
(VIRGINIA)--LAKES--ENVIRONMENTAL
ASPECTS--FAIR LAKES OFFICE PARK
  A lake for many purposes / David
    Cheek.
    Lake water used for heating and
    cooling of mixed-used office
    complex in Fairfax Co., Va.
    DEVELOPMENT 1990 Sept.-Oct., v.21,
    no.5, p.14-15, diagr., photos.,
    secn.

UNITED STATES--FAIRFAX COUNTY
(VIRGINIA)--OFFICE COMPLEXES--
HEATING AND VENTILATION--FAIR LAKES
OFFICE PARK
  A lake for many purposes / David
    Cheek.
    Lake water used for heating and
    cooling of mixed-used office
    complex in Fairfax Co., Va.
    DEVELOPMENT 1990 Sept.-Oct., v.21,
    no.5, p.14-15, diagr., photos.,
    secn.

UNITED STATES--FAIRFAX COUNTY
(VIRGINIA)--WATERWORKS--FAIR LAKES
OFFICE PARK
  A lake for many purposes / David
    Cheek.
    Lake water used for heating and
    cooling of mixed-used office
    complex in Fairfax Co., Va.
    DEVELOPMENT 1990 Sept.-Oct., v.21,
    no.5, p.14-15, diagr., photos.,
    secn.

UNITED STATES--FAIRFIELD BAY
(ARKANSAS)--HOUSES--20TH CENTURY--
WATSON HOUSE
  Jones + Jennings: Watson residence,
    testimonianza organica = organic
    testimony.
    Watson house, Fairfield Bay, Ark.
    ARCHITETTURA: CRONACHE E STORIA
    1990 Sept., v.36, no.9(419),
    p.642-643, elev., photos., plans.
  Solid gold: AIA's gold medalist is
    honored for his distinctive
    American design / Robert A. Ivy,
    Jr.
    The work of gold medalist Fay
    Jones: Watson house Fairfield Bay,
    Ark.; Worship center at Thorncrown
    Chapel, Eureka Springs, Ark.;
    Pinecote Pavilion, Picayune, Miss.
    (Continued next column)

UNITED STATES--FAIRFIELD BAY
(ARKANSAS)--HOUSES--20TH CENTURY--
WATSON HOUSE (CONTINUED)
  Solid gold: AIA's... (CONTINUED)
    ARCHITECTURE: THE AIA JOURNAL 1990
    Mar., v.79, no.3, p.82-[89],
    port., elev., photos., plan.

UNITED STATES--FAIRFIELD COUNTY
(CONNECTICUT)--HOUSES--VICTORIAN--
ALTERATIONS AND ADDITIONS--NAFF
HOUSE
  Past perfected / Elizabeth H.
    Hunter.
    Family-room addition to Victorian
    house in Fairfield Co., Conn.
    Owner and designer: Sue Naff.
    Kitchen designer: Beverly Ellsley.
    HOUSE BEAUTIFUL 1990 Sept., v.132,
    no.9, p.80-83, photos., plan.

UNITED STATES--FAIRFIELD (IOWA)--
HOUSES--20TH CENTURY--MARCUS HOUSE
  A dot on the horizon: the Marcus
    residence / Robert Tibbetts.
    In Fairfield, Iowa. Architects:
    Lawlor/Weller Design Group.
    IOWA ARCHITECT 1990 Summer, v.39,
    no.2, p.28-[31], photos., plans.

UNITED STATES--FALLS CHURCH
(VIRGINIA)--KIOSKS--ONE CAMBRIDGE
COURT
  [Concierge-security kiosk] / Kristen
    Richards.
    Located in atrium of Falls Church,
    Virginia office building, One
    Cambridge Court. Architect: Todd
    Lee.
    INTERIORS 1990 Oct., v.150, no.3,
    p.20-21, photo., secn.

UNITED STATES--FARMERS BRANCH
(TEXAS)--PLAYGROUNDS--ALL CHILDREN'S
PLAYGROUND
  Designing play for all / Frances
    Arroyo.
    The "All Children's Playground" in
    Farmers Branch, Texas.
    PARKS & RECREATION 1990 Aug.,
    v.25, no.8, p.40-43, ports.,
    photos.

UNITED STATES--FARMHOUSES--19TH
CENTURY--SOCIOLOGICAL ASPECTS
  Families and farmhouses in
    Nineteenth-century America [by]
    Sally McMurry [book review] /
    Bernard L. Herman.
    WINTERTHUR PORTFOLIO 1990 Autumn,
    v.25, no.2-3, p.194-196, refs.
  Families and farmhouses in
    nineteenth-century America:
    vernacular design and social
    change [by] Sally McMurry [book
    review] / J. Ritchie Garrison.
    SOCIETY OF ARCHITECTURAL
    HISTORIANS. JOURNAL 1990 Sept.,
    v.49, no.3, p.353-354.

UNITED STATES--FEDERAL AID TO
COMMUNITY DEVELOPMENT
  Creating more dynamic public
    housing: a modest proposal /
    Frederick Brown.
    JOURNAL OF HOUSING 1990 Nov-Dec.,
    v.47, no.6, p.309-11,314-315,
    charts, ports.

UNITED STATES--FENWICK (CONNECTICUT)--
HOUSES--INTERIOR DESIGN--HEPBURN
HOUSE
  Katharine Hepburn: four-time Best
    Actress in New York, Connecticut
    and California / A. Scott Berg.
    ARCHITECTURAL DIGEST 1990 Apr.,
    v.47, no.4, p.192-[197],292,294,
    ports., photos.

UNITED STATES--FERNDALE (CALIFORNIA)--
ARCHITECTURE--VICTORIAN
  Victoriana West: California's
    Humboldt County claims some of the
    finest Victorian architecture in
    the country / Suzie Boss.
    HISTORIC PRESERVATION 1990
    Jan.-Feb., v.42, no.1, p.60-63,
    photos.

UNITED STATES--FERNDALE (CALIFORNIA)--
HISTORIC HOUSE MUSEUMS--LINDEN HALL
  Victorian summer travel.
    Features buildings in Ferndale,
    Calif. (including Linden Hall),
    the Olallieberry Inn, Cambria,
    Calif., and Patton House Inn,
    Wooster, Ark.
    VICTORIAN HOMES 1990 Summer, v.9,
    no.3, p.[65]-70,72,74, photos.

UNITED STATES--FESTIVAL MARKETPLACES
  Urban alchemist: Benjamin Thompson
    turns downtown decay into gold /
    Andrea Oppenheimer Dean.
    HISTORIC PRESERVATION 1990
    July-Aug., v.42, no.4, p.12-15,
    port.

UNITED STATES--FILM SETS
  Anton Furst: architecture at the
    movies.
    COLUMBIA UNIVERSITY. GRADUATE
    SCHOOL OF ARCHITECTURE, PLANNING
    AND PRESERVATION. NEWSLINE 1990
    Feb., v.2, no.5, p.2, dwgs.,
    port., photos.
  Lights, camera, Living room/ Pilar
    Viladas.
    Interior sets for the movies of
    Merchant and Ivory.
    HOUSE & GARDEN 1990 Sept., v.162,
    no.9, p.[160-167], ports.,
    photos.,

UNITED STATES--FINLAND (MINNESOTA)--
SCHOOLS--SPECIAL--WOLF RIDGE
ENVIRONMENTAL LEARNING CENTER
  Rooms with a view: Setter Leach &
    Lindstrom gives young people a
    front-row seat in nature's
    classroom.
    Wolf Ridge Environmental Learning
    Center, Finland, Minnesota.
    ARCHITECTURE MINNESOTA 1990
    Sept.-Oct., v.16, no.5, p.26-29,
    photos., site plan.

UNITED STATES--FIREBOATS--HISTORY
  Dogwatch: [fireboats] / James R.
    Delgado.
    Reviews history of fireboats in
    the US since 1866.
    CRM BULLETIN: A NATIONAL PARK
    SERVICE TECHNICAL BULLETIN 1989,
    v.12, no.6, p.9-10, dwgs., photo.

UNITED STATES--FISHERS ISLAND (NEW
YORK)--HOUSES--HOUSE AT WILDERNESS
POINT
  House at Wilderness Point, Fishers
    Island, New York, 1986-.
    Shingle style house. Architects:
    Robert A.M. Stern Architects. Text
    in Japanese and English.
    GA HOUSES 1990 Mar., no.28,
    p.108-109, elevs., plan, secns.,
    site plan.

UNITED STATES--FISHERS ISLAND (NEW
YORK)--VACATION HOUSES--MCKIM HOUSE
  Haunted house [McKim house, Fishers
    Island, NY] / Thomas Fisher.
    Vacation house. Architects: Mark
    Simon and Leonard Wyeth of
    Centerbrook Architects.
    PROGRESSIVE ARCHITECTURE 1990
    Nov., v.71, no.12, p.70-73,
    photos., plans, secn., site plan.

UNITED STATES--FLEMINGTON (NEW
JERSEY)--RESIDENTIAL GARDENS--
WOODRUFF GARDEN
  Perennially surprising / Walter
    Chandoha.
    Residential garden in Flemington,
    N.J.
    HOUSE BEAUTIFUL 1990 Aug., v.132,
    no.8, p.[64-67], photos., plan.

UNITED STATES--FLOORS--18TH CENTURY--
WOODEN
  Notes on historic flooring: an 18th
    century method for making high
    quality wooden flooring from
    boards of irregular thickness /
    Lee H. Nelson.
    CRM BULLETIN: A NATIONAL PARK
    SERVICE TECHNICAL BULLETIN 1990,
    v.13, no.4, p.27-28, dwg., photo.,
    secns.

UNITED STATES--FLORIDA--CITIES AND
TOWNS--GROWTH
  Ideal urban form and visions of the
    good life: Florida's growth
    management dilemma / Ivonne
    Audirac, Anne H. Shermyen, Marc T.
    Smith.
    AMERICAN PLANNING ASSOCIATION.
    JOURNAL 1990 Autumn, v.56, no.4,
    p.470-482, photos., tables, aerial
    photos., refs.

UNITED STATES--FLORIDA--CITY
PLANNING--ENVIRONMENTAL ASPECTS
  Ideal urban form and visions of the
    good life: Florida's growth
    management dilemma / Ivonne
    Audirac, Anne H. Shermyen, Marc T.
    Smith.
    AMERICAN PLANNING ASSOCIATION.
    JOURNAL 1990 Autumn, v.56, no.4,
    p.470-482, photos., tables, aerial
    photos., refs.

UNITED STATES (FLORIDA)--CONSTRUCTION
INDUSTRY
  Down to the wire in Florida / John
    Koenig.
    Growth management legislation in
    Fla.
    PLANNING 1990 Oct., v.56, no.10,
    p.4-11, port., maps, photos.,
    sketch, aerial photo

UNITED STATES--FLORIDA--ENVIRONMENTAL
PROTECTION
  Balancing new development with
    conservation of wetlands in
    Florida / James R. Brindell.
    URBAN LAW AND POLICY 1988, v.9,
    no.4, p.331-344, biblio.

UNITED STATES--FLORIDA--HOUSES--
ARCHITECT'S--VILLARDEA (DOGGETT
HOUSE)
  Modern translation: ancient Persian
    architecture flavors a Florida
    villa / Colin Campbell.
    Home of architect Jane Davis
    Doggett, called Villardea.
    SOUTHERN ACCENTS 1990 July-Aug.,
    v.13, no.6, p.[66-75], port.,
    photos.

UNITED STATES--FLORIDA--HOUSES--
GRAYSON HOUSE
  Coming in from the sun [Florida
    house].
    Interior designer: William
    Hodgins.
    HOUSE BEAUTIFUL 1986 June, v.128,
    no.6, p.[76-81], photos.

UNITED STATES--FLORIDA--HOUSES--
INTERIOR DESIGN
  Tropical verve in Florida: scale and
    spirit shape a residence on the
    Gulf of Mexico / Gael Greene.
    Architect: Kasimir Korybut.
    Interior designer: Thomas Britt.
    ARCHITECTURAL DIGEST 1990 July,
    v.47, no.7, p.84-91, photos.

UNITED STATES (FLORIDA)--HOUSES--
STUDENT PROJECTS
  Design for sustainability at Seaside
    / Gary Coates.
    Student design studio projects.
    OZ / COLLEGE OF ARCHITECTURE AND
    DESIGN, KANSAS STATE UNIVERSITY
    1989, v.11, p.48-51, elevs.,
    plans, secn., site plans, refs.

UNITED STATES--FLORIDA--HOUSING
  Ideal urban form and visions of the
    good life: Florida's growth
    management dilemma / Ivonne
    Audirac, Anne H. Shermyen, Marc T.
    Smith.
    AMERICAN PLANNING ASSOCIATION.
    JOURNAL 1990 Autumn, v.56, no.4,
    p.470-482, photos., tables, aerial
    photos., refs.

UNITED STATES--FLORIDA--ISLANDS
  Architecture on the edge / Stephen
    D. Schreiber.
    On the landscape in South Florida
    and the boundaries (barrier
    islands, coastal ridge and
    landfill) that have influenced the
    constructed environment.
    CRIT 1990 Spring, no.24, p.16-20,
    refs.

UNITED STATES--FLORIDA KEYS
(FLORIDA)--UNDERWATER ARCHAEOLOGY--
SAN PEDRO WRECK SITE
  Establishing an underwater
    archaeological preserve in the
    Florida Keys: a case study [San
    Pedro wreck site] / Roger C.
    Smith, Robert Finegold, Eric
    Stephens.
    The New Spain Fleet was wrecked
    along the Florida Keys in 1733.
                      (Continued next page)

UNITED STATES--FORT WORTH (TEXAS)--
MUSEUMS--ART--ALTERATIONS AND
ADDITIONS--KIMBELL ART MUSEUM
(CONTINUED)
Giurgola's Kimbell addition draws
fire / Barbara L. Koerble.
ARCHITECTURE: THE AIA JOURNAL 1990
Jan., v.79, no.1, p.[35]-36,
photo.
Kimbell addition plea [letter] /
Philip Johnson...et al.
Copy of letter sent to Mrs. Ben J.
Fortson, director of the Kimbell
Art Foundation which calls for a
reconsideration of the addition
proposal.
PROGRESSIVE ARCHITECTURE 1990
Jan., v.71, no.1, p.9.
Kimbell plan draws prominent
criticism / Barbara L. Koerble.
Opposition to proposed addition to
Kimbell Art Museum. Architect:
Romaldo Giurgola.
TEXAS ARCHITECT 1990 Jan.-Feb.,
v.40, no.1, p.10, dwg.
Kimbell plans ambushed in New York /
Mark Alden Branch.
On the forum sponsored by New
York's Architectural League on
Mitchell Giurgola's proposed
addition to the Louis
Kahn-designed Kimbell Art Museum,
Fort Worth, TX.
PROGRESSIVE ARCHITECTURE 1990
Mar., v.71, no.3, p.23, model.
Museumserweiterung -- Imitation als
Architektursprache.
Kimbell Art Museum, Ft. Worth,
Tex.; Fundacio Miro, Barcelona;
and the Jewish Museum, New York.
Includes English summary.
BAUMEISTER 1990 Nov., v.87, no.11,
p.44-47, dwgs., models, photos.,
plans.
Report: Kimbell Art Museum expansion
abandoned / Barbara L. Koerble.
Original architect: Louis I. Kahn;
architects of proposed addition:
Mitchell Giurgola and Thorp. Text
in Japanese and English.
ARCHITECTURE AND URBANISM 1990
May, no.5(236), p.4-5, photo.
Report: Kimbell Art Museum expansion
/ Barbara Koerble.
Original architect: Louis I. Kahn;
architects of addition: Mitchell
Giurgola and Thorp. Text in
Japanese and English.
ARCHITECTURE AND URBANISM 1990
Feb., no.2(233), p.4-8, photos.,
plan, site plan.

UNITED STATES--FOUNTAIN HILLS
(ARIZONA)--HOUSES
Kamal Amin: dal Cairo all'Arizona,
sette opere organiche = from Cairo
to Arizona, seven organic works.
Houses in Va. and Ariz. and
medical centers in Tempe and
Scottsdale Ariz.
ARCHITETTURA: CRONACHE E STORIA
1990 Sept., v.36, no.9(419),
p.[612-634], dets., photos.,
plans, secns., site plans.

UNITED STATES--FRANKLIN (MICHIGAN)--
FARMHOUSES--GREEK REVIVAL--
CONSERVATION AND RESTORATION--
JOHNSON HOUSE
Greek Revival tragicomedy / Ruth
Mossok Johnson.
1840 farmhouse moved to Franklin,
MI.
OLD-HOUSE JOURNAL 1990 July-Aug,
v.18, no.4, p.53-56, photos.

UNITED STATES--FRANKLIN VILLAGE
(MICHIGAN)--HOUSES--19TH CENTURY--
ALTERATIONS AND ADDITIONS
Bridging space and time / Dale
Northup.
Addition to an 1859 farmhouse,
Franklin Village, Mich. Architect:
William Hartman.
INLAND ARCHITECT 1990 Mar.-Apr.,
v.34, no.2, p.44-45, photos.,
plan.

UNITED STATES--FREDRICKSBURG
(VIRGINIA)--WEEKEND HOUSES--HORNE
HOUSE
Designer's retreat. [Horne house,
Fredricksburg, Va.].
Interior designer: C. Larry Horne.
COLONIAL HOMES 1990 Oct., v.16,
no.5, p.[65]-71, photos.

UNITED STATES--FRESNO (CALIFORNIA)--
HOUSES--20TH CENTURY--SIMPSON HOUSE
Arthur Dyson: un architettura "del
luogo e del tempo" = An
architecture "of site and time".
Three U.S. houses.
ARCHITETTURA: CRONACHE E STORIA
1990 Oct., v.36, no.10(420),
p.[698]-[714], photos., plans,
secns.

UNITED STATES--FURNITURE--20TH CENTURY
Crafting a style / Patricia Conway.
Washington, D.C. apartment of Anne
and Ronald Abramson, collectors of
modern handmade furniture.
Interior designer: David M.
Schwarz/Architectural Services.
HOUSE & GARDEN 1990 Aug., v.162,
no.8, p.[118]-121,148, photos.

UNITED STATES--GAINESVILLE (FLORIDA)--
MEDICAL SCHOOLS--UNIVERSITY OF
FLORIDA--J. HILLIS MILLER HEALTH
CENTER
Academic Research Building, J.
Hillis Health Center, University
of Florida, Gainesville, Florida,
USA, 1990.
Architects: Hellmuth, Obata &
Kassabaum. Text in Japanese and
English.
ARCHITECTURE AND URBANISM 1990
Dec., no.12 extra edition,
p.172-177, photos., plan.

UNITED STATES--GAITHERSBURG
(MARYLAND)--NEW TOWNS--THE KENTLANDS
Breaking the code: urban design
portfolio / Beth Dunlop.
Small-town alternatives to
suburban sprawl, as offered by
Andres Duany and Elizabeth
Plater-Zyberk.
ARCHITECTURE: THE AIA JOURNAL 1990
Apr., v.79, no.4, p.80-83, ill.,
elev., plans, site plans.

UNITED STATES--GALVESTON ISLAND
(TEXAS)--BEACH HOUSES--CALDWELL
BEACH HOUSE
Houston design portfolio: slow
recovery.
Sesquicentennial Park (Team HOU);
Caldwell house (Natalye Appel);
Court at Museums Gate (Josiah
Baker); Gilliland house (Peter Jay
Zweig Architects); Finnell house
(Wittenberg Partnership); and St.
Mary's Episcopal Church (Gerald
Moorhead).
ARCHITECTURE: THE AIA JOURNAL 1990
Apr., v.79, no.4, p.54-73,
axonometric views, ill., elev.,
photos., plans, secns., site
plans.

UNITED STATES--GALVESTON (TEXAS)--
ARCHES--TEMPORARY--MARITIME ARCH
Rossi arch unveiled in Galveston /
Gerald Moorhead.
Maritime Arch. Architect: Aldo
Rossi.
PROGRESSIVE ARCHITECTURE 1990
Apr., v.71, no.4, p.29, photo.

UNITED STATES--GALVESTON (TEXAS)--
ARCHITECTURE--VICTORIAN
Building images: the pen and ink
drawings of Tom McNeff / Teresa
Byrne-Dodge.
A Houston artist and graphic
designer does drawings with the
quality of an engraving. Shown are
illustrations of 19th-cent.
Galveston architecture.
SOUTHERN ACCENTS 1989 July-Aug.,
v.12, no.4, p.128L-128R, dwgs.

UNITED STATES--GALVESTON (TEXAS)--
BOTANICAL GARDENS--MOODY GARDENS
The landscape of civilization as
experienced in the Moody
Historical Gardens [by] Geoffrey
Jellicoe [book review] / Sandra
Morris.
AA FILES 1990 Spring, no.19,
p.111,
Tree wishes [Sir Geoffrey Jellicoe]
/ Louise Rogers.
Latest work in the large oeuvre of
British landscape architect Sir
Geoffrey Jellicoe at Moody
Gardens, Galveston, Texas.
ARCHITECTS' JOURNAL 1990 Feb.14,
v.191, no.7, p.28-29, port.

UNITED STATES--GALVESTON (TEXAS)--
CAST-IRON FRONTS (ARCHITECTURE)--
RENAISSANCE REVIVAL
The Tremont House: an anchor of
architectural renewal in Galveston
/ Teresa Byrne-Dodge.
1879 block-long Renaissance
revival building on Ship
Mechanic's Row, notable for its
cast-iron facade. It was recently
renovated for use as a hotel.
Architects for renovation: Ford,
Powell and Carson.
SOUTHERN ACCENTS 1989 July-Aug.,
v.12, no.4, p.120-123, photos.

UNITED STATES--GALVESTON (TEXAS)--
HOTELS--TREMONT HOUSE
The Tremont House: an anchor of
architectural renewal in Galveston
/ Teresa Byrne-Dodge.
1879 block-long Renaissance
revival building on Ship
Mechanic's Row, notable for its
cast-iron facade. It was recently
renovated for use as a hotel.
Architects for renovation: Ford,
Powell and Carson.
SOUTHERN ACCENTS 1989 July-Aug.,
v.12, no.4, p.120-123, photos.

UNITED STATES--GALVESTON (TEXAS)--
MERCANTILE BUILDINGS--RENAISSANCE
REVIVAL--LEON & H. BLUM BUILDING
The Tremont House: an anchor of
architectural renewal in Galveston
/ Teresa Byrne-Dodge.
1879 block-long Renaissance
revival building on Ship
Mechanic's Row, notable for its
cast-iron facade. It was recently
renovated for use as a hotel.
Architects for renovation: Ford,
Powell and Carson.
SOUTHERN ACCENTS 1989 July-Aug.,
v.12, no.4, p.120-123, photos.

UNITED STATES--GARDEN CITIES--HISTORY
Developing and financing the 'garden
metropolis': urban planning and
housing policy in
twentieth-century America / Marc
A. Weiss.
"Examines the evolution of garden
city ideas in the U.S. during the
20th cent.", with emphasis on "the
central role of Thomas Adams, the
British planner who served as a
leading proponent of the garden
metropolis in the U.S.".
PLANNING PERSPECTIVES: PP 1990
Sept., v.5, no.3, p.307-319, refs.

UNITED STATES--GARDENS
Regional style: eco-logic at work.
A brief survey of six
"environmental" gardens in the
U.S. Landscape architects: Steven
K. Domigan, Edith Eddleman, Ron
Lutsco, Steve Trudnak, James Weht,
and David Cropp.
GARDEN DESIGN 1990 spring, v.9,
no.1, p.46-59, photos., site
plans, sketch.

UNITED STATES--GARDENS--20TH CENTURY
Garten der Zukunft? / Elke von
Radziewsky, Vera Graaf.
Features work by the following
American landscape architects:
Peter Walker, Martha Schwartz,
George Hargreaves, and Michael Van
Valkenburgh. english summary,
p.2-3.
ARCHITEKTUR & WOHNEN 1990
Oct.-Nov., no.5, p.90-[98],100,
ports., photos.

UNITED STATES--GARDENS--ENVIRONMENTAL
ASPECTS
Healing the Earth: how 20 years of
environmentalism have changed
American gardening / Cheryl Weber.
GARDEN DESIGN 1990 Spring, v.9,
no.1, p.30-35, photos.

UNITED STATES--GARDENS IN ART
Reminiscence and revival: the
old-fashioned garden, 1890-1910 /
Virginia Tuttle Clayton.
Discusses horticultural nostalgia
and a number of garden books, and
includes works by C. Hassam and
others.
ANTIQUES 1990 Apr., v.137, no.4,
p.[892]-905, photos., refs.

UNITED STATES--GARDENS--ITALIANATE--
DIRECTORIES
Published records of Italianate
gardens in America / Richard G.
Kenworthy.
A state-by-state listing of
gardens flourishing ca.1840-1940.
JOURNAL OF GARDEN HISTORY 1990
Jan.-Mar., v.10, no.1, p.[10]-70,
det., photos, plans, refs.

UNITED STATES--GASOLINE STATIONS
The future of pumping up / Philip
Berger.
On the design of gas stations,
particularly the Vista project by
PRAXIS Architects of San
Francisco.
INLAND ARCHITECT 1990 July-Aug.,
v.34, no.4, p.13,17, dwgs., photo.

UNITED STATES--GAY HEAD
(MASSACHUSETTS)--WEEKEND HOUSES--
ARCHITECTS'--KALKIN HOUSE
Architecture: Adam Kalkin / Robert
Campbell.
Kalkin weekend house in Gay Head,
Mass. composed of a 1820s Vermont
barn and steel industrial
warehouse, both of which were
shipped to the site. Architect:
Adam Kalkin.
ARCHITECTURAL DIGEST 1990 June,
v.47, no.6, p.172-177, port.,
model, photos.

UNITED STATES--GEOGRAPHIC INFORMATION
SYSTEMS
The evolution of spatial modeling in
the USA / Richard K. Brail.
EKISTICS 1989 Sept.-Dec., v.56,
no.338-339, p.249-253, refs.

UNITED STATES--GEOLOGY--HISTORY
Geology NHL theme study / Harry A.
Butowsky.
A new theme study by the National
Park Service's NHL Survey.
CRM BULLETIN: A NATIONAL PARK
SERVICE TECHNICAL BULLETIN 1990,
v.13, no.1, p.8-9, photos.

UNITED STATES--GEORGETOWN (COLORADO)--
MINING TOWNS
Looking for the mother lode: hard
lessons learned by the NPS /
Ronald W. Johnson, John C. Paige.
Describes controversy over a
National Park Service study for a
new National Historic Landmark in
Georgetown and Silver Plume,
Colo., 50 miles west of Denver.
CRM BULLETIN: A NATIONAL PARK
SERVICE TECHNICAL BULLETIN 1990,
v.13, no.4, p.18-20,

UNITED STATES--GEORGETOWN (TEXAS)--
CITY PLANNING
Zoning with intensity [Georgetown,
Texas] / Hildy L. Kingma.
PLANNING 1990 Oct., v.56, no.10,
p.18-21, graph, photos., plan.

UNITED STATES--GEORGETOWN (TEXAS)--
COMPREHENSIVE PLANS
Zoning with intensity [Georgetown,
Texas] / Hildy L. Kingma.
PLANNING 1990 Oct., v.56, no.10,
p.18-21, graph, photos., plan.

UNITED STATES--GEORGETOWN (TEXAS)--
ZONING
Zoning with intensity [Georgetown,
Texas] / Hildy L. Kingma.
PLANNING 1990 Oct., v.56, no.10,
p.18-21, graph, photos., plan.

UNITED STATES--GEORGIA--CITY PLANNING
Growth strategies: the new planning
game in Georgia / Arthur C.
Nelson.
CAROLINA PLANNING 1990 Fall, v.16,
no.2, p.4-8, port., map, table.

UNITED STATES--GEORGIA--LAND USE
Growth strategies: the new planning
game in Georgia / Arthur C.
Nelson.
CAROLINA PLANNING 1990 Fall, v.16,
no.2, p.4-8, port., map, table.

UNITED STATES--GEORGIA--REGIONAL
PLANNING
Growth strategies: the new planning
game in Georgia / Arthur C.
Nelson.
CAROLINA PLANNING 1990 Fall, v.16,
no.2, p.4-8, port., map, table.

UNITED STATES--GEYSERVILLE
(CALIFORNIA)--HEATING PLANTS--
PACIFIC GAS & ELECTRIC COMPANY
1990 AIA Component Awards: San
Francisco Chapter.
Three awards, one photo each.
ARCHITECTURE: THE MAGAZINE OF THE
AMERICAN INSTITUTE OF ARCHITECTS
1990 May, v.79, no.5, p.52,
photos.

UNITED STATES--GILLESPIE COUNTY
(TEXAS)--SCHOOLS--19TH CENTURY--
MORRIS RANCH SCHOOLHOUSE
The best little schoolhouse in Texas
/ Nancy Holmes.
On the Morris Ranch Schoolhouse,
built in 1893, near
Fredericksburg, TX. Architect:
Alfred Giles. The school is now
home to Frances Billup.
CONNOISSEUR 1990 May, v.220,
no.940, p.92-[97],148, port.,
photos.

UNITED STATES--GLASTONBURY
(CONNECTICUT)--HOUSES--COLONIAL--
JONATHAN HALE HOUSE
Designer at home [Jonathan Hale
House, Glastonbury, Conn.].
1750s house, home of Stuart and
Holly Holden.
COLONIAL HOMES 1990 Apr., v.16,
no.2, p.47-[54], port., photos.

UNITED STATES--GLASTONBURY
(CONNECTICUT)--SHOPPING CENTERS--
SHOPS AT SOMERSET SQUARE
Una plaza a la francesa: centro
comercial en Glastonbury,
Connecticut = A French-like
square.
Features shops at Somerset Square.
Architects: Robert A.M. Stern
Architects. English text, p.86.
A & V 1990, no.21, p.42-45,
elevs., maps, photos., site plans,
aerial photo.

UNITED STATES--GLENCOE (ILLINOIS)--
COUNTRY CLUBS--ALTERATIONS AND
ADDITIONS--LAKE SHORE COUNTRY CLUB
History in the making / Justin
Henderson.
Interiors of the renovated 1911
Lake Shore Country Club, Glencoe
Ill. Original architect: Howard
van Doren Shaw. Renovation
architect: John Vinci.
INTERIORS 1990 June, v.149, no.11,
p.100-103, photos., plan.

UNITED STATES--GLENDALE (ILLINOIS)--
POST OFFICES
Oh, say can you see... the post
office / Philip Berger.
In Glendale Heights, Ill.
Architect: Ross Barney/Jankowski
Architects.
INLAND ARCHITECT 1990 May-June,
v.34, no.3, p.17,20, photos.

UNITED STATES--GLENVIEW (ILLINOIS)--
GASOLINE STATIONS--MUNICIPAL FUELING
FACILITY
P/A Portfolio: the Chicago School:
today's curriculum / Philip
Arcidi.
Features two projects: Municipal
Fueling Facility, Glenview, Ill.,
architects: Lubotsky Metter
Worthington & Law; Illinois Bell
Telephone Remote Switching Unit,
Lincolnshire, Ill., architects:
Holabird and Root.
PROGRESSIVE ARCHITECTURE 1990
Feb., v.71, no.2, p.112-115,
photos., plan, site plan.

UNITED STATES--GLENVIEW (ILLINOIS)--
HOUSES--GOTHIC REVIVAL--KENNICOTT
HOUSE
Kennicott's Grove / David Newton.
250-acre estate in Glenview, Ill.
has one of the state's few
remaining praire groves. It is now
a national landmark and its Gothic
revival house has been restored as
a museum.
HISTORIC ILLINOIS 1990 Feb., v.12,
no.5, p.4-7, ports., photos.

UNITED STATES--GOOCHLAND COUNTY
(VIRGINIA)--HOUSES--20TH CENTURY--
GOSPODNETIC HOUSE
White house: Gospodnetic house,
Goochland County, Virginia / Lynn
Nesmith.
Interplan, Architect.
ARCHITECTURE: THE AIA JOURNAL 1990
Mar., v.79, no.3, p.146-149,
elevs., plans, secns.

UNITED STATES--GRAIN ELEVATORS--
ALTERATIONS AND ADDITIONS
Turning grain elevators into
prisons?
Proposal by The Eggers Group (TEG)
for additional prison space in New
York State, with applications
elsewhere.
URBAN LAND 1990 Jan., v.49, no.1,
p.28, secn.

UNITED STATES--GRANADA HILLS
(CALIFORNIA)--STORES--LIGHTING--
AMERICAN HOME VIDEO STORE
Lighting: American Home Video Store
in Granada Hills, Ca. / Justin
Henderson, Peter Barna.
Interior designer: Byron B. Savage
III.
INTERIORS 1989 Feb., v.148, no.7,
p.54-55, photos., plan.

UNITED STATES--GRAND MARAIS
(MINNESOTA)--LODGES--NANIBOUJOU
LODGE
Superior lodgings: Minnesota's
venerable Naniboujou Lodge / Karin
Winegar.
HOUSE & GARDEN 1990 Feb., v.162,
no.2, p.68, photos.

UNITED STATES--GRAND RAPIDS
(MICHIGAN)--CORPORATE OFFICE
BUILDINGS--STEELCASE CORPORATE
DEVELOPMENT CENTER
Steelcase's practical Pyramid /
Michael J. P. Smith.
The Corporate Development Center,
Grand Rapids, Mich. Architect:
WBDC Group and Donald J. Koster.
INLAND ARCHITECT 1990 Nov.-Dec.,
v.34, no.6, p.19-20, photo.,
secn., aerial photo.

UNITED STATES--GRAND RAPIDS
(MICHIGAN)--HOUSES--PRAIRIE SCHOOL--
CONSERVATION AND RESTORATION--MEYER
MAY HOUSE
Das Meyer May House in seiner
Umgebung: exzellente Restaurierung
eines "prairie house" von F.L.
Wright in Grand Rapids, Michigan /
Vincent Scully.
Funded by The Steelcase Co.
ARCHITEKTUR, INNENARCHITEKTUR,
TECHNISCHER AUSBAU 1990 Jan.-Feb.,
v.98, no.1-2, p.44-50, photos.,
plans.
The Wright way: restoration of the
Meyer May house / Amy Dana.
1909 house in Grand Rapids, Mich.,
now owned by Steelcase, Inc.
Original architect: Frank Lloyd
Wright. Restoration architects:
Tilton & Lewis Associates.
INTERIORS 1990 Jan., v.149, no.6,
p.160-[163], photos., plan.

UNITED STATES--GRAND RAPIDS
(MICHIGAN)--OFFICES--LIGHTING--
STEELCASE CORPORATE DEVELOPMENT
CENTER
Shadow free: new compact fluorescent
lamps and an even-newer indirect
lighting scheme / Joan F.
Blatterman.
Skylit spaces of Steelcase's
Corporate Development Center near
Grand Rapids. Architects: The WBDC
Group.
ARCHITECTURAL RECORD 1990 Mar.,
v.178, no.3, p.119-121, ill.,
photos.

UNITED STATES--GRANT COUNTY (NEW
MEXICO)--RANCHES--PRE-COLUMBIAN--
RUINED, EXTINCT, ETC.--NAN RANCH
RUIN
A Mimbres burial with associated
colon remains from the NAN ranch
ruin, New Mexico / Harry J.
Shafer, Marianne Marek, Karl J,
Reinhard.
A find dating from the 11th cent.,
in Grant County.
JOURNAL OF FIELD ARCHAEOLOGY 1989
Spring, v.16, no.1, p.17-30, map,
photos., site plan, tables,
biblio.

UNITED STATES--GRASS VALLEY
(CALIFORNIA)--COUNTRY HOUSES--19TH
CENTURY--EMPIRE MINE COTTAGE
Celebrating the holidays in Gold
Mine Country / Maureen Gilmer.
Features two northern California
buildings: Empire Mine Cottage,
Grass Valley (architect: Willis
Polk) and Red Castle Inn, Nevada
City (a brick Gothic revival house
on "Prospect Hill" built in 1857
for John Williams).
VICTORIAN HOMES 1990 Holidays,
v.9, no.5, p.38-[45], photos.

UNITED STATES--GREAT NECK (NEW YORK)--
PLAYGROUNDS
Spray pools: no wading / Richard A.
Arenella.
Spotlights a facility in Great
Neck, L.I. Project designers:
Sear-Brown Group.
PARKS & RECREATION 1990 Nov.,
v.25, no.11, p.30-33,71, ports.,
photos.

UNITED STATES--GREAT NECK (NEW YORK)--
POOLS
Spray pools: no wading / Richard A.
Arenella.
Spotlights a facility in Great
Neck, L.I. Project designers:
Sear-Brown Group.
PARKS & RECREATION 1990 Nov.,
v.25, no.11, p.30-33,71, ports.,
photos.

UNITED STATES--GREAT NECK (NEW YORK)--
WATERPARKS
Spray pools: no wading / Richard A.
Arenella.
Spotlights a facility in Great
Neck, L.I. Project designers:
Sear-Brown Group.
PARKS & RECREATION 1990 Nov.,
v.25, no.11, p.30-33,71, ports.,
photos.

UNITED STATES--GREAT SALT LAKE
(UTAH)--SALOONS--SALOON FOR JESSE
JAMES
Ins Gewicht fallend. Zwei
Balanceakte von Douglas Darden =
Tipping scales. Two balancing acts
by Douglas Darden.
Contents: Project for saloon,
Great Salt Lake, Utah --Project
for Temple Forgetful, at Romun
Romanum, Rome. Architect: Douglas
Darden.
DAIDALOS 1990 Sept.15, no.37,
p.100-105, dwg., elevs., model,
plans, secn.

UNITED STATES--GREENBELT CITIES
Clarence Stein and the greenbelt towns: settling for less / K. C. Parsons.
Architect and planner Clarence S. Stein's role in the formation of greenbelt towns during the New Deal.
AMERICAN PLANNING ASSOCIATION. JOURNAL 1990 Spring, v.56, no.2, p.161-183, dwg., ports., photo., plans, refs.

UNITED STATES--GREENBRAE (CALIFORNIA)--HOSPITALS--ALTERATIONS AND ADDITIONS--MARIN GENERAL HOSPITAL
Targeting treatment: Building Types Study 680, hospitals.
Uses 3 examples: Freeport Hospital Health Care Village, Kitchener, Ont. (NORR Partnership); Marin General Hospital Addition, Greenbrae, Calif. (Kaplan, McLaughlin, Diaz, Architects); and Lake Pavilion/Family Birth Center, Baptist Hospital of Miami (Ritchie Organization).
ARCHITECTURAL RECORD 1990 June, v.178, no.7, p.87-101, ill., photos., plans, site plans, aerial photo.

UNITED STATES--GREENSBORO (NORTH CAROLINA)--HOUSES--20TH CENTURY-- ALTERATIONS AND ADDITIONS--RAPP HOUSE
Source of civic pride: stunning addition for a well-loved Greensboro home / Susannah M. Wilson.
Rapp house. Architect: Bruce G. Sanders, interior designer Lindsay Henderson.
SOUTHERN ACCENTS 1990 Oct., v.13, no.8, p.106-111, port., photos.

UNITED STATES--GREENWAYS
The paths less traveled: a wrapup on the nations's greenways / Barry Didato.
Includes inset article: "How they did it in Boise and Denver", by Ruth Knack.
PLANNING 1990 Jan., v.56, no.1, p.6-10, ill., photos.

UNITED STATES--GREENWICH (CONNECTICUT)--HOUSES--19TH CENTURY--ALTERATIONS AND ADDITIONS-- HASCOE HOUSE
Intimate grandeur on the water: Shope Reno Wharton gives new life to a Connecticut mansion / Paul Goldberger.
Interiors of renovated 1880 waterfront home in Greenwich. Landmarked pedestrian bridge designed by John Augustus Roebling also on the site linking shore to nearby dock.
ARCHITECTURAL DIGEST 1990 Dec., v.47, no.13, p.[152-159], port., photos., plan.

UNITED STATES--GREENWICH (CONNECTICUT)--PEDESTRIAN BRIDGES-- 19TH CENTURY
Intimate grandeur on the water: Shope Reno Wharton gives new life to a Connecticut mansion / Paul Goldberger.
Interiors of renovated 1880 waterfront home in Greenwich. Landmarked pedestrian bridge designed by John Augustus Roebling also on the site linking shore to nearby dock.
ARCHITECTURAL DIGEST 1990 Dec., v.47, no.13, p.[152-159], port., photos., plan.

UNITED STATES--GRISWOLD (CONNECTICUT)--FARMHOUSES-- COLONIAL--CONSERVATION AND RESTORATION--VELEZ HOUSE
Connecticut yankee [Velez house, Griswold, Conn.].
The 1760 farmhouse has been recently restored.
COLONIAL HOMES 1990 June, v.16, no.3, p.61-67,146, photos.

UNITED STATES--GROUNDS--CONSERVATION AND RESTORATION
Principles for preserving historic plant material / Lauren Meier, Nora Mitchell.
Includes a section on preservation issues for living historic fabric, definitions for seven treatments, sources of additional information, and a bibliography.
CRM BULLETIN: A NATIONAL PARK SERVICE TECHNICAL BULLETIN 1990, v.13, no.6, p.17-24, photos., aerial photo., refs.

UNITED STATES--GROUP HOMES--LAW AND LEGISLATION
Saying yes to group homes / Thomas P. Smith.
Assessing local planning and zoning compliance.
PLANNING 1989 Dec., v.55, no.12, p.24-26, ports.

UNITED STATES--GUILFORD (CONNECTICUT)--HOUSES--COLONIAL-- JARED LEETE HOUSE
Guilford heirlooms. [Jared Leete House, Guilford, Conn.].
Built ca. 1774; now home to Guilford Forge Heirlooms.
COLONIAL HOMES 1990 Oct., v.16, no.5, p.[82]-87, ports., photos.

UNITED STATES--GUTHRIE (OKLAHOMA)-- BANKS--ALTERATIONS AND ADDITIONS-- GUTHRIE SAVINGS BANK
The Harrison House: a Victorian past reborn in Guthrie, Oklahoma / Norma McCutcheon.
Built in 1902 as a bank; now operated as a bed and breakfast inn. Located at 124 W. Harrison.
VICTORIAN HOMES 1990 Spring, v.9, no.2, p.86-88, photos.

UNITED STATES--GUTHRIE (OKLAHOMA)-- INNS--HARRISON HOUSE
The Harrison House: a Victorian past reborn in Guthrie, Oklahoma / Norma McCutcheon.
Built in 1902 as a bank; now operated as a bed and breakfast inn. Located at 124 W. Harrison.
VICTORIAN HOMES 1990 Spring, v.9, no.2, p.86-88, photos.

UNITED STATES--HABITAT--CONSERVATION AND RESTORATION
Habitats go home: replanting "wild" areas on residential sites / Georgia Tasker.
GARDEN DESIGN 1990 Spring, v.9, no.1, p.[36-45], photos., secns., site plan.
Regional style: eco-logic at work.
A brief survey of six "environmental" gardens in the U.S. Landscape architects: Steven K. Domigan, Edith Eddleman, Ron Lutsco, Steve Trudnak, James Weht, and David Cropp.
GARDEN DESIGN 1990 spring, v.9, no.1, p.46-59, photos., site plans, sketch.

UNITED STATES--HAMILTON TOWNSHIP (NEW JERSEY)--COUNTRY HOUSES--19TH CENTURY--KUSER FARM MANSION
A Victorian summer home: the Kuser Farm Mansion / Russell Roberts.
Built in 1892, in Hamilton Township, near Trenton, N.J.
VICTORIAN HOMES 1990 Summer, v.9, no.3, p.[50]-53, dets., photos.

UNITED STATES--HAMPTONS (NEW YORK)-- WEEKEND HOUSES--INTERIOR DESIGN
Primary motifs: William Diamond and Anthony Baratta rejuvenate a Victorian cottage with bold color and an eye for period detail / Sherrye Henry.
Interiors of a weekend house in the Hamptons.
HOUSE & GARDEN 1990 Aug., v.162, no.8, p.[80-87],153, photos.

UNITED STATES--HANOVER COUNTY (VIRGINIA)--FARMHOUSES--LOCKWOOD
Moving history: the struggle over Virginia must not end in "backsliding" / S. Watts Taylor.
Lockwood, Robert E. Lee's headquarters, has been sold to Media General which wants to move the house and this is being opposed.
PRESERVATION NEWS 1990 June, v.30, no.6, p.5, port., photo.

UNITED STATES--HANOVER (NEW HAMPSHIRE)--UNIVERSITIES AND COLLEGES--BUILDINGS--ALTERATIONS AND ADDITIONS--DARTMOUTH COLLEGE--THAYER SCHOOL OF ENGINEERING
Doble lenguaje: escuela de Ingenieria Thayer, New Hampshire = A two-fold language.
Addition ot the Thayer School of Engineering, Dartmouth College, Hanover, NH. Architects: Venturi, Scott Brown and Associates. English text, p.86.
A & V 1990, no.21, p.46-48, dwgs., elevs., models, plans, secn., site plans, sketches.

UNITED STATES--HARDING TOWNSHIP (NEW
JERSEY)--HOUSES--GROTTA HOUSE
Grotta Residence, Harding Township,
New Jersey, 1984-89.
Architects: Richard Meier &
Partners. Text in Japanese and
English.
GA HOUSES 1990 Mar., no.28,
p.46-47, axonometric view, plans,
site plan.

UNITED STATES--HARMON MEADOW (NEW
JERSEY)--PUBLISHING OFFICES--
INTERIOR DESIGN--MURDOCH MAGAZINES
Murdoch: Haines Lundberg Waehler
consolidates quarters / Edie Lee
Cohen.
Features new offices in Harmon
Meadow, N.J.
INTERIOR DESIGN 1990 Oct., v.61,
no.14, p.[234-239], photos.,
plans.

UNITED STATES--HARTFORD
(CONNECTICUT)--ARCHITECTURE
Architecture in the United States
[book review] / Rhodri Windsor
Liscombe, John Vincent Boyer,
William G. Farrar, IV, Robert
Winter.
Review of Charleston antebellum
architecture and civic destiny, by
Kenneth Severens; Structures and
styles: guided tours of Hartford
architecture, by Gregory E.
Andrews and David F. Ransom;
Vernacular architecture in
southern Illinois, by John M.
Coggeshall and Jo Anne Nast; and
Bruce Goff: toward aboslute
architecture, by David Delong.
SOCIETY OF ARCHITECTURAL
HISTORIANS. JOURNAL 1990 Mar.,
v.49, no.1, p.115-120,

UNITED STATES--HARTFORD
(CONNECTICUT)--BUILDINGS--19TH
CENTURY--CHENEY BLOCK
Hartford under siege: an editorial
report / Catherine Lynn.
On plans to demolish a number of
buildings for the new "Hartford
Town Center," including the Cheney
Block.
CONNECTICUT PRESERVATION NEWS 1989
July-Aug., v.12, no.4, p.[1]-2,
photo.

UNITED STATES--HARTFORD
(CONNECTICUT)--CULTURAL CENTERS--
UNIVERSITY OF HARTFORD--HARRY JACK
GRAY CENTER
Positive space: Tai Soo Kim's
multifaceted new complex presents
the University of Hartford with a
lively hub for cultural activities
/ Margaret Gaskie.
ARCHITECTURAL RECORD 1990 Feb.,
v.178, no.2, p.104-109, elevs.,
photos., plans, secns., site plans.

UNITED STATES--HARTFORD
(CONNECTICUT)--ENERGY EFFICIENT
BUILDINGS
Designing for energy efficiency /
Frank Juliano.
New energy-efficient design for a
Victorian-style house in Hartford,
Conn.
VICTORIAN HOMES 1990 Winter, v.9,
no.1, p.56-57, photos.

UNITED STATES--HARTFORD
(CONNECTICUT)--HISTORIC BUILDINGS--
DEMOLITION
Hartford under siege: an editorial
report / Catherine Lynn.
On plans to demolish a number of
buildings for the new "Hartford
Town Center," including the Cheney
Block.
CONNECTICUT PRESERVATION NEWS 1989
July-Aug., v.12, no.4, p.[1]-2,
photo.

UNITED STATES--HARTFORD
(CONNECTICUT)--HOUSES--VICTORIAN
REVIVAL--LAWSON HOUSE
Designing for energy efficiency /
Frank Juliano.
New energy-efficient design for a
Victorian-style house in Hartford,
Conn.
VICTORIAN HOMES 1990 Winter, v.9,
no.1, p.56-57, photos.

UNITED STATES--HARTFORD
(CONNECTICUT)--UNIVERSITIES AND
COLLEGES--BUILDINGS--UNIVERSITY OF
HARTFORD--HARRY JACK GRAY CENTER
Positive space: Tai Soo Kim's
multifaceted new complex presents
the University of Hartford with a
lively hub for cultural activities
/ Margaret Gaskie.
ARCHITECTURAL RECORD 1990 Feb.,
v.178, no.2, p.104-109, elevs.,
photos., plans, secns., site plan.

UNITED STATES--HAWAII--ARCHITECTURE--
PREHISTORIC
Monumental architecture and power in
Polynesian chiefdoms: a comparison
of Tonga and Hawaii / P.V. Kirch.
WORLD ARCHAEOLOGY 1990 Oct., v.22,
no.2, p.206-222, charts, maps,
table, aerial photo., biblio.

UNITED STATES--HEALDSBURG
(CALIFORNIA)--HOUSES
1990 AIA Component Awards: San
Francisco Chapter.
Three awards, one photo each.
ARCHITECTURE: THE MAGAZINE OF THE
AMERICAN INSTITUTE OF ARCHITECTS
1990 May, v.79, no.5, p.52,
photos.

UNITED STATES--HEALDSBURG
(CALIFORNIA)--HOUSES--SCHREYER HOUSE
Jennings and Stout Architects:
Schreyer residence, Healdsburg,
California, 1982-90.
Text in Japanese and English.
GA HOUSES 1990 Dec., no.30,
p.[136]-145, elevs., photos.,
plans, secns.

UNITED STATES--HEARY COUNTY
(INDIANA)--FARMS--VIEWS
Environmental cognition: the
prediction of preference in rural
Indiana / H. Randy Gimblett.
Research on the perception of
landscape, using a rural site in
Heary County, Ind. Includes
abstract.
JOURNAL OF ARCHITECTURAL AND
PLANNING RESEARCH 1990 Autumn,
v.7, no.3, p.222-234, photos.,
biblio.

UNITED STATES--HENNEPIN COUNTY
(MINNESOTA)--PLAYGROUNDS
Learning by the seat of your pants:
kids find a jungle gym to match
their imaginations at Hennepin
County regional parks.
Pictured is "Chutes and Ladders,"
a playground at Hyland Lake Parks
Reserve, Bloomington, Minn.
Landscape architect: Don King.
ARCHITECTURE MINNESOTA 1990
Sept.-Oct., v.16, no.5, p.32-33,
photos.

UNITED STATES--HERNDON (VIRGINIA)--
RESEARCH FACILITIES--CENTER FOR
INNOVATIVE TECHNOLOGY
Center for Innovative Technology,
Fairfax and Loudoun Counties,
Virginia: Arquitectonica,
Ward/Hall Associates.
Built 1989. Text in Japanese and
English.
GA DOCUMENT 1990 May, no.26,
p.[48]-55, photos., secn., site
plans.

UNITED STATES--HIGHLAND PARK
(ILLINOIS)--CAFES--INTERIOR DESIGN--
PINUCCIO
Cafe bravissimo / Justin Henderson.
Interiors of Pinuccio, cafe,
Highland Park, Ill. Architect:
Dario Tainer.
INTERIORS 1990 June, v.149, no.11,
p.104-[105], photos., plan.

UNITED STATES--HIGHLAND PARK
(ILLINOIS)--CITY HALLS--CONSERVATION
AND RESTORATION
Highland Park restoration project
completed: citizen "watchfulness"
salvation of City Hall cupola /
Maureen Nicolazzi, Mary Beth
Herr-Brandstrader.
Restoration of 1931 cupola.
HISTORIC ILLINOIS 1990 Dec., v.13,
no.4, p.4-5, photos.

UNITED STATES--HIGHLAND PARK
(ILLINOIS)--CUPOLAS--CONSERVATION
AND RESTORATION--CITY HALL
Highland Park restoration project
completed: citizen "watchfulness"
salvation of City Hall cupola /
Maureen Nicolazzi, Mary Beth
Herr-Brandstrader.
Restoration of 1931 cupola.
HISTORIC ILLINOIS 1990 Dec., v.13,
no.4, p.4-5, photos.

UNITED STATES--HIGHLAND PARK
(ILLINOIS)--HOUSES
Shingle style on the inland sea /
Karen E. Klages.
House in Highland Park, Ill.,
overlooking Lake Michigan.
Architect: Stuart Cohen and Anders
Nereim Architects.
INLAND ARCHITECT 1990 Mar.-Apr.,
v.34, no.2, p.46-49, photos.,
plans.
Wohnhaus Private Residence in
Highland Park.
Architects: Stuart Cohen &
Associates. Includes statement by
Cohen on his practice.
DEUTSCHE BAUZEITSCHRIFT 1990 May,
v.38, no.5, p.[650]-654, dets.,
dwgs., photos., plans, secn.,
sketches.

UNITED STATES--HIGHLAND PARK
  (ILLINOIS)--HOUSES--20TH CENTURY
  Una fetta di paradiso / Gilberto
  Oneto.
  House and gardens in Highland
  Park, Ill. Architects: The
  Dirsmith Group.
  VILLE GIARDINI 1990 May, no.248,
  p.62-69, dwgs., photos., aerial
  photos.

UNITED STATES--HIGHLAND PARK
  (ILLINOIS)--RESIDENTIAL GARDENS
  Una fetta di paradiso / Gilberto
  Oneto.
  House and gardens in Highland
  Park, Ill. Architects: The
  Dirsmith Group.
  VILLE GIARDINI 1990 May, no.248,
  p.62-69, dwgs., photos., aerial
  photos.

UNITED STATES--HINSDALE (ILLINOIS)--
  HOUSES
  The Zook look: a suburban fantasy /
  Michael J.P. Smith.
  Houses and stained glass windows
  by Hinsdale, Ill. architect:
  Roscoe Harold Zook (d.1949).
  INLAND ARCHITECT 1990 Mar.-Apr.,
  v.34, no.2, p.26, photos.

UNITED STATES--HISTORIC BUILDINGS--
  20TH CENTURY--EVALUATION
  Guidelines for evaluating and
  nominating properties that have
  achieved significance within the
  last fifty years / Marcella
  Sherfy, W. Ray Luce.
  NATIONAL REGISTER BULLETIN [1989],
  no.22, p.[1]-11, photos.

UNITED STATES--HISTORIC BUILDINGS--
  DIRECTORIES
  Historic houses, landmarks and
  museums: New England.
  A partial listing, the first in a
  series of five.
  ANTIQUES 1990 Apr., v.137, no.4,
  p.956-958, maps.

UNITED STATES--HISTORIC BUILDINGS--
  EVALUATION
  Guidelines for evaluating and
  documenting traditional cultural
  properties / Patricia L. Parker,
  Thomas F. King.
  How to evaluate the "traditional
  cultural significance" of a
  historic place.
  NATIONAL REGISTER BULLETIN [1990],
  no.38, entire issue (22 p.),
  photos., biblios., refs.

UNITED STATES--HISTORIC BUILDINGS--
  INVENTORIES
  HABS/HAER: a user's guide / Robert
  J. Kapsch.
  ASSOCIATION FOR PRESERVATION
  TECHNOLOGY. BULLETIN 1990, v.22,
  no.1-2, p.21-34, axonometric
  views, dets., elev., secns.,
  tables, isometric dwg., refs.
  Der Historic American Buildings
  Survey / Margaret Thomas Will.
  OSTERREICHISCHE ZEITSCHRIFT FUR
  KUNST UND DENKMALPFLEGE 1988,
  v.42, no.1-2, p.58-66, elevs.,
  photos., plans, secns., isometric
  dwg., refs.

UNITED STATES--HISTORIC BUILDINGS--
  MAINTENANCE AND REPAIR
  Lead-based paint in historic
  buildings / Camille M. Martone,
  Sharon C. Park.
  Discusses health hazards,
  detection, and abatement, and
  includes recommendations and
  precautions and a list of
  organizations and research sources
  for abatement.
  CRM BULLETIN: A NATIONAL PARK
  SERVICE TECHNICAL BULLETIN 1990,
  v.13, no.1, p.23-30, photo., refs.
  Rising damp in historic buildings
  II: case studies / Sharon C. Park.
  "Preservation Technology Update".
  CRM BULLETIN: A NATIONAL PARK
  SERVICE TECHNICAL BULLETIN 1990,
  v.13, no.3, p.23-27, photos.

UNITED STATES--HISTORIC BUILDINGS--
  MAINTENANCE AND REPAIR--STANDARDS
  The use of fire-rated wooden
  shingles on historic buidings /
  Sharon C. Park.
  Includes information on four
  organizations in the U.S. able to
  provide additional information.
  CRM BULLETIN: A NATIONAL PARK
  SERVICE TECHNICAL BULLETIN 1989,
  v.12, no.6, p.15-17, photo.

UNITED STATES--HISTORIC BUILDINGS--
  STUCCO--MAINTENANCE AND REPAIR
  Preservation and repair of historic
  stucco / Anne Grimmer.
  Adapted from a forthcoming
  "Preservation Brief".
  CRM BULLETIN: A NATIONAL PARK
  SERVICE TECHNICAL BULLETIN 1989,
  v.12, no.6, p.18-20, photos.

UNITED STATES--HISTORIC HOUSE
  MUSEUMS--VANDERBILT MANSIONS
  A surfeit of riches [book review].
  Review of: The Vanderbilts, by
  Jerry E. Patterson, 1990.
  COLONIAL HOMES 1990 June, v.16,
  no.3, p.16-28, dwgs., ports.,
  photos., engr.

UNITED STATES--HISTORIC LANDSCAPES--
  DOCUMENTATION
  Guidelines for evaluating and
  documenting rural historic
  landscapes / Linda Flint
  McClelland and J. Timothy Keller,
  Genevieve P. Keller, Robert Z.
  Melnick.
  NATIONAL REGISTER BULLETIN [1990],
  no.30, 33p., photos., maps, aerial
  photos., biblio.

UNITED STATES--HISTORIC LANDSCAPES--
  EVALUATION
  Guidelines for evaluating and
  documenting rural historic
  landscapes / Linda Flint
  McClelland and J. Timothy Keller,
  Genevieve P. Keller, Robert Z.
  Melnick.
  NATIONAL REGISTER BULLETIN [1990],
  no.30, 33p., photos., maps, aerial
  photos., biblio.

UNITED STATES--HISTORIC LANDSCAPES--
  STANDARDS
  The NPS Historic Landscape
  Initiative: developing national
  standards for the treatment of
  historic landscapes / Lauren G.
  Meier.
  CRM BULLETIN: A NATIONAL PARK
  SERVICE TECHNICAL BULLETIN 1990,
  v.13, no.2, p.12-13, biblio.

UNITED STATES--HISTORIC PRESERVATION
  Preserving African American
  heritage.
  PRESERVATION PERSPECTIVE NJ 1990
  May-June, v.9, no.3, p.[1]-2,
  photos.
  Who will care in the 1990s?: ethnic
  diversity will play a greater role
  in the preservation movement,
  particularly in urban
  neighborhoods / Michael A. Tomlan.
  PRESERVATION FORUM 1990 Winter,
  v.3, no.4, p.20-21, ill.

UNITED STATES--HISTORIC PRESERVATION--
  CONGRESSES
  Three perspectives on preservation
  planning / Bruce J. Noble, Jr.
  Summarizes three presentations
  about improving state and Federal
  management of cultural resources
  at the Preservation Challenges for
  the 1990s conference, held in
  Washington, June 5-7, 1990.
  Speakers were Pat Stein, Judy
  Propper, and Brit Storey.
  CRM BULLETIN: A NATIONAL PARK
  SERVICE TECHNICAL BULLETIN 1990,
  v.13, no.5, p.5-6, 17,

UNITED STATES--HISTORIC PRESERVATION--
  ECONOMIC ASPECTS
  The business of preservation is
  bullish and diverse / Sally
  Oldham.
  "Preservation's popular success
  has resulted in dramatic benefits
  for an ever-broadening industry."
  PRESERVATION FORUM 1990 Winter,
  v.3, no.4, p.14-19, graph, ill.,
  photos., refs.

UNITED STATES--HISTORIC PRESERVATION--
  METHODOLOGY
  Computer news: automation in the
  states / Betsy Chittenden.
  Report on two recent government
  studies of methods used in state
  historic preservation offices,
  including GIS, CAD, and AIPS
  (Automated Information Programs
  System).
  CRM BULLETIN: A NATIONAL PARK
  SERVICE TECHNICAL BULLETIN 1990,
  v.13, no.4, p.32.
  Design review and historic
  preservation / Michael B. Jackson.
  INLAND ARCHITECT 1990 Sept.-Oct.,
  v.34, no.5, p.104,99, dwg., photo.
  Federal Preservation Forum / Brit
  Allan Storey.
  Report on a meeting held in
  Denver, December (?) 1989, for the
  purpose of organizing the FPF,
  with objectives "To enhance the
  quality, efficiency, and economy
  in ...Federal historic
  preservation programs."
  CRM BULLETIN: A NATIONAL PARK
  SERVICE TECHNICAL BULLETIN 1990,
  v.13, no.5, p.7,

UNITED STATES--HISTORIC SITES
  Geology NHL theme study / Harry A.
  Butowsky.
    A new theme study by the National
    Park Service's NHL Survey.
    CRM BULLETIN: A NATIONAL PARK
    SERVICE TECHNICAL BULLETIN 1990,
    v.13, no.1, p.8-9, photos.

UNITED STATES--HISTORIC SITES--
CONSERVATION AND RESTORATION
  Principles for preserving historic
  plant material / Lauren Meier,
  Nora Mitchell.
    Includes a section on preservation
    issues for living historic fabric,
    definitions for seven treatments,
    sources of additional information,
    and a bibliography.
    CRM BULLETIN: A NATIONAL PARK
    SERVICE TECHNICAL BULLETIN 1990,
    v.13, no.6, p.17-24, photos.,
    aerial photo., refs.

UNITED STATES--HISTORIC SITES--
SOCIOLOGICAL ASPECTS
  Interpretation.
    Nine articles on historic site
    methods. Authors: Sandra S. Weber,
    F.A. Ketterson, Marcella Sherfy,
    Edward Tabor Linenthal, Raymond H.
    Thompson, Michael E. Whatley,
    Marie T. Myers, Karen
    Sweeny-Justice, Kathleen Hunter.
    CRM BULLETIN: A NATIONAL PARK
    SERVICE TECHNICAL BULLETIN 1990,
    v.13, no.3, p.1-21, photos.

UNITED STATES--HISTORY--AFRICAN
AMERICAN
  Preserving African American
  heritage.
    PRESERVATION PERSPECTIVE NJ 1990
    May-June, v.9, no.3, p.[1]-2,
    photos.

UNITED STATES--HOBOKEN (NEW JERSEY)--
MULTI-USE COMPLEXES
  Hoboken's waterfront: a simple twist
  of fate / Christ Mitchell.
    Planner: Stanton Eckstut.
    METROPOLIS 1990 Mar., v.9, no.7,
    p.17-19, photo.

UNITED STATES--HOBOKEN (NEW JERSEY)--
WATERFRONTS
  Hoboken's waterfront: a simple twist
  of fate / Christ Mitchell.
    Planner: Stanton Eckstut.
    METROPOLIS 1990 Mar., v.9, no.7,
    p.17-19, photo.

UNITED STATES--HOLLAND (MICHIGAN)--
INDUSTRIAL PARKS--HERMANN MILLER
DESIGN YARD
  A non-precious image / Jim Murphy.
    On the Hermann Miller Design Yard,
    Holland, Michigan. Architects:
    Meyer, Scherer & Rockcastle.
    PROGRESSIVE ARCHITECTURE 1990
    Feb., v.71, no.2, p.98-[105],
    dwg., photos., site plan.

UNITED STATES--HOLLYWOOD
(CALIFORNIA)--ARCHITECTURE
  Hollywood legacies of Wallace Neff,
  James E. Dolena, Roland E. Coate
  and Paul Williams / Michael Webb.
    ARCHITECTURAL DIGEST 1990 Apr.,
    v.47, no.4, p.36,40,42,46,48,
    dwg., ports., photos.

UNITED STATES--HOLLYWOOD
(CALIFORNIA)--BUNGALOWS--ALTERATIONS
AND ADDITIONS--GRAU HOUSE
  Pigments of her imagination,
  [Claudia Grau] / B. Colin Hamblin.
    Alterations to her bungalow in
    Hollywood, Calif., by fashion
    designer Claudia Grau.
    METROPOLITAN HOME 1990 Sept.,
    v.22, no.9, p.135-140, port.,
    photos.

UNITED STATES--HOLLYWOOD
(CALIFORNIA)--FAST-FOOD
RESTAURANTS--HAMBURGER HAMLET
  Zimmerman/Stafford, Hamburger
  Hamlet, Hollywood / Francesca
  Garcia-marquez.
    Text in Italian and English.
    DOMUS 1990 Mar., no.714, p.[6-7],
    axonometric view, dets., photos.,
    plan, secn.

UNITED STATES--HOLLYWOOD
(CALIFORNIA)--HOTELS--GARDEN OF
ALLAH
  Tales from the Garden of Allah /
  Garson Kanin.
    On the Hollywood hotel which was
    popular with screen stars of the
    1930s and 40s.
    ARCHITECTURAL DIGEST 1990 Apr.,
    v.47, no.4, p.54-66, ports.,
    photo.

UNITED STATES--HOLLYWOOD
(CALIFORNIA)--HOUSES--20TH CENTURY
  Architetture per il sito: la casa
  canyon = Site-friendly
  architecture: the canyon house.
    Two single-family houses in the
    Hollywood Hills. Architects: Hank
    Koning and Julie Eizenberg.
    ABITARE 1990 Apr., no.284,
    p.140-147, photos., plans, secns.,
    site plan, sketch.

UNITED STATES--HOLLYWOOD
(CALIFORNIA)--HOUSES--20TH CENTURY--
CONSERVATION AND RESTORATION--STORER
HOUSE
  Wright in Hollywood: a historic
  Frank Lloyd Wright house is
  brought back to life by film
  producer Joel Silver / Pilar
  Viladas.
    The 1923 Storer house. Architect
    for the restoration: Eric Wright.
    HOUSE & GARDEN 1990 Feb., v.162,
    no.2, p.[78]-87, port., photos.

UNITED STATES--HOLLYWOOD
(CALIFORNIA)--HOUSES--GEORGIAN
REVIVAL--COLBERT HOUSE
  Claudette Colbert: Best Actress for
  It happened one night / Jennifer
  Allen.
    Features her 1935 Georgian revival
    home in the Holmby Hills.
    Architect: Lloyd Wright.
    ARCHITECTURAL DIGEST 1990 Apr.,
    v.47, no.4, p.[226]-229, ports.,
    photos.

UNITED STATES--HOLLYWOOD
(CALIFORNIA)--HOUSES--SPANISH
COLONIAL REVIVAL--INTERIOR DESIGN--
DEMILLE HOUSE
  Cecil B. De Mille: Hollywood
  residence of a master showman /
  Michael Webb.
    Located in Laughlin Park.
    ARCHITECTURAL DIGEST 1990 Apr.,
    v.47, no.4, p.136-[139],282,
    port., photos.

UNITED STATES--HOLLYWOOD
(CALIFORNIA)--HOUSES--THAMES HOUSE
  Hodgetts and Fung Design Associates
  [houses].
    Contents: Viso residence,
    Hollywood Hills, California,
    design: 1988-89 -- Thames
    residence, Laurel Canyon,
    Hollywood, CAlifornia, design:
    1986-87. Architects: Hodgetts and
    Fung Design Associates. Text in
    Japanese and English.
    GA HOUSES 1990 Mar., no.28,
    p.96-99, dwgs., elevs., plans,
    secns.

UNITED STATES--HOLLYWOOD
(CALIFORNIA)--INTERIOR DESIGN
  Decorating's leading man: actor
  William Haines left the screen to
  become the film capital's star
  designer / Pilar Viladas.
    From the early 1930s until his
    death in 1973, Haines designed
    houses for Hollywood stars.
    HOUSE & GARDEN 1990 Aug., v.162,
    no.8, p.[100-108],151, ports.,
    photos.

UNITED STATES--HOLLYWOOD
(CALIFORNIA)--MANSIONS--SPANISH
MEDITERRANEAN REVIVAL--SENNETT
ESTATE
  Plans for the original Hollywood
  dream palace / Charles Lockwood.
    On the unexecuted designs for Mike
    Sennett's Hollywood Hills estate.
    Architect: John De Lario.
    ARCHITECTURAL DIGEST 1990 Apr.,
    v.47, no.4, p.90,94, dwg., port.

UNITED STATES--HOLLYWOOD
(CALIFORNIA)--RANCH-HOUSES--MELVYN
DOUGLAS HOUSE
  Melvyn Douglas: a hilltop house for
  the Best Supporting Actor in Hud
  and Being There / Jeffrey Simpson.
    Features 1938 ranch-style home in
    the Hollywood Hills designed by
    Roland E. Coate.
    ARCHITECTURAL DIGEST 1990 Apr.,
    v.47, no.4, p.212-213,296, port.,
    photos.

UNITED STATES--HOLLYWOOD (FLORIDA)--
CORPORATE OFFICE BUILDINGS--
PRESIDENTIAL CIRCLE (F. ROONEY INC.)
"Presidential Circle"
    Verwaltungsgebaude in Hollywood
    [Florida].
    F. Rooney Inc. corporate office
    building. Architects: Barretta &
    Associates.
    DEUTSCHE BAUZEITSCHRIFT 1990 June,
    v.38, no.6, p.831-838, dets.,
    photos., plans.

UNITED STATES--HOLLYWOOD HILLS
(CALIFORNIA)--HOUSES--SLOPING
SITES--VISO HOUSE
Hodgetts and Fung Design Associates
[houses].
Contents: Viso residence,
Hollywood Hills, California,
design: 1988-89 -- Thames
residence, Laurel Canyon,
Hollywood, CAlifornia, design:
1986-87. Architects: Hodgetts and
Fung Design Associates. Text in
Japanese and English.
GA HOUSES 1990 Mar., no.28,
p.96-99, dwgs., elevs., plans,
secns.

UNITED STATES--HOLYOKE
(MASSACHUSETTS)--MERRY-GO-ROUNDS--
CONSERVATION AND RESTORATION--
MOUNTAIN PARK CAROUSEL
Preservation in the round: Mountain
Park carousel, Holyoke, Mass. /
Nancy Levinson.
PRESERVATION NEWS 1990 May, v.30,
no.5, p.3,13, photo.

UNITED STATES--HOME OWNERSHIP
Homeownership: whose [sic] got to
have it? / Chester Hartman.
CITY LIMITS 1990 May, v.15, no.5,
p.19-20, port.

UNITED STATES--HOMELESSNESS
Housing for the homeless: can it be
done here? / T.P. Foder, L.S.
Grossman.
URBAN LAW AND POLICY 1988, v.9,
no.5, p.453-464, refs.

UNITED STATES--HOMELESSNESS--19TH
CENTURY
Homeless men and housing policy in
urban America, 1850-1920 / John C.
Schneider.
URBAN STUDIES 1989 Feb., v.26,
no.1, p.90-99, refs.

UNITED STATES--HOMELESSNESS--20TH
CENTURY
Homeless men and housing policy in
urban America, 1850-1920 / John C.
Schneider.
URBAN STUDIES 1989 Feb., v.26,
no.1, p.90-99, refs.

UNITED STATES--HONOLULU (HAWAII)--
CITIES AND TOWNS
City profile: Honolulu / Karl E.
Kim, Kem Lowry.
CITIES 1990 Nov., v.7, no.4,
p.274-282, maps, photos., refs.

UNITED STATES--HONOLULU (HAWAII)--CITY
PLANNING
City profile: Honolulu / Karl E.
Kim, Kem Lowry.
CITIES 1990 Nov., v.7, no.4,
p.274-282, maps, photos., refs.
Lewis Mumford's vision for Honolulu
- and perhaps a few other cities!
/ Gerald Hodge.
1938 planning report by Lewis
Mumford for Honolulu.
CITY MAGAZINE 1990 Summer, v.11,
no.4, p.33-36, port., photos.

UNITED STATES--HONOLULU (HAWAII)--
HOTELS--BEAUX-ARTS--CONSERVATION AND
RESTORATION--SHERATON MOANA
SURFRIDER
A new moon over Moana / Paula Rice
Jackson.
Features the restored interiors of
the 1901 Sheraton Moana Surfrider,
Honolulu. Original architect:
Oliver P. Traphagen. Restoration
architect: Virginia D. Murison.
INTERIORS 1990 Oct., v.150, no.3,
p.68-[71], photos.

UNITED STATES--HONOLULU (HAWAII)--LAND
USE--ECONOMIC ASPECTS
Urban land price: the extraordinary
case of Honolulu, Hawaii / Louis
A. Rose, Sumner J. La Croix.
URBAN STUDIES 1989 June, v.26,
no.3, p.301-314, tables, refs.

UNITED STATES--HONOLULU (HAWAII)--LAND
VALUES
Urban land price: the extraordinary
case of Honolulu, Hawaii / Louis
A. Rose, Sumner J. La Croix.
URBAN STUDIES 1989 June, v.26,
no.3, p.301-314, tables, refs.

UNITED STATES--HOPE (NEW JERSEY)--
INNS--COLONIAL--INN AT MILLRACE POND
Inn at Millrace Pond [Hope, N. J.].
COLONIAL HOMES 1990 Apr., v.16,
no.2, p.[120]-128, photos.

UNITED STATES--HOTELS--ALTERATIONS AND
ADDITIONS--INTERIOR DESIGN--ATLANTIC
CITY (NEW JERSEY)--BALLY'S PARK
PLACE CASINO HOTEL
Casino royale.
Interiors of guest tower addition
to Bally's Park Place Casino
Hotel, Atlantic City, N.J.
Interior designers: Kohn,
Pedersen, Fox, Conway Associates.
INTERIORS 1990 Sept., v.149,
no.14, p.110-[111], photos., plan.

UNITED STATES--HOTELS--ECONOMIC
ASPECTS
Hotel market: battered but still
showing signs of life / Harold
Kelman, Jane S. Everhart.
Features recent hotel/conference
center projects.
REAL ESTATE FORUM 1990 Nov., v.45,
no.11, p.88-90,92,94,96-102,104,
dwgs., ports., photos.

UNITED STATES--HOUSES--19TH CENTURY
Portraits of American architecture
[book review].
Review of book by Harry Devlin.
VICTORIAN HOMES 1990 Spring, v.9,
no.2, p.68-69, ill.

UNITED STATES--HOUSES--20TH CENTURY
Coming home to America.
A selection of six recent American
houses that reflect various
styles; articles are indexed
separately.
METROPOLITAN HOME 1990 July, v.22,
no.7, p.45-[75],
Record houses 1990: Building types
study 678.
Yearly issue devoted to 12 recent
houses by American architects,
each indexed separately.
ARCHITECTURAL RECORD 1990
Mid-Apr., v.178, no.5, p.33-102,
(Continued next column)

UNITED STATES--HOUSES--20TH CENTURY
(CONTINUED)
Record houses 1990:... (CONTINUED)
axonometric views, dwg., photos.,
plans, secns., site plans.

UNITED STATES--HOUSES--20TH CENTURY--
INTERIOR DESIGN
Let the sunshine in: Ogden Codman
unstuffed the overstuffed /
Mitchell Owens.
ELLE DECOR 1990 May, v.1, no.4,
p.28,32, ill., port., photos.

UNITED STATES--HOUSES--20TH CENTURY--
LOS ANGELES (CALIFORNIA)--
EXHIBITIONS
Utopia in the Suburbs [exhibition
review] / Douglas R. Suisman.
Exhibition "Blueprints for Modern
Living," MOCA, Los Angeles, Oct.
17, 1989-Feb. 17, 1990.
ART IN AMERICA 1990 Mar., v.78,
no.3, p.184-193, models, photos.

UNITED STATES--HOUSES--COLONIAL
REVIVAL
Early Colonial Revival / James C.
Massey, Shirley Maxwell.
OLD-HOUSE JOURNAL 1990 Mar.-Apr.,
v.18, no.2, p.45-50, ill.,
photos., plans.

UNITED STATES--HOUSES--CONSERVATION
AND RESTORATION
Winning big: the fourteen winners of
the Trust's 1989 Great American
Home Awards / Jane Gillette.
Grand prize to Robert Hodges for
the renovation of the French
Creole Joseph Kleinpeter House in
Baton Rouge, La.
HISTORIC PRESERVATION 1990
Jan.-Feb., v.42, no.1, p.42-51,
photos.

UNITED STATES--HOUSES--CRAFTSMAN
Arts & crafts houses / James C.
Massey, Shirley Maxwell.
OLD-HOUSE JOURNAL 1990 May-June,
v.18, no.3, p.48-52, dwg., photos.

UNITED STATES--HOUSES--INTERIOR DESIGN
Thematic continuity: informal spaces
designed for contemporary art /
Suzanne Stephens.
Interiors of Northeast home
designed by Thomas Britt.
ARCHITECTURAL DIGEST 1990 Feb.,
v.47, no.2, p.[148]-155, photos.

UNITED STATES--HOUSES--LOG
Log houses in America / J. Randall
Cotton.
OLD-HOUSE JOURNAL 1990 Jan.-Feb.,
v.18, no.1, p.37-44, dets., dwgs.,
photos., plans.

UNITED STATES--HOUSES--PRAIRIE SCHOOL
The Prairie School / James C.
Massey, Shirley Maxwell.
OLD-HOUSE JOURNAL 1990 July-Aug,
v.18, no.4, p.[47]-52, dwgs.,
photos., plans.

UNITED STATES--HOUSES--PREFABRICATED
Pre-cut houses: "catalog homes" /
James C. Massey & Shirley Maxwell.
Mail-order kit houses flourished
from 1900 to 1940.
OLD-HOUSE JOURNAL 1990 Nov.-Dec.,
v.18, no.6, p.36-41, ill., photos.

UNITED STATES--HOUSES--SMALL
Builder style: America's little
houses / James C. Massey, Shirley
Maxwell.
Homestead, Foursquare, Cottage,
and Bungalow styles.
OLD-HOUSE JOURNAL 1990 Sept.-Oct.,
v.18, no.5, p.45-49, ill., photos.

UNITED STATES--HOUSING
The flexible house: designing for
changing needs / Deborah A. Howe.
AMERICAN PLANNING ASSOCIATION.
JOURNAL 1990 Winter, v.56, no.1,
p.69-76, dwg., plans, site plan,
refs.

UNITED STATES--HOUSING--20TH CENTURY--
PUBLIC
The British roots of American
housing / Gerald Daly.
JOURNAL OF URBAN HISTORY 1989
Aug., v.15, no.4, p.399-434,
chart, photos., plans, tables,
refs.

UNITED STATES--HOUSING--AWARDS AND
PRIZES
The NAHRO H/CD Excellence Awards.
National Association of Housing
and Redevelopment Officials.
Eleven awards given in 1989.
JOURNAL OF HOUSING 1990 Jan.-Feb.,
v.47, no.1, p.30-44, photos.

UNITED STATES--HOUSING--ECONOMIC
ASPECTS
Financing community: methods for
assessing residential credit
disparites, market barriers, and
institutional reinvestment
performance in the metropolis /
Anne B. Shlay.
JOURNAL OF URBAN AFFAIRS 1988,
v.11, no.3, p.[201]-223, charts,
tables, refs.

UNITED STATES--HOUSING FOR ELDERLY
The potential market for housing
among older Americans / Karen
Martin Gibler.
REAL ESTATE ISSUES 1989
Fall-Winter, v.14, no.2, p.33-38,
ill., refs.

UNITED STATES--HOUSING FOR ELDERLY--
MAINTENANCE AND REPAIR--WISCONSIN
Home maintenance behavior and the
elderly / John Merrill.
Wisconsin case study.
HOUSING AND SOCIETY 1989, v.16,
no.3, p.[53]-36, charts, tables,
refs.

UNITED STATES--HOUSING FOR ELDERLY--
RESEARCH
Providing for the housing needs of
the elderly / Raymond J. Burby,
William M. Rohe.
AMERICAN PLANNING ASSOCIATION.
JOURNAL 1990 Summer, v.56, no.3,
p.324-340, diagrs., photo.,
tables, refs.

UNITED STATES--HOUSING FOR
HANDICAPPED--LAW AND LEGISLATION
Saying yes to group homes / Thomas
P. Smith.
Assessing local planning and
zoning compliance.
PLANNING 1989 Dec., v.55, no.12,
p.24-26, ports.

UNITED STATES--HOUSING FOR HOMELESS
Housing for the homeless: can it be
done here? / T.P. Foder, L.S.
Grossman.
URBAN LAW AND POLICY 1988, v.9,
no.5, p.453-464, refs.

UNITED STATES--HOUSING--LAW AND
LEGISLATION--HOUSING ACT OF 1949
A conversation with Lawrence M. Cox
[interview].
Housing administrator and former
president of the National Assn. of
Housing Officials (later NAHRO).
JOURNAL OF HOUSING 1989 July-Aug.,
v.46, no.4, p.176-179, ports.

UNITED STATES--HOUSING POLICY
Creating more dynamic public
housing: a modest proposal /
Frederick Brown.
JOURNAL OF HOUSING 1990 Nov-Dec.,
v.47, no.6, p.309-11,314-315,
charts, ports.
Homeless men and housing policy in
urban America, 1850-1920 / John C.
Schneider.
URBAN STUDIES 1989 Feb., v.26,
no.1, p.90-99, refs.
Housing for the homeless: can it be
done here? / T.P. Foder, L.S.
Grossman.
URBAN LAW AND POLICY 1988, v.9,
no.5, p.453-464, refs.
Jobs and housing: the search for
balance / Lloyd W. Bookout.
Studies the locational
relationship between jobs and
housing to determine whether
public policies can or should be
implemented to encourage closer
proximity between the two.
URBAN LAND 1990 Oct., v.49, no.10,
p.5-9, photo.
Scientific urban planning and the
ordering of daily life: the first
"war housing" experiment in the
United States, 1917-1919 /
Christian Topalov.
JOURNAL OF URBAN HISTORY 1990
Nov., v.17, no.1, p.14-45, maps,
photos., aerial photo., refs.

UNITED STATES--HOUSING POLICY--20TH
CENTURY
Developing and financing the 'garden
metropolis': urban planning and
housing policy in
twentieth-century America / Marc
A. Weiss.
"Examines the evolution of garden
city ideas in the U.S. during the
20th cent.", with emphasis on "the
central role of Thomas Adams, the
British planner who served as a
leading proponent of the garden
metropolis in the U.S.".
PLANNING PERSPECTIVES: PP 1990
Sept., v.5, no.3, p.307-319, refs.

UNITED STATES--HOUSING POLICY--HISTORY
A conversation with Lawrence M. Cox
[interview].
Housing administrator and former
president of the National Assn. of
Housing Officials (later NAHRO).
JOURNAL OF HOUSING 1989 July-Aug.,
v.46, no.4, p.176-179, ports.

UNITED STATES--HOUSING--PUBLIC
Options to conventional public
management / William Peterman.
JOURNAL OF URBAN AFFAIRS 1989,
v.11, no.1, p.[53]-68, charts,
refs.
Private owners of subsidized housing
vs. public goals: conflicting
interests in resyndication /
Rachel G. Bratt.
AMERICAN PLANNING ASSOCIATION.
JOURNAL 1987 Summer, v.53, no.3,
p.328-336, table, biblio., refs.
What should be done with the public
housing program? / Charles E.
Connerly.
AMERICAN PLANNING ASSOCIATION.
JOURNAL 1986 Spring, v.52, no.2,
p.142-155, photos., table,
biblio., refs.

UNITED STATES--HOUSING--PUBLIC--
PSYCHOLOGICAL ASPECTS
Improving the image of public
housing / John G. Hayes.
JOURNAL OF HOUSING 1990
Sept.-Oct., v.47, no.5, p.265-266,
268,270-273,

UNITED STATES--HOUSING--PUBLIC--
SOCIOLOGICAL ASPECTS
Creating more dynamic public
housing: a modest proposal /
Frederick Brown.
JOURNAL OF HOUSING 1990 Nov-Dec.,
v.47, no.6, p.309-11,314-315,
charts, ports.

UNITED STATES--HOUSING--SOCIOLOGICAL
ASPECTS
Building domestic liberty: Charlotte
Perkins Gilman's architectural
feminism [by] Polly Wynn Allen
[book review] / Kate Roberts.
WINTERTHUR PORTFOLIO 1990 Autumn,
v.25, no.2-3, p.196-198, refs.
Why higher income households move to
central cities / Daphne Spain.
JOURNAL OF URBAN AFFAIRS 1989,
v.11, no.3, p.[283]-299, tables,
refs.

UNITED STATES--HOUSING--SOCIOLOGICAL
ASPECTS--INFLUENCE
Residents participation and
grass-roots movements in the
United States [part 1] / Sachiko
Wakasugi.
Subtitle: A study on housing and
neighborhood-community planning by
residents. Text in Japanese;
English summary, p.87.
NIHON KENCHIKU GAKKAI KEIKAKUKEI
RONBUN HOKOKU SHU = JOURNAL OF
ARCHITECTURE, PLANNING AND
ENVIRONMENTAL ENGINEERING 1990
Apr., no.4(410), p.87-97, graphs,
tables, refs.

UNITED STATES--HOUSING SUBSIDIES
Lack of affordable housing spurs
employer-supported housing
programs / Myron P. Curzan, Amanda
Carney.
URBAN LAND 1989 July, v.48, no.7,
p.5-11, chart, photos.

UNITED STATES--HOUSTON (TEXAS)--
APARTMENT COMPLEXES--COURT AT
MUSEUMS GATE
Houston design portfolio: slow
recovery.
Sesquicentennial Park (Team HOU);
Caldwell house (Natalye Appel);
Court at Museums Gate (Josiah
Baker); Gilliland house (Peter Jay
Zweig Architects); Finnell house
(Wittenberg Partnership); and St.
Mary's Episcopal Church (Gerald
Moorhead).
ARCHITECTURE: THE AIA JOURNAL 1990
Apr., v.79, no.4, p.54-73,
axonometric views, ill., elev.,
photos., plans, secns., site
plans.

UNITED STATES--HOUSTON (TEXAS)--
APARTMENTS--INTERIOR DESIGN--ROLLINS
APARTMENT
Tranquility base: serene livability
in a Houston high rise / Nan Booth
Simpson.
Interior designer: Kelly Gale
Amen.
SOUTHERN ACCENTS 1990 May, v.13,
no.4, p.[128]-134, port., photos.

UNITED STATES--HOUSTON (TEXAS)--
ARCHITECTURE
Four projects [Carlos Jimenez].
In Houston, Texas. Spanish,
English text.
QUADERNS D'ARQUITECTURA I
URBANISME 1990 Jan.-Feb.-Mar.,
no.184, p.64-65, photos., plans.

UNITED STATES--HOUSTON (TEXAS)--
ARCHITECTURE--MAYAN REVIVAL
Mayan Revival revival: on the plains
of Texas, Precolumbian motifs rise
again / Alison Cook.
HOUSE & GARDEN 1990 Jan., v.162,
no.1, p.30,33, photos.

UNITED STATES--HOUSTON (TEXAS)--BARS
(EATING AND DRINKING
ESTABLISHMENTS)--OVATIONS
Interiors: a space for Ovations.
Ovations, a classical-music
performing space and bar in
Houston. Architects: Cisneros
Underhill.
TEXAS ARCHITECT 1990 Jan.-Feb.,
v.40, no.1, p.42-43, photos.,
plan, secns.

UNITED STATES--HOUSTON (TEXAS)--BUS
STATIONS
Metro's park-and-rides: busing up to
rail / Bruce C. Webb.
CITE: THE ARCHITECTURE AND DESIGN
REVIEW OF HOUSTON 1990 Fall,
no.25, p.12-13, photos.

UNITED STATES--HOUSTON (TEXAS)--CITIES
AND TOWNS
Houston: el eco de las autopistas /
Carlos Jimenez.
Spanish, English text.
QUADERNS D'ARQUITECTURA I
URBANISME 1990 Jan.-Feb.-Mar.,
no.184, p.114-[119], map, photos.

UNITED STATES--HOUSTON (TEXAS)--CITIES
AND TWONS--GROWTH--POLITICAL ASPECTS
The Houston growth coalition in
"boom" and "bust" / Albert
Schaffer.
JOURNAL OF URBAN AFFAIRS 1989,
v.11, no.1, p.[21]-38, refs.

UNITED STATES--HOUSTON (TEXAS)--CITY
PLANNING
Cite interviews planning comission
chairman Burdette Keeland
[interview] / Joel Warren Barna.
CITE: THE ARCHITECTURE AND DESIGN
REVIEW OF HOUSTON 1990 Fall,
no.25, p.24-25, port.

UNITED STATES--HOUSTON (TEXAS)--CITY
PLANNING--FOUNDERS PARK
Preservation: flap over Houston
historic district / Joel Warren
Barna.
Proposal to redevelop Freedmen's
Town/Fourth Ward to create
Founders Park, a new multi-use
development. Architects: Phillips
& Brown, EDI Architects.
Consultants: Andres Duany,
Elizabeth Plater-Zyberk.
PROGRESSIVE ARCHITECTURE 1990
June, v.71, no.6, p.30, ill.

UNITED STATES--HOUSTON (TEXAS)--
ENCLOSED STADIUMS--ASTRODOME
Il Duomo: people once compared the
Astrodome to Rome's monuments.
Now the Dome has itself become an
archetypal social form / Douglas
Pegues Harvey.
Opened Apr.9, 1965. Architects:
Lloyd & Morgan; Wilson, Morris,
Crain & Anderson.
TEXAS ARCHITECT 1990 May-June,
v.40, no.3, p.30-33, port.,
photos., aerial photos.

UNITED STATES--HOUSTON (TEXAS)--
GARDENS--BAYOU BEND GARDENS
Bayou Bend: the plan and history of
the gardens / David B. Warren.
Houston estate of the Hogg family.
Landscape designer: Ellen Shipman.
MUSEUM OF FINE ARTS, HOUSTON.
BULLETIN - THE MUSEUM OF FINE
ARTS, HOUSTON 1989 Winter-Spring,
v.12, no.2, p.66-93, ports.,
photos., plan.

UNITED STATES--HOUSTON (TEXAS)--HEALTH
CARE BUILDINGS
A well-healed building boom: ... the
market for health-care
architecture in Houston has never
been stronger / Joel Warren Barna.
TEXAS ARCHITECT 1990 May-June,
v.40, no.3, p.34-39, ill., dwgs.,
model, photos, plans, site plan.

UNITED STATES--HOUSTON (TEXAS)--
HISTORIC DISTRICTS--FREEDMEN'S TOWN
/ FOURTH WARD
Preservation: flap over Houston
historic district / Joel Warren
Barna.
Proposal to redevelop Freedmen's
Town/Fourth Ward to create
Founders Park, a new multi-use
development. Architects: Phillips
& Brown, EDI Architects.
Consultants: Andres Duany,
Elizabeth Plater-Zyberk.
PROGRESSIVE ARCHITECTURE 1990
June, v.71, no.6, p.30, ill.

UNITED STATES--HOUSTON (TEXAS)--
HISTORIC PRESERVATION
Preservation update: downtown
Houston / Raphael Longoria.
CITE: THE ARCHITECTURE AND DESIGN
REVIEW OF HOUSTON 1990 Fall,
no.25, p.5, photos., ref.

UNITED STATES--HOUSTON (TEXAS)--
HOSPITALS
A well-healed building boom: ... the
market for health-care
architecture in Houston has never
been stronger / Joel Warren Barna.
TEXAS ARCHITECT 1990 May-June,
v.40, no.3, p.34-39, ill., dwgs.,
model, photos, plans, site plan.

UNITED STATES--HOUSTON (TEXAS)--
HOUSES--20TH CENTURY--BUFFALO BAYOU
HOUSE
Blue Bayou: House Along the Bayou,
Houston, Texas / Grace Anderson.
Architect: Carlos Jimenez.
ARCHITECTURAL RECORD 1990
Mid-Apr., v.178, no.5, p.48-51,
photos., plans, site plan.
Light geometry: Houston architect
Carlos Jimenez creates a strong
but quiet counterpoint to the
opulence of River Oaks / David
Dillon.
HOUSE & GARDEN 1990 Mar., v.162,
no.3, p.[168]-173,209, photos.

UNITED STATES--HOUSTON (TEXAS)--
HOUSES--FINNELL HOUSE
Houston design portfolio: slow
recovery.
Sesquicentennial Park (Team HOU);
Caldwell house (Natalye Appel);
Court at Museums Gate (Josiah
Baker); Gilliland house (Peter Jay
Zweig Architects); Finnell house
(Wittenberg Partnership); and St.
Mary's Episcopal Church (Gerald
Moorhead).
ARCHITECTURE: THE AIA JOURNAL 1990
Apr., v.79, no.4, p.54-73,
axonometric views, ill., elev.,
photos., plans, secns., site
plans.

UNITED STATES--HOUSTON (TEXAS)--
HOUSES--INTERIOR DESIGN--ANDERSON
HOUSE
Sociable structure: a Houston home
designed for entertaining / Nan
Booth Simpson.
Anderson house. Architect: Joe
Carroll Williams.
SOUTHERN ACCENTS 1990 Oct., v.13,
no.8, p.[98]-105, ports., photos.

UNITED STATES--HOUSTON (TEXAS)--
HOUSES--INTERIOR DESIGN--FARISH
HOUSE
'80s glamour for a '50s ranch
[Houston] / Katrin Tolleson.
House of interior designer Stephen
Farish.
HOUSE BEAUTIFUL 1986 May, v.128,
no.5, p.84-[87], photos.

UNITED STATES--HOUSTON (TEXAS)--
HOUSES--INTERIOR DESIGN--LEVY HOUSE
Ancient meets avant-garde: in
Houston, an extraordinary
collection begged an extraordinary
setting / Nan Booth Simpson.
Levy house interiors.
Architectural designer: Larry S.
Davis.
SOUTHERN ACCENTS 1989 May-June,
v.12, no.3, p.[164]-173, photos.

UNITED STATES--HOUSTON (TEXAS)--
HOUSES--INTERIOR DESIGN--ZILKHA
HOUSE
Playful formality: a Houston home
packed with personal treasures /
Nan Booth Simpson.
Home of Cristina Zilkha. Interior
design: Letelier-Rock Design.
SOUTHERN ACCENTS 1990 Sept., v.13,
no.7, p.[68]-79, port., photos.

UNITED STATES--HOUSTON (TEXAS)--
HOUSES--ROTHWELL HOUSE
Rothwell House, Houston, Texas,
design: 1988-89; construction:
1990.
Architects: Taft Architects. Text
in Japanese and English.
GA HOUSES 1990 Mar., no.28,
p.114-115, model, plans, secns.

UNITED STATES--HOUSTON (TEXAS)--
HOUSING--PUBLIC--MAINTENANCE AND
REPAIR--ALLEN PARKWAY VILLAGE
Fourth Ward and the siege of Allen
Parkway Village / Rives Taylor.
Part 1: What HACH hath wrought.
Part 2: The Planning Department
and Fourth Ward.
CITE: THE ARCHITECTURE AND DESIGN
REVIEW OF HOUSTON 1990 Fall,
no.25, p.6-11,31, photo., aerial
photo., refs.

UNITED STATES--HOUSTON (TEXAS)--
MUSEUMS--ART--ALTERATIONS AND
ADDITIONS--MUSEUM OF FINE ARTS
Lillie and Hugh Roy Cullen Sculpture
Garden.
Whole issue. Created by Isamu
Noguchi.
MUSEUM OF FINE ARTS, HOUSTON.
BULLETIN - THE MUSEUM OF FINE
ARTS, HOUSTON 1986 Summer, v.9,
no.3, p.[2]-32. photos.

UNITED STATES--HOUSTON (TEXAS)--
MUSEUMS--ART--MENIL COLLECTION
Menil Museum, Houston (Texas),
1981-83.
Architects: Piano & Fitzgerald.
Engineers: Ove Arup & Partners.
ARCH PLUS 1990 Jan., no.102,
p.37-[41], dwg., model, photos.,
secns., sketches.

UNITED STATES--HOUSTON (TEXAS)--
MUSEUMS--SCIENCE--ALTERATIONS AND
ADDITIONS--HOUSTON MUSEUM OF NATURAL
SCIENCE
I-maxing out: addition to the
Houston Museum of Natural Science
/ Geoffrey Brune.
New facilities added in 1989.
Architects: Hoover & Furr; 3D/I.
CITE: THE ARCHITECTURE AND DESIGN
REVIEW OF HOUSTON 1990 Fall,
no.25, p.25, photos., site plan.

UNITED STATES--HOUSTON (TEXAS)--MUSIC
ROOMS--OVATIONS
Interiors: a space for Ovations.
Ovations, a classical-music
performing space and bar in
Houston. Architects: Cisneros
Underhill.
TEXAS ARCHITECT 1990 Jan.-Feb.,
v.40, no.1, p.42-43, photos.,
plan, secns.

UNITED STATES--HOUSTON (TEXAS)--
NEIGHBORHOODS--CONSERVATION AND
RESTORATION--FOURTH WARD
Fourth Ward and the siege of Allen
Parkway Village / Rives Taylor.
Part 1: What HACH hath wrought.
Part 2: The Planning Department
and Fourth Ward.
CITE: THE ARCHITECTURE AND DESIGN
REVIEW OF HOUSTON 1990 Fall,
no.25, p.6-11,31, photo., aerial
photo., refs.

UNITED STATES--HOUSTON (TEXAS)--
OFFICES--INTERIOR DESIGN--BERG &
ANDROPHY
Interiors.
Contents: Berg & Androphy Law
Offices, Houston (William F. Stern
and Associates); Majestic Diner,
Austin (STUDIO Texas); and, El
Centro College Student Center,
Dallas (Oglesby Group).
TEXAS ARCHITECT 1990 Sept.-Oct.,
v.40, no.5, p.40-43, photos.,
plans.

UNITED STATES--HOUSTON (TEXAS)--
OFFICES--INTERIOR DESIGN--FIRST
BOSTON
First Boston / Edie Lee Cohen.
Interiors of Houston offices.
Interior designers: Total Concept
Inc.
INTERIOR DESIGN 1990 June, v.61,
no.9, p.252-[253], photos.

UNITED STATES--HOUSTON (TEXAS)--
OUTDOOR SCULPTURE
Why a mouse?: public art in Houston
/ William Howze.
Includes "Index of public art in
Houston", listing some 170 works.
CITE: THE ARCHITECTURE AND DESIGN
REVIEW OF HOUSTON 1990 Fall,
no.25, p.17-21, cover, photos.

UNITED STATES--HOUSTON (TEXAS)--
PARKS--SESQUICENTENNIAL PARK
Houston Park phased into reality /
Peter Papademetriou.
Phase I of Sesquicentennial Park
completed. Architects: Team HOU.
PROGRESSIVE ARCHITECTURE 1990
Feb., v.71, no.1, p.24, photo.

UNITED STATES--HOUSTON (TEXAS)--
PARKS--SESQUICENTENNIAL PARK
(CONTINUED)
Public places for American cities:
three projects / Rodolfo Machado.
Includes Times Square Tower, New
York (1984); Pershing Square, Los
Angeles (1986); and
Sesquicentennial Park, Houston
(1986).
ASSEMBLAGE 1988 June, no.6,
p.[98]-113, axonometric views,
dets., dwgs., elevs., model,
photos., plans, secns., site
plans.
Special feature: Machado and
Silvetti.
Contents: Brief history.--
Statement / R. Machado, J.
Silvetti.-- The material force of
the architectural imagination / K.
Michael Hays.-- Works: Portantina,
New York, N.Y., 1986.-- Steps of
Providence, Rhode Island School of
Design, Providence, R.I., 1975.--
Municipal cemetery,
Polizzi-Generosa, Sicily, 1986.--
Sesquicentennial Park, Houston,
Tex., 1986.-- Central
transportation facility "la Porta
Meridionale," Palermo, Sicily,
1987.-- Four public squares,
Leonforte, Sicily, 1983. Text in
Japanese and English.
ARCHITECTURE AND URBANISM 1990
Apr., no.4(235), p.65-138,
axonometric views, elevs., models,
photos., plans, secns., site
plans.

UNITED STATES--HOUSTON (TEXAS)--
PEDESTRIAN TUNNELS
Die Tunnels der Liebe: Unterhalb von
Houston / Richard Ingersoll.
ARCHITHESE 1990 Jan.-Feb., v.20,
no.1, p.28-30, map, photos., refs.

UNITED STATES--HOUSTON (TEXAS)--PERIOD
ROOMS--BAYOU BEND
Ima Hogg and Bayou Blend: a history:
the interiors / David B. Warren.
Early American interiors of Bayou
Bend, home of Ima Hogg, and now
part of the Museum of Fine Arts,
Houston.
MUSEUM OF FINE ARTS, HOUSTON.
BULLETIN - THE MUSEUM OF FINE
ARTS, HOUSTON 1988 Fall, v.12,
no.1, p.2-63, ill., ports.,
photos., engrs.

UNITED STATES--HOUSTON (TEXAS)--PUBLIC
ART--DIRECTORIES
Why a mouse?: public art in Houston
/ William Howze.
Includes "Index of public art in
Houston", listing some 170 works.
CITE: THE ARCHITECTURE AND DESIGN
REVIEW OF HOUSTON 1990 Fall,
no.25, p.17-21, cover, photos.

UNITED STATES--HOUSTON (TEXAS)--
RAILROADS
Rail plans for Houston, Dallas /
Joel Warren Barna.
PROGRESSIVE ARCHITECTURE 1990
Aug., v.71, no.8, p.32,37, plan.

UNITED STATES--HOUSTON (TEXAS)--
RESIDENTIAL GARDENS--JUDGE GARDEN
Classicism's light new touch /
Carolyn Ulrich.
Small residential backyard gardens
in Chicago, New Haven, Houston,
and Washington, D.C. Landscape
architects: Timothy Lally, Ralph
Synnestvedt, Jr., Paul Bailey,
Douglas Kycia, McDugald-Steele,
Lanson Jones, and Jane Macleish.
GARDEN DESIGN 1990 autumn, v.9,
no.3, p.[30-37], photos.

UNITED STATES--HOUSTON (TEXAS)--
SCULPTURE GARDENS--MUSEUM OF FINE
ARTS--LILLIE AND HUGH ROY CULLEN
SCULPTURE GARDEN
Lillie and Hugh Roy Cullen Sculpture
Garden.
Whole issue. Created by Isamu
Noguchi.
MUSEUM OF FINE ARTS, HOUSTON.
BULLETIN - THE MUSEUM OF FINE
ARTS, HOUSTON 1986 Summer, v.9,
no.3, p.[2]-32, photos.

UNITED STATES--HOUSTON (TEXAS)--
STORES--INTERIOR DESIGN--HERMES
Hermes / Karen Maserjian.
Houston boutique in the Pavillon
Shopping Galleria. Architects:
Rena Dumas Architecture
Interieure, Whisler-Patri
Architects.
INTERIOR DESIGN 1990 June, v.61,
no.9, p.250-[251], photos.

UNITED STATES--HOUSTON (TEXAS)--
STUDENT UNIONS--ALTERATIONS AND
ADDITIONS--RICE UNIVERSITY--LEY
STUDENT CENTER
Special feature: recent works of
Cesar Pelli.
Contents: Editor's introduction--
Architects' statement / Cesar
Pelli-- Essay: Urban iconography
and the medium of architecture /
Gavin Macrae-Gibson, p.130-137--
Works: World Financial Center--
Norwest Tower-- Pacific Design
Center expansion-- Mattatuck
Museum-- Ley Student Center
expansion, Rice University-- Yale
Center for Molecular Medicine,
Yale University-- Carnegie Hall
tower-- Sunarhauserman
headquarters-- Fan Pier master
plan. Architects: Cesar Pelli &
Associates. Text in Japanese and
English.
ARCHITECTURE AND URBANISM 1990
Feb., no.2(233), p.[59]-148,
dwgs., elevs., photos., plans,
secns., site plans.

UNITED STATES--HOUSTON (TEXAS)--
TRANSIT SYSTEMS--METRO
Metro's park-and-rides: busing up to
rail / Bruce C. Webb.
CITE: THE ARCHITECTURE AND DESIGN
REVIEW OF HOUSTON 1990 Fall,
no.25, p.12-13, photos.
Trains, planes, and automobiles /
Joel Warren Barna.
Mass transit rail lines in Dallas
and Houston.
TEXAS ARCHITECT 1990 Mar.-Apr.,
v.40, no.2, p.22-29, dwgs.,
models, maps, photos., site plans.

UNITED STATES--HOUSTON (TEXAS)--URBAN
PARKS--SESQUICENTENNIAL PARK
Houston design portfolio: slow
recovery.
Sesquicentennial Park (Team HOU);
Caldwell house (Natalye Appel);
Court at Museums Gate (Josiah
Baker); Gilliland house (Peter Jay
Zweig Architects); Finnell house
(Wittenberg Partnership); and St.
Mary's Episcopal Church (Gerald
Moorhead).
ARCHITECTURE: THE AIA JOURNAL 1990
Apr., v.79, no.4, p.54-73,
axonometric views, ill., elev.,
photos., plans, secns., site
plans.

UNITED STATES--HUDSON RIVER VALLEY
(NEW YORK)--COUNTRY HOUSES--INTERIOR
DESIGN--MARINACCIO HOUSE
American country Zen: James and
Marilyn Marinaccio's Hudson River
Valley retreat / Steven M.L.
Aronson.
Features interiors of renovated
ice house on Philip J. Schuyler's
late 18th cent. estate, The Grove.
Owners have added teahouse and
gazebo.
ARCHITECTURAL DIGEST 1990 June,
v.47, no.6, p.[106]-113,212,
port., photos.

UNITED STATES--HUDSON RIVER VALLEY
(NEW YORK)--GUEST HOUSES--INTERIOR
DESIGN--SYLVANIA
Hudson River carriage house:
renewing Charles A. Platt's
historic design in New York State
/ Suzanne Stephens.
Features interiors of renovated
carriage house on Platt's 1904-09
Sylvania estate.
ARCHITECTURAL DIGEST 1990 June,
v.47, no.6, p.[150]-157,220,
photos.

UNITED STATES--HUDSON RIVER VALLEY
(NEW YORK)--HISTORIC BUILDINGS
Sleepy Hollow legends / Brooke
Astor.
A history of the Hudson River
Valley and its historic buildings.
HOUSE & GARDEN 1990 Aug., v.162,
no.8, p.[40,42], photos.

UNITED STATES--HUMBOLDT COUNTY
(CALIFORNIA)--ARCHITECTURE--
VICTORIAN
Victoriana West: California's
Humboldt County claims some of the
finest Victorian architecture in
the country / Suzie Boss.
HISTORIC PRESERVATION 1990
Jan.-Feb., v.42, no.1, p.60-63,
photos.

UNITED STATES--HUNTINGTON (NEW YORK)--
MODEL HOUSES--METAL--CONSERVATION
AND RESTORATION--ALUMINAIRE HOUSE
(WALLACE K. HARRISON HOUSE)
A. Laurence Kocher, Albert Frey: the
Aluminaire house, 1930-31 /
documentation by Joseph Rosa.
On the full-scale model house,
exhibited in New York, reassembled
on the Harrison estate in
Huntington, and moved to Central
Islip in the late 1980s.
ASSEMBLAGE 1990 Apr., no.11,
p.[58]-69, axonometric view,
(Continued next column)

UNITED STATES--HUNTINGTON (NEW YORK)--
MODEL HOUSES--METAL--CONSERVATION
AND RESTORATION--ALUMINAIRE HOUSE
(WALLACE K. HARRISON HOUSE)
(CONTINUED)
A. Laurence Kocher,....(CONTINUED)
dwgs., photos., plans, sketches,
refs.

UNITED STATES--ILLINOIS--HOUSES
Unconventional wit near Chicago:
Stanley Tigerman infuses a
suburban house with playful
complexities / Kurt Andersen.
ARCHITECTURAL DIGEST 1990 Dec.,
v.47, no.13, p.[124-129], 220,
port., photos., plan.

UNITED STATES--ILLINOIS--REAL ESTATE
AGENTS--ECONOMIC ASPECTS
Why do some real estate salespeople
earn more than others? / James R.
Follain, Terry Lutes, David A.
Meier.
THE JOURNAL OF REAL ESTATE
RESEARCH 1987 Fall, v.2, no.1,
p.73-81, chart, tables.

UNITED STATES--ILLINOIS--SHOPPING
CENTERS--TOWN SQUARE WHEATON
Robert Stern vs. Wayne's world /
Michael J.P. Smith.
Town Square Wheaton, a shopping
center under construction late in
1990 in a Chicago suburb.
INLAND ARCHITECT 1990 July-Aug.,
v.34, no.4, p.20,22, elev., site
plan.

UNITED STATES--ILLINOIS--TELEPHONE
BUILDINGS--ILLINOIS BELL TELEPHONE
Switching & changing / Michael J. P.
Smith.
Survey of buildings for Illinois
Bell Telephone (IBT) over 70
years, including several by
Holabird & Root and Holabird and
Roche.
INLAND ARCHITECT 1990 Nov.-Dec.,
v.34, no.6, p.42-47, dwg., photos.

UNITED STATES--ILLINOIS--VERNACULAR
ARCHITECTURE
Architecture in the United States
[book review] / Rhodri Windsor
Liscombe, John Vincent Boyer,
William G. Farrar, IV, Robert
Winter.
Review of Charleston antebellum
architecture and civic destiny, by
Kenneth Severens; Structures and
styles: guided tours of Hartford
architecture, by Gregory E.
Andrews and David F. Ransom;
Vernacular architecture in
southern Illinois, by John M.
Coggeshall and Jo Anne Nast; and
Bruce Goff: toward aboslute
architecture, by David Delong.
SOCIETY OF ARCHITECTURAL
HISTORIANS. JOURNAL 1990 Mar.,
v.49, no.1, p.115-120,

UNITED STATES--INDEPENDENCE
(MISSOURI)--CHURCHES--SPIRAL--
REORGANIZED CHURCH OF JESUS CHRIST
OF LATTER DAY SAINTS
The Temple: reorganized Church of
Jesus Christ of Latter Day Saints,
Independence, Missouri, USA, 1993.
Project for spiral form structure;
Hellmuth, Obata & Kassabaum. Text
in Japanese and English.
ARCHITECTURE AND URBANISM 1990
Dec., no.12 extra edition,
p.196-[199], dwgs., plans, secn.,
site plan.

UNITED STATES--INDIANAPOLIS
(INDIANA)--ESPLANADES--WHITE RIVER
PARK--RIVERFRONT PROMENADE
Urban Camouflage: Portfolio:
Danadjieva & Koenig Associates /
Andrea Oppenheimer Dean.
An architecture and landscape
architecture firm with offices in
Tiburon, Calif., and Bellevue,
Wash. contents: Freeway Air Rights
Development, Seattle; and
Riverfront Promenade, White River
Park, Indianapolis.
ARCHITECTURE: THE MAGAZINE OF THE
AMERICAN INSTITUTE OF ARCHITECTS
1990 Aug., v.79, no.8, p.60-65,
model, photos., site plans, aerial
photo.

UNITED STATES--INDIANAPOLIS
(INDIANA)--HOUSES--WEISZ HOUSE
Propagating the postmodern / Jayne
Merkel.
The Weisz residence, located
outside Indianapolis. Architect:
Paul Muller.
INLAND ARCHITECT 1990 Mar.-Apr.,
v.34, no.2, p.50-52, elev.,
photos., plans.

UNITED STATES--INDUSTRIAL BUILDINGS--
19TH CENTURYXTYPOLOGY
Artificial refrigeration and the
architecture of 19th-century
American breweries / Susan K.
Appel.
SOCIETY FOR INDUSTRIAL ARCHEOLOGY.
JOURNAL 1990, v.16, no.1, p.21-38,
ill., dwgs., photo., secns., refs.

UNITED STATES--INDUSTRIAL BUILDINGS--
AWARDS AND PRIZES
Design 90: NAIOP's Annual
Design/Development Awards Program.
DEVELOPMENT 1990 Nov.-Dec., v.21,
no.6, p.[6]-10, photos.

UNITED STATES--INDUSTRIAL BUILDINGS--
INFLUENCE
Genombrott forflyttat [book review]
/ Johan Radberg.
Reviews Den rationella fabriken-om
funktionalismens rotter, a
dissertation by Lisa Brunnstrom,
and A separate Atlantljr UD
industrial building and European
modern architecture, by Reyner
Banham.
ARKITEKTUR: THE SWEDISH REVIEW OF
ARCHITECTURE 1990 Dec., v.90,
no.10, p.55-58, elevs., photos.,
plans., table.

UNITED STATES--INDUSTRIAL DESIGN--
ENVIRONMENTAL ASPECTS
Who says you can't change the world?
/ Cynthia Chapin Davidson.
INLAND ARCHITECT 1990 Mar.-Apr.,
v.34, no.2, p.23, Commentary on
Earth Day (Apr.22,1990) and the
Green Pledge. Announces a new
dept. in this journal, "Earth",
concerning environmentally safe
products.

UNITED STATES--INDUSTRIAL DESIGN--
SOCIOLOGICAL ASPECTS
Streamlining with friction: an
exhibition review / Jane Webb
Smith.
"Streamlining America", at the
Henry Ford Museum, Dearborn,
Mich., Sept.1986-Dec.1989,
attempted to show how a concept
"became a system of social values
as well as a marketing tool...in
the 1930s".
WINTERTHUR PORTFOLIO 1990 Spring,
v.25, no.1, p.[55]-66, photos.,
refs.

UNITED STATES--INDUSTRIAL HOUSING
Scientific urban planning and the
ordering of daily life: the first
"war housing" experiment in the
United States, 1917-1919 /
Christian Topalov.
JOURNAL OF URBAN HISTORY 1990
Nov., v.17, no.1, p.14-45, maps,
photos., aerial photo., refs.

UNITED STATES--INFORMATION TECHNOLOGY
The evolution of spatial modeling in
the USA / Richard K. Brail.
EKISTICS 1989 Sept.-Dec., v.56,
no.338-339, p.249-253, refs.

UNITED STATES--INFRASTRUCTURE--HISTORY
The networked city: a Euro-American
review [book review] / Eugene P.
Moehring.
Review of: Technology and the rise
of the networked city in Europe
and America, ed. by Joel A. Tarr
and Gabriel Dupuy, 1988.
JOURNAL OF URBAN HISTORY 1990
Nov., v.17, no.1, p.88-97, refs.

UNITED STATES--INFRASTRUCTURE--
MAINTENANCE AND REPAIR
Infrastructure policy: repetitive
studies uneven response, next
steps / Marshall Kaplan.
URBAN AFFAIRS QUARTERLY 1990 Mar.,
v.25, no.3, p.371-388, table,
refs.

UNITED STATES--INSTALLATION WORKS
Lebbeus Woods: architecture rising /
Michael Sorkin.
COLUMBIA UNIVERSITY. GRADUATE
SCHOOL OF ARCHITECTURE, PLANNING
AND PRESERVATION NEWSLINE 1990
Nov., v.3, no.3, p.4, dwgs.,
model.

UNITED STATES--INTERIOR DESIGN
The reign of English decorating /
Nancy Goslee Power.
Particularly the style of John
Fowler.
HOUSE BEAUTIFUL 1986 June, v.128,
no.6, p.58-[65], dwg., ports.,
photos.

UNITED STATES--INTERIOR DESIGN--20TH
CENTURY
Louis Rorimer: nonresidential
interior design / Leslie Pina.
President of Rorimer-Brooks,
1910-1939.
WINTERTHUR PORTFOLIO 1990 Autumn,
v.25, no.2-3, p.[157]-176, photos.
What your rooms will be wearing next
year / Julie V. Iovine.
Window treatments, furniture,
tableware, and upholstery fabrics
for the 1990s.
METROPOLITAN HOME 1990 Nov., v.22,
no.11, p.131-144, dwgs., photos.

UNITED STATES--INTERIOR DESIGN--20TH
CENTURY--EXHIBITIONS
Streamlining with friction: an
exhibition review / Jane Webb
Smith.
"Streamlining America", at the
Henry Ford Museum, Dearborn,
Mich., Sept.1986-Dec.1989,
attempted to show how a concept
"became a system of social values
as well as a marketing tool...in
the 1930s".
WINTERTHUR PORTFOLIO 1990 Spring,
v.25, no.1, p.[55]-66, photos.,
refs.

UNITED STATES--INTERIOR DESIGN--
COLONIAL
The American way: the early
interiors of the American Museum
in Britain / Maureen Connett.
TRADITIONAL HOMES 1990 July, v.6,
no.10, p.53-54, photos.

UNITED STATES--INTERIOR DESIGN--
PSYCHOLOGICAL ASPECTS
Everything's coming up country /
Elaine Greene.
Group discussion on the continuing
popularity of American country
style. Participants: JoAnn
Barwick, Dr. Arlene Kagle,
Margaret Kennedy, and Elaine
Greene.
HOUSE BEAUTIFUL 1990 Mar., v.132,
no.3, p.80-83, photos.

UNITED STATES--INTERIOR LIGHTING--
VICTORIAN
How much light do you need? / Nadja
Maril.
VICTORIAN HOMES 1990 Summer, v.9,
no.3, p.20-21, ill., dwg.

UNITED STATES--IOWA--ARCHITECTURE--
AWARDS AND PRIZES
1989 Design Award Winners [Iowa
Chapter A.I.A.].
Ten winning projects, each indexed
separately.
IOWA ARCHITECT 1990 Spring, v.39,
no.1, p.9-[25], photos., plans,
site plan.

UNITED STATES--IOWA--BUILDINGS--
STUDENT PROJECTS
A portfolio of achievement: student
work, Iowa State University / Herb
Gottfried.
IOWA ARCHITECT 1990 Fall, v.39,
no.3, p.34-38, elevs., models,
plans, secns.

UNITED STATES--IOWA CITY (IOWA)--
HOUSES--ARCHITECTS'--MEISEL HOUSE
An in-town vacation home: Meisel
Residence / Judith Ann McClure.
In Iowa City. Architect: Martin
Meisel.
IOWA ARCHITECT 1990 Summer, v.39,
no.2, p.24-[27], photos., plans,
secn.

UNITED STATES--IOWA CITY (IOWA)--
LABORATORIES--UNIVERSITY OF IOWA--
LASER LABORATORY BUILDING
Frank O. Gehry.
Entire issue devoted to the work
of this American architect.
Criticism by A. Zaera Polo and
David Cohn. 15 projects and
buildings from 1987-1990 featured.
Text in Spanish and English.
EL CROQUIS 1990 Nov., v.9, no.45,
p.1-124, ports., elevs., models,
photos., plans, secns., site
plans, refs.
La habilidad de maquetista:
laboratorios laser de la
universidad de Iowa, Iowa City,
Iowa, 1987-1992.
Architects: Frank O. Gehry and
Associates. English summary,
p.87-88.
A & V 1990, no.25, p.68-69,
elevs., models, secns., site plan.

UNITED STATES--IOWA CITY (IOWA)--
RESEARCH FACILITIES--UNIVERSITY OF
IOWA--JOHN W. ECKSTEIN MEDICAL
RESEARCH BUILDING
Stepping ahead: the John W. Eckstein
Medical Research Building, the
University of Iowa College of
Medicine / Robert Tibbetts.
Architects/engineers: Hansen Lind
Meyer.
IOWA ARCHITECT 1990 Fall, v.39,
no.3, p.20-21, photos., plan.

UNITED STATES--IOWA CITY (IOWA)--
UNIVERSITIES AND COLLEGES--
BUILDINGS--FIELDHOUSE
Body buildings: designing multi-use
campus recreational facilities /
Martha Huntington.
Univ. of Mo. Recreation Facility
and Univ. of Iowa Fieldhouse.
IOWA ARCHITECT 1990 Fall, v.39,
no.3, p.26-31, dwg., photos.,
plan, isometric dwg.

UNITED STATES--IOWA CITY (IOWA)--
UNIVERSITIES AND COLLEGES--
BUILDINGS--UNIVERSITY OF IOWA--LASER
LABORATORY BUILDING
La habilidad de maquetista:
laboratorios laser de la
universidad de Iowa, Iowa City,
Iowa, 1987-1992.
Architects: Frank O. Gehry and
Associates. English summary,
p.87-88.
A & V 1990, no.25, p.68-69,
elevs., models, secns., site plan.

UNITED STATES--IOWA CITY (IOWA)--
UNIVERSITIES AND COLLEGES--
UNIVERSITY OF IOWA--LASER LABORATORY
BUILDING
Frank O. Gehry.
Entire issue devoted to the work
of this American architect.
Criticism by A. Zaera Polo and
David Cohn. 15 projects and
buildings from 1987-1990 featured.
Text in Spanish and English.
EL CROQUIS 1990 Nov., v.9, no.45,
p.1-124, ports., elevs., models,
photos., plans, secns., site
plans, refs.

UNITED STATES--IOWA--HOUSES--
ARCHITECTS'--FINDLAY HOUSE
Welcoming seclusion: Findlay
residence / Martha Huntington.
In Boone Co., Iowa. Architect:
Robert A. Findlay.
IOWA ARCHITECT 1990 Summer, v.39,
no.2, p.10-13, axonometric views,
dets., elevs., photos.

UNITED STATES--IOWA--LANDSCAPES
Precise, anonymous, enigmatic: on
architecture of the rural
landscape in Iowa / David Heymann.
IOWA ARCHITECT 1990 Winter, v.39,
no.4, p.28-35, photos.

UNITED STATES--IOWA--MAIN STREETS
Town squares: community identity /
Robert A. Findlay.
The Iowa Town Squares program.
IOWA ARCHITECT 1989 Winter, v.38,
no.5, p.[15-17], ill., photo,
sketch, aerial photo.

UNITED STATES--IOWA--PLAZAS
Town squares: community identity /
Robert A. Findlay.
The Iowa Town Squares program.
IOWA ARCHITECT 1989 Winter, v.38,
no.5, p.[15-17], ill., photo,
sketch, aerial photo.

UNITED STATES--IOWA--RURAL BUILDINGS
Precise, anonymous, enigmatic: on
architecture of the rural
landscape in Iowa / David Heymann.
IOWA ARCHITECT 1990 Winter, v.39,
no.4, p.28-35, photos.

UNITED STATES--IOWA--RURAL DEVELOPMENT
Hanging together [small town
clusters for rural development] /
Jim Schwab.
Examples in Iowa and Canada.
PLANNING 1990 Jan., v.56, no.1,
p.24-25, photos., aerial photo.

UNITED STATES--IOWA--UNIVERSITIES AND
COLLEGES--BUILDINGS
Learning environments: one student's
view of Iowa's academic
architecture / Greg Lehman.
Introduction to theme issue: seven
articles indexed separately.
IOWA ARCHITECT 1990 Fall, v.39,
no.3, p.11,

UNITED STATES--IPSWICH
(MASSACHUSETTS)--HOUSES--COLONIAL--
POLLY DOLE HOUSE (UPDIKE HOUSE)
The houses of Ipswich / John Updike.
Author's recollections of his
former home, the 1686 Polly Dole
House. Ipswich. Mass.
ARCHITECTURAL DIGEST 1990 June,
v.47, no.6, p.26,30,32, photos.

UNITED STATES--IRVINE (CALIFORNIA)--
CAMPUSES--UNIVERSITY OF CALIFORNIA
AT IRVINE
The academic village in exurbia:
David Neuman has moved on to Palo
Alto, where he is now campus
architect at Stanford / Aaron
Betsky.
ARCHITECTURAL RECORD 1990 Apr.,
v.178, no.4, p.49-53, port.,
photos.
Utopia revised: at the University of
California at Irvine, the struggle
to adapt the unyielding geometry
of the campus continues / John
Parman.
On William Pereira's 1963 master
plan, and subsequent buildings by
other architects.
ARCHITECTURE: THE AIA JOURNAL 1990
Jan., v.79, no.1, p.66-77, dwg.,
elev., photos., plans, site plans.

UNITED STATES--IRVINE (CALIFORNIA)--
LIBRARIES--UNIVERSITY AND COLLEGE--
UNIVERSITY OF CALIFORNIA, IRVINE--
SCIENCE LIBRARY
Projects: James Stirling Michael
Wilford & Associates / Thomas
Fisher.
Features four recent projects:
Science library, University of
California, Irvine; office
building development around the
Seville stadium; competition entry
for the Tokyo International Forum;
and the Venice Biennale bookstore.
PROGRESSIVE ARCHITECTURE 1990
Dec., v.71, no.13, p.96-98,
axonometric view, models, plans,
secns., site plans.
Science library, University of
California at Irvine, Los Angeles,
U.S.A.
Architects: James Stirling,
Michael Wilford and Associates.
Text in Japanese and English.
ARCHITECTURE AND URBANISM 1990
May, no.5 extra edition,
p.182-191, axonometric view,
elevs., model, plans, secn., site
plan.

UNITED STATES--IRVINE (CALIFORNIA)--
UNIVERSITIES AND COLLEGES--
BUILDINGS--UNIVERSITY OF CALIFORNIA
AT IRVINE
Utopia revised: at the University of
California at Irvine, the struggle
to adapt the unyielding geometry
of the campus continues / John
Parman.
On William Pereira's 1963 master
plan, and subsequent buildings by
other architects.
ARCHITECTURE: THE AIA JOURNAL 1990
Jan., v.79, no.1, p.66-77, dwg.,
elev., photos., plans, site plans.

UNITED STATES--IRWINDALE
(CALIFORNIA)--ATRIUMS--HOME SAVINGS
OF AMERICA
Banking by waterfall / Karin Tetlow.
On the atrium in the corporate
headquarters of Home Savings of
America, Irwindale, Calif.
Interior designers: PHH
Environments.
INTERIORS 1990 Apr., v.149, no.9,
p.94-[95], photos.

UNITED STATES--IRWINDALE
(CALIFORNIA)--CORPORATE OFFICE
BUILDINGS--INTERIOR DESIGN--HOME
SAVINGS OF AMERICA
Banking by waterfall / Karin Tetlow.
On the atrium in the corporate
headquarters of Home Savings of
America, Irwindale, Calif.
Interior designers: PHH
Environments.
INTERIORS 1990 Apr., v.149, no.9,
p.94-[95], photos.

UNITED STATES--ITHACA (NEW YORK)--
CENTERS FOR THE PERFORMING ARTS--
CORNELL UNIVERSITY--PERFORMING ARTS
CENTER
Center for the Performing Arts,
Cornell University, Ithaca, New
York, 1982-88.
Architects: James Stirling,
Michael Wilford & Associates, with
Wank adams Slavin Associates. Text
in Japanese and English.
GA DOCUMENT 1990 May, no.26,
p.68-[79], elevs., photos., plans,
secns., site plan.
Performing Arts Centre, Cornell
University, New York, U.S.A.,
1983-1988.
Architects: James Stirling,
Michael Wilford and Associates.
Text in Japanese and English.
Includes essay: In the classic
vein: the sky line / Brendan Gill.
ARCHITECTURE AND URBANISM 1990
May, no.5 extra edition, p.68-107,
photos., plans, secns., site plan.
Le revers du decor: Centre d'arts du
spectacle de l'Universite Cornell,
Ithaca, New York.
Performing Arts Center, Cornell
University. Architects: James
Stirling, Michael Wilford and
Associates with Wank Adams Slavin
Associates. English summary,
p.153. Spanish summary, p.199.
TECHNIQUES ET ARCHITECTURE 1990
Apr.-May, no.389, p.149-153,
photos., plans, secns.

UNITED STATES--ITHACA (NEW YORK)--
HOUSES--20TH CENTURY--SAGAN HOUSE
Casa Dr. Carl Sagan, Ithaca,
E.E.U.U.
Architects: Guillermo Jullian de
la Fuente, Ann M.
Pendleton-Jullian.
CA: REVISTA OFICIAL DEL COLEGIO DE
ARQUITECTOS DE CHILE 1989
Apr.-June. no.56, p.[38]-45,
dwgs., port., elevs., models,
plans, secns., site plan.

UNITED STATES--ITHACA (NEW YORK)--
UNIVERSITIES AND COLLEGES--
BUILDINGS--CORNELL UNIVERSITY--
PERFORMING ARTS CENTER
Center for the Performing Arts,
Cornell University, Ithaca, New
York, 1982-88.
Architects: James Stirling,
Michael Wilford & Associates, with
Wank adams Slavin Associates. Text
in Japanese and English.
GA DOCUMENT 1990 May, no.26,
p.68-[79], elevs., photos., plans,
secns., site plan.
Performing Arts Centre, Cornell
University, New York, U.S.A.,
1983-1988.
Architects: James Stirling,
Michael Wilford and Associates.
Text in Japanese and English.
Includes essay: In the classic
vein: the sky line / Brendan Gill.
ARCHITECTURE AND URBANISM 1990
May, no.5 extra edition, p.68-107,
photos., plans, secns., site plan.
Le revers du decor: Centre d'arts du
spectacle de l'Universite Cornell,
Ithaca, New York.
Performing Arts Center, Cornell
University. Architects: James
Stirling, Michael Wilford and
Associates with Wank Adams Slavin
Associates. English summary,
p.153. Spanish summary, p.199.
TECHNIQUES ET ARCHITECTURE 1990
Apr.-May, no.389, p.149-153,
photos., plans, secns.

UNITED STATES--JACKSON COUNTY
(ILLINOIS)--GRANGES (FRATERNAL
BUILDINGS)--20TH CENTURY
Jackson County Landmark: Grange Hall
/ Barbara Ulrich.
Built in 1912.
HISTORIC ILLINOIS 1990 Oct., v.13,
no.3, p.6-7, photos.

UNITED STATES--JACKSONVILLE BEACH
(FLORIDA)--CHURCHES--20TH CENTURY--
BEACH UNITED METHODIST CHURCH
To gather together: Building types
study 674: religious buildings /
Margaret Gaskie.
Four projects: Gates of the Grove
Synagogue, East Hampton, N.Y.
(Norman Jaffe); Beach United
Methodist Church, Jacksonville
Beach, Fla. (William Morgan
Architects); Blackhawk Bapist
Church, Fort Wayne, Ind.(Harding
Assoc.); and St. Peter's Catholic
Church, Olney, Md. (Hugh N.
Jacobsen).
ARCHITECTURAL RECORD 1990 Jan.,
v.178, no.1, 123-135, elevs.,
photos., plans, secns., site
plans.

UNITED STATES--JACKSONVILLE
(FLORIDA)--AFFORDABLE HOUSING
Springfield's renaissance: the
National Trust joins community
leaders in reviving Jacksonville,
Florida's historic Springfield
sector and shapes a model of
affordable housing / Eddie
Nickens.
HISTORIC PRESERVATION 1990
Jan.-Feb., v.42, no.1, p.30-[35],
68, photos.

UNITED STATES--JACKSONVILLE
(FLORIDA)--HISTORIC DISTRICTS--
SPRINGFIELD HISTORIC DISTRICT
Springfield's renaissance: the
National Trust joins community
leaders in reviving Jacksonville,
Florida's historic Springfield
sector and shapes a model of
affordable housing / Eddie
Nickens.
HISTORIC PRESERVATION 1990
Jan.-Feb., v.42, no.1, p.30-[35],
68, photos.

UNITED STATES--JACKSONVILLE
(FLORIDA)--RESTAURANTS
Forme zoomorfiche e spazi che
respirano: quattro esempi di
modellato di Kendrick Bangs
Kellogg. / Marisa Cerruti.
Restaurant, Jacksonville, Fl; Yen
house, La Jolla, CA; Gordon house,
san Diego, CA; restaurant, Rancho
Mirage, CA. English, French,
German, Spanish summaries, p.118.
ARCHITETTURA: CRONACHE E STORIA
1987 Feb., v.33, no.2(376),
p.[116]-126, photos., plans, site
plans.

UNITED STATES--JACKSONVILLE
(FLORIDA)--YACHT CLUBS--EPPING
FOREST YACHT CLUB
Southern traditions: preservation
efforts in today's South show new
interest in 20th-century
landmarks, as well as earlier ones
/ Clifford A. Pearson.
A portfolio of Southeast projects:
Epping Forest Yacht Club,
Jacksonville, Fla. (Pappas
Associates); Freedom Tower, Miami
(Heisenbottle Architects);
Venetian Pool, Coral Gables, Fla.
(H. Carlton Decker & Assoc.);
Howard Memorial Library, New
Orleans (E. Barron, M. Toups); and
Linden Row Inn, Richmond, Va.
(Glave Newman Anderson).
ARCHITECTURAL RECORD 1990 Mar.,
v.178, no.3, p.66-75, photos.,
plans, site plans.

UNITED STATES--JACKSONVILLE
(FLORIDA)--YACHT CLUBS--INTERIOR
DESIGN--EPPING FOREST YACHT CLUB
Epping Forest Yacht Club / Judith
Nasatir.
1926 du Pont mansion converted to
yacht club, Jacksonville, Fla.
Original architect: Harold
Saxelbye. Conversion architects:
Pappa Associates. Interior
designers: Catlin Interiors.
INTERIOR DESIGN 1990 June, v.61,
no.9, p.208-[213], photos., plan.

UNITED STATES--JERSEY CITY (NEW
JERSEY)--BANKS--NATIONAL WESTMINSTER
BANK NEW JERSEY
National Westminster Bank New
Jersey, Jersey City, New Jersey.
Architects: Grad Partnership.
ARCHITECTURE NEW JERSEY 1990,
v.26, no.6, p.14, photos.

UNITED STATES--JERSEY CITY (NEW
JERSEY)--COMPUTER CENTERS--RECRUIT
NEWPORT CENTER
New concept offers tenants
'plug-ready' data center.
Recruit Newport Center, Jersey
City, N.J.
REAL ESTATE FORUM 1990 Jan., v.45,
no.1, p.49, photo.

UNITED STATES--JERSEY CITY (NEW
JERSEY)--CORPORATE OFFICE
BUILDINGS--NATIONAL WESTMINSTER BANK
NEW JERSEY
National Westminster Bank New
Jersey, Jersey City, New Jersey.
Architects: Grad Partnership.
ARCHITECTURE NEW JERSEY 1990,
v.26, no.6, p.14, photos.

UNITED STATES--JERSEY CITY (NEW
JERSEY)--INTELLIGENT BUILDINGS--
NEWPORT FINANCIAL CENTER
Newport Financial Center / Jane
Everhart.
"Intelligent" office building on
the New Jersey side of the Hudson
River offers a "fail-safe power
supply" and spectacular views of
Manhattan.
REAL ESTATE FORUM 1990 Dec., v.45,
no.12, p.62-64,66,68,70,72,74,76,
ports., photos.

UNITED STATES--JERSEY CITY (NEW
JERSEY)--INTELLIGENT BUILDINGS--
RECRUIT NEWPORT CENTER
New concept offers tenants
'plug-ready' data center.
Recruit Newport Center, Jersey
City, N.J.
REAL ESTATE FORUM 1990 Jan., v.45,
no.1, p.49, photo.

UNITED STATES--JERSEY CITY (NEW
JERSEY)--LOFTS--ARCHITECTS'--ANDERS
LOFT
Great stories.
Feature section on ca.15 recent
American houses, including ones by
architects Andy Dean, in S.
Dartmouth, Mass.; Peter Anders, in
Jersey City, N.J.; Chip Arena, in
Chestertown, Md.; Cory Buckner and
Nicholas Roberts, in Malibu,
Calif.; Robby Reid, in Tempe,
Ariz.
METROPOLITAN HOME 1990 Feb., v.22,
no.2, p.125-166, photos., ports.

UNITED STATES--JERSEY CITY (NEW
JERSEY)--OFFICE BUILDINGS--RECRUIT
NEWPORT CENTER
New concept offers tenants
'plug-ready' data center.
Recruit Newport Center, Jersey
City, N.J.
REAL ESTATE FORUM 1990 Jan., v.45,
no.1, p.49, photo.

UNITED STATES--JERSEY CITY (NEW
JERSEY)--OFFICE COMPLEXES--NEWPORT
FINANCIAL CENTER
Newport Financial Center / Jane
Everhart.
"Intelligent" office building on
the New Jersey side of the Hudson
River offers a "fail-safe power
supply" and spectacular views of
Manhattan.
REAL ESTATE FORUM 1990 Dec., v.45,
no.12, p.62-64,66,68,70,72,74,76,
ports., photos.

UNITED STATES--JERSEY CITY (TEXAS)--
WINDOWS--STAINED GLASS--SAINT
MAXIMILIAN KOLBE CATHOLIC CHURCH
Glass with a conscience / David V.
Meumier.
Windows commemorating the
Holocaust at St. Maximilian Kolbe
Catholic Church, Jersey Village,
Tex. Artist: Gene Hester of
Genesis Art Glass Studio.
STAINED GLASS QUARTERLY 1989
Summer, v.84, no.2, p.117-119,
photos.

UNITED STATES--JERSEYVILLE
(ILLINOIS)--HOUSEBARNS--19TH
CENTURY--SCHWARZ-KRUEGER HOUSEBARN
The Schwarz-Krueger wine
cellar-housebarn / H. Wayne Price.
Built in 1868 near Jerseyville,
Ill. by a German immigrant.
PIONEER AMERICA SOCIETY
TRANSACTIONS 1989, v.12, p.39-46,
dwgs., photos., plans, secns.,
refs.

UNITED STATES--JERSEYVILLE
(ILLINOIS)--WINE CELLARS--19TH
CENTURY--SCHWARZ-KRUEGER WINE CELLAR
The Schwarz-Krueger wine
cellar-housebarn / H. Wayne Price.
Built in 1868 near Jerseyville,
Ill. by a German immigrant.
PIONEER AMERICA SOCIETY
TRANSACTIONS 1989, v.12, p.39-46,
dwgs., photos., plans, secns.,
refs.

UNITED STATES--JIM THORPE
(PENNSYLVANIA)--BED-AND-BREAKFAST
GUEST HOUSES--HANDWERK INN
Historic Jim Thorpe, Pennsylvania /
Deborah Barcan.
Contents: The Harry Packer
Mansion, a bed & breakfast inn.--
The Asa Packer Mansion, a historic
Italianate museum.
VICTORIAN HOMES 1990 Spring, v.9,
no.2, p.[36]-43, port., photos.

UNITED STATES--JIM THORPE
(PENNSYLVANIA)--CITIES AND TOWNS--
MAUCH CHUNK
Genius loci of Jim Thorpe,
Pennsylvania.
One of six urban design reports
included in special issue, Urban
Concepts. Extracted from a 1979
study of the Mauch Chunk Historic
District. Architects: Venturi
Rauch and Scott Brown Architects
and Planners.
ARCHITECTURAL DESIGN 1990, v.60,
no.1-2, p.52-57, elevs., photos.,
site plan.

UNITED STATES--JIM THORPE
(PENNSYLVANIA)--HISTORIC DISTRICTS
P/A awards update: the perils of
preservation planning / Thomas
Fisher.
Report on five preservation plans
for historic districts in the
following areas: Miami Beach,
Fla.; Rugby, Tenn.; Princeton, NJ;
Jim Thorpe, Pa. and Lowell, Mass.
PROGRESSIVE ARCHITECTURE 1990
June, v.71, no.6, p.100-105, ill.,
models, photos., plans, site plan.

UNITED STATES--JIM THORPE
(PENNSYLVANIA)--MANSIONS--
ITALIANATE--ASA PACKER MANSION
Historic Jim Thorpe, Pennsylvania /
Deborah Barcan.
Contents: The Harry Packer
Mansion, a bed & breakfast inn.--
The Asa Packer Mansion, a historic
Italianate museum.
VICTORIAN HOMES 1990 Spring, v.9,
no.2, p.[36]-43, port., photos.

UNITED STATES--JIM THORPE
(PENNSYLVANIA)--MANSIONS--SECOND
EMPIRE--HARRY PACKER MANSION
Historic Jim Thorpe, Pennsylvania /
Deborah Barcan.
Contents: The Harry Packer
Mansion, a bed & breakfast inn.--
The Asa Packer Mansion, a historic
Italianate museum.
VICTORIAN HOMES 1990 Spring, v.9,
no.2, p.[36]-43, port., photos.

UNITED STATES--JOHNS ISLAND (SOUTH
CAROLINA)--HOUSES--REID HOUSE
[Reid house and Waterside Inn, South
Carolina].
Contents: Reid house, John Island,
South Carolina -- Middleton Inn,
Charleston, South Carolina.
Architects: Clark & Menefee.
9H 1989, no.8, p.104-109, photos.,
plans, secns., site plan.

UNITED STATES--JOHNSTOWN
(PENNSYLVANIA)--CORPORATE OFFICE
BUILDINGS--CROWN AMERICAN
CORPORATION
Crown American Corporate Office
Building, Johnstown, Pennsylvania:
Michael Graves, Architect.
Design, 1985-88; built 1989. Text
in Japanese and English.
GA DOCUMENT 1990 May, no.26,
p.[92-105], photos., plans, secn.,
site plan.
Gravesian images: for the Johnstown,
Pennsylvania headquarters of Crown
American Corporation, Michael
Graves used classical forms /
Karen D. Stein.
ARCHITECTURAL RECORD 1990 Feb.,
v.178, no.2, p.76-83, photos.,
plans, secn.

UNITED STATES--JOHNSTOWN
(PENNSYLVANIA)--CORPORATE OFFICE
BUILDINGS--INTERIOR DESIGN--CROWN
AMERICAN CORPORATION.
Crowning touch / Paula Rice Jackson.
Focus on the interiors of Crown
American Corp. headquarters,
Johnstwon, Penn. Architects:
Michael Graves Architect.
INTERIORS 1990 Mar., v.149, no.8,
p.116-[123], port., photos., plan.

UNITED STATES--JONESBORO (GEORGIA)--
LIBRARIES--PUBLIC--CLAYTON COUNTY
LIBRARY
Clayton County Headquarters Library,
Jonesboro, Georgia.
Architects: Scogin, Elam & Bray
Architects. Spanish, English text.
QUADERNS D'ARQUITECTURA I
URBANISME 1990 Jan.-Feb.-Mar.,
no.184, p.52-55, photos., plans,
secns., site plan.

UNITED STATES--JONESBORO (GEORGIA)--
LIBRARIES--PUBLIC--CLAYTON COUNTY
LIBRARY (CONTINUED)
Scogin Elam and Bray.
Features four projects in Georgia:
Clayton County Library, Jonesboro;
Buckhead Branch Library, Atlanta;
Chmar house, Atlanta; and Turner
Village, Candler School of
Theology, Emory Univ., Atlanta.
English summaries.
ARCHITECTURE D'AUJOURD'HUI 1990
Oct., no.271, p.134-144, elevs.,
models, photos., plans, secns.,
site plans.
Scogin, Elam, Bray: Clayton County
Library, Jonesboro, Georgia, 1988.
Architects: Scogin, Elam & Bray,
Architects.
9H 1989, no.8, p.94-98, elevs.,
photos., plan, secns., site plan.

UNITED STATES--JOSHUA TREE
(CALIFORNIA)--HOUSES--MONUMENT
Josh Schweitzer.
Features desert home, the
Monument, Joshua Tree, Calif.
English summary.
ARCHITECTURE D'AUJOURD'HUI 1990
Oct., no.271, p.164-[167],
axonometric view, photos., plan.

UNITED STATES--JOSHUA TREE
(CALIFORNIA)--WEEKEND HOUSES--
ARCHITECTS'--SCHWEITZER HOUSE
The new frontier [house, Joshua
Tree, Calif.] / Charles Gandee.
Architect: Josh Schweitzer.
HOUSE & GARDEN 1990 June, v.162,
no.6, p.[120-125], port., photos.
Non sono "tesseracts" pero... = They
aren't "tesseracts" but...
[weekend house, Joshua Tree,
Calif.].
Architect: Josh Sweitzer.
ARCHITETTURA: CRONACHE E STORIA
1990 Nov., v.36, no.11(421),
p.800-801, axonometric view,
photos., plan.

UNITED STATES--JOSHUA TREE
(CALIFORNIA)--WEEKEND HOUSES--
ARCHITECTS'--THE MONUMENT
(SCHWEITZER HOUSE)
Desert Bloom: The Monument, Joshua
Tree, California / Aaron Betsky.
The Architect's weekend house.
Architects: Schweitzer BIM.
ARCHITECTURAL RECORD 1990
Mid-Apr., v.178, no.5, p.[64-69],
axonometric view, photos., plan.
Valley of the lost house / Michael
Webb.
The Monument (Schweitzer) house;
architects: Schweitzer BIM.
BLUEPRINT (LONDON, ENGLAND) 1990
July-Aug., no.69, p.24-25, photos.

UNITED STATES--JOSHUA TREE
(CALIFORNIA)--WEEKEND HOUSES--
MONUMENT
Schweitzer BIM: the Monument, Joshua
Tree, California, 1987-90.
Desert retreat. Text in Japanese
and English.
GA HOUSES 1990 Dec., no.30,
p.126-133, axonometric views,
photos., plan.

UNITED STATES--JULIAN (CALIFORNIA)--
POST OFFICES
Western front: Julian Main Post
Office, Julian, California.
Architects: Keniston & Mosher.
ARCHITECTURAL RECORD 1990 Nov.,
v.178, no.12, p.94-95, photos.,
plan.

UNITED STATES--KANSAS CITY
(MISSOURI)--CONVENTION FACILITIES--
ALTERATIONS AND ADDITIONS--BARTLE
HALL
Strung up in Kansas City [Missouri]
/ Barbara K. Hower.
Expansion plans for Bartle Hall
convention center. Architects:
HNTB and PBNI.
INLAND ARCHITECT 1990 Sept.-Oct.,
v.34, no.5, p.20,23, model.

UNITED STATES--KANSAS CITY
(MISSOURI)--ENVIRONMENTAL PROTECTION
Architects and the environment /
Lawrence Goldblatt.
On the efforts of Bob Berkebile
(Kansas City, Mo., AIA Chapter
president) and other Kansas
architects to preserve the
environment.
INLAND ARCHITECT 1990 July-Aug.,
v.34, no.4, p.7, aerial photo.

UNITED STATES--KANSAS CITY
(MISSOURI)--HOUSING FOR HOMELESS--
COMPETITIONS
Housing Kansas City's homeless /
Lawrence Goldblatt.
On a 1989 competition entitled
Affordable Family Housing, for
4-unit buildings. Sponsor: Kansas
City Chapter AIA. Winner: Powers
Associates. Second prize:
Arkhitekton.
INLAND ARCHITECT 1990 Jan.-Feb.,
v.34, no.1, p.[70-73], elev.,
plans.

UNITED STATES--KANSAS CITY
(MISSOURI)--MULTI-USE BUILDINGS--
STUDENT PROJECTS--GARMENT DISTRICT
Adaptive reuse: fifth year interior
architecture studio.
Reshaping the Garment District,
Kansas City, Mo.
OZ / COLLEGE OF ARCHITECTURE AND
DESIGN, KANSAS STATE UNIVERSITY
1989, v.11, p.56-57, dwgs., plans.

UNITED STATES--KANSAS CITY
(MISSOURI)--PARKS--PSYCHOLOGICAL
ASPECTS--RICHARD AND ANNETTE BLOCH
CANCER SURVIVOR PARK
Parks with a purpose [Bloch Cancer
Survivor Park] / Leonard Ehrler.
The Richard and Annette Bloch
Cancer Survivor Park in Kansas
City, Mo.; designed by
LandCorp-Ehrler (landscape
architects) and Milosav Cekic
Architects. Sculptures by Victor
Salmones.
PARKS & RECREATION 1990 July,
v.25, no.7, p.50-52,79, dwgs.,
elevs., plans.

UNITED STATES--KANSAS CITY
(MISSOURI)--RAISED PEDESTRIAN
WALKWAYS--THE LINK
Accurate reflections: glass,
detailing components / Marc S.
Harriman.
Contents: The Link, Kansas City
(Zimmer Gunsul Frasca
Partnership); 3M Austin Center,
Tex. (CRSS); Dakin Building, San
Francisco (Theodore Brown &
Partners).
ARCHITECTURE: THE MAGAZINE OF THE
AMERICAN INSTITUTE OF ARCHITECTS
1990 Aug., v.79, no.8, p.87-93,
dets., photos., elevs.

UNITED STATES--KANSAS CITY
(MISSOURI)--STORES--JEWELRY--MEASE
JEWELERS
Mease mystique / Robert Tibbetts.
Mease jewelry store, Kansas City,
Mo. Architects: Herbert Lewis
Kruse Blunck Architecture.
IOWA ARCHITECT 1990 Spring, v.39,
no.1, p.12-[13], photos., plan.

UNITED STATES--KANSAS CITY
(MISSOURI)--THEME PARKS--RICHARD AND
ANNETTE BLOCH CANCER SURVIVOR PARK
Parks with a purpose [Bloch Cancer
Survivor Park] / Leonard Ehrler.
The Richard and Annette Bloch
Cancer Survivor Park in Kansas
City, Mo.; designed by
LandCorp-Ehrler (landscape
architects) and Milosav Cekic
Architects. Sculptures by Victor
Salmones.
PARKS & RECREATION 1990 July,
v.25, no.7, p.50-52,79, dwgs.,
elevs., plans.

UNITED STATES--KENT (OHIO)--MONUMENTS
AND MEMORIALS--COMPETITIONS--KENT
STATE UNIVERSITY--MAY 4 MEMORIAL
The persistence of memory and Kent
State / Stanley Mathews.
On the design competition and the
final memorial design by Bruno
Ast, commemorating events of May
4, 1970.
INLAND ARCHITECT 1990 July-Aug.,
v.34, no.4, p.22-27, model,
photos., site plan.

UNITED STATES--KENTUCKY--CAVES--
MAMMOTH CAVE NATIONAL PARK
The Mammoth Cave National Park
Planning Project: cooperative
SHPO-Federal agency cultural
resource management / Bruce J.
Noble, Jr.
CRM BULLETIN: A NATIONAL PARK
SERVICE TECHNICAL BULLETIN 1990,
v.13, no.6, p.9-11,

UNITED STATES--KENTUCKY--LANDSCAPE
ARCHITECTURE--RESEARCH
Crafting the landscape symbol
vocabulary for a regional image:
the case of the Kentucky Bluegrass
/ Karl Raitz, Dorn VanDommelen.
LANDSCAPE JOURNAL 1990 Fall, v.9,
no.2, p.109, photos., elevs., map,
refs.

UNITED STATES--KENTUCKY--LANDSCAPE
ARCHITECTURE--SYMBOLIC ASPECTS
Creating the landscape symbol
vocabulary for a regional image:
the case of the Kentucky Bluegrass
/ Karl Raitz, Dorn VanDommelen.
LANDSCAPE JOURNAL 1990 Fall, v.9,
no.2, p.109, photos., elevs., map,
refs.

UNITED STATES--KENWOOD (MINNESOTA)--
HOUSES--20TH CENTURY--ALTERATIONS
AND ADDITIONS--MONDALE HOUSE
Room to breathe: an 83-year-old
Kenwood house rediscovers a
fountain of youth in space and
light.
Additions to Mondale house.
Architect: Martha Yunker.
ARCHITECTURE MINNESOTA 1990
May-June, v.16, no.3, p.54-57,
photos.

UNITED STATES--KEWANEE (ILLINOIS)--
HISTORIC HOUSE MUSEUMS--WOODLAND
PALACE
Kewanee's Woodland Palace / Cynthia
A. Fuener.
1890s house with engineering and
mechanical innovations, designed
by Frederick Francis.
HISTORIC ILLINOIS 1990 June, v.13,
no.1, p.[1]-5, ports., photos.

UNITED STATES--KEWANEE (ILLINOIS)--
HOUSES--19TH CENTURY--WOODLAND
PALACE
Kewanee's Woodland Palace / Cynthia
A. Fuener.
1890s house with engineering and
mechanical innovations, designed
by Frederick Francis.
HISTORIC ILLINOIS 1990 June, v.13,
no.1, p.[1]-5, ports., photos.

UNITED STATES--KEY WEST (FLORIDA)--
HISTORIC HOUSE MUSEUMS--AUDUBON
HOUSE
120 miles out to sea: Key West.
Includes Hemingway's home, Casa
Marina Hotel, the Wrecker's House,
the Audubon House, and the Curry
Mansion.
COLONIAL HOMES 1990 Aug., v.16,
no.4, p.88-[109],118, photos.

UNITED STATES--KEY WEST (FLORIDA)--
HISTORIC HOUSE MUSEUMS--WRECKER'S
MUSEUM
120 miles out to sea: Key West.
Includes Hemingway's home, Casa
Marina Hotel, the Wrecker's House,
the Audubon House, and the Curry
Mansion.
COLONIAL HOMES 1990 Aug., v.16,
no.4, p.88-[109],118, photos.

UNITED STATES--KEY WEST (FLORIDA)--
HOTELS--SPANISH COLONIAL REVIVAL--
MARRIOTT CASA MARINA RESORT
120 miles out to sea: Key West.
Includes Hemingway's home, Casa
Marina Hotel, the Wrecker's House,
the Audubon House, and the Curry
Mansion.
COLONIAL HOMES 1990 Aug., v.16,
no.4, p.88-[109],118, photos.

UNITED STATES--KEY WEST (FLORIDA)--
HOUSES--19TH CENTURY--WRECKER'S
HOUSE
120 miles out to sea: Key West.
Includes Hemingway's home, Casa
Marina Hotel, the Wrecker's House,
the Audubon House, and the Curry
Mansion.
COLONIAL HOMES 1990 Aug., v.16,
no.4, p.88-[109],118, photos.

UNITED STATES--KEY WEST (FLORIDA)--
HOUSES--SPANISH COLONIAL REVIVAL--
HEMINGWAY HOUSE
120 miles out to sea: Key West.
Includes Hemingway's home, Casa
Marina Hotel, the Wrecker's House,
the Audubon House, and the Curry
Mansion.
COLONIAL HOMES 1990 Aug., v.16,
no.4, p.88-[109],118, photos.

UNITED STATES--KEY WEST (FLORIDA)--
MANSIONS--19TH CENTURY--AUDUBON
HOUSE
120 miles out to sea: Key West.
Includes Hemingway's home, Casa
Marina Hotel, the Wrecker's House,
the Audubon House, and the Curry
Mansion.
COLONIAL HOMES 1990 Aug., v.16,
no.4, p.88-[109],118, photos.

UNITED STATES--KEY WEST (FLORIDA)--
MANSIONS--VICTORIAN--CURRY MANSION
120 miles out to sea: Key West.
Includes Hemingway's home, Casa
Marina Hotel, the Wrecker's House,
the Audubon House, and the Curry
Mansion.
COLONIAL HOMES 1990 Aug., v.16,
no.4, p.88-[109],118, photos.

UNITED STATES--KINGS POINT (NEW
YORK)--GUEST HOUSES--INTERIOR DESIGN
American playhouse: inventive
solutions for a Long Island guest
cottage / Brooks Peters.
Interiors of Kings Point guest
house with interior pool.
Interior designer: Michael de
Santis.
ARCHITECTURAL DIGEST 1990 Sept.,
v.47, no.10, p.202-205, photos.

UNITED STATES--KIRKLAND (WASHINGTON)--
SUPERMARKETS--LARRY'S MARKET
Northwest passage: regional
portfolio: the Pacific Northwest.
Six recent projects: Two Union
Sq., Seattle (NBBJ Group);
Washington Mutual Tower, Seattle
(Kohn Pedersen Fox, McKinley
Architects); Pacific First Centre,
Seattle (Callison Partnership);
Evergreen State College Studio
addition, Olympia (Miller/Hull
Partnership); Larry's Market,
Kirkland, Wash. (Carlson/Ferrin);
and Andover Park, Beaverton, Ore.
(Fisher-Friedman Associates).
ARCHITECTURAL RECORD 1990 May,
v.178, no.6, p.84-93, dwg.,
photos., plans, secns., site
plans.

UNITED STATES--KITCHEN GARDENS--
HISTORY
American adaptations / Mary Forsell.
The American kitchen garden as
created by European immigrants.
GARDEN DESIGN 1990 summer, v.9,
no.2, p.[36-43], photos.

UNITED STATES--KITCHENS--20TH CENTURY
My modern kitchen [1950s] / Martha
Kaplan.
Subtitle: Gadgets for a world when
babies were booming, wars were
cold, and chromium was hot.
ART & ANTIQUES 1990 Jan., v.7,
no.1, p.[76]-81, photos.

UNITED STATES--KNOXVILLE (TENNESSEE)--
TOWNSCAPES--EVALUATION
The evaluative image of the city /
Jack L. Nasar.
Methods for determining how the
public evaluates the cityscape,
providing the basis for a visual
plan. Examples from Knoxville and
Chattanooga, Tenn.
AMERICAN PLANNING ASSOCIATION
JOURNAL 1990 Winter, v.56, no.1,
p.41-53, maps, tables, aerial
photos., refs.

UNITED STATES--KOHLER (WISCONSIN)--
SHOWROOMS--DESIGN--KOHLER DESIGN
CENTER
Fresh ideas from Kohler / Karen
Maserjian.
Features showrooms at the Kohler
Design Center, Kohler, Wisc.
INTERIOR DESIGN 1990 Apr., v.61,
no.6, p.210-[211], photos.

UNITED STATES--KONA (HAWAII)--HOUSES--
KONA HOUSE
Meet the architect: Kendrick Bangs
Kellogg.
Contents: Essay: Natural
vernacular / Kay Kaiser,--
Introduction / Ken Kellogg,--
Works: Wing Sweep house, Riverside
County, CA,--Yen house, 1981,
Westway house, 1979, Atoll house,
1973, all in La Jolla, CA --
Pacific Beach house, San Diego,
CA, 1972,--Kona house, Kona Coast,
Hawaii, 1962. Text in Japanese and
English.
GA HOUSES 1990 July, no.29,
p.[22]-71, axonometric views,
port., photos., plans, secns.,
site plans.

UNITED STATES--LA CROSSE (WISCONSIN)--
AIRPORT TERMINALS--LA CROSSE AIRPORT
Plane and simple: a gleaming new
terminal creates a memorable
gateway to a small city / Lynn
Nesmith.
La Crosse Airport, Wisc.
Architect: HSR Associates.
ARCHITECTURE: THE AIA JOURNAL 1990
Feb., v.79, no.2, p.[72]-75,
elev., photos., plans.

UNITED STATES--LA JOLLA (CALIFORNIA)--
HOTELS--INTERIOR DESIGN--HYATT
REGENCY
Roman holiday / Nayana Currimbhoy.
Hyatt Regency, La Jolla,
California. Architect/Interior
designer: Michael Graves.
INTERIORS 1990 Oct., v.150, no.3,
p.56-[61], dwg., photos., site
plan.

UNITED STATES--LA JOLLA (CALIFORNIA)--
HOUSES--ATOLL HOUSE
Meet the architect: Kendrick Bangs
Kellogg.
Contents: Essay: Natural
vernacular / Kay Kaiser,--
Introduction / Ken Kellogg,--
Works: Wing Sweep house, Riverside
County, CA,--Yen house, 1981,
Westway house, 1979, Atoll house,
1973, all in La Jolla, CA --
Pacific Beach house, San Diego,
CA, 1972,--Kona house, Kona Coast,
Hawaii, 1962. Text in Japanese and
English.
GA HOUSES 1990 July, no.29,
p.[22]-71, axonometric views,
port., photos., plans, secns.,
site plans.

UNITED STATES--LA JOLLA (CALIFORNIA)--
HOUSES--NAIMAN HOUSE
Michael Graves Architect [houses].
Contents: Naiman house, La Jolla,
California, design: 1988-89 --
Henry house, Rheinbeck, New York,
design: 1987-89. Architect:
Michael Graves. Text in Japanese
and English.
GA HOUSES 1990 Mar., no.28,
p.104-107, elevs., models, plans,
secns.

UNITED STATES--LA JOLLA (CALIFORNIA)--
HOUSES--WESTWAY HOUSE
Meet the architect: Kendrick Bangs
Kellogg.
Contents: Essay: Natural
vernacular / Kay Kaiser,--
Introduction / Ken Kellogg,--
Works: Wing Sweep house, Riverside
County, CA,--Yen house, 1981,
Westway house, 1979, Atoll house,
1973, all in La Jolla, CA --
Pacific Beach house, San Diego,
CA, 1972,--Kona house, Kona Coast,
Hawaii, 1962. Text in Japanese and
English.
GA HOUSES 1990 July, no.29,
p.[22]-71, axonometric views,
port., photos., plans, secns.,
site plans.

UNITED STATES--LA JOLLA (CALIFORNIA)--
HOUSES--YEN HOUSE
Forme zoomorfiche e spazi che
respirano: quattro esempi di
modellato di Kendrick Bangs
Kellogg. / Marisa Cerruti.
Restaurant, Jacksonville, Fl; Yen
house, La Jolla, CA; Gordon house,
san Diego, CA; restaurant, Rancho
Mirage, CA. English, French,
German, Spanish summaries, p.118.
ARCHITETTURA: CRONACHE E STORIA
1987 Feb., v.33, no.2(376),
p.[116]-126, photos., plans, site
plans.
Meet the architect: Kendrick Bangs
Kellogg.
Contents: Essay: Natural
vernacular / Kay Kaiser,--
Introduction / Ken Kellogg,--
Works: Wing Sweep house, Riverside
County, CA,--Yen house, 1981,
Westway house, 1979, Atoll house,
1973, all in La Jolla, CA --
Pacific Beach house, San Diego,
CA, 1972,--Kona house, Kona Coast,
Hawaii, 1962. Text in Japanese and
English.
GA HOUSES 1990 July, no.29,
(Continued next column)

UNITED STATES--LA JOLLA (CALIFORNIA)--
HOUSES--YEN HOUSE (CONTINUED)
Meet the architect:...(CONTINUED)
p.[22]-71, axonometric views,
port., photos., plans, secns.,
site plans.

UNITED STATES--LA JOLLA (CALIFORNIA)--
LABORATORIES--MEDICAL--SALK
INSTITUTE
Horizons into the future / Jonas
Salk.
A personal reminiscence about the
author's collaboration with Kahn
on the design of the Salk
Institute for Biological Studies,
La Jolla, Calif.
ART & ANTIQUES 1990 Dec., v.7,
no.10, p.[66]-67,116-117, port.
Il Salk Institute di Louis Kahn a La
Jolla = Louis Kahn's Salk
Institute at La Jolla / Pierluigi
Molteni.
FRAMES, PORTE & FINESTRE 1990
Jan.-Mar., no.26, p.54-59,
photos., plan.
A sense of where you are [Salk
Institute] / Patrick Pacheco.
Architects: Louis I. Kahn.
ART & ANTIQUES 1990 Dec., v.7,
no.10, p.68-[73],117-118, ports.,
photos.

UNITED STATES--LA JOLLA (CALIFORNIA)--
MULTI-USE COMPLEXES--AVENTINE
Grand illusion: the Aventine, La
Jolla, California, Michael Graves,
Architect / Leon Whiteson.
Mixed-use complex.
ARCHITECTURE: THE MAGAZINE OF THE
AMERICAN INSTITUTE OF ARCHITECTS
1990 Aug., v.79, no.8, p.[66]-71,
elev., photos., plan, site plan.

UNITED STATES--LA QUINTA
(CALIFORNIA)--MANSIONS--20TH
CENTURY--GRIFFIN HOUSE
Merv plays the desert / Charles
Gandee.
160-acre desert ranch, La Quinta,
Calif., designed for Merv Griffin
by Waldo Fernandez.
HOUSE & GARDEN 1990 Aug., v.162,
no.8, p.[68]-75, ports., photos.

UNITED STATES--LA QUINTA
(CALIFORNIA)--RANCHES--GRIFFIN RANCH
Merv plays the desert / Charles
Gandee.
160-acre desert ranch, La Quinta,
Calif., designed for Merv Griffin
by Waldo Fernandez.
HOUSE & GARDEN 1990 Aug., v.162,
no.8, p.[68]-75, ports., photos.

UNITED STATES--LABORATORIES
Inquiry: laboratories / Philip
Arcidi.
Portfolio of seven different types
of laboratory buildings in the
U.S.
PROGRESSIVE ARCHITECTURE 1990
Aug., v.71, no.8, p.98-105, model,
photos., plans, secns.

UNITED STATES--LAC QUI PARLE COUNTY
(MINNESOTA)--PAVILIONS--PRAIRIE
PAVILION
Quiet spirit: Prairie Pavilion, Lac
Qui Parle County, Minnesota /
Bruce N. Wright.
The Stageberg Partners,
Architects.
ARCHITECTURE: THE AIA JOURNAL 1990
Mar., v.79, no.3, p.154-[157],
photos., site plan.

UNITED STATES--LACKAWANNA (NEW YORK)--
STEEL MILLS--BETHLEHEM STEEL
The work of rolling rails in the 32"
mill at Bethlehem Steel's
Lackawanna Plant: industrial
archeology and labor history /
Thomas E. Leary.
SOCIETY FOR INDUSTRIAL ARCHEOLOGY.
JOURNAL 1990, v.16, no.1, p.39-54,
dwgs., photos., plans, refs.

UNITED STATES--LAFAYETTE (INDIANA)--
HOUSES--SECOND EMPIRE--CABLE BALL
HOUSE
The Cable Ball Home in Indiana /
Kathy Kastilahn.
1859 Second Empire house in
Lafayette.
VICTORIAN HOMES 1990 Winter, v.9,
no.1, p.[30-37], dets., photos.

UNITED STATES--LAKE BLUFF (ILLINOIS)--
WEEKEND HOUSES--ARCHITECTS'--CHICKEN
COOP (BOOTH HOUSE)
Free-range architecture: The Chicken
Coop, Lake Bluff, Illinois /
Clifford A. Pearson.
Weekend house of architect
Laurence Booth. Architects: Booth
Hansen & Associates.
ARCHITECTURAL RECORD 1990
Mid-Apr., v.178, no.5, p.84-87,
dwg., photos., plan.
Laurence Booth - Project in
Illinois.
Booth Weekend House, Lake
Bluff.Includes short article by
Booth. In Annaherung an eine
amerikanische Architektur.
Architect: Larry Booth of Booth
Hansen & Associates.
DEUTSCHE BAUZEITSCHRIFT 1990 May,
v.38, no.5, p.[655]-660, dets.,
photos., plan, site plans.

UNITED STATES--LAKE BUENA VISTA
(FLORIDA)--HOTELS--GRAND FLORIDIAN
HOTEL
Continuing a grand tradition: the
Grand Floridian Beach Resort, Lake
Buena Vista, Florida, Wimberly
Allison Tong & Goo, Architects.
ARCHITECTURAL RECORD 1990 Feb.,
v.178, no.2, p.118-121, photos.,
plans, secns., site plan.

UNITED STATES--LAKE BUENA VISTA
(FLORIDA)--RESORTS--GRAND FLORIDIAN
BEACH RESORT
Continuing a grand tradition: the
Grand Floridian Beach Resort, Lake
Buena Vista, Florida, Wimberly
Allison Tong & Goo, Architects.
ARCHITECTURAL RECORD 1990 Feb.,
v.178, no.2, p.118-121, photos.,
plans, secns., site plan.

UNITED STATES--LAKE ELSINORE
(CALIFORNIA)--TOURISM
Managing growth by tourism planning:
the example of Lake Elsinore,
California / Roger W. Mobley, Marc
L. Miller.
URBAN LAND 1990 May, v.49, no.5,
p.17-20, map, plan, aerial photos.

UNITED STATES--LAKE FOREST
(ILLINOIS)--HOUSES--ARCHITECTS'--
RAGDALE
Ragdale, an architect's dream home /
Cynthia A. Fuener.
Architect Howard Van Doren Shaw's
home, Lake Forest, Ill., built
1896.
HISTORIC ILLINOIS 1990 Dec., v.13,
no.4, p.10-12.

UNITED STATES--LAKE JACKSON (TEXAS)--
HOUSES--GILLILAND HOUSE
Houston design portfolio: slow
recovery.
Sesquicentennial Park (Team HOU);
Caldwell house (Natalye Appel);
Court at Museums Gate (Josiah
Baker); Gilliland house (Peter Jay
Zweig Architects); Finnell house
(Wittenberg Partnership); and St.
Mary's Episcopal Church (Gerald
Moorhead).
ARCHITECTURE: THE AIA JOURNAL 1990
Apr., v.79, no.4, p.54-73,
axonometric views, ill., elev.,
photos., plans, secns., site
plans.

UNITED STATES--LAKE MINNETONKA
(MINNESOTA)--HOTELS--QUEEN ANNE
STYLE--RUINED, EXTINCT, ETC.--HOTEL
LAFAYETTE
Lost Minnesota: the Hotel Lafayette
on the shores of Lake Minnetonka,
1882-1897 / Jack El-Hai.
Architect: James H. Brodie.
ARCHITECTURE MINNESOTA 1990
July-Aug., v.16, no.4, p.66,
photo.

UNITED STATES--LAKE MINNETONKA
(MINNESOTA)--VACATION HOUSES
On the lakes of "Big Water": a
sampling of Lake Minnetonka
architecture by boat / Eric
Kudalis.
ARCHITECTURE MINNESOTA 1990
July-Aug., v.16, no.4, p.24-31,
photos.

UNITED STATES--LAKE POKEGAMA
(MINNESOTA)--HOUSES--20TH CENTURY--
THOMPSON HOUSE
Learning from Lundie: a north-woods
house reinterprets its
Scandanavian roots / Adelheid
Fischer.
Thompson house, Lake Pokegama,
Minn. Architect: David Salmela.
ARCHITECTURE MINNESOTA 1990
July-Aug., v.16, no.4, p.40-43,
dwg., photos.

UNITED STATES--LAKE RABUN (GEORGIA)--
VACATION HOUSES--JENNINGS HOUSE
A house by a lake / Marybeth Weston.
Georgia vacation home of American
artist Comer Jennings. Architects:
Spitzmiller & Norris.
HOUSE BEAUTIFUL 1990 Aug., v.132,
no.8, p.[42]-48, port., photos.

UNITED STATES--LAKE SUPERIOR--
OBSERVATION TOWERS
Un belvedre sul lago = A belvedere
overlooking the lake.
Project for observations towers on
Lake Superior; architects: Ann
Cederna and Douglas Frederick.
L'ARCA 1990 Sept., no.41
suppl.l'Arca 2, p.100, models.
Four orders in gold and
stone/observation decks, I, II,
and III.
Contents: Jewelry series: ring,
pendant, earring and armband --
Observation decks for lakeside
park on Lake Superior. Architects:
Ann Cederna and Douglas Frederick.
Text in Japanese and English.
ARCHITECTURE AND URBANISM 1990
Dec., no.12(243), p.56-[65],
models, photos.

UNITED STATES--LAKE TAHOE
(CALIFORNIA)--LODGES--INTERIOR
DESIGN
Lake Tahoe retreat / Edie Lee Cohen.
Interiors of enlarged vacation
home. Architects: Backen, Arrigoni
and Ross. Interior designers:
Pfister Partnership.
INTERIOR DESIGN 1990 Oct., v.61,
no.14, p.224-[233], photos.

UNITED STATES--LAKE TAHOE
(CALIFORNIA)--VACATION HOUSES--
INTERIOR DESIGN
Lake Tahoe retreat / Edie Lee Cohen.
Interiors of enlarged vacation
home. Architects: Backen, Arrigoni
and Ross. Interior designers:
Pfister Partnership.
INTERIOR DESIGN 1990 Oct., v.61,
no.14, p.224-[233], photos.

UNITED STATES--LAKE VERMILION
(MINNESOTA)--GAMBLING CASINOS--
FORTUNE BAY BINGO CASINO
Bingo. An Indian reservation places
its bets on winning design.
Fortune Bay Bingo Casino, designed
by Architectural Resources.
ARCHITECTURE MINNESOTA 1990
Sept.-Oct., v.16, no.5, p.44-45,
photos.

UNITED STATES--LAKE WALES (FLORIDA)--
HOUSES--SPANISH COLONIAL REVIVAL--
PINEWOOD
Pinewood, Iron Mountain's secret
garden: Mediterranean revival in
the Olmsted tradition / Derek
Fell.
Near Lake Wales, Fla. Landscape
architect: William L. Phillips;
architect: Charles R. Wait.
SOUTHERN ACCENTS 1990 Sept., v.13,
no.7, p.90-[95], photos.

UNITED STATES--LAKELAND (FLORIDA)--
CAMPUSES--CONSERVATION AND
RESTORATION--FLORIDA SOUTHERN
COLLEGE
Restoration for Florida Southern /
Judy Donohue.
Program to restore all campus
buildings designed by Frank Lloyd
Wright between 1938 and 1958.
Restoration architects: L.D.
Astorino & Associates.
PROGRESSIVE ARCHITECTURE 1990
Apr., v.71, no.4, p.30-31, photos.

UNITED STATES--LAKELAND (FLORIDA)--
UNIVERSITIES AND COLLEGES--
BUILDINGS--CONSERVATION AND
RESTORATION--FLORIDA SOUTHERN
COLLEGE
Restoration for Florida Southern /
Judy Donohue.
Program to restore all campus
buildings designed by Frank Lloyd
Wright between 1938 and 1958.
Restoration architects: L.D.
Astorino & Associates.
PROGRESSIVE ARCHITECTURE 1990
Apr., v.71, no.4, p.30-31, photos.

UNITED STATES--LAKEVIEW (ARKANSAS)--
HOUSING DEVELOPMENTS--LAKEVIEW
ESTATES
Country living: a Mississippi
architect designs dignified
dwellings for the rural poor /
Robert A. Ivy.
Affordable housing in Arkansas
designed by Billy Wenzil: Lakeview
Estates; Prototype FHA Housing;
Keystone Apts.; and DeQueen
Villas.
ARCHITECTURE: THE MAGAZINE OF THE
AMERICAN INSTITUTE OF ARCHITECTS
1990 July, v.79, no.7, p.[68]-73,
elevs., photos., site plans.

UNITED STATES--LAKEVILLE
(MASSACHUSETTS)--WAREHOUSES--
TALBOT'S DISTRIBUTION CENTER
I luoghi del lavoro: un esempio
contemporeano nel Massachusetts =
Talbots Distribution Center,
Lakeville, Mass. / Stefania
Mornati.
Architects: Symmes Maini & McKee
Associates. Includes English
translation. French, German, and
Spanish summaries, p.4.
L'INDUSTRIA DELLE COSTRUZIONI 1990
Apr., v.24, no.222, p.37-[43],
dwgs., photos., site plan.

UNITED STATES--LAMBERTVILLE (NEW
JERSEY)--WEEKEND HOUSES--MILL HOUSE
Amicable separation: Mill House
Casino, Lambertville, New Jersey
Keenen/Riley, Architects / Deborah
K. Dietsch.
600-sq.-ft. freestanding casino
for playing pool.
ARCHITECTURE: THE MAGAZINE OF THE
AMERICAN INSTITUTE OF ARCHITECTS
1990 Aug., v.79, no.8, p.56-59,
photos., plans.
Una casa per i giochi di
Keenen-Riley / Kenneth Frampton.
Reuse of stone foundations from a
mill site, for small home and
gazebo. Captions in Italian and
English.
CASABELLA 1990 Oct., v.54, no.572,
p.34-35, elevs., photos., plans,
site plan.
Mill house casino, Lambertville, New
Jersey.
Architects: Keenen Riley. Text in
Japanese and English.
ARCHITECTURE AND URBANISM 1990
Dec., no.12(243), p.32-[39],
photos., plans.

UNITED STATES--LAMPS--VICTORIAN
A look at lighting: practical ideas
for your home.
A section with articles on style,
lamps as investments, restoration,
purchasing, and reproductions.
VICTORIAN HOMES 1990 Spring, v.9,
no.2, p.73-85,98, dwgs., photos.

UNITED STATES--LANCASTER
(PENNSYLVANIA)--RELIGIOUS
COMMUNITIES
Un paradiso provvisorio = A
"provisional paradise" / Michael
S. A. Dechert.
On the Mennonite- Amish community
in Lancaster, Pennsylvania. Text
in Italian and English.
SPAZIO E SOCIETA 1990 July-Sept.,
v.13, no.51, p.58-67, photos.

UNITED STATES--LAND USE--STUDY AND
TEACHING
Specialized land use curricula in
urban planning graduate programs /
Donald Miller, Frank Westerlund.
In North America.
JOURNAL OF PLANNING EDUCATION AND
RESEARCH 1990 summer, v.9, no.3,
p.203-206, tables, refs.

UNITED STATES--LANDFILLS--
ENVIRONMENTAL ASPECTS
Putting the squeeze on America's
land fills / Dan Treadaway.
AMERICAN CITY & COUNTY 1989 Aug.,
v.104, no.8, p.42-50, ill., port.

UNITED STATES--LANDMARK BUILDINGS--
20TH CENTURY--EVALUATION
Guidelines for evaluating and
nominating properties that have
achieved significance within the
last fifty years / Marcella
Sherfy, W. Ray Luce.
NATIONAL REGISTER BULLETIN [1989],
no.22, p.[1]-11, photos.

UNITED STATES--LANDMARKS (MARKERS)--
INVENTORIES
Geology NHL theme study / Harry A.
Butowsky.
A new theme study by the National
Park Service's NHL Survey.
CRM BULLETIN: A NATIONAL PARK
SERVICE TECHNICAL BULLETIN 1990,
v.13, no.1, p.8-9, photos.

UNITED STATES--LANDSCAPE
Pragmatism in paradise: technology
and the American landscape /
Robert L . Thayer, Jr.
LANDSCAPE 1990, v.30, no.3,
p.1-11, diagr., photos., table,
biblio.

UNITED STATES--LANDSCAPE--20TH CENTURY
Modern pastoralism and the middle
landscape / Peter G. Rowe.
OZ / COLLEGE OF ARCHITECTURE AND
DESIGN, KANSAS STATE UNIVERSITY
1989, v.11, p.4-9, ill., model,
photos., site plans, aerial
photos., biblio.

UNITED STATES--LANDSCAPE ARCHITECTURE
American landscape architecture:
designers and places [book review]
/ Cecelia Paine.
LANDSCAPE ARCHITECTURAL REVIEW
1990 May, v.11, no.2, p.25-27,
Wide spaces and widening chaos /
Laurie Olin.
Profile of eight Americans,
outside the profession, who have
influenced landscape architects
and landscape architecture.
LANDSCAPE ARCHITECTURE 1990 Oct.,
v.80, no.10, p.[76]-83, dwgs.,
ports.

UNITED STATES--LANDSCAPE
ARCHITECTURE--20TH CENTURY
Garten der Zukunft? / Elke von
Radziewsky, Vera Graaf.
Features work by the following
American landscape architects:
Peter Walker, Martha Schwartz,
George Hargreaves, and Michael Van
Valkenburgh. english summary,
p.2-3.
ARCHITEKTUR & WOHNEN 1990
Oct.-Nov., no.5, p.90-[98],100,
ports., photos.
"Schutzt die Garten vor den
Designern!" [interview] / Elke von
Radziewsky.
Alexandre Chemetoff's thoughts on
contemporary American garden
design.
ARCHITEKTUR & WOHNEN 1990
Oct.-Nov., no.5, p.104, port.

UNITED STATES--LANDSCAPE
ARCHITECTURE--20TH CENTURY--
POLITICAL ASPECTS
Hope & prophecy: how the New Deal
spurred the rise of public
practice / Warren T. Byrd.
On the changing stature of the
profession of landscape
architecture from 1933-1942.
LANDSCAPE ARCHITECTURE 1990 Oct.,
v.80, no.10, p.84-89, dwgs.,
elevs., photos., aerial photo.

UNITED STATES--LANDSCAPE
ARCHITECTURE--AWARDS AND PRIZES
1990 awards [ASLA].
Features winners in four
categories: design (11), planning
and analysis (10), communications
(8), and research (1). Includes 3
student projects.
LANDSCAPE ARCHITECTURE 1990 Nov.,
v.80, no.11, p.[33]-69, photos.,
models, plans, site plans.

UNITED STATES--LANDSCAPE
ARCHITECTURE--STUDENT PROJECTS
Pro bono pedagogy / Vernon Mays.
On student community service
projects.
LANDSCAPE ARCHITECTURE 1990 Sept.,
v.80, no.9, p.64-67, dwg., photos.

UNITED STATES--LANDSCAPE--EVALUATION
ACADIA NATIONAL PARK (MAINE)
Vista management in Acadia National
Park / Eckart Lange.
In Maine.
LANDSCAPE AND URBAN PLANNING 1990
Dec., v.19, no.4, p.353-376,
chart, maps, photos., plans,
secns., tables, refs.

UNITED STATES--LANDSCAPE--INVENTORIES
Published records of Italianate
gardens in America / Richard G.
Kenworthy.
A state-by-state listing of
gardens flourishing ca.1840-1940.
JOURNAL OF GARDEN HISTORY 1990
Jan.-Mar., v.10, no.1, p.[10]-70,
det., photos, plans, refs.

UNITED STATES--LANDSCAPE PROTECTION
Beyond buildings: by setting its
sights on a humbler past,
preservation may offer the key to
a better future / Linda Mack.
On the increasing recognition of
"vernacular landscapes."
ARCHITECTURE MINNESOTA 1990
July-Aug., v.16, no.4, p.9,60-61,
dwgs.

UNITED STATES--LANDSCAPE PROTECTION--
METHODOLOGY
Park Cultural Landscape[s] Workshop
/ Robert R. Page.
Held Sept.18-20,1990 in
Alexandria, Va. Sponsor: National
Park Service, Park Historic
Architecture Division.
CRM BULLETIN: A NATIONAL PARK
SERVICE TECHNICAL BULLETIN 1990,
v.13, no.6, p.25,

UNITED STATES--LANDSCAPES--
EVALUATION--ACADIA NATIONAL PARK
(MAINE)
Toward a sustainable landscape with
high visual preference and high
ecological integrity: the Loop
Road in Acadia National Park,
U.S.A. / Carl Steinitz.
LANDSCAPE AND URBAN PLANNING 1990
June, v.19, no.3, p.213-250, maps,
graphs, photos., tables, refs.

UNITED STATES--LANHAM (MARYLAND)--
STORAGE FACILITIES--MUSEUM AND
ARCHAEOLOGICAL REGIONAL STORAGE
FACILITY
A trip to MARS / Pam West.
The new Museum and Archaeological
Regional Storage Facility, in
Lanham, Md. serves the parks and
institutions within the National
Capital Region (NCR).
CRM BULLETIN: A NATIONAL PARK
SERVICE TECHNICAL BULLETIN 1990,
v.13, no.5, p.9,17,

UNITED STATES--LANSDOWNE
(PENNSYLVANIA)--HOUSES--QUEEN ANNE
STYLE--CONSERVATION AND
RESTORATION--SCHULTZ HOUSE
Queen Anne restoration: a royal
tribulation / Suzanne LaRosa.
House of Matt & Judie Schultz,
Lansdowne, Penn.
OLD-HOUSE JOURNAL 1990 Mar.-Apr.,
v.18, no.2, p.58-62, port.,
photos.

UNITED STATES--LANSING (MICHIGAN)--
CAPITOLS--RENAISSANCE REVIVAL--
CONSERVATION AND RESTORATION--SENATE
CHAMBERS
Sound restoration / Michael Wagner.
On the restoration and acoustic
work done on the 1878 Senate
Chambers of the Michigan State
capitol, Lansing. Original
architect: Elijah E. Meyers [sic].
Restoration architect: Richard
(Continued next page)

UNITED STATES--LANSING (MICHIGAN)--
CAPITOLS--RENAISSANCE REVIVAL--
CONSERVATION AND RESTORATION--SENATE
CHAMBERS (CONTINUED)
Sound restoration /...(CONTINUED)
Frank. Acoustics: Jaffe Acoustics.
INTERIORS 1390 July, v.149, no.12,
p.34, diagr., photos.

UNITED STATES--LARAMIE (WYOMING)--
MUSEUMS--ART--UNIVERSITY OF
WYOMING--AMERICAN HERITAGE CENTER
AND ART MUSEUM
American Heritage Center and Art
Museum.
Located on the University of
Wyoming campus, Laramie.
Architects: Antoine Predock
Architect.
PROGRESSIVE ARCHITECTURE 1990
Jan., v.71, no.1, p.96-98, models,
plans, secn., site plans.
Un centro per la memoria collettiva:
American Heritage Center, Laramie
/ Maurizio Cecchetti.
Architects: Antoine Predock
Architect.
L'ARCA 1990 Oct., no.42, p.40-47,
1 folded leaf, dwgs., model,
plans, site plan.

UNITED STATES--LAS COLINAS (TEXAS)--
NEW TOWNS
Las Colinas revisited / David
Dillon.
Texas new town that is now the
corporate headquarters for Exxon.
PLANNING 1989 Dec., v.55, no.12,
p.6-11, map, photos., aerial
photos.

UNITED STATES--LAS COLINAS (TEXAS)--
TRANSIT SYSTEMS--AREA PERSONAL
TRANSIT (APT)
The power of the people mover: Las
Colinas and the Area Personal
Transit System / John w. Kapala.
Transportation system devised for
Texas new town Las Colinas.
DEVELOPMENT 1990 July-Aug., v.21,
no.4, p.14-16, port., photos.

UNITED STATES--LAS VEGAS (NEVADA)--
CITIES AND TOWNS
Neon high noon: Viva Las Vegas /
Guilllermo Cabrera Infante.
FMR 1990 Apr., v.9, no.43,
p.21-40, photos.
Relearning from Las Vegas / Steven
Izenour, David A. Dashiell.
A return to Las Vegas to evaluate
how the strip has changed.
ARCHITECTURE: THE AIA JOURNAL 1990
Oct., v.79, no.10, p.[46-51],
photos.

UNITED STATES--LAS VEGAS (NEVADA)--
CITY PLANNING
Relearning from Las Vegas / Steven
Izenour, David A. Dashiell.
A return to Las Vegas to evaluate
how the strip has changed.
ARCHITECTURE: THE AIA JOURNAL 1990
Oct., v.79, no.10, p.[46-51],
photos.

UNITED STATES--LAS VEGAS (NEVADA)--
GAMBLING CASINOS
Commercial vernacular in Las Vegas /
Steve Izenour, David A. Dashiell
III.
Update on the state of the Las
Vegas Strip.
RASSEGNA 1990 Sept., v.12,
no.43/3, p.80-88, photos.

UNITED STATES--LAS VEGAS (NEVADA)--
LIBRARIES--PUBLIC--LAS VEGAS LIBRARY
Down the strip: Las Vegas
Library/Discovery Museum / Karen
D. Stein.
Antoine Predock, Architect.
ARCHITECTURAL RECORD 1990 Oct.,
v.178, no.11, p.68-[75],
axonometric view, photos., plans.

UNITED STATES--LAS VEGAS (NEVADA)--
MUSEUMS--CHILDREN'S--DISCOVERY
MUSEUM
Down the strip: Las Vegas
Library/Discovery Museum / Karen
D. Stein.
Antoine Predock, Architect.
ARCHITECTURAL RECORD 1990 Oct.,
v.178, no.11, p.68-[75],
axonometric view, photos., plans.

UNITED STATES--LAS VEGAS (NEVADA)--
OFFICE BUILDINGS--MINAMI OFFICE
TOWER
Minami office tower, Las Vegas,
Nevade, USA, 1991.
Proposed 36 story building;
architects: Helmuth, Obata &
Kassabaum. Text in Japanese and
English.
ARCHITECTURE AND URBANISM 1990
Dec., no.12 extra edition,
p.85-[89], dwgs., plans, secns.

UNITED STATES--LAS VEGAS (NEVADA)--
RETIREMENT COMMUNITIES--SUN CITY
SUMMERLIN
Expensive-looking housing that's
not.
Sun City Summerlin retirement
community, Las Vegas, Nev.
Architects: Richardson Nagy
Martin.
URBAN LAND 1990 Jan., no.1,
p.30-31, photos., plan.

UNITED STATES--LAS VEGAS (NEVADA)--
SIGNS AND SIGN-BOARDS
Commercial vernacular in Las Vegas /
Steve Izenour, David A. Dashiell
III.
Update on the state of the Las
Vegas Strip.
RASSEGNA 1990 Sept., v.12,
no.43/3, p.80-88, photos.

UNITED STATES--LAS VEGAS (NEVADA)--
SIGNS AND SIGN-BOARDS--NEON
Neon high noon: Viva Las Vegas /
Guilllermo Cabrera Infante.
FMR 1990 Apr., v.9, no.43,
p.21-40, photos.

UNITED STATES--LAS VEGAS (NEVADA)--
STREETS--LAS VEGAS STRIP
Commercial vernacular in Las Vegas /
Steve Izenour, David A. Dashiell
III.
Update on the state of the Las
Vegas Strip.
RASSEGNA 1990 Sept., v.12,
no.43/3, p.80-88, photos.

UNITED STATES--LAS VEGAS (NEVADA)--
STRIP RETAIL CENTERS
Relearning from Las Vegas / Steven
Izenour, David A. Dashiell.
A return to Las Vegas to evaluate
how the strip has changed.
ARCHITECTURE: THE AIA JOURNAL 1990
Oct., v.79, no.10, p.[46-51],
photos.

UNITED STATES--LAWRENCE (KANSAS)--
HOUSES--19TH CENTURY--CONSERVATION
AND RESTORATION--BENEDICT HOUSE
Preservation victory: Kansan Dan
Rockhill rescues Lawrence landmark
[Benedict House] / Janet Majure.
Built in 1869 or 1870.
PRESERVATION NEWS 1990 Mar., v.30,
no.3, p.12-13, ports., photos.

UNITED STATES--LEE COUNTY (GEORGIA)--
HOUSES--19TH CENTURY--CONSERVATION
AND RESTORATION--RAGAN-LONG HOUSE
Georgia vignettes: antebellum
artistry.
19th-cent. Ragan-Long house, Lee
Co., Ga., now home to Bruce and
Hope Campbell.
COLONIAL HOMES 1990 Oct., v.16,
no.5, p.[102-107],154, photos.

UNITED STATES--LEXINGTON (KENTUCKY)--
HOUSES--19TH CENTURY--CONSERVATION
AND RESTORATION--POPE HOUSE
Kentuckians revive rare gem by
Latrobe [John Pope house,
Lexington, Ky.] / Arnold Berke.
Built 1811, Benjamin Henry
Latrobe, architect. Includes
column "Young and full of
imagination" which describes the
two surviving houses Latrobe
designed in England.
PRESERVATION NEWS 1990 June, v.30,
no.6, p.1,19, dwg., photos.

UNITED STATES--LEXINGTON (KENTUCKY)--
HOUSES--MILLER HOUSE
Miller House, Lexington, Kentucky,
design: 1989; under construction /
Jose Oubrerie.
Architects: Jose Oubrerie and
Atelier Wylde-Oubrerie. Text in
English and Japanese.
GA HOUSES 1990 Mar., no.28,
p.78-79, elev., model, plans,
secns.

UNITED STATES--LIGHTHOUSES--
DOCUMENTATION
Guidelines for evaluating and
documenting historic aids to
navigation / James P. Delgado,
Kevin J. Foster.
NATIONAL REGISTER BULLETIN [1990],
no.34, 17p., photos., aerial
photo., biblio.

UNITED STATES--LIGHTHOUSES--EVALUATION
Guidelines for evaluating and
documenting historic aids to
navigation / James P. Delgado,
Kevin J. Foster.
NATIONAL REGISTER BULLETIN [1990],
no.34, 17p., photos., aerial
photo., biblio.

UNITED STATES--LOS ALTOS
(CALIFORNIA)--HOUSES--ALTERATIONS
AND ADDITIONS--SEYMOUR HOUSE
Bart Prince: the sculptural drama of
a Los Altos, California, addition
and remodel.
Remodeled central section of
Seymour house built of wood,
plastic and glass allows lots of
natural light to filter in.
ARCHITECTURAL DIGEST 1990 Feb.,
v.47, no.2, p.106-107, elev.,
photos.

UNITED STATES--LOS ANGELES
(CALIFORNIA)--AFFORDABLE HOUSING
Carlyle Hall joins CRA [interview].
His thoughts on the goals and
policies of the Community
Redevelopment Agency, which
focuses on affordable housing.
L. A. ARCHITECT 1990 Mar., p.7.

UNITED STATES--LOS ANGELES
(CALIFORNIA)--AFFORDABLE HOUSING--
HISTORY
"Low cost houses" und CRA / Diane
Ghirardo.
Changing definitions of "low cost
housing" from the 1950s through
the 1980s in Los Angeles.
Includes 3 "affordable" projects
by Koning & Eizenberg Architects.
Text in German; summaries in
German, French and English.
WERK, BAUEN + WOHNEN 1990
July-Aug., no.7-8, p.58-61,
photos., plans.

UNITED STATES--LOS ANGELES
(CALIFORNIA)--APARTMENT COMPLEXES--
COMPETITIONS
New case study housing: MoCA housing
competition, Franklin and La Brea,
Hollywood, 1988.
Competition for design of 40 units
of housing. Architects: Adele
Naude Santos (first prize),
Hodgetts & Fung, Eric Owen Moss.
Text in Japanese and English.
GA HOUSES 1990 July, no.29,
p.16-21, elevs., plan, secn., site
plan.

UNITED STATES--LOS ANGELES
(CALIFORNIA)--ARCHITECTURE--20TH
CENTURY
La citta come una pasticceria ...
Los Angeles / Paolo Riani.
VILLE GIARDINI 1990 Jan., no.244,
p.30-33, photos.
Core concerns / Donald J. Canty.
A report on Los Angeles, 15 years
after the introduction of a
downtown urban renewal plan.
ARCHITECTURAL RECORD 1990 June,
v.178, no.7, p.58-65, dwgs.,
models, maps, photos.
Los Angeles.
Theme issue devoted to new
architecture in Los Angeles,
Calif. 18 articles indexed
separately.
WERK, BAUEN + WOHNEN 1990
July-Aug., no.7-8, entire issue
(73p.), axonometric views, ill.,
dwgs., photos., plans, secns.,
site plans, sketches, aerial
photos., refs.

UNITED STATES--LOS ANGELES
(CALIFORNIA)--ARCHITECTURE--20TH
CENTURY (CONTINUED)
Morphosis: L.A. beat / Antti Ahlava.
Report on a lecture given by Thom
Mayne in Helsinki, 3 Oct.1989.
ARKKITEHTI 1989, v.86, no.8,
p.20-21, models, photos., plans.
Neues aus L.A.: zu vier Tendenzen
der Architektur in Los Angeles /
Werner Lang.
BAUMEISTER 1990 Oct., v.87, no.10,
p.36-41, model, photos., plans,
secns.

UNITED STATES--LOS ANGELES
(CALIFORNIA)--ART CENTERS--J. PAUL
GETTY FINE ARTS CENTER
In costruzione il Paul Getty Center
di Los Angeles / D. Mandolesi.
Architect: Richard Meier.
L'INDUSTRIA DELLE COSTRUZIONI 1990
Oct., v.24, no.228, p.71, site
plans.
Invisible acropolis / Diane
Ghirardo.
Richard Meier's proposal for the
J. Paul Getty Fine Arts Center in
Santa Monica. "Examines...the
elitist assumptions it envitably
endorses."
ARCHITECTURAL REVIEW 1990 June,
v.187, no.1120, p.92-95, models,
map, photos.
J. Paul Getty a Los Angeles di
Richard Meier.
CASABELLA 1990 Apr., v.54, no.567,
p.32-33, axonometric view, elev.,
model, plan, site plans.
Newly published drawings of Richard
Meier's Getty Center / Mark Alden
Branch.
Drawings were recently published
in: Richard Meier: building for
art (Birkhauser, Boston).
PROGRESSIVE ARCHITECTURE 1990
Aug., v.71, no.8, p.119-121,
axonometric view, diagrs., elevs.,
plan, secn., site plan.

UNITED STATES--LOS ANGELES
(CALIFORNIA)--ART GALLERIES--MARGO
LEAVIN GALLERY
Oldenburg/Van Bruggen: il coltello
affetta muro.
The Margo Leavin Gallery, Los
Angeles, a converted post office,
features a work by artists Claes
Oldenburg and Coosje van Bruggen.
In Italian and English.
DOMUS 1990 May, no.716, p.[14-15],
dwgs., photos.

UNITED STATES--LOS ANGELES
(CALIFORNIA)--ARTISTS' STUDIOS--
HERMAN STUDIO
Herman residence and studio, Los
Angeles, 1986.
Architect: Frederick Fisher.
WERK, BAUEN + WOHNEN 1990
July-Aug., no.7-8, p.32-35,
photos., plans, secn.
Herman residence and studio, Los
Angeles, California.
Architect: Frederick Fisher.
Spanish, English text.
QUADERNS D'ARQUITECTURA I
URBANISME 1990 Jan.-Feb.-Mar.,
no.184, p.46, photos., plans,
secn.

UNITED STATES--LOS ANGELES
(CALIFORNIA)--AUDITORIUMS, CONCERT
HALLS--ALTERATIONS AND ADDITIONS--
COMPETITIONS--PAN PACIFIC AUDITORIUM
Real Problems result / Steven
Geoffrion, Robert Leach.
Winners of the 1990 Real Problems
competitions, which focused on the
adaptive reuse of the Pan Pacific
Auditorium. Winners: Douglas Sung,
Anthony Cheung.
L. A. ARCHITECT 1990 Mar., p.1,
elev., plan, secn.

UNITED STATES--LOS ANGELES
(CALIFORNIA)--AUDITORIUMS, CONCERT
HALLS--COMPETITIONS--WALT DISNEY
CONCERT HALL
Los Angeles Philharmonic Hall, Los
Angeles, U.S.A., 1988.
Architects: James Stirling,
Michael Wilford and Associates.
Text in Japanese and English.
ARCHITECTURE AND URBANISM 1990
May, no.5 extra edition,
p.204-217, axonometric views,
elevs., models, photo., plans,
secns., site plans.
Rafael Moneo: today's American
architecture.
Report on the Gropius Lecture,
given Apr.25, 1990, in which Moneo
examined two projects: Symphony
Hall, Philadelphia (Venturi Scott
Brown and Associates) and Disney
Concert Hall, Los Angeles (Frank
Gehry and Associates).
GSD NEWS / HARVARD UNIVERSITY.
GRADUATE SCHOOL OF DESIGN 1990
Summer-Fall, v.19, no.1, p.13-14.
Walt Disney concert hall, Los
Angeles, 1988.
Architects: Frank O. Gehry &
Associates. Includes essay: The
snake and the fish on the hill:
Frank O. Gehry's project for the
Walt Disney Concert Hall in Los
Angeles /Kurt W. Forster. Text in
Japanese and English.
ARCHITECTURE AND URBANISM 1990
Aug., no.8(239), p.[33]-52, model,
plans, secn., site plan, sketches.

UNITED STATES--LOS ANGELES
(CALIFORNIA)--AUDITORIUMS, CONCERT
HALLS--PERFORMING ARTS PAVILION
Performing Arts Pavilion.
Part of an arts park in Los
Angeles, the pavilion will contain
two theaters. Architects:
Morphosis, Coop Himmelblau and
Burton & Spitz.
PROGRESSIVE ARCHITECTURE 1990
Jan., v.71, no.1, p.107-109,
models, map, plans, secns.,
sketch.

UNITED STATES--LOS ANGELES
(CALIFORNIA)--AUDITORIUMS, CONCERT
HALLS--WALT DISNEY CONCERT HALL
Frank O. Gehry.
Entire issue devoted to the work
of this American architect.
Criticism by A. Zaera Polo and
David Cohn. 15 projects and
buildings from 1987-1990 featured.
Text in Spanish and English.
EL CROQUIS 1990 Nov., v.9, no.45,
p.1-124, ports., elevs., models,
photos., plans, secns., site
plans, refs.

UNITED STATES--LOS ANGELES
(CALIFORNIA)--AUDITORIUMS, CONCERT
HALLS--WALT DISNEY CONCERT HALL
(CONTINUED)
La musica de Los Angeles: sala de
conciertos Walt Disney, Los
Angeles, California, 1989-1995.
Architects: Frank O. Gehry and
Associates. English summary, p.88.
A & V 1990, no.25, p.76-77,
models, plans, secn.
La serpiente y el pez en la colina:
el auditorio de Gehry / Kurt W.
Forster.
Disney Concert Hall, Los Angeles.
ARQUITECTURA VIVA 1990 Jan.-Feb.,
no.10, p.27-31, dwg., models,
photos., sketches.

UNITED STATES--LOS ANGELES
(CALIFORNIA)--BATHROOMS--INTERIOR
DESIGN--ORR HOUSE
L.A. luxe / Paddy Calistro.
Bathroom for Hollywood writer.
Architect: Van-Martin Rowe.
HOUSE BEAUTIFUL 1990 May, v.132,
no.5, p.78-[79], photos., plan.

UNITED STATES--LOS ANGELES
(CALIFORNIA)--CAMPUSES--UNIVERSITY
OF CALIFORNIA, LOS ANGELES
UCLA plans for the future
[interview].
Interview with Charles Oakley,
UCLA's campus architect.
L. A. ARCHITECT 1990 May, p.5,

UNITED STATES--LOS ANGELES
(CALIFORNIA)--CENTRAL BUSINESS
DISTRICTS
Core concerns / Donald J. Canty.
A report on Los Angeles, 15 years
after the introduction of a
downtown urban renewal plan.
ARCHITECTURAL RECORD 1990 June,
v.178, no.7, p.58-65, dwgs.,
models, maps, photos.

UNITED STATES--LOS ANGELES
(CALIFORNIA)--CITIES AND TOWNS
Sichtbare und unsichtbare Strukturen
= Structures visibles et
invisibles = Phenomenal and
imaginative structures.
On the chaotic urban structure of
Los Angeles. Text in German;
summaries and captions in German,
French and English.
WERK, BAUEN + WOHNEN 1990
July-Aug., no.7-8, p.4-17, maps,
photos., site plans, sketches,
aerial photos.

UNITED STATES--LOS ANGELES
(CALIFORNIA)--CITY PLANNING
LA, DAPT: a progress report / Arthur
Golding.
On the work of the Los Angeles
Design Action Planning Team: a pro
bono group which holds workshops
and writes recommendations on
urban design in different areas of
the city.
L.A. ARCHITECT 1990 Feb., p.[8]-9,
map.

UNITED STATES--LOS ANGELES
(CALIFORNIA)--CITY PLANNING--CENTRAL
CITY WEST
L.A.'s Central City West plan
accents enlightened development /
Leon Whiteson.
Successful public-private
partnership for the development of
the Central City West district of
Los Angeles.
URBAN LAND 1990 Dec., v.49, no.12,
p.10-15, dwgs., site plans.

UNITED STATES--LOS ANGELES
(CALIFORNIA)--CITY PLANNING--
COMPETITIONS--BUNKER HILL
Planning and urban design
competition / Ernest R. Alexander,
Lawrence P. Witzling, guest
editors.
Seven articles, including one on a
mixed-use project for Bunker Hill
in Los Angeles. Authors: Jeffrey
E. Ollswang, Tridib Banerjee,
Anastasia Loukaitou-Sideris,
Joanna Eley, Dennis J. Casper,
Ruth Eckdish Knack, Andrew D.
Seidel.
JOURNAL OF ARCHITECTURAL AND
PLANNING RESEARCH 1990 Summer,
v.7, no.2, p.91-180, charts, site
plans, biblios., refs.

UNITED STATES--LOS ANGELES
(CALIFORNIA)--CITY PLANNING--
CONGRESSES
Special issue: redesigning the
region.
Looks at the issues addressed by
the Regional Urban Design
Conference, held Oct.4-6, Santa
Monica, Calif.
L.A. ARCHITECT 1990 Oct., entire
issue, maps, photos., aerial
photos.

UNITED STATES--LOS ANGELES
(CALIFORNIA)--CITY PLANNING--
METAPOLIS
Four projects of Aks Runo.
Contents: "Metapolis" Los Angeles
project, 1987 -- Olympic West
office towers, Los Angeles, 1988
-- Tokyo International Forum,
Tokyo, 1989 -- Alexandria Library
project, Egypt, 1989. Architects:
Aks Runo, Bahram Shirdel and
Andrew Zago. Text in Japanese and
English.
ARCHITECTURE AND URBANISM 1990
June, no.6(237), p.[7]-28, elevs.,
models, plans, site plan.

UNITED STATES--LOS ANGELES
(CALIFORNIA)--CITY PLANNING--
WESTWOOD
Planning Westwood / Pat Smith ... et
al.
L. A. ARCHITECT 1990 May, p.1,8-9,
map, site plan.

UNITED STATES--LOS ANGELES
(CALIFORNIA)--COMPREHENSIVE PLANS--
CENTRAL CITY WEST
L.A.'s Central City West plan
accents enlightened development /
Leon Whiteson.
Successful public-private
partnership for the development of
the Central City West district of
Los Angeles.
URBAN LAND 1990 Dec., v.49, no.12,
(Continued next column)

UNITED STATES--LOS ANGELES
(CALIFORNIA)--COMPREHENSIVE PLANS--
CENTRAL CITY WEST (CONTINUED)
L.A.'s Central City...(CONTINUED)
p.10-15, dwgs., site plans.

UNITED STATES--LOS ANGELES
(CALIFORNIA)--CONFERENCE ROOMS--
INTERIOR DESIGN--BOSTON COMPANY
The Boston Company / Mayer Rus.
Office interiors on lobby level in
one of the towers in California
Plaza, Los Angeles. Architects for
tower: Arthur Erickson Architects.
Interior designers for offices:
Francisco Kripacz, Arthur Erickson
Architects.
INTERIOR DESIGN 1990 Feb., v.61,
no.3, p.188-[189], photos., plan.

UNITED STATES--LOS ANGELES
(CALIFORNIA)--CORPORATE OFFICE
BUILDINGS--HOME SAVINGS OF AMERICA
TOWER
In good standing: Home Savings of
America Tower, Los Angeles /
Donald London.
Architect: Albert C. Martin &
Associates. Lobby murals by
Richard Haas.
ARCHITECTURAL RECORD 1990 Feb.,
v.178, no.2, p.94-97, elev.,
photos., plan, secn.

UNITED STATES--LOS ANGELES
(CALIFORNIA)--COTTAGES--INTERIOR
DESIGN--MASON - CARLISLE HOUSE
Double billing ... a California
cottage / Pilar Viladas.
Home of Morgan Mason and Belinda
Carlisle, Los Angeles. Designer:
Brian Murphy.
HOUSE & GARDEN 1990 June, v.162,
no.6, p.[126-131], port., photos.

UNITED STATES--LOS ANGELES
(CALIFORNIA)--CULTURAL CENTERS--
STUDENT PROJECTS--LOS ANGELES ART
PARK
Experimentation as Modus Operandi:
an investigation of design
process: the Los Angele Art Park /
Marc Angelil.
JOURNAL OF ARCHITECTURAL EDUCATION
1990 Nov., v.44, no.1, p.37-48,
dwgs., models, refs.

UNITED STATES--LOS ANGELES
(CALIFORNIA)--CULTURAL DISTRICTS--
LOS ANGELES ARTS PARK
Los Angeles Arts Park.
Competition entry. Architects:
Smith-Miller + Hawkinson. Spanish,
English text.
QUADERNS D'ARQUITECTURA I
URBANISME 1990 Jan.-Feb.-Mar.,
no.184, p.74-[77], models, site
plan.
The Los Angeles Arts Park / Philip
Arcidi.
Features five projects by the
following architects: Tod
Williams, Billie Tsien &
Associates, Mark Mack, Hodgetts
and Fung Design Associates, Adele
Naude Santos and Morphosis.
PROGRESSIVE ARCHITECTURE 1990
Sept., v.71, no.9, p.143-146.,
axonometric views, ill., models,
plans, secns., site plan.

UNITED STATES--LOS ANGELES
(CALIFORNIA)--CULTURAL DISTRICTS--
LOS ANGELES ARTS PARK (CONTINUED)
Tod Williams - Billie Tsien
[interview] / Kate Nesbitt.
Illustrates three projects: Arts
Park Center, Los Angeles; Feinberg
Hall, Princeton University; Tarlo
House, Sagaponack, N.Y. In Danish
and English.
SKALA 1990, no.20, p.34-39,
models, photos., refs.

UNITED STATES--LOS ANGELES
(CALIFORNIA)--DESIGN CENTERS--
ALTERATIONS AND ADDITIONS--PACIFIC
DESIGN CENTER
L'ampliamento del Pacific Design
Center a Hollywood = Pacific
Design Center, Phase II, West
Hollywood, Calif. / Silvano
Stucchi.
Architects: Cesar Pelli &
Associates, Gruen Associates. In
Italian and English; French,
German and Spanish summaries, p.4.
L'INDUSTRIA DELLE COSTRUZIONI 1990
June, v.24, no.224, p.32-37,4,
elev., photos., plans, secns.,
site plans.
Special feature: recent works of
Cesar Pelli.
Contents: Editor's introduction--
Architects' statement / Cesar
Pelli-- Essay: Urban iconography
and the medium of architecture /
Gavin Macrae-Gibson, p.130-137--
Works: World Financial Center--
Norwest Tower-- Pacific Design
Center expansion-- Mattatuck
Museum-- Ley Student Center
expansion, Rice University-- Yale
Center for Molecular Medicine,
Yale University-- Carnegie Hall
tower-- Sunarhauserman
headquarters-- Fan Pier master
plan. Architects: Cesar Pelli &
Associates. Text in Japanese and
English.
ARCHITECTURE AND URBANISM 1990
Feb., no.2(233), p.[59]-148,
dwgs., elevs., photos., plans,
secns., site plans.

UNITED STATES--LOS ANGELES
(CALIFORNIA)--ENDANGERED PLACES--LOS
ANGELES MEMORIAL COLISEUM
L.A. stadium threatened [Los Angeles
Memorial Coliseum] / Rachel S.
Cox.
Designed by John Parkinson and
Donald B. Parkinson, and completed
in 1923.
PRESERVATION NEWS 1990 Mar., v.30,
no.3, p.1,11, dwg., photo.

UNITED STATES--LOS ANGELES
(CALIFORNIA)--ENTRANCES--GLASS--
GRAND PLACE TOWER
Steel and glass bring form to light
/ James S. Russell.
Two examples of glass lobby
entrances: Los Angeles Center
(Johnson, Fain and Pereira) and
Grand Place Tower, Los Angeles
(SOM). Engineers: Ove Arup
Partnership; designers: James
Carpenter Design Associates.
ARCHITECTURAL RECORD axonometric
views, dets., dwgs., models.

UNITED STATES--LOS ANGELES
(CALIFORNIA)--ENTRANCES--GLASS--LOS
ANGELES CENTER
Steel and glass bring form to light
/ James S. Russell.
Two examples of glass lobby
entrances: Los Angeles Center
(Johnson, Fain and Pereira) and
Grand Place Tower, Los Angeles
(SOM). Engineers: Ove Arup
Partnership; designers: James
Carpenter Design Associates.
ARCHITECTURAL RECORD axonometric
views, dets., dwgs., models.

UNITED STATES--LOS ANGELES
(CALIFORNIA)--ETHNIC NEIGHBORHOODS
Power of Place / Jane Brown
Gillette.
The Power of Place, a small,
nonprofit organization in Los
Angeles, has developed 9 sites
associated with the city's ethnic
history.
HISTORIC PRESERVATION 1990
July-Aug., v.42, no.4, p.44-49,
70-71, ports., photos.

UNITED STATES--LOS ANGELES
(CALIFORNIA)--FAST-FOOD
RESTAURANTS--KENTUCKY FRIED CHICKEN
Funky chicken / Michael Webb.
Kentucky Fried Chicken restaurant,
Los Angeles; architects: Grinstein
- Daniels.
BLUEPRINT (LONDON, ENGLAND) 1990
Sept., no.70, p.38-39, photos.
Kentucky home: Kentucky Fried
Chicken, Los Angeles, California,
Grinstein/Daniels, Architects /
Leon Whiteson.
ARCHITECTURE: THE AIA JOURNAL 1990
Oct., v.79, no.10, p.52-55,
photos., plans, secns., site plan.

UNITED STATES--LOS ANGELES
(CALIFORNIA)--HISTORIC PRESERVATION
Power of Place / Jane Brown
Gillette.
The Power of Place, a small,
nonprofit organization in Los
Angeles, has developed 9 sites
associated with the city's ethnic
history.
HISTORIC PRESERVATION 1990
July-Aug., v.42, no.4, p.44-49,
70-71, ports., photos.

UNITED STATES--LOS ANGELES
(CALIFORNIA)--HOTELS--INTERIOR
DESIGN--CHECKERS
Checkers - small wonder in Los
Angeles / Michael Webb.
Features renovated interiors of
1920s hotel in downtown L.A.
Architects: Eric B. Holtsmark,
Kaplan McLauglin Diaz. Interior
designer: James Northcutt.
ARCHITECTURAL DIGEST 1990 Oct.,
v.47, no.11, p.[198],[199],164,
photos.

UNITED STATES--LOS ANGELES
(CALIFORNIA)--HOUSES--20TH CENTURY
De-strutturazione a piu livelli:
casa a Los Angeles.
Architect: Dean Nota.
ARCHITETTURA: CRONACHE E STORIA
1990 Mar., v.36, no.3(413),
p.210-211, photos, plans, secn.

UNITED STATES--LOS ANGELES
(CALIFORNIA)--HOUSES--20TH CENTURY
(CONTINUED)
Metal-frame houses of the Modern
Movement in Los Angeles, Part 2 /
Neil Jackson.
"The style that nearly...".
Appendix lists 44 works by
architect's name, including
several Case Study Houses, by
Craig Ellwood, Pierre Koenig,
Raphael Soriano, and others.
ARCHITECTURAL HISTORY 1990, v.33,
p.[167-187], dwgs., photos.,
plans, site plans, refs.
Moderne Wohnbauarchitektur =
L'architecture d'habitat moderne =
Modern domestic architecture /
Judith Sheine.
A selection of Los Angeles houses
dating from 1913-1959. Text in
German; summaries in German,
French, and English.
WERK, BAUEN + WOHNEN 1990
July-Aug., no.7-8, p.46-53, dwg.,
photos., plan, refs.

UNITED STATES--LOS ANGELES
(CALIFORNIA)--HOUSES--20TH CENTURY--
EXHIBITIONS
Blueprints for modern living:
exhibition at the Museum of
Contemporary Art, Los Angeles,
Oct.17, 1989-Feb.18, 1990
[exhibition review].
Installation architects: Hodgetts
& Fung. Text in Japanese and
English.
GA HOUSES 1990 July, no.29,
p.8-15, dwgs., elevs., photos.
Blueprints for modern living:
history and legacy of the Case
Study Houses: Museum of
Contemporary Art, Los Angeles, 17
October-18 February 1990
[exhibition review] / Mary Banham.
AA FILES 1990 Autumn, no.20,
p.77-82, axonometric view,
photos., plan, refs.
California case study: Blueprints
for modern living: history and
legacy of the Case Study Houses,
edited by Elizabeth A. T. Smith
[book review] / Ivor Richards.
Accompanies exhibition at the
Museum of Contemporary art, Los
Angeles 17 Oct.1989 - 18 Feb.1990.
ARCHITECTS' JOURNAL 1990 Oct.3,
v.192, no.14, p.71, photo.
Das Case-Study Programm: eine
Ruckschau auf die Kalifornische
Moderne nach 1945 / Werner Lang.
BAUMEISTER 1990 Apr., v.87, no.4,
p.54-59, photos.
Dogmas modernos: las "casa modelo"
Californias [exhibition review] /
Richard Ingersoll.
ARQUITECTURA VIVA 1990 Mar.-Apr.,
no.11, p.53-55, dwgs., photos
Eames design: the work of the office
of Charles and Ray Eames [and]
Blueprints for modern living:
history and legacy of the Case
Study houses [book review] / Pat
Kirkham.
Review of the 1989 book by John
and Marilyn Newhart and of the
1989 catalogue by the Museum of
Contemporary Art, Los Angeles.
JOURNAL OF DESIGN HISTORY 1990,
v.3, no.2-3, p.186-191, photos.,
refs.

UNITED STATES--LOS ANGELES
(CALIFORNIA)--HOUSES--20TH CENTURY--
HERMAN HOUSE
Herman residence and studio, Los
Angeles, 1986.
Architect: Frederick Fisher.
WERK, BAUEN + WOHNEN 1990
July-Aug., no.7-8, p.32-35,
photos., plans, secn.

UNITED STATES--LOS ANGELES
(CALIFORNIA)--HOUSES--20TH CENTURY--
MILLER HOUSE
Nel cielo sopra Los Angeles / Paolo
Riani.
Miller house in Laurel Canyon.
Architect: Paolo Riani.
VILLE GIARDINI 1990 May, no.248,
p.[10]-15, ill., photos., plans,
secn.

UNITED STATES--LOS ANGELES
(CALIFORNIA)--HOUSES--20TH CENTURY--
SCHNABEL HOUSE
Casa come villaggio: Schnabel
residence di Frank O. Gehry.
In Los Angeles, Calif.
ARCHITETTURA; CRONACHE E STORIA
1990 June, v.36, no.6(416),
p.443-445, photos., plans, secn.
Haus Schnabel, Los Angeles, 1988 /
Dagmar Richter.
Architect: Frank O. Gehry & Assoc.
WERK, BAUEN + WOHNEN 1990
July-Aug., no.7-8, p.36-39, elev.,
photos., plans, secn.

UNITED STATES--LOS ANGELES
(CALIFORNIA)--HOUSES--20TH CENTURY--
SILVERTOP
Silvertop house, Los Angeles, 1963.
Architect: John Lautner.
WERK, BAUEN + WOHNEN 1990
July-Aug., no.7-8, p.64-67,
elevs., photos., plans, site plan.

UNITED STATES--LOS ANGELES
(CALIFORNIA)--HOUSES--20TH CENTURY--
VASA HOUSE
Technik und Poesie: Haus Vasa in
West-Los Angeles (1984-1985).
Architects: Jurg Lang, Helmut C.
Schulitz.
ARCHITEKTUR, INNENARCHITEKTUR,
TECHNISCHER AUSBAU 1990 Jan.-Feb.,
v.98, no.1-2, p.18-21, dets.,
photos., plans, secns.

UNITED STATES--LOS ANGELES
(CALIFORNIA)--HOUSES--ALTERATIONS
AND ADDITIONS
Greffe et graphisme: extension d'une
maison a Los Angeles / Claudine
Mulard.
Architect: Frank Israel. English
summary, p.47.
ARCHITECTURE INTERIEURE CREE 1990
Feb., no.234, p.96-[99], elevs.,
photos., site plan.

UNITED STATES--LOS ANGELES
(CALIFORNIA)--HOUSES--ALTERATIONS
AND ADDITIONS--CDLT 1,2
Morphosis [houses].
Contents: CDLT 1,2, Los Angeles,
Calif., 1987-89.-- Was house,
Beverly Hills, Calif., 1988.--
Sixth Street house, Santa Monica,
Calif., 1986. Text in Japanese and
English.
GA HOUSES 1990 Mar., no.28,
p.6-19, axonometric views.,
elevs., models., plans, secns.

UNITED STATES--LOS ANGELES
(CALIFORNIA)--HOUSES--ALTERATIONS
AND ADDITIONS--LAUREL CANYON HOUSE
Sapore di messico [house, Laurel
Canyon, Los Angeles] / Lucia Bisi.
Architect: Steven Burr Williams.
VILLE GIARDINI 1990 Apr., no.247,
p.12-17, photos, plan.

UNITED STATES--LOS ANGELES
(CALIFORNIA)--HOUSES--ALTERATIONS
AND ADDITIONS--REICHEL - SINGER
HOUSE
Kitchens that cook: hot news, cool
choices / Julie V. Iovine.
Five projects, including an
expansion of the Sprecher house,
Los Angeles (architect: Michele
Saee); a Connecticut kitchen
renovation (architect: Louis
Mackall); Reichel-Singer house
conversion, Los Angeles (designer:
Josh Schweitzer); Sagalyn kitchen
(architect: Scott Simons); Laurie
and Maurie Williams' kitchen
renovation, Ore.
METROPOLITAN HOME 1990 May, v.22,
no.5, p.[123-136], det., photos.

UNITED STATES--LOS ANGELES
(CALIFORNIA)--HOUSES--ARCHITECTS'--
NEUTRA HOUSE
A living landmark of early
California modernism / Thomas S.
Hines.
Richard Neutra's 1932 home in Los
Angeles, also called the Van der
Leeuw Research House or VDL house.
House was nearly destroyed by fire
in 1963 and rebuilt.
ARCHITECTURAL DIGEST 1990 May,
v.47, no.5, p.56-66, port.,
photos.

UNITED STATES--LOS ANGELES
(CALIFORNIA)--HOUSES--ARCHITECTS'--
OJEDA HOUSE
Homesteading, the L.A. way / Julie
V. Iovine.
The stucco house (a cube) of
architect Ruben Ojeda.
METROPOLITAN HOME 1990 Sept.,
v.22, no.9, p.125-[129], ports.,
photos.

UNITED STATES--LOS ANGELES
(CALIFORNIA)--HOUSES--CHINESE
The house of the butterfly: Bob Ray
Offenhauser evokes the spirit of
ancient China in Los Angeles /
Michael Webb.
Chinese-style home modeled on
restored Ming home in Suzhou,
China. Interior designer: Harvey
Ackerman.
ARCHITECTURAL DIGEST 1990 Dec.,
v.47, no.13, p.[166]-175,228,
port., photos., site plan.

UNITED STATES--LOS ANGELES
(CALIFORNIA)--HOUSES--CRAFTSMAN--
INTERIOR DESIGN--TOTAH HOUSE
Der Stil-Virtuose / Vera Graaf.
Interiors of furniture designer
Larry Totah's craftsman-style home
in Los Angeles. English summary,
p.2.
ARCHITEKTUR & WOHNEN 1990
Oct.-Nov., no.5, p.56-64, port.,
photos.

UNITED STATES--LOS ANGELES
(CALIFORNIA)--HOUSES--HERMAN HOUSE
Herman residence and studio, Los
Angeles, California.
Architect: Frederick Fisher.
Spanish, English text.
QUADERNS D'ARQUITECTURA I
URBANISME 1990 Jan.-Feb.-Mar.,
no.184, p.46, photos., plans,
secn.

UNITED STATES--LOS ANGELES
(CALIFORNIA)--HOUSES--INTERIOR
DESIGN--CORCORAN HOUSE
Color makes a splash / Timothy J.
Ward.
Two interiors by designer Gregory
Evans: Dagny Corcoran house, Los
Angeles, and David Hockney beach
house, Calif.
METROPOLITAN HOME 1990 June, v.22,
no.6, p.73-[81], port., photos.

UNITED STATES--LOS ANGELES
(CALIFORNIA)--HOUSES--INTERIOR
DESIGN--CUKOR HOUSE (KERSTING IRVING
HOUSE)
The legend lives on: the
redecoration of George Cukor's
house evokes a golden era of the
silver screen / Leo Lerman.
Now home of Lynn von Kersting and
Richard Irving. Interior
designers: Von Kersting/Smith.
HOUSE & GARDEN 1990 Jan., v.162,
no.1, p.[60-69],146, port.,
photos.

UNITED STATES--LOS ANGELES
(CALIFORNIA)--HOUSES--INTERIOR
DESIGN--DUQUETTE HOUSE
One man's magic / Elizabeth Venant.
Features interiors of designer
Tony Duquette's home in Los
Angeles.
CONNOISSEUR 1990 Dec., v.220,
no.947, p.132-[138], ports.,
photos.

UNITED STATES--LOS ANGELES
(CALIFORNIA)--HOUSES--INTERIOR
DESIGN--FELDMAN HOUSE
A Dolena legacy: refurbishing the
architect's classic house in Los
Angeles / Bruce David Cohen.
Interiors of 1930s James Dolena
house owned by Mark and Marcie
Feldman. Interior designer: Craig
Wright.
ARCHITECTURAL DIGEST 1990 Sept.,
v.47, no.10, p.[164-171],227.

UNITED STATES--LOS ANGELES
(CALIFORNIA)--HOUSES--INTERIOR
DESIGN--HEPBURN HOUSE
Katharine Hepburn: four-time Best
Actress in New York, Connecticut
and California / A. Scott Berg.
ARCHITECTURAL DIGEST 1990 Apr.,
v.47, no.4, p.192-[197],292,294,
ports., photos.

UNITED STATES--LOS ANGELES
(CALIFORNIA)--HOUSES--INTERIOR
DESIGN--RAVETCH FRANK HOUSE
Irving Ravetch and Harriet Frank
Jr.: Best Screenplay nominees for
Hud and Norma Rae in Los Angeles /
Michael Frank.
Features home interiors.
ARCHITECTURAL DIGEST 1990 Apr.,
v.47, no.4, p.266-[269],312,
port., photos.

UNITED STATES--LOS ANGELES
(CALIFORNIA)--LAW OFFICES--INTERIOR
DESIGN--QUINN, KULLY & MORROW
Quinn, Kully & Morrow / Monica
Geran.
Interior of Los Angeles law
offices designed by Gensler and
Associates.
INTERIOR DESIGN 1990 Jan., v.61,
no.1, p.152-[155], photos., plan.

UNITED STATES--LOS ANGELES
(CALIFORNIA)--LIGHT RAIL TRANSIT
Building a light rail line means
making passengers happy.
Focus on Neil Peterson, executive
director of the Los Angeles County
Transportation Commission.
METRO MAGAZINE 1990 May-June,
v.86, no.3, p.38-39, port., photo.
L.A. light rail opening is just the
beginning / Lenny Levine.
First 22 miles of the projected
150-mile light rail transit system
for Los Angeles County.
METRO MAGAZINE 1990 May-June,
v.86, no.3, p.22-36, ports., map,
photo.
Light rail: the trolley reborn /
Walter Scott Perry.
On the Los Angeles Metrolight rail
project.
L. A. ARCHITECT 1990 July-Aug.,
p.5, dwg., photos.

UNITED STATES--LOS ANGELES
(CALIFORNIA)--LOBBIES--HOME SAVINGS
OF AMERICA TOWER
In good standing: Home Savings of
America Tower, Los Angeles /
Donald London.
Architect: Albert C. Martin &
Associates. Lobby murals by
Richard Haas.
ARCHITECTURAL RECORD 1990 Feb.,
v.178, no.2, p.94-97, elev.,
photos., plan, secn.

UNITED STATES--LOS ANGELES
(CALIFORNIA)--MONUMENTS AND
MEMORIALS--COMPETITIONS--STEEL
CLOUDS (GATEWAY)
Kilpailut: monumentin dekonstruointi
= Deconstruction of a monument /
Juhani Pallasmaa.
On the 1988 international
competition for a monument in Los
Angeles. Winners: Hani Rashid
Studio Asymptote. Second prize:
Kunnapu, Padrik and Siim.
Includes English translation.
ARKKITEHTI 1989, v.86, no.7,
p.79-85, cover, axonometric view,
dwgs., models. plan, secns.
Three projects by Studio Asymptote:
Hani Rashid, Lise Anne Couture.
Contents: Architects' statement,
by Hani Rashid & Lise Anne
Couture.--Project 1: Concorso da
Commune di Lanciano, Italy,
1987.--Project 2: Los Angeles West
Coast Gateway, Los Angeles, CA.--
Project 3: The Alexandria Library,
Alexandria, Egypt.--Brief history.
Text in Japanese and English.
ARCHITECTURE AND URBANISM 1989
Dec., no.12(231), p.[5]-28, dwgs.,
elevs., model, plans, secns., site
plans.

UNITED STATES--LOS ANGELES
(CALIFORNIA)--MONUMENTS AND
MEMORIALS--COMPETITIONS--VESSEL
(GATEWAY)
Projects by Dagmar Richter / Ulrich
Hinrichsmeyer.
Contents: "The Vessel" Los Angeles
Gateway competition [3rd prize]--
Berlin III, Germany, 1988 --
Advertising agency Grey,
Dusseldorf, Germany, 1988 --
Gallery UND, Dusseldorf, W.
Germany, 1987 -- Artists' housing
in Boston, Mass., 1987 -- Town
Hall for Kassel, W. Germany, 1986
-- Museum for the Brothers Grimm,
Kassel, W. Germany, 1986 -- A gate
for an ancient city, Paestum,
Italy, 1985 -- Sound space for
Meredith Monk, music by Meredith
Monk "Dolmen music," Salzburg,
Austria, 1985. Architects: Dagmar
Richter, Ulrich Hinrichsmeyer, MAX
1, MAX 2. Text in Japanese and
English.
ARCHITECTURE AND URBANISM 1990
Feb., no.2(233), p.34-58,
axonometric views, elevs., models,
photos., plans, secns.

UNITED STATES--LOS ANGELES
(CALIFORNIA)--MONUMENTS AND
MEMORIALS--CONO-CIELO
Il linguaggio della materia = The
language of materials / Andrea
Campioli.
Stone designs: Cono-cielo
monument, Los Angeles, 1988 --
Project for headquarters of
Internazionale Marmi e Macchine,
Carrara, Italy. Architect: Angelo
Mangiarotti.
L'ARCA 1990 Dec., no.44,
p.68-[75], dwgs., model, photos.,
plans.

UNITED STATES--LOS ANGELES
(CALIFORNIA)--MULTI-USE COMPLEXES--
GRAND AVENUE PLAZA
Special feature: Richard Keating:
years at SOM 1976-1990.
Essays: Editor's introduction /
Toshio Nakamura --Architect's
statement --Richard Keating and
the varieties of Modernism / John
Pastier --Works: Columbia Savings
& Loan, Beverly Hills, CA --Grand
Avenue Plaza, Los Angeles, CA,
1992 --Latham Watkins law offices,
Los Angeles, CA, 1989 --Gas Tower,
Los Angeles, CA, 1992 --Ocean
Boulevard Condominiums, Long
Beach, CA, 1989 --Tower City
Center competition, Cleveland,
Ohio, 1989 --Canon Building,
Beverly Hills, CA --Tokyo
International Forum honorable
mention project, Tokyo, Japan,
1989 --Katsuura Condominiums,
Katsuura, Japan, 1992. Architects:
Richard Keating of Skidmore,
Owings & Merrill and Keating Mann
Jernigan Rottet Architecture and
Interiors. Text in Japanese and
English.
ARCHITECTURE AND URBANISM 1990
Oct., no.10(241), p.58-128,
axonometric views, elevs.,
photos., plans.

UNITED STATES--LOS ANGELES
(CALIFORNIA)--MUSEUMS--ART--MUSEUM
OF CONTEMPORARY ART
From the body of the prince to
Mickey Mouse / Jo-anne Berelowitz.
Theoretical essay on the
postmodern museum. Focus on the
Museum of Contemporary Art, Los
Angeles and the Massachusetts
Museum of Contemporary Art (Mass
MoCA), North Adams, Mass.
OXFORD ART JOURNAL 1990, v.13,
no.2, p.70-84, dwgs., maps,
photos., aerial photo., biblio.,
refs.

UNITED STATES--LOS ANGELES
(CALIFORNIA)--OFFICE BUILDINGS--
CENTER WEST
Center West: gateway to Westwood? /
Carlton Davis.
Office building. Architect:
Mitchell Giurgola Architects.
L. A. ARCHITECT 1990 May, p.6,
photos., plans, secn.
Good taste: Center West, Los
Angeles, California,
Mitchell/Giurgola Architects.
23-story tower atop a 3-story
retail and parking podium.
ARCHITECTURAL RECORD 1990 Oct.,
v.178, no.11, p.90-[93], photos.,
plans, secn.

UNITED STATES--LOS ANGELES
(CALIFORNIA)--OFFICE BUILDINGS--GAS
COMPANY TOWER
Special feature: Richard Keating:
years at SOM 1976-1990.
Essays: Editor's introduction /
Toshio Nakamura --Architect's
statement --Richard Keating and
the varieties of Modernism / John
Pastier --Works: Columbia Savings
& Loan, Beverly Hills, CA --Grand
Avenue Plaza, Los Angeles, CA,
1992 --Latham Watkins law offices,
Los Angeles, CA, 1989 --Gas Tower,
Los Angeles, CA, 1992 --Ocean
Boulevard Condominiums, Long
Beach, CA, 1989 --Tower City
Center competition, Cleveland,
Ohio, 1989 --Canon Building,
Beverly Hills, CA --Tokyo
International Forum honorable
mention project, Tokyo, Japan,
1989 --Katsuura Condominiums,
Katsuura, Japan, 1992. Architects:
Richard Keating of Skidmore,
Owings & Merrill and Keating Mann
Jernigan Rottet Architecture and
Interiors. Text in Japanese and
English.
ARCHITECTURE AND URBANISM 1990
Oct., no.10(241), p.58-128,
axonometric views, elevs.,
photos., plans.

UNITED STATES--LOS ANGELES
(CALIFORNIA)--OFFICE BUILDINGS--
OLYMPIC WEST
Four projects of Aks Runo.
Contents: "Metapolis" Los Angeles
project, 1987 -- Olympic West
office towers, Los Angeles, 1988
-- Tokyo International Forum,
Tokyo, 1989 -- Alexandria Library
project, Egypt, 1989. Architects:
Aks Runo, Bahram Shirdel and
Andrew Zago. Text in Japanese and
English.
ARCHITECTURE AND URBANISM 1990
(Continued next page)

UNITED STATES--LOS ANGELES
(CALIFORNIA)--OFFICE BUILDINGS--
OLYMPIC WEST (CONTINUED)
Four projects of Aks...(CONTINUED)
June, no.6(237), p.[7]-28, elevs.,
models, plans, site plan.
Projekt Olympic-West-Burohauser,
1988.
Architects: Bahram Shirdel, Andrew
Zago.
WERK, BAUEN + WOHNEN 1990
July-Aug., no.7-8, p.56-57,
models, plans.

UNITED STATES--LOS ANGELES
(CALIFORNIA)--OFFICES--865 SOUTH
FIGUERA--MANULIFE LEASING CENTER
Soft-tech / Karin Tetlow.
On the Manulife Leasing Center
located in the new Los Angeles
office tower at 865 South
Figueroa. Architects: Albert C.
Martin and Associates.
INTERIORS 1990 June, v.149, no.11,
p.48, diagr., photo., secn.

UNITED STATES--LOS ANGELES
(CALIFORNIA)--OFFICES--INTERIOR
DESIGN--BOSTON COMPANY
The Boston Company / Mayer Rus.
Office interiors on lobby level in
one of the towers in California
Plaza, Los Angeles. Architects for
tower: Arthur Erickson Architects.
Interior designers for offices:
Francisco Kripacz, Arthur Erickson
Architects.
INTERIOR DESIGN 1990 Feb., v.61,
no.3, p.188-[189], photos., plan.

UNITED STATES--LOS ANGELES
(CALIFORNIA)--PHOTOGRAPHERS' STUDIOS
Studio fotografico a Los Angeles =
Photography studio, Los Angeles.
Conversion of two-story industrial
building into photographer's
studio; architect: Frederick
Fisher.
LOTUS INTERNATIONAL 1990, no.66,
p.80-83, axonometric views,
photos.

UNITED STATES--LOS ANGELES
(CALIFORNIA)--PHOTOGRAPHERS'
STUDIOS--HANAUER STUDIO
Schweitzer BIM: Mark Hanauer Studio,
Los Angeles, California, 1988-89.
Text in Japanese and English.
GA HOUSES 1990 Dec., no.30,
p.134-135, axonometric view,
photos., plan.

UNITED STATES--LOS ANGELES
(CALIFORNIA)--PLAZAS--PERSHING
SQUARE
Public places for American cities:
three projects / Rodolfo Machado.
Includes Times Square Tower, New
York (1984); Pershing Square, Los
Angeles (1986); and
Sesquicentennial Park, Houston
(1986).
ASSEMBLAGE 1990 June, no.6,
p.[98]-113, axonometric views,
dets., dwgs., elevs., model,
photos., plans., secns., site
plans.

UNITED STATES--LOS ANGELES
(CALIFORNIA)--POWER PLANTS--
UNIVERSITY OF CALIFORNIA, LOS
ANGELES
Central chiller plant.
Central chiller/ cogeneration
plant for the University of
California, Los Angeles campus.
Architects: Holt Hinshaw Pfau
Jones.
PROGRESSIVE ARCHITECTURE 1990
Jan., v.71, no.1, p.99-101,
elevs., model, plan, secn., site
plan.

UNITED STATES--LOS ANGELES
(CALIFORNIA)--RANCH HOUSES--
ALTERATIONS AND ADDITIONS--SPRECHER
HOUSE
Kitchens that cook: hot news, cool
choices / Julie V. Iovine.
Five projects, including an
expansion of the Sprecher house,
Los Angeles (architect: Michele
Saee); a Connecticut kitchen
renovation (architect: Louis
Mackall); Reichel-Singer house
conversion, Los Angeles (designer:
Josh Schweitzer); Sagalyn kitchen
(architect: Scott Simons); Laurie
and Maurie Williams' kitchen
renovation, Ore.
METROPOLITAN HOME 1990 May, v.22,
no.5, p.[123-136], det., photos.

UNITED STATES--LOS ANGELES
(CALIFORNIA)--REAL ESTATE
DEVELOPMENT
The community concerns of
developers: a personal philosophy
/ Robert F. Maguire.
Examples of Playa-Vista, a
development area south of Los
Angeles Int'l. Airport and the L.
A. Public Library. Developers and
planners: Maguire Thomas Partners.
URBAN LAND 1990 Apr., v.49, no.4,
p.12-15, models, photo., site
plan.

UNITED STATES--LOS ANGELES
(CALIFORNIA)--REGIONAL PLANNING--
CONGRESSES
Special issue: redesigning the
region.
Looks at the issues addressed by
the Regional Urban Design
Conference, held Oct.4-6, Santa
Monica, Calif.
L.A. ARCHITECT 1990 Oct., entire
issue, maps, photos., aerial
photos.

UNITED STATES--LOS ANGELES
(CALIFORNIA)--RESIDENTIAL GARDENS
Welcome to the backyard California /
Erica Goebel.
Gardens in San Francisco, Los
Angeles and Santa Barbara.
Landscape architects: Peter Jane
Pedersen, Calvin Abe & Assoc. with
Ron McCoy, Isabelle Greene, Ron
Lutsko, and Dennis Shaw.
GARDEN DESIGN 1990 autumn, v.9,
no.3, p.[38-45], photos.

UNITED STATES--LOS ANGELES
(CALIFORNIA)--RESTAURANTS
Cafe Society: Los Angeles serves up
a fresh selection of fashionable
restaurants where diners can go to
be pampered and entertained /
Michael Webb.
METROPOLIS 1990 Jan.-Feb., v.9,
no.6, p.60-65,79, photos.

UNITED STATES--LOS ANGELES
(CALIFORNIA)--RESTAURANTS--INTERIOR
DESIGN--ATLAS BAR AND GRILL
Heavenly cast / Lisa S. Cohen.
Interiors of the Atlas Bar and
Grill, Los Angeles. Architect: Ron
Meyers.
INTERIORS 1990 July, v.149, no.12,
p.94-[95], photos., plan.

UNITED STATES--LOS ANGELES
(CALIFORNIA)--RESTAURANTS--INTERIOR
DESIGN--BICE
Baci for Bice / Justin Henderson.
Interiors of Bice restaurant, Los
Angeles, which features an
"updated version of Italian Art
Deco of the 1920s and 1930s."
Designer: Adam Tihany.
INTERIORS 1990 Nov., v.150, no.4,
p.64-[65], photos., plan.

UNITED STATES--LOS ANGELES
(CALIFORNIA)--RESTAURANTS--INTERIOR
DESIGN--MELROSE BAR & GRILL
Melrose Bar & Grill / Mayer Rus.
Interiors of revamped restaurant
in the Pacific Design Center, Los
Angeles. Interior designer: Irwin
N. Stroll.
INTERIOR DESIGN 1990 Feb., v.61,
no.3, p.224-[225], photos.

UNITED STATES--LOS ANGELES
(CALIFORNIA)--RESTAURANTS--
TEMPORARY--PACIFIC DESIGN CENTER--
CAFE MILLENNIUM
Movable feast / Justin Henderson.
Student Ken Jacobsen designs a
temporary restaurant at the
Pacific Design Center, Los
Angeles, for Westweek 1990.
INTERIORS 1990 July, v.149, no.12,
p.62-[63], photos.

UNITED STATES--LOS ANGELES
(CALIFORNIA)--SHOPPING MALLS--
ALTERATIONS AND ADDITIONS--CENTURY
CITY SHOPPING CENTER
Mall wonder / Michelle Huneven.
Features renovated Century City
Shopping Center, Los Angeles.
Architect: Benjamin Thompson.
CONNOISSEUR 1990 Feb., v.220,
no.937, p.90-93, photos.

UNITED STATES--LOS ANGELES
(CALIFORNIA)--SHOWROOMS--CLOTHING--
LEON MAX
Show room in L.A.: Leon Max
show-room, 127, East Ninth Street,
Los Angeles / Birgit C. Dietsch.
Architect: Morphosis.
BAUWELT 1990 Sept.7, v.81, no.34,
p.1690-1691, photos., plans.

(Continued next page)

UNITED STATES--LOW INCOME HOUSING
                    (CONTINUED)
  Good work:...(CONTINUED)
    landscape architect: Michael
    Weinmayr; Scattered site housing
    (Madison, N.J.), architects: The
    Hillier Group; Diamond Park
    Housing (Philadelphia, Pa.),
    architects: Cecil Baker &
    Associates; DeSmet Apartments
    (Florissant, Mo.), architects:
    Henderson Group; Callahan Oaks
    (Orlando, Fla), architects:
    Fugleberg Koch; Mission Hill
    (Boston, Mass.), architects:
    Vitols Associates, landscape
    architects: Pryor/Geller; and
    Glenardon Apartments (Glenardon,
    Md.), architects: CHK Architects
    and Planners.
    JOURNAL OF HOUSING 1989 July-Aug.,
    v.46, no.4, p.196-201, dwg.,
    photos.
  Good works [low and moderate income
    housing].
    Eleven projects in the United
    States.
    JOURNAL OF HOUSING 1990 July-Aug.,
    v.47, no.4, p.196-199,202-205,
    photos.

UNITED STATES--LOWELL
  (MASSACHUSETTS)--HISTORIC DISTRICTS
  P/A awards update: the perils of
    preservation planning / Thomas
    Fisher.
    Report on five preservation plans
    for historic districts in the
    following areas: Miami Beach,
    Fla.; Rugby, Tenn,; Princeton, NJ;
    Jim Thorpe, Pa. and Lowell, Mass.
    PROGRESSIVE ARCHITECTURE 1990
    June, v.71, no.6, p.100-105, ill.,
    models, photos., plans, site plan.

UNITED STATES--LYME (CONNECTICUT)--
  HOUSES--CONSERVATION AND RESTORATION
  Old house heroics / Jane Geniesse.
    Endangered historic New England
    houses are dismantled, moved, and
    reassembled in Lyme, Conn. by
    preservationists Bill Oberg and
    H.P. "Skip" Broom.
    HOUSE BEAUTIFUL 1990 Sept., v.132,
    no.9, p.66-70,126, dets., ports.,
    photos.

UNITED STATES--LYME (NEW HAMPSHIRE)--
  BED-AND-BREAKFAST GUEST HOUSES--
  MARJORIE'S HOUSE BED & BREAKFAST
  Marjorie's house [Lyme, N.H.].
    Bed & breakfast inn in a 1772
    house.
    COLONIAL HOMES 1990 Aug., v.16,
    no.4, p.[66]-69, dets., photos.

UNITED STATES--LYME (NEW HAMPSHIRE)--
  HOUSES--COLONIAL--BARRY HOUSE
  Marjorie's house [Lyme, N.H.].
    Bed & breakfast inn in a 1772
    house.
    COLONIAL HOMES 1990 Aug., v.16,
    no.4, p.[66]-69, dets., photos.

UNITED STATES--LYNCHBURG (VIRGINIA)--
  COUNTRY HOUSES--PALLADIAN--POPLAR
  FOREST
  Thomas Jefferson's Poplar Forest:
    the mathematics of an ideal villa
    / C. Allan Brown.
    Poplar Forest, 7 mi. west of
    Lynchburg, Va., was Jefferson's
    country retreat. The
    Palladian-style villa was built
    1806-09.
    JOURNAL OF GARDEN HISTORY 1990
    Apr.-June, v.10, no.2, p.117-139,
    diagr., ill., elev., photos.,
    plans, site plans, engr., refs.

UNITED STATES--LYNCHBURG (VIRGINIA)--
  GARDENS--19TH CENTURY--POPLAR FOREST
  Thomas Jefferson's Poplar Forest:
    the mathematics of an ideal villa
    / C. Allan Brown.
    Poplar Forest, 7 mi. west of
    Lynchburg, Va., was Jefferson's
    country retreat. The
    Palladian-style villa was built
    1806-09.
    JOURNAL OF GARDEN HISTORY 1990
    Apr.-June, v.10, no.2, p.117-139,
    diagr., ill., elev., photos.,
    plans, site plans, engr., refs.

UNITED STATES--LYNDHURST (OHIO)--
  OFFICE BUILDINGS--LANDERBROOK PLACE
  An office building with a stainless
    reputation / Carol Poh Miller.
    Landerbrook Place in Lyndhurst,
    outside of Cleveland, Ohio.
    Exterior cladding is of corrugated
    stainless steel panels. Architect:
    Gerald J. Payto.
    INLAND ARCHITECT 1990 Nov.-Dec.,
    v.34, no.6, p.9,12, photos., plan.

UNITED STATES--MACKINAC ISLAND
  (MICHIGAN)--HOUSES--INTERIOR
  DESIGN--CORNER COTTAGE (MUSSER
  HOUSE)
  Mackinac vistas: a new spirit for
    the Grand Hotel owners' island
    cottage in Michigan / John Taylor.
    Features the interiors of Dan and
    Amelia Musser's home, Corner
    Cottage, on Mackinac Island.
    Interior designer: Carleton Varney
    of Dorothy Draper & Co.
    ARCHITECTURAL DIGEST 1990 Aug.,
    v.47, no.8, p.[166-174], photos.

UNITED STATES--MACKINAC ISLAND
  (MICHIGAN)--RESORTS--VICTORIAN
  Back to Mackinac ... an island in
    the Great Lakes / Edmund White.
    Intact Victorian resort on this
    northern Mich. island.
    HOUSE & GARDEN 1990 June, v.162,
    no.6, p.158-[169], photos.

UNITED STATES--MADISON (MISSISSIPPI)--
  COTTAGES--CHAMPION COTTAGE
  Ictta natura a visu aperto: opere
    californiane di Robert K.
    Overstreet.
    Darbee House, Berkeley;
    architect's house, Corte Madera;
    Cottage Champion, Madison, Miss.;
    house over water, Sausalito;
    mausoleum, Colma; restaurant.
    Summaries in English, French
    German, and Spanish.
    ARCHITETTURA; CRONACHE E STORIA
    1990 Jan., v.36, no.1(411),
    p.[32]-42, dwgs., photos., plans,
    secns.

UNITED STATES--MAINE--HOUSES
  John Calvin Stevens: domestic
    architecture, 1890-1930 [by] John
    Calvin Stevens II, Earle G.
    Shettleworth, Jr. [book review] /
    William David Barry.
    LANDMARKS OBSERVER 1990 Fall,
    v.16, no.4, p.10, photo.

UNITED STATES--MAINE--HOUSES--19TH
  CENTURY--WELLIVER HOUSE
  Nature study: the Maine woods
    provide a fertile landscape for
    painter Neil Welliver / Mark
    Strand.
    Studio and house.
    HOUSE & GARDEN 1990 June, v.162,
    no.6, p.108-[115],172, port.,
    photos.

UNITED STATES--MAINE--HOUSES--
  CONSERVATION AND RESTORATION
  Linda Griffin "she moves houses" /
    Linda Murnik.
    Resident of Windham, Maine,
    restores houses.
    LANDMARKS OBSERVER 1990 Fall,
    v.16, no.4, p.13, port.

UNITED STATES--MAINE--HOUSES--INTERIOR
  DESIGN
  Maine tradition / Caroline Seebohm.
    Interior decorator: Nancy
    Pierrepont.
    HOUSE & GARDEN 1990 Aug., v.162,
    no.8, p.[128-133], port., photos.

UNITED STATES--MAINE--HOUSES--RUSTIC--
  CHANNING HOUSE
  Maine attraction: offstage, Stockard
    Channing is drawn to New England's
    rugged coast / Vance Muse.
    HOUSE & GARDEN 1990 July, v.162,
    no.7, p.[70-75], port., photos.

UNITED STATES--MAINE--LANDSCAPE
  ARCHITECTURE--19TH CENTURY
  Olmsted alliance hopes to revitalize
    Maine's historic parks / Elizabeth
    Igleheart.
    On the formation in 1990 of the
    Maine Olmsted Alliance for Parks
    and Landscapes (MOAPL), to support
    preservation efforts at 141
    Olmsted project sited within the
    state.
    LANDMARKS OBSERVER 1990 Fall,
    v.16, no.4, p.14, photo.

UNITED STATES--MAINE--SAILBOATS--
  CONSERVATION AND RESTORATION
  Windjammer days / Christina Tree.
    The preservation of Maine's
    windjammer fleets.
    HISTORIC PRESERVATION 1990
    July-Aug., v.42, no.4, p.[22-29],
    photos.

UNITED STATES--MAINE--VERNACULAR
  ARCHITECTURE--19TH CENTURY--
  INFLUENCE
  Harboring tradition: for a new
    marine museum on the coast of
    Maine, architect Winton Scott was
    inspired by the powerful
    industrial vernacular of a local
    19th-century foundry / Nancy
    Levinson.
    The Maine Maritime Museum, Bath.
    ARCHITECTURAL RECORD 1990 June,
    v.178, no.7, p.72-[75], photos,
    plans, secn.

UNITED STATES--MALIBU (CALIFORNIA)--
BEACH HOUSES
Contemporary castle, Malibu,
California, completion: 1989.
Architect: John Lautner. Text in
Japanese and English.
GA HOUSES 1990 Mar., no.28,
p.110-113, model, plan, secns.

UNITED STATES--MALIBU (CALIFORNIA)--
BEACH HOUSES--20TH CENTURY--STEVENS
HOUSE
Stevens house, Malibu-Beach, 1968.
Architect: John Lautner.
WERK, BAUEN + WOHNEN 1990
July-Aug., no.7-8, p.62-63,
photos., plans, secns.

UNITED STATES--MALIBU (CALIFORNIA)--
BEACH HOUSES--INTERIOR DESIGN--IRMAS
HOUSE
Malibu spaces / Irene Borger.
Interiors of minimalist-style
beach house in Malibu Colony owned
by Audrey and Sydney Irmas.
Architect: Jack Lionel Warner.
Interior design: Judy Wilder.
ARCHITECTURAL DIGEST 1990 May,
v.47, no.5, p.152-[161],260,
port., photos.

UNITED STATES--MALIBU (CALIFORNIA)--
BEACH HOUSES--LIGHTING--IRMAS HOUSE
Razzle-Dazzle on the beach:
high-tech highlights the abstract
forms of a Malibu beach house /
Aaron Betsky.
Irmus house. Architect: Warren
Gray; lighting designer: David
Steinitz.
ARCHITECTURAL RECORD 1990 Aug.,
v.178, no.9 suppl., p.[16-19],
photos.

UNITED STATES--MALIBU (CALIFORNIA)--
COTTAGES--INTERIOR DESIGN--DERN
HOUSE (ROSE COTTAGE)
Coming home: for Bruce and Andrea
Dern, Malibu cottage offers a
welcome respite from life in
Hollywood / Buffy Birrittella.
HOUSE & GARDEN 1990 July, v.162,
no.7, p.[116-121], port., photos.

UNITED STATES--MALIBU (CALIFORNIA)--
DUPLEX HOUSES--SEACLIFF
The coastal condition: regional
portfolio: California housing /
Paul M. Sachner.
The first of a series of regional
portfolios, on 5 multifamily
projects: Armacost Duplex, Los
Angeles [Rebecca Binder]; 14-16
Leroy Pl., San Francisco (Hood
Miller); 1150 Lombard St., San
Francisco (Hood Miller); Meadow
Court, San Mateo (David Baker
Assoc.); and Seacliff, Malibu
(Kanner Associates).
ARCHITECTURAL RECORD 1990 Jan.,
v.178, no.1, p.90-99, elevs.,
photos., plans, secns., site
plans.

UNITED STATES--MALIBU (CALIFORNIA)--
HOUSES
Sette conferme di John Lautner delle
sette invarianti dell'architettura
moderna.
7 projects: Turner house, Aspen,
CO; Walstrom house, Los Angeles,
CA; Reiner house Los Angeles;
Arango house, Acapulco, Mexico;
house, Malibu, CA; children's
rehab center, Woodland Hills, CA;
house at Lechuza Point, Malibu.
English, French, German, Spanish
summaries.
ARCHITETTURA: CRONACHE E STORIA
1987 Jan., v.33, no.1(375),
p.[22]-40, photos., plans, secns.,
site plans.

UNITED STATES--MALIBU (CALIFORNIA)--
HOUSES--ACKERBERG HOUSE
Luxusdampfer am Strand / Vera Graaf.
On the Ackerberg house, Malibu,
Calif. Architect: Richard Meier.
ARCHITEKTUR & WOHNEN 1990
June-July, no.3, p.22-28,
axonometric view, port., photos.

UNITED STATES--MALIBU (CALIFORNIA)--
HOUSES--ARCHITECTS'--BUCKNER -
ROBERTS HOUSE
Great stories.
Feature section on ca.15 recent
American houses, including ones by
architects Andy Dean, in S.
Dartmouth, Mass.; Peter Anders, in
Jersey City, N.J.; Chip Arena, in
Chestertown, Md.; Cory Buckner and
Nicholas Roberts, in Malibu,
Calif.; Robby Reid, in Tempe,
Ariz.
METROPOLITAN HOME 1990 Feb., v.22,
no.2, p.125-166, photos., ports.

UNITED STATES--MALIBU (CALIFORNIA)--
HOUSES--ARCHITECTS'--DAZZAN HOUSE
Giorgio Dazzan: a contemporary
Malibu residence with a Pacific
orientation / Leon Whiteson.
Features architect's home.
ARCHITECTURAL DIGEST 1990 Sept.,
v.47, no.10, p.[82-85],106,
axonometric view, port., photos.

UNITED STATES--MALIBU (CALIFORNIA)--
HOUSES--SIDLEY HOUSE
Edward R. Niles Architect [houses].
Contents: Sidley house, Malibu,
Calif., 1985-87 -- Wilen house,
Malibu, Calif., design: 1988.
Architect: Edward R. Niles. Text
in Japanese and English.
GA HOUSES 1990 Mar., no.28,
p.86-89, axonometric view, elevs.,
model, plans, secn., site plans.

UNITED STATES--MALIBU (CALIFORNIA)--
HOUSES--SLOPING SITES--OPEN HOUSE
COOP Himmelblau: Open House, Malibu,
California, design: 1989-90;
completion: 1991 (est.).
Architects: COOP Himmelblau - Wolf
D. Prix, H. Swiczinsky. Text in
Japanese and English.
GA HOUSES 1990 Mar., no.28,
p.42-45, models, plans, secns.,
site plan.

UNITED STATES--MALIBU (CALIFORNIA)--
HOUSES--SPANISH COLONIAL REVIVAL
Moore Ruble Yudell: a Malibu
residence rooted in California's
Spanish Colonial traditions / Leon
Whiteson.
Cliffside residence. Architects:
Moore, Ruble, Yudell.
ARCHITECTURAL DIGEST 1990 Feb.,
v.47, no.2, p.[86]-91,114, port.,
photos.

UNITED STATES--MALIBU (CALIFORNIA)--
HOUSES--SPANISH COLONIAL REVIVAL--
INTERIOR DESIGN--LANDON HOUSE
Architectural Digest visits: Michael
Landon / Harry Hurt III.
Features interiors of Spanish
colonial revival home located ten
mi. north of Malibu. Architect:
Robert L. Earl. Interior designer:
Ron Wilson.
ARCHITECTURAL DIGEST 1990 July,
v.47, no.7, p.[110-117],176,
port., photos.

UNITED STATES--MALIBU (CALIFORNIA)--
HOUSES--WILEN HOUSE
Edward R. Niles Architect [houses].
Contents: Sidley house, Malibu,
Calif., 1985-87 -- Wilen house,
Malibu, Calif., design: 1988.
Architect: Edward R. Niles. Text
in Japanese and English.
GA HOUSES 1990 Mar., no.28,
p.86-89, axonometric view, elevs.,
model, plans, secn., site plans.

UNITED STATES--MALIBU (CALIFORNIA)--
PAVILIONS--DUQUETTE PAVILIONS
A jeweled setting: glittering
souvenirs of Hollywood adorn the
mountaintop pavilions of legendary
California designer Tony Duquette
/ Wendy Goodman.
The Duquette ranch, Malibu, Calif.
HOUSE & GARDEN 1990 Dec., v.162,
no.12, p.[136-143], ports.,
photos.

UNITED STATES--MANCHESTER-BY-THE-SEA
(MASSACHUSETTS)--HISTORIC
BUILDINGS--CONSERVATION AND
RESTORATION
Shingle-minded pursuits: a
Massachusetts town is
rediscovering its legacy of master
builders / Vincent Scully.
On the work of preservation
architect Stephen Roberts Holt in
Manchester-by-the-Sea.
HOUSE & GARDEN 1990 Nov., v.162,
no.11, p.[57]-66, dwgs., port.,
photos.

UNITED STATES--MANHASSET (NEW YORK)--
STORES--CLOTHING--INTERIOR DESIGN--
BARNEYS NEW YORK
Shop right / Karin Tetlow.
The interiors of four Barneys New
York stores located in suburban
malls. Architects: Rosenblum Harb
Architects.
INTERIORS 1990 July, v.149, no.12,
p.82-89, photos., plans.

UNITED STATES--MANHATTAN BEACH
(CALIFORNIA)--BEACH HOUSES--ROSS
HOUSE
Ross Residence, Manhattan Beach,
California, design: 1988-89; under
construction / Dean Nota.
Architects: Dean A. Nota and
Robert J. Bridges. Text in
Japanese and English.
GA HOUSES 1990 Mar., no.28,
p.83-85.

UNITED STATES--MANSIONS--VANDERBILT
MANSIONS
A surfeit of riches [book review].
Review of: The Vanderbilts, by
Jerry E. Patterson, 1990.
COLONIAL HOMES 1990 June, v.16,
no.3, p.16-28, dwgs., ports.,
photos., engr.

UNITED STATES--MARFA (TEXAS)--
MUSEUMS--ART--DIA ART FOUNDATION
Ristrutturazione di Fort Russel,
Texas = Renovation of Fort
Russell, Texas.
Military buildings of Fort Russell
military base renovated to house
Dia Art Foundation by Donald Judd.
LOTUS INTERNATIONAL 1990, no.66,
p.28-35, photos., plans, site
plans.

UNITED STATES--MARIN COUNTY
(CALIFORNIA)--HOUSES--INTERIOR
DESIGN--MELANIE MARTIN HOUSE
West Coast rustic / Jane Margolies.
Marin County (Ca.) house of
fashion designer Melanie Martin.
Portrait on p.41.
HOUSE BEAUTIFUL 1990 Aug., v.132,
no.8, p.41,58-63, port., photos.

UNITED STATES--MARINA DEL REY
(CALIFORNIA)--CEILINGS--ANGELI MARE
Out on a limb / Ziva Freiman.
Focus on two Marina del Rey
projects by Michele Saee of
Building: Ecru clothing store,
and Angeli Mare restaurant.
Includes selected detail article
on the ceiling structure of the
restaurant.
PROGRESSIVE ARCHITECTURE 1990
Apr., v.71, no.4, p.108-116,
dets., photos., plans, secns.

UNITED STATES--MARINA DEL REY
(CALIFORNIA)--RESTAURANTS--ANGELI
MARE
Out on a limb / Ziva Freiman.
Focus on two Marina del Rey
projects by Michele Saee of
Building: Ecru clothing store,
and Angeli Mare restaurant.
Includes selected detail article
on the ceiling structure of the
restaurant.
PROGRESSIVE ARCHITECTURE 1990
Apr., v.71, no.4, p.108-116,
dets., photos., plans, secns.

UNITED STATES--MARINA DEL REY
(CALIFORNIA)--STORES--CLOTHING--ECRU
Le corps en morceaux d'architecture.
Features Ecru Clothing store,
Marina del Rey, Calif. Architect:
Michele Saee.
ARCHITECTURE INTERIEURE CREE 1990
Oct.-Nov., no.239, p.138-[139],
photos.

UNITED STATES--MARINA DEL REY
(CALIFORNIA)--STORES--CLOTHING--ECRU
(CONTINUED)
Out on a limb / Ziva Freiman.
Focus on two Marina del Rey
projects by Michele Saee of
Building: Ecru clothing store,
and Angeli Mare restaurant.
Includes selected detail article
on the ceiling structure of the
restaurant.
PROGRESSIVE ARCHITECTURE 1990
Apr., v.71, no.4, p.108-116,
dets., photos., plans, secns.

UNITED STATES--MARION (VIRGINIA)--
HOUSES
Kamal Amin: dal Cairo all'Arizona,
sette opere organiche = from Cairo
to Arizona, seven organic works.
Houses in Va. and Ariz. and
medical centers in Tempe and
Scottsdale, Ariz.
ARCHITETTURA: CRONACHE E STORIA
1990 Sept., v.36, no.9(419),
p.[612-634], dets., photos.,
plans, secns., site plans.

UNITED STATES--MARSEILLE (ILLINOIS)--
HYDROELECTRIC POWER PLANTS--
NEOCLASSICAL--MARSEILLES HYDRO POWER
STATION
Marseilles Hydro Power Station
powered early transportation
system / Charles E. Spets.
Opened in 1911 and operated until
1988. Now on the National Register
of Historic Places. Designed in
Classical Revival style by
engineer C.W. Humphrey.
HISTORIC ILLINOIS 1990 Feb., v.12,
no.5, p.[1]-3,12-14, map, aerial
photo.

UNITED STATES--MARTHA'S VINEYARD
(MASSACHUSETTS)--BEACH HOUSES--
POLLAN HOUSE
Sea change: Charles Myer's vineyard
makeover: from sea shack to beach
cottage / Victoria Geibel.
ELLE DECOR 1990 June-July, v.1,
no.5, p.[116-125], photos.

UNITED STATES--MARYLAND--HOUSES
Architecture: Cesar Pelli / Michael
Webb.
Features home in Maryland whose
"central concept is the
organization of a complex of
functional pavilions along an
interior street--the gallery."
Architect: Cesar Pelli.
ARCHITECTURAL DIGEST 1990 July,
v.47, no.7, p.124-[129],178,
photos., plan.

UNITED STATES--MARYLAND--HOUSES--17TH
CENTURY--CONSERVATION AND
RESTORATION--BOUNDS LOTT
Bounds Lott: humble authenticity in
one of Maryland's oldest homes /
Susan Stiles Dowell.
Restored 17th-cent. house on
Maryland's Eastern Shore, home of
Robert Withey.
SOUTHERN ACCENTS 1990 Nov., v.13,
no.9, p.[70-79], photos.

UNITED STATES--MASON NECK (VIRGINIA)--
PLANTATION HOUSES--18TH CENTURY--
GUNSTON HALL
Tidewater treasure ... Gunston Hall
/ Martin Filler.
Mansion built in 1755-59 by George
Mason features wood carving
William Buckland.
HOUSE & GARDEN 1990 Nov., v.162,
no.11, p.132-[139],231, ports.,
photos., aerial photo.

UNITED STATES--MASSACHUSETTS--
CEMETERIES--CONSERVATION AND
RESTORATION
Burying ground preservation /
Dominique Woodall.
BOSTON PRESERVATION ALLIANCE
LETTER 1990 Feb., v.11, no.2, p.6,
photo.

UNITED STATES--MASSACHUSETTS--OPEN
SPACES--LAW AND LEGISLATION
"An act protecting open spaces."
On a proposal in the Massachusetts
Senate, to bar approval by local
authorities of new buidings tall
enough to shadow historic open
spaces.
BOSTON PRESERVATION ALLIANCE
LETTER 1990 May, v.11, no.3, p.1,
ill.

UNITED STATES--MASSAPEQUA (NEW YORK)--
BANKS--INTERIOR DESIGN--GREEN POINT
SAVINGS BANK
Green point Savings Bank
[Massapequa, N.Y.] / Mayer, Kus.
Interior designers: Sanford
Hanauer.
INTERIOR DESIGN 1990 Feb., v.61,
no.3, p.178-[179], photos., plan.

UNITED STATES--MATTESON (ILLINOIS)--
BRIDGES
Matteson plan bridges the gap /
Annemarie Mannion.
Plan by RTLK Associates for an
expanding Illinois town that is
bisected by Interstate 57.
INLAND ARCHITECT 1990 May-June,
v.34, no.3, p.84-[88], maps.

UNITED STATES--MATTESON (ILLINOIS)--
CITIES AND TOWNS--GROWTH
Matteson plan bridges the gap /
Annemarie Mannion.
Plan by RTLK Associates for an
expanding Illinois town that is
bisected by Interstate 57.
INLAND ARCHITECT 1990 May-June,
v.34, no.3, p.84-[88], maps.

UNITED STATES--MATTESON (ILLINOIS)--
LIBRARIES--PUBLIC--COMPETITIONS--
MATTESON LIBRARY
Matteson Library winner announced /
Annemarie Mannion.
INLAND ARCHITECT 1990 July-Aug.,
v.34, no.4, p.74-76, axonometric
view, plans.
Matteson Public Library design
competition entry.
Two projects by Richard Herman
Schroeder & Associates, and Jay D.
Measley Architects.
ARCHITECTURE NEW JERSEY 1990,
v.26, no.3, p.16-17, axonometric
views, elevs., plans.

UNITED STATES--MATTESON (ILLINOIS)--
ROADS--INTERSTATE 57
Matteson plan bridges the gap /
Annemarie Mannion.
Plan by RTLK Associates for an
expanding Illinois town that is
bisected by Interstate 57.
INLAND ARCHITECT 1990 May-June,
v.34, no.3, p.84-[88], maps.

UNITED STATES--MAYORS--HOLLAND, ART
Profile of a leader: Trenton's Art
Holland: a leader of mayors / Dan
Treadaway.
AMERICAN CITY & COUNTY 1989 June,
v.104, no.6, p.58-60, port.

UNITED STATES--MEMPHIS (TENNESSEE)--
CORPORATE OFFICE BUILDINGS--FEDERAL
EXPRESS
Verwaltungsgebaude Corporate Place
in Memphis, Tennessee.
On the Federal Express corporate
headquarters in the corporate
place office complex. Architects:
Nagle Hartray & Associates.
Includes commentary by James
Nagle.
DEUTSCHE BAUZEITSCHRIFT 1990 May,
v.38, no.5, p.675-680, dets.,
photos., plans, site plans.

UNITED STATES--MEMPHIS (TENNESSEE)--
HOUSES--INTERIOR DESIGN--NEWMAN
HOUSE
Memphis original / Susannah M.
Wilson.
Newman house interiors by Kay B.
Newman.
SOUTHERN ACCENTS 1990 Sept., v.13,
no.7, p.80-85, photos.

UNITED STATES--MEMPHIS (TENNESSEE)--
LIGHTING--ARCHITECTURAL AND
DECORATIVE--RIDGEWAY CENTER--REGALIA
Signs: the difference between night
and day.
Example at Ridgeway Center office
park in Memphis, Tenn. Signage and
lighting designers: Lorenc Design.
URBAN LAND 1990 Apr., v.49, no.4,
p.26-27, photos., site plan.

UNITED STATES--MEMPHIS (TENNESSEE)--
MUSEUMS--ART--ALTERATIONS AND
ADDITIONS--MEMPHIS BROOKS MUSEUM
Modernism with manners: Memphis
Brooks Museum, Memphis, Tennessee
/ Robert A. Ivy, Jr.
Addition to art museum.
Architects: SOM/Houston; Lee Askew
Nixon Ferguson & Wolfe.
ARCHITECTURE: THE AIA JOURNAL 1990
Mar., v.79, no.3, p.[122]-127,
photos., plans.
P/A Awards update: a graceful
takeover / Jim Murphy.
On the addition to the Memphis
Brooks Museum, Memphis.
Architects: Skidmore, Owings &
Merril, Houston with Lee Askew
Nixon Ferguson & Wolfe.
PROGRESSIVE ARCHITECTURE 1990 May,
v.71, no.5, p.103-105, photos.,
plans.

UNITED STATES--MEMPHIS (TENNESSEE)--
OFFICE COMPLEXES--CORPORATE PLACE
Verwaltungsgebaude Corporate Place
in Memphis, Tennessee.
On the Federal Express corporate
headquarters in the corporate
place office complex. Architects:
Nagle Hartray & Associates.
Includes commentary by James
Nagle.
DEUTSCHE BAUZEITSCHRIFT 1990 May,
v.38, no.5, p.675-680, dets.,
photos., plans, site plans.

UNITED STATES--MEMPHIS (TENNESSEE)--
SIGNS AND SIGNBOARDS--RIDGEWAY
CENTER--REGALIA
Signs: the difference between night
and day.
Example at Ridgeway Center office
park in Memphis, Tenn. Signage and
lighting designers: Lorenc Design.
URBAN LAND 1990 Apr., v.49, no.4,
p.26-27, photos., site plan.

UNITED STATES--MEMPHIS (TENNESSEE)--
STREETS--ALTERATIONS AND ADDITIONS--
BEALE STREET
Peabody Place & Beale Street,
downtown Memphis.
One of six urban design reports
included in special issue, Urban
Concepts. Extracted from a 1987
Center City Development Plan for
Downtown Memphis.
ARCHITECTURAL DESIGN 1990, v.60,
no.1-2, p.76-87, dwgs., maps,
photos., sketches, aerial photos.

UNITED STATES--MEMPHIS (TENNESSEE)--
STREETS--ALTERATIONS AND ADDITIONS--
PEABODY PLACE
Peabody Place & Beale Street,
downtown Memphis.
One of six urban design reports
included in special issue, Urban
Concepts. Extracted from a 1987
Center City Development Plan for
Downtown Memphis.
ARCHITECTURAL DESIGN 1990, v.60,
no.1-2, p.76-87, dwgs., maps,
photos., sketches, aerial photos.

UNITED STATES--MEMPHIS (TENNESSEE)--
TOWNHOUSES--INTERIOR DESIGN--HICKMAN
THOMLEY HOUSE
Subtle evolution: the ever-changing
town house of two Memphis
designers / Susannah M. Wilson.
Interior designers and owners:
Steven Hickman and Tom Thomley.
Architect for the remodeling:
Oscar E. Menzer.
SOUTHERN ACCENTS 1990 Oct., v.13,
no.8, p.[124]-130, photos.

UNITED STATES--MEMPHIS (TENNESSEE)--
UNIVERSITIES AND COLLEGES--
BUILDINGS--GOTHIC REVIVAL--RHODES
COLLEGE
"So good a design": the Colonial
campus of the College of William
and Mary, Its history, background
and legacy [by] James D. Kornwolf
[book review] / Howard Davis.
Review also covers Collegiate
Gothic: the architecture of Rhodes
College, by William Morgan.
WINTERTHUR PORTFOLIO 1990 Winter,
v.25, no.4, p.[289]-292.

UNITED STATES--MEMPHIS (TENNESSEE)--
WATERFRONTS
Peabody Place & Beale Street,
downtown Memphis.
One of six urban design reports
included in special issue, Urban
Concepts. Extracted from a 1987
Center City Development Plan for
Downtown Memphis.
ARCHITECTURAL DESIGN 1990, v.60,
no.1-2, p.76-87, dwgs., maps,
photos., sketches, aerial photos.

UNITED STATES--MENLO PARK
(CALIFORNIA)--BANKS--INTERIOR
DESIGN--RAYCHEM
Telling details / Lisa S. Cohen.
The teller's station Raychem
Corp's credit union facilily,
Menlo Park, CA. Architects: Simon
Martin-Vegue Winkelstein Moris.
INTERIORS 1990 May, v.149, no.10,
p.38-39, dets., photo., plan,
secn., elev.

UNITED STATES--MENLO PARK
(CALIFORNIA)--CORPORATE OFFICE
BUILDINGS--INTERIOR DESIGN--RAYCHEM
Upping the profile / Michael Wagner.
On the award-winning Raychem
headquarters worldwide. Architects
for Menlo Park headquarters: Cabak
Randall Jasper Griffiths
Associates. Interior designers:
Simon Martin-Vegue Winkelstein
Moris.
INTERIORS 1990 May, v.149, no.10,
p.178-191, dwgs., models, photos.,
plans, site plan.

UNITED STATES--MENLO PARK
(CALIFORNIA)--RESEARCH FACILITIES--
AT&T SOFTWARE LAB
Down to the wire:
telecommunications: AT&T Software
Lab, Menlo Park, California /
Karin Tetlow.
Architect: George W. Famous.
ARCHITECTURE: THE MAGAZINE OF THE
AMERICAN INSTITUTE OF ARCHITECTS
1990 May, v.79, no.5, p.119-122,
photos., plans.

UNITED STATES--METAMORA (ILLINOIS)--
BARNS--19TH CENTURY--CONSERVATION
AND RESTORATION--MENNONITE HISTORY
CENTER--SUTTER BARN
Barn raising at Metamora: a
photographic essay.
Re-erection of the 1868 Sutter
barn at the Mennonite History
Center, west of Metamora, Ill.
MATERIAL CULTURE 1989 Spring,
v.21, no.1, p.47-56, photos.

UNITED STATES--METROPOLITAN AREAS
Urban cores: development trends and
real estate opportunities in the
1990s / Christopher B. Leinberger.
URBAN LAND 1990 Dec., v.49, no.12,
p.4-9, photo., table, aerial
photos.

UNITED STATES--MIAMI BEACH (FLORIDA)--
ARCHITECTURE--ART DECO--CONSERVATION
AND RESTORATION
Barbara Baer Capitman dies
[obituary].
A champion of Art-deco-style
architecture in Miami Beach, died
Mar.29,1990.
PRESERVATION NEWS 1990 May, v.30,
(Continued next page)

UNITED STATES--MIAMI BEACH (FLORIDA)--
ARCHITECTURE--ART DECO--CONSERVATION
AND RESTORATION (CONTINUED)
Barbara Baer Capitman...(CONTINUED)
no.5, p.3,19, port.
Tropical deco [Miami Beach] / Mary
Halnan.
Art deco district of Miami Beach.
ARCHITECTS' JOURNAL 1990 Feb.21,
v.191, no.8, p.24-29, photos.

UNITED STATES--MIAMI BEACH (FLORIDA)--
CONVENTION FACILITIES--ALTERATIONS
AND ADDITIONS--MIAMI BEACH
CONVENTION CENTER
Taming the Behemoth: Building Types
Study 676: convention centers /
Margaret Gaskie.
San Jose, Calif., Convention
Center (MGA Partners); Sydney,
Australia, Convention Center (John
Andrews International); Adelaide,
Australia, Convention Center (John
Andrews International); and Miami
Beach Convention Center expansion
(Thompson, Ventulett, Stainback &
Associates).
ARCHITECTURAL RECORD 1990 Mar.,
v.178, no.3, p.99-113, photo.,
plans, secns., site plans.

UNITED STATES--MIAMI BEACH (FLORIDA)--
HISTORIC DISTRICTS
P/A awards update: the perils of
preservation planning / Thomas
Fisher.
Report on five preservation plans
for historic districts in the
following areas: Miami Beach,
Fla.; Rugby, Tenn,; Princeton, NJ;
Jim Thorpe, Pa. and Lowell, Mass.
PROGRESSIVE ARCHITECTURE 1990
June, v.71, no.6, p.100-105, ill.,
models, photos., plans, site plan.

UNITED STATES--MIAMI BEACH (FLORIDA)--
HISTORIC DISTRICTS--ART DECO
DISTRICT
Tropical deco [Miami Beach] / Mary
Halnan.
Art deco district of Miami Beach.
ARCHITECTS' JOURNAL 1990 Feb.21,
v.191, no.8, p.24-29, photos.

UNITED STATES--MIAMI BEACH (FLORIDA)--
STREETS--ALTERATIONS AND ADDITIONS--
WASHINGTON AVENUE
Washington Avenue, Miami Beach.
One of six urban design reports
included in special issue, Urban
Concepts. Extracted from a 1979
plan for the revitalisation of the
neighborhood. Architects: Venturi
and Rauch.
ARCHITECTURAL DESIGN 1990, v.60,
no.1-2, p.70-75, dwgs., elevs.,
photos., site plans.

UNITED STATES--MIAMI (FLORIDA)--
APARTMENTS--INTERIOR DESIGN--JOHNSON
GRIFFITH APARTMENT
Don Johnson and Melanie Griffith:
the "Vice" aesthetic recast in the
actors' Miami apartment / Beth
Dunlop.
Interior designer: Sam Robin.
ARCHITECTURAL DIGEST 1990 July,
v.47, no.7, p.150-[155],184,
port., photos.

UNITED STATES--MIAMI (FLORIDA)--
ARCHITECTURE--ART DECO--CONSERVATION
AND RESTORATION
Miami nice: in the pink again /
Carol Isaak Barden.
SOUTHERN ACCENTS 1990 Sept., v.13,
no.7, p.124-127, photos.
Will success kill the Deco district?
/ Michael Warren.
"A recent plan aimed at producing
convention hotels in Miami Beach's
colorful historic district has
some preservationists up in arms."
PLANNING 1990 Feb., v.56, no.2,
p.21-24, ports., elev., map,
photos.

UNITED STATES--MIAMI (FLORIDA)--
ARCHITECTURE--HISTORY
Architecture on the edge / Stephen
D. Schreiber.
On the landscape in South Florida
and the boundaries (barrier
islands, coastal ridge and
landfill) that have influenced the
constructed ewnvironment.
CRIT 1990 Spring, no.24, p.16-20,
refs.

UNITED STATES--MIAMI (FLORIDA)--
BANKS--INTERIOR DESIGN--CAPITAL BANK
Miami white: in the Capital Bank,
Gensler and Associates, Architects
create a winning design / Nayana
Currimbhoy.
Located in Miami, Florida.
INTERIORS 1990 Jan., v.149, no.6,
p.138-141, photos., plan.

UNITED STATES--MIAMI (FLORIDA)--
CORPORATE OFFICE BUILDINGS--BURGER
KING CORPORATION
Burger King Corporation World
Headquarters, Miami, Florida, USA,
1987.
Architects: Hellmuth, Obata &
Kassabaum; chief architect: Gyo
Obata. Text in Japanese and
English.
ARCHITECTURE AND URBANISM 1990
Dec., no.12 extra edition,
p.104-113, elevs., photos., plans,
site plan.

UNITED STATES--MIAMI (FLORIDA)--
FOUNTAINS
Fruit of the boom / Allan
Schwartzman.
Fountain designed by Claes
Oldenburg and Coosje van Bruggen
for a Miami plaza.
HOUSE & GARDEN 1990 Nov., v.162,
no.11, p.[202]-203, photos.

UNITED STATES--MIAMI (FLORIDA)--
HISTORIC DISTRICTS--CONSERVATION AND
RESTORATION--ART DECO DISTRICT
Will success kill the Deco district?
/ Michael Warren.
"A recent plan aimed at producing
convention hotels in Miami Beach's
colorful historic district has
some preservationists up in arms."
PLANNING 1990 Feb., v.56, no.2,
p.21-24, ports., elev., map,
photos.

UNITED STATES--MIAMI (FLORIDA)--
HOSPITALS--MATERNITY--BAPTIST
HOSPITAL OF MIAMI--LAKE PAVILION /
FAMILY BIRTH CENTER
Targeting treatment: Building Types
Study 680, hospitals.
Uses 3 examples: Freeport Hospital
Health Care Village, Kitchener,
Ont. (NORR Partnership); Marin
General Hospital Addition,
Greenbrae, Calif. (Kaplan,
McLaughlin, Diaz, Architects); and
Lake Pavilion/Family Birth Center,
Baptist Hospital of Miami (Ritchie
Organization).
ARCHITECTURAL RECORD 1990 June,
v.178, no.7, p.87-101, ill.,
photos., plans, site plans, aerial
photo.

UNITED STATES--MIAMI (FLORIDA)--
HOUSES--ARCHITECTS'--SPEAR -
FORT-BRESCIA HOUSE
Arquitectonica at home: Laurinda
Spear and Bernardo Fort-Brescia's
Miami residence / Beth Dunlop.
Located in Coconut Grove.
ARCHITECTURAL DIGEST 1990 Dec.,
v.47, no.13, p.42,46,50,54, port.,
photos.

UNITED STATES--MIAMI (FLORIDA)--
MARKETS--CARIBBEAN MARKETPLACE
Caribbean recall: Caribbean
Marketplace, Miami, Florida,
Charles Harrison Pawley, architect
/ Beth Dunlop.
ARCHITECTURAL RECORD 1990 Nov.,
v.178, no.12, p.90-[93], photos.,
plans, secns.

UNITED STATES--MIAMI (FLORIDA)--
MULTI-USE COMPLEXES--BRICKELL
GATEWAY
Brickell Gateway, Miami, Florida,
USA.
Project for high-rise mixed-use
complex. Architects: Hellmuth,
Obata & Kassabaum. Text in
Japanese and English.
ARCHITECTURE AND URBANISM 1990
Dec., no.12 extra edition,
p.204-[207], dwgs., elev., plans.

UNITED STATES--MIAMI (FLORIDA)--OFFICE
BUILDINGS--ART DECO--CONSERVATION
AND RESTORATION--FREEDOM TOWER
Southern traditions: preservation
efforts in today's South show new
interest in 20th-century
landmarks, as well as earlier ones
/ Clifford A. Pearson.
A portfolio of Southeast projects:
Epping Forest Yacht Club,
Jacksonville, Fla. (Pappas
Associates); Freedom Tower, Miami
(Heisenbottle Architects);
Venetian Pool, Coral Gables, Fla.
(H. Carlton Decker & Assoc.);
Howard Memorial Library, New
Orleans (E. Barron, M. Toups); and
Linden Row Inn, Richmond, Va.
(Glave Newman Anderson).
ARCHITECTURAL RECORD 1990 Mar.,
v.178, no.3, p.66-75, photos.,
plans, site plans.

UNITED STATES--MIAMI (FLORIDA)--
OFFICES--INTERIOR DESIGN--CODINA
GROUP
Codina Group / Monica Geran.
Miami real estate developer's
office designed by Joyce Snoweiss
Design Group.
INTERIOR DESIGN 1990 Jan., v.61,
no.1, p.196-[199], photos., plans.

UNITED STATES--MIAMI (FLORIDA)--REAL
ESTATE DEVELOPMENT
Miami nice: in the pink again /
Carol Isaak Barden.
SOUTHERN ACCENTS 1990 Sept., v.13,
no.7, p.124-127, photos.

UNITED STATES--MIAMI LAKES (FLORIDA)--
NEW TOWNS
Pumping up suburban downtowns /
Philip Langdon.
Examples in Reston, Va., Miami
Lakes, Fla., and Buffalo Grove,
Ill.
PLANNING 1990 July, v.56, no.7,
p.22-28, dwg., model, map,
photos., plans, aerial photo.

UNITED STATES--MICHIGAN--BUNGALOWS--
ALTERATIONS AND ADDITIONS
A prairie home solution / Victoria
Lautman.
Renovation of a 1920s bungalow on
Lake Michigan. Architect: Peter
Landon.
METROPOLITAN HOME 1990 July, v.22,
no.7, p.46-[51], photos.

UNITED STATES--MICHIGAN--GARDENS
Oggetti della memoria nel giardino:
un insolito in Michigan / Elisa
Dal Canto.
A garden in Mich.
VILLE GIARDINI 1990 Jan., no.244,
p.60-65, photos.

UNITED STATES--MICHIGAN--HOUSES
Palladian abstractions: Hugh Newell
Jacobsen's light-washed design in
Michigan / Robert Campbell.
Lakeside residence near Detroit is
a contemporary version of James
River plantation houses. Interior
designers: Ingles & Associates.
ARCHITECTURAL DIGEST 1990 Dec.,
v.47, no.13, p.[144-151],226,
port., photos., plan.

UNITED STATES--MICHIGAN--HURON
VALLEY--RESIDENTIAL GARDENS
Acquattato nel paesaggio: nel fianco
di una collina del Michigan /
Gilberto Oneto.
Gardens of a house in the Huron
Valley. Landscape architect:
Charles Cares.
VILLE GIARDINI 1990 Feb., no.245,
p.[64]-67, photos.

UNITED STATES--MICHIGAN--SWIMMING
POOLS
Acquattato nel paesaggio: nel fianco
di una collina del Michigan /
Gilberto Oneto.
Gardens of a house in the Huron
Valley. Landscape architect:
Charles Cares.
VILLE GIARDINI 1990 Feb., no.245,
p.[64]-67, photos.

UNITED STATES--MICHIGAN--VACATION
HOUSES--ALTERATIONS AND ADDITIONS
A prairie home solution / Victoria
Lautman.
Renovation of a 1920s bungalow on
Lake Michigan. Architect: Peter
Landon.
METROPOLITAN HOME 1990 July, v.22,
no.7, p.46-[51], photos.

UNITED STATES--MICHIGAN--WEEKEND
HOUSES
Architetture per il sito: la casa
nel bosco = Site-friendly
architecture: the house in the
wood.
Weekend house near Lake Michigan.
Architects: Pappageorge Haymes.
ABITARE 1990 Apr., no.284,
p.164-169, elevs., photos., plans,
site plan.

UNITED STATES--MICHIGAN--WEEKEND
HOUSES--ARCHITECTS'--GIBBONS - OLLIS
HOUSE
On a whim and a prairie
[Gibbons-Ollis house] / Victoria
Lautman.
A six-room weekend house, located
in rural Mich. and influenced by
Palladio. Architect: Rick Gibbons.
METROPOLITAN HOME 1990 June, v.22,
no.6, p.96-[101], port., photos.

UNITED STATES--MIDDLEBURG (VIRGINIA)--
HOUSES--INTERIOR DESIGN
In pursuit of the fox: at home in
Virginia's hunt country / Susannah
M. Wilson.
SOUTHERN ACCENTS 1990 Oct., v.13,
no.8, p.112-119, photos.

UNITED STATES--MIDDLETOWN (DELAWARE)--
BOATHOUSES--SAINT ANDREW'S SCHOOL
BOATHOUSE
Wood craft: Boathouse, St. Andrew's
School, Middletown, Delaware.
Architect: Richard Conway Meyer.
ARCHITECTURAL RECORD 1990 July,
v.178, no.8, p.58-59, photos.,
isometric dwg.

UNITED STATES--MIDWEST--ARCHITECTURE--
20TH CENTURY
Regional portfolio: the Midwest.
Six recent buildings, each indexed
separately.
ARCHITECTURE: THE AIA JOURNAL 1990
Feb., v.79, no.2, p.[68-87],
elev., model, photos, plans.

UNITED STATES--MIDWEST--ARCHITECTURE--
AWARDS AND PRIZES
Caretakers of time-proven beliefs:
The Central States Regional Awards
[1989] / Lynn Spears.
15 premiated projects in Iowa,
Nebr., Mo., and Okla.
IOWA ARCHITECT 1990 Spring, v.39,
no.1, p.26-35, photos.

UNITED STATES--MIDWEST--HOUSES
Midwest houses 3.
The third issue to focus on
residential design. The eight
articles are indexed separately.
INLAND ARCHITECT 1990 Mar.-Apr.,
v.34, no.2, p.31-55, ill., photos.

UNITED STATES--MIDWEST--HOUSING--
ALTERATIONS AND ADDITIONS--
SOCIOLOGICAL ASPECTS
Housing adjustments of rural
households: decisions and
consequences / Kathleen Ann Lodl,
E. Raedene Combs.
Housing adjustments (e.g.,
remodelling, changing residence)
in the Midwest.
HOUSING AND SOCIETY 1989, v.16,
no.3, p.13-22, chart, tables,
refs.

UNITED STATES--MILITARY BASES
Picking up the pieces [military
bases] / Robert Guskind.
Adaptive reuse of military bases
closed by the U.S. Dept. of
Defense.
PLANNING 1990 June, v.56, no.6,
p.12-16, photos., aerial photos.

UNITED STATES--MILITARY HOUSING
Military family housing: the older
public housing program / Chester
Hartman, Robin Drayer.
HOUSING AND SOCIETY 1990, v.17,
no.3, p.67-78, refs.

UNITED STATES--MILLBROOK (NEW YORK)--
HOUSES--GREEK REVIVAL--INTERIOR
DESIGN--OWEN HOUSE
A Classical education: restoring a
Greek Revival house in the Hudson
River Valley / John Gruen.
Interiors of restored home in
Millbrook, NY, owned and designed
by Sylvia Owen.
ARCHITECTURAL DIGEST 1990 June,
v.47, no.6, p.182-185, photos.

UNITED STATES--MILTON
(MASSACHUSETTS)--STUDENT UNIONS--
MILTON ACADEMY
Low budget, high power / Justin
Henderson.
On the student center at Milton
Academy, Milton, Mass. Architect:
Cameron Roberts.
INTERIORS 1990 June, v.149, no.11,
p.134-[135], photos., plan.

UNITED STATES--MILWAUKEE (WISCONSIN)--
ARCADES--MILWAUKEE CENTER
The Arcade: a forgotten urban type /
Robert Beckley.
Emphasis is on the Milwaukee
Center, which began as a
collaboration between MRT and
Beckley/Myers Architects.
INLAND ARCHITECT 1990 July-Aug.,
v.34, no.4, p.[52]-57, ill.,
model, photos., site plan.

UNITED STATES--MILWAUKEE (WISCONSIN)--
ARCHITECTURE
Milwaukee.
Feature section. Partial contents:
Milwaukee, in praise of the
commonplace, by Linda R. Krause.--
Way finding: exploring the
Milwaukee image, by Cynthia Chapin
Davidson. A third article is
separately indexed.
INLAND ARCHITECT 1990 July-Aug.,
v.34, no.4, p.31-51, dwgs.,
photos.

UNITED STATES--MILWAUKEE (WISCONSIN)--
CENTRAL BUSINESS DISTRICTS
Regional portfolio: The Midwest: a
tale of two cities / Clifford A.
Pearson.
Minneapolis and Milwaukee have
become two of the most livable
cities in the U.S. Contents: 100
E. Wisconsin Ave., Milwaukee
(Clark Tribble Harris & Li
Architects); Milwaukee Repertory
Theater (Beckley/Myers
Architects);5th St. Parking
Facility, Minneapolis (Stageberg
Partners); Valspar Varnish Factory
renovation, Minneapolis (Meyer,
Scherer & Rockcastle); and the
Ceresota, Minneapolis (Ellerbe
Becket).
ARCHITECTURAL RECORD 1990 Aug.,
v.178, no.9, p.62-71, axonometric
view, photos., plans, secns., site
plans.

UNITED STATES--MILWAUKEE (WISCONSIN)--
CENTRAL BUSINESS DISTRICTS--
ALTERATIONS AND ADDITIONS--
COMPETITIONS
The future of the industrial city /
Joel Warren Barna.
City planning proposals for
renewal of the Milwaukee, Wisc.
downtown area.
TEXAS ARCHITECT 1990 Mar.-Apr.,
v.40, no.2, p.30-35, map, site
plans.

UNITED STATES--MILWAUKEE (WISCONSIN)--
CITIES AND TOWNS--GROWTH
Milwaukee.
Feature section. Partial contents:
Milwaukee, in praise of the
commonplace, by Linda R. Krause.--
Way finding: exploring the
Milwaukee image, by Cynthia Chapin
Davidson. A third article is
separately indexed.
INLAND ARCHITECT 1990 July-Aug.,
v.34, no.4, p.31-51, dwgs.,
photos.

UNITED STATES--MILWAUKEE (WISCONSIN)--
CITY PLANNING--COMPETITIONS
The International City Design
Competition / Jeffrey E. Ollswang.
Sponsored by the University of
Wisconsin, Milwaukee. Contents:
Incremental utopias, by Allan B.
Jacobs; Cities of culture, cities
of places, by Carlos Tejeda; let
Milwaukee be Milwaukee, by Cynthia
Weese; Solutions in search of a
problem, by Amos Rapoport; and
Places are not impositions, by
William Turnbull, Jr.
PLACES 1990 Winter, v.6, no.2,
p.32-47, axonometric views, dwgs.,
map, photos., plans, site plans,
aerial photo., refs.

UNITED STATES--MILWAUKEE (WISCONSIN)--
CITY PLANNING--ITALIAN COMMUNITY
CENTER
L'Italian Community Center di
Milwaukee = The Italian Community
Center in Milwaukee / Philippe
Vernier.
15 acre redevelopment project;
architects: Bonifica spa (Gruppo
Iri-Italstat).
L'ARCA 1990 July-Aug., no.40,
p.12-19, dwgs., site plans,
sketches, aerial photo.

UNITED STATES--MILWAUKEE (WISCONSIN)--
ENCLOSED STADIUMS--BRADLEY CENTER
Bradley Center Arena, Milwaukee,
Wisconsin, USA, 1988.
Architects: Hellmuth, Obata &
Kassabaum. Text in Japanese and
English.
ARCHITECTURE AND URBANISM 1990
Dec., no.12 extra edition,
p.126-[131], photos., plans, site
plan.

UNITED STATES--MILWAUKEE (WISCONSIN)--
HOUSES--INTERIOR DESIGN--TOWER OF
BABEL
The house with a heart of stone /
Victor M. Cassidy.
Home near Milwaukee, Wisc., which
was constructed around massive
stone sculpture, Tower of Babel.
Architect: Charles Moore. Artist:
Dan Yarbrough.
CONNOISSEUR 1990 May, v.220,
no.940, p.104-107,148, axonometric
view, port., photos.

UNITED STATES--MILWAUKEE (WISCONSIN)--
OFFICE BUILDINGS--100 EAST WISCONSIN
AVENUE
Regional portfolio: The Midwest: a
tale of two cities / Clifford A.
Pearson.
Minneapolis and Milwaukee have
become two of the most livable
cities in the U.S. Contents: 100
E. Wisconsin Ave., Milwaukee
(Clark Tribble Harris & Li
Architects); Milwaukee Repertory
Theater (Beckley/Myers
Architects);5th St. Parking
Facility, Minneapolis (Stageberg
Partners); Valspar Varnish Factory
renovation, Minneapolis (Meyer,
Scherer & Rockcastle); and the
Ceresota, Minneapolis (Ellerbe
Becket).
ARCHITECTURAL RECORD 1990 Aug.,
v.178, no.9, p.62-71, axonometric
view, photos., plans, secns., site
plans.

UNITED STATES--MILWAUKEE (WISCONSIN)--
RESTAURANTS--INTERIOR DESIGN--DKC'S
ARMADILLO BAR AND GRILL
Wisconsin getaways: urban chic,
rural retreat / Karen E. Klages.
Two interiors: DKC's Armadillo Bar
and Grill, Milwaukee (architect:
Kubala Washatko Architects), and
The Inn at Pine Terrace,
Oconomowoc (designer: Zimmerman
Design Group).
INLAND ARCHITECT 1990 July-Aug.,
v.34, no.4, p.4-[5], photos.,
plan.

UNITED STATES--MILWAUKEE (WISCONSIN)--
SCULPTURE--STONE--TOWER OF BABEL
The house with a heart of stone /
Victor M. Cassidy.
Home near Milwaukee, Wisc., which
was constructed around massive
stone sculpture, Tower of Babel.
Architect: Charles Moore. Artist:
Dan Yarbrough.
CONNOISSEUR 1990 May, v.220,
no.940, p.104-107,148, axonometric
view, port., photos.

UNITED STATES--MILWAUKEE (WISCONSIN)--
THEATERS--MILWAUKEE REPERTORY
THEATER
Regional portfolio: The Midwest: a
tale of two cities / Clifford A.
Pearson.
Minneapolis and Milwaukee have
become two of the most livable
cities in the U.S. Contents: 100
E. Wisconsin Ave., Milwaukee
(Clark Tribble Harris & Li
Architects); Milwaukee Repertory
Theater (Beckley/Myers
Architects);5th St. Parking
Facility, Minneapolis (Stageberg
Partners); Valspar Varnish Factory
renovation, Minneapolis (Meyer,
Scherer & Rockcastle); and the
Ceresota, Minneapolis (Ellerbe
Becket).
ARCHITECTURAL RECORD 1990 Aug.,
v.178, no.9, p.62-71, axonometric
view, photos., plans, secns., site
plans.

UNITED STATES--MILWAUKEE (WISCONSIN)--
URBAN FRINGES
The future of the industrial city /
Joel Warren Barna.
City planning proposals for
renewal of the Milwaukee, Wisc.
downtown area.
TEXAS ARCHITECT 1990 Mar.-Apr.,
v.40, no.2, p.30-35, map, site
plans.

UNITED STATES--MINEOLA (NEW YORK)--
BANKS--INTERIOR DESIGN--CENTRAL
FEDERAL SAVINGS BANK
The color of money / Nayana
Currimbhoy.
Interiors of Central Federal
Savings Bank, Mineola, NY.
Architects: Swanke Hayden Connell.
INTERIORS 1990 Apr., v.149, no.9,
p.96-[99], photos., plan.

UNITED STATES--MINES--HISTORY--
CONGRESSES
Historic mining resources conference
/ Robert L. Spade.
Report on conference held Jan.1989
at Death Valley National Monument.
CRM BULLETIN: A NATIONAL PARK
SERVICE TECHNICAL BULLETIN 1990,
v.13, no.4, p.16-18,

UNITED STATES--MINNEAPOLIS
(MINNESOTA)--AMUSEMENT PARKS--
WONDERLAND
Lost Minnesota: Wonderland's Beacon
Tower, Minneapolis, 1905-1911 /
Jack El-Hai.
Amusement park tower, built 1905;
razed in 1911.
ARCHITECTURE MINNESOTA 1990
Sept.-Oct., v.16, no.5, p.72,
photo.

UNITED STATES--MINNEAPOLIS
(MINNESOTA)--ARMORIES--KENWOOD
ARMORY
Lost Minnesota: the Kenwood Armory,
Minneapolis, 1907-1934 / Jack
El-Hai.
ARCHITECTURE MINNESOTA 1990
Mar.-Apr., v.16, no.2, p.68,
photo.

UNITED STATES--MINNEAPOLIS
(MINNESOTA)--ARMORIES--MINNEAPOLIS
NATIONAL GUARD ARMORY
Endangered species: can the
Minneapolis Armory beat the
wrecking ball? / Jack El-Hai.
At 4th Ave. and 6th St. South.
Built 1935. Architect Major F.C.
Bettenburg.
ARCHITECTURE MINNESOTA 1990
Mar.-Apr., v.16, no.2, p.[48]-51,
photos.
On guard for Minneapolis Moderne:
Minneapolis National Guard Armory
/ Jim Leinfelder.
Armory built 1935 by the Minnesota
National Guard through the Public
Works Administration (PWA).
Hennepin County plans to raze the
armory and build a jail.
PRESERVATION NEWS 1990 Feb., v.30,
no.2, p.3, photo.

UNITED STATES--MINNEAPOLIS
(MINNESOTA)--ATRIUMS--GAVIIDAE
COMMON
Fantasy framework: details / Bill
Beyer.
The atrium of the Gaviidae Common
shopping center, Minneapolis,
designed by Cesar Pelli &
Associates.
ARCHITECTURE MINNESOTA 1990
Jan.-Feb., v.16, no.1, p.47, det.,
photo.

UNITED STATES--MINNEAPOLIS
(MINNESOTA)--CENTRAL BUSINESS
DISTRICTS
Regional portfolio: The Midwest: a
tale of two cities / Clifford A.
Pearson.
Minneapolis and Milwaukee have
become two of the most livable
cities in the U.S. Contents: 100
E. Wisconsin Ave., Milwaukee
(Clark Tribble Harris & Li
Architects); Milwaukee Repertory
Theater (Beckley/Myers
Architects);5th St. Parking
Facility, Minneapolis (Stageberg
Partners); Valspar Varnish Factory
renovation, Minneapolis (Meyer,
Scherer & Rockcastle); and the
Ceresota, Minneapolis (Ellerbe
Becket).
ARCHITECTURAL RECORD 1990 Aug.,
v.178, no.9, p.62-71, axonometric
view, photos., plans, secns., site
plans.

UNITED STATES--MINNEAPOLIS
(MINNESOTA)--CENTRAL BUSINESS
DISTRICTS--HENNEPIN AVENUE
Ray Harris: meeting development
opportunities in Minneapolis /
Eric Kudalis.
Developer hopes to revitalize
Hennepin Ave. in downtown
Minneapolis with E Block, a
mixed-use entertainment complex.
Architects: Jerde Partnership with
Korsunsky Krank Erickson.
ARCHITECTURE MINNESOTA 1990
Jan.-Feb., v.16, no.1, p.15,63,
dwg., port.

UNITED STATES--MINNEAPOLIS
(MINNESOTA)--CHURCHES--19TH
CENTURY--SAINT MARY'S RUSSIAN
ORTHODOX GREEK CATHOLIC CHURCH
Lost Minnesota: St. Mary's Russian
Orthodox Greek Catholic Church,
1888-1904 / Jack El-Hai.
Once in Minneapolis, at Fifth St.
and 17th Ave. N.E., it burned in
1904.
ARCHITECTURE MINNESOTA 1990
Nov.-Dec., v.16, no.6, p.74,
photo.

UNITED STATES--MINNEAPOLIS
(MINNESOTA)--CITIES AND TOWNS
NAHR in the Twin Cities / J. Marilyn
Henry.
JOURNAL OF HOUSING 1990
Sept.-Oct., v.47, no.5, p.251-255,
258-260,262-264, photos., aerial
photos.

UNITED STATES--MINNEAPOLIS
(MINNESOTA)--CITY PLANNING
Unbuilt Minnesota: Venturi, Rauch &
Scott Brown's 1981 redesign
proposal for Hennepin Avenue /
Robert Gerloff.
ARCHITECTURE MINNESOTA 1990
July-Aug., v.16, no.4, p.49, ill.

UNITED STATES--MINNEAPOLIS
(MINNESOTA)--COTTAGES--ALTERATIONS
AND ADDITIONS--ANDERSON HOUSE
The raw stuff: creative dreaming
makes for artful getaway under the
eaves.
Renovated attic of a 1931
Minneapolis cottage.
ARCHITECTURE MINNESOTA 1990
May-June, v.16, no.3, p.42-45,
photos.

UNITED STATES--MINNEAPOLIS
(MINNESOTA)--DEPARTMENT STORES--
RUINED, EXTINCT, ETC.--DONALDSON'S
Lost Minnesota: the Donaldson Block,
Minneapolis, built 1888-1924,
demolished 1982 / Paul Clifford
Larson.
A block of retail buildings,
including Donaldson's department
store.
ARCHITECTURE MINNESOTA 1990
Jan.-Feb., v.16, no.1, p.64,
photo.

UNITED STATES--MINNEAPOLIS
(MINNESOTA)--EXHIBITIONS--ART INTO
LIFE: RUSSIAN CONSTRUCTIVISM 1914-32
Art into life. Russian
Constructivism 1914-32 [exhibition
review] / Bruce N. Wright.
At the Walker Art Center and
elsewhere.
INLAND ARCHITECT 1990 Nov.-Dec.,
v.34, no.6, p.57-62, models.

UNITED STATES--MINNEAPOLIS
(MINNESOTA)--FACTORIES--ALTERATIONS
AND ADDITIONS--VALSPAR VARNISH
FACTORY
Regional portfolio: The Midwest: a
tale of two cities / Clifford A.
Pearson.
Minneapolis and Milwaukee have
become two of the most livable
cities in the U.S. Contents: 100
E. Wisconsin Ave., Milwaukee
(Clark Tribble Harris & Li
Architects); Milwaukee Repertory
(Continued next column)

UNITED STATES--MINNEAPOLIS
(MINNESOTA)--FACTORIES--ALTERATIONS
AND ADDITIONS--VALSPAR VARNISH
FACTORY (CONTINUED)
Regional portfolio:...(CONTINUED)
Theater (Beckley/Myers
Architects);5th St. Parking
Facility, Minneapolis (Stageberg
Partners); Valspar Varnish Factory
renovation, Minneapolis (Meyer,
Scherer & Rockcastle); and the
Ceresota, Minneapolis (Ellerbe
Becket).
ARCHITECTURAL RECORD 1990 Aug.,
v.178, no.9, p.62-71, axonometric
view, photos., plans, secns., site
plans.

UNITED STATES--MINNEAPOLIS
(MINNESOTA)--HOUSES
Playing with form and scale / Bruce
N. Wright.
House in a Minneapolis suburb,
built on the foundations of a
1950s modernist house. Architect:
Meyer, Scherer & Rockcastle.
INLAND ARCHITECT 1990 Mar.-Apr.,
v.34, no.2, p.34-36, axonometric
view, photos., plans.

UNITED STATES--MINNEAPOLIS
(MINNESOTA)--HOUSES--20TH CENTURY--
ALTERATIONS AND ADDITIONS--REINSTEIN
HOUSE
Neoclassical update:
turn-of-the-century house provides
classical charm with a
contemporary twist.
Reinstein House renovation near
Lake of the Isles in Minneapolis.
Architect: Martha Yunker.
ARCHITECTURE MINNESOTA 1990
May-June, v.16, no.3, p.46-49,
photos.

UNITED STATES--MINNEAPOLIS
(MINNESOTA)--HOUSES--20TH CENTURY--
BLACKBOURN HOUSE
Unbuilt Minnesota / Robert Gerloff.
Two designs for a Minneapolis
house for a 1938 Life magazine
article. Architects: Royal Barry
Wills, Frank Lloyd Wright. The
Wills design was built in
Minneapolis, and the Wright design
built at Two Rivers, Wisc.
ARCHITECTURE MINNESOTA 1990
May-June, v.16, no.3, p.67,
models.

UNITED STATES-- MINNEAPOLIS
(MINNESOTA)--HOUSES--ALTERATIONS AND
ADDITIONS--AHLES YUNKER HOUSE
Movie makeover.
Makeover of architects' house for
use as a film set.
ARCHITECTURE MINNESOTA 1990
May-June, v.16, no.3, p.64-65,
photos.

UNITED STATES--MINNEAPOLIS
(MINNESOTA)--HOUSES--BROWN - LELLMAN
HOUSE
Treetop building blocks / Bruce N.
Wright.
The Brown/Lellman house in the
Minnehaha Creek area of
Minneapolis. Architect: Meyer,
Scherer & Rockcastle.
INLAND ARCHITECT 1990 Mar.-Apr.,
v.34, no.2, p.37-39, elevs.,
photos., plans.

UNITED STATES--MINNEAPOLIS
(MINNESOTA)--HOUSES--PRAIRIE
SCHOOL--LAKE PLACE (PURCELL HOUSE)
Prairie School Minnesota style /
Larry Millett.
   The Purcell-Cutts House, located
   one block from Lake of the Isles.
   Built in 1913 and owned by the
   Minneapolis Institute of Arts
   since 1985. Architects: William
   Gray Purcell and George Grant
   Elmslie.
   INLAND ARCHITECT 1990 Nov.-Dec.,
   v.34, no.6, p.12,15, photos.

UNITED STATES--MINNEAPOLIS
(MINNESOTA)--HOUSING
NAHR in the Twin Cities / J. Marilyn
Henry.
   JOURNAL OF HOUSING 1990
   Sept.-Oct., v.47, no.5, p.251-255,
   258-260,262-264, photos., aerial
   photos.

UNITED STATES--MINNEAPOLIS
(MINNESOTA)--MULTI-USE BUILDINGS--
NEOCLASSICAL--YOUNG QUINLAN BUILDING
Young Quinlan reborn: a Minneapolis
landmark launches a fresh approach
to old grandeur.
   Retail/office building built in
   1926. Architect: Frederick
   Ackerman with Magney and Tusler.
   Renovations by Ellerbe Becket.
   ARCHITECTURE MINNESOTA 1990
   Jan.-Feb., v.16, no.1, p.[22]-29,
   port., photos.

UNITED STATES--MINNEAPOLIS
(MINNESOTA)--MULTI-USE COMPLEXES--E
BLOCK
Ray Harris: meeting development
opportunities in Minneapolis /
Eric Kudalis.
   Developer hopes to revitalize
   Hennepin Ave. in downtown
   Minneapolis with E Block, a
   mixed-use entertainment complex.
   Architects: Jerde Partnership with
   Korsunsky Krank Erickson.
   ARCHITECTURE MINNESOTA 1990
   Jan.-Feb., v.16, no.1, p.15,63,
   dwg., port.

UNITED STATES--MINNEAPOLIS
(MINNESOTA)--MUSEUMS--ART--WALKER
ART CENTER
Symposium: architecture on exhibit.
   Seven architectural curators
   respond to questions about
   exhibiting architecture at their
   institutions; Mildred Friedman,
   Walker Art Center; Georges
   Teyssot, Milan Triennale; John
   Zukowsky, Art Insitute of Chicago;
   Paolo Polledri, San Francisco
   Museum of Modern Art; Stuart
   Wrede, Museum of Modern Art, New
   York; Ulriche Jehle-Schulte
   Strathaus, Architekturmuseum
   Basel; Francois Burkhardt, Centre
   Creation Industrielle, Centre
   Pompidou, Paris.
   DESIGN BOOK REVIEW 1989 summer,
   no.16, p.23-32, photos.

UNITED STATES--MINNEAPOLIS
(MINNESOTA)--OFFICE BUILDINGS--
CERESOTA
Regional portfolio: The Midwest: a
tale of two cities / Clifford A.
Pearson.
   Minneapolis and Milwaukee have
   become two of the most livable
   cities in the U.S. Contents: 100
   E. Wisconsin Ave., Milwaukee
   (Clark Tribble Harris & Li
   Architects); Milwaukee Repertory
   Theater (Beckley/Myers
   Architects);5th St. Parking
   Facility, Minneapolis (Stageberg
   Partners); Valspar Varnish Factory
   renovation, Minneapolis (Meyer,
   Scherer & Rockcastle); and the
   Ceresota, Minneapolis (Ellerbe
   Becket).
   ARCHITECTURAL RECORD 1990 Aug.,
   v.178, no.9, p.62-71, axonometric
   view, photos., plans, secns., site
   plans.

UNITED STATES--MINNEAPOLIS
(MINNESOTA)--OFFICE BUILDINGS--
NORWEST CENTER
Collaborative art / Amy Dana.
   Interiors of Norwest Corp.
   corporate offices, Minneapolis,
   Minn. Interior designers: STUDIOS.
   Architect: Cesar Pelli.
   INTERIORS 1990 June, v.149, no.11,
   p.108-119, ports., photos., plans,
   models.
11 Norwest Center a Minneapolis =
Norwest Center tower, Minneapolis,
Minn. / Silvano Stucchi.
   Architect: Cesar Pelli &
   Associates. Includes English
   translation; French, German and
   Spanish summaries, p.[3-4].
   L'INDUSTRIA DELLE COSTRUZIONI 1990
   Oct., v.24, no.228, p.32-37,
   elev., photos., plans, site plan.
Special feature: recent works of
Cesar Pelli.
   Contents: Editor's introduction--
   Architects' statement / Cesar
   Pelli-- Essay: Urban iconography
   and the medium of architecture /
   Gavin Macrae-Gibson, p.130-137--
   Works: World Financial Center--
   Norwest Tower-- Pacific Design
   Center expansion-- Mattatuck
   Museum-- Ley Student Center
   expansion, Rice University-- Yale
   Center for Molecular Medicine,
   Yale University-- Carnegie Hall
   tower-- Sunarhauserman
   headquarters-- Fan Pier master
   plan. Architects: Cesar Pelli &
   Associates. Text in Japanese and
   English.
   ARCHITECTURE AND URBANISM 1990
   Feb., no.2(233), p.[59]-148,
   dwgs., elevs., photos., plans,
   secns., site plans.
Urban Icon: Norwest Center refines
and enervates - and is haunted by
- an historical type / Edward W.
Wolner.
   A 57-story tower in Minneapolis,
   incorporating fragments form the
   former Norwest Bank Building.
   Architect: Cesar Pelli.
   INLAND ARCHITECT 1990 Jan.-Feb.,
   v.34, no.1, p.44-48, elev.,
   photos.

UNITED STATES--MINNEAPOLIS
(MINNESOTA)--OFFICES--ARCHITECTS'--
ALTERATIONS AND ADDITIONS--
ARCHITECTURAL ALLIANCE
From warehouse to playhouse; three
local office designs take the
routine out of the 9-to-5 realm /
Sandra LaWall Lipschultz.
   Duffy Design Group offices
   (architect: Rob Reis);
   Architectural Alliance addition
   (architects: Ketcham, Lackens, De
   Angelo); and Janz/Abrahamson
   office (architects: Hammel Green
   and Abrahamson). All in
   Minneapolis.
   ARCHITECTURE MINNESOTA 1990
   Nov.-Dec., v.16, no.6, p.46-51,
   photos.

UNITED STATES--MINNEAPOLIS
(MINNESOTA)--OFFICES--DUFFY DESIGN
GROUP
From warehouse to playhouse; three
local office designs take the
routine out of the 9-to-5 realm /
Sandra LaWall Lipschultz.
   Duffy Design Group offices
   (architect: Rob Reis);
   Architectural Alliance addition
   (architects: Ketcham, Lackens, De
   Angelo); and Janz/Abrahamson
   office (architects: Hammel Green
   and Abrahamson). All in
   Minneapolis.
   ARCHITECTURE MINNESOTA 1990
   Nov.-Dec., v.16, no.6, p.46-51,
   photos.

UNITED STATES--MINNEAPOLIS
(MINNESOTA)--OFFICES--INTERIOR
DESIGN--DUFFY DESIGN GROUP
Incarnation on the waterfront /
Bruce N. Wright.
   Renovation of an 1887 warehouse at
   315 First Avenue, Minneapolis for
   apartments, bar and restaurant,
   and offices of the Duffy Design
   Group. Architect: Johnson/Reis &
   Associates.
   INLAND ARCHITECT 1990 Sept.-Oct.,
   v.34, no.5, p.6-7, axonometric
   view, photos.

UNITED STATES--MINNEAPOLIS
(MINNESOTA)--OFFICES--INTERIOR
DESIGN--NORWEST CORPORATION
Collaborative art / Amy Dana.
   Interiors of Norwest Corp.
   corporate offices, Minneapolis,
   Minn. Interior designers: STUDIOS.
   Architect: Cesar Pelli.
   INTERIORS 1990 June, v.149, no.11,
   p.108-119, ports., photos., plans,
   models.

UNITED STATES--MINNEAPOLIS
(MINNESOTA)--OFFICES--JANZ
ABRAHAMSON
From warehouse to playhouse; three
local office designs take the
routine out of the 9-to-5 realm /
Sandra LaWall Lipschultz.
   Duffy Design Group offices
   (architect: Rob Reis);
   Architectural Alliance addition
   (architects: Ketcham, Lackens, De
   Angelo); and Janz/Abrahamson
   office (architects: Hammel Green
   and Abrahamson). All in
   Minneapolis.
   ARCHITECTURE MINNESOTA 1990
(Continued next page)

UNITED STATES--MINNEAPOLIS
(MINNESOTA)--OFFICES--JANZ
ABRAHAMSON (CONTINUED)
From warehouse to...(CONTINUED)
Nov.-Dec., v.16, no.6, p.46-51,
photos.

UNITED STATES--MINNEAPOLIS
(MINNESOTA)--PARK BUILDINGS--LAKE
HARRIET
Hot dog! Refectory continues Lake
Harriet tradition of whimsical
architecture.
Concession stand in a Minneapolis
park. Architect: Milo Thompson of
Bentz/Thompson/Rietow.
ARCHITECTURE MINNESOTA 1990
Sept.-Oct., v.16, no.5, p.42-43,
photos.

UNITED STATES--MINNEAPOLIS
(MINNESOTA)--PARKING GARAGES--5TH
STREET PARKING/TRANSIT FACILITY
Regional portfolio: The Midwest: a
tale of two cities / Clifford A.
Pearson.
Minneapolis and Milwaukee have
become two of the most livable
cities in the U.S. Contents: 100
E. Wisconsin Ave., Milwaukee
(Clark Tribble Harris & Li
Architects); Milwaukee Repertory
Theater (Beckley/Myers
Architects);5th St. Parking
Facility, Minneapolis (Stageberg
Partners); Valspar Varnish Factory
renovation, Minneapolis (Meyer,
Scherer & Rockcastle); and the
Ceresota, Minneapolis (Ellerbe
Becket).
ARCHITECTURAL RECORD 1990 Aug.,
v.178, no.9, p.62-71, axonometric
view, photos., plans, secns., site
plans.

UNITED STATES--MINNEAPOLIS
(MINNESOTA)--PEDESTRIAN BRIDGES--
IRENE HIXON WHITNEY BRIDGE
Bridges as artful spaces / Terry
Jill Lassar.
Irene Hixon Whitney Bridge, a
pedestrian bridge in Minneapolis.
Bridge designer is sculptor Siah
Armajani.
URBAN LAND 1990 Nov., v.49, no.11,
p.32-33, photos., aerial photo..

UNITED STATES--MINNEAPOLIS
(MINNESOTA)--RAISED PEDESTRIAN
WALKWAYS--SKYWAY
Skyway-Systeme-ein Vorbild fur
unsere Stadte? / Barbara Hahn.
BAUWELT 1990 Mar.9, v.81, no.10,
p.434-440, maps, photos.

UNITED STATES--MINNEAPOLIS
(MINNESOTA)--REFECTORIES--LAKE
HARRIET
Hot dog! Refectory continues Lake
Harriet tradition of whimsical
architecture.
Concession stand in a Minneapolis
park. Architect: Milo Thompson of
Bentz/Thompson/Rietow.
ARCHITECTURE MINNESOTA 1990
Sept.-Oct., v.16, no.5, p.42-43,
photos.

UNITED STATES--MINNEAPOLIS
(MINNESOTA)--RESIDENTIAL GARDENS--
OSLUND GARDEN
Articulating winter / Cheryl Weber.
Plan for a garden in the backyard
of landscape architect Tom
Oslund's home in Minneapolis.
GARDEN DESIGN 1990 autumn, v.9,
no.3, p.70-72, axonometric view,
port., plan.

UNITED STATES--MINNEAPOLIS
(MINNESOTA)--SCHOOLS OF
ARCHITECTURE--ALTERATIONS AND
ADDITIONS--UNIVERSITY OF MINNESOTA--
SCHOOL OF ARCHITECTURE AND LANDSCAPE
ARCHITECTURE
School of Architecture.
Addition and renovation of the
School of Architecture and
Landscape Architecture, University
of Minnesota, Minneapolis. Design
architects: Steven Holl
Architects. Project architects:
Ellerbe Becket.
PROGRESSIVE ARCHITECTURE 1990
Jan., v.71, no.1, p.83-85,
axonometric view, models, plans,
secn., site plan.
Steven Holl.
Features four projects: P House,
Dallas; apartment house, Fukuoka,
Japan; American Memorial Library
extension competition entry,
Berlin; and the addition to the
School of Architecture, Univ. of
Minn., Minneapolis. English
summaries.
ARCHITECTURE D'AUJOURD'HUI 1990
Oct., no.271, p.122-126, dwgs.,
models, plan, secns., site plan.

UNITED STATES--MINNEAPOLIS
(MINNESOTA)--SHOPPING ARCADES--
GAVIIDAE COMMON
Nicollet's new neighbor: Gaviidae
Common establishes uncommon
standards for retail design / Kira
Obolensky.
Minneapolis shopping center.
Architects: Cesar Pelli &
Associates.
ARCHITECTURE MINNESOTA 1990
Jan.-Feb., v.16, no.1, p.32-33,
photos.

UNITED STATES--MINNEAPOLIS
(MINNESOTA)--SHOPPING CENTERS--
GAVIIDAE COMMON
Nicollet's new neighbor: Gaviidae
Common establishes uncommon
standards for retail design / Kira
Obolensky.
Minneapolis shopping center.
Architects: Cesar Pelli &
Associates.
ARCHITECTURE MINNESOTA 1990
Jan.-Feb., v.16, no.1, p.32-33,
photos.

UNITED STATES--MINNEAPOLIS
(MINNESOTA)--STORE FRONTS--MTC
TRANSIT STORE
Busing it: Shea Architects gives MTC
a lift.
The MTC Transit Store,
Minneapolis.
ARCHITECTURE MINNESOTA 1990
Sept.-Oct., v.16, no.5, p.46-47,
photos.

UNITED STATES--MINNEAPOLIS
(MINNESOTA)--STORES--CENTURY STUDIOS
A place of one's own [Century
Studios, Minneapolis].
Stained glass showroom and studio,
specializing in reproduction of
Tiffany lampshades.
ARCHITECTURE MINNESOTA 1990
May-June, v.16, no.3, p.31, port.

UNITED STATES--MINNEAPOLIS
(MINNESOTA)--STORES--CLOTHING--
AVALANCHE
When less is more: Avalanche's
minimalism sets the stage for the
fine art of retailing.
Clothing store, Minneapolis.
Designer: Steve Andersen.
ARCHITECTURE MINNESOTA 1990
Jan.-Feb., v.16, no.1, p.34-35,
photos.

UNITED STATES--MINNEAPOLIS
(MINNESOTA)--STORES--CLOTHING--
INTOTO
Gauging good design: InToto takes a
fresh angle on retail.
Minneapolis clothing store in
renovated house. Architect:
Daniel Larson; designer: Timothy
Huff.
ARCHITECTURE MINNESOTA 1990
Jan.-Feb., v.16, no.1, p.36-37,
photos.

UNITED STATES--MINNEAPOLIS
(MINNESOTA)--STORES--JEWELRY--
S-VINCENT
Lean elegance: a jeweler's studio
functions as both showroom and
gallery.
S-Vincent, Minneapolis store.
Architect: Gary Johnson.
ARCHITECTURE MINNESOTA 1990
Jan.-Feb., v.16, no.1, p.30-31,
photos.

UNITED STATES--MINNEAPOLIS
(MINNESOTA)--STORES--MTC TRANSIT
STORE
Busing it: Shea Architects gives MTC
a lift.
The MTC Transit Store,
Minneapolis.
ARCHITECTURE MINNESOTA 1990
Sept.-Oct., v.16, no.5, p.46-47,
photos.

UNITED STATES--MINNEAPOLIS
(MINNESOTA)--STREETS--ALTERATIONS
AND ADDITIONS--HENNEPIN AVENUE
Hennepin Avenue, Minneapolis.
One of six urban design reports
included in special issue, Urban
Concepts. Extracted from a 1981
plan by Denise Scott Brown, in
collaboration with
Bennett-Ringrose-Wolsfeld-Jarvis-G
ardner and Williams/O'Brien
Associates.
ARCHITECTURAL DESIGN 1990, v.60,
no.1-2. p.62-69, dwgs., elev.,
photos., site plans, sketches.
Unbuilt Minnesota: Venturi, Rauch &
Scott Brown's 1981 redesign
proposal for Hennepin Avenue /
Robert Gerloff.
ARCHITECTURE MINNESOTA 1990
July-Aug., v.16, no.4, p.49, ill.

UNITED STATES--MINNEAPOLIS
(MINNESOTA)--TALL BUILDINGS
Four new skyscrapers in Minneapolis
/ Larry Millett.
Architects: I. M. Pei,
Ellerbe-Becket, Lohan Associates,
and Walsh-Bishop Associates.
INLAND ARCHITECT 1990 Jan.-Feb.,
v.34, no.1, p.[19]-22, ill., dwg.,
elev., model.

UNITED STATES--MINNEAPOLIS
(MINNESOTA)--TOWERS--WONDERLAND
BEACON TOWER
Lost Minnesota: Wonderland's Beacon
Tower, Minneapolis, 1905-1911 /
Jack El-Hai.
Amusement park tower, built 1905;
razed in 1911.
ARCHITECTURE MINNESOTA 1990
Sept.-Oct., v.16, no.5, p.72,
photo.

UNITED STATES--MINNEAPOLIS
(MINNESOTA)--WAREHOUSES--19TH
CENTURY--ALTERATIONS AND ADDITIONS--
315 FIRST AVENUE
Incarnation on the waterfront /
Bruce N. Wright.
Renovation of an 1887 warehouse at
315 First Avenue, Minneapolis for
apartments, bar and restaurant,
and offices of the Duffy Design
Group. Architect: Johnson/Reis &
Associates.
INLAND ARCHITECT 1990 Sept.-Oct.,
v.34, no.5, p.6-7, axonometric
view, photos.

UNITED STATES--MINNESOTA--BUILDINGS--
AWARDS AND PRIZES
1989 MSAIA Honor Awards.
Five awards.
ARCHITECTURE MINNESOTA 1990
Mar.-Apr., v.16, no.2, p.22-[25],
photos.

UNITED STATES--MINNESOTA--BUILDINGS--
LOG
Homes on the range / Bill Beyer.
Details of corner timbering in log
buildings built by Finnish
settlers in the Iron Range of
Minn.
ARCHITECTURE MINNESOTA 1990
July-Aug., v.16, no.4, p.47, dets.

UNITED STATES--MINNESOTA--HUTS
Little house on the ice.
Minn. ice-fishing huts.
ARCHITECTURE MINNESOTA 1990
Jan.-Feb., v.16, no.1, p.[42-45],
photos.

UNITED STATES--MINNESOTA--INTERIOR
DESIGN--AWARDS AND PRIZES
1989 MSAIA Interior Design Awards.
Nine premiated projects.
ARCHITECTURE MINNESOTA 1990
Mar.-Apr., v.16, no.2, p.[26]-31,
photos.

UNITED STATES--MINNESOTA--LANDSCAPE
ARCHITECTURE
Prairie Restorations: a Minnesota
landscape alternative redefines
the meaning of home turf /
Adelheid Fischer.
Native-plant landscaping by Ron
Bowen of Prairie Restorations.
ARCHITECTURE MINNESOTA 1990
Mar.-Apr., v.16, no.2, p.17, 65,
(Continued next column)

UNITED STATES--MINNESOTA--LANDSCAPE
ARCHITECTURE (CONTINUED)
Prairie Restorations:... (CONTINUED)
67, photos.

UNITED STATES--MINNESOTA--OUTHOUSES
Into the woods [outhouses].
ARCHITECTURE MINNESOTA 1990
July-Aug., v.16, no.4, p.12-13,
photos.

UNITED STATES--MINNESOTA--PAVILIONS--
MICHAELSON HOUSE
A place of one's own / Adelheid
Fischer.
Pavilion and porch at a farmhouse
in Minnesota. Architect: James
Stageberg.
ARCHITECTURE MINNESOTA 1990
Mar.-Apr., v.16, no.2, p.19,
port., photos.

UNITED STATES--MINNESOTA--PLANTS
Prairie Restorations: a Minnesota
landscape alternative redefines
the meaning of home turf /
Adelheid Fischer.
Native-plant landscaping by Ron
Bowen of Prairie Restorations.
ARCHITECTURE MINNESOTA 1990
Mar.-Apr., v.16, no.2, p.17, 65,
67, photos.

UNITED STATES--MINNESOTA--PORCHES--
MICHAELSON HOUSE
A place of one's own / Adelheid
Fischer.
Pavilion and porch at a farmhouse
in Minnesota. Architect: James
Stageberg.
ARCHITECTURE MINNESOTA 1990
Mar.-Apr., v.16, no.2, p.19,
port., photos.

UNITED STATES--MINNESOTA--UNEXECUTED
DESIGNS
Unbuilt Minnesota: a glimpse of what
might have been / Robert Gorloff.
Unbuilt projects for Minn. sites,
1891-1989.
ARCHITECTURE MINNESOTA 1990
Mar.-Apr., v.16, no.2, p.[42]-47,
dwgs., elev., models.

UNITED STATES--MINNESOTA--VERNACULAR
ARCHITECTURE
Into the woods [outhouses].
ARCHITECTURE MINNESOTA 1990
July-Aug., v.16, no.4, p.12-13,
photos.
Little house on the ice.
Minn. ice-fishing huts.
ARCHITECTURE MINNESOTA 1990
Jan.-Feb., v.16, no.1, p.[42-45],
photos.

UNITED STATES--MISSION CHURCHES--
SPANISH COLONIAL
Spanish missions [in the U.S.] /
Antoinette J. Lee
This article lists and describes
the Spanish missions in the U.S.
Southwest and advocates that
several be placed on the World
Heritage List.
ASSOCIATION FOR PRESERVATION
TECHNOLOGY. BULLETIN 1990, v.22,
no.3, cover, p.42-54, photos.,
plans, axonometric view, refs.,
site lan, maps, elevs.

UNITED STATES--MISSISSIPPI RIVER
VALLEY--CITIES AND TOWNS
Along the lazy river / David Dillon.
"Expedition of the Fourth Coast"
summer study tour of cities and
towns along the Mississippi River
by Univ. of Minnesota planning
students.
PLANNING 1990 Nov., v.56, no.11,
p.20-23, ports., photos.,
sketches, aerial photo.
Expedition of the Fourth Coast /
Mary Henderson Gass.
Report on a six-week trip on the
Mississippi River run by the Univ.
of Minnesota Design Center for
American Urban Landscape.
INLAND ARCHITECT 1990 Nov.-Dec.,
v.34, no.6, p.63-66, dwgs.

UNITED STATES--MISSISSIPPI RIVER
VALLEY--TOURS--EXPEDITION OF THE
FOURTH COAST
Along the lazy river / David Dillon.
"Expedition of the Fourth Coast"
summer study tour of cities and
towns along the Mississippi River
by Univ. of Minnesota planning
students.
PLANNING 1990 Nov., v.56, no.11,
p.20-23, ports., photos.,
sketches, aerial photo.

UNITED STATES--MISSISSIPPI RIVER--
WATERFRONTS
Along the lazy river / David Dillon.
"Expedition of the Fourth Coast"
summer study tour of cities and
towns along the Mississippi River
by Univ. of Minnesota planning
students.
PLANNING 1990 Nov., v.56, no.11,
p.20-23, ports., photos.,
sketches, aerial photo.
Expedition of the Fourth Coast /
Mary Henderson Gass.
Report on a six-week trip on the
Mississippi River run by the Univ.
of Minnesota Design Center for
American Urban Landscape.
INLAND ARCHITECT 1990 Nov.-Dec.,
v.34, no.6, p.63-66, dwgs.

UNITED STATES--MISSOULA (MONTANA)--
SPORTS FACILITIES--WESTERN MONTANA
SPORTS MEDICINE AND FITNESS CENTER
George Oommen Cambridge,
Massachusetts.
Four projects: Briggs Athletic
Centre, Malkin Athletic Centre,
and McCurdy Track, at Harvard
University; Western Montana Sports
Medicine and Fitness Centre,
Missoula.
ARCHITECTURE + DESIGN 1990
Jan.-Feb., v.7, no.1, p.32-37,
photos., plans, aerial photos.

UNITED STATES--MOBILE HOME PARKS
Immobile homes / Ruth Eckdish Knack.
Mobile home developments, and
innovations in their design.
PLANNING 1990 Dec., v.56, no.12,
p.4-9, dwgs., elev., photos.,
plans, aerial photo.

UNITED STATES--MOBILE HOMES
Immobile homes / Ruth Eckdish Knack.
Mobile home developments, and
innovations in their design.
PLANNING 1990 Dec., v.56, no.12,
p.4-9, dwgs., elev., photos.,
plans, aerial photo.

UNITED STATES--MONMOUTH COUNTY (NEW
JERSEY)--OPEN SPACES--CONSERVATION
AND RESTORATION
Planning for resource protection in
Monmouth County / Faith S. Hahn.
Open space preservation in New
Jersey county.
PRESERVATION PERSPECTIVE NJ 1990
Jan.-Feb., v.9, no.1, p.[1]-2,
photo.

UNITED STATES--MONTANA--
FORTIFICATION--19TH CENTURY--
CONSERVATION AND RESTORATION--FORT
UNION
The great reconstruction
controversy: a debate and
discussion.
Reproduces a letter by Paul R.
Huey and a reply by William J.
Hunt, about Hunt's article in the
Feb. 1989 issue of this bulletin,
followed by an essay by Barry
Mackintosh on NPS policy and
practice.
CRM BULLETIN: A NATIONAL PARK
SERVICE TECHNICAL BULLETIN 1990,
v.13, no.1, p.[1]-7,14, dwg.,
photo.

UNITED STATES--MONTAUK (NEW YORK)--
COTTAGES--19TH CENTURY--INTERIOR
DESIGN--INGRAO COTTAGE
Romancing the stone: a Montauk
cottage... / Rebecca Johnson.
19th cent. stone cottage belonging
to Tony Ingrao.
HOUSE & GARDEN 1990 May, v.162,
no.5, p.[186-191], port., photos.

UNITED STATES--MONTECITO
(CALIFORNIA)--GARDENS--LOTUSLAND
Lotusland: a first view of America's
most exotic garden / Maggie
Keswick.
On the late Ganna Walska's
thirty-seven-acre garden in
Montecito, Ca.
CONNOISSEUR 1990 Oct., v.220,
no.945, p.98-[103],156, port.,
photos.

UNITED STATES--MONTECITO
(CALIFORNIA)--HOUSES--16TH CENTURY--
JANSEN HOUSE
English country West / Rhoda Jaffin
Murphy.
English Tudor farmhouse
transported and reconstructed in
Montecito, Calif. Interior design
by Ann James.
HOUSE BEAUTIFUL 1990 Apr., v.132,
no.4, p.67-73, photos., plan.

UNITED STATES--MONTECITO
(CALIFORNIA)--HOUSES--CRAWFORD HOUSE
Cristallisation du temps: maisons en
Californie, USA.
On the residential work of
Morphosis. Focus on the Was House
(1988), Los Angeles, and Crawford
House (1988), Montecito. Summaries
in English and Spanish.
TECHNIQUES ET ARCHITECTURE 1990
(Continued next column)

UNITED STATES--MONTECITO
(CALIFORNIA)--HOUSES--CRAWFORD HOUSE
(CONTINUED)
Cristallisation du...(CONTINUED)
June-July, no.390, p.106-[111],
180-181, models, plans.

UNITED STATES--MONTECITO
(CALIFORNIA)--HOUSES--INTERIOR
DESIGN--LAS TEJAS
Classical order / Charles Gandee.
Las Tejas, Montecito, Calif., was
inspired by the Villa Farnese.
Interior designer: John Saladino.
HOUSE & GARDEN 1990 Sept., v.162,
no.9, p.186-[195], port., photos.

UNITED STATES--MONTEREY COUNTY
(CALIFORNIA)--LOG-END HOUSES--19TH
CENTURY--EL SUR ANDREW MOLERA STATE
PARK--COOPER HOUSE
A New England log house on the
central California coast /
Kathleen E. Davis.
In Andrew Molera State Park, south
of Monterey, and at the heart of
El Sur land grant (1834). Built
by or for J.B.R. Cooper and
converted to a barn by 1891.
MATERIAL CULTURE 1989 Fall, v.21,
no.3, p.27-39, port., maps,
photos., plan., table, biblio.

UNITED STATES--MONTGOMERY (ALABAMA)--
HOUSES--INTERIOR DESIGN--FRANCO
HOUSE
Distinctive vision: a Montgomery
designer blazes her own trail /
Susannah M. Wilson.
Home of interior designer Anne
Franco. Architects: Barganier
McKee Sims.
SOUTHERN ACCENTS 1990 July-Aug.,
v.13, no.6, p.[88-95], port.,
photos.

UNITED STATES--MONTGOMERY (ALABAMA)--
MUSEUMS--ART--MONTGOMERY MUSEUM OF
FINE ARTS
Gift of site: Winton Blount endows
the Montgomery Museum with more
than art / Laura C. Lieberman.
The new home of the Montgomery
Museum of Fine Arts. Architects:
Barganier McKee Sims.
SOUTHERN ACCENTS 1989 Mar.-Apr.,
v.12, no.2, p.186-189, ill.,
port., photos.

UNITED STATES--MONTGOMERY COUNTY
(MARYLAND)--HOUSING DEVELOPMENTS--
TIMBERLAWN CRESCENT
Mixing incomes at Timberlawn
Crescent / Tom Doerr, Joyce
Siegel.
83-unit housing development in
Montgomery Co., Md., outside
Washington, D.C. Architects:
Larry Kester of Architects
Collective.
URBAN LAND 1990 Apr., v.49, no.4,
p.8-11, photos., table, site plan.

UNITED STATES--MONTGOMERY COUNTY
(MARYLAND)--HOUSING--PUBLIC--
TIMBERLAWN CRESCENT
Mixing incomes at Timberlawn
Crescent / Tom Doerr, Joyce
Siegel.
83-unit housing development in
Montgomery Co., Md., outside
Washington, D.C. Architects:
(Continued next column)

UNITED STATES--MONTGOMERY COUNTY
(MARYLAND)--HOUSING--PUBLIC--
TIMBERLAWN CRESCENT (CONTINUED)
Mixing incomes at...(CONTINUED)
Larry Kester of Architects
Collective.
URBAN LAND 1990 Apr., v.49, no.4,
p.8-11, photos., table, site plan.

UNITED STATES--MONTICELLO
(MINNESOTA)--PLAYGROUNDS
Designs in good citizenship:
Monticello builds a sense of
community by building a
playground.
Playground incorporating features
for the handicapped, in
Monticello, Minnesota. Architect:
Robert Leathers.
ARCHITECTURE MINNESOTA 1990
Sept.-Oct., v.16, no.5, p.30-31,
photos.

UNITED STATES--MONTROSE (CALIFORNIA)--
PARKS--MONTROSE PARK
Catch basin transformed into park.
Flood control catch basin in
Montrose, Ca. transformed into
popular, award-winning park.
AMERICAN CITY & COUNTY 1990 Mar.,
v.105, no.3, p.[33], photo.

UNITED STATES--MONTROSE (CALIFORNIA)--
RECREATION AREAS--MONTROSE PARK
Catch basin transformed into park.
Flood control catch basin in
Montrose, Ca. transformed into
popular, award-winning park.
AMERICAN CITY & COUNTY 1990 Mar.,
v.105, no.3, p.[33], photo.

UNITED STATES--MONUMENTS AND MEMORIALS
Toward a new language of form: Karl
Bitter and the beginnings of
archaism in American sculpture /
Susan Rather.
Examples include reliefs and
memorials from the 1900-1915
period.
WINTERTHUR PORTFOLIO 1990 Spring,
v.25, no.1, p.[1]-19, photos.,
refs.

UNITED STATES--MORENO VALLEY
(CALIFORNIA)--AFFORDABLE HOUSING
The long commute / William Fulton.
Affordable housing in the suburbs
of Moreno Valley, Ca. requires
long commuting time and distance
to work.
PLANNING 1990 July, v.56, no.7,
p.4-10, map, photos., aerial
photo.

UNITED STATES--MORENO VALLEY
(CALIFORNIA)--SUBURBS--GROWTH
The long commute / William Fulton.
Affordable housing in the suburbs
of Moreno Valley, Ca. requires
long commuting time and distance
to work.
PLANNING 1990 July, v.56, no.7,
p.4-10, map, photos., aerial
photo.

UNITED STATES--MORRISTOWN PLAINS (NEW
JERSEY)--CRISIS SHELTERS--INTERIOR
DESIGN--JERSEY BATTERED WOMEN'S
SERVICE
A sense of dignity / Alice Feiring.
On the renovation of the Jersey
Battered Women's Service,
Morristown Plains, NJ. New Jersey
ASID coordinated the project.
INTERIORS 1990 Oct., v.150, no.3,
p.80-81, port., photos.

UNITED STATES--MORRISVILLE
(PENNSYLVANIA)--HOUSES--19TH
CENTURY--STONE--ALTERATIONS AND
ADDITIONS--MAYER HOUSE
Collectors' keepsake.
Restoration of 19th cent.
fieldstone house in Morrisville,
Pa. Consulting architect for
restoration and additions: Edwin
Brumbaugh.
COLONIAL HOMES 1990 Feb., v.16,
no.1, p.51-59, port., photos.

UNITED STATES--MORRISVILLE
(PENNSYLVANIA)--HOUSES--19TH
CENTURY--STONE--CONSERVATION AND
RESTORATION--MAYER HOUSE
Collectors' keepsake.
Restoration of 19th cent.
fieldstone house in Morrisville,
Pa. Consulting architect for
restoration and additions: Edwin
Brumbaugh.
COLONIAL HOMES 1990 Feb., v.16,
no.1, p.51-59, port., photos.

UNITED STATES--MOULTRIE (GEORGIA)--
HOUSES--GREEK REVIVAL--IRIS COURT
Georgia vignettes: Iris Court.
Greek revival house built 1853;
its original site was in Albany,
but it was moved to Moultrie in
1965. Restoration architect:
Edward Vason Jones.
COLONIAL HOMES 1990 Oct., v.16,
no.5, p.[108-117],154, photos.

UNITED STATES--MOUNT PISGAH NATIONAL
FOREST (NORTH CAROLINA)--
ARBORETUMS--STUDENT PROJECTS--NORTH
CAROLINA ARBORETUM
Designs for the North Carolina
Arboretum.
A landscape design studio for
students of Linda Jewell.
Location: Mount Pisgah National
Forest.
GSD NEWS / HARVARD UNIVERSITY.
GRADUATE SCHOOL OF DESIGN 1990
Spring, v.18, no.4, p.11, dwg.,
site plans.

UNITED STATES--MOUNTAIN HOME
(ARKANSAS)--LOW INCOME HOUSING--
KEYSTONE APARTMENTS
Country living: a Mississippi
architect designs dignified
dwellings for the rural poor /
Robert A. Ivy.
Affordable housing in Arkansas
designed by Billy Wenzil; Lakeview
Estates; Prototype FHA Housing;
Keystone Apts.; and DeQueen
Villas.
ARCHITECTURE: THE MAGAZINE OF THE
AMERICAN INSTITUTE OF ARCHITECTS
1990 July, v.79, no.7, p.[68]-73,
elevs., photos., site plans.

UNITED STATES--MOUNTAIN HOUSE
(CALIFORNIA)--CITY HALLS
Inventing village hall / Bruce W.
Liedstrand.
Municipal services considered for
new towns. Example of Mountain
House, a new town near San
Francisco. Planners: Liedstrand
Associates.
URBAN LAND 1990 Feb, v.49, no.2,
p.32-33, sketches.

UNITED STATES--MOUNTAIN HOUSE
(CALIFORNIA)--NEW TOWNS
Inventing village hall / Bruce W.
Liedstrand.
Municipal services considered for
new towns. Example of Mountain
House, a new town near San
Francisco. Planners: Liedstrand
Associates.
URBAN LAND 1990 Feb, v.49, no.2,
p.32-33, sketches.

UNITED STATES--MOUNTAIN HOUSE
(CALIFORNIA)--PUBLIC SERVICES
Inventing village hall / Bruce W.
Liedstrand.
Municipal services considered for
new towns. Example of Mountain
House, a new town near San
Francisco. Planners: Liedstrand
Associates.
URBAN LAND 1990 Feb, v.49, no.2,
p.32-33, sketches.

UNITED STATES--MOUNTAIN VIEW
(CALIFORNIA)--CORPORATE OFFICE
BUILDINGS--SILICON GRAPHICS COMPUTER
SYSTEMS
Silicon Graphics / Edie Lee Cohen.
On the new corporate headquarters
for Silicon Graphics Computer
Systems, Mountain View, Calif.
Architects: STUDIOS.
INTERIOR DESIGN 1990 Apr., v.61,
no.6, p.166-[171], dwg., photos.,
plan.

UNITED STATES--MOVIE THEATERS--BARABOO
(WISCONSIN)--AL. RINGLING THEATRE
The Al. Ringling Theatre, Baraboo,
Wisconsin, 1915-1990 [Historic
American Building Survey, HABS
No.WIS-261].
Rapp and Rapp, architects.
THEATRE HISTORICAL SOCIETY. ANNUAL
1990, v.17, cover, p.1-24, ill.,
dwgs., port., photos., plans.

UNITED STATES--MUNCIE (INDIANA)--
COMPUTER CENTERS--BALL STATE
UNIVERSITY--COLLEGE OF ARCHITECTURE
AND PLANNING--COMPUTER GRAPHICS
LABORATORY
Linking perception research, visual
simulations and dynamic modeling
within a GIS framework: the Ball
State experience / Randy Gimblett.
COMPUTERS, ENVIRONMENT AND URBAN
SYSTEMS 1989 v.13, no.2,
p.109-123, figs., refs.

UNITED STATES--MUSEUM TECHNIQUES
Interpretation.
Nine articles on historic site
methods. Authors: Sandra S. Weber,
F.A. Ketterson, Marcella Sherfy,
Edward Tabor Linenthal, Raymond H.
Thompson, Michael E. Whatley,
Marie T. Myers, Karen
Sweeny-Justice, Kathleen Hunter.
CRM BULLETIN: A NATIONAL PARK
SERVICE TECHNICAL BULLETIN 1990,
v.13, no.3, p.1-21, photos.

UNITED STATES--MUSEUMS--20TH CENTURY
Tempo di musei: una conversazione a
tre voci = Museum time: a 3-voice
conversation / Carlo Bertelli,
Rossana Bossaglia, Fulvio Irace.
Discussion of the "museum
phenomenon" of the 1980s.
ABITARE 1990 Sept., no.288,
p.274-291, axonometric views,
ill., dwgs., models, photos.,
plans, secns., site plans,
sketches.
Vielfaltig wie widerspruchlich: die
Museumslandschaft der USA / Holger
Fischer.
DEUTSCHE BAUZEITUNG 1990 Apr.,
v.124, no.4, p.171-176, photos.

UNITED STATES--MUSEUMS--HISTORICAL--
DIRECTORIES
Historic houses, landmarks and
museums: New England.
A partial listing, the first in a
series of five.
ANTIQUES 1990 Apr., v.137, no.4,
p.956-958, maps.

UNITED STATES--MYSTIC (CONNECTICUT)--
INNS--18TH CENTURY--CONSERVATION AND
RESTORATION--CAPT. DANIEL PACKER
INNE
Capt. Daniel Packer Inne [Mystic,
Conn.].
1756 tavern and inn, restored by
Dick Kiley.
COLONIAL HOMES 1990 Oct., v.16,
no.5, p.140-[144],146, ports.,
photos.

UNITED STATES--NAGS HEAD (NORTH
CAROLINA)--CITY PLANNING
Pre-storm mitigation and post-storm
reconstruction: a plan for Nags
Head / Bruce M. Bortz.
Innovative planning efforts in the
field of hurricane and storm
mitigation by the town of Nags
Head, N.C.
CAROLINA PLANNING 1990 Fall, v.16,
no.2, p.15-18, map, photos.

UNITED STATES--NAGS HEAD (NORTH
CAROLINA)--NATURAL DISASTERS
Pre-storm mitigation and post-storm
reconstruction: a plan for Nags
Head / Bruce M. Bortz.
Innovative planning efforts in the
field of hurricane and storm
mitigation by the town of Nags
Head, N.C.
CAROLINA PLANNING 1990 Fall, v.16,
no.2, p.15-18, map, photos.

UNITED STATES--NANTUCKET
(MASSACHUSETTS)--BEACH HOUSES--
INTERIOR DESIGN
Nantucket Lookout: Mark Hampton
decorates a turn-of-the-century
beach house with a view toward
family tradition / Amy Fine
Collins.
HOUSE & GARDEN 1990 July, v.162,
no.7, p.[90-95],136, photo.

UNITED STATES--NANTUCKET
(MASSACHUSETTS)--HOUSES--FEDERAL--
INTERIOR DESIGN
Nantucket federal: Robert Denning
evokes the discreet luxury of
Nantucket's seafaring days in an
1807 house / Diane Lilly di
Costanzo.
HOUSE & GARDEN 1990 June, v.162,
no.6, p.[140-147], photos.

UNITED STATES--NANTUCKET
(MASSACHUSETTS)--HOUSES--INTERIOR
DESIGN--SLOVER HOUSE
Finishing touches: a master of faux
finishes surrounds herself with
the real thing in her Nantucket
house / Marcelle Clements.
Dorothy Slover's 19th-cent. house
on Main St.
HOUSE & GARDEN 1990 July, v.162,
no.7, p.[52-59], port., photos.

UNITED STATES--NANTUCKET
(MASSACHUSETTS)--VACATION HOUSES--
ROBERT HOUSE
Contemporary clapboard on a
Nantucket pond / Brendan Gill.
Vacation house owned by Rita and
Samuel Robert. Architect: Edward
F. Knowles.
ARCHITECTURAL DIGEST 1990 Aug.,
v.47, no.8, p.[124]-131,180,
photos.

UNITED STATES--NAPA (CALIFORNIA)--
PEDESTRIAN MALLS--NAPA TOWN CENTER
Reshuffling the deck: Building Types
Study 677: Retail facilities /
Clifford A. Pearson.
Fashion Island, Newport Beach,
Calif. (Jerde Partnership), North
Pier, Chicago (Booth Hansen &
Assoc., The Austin Co.); Napa Town
Center, Napa Calif. (Field Paoli
Architects); and A & S Plaza, New
York City (RTKL Assoc.).
ARCHITECTURAL RECORD 1990 Apr.,
v.178, no.4, p.97-111, photos.,
plans, secns., site plans.

UNITED STATES--NAPA (CALIFORNIA)--
SHOPPING CENTERS--NAPA TOWN CENTER
Reshuffling the deck: Building Types
Study 677: Retail facilities /
Clifford A. Pearson.
Fashion Island, Newport Beach,
Calif. (Jerde Partnership), North
Pier, Chicago (Booth Hansen &
Assoc., The Austin Co.); Napa Town
Center, Napa Calif. (Field Paoli
Architects); and A & S Plaza, New
York City (RTKL Assoc.).
ARCHITECTURAL RECORD 1990 Apr.,
v.178, no.4, p.97-111, photos.,
plans, secns., site plans.

UNITED STATES--NAPA VALLEY
(CALIFORNIA)--COUNTRY HOUSES--
SPANISH MEDITERRANEAN REVIVAL--
INTERIOR DESIGN--MAKAROVA KARKAR
HOUSE
Architectural digest visits: Natalia
Makarova / Robert Fizdale.
Interiors of Mediterranean-style
country house near Mount St.
Helena in the Napa Valley.
Architect: Charles Bass, Robert
Keenan.
ARCHITECTURAL DIGEST 1990 May,
v.47, no.5, p.194-[199],268,
port., photos.

UNITED STATES--NAPA VALLEY
(CALIFORNIA)--HOUSES--INTERIOR
DESIGN
A world of her own / Monica Geran.
Features interiors of renovated
condominium in the Napa Valley.
Interior designer: Thomas
Bartlett.
INTERIOR DESIGN 1990 Mar., v.61,
no.5, p.168-[171], photos., plan.

UNITED STATES--NASHUA (NEW
HAMPSHIRE)--SCHOOLS--ELEMENTARY--
ALTERATIONS AND ADDITIONS--MOUNT
PLEASANT ELEMENTARY SCHOOL
A lesson in tectonics / Thomas
Fisher.
On the gymnasium and classroom
additions to the 1920s Mount
Pleasant Elementary School,
Nashua, N.H. Architects: TAMS
Consultants. Includes Selected
Detail article on a wall section
of the addition.
PROGRESSIVE ARCHITECTURE 1990
Aug., v.71, no.8, p.110-112, det.,
photos., plans.

UNITED STATES--NASHVILLE (TENNESSEE)--
APARTMENT COMPLEXES--RIVERFRONT
APARTMENTS
All'ombra dei grattacieli fra i
reperti del produrre / Nicola
Anguilano.
148-unit housing development in a
former industrial area of
Nashville, Tenn. Architects: Tuck
Hinton Everton.
VILLE GIARDINI 1990 Sept., no.251,
p.10-17, axonometric views, dwgs.,
photos., plans, secns., site
plans.
Riverfront Apartments, Nashville.
Architects: Tuck Hinton Everton
Architects. Text in Italian and
English.
LOTUS INTERNATIONAL 1990, no.66,
p.58-65, axonometric views,
elevs., photos., plans, site plan.

UNITED STATES--NASHVILLE (TENNESSEE)--
GARAGES--ALTERATIONS AND ADDITIONS--
BELLE MEADE APARTMENT GARAGE
Belle Meade metamorphosis: revival
of an abandoned apartment garage /
Joan Fisch Gallivan.
Originally the 1915 garage for
Nashville apartment house, the
structure has been turned into a
Tudor-style home for Clare and
Hunter Armistead. Architect:
Bryant Glasgow; interior designer:
William N. Knox.
SOUTHERN ACCENTS 1989 Mar.-Apr.,
v.12, no.2, p.[119]-123, photos.

UNITED STATES--NASHVILLE (TENNESSEE)--
HOUSES--ARMISTEAD HOUSE
Belle Meade metamorphosis: revival
of an abandoned apartment garage /
Joan Fisch Gallivan.
Originally the 1915 garage for
Nashville apartment house, the
structure has been turned into a
Tudor-style home for Clare and
Hunter Armistead. Architect:
Bryant Glasgow; interior designer:
William N. Knox.
SOUTHERN ACCENTS 1989 Mar.-Apr.,
v.12, no.2, p.[119]-123, photos.

UNITED STATES--NASHVILLE (TENNESSEE)--
HOUSES--INTERIOR DESIGN--BOXWOOD
Belle Meade's Boxwood / Betsa Marsh.
House and garden of 1914 Georgian
revival home of the Flemings,
Nashville, Tenn. Landscape
architect: Ben Page. Architect:
C.A. Platt.
SOUTHERN ACCENTS 1990 May, v.13,
no.4, p.86-[95], port., photos.

UNITED STATES--NASHVILLE (TENNESSEE)--
RESIDENTIAL GARDENS--BOXWOOD
Belle Meade's Boxwood / Betsa Marsh.
House and garden of 1914 Georgian
revival home of the Flemings,
Nashville, Tenn. Landscape
architect: Ben Page. Architect:
C.A. Platt.
SOUTHERN ACCENTS 1990 May, v.13,
no.4, p.86-[95], port., photos.

UNITED STATES--NASHVILLE (TENNESSEE)--
SPORTS FACILITIES--CENTENNIAL
SPORTSPLEX
Centennial Sportsplex: a win-win
scenario / Julie C. Pursell.
Centennial Sportsplex, Nashville,
Tenn. Architects: Thomas, Miller &
Partners.
PARKS & RECREATION 1990 Dec.,
v.25, no.12, p.22-27,56, photos.
Water and ice: Centennial
Sportsplex, Nashville Tennessee,
Thomas, Miller & Partners,
Architects / Robert A. Ivy.
ARCHITECTURE: THE MAGAZINE OF THE
AMERICAN INSTITUTE OF ARCHITECTS
1990 Aug., v.79, no.8, p.[76]-79,
photos., plans, site plan.

UNITED STATES--NASHVILLE (TENNESSEE)--
WATERFRONT BUILDINGS--RIVERFRONT
APARTMENTS
All'ombra dei grattacieli fra i
reperti del produrre / Nicola
Anguilano.
148-unit housing development in a
former industrial area of
Nashville, Tenn. Architects: Tuck
Hinton Everton.
VILLE GIARDINI 1990 Sept., no.251,
p.10-17, axonometric views, dwgs.,
photos., plans, secns., site
plans.

UNITED STATES--NASSAU COUNTY (NEW
YORK)--HOUSES--INTERIOR DESIGN
Timeless charm: Kevin McNamara has
decorated the setting for his
clients changing lives' over two
decades / Penelope Green.
Georgian-style house in Nassau
Co., N.Y.
HOUSE & GARDEN 1990 Mar., v.162,
no.3, p.[130-135], photos.

UNITED STATES--NATCHEZ (MISSISSIPPI)--
GARDENS--ELM COURT
Gardens: Elms Cout / Irene Borger.
Gardens on the grounds of the
circa 1836 Greek Revival residence
of Grace McKitt-ick MacNeil in
Natchez, Mississippi. Landscape
architect: William Garbo.
ARCHITECTURAL DIGEST 1990 Feb.,
v.47, no.2, p.[228-234],244,
photos.

UNITED STATES--NATCHEZ (MISSISSIPPI)--
HISTORIC HOUSE MUSEUMS--MELROSE
Pride of Natchez: Melrose and its
remarkably complete original
furnishings / Allen Freeman.
12-room Greek Revival mansion,
designed by Jacob Byers and built
in 1845.
HISTORIC PRESERVATION 1990
May-June, v.42, no.3, p.[30]-35,
photos.

UNITED STATES--NATCHEZ (MISSISSIPPI)--
MANSIONS--GREEK REVIVAL--MELROSE
Pride of Natchez: Melrose and its
remarkably complete original
furnishings / Allen Freeman.
12-room Greek Revival mansion,
designed by Jacob Byers and built
in 1845.
HISTORIC PRESERVATION 1990
May-June, v.42, no.3, p.[30]-35,
photos.

UNITED STATES--NATCHEZ (MISSISSIPPI)--
PLANTATION HOUSES--INTERIOR DESIGN--
THE BURN
Natchez decorative arts.
On the Historic Natchez
Collection, a collection of
reproduction furniture and
accessories found in Natchez
plantation houses. They are shown
in The Burn, a renovated manor
house.
COLONIAL HOMES 1990 Oct., v.16,
no.5, p.[122-131],155, photos.

UNITED STATES--NATICK
(MASSACHUSETTS)--KITCHENS--
ALTERATIONS AND ADDITIONS
Dirigo Design: a contemporary
kitchen renovation / Karen
Maserjian.
Renovation of ca. 1910 kitchen in
19th cent. house in Natick, Mass.
INTERIOR DESIGN 1990 July, v.61,
no.10, p.174-[175], photos.

UNITED STATES. NATIONAL AERONAUTICS
AND SPACE ADMINISTRATION
Design goes to space: NASA and a
program at the University of
Houston are developing innovative
structures for living in space /
Karin Tetlow.
The Sasakawa International Center
for Space Architecture is working
on NASA's latest program, Space
Station Freedom.
ARCHITECTURE: THE MAGAZINE OF THE
AMERICAN INSTITUTE OF ARCHITECTS
1990 May, v.79, no.5, p.[98]-101,
ill., model.
Home, sweet space station / Joel
Warren Barna.
Students at the Sasakawa
International Center for Space
Architecture at the Univ. of
Houston face the problems of
(Continued next column)

UNITED STATES. NATIONAL AERONAUTICS
AND SPACE ADMINISTRATION
(CONTINUED)
Home, sweet space...(CONTINUED)
long-term habitation elsewhere in
the solar system.
TEXAS ARCHITECT 1990 May-June,
v.40, no.3, p.26-29, ill., dwgs.,
models.

UNITED STATES. NATIONAL PARK SERVICE
The great reconstruction
controversy: a debate and
discussion.
Reproduces a letter by Paul R.
Huey and a reply by William J.
Hunt, about Hunt's article in the
Feb. 1989 issue of this bulletin,
followed by an essay by Barry
Mackintosh on NPS policy and
practice.
CRM BULLETIN: A NATIONAL PARK
SERVICE TECHNICAL BULLETIN 1990,
v.13, no.1, p.[1]-7,14, dwg.,
photo.
The NPS Historic Landscape
Initiative: developing national
standards for the treatment of
historic landscapes / Lauren G.
Meier.
CRM BULLETIN: A NATIONAL PARK
SERVICE TECHNICAL BULLETIN 1990,
v.13, no.2, p.12-13, biblio.
NPS' super database of databases,
COMMON, where are you today?
Reprinted from Pointers, a
quarterly newsletter of the
Information and Data Systems
Division, NPS, v.4, no.1.
CRM BULLETIN: A NATIONAL PARK
SERVICE TECHNICAL BULLETIN 1990,
v.13, no.2, p.6,
NPS surveys yield data on the
effects of Hurricane Hugo / Thomas
A. Vitanza.
CRM BULLETIN: A NATIONAL PARK
SERVICE TECHNICAL BULLETIN 1990,
v.13, no.1, p.12-14, photos.,
aerial photos.
Partnership for preservation: an
Alaskan case study / Kate Lidfors.
Documentation and inventory of 171
objects, at the Church of the Holy
Ascension (1894), Unalaska.
CRM BULLETIN: A NATIONAL PARK
SERVICE TECHNICAL BULLETIN 1990,
v.13, no.6, p.13-15, port.,
photos.
You call this a national park? /
James Krohe.
Small urban parks form part of the
national parks system.
PLANNING 1990 Aug., v.56, no.8,
p.4-10, maps, photos., plan.

UNITED STATES. NATIONAL PARK SERVICE.
PARK HISTORIC ARCHITECTURE
DIVISION--CONGRESSES
Park Cultural Landscape[s] Workshop
/ Robert R. Page.
Held Sept.18-20,1990 in
Alexandria, Va. Sponsor: National
Park Service, Park Historic
Architecture Division.
CRM BULLETIN: A NATIONAL PARK
SERVICE TECHNICAL BULLETIN 1990,
v.13, no.6, p.25,

UNITED STATES--NATIONAL PARKS AND
RESERVES
Geology NHL theme study / Harry A.
Butowsky.
A new theme study by the National
Park Service's NHL Survey.
CRM BULLETIN: A NATIONAL PARK
SERVICE TECHNICAL BULLETIN 1990,
v.13, no.1, p.8-9, photos.
NPS' super database of databases,
COMMON, where are you today?
Reprinted from Pointers, a
quarterly newsletter of the
Information and Data Systems
Division, NPS, v.4, no.1.
CRM BULLETIN: A NATIONAL PARK
SERVICE TECHNICAL BULLETIN 1990,
v.13, no.2, p.6,
You call this a national park? /
James Krohe.
Small urban parks form part of the
national parks system.
PLANNING 1990 Aug., v.56, no.8,
p.4-10, maps, photos., plan.

UNITED STATES--NATIONAL PARKS AND
RESERVES--ACADIA NATIONAL PARK
(MAINE)
Toward a sustainable landscape with
high visual preference and high
ecological integrity: the Loop
Road in Acadia National Park,
U.S.A. / Carl Steinitz.
LANDSCAPE AND URBAN PLANNING 1990
June, v.19, no.3, p.213-250, maps,
graphs, photos., tables, refs.
Vista management in Acadia National
Park / Eckart Lange.
In Maine.
LANDSCAPE AND URBAN PLANNING 1990
Dec., v.19, no.4, p.353-376,
chart, maps, photos., plans,
secns., tables, refs.

UNITED STATES. NATIONAL PARKS SERVICE
NPS helps Charleston after Hugo.
CRM BULLETIN: A NATIONAL PARK
SERVICE TECHNICAL BULLETIN 1989,
v.12, no.6, p.11-14,cover, photos.

UNITED STATES--NATURAL DISASTERS
In the wake of the quake [northern
California] / John King.
Includes inset article: "Waiting
for the big one", by Jim Schwab;
on natural disasters around the
country.
PLANNING 1989 Dec., v.55, no.12,
p.12-17, ports., model, maps,
photos.

UNITED STATES--NAVASOTA (TEXAS)--
BED-AND-BREAKFAST GUEST HOUSES--
CASTLE INN
Texas castle / Candace Leslie.
1893 Victorian mansion in
Navasota, Texas, now a
bed-and-breakfast inn.
VICTORIAN HOMES 1990 Winter, v.9,
no.1, p.66-69, photos.

UNITED STATES--NAVASOTA (TEXAS)--
HOUSES--VICTORIAN--CONSERVATION AND
RESTORATION--THE CASTLE
Texas castle / Candace Leslie.
1893 Victorian mansion in
Navasota, Texas, now a
bed-and-breakfast inn.
VICTORIAN HOMES 1990 Winter, v.9,
no.1, p.66-69, photos.

UNITED STATES--NAZARETH
(PENNSYLVANIA)--HOUSES--FUISZ HOUSE
Turner Brooks: [three houses and
drawings].
Contents: House with two studios,
Sharon, Conn.,-- Fuisz house,
Nazareth, Pa.,--Sheldon house,
Shelburne, Vermont. Architect:
Turner Brooks, with Greg Clawson.
Text in Japanese and English.
GA HOUSES 1990 July, no.29,
p.148-159.

UNITED STATES--NEIGHBORHOODS--
POLITICAL ASPECTS
Power, planning and conflict /
Charles Hoch, guest editor.
Special issue. Contents: Power,
planning and conflict, by C. Hoch
-- Planners in conflict:
experience and perceptions in
California, by Linda C. Dalton --
Neighborhood redevelopment: the
planner's role in conflict
management, by Sanda Kaufman --
Environmental movement politics,
mandates to plan, and professional
planners..., by Sy Adler --
Passion, reason and power: the
rhetorics of electric power
planning in Chicago, by J.A.
Throgmorton.
JOURNAL OF ARCHITECTURAL AND
PLANNING RESEARCH 1990 Winter, v.7
no.4, p.271-350, graph, tables,
biblios., refs.

UNITED STATES--NETHERLANDS--LEIDEN--
DOLLHOUSES--17TH CENTURY--PETRONELLA
DE LA COURT DOLLHOUSE
The dolls' house of Petronella de la
Court / Shirley Glubok.
Dates from 17th-cent. Leiden; now
in the Centraal Museum in Utrecht.
ANTIQUES 1990 Feb., v.137, no.2,
p.[488]-501, photos.

UNITED STATES--NEVADA CITY
(CALIFORNIA)--HOUSES--BRICK--GOTHIC
REVIVAL--WILLIAMS HOUSE (RED CASTLE
INN)
Celebrating the holidays in Gold
Mine Country / Maureen Gilmer.
Features two northern California
buildings: Empire Mine Cottage,
Grass Valley (architect: Willis
Polk) and Red Castle Inn, Nevada
City (a brick Gothic revival house
on "Prospect Hill" built in 1857
for John Williams).
VICTORIAN HOMES 1990 Holidays,
v.9, no.5, p.38-[45], photos.

UNITED STATES--NEW ALBANY (OHIO)--
HOUSING DEVELOPMENTS--GEORGIAN
REVIVAL
Georgian on their minds: a new
community draws on the classic
architecture and landscape of
America's rural past / Douglas
Brenner.
The projected 5,000-acre community
in and around the old town of New
Albany, Ohio.
HOUSE & GARDEN 1990 Nov., v.162,
no.11, p.110,112, port., elevs.,
site plan.

UNITED STATES--NEW ALBANY (OHIO)--NEW
TOWNS
Georgian on their minds: a new
community draws on the classic
architecture and landscape of
America's rural past / Douglas
Brenner.
The projected 5,000-acre community
in and around the old town of New
Albany, Ohio.
HOUSE & GARDEN 1990 Nov., v.162,
no.11, p.110,112, port., elevs.,
site plan.
Unlimited vision [Leslie Wexner] /
Lynn Nesmith.
Buildings designed under the
patronage of Wexner. Architects:
Beyer Blinder Belle and Graham
Gund Architects; Jaquelin
Robertson, Hanna / Olin.
ARCHITECTURE: THE AIA JOURNAL 1990
Dec., v.79, no.12, p.[66]-73,
elevs., photos., plans, site
plans.

UNITED STATES--NEW BEDFORD
(MASSACHUSETTS)--ARCHIVES--NEW
BEDFORD FREE PUBLIC LIBRARY
New Bedford Free Public Library.
On landscape-related materials in
the southeatern Mass. collection,
including those from the local
horticultural society.
NEWSLETTER / THE CATALOGUE OF
LANDSCAPE RECORDS IN THE UNITED
STATES 1990 Fall, v.4, no.2,
p.[1-2].

UNITED STATES--NEW BERN (NORTH
CAROLINA)--ARCHITECTURE
The historic architecture of New
Bern and Craven County, North
Carolina [by] Peter B. Sandbeck
[book review] / Carl Lounsbury.
SOCIETY OF ARCHITECTURAL
HISTORIANS. JOURNAL 1990 Sept.,
v.49, no.3, p.344-345.

UNITED STATES--NEW BRUNSWICK (NEW
JERSEY)--ATRIUMS--NEW BRUNSWICK
CULTURAL CENTER ATRIUM
New Brunswick Cultural Center
Atrium, New Brunswick, New Jersey.
Architects: Rothe-Johnson
Associates.
ARCHITECTURE NEW JERSEY 1990,
v.26, no.3, p.13, elev., plan.

UNITED STATES--NEW BRUNSWICK (NEW
JERSEY)--CULTURAL CENTERS--NEW
BRUNSWICK CULTURAL CENTER
New Brunswick Cultural Center
Atrium, New Brunswick, New Jersey.
Architects: Rothe-Johnson
Associates.
ARCHITECTURE NEW JERSEY 1990,
v.26, no.3, p.13, elev., plan.

UNITED STATES--NEW BRUNSWICK (NEW
JERSEY)--OFFICE COMPLEXES--GOLDEN
TRIANGLE PLAZA
Golden Triangle Plaza, New
Brunswick, New Jersey.
Office complex. Architects:
Rothe-Johnson Associates.
ARCHITECTURE NEW JERSEY 1989,
v.25, no.3, p.10-11, photos., site
plan, aerial photo.

UNITED STATES--NEW CASTLE COUNTY
(DELAWARE)--HOUSES
Special feature: Venturi Scott Brown
and Associates.
Contents: Brief history-- Works:
Primate Center, Philadelphia
Zoological Garden.-- Lewis Thomas
Laboratory for Molecular Biology,
Princeton University, 1986.--
Malcolm S. Forbes Jr. College,
Princeton University, 1984.--
Gordon Wu Hall, Princeton
University, 1983.-- Venturi house,
Philadelphia, 1974-present.--
Izenour house, Stony Creek, Conn.,
1984.-- House in New Castle
County, Delaware, 1983.--
Coxe-Hayden house, Block Island,
R.I., 1981.-- Tarble Student
Center, Swarthmore College,
1985.-- Tree House, Philadelphia
Zoo, 1985.-- Welcome Park,
Philadelphia, 1982.-- Decorative
designs.-- Essay: "Body language"
and artifice: on some recent
designs by Venturi Scott Brown and
Associates. Text in Japanese and
English.
ARCHITECTURE AND URBANISM 1990
June, no.6(237), p.[39]-150,
ports., elevs., photos., plans,
secns., site plans.

UNITED STATES--NEW ENGLAND--
ARCHITECTURE--COLONIAL--ECONOMIC
ASPECTS
Bawns and beliefs: architecture,
commerce, and conversion in early
New England / Robert Blair St.
George.
Appendix is an excerpt from a 17th
century document, "The building
and enclosing of our countrie
farm".
WINTERTHUR PORTFOLIO 1990 Winter,
v.25, no.4, p.[241]-287, dwgs.,
photos., plans, engrs., refs.

UNITED STATES--NEW ENGLAND--
BUILDINGS--COLONIAL--CONSERVATION
AND RESTORATION
The resurrectionist: Stephen Mack
brings new life to endangered
eighteenth--century houses / Allen
Freeman.
The Rhode Island craftsman
disassembles and reconstructs
colonial buildings that would
otherwise be destroyed.
HISTORIC PRESERVATION 1990
July-Aug., v.42, no.4, p.[30-37],
port., photos.

UNITED STATES--NEW ENGLAND--CITIES AND
TOWNS--GROWTH
Growth and the loss of regional
character / J. Mark Davidson
Schuster.
Includes inset article on village
centers in New England.
PLACES 1990 Spring, v.6, no.3,
p.78-87, photos., plans, refs.

UNITED STATES--NEW ENGLAND--COMMUNITY
DEVELOPMENT
Growth and the loss of regional
character / J. Mark Davidson
Schuster.
Includes inset article on village
centers in New England.
PLACES 1990 Spring, v.6, no.3,
p.78-87, photos., plans, refs.

UNITED STATES--NEW ENGLAND--ENDANGERED
PLACES
The resurrectionist: Stephen Mack
brings new life to endangered
eighteenth--century houses / Allen
Freeman.
The Rhode Island craftsman
disassembles and reconstructs
colonial buildings that would
otherwise be destroyed.
HISTORIC PRESERVATION 1990
July-Aug., v.42, no.4, p.[30-37],
port., photos.

UNITED STATES--NEW ENGLAND--REGIONAL
PLANNING
Growth and the loss of regional
character / J. Mark Davidson
Schuster.
Includes inset article on village
centers in New England.
PLACES 1990 Spring, v.6, no.3,
p.78-87, photos., plans, refs.

UNITED STATES--NEW ENGLAND--VERNACULAR
ARCHITECTURE--17TH CENTURY
Bawns and beliefs: architecture,
commerce, and conversion in early
New England / Robert Blair St.
George.
Appendix is an excerpt from a 17th
century document, "The building
and enclosing of our countrie
farm".
WINTERTHUR PORTFOLIO 1990 Winter,
v.25, no.4, p.[241]-287, dwgs.,
photos., plans, engrs., refs.

UNITED STATES--NEW ENGLAND--VILLAGES--
CONSERVATION AND RESTORATION
Growth and the loss of regional
character / J. Mark Davidson
Schuster.
Includes inset article on village
centers in New England.
PLACES 1990 Spring, v.6, no.3,
p.78-87, photos., plans, refs.

UNITED STATES--NEW HAMPSHIRE--
BATHHOUSES
New England natatorium: rustic
poolhouse addition to a New
Hampshire farmhouse / Suzanne
Stephens.
Addition to 1770's Cape-style
farmhouse. Architect: Jon Evans.
ARCHITECTURAL DIGEST 1990 June,
v.47, no.6, p.[204-207],226,
phots.

UNITED STATES--NEW HAMPSHIRE--
FARMHOUSES--18TH CENTURY--
ALTERATIONS AND ADDITIONS
New England natatorium: rustic
poolhouse addition to a New
Hampshire farmhouse / Suzanne
Stephens.
Addition to 1770's Cape-style
farmhouse. Architect: Jon Evans.
ARCHITECTURAL DIGEST 1990 June,
v.47, no.6, p.[204-207],226,
phots.

UNITED STATES--NEW HAMPSHIRE--HOUSES--
SMALL--WHARTON-MCKEE HOUSE
New slant on the small house [New
Hampshire] / Susan Zevon.
Architects: Amsler Hagenah
MacLean, Architects.
HOUSE BEAUTIFUL 1986 June, v.128,
no.6, p.[72-75], photos., plans.

UNITED STATES--NEW HAMPSHIRE--SWIMMING
POOLS
New England natatorium: rustic
poolhouse addition to a New
Hampshire farmhouse / Suzanne
Stephens.
Addition to 1770's Cape-style
farmhouse. Architect: Jon Evans.
ARCHITECTURAL DIGEST 1990 June,
v.47, no.6, p.[204-207],226,
phots.

UNITED STATES--NEW HAVEN
(CONNECTICUT)--ARCHITECTURE--20TH
CENTURY
A model city remodeled / Marc
Wortman.
Survey of new building in New
Haven, Connecticut.
PROGRESSIVE ARCHITECTURE 1990
Jan., v.71, no.1, p.39-40,42,
elev., models, photos.

UNITED STATES--NEW HAVEN
(CONNECTICUT)--ARCHITECTURE--STUDY
AND TEACHING--YALE UNIVERSITY--
SCHOOL OF ARCHITECTURE
[Student projects 1988-1989].
YALE UNIVERSITY. SCHOOL OF
ARCHITECTURE. RETROSPECTA
1988-1989, p.[1-27], dwgs.,
ports., elevs., models, photos.,
secns.
[Student projects 1989-1990].
YALE UNIVERSITY. SCHOOL OF
ARCHITECTURE. RETROSPECTA
1989-1990, p.[1-27], ports.,
elevs., models, photos., plans,
secns., site plans.

UNITED STATES--NEW HAVEN
(CONNECTICUT)--HOSPITALS--
PSYCHIATRIC--YALE PSYCHIATRIC
INSTITUTE
Colores terapeuticos: Instituto
Psiquiatrico de Yale, New Haven,
Connecticut, 1985-1989.
Architects: Frank O. Gehry and
Associates. English summary, p.87.
A & V 1990, no.25, p.50-55,
elevs., model, photos., plans,
secns., site plans, sketches.
A new idea in New Haven [Yale
Psychiatric Institute] / Diana
Scott.
Residential treatment center for
mentally ill young adults and
adolescents. Architects: Frank O.
Gehry and Allan Dehar.
METROPOLIS 1990 Apr., v.9, no.8,
p.18-19, photo.
A village of healing: Yale
Psychiatric Institute, New Haven,
Connecticut / Michael J. Crosbie.
Architects: Frank O. Gehry &
Associates, Allan Dehar
Associates.
ARCHITECTURE: THE AIA JOURNAL 1990
Mar., v.79, no.3, p.[114]-121,
photos., plans, site plan

UNITED STATES--NEW HAVEN
(CONNECTICUT)--RESIDENTIAL GARDENS--
TYLER GARDEN
Classicism's light new touch /
Carolyn Ulrich.
Small residential backyard gardens
in Chicago, New Haven, Houston,
and Washington, D.C. Landscape
architects: Timothy Lally, Ralph
Synnestvedt, Jr., Paul Bailey,
Douglas Kycia, McDugald-Steele,
Lanson Jones, and Jane Macleish.
GARDEN DESIGN 1990 autumn, v.9,
no.3, p.[30-37], photos.

UNITED STATES--NEW HAVEN
(CONNECTICUT)--UNIVERSITIES AND
COLLEGES--BUILDINGS--YALE
UNIVERSITY--YALE PSYCHIATRIC
INSTITUTE
Colores terapeuticos: Instituto
Psiquiatrico de Yale, New Haven,
Connecticut, 1985-1989.
Architects: Frank O. Gehry and
Associates. English summary, p.87.
A & V 1990, no.25, p.50-55,
elevs., model, photos., plans,
secns., site plans, sketches.
Frank O. Gehry.
Entire issue devoted to the work
of this American architect.
Criticism by A. Zaera Polo and
David Cohn. 15 projects and
buildings from 1987-1990 featured.
Text in Spanish and English.
EL CROQUIS 1990 Nov., v.9, no.45,
p.1-124, ports., elevs., models,
photos., plans, secns., site
plans, refs.
A new idea in New Haven [Yale
Psychiatric Institute] / Diana
Scott.
Residential treatment center for
mentally ill young adults and
adolescents. Architects: Frank O.
Gehry and Allan Dehar.
METROPOLIS 1990 Apr., v.9, no.8,
p.18-19, photo.
A village of healing: Yale
Psychiatric Institute, New Haven,
Connecticut / Michael J. Crosbie.
Architects: Frank O. Gehry &
Associates, Allan Dehar
Associates.
ARCHITECTURE: THE AIA JOURNAL 1990
Mar., v.79, no.3, p.[114]-121,
photos., plans, site plan.

UNITED STATES--NEW HOPE
(PENNSYLVANIA)--APARTMENT HOUSES--
WATERWORKS
The search continues: building types
study 681, multifamily housing /
Donald J. Canty.
Four low-rise condominium
projects: The Waterworks, New
Hope, Penn. (Cecil Baker &
Associates, Architects); Back of
the Hill Rowhouses, Boston
(William Rawn Associates,
Architects); Samoset Resort and
Village, Rockport, Me. (Sasaki
Associates, Architects); and
Parkview Commons, San Francisco
(David Baker Architects).
ARCHITECTURAL RECORD 1990 July,
v.178, no.8, p.15-87, axonometric
views, elev., photos., plans, site
plans.

UNITED STATES--NEW HOPE
(PENNSYLVANIA)--FACTORIES--
ALTERATIONS AND ADDITIONS--UNION
PAPER MILL
The search continues: building types
study 681, multifamily housing /
Donald J. Canty.
Four low-rise condominium
projects: The Waterworks, New
Hope, Penn. (Cecil Baker &
Associates, Architects); Back of
the Hill Rowhouses, Boston
(William Rawn Associates,
Architects); Samoset Resort and
Village, Rockport, Me. (Sasaki
Associates, Architects); and
Parkview Commons, San Francisco
(David Baker Architects).
ARCHITECTURAL RECORD 1990 July,
v.178, no.8, p.15-87, axonometric
views, elev., photos., plans, site
plans.

UNITED STATES--NEW HOPE
(PENNSYLVANIA)--HOUSES--20TH CENTURY
Bucks County manor.
New house which resembles a
Colonial Stone farmhouse, Penn.
Architect: Richard Yarnall.
Interior designers: D'Aquino
Humphreys Interiors.
COLONIAL HOMES 1990 Aug., v.16,
no.4, p.33-[39], dets., photos.

UNITED STATES--NEW HOPE
(PENNSYLVANIA)--LOG-END HOUSES--19TH
CENTURY--CONSERVATION AND
RESTORATION--HILD - BELL HOUSE
Collector's addition / Dylan Landis.
Renovation of an 1880s log house
in New Hope, Penn., by antique
dealers Ed Hild and Patrick Bell.
METROPOLITAN HOME 1990 Oct., v.22,
no.10, p.150-155, port., photos.

UNITED STATES--NEW JERSEY--
ARCHITECTURE
Current work.
Fourteen projects recently
completed or currently on the
boards by N.J. architects.
ARCHITECTURE NEW JERSEY 1990,
v.26, no.2, p.9-20, axonometric
views, dets., dwgs., elevs.,
models, photos., plans, site
plans.
Urban design.
Seven current projects in New
Jersey cities, separately indexed.
ARCHITECTURE NEW JERSEY 1989,
v.25, no.3 p.5-12, axonometric
views, dwgs., photos., plans,
sketches.

UNITED STATES--NEW JERSEY--
ARCHITECTURE--AWARDS AND PRIZES
Design awards [New Jersey Society of
Architects 1989 Design Awards
Competition].
Excellence in architecture awards
to The Hillier Group; Frederick
Schmitt; Michael Graves; Short and
Ford; Venturi, Rauch and Scott
Brown. Other awards also included.
ARCHITECTURE NEW JERSEY 1990,
v.26, no.1, p.9-24, axonometric
view, dwgs., elevs., models,
photos., plans, secns.

UNITED STATES--NEW JERSEY--
ARCHITECTURE--CONSERVATION AND
RESTORATION
State focus on preservation for the
1990s.
In New Jersey.
PRESERVATION PERSPECTIVE NJ 1990
July-Aug., v.9, no.4, p.[1]-2,
photo.

UNITED STATES--NEW JERSEY--
ARCHITECTURE--CONSERVATION AND
RESTORATION--LAW AND LEGISLATION
Noteworthy preservation-related
court decisions.
In New Jersey.
PRESERVATION PERSPECTIVE NJ 1990
Nov.-Dec., v.9, no.6, p.[1]-2,
photo.

UNITED STATES--NEW JERSEY--BUILDINGS--
ALTERATIONS AND ADDITIONS
Additions and alterations / Regan
Young, Robert Cerutti.
On the architect's job of adding
to existing structures. Examples
of 12 projects in and near New
Jersey by New Jersey architects:
Katz Novoa Architects and
Planners; John DeFazio; Michael
Burns; Frederick Schmitt; Michael
Ryan Architects; Sykes O'Connor
Salerno Hazaveh; Parette and
Associates; Nadaskay Kopelson;
Michael Graves; Carla Bonacci;
Robert N. Auld; and Albert F.
Zaccone.
ARCHITECTURE NEW JERSEY 1990,
v.26, no.5, p.9-22, axonometric
view, ill., elevs., models,
photos., plans, secn.

UNITED STATES--NEW JERSEY--HISTORIC
BUILDINGS--INVENTORIES
Updating the state and national
registers.
New listings of historic
properties in New Jersey.
PRESERVATION PERSPECTIVE NJ 1990
July-Aug., v.9, no.4, p.2-5,
photos.

UNITED STATES--NEW JERSEY--HISTORIC
DISTRICTS--INVENTORIES
Updating the state and national
registers.
New listings of historic
properties in New Jersey.
PRESERVATION PERSPECTIVE NJ 1990
July-Aug., v.9, no.4, p.2-5,
photos.

UNITED STATES--NEW JERSEY--HISTORIC
PRESERVATION
State focus on preservation for the
1990s.
In New Jersey.
PRESERVATION PERSPECTIVE NJ 1990
July-Aug., v.9, no.4, p.[1]-2,
photo.

UNITED STATES--NEW JERSEY--HISTORIC
PRESERVATION--LAW AND LEGISLATION
Noteworthy preservation-related
court decisions.
In New Jersey.
PRESERVATION PERSPECTIVE NJ 1990
Nov.-Dec., v.9, no.6, p.[1]-2,
photo.

UNITED STATES--NEW JERSEY--HISTORIC
SITES--INVENTORIES
Updating the state and national
registers.
New listings of historic
properties in New Jersey.
PRESERVATION PERSPECTIVE NJ 1990
July-Aug., v.9, no.4, p.2-5,
photos.

UNITED STATES--NEW JERSEY--HOUSES
Remaking the Mediterranean style /
Robert Campbell.
Italianate-style home near the New
Jersey shore. Architects: Robert
A. M. Stern with Thomas A.
Kligerman.
ARCHITECTURAL DIGEST 1990 Dec.,
v.47, no.13, p.[102]-111,218,
axonometric view, port., photos.

UNITED STATES--NEW JERSEY--HOUSES--
20TH CENTURY--GROTTA HOUSE
Modern idyll: architect Richard
Meier's vision of the contemporary
country house takes an a classical
outlook / Martin Filler.
The Grotta house, northern N.J.
HOUSE & GARDEN 1990 June, v.162,
no.6, p.150-[157], port., photos.

UNITED STATES--NEW JERSEY--HOUSES--
DUTCH COLONIAL
Later Dutch houses of New York & New
Jersey / Russell Gilmore.
Examples from the 1770s.
OLD-HOUSE JOURNAL 1990 Mar.-Apr.,
v.18, no.2, back cover, photos.

UNITED STATES--NEW JERSEY--HOUSES--
GROTTA HOUSE
A collaboration [Grotta house,
northern New Jersey] / Jim Murphy.
Architects: Richard Meier and
Partners.
PROGRESSIVE ARCHITECTURE 1990
Nov., v.71, no.12, p.90-[95],
det., photos., plans, site plan.
Richard Meier & Partners: Grotta
residence, Harding Township, New
Jersey, 1984-89.
Architects: Richard Meier &
Partners. Text in Japanese and
English.
GA HOUSES 1990 Dec., no.30,
p.8-31, axonometric view, photos.,
plans, site plan.

UNITED STATES--NEW JERSEY--INTERIOR
DESIGN
Interiors.
Introduces recent interiors by New
Jersey architects and designers;
some separately indexed.
ARCHITECTURE NEW JERSEY 1990 v.26,
no.6, p.9-18, photos., plans.

UNITED STATES--NEW JERSEY--LAND USE--
PINELANDS
Development versus the environment:
the Pinelands / Robert Bembridge.
In southern New Jersey.
ARCHITECTURE NEW JERSEY 1990,
v.26, no.5, p.33,35,38.

UNITED STATES--NEW JERSEY--NATIONAL
PARKS AND RESERVES--PINELANDS
Development versus the environment:
the Pinelands / Robert Bembridge.
In southern New Jersey.
ARCHITECTURE NEW JERSEY 1990,
v.26, no.5, p.33,35,38,

UNITED STATES--NEW JERSEY--PUBLIC
BUILDINGS
Civic architecture.
Ten projects designed by New
Jersey architects, most within the
state; some separately indexed.
ARCHITECTURE NEW JERSEY 1990,
v.26, no.3, p.9-19, axonometric
views, dwgs., elevs., models,
photos., plans, secns., sketch.
Government as client / Nora
Odendahl.
In New Jersey.
ARCHITECTURE NEW JERSEY 1990,
v.26, no.3, p.20-21,25-28,30,

UNITED STATES--NEW JERSEY--PUBLIC
BUILDINGS--CONSERVATION AND
RESTORATION
Government as client / Nora
Odendahl.
In New Jersey.
ARCHITECTURE NEW JERSEY 1990,
v.26, no.3, p.20-21,25-28,30,

UNITED STATES--NEW JERSEY--STORES--
CLOTHING--INTERIOR DESIGN--LAST CALL
Interiors studio / Jean Gorman.
Interiors of Neiman Marcus
clearance center, Last Call, in
New Jersey shopping mall. Interior
designers: Hermanovski Lauck.
INTERIORS 1990 Sept., v.149,
no.14, p.24, photos.

UNITED STATES--NEW JERSEY--VERNACULAR
ARCHITECTURE--18TH CENTURY
Later Dutch houses of New York & New
Jersey / Russell Gilmore.
Examples from the 1770s.
OLD-HOUSE JOURNAL 1990 Mar.-Apr.,
v.18, no.2, back cover, photos.

UNITED STATES--NEW LONDON
(CONNECTICUT)--HOUSES--VICTORIAN--
INTERIOR DESIGN
Creating a Victorian workplace:
converting an old wreck to
beautiful Victorian offices / John
Kosmer.
Law office in New London, Conn.,
for Charles Irving, Nancy Dubicki,
and Garon Camassar.
VICTORIAN HOMES 1990 Spring, v.9,
no.2, p.56-59, photos.

UNITED STATES--NEW LONDON
(CONNECTICUT)--LAW OFFICES--INTERIOR
DESIGN--IRVING - DUBICKI - CAMASSAR
OFFICE
Creating a Victorian workplace:
converting an old wreck to
beautiful Victorian offices / John
Kosmer.
Law office in New London, Conn.,
for Charles Irving, Nancy Dubicki,
and Garon Camassar.
VICTORIAN HOMES 1990 Spring, v.9,
no.2, p.56-59, photos.

UNITED STATES--NEW MEXICO--BOOMTOWNS
Oil patch shacks: boom town housing
in New Mexico's little Texas /
Boyd C. Pratt.
TRIGLYPH 1989-1990 Winter, no.9,
p.34-47, maps, photos., refs.

UNITED STATES--NEW MEXICO--CEMETERIES
Sacred places of the Southwest /
Laura Sue Sanborn.
On camposantos, burial grounds of
Hispanic Catholics in the American
Southwest.
PLACES 1990 Fall, v.7, no.1,
p.[42]-49, photos.

UNITED STATES--NEW MEXICO--
FORTIFICATION--ADOBE--CONSERVATION
AND RESTORATION--FORT SELDEN STATE
MONUMENT
The Fort Selden adobe text wall
project / Michael Romero Taylor.
ASSOCIATION FOR PRESERVATION
TECHNOLOGY. BULLETIN 1990, v.22,
no.3, p.35-41, photos., tables,
refs.
Stabilization of Fort Selden's ruins
/ Thomas J. Caperton.
ASSOCIATION FOR PRESERVATION
TECHNOLOGY. BULLETIN 1990, v.22,
no.3, p.30-34, photos., refs.

UNITED STATES--NEW MEXICO--HOUSES--
SANTA FE STYLE
Santa Fe style revisited- with
credits! Santa Fe design: book
review / Robert W. Peters.
Review of a book by Elmo Baca,
Suzanne Deats, and others, 1990.
NEW MEXICO ARCHITECTURE 1990
Sept.-Dec., v.31, no.5-6, p.15-16,

UNITED STATES--NEW MEXICO--HOUSING
Oil patch shacks: boom town housing
in New Mexico's little Texas /
Boyd C. Pratt.
TRIGLYPH 1989-1990 Winter, no.9,
p.34-47, maps, photos., refs.

UNITED STATES--NEW MEXICO--HUNTING
LODGES--VERMEJO PARK RANCH--CASA
GRANDE
Sport and splendor: New Mexico's
spectacular Vermejo Park Ranch /
Samuel Young.
A restored gilded-age wilderness
retreat.
SOUTHERN ACCENTS 1990 July-Aug.,
v.13, no.6, p.110-113, photos.

UNITED STATES--NEW MEXICO--MISSION
CHURCHES--SPANISH COLONIAL--ADOBE--
CONSERVATION AND RESTORATION
The importance of vernacular
traditions [adobe churches, New
Mexico] / Anita Rodriquez,
Katherine Pettus.
Restoration of the early adobe
churches.
ASSOCIATION FOR PRESERVATION
TECHNOLOGY BULLETIN 1990, v.22,
no.3, p.2-4, photos., refs.

UNITED STATES--NEW MEXICO--MISSION
CHURCHES--SPANISH COLONIAL--SALINAS
PUEBLO MISSIONS NATIONAL MONUMENT--
SAN GREGORIO DE ABO
"We've got it, Tom", the search for
the first church of Abo [San
Gregorio de Abo, New Mexico] /
James E. Ivey.
ASSOCIATION FOR PRESERVATION
TECHNOLOGY. BULLETIN 1990, v.22,
no.3, p.73-79, photos.,
axonometric views, plans, refs.

UNITED STATES--NEW MEXICO--PUEBLOS--
CONSERVATION AND RESTORATION--ACOMA
SKY CITY
Rebuilding Acoma Sky City [pueblo in
New Mexico] / Paul G. McHenry, Jr.
ASSOCIATION FOR PRESERVATION
TECHNOLOGY. BULLETIN 1990, v.22,
no.3, p.55-64, 80, photos.,
elevs., refs., site plan, diagr.

UNITED STATES--NEW MEXICO--SACRED
SITES
Sacred places of the Southwest /
Laura Sue Sanborn.
On camposantos, burial grounds of
Hispanic Catholics in the American
Southwest.
PLACES 1990 Fall, v.7, no.1,
p.[42]-49, photos.

UNITED STATES--NEW MEXICO--SHOTGUN
HOUSES
Oil patch shacks: boom town housing
in New Mexico's little Texas /
Boyd C. Pratt.
TRIGLYPH 1989-1990 Winter, no.9,
p.34-47, maps, photos., refs.

UNITED STATES--NEW ORLEANS
(LOUISIANA)--APARTMENT HOUSES--
FLINT-GOODRIDGE APARTMENTS
"Something spectacular" Kemp
dedicates New Orleans housing
rehab [Flint-Goodridge Apartments,
formerly Flint-Goodridge
Hospital].
Originally built 1932.
PRESERVATION NEWS 1990 Mar., v.30,
no.3, p.1, ports., photo.

UNITED STATES--NEW ORLEANS
(LOUISIANA)--ARCHITECTURAL
DRAWINGS--19TH CENTURY--
COLLECTIONS--NOTARIAL ARCHIVES--PLAN
BOOK COLLECTION
The Notarial Archives of New
Orleans.
Includes the Plan Book Collection,
including several thousand
19th-cent. watercolors and site
plans.
NEWSLETTER / THE CATALOGUE OF
LANDSCAPE RECORDS IN THE UNITED
STATES 1990 Fall, v.4, no.2,
p.[2-3],

UNITED STATES--NEW ORLEANS
(LOUISIANA)--ARCHIVES--NOTARIAL
ARCHIVES
The Notarial Archives of New
Orleans.
Includes the Plan Book Collection,
including several thousand
19th-cent. watercolors and site
plans.
NEWSLETTER / THE CATALOGUE OF
LANDSCAPE RECORDS IN THE UNITED
STATES 1990 Fall, v.4, no.2,
p.[2-3],

UNITED STATES--NEW ORLEANS
(LOUISIANA)--ART GALLERIES--628
GALLERY
L'accademia New Orleans = The
academy: New Orleans.
628 Gallery features painted
furniture done by teenagers.
ABITARE 1990 Jan., no.281,
p.116-119, ports., photos.

UNITED STATES--NEW ORLEANS
(LOUISIANA)--HOTELS--HOTEL MAISON DE
VILLE
Hotel Maison de Ville: warm
hospitality in romantic New
Orleans / Susannah M. Wilson.
Originally a townhouse, in the
French Quarter.
SOUTHERN ACCENTS 1989 Nov.-Dec.,
v.12, no.6, p.180-185, port.,
photos.

UNITED STATES--NEW ORLEANS
(LOUISIANA)--HOUSES--19TH CENTURY--
INTERIOR DESIGN--SMITH HOUSE
Garden District romance: dreamy
design in the finest New Orleans
tradition / Joan Goldberger.
Interiors of 19th-cent. Smith
house on St. Charles Ave. Interior
designer: Nicholas Haslam.
SOUTHERN ACCENTS 1989 May-June,
v.12, no.3, p.[122]-129, port.,
photos.

UNITED STATES--NEW ORLEANS
(LOUISIANA)--HOUSES--INTERIOR DESIGN
Exuberant French flair: a home
fine-tuned to a New Orleans family
/ Susannah M. Wilson.
House interiors. Architect: Barry
M. Fox; interior designer: Lucile
Andrus.
SOUTHERN ACCENTS 1989 Nov.-Dec.,
v.12, no.6, p.136-141, photos.

UNITED STATES--NEW ORLEANS
(LOUISIANA)--HOUSES--ITALIANATE--
CONSERVATION AND RESTORATION--
GLEASON-EWIN HOUSE (CHRISTOVICH
HOUSE)
New Orleans elan: the restoration of
this nineteenth-century residence
marked a unique new beginning for
its owners / Anne Elizabeth
Powell.
The Gleason-Ewin house in the
Garden district, now the
Christovich home. Original
architect (1853): Isaac Thayer.
HISTORIC PRESERVATION 1990
Jan.-Feb., v.42, no.1, p.24-[29],
photos.

UNITED STATES--NEW ORLEANS
(LOUISIANA)--LIBRARIES--CONSERVATION
AND RESTORATION--HOWARD MEMORIAL
LIBRARY
Southern traditions: preservation
efforts in today's South show new
interest in 20th-century
landmarks, as well as earlier ones
/ Clifford A. Pearson.
A portfolio of Southeast projects:
Epping Forest Yacht Club,
Jacksonville, Fla. (Pappas
Associates); Freedom Tower, Miami
(Heisenbottle Architects);
Venetian Pool, Coral Gables, Fla.
(H. Carlton Decker & Assoc.);
Howard Memorial Library, New
Orleans (E. Barron, M. Toups); and
(Continued next column)

UNITED STATES--NEW ORLEANS
(LOUISIANA)--LIBRARIES--CONSERVATION
AND RESTORATION--HOWARD MEMORIAL
LIBRARY
Southern traditions:...(CONTINUED)
Linden Row Inn, Richmond, Va.
(Glave Newman Anderson).
ARCHITECTURAL RECORD 1990 Mar.,
v.178, no.3, p.66-75, photos.,
plans, site plans.

UNITED STATES--NEW ORLEANS
(LOUISIANA)--OFFICES--INTERIOR
DESIGN--BAUERLEIN
Imaging an image-maker / Kristen
Richards.
Interiors of the Bauerlein ad
agency, New Orleans. Interior
designers: Chrestia & Staub.
INTERIORS 1990 June, v.149, no.11,
p.24, photos., plan.

UNITED STATES--NEW ORLEANS
(LOUISIANA)--STREETCAR SYSTEMS--
CONSERVATION AND RESTORATION
Transit transformation; New Orleans
revives street lines / Thomas W.
Sweeney.
PRESERVATION NEWS 1990 Jan., v.30,
no.1, p.1,3,20, photos.

UNITED STATES--NEW ORLEANS
(LOUISIANA)--TOWNHOUSES--19TH
CENTURY--KAVANAUGH HOUSE
Latitudes of the sun: a
nineteenth-century town house in
the Marigny / Susannah M. Wilson.
Architectural renovation by Frank
W. Masson. Interior designer:
Decorations-Lucullus.
SOUTHERN ACCENTS 1990 June, v.13,
no.5, p.[70-81], photos.

UNITED STATES--NEW PALTZ (NEW YORK)--
HOUSES--GREEK REVIVAL--BARTSCH HOUSE
Hudson Valley scenes: painter's
magic.
Ca. 1835 Greek Revival style
house, home of artist William
Bartsch.
COLONIAL HOMES 1990 June, v.16,
no.3, p.128-133, port., photos.

UNITED STATES--NEW PRESTON
(CONNECTICUT)--ANTIQUE SHOPS
An antiquer's street of dreams / Kim
Waller.
Antique shops in New Preston,
Connecticut.
HOUSE BEAUTIFUL 1990 Oct., v.132,
no.10, p.35-36,42,46,48, ports.,
photos.

UNITED STATES--NEW RIVER (ARIZONA)--
HOUSES--MURRAY HOUSE
A desert lookout [Murray house, New
River, AZ] / Philip Arcidi.
Architects: William Bruder.
PROGRESSIVE ARCHITECTURE 1990
Nov., v.71, no.12, p.74-77,
photos., plan, secn., site plan.

UNITED STATES--NEW ROCHELLE (NEW
YORK)--HISTORIC HOUSE MUSEUMS--
COLONIAL--THOMAS PAINE HOUSE
Thomas Paine: the times that tried
his soul.
18th-cent. cottage in New
Rochelle, N.Y.
COLONIAL HOMES 1990 Apr., v.16,
no.2, p.56-59,130-131,136, port.,
photos.

UNITED STATES--NEW TOWNS
Beyond gridlock: looking for the new
suburban city / Joseph. E. Brown,
Michael E. Hickok.
Problems of definition for
"suburban urbanization", and the
transportation issues involved.
DEVELOPMENT 1990 July-Aug., v.21,
no.4, p.17-20, ill., dwgs.,
photos.
Breaking the code: urban design
portfolio / Beth Dunlop.
Small-town alternatives to
suburban sprawl, as offered by
Andres Duany and Elizabeth
Plater-Zyberk.
ARCHITECTURE: THE AIA JOURNAL 1990
Apr., v.79, no.4, p.80-83, ill.,
elev., plans, site plans.
Clarence Stein and the greenbelt
towns: settling for less / K. C.
Parsons.
Architect and planner Clarence S.
Stein's role in the formation of
greenbelt towns during the New
Deal.
AMERICAN PLANNING ASSOCIATION.
JOURNAL 1990 Spring, v.56, no.2,
p.161-183, dwg., ports., photo.,
plans, refs.
Urban cores: development trends and
real estate opportunities in the
1990s / Christopher B. Leinberger.
URBAN LAND 1990 Dec., v.49, no.12,
p.4-9, photo., table, aerial
photos.

UNITED STATES--NEW YORK--HISTORIC
PRESERVATION--ECONOMIC ASPECTS
Government partnership funds
preservation programs / Lucy A.
Breyer.
On 23 N.Y. State communities that
have become Certified Loval
Governments (CLGs).
PRESERVATION LEAGUE OF NEW YORK
STATE. NEWSLETTER 1990 Fall, v.16,
no.2, p.6-9, photos., engr.

UNITED STATES--NEW YORK--HOUSES--
GEORGIAN--ALTERATIONS AND
ADDITIONS--KLEBANOFF HOUSE
Georgian grace simplified [NY house
addition].
Architects: BumpZoid. Interior
designer: Susan Bishop.
HOUSE BEAUTIFUL 1986 June, v.128,
no.6, p.50-[59], photos.

UNITED STATES--NEW YORK (NEW YORK)--
AFFORDABLE HOUSING
Built to last? / Jeffrey Hoff.
Suburban-style housing in New
York.
CITY LIMITS 1990 Aug.-Sept., v.15,
no.7, p.9-10, port.
Rebels with a cause? / Doug
Turetsky.
Squatters in vacant New York City
buildings.
CITY LIMITS 1990 Apr., v.15, no.4,
p.12-15, ports., photos.

UNITED STATES--NEW YORK (NEW YORK)--
ANTIQUE SHOPS
The "fun part" of decorating / Jane
Margolies.
Interior designers Simone Feldman
and Victoria Hagan shop for
antiques in New York.
HOUSE BEAUTIFUL 1990 Sept., v.132,
no.9, p.28,32, ports., photos.

UNITED STATES--NEW YORK (NEW YORK)--
ANTIQUE SHOPS--JOHN ROSSELLI
ANTIQUES
Master of the fabulous faux / Sally
Clark.
Profile of antiques dealer and
producer of furniture
reproductions: John Rosselli.
HOUSE BEAUTIFUL 1990 Nov., v.132,
no.11, p.27-28, port., photo.

UNITED STATES--NEW YORK (NEW YORK)--
APARTMENT HOUSES--180 EAST 70TH
STREET
180 East 70th Street residential
building, New York, New York,
1984-86.
Architects: Kohn Pedersen Fox
Associates.
PROCESS: ARCHITECTURE 1989 Nov.,
no.86, p.48-49, elevs., photos.,
secn.

UNITED STATES--NEW YORK (NEW YORK)--
APARTMENT HOUSES--511 WEST 133RD
STREET
Vacant lots proposal: site #7, 511
West 133rd Street, Harlem,
Manhattan: Tod Williams and Billie
Tsien.
OZ / COLLEGE OF ARCHITECTURE AND
DESIGN, KANSAS STATE UNIVERSITY
1989, v.11, p.36-37, ill., models,
plan.

UNITED STATES--NEW YORK (NEW YORK)--
APARTMENT HOUSES--ARCHIVE
Avinash K. Malhotra, New York.
Three projects: Bleecker Court,
New York (1981); International
Plaza, New York (1984); and The
Archive, New York (1989); original
architect: Willoughby J. Edbrooke.
Developer: Rockrose Development
Corp.
ARCHITECTURE + DESIGN 1990
Jan.-Feb., v.7, no.1, p.24-31,
dwgs., photos., plans, secns.

UNITED STATES--NEW YORK (NEW YORK)--
APARTMENT HOUSES--BLEECKER COURT
Avinash K. Malhotra, New York.
Three projects: Bleecker Court,
New York (1981); International
Plaza, New York (1984); and The
Archive, New York (1989); original
architect: Willoughby J. Edbrooke.
Developer: Rockrose Development
Corp.
ARCHITECTURE + DESIGN 1990
Jan.-Feb., v.7, no.1, p.24-31,
dwgs., photos., plans, secns.

UNITED STATES--NEW YORK (NEW YORK)--
APARTMENT HOUSES--INTERNATIONAL
PLAZA
Avinash K. Malhotra, New York.
Three projects: Bleecker Court,
New York (1981); International
Plaza, New York (1984); and The
Archive, New York (1989); original
architect: Willoughby J. Edbrooke.
Developer: Rockrose Development
Corp.
ARCHITECTURE + DESIGN 1990
Jan.-Feb., v.7, no.1, p.24-31,
dwgs., photos., plans, secns.

UNITED STATES--NEW YORK (NEW YORK)--
APARTMENT HOUSES--NEW YORK CANCER
HOSPITAL (2 WEST 106TH STREET AND
CENTRAL PARK WEST)
The rise of Manhattan Valley /
Andrew White.
A landmark building, the New York
Cancer Hospital, at 2 W. 106 St.&
Central Park W., built by John J.
Astor in 1884, will be converted
to luxury housing with the
addition of a 27-story tower.
Original architect: Charles
Haight. Tower architect: Victor
Caliandro.
METROPOLIS 1990 Jan.-Feb., v.9,
no.6, p.16-18, photo.

UNITED STATES--NEW YORK (NEW YORK)--
APARTMENT HOUSES--WORLDWIDE PLAZA
Urban civility: Worldwide Plaza, New
York City, New York / Andrea
Oppenheimer Dean.
Architects: SOM/New York; Frank
Williams & Associates.
ARCHITECTURE: THE AIA JOURNAL 1990
Apr., v.79, no.4, p.[84-89],
photos., site plans, aerial photo.

UNITED STATES NEW YORK (NEW YORK)--
APARTMENTS
Apartment, New York, NY.
In the Police Building.
Architects: Smith-Miller +
Hawkinson. Spanish, English text.
QUADERNS D'ARQUITECTURA I
URBANISME 1990 Jan.-Feb.-Mar.,
no.184, p.70-[71], axonometric
view, photos., plans.
Material witness: Manhattan
apartment, New York City, Hariri &
Hariri / Victoria Geibel.
ARCHITECTURE: THE MAGAZINE OF THE
AMERICAN INSTITUTE OF ARCHITECTS
1990 June, v.79, no.6, p.[64-67],
photos., plan.
Rationnel et lyrique: appartement a
New York.
Architects: Frank Lupo and Daniel
Rowen. English summary, p.52.
ARCHITECTURE INTERIEURE CREE 1990
Feb., no.234, p.148-[151], photos.
The writing on the wall: architect
Frederic Schwartz left no surface
untouched in the Central Park West
apartment of a young collector /
Charles Gandee.
HOUSE & GARDEN 1990 Feb., v.162,
no.2, p.142-[147],162, photos.

UNITED STATES--NEW YORK (NEW YORK)--
APARTMENTS--ALTERATIONS AND
ADDITIONS
Great rooms / Anne Foxley.
The basement room of a New York
City apartment is transformed into
a living room. Interior designers
Carl D'Aquino and Geordi
Humphreys. Architect: Paul Laird.
HOUSE & GARDEN 1990 Dec., v.162,
no.12, p.[101]-103, photos.
Manhattan merger / Edie Lee Cohen.
Fusion of three apartments into
one within the Metropolitan Tower,
New York. Architects: Tod
Williams. Billie Tsien &
Associates.
INTERIOR DESIGN 1990 Sept., v.61,
no.12, p.216 [221], photos.,
plans.

UNITED STATES--NEW YORK (NEW YORK)--
APARTMENTS--ARCHITECTS'--HARIRI
APARTMENT
Sibling revelry: high touch, high
tech [Hariri apartment] / Julie V.
Iovine.
In midtown Manhattan, designed by
owners Gisue and Mojgan Hariri.
METROPOLITAN HOME 1990 Aug., v.22,
no.8, p.138-140, port., photos.

UNITED STATES--NEW YORK (NEW YORK)--
APARTMENTS--ARCHITECTS'--RANALLI
APARTMENT
Special feature: George Ranalli.
Contents: Essays: George Ranalli
statement: elements of
architecture/ George Ranalli--
Autonomous structures/ Ross
Miller--Interview: George Ranalli/
Ross Miller--Works 1979-1989:
Callender school renovation,
Newport, R.I.--Ranalli studio
apartment, New York City,
1982-83--Peak competition project,
Hong Kong, 1982--Paris Opera
competition project, 1983--Chicago
Tribune competition project,
1980--Times Tower competition
project, 1984--New York loft,
1985-86--Valentine chair--House
addition for "G" family,
Westchester, New York, 1987-88--
Conversion of barn to residence,
Red Hook, N.Y., 1988-89--K project
"Tower of Silence," Tokyo, Japan,
1989. Text in Japanese and
English.
ARCHITECTURE AND URBANISM 1990
Aug., no.8(239), p.[71-136],
axonometric views, port., elevs.,
models, photos., plans, secns.,
site plans.

UNITED STATES--NEW YORK (NEW YORK)--
APARTMENTS--INTERIOR DESIGN
Art is in the heart: Garrett Dangler
designs residential interiors /
Monica Geran.
Interiors of Manhattan apartment.
Architect: Blaine D. Bershad.
INTERIOR DESIGN 1990 Sept., v.61,
no.12, p.212-[215], photos., plan.
The big picture / Monica Geran.
Interiors of New York apartment
for contemporary art collectors
designed by Shelton, Mindel
Associates.
INTERIOR DESIGN 1990 Jan., v.61,
no.1, p.156-[165], photos., plans.
Carte Blanche / Monica Geran.
Apartment interiors in New York's
Metropolitan Tower. Interior
designer: Juan Montoya.
INTERIOR DESIGN 1990 Feb., v.61,
no.3, p.202-[209], photos., plan.
A Central Park masterpiece / Stephen
M. L. Aronson.
Interiors of New York apartment
designed by Non Bradshaw of
Bradshaw-De Palma.
ARCHITECTURAL DIGEST 1990 Nov.,
v.47, no.12, p.[206-217], 302,
photos.
City lights: Gary Hager of
Parish-Hadley finds inspiration in
a Manhattan panorama / Nancy Marx
Better.
HOUSE & GARDEN 1990 Feb., v.162,
no.2, p.104-107, photos.

UNITED STATES--NEW YORK (NEW YORK)--
APARTMENTS--INTERIOR DESIGN
(CONTINUED)
Earth, wind, and furniture / Andrea
Loukin.
Interiors of renovated 2,000 sq.
ft. New York apartment. Architect:
David Woolf.
INTERIOR DESIGN 1990 Mar., v.61,
no.5, p.172-[175], photos., plans.
Export quality: Colefax & Fowler's
very English style in successfully
transported to Manhattan apartment
/ Sherrye Henry.
HOUSE & GARDEN 1990 Nov., v.162,
no.11, p.[196-201],232, photos.
Fine on Fifth / Edie Lee Cohen.
Interiors of New York City
apartment. Interior designer:
Carl Hribar.
INTERIOR DESIGN 1990 Apr., v.61,
no.6, p.224-[229], photos., plan.
Library for living / Edie Lee Cohen.
Interiors of small Manhattan
apartment designed by John
Saladino.
INTERIOR DESIGN 1990 Dec., v.61,
no.16, p.138-[141], photos., plan.
Park Avenue country: modifying
English traditions in a prewar
apartment / Suzanne Stephens.
Interiors of New York duplex.
Interior designer: Bunny Williams.
ARCHITECTURAL DIGEST 1990 Nov.,
v.47, no.12, p.224-[231], port.,
photos.
Park Avenue living / Edie Lee Cohen.
Interiors of New York apartment.
Interior designers: Ohrbach
Jacobson.
INTERIOR DESIGN 1990 Feb., v.61,
no.3, p.[190-195], photos., plan.
Park Avenue thoroughbred / Judith
Thurman.
1929 New York apartment interiors
designed by Robert Bray and
Michael Schaible.
ARCHITECTURAL DIGEST 1990 Mar.,
v.47, no.3, p.[158]-165, photos.
Period splendor on Fifth: / Thomas
Mallon. Eighteenth-century French
style inspires a metropolitan
design.
Interiors of New York apartment.
Interior designers: Robert
Metzger, Michael Christiano.
ARCHITECTURAL DIGEST 1990 Nov.,
v.47, no.12, p.[256-263],312,
photos.
Pet project: Ned Marshall unleashes
his talents in the duplex of an
old friend and her four-footed
companions / Peter Haldeman.
Park Ave. apartment, New York
City.
HOUSE & GARDEN 1990 Dec., v.162,
no.12, p.[166]-171, port., photos.
Pfister finesse: Charles Pfister's
latest designs strike a masterly
balance between the classic and
the modern / Pilar Viladas.
The designer's own apartment in
San Francisco, and a New York City
apartment.
HOUSE & GARDEN 1990 July, v.162,
no.7, p.[124]-131, port., photos.
Regency swagger / Jonathan Etra.
New York apartment decorated by
Irvine & Fleming.
HOUSE & GARDEN 1990 Sept., v.162,
no.9, p.138-[141], photos.

UNITED STATES--NEW YORK (NEW YORK)--
APARTMENTS--INTERIOR DESIGN
(CONTINUED)
Restrained glamour for the city /
Peter Carlsen.
Interiors of New York apartment
overlooking Central Park.
Interior designers: Jay Spectre,
Geoffrey N. Bradfield.
ARCHITECTURAL DIGEST 1990 Nov.,
v.47, no.12, p.264-[271], 312,
photos.
Shifting focus: design partners
Brian Stoner and John Hutton take
a new perspective on classic forms
in a downtown apartment / Victoria
Geibel.
HOUSE & GARDEN 1990 Oct., v.162,
no.10, p.192-[197], port., photos.
A tailored setting: scale and
proportion define a Manhattan
apartment / John Gruen.
Interiors designed by Bebe
Winkler.
ARCHITECTURAL DIGEST 1990 Feb.,
v.47, no.2, p.[222-227], photos.
View from the top / Edie Lee Cohen.
Interiors of Manhattan apartment.
Architect: R. Scott Bromley.
INTERIOR DESIGN 1990 June, v.61,
no.9, p.[230-235], photos., plan.
Viewpoints / Monica Geran.
Interiors of midtown New York
apartment. Interior designers:
Space Design Group.
INTERIOR DESIGN 1990 Nov., v.61,
no.15, p.194-[199], photos., plan.

UNITED STATES--NEW YORK (NEW YORK)--
APARTMENTS--INTERIOR DESIGN--
ADLERSBERG APARTMENT
Poetry in a box / Donna Sapolin.
Renovation of apartment for Jay
Adlersberg. Architect: Margaret
Helfand.
METROPOLITAN HOME 1990 Oct., v.22,
no.10, p.[156]-160, port., photos.

UNITED STATES--NEW YORK (NEW YORK)--
APARTMENTS--INTERIOR DESIGN--ALTMAN
APARTMENT
Architectural Digest visits: Kathryn
and Robert Altman / Steven M.L.
Aronson.
Interiors of New York apartment.
Interior designers: Richard
Gillette, Stephen Shadley.
Renovation architect: David Gura.
ARCHITECTURAL DIGEST 1990 Mar.,
v.47, no.3, p.212-219,250, photos.

UNITED STATES--NEW YORK (NEW YORK)--
APARTMENTS--INTERIOR DESIGN--BAILEY
APARTMENT
Master course [Lee Bailey apartment]
/ Elaine Greene.
Manhattan loft apartment of food
and entertaining author Lee
Bailey.
HOUSE BEAUTIFUL 1990 Feb., v.132,
no.2, p.93-99, port., photos.

UNITED STATES--NEW YORK (NEW YORK)--
APARTMENTS--INTERIOR DESIGN--BEEKMAN
PLACE TRIPLEX
Smith-Miller & Hawkinson [houses].
Contents: House and studio
building, South Hampton, New York,
design: 1987-88 -- Beekman Place
townhouse triplex. New York, N.Y.,
design: 1988-89. Architects:
Smith-Miller Hawkinson Architects.
(Continued next column)

UNITED STATES--NEW YORK (NEW YORK)--
APARTMENTS--INTERIOR DESIGN--BEEKMAN
PLACE TRIPLEX (CONTINUED)
Smith-Miller &...(CONTINUED)
Text in Japanese and English.
GA HOUSES 1990 Mar., no.28,
p.92-93, axonometric views,.
model, plans.

UNITED STATES--NEW YORK (NEW YORK)--
APARTMENTS--INTERIOR DESIGN--BRYNNER
APARTMENT
Before and after: urban renewal on
high, transforming Kathy Brynner's
East Side apartment / Manuela
Hoelterhoff.
Interiors of New York apartment.
Interior designer: Vicente Wolf.
ARCHITECTURAL DIGEST 1990 Nov.,
v.47, no.12, p.278-[285], photos.

UNITED STATES--NEW YORK (NEW YORK)--
APARTMENTS--INTERIOR DESIGN--BUCK
APARTMENT
Lost and found / Joan Juliet Buck.
New York apartment of the author.
HOUSE & GARDEN 1990 Mar., v.162,
no.3, p.146-149, port., photos.

UNITED STATES--NEW YORK (NEW YORK)--
APARTMENTS--INTERIOR DESIGN--CANE
APARTMENT
Positive altitude: the skyline's the
limit in the apartment Robert
Currie designed for two New York
collectors / Joseph Giovannini.
HOUSE & GARDEN 1990 Dec., v.162,
no.12, p.[150-153], photos.

UNITED STATES--NEW YORK (NEW YORK)--
APARTMENTS--INTERIOR DESIGN--CLARK
APARTMENT
New York premiere: woman-about-town
Kitty Hawks makes her debut as a
decorator in a West Side duplex
for a Wall Streeter / Charles
Gandee.
HOUSE & GARDEN 1990 Oct., v.162,
no.10, p.[208-211],252, port.,
photos.

UNITED STATES--NEW YORK (NEW YORK)--
APARTMENTS--INTERIOR DESIGN--DAVIES
APARTMENT
Naive melody in Manhattan / Steven
M. L. Aronson.
Interiors of David Davies
apartment with a focus on his
American folk art collection.
ARCHITECTURAL DIGEST 1990 Oct,
v.47, no.11, p.244-249,290,
photos.

UNITED STATES--NEW YORK (NEW YORK)--
APARTMENTS--INTERIOR DESIGN--DENNING
AND FOURCADE APARTMENT
Drawn to scale: in their midtown
suite, Robert Denning and Vincent
Fourcade show that grandeur comes
in all sizes / Rosamond Bernier.
HOUSE & GARDEN 1990 Oct., v.162,
no.10, p.[198]-203, ill., port.,
photos.

UNITED STATES--NEW YORK (NEW YORK)--
APARTMENTS--INTERIOR DESIGN--DENNIS
APARTMENT
Definitive details: a Gramercy Park
apartment / Heather Smith
MacIsaac.
Architect: Alan Buchsbaum.
HOUSE & GARDEN 1990 Oct., v.162,
no.10, p.204-207, port., photos.

UNITED STATES--NEW YORK (NEW YORK)--
APARTMENTS--INTERIOR DESIGN--DWORK
APARTMENT
Elements of style in SoHo: a
designer's duplex in a renovated
police headquarters / Brooks
Peters.
Features interior designer Melvin
Dwork's New York apartment.
ARCHITECTURAL DIGEST 1990 Nov.,
v.47, no.12, p.232-[237], photos.

UNITED STATES--NEW YORK (NEW YORK)--
APARTMENTS--INTERIOR DESIGN--
EMMERLING APARTMENT
An urban homestead / Allison
Percival, Glenn Harrell.
Interior of designer Mary
Emmerling's New York City
apartment.
HOUSE BEAUTIFUL 1990 Nov., v.132,
no.11, p.[98]-103, port., photos.

UNITED STATES--NEW YORK (NEW YORK)--
APARTMENTS--INTERIOR DESIGN--FIFTH
AVENUE
Central Park East: architects Peter
Shelton and Lee Mindel bring the
park indoors in their decoration
of an Upper Fifth Avenue apartment
/ Joan Kron.
HOUSE & GARDEN 1990 Oct., v.162,
no.10, p.[230-235], port., photos.

UNITED STATES--NEW YORK (NEW YORK)--
APARTMENTS--INTERIOR DESIGN--FLYNN
APARTMENT
The essential D'Urso / Charles
Gandee.
A Greenwich Village apartment
decorated by Jor D'Urso.
HOUSE & GARDEN 1990 Sept., v.162,
no.9, p.[144-149], photos.

UNITED STATES--NEW YORK (NEW YORK)--
APARTMENTS--INTERIOR DESIGN--GILMOUR
APARTMENT
Chateau Manhattan / Christopher
Petkanas.
Gilmour duplex apartment.
Interior decorator: Richard Lowell
Neas.
HOUSE & GARDEN 1990 Sept., v.162,
no.9, p.150-153, photos.

UNITED STATES--NEW YORK (NEW YORK)--
APARTMENTS--INTERIOR DESIGN--GISH
APARTMENT
Lillian Gish: Birth of a nation's
epochal star in New York / Peter
Carlsen.
Features interiors of her
Manhattan apartment.
ARCHITECTURAL DIGEST 1990 Apr.,
v.47, no.4, p.238-239, port.,
photos.

UNITED STATES--NEW YORK (NEW YORK)--
APARTMENTS--INTERIOR DESIGN--
GREENWICH VILLAGE
Home work / Judith Jacobson.
Home office interiors in Greenwich
Village, New York. Architect:
Michael Rubin.
INTERIOR DESIGN 1990 Feb., v.61,
no.3, p.196-[197], photos., plan.

UNITED STATES--NEW YORK (NEW YORK)--
APARTMENTS--INTERIOR DESIGN--HARING
DUPLEX
Keith Haring: the legacy lives on /
Richard Lacayo.
Includes views of the interior of
his Greenwich Village duplex.
METROPOLITAN HOME 1990 Sept.,
v.22, no.9, p.97-102,150, port.,
photos.

UNITED STATES--NEW YORK (NEW YORK)--
APARTMENTS--INTERIOR DESIGN--
HATHAWAY APARTMENT
The Phillips collection: Sotheby's
French furniture expert Phillips
Hathaway lives among the finds of
a lifetime / Kent Black.
Park Ave. apt. Architect-interior
designer: M Group.
HOUSE & GARDEN 1990 Feb., v.162,
no.2, p.138-141, port., photos.

UNITED STATES--NEW YORK (NEW YORK)--
APARTMENTS--INTERIOR DESIGN--HOVIS
APARTMENT
Host of the town / Brooke Hayward.
Apartment of food writer Gene
Hovis in New York City.
HOUSE & GARDEN 1990 Dec., v.162,
no.12, p.[130-135],188, ports.,
photos.

UNITED STATES--NEW YORK (NEW YORK)--
APARTMENTS--INTERIOR DESIGN--HOWARD
APARTMENT
All in the family ... Gramercy Park
apartment / Charles MacLean.
Home of Philip and Alexandra
Howard. Architect: Richard Nash
Gould, interior designer: Justine
Cushing.
HOUSE & GARDEN 1990 Dec., v.162,
no.12, p.116-[121],190, ports.,
photos.

UNITED STATES--NEW YORK (NEW YORK)--
APARTMENTS--INTERIOR DESIGN--JONES
APARTMENT
West Side exoticism: evocative
textures and cultural allusions
for Felicia Jones / Patricia
Warner.
Interiors of New York apartment.
Interior designers. Richard
Gillette, Stephen Shadley.
ARCHITECTURAL DIGEST 1990 Nov.,
v.47, no.12, p.[292-298],316,
port., photos.

UNITED STATES--NEW YORK (NEW YORK)--
APARTMENTS--INTERIOR DESIGN--M LOFT
Transfigured by art and glass /
Philip Arcidi.
Focus on large glass display cases
in the interior of New York
apartment in 19th cent. former
warehouse. Architects: Kolatan
McDonald Studio.
PROGRESSIVE ARCHITECTURE 1990
Sept., v.71, no.9, p.126-127,
photos., plan.

UNITED STATES--NEW YORK (NEW YORK)--
APARTMENTS--INTERIOR DESIGN--
MAGNUSSON APARTMENT
Cultural roots / Edie Lee cohen.
Interiors of Carl and Emanuela
Magnussons New York apartment.
INTERIOR DESIGN 1990 Nov., v.61,
no.15, p.204-[209], photos.,
plans.

UNITED STATES--NEW YORK (NEW YORK)--
APARTMENTS--INTERIOR DESIGN--MALONEY
APARTMENT
High-rise heaven / Donna Sapolin.
Studio apartment of designer Carey
Maloney of the M (Group).
METROPOLITAN HOME 1990 Dec., v.22,
no.12, p.120-[121], photos.

UNITED STATES--NEW YORK (NEW YORK)--
APARTMENTS--INTERIOR DESIGN--MANSOUR
APARTMENT
Design's hidden persuader [James
Mansour] / Julie V. Iovine.
METROPOLITAN HOME 1990 Sept.,
v.22, no.9, p.114-[119], port.,
photos.

UNITED STATES--NEW YORK (NEW YORK)--
APARTMENTS--INTERIOR DESIGN--
MARTINEZ APARTMENT
Taste of Mexico: haute couture in an
East Side duplex / Caroline
Rennolds Milbank.
Interiors of Zarela Martinez's New
York apartment. Interior
designers: Mary McFadden, Kohle
Yohannan.
ARCHITECTURAL DIGEST 1990 Nov.,
v.47, no.12, p.[250]-255, 312,
port., photos.

UNITED STATES--NEW YORK (NEW YORK)--
APARTMENTS--INTERIOR DESIGN--MINELLI
APARTMENT
Liza Minelli: Cabaret's Best Actress
at home in New York / Peter
Carlsen.
Interior designer: Timothy
MacDonald.
ARCHITECTURAL DIGEST 1990 Apr.,
v.47, no.4, p.[244]-247, port.,
photos.

UNITED STATES--NEW YORK (NEW YORK)--
APARTMENTS--INTERIOR DESIGN--NYE
APARTMENT
Gotham romance: in her grand Fifth
Avenue apartment, decorator Hethea
Nye indulges her taste for luxury
/ Andrew Solomon.
HOUSE & GARDEN 1990 Oct., v.162,
no.10, p.[164-171], photos., port.

UNITED STATES--NEW YORK (NEW YORK)--
APARTMENTS--INTERIOR DESIGN--PETRIE
APARTMENT
The height of elegance: Milton and
Carroll Petrie moved five floors
up without leaving home / Pilar
Viladas.
Interior designers David Easton,
John Christensen, Denning &
Fourcade, Pauline Boardman.
HOUSE & GARDEN 1990 Feb., v.162,
no.2, p.116-121, port., photos.

UNITED STATES--NEW YORK (NEW YORK)--
APARTMENTS--INTERIOR DESIGN--
PINCUS-WITTEN / HECHT APARTMENT
Hide and seek: Robert Pincus-Witten
and Leon Hecht keep some of their
favorite treasures out of sight /
Douglas Brenner.
HOUSE & GARDEN 1990 May, v.162,
no.5, p.122,124, port., photos.

UNITED STATES--NEW YORK (NEW YORK)--
APARTMENTS--INTERIOR DESIGN--REVSON
APARTMENT
White nights in New York / Aileen
Mehle.
Interiors of Lyn Revson's New York
apartment. Interior designer: Mark
Hampton.
ARCHITECTURAL DIGEST 1990 Nov.,
v.47, no.12, p.218-[223],306,
port., photos.

UNITED STATES--NEW YORK (NEW YORK)--
APARTMENTS--INTERIOR DESIGN--SCHIANO
APARTMENT
Style Diva: at home on Park Avenue,
Vanity Fair's Marina Schiano
displays flair for drama / Gini
Alhadeff.
HOUSE & GARDEN 1990 Oct., v.162,
no.10, p.[172]-175, ports.,
photos.

UNITED STATES--NEW YORK (NEW YORK)--
APARTMENTS--INTERIOR DESIGN--SHAPIRO
FIELDS APARTMENT
Kolatan McDonald Studio
[apartments].
Contents: Apartment for an actor
dancer, Mott Street, New York,
N.Y. -- Shapiro Fields apartment,
Broadway & Riverside Drive, New
York, N.Y. Architects: Kolatan
McDonald Studio. Text in Japanese
and English.
GA HOUSES 1990 Mar., no.28,
p.72-74, axonmetric views, dwgs.,
plans.

UNITED STATES--NEW YORK (NEW YORK)--
APARTMENTS--INTERIOR DESIGN--SHORT
APARTMENT
Architectural digest visits: Bobby
Short / Judith Thurman.
Interiors of New York apartment.
ARCHITECTURAL DIGEST 1990 Nov.,
v.47, no.12, p.238-[243], ports.,
photos.

UNITED STATES--NEW YORK (NEW YORK)--
APARTMENTS--INTERIOR DESIGN--SOLOMON
APARTMENT
Revisiting the gilded age /
Christopher Finch.
Interiors of New York apartment
owned by Gregg Solomon. Interior
designer: Thomas Britt.
ARCHITECTURAL DIGEST 1990 Nov.,
v.47, no.12, p.196-[205], photos.

UNITED STATES--NEW YORK (NEW YORK)--
APARTMENTS--INTERIOR DESIGN--THOMSON
APARTMENT
Virgil's elegy: Virgil Thomson's
apartment in the Hotel Chelsea /
John Russell.
HOUSE & GARDEN 1990 Oct., v.162,
no.10, p.66,74,78, port., photos.

UNITED STATES--NEW YORK (NEW YORK)--
APARTMENTS--INTERIOR DESIGN--VON
FURSTENBERG APARTMENT
Uptown updated: discovering the new
old world / Richard Lacayo.
The apartment of fashion designer
Diane von Furstenberg on the Upper
East Side, New York. Interior
designer: Jean-Paul Beaujard.
METROPOLITAN HOME 1990 Aug., v.22,
no.8, p.[120]-123, port., photos.

UNITED STATES--NEW YORK (NEW YORK)--
APARTMENTS--INTERIOR DESIGN--WALKER
APARTMENT
Private stock: Jeff Walker, a vice
president of Ralph Lauren, creates
a look of his own at home / Peter
Wilkinson.
New York apartment.
HOUSE & GARDEN 1990 Mar., v.162,
no.3, p.158-[161], port., photos.

UNITED STATES--NEW YORK (NEW YORK)--
APARTMENTS--INTERIOR DESIGN--
WILLIAMS APARTMENT
A la refurb du temps perdu / Carol
Prisant.
Features Lillian Williams' 18th
cent. French interiors in her New
York apartment.
THE WORLD OF INTERIORS 1990 Sept.,
p.[130-141], photos.

UNITED STATES--NEW YORK (NEW YORK)--
APARTMENTS--SAMARAS APARTMENT
The Samaras spectrum: high above
Manhattan, artist Lucas Samaras
puts a spin on his own color wheel
/ Ingrid Sischy.
HOUSE & GARDEN 1990 Dec., v.162,
no.12, p.[122-129],191, port.,
photos.

UNITED STATES--NEW YORK (NEW YORK)--
APARTMENTS--SCHNEIDER APARTMENT
La scala ibrida = Existing spaces,
modern day designs: the hybrid
staircase.
Renovation of an apartment in
Manhattan's SoHo District.
Architects: Gisue and Mojgan
Hariri.
ABITARE 1990 Nov., no.290,
p.116-121, photos., plans.

UNITED STATES--NEW YORK (NEW YORK)--
APARTMENTS--SMALL--INTERIOR DESIGN--
NEAS APARTMENT
The Richard Neas trilogy: the
decorator's one-room New York
pied-a terre / Penelope Green.
HOUSE & GARDEN 1990 May, v.162,
no.5, p.[196]-201,220, port.,
photos.

UNITED STATES--NEW YORK (NEW YORK)--
ARCHITECTURE--19TH CENTURY
Manhattan manners, architecture and
style 1850-1900 [by] M. Christine
Boyer [book review] / Sergio
Stenti.
Published 1985.
STORIA DELLA CITTA 1989 Jan.-Mar.,
v.14, no.49, p.83-85, map, photos.

UNITED STATES--NEW YORK (NEW YORK)--
ARCHITECTURE--20TH CENTURY
New York architectuur [book review]
/ Dirk Baalman.
Review of 1989 monograph by
Heinrich Klotz.
DE ARCHITECT 1989 Dec., v.20,
no.12, p.62-63, photo.
The prospects of pluralism /
Christian Norberg-Schulz.
New York is described as the first
pluralistic city.
ARCHITECTURAL DESIGN 1989, v.59,
no.11-12, p.viii-xiii, axonometric
views, dwg., model, photos.,
secns., aerial photo.

UNITED STATES--NEW YORK (NEW YORK)--
ARCHITECTURE--HISTORY
New York 1930: Architecture and
urbanism between the two world
wars [book review] / Auke van der
Woud.
Authors are Robert A.M. Stern,
Gregory Gilmartin, Thomas Mellins.
ARCHIS 1990 Jan., no.1, p.56,
photo.

UNITED STATES--NEW YORK (NEW YORK)--
ARCHITECTURE--STUDY AND TEACHING--
COLUMBIA UNIVERSITY
Studying Japanese architecture at
Columbia University: Nikken Sekkei
supports new Headquarters.
Headquarters for Advanced Studies
in Japanese Architecture.
JAPAN ARCHITECT 1990 Jan., v.65,
no.1(393), p.5.

UNITED STATES--NEW YORK (NEW YORK)--
ARCHIVE BUILDINGS--ROMANESQUE
REVIVAL--ALTERATIONS AND ADDITIONS--
FEDERAL ARCHIVES BUILDING
Avinash K. Malhotra, New York.
Three projects: Bleecker Court,
New York (1981); International
Plaza, New York (1984); and The
Archive, New York (1989); original
architect: Willoughby J. Edbrooke.
Developer: Rockrose Development
Corp.
ARCHITECTURE + DESIGN 1990
Jan.-Feb., v.7, no.1, p.24-31,
dwgs., photos., plans, secns.

UNITED STATES--NEW YORK (NEW YORK)--
ART GALLERIES--CHALK-VERMILION
GALLERY
Chalk-Vermilion Gallery, New York,
NY.
Architects: Smith-Miller +
Hawkinson. Spanish, English text.
QUADERNS D'ARQUITECTURA I
URBANISME 1990 Jan.-Feb.-Mar.,
no.184, p.68-[69], axonometric
views, photos.
SoHo Gallery, Wooster Street, N.Y.
Renovation of loft space to house
art gallery; architects:
Smith-Miller + Hawkinson
Architects. Text in Italian and
English.
LOTUS INTERNATIONAL 1990, no.66,
p.40-45, axonometric views,
photos., plans.

UNITED STATES--NEW YORK (NEW YORK)--
ARTISTS' STUDIOS
La nascita del "loft lifestyle": the
seventies = The creation of a
"loft lifestyle": the seventies /
Sharon Zukin.
LOTUS INTERNATIONAL 1990, no.66,
p.16-27, ports., photos., refs.

UNITED STATES--NEW YORK (NEW YORK)--
ARTISTS' STUDIOS--CLOCKTOWER
Manhattan's arena for aesthetic
melodrama / Brendan Gill.
On the Clocktower and P.S. 1
artists' studios and exhibition
space administered by the
Institute for Contemporary Art.
ARCHITECTURAL DIGEST 1990 Nov.,
v.47, no.12, p.44-[54], port.,
photos.

UNITED STATES--NEW YORK (NEW YORK)--
ARTISTS' STUDIOS--MACDOUGAL ALLEY
New York's art alley de luxe:
MacDougal Alley / Avis Berman.
History of artists living on this
street.
ARCHITECTURAL DIGEST 1990 Nov.,
v.47, no.12, p.178,182,186,190,
192, photos.

UNITED STATES--NEW YORK (NEW YORK)--
ARTISTS' STUDIOS--SOHO
SoHo art lofts / Germano Celant.
Text in Italian and English.
LOTUS INTERNATIONAL 1990, no.66,
p.7-15, photos.

UNITED STATES--NEW YORK (NEW YORK)--
ATRIUMS--WINTER GARDEN
Acoustics: [Winter Garden] / Michael
Wagner.
On the acoustics in the Winter
Garden atrium, New York City.
Architects: Cesar Pelli &
Associates. Acoustics: Smith,
Fause & Associates.
INTERIORS 1990 Dec., v.150, no.5,
p.33, photo., plan.

UNITED STATES--NEW YORK (NEW YORK)--
BANKS--INTERIOR DESIGN--
CREDITANSTALT
Creditanstalt: Janko Rasic
Associates Architects design the
Austrian bank's New York spaces /
Monica Geran.
INTERIOR DESIGN 1990 May, v.61,
no.7, p.260-[265], photos., plans.

UNITED STATES--NEW YORK (NEW YORK)--
BANKS--INTERIOR DESIGN--U.S. TRUST
U.S. Trust / Andrea Loukin.
Interiors of New York branch
office. Interior designers:
Mancini Duffy.
INTERIOR DESIGN 1990 Feb., v.61,
no.3, p.184-[187], photos., plan.

UNITED STATES--NEW YORK (NEW YORK)--
BEDROOMS--INTERIOR DESIGN--VARNEY
APARTMENT
As pretty as she pleases / Elaine
Greene.
Bedroom of home-furnishings
executive Suzanne Varney.
HOUSE BEAUTIFUL 1990 Apr., v.132,
no.4, p.[84-85], port., photos.

UNITED STATES--NEW YORK (NEW YORK)--
BOTANICAL GARDENS--NEW YORK
BOTANICAL GARDEN
Beauty and the Bronx: the New York
Botanical Garden / Paula Deitz.
Features a rose garden designed by
Beatrix Jones Farrand.
HOUSE & GARDEN 1990 Oct., v.162,
no.10, p.[202]-225,252, photos.

UNITED STATES--NEW YORK (NEW YORK)--
BRASSERIES--INTERIOR DESIGN--LA CITE
La Cite: Arnold Syrop Associates
designs a festive New York
brasserie / Mayer Rus.
Located in the Time-Life Building.
INTERIOR DESIGN 1990 Sept., v.61,
no.12, p.178-181, photos., plan.

UNITED STATES--NEW YORK (NEW YORK)--
BROADCASTING STUDIOS--ABC
Television romance / Victoria
Geibel.
New York Buildings for American
Broadcasting Co. designed by Kohn
Pedersen Fox Associates.
ARCHITECTURE: THE AIA JOURNAL 1990
Dec., v.79, no.12, p.56-[59],
models, photos., plans, site
plans.

UNITED STATES--NEW YORK (NEW YORK)--
BROWNSTONES
The East Side brownstone - a
Cinderella story / Louis
Auchincloss.
On the history of New York
brownstones.
ARCHITECTURAL DIGEST 1990 Nov.,
v.47, no.12, p.35,38,40, port.,
photos.

UNITED STATES--NEW YORK (NEW YORK)--
BROWNSTONES--INTERIOR DESIGN--
STEINEM HOUSE
Ms. Steinem on the home front /
Gloria Steinem.
The writer's recently decorated
NYC brownstone. Interior designer
Filippa Naess.
HOUSE & GARDEN 1990 Oct., v.162,
no.10, p.[180]-185, port., photos.

UNITED STATES--NEW YORK (NEW YORK)--
BUILDING CODES
Big Apple barriers: specifying
lighting for projects in New York
City poses obstacles / Peter
Barna, Justin Henderson.
ARCHITECTURE: THE AIA JOURNAL 1990
Mar., v.79, no.3, p.197-198, ill.

UNITED STATES--NEW YORK (NEW YORK)--
BUILDING DIRECTORIES--WORLD
FINANCIAL CENTER
Building directories go futuristic /
Alan Levinsohn.
Three-dimensional and
video-interactive displays
featured at the World Financial
Center in New York.
REAL ESTATE FORUM 1990 July, v.45,
no.7, p.22, photos.

UNITED STATES--NEW YORK (NEW YORK)--
BUILDING MANAGEMENT
Resource recovery? [New York
City-owned buildings] / Lisa
Glazer.
Policy to maintain and repair
city-owned buildings implemented
by the Division of Property
Management.
CITY LIMITS 1990 Mar., v.15, no.3,
p.17-20, graph, port.

UNITED STATES--NEW YORK (NEW YORK)--
BUILDINGS--HEIGHT RESTRICTIONS--
UPPER EAST SIDE
Oculus Special Feature Committee on
Zoning on the Upper East Side:
Part II.
Shows interpretations for 4 sites,
by James Gauer, Marilyn Taylor,
Peter Samton, and Peter De Witt.
OCULUS 1990 Sept., v.53, no.1,
p.6-10, dwgs., ports., elevs.,
models, map, plans.

UNITED STATES--NEW YORK (NEW YORK)--
CAFES--CAFE NEWS (10 AVENUE A)
Neighborhood newcomers / Regina S.
Baraban.
Review of 3 NYC neighborhood
restaurants.
METROPOLIS 1990 Sept., v.10, no.2,
p.31, photos.

UNITED STATES--NEW YORK (NEW YORK)--
CAFETERIAS--INTERIOR DESIGN
Employee satisfaction.
Interiors of New York publishing
house cafeteria. Interior
designers: Kohn, Pedersen, Fox,
Conway Associates.
INTERIORS 1990 Sept., v.149,
no.14, p.114-[115], photo., plan.

UNITED STATES--NEW YORK (NEW YORK)--
CENTRAL BUSINESS DISTRICTS--GRAND
CENTRAL DISTRICT
The Grand Central partnership:
taking the initiative in
revitalizing a commercial area /
Barbara M. Walker.
URBAN LAND 1990 July, v.49, no.7,
p.12-15, map, photos.

UNITED STATES--NEW YORK (NEW YORK)--
CHINATOWNS--CHINATOWN
The once invisible city: Chinatown
... / Braden Phillips.
METROPOLIS 1990 Jan.-Feb., v.9,
no.6, p.[80]-85,95, photos.

UNITED STATES--NEW YORK (NEW YORK)--
CHURCHES--19TH CENTURY--CONSERVATION
AND RESTORATION--CHURCH OF THE
COVENANT
"Landmarking comes to Covenant"
[church, New York] / Ron Wilkoc.
Describes a cooperative process
for landmarking religious
buildings. Built in 1871 and 1927
and located at 310 East 42nd St.
COMMON BOND 1990 Fall, v.6, no.4,
p.2-4, dwg., photos.

UNITED STATES--NEW YORK (NEW YORK)--
CHURCHES--19TH CENTURY--CONSERVATION
AND RESTORATION--MARINERS' TEMPLE
BAPTIST CHURCH
Mariners' Temple Baptist Church:
we're building for our future /
Landmarks Committee of Mariners'
Temple.
A 150-year old brownstone church
located at Three Herry Street, New
York.
COMMON BOND 1990 Summer, v.6,
no.3, p.2-4, photos.

UNITED STATES--NEW YORK (NEW YORK)--
CHURCHES--ALTERATIONS AND
ADDITIONS--SAINT BARTHOLOMEW'S
CHURCH
Court denies St. Bart's plea: St.
Bartholomew's Church, New York /
Amy Worden.
PRESERVATION NEWS 1990 Feb., v.30,
no.2, p.1,22, photo.
St. Bart's revisited: Court upholds
landmark designation.
On Park Avenue, Manhattan, N.Y.
PRESERVATION LEAGUE OF NEW YORK
STATE. NEWSLETTER 1990-1991
Winter, v.16, no.3, p.[1], photos.

UNITED STATES--NEW YORK (NEW YORK)--
CHURCHES--CONSERVATION AND
RESTORATION--CHURCH OF THE HOLY
APOSTLES
New York church strives for
preservation and service [Church
of the Holy Apostles] / Jane
Gillette.
Architect: Minard Lafever, 1848.
PRESERVATION NEWS 1990 Apr., v.30,
no.4, p.8,17, photo.

UNITED STATES--NEW YORK (NEW YORK)--
CHURCHES--GOTHIC REVIVAL--
CONSERVATION AND RESTORATION--
ANNUNCIATION GREEK ORTHODOX CHURCH
Ask the Technical Preservation
Services Center: [internal
leaders].
Advice on downspouts located in
wall cavities and the prevention
of water damage in older
buildings. The example used is
the Annunciation Greek Orthodox
Church, W.91st. St., New York.
COMMON BOND 1990 Summer, v.6,
no.3, p.7-9, photos.

UNITED STATES--NEW YORK (NEW YORK)--
CITIES AND TOWNS
Aesthete in the city / David
Carrier.
ARTS MAGAZINE 1990 Apr., v.64,
no.8, p.67-73, refs.

UNITED STATES--NEW YORK (NEW YORK)--
CITIES AND TOWNS--19TH CENTURY
Manhattan manners, architecture and
style 1850-1900 [by] M. Christine
Boyer [book review] / Sergio
Stenti.
Published 1985.
STORIA DELLA CITTA 1989 Jan.-Mar.,
v.14, no.49, p.83-85, map, photos.

UNITED STATES--NEW YORK (NEW YORK)--
CITIES AND TOWNS--20TH CENTURY--
VIEWS
The skies of New York: rediscovering
John Button, metropolitan intimist
/ Hilton Kramer.
On the American painter
(1929-1982), in conjunction with a
1989 traveling exhibition.
ART & ANTIQUES 1990 Apr., v.7,
no.4, p.139-140, photo.

UNITED STATES--NEW YORK (NEW YORK)--
CITIES AND TOWNS--21ST CENTURY
Center for New York City's Future: a
different vision / Paul S. Byard.
Brief commentary on the vision
behind the newly-formed Center at
the University's architecture
school.
COLUMBIA UNIVERSITY. GRADUATE
SCHOOL OF ARCHITECTURE, PLANNING,
AND PRESERVATION. NEWSLINE 1990
Dec.-1991 Jan., v.3, no.4, p.6,
port.

UNITED STATES--NEW YORK (NEW YORK)--
CITIES AND TOWNS--ENVIRONMENTAL
ASPECTS
Hope for the city ... and some
practical advice [book review] /
Lynda Crawford.
Review of: The New York
Environment Book, by Eric A.
Goldstein and Mark A. Izeman; pub.
1990.
CITY LIMITS 1990 Oct., v.15, no.8,
p.23.

UNITED STATES--NEW YORK (NEW YORK)--
CITIES AND TOWNS--GROWTH
Future of New York as a global
center / Sigurd Grava.
COLUMBIA UNIVERSITY. GRADUATE
SCHOOL OF ARCHITECTURE, PLANNING
AND PRESERVATION. NEWSLINE 1990
Nov., v.3, no.3, p.7, ill., port.,
site plans.

UNITED STATES--NEW YORK (NEW YORK)--
CITIES AND TOWNS--VIEWS
The "New New York" and the Park Row
Building: American artists view
an icon of the modern age / Erica
E. Hirshler.
Architect: R. H. Robertson.
AMERICAN ART JOURNAL 1989, v.21,
no.4, p.26-45, ill., photo.

UNITED STATES--NEW YORK (NEW YORK)--
CITY PLANNING
Delirious New York / Rem Koolhaas.
ARCH PLUS 1990 Oct., no.105-106,
p.58-67, ill., dwgs., photos.,
plans, site plans, aerial photos.
Economic restructuring and the
politics of land use planning in
New York City / Norman I.
Fainstein, Susan S. Fainstein.
AMERICAN PLANNING ASSOCIATION.
JOURNAL 1987 Spring, v.53, no.2,
p.237-248, graphs, map, photos.,
biblio., refs.
An interview with Ron Shiffman.
Mr. Shiffman is the director of
the Pratt Center for Community and
Environmental Development at Pratt
Institute and a member of the New
York City Planning Commission.
VILLAGE VIEWS 1990, v.6, no.2,
p.5-59, port., photos.

UNITED STATES--NEW YORK (NEW YORK)--
CITY PLANNING (CONTINUED)
Parkway, beach and promenade: Robert
Moses' regional vision / Todd W.
Bressi.
Essay on the 100th anniversary of
the birth of Robert Moses.
PLACES 1990 Winter, v.6, no.2,
p.90-91, map, photo.
The planning man [Richard Schaffer]
/ Eve Heyn.
New York's first professional
planner to head the City Planning
Commission was formerly dean of
Columbia University's school of
urban planning. Also profiled are
the members of the City Planning
Commission.
CITY LIMITS 1990 Nov., v.15, no.9,
p.20-23, ports.
Post-industrial planning in New
York, Paris, and London / H. V.
Savitch.
AMERICAN PLANNING ASSOCIATION.
JOURNAL 1987 Winter, v.53, no.1,
p.80-91, maps, biblio., refs.
Regional conflict in the New York
metropolis: the legend of Robert
Moses and the power of the Port
Authority / Jameson W. Doig.
URBAN STUDIES 1990 Apr., v.27,
no.2, p.201-232, map, refs.

UNITED STATES--NEW YORK (NEW YORK)--
CITY PLANNING--BATTERY PARK CITY
Interiors platform / Sylvia Lavin.
On the "effect of the Battery Park
City Development on the Manhattan
landscape."
INTERIORS 1989 Feb., v.148, no.7,
p.16,20,22,24.
Poetry & Public Service / Ken
Johnson.
Integrating public art at Battery
Park City Plaza.
ART IN AMERICA 1990 Mar., v.78,
no.3, p.160-163,219, photos.

UNITED STATES--NEW YORK (NEW YORK)--
CITY PLANNING--BATTERY PARK CITY--
NORTH RESIDENTIAL AREA
Waterfront neighborhood.
On the North Residential Area of
Battery Park City, New York, which
will contain 3500-4000 residential
units, 3000-student high school
and 1.5 million square feet of
office space. Architects: Cooper,
Robertson & Partners.
PROGRESSIVE ARCHITECTURE 1990
Jan., v.71, no.1, p.120-121,
model, site plans, sketch.

UNITED STATES--NEW YORK (NEW YORK)--
CITY PLANNING--CITIZEN PARTICIPATION
Cities build coalitions with clout.
Citizen participation and
political activism in New York,
Birmingham, Ala., and San
Francisco.
ARCHITECTS' JOURNAL 1990 Mar.14,
v.191, no.11, p.50-57, elev.,
photos., aerial photos.

UNITED STATES--NEW YORK (NEW YORK)--
DORMITORIES--ALTERATIONS AND
ADDITIONS--UNION THEOLOGICAL
SEMINARY--HASTINGS HALL
(CONTINUED)
Special feature:...(CONTINUED)
houses, Bard College, Annandale,
N.Y. --Hastings Hall, Union
Theological Seminary, New York,
N.Y. --IBM-ISG North Central
Marketing Division headquarters,
White Plains, N.Y. --Seaman's
Church Institute, New York, N.Y.
--Yerba Buena Gardens Theater, San
Francisco, Calif. --National
Inventors Hall of Fame, Akron,
Ohio --New York University Medical
Center Biomolecular Research
building, New York, N.Y. --
Biographies of James S. Polshek,
Joseph L. Fleischer, Timothy P.
Hartung, and James G. Garrison,
p.126. Architects: James Stewart
Polshek & Partners. Text in
Japanese and English.
ARCHITECTURE AND URBANISM 1990
Nov., no.11(242), p.62-126,
axonometric views, models,
photos., plans, secns., site
plans.

UNITED STATES--NEW YORK (NEW YORK)--
DORMITORIES--BARNARD COLLEGE--
CENTENNIAL HALL
Special feature: James Polshek.
Contents: Introduction / Toshio
Nakamura --Architects' statement /
James S. Polshek and James G.
Garrison: --Works & projects:
United States Embassy, Muscat,
Oman --Centennial Hall, Barnard
College, New York, N.Y. --Alumni
houses, Bard College, Annandale,
N.Y. --Hastings Hall, Union
Theological Seminary, New York,
N.Y. --IBM-ISG North Central
Marketing Division headquarters,
White Plains, N.Y. --Seaman's
Church Institute, New York, N.Y.
--Yerba Buena Gardens Theater, San
Francisco, Calif. --National
Inventors Hall of Fame, Akron,
Ohio --New York University Medical
Center Biomolecular Research
building, New York, N.Y. --
Biographies of James S. Polshek,
Joseph L. Fleischer, Timothy P.
Hartung, and James G. Garrison,
p.126. Architects: James Stewart
Polshek & Partners. Text in
Japanese and English.
ARCHITECTURE AND URBANISM 1990
Nov., no.11(242), p.62-126,
axonometric views, models,
photos., plans, secns., site
plans.

UNITED STATES--NEW YORK (NEW YORK)--
DORMITORIES--COLUMBIA UNIVERSITY--
MORRIS A. SCHAPIRO RESIDENCE HALL
West Side study: Morris A. Schapiro
Residence Hall, Columbia
University, New York City, Gruzen
Samten Steinglass Architects /
Rosanna G. Liebman.
Principal designer: Scott Keller.
ARCHITECTURE: THE AIA JOURNAL 1990
Jan., v.79, no.1, p.[90]-91,
photos., plans.

UNITED STATES--NEW YORK (NEW YORK)--
EMPLOYEES' BUILDINGS AND
FACILITIES--INTERIOR DESIGN
Employee satisfaction.
Interiors of New York publishing
house cafeteria. Interior
designers: Kohn, Pedersen, Fox,
Conway Associates.
INTERIORS 1990 Sept., v.149,
no.14, p.114-[115], photo., plan.

UNITED STATES--NEW YORK (NEW YORK)--
ENTRANCE HALLS--CHURCH OF SAINT PAUL
THE APOSTLE
On the threshold: a tiny vestibule
designed by Leo J. Blackman makes
a smooth transition from outdoors
to indoors, and medieval to modern
/ Clifford A. Pearson.
Vestibule for St. Paul the
Apostle, in Manhattan.
ARCHITECTURAL RECORD 1990 Oct.,
v.178, no.11, p.76-[77], photos.,
plan.

UNITED STATES--NEW YORK (NEW YORK)--
EXHIBITION BUILDINGS--FINNISH
PAVILION
Finnischer Pavillon, Weltausstellung
New York 1939 / Stefan Middeler.
Architect: Alvar Aalto.
DER ARCHITEKT 1990 Dec., no.12,
p.581, dwg., refs.
Paisajes arquitectonicos: seis
maestros, seis imagenes / Ezra
Stoller.
Six landmark buildings by
Corbusier, Alvar Aalto, F.L.
Wright, Mies, Gordon Bunshaft, and
Richard Meier.
ARQUITECTURA VIVA 1990 May-June,
no.12, p.36-39, photos.

UNITED STATES--NEW YORK (NEW YORK)--
FACADES--CONSERVATION AND
RESTORATION--BLEECKER COURT
Avinash K. Malhotra, New York.
Three projects: Bleecker Court,
New York (1981); International
Plaza, New York (1984); and The
Archive, New York (1989); original
architect: Willoughby J. Edbrooke.
Developer: Rockrose Development
Corp.
ARCHITECTURE + DESIGN 1990
Jan.-Feb., v.7, no.1, p.24-31,
dwgs., photos., plans, secns.

UNITED STATES--NEW YORK (NEW YORK)--
FLORIST SHOPS--INTERIOR DESIGN--
BROADWAY FLORAL EXCHANGE
Broadway Floral: Theo David's Shop
in the Financial District / Edie
Lee Cohen.
Interiors of renovated New York
florist shop. Architect: Theo.
David & Associates.
INTERIOR DESIGN 1990 Sept., v.61,
no.12, p.200-[201], axonometric
view, photos., isometric dwg.

UNITED STATES--NEW YORK (NEW YORK)--
GARDENS--CHINESE--ASTOR COURT
Ein Garten als Museumsobjekt:
Probleme und Gedanken am Beispiel
eines chinesischen Gartens im
Metropolitan Museum of Art in New
York / Norbert Schindler.
GARTEN UND LANDSCHAFT 1990, v.100,
no.4, p.4-6, photos.

UNITED STATES--NEW YORK (NEW YORK)--
GAZEBOS--BATTERY PARK CITY--
NORTHPARK PAVILION
North Park Pavilion en Battery Park
City New York = North Park
Pavilion in Battery Park City New
York / Demetri Porphyrios.
Architect: Demetri Porphyrios.
COMPOSICION ARQUITECTONICA, ART &
ARCHITECTURE 1990 June, no.6,
p.[61]-70, dwg., elevs., plan,
secn., site plan, sketches, aerial
photo.

UNITED STATES--NEW YORK (NEW YORK)--
GENTRIFICATION--HARLEM
Harlem: a new renaissance? / Mark W.
Griffith, Errol T. Louis.
CITY LIMITS 1990 Oct., v.15, no.8,
p.16-19, port., photos.

UNITED STATES--NEW YORK (NEW YORK)--
HEALTH CLUBS--PLUS ONE FITNESS
CLINIC
Plus One: an exercise/health care
center in downtown New York /
Monica Geran.
Architect/interior designer: James
Biber.
INTERIOR DESIGN 1990 Mar., v.61,
no.5, p.206-[209], photos., plans.

UNITED STATES--NEW YORK (NEW YORK)--
HISTORIC DISTRICTS--LONGWOOD
HISTORIC DISTRICT
An interview with Thom Bess.
Mr. Bess represents the Longwood
Historic District in the Bronx.
VILLAGE VIEWS 1990, v.6, no.1,
p.[50]-63, port., photos.

UNITED STATES--NEW YORK (NEW YORK)--
HISTORIC HOUSE MUSEUMS--MORRIS-JUMEL
MANSION
Renewed life for colonial Manhattan
landmark [Morris-Jumel Mansion].
Located on W.160th St., east of
St. Nicholas Avenue. Built in
1765, opened as a museum in 1904,
and under restoration since
Sept.1990. Restoration team
supervisor: Don DeFillo. Project
architect: Jan Hird Pokorny.
Supervising architect: Blumberg &
Butter.
PRESERVATION LEAGUE OF NEW YORK
STATE. NEWSLETTER 1990-1991
Winter, v.16, no.3, p.4-5,
photos., plan.

UNITED STATES--NEW YORK (NEW YORK)--
HISTORIC PRESERVATION
The Historic City Report: ignoring
the lessons of history / Anthony
Max Tung.
Includes text of the report "New
York: The Historic City", prepared
by The NYC Landmarks Preservation
Commission, Feb.6,1989.
VILLAGE VIEWS 1989, v.5, no.4,
p.2-55, chart., graphs, port.

UNITED STATES--NEW YORK (NEW YORK)--
HISTORIC PRESERVATION--HARLEM
An interview with Horace Carter.
An interview with the head of the
Emanuel Pieterson Historical
Society about preservation efforts
in Harlem.
VILLAGE VIEWS 1990, v.6, no.1,
p.[24]-49, port., photos.

UNITED STATES--NEW YORK (NEW YORK)--
HISTORIC PRESERVATION--HISTORY
25 years of landmarking New York
City / Jacqueline Rivkin.
On the Landmarks Preservation
Commission.
METROPOLIS 1990 May, v.9, no.9,
p.28-31, ill., photo.

UNITED STATES--NEW YORK (NEW YORK)--
HOME OWNERSHIP
Built to last? / Jeffrey Hoff.
Suburban-style housing in New
York.
CITY LIMITS 1990 Aug.-Sept., v.15,
no.7, p.9-10, port.

UNITED STATES--NEW YORK (NEW YORK)--
HOMELESSNESS
Exhibition review: Street
performance; The Homeless Vehicle
Project / Graham Shane.
A rollable cart designed by
Krzystof Wodiczko and Rudolph
Luria.
JOURNAL OF ARCHITECTURAL EDUCATION
1990 summer, v.43, no.4, p.37-42,
elevs., models, photos., plans.
Teatro di strada: progetto di
veicolo per senzatetto = street
performance: the homeless vehicle
project / Grahame Shane.
Text in English and Italian.
SPAZIO E SOCIETA 1990 Oct.-Dec.,
v.13, no.52, p.46-53, dwgs.,
models, photos.

UNITED STATES--NEW YORK (NEW YORK)--
HOMELESSNESS--MATHEMATICAL MODELS
"Homelessness," contagious
destruction of housing, and
municipal service cuts in New York
City: 2, dynamics of a housing
famine / R. Wallace.
ENVIRONMENT AND PLANNING A 1990
Jan., v.22, no.1, p.5-15, graphs,
refs.

UNITED STATES--NEW YORK (NEW YORK)--
HOSPITALS--INTERIOR DESIGN--NEW YORK
UNIVERSITY MEDICAL CENTER
NYU Medical Center / Monica Geran.
Features one of the twenty luxury
suites designed by Charles P.
Swerz Interior Design.
INTERIOR DESIGN 1990 Nov., v.61,
no.15, p.188-[189], photos., plan.

UNITED STATES--NEW YORK (NEW YORK)--
HOSTELS--NEW YORK INTERNATIONAL
AYH-HOSTEL
New York gets hostel / Michele
Herman.
The New York International
AYH-Hostel, at 891 Amsterdam Ave.
between 103rd and 104th Sts., is
in a renovated Richard Morris Hunt
building (1883). Architects for
the renovation: Larsen Associates.
METROPOLIS 1990 May, v.9, no.9,
p.27-28, photos.

UNITED STATES--NEW YORK (NEW YORK)--
HOTELS--ALTERATIONS AND ADDITIONS--
ROYALTON HOTEL
Royalton Hotel, New York / Birgit
Dietsch.
Renovations to hotel on West 44th
St. Architect: Philippe Starck.
BAUWELT 1990 Mar.30, v.81, no.12,
p.530-531, photos., plans.

UNITED STATES--NEW YORK (NEW YORK)--
HOTELS--EMBASSY SUITES
Embassy Suites Times Square.
New York 460-room hotel built
around a landmarked theater
interior. Architects: Fox & Fowle
Architects.
PROGRESSIVE ARCHITECTURE 1990
Jan., v.71, no.1, p.102-103,
axonometric view, elevs., plans,
site plan.
When there's no place to go but up /
James S. Russell.
On collaboration between
architects and engineers to build
over, around, and through existing
buildings. Features 3 recent
projects: Presbyterian-University
Hospital, Pittsburgh; 1675
Broadway, New York City; and
Embassy Suites, New York City.
ARCHITECTURAL RECORD 1990 Sept.,
v.178, no.10, p.160-163, models,
photos., plans, secn., isometric
dwgs.

UNITED STATES--NEW YORK (NEW YORK)--
HOTELS--INTERIOR DESIGN
Dinner at the Inn / Regina S.
Baraban.
A review of 3 new hotel
restaurants in Manhattan.
METROPOLIS 1990 Nov., v.10, no.4,
p.25, photos.

UNITED STATES--NEW YORK (NEW YORK)--
HOTELS--INTERIOR DESIGN--MORGANS
Far-out inns / Regina S. Baraban.
Ian Schrager's new Manhattan
hotels for hip travellers.
METROPOLIS 1990 Nov., v.10, no.4,
p.48-[53], photos., model.
A new age of less is more / Layla
Dawson.
Features two hotel interiors
designed by Andree Putman: Hotel
in Wasserturm, Cologne and Morgans
Hotel, New York.
BUILDING DESIGN 1990 Apr.20,
no.982, p.34-37, dwgs., photos.

UNITED STATES--NEW YORK (NEW YORK)--
HOTELS--INTERIOR DESIGN--PARAMOUNT
HOTEL
Far-out inns / Regina S. Baraban.
Ian Schrager's new Manhattan
hotels for hip travellers.
METROPOLIS 1990 Nov., v.10, no.4,
p.48-[53], photos., model.
For Ian Schrager, design is
paramount / Fred A. Bernstein.
Renovation and interior design of
Paramount Hotel, at Eight Ave. and
46th St., New York by Schrager and
Philippe Starck.
METROPOLITAN HOME 1990 Nov., v.22,
no.11, p.63-[70],164, port.,
photos.
Paramount / Edie Lee Cohen.
Interiors of the new York hotel
designed by Philippe Starck.
INTERIOR DESIGN 1990 Dec., v.61,
no.16, p.142 [147], photos.,
plans.
Paramount Hotel.
Features interiors of New York
hotel designed by Philippe Starck.
Includes interview with hotel
owner, Ian Schrager. English
summary, p.215.
ARCHITECTURE INTERIEURE CREE 1990
Oct.-Nov., no.239, p.146-151,
photos.

UNITED STATES--NEW YORK (NEW YORK)--
HOTELS--INTERIOR DESIGN--ROYALTON
Far-out inns / Regina S. Baraban.
Ian Schrager's new Manhattan
hotels for hip travellers.
METROPOLIS 1990 Nov., v.10, no.4,
p.48-[53], photos., model.

UNITED STATES--NEW YORK (NEW YORK)--
HOTELS--RIGHA ROYAL HOTEL
Designing the super-thin new
buildings / James S. Russell.
Features 6 projects for tall
buildings in New York City,
Chicago and Paris.
ARCHITECTURAL RECORD 1990 Oct.,
v.178, no.11, p.105-109,
axonometric views, elev., models,
photos., plans.

UNITED STATES--NEW YORK (NEW YORK)--
HOUSES--19TH CENTURY--MAITLAND
ARMSTRONG HOUSE (58 WEST 10TH
STREET)
Maitland Armstrong's historic house
burns / Robert O. Jones.
Home of stained glass artist
(1836-1918) at 58 W. 10th St., New
York City burned Jan.3, 1989. The
house is being remodeled as
offices for NYU.
STAINED GLASS QUARTERLY 1989
Spring, v.84, no.1, p.42, photo.

UNITED STATES--NEW YORK (NEW YORK)--
HOUSES--OFFICIAL RESIDENCES--
CONSERVATION AND RESTORATION--GRACIE
MANSION
Gracie Mansion / Chippy Irvine.
On a five-year renovation to the
1799 mansion, home of New York's
mayor. Probable architect: Ezra
Weeks.
ART & ANTIQUES 1990 Jan., v.7,
no.1, p.82-87, photos., engr.

UNITED STATES--NEW YORK (NEW YORK)--
HOUSING--ARVERNE
Taming the city edge: urban design
portfolio / Andrea Oppenheimer
Dean.
The latest frontier--"outcities."
Mission Bay, San Francisco;
Downtown Norfolk, Va; Carr Norfolk
Southern Project, Alexandria, Va.;
and Arverne, New York City.
ARCHITECTURE: THE AIA JOURNAL 1990
Apr., v.79, no.4, p.[74]-79,147,
ill., model, plans, sketches,
aerial photos.

UNITED STATES--NEW YORK (NEW YORK)--
HOUSING DEVELOPMENTS--ROOSEVELT
ISLAND--SOUTHTOWN
Roosevelt Island's urban planning
lab / Jeffrey Hoff.
Southtown, a 1,956-unit 19-acre
mixed-income housing development.
Orig. architects of masterplan
(1969): Philip Johnson and John
Burgee. Additional architects:
Raquel Ramati Associates, Davis,
Brody & Associates.
METROPOLIS 1990 Jan.-Feb., v.9,
no.6, p.14-16, dwg.

UNITED STATES--NEW YORK (NEW YORK)--
HOUSING--EXHIBITIONS
Home New York home / Donald
Albrecht.
On "Home, a Place in the World," a
series of workshops, film programs
and exhibitions held in New York
City.
ARCHITECTURE: THE AIA JOURNAL 1990
Dec., v.79, no.12, p.24,26,
elevs., photos.

UNITED STATES--NEW YORK (NEW YORK)--
HOUSING FOR ELDERLY
No place like home / Marguerite
Holloway.
Residences known as "adult homes"
are a growing repository for the
homeless in New York City.
CITY LIMITS 1990 Mar., v.15, no.3,
p.10-13, ports., photos.

UNITED STATES--NEW YORK (NEW YORK)--
HOUSING FOR HANDICAPPED
No place like home / Marguerite
Holloway.
Residences known as "adult homes"
are a growing repository for the
homeless in New York City.
CITY LIMITS 1990 Mar., v.15, no.3,
p.10-13, ports., photos.

UNITED STATES--NEW YORK (NEW YORK)--
HOUSING FOR HOMELESS
Housing the homeless: high quality
apartments for the desiring few /
Lisa Glaser.
In New York City.
CITY LIMITS 1990 Oct., v.15, no.8,
p.20-21, photo.
Making a house a home / Jeffrey
Hoff.
Projects by architects to provide
"real homes" for the homeless in
NYC.
METROPOLIS 1990 Sept., v.10, no.2,
p.46-[51],79-81, elev., model,
photos., plans.
Mixed blessings: life after the
welfare hotels / Lisa Glazer.
New York City.
CITY LIMITS 1990 Feb., v.15, no.2,
p.8-13, ports., photos.
No place like home / Marguerite
Holloway.
Residences known as "adult homes"
are a growing repository for the
homeless in New York City.
CITY LIMITS 1990 Mar., v.15, no.3,
p.10-13, ports., photos.

UNITED STATES--NEW YORK (NEW YORK)--
HOUSING FOR HOMELESS--HOMELESS
VEHICLE PROJECT
Exhibition review: Street
performance; The Homeless Vehicle
Project / Graham Shane.
A rollable cart designed by
Krzystof Wodiczko and Rudolph
Luria.
JOURNAL OF ARCHITECTURAL EDUCATION
1990 summer, v.43, no.4, p.37-42,
elevs., models, photos., plans.
Teatro di strada: progetto di
veicolo per senzatetto = street
performance: the homeless vehicle
project / Grahame Shane.
Text in English and Italian.
SPAZIO E SOCIETA 1990 Oct.-Dec.,
v.13, no.52, p.46-53, dwgs.,
models, photos.

UNITED STATES--NEW YORK (NEW YORK)--
HOUSING--LOW-RISE
Context is everything / Sandy
Hornick.
Amendments to New York City's
zoning resolution allows for
increased lower density areas for
low-rise neighborhood housing.
PLANNING 1990 Dec., v.56, no.12,
p.22-26, diagrs., dwg., photo.,
secn.

UNITED STATES--NEW YORK (NEW YORK)--
HOUSING POLICY
Housing New York: a coalition
platform.
Proposal written and adopted by an
ad hoc coalition of more than 50
neighborhood housing groups and
individuals in New York City;
presented to the transition team
of Mayor David Dinkins, it
addresses the severe housing
crisis in the city.
CITY LIMITS 1990 Jan., v.15, no.1,
p.22-24.
Mixed blessings: life after the
welfare hotels / Lisa Glazer.
New York City.
CITY LIMITS 1990 Feb., v.15, no.2,
p.8-13, ports., photos.
On the record: housing commissioner
Felice Michetti [interview].
Includes a glossary of housing
terms used by the N.Y.C. Dept. of
Housing Preservation and
Development.
CITY LIMITS 1990 Oct., v.15, no.8,
p.8-11, port.
Resource recovery? [New York
City-owned buildings] / Lisa
Glazer.
Policy to maintain and repair
city-owned buildings implemented
by the Division of Property
Management.
CITY LIMITS 1990 Mar., v.15, no.3,
p.17-20, graph, port.

UNITED STATES--NEW YORK (NEW YORK)--
HOUSING PROJECTS--CLINTON
Mid-Manhattan Urban Renewal.
On the Clinton Community master
plan. Architects: Peterson,
Littenberg Architects.
PROGRESSIVE ARCHITECTURE 1990
Jan., v.71, no.1, p.110-112,
axonometric views, dwg., maps.

UNITED STATES--NEW YORK (NEW YORK)--
HOUSING--PUBLIC--MAINTENANCE AND
REPAIR
Resource recovery? [New York
City-owned buildings] / Lisa
Glazer.
Policy to maintain and repair
city-owned buildings implemented
by the Division of Property
Management.
CITY LIMITS 1990 Mar., v.15, no.3,
p.17-20, graph, port.

UNITED STATES--NEW YORK (NEW YORK)--
IMMIGRATION STATIONS--CONSERVATION
AND RESTORATION--ELLIS ISLAND
Celebrating an island artifact ...
Ellis Island / Cynthia Owen
Philip.
On the recent renovation of the
Main Building for use as a museum
of immigration.
ARCHAEOLOGY 1990 Sept.-Oct., v.43,
(Continued next column)

UNITED STATES--NEW YORK (NEW YORK)--
IMMIGRATION STATIONS--CONSERVATION
AND RESTORATION--ELLIS ISLAND)
(CONTINUED)
Celebrating an island...(CONTINUED)
no.5, p.[44]-51, dwgs., photos.,
site plan.
Coming home: Ellis Island, the
museum / Barbara Flanagan.
Architects: Beyer Blinder Belle
and Notter Finegold + Alexander.
METROPOLITAN HOME 1990 Aug., v.22,
no.8, p.82,84,86, photos.
Ellis Island, 1980s shrine / John
Morris Dixon.
Original architects: Boring &
Tilton. Restoration architects:
Beyer Blinder Belle, Architects
and Planners, Notter Finegold &
Alexander.
PROGRESSIVE ARCHITECTURE 1990
Nov., v.71, no.12, p.23-24,
photos.
Ellis Island - das nationale
Einwanderermuseum der USA.
Architects for the restoration:
Beyer, Blinder, Belle; Notter,
Finegold and Alexander.
BAUWELT 1990 Nov.23, v.81, no.44,
p.2190-2191, photos.
Ellis Island reopens as museum /
Jane Holtz Kay.
Architects: Beyer Blinder Belle.
ARCHITECTURE: THE AIA JOURNAL 1990
Nov., v.79, no.11, p.21-24,
photos.
Our threshold of liberty [Ellis
Island].
The renovated immigration facility
will reopen to visitors in fall of
1990.
COLONIAL HOMES 1990 June, v.16,
no.3, p.[34-40]., photos.
Reopening America's gates [Ellis
Island] / Clifford A. Pearson.
Ellis Island Immigration Center
has been renovated by Beyer
Blinder Belle and Notter Finegold
+ Alexander.
ARCHITECTURAL RECORD 1990 July,
v.178, no.8, p.[46]-57, dets.,
photos., plans, secns.

UNITED STATES--NEW YORK (NEW YORK)--
KITCHENS
The urban kitchen / Victoria Geibel.
Some NYC kitchens. Architects:
David Spiker, Michael Wolfe, James
Hong, David Estreich, Warren
James.
METROPOLIS 1990 Apr., v.9, no.8,
p.52-57, photos.

UNITED STATES--NEW YORK (NEW YORK)--
LABORATORIES--MEDICAL--NEW YORK
UNIVERSITY MEDICAL CENTER
Special feature: James Polshek.
Contents: Introduction / Toshio
Nakamura --Architects' statement /
James S. Polshek and James G.
Garrison: --Works & projects:
United States Embassy, Muscat,
Oman --Centennial Hall, Barnard
College, New York, N.Y. --Alumni
houses, Bard College, Annandale,
N.Y. --Hastings Hall, Union
Theological Seminary, New York,
N.Y. --IBM-ISG North Central
Marketing Division headquarters,
White Plains, N.Y. --Seaman's
Church Institute, New York, N.Y.
--Yerba Buena Gardens Theater, San
(Continued next page)

UNITED STATES--NEW YORK (NEW YORK)--
LABORATORIES--MEDICAL--NEW YORK
UNIVERSITY MEDICAL CENTER
(CONTINUED)
Special feature:...(CONTINUED)
Francisco, Calif. --National
Inventors Hall of Fame, Akron,
Ohio --New York University Medical
Center Biomolecular Research
building, New York, N.Y. --
Biographies of James S. Polshek,
Joseph L. Fleischer, Timothy P.
Hartung, and James G. Garrison,
p.126. Architects: James Stewart
Polshek & Partners. Text in
Japanese and English.
ARCHITECTURE AND URBANISM 1990
Nov., no.11(242), p.62-126,
axonometric views, models,
photos., plans, secns., site
plans.

UNITED STATES--NEW YORK (NEW YORK)--
LAND ART--EXCAVATION I
Arte como arquitectura como ciudad =
Art-as-architecture-as-town /
Sandro Marpillero.
Art and architecture as civic
design in the U.S. Three projects
illustrated: Plaza Park, San Jose,
Calif.; projects by Eric Ungers,
and Marina Linear Park, San
Diego. In Spanish and English.
ARQUITECTURA 1990 July-Aug., v.72,
no.285, p.126-137, elevs., models,
photos., plans, secns., site
plans.

UNITED STATES--NEW YORK (NEW YORK)--
LAND USE
Economic restructuring and the
politics of land use planning in
New York City / Norman I.
Fainstein, Susan S. Fainstein.
AMERICAN PLANNING ASSOCIATION.
JOURNAL 1987 Spring, v.53, no.2,
p.237-248, graphs, map, photos.,
biblio., refs.

UNITED STATES--NEW YORK (NEW YORK)--
LAND USE--LAW AND LEGISLATION
A user's guide to Charter process /
Todd W. Bressi.
Effects of the proposed revision
to the City Charter on land use in
New York.
CITY LIMITS 1990 Feb., v.15, no.2,
p.18-19.

UNITED STATES--NEW YORK (NEW YORK)--
LANDMARK BUILDINGS
The Historic City Report: ignoring
the lessons of history / Anthony
Max Tung.
Includes text of the report "New
York: The Historic City", prepared
by The NYC Landmarks Preservation
Commission, Feb.6,1989.
VILLAGE VIEWS 1989, v.5, no.4,
p.2-55, chart, graphs, port.

UNITED STATES--NEW YORK (NEW YORK)--
LANDMARK BUILDINGS--19TH CENTURY--
ALTERATIONS AND ADDITIONS--NEW YORK
CANCER HOSPITAL (2 WEST 106TH STREET
AND CENTRAL PARK WEST)
The rise of Manhattan Valley /
Andrew White.
A landmark building, the New York
Cancer Hospital, at 2 W. 106 St.&
Central Park W., built by John J.
Astor in 1884, will be converted
(Continued next column)

UNITED STATES--NEW YORK (NEW YORK)--
LANDMARK BUILDINGS--19TH CENTURY--
ALTERATIONS AND ADDITIONS--NEW YORK
CANCER HOSPITAL (2 WEST 106TH STREET
AND CENTRAL PARK WEST) (CONTINUED)
The rise of Manhattan...(CONTINUED)
to luxury housing with the
addition of a 27-story tower.
Original architect: Charles
Haight. Tower architect: Victor
Caliandro.
METROPOLIS 1990 Jan.-Feb., v.9,
no.6, p.16-18, photo.

UNITED STATES--NEW YORK (NEW YORK)--
LANDMARK BUILDINGS--CONSERVATION AND
RESTORATION--ECONOMIC ASPECTS
Enhancing the value of vintage
buildings / Brian Marlowe.
Examples of older commercial
buildings in New York.
REAL ESTATE FORUM 1990 Oct., v.45,
no.10, p.182-183, photos.

UNITED STATES--NEW YORK (NEW YORK)--
LANDMARK BUILDINGS--CONSERVATION AND
RESTORATION--HARLEM--HAMILTON
HEIGHTS
Harlem heritage: some of Manhattan's
finest landmarks stand on the
island's historic heights / Paul
M. Sachner.
HOUSE & GARDEN 1990 Oct., v.162,
no.10, p.118,[120], port., photos.

UNITED STATES--NEW YORK (NEW YORK)--
LANDMARK BUILDINGS--GREENWICH
VILLAGE
An interview with Ron Shiffman.
Mr. Shiffman is the director of
the Pratt Center for Community and
Environmental Development at Pratt
Institute and a member of the New
York City Planning Commission.
VILLAGE VIEWS 1990, v.6, no.2,
p.5-59, port., photos.

UNITED STATES--NEW YORK (NEW YORK)--
LANDMARK BUILDINGS--HARLEM
An interview with Horace Carter.
An interview with the head of the
Emanuel Pieterson Historical
Society about preservation efforts
in Harlem.
VILLAGE VIEWS 1990, v.6, no.1,
p.[24]-49, port., photos.

UNITED STATES--NEW YORK (NEW YORK)--
LANDMARK BUILDINGS--LAW AND
LEGISLATION--SAINT BARTHOLOMEW'S
CHURCH
Court denies St. Bart's plea: St.
Bartholomew's Church, New York /
Amy Worden.
PRESERVATION NEWS 1990 Feb., v.30,
no.2, p.1,22, photo.
St. Bart's revisited: Court upholds
landmark designation.
On Park Avenue, Manhattan, N.Y.
PRESERVATION LEAGUE OF NEW YORK
STATE. NEWSLETTER 1990-1991
Winter, v.16, no.3, p.[1], photos.

UNITED STATES--NEW YORK (NEW YORK)--
LANDMARK BUILDNGS--POLITICAL
ASPECTS
An interview with Reverend Timothy
Mitchell.
On his efforts to preserve the
Latimer House, in Flushing,
Queens, home of African-American
inventor Lewis Latimer.
VILLAGE VIEWS 1990, v.6, no.1,
p.[4]-23, port., photos.

UNITED STATES--NEW YORK (NEW YORK)--
LAW OFFICES--INTERIOR DESIGN--
MILGRIM, THOMAJAN & LEE
Legal renaissance / Amy Dana.
Features interiors of Wall Street
Law firm, Milgrim, Thomajan & Lee.
Interior designers: Kohn,
Pedersen, Fox, Conway Associates.
INTERIORS 1990 Sept., v.149,
no.14, p.116-[117], photos., plan.

UNITED STATES--NEW YORK (NEW YORK)--
LAW OFFICES--INTERIOR DESIGN--
SIMPSON THACHER & BARTLETT
Legal ease / Amy Dana.
Interiors of the New York City
headquarters of the law firm
Simpson, Thacher & Bartlett.
Interior designers: Rosen Perry
Preston.
INTERIORS 1990 Mar., v.149, no.8,
p.110-[115], photos., plan.

UNITED STATES--NEW YORK (NEW YORK)--
LIBRARIES--LAW--NEW YORK
UNIVERSITY--LAW SCHOOL LIBRARY
Places to learn: New York University
Law School, Washington Square,
West Third Street, New York, New
York.
Contents: Mercer Residence Hall --
D'Agostino Hall -- Law Library.
Architects: Benjamin Thompson &
Associates. Text in Japanese and
English.
PROCESS: ARCHITECTURE 1990 June,
no.89, p.80-83, photos., secn.,
site plan.

UNITED STATES--NEW YORK (NEW YORK)--
LIBRARIES--PUBLIC
Library reading / Mary Pat Akers.
Carnegie-funded public libraries
in NYC.
METROPOLIS 1990 Sept., v.10, no.2,
p.86-93, photos.

UNITED STATES--NEW YORK (NEW YORK)--
LOBBIES
Back in the public domain / Kriti
Siderakis.
New York City lobbies.
METROPOLIS 1990 Oct., v.10, no.3,
p.[68-73],87, dwg., photos.

UNITED STATES--NEW YORK (NEW YORK)--
LOBBIES--INTERIOR DESIGN--UNION BANK
OF SWITZERLAND
Union Bank of Switzerland / Monica
Geran.
Interiors of lobby level of
private New York bank. Interior
designers: Gensler and Associates,
Architects.
INTERIOR DESIGN 1990 Feb., v.61,
no.3, p.172-[177], photos., plan.

UNITED STATES--NEW YORK (NEW YORK)--
MERRY-GO ROUNDS
Roundabout [New York City carousels]
/ Lisa English.
METROPOLIS 1990 July-Aug., v.10,
no.1, p.[56-61],69, photos.

UNITED STATES--NEW YORK (NEW YORK)--
MODEL APARTMENTS--INTERIOR DESIGN
Tropics in the city / Karen
Maserjian.
Interiors of model apartment in
New York. Interior designer:
Thomas Britt.
INTERIOR DESIGN 1990 Oct., v.61,
no.14, p.[218-223], photos., plan.

UNITED STATES--NEW YORK (NEW YORK)--
MODEL APARTMENTS--INTERIOR DESIGN--
EAST 65TH STREET
Runaway model / Mayer Rus.
Interiors of model apartments on
East 65th Street, New York.
Interior designers: Robert
Metzger, Michael Christiano.
INTERIOR DESIGN 1990 Jan., v.61,
no.1, p.166-[167], photos.

UNITED STATES--NEW YORK (NEW YORK)--
MODEL APARTMENTS--POLICE BUILDING
Next year's model / Mark Alden
Branch.
Features model apartment in the
Police Building, which once housed
the New York Police Department.
Architects: Smith-Miller +
Hawkinson Architects.
PROGRESSIVE ARCHITECTURE 1990
Sept., v.71, no.9, p.128-129,
photos., plan.

UNITED STATES--NEW YORK (NEW YORK)--
MODEL HOUSES--UNDERGROUND--
UNDERGROUND HOUSE
Il domestico in guerra = Domesticity
at war / Beatriz Colomina.
Discusses the 1964-1965 New York
World's Fair, the Underground Home
and other exhibits, Michael Webb's
Slow House, and Donna Robertson's
Room in the City. In Italian and
English.
OTTAGONO 1990 Dec., no.97,
p.24-[49], ill., dwgs., models,
photos., plans, secn., refs.

UNITED STATES--NEW YORK (NEW YORK)--
MONUMENTS AND MEMORIALS
Architectural history and urban
history: a difficult marriage
[book review] / Joseph L. Arnold.
Review essay of Charleston:
antebellum architecture and civic
destiny, by Kenneth Severens; and
Public sculpture and the civic
ideal in New York City, 1890-1930,
by Michele Bogart.
JOURNAL OF URBAN HISTORY 1990
Nov., v.17, no.1, p.70-78, refs.
Public sculpture and the civic ideal
in New York City [b] Michele H.
Bogart [book review] / Eric J.
Sandeen.
WINTERTHUR PORTFOLIO 1990 Autumn,
v.25, no.2-3, p.209-212, refs.

UNITED STATES--NEW YORK (NEW YORK)--
MULTI-USE BUILDINGS--CITYSPIRE
Designing the super-thin new
buildings / James S. Russell.
Features 6 projects for tall
buildings in New York City,
Chicago and Paris.
ARCHITECTURAL RECORD 1990 Oct.,
v.178, no.11, p.105-109,
axonometric views, elev., models,
photos., plans.

UNITED STATES--NEW YORK (NEW YORK)--
MULTI-USE COMPLEXES--BATTERY PARK
CITY
Battery Park City's brave new world
/ Paul Goldberger.
Master plan: Cooper Eckstut
Associates.
ARCHITECTURAL DIGEST 1990 Nov.,
v.47, no.12, p.144,146,148, maps,
photos.

UNITED STATES--NEW YORK (NEW YORK)--
MULTI-USE COMPLEXES--MADISON SQUARE
GARDEN SITE
Madison Square Garden Site
Redevelopment.
Architect: Thomas Phifer, Richard
Meier & Partners.
OZ / COLLEGE OF ARCHITECTURE AND
DESIGN, KANSAS STATE UNIVERSITY
1989, v.11, p.40-41, models,
plans.

UNITED STATES--NEW YORK (NEW YORK)--
MULTI-USE COMPLEXES--MANHATTAN WEST
Wild, riled West / Tom McGhee.
Manhattan West, a mixed-use
development, was approved in Feb.
by the NYC Board of Estimate.
Architects: Buck/Cane, with
Schuman Lichtenstein Claman &
Efron.
METROPOLIS 1990 Sept., v.10, no.2,
p.22-25,

UNITED STATES--NEW YORK (NEW YORK)--
MULTI-USE COMPLEXES--RIVERSIDE SOUTH
Dumping Trump City: the sequel /
Craig Whitaker.
Two alternate schemes for the Penn
Yards site are presented, the
Willen/Gutman proposal and the
Riedner/Wasserman proposal.
OCULUS 1990 Oct., v.53, no.2,
p.6-11, dwgs., ports., elevs.,
models, site plans.

UNITED STATES--NEW YORK (NEW YORK)--
MULTI-USE COMPLEXES--TRUMP CITY
Dumping Trump City: the sequel /
Craig Whitaker.
Two alternate schemes for the Penn
Yards site are presented, the
Willen/Gutman proposal and the
Riedner/Wasserman proposal.
OCULUS 1990 Oct., v.53, no.2,
p.6-11, dwgs., ports., elevs.,
models, site plans.
Trump redux / Bret Senft.
A discussion of the present status
of Donald Trump's proposed
development on Manhattan's west
side.
METROPOLIS 1990 Nov., v.10, no.4,
p.17-18, aerial photo.

UNITED STATES--NEW YORK (NEW YORK)--
MULTI-USE COMPLEXES--WORLDWIDE PLAZA
Urban civility: Worldwide Plaza, New
York City, New York / Andrea
Oppenheimer Dean.
Architects: SOM/New York; Frank
Williams & Associates.
ARCHITECTURE: THE AIA JOURNAL 1990
Apr., v.79, no.4, p.[84-89],
photos., site plans, aerial photo.

UNITED STATES--NEW YORK (NEW YORK)--
MUNICIPAL BUILDINGS--BEAUX-ARTS--
CONSERVATION AND RESTORATION--
MUNICIPAL BUILDING
Restoration the old-fashioned way /
James S. Russell.
Stone repairs of the 1914 New York
Municipal Building, designed by
McKim Mead & White. Restoration
architects: Wank Adams Slavin
Associates.
ARCHITECTURAL RECORD 1990 Mar.,
v.178, no.3, p.124-127, dets.,
photos., secn.

UNITED STATES--NEW YORK (NEW YORK)--
MUNICIPAL BUILDINGS--CONSERVATION
AND RESTORATION--MUNICIPAL BUILDING
Linking preservation to
architectural design [Wank Adams
Slavin Associates] / Clem Labine.
Their Preservation Department's
projects include Fallingwater and
the New York Municipal Building.
CLEM LABINE'S TRADITIONAL BUILDING
1990 Mar.-Apr., v.3, no.2,
p.5.24-25, ports., photos.

UNITED STATES--NEW YORK (NEW YORK)--
MUSEUM OF MODERN ART--MUSEUMS--ART
"Arte della macchina" e "oggetti
utili" tra MoMA e Metropolitan =
"Machine Art" and "useful objects"
from MoMA to the Metropolitan /
Patricia Phillips.
OTTAGONO 1990 June, no.95,
p.105-[117], photos., refs.

UNITED STATES--NEW YORK (NEW YORK)--
MUSEUMS--ART--ALTERATIONS AND
ADDITIONS--SOLOMON R. GUGGENHEIM
MUSEUM
Commentary: adding to icons / Ross
Miller.
On the controversy surrounding the
additions to the Whitney,
Guggenheim and Kimbell Museums.
PROGRESSIVE ARCHITECTURE 1990
June, v.71, no.6, p.124-125,
axonometric view, elev., models.
Renewing our modern legacy / Andrea
Oppenheimer Dean.
Four additions to buildings of the
1950s and 1960s.
ARCHITECTURE: THE AIA JOURNAL 1990
Nov., v.79, no.11, p.66-69, ill.,
elevs., models, photos.

UNITED STATES--NEW YORK (NEW YORK)--
MUSEUMS--ART--ALTERATIONS AND
ADDITIONS--STUDENT PROJECTS--SOLOMON
R. GUGGENHEIM MUSEUM
Erweiterung des Solomon Guggenheim
Museums New York: Diplomarbeit van
Alexa Hartig.
Student project from TH Darmstadt.
DEUTSCHE BAUZEITUNG 1990 Jan.,
v.124, no.1, p.112-113, model,
plans, secns.

UNITED STATES--NEW YORK (NEW YORK)--
MUSEUMS--ART--ALTERATIONS AND
ADDITIONS--WHITNEY MUSEUM OF
AMERICAN ART
Commentary: adding to icons / Ross
    Miller.
    On the controversy surrounding the
    additions to the Whitney,
    Guggenheim and Kimbell Museums.
    PROGRESSIVE ARCHITECTURE 1990
    June, v.71, no.6, p.124-125,
    axonometric view, elev., models.

UNITED STATES--NEW YORK (NEW YORK)--
MUSEUMS--ART--LIGHTING--SOLOMON R.
GUGGENHEIM MUSEUM
Lighting Wright: how the new
    Guggenheim Museum galleries will
    be illuminated / Peter Barna,
    Justin Henderson.
    ARCHITECTURE: THE AIA JOURNAL 1990
    Mar., v.79, no.3, p.191-195,
    elev., models, photos., plans,
    secn.

UNITED STATES--NEW YORK (NEW YORK)--
MUSEUMS--ART--MUSEUM OF MODERN ART
Symposium: architecture on exhibit.
    Seven architectural curators
    respond to questions about
    exhibiting architecture at their
    institutions; Mildred Friedman,
    Walker Art Center; Georges
    Teyssot, Milan Triennale; John
    Zukowsky, Art Insitute of Chicago;
    Paolo Polledri, San Francisco
    Museum of Modern Art; Stuart
    Wrede, Museum of Modern Art, New
    York; Ulriche Jehle-Schulte
    Strathaus, Architekturmuseum,
    Basel; Francois Burkhardt, Centre
    Creation Industrielle, Centre
    Pompidou, Paris.
    DESIGN BOOK REVIEW 1989 summer,
    no.16, p.23-32, photos.

UNITED STATES--NEW YORK (NEW YORK)--
MUSEUMS--ART--SOLOMON R. GUGGENHEIM
MUSEUM
Paisajes arquitectonicos: seis
    maestros, seis imagenes / Ezra
    Stoller.
    Six landmark buildings by
    Corbusier, Alvar Aalto, F.L.
    Wright, Mies, Gordon Bunshaft, and
    Richard Meier.
    ARQUITECTURA VIVA 1990 May-June,
    no.12, p.36-39, photos.

UNITED STATES--NEW YORK (NEW YORK)--
MUSEUMS--CHILDREN'S--CHILDREN'S
MUSEUM OF MANHATTAN
New school of thought: a New York
    City children's museum boasts an
    interior landscape that marries
    learning and play / David Masello.
    Children's Museum of Manhattan, W.
    83rd St., New York City, housed in
    a 1920's school. Architects: Paul
    Segal Associates.
    ARCHITECTURAL RECORD 1990 July,
    v.178, no.8, p.68-[71], photos.,
    plans, secns.

UNITED STATES--NEW YORK (NEW YORK)--
MUSEUMS--DESIGN--COOPER HEWITT
MUSEUM
The art of the design museum /
    Karrie Jacobs.
    Features the Vitra Design Museum,
    the London Design Museum, and the
    Cooper-Hewitt Museum.
    METROPOLIS 1990 Dec., v.50, no.5,
    p.38-43,63-69, photos.

UNITED STATES--NEW YORK (NEW YORK)--
MUSEUMS--HISTORICAL--ALTERATIONS AND
ADDITIONS--JEWISH MUSEUM
Museumserweiterung -- Imitation als
    Architektursprache.
    Kimbell Art Museum, Ft. Worth,
    Tex.; Fundacio Miro, Barcelona;
    and the Jewish Museum, New York.
    Includes English summary.
    BAUMEISTER 1990 Nov., v.87, no.11,
    p.44-47, dwgs., models, photos.,
    plans.

UNITED STATES--NEW YORK (NEW YORK)--
MUSEUMS--HISTORICAL--ELLIS ISLAND
MUSEUM
Celebrating an island artifact ...
    Ellis Island / Cynthia Owen
    Philip.
    On the recent renovation of the
    Main Building for use as a museum
    of immigration.
    ARCHAEOLOGY 1990 Sept.-Oct., v.43,
    no.5, p.[44]-51, dwgs., photos.,
    site plan.
Coming home: Ellis Island, the
    museum / Barbara Flanagan.
    Architects: Beyer Blinder Belle
    and Notter Finegold + Alexander.
    METROPOLITAN HOME 1990 Aug., v.22,
    no.8, p.82,84,86, photos.
Ellis Island, 1980s shrine / John
    Morris Dixon.
    Original architects: Boring &
    Tilton. Restoration architects:
    Beyer Blinder Belle, Architects
    and Planners, Notter Finegold &
    Alexander.
    PROGRESSIVE ARCHITECTURE 1990
    Nov., v.71, no.12, p.23-24,
    photos.
Ellis Island - das nationale
    Einwanderermuseum der USA.
    Architects for the restoration:
    Beyer, Blinder, Belle; Notter,
    Finegold and Alexander.
    BAUWELT 1990 Nov.23, v.81, no.44,
    p.2190-2191, photos.
Ellis Island reopens as museum /
    Jane Holtz Kay.
    Architects: Beyer Blinder Belle.
    ARCHITECTURE: THE AIA JOURNAL 1990
    Nov., v.79, no.11, p.21-24,
    photos.
Reopening America's gates [Ellis
    Island] / Clifford A. Pearson.
    Ellis Island Immigration Center
    has been renovated by Beyer
    Blinder Belle and Notter Finegold
    + Alexander.
    ARCHITECTURAL RECORD 1990 July,
    v.178, no.8, p.[46]-57, dets.,
    photos., plans, secns.

UNITED STATES--NEW YORK (NEW YORK)--
MUSEUMS--HISTORICAL--ELLIS
ISLANDMUSEUM
Our threshold of liberty [Ellis
    Island].
    The renovated immigration facility
    will reopen to visitors in fall of
    1990.
    COLONIAL HOMES 1990 June, v.16,
    no.3, p.[34-40]., photos.

UNITED STATES--NEW YORK (NEW YORK)--
MUSEUMS--HISTORICAL--NATIONAL MUSEUM
OF IMMIGRATION
Immigration returns to Ellis Island
    / Jeffrey Hoff, Steven Saltzman.
    On the new National Museum of
    Immigration, which opens Sept.10,
    1990. Original architects: Boring
    & Tilton; restoration architects:
    Notter Finegold & Alexander, Beyer
    Blinder Belle.
    METROPOLIS 1990 Sept., v.10 no.2,
    p.19-22, photos.

UNITED STATES--NEW YORK (NEW YORK)--
NEIGHBORHOODS
Context is everything / Sandy
    Hornick.
    Amendments to New York City's
    zoning resolution allows for
    increased lower density areas for
    low-rise neighborhood housing.
    PLANNING 1990 Dec., v.56, no.12,
    p.22-26, diagrs., dwg., photo.,
    secn.

UNITED STATES--NEW YORK (NEW YORK)--
NEIGHBORHOODS--BATTERY PARK CITY
Battery Park City's brave new world
    / Paul Goldberger.
    Master plan: Cooper Eckstut
    Associates.
    ARCHITECTURAL DIGEST 1990 Nov.,
    v.47, no.12, p.144,146,148, maps,
    photos.

UNITED STATES--NEW YORK (NEW YORK)--
NEIGHBORHOODS--NEWSPAPER ROW
The fourth estate's former home /
    Michele Herman.
    Until the beginning of the 20th
    cent. virtually all of New York's
    newspapers were published in a few
    blocks just east of City Hall
    Park, known as Newspaper Row and
    Printing House Square.
    METROPOLIS 1990 Mar., v.9, no.7,
    p.[64-67],74-75, photos., aerial
    photo.

UNITED STATES--NEW YORK (NEW YORK)--
NEIGHBORHOODS--PRINTING HOUSE SQUARE
The fourth estate's former home /
    Michele Herman.
    Until the beginning of the 20th
    cent. virtually all of New York's
    newspapers were published in a few
    blocks just east of City Hall
    Park, known as Newspaper Row and
    Printing House Square.
    METROPOLIS 1990 Mar., v.9, no.7,
    p.[64-67],74-75, photos., aerial
    photo.

UNITED STATES--NEW YORK (NEW YORK)--
NEIGHBORHOODS--SOHO
Il quartiere di SoHo e il loft
   district: la nuova vita dei loft
   building = The SoHo area and the
   loft district: the new life of old
   buildings / Kaisa Broner.
   LOTUS INTERNATIONAL 1990, no.66,
   p.92-127, elevs., maps, photos.,
   plans, site plans, refs.

UNITED STATES--NEW YORK (NEW YORK)--
NEIGHBORHOODS--TRIBECA
Preserving a New York neighborhood's
   unique identity / Suzanne
   Stephens.
   On Tribeca.
   ARCHITECTURAL DIGEST 1990 Nov.,
   v.47, no.12, p.76,78,82,86,
   90-[91], port., photos.

UNITED STATES--NEW YORK (NEW YORK)--
NEWSPAPER BUILDINGS
The fourth estate's former home /
   Michele Herman.
   Until the beginning of the 20th
   cent. virtually all of New York's
   newspapers were published in a few
   blocks just east of City Hall
   Park, known as Newspaper Row and
   Printing House Square.
   METROPOLIS 1990 Mar., v.9, no.7,
   p.[64-67],74-75, photos., aerial
   photo.

UNITED STATES--NEW YORK (NEW YORK)--
NIGHTCLUBS--INTERIOR DESIGN--
BUILDING (POWERHOUSE)
Building: a nightclub / Justin
   Henderson.
   Interiors of New York nightclub,
   a.k.a. Powerhouse.
   INTERIORS 1990 Sept., v.149,
   no.14, p.126-127, photos.

UNITED STATES--NEW YORK (NEW YORK)--
NURSING HOMES--MOUNT SINAI MEDICAL
CENTER NURSING CENTER
AIDS and architecture / Alexander
   Farnsworth.
   Designing facilities to care for
   AIDS patients. Features a design
   for a nursing center to be
   operated by Mt. Sinai Medical
   Center. Architects: Norman
   Rosenfeld Architects.
   METROPOLIS 1990 Dec., v.50, no.5,
   p.21-23, dwgs.

UNITED STATES--NEW YORK (NEW YORK)--
OFFICE BUILDINGS--19TH CENTURY--
COOGAN BUILDING
Il Coogan Building: un edificio a
   rischio / Tom Killian.
   In New York; built 1875-1876.
   Architect: Alfred H. Thorp.
   CASABELLA 1990 May, v.54, no.568,
   p.32, photo.

UNITED STATES--NEW YORK (NEW YORK)--
OFFICE BUILDINGS--20TH CENTURY--
CONSERVATION AND RESTORATION--LEVER
HOUSE
Saving face: preservation: curtain
   wall restoration / Theodore H. M.
   Prudon.
   Cites four examples: the Woolworth
   Building, Hallidie Buildings,
   Commonwealth Building, Lever
   House.
   ARCHITECTURE: THE AIA JOURNAL 1990
   Nov., v.79, no.11, p.105-110,114,
   dwgs., dets., photos.

UNITED STATES--NEW YORK (NEW YORK)--
OFFICE BUILDINGS--20TH CENTURY--
CONSERVATION AND RESTORATION--
WOOLWORTH BUILDING
Saving face: preservation: curtain
   wall restoration / Theodore H. M.
   Prudon.
   Cites four examples: the Woolworth
   Building, Hallidie Buildings,
   Commonwealth Building, Lever
   House.
   ARCHITECTURE: THE AIA JOURNAL 1990
   Nov., v.79, no.11, p.105-110,114,
   dwgs., dets., photos.

UNITED STATES--NEW YORK (NEW YORK)--
OFFICE BUILDINGS--420 FIFTH AVENUE
Manhattan's 420 Fifth Avenue /
   Patric Dolan.
   Architects: Brennan Beer Gorman;
   developers: The Hammerson Group.
   REAL ESTATE FORUM 1990 Apr., v.45,
   no.4, p.50-56, port., photos.

UNITED STATES--NEW YORK (NEW YORK)--
OFFICE BUILDINGS--712 FIFTH AVENUE
Designing the super-thin new
   buildings / James S. Russell.
   Features 6 projects for tall
   buildings in New York City,
   Chicago and Paris.
   ARCHITECTURAL RECORD 1990 Oct.,
   v.178, no.11, p.105-109,
   axonometric views, elev., models,
   photos., plans.

UNITED STATES--NEW YORK (NEW YORK)--
OFFICE BUILDINGS--1675 BROADWAY
When there's no place to go but up /
   James S. Russell.
   On collaboration between
   architects and engineers to build
   over, around, and through existing
   buildings. Features 3 recent
   projects: Presbyterian-University
   Hospital, Pittsburgh; 1675
   Broadway, New York City; and
   Embassy Suites, New York City.
   ARCHITECTURAL RECORD 1990 Sept.,
   v.178, no.10, p.160-163, models,
   photos., plans, secn., isometric
   dwgs.

UNITED STATES--NEW YORK (NEW YORK)--
OFFICE BUILDINGS--ALTERATIONS AND
ADDITIONS
Office renovation in midtown
   Manhattan: lessons learned /
   Jacques N. Gordon, Liseann Shea.
   In the late 1980s.
   URBAN LAND 1990 Jan., v.49, no.1,
   p.6-10, graph, map, photos.,
   tables.

UNITED STATES--NEW YORK (NEW YORK)--
OFFICE BUILDINGS--ALTERATIONS AND
ADDITIONS--ROCKEFELLER CENTER
The Center moves west / Andrew
   White.
   Rockefeller Plaza West, a planned
   skyscraper addition to Rockefeller
   Center. Architects: Kohn Pedersen
   Fox.
   METROPOLIS 1990 Oct., v.10, no.3,
   p.26-29, model.

UNITED STATES--NEW YORK (NEW YORK)--
OFFICE BUILDINGS--BRILL BUILDING
The Brill Building was ... / Karrie
   Jacobs.
   At Broadway & 49th St., NYC, built
   1930. Architect: Victor Bark Jr.
   METROPOLIS 1990 Oct., v.10, no.3,
   p.[74]-77, 93, ports., photos.

UNITED STATES--NEW YORK (NEW YORK)--
OFFICE BUILDINGS--CARNEGIE HALL
TOWER
Special feature: recent works of
   Cesar Pelli.
   Contents: Editor's introduction--
   Architects' statement / Cesar
   Pelli-- Essay: Urban iconography
   and the medium of architecture /
   Gavin Macrae-Gibson, p.130-137--
   Works: World Financial Center--
   Norwest Tower-- Pacific Design
   Center expansion-- Mattatuck
   Museum-- Ley Student Center
   expansion, Rice University-- Yale
   Center for Molecular Medicine,
   Yale University-- Carnegie Hall
   tower-- Sunarhauserman
   headquarters-- Fan Pier master
   plan. Architects: Cesar Pelli &
   Associates. Text in Japanese and
   English.
   ARCHITECTURE AND URBANISM 1990
   Feb., no.2(233), p.[59]-148,
   dwgs., elevs., photos., plans,
   secns., site plans.

UNITED STATES--NEW YORK (NEW YORK)--
OFFICE BUILDINGS--PARK ROW BUILDING
The "New New York" and the Park Row
   Building: American artists view
   an icon of the modern age / Erica
   E. Hirshler.
   Architect: R. H. Robertson.
   AMERICAN ART JOURNAL 1989, v.21,
   no.4, p.26-45, ill., photo.

UNITED STATES--NEW YORK (NEW YORK)--
OFFICE BUILDINGS--ROCKEFELLER PLAZA
WEST
The Center moves west / Andrew
   White.
   Rockefeller Plaza West, a planned
   skyscraper addition to Rockefeller
   Center. Architects: Kohn Pedersen
   Fox.
   METROPOLIS 1990 Oct., v.10, no.3,
   p.26-29, model.
Rockefeller Plaza West, New York,
   New York, 1993.
   Site: Seventh Ave. between 49th &
   50th St.; architects: Kohn
   Pedersen Fox Associates. Text in
   Japanese and English.
   PROCESS: ARCHITECTURE 1989 Nov.,
   no.86, p.122-125, elevs., model,
   plans, secn., site plan.

UNITED STATES--NEW YORK (NEW YORK)--
OFFICE BUILDINGS--SEAGRAM BUILDING
Paisajes arquitectónicos: seis
   maestros, seis imagenes / Ezra
   Stoller.
   Six landmark buildings by
   Corbusier, Alvar Aalto, F.L.
   Wright, Mies, Gordon Bunshaft, and
   Richard Meier.
   ARQUITECTURA VIVA 1990 May-June,
   no.12, p.36-39, photos.

UNITED STATES--NEW YORK (NEW YORK)--
OFFICE COMPLEXES--WORLD FINANCIAL
CENTER
Special feature: recent works of
Cesar Pelli.
Contents: Editor's introduction--
Architects' statement / Cesar
Pelli-- Essay: Urban iconography
and the medium of architecture /
Gavin Macrae-Gibson, p.130-137--
Works: World Financial Center--
Norwest Tower-- Pacific Design
Center expansion-- Mattatuck
Museum-- Ley Student Center
expansion, Rice University-- Yale
Center for Molecular Medicine,
Yale University-- Carnegie Hall
tower-- Sunarhauserman
headquarters-- Fan Pier master
plan. Architects: Cesar Pelli &
Associates. Text in Japanese and
English.
ARCHITECTURE AND URBANISM 1990
Feb., no.2(233), p.[59]-148,
dwgs., elevs., photos., plans,
secns., site plans.

UNITED STATES--NEW YORK (NEW YORK)--
OFFICES--AMERICAN RE-INSURANCE
COMPANY
American Re-Insurance Company
offices, New York, New York.
Architects: The Hillier Group.
ARCHITECTURE NEW JERSEY 1990,
v.26, no.6, p.17, photos., plan.

UNITED STATES--NEW YORK (NEW YORK)--
OFFICES--ARCHITECTS'--INTERIOR
DESIGN--SWANKE HAYDEN CONNELL
ARCHITECTS
Swanke Hayden Connell: the firm
builds a building for its New York
headquarters / Edie Lee Cohen.
Office interiors.
INTERIOR DESIGN 1990 July, v.61,
no.10, p.[148-153], photos.,
plans.

UNITED STATES--NEW YORK (NEW YORK)--
OFFICES--ARDT-L
Implied movement: Henry Smith-Miller
and Laurie Hawkinson stress
program and suggest motion in a
pair of interiors / Victoria
Geibel.
ARDT-L Offices, Moss/Getchel Loft,
60th in New York City.
ARCHITECTURE: THE MAGAZINE OF THE
AMERICAN INSTITUTE OF ARCHITECTS
1990 June, v.79, no.6, p.80-85,
axonometric views, photos., plans.

UNITED STATES--NEW YORK (NEW YORK)--
OFFICES--DESIGNERS'--NAOMI LEFF AND
ASSOCIATES
Naomi Leff and Associates / Edie Lee
Cohen.
Interiors of N. Y. C. design firm
offices.
INTERIOR DESIGN 1990 July, v.61,
no.10, p.158-[161], axonometric
view, photos.

UNITED STATES--NEW YORK (NEW YORK)--
OFFICES--INTERIOR DESIGN--AJ
CONTRACTING
An inside job [AJ Contracting] /
Alice Feiring.
Interiors of New York executive
offices. Designer: John Chaloner.
INTERIORS 1990 Sept., v.149,
no.14, p.118-121, photos., plan.

UNITED STATES--NEW YORK (NEW YORK)--
OFFICES--INTERIOR DESIGN--BEAR
STEARNS & CO.
Bear Stearns & Co. / Monica Geran.
Features company president's new
office in midtown New York
designed by Eric Bernard.
INTERIOR DESIGN 1990 Mar., v.61,
no.5, p.[194]-195, photos., plan.

UNITED STATES--NEW YORK (NEW YORK)--
OFFICES--INTERIOR DESIGN--C.J.
LAWRENCE, MORGAN GRENFELL INC.
Trading up.
On interiors of New York financial
services company, C.J. Lawrence,
Morgan Grenfell Inc. Interior
designers: Kohn, Pedersen, Fox,
Conway Associates.
INTERIORS 1990 Sept., v.149,
no.14, p.112-[113],

UNITED STATES--NEW YORK (NEW YORK)--
OFFICES--INTERIOR DESIGN--CAPITAL
CITIES/ABC
Capital ideas [Capital Cities/ABC
offices, NYC].
Features interiors of Capital
Cities/ABC New York offices.
Interior designers: Kohn,
Pedersen, Fox, Conway Associates.
INTERIORS 1990 Sept., v.149,
no.14, p.108-[109], photos., plan.

UNITED STATES--NEW YORK (NEW YORK)--
OFFICES--INTERIOR DESIGN--CITICORP
Citicorp / Monica Geran.
Features interiors of one division
of Citicorp in their NYC Citicorp
Center. Interior designers: PHH
Environments.
INTERIOR DESIGN 1990 Sept., v.61,
no.12, p.[202-205], photos., plan.

UNITED STATES--NEW YORK (NEW YORK)--
OFFICES--INTERIOR DESIGN--
COMMERZBANK
Commerzbank: Owen & Mandolfo designs
the New York offices of the German
bank's Capital Markets division /
Mayer Rus.
INTERIOR DESIGN 1990 May, v.61,
no.7, p.250-[251], photos., plan.

UNITED STATES--NEW YORK (NEW YORK)--
OFFICES--INTERIOR DESIGN--COX & CO.
Detailed expansion / Kristen
Richards.
Features offices for two tenants
in a open loft in New York.
Architects: Phillips Janson Group.
INTERIORS 1990 Aug., v.149, no.13,
p.110-[111], photos.

UNITED STATES--NEW YORK (NEW YORK)--
OFFICES--INTERIOR DESIGN--DETAILS
Detailed expansion / Kristen
Richards.
Features offices for two tenants
in a open loft in New York.
Architects: Phillips Janson Group.
INTERIORS 1990 Aug., v.149, no.13,
p.110-[111], photos.

UNITED STATES--NEW YORK (NEW YORK)--
OFFICES--INTERIOR DESIGN--KOBE STEEL
USA
Kobe Steel USA / Monica Geran.
Interiors of New York headquarters
designed by the Interior Design
Division of Kajima International.
INTERIOR DESIGN 1990 Sept., v.61,
no.12, p.208-211, photos., plan.

UNITED STATES--NEW YORK (NEW YORK)--
OFFICES--INTERIOR DESIGN--LEVINE,
HUNTLEY, SCHMIDT & BEAVER.
LHS & B: New York ad agency by R.M.
Kliment & Frances Halsband
Architects.
Interiors of Levine, Hungley,
Schmidt & Beaver.
INTERIOR DESIGN 1990 June, v.61,
no.9, p.214-[219], photos., plans,
secn.

UNITED STATES--NEW YORK (NEW YORK)--
OFFICES--INTERIOR DESIGN--MURPHY &
DURIEU
Murphy & Durieu: the New York
brokerage firm's spaces by Searl
Design Inc. / Monica Geran.
INTERIOR DESIGN 1990 May, v.61,
no.7, p.256-[259], photos., plan.

UNITED STATES--NEW YORK (NEW YORK)--
OFFICES--INTERIOR DESIGN--NATIONAL
BROADCASTING COMPANY
NBC gets centered / Kristen
Richards.
Renovations of environmental
control center office in NBC's
Rockefeller Center offices.
Architect: Michael Wolfe.
INTERIORS 1990 Nov., v.150, no.4,
p.46-47, photos., plan.

UNITED STATES--NEW YORK (NEW YORK)--
OFFICES--INTERIOR DESIGN--NETWORK
GUARDIAN CENTER (NEW YORK TELEPHONE)
High gloss, high gloss / Nayana
Currimbhoy.
Features office interiors of New
York Telephone's Network Guardian
Center, New York, which includes a
monitoring station, marketing
offices and support areas.
Architects: Louis R. Morandi
Architect.
INTERIORS 1990 Nov., v.150, no.4,
p.48-51, photos., plan.

UNITED STATES--NEW YORK (NEW YORK)--
OFFICES--INTERIOR DESIGN--NW AYER
Accounts playable / Alice Feiring.
Interiors of advertising agency,
NW Ayer's world headquarters in
New York, which includes special
studio facilities. Interior
designers: Mancini Duffy.
INTERIORS 1990 Nov., v.150, no.4,
p.44-45, photos., plan.

UNITED STATES--NEW YORK (NEW YORK)--
OFFICES--INTERIOR DESIGN--ROSHAK &
COMPANY
High design, low budget / Angi
Bates.
Interiors of New York graphic
designer recruiting firm, Roshak &
Co. Architects: Zivkovic
Associates.
INTERIORS 1990 May, v.149, no.10,
p.32, photos., plan.

UNITED STATES--NEW YORK (NEW YORK)--
OFFICES--INTERIOR DESIGN--S & R
LITHO
S & R Litho / Monica Geran.
Interiors of New York offices.
Architects: Herbert Beckhard Frank
Richlan & Associates.
INTERIOR DESIGN 1990 Sept., v.61,
no.12, p.206-[207], photos., plan.

UNITED STATES--NEW YORK (NEW YORK)--
OFFICES--INTERIOR DESIGN--SOFT-COM
Soft-Com / Edie Lee Cohen.
Offices for computer software
concern, New York, NY. Architects:
William Green & Associates.
INTERIOR DESIGN 1990 June, v.61,
no.9, p.220-[223], photos., plan.

UNITED STATES--NEW YORK (NEW YORK)--
OFFICES--INTERIOR DESIGN--WORKMAN
PUBLISHING COMPANY
Workman: a New York publisher's
office by Mayers & Schiff / Monica
Geran.
INTERIOR DESIGN 1990 Mar., v.61,
no.5, p.196-[199], photos., plan.

UNITED STATES--NEW YORK (NEW YORK)--
OFFICES--INTERIOR DESIGN--WYSE
ADVERTISING
Wyse Advertising: Armstrong Cumming
Architects design, the agency's
relocated New York offices / Mayer
Rus.
INTERIOR DESIGN 1990 May, v.61,
no.7, p.252-[255], photos., plan.

UNITED STATES--NEW YORK (NEW YORK)--
OPEN SPACES
Using vacant land to reshape
American cities / Tom Fox.
PLACES 1989 Fall, v.6, no.1,
p.78-81, ports., models, map,
secn., ref.

UNITED STATES--NEW YORK (NEW YORK)--
PARISH HALLS--TUDOR REVIVAL--CHURCH
OF THE COVENANT--FELLOWSHIP HALL
"Landmarking comes to Covenant"
[church, New York] / Ron Wilkoc.
Describes a cooperative process
for landmarking religious
buildings. Built in 1871 and 1927
and located at 310 East 42nd St.
COMMON BOND 1990 Fall, v.6, no.4,
p.2-4, dwg., photos.

UNITED STATES--NEW YORK (NEW YORK)--
PARK BUILDINGS--CENTRAL PARK--HARLEM
MEER
Up in Central Park on the shore of
Harlem Meer.
Design for a three-building
complex for restaurant, boat
rental and discovery center.
Architects: Buttrick White &
Burtis.
ARCHITECTURAL RECORD 1990 Mar.,
v.178, no.3, p.19, plan.

UNITED STATES--NEW YORK (NEW YORK)--
PARKS--CONSERVATION AND
RESTORATION--FORT WASHINGTON PARK
Reviving city parks / Joseph P.
Griffith.
On efforts to restore two of upper
Manhattan's park pavilions:
Riverside Park Viewing Pavilion
(1919) and Fort Washington
Pavilion (1925). Architect of the
Riverside Park Pavilion: Theodore
(Continued next column)

UNITED STATES--NEW YORK (NEW YORK)--
PARKS--CONSERVATION AND
RESTORATION--FORT WASHINGTON PARK
(CONTINUED)
Reviving city parks /...(CONTINUED)
E. Videto.
METROPOLIS 1990 May, v.9, no.9,
p.31-33.

UNITED STATES--NEW YORK (NEW YORK)--
PARKS--CONSERVATION AND
RESTORATION--RIVERSIDE PARK
Reviving city parks / Joseph P.
Griffith.
On efforts to restore two of upper
Manhattan's park pavilions:
Riverside Park Viewing Pavilion
(1919) and Fort Washington
Pavilion (1925). Architect of the
Riverside Park Pavilion: Theodore
E. Videto.
METROPOLIS 1990 May, v.9, no.9,
p.31-33.

UNITED STATES--NEW YORK (NEW YORK)--
PAVILIONS--20TH CENTURY--
CONSERVATION AND RESTORATION--FORT
WASHINGTON PAVILION
Reviving city parks / Joseph P.
Griffith.
On efforts to restore two of upper
Manhattan's park pavilions:
Riverside Park Viewing Pavilion
(1919) and Fort Washington
Pavilion (1925). Architect of the
Riverside Park Pavilion: Theodore
E. Videto.
METROPOLIS 1990 May, v.9, no.9,
p.31-33.

UNITED STATES--NEW YORK (NEW YORK)--
PAVILIONS--20TH CENTURY--
CONSERVATION AND RESTORATION--
RIVERSIDE PARK VIEWING PAVILION
Reviving city parks / Joseph P.
Griffith.
On efforts to restore two of upper
Manhattan's park pavilions:
Riverside Park Viewing Pavilion
(1919) and Fort Washington
Pavilion (1925). Architect of the
Riverside Park Pavilion: Theodore
E. Videto.
METROPOLIS 1990 May, v.9, no.9,
p.31-33.

UNITED STATES--NEW YORK (NEW YORK)--
PAVILIONS--BATTERY PARK CITY--NORTH
PARK PAVILION
North Park Pavilion en Battery Park
City New York = North Park
Pavilion in Battery Park City New
York / Demetri Porphyrios.
Architect: Demetri Porphyrios.
COMPOSICION ARQUITECTONICA, ART &
ARCHITECTURE 1990 June, no.6,
p.[61]-70, dwg., elevs., plan,
secn., site plan, sketches, aerial
photo.

UNITED STATES--NEW YORK (NEW YORK)--
PENTHOUSES
Ipotesi per un gemellaggio: triplex
penthouse a New York e a Bologna /
Glauco Gresleri.
Architects: Steven Forman (NYC);
Glauco Gresleri (Bologna).
PARAMETRO 1990 Nov.-Dec., no.181,
p.84-91, axonometric views, dets.,
models, photos., plans, secns.

UNITED STATES--NEW YORK (NEW YORK)--
PENTHOUSES (CONTINUED)
Penthouse suite: Manhattan Triplex
Apartment, New York City, Steven
Forman, architect / Karen D.
Stein.
ARCHITECTURAL RECORD 1990 Sept.,
v.178, no.10, p.110-[117],
axonometric views, photos.

UNITED STATES--NEW YORK (NEW YORK)--
PENTHOUSES--ALTERATIONS AND
ADDITIONS
Supported in detail / Philip Arcidi.
Renovation of Park Ave. penthouse,
NYC. Interior architects: Deamer
Phillips Architecture.
PROGRESSIVE ARCHITECTURE 1990
Dec., v.71, no.13, p.86-89,
photos., plan.

UNITED STATES--NEW YORK (NEW YORK)--
PENTHOUSES--INTERIOR DESIGN
Exercise in logic / Edie Lee Cohen.
Interiors of Chelsea penthouse,
New York. Architect: Ian J. Cohn.
INTERIOR DESIGN 1990 May, v.61,
no.7, p.288-[293], photos., plans.
New York sur les toits.
Interiors of three-level penthouse
apartment in New York. Architect:
Steven Forman.
TECHNIQUES ET ARCHITECTURE 1990
Oct.-Nov., no.392, p.149-152,
axonometric views, model, photos.,
plan.

UNITED STATES--NEW YORK (NEW YORK)--
PENTHOUSES--INTERIOR DESIGN--DENTE
PENTHOUSE
Spare but not spartan: Barbara Dente
does the white thing / Michele
Herman.
Greenwich Village penthouse
interiors.
ELLE DECOR 1990 Apr., v.1, no.3,
p.126-131, photos.

UNITED STATES--NEW YORK (NEW YORK)--
PENTHOUSES--INTERIOR DESIGN--KRAMER
PENTHOUSE
A moss garden / Jim Murphy.
Focus on the lighting of the
Kramer penthouse, New York.
Architect: Michael Kalil.
PROGRESSIVE ARCHITECTURE 1990
Sept., v.71, no.9, p.104-[109],
photos., plan.

UNITED STATES--NEW YORK (NEW YORK)--
PENTHOUSES--INTERIOR DESIGN--LEONE
PENTHOUSE
Gramercy Park penthouse / Edie Lee
Cohen.
Interiors of Vivien Leone's
penthouse apartment and terraces
in New York's Gramercy Park Hotel.
Interior designer: Clodagh.
INTERIOR DESIGN 1990 Feb., v.61,
no.3, p.198-201, port., photos.,
plan.

UNITED STATES--NEW YORK (NEW YORK)--
PENTHOUSES--ZABAR PENTHOUSE
A new leaf: Abbie Zabar's art and
writing branch out beyond the
topiary in her Fifth Avenue
penthouse / Celia McGee.
HOUSE & GARDEN 1990 May, v.162,
no.5, p.118,[120], port., photos.

UNITED STATES--NEW YORK (NEW YORK)--
REAL ESTATE DEVELOPMENT--BATTERY
PARK CITY
Interiors platform / Sylvia Lavin.
On the "effect of the Battery Park
City Development on the Manhattan
landscape."
INTERIORS 1989 Feb., v.148, no.7,
p.16,20,22,24,

UNITED STATES--NEW YORK (NEW YORK)--
REAL ESTATE DEVELOPMENT--POLITICAL
ASPECTS
The RFP process: the rules of the
game / Todd W. Bressi.
CITY LIMITS 1990 May, v.15, no.5,
p.9-11, port., photo.

UNITED STATES--NEW YORK (NEW YORK)--
REAL ESTATE DEVELOPMENT--TIMES
SQUARE AREA
Times Square, New York City: la
costruzione di un problema
ingovernabile (1967/1987) = Times
Square: an unmanageable problem in
the making / Paolo Fareri.
In Italian; English summary,
p.121, 124.
URBANISTICA 1989 Oct., no.96,
p.7-20, 121, 124, elevs., maps,
photos., plans, biblio.

UNITED STATES--NEW YORK (NEW YORK)--
RESIDENTIAL GARDENS--JONES WOOD
A secret garden: twin rows of town
houses conceal a quiet piece of
old New York / William Bryant
Logan.
Jones Wood, a communal garden off
Third Ave., begun in 1919 and
recently restored.
HOUSE & GARDEN 1990 Oct., v.162,
no.10, p.[124],126, photos.

UNITED STATES--NEW YORK (NEW YORK)--
RESTAURANTS--BAROLO (398 WEST
BROADWAY)
Best dressed restaurants: Barolo /
Regina S. Baraban.
At 398 West Broadway, New York
City. Architects: Studio MORSA.
METROPOLIS 1990 July-Aug., v.10,
no.1, p.27, photos.

UNITED STATES--NEW YORK (NEW YORK)--
RESTAURANTS--BLUE LIGHT (242 EAST
58TH STREET)
Neighborhood newcomers / Regina S.
Baraban.
Review of 3 NYC neighborhood
restaurants.
METROPOLIS 1990 Sept., v.10, no.2,
p.31, photos.

UNITED STATES--NEW YORK (NEW YORK)--
RESTAURANTS--COFFEE SHOP (29 UNION
SQUARE WEST)
Neighborhood newcomers / Regina S.
Baraban.
Review of 3 NYC neighborhood
restaurants.
METROPOLIS 1990 Sept., v.10, no.2,
p.31, photos.

UNITED STATES--NEW YORK (NEW YORK)--
RESTAURANTS--ELDORADO PETIT
Eldorado Petit / Regina S. Baraban.
New York restaurant. Architects:
Jaime Tressera, Roberto Paulee.
METROPOLIS 1990 Oct., v.10, no.3,
p.35, photos.

UNITED STATES--NEW YORK (NEW YORK)--
RESTAURANTS--INTERIOR DESIGN--
AUREOLE
Best dressed restaurants: Aureole /
Regina S. Baraban.
At 34 E. 61st St., New York City.
Interior architect: John Harding.
METROPOLIS 1990 Mar., v.9, no.7,
p.24, photos.

UNITED STATES--NEW YORK (NEW YORK)--
RESTAURANTS--INTERIOR DESIGN--REMI
Remi redux / Edie Lee Cohen.
Interiors of relocated New York
restaurant, Remi. Interior
designer: Adam Tihany.
INTERIOR DESIGN 1990 Sept., v.61,
no.12, p.182-[185], photos., plan.

UNITED STATES--NEW YORK (NEW YORK)--
RESTAURANTS--LA CITE
Best dressed restaurants: La Cite /
Regina S. Baraban.
Restaurant and grill at 120 W.
51st St., Manhattan. Architect:
Arnold Syrop. Interior designer:
Joanne Syrop.
METROPOLIS 1990 Apr., v.9, no.8,
p.29, photo.

UNITED STATES--NEW YORK (NEW YORK)--
RESTAURANTS--POIRET
Best dressed restaurants: Poiret /
Regina S. Baraban.
At 474 Columbus Ave., New York
City. Interior designer: Nancy
Mah.
METROPOLIS 1990 May, v.9, no.9,
p.43, photos.

UNITED STATES--NEW YORK (NEW YORK)--
RESTAURANTS--REMI
Best dressed restaurants: Remi /
Regina S. Baraban.
At 145 W. 53rd St., New York.
Designer: Adam Tihany.
METROPOLIS 1990 Dec., v.10, no.5,
p.31, photos.

UNITED STATES--NEW YORK (NEW YORK)--
RESTAURANTS--TROUVAILLE
Best dressed restaurants: Trouvaille
/ Regina S. Baraban.
Renovated turn-of-the-century
tavern. At 174 Grand St., New
York. Interior designer: Lydia
DePolo of DePolo-Dunbar.
METROPOLIS 1990 June, v.9, no.10,
p.31, photos.

UNITED STATES--NEW YORK (NEW YORK)--
ROOF GARDENS--SANTASIERO GARDEN
A stargazer's garden: decorator
Anthony Santasiero went through
the roof of his Central Park West
penthouse to open a view of trees
and sky / Anthony Santasiero.
Landscape architect: Bruce Kelly.
HOUSE & GARDEN 1990 Oct., v.162,
no.10, p.[176]-179,251, photos.

UNITED STATES--NEW YORK (NEW YORK)--
ROOF TERRACES--SANTASIERO GARDEN
A stargazer's garden: decorator
Anthony Santasiero went through
the roof of his Central Park West
penthouse to open a view of trees
and sky / Anthony Santasiero.
Landscape architect: Bruce Kelly.
HOUSE & GARDEN 1990 Oct., v.162,
no.10, p.[176]-179,251, photos.

UNITED STATES--NEW YORK (NEW YORK)--
ROOMS--INTERIOR DESIGN--NEW YORK
UNIVERSITY MEDICAL CENTER
NYU Medical Center / Monica Geran.
Features one of the twenty luxury
suites designed by Charles P.
Swerz Interior Design.
INTERIOR DESIGN 1990 Nov., v.61,
no.15, p.188-[189], photos., plan.

UNITED STATES--NEW YORK (NEW YORK)--
ROW HOUSES--ALTERATIONS AND
ADDITIONS--HAYES HOUSE
Hayes & Co. [Hayes townhouse, New
York City] / Tom Wolfe.
Renovated Upper East Side row
house. Architects: Turner Brooks,
Ross Anderson; interior designer:
Chester Cleaver.
HOUSE & GARDEN 1990 Oct., v.162,
no.10, p.[156-163], port., photos.

UNITED STATES--NEW YORK (NEW YORK)--
ROW HOUSES--GREEK REVIVAL--
CONSERVATION AND RESTORATION--FORBES
- HARRISON HOUSE
A classical revision.
Restoration of a Greek revival row
house in Greenwich Village, New
York, home of Tim Forbes and Anne
Harrison. Architects for
restoration: DiDonno Associates.
HISTORIC PRESERVATION 1990
Mar.-Apr., v.42, no.2, p.[46]-53,
port., photos.

UNITED STATES--NEW YORK (NEW YORK)--
ROW HOUSES--INTERIOR DESIGN--FORD -
BALAZS HOUSE
Uptown downtown: Alison Spear
redesigned a Greenwich Village
town house to accomodate the
unusual domestic needs of modeling
mogul Katie Ford and entrepeneur
Andre Balazs / Brad Gooch.
HOUSE & GARDEN 1990 Oct., v.162,
no.10, p.214-219, ports., photos.

UNITED STATES--NEW YORK (NEW YORK)--
SCHOOLS--ALTERATIONS AND ADDITIONS
New York City schools: small is
better / Abby Bussel.
On the hypothetical design study
project and exhibition, New
Schools for New York, sponsored by
the Architectrual League of New
York and the Public Education
Association.
PROGRESSIVE ARCHITECTURE 1990
Mar., v.71, no.3, p.24-25, secn.

UNITED STATES--NEW YORK (NEW YORK)--
SCHOOLS--DANCE--ALVIN AILEY AMERICAN
DANCE CENTER
A sensuous space / Jean Gorman.
Features the Alvin Ailey American
Dance Center, New York, NY.
Architects: R.M. Kliment & Frances
Halsband Architects.
INTERIORS 1990 Dec., v.150, no.5,
p.78-81, axonometric view, photos.

UNITED STATES--NEW YORK (NEW YORK)--
STORES--CLOTHING--INTERIOR DESIGN--
SOHO SURPLUS
Forms and function / Amy Dana.
Interiors of SoHo Surplus clothing
store, New York. Architects:
Deborah Weintraub and Townsend
Moore.
INTERIORS 1990 July, v.149, no.12,
p.92-[93], photos.

UNITED STATES--NEW YORK (NEW YORK)--
STORES--CLOTHING--INTERIOR DESIGN--
ZARA INTERNATIONAL
Zara International / Edie Lee Cohen.
Interiors of two-level clothing
store in Manhattan. Interior
designers: ISD Inc.
INTERIOR DESIGN 1990 Nov., v.61,
no.15, p.168-171, photos., plans.

UNITED STATES--NEW YORK (NEW YORK)--
STORES--INTERIOR DESIGN--PORTANTINA
Special feature: Machado and
Silvetti.
Contents: Brief history.--
Statement / R. Machado, J.
Silvetti.-- The material force of
the architectural imagination / K.
Michael Hays.-- Works: Portantina,
New York, N.Y., 1986.-- Steps of
Providence, Rhode Island School of
Design, Providence, R.I., 1975.--
Municipal cemetery,
Polizzi-Generosa, Sicily, 1986.--
Sesquicentennial Park, Houston,
Tex., 1986.-- Central
transportation facility "la Porta
Meridionale," Palermo, Sicily,
1987.-- Four public squares,
Leonforte, Sicily, 1983. Text in
Japanese and English.
ARCHITECTURE AND URBANISM 1990
Apr., no.4(235), p.65-138,
axonometric views, elevs., models,
photos., plans, secns., site
plans.

UNITED STATES--NEW YORK (NEW YORK)--
STORES--INTERIOR DESIGN--SOHO
For galleriet / Anja Hubener, Bror
Karlsson.
Interiors of four SoHo boutiques:
Knoll International, Parachute,
Comme des Garcons, Yohji Yamamoto.
ARKITEKTUR: THE SWEDISH REVIEW OF
ARCHITECTURE 1990 May, v.90, no.4,
p.42-47, photos., plan.

UNITED STATES--NEW YORK (NEW YORK)--
STORES--JEWELRY--BULGARI
730 Fifth Avenue, New York = Il
nuovo negozio Bulgari / Paul
Goldberger.
Architects: Piero Sartogo
Architetti Associati: Piero
Sartogo and Nathalie Grenon.
L'ARCA 1990 Apr., no.37, p.72-79,
elevs., photos, plans, secn.
730 Fifth Avenue, New York / Paul
Goldberger and Richard Reid.
Bulgari shop, Crown Building.
Architect: Piero Sartogo.
L'ARCA 1990 June, no.39 suppl.,
p.[1]-61, dets., elevs., photos.

UNITED STATES--NEW YORK (NEW YORK)--
STORES--JEWELRY--EBEL
Ebel, here.
On the Manhattan shop and
headquarters. Architect: Andree
Putman.
INTERIOR DESIGN 1990 Mar., v.61,
no.5, p.154-[157], photos.

UNITED STATES--NEW YORK (NEW YORK)--
STORES--JEWELRY--INTERIOR DESIGN--
NIESSING
Niessing / Edie Lee Cohen.
Interiors of jewelry store on
Madison Ave., New York.
Architect: Toshiko Mori.
INTERIOR DESIGN 1990 Sept., v.61,
no.12, p.186-189, dwg., photos.

UNITED STATES--NEW YORK (NEW YORK)--
STORES--MOMA DESIGN STORE
MoMA store / Edie Lee Cohen.
Museum of Modern Art Design Store,
New York. Architects: Hambrecht
Terrell International.
INTERIOR DESIGN 1990 June, v.61,
no.9, p.258-[261], photos., plan.

UNITED STATES--NEW YORK (NEW YORK)--
STORES--SHOE--INTERIOR DESIGN--OTTO
TOOTSI PLOHOUND
Mind over matter / Ziva Freiman.
On the interiors of the Otto
Tootsi Plohound shoe store,
Manhattan. Designer: Walz
Design.
PROGRESSIVE ARCHITECTURE 1990
Feb., v.71, no.2, p.106-111,
photos., plan, sketches.

UNITED STATES--NEW YORK (NEW YORK)--
STREETS--CLEANING
Scorecard: New York recherche
proprete desesperement: evaluation
et conscience civique / Michel
Conan.
Keeping New York's streets clean
despite fiscal cutbacks. In
French; summaries in French,
English, Spanish and German
pp.[123]-125.
LES ANNALES DE LA RECHERCHE
URBAINE 1990 June-July, no.47,
p.34-44, photos., refs.

UNITED STATES--NEW YORK (NEW YORK)--
STUDENT HOUSING--COOPER UNION FOR
THE ADVANCEMENT OF SCIENCE AND ART
Bones and skin: competition for
student housing, Cooper Union, New
York, 1989 / Diane Lewis.
Architect: Diane Lewis.
AA FILES 1990 Autumn, no.20,
p.42-45, elevs., plans, secn.,
aerial photo.

UNITED STATES--NEW YORK (NEW YORK)--
STUDENT HOUSING--NEW YORK
UNIVERSITY--FILOMEN D'AGOSTINO HALL
Places to learn: New York University
Law School, Washington Square,
West Third Street, New York, New
York.
Contents: Mercer Residence Hall --
D'Agostino Hall -- Law Library.
Architects: Benjamin Thompson &
Associates. Text in Japanese and
English.
PROCESS: ARCHITECTURE 1990 June,
no.89, p.80-83, photos., secn.,
site plan.

UNITED STATES--NEW YORK (NEW YORK)--
SUBWAYS--MAINTENANCE AND REPAIR
Is New York's transit off track? /
Margaret Mittelbach.
Maintenance and repair of New
York's subways and stations is a
continuing problem.
CITY LIMITS 1990 Dec., v.15,
no.10, p.8-11, ports., photos.

UNITED STATES--NEW YORK (NEW YORK)--
SUBWAYS--STATIONS--INTERVALE AVENUE
Transportation blues / Alexander
Farnsworth.
The Intervale Ave. subway stop, in
the South Bronx, closed due to
vandalism, will be rebuilt and
opened in 2 1/2 years.
METROPOLIS 1990 July-Aug., v.10,
no.1, p.17-18, photos.

UNITED STATES--NEW YORK (NEW YORK)--
SUBWAYS--STATIONS--MAINTENANCE AND
REPAIR
Is New York's transit off track? /
Margaret Mittelbach.
Maintenance and repair of New
York's subways and stations is a
continuing problem.
CITY LIMITS 1990 Dec., v.15,
no.10, p.8-11, ports., photos.

UNITED STATES--NEW YORK (NEW YORK)--
SUPERMARKETS
Starving for supermarkets / Eve
Heyn.
Shortage of supermarkets in some
New York City neighborhoods. Inset
article by Erika Mallin.
CITY LIMITS 1990 Aug.-Sept., v.15,
no.7, p.22-25, photo., table.

UNITED STATES--NEW YORK (NEW YORK)--
SYNAGOGUES--19TH CENTURY--
CONSERVATION AND RESTORATION--
ELDRIDGE STREET SYNAGOGUE
Preservation profile: The Eldridge
Street Synagogue / Bill Moyers.
Text of a talk given on the 100th
anniversary of the synagogue
(Congregation Khal Adas Jeshurun
with Anshe Lubz) located at 12-16
Eldridge St., New York.
COMMON BOND 1989 Fall, v.5, no.4,
p.2-4, cover, elev., photos.

UNITED STATES--NEW YORK (NEW YORK)--
SYNAGOGUES--HISTORY
Synagogue architecture in New York:
an interview with Joy Kestenbaum /
Ronald Kopnicki.
VILLAGE VIEWS 1989, v.5, no.4,
p.[56]-79, photos.

UNITED STATES--NEW YORK (NEW YORK)--
TALL BUILDINGS
Brute force and ignorance:
Skyscraper [by] Karl Sabbagh [book
review] / Hugh Aldersey-Williams.
BLUEPRINT (LONDON, ENGLAND) 1990
Feb., no.64, p.51, port.
Delirious New York / Rem Koolhaas.
ARCH PLUS 1990 Oct., no.105-106,
p.58-67, ill., dwgs., photos.,
plans, site plans, aerial photos.

UNITED STATES--NEW YORK (NEW YORK)--
TALL BUILDINGS--CARNEGIE TOWER
Designing the super-thin new
buildings / James S. Russell.
Features 6 projects for tall
buildings in New York City,
Chicago and Paris.
ARCHITECTURAL RECORD 1990 Oct.,
v.178, no.11, p.105-109,
axonometric views, elev., models,
photos., plans.

UNITED STATES--NEW YORK (NEW YORK)--
TALL BUILDINGS--EQUITABLE BUILDING
A reconsideration of the Equitable
Building in New York / Sally Kitt
Chappell.
On ideologies surrounding the 1916
zoning movement, elevator
engineering, and management
techniques used in the 1912-1915
building, located at 120 S.
Broadway (architect: E.R. Graham).
Includes abstract.
SOCIETY OF ARCHITECTURAL
HISTORIANS. JOURNAL 1990 Mar.,
v.49, no.1, p.90-95, dwg.,
photos., refs.

UNITED STATES--NEW YORK (NEW YORK)--
TALL BUILDINGS--INFLUENCE
Monument 22 / Claes Caldenby.
Develops 11 arguments for or
against multi-storey buildings and
uses Ralph Erskine's building
Lilla Bommen in Gothenburg as an
example.
ARKITEKTUR: THE SWEDISH REVIEW OF
ARCHITECTURE 1990 May, v.90, no.4,
p.3-11, dwgs., elevs., models,
photos., plans, site plans,
isometric dwg., aerial photo.

UNITED STATES--NEW YORK (NEW YORK)--
TALL BUILDINGS--TIMES SQUARE TOWER
Public places for American cities:
three projects / Rodolfo Machado.
Includes Times Square Tower, New
York (1984); Pershing Square, Los
Angeles (1986); and
Sesquicentennial Park, Houston
(1986).
ASSEMBLAGE 1988 June, no.6,
p.[98]-113, axonometric views,
dets., dwgs., elevs., model,
photos., plans, secns., site
plans.

UNITED STATES--NEW YORK (NEW YORK)--
TELEVISION STATIONS--ABC
ABC phase II, office, studio
building, New York, New York,
1984-86.
Architects: Kohn Pedersen Fox
Associates; partner in charge:
Sheldon Fox.
PROCESS: ARCHITECTURE 1989 Nov.,
no.86, p.44-45, axonometric view,
elev., photos.
Television romance / Victoria
Geibel.
New York Buildings for American
Broadcasting Co. designed by Kohn
Pedersen Fox Associates.
ARCHITECTURE: THE AIA JOURNAL 1990
Dec., v.79, no.12, p.56-[59],
models, photos., plans, site
plans.

UNITED STATES--NEW YORK (NEW YORK)--
TENEMENT HOUSES--CONSERVATION AND
RESTORATION--250-254 EAST 4TH STREET
A housing enterprise / Peter Slatin.
The Enterprise Foundation and
LESCH, a community group, have
renovated 3 tenement buildings at
250-254 East 4th St. on the Lower
East Side of Manhattan.
METROPOLIS 1990 July-Aug., v.10,
no.1, p.18-20, photo.

UNITED STATES--NEW YORK (NEW YORK)--
TENSILE STRUCTURES--TEMPORARY--
BATTERY PARK CITY--WINTER GARDEN
Dramatic tension: temporary
performance structures in the
Winter Garden, Battery Park City /
Justin Henderson.
Architect: FTL Associates.
INTERIORS 1990 Jan., v.149, no.6,
p.154-[155], photos., plan.

UNITED STATES--NEW YORK (NEW YORK)--
THEATERS
The theaters of Herts and Tallant /
Bill Morrison.
MARQUEE 1990, v.22, no.4, cover,
p.3-22, ill., dwg., ports.,
photos., plan.

UNITED STATES--NEW YORK (NEW YORK)--
THEATERS--VICTORY
Teaching Times Square a lesson /
Andrew Mandel, Jacqueline Thaw.
While Times Square awaits
redevelopment, the theater group
En-Garde Arts performs "Crowbar"
in one of the area's saved
theaters, the Victory.
PLACES 1990 Summer, v.6, no.4,
p.[91-92], det., photos.

UNITED STATES--NEW YORK (NEW YORK)--
TOWNHOUSES--INTERIOR DESIGN
In Greenwich Village: amiable
sophistication defines an 1840s
town house / John Taylor.
Interior designer: Thomas Fleming
of Irvine & Fleming.
ARCHITECTURAL DIGEST 1990 Nov.,
v.47, no.12, p.286-291,316,

UNITED STATES--NEW YORK (NEW YORK)--
TOWNHOUSES--INTERIOR DESIGN--HEPBURN
HOUSE
Katharine Hepburn: four-time Best
Actress in New York, Connecticut
and California / A. Scott Berg.
ARCHITECTURAL DIGEST 1990 Apr.,
v.47, no.4, p.192-[197],292,294,
ports., photos.

UNITED STATES--NEW YORK (NEW YORK)--
TOWNHOUSES--INTERIOR DESIGN--
NUNNERLEY HOUSE
Manhattan moderne: where glamour
gets gutsy [Nunnerley townhouse] /
Julie V. Iovine.
Interior design of Upper East Side
home. Interior designer and owner:
Sandra Nunnerley./
METROPOLITAN HOME 1990 Aug., v.22,
no.8, p.124-[125], port., photos.

UNITED STATES--NEW YORK (NEW YORK)--
UNIVERSITIES AND COLLEGES--
BUILDINGS--COLUMBIA UNIVERSITY--
CENTER FOR ENGINEERING AND PHYSICAL
SCIENCE RESEARCH
Columbia University Center for
Engineering and Physical Science
Research, New York, New York, USA,
1991.
Architects: Hellmuth, Obata &
Kassabaum. Text in Japanese and
English.
ARCHITECTURE AND URBANISM 1990
Dec., no.12 extra edition,
p.178-181, axonometric view,
dwgs., plans, site plan.

UNITED STATES--NEW YORK (NEW YORK)--
UNIVERSITIES AND COLLEGES--
BUILDINGS--COLUMBIA UNIVERSITY--
MORRIS A. SCHAPIRO RESIDENCE HALL
West Side study: Morris A. Schapiro
Residence Hall, Columbia
University, New York City, Gruzen
Samten Steinglass Architects /
Rosanna G. Liebman.
Principal designer: Scott Keller.
ARCHITECTURE: THE AIA JOURNAL 1990
Jan., v.79, no.1, p.[90]-91,
photos., plans.

UNITED STATES--NEW YORK (NEW YORK)--
URBAN PARKS--CONSERVATION AND
RESTORATION--BRYANT PARK
Bryant Park plans proceed / Albert
Amateau, Steven Saltzman.
Restoration to enter final phase
in winter of 1990, to be completed
in spring of 1991. Landscape
architects: Hanna/Olin.
METROPOLIS 1990 Jan.-Feb., v.9,
no.6, p.13-14, elev., photos.

UNITED STATES--NEW YORK (NEW YORK)--
URBAN RENEWAL
New York--Phonix in der Asche? /
Wilma R. Albrecht.
ALTE STADT 1989, v.16 no.4,
p.[607]-609, refs.

UNITED STATES--NEW YORK (NEW YORK)--
URBAN RENEWAL--42ND STREET
REDEVELOPMENT PROJECT
Is bigger still better? / Doug
Turetsky.
Large developments at the Hunters
Point waterfront in Queens and in
Times Square are about to begin
construction despite slack in real
estate market.
CITY LIMITS 1990 Aug.-Sept., v.15,
no.7, p.12-15, port., photo.

UNITED STATES--NEW YORK (NEW YORK)--
URBAN RENEWAL--HARLEM
Harlem: a new renaissance? / Mark W.
Griffith, Errol T. Louis.
CITY LIMITS 1990 Oct., v.15, no.8,
p.16-19, port., photos.

UNITED STATES--NEW YORK (NEW YORK)--
URBAN RENEWAL--TIMES SQUARE AREA
Teaching Times Square a lesson /
Andrew Mandel, Jacqueline Thaw.
While Times Square awaits
redevelopment, the theater group
En-Garde Arts performs "Crowbar"
in one of the area's saved
theaters, the Victory.
PLACES 1990 Summer, v.6, no.4,
p.[91-92], det., photos.

AVERY INDEX TO ARCHITECTURAL PERIODICALS

UNITED STATES--NEW YORK (NEW YORK)--
URBAN RENEWAL--TIMES SQUARE AREA
(CONTINUED)
Times Square, New York City: la
costruzione di un problema
ingovernabile (1967/1987) = Times
Square: an unmanageable problem in
the making / Paolo Fareri.
In Italian; English summary,
p.121, 124.
URBANISTICA 1989 Oct., no.96,
p.7-20, 121, 124, elevs., maps,
photos., plans, biblio.

UNITED STATES--NEW YORK (NEW YORK)--
VANDALISM--SOUTH BRONX
Transportation blues / Alexander
Farnsworth.
The Intervale Ave. subway stop, in
the South Bronx, closed due to
vandalism, will be rebuilt and
opened in 2 1/2 years.
METROPOLIS 1990 July-Aug., v.10,
no.1, p.17-18, photos.

UNITED STATES--NEW YORK (NEW YORK)--
WATER TUNNELS
Visible city: water: New York's
complicated water system / Daniel
S. Levy.
METROPOLIS 1990 June, v.9, no.10,
p.78-84, photos.

UNITED STATES--NEW YORK (NEW YORK)--
WINDOWS--STAINED GLASS
Divine light ... Louis Comfort
Tiffany / Steven Saltzman.
Tiffany windows in New York City.
METROPOLIS 1990 May, v.9, no.9,
p.92-95,119-123, photos.

UNITED STATES--NEW YORK (NEW YORK)--
WORLD FAIRS--NEW YORK WORLD'S FAIR
1964
Il domestico in guerra = Domesticity
at war / Beatriz Colomina.
Discusses the 1964-1965 New York
World's Fair, the Underground Home
and other exhibits, Michael Webb's
Slow House, and Donna Robertson's
Room in the City. In Italian and
English.
OTTAGONO 1990 Dec., no.97,
p.24-[49], ill., dwgs., models,
photos., plans, secn., refs.

UNITED STATES--NEW YORK (NEW YORK)--
WORLD FAIRS--NEW YORK'S WORLD'S FAIR
1939--EXHIBITIONS
Back to the future [exhibition
review] / Julian Holder.
On the exhibition, Selling the
world of tomorrow, on view at the
Museum of the City of New York.
BUILDING DESIGN 1990 June 15,
no.990, p.30-31, dwgs., photos.

UNITED STATES--NEW YORK (NEW YORK)--
ZONING LAW
Context is everything / Sandy
Hornick.
Amendments to New York City's
zoning resolution allows for
increased lower density areas for
low-rise neighborhood housing.
PLANNING 1990 Dec., v.56, no.12,
p.22-26, diagrs., dwg., photo.,
secn.

UNITED STATES--NEW YORK (NEW YORK)--
ZONING LAW (CONTINUED)
A user's guide to Charter process /
Todd W. Bressi.
Effects of the proposed revision
to the City Charter on land use in
New York.
CITY LIMITS 1990 Feb., v.15, no.2,
p.18-19.

UNITED STATES--NEW YORK (NEW YORK)--
ZONING--UPPER EAST SIDE
Oculus Special Feature Committee on
Zoning on the Upper East Side:
Part II.
Shows interpretations for 4 sites,
by James Gauer, Marilyn Taylor,
Peter Samton, and Peter De Witt.
OCULUS 1990 Sept., v.53, no.1,
p.6-10, dwgs., ports., elevs.,
models, map, plans.

UNITED STATES--NEW YORK (NEW YORK)--
ZOOS--ALTERATIONS AND ADDITIONS--
CENTRAL PARK ZOO
Central Park Zoo, New York, New
York, 1988 / Kevin Roche.
Architects: Kevin Roche, John
Dinkeloo and Associates. Text in
Japanese and English.
ARCHITECTURE AND URBANISM 1990
Apr., no.4(235), p.[26]-39,
photos., site plan.

UNITED STATES--NEW YORK (NEW YORK)I--
LOFTS--LOFT M
Stanza del collezionista, loft "M",
N.Y. = Collector's room, "M" loft,
N.Y.
Architects: Ayse Sulan Kolatan and
William J. MacDonald.
LOTUS INTERNATIONAL 1990, no.66,
p.52-57, elevs., photos., plans,
secns.

UNITED STATES--NEW YORK (STATE)--
GARDENS--GREEK REVIVAL--LONG GARDEN
Taking the long view / Gregory Long.
The author's Greek revival garden
in central New York State.
HOUSE & GARDEN 1990 Nov., v.162,
no.11, p.[178-183],230, port.,
photos.

UNITED STATES--NEW YORK (STATE)--
HISTORIC PRESERVATION--AWARDS AND
PRIZES
Seventh annual Preservation League
awards presented.
Twelve private sector awards
presented on May 5, 1990 at the
17th annual conference.
PRESERVATION LEAGUE OF NEW YORK
STATE. NEWSLETTER 1990 Spring,
v.16, no.1, p.8, ports.

UNITED STATES--NEW YORK STATE--
HISTORIC PRESERVATION--CITIZEN
PARTICIPATION
Elmendorph Inn reopens.
Located at 43-45 N.Broadway, Red
Hook.
PRESERVATION LEAGUE OF NEW YORK
STATE. NEWSLETTER 1990-1991
Winter, v.16, no.3, p.6-7, photos.

UNITED STATES--NEW YORK (STATE)--
HISTORIC PRESERVATION --CONGRESSES
Preservation conference held in
Thousand Islands.
PRESERVATION LEAGUE OF NEW YORK
STATE. NEWSLETTER 1990 Spring,
v.16, no.1, p.3, ports., photo.

UNITED STATES--NEW YORK (STATE)--
HOUSES--19TH CENTURY
Residential building materials in
New York State, 1855-1875 / Brian
Coffey, Allen G. Noble.
MATERIAL CULTURE 1989 Spring,
v.21, no.1, p.2-21, dwgs., maps,
tables, refs.

UNITED STATES--NEW YORK (STATE)--
HOUSES--DUTCH COLONIAL
Later Dutch houses of New York & New
Jersey / Russell Gilmore.
Examples from the 1770s.
OLD-HOUSE JOURNAL 1990 Mar.-Apr.,
v.18, no.2, back cover, photos.

UNITED STATES--NEW YORK (STATE)--
HOUSES--INTERIOR DESIGN
Star quality: in an East Coast
retreat for one of Hollywood's
hottest properties... / Charles
Gandee.
Decorated with furniture from the
1940's and 1950's. Interior
decorators: Gillette-Shadley.
HOUSE & GARDEN 1990 May, v.162,
no.5, p.[150-157], photos.

UNITED STATES--NEW YORK (STATE)--LOW
INCOME HOUSING--ENVIRONMENTAL
ASPECTS
Local building officials and rental
housing energy efficiency / Joseph
Laquatra.
Study done in New York State.
HOUSING AND SOCIETY 1990, v.17,
no.3, p.47-56, tables, refs.

UNITED STATES--NEW YORK (STATE)--
RENTAL HOUSING--ENVIRONMENTAL
ASPECTS
Local building officials and rental
housing energy efficiency / Joseph
Laquatra.
Study done in New York State.
HOUSING AND SOCIETY 1990, v.17,
no.3, p.47-56, tables, refs.

UNITED STATES--NEW YORK (STATE)--
RESIDENTIAL GARDENS
Pretty as a picket: classic white
fences ... / Bob Felner.
Residential garden designed by
landscape architect Bruce Kelly.
HOUSE & GARDEN 1990 Mar., v.162,
no.3, p.124-[129], photos.

UNITED STATES--NEW YORK (STATE)--
RETREAT CENTERS--OBSIDIUM
On paper: living in obsidium.
A proposal to reuse an abandoned
missile silo as a "rural retreat
for urban dwellers." Architects:
James E. Langford and Sandi
Hubbard.
TEXAS ARCHITECT 1990 Nov-Dec.,
v.40, no.6, p.82, dwg., secns.

UNITED STATES--NEW YORK (STATE)--
VERNACULAR ARCHITECTURE--18TH
CENTURY
Later Dutch houses of New York & New
Jersey / Russell Gilmore.
Examples from the 1770s.
OLD-HOUSE JOURNAL 1990 Mar.-Apr.,
v.18, no.2, back cover, photos.

UNITED STATES--NEW YORK (STATE)--
WEEKEND HOUSES--INTERIOR DESIGN--
CAHAN - MIRABELLA HOUSE (VILLA SANTO
GUGLIELMO)
Villa Santo Guglielmo: Grace
Mirabella and Dr. William Cahan's
New York State residence / Judith
Thurman.
Architect: Alexander Gorlin.
ARCHITECTURAL DIGEST 1990 Feb.,
v.47, no.2, p.[164-169],238,
photos.

UNITED STATES--NEWARK (NEW JERSEY)--
APARTMENT COMPLEXES--POLK STREET
CONDOMINIUMS
Polk Street Condominiums, Newark,
New Jersey.
Architects: Barrett Allen
Ginsberg.
ARCHITECTURE NEW JERSEY 1989,
v.25, no.3, p.9, plans, site plan.

UNITED STATES--NEWARK (NEW JERSEY)--
CENTERS FOR THE PERFORMING ARTS--NEW
JERSEY CENTER FOR THE PERFORMING
ARTS
"Make no little plans..." The New
Jersey Center for the Performing
Arts / Sharon Ayn McHugh.
Planned for a 12-acre waterfront
site in Newark. Master plan by
James Stewart Polshek and SOM.
ARCHITECTURE NEW JERSEY 1990,
v.26, no.3, p.22, dwgs.

UNITED STATES--NEWARK (NEW JERSEY)--
CENTRAL BUSINESS DISTRICTS
Update on Newark: the doughnut hole
has been filled / Bruce Hendler.
URBAN LAND 1990 Apr., v.49, no.4,
p.22-23, axonometric view, tables.

UNITED STATES--NEWARK (NEW JERSEY)--
COURTHOUSES--MARTIN LUTHER KING JR.
FEDERAL OFFICE BUILDING AND
COURTHOUSE
Martin Luther King Jr. Federal
Office Building and Courthouse,
Newark, New Jersey.
Architects: The Grad Partnership.
ARCHITECTURE NEW JERSEY 1990,
v.26, no.3, p.10-11, axonometric
view, dwgs., model, secn.

UNITED STATES--NEWARK (NEW JERSEY)--
LABOR UNION BUILDINGS
Light-filled heavy metal ...
professional services building
near Newark, New Jersey / M.
Stephanie Stubbs.
Arrchitects: Ronald Schmidt &
Associates.
ARCHITECTURE: THE AIA JOURNAL 1990
Jan., v.79, no.1, p.128-129,
dets., photos., secn.

UNITED STATES--NEWARK (NEW JERSEY)--
LAW SCHOOLS--SETON HALL UNIVERSITY
LAW SCHOOL
Newark Centre for Commerce &
Education, Newark, New Jersey.
Includes Seton Hall University Law
School. Architects: The Grad
Partnership.
ARCHITECTURE NEW JERSEY 1989,
v.25, no.3, p.6-7, dwg., plans.

UNITED STATES--NEWARK (NEW JERSEY)--
MUSEUMS--ART--ALTERATIONS AND
ADDITIONS--NEWARK MUSEUM
The edifice complex / Peter C.
Papademetriou.
On the renovated Newark Museum.
Architect: Michael Graves.
CONNOISSEUR 1990 Mar., v.220,
no.938, p.30,32, photo.
Four not-so-easy pieces / Peter C.
Papademetriou.
Features remodeled Newark Museum,
Newark, NJ. Architects: Michael
Graves Architect.
PROGRESSIVE ARCHITECTURE 1990
Mar., v.71, no.3, p.88-[95],
model, photos., plans.
The Newark Museum reopens / Nora
Odendahl.
Renovation by Michael Graves.
ARCHITECTURE NEW JERSEY 1990,
v.26, no.2, p.21-23, photos.

UNITED STATES--NEWARK (NEW JERSEY)--
OFFICE BUILDINGS--NEWARK CENTRE FOR
COMMERCE & EDUCATION
Newark Centre for Commerce &
Education, Newark, New Jersey.
Includes Seton Hall University Law
School. Architects: The Grad
Partnership.
ARCHITECTURE NEW JERSEY 1989,
v.25, no.3, p.6-7, dwg., plans.

UNITED STATES--NEWARK (NEW JERSEY)--
PARKS--CONSERVATION AND
RESTORATION--BRANCH BROOK PARK
Reviving Newark's Branch Brook Park.
First county park in U.S., c.1895.
PRESERVATION PERSPECTIVE NJ 1990
May-June, v.9, no.3, p.4-5, photo.

UNITED STATES--NEWARK (NEW JERSEY)--
PUBLIC BUILDINGS--MARTIN LUTHER KING
JR. FEDERAL OFFICE BUILDING AND
COURTHOUSE
Martin Luther King Jr. Federal
Office Building and Courthouse,
Newark, New Jersey.
Architects: The Grad Partnership.
ARCHITECTURE NEW JERSEY 1990,
v.26, no.3, p.10-11, axonometric
view, dwgs., model, secn.

UNITED STATES--NEWARK (NEW JERSEY)--
REAL ESTATE DEVELOPMENT
Update on Newark: the doughnut hole
has been filled / Bruce Hendler.
URBAN LAND 1990 Apr., v.49, no.4,
p.22-23, axonometric view, tables.

UNITED STATES--NEWARK (NEW JERSEY)--
URBAN RENEWAL
Update on Newark: the doughnut hole
has been filled / Bruce Hendler.
URBAN LAND 1990 Apr., v.49, no.4,
p.22-23, axonometric view, tables.

UNITED STATES--NEWCOMB (NEW YORK)--
CAMPS--19TH CENTURY--CAMP SANTANONI
Summer hike to Adirondack Great
Camp.
Held in July 1990 at Camp
Santanoni, Newcomb, NY. Built
1888-1890. Architect: Robert H.
Robertson.
PRESERVATION LEAGUE OF NEW YORK
STATE. NEWSLETTER 1990 Fall, v.16,
no.2, p.3, photos.

UNITED STATES--NEWPORT BEACH
(CALIFORNIA)--HOTELS--FOUR SEASONS
HOTEL
The Four Seasons in Newport Beach,
California integrates luxury with
an informal West Coast style /
Justin Henderson.
Hotel architects: Wimberly,
Whisenand, Allison, Tong & Goo.
Interior designer: James Northcutt
Associates.
INTERIORS 1989 Feb., v.148, no.7,
p.46-47, photos.

UNITED STATES--NEWPORT BEACH
(CALIFORNIA)--MUSEUMS--ART--NEWPORT
HARBOR ART MUSEUM
Projects: Museums / Mark Alden
Branch.
On five new museums: United States
Holocaust Memorial Museum,
Washington D.C.; Massachusetts
Museum of Contemporary Art, North
Adams Mass.; Seattle Art Museum;
Museo de Arte Contemporaneo,
Barcelona; and the Newport Harbor
Art Museum, Newport Beach, Calif.
PROGRESSIVE ARCHITECTURE 1990 May,
v.71, no.5, p.124-128, axonometric
view, models, photos., plans,
secns., site plans, aerial photo.

UNITED STATES--NEWPORT BEACH
(CALIFORNIA)--SHOPPING MALLS--
FASHION ISLAND
Reshuffling the deck: Building Types
Study 677: Retail facilities /
Clifford A. Pearson.
Fashion Island, Newport Beach,
Calif. (Jerde Partnership), North
Pier, Chicago (Booth Hansen &
Assoc., The Austin Co.); Napa Town
Center, Napa Calif. (Field Paoli
Architects); and A & S Plaza, New
York City (RTKL Assoc.).
ARCHITECTURAL RECORD 1990 Apr.,
v.178, no.4, p.97-111, photos.,
plans, secns., site plans.

UNITED STATES--NEWPORT (RHODE
ISLAND)--APARTMENT HOUSES--CALLENDER
SCHOOL
Special feature: George Ranalli.
Contents: Essays: George Ranalli
statement: elements of
architecture/ George Ranalli--
Autonomous structures/ Ross
Miller--Interview: George Ranalli/
Ross Miller--Works 1979-1989:
Callender school renovation,
Newport, R.I.--Ranalli studio
apartment, New York City,
1982-83--Peak competition project,
Hong Kong, 1982--Paris Opera
competition project, 1983--Chicago
Tribune competition project,
1980--Times Tower competition
project, 1984--New York loft,
1985-86--Valentine chair--House
addition for "G" family,
(Continued next page)

UNITED STATES--NEWPORT (RHODE ISLAND)--APARTMENT HOUSES--CALLENDER SCHOOL (CONTINUED)
Special feature:...(CONTINUED)
Westchester, New York, 1987-88--Conversion of barn to residence, Red Hook, N.Y., 1988-89--K project "Tower of Silence," Tokyo, Japan, 1989. Text in Japanese and English.
ARCHITECTURE AND URBANISM 1990 Aug., no.8(239), p.[71-136], axonometric views, port., elevs., models, photos., plans, secns., site plans.

UNITED STATES--NEWPORT (RHODE ISLAND)--HOUSES--INTERIOR DESIGN--WAYNE HOUSE
John Wayne: Best Actor for True grit in Newport Beach / Sam Burchell.
Features home interiors.
ARCHITECTURAL DIGEST 1990 Apr., v.47, no.4, p.240-241,304, port., photos.

UNITED STATES--NEWPORT (RHODE ISLAND)--RESORTS--SUMMER
A new golden age for Newport / Walter McQuade.
Profile of the seaside resort.
CONNOISSEUR 1990 June, v.220, no.940, p.61-73,124-125, photos.

UNITED STATES--NEWPORT (RHODE ISLAND)--SEASIDE TOWNS
A new golden age for Newport / Walter McQuade.
Profile of the seaside resort.
CONNOISSEUR 1990 June, v.220, no.940, p.61-73,124-125, photos.

UNITED STATES--NIAGARA FALLS (NEW YORK)--FORTIFICATION--OLD FORT NIAGARA
A fort called Niagara / Stuart D. Scott, Patricia Kay Scott.
Originally estab. in 1688 and recently excavated.
ARCHAEOLOGY 1990 Jan.-Feb., v.43, no.1, p.64-66,84, ill., site plans, aerial photo.

UNITED STATES--NIWOT (COLORADO)--OWNER-BUILT HOUSES--AFFLECK HOUSE
Country Victorian / Carla F. Black.
House by builder Bob Affleck and interior designer Carol Affleck, in Niwot, Colorado.
VICTORIAN HOMES 1990 Summer, v.9, no.3, p.33-37, dets., port., photos.

UNITED STATES--NORFOLK (CONNECTICUT)--SUMMER HOUSES--ALTERATIONS AND ADDITIONS--GILL HOUSE
Wright and wrong in a Connecticut country house / Brendan Gill.
Author's recollections of his repeated alterations to his summer house in Norfolk, Ct., including his remodeling efforts after Frank Lloyd Wright's Usonian houses.
ARCHITECTURAL DIGEST 1990 June, v.47, no.6, p.34,[40-41],44, ill., port.

UNITED STATES--NORFOLK (MICHIGAN)--APARTMENTS--CRAFTSMAN--INTERIOR DESIGN--COOPER APARTMENT
The apartment over the store / Tom H. Gerhardt.
The home of Ken and Ruth Cooper, in a 1910 concrete block store, Norwalk, Mich., built by Pete Schneider.
VICTORIAN HOMES 1990 Fall, v.9, no.4, p.39-45, photos.

UNITED STATES--NORFOLK (VIRGINIA)--CENTRAL BUSINESS DISTRICTS
Taming the city edge: urban design portfolio / Andrea Oppenheimer Dean.
The latest frontier--"outcities." Mission Bay, San Francisco; Downtown Norfolk, Va; Carr Norfolk Southern Project, Alexandria, Va.; and Arverne, New York City.
ARCHITECTURE: THE AIA JOURNAL 1990 Apr., v.79, no.4, p.[74]-79,147, ill., model, plans, sketches, aerial photos.

UNITED STATES--NORFOLK (VIRGINIA)--DISTRICTS
Managing downtown revitalization by district / Maureen Atkinson, John Williams.
Distinguishes the various types of downtown districts which can be targeted for revitalization; examples in Toronto and Norfolk.
URBAN LAND 1990 Sept., v.49, no.9, p.2-6, photos., plans.

UNITED STATES--NORFOLK (VIRGINIA)--HOUSING
Focus on Norfolk, Virginia.
Ghent Square and the Scattered Site Infill Housing Program.
JOURNAL OF HOUSING 1990 Mar.-Apr., v.47, no.2, p.101-104, photos.

UNITED STATES--NORFOLK (VIRGINIA)--MUSEUMS--ART--ALTERATIONS AND ADDITIONS--CHRYSLER MUSEUM
Chrysler Museum renewed: an architectural transformation daring in its sensitivity / Benjamin Forgey.
Expansion and renovation of 1933 museum in Norfolk, Va. by Hartman-Cox Architects.
SOUTHERN ACCENTS 1989 Nov.-Dec., v.12, no.6, p.72-[80], photos.

UNITED STATES--NORFOLK (VIRGINIA)--URBAN RENEWAL
Focus on Norfolk, Virginia.
Ghent Square and the Scattered Site Infill Housing Program.
JOURNAL OF HOUSING 1990 Mar.-Apr., v.47, no.2, p.101-104, photos.

UNITED STATES--NORTH ADAMS (MASSACHUSETTS)--MUSEUMS--ART--MASSACHUSETTS MUSEUM OF CONTEMPORARY ART
From the body of the prince to Mickey Mouse / Jo-anne Berelowitz.
Theoretical essay on the postmodern museum. Focus on the Museum of Contemporary Art, Los Angeles and the Massachusetts Museum of Contemporary Art (Mass MoCA), North Adams, Mass.
OXFORD ART JOURNAL 1990, v.13, no.2, p.70-84, dwgs., maps,
(Continued next column)

UNITED STATES--NORTH ADAMS (MASSACHUSETTS)--MUSEUMS--ART--MASSACHUSETTS MUSEUM OF CONTEMPORARY ART (CONTINUED)
From the body of the...(CONTINUED)
photos., aerial photo., biblio., refs.
Museum as multinational: a new Guggenheim in Salzburg designed by Hans Hollein and a new contemporary art complex in a Massachusetts factory... / Michael Wise, Jillian Burt.
Proposed Massachusetts Museum of Contemporary Art, North Adams, Mass.; architects: Frank Gehry, Robert Venturi and David Childs.
BLUEPRINT (LONDON, ENGLAND) 1990 Oct., no.71, p.44-48, axonometric views, models, photos.
Projects: Museums / Mark Alden Branch.
On five new museums: United States Holocaust Memorial Museum, Washington D.C.; Massachusetts Museum of Contemporary Art, North Adams Mass.; Seattle Art Museum; Museo de Arte Contemporaneo, Barcelona; and the Newport Harbor Art Museum, Newport Beach, Calif.
PROGRESSIVE ARCHITECTURE 1990 May, v.71, no.5, p.124-128, axonometric view, models, photos., plans, secns., site plans, aerial photo.

UNITED STATES--NORTH CAROLINA--COURTHOUSES--19TH CENTURY
Raised courthouse in North Carolina / Daniel Fagg, Jr.
Built in Duplin and Wayne counties in the early 19th cent.
MATERIAL CULTURE 1989 Fall, v.21, no.3, p.1-8, plans, site plans, biblio.

UNITED STATES--NORTH CAROLINA--DRAINING
A report card on urban erosion and sedimentation control in North Carolina / Raymond J. Burby...et al.
CAROLINA PLANNING 1990 Fall, v.16, no.2, p.28-36, graphs, map, photos., tables, refs.

UNITED STATES--NORTH CAROLINA--HOUSES--TYPOLOGY
Pride and prejudice: the Appalachian boxed house in southwestern North Carolina / Michael Ann Williams.
WINTERTHUR PORTFOLIO 1990 Winter, v.25, no.4, p.[217]-230, photos., refs.

UNITED STATES--NORTH DAKOTA--FORTIFICATION--19TH CENTURY--CONSERVATION AND RESTORATION--FORT UNION
The great reconstruction controversy: a debate and discussion.
Reproduces a letter by Paul R. Huey and a reply by William J. Hunt, about Hunt's article in the Feb. 1989 issue of this bulletin, followed by an essay by Barry Mackintosh on NPS policy and practice.
CRM BULLETIN: A NATIONAL PARK SERVICE TECHNICAL BULLETIN 1990, v.13, no.1, p.[1]-7,14, dwg., photo.

UNITED STATES--NORTH PROVIDENCE (RHODE ISLAND)--FRAMING--19TH CENTURY--WOODEN--ALLENDALE MILL
The 1822 Allendale mill and slow-burning construction: a case study in the transmission of an architectural technology / Richard M. Candee.
On the framing technique used in Zachariah Allen's textile mill in North Providence, RI.
SOCIETY FOR INDUSTRIAL ARCHEOLOGY. JOURNAL 1989, v.15, no.1, p.21-34, dets., elevs., photos., plans, secns., engrs., refs.

UNITED STATES--NORTH PROVIDENCE (RHODE ISLAND)--TEXTILE MILLS--19TH CENTURY--ALLENDALE MILL
The 1822 Allendale mill and slow-burning construction: a case study in the transmission of an architectural technology / Richard M. Candee.
On the framing technique used in Zachariah Allen's textile mill in North Providence, RI.
SOCIETY FOR INDUSTRIAL ARCHEOLOGY. JOURNAL 1989, v.15, no.1, p.21-34, dets., elevs., photos., plans, secns., engrs., refs.

UNITED STATES--NORTHBROOK (ILLINOIS)--CORPORATE OFFICE BUILDINGS--CRATE & BARREL
Shop and shine / Karin Tetlow.
On award-winning design of Crate & Barrel's corporate headquarters in Northbrook, Ill. Architects: Solomon Cordwell Buenz.
INTERIORS 1990 May, v.149, no.10, p.206-[219], dwgs., photos., plan.

UNITED STATES--NORTON (MASSACHUSETTS)--STUDENT UNIONS--WHEATON COLLEGE--BALFOUR-HOOD CAMPUS CENTER
A mending wall: Balfour-Hood Campus Center, Wheaton College, Norton Massachusetts / Michael J. Crosbie.
Amsler Hagenah MacLean Architects with Robert Neiley Architects.
ARCHITECTURE: THE AIA JOURNAL 1990 Jan., v.79, no.1, p.82-83, photos.

UNITED STATES--NORWELL (MASSACHUSETTS)--CEMETERIES--18TH CENTURY--CONSERVATION AND RESTORATION
Burial ground controversy prompted by development: Part II / Charles E. Rounds, Jr.
In Norwell, Mass. Part I was published in the Nov.1989 issue of this newsletter.
BOSTON PRESERVATION ALLIANCE LETTER 1990 Jan., v.11, no.1, p.7-8, photo.

UNITED STATES--OAHU (HAWAII)--PLANTATIONS (SETTLEMENT AREAS)--CONSERVATION AND RESTORATION--EWA PLANTATION
Forever Ewa: Hawaiians hope to save once-proud plantation [Ewa Sugar Plantation, near Honolulu] / Rodney N. Smith.
PRESERVATION NEWS 1990 June, v.30, no.6, p.1,19, port., photos.

UNITED STATES--OAK BROOK (ILLINOIS)--RESTAURANTS--INTERIOR DESIGN--ZARROSTA GRILL
Zarrosta Grill / Edie Lee Cohen.
Interiors of Oak Brook, Ill. restaurant. Architects: Aumiller Youngquist.
INTERIOR DESIGN 1990 Feb., v.61, no.3, p.[218-219], photos.

UNITED STATES--OAK PARK (ILLINOIS)--BIRTHING ROOMS--INTERIOR DESIGN--WEST SUBURBAN HOSPITAL--MARGARET HOUCK FAMILY BIRTHING CENTER
Birthing center / Judith Davidsen.
Interiors of the Margaret Houck Family Birthing Center, West Suburban Hospital, Oak Park, Ill. Architects/ Interior designers: Loebl Schlossman and Hackl.
INTERIOR DESIGN 1990 Nov., v.61, no.15, p.190-193, photos., plan.

UNITED STATES--OAK PARK (ILLINOIS)--OPERATING ROOMS--INTERIOR DESIGN--WEST SUBURBAN HOSPITAL--MARGARET HOUCK FAMILY BIRTHING CENTER
Birthing center / Judith Davidsen.
Interiors of the Margaret Houck Family Birthing Center, West Suburban Hospital, Oak Park, Ill. Architects/ Interior designers: Loebl Schlossman and Hackl.
INTERIOR DESIGN 1990 Nov., v.61, no.15, p.190-193, photos., plan.

UNITED STATES--OAKLAND (CALIFORNIA)--HOUSES--CRAFTSMAN--INTERIOR DESIGN--SMITH HOME
Southwest sizzle: a colorful display of folk art energizes a California Craftsman cottage / Jane Margolies.
1917 mail-order Craftsman bungalow in Oakland, Ca.
HOUSE BEAUTIFUL 1990 May, v.132, no.5, p.[64-69], ports., photos.

UNITED STATES--OAKLAND (CALIFORNIA)--HOUSES--SLOPING SITES--GREWAL HOUSE
Grewal Residence, Oakland, California, design: 1988.
Architect: Stanley Saitowitz. Text in Japanese and English.
GA HOUSES 1990 Mar., no.28, p.82, elevs., model, plan, secns.

UNITED STATES--OAKLAND (CALIFORNIA)--MARKETS--ROCKRIDGE MARKET HALL
The making of a market / Herb Childress.
Rockridge Market Hall, Oakland, Ca. Architect and developer: Peter and Anthony Wilson (Wilson Associates).
PLACES 1990 Fall, v.7, no.1, p.50-63, dets., elev., photos., plans, aerial photos.

UNITED STATES--OAKLAND (CALIFORNIA)--MOVIE THEATERS--FOX OAKLAND THEATRE
Fox hunting in Oakland: hunters are stalking the rare Oakland Fox [Fox Oakland Theatre] / Herb Stockinger.
The Fox Oakland Theatre was completed in 1928, Weeks and Day, architects.
MARQUEE 1990, v.22, no.3, p.3-6, photos., secn.

UNITED STATES--OAKLAND (CALIFORNIA)--OFFICES--INTERIOR DESIGN--AT&T REMOTE WORK CENTER
Remote area ambiance / Karin Tetlow.
On the design of the AT&T Remote Work Center, Oakland, Calif. Architect: George W. Famous.
INTERIORS 1990 Mar., v.149, no.8, p.36, photo., isometric dwg.

UNITED STATES--OBERLIN (OHIO)--GAS HOLDERS--19TH CENTURY
Running on empty.
Historic 1889 gasholder house in Oberlin, Ohio, which once held coal gas, is threatened with demolition.
HISTORIC PRESERVATION 1990 July-Aug., v.42, no.4, p.[80], photo.

UNITED STATES--OCEAN CITY (MARYLAND)--SEASIDE TOWNS
Bay patrol: a Maryland coastal community fends off developers / Jeff Weintraub, Mary Lou Gallagher.
In Worcester County, Maryland, on the mainland across from Ocean City.
PLANNING 1990 Oct., v.56, no.10, p.22-23, maps, photos., aerial photo.

UNITED STATES--OCEAN CITY (NEW JERSEY)--RECREATION AREAS--MAINTENANCE AND REPAIR
Building a home-court advantage / John Kutch.
Tennis courts and recreational areas in Ocean City, N.J.
PARKS & RECREATION 1990 July, v.25, no.7, p.38-41, photos.

UNITED STATES--OCEAN CITY (NEW JERSEY)--TENNIS COURTS--MAINTENANCE AND REPAIR
Building a home-court advantage / John Kutch.
Tennis courts and recreational areas in Ocean City, N.J.
PARKS & RECREATION 1990 July, v.25, no.7, p.38-41, photos.

UNITED STATES--OCEANSIDE (CALIFORNIA)--CIVIC CENTERS--OCEANSIDE CIVIC CENTER
Homage to Gill: Oceanside Civic Center, Oceanside, California, Charles W. Moore/Urban Innovations Group, Architects.
ARCHITECTURAL RECORD 1990 Nov., v.178, no.12, p.[76]-81, elevs., photos., plans, site plan.

UNITED STATES--OCEANSIDE (CALIFORNIA)--INDUSTRIAL BUILDINGS--OCEANSIDE CONTOL FACILITY
Site-sensitive technology: Simon Martin Vegue Winkelstein Moris of San Francisco.
Three designs for projects that meld high technology and sensitive design: Oceanside Control Facility, Contra Costa Water Treatment complex, and addition to Lawrence Hall.
ARCHITECTURE: THE MAGAZINE OF THE AMERICAN INSTITUTE OF ARCHITECTS 1990 May, v.79, no.5, p.48, elev., models, secn.

UNITED STATES--OCONOMOWOC
(WISCONSIN)--INNS--INTERIOR DESIGN--
INN AT PINE TERRACE
    Wisconsin getaways: urban chic,
    rural retreat / Karen E. Klages.
    Two interiors: DKC's Armadillo Bar
    and Grill, Milwaukee (architect:
    Kubala Washatko Architects), and
    The Inn at Pine Terrace,
    Oconomowoc (designer: Zimmerman
    Design Group).
    INLAND ARCHITECT 1990 July-Aug.,
    v.34, no.4, p.4-[5], photos.,
    plan.

UNITED STATES--OFFICE BUILDINGS--
AWARDS AND PRIZES
    Design 90: NAIOP's Annual
    Design/Development Awards Program.
    DEVELOPMENT 1990 Nov.-Dec., v.21,
    no.6, p.[6]-10, photos.

UNITED STATES--OFFICE FURNITURE
    Steelcase's practical Pyramid /
    Michael J. P. Smith.
    The Corporate Development Center,
    Grand Rapids, Mich. Architect:
    WBDC Group and Donald J. Koster.
    INLAND ARCHITECT 1990 Nov.-Dec.,
    v.34, no.6, p.19-20, photo.,
    secn., aerial photo.

UNITED STATES--OHIO--CITY PLANNING--
STUDY AND TEACHING
    Encouraging regional cooperation
    among state university planning
    departments: Ohio's
    inter-institutional research
    consortium / Terry F. Buss.
    JOURNAL OF PLANNING EDUCATION AND
    RESEARCH 1990 Fall, v.10, no.1,
    p.71-74, refs.

UNITED STATES--OKLAHOMA CITY
(OKLAHOMA)--BOTANICAL GARDENS--
MYRIAD GARDENS
    I tropici nel vento: orto botanico a
    Oklahoma City.
    Myriad Gardens Crystal Bridge.
    Architects: Conklin Rossant.
    ARCHITETTURA; CRONACHE E STORIA
    1990 Mar., v.36, no.3(413),
    p.208-209, ill., photos, plans,
    secn., site plan.

UNITED STATES--OKLAHOMA CITY
(OKLAHOMA)--CHURCHES--ALTERATIONS
AND ADDITIONS--MAYWOOD PRESBYTERIAN
CHURCH
    Church revival: Stiles Circle
    Corporate Headquarters, Oklahoma
    City, Oklahoma, HTB, Inc.,
    Architects / Amy Gray Light.
    Adaptive reuse of a 1907 church.
    ARCHITECTURE: THE AIA JOURNAL 1990
    Nov., v.79, no.11, p.90-93,
    photos., plans, secns., sketches.

UNITED STATES--OKLAHOMA CITY
(OKLAHOMA)--CORPORATE OFFICE
BUILDINGS--STILES CIRCLE CORPORATE
HEADQUARTERS
    Church revival: Stiles Circle
    Corporate Headquarters, Oklahoma
    City, Oklahoma, HTB, Inc.,
    Architects / Amy Gray Light.
    Adaptive reuse of a 1907 church.
    ARCHITECTURE: THE AIA JOURNAL 1990
    Nov., v.79, no.11, p.90-93,
    photos., plans, secns., sketches.

UNITED STATES--OKLAHOMA CITY
(OKLAHOMA)--GREENHOUSES--MYRIAD
GARDENS CRYSTAL BRIDGE
    I tropici nel vento: orto botanico a
    Oklahoma City.
    Myriad Gardens Crystal Bridge.
    Architects: Conklin Rossant.
    ARCHITETTURA; CRONACHE E STORIA
    1990 Mar., v.36, no.3(413),
    p.208-209, ill., photos, plans,
    secn., site plan.

UNITED STATES--OKLAHOMA CITY
(OKLAHOMA)--HOUSES--ARCHITECTS'--
ALTERATIONS AND ADDITIONS--VILLA
BELL (ELLIOTT HOUSE)
    Villa Bell / Mayer Rus.
    Renovated interiors of 1920 home
    in Oklahoma City owned and
    renovated by Rand Elliott. The
    home was originally built for
    Richard Robert Bell.
    INTERIOR DESIGN 1990 July, v.61,
    no.10, p.140-[143], photos.,
    plans.

UNITED STATES--OKLAHOMA CITY
(OKLAHOMA)--PEDESTRIAN BRIDGES--
GLASS--MYRIAD GARDENS CRYSTAL BRIDGE
    I tropici nel vento: orto botanico a
    Oklahoma City.
    Myriad Gardens Crystal Bridge.
    Architects: Conklin Rossant.
    ARCHITETTURA; CRONACHE E STORIA
    1990 Mar., v.36, no.3(413),
    p.208-209, ill., photos, plans,
    secn., site plan.

UNITED STATES--OKLAHOMA CITY
(OKLAHOMA)--RACETRACKS--REMINGTON
PARK RACETRACK
    The Chalk Horse / Monica Geran.
    Interiors of penthouse
    suite/lounge owned by Ackerman
    Hood and McQueen Advertising at
    the Remington Park Racetrack,
    Oklahoma City, Okla. Interior
    designers: Elliott & Associates
    Architects.
    INTERIOR DESIGN 1990 June, v.61,
    no.9, p.202-[203], photos., plan.

UNITED STATES--OKLAHOMA CITY
(OKLAHOMA)--SCHOOLS--DANCE--BALLET
OKLAHOMA
    Ballet fairy tale / Kristen
    Richards.
    Oklahoma City industrial building
    converted into dance school for
    the Ballet Oklahoma. Renovation
    architects: Elliott + Associates
    Architects.
    INTERIORS 1990 Dec., v.150, no.5,
    p.84-[87], photos., plan.

UNITED STATES--OKLAHOMA CITY
(OKLAHOMA)--TELEPHONE BUILDINGS--
ALTERATIONS AND ADDITIONS--
SOUTHWESTERN BELL
    Communications Tone / Ralph Yellow.
    Features interiors of renovated
    Southwestern Bell's Communications
    Center, Oklahoma City, OK.
    Architects: HTB.
    INTERIORS 1990 Nov., v.150, no.4,
    p.52-[55], photos., plan.

UNITED STATES--OKLAHOMA CITY
(OKLAHOMA)--THEATERS--ALTERATIONS
AND ADDITIONS--MUMMERS THEATER
    A mummers' tale: a true life story /
    Barbara Koerble.
    Functional improvements planned
    for the Mummers Theater (1971),
    Oklahoma City. Original
    architect: John Johansen.
    Renovation architect: Elliott &
    Associates.
    CITE: THE ARCHITECTURE AND DESIGN
    REVIEW OF HOUSTON 1990 Fall,
    no.25, p.14-17, model, photos.,
    plan, secn., refs.

UNITED STATES--OKLAHOMA CITY
(OKLAHOMA)--THEATERS--ALTERATIONS
AND ADDITIONS--STAGE CENTER
    Renewing our modern legacy / Andrea
    Oppenheimer Dean.
    Four additions to buildings of the
    1950s and 1960s.
    ARCHITECTURE: THE AIA JOURNAL 1990
    Nov., v.79, no.11, p.66-69, ill.,
    elevs., models, photos.

UNITED STATES--OKLAHOMA CITY
(OKLAHOMA)--V.I.P. LOUNGES--INTERIOR
DESIGN--REMINGTON PARK RACETRACK--
CHALK HORSE
    The Chalk Horse / Monica Geran.
    Interiors of penthouse
    suite/lounge owned by Ackerman
    Hood and McQueen Advertising at
    the Remington Park Racetrack,
    Oklahoma City, Okla. Interior
    designers: Elliott & Associates
    Architects.
    INTERIOR DESIGN 1990 June, v.61,
    no.9, p.202-[203], photos., plan.

UNITED STATES--OLD SAYBROOK
(CONNECTICUT)--HOUSES--17TH
CENTURY--ELISHA BUSHNELL HOUSE
    Old Saybrook: plans for development
    on Bushnell site have come a long
    way.
    New plans for a shopping area
    incorporate the 17th-cent. Elisha
    Bushnell house.
    CONNECTICUT PRESERVATION NEWS 1989
    July-Aug., v.12, no.4, p.8-9,
    dwg., site plans.

UNITED STATES--OLD SAYBROOK
(CONNECTICUT)--SHOPPING CENTERS--
SAYBROOK SHOPS
    Old Saybrook: plans for development
    on Bushnell site have come a long
    way.
    New plans for a shopping area
    incorporate the 17th-cent. Elisha
    Bushnell house.
    CONNECTICUT PRESERVATION NEWS 1989
    July-Aug., v.12, no.4, p.8-9,
    dwg., site plans.

UNITED STATES--OLNEY (MARYLAND)--
CHURCHES--20TH CENTURY--SAINT
PETER'S CATHOLIC CHURCH
    To gather together: Building types
    study 674. religious buildings /
    Margaret Gaskie.
    Four projects: Gates of the Grove
    Synagogue, East Hampton, N.Y.
    (Norman Jaffe); Beach United
    Methodist Church, Jacksonville
    Beach, Fla. (William Morgan
    Architects); Blackhawk Bapist
    Church, Fort Wayne, Ind. (Harding
    Assoc.); and St. Peter's Catholic
    (Continued next page)

UNITED STATES--OLNEY (MARYLAND)--
CHURCHES--20TH CENTURY--SAINT
PETER'S CATHOLIC CHURCH
(CONTINUED)
To gather together:... (CONTINUED)
Church, Olney, Md. (Hugh N.
Jacobsen).
ARCHITECTURAL RECORD 1990 Jan.,
v.178, no.1, 123-135, elevs.,
photos., plans, secns., site
plans.

UNITED STATES--OMAHA (NEBRASKA)--
BUILDINGS--DEMOLITION--JOBBERS
CANYON
Farewell, Jobbers Canyon, but the
battle may continue in the courts
/ Arnold Berke.
"Jobbers Canyon, the historic
warehouse district in Omaha,
Nebr., ... has been virtually
wiped off the map."
PRESERVATION NEWS 1990 Jan., v.30,
no.1, p.7, photos.

UNITED STATES--OMAHA (NEBRASKA)--
HISTORIC DISTRICTS--JOBBERS CANYON
Farewell, Jobbers Canyon, but the
battle may continue in the courts
/ Arnold Berke.
"Jobbers Canyon, the historic
warehouse district in Omaha,
Nebr., ... has been virtually
wiped off the map."
PRESERVATION NEWS 1990 Jan., v.30,
no.1, p.7, photos.

UNITED STATES--OPEN SPACES
Ecology and aesthetics / Michael
Laurie.
On the design of open space.
PLACES 1989 Fall, v.6, no.1,
p.48-51, photos.
The urban garden as public space /
Mark Francis.
PLACES 1989 Fall, v.6, no.1,
p.52-59, photos., plan, aerial
photo., refs.

UNITED STATES--OPEN SPACES--
CONSERVATION AND RESTORATION
You call this a national park? /
James Krohe.
Small urban parks form part of the
national parks system.
PLANNING 1990 Aug., v.56, no.8,
p.4-10, maps, photos., plan.

UNITED STATES--OPEN SPACES--
PSYCHOLOGICAL ASPECTS
Women and downtown open spaces /
Louise Mozingo.
"Focus on issues designers should
consider in order to make downtown
open spaces more acceptable to
women users."
PLACES 1989 Fall, v.6, no.1,
p.38-47, maps, photos., site
plans, refs.

UNITED STATES--OPEN SPACES--
SOCIOLOGICAL ASPECTS
Social values in open space design /
Randolph T. Hester.
PLACES 1989 Fall, v.6, no.1,
p.68-[77], charts., diagrs.,
photos., plans, secns., aerial
photo.

UNITED STATES--OREGON--CITY PLANNING--
LAW AND LEGISLATION
Blazing new planning trails in
Oregon / Arthur C. Nelson.
Land use and planning regulations
mandated by the Oregon Land
Conservation and Development
Commission, created in 1973.
URBAN LAND 1990 Aug., v.49, no.8,
p.32-35, plans.

UNITED STATES--OREGON--HOUSES--
ALTERATIONS AND ADDITIONS--WILLIAMS
HOUSE
Kitchens that cook: hot news, cool
choices / Julie V. Iovine.
Five projects, including an
expansion of the Sprecher house,
Los Angeles (architect: Michele
Saee); a Connecticut kitchen
renovation (architect: Louis
Mackall); Reichel-Singer house
conversion, Los Angeles (designer:
Josh Schweitzer); Sagalyn kitchen
(architect: Scott Simons); Laurie
and Maurie Williams' kitchen
renovation, Ore.
METROPOLITAN HOME 1990 May, v.22,
no.5, p.[123-136], det., photos.

UNITED STATES--OREGON--HOUSING POLICY
State land use planning and
inclusionary zoning: evidence from
Oregon / Gerrit Knaap.
JOURNAL OF PLANNING EDUCATION AND
RESEARCH 1990 Fall, v.10, no.1,
p.39-46, refs.

UNITED STATES--OREGON--LAND USE
Self-interest and voter support for
Oregon's land use controls /
Gerrit J. Knaap.
AMERICAN PLANNING ASSOCIATION.
JOURNAL 1987 Winter, v.53, no.1,
p.92-97, tables, biblio., refs.

UNITED STATES--OREGON--LAND USE--LAW
AND LEGISLATION
Blazing new planning trails in
Oregon / Arthur C. Nelson.
Land use and planning regulations
mandated by the Oregon Land
Conservation and Development
Commission, created in 1973.
URBAN LAND 1990 Aug., v.49, no.8,
p.32-35, plans.

UNITED STATES--OREGON--LAND USE--
POLITICAL ASPECTS
State land use planning and
inclusionary zoning: evidence from
Oregon / Gerrit Knaap.
JOURNAL OF PLANNING EDUCATION AND
RESEARCH 1990 Fall, v.10, no.1,
p.39-46, refs.

UNITED STATES--OREGON--LOW INCOME
HOUSING--POLITICAL ASPECTS
State land use planning and
inclusionary zoning: evidence from
Oregon / Gerrit Knaap.
JOURNAL OF PLANNING EDUCATION AND
RESEARCH 1990 Fall, v.10, no.1,
p.39-46, refs.

UNITED STATES--OREGON--REGIONAL
PLANNING
State land use planning and
inclusionary zoning: evidence from
Oregon / Gerrit Knaap.
JOURNAL OF PLANNING EDUCATION AND
RESEARCH 1990 Fall, v.10, no.1,
p.39-46, refs.

UNITED STATES--OREGON--REGIONAL
PLANNING--LAW AND LEGISLATION
Blazing new planning trails in
Oregon / Arthur C. Nelson.
Land use and planning regulations
mandated by the Oregon Land
Conservation and Development
Commission, created in 1973.
URBAN LAND 1990 Aug., v.49, no.8,
p.32-35, plans.

UNITED STATES--ORGANIC ARCHITECTURE
Organic agenda / Jeffrey Cook.
On the future of organic
architecture in the U.S.
BUILDING DESIGN 1990 Aug.24,
no.1000, p.13, photos.

UNITED STATES--ORINDA (CALIFORNIA)--
HOUSES--INTERIOR DESIGN--HEADY HOUSE
In an Eastern garden: a Japanese
landscape enfolds a northern
California residence / Howard
Junker.
Interiors and gardens of Joan and
James Heady's home in Orinda.
Interior designer: John Wheatman.
Landscape architect: Kimio Kimura.
ARCHITECTURAL DIGEST 1990 Sept.,
v.47, no.10, p.[178-183], photos.

UNITED STATES--ORINDA (CALIFORNIA)--
RESIDENTIAL GARDENS--HEADY HOUSE
In an Eastern garden: a Japanese
landscape enfolds a northern
California residence / Howard
Junker.
Interiors and gardens of Joan and
James Heady's home in Orinda.
Interior designer: John Wheatman.
Landscape architect: Kimio Kimura.
ARCHITECTURAL DIGEST 1990 Sept.,
v.47, no.10, p.[178-183], photos.

UNITED STATES--ORLAND PARK
(ILLINOIS)--CIVIC CENTERS--ORLAND
PARK VILLAGE CENTER
The place of government: Orland Park
Village Center, Orland Park,
Illinois / Thomas Fisher.
Complex includes village hall,
civic center and recreation
building. Architects: Perkins &
Will. Design pricipal: Ralph
Johnson.
PROGRESSIVE ARCHITECTURE 1990
Oct., v.71, no.10, p.66-77, dets.,
dwg., photos., plans, site plans.

UNITED STATES--ORLANDO (FLORIDA)--
AFFORDABLE HOUSING
The housing connection: Orlando
takes a hands-on approach to
affordable housing / S. Renee
Mitchell.
PLANNING 1990 Sept., v.56, no.9,
p.18-19, photo.

UNITED STATES--ORLANDO (FLORIDA)--
AIRPORTS--ALTERATIONS AND
ADDITIONS--ORLAND INTERNATIONAL
AIRPORT
Ideas in flight: expanding the
Orlando International Airport.
An advertisement for AutoCAD,
using KBJ Architects project for
the airport expansion.
ARCHITECTURAL RECORD 1990 June,
v.178, no.7, p.A1-A20 (special
advertising section), ill.,
elevs., photos, plans, site plans.

UNITED STATES--ORLANDO (FLORIDA)--CITY
PLANNING--CITY COMMONS
Orlando's City Commons: a model
public/private venture / Lewis
Oliver, Eric Smart.
Major 7-acre development,
including a new city hall, public
park and plaza, commercial office
and retail space, and parking in
Orlando's Southern Gateway area.
Planners: Project for Public
Spaces (PPS, Inc.), and Heller &
Leake; architects for the city
hall: HKS and CRS Sirrine.
URBAN LAND 1990 Jan., v.49, no.1,
p.21-25, dwg., site plan, aerial
photo.

UNITED STATES--ORLANDO (FLORIDA)--
COMPREHENSIVE PLANS--CITY COMMONS
Orlando's City Commons: a model
public/private venture / Lewis
Oliver, Eric Smart.
Major 7-acre development,
including a new city hall, public
park and plaza, commercial office
and retail space, and parking in
Orlando's Southern Gateway area.
Planners: Project for Public
Spaces (PPS, Inc.), and Heller &
Leake; architects for the city
hall: HKS and CRS Sirrine.
URBAN LAND 1990 Jan., v.49, no.1,
p.21-25, dwg., site plan, aerial
photo.

UNITED STATES--ORLANDO (FLORIDA)--FILM
SETS--UNIVERSAL STUDIOS FLORIDA
Universal attractions: Ellerbe
Becket goes Hollywood with Florida
theme park.
Universal Studios Florida in
Orlando.
ARCHITECTURE MINNESOTA 1990
Nov.-Dec., v.16, no.6, p.30-33,53,
ill., photos.

UNITED STATES--ORLANDO (FLORIDA)--
FILMMAKERS' STUDIOS--UNIVERSAL
STUDIOS FLORIDA
Universal attractions: Ellerbe
Becket goes Hollywood with Florida
theme park.
Universal Studios Florida in
Orlando.
ARCHITECTURE MINNESOTA 1990
NOV.-DEC., v.16, no.6, p.30-33,53,
ill., photos.

UNITED STATES--ORLANDO (FLORIDA)--NEW
TOWNS--AVALON PARK
Breaking the code: urban design
portfolio / Beth Dunlop.
Small-town alternatives to
suburban sprawl, as offered by
Andres Duany and Elizabeth
Plater-Zyberk.
ARCHITECTURE: THE AIA JOURNAL 1990
(Continued next column)

UNITED STATES--ORLANDO (FLORIDA)--NEW
TOWNS--AVALON PARK (CONTINUED)
Breaking the code:... (CONTINUED)
Apr., v.79, no.4, p.80-83, ill.,
elev., plans, site plans.

UNITED STATES--ORLANDO (FLORIDA)--
PRISONS--33RD STREET CORRECTIONAL
CENTER
Orange County Correctional Center
[Florida].
Architects: Architects Design
Group of Florida. English, French,
German, Spanish summaries, p.112.
ARCHITETTURA: CRONACHE E STORIA
1987 Feb., v.33, no.2(376),
p.112-115, axonometric view,
photos., plans, site plan.

UNITED STATES--ORLANDO (FLORIDA)--REAL
ESTATE DEVELOPMENT--CITY COMMONS
Orlando's City Commons: a model
public/private venture / Lewis
Oliver, Eric Smart.
Major 7-acre development,
including a new city hall, public
park and plaza, commercial office
and retail space, and parking in
Orlando's Southern Gateway area.
Planners: Project for Public
Spaces (PPS, Inc.), and Heller &
Leake; architects for the city
hall: HKS and CRS Sirrine.
URBAN LAND 1990 Jan., v.49, no.1,
p.21-25, dwg., site plan, aerial
photo.

UNITED STATES--ORLANDO (FLORIDA)--
THEME PARKS--UNIVERSAL STUDIOS
FLORIDA
Universal attractions: Ellerbe
Becket goes Hollywood with Florida
theme park.
Universal Studios Florida in
Orlando.
ARCHITECTURE MINNESOTA 1990
Nov.-Dec., v.16, no.6, p.30-33,53,
ill., photos.

UNITED STATES--ORLEAN (VIRGINIA)--
HOUSING DEVELOPMENTS--VARZARA HILLS
Drawing on tradition: Julian Kulski
finds inspiration in the landscape
and architectural history of
Virginia / Jane Gillette.
On Varzara Hills, an exclusive,
planned development of 15 houses.
HISTORIC PRESERVATION 1990
Mar.-Apr., v.42, no.2, p.12-15,
port.

UNITED STATES--OSAWATOMIE (KANSAS)--
PSYCHIATRIC HOSPITALS--19TH
CENTURY--OSAWATOMIE STATE HOSPITAL
Keeping 'Old Main' alive; Kansas
dispute need to save historic
state hospital [Osawatomie State
Hospital, Osawatomie, Kansas] /
Janet Majure.
Built between 1867-1890.
PRESERVATION NEWS 1990 Jan., v.30,
no.1, p.1,6, port., photo.

UNITED STATES--OYSTER BAY (NEW YORK)--
HOUSES--INTERIOR DESIGN--FERGUSON
HOUSE
A Long Island, une maison au rythme
des saisons.
Interior designer Barry Ferguson's
home in Oyster Bay, which was
formerly a stable on the Roosevelt
estate. English summary, p.III.
MAISON FRANCAISE 1990 Apr.,
no.435, p.[72-81], port., photos.

UNITED STATES--OYSTER BAY (NEW YORK)--
HOUSES--INTERIOR DESIGN--HORST HOUSE
Portratist der feinen Welt / Vera
Graaf.
Features the interiors of Horst's
house in Oyster Bay, Long Island,
NY. English summary, p.3.
ARCHITEKTUR & WOHNEN 1990
Dec.-1991 Jan., no.6, p.74-[78],
port., photos.

UNITED STATES--OZARK MOUNTAINS--
HOUSES--SANDSTONE
Vernacular houses: Ozark giraffes /
Stephen B. Jordan.
Sandstone houses with painted
mortar were built 1920-1940 and
are found in Ark., Mo. and Okla.
OLD-HOUSE JOURNAL 1990 Jan.-Feb.,
v.18, no.1, p.back cover, photos.

UNITED STATES--OZARK MOUNTAINS--
VERNACULAR ARCHITECTURE--20TH
CENTURY
Vernacular houses: Ozark giraffes /
Stephen B. Jordan.
Sandstone houses with painted
mortar were built 1920-1940 and
are found in Ark., Mo. and Okla.
OLD-HOUSE JOURNAL 1990 Jan.-Feb.,
v.18, no.1, p.back cover, photos.

UNITED STATES--PACIFIC NORTHWEST--
NATIONAL PARKS AND RESERVES--
COLUMBIA GORGE NATIONAL SCENIC AREA
Power, planning and conflict /
Charles Hoch, guest editor.
Special issue. Contents: Power,
planning and conflict, by C. Hoch
-- Planners in conflict:
experience and perceptions in
California, by Linda C. Dalton --
Neighborhood redevelopment: the
planner's role in conflict
management, by Sanda Kaufman --
Environmental movement politics,
mandates to plan, and professional
planners..., by Sy Adler --
Passion, reason and power: the
rhetorics of electric power
planning in Chicago, by J.A.
Throgmorton.
JOURNAL OF ARCHITECTURAL AND
PLANNING RESEARCH 1990 Winter, v.7
no.4, p.271-350, graph, tables,
biblios., refs.

UNITED STATES--PAINTING--19TH CENTURY
A visitable past: views of Venice by
American artists, 1860-1915 [by]
Margaretta M. Revell [book review]
/ Betsy Fahlman.
WINTERTHUR PORTFOLIO 1990 Winter,
v.25, no.4, p.300-303, refs.

UNITED STATES--PALM BEACH COUNTY
(FLORIDA)--BUS SHELTERS--ECONOMIC
ASPECTS
 Protective revenue [bus shelters] /
 Angela Bellucci.
 Revenue-producing aspects of bus
 shelters.
 MASS TRANSIT 1990 Apr., v.17,
 no.4, p.26, photos.

UNITED STATES--PALM BEACH (FLORIDA)--
APARTMENTS--INTERIOR DESIGN
 Classical grace in Palm Beach /
 Jeffrey Simpson.
 Apartment interiors designed by
 William Hodgins.
 ARCHITECTURAL DIGEST 1990 Oct,
 v.47, no.11, p.[188-195], photos.

UNITED STATES--PALM BEACH (FLORIDA)--
APARTMENTS--INTERIOR DESIGN--SACHS
APARTMENT
 Reflected glories in Palm Beach /
 Jeffrey Simpson.
 Features interiors of Rose Sach's
 Palm Beach apartment. Interior
 designers: Robert Metzger, Michael
 Christiano.
 ARCHITECTURAL DIGEST 1990 Mar.,
 v.47, no.3, p.[172]-179, photos.

UNITED STATES--PALM BEACH (FLORIDA)--
ART GALLERIES--INTERIOR DESIGN--
HOLSTEIN GALLERIES
 Holstein Galleries / Edie Lee Cohen.
 Interiors of Palm Beach art glass
 gallery designed by Mario
 Echeverria.
 INTERIOR DESIGN 1990 Jan., v.61,
 no.1, p.200-[201], photos. plan.

UNITED STATES--PALM BEACH (FLORIDA)--
HISTORIC HOUSE MUSEUMS--HENRY
MORRISON FLAGLER MUSEUM
 Flagler of Florida.
 Whitehall, the 1901 Palm Beach
 mansion of developer Henry
 Morrison Flagler. Architects:
 Carrere & Hastings. Interior
 designers: Pottier and Stymes. It
 is now a museum.
 COLONIAL HOMES 1990 Aug., v.16,
 no.4, p.84-[87],118, port.,
 photos.

UNITED STATES--PALM BEACH (FLORIDA)--
HOUSES--INTERIOR DESIGN
 Regent park gem / Susannah M.
 Wilson.
 Palm Beach house. Architect:
 Clarence Mack. Interior designer:
 Dan Carithers.
 SOUTHERN ACCENTS 1990 May, v.13,
 no.4, p.[96]-105, photos.

UNITED STATES--PALM BEACH (FLORIDA)--
MANSIONS--BEAUX-ARTS--WHITEHALL
 Flagler of Florida.
 Whitehall, the 1901 Palm Beach
 mansion of developer Henry
 Morrison Flagler. Architects:
 Carrere & Hastings. Interior
 designers: Pottier and Stymes. It
 is now a museum.
 COLONIAL HOMES 1990 Aug., v.16,
 no.4, p.84-[87],118, port.,
 photos.

UNITED STATES--PALM BEACH (FLORIDA)--
NEW TOWNS--WELLINGTON
 Breaking the code: urban design
 portfolio / Beth Dunlop.
 Small-town alternatives to
 suburban sprawl, as offered by
 Andres Duany and Elizabeth
 Plater-Zyberk.
 ARCHITECTURE: THE AIA JOURNAL 1990
 Apr., v.79, no.4, p.80-83, ill.,
 elev., plans, site plans.

UNITED STATES--PALM BEACH (FLORIDA)--
TOWNHOUSES--INTERIOR DESIGN--HORN
HOUSE
 Tropical trompe l'oeil: Steve and
 Linda Horn's town house in Palm
 Beach / Steven M. L. Aronson.
 ARCHITECTURAL DIGEST 1990 Feb.,
 v.47, no.2, p.704-709, port.,
 photos.

UNITED STATES--PALM SPRINGS
(CALIFORNIA)--ENERGY CONSERVATION
 Community energy planning: winds of
 change from the San Gorgonio Pass
 / James A. Throgmorton.
 AMERICAN PLANNING ASSOCIATION.
 JOURNAL 1987 Summer, v.53, no.3,
 p.358-367, maps, photo., biblio.,
 refs.

UNITED STATES--PALM SPRINGS
(CALIFORNIA)--WEEKEND HOUSES--
INTERIOR DESIGN--RON WILSON HOUSE
 Creating an oasis / Rhoda Jaffin
 Murphy.
 Weekend house of interior designer
 Ron Wilson in Palm Springs, Calif.
 HOUSE BEAUTIFUL 1990 Feb., v.132,
 no.2, p.80-[87], photos.

UNITED STATES--PALO ALTO
(CALIFORNIA)--OFFICES--DESIGNERS'--
HODNICK DESIGN, LUNAR DESIGN
 Double take: Hodnick Design creates
 an all-for-one interior that
 accommodates two professions'
 needs / Paula Rice Jackson.
 Features the Palo Alto offices
 shared by Hodnick Design and Lunar
 Design.
 INTERIORS 1989 Feb., v.148, no.7,
 p.[140]-141, photos., plan.

UNITED STATES--PALO ALTO
(CALIFORNIA)--UNIVERSITIES AND
COLLEGES--BUILDINGS--STANFORD
UNIVERSITY--GRADUATE SCHOOL OF
BUSINESS
 University of Stanford, Graduate
 School of Business expansion
 facility, Palo Alto, California,
 1984-88.
 Architects: Kohn Pedersen Fox
 Associates; partner in charge: A.
 Eugene Kohn.
 PROCESS: ARCHITECTURE 1989 Nov.,
 no.86, p.58-59, elevs., photos.,
 plan.

UNITED STATES--PARADISE VALLEY
(ARIZONA)--HOUSES--20TH CENTURY--
ZUBER HOUSE
 Raising Arizona: Zuber house,
 Paradise Valley, Arizona / Karen
 D. Stein.
 Architect: Antoine Predock.
 ARCHITECTURAL RECORD 1990
 Mid-Apr., v.178, no.5, p.[88]-95,
 axonometric views, photos., plans.

UNITED STATES--PARADISE VALLEY
(ARIZONA)--HOUSES--HOUSE V
 House in Paradise Valley, Arizona /
 Douglas B. Sydnor.
 House V. Architect: Douglas B.
 Sydnor of Sydnor Architects.
 TRIGLYPH 1990 Summer, no.10,
 p.28-32, photos., secns., site
 plan.

UNITED STATES--PARADISE VALLEY
(ARIZONA)--HOUSES--ZUBER HOUSE
 Antoine Predock.
 Features the Zuber house, Paradise
 Valley, AZ and the Fine Arts
 Center. Univ. of Arizona, Tempe.
 English summary.
 ARCHITECTURE D'AUJOURD'HUI 1990
 Oct., no.271, p.177-187,
 axonometric view, photos., plans,
 secn.

UNITED STATES--PARK RIDGE (NEW
JERSEY)--CORPORATE OFFICE
BUILDINGS--HERTZ CORPORATE
HEADQUARTERS
 Hertz Corporate Headquarters, Park
 Ridge, New Jersey.
 Berger Associates, Architects and
 Planners.
 ARCHITECTURE NEW JERSEY 1990,
 v.26, no.6., p.12, photos., plan.

UNITED STATES--PARKS--STANDARDS
 Park standards are up in the air /
 James Krohe.
 National guidelines for parks and
 recreation areas are criticized.
 PLANNING 1990 Dec., v.56, no.12,
 p.10-13, ill., photos., plan.

UNITED STATES--PARSIPPANY (NEW
JERSEY)--HISTORIC HOUSE MUSEUMS--
CONSERVATION AND RESTORATION--
CRAFTSMAN FARMS
 Craftsman Farms set to open,
 meanwhile, the hunt for Stickley
 pieces goes on [Parsippany, N.J.]
 / Patricia Herold.
 PRESERVATION NEWS 1990 Apr., v.30,
 no.4, p.6,23, photos.

UNITED STATES--PARSIPPANY-TROY HILLS
(NEW JERSEY)--HOUSES--CRAFTSMAN--
CONSERVATION AND RESTORATION--
CRAFTSMAN FARMS
 Preservation: Stickley's Craftsman
 Farms / Abby Bussel.
 1907 home and five other original
 craftsman buildings in
 Parsippany-Troy Hills, N.J. to be
 restored.
 PROGRESSIVE ARCHITECTURE 1990
 June, v.71, no.6, p.26, photo.

UNITED STATES--PASADENA (CALIFORNIA)--
CITY PLANNING
 Emerald City [Pasadena, Calif.] /
 Daniel Solomon, Susan Haviland.
 OZ / COLLEGE OF ARCHITECTURE AND
 DESIGN, KANSAS STATE UNIVERSITY
 1989, v.11, p.42-45, dwgs.,
 photos., plans, site plans.

UNITED STATES--PASADENA (CALIFORNIA)--
COURTYARDS--COMPETITIONS--PASADENA
POLICE BUILDING
Conceiving a courtyard / Marc Pally.
Pasadena Police Building Public
Art Project competition sponsored
by the Pasadena Arts Commission.
Winning landscape architects:
Douglas and Regula Campbell
(Campbell and Campbell); winning
artist: Robert Irwin. Additional
entries included.
PLACES 1990 Spring, v.6, no.3,
p.4-17, ill., dwgs., elev.,
models, plans, sketch.

UNITED STATES--PASADENA (CALIFORNIA)--
GARDENS
Emerald City [Pasadena, Calif.] /
Daniel Solomon, Susan Haviland.
OZ / COLLEGE OF ARCHITECTURE AND
DESIGN, KANSAS STATE UNIVERSITY
1989, v.11, p.42-45, dwgs.,
photos., plans, site plans.

UNITED STATES--PASADENA (CALIFORNIA)--
PARKING GARAGES
Putting parking in its place / Susan
Haviland.
In residential areas; example of
Pasadena, Ca.
PLACES 1990 Spring, v.6, no.3,
p.88-91, photos., plans.

UNITED STATES--PASADENA (CALIFORNIA)--
ZONING LAW
Emerald City [Pasadena, Calif.] /
Daniel Solomon, Susan Haviland.
OZ / COLLEGE OF ARCHITECTURE AND
DESIGN, KANSAS STATE UNIVERSITY
1989, v.11, p.42-45, dwgs.,
photos., plans, site plans.

UNITED STATES--PASADENA (MARYLAND)--
PLAYGROUNDS--LAKE WATERFORD PARK
PLAYGROUND
A community takes charge / Lisa
Shore.
Creation of a playground in Lake
Waterford Park, Pasadena, Md.
PARKS & RECREATION 1990 Aug.,
v.25, no.8, p.30-35,71, photos.

UNITED STATES--PATERSON (NEW JERSEY)--
PUBLIC BUILDINGS--FEDERAL OFFICE
BUILDING
Federal Office Builidng, Paterson,
New Jersey.
Chapman and Biber, Architects and
Planners.
ARCHITECTURE NEW JERSEY 1990,
v.26, no.3, p.12, model, plan.

UNITED STATES--PEDESTRIAN FACILITIES--
SOCIOLOGICAL ASPECTS
Patterns of behavior in urban public
spaces / Jack L. Nasas, A. Rengin
Yurdakul.
Includes abstract.
JOURNAL OF ARCHITECTURAL AND
PLANNING RESEARCH 1990 Spring,
v.7, no.1, p.71-85, charts,
diagrs., photos, biblio.

UNITED STATES--PEDESTRIAN MALLS
European models and American
realities: a perspective on urban
design / Judith A. Martin.
LANDSCAPE 1990, v.30, no.3,
p.36-43, photos, biblio.

UNITED STATES--PEDESTRIAN MALLS
(CONTINUED)
From street to mall and back again /
Lawrence O. Houston.
Bulldozing pedestrian malls.
PLANNING 1990 June, v.56, no.6,
p.4-10, dwg., ports., photos.,
plans.
The status of the pedestrian mall in
American downtowns / Kent A.
Robertson.
URBAN AFFAIRS QUARTERLY 1990 Dec.,
v.26, no.2, p.250-273, photos.,
tables.

UNITED STATES--PEDESTRIAN STREETS
The status of the pedestrian mall in
American downtowns / Kent A.
Robertson.
URBAN AFFAIRS QUARTERLY 1990 Dec.,
v.26, no.2, p.250-273, photos.,
tables.

UNITED STATES--PENNSYLVANIA--CABINS--
CAMP TWEEDALE
Winter quarters: a year-round cabin
complex makes camping an event for
all seasons / Margaret Gaskie.
Girl Scout cabin complex, Camp
Tweedale, Lower Oxford township,
Penn. Susan Maxman Architects.
ARCHITECTURAL RECORD 1990 July,
v.178, no.8, p.64-67, photos.,
plans, secns., site plan.

UNITED STATES--PENNSYLVANIA--CAMPS--
CAMP TWEEDALE
Winter quarters: a year-round cabin
complex makes camping an event for
all seasons / Margaret Gaskie.
Girl Scout cabin complex, Camp
Tweedale, Lower Oxford township,
Penn. Susan Maxman Architects.
ARCHITECTURAL RECORD 1990 July,
v.178, no.8, p.64-67, photos.,
plans, secns., site plan.

UNITED STATES--PENNSYLVANIA--
DECORATION AND ORNAMENT
Hex-sign designs.
Examples of Pennsylvania Dutch hex
signs.
COLONIAL HOMES 1990 Oct., v.16,
no.5, p.44-48, ill., photos.

UNITED STATES--PENNSYLVANIA--FARM
BUILDINGS
Un paradiso provvisorio = A
"provisional paradise" / Michael
S. A. Dechert.
On the Mennonite- Amish community
in Lancaster, Pennsylvania. Text
in Italian and English.
SPAZIO E SOCIETA 1990 July-Sept.,
v.13, no.51, p.58-67, photos.

UNITED STATES--PENNSYLVANIA--
FARMHOUSES--ALTERATIONS AND
ADDITIONS
Formed anew: Amish religious
community expressed in "frontless"
houses and concentric farm plans /
Charles Bergengren.
VIA 1990, no.10, p.[146]-163,
photos., plans, sketches, refs.

UNITED STATES--PENNSYLVANIA--HOUSES--
INTERIOR DESIGN--FROVA HOUSE
Sensuous Modernism: Jeffrey Bilhuber
distills the luxurious simplicity
of the twenties in a house for the
nineties / Andrew Solomon.
Frova house, eastern Penn.
HOUSE & GARDEN 1990 May, v.162,
no.5, p.[128]-135,212, port.,
photos.

UNITED STATES--PENNSYLVANIA--
RESIDENTIAL GARDENS--HARRIS GARDEN
A Pennsylvania palette / Senga
Mortimer.
Gardens of artist Penelope Harris.
HOUSE & GARDEN 1990 May, v.162,
no.5, p.[158-165], port., photos.

UNITED STATES--PENNSYLVANIA--SIGNS AND
SIGN-BOARDS
Hex-sign designs.
Examples of Pennsylvania Dutch hex
signs.
COLONIAL HOMES 1990 Oct., v.16,
no.5, p.44-48, ill., photos.

UNITED STATES--PENSACOLA (FLORIDA)--
COTTAGES--19TH CENTURY
Vernacular houses: Pensacola Creole
cottages / Diana Jarvis Godwin.
OLD-HOUSE JOURNAL 1990 July-Aug,
v.18, no.4, p.[4] of cover,
photos., plan.

UNITED STATES--PENSACOLA (FLORIDA)--
VERNACULAR ARCHITECTURE
Vernacular houses: Pensacola Creole
cottages / Diana Jarvis Godwin.
OLD-HOUSE JOURNAL 1990 July-Aug,
v.18, no.4, p.[4] of cover,
photos., plan.

UNITED STATES--PEORIA (ILLINOIS)--
CHURCHES--WESTMINSTER PRESBYTERIAN
CHURCH
Prairie resurrection: a new church
rises like a phoenix from the
ashes of a devastating fire / Lynn
Nesmith.
Westminster Presbyterian Church,
Peoria, Ill. Architects: Weese
Langley Weese.
ARCHITECTURE: THE AIA JOURNAL 1990
Feb., v.79, no.2, p.[68-70],
photos., plan, secn.
Westminster Church in Peoria [IL].
Architects: Weese Langley Weese.
Includes short article,
Architektur als intuitiver
Prozess, by Benjamin Weese.
DEUTSCHE BAUZEITSCHRIFT 1990 May,
v.38, no.5, p.665-670, det.,
photos., plans, secns., sketches.

UNITED STATES--PERIODICALS
La presse architecturale aux
Etats-Unis, 1870-1910 / David Van
Zanten, Mary Woods.
REVUE DE L'ART 1990, no.89,
p.19-28, photos., plans, engrs.

UNITED STATES--PETALUMA (CALIFORNIA)--
AFFORDABLE HOUSING
Must growth restrictions eliminate
moderate-priced housing? / Thomas
I. Miller.
Cases cited: Boulder, CO;
Petaluma, CA.
AMERICAN PLANNING ASSOCIATION.
JOURNAL 1986 Summer, v.52, no.3,
p.319-325, maps, photo., tables,
biblio., refs.

UNITED STATES--PHEONIX (ARIZONA)--
CORPORATE OFFICE BUILDINGS--
ALTERATIONS AND ADDITIONS--PHOENIX
CITY SQUARE--3800 TOWER
    3800 Tower, Phoenix City Square:
    NAIOP grand award winner for
    remodel and restoration.
    Architects: Cornoyer-Hedrick.
    DEVELOPMENT 1990 Jan.-Feb., v.21,
    no.1, p.[20], photos.

UNITED STATES--PHILADELPHIA
(PENNSYLVANIA)--APARTMENT HOUSES--
DRAKE TOWER
    Interior storms for steel casement
    windows: the Drake Hotel (Drake
    Tower), Philadelphia, Pennsylvania
    / Charles E. Fisher, Christina
    Henry.
    PRESERVATION TECH NOTES 1986 Nov.,
    no.20, p.1-6, diagr., photos.

UNITED STATES--PHILADELPHIA
(PENNSYLVANIA)--ARCHITECTURE--
COMPETITIONS--CERTAINTEED AWARD FOR
CITY VISIONS
    City Visions put life in good ideas.
    "City Visions" competitions
    sponsored by Philadelphia's
    Foundation for Architecture
    inspire similar projects in civic
    excellence in Boston.
    ARCHITECTS' JOURNAL 1990 Mar.14,
    v.191, no.11, p.38-39,41,43-45,
    dwgs., port., photos., plans,
    secn., sketch.

UNITED STATES--PHILADELPHIA
(PENNSYLVANIA)--AUDITORIUMS, CONCERT
HALLS--19TH CENTURY--MAINTENANCE AND
REPAIR--PHILADELPHIA ACADEMY OF
MUSIC
    A sudden unusual force: a close call
    in Philadelphia raises disturbing
    questions / Nancy Levinson.
    The Philadelphia Academy of Music
    needed emergency repair when 2
    roof trusses failed. Original
    architects: LeBrun and Runge.
    Structural engineers: Keast &
    Hood.
    ARCHITECTURAL RECORD 1990 Feb.,
    v.178, no.2, p.146-147,174,
    photos., secns.

UNITED STATES--PHILADELPHIA
(PENNSYLVANIA)--AUDITORIUMS, CONCERT
HALLS--PHILADELPHIA ORCHESTRA HALL
    Philadelphia Orchestra Hall en
    Philadelphia Pennsylvania =
    Philadelphia Orchestra Hall in
    Philadelphia Pennsylvania.
    Architects: Venturi Scott Brown
    and Associates. Text in Spanish
    and English.
    COMPOSICION ARQUITECTONICA, ART &
    ARCHITECTURE 1989 Oct., no.4,
    p.[61]-78, dwgs., elevs., models,
    plans, site plans.
    Rafael Moneo: today's American
    architecture.
    Report on the Gropius Lecture,
    given Apr.25, 1990, in which Moneo
    examined two projects: Symphony
    Hall, Philadelphia (Venturi Scott
    Brown and Associates) and Disney
    Concert Hall, Los Angeles (Frank
    Gehry and Associates).
    GSD NEWS / HARVARD UNIVERSITY.
    GRADUATE SCHOOL OF DESIGN 1990
    Summer-Fall, v.19, no.1, p.13-14.

UNITED STATES--PHILADELPHIA
(PENNSYLVANIA)--AUDITORIUMS, CONCERT
HALLS--PHILADELPHIA ORCHESTRA HALL
(CONTINUED)
    Venturi et Scott Brown a
    Philadelphie / Bruno Suner.
    On the Philadelphia Orchestra
    Hall. English summary, p.176-177.
    ARCHITECTURE D'AUJOURD'HUI 1990
    Apr., no.268, p.175-177, dwgs.,
    model., plans, secn., site plan.

UNITED STATES--PHILADELPHIA
(PENNSYLVANIA)--CHURCHES--GOTHIC
REVIVAL--SWEDENBORGIAN CHURCH
    Healthy revival / Kristen Richards.
    Philadelphia Gothic revival church
    (1881) converted to corporate
    headquarters for Graduate Health
    System. Original architect:
    Theophilus P. Chandler. Conversion
    architects: Mark B. Thompson
    Associates. Interior designers:
    Richard Mark Design.
    INTERIORS 1990 Mar., v.149, no.8,
    p.124-[127], photos., plan.

UNITED STATES--PHILADELPHIA
(PENNSYLVANIA)--CITY PLANNING
    Le case di Filadelfia / Federico D.
    Moccia.
    English, French, German, Spanish
    summaries p.127-128.
    STORIA DELLA CITTA 1989 Jan.-Mar.,
    v.14, no.49, p.43-82, axonometric
    views, dets., elevs., maps,
    photos., plans, secns., biblio.,
    refs.

UNITED STATES--PHILADELPHIA
(PENNSYLVANIA)--CITY PLANNING--
CITIZEN PARTICIPATION
    City Visions put life in good ideas.
    "City Visions" competitions
    sponsored by Philadelphia's
    Foundation for Architecture
    inspire similar projects in civic
    excellence in Boston.
    ARCHITECTS' JOURNAL 1990 Mar.14,
    v.191, no.11, p.38-39,41,43-45,
    dwgs., port., photos., plans,
    secn., sketch.

UNITED STATES--PHILADELPHIA
(PENNSYLVANIA)--COMMUNICATIONS
COMPLEXES--TOWERS PERRIN DATA CENTER
    Towers Perrin Data Center,
    Philadelphia, Pennsylvania.
    Architects: The Hillier Group.
    ARCHITECTURE NEW JERSEY 1990,
    v.26, no.6, p.16, photos.

UNITED STATES--PHILADELPHIA
(PENNSYLVANIA)--COMPUTER CENTERS--
TOWERS PERRIN DATA CENTER
    Towers Perrin Data Center,
    Philadelphia, Pennsylvania.
    Architects: The Hillier Group.
    ARCHITECTURE NEW JERSEY 1990,
    v.26, no.6, p.16, photos.

UNITED STATES--PHILADELPHIA
(PENNSYLVANIA)--CONVENTION
FACILITIES--PHILADELPHIA CONVENTION
CENTER
    A third life for the Reading
    Terminal Market / David O'Neil.
    Conversion of Philadelphia's
    Reading Terminal, incorporating
    the farmers market, into a
    convention center.
    PLACES 1990 Summer, v.6, no.4,
    (Continued next column)

UNITED STATES--PHILADELPHIA
(PENNSYLVANIA)--CONVENTION
FACILITIES--PHILADELPHIA CONVENTION
CENTER (CONTINUED)
    A third life for the...(CONTINUED)
    p.93, photos.

UNITED STATES--PHILADELPHIA
(PENNSYLVANIA)--CORPORATE OFFICE
BUILDINGS--INTERIOR DESIGN--GRADUATE
HEALTH SYSTEM
    Healthy revival / Kristen Richards.
    Philadelphia Gothic revival church
    (1881) converted to corporate
    headquarters for Graduate Health
    System. Original architect:
    Theophilus P. Chandler. Conversion
    architects: Mark B. Thompson
    Associates. Interior designers:
    Richard Mark Design.
    INTERIORS 1990 Mar., v.149, no.8,
    p.124-[127], photos., plan.

UNITED STATES--PHILADELPHIA
(PENNSYLVANIA)--CORPORATE OFFICE
BUILDINGS--PHILADELPHIA SAVINGS FUND
SOCIETY BUILDING
    Two expressions of functionalism /
    Brian Melnik.
    The Philadelphia Savings Fund
    Society (PSFS) by George Howe and
    William Lescaze (1932) and Lloyd's
    of London by Richard Rogers
    (1986).
    CRIT 1990 Spring, no.24, p.40-43,
    refs.

UNITED STATES--PHILADELPHIA
(PENNSYLVANIA)--COUNTRY HOUSES
    Along that green embowered track
    [Main Line area, Penn.] / Clive
    Aslet.
    Country houses in this suburban
    area west of Philadelphia.
    COUNTRY LIFE 1990 Apr.26, v.184,
    no.17, p.118-121, ill., photos.

UNITED STATES--PHILADELPHIA
(PENNSYLVANIA)--FARMERS' MARKETS--
CONSERVATION AND RESTORATION--
READING TERMINAL MARKET
    A third life for the Reading
    Terminal Market / David O'Neil.
    Conversion of Philadelphia's
    Reading Terminal, incorporating
    the farmers market, into a
    convention center.
    PLACES 1990 Summer, v.6, no.4,
    p.93, photos.

UNITED STATES--PHILADELPHIA
(PENNSYLVANIA)--GARDENS--VICTORIAN--
EBENEZER MAXWELL MANSION
    Victorian gardens, where inspiration
    grows: the Ebenezer Maxwell
    Mansion in Philadelphia / Kathy S.
    Moses.
    Landscape architect for
    renovation: Reed L. Engle.
    VICTORIAN HOMES 1990 Winter, v.9,
    no.1, p.24-29, ill., photos.,
    biblio.

UNITED STATES--PHILADELPHIA
(PENNSYLVANIA)--GENTRIFICATION
Trajectories of neighborhood change:
the case of gentrification / R. A.
Beauregard.
In post-war Philadelphia.
ENVIRONMENT AND PLANNING A 1990
July, v.22, no.7, p.855-874, map,
tables, refs.

UNITED STATES--PHILADELPHIA
(PENNSYLVANIA)--HOSPITALS--
CHILDREN'S--INTERIOR DESIGN--
CHILDREN'S SEASHORE HOUSE
Healing comfort / Nayana Currimbhoy.
Focus on the interiors of the
children's Seashore House, a
pediatric convalescent center,
Philadelphia. Architects: Geddes
Brecher Qualls Cunningham
Architects. Interior designers:
Daroff Design.
INTERIORS 1990 Dec., v.150, no.5,
p.70-[73], photos., plan.

UNITED STATES--PHILADELPHIA
(PENNSYLVANIA)--HOUSES
Le case di Filadelfia / Federico D.
Moccia.
English, French, German, Spanish
summaries p.127-128.
STORIA DELLA CITTA 1989 Jan.-Mar.,
v.14, no.49, p.43-82, axonometric
views, dets., elevs., maps,
photos., plans, secns., biblio.,
refs.

UNITED STATES--PHILADELPHIA
(PENNSYLVANIA)--HOUSES--
ARCHITECTS'--VENTURI HOUSE
Special feature: Venturi Scott Brown
and Associates.
Contents: Brief history-- Works:
Primate Center, Philadelphia
Zoological Garden.-- Lewis Thomas
Laboratory for Molecular Biology,
Princeton University, 1986.--
Malcolm S. Forbes Jr. College,
Princeton University, 1984.--
Gordon Wu Hall, Princeton
University, 1983.-- Venturi house,
Philadelphia, 1974-present.--
Izenour house, Stony Creek, Conn.,
1984.-- House in New Castle
County, Delaware, 1983.--
Coxe-Hayden house, Block Island,
R.I., 1981.-- Tarble Student
Center, Swarthmore College,
1985.-- Tree House, Philadelphia
Zoo, 1985.-- Welcome Park,
Philadelphia, 1982.-- Decorative
designs.-- Essay: "Body language"
and artifice: on some recent
designs by Venturi Scott Brown and
Associates. Text in Japanese and
English.
ARCHITECTURE AND URBANISM 1990
June, no.6(237), p.[39]-150,
ports., elevs., photos., plans,
secns., site plans.

UNITED STATES--PHILADELPHIA
(PENNSYLVANIA)--LABORATORIES--
MEDICAL--UNIVERSITY OF
PENNSYLVANIA--SCHOOL OF MEDICINE--
CLINICAL RESEARCH BUILDING
Clinical research building School of
Medicine en University of
Pennsylvania Philadelphia
Pennsylvania = Clinical research
building School of Medicine at
University of Pennsylvania
(Continued next column)

UNITED STATES--PHILADELPHIA
(PENNSYLVANIA)--LABORATORIES--
MEDICAL--UNIVERSITY OF
PENNSYLVANIA--SCHOOL OF MEDICINE--
CLINICAL RESEARCH BUILDING
(CONTINUED)
Clinical research...(CONTINUED)
Philadelphia Pennsylvania.
Architects: Venturi, Scott Brown
and Associates.
COMPOSICION ARQUITECTONICA, ART &
ARCHITECTURE 1989 Oct., no.4,
p.[79]-84, elevs., model, photos.,
site plan.

UNITED STATES--PHILADELPHIA
(PENNSYLVANIA)--LAW OFFICES--
LIGHTING--HANGLEY CONNOLLY EPSTEIN
CHICCO FOXMAN AND EWING
Shedding light on the law / Justin
Henderson, Peter Barna.
Lighting for Philadelphia law
offices. Interior designers:
Daroff Design. Lighting Designer:
Gary Steffy.
INTERIORS 1990 Jan., v.149, no.6,
p.52, dets., photos., plan.

UNITED STATES--PHILADELPHIA
(PENNSYLVANIA)--MODEL APARTMENTS--
INTERIOR DESIGN
Less does more: Rodgers Design Group
integrates ample storage into a
small Philadelphia model apartment
/ Monica Geran.
INTERIOR DESIGN 1990 May, v.61,
no.7, p.294-[295], photos., plan.

UNITED STATES--PHILADELPHIA
(PENNSYLVANIA)--MULTI-USE
COMPLEXES--PENN'S LANDING
Landing on its feet: Penn's Landing
in Philadelphia has been on the
boards for nearly three decades /
Clifford A. Pearson.
The latest plan, by architects
Bower Lewis Thrower.
ARCHITECTURAL RECORD 1990 Feb.,
v.178, no.2, p.65-67, models, site
plans.

UNITED STATES--PHILADELPHIA
(PENNSYLVANIA)--MUSEUMS--SCIENCE--
ALTERATIONS AND ADDITIONS--FUTURES
CENTER
"New Kid" on Philly's Franklin
Parkway / Donald Prowler.
On the 1933 Franklin Institute's
new Futures Center addition.
Original architect: John T.
Windrim. Architects for the
addition: Geddes Brecher Qualls
Cunningham Architects.
PROGRESSIVE ARCHITECTURE 1990
Sept., v.71, no.9, p.25, photos.

UNITED STATES--PHILADELPHIA
(PENNSYLVANIA)--NEIGHBORHOODS
Trajectories of neighborhood change:
the case of gentrification / R. A.
Beauregard.
In post-war Philadelphia.
ENVIRONMENT AND PLANNING A 1990
July, v.22, no.7, p.855-874, map,
tables, refs.

UNITED STATES--PHILADELPHIA
(PENNSYLVANIA)--OFFICE BUILDINGS--
ALTERATIONS AND ADDITIONS--100 EAST
PRATT STREET
Renewing our modern legacy / Andrea
Oppenheimer Dean.
Four additions to buildings of the
1950s and 1960s.
ARCHITECTURE: THE AIA JOURNAL 1990
Nov., v.79, no.11, p.66-69, ill.,
elevs., models, photos.

UNITED STATES--PHILADELPHIA
(PENNSYLVANIA)--OFFICE BUILDINGS--
MELLON BANK CENTER
Mellon Bank Center, Philadelphia,
Pennsylvania, 1990.
53-storey building; architects:
Kohn Pedersen Fox Associates. Text
in Japanese and English.
PROCESS: ARCHITECTURE 1989 Nov.,
no.86, p.74-77, dwgs., elev.,
model, plans, secn.

UNITED STATES--PHILADELPHIA
(PENNSYLVANIA)=--PARKWAYS--BENJAMIN
FRANKLIN PARKWAY
Building the City Beautiful: the
Benjamin Franklin Parkway and the
Philadelphia Museum of Art [by]
David B. Brownlee [book review] /
Leonard K. Eaton.
Book published in conjunction with
the 1989 exhibition at the
Philadelphia Museum of Art.
WINTERTHUR PORTFOLIO 1990 Winter,
v.25, no.4, p.305-307,
The City Beautiful movement [by]
William H. Wilson [and] Building
the City Beautiful [by] David
Brownlee [book review] / Daniel
Bluestone.
Brownlee's book studies the
Benjamin Franklin Parkway, and the
Philadelphia Museum of Art and was
published on the occasion of an
exhibition there, Sept.9-Nov.26,
1989.
SOCIETY OF ARCHITECTURAL
HISTORIANS. JOURNAL 1990 Dec.,
v.49, no.4, p.455-457,

UNITED STATES--PHILADELPHIA
(PENNSYLVANIA)--PLAZAS--WELCOME PARK
Special feature: Venturi Scott Brown
and Associates.
Contents: Brief history-- Works:
Primate Center, Philadelphia
Zoological Garden.-- Lewis Thomas
Laboratory for Molecular Biology,
Princeton University, 1986.--
Malcolm S. Forbes Jr. College,
Princeton University, 1984.--
Gordon Wu Hall, Princeton
University, 1983.-- Venturi house,
Philadelphia, 1974-present.--
Izenour house, Stony Creek, Conn.,
1984.-- House in New Castle
County, Delaware, 1983.--
Coxe-Hayden house, Block Island,
R.I., 1981.-- Tarble Student
Center, Swarthmore College,
1985.-- Tree House, Philadelphia
Zoo, 1985.-- Welcome Park,
Philadelphia, 1982.-- Decorative
designs.-- Essay: "Body language"
and artifice: on some recent
designs by Venturi Scott Brown and
Associates. Text in Japanese and
English.
ARCHITECTURE AND URBANISM 1990
June, no.6(237), p.[39]-150,
(Continued next page)

UNITED STATES--PHILADELPHIA
(PENNSYLVANIA)--PLAZAS--WELCOME PARK
(CONTINUED)
Special feature:...(CONTINUED)
ports., elevs., photos., plans,
secns., site plans.

UNITED STATES--PHILADELPHIA
(PENNSYLVANIA)--RAILROAD TERMINALS--
ALTERATIONS AND ADDITIONS--READING
TERMINAL
A third life for the Reading
Terminal Market / David O'Neil.
Conversion of Philadelphia's
Reading Terminal, incorporating
the farmers market, into a
convention center.
PLACES 1990 Summer, v.6, no.4,
p.93, photos.

UNITED STATES--PHILADELPHIA
(PENNSYLVANIA)--RESIDENTIAL
GARDENS--HEDGLEIGH SPRING (CRESSON
GARDEN)
A growing legacy / Ken Druse.
82-year-old residential garden at
Hedgleigh Spring, near
Philadelphia. Gardner: Charles
Cresson.
HOUSE BEAUTIFUL 1990 Oct., v.132,
no.10, p.100-103, photos., plan.

UNITED STATES--PHILADELPHIA
(PENNSYLVANIA)--STAIRWAYS--COMCAST
Elegant stairway / Lisa S. Cohen.
Features stairway designed by
Karen Daroff for the Comcast
Corporation offices in
Philadelphia.
INTERIORS 1990 Jan., v.149, no.6,
p.40-41, dets., photo.

UNITED STATES--PHILADELPHIA
(PENNSYLVANIA)--STORES--INTERIOR
DESIGN--WINE RESERVE
The Wine Reserve, Philadelphia,
Pennsylvania.
Store and display area for the
Pennsylvania State Liquor Board.
Interiors by Boyd & Associates.
ARCHITECTURE NEW JERSEY 1990 v.26,
no.6, p.10, photos.

UNITED STATES--PHILADELPHIA
(PENNSYLVANIA)--STREETS--BROAD
STREET
A broad perspective: Philadelphia's
Broad Street claims a rich
architectural diversity / Thomas
Hine.
HISTORIC PRESERVATION 1990
July-Aug., v.42, no.4, p.16-19,
photo.

UNITED STATES--PHILADELPHIA
(PENNSYLVANIA)--TOWNHOUSES--
FEDERAL--ALTERATIONS AND ADDITIONS
Sculpturing space / Judith Nasatir.
Renovation of 1860 Federal-style
townhouse near Rittenhouse Square,
Philadelphia. Architects: Kieran
Timberlake Harris.
INTERIOR DESIGN 1990 Mar., v.61,
no.5, p.164-[167], model, photos.,
plans.

UNITED STATES--PHILADELPHIA
(PENNSYLVANIA)--UNIVERSITIES AND
COLLEGES--BUILDINGS--UNIVERSITY OF
PENNSYLVANIA
Un nuovo edificio per l'Universita
della Pennsylvania = A new
building for the Pennsylvania /
Silvano Stucchi.
An information center and office
building between 34th St. and
Walnut St., completed 1985.
Architects: Geddes, Brecher,
Qualls, Cunningham.
L'INDUSTRIA DELLE COSTRUZIONI 1990
Feb., v.24, no.220, p.22-27,
photos., plans, secn., site plan.

UNITED STATES--PHILADELPHIA
(PENNSYLVANIA--UNIVERSITIES AND
COLLEGES--BUILDINGS--UNIVERSITY OF
PENNSYLVANIA--SCHOOL OF MEDICINE--
CLINICAL RESEARCH BUILDING
Clinical research building School of
Medicine en University of
Pennsylvania Philadelphia
Pennsylvania = Clinical research
building School of Medicine at
University of Pennsylvania
Philadelphia Pennsylvania.
Architects: Venturi, Scott Brown
and Associates.
COMPOSICION ARQUITECTONICA, ART &
ARCHITECTURE 1989 Oct., no.4,
p.[79]-84, elevs., model, photos.,
site plan.

UNITED STATES--PHILADELPHIA
(PENNSYLVANIA)--WATERFRONT
BUILDINGS--PENN'S LANDING
Landing on its feet: Penn's Landing
in Philadelphia has been on the
boards for nearly three decades /
Clifford A. Pearson.
The latest plan, by architects
Bower Lewis Thrower.
ARCHITECTURAL RECORD 1990 Feb.,
v.178, no.2, p.65-67, models, site
plans.

UNITED STATES--PHILADELPHIA
(PENNSYLVANIA)--WINE CELLARS--WINE
RESERVE
The Wine Reserve, Philadelphia,
Pennsylvania.
Store and display area for the
Pennsylvania State Liquor Board.
Interiors by Boyd & Associates.
ARCHITECTURE NEW JERSEY 1990 v.26,
no.6, p.10, photos.

UNITED STATES--PHILADELPHIA
(PENNSYLVANIA)--ZOOS--PHILADELPHIA
ZOOLOGICAL GARDEN--WORLD OF PRIMATES
Special feature: Venturi Scott Brown
and Associates.
Contents: Brief history-- Works:
Primate Center, Philadelphia
Zoological Garden.-- Lewis Thomas
Laboratory for Molecular Biology,
Princeton University, 1986.--
Malcolm S. Forbes Jr. College,
Princeton University, 1984.--
Gordon Wu Hall, Princeton
University, 1983.-- Venturi house,
Philadelphia, 1974-present.--
Izenour house, Stony Creek, Conn.,
1984.-- House in New Castle
County, Delaware, 1983.--
Coxe-Hayden house, Block Island,
R.I., 1981.-- Tarble Student
Center, Swarthmore College,
1985.-- Tree House, Philadelphia
(Continued next column)

UNITED STATES--PHILADELPHIA
(PENNSYLVANIA)--ZOOS--PHILADELPHIA
ZOOLOGICAL GARDEN--WORLD OF PRIMATES
(CONTINUED)
Special feature:...(CONTINUED)
Zoo, 1985.-- Welcome Park,
Philadelphia, 1982.-- Decorative
designs.-- Essay: "Body language"
and artifice: on some recent
designs by Venturi Scott Brown and
Associates. Text in Japanese and
English.
ARCHITECTURE AND URBANISM 1990
June, no.6(237), p.[39]-150,
ports., elevs., photos., plans,
secns., site plans.

UNITED STATES--PHILADEPHIA
(PENNSYLVANIA)--URBAN BEAUTIFICATION
The City Beautiful movement [by]
William H. Wilson [and] Building
the City Beautiful [by] David
Brownlee [book review] / Daniel
Bluestone.
Brownlee's book studies the
Benjamin Franklin Parkway, and the
Philadelphia Museum of Art and was
published on the occasion of an
exhibition there, Sept.9-Nov.26,
1989.
SOCIETY OF ARCHITECTURAL
HISTORIANS. JOURNAL 1990 Dec.,
v.49, no.4, p.455-457,

UNITED STATES--PHOENIX (ARIZONA)--BUS
SHELTERS--ENVIRONMENTAL ASPECTS
Phoenix bus riders don't swelter in
the shelter / Lenny Levine.
'Cool tower' technology drops
outdoor temperatures 30 degrees in
open-air bus shelters.
METRO MAGAZINE 1990 July-Aug,
v.86, no.4, p.38-39, photo.

UNITED STATES--PHOENIX (ARIZONA)--CAR
WASHES--WEISS GUYS CAR WASH
Clean sweep: Weiss Guys Car Wash
Phoenix, Arizona / Heidi
Landecker.
Architects: William P. Bruder.
ARCHITECTURE: THE AIA JOURNAL 1990
Oct., v.79, no.10, p.56-57,
photos., plan, secn.

UNITED STATES--PHOENIX (ARIZONA)--
CITIES AND TOWNS
Phoenix: heritage and hospitality
southwest sytle / Marie Chapple
Camacho.
PARKS & RECREATION 1990 June,
v.25, no.6, p.38-42,84, photos.,
aerial photos.

UNITED STATES--PHOENIX (ARIZONA)--
HISTORIC HOUSE MUSEUMS--HERITAGE
SQUARE
The Rosson House [Heritage Square] /
Barbara Yost.
Built in 1895 in Phoenix, Ariz.
Architect: A.P. Petit. Restored in
the late 1970s and now open to the
public.
VICTORIAN HOMES 1990 summer, v.9,
no.3, p.[44]-49, dets., photos.

UNITED STATES--PHOENIX (ARIZONA)--
MANSIONS--19TH CENTURY--CONSERVATION
AND RESTORATION--ROSSON HOUSE
The Rosson House [Heritage Square] /
Barbara Yost.
Built in 1895 in Phoenix, Ariz.
Architect: A.P. Petit. Restored in
the late 1970s and now open to the
public.
VICTORIAN HOMES 1990 summer, v.9,
no.3, p.[44]-49, dets., photos.

UNITED STATES--PHOENIX (ARIZONA)--
RESIDENTIAL GARDENS--RESEARCH
Modeling residential landscape water
and energy use to evaluate water
conservation policies / E. Gregory
McPherson.
Data derived from computer
simulations using three types of
residential gardens, xeriscapes,
zeroscapes and mesiscapes, in
Phoenix and Tucson.
LANDSCAPE JOURNAL 1990 Fall, v.9,
no.2, p.122-134, photo., plans,
tables, refs.

UNITED STATES--PHOENIX (ARIZONA)--
WATER CONSERVATION--RESEARCH
Modeling residential landscape water
and energy use to evaluate water
conservation policies / E. Gregory
McPherson.
Data derived from computer
simulations using three types of
residential gardens, xeriscapes,
zeroscapes and mesiscapes, in
Phoenix and Tucson.
LANDSCAPE JOURNAL 1990 Fall, v.9,
no.2, p.122-134, photo., plans,
tables, refs.

UNITED STATES--PHOENIX (ARIZONA)--
XERISCAPES--RESEARCH
Modeling residential landscape water
and energy use to evaluate water
conservation policies / E. Gregory
McPherson.
Data derived from computer
simulations using three types of
residential gardens, xeriscapes,
zeroscapes and mesiscapes, in
Phoenix and Tucson.
LANDSCAPE JOURNAL 1990 Fall, v.9,
no.2, p.122-134, photo., plans,
tables, refs.

UNITED STATES--PHOTOGRAPHY--
ARCHITECTURAL
American portfolio / Manolo
Laguillo.
All photos, brief captions in
Spanish and English.
QUADERNS D'ARQUITECTURA I
URBANISME 1990 Jan.-Feb.-Mar.,
no.184, p.98-103, photos.

UNITED STATES--PICAYUNE
(MISSISSIPPI)--PAVILIONS--PINECOTE
PAVILION
Solid gold: AIA's gold medalist is
honored for his distinctive
American design / Robert A. Ivy,
Jr.
The work of gold medalist Fay
Jones: Watson house Fairfield Bay,
Ark.; Worship center at Thorncrown
Chapel, Eureka Springs, Ark.;
Pinecote Pavilion, Picayune, Miss.
ARCHITECTURE: THE AIA JOURNAL 1990
Mar., v.79, no.3, p.82-[89],
port., elev., photos., plan.

UNITED STATES--PIEDMONT (CALIFORNIA)--
HOUSES--ITALIANATE--INTERIOR DESIGN
A classical refrain: aristocratic
patina of a 1920s residence in
California / Howard Junker.
Features interiors of renovated
Italianate home in Piedmont
designed in 1925 by Albert Farr.
Interior designer: Anthony Hail.
ARCHITECTURAL DIGEST 1990 May,
v.47, no.5, p.250-[256], photos.

UNITED STATES--PINNACLE PEAK
(ARIZONA)--HOUSES
Kamal Amin: dal Cairo all'Arizona,
sette opere organiche = from Cairo
to Arizona, seven organic works.
Houses in Va. and Ariz. and
medical centers in Tempe and
Scottsdale, Ariz.
ARCHITETTURA: CRONACHE E STORIA
1990 Sept., v.36, no.9(419),
p.[612-634], dets., photos.,
plans, secns., site plans.

UNITED STATES--PITTSBURGH
(PENNSYLVANIA)--BUILDINGS--
DEMOLITION--SAINT PETER'S EPISCOPAL
CHURCH
"This is a tragedy" Pittsburgh's
oldest church is demolished [St.
Peter's Episcopal Church] / Thomas
Fiorina.
Built 1852; John Notman,
architect.
PRESERVATION NEWS 1990 Mar., v.30,
no.3, p.3, photo.

UNITED STATES--PITTSBURGH
(PENNSYLVANIA)--CHURCHES--19TH
CENTURY--SAINT PETER'S EPISCOPAL
CHURCH
"This is a tragedy" Pittsburgh's
oldest church is demolished [St.
Peter's Episcopal Church] / Thomas
Fiorina.
Built 1852; John Notman,
architect.
PRESERVATION NEWS 1990 Mar., v.30,
no.3, p.3, photo.

UNITED STATES--PITTSBURGH
(PENNSYLVANIA)--CITIES AND TOWNS--
ECONOMIC ASPECTS
Symposium: public-private
partnerships for economic
development in the Pittsburgh
region.
Five articles.
AMERICAN PLANNING ASSOCIATION.
JOURNAL 1987 Autumn, v.53, no.4,
p.430-477, maps, photos., tables,
biblios., refs.

UNITED STATES--PITTSBURGH
(PENNSYLVANIA)--CULTURAL CENTERS--
BEAUX-ARTS--CONSERVATION AND
RESTORATION--CARNEGIE
Technics: cleaning the Carnegie /
John Bundar, Judith Selwyn.
Built 1895 and later expanded.
Original architects: Longfellow,
Alden and Harlow. Restoration
architects: Williams Trebilcock
Whitehead. Preservation
consultants: Preservation
Technology Associates.
PROGRESSIVE ARCHITECTURE 1990
Oct., v.71, no.10, p.38-41,
photos., aerial photo.

UNITED STATES--PITTSBURGH
(PENNSYLVANIA)--HISTORIC HOUSE
MUSEUMS--CLAYTON
The Frick family's Clayton House:
Thierry Despont restores
Pittsburgh's grand estate / Susan
Mary Alsop.
Features restored interiors of the
1860's Italianate home, later
remodeled in 1891 by Frederick J.
Osterling. The home is now opened
to the public as a house museum.
ARCHITECTURAL DIGEST 1990 Dec.,
v.47, no.13, p.[140-143], 222,
port., photos.

UNITED STATES--PITTSBURGH
(PENNSYLVANIA)--HOSPITALS--
PRESBYTERIAN-UNIVERSITY HOSPITAL
When there's no place to go but up /
James S. Russell.
On collaboration between
architects and engineers to build
over, around, and through existing
buildings. Features 3 recent
projects: Presbyterian-University
Hospital, Pittsburgh; 1675
Broadway, New York City; and
Embassy Suites, New York City.
ARCHITECTURAL RECORD 1990 Sept.,
v.178, no.10, p.160-163, models,
photos., plans, secn., isometric
dwgs.

UNITED STATES--PITTSBURGH
(PENNSYLVANIA)--HOUSES
Pittsburgh folk: designing to suit a
spirited collection / Jeffrey
Simpson.
Interiors of Pittsburgh home
feature owners' collection of folk
art. Interior designer: Charles E.
Bolton.
ARCHITECTURAL DIGEST 1990 June,
v.47, no.6, p.[118]-127,218,
port., photos.

UNITED STATES--PITTSBURGH
(PENNSYLVANIA)--HOUSES--GIOVANNITI
HOUSE
Paisajes arquitectonicos: seis
maestros, seis imagenes / Ezra
Stoller.
Six landmark buildings by
Corbusier, Alvar Aalto, F.L.
Wright, Mies, Gordon Bunshaft, and
Richard Meier.
ARQUITECTURA VIVA 1990 May-June,
no.12, p.36-39, photos.

UNITED STATES--PITTSBURGH
(PENNSYLVANIA)--HOUSING FOR
ELDERLY--BENNETT PLACE HOUSING FOR
THE ELDERLY
Housing America / Andrea Oppenheimer
Dean.
Introductory article in theme
issue discusses the reasons for
the rise in homelessness in the
U.S. Cites 4 specific projects:
Shorehaven, Bronx, N.Y. (Liebman
Melting Partnership); Spring
Creek, Brooklyn, N.Y. (Liebman
Melting Partnership and Costas
Kondylis Architects); Turning
Point, San Mateo, Calif. (David
Baker Architects); and Bennett
Place Housing for the Elderly,
Pittsburgh, Pa. (Arthur Lubetz
Assoc.).
ARCHITECTURE: THE MAGAZINE OF THE
AMERICAN INSTITUTE OF ARCHITECTS
(Continued next page)

UNITED STATES--PITTSBURGH
(PENNSYLVANIA)--HOUSING FOR
ELDERLY--BENNETT PLACE HOUSING FOR
THE ELDERLY (CONTINUED)
Housing America /...(CONTINUED)
1990 July, v.79, no.7, p.51-55,
photos., plans, site plans.

UNITED STATES--PITTSBURGH
(PENNSYLVANIA)--RESEARCH
FACILITIES--CARNEGIE MELLON RESEARCH
INSTITUTE
Peter Eisenman.
Most of the issue devoted to this
architect. Nine projects featured.
Includes interview with David
Cohn. Text in Spanish and English.
EL CROQUIS 1989 Dec., v.8, no.41,
p.4-126,cover, axonometric views,
ill., dwgs., ports., elevs.,
models, photos., plans, secns.,
refs.
Peter Eisenman: der Kubus und seine
Abweichungen = Peter Eisenman: the
cube and its deviations / Werner
Oechslin.
Text in German and English.
DAIDALOS 1990 Mar.15, no.35,
p.46-57, ill., elevs., model,
plans, refs.

UNITED STATES--PITTSBURGH
(PENNSYLVANIA)--RESEARCH
FACILITIES--CARNEGIE-MELLON
UNIVERSITY--CARNEGIE-MELLON RESEARCH
INSTITUTE
Carnegie Mellon Research Institute.
Part of the Pittsburgh Technology
Center, Pittsburgh. Architects:
Eisenman Architects.
PROGRESSIVE ARCHITECTURE 1990
Jan., v.71, no.1, p.104-106,
dwgs., elev., model, plans,
secns., site plan.

UNITED STATES--PITTSBURGH
(PENNSYLVANIA)--RESEARCH
FACILITIES--CARNEGIE-MELLON
UNIVERSITY--SOFTWARE ENGINEERING
INSTITUTE
Planning and elaboration / Royce M.
Earnest.
On the Software Engineering
Institute at Carnegie Mellon
University, Pittsburgh.
Architects: Bohlin Powell Larkin
Cywinski, with Burt Hill Kosar
Rittelman Associates.
OZ / COLLEGE OF ARCHITECTURE AND
DESIGN, KANSAS STATE UNIVERSITY
1989, v.11, p.10-11, dwg.,
photos., site plan.

UNITED STATES--PITTSBURGH
(PENNSYLVANIA)--SYNAGOGUES--
CONSERVATION AND RESTORATION--RODEF
SHALOM SYNAGOGUE
Delineating waterproofing / James S.
Russell.
Drawings of flashing details for
two restoration projects by
Ehrenkrantz, Eckstut & Whitelaw.
ARCHITECTURAL RECORD 1990 Aug.,
v.178, no.9, p.100-103, photo.

UNITED STATES--PITTSFIELD
(MASSACHUSETTS)--MODEL HOUSES--
LIVING ENVIRONMENTS
Breaking ground / Michael Wagner.
Three projects: Kitchener, Ontario
city hall, architects: Kuwabara
Payne Mckenna Blumberg Architects;
Convocation Center, Amherst
College, Amherst, Mass.,
architects: Cambridge Seven
Associates; model home, part of
Living Environments program by GE
Plastics.
INTERIORS 1990 Feb., v.149, no.7,
p.128, dwgs.
GE Plastics concept house / David H.
George.
GE Plastics Living Environments
concept house in Pittsfield Mass.;
Architects: Richardson Nagy
Martin.
URBAN LAND 1990 July, v.49, no.7,
p.20-21, photo.
Inaugurata a Pittsfield la "Casa del
futuro".
Prototype house by GE Plastics.
L'INDUSTRIA DELLE COSTRUZIONI 1990
Mar., v.24, no.221, p.78, photo.
Plastic for the people / Forrest
Wilson.
On General Electric's "Plastic"
house, a lab built like a home to
test housing systems, Pittsfield,
Mass. Architect: David George, of
Richardson Nagy Martin.
ARCHITECTURE: THE AIA JOURNAL 1990
Mar., v.79, no.3, p.165-168,
photos.
Plastic showpiece / Denise Chevin.
Living Environment, a prototype
house by GE Plastics, located in
Pittsfield, Mass. A model was
illustrated in Building, 19
Jan.1990, p.23. Architect:
Richardson Nagy Martin.
BUILDING 1990 Jan.26, v.255, no.4,
p.74-75, photos.

UNITED STATES--PITTSFIELD
(MASSACHUSETTS)--PROTOTYPE
BUILDINGS--LIVING ENVIRONMENTS
Plastic for the people / Forrest
Wilson.
On General Electric's "Plastic"
house, a lab built like a home to
test housing systems, Pittsfield,
Mass. Architect: David George, of
Richardson Nagy Martin.
ARCHITECTURE: THE AIA JOURNAL 1990
Mar., v.79, no.3, p.165-168,
photos.

UNITED STATES--PLAINS (GEORGIA)--
HISTORIC SITES--JIMMY CARTER
NATIONAL HISTORIC SITE
A visual recording / Jim Small.
On an audio-visual recording in
1988 with former president Jimmy
Carter, in conjunction with the
future development of the Jimmy
Carter National Historic Site,
Plains, Ga.
CRM BULLETIN: A NATIONAL PARK
SERVICE TECHNICAL BULLETIN 1990,
v.13, no.2, p.[1],4-5, photo.

UNITED STATES--PLAINS (GEORGIA)--
HOUSES--CARTER HOUSE
A visual recording / Jim Small.
On an audio-visual recording in
1988 with former president Jimmy
Carter, in conjunction with the
future development of the Jimmy
Carter National Historic Site,
Plains, Ga.
CRM BULLETIN: A NATIONAL PARK
SERVICE TECHNICAL BULLETIN 1990,
v.13, no.2, p.[1],4-5, photo.

UNITED STATES--PLANO (TEXAS)--CONTROL
ROOMS--LIGHTING--ELECTRONIC DATA
SYSTEMS
A well-lighted space: David Mintz's
solution for the state-of-the-art
control room at Electronic Data
System's headquarters / David
Masello.
In Plano, Tex.
ARCHITECTURAL RECORD 1990 Aug.,
v.178, no.9 suppl., p.35-36, det.,
port., photo.

UNITED STATES--PLANO (TEXAS)--
CORPORATE OFFICE BUILDINGS--INTERIOR
DESIGN--ARCO INTERNATIONAL OIL & GAS
Arco in Texas / Edie Lee Cohen.
Interiors of recently consolidated
headquarters of Arco International
Oil & Gas in Plano.
Architects/Interior designers: PHH
Environments.
INTERIOR DESIGN 1990 Mar., v.61,
no.5, p.190-[193], photos., plan.

UNITED STATES--PLANTATION HOUSES--18TH
CENTURY--INFLUENCE
Palladian abstractions: Hugh Newell
Jacobsen's light-washed design in
Michigan / Robert Campbell.
Lakeside residence near Detroit is
a contemporary version of James
River plantation houses. Interior
designers: Ingles & Associates.
ARCHITECTURAL DIGEST 1990 Dec.,
v.47, no.13, p.[144-151],226,
port., photos., plan.

UNITED STATES--PLATTSBURGH (NEW
YORK)--LAUNCH TOWERS--ATLAS PROJECT
Tief gestapelt.
Introduction to feature of issue
devoted to military topics, which
includes an article on "Das Atlas
Projekt" (Plattsburgh, N.Y.),
p.1608-1611. Several articles are
indexed separately.
BAUWELT 1990 Sept.1, v.81, no.33,
p.1597, cover, photos.

UNITED STATES--PLAYGROUNDS--
MAINTENANCE AND REPAIR
Playground safety update / Frances
Wallach.
PARKS & RECREATION 1990 Aug.,
v.25, no.8, p.46-[50], photos.

UNITED STATES--PLAYGROUNDS--STANDARDS
Playground safety update / Frances
Wallach.
PARKS & RECREATION 1990 Aug.,
v.25, no.8, p.46-[50], photos.

UNITED STATES--PORTSMOUTH (NEW
HAMPSHIRE)--HISTORIC DISTRICTS--
STRAWBERY BANKE
    Waterfront hamlet: Strawbery Banke
    [New Hampshire].
        Features four Colonial buildings
        in this neighborhood of
        Portsmouth, N.H.
        COLONIAL HOMES 1990 Dec., v.16,
        no.6, p.[98]-121,146-147, photos.

UNITED STATES--PORTSMOUTH (NEW
HAMPSHIRE)--HOUSES--COLONIAL--CHASE
HOUSE
    Waterfront hamlet: Strawbery Banke
    [New Hampshire].
        Features four Colonial buildings
        in this neighborhood of
        Portsmouth, N.H.
        COLONIAL HOMES 1990 Dec., v.16,
        no.6, p.[98]-121,146-147, photos.

UNITED STATES--PORTSMOUTH (NEW
HAMPSHIRE)--HOUSES--COLONIAL--WALSH
HOUSE
    Waterfront hamlet: Strawbery Banke
    [New Hampshire].
        Features four Colonial buildings
        in this neighborhood of
        Portsmouth, N.H.
        COLONIAL HOMES 1990 Dec., v.16,
        no.6, p.[98]-121,146-147, photos.

UNITED STATES--PORTSMOUTH (NEW
HAMPSHIRE)--MANSIONS--FEDERAL--
ICHABOD GOODWIN MANSION
    Waterfront hamlet: Strawbery Banke
    [New Hampshire].
        Features four Colonial buildings
        in this neighborhood of
        Portsmouth, N.H.
        COLONIAL HOMES 1990 Dec., v.16,
        no.6, p.[98]-121,146-147, photos.

UNITED STATES--POUGHKEEPSIE (NEW
YORK)--CHURCHES--MAINTENANCE AND
REPAIR--SAINT JOHN THE BAPTIST
[Snow and ice slides]
    Example used is the St. John the
    Baptist church, Poughkeepsie, New
    York, which recently had its roof
    repaired.
    COMMON BOND 1989 Fall, v.5, no.4,
    p.4-6, ill., photos., secns.

UNITED STATES--POUGHKEEPSIE (NEW
YORK)--LANDSCAPE GARDENS--19TH
CENTURY--SPRINGSIDE
    Springside: A. J. Downing's only
    extant garden / Robert M. Toole.
    Located in Poughkeepsie, N.Y.
    JOURNAL OF GARDEN HISTORY 1989
    Jan.-Mar., v.9, no.1, p.[20]-39,
    dwgs., ports., elevs., photos.,
    plans, site plans, refs.

UNITED STATES--POUND RIDGE (NEW
YORK)--HOUSES--DRAKE HOUSE
    Legno come essenza / Marinetta
    Nunziante.
    Drake House, Pound Ridge, N.Y.
    Architect: Alfredo De Vido.
    VILLE GIARDINI 1990 Oct., no.252,
    p.18-23, photos., plans.

UNITED STATES--PRAIRIE DU PONT
(ILLINOIS)--HOUSES--18TH CENTURY--
LOG--PIERRE MARTIN HOUSE (BOISMENUE
HOUSE)
    The Pierre Martin House / Cynthia A.
    Fuener.
        1790 Pierre Martin/Boismenue
        house, near Cahokia, Ill., built
        by French Canadians in a French
        Creole "poteaux sur solle
        (post-on-sill)" construction.
        HISTORIC ILLINOIS 1990 Feb., v.12,
        no.5, p.8-9,11, photos., plan.

UNITED STATES--PRAIRIE DU PONT
(ILLINOIS)--HOUSES--FRENCH
COLONIAL--PIERRE MARTIN HOUSE
(BOISMENUE HOUSE)
    The Pierre Martin House / Cynthia A.
    Fuener.
        1790 Pierre Martin/Boismenue
        house, near Cahokia, Ill., built
        by French Canadians in a French
        Creole "poteaux sur solle
        (post-on-sill)" construction.
        HISTORIC ILLINOIS 1990 Feb., v.12,
        no.5, p.8-9,11, photos., plan.

UNITED STATES--PRINCE GEORGE'S COUNTY
(MARYLAND)--APARTMENT COMPLEXES--
SECURITY MEASURES--GLENARDEN
APARTMENTS
    Fighting crime: an architectural
    approach / Richard Tell.
        Rehabilitation of 577 units at
        Glenarden Apartments, a government
        subsidized housing complex in
        Prince George's Co., Md., for
        crime prevention. Rehabilitation
        architects: CHK Architects.
        JOURNAL OF HOUSING 1990 July-Aug.,
        v.47, no.4, p.207-212, dwg.,
        photos.

UNITED STATES--PRINCETON (NEW
JERSEY)--CENTRAL BUSINESS DISTRICTS
    Princeton, New Jersey.
        One of six urban design reports
        included in special issue, Urban
        Concepts. Extracted from a 1979
        study for the Borough of
        Princeton. Features the Palmer
        Square complex. Architects:
        Venturi, Rauch and Scott Brown.
        ARCHITECTURAL DESIGN 1990, v.60,
        no.1-2, p.58-61, dwg., photo.,
        site plan, table.

UNITED STATES--PRINCETON (NEW
JERSEY)--DORMITORIES--PRINCETON
UNIVERSITY--CLASS OF 1927 CLAPP HALL
    Alloggi universitari a Princeton =
    Class of 1927 - Clapp Hall,
    Princeton University, New Jersey /
    Silvano Stucchi.
        Architect: Koetter, Kim &
        Associates. in Italian and
        English; French, German and
        Spanish summaries, p.3-4.
        L'INDUSTRIA DELLE COSTRUZIONI 1990
        June, v.24, no.224, p.26-31,3-4,
        dwgs., elevs., photos., plans,
        site plan.

UNITED STATES--PRINCETON (NEW
JERSEY)--DORMITORIES--PRINCETON
UNIVERSITY--FEINBERG HALL
    Tod Williams - Billie Tsien
    [interview] / Kate Nesbitt.
        Illustrates three projects: Arts
        Park Center, Los Angeles; Feinberg
        Hall, Princeton University; Tarlo
        House, Sagaponack, N.Y. In Danish
        and English.
        SKALA 1990, no.20, p.34-39,
        models, photos., refs.

UNITED STATES--PRINCETON (NEW
JERSEY)--HISTORIC DISTRICTS--PALMER
SQUARE
    P/A awards update: the perils of
    preservation planning / Thomas
    Fisher.
        Report on five preservation plans
        for historic districts in the
        following areas: Miami Beach,
        Fla.; Rugby, Tenn,; Princeton, NJ;
        Jim Thorpe, Pa. and Lowell, Mass.
        PROGRESSIVE ARCHITECTURE 1990
        June, v.71, no.6, p.100-105, ill.,
        models, photos., plans, site plan.

UNITED STATES--PRINCETON (NEW
JERSEY)--HOUSES
    Breaking away / Monica Geran.
        Home in Princeton, NJ. Architects:
        Shelton, Mindel Associates.
        INTERIOR DESIGN 1990 June, v.61,
        no.9, p.236-[243], axonometric
        view, photos., plan.

UNITED STATES--PRINCETON (NEW
JERSEY)--HOUSES--FEN HOUSE
    Peter Waldman Architects [houses].
        Contents: Wetcher house: a fable
        of the Stegosaurus and the Trojan
        horse, Bay Oaks, Texas, desgin:
        1989 -- Fen house: a text for
        nomads, surveyors and lunatics,
        Princeton, N.J., design: 1988-89.
        Architects: Peter Waldman
        Architects. Text in Japanese and
        English.
        GA HOUSES 1990 Mar., no.28,
        p.120-127, elevs., models, plans,
        secns.

UNITED STATES--PRINCETON (NEW
JERSEY)--LABORATORIES--BIOLOGICAL--
PRINCETON UNIVERSITY--LOUIS THOMAS
LABORATORIES OF MOLECULAR BIOLOGY
    Special feature: Venturi Scott Brown
    and Associates.
        Contents: Brief history-- Works:
        Primate Center, Philadelphia
        Zoological Garden.-- Lewis Thomas
        Laboratory for Molecular Biology,
        Princeton University, 1986.--
        Malcolm S. Forbes Jr. College,
        Princeton University, 1984.--
        Gordon Wu Hall, Princeton
        University, 1983.-- Venturi house,
        Philadelphia, 1974-present.--
        Izenour house, Stony Creek, Conn.,
        1984.-- House in New Castle
        County, Delaware, 1983.--
        Coxe-Hayden house, Block Island,
        R.I., 1981.-- Tarble Student
        Center, Swarthmore College,
        1985.-- Tree House, Philadelphia
        Zoo, 1985.-- Welcome Park,
        Philadelphia, 1982.-- Decorative
        designs.-- Essay: "Body language"
        and artifice: on some recent
        designs by Venturi Scott Brown and
        Associates. Text in Japanese and
        (Continued next page)

UNITED STATES--PROVIDENCE (RHODE
ISLAND)--PLAZAS--RHODE ISLAND SCHOOL
OF DESIGN (CONTINUED)
Special feature:... (CONTINUED)
ARCHITECTURE AND URBANISM 1990
Apr., no.4(235), p.65-138,
axonometric views, elevs., models,
photos., plans, secns., site
plans.

UNITED STATES--PROVIDENCE (RHODE
ISLAND)--UNIVERSITIES AND COLLEGES--
BUILDINGS--BROWN UNIVERSITY--SALOMON
CENTER FOR TEACHING
Building Types Study 682: Campus
buildings: Extracurricular
education / Grace Anderson.
Four recently-completed buildings:
Salomon Center for Teaching, Brown
Univ. (Goody, Clancy & Assoc.);
Psychology Building, Vanderbilt
Univ. (Stubbins Assoc.);
Centennial Performing Arts Center,
Westminster School, Simsbury Conn.
(Graham Gund Architects); and
Price Center, Univ. of Calif. at
San Diego (Kaplan/McLaughlin/Diaz
Architects).
ARCHITECTURAL RECORD 1990 Aug.,
v.178, no.9, p.83-[95], elevs.,
photos., plans, secns., site
plans.

UNITED STATES--PUBLIC ART
Arte como arquitectura como ciudad =
Art-as-architecture-as-town /
Sandro Marpillero.
Art and architecture as civic
design in the U.S. Three projects
illustrated: Plaza Park, San Jose,
Calif.; projects by Eric Ungers,
and Marina Linear Park, San
Diego. In Spanish and English.
ARQUITECTURA 1990 July-Aug., v.72,
no.285, p.126-137, elevs., models,
photos., plans, secns., site
plans.

UNITED STATES--PUBLIC BUILDINGS--
MAINTENANCE AND REPAIR
Building support for public
buildings / Tim Darnell.
Argues for the need to
consistently maintain public
buildings, or to adapt them to new
uses.
AMERICAN CITY & COUNTY 1990 Jan.,
v.105, no.1, p.56-58,60, sketch.

UNITED STATES--PUBLIC HOUSING--
CRITICISM
Planning problems in post-war public
housing / Gerald P. Daly.
OPEN HOUSE INTERNATIONAL 1988,
v.13, no.3, p.36-40, ill., photos,
refs.

UNITED STATES--PUBLIC HOUSING--LAW AND
LEGISLATION--HOUSING AND COMMUNITY
DEVELOPMENT ACT OF 1987
The organizational strengths and
weaknesses of resident-managed
public housing sites in the United
States / Daniel J. Monti.
JOURNAL OF URBAN AFFAIRS 1989,
v.11, no.1, p.[39]-52, refs.

UNITED STATES--PUBLIC SERVICES--
HISTORY
Rediscovering the active city [book
review] / Terrence J. McDonald.
Review of: America becomes urban,
the development of U.S. cities and
towns, 1780-1980, by Eric H.
Monkkonen, Berkeley, 1988.
JOURNAL OF URBAN HISTORY 1990 May,
v.16, no.3, p.304-311, refs.

UNITED STATES--PUGET SOUND
(WASHINGTON)--HOUSES
Architecture: Arthur Erickson /
Douglas Gantenbein.
On a Northwest-style home on Puget
Sound, Washington.
ARCHITECTURAL DIGEST 1990 Mar.,
v.47, no.3, p.[220-227],258,
photos.

UNITED STATES--QUAGUE (NEW YORK)--
HOUSES--FELDMAN HOUSE
Feldman Residence, Quague, New York,
design: 1989; contruction: 1990.
Architects: Kiss + Zwigard. Text
in Japanese and English.
GA HOUSES 1990 Mar., no.28,
p.100-101, elevs., model, plans,
secns.

UNITED STATES--QUEENS (NEW YORK)--
HOUSING PROJECTS--ARVERNE
Abandoned Arverne Beach to be
revived / Julie Meidinger.
On new housing project in Queens,
N.Y. Architects: Ehrenkrantz,
Eckstut & Whitelaw, Liebman
Melting Partnership.
PROGRESSIVE ARCHITECTURE 1990
Feb., v.71, no.2, p.23, dwg., site
plan.

UNITED STATES--QUEENS (NEW YORK)--
MUSEUMS--ART--NOGUCHI MUSEUM
Lugar y memoria: el legado Noguchi /
Rosanna Liebman.
His studio, now a museum, in Long
Island City, Queens, N.Y.
ARQUITECTURA VIVA 1990 Nov.-Dec.,
no.15, p.35-37, port., photos.,
plans.

UNITED STATES--QUEENS (NEW YORK)--
NEIGHBORHOODS--HUNTERS POINT
Getting to the Point: a strange mix
of industrial and residential
buildings, the quiet Queens
neighborhood known as Hunters
Point is in for a change / Michele
Herman.
METROPOLIS 1990 Oct., v.10, no.3,
p.106-119, photos.

UNITED STATES--QUEENS (NEW YORK)--
SHOWROOMS--FURNITURE--INTERIOR
DESIGN--BRIGHT CHAIR CO.
Bright Chair Co.: ISD Incorporated
revitalizes the firm's existing
showroom / Monica Geran.
Located in the IDCNY.
INTERIOR DESIGN 1990 Sept., v.61,
no.12, p.236-[237], dwg., photos.

UNITED STATES--QUEENS (NEW YORK)--
SHOWROOMS--FURNITURE--TEMPORARY--
VECTA
Breaking down the wall: Morphosis
creates a mystifying temporary
exhibition for Vecta at the IDCNY
in New York / Michael Wagner.
INTERIORS 1990 Jan., v.149, no.6,
p.146-147, photos., plan.
Stuhle am laufende Baud / Birgit C.
Dietsch.
Two furniture showrooms for Vecta:
New York and Los Angeles.
Architect: Morphosis.
BAUWELT 1990 Sept.7, v.81, no.34,
p.1687-1689, photos., plan.

UNITED STATES--QUEENS (NEW YORK)--
SHOWROOMS--INTERIOR DESIGN--AMERICAN
STANDARD
American Standard / Monica Geran.
Interiors of IDCNY showroom
designed by Tigerman McCurry.
INTERIOR DESIGN 1990 Sept., v.61,
no.12, p.238-[241], dwgs., photos.

UNITED STATES--QUEENS (NEW YORK)--
SHOWROOMS--TEMPORARY--AMERICAN
STANDARD
Shower of angels / Michael Wagner.
Temporary bathroom fixtures
showroom for American Standard,
IDCNY. Architects: Tigerman
McCurry.
INTERIORS 1990 July, v.149, no.12,
p.76-[77], photos.

UNITED STATES--QUEENS (NEW YORK)--
SHOWROOMS--TEMPORARY--LACKAWANNA
LEATHER
Lackawanna Leather: a temporary
exhibit adjunct designed by Andrew
Belschner Joseph Vincent / Monica
Geran.
Designed on the occasion of the
1989 Designers' Saturday.
INTERIOR DESIGN 1990 Sept., v.61,
no.12, p.232-235, photos., plan.

UNITED STATES--QUEENS (NEW YORK)--
WATERFRONT BUILDINGS--ARVERNE
Setting the table in Arverne /
Jacqueline Rivkin.
Waterfront housing development
planned by the city for this area
of Queens. Developer: Oceanview
Associates. Architects: Liebman
Melting Partnership; Ehrenkrantz,
Eckstut & Whitelaw.
METROPOLIS 1990 June, v.9, no.10,
p.19-21, dwg.

UNITED STATES--QUEENS (NEW YORK)--
WATERFRONTS--HUNTER'S POINT
Is bigger still better? / Doug
Turetsky.
Large developments at the Hunters
Point waterfront in Queens and in
Times Square are about to begin
construction despite slack in real
estate market.
CITY LIMITS 1990 Aug.-Sept., v.15,
no.7, p.12-15, port., photo.

UNITED STATES--QUENNS (NEW YORK)--
HOUSING DEVELOPMENTS--ARVERNE
Setting the table in Arverne /
Jacqueline Rivkin.
Waterfront housing development
planned by the city for this area
of Queens. Developer: Oceanview
Associates. Architects: Liebman
Melting Partnership; Ehrenkrantz,
Eckstut & Whitelaw.
METROPOLIS 1990 June, v.9, no.10,
p.19-21, dwg.

UNITED STATES--QUINCY (ILLINOIS)--
HOUSES--19TH CENTURY--EELLS HOUSE
(415 JERSEY STREET)
Richard Eells, Quincy abolitionist /
Vincent P. Gauthier, Janet Gates
Conover.
Greek revival house at 415 Jersey
St., built in early 1800s and
modified to an Italianate style in
the 1850s.
HISTORIC ILLINOIS 1990 Oct., v.13,
no.3, p.8-11, photos.

UNITED STATES--QUINCY (ILLINOIS)--
HOUSES--QUEEN ANNE STYLE--
CONSERVATION AND RESTORATION--
MUSSELMAN HOUSE
"Gem City" house sparkles again /
David Newton.
Restoration of the 1888 Musselman
house in Quincy.
HISTORIC ILLINOIS 1990 June, v.13,
no.1, p.8-9.

UNITED STATES--QUINCY
(MASSACHUSETTS)--MENTAL HEALTH
FACILITIES--QUINCY MENTAL HEALTH
CENTER
Mental health center POE.
Report on the Quincy Mental Health
center prepared by Welch & Epp
Associates.
PROGRESSIVE ARCHITECTURE 1990
Jan., v.71, no.1, p.122, plan.

UNITED STATES--RACINE (WISCONSIN)--
CORPORATE OFFICE BUILDINGS--S.C.
JOHNSON & SON ADMINISTRATION
BUILDING
Le gratte-ciel en verre / Frank
Lloyd Wright.
Excerpt from Mon autobiographie,
by Frank Lloyd Wright, Editions
Plon, 1955, on the Johnson Wax
Laboratory Tower in Racine Wisc.
English summary, p.65. Spanish
summary, p.168.
TECHNIQUES ET ARCHITECTURE 1990
Aug.-Sept., no.391, p.64-65, dwg.,
photo., plan, secn.

UNITED STATES--RACINE (WISCONSIN)--
HOUSES--PRAIRIE SCHOOL--WINGSPREAD
"Wingspread", l'ultima prairi house
di Frank Lloyd Wright =
"Wingspread", Frank Lloyd Wright's
last prairie house / Rumori to
Apostolo.
Built in 1937, north of Racine,
Wisc., for Herbert Fisk Johnson.
FRAMES, PORTE & FINESTRE 1990
Apr.-June, no.27, p.56-63, dwg.,
port., maps, photos., plan.

UNITED STATES--RACINE (WISCONSIN)--
TALL BUILDINGS--S.C. JOHNSON & SON
ADMINISTRATION BUILDING
Le gratte-ciel en verre / Frank
Lloyd Wright.
Excerpt from Mon autobiographie,
by Frank Lloyd Wright, Editions
Plon, 1955, on the Johnson Wax
Laboratory Tower in Racine Wisc.
English summary, p.65. Spanish
summary, p.168.
TECHNIQUES ET ARCHITECTURE 1990
Aug.-Sept., no.391, p.64-65, dwg.,
photo., plan, secn.

UNITED STATES--RALEIGH (NORTH
CAROLINA)--GREENWAYS
Greenway use and users: an
examination of Raleigh and
Charlotte greenways / Owen J.
Furuseth, Robert E. Altman.
CAROLINA PLANNING 1990 Fall, v.16,
no.2, p.37-43, maps, photo.,
tables, refs.

UNITED STATES--RANCH HOUSES--
ALTERATIONS AND ADDITIONS
Installing a long-span header / Matt
Holmstrom.
Alteration of a load-bearing wall
for an addition to a ranch house;
location is unspecified.
FINE HOMEBUILDING 1989 Aug.,
no.55, p.75-[77], det., photos.

UNITED STATES--RANCHO MIRAGE
(CALIFORNIA)--RESTAURANTS
Forme zoomorfiche e spazi che
respirano: quattro esempi di
modellato di Kendrick Bangs
Kellogg. / Marisa Cerruti.
Restaurant, Jacksonville, Fl; Yen
house, La Jolla, CA; Gordon house,
san Diego, CA; restaurant, Rancho
Mirage, CA. English, French,
German, Spanish summaries, p.118.
ARCHITETTURA: CRONACHE E STORIA
1987 Feb., v.33, no.2(376),
p.[116]-126, photos., plans, site
plans.

UNITED STATES--REAL ESTATE DEVELOPMENT
Urban cores: development trends and
real estate opportunities in the
1990s / Christopher B. Leinberger.
URBAN LAND 1990 Dec., v.49, no.12,
p.4-9, photo., table, aerial
photos.

UNITED STATES--RECREATION AREAS--
STANDARDS
Park standards are up in the air /
James Krohe.
National guidelines for parks and
recreation areas are criticized.
PLANNING 1990 Dec., v.56, no.12,
p.10-13, ill., photos., plan.

UNITED STATES--RED BANK (NEW JERSEY)--
HOUSES--BLUFFS
The Bluffs, Red Bank, New Jersey.
Luxury riverside housing units,
some incorporated into existing
Victorian mansions. Architect:
Jerome Morley Larson.
ARCHITECTURE NEW JERSEY 1989,
v.25, no.3, p.8, photo.

UNITED STATES--RED BANK (NEW JERSEY)--
WATERFRONT BUILDINGS--BLUFFS
The Bluffs, Red Bank, New Jersey.
Luxury riverside housing units,
some incorporated into existing
Victorian mansions. Architect:
Jerome Morley Larson.
ARCHITECTURE NEW JERSEY 1989,
v.25, no.3, p.8, photo.

UNITED STATES--RED HOOK (NEW YORK)--
HOUSES
George Ranalli: barn for "a" family
a Red Hook, New York.
Text in Italian and English.
DOMUS 1990 Nov., no.721, p.12-13,
models, photos., plans, secns.,
sketches.

UNITED STATES--RED HOOK (NEW YORK)--
INNS--18TH CENTURY--CONSERVATION AND
RESTORATION--ELMENDORPH INN
Elmendorph Inn reopens.
Located at 43-45 N.Broadway, Red
Hook.
PRESERVATION LEAGUE OF NEW YORK
STATE. NEWSLETTER 1990-1991
Winter, v.16, no.3, p.6-7, photos.

UNITED STATES--REDWOOD CITY
(CALIFORNIA)--CORPORATE OFFICE
BUILDINGS--INTERIOR DESIGN--NEXT,
INC.
Next, Inc. / Judith Nasatir.
Interiors of corporate
headquarters, Redwood City, Calif.
Interior designers: Whisler Patri.
INTERIOR DESIGN 1990 Nov., v.61,
no.15, p.176-[179], photos.,
plans.

UNITED STATES--REGIONAL PLANNING
The evolution of spatial modeling in
the USA / Richard K. Brail.
EKISTICS 1989 Sept.-Dec., v.56,
no.338-339, p.249-253, refs.
Regional approaches gaining ground /
Joy McIlwain.
AMERICAN CITY & COUNTY 1989 Aug.,
v.104, no.8, p.38-41, ill.

UNITED STATES--REGIONALISM
Regional style: eco-logic at work.
A brief survey of six
"environmental" gardens in the
U.S. Landscape architects: Steven
K. Domigan, Edith Eddleman, Ron
Lutsco, Steve Trudnak, James Weht,
and David Cropp.
GARDEN DESIGN 1990 spring, v.9,
no.1, p.46-59, photos., site
plans, sketch.

UNITED STATES--RELIEF (SCULPTURE)
Toward a new language of form: Karl
Bitter and the beginnings of
archaism in American sculpture /
Susan Rather.
Examples include reliefs and
memorials from the 1900-1915
period.
WINTERTHUR PORTFOLIO 1990 Spring,
v.25, no.1, p.[1]-19, photos.,
refs.

UNITED STATES--RELIGIOUS BUILDINGS--
DOCUMENTATION
Documentation projects, part 1:
Photography / Neal A. Vogel,
Christopher Jenks.
Techniques for photo-documentation
of histcric buildings. Examples
include the Church of St. John the
Evangelist, Stockport, N.Y.
COMMON BOND 1990 Fall, v.6, no.4,
p.4-7, photos.

UNITED STATES--RESEARCH FACILITIES--
CONSERVATION AND RESTORATION--
POLITICAL ASPECTS
Making technological facilities NHLs
[part I] / Harry Butowsky.
Includes "The designation of
technological facilities as
National Historic Landmarks: a
report", covering the application
of the Historic Preservation Act
of 1966 to NASA properties and
observatories, such as those in
Pasadena, San Diego County, and
Cleveland.
CRM BULLETIN: A NATIONAL PARK
SERVICE TECHNICAL BULLETIN 1989,
v.12, no.6, p.1-4, dwg., photos.

UNITED STATES--RESIDENTIAL GARDENS
Lot, yard, and garden: American
distinctions / Paul Groth.
LANDSCAPE 1990 v.30, no.3,
p.29-35, diagrs., photos., biblio.

UNITED STATES--RESIDENTIAL GARDENS--
20TH CENTURY--EXHIBITIONS
Modernist landscapes: the
adventurous gardens of Fletcher
Steele stretched the aesthetic
boundaries of early twentieth
century design [exhibition review]
/ Mac Griswold.
Exhibition through Mar. 30 at the
Paine Webber Art Gallery, New
York.
HOUSE & GARDEN 1990 Mar., v.162,
no.3, p.116-[118], photos., port.,
secn.

UNITED STATES--RESIDENTIAL MOBILITY
The exurbanization of America and
its planning policy implications /
Arthur C. Nelson, Kenneth J.
Dueker.
JOURNAL OF PLANNING EDUCATION AND
RESEARCH 1990 Winter, v.9, no.2,
p.91-100, table, refs.

UNITED STATES--RESTAURANTS--INTERIOR
DESIGN--NEW YORK (NEW YORK)
Dinner at the Inn / Regina S.
Baraban.
A review of 3 new hotel
restaurants in Manhattan.
METROPOLIS 1990 Nov., v.10, no.4,
p.25, photos.

UNITED STATES--RESTON (VIRGINIA)--NEW
TOWNS
Las nuevas ciudades americanas (II):
ciudades de promocion privada =
Private enterprise towns / Abel
Enguita.
Example of Reston, Va. English
summary, p.82.
URBANISMO / COAM 1989 Sept., no.8,
p.73-82, dwg., maps, photo., plan,
tables, aerial photos.

UNITED STATES--RESTON (VIRGINIA)--NEW
TOWNS (CONTINUED)
Pumping up suburban downtowns /
Philip Langdon.
Examples in Reston, Va., Miami
Lakes, Fla., and Buffalo Grove,
Ill.
PLANNING 1990 July, v.56, no.7,
p.22-28, dwg., model, map,
photos., plans, aerial photo.

UNITED STATES--RHEINBECK (NEW YORK)--
WEEKEND HOUSES--HENRY HOUSE
Michael Graves Architect [houses].
Contents: Naiman house, La Jolla,
California, design: 1988-89 --
Henry house, Rheinbeck, New York,
design: 1987-89. Architect:
Michael Graves. Text in Japanese
and English.
GA HOUSES 1990 Mar., no.28,
p.104-107, elevs., models, plans,
secns.

UNITED STATES--RHINEBECK (NEW YORK)--
HOUSES--GOTHIC REVIVAL--INTERIOR
DESIGN--BEEKMAN ARMS--DELAMATER
HOUSE
Country-cottage revival / Jane
Margolies.
New interior furnishings by
Carolyn Gutilla for the Delamater
House, designed in 1844 by A. J.
Davis, now part of the Beekman
Arms inn, in Rhinebeck, N. Y.
HOUSE BEAUTIFUL 1990 Jan., v.132,
no.1, p.41-[45], photos.

UNITED STATES--RHINEBECK (NEW YORK)--
HOUSES--QUEEN ANNE STYLE--
WILDERSTEIN
Wilderstein: a loved and lived-in
family home in Rhinebeck, New York
/ Anne Needham.
Queen Anne style house completed
in the 1880s. Interior by J.B.
Tiffany; grounds by Calvert Vaux;
architect for exterior, Arnout
Cannon. Current owner: Wilderstein
Foundation.
VICTORIAN HOMES 1990 summer, v.9,
no.3, p.54-57, ill., photos.

UNITED STATES--RHINEBECK (NEW YORK)--
INNS--INTERIOR DESIGN--BEEKMAN
ARMS--DELAMATER HOUSE
Country-cottage revival / Jane
Margolies.
New interior furnishings by
Carolyn Gutilla for the Delamater
House, designed in 1844 by A. J.
Davis, now part of the Beekman
Arms inn, in Rhinebeck, N. Y.
HOUSE BEAUTIFUL 1990 Jan., v.132,
no.1, p.41-[45], photos.

UNITED STATES--RICHLAND CENTER
(WISCONSIN)--HOUSES--20TH CENTURY--
BARRET-TUXFORD HOUSE
Arthur Dyson: un architettura "del
luogo e del tempo" = An
architecture "of site and time".
Three U.S. houses.
ARCHITETTURA: CRONACHE E STORIA
1990 Oct., v.36, no.10(420),
p.[698]-[714], photos., plans,
secns.

UNITED STATES--RICHMOND
(MASSACHUSETTS)--COUNTRY HOUSES--
FEDERAL--INTERIOR DESIGN--GOODWOOD
(MOLYNEUX HOUSE)
A continental Yankee: interior drama
marks a designer's historic
federal estate in the Berkshires /
Peter Carlsen.
Interiors of Goodwood, Juan Pablo
Molyneux's 1792 country house in
Richmond, Mass.
ARCHITECTURAL DIGEST 1990 Feb.,
v.47, no.2, p.194-203, port.,
photos.

UNITED STATES--RICHMOND (VIRGINIA)--
GARDENS--VIRGINIA HOUSE
Roots of traditionalism: an
old-world garden at Virginia house
/ Derek Fell.
English-style gardens of 1920s
mansion in Richmon, Va.
SOUTHERN ACCENTS 1989 Mar.-Apr.,
v.12, no.2, p.[124-133], photos.

UNITED STATES--RICHMOND (VIRGINIA)--
HISTORIC HOUSE MUSEUMS--
WICKHAM-VALENTINE HOUSE
Behind-the-scenes job: conservators
turn sleuthhounds at Richmond's
Valentine Museum / Philip Morris.
Paint research and restoration at
the 1812 Wickham-Valentine House.
Restoration architects: Charles
Phillips, Paul Buchanan.
SOUTHERN ACCENTS 1989 Mar.-Apr.,
v.12, no.2, p.86-94, photos.

UNITED STATES--RICHMOND (VIRGINIA)--
INNS--LINDEN ROW INN
Southern traditions: preservation
efforts in today's South show new
interest in 20th-century
landmarks, as well as earlier ones
/ Clifford A. Pearson.
A portfolio of Southeast projects:
Epping Forest Yacht Club,
Jacksonville, Fla. (Pappas
Associates); Freedom Tower, Miami
(Heisenbottle Architects);
Venetian Pool, Coral Gables, Fla.
(H. Carlton Decker & Assoc.);
Howard Memorial Library, New
Orleans (E. Barron, M. Toups); and
Linden Row Inn, Richmond, Va.
(Glave Newman Anderson).
ARCHITECTURAL RECORD 1990 Mar.,
v.178, no.3, p.66-75, photos.,
plans, site plans.

UNITED STATES--RICHMOND (VIRGINIA)--
MURAL PAINTING AND DECORATION--
NEOCLASSICAL--CONSERVATION AND
RESTORATION--WICKHAM-VALENTINE HOUSE
Behind-the-scenes job: conservators
turn sleuthhounds at Richmond's
Valentine Museum / Philip Morris.
Paint research and restoration at
the 1812 Wickham-Valentine House.
Restoration architects: Charles
Phillips, Paul Buchanan.
SOUTHERN ACCENTS 1989 Mar.-Apr.,
v.12, no.2, p.86-94, photos.

UNITED STATES--RICHMOND (VIRGINIA)--
MUSEUMS--ART--VIRGINIA MUSEUM OF
FINE ARTS
  Virginia Museum of Fine Arts.
  Feature, with articles on the
  collections. Includes an introd.,
  by Paul N. Perrot, illustrated
  with photos. of the original
  building (1936, by Peebles and
  Ferguson) and the West wing (1985,
  Hardy Holzman Pfeiffer
  Associates).
  ANTIQUES 1990 Aug., v.138, no.2,
  p.[250]-313, photos.

UNITED STATES--RICHMOND (VIRGINIA)--
TOWNHOUSES--GREEK REVIVAL--
CONSERVATION AND RESTORATION--
FRANKLIN STREET
  Southern traditions: preservation
  efforts in today's South show new
  interest in 20th-century
  landmarks, as well as earlier ones
  / Clifford A. Pearson.
  A portfolio of Southeast projects:
  Epping Forest Yacht Club,
  Jacksonville, Fla. (Pappas
  Associates); Freedom Tower, Miami
  (Heisenbottle Architects);
  Venetian Pool, Coral Gables, Fla.
  (H. Carlton Decker & Assoc.);
  Howard Memorial Library, New
  Orleans (E. Barron, M. Toups); and
  Linden Row Inn, Richmond, Va.
  (Glave Newman Anderson).
  ARCHITECTURAL RECORD 1990 Mar.,
  v.178, no.3, p.66-75, photos.,
  plans, site plans.

UNITED STATES--RIDGWAY (COLORADO)--
VACATION HOUSES--WOLF HOUSE
  Bravo Ettore! Sottsass builds an
  American dream house / Richard
  Lacayo.
  Vacation house for Daniel Wolf
  near Telluride, Colo.
  METROPOLITAN HOME 1990 Nov., v.22,
  no.11, p.115-125, dwg., port.,
  photos.
  New frontier: Wolf house, Ridgway,
  Colorado, Sottsass Associati,
  architect / Karen D. Stein.
  ARCHITECTURAL RECORD 1990 Oct.,
  v.178, no.11, p.78-83, elev.,
  photos., plans.

UNITED STATES--RIVERSIDE
(CALIFORNIA)--MUSEUMS--PHOTOGRAPHY--
CALIFORNIA MUSEUM OF PHOTOGRAPHY
  In the mind's eye / Ziva Freiman.
  Former Kress dept. store in
  Riverside, Calif. converted into
  the California Museum of
  Photography. Architect: Stanley
  Saitowitz. Includes Selected
  Detail article on the steel
  staircase in the museum.
  PROGRESSIVE ARCHITECTURE 1990
  Sept., v.71, no.9, p.130-136,
  dets., ill., dwgs., photos.,
  plans.

UNITED STATES--RIVERSIDE COUNTY
(CALIFORNIA)--HOUSES--WING SWEEP
HOUSE
  Kendrick Bangs Kellogg [houses].
  Contents: Doolittle house "Wing
  Walk," Sin Barnyards County, [sic]
  CA, 1988 --Bailey house, San Diego
  County, CA, 1985 --Wing Sweep
  house, Riverside County, CA, 1986.
  Text in Japanese and English.
  (Continued next column)

UNITED STATES--RIVERSIDE COUNTY
(CALIFORNIA)--HOUSES--WING SWEEP
HOUSE (CONTINUED)
  Kendrick Bangs...(CONTINUED)
  GA HOUSES 1990 Mar., no.28,
  p.136-139, models, plans, site
  plans.
  Meet the architect: Kendrick Bangs
  Kellogg.
  Contents: Essay: Natural
  vernacular / Kay Kaiser,--
  Introduction / Ken Kellogg,--
  Works: Wing Sweep house, Riverside
  County, CA,--Yen house, 1981,
  Westway house, 1979, Atoll house,
  1973, all in La Jolla, CA --
  Pacific Beach house, San Diego,
  CA, 1972,--Kona house, Kona Coast,
  Hawaii, 1962. Text in Japanese and
  English.
  GA HOUSES 1990 July, no.29,
  p.[22]-71, axonometric views,
  port., photos., plans, secns.,
  site plans.

UNITED STATES--RIVERWOODS (ILLINOIS)--
CORPORATE OFFICE BUILDINGS--DEAN
WITTER FINANCIAL SERVICES GROUP
  Company manners: Dean Witter
  Financial Services Group,
  Riverwoods Corporate Place,
  Riverwoods, Illinois, Lohan
  Associates, Architects / Margaret
  Gaskie.
  ARCHITECTURAL RECORD 1990 Sept.,
  v.178, no.10, p.88-93, dets.,
  photos., plans.

UNITED STATES--ROADS
  On the road / Kristian Berg,
  Lars-Eric Jonsson.
  Roadside architecture in the U.S.
  ARKITEKTUR: THE SWEDISH REVIEW OF
  ARCHITECTURE 1990 Nov., v.90,
  no.9, p.12-19, dwg., photos.,
  aerial photos., biblio.

UNITED STATES--ROADS--ECONOMIC ASPECTS
  Toll roads: a new direction for US
  highways? / Elizabeth Deakin.
  BUILT ENVIRONMENT 1989, v.15,
  no.3-4, p.185-194, refs.

UNITED STATES--ROADSIDES
  On the road / Kristian Berg,
  Lars-Eric Jonsson.
  Roadside architecture in the U.S.
  ARKITEKTUR: THE SWEDISH REVIEW OF
  ARCHITECTURE 1990 Nov., v.90,
  no.9, p.12-19, dwg., photos.,
  aerial photos., biblio.

UNITED STATES--ROCHESTER (MICHIGAN)--
SCHOOLS--ELEMENTARY--ALTERATIONS AND
ADDITIONS--GAGE ELEMENTARY SCHOOL
  Making the grade: ATS & R advances a
  1950's elementary school to the
  head of its class.
  Gage Elementary School, Rochester,
  Minn.
  ARCHITECTURE MINNESOTA 1990
  Sept.-Oct., v.16, no.5, p.24-25,
  photos.

UNITED STATES--ROCHESTER (NEW YORK)--
HISTORIC HOUSE MUSEUMS--GEORGE
EASTMAN HOUSE
  Photo finish: vintage photos aid
  restoration of Eastman House
  [George Eastman House, Rochester,
  N.Y.] / Sebby Wilson Jacobson.
  McKim Mead and White designed the
  public rooms, built 1904-05.
  William Seale supervised its
  recent restoration.
  PRESERVATION NEWS 1990 Apr., v.30,
  no.4, p.7, port., photos.

UNITED STATES--ROCK ISLAND
(ILLINOIS)--UNIVERSITIES AND
COLLEGES--BUILDINGS--AUGUSTANA
COLLEGE--OLD MAIN
  Augustana College's Old Main: a
  Swedish center / David Newton.
  In Rock Island, Ill., completed in
  1893. Architect: E.S. Hammatt.
  HISTORIC ILLINOIS 1990 Dec., v.13,
  no.4, p.6-9, dwg., photos.

UNITED STATES--ROCKINGHAM (VERMONT)--
HOUSES--GEORGIAN--STEPHEN-DOUGLAS
ANTIQUES
  Collectors' choice.
  Antique shop in Rockingham, Vt.,
  housed in an 18th-cent. Georgian
  house.
  COLONIAL HOMES 1990 Aug., v.16,
  no.4, p.[52]-59, photos.

UNITED STATES--ROCKLIN (CALIFORNIA)--
FACTORIES--FURNITURE--HERMAN MILLER
WESTERN REGION MANUFACTURING AND
DISTRIBUTION FACILITY
  City on a hill...Herman Miller's new
  factory / Karen D. Stein.
  The Western Region Manufacturing
  and Distribution Facility,
  Rocklin, Calif. Architect: Frank
  O. Gehry & Associates; consulting
  architect: Tigerman McCurry
  Architects; assoc. architect:
  Dreyfuss and Blackford; landscape
  architects: Peter Walker / Martha
  Schwartz.
  ARCHITECTURAL RECORD 1990 Jan.,
  v.178, no.1, p.108-115, elev.,
  photos., plan, secns., site plan.
  Etat, prospectives et
  representations de l'industrie
  europeenne du bureau.
  On the office furniture industry.
  Features four showrooms and a
  factory by the following
  architects: Frank Gehry, Afra and
  Tobia Scarpa, Pierluigi Cerri and
  Paolo Ferrari. English summary,
  p.182-183.
  ARCHITECTURE INTERIEURE CREE 1990
  Apr.-May, no.236, p.[138-157],153,
  ports., elev., photos., plans,
  site plan.
  Frank O. Gehry.
  Entire issue devoted to the work
  of this American architect.
  Criticism by A. Zaera Polo and
  David Cohn. 15 projects and
  buildings from 1987-1990 featured.
  Text in Spanish and English.
  EL CROQUIS 1990 Nov., v.9, no.45,
  p.1-124, ports., elevs., models,
  photos., plans, secns., site
  plans, refs.

UNITED STATES--ROCKLIN (CALIFORNIA)--
FACTORIES--FURNITURE--HERMAN MILLER
WESTERN REGION MANUFACTURING AND
DISTRIBUTION FACILITY (CONTINUED)
Heavy Metal fur Herman Miller:
Mobelfabrik in Rocklin,
Kalifornien.
Architect: Frank Gehry.
BAUWELT 1990 Sept.7, v.81, no.34,
p.1670-1681,cover, photos., site
plan.
Paesaggi attorno al lavoro:
Sacramento, California: Herman
Miller = Landscapes of labour:
Herman Miller, in Sacramento,
California.
Furniture factory in Rocklin.
Architects: Frank O. Gehry &
Associates; Tigerman, Fugman &
McCurry. Landscape architects:
Peter Walker and Martha Schwartz.
ABITARE 1990 Oct., no.289,
p.244-255, elev., photos., plans,
secns., site plan.
El templo de cobre: factoria y
almacen Herman Miller, Rocklin,
California, 1985-1989.
Herman Miller Western Region
Manufacturing and Distribution
Facility. Architects: Frank O.
Gehry and Associates. English
text, p.86.
A & V 1990, no.25, p.36-41,
elevs., photos., plan, site plan,
sketches.

UNITED STATES--ROCKLIN (CALIFORNIA)--
GROUNDS--HERMAN MILLER
Prati e rocce intorno alla fabbrica
di Gehry: Landscaping per la
Herman Miller a Rockland [sic],
California, Peter Walker e Martha
Schwartz.
ARCHITETTURA; CRONACHE E STORIA
1990 Feb., v.36, no.2(412), p.134,
photos., site plan.

UNITED STATES--ROCKPORT (MAINE)--GOLF
COURSE COMMUNITIES--SAMOSET RESORT
AND VILLAGE
The search continues: building types
study 681, multifamily housing /
Donald J. Canty.
Four low-rise condominium
projects: The Waterworks, New
Hope, Penn. (Cecil Baker &
Associates, Architects); Back of
the Hill Rowhouses, Boston
(William Rawn Associates,
Architects); Samoset Resort and
Village, Rockport, Me. (Sasaki
Associates, Architects); and
Parkview Commons, San Francisco
(David Baker Architects).
ARCHITECTURAL RECORD 1990 July,
v.178, no.8, p.15-87, axonometric
views, elev., photos., plans, site
plans.

UNITED STATES--ROOSEVELT (NEW
JERSEY)--HOUSES--SOLAR--ROOSEVELT
SENIOR CITIZENS HOUSING
Una comunita solare per la terza eta
/ Elisa Dal Canto.
Housing for elderly, Roosevelt,
N.J. Architects: Kelbaugh & Lee.
VILLE GIARDINI 1990 Feb., no.245,
p.2-7, photos., plans, site plan.

UNITED STATES--ROOSEVELT (NEW
JERSEY)--HOUSING FOR ELDERLY--
ROOSEVELT SENIOR CITIZENS HOUSING
Una comunita solare per la terza eta
/ Elisa Dal Canto.
Housing for elderly, Roosevelt,
N.J. Architects: Kelbaugh & Lee.
VILLE GIARDINI 1990 Feb., no.245,
p.2-7, photos., plans, site plan.

UNITED STATES--ROSEMONT (ILLINOIS)--
OFFICE BUILDINGS--ONE O'HARE CENTER
One O'Hare Center, office building,
Rosemont, Illinois, 1984-86.
Architects: Kohn Pedersen Fox
Associates.
PROCESS: ARCHITECTURE 1989 Nov.,
no.86, p.42-43, elev., photos.,
plan.

UNITED STATES--ROSEMOUNT (ILLINOIS)--
METALWORK--ONE O'HARE CENTER
An affinity for ornament: the work
of Kohn Pedersen Fox... / Donald
London.
Decorative uses of metal on 4
recent projects: 225 W. Wacker
Dr., Chicago; 101 Federal St.,
Boston; 1 O'Hare Center,
Rosemount, Ill., and 900 N.
Michigan Ave., Chicago.
ARCHITECTURAL RECORD 1990 May,
v.178, no.6, p.121-125,
axonometric view, dets., elevs.,
photos., secns.

UNITED STATES--ROSS (CALIFORNIA)--
HOUSES--INTERIOR DESIGN
North of the Golden Gate / Joan
Chatfield-Taylor.
Interiors of renovated 1960 home
in Ross, Calif. Interior designer:
Ronald Crosetti.
ARCHITECTURAL DIGEST 1990 Oct.,
v.47, no.11, p.[264-269], photos.

UNITED STATES--ROSS VALLEY
(CALIFORNIA)--HOUSES--SNODGRASS
HOUSE
Professional metamorphosis: as his
own client, designer Warren
Snodgrass practices many
disciplines / Monica Geran.
Features Snodgrass house, Ross
Valley, Calif. Architect: David
Williams.
INTERIOR DESIGN 1990 May, v.61,
no.7, p.296-[301], photos., plan.

UNITED STATES--ROSSLYN (VIRGINIA)--
OFFICE BUILDINGS--POTOMAC TOWER
Escaping the box: ... Washington's
12 Best office buildings / James
Goode.
1718 Connecticut Ave., NW (David
M. Schwarz); 1250 24th St., NW
(Don Hisaka & Assoc.); Republic
Place (Keyes, Condon, Florance);
Potomac Tower (Pei Cobb Freed &
Partners); 317 Massachusetts Ave.,
NE (Weinstein Assoc.); 816
Connnecticut Ave., NW (Shalom
Baranes Assoc.); Franklin Square
(Phillip Johnson & John Burgee);
500 E St., SW (Kohn Pedersen Fox
Assoc.); Jefferson Court (SOM);
1001 Pennsylvania Ave., NW
(Hartman-Cox); 2631 Connecticut
Ave., NW (Martin & Jones).
MUSEUM & ARTS WASHINGTON 1990
Mar.-Apr., v.6, no.2, p.[58-65],
140, photos.

UNITED STATES--ROXBURY (CONNECTICUT)--
GARDENS--WOOSTER GARDEN
Out of bounds: designer Peter
Wooster disregards the conventions
of rural gentility in his
Connecticut compound / Mac
Griswold.
HOUSE & GARDEN 1990 June, v.162,
no.6, p.[132-139], port., photos.

UNITED STATES--ROXBURY (CONNECTICUT)--
HOUSES--CLOVER KNOLL
The house on Clover Knoll / Jim
Picton.
House for the builder-author's
parents, in Roxbury, Conn.
Includes a rooftop "gazebo."
Architect: Richard Donahoe.
FINE HOMEBUILDING 1989 Aug.,
no.55, p.82-87, photos., plans.

UNITED STATES--ROXBURY (CONNECTICUT)--
HOUSES--MARTINELLI HOUSE
Martinelli residence, Roxbury,
Connecticut.
Architect: Anthony Ames Architect.
Text in Japanese and English.
GA HOUSES 1990 July, no.29,
p.126-133, elevs., photos., plans,
site plan.

UNITED STATES--RUGBY (TENNESSEE)--
HISTORIC DISTRICTS
P/A awards update: the perils of
preservation planning / Thomas
Fisher.
Report on five preservation plans
for historic districts in the
following areas: Miami Beach,
Fla.; Rugby, Tenn.; Princeton, NJ;
Jim Thorpe, Pa. and Lowell, Mass.
PROGRESSIVE ARCHITECTURE 1990
June, v.71, no.6, p.100-105, ill.,
models, photos., plans, site plan.

UNITED STATES--RURAL LAND USE
The exurbanization of America and
its planning policy implications /
Arthur C. Nelson, Kenneth J.
Dueker.
JOURNAL OF PLANNING EDUCATION AND
RESEARCH 1990 Winter, v.9, no.2,
p.91-100, table, refs.

UNITED STATES--RUSH COUNTY (INDIANA)--
BARNS--CONSERVATION AND
RESTORATION--ARNOLD FARM
Indiana farm wins in Trust's BARN
AGAIN! program [Arnold Farm, Rush
Co.].
PRESERVATION NEWS 1990 May, v.30,
no.5, p.16,19, ports.

UNITED STATES--RUSH COUNTY (INDIANA)--
FARM BUILDINGS--CONSERVATION AND
RESTORATION--ARNOLD FARM
Indiana farm wins in Trust's BARN
AGAIN! program [Arnold Farm, Rush
Co.].
PRESERVATION NEWS 1990 May, v.30,
no.5, p.16,19, ports.

UNITED STATES--RUTHERFORD
(CALIFORNIA)--HOUSES--20TH CENTURY--
NAPA HOUSE (ANDERSON HOUSE)
High country: The Napa house,
Rutherford, California / Margaret
Gaskie.
Anderson's house. Architects:
Anderson Schwartz Architects.
ARCHITECTURAL RECORD 1990
Mid-Apr., v.178, no.5, p.96-[101],
elev., photos., plans.

UNITED STATES--SACRAMENTO
(CALIFORNIA)--CORPORATE OFFICE
BUILDINGS--WELLS FARGO CENTER
Wells Fargo Center at Capitol Mall,
Sacramento, California, USA, 1991.
Architects: Hellmuth, Obata &
Kassabaum. Text in Japanese and
English.
ARCHITECTURE AND URBANISM 1990
Dec., no.12 extra edition,
p.183-[185], elev., photos., plan.

UNITED STATES--SACRAMENTO
(CALIFORNIA)--HISTORIC HOUSE
MUSEUMS--CONSERVATION AND
RESTORATION--LELAND STANFORD HOUSE
A systematic approach to historic
structures reports / Thomas
Winter, Peter Schulz.
ASSOCIATION FOR PRESERVATION
TECHNOLOGY. BULLETIN 1990, v.22,
no.1-2, p.142-148, ill., photos.,
tables, refs.

UNITED STATES--SACRAMENTO
(CALIFORNIA)--MULTI-USE COMPLEXES--
LAGUNA WEST PROJECT
Cities to walk in: Laguna West
Project / Todd W. Bressi.
The concept of "pedestrian
pockets" in urban centers, as
developed by Peter Calthorpe and
Dan Solomon.
METROPOLIS 1990 Mar., v.9, no.7,
p.54-58, dwgs., site plans.

UNITED STATES--SACRAMENTO
(CALIFORNIA)--OFFICE BUILDINGS--
COMPETITIONS
Design over build in Sacramento /
Gary Delsohn.
PROGRESSIVE ARCHITECTURE 1990
Jan., v.71, no.1, p.30,32, model.

UNITED STATES--SAG HARBOR (NEW YORK)--
CITIES AND TOWNS
Sag Harbor, an American beauty /
Wilfrid Sheed.
ARCHITECTURAL DIGEST 1990 May,
v.47, no.5, p.29-40, photos.

UNITED STATES--SAG HARBOR (NEW YORK)--
WEEKEND HOUSES--INTERIOR DESIGN--
MOSES - PERLMAN HOUSE
A perfect fit: Rebecca Moses / Julie
V. Iovine.
Interior of weekend house in Sag
Harbor, N.Y., owned by the fashion
designer and her husband Louis
Perlman.
METROPOLITAN HOME 1990 June, v.22,
no.6, p.82-[87], ports., photos.

UNITED STATES--SAGAPONACK (NEW YORK)--
COUNTRY HOUSES--STAINLESS STEEL
William B. Gleckman: stainless-steel
siding for a cedar-lined country
house in Sagaponack / Suzanne
Stephens.
ARCHITECTURAL DIGEST 1990 Feb.,
v.47, no.2, p.98-[103], port.,
photos.

UNITED STATES--SAGAPONACK (NEW YORK)--
RESIDENTIAL GARDENS--DASH GARDEN
A painter's eye in the garden
[Robert Dash] / William L.
Hamilton.
Located on "Madoo" in Sagaponack,
Long Island, N.Y.
ART & ANTIQUES 1990 Summer,
p.55-56, port., photos.

UNITED STATES--SAINT AUGUSTINE
(FLORIDA)--HISTORIC BUILDINGS
Quixotic Saint Augustine: remaking
history for commerce / Beth
Dunlop.
SOUTHERN ACCENTS 1990 July-Aug.,
v.13, no.6, p.46-50, photos.

UNITED STATES--SAINT LOUIS
(MISSOURI)--ARTS DISTRICTS--GRAND
CENTER
Street as stage: the reviving
performing arts district in St.
Louis / Mary Henderson Gass.
Grand Center, between Grand Ave.
and Lincoln Blvd., has been
revitalized since 1980 by the City
Center Redevelopment Corporation,
under Richard Gaddes.
INLAND ARCHITECT 1990 Sept.-Oct.,
v.34, no.5, p.52-56, models,
secns., site plans.

UNITED STATES--SAINT LOUIS
(MISSOURI)--CHAPELS--PRIORY CHAPEL
Priory Chapel, St. Louis, Missouri,
USA.
Built 1962. Architect: Gyo Obata
of Hellmuth, Obata & Kassabaum.
Text in Japanese and English.
ARCHITECTURE AND URBANISM 1990
Dec., no.12 extra edition,
p.22-27,227, photos., secn., site
plan.

UNITED STATES--SAINT LOUIS
(MISSOURI)--CITY PLANNING--ECONOMIC
ASPECTS
Economics, politics and city design
/ Vincent C. Schoemehl.
The Mayor of St. Louis describes
his experiences in planning and
development after participating in
the Mayors' Institute for City
Design.
PLACES 1990 Summer, v.6, no.4,
p.14-21, photos.

UNITED STATES--SAINT LOUIS
(MISSOURI)--CITY PLANNING--HISTORY
The formation of urban
infrastructure through
nongovernmental planning: the
private places of St. Louis,
1869-1920 / David T. Beito, Bruce
Smith.
Examples drawn from the work of
architect Julius Pitzman.
JOURNAL OF URBAN HISTORY 1990 May,
v.16, no.3, p.263-303, photos.,
site plans, refs.
The persistence of vision: a century
of civic progress in St. Louis /
Tom Martinson.
PLACES 1990 Summer, v.6, no.4,
p.[22]-33, axonometric views,
dwg., photos., plans, aerial
photos.

UNITED STATES--SAINT LOUIS
(MISSOURI)--CITY PLANNING--POLITICAL
ASPECTS
Economics, politics and city design
/ Vincent C. Schoemehl.
The Mayor of St. Louis describes
his experiences in planning and
development after participating in
the Mayors' Institute for City
Design.
PLACES 1990 Summer, v.6, no.4,
p.14-21, photos.

UNITED STATES--SAINT LOUIS
(MISSOURI)--COMPREHENSIVE PLANS
The persistence of vision: a century
of civic progress in St. Louis /
Tom Martinson.
PLACES 1990 Summer, v.6, no.4,
p.[22]-33, axonometric views,
dwg., photos., plans, aerial
photos.

UNITED STATES--SAINT LOUIS
(MISSOURI)--CONVENTION FACILITIES--
ALTERATIONS AND ADDITIONS--CERVANTES
CONVENTION CENTER
Cervantes Convention Center
expansion & domed stadium, St.
Louis, Missouri, USA, 1993.
Architects: Hellmuth, Obata &
Kassabaum, with Kennedy Associates
Architects, Inc. Text in Japanese
and English.
ARCHITECTURE AND URBANISM 1990
Dec., no.12 extra edition,
p.192-195, dwgs., plan.

UNITED STATES--SAINT LOUIS
(MISSOURI)--INFRASTRUCTURE
The formation of urban
infrastructure through
nongovernmental planning: the
private places of St. Louis,
1869-1920 / David T. Beito, Bruce
Smith.
Examples drawn from the work of
architect Julius Pitzman.
JOURNAL OF URBAN HISTORY 1990 May,
v.16, no.3, p.263-303, photos.,
site plans, refs.

UNITED STATES--SAINT LOUIS
(MISSOURI)--MONUMENTS AND
MEMORIALS--JEFFERSON NATIONAL
EXPANSION MEMORIAL (GATEWAY ARCH)
Gateway Arch wins 25-year award.
Jefferson National Expansion
Memorial, St. Louis. Architect:
Eero Saarinen.
PROGRESSIVE ARCHITECTURE 1990
Mar., v.71, no.3, p.25, photo.

UNITED STATES--SAINT LOUIS
(MISSOURI)--NEIGHBORHOODS
The formation of urban
infrastructure through
nongovernmental planning: the
private places of St. Louis,
1869-1920 / David T. Beito, Bruce
Smith.
Examples drawn from the work of
architect Julius Pitzman.
JOURNAL OF URBAN HISTORY 1990 May,
v.16, no.3, p.263-303, photos.,
site plans, refs.

UNITED STATES--SAINT LOUIS
(MISSOURI)--OFFICE BUILDINGS--
METROPOLITAN SQUARE
Metropolitan Square, St. Louis,
Missouri, USA, 1989.
USA. Extra office buildings
architects: Hellmuth, Obata &
Kassabaum. Text in Japanese and
English.
ARCHITECTURE AND URBANISM 1990
Dec., no.12 extra edition
p.142-151, photos., plans.

UNITED STATES--SAINT LOUIS
(MISSOURI)--PENTHOUSES
Pent house en St. Louis, Missouri:
Mario Corea, D. Gray y D. Davis,
arquitectos.
Spanish, English text.
ON DISENO 1990, no.108, p.146-153,
axonometric views, photos., plans.

UNITED STATES--SAINT LOUIS
(MISSOURI)--RAILROAD STATIONS--19TH
CENTURY--ALTERATIONS AND ADDITIONS--
UNION STATION
St. Louis Union Station, St. Louis,
USA = St. Louis Union Station, St.
Louis, USA.
Conversion of 1894 station
combines historic renovation with
new construction. Architects: HOK,
Inc.
ARCHITEKTUR + WETTBEWERBE 1989
Dec., no.140, p.12-13, photos.,
site plan, aerial photo.

UNITED STATES--SAINT LOUIS
(MISSOURI)--REAL ESTATE DEVELOPMENT
The new spirit of St. Louis / Patric
Dolan.
REAL ESTATE FORUM 1990 Apr., v.45,
no.4, p.[118]-140, graphs, ill.,
model, photos., sketch, table,
aerial photo.

UNITED STATES--SAINT LOUIS
(MISSOURI)--ROW HOUSES--FEDERAL--
FIELD HOUSE
The Eugene Field House and Toy
Mansion in St. Louis, Missouri /
John Scholz.
Federal-style row house, built in
1845.
VICTORIAN HOMES 1990 Holidays,
v.9, no.5, p.26, photos.

UNITED STATES--SAINT LOUIS
(MISSOURI)--STORES--GREETING GALLERY
The Greeting Gallery, Missouri:
Mario Corea y D. Gray,
arquitectos.
Spanish, English text.
ON DISENO 1990, no.108, p.140-145,
dwg., photos., plan.

UNITED STATES--SAINT LOUIS
(MISSOURI)--ZOOS--SAINT LOUIS ZOO--
LIVING WORLD
The Living World, St. Louis Zoo,
Saint Louis, Missouri, USA, 1989.
Architects: Hellmuth, Obata &
Kassabaum. Text in Japanese and
English.
ARCHITECTURE AND URBANISM 1990
Dec., no.12 extra edition,
p.152-161, photos., plans, site
plan.

UNITED STATES--SAINT MARY'S COUNTY
(MARYLAND)--PLANTATION HOUSES--18TH
CENTURY--CONSERVATION AND
RESTORATION--BATCHELOR'S HOPE
Enhancing a legacy: Trust guides
historic Maryland house into the
future [Batchelor's Hope, St.
Mary's County] / Thomas W.
Sweeney.
"One of southern Maryland's most
unusual, and charming, small
18th-century houses has been given
by Walter and Elizabeth Simpson to
the National Trust..."
PRESERVATION NEWS 1990 June, v.30,
no.6, p.3,15, photos.

UNITED STATES--SAINT PAUL
(MINNESOTA)--CITIES AND TOWNS
NAHR in the Twin Cities / J. Marilyn
Henry.
JOURNAL OF HOUSING 1990
Sept.-Oct., v.47, no.5, p.251-255,
258-260,262-264, photos., aerial
photos.

UNITED STATES--SAINT PAUL
(MINNESOTA)--CORPORATE OFFICE
BUILDINGS--ST. PAUL COMPANIES
St. Paul Companies corporate
headquarters, St. Paul, Minnesota,
1991.
Proposed building adjacent to
existing headquarters; architects:
Kohn Pedersen Fox Associates. Text
in Japanese and English.
PROCESS: ARCHITECTURE 1989 Nov.,
no.86, p.106-109, elevs., model,
plans, secns., site plan,
sketches.

UNITED STATES--SAINT PAUL
(MINNESOTA)--HOUSES--OFFICIAL
RESIDENCES--GOVERNOR'S RESIDENCE
A living room for Minnesota: the
Governor's Residence offers
visitors a Minnesota-style welcome
with some of the graciousness of
an English country retreat /
Sandra LaWall Lipschultz.
1910 house at 1006 Summit Ave.,
St. Paul, was recently renovated.
Original architect: William
Channing.
ARCHITECTURE MINNESOTA 1990
May-June, v.16, no.3, p.58-61,
photos.

UNITED STATES--SAINT PAUL
(MINNESOTA)--HOUSES--VICTORIAN--
CONSERVATION AND RESTORATION--IRVINE
HOUSE (1006 SUMMIT AVENUE)
A living room for Minnesota: the
Governor's Residence offers
visitors a Minnesota-style welcome
with some of the graciousness of
an English country retreat /
Sandra LaWall Lipschultz.
1910 house at 1006 Summit Ave.,
St. Paul, was recently renovated.
Original architect: William
Channing.
ARCHITECTURE MINNESOTA 1990
May-June, v.16, no.3, p.58-61,
photos.

UNITED STATES--SAINT PAUL
(MINNESOTA)--HOUSING
NAHR in the Twin Cities / J. Marilyn
Henry.
JOURNAL OF HOUSING 1990
Sept.-Oct., v.47, no.5, p.251-255,
258-260,262-264, photos., aerial
photos.

UNITED STATES--SAINT PAUL
(MINNESOTA)--MUSEUMS--CHILDREN'S--
CHILDREN'S MUSEUM
Playing house: new exhibits at St.
Paul's Children's Museum teach
kids about the nuts and bolts of
residential design.
Architects: Meyer, Scherer and
Rockcastle and Winsor/Faricy
Architects.
ARCHITECTURE MINNESOTA 1990
Sept.-Oct., v.16, no.5, p.34-37,
photos.

UNITED STATES--SAINT PAUL
(MINNESOTA)--THEATERS--ORDWAY MUSIC
THEATER
Places for performance: Ordway Music
Theatre, St. Paul, Minnesota.
Architects: Benjamin Thompson &
Associates. Text in Japanese and
English.
PROCESS: ARCHITECTURE 1990 June
no.89, p.124-127, photos., plans.

UNITED STATES--SALEM (MASSACHUSETTS)--
ARCHIVES--ESSEX INSTITUTE
The Essex Institute [Salem, Mass].
Profile of the agency, founded in
1821, which maintains eight
historic houses and a collection
of over 40,000 artifacts and
documents of regional
significance.
NEWSLETTER / THE CATALOGUE OF
LANDSCAPE RECORDS IN THE UNITED
STATES 1990 Winter, v.3, no.3,
p.[1-2],

UNITED STATES--SALEM (MASSACHUSETTS)--
HOUSES--19TH CENTURY--
GARDNER-PINGREE HOUSE
The Gardner-Pingree House, Salem,
Massachusetts / Dean Lahikainen.
Built 1804-1806 after plans by
Samuel McIntire.
ANTIQUES 1990 Mar., v.137, no.3,
p.718-729, dwg., port., photos.,
plan, refs.

UNITED STATES--SALEM (OREGON)--CITIES
AND TOWNS--GROWTH
Using land markets to evaluate urban
containment programs / Arthur C.
Nelson.
Case study: Salem, Oregon.
AMERICAN PLANNING ASSOCIATION.
JOURNAL 1986 Spring, v.52, no.2,
p.156-171, graphs, maps, photo.,
tables, biblio., refs.

UNITED STATES--SALEM (OREGON)--LAND
USE
Using land markets to evaluate urban
containment programs / Arthur C.
Nelson.
Case study: Salem, Oregon.
AMERICAN PLANNING ASSOCIATION.
JOURNAL 1986 Spring, v.52, no.2,
p.156-171, graphs, maps, photo.,
tables, biblio., refs.

UNITED STATES--SALISBURY
(CONNECTICUT)--HISTORIC DISTRICTS
Education a major project of
Salisbury Local Historic District
Commission / Lou V. Burgess.
CONNECTICUT PRESERVATION NEWS 1990
Sept.-Oct., v.13, no.5, p.11,
photos.

UNITED STATES--SAN ANTONIO (TEXAS)--
DRIVE-IN BANKS--FROST MOTOR BANK AND
PLAZA
Frost Motor Bank and Plaza, San
Antonio.
Architects: Jones & Kell.
TEXAS ARCHITECT 1990 Jan.-Feb.,
v.40, no.1, p.35, photos., aerial
photo.

UNITED STATES--SAN ANTONIO (TEXAS)--
GREENHOUSES--SAN ANTONIO BOTANICAL
GARDEN--LUCILE HALSELL CONSERVATORY
Un paraiso enterrado: Ambasz en San
Antonio / Peter Buchanan.
Urban garden in Texas.
ARQUITECTURA VIVA 1990 Sept.-Oct.,
no.14, p.16-20, photos., plans,
secns., site plan.

UNITED STATES--SAN ANTONIO (TEXAS)--
LIBRARIES (ROOMS AND SPACES)--
OAKWELL--TOBIN LIBRARY
Scholar's workroom: Robert Tobin's
Medicean library at Oakwell /
David Dillon.
Private library in San Antonio,
designed in 1968 by Roger Rasbach.
SOUTHERN ACCENTS 1989 Nov.-Dec.,
v.12, no.6, p.106-113, port.,
photos.

UNITED STATES--SAN ANTONIO (TEXAS)--
MOVIE THEATERS--SPANISH
MEDITERRANEAN REVIVAL--CONSERVATION
AND RESTORATION--MAJESTIC THEATER
Restoring dreams / Mark Alden
Branch, Abby Bussel.
On the restoration of six 1920-30s
American movie palaces.
PROGRESSIVE ARCHITECTURE 1990
June, v.71, no.6, p.92-99,
photos., plans, secns.

UNITED STATES--SAN ANTONIO (TEXAS)--
PLAZAS--FROST MOTOR BANK AND PLAZA
Frost Motor Bank and Plaza, San
Antonio.
Architects: Jones & Kell.
TEXAS ARCHITECT 1990 Jan.-Feb.,
v.40, no.1, p.35, photos., aerial
photo.

UNITED STATES--SAN ANTONIO (TEXAS)--
WEEKEND HOUSES--LAKE CANYON HOUSE
Canyon Lake house.
Weekend house near San Antonio.
Lake/Flato Architects.
TEXAS ARCHITECT 1990 Jan.-Feb.,
v.40, no.1, p.25, photos., plans,
secn., site plan.

UNITED STATES--SAN DIEGO
(CALIFORNIA)--AFFORDABLE HOUSING
SRO revival: a hybrid building type
profitably solves San Diego's
housing problem / Karin Tetlow.
Five single room occupancy hotels.
Architects: Rob Wellington
Quigley, Jackson and Associates.
ARCHITECTURE: THE MAGAZINE OF THE
AMERICAN INSTITUTE OF ARCHITECTS
1990 July, v.79, no.7, p.60-63,
ill., photos., plans.

UNITED STATES--SAN DIEGO
(CALIFORNIA)--AMPHITHEATERS--SMALL
Dramatically designed: in San Diego,
a very theatrical garden / Carolyn
Hufbauer.
Small garden theatre designed by
Judith Munk.
GARDEN DESIGN 1990 Spring, v.9,
no.1, p.77-80, site plan, photos.

UNITED STATES--SAN DIEGO
(CALIFORNIA)--ARCHITECTURE--20TH
CENTURY
Houses of the mind: Lara breaks down
art-architcture barriers
[interview].
Interview with the artist, on his
selection of sites for his work
and architecture in San Diego and
elsewhere.
CARTOUCHE 1990 Spring, v.20,
p.8-9, axonometric views, photos.

UNITED STATES--SAN DIEGO
(CALIFORNIA)--ARCHITECTURE--STUDY
AND TEACHING--UNIVERSITY OF
CALIFORNIA, SAN DIEGO
Shaping the city: international
names to be featured at UCSD
symposium.
On the five speakers scheduled for
a May 5, 1990 conference and plans
for the Fall 1992 opening of the
San Diego architecture school.
CARTOUCHE 1990 Spring, v.20, p.5,
photo.

UNITED STATES--SAN DIEGO
(CALIFORNIA)--BEACH HOUSES--PACIFIC
BEACH HOUSE
Meet the architect: Kendrick Bangs
Kellogg.
Contents: Essay: Natural
vernacular / Kay Kaiser,--
Introduction / Ken Kellogg,--
Works: Wing Sweep house, Riverside
County, CA,--Yen house, 1981,
Westway house, 1979, Atoll house,
1973, all in La Jolla, CA --
Pacific Beach house, San Diego,
CA, 1972,--Kona house, Kona Coast,
Hawaii, 1962. Text in Japanese and
English.
GA HOUSES 1990 July, no.29,
p.[22]-71, axonometric views,
port., photos., plans, secns.,
site plans.

UNITED STATES--SAN DIEGO
(CALIFORNIA)--BOOKSTORES--LOMA
THEATER BOOKSTAR
Interiors.
Three projects: Loma Theater
Bookstar, San Diego (Alamo
Architects); Bank of Nova Scotia,
Toronto (Gensler and Associates);
and The Forum, Scottsdale, Ariz.
(James, Harwick + Partners).
TEXAS ARCHITECT 1990 Nov-Dec.,
v.40, no.6, p.60-63, photos.,
plans.

UNITED STATES--SAN DIEGO
(CALIFORNIA)--CENTRAL BUSINESS
DISTRICTS
A downtown boulevard? [interview] /
Ralph Roesling.
On the Centre City Planning
Committee (CCPC) activity in San
Diego, including an interview with
councilman Ron Roberts.
CARTOUCHE 1990 Winter, v.19,
p.6-7, dwg., map, aerial photo.

UNITED STATES--SAN DIEGO
(CALIFORNIA)--CITIES AND TOWNS--
GROWTH
City profile: San Diego / Nico
Calavita, Roger Caves.
CITIES 1990 May, v.7, no.2,
p.90-98, maps, photos., table,
refs.

UNITED STATES--SAN DIEGO
(CALIFORNIA)--CITY PLANNING--CITIZEN
PARTICIPATION--HILLCREST--UPTOWN
DISTRICT
Uptown District, San Diego: looking
at the future of mixed-use
development in American cities /
Janice Fillip.
Residential and commercial project
in the Hillcrest section.
Architects: SGPA Planning and
Architecture and Lorimer-Case;
landscape architects Karen
Scarborough, with Roger Deweese,
Inc.
URBAN LAND 1990 June, v.49, no.6,
p.2-7, photos., site plan, aerial
photo.

UNITED STATES--SAN DIEGO
(CALIFORNIA)--CONVENTION
FACILITIES--SAN DIEGO CONVENTION
CENTER
Glitter by the bay: San Diego
Convention Center, San Diego,
California / Donald J. Canty.
Arthur Erickson Architects; Deems
Lewis McKinley; with Loschky,
Marquardt & Nesholm, joint-venture
architects.
ARCHITECTURAL RECORD 1990 Aug.,
v.178, no.9, p.[54-61], photos.,
plans, secns., site plans.

UNITED STATES--SAN DIEGO
(CALIFORNIA)--DISTRICTS--HILLCREST--
UPTOWN DISTRICT
Urban delight: a 14-acre "new town"
has been sensitively inserted into
one of San Diego's most
distinctive neighborhoods / Donald
J. Canty.
Uptown District, in the Hillcrest
neighborhood. Architects: SGPA.
ARCHITECTURAL RECORD 1990 Oct.,
v.178, no.11, p.62-[67], map,
photos.

UNITED STATES--SAN DIEGO
(CALIFORNIA)--ENVIRONMENTAL POLICY
San Diego's environmental planning
process ten years later / Hamid
Shirvani, Michael Stepner.
AMERICAN PLANNING ASSOCIATION.
JOURNAL 1986 Spring, v.52, no.2,
p.212-219, dwgs., maps, biblio.

UNITED STATES--SAN DIEGO
(CALIFORNIA)--HOUSES--ARCHITECTS'--
DALRYMPLE HOUSE
Bringing up baby / Mark Alden
Branch.
Features the Dalrymple house, Home
Sweet Home, San Diego.
Architects: Pacific Associates,
Planners Architects. Richard
Dalrymple, project designer.
PROGRESSIVE ARCHITECTURE 1990
Nov., v.71, no.12, p.58-63,
elevs., photos., plans.

UNITED STATES--SAN DIEGO
(CALIFORNIA)--HOUSES--ARCHITECTS'--
DALRYMPLE HOUSE (CONTINUED)
Home sweet home, San Diego,
California, design 1983-85;
construction 1985-.
Architects: Pacific Associates,
Planners Architects. Text in
Japanese and English.
GA HOUSES 1990 Mar., no.28,
p.75-77. dwgs., elevs., plans,
isometric dwg.

UNITED STATES--SAN DIEGO
(CALIFORNIA)--HOUSES--GORDON HOUSE
Forme zoomorfiche e spazi che
respirano: quattro esempi di
modellato di Kendrick Bangs
Kellogg. / Marisa Cerruti.
Restaurant, Jacksonville, Fl; Yen
house, La Jolla, CA; Gordon house,
san Diego, CA; restaurant, Rancho
Mirage, CA. English, French,
German, Spanish summaries, p.118.
ARCHITETTURA: CRONACHE E STORIA
1987 Feb., v.33, no.2(376),
p.[116]-126, photos., plans, site
plans.

UNITED STATES--SAN DIEGO
(CALIFORNIA)--HOUSES--REED HOUSE
Reed residence, San Diego,
California, 1987-89.
Architect: Rob Wellington Quigley.
Text in Japanese and English.
GA HOUSES 1990 July, no.29,
p.[138]-143, photos., plans.

UNITED STATES--SAN DIEGO
(CALIFORNIA)--HOUSES--SLOPING
SITES--AJAX
Tom Grondona [houses].
Contents: Vicolo house, San Diego,
Calif., design: 1985 -- Ajax
house, San Diego, Calif., design:
1980. Architect: Tom Grondona.
Text in Japanese and English.
GA HOUSES 1990 Mar., no.28,
p.116-119, models,plans, site
plans.

UNITED STATES--SAN DIEGO
(CALIFORNIA)--HOUSES--SLOPING
SITES--VICOLO
Tom Grondona [houses].
Contents: Vicolo house, San Diego,
Calif., design: 1985 -- Ajax
house, San Diego, Calif., design:
1980. Architect: Tom Grondona.
Text in Japanese and English.
GA HOUSES 1990 Mar., no.28,
p.116-119, models,plans, site
plans.

UNITED STATES--SAN DIEGO
(CALIFORNIA)--HOUSING DEVELOPMENTS--
UPTOWN DISTRICT
Urban delight: a 14-acre "new town"
has been sensitively inserted into
one of San Diego's most
distinctive neighborhoods / Donald
J. Canty.
Uptown District, in the Hillcrest
neighborhood. Architects: SGPA.
ARCHITECTURAL RECORD 1990 Oct.,
v.178, no.11, p.62-[67], map,
photos.

UNITED STATES--SAN DIEGO
(CALIFORNIA)--LANDSCAPE
ARCHITECTURE--20TH CENTURY
San Diego: conquering arid obstacles
/ Kathy Day.
Survey of recent water-conscious
landscape projects in San Diego.
LANDSCAPE ARCHITECTURE 1990 Oct.,
v.80, no.10, p.54,56,58, photos.

UNITED STATES--SAN DIEGO
(CALIFORNIA)--LIBRARIES--UNIVERSITY
AND COLLEGE--ALTERATIONS AND
ADDITIONS--UNIVERSITY OF CALIFORNIA,
SAN DIEGO
Un perimetro di cristallo per
l'Universita di San Diego = A
crystal perimeter for San Diego
University / Maurizio Vitta.
Underground extension to library
designed by William Pereira;
architects of extension: Gunnar
Birkerts & Associates.
L'ARCA 1990 Apr., no.37, p.42-47,
axonometric view, photos., plans,
secns.

UNITED STATES--SAN DIEGO
(CALIFORNIA)--PARKS--MARINA LINEAR
PARK
Arte como arquitectura como ciudad =
Art-as-architecture-as-town /
Sandro Marpillero.
Art and architecture as civic
design in the U.S. Three projects
illustrated: Plaza Park, San Jose,
Calif.; projects by Eric Ungers,
and Marina Linear Park, San
Diego. In Spanish and English.
ARQUITECTURA 1990 July-Aug., v.72,
no.285, p.126-137, elevs., models,
photos., plans, secns., site
plans.
The Linear Park: will it salvage
pedestrian dignity on Harbor
Drive? [interview] / Dirk Sutro.
In San Diego. Landscape
architects: Peter Walker and
Martha Schwartz with the Austin
Hansen Group.
CARTOUCHE 1990 Winter, v.19,
p.10-11, maps, photos.

UNITED STATES--SAN DIEGO
(CALIFORNIA)--PLAZAS--HORTON PLAZA
Reclaiming the streets: Horton Plaza
versus the need for a new retail
vision / Frank Wolden.
On various design concepts
presented for a pocket of retail
development in San Diego.
CARTOUCHE 1990 Winter, v.19,
p.8-9, dwgs., photos.
Reinventing the square: everyone
knows that corporate plazas are
all wrong ... / Michael Webb.
Examples of corporate plazas as
civic spaces in Calif., especially
Horton Plaza, San Diego, and
Levi's Plaza, San Fransisco.
METROPOLIS 1990 Mar., v.9, no.7,
p.[50]-53,62-63, ill., photos.,
aerial photo.

UNITED STATES--SAN DIEGO
(CALIFORNIA)--QUARTERS (DISTRICTS)--
MARINA DISTRICT
The downtown neighborhood: growing a
sense of place in an urban desert
/ Tyler Gibbs.
On the Marina Planned District
Ordinance (PDO) in San Diego.
CARTOUCHE 1990 Winter, v.19,
p.4-5, dwgs.

UNITED STATES--SAN DIEGO
(CALIFORNIA)--REAL ESTATE
DEVELOPMENT--HILLCREST--UPTOWN
DISTRICT
Uptown District, San Diego: looking
at the future of mixed-use
development in American cities /
Janice Fillip.
Residential and commercial project
in the Hillcrest section.
Architects: SGPA Planning and
Architecture and Lorimer-Case;
landscape architects Karen
Scarborough, with Roger Deweese,
Inc.
URBAN LAND 1990 June, v.49, no.6,
p.2-7, photos., site plan, aerial
photo.

UNITED STATES--SAN DIEGO
(CALIFORNIA)--RESIDENTIAL GARDENS--
MUNK GARDEN
Dramatically designed: in San Diego,
a very theatrical garden / Carolyn
Hufbauer.
Small garden theatre designed by
Judith Munk.
GARDEN DESIGN 1990 Spring, v.9,
no.1, p.77-80, site plan, photos.

UNITED STATES--SAN DIEGO
(CALIFORNIA)--SINGLE ROOM OCCUPANCY
HOTELS
SRO revival: a hybrid building type
profitably solves San Diego's
housing problem / Karin Tetlow.
Five single room occupancy hotels.
Architects: Rob Wellington
Quigley, Jackson and Associates.
ARCHITECTURE: THE MAGAZINE OF THE
AMERICAN INSTITUTE OF ARCHITECTS
1990 July, v.79, no.7, p.60-63,
ill., photos., plans.

UNITED STATES--SAN DIEGO
(CALIFORNIA)--STREETS--BROADWAY
CIRCLE
Reclaiming the streets: Horton Plaza
versus the need for a new retail
vision / Frank Wolden.
On various design concepts
presented for a pocket of retail
development in San Diego.
CARTOUCHE 1990 Winter, v.19,
p.8-9, dwgs., photos.

UNITED STATES--SAN DIEGO
(CALIFORNIA)--STUDENT UNIONS--
UNIVERSITY OF CALIFORNIA AT SAN
DIEGO--PRICE CENTER
Building Types Study 682: Campus
buildings: Extracurricular
education / Grace Anderson.
Four recently-completed buildings:
Salomon Center for Teaching, Brown
Univ. (Goody, Clancy & Assoc.);
Psychology Building, Vanderbilt
Univ. (Stubbins Assoc.);
Centennial Performing Arts Center,
Westminster School, Simsbury Conn.
(Graham Gund Architects); and
(Continued next page)

UNITED STATES--SAN DIEGO
(CALIFORNIA)--STUDENT UNIONS--
UNIVERSITY OF CALIFORNIA AT SAN
DIEGO--PRICE CENTER (CONTINUED)
Building Types Study...(CONTINUED)
Price Center, Univ. of Calif. at
San Diego (Kaplan/McLaughlin/Diaz
Architects).
ARCHITECTURAL RECORD 1990 Aug.,
v.178, no.9, p.83-[95], elevs.,
photos., plans, secns., site
plans.

UNITED STATES--SAN DIEGO
(CALIFORNIA)--THEATERS--OPEN-AIR--
MUNK GARDEN THEATER
Dramatically designed: in San Diego,
a very theatrical garden / Carolyn
Hufbauer.
Small garden theatre designed by
Judith Munk.
GARDEN DESIGN 1990 Spring, v.9,
no.1, p.77-80, site plan, photos.

UNITED STATES--SAN DIEGO
(CALIFORNIA)--UNIVERSITIES AND
COLLEGES--BUILDINGS--UNIVERSITY OF
CALIFORNIA AT SAN DIEGO--PRICE
CENTER
Building Types Study 682: Campus
buildings: Extracurricular
education / Grace Anderson.
Four recently-completed buildings:
Salomon Center for Teaching, Brown
Univ. (Goody, Clancy & Assoc.);
Psychology Building, Vanderbilt
Univ. (Stubbins Assoc.);
Centennial Performing Arts Center,
Westminster School, Simsbury Conn.
(Graham Gund Architects); and
Price Center, Univ. of Calif. at
San Diego (Kaplan/McLaughlin/Diaz
Architects).
ARCHITECTURAL RECORD 1990 Aug.,
v.178, no.9, p.83-[95], elevs.,
photos., plans, secns., site
plans.

UNITED STATES--SAN DIEGO
(CALIFORNIA)--WATERFRONTS--
ALTERATIONS AND ADDITIONS
A downtown boulevard? [interview] /
Ralph Roesling.
On the Centre City Planning
Committee (CCPC) activity in San
Diego, including an interview with
councilman Ron Roberts.
CARTOUCHE 1990 Winter, v.19,
p.6-7, dwg., map, aerial photo.

UNITED STATES--SAN DIEGO
(CALIFORNIA)--XERISCAPES
San Diego: conquering arid obstacles
/ Kathy Day.
Survey of recent water-conscious
landscape projects in San Diego.
LANDSCAPE ARCHITECTURE 1990 Oct.,
v.80, no.10, p.54,56,58, photos.

UNITED STATES--SAN DIEGO COUNTY
(CALIFORNIA)--HOUSES--BAILEY HOUSE
Kendrick Bangs Kellogg [houses].
Contents: Doolittle house "Wing
Walk," Sin Barnyards County, [sic]
CA, 1988 --Bailey house, San Diego
County, CA, 1985 --Wing Sweep
house, Riverside County, CA, 1986.
Text in Japanese and English.
GA HOUSES 1990 Mar., no.28,
p.136-139, models, plans, site
plans.

UNITED STATES--SAN FRANCISCO BAY AREA
(CALIFORNIA)--GREENBELTS
The open space police / Steven H.
Heimoff, John King.
Maintaining open space near San
Francisco: the East Bay park
district and the Bay Area
greenbelt.
PLANNING 1990 Sept., v.56, no.9,
p.20-24, maps, photos.

UNITED STATES--SAN FRANCISCO BAY AREA
(CALIFORNIA)--LAND USE
Land use around suburban transit
stations / Henry Moon.
Land uses around 20 stations in
suburban Washington, D.C. and San
Francisco/Oakland.
TRANSPORTATION 1990, v.17, no.1,
p.67-88, diagrs., graphs, maps,
tables, aerial photos., refs.

UNITED STATES--SAN FRANCISCO BAY AREA
(CALIFORNIA)--OPEN SPACES
The open space police / Steven H.
Heimoff, John King.
Maintaining open space near San
Francisco: the East Bay park
district and the Bay Area
greenbelt.
PLANNING 1990 Sept., v.56, no.9,
p.20-24, maps, photos.

UNITED STATES--SAN FRANCISCO BAY AREA
(CALIFORNIA)--TRANSIT SYSTEMS--BAY
AREA RAPID TRANSIT (BART)
Land use around suburban transit
stations / Henry Moon.
Land uses around 20 stations in
suburban Washington, D.C. and San
Francisco/Oakland.
TRANSPORTATION 1990, v.17, no.1,
p.67-88, diagrs., graphs, maps,
tables, aerial photos., refs.
Transit system meets crisis / John
McCloud.
Effect of 1989 earthquake on BART,
the Bay Area Rapid Transit system
serving San Francisco and
surrounding area.
AMERICAN CITY & COUNTY 1989 Dec.,
v.104, no.12, p.28, 30, 32,

UNITED STATES--SAN FRANCISCO
(CALIFORNIA)--AFFORDABLE HOUSING
Bridging the housing gap / John
King.
Affordable housing in San
Francisco.
PLANNING 1990 Feb., v.56, no.2,
p.16-19, ports., map, photos.,
plan.

UNITED STATES--SAN FRANCISCO
(CALIFORNIA)--ANTIQUE SHOPS--OBIKO
Style's fairest trader [Sandra
Sakata] / Diane Dorrans Saeks.
Includes views of the designer's
San Francisco apartment and her
boutique, Obiko.
METROPOLITAN HOME 1990 Sept.,
v.22, no.9, p.120-123, port.,
photos.

UNITED STATES--SAN FRANCISCO
(CALIFORNIA)--APARTMENT HOUSES--1150
LOMBARD STREET (THE LOMBARDIA)
The coastal condition: regional
portfolio: California housing /
Paul M. Sachner.
The first of a series of regional
portfolios, on 5 multifamily
projects: Armacost Duplex, Los
Angeles [Rebecca Binder]; 14-16
Leroy Pl., San Francisco (Hood
Miller); 1150 Lombard St., San
Francisco (Hood Miller); Meadow
Court, San Mateo (David Baker
Assoc.); and Seacliff, Malibu
(Kanner Associates).
ARCHITECTURAL RECORD 1990 Jan.,
v.178, no.1, p.90-99, elevs.,
photos., plans, secns., site
plans.

UNITED STATES--SAN FRANCISCO
(CALIFORNIA)--APARTMENTS--INTERIOR
DESIGN--DOAN APARTMENT
Grand illusion by the Bay:
recreating a Genoese Palazzo in
San Francisco / Jeffrey Simpson.
Interiors of Doan apartment.
Interior designers: Valerian
Rybar, Jean-Francois Daigre.
ARCHITECTURAL DIGEST 1990 Feb.,
v.47, no.2, p.170-[179], photos.

UNITED STATES--SAN FRANCISCO
(CALIFORNIA)--APARTMENTS--INTERIOR
DESIGN--FRIIA APARTMENT
The Beaux Arts on Nob Hill / Joan
Chatfield-Taylor.
Interiors of Vincent Friia's San
Francisco apartment. Interior
designers: Albert Hadley and Gary
Hager of Parish-Hadley Associates.
ARCHITECTURAL DIGEST 1990 May,
v.47, no.5, p.[232-237], photos.

UNITED STATES--SAN FRANCISCO
(CALIFORNIA)--APARTMENTS--INTERIOR
DESIGN--PFISTER APARTMENT
How he lives: the San Francisco
residence of Charles Pfister /
Edie Lee Cohen.
The interior designer's apartment
on Nob Hill.
INTERIOR DESIGN 1990 July, v.61,
no.10, p.[132-139], photos., plan.
Pfister finesse: Charles Pfister's
latest designs strike a masterly
balance between the classic and
the modern / Pilar Viladas.
The designer's own apartment in
San Francisco, and a New York City
apartment.
HOUSE & GARDEN 1990 July, v.162,
no.7, p.[124]-131, port., photos.

UNITED STATES--SAN FRANCISCO
(CALIFORNIA)--APARTMENTS--INTERIOR
DESIGN--SAKATA APARTMENT
Style's fairest trader [Sandra
Sakata] / Diane Dorrans Saeks.
Includes views of the designer's
San Francisco apartment and her
boutique, Obiko.
METROPOLITAN HOME 1990 Sept.,
v.22, no.9, p.120-123, port.,
photos.

UNITED STATES--SAN FRANCISCO
(CALIFORNIA)--BANKS--INTERIOR
DESIGN--IMPERIAL BANK
Imperial Bank, San Francisco /
Monica Geran.
Features interiors of regional
headquarters. Architects/Interior
designers: Aston Pereira &
Associates.
INTERIOR DESIGN 1990 Apr., v.61,
no.6, p.176-[181], photos., plan,
secn.

UNITED STATES--SAN FRANCISCO
(CALIFORNIA)--BANKS--NEOCLASSICAL--
CONSERVATION AND RESTORATION--
FEDERAL RESERVE BANK BUILDING
Money in the bank: the restored Old
Fed lends classic counterpoint to
a modern San Francisco complex /
Kim Keister.
The 1920s Federal Reserve Bank
Building is now restored and is
the centerpiece of Embarcadero
West, a John C. Portman project.
Original architect: George Kelham.
Architects for restoration:
Kaplan, McLaughlin, and Diaz.
HISTORIC PRESERVATION 1990
Mar.-Apr., v.42, no.2, p.56-59,
photo.

UNITED STATES--SAN FRANCISCO
(CALIFORNIA)--BUILDINGS--GLASS
BLOCK--DIAMOND AND JEWELRY MART
Building with blocks / Sally B.
Woodbridge.
Diamond and Jewelry Mart, San
Francisco, features glass block
walls. Architects: Tanner Leddy
Maytum Stacy, Architects.
PROGRESSIVE ARCHITECTURE 1990
Dec., v.71, no.13, p.74-75,
photos., plan.

UNITED STATES--SAN FRANCISCO
(CALIFORNIA)--CITIES AND TOWNS--21ST
CENTURY--EXHIBITIONS
Artists afraid of their city:
Visionary San Francisco, San
Francisco Museum of Modern Art
[exhibition review] / Diana
Ketcham.
BLUEPRINT (LONDON, ENGLAND) 1990
Sept., no.70, p.57, ill.
California dreamers: an exhibition
looks backward and forward at
visionary schemes for San
Francisco [exhibition review] /
Thomas Hine.
"Visionary San Francisco", at the
San Francisco Museum of Modern
Art, June 14-Aug. 26.
HOUSE & GARDEN 1990 July, v.162,
no.7, p.[32],34, ill.
Dreaming by the Bay [exhibition
review] / Michael Webb.
"Visionary San Francisco", at the
San Francisco Musuem of Modern
Art, June 14-Aug. 26.
METROPOLIS 1990 July-Aug., v.10,
no.1, p.50-55,75, ill., dwgs.
"Visionary San Francisco": una
mostra tra sogno e realta
[exhibition review] / L.
Prestinenza Puglisi.
Exhibition at the Museum of Modern
Art, in San Francisco.
L'INDUSTRIA DELLE COSTRUZIONI 1990
Dec., v.24, no.230, p.60-61,
axonometric view, ill., models,
aerial photo.

UNITED STATES--SAN FRANCISCO
(CALIFORNIA)--CITY PLANNING
Economic growth or environmental
protection? The San Francsico
experience / Amit K. Ghosh.
Paper presented at the
International Conference on Local
Planning, Sydney, Australia, March
1990, "From Images to
Achievements."
AUSTRALIAN PLANNER: JOURNAL OF THE
ROYAL AUSTRALIA PLANNING INSTITUTE
1990 June, v.28, no.2, p.23-25.
Economic growth or environmental
protection? The San Francisco
experience / Amit K. Ghosh.
Paper presented at the
International Conference on Local
Planning, Sydney, Australia, March
1990, "From Images to
Achievements."
AUSTRALIAN PLANNER: JOURNAL OF THE
ROYAL AUSTRALIAN PLANNING
INSTITUTE 1990 June, v.28, no.2,
p.23-25.
Linking downtown development to
broader community goals: an
analysis of linkage policy in
three cities / W. Dennis Keating.
San Francisco, Santa Monica and
Boston.
AMERICAN PLANNING ASSOCIATION.
JOURNAL 1986 Spring, v.52, no.2,
p.133-141, biblio., refs.

UNITED STATES--SAN FRANCISCO
(CALIFORNIA)--CITY PLANNING--CITIZEN
PARTICIPATION
Cities build coalitions with clout.
Citizen participation and
political activism in New York,
Birmingham, Ala., and San
Francisco.
ARCHITECTS' JOURNAL 1990 Mar.14,
v.191, no.11, p.50-57, elev.,
photos., aerial photos.

UNITED STATES--SAN FRANCISCO
(CALIFORNIA)--CITY PLANNING--MISSION
BAY
Urban issues: Mission Bay / Sally
B. Woodbridge.
On the four plans proposed during
the 1980s for San Francisco's
Mission Bay. Includes plans by
John Carl Warnecke (1980), I.M.
Pei/Wallace Roberts & Todd (1985),
EDAW et al. (Mission Bay Planning
Team, 1987) and SOM (1989).
PROGRESSIVE ARCHITECTURE 1990 May,
v.71, no.5, p.121-122, figs.,
plans, site plans.

UNITED STATES--SAN FRANCISCO
(CALIFORNIA)--COMPREHENSIVE PLANS
Economic growth or environmental
protection? The San Francisco
experience / Amit K. Ghosh.
Paper presented at the
International Conference on Local
Planning, Sydney, Australia, March
1990, "From Images to
Achievements."
AUSTRALIAN PLANNER: JOURNAL OF THE
ROYAL AUSTRALIAN PLANNING
INSTITUTE 1990 June, v.28, no.2,
p.23-25.
Economic growth or environmental
protection? The San Francsico
experience / Amit K. Ghosh.
Paper presented at the
International Conference on Local
(Continued next column)

UNITED STATES--SAN FRANCISCO
(CALIFORNIA)--COMPREHENSIVE PLANS
(CONTINUED)
Economic growth or... (CONTINUED)
Planning, Sydney, Australia, March
1990, "From Images to
Achievements."
AUSTRALIAN PLANNER: JOURNAL OF THE
ROYAL AUSTRALIA PLANNING INSTITUTE
1990 June, v.28, no.2, p.23-25.

UNITED STATES--SAN FRANCISCO
(CALIFORNIA)--CONVENTION
FACILITIES--UNDERGROUND--MOSCONE
CONVENTION CENTER
George R. Moscone Convention Center,
San Francisco, California, USA,
1981.
Architects: Hellmuth, Obata &
Kassabaum, with Jack Young &
Associates. Text in Japanese and
English.
ARCHITECTURE AND URBANISM 1990
Dec., no.12 extra edition,
p.48-[57], photos., secn., site
plan.

UNITED STATES--SAN FRANCISCO
(CALIFORNIA)--COURTYARD HOUSES--
CASTRO COMMONS
American housing 1980-1990 / James
Tice.
Features: Castro Common, San
Francisco (Daniel Solomon, Paulett
Taggart); Sun-Tech Housing, Santa
Monica (Steve Andre, David Van
Hoy); Pacific Townhouses, Santa
Monica (Rebecca Binder, James
Stafford); Hoyt Square
Condominiums, Portland, OR (Robert
S. Leeb). Text in Italian and
English.
METAMORFOSI 1989, no.12, p.38-51,
axonometric views, models,
photos., plans, secns.

UNITED STATES--SAN FRANCISCO
(CALIFORNIA)--CULTURAL CENTERS--
VISUAL ARTS CENTER
Un japones mediterraneo: Maki en San
Francisco / Josep Maria Montaner.
Visual Arts Center.
ARQUITECTURA VIVA 1990 July-Aug.,
no.13, p.24-27, ill., models,
plans, secns., site plan.
Special edition: city and collective
forms.
Features nine projects including
competition entries and works in
progress by Maki and Associates,
1989-1992. Includes dialogue:
Architecture, city, public spirit,
by Riichi Miyake and Fumihiko
Maki. English summary, p.27.
KENCHIKU BUNKA 1990 June, v.45,
no.524, p.31-112, dwgs., ports.,
elevs., models, photos., plans,
secns., site plans, sketches.
Yerba Buena Gardens Visual Arts
Center, San Francisco, U.S.A.,
1992 / Fumihiko Maki.
Architects: Maki and Associates.
JAPAN ARCHITECT 1990 Aug.-Sept.,
v.65, no.8-9(400-401), p.72-77,
ill., elev., models, plans,
secns., site plan, sketches.

UNITED STATES--SAN FRANCISCO
(CALIFORNIA)--DENSITY
Density perception on residential
streets / James R. Bergdoll, Rick
W. Williams.
Study to examine which physical
characteristics influence people's
perception of density on urban
residential streets; examples
taken from San Francisco, Ca.
BERKELEY PLANNING JOURNAL 1990,
v.5, p.15-38, ill., elevs., map,
photos., plans, tables, biblio.

UNITED STATES--SAN FRANCISCO
(CALIFORNIA)--EARTHQUAKES AND
BUILDING
Bi-coastal disaster assistance /
Michael Adlerstein.
Report on assistance efforts made
by the NPS in Charleston, S.C.
after the Sept. 22, 1989 hurricane
and in San Francisco after the
Oct. 1989 Loma Prieta earthquake.
CRM BULLETIN: A NATIONAL PARK
SERVICE TECHNICAL BULLETIN 1990,
v.13, no.1, p.10-12,
History on the mend: Hugo, quake
victims work to save and rebuild /
Arnold Berke, Thomas W. Sweeney.
Reports on preservation efforts
following Hurricane Hugo and
northern California's earthquake.
PRESERVATION NEWS 1990 May, v.30,
no.5, p.1,18, photos.

UNITED STATES--SAN FRANCISCO
(CALIFORNIA)--GARDENS
Maybeck's landscapes / Dianne
Harris.
JOURNAL OF GARDEN HISTORY 1990
July-Sept., v.10, no.2, p.145-161,
ill., dwgs., port., elevs.,
photos., plans, secn., refs.

UNITED STATES--SAN FRANCISCO
(CALIFORNIA)--GRID PLAN CITIES
Where Gaia and Duranos make love /
Bruno Queysanne.
The author experiences the
"richness of...spatiality" in the
meeting of Earth and Sky in his
views of Pienza and San Francisco.
PLACES 1990 Winter, v.6, no.2,
p.4-6, photos., refs.

UNITED STATES--SAN FRANCISCO
(CALIFORNIA)--HOTELS--INTERIOR
DESIGN--PARK HYATT
Park Hyatt: Hirsch/Bedner and
Associates plays out a series of
contrasts for a hotel in San
Francisco / Mayer Rus.
INTERIOR DESIGN 1990 Apr., v.61,
no.6, p.[196-201], photos., plans.

UNITED STATES--SAN FRANCISCO
(CALIFORNIA)--HOUSES--20TH CENTURY
Per una brillante e cosciente
modernita / Lucio Blasi.
House in San Francisco suburbs.
Architect: Bill Stout.
VILLE GIARDINI 1990 Jan., no.244,
p.2-9, photos., plans, secns.

UNITED STATES--SAN FRANCISCO
(CALIFORNIA)--HOUSES--ARCHITECTS'--
STOUT - TAGGART HOUSE
Case con vista: San Francisco, un
osservatorio attraverso i tetti =
Houses with a view: San Francisco,
an observatory through the
rooftops.
Renovation of a Victorian cottage
in North Beach, now the home of
the architects, Bill Stout and
Paulett Taggart.
ABITARE 1990 Oct., no.289.
p.214-[221], axonometric view,
photos., plans.

UNITED STATES--SAN FRANCISCO
(CALIFORNIA)--HOUSES--GLEENSON JEAN
RENAUD HOUSE
Fortement symetrique: residence a
San Francisco / Claudine Mulard.
Gleenson Jean Renaud house.
Architects: Daniel Solomon and
Associates. English summary,
p.52.
ARCHITECTURE INTERIEURE CREE 1990
Feb., no.234, p.[156-159],
photos., plan.

UNITED STATES--SAN FRANCISCO
(CALIFORNIA)--HOUSES--INTERIOR
DESIGN
Sleek house / Mayer Rus.
Industrial building converted into
a house in San Francisco's North
Beach. Archiects: Tanner Leddy
Maytum Stacy, Architects.
INTERIOR DESIGN 1990 Apr., v.61,
no.6, p.212-[217], photos., plans,
secns.

UNITED STATES--SAN FRANCISCO
(CALIFORNIA)--HOUSES--INTERIOR
DESIGN--BOWES HOUSE
Art with a view: a San Francisco
house decorated by the late
Michael Taylor / William P.
Rayner.
HOUSE & GARDEN 1990 May, v.162,
no.5, p.[202-209], port., plans.

UNITED STATES--SAN FRANCISCO
(CALIFORNIA)--HOUSES--INTERIOR
DESIGN--HENDERSON HOUSE
Contemporary eclat: a collector's
San Francisco residence / Joan
Chatfield-Taylor.
Features Wellington Henderson's
home designed by Sandy Walker.
ARCHITECTURAL DIGEST 1990 Sept.,
v.47, no.10, p.142-149, ports.,
photos.

UNITED STATES--SAN FRANCISCO
(CALIFORNIA)--HOUSES--SHINGLE
STYLE--ALTERATIONS AND ADDITIONS--
BERGGRUEN HOUSE
Architecture: Robert A. M. Stern /
Paul Goldberger.
Features renovated Bay Area
Shingle style home in San
Francisco owned by John and
Gretchen Berggruen. Renovation
architects: Robert A. M. Stern
Architects.
ARCHITECTURAL DIGEST 1990 Oct.,
v.47, no.11, p.[196-205], photos.
Rising to the occasion [Berggruen
house, San Francisco] / Sally
Woodbridge.
Renovation of shingle style home.
Architects: Robert A. M. Stern
(Continued next column)

UNITED STATES--SAN FRANCISCO
(CALIFORNIA)--HOUSES--SHINGLE
STYLE--ALTERATIONS AND ADDITIONS--
BERGGRUEN HOUSE (CONTINUED)
Rising to the...(CONTINUED)
Architects.
PROGRESSIVE ARCHITECTURE 1990
Nov., v.71, no.12, p.80-85,
photos., plans, secns., site plan.

UNITED STATES--SAN FRANCISCO
(CALIFORNIA)--HOUSING
After the quake: how H/CD officials
responded to the San Francisco
disaster / Pat Soberanis.
JOURNAL OF HOUSING 1990
Sept.-Oct., v.47, no.5, p.276-277,
279, port., photo.

UNITED STATES--SAN FRANCISCO
(CALIFORNIA)--HOUSING COMPLEXES--
PARKVIEW COMMONS
The search continues: building types
study 681, multifamily housing /
Donald J. Canty.
Four low-rise condominium
projects: The Waterworks, New
Hope, Penn. (Cecil Baker &
Associates, Architects); Back of
the Hill Rowhouses, Boston
(William Rawn Associates,
Architects); Samoset Resort and
Village, Rockport, Me. (Sasaki
Associates, Architects); and
Parkview Commons, San Francisco
(David Baker Architects).
ARCHITECTURAL RECORD 1990 July,
v.178, no.8, p.15-87, axonometric
views, elev., photos., plans, site
plans.

UNITED STATES--SAN FRANCISCO
(CALIFORNIA)--KITCHENS--INTERIOR
DESIGN--WOLLACK HOUSE
Kitchen strategies / Sally Clark.
Customized kitchen in 1902 San
Francisco house. Designer: Daen
Scheiber.
HOUSE BEAUTIFUL 1990 Dec., v.132,
no.12, p.64-67, ports., photos.,
plan.

UNITED STATES--SAN FRANCISCO
(CALIFORNIA)--LANDSCAPE
Maybeck's landscapes / Dianne
Harris.
JOURNAL OF GARDEN HISTORY 1990
July-Sept., v.10, no.2, p.145-161,
ill., dwgs., port., elevs.,
photos., plans, secn., refs.

UNITED STATES--SAN FRANCISCO
(CALIFORNIA)--LAW OFFICES--INTERIOR
DESIGN--FOLGER & LEVIN
Folger & Levin / Monica Geran.
Interiors of San Francisco law
offices designed by Orlando
Diaz-Azcuy Associates.
INTERIOR DESIGN 1990 May, v.61,
no.7, p.144-[149], photos., plan.

UNITED STATES--SAN FRANCISCO
(CALIFORNIA)--LOFTS--BONAURO LOFT
Portrait of an artist ...
transformation of a South of
Market warehouse into the loft of
a graphic artist, San Francisco /
Karen Stein.
Architects: John Randolph, Bruce
Tomb, of the Interim Office of
Architecture.
ARCHITECTURAL RECORD 1990 Apr.,
(Continued next page)

UNITED STATES--SAN FRANCISCO
(CALIFORNIA)--REAL ESTATE
DEVELOPMENT--MISSION BAY
(CONTINUED)
Urban issues: ...(CONTINUED)
EDAW et al. (Mission Bay Planning
Team, 1987) and SOM (1989).
PROGRESSIVE ARCHITECTURE 1990 May,
v.71, no.5, p.121-122, figs.,
plans, site plans.

UNITED STATES--SAN FRANCISCO
(CALIFORNIA)--RESEARCH FACILITIES--
GENETECH
Light on main street / Alice
Feiring.
Features Genetech's renovated
research building, San Francisco.
Architects: MBT Associates.
INTERIORS 1990 Dec., v.150, no.5,
p.66-69, photos., plan, secn.

UNITED STATES--SAN FRANCISCO
(CALIFORNIA)--RESIDENTIAL GARDENS--
SMALL--EPSTEIN GARDEN
Welcome to the backyard California /
Erica Goebel.
Gardens in San Francisco, Los
Angeles and Santa Barbara.
Landscape architects: Peder Jens
Pedersen, Calvin Abe & Assoc. with
Ron McCoy, Isabelle Greene, Ron
Lutsko, and Dennis Shaw.
GARDEN DESIGN 1990 autumn, v.9,
no.3, p.[38-45], photos.

UNITED STATES--SAN FRANCISCO
(CALIFORNIA)--RESTAURANTS--INTERIOR
DESIGN--SQUARE ONE
Square One recombinant / Lois Wagner
Green.
On the remodeled interiors of
Square One restaurant, San
Francisco. Interior designers:
Andrew Belschner Joseph Vincent
Design Partnership. Original
architect: Charles Pfister.
INTERIOR DESIGN 1990 Apr., v.61,
no.6, p.[162-165], photos., plan.

UNITED STATES--SAN FRANCISCO
(CALIFORNIA)--RESTAURANTS--MONSOON
RESTAURANT
Golden gateway: Monsoon Restaurant,
San Francisco, California, Mack
Architects / Lynn Nesmith.
ARCHITECTURE: THE MAGAZINE OF THE
AMERICAN INSTITUTE OF ARCHITECTS
1990 June, v.79, no.6, p.78-79,
photos., plan.

UNITED STATES--SAN FRANCISCO
(CALIFORNIA)--ROW HOUSES--14-16
LEROY PLACE
The coastal condition: regional
portfolio: California housing /
Paul M. Sachner.
The first of a series of regional
portfolios, on 5 multifamily
projects, Altadena Duplex, Los
Angeles [Rebecca Binder]; 14-16
Leroy Pl., San Francisco (Hood
Miller); 1150 Lombard St., San
Francisco (Hood Miller); Meadow
Court, San Mateo (David Baker
Assoc.); and Seacliff, Malibu
(Kanner Associates).
ARCHITECTURAL RECORD 1990 Jan.,
v.178, no.1, p.90-99, elevs.,
photos., plans, secns., site
plans.

UNITED STATES--SAN FRANCISCO
(CALIFORNIA)--SCHOOLS--ELEMENTARY--
ALTERATIONS AND ADDITIONS--WALDORF
SCHOOL
Lessons in civility: two schools in
San Francisco exemplify the
multiple challenges of melding new
construction and existing
buildings into a single entity /
Donald J. Canty.
The Waldorf School, by Tanner
Leddy Maytum Stacy Architects; and
the San Francisco Day School, by
Simon Martin-Vegue Winkelstein
Moris.
ARCHITECTURAL RECORD 1990 Mar.,
v.178, no.3, p.84-91, elevs.,
photos., plans, secn., site plans.

UNITED STATES--SAN FRANCISCO
(CALIFORNIA)--SCHOOLS--ELEMENTARY--
SAN FRANCISCO DAY SCHOOL
Lessons in civility: two schools in
San Francisco exemplify the
multiple challenges of melding new
construction and existing
buildings into a single entity /
Donald J. Canty.
The Waldorf School, by Tanner
Leddy Maytum Stacy Architects; and
the San Francisco Day School, by
Simon Martin-Vegue Winkelstein
Moris.
ARCHITECTURAL RECORD 1990 Mar.,
v.178, no.3, p.84-91, elevs.,
photos., plans, secn., site plans.

UNITED STATES--SAN FRANCISCO
(CALIFORNIA)--SEWAGE DISPOSAL
PLANTS--UNDERGROUND--OCEANSIDE WATER
POLLUTION CONTROL PLANT
Rehabilitating the earth, San
Francisco-style / Kerry J. Dawson.
On the joint-use site of the
Oceanside Water Pollution Control
Plant and the addition to the San
Francisco Zoo. Landscape
architects: Royston Hanamoto Alley
and Abey, Landscape Architects.
LANDSCAPE ARCHITECTURE 1990 Dec.,
v.80, no.12, p.60-61, elev., site
plan, aerial photo.

UNITED STATES--SAN FRANCISCO
(CALIFORNIA)--SHOWROOMS--DIAMOND AND
JEWELRY MART
Building with blocks / Sally B.
Woodbridge.
Diamond and Jewelry Mart, San
Francisco, features glass block
walls. Architects: Tanner Leddy
Maytum Stacy, Architects.
PROGRESSIVE ARCHITECTURE 1990
Dec., v.71, no.13, p.74-75,
photos., plan.

UNITED STATES--SAN FRANCISCO
(CALIFORNIA)--STAIRWAYS--SBG
PARTNERS
Uhuru Clinic Geri Graesdeicher's in San
Francisco, USA = Converted grain
warehouse in San Francisco, USA.
Details of the stairway.
Architects: Richard Fernau, Laura
Hartman & Partner.
DETAIL 1990 Apr.-May, v.30, no.2,
p.148-149, axonometric view,
dets., photos.

UNITED STATES--SAN FRANCISCO
(CALIFORNIA)--STORES--CLOTHING--
INTERIOR DESIGN--JASMIN BY
APPOINTMENT
Jasmin by Appointment / Lois Wagner
Green.
Interiors of San Francisco fashion
boutique. Interior designer:
Bradley Rytz.
INTERIOR DESIGN 1990 Apr., v.61,
no.6, p.[182-185], photos., plans.

UNITED STATES--SAN FRANCISCO
(CALIFORNIA)--STREETS--BROADWAY
Broadway and Columbus / Larrisa
Bilaniuk...et al.
Intersection in San Francisco.
PLACES 1990 Winter, v.6, no.2,
p.72-79, photos., plan, sketches.

UNITED STATES--SAN FRANCISCO
(CALIFORNIA)--STREETS--COLUMBUS
AVENUE
Broadway and Columbus / Larrisa
Bilaniuk...et al.
Intersection in San Francisco.
PLACES 1990 Winter, v.6, no.2,
p.72-79, photos., plan, sketches.

UNITED STATES--SAN FRANCISCO
(CALIFORNIA)--THEATERS--YERBA BUENA
THEATER
Special feature: James Polshek.
Contents: Introduction / Toshio
Nakamura --Architects' statement /
James S. Polshek and James G.
Garrison: --Works & projects:
United States Embassy, Muscat,
Oman --Centennial Hall, Barnard
College, New York, N.Y. --Alumni
houses, Bard College, Annandale,
N.Y. --Hastings Hall, Union
Theological Seminary, New York,
N.Y. --IBM-ISG North Central
Marketing Division headquarters,
White Plains, N.Y. --Seaman's
Church Institute, New York, N.Y.
--Yerba Buena Gardens Theater, San
Francisco, Calif. --National
Inventors Hall of Fame, Akron,
Ohio --New York University Medical
Center Biomolecular Research
building, New York, N.Y. --
Biographies of James S. Polshek,
Joseph L. Fleischer, Timothy P.
Hartung, and James G. Garrison,
p.126. Architects: James Stewart
Polshek & Partners. Text in
Japanese and English.
ARCHITECTURE AND URBANISM 1990
Nov., no.11(242), p.62-126,
axonometric views, models,
photos., plans, secns., site
plans.

UNITED STATES--SAN FRANCISCO
(CALIFORNIA)--TOWNSCAPES
Where Gaia and Duranos make love /
Bruno Queysanne.
The author experienced the
"richness of...spatiality" in the
meeting of Earth and Sky in his
views of Pienza and San Francisco.
PLACES 1990 Winter, v.6, no.2,
p.4-6, photos., refs.

UNITED STATES--SAN FRANCISCO
(CALIFORNIA)--ZOOS--ALTERATIONS AND
ADDITIONS--SAN FRANCISCO ZOO
Rehabilitating the earth, San
Francisco-style / Kerry J. Dawson.
On the joint-use site of the
Oceanside Water Pollution Control
Plant and the addition to the San
Francisco Zoo. Landscape
architects: Roysten Hanamoto Alley
and Abey, Landscape Architects.
LANDSCAPE ARCHITECTURE 1990 Dec.,
v.80, no.12, p.60-61, elev., site
plan, aerial photo.

UNITED STATES--SAN FRANCISCO
(CALIFORNIA)I--DECORATORS' SHOW
HOUSES--SAN FRANCSISCO DECORATOR
SHOWCASE 1990
Cloud-nine kitchen / Kirsten
Harwood, Glenn Harrell.
Kitchen designed for the 1990 San
Francisco Decorator Showcase by
Agnes Bourne.
HOUSE BEAUTIFUL 1990 Nov., v.132,
no.11, p.116-[119], photos., plan.

UNITED STATES--SAN JOSE (CALIFORNIA)--
CENTRAL BUSINESS DISTRICTS
At home in San Jose / Donald J.
Canty.
Urban renewal in San Jose, Calif.,
under the direction of architects
Frank Taylor and Tom Aidala.
ARCHITECTURAL RECORD 1990 Sept.,
v.178, no.10, p.132-137, model,
map, photos., aerial photos.

UNITED STATES--SAN JOSE (CALIFORNIA)--
CITY PLANNING
At home in San Jose / Donald J.
Canty.
Urban renewal in San Jose, Calif.,
under the direction of architects
Frank Taylor and Tom Aidala.
ARCHITECTURAL RECORD 1990 Sept.,
v.178, no.10, p.132-137, model,
map, photos., aerial photos.

UNITED STATES--SAN JOSE (CALIFORNIA)--
CONVENTION FACILITIES--SAN JOSE
CONVENTION CENTER
Taming the Behemoth: Building Types
Study 676: convention centers /
Margaret Gaskie.
San Jose, Calif., Convention
Center (MGA Partners); Sydney,
Australia, Convention Center (John
Andrews International); Adelaide,
Australia, Convention Center (John
Andrews International); and Miami
Beach Convention Center expansion
(Thompson, Ventulett, Stainback &
Associates).
ARCHITECTURAL RECORD 1990 Mar.,
v.178, no.3, p.99-113, photo.,
plans, secns., site plans.

UNITED STATES--SAN JOSE (CALIFORNIA)--
HOSPITALS--INTERIOR DESIGN--
PLANETREE MODEL HOSPITAL
Healing revolution / Michael Wagner.
Interiors of the 25-bed Planetree
Model Hospital Unit at the San
Jose Medical Center, Calif.
Architects: John Liu and Marc
Schweitzer, Interior designers:
Victoria Fay & Associates.
INTERIORS 1990 Dec., v.150, no.5,
p.96-97, photos., plan.

UNITED STATES--SAN JOSE (CALIFORNIA)--
HOTELS--FAIRMONT HOTEL
Fairmont Hotel, San Jose,
California, USA, 1987.
Architects: Gyo Obata of Hellmuth,
Obata & Kassabaum. Text in
Japanese and English.
ARCHITECTURE AND URBANISM 1990
Dec., no.12 extra edition,
p.92-[97], photos., plans.

UNITED STATES--SAN JOSE (CALIFORNIA)--
OFFICES--INTERIOR DESIGN--APPLE
COMPUTER
Apple computer / Edie Lee Cohen.
Interiors of western operations
headquarters, San Jose, Calif.
Architects: Simon Martin-Vegue
Winkelstein Moris.
INTERIOR DESIGN 1990 Apr., v.61,
no.6, p.[190-195], photos., plan.

UNITED STATES--SAN JOSE (CALIFORNIA)--
PARKS--PLAZA PARK
Arte como arquitectura como ciudad =
Art-as-architecture-as-town /
Sandro Marpillero.
Art and architecture as civic
design in the U.S. Three projects
illustrated: Plaza Park, San Jose,
Calif.; projects by Eric Ungers,
and Marina Linear Park, San
Diego. In Spanish and English.
ARQUITECTURA 1990 July-Aug., v.72,
no.285, p.126-137, elevs., models,
photos., plans, secns., site
plans.

UNITED STATES--SAN JUAN CAPISTRANO
(CALIFORNIA)--COTTAGES--INTERIOR
DESIGN--DURENBERGER HOUSE
Worldly wizardry [cottage interiors]
/ Glenn Harrell.
Cottage of California antiques
dealer G.R. Durenberger.
HOUSE BEAUTIFUL 1990 Sept., v.132,
no.9, p.58-[63], port., photos.

UNITED STATES--SAN JUAN ISLANDS
(WASHINGTON)--COMMUNITY CENTERS--SAN
JUAN COMMUNITY THEATER
Island stage / Justin Henderson.
On the San Juan Community Theater
in Friday Harbor, San Juan Island,
Wash. Architects: Bumgardner
Architects.
INTERIORS 1990 Dec., v.150, no.5,
p.82-[83], photos., plan.

UNITED STATES--SAN MATEO
(CALIFORNIA)--HOUSING FOR HOMELESS--
TURNING POINT
Housing America / Andrea Oppenheimer
Dean.
Introductory article in theme
issue discusses the reasons for
the rise in homelessness in the
U.S. Cites 4 specific projects:
Shorehaven, Bronx, N.Y. (Liebman
Melting Partnership); Spring
Creek, Brooklyn, N.Y. (Liebman
Melting Partnership and Costas
Kondylis Architects); Turning
Point, San Mateo, Calif. (David
Baker Architects); and Bennett
Place Housing for the Elderly,
Pittsburgh, Pa. (Arthur Lubetz
Assoc.).
ARCHITECTURE: THE MAGAZINE OF THE
AMERICAN INSTITUTE OF ARCHITECTS
1990 July, v.79, no.7, p.51-55,
photos., plans, site plans.

UNITED STATES--SAN MATEO
(CALIFORNIA)--TOWNHOUSES--MEADOW
COURT
The coastal condition: regional
portfolio: California housing /
Paul M. Sachner.
The first of a series of regional
portfolios, on 5 multifamily
projects: Armacost Duplex, Los
Angeles [Rebecca Binder]; 14-16
Leroy Pl., San Francisco (Hood
Miller); 1150 Lombard St., San
Francisco (Hood Miller); Meadow
Court, San Mateo (David Baker
Assoc.); and Seacliff, Malibu
(Kanner Associates).
ARCHITECTURAL RECORD 1990 Jan.,
v.178, no.1, p.90-99, elevs.,
photos., plans, secns., site
plans.

UNITED STATES--SAN RAFAEL
(CALIFORNIA)--CIVIC CENTERS--
ALTERATIONS AND ADDITIONS--MARIN
COUNTY CIVIC CENTER
Where will it go? Marin Countians
debate jail at Wright landmark
[Marin County Civic Center, San
Rafael, Calif.] / Kim Keister.
HOK, Inc., architects.
PRESERVATION NEWS 1990 Apr., v.30,
no.4, p.3,17, port., photo.
Wright done wrong / Lynn Nesmith.
On proposed addition to Frank
Lloyd Wright's Marin County Civic
Center. Architects: HOK.
ARCHITECTURE: THE AIA JOURNAL 1990
Apr., v.79, no.4, p.[35], photos.

UNITED STATES--SANDERSVILLE
(GEORGIA)--CORPORATE OFFICE
BUILDINGS--THIELE KAOLIN
Industrial complex: Thiele Kaolin
Headquarters Sandersville,
Georgia.
Architects: Lord Aeck & Sargent.
ARCHITECTURE: THE AIA JOURNAL 1990
Oct., v.79, no.10, p.[76-79],
photos., plans, site plans.

UNITED STATES--SANGER (CALIFORNIA)--
HOUSES--20TH CENTURY--LENCIONI HOUSE
Arthur Dyson: un architettura "del
luogo e del tempo" = An
architecture "of site and time".
Three U.S. houses.
ARCHITETTURA: CRONACHE E STORIA
1990 Oct., v.36, no.10(420),
p.[698]-[714], photos., plans,
secns.

UNITED STATES--SANIBEL ISLAND
(FLORIDA)--VACATION HOUSES--
ARCHITECTS'--CASA CAMELEON
(SOLFISBURG-YELIN HOUSE)
A Sanikel cameleon / Beth Dunlop.
Architects' vacation house, Casa
Cameleon on Sanibel Island, Fla.
Architects: Roy J. Solfisburg.
ARCHITECTURAL DIGEST 1990 Aug.,
v.47, no.8, p.138-[143], photos.

UNITED STATES--SANTA BARBARA
(CALIFORNIA)--HOTELS--SPANISH
MEDITERRANEAN REVIVAL--INTERIOR
DESIGN--FOUR SEASONS BILTMORE
Four Seasons Biltmore / Edie Lee
Cohen.
Features renovated interiors of
1927 Santa Barbara hotel.
Original architect: Reginald
Johnson. Renovation
architects/interior designers:
James Northcutt Associates.
INTERIOR DESIGN 1990 Feb., v.61,
no.3, p.210-[217], photos., plan.

UNITED STATES--SANTA BARBARA
(CALIFORNIA)--RESIDENTIAL GARDENS
Welcome to the backyard California /
Erica Goebel.
Gardens in San Francisco, Los
Angeles and Santa Barbara.
Landscape architects: Peder Jens
Pedersen, Calvin Abe & Assoc. with
Ron McCoy, Isabelle Greene, Ron
Lutsko, and Dennis Shaw.
GARDEN DESIGN 1990 autumn, v.9,
no.3, p.[38-45], photos.

UNITED STATES--SANTA CLARA
(CALIFORNIA)--OFFICES--INTERIOR
DESIGN--APPLE COMPUTER, MONROE
CAMPUS
Apple Computer / Monica Geran.
Interiors of satellite extension
for engineering groups on the
Monroe Campus, Santa Clara, Calif.
Architects: Gensler and
Associates, Architects.
INTERIOR DESIGN 1990 Nov., v.61,
no.15, p.160-[165], photos., plan.

UNITED STATES--SANTA CLARA COUNTY
(CALIFORNIA)--INDUSTRIES, LOCATION
OF
Silicon Valley y Route 128: ¿
prototipos regionales o
excepciones historicas? / Annalee
Saxenian.
Concentrations of technology-based
industries in northern California
and suburban Boston. In Spanish;
English summary p.57.
URBANISMO / COAM 1990 Sept.,
no.11, p.46-57, maps, photos.,
aerial photos.

UNITED STATES--SANTA CLARA (NEW
MEXICO)--ARCHITECTURE--NATIVE
AMERICAN--SOCOIOLOGICAL ASPECTS
Conflicting landscape values: the
Santa Clara Pueblo and day school
/ Rina Swentzell.
PLACES 1990 Fall, v.7, no.1,
p.[18]-27, photos., plans, refs.

UNITED STATES--SANTA CRUZ
(CALIFORNIA)--FARMHOUSES--GREGORY
HOUSE
An indigenous thing: the story of
William Wurster and the Gregory
farmhouse / Daniel P. Gregory.
Includes contributions by Joseph
P. Esherick, Morley Baer, Lawrence
B. Anderson, and Robert A. M.
Stern.
PLACES 1990 Fall, v.7, no.1,
p.78-93, ill., elev., photos.,
plans, refs.

UNITED STATES--SANTA CRUZ
(CALIFORNIA)--SHOPPING MALLS--
PACIFIC GARDEN MALL
Post-earthquake placemaking in
downtown Santa Cruz / James E.
Pepper.
Destruction of the Pacific Garden
Mall in Santa Cruz by a
seven-tent, 34,000 sq. ft.
temporary complex known as the
Phoenix Pavilions.
PLACES 1990 Spring, v.6, no.3,
p.92-93, photos., plans.

UNITED STATES--SANTA CRUZ
(CALIFORNIA)--SHOPPING MALLS--
TEMPORARY--PHOENIX PAVILIONS
Post-earthquake placemaking in
downtown Santa Cruz / James E.
Pepper.
Destruction of the Pacific Garden
Mall in Santa Cruz by a
seven-tent, 34,000 sq. ft.
temporary complex known as the
Phoenix Pavilions.
PLACES 1990 Spring, v.6, no.3,
p.92-93, photos., plans.

UNITED STATES--SANTA CRUZ
(CALIFORNIA)--STUDENT UNIONS--
UNIVERSITY OF CALIFORNIA, SANTA CRUZ
Centre of gravitas / John Ellis.
Student Center, U.C. Santa Cruz.
Architects: Fernau and Hartman.
ARCHITECTURAL REVIEW 1990 Nov.,
v.188, no.1125, p.64-67, map,
photos., plans, secns., site plan.
A regionalist union / Sally
Woodbridge.
Student Center, U.C. Santa Cruz.
Architects: Fernau and Hartman.
PROGRESSIVE ARCHITECTURE 1990
June, v.71, no.6, p.106-113,
photo., plans, site plan.

UNITED STATES--SANTA CRUZ
(CALIFORNIA)--TENT STRUCTURES--
PHOENIX PAVILIONS
Post-earthquake placemaking in
downtown Santa Cruz / James E.
Pepper.
Destruction of the Pacific Garden
Mall in Santa Cruz by a
seven-tent, 34,000 sq. ft.
temporary complex known as the
Phoenix Pavilions.
PLACES 1990 Spring, v.6, no.3,
p.92-93, photos., plans.

UNITED STATES--SANTA CRUZ
(CALIFORNIA)--UNIVERSITIES AND
COLLEGES--BUILDINGS--ALTERATIONS AND
ADDITIONS--UNIVERSITY OF CALIFORNIA,
SANTA CRUZ--LAWRENCE HALL
Site-sensitive technology: Simon
Martin Vegue Winkelstein Moris of
San Francisco.
Three designs for projects that
meld high technology and sensitive
design: Hearst Mining Center,
Facility, Contra Costa Water
Treatment complex, and addition to
Lawrence Hall.
ARCHITECTURE: THE MAGAZINE OF THE
AMERICAN INSTITUTE OF ARCHITECTS
1990 May, v.79, no.5, p.48, elev.,
models, secn.

UNITED STATES--SANTA CRUZ
(CALIFORNIA)--UNIVERSITIES AND
COLLEGES--BUILDINGS--UNIVERSITY OF
CALIFORNIA, SANTA CRUZ--STUDENT
CENTER
Centre of gravitas / John Ellis.
Student Center, U.C. Santa Cruz.
Architects: Fernau and Hartman.
ARCHITECTURAL REVIEW 1990 Nov.,
v.188, no.1125, p.64-67, map,
photos., plans, secns., site plan.
A regionalist union / Sally
Woodbridge.
Student Center, U.C. Santa Cruz.
Architects: Fernau and Hartman.
PROGRESSIVE ARCHITECTURE 1990
June, v.71, no.6, p.106-113,
photo., plans, site plan.

UNITED STATES--SANTA FE (NEW MEXICO)--
ART GALLERIES
A collector's Santa Fe / Elizabeth
Tallent.
Profile of 13 art galleries in
Santa Fe specializing in Native
American arts.
ARCHITECTURAL DIGEST 1990 May,
v.47, no.5, p.102-110, photos.

UNITED STATES--SANTA FE (NEW MEXICO)--
CITIES AND TOWNS
The city different: Santa Fe has
charm, and Old-world feel--and an
identity crisis / Joy Waldron
Murphy.
HISTORIC PRESERVATION 1990
Mar.-Apr., v.42, no.2, p.16-19,
photo.

UNITED STATES--SANTA FE (NEW MEXICO)--
HEALTH CARE BUILDINGS--SANTA FE
IMAGING CENTER
Santa Fe Imaging Center, Santa Fe,
New Mexico.
Medical building. Architects:
Holmes Sabatini Eeds.
NEW MEXICO ARCHITECTURE 1990
Jan.-Apr., v.31, no.1-2, p.9-13,
axonometric view, dwgs., photos.,
site plan.

UNITED STATES--SANTA FE (NEW MEXICO)--
HISTORIC DISTRICTS--WESTSIDE
GUADALUPE HISTORIC DISTRICT
Santa Fe's Westside/Guadalupe
Historic District: Hispanic
vernacular versus Pueblo revival /
Beverly Spears.
NEW MEXICO ARCHITECTURE 1990
Sept.-Dec., v.31, no.5-6, p.9-13,
cover, photos.

UNITED STATES--SANTA FE (NEW MEXICO)--
HOUSES--ADOBE--MOSES HOUSE
Harmonious spaces: an artist's
hideaway in Santa Fe / W. Dean
Gillette.
Adobe house of Forrest Moses.
SOUTHERN ACCENTS 1990 June, v.13,
no.6, p.[74]-80 photos.

UNITED STATES--SANTA FE (NEW MEXICO)--
HOUSES--ADOBE--POTTERY HOUSE
Legacy of F.L.Wright: unfinished
plans realized.
Boulder House, Beverly Hills,
Calif.(1951) and Pottery House,
Santa Fe(1939-1942?). Text in
Japanese. Architects of record:
Taliesin Associated Architects of
the Frank Lloyd Wright Foundation.
SPACE DESIGN 1990 Aug., no.311,
(Continued next page)

UNITED STATES--SANTA FE (NEW MEXICO)--
HOUSES--ADOBE--POTTERY HOUSE
(CONTINUED)
Legacy of F.L.Wright:...(CONTINUED)
p.69-76, dwgs., map, photos., site
plans.

UNITED STATES--SANTA FE (NEW MEXICO)--
HOUSES--INTERIOR DESIGN--HACKMAN
HOUSE
Gene Hackman: Santa Fe spaces for
The French Connections's Best
Actor / Joan Chatfield-Taylor.
Features interiors of home
redesigned by Stephen Samuelson
and Harry Daple. Interior
designers: Ken Figueredo and Glynn
Gomez.
ARCHITECTURAL DIGEST 1990 Apr.,
v.47, no.4, p.250-251,312, port.,
photos.

UNITED STATES--SANTA FE (NEW MEXICO)--
MUSEUMS--ART
Thrice blessed: Santa Fe's museums
weave a multicultural tapestry /
Nan Booth Simpson.
SOUTHERN ACCENTS 1989 May-June,
v.12, no.3, p.200-B-200-T, ill.,
photos.

UNITED STATES--SANTA FE (NEW MEXICO)--
VERNACULAR ARCHITECTURE--SANTA FE
STYLE
Santa Fe's Westside/Guadalupe
Historic District: Hispanic
vernacular versus Pueblo revival /
Beverly Spears.
NEW MEXICO ARCHITECTURE 1990
Sept.-Dec., v.31, no.5-6, p.9-13,
cover, photos.

UNITED STATES--SANTA MONICA
(CALIFORNIA)--AFFORDABLE HOUSING
"Low cost houses" und CRA / Diane
Ghirardo.
Changing definitions of "low cost
housing" from the 1950s through
the 1980s in Los Angeles.
Includes 3 "affordable" projects
by Koning & Eizenberg Architects.
Text in German; summaries in
German, French and English.
WERK, BAUEN + WOHNEN 1990
July-Aug., no.7-8, p.58-61,
photos., plans.

UNITED STATES--SANTA MONICA
(CALIFORNIA)--ARCHITECTURE--STUDY
AND TEACHING--SOUTHERN CALIFORNIA
INSTITUTE OF ARCHITECTURE
Recent student work (and a few
comments) from SCI-ARC.
Includes discussion of the
architecture program at the
Southern California Institute of
Architecture.
L. A. ARCHITECT 1990 July-Aug.,
p.6-7, dwgs., models, sketch.

UNITED STATES--SANTA MONICA
(CALIFORNIA)--ART GALLERIES--MEYERS
- BLOOM GALLERY
From autos to art: Architect
Frederick Fisher's pure and simple
design for the Meyers-Bloom
Gallery / Justin Henderson.
Located in former auto showroom,
Santa Monica.
INTERIORS 1989 Feb., v.148, no.7,
p.136-[137], axonometric view,
photos.

UNITED STATES--SANTA MONICA
(CALIFORNIA)--BEACH HOUSES--INTERIOR
DESIGN--THALBERG SHEARER HOUSE
Norma Shearer and Irving G.
Thalberg: the Santa Monica beach
house of a Hollywood genius and
his leading lady / Richard
Schickel.
ARCHITECTURAL DIGEST 1990 Apr.,
v.47, no.4, p.218-[221],300,
ports., photos.

UNITED STATES--SANTA MONICA
(CALIFORNIA)--BEACH HOUSES--SPANISH
COLONIAL REVIVAL--MAYER HOUSE
Louis B. Mayer: MGM archetypal
studio head at home / A. Scott
Berg.
On Mayer's beach house in Santa
Monica.
ARCHITECTURAL DIGEST 1990 Apr.,
v.47, no.4, p.144-145,284, ports.,
photos.

UNITED STATES--SANTA MONICA
(CALIFORNIA)--CITY PLANNING
Linking downtown development to
broader community goals: an
analysis of linkage policy in
three cities / W. Dennis Keating.
San Francisco, Santa Monica and
Boston.
AMERICAN PLANNING ASSOCIATION.
JOURNAL 1986 Spring, v.52, no.2,
p.133-141, biblio., refs.

UNITED STATES--SANTA MONICA
(CALIFORNIA)--CULTURAL CENTERS--
PETER BOXENBAUM ARTS EDUCATION
CENTRE
Street life: Boxenbaum Arts
Education Centre, Santa Monica,
California, Moore Ruble Yudell
Architects / Lynn Nesmith.
ARCHITECTURE: THE MAGAZINE OF THE
AMERICAN INSTITUTE OF ARCHITECTS
1990 June, v.79, no.6, p.60-63,
elev., photos., plans, secns.

UNITED STATES--SANTA MONICA
(CALIFORNIA)--HOTELS--INTERIOR
DESIGN--LOEWS SANTA MONICA BEACH
HOTEL
Loews Santa Monica / Monica Geran.
Features interiors of new beach
hotel. Interior designers; Barry
Design Associates. Architects:
Archisystems International.
INTERIOR DESIGN 1990 Apr., v.61,
no.6, p.172-[175], photos., plan.

UNITED STATES--SANTA MONICA
(CALIFORNIA)--HOUSES--ALTERATIONS
AND ADDITIONS--SIXTH STREET HOUSE
Morphosis [houses].
Contents: CDLT 1,2, Los Angeles,
Calif., 1987-89.-- Was house,
Beverly Hills, Calif., 1988.--
Sixth Street house, Santa Monica,
Calif., 1986. Text in Japanese and
English.
GA HOUSES 1990 Mar., no.28,
p.6-19, axonometric views.,
elevs., models., plans., secns.

UNITED STATES--SANTA MONICA
(CALIFORNIA)--HOUSES--ARCHITECTS'--
KONING EIZENBERG HOUSE
Blueprint for the new family home /
Julie V. Iovine.
Home of architects Julie Eizenberg
and Hank Koning, Santa Monica,
Calif.
METROPOLITAN HOME 1990 Dec., v.22,
no.12, p.112-[119], photos.,
aerial photo.
Crystalline LA / Anthony Paine.
Features the Koning Eizenberg
house in Santa Monica. Architects:
Hank Koning and Julie Eizenberg.
ARCHITECTURAL REVIEW 1990 Apr.,
v.187, no.1118, p.94-96, elev.,
photos., plans, secn., site plan.
Enclave californienne: maison a
Santa Monica / Claudine Mulard.
Koning Eizenberg house.
Architects: Koning Eizenberg
Architecture. English summary,
p.47.
ARCHITECTURE INTERIEURE CREE 1990
Feb., no.234, p.[92]-95, elevs.,
photos., plans, site plan.
Into the garden: Koning Eizenberg
house, Santa Monica, California /
Michael Webb.
Koning Eizenberg Architecture.
ARCHITECTURE: THE AIA JOURNAL 1990
Mar., v.79, no.3, p.[136-141],
photos., plans.

UNITED STATES--SANTA MONICA
(CALIFORNIA)--HOUSES--INTERIOR
DESIGN--POWER HOUSE
Living the California life /
Elizabeth Gaynor.
Home of interior and garden
designer Nancy Goslee Power, Santa
Monica.
HOUSE BEAUTIFUL 1990 May, v.132,
no.5, p.56-63, ports., photos.

UNITED STATES--SANTA MONICA
(CALIFORNIA)--HOUSES--SUMMERS HOUSE
Mack Architects [houses].
Contents: Summers residence, Santa
Monica, Calif., 1989 -- Kashii
district housing, Fukuoka, Japan,
1988-90. Architects: Mack
Architects. Text in Japanese and
English.
GA HOUSES 1990 Mar., no.28,
p.34-41, axonometric views,
elevs., models, plans, site plans.
Mark Mack.
Most of issue devoted to the work
of this California-based
architect. Includes an interview
with David Cohn. Text in Spanish
and English.
EL CROQUIS 1990 Mar., v.9, no.42,
p.4-62, axonometric views, ill.,
dwgs., port., elevs., models,
photos., plans, secns., site
plans, refs.

UNITED STATES--SANTA MONICA
(CALIFORNIA)--HOUSES--WHITNEY HOUSE
Mark Mack.
Most of issue devoted to the work
of this California-based
architect. Includes an interview
with David Cohn. Text in Spanish
and English.
EL CROQUIS 1990 Mar., v.9, no.42,
p.4-62, axonometric views, ill.,
dwgs., port., elevs., models,
photos., plans, secns., site
plans, refs.

UNITED STATES--SANTA MONICA
(CALIFORNIA)--HOUSES--WHITNEY HOUSE
(CONTINUED)
Relectures: maisons a Los Angeles et
San Francisco, USA.
On two houses by Mark Mack: Baum
house, Berkeley and Whitney house,
Santa Monica. Summaries in English
and Spanish.
TECHNIQUES ET ARCHITECTURE 1990
June-July, no.390, p.112-118,181,
axonometric view, photos., plans,
elevs.

UNITED STATES--SANTA MONICA
(CALIFORNIA)--MULTI-USE COMPLEXES--
EDGEMAR
Frank O. Gehry.
Entire issue devoted to the work
of this American architect.
Criticism by A. Zaera Polo and
David Cohn. 15 projects and
buildings from 1987-1990 featured.
Text in Spanish and English.
EL CROQUIS 1990 Nov., v.9, no.45,
p.1-124, ports., elevs., models,
photos., plans, secns., site
plans, refs.

UNITED STATES--SANTA MONICA
(CALIFORNIA)--MULTI-USE COMPLEXES--
SANTA MONICA MUSEUM OF ART
La formula del desorden: museo de
arte y centro comercial Edgemar,
Santa Monica, California,
1984-1988.
On the Edgemar multi-use complex
which contains the Santa Monica
Museum of Art. Architect: Frank O.
Gehry. English text, p.86.
A & V 1990, no.25, p.30-35, dets.,
elevs., photos., plan, secn., site
plan.

UNITED STATES--SANTA MONICA
(CALIFORNIA)--MUSEUMS--ART--SANTA
MONICA MUSEUM OF ART
Apparentemente casuale: Frank Gehry,
Museo a Santa Monica.
ARCHITETTURA; CRONACHE E STORIA
1990 Feb., v.36, no.2(412),
p.123-125, axonometric view,
photos., plans, secn.
La formula del desorden: museo de
arte y centro comercial Edgemar,
Santa Monica, California,
1984-1988.
On the Edgemar multi-use complex
which contains the Santa Monica
Museum of Art. Architect: Frank O.
Gehry. English text, p.86.
A & V 1990, no.25, p.30-35, dets.,
elevs., photos., plan, secn., site
plan.

UNITED STATES--SANTA MONICA
(CALIFORNIA)--RESIDENTIAL GARDENS--
POWER GARDEN
Living the California life /
Elizabeth Caymer.
Home of interior and garden
designer Nancy Goslee Power, Santa
Monica.
HOUSE BEAUTIFUL 1990 May, v.132,
no.5, p.56-63, ports., photos.

UNITED STATES--SANTA MONICA
(CALIFORNIA)--RESTAURANTS--INTERIOR
DESIGN--DC-3
Flying sculpture: designers Solberg
& Lowe Architects creates DC-3 /
Michael Wagner.
Interiors of Santa Monica
restaurant DC-3. Collaborating
artist/designer: Charles Arnoldi.
INTERIORS 1990 Jan., v.149, no.6,
p.156-157, photos., plan.

UNITED STATES--SANTA MONICA
(CALIFORNIA)--STUDENT PROJECTS--
SOUTHERN CALIFORNIA INSTITUTE OF
ARCHITECTURE
Recent student work (and a few
comments) from SCI-ARC.
Includes discussion of the
architecture program at the
Southern California Institute of
Architecture.
L. A. ARCHITECT 1990 July-Aug.,
p.6-7, dwgs., models, sketch.

UNITED STATES--SANTA MONICA
(CALIFORNIA)--TOWNHOUSES--PACIFIC
TOWNHOUSES
American housing 1980-1990 / James
Tice.
Features: Castro Common, San
Francisco (Daniel Solomon, Paulett
Taggart); Sun-Tech Housing, Santa
Monica (Steve Andre, David Van
Hoy); Pacific Townhouses, Santa
Monica (Rebecca Binder, James
Stafford); Hoyt Square
Condominiums, Portland, OR (Robert
S. Leeb). Text in Italian and
English.
METAMORFOSI 1989, no.12, p.38-51,
axonometric views, models,
photos., plans, secns.

UNITED STATES--SANTA MONICA
(CALIFORNIA)--TOWNHOUSES--SUN-TECH
TOWNHOUSES
American housing 1980-1990 / James
Tice.
Features: Castro Common, San
Francisco (Daniel Solomon, Paulett
Taggart); Sun-Tech Housing, Santa
Monica (Steve Andre, David Van
Hoy); Pacific Townhouses, Santa
Monica (Rebecca Binder, James
Stafford); Hoyt Square
Condominiums, Portland, OR (Robert
S. Leeb). Text in Italian and
English.
METAMORFOSI 1989, no.12, p.38-51,
axonometric views, models,
photos., plans, secns.

UNITED STATES--SANTA ROSA
(CALIFORNIA)--PRISONS--SONOMA COUNTY
DETENTION FACILITY
Courts help shape jail design:
Sonoma County Detention Facility,
Santa Rosa, California.
Architects: The Ehrenkrantz Group.
ARCHITECTURAL RECORD 1990 Sept.,
v.178, no.10, p.146-147, photos.,
plans, site plan.

UNITED STATES--SARASOTA (FLORIDA)--
HOUSES--LONGBOAT KEY
Two houses / Preston Scott Cohen.
House on Longboat Key and House on
Siesta Key, both near Sarasota,
Fla., and designed by the author.
ASSEMBLAGE 1990 Dec., no.13,
p.[72]-87, dwgs., models, plans,
secns., site plans.

UNITED STATES--SARASOTA (FLORIDA)--
HOUSES--SIESTA KEY
Two houses / Preston Scott Cohen.
House on Longboat Key and House on
Siesta Key, both near Sarasota,
Fla., and designed by the author.
ASSEMBLAGE 1990 Dec., no.13,
p.[72]-87, dwgs., models, plans,
secns., site plans.

UNITED STATES--SAUSALITO
(CALIFORNIA)--HOUSES
Nella natura a viso aperto: opere
californiane di Robert K.
Overstreet.
Barbee House, Berkeley;
architect's house, Corte Madera;
Cottage Champion, Madison, Miss.;
house over water, Sausalito;
mausoleum, Colma; restaurant.
Summaries in English, French,
German, and Spanish.
ARCHITETTURA; CRONACHE E STORIA
1990 Jan., v.36, no.1(411),
p.[32]-42, dwgs., photos., plans,
secns.

UNITED STATES--SAUSALITO
(CALIFORNIA)--HOUSES--GERHARDT HOUSE
Mark Mack.
Most of issue devoted to the work
of this California-based
architect. Includes an interview
with David Cohn. Text in Spanish
and English.
EL CROQUIS 1990 Mar., v.9, no.42,
p.4-62, axonometric views, ill.,
dwgs., port., elevs., models,
photos., plans, secns., site
plans, refs.

UNITED STATES--SCALES MOUND
(ILLINOIS)--HISTORIC DISTRICTS
Scales Mound Historic District /
Floyd Mansberger.
HISTORIC ILLINOIS 1990 Dec., v.13,
no.4, p.[1]-3,14, photos.

UNITED STATES--SCALES MOUND
(ILLINOIS)--VILLAGES--19TH CENTURY
Scales Mound Historic District /
Floyd Mansberger.
HISTORIC ILLINOIS 1990 Dec., v.13,
no.4, p.[1]-3,14, photos.

UNITED STATES--SCOTTSDALE (ARIZONA)--
CLUBHOUSES--INTERIOR DESIGN--DESERT
MOUNTAIN GOLF CLUBHOUSE
Western magic [Desert Mountain Golf
Clubhouse] / Justin Henderson.
Near Scottsdale, Az. Architect:
Robert Bacon of Studio b. Interior
designers: D. Eric Bron and
Dorothy Bron of Lescher and
Mahoney/DLR Group.
INTERIORS 1990 Oct., v.150, no.3,
p.64-[67], photos., plan.

UNITED STATES--SCOTTSDALE (ARIZONA)--
HOTELS--HYATT REGENCY
Breaking new ground in the desert:
Hyatt Regency, Scottsdale,
Arizona, Hornberger Worstell &
Associates, architects.
Landscape architects: SWA Group.
ARCHITECTURAL RECORD 1990 Feb.,
v.178, no.2, p.122-125, photos.,
plan, site plan.

UNITED STATES--SCOTTSDALE (ARIZONA)--
HOUSES
Kamal Amin: dal Cairo all'Arizona,
sette opere organiche = from Cairo
to Arizona, seven organic works.
Houses in Va. and Ariz. and
medical centers in Tempe and
Scottsdale, Ariz.
ARCHITETTURA: CRONACHE E STORIA
1990 Sept., v.36, no.9(419),
p.[612-634], dets., photos.,
plans, secns., site plans.

UNITED STATES--SCOTTSDALE (ARIZONA)--
MEDICAL CENTERS--CARDIOVASCULAR
CENTER
Kamal Amin: dal Cairo all'Arizona,
sette opere organiche = from Cairo
to Arizona, seven organic works.
Houses in Va. and Ariz. and
medical centers in Tempe and
Scottsdale, Ariz.
ARCHITETTURA: CRONACHE E STORIA
1990 Sept., v.36, no.9(419),
p.[612-634], dets., photos.,
plans, secns., site plans.

UNITED STATES--SCOTTSDALE (ARIZONA)--
OFFICE BUILDINGS--INTERIOR DESIGN--
FORUM
Interiors.
Three projects: Loma Theater
Bookstar, San Diego (Alamo
Architects); Bank of Nova Scotia,
Toronto (Gensler and Associates);
and The Forum, Scottsdale, Ariz.
(James, Harwick + Partners).
TEXAS ARCHITECT 1990 Nov-Dec.,
v.40, no.6, p.60-63, photos.,
plans.

UNITED STATES--SEA ISLAND (GEORGIA)--
HOUSES--EUGENE O'NEILL HOUSE (CASA
GENOTTA)
Sea Island sanctuary: Eugene
O'Neill's former workspace-retreat
/ Susannah M. Wilson.
Architect: Francis Abreau.
Landscape designer: T. Miesse
Baumgardner.
SOUTHERN ACCENTS 1990 June, v.13,
no.5, p.54-[61], photos.

UNITED STATES--SEA ISLAND (GEORGIA)--
VACATION HOUSES--MAISON DU CYGNE
(ANDERSON HOUSE)
Maison du Cygne: metamorphosis on
the Georgia Coast / Helen C.
Griffith.
Rosemary Anderson house, Sea
Island. Architect for renovations:
John Shackelford of William Frank
McCall Architects and Interior
Designer: Elizabeth Tucker.
SOUTHERN ACCENTS 1990 July-Aug.,
v.13, no.6, p.76-83, photos.

UNITED STATES--SEASIDE (FLORIDA)--
BELVEDERES
''Belvederes' en el golfo: casa y
torre en Seaside, Florida =
Belvederes by the Gulf.
On Leon Krier's summer house.
English text, p.87.
A & V 1990, no.21, p.54-57, dwgs.,
elevs., photos., plans.

UNITED STATES--SEASIDE (FLORIDA)--
HOUSES--ARCHITECTS'--CASASCO HOUSE
Seaside story / Julie V. Iovine.
House in Seaside, Fla. Architect:
Victoria Casasco.
METROPOLITAN HOME 1990 July, v.22,
no.7, p.70-[75], photos.

UNITED STATES--SEASIDE (FLORIDA)--
HOUSES--ARCHITECTS'--CHATHAM HOUSE
Architecture for the '90s.
Holt Hinshaw Pfau Jones, Astronaut
Memorial, San Francisco--Henry
Myerberg, house in Vieques, P.R.--
Walter Chatham, house in Seaside,
Fla.--Carrie Glassman Shoemake,
house near Austin, Tex.--Mark
Domiteaux, house in Tex.--Frank
Lupo, Daniel Rowan, loft in NYC--
Michael Codwell, 4 projects in New
England.
METROPOLITAN HOME 1990 Jan., v.22,
no.1, p.[72]-96, ports., photos.

UNITED STATES--SEASIDE (FLORIDA)--
HOUSES--ARCHITECTS'--KRIER HOUSE
''Belvederes' en el golfo: casa y
torre en Seaside, Florida =
Belvederes by the Gulf.
On Leon Krier's summer house.
English text, p.87.
A & V 1990, no.21, p.54-57, dwgs.,
elevs., photos., plans.
La casa de Leon Krier en Seaside,
Florida = The house of Leon Krier
at Seaside, Florida / Leon Krier,
Miguel Garay.
Text in Spanish and English.
COMPOSICION ARQUITECTONICA, ART &
ARCHITECTURE 1989 June, no.3,
p.[39]-72, dets., elevs., photos.,
plans, site plan, sketches, aerial
photos.
Temple contempo [Seaside, Florida] /
Julie V. Iovine.
House by Leon Krier.
METROPOLITAN HOME 1990 July, v.22,
no.7, p.[67]-69, photos.

UNITED STATES--SEASIDE (FLORIDA)--
HOUSES--FORSYTHE HOUSE
Forsythe House, Seaside, Florida,
design: 1989; completion: 1990
(est.).
Architect: Walter F. Chatham. Text
in Japanese and English.
GA HOUSES 1990 Mar., no.28,
p.80-81, elevs., model, plans,
secns.

UNITED STATES--SEASIDE (FLORIDA)--NEW
TOWNS
Design for sustainability at Seaside
/ Gary Coates.
Student design studio projects.
OZ / COLLEGE OF ARCHITECTURE AND
DESIGN, KANSAS STATE UNIVERSITY
1989, v.11, p.48-51, elevs.,
plans, secn., site plans, refs.

UNITED STATES--SEASIDE (FLORIDA)--NEW
TOWNS (CONTINUED)
The Seaside story [Fla.] / Robert
Davis.
OZ / COLLEGE OF ARCHITECTURE AND
DESIGN, KANSAS STATE UNIVERSITY
1989, v.11, p.46-47, photo.

UNITED STATES--SEASIDE (FLORIDA)--
SEASIDE TOWNS
Howdee, Charlie! / Thomas
Thiis-Evensen.
On Prince Charles opinions on
architecture, Paternoster Square
proposals, and buildings in
Seaside, Fla.
ARKITEKTEN 1990 Mar., v.92, no.3,
p.80-85, dwgs., elevs., models,
photos., secns.
Seaside, Florida / Jorgen Loeb.
Planning by Andres Duany and
Elizabeth Plater Zyberk.
ARKITEKTUR: THE SWEDISH REVIEW OF
ARCHITECTURE 1990 Dec., v.90,
no.10, p.52-53, maps, photos.
The Seaside story [Fla.] / Robert
Davis.
OZ / COLLEGE OF ARCHITECTURE AND
DESIGN, KANSAS STATE UNIVERSITY
1989, v.11, p.46-47, photo.

UNITED STATES--SEASIDE (FLORIDA)--
TOWERS
''Belvederes' en el golfo: casa y
torre en Seaside, Florida =
Belvederes by the Gulf.
On Leon Krier's summer house.
English text, p.87.
A & V 1990, no.21, p.54-57, dwgs.,
elevs., photos., plans.

UNITED STATES--SEATTLE (WASHINGTON)--
APARTMENTS--ARCHITECTS'--INTERIOR
DESIGN--OLSON APARTMENT
James Olson: melding art and
architecture in an urban Seattle
apartment / Jon Krakauer.
Focus on interiors. Architects:
James Olson.
ARCHITECTURAL DIGEST 1990 Feb.,
v.47, no.2, p.92-[95], port.,
photos., plan, secn.

UNITED STATES--SEATTLE (WASHINGTON)--
ART GALLERIES--CASA U-BETCHA
A mad mix of archi-Tex-Mex: Casa
U-Betcha by Winn Architecture /
Justin Henderson.
Restaurant/art gallery located in
Seattle.
INTERIORS 1990 Jan., v.149, no.6,
p.158-[159], photos., plan.

UNITED STATES--SEATTLE (WASHINGTON)--
BUILDINGS--HEIGHT RESTRICTIONS
Seattle in CAPtivity / Casey Corr.
Slow-growth initiative in Seattle
known as the Citizens' Alternative
Plan (CAP).
PLANNING 1990 Jan., v.56, no.1,
p.18-21, ill., dwgs., photos.

UNITED STATES--SEATTLE (WASHINGTON)--
BUS STATIONS
Seattle Metro Tunnel:
state-of-the-art maintenance /
Richard Locke.
Underground transportation tunnel
for downtown Seattle will
accomodate buses and light rail,
and be serviced by five passenger
stations. Designers and engineers:
(Continued next page)

UNITED STATES--SEATTLE (WASHINGTON)--
OFFICES--ALTERATIONS AND ADDITIONS--
AVCON INC.
New image / Amy Dana.
    Addition to Avcon Inc.'s offices
    in warehouse space in Seattle's
    Pioneer Square.
    Architects/Interior designers:
    Callison Parnership.
    INTERIORS 1990 Feb., v.149, no.7,
    p.114-[115], photos., plan.

UNITED STATES--SEATTLE (WASHINGTON)--
OFFICES--INTERIOR DESIGN--GNA
Sails in the sky / Justin Henderson.
    On the interiors of the GNA
    offices, Seattle, located in the
    Two Union Square Building.
    Architects for building: NBBJ
    Architects. Interior designers:
    for building BSD, NBBJ's interior
    architecture group.
    INTERIORS 1990 Feb., v.149, no.7,
    p.108-109, photos., plan.

UNITED STATES--SEATTLE (WASHINGTON)--
RESTAURANTS--INTERIOR DESIGN--CASA
U-BETCHA
A mad mix of archi-Tex-Mex: Casa
U-Betcha by Winn Architecture /
Justin Henderson.
    Restaurant/art gallery located in
    Seattle.
    INTERIORS 1990 Jan., v.149, no.6,
    p.158-[159], photos., plan.

UNITED STATES--SEATTLE (WASHINGTON)--
ROADS
Stadt und Verkehr.
    Special issue on towns and
    traffic. 22 projects illustrated.
    English summary, p.53.
    BAUMEISTER 1990 Aug., v.87, no.8,
    p.13-53, dwgs., models, photos.,
    plans, secns., site plans, aerial
    photos.

UNITED STATES--SEATTLE (WASHINGTON)--
STORES--INTERIOR DESIGN--IL VECCHIO
Functional art / Justin Henderson.
    Il Vecchio, Seattle, a custom
    bicycle shop includes repair
    workshop. Architects: Edward
    Weinstein Associates Architects.
    INTERIORS 1990 Feb., v.149, no.7,
    p.116-[117], axonometric view,
    photos.

UNITED STATES--SEATTLE (WASHINGTON)--
STORES--JEWELRY--LIGHTING--MONROE
JEWELERS
Jewel box: Monroe Jewelers, Seattle,
Washington / Donald J. Canty.
    Interior lighting. Architect:
    Olson/Sundberg.
    ARCHITECTURAL RECORD 1990 Aug.,
    v.178, no.9 suppl., p.14-[15],
    photos., plan.

UNITED STATES--SEATTLE (WASHINGTON)--
TRANSPORTATION PLANNING
Seattle Metro Tunnel:
    state-of-the-art maintenance /
    Richard Locke.
    Underground transportation tunnel
    for downtown Seattle will
    accomodate buses and light rail,
    and be serviced by five passenger
    stations. Designers and engineers:
    Parsons, Brinckerhoff, Quade &
    Douglas.
    MASS TRANSIT 1990 Sept.-Oct.,
        (Continued next column)

UNITED STATES--SEATTLE (WASHINGTON)--
TRANSPORTATION PLANNING
    (CONTINUED)
Seattle Metro Tunnel: (CONTINUED)
    v.17, no.9-10, p.24,26, photo.

UNITED STATES--SEATTLE (WASHINGTON)--
TUNNELS--METRO TUNNEL
Seattle Metro Tunnel:
    state-of-the-art maintenance /
    Richard Locke.
    Underground transportation tunnel
    for downtown Seattle will
    accomodate buses and light rail,
    and be serviced by five passenger
    stations. Designers and engineers:
    Parsons, Brinckerhoff, Quade &
    Douglas.
    MASS TRANSIT 1990 Sept.-Oct.,
    v.17, no.9-10, p.24,26, photo.

UNITED STATES--SEATTLE (WASHINGTON)--
URBAN PARKS--FREEWAY PARK
Urban Camouflage: Portfolio:
Danadjieva & Koenig Associates /
Andrea Oppenheimer Dean.
    An architecture and landscape
    architecture firm with offices in
    Tiburon, Calif., and Bellevue,
    Wash. contents: Freeway Air Rights
    Development, Seattle; and
    Riverfront Promenade, White River
    Park, Indianapolis.
    ARCHITECTURE: THE MAGAZINE OF THE
    AMERICAN INSTITUTE OF ARCHITECTS
    1990 Aug., v.79, no.8, p.60-65,
    model, photos., site plans, aerial
    photo.

UNITED STATES--SECAUCUS (NEW JERSEY)--
MULTI-USE COMPLEXES--ALLIED JUNCTION
All aboard at Allied Junction: a
    public-private partnership spurs
    the planning of the New Jersey
    transit link / Bruce Ross.
    New transportation hub planned for
    northern New Jersey. Commercial
    complex and transfer station
    architects: Brennan Beer Gorman
    Architects.
    MASS TRANSIT 1990 Apr., v.17,
    no.4, p.22-23, dwg.

UNITED STATES--SECAUCUS (NEW JERSEY)--
TRANSPORTATION BUILDINGS--ALLIED
JUNCTION
All aboard at Allied Junction: a
    public-private partnership spurs
    the planning of the New Jersey
    transit link / Bruce Ross.
    New transportation hub planned for
    northern New Jersey. Commercial
    complex and transfer station
    architects: Brennan Beer Gorman
    Architects.
    MASS TRANSIT 1990 Apr., v.17,
    no.4, p.22-23, dwg.

UNITED STATES--SHARON (CONNECTICUT)--
HOUSES--HOUSE WITH TWO STUDIOS
Turner Brooks: [three houses and
drawings].
    Contents: House with two studios,
    Sharon, Conn.,-- Fuisz house,
    Nazareth, Pa.,--Sheldon house,
    Shelburne, Vermont. Architect:
    Turner Brooks, with Greg Clawson.
    Text in Japanese and English.
    GA HOUSES 1990 July, no.29,
    p.148-159,

UNITED STATES--SHELBURNE (VERMONT)--
HOUSES--SHELDON HOUSE
Turner Brooks: [three houses and
drawings].
    Contents: House with two studios,
    Sharon, Conn.,-- Fuisz house,
    Nazareth, Pa.,--Sheldon house,
    Shelburne, Vermont. Architect:
    Turner Brooks, with Greg Clawson.
    Text in Japanese and English.
    GA HOUSES 1990 July, no.29,
    p.148-159,

UNITED STATES--SHELBY COUNTY
(ALABAMA)--CITY PLANNING
The trials of Connie Cooper / Nancy
    Wilstach, Kent Faulk, Lou Ann Ray.
    American Planning Assn.
    president-elect and her practice
    in Shelby Co., Ala.
    PLANNING 1990 Nov., v.56, no.11,
    p.12-14, map, port.

UNITED STATES--SHELTER ISLAND (NEW
YORK)--STUDIOS--PEDERSEN HOUSE
Formal axis in weekend clothes /
    Mark Alden Branch.
    Features architect William
    Pedersen's renovated 80-year-old
    weekend home and studio on Shelter
    Island, NY.
    PROGRESSIVE ARCHITECTURE 1990
    Nov., v.71, no.12, p.86-89,
    photos., plans, secn., site plan.

UNITED STATES--SHELTER ISLAND (NEW
YORK)--WEEKEND HOUSES--ARCHITECTS'--
ALTERATIONS AND ADDITIONS--PEDERSEN
HOUSE
Formal axis in weekend clothes /
    Mark Alden Branch.
    Features architect William
    Pedersen's renovated 80-year-old
    weekend home and studio on Shelter
    Island, NY.
    PROGRESSIVE ARCHITECTURE 1990
    Nov., v.71, no.12, p.86-89,
    photos., plans, secn., site plan.

UNITED STATES--SHENANDOAH (IOWA)--
CITIES AND TOWNS
The value (s) of the small town.
    Shenandoah, Iowa / Lynn Spears.
    IOWA ARCHITECT 1990 Winter, v.39,
    no.4, p.26-27, photos.

UNITED STATES--SHERBURNE (NEW YORK)--
CITY PLANNING--CITIZEN PARTICIPATION
Main Street revitalization: a
    success story / Joyce Nazzitto
    Steward.
    PLANNING NEWS 1990 July-Aug.,
    v.54, no.4, p.3-4,

UNITED STATES--SHERBURNE (NEW YORK)--
MAIN STREETS--CONSERVATION AND
RESTORATION
Main Street revitalization: a
    success story / Joyce Nazzitto
    Steward.
    PLANNING NEWS 1990 July-Aug.,
    v.54, no.4, p.3-4,

UNITED STATES--SHERBURNE (NEW YORK)--
VILLAGES--CONSERVATION AND
RESTORATION
Main Street revitalization: a
    success story / Joyce Nazzitto
    Steward.
    PLANNING NEWS 1990 July-Aug.,
    v.54, no.4, p.3-4,

UNITED STATES--SHERIDAN (OREGON)--
PRISONS--FEDERAL CORRECTIONAL
INSTITUTION
  Frontier justice redefined: Federal
  Correctional Institution,
  Sheridan, Oregon.
  Architects: Zimmer Gunsul Frasca
  Partnership.
  ARCHITECTURAL RECORD 1990 Sept.,
  v.178, no.10, p.142-145,
  axonometric views, photos., plans,
  secns., site plan.

UNITED STATES--SHOREVIEW (MINNESOTA)--
HOUSES--20TH CENTURY--ALTERATIONS
AND ADDITIONS--LAW HOUSE
  Rethinking the ranch: a 1950s tract
  home gets its priorities straight.
  Law house, Shoreview. Architect:
  Kelly Davis, of McGuire Engler
  Davis Architects.
  ARCHITECTURE MINNESOTA 1990
  May-June, v.16, no.3, p.50-53,
  photos.

UNITED STATES--SHORT HILLS (NEW
JERSEY)--STORES--CLOTHING--INTERIOR
DESIGN--BARNEYS NEW YORK
  Shop right / Karin Tetlow.
  The interiors of four Barneys New
  York stores located in suburban
  malls. Architects: Rosenblum Harb
  Architects.
  INTERIORS 1990 July, v.149, no.12,
  p.82-89, photos., plans.

UNITED STATES--SHOWROOMS--DU PONT
RESOURCE CENTER
  Du Pont Resource Center / Monica
  Geran.
  Multi-media showroom,
  "communications complex." Interior
  designers: Eva Maddox Associates.
  INTERIOR DESIGN 1990 Nov., v.61,
  no.15, p.144-[147], photos., plan.

UNITED STATES--SILICON VALLEY
(CALIFORNIA)--INDUSTRIAL PARKS
  Vingt ans de gestation, trente de
  maturite en Californie: la genese
  de la Silicon Valley / Yann
  Couvidat.
  The development of industrial and
  research parks in California's
  Silicon Valley. French, English,
  German and Spanish summaries,
  p.[123]-126.
  LES ANNALES DE LA RECHERCHE
  URBAINE 1990 Mar.-Apr., no.46,
  p.[31]-38, photos., refs.

UNITED STATES--SILICON VALLEY
(CALIFORNIA)--RESEARCH PARKS
  Vingt ans de gestation, trente de
  maturite en Californie: la genese
  de la Silicon Valley / Yann
  Couvidat.
  The development of industrial and
  research parks in California's
  Silicon Valley. French, English,
  German and Spanish summaries,
  p.[123]-126.
  LES ANNALES DE LA RECHERCHE
  URBAINE 1990 Mar.-Apr., no.46,
  p.[31]-38, photos., refs.

UNITED STATES--SILOS
  Turning grain elevators into
  prisons?
  Proposal by The Eggers Group (TEG)
  for additional prison space in New
  York State, with applications
  elsewhere.
  URBAN LAND 1990 Jan., v.49, no.1,
  p.28, secn.

UNITED STATES--SILVER PLUME
(COLORADO)--MINING TOWNS
  Looking for the mother lode: hard
  lessons learned by the NPS /
  Ronald W. Johnson, John C. Paige.
  Describes controversy over a
  National Park Service study for a
  new National Historic Landmark in
  Georgetown and Silver Plume,
  Colo., 50 miles west of Denver.
  CRM BULLETIN: A NATIONAL PARK
  SERVICE TECHNICAL BULLETIN 1990,
  v.13, no.4, p.18-20.

UNITED STATES--SIMSBURY
(CONNECTICUT)--CENTERS FOR THE
PERFORMING ARTS--WESTMINSTER
SCHOOL--CENTENNIAL PERFORMING ARTS
CENTER
  Building Types Study 682: Campus
  buildings: Extracurricular
  education / Grace Anderson.
  Four recently-completed buildings:
  Salomon Center for Teaching, Brown
  Univ. (Goody, Clancy & Assoc.);
  Psychology Building, Vanderbilt
  Univ. (Stubbins Assoc.);
  Centennial Performing Arts Center,
  Westminster School, Simsbury Conn.
  (Graham Gund Architects); and
  Price Center, Univ. of Calif. at
  San Diego (Kaplan/McLaughlin/Diaz
  Architects).
  ARCHITECTURAL RECORD 1990 Aug.,
  v.178, no.9, p.83-[95], elevs.,
  photos., plans, secns., site
  plans.

UNITED STATES--SIMSBURY
(CONNECTICUT)--SCHOOLS--SECONDARY--
WESTMINSTER SCHOOL
  Building Types Study 682: Campus
  buildings: Extracurricular
  education / Grace Anderson.
  Four recently-completed buildings:
  Salomon Center for Teaching, Brown
  Univ. (Goody, Clancy & Assoc.);
  Psychology Building, Vanderbilt
  Univ. (Stubbins Assoc.);
  Centennial Performing Arts Center,
  Westminster School, Simsbury Conn.
  (Graham Gund Architects); and
  Price Center, Univ. of Calif. at
  San Diego (Kaplan/McLaughlin/Diaz
  Architects).
  ARCHITECTURAL RECORD 1990 Aug.,
  v.178, no.9, p.83-[95], elevs.,
  photos., plans, secns., site
  plans.

UNITED STATES--SKIDAWAY ISLAND
(GEORGIA)--HOUSES--20TH CENTURY--
MOORE HOUSE
  Halcyon views: sparkling style for
  an island home.
  Moore house, Skidaway Island, Ga.
  Architect: Harry A. MacEwen;
  interior designer: Joci Firth.
  SOUTHERN ACCENTS 1989 July-Aug.,
  v.12, no.4, p.72-81, photos.

UNITED STATES--SMITHFIELD (VIRGINIA)--
HOUSES--COLONIAL--MARCH HOUSE
  Virginia belle, [March house,
  Smithfield, Va.].
  Brick house built 1809 and
  recently restored. Restoration
  consultant: Hugh Weaver.
  COLONIAL HOMES 1990 June, v.16,
  no.3, p.68-[75],146,150, photos.

UNITED STATES--SOMERS (NEW YORK)--
CORPORATE OFFICE BUILDINGS--INTERIOR
DESIGN--PEPSI-COLA WORLDWIDE
BEVERAGES
  Pepsi's new generation / Karin
  Tetlow.
  Interiors of Pepsi-Cola Worldwide
  Beverages headquarters, Somers,
  N.Y. Interior designers: Rosen
  Perry Preston.
  INTERIORS 1990 Mar., v.149, no.8,
  p.102-[109], photos., plan.

UNITED STATES--SONOMA (CALIFORNIA)--
HOUSES--FLAX HOUSE
  Pueblo for two / Kate Simonne.
  Sonoma, Calif., house resembles
  adobe village. Architect: Don
  Sandy of Sandy & Babcock;
  landscape architects: Garden
  Design.
  HOUSE BEAUTIFUL 1990 May, v.132,
  no.5, p.70-[77], dets., ports.,
  photos., plan.

UNITED STATES--SONOMA COUNTY
(CALIFORNIA)--HOUSES
  Richard Hedman and Andrew Jaszewski:
  Palladian forms defined by
  corrugated metal in a Sonoma
  County villa.
  "Contemporary Palladian" home.
  ARCHITECTURAL DIGEST 1990 Sept.,
  v.47, no.10, p.[92-93], port.,
  photos.

UNITED STATES--SOUTH CAROLINA--
GARDENS--MAGNOLIA PLANTATION
  Gardens: Magnolia Plantation / James
  S. Wamsley.
  Located along the banks of the
  Ashley River near Charleston, the
  garden dates back to the 1840s and
  has been owned by the Hastie
  family since 1680.
  ARCHITECTURAL DIGEST 1990 May,
  v.47, no.5, p.244-249,282, photos.

UNITED STATES--SOUTH CAROLINA--LOG
CABINS--INTERIOR DESIGN--KEY HOUSE
  Blue Ridge roots ... a designer's
  South Carolina cabin / Wendy
  Mallinson.
  Bill Key's retreat.
  SOUTHERN ACCENTS 1990 Sept., v.13,
  no.7, p.110-114, photos.

UNITED STATES--SOUTH CAROLINA--WEEKEND
HOUSES--INTERIOR DESIGN--KEY HOUSE
  Blue Ridge roots ... a designer's
  South Carolina cabin / Wendy
  Mallinson.
  Bill Key's retreat.
  SOUTHERN ACCENTS 1990 Sept., v.13,
  no.7, p.110-114, photos.

UNITED STATES--SOUTH DARTMOUTH
(MASSACHUSETTS)--HOUSES--
ARCHITECTS'--DEAN HOUSE
Great stories.
Feature section on ca.15 recent
American houses, including ones by
architects Andy Dean, in S.
Dartmouth, Mass.; Peter Anders, in
Jersey City, N.J.; Chip Arena, in
Chestertown, Md.; Cory Buckner and
Nicholas Roberts, in Malibu,
Calif.; Robby Reid, in Tempe,
Ariz.
METROPOLITAN HOME 1990 Feb., v.22,
no.2, p.125-166, photos., ports.

UNITED STATES--SOUTHAMPTON (NEW
YORK)--HOUSES
American revolutionary / Michael
McDonough.
House designed by the architect
author for site near Shinnecock
Bay, Southampton, N.Y.
METROPOLITAN HOME 1990 May, v.22,
no.5, p.103-[109],150, dets.,
photos.
Smith-Miller & Hawkinson [houses].
Contents: House and studio
building, South Hampton, New York,
design: 1987-88 -- Beekman Place
townhouse triplex, New York, N.Y.,
design: 1988-89. Architects:
Smith-Miller Hawkinson Architects.
Text in Japanese and English.
GA HOUSES 1990 Mar., no.28,
p.92-93, axonometric views,.
model, plans.

UNITED STATES--SOUTHAMPTON (NEW
YORK)--HOUSES--INTERIOR DESIGN--SWID
HOUSE
Country's new light ... a
Southampton house decorated by
Stephen Sills / Charles Gandee.
House of Nan Swid.
HOUSE & GARDEN 1990 June, v.162,
no.6, p.[90-99],172, port.,
photos.

UNITED STATES--SOUTHAMPTON (NEW
YORK)--SUMMER HOUSES--INTERIOR
DESIGN--SALOMON HOUSE
Beachside fantasy / Glenn Harrell.
Summer house of New York decorator
David Salomon in Southampton, N.Y.
HOUSE BEAUTIFUL 1990 July, v.132,
no.7, p.[44]-49, port., photos.

UNITED STATES--SOUTHAMPTON (NEW
YORK)--WEEKEND HOUSES--INTERIOR
DESIGN--HACKETT HOUSE
Southampton character study:
updating a historic summer estate
on Long Island / John Taylor.
Interiors of Brue and Joann
Hackett's renovated ca. 1913
weekend house. Interior designer:
Mary Meehan. Renavation architect:
Richard Sawicki. Landscape
architect: Elise DeBoeck Deans.
ARCHITECTURAL DIGEST 1990 May,
v.47, no.5, p.[178-185], port.,
photos.

UNITED STATES--SOUTHBURY
(CONNECTICUT)--CORPORATE OFFICE
BUILDINGS--IBM
Places to work: IBM Corporation
headquarters, staff offices and
conference center, Southbury,
Connecticut.
Architects: Benjamin Thompson &
Associates. Text in Japanese and
English.
PROCESS: ARCHITECTURE 1990 June,
no.89, p.90-92,

UNITED STATES--SOUTHERN STATES--
BATTLEFIELDS--19TH CENTURY--
CONSERVATION AND RESTORATION
Protecting battlefields: American
Battlefield Protection Program.
Includes a list of c. 20 priority
Civil War battlefields.
CRM BULLETIN: A NATIONAL PARK
SERVICE TECHNICAL BULLETIN 1990,
v.13, no.5, p.1-2, map, aeriel
photo.

UNITED STATES--SOUTHERN STATES--
REGIONALISM
Down at the crossroads: a regional
design finds a strong new voice /
Robert Ivy.
Regional-style building in the
South.
SOUTHERN ACCENTS 1990 May, v.13,
no.4, p.52-60, photos.

UNITED STATES--SOUTHLAKE (TEXAS)--
OFFICE PARKS--SOLANA (IBM)
I fasti dell'elettronica = The
glorious deeds of electronics
[Westlake/Southlake for IBM,
Solana, Texas].
Architects: Mitchell Giurgola:
Legorreta, Leason Pomeroy Assoc.
ARCHITETTURA: CRONACHE E STORIA
1990 Oct., v.36, no.10(420),
p.724-726, photos., plan, site
plans.
"Solana": Business Park in
Westlake/Southlake, Texas.
Architects: Mitchell Giurgola
Architects: Legorreta Arquitectos;
Leason Pomeroy. Includes English
summary.
BAUMEISTER 1990 Apr., v.87, no.4,
p.32-41, photos., plans, site
plans.

UNITED STATES--SOUTHPORT (NEW YORK)--
HOUSES--EISENBERG HOUSE
Eisenberg residence, Hampton Bays,
Long Island.
Architects: Tod Williams, Billie
Tsien & Associates. Spanish,
English text.
QUADERNS D'ARQUITECTURA I
URBANISME 1990 Jan.-Feb.-Mar.,
no.184, p.66-[67], photos., plan,
secn.

UNITED STATES--SOUTHWEST--KIVAS--
NATIVE AMERICAN
Large-scale integrative facilities
in tribal societies:
cross-cultural and southwestern
U.S. examples / Michael A. Adler,
Richard H. Wilshusen.
Includes discussion of the kiva in
the U.S. Southwest.
WORLD ARCHAEOLOGY 1990 Oct., v.22,
no.2, p.133-146, graph, elev.,
map, plan, table, biblio.

UNITED STATES--SOUTHWEST--PIT
DWELLINGS--ANASAZI
Pit structure abandonment in the
Four Corners region of the
American Southwest: late
Basketmaker III and Pueblo I
periods / Catherine M. Cameron.
An examination of data from 88
Anasazi pit structures dating from
ca. 500 to 900 A.C.
JOURNAL OF FIELD ARCHAEOLOGY 1990
Spring, v.17, no.1, p.27-37, dwg.,
map, tables, biblio.

UNITED STATES--SPOKANE (WASHINGTON)--
MOVIE THEATERS
The Spokane spectacle [theaters
constructed in Spokane,
Washington, 1883-1983] / George L.
Lufkin.
MARQUEE 1990, v.22, no.1, cover,
p.3-16, photos.

UNITED STATES--SPOKANE (WASHINGTON)--
THEATERS
The Spokane spectacle [theaters
constructed in Spokane,
Washington, 1883-1983] / George L.
Lufkin.
MARQUEE 1990, v.22, no.1, cover,
p.3-16, photos.

UNITED STATES--SPRINGFIELD
(ILLINOIS)--EXCAVATIONS
(ARCHAEOLOGY)--LINCOLN HOME
Archaeology's contribution to
Lincoln Home restoration / Vergil
E. Noble.
Excavations at the Springfield
Site, 1987-1988.
HISTORIC ILLINOIS 1989 Aug., v.12,
no.2, p.4-7, photos.

UNITED STATES--SPRINGFIELD
(ILLINOIS)--HISTORIC HOUSE MUSEUMS--
LINCOLN HOME
Archaeology's contribution to
Lincoln Home restoration / Vergil
E. Noble.
Excavations at the Springfield
Site, 1987-1988.
HISTORIC ILLINOIS 1989 Aug., v.12,
no.2, p.4-7, photos.

UNITED STATES--SPRINGFIELD
(ILLINOIS)--HISTORIC SITES--
DANA-THOMAS HOUSE
A Wright restoration: the
Dana-Thomas House reopens / Dennis
McFadden.
Completed in 1904 and now a State
Historic Site, Springfield, Ill.
INLAND ARCHITECT 1990 Sept.-Oct.,
v.34, no.5, p.[31-39], dwgs.,
photos., plan, secn.

UNITED STATES--SPRINGFIELD
(ILLINOIS)--HOUSES--CONSERVATION AND
RESTORATION--DANA-THOMAS HOUSE
A Wright restoration: the
Dana-Thomas House reopens / Dennis
McFadden.
Completed in 1904 and now a State
Historic Site, Springfield, Ill.
INLAND ARCHITECT 1990 Sept.-Oct.,
v.34, no.5, p.[31-39], dwgs.,
photos., plan, secn.

UNITED STATES--SPRINGFIELD
(MISSOURI)--HOUSES--CONSERVATION AND
RESTORATION--DANA-THOMAS HOUSE
  Dana-Thomas House reopens / David
    Blanchette.
    1904 house in Springfield, Ill.
    has been restored to its 1910
    appearance and is open to the
    public. Architect: Frank Lloyd
    Wright. Restoration architects:
    Hasbrouck Peterson Associates.
    HISTORIC ILLINOIS 1990 Oct., v.13,
    no.3, p.14,

UNITED STATES--SPRINGS (NEW YORK)--
FORMAL GARDENS--LIEBER GARDEN
  Planting between the lines: Gus and
    Judith Lieber's garden / Patricia
    Thorpe.
    In Springs, Long Island, N.Y.
    HOUSE & GARDEN 1990 Aug., v.162,
    no.8, p.122-[127],151, ports.,
    photos.

UNITED STATES--SPRINGS (NEW YORK)--
PARTERRES--LIEBER GARDEN
  Planting between the lines: Gus and
    Judith Lieber's garden / Patricia
    Thorpe.
    In Springs, Long Island, N.Y.
    HOUSE & GARDEN 1990 Aug., v.162,
    no.8, p.122-[127],151, ports.,
    photos.

UNITED STATES--ST. JOHN THE BAPTIST
PARISH (LOUISIANA)--PLANTATION
HOUSES--WHITNEY PLANTATION
  Plastics: new crop at landmark
    plantation? [Whitney Plantation,
    St. John the Baptist Parish,
    Wallace, La.] / Thomas W. Sweeney.
    "One of Louisiana's most important
    early plantation houses may be
    purchased by a Taiwanese plastics
    company for the site of proposed
    rayon fiber plant..."
    PRESERVATION NEWS 1990 Apr., v.30,
    no.4, p.1,23, photos.

UNITED STATES--STENCIL WORK
  Stencil deigns for a room with
    personality [Decorating a teen's
    room, Part II].
    VICTORIAN HOMES 1990 Summer, v.9,
    no.3, p.58-63,78-79, diagrs.,
    photos.

UNITED STATES--STILLWATER
(MINNESOTA)--ARTISTS' STUDIOS--
MACKENZIE STUDIO
  A place of one's own [pottery
    workshop].
    Showroom of potter Warren
    MacKenzie in Stillwater, Minn.
    Architect: Michael McGuire.
    ARCHITECTURE MINNESOTA 1990
    Jan.-Feb., v.16, no.1, p.19,
    port., photo.

UNITED STATES--STINSON BEACH
(CALIFORNIA)--BEACH HOUSES--MCDONALD
HOUSE
  A different wavelength: the curves
    of a California beach house
    express architect Stanley
    Saitowitz's sense of place / Pilar
    Viladas.
    The McDonald house, Stinson Beach.
    HOUSE & GARDEN 1990 Aug., v.162,
    no.8, p.[108]-111, photos.

UNITED STATES--STINSON BEACH
(CALIFORNIA)--BEACH HOUSES--MCDONALD
HOUSE (CONTINUED)
  McDonald residence, Stinson Beach,
    California, 1987-88.
    Architect: Stanley Saitowitz.
    Text in Japanese and English.
    GA HOUSES 1990 July, no.29,
    p.[120]-125, elevs., photos.,
    plan.
  The perfect wave: McDonald House,
    Stinson Beach, California / Donald
    J. Canty.
    Architect: The Stanley Saitowitz
    Office.
    ARCHITECTURAL RECORD 1990
    Mid-Apr., v.178, no.5, p.[52]-57,
    elev., photos., plan.
  Stanley Saitowitz.
    Features two projects: Di Napoli,
    Los Gatos, Calif. and McDonald
    beach house, Stinson Beach, Calif.
    English summary.
    ARCHITECTURE D'AUJOURD'HUI 1990
    Oct., no.271, p.168-170,
    axonometric views, photos., site
    plan.

UNITED STATES--STOCKBRIDGE
(MASSACHUSETTS)--ARCHITECTURE
  Berkshire byway: Stockbridge, Mass.
    Four articles: Berkshire byway;
    Red Lion Inn (1773); Mission House
    (1739); and Sculptor's sanctuary
    (home of Daniel Chester French,
    b.1898-1900). Architect of D.C.
    French house: Henry Bacon.
    COLONIAL HOMES 1990 Feb., v.16,
    no.1, p.[76]-107,136,138,140,
    dwgs., ports., photos.

UNITED STATES--STOCKBRIDGE
(MASSACHUSETTS)--ARTISTS' STUDIOS--
CHESTERWOOD (DANIEL CHESTER FRENCH
STUDIO)
  Berkshire byway: Stockbridge, Mass.
    Four articles: Berkshire byway;
    Red Lion Inn (1773); Mission House
    (1739); and Sculptor's sanctuary
    (home of Daniel Chester French,
    b.1898-1900). Architect of D.C.
    French house: Henry Bacon.
    COLONIAL HOMES 1990 Feb., v.16,
    no.1, p.[76]-107,136,138,140,
    dwgs., ports., photos.

UNITED STATES--STOCKBRIDGE
(MASSACHUSETTS)--HISTORIC
BUILDINGS--18TH CENTURY--MISSION
HOUSE
  Berkshire byway: Stockbridge, Mass.
    Four articles: Berkshire byway;
    Red Lion Inn (1773); Mission House
    (1739); and Sculptor's sanctuary
    (home of Daniel Chester French,
    b.1898-1900). Architect of D.C.
    French house: Henry Bacon.
    COLONIAL HOMES 1990 Feb., v.16,
    no.1, p.[76]-107,136,138,140,
    dwgs., ports., photos.

UNITED STATES--STOCKBRIDGE
(MASSACHUSETTS)--HOUSES--CHESTERWOOD
(DANIEL CHESTER FRENCH HOUSE)
  Berkshire byway: Stockbridge, Mass.
    Four articles: Berkshire byway;
    Red Lion Inn (1773); Mission House
    (1739); and Sculptor's sanctuary
    (home of Daniel Chester French,
    b.1898-1900). Architect of D.C.
    French house: Henry Bacon.
    COLONIAL HOMES 1990 Feb., v.16,
    (Continued next column)

UNITED STATES--STOCKBRIDGE
(MASSACHUSETTS)--HOUSES--CHESTERWOOD
(DANIEL CHESTER FRENCH HOUSE)
(CONTINUED)
  Berkshire byway:...(CONTINUED)
    no.1, p.[76]-107,136,138,140,
    dwgs., ports., photos.
  Life-size canvases / Eleanor Berman.
    Houses of painters and sculptors:
    Daniel Chester French (designed
    with architect Henry Bacon);
    Augustus Saint-Gaudens; Frida
    Kahlo; Evelyn and Frederic
    Bartlett.
    HOUSE BEAUTIFUL 1990 July, v.132,
    no.7, p.30,32, photos.

UNITED STATES--STOCKBRIDGE
(MASSACHUSETTS)--INNS--18TH
CENTURY--RED LION INN
  Berkshire byway: Stockbridge, Mass.
    Four articles: Berkshire byway;
    Red Lion Inn (1773); Mission House
    (1739); and Sculptor's sanctuary
    (home of Daniel Chester French,
    b.1898-1900). Architect of D.C.
    French house: Henry Bacon.
    COLONIAL HOMES 1990 Feb., v.16,
    no.1, p.[76]-107,136,138,140,
    dwgs., ports., photos.

UNITED STATES--STOCKBRIDGE
(MASSACHUSETTS)--VILLAGES
  Berkshire byway: Stockbridge, Mass.
    Four articles: Berkshire byway;
    Red Lion Inn (1773); Mission House
    (1739); and Sculptor's sanctuary
    (home of Daniel Chester French,
    b.1898-1900). Architect of D.C.
    French house: Henry Bacon.
    COLONIAL HOMES 1990 Feb., v.16,
    no.1, p.[76]-107,136,138,140,
    dwgs., ports., photos.

UNITED STATES--STOCKHOLM (WISCONSIN)--
HOUSES--ARCHITECTS'--WIND WHISTLE
(TOTH-STAGEBERG HOUSE)
  Crayon-colored dream house / Susan
    Allen Toth.
    Wisconsin weekend house designed
    by James Stageberg.
    HOUSE BEAUTIFUL 1990 Apr., v.132,
    no.4, p.[94]-95,121, photos.,
    secn.

UNITED STATES--STOCKHOLM (WISCONSIN)--
WEEKEND HOUSES--WIND WHISTLE
(TOTH-STAGEBERG HOUSE)
  Crayon-colored dream house / Susan
    Allen Toth.
    Wisconsin weekend house designed
    by James Stageberg.
    HOUSE BEAUTIFUL 1990 Apr., v.132,
    no.4, p.[94]-95,121, photos.,
    secn.

UNITED STATES--STOCKPORT (NEW YORK)--
CHURCHES--GOTHIC REVIVAL--SAINT JOHN
THE EVANGELIST
  Documentation projects; part 1:
    Photography / Neal A. Vogel,
    Christopher Jenks.
    Techniques for photo-documentation
    of historic buildings. Examples
    include the Church of St. John the
    Evangelist, Stockport, N.Y.
    COMMON BOND 1990 Fall, v.6, no.4,
    p.4-7, photos.

UNITED STATES--STOCKTON (NEW JERSEY)--
INNS--18TH CENTURY--STOCKTON INN
There's a small hotel [Stockton, N.J.].
   The Stockton Inn on the Delaware River, built 1710.
   COLONIAL HOMES 1990 Feb., v.16, no.1, p.122-130,132, ill., photos.

UNITED STATES--STONINGTON (CONNECTICUT)--COTTAGES--INTERIOR DESIGN--GEORGINA FAIRHOLME COTTAGE
Cottage industry / Allison Percival, Glenn Harrell.
   Connecticut country home of interior designer Georgina Fairholme.
   HOUSE BEAUTIFUL 1990 Nov., v.132, no.11, p.[108]-[113], port., photos.

UNITED STATES--STONY CREEK (CONNECTICUT)--HOUSES--IZENOUR HOUSE
Special feature: Venturi Scott Brown and Associates.
   Contents: Brief history-- Works: Primate Center, Philadelphia Zoological Garden.-- Lewis Thomas Laboratory for Molecular Biology, Princeton University, 1986.-- Malcolm S. Forbes Jr. College, Princeton University, 1984.-- Gordon Wu Hall, Princeton University, 1983.-- Venturi house, Philadelphia, 1974-present.-- Izenour house, Stony Creek, Conn., 1984.-- House in New Castle County, Delaware, 1983.-- Coxe-Hayden house, Block Island, R.I., 1981.-- Tarble Student Center, Swarthmore College, 1985.-- Tree House, Philadelphia Zoo, 1985.-- Welcome Park, Philadelphia, 1982.-- Decorative designs.-- Essay: "Body language" and artifice: on some recent designs by Venturi Scott Brown and Associates. Text in Japanese and English.
   ARCHITECTURE AND URBANISM 1990 June, no.6(237), p.[39]-150, ports., elevs., photos., plans, secns., site plans.

UNITED STATES--STORAGE TANKS--UNDERGROUND--ENVIRONMENTAL ASPECTS
Underground storage tanks: Subtitle 1 responsibilities / Edward Cichon.
   AMERICAN CITY & COUNTY 1990 June, v.105, no.6, p.46,48,50, photo.

UNITED STATES--STORAGE TANKS--UNDERGROUND--LAW AND LEGISLATION
Beware of underground storage tanks / Joseph B. Pereles.
   DEVELOPMENT 1990 May-June, v.21, no.3, p.10-12, port., photos.
Underground storage tanks: Subtitle 1 responsibilities / Edward Cichon.
   AMERICAN CITY & COUNTY 1990 June, v.105, no.6, p.46,48,50, photo.

UNITED STATES--STORRS (CONNECTICUT)--UNIVERSITIES AND COLLEGES--BUILDINGS--ALUMNI HOUSE
Across the grain: a university building offers lessons in detailing wood / Douglas E. Gordon, M. Stephanie Stubbs.
   Alumni house, Univ. of Conn. Architects: Shope Reno Wharton Associates.
   ARCHITECTURE: THE AIA JOURNAL 1990 Apr., v.79, no.4, p.95-97, dets., photos., secn.

UNITED STATES--STOVES--19TH CENTURY
"We have got a very good cooking stove"; advertising, design, and consumer response to the cookstove, 1815-1880 / Priscilla J. Brewer.
   In the U.S.
   WINTERTHUR PORTFOLIO 1990 Spring, v.25, no.1, p.[35]-54, ill., photos., engrs., refs.

UNITED STATES--STRATTON MOUNTAIN (VERMONT)--HOUSES--CARWILL HOUSE
Carwill house, Stratton Mountain, Vermont, 1990.
   Architects: Kohn Pedersen Fox Associates. Clients: Mr. & Mrs. William Stutt. Text Japanese and English.
   PROCESS: ARCHITECTURE 1989 Nov., no.86, p.134-136, axonometric view, elevs., plans, secns., site plan.

UNITED STATES--STREETS--RESEARCH
Patterns of behavior in urban public spaces / Jack L. Nasas, A. Rengin Yurdakul.
   Includes abstract.
   JOURNAL OF ARCHITECTURAL AND PLANNING RESEARCH 1990 Spring, v.7, no.1, p.71-85, charts, diagrs., photos, biblio.

UNITED STATES--STREETS--SOCIOLOGICAL ASPECTS
Taking it to the streets: expert prescriptions for healthy urban arteries / Jane Jacobs.
   Includes "The sensory street", an excerpt from City: Rediscovering the Center, by William Whyte.
   CARTOUCHE 1990 Winter, v.19, p.14-16,

UNITED STATES--SUBURBS
Breaking the code: urban design portfolio / Beth Dunlop.
   Small-town alternatives to suburban sprawl, as offered by Andres Duany and Elizabeth Plater-Zyberk.
   ARCHITECTURE: THE AIA JOURNAL 1990 Apr., v.79, no.4, p.80-83, ill., elev., plans, site plans.
Repent, ye sinners, repent / Ruth Eckdish Knack.
   PLANNING 1989 Aug., v.55, no.8, p.4-8, diagr., port., photos., plans.

UNITED STATES--SUBURBS--GROWTH
Beyond gridlock: looking for the new suburban city / Joseph. E. Brown, Michael E. Hickok.
   Problems of definition for "suburban urbanization", and the transportation issues involved.
(Continued next column)

UNITED STATES--SUBURBS--GROWTH
(CONTINUED)
Beyond gridlock:...(CONTINUED)
   DEVELOPMENT 1990 July-Aug., v.21, no.4, p.17-20, ill., dwgs., photos.
Pumping up suburban downtowns / Philip Langdon.
   Examples in Reston, Va., Miami Lakes, Fla., and Buffalo Grove, Ill.
   PLANNING 1990 July, v.56, no.7, p.22-28, dwg., model, map, photos., plans, aerial photo.

UNITED STATES--SUN VALLEY (IDAHO)--VACATION HOUSES
Bart Prince Architect [houses].
   Contents: Vacation house, Sun Valley, Ida., design: 1988-89 -- Barbi Benton George Gradow family residence, Aspen, Colo., design: 1989. Text in Japanese and English.
   GA HOUSES 1990 Mar., no.28, p.128-133, elevs., models, plans, secns.

UNITED STATES--SUNLAND PARK (NEW MEXICO)--SCHOOLS--SECONDARY--CAPITAL HIGH SCHOOL
Una scuola nel deserto del Nuovo Messico = Riverside School in Sunland Park, New Mexico / Silvano Stucchi.
   Architects: Perkins & Will. Includes English translation; French, German, and Spanish summaries, p.4.
   L'INDUSTRIA DELLE COSTRUZIONI 1990 Jan., v.24, no.219, p.32-37,cover, axonometric views, dwgs., elev., photos., plans, site plan.

UNITED STATES--SUNNYVALE (CALIFORNIA)--OFFICE BUILDINGS--LOCKHEED BUILDING 157
Successfully daylighting a large commercial building: a case study of Lockheed Building 157 / Charles c. Benton, Marc Fountain.
   Architects: Leo A. Daly Co. Includes recommended reading.
   PROGRESSIVE ARCHITECTURE 1990 Nov., v.71, no.12, p.119-121, det., graphs, photo., plan, secns., biblios.

UNITED STATES--SUNSET BEACH (NORTH CAROLINA)--BRIDGES
A bridge to the past: swimming against the tide of development at Sunset Beach [N.C.] / Lynn Nesmith.
   A barrier island community's effort to control overbuilding.
   SOUTHERN ACCENTS 1990 Oct., v.13, no.8, p.50-[56], photos.

UNITED STATES--SUNSET BEACH (NORTH CAROLINA)--CONSERVATION OF NATURAL RESOURCES
A bridge to the past: swimming against the tide of development at Sunset Beach [N.C.] / Lynn Nesmith.
   A barrier island community's effort to control overbuilding.
   SOUTHERN ACCENTS 1990 Oct., v.13, no.8, p.50-[56], photos.

UNITED STATES--SUNSET BEACH (NORTH
CAROLINA)--REAL ESTATE DEVELOPMENT
A bridge to the past: swimming
against the tide of development at
Sunset Beach [N.C.] / Lynn
Nesmith.
A barrier island community's
effort to control overbuilding.
SOUTHERN ACCENTS 1990 Oct., v.13,
no.8, p.50-[56], photos.

UNITED STATES--SUTTER COUNTY
(CALIFORNIA)--HOUSES--19TH CENTURY--
INTERIOR DESIGN--WINSHIP HOUSE
Mrs. Winship's house in Sutter
County, California / Maureen
Gilmer.
Built in the 1880s and expanded in
the 1950s.
VICTORIAN HOMES 1990 Spring, v.9,
no.2, p.70-72, dwg., photos.

UNITED STATES--SWARTHMORE
(PENNSYLVANIA)--STUDENT UNIONS--
SWARTHMORE COLLEGE--TARBLE STUDENT
CENTER
Special feature: Venturi Scott Brown
and Associates.
Contents: Brief history-- Works:
Primate Center, Philadelphia
Zoological Garden.-- Lewis Thomas
Laboratory for Molecular Biology,
Princeton University, 1986.--
Malcolm S. Forbes Jr. College,
Princeton University, 1984.--
Gordon Wu Hall, Princeton
University, 1983.-- Venturi house,
Philadelphia, 1974-present.--
Izenour house, Stony Creek, Conn.,
1984.-- House in New Castle
County, Delaware, 1983.--
Coxe-Hayden house, Block Island,
R.I., 1981.-- Tarble Student
Center, Swarthmore College,
1985.-- Tree House, Philadelphia
Zoo, 1985.-- Welcome Park,
Philadelphia, 1982.-- Decorative
designs.-- Essay: "Body language"
and artifice: on some recent
designs by Venturi Scott Brown and
Associates. Text in Japanese and
English.
ARCHITECTURE AND URBANISM 1990
June, no.6(237), p.[39]-150,
ports., elevs., photos., plans,
secns., site plans.

UNITED STATES--SWEET GRASS COUNTY
(WYOMING)--RANCH HOUSES--LOG--RAW
DEAL RANCH (MCGUANE HOUSE)
McGuane Country: the novelist stakes
his claim in Sweet Grass County,
Montana / William Hjortsberg.
HOUSE & GARDEN 1990 Mar., v.162,
no.3, p.[136]-141,202, port.,
photos.

UNITED STATES--TACOMA (WASHINGTON)--
CORPORATE OFFICE BUILDINGS--FRANK
RUSSELL WORLD HEADQUARTERS
Mountain magic / Justin Henderson.
Wyatt Stapper Architects draw on
regional motifs for the siting,
structure and spatial organization
of the Frank Russell World
Headquarters, Tacoma, Wash.
INTERIORS 1990 Feb., v.149, no.7,
p.110-113, axonometric view,
photos.

UNITED STATES--TALL BUILDINGS--ROUND
Turning grain elevators into
prisons?
Proposal by The Eggers Group (TEG)
for additional prison space in New
York State, with applications
elsewhere.
URBAN LAND 1990 Jan., v.49, no.1,
p.28, secn.

UNITED STATES--TALLAHASSEE (FLORIDA)--
COMPREHENSIVE PLANS
Down to the wire in Florida / John
Koenig.
Growth management legislation in
Fla.
PLANNING 1990 Oct., v.56, no.10,
p.4-11, port., maps, photos.,
sketch, aerial photo.

UNITED STATES--TAMPA (FLORIDA)--
APARTMENT HOUSES--BAYSHORE ON THE
BOULEVARD
Bayshore on the Boulevard, Tampa,
Fla.
Speculative housing project.
Architect: Josiah R. Baker of
OAD.
TEXAS ARCHITECT 1990 Jan.-Feb.,
v.40, no.1, p.31, axonometric
view, photos.
Discovery: alloggia Tampa, Florida.
Architect: Josiah R. Baker.
ARCHITETTURA; CRONACHE E STORIA
1990 May, v.36, no.5(415),
p.366-367, axonometric view,
photos., plan.

UNITED STATES--TAMPA (FLORIDA)--
BANKS--INTERIOR DESIGN--NCNB
NATIONAL BANK
Banking on proportion: a
mathematical system for NCNB
National Bank / Michael Wagner.
Bank located in Tampa, Fl. was
designed using a mathematical
system based on a series of
logarithms developed by 13th cent.
Italian mathematician Leonardo
Fibonacci. Architect: Harry C.
Wolf. Interior designers:
Associated Space Design.
INTERIORS 1990 Jan., v.149, no.6,
p.136-[137], photos., plan.

UNITED STATES--TAMPA (FLORIDA)--
CORPORATE OFFICE BUILDINGS--ROUND--
NORTH CAROLINA NATIONAL BANK
Completato l'edificio per la NCBN a
Tampa in Florida.
The North Carolina National Bank.
Architect: Harry Wolf.
CASABELLA 1990 Mar., v.54, no.566,
p.33, photos.

UNITED STATES--TAMPA (FLORIDA)--
GRILLES
The how-to's of tree grating / Diana
Kyle.
Functional and decorative tree
grates for maintaining city trees
in Tampa, Fla.
PARKS & RECREATION 1990 Jan.,
v.25, no.1, p.76-82, ill., photos.

UNITED STATES--TAMPA (FLORIDA)--URBAN
FORESTRY
The how-to's of tree grating / Diana
Kyle.
Functional and decorative tree
grates for maintaining city trees
in Tampa, Fla.
PARKS & RECREATION 1990 Jan.,
v.25, no.1, p.76-82, ill., photos.

UNITED STATES--TAPPAN (NEW YORK)--
TAVERNS--COLONIAL--CONSERVATION AND
RESTORATION--OLD '76 HOUSE
In the spirit of '76: Tappan, New
York's Old '76 House is once again
a quiet country tavern / Betsy
Dance.
HISTORIC PRESERVATION 1990
May-June, v.42, no.3, p.52-55,
photos.

UNITED STATES--TARBORO (NORTH
CAROLINA)--CITY PLANNING
Downtown revitalization and historic
preservation in small town
America: a case study of Tarboro,
North Carolina / E. Watson Brown,
Wes Hankins.
CAROLINA PLANNING 1990 Fall, v.16,
no.2, p.50-54, photos., refs.

UNITED STATES--TARBORO (NORTH
CAROLINA)--HISTORIC DISTRICTS--
CONSERVATION AND RESTORATION
Downtown revitalization and historic
preservation in small town
America: a case study of Tarboro,
North Carolina / E. Watson Brown,
Wes Hankins.
CAROLINA PLANNING 1990 Fall, v.16,
no.2, p.50-54, photos., refs.

UNITED STATES--TARBORO (NORTH
CAROLINA)--URBAN RENEWAL
Downtown revitalization and historic
preservation in small town
America: a case study of Tarboro,
North Carolina / E. Watson Brown,
Wes Hankins.
CAROLINA PLANNING 1990 Fall, v.16,
no.2, p.50-54, photos., refs.

UNITED STATES--TARRYTOWN (NEW YORK)--
COUNTRY HOUSES--19TH CENTURY--
SUNNYSIDE (IRVING HOUSE)
Christmas at Sleepy Hollow / Deborah
Barcan.
On decorations at Sunnyside, the
1836 home of Wahington Irving,
near Tarrytown, N.Y.
VICTORIAN HOMES 1990 Holidays,
v.9, no.5, p.[46]-51, photos.

UNITED STATES--TAYLORSTOWN
(VIRGINIA)--FLOUR MILLS--18TH
CENTURY--ALTERATIONS AND ADDITIONS--
BOUCHARD-YECK HOUSE
At home in a 1730 gristmill / Rhoda
Jaffin Murphy.
Home of interior designers Ed
Bouchard and Bud Yeck in converted
Virginia gristmill.
HOUSE BEAUTIFUL 1990 June, v.132,
no.6, p.82-89, photos.

UNITED STATES--TRENTON (NEW JERSEY)--
CITY PLANNING (CONTINUED)
Trenton: recalled to...(CONTINUED)
axonometric views, graph, dwgs.,
map, photos.

UNITED STATES--TRENTON (NEW JERSEY)--
UNIVERSITIES AND COLLEGES--
BUILDINGS--ALTERATIONS AND
ADDITIONS--MERCER COUNTY COMMUNITY
COLLEGE--KERNEY CENTER
Kerney Center, Mercer County
Community College, Trenton, New
Jersey.
Addition to 1968 brick building.
Architects: Clarke & Caton.
ARCHITECTURE NEW JERSEY 1989,
v.25, no.3, p.12, dwg.

UNITED STATES--TRENTON (NEW JERSEY)--
URBAN RENEWAL
Trenton: recalled to life / Nora
Odendahl, Sharon Ayn McHugh,
Robert D. Cerutti.
Includes inset article on the
Capital City Renaissance Plan, by
Sharon Ayn McHugh.
ARCHITECTURE NEW JERSEY 1989,
v.25, no.3, p.13-22, 29,
axonometric views, graph, dwgs.,
map, photos.

UNITED STATES--TRENTON (NEW JERSEY)--
WATERFRONTS
Trenton: recalled to life / Nora
Odendahl, Sharon Ayn McHugh,
Robert D. Cerutti.
Includes inset article on the
Capital City Renaissance Plan, by
Sharon Ayn McHugh.
ARCHITECTURE NEW JERSEY 1989,
v.25, no.3, p.13-22, 29,
axonometric views, graph, dwgs.,
map, photos.

UNITED STATES--TRIPLE-DECKER HOUSES
Rediscovering the three decker house
/ Howard Husock.
Potential of "the common New
England three family houses or
'three deckers" in the search for
more private low- and
moderate-income housing.
THE PUBLIC INTEREST 1990 Winter,
no.98, p.49-60, tables, refs.

UNITED STATES--TROY (MICHIGAN)--OFFICE
BUILDINGS--LIBERTY CENTER
L'ha spezzato un serpente = Split by
a snake [Liberty Center, Troy,
Mich.].
Architects: Rossetti Associates.
ARCHITETTURA: CRONACHE E STORIA
1990 Sept., v.36, no.9(419),
p.635-639, photos., plans, sketch.
A separate piece: Liberty Center,
Troy Michigan / Robert a. Benson.
Pair of 6-storey office buildings.
Architects: Rossetti Associates.
ARCHITECTURE: THE AIA JOURNAL 1990
Feb., v.79, no.2, p.86-[87],
photos, plan.

UNITED STATES--TROY (NEW YORK)--
IRONWORK--ARCHITECTURAL
Ornamental ironwork in Albany and
Troy / Diana S. Waite.
Excerpt from Ornamental ironwork:
two centuries of craftsmanship in
Albany and Troy, New York.
PRESERVATION LEAGUE OF NEW YORK
STATE. NEWSLETTER 1990 Spring,
(Continued next column)

UNITED STATES--TROY (NEW YORK)--
IRONWORK--ARCHITECTURAL
(CONTINUED)
Ornamental ironwork...(CONTINUED)
v.16, no.1 p.4-5, photos.

UNITED STATES--TUCSON (ARIZONA)--
RESIDENTIAL GARDENS--RESEARCH
Modeling residential landscape water
and energy use to evaluate water
conservation policies / E. Gregory
McPherson.
Data derived from computer
simulations using three types of
residential gardens, xeriscapes,
zeroscapes and mesiscapes, in
Phoenix and Tucson.
LANDSCAPE JOURNAL 1990 Fall, v.9,
no.2, p.122-134, photo., plans,
tables, refs.

UNITED STATES--TUCSON (ARIZONA)--WATER
CONSERVATION--RESEARCH
Modeling residential landscape water
and energy use to evaluate water
conservation policies / E. Gregory
McPherson.
Data derived from computer
simulations using three types of
residential gardens, xeriscapes,
zeroscapes and mesiscapes, in
Phoenix and Tucson.
LANDSCAPE JOURNAL 1990 Fall, v.9,
no.2, p.122-134, photo., plans,
tables, refs.

UNITED STATES--TUCSON (ARIZONA)--
XERISCAPES--RESEARCH
Modeling residential landscape water
and energy use to evaluate water
conservation policies / E. Gregory
McPherson.
Data derived from computer
simulations using three types of
residential gardens, xeriscapes,
zeroscapes and mesiscapes, in
Phoenix and Tucson.
LANDSCAPE JOURNAL 1990 Fall, v.9,
no.2, p.122-134, photo., plans,
tables, refs.

UNITED STATES--TUNBRIDGE (VERMONT)--
FARM BUILDINGS
Searching for quality of life / John
Stickney.
A linen business headquarters in
farm buildings, Tunbridge, Vt.
METROPOLITAN HOME 1990 Dec., v.22,
no.12, p.101-111, port., photos.

UNITED STATES--TUSCUMBRIA (ALABAMA)--
COUNTRY HOUSES--CONSERVATION AND
RESTORATION--BELLE MONT
The restoration of "Belle Mont" /
Harvie P. Jones.
A ca.1823 country house located
near Tuscumbria, Alabama. Replicas
of architectural details recreated
from HABS photographs and drawings
differ significantly from the
originals.
ASSOCIATION FOR PRESERVATION
TECHNOLOGY BULLETIN 1990, v.22,
no.1-2, p.156-157, det., elev.,
photos.

UNITED STATES--TUXEDO PARK (NEW
YORK)--CITIES AND TOWNS
Tuxedo Park [New York] / Norma
Skurka.
Original planner: Pierre
Lorillard.
HOUSE BEAUTIFUL 1986 May, v.128,
no.5, p.68-77, photos.

UNITED STATES--TUXEDO PARK (NEW
YORK)--HOUSES--INTERIOR DESIGN--
BRADFIELD HOUSE
In Tuxedo Park: fanciful themes
enrich a designer's New York dream
house / John Taylor.
Interior designer: Geoffrey
Bradfield.
ARCHITECTURAL DIGEST 1990 July,
v.47, no.7, p.130-137,184, port.,
photos.

UNITED STATES--TWO RIVERS
(WISCONSIN)--HOUSES--20TH CENTURY--
SCHWARTZ HOUSE
Unbuilt Minnesota / Robert Gerloff.
Two designs for a Minneapolis
house for a 1938 Life magazine
article. Architects: Royal Barry
Wills, Frank Lloyd Wright. The
Wills design was built in
Minneapolis, and the Wright design
built at Two Rivers, Wisc.
ARCHITECTURE MINNESOTA 1990
May-June, v.16, no.3, p.67,
models.

UNITED STATES--UNALASKA (ALASKA)--
CHURCH DECORATION AND ORNAMENT--
INVENTORIES
Partnership for preservation: an
Alaskan case study / Kate Lidfors.
Documentation and inventory of 171
objects, at the Church of the Holy
Ascension (1894), Unalaska.
CRM BULLETIN: A NATIONAL PARK
SERVICE TECHNICAL BULLETIN 1990,
v.13, no.6, p.13-15, port.,
photos.

UNITED STATES--UNALASKA (ALASKA)--
CHURCHES--19TH CENTURY--CONSERVATION
AND RESTORATION--CHURCH OF THE HOLY
ASCENSION
Partnership for preservation: an
Alaskan case study / Kate Lidfors.
Documentation and inventory of 171
objects, at the Church of the Holy
Ascension (1894), Unalaska.
CRM BULLETIN: A NATIONAL PARK
SERVICE TECHNICAL BULLETIN 1990,
v.13, no.6, p.13-15, port.,
photos.

UNITED STATES--UNION (MAINE)--HOUSES--
18TH CENTURY--EBENEZER ALDEN HOUSE
The Ebenezer Alden House, Union,
Maine / William Nathaniel Banks.
Built 1797-1800. Builder:
Ebenezer Dunton. Current owners:
Joseph and Hazel Marcus.
ANTIQUES 1990 July, v.138, no.1,
p.134-[141], dwg., photos., refs.

UNITED STATES--UNIVERSITIES AND
COLLEGES--BUILDINGS
Boom and reverberation: a new crop
of academic buildings considers
context and campus life / Richard
Bender.
ARCHITECTURE: THE AIA JOURNAL 1990
Jan., v.79, no.1, p.58-59, photos.

UNITED STATES--URBAN BEAUTIFICATION--
20TH CENTURY
Building the City Beautiful: the
Benjamin Franklin Parkway and the
Philadelphia Museum of Art [by]
David B. Brownlee [book review] /
Leonard K. Eaton.
Book published in conjunction with
the 1989 exhibition at the
Philadelphia Museum of Art.
WINTERTHUR PORTFOLIO 1990 Winter,
v.25, no.4, p.305-307.
The City Beautiful movement [by]
William H. Wilson [and] Building
the City Beautiful [by] David
Brownlee [book review] / Daniel
Bluestone.
Brownlee's book studies the
Benjamin Franklin Parkway, and the
Philadelphia Museum of Art and was
published on the occasion of an
exhibition there, Sept.9-Nov.26,
1989.
SOCIETY OF ARCHITECTURAL
HISTORIANS. JOURNAL 1990 Dec.,
v.49, no.4, p.455-457.
The City Beautiful movement [by]
William H. Wilson [book review] /
Charlotte Vestal Brown.
WINTERTHUR PORTFOLIO 1990 Autumn,
v.25, no.2-3, p.207-208,

UNITED STATES--URBAN DESIGN
Urban concepts [Architectural design
profile 83] / Denise Scott Brown.
Contents: Paralipomena in urban
design.-- Between three stools.--
Public realm, public sector and
the public interest in urban
design.-- Rise and fall of
community architecture.-- Urban
design reports [six, indexed
separately]. Includes a discussion
with Martin Pawley, Simon Jenkins,
Robert Thorne, Jake Brown, Ken
Powell, Charles Jencks, and John
Thompson.
ARCHITECTURAL DESIGN 1990, v.60,
no.1-2, p.[1]-96, dwgs., elevs.,
photos., site plans, aerial
photos., biblio., refs.

UNITED STATES--URBAN FORESTRY
The urban garden as public space /
Mark Francis.
PLACES 1989 Fall, v.6, no.1,
p.52-59, photos., plan, aerial
photo., refs.

UNITED STATES--URBAN FRINGES
Beyond gridlock: looking for the new
suburban city / Joseph. E. Brown,
Michael E. Hickok.
Problems of definition for
"suburban urbanization", and the
transportation issues involved.
DEVELOPMENT 1990 July-Aug., v.21,
no.4, p.17-20, ill., dwgs.,
photos.
Modern pastoralism and the middle
landscape / Peter G. Rowe.
OZ / COLLEGE OF ARCHITECTURE AND
DESIGN, KANSAS STATE UNIVERSITY
1989, v.11, p.4-9, ill., model,
photos., site plans, aerial
photos., biblio.
Taming the city edge: urban design
portfolio / Andrea Oppenheimer
Dean
The latest frontier--"outcities."
Mission Bay, San Francisco;
Downtown Norfolk, Va; Carr Norfolk
(Continued next column)

UNITED STATES--URBAN FRINGES
(CONTINUED)
Taming the city edge:...(CONTINUED)
Southern Project, Alexandria, Va.;
and Arverne, New York City.
ARCHITECTURE: THE AIA JOURNAL 1990
Apr., v.79, no.4, p.[74]-79,147,
ill., model, plans, sketches,
aerial photos.

UNITED STATES--URBAN PARKS
You call this a national park? /
James Krohe.
Small urban parks form part of the
national parks system.
PLANNING 1990 Aug., v.56, no.8,
p.4-10, maps, photos., plan.

UNITED STATES--URBAN RENEWAL
American downtowns: past and present
attempts at revitalization /
Robert J. Carey.
BUILT ENVIRONMENT 1988, v.14,
no.1, p.47-59, graphs, photos,
tables, refs.
Urban renewal: Downtown inc.: how
America rebuilds cities, by
Bernard J. Frieden and Lynne B.
Sagalyn [book review] / Francis
Tibbalds.
ROYAL SOCIETY OF ARTS, LONDON. RSA
JOURNAL 1990 Dec., v.139, no.5413,
p.947.

UNITED STATES--URBAN RENEWAL--HISTORY
Urban renewal: an administrator
remembers / Charles L. Farris.
The author looks back on 40 years
of urban renewal in the U.S.
JOURNAL OF HOUSING 1989 July-Aug.,
v.46, no.4, p.169-171,173-174,
178-179, port., photo., aerial
photo.

UNITED STATES--URBAN VILLAGES
Recapturing vitality with new urban
villages / William Kearns, Thomas
E. McDonough.
DEVELOPMENT 1989 Nov.-Dec., v.20,
no.6, p.10-11, photo.

UNITED STATES--URBANA-CHAMPAIGN
(ILLINOIS)--ASTRONOMICAL
OBSERVATORIES--UNIVERSITY OF
ILLINOIS--ASTRONOMICAL OBSERVATORY
The University of Illinois
Observatory / David Newton.
Installed in 1896. Architect:
Charles A. Gunn.
HISTORIC ILLINOIS 1990 Oct., v.13,
no.3, p.[1]-5, photos.

UNITED STATES--URBANA-CHAMPAIGN
(ILLINOIS)--AUDITORIUMS, CONCERT
HALLS--CONSERVATION AND
RESTORATION--UNIVERSITY OF
ILLINOIS--FOELLINGER AUDITORIUM
Crowning history with metalsmith
Hank Hart / Thomas W. Sweeney.
Restoration of the copper dome of
the Foellinger Auditorium,
University of Ill.
PRESERVATION NEWS 1990 June, v.30,
no.6, p.8-9, ports., photos.

UNITED STATES--URBANA-CHAMPAIGN
(ILLINOIS)--ROOFS--COPPER--
UNIVERSITY OF ILLINOIS--FOELLINGER
AUDITORIUM
Crowning history with metalsmith
Hank Hart / Thomas W. Sweeney.
Restoration of the copper dome of
the Foellinger Auditorium,
University of Ill.
PRESERVATION NEWS 1990 June, v.30,
no.6, p.8-9, ports., photos.

UNITED STATES--URBANA-CHAMPAIGN
(ILLINOIS)--UNIVERSITIES AND
COLLEGES--BUILDINGS--UNIVERSITY OF
ILLINOIS
The University of Illinois
Observatory / David Newton.
Installed in 1896. Architect:
Charles A. Gunn.
HISTORIC ILLINOIS 1990 Oct., v.13,
no.3, p.[1]-5, photos.

UNITED STATES--USEPPA ISLAND
(FLORIDA)--BEACH HOUSES--BARKER
HOUSE
Sunstruck: Useppa's mesmerizing
appeal.
Barker house, on Useppa Island,
off the s.w. Fla. coast. Interior
designer: Terry Leet.
SOUTHERN ACCENTS 1989 July-Aug.,
v.12, no.4, p.114-118, photos.

UNITED STATES--VAN DEUSENVILLE
(MASSACHUSETTS)--HOUSES--INTERIOR
DESIGN--WOLFMAN GOLD HOUSE
Household effects: the country
retreat of tabletop entrepreneurs
Peri Wolfman and Charley Gold /
Linda Ellerbee.
Interiors of house in Van
Deusenville, Mass.
HOUSE & GARDEN 1990 July, v.162,
no.7, p.[76-79], port., photos.

UNITED STATES--VENICE (CALIFORNIA)--
ATHLETIC CLUBS--GOLD'S GYM
Gold's Gym in Venice, Ca. / Ann
Bergren.
Includes portions of interviews
with Ed Connors (owner), Jeffrey
Kipnis, Langston Hardaway, Michael
Rotondi.
ASSEMBLAGE 1990 Dec., no.13,
p.[6]-33, photos., refs.

UNITED STATES--VENICE (CALIFORNIA)--
BEACH HOUSES
Antoine Predock: Venice house,
Venice, California, 1988-90.
Architect: Antoine Predock. Text
in Japanese and English.
GA HOUSES 1990 Dec., no.30,
p.118-121, dwg., photos., plans.

UNITED STATES--VENICE (CALIFORNIA)--
BEACH HOUSES--CONCRETE
Dynamics of Venice Beach: Antoine
Predock synthesizes the natural
and urban energies of a singular
site / Sylvia Lavin.
Concrete beach house in Venice,
Calif.
ARCHITECTURAL DIGEST 1990 Dec.,
v.47, no.13, p.[120-123], 218,
port., photos., plans.

UNITED STATES--VENICE (CALIFORNIA)--
CORPORATE OFFICE BUILDINGS--
CHIAT/DAY
Lentes de aumento: edificio
Chiat/Day en Main Street, Venice,
California, 1984-1991.
Office building features giant
binoculars designed by Claes
Oldenburg and Coosje van Bruggen.
Architects: Frank O. Gehry and
Associates. English summary, p.88.
A & V 1990, no.25, p.70-71,
models, plans, site plan.

UNITED STATES--VENICE (CALIFORNIA)--
HOUSES--HOPPER HOUSE
Hopper residence, Venice,
California.
Architects: BAM Construction
Design. Spanish, English text.
QUADERNS D'ARQUITECTURA I
URBANISME 1990 Jan.-Feb.-Mar.,
no.184, p.42-[45], photos., plans,
secn.

UNITED STATES--VENICE (CALIFORNIA)--
HOUSES--WINDWARD CIRCLE ARTS
BUILDING
A Venice, quasi una piazza = Urban
realizations: the almost piazza in
Venice, California / Anne-Marie
Dubois Dumee.
Windward Circle, an area around a
traffic roundabout; includes a
shopping center, an office
building, and a house for an
artist. Architect: Steven Ehrlich.
ABITARE 1990 Apr., no.284,
p.176-183, dwgs., elevs., photos.,
secn., site plan, aerial photo.

UNITED STATES--VENICE (CALIFORNIA)--
MULTI-USE BUILDINGS--MAIN STREET
BUILDING
Frank O. Gehry.
Entire issue devoted to the work
of this American architect.
Criticism by A. Zaera Polo and
David Cohn. 15 projects and
buildings from 1987-1990 featured.
Text in Spanish and English.
EL CROQUIS 1990 Nov., v.9, no.45,
p.1-124, ports., elevs., models,
photos., plans, secns., site
plans, refs.

UNITED STATES--VENICE (CALIFORNIA)--
MULTI-USE BUILDINGS--RACE THROUGH
THE CLOUDS
A Venice, quasi una piazza = Urban
realizations: the almost piazza in
Venice, California / Anne-Marie
Dubois Dumee.
Windward Circle, an area around a
traffic roundabout; includes a
shopping center, an office
building, and a house for an
artist. Architect: Steven Ehrlich.
ABITARE 1990 Apr., no.284,
p.176-183, dwgs., elevs., photos.,
secn., site plan, aerial photo.

UNITED STATES--VENICE (CALIFORNIA)--
OFFICE BUILDINGS--KEITH BRIGHT AND
ASSOCIATES
Bright and Associates, Venice, 1989
[Calif.].
Renovated office building at 901
W. Washington Blvd. Archiect:
Franklin D. Israel.
WERK, BAUEN + WOHNEN 1990
July-Aug., no.7-8, p.28-30,
axonometric view, photos., plans.

UNITED STATES--VENICE (CALIFORNIA)--
OFFICE BUILDINGS--KEITH BRIGHT AND
ASSOCIATES (CONTINUED)
Franklin D. Israel.
Features the Keith Bright and
Associates office building,
Venice, Calif. and the
Berry-Arango house, Beverly Hills.
English summary.
ARCHITECTURE D'AUJOURD'HUI 1990
Oct., no.271, p.159-163,
axonometric views, elev., photos.,
plans, secn.

UNITED STATES--VENICE (CALIFORNIA)--
OFFICES--DESIGNERS'--ALTERATIONS AND
ADDITIONS--EAMES OFFICE
Within a hallowed shell / John
Morris Dixon.
New design offices for Bright &
Associates inside former Eames
studio, Venice, Calif.
Architects: Franklin D. Israel,
Design Associates.
PROGRESSIVE ARCHITECTURE 1990
Sept., v.71, no.9, p.96-[103],
axonometric view, photos., plans,
site plan, isometric dwg.

UNITED STATES--VENICE (CALIFORNIA)--
OFFICES--DESIGNERS'--BRIGHT &
ASSOCIATES
Within a hallowed shell / John
Morris Dixon.
New design offices for Bright &
Associates inside former Eames
studio, Venice, Calif.
Architects: Franklin D. Israel,
Design Associates.
PROGRESSIVE ARCHITECTURE 1990
Sept., v.71, no.9, p.96-[103],
axonometric view, photos., plans,
site plan, isometric dwg.

UNITED STATES--VENICE (CALIFORNIA)--
PLAZAS--WINDWARD CIRCLE
A Venice, quasi una piazza = Urban
realizations: the almost piazza in
Venice, California / Anne-Marie
Dubois Dumee.
Windward Circle, an area around a
traffic roundabout; includes a
shopping center, an office
building, and a house for an
artist. Architect: Steven Ehrlich.
ABITARE 1990 Apr., no.284,
p.176-183, dwgs., elevs., photos.,
secn., site plan, aerial photo.

UNITED STATES--VENICE (CALIFORNIA)--
SHOPPING CENTERS--ACE MARKET PLACE
A Venice, quasi una piazza = Urban
realizations: the almost piazza in
Venice, California / Anne-Marie
Dubois Dumee.
Windward Circle, an area around a
traffic roundabout; includes a
shopping center, an office
building, and a house for an
artist. Architect: Steven Ehrlich.
ABITARE 1990 Apr., no.284,
p.176-183, dwgs., elevs., photos.,
secn., site plan, aerial photo.

UNITED STATES--VERMONT--INNS--
COLONIAL--WEATHERSFIELD INN
Weathersfield Inn.
House built ca. 1794, now an inn
in central Vermont.
COLONIAL HOMES 1990 Dec., v.16,
no.6, p.[130-138], photos.

UNITED STATES--VERNACULAR ARCHITECTURE
Builder style: America's little
houses / James C. Massey, Shirley
Maxwell.
Homestead, Foursquare, Cottage,
and Bungalow styles.
OLD-HOUSE JOURNAL 1990 Sept.-Oct.,
v.18, no.5, p.45-49, ill., photos.
Luoghi di bellezza fotografati /
Bruce J. Archer.
Photographs of American roadside
beauty salons by John Margolies.
Text in Italian and English.
DOMUS 1990 Jan., no.712, p.8-9,
photos.

UNITED STATES--VERNACULAR
ARCHITECTURE--19TH CENTURY--
SOCIOLOGICAL ASPECTS
Families and farmhouses in
Nineteenth-century America [by]
Sally McMurry [book review] /
Bernard L. Herman.
WINTERTHUR PORTFOLIO 1990 Autumn,
v.25, no.2-3, p.194-196, refs.
Families and farmhouses in
nineteenth-century America:
vernacular design and social
change [by] Sally McMurry [book
review] / J. Ritchie Garrison.
SOCIETY OF ARCHITECTURAL
HISTORIANS. JOURNAL 1990 Sept.,
v.49, no.3, p.353-354,

UNITED STATES--VERNACULAR
ARCHITECTURE--ADDRESSES, ESSAYS,
LECTURES
Perspectives in vernacular
architecture, III [edited by]
Thomas Carter and Bernard L.
Herman [book review] / Richard M.
Candee.
Review of volume of 18 essays
originally presented as papers at
the 1985, 1986, and 1987
Perspectives in Vernacular
Architecture conferences.
WINTERTHUR PORTFOLIO 1990 Autumn,
v.25, no.2-3, p.191-194,

UNITED STATES--VERNACULAR
ARCHITECTURE--SOCIOLOGICAL ASPECTS
Using ethnic history to understand
urban landscapes / Dolores Hayden.
PLACES 1990 Fall, v.7, no.1,
p.[10]-17, photos., refs.

UNITED STATES--VICKSBURG
(MISSISSIPPI)--INNS--CEDAR GROVE
Cedar Grove: remembered southern
grandeur in Vicksburg / Derro
Evans.
Antebellum mansion, now an inn.
SOUTHERN ACCENTS 1989 May-June,
v.12, no.3, p.216-221, photos.

UNITED STATES--VICKSBURG
(MISSISSIPPI)--MANSIONS--INTERIOR
DESIGN--CEDAR GROVE
Cedar Grove: remembered southern
grandeur in Vicksburg / Derro
Evans.
Antebellum mansion, now an inn.
SOUTHERN ACCENTS 1989 May-June,
v.12, no.3, p.216-221, photos.

UNITED STATES--VIENNA (VIRGINIA)--
CORPORATE OFFICE BUILDINGS--INTERIOR
DESIGN--METROPOLITAN PARTNERSHIP
Luxury selling / Alice S. Feiring.
Interiors of Metropolitan
Partnership headquarters, a real
estate development co., Vienna,
Va. Architects: Gensler and
Associates, Architects.
INTERIORS 1990 Apr., v.149, no.9,
p.82-85, photos., plan.

UNITED STATES--VILLAGES OF KAPOLEI
(HAWAII)--AFFORDABLE HOUSING
Affordable housing "Hawaiian" style.
On the Villages of Kapolei site,
near Honolulu.
JOURNAL OF HOUSING 1990 May-June,
v.47, no.3, p.170-174, dwg.,
port., photos.

UNITED STATES--VIRGINIA--
BATTLEFIELDS--MANASSAS NATIONAL
BATTLEFIELD PARK
Manassas settlement drags on.
Controversy over development of a
100-acre site adjacent to the Va.
park.
PRESERVATION NEWS 1990 Feb., v.30,
no.2, p.6, photo.

UNITED STATES--VIRGINIA--CAMPUS
PLANNING--18TH CENTURY
"So good a design": the Colonial
campus of the College of William
and Mary, its history, background
and legacy [by] James D. Kornwolf
[book review] / Howard Davis.
Review also covers Collegiate
Gothic: the architecture of Rhodes
College, by William Morgan.
WINTERTHUR PORTFOLIO 1990 Winter,
v.25, no.4, p.[289]-292,

UNITED STATES--VIRGINIA--COUNTRY
HOUSES--18TH CENTURY--MONTICELLO
Mountain aerie: Monticello reveals
Thomas Jefferson's visionary
genius / Susan Stiles Dowell.
House begun in 1769.
SOUTHERN ACCENTS 1989 Nov.-Dec.,
v.12, no.6, p.142-149, photos.

UNITED STATES--VIRGINIA--COUNTRY
HOUSES--WILLOW OAKS (HARRIMAN HOUSE)
Pamela Harriman's Willow Oaks: an
English garden in the Virigina
countryside / Prudence Squier.
SOUTHERN ACCENTS 1990 May, v,13,
no.4, p.[120] 127, port., photos.

UNITED STATES--VIRGINIA--KITCHEN
GARDENS--17TH CENTURY--BACON'S
CASTLE
History unearthed: a team of experts
returns the garden of Bacon's
Castle to national prominence /
Kathleen McCormick.
English Renaissance-style garden
of a plantation house in VA.
Landscape architecture for
restoration: Rudy Favretti.
(Continued next column)

UNITED STATES--VIRGINIA--KITCHEN
GARDENS--17TH CENTURY--BACON'S
CASTLE (CONTINUED)
History unearthed: a...(CONTINUED)
HISTORIC PRESERVATION 1990
July-Aug., v.42, no.4, p.58-[61],
photo.

UNITED STATES--VIRGINIA--PLANTATION
HOUSES--GEORGIAN--INTERIOR DESIGN--
WESTOVER PLANTATION
Westover Plantation:
eighteenth-century accolades still
ring true / Lucy Putnam Post.
Georgian mansion built 1730-34, on
the banks of the James River in
Tidewater Va.
SOUTHERN ACCENTS 1989 July-Aug.,
v.12, no.4, p.108-[113], photos.

UNITED STATES--VIRGINIA--RESIDENTIAL
GARDENS--WILLOW OAKS
Pamela Harriman's Willow Oaks: an
English garden in the Virigina
countryside / Prudence Squier.
SOUTHERN ACCENTS 1990 May, v.13,
no.4, p.[120]-127, port., photos.

UNITED STATES--VIRGINIA--ZONING
Downzoning: an unprecedented
developers' victory.
DEVELOPMENT 1990 Sept.-Oct., v.21,
no.5, p.28-29,

UNITED STATES--WAINSCOTT (NEW YORK)--
HOUSES--INTERIOR DESIGN--BANTRY
HOUSE
Weekends in Wainscott / Bob Felner.
Interior renovations of a Long
Island farmhouse by owner Bryan
Bantry. Interior decorator: Tinka
Topping.
HOUSE & GARDEN 1990 Aug. v.162,
no.8, p.[112-117], photos.

UNITED STATES--WAKEENEY (KANSAS)--
HOUSES--LANG HOUSE
Kansas prairie schooner / Michael
J.P. Smith.
The Lang residence, WaKeeney, Kan.
Architect: Gastinger Rees Walker
Architects.
INLAND ARCHITECT 1990 Mar.-Apr.,
v.34, no.2, p.40-43, photos.,
plans.

UNITED STATES--WALLINGFORD
(CONNECTICUT)--SCHOOLS--BOARDING--
CHOATE ROSEMARY HALL--SCIENCE CENTER
Bridging science with art: Science
Center, Choate Rosemary Hall,
Wallingford, Connecticut, Pei Cobb
Freed & Partners, Architects /
Michael J. Crosbie.
ARCHITECTURE: THE AIA JOURNAL 1990
Feb., v.79, no.2, p.[50-55],
axonometric view, elev., photos,
plans, secns., site plans.
Pei Cobb Freed & Partners: un
legamento dinamico = a dynamic
ligament.
Science Center, Wallingford, Ct.
ARCHITETTURA: CRONACHE E STORIA
1990 Sept., v.36, no.9(419),
p.640-641, axonometric view,
photos., secn., site plan.

UNITED STATES--WALLS--STUCCO--
CONSERVATION AND RESTORATION
Preservation and repair of historic
stucco / Anne Grimmer.
Adapted from a forthcoming
"Preservation Brief".
CRM BULLETIN: A NATIONAL PARK
SERVICE TECHNICAL BULLETIN 1989,
v.12, no.6, p.18-20, photos.

UNITED STATES--WALPOLE
(MASSACHUSETTS)--HOUSES--COLONIAL--
BELLOWS HOUSE
Dealers' retreat [Bellows house,
Walpole, N.H.].
Colonial house belonging to Roman
Farquhar.
COLONIAL HOMES 1990 Aug., v.16,
no.4, p.60-[65]5, photos.

UNITED STATES--WALT DISNEY WORLD
(FLORIDA)--CARPETS--SWAN HOTEL
Product design 465-foot dash / Alice
Feiring.
On the Michael Graves carpet for
the Walt Disney World Swan Hotel,
Orlando.
INTERIORS 1990 Aug., v.149, no.13,
p.100, photos., sketches.

UNITED STATES--WALT DISNEY WORLD
(FLORIDA)--CORPORATE OFFICE
BUILDINGS--CASTING CENTER
A touch of magic: Robert A.M.
Stern's fantasy world for the Walt
Disney World Casting Center in
Orlando, Florida / Nayana
Currimbhoy.
INTERIORS 1990 Jan., v.149, no.6,
p.130-[133], photos., plan.

UNITED STATES--WALT DISNEY WORLD
(FLORIDA)--HOTELS--DOLPHIN HOTEL
Fish story [Walt Disney World
Dolphin Hotel] / Mark Alden
Branch.
Architect: Michael Graves.
PROGRESSIVE ARCHITECTURE 1990
Oct., v.71, no.10, p.82-89,
photos., plans, site plan.
Mickey Mouse architecture / Penny
McGuire.
On the Walt Disney World Dolphin
and Swan hotels, Orlando, Florida.
Architect: Michael Graves.
ARCHITECTURAL REVIEW 1990 Aug.,
v.188, no.1122, p.4,9, photos.
Taking the Mickey seriously / Graham
Ridout.
The Walt Disney World Dolphin
Hotel. Architect: Michael Graves.
BUILDING 1990 July 6, v.255,
no.27, p.56-60, port., photos.,
serial photo.
Walt Disney World Swan and Dolphin
Hotels, Lake Buena Vista, Florida:
Michael Graves, Architect.
Under construction. Text in
Japanese and English.
GA DOCUMENT 1990 May, no.26,
p.[90-91], photos.

UNITED STATES--WALT DISNEY WORLD
(FLORIDA)--HOTELS--SWAN HOTEL
Animal spirits / Vincent Scully.
Focus on the Walt Disney World
Swan Hotel by Michael Graves.
PROGRESSIVE ARCHITECTURE 1990
Oct., v.71, no.10, p.90-91,
photos.

UNITED STATES--WALT DISNEY WORLD
(FLORIDA)--HOTELS--SWAN HOTEL
(CONTINUED)
Graves just wants to have fun /
Arlene Hirst.
Features the resort and convention
center at Walt Disney World,
including the Swan Hotel, as well
as furniture.
METROPOLITAN HOME 1990 Mar., v.22,
no.3, p.28,30, photos.
Mickey Mouse architecture / Penny
McGuire.
On the Walt Disney World Dolphin
and Swan hotels, Orlando, Florida.
Architect: Michael Graves.
ARCHITECTURAL REVIEW 1990 Aug.,
v.188, no.1122, p.4,9, photos.
Story time / Mark Alden Branch.
On the Walt Disney World Swan
Hotel. Architects: Michael Graves
Architect.
PROGRESSIVE ARCHITECTURE 1990
Mar., v.71, no.3, p.[76]-83,
model, photos., plans.
Swan's way ... Swan Hotel at
Orlando's Disney World / Charles
Gandee.
Architect: Michael Graves.
HOUSE & GARDEN 1990 Mar., v.162,
no.3, p.[142-145], port., photos.
Walt Disney World Swan and Dolphin
Hotels, Lake Buena Vista, Florida:
Michael Graves, Architect.
Under construction. Text in
Japanese and English.
GA DOCUMENT 1990 May, no.26,
p.[90-91], photos.

UNITED STATES--WALT DISNEY WORLD
(FLORIDA)--OFFICE BUILDINGS
Arata Isozaki / Jun Aoki.
Contents: Art Tower, Mito,
Ibaraki, design: 1986-88;
construction: 1988-90 -- Walt
Disney World office building,
Orlando, Fla., design: 1987-89;
completion: Dec.1990. Text in
Japanese and English.
GA DOCUMENT 1990 Apr., no.25,
p.[74]-[91], elevs., models,
photos., plans, secns., site plan.

UNITED STATES--WALT DISNEY WORLD
(FLORIDA)--SCULPTURE--
ARCHITECTURAL--SWAN HOTEL
Swan statues, Swan Hotel, Walt
Disney World Lake Buena Vista,
Florida.
Architects: Michael Graves
Architect.
PROGRESSIVE ARCHITECTURE 1990
Mar., v.71, no.3, p.119, det.,
dwgs., photo., secn.

UNITED STATES--WALT DISNEY WORLD
(FLORIDA)--THEME PARKS
Animal spirits / Vincent Scully.
Focus on the Walt Disney World
Swan Hotel by Michael Graves.
PROGRESSIVE ARCHITECTURE 1990
Oct., v.71, no.10, p.90-91,
photos.
Why (and how) does Disney do it? /
Mark Alden Branch.
Focus on work of Robert A. M.
Stern and Michael Graves at Disney
World, Orlando, Florida.
PROGRESSIVE ARCHITECTURE 1990
Oct., v.71, no.10, p.78-81,
photos., models.

UNITED STATES--WALT DISNEY WORLD
(FLORIDA)--THEME PARKS--EPCOT--
FUTURE WORLD
The end of the future: at Walt
Disney's Epcot... / Karrie Jacobs.
METROPOLIS 1990 Jan.-Feb., v.9,
no.6, p.[52-59],73,75, port.,
photos.

UNITED STATES--WARREN (VERMONT)--
SCHOOLS OF ARCHITECTURE--
YESTERMORROW DESIGN / BUILD SCHOOL
Travel: a home-building vacation in
Vermont / Jane Margolies.
Yestermorrow Design / Build
School.
HOUSE BEAUTIFUL 1986 May, v.128,
no.5, p.41-42,46, photo.

UNITED STATES--WARWICK (NEW YORK)--
FARMHOUSES--19TH CENTURY--
CONSERVATION AND RESTORATION
Hudson Valley scenes: Vail House
Inn.
At Warwick, N.Y., in a 19th-cent.
farmhouse. Architect for
renovation: Thomas DeGraw.
Interior designer: Michael
Bertolini.
COLONIAL HOMES 1990 June, v.16,
no.3, p.134-140,142, port.,
photos.

UNITED STATES--WARWICK (NEW YORK)--
RESTAURANTS--INTERIOR DESIGN--VAIL
HOUSE INN
Hudson Valley scenes: Vail House
Inn.
At Warwick, N.Y., in a 19th-cent.
farmhouse. Architect for
renovation: Thomas DeGraw.
Interior designer: Michael
Bertolini.
COLONIAL HOMES 1990 June, v.16,
no.3, p.134-140,142, port.,
photos.

UNITED STATES--WASHINGTON (DC)--
RESIDENTIAL GARDENS--NEOCLASSICAL--
MACLEISH GARDEN
Classicism's light new touch /
Carolyn Ulrich.
Small residential backyard gardens
in Chicago, New Haven, Houston,
and Washington, D.C. Landscape
architects: Timothy Lally, Ralph
Synnestvedt, Jr., Paul Bailey,
Douglas Kycia, McDugald-Steele,
Lanson Jones, and Jane Macleish.
GARDEN DESIGN 1990 autumn, v.9,
no.3, p.[30-37], photos.

UNITED STATES--WASHINGTON (DISTRICT OF
COLUMBIA)--APARTMENT HOUSES--
SARATOGA
The best and worst of Washington,
D.C. / Donald J. Canty.
A brief history of 4 decades of
architecture and planning.
Includes Franklin Sq. (John Burgee
Architects (with Philip Johnson);
a development by Keyes Condon
Florance; the Saratoga (David M.
Schwarz).
ARCHITECTURAL RECORD 1990 Feb.,
v.178, no.2, p.98-103, ill.,
photos., plans, site plan.

UNITED STATES--WASHINGTON (DISTRICT OF
COLUMBIA)--APARTMENTS--INTERIOR
DESIGN--ABRAMSON APARTMENT
Crafting a style / Patricia Conway.
Washington, D.C. apartment of Anne
and Ronald Abramson, collectors of
modern handmade furniture.
Interior designer: David M.
Schwarz/Architectural Services.
HOUSE & GARDEN 1990 Aug., v.162,
no.8, p.[118]-121,148, photos.

UNITED STATES--WASHINGTON (DISTRICT OF
COLUMBIA)--ARCHITECTURE--20TH
CENTURY
Overview: ... the pros and cons of
D. C.'s architectural scene /
Ralph Bennett.
MUSEUM & ARTS WASHINGTON 1990
Mar.-Apr., v.6, no.2, p.[52],57,
ports.

UNITED STATES--WASHINGTON (DISTRICT OF
COLUMBIA)--ARCHITECTURE--20TH
CENTURY--CRITICISM
The best and worst of Washington,
D.C. / Donald J. Canty.
A brief history of 4 decades of
architecture and planning.
Includes Franklin Sq. (John Burgee
Architects (with Philip Johnson);
a development by Keyes Condon
Florance; the Saratoga (David M.
Schwarz).
ARCHITECTURAL RECORD 1990 Feb.,
v.178, no.2, p.98-103, ill.,
photos., plans, site plan.

UNITED STATES--WASHINGTON (DISTRICT OF
COLUMBIA)--BANKS--COMPETITIONS--
WORLD BANK
Kohn Pedersen Fox wins World Bank /
Thomas Vonier.
Competition to design bank on
Pennsylvania Avenue site,
Washington, D.C.
PROGRESSIVE ARCHITECTURE 1990
July, v.71, no.7, p.23-24, model.

UNITED STATES--WASHINGTON (DISTRICT OF
COLUMBIA)--BANKS--CONSERVATION AND
RESTORATION--RIGGS BANK (FARMERS AND
MECHANICS BANK)
"Proud of what I've done": Romanian
emigre blossoms in new world /
Thomas W. Sweeney.
Aurelian Ilie, a specialist in
marbleizing, scagliola and
stenciling, has restored the
painted interior finish of Union
Station, Wahington, D.C., and the
Riggs Bank (formerly Farmers and
Mechanics Bank), Georgetown, D.C.
PRESERVATION NEWS 1990 Feb., v.30,
no.2, p.14-15, ports., photos.

UNITED STATES--WASHINGTON (DISTRICT OF
COLUMBIA)--BANKS--INTERIOR DESIGN--
SECOND NATIONAL FEDERAL SAVINGS BANK
Second National Bank [Washington,
D.C.] / Judith Nasatir.
Interior designer: Ethel
Armstrong-Merrigan.
INTERIOR DESIGN 1990 Feb., v.61,
no.3, p180-[183], photos., plan.

UNITED STATES--WASHINGTON (DISTRICT OF COLUMBIA)--BANKS--WORLD BANK "J" BUILDING
World Bank "J" Building, Washington, D.C., USA, 1987.
Architects: Hellmuth, Obata & Kassabaum; chief architect: Gyo Obata. Text in Japanese and English.
ARCHITECTURE AND URBANISM 1990 Dec., no.12 extra edition, p.114-119, photos., plans, secn.

UNITED STATES--WASHINGTON (DISTRICT OF COLUMBIA)--CAMPUS PLANNING--CITIZEN PARTICIPATION--AMERICAN UNIVERSITY
The American University campus plan: a lesson in neighborhood relations / Whayne S. Quin, Edward L. Donohue.
In Washington, D.C.
URBAN LAND 1990 Dec., v.49, no.12, p.2-3, elev.

UNITED STATES--WASHINGTON (DISTRICT OF COLUMBIA)--CAPITOLS--CONSERVATION AND RESTORATION--UNITED STATES CAPITOL
George White, Architect of the Capitol / Donald J. Canty.
ARCHITECTURAL RECORD 1990 June, v.178, no.7, p.43-44, port., model, photo.

UNITED STATES--WASHINGTON (DISTRICT OF COLUMBIA)--CHANCERIES--CANADIAN CHANCERY
The new Canadian chancery: 501 Pennsylvania Avenue, Washington, D.C. / Cornelia Hahn Oberlander.
A u-shape building with courtyard and hanging gardens. Landscape architects: the author and Arthur Erikson Architects. Architect: Arthur Erickson. Includes French summary.
LANDSCAPE ARCHITECTURAL REVIEW 1990 Oct., v.11, no.4, p.6-7, photos., secn.

UNITED STATES--WASHINGTON (DISTRICT OF COLUMBIA)--CITY PLANNING
Un plan para la mejora ambiental de las avenidas Constitution e Independence de Washington / Abel Enguita.
URBANISMO / COAM 1990 May, no.10, p.118-127, charts, dwgs., photos., plans, secns., aerial photo.

UNITED STATES--WASHINGTON (DISTRICT OF COLUMBIA)--CITY PLANNING--20TH CENTURY
The best and worst of Washington, D.C. / Donald J. Canty.
A brief history of 4 decades of architecture and planning.
Includes Franklin Sq. (John Burgee Architects (with Philip Johnson); a development by Hoyes Gordon Florance; the Saratoga (David M. Schwarz).
ARCHITECTURAL RECORD 1990 Feb., v.178, no.2, p.98-103, ill., photos., plans, site plan.

UNITED STATES--WASHINGTON (DISTRICT OF COLUMBIA)--CITY PLANNING--20TH CENTURY--POLITICAL ASPECTS
The ideal of a "model city": federal social policy for the District of Columbia, 1905-1909 / Robert Harrison.
JOURNAL OF URBAN HISTORY 1989 Aug., v.15, no.4, p.435-463, refs.

UNITED STATES--WASHINGTON (DISTRICT OF COLUMBIA)--COLUMNS--UNITED STATES NATIONAL ARBORETUM
Capitol columns stand again / Thomas Vonier.
22 sandstone Corinthian columns from the East Portico of the U.S. Capitol installed and U.S. National Arboretum. Landscape architects: EDAW.
PROGRESSIVE ARCHITECTURE 1990 Sept., v.71, no.9, p.27, photo.

UNITED STATES--WASHINGTON (DISTRICT OF COLUMBIA)--COMPREHENSIVE PLANS
Un plan para la mejora ambiental de las avenidas Constitution e Independence de Washington / Abel Enguita.
URBANISMO / COAM 1990 May, no.10, p.118-127, charts, dwgs., photos., plans, secns., aerial photo.

UNITED STATES--WASHINGTON (DISTRICT OF COLUMBIA)--CONFERENCE ROOMS--NATIONAL CONFERENCE OF CATHOLIC BISHOPS - UNITED STATES CATHOLIC CONFERENCE
[Conference room, National Conference of Catholic Bishops] / Michael Wagner.
Focus on architectural acoustics in Washington D.C. headquarters designed by Leo A. Daly Co. Designers: Jaffe Acoustics.
INTERIORS 1990 Oct., v.150, no.3, p.26, photo., secn.

UNITED STATES--WASHINGTON (DISTRICT OF COLUMBIA)--CORPORATE OFFICE BUILDINGS--INTERIOR DESIGN--US WEST
Corporate trail blazers / Kristen Richards.
Interiors of US West headquarters, Washington, D.C. Architects: Ronn Jaffe Associates.
INTERIORS 1990 Apr., v.149, no.9, p.[86-89], photos., plan.

UNITED STATES--WASHINGTON (DISTRICT OF COLUMBIA)--DINING ROOMS--NEOCLASSICAL--UNITED STATES DEPARTMENT OF STATE
La grandilocuencia de lo imperial: Comedor Benjamin Franklin, Washington.
Benjamin Franklin Dining Room, Dept. of State, Washington, D.C. Architects: John Blatteau Associates Architects. English Summary, p. 88.
A & V 1990, no.21, p.68-71, dets., dwgs., elevs., photos., secns.

UNITED STATES--WASHINGTON (DISTRICT OF COLUMBIA)--EMBASSIES--CANADIAN CHANCERY
Federal style: Canadian Chancery Washington D. C. Arthur Erickson Architects / Peter Blake.
ARCHITECTURAL RECORD 1990 Mar., v.178, no.3, p.58-65, elevs., photos., plans, secns.

UNITED STATES--WASHINGTON (DISTRICT OF COLUMBIA)--FORMAL GARDENS--PROSPECT HOUSE
Hospitality on the Potomac: the convivial formal garden of Georgetown's Prospect House / Bettz Burr.
Gardens of a house built in 1788. Landscape architect: Mina Bruce Haldeman.
SOUTHERN ACCENTS 1989 May-June, v.12, no.3, p.130-137, photos.

UNITED STATES--WASHINGTON (DISTRICT OF COLUMBIA)--GARDENS--JAPANESE--HILLWOOD JAPANESE GARDEN
A fine and private place: Marjorie Merriweather Post's Japanese garden at Hillwood / Susan Stiles Dowell.
Washington, D.C. estate, now open to the public. Designer: Shogo J. Myaida.
SOUTHERN ACCENTS 1990 Oct., v.13, no.8, p.[92-97], photos.

UNITED STATES--WASHINGTON (DISTRICT OF COLUMBIA)--GENTRIFICATION--ECONOMIC ASPECTS
D.C. study finds preservation not linked to gentrification.
Report of recent study: The impact of historic district designation in Washington, D.C., in Public investment, a special edition of the PAS memo.
AMERICAN PLANNING ASSOCIATION. PLANNING ADVISORY SERVICE. PAS MEMO 1990 Mar., p.[1]-2, photo.

UNITED STATES--WASHINGTON (DISTRICT OF COLUMBIA)--HISTORIC DISTRICTS--ECONOMIC ASPECTS
D.C. study finds preservation not linked to gentrification.
Report of recent study: The impact of historic district designation in Washington, D.C., in Public investment, a special edition of the PAS memo.
AMERICAN PLANNING ASSOCIATION. PLANNING ADVISORY SERVICE. PAS MEMO 1990 Mar., p.[1]-2, photo.

UNITED STATES--WASHINGTON (DISTRICT OF COLUMBIA)--HISTORIC HOUSE MUSEUMS--BELL HOUSE
Making Bell House sound: U.S. WEST restores Georgetown landmark / Thomas W. Sweeney
The 1853 house, bought in 1881 by Alexander Graham Bell as a residence for his father, has been acquired by U.S. WEST, the telephone company, and restored under the supervision of Bette Anderson.
PRESERVATION NEWS 1990 Feb., v.30, no.2, p.7,16, photos.

UNITED STATES--WASHINGTON (DISTRICT OF
COLUMBIA)--HISTORIC PRESERVATION
Redefining urban renewal: for
   Hartman-Cox the zeitgeist is
   preservation / Andrea Oppenheimer
   Dean.
   HISTORIC PRESERVATION 1990
   May-June, v.42, no.3, p.12,14-15,
   port.

UNITED STATES--WASHINGTON (DISTRICT OF
COLUMBIA)--HOSPITALS--CHILDREN'S--
HOSPITAL FOR SICK CHILDREN
Preservation and pediatrics: battle
   heats up over future of D.C.
   hospital [Hospital for Sick
   Children] / Allen Freeman.
   Built 1920; Nathan C. Wyeth,
   architect.
   PRESERVATION NEWS 1990 Apr., v.30,
   no.4, p.3,23, photo.

UNITED STATES--WASHINGTON (DISTRICT OF
COLUMBIA)--HOUSES--18TH CENTURY--
CONSERVATION AND RESTORATION--
OCTAGON
Anatomy of a restoration: the
   meticulous preservation of The
   Octagon, one of America's most
   remarkable homes / Alice L.
   Powers.
   Designed in 1798 by William
   Thornton, the architect of the
   U.S. Capitol, it is now an
   architectural museum.
   HISTORIC PRESERVATION 1990
   Mar.-Apr., v.42, no.2, p.[38-43],
   74, photos.

UNITED STATES--WASHINGTON (DISTRICT OF
COLUMBIA)--HOUSES--ARCHITECTS'--
DEMETRIOU - ADAMSTEIN HOUSE
Great transformations.
   Alterations to a 1940s colonial
   brick house in Washington, D.C.
   Architects and owners: Olivia
   Demetriou and Theodore Adamstein.
   METROPOLITAN HOME 1990 Oct., v.22,
   no.10, p.[124]-129, photos.

UNITED STATES--WASHINGTON (DISTRICT OF
COLUMBIA)--HOUSES--COLONIAL
REVIVAL--ALTERATIONS AND ADDITIONS--
DEMETRIOU - ADAMSTEIN HOUSE
Great transformations.
   Alterations to a 1940s colonial
   brick house in Washington, D.C.
   Architects and owners: Olivia
   Demetriou and Theodore Adamstein.
   METROPOLITAN HOME 1990 Oct., v.22,
   no.10, p.[124]-129, photos.

UNITED STATES--WASHINGTON (DISTRICT OF
COLUMBIA)--HOUSES--GEORGIAN--
ALTERATIONS AND ADDITIONS
Merging with the garden / Susan
   Zevon.
   Back addition to Georgian house in
   Washington, D.C. Architects for
   addition: Hartman-Cox; interior
   designers: Oz Interiors.
   HOUSE BEAUTIFUL 1990 Sept., v.132,
   no.9, p.111-118, photos., plan.

UNITED STATES--WASHINGTON (DISTRICT OF
COLUMBIA)--HOUSES--INTERIOR DESIGN
Harmonies of art: the result is more
   than the sum of its parts / Susan
   Stiles Dowell.
   Georgetown town house interiors.
   Interior designer: Anthony Childs.
   SOUTHERN ACCENTS 1989 Nov.-Dec.,
   v.12, no.6, p.[120]-125, photos.

UNITED STATES--WASHINGTON (DISTRICT OF
COLUMBIA)--HOUSES--INTERIOR DESIGN--
BLAIR HOUSE
Blair house: royally refurbished to
   receive the President's guests /
   Lucy Putnam Post.
   Restoration of the 19th-cent.
   official guest residence of the
   U.S. president. Interior
   decorators: Mark Hampton and Mario
   Buatta.
   SOUTHERN ACCENTS 1989 Mar.-Apr.,
   v.12, no.2, p.106-117, photos.

UNITED STATES--WASHINGTON (DISTRICT OF
COLUMBIA)--HOUSES--INTERIOR DESIGN--
CROSS HOUSE
Stretching the canvas.
   Interior of the home of artist
   Rebecca Cross, Washington, D.C.
   METROPOLITAN HOME 1990 Sept.,
   v.22, no.9, p.110-[113], port.,
   photos.

UNITED STATES--WASHINGTON (DISTRICT OF
COLUMBIA)--HOUSES--INTERIOR DESIGN--
PHEASANT HOUSE
Far from the maddening crowd:
   Italian architecture and a county
   garden set this Georgetown
   gatehouse apart / Susan Stiles
   Dowell.
   Home of interior designer Thomas
   Pheasant.
   SOUTHERN ACCENTS 1989 July-Aug.,
   v.12, no.4, p.88-93, port.,
   photos.

UNITED STATES--WASHINGTON (DISTRICT OF
COLUMBIA)--HOUSES--INTERIOR DESIGN--
QUINN BRADLEE HOUSE
Quinn-tessential favorite: the
   Georgetown living room of Sally
   Quinn and Ben Bradlee / Susan
   Stiles Dowell.
   SOUTHERN ACCENTS 1990 Sept., v.13,
   no.7, p.86-[88], port., photos.

UNITED STATES--WASHINGTON (DISTRICT OF
COLUMBIA)--LAND USE
Land use around suburban transit
   stations / Henry Moon.
   Land uses around 20 stations in
   suburban Washington, D.C. and San
   Francisco/Oakland.
   TRANSPORTATION 1990, v.17, no.1,
   p.67-88, diagrs., graphs, maps,
   tables, aerial photos., refs.

UNITED STATES--WASHINGTON (DISTRICT OF
COLUMBIA)--LAW OFFICES--INTERIOR
DESIGN--ROGOVIN, HUGE & SCHILLER
Legal maneuvers / Michael Wagner.
   On the law offices of Rogovin,
   Huge & Schiller, Washington, D.C.
   Architects: STUDIOS.
   INTERIORS 1990 Apr., v.149, no.9,
   p.70-[73], axonometric view,
   photos.

UNITED STATES--WASHINGTON (DISTRICT OF
COLUMBIA)--MONUMENTS AND MEMORIALS--
LINCOLN PARK--EMANCIPATION STATUE
Emancipation statue, Lincoln Park /
   Marilyn W. Nickels.
   Sculptor: Thomas Ball. Designed
   after 1865 and dedicated in 1876.
   CRM BULLETIN: A NATIONAL PARK
   SERVICE TECHNICAL BULLETIN 1990,
   v.13, no.1, p.19-21, port., photo.

UNITED STATES--WASHINGTON (DISTRICT OF
COLUMBIA)--MULTI-USE BUILDINGS--1001
PENNSYLVANIA AVENUE, NW
Escaping the box: ... Washington's
   12 Best office buildings / James
   Goode.
   1718 Connecticut Ave., NW (David
   M. Schwarz); 1250 24th St., NW
   (Don Hisaka & Assoc.); Republic
   Place (Keyes, Condon, Florance);
   Potomac Tower (Pei Cobb Freed &
   Partners); 317 Massachusetts Ave.,
   NE (Weinstein Assoc.); 816
   Connnecticut Ave., NW (Shalom
   Baranes Assoc.); Franklin Square
   (Phillip Johnson & John Burgee);
   500 E St., SW (Kohn Pedersen Fox
   Assoc.); Jefferson Court (SOM);
   1001 Pennsylvania Ave., NW
   (Hartman-Cox); 2631 Connecticut
   Ave., NW (Martin & Jones).
   MUSEUM & ARTS WASHINGTON 1990
   Mar.-Apr., v.6, no.2, p.[58-65],
   140, photos.

UNITED STATES--WASHINGTON (DISTRICT OF
COLUMBIA)--MULTI-USE COMPLEXES--16TH
STREET
The best and worst of Washington,
   D.C. / Donald J. Canty.
   A brief history of 4 decades of
   architecture and planning.
   Includes Franklin Sq. (John Burgee
   Architects (with Philip Johnson);
   a development by Keyes Condon
   Florance; the Saratoga (David M.
   Schwarz).
   ARCHITECTURAL RECORD 1990 Feb.,
   v.178, no.2, p.98-103, ill.,
   photos., plans, site plan.

UNITED STATES--WASHINGTON (DISTRICT OF
COLUMBIA)--MURAL PAINTING AND
DECORATION--20TH CENTURY--WALDRON
HOUSE
Overhead, the valiant ceiling:
   gazing upward at a brilliant
   mural.
   Mural in Washington, D.C., home of
   Bob Waldron, painted by Dana
   Westring.
   SOUTHERN ACCENTS 1990 June, v.13,
   no.5, p.128, photo.

UNITED STATES--WASHINGTON (DISTRICT OF
COLUMBIA)--MUSEUMS--AERONAUTICAL--
ALTERATIONS AND ADDITIONS--NATIONAL
AIR AND SPACE MUSEUM
National Air and Space Museum, the
   Smithsonian Institution,
   Washington, D.C., USA, 1976.
   Architects: Hellmuth, Obata &
   Kassabaum. Text in Japanese and
   English.
   ARCHITECTURE AND URBANISM 1990
   Dec., no.12 extra edition,
   p.32-[39], elevs., photos., plan,
   secn., site plan.

UNITED STATES--WASHINGTON (DISTRICT OF COLUMBIA)--MUSEUMS--ARCHITECTURAL--OCTAGON
Anatomy of a restoration: the meticulous preservation of The Octagon, one of America's most remarkable homes / Alice L. Powers.
Designed in 1798 by William Thornton, the architect of the U.S. Capitol, it is now an architectural museum.
HISTORIC PRESERVATION 1990 Mar.-Apr., v.42, no.2, p.[38-43], 74, photos.

UNITED STATES--WASHINGTON (DISTRICT OF COLUMBIA)--MUSEUMS--ART--ALTERATIONS AND ADDITIONS--DUMBARTON OAKS--COURTYARD GALLERY OF THE BYZANTINE COLLECTION
Seamless addition: Courtyard Gallery, Dumbarton Oaks, Washington, D.C., Hartman-Cox Architects / Andrea Oppenheimer Dean.
ARCHITECTURE: THE MAGAZINE OF THE AMERICAN INSTITUTE OF ARCHITECTS 1990 June, v.79, no.6, p.[74]-77, photos., plans, secns.

UNITED STATES--WASHINGTON (DISTRICT OF COLUMBIA)--MUSEUMS--ART--HIRSHHORN MUSEUM
Paisajes arquitectonicos: seis maestros, seis imagenes / Ezra Stoller.
Six landmark buildings by Corbusier, Alvar Aalto, F.L. Wright, Mies, Gordon Bunshaft, and Richard Meier.
ARQUITECTURA VIVA 1990 May-June, no.12, p.36-39, photos.

UNITED STATES--WASHINGTON (DISTRICT OF COLUMBIA)--MUSEUMS--ART--NATIONAL MUSEUM OF WOMEN IN THE ARTS
Big names and bright lights: grass roots success for the National Museum of Women in the Arts / Susan Stiles Dowell.
In the former 1907 Masonic Order headquarter, Washington, D.C.
SOUTHERN ACCENTS 1989 May-June, v.12, no.3, p.76-80, ports., photo.

UNITED STATES--WASHINGTON (DISTRICT OF COLUMBIA)--MUSEUMS--HISTORICAL--UNITED STATES HOLOCAUST MEMORIAL MUSEUM
Projects: Museums / Mark Alden Branch.
On five new museums: United States Holocaust Memorial Museum, Washington D.C.; Massachusetts Museum of Contemporary Art, North Adams Mass.; Seattle Art Museum; Museo de Arte Contemporaneo, Barcelona; and the Newport Harbor Art Museum, Newport Beach, Calif.
PROGRESSIVE ARCHITECTURE 1990 May, v.71, no.5, p.124-128, axonometric view, models, photos., plans, secns., site plans, aerial photo.

UNITED STATES--WASHINGTON (DISTRICT OF COLUMBIA)--OFFICE BUILDINGS--317 MASSACHUSETTS AVENUE, NE
Escaping the box: ... Washington's 12 Best office buildings / James Goode.
1718 Connecticut Ave., NW (David M. Schwarz); 1250 24th St., NW (Don Hisaka & Assoc.); Republic Place (Keyes, Condon, Florance); Potomac Tower (Pei Cobb Freed & Partners); 317 Massachusetts Ave., NE (Weinstein Assoc.); 816 Connnecticut Ave., NW (Shalom Baranes Assoc.); Franklin Square (Phillip Johnson & John Burgee); 500 E St., SW (Kohn Pedersen Fox Assoc.); Jefferson Court (SOM); 1001 Pennsylvania Ave., NW (Hartman-Cox); 2631 Connecticut Ave., NW (Martin & Jones).
MUSEUM & ARTS WASHINGTON 1990 Mar.-Apr., v.6, no.2, p.[58-65], 140, photos.

UNITED STATES--WASHINGTON (DISTRICT OF COLUMBIA)--OFFICE BUILDINGS--500 E STREET, SW
500 E Street S.W. office building, Washington, D.C., 1984-87.
Architects: Kohn Pedersen Fox Associates; partner in charge: A. Eugene Kohn.
PROCESS: ARCHITECTURE 1989 Nov., no.86, p.60-63, dwg., elevs., photos.
Escaping the box: ... Washington's 12 Best office buildings / James Goode.
1718 Connecticut Ave., NW (David M. Schwarz); 1250 24th St., NW (Don Hisaka & Assoc.); Republic Place (Keyes, Condon, Florance); Potomac Tower (Pei Cobb Freed & Partners); 317 Massachusetts Ave., NE (Weinstein Assoc.); 816 Connnecticut Ave., NW (Shalom Baranes Assoc.); Franklin Square (Phillip Johnson & John Burgee); 500 E St., SW (Kohn Pedersen Fox Assoc.); Jefferson Court (SOM); 1001 Pennsylvania Ave., NW (Hartman-Cox); 2631 Connecticut Ave., NW (Martin & Jones).
MUSEUM & ARTS WASHINGTON 1990 Mar.-Apr., v.6, no.2, p.[58-65], 140, photos.

UNITED STATES--WASHINGTON (DISTRICT OF COLUMBIA)--OFFICE BUILDINGS--816 CONNECTICUT AVENUE, NW
Escaping the box: ... Washington's 12 Best office buildings / James Goode.
1718 Connecticut Ave., NW (David M. Schwarz); 1250 24th St., NW (Don Hisaka & Assoc.); Republic Place (Keyes, Condon, Florance); Potomac Tower (Pei Cobb Freed & Partners); 317 Massachusetts Ave., NE (Weinstein Assoc.); 816 Connnecticut Ave., NW (Shalom Baranes Assoc.); Franklin Square (Phillip Johnson & John Burgee); 500 E St., SW (Kohn Pedersen Fox Assoc.); Jefferson Court (SOM); 1001 Pennsylvania Ave., NW (Hartman-Cox); 2631 Connecticut Ave., NW (Martin & Jones).
MUSEUM & ARTS WASHINGTON 1990 Mar.-Apr., v.6, no.2, p.[58-65], 140, photos.

UNITED STATES--WASHINGTON (DISTRICT OF COLUMBIA)--OFFICE BUILDINGS--1250 24TH STREET, NW
Escaping the box: ... Washington's 12 Best office buildings / James Goode.
1718 Connecticut Ave., NW (David M. Schwarz); 1250 24th St., NW (Don Hisaka & Assoc.); Republic Place (Keyes, Condon, Florance); Potomac Tower (Pei Cobb Freed & Partners); 317 Massachusetts Ave., NE (Weinstein Assoc.); 816 Connnecticut Ave., NW (Shalom Baranes Assoc.); Franklin Square (Phillip Johnson & John Burgee); 500 E St., SW (Kohn Pedersen Fox Assoc.); Jefferson Court (SOM); 1001 Pennsylvania Ave., NW (Hartman-Cox); 2631 Connecticut Ave., NW (Martin & Jones).
MUSEUM & ARTS WASHINGTON 1990 Mar.-Apr., v.6, no.2, p.[58-65], 140, photos.

UNITED STATES--WASHINGTON (DISTRICT OF COLUMBIA)--OFFICE BUILDINGS--1718 CONNECTICUT AVENUE
Escaping the box: ... Washington's 12 Best office buildings / James Goode.
1718 Connecticut Ave., NW (David M. Schwarz); 1250 24th St., NW (Don Hisaka & Assoc.); Republic Place (Keyes, Condon, Florance); Potomac Tower (Pei Cobb Freed & Partners); 317 Massachusetts Ave., NE (Weinstein Assoc.); 816 Connnecticut Ave., NW (Shalom Baranes Assoc.); Franklin Square (Phillip Johnson & John Burgee); 500 E St., SW (Kohn Pedersen Fox Assoc.); Jefferson Court (SOM); 1001 Pennsylvania Ave., NW (Hartman-Cox); 2631 Connecticut Ave., NW (Martin & Jones).
MUSEUM & ARTS WASHINGTON 1990 Mar.-Apr., v.6, no.2, p.[58-65], 140, photos.

UNITED STATES--WASHINGTON (DISTRICT OF COLUMBIA)--OFFICE BUILDINGS--2631 CONNECTICUT AVENUE, NW
Escaping the box: ... Washington's 12 Best office buildings / James Goode.
1718 Connecticut Ave., NW (David M. Schwarz); 1250 24th St., NW (Don Hisaka & Assoc.); Republic Place (Keyes, Condon, Florance); Potomac Tower (Pei Cobb Freed & Partners); 317 Massachusetts Ave., NE (Weinstein Assoc.); 816 Connnecticut Ave., NW (Shalom Baranes Assoc.); Franklin Square (Phillip Johnson & John Burgee); 500 E St., SW (Kohn Pedersen Fox Assoc.); Jefferson Court (SOM); 1001 Pennsylvania Ave., NW (Hartman-Cox); 2631 Connecticut Ave., NW (Martin & Jones).
MUSEUM & ARTS WASHINGTON 1990 Mar.-Apr., v.6, no.2, p.[58-65], 140, photos.

UNITED STATES--WASHINGTON (DISTRICT OF
COLUMBIA)--STREETS--INDEPENDENCE
AVENUE
Un plan para la mejora ambiental de
las avenidas Constitution e
Independence de Washington / Abel
Enguita.
URBANISMO / COAM 1990 May, no.10,
p.118-127, charts, dwgs., photos.,
plans, secns., aerial photo.

UNITED STATES--WASHINGTON (DISTRICT OF
COLUMBIA)--THEATERS--STAGE-SETTING
AND SCENERY--TEMPORARY--CITADEL
SOUNDSTAGE
Setting a marriage / Justin
Henderson.
Stage sets for a wedding held in
the Citadel Soundstage,
Washington, D.C. Architects: David
M. Schwarz Architectural Services.
INTERIORS 1990 Apr., v.149, no.9,
p.90-[93], photos., plans.

UNITED STATES--WASHINGTON (DISTRICT OF
COLUMBIA)--TOWNHOUSES--INTERIOR
DESIGN--POLING HOUSE
Textural context: Marilyn Poling's
subtle new direction in design /
Susan Stiles Dowell.
House in the Kalorama district of
Washington, D.C.
SOUTHERN ACCENTS 1990 June, v.13,
no.5, p.[90]-96, dets., photos.

UNITED STATES--WASHINGTON (DISTRICT OF
COLUMBIA)--TRANSIT SYSTEMS--METRO
Land use around suburban transit
stations / Henry Moon.
Land uses around 20 stations in
suburban Washington, D.C. and San
Francisco/Oakland.
TRANSPORTATION 1990, v.17, no.1,
p.67-88, diagrs., graphs, maps,
tables, aerial photos., refs.

UNITED STATES--WASHINGTON (DISTRICT OF
COLUMBIA)--WATER TREATMENT PLANTS--
19TH CENTURY--MCMILLAN RESERVOIR
Sand castles / Thomas W. Sweeney.
McMillan Reservoir site and park,
Washington, D.C., threatened by
development. Landscape architect:
Frederick Law Olmstead, Jr.
HISTORIC PRESERVATION 1990
July-Aug., v.42, no.4, p.38-[43],
72, photos.

UNITED STATES--WASHINGTON (DISTRICT OF
COLUMBIA)--WINDOWS--STAINED GLASS--
US WEST CORPORATION
Western window / Lisa Cohen.
Stained glass window in the
Washington, D.C. branch of US West
Corp. Designers: Ronn Jaffe
Associates.
INTERIORS 1990 Apr., v.149, no.9,
p.28, dwg., photo.

UNITED STATES--WASHINGTON ISLAND
(WISCONSIN)--SUMMER HOUSES--BENNETT
HOUSE
Town and country [two houses by
Frederick Phillips & Associates] /
Clifford A. Pearson.
Phillips Townhouse, Chicago; and
Bennett house, Washington Island,
Wisc.
ARCHITECTURAL RECORD 1990
Mid-Apr., v.178, no.5, p.68-63,
photos., plans, secns.

UNITED STATES--WASHINGTON ISLAND
(WISCONSIN)--VACATION HOUSES--
PHILLIPS HOUSE
The psychology of small / Cynthia
Chapin Davidson.
A 1200- square foot vacation house
designed by Frederick Phillips for
his parents, on Washington Island,
Wisc.
INLAND ARCHITECT 1990 Mar.-Apr.,
v.34, no.2, p.32-33, photos.,
plans.

UNITED STATES--WASHOE COUNTY
(NEVADA)--INFRASTRUCTURE--
MAINTENANCE AND REPAIR
Washoe County, Nevada / Tracy
Burrows.
Winner of 1990 Current Topic Award
for GIS data applied to capital
improvements program (CIP)
planning for the county.
PLANNING 1990 Mar., v.56, no.3,
p.[10], map.

UNITED STATES--WATER QUALITY
MANAGEMENT
Stormwater management for the 1990s
/ Larry Roesner, Robert Matthews.
AMERICAN CITY & COUNTY 1990 Feb.,
v.105, no.2, p.44,46,48,50,52-54,
photos.

UNITED STATES--WATERBURY
(CONNECTICUT)--MUSEUMS--HISTORICAL--
MATTATUCK MUSEUM
Special feature: recent works of
Cesar Pelli.
Contents: Editor's introduction--
Architects' statement / Cesar
Pelli-- Essay: Urban iconography
and the medium of architecture /
Gavin Macrae-Gibson, p.130-137--
Works: World Financial Center--
Norwest Tower-- Pacific Design
Center expansion-- Mattatuck
Museum-- Ley Student Center
expansion, Rice University-- Yale
Center for Molecular Medicine,
Yale University-- Carnegie Hall
tower-- Sunarhauserman
headquarters-- Fan Pier master
plan. Architects: Cesar Pelli &
Associates. Text in Japanese and
English.
ARCHITECTURE AND URBANISM 1990
Feb., no.2(233), p.[59]-148,
dwgs., elevs., photos., plans,
secns., site plans.

UNITED STATES--WATERFRONTS
Whose waterfront is it, anyway? /
Ann Breen, Dick Rigby.
Access issues in waterfront
development and the public
interest.
PLANNING 1990 Feb., v.56, no.2,
p.10-12, photos., site plan.

UNITED STATES--WATERVILLE VALLEY (NEW
HAMPSHIRE)--HOTELS--GOLDEN EAGLE
LODGE
Town and country: Golden Eagle Lodge
and Waterville Valley Town Square,
Waterville Valley, New Hampshire,
Graham Gund Architects.
ARCHITECTURAL RECORD 1990 Feb.,
v.178, no.2, p.128-131, photos.,
plans, site plan.

UNITED STATES--WATERVILLE VALLEY (NEW
HAMPSHIRE)--MULTI-USE COMPLEXES--
WATERVILLE VALLEY TOWN SQUARE
Town and country: Golden Eagle Lodge
and Waterville Valley Town Square,
Waterville Valley, New Hampshire,
Graham Gund Architects.
ARCHITECTURAL RECORD 1990 Feb.,
v.178, no.2, p.128-131, photos.,
plans, site plan.

UNITED STATES--WATERVLIET--MEETING
HOUSES--19TH CENTURY--CONSERVATION
AND RESTORATION--WATERVLIET SHAKER
COMMUNITY
Meeting house nucleus of Watervliet
Shaker community / Diane
Conroy-LaCivita.
Built in 1848 and currently under
restoration.
PRESERVATION LEAGUE OF NEW YORK
STATE. NEWSLETTER 1990 Spring,
v.16, no.1, p.6-7, elevs., photo.

UNITED STATES--WATSONVILLE
(CALIFORNIA)--CITY PLANNING
Small town revitalization: lessons
from Watsonville, California /
Michael Stanton.
Small town devastated by the
Oct.17, 1989 California earthquake
is replanned.
URBAN LAND 1990 Nov., v.49, no.11,
p.20-24, photo., plan, sketches.

UNITED STATES--WATTS--SHOPPING
CENTERS--SECURITY MEASURES--LOS
ANGELES (CALIFORNIA)
Security works: shopping enclaves
bring hope, investment to blighted
inner-city neighborhoods / Richard
M. Titus.
High security retail centers in
the Watts section of Los Angeles,
and elsewhere.
URBAN LAND 1990 Feb., v.49, no.1,
p.2-5, photos.

UNITED STATES--WAYZATA (MINNESOTA)--
GUEST HOUSES--WINTON GUEST HOUSE
Frank O. Gehry.
Entire issue devoted to the work
of this American architect.
Criticism by A. Zaera Polo and
David Cohn. 15 projects and
buildings from 1987-1990 featured.
Text in Spanish and English.
EL CROQUIS 1990 Nov., v.9, no.45,
p.1-124, ports., elevs., models,
photos., plans, secns., site
plans, refs.
Jugar a las cuatro esquinas: casa de
invitados, residencia Winton,
Wayzata, Minnesota, 1983-1987.
Architect: Frank O. Gehry. English
text, p.86.
A & V 1990, no.25, p.18-23, dets.,
models, photos., secns., site
plan, sketches.

UNITED STATES--WEST AUSTIN (TEXAS)--
RESEARCH FACILITIES--3M AUSTIN
CENTER
Accurate reflections: glass,
detailing components / Marc S.
Harriman.
Contents: The Link, Kansas City
(Zimmer Gunsul Frasca
Partnership); 3M Austin Center,
Tex. (CRSS); Dakin Building, San
Francisco (Theodore Brown &
Partners).
(Continued next page)

UNITED STATES--WEST AUSTIN (TEXAS)--
RESEARCH FACILITIES--3M AUSTIN
CENTER (CONTINUED)
    Accurate reflections:...(CONTINUED)
    ARCHITECTURE: THE MAGAZINE OF THE
    AMERICAN INSTITUTE OF ARCHITECTS
    1990 Aug., v.79, no.8, p.87-93,
    dets., photos., elevs.

UNITED STATES--WEST DES MOINES
(IOWA)--HOUSES--20TH CENTURY--
JOHNSTON HOUSE
    Tailored to suit: Johnston residence
    / J. Mark Schmidt.
    West Des Moines, Iowa. Architect:
    Lon Sinclair.
    IOWA ARCHITECT 1990 Summer, v.39,
    no.2, p.18-[19], photos., plan.

UNITED STATES--WEST DES MOINES
(IOWA)--OFFICES--ALTERATIONS AND
ADDITIONS--STILWELL JUNIOR HIGH
SCHOOL
    Stilwell Junior High School: School
    daze / Linda Mason Hunter.
    Remodeling of principal's office.
    Architects: Stouffer and Smith.
    IOWA ARCHITECT 1990 Spring, v.39,
    no.1, p.18-[19], photos., plan.

UNITED STATES--WEST HOLLYWOOD
(CALIFORNIA)--CORPORATE OFFICE
BUILDINGS--HEMDALE FILM CORPORATION
    Change in scene: Hemdale Film
    Corporation, West Hollywood,
    California, Hodgetts & Fung Design
    Associates, Architects / Aaron
    Betsky.
    ARCHITECTURAL RECORD 1990 Sept.,
    v.178, no.10, p.104-[111], dwgs.,
    photos., plans, secn.

UNITED STATES--WEST LAGUNA
(CALIFORNIA)--PEDESTRIANS
    The first pedestrian pocket / Gary
    Delsohn.
    Designing the suburbs for
    pedestrians in West Laguna, Ca.
    Architect: Peter Calthorpe.
    PLANNING 1989 Dec., v.55, no.12,
    p.20-22, plans, sketches.

UNITED STATES--WEST LAGUNA
(CALIFORNIA)--SUBURBS
    The first pedestrian pocket / Gary
    Delsohn.
    Designing the suburbs for
    pedestrians in West Laguna, Ca.
    Architect: Peter Calthorpe.
    PLANNING 1989 Dec., v.55, no.12,
    p.20-22, plans, sketches.

UNITED STATES--WEST LOS ANGELES
(CALIFORNIA)--HOUSES--HOUSE T & L
    House T & L, West Los Angeles,
    California, design: 1989;
    completion:1990 (est.).
    Architect: Eric Owen Moss. Text in
    Japanese and English.
    GA HOUSES 1990 Mar., no.28,
    p.54-57, elevs., model, plans,
    secns.

UNITED STATES--WEST PALM BEACH
(FLORIDA)--CAMPUSES--PALM BEACH
ATLANTIC COLLEGE
    Live and learn: Palm Beach Atlantic
    College / Joyce Dutson.
    Architects and planners: James T.
    Biehle, H. Stewart Thompson.
    ARCHITECTURE: THE AIA JOURNAL 1990
    Jan., v.79, no.1, p.115-116,
    photo., site plans.

UNITED STATES--WEST VIRGINIA--HOUSES--
ARCHITECTS'--PRICE HOUSE
    Architecture.
    Features Ando's Church of Light,
    Osaka; Ikko Tanaka's house; Shoji
    and Masako Hayashi; Atsushi
    Kitagawara; Travis Price and his
    home in the Appalachians, W. Va.
    METROPOLITAN HOME 1990 Mar., v.22,
    no.3, p.97-112, 127-133, ports.,
    photos.

UNITED STATES--WESTCHESTER COUNTY (NEW
YORK)--HOUSES
    Contemporary tradition: a
    multifaceted design for a
    Westchester County residence by
    Peter L. Gluck / Suzanne Stephens.
    3-story home facing Long Island
    Sound.
    ARCHITECTURAL DIGEST 1990 Dec.,
    v.47, no.13, p.[190-196], 230,
    dwg., port., photos.

UNITED STATES--WESTCHESTER COUNTY (NEW
YORK)--HOUSES--19TH CENTURY--
ALTERATIONS AND ADDITIONS--LENNEY
HOUSE
    A classical solution / Elizabeth H.
    Hunter.
    Screened porch replaced by room
    addition with many French doors;
    architect; Raymond Skorupa;
    owner/interior designer: Leah
    Lenney.
    HOUSE BEAUTIFUL 1990 Aug., v.132,
    no.8, p.41,76, port., photos.

UNITED STATES--WESTCHESTER COUNTY (NEW
YORK)--HOUSES--ALTERATIONS AND
ADDITIONS
    Special feature: George Ranalli.
    Contents: Essays: George Ranalli
    statement: elements of
    architecture/ George Ranalli--
    Autonomous structures/ Ross
    Miller--Interview: George Ranalli/
    Ross Miller--Works 1979-1989:
    Callender school renovation,
    Newport, R.I.--Ranalli studio
    apartment, New York City,
    1982-83--Peak competition project,
    Hong Kong, 1982--Paris Opera
    competition project, 1983--Chicago
    Tribune competition project,
    1980--Times Tower competition
    project, 1984--New York loft,
    1985-86--Valentine chair--House
    addition for "G" family,
    Westchester, New York, 1987-88--
    Conversion of barn to residence,
    Red Hook, N.Y., 1988-89--K project
    "Tower of Silence," Tokyo, Japan,
    1989. Text in Japanese and
    English.
    ARCHITECTURE AND URBANISM 1990
    Aug., no.8(239), p.[71-136],
    axonometric views, port., elevs.,
    models, photos., plans, secns.,
    site plans.

UNITED STATES--WESTCHESTER COUNTY (NEW
YORK)--HOUSES--INTERIOR DESIGN
    Modified modern: traditional touches
    for contemporary collectors in New
    York / Hunter Drohojowska.
    Interiors of Westchester Co. home.
    Interior designers: Robert
    Metzger, Michael Christiano.
    ARCHITECTURAL DIGEST 1990 July,
    v.47, no.7, p.[102-109],176,
    photos.

UNITED STATES--WESTLAKE (TEXAS)--
HOTELS--SOLANA MARRIOTT HOTEL
    Of the land: Solana Marriott Hotel,
    Westlake, Texas: Legorreta
    Arquitectos and Skidmore, Owings &
    Merrill/Los Angeles / David
    Dillon.
    ARCHITECTURE: THE AIA JOURNAL 1990
    Nov., v.79, no.11, p.[94-101],
    photos., plan.

UNITED STATES--WESTLAKE (TEXAS)--
OFFICE PARKS--SOLANA (IBM)
    I fasti dell'elettronica = The
    glorious deeds of electronics
    [Westlake/Southlake for IBM,
    Solana, Texas].
    Architects: Mitchell Giurgola:
    Legorreta, Leason Pomeroy Assoc.
    ARCHITETTURA: CRONACHE E STORIA
    1990 Oct., v.36, no.10(420),
    p.724-726, photos., plan, site
    plans.
    "Solana": Business Park in
    Westlake/Southlake, Texas.
    Architects: Mitchell Giurgola
    Architects: Legorreta Arquitectos;
    Leason Pomeroy. Includes English
    summary.
    BAUMEISTER 1990 Apr., v.87, no.4,
    p.32-41, photos., plans, site
    plans.

UNITED STATES--WESTPORT
(CONNECTICUT)--HOUSES--ALTERATIONS
AND ADDITIONS
    Infusion of charm / Susan Zevon.
    Additions to house in Westport,
    Connecticut. Architects:
    Rosenblum/Harb Architects.
    HOUSE BEAUTIFUL 1990 Oct., v.132,
    no.10, p.112-115, dets., photos.,
    plan.

UNITED STATES--WESTPORT
(CONNECTICUT)--WEEKEND HOUSES--
ALTERATIONS AND ADDITIONS
    Infusion of charm / Susan Zevon.
    Additions to house in Westport,
    Connecticut. Architects:
    Rosenblum/Harb Architects.
    HOUSE BEAUTIFUL 1990 Oct., v.132,
    no.10, p.112-115, dets., photos.,
    plan.

UNITED STATES--WHIDBEY ISLAND
(WASHINGTON)--INNS--INN AT LANGLEY
    Pacific rim regionalism: the Inn at
    Langley, Whidbey Island,
    Washington, Gaylord Grainger Libby
    O'Brien-Smith Architects.
    ARCHITECTURAL RECORD 1990 Feb.,
    v.178, no.2, p.126-127, photos.,
    plan, secn.

UNITED STATES--WHITE BEAR LAKE
(MINNESOTA)--CHURCHES--CONSERVATION
AND RESTORATION--SAINT MARY OF THE
LAKE
    Detail / Bill Beyer.
    Minn. limestone used in exterior
    restoration of St. Mary of the
    Lake Church in White Bear Lake.
    ARCHITECTURE MINNESOTA 1990
    Mar.-Apr., v.16, no.2, p.53,
    photos.

UNITED STATES--WHITE PLAINS (NEW YORK)--OFFICE BUILDINGS--IBM
Special feature: James Polshek. Contents: Introduction / Toshio Nakamura --Architects' statement / James S. Polshek and James G. Garrison: --Works & projects: United States Embassy, Muscat, Oman --Centennial Hall, Barnard College, New York, N.Y. --Alumni houses, Bard College, Annandale, N.Y. --Hastings Hall, Union Theological Seminary, New York, N.Y. --IBM-ISG North Central Marketing Division headquarters, White Plains, N.Y. --Seaman's Church Institute, New York, N.Y. --Yerba Buena Gardens Theater, San Francisco, Calif. --National Inventors Hall of Fame, Akron, Ohio --New York University Medical Center Biomolecular Research building, New York, N.Y. --Biographies of James S. Polshek, Joseph L. Fleischer, Timothy P. Hartung, and James G. Garrison, p.126. Architects: James Stewart Polshek & Partners. Text in Japanese and English.
ARCHITECTURE AND URBANISM 1990 Nov., no.11(242), p.62-126, axonometric views, models, photos., plans, secns., site plans.

UNITED STATES--WHITE PLAINS (NEW YORK)--PUBLIC BUILDINGS--PUBLIC SAFETY BUILDING
Public Safety Building, White Plains, New York.
Geddes Brecher Qualls Cunningham. architects.
ARCHITECTURE NEW JERSEY 1990, v.26, no.3, p.18-19, axonometric view, dwg., photos., plan, sketch.

UNITED STATES--WILLIAMSBURG (VIRGINIA)--CAMPUSES--HISTORY--COLLEGE OF WILLIAM AND MARY
"So good a design": a William and Mary garden at William and Mary / James D. Kornwolf.
18th-cent. garden at the college in Va. reflects the Anglo-Dutch taste associated with King William and Queen Mary.
JOURNAL OF GARDEN HISTORY 1990 July-Sept., v.10, no.2, p.173-188, elevs., maps, plans, site plans, engrs., refs.

UNITED STATES--WILLIAMSBURG (VIRGINIA)--CAPITOLS--COLONIAL REVIVAL--COLONIAL WILLIAMSBURG
Beaux-Arts ideals and colonial reality: the reconstruction of Williamsburg's Capitol, 1928-1934 / Carl R. Lounsbury.
Architect: Perry, Shaw & Hepburn. Includes abstract.
SOCIETY OF ARCHITECTURAL HISTORIANS. JOURNAL 1990 Dec., v.49, no.4, p.373-389, elevs., photos., plans, refs.

UNITED STATES--WILLIAMSBURG (VIRGINIA)--FURNITURE--18TH CENTURY--COLLECTIONS--HENNAGE COLLECTION
Living with antiques: the American furniture collection of Joseph and June Hennage of Williamsburg, Virginia / Wendell and Elisabeth Garrett.
In "a modern Georgian house," South England St., completed in 1989. Architects: Richard Newlon and Floyd Johnson.
ANTIQUES 1990 Dec., v.138, no.6, p.1228-1239, photos., refs.

UNITED STATES--WILLIAMSBURG (VIRGINIA)--GARDENS--COLONIAL--COLLEGE OF WILLIAM AND MARY
"So good a design": a William and Mary garden at William and Mary / James D. Kornwolf.
18th-cent. garden at the college in Va. reflects the Anglo-Dutch taste associated with King William and Queen Mary.
JOURNAL OF GARDEN HISTORY 1990 July-Sept., v.10, no.2, p.173-188, elevs., maps, plans, site plans, engrs., refs.

UNITED STATES--WILLIAMSBURG (VIRGINIA)--HOUSES--COLONIAL REPRODUCTIONS--EBENEEZER EWING HOUSE
Williamsburg cottage.
Modern house in a Colonial style, built by Vira Goldman of Hladun/Goldman.
COLONIAL HOMES 1990 Aug., v.16, no.4, p.[40-43], photos.

UNITED STATES--WILLIAMSBURG (VIRGINIA)--HOUSES--GEORGIAN REVIVAL--HENNAGE HOUSE
Living with antiques: the American furniture collection of Joseph and June Hennage of Williamsburg, Virginia / Wendell and Elisabeth Garrett.
In "a modern Georgian house," South England St., completed in 1989. Architects: Richard Newlon and Floyd Johnson.
ANTIQUES 1990 Dec., v.138, no.6, p.1228-1239, photos., refs.

UNITED STATES--WILLIAMSBURG (VIRGINIA)--MUSEUM VILLAGES--COLONIAL WILLIAMSBURG
Forum: social responsibility and the American history museum / Edward A. Chapell.
Explores "some of the current strengths, problems, and needs of history museums...", with reference to Colonial Williamsburg Foundation and other museums.
WINTERTHUR PORTFOLIO 1989 Winter, v.24, no.4, p.[247]-265, photos., refs.

UNITED STATES--WILLIAMSBURG (VIRGINIA)--UNIVERSITIES AND COLLEGES--BUILDINGS--COLONIAL--COLLEGE OF WILLIAM AND MARY
"So good a design": the Colonial campus of the College of William and Mary, Its history, background and legacy [by] James D. Kornwolf [book review] / Howard Davis.
Review also covers Collegiate Gothic: the architecture of Rhodes
(Continued next column)

UNITED STATES--WILLIAMSBURG (VIRGINIA)--UNIVERSITIES AND COLLEGES--BUILDINGS--COLONIAL--COLLEGE OF WILLIAM AND MARY (CONTINUED)
"So good a design":...(CONTINUED) College, by William Morgan.
WINTERTHUR PORTFOLIO 1990 Winter, v.25, no.4, p.[289]-292,

UNITED STATES--WILLIAMSPORT (INDIANA)--HOUSES--INTERIOR DESIGN--COTTRELL HOUSE
Looking homeward: a designer's return to a classic Indiana house / Hunter Drohojowska.
Features interiors of interior designer John Cottrell's 1842 home in Williamsport.
ARCHITECTURAL DIGEST 1990 June, v.47, no.6, p.[164-171],220, photos.

UNITED STATES--WILMINGTON (DELAWARE)--RECREATION AREAS
Waterfront + renovation = recreation / Christy C. McEvilly.
PARKS & RECREATION 1989 July, v.24, no.7, p.34-36,75, photos.

UNITED STATES--WILMINGTON (DELAWARE)--RESIDENTIAL GARDENS
Mummy's follies: curious undertakings yield dramatic results for a Delaware gardener / Susan Stiles Dowell.
Landscape architect: Herbert Plankinton.
SOUTHERN ACCENTS 1989 May-June, v.12, no.3, p.[174]-179, photos.

UNITED STATES--WILMINGTON (DELAWARE)--WATERFRONTS--CONSERVATION AND RESTORATION
Waterfront + renovation = recreation / Christy C. McEvilly.
PARKS & RECREATION 1989 July, v.24, no.7, p.34-36,75, photos.

UNITED STATES--WILSON (NORTH CAROLINA)--HOUSES--INTERIOR DESIGN--BROWN HOUSE
A Louisiana transplant: North Carolina home with a French accent.
Brown house interiors, Wilson, N.C. Architectural designer: Robert Smith.
SOUTHERN ACCENTS 1989 May-June, v.12, no.3, p.154-159, photos.

UNITED STATES--WILTON (CONNECTICUT)--OFFICES--INTERIOR DESIGN--DELOITTE & TOUCHE HEADQUARTERS
Dressing for the office: Building Types Study 679: commercial interiors / Karen D. Stein.
Three projects: Vogue conference room (Tod Williams, Billie Tsien); Spy offices (Chan and Mohney); and Deloitte & Touche Headquarters (Peter Pran and Carlos Zapata for Ellerbe Becket).
ARCHITECTURAL RECORD 1990 May, v.178, no.6, p.103-115, photos., plans, secn.

UNITED STATES--WINDHAM (VERMONT)--
HOUSES--ARCHITECTS'--SHANNON HOUSE
  Shannon house, Windham, Vermont,
    design: 1986; completion: 1990
    (est.).
    Architect & owner: Robert Foote
    Shannon. Text in Japanese and
    English.
    GA HOUSES 1990 Mar., no.28,
    p.134-135, elev., plans, secns.

UNITED STATES--WINONA (MINNESOTA)--
HOUSES--PRAIRIE SCHOOL--ROCKLEDGE
  Lost Minnesota: Rockledge, Winona,
    Minn., 1911-1987 / Jack El-Hai.
    1911 house, razed in 1987.
    Architect: George Washington
    Maher.
    ARCHITECTURE MINNESOTA 1990
    May-June, v.16, no.3, p.118,
    photo.

UNITED STATES--WINSTON-SALEM (NORTH
CAROLINA)--ARENAS--LAWRENCE JOEL
VETERANS MEMORIAL COLISEUM
  Slam-dunk: a new coliseum scores big
    on design.
    The Lawrence Joel Veterans
    Memorial Coliseum in Winston
    Salem, N.C. Architect: Don Eyberg
    of Ellerbe Becket.
    ARCHITECTURE MINNESOTA 1990
    Nov.-Dec., v.16, no.6, p.36-37,
    photos.

UNITED STATES--WINSTON-SALEM (NORTH
CAROLINA)--PERIOD ROOMS--COLONIAL--
MUSEUM OF EARLY SOUTHERN DECORATIVE
ARTS
  Collective genius: one of the finest
    decorative-arts museums in America
    / Rick Mashburn.
    The Museum of Early Southern
    Decorative Arts, Winston-Salem,
    N.C.
    HISTORIC PRESERVATION 1990
    July-Aug., v.42, no.4, p.[50-55],
    port., photos.

UNITED STATES--WISCONSIN--BUILDING
MATERIALS
  The character of place: building
    materials and architectural
    characteristics in Eau Claire,
    Wisconsin / Ingolf Vogeler.
    Analysis of house styles
    (1860's-1970's) using field
    observations and data obtained
    from the assessor's office.
    MATERIAL CULTURE 1990 Spring,
    v.22, no.1, p.1-21, graphs, maps,
    biblio.

UNITED STATES--WOODBRIDGE (NEW
JERSEY)--OFFICES--WICK BUILDERS
CORPORATE OFFICES
  Wick Builders Corporate Offices,
    Woodbridge, New Jersey.
    Architects: The Kellner Group.
    ARCHITECTURE NEW JERSEY 1990,
    v.26, no.6., p.13, photos.

UNITED STATES--WOODLAND HILLS
(CALIFORNIA)--HOUSES--SLOPING
SITES--KUSTIN HOUSE
  Vancouver, Patricia et John Patkau.
    Features four houses: Porter-Van
    den Bosch house, Toronto; Kustin
    house, Woodland Hills, Ca.; Greene
    house, West Vancouver, B.C. and
    Appleton house, Victoria, B.C.
    English summaries.
                (Continued next column)

UNITED STATES--WOODLAND HILLS
(CALIFORNIA)--HOUSES--SLOPING
SITES--KUSTIN HOUSE (CONTINUED)
  Vancouver, Patricia...(CONTINUED)
    ARCHITECTURE D'AUJOURD'HUI 1990
    Sept., no.270, p.148-162,
    axonometric views, dets., ports.,
    elevs., models, photos., plans,
    secns.

UNITED STATES--WOODLAND HILLS
(CALIFORNIA)--HOUSES--STRUCKUS HOUSE
  Sculpture "to be lived in," Woodland
    Hills, California, 1979-87.
    Includes essay: Al Struckus house
    by Bruce Goff / Bart Prince.
    Architects: Bruce Goff and Frank
    Purtill (associate architect).
    Text in Japanese and English.
    GA HOUSES 1990 July, no.29,
    p.72-81, photos., plans, site
    plan.

UNITED STATES--WOODLAND HILLS
(CALIFORNIA)--REHABILITATION CENTERS
  Sette conferme di John Lautner delle
    sette invarianti dell'architettura
    moderna.
    7 projects: Turner house, Aspen,
    CO; Walstrom house, Los Angeles,
    CA; Reiner house Los Angeles;
    Arango house, Acapulco, Mexico;
    house, Malibu, CA; children's
    rehab center, Woodland Hills, CA;
    house at Lechuza Point, Malibu.
    English, French, German, Spanish
    summaries.
    ARCHITETTURA: CRONACHE E STORIA
    1987 Jan., v.33, no.1(375),
    p.[22]-40, photos., plans, secns.,
    site plans.

UNITED STATES--WOODSIDE (CALIFORNIA)--
HOUSES--KELLY HOUSE
  Classico e vernacolo / Marinetta
    Nunziate.
    The Kelly house, Woodside, Calif.
    (1987). Architect: Mark Mack.
    VILLE GIARDINI 1990 Mar., no.246,
    p.20-29, photos, plans.

UNITED STATES--WOODSTOCK (VERMONT)--
WEEKEND HOUSES--INTERIOR DESIGN
  Shaker show / Monica Geran.
    Interiors of weekend/holiday
    retreat in Woodstock, Vt. designed
    by Sandra Nunnerley.
    INTERIOR DESIGN 1990 Jan., v.61,
    no.1, p.172-[175], photos., plans.

UNITED STATES--WOOSTER (ARKANSAS)--
BED-AND-BREAKFAST GUEST HOUSES--
PATTON HOUSE INN
  Victorian summer travel.
    Features buildings in Ferndale,
    Calif. (including Linden Hall),
    the Olallieberry Inn, Cambria,
    Calif., and Patton House Inn,
    Wooster, Ark.
    VICTORIAN HOMES 1990 Summer, v.9,
    no.3, p.[65]-70,72,74, photos.

UNITED STATES--WORCESTER COUNTY
(MARYLAND)--REAL ESTATE
DEVELOPMENT--ENVIRONMENTAL ASPECTS
  Bay patrol: a Maryland coastal
    community fends off developers /
    Jeff Weintraub, Mary Lou
    Gallagher.
    In Worcester County, Maryland, on
    the mainland across from Ocean
    City.
                (Continued next column)

UNITED STATES--WORCESTER COUNTY
(MARYLAND)--REAL ESTATE
DEVELOPMENT--ENVIRONMENTAL ASPECTS
                        (CONTINUED)
  Bay patrol: a...(CONTINUED)
    PLANNING 1990 Oct., v.56, no.10,
    p.22-23, maps, photos., aerial
    photo.

UNITED STATES--WORCESTER COUNTY
(MARYLAND)--WATERFRONTS--
ENVIRONMENTAL ASPECTS
  Bay patrol: a Maryland coastal
    community fends off developers /
    Jeff Weintraub, Mary Lou
    Gallagher.
    In Worcester County, Maryland, on
    the mainland across from Ocean
    City.
    PLANNING 1990 Oct., v.56, no.10,
    p.22-23, maps, photos., aerial
    photo.

UNITED STATES--WORCESTER COUNTY
(MARYLAND)--WETLANDS
  Bay patrol: a Maryland coastal
    community fends off developers /
    Jeff Weintraub, Mary Lou
    Gallagher.
    In Worcester County, Maryland, on
    the mainland across from Ocean
    City.
    PLANNING 1990 Oct., v.56, no.10,
    p.22-23, maps, photos., aerial
    photo.

UNITED STATES--WORLD TRADE CENTERS
  World trade centers: made to order
    for today's truly global
    marketplace / Harold Kelman.
    In Boston, New York, Washington,
    Chicago, and other United States
    cities.
    REAL ESTATE FORUM 1990 Mar., v.45,
    no.3, p.94-102, dwgs., elevs.,
    photos., aerial photo.

UNITED STATES--WYOMING--WINTER SPORTS
FACILITIES--SNOWY RANGE SKI AREA
  Snowy Range ski resort: an
    illustration of GIS planning
    principles / Rosalyn Johnson, Jon
    Bryan Burley.
    Evaluatin of expansion
    possibilities for a 500-acre site
    located in southeastern Wyoming,
    30 miles west of Laramie.
    Includes French summary.
    LANDSCAPE ARCHITECTURAL REVIEW
    1990 Mar., v.11, no.1, p.15-18,
    maps, biblio.

UNITED STATES--XERISCAPES
  Regional style: eco-logic at work.
    A brief survey of six
    "environmental" gardens in the
    U.S. Landscape architects: Steven
    K. Domigan, Edith Eddleman, Ron
    Lutsco, Steve Trudnak, James Weht,
    and David Cropp.
    GARDEN DESIGN 1990 spring, v.9,
    no.1, p.46-59, photos., site
    plans, sketch.

UNITED STATES--YARDS
  Lot, yard, and garden: American
    distinctions / Paul Groth.
    LANDSCAPE 1990, v.30, no.3,
    p.29-35, diagrs., photos., biblio.

UNITED STATES--YARMOUTH (MAINE)--
CITIES AND TOWNS--GROWTH
A village copes with growth
[Yarmouth, Maine] / Margaret W.
Soule.
LANDMARKS OBSERVER 1990 Spring,
v.16, no.3, p.3-5,1, ports.,
photos.

UNITED STATES--YARMOUTH (MAINE)--MAIN
STREETS
A village copes with growth
[Yarmouth, Maine] / Margaret W.
Soule.
LANDMARKS OBSERVER 1990 Spring,
v.16, no.3, p.3-5,1, ports.,
photos.

UNITED STATES--YEMASSEE (SOUTH
CAROLINA)--MANSIONS--GEORGIAN
REVIVAL--INTERIOR DESIGN--CHEROKEE
PLANTATION (UPDYKE HOUSE)
Cherokee Plantation: new life for a
South Carolina estate / James S.
Wamsley.
Interiors of 1930-31 Georgian
revival mansion owned by Carol and
Randolph Updyke on 3800-acre
plantation near Yemassee.
Interior designers: Judie and
Bennett Weinstock.
ARCHITECTURAL DIGEST 1990 June,
v.47, no.6, p.138-[143], photos.

UNITED STATES--YORK COUNTY
(PENNSYLVANIA)--HOUSES--CONSERVATION
AND RESTORATION--HAINES SHOE HOUSE
Shoe house: a perfect fit? [Haines
Shoe House, York County, Pa.] /
Thomas W. Sweeney.
Mahlon Haines built his Shoe House
in 1948 to advertise his shoe
business.
PRESERVATION NEWS 1989 Dec., v.29,
no.12, p.1,17, port., photo.

UNITED STATES--YORK (PENNSYLVANIA)--
TIMBER-FRAMED BUILDINGS
Catering for charity [review] / Tom
Woolley.
"Raising the roof", television
program aired on the BBC showed
volunteers constructing two
timber-framed houses in three days
in York, Pa.
ARCHITECTS' JOURNAL 1990
Aug.22-29, v.192, no.7-8, p.71,
ports.

UNITED STATES--YORKTOWN (NEW YORK)--
REHABILITATION CENTERS--INTERIOR
DESIGN--ARC WEST TREATMENT CENTER
ARC West / Monica Geran.
Interiors of renovated and
expanded addiction recovery center
in Yorktown, NY. Architects/
Interior designers: Salsano
Associates.
INTERIOR DESIGN 1990 Nov., v.61,
no.15, p.184-[187], photos,
plans.

UNITED STATES--YOUNGSTOWN (OHIO)--
MUSEUMS--HISTORICAL--HISTORICAL
CENTER OF INDUSTRY AND LABOR
Historical Center of Industry and
Labor, Youngstown, Ohio: Michael
Graves, Architect.
Design: 1985-88, completion: 1989.
Associate architects: Raymond J.
Jaminet & Partners. Text in
Japanese and English.
(Continued next column)

UNITED STATES--YOUNGSTOWN (OHIO)--
MUSEUMS--HISTORICAL--HISTORICAL
CENTER OF INDUSTRY AND LABOR
(CONTINUED)
Historical Center of...(CONTINUED)
GA DOCUMENT 1990 May, no.26,
p.106-113, elevs., photos., plans,
secns., site plan.
Museo della storia dell'Industria a
Youngstown = Youngstown's Museum
of Industry, Ohio / Silvano
Stucchi.
Architect: Michael Graves. In
English and Italian; summaries in
French, German and Spanish, p.4.
L'INDUSTRIA DELLE COSTRUZIONI 1990
Nov., v.24, no.229, p.38-43,
elev., photos., plans, secn.
Steel industry enshrined / Philip
Arcidi.
On the Historical Center of
Industry and Labor, Youngstown,
OH. Architects: Michael Graves
Architect; Raymond J. Jaminet &
Partners, Architects.
PROGRESSIVE ARCHITECTURE 1990
Mar., v.71, no.3, p.84-87, model,
photos., plans, secn.

UNITED STATES--YUKON (OKLAHOMA)--
BANKS--BANK OF OKLAHOMA
On the corner: Bank of Oklahoma,
Yukon, Oklahoma, Elliott +
Associates Architects / Deborah K.
Dietsch.
ARCHITECTURE: THE AIA JOURNAL 1990
Oct., v.79, no.10, p.[58]-59,
photos., plan.

UNITED STATES--ZAVALA COUNTY (TEXAS)--
WEEKEND HOUSES--SOUTH BURKE RANCH
HEADQUARTERS
South Burke Ranch Headquarters.
In Zavala Co. Lake Flato
Architects.
TEXAS ARCHITECT 1990 Jan.-Feb.,
v.40, no.1, p.26, photos., plan,
site plan.

UNITED STATES--ZONING
Let the sun shine in: how zoning to
preserve light is significantly
affecting cities across the U.S. /
Terry Jill Lassar.
ARCHITECTURE: THE MAGAZINE OF THE
AMERICAN INSTITUTE OF ARCHITECTS
1990 May, v.79, no.5, p.102-105,
155-156,159, ill., map, diagr.
Zoning today: a time for reckoning /
Charles M. Haar, Jerold S. Kayden.
Succinct, critical analysis of
zoning.
PLANNING 1989 June, v.55, no.6,
p.20-21, ill.

UNITED STATES--ZONING LAW
Zoning today: a time for reckoning /
Charles M. Haar, Jerold S. Kayden.
Succinct, critical analysis of
zoning.
PLANNING 1989 June, v.55, no.6,
p.20-21, ill.

UNIVERSITA DI FIRENZE. FACOLTA DI
ARCHITETTURA
Architettura Firenze.
A suppl. on the Facolta di
architettura di Firenze. Features
interviews with 9 professors.
MODO 1990 Aug.-Sept., v.13,
no.125, p.I-XV, dwgs., ports.,
model, site plan.

UNIVERSITA DI NAPOLI. FACOLTA DI
ARCHITETTURA
Architettura Napoli.
Special inserted suppl. on the
Naples architecture school
features interviews with the
faculty.
MODO 1990 May, v.13, no.123
(suppl.), p.I-XVI,

UNIVERSITA DI PARMA. CENTRO STUDI E
ARCHIVIO DELLA COMMUNICAZIONE
Marcello Nizzoli: una mostra a
Reggio Emilia [exhibition review].
Organized by the CSAG of the
Universita di Parma.
L'INDUSTRIA DELLE COSTRUZIONI 1990
Feb., v.24, no.220, p.64-65,
dwgs., model, photos.

UNIVERSITA DI ROMA. FACOLTA DI
ARCHITETTURA--EXHIBITIONS
Le architetture dei Pietila a Roma
[exhibition review].
Exhibition at the Universita di
Roma.
L'INDUSTRIA DELLE COSTRUZIONI 1990
Feb., v.24, no.220, p.66-67,
photos., secns., sketch.

UNIVERSITAT STUTTGART
Infrastructure planning: the
difficult growth of a study
program / Francisco J. Luciano.
Masters degree program at the
University of Stuttgart for Third
World applications.
EKISTICS 1988 Jan.-June, v.55,
no.328-330, p.48-51, graphs,
table.

UNIVERSITE DE MONTREAL. ECOLE
D'ARCHITECTURE DE PAYSAGE--
CONGRESSES
Congres '89 atelier thematique:
l'avenir des berges, le fleuve
St.-Laurent / Irene Cinq-Mars.
The author is director of the
Ecole d'architecture de paysage,
Universite de Montreal.
LANDSCAPE ARCHITECTURAL REVIEW
1990 Mar., v.11, no.1, p.25,27,

UNIVERSITIES AND COLLEGES
See also ART SCHOOLS
See also CAMPUS PLANNING
See also CAMPUSES
See also CONSERVATORIES OF MUSIC
See also LAW SCHOOLS
See also MEDICAL SCHOOLS
See also SCHOOLS OF ARCHITECTURE
See also VETERINARY COLLEGES

UNIVERSITIES AND COLLEGES - BUILDINGS
See also ALUMNI CENTERS
See also CAMPUSES
See also DORMITORIES
See also FACULTY HOUSING
See also LIBRARIES - UNIVERSITY AND
COLLEGE
See also STUDENT HOUSING
See also STUDENT UNIONS
See also UNIVERSITY MUSEUMS

UNIVERSITIES AND COLLEGES--BUILDINGS--
AUSTRALIA--CANBERRA--TUGGERANONG
COLLEGE
Tuggeranong College and Town Centre
Library.
In Canberra. Architects: Edwards
Madigan Torzillo Briggs.
ARCHITECTURE AUSTRALIA 1990 July,
v.79, no.6, p.46-47, photos.,
plan.

UNIVERSITIES AND COLLEGES--BUILDINGS--
AUSTRALIA--DANDENONG--DANDENONG
COLLEGE
Dandenong College of TAFE stage III:
Edmond & Corrigan Pty Ltd;
Ministry of Housing &
Construction.
ARCHITECTURE AUSTRALIA 1989 Dec.,
v.78, no.11, p.42, photos., plan.

UNIVERSITIES AND COLLEGES--BUILDINGS--
AUSTRALIA--QUEENSLAND--BOND
UNIVERSITY
Bond University Library, Humanities
and Administration Buildings / Jun
Aoki.
Located in Queensland, Australia.
Completion date: Oct.,1989.
Architects: Arata Isozaki &
Associates.
JAPAN ARCHITECT 1990 Oct., v.65,
no.10(402), p.[45]-51, photos.,
plans, secn., site plan, aerial
photo.
Daryl Jackson: four projects / Daryl
Jackson.
The Australian Film, Television
and Radio School, North Ryde, NSW;
Bond University, Queensland;
Penguin Parade, Phillip Island,
Victoria; and Australian Chancery,
Riyadh, Saudi Arabia.
ARCHITECTURE AUSTRALIA 1990 Mar.,
v.79, no.2, p.27-42, dets., dwgs.,
photos., plans, secns., site
plans, aerial photo.

UNIVERSITIES AND COLLEGES--BUILDINGS--
AUSTRALIA--TENTERFIELD--TENTERFIELD
COLLEGE OF TAFE
New educational buildings.
Three projects designed by the New
South Wales Government Architect,
L.D. Kelly, for small communities.
ARCHITECTURE AUSTRALIA 1990 July,
v.79, no.6, p.48-50, photos.,
plans.

UNIVERSITIES AND COLLEGES--BUILDINGS--
AUSTRIA--GRAZ--TECHNISCHES
UNIVERSITAT--INSTITUT FUR BIOCHEMIE
UND BIOTECHNOLOGIE
Il caos si ferma al dettaglio:
Istituto di Biochimica e
Biotecnologia a Graz.
Architects: Michael and Karla
Szyszkowitz.
ARCHITETTURA; CRONACHE E STORIA
1990 Apr., v.36, no.4(414),
p.286-287, axonometric view,
elev., photos., plan, sketch.

UNIVERSITIES AND COLLEGES--BUILDINGS--
CANADA--MONTREAL (QUEBEC)--
UNIVERSITE DE MONTREAL--PAVILLON
PRINCIPAL
Graphisme et praxis chez Ernest
Cormier, "architecte et
ingenieur-constructeur": le
"pavillon principal" de
l'Universite de Montreal /
Isabelle Gournay.
RACAR: REVUE D'ART CANADIENNE.
CANADIAN ART REVIEW 1989, v.16,
no.2, p.161-164,273-287, dets.,
dwgs., elevs., model, plans, site
plans, refs.

UNIVERSITIES AND COLLEGES--BUILDINGS--
CANADA--TORONTO (ONTARIO)--
UNIVERSITY OF TORONTO--EARTH
SCIENCES CENTRE
Il centro di scienze naturali di
Toronto = Earth sciences centre,
Toronto / Lucia Bisi.
Architects: Bergman & Hamann, A.
J. Diamond, Donald Schmitt and
Company.
L'ARCA 1990 Apr., no.37, p.26-33,
dets., elevs., photos, plans,
secns., site plan.
Earth Sciences Centre, University of
Toronto / Trevor Boddy.
A joint venture by Bregman &
Hamann Architects and A.J.
Diamond, Donald Schmitt and Co.
CANADIAN ARCHITECT 1990 May, v.35,
no.5, p.28-35, elevs., photos,
plans, site plans.
Town and gown [Earth Sciences
Centre, University of Toronto] /
Brian Carter.
Architects: Bregman and Hamann;
A.J. Diamond, Donald Schmitt and
Company.
ARCHITECTS' JOURNAL 1990 Aug.8,
v.192, no.6, p.28-33, photos.,
plans, site plan.

UNIVERSITIES AND COLLEGES--BUILDINGS--
CANADA--TRENT (ONTARIO)--TRENT
UNIVERSITY--ENVIRONMENTAL SCIENCES
BUILDING
The Canadian Architect 1990 22nd
Annual Awards of Excellence.
Eight awards. Architects: Steven
Fong, A.J. Diamond, Donald Schmitt
& Co. with Kolker Kolker Epstein
Architects, Meltzer Igra
Architects, Bugod Figueiredo
Krendel Architects, Peter Cardew
Architects, Richard Henriquez
Architect, Laszlo Nemeth Assoc.,
Kearns Mancini Architects, Patkan
Architects, Saucier + Perrotte,
and Kuwabara Payne McKenna
Blumberg.
CANADIAN ARCHITECT 1990 Dec.,
v.35, no.12, p.9-24,29, dwgs.,
elevs., models, plans, secns.,
site plans.

UNIVERSITIES AND COLLEGES--BUILDINGS--
CANADA--WATERLOO (ONTARIO)--
UNIVERSITY OF WATERLOO--WILLIAM
DAVIS COMPUTER RESEARCH CENTRE
Beauty and the beast at the
University of Waterloo / Brian
Komonko.
William Davis Computer Research
Centre at the Univ. of Waterloo
(Ontario, Canada); architects:
IKOY.
CITY MAGAZINE 1989 Summer-Fall,
(Continued next column)

UNIVERSITIES AND COLLEGES--BUILDINGS--
CANADA--WATERLOO (ONTARIO)--
UNIVERSITY OF WATERLOO--WILLIAM
DAVIS COMPUTER RESEARCH CENTRE
(CONTINUED)
Beauty and the beast...(CONTINUED)
v.11, no.1, p.10, photos.
Il computer vi unira: "Computer
Research Center" dell'Universita
di Waterloo, Ontario.
Architect: Mathers & Haldenby,
IKOY Partnership.
ARCHITETTURA; CRONACHE E STORIA
1990 Apr., v.36, no.4(414),
p.288-289, dwg., photos., plan,
secn.

UNIVERSITIES AND COLLEGES--BUILDINGS--
CEYLON--MATARA--RUHUNU UNIVERSITY
The architecture of Geoffrey Bawa,
an intimacy of experience and
expression.
Features four projects: Madura
Club, Madura, Iadia; Triton Hotel,
Ahungalla, Sri Lanka; New
Parliamentary complex, Sri
Jayawardenepura, Kotte; Ruhuna
University, Matara.
ARCHITECTURE + DESIGN 1990
Mar.-Apr., v.7, no.2, p.57-71,
dwg., photos., plans, secns., site
plans, sketches.

UNIVERSITIES AND COLLEGES--BUILDINGS--
CHILE--SANTIAGO--UNIVERSIDAD
CATOLICA DE CHILE--CENTRO DE
EXTENSION
Centro de extension de la pontificia
universidad catolica de Chile.
Architects: Jose Antonio Gomez L.,
Montserrat Palmer, and Teodoro
Fernandez.
ARQ 1990 Mar., no.14, p.8-15,
dets., photos., plans, secns.

UNIVERSITIES AND COLLEGES--BUILDINGS--
COLONIAL--UNITED STATES--
WILLIAMSBURG (VIRGINIA)--COLLEGE OF
WILLIAM AND MARY
"So good a design": the Colonial
campus of the College of William
and Mary, Its history, background
and legacy [by] James D. Kornwolf
[book review] / Howard Davis.
Review also covers Collegiate
Gothic: the architecture of Rhodes
College, by William Morgan.
WINTERTHUR PORTFOLIO 1990 Winter,
v.25, no.4, p.[289]-292,

UNIVERSITIES AND COLLEGES--BUILDINGS--
COMPETITIONS--AUSTRALIA--PERTH--
UNIVERSITY OF WESTERN AUSTRALIA--
ZOOLOGY BUILDING
Five architects' ideas for a new
university building / Frank
Roberts.
Competition for new zoology
building, University of Western
Australia, Perth. Winning
architects: R.J. Ferguson &
Associates.
THE ARCHITECT, W.A.: THE OFFICIAL
JOURNAL OF THE ROYAL AUSTRALIAN
INSTITUTE OF ARCHITECTS, W.A.
CHAPTER 1990, v.30, no.4, p.7-9,
elevs., site plan.

UNIVERSITIES AND COLLEGES--BUILDINGS--
COMPETITIONS--GERMANY (WEST)--
BERLIN--FREIE UNIVERSITAT
Une lecon d'anatomie berlinoise /
Corinne Jacquand.
Features the winning design in the
competition for Anatomy Institute
at the Freie Universitat, Berlin.
Architect: Paul Ziegert.
ARCHITECTURE D'AUJOURD'HUI 1990
Feb., no.267, p.50-51, dwgs.,
elevs., models, plan, site plan.

UNIVERSITIES AND COLLEGES--BUILDINGS--
COMPETITIONS--SPAIN--SALAMANCA--
UNIVERSIDAD SALAMANCA
Concurso de anteproyectos para el
campus de ciencas
juridicas-sociales y empresiales,
Univ. Salamanca, Nov. 1989.
First prize to Luis Garcia Gil, et
al..
ARQUITECTURA 1990 Jan.-Feb., v.72,
no.282, p.18-19, elevs., plans,
site plan.

UNIVERSITIES AND COLLEGES--BUILDINGS--
COMPETITIONS--UNITED STATES--
COLUMBUS (OHIO)--OHIO STATE
UNIVERSITY--WEXNER CENTER FOR THE
VISUAL ARTS
Conflicto de intereses: el concurso
para el Wexner Center / Alan
Colquhoun.
ARQUITECTURA VIVA 1990 Mar.-Apr.,
no.11, p.24-26, axonometric view,
dwgs., elevs., models.

UNIVERSITIES AND COLLEGES--BUILDINGS--
CONSERVATION AND RESTORATION--UNITED
STATES--CHARLOTTESVILLE (VIRGINIA)--
UNIVERSITY OF VIRGINIA--ACADEMICAL
VILLAGE
"The Academical Village of Thomas
Jefferson" / James Murray Howard.
On the restoration of these
buildings which are part of the
Univ. of Virginia, Charlottesville
campus. Summaries in French,
Italian and Spanish.
ICOMOS INFORMATION 1989 Oct.-Dec.,
no.4, p.19-25, dwg., port.,
photos., site plan, refs.

UNIVERSITIES AND COLLEGES--BUILDINGS--
CONSERVATION AND RESTORATION--UNITED
STATES--LAKELAND (FLORIDA)--FLORIDA
SOUTHERN COLLEGE
Restoration for Florida Southern /
Judy Donohue.
Program to restore all campus
buildings designed by Frank Lloyd
Wright between 1938 and 1958.
Restoration architects: L.D.
Astorino & Associates.
PROGRESSIVE ARCHITECTURE 1990
Apr., v.71, no.4, p.30-31, photos.

UNIVERSITIES AND COLLEGES--BUILDINGS--
ENGLAND--ASCOT--IMPERIAL COLLEGE--
CENTRE FOR POPULATION BIOLOGY
Baby biosphere / Denise Chevin.
Research facilities, including
Ecotron house, at the Center for
Population Biology, at Imperial
College, in Ascot, Berkshire,
including chambers for ecological
studies.
BUILDING 1990 Nov.16, v.255,
no.45, p.88-89, photos., secn.

UNIVERSITIES AND COLLEGES--BUILDINGS--
ENGLAND--BRISTOL--UNIVERSITY OF
BRISTOL--FACULTY OF ARTS
Phased faculty: Arts Faculty,
Bristol.
Contents: Appraisal, by Richard
Weston; Economic appraisal, cost
comment, by Roger Barbrook; Cost
analysis; Raised walkway:
Education building, MacCormac
Jamieson Prichard and Wright.
ARCHITECTS' JOURNAL 1990 Jan.31,
v.191, no.5, p.33-48,53-55, dets.,
photos., plans, secns., site plan,
table, isometric dwg., aerial
photo., refs.

UNIVERSITIES AND COLLEGES--BUILDINGS--
ENGLAND--CAMBRIDGE--CAMBRIDGE
UNIVERSITY--TRINITY COLLEGE--BLUE
BOAR COURT
College tradition: Blue Boar Court.
Student housing for Trinity
College, Cambridge. Architects:
MacCormac, Jamieson, Prichard &
Wright. Contents: Appraisal, by
Peter Wislocki; Cost comment, by
Roger Barbrook; External Wall,
hall of residence, MJPW
Architects.
ARCHITECTS' JOURNAL 1990 Dec.5,
v.192, no.23, p.31-39,41-43,47-49,
axonometric view, dets., elev.,
model, photos., plans, secns.,
site plan.

UNIVERSITIES AND COLLEGES--BUILDINGS--
ENGLAND--CIRENCESTER--ROYAL
AGRICULTURAL COLLEGE--BLEDISLOE
COURT
Roof and external walls: hall of
residence: David Lea.
Bledisloe Court residence hall,
Royal Agricultural College,
Cirencester. The use of local
stone for exterior walls, roof
tiles and window mullions allows
this 1983 building to age
gracefully in its Cotswold
setting.
ARCHITECTS' JOURNAL 1990 Sept.26,
v.192, no.13, p.55-57, dets.,
photo., secns.

UNIVERSITIES AND COLLEGES--BUILDINGS--
ENGLAND--HIGHFIELD--UNIVERSITY OF
SOUTHAMPTON--MANAGEMENT SCHOOL
Finishing school: Southhampton
University Management School.
Located in Chilworth Research
Park. Interior designer: Merchant
Design International.
BUILDING 1990 Dec.7, v.255, no.48,
p.74-75,

UNIVERSITIES AND COLLEGES--BUILDINGS--
ENGLAND--LIVERPOOL--LIVERPOOL
UNIVERSITY--SCHOOL OF ARCHITECTURE
AND BUILDING ENGINEERING
Hochschule fur Architektur und
Hochbautechnik in Liverpool =
University School of Architecture
and Building Engineeringg in
Liverpool.
Architects: Dave King and Rod
McAllister with Gerald Beech
Partnership.
DETAIL 1990 Dec.,-1991 Jan., v.30,
no.6, p.614-619, dets., photos.,
plans, secns., site plan.

UNIVERSITIES AND COLLEGES--BUILDINGS--
ENGLAND--LONDON--UNIVERSITY OF
LONDON--COURTAULD INSTITUTE OF ART
Art into architecture / Dan
Cruickshank, Peter Wilson.
Conversion of Somerset House on
the Strand, London, into the new
location for the Courtauld
Institute of Art and the Witt
Library. Architects for the
conversion: Green Lloyd Architects
and Christopher Firmstone;
original architect: Sir William
Chambers. Includes separate
article on the student cafeteria,
p.55-57.
ARCHITECTS' JOURNAL 1990 Oct.31,
v.192, no.18, p.34-[41],44-49,
55-57, dets., ill., photos.,
plans, secns.
Courtauld: changement d'adresse /
Jeanne-Marie de Broglie.
On the installation of the
Courtauld Institute in Somerset
House (1774-1780), London.
Original architect: Sir William
Chambers.
CONNAISSANCE DES ARTS 1990 Sept.,
no.463, p.[142]-151, photos.
Putting art in the vaults / Kenneth
Powell.
On two London projects: the
conversion of Somerset House,
designed by Sir William Chambers,
into space for the Courtauld
Institute and Galleries and the
expansion and restoration of the
underground vaults of the Royal
Society of Arts.
RIBA JOURNAL 1990 Aug., v.97,
no.8, p.48-51,54-56, photos.,
secns.
Somerset House, London: the
Courtauld Institute / Richard
Haslam.
Restoration of North Block of
Somerset House, in the Strand, to
house the Courtauld Institute and
its picture collection. Original
architect: Sir William Chambers;
restoration architect: Christopher
Firmstone.
COUNTRY LIFE 1990 June 21, v.184,
no.25, p.114-117, photos., plan.

UNIVERSITIES AND COLLEGES--BUILDINGS--
ENGLAND--LONDON--UNIVERSITY OF
LONDON--QUEEN MARY AND WESTFIELD
COLLEGE
Halls of residence 2: case studies.
Student accomodation in Glasgow,
Edinburgh, and east London.
Architects: MacCormac Jamieson
Prichard for Queen Mary and
Westfield College, University of
London; The Kennedy Partership for
Forbes Hall, University of
Strathclyde, Glasgow; and Davis
Duncan Partnership for Robertson's
Close, University of Edinburgh.
ARCHITECTS' JOURNAL 1990 Aug.1,
v.192, no.5, p.49-53, axonometric
view, photos., plans, secn., site
plans.

UNIVERSITIES AND COLLEGES--BUILDINGS--
ENGLAND--LONDON--UNIVERSITY OF
LONDON--WESTFIELD COLLEGE--
INFORMATICS TECHNOLOGY LABORATORY
Informatics Teaching Laboratory.
At Westfield College, University
of London, on Mile End Road; for
the study of computer science.
Architect: MacCormac Jamieson
Prichard.
BUILDING 1990 Feb.23, v.255, no.8,
p.57-64, det., photos., plans,
secn., site plan, tables.

UNIVERSITIES AND COLLEGES--BUILDINGS--
ENGLAND--NORWICH--UNIVERSITY OF EAST
ANGLIA
Planning authority / John Welsh.
On Rick Mather Architects'
development plan for the
University of East Anglia,
Norwich.
BUILDING DESIGN 1990 Nov.9,
no.1011, p.10-11, dwgs., models,
plans, secns., site plans.

UNIVERSITIES AND COLLEGES--BUILDINGS--
ENGLAND--OXFORD--OXFORD UNIVERSITY--
MAGDALEN COLLEGE
An auspicious alliance: Pugin,
Bloxam, and the Magdalen
Commissions / Leon B. Litvack.
Sequel to an article publ. in
JSAH, 1986, v.45, p.358-373.
Surveys the history of two small
commissions (Magdalen College
gateway and the Church of Saint
Lawrence, Tubney). Includes
abstract.
SOCIETY OF ARCHITECTURAL
HISTORIANS. JOURNAL 1990 June,
v.49, no.2, p.154-160, dets.,
dwgs., photos., plans, secns.,
refs.

UNIVERSITIES AND COLLEGES--BUILDINGS--
ENGLAND--OXFORD--OXFORD UNIVERSITY--
SAINT JOHN'S COLLEGE
College developments.
Looks at St. John's College,
Oxford, by Richard MacCormac to
examine the principles put forward
by the architect in his bid for
the RIBA presidency within his own
work.
ARCHITECTS' JOURNAL 1990 Nov.14,
v.192, no.20, p.14-17, dwgs.,
elevs., model, photo., plans, site
plans.

UNIVERSITIES AND COLLEGES--BUILDINGS--
ENGLAND--OXFORD--OXFORD UNIVERSITY--
SAINT JOHN'S COLLEGE--CANTERBURY
QUADRANGLE
The Canterbury Quadrangle, St.
John's College, Oxford [by] Howard
Colvin [book review] / Ivor
Bulmer-Thomas.
ANCIENT MONUMENTS SOCIETY.
TRANSACTIONS 1990, new ser.,v.34,
p 200,

UNIVERSITIES AND COLLEGES--BUILDINGS--
ENGLAND--PORTSMOUTH--PORTSMOUTH
POLYTECHNIC
Second thoughts [Portsmouth
Polytechnic Library, Phase 2] /
Richard Weston.
13 years separate the design and
construction of the first and
second phases of Frewen Library,
Portsmouth Polytechnic (Eng.).
(Continued next column)

UNIVERSITIES AND COLLEGES--BUILDINGS--
ENGLAND--PORTSMOUTH--PORTSMOUTH
POLYTECHNIC (CONTiNUED)
Second thoughts... (CONTINUED)
Architects: Ahrends Burton and
Koralek.
ARCHITECTS' JOURNAL 1990 Jan.24,
v.191, no.4, p.44-51, elevs.,
photos., secns., site plans,
sketch. aerial photo.

UNIVERSITIES AND COLLEGES--BUILDINGS--
FRANCE--DUNKIRK--INSTITUT
UNIVERSITAIRE DE TECHNOLOGIE--POLE
UNIVERSITAIRE
Universite de la Citadelle
Dunkerque.
On the Pole universitaire, at the
Institut Universitaire de
technologie, Dunkirk. Architects:
Architecture Studio.
TECHNIQUES ET ARCHITECTURE 1990
Dec.-1991 Jan., no.393, p.15-19,
photos., plans, secns., site
plans, aerial photos.

UNIVERSITIES AND COLLEGES--BUILDINGS--
FRANCE--MAS-D'AZIL
Fins de chantier.
Contents: Apartment house:
20-28, rue Ramponneau, Paris;
architect: Fernando Montes --
Showroom building, Kita-Aoyama,
Tokyo, Japan; architect: Fumihiko
Maki -- College du Mas-d'Azil,
Ariege, France; architects:
Joseph Almudever and Christian
Lefebvre.
LE MONITEUR ARCHITECTURE AMC 1990
Apr., no.10, p.15-21, axonometric
view, photos., plans, secn.

UNIVERSITIES AND COLLEGES--BUILDINGS--
GERMANY (WEST)--AACHEN--TECHNISCHE
HOCHSCHULE AACHEN--MEDIZINISCHE
FAKULTAT
Darum Sichtinstallation:
medizinische Fakultat der
Technischen Hochschule Aachen.
Architects: Jurgen Kunz with Paul
Troger and Wolfgang Weber.
Includes English summary.
DETAIL 1990 Dec.-1991 Jan., v.30,
no.6, p.581-584, dwgs., photos.,
secns., isometric dwgs.

UNIVERSITIES AND COLLEGES--BUILDINGS--
GERMANY (WEST)--BREMERHAVEN--
CARLSBURG HOCHSCHULE
Carlsburg-Hochschule in Bremerhaven:
2. Bauabschnitt.
Architects: Gottfried Bohm, Gunter
Kaesbach. Includes English
summary.
BAUMEISTER 1990 Mar., v.87, no.3,
p.30-31, photos., plans, secns.,
site plans.

UNIVERSITIES AND COLLEGES--BUILDINGS--
GERMANY (WEST)--EICHSTATT--
KATHOLISCHE UNIVERSITAT FACULTY FOR
JOURNALISM AND PSYCHOLOGY
Restauro e trasformazione dell
storico orfanotrofio di Eichstatt:
karljosef Schattner / Gilberto
Botti.
Text in Italian and English.
DOMUS 1990 Apr., no.715,
p.[52-57], axonometric view,
elev., photos, plans, site plan.

UNIVERSITIES AND COLLEGES--BUILDINGS--
GERMANY (WEST)--FRANKFURT AM MAIN--
UNIVERSITAT FRANKFURT--BIOZENTRUM
Peter Eisenman.
Most of the issue devoted to this
architect. Nine projects featured.
Includes interview with David
Cohn. Text in Spanish and English.
EL CROQUIS 1989 Dec., v.8, no.41,
p.4-126,cover, axonometric views,
ill., dwgs., ports., elevs.,
models, photos., plans, secns.,
refs.

UNIVERSITIES AND COLLEGES--BUILDINGS--
GERMANY (WEST)--FREISING--
WEIHENSTEPHEN
Lebensmitteltechnikum in
Freising-Weihenstephen = College
for Food Technology in
Freising-Weihenstephen.
Architects: H. Geierstanger, W.
Hurmer, J.A. Adam, et al.
DETAIL 1990 Dec.-1991 Jan., v.30,
no.6, p.SI-SIV, dets., elevs.,
photos., plans, secn., site plan.

UNIVERSITIES AND COLLEGES--BUILDINGS--
GERMANY (WEST)--INGOLSTADT--
KATHOLISCHE UNIVERSITAT EICHSTATT--
WIRTSCHAFTSWISSENSCHAFTLICHE
FAKULTAT
Ingolstadt: Bibliothek statt Kirche.
Renovations and conversion of
church and adjacent building at
Stiftung Katholische Universitat
Eichstatt. Architect: Wilhelm
Kucker.
BAUWELT 1990 Mar.16, v.81, no.11,
p.512-515, photos., plan, secns.,
site plan.

UNIVERSITIES AND COLLEGES--BUILDINGS--
GERMANY (WEST)--INGOLSTADT--
ZKATOLISCHE UNIVERSITAT EICHSTATT--
WIRTSCHAFTSWISSENSCHAFTLICHE
FAKULTAT
Wirtschaftswissenschaftliche
Fakultat der Universitat
Eichstatt, Ingolstadt = Faculty of
Economics at the University of
Eichstatt.
Architect: Wilhelm Kucker.
DETAIL 1990 Oct.-Nov., v.30, no.5,
p.SI-SIV,504, dets., photos.,
plans, secn., site plan.

UNIVERSITIES AND COLLEGES--BUILDINGS--
GERMANY (WEST)--KIEL--
CHRISTIAN-ALBRECHTS-UNIVERSITAT--
GEOMAR
Forschungszentrum GEOMAR.
On the 1987 competition for new
fscility for the Forschungszentrum
fur Marine Geowissenschaften, at
the Christian-Albrechts-Universita
t, Kiel. First prize entry by
Walter Kleine, Jurgen Ripken, and
Sigrid Kleine.
BAUWELT 1990 Apr.13, v.81, no.14,
p.702-703, site plan.

UNIVERSITIES AND COLLEGES--BUILDINGS--
GERMANY (WEST)--MANNHEIM--
UNIVERSITAT MANNHEIM
Architektur unterwegs.
Three projects: Horsaal und
Bibliotheksgebaude A3, Universitat
Mannheim (architect: Gottfr.
Bohm); Colonia-Victoire
Versicherung, Cologne (architects:
Architekten Dansard, Kalenborn &
(Continued next page)

UNIVERSITIES AND COLLEGES--BUILDINGS--
GERMANY (WEST)--MANNHEIM--
UNIVERSITAT MANNHEIM (CONTINUED)
Architektur unterwegs. (CONTINUED)
Partner, and BHLM Architekten
Stadtplaner); Brunnangerhalle
Starnberg (architects: Moritz
Hauschild, Rudiger Fritsch).
DEUTSCHES ARCHITEKTENBLATT 1990
Dec.1, v.22, no.12, p.1835-1838,
photos., plans.

UNIVERSITIES AND COLLEGES--BUILDINGS--
GERMANY (WEST)--REUTLINGEN--
UNIVERSITAT--MUSIKWISSENSCHAFTLICHES
INSTITUT
Pfleghof: Umbau des
Musikwissenschaftlichen Instituts
der Universitat.
Interior renovations to a late
15th-cent. building. Architect:
Dieter Hauser.
BAUWELT 1990 Jan.19, v.81, no.2-3,
p.80-82, photos., plans, secns.

UNIVERSITIES AND COLLEGES--BUILDINGS--
GERMANY (WEST)--STUTTGART--
UNIVERSITAT HOHENHEIM
Vierlinge: neue Instituts- und
Horsaalgebaude fur die Universitat
Hohenheim.
Architects: Drei Architekten und
Partner.
ARCHITEKTUR, INNENARCHITEKTUR,
TECHNISCHER AUSBAU 1990 Oct.,
v.98, no.10, p.42-46, photos.,
plans, secn., site plans.

UNIVERSITIES AND COLLEGES--BUILDINGS--
GOTHIC REVIVAL--UNITED STATES--
MEMPHIS (TENNESSEE)--RHODES COLLEGE
"So good a design": the Colonial
campus of the College of William
and Mary, Its history, background
and legacy [by] James D. Kornwolf
[book review] / Howard Davis.
Review also covers Collegiate
Gothic: the architecture of Rhodes
College, by William Morgan.
WINTERTHUR PORTFOLIO 1990 Winter,
v.25, no.4, p.[289]-292,

UNIVERSITIES AND COLLEGES--BUILDINGS--
HONG KONG--HONG KONG POLYTECHNIC
A learning experience [Hong Kong
Polytechnic's new entrance
building].
Architects: Leigh & Orange.
ASIAN ARCHITECT AND CONTRACTOR
1989 Sept., v.19, no.9, p.44,
photos.

UNIVERSITIES AND COLLEGES--BUILDINGS--
INDIA--DHARWAD--SHRI DHARMASTHALA
MANJUNATHESHWARA INSTITUTE OF
ENGINEERING AND TECHNOLOGY
Shri Dharmasthala Manjunatheshwara
Institute of Engineering and
Technology, Dharwad, Karnataka /
Shirish Beri.
Completed in 1988. Architect:
Shirish Beri.
ARCHITECTURE + DESIGN 1990
May-June, v.7, no.3, p.32-37,
photos., plan, secns., site plan.

UNIVERSITIES AND COLLEGES--BUILDINGS--
INDIA--NEW DELHI--UNIVERSITY OF NEW
DELHI--CENTRAL INSTITUTE OF
EDUCATIONAL TECHNOLOGY
Istituto centrale di technologia per
l'educazione presso Delhi.
Built 1988-1990. Architects: Raj
Rewal Associates.
CASABELLA 1990 July-Aug., v.54,
no.570, p.26-27, axonometric view,
elevs., photos., plan, secn.
E qualcosa di moghuli: Raj Rewal,
Istituto universitario di Scienza
della communicazione, Nuova Delhi.
ARCHITETTURA; CRONACHE E STORIA
1990 Jan., v.36, no.1(411),
p.48-49, axonometric views,
photos.
Rewal Rasa / Dan Cruickshank.
On the Central Institute of
Educational Technology, New Delhi.
Architect: Raj Rewal.
ARCHITECTURAL REVIEW 1990 Jan.,
v.187, no.1115, p.[56]-59,
axonometric view, photos.

UNIVERSITIES AND COLLEGES--BUILDINGS--
ISRAEL--HAIFA--BLOOMFIELD BUILDING
"Bloomfield Building" nel
Politecnico di Haifa.
Architects: Yacov Rechter, Chaim
Ben Ari. Summaries in English,
French, German, and Spanish.
ARCHITETTURA; CRONACHE E STORIA
1990 June, v.36, no.6(416),
p.434-[442], photos., plans,
secn., site plans.

UNIVERSITIES AND COLLEGES--BUILDINGS--
ITALY--AQUILA--UNIVERSITARE
L'AQUILA--FACOLTA DI SCIENZE
La Facolta di Scienze a L'Aquila =
The Science Faculty of L'Aquila /
Maurizio Vitta.
Architects: Guido Gigli, Bruno
Remotti, Ludovico Rolli.
L'ARCA 1990 July-Aug., no.40,
p.66-73, photos., plans, secn.

UNIVERSITIES AND COLLEGES--BUILDINGS--
ITALY--BOLOGNA--UNIVERSITA DI
BOLOGNA--BATTIFERRO
Sozialwohnungen und
Studentenwohnungen in Battiffero.
Built for the University of
Bologna, 1984-1987. Architect:
Gianfranco Dall'Erba.
BAUWELT 1990 Apr.6, v.81, no.13,
p.676-677, photos., plans, secn.

UNIVERSITIES AND COLLEGES--BUILDINGS--
ITALY--BOLOGNA--UNIVERSITA DI
BOLOGNA--ZIEGELI VIA RONCAGLIO
Studentenwohnungen in der ehemaligen
Ziegeli Via Roncaglio.
Built for the University of
Bologna, 1984-1988. Architect:
Sandro Breschi.
BAUWELT 1990 Apr.6, v.81, no.13,
p.674-675, elevs., photos., plans,
secn.

UNIVERSITIES AND COLLEGES--BUILDINGS--
ITALY--MILAN--ISTITUTO UNIVERSITARIO
DI LINGUE MODERNE
A Milano, ritorno alla
"universitas".
Classroom, office and library
buildings planned for the I.U.L.M.
Architects: Lorenzo and Roberto
Guiducci.
L'INDUSTRIA DELLE COSTRUZIONI 1990
(Continued next column)

UNIVERSITIES AND COLLEGES--BUILDINGS--
ITALY--MILAN--ISTITUTO UNIVERSITARIO
DI LINGUE MODERNE (CONTINUED)
A Milano, ritorno alla (CONTINUED)
Dec. v.24, no.230, p.66-67, dwgs.,
elevs., plans, secn.

UNIVERSITIES AND COLLEGES--BUILDINGS--
ITALY--PESCARA
Complesso universitario a Pescara /
Giovanni Klaus Koenig.
Architects: Franco Donato, Leo
Giubilei. Summaries in English,
French, erman, and Spanish.
ARCHITETTURA; CRONACHE E STORIA
1990 Apr., v.36, no.4(414)
p.[246]-261, elevs., photos.,
plans, secns., site plan.

UNIVERSITIES AND COLLEGES--BUILDINGS--
JAPAN--INBA--TOKYO CHRISTIAN
COLLEGE--CHAPEL
Tokyo Christian College Chapel / Jun
Aoki.
Located in Inba, Chiba Prefecture.
Completion date: May 1989.
Architects: Arata Isozaki &
Associates.
JAPAN ARCHITECT 1990 Oct., v.65,
no.10(402), p.52-57, photos.,
plna, secns.

UNIVERSITIES AND COLLEGES--BUILDINGS--
JAPAN--KOBE--KOBE INSTITUTE OF ART
TECHNOLOGY
Kobe Institute of Art Technology.
Established in 1989. Architects:
Yasumi Yoshitake, Shigefumi
Suzuki. English summary, p.23.
KENCHIKU BUNKA 1990 Mar., v.45,
no.521, p.111-122, diagr.,
photos., plans, elevs., site
plans, sketches.

UNIVERSITIES AND COLLEGES--BUILDINGS--
JAPAN--KOBE--SAINT CATHERINE'S
COLLEGE--KOBE INSTITUTE
St. Catherine's at Kobe / Dan
Cruickshank.
First Oxford University building
constructed outside of the city is
St. Catherine's College in Kobe,
Japan. Troughton McAslan
Architects.
ARCHITECTS' JOURNAL 1990 Nov.7,
v.192, no.19, p.26-29, axonometric
view, dwgs., elev., models, secn.

UNIVERSITIES AND COLLEGES--BUILDINGS--
JAPAN--OMIYA--SHIBAURA INSTITUTE OF
TECHNOLOGY--SAITO MEMORIAL HALL
Takefumi Aida / Takefumi Aida.
Contents: War Dead Memorial Park,
Tokyo, design: 1987; construction:
1987-88 -- Saito Memorial Hall,
Shibaura Institute of Technology,
Omiya, Saitama, Japan, design:
1989; completion: Sept.1990. Text
in Japanese and English.
GA DOCUMENT 1990 Apr., no.25,
p.12-17, axonometric views,
elevs., models, photos., plans.

UNIVERSITIES AND COLLEGES--BUILDINGS--
JAPAN--TOKYO--AOYAMA TECHNICAL
COLLEGE
Liberta e indipendenza [Aoyama
Technical College, Tokyo] / Makoto
Sei Watanabe.
Architect: Makoto Sei Watanabe.
MODO 1990 Dec., v.13, no.128,
p.52-53, photos.

UNIVERSITIES AND COLLEGES--BUILDINGS--
JAPAN--TOKYO--MUSASHINO WOMEN'S
COLLEGE--GREEN HALL
Hiroshi Hara & Atelier O: Musashino
Women's College, Green Hall, Hoya,
Tokyo, Japan, design: 1988-89;
construction: 1989-90.
Text in Japanese and English.
GA DOCUMENT 1990 Sept., no.27,
p.96-105, elevs., photos., plans,
secns.
Special edition I: scene scheme of
learning.
Features two projects by Hiroshi
Hara and Atelier O: Takezono-Nishi
primary school, Tsukuba and Green
Hall, Musashino Women's College.
Includes essay by Hara, entitled:
From "Note for Modality." English
summary, p.23.
KENCHIKU BUNKA 1990 Sept., v.45,
no.527, p.25-56, axonometric
views, elevs., photos., plans,
secns., site plans.
Special edition I: urban modal
inductor.
Features five projects by Hiroshi
Hara and Atelier O. English
summary, p.23.
KENCHIKU BUNKA 1990 Mar., v.45,
no.521, p.33-68, axonometric
views, ill., models, photos.,
plans, secns., sketch.

UNIVERSITIES AND COLLEGES--BUILDINGS--
JAPAN--TOKYO--MUSASHINO WOMEN'S
COLLEGE--KINDERGARDEN
Special edition I: urban modal
inductor.
Features five projects by Hiroshi
Hara and Atelier O. English
summary, p.23.
KENCHIKU BUNKA 1990 Mar., v.45,
no.521, p.33-68, axonometric
views, ill., models, photos.,
plans, secns., sketch.

UNIVERSITIES AND COLLEGES--BUILDINGS--
JAPAN--TOKYO--TOKYO INSTITUTE OF
TECHNOLOGY--CENTENNIAL HALL
Tokyo, die Schonheit des Chaos /
Kazuo Shinohara.
Centennial Hall, an art building
for the Tokyo Institute of
Technology. Architect: K.
Shinohara.
ARCH PLUS 1990 Oct., no.105-106,
p.48-50, elevs., photos., plans,
secns., site plans.

UNIVERSITIES AND COLLEGES--BUILDINGS--
MIDDLE EAST
Building for higher education in the
Gulf / Kamal El Kafrawi.
Introduction to section with five
articles (indexed separately).
MIMAR: ARCHITECTURE IN DEVELOPMENT
1990 Dec., v.10, no.4(37), p.23,

UNIVERSITIES AND COLLEGES--BUILDINGS--
NETHERLANDS--HAGUE--HAAGSE
HOGESCHOOL
Haagse Hogeschool kiest PRO.
Model and drawing by Atelier PRO
for plaza and oval administrative
building in The Hague.
DE ARCHITECT 1990 Oct., v.21,
no.10, p.36-37, dwg., model.

UNIVERSITIES AND COLLEGES--BUILDINGS--
OMAN--SULTAN QABOOS UNIVERSITY
Sultan Qaboos University, Oman.
Located in Al Khwad; completed in
1986. Architect: YRM
International.
MIMAR: ARCHITECTURE IN DEVELOPMENT
1990 Dec., v.10, no.4(37),
p.46-49, photos., site plan,
aerial photo.

UNIVERSITIES AND COLLEGES--BUILDINGS--
PAKISTAN--LAHORE--LAHORE UNIVERSITY
OF MANAGEMENT SCIENCES
Lahore University of Management
Sciences / Murlidhar Dawani.
Includes Academic block and
student housing. Architects: Habib
Fida Ali, Husnain Lotia, Ali
Naqvi, Mansoor Ghanchi. Expected
completion date for Phase I:1992.
MIMAR: ARCHITECTURE IN DEVELOPMENT
1990 Dec., v.10, no.4(37),
p.40-[45], dwgs., models, plan,
site plan.

UNIVERSITIES AND COLLEGES--BUILDINGS--
SAUDI ARABIA--RIYADH--KING SAUD
UNIVERSITY
King Saud University, Riyadh, Saudi
Arabia, 1984.
Architects: Gyo Obata of Hellmuth,
Obata & Kassabaum, with Gollins
Melvin Ward Partnership. Text in
Japanese and English.
ARCHITECTURE AND URBANISM 1990
Dec., no.12 extra edition,
p.40-[47], photos., secn., site
plan.

UNIVERSITIES AND COLLEGES--BUILDINGS--
SCOTLAND--EDINBURGH--UNIVERSITY OF
EDINBURGH--ROBERTSON'S CLOSE
Halls of residence 2: case studies.
Student accomodation in Glasgow,
Edinburgh, and east London.
Architects: MacCormac Jamieson
Prichard for Queen Mary and
Westfield College, University of
London; The Kennedy Partership for
Forbes Hall, University of
Strathclyde, Glasgow; and Davis
Duncan Partnership for Robertson's
Close, University of Edinburgh.
ARCHITECTS' JOURNAL 1990 Aug.1,
v.192, no.5, p.49-53, axonometric
view, photos., plans, secn., site
plans.

UNIVERSITIES AND COLLEGES--BUILDINGS--
SCOTLAND--GLASGOW--UNIVERSITY OF
STRATHCLYDE--FORBES HALL
Halls of residence 2: case studies.
Student accomodation in Glasgow,
Edinburgh, and east London.
Architects: MacCormac Jamieson
Prichard for Queen Mary and
Westfield College, University of
London; The Kennedy Partership for
Forbes Hall, University of
Strathclyde, Glasgow; and Davis
Duncan Partnership for Robertson's
(Continued next column)

UNIVERSITIES AND COLLEGES--BUILDINGS--
SCOTLAND--GLASGOW--UNIVERSITY OF
STRATHCLYDE--FORBES HALL
(CONTINUED)
Halls of residence 2:...(CONTINUED)
Close, University of Edinburgh.
ARCHITECTS' JOURNAL 1990 Aug.1,
v.192, no.5, p.49-53, axonometric
view, photos., plans, secn., site
plans.

UNIVERSITIES AND COLLEGES--BUILDINGS--
SOUTH AFRICA--DURBAN--UNIVERSITY OF
SOUTH AFRICA--DURBAN REGIONAL OFFICE
UNISA, Durban regional offices.
Offices of the University of South
Africa contain seminar and
examination facilities,
administrative offices and
library. Architects: Brian
Sandrock Architects.
ARCHITECT & BUILDER 1989 July,
p.2-5, elev., photos., plans.

UNIVERSITIES AND COLLEGES--BUILDINGS--
SPAIN--BARCELONA--UNIVERSIDAD
POLITECNICA BARCELONA
Biblioteca y departamentos; U.
Politecnica Barcelona, 1989-90.
Architect: Jose Llinas.
ARQUITECTURA 1990 Jan.-Feb., v.72,
no.282, p.122-129, elevs.,
photos., plans, secns.

UNIVERSITIES AND COLLEGES--BUILDINGS--
SWITZERLAND--BERN--LEHRGEBAUDE DER
VET.-MED.
Lehrgebaude der Vet.-Med. Fakultat
Universitat Bern, 1989/90.
Architect: Franz Oswald.
WERK, BAUEN + WOHNEN 1989 Dec.,
no.12, p.53, dwgs., elev., plan,
secn., site plan.

UNIVERSITIES AND COLLEGES--BUILDINGS--
UNITED STATES
Boom and reverberation: a new crop
of academic buildings considers
context and campus life / Richard
Bender.
ARCHITECTURE: THE AIA JOURNAL 1990
Jan., v.79, no.1, p.58-59, photos.

UNIVERSITIES AND COLLEGES--BUILDINGS--
UNITED STATES--AMES (IOWA)--IOWA
STATE UNIVERSITY--AGRONOMY HALL
A future with a past: Agronomy Hall,
Iowa State University / Martha
Huntington.
In Ames. Architects: RDG
Bussard/Dikis.
IOWA ARCHITECT 1990 Fall, v.39,
no.3, p.22-[25], photos., plans,
site plan.

UNIVERSITIES AND COLLEGES--BUILDINGS--
UNITED STATES--AMES (IOWA)--IOWA
STATE UNIVERSITY--MOLECULAR BIOLOGY
BUILDING
Becoding nature in Ames / Barbara H.
Hower.
The Molecular Biology Building at
Iowa State University. Architects:
Hansen Lind Meyer.
INLAND ARCHITECT 1990 Sept.-Oct.,
v.34, no.5, p.12, dwgs.

UNIVERSITIES AND COLLEGES--BUILDINGS--
UNITED STATES--AMHERST
(MASSACHUSETTS)--AMHERST COLLEGE--
CONVOCATION CENTER
Breaking ground / Michael Wagner.
Three projects: Kitchener, Ontario
city hall, architects: Kuwabara
Payne Mckenna Blumberg Architects;
Convocation Center, Amherst
College, Amherst, Mass.,
architects: Cambridge Seven
Associates; model home, part of
Living Environments program by GE
Plastics.
INTERIORS 1990 Feb., v.149, no.7,
p.128, dwgs.

UNIVERSITIES AND COLLEGES--BUILDINGS--
UNITED STATES--APPLETON
(WISCONSIN)--LAWRENCE UNIVERSITY--
WRISTON ART CENTER
For art's sake: Wriston Art Center,
Lawrence University, Appleton,
Wisconsin, Centerbrook Architects
/ Lynn Nesmith.
ARCHITECTURE: THE AIA JOURNAL 1990
Jan., v.79, no.1, p.[84]-89,
photos., plans, site plan.

UNIVERSITIES AND COLLEGES--BUILDINGS--
UNITED STATES--ATLANTA (GEORGIA)--
EMORY UNIVERSITY--D. ABBOTT TURNER
CENTER
Focal point: [D. Abbott Turner
Center, Emory University] / Jim
Murphy.
On the community center of the
Candler School of Theology.
Includes small chapel and the
renovated Turner Village Housing.
Architects: Scogin, Elam & Bray,
Architects.
PROGRESSIVE ARCHITECTURE 1990
Dec., v.71, no.13, p.66-73, dets.,
photos., plan, site plan.

UNIVERSITIES AND COLLEGES--BUILDINGS--
UNITED STATES--ATLANTA (GEORGIA)--
EMORY UNIVERSITY--TURNER VILLAGE
Scogin Elam and Bray.
Features four projects in Georgia:
Clayton County Library, Jonesboro;
Buckhead Branch Library, Atlanta;
Chmar house, Atlanta; and Turner
Village, Candler School of
Theology, Emory Univ., Atlanta.
English summaries.
ARCHITECTURE D'AUJOURD'HUI 1990
Oct., no.271, p.134-144, elevs.,
models, photos., plans, secns.,
site plans.

UNIVERSITIES AND COLLEGES--BUILDINGS--
UNITED STATES--AUSTIN (TEXAS)--
UNIVERSITY OF TEXAS AT AUSTIN--
ALUMNI CENTER
Alumni center adds more and Moore /
Ray Don Tilley.
The UT Austin Alumni Center
addition. Architects: Charles
Moore, Richard Dodge, and Jessen
Inc.
TEXAS ARCHITECT 1990 July-Aug.,
v.40, no.4, p.59, dwgs., site
plan.

UNIVERSITIES AND COLLEGES--BUILDINGS--
UNITED STATES--BOSTON
(MASSACHUSETTS)--HARVARD
UNIVERSITY--SHAD HALL
Academic fitness: Shad Hall, Harvard
University, Boston, Massachusetts
/ Robert Campbell.
Athletic center for the Graduate
School of Business Administration.
Architects: Kallmann, McKinnell &
Wood.
ARCHITECTURE: THE AIA JOURNAL 1990
Mar., v.79, no.3, p.128-133,
elevs., photos., secns., site
plan.

UNIVERSITIES AND COLLEGES--BUILDINGS--
UNITED STATES--BOSTON
(MASSACHUSETTS)--NORTHEASTERN
UNIVERSITY BOATHOUSE
Team spirit: Northeastern University
Boathouse, Boston, Massachusetts,
Graham Gund Architects / Michael
J. Crosbie.
ARCHITECTURE: THE MAGAZINE OF THE
AMERICAN INSTITUTE OF ARCHITECTS
1990 Aug., v.79, no.8, p.72-75,
photos., plans, site plan.

UNIVERSITIES AND COLLEGES--BUILDINGS--
UNITED STATES--BRUNSWICK (MAINE)--
BOWDOIN COLLEGE
The architecture of Bowdoin College
[by] Patricia McGraw Anderson
[book review] / Margaret Henderson
Floyd.
SOCIETY OF ARCHITECTURAL
HISTORIANS. JOURNAL 1990 Sept.,
v.49, no.3, p.346-347.

UNIVERSITIES AND COLLEGES--BUILDINGS--
UNITED STATES--CAMBRIDGE
(MASSACHUSETTS)--HARVARD UNIVERSITY
George Oommen Cambridge,
Massachusetts.
Four projects: Briggs Athletic
Centre, Malkin Athletic Centre,
and McCurdy Track, at Harvard
University; Western Montana Sports
Medicine and Fitness Centre,
Missoula.
ARCHITECTURE + DESIGN 1990
Jan.-Feb., v.7, no.1, p.32-37,
photos., plans, aerial photos.

UNIVERSITIES AND COLLEGES--BUILDINGS--
UNITED STATES--CAMBRIDGE
(MASSACHUSETTS)--HARVARD
UNIVERSITY--SHAD HALL
A gym shapes up: Shad Hall, Boston,
Massachusetts, Harvard University
/ James S. Russell.
Architects: Kallmann, McKinnell &
Wood.
ARCHITECTURAL RECORD 1990 May,
v.178, no.6, p.78-[83], det.,
photos., plans, secns., site plan.

UNIVERSITIES AND COLLEGES--BUILDINGS--
UNITED STATES--CEDAR RAPIDS (IOWA)--
UNIVERSITY OF NORTHERN IOWA--
COMMUNICATIONS ART CENTER
UNI Communications Art Building:
Campus collage / Robert Tibbetts.
At the University of Northern
Iowa, Cedar Rapids. Architects:
RDG Bussard Dikis Associates.
IOWA ARCHITECT 1990 Spring, v.39,
no.1, p.20-21, photos., site plan.

UNIVERSITIES AND COLLEGES--BUILDINGS--
UNITED STATES--CINCINNATI (OHIO)--
UNIVERSITY OF CINCINNATI--COLLEGE OF
DESIGN, ARCHITECTURE, ART AND
PLANNING
Special feature: recent works of
Peter Eisenman.
Contents: Editor's introduction.--
Essays: Peter Eisenman: releasing
time imprisoned in space / Tadao
Ando.-- A framework for the future
/ Kurt W. Forster.-- Four notes on
the recent architecture of Peter
Eisenman / Ignasi de
Sola-Morales.-- A matter of
respect.-- Works: Wexner Center
for the Visual Arts, Ohio State
University.-- Columbus Convention
Center.-- Banyoles Olympic Hotel
competition.-- College of Design,
Architecture, Art and Planning,
University of Cincinnati.--
Interview: Peter Eisenman / Jeff
Kipnis. Text in Japanese and
English.
ARCHITECTURE AND URBANISM 1990
Jan., no.1(232), p.[7]-182,
axonometric views, elevs., models,
photos., plans, secns., sketches.

UNIVERSITIES AND COLLEGES--BUILDINGS--
UNITED STATES--CINCINNATTI (OHIO)--
UNIVERSITY OF CINCINNATTI--COLLEGE
OF DESIGN, ARCHITECTURE, ART AND
PLANNING
Taking risks: Eisenman in Ohio /
Cynthia Chapin Davidson.
On form and the depiction of
movement in the Columbus
Convention Center; the College of
Design, Architecture, Art &
Planning (DAAP) at the University
of Cincinnati; and the Wexner
Center at Ohio State University.
INLAND ARCHITECT 1990 May-June,
v.34, no.3, p.[44]-51, dwgs.,
elevs., models, plans, secns.,
site plans.

UNIVERSITIES AND COLLEGES--BUILDINGS--
UNITED STATES--CLINTON (NEW YORK)--
HAMILTON COLLEGE--WILLIAM M. BRISTOL
JR. NATATORIUM
Aquatic art: William M. Bristol Jr.
Natatorium, Hamilton College,
Clinton, New York / Margaret
Gaskie.
Architects: Perry Dean Rogers &
Partners.
ARCHITECTURAL RECORD 1990 Apr.,
v.178, no.4, p.84-[89], elev.,
photos., plan, secns., site plans.

UNIVERSITIES AND COLLEGES--BUILDINGS--
UNITED STATES--COLUMBIA (MISSOURI)--
UNIVERSITY OF MISSOURI--STUDENT
RECREATION CENTER
Body buildings: designing multi-use
campus recreational facilities /
Martha Huntington.
Univ. of Mo. Recreation Facility
and Univ. of Iowa Fieldhouse.
IOWA ARCHITECT 1990 Fall, v.39,
no.3, p.26-31, dwg., photos.,
plan, isometric dwg.

UNIVERSITIES AND COLLEGES--BUILDINGS--
UNITED STATES--COLUMBUS (OHIO)--OHIO
STATE UNIVERSITY--WEXNER CENTER FOR
THE VISUAL ARTS
Gebouw als gebeurtenis: Peter
Eisenmans Wexner Center for the
Visual Arts / Marian van der
Waals.
In Columbus, Ohio.
DE ARCHITECT 1990 May, v.21, no.5,
p.51-55, axonometric views,
photos., plans, site plans.
The grid and the grain / Diane
Ghirardo.
Wexner Center for the Visual Arts.
Ohio State Univ., Columbus.
Architects: Peter Eisenman,
Richard Trott.
ARCHITECTURAL REVIEW 1990 June,
v.187, no.1120, p.79-86, map,
photos, plans, secn., aerial
photo.
Un manifesto decostruttivista = A
deconstructivist manifesto [Wexner
Center for the Visual Arts, Ohio
State University].
Architects: Peter Eisenman, with
Richard Trott and Arthur Baker.
ARCHITETTURA; CRONACHE E STORIA
1990 July-Aug., v.36,
no.7-8(417-418), p.553-555,
photos., plans, aerial photo.
Peter Eisenman.
Most of the issue devoted to this
architect. Nine projects featured.
Includes interview with David
Cohn. Text in Spanish and English.
EL CROQUIS 1989 Dec., v.8, no.41,
p.4-126,cover, axonometric views,
ill., dwgs., ports., elevs.,
models, photos., plans, secns.,
refs.
Peter Eisenman: Wexner Center for
the Visual Arts, Columbus, Ohio /
R.E. Somol.
In Italian and English.
DOMUS 1990 Jan., no.712,
p.[38-47], dets., elevs., photos,
plans, secns., site plans,
sketches.
Special feature: recent works of
Peter Eisenman.
Contents: Editor's introduction.--
Essays: Peter Eisenman: releasing
time imprisoned in space / Tadao
Ando.-- A framework for the future
/ Kurt W. Forster.-- Four notes on
the recent architecture of Peter
Eisenman / Ignasi de
Sola-Morales.-- A matter of
respect.-- Works: Wexner Center
for the Visual Arts, Ohio State
University.-- Columbus Convention
Center.-- Banyoles Olympic Hotel
competition.-- College of Design,
Architecture, Art and Planning,
University of Cincinnati.--
Interview: Peter Eisenman / Jeff
Kipnis. Text in Japanese and
English.
ARCHITECTURE AND URBANISM 1990
Jan., no.1(232), p.[7]-182,
axonometric views, elevs., models,
photos., plans, secns., sketches.
Strukturalistiske spidsfindigheder--
om Wexner-centret for visuel kunst
/ Fleming Skude.
Architect: Peter Eisenman.
Reprinted from Progressive
architecture, 1989, no.10.
ARKITEKTUR DK 1990, v.34, no.1-2,
p.A2-A12, dwgs., photo., plan,
site plan.

UNIVERSITIES AND COLLEGES--BUILDINGS--
UNITED STATES--COLUMBUS (OHIO)--OHIO
STATE UNIVERSITY--WEXNER CENTER FOR
THE VISUAL ARTS (CONTINUED)
Taking risks: Eisenman in Ohio /
Cynthia Chapin Davidson.
On form and the depiction of
movement in the Columbus
Convention Center; the College of
Design, Architecture, Art &
Planning (DAAP) at the University
of Cincinnati; and the Wexner
Center at Ohio State University.
INLAND ARCHITECT 1990 May-June,
v.34, no.3, p.[44]-51, dwgs.,
elevs., models, plans, secns.,
site plans.
Teoria y deleite: las abstracciones
de Eisenman / Vincent Scully.
The Wexner Center for the Visual
Arts, Ohio State University.
ARQUITECTURA VIVA 1990 Mar.-Apr.,
no.11, p.27-31, photos, plans.
Wexing eloquent in Columbus / Robert
Benson.
The Wexner Center for the Visual
Arts, Ohio State University.
Architect: Peter Eisenman.
INLAND ARCHITECT 1990 May-June,
v.34, no.3, p.34-43, photos.,
plans, aerial photo.
Wexner Center for the Visual Arts
[Architectural Design Profile 82].
Feature of issue. Includes "A
personal note," by Philip Johnson;
"Eisenman's White holes," by
Charles Jencks; "Between the
sphere and the labyrinth," by R.
E. Somol; "A framework for the
future," by Kurt W. Forster.
ARCHITECTURAL DESIGN 1989, v.59,
no.11-12, p.[1]-80, back cover,
axonometric views, port., photos.,
plans, secns., site plans,
sketches, aerial photos., refs.
The Wexner fragments for the visual
arts / Kay Bea Jones.
Criticism of the Wexner Center for
the Visual Arts at Ohio State
Univ. Architect: Peter Eisenman.
JOURNAL OF ARCHITECTURAL EDUCATION
1990 Spring, v.43, no.3, p.34-38,
photos., refs.
Wexner-Zentrum der visuellen Kunste
und Bibliothek in Columbus/Ohio,
USA = Wexner Centre for the Visual
Arts and Fine Arts Library in
Columbus/Ohio, USA.
Architects: Peter Eisenman,
Richard Trott.
ARCHITEKTUR + WETTBEWERBE 1990
Sept., no.143, p.6-7, photos.,
plan.

UNIVERSITIES AND COLLEGES--BUILDINGS--
UNITED STATES--CORPUS CHRISTI
(TEXAS)--DEL MAR COLLEGE--FINE ARTS
CENTER
A vaulted spine at Del Mar College /
Joel Warren Barna.
Del Mar College Fine Arts Center,
Corpus Christi. Architects: Kipp,
Richter & Associates.
TEXAS ARCHITECT 1990 July-Aug.,
v.40, no.4, p.48, photos., plan,
site plan.

UNIVERSITIES AND COLLEGES--BUILDINGS--
UNITED STATES--DENVER (COLORADO)--
UNIVERSITY OF COLORADO, DENVER--
AURARIA HIGHER EDUCATION CENTER--
NORTH CLASSROOM BUILDING
Nuove aule per l'Universita del
Colorado = North Classroom
Building, Denver, Colorado /
Silvano Stucchi.
At the Auraria Higher Education
Center. Architect: Hoover Berg
Desmond. Includes English
translation; French, German and
Spanish summaries, p.[4].
L'INDUSTRIA DELLE COSTRUZIONI 1990
Oct., v.24, no.228, p.28-31,
photos., plans, site plans.
Una parete che invece si apre:
Blocco di aule per L'universita di
Denver, Colorado.
Architects: Studio Hoover Berg
Desmond.
ARCHITETTURA; CRONACHE E STORIA
1990 Apr., v.36, no.4(414),
p.284-285, axonometric view,
photos., site plan.

UNIVERSITIES AND COLLEGES--BUILDINGS--
UNITED STATES--DES MOINES (IOWA)--
DRAKE UNIVERSITY--LAW SCHOOL LEGAL
CLINIC
Legal precedence: Law School Legal
Clinic, Drake University, Des
Moines, Iowa / Robert Tibbetts.
Architects: Herbert Lewis Kruse
Blunck Architecture.
ARCHITECTURE: THE AIA JOURNAL 1990
Feb., v.79, no.2, p.84-85, photos,
plans.

UNIVERSITIES AND COLLEGES--BUILDINGS--
UNITED STATES--HARTFORD
(CONNECTICUT)--UNIVERSITY OF
HARTFORD--HARRY JACK GRAY CENTER
Positive space: Tai Soo Kim's
multifaceted new complex presents
the University of Hartford with a
lively hub for cultural activities
/ Margaret Gaskie.
ARCHITECTURAL RECORD 1990 Feb.,
v.178, no.2, p.104-109, elevs.,
photos., plans, secns., site plan.

UNIVERSITIES AND COLLEGES--BUILDINGS--
UNITED STATES--IOWA
Learning environments: one student's
view of Iowa's academic
architecture / Greg Lehman.
Introduction to theme issue: seven
articles indexed separately.
IOWA ARCHITECT 1990 Fall, v.39,
no.3, p.11.

UNIVERSITIES AND COLLEGES--BUILDINGS--
UNITED STATES--IOWA CITY (IOWA)--
FIELDHOUSE
Body buildings: designing multi-use
campus recreational facilities /
Martha Huntington.
Univ. of Iowa Recreation Facility
and Univ. of Iowa Fieldhouse.
IOWA ARCHITECT 1990 Fall, v.39,
no.3, p.26-31, dwg., photos.,
plan, isometric dwg.

UNIVERSITIES AND COLLEGES--BUILDINGS--
UNITED STATES--IOWA CITY (IOWA)--
UNIVERSITY OF IOWA--LASER LABORATORY
BUILDING
La habilidad de maquetista:
laboratorios laser de la
universidad de Iowa, Iowa City,
Iowa, 1987-1992.
Architects: Frank O. Gehry and
Associates. English summary,
p.87-88.
A & V 1990, no.25, p.68-69,
elevs., models, secns., site plan.

UNIVERSITIES AND COLLEGES--BUILDINGS--
UNITED STATES--IRVINE (CALIFORNIA)--
UNIVERSITY OF CALIFORNIA AT IRVINE
Utopia revised: at the University of
California at Irvine, the struggle
to adapt the unyielding geometry
of the campus continues / John
Parman.
On William Pereira's 1963 master
plan, and subsequent buildings by
other architects.
ARCHITECTURE: THE AIA JOURNAL 1990
Jan., v.79, no.1, p.66-77, dwg.,
elev., photos., plans, site plans.

UNIVERSITIES AND COLLEGES--BUILDINGS--
UNITED STATES--ITHACA (NEW YORK)--
CORNELL UNIVERSITY--PERFORMING ARTS
CENTER
Center for the Performing Arts,
Cornell University, Ithaca, New
York, 1982-88.
Architects: James Stirling,
Michael Wilford & Associates, with
Wank adams Slavin Associates. Text
in Japanese and English.
GA DOCUMENT 1990 May, no.26,
p.68-[79], elevs., photos., plans,
secns., site plan.
Performing Arts Centre, Cornell
University, New York, U.S.A.,
1983-1988.
Architects: James Stirling,
Michael Wilford and Associates.
Text in Japanese and English.
Includes essay: In the classic
vein: the sky line / Brendan Gill.
ARCHITECTURE AND URBANISM 1990
May, no.5 extra edition, p.68-107,
photos., plans, secns., site plan.
Le revers du decor: Centre d'arts du
spectacle de l'Universite Cornell,
Ithaca, New York.
Performing Arts Center, Cornell
University. Architects: James
Stirling, Michael Wilford and
Associates with Wank Adams Slavin
Associates. English summary,
p.153. Spanish summary, p.199.
TECHNIQUES ET ARCHITECTURE 1990
Apr.-May, no.389, p.149-153,
photos., plans, secns.

UNIVERSITIES AND COLLEGES--BUILDINGS--
UNITED STATES--NEW HAVEN
(CONNECTICUT)--YALE UNIVERSITY--YALE
PSYCHIATRIC INSTITUTE
Colores terapeuticos: Instituto
Psiquiatrico de Yale, New Haven,
Connecticut, 1985-1989.
Architects: Frank O. Gehry and
Associates. English summary, p.87.
A & V 1990, no.25, p.50-55,
elevs., model, photos., plans,
secns., site plans, sketches.

UNIVERSITIES AND COLLEGES--BUILDINGS--
UNITED STATES--NEW HAVEN
(CONNECTICUT)--YALE UNIVERSITY--YALE
PSYCHIATRIC INSTITUTE (CONTINUED)
Frank O. Gehry.
Entire issue devoted to the work
of this American architect.
Criticism by A. Zaera Polo and
David Cohn. 15 projects and
buildings from 1987-1990 featured.
Text in Spanish and English.
EL CROQUIS 1990 Nov., v.9, no.45,
p.1-124, ports., elevs., models,
photos., plans, secns., site
plans, refs.
A new idea in New Haven [Yale
Psychiatric Institute] / Diana
Scott.
Residential treatment center for
mentally ill young adults and
adolescents. Architects: Frank O.
Gehry and Allan Dehar.
METROPOLIS 1990 Apr., v.9, no.8,
p.18-19, photo.
A village of healing: Yale
Psychiatric Institute, New Haven,
Connecticut / Michael J. Crosbie.
Architects: Frank O. Gehry &
Associates, Allan Dehar
Associates.
ARCHITECTURE: THE AIA JOURNAL 1990
Mar., v.79, no.3, p.[114]-121,
photos., plans, site plan.

UNIVERSITIES AND COLLEGES--BUILDINGS--
UNITED STATES--NEW YORK (NEW YORK)--
COLUMBIA UNIVERSITY--CENTER FOR
ENGINEERING AND PHYSICAL SCIENCE
RESEARCH
Columbia University Center for
Engineering and Physical Science
Research, New York, New York, USA,
1991.
Architects: Hellmuth, Obata &
Kassabaum. Text in Japanese and
English.
ARCHITECTURE AND URBANISM 1990
Dec., no.12 extra edition,
p.178-181, axonometric view,
dwgs., plans, site plan.

UNIVERSITIES AND COLLEGES--BUILDINGS--
UNITED STATES--NEW YORK (NEW YORK)--
COLUMBIA UNIVERSITY--MORRIS A.
SCHAPIRO RESIDENCE HALL
West Side study: Morris A. Schapiro
Residence Hall, Columbia
University, New York City, Gruzen
Samten Steinglass Architects /
Rosanna G. Liebman.
Principal designer: Scott Keller.
ARCHITECTURE: THE AIA JOURNAL 1990
Jan., v.79, no.1, p.[90]-91,
photos., plans.

UNIVERSITIES AND COLLEGES--BUILDINGS--
UNITED STATES--PALO ALTO
(CALIFORNIA)--STANFORD UNIVERSITY--
GRADUATE SCHOOL OF BUSINESS
University of Stanford, Graduate
School of Business expansion
facility, Palo Alto, California,
1984-88.
Architects: Kohn Pedersen Fox
Associates; partner in charge: A.
Eugene Kohn.
PROCESS: ARCHITECTURE 1989 Nov.,
no.86, p.58-59, elevs., photos.,
plan.

UNIVERSITIES AND COLLEGES--BUILDINGS--
UNITED STATES--PHILADELPHIA
(PENNSYLVANIA)--UNIVERSITY OF
PENNSYLVANIA
Un nuovo edificio per l'Universita
della Pennsylvania = A new
building for the Pennsylvania /
Silvano Stucchi.
An information center and office
building between 34th St. and
Walnut St., completed 1985.
Architects: Geddes, Brecher,
Qualls, Cunningham.
L'INDUSTRIA DELLE COSTRUZIONI 1990
Feb., v.24, no.220, p.22-27,
photos., plans, secn., site plan.

UNIVERSITIES AND COLLEGES--BUILDINGS--
UNITED STATES--PHILADELPHIA
(PENNSYLVANIA--UNIVERSITY OF
PENNSYLVANIA--SCHOOL OF MEDICINE--
CLINICAL RESEARCH BUILDING
Clinical research building School of
Medicine en University of
Pennsylvania Philadelphia
Pennsylvania = Clinical research
building School of Medicine at
University of Pennsylvania
Philadelphia Pennsylvania.
Architects: Venturi, Scott Brown
and Associates.
COMPOSICION ARQUITECTONICA, ART &
ARCHITECTURE 1989 Oct., no.4,
p.[79]-84, elevs., model, photos.,
site plan.

UNIVERSITIES AND COLLEGES--BUILDINGS--
UNITED STATES--PRINCETON (NEW
JERSEY)--PRINCETON UNIVERSITY--
COMPUTER SCIENCE BUILDING
Computer talk: Computer Science
Building, Princeton University,
Princeton, New Jersey, R.M.
Kliment & Frances Halsband
Architects / Margaret Gaskie.
ARCHITECTURAL RECORD 1990 Sept.,
v.178, no.10, p.122-127,
axonometric views, photos., plans,
s ecn., site plan.

UNIVERSITIES AND COLLEGES--BUILDINGS--
UNITED STATES--PRINCETON (NEW
JERSEY)--PRINCETON UNIVERSITY--
GORDON WU HALL
Gordon Wu Hall Butler College en
Princeton University Princeton,
New Jersey = Gordon Wu Hall Butler
College at Princeton University
Princeton New Jersey.
Architects: Venturi, Rauch and
Scott Brown. Text in Spanish and
English.
COMPOSICION ARQUITECTONICA, ART &
ARCHITECTURE 1989 Oct., no.4,
p.[41]-52, elevs., photos., plans,
secns.
Special feature: Venturi Scott Brown
and Associates.
Contents: Brief history-- Works:
Primate Center, Philadelphia
Zoological Garden.-- Lewis Thomas
Laboratory for Molecular Biology,
Princeton University, 1986.--
Malcolm S. Forbes Jr. College,
Princeton University, 1984.--
Gordon Wu Hall, Princeton
University, 1983.-- Venturi house,
Philadelphia, 1974-present.--
Izenour house, Stony Creek, Conn.,
1984.-- House in New Castle
County, Delaware, 1983.--
Coxe-Hayden house, Block Island,
(Continued next page)

UNIVERSITIES AND COLLEGES--BUILDINGS--
UNITED STATES--PRINCETON (NEW
JERSEY)--PRINCETON UNIVERSITY--
GORDON WU HALL (CONTINUED)
Special feature:...(CONTINUED)
R.I., 1981.-- Tarble Student
Center, Swarthmore College,
1985.-- Tree House, Philadelphia
Zoo, 1985.-- Welcome Park,
Philadelphia, 1982.-- Decorative
designs.-- Essay: "Body language"
and artifice: on some recent
designs by Venturi Scott Brown and
Associates. Text in Japanese and
English.
ARCHITECTURE AND URBANISM 1990
June, no.6(237), p.[39]-150,
ports., elevs., photos., plans,
secns., site plans.

UNIVERSITIES AND COLLEGES--BUILDINGS--
UNITED STATES--PRINCETON (NEW
JERSEY)--PRINCETON UNIVERSITY--
MALCOLM S. FORBES JR. COLLEGE
Special feature: Venturi Scott Brown
and Associates.
Contents: Brief history-- Works:
Primate Center, Philadelphia
Zoological Garden.-- Lewis Thomas
Laboratory for Molecular Biology,
Princeton University, 1986.--
Malcolm S. Forbes Jr. College,
Princeton University, 1984.--
Gordon Wu Hall, Princeton
University, 1983.-- Venturi house,
Philadelphia, 1974-present.--
Izenour house, Stony Creek, Conn.,
1984.-- House in New Castle
County, Delaware, 1983.--
Coxe-Hayden house, Block Island,
R.I., 1981.-- Tarble Student
Center, Swarthmore College,
1985.-- Tree House, Philadelphia
Zoo, 1985.-- Welcome Park,
Philadelphia, 1982.-- Decorative
designs.-- Essay: "Body language"
and artifice: on some recent
designs by Venturi Scott Brown and
Associates. Text in Japanese and
English.
ARCHITECTURE AND URBANISM 1990
June, no.6(237), p.[39]-150,
ports., elevs., photos., plans,
secns., site plans.

UNIVERSITIES AND COLLEGES--BUILDINGS--
UNITED STATES--PROVIDENCE (RHODE
ISLAND)--BROWN UNIVERSITY--SALOMON
CENTER FOR TEACHING
Building Types Study 682: Campus
buildings: Extracurricular
education / Grace Anderson.
Four recently-completed buildings:
Salomon Center for Teaching, Brown
Univ. (Goody, Clancy & Assoc.);
Psychology Building, Vanderbilt
Univ. (Stubbins Assoc.);
Centennial Performing Arts Center,
Westminster School, Simsbury Conn.
(Graham Gund Architects); and
Price Center, Univ. of Calif. at
San Diego (Kaplan/McLaughlin/Diaz
Architects).
ARCHITECTURAL RECORD 1990 Aug.,
v.178, no.9, p.83-[95], elevs.,
photos., plans, secns., site
plans.

UNIVERSITIES AND COLLEGES--BUILDINGS--
UNITED STATES--ROCK ISLAND
(ILLINOIS)--AUGUSTANA COLLEGE--OLD
MAIN
Augustana College's Old Main: a
Swedish center / David Newton.
In Rock Island, Ill., completed in
1893. Architect: E.S. Hammatt.
HISTORIC ILLINOIS 1990 Dec., v.13,
no.4, p.6-9, dwg., photos.

UNIVERSITIES AND COLLEGES--BUILDINGS--
UNITED STATES--SAN DIEGO
(CALIFORNIA)--UNIVERSITY OF
CALIFORNIA AT SAN DIEGO--PRICE
CENTER
Building Types Study 682: Campus
buildings: Extracurricular
education / Grace Anderson.
Four recently-completed buildings:
Salomon Center for Teaching, Brown
Univ. (Goody, Clancy & Assoc.);
Psychology Building, Vanderbilt
Univ. (Stubbins Assoc.);
Centennial Performing Arts Center,
Westminster School, Simsbury Conn.
(Graham Gund Architects); and
Price Center, Univ. of Calif. at
San Diego (Kaplan/McLaughlin/Diaz
Architects).
ARCHITECTURAL RECORD 1990 Aug.,
v.178, no.9, p.83-[95], elevs.,
photos., plans, secns., site
plans.

UNIVERSITIES AND COLLEGES--BUILDINGS--
UNITED STATES--SANTA CRUZ
(CALIFORNIA)--UNIVERSITY OF
CALIFORNIA, SANTA CRUZ--STUDENT
CENTER
Centre of gravitas / John Ellis.
Student Center, U.C. Santa Cruz.
Architects: Fernau and Hartman.
ARCHITECTURAL REVIEW 1990 Nov.,
v.188, no.1125, p.64-67, map,
photos., plans, secns., site plan.
A regionalist union / Sally
Woodbridge.
Student Center, U.C. Santa Cruz.
Architects: Fernau and Hartman.
PROGRESSIVE ARCHITECTURE 1990
June, v.71, no.6, p.106-113,
photo., plans, site plan.

UNIVERSITIES AND COLLEGES--BUILDINGS--
UNITED STATES--STORRS
(CONNECTICUT)--ALUMNI HOUSE
Across the grain: a university
building offers lessons in
detailing wood / Douglas E.
Gordon, M. Stephanie Stubbs.
Alumni house, Univ. of Conn.
Architects: Shope Reno Wharton
Associates.
ARCHITECTURE: THE AIA JOURNAL 1990
Apr., v.79, no.4, p.95-97, dets.,
photos., secn.

UNIVERSITIES AND COLLEGES--BUILDINGS--
UNITED STATES--TEMPE (ARIZONA)--
ARIZONA STATE UNIVERSITY
Desert blooms: a trio of engaging
buildings breaks Arizona State
University's arid architectural
tradition / Lawrence W. Cheek.
Fine Arts Center (Antoine Predock
Architect); Hayden Library
Expansion (Sasaki Associates); and
College of Architecture and
Environmental Design (Hillier
Group).
ARCHITECTURE: THE AIA JOURNAL 1990
(Continued next column)

UNIVERSITIES AND COLLEGES--BUILDINGS--
UNITED STATES--TEMPE (ARIZONA)--
ARIZONA STATE UNIVERSITY
(CONTINUED)
Desert blooms: a trio...(CONTINUED)
Jan., v.79, no.1, p.92-97,
photos., plan, secn., site plan,
aerial photo.

UNIVERSITIES AND COLLEGES--BUILDINGS--
UNITED STATES--TEMPE (ARIZONA)--
ARIZONA STATE UNIVERSITY--FINE ARTS
CENTER
Antoine Predock.
Features the Zuber house, Paradise
Valley, AZ and the Fine Arts
Center. Univ. of Arizona, Tempe.
English summary.
ARCHITECTURE D'AUJOURD'HUI 1990
Oct., no.271, p.177-187,
axonometric view, photos., plans,
secn.
Tutti i sensi in gioco: Antoine
Predock, Centro di belle arti per
l'Universita dell'Arizona.
ARCHITETTURA; CRONACHE E STORIA
1990 Jan., v.36, no.1(411),
p.52-53, photos., plans, site
plan, aerial photo.

UNIVERSITIES AND COLLEGES--BUILDINGS--
UNITED STATES--TEMPE (ARIZONA)--
ARIZONA STATE UNIVERSITY--
GRADY-GAMMAGE AUDITORIUM
The Wright way: restoring a pair of
landmark structures / Amy Gray
Light.
Repairs using the latest
developments in roofing and
sealant technologies, for the
Grady-Gammage Auditorium at Ariz.
State Univ. and for the Affleck
House in Bloomfield Hills, Mich.
ARCHITECTURE: THE AIA JOURNAL 1990
Nov., v.79, no.11, p.153, photos.

UNIVERSITIES AND COLLEGES--BUILDINGS--
UNITED STATES--TEMPE (ARIZONA)--
UNIVERSITY OF ARIZONA--FINE ARTS
CENTER
El desierto edificado: Predock,
centro de arte en Arizona / Sylvia
Lavin.
Fine Arts Center of the Univ. of
Ariz., Tempe.
ARQUITECTURA VIVA 1990 Nov.-Dec.,
no.15, p.24-28, dwgs., photos.,
plans.

UNIVERSITIES AND COLLEGES--BUILDINGS--
UNITED STATES--URBANA-CHAMPAIGN
(ILLINOIS)--UNIVERSITY OF ILLINOIS
The University of Illinois
Observatory / David Newton.
Installed in 1896. Architect:
Charles A. Gunn.
HISTORIC ILLINOIS 1990 Oct., v.13,
no.3, p.[1]-5, photos.

UNIVERSITIES AND COLLEGES--BUILDINGS--
WALES--CARDIFF--UNIVERSITY OF WALES.
COLLEGE OF CARDIFF--FACULTY BUILDING
Faculty building, Cardiff.
The first of six new buildings for
the Univ. of Wales. Architect: Wyn
Thomas + Partners.
BUILDING 1990 Jan.26, v.255, no.4,
p.63-70, det., photos., plans,
secns., site plan, table.

UNIVERSITIES AND COLLEGES--BUILDINGS--
WOODEN--ENGLAND--DORSET--HOOKE PARK
COLLEGE
Holzern: drei Holzbauten fur das
Hooke Park College, Dorset.
Architects: Ahrends, Burton and
Koralek; with Frei Otto.
DEUTSCHE BAUZEITUNG 1990 July,
v.124, no.7, p.112-114, dets.,
photos., isometric dwg.

UNIVERSITIES AND COLLEGES--CANADA--
MONTREAL (QUEBEC)--UNIVERSITE DE
MONTREAL--EXHIBITIONS
Ernest Cormier: a towering talent
[exhibition review] / Tim
Morawetz.
"Ernest Cormier and the Universite
de Montreal," at the Canadian
Centre for Architecture, until
Oct.14.
CANADIAN ARCHITECT 1990 July,
v.35, no.7, p.28-29, ill., port.,
photos., aerial photo.

UNIVERSITIES AND COLLEGES--
COMPETITIONS--BUILDINGS--ENGLAND--
CAMBRIDGE--CHURCHILL COLLEGE
Cambridge / Esben Larsen.
Competition entry by Henning
Larsens Tegnestue for conference
center at Churchill College.
ARKITEKTEN 1990 Feb., v.92, no.2,
p.64-65, model, plans, secn.

UNIVERSITIES AND COLLEGES--ENGLAND--
BRADFORD--BRADFORD CITY
TECHNOLOGICAL COLLEGE
Back to school.
On the Bradford City Technological
College. Architects: John Brunton
Partnership.
BUILDING DESIGN 1989 Oct., suppl.,
p.44, dwgs., model.

UNIVERSITIES AND COLLEGES--EUROPE
Geography of universities in Western
Europe / Serge Vassal.
Spatial dynamics of university
location.
EKISTICS 1988 Jan.-June, v.55,
no.328-330, p.146-152, maps,
plans, refs.
Geography of universities in Western
Europe / Serge Vassal.
Spatial dynamics of university
location.
EKISTICS 1988 Jan.-June, v.55,
no.328-330, p.146-152, maps,
plans, refs.

UNIVERSITIES AND COLLEGES--FRANCE--
PARIS
Un college a Parigi = College in
Paris.
At the corner of Rue Balard and
Rue St.-Charles. Architects:
Olivier Brenac, Xavier Gonzalez,
Pascale Guedot.
ARCHITETTURA: CRONACHE E STORIA
1990 Sept., v.36, no.9(419),
p.636-637, photos., plans, sketch.

UNIVERSITIES AND COLLEGES--GERMANY
(WEST)--BREMEN--TECHNOLOGIEPARK
UNIVERSITAT BREMEN
Technologiepark Universitat Bremen.
Architects: Gert Schulze and
Heinrich Campe; Hochbauamt Bremen;
Wolfram Dahms; Haslob Hartlich
Schutz; Oswald M. Ungers;
Rosengart + Partner; Kurt Schmidt.
(Continued next column)

UNIVERSITIES AND COLLEGES--GERMANY
(WEST)--BREMEN--TECHNOLOGIEPARK
UNIVERSITAT BREMEN (CONTINUED)
Technologiepark...(CONTINUED)
Includes English summary.
BAUMEISTER 1990 Dec., v.87, no.12,
p.32-41, photos., plans, secns.,
site plans, aerial photos.

UNIVERSITIES AND COLLEGES--ITALY--
MILAN--POLITECNICO DI MILANO--NUOVO
POLITECNICO ALLA BOVISA
Milano: nuovo politecnico alla
Bovisa.
Plans for a new branch of the
Milan Polytechnic in the Bovisa
district. Architects: Baffa,
Battisti, Canella, Crotti, Grassi,
Grisotti, Mantero, Monestiroli,
Nicolin, Vigano.
DOMUS 1990 Sept., no.719,
p.[18-20], dwgs., elevs., plans,
site plans.

UNIVERSITIES AND COLLEGES--
SOCIOLOGICAL ASPECTS--EUROPE
Universita: le condizioni della
futura autonomia [editorial] /
Vittorio Gregotti.
Includes English summary.
CASABELLA 1990 Mar., v.54, no.566,
p.2-3,63.

UNIVERSITIES AND COLLEGES--STUDENT
PROJECTS--AUSTRALIA--FREMANTLE--
CATHOLIC UNIVERSITY
Catholic University.
University in Fremantle was the
final year project undertaken in
1988 at the School of
Architecture, University of
Western Australia.
THE ARCHITECT, W.A.: THE OFFICIAL
JOURNAL OF THE ROYAL AUSTRALIAN
INSTITUTE OF ARCHITECTS, W.A.
CHAPTER 1989, v.30, no.1, p.14-16,
axonometric view, dgws., port.,
site plan.

UNIVERSITIES AND COLLEGES--UNITED
STATES--IOWA CITY (IOWA)--UNIVERSITY
OF IOWA--LASER LABORATORY BUILDING
Frank O. Gehry.
Entire issue devoted to the work
of this American architect.
Criticism by A. Zaera Polo and
David Cohn. 15 projects and
buildings from 1987-1990 featured.
Text in Spanish and English.
EL CROQUIS 1990 Nov., v.9, no.45,
p.1-124, ports., elevs., models,
photos., plans, secns., site
plans, refs.

UNIVERSITIES AND COLLEGES--UNITED
STATES--LOS ANGELES (CALIFORNIA)--
UNIVERSITY OF CALIFORNIA, LOS
ANGELES
UCLA plans for the future
[interview].
Interview with Charles Oakley,
UCLA's campus architect.
L. A. ARCHITECT 1990 May, p.5.

UNIVERSITY MUSEUMS--UNITED STATES--
ATLANTA (GEORGIA)--EMORY
UNIVERSITY--MUSEUM OF ART AND
ARCHAEOLOGY
Museum of Art and Archeology, Emory
University, Atlanta, Georgia.
Michael Graves, architect.
ARCHITECTURE NEW JERSEY 1990.
v.26, no.6, p.11, photos.

UNIVERSITY OF ARIZONA. DISABILITY
RESOURCE CENTER
Breaking down barriers / Lawrence W.
Cheek.
The Disability Resource Center at
the Univ. of Ariz., Tuscon, offers
students awareness training.
ARCHITECTURE: THE AIA JOURNAL 1990
Jan., v.79, no.1, p.113-114,
photos.

UNIVERSITY OF ARKANSAS (FAYETTEVILLE
CAMPUS). CENTER FOR DESIGN MEDIA AND
ENVIRONMENTAL RESEARCH
Computer-generated video explains
design / Karen Cordes.
A project initiated by Prof. H.
Gordon Brooks at the University of
Ark. uses computerized animation
graphics and electronic image
processing.
ARCHITECTURAL RECORD 1990 Sept.,
v.178, no.10, p.180-181, ill.

UNIVERSITY OF BATH. SCHOOL OF
ARCHITECTURE AND BUILDING
ENGINEERING
The crow and the clown: A case for
Aalto / Neil Parkyn.
One-day 'Focus' conference at Bath
University School of Architecture
and Building Engineering on Alvar
Aalto, held 19 May 1990.
ARCHITECTS' JOURNAL 1990 June 6,
v.191, no.23, p.74-75, photos.

UNIVERSITY OF HOUSTON. SASAKAWA
INTERNATIONAL CENTER FOR SPACE
ARCHITECTURE
Design goes to space: NASA and a
program at the University of
Houston are developing innovative
structures for living in space /
Karin Tetlow.
The Sasakawa International Center
for Space Architecture is working
on NASA's latest program, Space
Station Freedom.
ARCHITECTURE: THE MAGAZINE OF THE
AMERICAN INSTITUTE OF ARCHITECTS
1990 May, v.79, no.5, p.[98]-101,
ill., model.
Home, sweet space station / Joel
Warren Barna.
Students at the Sasakawa
International Center for Space
Architecture at the Univ. of
Houston face the problems of
long-term habitation elsewhere in
the solar system.
TEXAS ARCHITECT 1990 May-June,
v.40, no.3, p.26-29, ill., dwgs.,
models.

UNIVERSITY OF MINNESOTA--DESIGN CENTER
FOR AMERICAN URBAN LANDSCAPE
Along the lazy river / David Dillon.
"Expedition of the Fourth Coast"
summer study tour of cities and
towns along the Mississippi River
by Univ. of Minnesota planning
students.
PLANNING 1990 Nov., v.56, no.11,
p.20-23, ports., photos.,
sketches, aerial photo.
Expedition of the Fourth Coast /
Mary Henderson Gass.
Report on a six-week trip on the
Mississippi River run by the Univ.
of Minnesota Design Center for
American Urban Landscape.
INLAND ARCHITECT 1990 Nov.-Dec.,
v.34, no.6, p.63-66, dwgs.

UNIVERSITY OF MINNESOTA. SCHOOL OF
ARCHITECTURE AND LANDSCAPE
ARCHITECTURE--EXHIBITIONS
Compte rendu du colloque
"l'avant-garde et le paysage:
peuvent-ils etre reconcilies?" /
Daniele Routaboule.
Report given in Montreal in May
1989 on a conference held in
Apr.1989 at the Univ. of
Minnesota, "The Avant-Garde and
the Landscape: Can They Be
Recnciled?". In French and
English.
LANDSCAPE ARCHITECTURAL REVIEW
1990 May, v.11, no.2, p.20-22,

UNIVERSITY OF NORTH CAROLINA. DEPT. OF
CITY AND REGIONAL PLANNING
An interview with John A. Parker /
Carolina Planning Staff.
Founder of the Dept. of City and
Regional Planning, University of
North Carolina at Chapel Hill.
CAROLINA PLANNING 1990 Fall,
v.16, no.2, p.2-3, port.

UNIVERSITY OF WISCONSIN--MILWAUKEE.
CENTER FOR ARCHITECTURE AND URBAN
PLANNING RESEARCH
Holding on to home.
On the report. Holding on to home:
designing environments for people
with dementia, prepared by the
Center for Architecture and Urban
Planning Research, University of
Wisconsin, Milwaukee and Kahler
Slater Torphy Architects.
PROGRESSIVE ARCHITECTURE 1990
Jan., v.71, no.1, p.124, dwg.

UNNERBACK, AXEL
Utsikt fran Vaderstads kyrka / Axel
Unnerback.
Analysis of church building in
Sweden 1760-1860, using Vaderstad
as an example and discussing
architects Carl Harleman, C.F.
Adelcrantz and Axel Nystrom.
Includes English summary.
BEBYGGELSEHISTORISK TIDSKRIFT
1989, no.17-18, p.141-160, elevs.,
photos., plans, secns., biblio.,
refs.

UNO, HIROZO
A growth in household and renovation
of houses [part i] / Hirozo Uno.
Subtitle: A study on the change in
housing and living style of
detached houses in Hokkaido. Text
in Japanese; English summary.
(Continued next column)

UNO, HIROZO (CONTINUED)
A growth in household...(CONTINUED)
p.99.
NIHON KENCHIKU GAKKAI KEIKAKUKEI
RONBUN HOKOKU SHU = JOURNAL OF
ARCHITECTURE, PLANNING AND
ENVIRONMENTAL ENGINEERING 1990
Apr., no.4(410), p.99-104, graphs,
plans, tables, refs.

UNREALIZED PROJECTS
See UNEXECUTED DESIGNS

UNWIN, RAYMOND, SIR, 1863-1940
Garden city: Letchworth: the first
garden city, by Mervyn Miller
[book review] / James Stevens
Curl.
ROYAL SOCIETY OF ARTS, LONDON. RSA
JOURNAL 1990 May, v.138, no.5406,
p.441-442.

UNWIN, RAYMOND, SIR, 1864-1940
The elusive green background:
Raymond Unwin and the Greater
London Regional Plan / Mervyn
Miller.
PLANNING PERSPECTIVES: PP 1989
Jan., v.4, no.1, p.[15]-44, port.,
plans, table, refs.

UPDIKE, JOHN
The houses of Ipswich / John Updike.
Author's recollections of his
former home, the 1686 Polly Dole
House. Ipswich. Mass.
ARCHITECTURAL DIGEST 1990 June,
v.47, no.6, p.26,30,32, photos.

UPM (FIRM)
Clinic in Hatano / Hajime Yatsuka.
Architects: Hajime Yatsuka, UPM.
JAPAN ARCHITECT 1990 July, v.65,
no.7(399), p.26-31, photos.,
plans, secn.

URANO, YOSHIMI
Heat and mass transfer at outside
surface of buildings / Akihito
Ozaki, et al.
Subtitle: Wind tunnel tests of
heat and mass transfer on
horizontal surfaces. English
summary, p.25.
NIHON KENCHIKU GAKKAI KEIKAKUKEI
RONBUN HOKOKU SHU = JOURNAL OF
ARCHITECTURE, PLANNING AND
ENVIRONMENTAL ENGINEERING 1990
Jan., no.1(407), p.11-25, charts,
diagrs., graphs, tables, refs.

URARTIAN
See "URARTIAN" AS A SUBHEADING AFTER
SPECIFIC BUILDING TYPES OR OTHER
MAIN HEADINGS.

URBAIN, PASCAL
Lycee technique du batiment,
Marseille.
Lycee Diderot. Architects: Bui
Kien Quoc with Pascal Urbain,
Bernard Desmoulin, Jean-Marc
Chancel. English summary, p.97;
Spanish summary, p.172.
TECHNIQUES ET ARCHITECTURE 1990
Oct.-Nov., no.392, p.94-97,
axonometric view, photos., plan,
site plan.

URBAN BEAUTIFICATION--20TH CENTURY--
UNITED STATES
Building the City Beautiful: the
Benjamin Franklin Parkway and the
Philadelphia Museum of Art [by]
David B. Brownlee [book review] /
Leonard K. Eaton.
Book published in conjunction with
the 1989 exhibition at the
Philadelphia Museum of Art.
WINTERTHUR PORTFOLIO 1990 Winter,
v.25, no.4, p.305-307.
The City Beautiful movement [by]
William H. Wilson [and] Building
the City Beautiful [by] David
Brownlee [book review] / Daniel
Bluestone.
Brownlee's book studies the
Benjamin Franklin Parkway, and the
Philadelphia Museum of Art and was
published on the occasion of an
exhibition there, Sept.9-Nov.26,
1989.
SOCIETY OF ARCHITECTURAL
HISTORIANS. JOURNAL 1990 Dec.,
v.49, no.4, p.455-457.
The City Beautiful movement [by]
William H. Wilson [book review] /
Charlotte Vestal Brown.
WINTERTHUR PORTFOLIO 1990 Autumn,
v.25, no.2-3, p.207-208.

URBAN BEAUTIFICATION--UNITED STATES--
PHILADEPHIA (PENNSYLVANIA)
The City Beautiful movement [by]
William H. Wilson [and] Building
the City Beautiful [by] David
Brownlee [book review] / Daniel
Bluestone.
Brownlee's book studies the
Benjamin Franklin Parkway, and the
Philadelphia Museum of Art and was
published on the occasion of an
exhibition there, Sept.9-Nov.26,
1989.
SOCIETY OF ARCHITECTURAL
HISTORIANS. JOURNAL 1990 Dec.,
v.49, no.4, p.455-457.

URBAN DESIGN
The current interest in urban
design: implications for planning
education in Australia / Stephen
Hamnet.
EKISTICS 1988 Jan.-June, v.55,
no.328-330, p.101-105, refs.
Design control: a call for a new
approach / Tony Hall.
In urban design.
THE PLANNER 1990 Oct.5, v.76,
no.39, p.14-18, photos., refs.
Discussion: mobility and urban space
design / Keijin Kamino, Nobuyuki
Hata, Tadahiko Higuchi.
THE WHEEL EXTENDED 1990, v.19,
no.3, p.8-15, dets., ill., ports.,
model, photos.
Economics, politics and city design
/ Vincent C. Schoemehl.
The Mayor of St. Louis describes
his experiences in planning and
development after participating in
the Mayors' Institute for City
Design.
PLACES 1990 Summer, v.6, no.4,
p.14-21, photos.
Open spaces and quality of urban
life / Michael Gregan.
LANDSCAPE DESIGN 1990 June,
no.191, p.12-14, photos., table,
refs.

URBAN DESIGN (CONTINUED)
The poetics of city and nature:
toward a new aesthetic for urban
design / Anne Whiston Spirn.
PLACES 1989 Fall, v.6, no.1,
p.82-93, dwg., photos., aerial
photo., refs.
La practica del disegno urbano = The
practice of urban design / Franco
Mancuso.
In Italian; English summary,
p.120-121.
URBANISTICA 1989 June, no.95,
p.11-14,120-121, ill., plans.
La qualita e il luogo / Marinetta
Nunziante.
VILLE GIARDINI 1990 Sept., no.251,
p.30-[33], dwgs., photos., plans,
secn.
Questions to ask a space / Ronald
Lee Fleming.
The author proposes a set of
questions to be asked by planners
and design reviewers when
evaluating a public space.
PLACES 1990 Summer, v.6, no.4,
p.12-13, aerial photo.
Reality as a discipline:
metropolitan architecture and
urban identity = La realidad como
disciplina: arquitectura
metropolitana y identidad urbana /
Fritz Neumeyer.
QUADERNS D'ARQUITECTURA I
URBANISME 1989 Oct.-Dec., no.183,
p.,136-143, dwgs., photos.
Thema: stad en landschap.
"Themanummer 40"; the five
articles on landscape design in
cities are indexed separately.
DE ARCHITECT THEMA 1990 Sept.,
v.21, no.9 suppl., p.3-49, ill.,
photos.
Toward an urban design manifesto /
Allan Jacobs, Donald Appleyard.
AMERICAN PLANNING ASSOCIATION.
JOURNAL 1987 Winter, v.53, no.1,
p.112-120,
Urban design.
Introduces 8-part series; parts
1-3 published in this issue.
Contents: 1: Introduction; 2: Key
words and phrases; 3: Ecological
urban design.
ARCHITECTS' JOURNAL 1990 Oct.24,
v.192, no.17, p.61-71, diagrs.,
graph, ill, dwgs., photos., plans,
refs.
Urban design 4: participation
techniques / Robert Cowan.
Fourth in series on urban design.
ARCHITECTS' JOURNAL 1990 Oct.31,
v.192, no.18, p.59-61, dwg.,
photo., sketches.
Urban design 5: regional identity /
Hildebrand Frey.
Maintaining city identity during
the process of urbanization and
growth. Fifth in series on urban
design.
ARCHITECTS' JOURNAL 1990 Oct.31,
v.192, no.18, p.63-65, photos.,
plans.
Urban design 7: new settlements /
Jon Rowland.
Seventh in series on urban design.
ARCHITECTS' JOURNAL 1990 Nov.7,
v.192, no.19, p.63-66, diagr.,
map, plans, site plans, aerial
photo., refs.

URBAN DESIGN (CONTINUED)
Urban planning and urban design /
John Toon.
EKISTICS 1988 Jan.-June, v.55,
no.328-330, p.95-105, refs.

URBAN DESIGN--17TH CENTURY--ENGLAND--
LONDON
Order and structure in urban design:
the plans for the rebuilding of
London after the Great Fire of
1666 / Julienne Hanson.
EKISTICS 1989 Jan.-Apr., v.56,
no.334-335, p.22-42, ill., maps,
plans, table, engrs., refs.

URBAN DESIGN--20TH CENTURY
Un'altra tradizione moderna: dalla
rottura dell'anno trenta al
progetto urbano moderno = Another
modern tradition: from the break
of 1930 to the modern urban
project / Manuel de Sola Morales.
Principal themes in urban planning
since the 1920s.
LOTUS INTERNATIONAL 1989, no.64,
p.6-31, ill., models, photos.,
site plans.
Space, culture and urban design in
late modernism and after / John
Peponis.
EKISTICS 1989 Jan.-Apr., v.56,
no.334-335, p.93-108, axonometric
view, diagrs., map, photos.,
plans, sketch, aerial photos.,
biblio.

URBAN DESIGN--20TH CENTURY--
NETHERLANDS--ROTTERDAM
Arquitectura de la nueva centralidad
= Architecture of the new
centrality / Joan Busquets.
Includes project for center of
Rotterdam.
QUADERNS D'ARQUITECTURA I
URBANISME 1989 Oct.-Dec., no.183,
p.105-112, dwgs., models, aerial
photos.

URBAN DESIGN--20TH CENTURY--SPAIN--
MADRID
Making the most of Madrid / Seamus
Filor.
Discussion of civic improvements
currently in progress in Madrid.
LANDSCAPE DESIGN 1990 June,
no.191, p.30-31, photos., refs.

URBAN DESIGN--COMPETITIONS
Planning and urban design
competition / Ernest R. Alexander,
Lawrence P. Witzling, guest
editors.
Seven articles, including one on a
mixed-use project for Bunker Hill
in Los Angeles. Authors: Jeffrey
E. Ollswang, Tridib Banerjee,
Anastasia Loukaitou-Sideris,
Joanna Eley, Dennis J. Casper,
Ruth Eckdish Knack, Andrew D.
Seidel.
JOURNAL OF ARCHITECTURAL AND
PLANNING RESEARCH 1990 Summer,
v.7, no.2, p.91-180, charts, site
plans, biblios., refs.

URBAN DESIGN--COMPETITIONS--JAPAN--
YOKOHAMA
Winners in the 2nd Yokohama Urban
Design International Competition.
Theme: revitalization of the
waterfront - Yokohama Kaigan Dori.
Includes 13 winning entries and
judges' commentary. First prize
winner: Shigeru Yoshino.
JAPAN ARCHITECT 1990 Oct., v.65,
no.10, p.71-76, dwgs., elevs.,
models, plan, secns.

URBAN DESIGN--CONGRESSES
Designing for new city limits / Mary
Halnan.
On the fifth annual conference of
the International Centre for
Studies in Urban Design, held in
Glasgow Sept. 1990.
ARCHITECTS' JOURNAL 1990 Oct.17,
v.192, no.16, p.15, photos.,
aerial photos.

URBAN DESIGN--CRITICISM
Design and evaluation of urban
design codes / Francis Tibbalds.
Paper presented at the
International Conference on local
Planning, Sydney, Australia, March
1990, "From Images to
Achievements." Critiques points
raised by Prince Charles
concerning architecture and city
planning.
AUSTRALIAN PLANNER: JOURNAL OF THE
ROYAL AUSTRALIAN PLANNING
INSTITUTE 1990 June, v.28, no.2,
p.40-44,
The ten commandments of
architectural and urban design /
John Punter.
An analysis and reply to ten
principles defined by the Prince
of Wales.
THE PLANNER 1990 Oct.5, v.76,
no.39, p.10-14, photos., table,
refs.

URBAN DESIGN--DENMARK--HILLEROD.
CAD-erfaringer / Dan Wajnman.
One of several articles in issue
entitled "Computer aided design".
Work illustrated urban design in
Odense and Hillerod, Denmark, by
the author and Ulrik Plesner.
ARKITEKTEN 1990 Sept., v.92,
no.13, p.433-436, ill., dwgs.

URBAN DESIGN--DENMARK--ODENSE
CAD-erfaringer / Dan Wajnman.
One of several articles in issue
entitled "Computer aided design".
Work illustrated urban design in
Odense and Hillerod, Denmark, by
the author and Ulrik Plesner.
ARKITEKTEN 1990 Sept., v.92,
no.13, p.433-436, ill., dwgs.

URBAN DESIGN--ENGLAND--CHELMSFORD
Generating urban design objectives
for local areas: a methodology and
case study application to
Chelmsford, Essex / A.C. Hall.
TOWN PLANNING REVIEW 1990 July,
v.61, no.3, p.287-309, dwgs., map,
photos., plans, site plan, refs.

URBAN FRINGES--CHILE--SANTIAGO
Vivienda social / Rodrigo Tapia.
Several projects for the outskirts
of Santiago.
ARQ 1990 Mar., no.14, p.16-31,
models, maps, photos., plans,
aerial photo.

URBAN FRINGES--CHINA--SHANGHAI
Satellite town development in
Shanghai, China: an overview /
Farhad Atash, Xinhao Wang.
Includes abstract.
JOURNAL OF ARCHITECTURAL AND
PLANNING RESEARCH 1990 Autumn,
v.7, no.3, p.245-259, maps, table.

URBAN FRINGES--CONGRESSES
Designing for new city limits / Mary
Halnan.
On the fifth annual conference of
the International Centre for
Studies in Urban Design, held in
Glasgow Sept. 1990.
ARCHITECTS' JOURNAL 1990 Oct.17,
v.192, no.16, p.15, photos.,
aerial photos.

URBAN FRINGES--FRANCE--PARIS
Coop Himmelblau: das Projekt
Melun-Senart / Dietmar Steiner.
Competition for a satellite town
on the outskirts of Paris.
BAUWELT 1990 Sept.28, v.81, no.36,
p.1832-1835, site plans.
Social woningsbouw en de ring rond
Parijs / Jean Francois Chiffard,
Yves Roujon.
The development of the periphery
of Paris in the 19th and early
20th centuries and work of the
Office of the HBM.
ARCHIS 1989 Oct., no.10, p.42-53,
maps, photos., plans, site plans,
aerial photo., refs.

URBAN FRINGES--GERMANY (WEST)--HAMBURG
Landwirtschaft am Stadtrand /
Andreas Brandt.
Agriculture in the urban fringe: a
demonstration project in Hamburg.
Includes English summary and
captions.
GARTEN UND LANDSCHAFT 1990, v.100,
no.4, p.46-50, photos., refs.

URBAN FRINGES--GREAT BRITAIN
Peripheral estates: not the sort of
place for planners? / David
Wright.
THE PLANNER 1990 Feb.16, v.76,
no.6, p.16, port.
Planners and peripheral estates /
Duncan Sim.
THE PLANNER 1990 Feb.16, v.76,
no.6, p.17-19, photos., refs.

URBAN FRINGES--GROWTH--CHINA--PEKING
Studies on Beijing's development
strategies / Zhao Dongri.
Covers population structure;
sub-centers, satellite towns,
urban region; water shortage;
traffic.
BUILDING IN CHINA 1989 Mar., v.2,
no.1, p.18-22, table.

URBAN FRINGES--HISTORY--ENGLAND
Ages of English design:
preservation, modernism and tales
of their history, 1926-1939 /
David Matless.
JOURNAL OF DESIGN HISTORY 1990,
v.3, no.4, p.203-212, ill., refs.

URBAN FRINGES--ITALY--FLORENCE
De periferie van Florence.
Feature section. Contents: La
Firenze brutta, by Ed Taverne.--
Beeld en werkelijkheid van een
stad en haar periferie, by Charles
van den Heuvel.--De verplaatsing
van een volksprobleem, by Francis
Prins.
ARCHIS 1989 Sept., no.9, p.27-53,
axonometric views, ill., elevs.,
maps, photos., plans, secns., site
plans, aerial photos., refs.

URBAN FRINGES--ITALY--ROME
Concorso sul tema "Quale periferia
per Roma capitale?".
L'INDUSTRIA DELLE COSTRUZIONI 1990
Mar., v.24, no.221, p.74-76, maps.

URBAN FRINGES--ITALY--ROME--ACILIA SUD
Acilia Sud: la riqualificazione
della periferia abusiva = Acilia
Sud: regeneration in self-help
housing suburbs / Alberto
Clementi.
Acilia Sud is a residential
outskirt of Rome/Ostia. In
Italian; English summary, p.122.
URBANISTICA 1989 Mar., no.94,
p.7-16,122, axonometric view,
photos., plans, site plans, refs.

URBAN FRINGES--NETHERLANDS--HAGUE
Fragmentatie in de periferie: de
"tapijtmetropool" van Willem - Jan
Neutelings / Hilde Heynen.
Text of the author's presentation
at a colloquium on "Fragmented
Spaces", held in Louvain, 26-28
Oct.1989. Features a project for
changes along the south edge of
The Hague.
ARCHIS 1990 Mar., no.3, p.16-21,
models, maps, refs.

URBAN FRINGES--SCOTLAND--GLASGOW
Development pressure in the
metropolitan fringe / Michael
Pacione.
Principally in Glasgow, Scotland.
LAND DEVELOPMENT STUDIES 1990 May,
v.7, no.2, p.69-82, maps, tables,
refs.

URBAN FRINGES--SWEDEN
Tema: externt.
Introduction to issue on "external
centers". Articles are indexed
separately. Commentary by Olof
Hultin, p.28. English
translation, p.55.
ARKITEKTUR: THE SWEDISH REVIEW OF
ARCHITECTURE 1990 Jan.-Feb., v.90,
no.1, p.2-3, cover, photo.

URBAN FRINGES--UNITED STATES
Beyond gridlock: looking for the new
suburban city / Joseph. E. Brown,
Michael E. Hickok.
Problems of definition for
"suburban urbanization", and the
transportation issues involved.
DEVELOPMENT 1990 July-Aug., v.21,
(Continued next column)

URBAN FRINGES--UNITED STATES
(CONTINUED)
Beyond gridlock:...(CONTINUED)
no.4, p.17-20, ill., dwgs.,
photos.
Modern pastoralism and the middle
landscape / Peter G. Rowe.
OZ / COLLEGE OF ARCHITECTURE AND
DESIGN, KANSAS STATE UNIVERSITY
1989, v.11, p.4-9, ill., model,
photos., site plans, aerial
photos., biblio.
Taming the city edge: urban design
portfolio / Andrea Oppenheimer
Dean.
The latest frontier--"outcities."
Mission Bay, San Francisco;
Downtown Norfolk, Va; Carr Norfolk
Southern Project, Alexandria, Va.;
and Arverne, New York City.
ARCHITECTURE: THE AIA JOURNAL 1990
Apr., v.79, no.4, p.[74]-79,147,
ill., model, plans, sketches,
aerial photos.

URBAN FRINGES--UNITED STATES--CHICAGO
(ILLINOIS)
The new main street / Robert
Bruegmann.
New office developments along
expressways west and north of
Chicago.
INLAND ARCHITECT 1990 Nov.-Dec.,
v.34, no.6, p.34-41, dwgs., map,
photos., site plans, aerial photo.

URBAN FRINGES--UNITED STATES--
MILWAUKEE (WISCONSIN)
The future of the industrial city /
Joel Warren Barna.
City planning proposals for
renewal of the Milwaukee, Wisc.
downtown area.
TEXAS ARCHITECT 1990 Mar.-Apr.,
v.40, no.2, p.30-35, map, site
plans.

URBAN INNOVATIONS GROUP
Homage to Gill: Oceanside Civic
Center, Oceanside, California,
Charles W. Moore/Urban Innovations
Group, Architects.
ARCHITECTURAL RECORD 1990 Nov.,
v.178, no.12, p.[76]-81, elevs.,
photos., plans, site plan.

URBAN LAND INSTITUTE--AWARDS AND
PRIZES
The 1990 ULI Awards for Excellence.
Seven awards for outstanding
development projects.
URBAN LAND 1990 Dec., v.49, no.12,
p.16-24, photos., aerial photos.

URBAN PARKS
Lat mellanrummen gronska! / Eivor
Bucht.
On the need for green spaces in
cities, in conjunction with an
international symposium in Almarp
Sweden, Aug. 1989. Includes
English summary and captions.
LANDSKAB 1990 Feb., v.71, no.1,
p.1-5,24, photos., refs.
Urban open space: from space to
place / Janice Morphet.
THE PLANNER 1990 Dec.14, v.76,
no.49, p.82-84, port., photos.

URBAN PARKS--ALTERATIONS AND
ADDITIONS--STUDENT PROJECTS--SPAIN--
MADRID--BUEN RETIRO
Parque y pabellon en el retiro =
Park and pavilion.
Student project by Asuncion
Agullo, 1989, for a park in
Madrid.
EL CROQUIS 1990 Mar., v.9, no.42,
p.169-174, elevs., plans, secns.

URBAN PARKS--CANADA--MONTREAL
(QUEBEC)--CANADIAN CENTRE FOR
ARCHITECTURE
Melvin Charney: giardino-scultura
del CCA a Montreal / Pierre
Restany.
In Italian and English.
DOMUS 1990 Jan., no.712, p.6-[7],
axonometric view, models, site
plans.

URBAN PARKS--CANADA--VANCOUVER
(BRITISH COLUMBIA)--ROBSON SQUARE
Robson Square in Vancouver, Kanada =
Robson Square in Vancouver,
Canada.
Urban park. Architects: Arthur
Erickson Architects.
ARCHITEKTUR + WETTBEWERBE 1990
Dec., no.144, p.12, photos.,
secn., site plan.

URBAN PARKS--COMPETITIONS--CANADA--
TORONTO (ONTARIO)--BAY ADELAIDE PARK
Six schemes for a downtown park:
Toronto's Bay Adelaide Park
competition....
1st prize to Baird/Sampson and
Milus Bollengberghe Topps
Watchorn. Illustrates five other
schemes as well.
CANADIAN ARCHITECT 1990 Nov.,
v.35, no.11, p.30-34, ill., dwgs.,
model, plans, site plans.

URBAN PARKS--CONSERVATION AND
RESTORATION--UNITED STATES--NEW YORK
(NEW YORK)--BRYANT PARK
Bryant Park plans proceed / Albert
Amateau, Steven Saltzman.
Restoration to enter final phase
in winter of 1990, to be completed
in spring of 1991. Landscape
architects: Hanna/Olin.
METROPOLIS 1990 Jan.-Feb., v.9,
no.6, p.13-14, elev., photos.

URBAN PARKS--ENGLAND--LONDON--
EXHIBITIONS
Capital pastime recorded [exhibition
review] / Tony Venison.
"London's Pride," exhibition at
the Museum of London, 1990.
COUNTRY LIFE 1990 May 10, v.184,
no.19, p.100-103, ill., photos.
Gardens of delight: London's pride:
the history of the capital's
gardens [exhibition review] /
Robert Harbison.
Exhibition at the Museum of London
until 12 Aug. 1990.
ARCHITECT'S JOURNAL 1990 May 16,
v.191, no.20, p.90-91, axonometric
view, ill., photo., plan.
London's gardens [exhibition
review].
"London's pride: the history of
the capital's gardens": the first
exhibition to trace the history
and evolution of London's parks
and gardens from medieval times to
(Continued next column)

URBAN PARKS--ENGLAND--LONDON--
EXHIBITIONS (CONTINUED)
London's gardens...(CONTINUED)
the present. Held at the Museum of
London until 12 Aug. 1990.
ROYAL SOCIETY OF ARTS, LONDON. RSA
JOURNAL 1990 July, v.138, no.5408,
p.564, photo.
London's pride: the History of the
Capital's Gardens exhibition held
at the Museum of London /May to 12
August 1990 [exhibition review] /
Robert Oresko.
LONDON JOURNAL 1990, v.15, no.2,
p.[155]-159, ref.

URBAN PARKS--GERMANY (WEST)
Neues Denken gefragt / Jurgen
Milchert.
Park use demands and environmental
awareness in Germany. English
summary and captions.
GARTEN UND LANDSCHAFT 1990, v.100,
no.11, p.25-32, photos., ref.

URBAN PARKS--GREAT BRITAIN
Greening the city: reclamation and
revival / Brian Clouston.
Compares Britain's tradition of
landscape architecture with
post-war developments elsewhere.
URBAN FUTURES 1989 Spring, v.2,
no.1, p.13-20, photos.

URBAN PARKS--GREECE--DRAMA--AYIA
VARVARA
The Ayia Varvara site project: a
case of urban landscape design /
M. Ananiadou-Tzimopoulou, D.A.
Fatouros.
A project involving the planning
and design of a cultural landscape
in a natural area incorporated
within the city of Drama in
northern Greece.
LANDSCAPE AND URBAN PLANNING 1990
Apr., v.19, no.1, p.69-97,
photos., plans, secns., site
plans, sketches, refs.

URBAN PARKS--ITALY--BOLOGNA
Stadtischer Park auf dem Gelande
einer ehemaligen Tabakfabrik in
Bologna, Italien = Urban park on
the area of a former tobacco
factory in Bologna, Italy.
Architects: Alessandro Anselmi,
Francesco Cellini, Andrea
Salvioni, Roberto Ugolini.
ARCHITEKTUR + WETTBEWERBE 1990
Dec., no.144, p.17, dwgs.

URBAN PARKS--JAPAN--NAGOYA--SHIROTORU
PARK
Motoo Yoshimura: creation of
contemporary Japanese gardens /
edited by Motoo Yoshimura and Dina
Yando Yoshimura.
Contents: Essay: Construction of
Japanese landscape gardens in the
age of urbanization / Motoo
Yoshimura --Works: Shirotori Park
--Shirotori Tea House garden --
Fukuda house garden, Kyoto --
Yoshida Steak House garden --Kyoto
Historical Museum garden --
Yamamoto Tea Shop & garden,
Shigaraki --World Orchid
Exhibition grounds, Tokyo --
Katsurazaka pedestrian footpath,
Kyoto --Osaka International
Exposition Memorial Park.
(Continued next column)

URBAN PARKS--JAPAN--NAGOYA--SHIROTORU
PARK (CONTINUED)
Motoo Yoshimura:...(CONTINUED)
Landscape architect: Motto
Yoshimura. Text in Japanese and
English.
PROCESS: ARCHITECTURE 1990 Sept.,
no.91, p.[1]-154, dwgs., port.,
photos., plans, secns., site
plans, aerial photos.

URBAN PARKS--MATHEMATICAL MODELS
The optimal provision of a central
park in a city / Chung-hsin Yang.
Chiefly equations.
JOURNAL OF REGIONAL SCIENCE 1990
Feb., v.30, no.1, p.15-36, diagr.,
graphs, refs.

URBAN PARKS--POLITICAL ASPECTS--
GERMANY (WEST)--FREIBURG
Wandel von Werten und Normen /
Bernhard Utz.
A case example of management
within the Freiburg parks dept.
English summary and captions.
GARTEN UND LANDSCHAFT 1990, v.100,
no.11, p.37-39, photos.

URBAN PARKS--SCOTLAND--GLASGOW
Greener Glasgow is child's play /
Ruth Owens.
West German environmental artist
Dieter Magnus has designed a park
and playground space in Glasgow
that is both urban park and water
garden.
ARCHITECTS' JOURNAL 1990 Feb.28,
v.191, no.9, p.17, port., model,
photos.

URBAN PARKS--SOCIOLOGICAL ASPECTS--
CHINA
Survey for resident needs for
outdoor activities / Bai Demao.
Survey of multi-unit households in
Unity Lake, Sturdy Pine, and
Zuojaizhuang, China.
BUILDING IN CHINA 1990 Mar., v.3,
no.1, p.3-15, graphs, tables,
plans.

URBAN PARKS--STANDARDS--CHINA
Standards.
Contents: XXI. Public transport in
cities. -- XXII.Road and bridge
engineering in urban areas. --
XXIII. Gardens and parks in urban
areas. -- XXIV.Urban environmental
sanitation. -- XXV. Urban disaster
mitigation.
BUILDING IN CHINA 1990 Mar., v.3,
no.1, p.46-48, tables.

URBAN PARKS--SWEDEN
La progettazione degli spazi aperti
nell'edilizia residenziale svedese
/ Eivor Bucht.
URBANISTICA 1989 Dec., no.97,
p.76-78, axonometric view, photos.

URBAN PARKS--UNITED STATES
You call this a national park? /
James Krohe.
Small urban parks form part of the
national parks system.
PLANNING 1990 Aug., v.56, no.8,
p.4-10, maps, photos., plan.

URBAN PARKS--UNITED STATES--DES MOINES
(IOWA)--PRINCIPAL PARK
Principal Park: a park with
principles / Debra Kurtz.
Urban park in downtown Des Moines.
Architects: Brooks Borg and
Skiles.
IOWA ARCHITECT 1989 Winter, v.38,
no.5, p.22-25, photos, site plan.

URBAN PARKS--UNITED STATES--HOUSTON
(TEXAS)--SESQUICENTENNIAL PARK
Houston design portfolio: slow
recovery.
Sesquicentennial Park (Team HOU);
Caldwell house (Natalye Appel);
Court at Museums Gate (Josiah
Baker); Gilliland house (Peter Jay
Zweig Architects); Finnell house
(Wittenberg Partnership); and St.
Mary's Episcopal Church (Gerald
Moorhead).
ARCHITECTURE: THE AIA JOURNAL 1990
Apr., v.79, no.4, p.54-73,
axonometric views, ill., elev.,
photos., plans, secns., site
plans.

URBAN PARKS--UNITED STATES--SEATTLE
(WASHINGTON)--FREEWAY PARK
Urban Camouflage: Portfolio:
Danadjieva & Koenig Associates /
Andrea Oppenheimer Dean.
An architecture and landscape
architecture firm with offices in
Tiburon, Calif., and Bellevue,
Wash. contents: Freeway Air Rights
Development, Seattle; and
Riverfront Promenade, White River
Park, Indianapolis.
ARCHITECTURE: THE MAGAZINE OF THE
AMERICAN INSTITUTE OF ARCHITECTS
1990 Aug., v.79, no.8, p.60-65,
model, photos., site plans, aerial
photo.

URBAN PLANNING
See CITY PLANNING

URBAN POPULATION MOVEMENTS
See RESIDENTIAL MOBILITY

URBAN RENEWAL
Dal recupero edilizio alla
riqualificazione urbana = From
building rehabilitation to urban
renewal / Maurizio Marcelloni.
In Italian; English summary, p.21.
URBANISTICA 1988 Nov., no.93,
p.6-21, axonometric views, model,
photos., plans.
Partners in urban regeneration /
John Fitz-Gerald.
Identifies different forms of
partnership.
THE PLANNER 1990 Dec.14, v.76,
no.49, p.79-81, port., photos.

URBAN RENEWAL--CHILE--SANTIAGO
Una estrategia democratica de
renovacion urbana residencial: el
caso de la comuna de Santiago /
Andres Necochea, Ana Maria Icaza.
EURE. REVISTA LATINOAMERICANA DE
ESTUDIOS URBANOS REGIONALES 1990
June, v.16, no.48, p.37-65, table,
refs.

URBAN RENEWAL--CHINA--SHENYANG
Comprehensive urban renewal of old
urban districts in Shenyang.
CHINA CITY PLANNING REVIEW 1988
Mar., v.4, no.1, p.15-32, maps,
plans, tables.

URBAN RENEWAL--CITIZEN PARTICIPATION
Zum Verhaltnis von Stadtebaupolitik
und Gesellschaftsstrategie aus
soziologischer Sicht / Bernd
Hunger.
Sociological aspects of town
planning. German, Russian,
English and French summaries,
p.55-56.
ARCHITEKTUR DER DDR 1990 Feb.,
v.38, no.2, p.9-10, charts.

URBAN RENEWAL--CITIZEN PARTICIPATION--
ECUADOR--QUITO
The historic centre of Quito,
Ecuador: a case study for the
application of some principles on
housing and participation /
Mauricio Moreno.
OPEN HOUSE INTERNATIONAL 1988,
v.13, no.4, p.12-24, diagrs.,
dwgs., plans, tables, refs.

URBAN RENEWAL--CUBA
Castro's Cuba is looking to CAG /
Robert Cowan.
RIBA's Community Architecture
Group (CAG) is invited to organize
a British architecture workshop in
Cuba to study urban renewal and
housing. The invitation comes from
UNIAC, the Cuban Union of
Architects.
ARCHITECTS' JOURNAL 1990 June 20,
v.191, no.25, p.14-15, ports.,
photos.

URBAN RENEWAL--DEVELOPING COUNTRIES
Feature: Rehabilitation of
inner-city areas.
HABITAT NEWS 1988 Dec., v.10,
no.3, p.46-49, chart.

URBAN RENEWAL--EGYPT--ISMAILIA
The effects of combined upgrading
and new development schemes on
housing patterns of the site: case
study of Ismailia project in Egypt
/ Hany B. Seraq-El-Din.
Award-winning housing project in
Ismailia city.
INTERNATIONAL JOURNAL FOR HOUSING
SCIENCE AND ITS APPLICATIONS 1990,
v.14, no.4, p.259-272, photos.,
site plan, refs.

URBAN RENEWAL--ENGLAND--LONDON--
DOCKLANDS
London Docklands: ouvriers, dockers
et yuppies: une nouvelle ville
internationale / Genevieve
Marotel, Alain Tarrius.
French, English, German, and
Spanish summaries, p.[123]-126.
LES ANNALES DE LA RECHERCHE
URBAINE 1990 Mar.-Apr., no.46,
p.[75]-86, map, photos., tables.

URBAN RENEWAL--ENGLAND--NEWCASTLE UPON
TYNE
The Newcastle initiative.
Theme issue. Contents: The
Newcastle initiative: a case study
of a city doing business with
business; The Theatre Village; Key
development issues; Vision and
strategy; Proposals, outline costs
and benefits; and Delivering
regeneration.
URBAN FUTURES 1989, v.2, no.3,
p.cover,1-48, charts, diagr.,
maps, photo., site plans,
sketches, aerial photo.

URBAN RENEWAL--ENGLAND--SALFORD
Lowry's landscape regenerated.
On the work of the Salford
Landscape Group, part of the 1984
urban renewal strategy for the
city.
LANDSCAPE DESIGN 1989 Nov.,
no.185, p.36-37,39-41, photos.,
refs.

URBAN RENEWAL--ENGLAND--SHEFFIELD
Inner city reconstruction -
Sheffield: a case study / Richard
D. Field, Clive Betts, Cedric
Green.
Report delivered to the Society 22
Nov.1989.
ROYAL SOCIETY OF ARTS, LONDON. RSA
JOURNAL 1990 Apr., v.138, no.5405,
p.343-353, photos.

URBAN RENEWAL--ENGLAND--THORNE
Thorne: a community fighting back /
Tony Aldous.
Urban renewal of Yorkshire market
town-turned-mining community.
URBAN FUTURES 1990 Spring, v.3,
no.1, p.40-45, photos., sketch.

URBAN RENEWAL--ENGLAND--WIGAN
Regeneration in action / John
Sloane.
In Wigan.
HOUSING AND PLANNING REVIEW 1990
Aug.-Sept., v.45, no.4, p.10-11,
photo.
"Why conserve Wigan?" / Adrian
Hardy.
HOUSING AND PLANNING REVIEW 1990
Aug.-Sept., v.45, no.4, p.13-14,
photos.

URBAN RENEWAL--ENGLAND--WIRRAL--
SUNNINGDALE COMMUNITY PROJECT
Sunningdale Community Project / John
Agass.
Urban renewal in Wirral,
Merseyside.
HOUSING REVIEW 1990 Mar.-Apr.,
v.39, no.2, p.41-42, sketch.

URBAN RENEWAL--FRANCE--SAINT-DIE DES
VOSGES
Vosges Vei ts.
Plan for the "green" urban renewal
of Saint-Die Des Vosges.
Architects: Jean Marie Hennin and
Nicolas Normier.
ARCHITECTURAL REVIEW 1990 Sept.,
v.188, no.1123, p.68-70,
axonometric view, elevs., models,
plans, secns., site plans,
isometric dwgs.

URBAN RENEWAL--GERMANY (EAST)--
THURINGEN
Erste Hilfe: die Hessenhilfe fur
Thuringen / Oliver G. Hamm.
DEUTSCHE BAUZEITUNG 1990 June,
v.124, no.6, p.81-84, ill., map,
photos.

URBAN RENEWAL--GERMANY (WEST)
Urban renewal policies and
back-to-the-city migration: the
case of West Germany / Jurgen
Friedrichs.
AMERICAN PLANNING ASSOCIATION.
JOURNAL 1987 Winter, v.53, no.1,
p.70-79, map, tables, biblio.,
refs.

URBAN RENEWAL--GERMANY (WEST)--
REGENSBURG
Baualtersplane zur Stadtsanierung:
Regensburg I-VIII [book review].
ZEITSCHRIFT FUR SCHWEIZERISCHE
ARCHAOLOGIE UND KUNSTGESCHICHTE
1989, v.46, no.1, p.106-108, refs.

URBAN RENEWAL--GREAT BRITAIN
Britain's Fair Towns: a national
competition proposal for
environmental and economic
regeneration of the smaller town /
Alan Simpson, Gerry Kemp.
URBAN FUTURES 1989 Spring, v.2,
no.1, p.5-12, axonometric view,
plans, sketches.
Expanding improvement areas / John
Morris.
HOUSING 1990 June-July, v.26,
no.5, p.41,43,45,47, photos.
National garden festival:
regeneration or degeneration? /
John Turner.
URBAN FUTURES 1989 Spring, v.2,
no.1, p.41-44, photos.
Planners and peripheral estates /
Duncan Sim.
THE PLANNER 1990 Feb.16, v.76,
no.6, p.17-19, photos., refs.
Urban renewal.
Special feature, publ. in
conjunction with the Countdown
Through the Nineties conference
sponsored by the British Urban
Regeneration Association.
BUILDING 1990 Feb.9, v.255, no.6,
p.55-66, ill., ports., photos.

URBAN RENEWAL--IRAN
Design participation in the context
of urban renewal / Amir Hossein
Afrassiabi.
URBAN FUTURES 1989 Summer, v.2,
no.2, p.24-32, chart., diagr.,
refs.

URBAN RENEWAL--ITALY
Dal recupero edilizio alla
riqualificazione urbana = From
building rehabilitation to urban
renewal / Maurizio Marcelloni.
In Italian; English summary, p.21.
URBANISTICA 1988 Nov., no.93,
p.6-21, axonometric views, model,
photos., plans.

URBAN RENEWAL--ITALY--GENOA
Milano, Torino e Genova: aree
industriali dismesse e piano =
Milan, Turin and Genoa: disused
industrial areas and urban plan /
Federico Oliva.
In Italian; English summary,
(Continued next column)

URBAN RENEWAL--ITALY--GENOA
(CONTINUED)
Milano, Torino e...(CONTINUED)
p.128.
URBANISTICA 1988 Nov., no.93,
p.104-121, 128, axonometric view,
dwg., maps, photos., plans, secn.,
site plans, refs.

URBAN RENEWAL--ITALY--MILAN
Milano, Torino e Genova: aree
industriali dismesse e piano =
Milan, Turin and Genoa: disused
industrial areas and urban plan /
Federico Oliva.
In Italian; English summary,
p.128.
URBANISTICA 1988 Nov., no.93,
p.104-121, 128, axonometric view,
dwg., maps, photos., plans, secn.,
site plans, refs.

URBAN RENEWAL--ITALY--TURIN
Milano, Torino e Genova: aree
industriali dismesse e piano =
Milan, Turin and Genoa: disused
industrial areas and urban plan /
Federico Oliva.
In Italian; English summary,
p.128.
URBANISTICA 1988 Nov., no.93,
p.104-121, 128, axonometric view,
dwg., maps, photos., plans, secn.,
site plans, refs.

URBAN RENEWAL--JAPAN--TOKYO
Study on the improvement of the
residential environment from the
acutual [sic] condition of
self-help housing improvement
action by owner-occupant in small
site detached and row houses
congested area / Masanori Koh.
Survey defines self-help housing
actions and proposes a policy.
Text in Japanese. Includes English
summary.
NIHON KENCHIKU GAKKAI KEIKAKUKEI
RONBUN HOKOKU SHU = JOURNAL OF
ARCHITECTURE, PLANNING AND
ENVIRONMENTAL ENGINEERING 1990
June [July], no.7(413), p.95-105,
maps, tables, refs.

URBAN RENEWAL--MEXICO--MEXICO CITY--
SANTA ANITA
The glories of Santa Anita: a
Mexican horror story / Sigismund
Engelkind Keeling.
Small town absorbed by Mexico
City, now a shantytown.
PROSPECT 1989, no.3, p.5-8, map,
photos.

URBAN RENEWAL--NETHERLANDS--ROTTERDAM
"Hai quel che disegni..." / Jacques
Nycolaas.
The 'Juniproject' and the urban
plan for Rotterdam. In Italian;
English summary, p.95.
URBANISTICA 1988 Nov., no.93,
p.44-48, 95, diagrs., plans, site
plans, refs.

URBAN RENEWAL--NEW ZEALAND--
CHRISTCHURCH
Pumping life into central city / Ken
Lawn.
Urban renewal in Christchurch, New
Zealand.
PLANNING QUARTERLY 1989 Sept.,
no.95, p.26-28, map, photo.

URBAN RENEWAL--NORTHERN IRELAND--
BELFAST
Making Belfast work / Bill Morrison.
THE PLANNER 1990 Dec.14, v.76,
no.49, p.32-35, port., photos.

URBAN RENEWAL--NORWAY--BERGEN
Stadterneuerung in Bergen / Arne
Smedsrig.
English summary and captions.
GARTEN UND LANDSCHAFT 1990, v.100,
no.8, p.56-60, photos., site
plans.

URBAN RENEWAL--POLITICAL ASPECTS
Le origini dell'urbanistica moderna:
Francia e Stati Uniti.
Contents: Ragione e visione: la
mentalita pianificatoria negli
Stati Uniti e l'indagine urbana,
1890-1930, by Christine Boyer.--
L'urbanistica come movimento
sociale: militanti e
professionisti del City Planning
negli Stati Uniti, 1909-1917, by
Christian Topalov.-- "Reconstituir
la cite": dalla concezione
organicistica della citta alla
riforma del quartiere popolare in
Francia nel primo quarto del
secolo, by Susanna Magri.-- La
genesi dell'urbanistica di piano e
la questione della modernizzazione
politica, 1900-1930, by Jean
Pierre Gaudin.
STORIA URBANA 1989 July-Dec.,
v.13, no.48-49, p.127-245, tables,
refs.

URBAN RENEWAL--POLITICAL ASPECTS--
GERMANY
Urban renewal under National
Socialism: practical policy and
political objectives in Hitler's
Germany / Ursula von Petz.
PLANNING PERSPECTIVES PP 1990 May,
v.5, no.2, p.169-187, ports.,
photos., plans, aerial photos.,
refs.

URBAN RENEWAL--SCOTLAND--GLASGOW
Fighting for funds / Ruth Owens.
Glasgow as "City of Culture 1990"
continues its regeneration
schemes.
ARCHITECTS' JOURNAL 1990 May 30,
v.191, no.22, p.26-27, 29,
sketches.
GEAR: la gestion des partenaires
publics de la renovation / Urlan
Wannop.
Urban renewal in Scotland's
Glasgow Eastern Area Renewal
(GEAR) project. French, English,
German and Spanish summaries,
p.[125]-127.
LES ANNALES DE LA RECHERCHE
URBAINE 1990 Oct., no.48,
p.[74]-85, port., photos., tables.
La genesi della citta
post-industriale [Glasgow} / W. F.
Lever.
In Italian.
URBANISTICA 1989 Oct., no.96,
p.109-112, photos., biblio.
IFHP study visit 'Glasgow (S)miles
Better' / Harry Bentham.
PROSPECT 1989, no.3, p.2-4,
photos.

URBAN RENEWAL--SCOTLAND--GLASGOW
(CONTINUED)
Infrastructure restoration as a tool
for stimulating urban renewal: the
Glasgow Canal / Kenneth J. Button,
David W. Pearce.
URBAN STUDIES 1989 Dec., v.26,
no.6, p.559-571, map., tables,
refs.
Revival urbano ovvero la riscoperta
della citta [Glasgow] / A. G.
Vogt.
In Italian; Italian and English
captions.
URBANISTICA 1989 Oct., no.96,
p.112-115, photos., aerial photo.,
refs.
La riqualificazione dell'east end:
il gear project / Raffaele
Paloscia.
The Glasgow Eastern Area Renewal
project (GEAR), an inner-city
urban renewal project. In Italian,
with Italian and English captions.
URBANISTICA 1989 Oct., no.96,
p.115-119, maps, photos., refs.

URBAN RENEWAL--SPAIN
Le politiche de recupero dei centri
storici nella Spagna degli anni
Ottanta = Spain's inner-city
rehabilitation policy for the
1980s / Francisco Pol.
In Italian; English captions;
English summary, p.124.
URBANISTICA 1989 Mar., no.94,
p.53-63, axonometric views, dwgs.,
elevs., model, photos., plans,
secns., aerial photos.

URBAN RENEWAL--SPAIN--MADRID
The Madrid neighborhood remodelling
programme: a case study / Robert
Chubb.
LAND DEVELOPMENT STUDIES 1989
Jan., v.6, no.1, p.[3]-11, biblio.

URBAN RENEWAL--STUDENT PROJECTS--
ITALY--NAPLES
Napoli, architettura e citta:
secondoi seminario di
progettazione / Uberto Siola.
On the 1990 International Seminar
on Architectural Design, "Naples,
Architecture and City." Presents
student projects for the
revitalization of 4 areas of
Naples. Text in Italian and
English.
DOMUS 1990 Dec., no.722,
p.[11]-[16], dwgs., elevs., model,
site plans.

URBAN RENEWAL--SWEDEN--GOTEBORG
Il porto che cambia = Converting the
port: Goteborg / Pietro Raffeone.
Abandoned harbor and shipyards to
be redeveloped. Architects: Ralph
Erskine; White Arkitekter; Pietro
Raffone; Arkitektlaget.
ABITARE 1990 July-Aug., no.287,
p.216-[223], dwg., model, photos.,
plan, site plans.

URBAN RENEWAL--TANZANIA--
DAR-ES-SALAAM--KARIKOO
Low cost urban renewal in Tanzania:
community participation in
Dar-Es Salaam / Sababu Kaitilla.
In the Kariakoo neighborhood.
CITIES 1990 Aug., v.7, no.3,
p.211-223, plans, tables, refs.

URBAN RENEWAL--UNITED STATES
American downtowns: past and present
attempts at revitalization /
Robert J. Carey.
BUILT ENVIRONMENT 1988, v.14,
no.1, p.47-59, graphs, photos,
tables, refs.
Urban renewal: Downtown inc.: how
America rebuilds cities, by
Bernard J. Frieden and Lynne B.
Sagalyn [book review] / Francis
Tibbalds.
ROYAL SOCIETY OF ARTS, LONDON. RSA
JOURNAL 1990 Dec., v.139, no.5413,
p.947,

URBAN RENEWAL--UNITED STATES--FORT
WAYNE (INDIANA)
An action plan for revitalizing
south central Fort Wayne / Diane
R. Suchman.
URBAN LAND 1990 Sept., v.49, no.9,
p.20-25, photos., plans.

URBAN RENEWAL--UNITED STATES--HISTORY
Urban renewal: an administrator
remembers / Charles L. Farris.
The author looks back on 40 years
of urban renewal in the U.S.
JOURNAL OF HOUSING 1989 July-Aug.,
v.46, no.4, p.169-171,173-174,
178-179, port., photo., aerial
photo.

URBAN RENEWAL--UNITED STATES--LOS
ANGELES (CALIFORNIA)
Core concerns / Donald J. Canty.
A report on Los Angeles, 15 years
after the introduction of a
downtown urban renewal plan.
ARCHITECTURAL RECORD 1990 June,
v.178, no.7, p.58-65, dwgs.,
models, maps, photos.

URBAN RENEWAL--UNITED STATES--NEW YORK
(NEW YORK)
New York--Phonix in der Asche? /
Wilma R. Albrecht.
ALTE STADT 1989, v.16 no.4,
p.[607]-609, refs.

URBAN RENEWAL--UNITED STATES--NEW YORK
(NEW YORK)--42ND STREET
REDEVELOPMENT PROJECT
Is bigger still better? / Doug
Turetsky.
Large developments at the Hunters
Point waterfront in Queens and in
Times Square are about to begin
construction despite slack in real
estate market.
CITY LIMITS 1990 Aug.-Sept., v.15,
no.7, p.12-15, port., photo.

URBAN RENEWAL--UNITED STATES--NEW YORK
(NEW YORK)--HARLEM
Harlem: a new renaissance? / Mark W.
Griffith, Errol T. Louis.
CITY LIMITS 1990 Oct., v.15, no.8,
p.16-19, port., photos.

URBAN RENEWAL--UNITED STATES--NEW YORK
(NEW YORK)--TIMES SQUARE AREA
Teaching Times Square a lesson /
Andrew Mandel, Jacqueline Thaw.
While Times Square awaits
redevelopment, the theater group
En-Garde Arts performs "Crowbar"
in one of the area's saved
theaters, the Victory.
PLACES 1990 Summer, v.6, no.4,
p.[91-92], det., photos.

URBAN RENEWAL--UNITED STATES--NEW YORK
(NEW YORK)--TIMES SQUARE AREA
(CONTINUED)
Times Square, New York City: la
costruzione di un problema
ingovernabile (1967/1987) = Times
Square: an unmanageable problem in
the making / Paolo Fareri.
In Italian; English summary,
p.121, 124.
URBANISTICA 1989 Oct., no.96,
p.7-20, 121, 124, elevs., maps,
photos., plans, biblio.

URBAN RENEWAL--UNITED STATES--NEWARK
(NEW JERSEY)
Update on Newark: the doughnut hole
has been filled / Bruce Hendler.
URBAN LAND 1990 Apr., v.49, no.4,
p.22-23, axonometric view, tables.

URBAN RENEWAL--UNITED STATES--NORFOLK
(VIRGINIA)
Focus on Norfolk, Virginia.
Ghent Square and the Scattered
Site Infill Housing Program.
JOURNAL OF HOUSING 1990 Mar.-Apr.,
v.47, no.2, p.101-104, photos.

URBAN RENEWAL--UNITED STATES--TARBORO
(NORTH CAROLINA)
Downtown revitalization and historic
preservation in small town
America: a case study of Tarboro,
North Carolina / E. Watson Brown,
Wes Hankins.
CAROLINA PLANNING 1990 Fall, v.16,
no.2, p.50-54, photos., refs.

URBAN RENEWAL--UNITED STATES--TRENTON
(NEW JERSEY)
Trenton: recalled to life / Nora
Odendahl, Sharon Ayn McHugh,
Robert D. Cerutti.
Includes inset article on the
Capital City Renaissance Plan, by
Sharon Ayn McHugh.
ARCHITECTURE NEW JERSEY 1989,
v.25, no.3, p.13-22, 29,
axonometric views, graph, dwgs.,
map, photos.

URBAN RENEWAL--WALES
Urban renewal in Wales: the role of
the Welsh Development Agency /
John H. Pavitt.
Councillors school opening
address, Town and Country Planning
Summer School, Swansea, Wales,
Sept. 1990.
THE PLANNER 1990 Dec.14, v.76,
no.49, p.70-74, charts, port.,
aerial photo.

URBAN RENEWAL--WALES--CARDIFF
Cardiff Bay development / David S.
Walton.
THE PLANNER 1990 Dec.14, v.76,
no.49, p.10-18, port., site plan,
sketches.

URBAN RENEWAL--WALES--SWANSEA
Swansea: regeneration of the city /
Trever M. Osborne.
THE PLANNER 1990 Dec.14, v.76,
no.49, p.7-9, port., photos.

URBAN TRANSIT
See TRANSIT SYSTEMS

URBAN TRANSPORTATION
See also CITY TRAFFIC
See also TRANSIT SYSTEMS
Le reti nella citta = Urban networks
/ Giuseppe Longhi.
Urban transportation systems.
L'ARCA 1990 Sept., no.41, p.4-7,
photos.

URBAN TRANSPORTATION--FRANCE--
ILE-DE-FRANCE
Las politicas de desplazamientos en
Ile-de-France = Transport policies
in the Ile-de-France / Pascale
Pecheur.
English summary, p.28.
URBANISMO / COAM 1990 May, no.10,
p.20-28, graph, ill., maps,
photos., plans, table.

URBAN TRANSPORTATION--SPAIN--SEVILLE
El trafico y el transporte en la
ciudad de Sevilla = Traffic and
transport in the city of Seville /
Miguel Durban.
English summary, p.47.
URBANISMO / COAM 1990 May, no.10,
p.38-47, maps, photos., plans,
aerial photos.

URBAN VILLAGES
Class A urban village cores from
scratch: the growing trend /
Christopher B. Leinberger.
REAL ESTATE ISSUES 1989
Fall-Winter, v.14, no.2, p.16-19,
ill.
The holy grid: a skeptic's view /
Sam Hall Kaplan.
The author "wonders whether 'the
urban village' is simply the
design idea of the month".
PLANNING 1990 Nov., v.56, no.11,
p.10-11, ill., photo., sketch.
Traditional neighborhood
development: will the traffic
work? / Walter Kulash, Joe Anglin,
David Marks.
DEVELOPMENT 1990 July-Aug., v.21,
no.4, p.21-24, ill., plans.

URBAN VILLAGES--UNITED STATES
Recapturing vitality with new urban
villages / William Kearns, Thomas
E. McDonough.
DEVELOPMENT 1989 Nov.-Dec., v.20,
no.6, p.10-11, photo.

URBANISM
See CITIES AND TOWNS

URBANISTS
See CITY PLANNERS

URBANIZATION
Du voisinage a l'urbanite: les
mobilites pietonnes / Jean-Marc
Offner.
Pedestrian spatial mobility.
French, English, and Spanish
summaries.
ESPACES ET SOCIETES 1988,
no.54-55, p.[69]-88, diagrs., site
plan, table, biblio.
Fragment als Srategie / Bernard
Leupen.
"Designing in the urban context of
the 90s." Text in German,
summaries in German, French and
(Continued next column)

URBANIZATION (CONTINUED)
Fragment als Srategie...(CONTINUED)
English. The works by Nouvel and
Koolhaas which follow are indexed
separately.
WERK, BAUEN + WOHNEN 1990 Mar.,
no.3, p.24-31, ill., model,
secns., site plans, refs.
Die Stadt sieht man nicht = The city
is not seen / Eberhard
Kulenkampff.
The perception of cities by their
inhabitants. Text in German and in
English.
DAIDALOS 1989 Dec.15, no.34,
p.30-47, photos.
Urban design 5: regional identity /
Hildebrand Frey.
Maintaining city identity during
the process of urbanization and
growth. Fifth in series on urban
design.
ARCHITECTS' JOURNAL 1990 Oct.31,
v.192, no.18, p.63-65, photos.,
plans.

URBANIZATION--17TH CENTURY--TURKEY--
ISTANBUL
Communal living in Ottoman Istanbul:
searching for the foundations of
an urban tradition / Rhoads
Murphey.
JOURNAL OF URBAN HISTORY 1990
Feb., v.16, no.2, p.115-131, refs.

URBANIZATION--18TH CENTURY--TURKEY--
ISTANBUL
Communal living in Ottoman Istanbul:
searching for the foundations of
an urban tradition / Rhoads
Murphey.
JOURNAL OF URBAN HISTORY 1990
Feb., v.16, no.2, p.115-131, refs.

URBANIZATION--19TH CENTURY--
SOCIOLOGICAL ASPECTS--ENGLAND--
LONDON
The spatial configuration of class
solidarity in London's West End
1792-1939 / P. J. Atkins.
URBAN HISTORY YEARBOOK 1990, v.17,
p.[36]-65, diagrs., graphs, maps,
tables, refs.

URBANIZATION--BRAZIL--SAO PAULO
A convivencia com a contradicao
metropolitana.
PROJETO 1990 Dec.-1991 Jan.,
no.137, p.A1-A24, elevs., maps,
photos., plans, secns., site
plans, tables, aerial photo.

URBANIZATION--CHINA
The cities of the USSR and China:
streets apart? / John Cole.
CITIES 1990 May, v.7, no.2,
p.159-168, graphs, map, photos.,
tables, refs.

URBANIZATION--DEVELOPING COUNTRIES
Controlled urbanisation: a planned
approach to the housing crisis /
Brian G. Field.
INTERNATIONAL JOURNAL FOR HOUSING
SCIENCE AND ITS APPLICATIONS 1989,
v.13, no.3, p.[233]-242, chart,
map, plan, refs.
New approaches in urban services
delivery: a comparison of emerging
experience in selected Asian
countries / Emiel A. Wegelin.
CITIES 1990 Aug., v.7, no.3,
(Continued next column)

URBANIZATION--DEVELOPING COUNTRIES
(CONTINUED)
New approaches in...(CONTINUED)
p.244-258, refs.
The Third World goes to town: will
U.S. policy catch up? / Coralie
Bryant.
Third World urbanization.
CITIES 1990 May, v.7, no.2,
p.125-132, refs.

URBANIZATION--DEVELOPING COUNTRIES--
CONGRESSES
World Habitat Day 1989 update:
"shelter and urbanization" theme
for 1990.
Sponsored by UNCHS (Habitat).
HABITAT NEWS 1990 Apr., v.12,
no.1, p.14-17, ill., ports.,
model, photos.

URBANIZATION--ECONOMIC ASPECTS
King of the city: global cities:
post-imperialism and the
internationalisation of London
[by] Anthony D. King [book review]
/ Peter Hall.
ARCHITECTS' JOURNAL 1990 Jan.31,
v.191, no.5, p.73-74,

URBANIZATION--ECUADOR--CUENCA
Cuenca, Ecuador: planner's dream or
speculator's delight? / Stella
Lowder.
THIRD WORLD PLANNING REVIEW 1990
May, v.12, no.2, p.[107]-130,
maps, tables, refs.

URBANIZATION--ENGLAND--LONDON
King of the city: global cities:
post-imperialism and the
internationalisation of London
[by] Anthony D. King [book review]
/ Peter Hall.
ARCHITECTS' JOURNAL 1990 Jan.31,
v.191, no.5, p.73-74,

URBANIZATION--ENVIRONMENTAL ASPECTS
The greenhouse effect and the city /
Patrick N. Troy.
AUSTRALIAN PLANNER: JOURNAL OF THE
ROYAL AUSTRALIAN PLANNING
INSTITUTE 1990 Mar., v.28, no.1,
p.17-22, biblio.

URBANIZATION--ENVIRONMENTAL ASPECTS--
UNITED STATES--LITTLE MIAMI RIVER
BASIN (OHIO)
The hydrologic effects of urban land
use: a case study of the Little
Miami River Basin / Susanna T.Y.
Tong.
LANDSCAPE AND URBAN PLANNING 1990
Apr., v.19, no.1, p.99-105,
graphs, tables, refs.

URBANIZATION--EUROPE
Libri recenti sulla storia delle
citta europee [book review] /
Lando Bortolotti.
Reviews three books: Storia della
citta europea dal 1000 al 1950; Le
citta e le mura; Storia
dell'urbanistica - L'Europa del
secondo dopo-guerra.
STORIA URBANA 1990 July-Sept.,
v.14, no.52, p.[195]-206, biblio.

URBANIZATION--GREECE--ATHENS
Positive aspects of Greek
urbanization: the case of Athens
by 1980 / Peter S. Allen.
EKISTICS 1986 May-Aug., v.53,
no.318-319, p.187-194, refs.

URBANIZATION--HISTORY--SCOTLAND
North of the border: The story of
Scotland's towns, by R. J.
Naismith [book review] / Jan
Magnus Fladmark.
ARCHITECTS' JOURNAL 1990 Sept.26,
v.192, no.13, p.79,

URBANIZATION--IRAN
Design participation in the context
of urban renewal / Amir Hossein
Afrassiabi.
URBAN FUTURES 1989 Summer, v.2,
no.2, p.24-32, chart., diagr.,
refs.

URBANIZATION--ITALY--TRENTO
Piano regolatore del Comune di
Trento: relazione generale.
City planning policies for the
expansion of Trent. Coordinators:
Marcello Vittorini, Giorgio
Trebbi. Summaries in French,
English, German, and Spanish, p.1.
Captions in Italian and English.
PARAMETRO 1990 Nov.-Dec., no.181,
p.16-51, maps, photos., plans,
site plans, tables, aerial photos.

URBANIZATION--ITALY--TURIN
Deconcentration urbaine et probleme
residentiel a Turin (Italie) /
Petros Petsimeris.
French, English and Spanish
summaries.
ESPACES ET SOCIETES 1988,
no.52-53. p.109-123, maps, refs.

URBANIZATION--NETHERLANDS--AMSTERDAM
Neues aus den Niederlanden = Du
nouveau des Pays-Bas = News from
the Netherlands.
Recent Dutch architecture and city
planning projects.
WERK, BAUEN + WOHNEN 1990
Jan.-Feb., no.1-2, p.18-64,
models, maps, photos., plans,
secns., site plans, aerial photos.

URBANIZATION--NETHERLANDS--HAGUE
Neues aus den Niederlanden = Du
nouveau des Pays-Bas = News from
the Netherlands.
Recent Dutch architecture and city
planning projects.
WERK, BAUEN + WOHNEN 1990
Jan.-Feb., no.1-2, p.18-64,
models, maps, photos., plans,
secns., site plans, aerial photos.

URBANIZATION--SOCIOLOGICAL ASPECTS
Urbanization as a phenomenon of
social history / T. U. Whipple.
OXFORD JOURNAL OF ARCHAEOLOGY 1989
July, v.8, no.2, p.167-177, refs.

URBANIZATION--SOUTH ASIA
New approaches in urban services
delivery: a comparison of emerging
experience in selected Asian
countries / Emiel A. Wegelin
CITIES 1990 Aug., v.7, no.3,
p.244-258, refs.

URBANIZATION--SOVIET UNION
The cities of the USSR and China:
streets apart? / John Cole.
CITIES 1990 May, v.7, no.2,
p.159-168, graphs, map, photos.,
tables, refs.

URBANIZATION--SWITZERLAND
Mitte des Mittellandes--Vakuum der
Schweiz?
Urbanization of midlands lying
between cities. Text in German;
summaries in German, French and
English.
WERK, BAUEN + WOHNEN 1990 May,
no.5, p.58-63, maps, photos.,
aerial photos., refs.

URBANIZATION--SYRIA
A decentralized approach to
urbanization: the case of Syria /
Riad G. Mahayni.
JOURNAL OF PLANNING EDUCATION AND
RESEARCH 1990 Winter, v.9, no.2,
p.117-125, map, tables, refs.

URBANIZATION--THEORY
Studying cities in their context /
Jan de Vries.
English and French summaries.
URBAN HISTORY REVIEW. REVUE
D'HISTOIRE URBAINE 1990 Feb.,
v.18, no.3, p.193-199, table,
refs.

URBANIZATION--THEORY--UNITED STATES
Flexible accumulation through
urbanization: reflections on
"Post-Modernism" in the American
City / David Harvey.
PERSPECTA 1990, no.26, p.251-272,
table, refs.

URBINI, NICOLETTA MAIOLI
Forte Stella a Monte Argentacio e la
Fortezza Spagnola di Porto Santo
Stefano: due diverse soluzioni
techniche nell'ambito della stesa
fuzione / Nicoletta Maioli Urbini.
BOLLETTINO D'ARTE 1990 May-June,
v.74 [76], no.61, p.61-88, ill.,
dwgs., elevs., maps, photos.,
plans, secns., refs.

URGELL, JOSEP
La arquitectura residencial de la
Villa Olimpica / Justo Isasi.
Includes 13 projects. English
summary, p.86.
A & V 1990, no.22, p.26-54, dets.,
ill., elevs., models, plans,
secns., site plans, sketches.

URINALS, PUBLIC
See REST ROOMS

URNS
See also VASES

URS MULLER, THOMAS RHODE UND PARTNER
Schutzenplatz in Salzgitter.
Architects: Urs Muller, Thomas
Rhode & Partner. Includes English
summary.
BAUMEISTER 1990 Oct., v.87, no.10,
p.42-45, photos., plans, secns.,
site plans.

URTOPIA INC.
Pharos Yk Yumura View Heim.
Apartment house with office on
first floor. Architects: Hideto
Horiike, Urtopia Inc. English
summary, p. 17.
KENCHIKU BUNKA 1990 Jan., v.45,
no.519, p.144-150, axonometric
view, photos., plans, secn.

USANDIZAGA CALPARSORO, MIGUEL MARIA
Crestas de perfil: palacio de
congresos y convenciones.
Convention facility for
Barcelona's Olympic village.
Architects: Jose Antonio Martinez
Lapena, Elias Torres Tur, Miguel
Maria Usandizaga Calparsoro.
English summary, p.88.
A & V 1990, no.22, p.78-80, dwgs.,
elevs., models, plans, secns.,
site plans.

USER PREFERENCE IN DESIGN
See PARTICIPATORY DESIGN

USHIDA, EISAKU
Echo Chamber / Kathryn Findlay,
Eisaku Ushida.
House, Tokyo. Architects: Ushida
Findlay Partnership.
JAPAN ARCHITECT 1990 Apr., v.65,
no.4(396), p.53-57, photos.,
plans, secn., site plan.

USHIDA FINDLAY PARTNERSHIP
Echo Chamber / Kathryn Findlay,
Eisaku Ushida.
House, Tokyo. Architects: Ushida
Findlay Partnership.
JAPAN ARCHITECT 1990 Apr., v.65,
no.4(396), p.53-57, photos.,
plans, secn., site plan.

USLEBER, JURGEN
Fernsehmuseum und Parkhaus in Mainz.
Competition winners. First prize:
Jurgen Usleber. Second prize:
Brigitte Fischer.
BAUWELT 1990 May 18, v.81, no.19,
p.932, secn., site plans.

USON SARDANA, CELIA
Un alfarje mudejar en la Iglesia de
la Virgen de Tobed / Celia Uson
Sardana, Ines Ducar Esteban.
Decorated ceiling.
SEMINARIO DE ARTE ARAGONES
1988-1989, v.42-43, p.5-46, dwgs.,
photos., refs.

USONIAN HOUSES--INFLUENCE
Wright and wrong in a Connecticut
country house / Brendan Gill.
Author's recollections of his
repeated alterations to his summer
house in Norfolk, Ct., including
his remodeling efforts after Frank
Lloyd Wright's Usonian houses.
ARCHITECTURAL DIGEST 1990 June,
v.47, no.6, p.34,[40-41],44, ill.,
port.

USSING, SUSANNE, 1940-
Arkitekturen pa Charlottenborg
[exhibition review].
Installation works by Susanne
Ussing, Carsten Hoff and others.
ARKITEKTEN 1989 Dec.12, v.91,
no.22, p.562-564, models, photos.

USTARROZ, ALBERTO
San Sebastian, concorso per un centro culturale / Alberto Ustarroz.
Projects by Juan N. Baldeweg, Mario Botta, Norman Foster, Arata Isozaki, Luis Pena, and Rafael Moneo (winner). Text in Italian and English.
DOMUS 1990 Dec., no.722, p.[48-55],XXIV, dwgs., elevs., models, plans, secns., site plans, aerial photos.

UTILITY PLANTS
See HEATING PLANTS

UTKIN, ILYA--EXHIBITIONS
Paper architects "build" in New York gallery [exhibition review] / Mark Alden Branch.
On the Paper Architects exhibition on view at Ronald Feldman Fine Arts, New York. Features drawings by Soviets Ilya Utkin and Alexander Brodsky.
PROGRESSIVE ARCHITECTURE 1990 May, v.71, no.5, p.25, ill., photo.
Visionary structures / Carl Little.
Exhibit at Ronald Feldman of Alexander Brodsky and Ilya Utkins fantasy assemblage and architectural drawings.
ART IN AMERICA 1990 Sept., v.78, no.9, p.178-179, photo.

UTOPIAN COMMUNITIES
See also UTOPIAS
See also COLLECTIVE SETTLEMENTS
Twin peaks / Joe Holyoak.
Traces the development of the tradition of the dispersed city which William Morris described in his 1890 essay, News from Nowhere. The essay appeared in the magazine Commonweal.
BUILDING DESIGN 1990 Nov.16, no.1011, p.22-23, dwgs., photos., site plans.

UTOPIAN COMMUNITIES--19TH CENTURY--FRANCE
L'exportation des modeles utopiques au XIXe siecle: la foi experimental des disciples / Annik Osmont.
French, English, Spanish and German summaries, p.[122]-124.
LES ANNALES DE LA RECHERCHE URBAINE 1989 [Mar.-Apr.], no.42, p.19-26, [122]-124, dwg., plans, engrs., refs.

UTOPIAN COMMUNITIES--SWEDEN--JARNA--RUDOLF STEINER SEMINARIET
Il paese dell'anima = A village for the soul: Jarna.
The Rudolf Steiner Seminary.
Architect: Erik Asmussen.
ABITARE 1990 July-Aug., no.287, p.208-215, dwgs., photos., plan, secns., site plan.

UTOPIAN COMMUNITIES--UNITED STATES--ARCOSANTI (ARIZONA)
Il mondo di Soleri = The world of Soleri / Michele Bazan Giordano.
Includes interview with Paolo Soleri.
L'ARCA 1990 Apr., no.37 suppl. l'Arca, p.100-101, photo.

UTOPIAN COMMUNITIES--UNITED STATES--ARCOSANTI (ARIZONA) (CONTINUED)
La ricerca di Paolo Soleri = Paolo Soleri's research / Luca Zevi.
Includes an interview.
ARCHITETTURA: CRONACHE E STORIA 1990 Dec., v.36, no.12(422), p.[838]-874, ill., dwgs., photos., plans, secns., site plans, sketches, aerial photos., biblio.

UTOPIAS
See also IDEAL CITIES
See also UTOPIAN COMMUNITIES
Innen Welt = Inner world / Gert Kahler.
Commentary on the unreal utopian environments within large urban complexes. Text in German and English.
DAIDALOS 1990 June 15, no.36, p.30-41, ill., elev., photos., plans, refs.
La ricerca di Paolo Soleri = Paolo Soleri's research / Luca Zevi.
Includes an interview.
ARCHITETTURA: CRONACHE E STORIA 1990 Dec., v.36, no.12(422), p.[838]-874, ill., dwgs., photos., plans, secns., site plans, sketches, aerial photos., biblio.
Twin peaks / Joe Holyoak.
Traces the development of the tradition of the dispersed city which William Morris described in his 1890 essay, News from Nowhere. The essay appeared in the magazine Commonweal.
BUILDING DESIGN 1990 Nov.16, no.1011, p.22-23, dwgs., photos., site plans.
Utopia e realismo nella concezione dell'intendenza di Auguste Comte / Mirella Larizza Lolli.
First presented at a conference on 18th and 19th-cent. provincialism and regionalism, Sept.1988.
STORIA URBANA 1989 Jan.-Mar., v.13, no.46, p.103-119, refs.
William Morris's legacy to planners / Dennis Hardy.
THE PLANNER 1990 July 27, v.76, no.29, p.11-14, ill., port., refs.

UTZ, BERNHARD
Wandel von Werten und Normen / Bernhard Utz.
A case example of management within the Freiburg parks dept. English summary and captions.
GARTEN UND LANDSCHAFT 1990, v.100, no.11, p.37-39, photos.

UTZON ASSOCIATES
Aeldre-, almennyttige og andelsboliger i Billund bymidte.
Projects for cluster housing in Billund, Denmark, by Nielsen, Nielsen & Nielsen; Arkitektgruppen i Aarhus; L. C. Johannsens Tegnestue; and Utzon Associates.
ARKITEKTEN 1989 Dec.12, v.91, no.22, p.553-558, axonometric views, elevs., plans, secns., site plans, sketches.
Hotelier til Kalvebod / Esben Larsen.
Six entries in a closed competition for a hotel project near Kalvebod Brygge, Copenhagen. Architects: Utzon Associates and H. Remmen Holding;
(Continued next column)

UTZON ASSOCIATES (CONTINUED)
Hotelier til Kalvebod...(CONTINUED)
Raaschou-Nielsen and J + F Johnston + Partners; Henning Larsen; PLH Arkitekter.
ARKITEKTEN 1990 Aug., v.92, no.11, p.350-353, elevs., models, secns., site plans, aerial photos.
Paustians hus / Christian Norberg-Schulz.
A furniture showroom and restaurant at Kalkbroenderilobskaj 2, Copenhagen. Architect: Utzon Associates. Includes commentary by Boje Lundgaard. Includes English and German captions and summaries.
ARKITEKTUR DK 1989, v.33, no.8, p.353-369, photos., plans, secns., site plans, sketches.

UTZON, JORN, 1919-
La "foresta" di Utzon a Copenhagen / Christian Norberg-Schultz.
The Paustian furniture showroom. Includes English captions.
CASABELLA 1990 Dec., v.54, no.574, p.38-39, photos., plan, secns., sketch.
PS: Jorn Utzon: Utzon pa nytt / Soren Thurell.
ARKITEKTUR: THE SWEDISH REVIEW OF ARCHITECTURE 1990 May, v.90, no.4, p.48-51, models, photos., plans, secns., biblio.

UTZON, LIN
Kunsten tilbage i arkitekturen / Adrian Carter.
On the career and work of Danish designer Lin Utzon. Includes English and German summaries.
ARKITEKTUR DK 1990, v.34, no.5, p.258-268, dwgs., ports., photos.

UYTENHAAK, RUDY
Een gebouw voor de stad: Woningbouw van Rudy Uytenhaak in Amsterdam / Arjen Oosterman.
Apartment house (De Droogbak) near railroad yard, located at Haarlemmer Hottuinenweg, Amsterdam. Built 1986-1989.
ARCHIS 1990 Mar., no.3, p.36-41, axonometric views, dwg., photos., plans, secn., site plan, refs.
Le logement social aux Pays-Bas / Didier Rebois.
Contents: Tiendplein housing complex, Rotterdam, architects: Architectengroep Mecanoo-- Droogbak housing complex, Amsterdam; architect: Rudy Uytenhaak-- Housing complex, Deventer; architect: Theo Bosch-- Interviews with Rein Geursten and Max Rissalada.
LE MONITEUR ARCHITECTURE AMC 1990 Nov., no.16, p.26-35, axonometric view, model, photos., plans, site plans.
Mit shief aufgesetzer Mutze und Brille: Wohnhaus mit Werkstatt in Zwolle.
Architect: Rudy Uytenhaak.
BAUWELT 1990 Oct.12, v.81, no.38, p.1940-1941, photos, plans, secn., site plan.

UYTENHAAK, RUDY (CONTINUED)

Neues aus Amsterdam: drei
amsterdamer Architekten und ihre
jungsten Beitrage zum sozialen
Wohnungsban / Gerrit Confurius.
The feature article in issue
entitled "Neues aus A'dam",
covering seven recent housing and
apartment projects by Paul de Ley,
Lucien Lafour, and Rudy Uytenhaak.
BAUWELT 1990 Aug.17, v.81, no.31,
p.1528-1547, axonometric views,
photos., plans, site plans.

Palazzo's in de Csaar Peter Buurt :
Uytenhaak introduceert nieuw
verkavelingstype / Hans
Stoutjesdijk.
A 141-unit apartment complex
located on Conradstraat,
Amsterdam. Completed in July 1990.
Architect: Rudy Uytenhaak.
DE ARCHITECT 1990 Sept., v.21,
no.9, p.100-105, elev., photos.,
plans, site plan.

Stijlvol in de nuances: woongebouw
"de Droogbak" van Rudy Uytenhaak /
Janny Rodermond.
A 96-unit apartment building on
the Haarlemmer Houttuinenweg,
Amsterdam. Opened in Dec. 1989.
DE ARCHITECT 1990 Feb., v.21,
no.2, p.30-37, cover, elev.,
photos., plans, secn., site plan.

Wohnungen in einer Feuerwache /
Gerrit Confurius.
Alterations for housing to a 1907
fire station, between Amstel and
Weesperplein, Amsterdam.
Renovation architect: Rudy
Uytenhaak.
BAUWELT 1990 July 13, v.81, no.26,
p.1332-1338, photos., plans, secn.

UYTTENHOVE, PIETER

40 Architekten onder de 40: de
"jonge garde" van Parijs
[exhibition review] / Pieter
Uyttenhove.
Exhibit at the IFA (Institut
francais d'architecture).
ARCHIS 1990 Dec., no.12, p.2-3,
ports.

Architectures publiques: de
vernieuwing van de traditie
[exhibition review] / Pieter
Uyttenhove.
Recent exhibition at the Centre
Georges Pompidou.
ARCHIS 1990 May, no.5, p.5-6,
photos., ref.

The garden city education of Belgian
planners around the First World
War / Pieter Uyttenhove.
Describes British efforts to
prepare Belgian planners for
post-war reconstruction following
the principles of the garden city
movement at the Town Planning
Conference on the Reconstruction
of Belgium, 11-16 Feb. 1915.
PLANNING PERSPECTIVES:* PP 1990
Sept., v.5, no.3, p.271-283, refs.

Le Grand Paris: de voorstad wordt
stad: stedebouw als roeping /
Pieter Uyttenhove.
ARCHIS 1989 Oct., no.10, p.22-31,
ill., maps, photos., aerial
photos., refs.

UYTTENHOVE, PIETER (CONTINUED)

Metropole 90: de wedren van de eeuu
[exhibition review] / Pieter
Uyttenhove.
Exhibition at the Pavillon de
l'Arsenal, Paris until June 3,
1990.
ARCHIS 1990 Apr., no.4, p.4-5,
photos., refs.

La metropole imaginaire: im atlas de
Paris [by] Bruno Fortier [book
review] / Pieter Uyttenhove.
In conjunction with the exhibition
at the Institut francais
d'architecture.
ARCHIS 1990 Dec., no.12, p.54-55,
ill.

Een nieuwe stad wordt volwassen:
Cergy-Pontoise 1969-1989
[exhibition review] / Pieter
Uyttenhove.
Exhibition at the Prefecture du
Val d'Oise until Nov.26, 1989.
ARCHIS 1989 Nov., no.11, p.2-3,
aerial photo., refs.

Parijs, twee denkwijzen / Pieter
Uyttenhove.
Introduction to four articles,
indexed separately.
ARCHIS 1989 Oct., no.10, p.13,
ill., map.

Stedebouw in de marge van de stud:
Seine Rieve Gauche in Parijs:
plannen vallen op hun plaats /
Pieter Uyttenhove.
Published in conjunction with an
exhibition at the Pavillon de
l'Arsenal, Paris, opening in Oct.
1990.
ARCHIS 1990 Oct., no.10, p.27-35,
dwgs., maps, photos., secns., site
plans, aerial photos., refs.

Tegenpolen van cultuur: American
Center en Maison de la Culture
Japon a Paris / Pieter Uyttenhove.
Architects: Frank Gehry; Mazayuki
Yamanaka and Kenneth Armstrong.
ARCHIS 1990 Nov., no.11, p.2-3,
models, ref.

Weer wat dichter bij oneindig:
Verlenging van de as Louvre - La
Defense en uitbreiding van
La-Defense Ouest. / Pieter
Uyttenhove.
ARCHIS 1990 Sept., no.9, p.6-7,
dwgs.

V.I.P. LOUNGES--INTERIOR DESIGN--
UNITED STATES--OKLAHOMA CITY
(OKLAHOMA)--REMINGTON PARK
RACETRACK--CHALK HORSE
The Chalk Horse / Monica Geran.
Interiors of penthouse
suite/lounge owned by Ackerman
Hood and McQueen Advertising at
the Remington Park Racetrack,
Oklahoma City, Okla. Interior
designers: Elliott & Associates
Architects.
INTERIOR DESIGN 1990 June, v.61,
no.9, p.202-[203], photos., plan.

VAASSEN, ELGIN
Ainmillers Glasfenster fur
Parliament Hall in Edinburgh und
eine unbekannte Aquarellskizze
Wilhelm von Kaulbachs von 1867
dafur / Elgin Vaassen.
Narrative of commission.
KUNST IN HESSEN UND AM MITTELRHEIN
1987, no.27, p.67-93, dwgs.,
photos., sketches, refs.

VACATION CAMPS
See also SUMMER CAMPS

VACATION HOUSES
See also BEACH HOUSES
See also CABINS
See also COTTAGES
See also COUNTRY HOUSES
See also SUMMER HOUSES
See also VILLAS
See also WEEKEND HOUSES

VACATION HOUSES--ALTERATIONS AND
ADDITIONS--AUSTRALIA--POINT LOOKOUT
Stradbroke lookout.
Features remodeled vacation home
with lookout platform, Point
Lookout, Stradbroke Island,
Queensland. Architects: Brit
Andresen, Timothy Hill.
ARCHITECTURAL REVIEW 1990 Apr.,
v.187, no.1118, p.73-[76],
axonometric views, photos.

VACATION HOUSES--ALTERATIONS AND
ADDITIONS--FRANCE--BRITTANY
Un abordage en Bretagne.
Vacation home addition.
Architects: Caroline Bapst, Bruno
Pantz. English summary, p.52.
ARCHITECTURE INTERIEURE CREE 1990
Feb., no.234, p.[126-127],
photos., plan.
Agrandissement d'une maison de
Bretagne.
Vacation home addition, Brittany.
Architects: Bruno Pantz, Caroline
Bapst-Failliot.
ARCHITECTURE D'AUJOURD'HUI 1990
Feb., no.267, p.55, photos.,
plans.

VACATION HOUSES--ALTERATIONS AND
ADDITIONS--UNITED STATES--MICHIGAN
A prairie home solution / Victoria
Lautman.
Renovation of a 1920s bungalow on
Lake Michigan. Architect: Peter
Landon.
METROPOLITAN HOME 1990 July, v.22,
no.7, p.46-[51], photos.

VACATION HOUSES--ARCHITECTS'--GREECE--
HYDRA--ANTONIADES HOUSE
Elpenorean architecture: space
through the "Odyssey" / Anthony C.
Antoniades.
Contents: Condominium in Saronis,
Greece.--Architects' residence in
Hydra, Greece.--Private chapel in
private garden, Andros Island,
Greece. Architect: Anthony C.
Antoniades. Text in Japanese and
English.
ARCHITECTURE AND URBANISM 1990
July, no.7(238), p.82-100,
axonometric views, elevs.,
photos., plans, secns.

VACATION HOUSES--ARCHITECTS'--SWEDEN
Arcaica e moderna [vacation house,
Sweden] / Elisa Dal Canto.
Architect: Karin Mattson-Nordin.
VILLE GIARDINI 1990 Apr., no.247,
p.18-21, photos, plan.

VACATION HOUSES--ARCHITECTS'--UNITED
STATES--SANIBEL ISLAND (FLORIDA)--
CASA CAMELEON (SOLFISBURG-YELIN
HOUSE)
A Sanikel cameleon / Beth Dunlop.
Architects' vacation house, Casa
Cameleon on Sanibel Island, Fla.
Architects: Roy J. Solfisburg.
ARCHITECTURAL DIGEST 1990 Aug.,
v.47, no.8, p.138-[143], photos.

VACATION HOUSES--AUSTRALIA--
PITTWATER--MACKEREL BEACH HOUSE
House at Pittwater: Alexander
Tzannes.
Located on Mackerel Beach.
ARCHITECTURE AUSTRALIA 1989 Dec.,
v.78, no.11, p.46, photos., secn.

VACATION HOUSES--BRAZIL--GAROPABA
Casa na praia de Garopaba / Julio
Ramos Collares.
Architect: J. Collares.
PROJETO 1990 Aug., no.134,
p.54-55, photos., plans, secn.,
sketches.

VACATION HOUSES--BRAZIL--UBATUBA--
RESIDENCIA WOISKY
Casa na praia Vermelha / Pepe Asbum.
Residencia Woisky's. Architect: P.
Asbum.
PROJETO 1990 Aug., no.134,
p.56-58, dwg., photos., site
plans.

VACATION HOUSES--CANADA--CALEDON
(ONTARIO)--ALEXANDER HOUSE
The Canadian Architect 1990 22nd
Annual Awards of Excellence.
Eight awards. Architects: Steven
Fong, A.J. Diamond, Donald Schmitt
& Co. with Kolker Kolker Epstein
Architects, Meltzer Igra
Architects, Bugod Figueiredo
Krendel Architects, Peter Cardew
Architects, Richard Henriquez
Architect, Laszlo Nemeth Assoc.,
Kearns Mancini Architects, Patkan
Architects, Saucier + Perrotte,
and Kuwabara Payne McKenna
Blumberg.
CANADIAN ARCHITECT 1990 Dec.,
v.35, no.12, p.9-24,29, dwgs.,
elevs., models, plans, secns.,
site plans.

VACATION HOUSES--DENMARK--LAESO
Traditional Laeso.
Holiday home on Danish island,
Laeso. Architect: Hanne Kjaerholm.
ARCHITECTURAL REVIEW 1990 Apr.,
v.187, no.1118, p.52-55, photos.,
plan, secn., site plan.

VACATION HOUSES--ECONOMIC ASPECTS--
ENGLAND
Building homes.
Articles on vacation houses,
resorts, marina development on the
Welsh coastline, golf course
communities, tourism in Eastern
Europe, and the second home
market.
BUILDING 1990 Aug.10, v.255,
no.32,suppl., p.3-22, map, photos.

VACATION HOUSES--ENVIRONMENTAL
ASPECTS--TURKEY
Problems and potentials of second
homes / Cemal Arkon.
On the Aegean coasts. (principally
Turkey).
INTERNATIONAL JOURNAL FOR HOUSING
SCIENCE AND ITS APPLICATIONS 1990,
v.14, no.1, p.065-070, map.

VACATION HOUSES--FRANCE--CORSICA
Wide open spaces [vacation house in
Corsica] / Francoise Labro.
Architect: Boguslaw Brzeckowski.
ELLE DECOR 1990 Apr., v.1, no.3,
p.[106-113], photos.

VACATION HOUSES--FRANCE--FINISTERE
Ti'lil: villa of the dunes / Claire
Touchard.
A ship-inspired house at
Finistere, Brittany. Architects:
Caroline Bapst, Bruno Pantz.
ELLE DECOR 1990 Mar., v.1, no.2,
p.[18]-24, axonometric view,
photos., plans.

VACATION HOUSES--FRANCE--LAC
D'HOSSEGOR
Sur le pont: maison sur le lac
d'Hossegor.
Architect: Jean-Philippe Pargade.
Summaries in English and Spanish.
TECHNIQUES ET ARCHITECTURE 1990
June-July, no.390, p.128-129,181,
elev., model, plans, secn.,
sketch.

VACATION HOUSES--FRANCE--MOLIETS
Ferienhaus in Moliets, Frankreich,
1989.
Architect: Marcel Ferrier.
WERK, BAUEN + WOHNEN 1989 Dec.,
no.12, p.47, axonometric view,
elev., photo., plan.

VACATION HOUSES--FRANCE--PERIGORD
The Gallic sense of home.
Perigord farmhouse.
HOUSE BEAUTIFUL 1990 Mar., v.132,
no.3, p.[68-71], photos.

VACATION HOUSES--INTERIOR DESIGN--
AUSTRALIA--CAMMERAY--HANNES HOUSE
Four by Seidler / Stanley
Abercrombie.
Features Seidler and Associates'
office addition, Sydney; Hannes
house, Cammeray; Capita Tower and
restaurant, Sydney.
INTERIOR DESIGN 1990 May, v.61,
no.7, p.210-[223], dwg., photos.,
plans, secns., site plan.

VACATION HOUSES--INTERIOR DESIGN--
BARBADOS--SAPCOTE HOUSE
   Playing with the past: Nicholas
   Haslam reinterprets a classic
   Caribbean pavilion by Oliver
   Messel / John Richardson.
   Decoration of a pavilion on
   Barbados.
   HOUSE & GARDEN 1990 Jan., v.162,
   no.1, p.[112-117],147, photos.

VACATION HOUSES--INTERIOR DESIGN--
FRANCE--PROVENCE--MOUSSIERE HOUSE
   Historische Entscheidung / Brigitte
   Forgeur.
   Features interiors of restored
   stone home in Provence, which is
   the vacation home of the Moussiere
   family. English summary, p.1.
   ARCHITEKTUR & WOHNEN 1990
   Aug.-Sept., no.4, p.20-[27],
   photos.

VACATION HOUSES--INTERIOR DESIGN--
FRANCE--SAINT-TROPEZ--MAZE HOUSE
   Jours tranquilles a Saint-Tropez /
   Gilles Dalliere.
   Features Daniele Maze's vacation
   house in Saint-Tropez.
   MAISON FRANCAISE 1990 July-Aug.,
   no.438, p.[48-57], photos.

VACATION HOUSES--INTERIOR DESIGN--
FRANCE--VAR
   L'ete et apres / Gilles Dalliere.
   Interiors of a vacation house in
   the Var.
   MAISON FRANCAISE 1990 July-Aug.,
   no.438, p.[78-85], dets., photos.

VACATION HOUSES--INTERIOR DESIGN--
GREECE--HYDRA--MCGUIRE HOUSE
   Housekeeping on Hydra / Adrian Cook.
   Interiors of John and Elinor
   McGuire's home on Hydra.
   Architect: Edward Tuttle.
   Interior renovation designer:
   Andrew Delfino.
   ARCHITECTURAL DIGEST 1990 Aug.,
   v.47, no.8, p.[144-149], photos.

VACATION HOUSES--INTERIOR DESIGN--
ITALY--GARGNANO--BONESI HOUSE
   Schone Aussicht fur Geschafte / Lina
   Kalin.
   Features Loredana and Nazzareno
   Bonesi's vacation house, in a
   former warehouse, Gargnano, Italy.
   ARCHITEKTUR & WOHNEN 1990
   Mar.-Apr., no.2,dp.[62]-65, port.,
   photos.

VACATION HOUSES--INTERIOR DESIGN--
UNITED STATES--BOCA RATON (FLORIDA)
   Pretty in peach; a Boca Raton
   condominium by R. Scott Bronley,
   AIA, of Bromley-Jacobsen / Edie
   Lee Cohen.
   INTERIOR DESIGN 1990 Apr., v.61,
   no.4, p.[210-213], photos., plans

VACATION HOUSES--INTERIOR DESIGN--
UNITED STATES--COLORADO
   Colorado spirit: infusing a
   southwestern-style vacation house
   with bold sophistication / Suzanne
   Stephens.
   Interior designer: Thomas Britt.
   ARCHITECTURAL DIGEST 1990 May,
   v.47, no.5, p.[172]-177, photos.

VACATION HOUSES--INTERIOR DESIGN--
UNITED STATES--LAKE TAHOE
(CALIFORNIA)
   Lake Tahoe retreat / Edie Lee Cohen.
   Interiors of enlarged vacation
   home. Architects: Backen, Arrigoni
   and Ross. Interior designers:
   Pfister Partnership.
   INTERIOR DESIGN 1990 Oct., v.61,
   no.14, p.224-[233], photos.

VACATION HOUSES--ITALY--KORTSCH
   Giovani architetti di montagna =
   Young mountain architects.
   Examples of work by South Tyrolean
   architects, Josef Kostner, Werner
   Tscholl, C. Mayr-Fingerle, and
   Walter Dietl.
   ABITARE 1990 Dec., no.291,
   p.116-133, photos., plans, secns.,
   elevs.

VACATION HOUSES--ITALY--PRAMOLLO
   L'armonico contrasto / Assunta
   Limardi.
   Vacation house in the mountains of
   the Piedmont, in the village of
   Pramollo. Architect: Bruno
   Arione.
   VILLE GIARDINI 1990 Dec., no.254,
   p.22-27, photos., plans, site
   plans.

VACATION HOUSES--ITALY--SAN GENESIO--
KOSTNER HOUSE
   Giovani architetti di montagna =
   Young mountain architects.
   Examples of work by South Tyrolean
   architects, Josef Kostner, Werner
   Tscholl, C. Mayr-Fingerle, and
   Walter Dietl.
   ABITARE 1990 Dec., no.291,
   p.116-133, photos., plans, secns.,
   elevs.

VACATION HOUSES--ITALY--SARDINIA--
COSTA SMERALDA
   Gut versteckt.... / Antje Suchting.
   Features home on the Costa
   Smeralda of Sardinia owned by a
   family from Hamburg.
   ARCHITEKTUR & WOHNEN 1990
   June-July, no.3, p.[52]-57, port.,
   photos.

VACATION HOUSES--ITALY--SARDINIA--
GALLURA
   A un passo dal mare = At a stone's
   throw from the sea.
   Five houses in Gallura, Sardinia.
   ABITARE 1990 May, no.285,
   p.158-[175], photos, plans,
   secns., site plans, aerial photos.

VACATION HOUSES--ITALY--SARDINIA--
PUNTA SARDEGNA
   A un passo dal mare = At a stone's
   throw from the sea.
   Five houses in Gallura, Sardinia.
   ABITARE 1990 May, no.285,
   p.158-[175], photos, plans,
   secns., site plans, aerial photos.

VACATION HOUSES--ITALY--VAL VENY
   La forma come invariabile / Ruggero
   Borghi.
   Vacation house in the mountains of
   Val Veny, Italy. Architect:
   Andrea Vecchi.
   VILLE GIARDINI 1990 Dec., no.254,
   p.10-15, photos., plans, secn.

VACATION HOUSES--JAPAN--KANAGAWA--
KITAMURA HOUSE
   The Kitamura vacation house,
   Kanagawa, [Japan], 1983.
   Architects: Kazumasa Yamashita,
   Architect and Associates. Text in
   Japanese and English.
   PROCESS: ARCHITECTURE 1989 Dec.,
   no.87, p.42-43, photos., plans,
   secn.

VACATION HOUSES--JAPAN--KIYOSATO
   Kiyosato-kaku / Satoko Shinohara.
   Mountain vacation house.
   Architects: Satoko Shinohara,
   Kengo Kuma.
   JAPAN ARCHITECT 1990 Apr., v.65,
   no.4 (396), p.58-62, elevs.,
   photos., site plan.

VACATION HOUSES--JAPAN--SAEKI-GUN--LA
VILLA A VOILE
   La villa a voile.
   Oceanfront vacation home
   Saeki-gun. Architects: Norihiko
   Dan, Aoshima Associates and
   Engineers. English summary, p.17.
   KENCHIKU BUNKA 1990 Jan., v.45,
   no.519, p.112-115, axonometric
   view, photos., ill., plans, secn.,
   sketches.
   La Villa a Voile / Norihiko Dan.
   Guesthouse/vacation house for the
   Penta Ocean Company, Saeki-gun,
   Nomijima Island, Hiroshima
   Prefecture. Architects: Norihiko
   Dan, Aoshima Architects and
   Engineers.
   JAPAN ARCHITECT 1990 Feb., v.65,
   no.2(394), p.26-31, axonometric
   view, photos., plans, secns.

VACATION HOUSES--JAPAN--
SARASHINA-GUN--HIJIRI VILLA
   Hijiri Villa / Osami Hamaguchi.
   Vacation house on slope of Mt.
   Hijiri. Architect: Osami
   Hamaguchi.
   JAPAN ARCHITECT 1990 Apr., v.65,
   no.4 (396), p.47-52, elev.,
   photos., plans, site plan.

VACATION HOUSES--NETHERLANDS--ALMERE--
POLDERBLIK
   Polder als uitgangspunt: lichtvoetig
   ontwerp van Teun Koolhaas /
   Liesbeth Melis.
   "Polderblik", house on stilts near
   water in Almere.
   DE ARCHITECT 1990 June, v.21,
   no.6, p.81-85, elevs., photos.,
   plans, secns.
   Vorubergehend Wohnen.
   Two of 17 houses designed for a
   "De Fantasie" competition in
   Almere in 1982: Haus Amfibie
   (architects: F.F. Holvast, D.E.
   van Worden) and Haus Polder-blik
   (architect: Teun Koolhaas).
   BAUWELT 1990 Nov. 2, v.81, no.41
   p.2096-2097, photos.

VACATION HOUSES--PORTUGAL--QUINTA DO
LAGO
   Giovane generazione portoghese:
   Eduardo Souto de Moura / Alexandre
   Alves Costa.
   Four projects from the mid-1980s:
   vacation house, Quinta do Lago,
   Algarve; exterior renovations,
   Casa Manuel Oliveira, Porto;
   renovation of houses, Geres;
      (Continued next page)

VACATION HOUSES--PORTUGAL--QUINTA DO
LAGO (CONTINUED)
Giovane generazione... (CONTINUED)
cultural center, Porto. Includes
English summary; captions in
Italian and English.
CASABELLA 1990 Jan., v.54, no.564,
p.4-15,59, axonometric views,
port., elevs., photos., plans,
secn., sketches, refs.

VACATION HOUSES--SAINT BARTHELEMY--
BARYSHNIKOV HOUSE
Mikhail Baryshnikov on St.
Barthelemy / Philippe Seulliet.
Features the interiors of
neighboring Mexican vernacular
style vacation houses owned by the
dancer. Architect: Rob Miles
Reincke. Interior designer: Bille
du Mesnil.
ARCHITECTURAL DIGEST 1990 Aug.,
v.47, no.8, p.132-137, photos.

VACATION HOUSES--SPAIN--IBIZA--CAP
MARTINET
Angles on Ibiza / Peter Buchanan.
Vacation house, Cap Martinet,
Ibiza, Spain. Architects: Jose
Antonio Martinez Lapena and Elias
Torres Tur.
ARCHITECTURAL REVIEW 1990 Apr.,
v.187, no.1118, p.56-[60],
photos., plans, secns.
Pour l'horizon: maison du Cap
Martinet, Ibiza, Baleares.
Architect: Elias Torres Tur, Jose
Antonio Martinez Lapena. Includes
English and Spanish summaries.
TECHNIQUES ET ARCHITECTURE 1990
June-July, no.390, p.90-[95],180,
elev., photos., plans, secns.

VACATION HOUSES--SPAIN--MAJORCA--
NEUENDORF HOUSE
Wohnskulptur / Gesa Engelschall.
Features Hans Neuendorf's vacation
house in Majorca. Architect:
Claudio Silvestrin.
ARCHITEKTUR & WOHNEN 1990
Dec.-1991 Jan., no.6, p.36-43,
port., photos., isometric dwg.

VACATION HOUSES--SWITZERLAND--GENOLIER
Colonie de vacances a Genolier
(Vaud).
Built 1987-89. Architect:
Pierre-Alain Renaud.
WERK, BAUEN + WOHNEN 1990 Dec.,
no.12, p.1-4(folded, at back),
dets., photos., plans, secns.,
site plan, isometric dwgs., aerial
photo.

VACATION HOUSES--THAILAND--BAN WART
NAM TON--BOEHM-BEZING HOUSE
Mystik auf Stelzen / Erdtrud
Muhlens.
Features Suhid and Diether von
Boehm-Bezing's vacation home in
Ban Wart Nam Ton, Thailand.
English summary, p.2.
ARCHITEKTUR & WOHNEN 1990
Aug.-Sept., no.4, p.48-53,
photos., plan.

VACATION HOUSES--UNITED STATES--
CALIFORNIA--SEA RANCH
Sea Ranch e i mari d'argento / Paolo
Riani.
Landscaping: Lawrence Halprin.
Architect: Charles Moore.
VILLE GIARDINI 1990 Apr., no.247,
p.32-35, ill., dwgs., photos.

VACATION HOUSES--UNITED STATES--
COLUMBIA RIVER VALLEY (WASHINGTON)
In the family way [vacation home,
Washington state] / Julie V.
Iovine.
A family compound, on the Columbia
River. Architect: Tiger Warren.
METROPOLITAN HOME 1990 June, v.22,
no.6, p.88-94, photo.

VACATION HOUSES--UNITED STATES--
CONNECTICUT
Shope Reno Wharton: a shingled
cottage / Suzanne Stephens.
Vacation home on Conn. island.
ARCHITECTURAL DIGEST 1990 Sept.,
v.47, no.10, p.[94-97],108,
photos., plans.

VACATION HOUSES--UNITED STATES--
CRESTED BUTTE (COLORADO)--SOUCHERAY
HOUSE
Home away from home: a Colorado
vacation house with a heart of
glass.
Soucheray house, Crested Butte.
Architect: Kelly Davis.
ARCHITECTURE MINNESOTA 1990
Nov.-Dec., v.16, no.6, p.34-35,
photos.

VACATION HOUSES--UNITED STATES--
FISHERS ISLAND (NEW YORK)--MCKIM
HOUSE
Haunted house [McKim house, Fishers
Island, NY] / Thomas Fisher.
Vacation house. Architects: Mark
Simon and Leonard Wyeth of
Centerbrook Architects.
PROGRESSIVE ARCHITECTURE 1990
Nov., v.71, no.12, p.70-73,
photos., plans, secn., site plan.

VACATION HOUSES--UNITED STATES--LAKE
MINNETONKA (MINNESOTA)
On the lakes of "Big Water": a
sampling of Lake Minnetonka
architecture by boat / Eric
Kudalis.
ARCHITECTURE MINNESOTA 1990
July-Aug., v.16, no.4, p.24-31,
photos.

VACATION HOUSES--UNITED STATES--LAKE
RABUN (GEORGIA)--JENNINGS HOUSE
A house by a lake / Marybeth Weston.
Georgia vacation home of American
artist Comer Jennings. Architects:
Spitzmiller & Norris.
HOUSE BEAUTIFUL 1990 Aug., v.132,
no.8, p.[42]-48, port., photos.

VACATION HOUSES--UNITED STATES--LOG
HILL MESA (COLORADO)
Interview: Ettore Sottsass.
On his plans for a "vacation
village" in Log Hill Mesa,
Colorado.
PROGRESSIVE ARCHITECTURE 1990
Nov., v.71, no.12, p.96-97, dwgs.,
photo., sketches.

VACATION HOUSES--UNITED STATES--
NANTUCKET (MASSACHUSETTS)--ROBERT
HOUSE
Contemporary clapboard on a
Nantucket pond / Brendan Gill.
Vacation house owned by Rita and
Samuel Robert. Architect: Edward
F. Knowles.
ARCHITECTURAL DIGEST 1990 Aug.,
v.47, no.8, p.[124]-131,180,
photos.

VACATION HOUSES--UNITED STATES--
RIDGWAY (COLORADO)--WOLF HOUSE
Bravo Ettore! Sottsass builds an
American dream house / Richard
Lacayo.
Vacation house for Daniel Wolf
near Telluride, Colo.
METROPOLITAN HOME 1990 Nov., v.22,
no.11, p.115-125, dwg., port.,
photos.
New frontier: Wolf house, Ridgway,
Colorado, Sottsass Associati,
architect / Karen D. Stein.
ARCHITECTURAL RECORD 1990 Oct.,
v.178, no.11, p.78-83, elev.,
photos., plans.

VACATION HOUSES--UNITED STATES--SEA
ISLAND (GEORGIA)--MAISON DU CYGNE
(ANDERSON HOUSE)
Maison du Cygne: metamorphosis on
the Georgia Coast / Helen C.
Griffith.
Rosemary Anderson house, Sea
Island. Architect for renovations:
John Shackelford of William Frank
McCall Architects and Interior
Designer: Elizabeth Tucker.
SOUTHERN ACCENTS 1990 July-Aug.,
v.13, no.6, p.76-83, photos.

VACATION HOUSES--UNITED STATES--
STOCKHOLM (WISCONSIN)--WIND WHISTLE
(TOTH-STAGEBERG HOUSE)
Crayon-colored dream house / Susan
Allen Toth.
Wisconsin weekend house designed
by James Stageberg.
HOUSE BEAUTIFUL 1990 Apr., v.132,
no.4, p.[94]-95,121, photos.,
secn.

VACATION HOUSES--UNITED STATES--SUN
VALLEY (IDAHO)
Bart Prince Architect [houses].
Contents: Vacation house, Sun
Valley, Ida., design: 1988-89 --
Barbi Benton George Gradow family
residence, Aspen, Colo., design:
1989. Text in Japanese and
English.
GA HOUSES 1990 Mar., no.28,
p.128-133, elevs., models, plans,
secns.

VACATION HOUSES--UNITED STATES--
WASHINGTON ISLAND (WISCONSIN)--
PHILLIPS HOUSE
The psychology of small / Cynthia
Chapin Davidson.
A 1200- square foot vacation house
designed by Frederick Phillips for
his parents, on Washington Island,
Wisc.
INLAND ARCHITECT 1990 Mar.-Apr.,
v.34, no.2, p.32-33, photos.,
plans.

VACATION HOUSES--UNITED STATES--WEST
BATH (MAINE)
Vacation house, West Bath, Main,
[United States].
Architects: Leers Weinzapfel
Associates. Text in Japanese and
English.
ARCHITECTURE AND URBANISM 1990
Dec., no.12(243), p.24-[31],
photos., plans, site plan.

VACATION HOUSES--WOODEN--FRANCE--
CORSICA--SPERONE--FELDMAN HOUSE
Fitting in wood: recent houses on
Corsica / Tom Higgins.
Features five cedarwood vacation
homes in Sperone. Architects:
Groupe d'Etudes Architecturales.
ARCHITECTURAL REVIEW 1990 May,
v.187, no.1119, p.79-82, photos,
plans, dets.

VACATION HOUSES--WOODEN--FRANCE--
CORSICA--SPERONE--OCKRENT HOUSE
Fitting in wood: recent houses on
Corsica / Tom Higgins.
Features five cedarwood vacation
homes in Sperone. Architects:
Groupe d'Etudes Architecturales.
ARCHITECTURAL REVIEW 1990 May,
v.187, no.1119, p.79-82, photos,
plans, dets.

VACATION HOUSES--WOODEN--FRANCE--
CORSICA--SPERONE--PICCOLI HOUSE
Fitting in wood: recent houses on
Corsica / Tom Higgins.
Features five cedarwood vacation
homes in Sperone. Architects:
Groupe d'Etudes Architecturales.
ARCHITECTURAL REVIEW 1990 May,
v.187, no.1119, p.79-82, photos,
plans, dets.

VACATION HOUSES--WOODEN--FRANCE--
CORSICA--SPERONE--ROUX HOUSE
Fitting in wood: recent houses on
Corsica / Tom Higgins.
Features five cedarwood vacation
homes in Sperone. Architects:
Groupe d'Etudes Architecturales.
ARCHITECTURAL REVIEW 1990 May,
v.187, no.1119, p.79-82, photos,
plans, dets.

VACATION HOUSES--WOODEN--FRANCE--
CORSICA--SPERONE--SEGUELA HOUSE
Fitting in wood: recent houses on
Corsica / Tom Higgins.
Features five cedarwood vacation
homes in Sperone. Architects:
Groupe d'Etudes Architecturales.
ARCHITECTURAL REVIEW 1990 May,
v.187, no.1119, p.79-82, photos,
plans, dets.

VACCARO, ALESSANDRA MELUCCO
Restauro e anastilosi: il caso
dell'Acropoli di Atene /
Alessandra Melucco Vaccaro.
PROSPETTIVA 1988 Apr.-1989 Jan.,
no.53-56, p.49-54, dwgs., photos.,
reconst. dwgs., refs.

VACCARO, GIUSEPPE, 1896-1979
La progettazione dell'E42: la prima
fase = The planning of the E42:
the first phase / Riccardo
Mariani.
The planning of the E42:
Esposizione Universale in Roma
1941-1942; architects: Giuseppe
(Continued next column)

VACCARO, GIUSEPPE, 1896-1979
(CONTINUED)
La progettazione...(CONTINUED)
Pagano, Marcello Piacentini, Luigi
Piccinato, Ettore Rossi, Luigi
Vietti, Adalberto Libera, Giuseppe
Terragni, Pietro Lingeri, Cesare
Cattaneo, Giovanni Guerrini,
Ernesto La Padula, Mario Romano,
Gian Luigi Banfi, Ludovico B. di
Belgioso, Gaetano Ciocca, Enrico
Peressutti, Ernesto N. Rogers,
Franco Albini, Ignazio Gardella,
Giancarlo Palanti, Giovanna
Romano, Luciano Baldessari,
Ernesto Saliva, Luigi Moretti,
Gino Pollini, Luigi Figini, and
Giuseppe Vaccaro.
LOTUS INTERNATIONAL 1990, no.67,
p.90-125, elevs., models, photos.,
plans, secns., site plans,
sketches, aerial photos.

VACCHINI, LIVIO, 1933-
Einfamilienhaus in Vogorno, 1985 /
Paulo Fumagalli.
Architect: Livio Vacchini.
WERK, BAUEN + WOHNEN 1990 Apr.,
no.4, p.29-33, elev., photos.,
plans.
Enfamiliehus i Vogorno.
Stone house on sloping site in
Switzerland. Architect: Livio
Vacchini.
ARKITEKTUR DK 1990, v.34, no.6,
p.A98-A99, photos., plans, elev.
Escola primaria cria a praca
principal da cidade.
In Montagnola, Switzerland.
Architect: Civio Vacchini.
PROJETO 1989 June, no.122,
p.44-50, elev, photos, plans,
secns., site plan.
Projet pour un batiment des Postes,
Locarno, 1989.
Architect: Livio Vacchini.
WERK, BAUEN + WOHNEN 1989 Dec.,
no.12, p.67, elevs., plan, site
plan.
Svizzera anni '90: tre culture, tre
architetture = Switzerland 1990:
three cultures, three
architectures / Paolo Fumagalli.
Features projects by Jacques
Herzog and Pierre de Meuron; Livio
Vacchini; Atelier 5; Willi Egli;
Mario Botta; Jean-Jacques Oberson;
Giancarlo Durisch; Aurelio
Galfetti; Luigi Snozzi; Roger
Diener; Atelier Cube; Matti,
Burgi, Ragaz; Schnebli, Ammann &
Partner; R. Luscher; V. Mangeat;
S. Calatrava, A. Amsler, and W.
Rueger; Mario Campi and Franco
Pessina; and Peter Zumthor.
Includes an article by Werner
Jehle, "The mountain: painters,
engineers, and architects." Text
in Italian and English.
ABITARE 1990 Nov., no.290,
p.150-191, axonometric views,
dets., ill., elevs., maps,
photos., plans, secns., site
plans, sketch, aerial photo.

VADASZ, GYORGY, 1933-
Special feature: Contemporary
Hungarian architecture / edited by
Dezend Dagner.
Works illustrated by architects:
Imre Makovecz, Gabor Mezei, Andras
Erdei, Sandor Devenyi, Attila
(Continued next column)

VADASZ, GYORGY, 1933- (CONTINUED)
Special feature: ...(CONTINUED)
Kovacs, Laszlo Saros, Tamas Nagy,
Gyorgy Csete, Peter Oltai, Istvan
Kistelegdi, Tibor Jankovics, Csasa
Bodonyi, Istvan Ferencz, Tamas
Noll, Beno Taba, Janos Golda,
Agnes Thoma, Jozsef Kerenyi,
Gyorgy Vadasz, Gyorgy Keves, Adam
Sylvester and Gabor Turanyi. Text
in Japanese and English.
ARCHITECTURE AND URBANISM 1990
Mar., no.3(234), p.7-126,
axonometric views, dwgs., elevs.,
photos., plans, secns.

VADMAN, DAVID R.
The state of facilities management:
New York moves ahead with
computerization in surveying 20
million square feet / David R.
Vadman.
Cannon developed an automated
system for New York State.
ARCHITECTURE: THE AIA JOURNAL 1990
Mar., v.79, no.3, p.[181]-182,
ill., photo., plans.

VAES, JAN
Riutilizzazione cristiana di edifici
dell'antichita classica: un
atlante = Christian reutilization
of the buildings of classical
antiquity / Jan Vaes.
LOTUS INTERNATIONAL 1990, no.65,
p.16-39, axonometric views, ill.,
plans, secns.

VAETH, J. GORDON
Zeppelin decor: the Graf Zeppelin
and the Hindenburg / J. Gordon
Vaeth.
Interior architect of the
Hindenberg: Frits Breuhaus.
JOURNAL OF DECORATIVE AND
PROPAGANDA ARTS 1990
Winter-Spring, no.15, p.48-[59],
ill., photos., plans, refs.

VAGO, PIERRE, 1910-
Europa und die Architekten / Pierre
Vago.
Statement, written in 1989, by the
French architect (b.1910).
DEUTSCHES ARCHITEKTENBLATT 1990
June 1, v.22, no.6, p.939.
Pierre et les debuts de
L'Architecture d'Aujourd'hui
1930-1940: entretien avec Pierre
Vago [interview] / Gilles Ragot.
REVUE DE L'ART 1990, no.89,
p.77-81, ill., refs.
Pour une autre approche de l'UIA /
Pierre Vago.
Open letter written in 1989 by the
founder and honorary president of
the International Union of
Architects.
ARCHITECTURE D'AUJOURD'HUI 1990
Apr., no.268, p.56, port.

VAGO, PIERRE, 1910---ADDRESSES,
ESSAYS, LECTURES
Pour une autre approche de l'UIA /
Pierre Vago.
Open letter written in 1989 by the
founder and honorary president of
the International Union of
Architects.
ARCHITECTURE D'AUJOURD'HUI 1990
Apr., no.268, p.56, port.

VAHJEN, HEIKO
    Im Oberharz: Betriebsgebaude fur die
    Funkubertragungsstelle Torfhaus.
    Built 1986-1987. Architects: Henze
    & Vahjen.
    DEUTSCHE BAUZEITUNG 1990 Dec.,
    v.124, no.12, p.38-39, photos.,
    plan, secn., site plan.
    Wohnen in Gemeinschaft: Postwohnheim
    in Hannover-Kleefeld.
    Architects: Henze + Vahjen.
    DEUTSCHE BAUZEITUNG 1990 Dec.,
    v.124, no.12, p.40-43, axonometric
    view, elevs., photos., plans,
    secn.

VAIZEY, MARINA
    Designing for theatre: British
    theatre design: the Modern age,
    edited by John Goodwin [book
    review] / Marina Vaizey.
    Scenery design and states sets.
    ROYAL SOCIETY OF ARTS, LONDON. RSA
    JOURNAL 1990 Apr., v.138, no.5405,
    p.375-376,

VAKIL, ANNA
    Integrative planning workshops: the
    Michigan experience / Anna Vakil,
    Robert W. Marans, Allan Feldt.
    JOURNAL OF PLANNING EDUCATION AND
    RESEARCH 1990 Fall, v.10, no.1,
    p.61-69, refs.

VAL, JOSEP, 1955-
    Hiding place / David Redhead.
    Interiors of a Barcelona
    restaurant, El Refugi. Architect:
    Jose Antonio Val.
    DESIGNERS' JOURNAL 1990 Feb.,
    no.54, p.68-70, photos., plans.
    Special feature: Commercial
    interiors in Barcelona.
    Contents: Between minimalism and
    Movid, by Naoki Inagawa -- Alfredo
    Arribas -- Josep Val and Xavier
    Vendrell -- Dani Freixes and
    Vicente Miranda -- Tonet Sunyer
    and Jordi Badia -- Eduard Samso --
    Ventura Valcarce and Carlos Valls.
    Includes interviews and
    biographical information and
    features 13 individual commercial
    projects. Text in Japanese.
    SPACE DESIGN 1990 Nov.,
    no.11(314), p.005-072, dets.,
    ports., photos., plans, secns.,
    refs.

VALANCES--WOODEN
    Window dressing / Kelly O'Connor.
    Wooden valences.
    HOUSE BEAUTIFUL 1990 Jan., v.132,
    no.1, p.86, photos.

VALCARCE, VENTURA
    Special feature: Commercial
    interiors in Barcelona.
    Contents: Between minimalism and
    Movid, by Naoki Inagawa -- Alfredo
    Arribas -- Josep Val and Xavier
    Vendrell -- Dani Freixes and
    Vicente Miranda -- Tonet Sunyer
    and Jordi Badia -- Eduard Samso --
    Ventura Valcarce and Carlos Valls.
    Includes interviews and
    biographical information and
    features 13 individual commercial
    projects. Text in Japanese.
    SPACE DESIGN 1990 Nov.,
    no.11(314), p.005-072, dets.,
    ports., photos., plans, secns.,
    refs.

VALDES, ALFONSO
    Jacobsen 4 - Espana 4 / Alfonso
    Valdes.
    Text in Spanish and English.
    ARQUITECTURA 1990 Mar.-June, v.72,
    no.283-284, p.140-151, elevs.,
    model, photos., plans.

VALDES CRUZ, LEONARDO
    Poesia y arquitectura: 2 proyectos
    de titulo en Cantalao.
    Projects by Leonardo Valdes Cruz
    and Sandra Bordoni Acuna, for an
    underground library and a writers'
    colony.
    ARQ 1989 Aug., no.13, p.16-24,
    dwgs., models, plans, secns.

VALE, BRENDA
    Build it green: superinsulation /
    Barrie Evans.
    Energy-efficient Woodchurch
    Medical Centre. Architects: Brenda
    and Robert Vale.
    ARCHITECTS' JOURNAL 1990 Mar.7,
    v.191, no.10, p.65-68, diagrs.,
    photos., plans, secns.

VALE, ROBERT
    Build it green: superinsulation /
    Barrie Evans.
    Energy-efficient Woodchurch
    Medical Centre. Architects: Brenda
    and Robert Vale.
    ARCHITECTS' JOURNAL 1990 Mar.7,
    v.191, no.10, p.65-68, diagrs.,
    photos., plans, secns.

VALEGGIA, ELIO
    Severa, al limite del bosco / Elisa
    Dal Canto.
    House in Vira, in the Ticino
    region of Switzerland. Architect:
    Elio Valeggia.
    VILLE GIARDINI 1990 May, no.248,
    p.30-35, photos., plans, secn.

VALENA, TOMAS
    Der Ort der Stadt: eine
    Wanderausstellung zur
    Wechselwirkung von Topographie und
    urbaner Form / Jorg Stabenow.
    Student projects at TU Munchen
    entitled "Stadt und Topographie,"
    directed by Tomas Valena, use
    Ljubljana as their basis.
    ARCH PLUS 1990 Apr., no.103,
    p.32-33, maps.
    Die Topo-Graphie und die Aneignung
    des Stadtraumes / Tomas Valena.
    DER ARCHITEKT 1990 Nov., no.11,
    p.502-508, photos., site plans,
    aerial photo.

VALENCIA--TELEVISION STATIONS--
TELEVISIO VALENCIANA
    La arquitectura de Vetges Tu:
    Mediterrania = The architecture of
    Vetges Tu: Mediterrania.
    Most of issue devoted to works by
    this Spanish firm. Contents:
    Jardin del Turia, Valencia;
    Televisio Valenciana; cementerio
    de Tavernes de la Valldigna;
    Centro escolar publico en Port de
    Sagunt; viviendas en quart de
    Poblet; estudio de detalle y
    vivendas en La Flota, Murcia; dos
    viviendas rehabilitadas en la
    huerta murciana; vestuarios en
    tavernes de la Valldigna,
    Valencia. Text in Italian and
    (Continued next column)

VALENCIA--TELEVISION STATIONS--
TELEVISIO VALENCIANA (CONTINUED)
    La arquitectura de...(CONTINUED)
    English.
    ON DISENO 1990, no.112(suppl.),
    p.113-191, axonometric views,
    ill., dwgs., elevs., models,
    photos., plans, site plans, aerial
    photos.

VALENTE, ILARIA
    A proposito di un libro su Milano
    [interview and review] / Stefano
    Boeri.
    Interview with Attilio Schemmari
    and discussion of a supplement to
    Domus, no.711 (Dec.1989) edited by
    Luca Basso Peressut and Ilaria
    Valente, "Milano: architetture per
    la citta 1980-1990".
    CASABELLA 1990 Apr., v.54, no.567,
    p.34-36, ill.

VALENTI, MARINA
    Jose Zanine Caldas: per atelier ...
    una foresta / Marina Valenti.
    ARCHITETTURA; CRONACHE E STORIA
    1990 May, v.36, no.5(415),
    p.[392]-395, port., model, photos.

VALENTIEN, CHRISTOPH
    Gestaltung ohne Okologie? /
    Christoph Valentien.
    On integrating the teaching of
    ecology in landscape design
    programs. Includes English
    summary.
    GARTEN UND LANDSCHAFT 1990, v.100,
    no.2, p.38-40, ill., photos.

VALENTIN, CHRISTOPH
    Verborgene Achsen. Geometrie im
    englischen Landschaftsgarten =
    Hidden axes. Geometry in English
    landscape gardens / Christoph
    Valentien, Peter Weyman.
    Design of Oppenweiler Castle
    grounds, Wurttemberg, 1790-98;
    landscape architect: Friedrich
    Ludwig von Sckell.
    DAIDALOS 1989 Dec.15, no.34,
    p.72-79, photos., site plans,
    refs.

VALENTIN, KARL
    Groszstadien 1990.
    Issue features stadiums. In
    addition to several articles
    indexed separately, includes
    essays by Felix Zwoch,
    Heinz-Joachim Fischer, Karl
    Valentin, Mara Pinardi, Marco
    Degl'Innocenti, and Ermanno
    Ranzani, and features the stadiums
    at Bari, Florence, Genoa, Milan,
    Palermo, Rome, Turin, and Udine.
    BAUWELT 1990 June 29, v.81, no.24,
    p.1202-1246, ill., elevs., models,
    photos., plans, secns., site
    plans, aerial photos.

VALENTIN, PETER
    Verborgene Achsen. Geometrie im
    englischen Landschaftsgarten =
    Hidden axes. Geometry in English
    landscape gardens / Christoph
    Valentien, Peter Weyman.
    Design of Oppenweiler Castle
    grounds, Wurttemberg, 1790-98;
    landscape architect: Friedrich
    Ludwig von Sckell.
    DAIDALOS 1989 Dec.15, no.34,
    (Continued next page)

VALENTIN, PETER (CONTINUED)
Verborgene Achsen....(CONTINUED)
p.72-79, photos., site plans,
refs.

VALENTYN, THOMAS VAN DEN
A deux pas de Beethoven: salle de
musique de chambre, Bonn, Rfa.
On the Kammersmusiksaal, Bonn.
Architects: Thomas van den
Valentyn, Klaus Muller. English
summmary, p.114. Spanish summary.
p.198.
TECHNIQUES ET ARCHITECTURE 1990
Apr.-May, no.389, p.112-115,
axonometric view, photos., plan,
secn.
Amenagement interieur / Elisabeth
Allain-Dupre and Odile Seyler.
Survey of recent interior design
in France. Includes interview
with Patrick Rubin. Several works
indexed seperately.
LE MONITEUR ARCHITECTURE AMC 1990
July-Aug., no.13, p.27-74,
axonometric views, photos. plans.
Exquisite Unterwelt: Weinstube und
Kirchenraum in Schloss Eichholz /
Ingeborg Flagge.
Architect: Thomas van den
Valentyn, with Klaus Muller.
ARCHITEKTUR, INNENARCHITEKTUR,
TECHNISCHER AUSBAU 1990 May, v.98,
no.5, p.12-16, axonometric view,
photos., secn.

VALERIO, LUCIA
Fra le austere mura del borgo
feudale / Lucia Valerio.
Castello di Spaltenna in Chianti
is now a hotel.
VILLE GIARDINI 1990 Nov., no.253,
p.8-15, photos.
Lo specchio dell'anima / Lucia
Valerio.
The Castello Juval, a medieval
castle in the South Tirol, is home
to mountaineer Reinhold Messner.
Architect for renovations: Karl
Spitaler.
VILLE GIARDINI 1990 Dec., no.254,
p.2-9, photos., secns., site plan.

VALJAKKA, ILMO
"Yhtyneet Kuvalehet" [sic] - United
Magazines - Verlagsgebaude in
Helsinki.
Architect: Ilmo Valjakka.
DEUTSCHE BAUZEITSCHRIFT 1990
Sept., v.38, no.9, p.1201-1208,
axonometric views, dwgs., photos.,
plans.

VALJAKKA, TIMO
Rakennuksia ilman rakennusta: Per
Kirkeby tunkeutuu kasitteiden
valiin / Timo Valjakka.
ARKKITEHTI 1989, v.86, no.8, p.19,
ill., photo.

VALK, A. VAN DER
Planning for rule and order in
Amsterdam / R. Postuma, A. van der
Valk, G. Wallagh.
BUILT ENVIRONMENT 1989, v.15,
no.1, p.17-27, plans, tables,
refs.

VALKAMA, ESKO
Arkitektur pa NordForm / Kim
Dirckinck-Holmfeld, Lard Nevald.
Model town houses for the summer
1990 exhibit in Malmo, by
Tegnestuen Vandkunsten, Gudrun
Molden and Per Hojgaard, Ori Merom
and Peter Hesselgren, Kari Kousma
and Esko Valkama, and Gudmundur
Jonsson.
ARKITEKTEN 1990 Nov., v.92, no.17,
p.540-545, photos., model, plans,
secns.

VALKENBURGH, MICHAEL VAN
Garten der Zukunft? / Elke von
Radziewsky, Vera Graaf.
Features work by the following
American landscape architects:
Peter Walker, Martha Schwartz,
George Hargreaves, and Michael Van
Valkenburgh. english summary,
p.2-3.
ARCHITEKTUR & WOHNEN 1990
Oct.-Nov., no.5, p.90-[98],100,
ports., photos.
Landscapes for the 21st century
[competition].
Features 15 winning projects,
which include descriptions in the
designers' own words. Competition
sponsored by "Landscape
Architecture". Includes articles
by the judges, Jory Johnson, M.
Paul Friedburg and James Wines.
LANDSCAPE ARCHITECTURE 1990 Dec.,
v.80, no.12, p.[32-54], ill.,
ports., site plans, aerial photo.
Michael Van Valkenburgh: Landscape
architecture as a design.
Profile of the landscape
architect, his recent projects,
and ideas presented in an Apr.18,
1990 lecture at Harvard.
GSD NEWS / HARVARD UNIVERSITY.
GRADUATE SCHOOL OF DESIGN 1990
Summer-Fall, v.19, no.1, p.13,
aerial photo.

VALLE, GINO, 1923-
Sul projetto di Gino Valle alla
Giudecca = On Gino Valle's project
at the Giudecca / Pierre Alain
Croset.
LOTUS INTERNATIONAL 1986, no.51
p.108-128, axonometric views,
dets., elevs., photos., secns.,
sketches.
Verwaltungsgebaude in Ivrea.
Office building by Gina Valle in
"Olivetti City". Includes English
summary.
BAUMEISTER 1990 June, v.87, no.6,
p.46-52, photos., plans, secns.,
site plans.

VALLE, GINO, 1923---EXHIBITIONS
Itinerari nell'architettura
[exhibition and book review] /
Candon Marpillorn
Review of 1989 monograph by
Pierre-Alain Croset and exhibition
held at the Basilica Palladiana in
Vicenza, 17 Mar.-25 Apr.1989.
Title: Gino Valle, progetti e
architettura. Captions in Italian
and English.
CASABELLA 1990 Jan., v.54, no.564,
p.31-32, port., photo.

VALLE, PATRIZIA
Centro scolastico distrettuale di
Dolo.
School designed and built
1978-1987. Architect: Valeriano
Pastor, with Silvio Paolini,
Renato Rizzi and Patrizia Valle.
Text in Italian and English.
ANFIONE ZETO 1989, v.1, no.1,
p.16-211, axonometric views,
port., elevs., photos., plans,
secns., site plans.
Silvio Paolini e Patrizia Valle:
Scuola media a Sambruson-Dolo
(VE), Ing. Luigi Muffato
(strutture) / Valeriano Pastor.
Text in Italian and English.
ANFIONE ZETO 1989, v.1, no.2-3,
p.256-277, axonometric view,
elevs., model, photos., plans,
secns., site plans.

VALLE PEREZ, JOSE CARLOS
Significacion de la Iglesia en el
panorama de la arquitectura de la
orden del Cister / Jose Carlos
Valle Perez.
Article in issue devoted to the
Iglesia del Monasterio de Santa
Maria la Real de Huelgas, in
Burgos, Spain.
REALES SITIOS 1990, v.27, no.105,
49-56,[1] folded leaf, photos.,
refs.

VALLEE, JEAN DE LA, 1620-1696
Forlorad fasadutsmyckning pa
Ulriksdal och Venngarn / Ingrid
Rosell.
On the 17th-cent. facade
decorations on the palaces of
Ulriksdal (Jakobsdal) and
Venngarn, Sweden, particularly the
role of architects Jean de la
Vallee and Matthias Holl.
Includes English summary.
KONSTHISTORISK TIDSKRIFT 1989,
v.58, no.4, p.[151]-156, engrs.,
refs.

VALLI, DARIO
Scuola media a Guanzate, Como =
Secondary school near Como /
Roberto Gamba.
Architects: Dorian Battaglia,
Augusto Roda, Dario Valli. In
Italian and English; French,
German, and Spanish summaries,
p.3.
L'INDUSTRIA DELLE COSTRUZIONI 1990
June, v.24, no.224, p.20-25,3,
dets., elevs., map, photos.,
plans, secns., site plan.

VALLIFUOCO, GIUSEPPE
Vallifuoco e Steingut: progetti e
opere recenti = The work of
Vallifuoco and Steingut /
Francesco Garofalo.
In English and Italian; summaries
in French, German, and Spanish,
p.3.
L'INDUSTRIA DELLE COSTRUZIONI 1990
Nov., v.24, no.229, p.6-21,
axonometric views, elevs., models,
photos., plans, secns., site
plans.

VALLINI, WALTER, 1935-
Michela formia, Walter Vallini: negozio Caravan ad Alba. Text in Italian and English. DOMUS 1990 Apr., no.715, p.[1-3], photos, plans, secn.

VALLS, CARLOS, 1951-
Special feature: Commercial interiors in Barcelona. Contents: Between minimalism and Movid, by Naoki Inagawa -- Alfredo Arribas -- Josep Val and Xavier Vendrell -- Dani Freixes and Vicente Miranda -- Tonet Sunyer and Jordi Badia -- Eduard Samso -- Ventura Valcarce and Carlos Valls. Includes interviews and biographical information and features 13 individual commercial projects. Text in Japanese. SPACE DESIGN 1990 Nov., no.11(314), p.005-072, dets., ports., photos., plans, secns., refs.

VALMARANA, MARIO DI
Historic architecture: the Villa Rotonda / Mario Di Valmarana. Restoration of Palladio's Villa Rotunda, Vicenza, begun around 1570. Work is being sponsored by the Valmarana family, which has owned it since 1911. ARCHITECTURAL DIGEST 1990 Jan., v.47, no.1, p.[142-147],176,179, ports., photos.

VALODE ET PISTRE
Bordeaux: le renouveau de l'Entrepot Laine / Beatrice Houzelle. On the conversion of a customs warehouse into an art museum, the Musee d'art contemporain de Bordeaux et Arc en Reve, Centre d'Architecture. Architects: Valode et Pistre. TECHNIQUES ET ARCHITECTURE 1990 Oct.-Nov., no.392, p.17-20, photos., plan, secn.
Centre de Recherche BULL Paris. Article emphasizes the atrium design. Architects: Valode et Pistre. LE MUR VIVANT 1990, no.96, p.19-24,cover, det., dwgs., elev., photos.
Le reel mis a nu / Jean-Paul Robert. Conversion of Bordeaux warehouse into a contemporary art museum. Renovation architects: Valode et Pistre. English summary, p.16-17. ARCHITECTURE D'AUJOURD'HUI 1990 Oct., no.271, p.13-18, photos., plans, secns.

VALPERGA, MAURIZIO, FL. 17TH CENT.
Il restauro di palazzo Valperga-Galleani a Torino = The restoration of Palazzo Valperga-Galleani in Turin / Piercarlo Poma. Original architect: Antonio Maurizio Valperga. Architect for restoration: Alfredo Panie. In Italian and English; French, German, and Spanish summaries, p.4. L'INDUSTRIA DELLE COSTRUZIONI 1990 June, v.24, no.224, p.38-49, dets., photos., plans, secns., engrs.

VALUE ENGINEERING
See COST BENEFIT ANALYSIS

VAN BERKEL EN BOS
Ben van Berkel ontwerp gevangenistuin: twee-dimensionaliteit als uitgangspunt / Liesbeth Melis. DE ARCHITECT 1989 Oct., v.20, no.10, p.119-121, dwg., photos., plan, sketches, biblio.
La citta e il suo fiume = The city and its river / Jef Vanreusel. Stad aan de stroom project designs from international competition for urban renewal of three areas of Antwerp; Quay, Islet and South; architects: Yves Lion, Manuel de Sola-Morales, Bob van Reeth, Beth Gali, Rem Koolhaas, Toyo Ito, Van Berkel & Bos, Van Veen & Van Meer, Bureau of Urban Design. Overall site plan: Spea - Ingegneria Europa (Gruppo-Italstat). L'ARCA 1990 Dec., no.44, p.32-43, models, map, photos., plans, site plans.

VAN DER LINDIN, GEERT
Het kasteeldomein Breivelde: een landschapstuin te Zottegem (Grotenberge) / Geert Van der Linden. The landscape garden of the Chateau de Grootenberge, in Belgium, constructed between 1885 and 1888. English summary, p.63. MONUMENTEN EN LANDSCHAPPEN 1990 Mar.-Apr., v.9, no.2, p.12-28, maps, photos., site plans, table, refs.

VAN EMPELEN, VAN AALDEREN
Vier parken voor beverwijk: meervoudige opdracht laat grote diversiteit zien / David Louwerse. Landscape designs by Lodewijk Wiegersma, Van Empelen/Van Aalderen, West 8, and Ecoplan. DE ARCHITECT THEMA 1990 Sept., v.21, no.9 suppl., p.37-43, dwgs., model, photo., site plans.

VAN HERK EN DE KLEIJN
Inspirerende verdichtingsbouw: Woningsbouwproject De Rade in Den Haag / Cees Zwinkels. A 74-unit apartment building completed Nov.1989. Architect: Van Herk en de Kleijn. DE ARCHITECT 1990 Jan., v.21, no.1, p.70-75, photos., plans, secn., site plans.
Niewbouwblokken retoucheren het straatbeeld: woningbouw in Middelland van Van Herk en De Kleijn / Joris Molenaar. Several apartment buildings in the West-Kruiskade area of Rotterdam, along Middellandstraat, Nieuwe Binnenweg and other streets. ARCHIS 1989 Sept., no.9, p.18-26, elevs., photos., plans, secns., site plans, aerial photo.
Reihenhauser, Suze Robertsonstraat in Den Haag, Niederlande = A strip of dwellings, Suze Robertsonstraat in The Hague, Netherlands. Apartment house. Architects: Van Herk en De Kleijn. ARCHITEKTUR + WETTBEWERBE 1990 June, no.142, p.21, photos., plans.

VAN HERK EN DE KLEIJN (CONTINUED)
Roze woonlint als groot gebaar: Van Herk & De Kleijn in Zuiderpolder Haarlem / Hans Stoutjesdijk. Housing project, completed in Dec.1989. DE ARCHITECT 1990 Apr., v.21, no.4, p.45-49, photos., plans, site plan.

VAN HEYNINGEN AND HAWARD ARCHITECTS
Back to school for competition winner. Van Heyningen and Haward wins a limited competition for the design of the King Alfred School in Golders Green, north London. Original school buildings by E.C. Kaufmann, 1934-5. ARCHITECTS' JOURNAL 1990 Aug.8, v.192, no.6 p.13, axomometric views, secns.
School prizes / Clare Melhuish. Features three entries in the competition for King Alfred's School, Golders Green, London. Winning architects: Van Heyningen and Haward Architects. Other entries by Weston Williamson Architects and Chris Wilkinson Architects. BUILDING DESIGN 1990 Sept.14, no.1003, p.30-31, axomometric view, dwgs., plans, site plans.

VAN VEEN & VAN MEER
La citta e il suo fiume = The city and its river / Jef Vanreusel. Stad aan de stroom project designs from international competition for urban renewal of three areas of Antwerp; Quay, Islet and South; architects: Yves Lion, Manuel de Sola-Morales, Bob van Reeth, Beth Gali, Rem Koolhaas, Toyo Ito, Van Berkel & Bos, Van Veen & Van Meer, Bureau of Urban Design. Overall site plan: Spea - Ingegneria Europa (Gruppo-Italstat). L'ARCA 1990 Dec., no.44, p.32-43, models, map, photos., plans, site plans.

VANBRUGH, JOHN, SIR, 1664-1726
Anatomy of a country house: Building of Castle Howard [book review] / Julian Bicknell. BLUEPRINT (LONDON, ENGLAND) 1990 Apr., no.66, p.66,68,
Diverting labyrinths / John Harris. Architect: Sir John Vanbrugh. COUNTRY LIFE 1990 Jan.11, v.184, no.2, p.62-65, ill., photos., site plans.

VANDALISM
See also DEFACEMENT
See also THEFT

VANDALISM--GREAT BRITAIN
Protective coatings and paint. A product feature with articles on water-based paints, intumescent coatings, and prevention of spray paint vandalism. BUILDING 1990 Sept.21, v.255, no.37, p.69-83, ill., photos.

VANDALISM--UNITED STATES--NEW YORK
(NEW YORK)--SOUTH BRONX
  Transportation blues / Alexander
    Farnsworth.
    The Intervale Ave. subway stop, in
    the South Bronx, closed due to
    vandalism, will be rebuilt and
    opened in 2 1/2 years.
    METROPOLIS 1990 July-Aug., v.10,
    no.1, p.17-18, photos.

VANDENBROEK, PAUL
  De "salette" of pronkkamer in het
    17de-eeuwse Brabantse burgerhuls:
    familie- en groesportretten als
    iconografische bron, omstreeks
    1640-1680 / Paul Vandenbroeck.
    Baroque interiors in genre
    paintings. English summary, p.64.
    MONUMENTEN EN LANDSCHAPPEN 1990
    Nov.-Dec., v.9, no.6, p.41-62,
    ill., refs.

VANDENHOVE, CHARLES, 1927-
  Een kunst van weinig woorden: vier
    ontwerpen van Bruno Albert,
    Charles Vandenhove en John Berhaut
    / Arthur Wortmann.
    Four Liege projects: design for
    the Hogere Handelsschool (1989),
    with Camille Ghysen; Le Balloir
    (1988-1991); La Maison Heureuse,
    Ans (1986-1989); Woning Sutoor,
    Embourg (1988-1989).
    ARCHIS 1990 July, no.7, p.15-24,
    elevs., photos., plans, secn.,
    refs.
  Vandenhove Verbouwt Haage
    Schouwburg.
    Renovation of the 1804 Koninklijke
    Schouwburg. Architect for
    renovation: Charles Vandenhove.
    DE ARCHITECT 1990 Mar., v.21,
    no.3, p.19, model.

VANDERBYL DESIGN
  Bernhardt Furniture / Judith
    Davidsen.
    Interiors of redesigned Chicago
    Merchandise Mart showroom.
    Interior designers: Vanderbyl
    Design.
    INTERIOR DESIGN 1990 Oct., v.61,
    no.14, p.248-[251], photos.,
    isometric dwg.
  Bernhardt, Los Angeles / Judith
    Nasatir.
    Interiors of furniture showroom in
    the Pacific Design Center, Los
    Angeles. Interior designers:
    Vanderbyl Design.
    INTERIOR DESIGN 1990 Feb., v.61,
    no.3, p.230-[233], axonometric
    view, photos.
  Designer's Design: Furniture and
    graphics designer Michael
    Vanderbyl's new offices / Paula
    Rice Jackson.
    Features Vanderbyl Design offices,
    San Francisco.
    INTERIORS 1989 Feb., v.148, no.7,
    p.130-134, axonometric view,
    photos.
  Shoebox drama on a shoestring budget
    / Kristen Richards.
    Features Bernhardt Furniture
    Showroom, Pacific Design Center,
    Los Angeles. Designers: Vanderbyl
    Design.
    INTERIORS 1990 Jan., v.149, no.6,
    p.164-165, photos., plan.

VANDERBYL, MICHAEL
  Designer's Design: Furniture and
    graphics designer Michael
    Vanderbyl's new offices / Paula
    Rice Jackson.
    Features Vanderbyl Design offices,
    San Francisco.
    INTERIORS 1989 Feb., v.148, no.7,
    p.130-134, axonometric view,
    photos.

VANDERSTAPPEN, HARRIE A.
  Written and unwritten: a new history
    of the Buddhist caves at Yungang
    [by] James O. Caswell [book
    review] / Harrie A. Vanderstappen.
    ARS ORIENTALIS 1989, v.19,
    p.125-127,

VANDOMMELEN, DORN
  Creating the landscape symbol
    vocabulary for a regional image:
    the case of the Kentucky Bluegrass
    / Karl Raitz, Dorn VanDommelen.
    LANDSCAPE JOURNAL 1990 Fall, v.9,
    no.2, p.109, photos., elevs., map,
    refs.

VANLAETHEM, FRANCE
  Le centenaire de la corporation
    professionnelle des architectes du
    Quebec / France Vanlaethem.
    ARQ: ARCHITECTURE/QUEBEC 1990
    June, no.55, p.50, biblio.
  Element d'un art de vivre: un
    pavillon de jardin a Toronto /
    France Vanlaethem.
    Architects: Brigitte Shim, Howard
    Sutcliffe.
    ARQ: ARCHITECTURE/QUEBEC 1990
    Oct., no.57, p.22, photos., plan.
  Les premiers programmes
    d'enseignement de l'architecture:
    le centenaire de la corporation
    professionnelle des architectes du
    Quebec / France Vanlaethem.
    ARQ: ARCHITECTURE/QUEBEC 1990
    Dec., no.58, p.35, dwg., refs.

VANN, JOHN
  Architects' pensions: what you can
    do / John Vann.
    British examples.
    ARCHITECTS' JOURNAL 1990 May 2,
    v.191, no.18, p.77-79, ill.

VANNUCCHI, GIANFRANCO
  Centro Empresarial Terra Brasilis,
    Sao Paulo.
    Architects: J. Koningsberger, G.
    Vannucchi.
    PROJETO 1990 Dec.-1991 Jan.,
    no.137, p.62-65, port., elevs.,
    photos., plans.

VANREUSEL, JEF
  La citta e il suo fiume = The city
    and its river / Jef Vanreusel.
    Stad aan de stroom project designs
    from international competition for
    urban renewal of three areas of
    Antwerp; Quay, Islet and South;
    architects: Yves Lion, Manuel de
    Sola-Morales, Bob van Reeth, Beth
    Gali, Rem Koolhaas, Toyo Ito, Van
    Berkel & Bos, Van Veen & Van Meer,
    Bureau of Urban Development.
    Overall site plan: Spea - Ingegneria
    Europa (Gruppe Italsteel).
    L'ARCA 1990 Dec., no.44, p.32-43,
    models, map, photos., plans, site
    plans.

VANVITELLI, LUIGI, 1700-1773
  Architecture in miniature:
    Vanvitelli / Cesare de Seta.
    Wooden scale models of Caserta,
    the palace of Charles of Bourbon.
    Architect: Luigi Vanvitelli; made
    by Antonio Rosz between 1756-1761.
    FMR 1990 Feb., v.9, no.42,
    p.81-96, ill., models.

VARALDO, GIUSEPPE, 1926-
  Mensa aziendale a Moncalerio, Torino
    = An office cafeteria in
    Moncalerio, Turin / Domenico
    Bagliani, Lauro Sassi.
    For the D.E.A. Company. Architect:
    Giuseppe Varaldo. In English and
    Italian; summaries in French,
    German and Spanish, p.3.
    L'INDUSTRIA DELLE COSTRUZIONI 1990
    Nov., v.24, no.229, p.22-27,
    axonometric views, photos.

VARANISHI, SATYA
  Ekamra Kshetra: Bhubaneshwar, Orissa
    / Satya Varanishi.
    A recent INTACH study "stresses
    the developmental requirements of
    the old town and indentifies
    almost twenty projects" for
    preservation work.
    ARCHITECTURE + DESIGN 1989
    Nov.-Dec., v.6, no.1, p.[74]-79,
    maps, photos.

VARDY, JOHN, D. 1765
  Spencer House, London / Gervase
    Jackson-Stops.
    Built 1756-1766 for the 1st Earl
    Spencer; architects: John Vardy,
    James "Athenian" Stuart, Henry
    Holland. Restoration architect:
    Rolfe Judd.
    COUNTRY LIFE 1990 Nov.29, v.184,
    no.48, p.42-47, photos.

VARGA, G.
  Erlebenswertes Buro-Ambiente: mit
    "Gesika Nova," ein Autohaus zeigt
    Flagge / Petra Lasar.
    Mercedes dealership, Stuttgart.
    Architects: W. Held, G. Varga.
    ARCHITEKTUR, INNENARCHITEKTUR,
    TECHNISCHER AUSBAU 1990 Apr.,
    v.98, no.4, p.100-102, photos.

VARGAS, EDUARDO
  Concurso Museo de Arte, Wolfsburg,
    Alemania.
    Architect: Eduardo Vargas H.
    CA: REVISTA OFICIAL DEL COLEGIO DE
    ARQUITECTOS DE CHILE 1989
    Apr.-June, no.56, p.[64-67],
    dwgs., port., elevs., model,
    plans, secns., site plans.

VARGAS, PAULO SERGIO DE PAULA
  Hotel Praia Sol, Serra, ES.
    Architects: P. Vargas, G.
    Apolinario.
    PROJETO 1990 Nov., no.136,
    p.45-47, photos., plans, secns.

VARINI, GIANFRANCO, 1939-
  Ansaloni-Varini: Scuola materna a
    pieve modolena (RE).
    In Italian and English.
    DOMUS 1990 May, no.716, p.[1]-3,
    dates., photos., plans, sketches.

VARINI, GIANFRANCO, 1939-
(CONTINUED)
Scuola materna a Villa Ospizio,
Reggio Emilia / Massimo Mussini.
Architects: Gianfranco Varini,
Eugenio Ansaloni. Summaries in
English, French, German and
Spanish. p.104.
ARCHITETTURA: CRONACHE E STORIA
1990 Feb., v.36, no.2(412),
p.104-109, axonometric view,
photos., plan, secn., site plan,
sketches.

VARLEY, H. PAUL
The Occident expressed / Ziva
Freiman.
One of two companion essays which
examine the work and influence of
foreign architects working in
Japan. Includes excerpt from
Japanese culture, by H. Paul
Varley, which reveals "how
Modernism and American models
affected Japanese attitudes and
lifestyles."
PROGRESSIVE ARCHITECTURE 1990 May,
v.71, no.5, p.108-117,122, ill.,
photos., plan, secn.

VARMING, KRISTOFFER NYROP, 1865-1936
Danmarks Natur - og
Laegevidenskabelige Bibliotek,
Kobenhavn.
Addition to a c.50-year old
university library at Norre Alle
49. Architects: Eva og Nils Koppel
- Gert Edstrand. Original
architect: Kristoffer Varming.
Includes English and German
captions and summaries.
ARKITEKTUR DK 1989, v.33, no.8,
p.388-392, elev., photos., site
plan.

VARNEY, CARLETON
Hall of Fame: celebrations and
memories [1990].
Profiles of twelve new inductees
into the Interior Design Hall of
Fame and the winners of three
special citations.
INTERIOR DESIGN 1990 Dec., v.61,
no.16, p.105-[125], ports.,
photos.
Mackinac vistas: a new spirit for
the Grand Hotel owners' island
cottage in Michigan / John Taylor.
Features the interiors of Dan and
Amelia Musser's home, Corner
Cottage, on Mackinac Island.
Interior designer: Carleton Varney
of Dorothy Draper & Co.
ARCHITECTURAL DIGEST 1990 Aug.,
v.47, no.8, p.[166-174], photos.
West Virginia governor's mansion /
Monica Geran.
Interiors of renovated
Georgian-style mansion in
Charleston. Original architect:
Walker Martens. Interior
designers: Carleton Varney of
Dorothy Draper & Co.
INTERIOR DESIGN 1990 Mar., v.61,
no.5, p.176-[183], photos., plan.

VARROQUIER, JEAN-CHRISTIAN
Siege social a Levallois / Brigitte
Fitoussi.
Auguste Thouard corporate office
building, Levallois-Perret.
Architects: Tessa de Saint
Blanquat, Christian Varroquier,
David Mary.
ARCHITECTURE D'AUJOURD'HUI 1990
Sept., no.270, p.197-198, photos.,
plans.

VASARI, GIORGIO, 1511-1574
The Brancacci Chapel / Umberto
Baldini.
The chapel in the church of the
Carmine in Florence has been
restored and opened to the public.
Features frescoes by Tommasino, or
Masolino, and by Masaccio.
Includes notes on the restoration
by Ornella Casazza and an essay by
Vasari on Masaccio.
FMR 1990 June, v.9, no.44,
p.57-88, ill.
Vasari e le stampe / Evelina Borea.
PROSPETTIVA 1989 Apr.-1990 Oct.,
no.57-60, p.18-38, engrs., refs.

VASCONCELLOS, MARIA JOSEFINA
Colonial e pos-moderno: quem nao
gostar reclame com o bispo.
Palacio Arquiepiscopal, Mariana,
Brazil (1983-87), Architects: Eolo
Maia, Maria J. de Vasconcellos,
Sylvio E. de Podesta.
PROJETO 1988 Nov., no.116,
p.60-66, dwgs., elevs., photos.,
plans, secns.

VASCONI, CLAUDE, 1940-
Actualites: concours Sextius
Mirabeau: le nouveau cours
d'Aix-en-Provence / Bruno Fortier.
Projects for urban renewal of
Sextius Mirabeau district;
architects: Oriol Bohigas
(winner), Alessandro Anselmi,
Patrick le Merdy, Alain Sarfati,
Gregotti Associati, Richard Rogers
and Partners, Christian de
Portzamparc, Jean Nouvel &
Emmanuel Cattani, Claude Vasconi,
Martorel Bohigas Mackay, Kurokawa,
Lopez, Bonell, Durand, Richard
Meier & Partners, Giancarlo de
Carlo.
LE MONITEUR ARCHITECTURE AMC 1990
Oct., no.15, p.7-9, models,
photo., aerial photo.
Actualites: un concours hors du
commun / Elisabeth Allain-Dupre.
Contents: Interview with Christian
Cleret, director of the
Etablissement public du Centre
international de Conferences--
Competition projects by architects
Stanislas Fiszer & Philippe
Guyard, Yves Lion & Alan Levitt,
Claude Vasconi, Jean Nouvel &
Emmanuel Cattani, Alain Domingo,
Bernard Dufournet, Alain Rihn,
Franck Hammoutene, Olivier Arene,
Christine Edeikins, Olivier
Chaslin, Alain Le Houedec, Luc
Weizmann, Alain Sarfati, Jean
Dubus, Jean-Pierre Loth, Christian
de Portzamparc, and Bertrand
Bonnier.
LE MONITEUR ARCHITECTURE AMC 1990
May, no.11, p.6-9, elevs., models,
plans, secns., site plans.

VASCONI, CLAUDE, 1940- (CONTINUED)
Angers Front de Maine.
Project for the right bank of the
Maine, to reconcile the two
approaches to Angers. Architect:
Cl. Vasconi.
LE MUR VIVANT 1990, no.95,
p.73-74, axonometric views, dwgs.,
elevs., plans, site plans.
Centro internazionale Congressi a
Parigi.
Winner: Francesco Soleri [i.e.,
Francis Soler]: Projects by Jean
Nouvel and Emmanuel Cattani,
Claude Vasconi, and others.
L'INDUSTRIA DELLE COSTRUZIONI 1990
Dec. v.24, no.230, p.70-72,
models, secns.
Claude Vasconi sur la Maine.
On Vasconi's project, "Vitrine de
l'Angers de l'an 2000" for the
development of the right bank area
of the Maine river in Angers.
ARCHITECTURE INTERIEURE CREE 1990
Apr.-May, no.236, p.28, dwgs.,
site plans.
La fortezza di Olympique 2000 =
Olympique 2000 citadel / Lucia
Bisi.
Project for Olympic village
housing for 1992 Winter Olympics
at Albertville, France; architect:
Claude Vasconi.
L'ARCA 1990 May, no.38 suppl.
l'Arca 2, p.97-98, elev., model,
site plan.
Hotel du departement Strasbourg.
Architects: Vasconi, Spitz, Lever,
Jacob, Lauber. Includes two other
projects by Claude Vasconi: Hotel
de Ville, Toulon and the Centre de
Chirurgie Hepatobiliaire, Hopital
Paul Brousse, Villejuif.
TECHNIQUES ET ARCHITECTURE 1990
Oct.-Nov., no.392, p.29-36,
axonometric view, det., elev.,
model, photos., plans, secns.,
site plan, aerial photo.
Konstruktive Intelligenz / Peter
Rice.
Includes a discussion by
architects G. Behnisch, C.
Vasconi, O. Aicher, J. Nouvel, H.
Schultiz & R. Rogers and engineers
S. Polonyi, P. Rice, and H.
Malotki.
ARCH PLUS 1990 Jan., no.102,
p.42-52, dets., photos.
Paroles et musique: Corum de
Montpellier.
Performing arts center,
Montpellier. Architect: Claude
Vasconi. English summary, p.97.
Spanish summary, p.198.
TECHNIQUES ET ARCHITECTURE 1990
Apr.-May, no.389, p.92-97,
diagrs., photos., plans, secns.,
site plan.
Quai Branly / Jean-Paul Robert.
Entries by 7 French firms in the
competition to design an
international conference center in
Paris near the Eiffel Tower.
Winning architect: Francois Soler.
Includes English summaries.
ARCHITECTURE D'AUJOURD'HUI 1990
Apr., no.268, p.[20]-38,
axonometric views, dwgs., ports.,
elev., models, photos., plans,
secns., aerial photo.

VASCONI, CLAUDE, 1940- (CONTINUED)
Sept projets pour le Quai Branly:
Centre de conferences
internationales.
Includes seven entries in the
competition for an international
conference center near the Quai
Branly, Paris. Winning architect:
Francis Soler.
TECHNIQUES ET ARCHITECTURE 1990
Apr.-May, no.389, p.17-26, dwgs.,
models, plans, secns., site plans,
aerial photo.
Tecnologia nel verde = Technology
opening up to nature / Lucia Bisi.
Thomson factory at
Marly-les-Valenciennes. Architect:
Claude Vasconi.
L'ARCA 1990 Mar., no.36, p.18-27,
dets., elevs., photos, plans,
secns., site plan.
Thomson LCC, Valenciennes.
Architect: Cl. Vasconi.
LE MUR VIVANT 1990, no.95,
p.32-36, axonometric views,
elevs., photos., secns.
Toulon: concours pour l'hotel de
ville.
Competition designs by Claude
Vasconi (winner); Fainsilber,
Petraccone, & Vodar; J. Donato;
Borde, Nothhelfer, Duchier; Andre
Stern; and Badani, Lefrancois,
Detroyat et Condroyer.
LE MONITEUR ARCHITECTURE AMC 1990
Apr., no.10, p.8-9, ill., models,
plans, secns., site plans.
Trasparenze controllate = Controlled
transparence.
Project for international
conference center on Quai Branly,
Paris; architect: Claude Vasconi.
L'ARCA 1990 Nov., no.43 suppl.
l'Arca 2, p.97-98, axonometric
view, elev., model, secns., site
plan.
Ultimo ponte a Parigi = The latest
bridge in Paris / Maurizio Vitta.
Competition projects for new
bridge over Seine; architects:
Claude Vasconi; Remy Butler and J.
V. Berlottier; Foster, Francis,
Jourda & Perraudin; Chemetov &
Huidobro; Dominique Perrault.
L'ARCA 1990 July-Aug., no.40,
p.20-29, 1 folded leaf, elevs.,
plans, secns., site plans.
Urban Mun / Frances Anderton.
On the Centre Republique,
Saint-Nazaire. Architect: Claude
Vasconi.
ARCHITECTURAL REVIEW 1990 Jan.,
v.187, no.1115, p.70-74, det.,
dwg., photos., plans, secns., site
plan.
Wohn- und Gewerbebebaung in Paris,
19. Bezirk, Frankreich =
Residential and commercial
buildings in Paris, 19th district,
France.
Competition. Winning architect:
Claude Vasconi. Text in German.
ARCHITEKTUR I WETTBEWERBE 1990
June, no.142, p.30-32, axonometric
views, dwgs., plans.

VASCONI, CLAUDE, 1940---EXHIBITIONS
Claude Vasconi all'INARCH di Roma
[exhibition review].
L'INDUSTRIA DELLE COSTRUZIONI 1990
Oct., v.24, no.228, p.66-67,
dets., photos.

VASCONI, SPITZ, LEVER, JACOB, LAUBER
Hotel du departement Strasbourg.
Architects: Vasconi, Spitz, Lever,
Jacob, Lauber. Includes two other
projects by Claude Vasconi: Hotel
de Ville, Toulon and the Centre de
Chirurgie Hepatobiliaire, Hopital
Paul Brousse, Villejuif.
TECHNIQUES ET ARCHITECTURE 1990
Oct.-Nov., no.392, p.29-36,
axonometric view, det., elev.,
model, photos., plans, secns.,
site plan, aerial photo.

VASQUEZ CONSUEGRO, GUILLERMO
Casa Rolando, Mairena del Aljarafe.
Architect: Giullermo Vasquez
Consuegra. Text in Italian and
English.
LOTUS INTERNATIONAL 1989, no.63,
p.34-41, axonometric views,
elevs., photos., plans, secn.

VASQUEZ DE CASTRO, ANTONIO, 1929-
Un pulso con la mole: Centro de Arte
Reina Sofia, Madrid.
Renovation of 18th cent. military
hospital into an art museum.
Architects: Antonio Vazquez de
Castro, Jose Luis Iniguez de
Onzono. English text, p.90.
A & V 1990, no.26, p.26-31,
elevs., photos., plans, site
plans.

VASS, ANDREAS
Neuorganisation des Zugangsbereichs
zur Alhambra, Granada, Spanien =
Reorganization of the areas
surrounding the new access to the
Alhambra, Granada, Spain.
International idea competition.
Features winning designs by Peter
Nigst, Erich Hubmann, Andreas
Vass, for the overall plan, and
the design for the Parque de los
Alijares and cemetery by Daniele
Vitale. Text in German.
ARCHITEKTUR + WETTBEWERBE 1990
Dec., no.144, p.56-58, dwgs.,
models, secns., site plans.

VASSAL, SERGE
Geography of universities in Western
Europe / Serge Vassal.
Spatial dynamics of university
location.
EKISTICS 1988 Jan.-June, v.55,
no.328-330, p.146-152, maps,
plans, refs.
Geography of universities in Western
Europe / Serge Vassal.
Spatial dynamics of university
location.
EKISTICS 1988 Jan.-June, v.55,
no.328-330, p.146-152, maps,
plans, refs.

VASSALLI, FRANCESCO
Aske Hall, Yorkshire - I: the seat
of the Marquess of Zetland / Giles
Worsley.
Architect: William Wakefield;
plasterer: Francesco Vassalli.
COUNTRY LIFE 1990 Mar.1, v.184,
(Continued next column)

VASSALLI, FRANCESCO (CONTINUED)
Aske Hall, Yorkshire...(CONTINUED)
no.9, p.80-83, ill., photos.

VASSEUR, ISABEL
Festival landmarks / Isabel Vasseur.
On the incorporation of outdoor
sculpture in the Gateshead
National Garden Festival 1990.
LANDSCAPE DESIGN 1990 July-Aug.,
no.192, p.40-41, photos.

VAU, LOUIS LE, 1612-1670--INFLUENCE
Le Chateau de Pennautier (Aude) /
Yves Bruand.
Built between 1670 and 1676, the
chateau was inspired by Le Vau's
design for Versailles. Alterations
made in 1847-1848 by local
architect Jean Champagne. English
summary, p.24.
GAZETTE DES BEAUX-ARTS 1990 Jan.,
ser.6,v.115, no.1452, p.[15]-24,
dets., dwgs., photos., plans, site
plan, refs.

VAUBAN, SEBASTIEN LE PRESTE DE,
1633-1707
Model cities / Jean Dethier.
On the collection of 17-19th cent.
model towns, which constitute the
musee des Plans en Relief, Hotel
National des Invalides, Paris. The
initial enterprise was begun in
1678 by Sebastien Vauban.
ARCHITECTURAL REVIEW 1990 May,
v.187, no.1119, p.89-92, models.

VAUDAGNA, MAURIZIO. ESTETICA DELLA
POLITICA.
Citta e politica nel fascismo [book
review] / Cristina Bianchetti.
Review of L'estetica della
politica: Europa e America negli
anni Trenta, a vol. of essays ed.
by M. Vaudagna. Captions in
Italian and English.
CASABELLA 1990 Jan., v.54, no.564,
p.35-36.

VAUDEVILLE, BERNARD
Les Tours de la Liberte / Bernard
Vaudeville, Brian Forster.
Temporary structures as monument
to the French Revolution
Bicentenary celebrations.
Architects: Jean-Marie Hennin and
Nicolas Normier.
THE ARUP JOURNAL 1989 Autumn,
v.24, no.3, p.17-19, dets.,
photos.

VAUGHAN, HENRY, 1845-1917
St. Margaret's Convent Chapel /
Kimberly A. Shilland.
Situated at Louisburg Square and
Pickney St., Boston. Designed in
1882 and completed in 1921.
Architect: Henry Vaughan.
BOSTON PRESERVATION ALLIANCE
LETTER 1990 Jan., v.11, no.1, p.3,
photo.

VAUGHN, STEPHANIE
Fanciful farm: Richard and Victoria
MacKenzie-Childs apply wit and
whimsy to design / Stephanie
Vaughn.
1810 farmhouse of designers, in
western N.Y. State.
HOUSE & GARDEN 1990 July, v.162,
no.7, p.[36,38], photos.

VAULTING
See VAULTS (ARCHITECTURE)

VAULTS (ARCHITECTURE)
See also FAN VAULTING (ARCHITECTURE)
See also RIBBED VAULTING
(ARCHITECTURE)
See also HYPOGEA
See also PITCHED-BRICK VAULTS
Erhebend: Gewolbe als Meisterwerke
der Geometrie / Ursula Baus.
DEUTSCHE BAUZEITUNG 1990 July,
v.124, no.7, p.14-23, photos.,
plan, secns., refs.

VAULTS (ARCHITECTURE)--18TH CENTURY--
ALTERATIONS AND ADDITIONS--ENGLAND--
LONDON--ROYAL SOCIETY OF ARTS
Converting the vaults and developing
the Society's house, 1977-1990 /
Sam Lloyd.
Conversion of 18th cent. vaults
for additional space for the Royal
Society of Arts, London.
Architects: Green Lloyd.
ROYAL SOCIETY OF ARTS, LONDON. RSA
JOURNAL 1990 Oct., v.138, no.5411,
p.734-737, photos., secn.
Putting art in the vaults / Kenneth
Powell.
On two London projects: the
conversion of Somerset House,
designed by Sir William Chambers,
into space for the Courtauld
Institute and Galleries and the
expansion and restoration of the
underground vaults of the Royal
Society of Arts.
RIBA JOURNAL 1990 Aug., v.97,
no.8, p.48-51,54-56, photos.,
secns.
Underworld society makes good.
Features renovated vault area
under the Royal Society of Arts
building, London. Architects:
Green Lloyd.
DESIGNERS' JOURNAL 1990 Sept.,
no.60, p.11, photos.
Vaults.
Opening of the RSA vaults by HRH
Prince Philip; expansion and
restoration of underground vaults
at headquarters of the Royal
Society of Arts, London.
Architects: Green Lloyd Adams.
ROYAL SOCIETY OF ARTS, LONDON. RSA
JOURNAL 1990 July, v.138, no.5408,
p.512-514, ports., photos.

VAULTS (ARCHITECTURE)--BRICK--17TH
CENTURY--ITALY--IRPINIA--CATTEDRALE
DI SANT'ANGELO DEI LOMBARDI--
RESEARCH
Effetti del terremoto sulle
strutture laterizie a volta /
Fabio Ortolani.
Report on an experiment with
brick-laying and earthquakes
carried out on a model, in the
restoration of the 17th cent.
Cattedrale Sant'Angelo dei
Lombardi in Irpinia. Summaries in
English, French, German, and
Spanish.
PALLADIO 1988 Dec., v.1, no.2,
p.143-146, dets., dwgs., photo.,
refs.

VAULTS (ARCHITECTURE)--BRICK--
RENAISSANCE--RESEARCH
Divagazioni sulle cupole con
spinapesce spiralimorfi / Antonino
Giuffre, Riccardo Migliari.
Follow-up on G. Zander's article,
Gli ottagoni di San Pietro
reconosciuti nel dis. arch Uff.
no. 1330, in Palladio, June 1988,
v.1, no.1, p.67-82. Summaries in
English, French, German, and
Spanish.
PALLADIO 1988 Dec., v.1, no.2,
p.147-148, dwgs., isometric dwg.

VAULTS (ARCHITECTURE)--FRANCE
Vaulted construction in French
Megalithic tombs / W.G. Cavanagh,
R.R. Laxton.
An analysis of vaults in passage
graves at Barnenez and Ile Carn,
in northwestern France. Includes
abstract.
OXFORD JOURNAL OF ARCHAEOLOGY 1990
July, v.9, no.2, p.141-167, maps,
photos., plans, secns., tables,
biblio.

VAULTS (ARCHITECTURE)--MUD--
ASSYRO-BABYLONIAN
Innovations in mud-brick: decorative
and structural techniques in
ancient Mesopotamia/ David Oates.
Focus on the Great Temple, Tell al
Rimah, ca. 1800 B.C.
WORLD ARCHAEOLOGY 1990 Feb., v.21,
no.3, p.[388]-406, axonometric
view, dets., map, photos., plans,
secns., reconst. dwgs., refs.

VAULTS (ARCHITECTURE)--RESEARCH--19TH
CENTURY--HISTORY
Sintesi storica sulla statica di
archi, volte e cupole nel XIX
secolo / Eduardo Benvenuto,
Massimo Corradi, Federico Foce.
Historical synthesis of the
scientific studies carried out
during the 19th cent. on the
statics of arches, vaults, and
masonry domes. Summaries in
English, French, German, and
Spanish.
PALLADIO 1988 Dec., v.1, no.2,
p.51-68, dets., diagrs., refs.

VAULTS (SEPULCHRAL)
See TOMBS

VAUPEL, BODIL
Bodil Vaupel / Adelheid Fischer.
Profile of Danish architect who
practices in Minneapolis.
ARCHITECTURE MINNESOTA 1990
May-June, v.16, no.3, p.25,80,
port.
A place of one's own.
A doll house built by architect
Bodil Vaupel and her daughters.
ARCHITECTURE MINNESOTA 1990
Sept.-Oct., v.16, no.5, p.21,
port., photo.

VAUX, CALVERT, 1824-1895
Wilderstein: a loved and lived-in
family home in Rhinebeck, New York
/ Anne Needham.
Queen Anne style house completed
in the 1880s. Interior by J.B.
Tiffany; grounds by Calvert Vaux;
architect for exterior, Arnout
Cannon. Current owner: Wilderstein
(Continued next column)

VAUX, CALVERT, 1824-1895 (CONTINUED)
Wilderstein: a loved... (CONTINUED)
Foundation.
VICTORIAN HOMES 1990 summer, v.9,
no.3, p.54-57, ill., photos.

VAVRA, Z.
Risanamento, restauro e rinso a
Praga = Rehabilitation,
restoration and reuse in Prague /
Fiamma Dinelli.
Describes four recent projects:
Belfry house in Old Town Square
(V. Pelzlbauer, A.Charvatova);
Prague National Theater (Z. Vavra,
F. Flasar); St. Agnes Monastery
(K. Kunca, J. Hlavaty); and an
entire street (P.Kupka, J.Blazck,
M. Lierova). Includes English
translation. French, German, and
Spanish summaries, p.4.
L'INDUSTRIA DELLE COSTRUZIONI 1990
Apr., v.24, no.222, p.44-51, det.,
photos., plans, aerial photo.

VAYER, LAJOS
Problemi iconologici nel ciclo di
affreschi di Piero della Francesca
ad Arezzo / Lajos Vayer.
Paper presented at the Qualita
ecclesiale nell'arte conference in
19889. Includes abstract in
English.
ARTE CRISTIANA 1990 Mar.-July,
v.78, no.737-738, p.161-168,
dets., photos.

VAZQUEZ CONSUEGRA, GUILLERMO
Al pie de la Giralda: Casa Santos,
Sevilla.
Architect: Guillermo Vazquez
Consuegra. English summary, p.92.
A & V 1990, no.24, p.76-80,
axonometric view, photos., plans,
secns., site plans.
Edificio di abitazioni Ramon y
Cajal, Siviglia = Ramon y Cajal
building, Seville.
38-unit four-storey apartment
house; architect: Guillermo
Vasquez Consuegra.
LOTUS INTERNATIONAL 1989, no.63,
p.42-49, axonometric views,
elevs., photos., plans, secns.,
site plans.
Institut fur Architektur in Sevilla,
E = Institute for Architecture in
Sevilla, E.
Details of the stairway.
Architect: G. Vasquez Consuegra.
DETAIL 1990 Apr.-May, v.30, no.2,
p.152-155, axonometric view,
dets., photos., secn.
Istituto di architettura di Siviglia
= Institute of architecture at
Seville.
Site: Patio de Banderas.
Architect: Guillermo Vasquez
Consuegra.
LOTUS INTERNATIONAL 1989, no.63,
p.50-55, photos., plans, secns.
Sanierung eines Wohngebaudes in
Sevilla = Refurbishment of a
residential building in Seville.
At Plaza del Pan and Calle Huelva.
Architect: G. Vazquez Consuegra.
DETAIL 1990 Oct.-Nov., v.30, no.5,
p.484-485, axonometric view, det.,
photos., plan, secn., site plan.

VELLY, MICHEL (CONTINUED)
Brittany builds /...(CONTINUED)
v.187, no.1119, p.74-78, elevs.,
photos., plans, secn., site plan,
isometric dwgs.

VELODROMES
See BICYCLE RACING TRACKS

VELSEN, KOEN VAN, 1952-
Architectuur van het verdwijnen:
Wiel Arets wint opdracht AHK /
Janny Rodermond.
The Amsterdamse Hogeschool voor de
Kunsten. Includes proposals by Van
Velsen and Teun Koolhaas.
DE ARCHITECT 1990 Dec., v.21,
no.12, p.42-47, models, plans,
site plans, aerial photos.
Double Dutch / Richard Weston.
New municipal library in Zeewolde,
Netherlands. Architect: Koen van
Velsen.
ARCHITECTS' JOURNAL 1990 June 27,
v.191, no.26, p.42-47, axonometric
views, photos., plans, secns.
External walls, library: Koen van
Velsen.
Exterior of municipal library in
Zeewolde, Netherlands, is composed
of various materials, including
concrete, galvanized steel and
polycarbonate glazing.
ARCHITECTS' JOURNAL 1990 June 27,
v.191, no.26, p.53-55, dets.,
photos., plan, secns.
Gooiland het modernste gebouw van
Nederland: Interieurverbouwing
door Koen van Velsen / Janny
Rodermond.
Renovation of the 1936 Grand Hotel
Gooiland. Original architect: J.
Duiker. Current architect: Van
Klooster (project architect: Koen
van Velsen).
DE ARCHITECT 1990 Sept., v.21,
no.9, p.[44]-55, photos., plans,
refs.
Gooiland: verplichte kost
[exhibition review] / Jeroen
Schilt.
On the restoration of Modern
Movement buildings in the
Netherlands, including Duiker's
Gooiland in Hilversum (restoration
architects: Van Klooster and Van
Velsen). Exhibition opened on
Sept. 27, 1990.
ARCHIS 1990 Nov., no.11, p.3,
photo.
Neues aus den Niederlanden = Du
nouveau des Pays-Bas = News from
the Netherlands.
Recent Dutch architecture and city
planning projects.
WERK, BAUEN + WOHNEN 1990
Jan.-Feb., no.1-2, p.18-64,
models, maps, photos., plans,
secns., site plans, aerial photos.
Een nooduitgang voor de
Zakelijkheid: Koen van Velsens
verbouwing van Hotel Gooiland /
Arthur Wortmann.
Opened in 1936. Architect: J.
Duiker. Renovation architects:
Architectenbureau Van Klooster.
ARCHIS 1990 Sept., no.9, p.38-45,
photos., plans, secn., refs.

VELSEN, KOEN VAN, 1952- (CONTINUED)
Offentliche Bucherei in Zeewolde,
Niederlande = Public library in
Zeewolde, the Netherlands.
Architect: Koen van Velsen.
ARCHITEKTUR + WETTBEWERBE 1990
Sept., no.143, p.15-16, photos.,
site plan.
Special feature 2. New wave of
architecture in the Netherlands.
Contents: The Works of Koen van
Velsen: Library in Zeewolde, Total
Design, Royal Army and Weapon
Museum, State Academy of Fine
Arts, Graphic artist's studio and
house, Portrait of Koen van
Velsen, by Shimpachiro Ishigami,
Residence Vinkeveen,
Photographer's house and studio,
Preconceptions are Hindrance, by
Hans van Dijk. The Works of Wiel
Arets: Academy of Art, Pharmacy
and house, Fashion shop, Pharmacy.
Text in Japanese.
SPACE DESIGN 1990 Aug., no.311,
p.25-60, dwgs., elevs., photos.,
plans, secns., site plans.
Theoreticus of practicus, ethicus of
idealist... : Architecten over de
dilemmas van het restaureren /
Joris Molenaar.
Theories on renovation, with
reference to the ideas of
Hubert-Jan Henket, Wytze Patijn,
Van Velsen, Van den Thillart,
Meindert Booy, Jaap Franso, Bertus
Mulder.
ARCHIS 1990 Sept., no.9, p.24-37,
models, photos., plan, refs.

VENANT, ELIZABETH
One man's magic / Elizabeth Venant.
Features interiors of designer
Tony Duquette's home in Los
Angeles.
CONNOISSEUR 1990 Dec., v.220,
no.947, p.132-[138], ports.,
photos.

VENDER, CLAUDIO
Casa Conti, Barlassina (Como):
Claudio Vender / Manolo De Giorgi,
Luigi Spinelli.
Built 1959. Text in Italian and
English.
DOMUS 1990 Sept., no.719,
p.[116-124], photos.,plans.

VENDRELL, XAVIER, 1955-
Special feature: Commercial
interiors in Barcelona.
Contents: Between minimalism and
Movid, by Naoki Inagawa -- Alfredo
Arribas -- Josep Val and Xavier
Vendrell -- Dani Freixes and
Vicente Miranda -- Tonet Sunyer
and Jordi Badia -- Eduard Samso --
Ventura Valcarce and Carlos Valls.
Includes interviews and
biographical information and
features 13 individual commercial
projects. Text in Japanese.
SPACE DESIGN 1990 Nov.,
no.11(314), p.005-072, dets.,
ports., photos., plans, secns.,
refs.

VENEER--WOODEN
Way through the woods / Aidan
Walker.
Discussion of the use of temperate
hardwoods in light of ecological
and economic concerns.
DESIGNERS' JOURNAL 1990 June,
no.58, p.58-60, ill.

VENERIS, ELIAS
Incursione suprematista nel
Mediterraneo: Therma Hotel, baia
di Gera, Lesbo = Suprematist
incursion in the Mediterranean:
Therma Hotel, Bay of Gera, Lesvos.
Architects: Elia Zenghelis, Ron
Steiner, Elias Veneris, Zoe
Zenghelis.
LOTUS INTERNATIONAL 1986, no.52,
p.30-39, axonometric views,
elevs., models, plans, secns.,
site plans.

VENETIAN BLINDS
Doors and windows.
Eleven articles, including ones on
blinds, clasps, locks, and fire
safety.
BUILDING 1990 Feb.23, v.255, no.8
suppl., p.3-55, photos.

VENEZIA, FRANCESCO, 1944-
Francesco Venezia: Public garden,
Gibellina, Sicily, 1988.
Incomplete building without roof
as partial ruin; architect:
Francesco Venezia.
9H 1989, no.8, p.88-93, photos.,
site plan, sketch.
Progetti recenti di Francesco
Venezia / Vittorio Savi, Giordano
Tironi.
Includes restoration of Buida Oli
waterfront, Alcoy, Spain;
renovation to Palazzo Faina
museum, Orvieto; competition entry
for gardens, Park de la Fontaine,
Nimes; and urban center
alterations, San Pietro a
Patierno, Naples. Includes
English captions and summary.
CASABELLA 1990 Mar., v.54, no.566,
p.4-17,59-60, axonometric view,
models, photos., plans, secns.,
site plans, sketches.
Progetto per il Padiglione Italia
alla Biennale di Venezia = Project
for the Italian Pavilion at the
Biennnale di Venezia / Francesco
Venezia.
Architect: Francesco Venezia.
ANFIONE ZETO 1989, v.1, no.1,
p.229-237,

VENEZUELA--CARACAS--EMBASSIES--UNITED
STATES EMBASSY
Safe diplomacy: security: new
safeguards established by the U.S.
State Department / Lynn Nesmith.
On 5 new U.S. embassy projects to
be built with security
requirements of the U.S. State
Dept. Foreign Buildings
Operations.
ARCHITECTURE: THE MAGAZINE OF THE
AMERICAN INSTITUTE OF ARCHITECTS
1990 May, v.79, no.5, p.78-83,
ill., elevs., models, secn., site
plans.

VENEZUELA--HOUSING--ECONOMIC ASPECTS
Human settlement patterns in
Venezuela: the contributions of
the formal and informal housing
sectors / Christine C. Cook.
HOUSING AND SOCIETY 1988, v.15,
no.2, p.126-144, photos, map,
plans, tables, refs.

VENEZUELA--HOUSING--SOCIOLOGICAL
ASPECTS
Human settlement patterns in
Venezuela: the contributions of
the formal and informal housing
sectors / Christine C. Cook.
HOUSING AND SOCIETY 1988, v.15,
no.2, p.126-144, photos, map,
plans, tables, refs.

VENEZUELA--JUDIBANA--COMPANY TOWNS
Cross-cultural explorations in a
company town: Judibana, Venezuela.
Exchange during spring and summer
1990 with the School of
Architecture at Simon Bolivar
University, Caracas, Venezuela.
Leaders: Alex Krieger, David
Gouverneur, Jose Miguel Roig.
Projects were for urban design of
the Lagover oil company town.
GSD NEWS / HARVARD UNIVERSITY.
GRADUATE SCHOOL OF DESIGN 1990
Summer-Fall, v.19, no.1, p.11,
photo., site plans.

VENISON, TONY
Capital pastime recorded [exhibition
review] / Tony Venison.
"London's Pride," exhibition at
the Museum of London, 1990.
COUNTRY LIFE 1990 May 10, v.184,
no.19, p.100-103, ill., photos.
A caprice well named / Tony Venison.
El Capricho landscape gardens,
outside Madrid.
COUNTRY LIFE 1990 Dec.20, v.184,
no.51, p.46-49, photos.
In the footsteps of the Tudors
[gardens of Penshurst Place] /
Tony Venison.
Site: 5 mi. west of Tunbridge,
Kent.
COUNTRY LIFE 1990 June 21, v.184,
no.25, p.124-129, photos.
A place for whimsy / Tony Venison.
COUNTRY LIFE 1990 Feb.2, v.184,
no.5, p.62-64, photos.
Stylish notions [gardens of Sutton
Park, Sutton-in-the-Forest] / Tony
Venison.
Georgian gardens. Garden
consultant: Percy Cane.
COUNTRY LIFE 1990 May 3, v.184,
no.18, p.148-151, photos., site
plan.
Topiary III: Clipsham Hall / Tony
Venison.
COUNTRY LIFE 1990 Jan.25, v.184,
no.4, p.96-97, photos.
Topiary V: gazetteer: British
gardens with outstanding topiary /
Tony Venison.
Includes list of houses with
locations and hours.
COUNTRY LIFE 1990 Feb.8, v.184,
no.6, p.72-75, photos.

VENN, AXEL
Ground rules / Axel Venn.
On carpet design in the UK, the
Continent and in the U.S.
DESIGN 1990 Jan., no.443, p.44-45,
photos.

VENO, KATSUHISA
Study on the architecture of the
original Golden Hall of Toji in
early Heian Era / Katsuhisa Veno.
Text in Japanese. Includes English
summary.
NIHON KENCHIKU GAKKAI KEIKAKUKEI
RONBUN HOKOKU SHU = JOURNAL OF
ARCHITECTURE, PLANNING AND
ENVIRONMENTAL ENGINEERING 1990
Sept., no.9(415), p.111-119, plan,
secn., table, refs.

VENTILATING BUILDINGS--AUSTRIA
Gli elefanti verdi de Eilfried Huth:
torri di ventilazione autostradale
in Austria.
ARCHITETTURA; CRONACHE E STORIA
1990 Mar., v.36, no.3(413), p.212,
photos, plan.

VENTILATION
See HVAC

VENTRE, FRANCIS T.
Regulation: a realization of social
ethics / Francis T. Ventre.
Ethics relating to design, in the
U.S.
VIA 1990, no.10, p.[50]-61, dets.,
photos., sketches, tables, refs.

VENTURI AND RAUCH
Washington Avenue, Miami Beach.
One of six urban design reports
included in special issue, Urban
Concepts. Extracted from a 1979
plan for the revitalisation of the
neighborhood. Architects: Venturi
and Rauch.
ARCHITECTURAL DESIGN 1990, v.60,
no.1-2, p.70-75, dwgs., elevs.,
photos., site plans.

VENTURI, MARCO
Stahlstadt cent'anni dopo / Marco
Venturi.
Report on an international
Conference held in Terni, 1-2
Dec.1989. Title: Le citta
siderurgiche europee: progetti di
trasformazione in atto.
CASABELLA 1990 May, v.54, no.568,
p.34-35, aerial photos.

VENTURI, RAUCH AND SCOTT BROWN
La batalla del posmoderno: pugna pro
un estilo de fin de siglo / Hugh
Honour.
Focus on the Sainsbury Wing
extension to the National Gallery,
London. Architects: Venturi, Rauch
and Scott Brown. English summary,
p.84-85.
A & V 1990, no.21, p.12-19, dets.,
dwgs., models, photos.
Design awards [New Jersey Society of
Architects 1989 Design Awards
Competition].
Excellence in architecture awards
to The Hillier Group; Frederick
Schmitt; Michael Graves; Short and
Ford; Venturi, Rauch and Scott
Brown. Other awards also included.
ARCHITECTURE NEW JERSEY 1990,
(Continued next column)

VENTURI, RAUCH AND SCOTT BROWN
                            (CONTINUED)
Design awards [New... (CONTINUED)
v.26, no.1, p.9-24, axonometric
view, dwgs., elevs., models,
photos., plans, secns.
Frontis.
Painting of the construction of
the new Sainsbury wing of the
National Gallery, London, by
Andrew Norris, house assistant at
BAL's Heinz Gallery. He plans to
record every aspect of
construction.
RIBA JOURNAL 1990 Mar., v.97,
no.3, p.5, dwg.
Genius loci of Jim Thorpe,
Pennsylvania.
One of six urban design reports
included in special issue, Urban
Concepts. Extracted from a 1979
study of the Mauch Chunk Historic
District. Architects: Venturi
Rauch and Scott Brown Architects
and Planners.
ARCHITECTURAL DESIGN 1990, v.60,
no.1-2, p.52-57, elevs., photos.,
site plan.
Gordon Wu Hall Butler College en
Princeton University Princeton,
New Jersey = Gordon Wu Hall Butler
College at Princeton University
Princeton New Jersey.
Architects: Venturi, Rauch and
Scott Brown. Text in Spanish and
English.
COMPOSICION ARQUITECTONICA, ART &
ARCHITECTURE 1989 Oct., no.4,
p.[41]-52, elevs., photos., plans,
secns.
House in Long Island, New York,
design: 1985-87; completion: 1990
(est.).
A shingle style summer house.
Architects: Venturi, Rauch and
Scott Brown. Text in Japanese and
English.
GA HOUSES 1990 Mar., no.28,
p.102-103, elevs., model, plans,
secns., site plan.
Laguna Gloria Art Museum en Austin
Texas = Laguna Gloria Art Museum
in Austin Texas.
Architects: Venturi, Rauch and
Scott Brown. Text in Spanish and
English.
COMPOSICION ARQUITECTONICA, ART &
ARCHITECTURE 1989 Oct., no.4,
p.[85]-96, dwgs., ports., elevs.,
plans, secns., site plans,
sketches.
Peabody Place & Beale Street,
downtown Memphis.
One of six urban design reports
included in special issue, Urban
Concepts. Extracted from a 1987
Center City Development Plan for
Downtown Memphis.
ARCHITECTURAL DESIGN 1990, v.60,
no.1-2, p.76-97, dwgs., maps,
photos., sketches, aerial photos.
Princeton, New Jersey.
One of six urban design reports
included in special issue, Urban
Concepts. Extracted from a 1979
study for the Borough of
Princeton. Features the Palmer
Square complex. Architects:
Venturi, Rauch and Scott Brown.
ARCHITECTURAL DESIGN 1990, v.60,
no.1-2, p.58-61, dwg., photo.,
site plan, table.

VENTURI, RAUCH AND SCOTT BROWN
(CONTINUED)
The Republic Square District,
Austin.
One of six urban design reports
included in special issue, Urban
Concepts. Extracted from a 1984
plan. Designers: Venturi, Rauch
and Scott Brown.
ARCHITECTURAL DESIGN 1990, v.60,
no.1-2, p.88-95, dwgs., elevs.,
maps, photos., sketches, aerial
photo.
Special feature: Venturi Scott Brown
and Associates.
Contents: Brief history-- Works:
Primate Center, Philadelphia
Zoological Garden.-- Lewis Thomas
Laboratory for Molecular Biology,
Princeton University, 1986.--
Malcolm S. Forbes Jr. College,
Princeton University, 1984.--
Gordon Wu Hall, Princeton
University, 1983.-- Venturi house,
Philadelphia, 1974-present.--
Izenour house, Stony Creek, Conn.,
1984.-- House in New Castle
County, Delaware, 1983.--
Coxe-Hayden house, Block Island,
R.I.-- 1981.-- Tarble Student
Center, Swarthmore College,
1985.-- Tree House, Philadelphia
Zoo, 1985.-- Welcome Park,
Philadelphia, 1982.-- Decorative
designs.-- Essay: "Body language"
and artifice: on some recent
designs by Venturi Scott Brown and
Associates. Text in Japanese and
English.
ARCHITECTURE AND URBANISM 1990
June, no.6(237), p.[39]-150,
ports., elevs., photos., plans,
secns., site plans.
Unbuilt Minnesota: Venturi, Rauch &
Scott Brown's 1981 redesign
proposal for Hennepin Avenue /
Robert Gerloff.
ARCHITECTURE MINNESOTA 1990
July-Aug., v.16, no.4, p.49, ill.
Venturi, Rauch & Scott Brown:
buildings and projects [by]
Stanislaus von Moos [book review]
/ Geert Bekaert.
ARCHIS 1989 Nov., no.11, p.53,
ill.

VENTURI, ROBERT, 1925-
Architecture prete une porter.
Jewelry designed by architects,
available through Palazzetti: A
book, Jewelry by Architects, is
available.
ARCHITECTURAL RECORD 1990 Nov.,
v.178, no.12, p.[135], photos.
La contraddizione decorata = The
decorated gap / Mark Wigley.
On Denise Scott-Brown and Robert
Venturi's work, including
"Complexity and contradiction in
architecture" and "Learning from
Las Vegas."
OTTAGONO 1990 Mar., no.94,
p.36-55, dwgs., elevs., models,
photos., plans, secns., sketches,
refs.
De la invencion a la convencion en
arquitectura = From invention to
convention in architecture /
Robert Venturi.
On the "architectural implications
of our archetypal museum." This
essay has been adapted from the
(Continued next column)

VENTURI, ROBERT, 1925- (CONTINUED)
De la invencion a la...(CONTINUED)
Thomas Cubitt Lecture presented to
the Royal Society of Arts in
London, April 1987. Text in
Spanish and English.
COMPOSICION ARQUITECTONICA, ART &
ARCHITECTURE 1989 Oct., no.4,
p.[25]-40, dwg., photos.
Ein Haus wie ein Dorf / Barbara
Friedrich.
On the Alessi house, Lago d'Orta,
Italy, designed by Alessandro
Mindini. Contributing architects:
Ricardo Dalisi, Ettore Sottsass,
Robert Venturi, Achille
Castiglioni, Frank O. Gehry, Aldo
Rossi and Milton Glaser.
ARCHITEKTUR & WOHNEN 1990
Feb.-Mar., no.1, p.30-38, ports.,
photos., plans.
HB architecture today: Robert
Venturi and Denise Scott Brown
[interview] / Barbaralee
Diamonstein.
HOUSE BEAUTIFUL 1986 May, v.128,
no.5, p.172, port., photo.
JA interview: Robert Venturi and
Denise Scott Brown / Toshio
Nakamura.
JAPAN ARCHITECT 1990 May, v.65,
no.5(397), p.6-8, ports.
Museum as multinational: a new
Guggenheim in Salzburg designed by
Hans Hollein and a new
contemporary art complex in a
Massachusetts factory... / Michael
Wise, Jillian Burt.
Proposed Massachusetts Museum of
Contemporary Art, North Adams,
Mass.; architects: Frank Gehry,
Robert Venturi and David Childs.
BLUEPRINT (LONDON, ENGLAND) 1990
Oct., no.71, p.44-48, axonometric
views, models, photos.
Re-evaluation: Esther McCoy and the
Second Generation / Robert
Venturi, Denise Scott Brown.
PROGRESSIVE ARCHITECTURE 1990
Feb., v.71, no.2, p.118-119,
photos.
Residential sculpture: It's in the
Mail / Kirk Von Blunck.
Mailboxes designed by Graves,
Venturi, and Selbert.
IOWA ARCHITECT 1990 Winter., v.39,
no.4, p.5, photos.
Robert Venturi and Denise Scott
Brown speak out on issues of urban
contextualism, postmodernism and
"willful disharmony" [interview] /
Kurt Andersen.
ARCHITECTURAL DIGEST 1990 Feb.,
v.47, no.2, p.68,72,74,78,82,
ports., elevs., model, photo.

VENTURI, ROBERT, 1925---ADDRESSES,
ESSAYS, LECTURES
The hermetic fallacy / Victoria A.
Laurence.
Essay on Robert Venturi's
"Complexity and contradiction in
architecture", architectural
criticism in the 1960s, and the
Modernist mission.
CRIT 1990 Spring, no.24, p.26-28,

VENTURI, ROBERT, 1925---INFLUENCE
Wide spaces and widening chaos /
Laurie Olin.
Profile of eight Americans,
outside the profession, who have
influenced landscape architects
and landscape architecture.
LANDSCAPE ARCHITECTURE 1990 Oct.,
v.80, no.10, p.[76]-83, dwgs.,
ports.

VENTURI, ROBERT, 1925-. KOMPLEXITAT
UND WIDERSPRUCH IN DER ARCHITEKTUR
Schichten und Geschichte [book
review] / Alois Martin Muller.
Reflections on two books: Der
Internationale Stil 1932 and,
Komplexitat und Widerspruch in der
Architektur.
ARCHITHESE 1990 July-Aug., v.20,
no.4, p.58-61,66,68, dwg., photo.,
refs.

VENTURI, ROBERT, 1925-. LEARNING FROM
LAS VEGAS
Learning from the Australian
ugliness / Ian Kelly.
Presented as a paper at the
Transition Tenth Anniversary
Conference-Robin Boyd and
Australian architectural
criticism: a reassessment, in
Melbourne, July,1989.
THE ARCHITECT, W.A.: THE OFFICIAL
JOURNAL OF THE ROYAL AUSTRALIAN
INSTITUTE OF ARCHITECTS, W.A.
CHAPTER 1989, v.29, no.4,
p.[36]-40, refs.
Relearning from Las Vegas / Steven
Izenour, David A. Dashiell.
A return to Las Vegas to evaluate
how the strip has changed.
ARCHITECTURE: THE AIA JOURNAL 1990
Oct., v.79, no.10, p.[46-51],
photos.

VENTURI, SCOTT BROWN AND ASSOCIATES
Casa a Long Island, N.Y.
Architects: Robert Venturi, Denise
Scott Brown. English summary,
p.31.
METAMORFOSI 1989, no.12, p.30-32,
photos., plans.
Clinical research building School of
Medicine en University of
Pennsylvania Philadelphia
Pennsylvania = Clinical research
building School of Medicine at
University of Pennsylvania
Philadelphia Pennsylvania.
Architects: Venturi, Scott Brown
and Associates.
COMPOSICION ARQUITECTONICA, ART &
ARCHITECTURE 1989 Oct., no.4,
p.[79]-84, elevs., model, photos.,
site plan.
La contraddizione decorata = The
decorated gap / Mark Wigley.
On Denise Scott-Brown and Robert
Venturi's work, including
"Complexity and contradiction in
architecture" and "Learning from
Las Vegas."
OTTAGONO 1990 Mar., no.94,
p.36-55, dwgs., elevs., models,
photos., plans, secns., sketches,
refs.
Design 100: the people, products,
ideas that shape our lives.
"Special issue." Architects
mentioned include Venturi and
Scott Brown, Robert A. M. Stern,
(Continued next page)

VENTURI, SCOTT BROWN AND ASSOCIATES
(CONTINUED)
Design 100: the... (CONTINUED)
Frank Gehry, Richard Meier,
Morphosis, Coop Himmelblau, Andres
Duany + Elizabeth Plater-Zyberk,
Stanley Tigerman and Margaret
McCurry, Eric Owen Moss, Charles
Warren, Michael Graves, Peter
Eisenman, and Lake/Flato
Architects.
METROPOLITAN HOME 1990 Apr., v.22,
no.4, p.[67-199], ports., photos.
Doble lenguaje: escuela de
Ingenieria Thayer, New Hampshire =
A two-fold language.
Addition ot the Thayer School of
Engineering, Dartmouth College,
Hanover, NH. Architects: Venturi,
Scott Brown and Associates.
English text, p.86.
A & V 1990, no.21, p.46-48, dwgs.,
elevs., models, plans, secn., site
plans, sketches.
In the coastal vernacular: a
residence by Robert Venturi and
Denise Scott Brown / Suzanne
Stephens.
Boat-shaped home overlooking Long
Island sound. Interior designer:
Dian Boone.
ARCHITECTURAL DIGEST 1990 Dec.,
v.47, no.13, p.[112-119], port.,
photos., plan.
Philadelphia Orchestra Hall en
Philadelphia Pennsylvania =
Philadelphia Orchestra Hall in
Philadelphia Pennsylvania.
Architects: Venturi Scott Brown
and Associates. Text in Spanish
and English.
COMPOSICION ARQUITECTONICA, ART &
ARCHITECTURE 1989 Oct., no.4,
p.[61]-78, dwgs., elevs., models,
plans, site plans.
Princeton Club / Judith Nasatir.
Features renovated interiors of
New York City club. Architects:
Venturi, Scott Brown and
Associates with Anderson Schwartz
Architects.
INTERIOR DESIGN 1990 Sept., v.61,
no.12, p.174-[177], elev.,
photos., plan.
Projecto para el concurso del
Pabellon USA para la Expo'92 de
Sevilla Spain = Project for the
competition of the USA Pavilion
for the Expo'92 in Sevilla Spain.
Architects: Venturi, Scott Brown
and Associates. Text in Spanish
and English.
COMPOSICION ARQUITECTONICA, ART &
ARCHITECTURE 1989 Oct., no.4,
p.[53]-60, dwgs., elevs., plans,
secns.
Projects: Museums / Mark Alden
Branch.
On five new museums: United States
Holocaust Memorial Museum,
Washington D.C.; Massachusetts
Museum of Contemporary Art, North
Adams Mass.; Seattle Art Museum;
Museo de Arte Contemporaneo,
Barcelona; and the Newport Harbor
Art Museum, Newport Beach, Calif.
PROGRESSIVE ARCHITECTURE 1990 May,
v.71, no.5, p.124-128, axonometric
view, models, photos., plans,
secns., site plans, aerial photo.

VENTURI, SCOTT BROWN AND ASSOCIATES
(CONTINUED)
Rafael Moneo: today's American
architecture.
Report on the Gropius Lecture,
given Apr.25, 1930, in which Moneo
examined two projects: Symphony
Hall, Philadelphia (Venturi Scott
Brown and Associates) and Disney
Concert Hall, Los Angeles (Frank
Gehry and Associates).
GSD NEWS / HARVARD UNIVERSITY.
GRADUATE SCHOOL OF DESIGN 1990
Summer-Fall, v.19, no.1, p.13-14.
Utopia revised: at the University of
California at Irvine, the struggle
to adapt the unyielding geometry
of the campus continues / John
Parman.
On William Pereira's 1963 master
plan, and subsequent buildings by
other architects.
ARCHITECTURE: THE AIA JOURNAL 1990
Jan., v.79, no.1, p.66-77, dwg.,
elev., photos., plans, site plans.
Venturi et Scott Brown a
Philadelphie / Bruno Suner.
On the Philadelphia Orchestra
Hall. English summary, p.176-177.
ARCHITECTURE D'AUJOURD'HUI 1990
Apr., no.268, p.175-177, dwgs.,
model., plans, secn., site plan.

VENTURINI, ANNALISA
Rovigo e le sue difese: indagini
stratigrafiche sulla porta di San
Bartolomeo (secc.XV-XIX) / Ugo
Soragni, Stefania Ferrari,
Annalisa Venturini.
Restoration of a city gate.
English, French, German, Spanish
summaries, p.125.
STORIA DELLA CITTA 1989 Apr.-June,
v.14, no.50, p.51-76, maps,
photos., plans, tables, reconst.
dwgs.

VENUTI, GIUSEPPE CAMPOS
Il piano di Firenze e il
dimensionamento previsionale /
Giovanni Astengo, Guiseppe Campos
Venuti.
Master plan for Florence.
URBANISTICA 1989 June, no.95,
p.28-36, det., maps, plans, site
plans, tables.
Progetto urbano I = Urban Project I
/ Stefano Boeri, Francesco
Infussi, Ugo Ischia.
City planning in Italian cities.
Contributions by: Augusto
Cagnardi, Giuseppe Campos Venuti,
Bruno Gabrielli, Cesare Macchi
Cassia, Luigi Mazza, Alberto Mioni
and Uberto Siola. In Italian;
Italian and English captions;
English summary, p.121.
URBANISTICA 1989 June, no.95,
p.57-72, 121, plans, ref.

VERA, ANDRE, 1881-1971
Les freres Vera et l'art des jardins
entre les deux guerres / Catherine
Gueissaz.
English summary, p.134.
HISTOIRE DE L'ART 1990 Dec.,
no.12, p.81-89, photos.. plans,
site plans, refs.

VERA, PAUL, 1882-1957
Les freres Vera et l'art des jardins
entre les deux guerres / Catherine
Gueissaz.
English summary, p.134.
HISTOIRE DE L'ART 1990 Dec.,
no.12, p.81-89, photos., plans,
site plans, refs.

VERANDAS
See PORCHES

VERBAKEL, JOS
Thema: bouwen en milieu.
"Themanummer 38", with articles on
energy efficient housing. Authors:
Cees Zwinkels, Wim Keijsers, Jos
Verbakel, Hans Groeneveld, Chiel
Boonstra, Peter Fraanje, Tjerk
Reijenga, Frans de Haas, Joop
Niesten.
DE ARCHITECT THEMA 1990 Mar.,
v.21, no.3 suppl., p.3-63,
axonometric views, graph, elevs.,
models, photos., plans, secns.,
site plans, tables, biblios.

VERBEEK, ALBERT. ROMANISCHE BAUKUNST
AN RHEIN UND MAAS
Romanische Baukunst an Rhein und
Maas [by] Hans Erich Kubach [and]
Albert Vaerbeek [book review] /
Warren Sanderson.
Review of the final interpretative
volume (4) of
Architekturgeschichte und
Kunstland-schaft.
SOCIETY OF ARCHITECTURAL
HISTORIANS. JOURNAL 1990 Dec.,
v.49, no.4, p.441-443,

VERDA, GIANMARIA
Place de Rome in Martigny, Schweiz =
Place de Rome in Martigny,
Switzerland.
Competition. First prize winners:
Sandro Cabrini, Bruno Keller,
Gianmaria Verda. Text in German.
ARCHITEKTUR + WETTBEWERBE 1990
Dec., no.144, p.84-87, elevs.,
models, site plans.

VERDE, RUTH
Niemeyer en libertad: el Memorial de
America Latina / Ruth Verde.
In Sao Paolo, Brazil.
ARQUITECTURA VIVA 1990 Sept.-Oct.,
no.14, p.34-35, photos., sketch.

VERDERBER, STEPHEN
Dimensions of person-environment
relationships in shelters for
victims of domestic violence / Ben
J. Refuerzo, Stephen Verderber.
A study of shelters for battered
women and children, conducted in
Los Angeles and New Orleans.
Includes abstract.
JOURNAL OF ARCHITECTURAL AND
PLANNING RESEARCH 1990 Spring,
v.7, no.1, p.33-52, charts,
diagrs., photos., biblio.

VERDU BELMONTE, CARLOS
Plan especial de conservacion y
reforma interior de Antequera /
Luis Machuca, Carlos Verdu.
URBANISMO / COAM 1990 Jan., no.9,
p.57-64, photo., plans, dwgs.,
elevs., chart, axonometric views.

VERDU, MIGUEL
Arquitecturas orquestadas: los
auditorios espanoles de los
noventa / Miguel Verdu.
Projects by Jose Maria Garcia de
Paredes, and others.
ARQUITECTURA VIVA 1990 Jan.-Feb.,
no.10, p.6-10, model, photo.,
secn., table.

VEREINIGUNG DER LANDESDENKMALPFLEGE
Identitat des Objekts.
Issue devoted to a conference held
in Fulda, 6-9 June 1988, by the
Vereinigung der
Landesdenkmalpfleger in der
Bundesrepublik Deutschland.
Includes articles by Gottfried
Kiesow, Hannes Eckert, Reinhard
Bentmann, and Claus Arendt. Five
other articles are indexed
separately.
DEUTSCHE KUNST UND DENKMALPFLEGE
1988, v.46, no.2, entire issue,
ill.

VEREY, ROSEMARY
The essence of an English garden
[Barnsley House] / Margaret Parke.
In the Cotswolds. Created by
Rosemary Verey,
HOUSE BEAUTIFUL 1986 May, v.128,
no.5, p.88-[91],142-143, port.,
photos.

VERGA, CORRADO
Ricordo di Corrado Verga / Maria
Luisa Gatti Perer.
ARTE LOMBARDA 1989, no.90-91,
p.178-182,

VERGE, GENE
Buster Keaton: an Italian villa for
the great stone face / Richard W.
Bann.
1925 home in Beverly Hills.
Architect: Gene Verge.
ARCHITECTURAL DIGEST 1990 Apr.,
v.47, no.4, p.140-143,282, port.,
photos.

VERGEBOARDS
See BARGE BOARDS

VERGNOLLE, ELAINE
Fortune et infortunes du chapiteau
corinthien dans le monde roman /
Elaine Vergnolle.
In France.
REVUE DE L'ART 1990, no.90,
p.21-34, photos.

VERHELST, KAREL
Het interieur van de abtsvleugel van
de voormalige abdij van
Sint-Truiden / Karel Verhelst.
The interior of the 18th-cent.
abbot's wing in the former abbey
of Sint-Truiden. English summary,
p.63.
MONUMENTEN EN LANDSCHAPPEN 1990
Jan.-Feb., v.9, no.1, p.25-40,
photos., plans, site plan, engrs.,
refs.

VERHEYEN, FONS
NWR - BouwRAI: Verzameling
vrijblijvende experimenten / Han
Mickel, Wijnand Looise.
Projects at the annual Dutch
building exhibition held in
Almere, by Fans Verheyen, Luzia
(Continued next column)

VERHEYEN, FONS (CONTINUED)
NWR - BouwRAI:...(CONTINUED)
Hartsuyker, Teun Koolhaas
Associates, Macanoo, and others.
DE ARCHITECT 1990 May, v.21, no.5,
p.44-49, dets., dwg., photos.,
plans.

VERMEULEN, PAUL
Gehavende stad aan de Stroom:
schadum over ideeenwedstrijd
Antwerpen water front / Paul
Vermeulen.
On a new initiative, beginning in
Dec.1989 for design solutions for
Dutch waterfronts.
ARCHIS 1990 Jan., no.1, p.6-7,
model, photo.
Haalbaarheid troef: Ideeenprijsvraag
Stad aan de Stroom geevalueerd /
Paul Vermeulen.
Projects discussed include that by
Toyo Ito.
ARCHIS 1990 Nov., no.11, p.6,
model.
Kunstwerken voor het collectief
geheugen: Greisch's bruggen over
de Maas en het Albertkanaal / Paul
Vermeulen.
Four bridges over the Maas and the
Albertkanaal: Ben-Ahin, Wandre,
Lanaye, and Hermalle.
ARCHIS 1990 July, no.7, p.31-39,
dwg., photos., secn., aerial
photos., refs.
Een onaf portret:
Loos-tentoonstelling in Wenen
[exhibition review] / Paul
Vermeulen.
ARCHIS 1990 Mar., no.3, p.12-15,
dwgs., elev., models, photo.,
refs.
Ontledigde tekens: de piramide van
Pei en de boog van Von Spreckelson
/ Paul Vermeulen.
ARCHIS 1989 Oct., no.10, p.14-21,
dwgs., models, photos., secns.,
site plans, engrs., refs.
Het realisme van De Koninck:
Ontwerpen van een belgisch
modernist [exhibition review] /
Paul Vermeulen.
Exhibit at the Fondation pour
l'Architecture, Brussels, until
Apr.8,1990.
ARCHIS 1990 Feb., no.2, p.4,
photos.
Sleutelen aan het Antwerpse trauma:
Stad aan de stroom:
stedebouwkundige prijsvraag voor
Antwerps havengebied / Paul
Vermeulen.
Competition entries by Manuel de
Sola-Morales, OMA, Toyo Ito, Beth
Gali, Ben van Berkel, Yves Lion,
Bob van Reeth.
ARCHIS 1990 Sept., no.9, p.46-51,
dwgs., models, maps, site plans,
refs.

VERNACULAR ARCHITECTURE
See also REGIONALISM
A comparative study of the miners'
homes in Cornwall, England and the
miners' homes of the Cornish in
Michigan / Mary Jo Rowell Brown,
Evelyn M. Franklin.
HOUSING AND SOCIETY 1988, v.15,
no.2, p.108-125, charts, maps,
photos, plans, refs.

VERNACULAR ARCHITECTURE (CONTINUED)
Vernacular architecture: what to
learn / Victor Papanek.
ARCHITECTURE SA = ARGITEKTUUR SA
1989 July-Aug., no.7-8, p.14-18,
photos, biblio.

VERNACULAR ARCHITECTURE--17TH
CENTURY--UNITED STATES--NEW ENGLAND
Bawns and beliefs: architecture,
commerce, and conversion in early
New England / Robert Blair St.
George.
Appendix is an excerpt from a 17th
century document, "The building
and enclosing of our countrie
farm".
WINTERTHUR PORTFOLIO 1990 Winter,
v.25, no.4, p.[241]-287, dwgs.,
photos., plans, engrs., refs.

VERNACULAR ARCHITECTURE--18TH
CENTURY--UNITED STATES--NEW JERSEY
Later Dutch houses of New York &
Jersey / Russell Gilmore.
Examples from the 1770s.
OLD-HOUSE JOURNAL 1990 Mar.-Apr.,
v.18, no.2, back cover, photos.

VERNACULAR ARCHITECTURE--18TH
CENTURY--UNITED STATES--NEW YORK
(STATE)
Later Dutch houses of New York & New
Jersey / Russell Gilmore.
Examples from the 1770s.
OLD-HOUSE JOURNAL 1990 Mar.-Apr.,
v.18, no.2, back cover, photos.

VERNACULAR ARCHITECTURE--19TH
CENTURY--SOCIOLOGICAL ASPECTS--
UNITED STATES
Families and farmhouses in
Nineteenth-century America [by]
Sally McMurry [book review] /
Bernard L. Herman.
WINTERTHUR PORTFOLIO 1990 Autumn,
v.25, no.2-3, p.194-196, refs.
Families and farmhouses in
nineteenth-century America:
vernacular design and social
change [by] Sally McMurry [book
review] / J. Ritchie Garrison.
SOCIETY OF ARCHITECTURAL
HISTORIANS. JOURNAL 1990 Sept.,
v.49, no.3, p.353-354,

VERNACULAR ARCHITECTURE--19TH
CENTURY--TRINIDAD
Home and colonial: flamboyance and
nostalgia among Trinidad's
townhouses / Len Mitchell.
TRADITIONAL HOMES 1990 Mar., v.6,
no.6, p.127-130, photos.

VERNACULAR ARCHITECTURE--19TH
CENTURY--UNITED STATES--BERKS COUNTY
(PENNSYLVANIA)
Vernacular Houses: two-door houses /
Michelle Nicholl.
One of the mast common house types
in western Berks Co., Penn.,
evolved from the traditional
Pennsylvania Deutsch farmhouse.
OLD-HOUSE JOURNAL 1990 May-June,
v.18, no.3, p.[4] of cover,
photos., plan.

VERNACULAR ARCHITECTURE--19TH CENTURY--UNITED STATES--MAINE--INFLUENCE
Harboring tradition: for a new marine museum on the coast of Maine, architect Winton Scott was inspired by the powerful industrial vernacular of a local 19th-century foundry / Nancy Levinson.
The Maine Maritime Museum, Bath.
ARCHITECTURAL RECORD 1990 June, v.178, no.7, p.72-[75], photos, plans, secn.

VERNACULAR ARCHITECTURE--19TH CENTURY--UNITED STATES--TENNESSEE
Vernacular houses: Middle Tennessee I-house / Claudette Stager, Elizabeth Straw.
A regional interpretation of the central-passage house, frequently embellished with Greek revival details, built from the 1820s to 1880s.
OLD-HOUSE JOURNAL 1990 Sept.-Oct., v.18, no.5, p.[4] of cover, photos., plan.

VERNACULAR ARCHITECTURE--20TH CENTURY--CRITICISM--JAPAN
"Japaneseness" among the Japanese architects who supported rationalism in the late 1920s and the 1930s / Hiroyasu Fujioka.
Text in Japanese. English summary, p.173.
NIHON KENCHIKU GAKKAI KEIKAKUKEI RONBUN HOKOKU SHU = JOURNAL OF ARCHITECTURE, PLANNING AND ENVIRONMENTAL ENGINEERING 1990 June, no.6(412), p.173-180, refs.

VERNACULAR ARCHITECTURE--20TH CENTURY--UNITED STATES--OZARK MOUNTAINS
Vernacular houses: Ozark giraffes / Stephen B. Jordan.
Sandstone houses with painted mortar were built 1920-1940 and are found in Ark., Mo. and Okla.
OLD-HOUSE JOURNAL 1990 Jan.-Feb., v.18, no.1, p.back cover, photos.

VERNACULAR ARCHITECTURE--AUSTRALIAN ABORIGINAL--INFLUENCE
Architetture per gli aborigeni = The dark side architectures for aborigines / Paolo Tombesi.
Features two projects: Mutitjulu Community Housing near Ayers Rock, architect: Paul Pholeros and the Aboriginal Alcoholic Rehabilitation Centre, Kinchela Creek, architect: Glenn Murcutt.
SPAZIO E SOCIETA 1990 Jan.-Mar., v.13, no.49, p.94-105, dwgs., elevs., models, photos., plans, secns., site plans.

VERNACULAR ARCHITECTURE--BRAZIL--AMAZUNIA--INFLUENCE
Retiro Tagaste, uma arquitectura para a Amazonia / Joao Castro Filho.
Retiro Tagaste, Ananincleua, Brazil. Architect: J. Castro Filho.
PROJETO 1990 Apr., no.130, p.106-111, photos., secns., site plan.

VERNACULAR ARCHITECTURE--CANADA
Byzantium on the prairies: the eccentric heritage of Father Philip Ruh / Robert Hunter.
The French priest was responsible for the building of numerous Ukrainian-style churches in Canada from 1913 through 1960.
CANADIAN HERITAGE 1990 spring, v.15, no.4, p.14-18,37,41,43, port., photos.

VERNACULAR ARCHITECTURE--CANADA--NOVA SCOTIA--INFLUENCE
Maritime journey / Brian Carter.
Features three contemporary "sheds" in Nova Scotia designed by Canadian architect Brian MacKay-Lyons and two recent projects in Halifax.
ARCHITECTURAL REVIEW 1990 Nov., v.188, no.1125, p.68-77, dwgs., elevs., photos., plans, secns., site plan.

VERNACULAR ARCHITECTURE--CHINA
Chinese architecture, palaces and Imperial gardens / Laurence G. Liu.
ARCHITECTURAL DESIGN 1989, v.59, no.11-12, p.XVI-XXX, photos.
The other China: China's vernacular architecture: house form and culture, by Ronald G. Knapp [book review] / Richard Weston.
ARCHITECTS' JOURNAL 1990 Mar.14, v.191, no.11, p.94, axonometric view.
Rammed citadels, wonders of South Fujian Province / Huang Hanmin.
On traditional four or five-story collective dwellings, their types, and shapes.
BUILDING IN CHINA 1989 Dec., v.2, no.4, p.29-36,28,inside cover, dwgs., port., map, photos., plans.

VERNACULAR ARCHITECTURE--CHINA--HUIZHOU
Vernacular dwellings in Huizhou / Zhou Yuangyang.
Houses in Anhui Province with white washed walls, small dark tiles, decorated gable walls, and ornamental carved window frames.
BUILDING IN CHINA 1990 Mar., v.3, no.1, p.27-29, [2 p. photos insert], photos.

VERNACULAR ARCHITECTURE--CONSERVATION AND RESTORATION--ENGLAND--WHITWELL
Renovation case history no.64: an example to us all.
Derbyshire Co. Council repaired 4 neglected houses in Whitwell.
TRADITIONAL HOMES 1990 Jan., v.6, no.4, p.22-28, dwgs., dets., photos., plans, secn.

VERNACULAR ARCHITECTURE DOCUMENTATION--AUSTRALIA--NEW SOUTH WALES
Recording vernacular rural structures in New South Wales / Peter Freeman.
ASSOCIATION FOR PRESERVATION TECHNOLOGY BULLETIN 1990, v.22, no.1-2, p.39-43, ill., map, photos., site plan, refs.

VERNACULAR ARCHITECTURE--ENGLAND--CHESHIRE
Vive la difference: the various regional styles of the Northwest of England / Bill Laws.
TRADITIONAL HOMES 1990 July, v.6, no.10, p.15-20, photos., refs.

VERNACULAR ARCHITECTURE--ENGLAND--COTSWOLDS
Vernacular architecture: limestone country / Andrew Sim.
Houses along the "Cotswold limestone belt" of England.
TRADITIONAL HOMES 1990 Aug., v.6, no.11, p.15-20, photos.

VERNACULAR ARCHITECTURE--ENGLAND--LANCASHIRE
Vive la difference: the various regional styles of the Northwest of England / Bill Laws.
TRADITIONAL HOMES 1990 July, v.6, no.10, p.15-20, photos., refs.

VERNACULAR ARCHITECTURE--ENGLAND--NORTH YORKSHIRE
Pastoral peace: the traditional housing of the sheep-farming areas of North Yorkshire / Bill Laws.
TRADITIONAL HOMES 1990 Apr., v.6, no.7, p.36-40, photos., biblios.

VERNACULAR ARCHITECTURE--ENGLAND--NORTHUMBERLAND
Vernacular architecture: feudal and far between / Andrew Sim.
A trip to the "landowner's landscape" of the far Northeast England, mostly featuring fortified sandstone houses of the upper classes.
TRADITIONAL HOMES 1990 Sept., v.6, no.12, p.89-92, photos.

VERNACULAR ARCHITECTURE--ENGLAND--WESTERN HOME COUNTIES
Vernacular architecture: home assortment: the varied buildings of the Western Home Counties / Andrew Sim.
The counties surrounding London.
TRADITIONAL HOMES 1990 June, v.6, no.9, p.33-36, photos, ref.

VERNACULAR ARCHITECTURE--FINLAND
Trond M E Dancke: Opp av ruinene, Gjenreisningen av Finnmark 1945-1960 [book review] / Ingebjorg Hage.
BEBYGGELSEHISTORISK TIDSKRIFT 1989, no.17-18, p.187-190, dwgs., plans.

VERNACULAR ARCHITECTURE FORUM (U.S.)
Perspectives in vernacular architecture, III [edited by] Thomas Carter and Bernard L. Herman [book review] / Richard M. Candee
Review of volume of 10 essays originally presented as papers at the 1985, 1986, and 1987 Perspectives in Vernacular Architecture conferences.
WINTERTHUR PORTFOLIO 1990 Autumn, v.25, no.2-3, p.191-194,

VERNACULAR ARCHITECTURE--FRANCE--
CEVENNES VALLEY
Rural society and protected area:
which dialogue? The case study of
Cevennes National Park and
Biosphere Reserve (France) /
Gerald Collin.
Reference is made to the form of
the vernacular architecture of the
area.
LANDSCAPE AND URBAN PLANNING 1990
May, v.19, no.2, p.173-180,
photos., refs.

VERNACULAR ARCHITECTURE--GERMANY
(EAST)--WAREN
Stadtbildsanierung durch Eigenheime
in Waren-Murits / Harald Korthals.
Examples of new houses and infill
homes that blend with existing
traditional structures in this
area of E. Germany. Architects:
Wolfgang Hermann (design), Harald
Korthals (project).
ARCHITEKTUR DER DDR 1989 Nov.,
v.38, no.11, p.26-28, elevs.,
photos., plan, secn.

VERNACULAR ARCHITECTURE--GREAT BRITAIN
The British Isles [book review].
Reviews of recent books on Inigo
Jones, Wren's design of St.
Paul's, John Claudius Loudon, six
vernacular topics. Reviewers: John
Bold, A. A. Tait, Anthony Quiney.
SOCIETY OF ARCHITECTURAL
HISTORIANS. JOURNAL 1990 June,
v.49, no.2, p.217-221,

VERNACULAR ARCHITECTURE--GREECE--
RHODES
"Pastori-architetti" dell'Isola di
Rodi / Roberta Maculan.
AREA 1989 July-Aug., v.9, no.47,
p.34-[39], photos.

VERNACULAR ARCHITECTURE--GREECE--
SANTORINI
Sudliches Licht: Kykladenarchitektur
auf der griechischen Insel
Santorin / Gerhard Ullmann.
DER ARCHITEKT 1990 Sept., no.9,
p.403-404, photos.

VERNACULAR ARCHITECTURE--GUINEA
Los mosquees peules du Fouta-Djalon,
l'exemple de Kamsa-Gawol /
Fracoise Doutreuwe, Bernard
Salvaing.
Discussion of 1980 mud mosque
complex in the Fouta Djallon
region of Guinea. Summaries in
English, Italian and Spanish.
ICOMOS INFORMATION 1990 Apr.-June,
no.2, p.17-29, maps, photos.,
plans, secns., site plan, biblio.,
refs.

VERNACULAR ARCHITECTURE--INDIA
A master builder: Amritbhai Sompura
[interview] / A. G. Krishna Menon.
The ca. 80-year old architect of
temples, also known by the surname
Trivedi.
ARCHITECTURE + DESIGN 1989
Nov.-Dec., v.6, no.1, p.121,123,
port., secn.
Ta'zia: ephemeral architecture in
India / Shakeel Hossain.
Ta'zias are decorative miniature
mausoleums used in festive
processions.
(Continued next column)

VERNACULAR ARCHITECTURE--INDIA
(CONTINUED)
Ta'zia: ephemeral...(CONTINUED)
MIMAR: ARCHITECTURE IN DEVELOPMENT
1990 June, v.10, no.2(35),
p.[10]-17, photos., refs.

VERNACULAR ARCHITECTURE--INDIA--
INFLUENCE
Indian reflection / Gautam Bhatia.
Seven homes in India which rely on
regional architecture and
craftsmen. Architects: Vasant and
Revathi Kamath, Romi Khosla,
Jaimini Mehta, Laurie Baker and
Ramu Katakham.
ARCHITECTURAL REVIEW 1990 Nov.,
v.188, no.1125, p.[82]-89, dwgs.,
elevs., photos., plans, secns.,
site plans.

VERNACULAR ARCHITECTURE--INDONESIA--
BALI
Amandari, Ubud, Bali.
A traditional style hotel in a
site selected to reflect the
cultural diversity of the
surroundings. Architect: Peter
Muller.
MIMAR: ARCHITECTURE IN DEVELOPMENT
1990 Sept., v.10, no.3(36),
p.24-[29], maps, photos., plan,
secn., site plan.

VERNACULAR ARCHITECTURE--IRELAND
Irish-vernacular architecture: an
illustration of semiotic analysis
/ Ann C. Ziebarth.
Studies "the interaction of
culture and design."
HOUSING AND SOCIETY 1990, v.17,
no.1, p.27-34, plans, refs.

VERNACULAR ARCHITECTURE--ISLAMIC
COUNTRIES
Hassan Fathy: the new
traditionalists / James Steele.
ARCHITECTURAL DESIGN 1989, v.59,
no.11-12, p.ii-vii, dwg., elevs.,
plan, secns., site plans.

VERNACULAR ARCHITECTURE--ITALY
Case come gioielli: il Neobarocco
Boemo / Alfredo Zappa.
Featuring the painted facades of
houses in the former province of
Bohemia.
VILLE GIARDINI 1990 July-Aug.,
no.250, p.[32]-41, photos.

VERNACULAR ARCHITECTURE--ITALY--
SARDINIA--INFLUENCE
Gut versteckt.... / Antje Suchting.
Features home on the Costa
Smeralda of Sardinia owned by a
family from Hamburg.
ARCHITEKTUR & WOHNEN 1990
June-July, no.3, p.[52]-57, port.,
photos.

VERNACULAR ARCHITECTURE--JAPAN
Representing traditional Japanese
architecture, part 3: Concepts of
architecture space within linear
perspective and cubism / J.
Lawrence Mattot.
Text in Japanese.
SPACE DESIGN 1990 Nov.,
no.11(314), p.089-092, axonometric
view, ill, photos., plan, refs.

VERNACULAR ARCHITECTURE--JAPAN
(CONTINUED)
Representing traditional Japanese
architecture, part 1: Introduction
/ J. Lawrence Matott.
Refers to influences on Frank
Lloyd Wright. Text in Japanese.
SPACE DESIGN 1990 July, no.310,
p.93-96, dwgs., photos., plans,
refs.
Representing traditional Japanese
architecture, part 2: Awareness of
Japanese space / J. Lawrence
Matott.
Text in Japanese.
SPACE DESIGN 1990 Oct.,
no.10(313), p.155-160, photos.,
plans, engrs., isometric dwgs.,
refs.
Representing traditional Japanese
architecture, part 4: Today's
media and spatial representation /
J. Lawrence Matott.
Text in Japanese.
SPACE DESIGN 1990 Dec.,
no.12(315), p.69-72, ill., refs.
Size and layout of structural
members about Japanese wooden
building systems / Takashi Oono.
"A research survey on carpenter's
or builder's knowledges [sic] and
skills to work about wooden
building systems in Tokyo and
Kanagawa (Part 2)". In Japanese;
English summary, p.17.
NIHON KENCHIKU GAKKAI KEIKAKUKEI
RONBUN HOKOKU SHU = JOURNAL OF
ARCHITECTURE, PLANNING AND
ENVIRONMENTAL ENGINEERING 1990
May, no.5(411), p.17-23, graphs,
plans, tables, refs.
Study on the historical evolution of
the town housing types in the
built-up area where Samurai
classes had inhabited in Edo area
/ Shingo Tamaki, Tatsuo Masuta.
"Case study in Kanazawa City, part
6". Text in Japanese. Includes
English summary.
NIHON KENCHIKU GAKKAI KEIKAKUKEI
RONBUN HOKOKU SHU = JOURNAL OF
ARCHITECTURE, PLANNING AND
ENVIRONMENTAL ENGINEERING 1990
June [July], no.7(413), p.49-60,
photos., plans, tables, refs.

VERNACULAR ARCHITECTURE--JAPAN--
INFLUENCE
New trends of Japanese-style
architecture.
Three new projects, indexed
separately.
JAPAN ARCHITECT 1990 May, v.65,
no.5(397), p.[9]-50, axonometric
view, dets., elevs., photos.,
plans, secns., site plan.

VERNACULAR ARCHITECTURE--JAPAN--KYOTO
The characteristics and developing
processes of the town houses in
Sonobe, and old castle town /
Osamu Oba.
Text in Japanese; English summary,
p.119.
NIHON KENCHIKU GAKKAI KEIKAKUKEI
RONBUN HOKOKU SHU = JOURNAL OF
ARCHITECTURE, PLANNING AND
ENVIRONMENTAL ENGINEERING 1990
June, no.6(412), p.119-131, maps,
plans, secns., tables, ref.

VERNACULAR ARCHITECTURE--KENYA
Journey in African savanna:
recollections of an unrecorded
continent / Shikiko Saito.
Text in Japanese.
SPACE DESIGN 1990 Dec.,
no.12(315), p.53-60, photos.

VERNACULAR ARCHITECTURE--KOREA--HAHOE
A research on the spatial
composition of the traditional
houses in Hahoe, Korea / Jeongsik
Cho, Kiyoshi Kawasaki, Masamai
Kobayashi.
"About classification of plan type
and spatial sparation for men and
women". Text in Japaenese;
includes English summary.
NIHON KENCHIKU GAKKAI KEIKAKUKEI
RONBUN HOKOKU SHU = JOURNAL OF
ARCHITECTURE, PLANNING AND
ENVIRONMENTAL ENGINEERING 1990
Nov., no.11(417), p.51-60, plans,
tables.

VERNACULAR ARCHITECTURE--LIBERIA
A land and life folk remembered:
Americo-Liberian folk architecture
[book review] / James Borchert.
Review of catalog by Svend E.
Holsoe and Bernard L. Herman,
published in conjunction with a
1988 exhibition.
WINTERTHUR PORTFOLIO 1990 Autumn,
v.25, no.2-3, p.199-201, refs.

VERNACULAR ARCHITECTURE--LIBYA
Oasis towns in Libyan arab
Jamahiriya, A special case-study:
Ghadames / Flemming Aalund.
Summaries in French, Italian and
Spanish.
ICOMOS INFORMATION 1989 Jan.-Mar.,
no.1, p.3-9, map, photos., plans,
secn., biblio.

VERNACULAR ARCHITECTURE--MALAWI
Bedre dansk byggeskik i Malawi /
Birthe Lauritsen.
Recent building supervised by
Danish architect Uffe Leinum.
ARKITEKTEN 1990 Mar., v.92, no.3,
p.98-99, dwgs., photos.

VERNACULAR ARCHITECTURE--MEXICO--
INFLUENCE
Mikhail Baryshnikov on St.
Barthelemy / Philippe Seulliet.
Features the interiors of
neighboring Mexican vernacular
style vacation houses owned by the
dancer. Architect: Rob Miles
Reincke. Interior designer: Bille
du Mesnil.
ARCHITECTURAL DIGEST 1990 Aug.,
v.47, no.8, p.132-137, photos.

VERNACULAR ARCHITECTURE--MUD--YEMEN
Building on the organic / Clare
Melhuish.
On the work of Dr. Samar Damluji
on Yemen's mud-brick architecture.
BUILDING DESIGN 1990 May 11,
no.985, p.28-33, elevs., photos.,
plans, secns.

VERNACULAR ARCHITECTURE--NEPAL
The merging of traditional and
modern cultures in Nepal / Onju
Roy.
ARCHITECTURE + DESIGN 1990
May-June, v.7, no.3, p.73-80,
maps, photos., plans, secns., site
plans.

VERNACULAR ARCHITECTURE--NIGERIA
Building in the Air and Tenere
Region, Niger / John Norton.
On building associated with a
conservation program for the
sub-Saharan strip.
MIMAR: ARCHITECTURE IN DEVELOPMENT
1990 Mar., v.10, no.1(34),
p.[50]-57, photos.

VERNACULAR ARCHITECTURE--NORWAY
Linked with the landscape: Norway's
delicately decorative buildings
have survived a tough history and
a harsh climate.
Fantoft Church; Bryggen Hansa
merchant's buildings; and the home
of Edvard Grieg.
TRADITIONAL HOMES 1990 Feb., v.6,
no.5, p.107-109, photos.

VERNACULAR ARCHITECTURE--NORWAY--
INFLUENCE
Nature trail / Ulf Gronvold.
On the Friluftshuset at Orre
beach, Norway, an information and
exhibition pavilion. Architect:
Per Line.
ARCHITECTURAL REVIEW 1990 Sept.,
v.188, no.1123, p.87-90, photos.,
plans, secns.

VERNACULAR ARCHITECTURE--SANTA FE
STYLE--UNITED STATES--SANTA FE (NEW
MEXICO)
Santa Fe's Westside/Guadalupe
Historic District: Hispanic
vernacular versus Pueblo revival /
Beverly Spears.
NEW MEXICO ARCHITECTURE 1990
Sept.-Dec., v.31, no.5-6, p.9-13,
cover, photos.

VERNACULAR ARCHITECTURE--SCOTLAND
Crofts to castles: the classic
dwelling types of the Highlands
and Islands / Geoffrey Stell.
TRADITIONAL HOMES 1990 Mar., v.6,
no.6, p.14-18, photos., biblio.
Scottish ancestral homes.
COLONIAL HOMES 1990 June, v.16,
no.3, p.[86-87],150, photos.
Vernacular architecture: Scottish
division: the homes of the border
/ Geoffrey Stell.
TRADITIONAL HOMES 1990 Jan., v.6,
no.4, p.16-20, photos., biblios.

VERNACULAR ARCHITECTURE--SCOTLAND--
CENTRAL LOWLANDS
Heart of stone: the unique character
of vernacular architecture in
Scotland's Central Lowlands /
Geoffrey Stell.
TRADITIONAL HOMES 1990 Feb., v.6,
no.5, p.35-39, photos., biblio.

VERNACULAR ARCHITECTURE--SCOTLAND--
INFLUENCE
James MacLaren / Alan Calder.
Townhouses in Bayswater, London,
and cottages in Glenlyon,
Scotland, by Arts and Crafts
architect James MacLaren.
Exhibition of the architect's
works at the Heinz Gallery,
London, beginning Jan.1990.
ARCHITECTS' JOURNAL 1990 Jan.17,
v.191, no.3, p.34-53, dets.,
dwgs., ports., photos., plans,
sketches, refs.
Modern history [Scandic Crown Hotel,
Edinburgh] / Malcolm Fraser.
250 bedroom hotel on Edinburgh's
Royal Mile. Architect: Ian Begg.
ARCHITECTS' JOURNAL 1990 Apr.25,
v.191, no.17, p.26-29, dwg.,
photos., plan, secns., site plan.
A new direction / Brian Edwards.
Addition to Scottish croft north
of Glasgow. Architects: McGurn
Logan Duncan & Opfer.
BUILDING DESIGN 1990 June 8,
no.989, p.20-23, elevs., photos.,
plans.

VERNACULAR ARCHITECTURE--SOCIOLOGICAL
ASPECTS--JAPAN
Study on the patterns and its
historical evolution process of
popular dwelling in the built-up
area where Samurai classes had
inhabited in Edo era / Tatsuo
Masuta.
Text in Japanese; English summary,
p.107.
NIHON KENCHIKU GAKKAI KEIKAKUKEI
RONBUN HOKOKU SHU = JOURNAL OF
ARCHITECTURE, PLANNING AND
ENVIRONMENTAL ENGINEERING 1990
Mar., no.3(409), p.95-107,
photos., plans, refs.

VERNACULAR ARCHITECTURE--SOCIOLOGICAL
ASPECTS--LEBANON
Reconstruction and cultural
considerations: the case of war
damaged villages in Lebanon /
Souheil El-Masri.
URBAN FUTURES 1989 Winter, v.2,
no.4, p.45-53, axonometric views,
charts, diagrs., maps, plans,
secns., sketches, tables, biblio.

VERNACULAR ARCHITECTURE--SOCIOLOGICAL
ASPECTS--UNITED STATES
Using ethnic history to understand
urban landscapes / Dolores Hayden.
PLACES 1990 Fall, v.7, no.1,
p.[10]-17, photos., refs.

VERNACULAR ARCHITECTURE--SOUTH AFRICA
Spazas of Khayelitsha / Martin Duys.
On the informal and improvisatory
nature of shops, called spazas in
Xhosa.
ADA: ARCHITECTURE, DESIGN, ART
1989, no.7, p.48-49, photos.

VERNACULAR ARCHITECTURE--SOUTH
AFRICA--HISTORY
Origins and diffusion of vernacular
architecture in Southern Africa /
Dennis Radford.
ARCHITECTURE SA = ARGITEKTUUR SA
1989 July-Aug., no.7-8, p.13-14,
elev., maps, photos, refs.

VERNACULAR ARCHITECTURE--SOUTH
AFRICA--NATAL
Gable and hip on street and farm:
Voortrekker houses in Natal /
Brian Kearney.
ARCHITECTURE SA = ARGITEKTUUR SA
1989 July-Aug., no.7-8, p.32-36,
dwg., site plan, refs.

VERNACULAR ARCHITECTURE--SOVIET
UNION--INFLUENCE
Russian reverie: Yves Saint Laurent
retreats to a dacha on his Norman
estate / Edmund White.
Russian-style dacha near his
chateau at Deauville.
HOUSE & GARDEN 1990 Jan., v.162,
no.1, p.[118-123],146, port.,
photos.

VERNACULAR ARCHITECTURE--SOVIET
UNION--SAMARKAND
Images of Samarkand / Klaus Herdeg.
On changes in Uzbek since the
author's visit in 1975.
MIMAR: ARCHITECTURE IN DEVELOPMENT
1990 Dec., v.10, no.4(37),
p.12-[19], axonometric view, map,
photos.

VERNACULAR ARCHITECTURE--SRI LANKA
Architecture Sri Lanka.
Feature of issue. Includes two
articles separately indexed;
Foreword by Ashok B. Lall; Trends
and transitions, by Anjalendran C.
and Rajiv Wanasundara; The Sri
Lankan vernacular; The eighties.
ARCHITECTURE + DESIGN 1990
Mar.-Apr., v.7, no.2, p.23-113,
dwgs., photos., plans, secns.,
site plans.

VERNACULAR ARCHITECTURE--STONE--
ENGLAND--SOUTH PENNINES
Vernacular architecture: industrial
legacy: the traditional stonework
of the South Pennines / Bill Laws.
TRADITIONAL HOMES 1990 May, v.6,
no.8, p.37-40, dets., photos.,
biblio.

VERNACULAR ARCHITECTURE--SWEDEN
A homemade house [Lilla Hyttnas] /
Witold Rybczynski.
The home of artist Carl Larsson
and his wife Karin, a traditional
log cabin in Sundborn, over 100
miles from Stockholm.
ART & ANTIQUES 1990 Dec., v.7,
no.10, p.[74]-81,120, ports.,
photos.

VERNACULAR ARCHITECTURE--SWEDEN--
GOTLAND
Gotland - an island in the Baltic
Sea / Rebecka Tarchys.
Views of traditional buildings and
related arts.
LIVING ARCHITECTURE 1990, no.9,
p.110-139, photos.

VERNACULAR ARCHITECTURE--SWITZERLAND--
ENGADINE
"Chesa" engadinese = An Engadin
"chesa".
Restoration of 17th-cent. Swiss
house. Architect: Hans-Jorg Ruch
of Ruch & Husler.
ABITARE 1990 Mar., no.283,
p.134-139, photos., plans, secn.

VERNACULAR ARCHITECTURE--SWITZERLAND--
FREIBURG
Jean-Pierre Anderegg: Die
Bauernhauser des Kantons Freiburg
[book review] / Peter F. Kopp.
ZEITSCHRIFT FUR SCHWEIZERISCHE
ARCHAOLOGIE UND KUNSTGESCHICHTE
1989, v.46, no.4, p.323-325, plan.

VERNACULAR ARCHITECTURE--THAILAND--
INFLUENCE
Mystik auf Stelzen / Erdtrud
Muhlens.
Features Suhid and Diether von
Boehm-Bezing's vacation home in
Ban Wart Nam Ton, Thailand.
English summary, p.2.
ARCHITEKTUR & WOHNEN 1990
Aug.-Sept., no.4, p.48-53,
photos., plan.

VERNACULAR ARCHITECTURE--THEORY
Mellan hem och Yttervarld / Mats
Widbom.
Report on a seminar on
ethnological aspects of domestic
architecture.
ARKITEKTUR: THE SWEDISH REVIEW OF
ARCHITECTURE 1990 Aug., v.90,
no.6, p.32-33, photo.

VERNACULAR ARCHITECTURE--TURKEY
Analysis of space in Turkish folk
houses / Tatsuya Yamamoto.
Text in Japanese.
SPACE DESIGN 1990 Feb., no.305,
p.45-68, dets., map, photos.,
plans, table.
Ayder Mezra: thematic variation in
middle meadow houses / Bill Boehm.
A typological study of seasonal
mountain houses in Turkey.
MIMAR: ARCHITECTURE IN DEVELOPMENT
1990 Sept., v.10, no.3(36),
p.13-17, photos., sketches.

VERNACULAR ARCHITECTURE--UNITED STATES
Builder style: America's little
houses / James C. Massey, Shirley
Maxwell.
Homestead, Foursquare, Cottage,
and Bungalow styles.
OLD-HOUSE JOURNAL 1990 Sept.-Oct.,
v.18, no.5, p.45-49, ill., photos.
Luoghi di bellezza fotografati /
Bruce J. Archer.
Photographs of American roadside
beauty salons by John Margolies.
Text in Italian and English.
DOMUS 1990 Jan., no.712, p.8-9,
photos.

VERNACULAR ARCHITECTURE--UNITED
STATES--ADDRESSES, ESSAYS, LECTURES
Perspectives in vernacular
architecture, III [edited by]
Thomas Carter and Bernard L.
Herman [book review] / Richard M.
Candee.
Review of volume of 18 essays
originally presented as papers at
the 1985, 1986, and 1987
Perspectives in Vernacular
Architecture conferences.
WINTERTHUR PORTFOLIO 1990 Autumn,
v.25, no.2-3, p.191-194,

VERNACULAR ARCHITECTURE--UNITED
STATES--EAU CLAIRE (WISCONSIN)
The character of place: building
materials and architectural
characteristics in Eau Claire,
Wisconsin / Ingolf Vogeler.
Analysis of house styles
(1860's-1970's) using field
observations and data obtained
from the assessor's office.
MATERIAL CULTURE 1990 Spring,
v.22, no.1, p.1-21, graphs, maps,
biblio.

VERNACULAR ARCHITECTURE--UNITED
STATES--EMBARASS (MINNESOTA)
Diamonds in the fields: a
northern-Minnesota town discovers
a national treasure in its unsung
architecture / Adelheid Fischer.
Log structures built by Finnish
settlers in Embarass, Minn.
ARCHITECTURE MINNESOTA 1990
July-Aug., v.16, no.4, p.32-39,
ports., photos.

VERNACULAR ARCHITECTURE--UNITED
STATES--ILLINOIS
Architecture in the United States
[book review] / Rhodri Windsor
Liscombe, John Vincent Boyer,
William G. Farrar, IV, Robert
Winter.
Review of Charleston antebellum
architecture and civic destiny, by
Kenneth Severens; Structures and
styles: guided tours of Hartford
architecture, by Gregory E.
Andrews and David F. Ransom;
Vernacular architecture in
southern Illinois, by John M.
Coggeshall and Jo Anne Nast; and
Bruce Goff: toward aboslute
architecture, by David Delong.
SOCIETY OF ARCHITECTURAL
HISTORIANS. JOURNAL 1990 Mar.,
v.49, no.1, p.115-120,

VERNACULAR ARCHITECTURE--UNITED
STATES--MINNESOTA
Into the woods [outhouses].
ARCHITECTURE MINNESOTA 1990
July-Aug., v.16, no.4, p.12-13,
photos.
Little house on the ice.
Minn. ice-fishing huts.
ARCHITECTURE MINNESOTA 1990
Jan.-Feb., v.16, no.1, p.[42-45],
photos.

VERNACULAR ARCHITECTURE--UNITED
STATES--NORTH CAROLINA
Pride and prejudice: the Appalachian
boxed house in southwestern North
Carolina / Michael Ann Williams.
WINTERTHUR PORTFOLIO 1990 Winter,
v.25, no.4, p.[217]-230, photos.,
refs.

VERNACULAR ARCHITECTURE--UNITED
STATES--PENSACOLA (FLORIDA)
Vernacular houses: Pensacola Creole
cottages / Diana Jarvis Godwin.
OLD-HOUSE JOURNAL 1990 July-Aug,
v.18, no.4, p.[4] of cover,
photos., plan.

VERNACULAR ARCHITECTURE--UNITED
STATES--SOUTHERN STATES
The complex origins of the American
domestic piazza-veranda-gallery /
Jay Edwards.
MATERIAL CULTURE 1989 Summer,
v.21, no.2, p.2-58, axonometric
views, dwgs., elev., maps,
photos., plans, engrs., biblio.

VERNACULAR ARCHITECTURE--YEMAN--SANAA
Bilder aus dem Jeman / Brigette
Hellgoth.
Views of buildings in Sanaa,
northwest Yemen.
BAUWELT 1990 Sept.14, v.81, no.35,
p.1722-1724, 1729-1731, photos.

VERNACULAR ARCHITECTURE--YEMEN
Cities and villages of the Yemen
Arab Republic / Satoshi Ueda.
Includes "The contemporary
significance of the Islamic city",
by Nobuhide Jinnai. Text in
Japanese.
SPACE DESIGN 1990 Sept., no.312,
p.077-088, maps, photos., plans,
secns., refs.

VERNACULAR ARCHITECTURE--YORUBA--
NIGERIA
The traditional housing of Yoruba
towns in south western Nigeria /
Ralph Mills-Tettey.
INTERNATIONAL JOURNAL FOR HOUSING
SCIENCE AND ITS APPLICATIONS 1990,
v.14, no.1, p.047-055, maps,
plans, secns., refs.

VERNES, MICHEL
Cuisines / Michel Vernes.
On kitchen history, design and
equipment. English summary,
p.215.
ARCHITECTURE INTERIEURE CREE 1990
Oct.-Nov., no.239, p.162-191,
ill., photos.
Cuisines / Michel Vernes.
On the history of kitchens.
ARCHITECTURE INTERIEURE CREE 1990
June-July, no.237, p.[80-89],
photos., engrs.

VERNIER, PHILIPPE
Al di la della facciata = Beyond the
facade / Philippe Vernier.
Contents: OXY building and
D-Hotel, Tokyo, Japan; architects:
Kiyoshi Sey Takeyama and Amphore
Architects and Associates.
Includes essay: From
trans-territory to another world:
OXY building and D-Hotel / Kiyoshi
Sey Takeyama. Text in Italian and
English.
L'ARCA 1990 Feb., no.35, p.12-23,
axonometric view, elevs., photos,
plans, secns.
L'Italian Community Center di
Milwaukee = The Italian Community
Center in Milwaukee / Philippe
Vernier.
15 acre redevelopment project;
architects: Bonifica spa (Gruppo
Iri-Italstat).
L'ARCA 1990 July-Aug., no.40,
p.12-19, dwgs., site plans,
sketches, aerial photo.

VERNIER, PHILIPPE (CONTINUED)
Il laboratorio per il mare = A
maritime laboratory / Philippe
Vernier.
Marine and fisheries laboratory at
Fano, Italy; architects: Mariano
Cantarini and Celio Francioni.
L'ARCA 1990 Dec., no.44, p.52-57,
elevs., photos., plans, secns.
Uno stadio nel parco = A stadium in
the park / Philippe Vernier.
Architects: Sergio Hutter, Toni
Cordero, Francesco Ossola.
L'ARCA 1990 May, no.38, p.66-73,
1folded leaf, axonometric views,
dets., dwgs., photos., plans,
secns.
Tokyo International Forum / Philippe
Vernier.
Winning competition project;
architect: Rafael Vinoly. Text in
Italian and English.
L'ARCA 1990 June, no.39, o.34-39,
dwgs., model, plans, site plan.

VERONESI, BARBARA
Costruire con il legno / Walter
Bianchi, Barbara Veronesi.
VILLE GIARDINI 1990 Sept., no.251,
p.[48]-51, dwg., photos.
Costruire con l'acciaio / Walter
Bianchi, Barbara Veronesi.
Examples of construction with
steel frames and glass.
VILLE GIARDINI 1990 May, no.248,
p.[54-59], figs., dwgs., photos.
La pietra, il mattone, il blocco
nelle costruzioni / Walter
Bianchi, Barbara Veronesi.
VILLE GIARDINI 1990 July-Aug.,
no.250, p.[60]-63, dwg., photos.

VERONESTI, BARBARA
Costruire con il cemento armato /
Walter Bianchi, Barbara Veronesi.
VILLE GIARDINI 1990 June, no.249,
p.48-53, ill., photos.

VERPOEST, LUC
Henry van de Velde [by] Klaus-Jurgen
Sembach [book review] / Luc
Verpoest.
ARCHIS 1990 May, no.5, p.52-53,
port., photos., refs.

VERPRAET, GILLES
Les theories americaines de
l'amenagement urbain: la question
des professions / Gilles Verpraet.
French, English, Spanish and
German summaries, p.246-252.
LES ANNALES DE LA RECHERCHE
URBAINE 1989 Dec., no.44-45,
p.15-25, [246]-247, 249, 251,
photos., biblio., refs.

VERSTEGEN, TON
Architectuurbeleid en kwaliteit /
Ton Verstegen.
One of several articles in
Themanummer 41: "Thema:
architectuur en macht." Discusses
policies of the VROM and WVC, and
the BNA, on the occasion of an
exhibition in summer 1988 in
Rotterdam.
DE ARCHITECT THEMA 1990 Nov.,
v.21, no.11 suppl., p.29-31,
photos., site plan, refs.

VERSTEGEN, TON (CONTINUED)
Ideeenprijsvraag herinrichting De
Brink in Deventer / Ton Verstegen.
On competition for design of the
green in Deventer. Winners: Hans
de Witte, Kees van de Broek.
ARCHIS 1990 July, no.7, p.7-8,
dwgs.
Oproepen tot bevlogenheid: Week van
de volkshuisvesting / Ton
Verstegen.
On a manifesto ("Women in de jaren
'90), by Werkgroep 5x5 and events
held Nov.22-24, 1989 at the
Kunsthal in Rotterdam about
housing.
ARCHIS 1990 Jan., no.1, p.12-13,
photo., aerial photo., ref.
Stadstimmeren in Rotterdam / Ton
Verstegen.
Changes on the waterfront,
including the Aelbrechtskade by
Adriaan Geuze.
ARCHIS 1990 Dec., no.12, p.3-4,
photos., refs.

VERT, JOAN CARLES
Vivienda unifamiliar en Alella:
Jordi Salvat y Joan Carles Vert,
arquitectos.
Spanish and English text.
ON DISENO 1989, no.106, p.110-117,
photos., plans, secns.

VESELY, DALIBOR
On the relevance of phenomenology /
Dalibor Vesely.
Based on a discussion in a Univ.
of Houston seminar held on 11
Dec.1984.
PRATT JOURNAL OF ARCHITECTURE
1988, v.2, p.59-62, port., ref.

VESTERGAARD, FLEMMING
Svend Otto Roloff 1907-1990
[obituary] / Flemming Vestergaard.
ARKITEKTEN 1990 Apr., v.92, no.5,
p.175,

VESTIBULES
See ENTRANCE HALLS

VESTPOCKET PARKS
See URBAN PARKS

VETERINARY COLLEGES--SPAIN--BARCELONA
Jordi Fabre e Merce Torras: Facolta
di veterinaria di Bellaterra
(Barcellona) / Duccio Malagamba.
Text in Italian and English.
DOMUS 1990 Apr., no.715, p.10-11,
xxii, axonometric view, elevs.,
photos, plan, site plan.

VETERINARY HOSPITALS
See HOSPITALS - VETERINARY

VETERINARY LABORATORIES
See LABORATORIES - VETERINARY

VETERINARY SCHOOLS
See VETERINARY COLLEGES

VETGES TU I MEDITERRANIA
La arquitectura de Vetges Tu:
Mediterrania = The architecture of
Vetges Tu: Mediterrania.
Most of issue devoted to works by
this Spanish firm. Contents:
Jardin del Turia, Valencia;
Televisio Valenciana; cementerio
de Tavernes de la Valldigna;
(Continued next page)

VETGES TU I MEDITERRANIA (CONTINUED)
La arquitectura de...(CONTINUED)
Centro escolar publico en Port de
Sagunt; viviendas en quart de
Poblet; estudio de detalle y
vivendas en La Flota, Murcia; dos
viviendas rehabilitadas en la
huerta murciana; vestuarios en
tavernes de la Valldigna,
Valencia. Text in Italian and
English.
ON DISENO 1990, no.112(suppl.),
p.113-191, axonometric views,
ill., dwgs., elevs., models,
photos., plans, site plans, aerial
photos.

VETSCH, WALTER
Projektwettbewerb Seeuferanlage
Pfaffikon SZ = Concours de projets
pour l'amenagement du bord du lac
a Pfaffikon SZ = Project
competition for lakeside
facilities at Pfaffikon SZ /
Christian Stern.
Winning project by Walter Vetsch.
ANTHOS 1989, v.28, no.4, p.39-42,
site plans, sketches.

VETTORETTO, LUCIANO
Elementi di continuita e di
mutamento nelle forme insediative
e nei paesaggi politico-sociali
del Veneto = Elements of
continuity and change in
settlement forms and in the
sociopolitical landscapes of the
Veneto region / Luciano
Vettoretto.
English summary, p.128.
URBANISTICA 1989 Oct., no.96,
p.75-83,128, maps, refs.

VEYSSIERE, JEAN-LOUIS
Actualities: concours semapa Paris
XIIIe: invention d'une rue /
Pascale Joffroy.
Competition projects for 660 unit
housing development at rues
Tolbiac & Nationale, Paris 13e.
Architects: Patrick Celeste &
Dominique Blanc (winners), Alain
Gignoux & Jean-Louis Veyssiere,
Vincent Renie & Jean-Christophe
Morisseau, Pierre Bolze & Simon
Rodriguez-Pages, Bruno J. Hubert &
Michel Roy.
LE MONITEUR ARCHITECTURE AMC 1990
Feb., no.8, p.10-11, axonometric
views, elevs., plans, site plans.

VIADUCTS
See also BRIDGES

VIADUCTS--ITALY--ROME--VIA TIBURTINA
Un intervento "modello" per Roma.
The Via Tiburtina viaduct, between
the Via dei Monti Tiburtini and
the Via F. Fiorentini.
L'INDUSTRIA DELLE COSTRUZIONI 1990
Oct., v.24, no.228, p.76-77,
photos., secn.

VIALA, HELENE
Pleins feux sur le bleu / Helene
Viala.
Interiors of Jean-Paul Barriol's
Paris apartment in the 11th
arrondisement, formerly a workshop
of a cabinetmaker. Interior
architects and designers: Henri
and Jacqueline Boiffils. English
(Continued next column)

VIALA, HELENE (CONTINUED)
Pleins feux sur le...(CONTINUED)
summary, p.111.
MAISON FRANCAISE 1990 Dec.,
no.442, p.[134-143], photos.

VIAPLANA, ALBERT
Archivo en blanco y negro: cronica
grafica de tres generaciones/
Francese Catala-Roca.
Six projects from 1951-1988, by
architects Antoni Gaudi, Barba
Corsini, Antoni de Moragas, Jose
Antonio Coderch, Josep Lluis Sert,
Helio Pinon y Albert Viaplana.
ARQUITECTURA VIVA 1990 May-June,
no.12, p.33-35, photos.
Fugas escalonadas: edificios de
oficinas Eurocity 2, 3 y 4 =
Vanishing steps.
Located along the calle Zamora,
Barcelona.
A & V 1990, no.22, p.60-61,
elevs., models, plans, site plan,
sketches.
Urban space [Barcelona].
Part of a special feature on
Spanish contemporary architecture.
Contents: Plaza Granollers, by
Albert Viaplana, Helio Pinon.--
Parc de L'Espanya Industrial, by
Luis Pena Ganchegui.--Funicular de
Vallvidrera, by Josep Llinas.--
Puente Bach de Roda, by Santiago
Calatrava.--Brief Histories. Text
in Japanese.
SPACE DESIGN 1990 May, no.308,
p.75-92, dets., ports., elevs.,
photos., plans, secns., sketch,
isometric dwg.

VIBRATION OF BUILDINGS
See BUILDINGS - VIBRATION

VICARAGES (BUILDINGS)
See PARSONAGES

VICARI, SERENA
Building Milan: alternative machines
of growth / Serena Vicari, Harvey
Molotch.
Transportation planning for
underground rapid transit in Milan
and the various forces which
influence decision-making.
English and French summaries.
INTERNATIONAL JOURNAL OF URBAN AND
REGIONAL RESEARCH 1990 Dec., v.14,
no.4, p.[602]-624, axonometric
view, plans, refs.

VICHET, CHRISTINE DE
Dans le socle du CNIT.
On the design of the Essec and
Palais des Congres, part of the
World Trade Center in the CNIT,
Paris. Architects: Christine De
Vichet, Philippe Noir.
ARCHITECTURE INTERIEURE CREE 1990
Apr.-May, no.236, p.[130]-133,
photos.
L'espace cercle lumiere.
Features the Philips Eclairage
showroom. Interior designers:
Philippe Noir, Christine de
Vichet.
TECHNIQUES ET ARCHITECTURE 1990
June-July, no.390, p.48, photos.

VICHET, CHRISTINE DE (CONTINUED)
Le Fouquet's Bastille.
Restaurant interiors, Paris.
Interior designers: Christine De
Vichet, Philippe Noir.
ARCHITECTURE INTERIEURE CREE 1990
Mar., no.235, p.124-[129], photos.

VICO, GIAMBATTISTA, 1668-1744.
PRINCIPI DI UNA SCIENZA NUOVA
Skiagraphy and the ipsum of
architecture / Donald Kunze.
The "architecture" of shadows.
VIA 1990, no.11, p.62-75, ill.,
refs.

VICTOR CALIANDRO ARCHITECTS
The rise of Manhattan Valley /
Andrew White.
A landmark building, the New York
Cancer Hospital, at 2 W. 106 St.&
Central Park W., built by John J.
Astor in 1884, will be converted
to luxury housing with the
addition of a 27-story tower.
Original architect: Charles
Haight. Tower architect: Victor
Caliandro.
METROPOLIS 1990 Jan.-Feb., v.9,
no.6, p.16-18, photo.

VICTORIA AND ALBERT MUSEUM--
EXHIBITIONS
Before the theme parks: Recording
Britain [exhibition review] / Paul
Hogarth.
Exhibition of British art
commissioned during WWII to record
Britain's endangered heritage,
held at the Victoria and Albert
Museum, London, through 18
Nov.1990. The war-time project was
organized by Kenneth Clark.
ROYAL SOCIETY OF ARTS, LONDON. RSA
JOURNAL 1990 Oct., v.138, no.5411,
p.786-787, ill.
Flexible friends: The plastics age:
from modernity to post-modernity
[exhibition review] / Fay Sweet.
Exhibition of plastic as a
building industrial and decorative
material at the Victoria and
Albert Museum, London, through 29
Apr. 1990.
ARCHITECTS' JOURNAL 1990 Feb.28,
v.191, no.9, p.78-79, photos.
Der Prinz und die Architekten
[exhibition and book review] /
Brian Hatton.
On "A Vision of Britain" at the
V&A Museum, London.
ARCHITHESE 1990 Jan.-Feb., v.20,
no.1, p.82-83, dwg., models, site
plans.
Traditional lines: Household
choices: design in domestic
consumption [exhibition review] /
Sebastian Conran.
Interior design exhibition at the
Victoria and Albert Museum,
London, through 1 July 1990.
ROYAL SOCIETY OF ARTS, LONDON. RSA
JOURNAL 1990 May, v.138, no.5406,
p.436-437, photos.

VICTORIA FAY & ASSOCIATES
Healing revolution / Michael Wagner.
Interiors of the 25-bed Planetree
Model Hospital Unit at the San
Jose Medical Center, Calif.
Architects: John Liu and Marc
Schweitzer, Interior designers:
Victoria Fay & Associates.
INTERIORS 1990 Dec., v.150, no.5,
p.96-97. photos., plan.

VICTORIAN
See "VICTORIAN" AS A SUBHEADING
AFTER SPECIFIC BUILDING TYPES OR
OTHER MAIN HEADINGS.

VICTORIAN REVIVAL
See "VICTORIAN REVIVAL" AS A
SUBHEADING AFTER SPECIFIC BUILDING
TYPES OR OTHER MAIN HEADINGS.

VICTORIAN SOCIETY
Doctor Holder's casebook: Julia Abel
Smith accompanies the Victorian
Society's caseworker on his
rounds.
Richard Holder is a caseworker for
the Victorian Society, Bedford
Park, London, and makes decisions
on building alteration requests.
TRADITIONAL HOMES 1990 Feb., v.6,
no.5, p.91-93, photos.

VIDARI, PIER PARIDE
La citta dell'ufficio:
self-contained workstations / Pier
Paride Vidari.
Olivetti research facility, Bari,
Italy. Architects: Luigi Giffone
and Luigi V. Mangano of Degw
Italia, with Michele De Lucchi of
Studio De Lucchi. Text in Italian
and English.
L'ARCA 1990 June, no.39, p.48-55,
elevs., model, plans, secns., site
plan.

VIDEO ARCADES--NETHERLANDS--GRONINGEN
What a wonderful world / Elke von
Radziewsky.
Features the five Video pavilions
in Groningen designed by the
following architects: Peter
Eisenman, Bernard Tschumi, Zaha
Hadid, Coop Himmelblau and Rem
Koolhaas. English summary, p.5.
ARCHITEKTUR & WOHNEN 1990
Dec.-1991 Jan., no.6, p.144-148,
photos.
What a wonderful world:
Videopaviljoens in Groningen / Jos
Roodbol.
Small pavilions at five sites.
Architects: Coop Himmelblau, Peter
Eisenman, Bernard Tschumi, Zaha
Hadid, and Rem Koolhaas.
DE ARCHITECT 1990 Oct., v.21,
no.10, p.54-59, photos., site
plan.

VIDEO DISCS
See VIDEODISCS

VIDEO RECORDINGS
Building homes: innovation.
Sections on Nordic housing
(Tampere, Vasteras, and Tromso),
housing procurement, videos for
presentations, a four star
timber-frame retirement complex in
South Harrow, conversion of a
former workhouse and hospital into
(Continued next column)

VIDEO RECORDINGS (CONTINUED)
Building homes:...(CONTINUED)
a mixed-use development
(architect: Burrell Foley
Associates).
BUILDING 1990 Oct. 12, v.255,
no.40, Suppl., entire issue,
photos., secn.
Computer-generated video explains
design / Karen Cordes.
A project initiated by Prof. H.
Gordon Brooks at the University of
Ark. uses computerized animation
graphics and electronic image
processing.
ARCHITECTURAL RECORD 1990 Sept.,
v.178, no.10, p.180-181, ill.
Design in motion: computers: video
presentations / Oliver R. Witte.
Integrating video with CADD is
changing the way architects
develop presentations.
ARCHITECTURE: THE AIA JOURNAL 1990
Nov., v.79, no.11, p.141-144,148,
ill., photo.
Recording historic environments with
still video cameras / Kurt Novak.
ASSOCIATION FOR PRESERVATION
TECHNOLOGY. BULLETIN 1990, v.22,
no.1-2, p.149-155, diagr.,
photos., refs.
Roll 'em / Karen Finucan.
The use of video tapes in planning
presentations. Includes a short
glossary of terms used in video
production.
PLANNING 1990 Aug., v.56, no.8,
p.12-17, ill., photos.
Videographic documentation,
analysis, and manipulation: a new
tool for cultural resource
management / G. Barrett Kennedy.
ASSOCIATION FOR PRESERVATION
TECHNOLOGY BULLETIN 1990, v.22,
no.1-2, p.97-103,
A visual recording / Jim Small.
On an audio-visual recording in
1988 with former president Jimmy
Carter, in conjunction with the
future development of the Jimmy
Carter National Historic Site,
Plains, Ga.
CRM BULLETIN: A NATIONAL PARK
SERVICE TECHNICAL BULLETIN 1990,
v.13, no.2, p.[1],4-5, photo.

VIDEODISKS
See VIDEODISCS

VIDEOS
See VIDEO RECORDINGS

VIDER, ELISE
Environmental theater ... the new
zoo / Elise Vider.
Coe Lee Robinson Roesch, a
landscape architecture firm
specializing in zoo design.
METROPOLIS 1990 June, v.9, no.10,
p.44-49, photos.

VIDETO, THEODORE E.
Reviving city parks / Joseph P.
Griffith.
On efforts to restore two of upper
Manhattan's park pavilions:
Riverside Park Viewing Pavilion
(1919) and Fort Washington
Pavilion (1925). Architect of the
Riverside Park Pavilion: Theodore
E. Videto.
METROPOLIS 1990 May, v.9, no.9,
p.31-33,

VIDLER, ANTHONY
The building in pain: the body and
architecture in post-modern
culture / Anthony Vidler.
The sensibility of architectural
objects as analogies of human
forms.
AA FILES 1990 Spring, no.19,
p.3-10, dwg., photos., refs.
Case per cyborg = Homes for cyborgs
/ Anthony Vidler.
OTTAGONO 1990 Sept., no.96,
p.[36]-55, ill., photos., refs.
Centro medico e casa d'abitazione,
Hapert/Olanda: Wiel Arets /
Anthony Vidler.
Text in Italian and English.
DOMUS 1990 Apr., no.715,
p.[38-45],xxiii, elevs., photos,
plans, secns., site plan, aerial
photo.
Dal tatuaggio al monile:
architettura come ornamento = From
tattoo to trinket: architecture as
adornment / Anthony Vidler.
OTTAGONO 1990 Mar., no.94,
p.16-35, models, photos., plans,
sketches, aerial photo., refs.
Notes on the sublime: from
Neoclassicism to Postmodernism /
Anthony Vidler.
With reference to Longinus, Burke,
Hegel and others.
THE PRINCETON JOURNAL 1988, v.3,
p.165-190, dwgs., elevs.

VIDLER, ANTHONY, 1941-
Theorizing the unhomely / Anthony
Vidler.
On the "uncanny qualities of
contemporary architecture."
COLUMBIA UNIVERSITY. GRADUATE
SCHOOL OF ARCHITECTURE, PLANNING
AND PRESERVATION. NEWSLINE 1990
Nov., v.3, no.3, p.3, photo.

VIDLER, ANTHONY, 1941-. LEDOUX
Ledoux [by] Anthony Vidler [book
review] / Geert Bekaert.
ARCHIS 1989 Oct., no.10, p.55,
ill.

VIDLER, ANTHONY, 1941-. WRITING ON THE
WALLS
The writing on the walls [by]
Anthony Vidler [book review] /
Richard Becherer.
JOURNAL OF ARCHITECTURAL EDUCATION
1990 Spring, v.43, no.3, p.43-45,
ill., plans, refs.

VIDO, MARCO
Daneri e Genova: Domus Itinerario
n.59 / Marco Brandolisio, Marco
Vido.
A guide to buildings in Genoa
designed by Luigi Carlo Daneri. In
Italian and English.
DOMUS 1990 July-Aug., no.718,
p.[4] folded p. at end of issue,
maps, photos., plans, secns.
Luigi Carlo Daneri, edifici alla
Foce Bisagno, Genova / Marco
Brandolisio, Marco Vido.
Housing complex built 1939-1958.
In Italian and English.
DOMUS 1990 July-Aug., no.718,
p.[80]-88, axonometric views,
ill., dwgs., elevs., photos.,
plans, secns., sketches.

VIEHL, ROLAND
Vom "Optiker-Laden" zum Augenoptiker
- Fachgeschaft: Zeitgemasse
Modernisierung in Wesel.
Architects: Ulrich Schmidt, Roland
Viehl.
ARCHITEKTUR, INNENARCHITEKTUR,
TECHNISCHER AUSBAU 1989 Sept.,
v.97, no.9, p.74-76, photos.,
plan.

VIEN, NGUYEN SI
Typhoon resistant building in
Vietnam / John Norton, Guillaume
Chantry, Nguyen Si Vien.
Describes a program begun in 1989
in three provinces aimed at
reducing damage.
MIMAR: ARCHITECTURE IN DEVELOPMENT
1990 Dec., v.10, no.4(37),
p.70-77, ill., photos., refs.

VIERKOTTER, ROLF
La vie en rose: Restaurant in
Munchen.
Interior architects: R.
Vierkotter, B. Lenz, W. Nowak, M.
Pappstein.
ARCHITEKTUR, INNENARCHITEKTUR,
TECHNISCHER AUSBAU 1990 June,
v.98, no.6, p.28-30, photos.,
plans.

VIERVANT, LEENDERT, 1752?-1801
Over saaiheid en opwindende eenvoud
/ Maarten Kloos.
Results of recent competition for
addition to Teylers Museum,
Haarlem. Winner: Hubert Jan Henk.
Original architect (1784):
Leendert Viervant.
ARCHIS 1990 July, no.7, p.2-3,
models, plan, secn., site plan.
Teleurstellende resultaten
prijsvraag Teylersmuseum /
Liesbeth Melis.
Results of an open competition for
an addition to the 1778 museum
(original architect: Leendert
Viervant). Winner: Hubert Jan
Henket. Includes three other
projects.
DE ARCHITECT 1990 July-Aug., v.21,
no.7-8, p.20-23, dwg., elev.,
models, plan.

VIETEN, WERNER, 1924-
Ev. Gemeindezentrum in Frechen -
Buschbell.
On the restoration of the 1741/42
parish church and the addition of
a parish hall. Original master
builder: Johannes Kribben.
Architects for restoration and
addition: Werner Vieten, Peter
Johnssen.
DEUTSCHE BAUZEITSCHRIFT 1990 July,
v.38, no.7, p.985-988, photos.,
plans, secns., site plans.

VIETNAM--BUILDINGS--ENVIRONMENTAL
ASPECTS
Typhoon resistant building in
Vietnam / John Norton, Guillaume
Chantry, Nguyen Si Vien.
Describes a program begun in 1989
in three provinces aimed at
reducing damage.
MIMAR: ARCHITECTURE IN DEVELOPMENT
1990 Dec., v.10, no.4(37),
p.70-77, ill., photos., refs.

VIETTI, LUIGI
La progettazione dell'E42: la prima
fase = The planning of the E42:
the first phase / Riccardo
Mariani.
The planning of the E42:
Esposizione Universale in Roma
1941-1942; architects: Giuseppe
Pagano, Marcello Piacentini, Luigi
Piccinato, Ettore Rossi, Luigi
Vietti, Adalberto Libera, Giuseppe
Terragni, Pietro Lingeri, Cesare
Cattaneo, Giovanni Guerrini,
Ernesto La Padula, Mario Romano,
Gian Luigi Banfi, Ludovico B. di
Belgioso, Gaetano Ciocca, Enrico
Peressutti, Ernesto N. Rogers,
Franco Albini, Ignazio Gardella,
Giancarlo Palanti, Giovanna
Romano, Luciano Baldessari,
Ernesto Saliva, Luigi Moretti,
Gino Pollini, Luigi Figini, and
Giuseppe Vaccaro.
LOTUS INTERNATIONAL 1990, no.67,
p.90-125, elevs., models, photos.,
plans, secns., site plans,
sketches, aerial photos.

VIEWS
See CITIES AND TOWNS - VIEWS

VIGANO, VITTORIANO, 1919-
Milano: nuovo politecnico alla
Bovisa.
Plans for a new branch of the
Milan Polytechnic in the Bovisa
district. Architects: Baffa,
Battisti, Canella, Crotti, Grassi,
Grisotti, Mantero, Monestiroli,
Nicolin, Vigano.
DOMUS 1990 Sept., no.719,
p.[18-20], dwgs., elevs., plans,
site plans.

VIGATO, JEAN-CLAUDE
Un eclectisme industrieux
[exhibition review] / Jean-Claude
Vigato.
Review of the exhibition, Tony
Garnier, 1869-1948, on view at the
CCI, Centre Georges Pompidou,
Paris, Mar. 7-May 28, 1990.
ARCHITECTURE D'AUJOURD'HUI 1990
Feb., no.267, p.36-38, ill.,
dwgs., sketches.
Lycee technique au Luxembourg /
Jean-Claude Vigato.
Located in Bonnevoie. Architects:
Atelier A & U.
ARCHITECTURE D'AUJOURD'HUI 1990
Oct., no.271, p.92-93, photos.,
plan.

VIGNE, EDMOND DE, 1839-1917
Egyptomanie fin de siecle: Le
Typhonium, demeure des peintres
Adrien Demont et Virginie
Demont-Breton / Annette Bourrut
Lacouture.
History of the 1891 Egyptian
revival home, Le Typhonium, in
Wissant, France. Original
architect: Edmond De Vigne. Later
additions in 1909-1911 designed by
artists/owners, Adrien Demont and
Virginie Demont-Breton.
SOCIETE DE L'HISTOIRE DE L'ART
FRANCAIS. BULLETIN 1990,
p.[277]-296, dwgs., photos.,
plans.

VIGNELLI ASSOCIATES
Purely Italian / Alice S. Feiring.
Poltrona Fran Showroom, Tolentino,
Italy. Interior designers:
Vignelli Associates.
INTERIORS 1990 Aug., v.149, no.13,
p.92-95, photos., plan.

VIGNELLI ASSOCIATES--EXHIBITIONS
New York stars of Eurostyle: Design
Vignelli [exhibition review] /
Hugh Aldersey-Williams.
Exhibition at Royal College of
Art, London.
BLUEPRINT (LONDON, ENGLAND) 1990
June, no.68, p.59-60, photo.

VIGNELLI, MASSIMO. HUGH NEWELL
JACOBSEN, ARCHITECT
Pavilion living: Hugh Newell
Jacobsen, architect [book review]
/ Sanford M. Nelson.
Book ed. by Massimo Vignelli, pub.
by AIA, 1990.
ARCHITECTURE: THE MAGAZINE OF THE
AMERICAN INSTITUTE OF ARCHITECTS
1990 June, v.79, no.6, p.43,46-47,
photo.

VIGNERON, PIERRE
Direction Generale des
Telecommunications Paris.
Located at 6, place d'Alleray, in
the 15th arr. Architect: P.
Vigneron.
LE MUR VIVANT 1990, no.95,
p.66-69, photos., plans, secn.

VIGNES, MARIA
Un "castel medieval" a l'ombre du
"Moulin-Rouge / Maria Vignes.
The house of Ernest Eymonaud, in
the Montparnasse section of Paris,
built in The Late 19th cent.
SITES ET MONUMENTS 1990, no.130,
p.11-13, photo.

VIGNOLA, GIACOMO BAROZZI DA,
1507-1573--INFLUENCE
Classical order / Charles Gandee.
Las Tejas, Montecito, Calif., was
inspired by the Villa Farnese.
Interior designer: John Saladino.
HOUSE & GARDEN 1990 Sept., v.162,
no.9, p.186-[195], port., photos.

VIGORELLI, VALERIO
La porta per una Cattedrale in
Africa [Burindi] / Valerio
Vigorelli.
Reliefs on doors of a new
cathedral in Ruanda-Urundi,
territory in East Central Africa.
ARTE CRISTIANA 1990 Nov-Dec.,
v.78, no.741, p.457-460, photos.,
refs.
La qualita ecclesiale nell'arte -
Architettura, liturgia, immagini:
la committenza della Chiesa ieri e
oggi / Valerio Vigorelli.
Introduction to issue devoted to
papers from congress cosponsored
by Arte cristiana and the
Universita Cattolica, 6-7
Feb.1989. Eight articles are
indexed separately.
ARTE CRISTIANA 1990 Mar.-July,
v.78, no.737-738, p.81-82, refs.

VIGUIER, JEAN-PAUL
Actualites: ciel de France a
Seville.
Project for French pavilion at
Exposicion Universal 1992;
architects: Jean-Paul Viguier,
Jean-Francois Jodry, Francois
Seigneur.
LE MONITEUR ARCHITECTURE AMC 1990
Apr., no.10, p.5, model, secn.
Details: architectes et industriels:
quel enjeu? / Jean-Pierre Menard.
Commentary on the collaboration of
architects and industry by
Jean-Paul Derel, Bernard Plattner,
Antoine Bres, Alain Boels,
Jean-Robert Mazaud, Paul Roger,
Jean-Marie Nunez, Jacques Bertoux,
Jean-Pierre Buffi, Jean Nouvel,
Jean-Paul Viguier and Roger
Baltus.
LE MONITEUR ARCHITECTURE AMC 1990
June, no.12, p.47-51, photos.
Park Citroen-Cevennes in Paris,
Frankreich = Park Citroen-Cevennes
in Paris, France.
Competition. Joint first prize
winners: Patrick Berger, Gilles
Clement; Jean-Paul Viguier,
Jean-Francois Jodry et Associes,
Alain Provost. Text in German.
ARCHITEKTUR + WETTBEWERBE 1990
Mar., no.141, p.70-73, dwgs.,
models, site plans.
Pavillon francais de Seville: cinq
projets pour l'exposition
universelle de 1992.
Winning architects: Jean-Paul
Viguier, Jean-Francois Jodry,
Francois Seigneur. English
summary, p.68. Spanish summary,
p.148.
TECHNIQUES ET ARCHITECTURE 1990
Mar., no.388, p.64-69, axonometric
view, dets., ill., dwgs., models,
plans, site plans..
Ein Quadrat im Himmel Spaniens:
Wettbewerb: Franzosischer Pavillon
fur die Expo 92 in Sevilla.
First prize: J.-P. Viguier, J.-F.
Jodry, F. Seigneur.
ARCH PLUS 1990 July, no.104,
p.34-35, dwg., models, plans,
secns.
Seville, tragi-comedie d'un concours
/ Frederique de Gravelaine.
On the competition for the French
pavilion for the 1992 Expo in
Seville. Winning architects:
Jean-Paul Viguier, Jean-Francois
Jodry and Francois Seigneur.
ARCHITECTURE D'AUJOURD'HUI 1990
June, no.269, p.16-20, ill.,
models, plans.

VIGUIER-JODRY ET ASSOCIES
Hidden depths / John Welsh.
On the French Pavilion for the
Exposicion Universal, Seville.
Architects: Viguier-Jodry et
Associes.
BUILDING DESIGN 1990 Mar.9,
no.976, p.12, models, plans,
secns.

VIKELAS, GIANNIS, 1931-
Yiannis Vikelas y la Fundacion
Goulandris de Atenas / Yves
Zimmermann.
Spanish, English text.
ON DISENO 1990, no.108, p.170-188,
photos., plans.

VIKING
See "VIKING" AS A SUBHEADING AFTER
SPECIFIC BUILDING TYPES OR OTHER
MAIN HEADINGS.

VILA RODRIGUEZ, RAFAEL
Il restauro della facciata di Casa
Mila "La Pedrera" = The
restoration of the facade of Casa
Mila / Rafael Villa [sic]
Rodriguez.
Restoration of 1906-1910 apartment
building at 92 Paseo de Gracia,
Barcelona. Original architect:
Antoni Gaudi Jornet. Architects
for restorations: Josef Emilio
Hernandez-Cros, Rafael Vila
Rodriguez.
FRAMES, PORTE & FINESTRE 1990
July-Sept., no.28, p.52-57,
photos.

VILADAS, PILAR
Buildings in a Box: an exhibition
explores the history of modern
architecture through Lincoln Logs,
Erector sets, and Tinkertoys
[exhibition review] / Pilar
Viladas.
"Buildings in Boxes" at the CCA,
Montreal, through Mar.1991.
HOUSE & GARDEN 1990 Dec., v.162,
no.12, p.54, ill., models.
Chicago Modern / Pilar Viladas.
Apartment renovation by Krueck &
Olsen.
HOUSE & GARDEN 1990 Nov., v.162,
no.11, p.[154-159], photos.
Cranked, curled and cantilevered /
Pilar Viladas.
On the Vitra Design Museum, Weil
am Rhein, Architect: Frank O.
Gehry. Includes short article by
Philip Arcidi which compares Gehry
and Hans Scharoun (1893-1972).
PROGRESSIVE ARCHITECTURE 1990 May,
v.71, no.5, p.94-[99], model,
photos., plans, secn., site plan.
Decorating's leading man: actor
William Haines left the screen to
become the film capital's star
designer / Pilar Viladas.
From the early 1930s until his
death in 1973, Haines designed
houses for Hollywood stars.
HOUSE & GARDEN 1990 Aug., v.162,
no.8, p.[100-108],151, ports.,
photos.
A different wavelength: the curves
of a California beach house
express architect Stanley
Saitowitz's sense of place / Pilar
Viladas.
The McDonald house, Stinson Beach.
HOUSE & GARDEN 1990 Aug., v.162,
no.8, p.[108]-111, photos.
Double billing ... a California
cottage / Pilar Viladas.
Home of Morgan Mason and Belinda
Carlisle, Los Angeles. Designer:
Brian Murphy.
HOUSE & GARDEN 1990 June, v.162,
no.6, p.[126-131], port., photos.

VILADAS, PILAR (CONTINUED)
The height of elegance: Milton and
Carroll Petrie moved five floors
up without leaving home / Pilar
Viladas.
Interior designers David Easton,
John Christensen, Denning &
Fourcade, Pauline Boardman.
HOUSE & GARDEN 1990 Feb., v.162,
no.2, p.116-121, port., photos.
Light in the forest: a Seattle
guesthouse by architect Jim Cutler
begins where nature leaves off /
Pilar Viladas.
HOUSE & GARDEN 1990 Dec., v.162,
no.12, p.[154-159], photos.
Lights, camera, Living room/ Pilar
Viladas.
Interior sets for the movies of
Merchant and Ivory.
HOUSE & GARDEN 1990 Sept., v.162,
no.9, p.[160-167], ports.,
photos.,
Pavilions on the edge: Frank Gehry
carves out an otherworldly
compound in a familiar Los Angeles
landscape / Pilar Viladas.
House of Rockwell and Marna
Schnabel, Brentwood.
HOUSE & GARDEN 1990 July, v.162,
no.7, p.60-[69],136, port.,
photos., plan.
Pfister finesse: Charles Pfister's
latest designs strike a masterly
balance between the classic and
the modern / Pilar Viladas.
The designer's own apartment in
San Francisco, and a New York City
apartment.
HOUSE & GARDEN 1990 July, v.162,
no.7, p.[124]-131, port., photos.
Private view / Pilar Viladas.
Milan apartment of Roberta Etro.
Architect: Piero Castellini.
HOUSE & GARDEN 1990 Apr., v.162,
no.4, p.[190]-195, port., photos.
Reluctant regionalists: architects
across America question whether
traditional forms are always
appropriate / Pilar Viladas.
HOUSE & GARDEN 1990 June, v.162,
no.6, p.48,53, ill.
Wright in Hollywood: a historic
Frank Lloyd Wright house is
brought back to life by film
producer Joel Silver / Pilar
Viladas.
The 1923 Storer house. Architect
for the restoration: Eric Wright.
HOUSE & GARDEN 1990 Feb., v.162,
no.2, p.[78]-87, port., photos.

VILALTA, RAMON
Concorsi: Faro Punta Aldea (Gran
Canaria) = Competitions: the Punta
Aldea Lighthouse (Gran Canaria).
The 1st prize awarded nationally
by the M.O.P.U. Architects: Rafael
Aranda, Carmen Pigem and Ramon
Vilalta
ANFIONE ZETO 1989, v.1, no.2-3,
p.298-303, ill., ports., elev.,
model, plans, site plan.

VILBY, KNUD
U-Landenes millionbyer: det er andet
end slum [book review] / Knud
Vilby.
Review of Pirater, bonder,
besaettere: Tredie Verden...., by
Lars Marcussen.
ARKITEKTEN 1990 June, v.92, no.8,
(Continued next page)

VILBY, KNUD (CONTINUED)
U-Landenes... (CONTINUED)
p.282-283, photos.

VILHJALMSSON, MANFRED
Anlaeg ved Det islandski
Nationalbibliotek / Reynir
Vilhjalmsson.
Landscaping by the author of
grounds in Reykjavik, for national
library begun in 1978 and not yet
complete. Architects: Manfred
Vilhjalmsson, Thorvaldur S.
Thorvaldsson. Includes English
trnaslation and captions.
LANDSKAB 1990 May, v.71, no.3-4,
p.1S1-1S4, photos., plan, site
plan.

VILHJALMSSON, REYNIR
Anlaeg ved Det islandski
Nationalbibliotek / Reynir
Vilhjalmsson.
Landscaping by the author of
grounds in Reykjavik, for national
library begun in 1978 and not yet
complete. Architects: Manfred
Vilhjalmsson, Thorvaldur S.
Thorvaldsson. Includes English
trnaslation and captions.
LANDSKAB 1990 May, v.71, no.3-4,
p.1S1-1S4, photos., plan, site
plan.

VILLA, ELENA
Un giardino allusivo: spazi
monofloreali / Elena Villa.
Gardens of Gerald Coke, in
Bentley, England.
VILLE GIARDINI 1990 Mar., no.246,
p.64-[67], photos.
Il giardino edoardiano: stanze a
cielo aperto / Elena Villa.
Walled garden at Polesden Lacey,
England, designed by Margaret
Helen Greville.
VILLE GIARDINI 1990 Mar., no.246,
p.[68]-71, photos.
Un giardino italiano in Normandia:
il gioiello di Brecy / Elena
Villa.
Baroque garden attributed to
Francois Mansart.
VILLE GIARDINI 1990 Dec., no.254,
p.56-59, photos.
Il giarino elisabettiano: siepi
arabescate / Elena Villa.
An English knot garden at Hatfield
House.
VILLE GIARDINI 1990 Mar., no.246,
p.72-75, photos.

VILLA SANZ, MARIANO DE LA
Rehabilitacion de Colegio de San
Esteban de Murcia: J. Plaza, E.
Sancho, V. Perez, M. de la Villa,
P. Sanmartin y S. Moreno.
Spanish, English text.
ON DISENO 1990, no.109, p.128-135,
photos., plans.

VILLA UGAS, MARIA DE PILAR DE LA
La arquitectura residencial de la
Villa Olimpica / Justo Isasi.
Includes 13 projects. English
summary, p.86.
A & V 1990, no.22, p.26-54, dets.,
ill., elevs., models, plans,
secns., site plans, sketches.

VILLAGE MUSEUMS
See MUSEUM VILLAGES

VILLAGES
See also CITIES AND TOWNS
See also HAMLETS
See also MUSEUM VILLAGES
Fragment als Verbrechen?: das
Rustikaldorfchen / H. P. Bartschi.
WERK, BAUEN + WOHNEN 1990 Nov.,
no.11, p.17, axonometric view,
elev., photos., plan, secn.

VILLAGES--19TH CENTURY--DENMARK--
TARNBY
Landboreformerne i Tarnby:
Aendringer i bebyggelse og
socialstruktur i en landsby taet
ved Kobenhavn ca. 1780-1830 /
Karl-Erik Frandsen.
A study of rural reforms in a
village near Copenhagen,
1780-1830. Includes English
summary.
BEBYGGELSEHISTORISK TIDSKRIFT
1989, no.17-18, p.15-30, maps,
graphs, photo., tables, refs.

VILLAGES--19TH CENTURY--UNITED
STATES--SCALES MOUND (ILLINOIS)
Scales Mound Historic District /
Floyd Mansberger.
HISTORIC ILLINOIS 1990 Dec., v.13,
no.4, p.[1]-3,14, photos.

VILLAGES--AZTEC--MEXICO--MORELOS
Architectural patterns at three
Aztec-period sites in Morelos,
Mexico / Michael E. Smith.
JOURNAL OF FIELD ARCHAEOLOGY 1989
Summer, v.16, no.2, p.185-203,
map, photos., plans, secn., site
plans, tables, biblio.

VILLAGES--COLONIAL--UNITED STATES--
LITCHFIELD (CONNECTICUT)
Litchfield, Conn.: vintage village.
Highlights four colonial homes in
this town; each indexed
separately.
COLONIAL HOMES 1990 Dec., v.16,
no.6, p.70-93,144, photos.

VILLAGES--CONSERVATION AND
RESTORATION--GERMANY (EAST)--
POTSDAM--RHINOWER LANDCHEN
Komplexe Umweltgestaltung im
Rhinower Landchen / Ruth Pape.
Regional environmental planning in
a small area of Potsdam. English,
French, German, and Russian
summaries, p.55-56.
ARCHITEKTUR DER DDR 1989 Dec.,
v.38, no.12, p.24-27, ill., map,
photos., plan, sketch.

VILLAGES--CONSERVATION AND
RESTORATION--GERMANY (WEST)
Dorfsanierung heute / G. Konieczny.
DEUTSCHE BAUZEITSCHRIFT 1990 June,
v.38, no.6, p.861-864, photos.,
secn.

VILLAGES--CONSERVATION AND
RESTORATION--UNITED STATES--NEW
ENGLAND
Growth and the loss of regional
character / J. Mark Davidson
Schuster.
Includes inset article on village
centers in New England.
PLACES 1990 Spring, v.6, no.3,
(Continued next column)

VILLAGES--CONSERVATION AND
RESTORATION--UNITED STATES--NEW
ENGLAND (CONTINUED)
Growth and the loss... (CONTINUED)
p.78-87, photos., plans, refs.

VILLAGES--CONSERVATION AND
RESTORATION--UNITED STATES--
SHERBURNE (NEW YORK)
Main Street revitalization: a
success story / Joyce Nazzitto
Steward.
PLANNING NEWS 1990 July-Aug.,
v.54, no.4, p.3-4,

VILLAGES--ECONOMIC ASPECTS--BANGLADESH
The Grameen Bank Housing Loan
project.
In villages in Bangladesh, since
1984.
MIMAR: ARCHITECTURE IN DEVELOPMENT
1990 Mar., v.10, no.1(34),
p.36-41, photos.

VILLAGES--INDIA--AKHAL
Akhal - brug af landskabet i en
bjerglandsby i Indien / Per
Diemer.
Land use in a small Kashmiri
village in northeastern India.
Includes English summary and
captions.
LANDSKAB 1990 Feb., v.71, no.1,
p.6-13,24, dwgs., maps, photos.,
plans, secns., site plans.

VILLAGES--JAPAN
Sukiya Yu.
Contents: Kazuhiro Ishii Architect
& Associates.--
"Village'ification" of Sukiya, by
Kazuhiro Ishii. Text in Japanese.
SPACE DESIGN 1990 Feb., no.305,
p.93-100, axonometric views,
dwgs., elevs., photos., plans,
secns.

VILLAGES--JAPAN--INFLUENCE
Takebe International House / Osamu
Ishiyama.
Lodging facilities for foreign
tourists, operated by Okayama
Prefecture, Mitsu-Gun. The plan is
modeled after old Japanese
villages. Architects: Ishiyama
Laboratory, Waseda University.
JAPAN ARCHITECT 1990 Nov.-Dec.,
v.65, no.11-12(403-404), p.52-59,
elevs., photos., plans, site plan.

VILLAGES--MEDIEVAL--ITALY--MONTARRENTI
Timeless Tuscany / Riccardo
Francovich, Richard Hodges.
Excavations of the Renaissance
village of Montarrenti.
ARCHAEOLOGY 1990 July-Aug., v.43,
no.4, p.58-59,77, maps, photos.

VILLAGES--RENAISSANCE--ITALY--
MONTARRENTI
Timeless Tuscany / Riccardo
Francovich, Richard Hodges.
Excavations of the Renaissance
village of Montarrenti.
ARCHAEOLOGY 1990 July-Aug., v.43,
no.4, p.58-59,77, maps, photos.

VILLAGES--ROMANIA
Les villages apres la
systematisation / Michel Parent.
On the future of Romanian villages
after the revolution in Dec. 1989.
MONUMENTS HISTORIQUES 1990
June-July, no.169, p.25-30,
photos., aerial photo.

VILLAGES--SOCIOLOGICAL ASPECTS--
LEBANON
Reconstruction and cultural
considerations: the case of war
damaged villages in Lebanon /
Souheil El-Masri.
URBAN FUTURES 1989 Winter, v.2,
no.4, p.45-53, axonometric views,
charts, diagrs., maps, plans,
secns., sketches, tables, biblio.

VILLAGES--SWEDEN--GAMMELSTAD
Le chiese, luoghi di aggregazione =
Churches, places of cohesion /
Carl Goran Bergman.
Markuskyran, Skarpnack, 1960 (S.
Lewerentz); church at Nacka (G.
Wickman; additions by Carl Nyren);
Gammelstad church.
ABITARE 1990 July-Aug., no.287,
p.184-189, elev., photos., plans,
site plan.

VILLAGES--UNITED STATES--EAST HAMPTON
(NEW YORK)
East Hampton, N. Y.: village by the
dunes.
COLONIAL HOMES 1990 Apr., v.16,
no.2, p.64-[67],136, map, photo.

VILLAGES--UNITED STATES--LOG HILL MESA
(COLORADO)
Interview: Ettore Sottsass.
On his plans for a "vacation
village" in Log Hill Mesa,
Colorado.
PROGRESSIVE ARCHITECTURE 1990
Nov., v.71, no.12, p.96-97, dwgs.,
photo., sketches.

VILLAGES--UNITED STATES--STOCKBRIDGE
(MASSACHUSETTS)
Berkshire byway: Stockbridge, Mass.
Four articles: Berkshire byway;
Red Lion Inn (1773); Mission House
(1739); and Sculptor's sanctuary
(home of Daniel Chester French,
b.1898-1900). Architect of D.C.
French house: Henry Bacon.
COLONIAL HOMES 1990 Feb., v.16,
no.1, p.[76]-107,136,138,140,
dwgs., ports., photos.

VILLANI, ENRICO, 1928-
Cassa di Risparmio con centro
servizi a Biella.
Architects: Enrico and Luca
Villani. Summaries in English,
French, German, and Spanish.
ARCHITETTURA; CRONACHE E STORIA
1990 June, v.36, no.6(416),
p.[426]-429, det., photos., plan,
site plan.
Cassa di Risparmio di Biella.
Architect: Enrico Villani.
Summaries in English, French and
Spanish.
ABACUS 1990 Oct.-Dec., v.6, no.24,
p.48-57, dets., dwg., elev.,
photos., secn., site plan.

VILLANI, LUCA, 1960-
Cassa di Risparmio con centro
servizi a Biella.
Architects: Enrico and Luca
Villani. Summaries in English,
French, German, and Spanish.
ARCHITETTURA; CRONACHE E STORIA
1990 June, v.36, no.6(416),
p.[426]-429, det., photos., plan,
site plan.

VILLANO, JOSEPH R., 1940-1990
Joseph R. Villano [obituary].
INTERIOR DESIGN 1990 July, v.61,
no.10, p.36.

VILLANOVA, ROSELYNE DE
La maison du retour au Portugal /
Roselyne de Villanova.
French, English, German and
Spanish summaries, p.[123]-126.
LES ANNALES DE LA RECHERCHE
URBAINE 1989 Mar.-Apr., no.41,
p.67-75, [123]-126, photos., refs.

VILLANUEVA BRANDT, CARLOS
Building bloc / Jose Manser.
On the original members of NATO,
Narrative Architecture Today:
Nigel Coates, Mark Prizeman,
Carlos Villanueva, Robert Mull,
Catrina Beevor, Peter Fleissig,
Melanie Sainsbury, Martin Benson
and Christina Norton.
DESIGNERS' JOURNAL 1990 June,
no.58, p.33-38, ports.
Character references / Hannah
Schlee.
Interiors of Bernard Van Meer's
London apartment. Interior
designer: Carlos Villanueva
Brandt.
THE WORLD OF INTERIORS 1990 May,
p.112-119, photos.

VILLANUEVA, JUAN DE, 1739-1811
La Casita del Principe, El Pardo: a
property of the Patrimonio
Nacional / Giles Worsley.
Built in 1784 for the future King
Carlos IV; architect: Juan de
Villanueva.
COUNTRY LIFE 1990 Dec.20, v.184,
no.51, p.56-61, photos.

VILLAS
See also COUNTRY HOUSES
Morality and reality: in search of
the better argument / Jon Michael
Schwarting.
On non-tangible aspects of
architectural discourse over
several centuries. Examples
include various villas and four
recent projects in New York by the
author.
VIA 1990, no.10, p.[62]-79,
diagrs., dwgs., models, photos.,
plans, sketches, refs.
The Villa: form and ideology of
country houses by James S.
Ackerman [book review] / Georgia
Clarke.
AA FILES 1990 Autumn, no.20,
p.106-107.

VILLAS--16TH CENTURY--INTERIOR
DESIGN--ITALY--VENETO--VILLA
MARCELLO
The Villa Marcello: a 16th-century
treasure in the Veneto / Peter
Lauritzen.
ARCHITECTURAL DIGEST 1990 Jan.,
v.47, no.1, p.98-105, port.,
photos.

VILLAS--17TH CENTURY--CONSERVATION AND
RESTORATION--ITALY--PARMA--VILLA
MAGNANI ROCCA
Protezione speciali per Villa
Magnani Rocca.
Dates from the 17th cent., in
Parma.
L'INDUSTRIA DELLE COSTRUZIONI 1990
Sept., v.24, no.227, p.71, photo.

VILLAS--17TH CENTURY--ITALY--BAGHERIA
Storia di villa: a bagheria nel
settecento / Ovidio Guaita.
Six villas in the area of
Bagheria, Italy.
VILLE GIARDINI 1990 Dec., no.254,
p.42-47, photos., aerial photos.

VILLAS--17TH CENTURY--ITALY--BOLLATE--
CASTELLAZZO
Il patrimonio storico: Villa
Lombarda = Historic heritage:
Lombard villa.
Castellazzo di Bollate, attrib. to
Giovanni Ruggeri.
ABITARE 1990 Dec., no.291,
p.134-[143], photos., aerial
photos.

VILLAS--17TH CENTURY--ITALY--ROME--
VILLA DORIA PAMPHILI
Villa Pamphilj nel passato vista da
un "giardiniere" / Stelvio
Coggiatti.
L'URBE: RIVISTA ROMANA DI STORIA,
ARTE, LETTERE, COSTUMANZE 1989
Jan.-Feb., v.52, nos.1-2, p.24-28,
photos.

VILLAS--17TH CENTURY--ITALY--ROME--
VILLA MISSORI
Un disegno di Borromini per la
"vigna" di Bernardino Missori /
Marina Carta.
On Borromini's design (dated ca.
1640s) for a villa for Bernardino
Missori, outside the Porta Pia,
Rome, which features a
concave-convex structure. The
author presents other contemporary
work by Borromini with similar
features. Summaries in English,
French, German and Spanish, p.157.
PALLADIO 1989 July-Dec., v.2,
no.4, p.69-76, dets., dwgs., refs.

VILLAS--19TH CENTURY--ALTERATIONS AND
ADDITIONS--ITALY--PUGLIA
La dolce vita: Transit Design
enhances a villa in Puglia / Edie
Lee Cohen.
Interiors of renovated 19th cent.
villa.
INTERIOR DESIGN 1990 Aug., v.61,
no.11, p.130-[135], photos., plan.

VILLAS--19TH CENTURY--ALTERATIONS AND
ADDITIONS--SPAIN--BARCELONA--TORRE
D'ALTURES (CASA DE LAS AIGUES)
Rehabilitacion de la Torre d'Altures
de Barcelona : Victor Argenti,
arquitecto.
Spanish, English text.
ON DISENO 1990, no.109, p.172-177,
photos., plans.

VILLAS--19TH CENTURY--AUSTRIA--
SALZKAMMERGUT--VILLA LANNA
Ein feudales Erbe / Jutta Kohout.
On the 1875 Villa Lanna in the
Salzkammergut, Austria, owned by
the Trauttenberg family.
Architect: Karl Tietz.
ARCHITEKTUR & WOHNEN 1990
Feb.-Mar., no.1, p.40-49, ports.,
photos., plans.

VILLAS--19TH CENTURY--CONSERVATION AND
RESTORATION--FRANCE--MONTREDON--
VILLA PASTRE
Keys of the city: the Villa Pastre
opens its doors to the guests of
Marseilles / Edmonde Charles-Roux.
Now the official guest house for
the city of Marseilles.
ELLE DECOR 1990 June-July, v.1,
no.5, p.90-[99], photos.

VILLAS--19TH CENTURY--INTERIOR
DESIGN--ITALY--TORRE DEL LAGO--VILLA
PUCCINI
Puccini's Torre del Lago / William
Weaver.
Interiors of turn-of-the-century
Villa near Viareggio.
ARCHITECTURAL DIGEST 1990 Jan.,
v.47, no.1, p.124-129, port.,
photos.

VILLAS--19TH CENTURY--ITALY--VARESE--
VILLA LA MOTTA
Sul lago nella quiete del grande
giardino / Lucia Bisi.
1850 Villa La Motta, now a hotel
near Varese, Italy. Original
architect: Giuseppe Balzaretto;
architect for the restoration:
Enrico Buzzi.
VILLE GIARDINI 1990 Nov., no.253,
p.2-7, photos.

VILLAS--19TH CENTURY--SWITZERLAND--
GENEVA--VILLA LA GORDANNE
Classical romance: a
nineteenth-century rotunda
encompasses a small but stately
realm / Christopher Simon Sykes.
Villa La Gordanne, overlooking
Lake Geneva was commissioned ca.
1800 as a copy of Belle Isle, an
18th-cent. house in the English
Lake District. Interior designer:
Tom Parr, of Colefax & Fowler.
HOUSE & GARDEN 1990 Mar., v.162,
no.3, p.188-195,211, port.,
photos.

VILLAS--20TH CENTURY--ALTERATIONS AND
ADDITIONS--ENGLAND--ARUNDEL--
BERESFORD-CLARK HOUSE
A sure hand [villa restoration] /
Elizabeth H. Hunter.
New additions, interiors and
gardens of 1912 villa near
Arundel, England, by owner and
interior designer Charles
Beresford-Clark.
HOUSE BEAUTIFUL 1990 July, v.132,
(Continued next column)

VILLAS--20TH CENTURY--ALTERATIONS AND
ADDITIONS--ENGLAND--ARUNDEL--
BERESFORD-CLARK HOUSE (CONTINUED)
A sure hand [villa...(CONTINUED)
no.7, p.35-42, port., photos.

VILLAS--20TH CENTURY--CONSERVATION AND
RESTORATION--ITALY--CAPRI--VILLA
MALAPARTE
L'Associazione Casa Malaparte.
On the formation of a group to
protect the 1938 house on a cliff
at Punta Massullo, Capri.
Architect: Adalberto Libera.
L'INDUSTRIA DELLE COSTRUZIONI 1990
Sept., v.24, no.227, p.62, photos.

VILLAS--20TH CENTURY--CONSERVATION AND
RESTORATION--SWITZERLAND--BURIER--
VILLA KENWIN
Ein Restaurationsversuch: die Villa
Kenwin in Burier/La Tour-de-Peilz
/ Gilles Barbey.
Architects: Hermann Henselmann
(1931), Giovanni Pezzoli (1987).
WERK, BAUEN + WOHNEN 1990 Oct.,
no.10, p.2-8, elevs., photos.,
plans, sketch., refs.

VILLAS--20TH CENTURY--FRANCE--CROIX--
VILLA CAVROIX
Croix purpose / Dennis Sharp.
On the endangered Villa Cavroix
(1931-1932), Croix, France.
Architect: Robert Mallet-Stevens.
BUILDING DESIGN 1990 Oct.19,
no.1008, p.20-21, elevs., photos.,
secn., site plan.
Une demeure 1930 / Suzanne Tise.
Villa Cavrois, Croix, France,
built in 1932; architect: Robert
Mallet-Stevens.
LE MONITEUR ARCHITECTURE AMC 1990
July-Aug., no.13, p.84-89,
photos., plans.
Peril en la demeure / Richard Klein.
On the Villa Cavrois, Croix, built
in 1932 by Robert Mallet-Stevens
which is now abandoned and falling
apart.
ARCHITECTURE D'AUJOURD'HUI 1990
Feb., no.267, p.23, photos.

VILLAS--20TH CENTURY--FRANCE--POISSY--
VILLA SAVOYE
Plan + coupe + elevation "propos sur
la villa Savoye et autres
edifications paralleles" / Pierre
Boudon.
Modernity in architecture, as
illustrated by Le Corbusier's
Villa Savoye. French, English and
Spanish summaries.
ESPACES ET SOCIETES 1988,
no.52-53, p.185-201, axonometric
view, diagrs., dwgs., refs.

VILLAS--20TH CENTURY--ITALY--BOLZANO
Giovani architetti di montagna =
Young mountain architects.
Examples of work by South Tyrolean
architects, Josef Kostner, Werner
Tscholl, C. Mayr-Fingerle, and
Walter Dietl.
ABITARE 1990 Dec., no.291,
p.116-133, photos., plans, secns.,
elevs.

VILLAS--20TH CENTURY--ITALY--IMOLA--
VILLA MUGGIA
Appelo per il recupero della Villa
Muggia di Bottoni e Pucci = Appeal
for the restoration of Villa
Muggia by Bottoni And Pucci.
Villa at Imola, Italy, built
1935-38.
DOMUS 1990 June, no.717, p.[18],
photos., secn.

VILLAS--ADDRESSES, ESSAYS, LECTURES
Essays, not essence: The villa: form
and ideology of country houses, by
James S. Ackerman [book review] /
Richard Hewlings.
ARCHITECTS' JOURNAL 1990 July 4,
v.192, no.1, p.73, photo.

VILLAS--ALTERATIONS AND ADDITIONS--
ITALY--CERNOBBIO--VILLA ERBA
Coperture vetrate per Villa Erba a
Cernobbio.
Architect: Mario Bellini.
L'INDUSTRIA DELLE COSTRUZIONI 1990
Sept., v.24, no.227, p.69, photos.

VILLAS--ART NOUVEAU--ITALY--
CALENZANO--VILLA PERAGALLO
A Prato, l'eclettica residenza
Peragallo / Ovidio Guaita.
Villa Peragallo, built early 20th
cent., in Calenzano, near
Florence. Architect: Enrico Dante
Fantappie.
VILLE GIARDINI 1990 Sept., no.251,
p.38-43, photos.

VILLAS--BAROQUE--ITALY--ROME--VILLA
PANIZZA
Documenti per il tardo barocco
romano: Casa Panizza e l'opera
dell'architetto Simone Felice
Delino / Mario Bevilacqua.
House dates from 1694-1700.
Summaries in English, French,
German and Spanish.
PALLADIO 1989 Jan.-June, no.3,
p.133-142, dwg., photos., plans,
engrs., refs.

VILLAS--BAROQUE--ITALY--SICILY--
BAGHERIA--VILLA PALAGONIA
Petrified in Palagonia / Martin
Gayford.
Focus on the Baroque sculptural
decoration added to the early 18th
cent. Villa Palagonia at Bagheria,
near Palermo. Architect: Maria
Tommaso Napoli.
THE WORLD OF INTERIORS 1990 Oct.,
p.[164-171], photos.

VILLAS--BAROQUE--RUINED, EXTINCT,
ETC.--ITALY--ROME--VILLA DEL PIGNETO
SACCHETTI
The villa del Pigneto Sacchetti /
Jorg M. Merz, Anthony F. Blunt.
Analysis of new documents suggests
the late 1630s through late 1640s
for Pietro da Cortona's work.
Includes abstract, and an
appendix, listing references in 13
manuscripts in a chronological
format from 1570-1686.
SOCIETY OF ARCHITECTURAL
HISTORIANS. JOURNAL 1990 Dec.,
v.49, no.4, p.390-406, dwgs.,
maps, plans, secns., engrs., refs.

VILLAS--INTERIOR DESIGN--SOUTH
AFRICA--HOUSE COLE (HERCULANEUM)
Paint magic / Penny Swift.
In conjunction with the author's
book, Plascon paint techniques,
discusses the use of paint in
interior design. Feature three
projects: Salvago boutique, Camp's
Bay, Cape Town (architect: Roger
Martin); "Herculaneum", home of
designer Jacqueline Cole; Floris
Smit Huijs restaurant, Cape Town
(interior decorator: Francois du
Plessis).
ADA: ARCHITECTURE, DESIGN, ART
1989, no.7, p.27-33, ports.,
photos.

VILLAS--INTERIOR DESIGN--SWITZERLAND--
LA CHAUX-DE-FONDS--VILLA SCHWOB
Ebel, abroad.
Features two projects by Andree
Putman: Ebel exhibition stand for
the 1985 Basel fair and the
restoration of Le Corbusier's
Villa Schwob in La Chaux-de-Fonds,
which serves as Ebel's main
headquarters. Includes photo of
billboard-facade of Ebel Paris
shop, now under construction.
INTERIOR DESIGN 1990 Mar., v.61,
no.5, p.158-[163], photos.

VILLAS--ITALIANATE--INTERIOR DESIGN--
UNITED STATES--COCONUT GROVE
(FLORIDA)--VIZCAYA
Coconut Grove rococo [Vizcaya,
Miami] / William L. Hamilton.
On the interiors of the 1914
villa. Designer: Paul Chalfin.
ART & ANTIQUES 1990 Oct., v.7,
no.7, p.116-120,139, photos.

VILLAS--ITALY--CAPRI--VILLA MALAPARTE
An italian writer's architectural
statement on Capri / Michael Webb.
On Curzio Malaparte's 1940 villa,
Villa Malaparte.
ARCHITECTURAL DIGEST 1990 Aug.,
v.47, no.8, p.46-59, photos.
Nature, surrealism, and folk design
methodology in the Casa Malaparte
/ Michael McDonough.
Architect: Adalberto Libera. Text
in Japanese and English.
ARCHITECTURE AND URBANISM 1990
Dec., no.12(243), p.3-14, dwgs.,
photos.

VILLAS--ITALY--INFLUENCE
Frank Lloyd Wright and the Italian
villa / Alexander Gorlin.
Text in Japanese and English.
ARCHITECTURE AND URBANISM 1990
Oct., no.10(241), p.44-57, dwgs.,
photos., plans, biblio., refs.

VILLAS--ITALY--ORENA--VILLA BORROMEO
Il parco della famiglia Borromeo ad
Oreno / Guistino De Lorenzo.
Lombardy garden begun in 1830.
Landscape architects; Adalberto
and Alessandro Borromeo.
VILLE GIARDINI 1990 Dec., no.254,
p.60-69, photos.

VILLAS--ITALY--OSIMO--MONTECERNO
Renaissance glories at Montecerno /
Peter Lauritzen.
Villa near Osimo is the ancestral
seat of the Fiorenzi family and is
home to Principessa Donatella
Colonna.
ARCHITECTURAL DIGEST 1990 Jan.,
v.47, no.1, p.64,64G,64L, port.,
photos.

VILLAS--ITALY--SANTA MARIA DI LEUCA
Ville al Mare di S. Maria di Leuca /
Ugo La Pietra.
Seaside villas in a Balnearic
village.
AREA 1989 July-Aug., v.9, no.47,
p.48-[53], photos.

VILLAS--ITALY--SETTIGNANO--VILLA I
TATTI
The legacy of I Tatti / Peter
Lauritzen.
On the history of Villa I Tatti,
Bernard Berenson's home in
Settignano. It now houses the
Harvard University Center for
Italian Renaissance Studies.
ARCHITECTURAL DIGEST 1990 Jan.,
v.47, no.1, p.112-117,168, port.,
photos.

VILLAS--ITALY--TUSCANY--VILLA
VIVIANI--ANECDOTES, FACETIAE,
SATIRE, ETC.
Un americano a Villa Viviani = an
American in Villa Viviani / Mark
Twain.
Excerpt from the Autobiography of
Mark Twain, Harper & Brothers, NY,
1959. Includes article on the
history of the villa. Twain
rented this villa in 1892. Text
in Italian and English.
SPAZIO E SOCIETA 1990 July-Sept.,
v.13, no.51, p.116-121, port.,
photos.

VILLAS--ITALY--TUSCANY--VILLA
VIVIANI--HISTORY
Un americano a Villa Viviani = an
American in Villa Viviani / Mark
Twain.
Excerpt from the Autobiography of
Mark Twain, Harper & Brothers, NY,
1959. Includes article on the
history of the villa. Twain
rented this villa in 1892. Text
in Italian and English.
SPAZIO E SOCIETA 1990 July-Sept.,
v.13, no.51, p.116-121, port.,
photos.

VILLAS--JAPAN--KANAGAWA
A villa on the cape, Kanangawa,
[Japan], 1989.
Architects: Kazumasa Yamashita,
Architect and Associates. Text in
Japanese and English.
PROCESS: ARCHITECTURE 1989 Dec.,
no.87, p.94-103, photos., plans,
secns., site plan.

VILLAS--MOROCCO--MARRAKESH--LA SOURCE
Retreat to Marrakesh: Patrick and
Martine Guerrand-Hermes leave the
modern world behind when they
escape to their villa in Morocco.
HOUSE & GARDEN 1990 Feb., v.162,
no.2, p.[94]-99, photos.

VILLAS--NEOCLASSICAL--ITALY--FLORENCE
Ville fiorentine: dalle dimore
barocche dei granduchi alle
residenze neoclassiche borghesi /
Ovidio Guaita.
VILLE GIARDINI 1990 Feb., no.245,
p.34-41, photos., engrs., aerial
photos.

VILLAS--RENAISSANCE--ALTERATIONS AND
ADDITIONS--ITALY--FLORENCE--VILLA LA
MASSA
Dove curva il fiume / Lucia Bisi.
Villa La Massa, just outside of
Florence, is now a hotel.
VILLE GIARDINI 1990 Nov., no.253,
p.30-31, photos.

VILLAS--RENAISSANCE--ALTERATIONS AND
ADDITIONS--ITALY--PALO LAZIALE--
VECCHIA POSTE
Sul mare fuori dal tempo / Marinetta
Nunziante.
The Vecchia Poste, at Palo
Laziale, Italy, now an exclusive
hotel.
VILLE GIARDINI 1990 Nov., no.253,
p.24-29, photos., aerial photo.

VILLAS--RENAISSANCE--CONSERVATION AND
RESTORATION--ITALY--ROME--VILLA
ALDOBRANDINI
Villa Aldobrandini a Monte
Magnanapoli nella seconda meta
dell' ottocento (I parte) / Carla
Benocci.
Nineteenth-century restoration of
the renaissance villa under the
direction of Giovanni Battista
Benedetti.
L'URBE: RIVISTA ROMANA DI STORIA,
ARTE, LETTERE, COSTUMANZE 1989
Sept.-Dec., v.52, no.5-6, p.24-38,
elevs., plans, tables, refs.

VILLAS--RENAISSANCE--CONSERVATION AND
RESTORATION--ITALY--ROME--VILLA
MATTEI AL CELIO
Il rinnovamento seicentesco della
Villa Mattei al Celio: Francesco
Peparelli, Andrea Saachi, Andrea
Lilli ed altri artisti / Carla
Benocci.
STORIA DELL'ARTE 1989, no.66,
p.[187]-196,pl.1-9, photos, plan,
engrs., refs.

VILLAS--RENAISSANCE--HISTORY--ITALY--
FRASCA--VILLA ALDOBRANDINI
Villa Aldobrandini a Monte
Magnanapoli nella prima meta
dell'Ottocento (II) / Carla
Benocci.
L'URBE: RIVISTA ROMANA DI STORIA,
ARTE, LETTERE, COSTUMANZE 1989
Jan.-Feb., v.52, nos.1-2, p.9-23,
ill., elev., photo., engrs., refs.

VILLAS--RENAISSANCE--ITALY
Palladio parade: Palladio's villas:
life in the Renaissance
countryside, by Paul Holberton
[book review] / Robert Tavernor.
ARCHITECTS' JOURNAL 1990 Sept.19,
v.192, no.12, p.87.
Storia di villa: nella campagna
romana / Ouidio Guaita.
Features five villas and gardens
near Rome.
VILLE GIARDINI 1990 Mar., no.246,
p.42-47, dwgs., elev., photos,
secn.

VILLAS--ROMAN--RUINED, EXTINCT, ETC.--
ISRAEL--REPHAIM VALLEY--EIN YAEL
  What's a Roman villa doing outside
  Jerusalem? / Gershon Edelstein.
  Ein Yael, the site of an ancient
  agricultural settlement in the
  Rephaim Valley, five miles west of
  Jerusalem.
  BIBLICAL ARCHAEOLOGY REVIEW 1990
  Nov.-Dec., v.16, no.6, p.32-42,
  photos., plans, secn., refs.

VILLAS--ROMAN--SOCIOLOGICAL ASPECTS--
GREAT BRITAIN
  The social significance of villa
  architecture in celtic north west
  Europe / Simon Clarke.
  With particular reference to
  interpretation of the upper Thames
  region. Includes abstract.
  OXFORD JOURNAL OF ARCHAEOLOGY 1990
  Nov., v.9, no.3, p.337-353,
  graphs, plans, tables, biblio.

VILLAS--SWITZERLAND--SAINT MORITZ--
OBERALPINA--VILLA BOHLER
  Tessenow a St. Moritz: requiem for
  Villa Bohler / Heinz Adamek.
  Demolition of villa built in
  1916-17 for Friedrich Bohler,:
  architect: Heinrich von Tessenow.
  Text in Italian and English.
  L'ARCA 1990 Mar., no.36, p.4-7,
  ill., photos, plan.

VILLES VIEILLES
  See OLD TOWNS

VILLETTE, OLIVIER
  Fins de chantier.
    Contents: Prison, Brest, France;
    architects: Remy Butler, Olivier
    Villette-- Police station,
    Roubaix, France; architects:
    Bernard Bassez, Claude Franck,
    Maite Rumeau-Bassez.
    LE MONITEUR ARCHITECTURE AMC 1990
    July-Aug., no.13, p.11-14,17-18,
    photos., plans.

VILLIERS, RINA DE
  Pretoria se argitektuur deur di Oe
  van Kunstenaars / Rina de
  Villiers.
  Pretoria as represented in art,
  especially by Jacob Hendrik
  Pierneef. In Africaans, with
  English summary.
  ARCHITECTURE SA = ARGITEKTUUR SA
  1989 May-June, no.5-6, p.19-22,
  ill., dwgs., sketches, engrs.

VILLIGER, JORG
  Siedlungsgarten in der Stadt Zurich:
  ein Pilotprojekt = Jardins dans
  les lotissements residentiels de
  Zurich: un projet pilote = Housing
  estate gardens in the city of
  Zurich: a pilot project / Felix
  Guhl, Jorg Villiger.
  ANTHOS 1989, v.28, no.4, p.14-17,

VINCI, JOHN
  History in the making / Justin
  Henderson.
  Interiors of the renovated 1911
  Lake Shore Country Club, Glencoe
  Ill. Original architect: Howard
  van Doren Shaw. Renovation
  architect: John Vinci.
  INTERIORS 1990 June, v.149, no.11,
  p.100-103, photos., plan.

VINCKEBOONS, PHILIP, 1607 OR 8-1678
  Philips Vingboons (1607-1678),
  architect [by] Koen Ottenheym
  [book review] / Herman van
  Bergeijk.
  ARCHIS 1990 Mar., no.3, p.54-55,
  ill., ref.
  Philips Vingboons [book review] /
  Karin Jongbloed.
  Reviews three 1989 monographs.
  DE ARCHITECT 1989 Oct., v.20,
  no.10, p.81, elev.

VINCKEBOONS, PHILIP, 1607 OR 8-1678--
EXHIBITIONS
  De familie Vingboons in het Paleis
  op de Dam [exhibition review] /
  Kees van der Ploeg.
  Review of Het Kunstbedrijf van de
  familie Vingboons, schilders,
  architecten en kaarttekenaars in
  de gouden eeuw, at the Paleis op
  de Dam, Amsterdam, until 3 Sept.
  1989. Includes drawings by
  Philips Vingboons.
  ARCHIS 1989 Aug., no.8, p.5-6,
  elevs.

VINDUM, KJELD
  Casa Stelling, Gammel Torv, 6,
  Copenhage, 1934-35: Una afilada
  esquina redonaeda / Kjeld Vindum.
  Five-story building for offices,
  shops, and an apartment.
  Architect: Arne Jacobsen. Text in
  Spanish and English.
  ARQUITECTURA 1990 Mar.-June, v.72,
  no.283-284, p.66-84, elevs.,
  photos., plans, refs.
  Set spraengte tempel / Kjeld Vindum.
  A legal building (courthouse) in
  Holstebro, Denmark. Architect:
  Nielsen, Nielsen & Nielsen.
  ARKITEKTEN 1990 Nov. v.92, no.16,
  p.524-527, axonometric view,
  elevs., models, plans, site plans,
  sketches.

VINES
  L'epiderme vegetable / Gilberto
  Oneto.
  Hanging gardens and vines.
  VILLE GIARDINI 1990 Apr., no.247,
  p.50-53, photos.
  Grune Wande: Fassaden lebendig
  gestalten / Klaus Werk.
  DEUTSCHE BAUZEITUNG 1990 Sept.,
  v.124, no.9, p.52-55, photos.,
  refs.
  Die lebende Fassade: Pflanzen und
  Technik der grunen Fassade / Hans
  Jurgen Krolkewicz.
  DEUTSCHE BAUZEITSCHRIFT 1990
  Sept., v.38, no.9, p.1259-1262,
  1265, dwgs., photos., refs.

VINOLY, RAFAEL, 1944-
  "It is unbelievable!" The Tokyo
  International Forum by Rafael
  Vinoly.
  Winning design by Vinoly.
  JAPAN ARCHITECT 1990 Jan., v.65,
  no.1(393), p.5, dwg., port.,
  models.
  Tokyo International Forum / Philippe
  Vernier.
  Winning competition project;
  architect: Rafael Vinoly. Text in
  Italian and English.
  L'ARCA 1990 June, no.39, o.34-39,
  dwgs., model, plans, site plan.

VINOLY, RAFAEL, 1944- (CONTINUED)
  Vinoly takes Tokyo forum / Mark
  Alden Branch.
  Rafael Vinoly wins competition for
  the design of the Tokyo
  International Forum.
  PROGRESSIVE ARCHITECTURE 1990
  Jan., v.71, no.1, p.27,32, dwgs.

VINT, ROBERT
  The restoration of San Xavier del
  Bac: Phase I / Robert Vint.
  Restoration of 1797 Spanish
  Colonial church, Bac, Ariz.
  Restoration architect: Eleazar
  Herreras. Architect of record:
  Robert Vint. Article focuses on
  the refinishing of the building's
  exterior.
  TRIGLYPH 1990 Summer, no.10,
  p.33-43, photos., secn., refs.

VINTS, L.
  Spitsbogen in Noord-Limburg / L.
  Vints.
  On neogothic churches in this area
  of Belgium.
  MONUMENTEN EN LANDSCHAPPEN 1990
  Sept.-Oct., v.9, no.5, p.9-11 (of
  M&L binnenkrant), det., ill.,
  elevs., photo., refs.

VIO, RICCARDO. SULLE TRACCE DI LE
CORBUSIER
  Le Corbusier e gli
  "architetti-autori" [book review]
  / Annalisa Avon.
  Review of Sulle tracce di Le
  Corbusier, edited by C. Palazzolo
  and R. Vio.
  CASABELLA 1990 Apr., v.54, no.567,
  p.28-29, sketch.

VIOLA, PAOLO
  Lignano Sabbiadoro, Il giardino dei
  labirinti = The garden of the
  labyrinths.
  Open-air theater and walkway in an
  Italian "tourist village."
  Architects: Studio Nizzoli (G.M.
  Oliveri, P. Viola).
  ARCHITETTURA: CRONACHE E STORIA
  1990 Nov., v.36, no.11(421),
  p.770-777, elevs., photos., plans,
  secns.

VIOLLET-LE-DUC, EUGENE EMMANUEL,
1814-1879
  Anthological excerpts from Gottfried
  Semper to Henri Focillon.
  Excerpts from eight writers' works
  on decoration and ornament.
  RASSEGNA 1990 Mar., v.12, no.41/1,
  p.77-88, ill.
  La decorazione come costruzione: un
  paradosso? = Decoration as
  building: a paradox? / Jacques
  Lucan.
  Discusses Viollet-le-Duc, August
  de Choisy, and other French
  theorists.
  OTTAGONO 1990 Mar., no.94,
  p.56-[67], axonometric views,
  dets., dwgs., elevs., photos.,
  refs.
  Derestoring Viollet-le-Duc: the
  battle of Saint-Sernin in Toulouse
  / Thomas W. Lyman.
  On controversy over recent
  evidence relating to the 1860
  restoration of the roof, and
  research and policy from ca. 1981.
  (Continued next page)

VIOLLET-LE-DUC, EUGENE EMMANUEL,
1814-1879 (CONTINUED)
Derestoring...(CONTINUED)
KUNSTCHRONIK 1990 June, v.43,
no.6, p.252-254, [1 p. of plates],
photo.
Restoring the stained glass of
Troyes Cathedral: the ambiguous
legacy of Viollet-le-Duc /
Elizabeth Carson Pastan.
Includes abstract.
GESTA 1990, v.29, no.2, p.155-166,
axonometric view, photos., engr.,
refs.
Saint Sernin de Toulouse:
restauration des couronnements et
toitures / Yves Boiret.
On the debate surrounding the
renovation/restoration of the
church roof designed by
Viollet-le-Duc between 1860 and
1879. It has been decided to
restore the roof to the pre-1860
state. Summaries in English,
Italian and Spanish.
ICOMOS INFORMATION 1990
July-Sept., no.3, p.3-11, dwgs.,
elevs., photos.

VIOLLET-LE-DUC, EUGENE EMMANUEL,
1814-1879--EXHIBITIONS
Saint-Sernin de Toulouse tresors et
metamorphoses [exhibition review].
Exhibition at the Musee
Saint-Raymond, Toulouse, on the
Romanesque basilica of
Saint-Sernin, through 14 Jan.1990.
Includes restoration work by E.
Viollet-le-Duc and Yves Boiret.
ARCHEOLOGIA 1989 Nov., no.251,
p.16-17, elev.

VIOLLET-LE-DUC, EUGENE EMMANUEL,
1814-1879--INFLUENCE
Der Entwurf als beherrschte Bewegung
= Le projet comme maitrise du
mouvement / Kenneth Frampton.
On the new Stadelhofen Bahnhof in
Zurich. Architects: Santiago
Calatrava, Jean Prouve.
ARCHITHESE 1990 Mar.-Apr., v.20,
no.2, p.52-69, dets., elevs.,
photos.. plans. secns.. sketches.

VION, PIERRE
Les artistes de l'entree de Louis
XIV en 1660 / Christoph Frank.
On the architects and artists of
the temporary structures erected
for Louis XIV's celebrated
procession through Paris on August
26, 1660, as recorded in archival
documents in the Archives
Nationals.
SOCIETE DE L'HISTOIRE DE L'ART
FRANCAIS. BULLETIN 1990,
p.[53]-74, dwgs., engrs., refs.

VIQUIER, JEAN-PAUL
Seville enfin / M.H. Contal.
Project for French pavilion for
the Exposicion Universal 1992.
Architects: Francois Seigneur,
Jean-Paul Viguier and
Jean-Francois Jodry.
ARCHITECTURE INTERIEURE CREE 1990
Mar., no.235, p.17, model, plan,
secn.

VIRGILE, CARLOS
Moving spirit / David Redhead.
Profile of Carlos Virgile and
Nigel Stone of Imagination.
DESIGNERS' JOURNAL 1990 Sept.,
no.60, p.90-91, port.

VIRGIN ISLANDS OF THE UNITED STATES--
BEACH HOUSES
Le capanne di Robinson [beach house,
Virgin Islands] / Luisa Basso.
Architect: Ron Dirsmith.
VILLE GIARDINI 1990 Apr., no.247,
p.30-31, photos, site plan.

VIRILIO, PAUL
De l'emprise des signes / Marie
Helene Contal.
Interview with Paul Virilio, Jean
Pierre Le Dantac and Patrice
Goulet about the new "architecture
of signs." English summary,
p.214.
ARCHITECTURE INTERIEURE CREE 1990
Oct.-Nov., no.239, p.[108]-114,
dwgs., ports., sketches.
L'inertie domotique / Paul Virilio.
Last article of a trilogy on "the
evolution of the status of
contemporary space." Summaries in
English and Spanish.
TECHNIQUES ET ARCHITECTURE 1990
June-July, no.390, p.119-121,181,
photo.

VIRILIO, PAUL, 1932-
La nouvelle domesticite / Paul
Virilio.
Text from Virilio's lecture at the
Universite du Quebec a Montreal in
1989.
ARQ: ARCHITECTURE/QUEBEC 1990
Oct., no.57, p.29-30,

VIRILIO, PAUL, 1932- --ADDRESSES,
ESSAYS, LECTURES
La nouvelle domesticite / Paul
Virilio.
Text from Virilio's lecture at the
Universite du Quebec a Montreal in
1989.
ARQ: ARCHITECTURE/QUEBEC 1990
Oct., no.57, p.29-30,

VIRLOGEUX, MICHEL
Travaux d'ingenieurs / Virginie
Picon-Lefebvre.
Structural engineering projects by
Michel Virolgeux, Marc Mimram,
Rene Greisch, Santiago Calatrava
and Peter Rice.
LE MONITEUR ARCHITECTURE AMC 1990
Oct., no.15, p.30-49, axonometric
views, ports., elev., photos.,
secns.

VIRNO, PAOLO
Un dedalo di parole: Per un'analisi
linguistica della metropoli /
Paolo Virno.
CASABELLA 1990 Apr., v.54, no.567,
p.37-39, ill.

VIRTA, KARI
Sinikello symmetry.
Sinikello day care center, Kuopio,
for the staff of Kuopio
University. Architect: Kari Virta.
ARCHITECTURAL REVIEW 1990 Mar.,
v.187, no.1117, p.84-87,
axonometric view, elevs., photos.,
plans, secns.

VISBY ARKITEKTGRUPP
KV triangeln, Visby / Annalena
Mosseen.
Renovation to shops and residences
on the Hastgatan, Sodra
Kyrkogatan, Smittens block.
Architect: Visby Arkitektgrupp.
Completed in 1988. Includes
commentary by Kristian Berg.
ARKITEKTUR: THE SWEDISH REVIEW OF
ARCHITECTURE 1990 Sept., v.90,
no.7, p.40-47, photos., plan, site
plans.

VISCONTI, VALERIA
Il piu recente progetto di Aldo Van
Eyck: diabolico maestro / Valeria
Visconti.
Convention complex for the
European Space Research and
Technology Centre, Noordwijk.
ARCHITETTURA; CRONACHE E STORIA
1990 Apr., v.36, no.4(414),
p.314-318, dets., ill., photos.,
plans, aerial photos.

VISIGOTH
See "VISIGOTH" AS A SUBHEADING AFTER
SPECIFIC BUILDING TYPES OR OTHER
MAIN HEADINGS.

VISIGOTHIC
See VISIGOTH

VISINTIN, FEDERICA
Plinio Marconi e il piano regolatore
generale di Verona, 1931-1954 /
Federica Visintin.
Planner: Plinio Marconi.
STORIA URBANA 1990 July-Sept.,
v.14, no.52, p.[137]-163, maps,
refs.

VISIONARY ARCHITECTURE
See FANTASTIC ARCHITECTURE

VISITORS' CENTERS
See also ARCHITECTURAL CENTERS
See also NATURE CENTERS

VISITORS' CENTERS--ALTERATIONS AND
ADDITIONS--SPAIN--BARCELONA--OFICINA
DE TURISMO
La redistribucion de una espacio
para una mayor funcionalidad:
David Gallego, Xavier de Pablo.
Remodeling of tourism information
office, Barcelona. English text,
p.184-185. In "On oficina," 1990
supplement issue.
ON DISENO 1990, suppl., p.94-97,
photos.

VISITORS' CENTERS--AUSTRALIA--KEMPSEY
Glenn Murcutt: Rakennuksia ja
suunnitelmia, Australia =
Buildings and projects, Australia.
Six projects: New Museum and
Tourist Information Office, South
Kempsey Park, Kempsey, N.S.W.;
Silver City Museum, Broken Hill,
N.S.W.; Magney Moruya house,
Bingie Point, N.S.W.; Eastaway and
Ball house, Glenorie; two
farmhouses. Includes English
translation.
ARKKITEHTI 1989, v.86, no.7,
p.52-67, inside front cover,
elevs., models, photos., plans,
secns., sketches, biblio.

VISITORS' CENTERS--COMPETITIONS--
DENMARK--DUPPEL--DYBBOL BANKE
Besogscenter pa Dybbol Banke
[Duppel].
A 1989 competition for a visitors'
center on a battlefield site in a
Danish village in Schleswig. First
prize: Michael Freddie, Ernst
Lohse. Second prize: Fogh &
Folner. Third prize: Hans Maar
Andersen.
ARKITEKTEN 1990 Aug., v.92, no.11,
p.360-371, axonometric views,
dwgs., elevs., models, maps,
photos., plans, secns., site
plans.

VISITORS' CENTERS--COMPETITIONS--
GERMANY (WEST)--ROTTWEIL--
ENERGIE-INFORMATIONS-CENTRUM
Konzentrierte Energie: Wettbewerb:
Energie-Informations centrum (EIC)
der Stadtwerke Rottweil.
1st prize: LOG ID, D. Schempp, K.
Miebach.
ARCH PLUS 1990 July, no.104, p.45,
model, plan, secns.

VISITORS' CENTERS--COMPETITIONS--
WALES--CARDIFF--CARDIFF CASTLE
Castle vistas [Cardiff Castle
visitors' center].
Competition entries for Cardiff
Castle visitors' center: Robert
Byron Associates; Greenfield
Midgley Architects; Pawson
Williams; Andy Foster; and
Katerina Ruedi.
ARCHITECTS' JOURNAL 1990 Aug.8,
v.192, no.6, p.20-25, dwgs.,
elevs., photo., plans, secns.,
site plan.

VISITORS' CENTERS--ENGLAND--GREAT
TORRINGTON--ROSEMOOR VISITOR CENTRE
Horticultural hospitality / Brian
Carter.
National garden and visitors'
center for the Royal Horticultural
Society near Bideford, Devon.
Landscape architect: Elizabeth
Banks Associates; visitors' center
architect: Ferguson Mann
Architects. Includes separate
article: "Roof, garden centre,
Ferguson Mann Architects",
p.49-51.
ARCHITECTS' JOURNAL 1990 Nov.28,
v.192, no.22, p.40-45, axonometric
views, dets., photos., plans,
secns., site plan, sketches.

VISITORS' CENTERS--FRANCE--CHINON--
MAISON DE LA CONFLUENCE
Si ... viaggiare! = Over the points,
on the road / Doriana O.
Mandrelli.
Contents: Cemetery at Civita
Castellana, Italy --Maison de la
Confluence, Chinon, France.
Architect: Massimiliano Fuksas.
L'ARCA 1990 Nov., no.43,
p.68-[79], dwgs., elevs., photos.,
plans.

VISITORS' CENTERS--FRANCE--MARQUEZE--
ECOMUSEE
Batiment d'accueil de l'Ecomusee de
Marqueze.
Architects: Olivier Brochet,
Emmanuel Lajus, Christine Pueyo.
English summary, p.127. Spanish
summary, p.173.
TECHNIQUES ET ARCHITECTURE 1990
Oct.-Nov., no.392, p.126-[127],
elev., photos., plan.

VISITORS' CENTERS--GERMANY (WEST)--
AACHEN--KAISERPLATZ
Kaiserplatz, Aschen, West Germany,
1987.
Project for Visitor's centers at
Roman baths site. Architects:
James Stirling, Michael Wilford
and Associates. Text in Japanese
and English.
ARCHITECTURE AND URBANISM 1990
May, no.5 extra edition,
p.172-181, photo., models, plans,
secns., site plans.

VISITORS' CENTERS--GERMANY (WEST)--
USINGEN--ERDFUNKSTELLE
Besucher-Pavillon:
Informationszentrum der
Erdfunkstelle Usingen.
Architects: Voigt und Herzog.
DEUTSCHE BAUZEITUNG 1990 Dec.,
v.124, no.12, p.56-58, dets.,
elevs., models, plans, secns.

VISITORS' CENTERS--ITALY--CROTONE--
CAPO COLONNA
L'ultima colonna = The last column /
Paolo Spada.
On the Capo Colonna archaeological
park and visitor center, Crotone,
Italy. Architects: Paolo Spada,
Italo Insolera, Tommaso Tedesco.
SPAZIO E SOCIETA 1990 Apr.-June,
v.13, no.50, p.112-119, maps,
photos., aerial photo.

VISITORS' CENTERS--JAPAN--ENIWA--
SAPPORO BREWERIES GUEST HOUSE
Toyo Ito: pavillon d'acceuil a
Hokkaido.
Sapporo Breweries Visitors'
center, Eniwa, Hokkaido.
ARCHITECTURE D'AUJOURD'HUI 1990
Oct., no.271, p.242-243, elev.,
photos., plan, site plan.
Toyo Ito / Toyo Ito.
Contents: Guest house for Sapporo
Breweries, Eniwa, Hokkaido,
design: 1987-88; construction:
1988-89 -- Project N, Tama, Tokyo,
design: 1988-89; completion: Mar.
1992. Text in Japanese and
English.
GA DOCUMENT 1990 Apr., no.25,
p.[92]-97, elev., model, photos.,
plans, site plan.

VISITORS' CENTERS--JAPAN--KOGA--KOGA
CITY VISITORS' PLAZA
Kunihiko Hayakawa / Kunihiko
Hayakawa.
Contents: Angle, Himeji, Hyogo,
design: 1986-87; construction:
1987-88 -- Koga City Visitor's
Plaza, design: 1989; completion:
1991. Text in Japanese and
English.
GA DOCUMENT 1990 Apr., no.25,
p.52-63, elevs., photos., plans,
secns., site plan.

VISITORS' CENTERS--JAPAN--SAGAMIHARA--
SAMAGIHARA PREFECTURAL PARK
Sagamihara Park Visitor Center,
Kanagawa, [Japan], 1985.
Architects: Kazumasa Yamashita,
Architect and Associates. Text in
Japanese and English.
PROCESS: ARCHITECTURE 1989 Dec.,
no.87, p.62-63, photos., plan,
secn.

VISITORS' CENTERS--JAPAN--TOKYO--TEPIA
E talvolta volano: Centro
d'informazioni "Tepia" in
Giappone: Maki & Associates.
ARCHITETTURA; CRONACHE E STORIA
1990 Feb., v.36, no.2(412),
p.130-131, photos., plan,
sketches.

VISITORS' CENTERS--NORWAY--ORRE--
FRILUFTSHUSET
Nature trail / Ulf Gronvold.
On the Friluftshuset at Orre
beach, Norway, an information and
exhibition pavilion. Architect:
Per Line.
ARCHITECTURAL REVIEW 1990 Sept.,
v.188, no.1123, p.87-90, photos.,
plans, secns.

VISITORS' CENTERS--SCOTLAND--CARDIFF
Star roll / John Welsh.
On the Cardiff Bay Visitors'
Center. Architects: Alsop &
Lyall.
BUILDING DESIGN 1990 Nov.2,
no.1010, p.16,33, dets., photos.,
secns., sketches.
[Three projects by Will Alsop] /
Jonathan Adams.
Contents: Visitors' center,
Cardiff, Scotland --Apartment
house, Hafenstrasse, Hamburg --
Hotel du Department, Marseilles,
France. Architect: William Alsop
of Alsop & Lyall.
AA FILES 1990 Autumn, no.20,
p.22-30, dwgs., elev., photos.,
secn.

VISITORS' CENTERS--SWITZERLAND--
GENEVA--EUROPEAN ORGANIZATION FOR
NUCLEAR RESEARCH (CERN)--MICROCOSM
Gaia, habitat interplanetario =
Gaia, an interplanetary habitat /
Michele Caldarelli.
Project for "Microcosm" visitors'
center; architect: Filippo Avalle.
L'ARCA 1990 Jan., no.34, p.92-96,
axonometric view, dwgs., model.

VISNICENKO, L.
Il complesso residenziale di via
Gorkij (Mosca) = Presentation of
the residential project in Gorki
street in Moscow / S. Svatin.
Built 1985-88. Architects: A.
Meerson, E. Podol'skaia, O. Palei,
L. Visnicenko.
METAMORFOSI 1988, no.11, p.53-56,
photos., site plans.

VISSER, WILMA
Bakema = Bakema.
Contents: Editorial, by Dick Apon.
The big scale, by Arjen Oosterman.
't Hool, twenty years of modern
living, by Tom Dubbelman. A
baker's cart in Buikslotermeer, by
Inge Timmermans. Bakema, by
Francis Strauven. Space for the
(Continued next page)

VISSER, WILMA (CONTINUED)
  Bakema = Bakema. (CONTINUED)
    pedestrian and the Friendships
    Model, by Wilma Visser. From the
    Euromast to the Dutch pavilion for
    Osaka, by Rob Dettingmeijer. And
    Bakema..., by Rob Dettingmeijer &
    Frans Hooijkaas. Biography. In
    Dutch and English.
    FORUM 1990 Sept., v.34, no.3,
    p.[1]-[49], dwgs., models,
    photos., secns., refs.

VISUAL POLLUTION
  See LANDSCAPE PROTECTION

VISUALLY HANDICAPPED - HOUSING
  See HOUSING FOR HANDICAPPED

VITALE, DANIELE, 1904-
  Neuorganisation des Zugangsbereichs
    zur Alhambra, Granada, Spanien =
    Reorganization of the areas
    surrounding the new access to the
    Alhambra, Granada, Spain.
    International idea competition.
    Features winning designs by Peter
    Nigst, Erich Hubmann, Andreas
    Vass, for the overall plan, and
    the design for the Parque de los
    Alijares and cemetery by Daniele
    Vitale. Text in German.
    ARCHITEKTUR + WETTBEWERBE 1990
    Dec., no.144, p.56-58, dwgs.,
    models, secns., site plans.

VITANZA, THOMAS A.
  NPS surveys yield data on the
    effects of Hurricane Hugo / Thomas
    A. Vitanza.
    CRM BULLETIN: A NATIONAL PARK
    SERVICE TECHNICAL BULLETIN 1990,
    v.13, no.1, p.12-14, photos.,
    aerial photos.

VITART, MYRTO
  Fringale de musees.
    On two museum renovation
    competitons: Musee des Beaux-Arts,
    Nancy, architects: Laurent
    Beaudouin, Sylvain Giacomazzi;
    Musee des Beaux-Arts, Lille,
    architects: Jean-Marc Ibos, Myrto
    Vitart.
    ARCHITECTURE D'AUJOURD'HUI 1990
    Oct., no.271, p.88-91, dwg.,
    elevs., plans, secns., sketch.
  Kulturzentrum ONYX in St. Herblain,
    Frankreich = Cultural centre ONYX
    in St. Herblain, France.
    Architects: Myrto Vitart, of Jean
    Nouvel et Associes.
    ARCHITEKTUR + WETTBEWERBE 1990
    Sept., no.143, p.13-14, photos.,
    plans, site plan.
  Kulturzentrum Onyx: St. Herblain
    Atlantis (Loire-Frankreich).
    Architects: Myrto Vitart for Jean
    Nouvel & assoc.
    ARCH PLUS 1990 Jan., no.103,
    p.54-56, photos., plans, secn.,
    site plan.
  De metal charol: centro cultural
    Onyx, de Myrto Vitart / Vicente
    Paton.
    ARQUITECTURA VIVA 1990 July-Aug.,
    no.13, p.28-31, dwg., elevs.,
    photos., plans, secn., site plan.

VITART, MYRTO (CONTINUED)
  Musee des Beaux-Arts de Lille.
    On the renovation of the museum.
    Architects: Jean-Marc Ibos, Myrto
    Vitart. English summary, p.129.
    Spanish summary, p.173.
    TECHNIQUES ET ARCHITECTURE 1990
    Oct.-Nov., no.392, p.128-129,
    dwg., plan, secns.
  Een Nouvel concept: cultureel
    centrum te Saint Herblain /
    Bernard Leupen.
    Located in a suburb of Nantes.
    Architect: Myrto Vitart of Jean
    Nouvel ' Associes.
    DE ARCHITECT 1989 Dec., v.20,
    no.12, p.85-89, photos., plans,
    secns., site plan.
  Quatre projects pour Lille / Arnauld
    Brejon de Lavergnee.
    On the competition for the
    renovation of the Musee des
    Beaux-Arts, Lille. Winning
    Architects: Jean-Marc Ibos, Myrto
    Vitart.
    CONNAISSANCE DES ARTS 1990
    July-Aug., no.461-462, p.23-25,
    dwg., photos., secn.

VITEK, ANTONIN, 1892-1979
  Bata architecture / Vladimir
    Slapeta.
    On the projects and architects
    sponsored by the Bata firm,
    particularly in Zlin.
    RASSEGNA 1990 Sept., v.12,
    no.43/3, p.70-79, dwgs., photos.
  Die "Bata"-Architektur oder die
    Architektur eines Unternehmens /
    Vladimir Slapeta.
    On the projects and architects
    sponsored by the firm Bat'a,
    especially in Czechoslovakia.
    BAUFORUM 1990, v.23, no.136,
    p.19-48,cover, dwgs., ports.,
    elevs., photos., plans, secns.,
    site plans, sketches, biblio.

VITELLOZZI, ANNIBALE
  Il nuovo Stadio Olimpico a Roma =
    The renovated Olympic Stadium in
    Rome / Giuseppe Nannerini.
    Project head: Annibale Vitellozzi
    et al. Project architect: Studio
    Zucker. Includes English
    translation; French, German and
    Spanish summaries p.[3].
    L'INDUSTRIA DELLE COSTRUZIONI 1990
    Oct., v.24, no.228, p.6-17, dets.,
    models, photos., plans, secns.

VITIELLO AND ASSOCIATES
  Eskaton Village: a lifecare project
    that made neighbors part of the
    development team / Deborah S.
    Brittan.
    Architects: Vitiello and
    Associates.
    URBAN LAND 1990 Feb, v.49, no.2,
    p.21-23, diagrs., plans, elevs.,
    site plans.

VITILLO, PIERGIORGIO
  Torino e Genova: una rassegna
    bibliografica / Laura Pogliani,
    Piergiorgio Vitillo.
    Bibliographies on Turin and Genoa;
    text in Italian.
    URBANISTICA 1988 Nov., no.93,
    p.101-103, biblio.

VITO, LUIGI DI
  Venosa: saggio per una carta storica
    del territorio comunale / Gregorio
    Angelini, Luigi di Vito,
    Antonietta Groia.
    English, French, German, Spanish
    summaries p.128.
    STORIA DELLA CITTA 1989 Jan.-Mar.,
    v.14, no.49, p.89-124, maps,
    engrs., refs.

VITOLS ASSOCIATES
  Good work: architects' designs for
    low-income housing.
    Seven projects: Washington Elms
    (Cambridge, Mass.), architects:
    Bruner/Cott & Associates,
    landscape architect: Michael
    Weinmayr; Scattered site housing
    (Madison, N.J.), architects: The
    Hillier Group; Diamond Park
    Housing (Philadelphia, Pa.),
    architects: Cecil Baker &
    Associates; DeSmet Apartments
    (Florissant, Mo.), architects:
    Henderson Group; Callahan Oaks
    (Orlando, Fla), architects:
    Fugleberg Koch; Mission Hill
    (Boston, Mass.), architects:
    Vitols Associates, landscape
    architects: Pryor/Geller; and
    Glenardon Apartments (Glenardon,
    Md.), architects: CHK Architects
    and Planners.
    JOURNAL OF HOUSING 1989 July-Aug.,
    v.46, no.4, p.196-201, dwg.,
    photos.

VITOU, ELISABETH. GABRIEL GUEVREKIAN,
1900-1970
  Gabriel Guevrekian (1900-1970): une
    autre architecture [by] Elisabeth
    Vilou, Dominique Deshoulieres,
    Hubert Jeanneau [book review] /
    Dorothee Imbert.
    SOCIETY OF ARCHITECTURAL
    HISTORIANS. JOURNAL 1990 Dec.,
    v.49, no.4, p.449-450,

VITRUVIUS POLLIO
  Excerpt: Dinocrates, architect.
    Excerpt from Vitruvius' intro. to
    Book II, "provides a glimpse of
    the golden age of marketing."
    PROGRESSIVE ARCHITECTURE 1990
    Apr., v.71, no.4, p.121, ill.
  Vitruvius and Roman theater design /
    Frank B. Sear.
    AMERICAN JOURNAL OF ARCHAEOLOGY
    1990 Apr., v.94, no.2, p.249-258,
    diagrs., plans, refs.

VITRUVIUS POLLIO. DE ARCHITECTURA
  Medietes et approximations chez
    Vitruve / Louis Frey.
    Focus on Vitruvius' Book III of De
    architectura. English summary,
    p.444.
    REVUE ARCHEOLOGIQUE 1990, no.2,
    p.[285]-330, diagrs., dwgs.,
    biblio., refs.
  The Simulachrum of Fabio Calvo: a
    view of Roman architecture
    all'antica in 1527 / Philip J.
    Jacks.
    The work of the antiquarian Calvo
    was "the first systematic attempt
    to visualize the urban formation
    of Rome in historical stages."
    Includes abstract.
    ART BULLETIN 1990 Sept., v.72,
    no.3, p.453-481, ill., photos.,
      (Continued next page)

VITRUVIUS POLLIO. DE ARCHITECTURA
                    (CONTINUED)
  The Simulachrum of...(CONTINUED)
  plans, engrs., secns., biblio.,
  refs.

VITTA, MAURIZIO
  Ambiguita e iconismo per l'industria
  = Ambiguity and iconism for
  industry / Maurizio Vitta.
  Pelli factory, Empoli; architect:
  Paolo Riani.
  L'ARCA 1990 Dec., no.44, p.58-63,
  photos., plans, secn.
  Il CED del Credito Italiano a Milano
  = Credito Italiano DPC centre in
  Milan / Maurizio Vitta.
  Data processing center between Via
  Trenno & Via Sant'Elia.
  Architects: Ignazio Gardella,
  Paolo Crescini. Text in Italian
  and English.
  L'ARCA 1990 Jan., no.34, p.74-81,
  axonometric view, photos., aerial
  photo.
  Un complesso per gli incontri:
  Makuhari Messe, Tokyo / Maurizio
  Vitta.
  Architects: Fumihiko Maki. Text in
  Italian and English.
  L'ARCA 1990 Sept., no.41, p.8-19,
  axonometric view, elevs., photos.,
  plans, secns.
  Il design e ergonomia = Design and
  ergonomics / John Wakefield,
  Maurizio Vitta.
  Focus on "Swing" office chair and
  "Stream" movable dividing wall;
  designer: Isao Hosoe.
  L'ARCA 1990 Oct., no.42, p.80-85,
  axonometric view, dwgs., elevs.,
  photos., plans.
  La Facolta di Scienze a L'Aquila =
  The Science Faculty of L'Aquila /
  Maurizio Vitta.
  Architects: Guido Gigli, Bruno
  Remotti, Ludovico Rolli.
  L'ARCA 1990 July-Aug., no.40,
  p.66-73, photos., plans, secn.
  Una foresta di metallo a Fujisawa:
  Shonandai Cultural Center /
  Maurizio Vitta.
  Architect: Itsuko Hasegawa.
  L'ARCA 1990 Oct., no.42, p.22-31,
  elevs., photos., plans.
  Il Gotico moderno di Gunnar Birkerts
  = Gunnar Birkerts' modern Gothic /
  Maurizio Vitta.
  On St. Peter's Lutheran Church,
  Columbus, Ind., designed in 1980
  and recently completed.
  L'ARCA 1990 Feb., no.35, p.24-33,
  elev., photos, plans, secns., site
  plans, sketch.
  Il gusto modo di far le cose = The
  right way of doing things /
  Maurizio Vitta.
  The architecture of Medieval
  monastic orders in Europe.
  L'ARCA 1990 Dec., no.44, p.4-9,
  photos., plans.
  Ieri e oggi le mura = The city and
  the walls [book review] / Maurizio
  Vitta.
  Review of La citta e le mura, ed.
  by Cesare De Seta. Text in Italian
  and English.
  L'ARCA 1990 Jan., no.34 suppl.
  press, p.109,

VITTA, MAURIZIO (CONTINUED)
  National Guard Sports Center, Khashm
  Alaan / Maurizio Vitta.
  Architect: Claudio Salocchi. Text
  in Italian and English.
  L'ARCA 1990 May, no.38, p.26-33,
  photos., plans, secns., site
  plans.
  Un ombrello per rifugio = An
  umbrella shelter / Maurizio Vitta.
  Transportable emergency shelter
  design; architects: Future
  Systems.
  L'ARCA 1990 Oct., no.42 suppl.
  l'Arca 2, p.97-98, dwgs., elevs.,
  photo.
  Per i diritti dell'uomo = Building
  for the Rights of Man / Maurizio
  Vitta.
  In Strasbourg, France. Architects:
  Richard Rogers Partnership. Text
  in Italian and English.
  L'ARCA 1990 Mar., no.36,
  p.[52]-59, elevs., model, plans,
  secn., site plan.
  Un perimetro di cristallo per
  l'Universita di San Diego = A
  crystal perimeter for San Diego
  University / Maurizio Vitta.
  Underground extension to library
  designed by William Pereira;
  architects of extension: Gunnar
  Birkerts & Associates.
  L'ARCA 1990 Apr., no.37, p.42-47,
  axonometric view, photos., plans,
  secns.
  Sobrieta "intelligente" nel cuore di
  Londra = "Intelligent" sobriety in
  the heart of London / Maurizio
  Vitta.
  News International building,
  Whitefriars Street, London
  project; architects: YRM
  Architects & Planners. Includes
  essay: Computers and global
  design. Text in Italian and
  English.
  L'ARCA 1990 June, no.39, p.20-33,
  dwgs., elevs., plans, secns., site
  plan.
  Spazio, luce, architettura = Space,
  light, architecture / Maurizio
  Vitta.
  L'ARCA 1990 Nov., no.43, p.1-[3],
  photo.
  Tra innocenza e narcisismo = Twixt
  innocence and narcissism [book
  review] / Maurizio Vitta.
  Review of L'Architettura di Gunnar
  Birkerts, by Kay Kaiser. Text in
  Italian and English.
  L'ARCA 1990 Jan., no.34 suppl.
  press, p.108, model.
  Ultimo ponte a Parigi = The latest
  bridge in Paris / Maurizio Vitta.
  Competition projects for new
  bridge over Seine; architects:
  Claude Vasconi; Remy Butler and J.
  V. Berlottier; Foster, Francis,
  Jourda & Perraudin; Chemetov &
  Huidobro; Dominique Perrault.
  L'ARCA 1990 July-Aug., no.40,
  p.20-29, 1 folded leaf, elevs.,
  plans, secns., site plans.

VITTADINI, MARIA ROSA
  Politiche per Venezia / Cristina
  Bianchetti, Chiara Merlini.
  Introduces eight articles on city
  planning in Venice. English
  summaries, p.124-126. Contents:
  Osservare le politiche per
                    (Continued next column)

VITTADINI, MARIA ROSA (CONTINUED)
  Politiche per Venezia...(CONTINUED)
  Venezia: perche?; Marittima e
  Arsenale nel contesto delle
  trasformazioni urbane a Venezia;
  Vedute della laguna; Il consorzio
  Venezia nuova, concessionario
  dello stato per le opere di
  salvaguardia di Venezia; La casa a
  Venezia; Infrastrutture per la
  mobilita (e l'uranistica) nella
  nuova dimensione di Venezia;
  Appunti sulla questione della
  metropolitana a Venezia; Alcuni
  limiti alla delegittimazione
  sociale delle istituzioni
  pubbliche di governo urbano.
  URBANISTICA 1990 Mar., no.98,
  p.33-86,124-126, graphs, maps,
  photos., plans, secn., site plan,
  tables, refs.
  Il Prg di Pistoia / Armando Barp,
  Maria Rosa Vittadini.
  Master plan for Pistoia. City
  planners: Armando Barp, Claudio
  Cicchetti, Sandro Pandolfo, Maria
  Rosa Vittadini. English summary.
  URBANISTICA 1989 June, no.95,
  p.19-21, plans.

VITTORINI, MARCELLO
  Piano regolatore del Comune di
  Trento: relazione generale.
  City planning policies for the
  expansion of Trent. Coordinators:
  Marcello Vittorini, Giorgio
  Trebbi. Summaries in French,
  English, German, and Spanish, p.1.
  Captions in Italian and English.
  PARAMETRO 1990 Nov.-Dec., no.181,
  p.16-51, maps, photos., plans,
  site plans, tables, aerial photos.

VIVALDI, RENATO
  Fundacion Santa Barbara, Mammola,
  Italia.
  Architects: Renato Vivaldi T.,
  Jorge Brunetto, Aldo Hidalgo H.,
  Adriana Perez P.
  CA: REVISTA OFICIAL DEL COLEGIO DE
  ARQUITECTOS DE CHILE 1989
  Apr.-June, no.56, p.[68]-71,
  dwgs., port., elev., map, photos.,
  plan, secns., site plan.

VIVIEN, JEAN-FRANCOIS
  Au-dela de la Grande Arche /
  Jean-Louis Pages, Jean-Francois
  Vivien.
  To develop the loop of the Seine
  from La Defense to Genovilliers.
  English, French and Spanish
  abstracts, p.3, English summary,
  p.24.
  CAHIERS DE L'INSTITUT
  D'AMENAGEMENT ET D'URBANISME DE LA
  REGION D'ILE-DE-FRANCE 1990 Jan.,
  no.92, p.9-24, maps, photo.,
  plans, site plans, sketch, aerial
  photos.

VLASTIMIL KOUBEK (FIRM)
  Square 456, Washington, D.C., 1991.
  Proposed building at 6th and E
  St., N.W.; architects: Kohn
  Pedersen Fox Associates and
  Vlastimil Koubek.
  PROCESS: ARCHITECTURE 1989 Nov.,
  no.86, p.86-89, elevs., model,
  plans, secns., site plan.

VLCEK, PAVEL
"Dientzenhoferuv skicar" a ceska
architektura 1640-1670 / Pavel
Vlcek.
Elevations and plans from the
"Dietzenhofers Sketchbook."
Includes German summary.
UMENI 1989, v.37, no.6, p.473-497,
elevs., plans, refs.
Kostel sv. Kateriny na novem meste
prazskem / Lubos Lancinger, Pavel
Vlcek.
Church of St. Catherine in
Prague's New Town. Architect:
K.I. Dietzenhofer.
UMENI 1989, v.37, no.6, p.553-556,
photos., plans, refs.

VLIET, NICK VAN
Dodoma, new capital of Tanzania: a
case of non-sustainable
development / Nick van Vliet.
LANDSCAPE ARCHITECTURAL REVIEW
1990 Oct., v.11, no.4, p.13-18,
maps, photos., biblios.
The game of wildlife conservation:
conflicts in the Serengeti / Nick
van Vliet.
An ecological entity of open and
wooded grasslands in northern
Tanzania and southwestern Kenya.
Includes French summary.
LANDSCAPE ARCHITECTURAL REVIEW
1990 Mar., v.11, no.1, p.6-12,
map, photos., biblios.

VLIS, MICHAEL VAN DER
"Discussies: winst voor
stedebouwkurdige kwaliteit"
[interview] / Marijke Prins.
A discussion with Michael Van der
Vlis, chief of the project for
development of the IJ-oevers area
of Amsterdam.
BOUW 1989 Aug.11, v.44, no.16,
p.10-12, diagrs., dwgs., port.,
map, secn.

VLUGT, MAURITS VAN DER
Application of geographic
information systems in Europe /
Henk J. Scholten, Maurits van der
Vlugt.
EKISTICS 1989 Sept.-Dec., v.56,
no.338-339, p.304-311, chart,
table, biblio.

VOCABULARY
See "VOCABULARY" AS A SUBHEADING
AFTER MAIN HEADINGS.

VOCATIONAL SCHOOLS
See SCHOOLS - VOCATIONAL

VOCATIONAL SCHOOLS--LUXEMBOURG--
BONNEVOIE
Lycee technique au Luxembourg /
Jean-Claude Vigato.
Located in Bonnevoie. Architects:
Atelier A.L.D.
ARCHITECTURE D'AUJOURD'HUI 1990
Oct., no.271, p.92-93, photos.,
plan.

VODAR, M.
Toulon: concours pour l'hotel de
ville.
Competition designs by Claude
Vasconi (winner); Fainsilber,
Petraccone, & Vodar; J. Donato;
Borde, Nothhelfer, Duchier; Andre
Stern; and Badani, Lefrancois,
(Continued next column)

VODAR, M. (CONTINUED)
Toulon: concours...(CONTINUED)
Detroyat et Condroyer.
LE MONITEUR ARCHITECTURE AMC 1990
Apr., no.10, p.8-9, ill., models,
plans, secns., site plans.

VOELKER, THEODORE
To gather together: Andover Town
Hall restoration / Paul M.
Sachner.
In Andover, Mass. Architects: Ann
Beha Associates. Original
architect (1855): Theodore
Voelker.
ARCHITECTURAL RECORD 1990 Nov.,
v.178, no.12, p.62-65, photos.,
plans, secn.

VOELKER, WILLIAM
Economics: whither the economy? /
William Voelker.
PROGRESSIVE ARCHITECTURE 1990
Dec., v.71, no.13, p.53.

VOGEL, NEAL A.
Documentation projects, part 1:
Photography / Neal A. Vogel,
Christopher Jenks.
Techniques for photo-documentation
of historic buildings. Examples
include the Church of St. John the
Evangelist, Stockport, N.Y.
COMMON BOND 1990 Fall, v.6, no.4,
p.4-7, photos.

VOGELER, INGOLF
The character of place: building
materials and architectural
characteristics in Eau Claire,
Wisconsin / Ingolf Vogeler.
Analysis of house styles
(1860's-1970's) using field
observations and data obtained
from the assessor's office.
MATERIAL CULTURE 1990 Spring,
v.22, no.1, p.1-21, graphs, maps,
biblio.

VOGLER, WERNER
Der spanische Konig als Stifter von
Pontifikalornaten fur den Abt von
St. Gallen im 17. und 18.
Jahrhundert / Werner Vogler.
French and Italian summaries.
UNSERE KUNSTDENKMALER 1989, v.40,
no.3, p.247, plan, engrs., refs.

VOGLIAZZO, MAURIZIO
Il Biocenter di Francoforte =
Frankfurt Biocenter / Maurizio
Vogliazzo.
Project for biological laboratory
at Frankfurt University;
architect: Peter Eisenman.
L'ARCA 1990 Nov., no.43, p.52-59,
dwgs., model, plans.
Un tunnel sulla stazione = The
Waterloo enclosure / Maurizio
Vogliazzo.
New international train terminal
of Waterloo Station, London.
Architects: Nicholas Grimshaw &
Partners. Structural engineers:
YRM, Anthony Hunt Associates. Text
in Italian and English.
L'ARCA 1990 Sept., no.41, p.26-39,
dwgs., models, photos., plans,
secns., site plan.

VOGT, A. G.
Islamic world architects at
Mackintosh School of Architecture
/ A.G. Vogt.
ARTS & THE ISLAMIC WORLD 1990
Autumn-Winter, no.19, p.105-107,
111, axonometric view, dwgs.,
maps, photos.
Revival urbano ovvero la riscoperta
della citta [Glasgow] / A. G.
Vogt.
In Italian; Italian and English
captions.
URBANISTICA 1989 Oct., no.96,
p.112-115, photos., aerial photo.,
refs.

VOGT-GOKNIL, ULYA
Der Kubus in der islamischen
Architektur = The cube in Islamic
architecture / Ulya Vogt-Goknil.
Text in German and English.
DAIDALOS 1990 Mar.15, no.35,
p.61-73, photos., plans, secn.,
refs.

VOIGT & HERZIG
Besucher-Pavillon:
Informationszentrum der
Erdfunkstelle Usingen.
Architects: Voigt und Herzog.
DEUTSCHE BAUZEITUNG 1990 Dec.,
v.124, no.12, p.56-58, dets.,
elevs., models, plans, secns.
Museum fur Volkerkunde in Frankfurt.
Competition projects by Richard
Meier (winner); O.M. Ungers; and
Voigt & Herzig; Becker, Grossman,
Meiler.
BAUMEISTER 1990 June, v.87, no.6,
p.40-45, axonometric views,
models, site plans.

VOIGT, EBERHARD, 1946-
LZ 127: Erweiterung des
Zeppelin-Museums in Neu-Isenburg.
Architects: Voigt und Herzig.
DEUTSCHE BAUZEITUNG 1990 Jan.,
v.124, no.1, p.46-48, photos.,
plans, secn., site plan.
Vielseitig: ein Portrait der
Architekten Eberhard Voigt und
Franz Herzig, Darmstadt.
DEUTSCHE BAUZEITUNG 1990 Apr.,
v.124, no.4, p.56-57, ill., dwg.,
photos.

VOIGT, WOLFGANG
Architettura dell'occupazione:
Francia e Germania 1940-1950 /
Jean-Louis Cohen, Hartmut Frank.
Contributions by Wolfgang Voigt,
Ulrich Hohns, and Remi Baudoui.
Includes English captions and
summary.
CASABELLA 1990 Apr., v.54, no.567,
p.40-63, axonometric view, ill.,
dwgs., elevs., models, maps,
photos., plans, site plans,
sketches, biblio., refs.
Brasilia in hartje Berlijn:
prijsvraag "Hauptstadte Berlin"
1957-1958 / Wolfgang Voigt.
Winners included Alison and Peter
Smithson, Marion Tournon-Branly.
ARCHIS 1990 Dec., no.12, p.4-5,
dwg., plan, site plan.

VON GERKAN, MARG UND PARTNER
(CONTINUED)
On the Elbe / Veronica Pease.
Multi-use building in Hamburg
contains architects' offices,
restaurant and art gallery.
Architects: Von Gerkan, Marg und
Partner.
ARCHITECTURAL REVIEW 1990 Dec.,
v.188, no.1126, p.39-43, dets.,
photos., plans, secns., site
plans.
Projekt "Elbeschlucht": Restaurant,
Architektenburo, Galerie und
Wohnhaus in Hamburg.
Built 1988-90. Architects:
Meinhard von Gerkan; von Gerkan,
Marg and Partner. Includes English
summary.
BAUMEISTER 1990 July, v.87, no.7,
p.54-59, photos., plans, secns.,
site plan.
Strassenkreuzer: Wohn- und
Geschaftschaus in Hamburg / Dirk
Meyhofer.
Architects: Von Gerkan, Marg und
Partner.
DEUTSCHE BAUZEITUNG 1990 May,
v.124, no.5, p.14-19, photos.,
plans, secn., site plan.
Toblerone: die Erweiterung des
Stuttgarter Flughafens:
Erlauterung und Kommentar.
Architects: von Gerkan, Marg und
Partner.
DEUTSCHE BAUZEITUNG 1990 Nov.,
v.124, no.11, p.40-49, dets.,
elevs., models, photos., plans,
secns., aerial photos.
Tokyo International Forum / Gerhard
G. Feldmeyer.
Features entries by Von Gerkan,
Marg und Partner and Hentrich
Petschnigg und Partner.
DEUTSCHE BAUZEITSCHRIFT 1990 Nov.,
v.38, no.11, p.1551-1555, dwgs.,
models, plans, secns., isometric
dwg.
Um den Globus...Flughafen in Japan,
den USA, Danemark und Deutschland
/ Ursula Baus.
Kansai Airport, Osaka (Renzo
Piano, Paul Andreu); O'Hare
Airport, Chicago (Helmut Jahn with
Epstein & Sons); Copenhagen
Airport, Kastrup (Holscher,
Axelsson, Sorensen); Flughafen
Hamburg, Fuhlsbuttel (Von Gerkan,
Marg und Partner); and Terminal
Ost, Frankfurt (Buro J. S. K).
DEUTSCHE BAUZEITUNG 1990 Nov.,
v.124, no.11, p.54-63, dwgs.,
elevs., models, photos., plans,
secns., site plans.
Umbau der Hauptverwaltung der
Bertelsmann AG / Horst Ludwig,
Achim Nagel.
Located in Gutersloh. Architects:
Von Gerkan, Marg und Partner.
DEUTSCHE BAUZEITSCHRIFT 1990 Oct.,
v.38, no.10, p.1417-1428, dets.,
photos., plans, secns., site
plans, tables.

VON KERSTING / SMITH
The legend lives on: the
redecoration of George Cukor's
house evokes a golden era of the
silver screen / Leo Lerman.
Now home of Lynn von Kersting and
Richard Irving. Interior
designers: Von Kersting/Smith.
(Continued next column)

VON KERSTING / SMITH (CONTINUED)
The legend lives on:...(CONTINUED)
HOUSE & GARDEN 1990 Jan., v.162,
no.1, p.[60-69],146, port.,
photos.

VONEY, WILLI
Wohn- und Geschaftshaus in Baden,
Wettbewerbsprojekt, 1988 (in
Ausfuhrung) / Willi Voney.
Architects: Burkhard & Mueller.
WERK, BAUEN + WOHNEN 1990 Apr.,
no.4, p.38-41, dwg., elevs.,
plans, secns., site plan.

VONIER, THOMAS
Capitol columns stand again / Thomas
Vonier.
22 sandstone Corinthian columns
from the East Portico of the U.S.
Capitol installed and U.S.
National Arboretum. Landscape
architects: EDAW.
PROGRESSIVE ARCHITECTURE 1990
Sept., v.71, no.9, p.27, photo.
Congress considers architectural
copyrights / Thomas Vonier.
On H.R. 3990, the Architectural
Works Copyright Protection Act of
1990.
PROGRESSIVE ARCHITECTURE 1990 May,
v.71, no.5, p.26,28,
IBM's architecture at Building
Museum [exhibition review] /
Thomas Vonier.
Part of the National Building
Museum's fourth annual design
award program. On view through
Sept. 1990.
PROGRESSIVE ARCHITECTURE 1990 May,
v.71, no.5, p.26, photos.
Kohn Pedersen Fox wins World Bank /
Thomas Vonier.
Competition to design bank on
Pennsylvania Avenue site,
Washington, D.C.
PROGRESSIVE ARCHITECTURE 1990
July, v.71, no.7, p.23-24, model.
P/A awards update: a two-fold
solution / Thomas Vonier, Philip
Arcidi.
The U.S. Embassy in Muscat, Oman
and the State Dept.'s Office of
Foreign Buildings Operation's
requirements for security design.
Architects: James Stewart Polshek
& Partners.
PROGRESSIVE ARCHITECTURE 1990
June, v.71, no.6, p.114-120,
elevs., photos., plans, secns.
UIA meeting in Montreal:
Archistroika / Thomas Vonier.
Report on 17th world congress of
the International Union of
Architects.
PROGRESSIVE ARCHITECTURE 1990
July, v.71, no.7, p.26.
Washington report [Justice
Department investigation of AIA] /
Thomas Vonier.
On the recent consent decree
involving claims that the AIA had
conspired to violate the Sherman
Antitrust Act.
PROGRESSIVE ARCHITECTURE 1990
Oct., v.71, no.10, p.23-24,
Woman's memorial design chosen /
Thomas Vonier.
Winning design for the entrance of
Arlington National Cemetary
incorporates glass prisms atop
existing Beaux-Arts hemicycle
(Continued next column)

VONIER, THOMAS (CONTINUED)
Woman's memorial...(CONTINUED)
designed by McKim, Mead and White.
Architects: Marion Gail Weiss,
Michael A. Manfredi. Alternate
winners: Teresa Norton, Cleveland
Harp.
PROGRESSIVE ARCHITECTURE 1990
Jan., v.71, no.1, p.30, models.

VONNAK, ARPAD
Zum 5. Mal "Wohnhaus des Jahres" in
Ungarn / Kalman Timon.
Six projects. Architects: Gabor
Farkas, Gyorgy Radvanyi, Ferenc
Lorincz, Jozsef Pinczei, Arpad
Vonnak, and Gyorgy Ruisz. German,
Russian, English and French
summaries, p.55-56.
ARCHITEKTUR DER DDR 1990 Feb.,
v.38, no.2, p.43-48, photos.,
plans.

VOORDT, THEO J.M. VAN DER
Building adaptable housing - from
theory to practice / Theo J. M.
van der Voordt.
On housing for the handicapped in
the Netherlands. Includes French
summary.
ARCHITECTURE & COMPORTEMENT =
ARCHITECTURE & BEHAVIOUR 1990,
v.6, no.1, p.17-37, figs., graph,
plans, tables, biblio.

VORHOELZER, ROBERT, 1884-1954--
EXHIBITIONS
Rudolf Vorhoelzer und Lois
Welzenbacher, zwei Ausstellungen
uber alternative Wege des Neuen
Bauens [exhibition review] / Jorg
Stabenow.
Exhibitions in Munich and
Innsbruck.
ARCH PLUS 1990 July, no.104,
p.14-15, models, photos., plans.

VORREITER, GABRIELE
El refugio de los nomadas: un cafe
de Toyo Ito / Gabriele Vorreiter.
Cafe Nomad, Tokyo.
ARQUITECTURA VIVA 1990 May-June,
no.12, p.57-59, photos., plans,
secns.

VOSS, HENRY
Gentofte-Vangede Idraetsforening /
Henry Voss.
Clubhouse for an athletic
association in a Copenhagen
suburb, completed in 1989.
Architect: Ole Ramsgaard Thomsen.
Includes English and German
summaries.
ARKITEKTUR DK 1990, v.34, no.7,
p.351-354, photos., plan, site
plan.
Knud Peter Harboe / Henry Voss.
Five projects: Villa for an art
collector; office building and
gym, Gl. Kongevej, Copenhagen;
Sophus Berendsen head-quarters,
Gladsaxe; apartment building at Pi
Alle 9-11, Fredericksberg; villa,
Holte. Includes English and
German summaries.
ARKITEKTUR DK 1990, v.34, no.6,
p.306-316, dwgs., photos., plans,
site plans.

VOTICKY, ROBERT
Designs on Europe / Robert Voticky.
Report on the RIBA seminar,
Building in Europe.
BUILDING DESIGN 1990 Apr.13,
no.981, p.20-23, photos.

VOUSSEAUX
See KEYSTONES

VOYE, LILIANE
Autour des "images de la ville".
Three articles: "Les images de la
ville: questions au
post-modernisme", by Liliane Voye;
"Images de la ville, images de la
vie", by Ch. Roy; and "Composer la
ville et ses images", by Michel
Conan. From special issue on
Raymond Ledrut 1969. French,
English and Spanish summaries.
ESPACES ET SOCIETES 1990,
no.57-58, p.71-119, diagrs.,
tables, refs.

VOYSEY, CHARLES F. A., 1857-1941
A designer's domain: inspiration on
the Voysey Room at the Geffrye
Museum / Maureen Connett.
Art nouveau period room in a
London museum.
TRADITIONAL HOMES 1990 Apr., v.6,
no.7, p.55-56, photos.

VOYSEY, CHARLES F. A., 1857-1941--
EXHIBITIONS
An eye for a line: Voysey and
decoration: drawings from the
collection of the British
Architectural Library. [exhibition
review] / Roderick Gradidge.
Exhibition held at the Heinz
Gallery, London through 27 Oct.
1990. Includes book review: The
decorative designs of C.F.A.
Voysey, by Stuart Durant.
ARCHITECTS' JOURNAL 1990 Oct.17,
v.192, no.16, p.94-95,97, ill.
Papered optimism: Voysey wallpaper
designs [exhibition review] /
Michael Hall.
Exhibition held at Heinz Gallery,
RIBA, Sept.-Oct. 1990.
COUNTRY LIFE 1990 Oct.11, v.184,
no.41, p.118, photo.
Versatile Voysey: Voysey and
decoration: drawings from the
collection of the British
Architectural Library [exhibition
review] / Trevor Gett.
Exhibition of drawings by Arts and
Crafts architect C.F.A. Voysey at
the RIBA Heinz Gallery, London 19
Sept. to 27 Oct. 1990.
ROYAL SOCIETY OF ARTS, LONDON. RSA
JOURNAL 1990 Dec., v.139, no.5413,
p.939-940, ill.

VOZENILEK, JIRI, 1909-1986
Bata architecture / Vladimir
Slapeta.
On the projects and architects
sponsored by the Bata firm,
particularly in Zlin.
RASSEGNA 1990 Sept., v.12,
no.43/3, p.70-79, dwgs., photos.
Die "Bata"-Architektur oder die
Architektur eines Unternehmens /
Vladimir Slapeta.
On the projects and architects
sponsored by the firm Bat'a,
especially in Czechoslovakia.
(Continued next column)

VOZENILEK, JIRI, 1909-1986
(CONTINUED)
Die...(CONTINUED)
BAUFORUM 1990, v.23, no.136,
p.19-48,cover, dwgs., ports.,
elevs., photos., plans, secns.,
site plans, sketches, biblio.

VREEZE, NOUD DE
Tussen marktmechanisme en politieke
idealen: de landelijke politiek en
de kwaliteit van dc
volkshuisvesting / Noud de Vreeze.
Reviews history of Dutch housing
policy under about ten ministers
during the past four decades.
ARCHIS 1990 Feb., no.2, p.21-28,
ports.

VRETBLAD, LASSE
Globen city, Stockholm / Sture
Koinberg, Lasse Vretblad.
Architects: Berg Arkitektkontor.
ARKITEKTUR: THE SWEDISH REVIEW OF
ARCHITECTURE 1990 Jan.-Feb., v.90,
no.1, p.22-29, photos., plans.

VRIES, HERMAN DE
Kunst per strekkende meter langs de
snelweg: geluidsscherm in
Amsterdam-Noord / Herman de Vries.
A 12 km.-long noise barrier along
highway A-10 in north Amsterdam,
by artist Pjotr van Oorschot and
landscape architect Ron Pfeiffer.
ARCHIS 1989 Sept., no.9, p.10-11,
axonometric view, photos.

VRIES, JAN DE
Studying cities in their context /
Jan de Vries.
English and French summaries.
URBAN HISTORY REVIEW. REVUE
D'HISTOIRE URBAINE 1990 Feb.,
v.18, no.3, p.193-199, table,
refs.

VRIJLANDT, P.
Vergezichten: thema's in de
landschapsarchitectuur / Eric
Luiten.
Problems and solutions in local,
regional and national landscape
planning. Examples are by K.
Kerkstra and P. Vrijlandt, C.
Harmsen and J.W. Jansens, B.
Olthof and W. Oerlemans.
ARCHIS 1990 Sept., no.9, p.11-16,
dwgs., maps, secn., biblio.

VROOM, M. J.
Changing agricultural landscapes of
Europe / M.J. Vroom.
Special issue, edited by M.J.
Vroom. "A selection from the
papers delivered at the Conference
organized by the Dutch Foundation:
'The future of the European
Landscape', under the auspices of
the International Federation of
Landscape Architects in Rotterdam,
9-11 May 1988."
LANDSCAPE AND URBAN PLANNING 1990
Feb., v.18, nos.3-4, p.179-353,
graphs, port., maps, photos.,
plans, sketches, refs.

VROOM, METO J.
Landscape planning in the
Netherlands: the role of
competitions / Vroom, M.J.
BUILT ENVIRONMENT 1990, v.16,
no.2, p.141-161, axonometric view,
graph, photos., maps, plans,
secns., refs.
Landscape planning: some European
perspectives / Meto J. Vroom.
Theme issue: six articles,
separately indexed.
BUILT ENVIRONMENT 1990, v.16,
no.2, p.89-91,

VURPAS, PIERRE
L'hotellerie en mouvement.
On the hotel industry. Includes
eight recent hotel projects.
English summary, p.162.
ARCHITECTURE INTERIEURE CREE 1990
Mar., no.235, p.48-83, dwgs.,
ports., photos., plans, isometric
dwgs.

VYBIRAL, JINDRICH
Architektura let 1850-1950 v Knove /
Jindrich Vybiral, Pavel Zatloukal.
Includes German summary.
UMENI 1990, v.38, no.6, p.521-533,
elev., photos., refs.

VYTLACIL, ANNE
Architecture: a place for women.
Contents: Room at the top? Sexism
and the star system in
architecture, by Denise Scott
Brown.--Educating for the future,
by Matilda McQuaid.--The studio
experience: differences for women
students, by Anne Vytlacil.
ARCHITECTURAL DESIGN 1990, v.60,
no.1-2, p.[X]-[XIV],

WAAL, ALLAN DE
Byens rum, historien og buggelysten / Allan de Waal, Grethe Silding. Presents Danish methods of town planning and preservation, using Roskilde and Nakskov as examples. ARKITEKTEN 1990 Apr., v.92, no.5, p.152-157, photos., site plans, sketches.

WAALS, MARIAN VAN DER
Gebouw als gebeurtenis: Peter Eisenmans Wexner Center for the Visual Arts / Marian van der Waals. In Columbus, Ohio. DE ARCHITECT 1990 May, v.21, no.5, p.51-55, axonometric views, photos., plans, site plans.

WACHENFELD & ENDERT
Architektur unterwegs.
Three projects: Commerzbank Bochum-Wattenschied, Bochum (architect: Bernd Fuldner); Sotronic Kabelsysteme GmbH, Baunach (architect: Michael Jockers); Institut fur offentliche verwaltung Nordrhein-Westfalen, Hilden (architect: Wachenfeld & Endert). DEUTSCHES ARCHITEKTENBLATT 1990 Mar.1, v.22, no.1, p.349-352, elevs., photos., plans.

WADA, YUKINOBU
Study on the method of local planning in France / Yuji Kusumoto, Nobuyoshi Fujimoto, Yukinobu Wada. Part 1: "Land use planning" for small communes. Text in Japanese; Enlgish summary. NIHON KENCHIKU GAKKAI KEIKAKUKEI RONBUN HOKOKU SHU = JOURNAL OF ARCHITECTURE, PLANNING AND ENVIRONMENTAL ENGINEERING 1990 Nov., no.11(417), p.87-98, map, site plan, tablkes, refs.

WAEGEMAN, T. G.
Le chateau de Rullingen / T.G. Waegeman. History of manor house located in Borgloon, Belgium. After fire in 1920, the manor was rebuilt in the brabancon neo-Renaissance style by the Belgian architect, Langerock. MAISONS D'HIER ET D'AUJOURD'HUI = DE WOONSTEDE DOOR DE EEUWEN HEEN 1990 June, no.86, p.42-48, map, photos., plan, refs.

WAERN, RASMUS
Egna Ogon & Andras [book review] / Rasmus Waern. Review of Varlden den lilla den stora: Lustvandringar i Klassicismens arkitektur och tradgardar, by Anna-Maria Blenow and Olle Svedberg, and Stader, byggnader..., byNils Erik Wickberg. ARKITEKTUR: THE SWEDISH REVIEW OF ARCHITECTURE 1990 Nov., v.90, no.9, p.55-57, dwg., photos. Svensk modell [book review] / Rasmus Waern. Review of Sven Markelius, arkitekt, by Eva Rudberg. ARKITEKTUR: THE SWEDISH REVIEW OF ARCHITECTURE 1990 June-July, v.90, (Continued next column)

WAERN, RASMUS (CONTINUED)
Svensk modell [book...(CONTINUED) no.5, p.50-52, port., plan, sketches. Vastra piren, Goteborg / Per Dahlin, Pietro Raffone. Restaurant, with triangular plan, on an Eriksberg pier. Architect: Arkitektlaget AB. Built 1989-1990. Includes commentary by Rasmus Waern. ARKITEKTUR: THE SWEDISH REVIEW OF ARCHITECTURE 1990 Nov., v.90, no.9, p.28-33, photos., plans, secn., site plan.

WAGMANN, GUNTER
Unterrichts- und Internatsgebaude in Grub bei Munchen, D = Seminar and boarding school building in Grub near Munich, G. New building for an agricultural training school. Architects: Helmut Gebhard, Bernhard Landbrecht, Gunter Wagmann. DETAIL 1990 Feb.-Mar., v.30, no.1, p.39-46, dets., photos., plans, secns.

WAGNER, FRIEDOLIN
Der Sonne zum Trotz / Friedolin Wagner. On Marchesa Liviana Taverna Gallerati-Scotti's garden in Torre San Lorenzo, Italy. ARCHITEKTUR & WOHNEN 1990 June-July, no.3, p.82-88, port., photos.

WAGNER, FRIEDRICH
Mies-van-der-Rohe-Preis 1990. Prize granted by the Aktiongemeinschaft Glas im Bau. First prize (Friedrich Wagner, for hall in Schwabisch Hall) and five other winners. BAUWELT 1990 May 25, v.81, no.20, p.974-975, photos. Mies-van-der-Rohe-Preis 1990. Winner: Friedrich Wagner. DEUTSCHE BAUZEITSCHRIFT 1990 June, v.38, no.6, p.788-789, photos.

WAGNER, FRITZ
Zug: Planung in einer Wohlstandsregion / Fritz Wagner. SCHWEIZER BAUMARKT 1989 Oct.2, no.13, p.ii-iv, photos.

WAGNER, HELMUT
Luftdichtigkeit und Feuchteschutz beim Steildach mit Dammung zwischer den Sparren / Helmut Wagner. DEUTSCHE BAUZEITSCHRIFT 1989 Dec., v.37, no.12, p.1639-1646, dets., graphs, tables.

WAGNER, HORST
Cleaner braaskm anlaga in Saarbrucken-Burbach. Architects: D. Trageser, H. Wagner. DEUTSCHE BAUZEITUNG 1990 Mar., v.124, no.3, p.36-39, axonometric view, photos., plan, secn.

WAGNER, JORG
Das Grabmal von Konig Antiochos 1. von Kommagene duf dem Nemrud Dag / Spencer Sahin, Jorg Wagner. ANTIKE WELT 1989, v.20, no.1, p.55-58, dwg., photos., refs.

WAGNER, MARTIN, 1947-
Ristratturazione a Vico Morcote (Canton Ticino) / Renzo Salmoiraghi. On the renovation of Villa Ruggia, the seat of the Southern California Institute of Architecture (SCI-ARC) school. Architect: Martin Wagner. English, French and Spanish summaries. ABACUS 1990 Apr.-June, v.6, no.22, p.34-43, axonometric views, dets., photos., plans, secns. Suisse: le credo de l'habitat groupe. Feature four projects: Castel Schmitten, Fribourg, architects: Martin Wagner, David and Samuel Spycher; Merzenacker project, Bern, architects: ARB Arbeitsgruppe; Habitat industriel, Givisiez, architect: Rodolphe Luscher and a multi-use building, Geneva, architect: Rodolpke Luscher and a multi-use building, Geneva, architect: Chantal Scaler. English summary, p.180. ARCHITECTURE INTERIEURE CREE 1990 June-July, no.237, p.[108]-119, dwgs., photos., secns.

WAGNER, MICHAEL
Acoustics / Michael Wagner. On a new electroacoustic device that simulates human hearing before construction begins. INTERIORS 1990 Sept., v.149, no.14, p.38, photo. Acoustics / Michael Wagner. On Almute, a new metal panel product by NDC, Ltd. which is becoming popular because of its acoustical properties. INTERIORS 1990 Nov., v.150, no.4, p.24, graph, photos. Acoustics: [Winter Garden] / Michael Wagner. On the acoustics in the Winter Garden atrium, New York City. Architects: Cesar Pelli & Associates. Acoustics: Smith, Fause & Associates. INTERIORS 1990 Dec., v.150, no.5, p.33, photo., plan. An amazing new performing arts center in California / Michael Wagner, Dennis Paoletti. Orange County Performing Arts Center, Costa Mesa, Calif. Architects: Caudill Rowlett Scott, Blue Rock Partnership. INTERIORS 1989 Feb., v.148, no.7, p.58, dwg., photo. Apple Corps / Michael Wagner. Feature interiors of Apple Computer's office in Washington, D.C. Architects: STUDIOS. INTERIORS 1990 Apr., v.149, no.9, p.78-[81], photos , plan. Banking on proportion: a mathematical system for NCNB National Bank / Michael Wagner. Bank located in Tampa, Fl. was designed using a mathematical (Continued next page)

WAGNER, MICHAEL (CONTINUED)
Banking on... (CONTINUED)
system based on a series of
logarithms developed by 13th cent.
Italian mathematician Leonardo
Fibonacci. Architect: Harry C.
Wolf. Interior designers:
Associated Space Design.
INTERIORS 1990 Jan., v.149, no.6,
p.136-[137], photos., plan.
Breaking down the wall: Morphosis
creates a mystifying temporary
exhibition for Vecta at the IDCNY
in New York / Michael Wagner.
INTERIORS 1990 Jan., v.149, no.6,
p.146-147, photos., plan.
Breaking ground / Michael Wagner.
Three projects: Kitchener, Ontario
city hall, architects: Kuwabara
Payne Mckenna Blumberg Architects;
Convocation Center, Amherst
College, Amherst, Mass.,
architects: Cambridge Seven
Associates; model home, part of
Living Environments program by GE
Plastics.
INTERIORS 1990 Feb., v.149, no.7,
p.128, dwgs.
[Conference room, National
Conference of Catholic Bishops] /
Michael Wagner.
Focus on architectural acoustics
in Washington D.C. headquarters
designed by Leo A. Daly Co.
Designers: Jaffe Acoustics.
INTERIORS 1990 Oct., v.150, no.3,
p.26, photo.
Flying sculpture: designers Solberg
& Lowe Architects creates DC-3 /
Michael Wagner.
Interiors of Santa Monica
restaurant DC-3. Collaborating
artist/designer: Charles Arnoldi.
INTERIORS 1990 Jan., v.149, no.6,
p.156-157, photos., plan.
A good mix [Hotel Inter-Continental,
Chicago] / Michael Wagner.
Restoration of eclectic 1929
building which was originally a
Shriners athletic club.
Restoration architects: Harry
Weese and Associates. Interior
designers: Design Continuum.
INTERIORS 1990 Oct., v.150, no.3,
p.34, photos.
Green for health / Michael Wagner.
On research project in the use of
house plants to remove toxic
pollutants in indoor air.
INTERIORS 1990 Oct., v.150, no.3,
p.76-[79], dwg., port., photos.,
tables.
Healing revolution / Michael Wagner.
Interiors of the 25-bed Planetree
Model Hospital Unit at the San
Jose Medical Center, Calif.
Architects: John Liu and Marc
Schweitzer, Interior designers:
Victoria Fay & Associates.
INTERIORS 1990 Dec., v.150, no.5,
p.96-97, photos., plan.
Indoor sound outdoors / Michael
Wagner.
Music pavilion, called the Charles
Ives Center Pavilion, Danbury
Conn. Architects: Kosinki
Associates with Jaffe Acoustics.
INTERIORS 1990 Feb., v.149, no.7,
p.58, photos., plan, secn.

WAGNER, MICHAEL (CONTINUED)
Legal maneuvers / Michael Wagner.
On the law offices of Rogovin,
Huge & Schiller, Washington, D.C.
Architects: STUDIOS.
INTERIORS 1990 Apr., v.149, no.9,
p.70-[73], axonometric view,
photos.
Lighting up Playboy / Michael
Wagner.
Interiors of Playboy Enterprises,
Chicago. Architects: Himmel Bonner
Architects.
INTERIORS 1990 June, v.149, no.11,
p.92-[99], photos., plans.
Making it to the top: circulation /
Michael Wagner.
On elevators and escalators.
ARCHITECTURE: THE MAGAZINE OF THE
AMERICAN INSTITUTE OF ARCHITECTS
1990 May, v.79, no.5, p.[86]-89,
dwg., elev., photos.
A New York state law requires
manufacturers of synthetic
interior finishes to test for
smoke toxicity / Michael Wagner.
INTERIORS 1989 Feb., v.148, no.7,
p.119, chart, table.
Newsworthy launching: Eva Maddox
Associates sets a new direction
for new selling with a trail
blazing prototype for Eastern
Lobby Shops / Michael Wagner.
Features prototype newsstand in the
Northwest train station, Chicago.
INTERIORS 1990 Jan., v.149, no.6,
p.144-[145], photos., plan.
Perestroikatachture [exhibition
review] / Michael Wagner.
Review of the traveling
exhibition, the socially
responsible environment USA/USSR
1980-1990. Sponsored by the Union
of Soviet Architects and the
Architects, Designers, and
Planners for Social Responsiblily.
INTERIORS 1990 Sept., v.149,
no.14, p.130-131, port., photos.
Re-psyched future / Michael Wagner.
On the recycling program at the
St. Louis offices of HOK, Inc.
INTERIORS 1990 Sept., v.149,
no.14, p.128-129, diagr., photos.
Reviving the senses / Michael
Wagner.
Redesigned control room of factory
belonging to Himont Srl Italia,
Ferrara. Architects/Interior
designers: Piera Scuri, Douglas
Skene.
INTERIORS 1990 Dec., v.150, no.5,
p.98-99, photos., plan.
Safety firsts: securing buildings
with electronic access control /
Michael Wagner.
ARCHITECTURE: THE AIA JOURNAL 1990
Apr., v.79, no.4, p.127-128,
diagrs., photos.
Shower of angels / Michael Wagner.
Temporary bathroom fixtures
showroom for American Standard,
IDCNY. Architects: Tigerman
McCurry.
INTERIORS 1990 July, v.149, no.12,
p.76-[77], photos.
Sound education / Michael Wagner.
On the conversion of a high school
gymnasium into a community and
high school theater, Dublin, Ohio.
Architects: SEM Partners with
Jaffe Acoustics.
INTERIORS 1990 Jan., v.149, no.6,
(Continued next column)

WAGNER, MICHAEL (CONTINUED)
Sound education /... (CONTINUED)
p.56, photo., plan, secn.
Sound government / Michael Wagner.
On the new state office building
in Columbus, Ohio, the Vern Riffe
Center, which includes three
performing arts theaters.
Architects: Bohm-NBBJ Architects,
Jaffe Acoustics.
INTERIORS 1990 Apr., v.149, no.9,
p.98, photo., secn.
Sound literature / Michael Wagner.
Bibliography on acoustics.
INTERIORS 1990 June, v.149, no.11,
p.54.
Sound perfect / Michael Wagner.
On the acoustical and
soundproofing work undertaken at
the Wexner Center for the Visual
Arts, Columbus, Ohio. Architects:
Peter Eisenman, Richard Trott with
Jaffe Acoustics.
INTERIORS 1990 May, v.149, no.10,
p.78, photo., plan.
Sound restoration / Michael Wagner.
On the restoration and acoustic
work done on the 1878 Senate
Chambers of the Michigan State
capitol, Lansing. Original
architect: Elijah E. Meyers [sic].
Restoration architect: Richard
Frank. Acoustics: Jaffe Acoustics.
INTERIORS 1990 July, v.149, no.12,
p.34, diagr., photos.
Tough legislation / Michael Wagner.
Focus on the Americans with
Disabilities Act (ADA).
INTERIORS 1990 Nov., v.150, no.4,
p.66-[67], photos.
Upping the profile / Michael Wagner.
On the award-winning Raychem
headquarters worldwide. Architects
for Menlo Park headquarters: Cabak
Randall Jasper Griffiths
Associates. Interior designers:
Simon Martin-Vegue Winkelstein
Moris.
INTERIORS 1990 May, v.149, no.10,
p.178-191, dwgs., models, photos.,
plans, site plan.
Wheeling and dealing / Michael
Wagner.
On the Herman Miller office
Pavilion, Washington, D.C.
Architects: STUDIOS.
INTERIORS 1990 Apr., v.149, no.9,
p.74-[77], photos., plan.

WAGNER, OTTO, 1841-1918
Architettura e statua tra Wiener
Secession e Jugendstil /
Alessandra Muntoni.
Including works by O. Wagner, J.
M. Olbrich, J. Hoffmann. English,
French, German, Spanish summaries,
p.138.
STORIA DELLA CITTA 1988 Oct.-Dec.,
v.13, no.48, p.69-82, dwgs.,
photos., refs.
Kakanian architect: Modern
architecture: a guidebook for his
students to this field of art by
Otto Wagner [book review] / James
Stevens Curl.
ROYAL SOCIETY OF ARTS, LONDON. RSA
JOURNAL 1990 Apr., v.138, no.5405,
p.378,

WAGNER, OTTO, 1841-1918 (CONTINUED)
Die Nussdorfer Wehr und Brucke: el
puente como espacio publico = Die
Nussdorfer wehr und Brucke: a
bridge as a public space / Joan
Roig.
On a project (1894-1898) by Otto
Wagner for the regulation of the
Danube Canal in Nussdorf Docks
near Vienna. Text in Spanish and
English.
ARQUITECTURA 1990 July-Aug., v.72,
no.285, p.112-117, ill., dwgs.,
elevs., photos., site plans, engr.

WAGNER, RICHARD, 1813-1883
The Munich Festival Theater letters
/ Sophie Gobran.
Never built, but functional as a
prototype for opera houses in
Central Europe. Article includes
excerpts from correspondence
between architect Gottfried Semper
and Richard Wagner.
PERSPECTA 1990, no.26, p.47-68,
ports., elev., models, map,
photos., plans, site plans, refs.

WAGNER, RICHARD, 1813-1883--INFLUENCE
Bavarian swan song: Castle
Neuschwanstein, Mad King Ludwig
II's Wagnerian shrine to Germanic
myth / Carrie Rickey.
ART & ANTIQUES 1990 May, v.7,
no.5, p.118-[125], photos.

WAGNER-RIEGER, RENATE, 1921-1980.
MITTELALTERLICHE ARCHITEKTUR IN
OSTERREICH
O stredoveke architekture v rakousku
[book review] / Jiri Kuthan.
Review of: Mittelalterliche
Architektur in Osterreich, by R.
Wagner-Rieger (Vienna: Pressehaus
St. Polten, 1988).
UMENI 1990, v.38, no.1, p.68-73,
photos.

WAGNER, WILLIAM J.
A Midwestern homestead house: living
the simple life / Linda Mason
Hunter.
Back porch addition to a 1910
house in Des Moines, Iowa.
Architect for addition: William J.
Wagner.
IOWA ARCHITECT 1990 Summer, v.39,
no.2, p.32-33, ill., photos.,
biblio.

WAGSTAFF, MICHAEL
Grant aided private sector housing
in the inner city; the Nottingham
experience / Roger Smith, Michael
Wagstaff.
THE PLANNER 1989 July, v.75,
no.11, p.9-10, table, refs.

WAHAB, IBRAHIM BIN
Urban transport in Kuala Lumpur /
Ibrahim Bin Wahab.
CITIES 1990 Aug., v.7, no.3,
p.236-243, graph, maps, tables,
refs.

WAIDE, W. L. (W. LEATH), 1910-1990
Obituary: W.L. Waide.
British city planner, died at age
80 on 9 Aug. 1990.
THE PLANNER 1990 Oct.12, v.76,
no.40, p.16,

WAINSCOTING--CONSERVATION AND
RESTORATION
Construction details & repairs:
wainscot / Gordon Bock.
Includes list of materials
suppliers.
OLD-HOUSE JOURNAL 1990 Jan.-Feb.,
v.18, no.1, p.30-36, dets.,
photos., secns.

WAINSCOTING--DIRECTORIES
A study in architectural paneling /
Clem Labine.
Contains architectural paneling
source list.
CLEM LABINE'S TRADITIONAL BUILDING
1990 Nov.-Dec., v.3, no.6, p.9-19,
ill., photos., tables.

WAINWRIGHT, CLIVE
Ardent simplicity / Clive
Wainwright.
Furnishings of Bishops Court
house, Devon; architect: William
White.
COUNTRY LIFE 1990 Oct.18 v.184,
no.42, p.150-151,154, photos.

WAINWRIGHT, CLIVE. ROMANTIC INTERIOR
The Romantic interior: the British
collector at home, 1750-1850 [by]
Clive Wainwright [book review] /
Pat Kirkham.
JOURNAL OF DESIGN HISTORY 1990,
v.3, no.4, p.235-238,

WAISMAN, MARINA
A arquitetura dos anos 80 e as
tendencias da nova decada.
An overview of international
architecture of the 1980s.
Includes essays by Ruth Verde
Zein, Marina Waisman, and and
Franco Purini.
PROJETO 1990 Jan.-Feb., no.129,
p.[65]-110, axonometric views,
dwgs., model, photos, plans,
aerial photos.
Cuestion de "divergencia": sobre el
regionalismo critico / Marina
Waisman.
ARQUITECTURA VIVA 1990 May-June,
no.12, p.43, photo., sketch.
Mario Roberto Alvarez: ein Vertreter
der Klassischen Moderne / Marina
Waisman.
DER ARCHITEKT 1990 Oct., no.10,
p.458-460, photos., secn.

WAIT, CHARLES R.
Pinewood, Iron Mountain's secret
garden: Mediterranean revival in
the Olmsted tradition / Derek
Fell.
Near Lake Wales, Fla. Landscape
architect: William L. Phillips;
architect: Charles R. Wait.
SOUTHERN ACCENTS 1990 Sept., v.13,
no.7, p.90-[95], photos.

WAITE, DIANA S.
Ornamental ironwork in Albany and
Troy / Diana S. Waite.
Excerpt from Ornamental ironwork:
two centuries of craftsmanship in
Albany and Troy, New York.
PRESERVATION LEAGUE OF NEW YORK
STATE. NEWSLETTER 1990 Spring,
v.16, no.1 p.4-5, photos.

WAJNMAN, DAN, 1947-
CAD-erfaringer / Dan Wajnman.
One of several articles in issue
entitled "Computer aided design".
Work illustrated urban design in
Odense and Hillerod, Denmark, by
the author and Ulrik Plesner.
ARKITEKTEN 1990 Sept., v.92,
no.13, p.433-436, ill., dwgs.

WAKABAYASHI, HIROYUKI
Escamuse / Hiroyuki Wakabayashi.
Two cotton warehouses in Suita,
Osaka Prefecture, converted to
house restaurant, Escamuse.
Architects: Hiroyuki Wakabayashi,
Architect and Associates.
JAPAN ARCHITECT 1990 Jan., v.65,
no.1(393), p.39-43, elevs.,
photos., plan, secns., site plan.

WAKASUGI, SACHIKO
Residents participation and
grass-roots movements in the
United States [part 1] / Sachiko
Wakasugi.
Subtitle: A study on housing and
neighborhood-community planning by
residents. Text in Japanese;
English summary, p.87.
NIHON KENCHIKU GAKKAI KEIKAKUKEI
RONBUN HOKOKU SHU = JOURNAL OF
ARCHITECTURE, PLANNING AND
ENVIRONMENTAL ENGINEERING 1990
Apr., no.4(410), p.87-97, graphs,
tables, refs.

WAKATSUKI, YUKITOSHI
Keio University Shonan Fujisawa
campus, Fujisawa, Kanagawa
Prefecture, 1993 / Yukitoshi
Wakatsuki.
Architects: Maki and Associates.
JAPAN ARCHITECT 1990 Aug.-Sept.,
v.65, no.8-9(400-401), p.66-71,
axonometric view, dwg., model,
photos., site plan.

WAKAYAMA, SHIGERU
The architectural space in
Makuranosousi / Shigeru Wakayama.
In Japanese; English summary,
p.89.
NIHON KENCHIKU GAKKAI KEIKAKUKEI
RONBUN HOKOKU SHU = JOURNAL OF
ARCHITECTURE, PLANNING AND
ENVIRONMENTAL ENGINEERING 1990
May, no.5(411), p.89-95, graphs,
tables, refs.
The space organization of
Genzimonogatani / Shigeru
Wakayama.
An analysis of "three parts of the
story", for "emotion and
organization of architectural
space". English summary, p.99.
NIHON KENCHIKU GAKKAI KEIKAKUKEI
RONBUN HOKOKU SHU = JOURNAL OF
ARCHITECTURE, PLANNING AND
ENVIRONMENTAL ENGINEERING 1990
Feb., no.2(408), p.93-99, charts.,
graphs, maps, tables, refs.

WAKEFIELD, JOHN
Il concorso di Marsiglia = Neck and
neck in Marseilles / John
Wakefield, William Alsop.
Competition projects for regional
government headquarters;
architects: Foster Associates,
Alsop & Lyall (winners).
L'ARCA 1990 Nov., no.43,
(Continued next page)

WAKEFIELD, JOHN (CONTINUED)
Il concorso di...(CONTINUED)
p.26-[41], dwgs., models, plans,
secns., site plan.
Il design e ergonomia = Design and
ergonomics / John Wakefield,
Maurizio Vitta.
Focus on "Swing" office chair and
"Stream" movable dividing wall;
designer: Isao Hosoe.
L'ARCA 1990 Oct., no.42, p.80-85,
axonometric view, dwgs., elevs.,
photos., plans.

WAKEFIELD, WILLIAM, D. 1730
Aske Hall, Yorkshire - I: the seat
of the Marquess of Zetland / Giles
Worsley.
Architect: William Wakefield;
plasterer: Francesco Vassalli.
COUNTRY LIFE 1990 Mar.1, v.184,
no.9, p.80-83, ill., photos.
Duncombe Park, Yorkshire - I: the
seat of Lord Feversham / Giles
Worsley.
Architects: William Wakefield,
Charles Barry, and William Young.
COUNTRY LIFE 1990 May 24, v.184,
no.21, p.116-121, dwg., photos.
Duncombe Park Yorkshire - II: the
seat of Lord Feversham / Giles
Worsley.
Architects: William Wakefield,
Charles Barry, William Young.
COUNTRY LIFE 1990 May 31, v.184,
no.22, p.138-143, ill., photo.

WALBANK, MARY E. HOSKINS
Pausanias, Octavia and Temple E at
Corinth / Mary E. Hoskins Walbank.
THE ANNUAL OF THE BRITISH SCHOOL
AT ATHENS 1989, no.84,
p.[361]-394, photos., plans, refs.

WALBAUM, PIERRE-HERVE
Other voices other lives / Barbara
Stoeltie.
Interiors of decorator
Pierre-Herve Walbaum's apartment
near the Tuileries in Paris.
THE WORLD OF INTERIORS 1990 Nov.,
p.106-[115], port., photos.
Sous l'empire d'une passion / Gilles
Dalliere.
Features Empire-style interiors of
interior designer Pierre Herve
Walbaum's Paris apartment.
English summary, p.III.
MAISON FRANCAISE 1990 Apr.,
no.435, p.[102-111], port.,
photos.

WALCOT, WILLIAM 1874-1943--EXHIBITIONS
The second coming: William Walcot
(1874-1943): magical impressions
[exhibition review] / Hermione
Hobhouse.
Exhibition of oils, watercolors,
drawings and etchings at the
Building Centre, London, until 31
May 1990.
ARCHITECTS' JOURNAL 1990 May 9,
v.191, no.19, p.89,91, ill.

WALDHOR, IVO
Kulturens restaurang, Lund / Marten
Duner, Ivo Waldhor.
Restaurant pavilion at
Tegnersplatsen 1 (1988-1989).
Architect: A-Plan Arkitektkontor
AB. Includes commentary by
Madeleine Brechensbauer Brandin.
(Continued next column)

WALDHOR, IVO (CONTINUED)
Kulturens restaurang,...(CONTINUED)
ARKITEKTUR: THE SWEDISH REVIEW OF
ARCHITECTURE 1990 Nov., v.90,
no.9, p.48-53, photos., plans,
site plan.

WALES--CARDIFF--ARCHITECTURE--STUDY
AND TEACHING--UNIVERSITY OF WALES
Arguments and facts: fifth year work
at the University of Wales /
Catherine Cooke, Ivor Richards.
Student projects for a Western
headquarter for a Soviet
newspaper, "Argumenty i Fakty -
Arguments and Facts".
ARCHITECTURAL DESIGN 1990, v.60,
no.3-4, p.94-96, models, plan,
secn.

WALES--CARDIFF--CASTLES--ALTERATIONS
AND ADDITIONS--CARDIFF CASTLE
Castle vistas [Cardiff Castle
visitors' center].
Competition entries for Cardiff
Castle visitors' center: Robert
Byron Associates; Greenfield
Midgley Architects; Pawson
Williams; Andy Foster; and
Katerina Ruedi.
ARCHITECTS' JOURNAL 1990 Aug.8,
v.192, no.6, p.20-25, dwgs.,
elevs., photo., plans, secns.,
site plan.

WALES--CARDIFF--COMPREHENSIVE PLANS--
CARDIFF BAY DEVELOPMENT
Cardiff Bay development / David S.
Walton.
THE PLANNER 1990 Dec.14, v.76,
no.49, p.10-18, port., site plan,
sketches.

WALES--CARDIFF--HOUSING--EVALUATION
Stock answers / Ian Monroe.
Stock Conditions Survey assesses
the quality of housing in Cardiff,
Wales.
HOUSING AND PLANNING REVIEW 1990
June-July, v.45, no.3, p.14,
photo.

WALES--CARDIFF--MUNICIPAL BUILDINGS--
SOUTH GLAMORGAN COUNTY HALL
Quality Brickwork Award 1990.
The fifth annual Brick Development
Association/Building magazine
awards. Presents the 12 regional
winners and the winning project:
South Glamorgan County Hall,
Cardiff (architect: County
Architect).
BUILDING 1990 June 1, v.255, no.22
suppl., p.3-25, photos.

WALES--CARDIFF--NATIONAL MUSEUMS--
ALTERATIONS AND ADDITIONS--NATIONAL
MUSEUM OF WALES
Exhibiting restraint [National
Museum of Wales extension] /
Graham Ridout.
On construction management (Apr.
1989-Mar. 1992) for the East Wing
and Courtyard extensions.
Architect: Alex Gordon Partners.
BUILDING 1990 July 20, v.255,
no.29, p.36-39, det., photos.

WALES--CARDIFF--REAL ESTATE
DEVELOPMENT--ENVIRONMENTAL ASPECTS--
CARDIFF BAY
Taming developers at Cardiff Bay /
Julian Dobson.
Environmental and flooding
concerns are bases for opposition
to proposed development in South
Cardiff, Wales.
HOUSING 1989 Dec.-1990 Jan., v.26,
no.10, p.24-27, ports., photos.

WALES--CARDIFF--UNIVERSITIES AND
COLLEGES--BUILDINGS--UNIVERSITY OF
WALES. COLLEGE OF CARDIFF--FACULTY
BUILDING
Faculty building, Cardiff.
The first of six new buildings for
the Univ. of Wales. Architect: Wyn
Thomas + Partners.
BUILDING 1990 Jan.26, v.255, no.4,
p.63-70, det., photos., plans,
secns., site plan, table.

WALES--CARDIFF--URBAN RENEWAL
Cardiff Bay development / David S.
Walton.
THE PLANNER 1990 Dec.14, v.76,
no.49, p.10-18, port., site plan,
sketches.

WALES--CARDIFF--VISITORS' CENTERS--
COMPETITIONS--CARDIFF CASTLE
Castle vistas [Cardiff Castle
visitors' center].
Competition entries for Cardiff
Castle visitors' center: Robert
Byron Associates; Greenfield
Midgley Architects; Pawson
Williams; Andy Foster; and
Katerina Ruedi.
ARCHITECTS' JOURNAL 1990 Aug.8,
v.192, no.6, p.20-25, dwgs.,
elevs., photo., plans, secns.,
site plan.

WALES--CARDIFF--WATERFRONTS
Cardiff Bay development / David S.
Walton.
THE PLANNER 1990 Dec.14, v.76,
no.49, p.10-18, port., site plan,
sketches.

WALES--CARDIFF--WATERFRONTS--CARDIFF
BAY
Taming developers at Cardiff Bay /
Julian Dobson.
Environmental and flooding
concerns are bases for opposition
to proposed development in South
Cardiff, Wales.
HOUSING 1989 Dec.-1990 Jan., v.26,
no.10, p.24-27, ports., photos.

WALES--CARDIGANSHIRE--LANDSCAPE
GARDENS--HADOD
Landscaping the sublime / Caroline
Kerkham.
Landscape Gardens at Hafod estate,
Cardiganshire, Wales; landscape
architect: Thomas Johnes.
COUNTRY LIFE 1990 Nov.29, v.184,
no.48, p.48-51, ill.

WALES--CAVISTER--GREENHOUSES--
POLYCARBONATE--WATERWAYS GARDEN
CENTRE
    Demountable structure: Garden
    Centre: Terry Farrell Partnership.
    Demountable greenhouse, now 10
    years old.
    ARCHITECTS' JOURNAL 1990 Jan.17,
    v.191, no.3, p.57-59, diagrs.,
    photos., plan, secn., isometric
    dwg.

WALES--CIRENCESTER--STUDENT HOUSING--
ROYAL AGRICULTURAL COLLEGE
    Gebaudebeispiel: Vorabdruck aus dem
    neuen Dachatlas Geneigte Dacher.
    Roof details from 4 projects:
    swimming center, Albstadt, W.G.
    (P.Siefert et al); housing
    development, Gebensdorf,
    Switzerland (C. Tognola, C.
    Stahel, D. Zulauf); student
    housing, Wales (D. Lea); and
    housing for handicapped,
    Eastleigh, England (D. White).
    DETAIL 1990 Feb.-Mar., v.30, no.1,
    p.[16-23], dets., elev., photos.,
    plans, secns., site plans.

WALES--COUNTRY HOUSES--18TH CENTURY--
HAFOD
    Thomas Johnes of Hafod / William
    Gibson.
    Forested estate and country house
    of Thomas Johnes in Cardiganshire,
    North Wales. House designed by
    Thomas Baldwin, with additional
    wings by John Nash. Article
    presented by the Study Group for
    the Society's History.
    ROYAL SOCIETY OF ARTS, LONDON. RSA
    JOURNAL 1990 June, v.138, no.5407,
    p.496-499, port., elev. refs.

WALES--EBBW VALE--BELVEDERES--GARDEN
FESTIVAL WALES 1992
    Coming out on top / John Welsh.
    BUILDING DESIGN 1990 Oct.26,
    no.1009, p.24-25, dwgs., plans,
    secns.

WALES--EBBW VALE--GARDEN SHOWS--GARDEN
FESTIVAL WALES 1992
    Coming out on top / John Welsh.
    BUILDING DESIGN 1990 Oct.26,
    no.1009, p.24-25, dwgs., plans,
    secns.
    Enter Ebbw Vale / Jane Porter.
    Report on the Ebbw Vale garden
    festival to be held May-Oct.,
    1992.
    LANDSCAPE DESIGN 1990 July-Aug.,
    no.192, p.46-48, photos., table.
    Not everything in the garden /
    Callum Murray.
    Ebbw Vale (Wales) will follow
    Gateshead and Glasgow as the site
    of Britain's next garden festival.
    ARCHITECTS' JOURNAL 1990 Oct.10,
    v.192, no.15, p.14-15, elev.,
    photos., plan.

WALES--ESTATES (AGRICULTURAL
COMPLEXES)--HAFOD
    Thomas Johnes of Hafod / William
    Gibson.
    Forested estate and country house
    of Thomas Johnes in Cardiganshire,
    North Wales. House designed by
    Thomas Baldwin, with additional
    wings by John Nash. Article
    presented by the Study Group for
                (Continued next column)

WALES--ESTATES (AGRICULTURAL
COMPLEXES)--HAFOD (CONTINUED)
    Thomas Johnes of...(CONTINUED)
    the Society's History.
    ROYAL SOCIETY OF ARTS, LONDON. RSA
    JOURNAL 1990 June, v.138, no.5407,
    p.496-499, port., elev. refs.

WALES--FLINT--FARMS--ROMAN--PENTRE
FARM
    Pentre farm Flint 1976-81: an
    official building in the Roman
    lead mining district / T.J.
    O'Leary, Kevin Blockley, Chris
    Musson.
    BAR BRITISH SERIES 1989, no.207,
    p.[i]-135, dwgs., photos., plans,
    site plans, tables, reconst.
    dwgs., biblio.

WALES--GLAMORGAN--COTTAGES--
INVENTORIES
    An inventory of the ancient
    monuments in Glamorgan: Volume IV:
    domestic architecture from the
    Reformation to the Industrial
    Revolution: Part II: farmhouses
    and cottages [book review] /
    Stuart Wrathmell.
    POST-MEDIEVAL ARCHAEOLOGY 1989,
    v.23, p.83-84,

WALES--GLAMORGAN--FARMHOUSES--
INVENTORIES
    An inventory of the ancient
    monuments in Glamorgan: Volume IV:
    domestic architecture from the
    Reformation to the Industrial
    Revolution: Part II: farmhouses
    and cottages [book review] /
    Stuart Wrathmell.
    POST-MEDIEVAL ARCHAEOLOGY 1989,
    v.23, p.83-84,

WALES--GLAMORGAN--HISTORIC BUILDINGS--
INVENTORIES
    An inventory of the ancient
    monuments in Glamorgan: Volume IV:
    domestic architecture from the
    Reformation to the Industrial
    Revolution: Part II: farmhouses
    and cottages [book review] /
    Stuart Wrathmell.
    POST-MEDIEVAL ARCHAEOLOGY 1989,
    v.23, p.83-84,

WALES--GWENT--GARDENS--CASTLE HOUSE
    In keeping with a Castle / Roddy
    Llewellyn.
    Castle House garden, Usk, Gwent,
    Wales.
    COUNTRY LIFE 1990 Sept.13, v.184,
    no.37, p.190-193, photos, site
    plan.

WALES--GWYNEDD--RESORTS--SEASIDE--
PORTMEIRION
    Visionary village: a Welsh architect
    conjures up a Mediterranean town
    on Cardigan Bay / Jan Morris.
    Sir Clough Williams-Ellis created
    the town of Portmeirion in the
    1920s and '30s.
    HOUSE & GARDEN 1990 Sept., v.162,
    no.9, p.82, port., photo.

WALES--HISTORIC BUILDINGS--
CONSERVATION AND RESTORATION
    The R.C.A.H.M. Wales in my time
    1949-89 / Peter Smith.
    Peter Smith is the Secretary of
    the Royal Commission on the
    Ancient and Historical Monuments
    of Wales.
    ANCIENT MONUMENTS SOCIETY.
    TRANSACTIONS 1990, new ser.,v.34,
    p.[29]-83, axonometric views,
    ill., dwgs., elevs., maps,
    photos., plans, secns., aerial
    photos., biblio., refs.

WALES--HISTORIC SITES--CONSERVATION
AND RESTORATION
    The R.C.A.H.M. Wales in my time
    1949-89 / Peter Smith.
    Peter Smith is the Secretary of
    the Royal Commission on the
    Ancient and Historical Monuments
    of Wales.
    ANCIENT MONUMENTS SOCIETY.
    TRANSACTIONS 1990, new ser.,v.34,
    p.[29]-83, axonometric views,
    ill., dwgs., elevs., maps,
    photos., plans, secns., aerial
    photos., biblio., refs.

WALES--HOUSES--TAYLOR HOUSE
    Scarpa and the mothers of invention
    / John Welsh.
    Barn in North Wales converted into
    house for architect's parents.
    Architects: Andrew Taylor, Pankaj
    Patel.
    BUILDING DESIGN 1990 Mar.2,
    no.975, p.12, axonometric view,
    det., elevs., plans, site plan.

WALES--MAPS
    The representation of industry on
    large-scale county maps of England
    and Wales 1700-c.1840 / David
    Smith.
    Includes summary.
    INDUSTRIAL ARCHAEOLOGY REVIEW 1990
    Spring, v.12, no.2, p.153-177,
    maps, photos., tables, refs.

WALES--MARINAS
    Building homes.
    Articles on vacation houses,
    resorts, marina development on the
    Welsh coastline, golf course
    communities, tourism in Eastern
    Europe, and the second home
    market.
    BUILDING 1990 Aug.10, v.255,
    no.32,suppl., p.3-22, map, photos.

WALES--MOLD--COUNTRY HOUSES--
JACOBEAN--PLAS TEG
    Bathed in splendour: Plas Teg, where
    eight distinctive bathrooms have
    been installed / Judi Goodwin.
    Bathrooms in a Jacobean Mansion
    near Mold, Wales.
    TRADITIONAL HOMES 1990 Apr., v.6,
    no.7, p.75-80, dwg., photos.

WALES--PONTYPOOL--IRON WORKS--NEATH
ABBEY IRON CO.
    The steam engines at Glym Pits
    Colliery, Pontypool: an
    archaeological investigation /
    Marilyn Palmer, Peter Neaverson.
    In South Wales. Surveyed in
    1988-1989. Article traces the
    evolution of pumping and winding
    systems manufactured by the Neath
                (Continued next page)

WALES--PONTYPOOL--IRON WORKS--NEATH
ABBEY IRON CO. (CONTINUED)
The steam engines at...(CONTINUED)
Abbey Iron Co. Includes abstract.
INDUSTRIAL ARCHAEOLOGY REVIEW 1990
Autumn, v.13, no.1, p.7-34,
photos., secns., refs.

WALES--PONTYPOOL--POWERHOUSES--19TH
CENTURY--GLYM PITS COLLIERY
The steam engines at Glym Pits
Colliery, Pontypool: an
archaeological investigation /
Marilyn Palmer, Peter Neaverson.
In South Wales. Surveyed in
1988-1989. Article traces the
evolution of pumping and winding
systems manufactured by the Neath
Abbey Iron Co. Includes abstract.
INDUSTRIAL ARCHAEOLOGY REVIEW 1990
Autumn, v.13, no.1, p.7-34,
photos., secns., refs.

WALES--PORTMEIRION--TOURIST TOWNS
Village of dreams: the holiday
village of Portmeirion in North
Wales / Vivien Bellamy.
TRADITIONAL HOMES 1990 Mar., v.6,
no.6, p.11-13, photos.

WALES--PRESTATYN--FARMS--IRON AGE
Prestatyn 1984-5: an Iron-age
farmstead and Romano-British
industrial settlement in North
Wales / Kevin Blockley.
BAR BRITISH SERIES 1989, no.210,
p.iii-231, graphs, dwgs., photos.,
plans, secns., site plans, tables,
reconst. dwgs., biblio.

WALES--PRESTATYN--SETTLEMENTS--ROMAN
Prestatyn 1984-5: an Iron-age
farmstead and Romano-British
industrial settlement in North
Wales / Kevin Blockley.
BAR BRITISH SERIES 1989, no.210,
p.iii-231, graphs, dwgs., photos.,
plans, secns., site plans, tables,
reconst. dwgs., biblio.

WALES--RHONDDA--AUDITORIUMS, CONCERT
HALLS--RHONDDA HERITAGE PARK
Hitting a highnote / Dan
Cruickshank.
Patel and Taylor's scheme for a
choral center in the Rhondda
Valley, Wales.
ARCHITECTS' JOURNAL 1990 Oct.24,
v.192, no.17, p.26-27, axonometric
view, elevs., plan, secn.

WALES--SOUTH GLAMORGAN--HOTELS--JANE
HODGE HOTEL
Jane Hodge Hotel.
In Trerhyngyel, South Glamorgan;
designed and run for the disabled
and their families. Client: John
Grooms Association for Disabled
People. Architect: Gerald Latter
Associates.
BUILDING 1990 Oct.26, v.255,
no.42, p.45-52, photos., plans,
secn., site plan, tables.

WALES--SWANSEA--CITY PLANNING
Swansea: regeneration of the city /
Trever M. Osborne.
THE PLANNER 1990 Dec.14, v.76,
no.49, p.7-9, port., photos.

WALES--SWANSEA--HOUSING DEVELOPMENTS--
COMPETITIONS--PENPLAS
Verdichteter Wohnungsbau in
Holzkonstruktion Penplas/Swansea,
Grossbritannien = Urbanbuild
timberframe housing,
Penplas/Swansea, Great Britain.
Competition. Winning architects:
PCKO Partnership. Text in German.
ARCHITEKTUR + WETTBEWERBE 1990
June, no.142, p.52-55, dwgs.,
elevs., maps, plans, site plans.

WALES--SWANSEA--TIMBER-FRAMED
BUILDINGS--COMPETITIONS--PENPLAS
Verdichteter Wohnungsbau in
Holzkonstruktion Penplas/Swansea,
Grossbritannien = Urbanbuild
timberframe housing,
Penplas/Swansea, Great Britain.
Competition. Winning architects:
PCKO Partnership. Text in German.
ARCHITEKTUR + WETTBEWERBE 1990
June, no.142, p.52-55, dwgs.,
elevs., maps, plans, site plans.

WALES--SWANSEA--URBAN RENEWAL
Swansea: regeneration of the city /
Trever M. Osborne.
THE PLANNER 1990 Dec.14, v.76,
no.49, p.7-9, port., photos.

WALES--URBAN RENEWAL
Urban renewal in Wales: the role of
the Welsh Development Agency /
John H. Pavitt.
Councillors school opening
address, Town and Country Planning
Summer School, Swansea, Wales,
Sept. 1990.
THE PLANNER 1990 Dec.14, v.76,
no.49, p.70-74, charts, port.,
aerial photo.

WALES--WEST GLAMORGAN--SETTLEMENTS--
BRONZE AGE--GOWER--CEFN BRYN
Cairns and "cairn fields": evidence
of early agriculture on Cefn Bryn,
Gower, West Glamorgan / Anthony H.
Ward.
Discusses "the nature of early
agriculture and its relationship
to ritual and settlement in the
local landscape."
LANDSCAPE HISTORY 1989, v.11,
p.[5]-18, diagrs., graphs, maps,
tables, biblio.

WALKER, AIDAN
Creative ear / Aidan Walker.
Profile of interior designer Paul
Mullins.
DESIGNERS' JOURNAL 1990 Apr.,
no.56, p.68-72, port., photos.,
plan.
Serious make belief / Aidan Walker.
Profile of Alberto Alessi.
DESIGNERS' JOURNAL 1990 Sept.,
no.60, p.16-[17], port.
Way through the woods / Aidan
Walker.
Discussion of the use of temperate
hardwoods in light of ecological
and economic concerns.
DESIGNERS' JOURNAL 1990 June,
no.58, p.58-60, ill.

WALKER ART CENTER--EXHIBITIONS
Architecture on display: Mildred
Friedman of the Walker Art Center
has brought architectectural
exhibitions into the third
dimension / Donald J. Canty.
ARCHITECTURAL RECORD 1990 Mar.,
v.178, no.3, p.45, 47, port.,
photos.
Art into life. Russian
Constructivism 1914-32 [exhibition
review] / Bruce N. Wright.
At the Walker Art Center and
elsewhere.
INLAND ARCHITECT 1990 Nov.-Dec.,
v.34, no.6, p.57-62, models.
Domestic arrangements at the Walker
[exhibition review] / Linda Mack.
Review of the installation by Tod
Williams, Billie Tsien and
Associates, part of the
Architecture Tomorrow series at
the Walker Art Center in
Minneapolis.
ARCHITECTURE: THE AIA JOURNAL 1990
Feb., v.79, no.2, p.20, photos,
plan.
Experiments in Domestic Arrangements
[exhibition review] / Larry
Millett.
Reviews the third of six exhibits
in the "Architecture Tomorrow"
series at the Walker Art Center,
Minneapolis. Presents a model
house, experimenting with
materials and elements.
Architects: Tod Williams, Billie
Tsien.
INLAND ARCHITECT 1990 Mar.-Apr.,
v.34, no.2, p.9,12, plan.
An interim report on the possible
future: Tod Williams and Billie
Tsien present an ambitious but
compromised vision of domestic
life at the Walker Art Center
[exhibition review].
ARCHITECTURAL RECORD 1990 Mar.,
v.178, no.3, p.49, photos., plan.
Tod Williams, Billie Tsien: Domestic
Arrangements.
The architects discuss their house
on exhibit at the Walker Art
Center and the Whitney Museum. In
Italian and English.
DOMUS 1990 June, no.717,
p.[58-65], photos., plan.
When Morphosis met the museum
[exhibition review] / Mason
Riddle.
"Three houses", an exhibition at
Walker Art Center, Minneapolis.
METROPOLIS 1990 July-Aug., v.10,
no.1, p.24, photos.

WALKER, BARBARA M.
The Grand Central partnership:
taking the initiative in
revitalizing a commercial area /
Barbara M. Walker.
URBAN LAND 1990 July, v.49, no.7,
p.12-15, map, photos.

WALKER, CHARLES
Mitigating the social costs of
private development: the
experience of linkage programmes
in the United States / Jon Dawson,
Charles Walker.
Considered with planning gain in
Britain.
TOWN PLANNING REVIEW 1990 Apr.,
v.61, no.2, p.157-170, refs.

WALKER, DAVID
Unearthed treasures: William T.C. Walker's Rome scholarship drawings 1937-9 [exhibition review] / David Walker.
Exhibition at the RIAS Gallery, Edinburgh, 30 July to 3 Aug. 1990.
ARCHITECTS' JOURNAL 1990 Aug.15. v.192, no.7, p.62-63, dwgs.
A wee celebration: For a wee country: architectural contributions to Scottish society since 1840 [exhibition review] / David Walker.
Exhibition to celebrate the 150th anniversary of the founding of the Royal Incorporation of Architects in Scotland's (RIAS) predecessor body, the Institute of Architects of Scotland. The exhibition is drawn from RIAS' drawings collection. Held in Parish Halls, Glasgow, through 18 Apr.1990, then on tour.
ARCHITECTS' JOURNAL 1990 Apr.4. v.191, no.14, p.88-90, dwgs., photo.
William Burn's fashionable functionalism / David Walker.
On the career of William Burn (1789-1870) and the important contribution he made to the planning of the Victorian country house.
RIBA JOURNAL 1990 Oct., v.97, no.10, p.44-47,50-51, dwgs., elev., photos., plan.

WALKER, DAVID A.
Documentation of historic museum vessels: Bureaucratic paperwork or vital working tool? / David A. Walker.
ASSOCIATION FOR PRESERVATION TECHNOLOGY BULLETIN 1990, v.22, no.1-2, p.104-108, photos., tables.

WALKER, DAVID M.
The work of kings: The architecture of the Scottish renaissance 1500-1600 [exhibition review] / David M. Walker.
Exhibition at the RIAS Gallery, Edinburgh, through 19 Sept. 1990.
ARCHITECTS' JOURNAL 1990 Sept.5, v.192, no.10, p.86-87, dwgs., elevs.

WALKER, DEREK
Kensington gore / Derek Walker.
On the changes in the architecture and interior design departments at the Royal College of Art.
BUILDING DESIGN 1990 Oct.5, no.1006, p.20-21, dwgs., models, secn.

WALKER GROUP
Renewal of department store.
Renovation of Japanese dept. store. Architects: Walker Group.
KENCHIKU BUNKA 1990 Jan., v.45, no.519, p.83, photos.

WALKER, KURT E.
Zuganglich: Neubau der Hauptverwaltung der Volksbank Baden-Baden EG.
Architects: Kurt E. Walker, Jorg D. Troldner.
ARCHITEKTUR, INNENARCHITEKTUR,
(Continued next column)

WALKER, KURT E. (CONTINUED)
Zuganglich: Neubau der (CONTINUED)
TECHNISCHER AUSBAU 1990 Dec., v.98, no.12, p.52-53, photos., plans.

WALKER, LESTER, 1930-
Victorian cottage [Catskill Mountains]
Architect: Lester Walker.
HOUSE BEAUTIFUL 1986 May, v.128, no.5, p.49-[61], photos., plans.

WALKER, PENELOPE
Bee boles in Kent / Penelope Walker.
Special structures, which survive in brick and stone, providing enclosures for early forms of bee hives known as "skeps"; they often appear as wall recesses.
ARCHAEOLOGIA CANTIANA 1988, v.106, p.107-127, map, photos., sketch, tables, refs.

WALKER, PETER, 1932-
Garten der Zukunft? / Elke von Radziewsky, Vera Graaf.
Features work by the following American landscape architects: Peter Walker, Martha Schwartz, George Hargreaves, and Michael Van Valkenburgh. english summary, p.2-3.
ARCHITEKTUR & WOHNEN 1990 Oct.-Nov., no.5, p.90-[98],100, ports., photos.

WALKER, RAY
Developing ideas: good design still counts / Ray Walker.
Maintaining design standards for volume housing.
HOUSING AND PLANNING REVIEW 1990 Feb.-Mar., v.45, no.1, p.15-17, sketches.

WALKER, SANDY
Contemporary eclat: a collector's San Francisco residence / Joan Chatfield-Taylor.
Features Wellington Henderson's home designed by Sandy Walker.
ARCHITECTURAL DIGEST 1990 Sept., v.47, no.10, p.142-149, ports., photos.

WALKER, STANSFELD THOMAS, 1902-1990
Stansfeld Thomas (Bob) Walker [obituary] / Graham Winteringham.
RIBA JOURNAL 1990 Sept., v.97 no.9, p.106,

WALKER, TOM
[Distinguished Leadership Awards 1990].
Winners of 1990 APA Awards: Norman Krumholz, Gov. Joe Frank Harris (Georgia), and Robert A Stone. The Diana Donald Award, for planning service on behalf of women, was awarded to Marsha Ritzdorf.
PLANNING 1990 Mar., v.56, no.3, p.[12]-14, ports.

WALKER, WILLIAM T. C.--EXHIBITIONS
Unearthed treasures: William T.C. Walker's Rome scholarship drawings 1937-9 [exhibition review] / David Walker.
Exhibition at the RIAS Gallery, Edinburgh, 30 July to 3 Aug. 1990.
ARCHITECTS' JOURNAL 1990 Aug.15.
(Continued next column)

WALKER, WILLIAM T. C.--EXHIBITIONS
(CONTINUED)
Unearthed treasures:...(CONTINUED)
v.192, no.7, p.62-63, dwgs.

WALKWAYS
See also BOARDWALKS
See also COVERED WALKS
See also GARDEN WALKS
See also PATHS
See also RAISED PEDESTRIAN WALKWAYS
See also SIDEWALKS

WALKWAYS--FRANCE--TOULOUSE
Si piega (in due sensi) per resistere = It bends (in two senses) in order to resist [Walkway, Toulouse, France].
Engineer: Marc Mimram.
ARCHITETTURA: CRONACHE E STORIA 1990 Nov., v.36, no.11(421), p.806, dwg., elev., photos., plan.

WALKWAYS--ITALY--LIGNANO SABBIADORO-- GIARDINO DEI LABIRINTI
Lignano Sabbiadoro, Il giardino dei labirinti = The garden of the labyrinths.
Open-air theater and walkway in an Italian "tourist village."
Architects: Studio Nizzoli (G.M. Oliveri, P. Viola).
ARCHITETTURA: CRONACHE E STORIA 1990 Nov., v.36, no.11(421), p.770-777, elevs., photos., plans, secns.

WALKWAYS--WOODEN--FRANCE--LORMONT
Construccio de fusta = Wooden construction.
Wooden walkway, Lormont, France.
Architect: Yves Ballot. Text in Catalan and English.
QUADERNS D'ARQUITECTURA I URBANISME 1988 July-Sept., no.178, p.[76-79], elevs., photos., secn.

WALL COVERINGS
Creating an individual environment [wall coverings] / Emer Hughes.
Irish examples.
PLAN: ARCHITECTURE + BUILDING DESIGN IN IRELAND 1990 Apr., v.29, no.4, p.36-42, photos.

WALL COVERINGS--DIRECTORIES
Historic wallcoverings [special report] / Eve M. Kahn.
Contains two directories of manufacturers of "historic" wall coverings and wallpapers.
CLEM LABINE'S TRADITIONAL BUILDING 1990 Jan-Feb., v.3, no.1, p.1, 5-13, ill., dwgs., photos., tables, biblios.

WALL COVERINGS--REPRODUCTIONS
Paper chase.
Wall coverings reproducing historical patterns.
HISTORIC PRESERVATION 1990 Jan.-Feb., v.42, no.1, p.36-39, ill.

WALL COVERINGS--UNITED STATES-- DIRECTORIES
Textile and wallcovering directory.
Listing of 346 manufacturers of contract textiles and wall coverings.
INTERIORS 1990 July, v.149, no.12, p.48-59, tables.

WALL, MARIA
Calculation of climatic conditions and energy requirements for a proposed glass roof: the abbey church ruins at Hamar, Norway / Maria Wall.
In Feb.1987 a competition was announced for a superstructure over the church ruins. Winning proposal was "Poetry of reason", by Kjell Lund and Nils Slaatto.
SWEDISH COUNCIL FOR BUILDING RESEARCH. DOCUMENT 1990, D19, p.[1]-27, graphs, dwg., photo., isometric dwg., biblio.

WALL SYSTEMS
ICF: brick system e Burdick group = Brick System meets the Burdick group.
Interior of IMC Investment Management Co., Trento, using a flexible wall system. Designer: Marcello Armani.
OTTAGONO 1990 Dec., no.97, p.144-147, photos., plan.

WALL SYSTEMS--CONTRACTS AND SPECIFICATIONS
Soffit option / Rodney Cooper.
Product survey of ceiling and partition systems.
DESIGNERS' JOURNAL 1990 July-Aug., no.59, p.34-36, photos.

WALL SYSTEMS--DIRECTORIES
Disappearing act [storage wall systems] / Anne Hadley.
Includes directory of storage wall system suppliers.
DESIGNERS' JOURNAL 1990 Apr., no.56, p.60-62,65,67, ill.

WALLACE-HADRILL, ANDREW
The social structure of the Roman house / Andrew Wallace-Hadrill.
Italian summary, p.[ix].
BRITISH SCHOOL AT ROME PAPERS OF THE BRITISH SCHOOL AT ROME 1988, v.56, p.[43]-97,pl.VI-X, axonometric view, diagrs., photos., plans, secns., refs.

WALLACE, R.
"Homelessness," contagious destruction of housing, and municipal service cuts in New York City: 2, dynamics of a housing famine / R. Wallace.
ENVIRONMENT AND PLANNING A 1990 Jan., v.22, no.1, p.5-15, graphs, refs.

WALLACE ROBERTS & TODD
Urban issues: Mission Bay / Sally B. Woodbridge.
On the four plans proposed during the 1980s for San Francisco's Mission Bay. Includes plans by John Carl Warnecke (1980), I.M. Pei/Wallace Roberts & Todd (1985), EDAW et al. (Mission Bay Planning Team, 1987) and SOM (1989).
PROGRESSIVE ARCHITECTURE 1990 May, v.71, no.5, p.121-122, figs., plans, site plans.

WALLACH, FRANCES
Playground safety update / Frances Wallach.
PARKS & RECREATION 1990 Aug., v.25, no.8, p.46-[50], photos.
Playgrounds.
Three articles regarding design considerations of playgrounds: "How many parts make a playground?", Sally McIntyre; "Designing a playground that fits", Asher Etkes; "Answers to your playground surface questions", Frances Wallach, Robert Heath.
PARKS & RECREATION 1989 Mar., v.24, no.3, p.26-38,62, photos.

WALLACH GLASS STUDIO
Decorative glass.
Jed and Christine Wallach execute architectural commissions in glass, using a unique "deep V" high-pressure sandblasting technique.
ARCHITECTURAL RECORD 1990 Apr., v.178, no.4, p.127, photos.

WALLAGH, G.
Planning for rule and order in Amsterdam / R. Postuma, A. van der Valk, G. Wallagh.
BUILT ENVIRONMENT 1989, v.15, no.1, p.17-27, plans, tables, refs.

WALLED GARDENS
See ENCLOSED GARDENS

WALLENSTEIN, SVEN-OLOV
Tema: fiktioner.
Introduction to issue on architecture and language. Includes five articles indexed separately and a sixth, Kubricks Rum, by Sven-Olov Wallenstein. English translation, p.63.
ARKITEKTUR: THE SWEDISH REVIEW OF ARCHITECTURE 1990 Mar., v.90, no.2, p.2-31, ill., photos.

WALLER, KIM
An antiquer's street of dreams / Kim Waller.
Antique shops in New Preston, Connecticut.
HOUSE BEAUTIFUL 1990 Oct., v.132, no.10, p.35-36,42,46,48, ports., photos.
A decorator's London: secret sources / Kim Waller.
Colefax and Fowler designer Imogen Taylor's choice of London antique shops.
HOUSE BEAUTIFUL 1990 May, v.132, no.5, p.88-91, ports., photos.
Puerto Rico's old-world charms / Kim Waller.
Small inns and guest houses.
HOUSE BEAUTIFUL 1990 Jan., v.132, no.1, p.28-30, photos.

WALLER, SYDNEY LANCASTER
The figure in leaded glass / Sydney Lancaster Waller.
In the works of David Wilson.
STAINED GLASS QUARTERLY 1989 Spring, v.84, no.1, p.25-32, photos.

WALLIS, WILLIAM JOHN
Hindsights: enhancing the backyard view--from inside the house / Mia Amato.
GARDEN DESIGN 1990 autumn, v.9, no.3, p.[50]-56, photos.

WALLPAPER
Creating an individual environment [wall coverings] / Emer Hughes.
Irish examples.
PLAN: ARCHITECTURE + BUILDING DESIGN IN IRELAND 1990 Apr., v.29, no.4, p.36-42, photos.
Deep friezes: the turn-of the century enthusiasm for wallpaper friezes / Christine Woods.
TRADITIONAL HOMES 1990 Nov., v.7, no.2, p.55-58, ill.
Ultimate panoramas / J.C. Suares.
On the panorama wallpapers produced by Zuber & Cie of Rixheim, France.
CONNOISSEUR 1990 July, v.220, no.942, p.60-[65],106-107, ill., photos.

WALLPAPER--19TH CENTURY
Edgewise / Sarah Howell.
Features British wallpaper border pattern book from around 1850. The book has been attributed to the Woollams firm.
THE WORLD OF INTERIORS 1990 Dec., p.114-121, photos.
William Morris and his wallpapers / Deborah Barcan.
Includes photos of Morris' house in Bexleyheath, designed by Philip Webb.
VICTORIAN HOMES 1990 Winter, v.9, no.1, p.38-43, dets., ports., photos.

WALLPAPER--19TH CENTURY--CONSERVATION AND RESTORATION
Brushing through the tulips: a Victorian stencilled wallcovering comes to life once more / Christine Woods.
Reproduction of "Tulip Garden", an 1890s design originally used in the billard room of a country house near Bushey Heath.
TRADITIONAL HOMES 1990 Oct., v.7, no.1, p.51-54, photos.

WALLPAPER--19TH CENTURY--REPRODUCTIONS
The Morris interior / John Burrows.
19th-cent.-style interiors featuring William Morris designs that are now available as reproductions. Includes list of suppliers of wallpapers,fabrics and carpets.
OLD-HOUSE JOURNAL 1990 Sept.-Oct., v.18, no.5, p.[56]-60, ill., port., photos.

WALLPAPER--20TH CENTURY--GREAT BRITAIN--EXHIBITIONS
Wallflowers: A popular art: British wallpapers, 1930-1960 [exhibition review] / Gillian Darley.
Exhibition at the Orleans House Gallery, Twickenham, through Feb.11, 1990; then the Whitworth Art Gallery, University of Manchester, 16 Mar.-28 Apr.1990.
ARCHITECTS' JOURNAL 1990 Jan.17, v.191, no.3, p.80-82, ill.

WALLPAPER--DIRECTORIES
Historic wallcoverings [special report] / Eve M. Kahn.
Contains two directories of manufacturers of "historic" wall coverings and wallpapers.
CLEM LABINE'S TRADITIONAL BUILDING 1990 Jan-Feb., v.3, no.1, p.1, 5-13, ill., dwgs., photos., tables, biblios.

WALLPAPER--GREAT BRITAIN--EXHIBITIONS
English wallpapers: Paper and paste: historic English wallpapers [exhibition review] / Edward Pond.
Exhibition at the Manchester City Art galleries through 3 Feb.1991.
ROYAL SOCIETY OF ARTS, LONDON. RSA JOURNAL 1990 Dec., v.139, no.5413, p.940-942, ill.
An eye for a line: Voysey and decoration: drawings from the collection of the British Architectural Library. [exhibition review] / Roderick Gradidge.
Exhibition held at the Heinz Gallery, London through 27 Oct. 1990. Includes book review: The decorative designs of C.F.A. Voysey, by Stuart Durant.
ARCHITECTS' JOURNAL 1990 Oct.17, v.192, no.16, p.94-95,97, ill.
Papered optimism: Voysey wallpaper designs [exhibition review] / Michael Hall.
Exhibition held at Heinz Gallery, RIBA, Sept.-Oct. 1990.
COUNTRY LIFE 1990 Oct.11, v.184, no.41, p.118, photo.
Versatile Voysey: Voysey and decoration: drawings from the collection of the British Architectural Library [exhibition review] / Trevor Gett.
Exhibition of drawings by Arts and Crafts architect C.F.A. Voysey at the RIBA Heinz Gallery, London 19 Sept. to 27 Oct. 1990.
ROYAL SOCIETY OF ARTS, LONDON. RSA JOURNAL 1990 Dec., v.139, no.5413, p.939-940, ill.

WALLPAPER--REPRODUCTIONS
Paper chase.
Wall coverings reproducing historical patterns.
HISTORIC PRESERVATION 1990 Jan.-Feb., v.42, no.1, p.36-39, ill.

WALLPAPER--VICTORIAN--REPRODUCTIONS
Home furnishings: decorating with a Victorian view / Nancy A. Ruhling.
VICTORIAN HOMES 1990 Winter, v.9, no.1, p.46-[51],78, photos.

WALLS
See also CITY WALLS
See also CURTAIN WALLS
See also DIAPHRAGM WALLS
See also EXTERIOR WALLS
See also HOT WALLS
See also INTERIOR WALLS
See also LOAD-BEARING WALLS
See also MASONRY
See also ORTHOSTATS
See also PANELS
See also PARTITIONS
See also PARTY WALLS
See also PIERCED WALLS
See also QIBLA WALLS
See also RETAINING WALLS
(Continued next column)

WALLS (CONTINUED)
See also CITY WALLS (CONTINUED)
See also SEAWALLS
See also SHEAR WALLS
See also WALL SYSTEMS
See also WALLS (FORTIFICATION)
Within these walls: the astonishing variety of walls which can enclose gardens / Dick Randall, Jean Randall.
TRADITIONAL HOMES 1990 Feb., v.6, no.5, p.[82]-86, photos., biblio.

WALLS--BRICK
Il ritorno della muratura portante / a cura di Alfredo Zappa.
VILLE GIARDINI 1990 Apr., no.247, p.[46]-49, diagrs., figs, ill., refs.

WALLS--BRICK--17TH CENTURY--ITALY--ROME
Tecniche murarie nelle fabbriche romane del 600 / Maria Cristina Boido.
L'INDUSTRIA DELLE COSTRUZIONI 1990 Dec., v.24, no.230, p.52-56, dwgs., elevs., biblio.

WALLS--BRICK--19TH CENTURY--UNITED STATES--ANDERSONVILLE (GEORGIA)--NATIONAL CEMETERY
Restoring a historic brick wall / Mark Ragan.
A five-foot wall built in 1878-1879 around the National Cemetery in Andersonville, Ga.
CRM BULLETIN: A NATIONAL PARK SERVICE TECHNICAL BULLETIN 1990, v.13, no.5, p.8, port.

WALLS--CONTRACTS AND SPECIFICATIONS--GREAT BRITAIN
Concrete products.
Supplement has eight articles, including ones on blocking sound, interior wall specifications, color in cladding, bricks, block paving, and foundation walls. Includes a guide to essential standards, approvals, contacts, and associations.
BUILDING 1990 June 29, v.255, no.26 suppl., p.3-23, photos., secn., table.

WALLS--DETAILS
"Complessita e contraddizioni" per un rivestimento in legno / Walter Bianchi, Mauro Colombo.
Corner details of a house in Zug, Switzerland. Architect: Bany Meier.
VILLE GIARDINI 1990 May, no.248, p.52-[53]', dets., photos., plan, secn.

WALLS (FORTIFICATION)
See also FORTIFICATION

WALLS (FORTIFICATION)--12TH CENTURY--FRANCE--PARIS
The Philip Augustas wall around Paris: eight centuries old this year and in need of help / Arthur Gillette.
Summaries in French, Italian and Spanish.
ICOMOS INFORMATION 1990 Apr.-June, no.2, p.9-16, map, photos.

WALLS (FORTIFICATION)--ANCIENT--EGYPT--NILE
Esquisse d'une typologie des villes fortifiees de l'Egypte pharaonique / Daniel Soulie.
HISTOIRE DE L'ART 1990 May, no.9-10, p.3-8, site plans, refs.

WALLS (FORTIFICATION)--EGYPTIAN--EGYPT--NILE
Esquisse d'une typologie des villes fortifiees de l'Egypte pharaonique / Daniel Soulie.
HISTOIRE DE L'ART 1990 May, no.9-10, p.3-8, site plans, refs.

WALLS (FORTIFICATION)--ROMAN--ITALY--TERRACINA
Osservazioni sulle mura di Terracina / Giorgio Ortolani.
Comparison of the building methods and typological characteristics of the Roman Walls in Terracina with contemporary buildings. Summaries in English, French, German and Spanish.
PALLADIO 1988 Dec., v.1, no.2, p.69-84, dets., dwg., elevs., photos., site plan, refs.

WALLS--GLASS
Die Domane von Mexx: Neubau eines Verwaltungsgebaudes bei Korschenbroich.
Architect: Sjoerd Soeters.
BAUWELT 1990 Sept.7, v.81, no.34, p.1666-1669, photos., plans.
Glazing.
"Technology special", with articles on craftsmanship, residential uses for high-tech glazing, fire-resistant glazing, and structural glazing.
BUILDING 1990 Dec.14, v.255, no.49, p.45-57, axonometric view, dwgs., photos., tables.
Der Saal im Saal: Umbau der Borse in Amsterdam / Mick Eekhout.
Addition of a small glass music hall for the Nederlands Philharmonisch Orkest within existing hall at the Borse. Original architect: H. P. Berlage. Current architect: Pieter Zaanen. One of two articles in issue entitled "Neu in Alt".
BAUWELT 1990 May 11, v.81, no.18, p.892-898,cover, ill., photos., plans.

WALLS--GLASS BLOCK
De l'hotel de police a l'hotel industriel.
Features two projects by Jerome Brunet and Eric Saunier: police station, Herouville-Saint-Clair and an industrial building, Paris. English summary, p.117. Spanish summary, p.173.
TECHNIQUES ET ARCHITECTURE 1990 Oct.-Nov., no.292, p.116-117, elev., photos., plans, secn., site plans.

WALLS--HAUSA--NIGERIA
Hausa walls / Oroma B.A. Nwanodi.
Social, economic and political factors, in northern Nigeria and southern Niger.
ARCHITECTURE + DESIGN 1990 July-Aug., v.7, no.4, p.73-85, dwgs., maps., photos., secns., site plans, refs.

WALLS--MAINTENANCE AND REPAIR
Bridging the gap: cavity walls /
John Fidler.
Includes a list of addresses.
TRADITIONAL HOMES 1990 Feb., v.6,
no.5, p.118-121, dets., photo.,
biblio.

WALLS--MASONRY
Making masonry walls look their best
/ Christine Beall.
ARCHITECTURAL RECORD 1990 Nov.,
v.178, no.12, p.112-113, photos.
Mauerwerk: Stand der Entwicklung /
W. Manns, K. Zeus.
DEUTSCHES ARCHITEKTENBLATT 1990
Sept.1, v.22, no.9, p.1359-1360,
dwgs., tables.

WALLS--PLASTER--CONSERVATION AND
RESTORATION
Repairing historic flat plaster:
Walls and ceilings / Marylee
MacDonald.
PRESERVATION BRIEFS 1989 Oct.,
no.21, p.1-14, diagrs., ill.,
photos., table, biblio.

WALLS--STORE
Garten aus Pflanzen und Stein /
Wolfgang Barth.
The use of store and vegetation in
landscape design should reflect
local conditions. Includes English
summary.
GARTEN UND LANDSCHAFT 1990, v.100,
no.5, p.29-32, photos., plans.

WALLS--STUCCO--CONSERVATION AND
RESTORATION--UNITED STATES
Preservation and repair of historic
stucco / Anne Grimmer.
Adapted from a forthcoming
"Preservation Brief".
CRM BULLETIN: A NATIONAL PARK
SERVICE TECHNICAL BULLETIN 1989,
v.12, no.6, p.18-20, photos.

WALPOLE, HORACE, 1717-1797
On the supposed Chineseness of the
English landscape garden / David
Jacques.
GARDEN HISTORY 1990 autumn, v.18,
no.2, p.[180]-191, ill., plan,
engrs., refs.

WALSH BISHOP ASSOCIATES
Four new skyscrapers in Minneapolis
/ Larry Millett.
Architects: I. M. Pei,
Ellerbe-Becket, Lohan Associates,
and Walsh-Bishop Associates.
INLAND ARCHITECT 1990 Jan.-Feb.,
v.34, no.1, p.[19]-22, ill., dwg.,
elev., model.

WALTER KNOLL & CO.
Plan furniture 1932-1938: the German
connection / Barbara Tilson.
A modernist experiment in the
manufacture and retail of
contemporary furnishings, founded
by Serge Chermayeff and involving
Franz Schuster and Walter Knoll &
Co.
JOURNAL OF DESIGN HISTORY 1990,
v.3, no.2-3, p.1435-155, photos.,
refs.

WALTERS, BRIAN
Hamburg airport stretches its wings
/ Brian Walters.
On the winning design to expand
Fuhlsbuttel airport. Architects:
von Gerkan, Marg und Partner.
BUILDING DESIGN 1990 Jan.19,
no.969, p.18, ill., models.
A new home for the Vasa / Brian
Walters.
On the Vasa Museum, Stockholm,
which was designed for a 17th
cent. Warship. Architects: Ove
Hidemark Goran M'ansson
Arkitektkontor.
BUILDING DESIGN 1990 Jan.19,
no.969, p.19, photos., secn.
Terminal solution / Brian Walters.
On the Stockholm downtown airline
terminal. Architects: Arken
Arkitekter, Ralph Erskine
Architect and Planner, Ahlquist &
Culjat and Tengboms
Arkitektkontor.
BUILDING DESIGN 1990 Apr.20,
no.982, p.42-43, photos.

WALTERS, DAVID
Form and content: the analysis of an
urban setting / David Walters.
Examines ideas of urban place by
the graphic analysis of Siena,
Italy.
OZ / COLLEGE OF ARCHITECTURE AND
DESIGN, KANSAS STATE UNIVERSITY
1989, v.11, p.24-27, maps.
A framework for theory in
architecture / David Walters.
REFLECTIONS: THE JOURNAL OF THE
SCHOOL OF ARCHITECTURE UNIVERSITY
OF ILLINOIS AT URBANA-CHAMPAIGN
1990 Spring, no.7, p.32-43, refs.

WALTERS, JONATHAN
Deco Moderne adapted: Des Moines's
famed Butler Mansion finds new
life as an advertising firm /
Jonathan Walters.
Original architect (1937): George
Kraetsch. Architects for
renovation: Wells, Woodburn, and
O'Neil.
HISTORIC PRESERVATION 1990
Jan.-Feb., v.42, no.1, p.64-65,
photo.

WALTMAN, MATTHEW
AA diploma honours 1989-90 / Raoul
Bunschoten, Wiel Arets, Stefano de
Martino, Peter Salter, Ron Herron,
Andrew Holmes and John Frazer.
Diploma prizes to Joel Segal, Voon
Yee Wong, Simon Hart, Toru Ogata,
Bobby Desai, Shin Egashira and
Matthew Waltman.
AA FILES 1990 Autumn, no.20,
p.95-101, dwgs., models, photo.

WALTON, DAVID S.
Cardiff Bay development / David S.
Walton.
THE PLANNER 1990 Dec.14, v.76,
no.49, p.10-18, port., site plan,
sketches.

WALTON DESIGN
Culinary criteria: the kitchen of an
exacting designer / Kit Wedd.
Designer: Rosa Lewis, of Walton
Design.
TRADITIONAL HOMES 1990 July, v.6,
no.10, p.[37-38], photos.

WALTON, TONY
Fortifications of the Taupo Campaign
/ Tony Walton.
19th cent. fortification built by
the government forces during the
Maori uprising.
HISTORIC PLACES IN NEW ZEALAND
1989 June, no.25, p.14-16, maps,
photos., site plans, aerial photo.

WALZ DESIGN
Mind over matter / Ziva Freiman.
On the interiors of the Otto
Tootsi Plohound shoe store,
Manhattan. Designer: Walz
Design.
PROGRESSIVE ARCHITECTURE 1990
Feb., v.71, no.2, p.106-111,
photos., plan, sketches.

WAMSLEY, JAMES S.
Cherokee Plantation: new life for a
South Carolina estate / James S.
Wamsley.
Interiors of 1930-31 Georgian
revival mansion owned by Carol and
Randolph Updyke on 3800-acre
plantation near Yemassee.
Interior designers: Judie and
Bennett Weinstock.
ARCHITECTURAL DIGEST 1990 June,
v.47, no.6, p.138-[143], photos.
Gardens: Magnolia Plantation / James
S. Wamsley.
Located along the banks of the
Ashley River near Charleston, the
garden dates back to the 1840s and
has been owned by the Hastie
family since 1680.
ARCHITECTURAL DIGEST 1990 May,
v.47, no.5, p.244-249,282, photos.

WANASUNDARA, ANJALENDRAN C.
Architecture Sri Lanka.
Feature of issue. Includes two
articles separately indexed;
Foreword by Ashok B. Lall; Trends
and transitions, by Anjalendran C.
and Rajiv Wanasundara; The Sri
Lankan vernacular; The eighties.
ARCHITECTURE + DESIGN 1990
Mar.-Apr., v.7, no.2, p.23-113,
dwgs., photos., plans, secns.,
site plans.

WANASUNDARA, RAJIV
Architecture Sri Lanka.
Feature of issue. Includes two
articles separately indexed;
Foreword by Ashok B. Lall; Trends
and transitions, by Anjalendran C.
and Rajiv Wanasundara; The Sri
Lankan vernacular; The eighties.
ARCHITECTURE + DESIGN 1990
Mar.-Apr., v.7, no.2, p.23-113,
dwgs., photos., plans, secns.,
site plans.

WANDEL, HUBERTUS
Erste Preise: Stadt- und Ortskerne.
Three projects: Innenstadt
Grevenbroich (architects: Ruth
Paffrath-Baureis, Heinrich
Schneider); Neckarstrasse
Stuttgart (architect: Gunter H.
Telian); Innenstadt Puttlingen
(architect: Hubertus Wandel).
DEUTSCHES ARCHITEKTENBLATT 1990
Nov.1, v.22, no.11, p.1699-1702,
dwgs., models, site plans.

WANG, NENGYUAN
Bridge construction in China / Wang Nengyuan.
BUILDING IN CHINA 1989 Sept., v.2, no.3, p.6-17,insert, dets., port., photos.

WANG, SHIH-YEH
Research and investigation on space attribute and space use on each floor of buildings in Tokyo / Shih-yeh Wang....[et al.].
Analysis of three categories of space: public and private, over and under, inner and outer. Text in Japanese; English summary, p.105.
NIHON KENCHIKU GAKKAI KEIKAKUKEI RONBUN HOKOKU SHU = JOURNAL OF ARCHITECTURE, PLANNING AND ENVIRONMENTAL ENGINEERING 1990 Apr., no.4(410), p.105-112, graphs, ill., maps, tables, refs.

WANG, TIANXI
National style and contextualism [Beidaihe resort hostel] / Wang Tianxi.
A new hostel at a summer resort in North China, by the Architectural Design Group of the Ministry of Construction.
BUILDING IN CHINA 1989 June, v.2, no.2, p.18-25, dwgs., photos., plans, secn.

WANG, WILFRIED
Un 'architettura di silenziose articolazioni: sull'opera di Peter Zumthor = An architecture of silent articulations on the work of Peter Zumthor / Wilfried Wang.
Works include Atelier Zumthor, Haldenstein, Switzerland (1987). In Italian and English.
OTTAGONO 1990 Dec., no.97, p.[48-80], dets., dwgs, elevs., photos., plans, secns.
Edificio per uffici B3 a Stockley Park, Londra: Foster Associates / Wilfried Wang.
Text in Italian and English.
DOMUS 1990 Feb., no.713, p.[29-37], axonometric views, dets., elevs., photos, plans, secns., site plan.
Peter Celsing e la classicita nel moderno / Wilfried Wang, Johan Celsing.
Includes a personal essay on the construction of the architect's villa in Drottningholm by his son. Text in Italian and English.
CASABELLA 1990 Oct., v.54, no.572, p.42-53,61-62, axonometric view, elevs., models, photos., plans, secns., site plan, sketches, aerial photo., refs.
Vasamuseet: Ett Masterverk.
Introduction to issue featuring the Stockholm museum built for the 17th-cent. Dutch ship. Architect: Mansson Dahlback Arkitektkontor. Includes essay by Marianne Dahlback and Goran Mansson, and commentary by Bengt O.H. Johansson, Brita Koefoed-Jespersen, and Wilfried Wang. English translations, p.61-62.
ARKITEKTUR: THE SWEDISH REVIEW OF ARCHITECTURE 1990 Oct., v.90,
(Continued next column)

WANG, WILFRIED (CONTINUED)
Vasamuseet: Ett...(CONTINUED)
no.8, p.2-35,cover, dets., elevs., photos., plans, secns., site plans.

WANG, XINHAO
Satellite town development in Shanghai, China: an overview / Farhad Atash, Xinhao Wang.
Includes abstract.
JOURNAL OF ARCHITECTURAL AND PLANNING RESEARCH 1990 Autumn, v.7, no.3, p.245-259, maps, table.

WANG, YUKUN
The dynamics of housing finance in China / Wang Yukun.
BUILDING IN CHINA 1989 Mar., v.2, no.1, p.9-17, charts, graphs, photos.

WANK ADAMS SLAVIN ASSOCIATES
Center for the Performing Arts, Cornell University, Ithaca, New York, 1982-88.
Architects: James Stirling, Michael Wilford & Associates, with Wank adams Slavin Associates. Text in Japanese and English.
GA DOCUMENT 1990 May, no.26, p.68-[79], elevs., photos., plans, secns., site plan.
Linking preservation to architectural design [Wank Adams Slavin Associates] / Clem Labine.
Their Preservation Department's projects include Fallingwater and the New York Municipal Building.
CLEM LABINE'S TRADITIONAL BUILDING 1990 Mar.-Apr., v.3, no.2, p.5.24-25, ports., photos.
Restoration the old-fashioned way / James S. Russell.
Stone repairs of the 1914 New York Municipal Building, designed by McKim Mead & White. Restoration architects: Wank Adams Slavin Associates.
ARCHITECTURAL RECORD 1990 Mar., v.178, no.3, p.124-127, dets., photos., secn.
Le revers du decor: Centre d'arts du spectacle de l'Universite Cornell, Ithaca, New York.
Performing Arts Center, Cornell University. Architects: James Stirling, Michael Wilford and Associates with Wank Adams Slavin Associates. English summary, p.153. Spanish summary, p.199.
TECHNIQUES ET ARCHITECTURE 1990 Apr.-May, no.389, p.149-153, photos., plans, secns.

WANNOP, URLAN
GEAR: la gestion des partenaires publics de la renovation / Urlan Wannop.
Urban renewal in Scotland's Glasgow Eastern Area Renewal (GEAR) project. French, English, German and Spanish summaries, p.[125]-127.
LES ANNALES DE LA RECHERCHE URBAINE 1990 Oct., no.48, p.[74]-85, port., photos., tables.

WAR DAMAGE TO BUILDINGS
See also BOMBINGS
Blast-free design: a computer modeling program simulates bomb attacks to minimize potential destruction... / Gregory Littleton.
On the BombCAD analysis system.
ARCHITECTURE: THE MAGAZINE OF THE AMERICAN INSTITUTE OF ARCHITECTS 1990 May, v.79, no.5, p.84-85, ill.
Northern France rebuilt / Paul Atterbury.
Rebuilt structures financed by German reparations after WWI in Pas-de-Calais region; architects: Louis Cordonnier, Pierre Paquet, Urbain Casson, Duval et Gonse, Louis Duthoit.
COUNTRY LIFE 1990 May 3, v.184, no.18, p.166-167,170, map, photos.

WAR DAMAGE TO BUILDINGS--ENGLAND--BRISTOL--EXHIBITIONS
What the censor saw: the West at war [exhibition review] / Sian Ellis.
"Exhibition of published and unpublished photographs by Jim Facey, the Bristol Evening Post's chief photographer during the Second World War and Photographer of the Year award winner..." Includes photographs censored during the war, and many of bomb-damaged buildings. Held at the Watershed, Bristol, through 8 Apr.1990.
ARCHITECTS' JOURNAL 1990 Mar.28, v.191, no.13, p.89-90, photo.

WAR DAMAGE TO BUILDINGS--FRANCE--REIMS
The reconstruction of Reims, 1919-30 / Hugh Clout.
PLANNING OUTLOOK 1989, v.32, no.1, p.23-34, diagrs., graph, maps, photos., site plans, table, refs.

WAR DAMAGE TO BUILDINGS--GERMANY (EAST)
Grossrachen: ein Dorf stirbt fur den Tagebau / Alexandra Staub.
BAUWELT 1990 July 20, v.81, no.27, p.1396-1397, photos.

WAR DAMAGE TO BUILDINGS--GERMANY (EAST)--LEIPZIG--VOLKSBAUKONFERENZ 1990
Trauer um Leipzig / Sebastian Redecke.
Text of the author's introduction to the Ersten Leipziger Volksbaukonferenz, held 6-7 Jan.1990. Concentrates on needs and plans for inner city reconstruction after 1945.
BAUWELT 1990 Mar.30, v.81, no.12, p.552-561, maps, photos.

WAR DAMAGE TO BUILDINGS--GERMANY (WEST)
Werner Durth, Niels Gutschow: Traume in Trummern / Gerd Albern.
Review of a 1988 book. Subtitle: "Planungen zum Wiederaufbau zerstorter Stadte in Westen Deutschlands, 1940-1950.
DEUTSCHE KUNST UND DENKMALPFLEGE 1989, v.47, no.2, p.150-161,

WAR DAMAGE TO BUILDINGS--GERMANY
(WEST) (CONTINUED)
Wiederaufbau 1945-1960 / Gerhard
Rabeler.
DEUTSCHE KUNST UND DENKMALPFLEGE
1989, v.47, no.2, p.114-128, ill.,
photos., site plans, biblio.

WAR DAMAGE TO BUILDINGS--GERMANY
(WEST)--HELGOLAND
Gedanken aum Wiederaufbau Helgolands
/ Niels Gutschow.
DEUTSCHE KUNST UND DENKMALPFLEGE
1989, v.47, no.2, p.129-147, dwg.,
ports., elevs., model, photos.,
plans, site plans, aerial photos.

WAR DAMAGE TO BUILDINGS--GREAT BRITAIN
Coventry nach dem 14.11.1940: 50
Jahre Stadtentwicklungsplanung /
Friedhelm Fischer.
BAUWELT 1990 Nov.16, v.81,
no.42-43, p.2118-2119, dwg., maps.

WAR DAMAGE TO BUILDINGS--LEBANON
Reconstruction and cultural
considerations: the case of war
damaged villages in Lebanon /
Souheil El-Masri.
URBAN FUTURES 1989 Winter, v.2,
no.4, p.45-53, axonometric views,
charts, diagrs., maps, plans,
secns., sketches, tables, biblio.

WAR DAMAGE TO BUILDINGS--POLAND
Der Wiederaufbau der historischen
Stadtzentren in Polen / Konstanty
Kalinowski.
Using Danzig as an example.
DEUTSCHE KUNST UND DENKMALPFLEGE
1989, v.47, no.2, p.102-113, maps,
photos., aerial photos., refs.

WAR DAMAGE TO BUILDINGS--RESEARCH
Street fighting [Copehill Down] /
Richard MacLean.
A model fighting village on
Salisbury Plain used for combat
training by the British Army.
BUILDING 1990 May 11, v.255,
no.19, p.26-27, photos., aerial
photo.

WAR MEMORIALS--19TH CENTURY--
SCOTLAND--GLASGOW--DUKE OF
WELLINGTON
Carlo Marochetti and the Glasgow
Wellington memorial / Philip
Ward-Jackson.
BURLINGTON MAGAZINE 1990 Dec.,
v.132, no.1053, p.851-862,
photos., engr., refs.

WAR MEMORIALS--20TH CENTURY--INDIA
Geddes and Mackintosh / James S.
McGrath.
Supplements the author's article
in no.50 of this journal,
concerning plans dating from 1915
to 1918 in association with town
planning surveysin India.
CHARLES RENNIE MACKINTOSH SOCIETY.
NEWSLETTER 1990 Spring, no.53,
p.5, dwg.

WAR MEMORIALS--AUSTRALIA
Il monumento mobile: la circolazione
e l'arte della memoria = The
mobile monument: circulation and
the suburban art of memory /
Deirdre Gilfedder.
PARAMETRO 1990 Jan.-Feb., no.176,
p.64-67, photos., refs.

WAR MEMORIALS--COMPETITIONS--UNITED
STATES--ARLINGTON (VIRGINIA)--
ARLINGTON NATIONAL CEMETERY--WOMEN
IN MILITARY SERVICE FOR AMERICA
MEMORIAL
In memoriam / Victoria Geibel.
On the design for a memorial to
honor American women who served in
the military, to be placed at
Arlington Cemetery. Architects:
Marion Gail Weiss and Michael A.
Manfredi.
METROPOLIS 1990 Jan.-Feb., v.9,
no.6, p.32, models.
Military Women's Memorial winner
announced / Douglas E. Gordon.
Winning design by Manfredi/Weiss.
ARCHITECTURE: THE AIA JOURNAL 1990
Jan., v.79, no.1, p.28, models.
Woman's memorial design chosen /
Thomas Vonier.
Winning design for the entrance of
Arlington National Cemetary
incorporates glass prisms atop
existing Beaux-Arts hemicycle
designed by McKim, Mead and White.
Architects: Marion Gail Weiss,
Michael A. Manfredi. Alternate
winners: Teresa Norton, Cleveland
Harp.
PROGRESSIVE ARCHITECTURE 1990
Jan., v.71, no.1, p.30, models.

WAR MEMORIALS--ITALY--SAN POLO DI
TORRILE
Paolo Zermani, monumento a S. Polo
di Torrile, Parma / Paolo Zermani.
Design for a war memorial. Text in
Italian and English.
DOMUS 1990 Jan., no.712,
p.12-[13], elevs., models, map,
plans, secns., site plan, sketch.

WAR MEMORIALS--JAPAN--TOKYO--WAR DEAD
MEMORIAL PARK
Takefumi Aida / Takefumi Aida.
Contents: War Dead Memorial Park,
Tokyo, design: 1987; construction:
1987-88 -- Saito Memorial Hall,
Shibaura Institute of Technology,
Omiya, Saitama, Japan, design:
1989; completion: Sept.1990. Text
in Japanese and English.
GA DOCUMENT 1990 Apr., no.25,
p.12-17, axonometric views,
elevs., models, photos., plans.

WAR MEMORIALS--SPAIN--BARCELONA--
FOSSAR DE LA PEDRERA
Barcellona, il Fossar de la Pedrera:
il recupero della memoria =
Barcelona, the Fossar de la
Pedrera: a reawareness of
memories.
A monument to the dead of the
Civil War, located in an abandoned
quarry. Architect: Beth Gali.
ABITARE 1990 Oct., no.289,
p.256-261, photos., site plan,
aerial photo.

WARD, A.
Ideology, culture and the design
studio / A. Ward.
"The political and psychological
neutrality of traditional studio
design processes is questioned,
and contrasted with the emerging
processes and value structures of
community design projects."
DESIGN STUDIES 1990 Jan., v.1,
no.11, p.10-16, refs.

WARD, ANTHONY H.
Cairns and "cairn fields": evidence
of early agriculture on Cefn Bryn,
Gower, West Glamorgan / Anthony H.
Ward.
Discusses "the nature of early
agriculture and its relationship
to ritual and settlement in the
local landscape."
LANDSCAPE HISTORY 1989, v.11,
p.[5]-18, diagrs., graphs, maps,
tables, biblio.

WARD, BASIL, 1902-1978
British modern architecture of the
30s: the work of Connell, Ward and
Lucas / Dennis Sharp.
Text in Japanese and English.
Includes a chronology of buildings
and projects, 1927-39.
ARCHITECTURE AND URBANISM 1990
Sept., no.9(240), p.37-50, ports.,
photos., refs.

WARD BOGARD AND ASSOCIATES
Denton County Courthouse.
Restoration of 1895 courthouse in
Denton. Original architect: W.
C. Dodson. Restoration architect:
Ward Bogard & Associates.
TEXAS ARCHITECT 1990 Jan.-Feb.,
v.40, no.1, p.33, photos.

WARD, COLIN
AJ Christmas books [book review].
Eight reviewers highlight their
choices for the best architecture
books of 1990.
ARCHITECTS' JOURNAL 1990 Dec.5,
v.192, no.23, p.66-69, ill.,
port., model, photos, plans, engr.
Housing matters: Octavia Hill by
Gillian Darley [book review] /
Colin Ward.
Biography of social reformer and
housing advocate. Co-founder of
the National Trust.
ARCHITECTS' JOURNAL 1990 Jan.31,
v.191, no.5, p.74, port.
Lewis Mumford 1895-1990 [obituary] /
Colin Ward.
CASABELLA 1990 June, v.54, no.569,
p.31, port.
Obituary: Lewis Mumford / Colin
Ward.
ARCHITECTURAL REVIEW 1990 Mar.,
v.187, no.1117, p.9, port.

WARD, COLIN. TALKING HOUSES
Plain speaking: Talking houses, by
Colin Ward [book review] / Alison
Ravetz.
ARCHITECTS' JOURNAL 1990 Oct.24,
v.192, no.17, p.82-83,

WARD, COLIN. WELCOME, THINNER CITY
City or cell? Welcome, thinner city,
by Colin Ward [book review] /
Robert Cowan.
ARCHITECTS' JOURNAL 1990 Feb.28,
v.191, no.9, p.76-77, photos.

WARD, DAVID C.
The Correspondence and miscellaneous
papers of Benjamin Henry Latrobe
[ed. by] John C. Van Horne [book
review] / David C. Ward.
Reviews the final volume, v.3,
1811-1820.
WINTERTHUR PORTFOLIO 1990 Winter,
v.25, no.4, p.297-300, ref.

WARD HALL ASSOCIATES
Center for Innovative Technology,
Fairfax and Loudoun Counties,
Virginia: Arquitectonica,
Ward/Hall Associates.
Built 1989. Text in Japanese and
English.
GA DOCUMENT 1990 May, no.26,
p.[48]-55, photos., secn., site
plans.

WARD-JACKSON, PHILIP
Carlo Marochetti and the Glasgow
Wellington memorial / Philip
Ward-Jackson.
BURLINGTON MAGAZINE 1990 Dec.,
v.132, no.1053, p.851-862,
photos., engr., refs.

WARD, JANET
Hurricanes require advance
preparation / Jennifer Carlile,
Janet Ward.
Preparedness plans for Charleston,
S.C., Biloxi, Miss., and New
Orleans, La.
AMERICAN CITY & COUNTY 1989 Dec.,
v.104, no.12, p.37-38, 41, port.
Oakland officials marshall resources
/ Don Ciandella, Janet Ward.
Effect of San Francisco earthquake
in Oakland, Ca.
AMERICAN CITY & COUNTY 1989 Dec.,
v.104, no.12, p.26-27, photo.
On top of the epicenter / Janet
Ward, Joe Morris, Jennifer
Carlile.
Residential communities of Santa
Cruz, Watsonville and Los Gatos,
CA., bore the brunt of the 1989
"San Francisco" earthquake.
AMERICAN CITY & COUNTY 1989 Dec.,
v.104, no.12, p.34-36,

WARD PERKINS, BRYAN. FROM CLASSICAL
ANTIQUITY TO THE MIDDLE AGES
From classical antiquity to the
Middle Ages: urban public building
in northern and central Italy
[book review] / Charles B.
McClendon.
SOCIETY OF ARCHITECTURAL
HISTORIANS, JOURNAL 1990 Mar.,
v.49, no.1, p.106-107.

WARD, STEPHEN V.
The garden city tradition
re-examined / Stephen V. Ward.
PLANNING PERSPECTIVES PP 1990
Sept., v.5, no.3, p.249-256, refs.

WARD, TIMOTHY J.
Color makes a splash / Timothy J.
Ward.
Two interiors by designer Gregory
Evans: Dagny Corcoran house, Los
Angeles, and David Hockney beach
house, Calif.
METROPOLITAN HOME 1990 June, v.22,
no.6, p.73-[81], port., photos.
Taming the wide-open spaces [loft,
New York] / Timothy J. Ward.
Interior designer: Peter
Wheelwright.
METROPOLITAN HOME 1990 Aug., v.22,
no.8, p.134-137, photos.

WARDLE, K. A.
Excavations at Assiros Toumba 1988:
a preliminary report / K.A.
Wardle.
THE ANNUAL OF THE BRITISH SCHOOL
AT ATHENS 1989, no.84,
p.[447]-463,pl.68-71, dwgs.,
photos., site plans, refs.

WARDS
See HOSPITAL WARDS

WARE, ISAAC, D. 1766. COMPLETE BODY OF
ARCHITECTURE
On the theory of order in Isaac
Ware's "A complete body of
architecture" / Kazuhike Hoshi.
Text in Japanese; English summary,
p.155.
NIHON KENCHIKU GAKKAI KEIKAKUKEI
RONBUN HOKOKU SHU = JOURNAL OF
ARCHITECTURE, PLANNING AND
ENVIRONMENTAL ENGINEERING 1990
Apr., no.4(410), p.155-164, dets.,
refs.

WAREHOUSES
See also DISTRIBUTION CENTERS
See also INDUSTRIAL BUILDINGS
See also STOREHOUSES
Build-to-suit automated distribution
centers spell opportunity for
developers / Donald A. Sigman.
Modern, large-scale, automated
regional distribution centers.
DEVELOPMENT 1990 Nov.-Dec., v.21,
no.6, p.34-36, port., photos.,
table.
Flexible building type responds to
industrial user needs / James P.
Nygaard.
"Flex" buildings, also known as
service centers, showroom
buildings, tech centers and
office/warehouse buildings, are
typically low-rise single or
multi-tenant buildings designed to
accommodate different amounts of
backroom and office space.
DEVELOPMENT 1990 Jan.-Feb., v.21,
no.1, p.21-22, port., photos.

WAREHOUSES--19TH CENTURY--ALTERATIONS
AND ADDITIONS--ENGLAND--LIVERPOOL--
ALBERT DOCK
Tempo di musei: Liverpool, la Tate
Gallery = Museum time: the Tate
Gallery, Liverpool.
Architects: James Stirling,
Michael Wilford and Associates.
ABITARE 1990 Sept., no.288,
p.268-273, photos., plans, secns.,

WAREHOUSES--19TH CENTURY--ALTERATIONS
AND ADDITIONS--UNITED STATES--
MINNEAPOLIS (MINNESOTA)--315 FIRST
AVENUE
Incarnation on the waterfront /
Bruce N. Wright.
Renovation of an 1887 warehouse at
315 First Avenue, Minneapolis for
apartments, bar and restaurant,
and offices of the Duffy Design
Group. Architect: Johnson/Reis &
Associates.
INLAND ARCHITECT 1990 Sept.-Oct.,
v.34, no.5, p.6-7, axonometric
view, photos.

WAREHOUSES--19TH CENTURY--BELGIUM--
ANTWERP
De Antwerpse pakhuizen en het
"Koninklijk Stapelhuis":
stedebouw-Kundige en
bouwconstructieve aspecten / Piet
Lombaerde.
19th and early 20th-cent.
warehouses in Antwerp are now
endangered due to the demolition
of the "Royal Entrepot". English
summary, p.75-76.
MONUMENTEN EN LANDSCHAPPEN 1990
July-Aug., v.9, no.4, p.53-63,
dwgs., elevs., photos., plans,
refs.

WAREHOUSES--19TH CENTURY--BELGIUM--
ANTWERP--KONINKLIJK STAPELHUIS
De Antwerpse pakhuizen en het
"Koninklijk Stapelhuis":
stedebouw-Kundige en
bouwconstructieve aspecten / Piet
Lombaerde.
19th and early 20th-cent.
warehouses in Antwerp are now
endangered due to the demolition
of the "Royal Entrepot". English
summary, p.75-76.
MONUMENTEN EN LANDSCHAPPEN 1990
July-Aug., v.9, no.4, p.53-63,
dwgs., elevs., photos., plans,
refs.

WAREHOUSES--ALTERATIONS AND
ADDITIONS--GERMANY (WEST)--HAMBURG
Denkmalpflege im Hafen? Technische
Kulturdenkmaler im Wandel /
Manfred F. Fischer.
ARCHITEKTUR + WETTBEWERBE 1989
Dec., no.140, p.2, port., photos.

WAREHOUSES--ALTERATIONS AND
ADDITIONS--UNITED STATES--CHICAGO
(ILLINOIS)--NORTH PIER
Reuse + retail = Razzmatazz / Paul
Glassman.
Adaptive reuse of North Pier, one
of the Pugh Warehouses along Ogden
Slip in Chicago, into a retail and
office complex. Completed in 1920.
Original architect: Christian
Albert Eckstrom. Architect:
Laurence Booth. Interior designer:
David Peterhans.
INLAND ARCHITECT 1990 Sept.-Oct.,
v.34, no.5, p.[48]-51, photos.,
plan.

WAREHOUSES--VICTORIAN--ALTERATIONS AND ADDITIONS--ENGLAND--LONDON
Elementary connection [57 Mansell St., London] /.Peter Weatherhead. Refurbishment of a Georgian townhouse, and of a Victorian warehouse behind it, and conversion into offices for an insurance company. Architect: Trehearne & Norman.
BUILDING 1990 Apr.13, v.255, no.15, p.46-48, photos.

WARHAFTIG, MYRA
Alex Baerwald: Berlin 1877 - Jerusalem 1930 [exhibition review] / Myra Warhaftig.
In conjunction with an exhibition in Haifa, Spring 1990.
BAUWELT 1990 Aug.24, v.81, no.32, p.1562-1564, photos.

WARKE, VAL K.
Education of an architect; [and] Tadao Ando: the Yale Studio & current works [book review] / Val K. Warke.
JOURNAL OF ARCHITECTURAL EDUCATION 1990 Summer, v.43, no.4, p.45-50, port., model, photo.

WARNER, ANDREW JACKSON, 1833-1910
Extraordinary efforts save Willard Chapel.
A Romanesque revival chapel and the adjoining Welch Memorial Building, built 1892-1894 are the only remaining buildings from Auburn Theological Seminary and have been purchased by the Cayuga County Community Preservation Committee. Architects: Andrew Jackson Warner.
PRESERVATION LEAGUE OF NEW YORK STATE. NEWSLETTER 1990 Spring, v.16, no.1, p.1-2, photos.

WARNER, JACK LIONEL
Malibu spaces / Irene Borger. Interiors of minimalist-style beach house in Malibu Colony owned by Audrey and Sydney Irmas. Architect: Jack Lionel Warner. Interior design: Judy Wilder.
ARCHITECTURAL DIGEST 1990 May, v.47, no.5, p.152-[161],260, port., photos.

WARNER, PATRICIA
Connecticut heritage: uncommon acquisitions in a former mill / Patricia Warner.
Interiors of renovated 1830's grist mill designed by Keith Irvine and Richard Keith Langham of Irvine & Fleming.
ARCHITECTURAL DIGEST 1990 June, v.47, no.6, p.[192-197], photos.
West Side exoticism: evocative textures and cultural allusions for Felicia Jones / Patricia Warner.
Interiors of New York apartment. Interior designers. Richard Gillette, Stephen Shadley.
ARCHITECTURAL DIGEST 1990 Nov., v.47, no.12, p.[292-298],316, port., photos.

WARNER, TIM
Inherited flair for rural harmony / Tim Warner.
Architectural designs of John Adey Repton, son of Humphrey.
COUNTRY LIFE 1990 Apr.12, v.184, no.15, p.92-95, ill., dwgs., elevs., map.

WARRELL, IAN
J.M.W. Turner at Petworth House, West Sussex / Ian Warrell.
Sketches done at and depicting scenes of the "House of Art".
ANTIQUES 1990 Apr., v.137, no.4, p.914-927,cover, photos.

WARREN AND WETMORE
Metro-North plans major renovation of Grand Central.
1913 building designed by Reed & Stem and Warren & Wetmore to receive a $400-million overhaul. Architects for renovation: Beyer Blinder Belle, Harry Weese & Associates.
ARCHITECTURAL RECORD 1990 June, v.178, no.7, p.21, secn.
Een plein voor een bibliotheek: bij de heraanleg van het Monseigneur Ladeuzeplein te Leuven / Mark Derez.
The library of the Catholic University in Louvain, Belgium, built 1921-28, and unrealized plans for a square in front. Architects: Warren and Wetmore. English summary, p.63.
MONUMENTEN EN LANDSCHAPPEN 1990 Mar.-Apr., v.9, no.2, p.29-54, ill., dwgs., ports., elevs., model, photos., plans, engrs., refs.
Preservation: Grand Central restoration / Philip Arcidi. 1913 terminal to receive $400 million for redevelopment/restoration. Original architects: Warren and Wetmore, Reed & Stem. Architects for renovation: Beyer Blinder Belle, Harry Weese & Associates.
PROGRESSIVE ARCHITECTURE 1990 June, v.71, no.6, p.26, secn.

WARREN, CHARLES
Design 100: the people, products, ideas that shape our lives. "Special issue." Architects mentioned include Venturi and Scott Brown, Robert A. M. Stern, Frank Gehry, Richard Meier, Morphosis, Coop Himmelblau, Andres Duany + Elizabeth Plater-Zyberk, Stanley Tigerman and Margaret McCurry, Eric Owen Moss, Charles Warren, Michael Graves, Peter Eisenman, and Lake/Flato Architects.
METROPOLITAN HOME 1990 Apr., v.22, no.4, p.[67-199], ports., photos.

WARREN, DAVID B.
Bayou Bend: the plan and history of the gardens / David B. Warren. Houston estate of the Hogg family. Landscape designer: Ellen Shipman.
MUSEUM OF FINE ARTS, HOUSTON. BULLETIN - THE MUSEUM OF FINE ARTS, HOUSTON 1989 Winter-Spring, v.12, no.2, p.66-93, ports., photos., plan.

WARREN, DAVID B. (CONTINUED)
Ima Hogg and Bayou Blend: a history: the interiors / David B. Warren. Early American interiors of Bayou Bend, home of Ima Hogg, and now part of the Museum of Fine Arts, Houston.
MUSEUM OF FINE ARTS, HOUSTON. BULLETIN - THE MUSEUM OF FINE ARTS, HOUSTON 1988 Fall, v.12, no.1, p.2-63, ill., ports., photos., engrs.

WARREN, MICHAEL
Will success kill the Deco district? / Michael Warren. "A recent plan aimed at producing convention hotels in Miami Beach's colorful historic district has some preservationists up in arms."
PLANNING 1990 Feb., v.56, no.2, p.21-24, ports., elev., map, photos.

WARREN, SUE
Pallant House, Chichester: a tale of restoration and benefaction / Sue Warren.
Queen Anne town house, built in 1713; now housing the 20th-cent. art collections of Walter Hussey and Charles Kearley.
APOLLO 1990 Nov., v.132, no.345, p.342-343, port., photo.

WARREN, TIGER
In the family way [vacation home, Washington state] / Julie V. Iovine.
A family compound, on the Columbia River. Architect: Tiger Warren.
METROPOLITAN HOME 1990 June, v.22, no.6, p.88-94, photo.

WARSZAWSKI, A.
The use of computer graphics as a scheduling tool / A. Retik, A. Warszawski, A. Banai.
BUILDING AND ENVIRONMENT 1990, v.25, no.2, p.133-142, dwgs., refs., diagrs.

WARTIAINEN, KAI
Holmenomradet, Norrkoping / Kai Wartiainen.
ARKITEKTUR: THE SWEDISH REVIEW OF ARCHITECTURE 1990 June-July, v.90, no.5, p.28-31, dwgs., elev., model, site plan, aerial photos.

WARUSFEL, OLIVIER
Acoustique previsionelle et simulation informatique / Jean-Pascal Jullien, Olivier Warusfel.
Acoustic forecasting. English summary, p.69. Spanish summary, p.197.
TECHNIQUES ET ARCHITECTURE 1990 Apr.-May, no.389, p.68-69, diagrs.

WASEDA DAIGAKU. ISHIYAMA LABORATORY
Takebe International House / Osamu Ishiyama.
Lodging facilities for foreign tourists, operated by Okayama Prefecture, Mitsu-Gun. The plan is modeled after old Japanese villages. Architects: Ishiyama Laboratory, Waseda University.
JAPAN ARCHITECT 1990 Nov.-Dec., v.65, no.11-12(403-404), p.52-59, elevs., photos., plans, site plan.

WASHETERIAS
See COIN-OPERATED LAUNDRIES

WASHINGTON ARCHITECTURAL GROUP
Current work.
Fourteen projects recently completed or currently on the boards by N.J. architects.
ARCHITECTURE NEW JERSEY 1990, v.26, no.2, p.9-20, axonometric views, dets., dwgs., elevs., models, photos., plans, site plans.

WASHINGTON UNIVERSITY (SAINT LOUIS, MO.). SCHOOL OF ARCHITECTURE
Washington University, Journal of Student Work, School of Architecture.
Entire issue devoted to studio projects.
APPROACH 1989, no.6, p.[1]-[95], axonometric views, dwgs., elevs., models, photos., plans, secn., site plans.

WASOWSKI, BARTLOMIEJ NATANIEL, 1617-1687
Udzial Bartlomieja Nataniela Wasowskiego W Budowie Kosciola Kolegium Jezuitow (Obecnie Farnego) w Poznaniu / Adam Malkiewicz.
His work at the Cathedral in Poznan. French summary, p.114.
FOLIA HISTORIAE ARTIUM 1990, v.26, p.87-[114], dwgs., photos., plans, secns., refs.

WASSARD, ERIK
Tema: Finansiering i det indre marked.
Theme includes editorial ("Ah Europe") and five articles on finance and economic matters within the EEC and their likely effect on the building industries. Authors: Erik Wassard, Jonas Moller, Eric Messerschmidt, and Kim Dirckinck-Holmfeld.
ARKITEKTEN 1990 Oct., v.92, no.15, p.[476]-499, graph, ports., maps, tables, aerial photo., refs.

WASSELL, DAVID G.
Tomorrow's landscape architects / David G. Wassell, Rod Edwards.
Summary of 1989 graduate work at Leeds Polytechnic and the Edinburgh College of Art.
LANDSCAPE DESIGN 1989 Nov., no.185, p.14-15, ill.

WASSERMAN, JOSEPH
Dumping Trump City: the sequel / Craig Whitaker.
Two alternate schemes for the Penn Yards site are presented, the Willen/Gutman proposal and the Riedner/Wasserman proposal.
OCULUS 1990 Oct., v.53, no.2, p.6-11, dwgs., ports., elevs., models, site plans.

WASSMAN, DEBRA
Best Small House 1990 / Susan Zevon, Katie Ridder.
Competition sponsored by HB and the American Wood Council. Winning house in Amenia, N.Y. by Jonathan Lanman and Debra Wassman of Trumbull Architects, N.Y.C.
(Continued next column)

WASSMAN, DEBRA (CONTINUED)
Best Small House 1990...(CONTINUED)
Interior designer: Paul Leonard.
HOUSE BEAUTIFUL 1990 Nov., v.132, no.11, p.81-91, photos., plans.

WASTE - DISPOSAL OF
See REFUSE AND REFUSE DISPOSAL

WASTE DISPOSAL PLANTS
See REFUSE DISPOSAL WORKS

WASTELAND
See also RECLAIMED LAND
Stadtbrachen sind Grunflachen / Ute Nolda.
Urban wasteland as an important recreational resource. Includes English summary.
GARTEN UND LANDSCHAFT 1990, v.100, no.9, p.27-32, diagr., graph, ill., map, photos., biblio.
The TOADS: a new American urban epidemic / Michael R. Greenberg, Frank J. Popper, Bernadette M. West.
"Temporarily obsolete abandoned derelict sites": deserted industrial sites and housing that become makeshift housing for the homeless, fire safety hazards and toxic waste sites.
URBAN AFFAIRS QUARTERLY 1990 Mar., v.25, no.3, p.435-454, tables, refs.

WASTEWATER RECLAMATION
See WATER REUSE

WATANABE, AKIRA
Internal logic in Tokyo: Akira Watanabe's small-scale oasis of dynamic space / Michael Webb.
Home in the Meguro district owned and designed by Watanabe, was home to Christian Charrat from 1983 to 1988.
ARCHITECTURAL DIGEST 1990 Dec., v.47, no.13, p.176-[181], port., photos., plan.
JIA Rookie Award to Akira Watanabe and Akira Kuryu.
The Japan Institute of Architects awards first Rookie Award.
JAPAN ARCHITECT 1990 Jan., v.65, no.1(393), p.4, port.

WATANABE, HIROSHI
Hiroshi Watanabe looks at the effect western architects are having in Japan / Hiroshi Watanabe.
PROGRESSIVE ARCHITECTURE 1990 May, v.71, no.5, p.113-117, photos., plans, secns., sketch.
Japan: monastic to fantastic / Hiroshi Watanabe.
Works by various architects.
ART IN AMERICA 1990 Apr., v.78, no.4, p.220-[227], photos.
Two landmarks for Tokyo / Hiroshi Watanabe, John Morris Dixon.
Two projects by Fumihiko Maki and Maki and Associates: Makuhari Messe, or Nippon Convention Center, and the Tokyo Metropolitan Gymnasium.
PROGRESSIVE ARCHITECTURE 1990 Aug., v.71, no.8, p.74-87, axonometric views, port., model, photos., plans, secns., site plan, aerial photos.

WATANABE, HISAKO
On the contemporary landscape, Part 1: Structure without design.
"Special series." Contents: Photographs by Toshiharu Kitajima. Text in Japanese.
SPACE DESIGN 1990 Sept., no.312, p.005-076, photos., map.

WATANABE, KATSUHIKO
Structures of Chok / Takayuki Kurotsu, Katsuhiko Watanabe.
"Quadrangle architecture of the royal buildings of Nepal, part 1". English summary, p.109.
NIHON KENCHIKU GAKKAI KEIKAKUKEI RONBUN HOKOKU SHU = JOURNAL OF ARCHITECTURE, PLANNING AND ENVIRONMENTAL ENGINEERING 1990 Feb., no.2(408), p.101-109, photos., plans, secns., site plans, refs.

WATANABE, MAKOTO, 1952-
Directions in urban housing, part I: Housing complexes--a topical study.
Contents: Discussion (Kunihiko Hayakawa, Makoto Motokura, Makoto Ueda).--Works (Hoichiro Itai + Section R Architects; Makoto Watanabe + Yoko Kinoshita + A. D. H.; Kunihiko Hayakawa; HEXA; Hiroshi Nishioka; Makoto Motokura + KENCHIKU Design Studio, Tokyo; Tadasu Ohe). Text in Japanese.
SPACE DESIGN 1990 Jan., no.304, p.05-52, axonometric views, elev., models, photos., plans, secns., site plans.
Liberta e indipendenza [Aoyama Technical College, Tokyo] / Makoto Sei Watanabe.
Architect: Makoto Sei Watanabe.
MODO 1990 Dec., v.13, no.128, p.52-53, photos.
Makoto Sei Watanabe: Project 9+1.
Includes essays by Watanabe and by Riichi Miyake. Text in Japanese.
SPACE DESIGN 1990 July, no.310, p.49-68, models, photos., secns.

WATANABE, TOSHIYUKI
Heat and mass transfer at outside surface of buildings / Akihito Ozaki, et al.
Subtitle: Wind tunnel tests of heat and mass transfer on horizontal surfaces. English summary, p.25.
NIHON KENCHIKU GAKKAI KEIKAKUKEI RONBUN HOKOKU SHU = JOURNAL OF ARCHITECTURE, PLANNING AND ENVIRONMENTAL ENGINEERING 1990 Jan., no.1(407), p.11-25, charts, diagrs., graphs, tables, refs.

WATANABE, TOYOKAZU, 1938-
Special contribution: Tokyo Budokan is not dynamism / Toyokazu Watanabe.
Text in Japanese.
KENCHIKU BUNKA 1990 Sept., v.45, no.527, p.181-184, photos.
Special edition II: architecture beyond imagination.
Features three recent works by Toyokazu Watanabe. Includes essay, Architecture beyond imagination. English summary, p.23.
KENCHIKU BUNKA 1990 Mar., v.45, no.521, p.123-144, elevs., models, photos., plans, secns.

WATANABE, YOKO
    A study reconstructing the
    settlement form of Doi-Kachu in
    Aki originated from the medieval
    castle town and its dwelling lots
    / Hirohisa Ito, Yoko Watanabe.
    "A study on spacial [sic]
    composition of Samurai houses of
    Doi in Aki district in the Fief of
    Tosa during the Edo period, Part
    1". Text in Japanese; includes
    English summary.
    NIHON KENCHIKU GAKKAI KEIKAKUKEI
    RONBUN HOKOKU SHU = JOURNAL OF
    ARCHITECTURE, PLANNING AND
    ENVIRONMENTAL ENGINEERING 1990
    Nov., no.11(417), p.127-136,
    plans, tables, refs.

WATER AND ARCHITECTURE
    See also CASCADES
    See also FOUNTAINS
    See also WATER FEATURES
    See also WATER GARDENS
    See also WATER SLIDES
    Using water to create a natural
    setting / Robert G. Lamphere.
    Followed by second article: One
    Cambridge Court's fountain:
    beautiful and intelligent, p.17.
    DEVELOPMENT 1990 Sept.-Oct., v.21,
    no.5, p.16, photos.
    Waterscapes: a creative evolution /
    Martin L. Epps.
    First of five articles on the use
    of water in development projects;
    some separately indexed.
    DEVELOPMENT 1990 Sept.-Oct., v.21,
    no.5, p.10-12, photos., aerial
    photo.

WATER AND ARCHITECTURE--SYMBOLIC
ASPECTS
    The Cairene sabil: form and meaning
    / Saleh Lamei Mostafa.
    MUQARNAS 1990, v.6, p.[33]-42,
    photos., refs.

WATER BUILDINGS--COMPETITIONS--GERMANY
(WEST)--HAMBURG--ERICUSSPITZE
    Deichtormarkt und Ericusspitze in
    Hamburg.
    Office building with two sides
    along the river. First prize: Jorg
    Friedrich.
    BAUWELT 1990 Aug.17, v.81, no.31,
    p.1516, model, plan, secn.

WATER CONSERVATION
    Visible city: water: New York's
    complicated water system / Daniel
    S. Levy.
    METROPOLIS 1990 June, v.9, no.10,
    p.78-84, photos.

WATER CONSERVATION--RESEARCH--UNITED
STATES--PHOENIX (ARIZONA)
    Modeling residential landscape water
    and energy use to evaluate water
    conservation policies / E. Gregory
    McPherson.
    Data derived from computer
    simulations using three types of
    residential gardens, xeriscapes,
    zeroscapes and mesiscapes, in
    Phoenix and Tucson.
    LANDSCAPE JOURNAL 1990 Fall, v.9,
    no.2, p.122-134, photo., plans,
    tables, refs.

WATER CONSERVATION--RESEARCH--UNITED
STATES--TUCSON (ARIZONA)
    Modeling residential landscape water
    and energy use to evaluate water
    conservation policies / E. Gregory
    McPherson.
    Data derived from computer
    simulations using three types of
    residential gardens, xeriscapes,
    zeroscapes and mesiscapes, in
    Phoenix and Tucson.
    LANDSCAPE JOURNAL 1990 Fall, v.9,
    no.2, p.122-134, photo., plans,
    tables, refs.

WATER-CONSERVING GARDENS
    See XERISCAPES

WATER FEATURES
    Fun for everyone: the aquatic
    formula / Alan Heuss.
    Aquatic recreation centers,
    including swimming pools, water
    slides, and other aquatic
    features.
    PARKS & RECREATION 1990 Nov.,
    v.25, no.11, p.34-38, photos.
    Using water to create a natural
    setting / Robert G. Lamphere.
    Followed by second article: One
    Cambridge Court's fountain:
    beautiful and intelligent, p.17.
    DEVELOPMENT 1990 Sept.-Oct., v.21,
    no.5, p.16, photos.
    A waterpark planner / Joshua L.
    Brener.
    PARKS & RECREATION 1990 Nov.,
    v.25, no.11, p.42-[44],71, photos.
    Waterscapes: a creative evolution /
    Martin L. Epps.
    First of five articles on the use
    of water in development projects;
    some separately indexed.
    DEVELOPMENT 1990 Sept.-Oct., v.21,
    no.5, p.10-12, photos., aerial
    photo.

WATER FUN PARKS
    See WATERPARKS

WATER GARDENS--FRANCE--MARLY
    Marly, jardin des eaux / Bruno
    Bentz.
    English summary, p.133.
    HISTOIRE DE L'ART 1990 Dec.,
    no.12, p.27-36, dets., photos.,
    plans, refs.

WATER GARDENS--JAPANESE--JAPAN--
KAMAKURA--ZUISEN TEMPLE
    The garden in Zuisen Temple,
    Kamakura, Japan: design form and
    phylogenetic meaning / Norris
    Brock Johnson.
    JOURNAL OF GARDEN HISTORY 1990
    Oct.-Dec., v.10, no.4, p.214-236,
    ill., dwgs., port., photos.,
    secn., refs.

WATER GARDENS--MOGHUL--INDIA--KASHMIR
    Adrift in a Mughal garden: seeing
    the vale of Kashmir from the deck
    of a houseboat / Elizabeth B.
    Moynihan.
    Shalamar Bagh, and other gardens.
    ARCHITECTURAL DIGEST 1990 May,
    v.47, no.5, p.90-95,118-119,122,
    map, photos.

WATER GARDENS--SCOTLAND--GLASGOW
    Greener Glasgow is child's play /
    Ruth Owens.
    West German environmental artist
    Dieter Magnus has designed a park
    and playground space in Glasgow
    that is both urban park and water
    garden.
    ARCHITECTS' JOURNAL 1990 Feb.28,
    v.191, no.9, p.17, port., model,
    photos.

WATER GARDENS--SWITZERLAND--SOMAZZO
    Trasgressione verde: divertimento da
    esterni nel canton Ticino /
    Gilberto Oneto.
    Water gardens of a house in
    Somazzo, Switzerland. Architect:
    Ivan Ruperti.
    VILLE GIARDINI 1990 Feb., no.245,
    p.[56]-63, photos.

WATER MILLS--ALTERATIONS AND
ADDITIONS--SPAIN--MURCIA
    Progetto per la ristrutturazione dei
    Mulini Vecchi di Murcia = Project
    for the reconversion of the old
    watermills of Murcia / Juan
    Navarro Baldeweg.
    Architects: Juan Navarro Baldeweg
    with Jose Maria Merce.
    LOTUS INTERNATIONAL 1986, no.52,
    p.26-29, elevs., model, photo.,
    plans, secns., site plans.

WATER MILLS--IRELAND
    The introduction of the vertical
    watermill into Ireland: some
    recent archaeological evidence /
    Colin Rynne.
    Includes abstract.
    MEDIEVAL ARCHAEOLOGY 1989, v.33,
    p.21-31, axonometric view, secns.,
    refs.

WATER PURIFICATION PLANTS
    See WATER TREATMENT PLANTS

WATER QUALITY MANAGEMENT--CHINA
    Standards [Current standards, codes
    & specifications for urban & rural
    development].
    Part XV: Urban water supply and
    sewage engineering. Part XVI:
    Urban water quality. Parts SVII
    and XVIII are under compilation.
    BUILDING IN CHINA 1989 Sept., v.2,
    no.3, p.52-53, tables.

WATER QUALITY MANAGEMENT--DEVELOPING
COUNTRIES
    Applying lessons from housing to
    meeting the challenge of water and
    sanitation for the urban poor /
    Tim Campbell.
    AMERICAN PLANNING ASSOCIATION.
    JOURNAL 1987 Spring, v.53, no.2,
    p.186-192, chart, photo., biblio.,
    refs.
    Water supply and wastewater
    treatment for low income housing
    projects / Percival R. Thomas.
    INTERNATIONAL JOURNAL FOR HOUSING
    SCIENCE AND ITS APPLICATIONS 1990,
    v.14, no.1, p.057-063, chart,
    secn., refs.

WATER QUALITY MANAGEMENT--STANDARDS--
CHINA
Standards.
The first of the ongoing standards
sections with new or revised
information. Contents:
I.Geotechnical investigation and
surveying.--II.Building
materials.--III.Building products
and elements.
BUILDING IN CHINA 1990 Sept., v.3,
no.3, p.52-53, tables.

WATER QUALITY MANAGEMENT--UNITED
STATES
Stormwater management for the 1990s
/ Larry Roesner, Robert Matthews.
AMERICAN CITY & COUNTY 1990 Feb.,
v.105, no.2, p.44,46,48,50,52-54,
photos.

WATER QUALITY MANAGEMENT--UNITED
STATES--LITTLE MIAMI RIVER BASIN
(OHIO)
The hydrologic effects of urban land
use: a case study of the Little
Miami River Basin / Susanna T.Y.
Tong.
LANDSCAPE AND URBAN PLANNING 1990
Apr., v.19, no.1, p.99-105,
graphs, tables, refs.

WATER RESOURCES DEVELOPMENT--CHINA
Studies on Beijing's development
strategies / Zhao Dongri.
Covers population structure;
sub-centers, satellite towns,
urban region; water shortage;
traffic.
BUILDING IN CHINA 1989 Mar., v.2,
no.1, p.18-22, table.

WATER REUSE
Reclaimed resources: building
systems: recycling wastewater /
Ray Don Tilley.
Plumbing systems that conserve and
reuse water.
ARCHITECTURE: THE AIA JOURNAL 1990
Dec., v.79, no.12, p.97-99,102,
dwgs., photos.

WATER SLIDES
Fun for everyone: the aquatic
formula / Alan Heuss.
Aquatic recreation centers,
including swimming pools, water
slides, and other aquatic
features.
PARKS & RECREATION 1990 Nov.,
v.25, no.11, p.34-38, photos.
A waterpark planner / Joshua L.
Brener.
PARKS & RECREATION 1990 Nov.,
v.25, no.11, p.42-[44],71, photos.

WATER TANKS--NEPAL
An ethno-archaeological
investigation into irrigation
agriculture and water systems in
mid-Western Nepal [part 5] /
Thomas M.C. Pinhorn.
Continued, from no.113. Covers
ancient water-conduits and water
tanks. Includes a small glossary.
PRACINA NEPALA 1989 Oct.-Nov.,
no.114, p.[18]-23, biblio.

WATER TOWERS--19TH CENTURY--BELGIUM
Eenheid in verscheidenheid: de
bouwgeschiedenis van watertorens /
Wim Van Craenenbroeck.
The history of modern water tower
construction, beginning in 1867.
English summary, p.76.
MONUMENTEN EN LANDSCHAPPEN 1990
July-Aug., v.9, no.4, p.64-74,
fig., photos., secn., refs.

WATER TOWERS--20TH CENTURY--BELGIUM
Eenheid in verscheidenheid: de
bouwgeschiedenis van watertorens /
Wim Van Craenenbroeck.
The history of modern water tower
construction, beginning in 1867.
English summary, p.76.
MONUMENTEN EN LANDSCHAPPEN 1990
July-Aug., v.9, no.4, p.64-74,
fig., photos., secn., refs.

WATER TOWERS--20TH CENTURY--RUINED
EXTINCT, ETC.--NETHERLANDS--
WASSENAAR
Fixatie op het functionalisme: het
eerste Docomomo-congres in
Eindhoven / Hans Ibelings.
Report on conference held by
association to preserve Modern
Movement buildings. Includes
photographs of the destruction of
a 1927 water tower in Wassenaar
(architect: J.P.L. Hendriks).
DE ARCHITECT 1990 Nov., v.21,
no.11, p.35-37, photos., refs.

WATER TOWERS--ALTERATIONS AND
ADDITIONS--GERMANY (WEST)--HAMBURG--
LOKSTEDT
Umbau eines Wasserturmes in Hamburg
Lokstedt = Conversion of a water
tower in Hamburg Lokstedt.
Conversion of water tower into a
house. Architects: Siegfried
Geisler, Schindel und Kahle.
ARCHITEKTUR + WETTBEWERBE 1989
Dec., no.140, p.25, photos., plan.

WATER TREATMENT PLANTS--19TH CENTURY--
UNITED STATES--WASHINGTON (DISTRICT
OF COLUMBIA)--MCMILLAN RESERVOIR
Sand castles / Thomas W. Sweeney.
McMillan Reservoir site and park,
Washington, D.C., threatened by
development. Landscape architect:
Frederick Law Olmstead, Jr.
HISTORIC PRESERVATION 1990
July-Aug., v.42, no.4, p.38-[43],
72, photos.

WATER TREATMENT PLANTS--ITALY--SALERNO
Disinquinamento del Golfo di Salerno
= A wastewater treatment plant for
the Salerno Gulf / Alessandro
Macchi.
Architects: Consorzio CONSAL.
L'INDUSTRIA DELLE COSTRUZIONI 1990
Oct., v.24, no.228, p.49-58,
cover, diagrs., graphs, map,
photos., site plan.

WATER TREATMENT PLANTS--NEW ZEALAND--
PORIRVA BASIN WASTEWATER TREATMENT
PLANT
The saga of Porirva wastewater / Tim
M. Davin.
Wastewater treatment plant near
Porirva Harbour, New Zealand.
PLANNING QUARTERLY 1989 Dec,
no.96, p.23-24, map, photo.

WATER TREATMENT PLANTS--SPAIN--
GUADARRAMA
Tres estaciones depuradoras de aguas
residuales = Three water
purification plants.
In Majadahonda, Guadarrama and
Villalba. Architects: Juan
Herreros, Inaki Abalos. Text in
Spanish and English.
QUADERNS D'ARQUITECTURA I
URBANISME 1988 July-Sept., no.178,
p.102-119, photos., plans, secn.,
site plan.

WATER TREATMENT PLANTS--SPAIN--
MAJADAHONDA
Tres estaciones depuradoras de aguas
residuales = Three water
purification plants.
In Majadahonda, Guadarrama and
Villalba. Architects: Juan
Herreros, Inaki Abalos. Text in
Spanish and English.
QUADERNS D'ARQUITECTURA I
URBANISME 1988 July-Sept., no.178,
p.102-119, photos., plans, secn.,
site plan.

WATER TREATMENT PLANTS--SPAIN--
VILLALBA
Tres estaciones depuradoras de aguas
residuales = Three water
purification plants.
In Majadahonda, Guadarrama and
Villalba. Architects: Juan
Herreros, Inaki Abalos. Text in
Spanish and English.
QUADERNS D'ARQUITECTURA I
URBANISME 1988 July-Sept., no.178,
p.102-119, photos., plans, secn.,
site plan.

WATER TREATMENT PLANTS--UNITED
STATES--CONTRA COSTA (CALIFORNIA)--
CONTRA COSTA WATER TREATMENT COMPLEX
Site-sensitive technology: Simon
Martin Vegue Winkelstein Moris of
San Francisco.
Three designs for projects that
meld high technology and sensitive
design: Oceanside Control
Facility, Contra Costa Water
Treatment complex, and addition to
Lawrence Hall.
ARCHITECTURE: THE MAGAZINE OF THE
AMERICAN INSTITUTE OF ARCHITECTS
1990 May, v.79, no.5, p.48, elev.,
models, secn.

WATER TUNNELS--ANCIENT--ISRAEL--JORDAN
VALLEY
Die Wasserversorgung geschichtlicher
Wustenfestungen am Jordantal /
Gunther Garbrecht, Jehuda Peleg.
ANTIKE WELT 1989, v.20, no.2,
p.2-20, graphs, maps, photos,
secn., site plans, refs.

WATER TUNNELS--UNITED STATES--NEW YORK
(NEW YORK)
Visible city: water: New York's
complicated water system / Daniel
S. Levy.
METROPOLIS 1990 June, v.9, no.10,
p.78-84, photos.

WATER-WHEELS
See WATERWHEELS

WATER WORKS
See WATERWORKS

WATERCOLOR AND INK WASH DRAWINGS
See also ARCHITECTURAL DRAWINGS

WATERCOLOR AND INK WASH DRAWINGS--16TH
CENTURY
La Sicilia del cinquecento nella
"Descrittione in diseguo" di
Camillo Camiliani / Marina
Scarlatta.
On the 300 16th cent. watercolor
and India ink drawings by
Camilliani which comprise the
historical and geographic
treatise, Descrittione della
Sicilia. Summaries in English,
French, German and Spanish.
PALLADIO 1988 Dec., v.1, no.2,
p.15-36, ill., dwgs., refs.

WATERCOLOR AND INK WASH DRAWINGS--
EXHIBITIONS
Daring watercolours: Hugh Buchanan
[exhibition review] / Christopher
Woodward.
Exhibition of architectural
watercolors by Scottish artist
Hugh Buchanan at the Francis Kyle
Gallery, London, through 1 Mar.
1990.
ARCHITECTS' JOURNAL 1990 Feb.21,
v.191, no.8, p.88-89, dwg.

WATERCOLORS
See WATERCOLOR AND INK WASH DRAWINGS

WATERCOURSES
See STREAMS

WATERFRONT BUILDINGS
See also SHIP TERMINALS
See also WATERFRONTS
How a small design firm works with
developers / Daniel Waterman.
Carrington Associates, a New York
firm works with Waterfront Invest,
a young development firm.
ARCHITECTURAL RECORD 1990 Feb.,
v.178, no.2, p.52-53, photos.,
model.

WATERFRONT BUILDINGS--ALTERATIONS AND
ADDITIONS--ENGLAND--LONDON--ANCHOR
BREWHOUSE
Thameside anchor.
19th cent. London brewery, Anchor
Brewhouse, converted into housing.
Architects: Pollard Thomas and
Edward.
ARCHITECTURAL REVIEW 1990 Oct.,
v.188, no.1124, p.81-84, elevs.,
photos., plans.

WATERFRONT BUILDINGS--ALTERATIONS AND
ADDITIONS--IRELAND--DUBLIN--30-32
SIR JOHN ROGERSON'S QUAY
Warehouse rock / John Olley.
Conversion of Dublin warehouse
into offices for Irish rock group
U2. Architects: Felim Dunne in
association with Beardsmore Yauner
Byrne. Second article features the
staircase, p.55-57.
ARCHITECTS' JOURNAL 1990 Nov.7,
v.192, no.19, p.38-47,55-57,
dets., photos., plans, secns.,
site plan, isometric dwg.

WATERFRONT BUILDINGS--ALTERATIONS AND
ADDITIONS--SWEDEN--NORRKOPING--
HOLMENOMRADET
Holmenomradet, Norrkoping / Kai
Wartiainen.
ARKITEKTUR: THE SWEDISH REVIEW OF
ARCHITECTURE 1990 June-July, v.90,
no.5, p.28-31, dwgs., elev.,
model, site plan, aerial photos.

WATERFRONT BUILDINGS--BELGIUM--ANTWERP
De Antwerpse pakhuizen en het
"Koninklijk Stapelhuis":
stedebouw-kundlge en
bouwconstructieve aspecten / Piet
Lombaerde.
19th and early 20th-cent.
warehouses in Antwerp are now
endangered due to the demolition
of the "Royal Entrepot". English
summary, p.75-76.
MONUMENTEN EN LANDSCHAPPEN 1990
July-Aug., v.9, no.4, p.53-63,
dwgs., elevs., photos., plans,
refs.

WATERFRONT BUILDINGS--BELGIUM--
ANTWERP--ISLET
In the mouth of the Scheldt.
On proposals by the Bureau for
Urban Design for the development
of the derelict dockland area,
Islet, in Antwerp.
ARCHITECTURAL REVIEW 1990 Dec.,
v.188, no.1126, p.50-53, dwgs.,
maps, site plans.

WATERFRONT BUILDINGS--BELGIUM--RUPEL
RIVER AREA
Een industrieel-archeologisch site
langs de Rupel / Hugo Lejon.
History of an industrial region
along the Rupel River in Belgium,
particularly in the town of Boom.
English summary, p.75.
MONUMENTEN EN LANDSCHAPPEN 1990
July-Aug., v.9, no.4, p.21-28,
ill., elev., map, photos., secns.,
site plan, engrs., refs.

WATERFRONT BUILDINGS--COMPETITIONS--
ENGLAND--LIVERPOOL--PIER HEAD
Liver line-up / Clare Melhuish.
Features five entries in the
competition for the redevelopment
of Pier Head, Liverpool.
Architects: David Marks, Julia
Barfield Architects; Allies and
Morrison; Cass Associates;
Austin-Smith: Lord; Tibbalds
Colbourne Partnership.
BUILDING DESIGN 1990 June 15,
no.990, p.18,20-22, dwgs., elevs.,
secns., site plans.

WATERFRONT BUILDINGS--COMPETITIONS--
ENGLAND--LONDON--ISLE OF DOGS
Appetite restored in Docklands /
John Welsh.
Features entries in a competition
for an isle of Dogs restaurant.
Winning architects: Rick Mather
Architects.
BUILDING DESIGN 1990 Mar.16,
no.977, p.10-11, secns., plan,
wxonometric views, elevs.,
sketches, isometric dwgs.

WATERFRONT BUILDINGS--COMPETITIONS--
GERMANY (WEST)--HAMBURG
Gutachterwettbewerb Kehrwiederspitze
/ Gert Kahler.
Competition entry for waterfront
buildings in Hamburg. Architects:
Kleffel Kohnholdt, and Kohn
Pedersen Fox.
BAUWELT 1990 Dec.7, v.81, no.46,
p.2292, model.
Hamburg und sein Hafen / Gert
Kahler.
The main article in issue on
Hamburg entitled "Tor zur Welt".
Reviews the harbor area buildings,
the Sandtorhafen-Speicherstadt
area, and three competitions.
Prize winners include Patshan
Winking Architekten; v. Gerkan,
Marg + Partner; Kleffel Kohnholdt;
Massimiliano Fuksas; Jorg
Friedrich; AC Architekten Contor;
ASW Architekten Silcher + Werner;
Rainer Wischhusen.
BAUWELT 1990 Dec.7, v.81, no.46,
p.2298-2317, dwgs., models,
photos., plans, secns., site
plans, aerial photos., refs.

WATERFRONT BUILDINGS--COMPETITIONS--
GERMANY (WEST)--REGENSBURG--
DONAUMARKT
Stadthalle Regensburg - Donaumarkt =
Civic Hall Regensburg -
Donaumarkt.
Competition. Architects: Kjaer &
Richter, Dan Christensen. Includes
two other entries. Text in German.
ARCHITEKTUR + WETTBEWERBE 1990
Sept., no.143, p.27-31, elevs.,
models, plans, secns., site plans.

WATERFRONT BUILDINGS--COMPETITIONS--
NORWAY--OSLO--AKER BRYGGE
Badezentrum "Aker Brygge" in Oslo,
Norwegen = Aqua-leisure centre
"Aker Brygge" in Oslo, Norway.
Competition for waterfront
multi-use complex. Winning
architects: Theo Bjerg, Palle
Dyreborg. Text in German.
ARCHITEKTUR + WETTBEWERBE 1990
Mar., no.141, p.37-41, elevs.,
models, plans, secns., site plans.

WATERFRONT BUILDINGS--ENGLAND--
LONDON--130-132 GROSVENOR ROAD
On the waterfront / Kester
Rattenbury.
On Richard Rogers' proposed
riverside office building at
130-132 Grosvenor Road, London.
BUILDING DESIGN 1990 Oct.19,
no.1008, p.12, models, sketches.

WATERFRONT BUILDINGS--ENGLAND--
LONDON--SHAD THAMES
Street wise [Shad Thames, London] /
Dan Cruickshank.
In the London Docklands
development area.
ARCHITECTS' JOURNAL 1990 May 16,
v.191, no.20, p.26-29, map,
photos.

WATERFRONT BUILDINGS--ENGLAND--
LONDON--THAMES QUAY
Stemming the tide / John Welsh.
On the Thames Quay office building
on the Isle of Dogs, London.
Architects: YRM Partnership.
BUILDING DESIGN 1990 Apr.13,
no.981, p.10, axonometric views,
photos., plan.

WATERFRONT BUILDINGS--FRANCE--
BORDEAUX--CATHEDRALE ENGLOUTIE
Water music / Clare Melhuish.
On the design for a riverscape
building in Bordeaux by Alsop &
Lyall.
BUILDING DESIGN 1990 May 4,
no.984, p.24, elev., ill., secn.,
site plan.

WATERFRONT BUILDINGS--GERMANY (WEST)--
HAMBURG--ALSTERPAVILLON
Erholungsinsel: der Alsterpavillon
in Hamburg / Karin von Behr.
DEUTSCHE BAUZEITUNG 1990 Oct.,
v.124, no.10, p.152-162, photos.,
plan, refs.

WATERFRONT BUILDINGS--GERMANY (WEST)--
HUSUM--RATHAUS
Rathaus am Hafen, Bauen am Ort: das
neue Rathaus am Binnenhafen in
Husum / Gert Kahler.
Architects: Dieter Patschan, Asmus
Werner, Bernhard Winking.
BAUWELT 1990 May 4, v.81, no.4,
p.840-843, elev., photos., plans,
secns., site plan.

WATERFRONT BUILDINGS--NETHERLANDS--
ROTTERDAM
Containers a quaix aux Pays-Bas.
Waterfront housing block,
Rotterdam. Architects: Herve
Daridan, Isabelle Manescau,
Jean-Marie Dancy, Francois
Marzelle, Edouard Steeg. English
summary, p.93; Spanish summary,
p.172.
TECHNIQUES ET ARCHITECTURE 1990
Oct.-Nov., no.392, p.92-93, dwg.,
elev., models.

WATERFRONT BUILDINGS--NETHERLANDS--
ROTTERDAM--AELBRECHTSKADE
Stadtstimmeren in Rotterdam / Ton
Verstegen.
Changes on the waterfront,
including the Aelbrechtskade by
Adriaan Geuze.
ARCHIS 1990 Dec., no.12, p.3-4,
photos., refs.

WATERFRONT BUILDINGS--NORWAY--OSLO--
AKER BRYGGE
Aker Brygge / Francis Duffy.
Waterfront multi-use development,
Oslo. Architect: Niels Torp.
ARCHITECTURAL REVIEW 1990 Aug.,
v.188, no.1122, p.[55]-62,
photos., plans, secn., site plan.
Til forsvar for Aker Brygge
[letter]/ Fredrik A.S. Torp, Kim
Dirckinck-Holmfeld.
Correspondence relating to an
article in the May 1990 issue of
this journal.
ARKITEKTEN 1990 July, v.92, no.9,
p.304, photos., aerial photo.

WATERFRONT BUILDINGS--NORWAY--OSLO--
AKER BRYGGE (CONTINUED)
Vetrati aggetti e ponti di Niels
Torp: "Aker Brygge" ad Oslo.
ARCHITETTURA; CRONACHE E STORIA
1990 Apr., v.36, no.4(414),
p.292-294, photos., site plan.

WATERFRONT BUILDINGS--SCOTLAND--
GLASGOW--CARRICK QUAY
Quay features / Brian Edwards.
On the new riverside housing
development Carrick Quay, Glasgow.
Architect: Davis Duncan
Partnership.
BUILDING DESIGN 1990 Oct.26,
no.1009, p.26, axonometric views,
photos., plans, secns.

WATERFRONT BUILDINGS--SPAIN--BARCELONA
Pabellones de cubierta: el puerto
olimpico = Deck pavilions.
On the Barcelona waterfront
buildings. Projects by Martorell,
Bohigas, Mackay, Puigdomenech,
including a sailing school,
reception building and athlete
housing. English text, p.88.
A & V 1990, no.22, p.66-69, dwg.,
elevs., models, plans, secns.,
site plans.

WATERFRONT BUILDINGS--UNITED STATES--
CAMDEN (NEW JERSEY)
Sharks and seals to Camden's rescue
/ Martin McNamara.
Projected waterfront development
for Camden, N.J.
METROPOLIS 1990 Oct., v.10, no.3,
p.25-26, model.

WATERFRONT BUILDINGS--UNITED STATES--
CHICAGO (ILLINOIS)--BURNHAM HARBOR
STATION
Snug harbor: Burnham Harbor Station,
Chicago, Illinois.
Public harbor station on the
lakefront. Architects: Chicago
Park District; William Latoza,
senior designer.
ARCHITECTURAL RECORD 1990 Nov.,
v.178, no.12, p.[82]-83, photos.,
plan.

WATERFRONT BUILDINGS--UNITED STATES--
NASHVILLE (TENNESSEE)--RIVERFRONT
APARTMENTS
All'ombra dei grattacieli fra i
reperti del produrre / Nicola
Anguilano.
148-unit housing development in a
former industrial area of
Nashville, Tenn. Architects: Tuck
Hinton Everton.
VILLE GIARDINI 1990 Sept., no.251,
p.10-17, axonometric views, dwgs.,
photos., plans, secns., site
plans.

WATERFRONT BUILDINGS--UNITED STATES--
PHILADELPHIA (PENNSYLVANIA)--PENN'S
LANDING
Landing on its feet: Penn's Landing
in Philadelphia has been on the
boards for nearly three decades /
Clifford A. Pearson.
The latest plan, by architects
Bower Lewis Thrower.
ARCHITECTURAL RECORD 1990 Feb.,
v.178, no.2, p.65-67, models, site
plans.

WATERFRONT BUILDINGS--UNITED STATES--
QUEENS (NEW YORK)--ARVERNE
Setting the table in Arverne /
Jacqueline Rivkin.
Waterfront housing development
planned by the city for this area
of Queens. Developer: Oceanview
Associates. Architects: Liebman
Melting Partnership; Ehrenkrantz,
Eckstut & Whitelaw.
METROPOLIS 1990 June, v.9, no.10,
p.19-21, dwg.

WATERFRONT BUILDINGS--UNITED STATES--
RED BANK (NEW JERSEY)--BLUFFS
The Bluffs, Red Bank, New Jersey.
Luxury riverside housing units,
some incorporated into existing
Victorian mansions. Architect:
Jerome Morley Larson.
ARCHITECTURE NEW JERSEY 1989,
v.25, no.3, p.8, photo.

WATERFRONT INVEST
How a small design firm works with
developers / Daniel Waterman.
Carrington Associates, a New York
firm works with Waterfront Invest,
a young development firm.
ARCHITECTURAL RECORD 1990 Feb.,
v.178, no.2, p.52-53, photos.,
model.

WATERFRONTS
See also WATERFRONT BUILDINGS
The abc's of waterfront planning /
Frederick H. Zeidman.
URBAN LAND 1989 June, v.48, no.6,
p.11-15, dwg., photos., site plan,
engr.
Leisure at the waterfront / Andrew
Thorburn.
THE PLANNER 1990 Apr.6, v.76,
no.13, p.18-19, photo.
Of second cities and ships at sea:
regulations guide development on
the waterfront / Richard J.
Bertman, Dan Pinck.
REAL ESTATE FINANCE 1990 Winter,
v.6, no.4, p.79-82, photo.

WATERFRONTS--19TH CENTURY--CANADA--
TORONTO (ONTARIO)--ASHBRIDGE'S BAY
Planning urban waterfront industrial
districts: Toronto's Ashbridge
Bay, 1889-1910 / Gene Desfor.
URBAN HISTORY REVIEW REVUE
D'HISTOIRE URBAINE 1988 Oct.,
v.17, no.2, p.77-91, axonometric
view, maps, photos., refs.

WATERFRONTS--20TH CENTURY--CANADA--
TORONTO (ONTARIO)
Port authorities as urban land
developers: the case of the
Toronto Harbour Commissioners and
their Outer Harbour Project,
1912-68 / Roy Merrens.
URBAN HISTORY REVIEW REVUE
D'HISTOIRE URBAINE 1988 Oct.,
v.17, no.2, p.92-105, axonometric
view, dwg., maps, photo., refs.

WATERFRONTS--20TH CENTURY--CANADA--
TORONTO (ONTARIO)--ASHBRIDGE'S BAY
Planning urban waterfront industrial
districts: Toronto's Ashbridge
Bay, 1889-1910 / Gene Desfor.
URBAN HISTORY REVIEW REVUE
D'HISTOIRE URBAINE 1988 Oct.,
v.17, no.2, p.77-91, axonometric
view, maps, photos., refs.

WATERFRONTS--ALTERATIONS AND
ADDITIONS--BELGIUM--ANTWERP
Antwerpen als trendvolger of
trendsetter: artefacten van het
collective geheugen / Han Meyer.
DE ARCHITECT 1990 Sept., v.21,
no.9, p.134-139, site plans,
aerial photo., refs.

WATERFRONTS--ALTERATIONS AND
ADDITIONS--BELGIUM--ANTWERP--ISLET
In the mouth of the Scheldt.
On proposals by the Bureau for
Urban Design for the development
of the derelict dockland area,
Islet, in Antwerp.
ARCHITECTURAL REVIEW 1990 Dec.,
v.188, no.1126, p.50-53, dwgs.,
maps, site plans.
Revitalising Antwerp / John Welsh.
Features winning design by Bureau
for Urban Design for the
renovation the old waterfront area
of Antwerp, called the "Islet".
BUILDING DESIGN 1990 July 6,
no.993, p.12, dwgs., site plans.

WATERFRONTS--ALTERATIONS AND
ADDITIONS--COMPETITIONS--DENMARK--
FAABORG
Faaborg havn.
Results of a 1989 ideas
competition for alterations to the
Danish harbor. First prize: Bo
Lautrup, Peter Dalsgaard, Lars
Juel Thiis Knudsen, Ib V. Nielsen.
Second prize: Jorn Boldsen. Third
prize: Thure Nielsen & Rubow.
ARKITEKTEN 1990 Apr., v.92, no.4,
p.120-130, dwgs., maps, photos.,
site plans.

WATERFRONTS--ALTERATIONS AND
ADDITIONS--COMPETITIONS--ITALY--
VENICE--PORTA PER VENEZIA
Concorso internazionale "Una porta
per Venezia".
Announcement of an international
competition for redesign of a
waterfront area Piazzale Roma in
Venice. Sponsors: Biennale di
Venezia, Amministrazione Comunale.
L'INDUSTRIA DELLE COSTRUZIONI 1990
Sept., v.24, no.227, p.61, site
plan, engr., aerial photo.

WATERFRONTS--ALTERATIONS AND
ADDITIONS--DENMARK--COPENHAGEN
Kobenhavn / Kim Dirckinck-Holmfeld.
ARKITEKTEN 1990 May, v.92, no.6,
p.[180]-187, model, maps, photos.

WATERFRONTS--ALTERATIONS AND
ADDITIONS--ENGLAND--LONDON--
DOCKLANDS
Pa djupa vatten / Ulla Harde.
Commentary on recent developments
at the Docklands, London.
ARKITEKTUR: THE SWEDISH REVIEW OF
ARCHITECTURE 1990 Sept., v.90,
no.7, p.54-57, dwg., elevs., maps,
photos., plan.

WATERFRONTS--ALTERATIONS AND
ADDITIONS--FRANCE--ANGERS--LA MAINE
Angers Front de Maine.
Project for the right bank of the
Maine, to reconcile the two
approaches to Angers. Architect:
Cl. Vasconi.
LE MUR VIVANT 1990, no.95,
p.73-74, axonometric views, dwgs.,
elevs., plans, site plans.

WATERFRONTS--ALTERATIONS AND
ADDITIONS--GERMANY (WEST)--HAMBURG--
SPEICHERSTADT
Amburgo: politiche urbane per la
citta portuale / Egbert Kossak,
Ullrich Schwarz.
The fourth annual Bauforum, an
open design seminar held in
Hamburg, Sept. 1989, focussing on
the Speicherstadt warehouse
district near the port. Includes
English summary; Captions in
Italian and English.
CASABELLA 1990 Jan., v.54, no.564,
p.44-51,61, models, maps, photos.,
secn., sketches, aerial photos.
Dock steady / John Welsh.
On Massimiliano Fuksas' proposal
for waterfront office building in
the Speicherstadt area, Hamburg.
BUILDING DESIGN 1990 Apr.13,
no.981, p.18-19, elevs., models,
plans, secns., site plans.

WATERFRONTS--ALTERATIONS AND
ADDITIONS--ITALY--ROME--LUNGOTEVERE
Il progetto integrato lungotevere =
Overall project for the Tiber
embankment / Galeazzo Ruspoli.
Proposed rehabilitation, Rome;
architect: Galeazzo Ruspoli.
L'ARCA 1990 July-Aug., no.40,
p.56-59, dwgs., maps, site plans.

WATERFRONTS--ALTERATIONS AND
ADDITIONS--NETHERLANDS--AMSTERDAM--
IJ-OEVERS
De IJ-oevers en het gevaar van
middelmatigheid / Donald Lambert.
ARCHIS 1990 Oct., no.10, p.22-26,
ill., dwgs., models, photo.,
aerial photos.

WATERFRONTS--ALTERATIONS AND
ADDITIONS--NETHERLANDS--HAGUE
Den Haag.
Contents: Den Haag zonder petten
en pruiken, by Cees Boekraad -- De
stad achter de duinen: Plannen
voor de Haagse stadsrand, by Miel
Karthaus -- Den Haag Centraal:
Plannen voor de binnenstad, by
Joos Aerts, Dick Bruyne -- Schone
eenheid: De 'Nieuwe Haagse
School', by Victor Freijser.
ARCHIS 1990 Feb., no.2, p.29-51,
dwgs., models, maps, photos.,
plans, secns., site plans, engrs.,
aerial photos.

WATERFRONTS--ALTERATIONS AND
ADDITIONS--NETHERLANDS--MAASTRICHT--
MAAS
De architectuur van de stad: een
kritiek op Coenens ontwerp voor
het Sphinx-Ceramiqueterrein /
Sjoerd Cusveller.
New plans for a district along the
river in Maastricht.
DE ARCHITECT 1990 Mar., v.21,
no.3, p.46-53, axonometric views,
ill., elevs., map, plans, site
plans, sketches, refs.

WATERFRONTS--ALTERATIONS AND
ADDITIONS--NETHERLANDS--MAASTRICHT--
SPHINX CERAMIQUETERREIN
Architectenkeuze Shpinx [sic]
Ceramiqueterrein rond.
An urban design project for
Maastricht by Jo Coenen.
DE ARCHITECT 1990 Oct., v.21,
no.10, p.35, site plan.

WATERFRONTS--ALTERATIONS AND
ADDITIONS--NORWAY--BAERUN
Veritasparken, Baerum / Ola Bettum.
A two-phase conversion of old
industrial area into an office
park. Landscape architects:
Hindhamar-Sundt-Thomassen.
Architects: Kjell Lund and Nils
Slaatto. Includes English
translation.
LANDSKAB 1990 May, v.71, no.3-4,
p.N-7-N-11, photos., secns., site
plans.

WATERFRONTS--ALTERATIONS AND
ADDITIONS--UNITED STATES--CHICAGO
(ILLINOIS)--CHICAGO RIVER
Making big plans for the Chicago
River / Howard S. Decker.
INLAND ARCHITECT 1990 July-Aug.,
v.34, no.4, p.9-10, photos., site
plan.

WATERFRONTS--ALTERATIONS AND
ADDITIONS--UNITED STATES--CINCINNATI
(OHIO)
From sow's ear to silk purse: an
unusual architect-client
relationship transforms an
abandoned waterfront in the
nation's Porkopolis into an
award-winning design.
The Cincinnati Gateway Sculpture,
at the entrance to the
Bicentennial Commons Park.
Sculptor: Andrew Leicester;
architects: Meyer, Scherer &
Rockcastle.
ARCHITECTURE MINNESOTA 1990
Nov.-Dec., v.16, no.6, p.38-41,
photos.

WATERFRONTS--ALTERATIONS AND
ADDITIONS--UNITED STATES--SAN DIEGO
(CALIFORNIA)
A downtown boulevard? [interview] /
Ralph Roesling.
On the Centre City Planning
Committee (CCPC) activity in San
Diego, including an interview with
councilman Ron Roberts.
CARTOUCHE 1990 Winter, v.19,
p.6-7, dwg., map, aerial photo.

WATERFRONTS--AUSTRALIA--PERTH
Questions to Cityvision [interview].
Interview with Bill Warnock of
City Vision on the proposed
Waterfront development plan for
Perth.
THE ARCHITECT, W.A.: THE OFFICIAL
JOURNAL OF THE ROYAL AUSTRALIAN
INSTITUTE OF ARCHITECTS, W.A.
CHAPTER 1989, v.30, no.1, p.26-29,
ports., photo., site plans.

WATERFRONTS--CANADA--NIAGARA FALLS
(ONTARIO)--QUEEN VICTORIA PARK
Ontario's Niagara parks.
On the plan to improve the
transportation and riverfront
development along the Canadian
shore of the Niagara River.
Architects: Moriyama and Teshima.
PROGRESSIVE ARCHITECTURE 1990
Jan., v.71, no.1, p.116-117, maps.

WATERFRONTS--CANADA--QUEBEC--SAINT
LAWRENCE RIVER
Congres '89 atelier thematique:
l'avenir des berges, le fleuve
St.-Laurent / Irene Cinq-Mars.
The author is director of the
Ecole d'architecture de paysage,
Universite de Montreal.
LANDSCAPE ARCHITECTURAL REVIEW
1990 Mar., v.11, no.1, p.25,27.

WATERFRONTS--CANADA--TORONTO (ONTARIO)
Developers play highrise hardball
all around Toronto's Dome / Jack
Layton.
Waterfront development vs. public
access to railway lands near
Toronto's domed stadium.
CITY MAGAZINE 1990 Summer, v.11,
no.4, p.8-9.

WATERFRONTS--COMPETITIONS--BELGIUM--
ANTWERP
Gehavende stad aan de Stroom:
schadum over ideeenwedstrijd
Antwerpen water front / Paul
Vermeulen.
On a new initiative, beginning in
Dec.1989 for design solutions for
Dutch waterfronts.
ARCHIS 1990 Jan., no.1, p.6-7,
model, photo.

WATERFRONTS--COMPETITIONS--BELGIUM--
ANTWERP--STAD AAN DE STROOM
La citta e il suo fiume = The city
and its river / Jef Vanreusel.
Stad aan de stroom project designs
from international competition for
urban renewal of three areas of
Antwerp; Quay, Islet and South;
architects: Yves Lion, Manuel de
Sola-Morales, Bob van Reeth, Beth
Gali, Rem Koolhaas, Toyo Ito, Van
Berkel & Bos, Van Veen & Van Meer,
Bureau of Urban Design. Overall
site plan: Spea - Ingegneria
Europa (Gruppo-Italstat).
L'ARCA 1990 Dec., no.44, p.32-43,
models, map, photos., plans, site
plans.

WATERFRONTS--COMPETITIONS--BELGIUM--
ANTWERP--STAD AAN DER STROOM
Haalbaarheid troef: Ideeenprijsvraag
Stad aan de Stroom geevalueerd /
Paul Vermeulen.
Projects discussed include that by
Toyo Ito.
ARCHIS 1990 Nov., no.11, p.6,
model.
Vermaning aan Antwerpen: Hou 'n stuk
haven in de staad / Hans Stevens.
Waterfront development, "Stad aan
de Stroom."
BOUW 1990 Oct.5, v.45, no.20,
p.22-24, photo., models, engr.

WATERFRONTS--COMPETITIONS--DENMARK--
AALBORG
Aalborg havnefront: idekonkurrence.
On a 1989 competition, cosponsored
by the city of Aalborg and the
DAL, for redesign of the city's
waterfront. Publishes seven
winning entries in two categories.
First prize: Lars Bjork Nielsen.
ARKITEKTEN 1989 Nov.28, v.91,
no.21, p.525-536, axonometric
views, dwgs., elevs., model, maps,
secns., site plans.

WATERFRONTS--COMPETITIONS--ENGLAND--
LIVERPOOL--PIER HEAD
Liver line-up / Clare Melhuish.
Features five entries in the
competition for the redevelopment
of Pier Head, Liverpool.
Architects: David Marks, Julia
Barfield Architects; Allies and
Morrison; Cass Associates;
Austin-Smith: Lord; Tibbalds
Colbourne Partnership.
BUILDING DESIGN 1990 June 15,
no.990, p.18,20-22, dwgs., elevs.,
secns., site plans.

WATERFRONTS--COMPETITIONS--JAPAN--
YOKOHAMA
Winners in the 2nd Yokohama Urban
Design International Competition.
Theme: revitalization of the
waterfront - Yokohama Kaigan Dori.
Includes 13 winning entries and
judges' commentary. First prize
winner: Shigeru Yoshino.
JAPAN ARCHITECT 1990 Oct., v.65,
no.10, p.71-76, dwgs., elevs.,
models, plan, secns.

WATERFRONTS--COMPETITIONS--
NETHERLANDS--DOMBURG--DORIMARE
De architect als joker:
Tentoonstelling in Domburg
[exhibition review] / Arthur
Wortmann.
Projects on exhibit, Sept.1989, at
the Dorimare recreation center in
Domburg, for development of the
waterfront. Architects: Wiel
Arets, Stephane Beel and Luc
Reuse, Ben van Berkel, Chris
Kempe.
ARCHIS 1990 Sept., no.9, p.4-5,
ill., model.

WATERFRONTS--COMPETITIONS--
SWITZERLAND--PFAFFIKON
Projektwettbewerb Seeuferanlage
Pfaffikon SZ = Concours de projets
pour l'amenagement du bord du lac
a Pfaffikon SZ = Project
competition for lakeside
facilities at Pfaffikon SZ /
Christian Stern.
Winning project by Walter Vetsch.
ANTHOS 1989, v.28, no.4, p.39-42,
site plans, sketches.

WATERFRONTS--CONSERVATION AND
RESTORATION--INDIA--BRINDAVAN
Ghats of Mathura and Vrindavan /
Rajat Ray.
Projects "to repair and restore
the physical attributes" of
riverfronts in the cultural area
of Brajbhumi.
ARCHITECTURE + DESIGN 1989
Nov.-Dec., v.6, no.1, p.[61]-69,
dets., ill., dwgs., maps, photos,
plans, secns., site plans.

WATERFRONTS--CONSERVATION AND
RESTORATION--INDIA--MUTTRA
Ghats of Mathura and Vrindavan /
Rajat Ray.
Projects "to repair and restore
the physical attributes" of
riverfronts in the cultural area
of Brajbhumi.
ARCHITECTURE + DESIGN 1989
Nov.-Dec., v.6, no.1, p.[61]-69,
dets., ill., dwgs., maps, photos,
plans, secns., site plans.

WATERFRONTS--CONSERVATION AND
RESTORATION--UNITED STATES--
WILMINGTON (DELAWARE)
Waterfront + renovation = recreation
/ Christy C. McEvilly.
PARKS & RECREATION 1989 July,
v.24, no.7, p.34-36,75, photos.

WATERFRONTS--ECONOMIC ASPECTS
Waterfront projects showing greater
recession resistance / Edward D.
Pasternak.
REAL ESTATE FORUM 1990 July, v.45,
no.7, p.264-273, dwgs., ports.,
photos., aerial photos.

WATERFRONTS--ECONOMIC ASPECTS--
ENGLAND--LONDON--DOCKLANDS
Royal abdication [Royal Docks] /
Martin Spring.
Strategy and economic setbacks for
the LDDC's development of the
Docklands.
BUILDING 1990 May 25, v.255,
no.21, p.24-25, map, photo.

WATERFRONTS--ENGLAND--LIVERPOOL--PIER
HEAD
Piering into the future of
Liverpool.
Redevelopment of Pier Head in
Liverpool. Proposals by Tibbalds
Colbourne Karski Williams; Allies
and Morrison; Austin Smith Lord;
Cass Associates; and David Marks
and Julia Barfield.
ARCHITECTS' JOURNAL 1990 June 13,
v.191, no.24, p.12, axonometric
view, dwgs.

WATERFRONTS--ENGLAND--LONDON--
GREENLAND DOCK
Hard landscaping, Greenland Dock,
Conran Roche Architects.
ARCHITECTS' JOURNAL 1990 Nov.14,
v.192, no.20, p.51-53, dets.,
photos., plans, secns.

WATERFRONTS--ENGLAND--LONDON--
GREENWICH
That's toytown says Greenwich /
Robert Cowan.
Masterplan for the last large
development site in London on the
Blackwall peninsula in Greenwich.
Architects/planners:
Llewelyn-Davies.
ARCHITECTS' JOURNAL 1990 Oct.24,
v.192, no.17, p.14, dwg., site
plan.

WATERFRONTS--ENGLAND--TYNE RIVER
Beyond the dreams of avarice / Dick
Foster, Colin Jubb, David Price.
Riverside development along the
Tyne (England).
URBAN FUTURES 1989 Spring, v.2,
no.1, p.21-27, ill., photos.,
refs.

WATERFRONTS--ENVIRONMENTAL ASPECTS--
CANADA--SASKATOON (SASKATCHEWAN)
Conserving the urban river corridor:
experience from Saskatoon /
Brijesh Mathur.
PLAN CANADA 1989 Sept., v.29,
no.5, p.43-49, photo., plans,
maps, refs.

WATERFRONTS--ENVIRONMENTAL ASPECTS--
FRANCE--PARIS--SEINE
Les inondations en region
d'Ile-de-France: prevenir ou
pallier / Alain Le Saux.
On flood prevention or alleviation
in the Paris and Seine River area,
with reference to the 1983 and
earlier floods. Includes English
abstract. English, French, and
Spanish summaries, p.3.
CAHIERS DE L'INSTITUT
D'AMENAGEMENT ET D'URBANISME DE LA
REGION D'ILE-DE-FRANCE 1989 Oct.,
no.91, p.47-64, photos., tables.

WATERFRONTS--ENVIRONMENTAL ASPECTS--
UNITED STATES--WORCESTER COUNTY
(MARYLAND)
Bay patrol: a Maryland coastal
community fends off developers /
Jeff Weintraub, Mary Lou
Gallagher.
In Worcester County, Maryland, on
the mainland across from Ocean
City.
PLANNING 1990 Oct., v.56, no.10,
p.22-23, maps, photos., aerial
photo.

WATERFRONTS--FRANCE--PARIS--RIVE
GAUCHE
Stedebouw in de marge van de stud:
Seine Rieve Gauche in Parijs:
plannen vallen op hun plaats /
Pieter Uyttenhove.
Published in conjunction with an
exhibition at the Pavillon de
l'Arsenal, Paris, opening in Oct.
1990.
ARCHIS 1990 Oct., no.10, p.27-35,
dwgs., maps, photos., secns., site
plans, aerial photos., refs.

WATERFRONTS--GERMANY (WEST)--
LUDWIGSHAFEN--RHEINUFER-SUD
Ludwigshafen - Rheinufer-Sud: ein
ganz normales
Stadtentwicklungsprojekt? / Gerd
Wilhelmus.
Discusses the site and proposals
by three firms: Ganz + Rolfes,
Zlonicky & Wachten, Albert Speer &
Partner.
BAUWELT 1990 Sept.28, v.81, no.36,
p.1793-1808, dwgs., elevs.,
models, maps, site plans.

WATERFRONTS--HISTORY--EUROPE
Il fiume e la citta / Renzo Dubbini.
Captions in Italian and English.
CASABELLA 1990 Oct., v.54, no.572,
p.26-29, ill., site plans, biblio.

WATERFRONTS--IRELAND--DERRY--FOYLE
DOCKS
Creating a landmark for Derry City /
Emer Hughes.
Proposed waterfront development
for Derry by graduate student in
design at the Univ. of Ulster,
Belfast, wins the 1989 Graduate
Designer Award.
(Continued next column)

WATERFRONTS--IRELAND--DERRY--FOYLE
DOCKS (CONTINUED)
Creating a landmark...(CONTINUED)
PLAN: ARCHITECTURE + INTERIOR
DESIGN IN IRELAND 1989 Nov., v.25,
no.11, p.17, ports., site plan.

WATERFRONTS--ITALY--RIMINI
La citta balneare: una proposta di
Emilio Ambasz per una architettura
marina a Rimini / Roberto
Semprini.
MODO 1990 Oct., v.13, no.126,
p.52-53, elev., model, site plan.

WATERFRONTS--KUWAIT--WATERFRONT PARK
Kuwait City waterfront development /
Brian Brace Taylor.
Completed in 1988. Consultants:
Ghazi Sultan, architect, Kuwait
Engineers Office; Sasaki
Associates, Boston.
MIMAR: ARCHITECTURE IN DEVELOPMENT
1990 Mar., v.10, no.1(34),
p.[12]-20, cover, map, photos.,
plans, secns., site plans.

WATERFRONTS--NETHERLANDS
Verstedelijking en
Landschapsontwikkeling: Villanova
onderzoekt nieuwe aanpak / Maurits
de Hoog.
Includes discussion of design of
several park areas and
waterfronts, and a comparison of
several port cities' plans.
DE ARCHITECT THEMA 1990 Sept.,
v.21, no.9 suppl., p.15-26, maps,
site plans, refs.

WATERFRONTS--NETHERLANDS--ROTTERDAM
Kop van Zuid e il futuro di
Rotterdam-sud / Jacques Nycolaas.
Waterfront development projects in
south Rotterdam. In Italian, with
Italian and English captions.
URBANISTICA 1988 Nov., no.93,
p.56-59, elevs., models, photo.,
plans.
Stadtstimmeren in Rotterdam / Ton
Verstegen.
Changes on the waterfront,
including the Aelbrechtskade by
Adriaan Geuze.
ARCHIS 1990 Dec., no.12, p.3-4,
photos., refs.

WATERFRONTS--NEW ZEALAND--AUCKLAND
A new future for Aukland's harbour
edge / Alan Bradbourne.
PLANNING QUARTERLY 1989 Dec,
no.96, p.15-18, dwgs., aerial
photo.

WATERFRONTS--NEW ZEALAND--AUCKLAND--
VIADUCT BASIN
A major facelift for the Viaduct
Basin [Auckland, N. Z.] / Brian
Healy.
PLANNING QUARTERLY 1989 Dec,
no.96, p.19-22, photos.

WATERFRONTS--NEW ZEALAND--MANUKAU
Manukau tries coastal management
planning / Glenda Dixon.
New Zealand waterfront
development.
PLANNING QUARTERLY 1989 Dec,
no.96, p.30-33, map, aerial
photos.

WATERFRONTS--NEW ZEALAND--MILFORD
SOUND
Development at the coast in Milford
Sound / Brian Coutts.
New Zealand.
PLANNING QUARTERLY 1989 Dec,
no.96, p.12-13, plan.

WATERFRONTS--NEW ZEALAND--WELLINGTON--
LAMBTON HARBOUR
Wellington's waterfront saga / Fiona
Christeller.
New Zealand.
PLANNING QUARTERLY 1989 Dec,
no.96, p.6-8, model.

WATERFRONTS--NEW ZEALAND--WELLINGTON--
LAMBTON HARBOUR DEVELOPMENT
Lambton Harbour Development [New
Zealand].
Model of the proposed development.
PLANNING QUARTERLY 1989 Dec,
no.96, p.4-5, model.
People versus concrete towers / J.
C. Horne.
Real estate development along
Wellington, New Zealand's Lambton
Harbour waterfront runs contrary
to citizens' preferences.
PLANNING QUARTERLY 1989 Dec,
no.96, p.9-10, photos.
Reply to the critics / Terry
McDavitt.
Response to preceding article on
development of Wellington's
Lambton Harbour.
PLANNING QUARTERLY 1989 Dec,
no.96, p.10-11, photos.

WATERFRONTS--SOUTH AFRICA--CAPE TOWN
Green and Sea Point draft policy /
Fabio Todeschini.
City planning for Cape Town areas,
by Todeschini and Japha.
ARCHITECTURE SA = ARGITEKTUUR SA
1989 May-June, no.5-6, p.42-[43],
graphs, elev., photos., secn.,
site plan, aerial photos.

WATERFRONTS--SPAIN--BARCELONA
El ensanche litoral: la Villa
Olimpica, historia de una idea /
Josep Maria Montaner.
English summary, p.83-85.
A & V 1990, no.22, p.16-24, dwgs.,
elevs., models, maps, plans,
aerial photos.
Pabellones de cubierta: el puerto
olimpico = Deck pavilions.
On the Barcelona waterfront
buildings. Projects by Martorell,
Bohigas, Mackay, Puigdomenech,
including a sailing school,
reception building and athlete
housing. English text, p.88.
A & V 1990, no.22, p.66-69, dwg.,
elevs., models, plans, secns.,
site plans.
Regisseurs van het moderne
stadsleven: Joan Busquets en
Manuel de Sola-Morales [Interview]
/ Han Meyer.
The second of two articles in an
issue featuring Barcelona.
DE ARCHITECT 1989 Oct., v.20,
no.10, p.56-61, cover, photos.,
secns., site plans.

WATERFRONTS--UNITED STATES
Whose waterfront is it, anyway? /
Ann Breen, Dick Rigby.
Access issues in waterfront
development and the public
interest.
PLANNING 1990 Feb., v.56, no.2,
p.10-12, photos., site plan.

WATERFRONTS--UNITED STATES--CHESAPEAKE
(VIRGINIA)--RIVER WALK
River Walk civic places.
On the series of gateways and
public spaces among a 484-acre
suburban community on the
Elizabeth River in Chesapeake, Va.
Architects: Eric R. Kuhne and
Associates.
PROGRESSIVE ARCHITECTURE 1990
Jan., v.71, no.1, p.113-115,
dwgs., elevs., photo., site plans.

WATERFRONTS--UNITED STATES--CHICAGO
(ILLINOIS)--CITYFRONT CENTER
Establishing a long-range framework
for development.
Cityfront Center, in Chicago.
Master plan proposed by Lohan
Associates.
URBAN LAND 1990 Oct., v.49, no.10,
p.32-33, models, photos.
Urban critique: Cityfront Center /
Cheryl Kent.
On the design guidelines for
Chicago development located on the
banks of the Chicago River.
Masterplanners: Alexander Cooper
& Partners.
PROGRESSIVE ARCHITECTURE 1990
Feb., v.71, no.2, p.121-122,
dwgs., photos., site plans.

WATERFRONTS--UNITED STATES--HOBOKEN
(NEW JERSEY)
Hoboken's waterfront: a simple twist
of fate / Christ Mitchell.
Planner: Stanton Eckstut.
METROPOLIS 1990 Mar., v.9, no.7,
p.17-19, photo.

WATERFRONTS--UNITED STATES--MEMPHIS
(TENNESSEE)
Peabody Place & Beale Street,
downtown Memphis.
One of six urban design reports
included in special issue, Urban
Concepts. Extracted from a 1987
Center City Development Plan for
Downtown Memphis.
ARCHITECTURAL DESIGN 1990, v.60,
no.1-2, p.76-87, dwgs., maps,
photos., sketches, aerial photos.

WATERFRONTS--UNITED STATES--
MISSISSIPPI RIVER
Along the lazy river / David Dillon.
"Expedition of the Fourth Coast"
summer study tour of cities and
towns along the Mississippi River
by Univ. of Minnesota planning
students.
PLANNING 1990 Nov., v.56, no.11,
p.20-23, ports., photos.,
sketches, aerial photo.
Expedition of the Fourth Coast /
Mary Henderson Gass.
Report on a six-week trip on the
Mississippi River run by the Univ.
of Minnesota Design Center for
American Urban Landscape.
INLAND ARCHITECT 1990 Nov.-Dec.,
v.34, no.6, p.63-66, dwgs.

WATERFRONTS--UNITED STATES--QUEENS
(NEW YORK)--HUNTER'S POINT
Is bigger still better? / Doug
Turetsky.
Large developments at the Hunters
Point waterfront in Queens and in
Times Square are about to begin
construction despite slack in real
estate market.
CITY LIMITS 1990 Aug.-Sept., v.15,
no.7, p.12-15, port., photo.

WATERFRONTS--UNITED STATES--TRENTON
(NEW JERSEY)
Trenton: recalled to life / Nora
Odendahl, Sharon Ayn McHugh,
Robert D. Cerutti.
Includes inset article on the
Capital City Renaissance Plan, by
Sharon Ayn McHugh.
ARCHITECTURE NEW JERSEY 1989,
v.25, no.3, p.13-22, 29,
axonometric views, graph, dwgs.,
map, photos.

WATERFRONTS--WALES--CARDIFF
Cardiff Bay development / David S.
Walton.
THE PLANNER 1990 Dec.14, v.76,
no.49, p.10-18, port., site plan,
sketches.

WATERFRONTS--WALES--CARDIFF--CARDIFF
BAY
Taming developers at Cardiff Bay /
Julian Dobson.
Environmental and flooding
concerns are bases for opposition
to proposed development in South
Cardiff, Wales.
HOUSING 1989 Dec.-1990 Jan., v.26,
no.10, p.24-27, ports., photos.

WATERING-PLACES
See SPAS

WATERMAN, DANIEL
How a small design firm works with
developers / Daniel Waterman.
Carrington Associates, a New York
firm works with Waterfront Invest,
a young development firm.
ARCHITECTURAL RECORD 1990 Feb.,
v.178, no.2, p.52-53, photos.,
model.

WATERPARKS
The complete aquatic guide / Alison
Osinski.
New building materials, equipment,
and design features for swimming
pools, water parks, etc.
PARKS & RECREATION 1990 Feb.,
v.25, no.2, p.36-43,83.
Fun for everyone: the aquatic
formula / Alan Heuss.
Aquatic recreation centers,
including swimming pools, water
slides, and other aquatic
features.
PARKS & RECREATION 1990 Nov.,
v.25, no.11, p.34-38, photos.
Life saving trends: waterparks lead
the way / Jeff Ellis.
Growth of the waterpark industry,
and the development of
state-of-the-art aquatic life
saving technology.
PARKS & RECREATION 1990 Feb.,
v.25, no.2, p.50-53, photos.

WATERPARKS (CONTINUED)
A waterpark planner / Joshua L.
Brener.
PARKS & RECREATION 1990 Nov.,
v.25, no.11, p.42-[44],71, photos.
Waterparks: sliding into fun and
profits / Suzanne McCormick.
PARKS & RECREATION 1990 Nov.,
v.25, no.11, p.46-49, photos.

WATERPARKS--GREAT BRITAIN
Buildings update: swimming pools 2:
case studies.
Second in series on British
swimming pools. Case studies of
The Rapids, Romsey, architects:
Sargent & Potiriadis; Ainslie
Park, architects: Faulkner Browns;
and Coral Reef, Bracknell,
architects: Sargent & Potiriadis.
ARCHITECTS' JOURNAL 1990 Oct.17,
v.192, no.16, p.69-75, photos.,
plans, site plans.

WATERPARKS--UNITED STATES--GREAT NECK
(NEW YORK)
Spray pools: no wading / Richard A.
Arenella.
Spotlights a facility in Great
Neck, L.I. Project designers:
Sear-Brown Group.
PARKS & RECREATION 1990 Nov.,
v.25, no.11, p.30-33,71, ports.,
photos.

WATERPROOFING
See also DAMPNESS IN BUILDINGS
Bauphysikalische Betrachtung der
Schutz-und
Instandsetzungsmassnahmen fur
Betonoberflachen / Heinz Klopfer.
Methods of evaluation and
maintenance of concrete surfaces.
DEUTSCHES ARCHITEKTENBLATT 1990
Jan.1, v.22, no.1, p.99-112,
dets., graphs, tables, refs.
Dammschicht schutzt die Abdichtung.
DEUTSCHES ARCHITEKTENBLATT 1990
Sept.1, v.22, no.9, p.1399, det.,
photos.
Zum Langzeitverhalten von
Umkehrdachern / Gunter Zimmermann.
Maintenance, alterations, and
waterproofing of flat roofs of
various materials.
DEUTSCHES ARCHITEKTENBLATT 1990
Oct.1, v.22, no.10, p.1559-1565,
photos., tables, refs.

WATERS, BRIAN
Aesthetic control / Brian Waters.
Author proposes the establishment
of architectural advisory panels
to advise local planning
committees.
RIBA JOURNAL 1990 June, v.97,
no.6, p.48-50, port., refs.

WATERS, CRAIG
Building regs determined: disabled
access 2 / Harry Hosker, Craig
Waters.
In Britain.
ARCHITECTS' JOURNAL 1990 June 20,
v.191, no.25, p.75-76, ill.
Building regs determined: disabled
access / Harry Hosker, Craig
Waters.
ARCHITECTS' JOURNAL 1990 June 13,
v.191, no.24, p.71-72, ill.

WATERS, CRAIG (CONTINUED)
Building regs determined: fire and
houses / Harry Hosker, Craig
Waters.
In Britain.
ARCHITECTS' JOURNAL 1990 Nov.21,
v.192, no.20, p.63-65,

WATERSHED (GALLERY)--EXHIBITIONS
What the censor saw: the West at war
[exhibition review] / Sian Ellis.
"Exhibition of published and
unpublished photographs by Jim
Facey, the Bristol Evening Post's
chief photographer during the
Second World War and Photographer
of the Year award winner..."
Includes photographs censored
during the war, and many of
bomb-damaged buildings. Held at
the Watershed, Bristol, through 8
Apr.1990.
ARCHITECTS' JOURNAL 1990 Mar.28,
v.191, no.13, p.89-90, photo.

WATERWORKS
See also CONDUITS
See also IRRIGATION WORKS
See also PUMPING STATIONS

WATERWORKS--GERMANY (WEST)--BIGGESEE
Reservoirs of goodwill / Owen D.
Manning.
On the Biggesee reservoir area in
Germany. Comparison made with
British water-engineering
landscapes.
LANDSCAPE DESIGN 1990 June,
no.191, p.16, photos.

WATERWORKS--JAPAN
The effects of layouts of covered
water works to the plot planning
of residential zones in castle
towns / Jun Hatano.
"The study of the town planning
method of Japanese castle towns
from its water work's point of
view IV". Text in Japanese;
includes English summary.
NIHON KENCHIKU GAKKAI KEIKAKUKEI
RONBUN HOKOKU SHU = JOURNAL OF
ARCHITECTURE, PLANNING AND
ENVIRONMENTAL ENGINEERING 1990
Oct., no.10(416), p.101-110,
diagr., graphs, maps, refs.
The effects of layouts of open water
works to the plot planning of
residential zones in castle towns
/ Jun Hatano.
Subtitle: The study of the town
planning method of Japanese castle
towns from its water work's points
of view III. English summary,
p.143.
NIHON KENCHIKU GAKKAI KEIKAKUKEI
RONBUN HOKOKU SHU = JOURNAL OF
ARCHITECTURE, PLANNING AND
ENVIRONMENTAL ENGINEERING 1990
Feb., no.8(408), p.133-143,
charts, site plans, refs.

WATERWORKS--ROMAN
Perspective on Roman technology /
Kevin Greene.
In light of recent research into
boats, vehicles, water-lifting
devices, and water mills. Includes
abstract.
OXFORD JOURNAL OF ARCHAEOLOGY 1990
July, v.9, no.2, p.209-219,

WATERWORKS--UNITED STATES--FAIRFAX
COUNTY (VIRGINIA)--FAIR LAKES OFFICE
PARK
A lake for many purposes / David
Cheek.
Lake water used for heating and
cooling of mixed-used office
complex in Fairfax Co., Va.
DEVELOPMENT 1990 Sept.-Oct., v.21,
no.5, p.14-15, diagr., photos.,
secn.

WATGE, JUVENAL
Prioridade para insercao no entorno
e insolacao: Edificio Curumim,
Porto Alegre.
Architects: F. Kiefer, J. Watge
Jr.
PROJETO 1989 June, no.122,
p.62-63, photos, plans.

WATKIN, DAVID
The migration of the palm: a
case-study of architectural
ornament as a vehicle of meaning /
David Watkin.
An examination of this motif, its
changing significance, and
revivals.
APOLLO 1990 Feb., v.131, no.336,
p.78-84, photos., engrs., refs.

WATKIN, DAVID, 1941-
Klassiek versus modern: David
Watkin: "Ik ben nu eenmaal geen
Hegeliaans determinist" / Hans
Ibelings, Erik de Jong.
ARCHIS 1990 May, no.5, p.31-35,
port., photos.

WATKINS, DAVID G.
El Walhalla = The Walhalla / David
J. Watkin.
Monument to the German nation,
1832-1842. Architect: Leo von
Klenze. Includes designs
submitted in the 1814-16
competition for the monument by
Karl Haller von Hallerstein, Karl
von Fischer and Daniel Ohlmuller.
COMPOSICION ARQUITECTONICA, ART &
ARCHITECTURE 1990 Feb., no.5,
p.[63]-92, ill., dwgs., elevs.,
photos., plans, secns., refs.

WATKINS, TREVOR
The origins of house and home? /
Trevor Watkins.
Excavations of neolithic
subterranean houses at the site of
Qermez Dere in northern Iraq.
WORLD ARCHAEOLOGY 1990 Feb., v.21,
no.3, p.[336]-347, axonometric
view, fig., dwg., map, plan, refs.

WATKINS, VICTOR
Horse sense [housing maintenance] /
Victor Watkins.
Responsibilities of landlord and
tenant for public housing
maintenance.
HOUSING AND PLANNING REVIEW 1989
Dec.-1990 Jan., v.44, no.6,
p.18-19, photo.

WATSON, DONALD R.
House at Graceville: Donald Watson.
ARCHITECTURE AUSTRALIA 1989 Dec.,
v.78, no.11, p.31-33, port.,
photos., plans.

WATSON, FIONA
"Every district should have one":
pioneer hospitals in the Scottish
Highlands / Fiona Watson.
Includes asylums and poorhouses.
THE JOURNAL AND ANNUAL REPORT /
THE SCOTTISH GEORGIAN SOCIETY FOR
THE STUDY AND PROTECTION OF
SCOTTISH ARCHITECTURE 1989, no.16,
p.43-54, photos., plan, engr.,
refs.

WATSON, ISOBEL. GENTLEMEN IN THE
BUILDING LINE: THE DEVELOPMENT OF
SOUTH HACKNEY
Gentleman in the building line: the
development of South Hackney [by]
Isobel Watson [book review] / F.
M. L. Thompson.
LONDON JOURNAL 1990, v.15, no.2,
p.186-187,

WATTAM, KEN
Playing a new tune: computer
strategy / Ken Wattam.
"Computers and telecommunications
have had their effect on the
building industry but have not
transformed the way the industry
operates. [This article looks at]
how computers could play a more
central role in business
strategy."
ARCHITECTS' JOURNAL 1990 July 18,
v.192, no.3, p.59-60, dwg., plan.

WATZMAN, HAIM
Restoring an "ancient pasture" /
Haim Watzman.
On the Neot Kedumim biblical park
and botanical research center.
Landscape architect: Hillel Omer.
LANDSCAPE ARCHITECTURE 1990 Sept.,
v.80, no.9, p.[36-37], photo.

WAUTHIER-WURMSER, BERNARD
Emboitements: maison a Bagnolet.
Group of 19th cent. cottages
converted to art collector's home.
Architects: Yves Tissier, Bernard
Wauthier-Wurmser. Summaries in
English and Spanish.
TECHNIQUES ET ARCHITECTURE 1990
June-July, no.390, p.72-73,179,
photos., plan, secn.
La maison reconsideree / Yves
Tissier, Bernard Wauthier-Wurmser.
Includes English and Spanish
summaries.
TECHNIQUES ET ARCHITECTURE 1990
June-July, no.390, p.104-105,180,
photos., refs.

WAVS
See BAOLIS

WAWROWSKY, HANS GUNTER
Edmonton Mall uberall? / Hans Gunter
Wawrowsky.
DER ARCHITEKT 1990 July-Aug.,
no.7-8, p.343, dwgs., photo.

WAWRZYNSKI, JACK
Polish planning in transition /
Jerzy Regulski, Jack Wawrzynski.
TOWN PLANNING REVIEW 1989 July,
v.60, no.3, p.247-269, maps,
photos., plan, aerial photo.,
refs.

WAY HOUSES
See POSTHOUSES

WAY, NEIL, 1963-
Neil Way; starting over / Alastair
Stewart.
British architect, formerly with
Peter Taylor Associates, in
Uckfield, Sussex.
BUILDING 1990 Nov.9, v.255, no.44,
p.44-45, port.

WAYMENT, HILARY
The Master of the Mass of Saint
Gregory Roundel / Hilary Wayment.
Identifies works of this anonymous
16th-cent. Netherlandish glass
painter.
OUD HOLLAND 1989, v.103, no.2,
p.61-96, ill., photos., plan,
biblios., refs.

WB & ASOCIADOS
Una propuesta a las necesidades
actuales: WB & Asociados.
Offices of advertising agency GGK,
Barcelona. English text, p.190. In
"On oficina", 1990 supplement
issue.
ON DISENO 1990, suppl., p.82-87,
photos.
Tecnologia y diseno para una oficina
futurista: WB & Asociados.
Offices of the Financial Futures
Market, Barcelona. English text,
p.189-190. In "On oficina," 1990
supplement issue.
ON DISENO 1990, suppl., p.72-81,
photos.

WBDC, INC.
Shadow free: new compact fluorescent
lamps and an even-newer indirect
lighting scheme / Joan F.
Blatterman.
Skylit spaces of Steelcase's
Corporate Development Center near
Grand Rapids. Architects: The WBDC
Group.
ARCHITECTURAL RECORD 1990 Mar.,
v.178, no.3, p.119-121, ill.,
photos.
Steelcase's practical Pyramid /
Michael J. P. Smith.
The Corporate Development Center,
Grand Rapids, Mich. Architect:
WBDC Group and Donald J. Koster.
INLAND ARCHITECT 1990 Nov.-Dec.,
v.34, no.6, p.19-20, photo.,
secn., aerial photo.

WEATHER STATIONS
See METEOROLOGICAL STATIONS

WEATHERBOARDING
See SIDING

WEATHERHEAD, PETER
Brightsite and beautiful / Peter
Weatherhead.
On the work of the Groundwork
Trust to encourage British
companies to participate in
schemes for environmental
regeneration.
BUILDING 1990 Mar.16, v.255,
no.11, p.64-65, photos.
Elementary connection [57 Mansell
St., London] / Peter Weatherhead.
Refurbishment of a Georgian
townhouse, and of a Victorian
warehouse behind it, and
(Continued next column)

WEATHERHEAD, PETER (CONTINUED)
Elementary connection...(CONTINUED)
conversion into offices for an
insurance company. Architect:
Trehearne & Norman.
BUILDING 1990 Apr.13, v.255,
no.15, p.46-48, photos.
Loggias to lodgings [East Banqueting
House, Chipping Campden] / Peter
Weatherhead.
Conversion of a 17th-cent. garden
loggia into vacation apartments.
BUILDING 1990 May 4, v.255, no.18,
p.58-60, photos.
Mills and boom / Peter Weatherhead.
SAVE Britain's Heritage is
campaigning to promote adaptive
reuse of old industrial buildings.
BUILDING 1990 June 29, v.255,
no.26, p.46-49, photos.
Souped up convertible [Le Capitole,
Nanterre] / Peter Weatherhead.
Conversion of a 1920s Citroen
factory into a mixed use
development, in Parc des
Fontaines. Architects: KLN.
BUILDING 1990 Jan.5, v.255, no.1,
p.44-48, photos.
Take your partners [Yorkshire Dance
Centre] / Peter Weatherhead.
Conversion of an Edwardian
warehouse in inner Leeds.
Architects: Allen Tod.
BUILDING 1990 Feb.23, v.255, no.8,
p.51-53, photos.
Trading in old silk ties [Merton
Abbey Mills] / Peter Weatherhead.
A derelict silk-printing works on
River Wandle, south London,
converted to new commercial uses.
Architects: John Dickinson and
Bryan Wells.
BUILDING 1990 Oct.5, v.255, no.39,
p.53-55, ill., photos.

WEATHERING OF BUILDINGS
Dreischichtige
Stahlbeton-Fassadenelemente:
Absturz einer Aussenschale.
DEUTSCHES ARCHITEKTENBLATT 1990
Sept.1, v.22, no.9, p.1383-1384,
det., photos., refs.
Gneisplatten als Terrassenbelag:
Braunfarbung durch eisenhaltige
Kieskorner / Gunter Zimmermann.
DEUTSCHES ARCHITEKTENBLATT 1990
Oct.1, v.22, no.10, p.1583,
photos.
Hinterluftete Fassadenbekleidung mit
Marmorplatten: Konkave Verformung,
Rissbildung Ausbruche / Will
Stocksiefen.
DEUTSCHES ARCHITEKTENBLATT 1990
July 1, v.22, no.7, p.1137,
photos.
Schaden an Belagen und Bekleidungen
aus Naturstein / Gunter
Zimmermann.
DEUTSCHES ARCHITEKTENBLATT 1990
Nov.1, v.22, no.11, p.1737-1742,
photos., det., refs.

WEATHERING OF BUILDINGS--GERMANY
(WEST)
Wandbekleidung aus hinterlufteten
Granitplatten: Beschadigung durch
Stoss und Schlag.
Damage to granite cladding, with
reference to W. German code DIN 18
515.
DEUTSCHES ARCHITEKTENBLATT 1990
May 1, v.22, no.5, p.811, photos.,
biblio.

WEATHERING OF BUILDINGS--JAMAICA
Repairing paradise [Jamaica].
Repairing hurricane-damaged homes
in Jamaica.
VOLUNTARY HOUSING 1990 May, v.23,
no.4, p.24-25, ports., photos.

WEATHERING OF BUILDINGS--JAPAN
A study on the transform-process of
the eaves-style of traditional
farmhouses from a point of view of
wind and snow damage at Kuroishi
Clan, Aomori prefecture / Toshiei
Tsukidate.
Text in Japanese. Includes English
summary.
NIHON KENCHIKU GAKKAI KEIKAKUKEI
RONBUN HOKOKU SHU = JOURNAL OF
ARCHITECTURE, PLANNING AND
ENVIRONMENTAL ENGINEERING 1990
Sept., no.9(415), p.153-160,
dets., map, photos., tables, refs.

WEATHERING OF BUILDINGS--RESEARCH
Conservation research proposal for
the Great Sphinx presented in
Cairo.
THE GETTY CONSERVATION INSTITUTE
NEWSLETTER 1990 Winter, v.5, no.1,
p.1-3, photos.
Influence of pollution on mortar and
concrete / Satish Chandra.
Analysis of effects of, and
remedies for, atmospheric gases,
using several bridges and tunnels
in Sweden as examples. Includes
Swedish summary.
SWEDISH COUNCIL FOR BUILDING
RESEARCH. DOCUMENT 1990, D6,
p.1-83, diagrs., graphs, photos.,
secn., table, biblio.

WEATHERPROOFING
See WEATHERTIGHTNESS

WEATHERSTRIPPING
See WEATHERSTRIPS

WEATHERTIGHTNESS
Umkehrdach eines Schulzentrums: Hohe
Feuchtegehalte der
Extruderschaumplatten.
DEUTSCHES ARCHITEKTENBLATT 1990
Dec.1, v.22, no.12, p.1889,
photos., refs.
Weatherproofing membranes on roofs:
felt and nonwoven fabric of rubber
and plastics / Enar Tornkvist.
SWEDISH COUNCIL FOR BUILDING
RESEARCH. DOCUMENT 1990, D22,
p.[1]-109, diagrs., photos.,
secns.

WEAVER, HUGH
Virginia belle, [March house,
Smithfield, Va.].
Brick house built 1809 and
recently restored. Restoration
consultant: Hugh Weaver.
COLONIAL HOMES 1990 June, v.16,
no.3, p.68-[75],146,150, photos.

WEAVER, LAWRENCE, SIR, 1876-1930--
BIBLIOGRAPHY
Lawrence Weaver,1876-1930: an
annotated bibliography [by]
Lawrence Trevelyan Weaver [book
review] / Susan E. Schnare.
SOCIETY OF ARCHITECTURAL
HISTORIANS. JOURNAL 1990 Dec.,
v.49, no.4, p.448-449,

WEAVER, LAWRENCE TREVELYAN. LAWRENCE
WEAVER 1876-1930: AN ANNOTATED
BIBLIOGRAPHY
Lawrence Weaver,1876-1930: an
annotated bibliography [by]
Lawrence Trevelyan Weaver [book
review] / Susan E. Schnare.
SOCIETY OF ARCHITECTURAL
HISTORIANS. JOURNAL 1990 Dec.,
v.49, no.4, p.448-449,

WEAVER, WILLIAM
A Fornasetti original / William
Weaver.
Interiors of Piero Fornasetti's
summer home outside of Varenna on
Lake Como. The villa was designed
1899 but the interiors were redone
by Fornasetti during the 1950s.
ARCHITECTURAL DIGEST 1990 Jan.,
v.47, no.1, p.130-[135],168,170,
port., photos.
Gardens: La Cassinella on Lake Como
/ William Weaver.
Gardens on the grounds of a
lakeside villa in Campo owned by
Giacomo Mantegazza were begun in
the 1920s by the owner's father.
ARCHITECTURAL DIGEST 1990 Sept.,
v.47, no.10, p.190-[195],234,
photos.
Greppo alla Fendi reclaiming a
hillside village in Umbria /
William Weaver.
Feature interiors of several
restored homes owned by the Fendi
familiy in the restored Village of
Greppolischieto.
ARCHITECTURAL DIGEST 1990 Jan.,
v.47, no.1, p.[106-111],164,
port., photos.
Puccini's Torre del Lago / William
Weaver.
Interiors of turn-of-the-century
Villa near Viareggio.
ARCHITECTURAL DIGEST 1990 Jan.,
v.47, no.1, p.124-129, port.,
photos.
Switzerland's La Cour de Ferme:
restoring a 17th-century chalet
near Gstaad / William Weaver.
Focus on the interiors of 1695
chalet owned by Scott and Valerie
Youmans.
ARCHITECTURAL DIGEST 1990 Oct,
v.47, no.11, p.[256]-263,294,
port., photos.

WEBB, BRUCE
All in fun: entertainment
architecture / Bruce Webb.
TEXAS ARCHITECT 1990 Sept.-Oct.,
v.40, no.5, p.26-[33], photos.

WEBB, JOHN, 1611-1672
Disneyland in Greenwich: the
restoration of the Queen's House /
John Harris.
Architects: Inigo Jones, John
Webb. Dates from the early 17th
century.
APOLLO 1990 Oct., v.132, no.344,
p.256-260, elev., photos.
Execution of an ideal / John Martin
Robinson.
Controversial and costly
restoration of the Queen's House,
Greenwich, by Inigo Jones.
Consultant architects for the
restoration: Thomas Ford &
Partners.
ARCHITECTS' JOURNAL 1990 July 4,
(Continued next column)

WEBB, JOHN, 1611-1672 (CONTINUED)
Execution of an ideal... (CONTINUED)
v.192, no.1, p.32-39,41, dwgs.,
photos., plans, secn., sketches.
A house fit for a queen / Richard
Wilcock.
On the restoration of the 1660s
interiors of the Queen's House,
Greenwich. Original architects:
Inigo Jones, later enlarged by
John Webb. Restoration architects:
Thomas Ford and Partners.
RIBA JOURNAL 1990 June, v.97,
no.6, p.71,73-74, photos.
Two successful restorations: Wilton
House and Frogmore House / Brian
Allen.
Architects: Isaac de Caus, John
Webb; James Wyatt, Hugh May.
APOLLO 1990 Nov., v.132, no.345,
p.336-339, photos., engr.

WEBB, MICHAEL
Architecture: Cesar Pelli / Michael
Webb.
Features home in Maryland whose
"central concept is the
organization of a complex of
functional pavilions along an
interior street--the gallery."
Architect: Cesar Pelli.
ARCHITECTURAL DIGEST 1990 July,
v.47, no.7, p.124-[129],178,
photos., plan.
Cafe Society: Los Angeles serves up
a fresh selection of fashionable
restaurants where diners can go to
be pampered and entertained /
Michael Webb.
METROPOLIS 1990 Jan.-Feb., v.9,
no.6, p.60-65,79, photos.
Cecil B. De Mille: Hollywood
residence of a master showman /
Michael Webb.
Located in Laughlin Park.
ARCHITECTURAL DIGEST 1990 Apr.,
v.47, no.4, p.136-[139],282,
port., photos.
Checkers - small wonder in Los
Angeles / Michael Webb.
Features renovated interiors of
1920s hotel in downtown L.A.
Architects: Eric B. Holtsmark,
Kaplan McLauglin Diaz. Interior
designer: James Northcutt.
ARCHITECTURAL DIGEST 1990 Oct.,
v.47, no.11, p.[100],[102],104,
photos.
Dreaming by the Bay [exhibition
review] / Michael Webb.
"Visionary San Francisco", at the
San Francisco Musuem of Modern
Art, June 14-Aug. 26.
METROPOLIS 1990 July-Aug., v.10,
no.1, p.50-55,75, ill., dwgs.
Funky chicken / Michael Webb.
Kentucky Fried Chicken restaurant,
Los Angeles; architects: Grinstein
- Daniels.
BLUEPRINT (LONDON, ENGLAND) 1990
Sept., no.70, p.34-35, photos.
Hollywood legacies of Wallace Neff,
James E. Dolena, Roland E. Coate
and Paul Williams / Michael Webb.
ARCHITECTURAL DIGEST 1990 Apr.,
v.47, no.4, p.36,40,42,46,48,
dwg., ports., photos.
The house of the butterfly: Bob Ray
Offenhauser evokes the spirit of
ancient China in Los Angeles /
Michael Webb.
Chinese-style home modeled on
(Continued next column)

WEBB, MICHAEL (CONTINUED)
The house of the... (CONTINUED)
restored Ming home in Suzhou,
China. Interior designer: Harvey
Ackerman.
ARCHITECTURAL DIGEST 1990 Dec.,
v.47, no.13, p.[166]-175,228,
port., photos., site plan.
Internal logic in Tokyo: Akira
Watanabe's small-scale oasis of
dynamic space / Michael Webb.
Home in the Meguro district owned
and designed by Watanabe, was home
to Christian Charrat from 1983 to
1988.
ARCHITECTURAL DIGEST 1990 Dec.,
v.47, no.13, p.176-[181], port.,
photos., plan.
Into the garden: Koning Eizenberg
house, Santa Monica, California /
Michael Webb.
Koning Eizenberg Architecture.
ARCHITECTURE: THE AIA JOURNAL 1990
Mar., v.79, no.3, p.[136-141],
photos., plans.
An italian writer's architectural
statement on Capri / Michael Webb.
On Curzio Malaparte's 1940 villa,
Villa Malaparte.
ARCHITECTURAL DIGEST 1990 Aug.,
v.47, no.8, p.46-59, photos.
Of a visionary nature: Bart Prince's
sculptural design for Joe and
Etsuko Price in California /
Michael Webb.
Beach-front residence in southern
California.
ARCHITECTURAL DIGEST 1990 Dec.,
v.47, no.13, p.[182]-189, 228,
ports., photos., plan.
Pioneering art director who brought
modernism to the movies / Michael
Webb.
On Cedric Gibbons.
ARCHITECTURAL DIGEST 1990 Apr.,
v.47, no.4, p.100,104,108,112,
port., photos.
Reinventing the square: everyone
knows that corporate plazas are
all wrong ... / Michael Webb.
Examples of corporate plazas as
civic spaces in Calif., especially
Horton Plaza, San Diego, and
Levi's Plaza, San Fransisco.
METROPOLIS 1990 Mar., v.9, no.7,
p.[50]-53,62-63, ill., photos.,
aerial photo.
Valley of the lost house / Michael
Webb.
The Monument (Schweitzer) house;
architects: Schweitzer BIM.
BLUEPRINT (LONDON, ENGLAND) 1990
July-Aug., no.69, p.24-25, photos.

WEBB, MICHAEL, 1937-
Il domestico in guerra = Domesticity
at war / Beatriz Colomina.
Discusses the 1964-1965 New York
World's Fair, the Underground Home
and other exhibits, Michael Webb's
Sina House, and Dying Robertson's
Room in the City. In Italian and
English.
OTTAGONO 1990 Dec., no.97,
p.24-[49], ill., dwgs., models,
photos., plans, secn., refs.

WEBB, PHILIP, 1831-1915
  William Morris and his wallpapers /
  Deborah Barcan.
  Includes photos of Morris' house
  in Bexleyheath, designed by Philip
  Webb.
  VICTORIAN HOMES 1990 Winter, v.9,
  no.1, p.38-43, dets., ports.,
  photos.

WEBBER STAUNTON AND SPAULDING
  Harold Lloyd: a renaissance palace
  for one of the silent era's great
  comic pioneers / Kevin Brownlow.
  Features Greenacres built in
  1927-28, Beverly Hills.
  Architects: Webber Staunton and
  Spaulding.
  ARCHITECTURAL DIGEST 1990 Apr.,
  v.47, no.4, p.160-[165], port.,
  photos.

WEBER, CHERYL
  Articulating winter / Cheryl Weber.
  Plan for a garden in the backyard
  of landscape architect Tom
  Oslund's home in Minneapolis.
  GARDEN DESIGN 1990 autumn, v.9,
  no.3, p.70-72, axonometric view,
  port., plan.
  Beyond the vegetable patch:
  foodscape design for the nineties
  / Cheryl Weber.
  GARDEN DESIGN 1990 summer, v.9,
  no.2, p.[44]-53, photos., plan.
  Healing the Earth: how 20 years of
  environmentalism have changed
  American gardening / Cheryl Weber.
  GARDEN DESIGN 1990 Spring, v.9,
  no.1, p.30-35, photos.
  Simple solutions / Cheryl Weber.
  Tiny backyard garden of Michael
  Dunham in Baltimore. Landscape
  designer: Michael McWilliams.
  GARDEN DESIGN 1990 autumn, v.9,
  no.3, p.46-49, photos., plan.

WEBER, FRITZ
  Gemeindeamt und Raiffeisenbank in
  Prutz/Tirol.
  Architect: Fritz Weber.
  DEUTSCHE BAUZEITSCHRIFT 1990 Feb.,
  v.38, no.2, p.223-230, axonometric
  views, dwgs., maps, photos.,
  plans, secns.

WEBER, HELMUT
  Anstriche in der Bausanierung /
  Helmut Weber.
  Conservation techniques and
  materials used in impregnating.
  DEUTSCHES ARCHITEKTENBLATT 1990
  Sept.1, v.22, no.9, p.1341-1344,
  diagrs., tables.

WEBER, JORG
  Erste Preise: Sozialbauten.
  Four projects: Altenpflegeheim
  Sachsenheim (architect: Ulli G.
  Hassig + Partner); Pflegeheim der
  Barmherzigen Bruder, Algasing
  Dorfen (architect: Jurgen Krug +
  Partner); Kinderzentrum
  Ludwigshafen am Rhein (architect:
  Erwin Morlock et al); conversion
  of Mullerwohnhaus to a meeting
  house, Ortschaft Sudhemmern
  (architect: Jorg Weber).
  DEUTSCHES ARCHITEKTENBLATT 1990
  June 1, v.22, no.6, p.931-934,
  elevs., models, plans, secns.,
  site plans.

WEBER, KARL-KLAUS
  Gestalterische Uberlegungen zu den
  Uberkuppelungstheorien des
  Zentralraumes der Piazza d'Oro in
  der Villa Hadrian bei Tivoli /
  Karl-Klaus Weber.
  ARCHITECTURA 1990, v.20, no.2,
  p.101-107, axonometric views,
  secns., reconst. dwgs., refs.

WEBER, MARIE-ANNE
  Odenser gagader / Marie-Anne Weber.
  Reorganization of central Odense
  and design of new pedestrian areas
  by Ginman Harboe Borup
  Landskabsarkitekter. Includes
  English translation and captions.
  LANDSKAB 1990 May, v.71, no.3-4,
  p.DK9-DK12, photos., site plans.

WEBER, MICHAEL
  Korperschall und Erschutterung /
  Michael Weber.
  DEUTSCHE BAUZEITSCHRIFT 1989 Dec.,
  v.37, no.12, p.1657-1658, graphs,
  dwgs.

WEBER, NICHOLAS FOX
  Alvar Aalto's living masterpiece in
  Finland / Nicholas Fox Weber.
  On the Villa Mairea, commissioned
  in 1937 by Harry and Maire
  Gullichsen. Located in Noormarkku.
  ARCHITECTURAL DIGEST 1990 Feb.,
  v.47, no.2, p.50,54,58,62, ports.,
  photos.
  Architectural Digest visits:
  Maximilian Schell / Nicholas Fox
  Weber.
  Focus on the art collection in his
  turn-of-the-century European home.
  ARCHITECTURAL DIGEST 1990 Sept.,
  v.47, no.10, p.184-[189],230,
  [232-233], ports., photos.
  Baroque splendors of Vienna's
  Schwarzenberg Palace / Nicholas
  Fox Weber.
  Design begun by Johann Lucas von
  Hildebrant in 1697, continued by
  Fischer von Erlach from 1720-1723
  and completed by his son in 1727.
  The palace is now both the private
  residence of Prince Karl Johannes
  von Schwarzenberg and a luxury
  hotel, the Hotel im Palais
  Schwarzenberg.
  ARCHITECTURAL DIGEST 1990 Sept.,
  v.47, no.10, p.116,122,126, port.,
  photos.
  A German Baroque villa devoted to
  the pursuit of pleasure / Nicholas
  Fox Weber.
  On the 1732 Schloss Favorite,
  Ludwigsburg. Architect: Donato
  Giuseppe Frisoni. Interiors
  remodeled between 1799 and 1801 by
  Nicolaus Friedrich Thouret.
  ARCHITECTURAL DIGEST 1990 May,
  v.47, no.5, p.134-146, photos.
  Historic houses: Johannes Brahms:
  the composer's summer sanctuary in
  Baden-Baden / Nicholas Fox Weber.
  An historic house museum in
  Lichtental.
  ARCHITECTURAL DIGEST 1990 July,
  v.47, no.7, p.58,62,64, port.,
  photos.
  Revisiting the landmark Tugendhat
  house / Nicholas Fox Weber.
  On the 1928-1930 home in Brno,
  Czechoslovakia. Architect: Ludwig
  Mies van der Rohe.
  (Continued next column)

WEBER, NICHOLAS FOX (CONTINUED)
  Revisiting the...(CONTINUED)
  ARCHITECTURAL DIGEST 1990 Oct.,
  v.47, no.11, p.74,78,82,84,[86],
  port., photos., sketch.

WEBER, OLAF
  Gestalterische Grundwerte der
  Architektur Thesen / Olaf Weber.
  ARCHITEKTUR DER DDR 1990 Jan.,
  v.38, no.1, p.41-44,

WEBER, PETER
  Neue Bauten von Peter Weber.
  House renovations in Wanna, Leer,
  and Worpswede, W. Germany;
  residential development in Bremen;
  and renovation of Strandhalle,
  Bremerhaven. Includes English
  summaries.
  BAUMEISTER 1990 Jan., v.87, no.1,
  p.17-37, dets., elevs., models,
  photos., plans, secns., site
  plans.

WEBER, SANDRA S.
  Interpretation.
  Nine articles on historic site
  methods. Authors: Sandra S. Weber,
  F.A. Ketterson, Marcella Sherfy,
  Edward Tabor Linenthal, Raymond H.
  Thompson, Michael E. Whatley,
  Marie T. Myers, Karen
  Sweeny-Justice, Kathleen Hunter.
  CRM BULLETIN: A NATIONAL PARK
  SERVICE TECHNICAL BULLETIN 1990,
  v.13, no.3, p.1-21, photos.

WEBER, THOMAS
  Gadara in der Dekapolis: deutsche
  Ausgrabungen bei Umm Qais in
  Nordjordanien 1986 bis 1988.
  Reports by Peter Cornelius Bol,
  Adolf Hoffmann, and Thomas Weber,
  and essays by Odile Dussart, Peter
  W. Herz, Susanne Kerner, Lee A.
  Maxwell, and Kevin Rielly.
  ARCHAOLOGISCHER ANZEIGER 1990,
  no.2, p.[193]-266, dets., photos.,
  elevs., map, plans, secns., site
  plans, refs.

WEBER, WOLFGANG
  Architektur unterwegs.
  Two projects: Produktions- und
  Lagerhalle der Brauerei
  Bischofshof, Regensburg
  (architect: Oswald Peithner);
  Clinic for forensic psychiatry,
  Duren (architects: Jurgen Kunz,
  Wolfgang Weber).
  DEUTSCHES ARCHITEKTENBLATT 1990
  Oct.1, v.22, no.10, p.1515-1518,
  elevs., photos., plans.
  Darum Sichtinstallation:
  medizinische Fakultat der
  Technischen Hochschule Aachen.
  Architects: Jurgen Kunz with Paul
  Troger and Wolfgang Weber.
  Includes English summary.
  DETAIL 1990 Dec.-1991 Jan., v.30,
  no.6, p.581-584, dwgs., photos.,
  secns., isometric dwgs.

WECKWERTH, HELMUT
  Ausbildung und Berufspraxis in der
  EG / Johannes von Korff, Helmut
  Weckwerth.
  On education and professional
  practice for landscape architects
  in the European Community.
  Includes English summary.
  (Continued next page)

WECKWERTH, HELMUT (CONTINUED)
Ausbildung und... (CONTINUED)
GARTEN UND LANDSCHAFT 1990, v.100, no.2, p.19-24, photos., tables, refs.

WEDD, KIT
Allied to design: a new competition is bringing style to the high street / Kit Wedd.
Young interior designers created a living room for a "young couple with a limited budget."
TRADITIONAL HOMES 1990 Mar., v.6, no.6, p.78-80, dwgs., photos.
Cathedral cottage: a picturesque home in Salisbury / Kit Wedd.
TRADITIONAL HOMES 1990 Apr., v.6, no.7, p.45-48, photos.
Conflicting demands: how a modern kitchen has been designed with respect for its historic setting / Kitt Wedd.
Renovation of an 1800 farmhouse kitchen in Kent.
TRADITIONAL HOMES 1990 Oct., v.7, no.1, p.33-34, photos.
Culinary criteria: the kitchen of an exacting designer / Kit Wedd.
Designer: Rosa Lewis, of Walton Design.
TRADITIONAL HOMES 1990 July, v.6, no.10, p.[37-38], photos.
Glasgow Boy: the enduring influence of Charles Rennie Mackintosh characterises a modern interior / Kit Wedd.
Reproductions of wallpaper and furniture.
TRADITIONAL HOMES 1990 June, v.6, no.9, p.[48]-49, photos.
Light fantastic: Kit Wedd recreates a sophisticated interior of the 1930's.
TRADITIONAL HOMES 1990 May, v.6, no.8, p.52-53, photos.
The mill's tale: an eighteenth century mill can still earn its keep today, thanks to a sensitive renovation: Renovation Case History no. 74 / Kit Wedd.
Maplehurst Mill, built 1756, is now the home of Kenneth and Heather Parker.
TRADITIONAL HOMES 1990 Dec., v.7, no.3, p.16-21, photos., plans, ref.
Renovation case history no. 72: Britannia rules, a Worcester townhouse made worthy of its historic setting once again / Kit Wedd.
1845 terraced house in Britannia Square, Worcester, England.
Architect for restoration: James Snell.
TRADITIONAL HOMES 1990 Oct., v.7, no.1, p.16-21, photos., plans.
Renovation case history no.73: a fine whim / Kit Wedd.
Stone farm buildings consolidated into a home in the village of Hartington.
TRADITIONAL HOMES 1990 Nov., v.7, no.2, p.22-27, photos., plans.
Simple addition: a Cambridgeshire farmhouse which has been sympathetically renovated and extended / Kit Wedd.
Home of Pamela Tudor-Craig.
TRADITIONAL HOMES 1990 June, v.6, no.9, p.39-42, photos.

WEDD, KIT (CONTINUED)
User friendly: the benefits of conservatory ownership / Kit Wedd.
TRADITIONAL HOMES 1990 June, v.6, no.9, p.91-96, photos.

WEDDING PALACES
See MARRIAGE HALLS

WEDEBRUNN, OLA
Planetariet / Ola Wedebrunn.
In conjunction with Knud Munk's Tycho Brahe Planetariet, discusses possible influences, including Bjernede Kirke (1900) and a 1907 project by P.V. Jensen.
ARKITEKTEN 1990 Aug., v.92, no.11, p.380, model, photos., refs.

WEEBER, CAREL, 1937-
De andere fabriek: Carel Weebers Huis van Bewaring in Rotterdam / Bart Lootsma.
The "De Schie" penitentiary, completed in 1989.
DE ARCHITECT 1990 Jan., v.21, no.1, p.40-47, cover, axonometric views, elev., photos., plans, secn., refs.
Carel Weeber [by] Ed Taverne [book review] / Johann Van de Beek.
DE ARCHITECT 1990 June, v.21, no.6, p.65-67, dwg., photos.
Gevangenis te Rotterdam.
Prison, built 1988-89. Architekten Cie. te Amsterdam, C. Weeber.
BOUW 1990 Oct.5, v.45, no.20, p.29-32, photos., elev., plans, site plan.
Ingekleurde schema's: Carel Weebers gevangenis in Rotterdam / Hans van Dijk.
The De Schie penitentiary, 1985-1989.
ARCHIS 1990 Jan., no.1, p.22-27, elevs., photos., plans, secns., site plans, refs.
Stedebouw in gefragmenteerde context: herinchting stationsgebied Voorburg door Carel Weeber / Wim Nijenhuis.
DE ARCHITECT 1989 Dec., v.20, no.12, p.68-73, photos., site plans.
Tre "congegni urbani" per Rotterdam / D. Mandolesi.
The Spijkenisse, Heemraadiaan, and De Akkers transit stations.
Architect: C. Weber, with C. Veerling.
L'INDUSTRIA DELLE COSTRUZIONI 1990 July-Aug., v.24, no.225-226, p.68-69, photos., secns., aerial photo.
"Vormgeving is amereel": een gesprele met Carel Weeber [interview] / Hans van Dijk, Rob de Graf.
ARCHIS 1990 Jan., no.1, p.28-31, port.

WEEBER, CAREL, 1937---EXHIBITIONS
Carel Weeber en het arrogante type [exhibition review] / Arthur Wortmann.
At the Nederlands Architectuurinstituut, Rotterdam, until May 13, 1990.
ARCHIS 1990 Apr., no.4, p.3, dwg., photo., refs.

WEEKEND HOUSES--ALTERATIONS AND ADDITIONS--UNITED STATES--WESTPORT (CONNECTICUT)
Infusion of charm / Susan Zevon.
Additions to house in Westport, Connecticut. Architects: Rosenblum/Harb Architects.
HOUSE BEAUTIFUL 1990 Oct., v.132, no.10, p.112-115, dets., photos., plan.

WEEKEND HOUSES--ARCHITECTS'--ALTERATIONS AND ADDITIONS--UNITED STATES--SHELTER ISLAND (NEW YORK)--PEDERSEN HOUSE
Formal axis in weekend clothes / Mark Alden Branch.
Features architect William Pedersen's renovated 80-year-old weekend home and studio on Shelter Island, NY.
PROGRESSIVE ARCHITECTURE 1990 Nov., v.71, no.12, p.86-89, photos., plans, secn., site plan.

WEEKEND HOUSES--ARCHITECTS'--FINLAND--HAILUOTO--JUNTUNEN HOUSE
Architetture per il sito: la casa sull'isola = Site-friendly architecture: the house on the island.
Weekend house of architect Veikko Juntunen, Hailuoto, Finland.
Architect: Risto Harju.
ABITARE 1990 Apr., no.284, p.170-175, photos., plan.

WEEKEND HOUSES--ARCHITECTS'--JAMAICA--PORT ANTONIO--CRYSTAL COVE (GOODMAN HOUSE)
American modernism transformed by the Jamaican vernacular / Suzanne Stephens.
On the work of Marvin Goodman in Jamaica, including his weekend house, Crystal Cove, in Port Antonio.
ARCHITECTURAL DIGEST 1990 Aug., v.47, no.8, p.62,68,74,[76], ill., photos.

WEEKEND HOUSES--ARCHITECTS'--UNITED STATES--GAY HEAD (MASSACHUSETTS)--KALKIN HOUSE
Architecture: Adam Kalkin / Robert Campbell.
Kalkin weekend house in Gay Head, Mass. composed of a 1820s Vermont barn and steel industrial warehouse, both of which were shipped to the site. Architect: Adam Kalkin.
ARCHITECTURAL DIGEST 1990 June, v.47, no.6, p.172-177, port., model, photos.

WEEKEND HOUSES--ARCHITECTS'--UNITED STATES--JOSHUA TREE (CALIFORNIA)--SCHWEITZER HOUSE
The new frontier [house, Joshua Tree, Calif.] / Charles Gandee.
Architect: Josh Schweitzer.
HOUSE & GARDEN 1990 June, v.162, no.6, p.[120-125], port., photos.
Non sono "tesseracts" pero... = They aren't "tesseracts" but... [weekend house, Joshua Tree, Calif.].
Architect: Josh Sweitzer.
ARCHITETTURA: CRONACHE E STORIA 1990 Nov., v.36, no.11(421), p.800-801, axonometric view, photos., plan.

WEEKEND HOUSES--ARCHITECTS'--UNITED
STATES--JOSHUA TREE (CALIFORNIA)--
THE MONUMENT (SCHWEITZER HOUSE)
Desert Bloom: The Monument, Joshua
Tree, California / Aaron Betsky.
The Architect's weekend house.
Architects: Schweitzer BIM.
ARCHITECTURAL RECORD 1990
Mid-Apr., v.178, no.5, p.[64-69],
axonometric view, photos., plan.
Valley of the lost house / Michael
Webb.
The Monument (Schweitzer) house;
architects: Schweitzer BIM.
BLUEPRINT (LONDON, ENGLAND) 1990
July-Aug., no.69, p.24-25, photos.

WEEKEND HOUSES--ARCHITECTS'--UNITED
STATES--LAKE BLUFF (ILLINOIS)--
CHICKEN COOP (BOOTH HOUSE)
Free-range architecture: The Chicken
Coop, Lake Bluff, Illinois /
Clifford A. Pearson.
Weekend house of architect
Laurence Booth. Architects: Booth
Hansen & Associates.
ARCHITECTURAL RECORD 1990
Mid-Apr., v.178, no.5, p.84-87,
dwg., photos., plan.
Laurence Booth - Project in
Illinois.
Booth Weekend House, Lake
Bluff.Includes short article by
Booth. In Annaherung an eine
amerikanische Architektur.
Architect: Larry Booth of Booth
Hansen & Associates.
DEUTSCHE BAUZEITSCHRIFT 1990 May,
v.38, no.5, p.[655]-660, dets.,
photos., plan, site plans.

WEEKEND HOUSES--ARCHITECTS'--UNITED
STATES--MICHIGAN--GIBBONS - OLLIS
HOUSE
On a whim and a prairie
[Gibbons-Ollis house] / Victoria
Lautman.
A six-room weekend house, located
in rural Mich. and influenced by
Palladio. Architect: Rick Gibbons.
METROPOLITAN HOME 1990 June, v.22,
no.6, p.96-[101], port., photos.

WEEKEND HOUSES--GERMANY (WEST)--
HAARDTGEBIRGE
Wohnhaus im Haardtgebirge.
Architect: Peter Sturzebecher.
Includes English summary.
BAUMEISTER 1990 Nov., v.87, no.11,
p.48-51, photos., plans, secns.,
isometric dwg.

WEEKEND HOUSES--GERMANY (WEST)--
PALATINATE
Ausgetuftelt prazise: Wochenendhaus
im Pfalzer Wald / Klaus-Dieter
Weiss.
Architect: Peter Sturzebecher.
BAUWELT 1990 Oct.12, v.81, no.38,
p.1930-1933, axonometric view,
elev., photos., plans, secn.

WEEKEND HOUSES--INTERIOR DESIGN
Joys of the cottage / Elizabeth H.
Hunter.
Interiors of weekend house
designed to give the feel of a
cottage. Interior designer John
Robert Moore II.
HOUSE BEAUTIFUL 1990 Feb., v.132,
no.2, p.[62]-67, photos.

WEEKEND HOUSES--INTERIOR DESIGN--
UNITED STATES--HAMPTONS (NEW YORK)
Primary motifs: William Diamond and
Anthony Baratta rejuvenate a
Victorian cottage with bold color
and an eye for period detail /
Sherrye Henry.
Interiors of a weekend house in
the Hamptons.
HOUSE & GARDEN 1990 Aug., v.162,
no.8, p.[80-87],153, photos.

WEEKEND HOUSES--INTERIOR DESIGN--
UNITED STATES--NEW YORK (STATE)--
CAHAN - MIRABELLA HOUSE (VILLA SANTO
GUGLIELMO)
Villa Santo Guglielmo: Grace
Mirabella and Dr. William Cahan's
New York State residence / Judith
Thurman.
Architect: Alexander Gorlin.
ARCHITECTURAL DIGEST 1990 Feb.,
v.47, no.2, p.[164-169],238,
photos.

WEEKEND HOUSES--INTERIOR DESIGN--
UNITED STATES--PALM SPRINGS
(CALIFORNIA)--RON WILSON HOUSE
Creating an oasis / Rhoda Jaffin
Murphy.
Weekend house of interior designer
Ron Wilson in Palm Springs, Calif.
HOUSE BEAUTIFUL 1990 Feb., v.132,
no.2, p.80-[87], photos.

WEEKEND HOUSES--INTERIOR DESIGN--
UNITED STATES--SAG HARBOR (NEW
YORK)--MOSES - PERLMAN HOUSE
A perfect fit: Rebecca Moses / Julie
V. Iovine.
Interior of weekend house in Sag
Harbor, N.Y., owned by the fashion
designer and her husband Louis
Perlman.
METROPOLITAN HOME 1990 June, v.22,
no.6, p.82-[87], ports., photos.

WEEKEND HOUSES--INTERIOR DESIGN--
UNITED STATES--SOUTH CAROLINA--KEY
HOUSE
Blue Ridge roots ... a designer's
South Carolina cabin / Wendy
Mallinson.
Bill Key's retreat.
SOUTHERN ACCENTS 1990 Sept., v.13,
no.7, p.110-114, photos.

WEEKEND HOUSES--INTERIOR DESIGN--
UNITED STATES--SOUTHAMPTON (NEW
YORK)--HACKETT HOUSE
Southampton character study:
updating a historic summer estate
on Long Island / John Taylor.
Interiors of Brue and Joann
Hackett's renovated ca. 1913
weekend house. Interior designer:
Mary Meehan. Renavation architect:
Richard Sawicki. Landscape
architect: Elise DeBoeck Deans.
ARCHITECTURAL DIGEST 1990 May,
v.47, no.5, p.[178-185], port.,
photos.

WEEKEND HOUSES--INTERIOR DESIGN--
UNITED STATES--WOODSTOCK (VERMONT)
Shaker show / Monica Geran.
Interiors of weekend/holiday
retreat in Woodstock, Vt. designed
by Sandra Nunnerley.
INTERIOR DESIGN 1990 Jan., v.61,
no.1, p.172-[175], photos., plans.

WEEKEND HOUSES--JAPAN--NAGANO--ABE
HOUSE
The Abe weekend house, Nagano,
[Japan], 1986.
Architects: Kazumasa Yamashita,
Architect and Associates. Text in
Japanese and English.
PROCESS: ARCHITECTURE 1989 Dec.,
no.87, p.70-73, photos., plans,
secn.

WEEKEND HOUSES--JAPAN--YAMANASHI--
PLATFORM
Residence Platform a Yamanashi.
Architect: Kazuyo Sejima.
Includes statement by architect.
English summary.
TECHNIQUES ET ARCHITECTURE 1990
June-July, no.390, p.140-141,
photos., plan, secn.

WEEKEND HOUSES--SLOPING SITES--
AUSTRIA--LAVANTEGG
Graz particularity / Peter Blundell
Jones.
Comparison of three recent houses
in the Graz area by Klaus Kada,
Volker Giencke and Hermann
Eisenkock.
ARCHITECTURAL REVIEW 1990 Apr.,
v.187, no.1118, p.36-51,
axonometric views, dwgs, elevs.,
photos., plans secns., site plans.

WEEKEND HOUSES--SLOPING SITES--SPAIN--
PUERTO DE SANTA MARIA--GUARDIOLA
HOUSE
Eisenman Architects [houses].
Contents: Guardiola house, Puerto
de Santa Maria, Cadiz, Spain, 1988
-- Social housing for 200,000th
home housing fesival at
Dedemsvaartweg, the Hague,
Netherlands, 1989. Architects:
Eisenman Architects. Text in
Japanese and English.
GA HOUSES 1990 Mar., no.28,
p.20-26, axonometric views, dwgs.,
models, photos., plans., secns.
Peter Eisenman.
Most of the issue devoted to this
architect. Nine projects featured.
Includes interview with David
Cohn. Text in Spanish and English.
EL CROQUIS 1989 Dec., v.8, no.41,
p.4-126,cover, axonometric views,
ill., dwgs., ports., elevs.,
models, photos., plans, secns.,
refs.

WEEKEND HOUSES--UNITED STATES--CANYON
LAKE (TEXAS)--SALGE HOUSE
Texas breeze [Salgo Lakehouse,
Canyon Lake, Texas] / Joel Warren
Barna.
Weekend house. Architects: Lake
Flato Architects.
PROGRESSIVE ARCHITECTURE 1990
Nov., v.71, no.12, p.78-79,
photos., plans.

WEEKEND HOUSES--UNITED STATES--DALLAS
COUNTY (IOWA)
Clear retreat / Mark E. Blunck.
Weekend house, Dallas Co., Iowa.
Architects: Wells Woodburn O'Neil.
IOWA ARCHITECT 1990 Spring, v.39,
no.1, p.10-[11], photos., plans.

WEEKEND HOUSES--UNITED STATES--EAST
HAMPTON (NEW YORK)
Architecture: Gwathmey Siegel &
Associates / Kurt Andersen.
East Hampton weekend house,
including guesthouse on 4-acre
beachfront site. Architect:
Charles Gwathmey.
ARCHITECTURAL DIGEST 1990 May,
v.47, no.5, p.[206-213],276,
photos., site plan.

WEEKEND HOUSES--UNITED STATES--
FREDRICKSBURG (VIRGINIA)--HORNE
HOUSE
Designer's retreat. [Horne house,
Fredricksburg, Va.].
Interior designer: C. Larry Horne.
COLONIAL HOMES 1990 Oct., v.16,
no.5, p.[65]-71, photos.

WEEKEND HOUSES--UNITED STATES--JOSHUA
TREE (CALIFORNIA)--MONUMENT
Schweitzer BIM: the Monument, Joshua
Tree, California, 1987-90.
Desert retreat. Text in Japanese
and English.
GA HOUSES 1990 Dec., no.30,
p.126-133, axonometric views,
photos., plan.

WEEKEND HOUSES--UNITED STATES--
LAMBERTVILLE (NEW JERSEY)--MILL
HOUSE
Amicable separation: Mill House
Casino, Lambertville, New Jersey
Keenen/Riley, Architects / Deborah
K. Dietsch.
600-sq.-ft. freestanding casino
for playing pool.
ARCHITECTURE: THE MAGAZINE OF THE
AMERICAN INSTITUTE OF ARCHITECTS
1990 Aug., v.79, no.8, p.56-59,
photos., plans.
Una casa per i giochi di
Keenen-Riley / Kenneth Frampton.
Reuse of stone foundations from a
mill site, for small home and
gazebo. Captions in Italian and
English.
CASABELLA 1990 Oct., v.54, no.572,
p.34-35, elevs., photos., plans,
site plan.
Mill house casino, Lambertville, New
Jersey.
Architects: Keenen Riley. Text in
Japanese and English.
ARCHITECTURE AND URBANISM 1990
Dec., no.12(243), p.32-[39],
photos., plans.

WEEKEND HOUSES--UNITED STATES--
MICHIGAN
Architetture per il sito: la casa
nel bosco = Site-friendly
architecture: the house in the
wood.
Weekend house near Lake Michigan.
Architects: Pappageorge Haymes.
ABITARE 1990 Apr., no.284,
p.164-169, elevs., photos., plans,
site plan.

WEEKEND HOUSES--UNITED STATES--
RHEINBECK (NEW YORK)--HENRY HOUSE
Michael Graves Architect [houses].
Contents: Naiman house, La Jolla,
California, design: 1988-89 --
Henry house, Rheinbeck, New York,
design: 1987-89. Architect:
Michael Graves. Text in Japanese
and English.
(Continued next column)

WEEKEND HOUSES--UNITED STATES--
RHEINBECK (NEW YORK)--HENRY HOUSE
(CONTINUED)
Michael Graves...(CONTINUED)
GA HOUSES 1990 Mar., no.28,
p.104-107, elevs., models, plans,
secns.

WEEKEND HOUSES--UNITED STATES--SAN
ANTONIO (TEXAS)--LAKE CANYON HOUSE
Canyon Lake house.
Weekend house near San Antonio.
Lake/Flato Architects.
TEXAS ARCHITECT 1990 Jan.-Feb.,
v.40, no.1, p.25, photos., plans,
secn., site plan.

WEEKEND HOUSES--UNITED STATES--
STOCKHOLM (WISCONSIN)--WIND WHISTLE
(TOTH-STAGEBERG HOUSE)
Crayon-colored dream house / Susan
Allen Toth.
Wisconsin weekend house designed
by James Stageberg.
HOUSE BEAUTIFUL 1990 Apr., v.132,
no.4, p.[94]-95,121, photos.,
secn.

WEEKEND HOUSES--UNITED STATES--ZAVALA
COUNTY (TEXAS)--SOUTH BURKE RANCH
HEADQUARTERS
South Burke Ranch Headquarters.
In Zavala Co. Lake Flato
Architects.
TEXAS ARCHITECT 1990 Jan.-Feb.,
v.40, no.1, p.26, photos., plan,
site plan.

WEEKS AND DAY
Fox hunting in Oakland: hunters are
stalking the rare Oakland Fox [Fox
Oakland Theatre] / Herb
Stockinger.
The Fox Oakland Theatre was
completed in 1928, Weeks and Day,
architects.
MARQUEE 1990, v.22, no.3, p.3-6,
photos., secn.

WEEKS, CHRISTOPHER
Realizing aromantic vision: a wave
of Spanish Revival architecture
swept across Southern California
during the 1920s, and Architect
Palmer Sabin rode it to success /
Christopher Weeks.
METROPOLIS 1990 Mar., v.9, no.7,
p.[44]-49,77,79,81, photos., ill.,
dwgs.

WEEKS, EZRA
Gracie Mansion / Chippy Irvine.
On a five-year renovation to the
1799 mansion, home of New York's
mayor. Probable architect: Ezra
Weeks.
ART & ANTIQUES 1990 Jan., v.7,
no.1, p.82-87, photos., engr.

WEESE, BENJAMIN H. 1929-
Westminster Church in Peoria [IL].
Architects: Weese Langley Weese.
Includes short article,
Architektur als intuitiver
Prozess, by Benjamin Weese.
DEUTSCHE BAUZEITSCHRIFT 1990 May,
v.38, no.5, p.665-670, det.,
photos., plans, secns., sketches.

WEESE, BENJAMIN H., 1929-
(CONTINUED)

WEESE, CYNTHIA
The International City Design
Competition / Jeffrey E. Ollswang.
Sponsored by the University of
Wisconsin, Milwaukee. Contents:
Incremental utopias, by Allan B.
Jacobs; Cities of culture, cities
of places, by Carlos Tejeda; let
Milwaukee be Milwaukee, by Cynthia
Weese; Solutions in search of a
problem, by Amos Rapoport; and
Places are not impositions, by
William Turnbull, Jr.
PLACES 1990 Winter, v.6, no.2,
p.32-47, axonometric views, dwgs.,
map, photos., plans, site plans,
aerial photo., refs.
Room at the Top? Sexism and the Star
System in Architecture / Denise
Scott Brown.
One of four sections in a special
feature on "Women in American
Architecture". English
translation, p.73-75.
SPACE DESIGN 1990 June, no.309,
p.54-71,73-75, dwgs., ports.,
elevs., photos., plans, secns.,
site plams, refs.

WEESE, HARRY, 1915-
New life for Chicago's Chinatown /
Annie Morse.
A 32-acre commercial residential
project by the Chinese American
Development Corporation (CADC) and
Link Programs (a division of the
Himmel Group). Phases I-III will
be completed 1991-c1997.
Architect: Harry Weese.
INLAND ARCHITECT 1990 Nov.-Dec.,
v.34, no.6, p.22, dwg.

WEESE LANGLEY WEESE
Prairie resurrection: a new church
rises like a phoenix from the
ashes of a devastating fire / Lynn
Nesmith.
Westminster Presbyterian Church,
Peoria, Ill. Architects: Weese
Langley Weese.
ARCHITECTURE: THE AIA JOURNAL 1990
Feb., v.79, no.2, p.[68-70],
photos., plan, secn.
Westminster Church in Peoria [IL].
Architects: Weese Langley Weese.
Includes short article,
Architektur als intuitiver
Prozess, by Benjamin Weese.
DEUTSCHE BAUZEITSCHRIFT 1990 May,
v.38, no.5, p.665-670, det.,
photos., plans, secns., sketches.

WEGELIN, EMIEL A.
New approaches in urban services
delivery: a comparison of emerging
experience in selected Asian
countries / Emiel A. Wegelin.
CITIES 1990 Aug., v.7, no.3,
p.244-258, refs.

WEGNER, REINHARD
Die Einrichtung des Alten Museums in
Berlin anmerkungen zu einem neu
entdeckten Schinkel-Dokument /
Reinhard Wegner.
JAHRBUCH DER BERLINER MUSEEN 1989
v.31, p.[105]-107, plans, engrs.,
refs.

WEHBERG LANGE EPPINGER SCHMIDTKE
Parlamentsvorzone Bonn = The approach area to Parliament, Bonn. Idea competition. Winning architects: Wehberg Lange Eppinger Schmidtke. Text in German. ARCHITEKTUR + WETTBEWERBE 1990 Dec., no.144, p.72-74, dwgs., site plans.

WEHT, JAMES
Regional style: eco-logic at work. A brief survey of six "environmental" gardens in the U.S. Landscape architects: Steven K. Domigan, Edith Eddleman, Ron Lutsco, Steve Trudnak, James Weht, and David Cropp. GARDEN DESIGN 1990 spring, v.9, no.1, p.46-59, photos., site plans, sketch.

WEI, CHEN
Heritage conservation: east and west / Chen Wei and Andreas Aass. Comparison of the approaches to heritage conservation in the West and in China, as exemplified in the Acropolis in Athens and the Confucius Temple Complex in Qufu. Summaries in French, Italian and Spanish. ICOMOS INFORMATION 1989 July-Aug., no.3, p.3-8, photos., plans, biblio.

WEI, LIAN
Aseismic design of buildings / Wei Lian. BUILDING IN CHINA 1989 Sept., v.2, no.3, p.17-23,5, charts, port, tables.

WEICKENMEIER, NORBERT
Uber den "Vorsatz zur Vitalitat" und dessen Folgen fur die Architektur / Norbert Weickenmeier. DER ARCHITEKT 1990 July-Aug., no.7-8, p.356-359, photos., plans, site plans, isometric dwg.
Von einer Architektur im "Geist der Zeit" / Norbert Weickenmeier. DER ARCHITEKT 1990 Jan., no.1, p.25-29, axonometric view, dwg., elev., plans, refs.

WEIDEGER, PAULA
England in bloom / Paula Weideger. English gardens open to the public. HOUSE BEAUTIFUL 1990 May, v.132, no.5, p.42-53,143, photos., biblio.

WEIGH-HOUSES
See WEIGH STATIONS

WEIGHING-HOUSES
See WEIGH STATIONS

WEIGHTS AND MEASURES
Run it down the field again, fellows / Grady Clay. The football field as a standard measurement, as illustrated in a wide variety of quotes. PLACES 1990 Summer, v.6, no.4, p.4-8, photo., plan, aerial photos.

WEILE, CHARLOTTE, 1951-
C7 Design, Kobenhavn. A small exhibition space for designer products, on Grabrodre Torv square. Architect: Charlotte Weile. Includes English caption. ARKITEKTUR DK 1990, v.34, no.3, p.132, photos., plan.

WEILL, MICHEL
Details: Logements: la rehabilitation / Jean-Pierre Menard. Contents: Restoration of Jean Zay Universite residence, Antony, France, built 1955-1958; original architect: Eugene Baudoin; renovation architect: Pierre Grandveaud-- Renovation of apartment complex "Les Buffets", Fontenay-aux-Roses, France, built 1958; original architects: Guy Lagneau, Michel Weill, Jean Dimitrijevic, Jean Perrottet; renovation architect: Jean Perrottet-- Renovation of la Viste housing complex, Marseille, France, built in 1959; original architect : Georges Candilis; renovaiton architect: Pierre Gangnet-- Renovation of apartment house, quartier du Haut-du-Lievre, Nancy, France, built 1956-62; original architect: Bernard Zehrfuss; renovation architect: Christian Sarfati. LE MONITEUR ARCHITECTURE AMC 1990 Nov., no.16, p.37-44, axonometric views, dets., ports., photos.
Reference: le Musee des Beaux-Arts du Havre / Joseph Abram. Built from 1958 to 1961: architects: Guy Lagneau, Michel Weill, Jean Dimitrijevic, Raymond Audigier, with Jean Prouve. LE MONITEUR ARCHITECTURE AMC 1990 Oct., no.15, p.50-64, model, photos., plans, secn.

WEIMA, WILLIAM
Le cheval de Troie et la ville assiegee / William Weima. Architectural model dealing with the new urban order. ARQ: ARCHITECTURE/QUEBEC 1990 June, no.55, p.46-47, models.

WEINBERG, W.
Post- und Fernmeldeamt in Rosenheim. Architects: Oberpostdirektion Munchen, H.L. Sopper, H. Winkler, W. Weinberg, F. Bauer. DEUTSCHE BAUZEITSCHRIFT 1990 Oct., v.38, no.10, p.1369-1377, dets., photos., plan, secn., site plans.

WEINBRENNER, EBERHARD, 1925-
Freie Architekten und offentliches Bauen / Eberhard Weinbrenner. Text of a talk given in Mar. 1990 at the Villa Vigoni, Comer See, on the role of the architect in a democratic society. DEUTSCHES ARCHITEKTENBLATT 1990 Oct.1, v.22, no.10, p.1519-1520, 1522,
Der Verfall der Stadte in der DDR. Issue features East German architecture. Contents: Wovon spricht die Architektur der DDR?, by Walter Kruger-- Blindes Fortschrittsdenken und boses
(Continued next column)

WEINBRENNER, EBERHARD, 1925-
(CONTINUED)
Der Verfall der...(CONTINUED) Erwachen, by Bruno Flierl-- Stadterhaltung in der DDR: Stand April 1990, by Peter Goralczyk-- Stadtzerstorung in... [10 cities]-- Schlicht und einfach nach GRW? [interview with Jan C. Bassenge, Joachim Ganz, Hans Kollhoff, Wolfgang Nagel, Michaele Schreyer, Eberhard Weinbrenner. BAUWELT 1990 May 18, v.81, no.19, p.938-961, maps, photos.

WEINBRENNER, ULRICH
Business-Domizil: das Dorint-Hotel in Frankfurt-Niederrad. Interior architects: U. Weinbrenner, M. Merz-Schulze. ARCHITEKTUR, INNENARCHITEKTUR, TECHNISCHER AUSBAU 1990 June, v.98, no.6, p.48-57, dwgs., elev., models, photos., plans.

WEINDEL, MICHAEL
Kindergarten "Don Bosco" in Waldbronn. Architect: Michael Weindel. DEUTSCHE BAUZEITSCHRIFT 1989 Dec., v.37, no.12, p.1621-1626, dets., photos., site plan.

WEINER, DEBORAH E. B.
The architecture of Victorian philanthropy: the settlement house as manorial residence / Deborah E. B. Weiner. Toynbee Hall, London. Architect: Elijah Hoole. ART HISTORY 1990 June, v.13, no.2, p.212-227, ill., photo., engrs., refs.

WEINGARDEN, LAUREN S.
American architects [book review]. Review of books on Louis Sullivan, Philip Trammell Shutze, Louis Kahn, and Gordon Bunshaft, by Lauren S. Weingarden, Keith Morgan, David B. Brownlee, and Franz Schulze. SOCIETY OF ARCHITECTURAL HISTORIANS. JOURNAL 1990 June, v.49, no.2, p.222-229,

WEINSTEIN, AMY
Urbanist without Portfolio: Notes on a career / by Jane Thompson. One of four sections in a special feature on "Women in American Architecture". Contents: Marion G. Weiss.-- Inea Elskop/1100 Architect. Billie Tsien.-- Patricia Sapinsley.--Alison Sky+Michelle Stone/SITE Projects, Inc.--Karen Bausman+Leslie Gill.-- Deborah Berke.--Amy Weinstein.-- Adele Naude Santos. English translation, p.73. SPACE DESIGN 1990 June, no.309, p.36-53,73, axonometric views, dwgs., ports., elevs., models, photos., plans, secns.

WEINSTEIN ASSOCIATES ARCHITECTS
Escaping the box: ... Washington's 12 Best office buildings / James Goode. 1718 Connecticut Ave., NW (David M. Schwarz); 1250 24th St., NW (Don Hisaka & Assoc.); Republic
(Continued next page)

WELBANK, MICHAEL (CONTINUED)
Michael Welbank,....(CONTINUED)
urban areas as mobility guidance
systems for visually-disabled
pedestrians.
THE PLANNER 1990 June 1, v.76,
no.21, p.21, port.

WELCH & EPP ASSOCIATES
Design for access.
On two projects/reports: Access
Improvements Workbook and Design
for Access Guidebook prepared by
Adaptive Environments, Inc. and
Welch & Epp Associates.
PROGRESSIVE ARCHITECTURE 1990
Jan., v.71, no.1, p.125, dwgs.
Mental health center POE.
Report on the Quincy Mental Health
center prepared by Welch & Epp
Associates.
PROGRESSIVE ARCHITECTURE 1990
Jan., v.71, no.1, p.122, plan.

WELCH, FRANK
A walk in Tuscany / Frank Welch.
TEXAS ARCHITECT 1990 July-Aug.,
v.40, no.4, p.42-45, photos.

WELCH, H.
Van Zandput tot recreatieplas: Plan
"Natte Broek" wint
ideeenprijsvraag / Helene Damen.
Results of the "Maanderplas"
competition for a site south of
Ede, Netherlands. Winners: H.
Jansen, T. Thus, H. Welch.
DE ARCHITECT 1989 Dec., v.20,
no.12, p.30-31, site plans.

WELCH, POLLY
Excellence in urban development:
preliminary findings from a review
of the Rudy Bruner Award program /
Robert G. Shibley, Polly Welch.
Describes the biennial Rudy Bruner
Award for Excellence in the Urban
Environment. Awarded in 1989 and
1989 for "urban development
projects that achieve a synthesis
of competing goals and values."
URBAN LAND 1990 Sept., v.49, no.9,
p.7-10, ill., photos.

WELDED WIRE REINFORCEMENT
Meshing about / Graham Ridout.
On the use of tailored fabric
reinforcement in place of
reinforcement bars in Britain.
BUILDING 1990 Dec.7, v.255, no.48,
p.66-67, photos.

WELLER & SEBASTIAN
Heim mit Wohngruppen: Wohnheim fur
Behinderte in Worth am Rhein.
Architects: Weller & Sebastian.
DEUTSCHE BAUZEITUNG 1990 Feb.,
v.124, no.2, p.40-43, photos.,
plan, rooms, site plan.

WELLER, PETER
Fachstudienreise der
Architektenkammer Rheinland-Pfalz
nach London vom 24. bis 27. August
1989: Bericht und Resumee / Peter
Weller.
Report on German architects' tour:
England/High Tech.
DEUTSCHES ARCHITEKTENBLATT 1990
Jan.1, v.22, no.1, p.18-20,
photos.

WELLER, SAM
Cemeteries - designing for the
public / Sam Weller.
Outlines flaws in modern cemetery
design in Britain.
LANDSCAPE DESIGN 1989 Oct.,
no.184, p.10-11, photos.

WELLER, SUSAN NEUBERGER
Law: protecting your designs / Susan
Neuberger Weller.
On copyrights, trademark law and
design patents.
PROGRESSIVE ARCHITECTURE 1990
Aug., v.71, no.8, p.63,

WELLS
See also BAOLIS

WELLS, BRYAN WILLIAM
Trading in old silk ties [Merton
Abbey Mills] / Peter Weatherhead.
A derelict silk-printing works on
River Wandle, south London,
converted to new commercial uses.
Architects: John Dickinson and
Bryan Wells.
BUILDING 1990 Oct.5, v.255, no.39,
p.53-55, ill., photos.

WELLS, DOUGLAS A.
Streamlined reborn in Des Moines /
Mark E. Blunck.
Restoration and addition to Butler
House, built in the 1930s at Fleur
Drive and Bell Ave., for use by
Kragie/Newell Advertising.
Restoration architects: Douglas A.
Wells and Michael J. Kastner.
INLAND ARCHITECT 1990 Mar.-Apr.,
v.34, no.2, p.65-[68], photos.

**WELLS, H. G. (HERBERT GEORGE),
1866-1946. THINGS TO COME**
"Things to come": la transparenza
del futuro / Paola Antonelli.
On the film set of H.G. Wells'
1935 sci-fi novel. Text in Italian
and English.
DOMUS 1990 Sept., no.719,
p.[90-97], photos.

**WELLS--ISLAMIC--EGYPT--CAIRO--SYMBOLIC
ASPECTS**
The Cairene sabil: form and meaning
/ Saleh Lamei Mostafa.
MUQARNAS 1990, v.6, p.[33]-42,
photos., refs.

WELLS, MATTHEW
Step by step / Jose Manser.
On the work of architect/engineer
Matthew Wells.
DESIGNERS' JOURNAL 1990 Feb.,
no.54, p.52-55, dwgs., port.

WELLS, TED
Hastings leads the way in the
marketplace yet again / Ted Wells.
Preservation of commercial center
of Hastings, New Zealand by
innovative traffic
redistribution, and pedestrian
mall. Children's play area
features concrete sheep.
PLANNING QUARTERLY 1989 Sept.,
no.95, p.29-33, ports., photos.,
plan, secns.

WELLS-THORPE, JOHN ARTHUR
Bristol: Parkyn's progress.
Higlights eight recent commercial
and office projects. Architects
include Thornton Hartnell, MWT,
BGP Group, Leslie Jones
Architects, Alec Freneh
Partnership, John Wells-Thorpe,
and Richard Hemingway.
BUILDING 1990 Aug.31, v.255,
no.34, p.28-33, port., map,
photos.

WELSH, BRUCE C.
Metro's park-and-rides: busing up to
rail / Bruce C. Webb.
CITE: THE ARCHITECTURE AND DESIGN
REVIEW OF HOUSTON 1990 Fall,
no.25, p.12-13, photos.

WELSH, JOHN
Acropolis addition / John Welsh.
Features seven British entries in
the competition for the Acropolis
Museum, Athens.
BUILDING DESIGN 1990 May 25,
no.987, p.28-35, elevs., models,
maps, plans, secns., site plans,
sketches.
All mod cons / John Welsh.
On 2-unit office building, Cobham
Mews Studios, Camden Town, London.
Architects: David Chipperfield
Associates.
BUILDING DESIGN 1990 Feb.9,
no.972, p.22-23, axonometric view,
elev., photos., plans.
Alpine snow job / John Welsh.
Features Richard Horden's design
for a transportable ski hut.
BUILDING DESIGN 1990 Oct.26,
no.1009, p.30, models, sketches.
Altered States / John Welsh.
On the work of Bulgarian architect
Damian Stoyanov.
BUILDING DESIGN 1990 Mar.16,
no.977, p.22-23, axonometric view,
elevs., model, plan.
Appetite restored in Docklands /
John Welsh.
Features entries in a competition
for an isle of Dogs restaurant.
Winning architects: Rick Mather
Architects.
BUILDING DESIGN 1990 Mar.16,
no.977, p.10-11, secns., plan,
wxonometric views, elevs.,
sketches, isometric dwgs.
Avoiding urban bad manners / John
Welsh.
Multi-use office block and
studio/workshops building on York
Way, London. Architects: Chassay
Last.
BUILDING DESIGN 1990 Jan.5,
no.967, p.10, axonometric view,
ill., elev., plan.
Behind the facade / John Welsh.
Renovation of London office
building housed in 18th cent.
residential building, 23 Gosfield
Street. Architects: Future Systems
Consultants.
BUILDING DESIGN 1990 Aug.10-17,
no.998-999, p.8, elevs., model,
plans, secn.
Big enough for Birmingham / John
Welsh.
Features winning design for the
Birmingham Star Site business
center. Architects: Derek Walker
Associates.

(Continued next page)

WELSH, JOHN (CONTINUED)
Part of the furniture / John Welsh.
On the Scott Howard headquarters
building on Pentonville Road,
London. It features a replica of
the Georgian facade of the church
which used to stand on the site.
Architects: Allies and Morrison.
BUILDING DESIGN 1990 Sept.7,
no.1002, p.18, elev., photos.,
plan, secn.
Patent success / John Welsh.
On the European Patent Office,
Europees Octrooibureau, the Hague.
Architects: Neutelings en
Roodbeen.
BUILDING DESIGN 1990 Mar.23,
no.978, p.24-27, dwgs., aerial
photo, models, elevs.
Patience rewarded / John Welsh.
On the Glasgow Royal Concert Hall.
Architects: Sir Leslie Martin with
Robert Matthew, Johnson-Marshall &
Partners.
BUILDING DESIGN 1990 Oct.12,
no.1007, p.10-11, model, photos.,
plans, secns., site plan.
Planning authority / John Welsh.
On Rick Mather Architects'
development plan for the
University of East Anglia,
Norwich.
BUILDING DESIGN 1990 Nov.9,
no.1011, p.10-11, dwgs., models,
plans, secns., site plans.
Power to the people - but less of it
[exhibition review] / John Welsh.
Review of the exhibition on the
work of ECD Partnership, on view
at Smiths Gallery, Covent Garden,
London, Jan.22 - Feb.3, 1990.
BUILDING DESIGN 1990 Jan.19,
no.969, p.2, ill.
Red tape works wonders / John Welsh.
Competition for the European
Patent Office, Europees
Octrooibureau, the Hague. Joint
finalists: Pysall und Stahrenberg
Architekten, W. J. Neutelings and
Frank R. Roodbeen.
BUILDING DESIGN 1990 Feb.2,
no.971, p.12-13, dwgs., models,
secns., site plan.
Revitalising Antwerp / John Welsh.
Features winning design by Bureau
for Urban Design for the
renovation the old waterfront area
of Antwerp, called the "Islet".
BUILDING DESIGN 1990 July 6,
no.993, p.12, dwgs., site plans.
Road house / John Welsh.
On the London nightclub,
Subterania. Architects: Madigan &
Donald.
BUILDING DESIGN 1989 Oct., suppl.,
p.20-21, axonometric views,
photos., plans.
Rousseau's contract / John Welsh.
On architect Jacques Rousseau's
home, Maison Coloniale, Montreal.
BUILDING DESIGN 1990 July 6,
no.993, p.24-25, photos., plans,
model.
Rural seating / John Welsh.
On the new Rovo factory, Lossburg,
Germany. Architects: Mann und
Partner.
BUILDING DESIGN 1990 June 1,
no.988, p.18, models, secns.

WELSH, JOHN (CONTINUED)
Scarpa and the mothers of invention
/ John Welsh.
Barn in North Wales converted into
house for architect's parents.
Architects: Andrew Taylor, Pankaj
Patel.
BUILDING DESIGN 1990 Mar.2,
no.975, p.12, axonometric view,
det., elevs., plans, site plan.
Seeking new trains of thought for
Waverley / John Welsh.
On the Waverley Street Station
Competition, Edinburgh. First
prize: Price & Cullen.
BUILDING DESIGN 1990 Feb.23,
no.974, p.12, dwgs., photos.
Shelf life / John Welsh.
On the design for the Venice
Biennale bookstore. Architect:
James Stirling.
BUILDING DESIGN 1990 June 29,
no.992, p.24-25, axonometric
views, dwgs., elevs., models,
secns., site plans, sketches.
Shelter that spun off from space /
John Welsh.
On the Universal Shelter, designed
with heat-retaining fabric and
collapsible ribs. Future Systems
Consultants.
BUILDING DESIGN 1990 Jan.19,
no.969, p.12, dwgs., elev.,
photo., isometric dwg.
Siena doorway / John Welsh.
On the winning design for the bank
headquarters and chamber of
commerce in Siena. Architects:
Martorell, Bohigas, Mackay.
BUILDING DESIGN 1990 Apr.6,
no.980, p.10, axonometric view,
dwgs.
Six for Seville / John Welsh.
Features six UK entries for the
Seville Expo European Community
Pavilion competition.
BUILDING DESIGN 1990 Jan.26,
no.970, p.18-21, ill., elevs.,
models, plan, secn.
Slings and arrows / John Welsh.
Report on Aldo van Eyck's address
at the RIBA.
BUILDING DESIGN 1990 June 29,
no.992, p.2, port.
Sloane neighbour / John Welsh.
On the Clearings III speculative
office building, London.
Architects: Stanton & Williams,
YRM Partnership.
BUILDING DESIGN 1990 Oct.26,
no.1009, p.12, photos., plans,
site plans.
Social engineering for Brighton Rock
/ John Welsh.
Features refurbished interiors of
Laings Bar, Brighton. Architect:
Alan Phillips.
BUILDING DESIGN 1989 Oct., suppl.,
p.5-6, photos.
Spare art / John Welsh.
Features J. P. Morgan bank,
Amsterdam. Architect: Wim G.
Quist.
BUILDING DESIGN 1990 May 4,
no.984, p.20-21, photos., plans,
secn., site plan.
Speaking for itself / John Welsh.
Features interiors of HHCL
offices, London. Architects:
Harper MacKay.
BUILDING DESIGN 1990 Mar.16,
no.977, p.38, photos., plan.

WELSH, JOHN (CONTINUED)
Star roll / John Welsh.
On the Cardiff Bay Visitors'
Center. Architects: Alsop &
Lyall.
BUILDING DESIGN 1990 Nov.2,
no.1010, p.16,33, dets., photos.,
secns., sketches.
Stemming the tide / John Welsh.
On the Thames Quay office building
on the Isle of Dogs, London.
Architects: YRM Partnership.
BUILDING DESIGN 1990 Apr.13,
no.981, p.10, axonometric views,
photos., plan.
Stirling exchange / John Welsh.
On the work of James Stirling on
the occasion of the exhibition of
his designs at the Galleria
Communale d'Arte Moderna, Bologna.
BUILDING DESIGN 1990 Oct.5,
no.1006, p.2, port.
Stitch in time / John Welsh.
Features the Fitch RS London
office building, formed by two
renovated warehouses. Architects:
Fitch Benoy.
BUILDING DESIGN 1990 Aug.31,
no.1001, p.8-9, axonometric views,
photos., plans, secn.
Tight line / John Welsh.
On the Ludgate master plan,
London. Masterplanners: RHWL. New
buildings by Skidmore, Owings &
Merrill, RHWL and John Outram
Partnership.
BUILDING DESIGN 1990 May 4,
no.984, p.32-33, dwgs., elevs.,
site plans.
Towering individuals / John Welsh.
On Office building and multi-use
block, north of Brook Green, West
London. Architects: Wickham &
Associates.
BUILDING DESIGN 1990 Jan.19,
no.969, p.22-23, axonometric
views, elevs., models, map, plans,
secns., site plan.
Turning Japanese / John Welsh.
On the II Palazzo hotel, Fukuoka,
Japan. Architect: Aldo Rossi.
BUILDING DESIGN 1990 Mar.16,
no.977, p.24-25, photos., plans,
secns.
Urban deliberation / John Welsh.
Jessica Square office development,
Wandsworth, London. Architects:
Munkenbeck & Marshall.
BUILDING DESIGN 1990 Apr.27,
no.983, p.22-23, axonometric
views, dwgs., models, plans, site
plans.
Water works / John Welsh.
Features winning design for
Genoa's Piazza Dante Competeition.
Architects: Machado and Silvetti.
BUILDING DESIGN 1990 Mar.23,
no.978, p.12, dwgs., site plans.
Where there's hope there's life /
John Welsh.
Features Hopewell Yard,
Camberwell, South London.
Architects: David Quigley
Architects.
BUILDING DESIGN 1990 Oct.26,
no.1009, p.16, photos., plans.
Winning Irish modesty / John Welsh.
Features seven winners of the New
Architecture Awards of the
Architectural Association of
Ireland.
BUILDING DESIGN 1990 Jan.12,
(Continued next page)

WESTON, RICHARD (CONTINUED)
Finnish feast: C. L. Engel:
architect and city planner,
1778-1840 [exhibition review] /
Richard Weston.
Exhibition in the Cathedral Crypt,
Helsinki, Aug. to 14 Sept. 1990.
ARCHITECTS' JOURNAL 1990 Sept.19,
v.192, no.12, p.84-85, dwgs.,
elev., plans, secn.
Finnish modernism: An architectural
present: seven approaches
[exhibition review] / Richard
Weston.
Exhibition at the Museum of
Finnish Architecture, Helsinki,
through 14 Sept. 1990, then
touring to Stockholm.
ARCHITECTS' JOURNAL 1990 Sept.12,
v.192, no.11, p.82-84, dwg.,
models, photos.
Kajaani culture / Richard Weston.
Kajaani cultural center.
Architect: Juha Leiviska.
ARCHITECTURAL REVIEW 1990 Mar.,
v.187, no.1117, p.67-71, elevs.,
models, photos., plans, secns.,
site plans.
The other China: China's vernacular
architecture: house form and
culture, by Ronald G. Knapp [book
review] / Richard Weston.
ARCHITECTS' JOURNAL 1990 Mar.14,
v.191, no.11, p.94, axonometric
view.
Second thoughts [Portsmouth
Polytechnic Library, Phase 2] /
Richard Weston.
13 years separate the design and
construction of the first and
second phases of Frewen Library,
Portsmouth Polytechnic (Eng.).
Architects: Ahrends Burton and
Koralek.
ARCHITECTS' JOURNAL 1990 Jan.24,
v.191, no.4, p.44-51, elevs.,
photos., secns., site plans,
sketch. aerial photo.

WESTON WILLIAMSON ARCHITECTS AND
DESIGNERS
Frontis [Marketplace, London] /
Richard Wilcock.
London warehouse near London
Bridge station, converted into
corporate office building for
Marketplace, an advertising
agency. Architects: Weston
Williamson.
RIBA JOURNAL 1990 Oct., v.97,
no.10, p.6-8, photos.
School prizes / Clare Melhuish.
Features three entries in the
competition for King Alfred's
School, Golders Green, London.
Winning architects: Van Heyningen
and Haward Architects. Other
entries by Weston Williamson
Architects and Chris Wilkinson
Architects.
BUILDING DESIGN 1990 Sept.14,
no.1003, p.30-31, axonometric
view, dwgs., plans, site plans.

WESTON WILLIAMSON ARCHITECTS AND
PLANNERS
Going into details / Clare Melhuish.
On the work of Weston Williamson
Architects and Designers.
BUILDING DESIGN 1990 Feb.23,
no.974, p.20-23, dwgs., photos.,
plan.

WESTPHAL, UWE
Architecture and advertising in
Third Reich Germany / Uwe
Westphal.
RASSEGNA 1990 Sept., v.12,
no.43/3, p.58-69, ill., photos.,
refs.

WESTPHALEN, JOSEPH V.
Im Namen der "Rose": Gesprache uber
die letzten Dinge / Joseph v.
Westphalen.
BAUWELT 1990 Jan.19, v.81, no.2-3,
p.111-115, photo.

WESTRING, DANA
Overhead, the valiant ceiling:
gazing upward at a brilliant
mural.
Mural in Washington, D.C., home of
Bob Waldron, painted by Dana
Westring.
SOUTHERN ACCENTS 1990 June, v.13,
no.5, p.128, photo.

WESTRUP, PETER
High Tech ubergestulpt:
Ortsvermittlungstelle in Frankfurt
am Main.
Architects: von Lamatsch-Kaempfe,
Westrup.
DEUTSCHE BAUZEITUNG 1990 Dec.,
v.124, no.12, p.18-21, axonometric
views, photos., plans, secns.
Mitten im Wohngebiet: Erweiterung
einer Ortsvermittlungsstelle bei
Hanau.
Architects: von Lamatsch-Kaempfe,
Westrup.
DEUTSCHE BAUZEITUNG 1990 Dec.,
v.124, no.12, p.22-23, axonometric
views, elevs., plan, secn.

WESTWOOD, COLIN, 1920-
Recorder of the broken wave / Robert
Elwall.
On the Colin Westwood Collection
in the British Architectural
Library's photographs collection.
RIBA JOURNAL 1990 Nov., v.97,
no.11, p.50-52, photos.

WETLANDS--CONSERVATION AND
RESTORATION--UNITED STATES--FAIR
OAKS (VIRGINIA)--HIGH RIDGE OFFICE
PARK
A stormwater pond is wetlands
mitigation amenity.
Stormwater management results in
expanded and protected wetlands
environment at High Ridge Office
Park, Fair Oaks, Va. Engineers and
designers: Greenhorne & O'Mara.
URBAN LAND 1990 Dec., v.49, no.12,
p.28-29, plan, secns.

WETLANDS--CONSERVATION AND
RESTORATION--UNITED STATES--FLORIDA
Balancing new development with
conservation of wetlands in
Florida / James R. Brindell.
URBAN LAW AND POLICY 1988, v.9,
no.4, p.331-344, biblio.

WETLANDS--UNITED STATES--WORCESTER
COUNTY (MARYLAND)
Bay patrol: a Maryland coastal
community fends off developers /
Jeff Weintraub, Mary Lou
Gallagher.
In Worcester County, Maryland, on
the mainland across from Ocean
City.
PLANNING 1990 Oct., v.56, no.10,
p.22-23, maps, photos., aerial
photo.

WEXNER, LESLIE H., 1937-
Unlimited vision [Leslie Wexner] /
Lynn Nesmith.
Buildings designed under the
patronage of Wexner. Architects:
Beyer Blinder Belle and Graham
Gund Architects; Jaquelin
Robertson, Hanna / Olin.
ARCHITECTURE: THE AIA JOURNAL 1990
Dec., v.79, no.12, p.[66]-73,
elevs., photos., plans, site
plans.

WEYMOUTH, VICTORIA
Edwardian revival: decorator Lady
Victoria Weymouth recalls the
gilded age in John Singer
Sargent's London house / Patrick
Kinmonth.
HOUSE & GARDEN 1990 May, v.162,
no.5, p.[172-177], port., photos.

WHALEN, MICHAEL E.
Defining buried features before
excavation: a case from the
American Southwest / Michael E.
Whalen.
On the appliction of soil coring
and augering techniques in a study
area known as the Hueco Bolson,
near El Paso, Tex. Includes
abstract.
JOURNAL OF FIELD ARCHAEOLOGY 1990
Fall, v.17, no.3, p.323-331,
graph, photos., site plans,
tables, biblio.

WHALLEY, ANDREW
Scottish sunhouse.
Features the Whalley house
(architect's parents) near the
Village of Dollar, Scotland, which
utilizes local materials and the
latest in glazing technology.
Architects: Fiona Galbraith,
Andrew Whalley.
ARCHITECTURAL REVIEW 1990 Dec.,
v.188, no.1126, p.[57]-61,
Una trave "reattiva" = Responsive
trusses / Christopher McCarthy,
Andrew Whalley.
Experimental "responsive truss"
design; architects: Fiona
Galbraith, Christopher McCarthy,
Andrew Whalley.
L'ARCA 1990 Oct., no.42, p.56-61,
diagrs., dwgs, model.
Warmender Kristall: Haus Whalley,
Kellyburn Bridge, Dollar,
Schottland.
Architects: Andrew Whalley, Fiona
Galbraith.
ARCH PLUS 1990 July, no.104, p.36,
dwgs., photos., plan, secn.

WHITE ARKITEKTER (CONTINUED)

Lilla Bommen, Goteborg / Ralph Erskine.
Multi-storey office building. Architects: Ralph Erskine and White Arkitekter. Includes commentary by Olof Hultin.
ARKITEKTUR: THE SWEDISH REVIEW OF ARCHITECTURE 1990 May, v.90, no.4, p.12-21, cover, photos., plans, secn., site plans.

Lundagard - ett tradfornyclseprojekt.
Competition for change to the 1746 plan by Harleman, with winning projects by Sven-Ingvar Andersson, White Arkitekter and Anders Johansson, and Jeppe Aagaard Andersen. Includes English captions and summary.
LANDSKAB 1990 Aug., v.71, no.5, p.59-70,76, dwgs., model, photos., plans.

Moderne kunst i tidligere el-vaerk / Lasse Freisleben.
Renovation of a 90-year old gasworks on Gasverksgatan/Stora Nygatan, Malmo, Sweden for use as an exhibition hall for modern art. Original architect: John Smedberg. Restoration architect: White Arkitekter.
ARKITEKTEN 1989 Dec.12, v.91, no.22, p.A544-A546, photos., plan.

Il porto che cambia = Converting the port: Goteborg / Pietro Raffeone.
Abandoned harbor and shipyards to be redeveloped. Architects: Ralph Erskine; White Arkitekter; Pietro Raffone; Arkitektlaget.
ABITARE 1990 July-Aug., no.287, p.216-[223], dwg., model, photos., plan, site plans.

Volvo Uddevalla / Gunnar Werner.
Automobile factory located at F d Uddevallavarvet. Architects: White arkitekter, Mitchell Giurgola Architects, AKOS arkitektkontor. Includes commentary by Anders Tornqvist and Peter Ullmark.
ARKITEKTUR: THE SWEDISH REVIEW OF ARCHITECTURE 1990 Jan.-Feb., v.90, no.1, p.38-47, photos., plans, site plans, sketches.

WHITE BUDD VAN NESS PARTNERSHIP

Supplanting the state-office stereotype / Joel Warren Barna.
Brown-Heatly State Office Building, Austin. Architects: White Budd Van Ness Partnership.
TEXAS ARCHITECT 1990 July-Aug., v.40, no.4, p.49, photos., plan.

WHITE, DAVID

Gebaudebeispiel: Vorabdruck aus dem neuen Dachatlas Geneigte Dacher.
Roof details from 4 projects: swimming center, Albstadt, W.G. (P.Siefert et al); housing development, Gebensdorf, Switzerland (C. Tognola, C. Stahel, D. Zulauf); student housing, Wales (D. Lea); and housing for handicapped, Eastleigh, England (D. White).
DETAIL 1990 Feb.-Mar., v.30, no.1, p.[16-23], dets., elev., photos., plans, secns., site plans.

WHITE, EDMUND

Back to Mackinac ... an island in the Great Lakes / Edmund White.
Intact Victorian resort on this northern Mich. island.
HOUSE & GARDEN 1990 June, v.162, no.6, p.158-[169], photos.

Russian reverie: Yves Saint Laurent retreats to a dacha on his Norman estate / Edmund White.
Russian-style dacha near his chateau at Deauville.
HOUSE & GARDEN 1990 Jan., v.162, no.1, p.[118-123],146, port., photos.

Sharp focus: an American photographer in Paris arranges the fragments of his domestic life / Edmund White.
The house of David Seidner.
HOUSE & GARDEN 1990 Feb., v.162, no.2, p.132-137, port., photos.

WHITE, GEORGE M. (GEORGE MALCOLM), 1920-

George White, Architect of the Capitol / Donald J. Canty.
ARCHITECTURAL RECORD 1990 June, v.178, no.7, p.43-44, port., model, photo.

WHITE, MICHAEL D.

Lighting: optical control and shielding / Michael D. White.
Emphasis on downlights.
INTERIOR DESIGN 1990 Mar., v.61, no.5, p.184-185, dwg.

WHITE, ROGER

Home counties child: Classical design in the late twentieth century: the recent work of Robert Adam [exhibition review] / Roger White.
Exhibition at the Heinz Gallery, London, through 20 Dec. 1990.
ARCHITECTS' JOURNAL 1990 Dec.12, v.192, no.24, p.54-55, ports., elev., photo., sketch.

WHITE, SAMUEL

How three architects market themselves / Nicholas J. Polites.
Marketing strategies of Samuel White, Leland Cott, and Hugh Jacobsen.
ARCHITECTURAL RECORD 1990 July, v.178, no.8, p.27-28, ports.

WHITE, WILLIAM, 1825-1900

Ardent simplicity / Clive Wainwright.
Furnishings of Bishops Court house, Devon; architect: William White.
COUNTRY LIFE 1990 Oct.18 v.184, no.42, p.150-151,154, photos.

Bishops Court, Devon / Chris Brooks.
Architect: William White.
COUNTRY LIFE 1990 Feb.15, v.184, no.7, p.54-58, photos.

WHITE, WILLIAM, 1925-1990

William (Bill) White [obituary] / Sid Tasker.
RIBA JOURNAL 1990 Dec., v.97, no.12, p.85.

WHITEHAND, J. W. R.

Development pressure, development control and suburban townscape change: case studies in south-east England / J. W. R. Whitehand.
TOWN PLANNING REVIEW 1989 Oct., v.60, no.4, p.403-420, map, photos., site plans, tables, refs.

WHITEHEAD, DAVID

Summer deadline for Moscow trio.
Three British competition entries for Moscow's Chamber Theatre Arts Centre in the Hermitage Gardens: Peter Baynes and David Whitehead; John Seifert; and Mills Beaumont Leavy (MBL).
ARCHITECTS' JOURNAL 1990 Sept.26, v.192, no.13, p.12-13, axonometric view, elev., model, secns., sketches.

WHITELEY, MARY

Les pieces privees de l'appartement du roi au chateau de Vincennes / Mary Whiteley.
BULLETIN MONUMENTAL 1990, v.148, no.1, p.[83]-85, plans.

WHITELEY, NIGEL

Banham and "Otherness": Reyner Banham (1922-1988) and his quest for an architecture autre / Nigel Whiteley.
ARCHITECTURAL HISTORY 1990, v.33, p.[188]-221, axonometric views, dwgs., photos., refs.

WHITEMAN, JOHN

Eat it! A dead fragment on how Louis Sullivan dies / John Whileman.
INLAND ARCHITECT 1990 May-June, v.34, no.3, p.111, photo.

WHITESELL, MIKE

Getting the lead out of bridge coatings / Mike Whitesell.
"Significant changes have taken place in terms of environmental regualtions governing bridge coatings."
AMERICAN CITY & COUNTY 1990 May, v.105, no.5, p.96-99.

WHITESON, LEON

Angeleno abstraction: Arango/Berry House, Los Angeles, California / Leon Whiteson.
Architect: Franklin D. Israel Design Associates.
ARCHITECTURE: THE AIA JOURNAL 1990 Mar., v.79, no.3, p.[150]-153, axonometric view, photos.

A feast for the eyes / Leon Whiteson.
On the Maple Drive Restaurant, Beverly Hills, Calif. Architects: L. Anthony Greenberg, Widom Wein Cohen.
PROGRESSIVE ARCHITECTURE 1990 Sept., v.71, no.9, p.116-[119], photos., plan.

Giorgio Dazzan: a contemporary Malibu residence with a Pacific orientation / Leon Whiteson.
Features architect's home.
ARCHITECTURAL DIGEST 1990 Sept., v.47, no.10, p.[82-85],106, axonometric view, port., photos.

WHITESON, LEON (CONTINUED)
Grand illusion: the Aventine, La
Jolla, California, Michael Graves,
Architect / Leon Whiteson.
Mixed-use complex.
ARCHITECTURE: THE MAGAZINE OF THE
AMERICAN INSTITUTE OF ARCHITECTS
1990 Aug., v.79, no.8, p.[66]-71,
elev., photos., plan, site plan.
Kentucky home: Kentucky Fried
Chicken, Los Angeles, California,
Grinstein/Daniels, Architects /
Leon Whiteson.
ARCHITECTURE: THE AIA JOURNAL 1990
Oct., v.79, no.10, p.52-55,
photos., plans, secns., site plan.
L.A.'s Central City West plan
accents enlightened development /
Leon Whiteson.
Successful public-private
partnership for the development of
the Central City West district of
Los Angeles.
URBAN LAND 1990 Dec., v.49, no.12,
p.10-15, dwgs., site plans.
Moore Ruble Yudell: a Malibu
residence rooted in California's
Spanish Colonial traditions / Leon
Whiteson.
Cliffside residence. Architects:
Moore, Ruble, Yudell.
ARCHITECTURAL DIGEST 1990 Feb.,
v.47, no.2, p.[86]-91,114, port.,
photos.

WHITNEY, DAVID
Structures for development
partnerships in the 1990s:
practice in West Yorkshire / David
Whitney, Graham Haughton.
THE PLANNER 1990 June 1, v.76,
no.21, p.15-19, photos., refs.

WHITNEY MUSEUM OF AMERICAN ART,
DOWNTOWN AT FEDERAL RESERVE PLAZA--
EXHIBITIONS
Sistemazioni domestiche = domestic
arrangements / Patricia Phillips.
On the second installation by Tod
Williams and Billie Tsien, at the
Whitney Museum of American Art
branch at Federal Plaza. In
Italian and English.
OTTAGONO 1990 Dec., no.97,
p.17-[23], models, photos.
Tod Williams, Billie Tsien: Domestic
Arrangements.
The architects discuss their house
on exhibit at the Walker Art
Center and the Whitney Museum. In
Italian and English.
DOMUS 1990 June, no.717,
p.[58-65], photos., plan.
Williams & Tsien's Walker
experiments [exhibition review] /
Bruce Wright.
On the exhibition, Domestic
Arrangements on view at the
Whitney Museum Downtown at Federal
Reserve Plaza, New York, Mar.
14-May 18, 1990.
PROGRESSIVE ARCHITECTURE 1990
Feb., v.71, no.2, p.24, photo.

WHITTED, MICHAEL
Whither GIS? / Michael Whitted.
Alternatives to GIS.
AMERICAN CITY & COUNTY 1990 Aug.,
v.105, no.8, p.52-[58], maps,
aerial photo.

WHITTEMORE, ELLEN
Exploring the elements of urban
design.
Student projects for two sites in
greater Boston, for Elements of
Urban Design course taught by
Peter G. Rowe and Ellen
Whittemore.
GSD NEWS / HARVARD UNIVERSITY.
GRADUATE SCHOOL OF DESIGN 1990
Spring, v.18, no.4, p.15, dwg.,
models, site plan.

WHITTINGTON, DALE
Planning in squatter settlements: an
interview with a community leader
/ Donald T. Lauria, Dale
Whittington.
In Latin America.
JOURNAL OF PLANNING EDUCATION AND
RESEARCH 1990 summer, v.9, no.3,
p.207-212.

WHITWORTH ART GALLERY--EXHIBITION
Wallflowers: A popular art: British
wallpapers, 1930-1960 [exhibition
review] / Gillian Darley.
Exhibition at the Orleans House
Gallery, Twickenham, through
Feb.11, 1990; then the Whitworth
Art Gallery, University of
Manchester, 16 Mar.-28 Apr.1990.
ARCHITECTS' JOURNAL 1990 Jan.17,
v.191, no.3, p.80-82, ill.

WHITZMAN, CAROLYN
Community and design: against the
solution St. James Town / Carolyn
Whitzman.
Problems with maintenance and
management of 1960s high-rise
residential development which
served as a prototype for Toronto
and other Canadian cities.
CITY MAGAZINE 1989 Summer-Fall,
v.11, no.1, p.32-36, photo., plan.

WHYSALL, PAUL
The Addison Act and the local
authority response: housing policy
formulation and implementation in
Nottingham 1917-1922 / Roger
Smith, Paul Whysall.
TOWN PLANNING REVIEW 1990 Apr.,
v.61, no.2, p.185-206, photos.,
plans, refs.

WHYTE, WILLIAM
Taking it to the streets: expert
prescriptions for healthy urban
arteries / Jane Jacobs.
Includes "The sensory street", an
excerpt from City; Rediscovering
the Center, by William Whyte.
CARTOUCHE 1990 Winter, v.19,
p.14-16.

WICH HOUSES
See SALT HOUSES

WICK, CLARA
Il museo nella fabbrica = Museum in
a factory / Clara Wick, Davide
Montovani.
Former sugar mill converted to
museum and display facility;
architects for conversion:
Giuseppe Gambirasio, Guglielmo
Zambrini, Loris Macci.
L'ARCA 1990 Feb., no.35, p.62-67,
axonometric view, elevs., photos,
secns.
Il progetto della luce "The lighting
project" / Clara Wick.
CAD software program to visualize
effects of lighting systems
developed by Philip Eindhoven
Laboratories. Text in Italian and
English.
L'ARCA 1990 June, no.39, p.84-85,
charts, photos.

WICKBERG, NILS ERIK
Nils Erik Wickbergin teemat /
Vilhelm Helander.
ARKKITEHTI 1989, v.86, no.7,
p.74-77, ill., port.

WICKBERG, NILS ERIK, 1909-. STADER,
BYGGNADER
Egna Ogon & Andras [book review] /
Rasmus Waern.
Review of Varlden den lilla den
stora: Lustvandringar i
Klassicismens arkitektur och
tradgardar, by Anna-Maria Blenow
and Olle Svedberg, and Stader,
byggnader..., by Nils Erik
Wickberg.
ARKITEKTUR: THE SWEDISH REVIEW OF
ARCHITECTURE 1990 Nov., v.90,
no.9, p.55-57, dwg., photos.

WICKE, HARALD
Gestaltung von Strassen, Gassen und
Platzen im Altstadtbereich von
Passau = Design of streets, alleys
and squares in the old town of
Passau.
Competition. Winning architects:
Werner Roth, Heinrich Schell,
Harald Wicke. Text in German.
ARCHITEKTUR + WETTBEWERBE 1990
Dec., no.144, p.64-67, site plans,
photos.

WICKHAM & ASSOCIATES
Towering individuals / John Welsh.
On Office building and multi-use
block, north of Brook Green, West
London. Architects: Wickham &
Associates.
BUILDING DESIGN 1990 Jan.19,
no.969, p.22-23, axonometric
views, elevs., models, map, plans,
secns., site plan.
Wickham in Waltham / Peter Davey.
Public housing, Waltham Forest,
London. Architects: Wickham &
Associates.
ARCHITECTURAL REVIEW 1990 Oct.,
v.188, no.1124, p.[59-64],
axonometric view, dwg., photos.,
plans, secns., site plans.

WICKMAN, GUSTAF, 1858-1916
Le chiese, luoghi di aggregazione =
Churches, places of cohesion /
Carl Goran Bergman.
Markuskyran, Skarphack, 1900 (D.
Lewerentz); church at Nacka (G.
Wickman; additions by Carl Nyren);
(Continued next page)

WICKMAN, GUSTAF, 1858-1916
(CONTINUED)
Le chiese, luoghi di...(CONTINUED)
Gammelstad church.
ABITARE 1990 July-Aug., no.287,
p.184-189, elev., photos., plans,
site plan.

WIDBOM, MATS
Mellan hem och Yttervarld / Mats
Widbom.
Report on a seminar on
ethnological aspects of domestic
architecture.
ARKITEKTUR: THE SWEDISH REVIEW OF
ARCHITECTURE 1990 Aug., v.90,
no.6, p.32-33, photo.

WIDDICOMBE, SARAH
Height without trees / Sarah
Widdicombe.
Garden structures. Includes a list
of suppliers.
TRADITIONAL HOMES 1990 May, v.6,
no.8, p.99-101, photos., biblio.

WIDMANN, SAMPO, 1942-
Architektur unterwegs.
Four projects: Austellungshalle
"Alter Bahnhof", Rosenheim
(architect: Joseph Karg); Rathaus
Husum am Binnenhafen, Husum
(architect: Patschan - Werner -
Winking); Schulpark
Gottingen-Weende, Gottingen
(landscape architect: Gunther
Quentin); Bayerische
Demonstrativbaum-assnahme,
Passau-Neustift (architect: Herman
Schroder & Sampo Widmann).
DEUTSCHES ARCHITEKTENBLATT 1990
May 1, v.22, no.5, p.727-730,
elevs., photos., plans, secn.,
site plans.
Aussegnungshalle in Eching.
Architects: Sampo Widmann, Stephan
Romero.
DEUTSCHE BAUZEITSCHRIFT 1990 Feb.,
v.38, no.2, p.199-204, dets.,
dwg., elevs., photos., plans.
Einfach gut: Haus eines Kunstlers,
Oberbeuern, Baden-Baden.
Architect: Sampo Widmann.
DEUTSCHE BAUZEITUNG 1990 Aug.,
v.124, no.8, p.14-21, dets.,
photos., secn.
In der Provinz: Gartenwohnanlage
Dietersheim / Oliver G. Hamm.
Architect: Sampo Widmann.
DEUTSCHE BAUZEITUNG 1990 Aug.,
v.124, no.8, p.22-25, elevs.,
photos., plans, secn.
Wohnhaus mit Atelier in Baden-Baden.
Built 1989. Architect: Sampo
Widmann. Includes English summary.
BAUMEISTER 1990 Jan., v.87, no.1,
p.56-58, photos., plans, secn.
Wohnungspolitische Konzepte:
Wohnungsbauprojekte / Rudi Kujath.
Section on many new housing
projects in Germany. Contents:
Berlin, by Rudi Kujath.--Koln, by
Uwe Kessler.--Bayern, by Dieter
Gutekunst.--Frankfurt, by Martin
Wentz.--Hannover, by Hanns
Adrian.--Der LEG
Nordrhein-Westfalen, by Roswitha
Sinz.--Anmerkungen..., by Hartmut
Grosshans. Among the architects
represented are Otto Steidle +
Partner; Andreas Brandt & Rudolf
Bottcher; Joachim Ganz, Walter
(Continued next column)

WIDMANN, SAMPO, 1942- (CONTINUED)
Wohnungspolitische...(CONTINUED)
Rolfes; Axel Schultes; Wolfgang
Scharlach and Rainer Wischhusen;
Rebecca Chestnutt et al; Hubertus
Hoffmann; Paul Petry; Hermann
Schroder, Sampo Widmann; Gerhart
Laage; Freed Ahrens.
BAUWELT 1990 Mar.30, v.81, no.12,
p.572-598, elevs., plans, secns.,
site plans, tables.

WIDMAYER, PETRA
Information, Design, und
Gesellschaft im zukunftigen Europa
/ Petra Widmayer.
Report on a seminar held on
Dec.8-9, 1989 in Darmstadt by the
Deutsche Werkbund e.V. Title:
Euro-Design - Information, Design,
Gesellschaft und Europa.
BAUWELT 1990 Jan.19, v.81, no.2-3,
p.61.
Interieur '90 in Kortrijk
[exhibition review] / Petra
Widmayer.
The 12th annual exhibit, held
Oct.18-28,1990.
BAUWELT 1990 Dec.1, v.81, no.45,
p.2237-2238.

WIDOM WEIN COHEN
Drawing to learn / Andrea Loukin.
On presentation drawings by the
firm Widom Wein Cohen. This is the
second article in a periodic
series on alternative techniques
used for presentation drawings.
INTERIOR DESIGN 1990 May, v.61,
no.7, p.224-227, dwgs.
A feast for the eyes / Leon
Whiteson.
On the Maple Drive Restaurant,
Beverly Hills, Calif. Architects:
L. Anthony Greenberg, Widom Wein
Cohen.
PROGRESSIVE ARCHITECTURE 1990
Sept., v.71, no.9, p.116-[119],
photos., plan.
Utopia revised: at the University of
California at Irvine, the struggle
to adapt the unyielding geometry
of the campus continues / John
Parman.
On William Pereira's 1963 master
plan, and subsequent buildings by
other architects.
ARCHITECTURE: THE AIA JOURNAL 1990
Jan., v.79, no.1, p.66-77, dwg.,
elev., photos., plans, site plans.

WIEBENGA, JAN GERKO, 1886-1974
Gered en toch verloren: restauratie
school Wiebenga Aalsmeer / Arjen
Oosterman, Dick Kuhn.
Built in 1930, restored in 1989.
DE ARCHITECT 1989 Oct., v.20,
no.10, p.95-99, port., photos.,
plans.

WIEDEWELT, JOHANNES, 1731-1802
Wiedewelts mindestotter i
Jaegerspris = Wiedewelt's memorial
columns in Jaegerspris / Else
Marie Bukdahl.
Subtitle: The sharp profile of
neoclassicism and the pre-Romantic
open space of cognition. Sculptor:
Johannes Wiedewelt. In Danish and
English.
SKALA 1990, no.22, p.d18-21,
photos., refs.

WIEGAND HOFFMANN, NANY
Good buys to Berlin / Tim Clark.
Interior of architect Nany Wiegand
Hoffman's apartment in Berlin.
THE WORLD OF INTERIORS 1990 Nov.,
p.[186]-193, port., photos.

WIEGERSMA, LODEWIJK
Vier parken voor beverwijk:
meervoudige opdracht laat grote
diversiteit zien / David Louwerse.
Landscape designs by Lodewijk
Wiegersma, Van Empelen/Van
Aalderen, West 8, and Ecoplan.
DE ARCHITECT THEMA 1990 Sept.,
v.21, no.9 suppl., p.37-43, dwgs.,
model, photo., site plans.

WIELAND, HORST
Bestandsaufnahme und Neuorientierung
in der DDR - von der
"Projektierung" zur "Planung" /
Horst Wieland.
DEUTSCHES ARCHITEKTENBLATT 1990
May 1, v.22, no.5, p.741-742,
chart.

WIEMER, WOLFGANG
Digitale Bildverarbeitung in der
Kunstwissenschaft: eine Datenbank
zur Proportionsanalyse
mittelalterlicher Kirchen /
Wolfgang Wiemer.
KUNSTCHRONIK 1990 Feb., v.43,
no.2, p.55-62,plate 3, chart,
biblio.

WIENANDS, RUDOLF
Beschwingt: Umbau der Hypo-Bank
Munchen-Sud.
Architects: Rudolf Wienands.
ARCHITEKTUR, INNENARCHITEKTUR,
TECHNISCHER AUSBAU 1990 Dec.,
v.98, no.12, p.38-41, elev.,
photos., plan.

WIERDA, SYTZE
Die onderbroke stad / S.W. le Roux,
D. Holm.
Pretoria's civic architecture
bears the stamp of Sytze Wierdz.
In Africaans, with English
summary.
ARCHITECTURE SA = ARGITEKTUUR SA
1989 May-June, no.5-6, p.30-34,
dets., dwg., photos., engr.,
biblio., refs.

WIERSMA, ERIK
De architect als koning in
Prinsenland / Wijnand Looise, Erik
Wiersma.
One of several articles in
Themanummer 41: "Thema:
architectuur en macht." Reviews
new buildings in a district in
Rotterdam.
DE ARCHITECT THEMA 1990 Nov.,
v.21, no.11 suppl., p.40-45,
model, photos., site plans.

WIESE-VON OFEN, IRENE
Das Wachstum steuern.
Issue devoted to recent city
planning projects in Germany.
Includes essays by Karl Ganser,
Ulrich Pfeiffer, and Irene
Wiese-von Ofen. Most articles
indexed separately.
BAUWELT 1990 Sept.28, v.81, no.36,
p.cover,[1782-1792],1814-1815,
ill.

WIESENTHAL, KONRAD
Ein Haus im Walde: Neubau eines
Wohnhauses in Sundern.
Jansen house. Architect: Konrad
Wiesenthal.
ARCHITEKTUR, INNENARCHITEKTUR,
TECHNISCHER AUSBAU 1990 Jan.-Feb.,
v.98, no.1-2, p.26-28, elevs.,
photos., plan.

WIESER, HARALD
Merkur-Market [Bad Voslau].
Architect: Harald Wieser.
BAUFORUM 1990, v.23, no.136,
p.62-63,85, photos., plans.

WIESLER, HERMANN
Architekturzitat als szenische Macht
/ Hermann Wiesler.
BAUWELT 1990 July 27, v.81, no.28,
p.1428-1433, dwg., photo., site
plans.

WIESNER, THOMAS, 1956-
Barcelona / Peder Boas Jensen ...
[et al.].
Theme of issue. Contents: By
eller OL, by Peder Boas Jensen and
Elith Juul Moller.-- Idraettens
arenaer, by Ebbe Melgaard.--
Kataloniens hovedstad, by Jorgen
Sestoft.-- Gensyn med Gaudi, by
Nils-Ole Lund.-- Parkerne i
Barcelona, by Jorgen Peder Hansen
and Anna Maria Indrio.-- Den
nordiske inspiration, by Nils-Ole
Lund.-- Ny katalansk arkitektur,
by Jan Christiansen and Gosta
Knudsen.-- Miralles og Pinos, by
Thomas Wiesner.
ARKITEKTEN 1990 May, v.92, no.7,
p.[212]-249,cover, axonometric
views, diagrs., maps, photos.,
secns., aerial photos., biblios.
Mietwohnungsbau in Deutschland:
Ideenwettbewerb 89.
Competition sponsored by Deutsches
Architektenblatt and
Transportbeton. First prize
winners (four projects): Merete
Ahnfeldt-Mollerup and Thomas
Wiesner, Nicola Kaiser and Jurgen
Reichstein, Fritz Matzinger, and
Robert Kapitonow. Eight additional
entries are illustrated.
DEUTSCHES ARCHITEKTENBLATT 1990
Jan.1, v.22, no.1, p.59-74,
axonometric views, dwgs., port.,
models, plans, secns., site plans.

WIG, SIDDHARTHA
Baron Palace, Cairo , Egypt / Veena
Wig, Siddhartha Wig.
Built in the late 1920s and
influenced by Hindu temples and
sculpture. Architects included
Alexander Marcel.
ARCHITECTURE + DESIGN 1990
July-Aug., v.7, no.4, p.16-17,
photos.

WIG, VEENA
Baron Palace, Cairo , Egypt / Veena
Wig, Siddhartha Wig.
Built in the late 1920s and
influenced by Hindu temples and
sculpture. Architects included
Alexander Marcel.
ARCHITECTURE + DESIGN 1990
July-Aug., v.7, no.4, p.16-17,
photos.

WIGGINS, LYNA L.
California planning agency
experiences with automated mapping
and geographic information systems
/ S.P. French, L.L. Wiggins.
ENVIRONMENT AND PLANNING B 1990
Oct., v.17, no.4, p.441-450,
tables, refs.
Computer adoption and use in
California planning agencies:
implications for education /
Steven P. French, Lyna L. Wiggins.
JOURNAL OF PLANNING EDUCATION AND
RESEARCH 1989 Winter, v.8, no.2,
p.97-108, charts, graphs, refs.

WIGGINS, LYNN L.
Planning with hypermedia: combining
text, graphics, sound, and video /
Lynn L. Wiggins, Michael J.
Shiffer.
AMERICAN PLANNING ASSOCIATION.
JOURNAL 1990 Spring, v.56, no.2,
p.226-235, ill., map, photos.,
refs.

WIGLEY, MARK
La contraddizione decorata = The
decorated gap / Mark Wigley.
On Denise Scott-Brown and Robert
Venturi's work, including
"Complexity and contradiction in
architecture" and "Learning from
Las Vegas."
OTTAGONO 1990 Mar., no.94,
p.36-55, dwgs., elevs., models,
photos., plans, secns., sketches,
refs.
La disciplina dell'architettura =
The discipline of architecture /
Mark Wigley.
OTTAGONO 1990 Sept., no.96,
p.19-27, ill., refs.

WIGREN, CHRISTOPHER
Ashford: farmland easement /
Christopphter Wigren.
30 acres of open farmland
surrounding 19th-cent. buildings
will be preserved.
CONNECTICUT PRESERVATION NEWS 1990
Jan.-Feb., v.13, no.1, p.4-5,
photo.
Preservation easements: how to keep
it safe after you've gone /
Christopher Wigren.
A contract made between a property
owner and a nonprofit organization
which gives the organization the
authority to restrict alterations
to the property.
CONNECTICUT PRESERVATION NEWS 1990
Jan.-Feb., v.13, no.1, p.5,

WIJDEVELD, HENDRICI THEODORI,
1885-1987
Nieuwe "billen van Wijdeveld".
Designs for block in the Indische
Buurt area of Amsterdam, after the
1970 one by H.T. Wijdeveld, by the
architects: Jo Coenen, Cees
Nagelkerke, and Duinker/van der
Torre.
DE ARCHITECT 1990 July-Aug., v.21,
no.7-8, p.12, dwgs.

WIJK, RIKKERT
Edilizia sociale in Olanda: Theo
Bosch, Paul de Ley, Lucien Lafour
e Rikkert Wijk = Social housing in
the Netherlands: Theo Bosch, Paul
de Ley, Lucien Lafour & Rikkert
Wijk / Matthijs de Boer.
Discussion of five projects.
SPAZIO E SOCIETA 1990 Oct.-Dec.,
v.13, no.52, p.30-45, ports.,
models, photos., plans, site
plans.
Lucien Lafour and Rikkert Wijk.
Features two housing projects:
Apartment house, Realeneiland,
Amsterdam; Social housing,
Abattoirterrein, Amsterdam.
ARCHITECTURAL REVIEW 1990 Feb.,
v.187, no.1116, p.90-97, photos.,
plans, secns., site plans.

WILBER, DONALD N.
Shiraz 1935 / Donald N. Wilber.
Religious structures.
IRAN 1989, v.27, p.125-128,plates,
plan, aerial photo., biblio.,
refs.

WILCOCK, RICHARD
Backing better bricks / Richard
Wilcock.
On the Guestling brickworks,
Hastings.
RIBA JOURNAL 1990 Aug., v.97,
no.8, p.61,65, photos.
A break with tradition / Richard
Wilcock.
Two London museum restaurants
designed by Tectus.
RIBA JOURNAL 1990 June, v.97,
no.6, p.57-58,60-61, photos.,
plans.
[Bricklayers Arms, London] / Richard
Wilcock.
Low-rise office / warehouse
development off Old Kent road,
London. Architects: Robshaw
Richmond.
RIBA JOURNAL 1990 Dec., v.97,
no.12, p.6-8, photos.
Doubling up on Danish standards /
Richard Wilcock.
On the Rockwool administration
building, Hedehusene. Architect:
Jens Arnfred.
RIBA JOURNAL 1990 Sept., v.97,
no.9, p.91-92, photos., plan,
secn.
Frontis [Marketplace, London] /
Richard Wilcock.
London warehouse near London
Bridge station, converted into
corporate office building for
Marketplace, an advertising
agency. Architects: Weston
Williamson.
RIBA JOURNAL 1990 Oct., v.97,
no.10, p.6-8, photos.
[Hopewell Yard, London] / Richard
Wilcock.
Multi-use building, Camberwell,
South London. Architects: David
Quigley Architects.
RIBA JOURNAL 1990 Nov., v.97,
no.11, p.[6]-8, photos.
A house fit for a queen / Richard
Wilcock.
On the restoration of the 1660s
interiors of the Queen's House,
Greenwich. Original architects:
Inigo Jones, later enlarged by
John Webb. Restoration architects:
(Continued next page)

WILKERSON, CHARLES K. NISHAPUR: SOME EARLY ISLAMIC BUILDINGS AND THEIR DECORATION
Nishapur: some early Islamic buildings and their decoration [by] Charles K. Wilkerson [book review] / Robert Hillenbrand. ORIENTAL ART 1989 Spring, v.35, no.1, p.44-46.

WILKINS, WILLIAM, 1778-1839
"A gallery worthy of the British people": James Pennethorne's designs for the National Gallery, 1845-1867 / Geoffrey Tyack. Plans for new galleries. Original architect: William Wilkins. ARCHITECTURAL HISTORY 1990, v.33, p.120-134, dwgs., plans, secns., site plans, refs.

WILKINSON, ALIX
Gardens in ancient Egypt: their locations and symbolism / Alix Wilkinson. JOURNAL OF GARDEN HISTORY 1990 Oct.-Dec., v.10, no.4, p.199-208, ill., model, refs.

WILKINSON, JEFF
New bathrooms in old houses / Jeff Wilkinson. OLD-HOUSE JOURNAL 1990 Sept.-Oct., v.18, no.5, p.[28-33], photos., plans.
The story of porches: an American tradition / Jeff Wilkinson. OLD-HOUSE JOURNAL 1990 July-Aug, v.18, no.4, p.30-37, dwgs., photos.
Who they were: Geo. Palliser / Jeff Wilkinson. 19th-cent. "mail-order architect" based in Bridgeport, Conn., then in New York City. OLD-HOUSE JOURNAL 1990 Nov.-Dec., v.18, no.6, p.18,20, elev., engr.
Who they were: Greene & Greene / Jeff Wilkinson. OLD-HOUSE JOURNAL 1990 July-Aug, v.18, no.4, p.26,28, port., photos.

WILKINSON, JOSEPH
When and how to hire a lighting designer / Joseph Wilkinson. ARCHITECTURAL RECORD 1990 Aug., v.178, no.9 suppl., p.8-11, photos.

WILKINSON, NATALIE
Who they were: Catharine Beecher / Natalie Wilkinson. Writer and social reformer, she wrote in 1841 Treatise on Domestic Economy. OLD-HOUSE JOURNAL 1990 Sept.-Oct., v.18, no.5, p.24,26, ill., port.

WILKINSON, PETER
Private stock: Jeff Walker, a vice president of Ralph Lauren, creates a look of his own at home / Peter Wilkinson. New York apartment. HOUSE & GARDEN 1990 Mar., v.162, no.3, p.158-[161], port., photos.

WILKOC, RON
"Landmarking comes to Covenant" [church, New York] / Ron Wilkoc. Describes a cooperative process for landmarking religious buildings. Built in 1871 and 1927 and located at 310 East 42nd St. COMMON BOND 1990 Fall, v.6, no.4, p.2-4, dwg., photos.

WILL, MARGARET THOMAS
Der Historic American Buildings Survey / Margaret Thomas Will. OSTERREICHISCHE ZEITSCHRIFT FUR KUNST UND DENKMALPFLEGE 1988, v.42, no.1-2, p.58-66, elevs., photos., plans, secns., isometric dwg., refs.

WILL, THOMAS
Im Kontext der modernen Stadt / Thomas Will, Jorg Stabenow. ARCH PLUS 1990 Oct., no.105-106, p.88-94, dwgs., models, photos., plans, aerial photos., refs.
Der Stadt auf den Grund gehen [exhibition review] / Thomas Will. Review of "Stadt und Topographie," at the Bayerische Akademie der Schonen Kunste, Munich, May 27-July 1, 1990. ARCHITHESE 1990 May-June, v.20, no.3, p.78-80, maps, engr., aerial photo., refs.

WILLCUT, CRAIG
Building high tech security systems / Craig Willcut, Martin Mancini. In corporate and research facilities. DEVELOPMENT 1990 May-June, v.21, no.3, p.26-27, photos.

WILLEN, PAUL
Dumping Trump City: the sequel / Craig Whitaker. Two alternate schemes for the Penn Yards site are presented, the Willen/Gutman proposal and the Riedner/Wasserman proposal. OCULUS 1990 Oct., v.53, no.2, p.6-11, dwgs., ports., elevs., models, site plans.

WILLENBECHER, JOHN, 1936-
The cat's meow: artist John Willenbecher creates model homes that make his clients purr / Iris Owens. Cat houses made from cardboard boxes. HOUSE & GARDEN 1990 June, v.162, no.6, p.82,84, photos.

WILLENSKY, ELLIOT, 1934-1990
Elliot Willensky [obituary]. PROGRESSIVE ARCHITECTURE 1990 Nov., v.71, no.12, p.26.

WILLIAM F. STERN AND ASSOCIATES
Interiors.
Contents: Berg & Androphy Law Offices, Houston (William F. Stern and Associates); Majestic Diner, Austin (STUDIO Texas); and, El Centro College Student Center, Dallas (Oglesby Group). TEXAS ARCHITECT 1990 Sept.-Oct., v.40, no.5, p.40-43, photos., plans.

WILLIAM FRANK MCCALL ARCHITECTS AND INTERIOR DESIGNERS
Georgian grace in Atlanta: renewing southern traditions for Charlotte and Rankin Smith / Jeffrey Simpson. Interiors of Georgian-style home in northwestern Atlanta. Architect: William Frank McCall. Interior designers: Betty Sherrill and Ethel Smith of McMillen. ARCHITECTURAL DIGEST 1990 May, v.47, no.5, p.220-225, photos.
Maison du Cygne: metamorphosis on the Georgia Coast / Helen C. Griffith. Rosemary Anderson house, Sea Island. Architect for renovations: John Shackelford of William Frank McCall Architects and Interior Designer: Elizabeth Tucker. SOUTHERN ACCENTS 1990 July-Aug., v.13, no.6, p.76-83, photos.

WILLIAM GREEN & ASSOCIATES
Soft-Com / Edie Lee Cohen. Offices for computer software concern, New York, NY. Architects: William Green & Associates. INTERIOR DESIGN 1990 June, v.61, no.9, p.220-[223], photos., plan.

WILLIAM H. BYRNE & SON
Mater Misericordiae Hospital, Dublin. Architects: William H. Byrne & Son. PLAN: ARCHITECTURE + BUILDING DESIGN IN IRELAND 1990 Mar., v.28, no.3, p.3-9, dwg., model, photos., plans.

WILLIAM KESSLER & ASSOCIATES
Due recenti opere di William Kessler = The Industrial Technology Institute in Ann-Arbor, and The State Library and Historical Museum in Lansing, Mich. / Stefania Mornati. The buildings opened in 1987 and 1989. L'INDUSTRIA DELLE COSTRUZIONI 1990 May, v.24, no.223, p.54-59,4, elevs., photos., plans.
Restoring dreams / Mark Alden Branch, Abby Bussel. On the restoration of six 1920-30s American movie palaces. PROGRESSIVE ARCHITECTURE 1990 June, v.71, no.6, p.92-99, photos., plans, secns.

WILLIAM L. PEREIRA ASSOCIATES
Un perimetro di cristallo per l'Universita di San Diego = A crystal perimeter for San Diego University / Maurizio Vitta. Underground extension to library designed by William Pereira; architects of extension: Gunnar Birkerts & Associates. L'ARCA 1990 Apr., no.37, p.42-47, axonometric view, photos., plans, secns.

WILLIAM MORGAN ARCHITECTS
To gather together: Building types study 674: religious buildings / Margaret Gaskie.
Four projects: Gates of the Grove Synagogue, East Hampton, N.Y. (Norman Jaffe); Beach United Methodist Church, Jacksonville Beach, Fla. (William Morgan Architects); Blackhawk Bapist Church, Fort Wayne, Ind.(Harding Assoc.); and St. Peter's Catholic Church, Olney, Md. (Hugh N. Jacobsen).
ARCHITECTURAL RECORD 1990 Jan., v.178, no.1, 123-135, elevs., photos., plans, secns., site plans.

WILLIAM NIMMO & PARTNERS
Hole at the hears [Lutyens House, London] / Dan Cruickshank.
"Massive internal reconstruction" of Britannic House, renamed Lutyens House, Finsbury Circus, London. Original architect: Edwin Lutyens; executive architects for reconstruction: William Nimmo & Partners; consultant architects: Peter Inskip and Peter Jenkins Architects.
ARCHITECTS' JOURNAL 1990 Jan.31, v.191, no.5, p.24-29, elev. photos., plans, secns., engr.

WILLIAM NYCUM ARCHITECTS
Hospital and Community Health Centre, Souris, P.E.I.
Architects: William Nycum Architects, the Dubois Plumb Partnership.
CANADIAN ARCHITECT 1990 Mar., v.35, no.3, p.33-35, elevs., photos., plans, site plan.

WILLIAM OF SENS
Some observations on the early flying buttress and choir triforium of Canterbury Cathedral / Yoshio Kusaba.
Dates from the late 1170s. Builder: William of Sens. Includes abstract.
GESTA 1989, v.28, no.2, p.175-189, fig., photos., plans, secns., refs.

WILLIAM RAWN ASSOCIATES
Front porch society: Battle Road Farm, Lincoln, Massachusetts, William Rawn Associates / Michael Leccese.
40-unit mixed-income complex.
ARCHITECTURE: THE MAGAZINE OF THE AMERICAN INSTITUTE OF ARCHITECTS 1990 July, v.79, no.7, p.[56]-59, photos., plans, site plans.
The search continues: building types study 681, multifamily housing / Donald J. Canty.
Four low-rise condominium projects: The Waterworks, New Hope, Penn. (Cecil Baker & Associates, Architects); Back of the Hill Rowhouses, Boston (William Rawn Associates, Architects); Samoset Resort and Village, Rockport, Me. (Sasaki Associates, Architects); and Parkview Commons, San Francisco (David Baker Architects).
ARCHITECTURAL RECORD 1990 July,
(Continued next column)

WILLIAM RAWN ASSOCIATES (CONTINUED)
The search continues:...(CONTINUED) v.178, no.8, p.15-87, axonometric views, elev., photos., plans, site plans.

WILLIAMS, ALLAN
L'evolution de la politique du logement au Portugal / Jorge Gaspar, Manuel C. Patricio, Allan Williams.
French, English and Spanish summaries.
ESPACES ET SOCIETES 1988, no.52-53, p.167-182, tables, biblio.

WILLIAMS, AMANCIO, 1913-1989
Una pasion argentina: Amancio Williams "in memoriam" [obituary] / Roberto Fernandez.
ARQUITECTURA VIVA 1990 Sept.-Oct., no.14, p.36-37, dwg., photos., plan.

WILLIAMS, ANTHONY
Ansdell Library / Anthony Williams.
A branch library in the Fylde district. Architects: Lancashire County Council.
BUILDING 1990 Nov.9, v.255, no.44, p.49-56, photos., plans, secns., site plan, table.

WILLIAMS, BUNNY
Park Avenue country: modifying English traditions in a prewar apartment / Suzanne Stephens.
Interiors of New York duplex. Interior designer: Bunny Williams.
ARCHITECTURAL DIGEST 1990 Nov., v.47, no.12, p.224-[231], port., photos.

WILLIAMS, COLIN
Mishmash mesh [Colin Williams] / Denise Chevin.
The founder and managing director of WOCAD, a British specialist CAD firm, on marketing and development of an AutoCAD-compatible system.
BUILDING 1990 Mar.2, v.255, no.9, p.50-51, dwgs., port.

WILLIAMS, DAVID W.
Professional metamorphosis: as his own client, designer Warren Snodgrass practices many disciplines / Monica Geran.
Features Snodgrass house, Ross Valley, Calif. Architect: David Williams.
INTERIOR DESIGN 1990 May, v.61, no.7, p.296-[301], photos., plan.

WILLIAMS-ELLIS, CLOUGH, SIR, 1883-1978
Visionary village: a Welsh architect conjures up a Mediterranean town on Cardigan Bay / Jan Morris.
Sir Clough Williams-Ellis created the town of Portmeirion in the 1920s and '30s.
HOUSE & GARDEN 1990 Sept., v.162, no.9, p.82, port., photo.

WILLIAMS, EVAN
Tropical punch / Justin Henderson.
The Grand Lido Hotel, Negril, Jamaica. Architects: Evan Williams with Design Collaborative. Interior designers: DC! International.
INTERIORS 1990 May, v.149, no.10, p.222-[225], photos.

WILLIAMS, G. B. A.
H. Reginald Ross [obituary] / G.B.A. Williams.
RIBA JOURNAL 1990 July, v.97, no.7, p.90.

WILLIAMS, GILBERT, 1914-1990
Gilbert Williams [obituary] / Roy Gosney.
RIBA JOURNAL 1990 Sept., v.97 no.9, p.106.

WILLIAMS, JOE CARROLL
Sociable structure: a Houston home designed for entertaining / Nan Booth Simpson.
Anderson house. Architect: Joe Carroll Williams.
SOUTHERN ACCENTS 1990 Oct., v.13, no.8, p.[98]-105, ports., photos.

WILLIAMS, JOHN
Managing downtown revitalization by district / Maureen Atkinson, John Williams.
Distinguishes the various types of downtown districts which can be targeted for revitalization; examples in Toronto and Norfolk.
URBAN LAND 1990 Sept., v.49, no.9, p.2-6, photos., plans.

WILLIAMS, KEITH
First steps / Keith Williams.
On the occasion of the exhibition Walking on glass, on the work of Pawson Williams. On view at the Blanc de Bierges Gallery, London, from Oct.27-Nov.2, 1990.
BUILDING DESIGN 1990 Oct.26, no.1009, p.34-35, dwgs.

WILLIAMS, MICHAEL ANN
Pride and prejudice: the Appalachian boxed house in southwestern North Carolina / Michael Ann Williams.
WINTERTHUR PORTFOLIO 1990 Winter, v.25, no.4, p.[217]-230, photos., refs.

WILLIAMS, O'BRIEN ASSOCIATES
Hennepin Avenue, Minneapolis.
One of six urban design reports included in special issue, Urban Concepts. Extracted from a 1981 plan by Denise Scott Brown, in collaboration with Bennett-Ringrose-Wolsfeld-Jarvis-Gardner and Williams/O'Brien Associates.
ARCHITECTURAL DESIGN 1990, v.60, no.1-2. p.62-69, dwgs., elev., photos., site plans, sketches.
Regional portfolio: The Midwest: a tale of two cities / Clifford A. Pearson.
Minneapolis and Milwaukee have become two of the most livable cities in the U.S. Contents: 100 E. Wisconsin Ave., Milwaukee (Clark Tribble Harris & Li Architects); Milwaukee Repertory
(Continued next page)

WILLIAMS, O'BRIEN ASSOCIATES
(CONTINUED)
Regional portfolio:...(CONTINUED)
Theater (Beckley/Myers
Architects);5th St. Parking
Facility, Minneapolis (Stageberg
Partners); Valspar Varnish Factory
renovation, Minneapolis (Meyer,
Scherer & Rockcastle); and the
Ceresota, Minneapolis (Ellerbe
Becket).
ARCHITECTURAL RECORD 1990 Aug.,
v.178, no.9, p.62-71, axonometric
view, photos., plans, secns., site
plans.

WILLIAMS, PAUL R., 1894-1980
Hollywood legacies of Wallace Neff,
James E. Dolena, Roland E. Coate
and Paul Williams / Michael Webb.
ARCHITECTURAL DIGEST 1990 Apr.,
v.47, no.4, p.36,40,42,46,48,
dwg., ports., photos.

WILLIAMS, RICHARD H.
Internationalizing planning
education, 1992 and the European
ERASMUS program / Richard H.
Williams.
JOURNAL OF PLANNING EDUCATION AND
RESEARCH 1990 Fall, v.10, no.1,
p.75-78, refs.

WILLIAMS, RICK W.
Density perception on residential
streets / James R. Bergdoll, Rick
W. Williams.
Study to examine which physical
characteristics influence people's
perception of density on urban
residential streets; examples
taken from San Francisco, Ca.
BERKELEY PLANNING JOURNAL 1990,
v.5, p.15-38, ill., elevs., map,
photos., plans, tables, biblio.

WILLIAMS, RONALD
Tropiques Nord, Montreal, Quebec:
un jardin tropical interieur / Ron
Williams, Lucie Begin.
12-story atrium containing a
tropical garden is the central
feature of the Tropics North
condominium project. Landscape
architects: Ron Williams and
Lucie Begin. In French and
English.
LANDSCAPE ARCHITECTURAL REVIEW
1989 Dec., v.10, no.5, p.16-17,
photos.

WILLIAMS, STEVEN BURR
Sapore di messico [house, Laurel
Canyon, Los Angeles] / Lucia Bisi.
Architect: Steven Burr Williams.
VILLE GIARDINI 1990 Apr., no.247,
p.12-17, photos, plan.

WILLIAMS, TOD, 1943-
Extending the architectural impulse
into interior design.
Features comments by Billie Tsien,
Michael Graves, Arthur Erickson,
Tod Williams, Fred Schwartz, Roger
Ferri, Allan Greenberg, Frank
Israel, and Christopher Rudolph.
ARCHITECTURAL DIGEST 1990 Dec.,
v.47, no.13, p.58,62,68,72,76,78,
photos.

WILLIAMS, TOD, 1943- (CONTINUED)
Tod Williams, Billie Tsien: Domestic
Arrangements.
The architects discuss their house
on exhibit at the Walker Art
Center and the Whitney Museum. In
Italian and English.
DOMUS 1990 June, no.717,
p.[58-65], photos., plan.
Tod Williams - Billie Tsien
[interview] / Kate Nesbitt.
Illustrates three projects: Arts
Park Center, Los Angeles; Feinberg
Hall, Princeton University; Tarlo
House, Sagaponack, N.Y. In Danish
and English.
SKALA 1990, no.20, p.34-39,
models, photos., refs.

WILLIAMS TREBILCOCK WHITEHEAD
Technics: cleaning the Carnegie /
John Dender, Judith Selwyn.
Built 1895 and later expanded.
Original architects: Longfellow,
Alden and Harlow. Restoration
architects: Williams Trebilcock
Whitehead. Preservation
consultants: Preservation
Technology Associates.
PROGRESSIVE ARCHITECTURE 1990
Oct., v.71, no.10, p.38-41,
photos., aerial photo.

WILLIAMS, WILL
Life in a northern practice / Will
Williams.
Profile of the Manchester
landscape architecture firm, Derek
Lovejoy and Partners.
LANDSCAPE DESIGN 1989 Nov.,
no.185, p.48-50, dwgs., model,
photos., aerial photos.

WILLIAMSON, ELIZABETH. GLASGOW
Guiding light: The buildings of
Scotland: Glasgow, by Elizabeth
Williamson, Anne Riches and
Malcolm Higgs [book review] /
Robert Thorne.
Review of Glasgow, by E.
Williamson, et al. In "The
Buildings of Scotland" series.
ARCHITECTS' JOURNAL 1990 May 30,
v.191, no.22, p.69-70, photos.,
aerial photo.

WILLIAMSON, I. P.
Land information systems in local
government: a case study / I. P.
Williamson, G. J. Hunter, F. J.
Leahy.
Computerized information
management system handling
graphical and textual land-related
data for Melbourne, Australia.
AUSTRALIAN PLANNER: JOURNAL OF THE
ROYAL AUSTRALIAN PLANNING
INSTITUTE 1989 Dec., v.27, no.4,
p.14-18, chart, refs.

WILLIAMSON, JOHN, 1905-1990
John Williamson [obituary].
INTERIOR DESIGN 1990 Aug., v.61,
no.11, p.30.

WILLIAMSON, NEIL
Free to design? / Neil Williamson.
On the issues involved in the
hiring of public landscape
architects (local authority) for
private sector developments in
Great Britain.
LANDSCAPE DESIGN 1989 Apr.,
no.179, p.49-50.

WILLIAMSON, PAUL
Early medieval wall painting and
painted sculpture in England / ed.
by Sharon Cather, David Park, Paul
Williamson.
Based on the proceedings of a
symposium at the Courtauld
Institute of Art, Feb. 1985.
BAR BRITISH SERIES 1990, no.216,
p.[1]-262, dwgs., photos., plans,
site plans, reconst. dwgs., refs.

WILLIS, DAN
Landscapes for the 21st century
[competition].
Features 15 winning projects,
which include descriptions in the
designers' own words. Competition
sponsored by "Landscape
Architecture". Includes articles
by the judges, Jory Johnson, M.
Paul Friedburg and James Wines.
LANDSCAPE ARCHITECTURE 1990 Dec.,
v.80, no.12, p.[32-54], ill.,
ports., site plans, aerial photo.

WILLIS, PETER
Earl De La Warr and the competition
for the Bexhill Pavilion, 1933-34
/ Russell Stevens, Peter Willis.
Includes discussion of the
controversy. Winners Erich
Mendelsohn and Serge Chermayeff.
ARCHITECTURAL HISTORY 1990, v.33,
p.[135-166], dwgs., ports.,
elevs., photos., plans, aerial
photos., refs.

WILLIS, TIM
With an eye to a feast / Tim Willis.
Focus on the 18th cent.-inspired
wall decorations in the restaurant
at Kenwood, London. Artist:
Christopher Boulter.
THE WORLD OF INTERIORS 1990 Oct.,
p.254-[259], photos.

WILLMOTT, PETER
Tasmanian trio / Rory Spence.
Features three projects in Hobart:
garden room, South Hobart,
architect: Jim Jones; house
addition, West Hobart, architect:
Leigh Woolley and studio house,
West Hobart, architect: Peter
Willmott.
ARCHITECTURAL REVIEW 1990 Apr.,
v.187, no.1118, p.87-[93],
photos., plans, secns., site
plans.

WILLOCK, ROGER. BULWARK OF EMPIRE
Bulwark of Empire, by Roger Willock
[book review] / Jonathan Coad.
Reprint of 1962 ed. on naval
fortifications at Bermuda.
POST-MEDIEVAL ARCHAEOLOGY 1989,
v.23, p.85-86.

WILLS, ROYAL BARRY
Unbuilt Minnesota / Robert Gerloff.
Two designs for a Minneapolis
house for a 1938 Life magazine
article. Architects: Royal Barry
Wills, Frank Lloyd Wright. The
Wills design was built in
Minneapolis, and the Wright design
built at Two Rivers, Wisc.
ARCHITECTURE MINNESOTA 1990
May-June, v.16, no.3, p.67,
models.

WILLSON, EDWARD JAMES, 1787-1854
Hainton Hall, Lincolnshire: the seat
of Mr. James Heneage / John Martin
Robinson.
Architects: Peter Atkinson,
William Emes, Edward James Wilson,
William Burn and Charles Morris.
COUNTRY LIFE 1990 July 12, v.184,
no.28, p.84-89, photos.

WILMOTH, STEPHEN
Cottage karma / Jody
Thompson-Kennedy, Kirsten Harwood.
Remodelled Carmel, Calif. cottage.
Renovation architect: Stephen
Wilmoth.
HOUSE BEAUTIFUL 1990 June, v.132,
no.6, p.72-75, photos.

WILMOTTE, JEAN-MICHEL
L'accueil et l'histoire.
Projects in three medieval French
towns which incorporate new
buildings into historic buildings.
Architect: Jean-Michel Wilmotte.
ARCHITECTURE INTERIEURE CREE 1990
Mar., no.235, p.28, dwgs.,
photos., secn.
L'alu s'expose.
On the Espace Technal showroom,
Toulouse. Architect: Jean-Michel
Wilmotte.
TECHNIQUES ET ARCHITECTURE 1990
June-July, no.390, p.169, photos.
[Amenagement interieur]: bureaux.
Contents: Office of president,
Region Champagne-Ardennes,
Chalons-sur-Marne, France;
architect: Henri Ciriani-- Office,
Ministere de Finances, Paris;
architect: Isabelle Hebey--
Office, 5 place de la Pergola,
Toulouse, France; architect:
Jean-Pierre Estrampes-- Office,
181 avenue Joliot-Curie, Nanterre,
France; architect: Alain Richard--
Bank interior, Bruges; architect:
Stephane Beel-- Office, Green
Movie, Milan, Italy; architect:
Carlo Santi.
LE MONITEUR ARCHITECTURE AMC 1990
July-Aug., no.13, p.46-57,
axonometric views, photos., plans.
[Amenagement interieur]: commerces.
Contents: Boutique Koshino, Paris
VIIIe; architect: Jean-Michel
Wilmotte-- Apple showroom, ave. de
la Grande Armee, Paris; architect:
Berbesson Racine et Associes--
Castelli showroom, Paris;
designer: Ronald Cecil Sportes--
Unifor furniture showroom, Milan,
Italy; architects: Afra & Tobia
Scarpa-- Boutique Jean-Louis
Imbert, Marseille, France;
architect: Rudy Ricciotti--
Recorded music store, Nantes,
France; architect: Studio Naco.
LE MONITEUR ARCHITECTURE AMC 1990
(Continued next column)

WILMOTTE, JEAN-MICHEL (CONTINUED)
[Amenagement... (CONTINUED)
July-Aug., no.13, p.36-45,
axonometric views, photos., plans.
L'avenir du Louvre / Jean Lebrat.
Includes interviews with I.M. Pei,
Jean-Michel Wilmotte and Michel
Macary.
CONNAISSANCE DES ARTS 1990
July-Aug., no.461-462, p.[50-67],
model, photos.
Interieurs: Toulouse: un espace du
profile.
Technal 3, rue des Arts.
Architects: Jean-Michel Wilmotte,
Massimo Quendolo.
LE MONITEUR ARCHITECTURE AMC 1990
May, no.11, p.18-20, axonometric
views, photos.
J-M Wilmotte.
Profile of Wilmotte; part of
obituary of the photographer Hans
Namuth.
CONNAISSANCE DES ARTS 1990 Dec.,
no.466, p.[74]-75, photo.
Objets bruts.
Technal showroom, Toulouse.
Interior architect: Jean-Michel
Wilmotte.
ARCHITECTURE INTERIEURE CREE 1990
Oct.-Nov., no.239, p.140-143,
photos.
Le restaurant Quick a Nimes.
Interiors of fast-food restaurant.
Interior designer: Jean-Michel
Wilmotte.
ARCHITECTURE INTERIEURE CREE 1990
Mar., no.235, p.[122-123], photos.
Sur le mode de la fugue.
Interiors of the Junko Koshino
boutique, Paris. Architect:
Jean-Michel Wilmotte.
ARCHITECTURE INTERIEURE CREE 1990
Oct.-Nov., no.239, p.132-133,
photos.

WILS, JAN, 1891-1972
De Papaverhof in ere hersteld:
renovatie in de geest van
oorspronkelijk ontwerp / Henk van
der Schoor.
On the 1920 design for the garden
apartment complex, the De Stijl
movement, F.L. Wright's influence,
and the recent restoration of the
buildings. Original architect: Jan
Wils. Renovation architect: J.
Franso.
DE ARCHITECT 1989 Dec., v.20,
no.12, p.92-99, dwg., photos.,
plans, secns., site plan.
De stijl van Jan Wils [book review]
/ Cees Boekraad.
Edited by Victor Freijser. Essays
by Jaap Franso et al.
ARCHIS 1990 Mar., no.3, p.55-56,
elev., plans, refs.

WILSHUSEN, RICHARD H.
Large-scale integrative facilities
in tribal societies:
cross-cultural and southwestern
U.S. examples / Michael A. Adler,
Richard H. Wilshusen.
Includes discussion of the kiva in
the U.S. Southwest.
WORLD ARCHAEOLOGY 1990 Oct., v.22,
no.2, p.133-146, graph, elev.,
map, plan, table, biblio.

WILSON, ALEX
An improved outlook: glass: window
developments / Alex Wilson.
ARCHITECTURE: THE MAGAZINE OF THE
AMERICAN INSTITUTE OF ARCHITECTS
1990 Aug., v.79, no.8, p.95-98,
dets., ill., tables.
Light duty: building systems:
alternative energies / Alex
Wilson.
Solar water heating and
photovoltaics.
ARCHITECTURE: THE AIA JOURNAL 1990
Dec., v.79, no.12, p.[81]-86,
graph, dwgs., photos.

WILSON ASSOCIATES
The making of a market / Herb
Childress.
Rockridge Market Hall, Oakland,
Ca. Architect and developer: Peter
and Anthony Wilson (Wilson
Associates).
PLACES 1990 Fall, v.7, no.1,
p.50-63, dets., elev., photos.,
plans, aerial photos.

WILSON, BEN
Mild man of the woods / Elspeth
Thompson.
Features wooden figurative
sculptures in Hadley Woods.
Artist: Ben Wilson.
THE WORLD OF INTERIORS 1990 June,
p.[146-155], port., photos.

WILSON, CHRISTOPHER. GOTHIC CATHEDRAL
Gothic revisionism: the Gothic
cathedral, by Christopher Wilson
[book review] / Andrew Saint.
Review of the Gothic cathedral, by
C. Wilson.
ARCHITECTS' JOURNAL 1990 Mar.28,
v.191, no.13, p.90-91, photos.

WILSON, COLIN ST. JOHN, 1922-
Marathon man / Kester Rattenbury.
Report on Colin St. John Wilson's
lecture at the RIBA, "Building the
British Library."
BUILDING DESIGN 1990 Nov.16,
no.1011, p.20, ill.
The modern tradition / kColin St.
John Wilson.
Features three recent urban
buildings by Gullichsen Kairamo
Vormala: Itakeskus Center,
Helsinki; cultural center,
Pieksamaki; and the Stockmann
department store, Helsinki.
ARCHITECTURAL REVIEW 1990 Mar.,
v.187, no.1117, p.37-[50], elevs.,
photos., plans, secns., site
plans, sketches.

WILSON, D. J.
Gravity driven counterflow through
an open door in a sealed room / D.
J. Wilson, D. E. Kiel.
BUILDING AND ENVIRONMENT 1990,
v.25, no.4, p.379-388, diagrs.,
graphs, plan, refs.

WILSON, DAVID
The figure in leaded glass / Sydney
Lancaster Waller.
In the works of David Wilson.
STAINED GLASS QUARTERLY 1989
Spring, v.84, no.1, p.25-32,
photos.

WINDOWS--STAINED GLASS--UNITED
STATES--WASHINGTON (DISTRICT OF
COLUMBIA)--US WEST CORPORATION
Western window / Lisa Cohen.
Stained glass window in the
Washington, D.C. branch of US West
Corp. Designers: Ronn Jaffe
Associates.
INTERIORS 1990 Apr., v.149, no.9,
p.28, dwg., photo.

WINDOWS--STANDARDS--CHINA
Standards.
The first of the ongoing standards
sections with new or revised
information. Contents:
I.Geotechnical investigation and
surveying.--II.Building
materials.--III.Building products
and elements.
BUILDING IN CHINA 1990 Sept., v.3,
no.3, p.52-53, tables.

WINDOWS--STANDARDS--GERMANY (WEST)
Neufassung von DIN 4109: richtige
Anwendung bei Planung und
Ausfuhrung des Schallschutzes von
Fenstern und Turen / Hans
Froehlich.
DEUTSCHES ARCHITEKTENBLATT 1990
June 1, v.22, no.6, p.969-975,
978, dets., graphs, tables.

WINDOWS--STUDENT PROJECTS
The window and the door: fourth
architecture studio.
Critic: Llewellyn Seibold.
OZ / COLLEGE OF ARCHITECTURE AND
DESIGN, KANSAS STATE UNIVERSITY
1989, v.11, p.52-53, det., models,
plan.

WINDOWS--WOODEN--MAINTENANCE AND
REPAIR--DENMARK
Bygningsbevaring pa losblade.
Techniques for repairing and
strengthening wooden windows.
ARKITEKTEN 1989 Nov.28, v.91,
no.21, p.540, dets., photos.

WINDRIM, JOHN TORREY, 1866-1934
"New Kid" on Philly's Franklin
Parkway / Donald Prowler.
On the 1933 Franklin Institute's
new Futures Center addition.
Original architect: John T.
Windrim. Architects for the
addition: Geddes Brecher Qualls
Cunningham Architects.
PROGRESSIVE ARCHITECTURE 1990
Sept., v.71, no.9, p.25, photos.

WINE CELLARS
See also BEER CELLARS

WINE CELLARS--19TH CENTURY--UNITED
STATES--JERSEYVILLE (ILLINOIS)--
SCHWARZ-KRUEGER WINE CELLAR
The Schwarz-Krueger wine
cellar-housebarn / H. Wayne Price.
Built in 1868 near Jerseyville,
Ill. by a German immigrant.
PIONEER AMERICA SOCIETY
TRANSACTIONS 1989, v.12, p.39-46,
dwgs., photos., plans, secns.,
refs.

WINE CELLARS--20TH CENTURY--GERMANY
(WEST)--TRIER--BISCHOFLICHE
WEINGUTER
Dokumente der Architektur des 20.
Jahrhunderts: Objekt:
Kellererweiterung der
Bischoflichen Weinguter in Trier.
Built 1968. Architect: Alois
Peitz.
DER ARCHITEKT 1990 May, no.5,
p.224, photos., plan.

WINE CELLARS--SPAIN--GARRAF--CASTILLO
DE GARRAF (BODEGAS GUELL)
Bodegas Guell in Garraf (1895-1901)
/ Manfred Speidel.
Former wine cellars built for Don
Eusebio Gell y Bacigalupa;
architect: Antoni Gaudi. Text in
Japanese and English.
ARCHITECTURE AND URBANISM 1990
July, no.7(238), p.50-[63],
elevs., photos., plans, secns.,
site plans, refs.

WINE CELLARS--SPAIN--SAN SADURNI DE
NOYA--CAVAS RAVENTOS BLANC
Archaic in Arcadia.
Features two wine-related projects
in Sant-Sadurni d'Anoia by Jaume
Bach and Gabriel Mora: Raventos
Blanc winery, and the school of
viticulture and enology.
ARCHITECTURAL REVIEW 1990 July,
v.188, no.1121, p.60-67, elevs.,
photos., plans, secns., site
plans, aerial photos.
Archaische Anklange an Arkadien:
Weinkellerei und Schule fur
Weinbau in Sant Sadurni d'Anota
[sic], 1986-1988.
Architects: Jaume Bach & Gabriel
Mora.
WERK, BAUEN + WOHNEN 1990 Nov.,
no.11, p.2-11, elevs., photos.,
plans, secns., site plans, aerial
photo.
Meister der sensuellen Form: neue
Arbeiten von Bach und Mora.
Three projects: Kindertagesstatte
"Torre Baldovina" in Santa Coloma
de Gramenet; Weinbausschule "Merce
Rosell" in Espiells; Weinkellerei
"Cavas Raventos Blanc" in Sant
Sadurni d'Anoia. One of four
articles on the theme "Barcelona
bauen".
BAUWELT 1990 Mar.2, v.81, no.9,
p.386-387, axonometric view,
plans, photos.
Spagna, Alto Penedes: le Cantine
Raventos i Blanc = Spain, Alto
Penedes: the Raventos i Blanc
Winery / Tamara Molinari.
Architects: Jaume Bach, Gabriel
Mora.
ABITARE 1990 June, no.286,
p.134-[141], photos, plans,
secns., site plan, aerial photo.

WINE CELLARS--UNITED STATES--
PHILADELPHIA (PENNSYLVANIA)--WINE
RESERVE
The Wine Reserve, Philadelphia,
Pennsylvania.
Store and display area for the
Pennsylvania State Liquor Board.
Interiors by Boyd & Associates.
ARCHITECTURE NEW JERSEY 1990 v.26,
no.6, p.10, photos.

WINEGAR, KARIN
Superior lodgings: Minnesota's
venerable Naniboujou Lodge / Karin
Winegar.
HOUSE & GARDEN 1990 Feb., v.162,
no.2, p.68, photos.

WINERIES--SPAIN--ALTO PENEDES--
CODORNIU
Spagna, Alto Penedes: le Cantine
Codorniu = Spain, Alto Penedes:
the Codoriu Winery / Tamara
Molirari.
Architect: Josep Puig i Cadafalch.
ABITARE 1990 June, no.286,
p.142-147, dwgs., photos.

WINERIES--SPAIN--SAN SADURNI DE NOYA--
CAVAS RAVENTOS BLANC
Archaic in Arcadia.
Features two wine-related projects
in Sant-Sadurni d'Anoia by Jaume
Bach and Gabriel Mora: Raventos
Blanc winery, and the school of
viticulture and enology.
ARCHITECTURAL REVIEW 1990 July,
v.188, no.1121, p.60-67, elevs.,
photos., plans, secns., site
plans, aerial photos.
Archaische Anklange an Arkadien:
Weinkellerei und Schule fur
Weinbau in Sant Sadurni d'Anota
[sic], 1986-1988.
Architects: Jaume Bach & Gabriel
Mora.
WERK, BAUEN + WOHNEN 1990 Nov.,
no.11, p.2-11, elevs., photos.,
plans, secns., site plans, aerial
photo.
Meister der sensuellen Form: neue
Arbeiten von Bach und Mora.
Three projects: Kindertagesstatte
"Torre Baldovina" in Santa Coloma
de Gramenet; Weinbausschule "Merce
Rosell" in Espiells; Weinkellerei
"Cavas Raventos Blanc" in Sant
Sadurni d'Anoia. One of four
articles on the theme "Barcelona
bauen".
BAUWELT 1990 Mar.2, v.81, no.9,
p.386-387, axonometric view,
plans, photos.
Spagna, Alto Penedes: le Cantine
Raventos i Blanc = Spain, Alto
Penedes: the Raventos i Blanc
Winery / Tamara Molinari.
Architects: Jaume Bach, Gabriel
Mora.
ABITARE 1990 June, no.286,
p.134-[141], photos, plans,
secns., site plan, aerial photo.

WINERIES--UNITED STATES--CALISTOGA
(CALIFORNIA)--CLOS PEGASE
Mitologia de colores: Bodegas Clos
Pegase en Napa Valley, California
= Colored mythologies.
Architect: Michael Graves. English
text, p.86.
A & V 1990, no.21, p.38-41, dwg.,
photos., secn., site plan.

WINES, JAMES, 1932-
Green architecture...The role of
architecture in the built
environment: a recent SITE
project... / James Wines.
The Four Continents Bridge,
Hiroshima, Japan. Principal
architect: Joshua Weinstein.
ARCHITECTURAL RECORD 1990 Apr.,
v.178, no.4, p.78-83,163, ill.,
photos., plan, secn.

WINES, JAMES, 1932- (CONTINUED)
Interview: James Wines, Joshua
Weinstein, SITE / Thomas Fisher.
On "their method of working and
the meaning of their
architecture."
PROGRESSIVE ARCHITECTURE 1990
Aug., v.71, no.8, p.116-117,
dwgs., port.
Landscapes for the 21st century
[competition].
Features 15 winning projects,
which include descriptions in the
designers' own words. Competition
sponsored by "Landscape
Architecture". Includes articles
by the judges, Jory Johnson, M.
Paul Friedburg and James Wines.
LANDSCAPE ARCHITECTURE 1990 Dec.,
v.80, no.12, p.[32-54], ill.,
ports., site plans, aerial photo.

WINGAERT, THIERRY VAN DE
Extension de la DRAC,
Aix-en-Provence.
Addition to the Direction
Regionale des Affaires Culturelles
building. Architect: Thierry van
de Wingaert. English summary,
p.78. Spanish summary, p.172.
TECHNIQUES ET ARCHITECTURE 1990
Oct.-Nov., no.392, p.78, dwg.,
plan, secn., site plan.
Fins de chantier / Joan Pascuale
Argente ... [et al.].
Contents: Former tannery converted
to association building,
Chatillon-sur-Indre, France;
architect: Thierry Van de
Wingaert.--Hospital Paul-Brousse,
Villejuif, France; architects:
Avant-Travaux.--Housing complex,
Barcelona, Spain; architects: Joan
Pascual Argente, Ramon Ausio
Mateu, Lluis Badenas Oradanos,
Joan Forgas Coll, Teresa Gimeno
Marin, Enric Serra Grau.
LE MONITEUR ARCHITECTURE AMC 1990
May, no.11, p.11-16, photos.,
plans.

WINGARDH & WINGARDH
Oijared Executive Country Club,
Oijared, Sweden, 1988.
Architects: Wingardh & Wingardh.
Includes essay: Arising out of the
ground / Claes Dreijer. Text in
Japanese and English.
ARCHITECTURE AND URBANISM 1990
July, no.7(238), p.[68]-81,
photos., plan, secn., site plan.
Oijared Klubhaus bei Gotborg,
Schweden = Oijared clubhouse near
Goteborg, Sweden.
Earth sheltered building.
Architects: Wingardh & Wingardh.
ARCHITEKTUR + WETTBEWERBE 1990
Mar., no.141, p.18-19, photos.,
plan, secn.

WINGARDH OCH WINGARDH OCH WILHELMSSON
White noise / David Redhead.
Interiors of the Scandic Crown
Hotel, Stockholm. Interior
designers: Wingardh och Wingardh
och Wilhelmsson.
DESIGNERS' JOURNAL 1990 June,
no.58, p.84-[87], photos., plan.

WINKEL, CAMIEL VAN
Gekooid: clips in pavilijoens /
Camiel van Winkel.
Five projects for "video clips"
(kiosks or pavilions) in
Groningen. Co-sponsor: Groninger
Museum. Architects: Zaha Hadid,
Peter Eisenman, Bernard Tschumi,
Rem Koolhaas, and Coop Himmelblau.
ARCHIS 1990 Oct., no.10, p.4-5,
photos.

WINKELMANN, DIETMAR
Innerstadtische Bebauung in
Mischbauweise im Stadtkern
Zwickaus / Dietmar Winkelmann.
New buildings on Hauptstrasse,
Zwickau.
ARCHITEKTUR DER DDR 1989 Dec.,
v.38, no.12, p.12-17, elevs.,
photos., plans, secns., site
plans.
Die Rekonstruktion des Zwickauer
Dunnebierhauses / Uwe Dassler,
Dietmar Winkelmann.
Built in 1480; restored 1980-1984
and used as a registrar's office.
English, French, German, and
Russian summaries, p.55-56.
ARCHITEKTUR DER DDR 1989 Dec.,
v.38, no.12, p.20-23, photos.,
plans, secns.

WINKELS, KARSTEN
"Die Stadt von morgen - planen fur
den Menschen" - Stadtvertragliche
Hauptverkehrstrasse = "The city of
tomorrow - planning for people" -
main thouroughfares that are
acceptable to a city.
Idea competition. Three joint
first prize winners: Hans-Rainer
Rung, Karsten Winkels; Albert
Moritz; Jochen Dittus, Siegfried
Volmer. Text in German.
ARCHITEKTUR + WETTBEWERBE 1990
Dec., no.144, p.75-78, photos.,
plans, secns., site plans.

WINKLER, ANDREAS, 1955-
Architekt contra Ladeneinrichter:
Cornelia Krause im Gesprach mit
Andreas Winkler [interview].
DEUTSCHE BAUZEITUNG 1990 Oct.,
v.124, no.10, p.46-51, axonometric
views, dets., port., photos.,
plans, secns.
Im spitzen Winkel: eine Apotheke in
Karlsruhe.
Architect: Andreas Winkler with
Dieter Scheeren.
ARCHITEKTUR, INNENARCHITEKTUR,
TECHNISCHER AUSBAU 1990 Nov.,
v.98, no.11, p.58-60, photos.,
plan, isometric dwg.
Mit Biss: Bistro "al dente" in
Karlsruhe.
Architects: Andreas Winkler with
Christoph Hildebrand.
DEUTSCHE BAUZEITUNG 1990 Oct.,
v.124, no.10, p.57-59, axonometric
view, photos.
Mit System: die Boutique "Calla Mode
Feminin" in Karlsruhe.
Architect: Andreas Winkler with
Barbara Grosse-Rhode.
ARCHITEKTUR, INNENARCHITEKTUR,
TECHNISCHER AUSBAU 1989 Sept.,
v.97, no.9, p.42-45, axonometric
view, dets., photos.

WINKLER, BEBE
A tailored setting: scale and
proportion define a Manhattan
apartment / John Gruen.
Interiors designed by Bebe
Winkler.
ARCH!TECTURAL DIGEST 1990 Feb.,
v.47, no.2, p.[222-227], photos.

WINKLER, BERNHARD
Piano della mobilita per la citta di
Bologna / Bernhard Winkler.
Article forms most of this issue.
Presents the traffic scheme for
Bologna proposed by Prof. Winkler.
Summaries in French, English,
German, and Spanish, p.1. Captions
in Italian and English. Includes
commentary by Claudio Sassi, and
German text on p.88-89.
PARAMETRO 1990 Mar.-Apr., no.177,
p.19-67,cover, dwgs., port., maps,
photos., site plans, tables,
engrs., aerial photos.

WINKLER, CLAUS, 1929-
Wohnen im Moosstefflfeld, Ebergsberg
/ Wolfgang Brauner, Gerhard Eber.
Housing and open space plan in
Ebersberg, Germany. Architects:
Winkler und Effinger. Includes
English summary and captions.
GARTEN UND LANDSCHAFT 1990, v.100,
no.4, p.26-29, photos., site
plans, isometric dwgs.

WINKLER, HARTMUT
Der Walkman-Effekt. Neue Konzepte
fur mobile Raume und
Klanfarchitekturen = The Walkman
effect. New concepts for mobile
spaces and sound architectures /
Christian W. Thomsen, Angela
Krewani, Hartmut Winkler.
Text in German and English.
DAIDALOS 1990 June 15, no.36,
p.52-61, ill., photos., refs.

WINKLER, HEINRICH
Neubau fur den Post- und
Fernmeldedienst, Rosenheim.
Architects: Oberpostdirektion
Munchen, Heinz Ludwig Sopper,
Heinrich Winkler.
BAUWELT 1990 Mar.16, v.81, no.11,
p.466, photos.
Post- und Fernmeldeamt in Rosenheim.
Architects: Oberpostdirektion
Munchen, H.L. Sopper, H. Winkler,
W. Weinberg, F. Bauer.
DEUTSCHE BAUZEITSCHRIFT 1990 Oct.,
v.38, no.10, p.1369-1377, dets.,
photos., plan, secn., site plans.

WINKLER, JOHN
Representing the body politic: the
theater of manhood in classical
Athens / John Winkler.
PERSPECTA 1990, no.26, p.215-228,
photos., plans, tables, aerial
photos., refs.

WINKLER, KLAUS
"Sedan-Rennfeld" in Pforzheim =
"Sedan-Rennfeld" in Pforzheim.
Competition for multi-use
building. Winning architect: Klaus
Winkler. Text in German.
ARCHITEKTUR + WETTBEWERBE 1990
June, no.142, p.46-51, dwgs.,
elevs., models, plans, site plans,
sketches.

WINN ARCHITECTURE
A mad mix of archi-Tex-Mex: Casa
U-Betcha by Winn Architecture /
Justin Henderson.
Restaurant/art gallery located in
Seattle.
INTERIORS 1990 Jan., v.149, no.6,
p.158-[159], photos., plan.

WINSKELL ARCHITECTS
Tynemouth station, [North Tyne
side].
Designed in 1882 by William Bell.
Restoration architect: Rock
Townsend with Winskell.
BUILDING 1990 Oct.12, v.255,
no.40, p.55-62, dets., photos.,
site plan, tables.

WINSOR FARICY ARCHITECTS
Playing house: new exhibits at St.
Paul's Children's Museum teach
kids about the nuts and bolts of
residential design.
Architects: Meyer, Scherer and
Rockcastle and Winsor/Faricy
Architects.
ARCHITECTURE MINNESOTA 1990
Sept.-Oct., v.16, no.5, p.34-37,
photos.

WINSTON, DENIS
Raise high the roof beam --
planner!: the Denis Winston
Memorial lecture 1990 / John Toon.
Presented at the International
Conference on Local Planning,
Sydney Australia.
AUSTRALIAN PLANNER: JOURNAL OF THE
ROYAL AUSTRALIAN PLANNING
INSTITUTE 1990 June, v.28, no.2,
p.45-48,

WINTER, FREDERICK A.
The underside of Manhattan /
Frederick A. Winter.
Recent urban archaeological work
in lower Manhattan, New York.
ARCHAEOLOGY 1990 May-June, v.43,
no.3, p.66-69, map.

WINTER GARDENS--ENVIRONMENTAL ASPECTS
Auswirkungen von Aussenwanden und
Wintergarten auf das Raumklima /
Gerd Hauser.
DEUTSCHES ARCHITEKTENBLATT 1990
Mar.1, v.22, no.1, p.393-398,
diagrs., graphs, tables, biblio.

WINTER GARDENS--MAINTENANCE AND REPAIR
Wintergarten: Grundlagen, Bauphysik
und Nutzung / Friedemann Stahl.
DEUTSCHE BAUZEITUNG 1990 May,
v.124, no.5, p.102-110, photo.,
tables, refs.

WINTER, HELMUT
Architektursymbolik zwischen gestern
und ubermorgen / Helmut Winter.
On a competition project for Expo
1992 in Seville, entitled
"Zeitraum." Architects: Keiser und
Muller.
ARCHITHESE 1990 July-Aug., v.20,
no.4, p.80-81,86, model, plan,
secn., isometric dwgs.

WINTER, JOHN
AJ Christmas books [book review].
Eight reviewers highlight their
choices for the best architecture
books of 1990.
ARCHITECTS' JOURNAL 1990 Dec.5,
v.192, no.23, p.66-69, ill.,
port., model, photos, plans, engr.
Shipshape / John Winter.
On the Vasamuseet, Stockholm.
Architects: Ove Hidemark Goran
M'ansson Arkitektkontor.
ARCHITECTURAL REVIEW. 1990 Aug.,
v.188, no.1122, p.9-10, photos.
Working with the masters / Peter
Wislocki, Bronagh Carey.
Veterans of legendary 20th century
architectural offices describe how
the masters designed: Adrian Gale
on Mies van der Rohe; John Winter
on Erno Goldfinger; Andre
Wogenscky on Le Corbusier; Trevor
Dannatt on Jane Drew and Maxwell
Fry; and Patrick Hodgkinson on
Alvar Aalto. Fourth article in
series "How architects design."
ARCHITECTS' JOURNAL 1990
Dec.19-26, v.192, no.25-26,
p.42-47, dwg., ports., models,
photos., plan, secn., sketches.

WINTER, KARIN
Ekero centrum / Ralph Erskine.
Built 1985-1990. Architect: Ralph
Erskine Architect Planner.
Includes commentary by Karin
Winter.
ARKITEKTUR: THE SWEDISH REVIEW OF
ARCHITECTURE 1990 Dec., v.90,
no.10, p.38-51, ill., photos.,
plan, site plans.

WINTER, ROBERT
Architecture in the United States
[book review] / Rhodri Windsor
Liscombe, John Vincent Boyer,
William G. Farrar, IV, Robert
Winter.
Review of Charleston antebellum
architecture and civic destiny, by
Kenneth Severens; Structures and
styles: guided tours of Hartford
architecture, by Gregory E.
Andrews and David F. Ransom;
Vernacular architecture in
southern Illinois, by John M.
Coggeshall and Jo Anne Nast; and
Bruce Goff: toward absolute
architecture, by David Delong.
SOCIETY OF ARCHITECTURAL
HISTORIANS. JOURNAL 1990 Mar.,
v.49, no.1, p.115-120,

WINTER SPORTS FACILITIES
See also SKATING RINKS
See also SKI LIFTS
See also SKI LODGES

WINTER SPORTS FACILITIES--
COMPETITIONS AUSTRIA--SAALBACH
Sport und Skistadion Saalbach,
Osterreich = Sports and ski
stadium Saalbach, Austria.
Competition. Winning architect:
Andreas Fellerer. Text in German.
ARCHITEKTUR + WETTBEWERBE 1990
Mar., no.141, p.88-91, dwgs.,
elevs., models, plans, secns.,
site plans.

WINTER SPORTS FACILITIES--FRANCE--
ALBERTVILLE
Jeux d'hiver stades d'ete / Pascale
Blin.
English summary, p.34-35. Spanish
summary, p.153.
TECHNIQUES ET ARCHITECTURE 1990
Dec.-1991 Jan., no.393, p.[30]-35,
dwgs., plans, secns., models,
sketches.

WINTER SPORTS FACILITIES--UNITED
STATES--WYOMING--SNOWY RANGE SKI
AREA
Snowy Range ski resort: an
illustration of GIS planning
principles / Rosalyn Johnson, Jon
Bryan Burley.
Evaluatin of expansion
possibilities for a 500-acre site
located in southeastern Wyoming,
30 miles west of Laramie.
Includes French summary.
LANDSCAPE ARCHITECTURAL REVIEW
1990 Mar., v.11, no.1, p.15-18,
maps, biblio.

WINTER, THOMAS
A systematic approach to historic
structures reports / Thomas
Winter, Peter Schulz.
ASSOCIATION FOR PRESERVATION
TECHNOLOGY. BULLETIN 1990, v.22,
no.1-2, p.142-148, ill., photos.,
tables, refs.

WINTERBOTTOM, DANIEL
Sculpted brick / Daniel
Winterbottom.
Features work by artists Ken
Williams and Walter Ritchie.
LANDSCAPE ARCHITECTURE 1990 Nov.,
v.80, no.11, p.76-77, photos.
Sculpted brick II / Daniel
Winterbottom.
Second article in two-part series
on the reemergence of sculpted
brick in landscape architectural
design.
LANDSCAPE ARCHITECTURE 1990 Dec.,
v.80, no.12, p.62-64, port.,
photos.

WINTERINGHAM, GRAHAM
Stansfeld Thomas (Bob) Walker
[obituary] / Graham Winteringham.
RIBA JOURNAL 1990 Sept., v.97
no.9, p.106,

WINTERMANS, FRANK, 1949-
Architecten ontwerpen
voetgangersbrug in Leiden /
Liesbeth Melis.
Three proposals for a new
footbridge over the Singel canal,
to replace a rustic one dating
from 1913. Architects: Evert
Kleijer, Frank and Paul
Wintermans, and Georges Descombes.
DE ARCHITECT 1989 Oct., v.20,
no.10, p.40-43, dwg., elev.,
photos., secns., site plan,
isometric dwg.

WINTERMANS, PAUL, 1950-
Architecten ontwerpen
voetgangersbrug in Leiden /
Liesbeth Melis.
Three proposals for a new
footbridge over the Singel canal,
to replace a rustic one dating
from 1913. Arcitects: Evert
(Continued next page)

WINTERMANS, PAUL, 1950- (CONTINUED)
Architecten ontwerpen (CONTINUED)
Kleijer, Frank and Paul
Wintermans, and Georges Descombes.
DE ARCHITECT 1989 Oct., v.20,
no.10, p.40-43, dwg., elev.,
photos., secns., site plan,
isometric dwg.

WINTON SCOTT ARCHITECTS
Harboring tradition: for a new
marine museum on the coast of
Maine, architect Winton Scott was
inspired by the powerful
industrial vernacular of a local
19th-century foundry / Nancy
Levinson.
The Maine Maritime Museum, Bath.
ARCHITECTURAL RECORD 1990 June,
v.178, no.7, p.72-[75], photos,
plans, secn.

WIRE FABRIC REINFORCEMENT
See WELDED WIRE FABRIC

WIRING
See also DATA TRANSMISSION SYSTEMS
Access floors: a way to handle the
cabling mess.
ARCHITECTURAL RECORD 1990 Sept.,
v.178, no.10, p.157-159,203,
dwgs., photos.
Big Apple barriers: specifying
lighting for projects in New York
City poses obstacles / Peter
Barna, Justin Henderson.
ARCHITECTURE: THE AIA JOURNAL 1990
Mar., v.79, no.3, p.197-198, ill.
Weiterverwendung von elektrischen
Installationen / Heinz Schmitz,
Norbert Stannek.
DEUTSCHES ARCHITEKTENBLATT 1990
Nov.1, v.22, no.11, p.1725-1726,
photos.

WIRING--UNDERGROUND
College ties / Denise Chevin.
Cambridge University will be
locating its fiber-optic cabling
network underground.
BUILDING 1990 Nov.23, v.255,
no.46, p.62-63, photos., site
plan.

WIRKKALA, MAARIA
Toisessa valossa: Ajatuksia
hiekkakasojen ja rakennustyomaiden
aarelta - In a different light /
Juha Ilonen.
On a performance ("At the same
time in another place") held at a
construction site in Ruoholahti,
27-29 Oct.1989. Artists: Maaria
Wirkkala, Jukka Mikkonen. Includes
English translation.
ARKKITEHTI 1989, v.86, no.8,
p.26-29, photos.

WIRNER, HELMUT
Unternehmerische Revitalisierung von
Industriegebieten / Helmut Wirner.
ARCHITEKTUR + WETTBEWERBE 1989
Dec., no.140, p.3, port., aerial
photo.

WIRSING, WERNER, 1919-
Architekturpreis Munchen fur Werner
Wirsing.
Prize awarded on 20 Sept.1989 by
the Landeshauptstadt Munchen.
DEUTSCHES ARCHITEKTENBLATT 1989
Dec.1, v.21, no.12, p.1777-1778,
port.

WIRSING, WERNER, 1919- (CONTINUED)
Ateliertreppe in einem Wohnhaus in
Grobenzell bei Munchen = Studio
staircase in a dwelling house in a
suburb of Munich.
Architect: Werner Wirsing.
DETAIL 1990 Apr.-May, v.30, no.2,
p.134-135, dets., photos., plan,
secn.

WIRTH, THOMAS
Naturgarten und Okohaus in Wurzburg
/ Thomas Pregnitzer, Thomas Wirth.
Architects: Peter Baumeister, Hans
Bieberstein.
GARTEN UND LANDSCHAFT 1990, v.100,
no.9, p.48,50-51, photos., site
plan.

WIRTZ, JACQUES
Erfullung eines langen Traums /
Barbara Dinoi.
Interiors of home west of Antwerp.
Architect: Marc Corbiau. Interior
designers: Paul Ibens, Claire
Bataille. Landscape architect:
Jacques Wirtz. English summary,
p.1-2.
ARCHITEKTUR & WOHNEN 1990
Oct.-Nov., no.5, p.[38]-44,
photos., plan, site plan.
Ein Palais fur die Provinz /
Brigitte Forgeur, Barbara
Friedrich.
Interiors of country house in
Brasschaat, Belgium. Architect:
Marc Corbiau. Interior designer:
Jean de Meulder. Landscape
architect: Jacques Wirtz.
ARCHITEKTUR & WOHNEN 1990
Mar.-Apr., no.2, p.20-28, photos.,
plan, site plan.

WIRZ, STEFAN
Landschaftsplanung.
Articles by Stefan Wirz, G.
Hahn-Herse, H-D Baaske, [et al.].
GARTEN UND LANDSCHAFT 1990, v.100,
no.1, p.27-63, cover, charts,
maps, photos., tables.

WISCHHUSEN, RAINER
Hamburg und sein Hafen / Gert
Kahler.
The main article in issue on
Hamburg entitled "Tor zur Welt".
Reviews the harbor area buildings,
the Sandtorhafen-Speicherstadt
area, and three competitions.
Prize winners include Patshan
Winking Architekten; v. Gerkan,
Marg + Partner; Kleffel Kohnholdt;
Massimiliano Fuksas; Jorg
Friedrich; AC Architekten Contor;
ASW Architekten Silcher + Werner;
Rainer Wischhusen.
BAUWELT 1990 Dec.7, v.81, no.46,
p.2298-2317, dwgs., models,
photos., plans, secns., site
plans, aerial photos., refs.
Wohnungspolitische Konzepte:
Wohnungsbauprojekte / Rudi Kujath.
Section on many new housing
projects in Germany. Contents:
Berlin, by Rudi Kujath.--Koln, by
Uwe Kessler.--Bayern, by Dieter
Gutekunst.--Frankfurt, by Martin
Wentz.--Hannover, by Hanns
Adrian.--Der LEG
Nordrhein-Westfalen, by Roswitha
Sinz.--Anmerkungen..., by Hartmut
Grosshans. Among the architects
(Continued next column)

WISCHHUSEN, RAINER (CONTINUED)
Wohnungspolitische...(CONTINUED)
represented are Otto Steidle +
Partner; Andreas Brandt & Rudolf
Bottcher; Joachim Ganz, Walter
Rolfes; Axel Schultes; Wolfgang
Scharlach und Rainer Wischhusen;
Rebecca Chestnutt et al; Hubertus
Hoffmann; Paul Petry; Hermann
Schroder, Sampo Widmann; Gerhart
Laage; Freed Ahrens.
BAUWELT 1990 Mar.30, v.81, no.12,
p.572-598, elevs., plans, secns.,
site plans, tables.

WISE, MICHAEL
Museum as multinational: a new
Guggenheim in Salzburg designed by
Hans Hollein and a new
contemporary art complex in a
Massachusetts factory... / Michael
Wise, Jillian Burt.
Proposed Massachusetts Museum of
Contemporary Art, North Adams,
Mass.; architects: Frank Gehry,
Robert Venturi and David Childs.
BLUEPRINT (LONDON, ENGLAND) 1990
Oct., no.71, p.44-48, axonometric
views, models, photos.

WISEMAN, S. J.
The human stage: English theatre
design, 1567-1640 [by] John Orrell
[book review] / S.J. Wiseman.
Reviewed with: The Boar's Head
Playhouse, by Herbert Berry.
LONDON JOURNAL 1990, v.15, no.1,
p.84-86.

WISLOCKI, PETER
College tradition: Blue Boar Court.
Student housing for Trinity
College, Cambridge. Architects:
MacCormac, Jamieson, Prichard &
Wright. Contents: Appraisal, by
Peter Wislocki; Cost comment, by
Roger Barbrook; External Wall,
hall of residence, MJPW
Architects.
ARCHITECTS' JOURNAL 1990 Dec.5,
v.192, no.23, p.31-39,41-43,47-49,
axonometric view, dets., elev.,
model, photos., plans, secns.,
site plan.
Ideal home / Peter Wislocki.
Modernist house of architect John
Jenkins in Highgate, north London.
Architects: John Jenkins and
Haverstock Associates.
ARCHITECTS' JOURNAL 1990 Sept.12,
v.192, no.11, p.40-45, photos.,
plans, secn.
Objets prouve: Jean Prouve,
'constructeur' [exhibition review]
/ Peter Wislocki.
Exhibition at the Centre Georges
Pompidou, Paris, through 28
Jan.1991.
ARCHITECTS' JOURNAL 1990
Dec.19-26, v.192, no.25-26,
p.54-55, dwg., photos.
Seine perspective: Japanese House of
Culture, Paris: exhibition of
competition entries [exhibition
review] / Peter Wislocki.
Held at the Pavillon de l'Arsenal
through 11 Nov. 1990. Exhibition
documented all 453 entries.
Winners: Masayuki Yamanaka,
Kenneth Armstrong, and Jennifer
Smith.
ARCHITECTS' JOURNAL 1990 Oct.24,
(Continued next page)

WITZLING, LAWRENCE P.
Planning and urban design
competition / Ernest R. Alexander,
Lawrence P. Witzling, guest
editors.
Seven articles, including one on a
mixed-use project for Bunker Hill
in Los Angeles. Authors: Jeffrey
E. Ollswang, Tridib Banerjee,
Anastasia Loukaitou-Sideris,
Joanna Eley, Dennis J. Casper,
Ruth Eckdish Knack, Andrew D.
Seidel.
JOURNAL OF ARCHITECTURAL AND
PLANNING RESEARCH 1990 Summer,
v.7, no.2, p.91-180, charts, site
plans, biblios., refs.

WODICZKO, KRZYSTOF, 1943-
Exhibition review: Street
performance; The Homeless Vehicle
Project / Graham Shane.
A rollable cart designed by
Krzystof Wodiczko and Rudolph
Luria.
JOURNAL OF ARCHITECTURAL EDUCATION
1990 summer, v.43, no.4, p.37-42,
elevs., models, photos., plans.

WODZ, KAZIMIERA
L'espace et la vie quotidienne d'un
quarter ouvrier (l'exemple de
Bogucice) / Kazimiera Wodz.
Describes the working-class
district of Bogucice, in Katowice
City, Poland. French, English and
Spanish summaries.
ESPACES ET SOCIETES 1988,
no.52-53. p.139-146, refs.

WOERUM, JENS
Edb pa Kunstakademiets Arkitektskole
/ Jens Woerum.
ARKITEKTEN 1990 Sept., v.92,
no.13, p.A266,

WOGENSCKY, ANDRE, 1916-
Working with the masters / Peter
Wislocki, Bronagh Carey.
Veterans of legendary 20th century
architectural offices describe how
the masters designed: Adrian Gale
on Mies van der Rohe; John Winter
on Erno Goldfinger; Andre
Wogenscky on Le Corbusier; Trevor
Dannatt on Jane Drew and Maxwell
Fry; and Patrick Hodgkinson on
Alvar Aalto. Fourth article in
series "How architects design."
ARCHITECTS' JOURNAL 1990
Dec.19-26, v.192, no.25-26,
p.42-47, dwg., ports., models,
photos., plan, secn., sketches.

WOHLERT, VILHELM, 1920-
Det kinesiske Lysthus.
The late 18th cent. Chinese
pavilion in the garden at
Frederiksberg Castle (architect:
Andreas Kirkerup). Restoration
architects: Ole Priskorn, Vilhelm
Wohlert. Includes an
art-historical commentary on the
restoration (by Claus M. Schmidt)
and English and German summaries.
ARKITEKTUR DK 1990, v.34, no.7,
p.344-350, elevs., photos., plans,
secns., site plans.

WOHLHAGE, KONRAD
Das Objeckt und die Stadt:
Erinnerung an eine Berliner
Tradition / Konrad Wohlhage.
ARCH PLUS 1990 Oct., no.105-106,
p.51-57, axonometric views, model,
maps, plans, site plans, aerial
photos., refs.
Sozialer Mietwohnungsbau Schlesische
Strasse/Taborstrasse in Berlin =
Social housing Schlesische
Strasse/Taborstrasse in Berlin.
Competition. Winning architects:
Hilde Leon, Konrad Wohlhage. Text
in German.
ARCHITEKTUR + WETTBEWERBE 1990
June, no.142, p.38-40, dwgs.,
elevs., models, plans.
Verwaltungsgebaude
Berlin-Wilmersdorf.
Competition winners: Hilde Leon,
Konrad Wohlhage.
BAUWELT 1990 Dec.14, v.81, no.47,
p.2332, model.

WOHLIN, ROLF
I Cadiz Ropar Ljuset ut Sig / Rolf
Wohlin.
ARKITEKTUR: THE SWEDISH REVIEW OF
ARCHITECTURE 1990 Apr., v.90,
no.3, p.46-49, photos.
Satt f till orm / Rolf Wohlin.
Essay on form in architecture,
illustrated with five photographs
of European structures.
ARKITEKTUR: THE SWEDISH REVIEW OF
ARCHITECTURE 1990 Dec., v.90,
no.10, p.26-31, photos.

WOJTOWICZ, ROBERT
Lewis Mumford: a life [by] Donald L.
Miller [book review] / Robert
Wojtowicz.
SOCIETY OF ARCHITECTURAL
HISTORIANS. JOURNAL 1990 Sept.,
v.49, no.3, p.351-352,

WOLDEN, FRANK
Reclaiming the streets: Horton Plaza
versus the need for a new retail
vision / Frank Wolden.
On various design concepts
presented for a pocket of retail
development in San Diego.
CARTOUCHE 1990 Winter, v.19,
p.8-9, dwgs., photos.

WOLF, HARRY C.
Banking on proportion: a
mathematical system for NCNB
National Bank / Michael Wagner.
Bank located in Tampa, Fl. was
designed using a mathematical
system based on a series of
logarithms developed by 13th cent.
Italian mathematician Leonardo
Fibonacci. Architect: Harry C.
Wolf. Interior designers:
Associated Space Design.
INTERIORS 1990 Jan., v.149, no.6,
p.136-[137], photos., plan.
Completato l'edificio per la NCBN a
Tampa in Florida.
The North Carolina National Bank.
Architect: Harry Wolf.
CASABELLA 1990 Mar., v.54, no.566,
p.33, photos.

WOLF, IGNAZ
Die Suchard-Hauser in Bludenz: ein
Nachruf / Johann Peer.
Built in the late 1800's as
workers' housing. Architect: Ignaz
Wolf.
OSTERREICHISCHE ZEITSCHRIFT FUR
KUNST UND DENKMALPFLEGE 1990,
v.44, no.1-2, p.87-92, elevs.,
photos., plans, secn., site plans,
refs.

WOLF, TOBIAS
Erste Preise: Verwaltungsbauten.
Four projects: Public exchange,
Meschede (architect: Helmut
Blocher); Rathaus, Harsefeld
(architect: Feldmann, Hofmann,
Rohde, Schurmeyer); Landratsamt
Giessen (architect: Rohrbach &
Partner); Stadtwerke Ettlingen
(architect: Tobias Wulf).
DEUTSCHES ARCHITEKTENBLATT 1990
Apr.1, v.22, no.4, p.531-534,
elevs., models, secn., site plans.

WOLF, URS
Locker angedichtet: Anmerkung zum
offentlichen Wettbewerb auf den
Rontgenareal im Zurcher
Industriequartier.
1st prize to Isa Sturm & Urs Wolf.
WERK, BAUEN + WOHNEN 1990 Dec.,
no.12, p.12, models, site plans.
Rontgenareal Zurich:
Projektwettbewerb.
Projects in a competition for a
mixed use complex in the area
around the Rontgenstrasse train
station. First prize to the
"Khan" project by Isa Sturm and
Urs Wolf.
SCHWEIZER BAUMARKT 1990 Oct.29,
v.25, no.13, p.[I]-IV, models.

WOLF, VICENTE
Before and after: urban renewal on
high, transforming Kathy Brynner's
East Side apartment / Manuela
Hoelterhoff.
Interiors of New York apartment.
Interior designer: Vicente Wolf.
ARCHITECTURAL DIGEST 1990 Nov.,
v.47, no.12, p.278-[285], photos.
Kips Bay [Decorator show house 1990]
/ Mayer Rus.
Selective survey of rooms in the
show house held in a Renaissance
revival townhouse on E. 76th St.
in New York.
INTERIOR DESIGN 1990 Sept., v.61,
no.12, p.222-231, photos.

WOLFE, MICHAEL
NBC gets centered / Kristen
Richards.
Renovations of environmental
control center office in NBC's
Rockefeller Center offices.
Architect: Michael Wolfe.
INTERIORS 1990 Nov., v.150, no.4,
p.46-47, photos., plan.
The urban kitchen / Victoria Geibel.
Some NYC kitchens. Architects:
David Spiker, Michael Wolfe, James
Hong, David Estreich, Warren
James.
METROPOLIS 1990 Apr., v.9, no.8,
p.52-57, photos.

WOLFE, TOM
    Hayes & Co. [Hayes townhouse, New
    York City] / Tom Wolfe.
    Renovated Upper East Side row
    house. Architects: Turner Brooks,
    Ross Anderson; interior designer:
    Chester Cleaver.
    HOUSE & GARDEN 1990 Oct., v.162,
    no.10, p.[156-163], port., photos.

WOLFENSBERGER, RUDOLF
    Der neue Uetlibergturm: Form,
    Konstruktion, Baustelle / Rudolf
    Wolfensberger.
    Built 1990.
    SCHWEIZER BAUMARKT 1990 Dec.10,
    v.25, no.15, p.IV-VI, port.,
    photos.

WOLFF, RENATE
    Oh la la, Lacroix / Renate Wolff.
    Interiors of the fashion designer
    Christian Lacroix's apartment in
    St. Germain, Paris. English
    summary, p.1.
    ARCHITEKTUR & WOHNEN 1990
    Oct.-Nov., no.5, p.24-34, port.,
    photos.

WOLFRUM, GERHARD
    Wohnhaus mit Arztpraxis in
    Lauterhofen, 1989 / Joachim
    Andreas Joedicke.
    Architects: Werner Brandl, Gerhard
    Wolfrum.
    WERK, BAUEN + WOHNEN 1990 June,
    no.6, p.74-76, photos., plans,
    secn.

WOLLWEBER, IMKE
    Harry Maasz; ein phantasievoller
    Gestalter / Imke Wollweber.
    Includes English summary.
    GARTEN UND LANDSCHAFT 1990, v.100,
    no.12, p.39-42, dwgs., ports.,
    photos., plan, site plan.

WOLNER, EDWARD W.
    Review of the 1989 annual meeting of
    the ASCA [sic] East Central Region
    / Edward Wolner.
    ACSA Conference entitled "Defining
    Architecture: an Autonomous or
    Interdisciplinary Endeavor?", held
    in Ann Arbor, Mich.
    JOURNAL OF ARCHITECTURAL EDUCATION
    1990 Spring, v.43, no.3, p.54-55.
    Urban icon: Norwest Center refines
    and enervates - and is haunted by
    - an historical type / Edward W.
    Wolner.
    A 57-story tower in Minneapolis,
    incorporating fragments form the
    former Norwest Bank Building.
    Architect: Cesar Pelli.
    INLAND ARCHITECT 1990 Jan.-Feb.,
    v.34, no.1, p.44-48, elev.,
    photos.

WOLODARSKI, ALEKSANDER
    Klarakuset, Stockholm / Bertil
    Rrodin, Dag Cavallius, Tony Rydh.
    An office and shopping building at
    Drottninggatan 33. Architect:
    Nyrens Arkitektkontor. Includes
    commentary by Aleksander
    Wolodarski (p.27-23) and an
    English translation (p.53-54).
    ARKITEKTUR: THE SWEDISH REVIEW OF
    ARCHITECTURE 1990 June-July, v.90,
    no.5, p.4-13, elevs., photos.,
    plans, secns., site plans.

WOLODARSKI, ALEKSANDER (CONTINUED)
    KV Sumpen, Stockholm / Bengt
    Lindroos.
    Office building with restaurant,
    on corner of the Sturegaten and
    Lastmakargatan. Architect: Bengt
    Lindroos Arkitektkontor. Includes
    commentary by Aleksander
    Wolodarski and English translation
    (p.53-54).
    ARKITEKTUR: THE SWEDISH REVIEW OF
    ARCHITECTURE 1990 June-July, v.90,
    no.5, p.14-23, det., elev.,
    photos., plans, secns., site plan.

WOLSCHKE-BUHLMAHN, JOACHIM
    Changes in the philosophy of garden
    architecture in the 20th century
    and their impact upon the social
    and spatial environment / Gert
    Groening, Joachim
    Wolschke-Bulmahn.
    JOURNAL OF GARDEN HISTORY 1989
    Apr.-June, v.9, no.2, p.[53]-70,
    photos., site plans, refs.

WOLSCHKE-BULMAN, JOACHIM
    Geschichte der Gartentheorie [by]
    Clemens Alexander Wimmer [book
    review] / Joachim Wolschke-Bulman.
    JOURNAL OF GARDEN HISTORY 1990
    Oct.-Dec., v.10, no.4, p.247-251,
    Review of a 1989 book. Text in
    English.

WOLZ, GUNTHER K.
    Mehrzweckhalle in
    Shorndorf-Oberberken.
    Architect: Gunther K. Wolz of
    Beyer, Weitbrecht, Wolz. Includes
    English summary.
    BAUMEISTER 1990 Oct., v.87, no.10,
    p.55-59, elev., photos., plans,
    secns., site plan.

WOLZ, JOHN L.
    30 years of full-service interior
    planning: Milo Kleinberg Design
    Associates, Inc. / John L. Wolz.
    Interior designers for corporate
    office space.
    REAL ESTATE FORUM 1989 Dec., v.44,
    no.12, p.74-82, ports., photos.

WOMEN AND ARCHITECTURE
    See ARCHITECTURE AND WOMEN

WOMEN AND PLANNING GROUP
    Planning with people in mind / Emer
    Hughes.
    Recommendations of the Women and
    Planning Group, an organization of
    women city planners in the Dublin
    region.
    PLAN: ARCHITECTURE AND BUILDING
    DESIGN IN IRELAND 1990 June, v.31,
    no.6, p.46-47, plan.

WOMEN ARCHITECTS
    See also WOMEN CITY PLANNERS
    See also WOMEN LANDSCAPE ARCHITECTS
    Architecture: a place for women.
    Contents: Room at the top? Sexism
    and the star system in
    architecture, by Denise Scott
    Brown.--Educating for the future,
    by Matilda McQuaid.--The studio
    experience: differences for women
    students, by Anne Vytlacil.
    ARCHITECTURAL DESIGN 1990, v.60,
    no.1-2, p.[X]-[XIV],

WOMEN ARCHITECTS (CONTINUED)
    The gender agenda / Clare Melhuish.
    On the group, Warm, Women as Role
    Models, a women's group initiated
    by architects Gail Waldman and
    Angela Jim.
    BUILDING DESIGN 1990 Oct.19,
    no.1008, p.27,
    Kicking against the pricks / Clare
    Lorenz.
    ON the author's research on
    contemporary women architects.
    BUILDING DESIGN 1990 Oct.19,
    no.1008, p.24-25, photos.
    Outside the inner circle: women in
    architecture [by] Clare Lorenz
    [book review] / Amanda Levete.
    BLUEPRINT (LONDON, ENGLAND) 1990
    Oct., no.71, p.53-54,
    Perspectives: the vital ingredient
    designers forgot / Vicky Wilson.
    Work of Women's Design Service,
    London.
    BLUEPRINT (LONDON, ENGLAND) 1990
    Mar., no.65, p.14,

WOMEN ARCHITECTS--CONGRESSES
    Women and Architecture / Anne
    Zimmerman.
    Report on a conference in San
    Diego.
    ARCHITECTURE: THE AIA JOURNAL 1990
    Apr., v.79, no.4, p.36, photo.

WOMEN ARCHITECTS--UNITED STATES
    Architecture: a place for women
    [book review] / Cheryl Robertson.
    SOCIETY OF ARCHITECTURAL
    HISTORIANS. JOURNAL 1990 Sept.,
    v.49, no.3, p.349-351,
    Conversations with Women Architects
    / Toshira Sato.
    One of four sections in a special
    feature on "Women in American
    Architecture". Contents: Julie
    Eizenberg.--Norma Sklarek/The
    Jerda Partnership.--Deborah
    Sussman.--Diane M. Caughey.--
    Pamela Burton+Katherine Spitz.--
    Dolores Hayden.--Sheila Levrant de
    Bretteville.
    SPACE DESIGN 1990 June, no.309,
    p.06-22, dwgs., ports., elev.,
    models, phgotos., plans, secn.
    Feminist Design / Sheila Levrant de
    Bretteville.
    One of four sections in a special
    feature on "Women in American
    Architecture". Contents: Lucia
    Howard/Ace Architects.--Susan M.
    Goltsman.--Andrea P. Leers+Jane
    Weinzapfel.--Ann M. Beha.--Jane
    Thompson/Benjamin Thompson &
    Associates.
    SPACE DESIGN 1990 June, no.309,
    p.23-35,72-73, dwgs., ports.,
    photos., plans, site plan.
    Room at the Top? Sexism and the Star
    System in Architecture / Denise
    Scott Brown.
    One of four sections in a special
    feature on "Women in American
    Architecture". English
    translation, p.73 75.
    SPACE DESIGN 1990 June, no.309,
    p.54-71,73-75, dwgs., ports.,
    elevs., photos., plans, secns.,
    site plams, refs.

WOMEN ARCHITECTS--UNITED STATES
                    (CONTINUED)
   Special feature: Women in American
   architecture / Toshiro Sato, guest
   editor.
   The four sections are indexed
   separately.
   SPACE DESIGN 1990 June, no.309,
   p.05-76, ill.
   Urbanist without Portfolio: Notes on
   a career / by Jane Thompson.
   One of four sections in a special
   feature on "Women in American
   Architecture". Contents: Marion G.
   Weiss.-- Inea Elskop/1100
   Architect. Billie Tsien.--
   Patricia Sapinsley.--Alison
   Sky+Michelle Stone/SITE Projects,
   Inc.--Karen Bausman+Leslie Gill.--
   Deborah Berke.--Amy Weinstein.--
   Adele Naude Santos. English
   translation, p.73.
   SPACE DESIGN 1990 June, no.309,
   p.36-53,73, axonometric views,
   dwgs., ports., elevs., models,
   photos., plans, secns.

WOMEN ARCHITECTS--UNITED STATES--LOS
ANGELES (CALIFORNIA)
   Breaking down the barriers: LA's
   minority and women architects /
   Ann Moore.
   L. A. ARCHITECT 1990 Feb.,
   p.[6]-7, photos., elev. plan.

WOMEN AS ARCHITECTS
   See WOMEN ARCHITECTS

WOMEN CITY PLANNERS
   Increasing minority and female
   representation in the profession:
   a call for diversity / Catherine
   L. Ross.
   JOURNAL OF PLANNING EDUCATION AND
   RESEARCH 1990 Winter, v.9, no.2,
   p.135-138, tables, refs.

WOMEN CITY PLANNERS--AUSTRALIA
   Where are the women planners? /
   Wendy Bell.
   Examines the Royal Australian
   Planning Institute.
   AUSTRALIAN PLANNER: JOURNAL OF THE
   ROYAL AUSTRALIAN PLANNING
   INSTITUTE 1990 Mar., v.28, no.1,
   p.32-35, refs.

WOMEN CITY PLANNERS--CANADA--WOMEN
PLAN TORONTO
   A voice for balance / Colleen Weir.
   Describes the activities of Women
   Plan Toronto, a group formed in
   1981 to "discover and serve the
   specific needs of women in the
   processes and results of city
   planning."
   CITY MAGAZINE 1989 Summer-Fall,
   v.11, no.1, p.7-9, photos.

WOMEN CITY PLANNERS--GREAT BRITAIN
   Training for planning / Diana
   Fitzsimons.
   Women as students in city
   planning.
   THE PLANNER 1990 Apr.13, v.76,
   no.14, p.29-30,

WOMEN CITY PLANNERS--IRELAND
   Planning with people in mind / Emer
   Hughes.
   Recommendations of the Women and
   Planning Group, an organization of
   woman city planners in the Dublin
   region.
   PLAN: ARCHITECTURE AND BUILDING
   DESIGN IN IRELAND 1990 June, v.31,
   no.6, p.46-47, plan.

WOMEN LANDSCAPE ARCHITECTS
   See also WOMEN ARCHITECTS

WOMEN LANDSCAPE ARCHITECTS--UNITED
STATES--PASADENA (CALIFORNIA)
   Landscaping the American dream: the
   gardens and film sets of Florence
   Yoch: 1890-1972 [by] James J. Yoch
   [book review] / David Gebhard.
   Discusses the contributions of
   Lucile Council, Yoch's partner.
   SOCIETY OF ARCHITECTURAL
   HISTORIANS. JOURNAL 1990 Dec.,
   v.49, no.4, p.450-452,

WOMEN PLAN TORONTO (ORGANIZATION)
   A voice for balance / Colleen Weir.
   Describes the activities of Women
   Plan Toronto, a group formed in
   1981 to "discover and serve the
   specific needs of women in the
   processes and results of city
   planning."
   CITY MAGAZINE 1989 Summer-Fall,
   v.11, no.1, p.7-9, photos.

WOMEN'S DESIGN SERVICE
   Perspectives: the vital ingredient
   designers forgot / Vicky Wilson.
   Work of Women's Design Service,
   London.
   BLUEPRINT (LONDON, ENGLAND) 1990
   Mar., no.65, p.14,

WOMEN'S MOVEMENT
   See FEMINISM

WOMEN'S SHELTERS
   See CRISIS SHELTERS

WOMERSLEY, J. LEWIS, 1910-1990
   Lewis Womersley [obituary].
   BUILDING DESIGN 1990 Nov.9,
   no.1011, p.5,
   Obituary: J. Lewis Womersley CBE /
   Anthony J. Pass.
   British city planner and
   architect.
   THE PLANNER 1990 Dec.14, v.76,
   no.49, p.XV,

WONDRA, HEINZ
   Der "Forellenweg" in Salzburg.
   Housing development. Architects:
   Rob Krier; Adolf Krischanitz;
   Franz Fonatsch, Heinz Wondra;
   Reiner Kaschl, Heide Muhlfellner;
   Aldo Rossi; Franz Demblin; Erwin
   Pontiller; and O.M. Ungers.
   Includes English summary.
   BAUMEISTER 1990 June, v.87, no.6,
   p.56-62, photos., plans, site
   plan, aerial photos.

WONG AND OUYANG AND ASSOCIATES
   Cranes were the key [Pacific Place
   project in Hong Kong].
   A two-tower multi-use complex.
   Architects: Wong and Ouyang.
   ASIAN ARCHITECT AND CONTRACTOR
   1989 Sept., v.19, no.9, p.[24]-28,
   photos.

WONG AND OUYANG AND ASSOCIATES
                    (CONTINUED)
   Rudolph: pompe di energia a
   Hong-Kong.
   Bond Centre. Architects: Paul
   Rudolph with Wong & Ouyang.
   ARCHITETTURA; CRONACHE E STORIA
   1989 Oct., v.35, no.10(408),
   p.734-735, photos., plans.

WONG, CHARLES C. C.
   Infrastructure and its effect on the
   environment / Charles C. C. Wong.
   ASIAN ARCHITECT AND CONTRACTOR
   1989 Aug., v.19, no.8, p.28,
   chart.

WONG, JOHN
   Using landscape architecture to
   address a civic space / Beth
   McKinney.
   Student projects for a 4.5-acre
   civic complex in Burnaby, B. C.,
   in a studio led by visiting
   critics William Callaway and John
   Wong.
   GSD NEWS / HARVARD UNIVERSITY.
   GRADUATE SCHOOL OF DESIGN 1990
   Winter, v.18, no.3, p.8, models,
   site plan.

WONG, PETER
   Specifying finish hardware / Peter
   Wong.
   CANADIAN ARCHITECT 1990 Apr.,
   v.35, no.4, p.57,

WONG, VOON YEE
   AA diploma honours 1989-90 / Raoul
   Bunschoten, Wiel Arets, Stefano de
   Martino, Peter Salter, Ron Herron,
   Andrew Holmes and John Frazer.
   Diploma prizes to Joel Segal, Voon
   Yee Wong, Simon Hart, Toru Ogata,
   Bobby Desai, Shin Egashira and
   Matthew Waltman.
   AA FILES 1990 Autumn, no.20,
   p.95-101, dwgs., models, photo.

WOO AND WILLIAMS
   Uncommon dwellings: Harvard faculty
   housing, Cambridge, Massachusetts,
   Woo + Williams, Architects /
   Robert Campbell.
   Townhouses.
   ARCHITECTURE: THE AIA JOURNAL 1990
   Jan., v.79, no.1, p.78-81,
   photos., plan, secns., site plan.

WOOD
   See also DRY ROT
   See also HARDWOOD
   See also LUMBER
   See also MILLWORK
   See also PARTICLE BOARD
   See also PLYWOOD
   See also "WOODEN" AS A SUBHEADING
   AFTER SPECIFIC BUILDING TYPES OR
   OTHER MAIN HEADINGS.
   Factors influencing the paintability
   of wood: literature search -
   summary - report / Erik Nilsson.
   Report of a search (date is
   unspecified) of chemistry,
   agriculture, surface coatings of
   wood databases.
   SWEDISH COUNCIL FOR BUILDING
   RESEARCH. DOCUMENT 1990, D11,
   p.1-24,

WOOD (CONTINUED)
Timber.
Special feature, with articles on conservation, quality, fiberboard, glulam, the variety of products, and drying of timber.
BUILDING 1990 Feb.16, v.255, no.7, p.61-72, graph, photos., table.

WOOD, BRYANT G.
Did the Israelites conquer Jericho? a new look at the archaeological evidence / Bryant G. Wood.
A revision of a paper presented at the Near East Archaeological Society meeting, South Hamilton, Mass., Dec. 4, 1987.
BIBLICAL ARCHAEOLOGY REVIEW 1990 Mar.-Apr., v.16, no.2, p.44-58, dwg., photos., secns., site plans, reconst. dwgs., aerial photo., refs.

WOOD BUILDINGS
See BUILDINGS - WOODEN

WOOD-CARVERS--DOCUMENTATION--JAPAN--TOYAMA PREFECTURE--INAMI
The Bansho-ya family of wood carving carpenter in Inami, Etchu: succession and work methods / Susumu Hyuga.
In the 18th and 19th centuries, in the Toyama prefecture. Text in Japanese; includes English summary.
NIHON KENCHIKU GAKKAI KEIKAKUKEI RONBUN HOKOKU SHU = JOURNAL OF ARCHITECTURE, PLANNING AND ENVIRONMENTAL ENGINEERING 1990 Nov., no.11(417), p.117-126, maps., tables.

WOOD - CONSERVATION AND RESTORATION
See WOOD - PRESERVATION

WOOD DECAY
See WOOD - DETERIORATION

WOOD - DETERIORATION
See also DRY ROT
See also WOOD - PRESERVATION

WOOD--ECONOMIC ASPECTS
The comparative study of building codes in Japan, the USA and Canada [part 2] / Hideyo Totani.
Subtitle: Japanese wood products trading practice named under SUPER 301 and the problems of Japanese domestic codes and standards.
Text in Japanese; English summary, p.45.
NIHON KENCHIKU GAKKAI KEIKAKUKEI RONBUN HOKOKU SHU = JOURNAL OF ARCHITECTURE, PLANNING AND ENVIRONMENTAL ENGINEERING 1990 Apr., no.4(410), p.45-52, table, refs.
Way through the woods / Aidan Walker.
Discussion of the use of temperate hardwoods in light of ecological and economic concerns.
DESIGNERS' JOURNAL 1990 June, no.58, p.58-60, ill.

WOOD--ECONOMIC ASPECTS--IRELAND
Timber: a growth industry? / Emer Hughes.
Irish timber industry.
PLAN: ARCHITECTURE & BUILDING DESIGN IN IRELAND 1990 Jan., v.27, no.1, p.26, photo.

WOOD--ENVIRONMENTAL ASPECTS
Forest rules OK / Graham Ridout.
On the Timber Trades Federation's campaign to promote the use of wood from renewable sources.
BUILDING 1990 Sept.28, v.255, no.38, p.61, tables.
How good is wood? / Timothy B. McDonald.
A series of articles on the environmental factors of wood and wood products.
ARCHITECTURAL RECORD 1990 Dec., v.178, no.13, p.39-45, charts, dwg., photo.

WOOD--FIREPROOFING
Under fire: new research on retardant-treated plywood fills in knowledge gaps / Timothy B. McDonald.
ARCHITECTURE: THE AIA JOURNAL 1990 Apr., v.79, no.4, p.99-100, figs.

WOOD-FRAME BUILDINGS
See STRUCTURAL FRAMES - WOODEN

WOOD-FRAME CONSTRUCTION
See STRUCTURAL FRAMES - WOODEN

WOOD INLAY
See MARQUETRY

WOOD, JOHN, 1704-1754
Flights of fancy.
Recreation of original early 18th cent. timber staircase in No.15 Queen Sq., Bath, designed by John Wood the Elder. Woodwork for new staircase by Donal Channer & Co.
ARCHITECTS' JOURNAL 1990 Sept.26, v.192, no.13, p.46-[47],49, axonometric view, elev., photos., secn.

WOOD, JOHN, 1728-1781
Luxushotel im Reihenhaus / Justin Thyme.
On the Royal Crescent, 18th cent. townhouses in Bath, which have been converted into a hotel. Original architect: John Wood.
ARCHITEKTUR & WOHNEN 1990 Dec.-1991 Jan., no.6, p.102-104, photos.

WOOD MARSH ARCHITECTURE
Up and coming in Melbourne / Hamish Lyon.
Four recent projects: "Home Sweet Home" exhibition (Philip Goad, architect); Lauriston Girls' School swimming complex (architects: Henderson and Lodge); Rabic House (Wood/Marsh Architecture); and Renaissance House (Architects: Perrott Lyon Mathieson).
ARCHITECTURE AUSTRALIA 1990 May, v.79, no.4, p.28-37, ill., models, photos., plans, site plan, aerial photo.

WOOD, PAUL
Winters of discontent / Paul Wood.
On Milton Keynes, England.
OXFORD ART JOURNAL 1990, v.13, no.1, p.89-94, photos.

WOOD - PRESERVATION
See also FIREPROOFING OF WOOD
See also WOOD - DETERIORATION
See also WOOD PRESERVATIVES
Le traitement curatif du bois dans le batiment.
Entire issue on wood conservation.
NOTE D'INFORMATION TECHNIQUE 1990, no.180, p.3-47, dwgs., photos., tables, biblio.

WOODALL, DOMINIQUE
Burying ground preservation / Dominique Woodall.
BOSTON PRESERVATION ALLIANCE LETTER 1990 Feb., v.11, no.2, p.6, photo.

WOODBRIDGE, SALLY
Building with blocks / Sally B. Woodbridge.
Diamond and Jewelry Mart, San Francisco, features glass block walls. Architects: Tanner Leddy Maytum Stacy, Architects.
PROGRESSIVE ARCHITECTURE 1990 Dec., v.71, no.13, p.74-75, photos., plan.
Quake damage to historic buildings / Sally Woodbridge.
On the efforts of the National Parks Service, the California Dept. of Parks and Recreation with the state office to Historic Preservation, to survey Northern California buildings damaged by the earthquake on Oct. 17, 1989.
PROGRESSIVE ARCHITECTURE 1990 Jan., v.71, no.1 p.29-30, photos.
A regionalist union / Sally Woodbridge.
Student Center, U.C. Santa Cruz. Architects: Fernau and Hartman.
PROGRESSIVE ARCHITECTURE 1990 June, v.71, no.6, p.106-113, photo., plans, site plan.
Rising to the occasion [Berggruen house, San Francisco] / Sally Woodbridge.
Renovation of shingle style home. Architects: Robert A. M. Stern Architects.
PROGRESSIVE ARCHITECTURE 1990 Nov., v.71, no.12, p.80-85, photos., plans, secns., site plan.
Urban issues: Mission Bay / Sally B. Woodbridge.
On the four plans proposed during the 1980s for San Francisco's Mission Bay. Includes plans by John Carl Warnecke (1980), I.M. Pei/Wallace Roberts & Todd (1985), EDAW et al. (Mission Bay Planning Team, 1987) and SOM (1989).
PROGRESSIVE ARCHITECTURE 1990 May, v.71, no.5, p.121-122, figs., plans, site plans.

WOODCARVERS--GREAT BRITAIN--REID, DICK
Chisel me timbers / Pat Garratt.
Profile of the firm Dick Reid, Stone and Wood Carver, York.
THE WORLD OF INTERIORS 1990 July-Aug., p.23,25-26, dets., port., photos.

WOODCARVING--EDO--JAPAN
Study on two families named Izumi and Takamatsu as the master-carver who belonged to Sakuzikata department of the Tokugawa Syogunate / Ryuichi Ito.
Text in Japanese; includes English summary.
NIHON KENCHIKU GAKKAI KEIKAKUKEI RONBUN HOKOKU SHU = JOURNAL OF ARCHITECTURE, PLANNING AND ENVIRONMENTAL ENGINEERING 1990 Aug., no.8(414), p.117-123, refs.

WOODEN
See "WOODEN" AS A SUBHEADING AFTER SPECIFIC BUILDING TYPES OR OTHER MAIN HEADINGS.

WOODFIN, THOMAS
Suite: luna de miel / Karen Hillier and Thomas Woodfin.
VIA 1990, no.11, p.124-133, photos.

WOODGER, AEDAN
Excavations in the Walbrook Valley / Duncan Lees, Aedan Woodger, Clive Orton.
Ancient London stream bed, site of Roman London.
LONDON ARCHAEOLOGIST 1989 Winter, v.6, no.5, p.115-119, axonometric view, diagr., photos., plan, site plans.

WOODHAM, TOM
The sheltering arbor: universal allure of a European standard / Tom Woodham.
SOUTHERN ACCENTS 1990 July-Aug., v.13, no.6, p.52-59, photos.

WOODROW, DAVID
Development control issues / David Woodrow.
THE PLANNER 1990 Feb.23, v.76, no.7, p.75-78, port.

WOODS, CHRISTINE
Brushing through the tulips: a Victorian stencilled wallcovering comes to life once more / Christine Woods.
Reproduction of "Tulip Garden", an 1890s design originally used in the billard room of a country house near Bushey Heath.
TRADITIONAL HOMES 1990 Oct., v.7, no.1, p.51-54, photos.
Deep friezes: the turn-of the century enthusiasm for wallpaper friezes / Christine Woods.
TRADITIONAL HOMES 1990 Nov., v.7, no.2, p.55-58, ill.

WOODS, LEBBEUS, 1940-
Architektur erhebt sich. Lebbeus Wood's Projekt Aerial Paris = Architecture rising. Lebbeus Wood's Aerial Paris project / Michael Sorkin.
Aerial Paris project, 1989; architect: Lebbeus Woods.
DAIDALOS 1990 Sept.15, no.37, p.118-121, dwgs.
Lebbeus Woods: architecture rising / Michael Sorkin.
COLUMBIA UNIVERSITY. GRADUATE SCHOOL OF ARCHITECTURE, PLANNING AND PRESERVATION. NEWSLINE 1990 Nov., v.3, no.3, p.4, dwgs., model.

WOODS, LEBBEUS, 1940- (CONTINUED)
Lebbeus Woods, RIEA, and its Berlin exhibition of experimental architecture [exhibition review] / Christian W. Thomsen.
Report on exhibition held at Aedes Gallery. Text in Japanese and English.
ARCHITECTURE AND URBANISM 1990 Oct., no.10(241), p.30-[43], dwgs., photos.

WOODS, MARY
La presse architecturale aux Etats-Unis, 1870-1910 / David Van Zanten, Mary Woods.
REVUE DE L'ART 1990, no.89, p.19-28, photos., plans, engrs.

WOODS, RICHARD, 1716?-1793
Air of irregularity / Tim Mowl.
Park laid out in 1760s for Sir Robert Throckmorton; landscape architect: Richard Woods.
COUNTRY LIFE 1990 Jan.11, v.184, no.2, p.58-61, photos.

WOODWARD, CHRISTOPHER
Daring watercolours: Hugh Buchanan [exhibition review] / Christopher Woodward.
Exhibition of architectural watercolors by Scottish artist Hugh Buchanan at the Francis Kyle Gallery, London, through 1 Mar. 1990.
ARCHITECTS' JOURNAL 1990 Feb.21, v.191, no.8, p.88-89, dwg.

WOODWARD, HIRAM W.
The Laksmana temple, Khajuraho, and its meanings / Hiram W. Woodward.
11th cent. temple. Focus on iconographic analysis of temple sculpture in light of certain texts.
ARS ORIENTALIS 1989, v.19, p.[27]-48, diagr., dwg., photos., plan, refs.

WOODWORK
Caja de piedra, corazon de madera: Ayuntamiento de Lesaka, Navarra. Restoration of 18th century City Hall, Lesaca, Spain. Architects: Alberto Ustarroz, Manuel Iniguez.
English summary, p.87.
A & V 1990, no.21, p.50-53, photos., plans, secns.
On the threshold: a tiny vestibule designed by Leo J. Blackman makes a smooth transition from outdoors to indoors, and medieval to modern / Clifford A. Pearson.
Vestibule for St. Paul the Apostle, in Manhattan.
ARCHITECTURAL RECORD 1990 Oct., v.178, no.11, p.76-[77], photos., plan.
Woodwork examination: how original joinery survives changing fashion / Michael Thornton.
TRADITIONAL HOMES 1990 Mar., v.6, no.6, p.89-93, dwgs., photos.

WOODWORK--15TH CENTURY--ITALY--ASCOLI
Giovanni di Stefano da Montelparo intagliatore marchigiano del sec. XV / Giuseppe Crocetti.
On the work of the woodcarver from Ascoli, ca. 1448-1456, on the choir of San Domenico, Fermo, and
(Continued next column)

WOODWORK--15TH CENTURY--ITALY--ASCOLI (CONTINUED)
Giovanni di Stefano...(CONTINUED)
on choir stalls at Santa Maria dei Servi di Colle Landone, Perugia. Includes English summary.
ARTE CRISTIANA 1989 Nov.-Dec., v.77, no.735, p.465-474, photos., refs.

WOODWORK--18TH CENTURY
Tidewater treasure ... Gunston Hall / Martin Filler.
Mansion built in 1755-59 by George Mason features wood carving William Buckland.
HOUSE & GARDEN 1990 Nov., v.162, no.11, p.132-[139],231, ports., photos., aerial photo.

WOODWORK--NEPAL
Architectural woodwork in Nepal / Shaphalya Amatya.
PRACINA NEPALA 1988 Dec.-1989 Jan., no.109, p.[1]-3,

WOODWORK--QING--CHINA--HANGZHOU
Hu Qing Yu Tang, a traditional Chinese pharmacy / Wu Jiamin.
In Hangzhou, Zhejiang province; built in 1876.
BUILDING IN CHINA 1990 Dec., v.3 no.4, p.39-44, insert{1p.}, port., photos., plan.

WOODWORKERS
See also FURNITURE WORKERS
See also WOOD-CARVERS

WOODWORKERS--17TH CENTURY--JAPAN
Study on carvers who belonged to the Tokugawa shogunate / Ryuichi Ito.
In Japanese; English summary, p.97.
NIHON KENCHIKU GAKKAI KEIKAKUKEI RONBUN HOKOKU SHU = JOURNAL OF ARCHITECTURE, PLANNING AND ENVIRONMENTAL ENGINEERING 1990 May, no.5(411), p.97-105, charts, refs.

WOODWORKERS--UNITED STATES--NAKASHIMA, GEORGE
George Nakashima [obituary].
INTERIOR DESIGN 1990 July, v.61, no.10, p.36,

WOODY, WILLIAM M.
Building corrosion-resistant parking structures / William M. Woody.
Includes inset article: "Strategic parking solutions", by Kenneth E. McCurdy and Nickitas F. Panayotou.
DEVELOPMENT 1990 Mar.-Apr., v.21, no.2, p.29-31,33, port., photos.

WOOLF, DAVID E.
Earth, wind, and furniture / Andrea Loukin.
Interiors of renovated 2,000 sq. ft. New York apartment. Architect: David Woolf.
INTERIOR DESIGN 1990 Mar., v.61, no.5, p.172-[175], photos., plans.

WOOLLEY, LEIGH
Tasmanian trio / Rory Spence.
Features three projects in Hobart: garden room, South Hobart, architect: Jim Jones; house addition, West Hobart, architect: Leigh Woolley and studio house,
(Continued next page)

WORLD FAIRS--SPAIN--SEVILLE--
EXPOSICION UNIVERSAL 1992
(CONTINUED)
Parkgestaltung auf dem Gelande der
Weltausstellung / Jose A. Mejias,
M. Cristina Andres.
Park design for Expo '92 on the
Isla de la Cartuja, Seville,
Spain. Includes English summary.
GARTEN UND LANDSCHAFT 1990, v.100,
no.3, p.55-66, map, photos, site
plan.
El recinto apresurado: Sevilla: la
cuenta atras de la Expo / Adela
Garcia-Herrera.
ARQUITECTURA VIVA 1990 Sept.-Oct.,
no.14, p.6-11, elevs., models,
secns.
Verdensudstillingen 1992: the Big
Bang i Sevilla / Martin Keiding.
ARKITEKTEN 1990 Jan., v.92, no.1,
p.18-19, photos.
Een verleden voor de toekomst: de
wereldtentoostelling in Sevilla
1992 / Arjen Oosterman.
ARCHIS 1990 Oct., no.10, p.13-21,
ill., dwgs., models, secns., site
plans, aerial photos.

WORLD FAIRS--UNITED STATES--CHICAGO
(ILLINOIS)
Sketches for the 1992 Chicago
World's Fair: John Hejduk and
Thomas Beeby.
PERSPECTA 1990, no.26, p.229-230,
sketches.

WORLD FAIRS--UNITED STATES--NEW YORK
(NEW YORK)--NEW YORK WORLD'S FAIR
1964
Il domestico in guerra = Domesticity
at war / Beatriz Colomina.
Discusses the 1964-1965 New York
World's Fair, the Underground Home
and other exhibits, Michael Webb's
Slow House, and Donna Robertson's
Room in the City. In Italian and
English.
OTTAGONO 1990 Dec., no.97,
p.24-[49], ill., dwgs., models,
photos., plans, secn., refs.

WORLD FAIRS--UNITED STATES--NEW YORK
(NEW YORK)--NEW YORK'S WORLD'S FAIR
1939--EXHIBITIONS
Back to the future [exhibition
review] / Julian Holder.
On the exhibition, Selling the
world of tomorrow, on view at the
Museum of the City of New York.
BUILDING DESIGN 1990 June 15,
no.990, p.30-31, dwgs., photos.

WORLD HERITAGE COMMITTEE
Spanish missions [in the U.S.] /
Antoinette J. Lee.
This aricle lists and describes
the Spanish missions in the U.S.
Southwest and advocates that
several be placed on the World
Heritage List.
ASSOCIATION FOR PRESERVATION
TECHNOLOGY. BULLETIN 1990, v.22,
no.3, cover, p.42-54, photos.,
plans, axonometric view, refs.,
site lan, maps, elevs.

WORLD MONUMENTS FUND (NEW YORK, N.Y.)
Restoring the Angkor Temples: a
struggle against nature and man /
Bonnie Burnham.
ART INTERNATIONAL 1990 Winter, new
ser., no.13, p.79-[83], photos.

WORLD TRADE CENTERS--BRAZIL--RIO DE
JANEIRO--CENTRO EMPRESARIAL
INTERNACIONAL RIO
Um edificio inteligente na regiao
portuaria: Centro Empresarial
Internacional Rio.
Architects: Edison and Edmundo
Musa.
PROJETO 1990 Aug., no.134,
p.36-39, photos., plans, secn.,
aerial photos.

WORLD TRADE CENTERS--CANADA--MONTREAL
(QUEBEC)--CENTRE DE COMMERCE MONDIAL
Le facadisme: le decor a l'envers!
Ou less is decor! / Dinu Bumbaru.
Report on the April 1989 Montreal
symposium of facadism. Includes
discussion on the use of facadism
in the Centre de Commerce Mondial
de Montreal. Summaries in English,
Italian and Spanish.
ICOMOS INFORMATION 1989 Oct.-Dec.,
no.4, p.11-18, photos., elev.
Quelques projets en cours de
realisation [Montreal].
Includes seven projects.
Architects: LeMoyne Lapointe
Magne, Werleman Guy McMahon,
Tolchinsky & Goodz, Kohn Pedersen
Fox Associates, Dan S. Hanganu,
Arcop Associates, Roy Provencher,
L'Atelier, JLP & Associes and
Blouin et associes.
ARQ: ARCHITECTURE/QUEBEC 1990
Apr., no.54, p.42-48, elevs.,
models, photos., plans, secns.,
site plans, refs.

WORLD TRADE CENTERS--ITALY--GENOA
World Trade Center a Genova: torre
nel complesso San Benigno.
Architects: Piero Gambacciani,
with R. Garibaldi and A. Messina.
Summaries in English, French,
German, and Spanish.
ARCHITETTURA; CRONACHE E STORIA
1990 June, v.36, no.6(416),
p.406-417, dets., map, photos.,
plans, secns., site plan.

WORLD TRADE CENTERS--POLAND--WARSAW--
WARSAW TRADE CENTER
William McDonough / Adelheid
Fischer.
On the New York architect and his
proposal for the Warsaw, Poland,
Trade Center.
ARCHITECTURE MINNESOTA 1990
Nov.-Dec., v.16, no.6, p.21,64,
port., model.

WORLD TRADE CENTERS--SWEDEN--
STOCKHOLM--WORLD TRADE CENTER
Stoccolma: le megastrutture =
Stockholm: mega-buildings.
The World Trade Center (Arken,
Erskine & Tengbom); The Globe
(Berg Arkitektkontor).
ABITARE 1990 July-Aug., no.287,
p.124-129, dwg., photos., plans,
secns., site plan, aerial photo.

WORLD TRADE CENTERS--SWEDEN--
STOCKHOLM--WORLD TRADE CENTER
(CONTINUED)
Tema: Glas i byggeriet.
Technical aspects of glass
construction, with reference to
the Cityterminalen/World Trade
Center in Stockholm (architects:
Arken, Erskine og Tengbom). Issue
includes other articles on glass,
indexed separately.
ARKITEKTEN 1990 June, v.92, no.8,
p.A178,A180, A182, diagr., photo.,
secn.

WORLD TRADE CENTERS--UNITED STATES
World trade centers: made to order
for today's truly global
marketplace / Harold Kelman.
In Boston, New York, Washington,
Chicago, and other United States
cities.
REAL ESTATE FORUM 1990 Mar., v.45,
no.3, p.94-102, dwgs., elevs.,
photos., aerial photo.

WORLD'S FAIRS
See WORLD FAIRS

WORLDWIDE APPROACH
See GLOBALISM

WORMELL, SEBASTIAN
Moving the baroque [book review] /
Sebastian Wormell.
Review of Joze Plecnik, Architect,
1872-1957, edited by Francois
Burkhardt, Claude Eveno and Boris
Podrecca, translated by Carol
Volk.
BUILDING DESIGN 1990 Apr.6,
no.980, p.34-35, photos., secn.

WORNER, NORBERT
Zum Tode des Architekten Hans
Magoley [obituary] / Norbert
Worner.
DER ARCHITEKT 1990 July-Aug.,
no.7-8, p.13.

WORNUM, GEORGE GREY, 1888-1957
Inside story: Kenneth Powell on
London property.
House at 39 Weymouth St., London;
architect: George Grey Wornum.
COUNTRY LIFE 1990 Nov.22, v.184,
no.47, p.108, photos.

WORRALL, L.
Information systems for urban and
regional planning in the United
Kingdom: a review / L. Worrrall.
ENVIRONMENT AND PLANNING B 1990
Oct., v.17, no.4, p.451-462,
chart, refs.

WORRINGER, WILHELM
Anthological excerpts from Gottfried
Semper to Henri Focillon.
Excerpts from eight writers' works
on decoration and ornament.
RASSEGNA 1990 Mar., v.12, no.41/1,
p.77-88, ill.

WORSLEY, GILES
Aske Hall, Yorkshire - I: the seat
of the Marquess of Zetland / Giles
Worsley.
Architect: William Wakefield;
plasterer: Francesco Vassalli.
COUNTRY LIFE 1990 Mar.1, v.184,
no.9, p.80-83, ill., photos.

WORSLEY, GILES (CONTINUED)

Aske Hall, Yorkshire - II: the seat of the Marquess of Zetland / Giles Worsley.
Architects: John Carr, Ignatius Bonomi, Claud Phillimore.
COUNTRY LIFE 1990 Mar.8, v.184, no.10, p.98-103, photos.

La Casita del Principe, El Pardo: a property of the Patrimonio Nacional / Giles Worsley.
Built in 1784 for the future King Carlos IV; architect: Juan de Villanueva.
COUNTRY LIFE 1990 Dec.20, v.184, no.51, p.56-61, photos.

Castello di Racconigi / Giles Worsley.
Seat of the princes of Carignano, Piedmont; architects: Guarino Guarini, Giovanni Battista Borra, Pelagio Palagi.
COUNTRY LIFE 1990 July 5, v.184, no.27, p.106-111, photos.

Designs of antiquity: Hawksmoor's London churches / Giles Worsley.
Architect: Nicholas Hawksmoor.
COUNTRY LIFE 1990 Oct.18 v.184, no.42, p.172,174, ill., photos.

Duncombe Park, Yorkshire - I: the seat of Lord Feversham / Giles Worsley.
Architects: William Wakefield, Charles Barry, and William Young.
COUNTRY LIFE 1990 May 24, v.184, no.21, p.116-121, dwg., photos.

Duncombe Park Yorkshire - II: the seat of Lord Feversham / Giles Worsley.
Architects: William Wakefield, Charles Barry, William Young.
COUNTRY LIFE 1990 May 31, v.184, no.22, p.138-143, ill., photo.

Impractical but proper / Giles Worsley.
The placement of kitchens in 17th and 18th cent. country houses.
COUNTRY LIFE 1990 Nov.22, v.184, no.47, p.54-57, dwgs., secns.

Is banality inevitable? / Giles Worsley.
Country Life commission for petrol station designs; designers: Glynn Boyd Harte, James Gorst, Murray John, Stephan Ryan, Alan Powers, and Roderick Gradidge.
COUNTRY LIFE 1990 Sept.20, v.184, no.38, p.140-143, dwgs., elevs., plans.

Nicholas Hawksmoor: a pioneer neo-Palladian? / Giles Worsley.
ARCHITECTURAL HISTORY 1990, v.33, p.[60]-74, dwgs., elevs., photos., secns., refs.

Oakwell Hall, Yorkshire: the property of Kirklees Metropolitan Council / Giles Worsley.
House built ca.1583 & altered in 17th century.
COUNTRY LIFE 1990 Jan.18, v.184, no.3, p.40-45, photos.

Riding on status: the stables at Houghton / Giles Worsley.
COUNTRY LIFE 1990 Sept.27, v.184, no.39, p.108-111, photos.

Rococo survival [Dalton Hall gardens] / Giles Worsley.
Gardens laid out in 1730s.
Gardeners: Richard North, Richard Davies, John Scott.
COUNTRY LIFE 1990 May 17, v.184, no.20, p.198-200, elevs., photos., site plans, engrs.

WORSLEY, GILES (CONTINUED)

Schooling movements / Giles Worsley.
The 17th century British horse riding houses.
COUNTRY LIFE 1990 Oct.4, v.184, no.40, p.158-160, photos., elevs., plan, secn.

Tales from Crummie-Toddie / Giles Worsley.
COUNTRY LIFE 1990 Aug.2, v.184, no.31, p.78-82, photos.

West Wycombe Park, Bucks: the seat of Sir Francis Dashwood and a property of the National Trust / Giles Worsley.
Neoclassical house remodelled between 1748-1771 by Sir Francis Dashwood.
COUNTRY LIFE 1990 Sept.6, v.184, no.36, p.112-117, photos.

Womersley Park, Yorkshire: the home of Hon. Martin and Mrs. Parsons / Giles Worsley.
COUNTRY LIFE 1990 Dec.13, v.184, no.50, p.42-45, photos.

WORSLEY, STEVEN

The Ipswich Horse Tram Depot / Steven Worsley.
History since 1880.
INDUSTRIAL ARCHAEOLOGY REVIEW 1990 Spring, v.12, no.2, p.145-152, photos., plan, secns., site plan, biblio., refs.

WORTMAN, MARC

Bofill plays the provinces / Marc Wortman.
A new, mixed-use neighborhood, called Antigone, in Montpellier, France.
ARCHITECTURAL RECORD 1990 July, v.178, no.8, p.41-42, ill., photos., site plan.

A model city remodeled / Marc Wortman.
Survey of new building in New Haven, Connecticut.
PROGRESSIVE ARCHITECTURE 1990 Jan., v.71, no.1, p.39-40,42, elev., models, photos.

WORTMANN, ARTHUR

Afscheid Koolhaas in teken van moed en wanhoop: symposium in Delft / Arthur Wortmann.
Report on conference held by the Technische Universiteit Delft, 27 Apr.1990, entitled "Hoe modern is de Nederlandse architectuur?"
Issue includes one article (separately indexed) from the symposium.
ARCHIS 1990 June, no.6, p.6-7.

Archiprix 1989 en de Wet van de Verliezende Winnaars / Arthur Wertmann.
On the presentation of the 1989 Dutch annual student awards, held on 18 Apr.1990 in Zoewolde.
ARCHIS 1990 May, no.5, p.2, ill.

De architect als joker:
Tentoonstelling in Domburg [exhibition review] / Arthur Wortmann.
Projects on exhibit, Sept.1989, at the Dorimare recreation center in Domburg, for development of the waterfront. Architects: Wiel Arets, Stephane Beel and Luc Reuse, Ben van Berkel, Chris Kempe.

(Continued next column)

WORTMANN, ARTHUR (CONTINUED)

De architect als joker: (CONTINUED)
ARCHIS 1990 Sept., no.9, p.4-5, ill., model.

Architecture and body [by] Scott marble et al. [book review] / Arthur Wortmann.
ARCHIS 1989 Nov., no.11, p.55, ill., ref.

De Archivaris [by] Francois Schuiten, Benoit Peeters [book review] / Arthur Wortmann.
ARCHIS 1990 Feb., no.2, p.54-55, dwg.

Carel Weeber en het arrogante type [exhibition review] / Arthur Wortmann.
At the Nederlands Architectuurinstituut, Rotterdam, until May 13, 1990.
ARCHIS 1990 Apr., no.4, p.3, dwg., photo., refs.

Geen rozen zonder doornon: de vierde Biennale jonge Nederlandse architecten / Arthur Wortmann.
"Follies voor de Floriade 1992", on exhibit until Feb.11, 1990 at the Nederlands Architectuurinstituut in Rotterdam.
ARCHIS 1990 Jan., no.1, p.8-11, models.

Een kunst van weinig woorden: vier ontwerpen van Bruno Albert, Charles Vandenhove en John Berhaut / Arthur Wortmann.
Four Liege projects: design for the Hogere Handelsschool (1989), with Camille Ghysen; Le Balloir (1988-1991); La Maison Heureuse, Ans (1986-1989); Woning Sutoor, Embourg (1988-1989).
ARCHIS 1990 July, no.7, p.15-24, elevs., photos., plans, secn., refs.

Een nooduitgang voor de Zakelijkheid: Koen van Velsens verbouwing van Hotel Gooiland / Arthur Wortmann.
Opened in 1936. Architect: J. Duiker. Renovation architects: Architectenbureau Van Klooster.
ARCHIS 1990 Sept., no.9, p.38-45, photos., plans, secn., refs.

De perfertie voorbij: Waarom Bert Dirrix de Prix de Rome voor architectuur won / Arthur Wortmann.
First prize: Bert Dirrix. Second prize: Roberto Meyer.
ARCHIS 1990 Oct., no.10, p.46-51, model, plans, secns., site plans, sketches.

Peter Eisenman: Recent projecten-recent projects [book review] / Arthur Wortmann.
Edited by Arie Graafland.
ARCHIS 1990 May, no.5, p.56-57, plans.

Prix de Rome deelnemers worden bedankt voor de moeite / Arthur Wortmann.
Dutch winners of the 1990 awards, announced on 4 May included Jules Beckers, Art Zaaijer, and Dirk Jan Postel.
ARCHIS 1990 June, no.6, p.2-3, axonometric view, plans.

WRIGHT, FRANK LLOYD, 1867-1959--
CORRESPONDENCE AND RECORDS
"Oh, Frahnk": FLW and Miriam Noel /
William Marlin.
Correspondence and memoirs by
Wright's second wife.
INLAND ARCHITECT 1990 Sept.-Oct.,
v.34, no.5, p.24,26,70,73, port.,
photos.

WRIGHT, FRANK LLOYD, 1867-1959--
EXHIBITIONS
Drawing the Wright way [exhibition
review] / Stanley Allan.
Review of exhibit at the Phoenix
Art Museum early in 1990, of 300
drawings from the Taliesin West
archives.
INLAND ARCHITECT 1990 May-June,
v.34, no.3, p.90-96, elev., secns.
Rare Wright drawings in Phoenix
[exhibition review] / Jeffrey
Cook.
Review of Frank Lloyd Wright
Drawings at the Phoenix Art Museum
until Apr.8, 1990.
PROGRESSIVE ARCHITECTURE 1990
Mar., v.71, no.3, p.23-24, dwg.
"...as you work, as you play": zur
Ausstellung von
Frank-Lloyd-Wright-Zeichnungen im
Phoenix Art Museum, Phoenix,
Arizona, 13.Januar bis 15.April
1990 [exhibition review] / Christa
Zeller.
WERK, BAUEN + WOHNEN 1990 June,
no.6, p.12-15, dwgs., elevs.,
photos.
Zeichnungen von Frank Lloyd Wright:
zu einer Ausstellung in Phoenix
[exhibition review].
Jan.13-Apr.8, 1990, Phoenix Art
Museum.
BAUMEISTER 1990 Jan., v.87, no.1,
p.64, dwgs.

WRIGHT, FRANK LLOYD, 1867-1959--
INFLUENCE
Cassina: vivere con un genio =
Living with genius.
Furniture modelled on F.L.
Wright's designs for the Robie
House and others.
OTTAGONO 1990 Sept., no.96,
p.164-[167], dwgs., photos.
De Papaverhof in ere hersteld:
renovatie in de geest van
oorspronkelijk ontwerp / Henk van
der Schoor.
On the 1920 design for the garden
apartment complex, the De Stijl
movement, F.L. Wright's influence,
and the recent restoration of the
buildings. Original architect: Jan
Wils. Renovation architect: J.
Franso.
DE ARCHITECT 1989 Dec., v.20,
no.12, p.92-99, dwg., photos.,
plans, secns., site plan.
Paranoia or conspiracy: a question
of Wright / Nicholas Davis.
Includes a response by Diane
Ghirardo.
JOURNAL OF ARCHITECTURAL EDUCATION
1990 Winter, v.43, no.2, p.62-64,
refs.
Quattro interpretazioni della
residenza in chiave organica.
Four houses by Ugo Bartorelli and
Ruggero Tacchini: at S. Maurizio
d'Opaglio, Gozzano, and
Borgomanero. Summaries in English,
(Continued next column)

WRIGHT, FRANK LLOYD, 1867-1959--
INFLUENCE (CONTINUED)
Quattro... (CONTINUED)
French, German, and Spanish.
ARCHITETTURA; CRONACHE E STORIA
1990 Apr., v.36, no.4(414),
p.[262]-269, photos., plans,
secns., site plans, aerial photo.
Wide spaces and widening chaos /
Laurie Olin.
Profile of eight Americans,
outside the profession, who have
influenced landscape architects
and landscape architecture.
LANDSCAPE ARCHITECTURE 1990 Oct.,
v.80, no.10, p.[76]-83, dwgs.,
ports.
Wright and wrong in a Connecticut
country house / Brendan Gill.
Author's recollections of his
repeated alterations to his summer
house in Norfolk, Ct., including
his remodeling efforts after Frank
Lloyd Wright's Usonian houses.
ARCHITECTURAL DIGEST 1990 June,
v.47, no.6, p.34,[40-41],44, ill.,
port.

WRIGHT, LLOYD, 1890-1978
Claudette Colbert: Best Actress for
It happened one night / Jennifer
Allen.
Features her 1935 Georgian revival
home in the Holmby Hills.
Architect: Lloyd Wright.
ARCHITECTURAL DIGEST 1990 Apr.,
v.47, no.4, p.[226]-229, ports.,
photos.
Lloyd Wright and the Lehigh Airport
competition / Howard Shubert.
RACAR: REVUE D'ART CANADIENNE.
CANADIAN ART REVIEW 1989, v.16,
no.2, p.165-170,288-297, dets.,
elevs., plans, site plans, refs.

WRIGHT, PENNY
Designer toys: The art and science
of Lego [exhibition review] /
Penny Wright.
Exhibition at the Science Museum,
London, through 30 April 1990.
ARCHITECTS' JOURNAL 1990 Apr.18,
v.191, no.16, p.85, photos.
No stone unturned: Unplanned
entertainment / Penny Wright.
Report of talk given 19 Oct. 1990
at the Architectural Association,
London, by Mark Fisher of Fisher
Park, designers of demountable
stage sets for performers such as
the Rolling Stones.
ARCHITECTS' JOURNAL 1990 Oct.31,
v.192, no.18, p.73,75, elev.,
photo.
Of tsars and arches: Glasgow's
Glasgow: a city within a city
[exhibition review] / Penny
Wright.
Organized by architect Douglas
Clelland in the railway arches
under Glasgow's Central Station.
Comprises "'the biggest temporary
exhibition' and the 'most
extensive audio-visual
presentation ever assembled for
one event' in Britain". Through 5
Nov.1990.
ARCHITECTS' JOURNAL 1990 May 30,
v.191, no.22, p.68-69, axonometric
view, photo., plan.

WRIGHT, STEPHEN
Visions for the Midlands / Michael
Dower.
Regional lectures on 'The Future
Countryside' delivered at
Kedleston Hall, Derbyshire 27 Apr.
1990. Includes two additional
lectures by Ian Bowler and Stephen
Wright.
ROYAL SOCIETY OF ARTS, LONDON. RSA
JOURNAL 1990 Dec., v.139, no.5413,
p.926-937, tables.

WRIGHT, SYLVIA HART. SOURCEBOOK OF
CONTEMPORARY NORTH AMERICAN
ARCHITECTURE FROM POSTWAR TO
POSTMODERN
Sourcebook of contemporary North
American architecture [book
review] / Hans van Dijk.
Covers the mid-20th cent. Author:
Sylvia Hart Wright.
ARCHIS 1989 Oct., no.10, p.56-57,
ill.

WRITING OF SPECIFICATIONS
See SPECIFICATION WRITING

WROUGHT-IRON
See WROUGHT IRON
See also "WROUGHT IRON" AS A
SUBHEADING AFTER SPECIFIC BUILDING
TYPES OR OTHER MAIN HEADINGS.

WT PARTNERSHIPS
Refurbishment: museums and
galleries.
Theme with seven articles,
including ones on the V & A
Museum, the McLellan Galleries in
Glasgow, and the Royal Academy of
Arts (architect: Foster
Associates).
BUILDING 1990 Sept.14, v.255,
no.36, suppl., p.[1]-47, dwg.,
photos., secn.

WU, JIAMIN
Hu Qing Yu Tang, a traditional
Chinese pharmacy / Wu Jiamin.
In Hangzhou, Zhejiang province;
built in 1876.
BUILDING IN CHINA 1990 Dec., v.3
no.4, p.39-44,insert{1p.}, port.,
photos., plan.

WU, MICHAEL Y.
Enclosed entity: Michael Wu's
addition to a suburban residence /
Edie Lee Cohen.
INTERIOR DESIGN 1990 May, v.61,
no.7, p.286-[287], axonometric
view, photos.

WU, ZAIYI
Ancient bridges in Suzhou / Wu
Zaiyi.
BUILDING IN CHINA 1990 June, v.3,
no.2 p.28-30,insert, port.,
photos.

WULZ, FREDRIK
Om tid eller plats.
Introduction to issue entitled
"Fasad", on the concept of
facades. Includes three articles
indexed separately and one
entitled "Vad ar en fasad?" by
Fredrik Wulz.
ARKITEKTUR: THE SWEDISH REVIEW OF
ARCHITECTURE 1990 June-July, v.90,
no.5, p.2-3,24-27, cover, photos.,
sketch.

WYLLIE & UFNAL CONSULTING ENGINEERS
  John Street Pedestrian Bridge,
    Toronto.
    To take baseball fans from Front
    St. to the SkyDome. Montgomery and
    Sisam Architects with Wyllie &
    Ufnal Consulting Engineers.
    CANADIAN ARCHITECT 1990 July,
    v.35, no.7, p.24-26, photos.

WYMAN, LANCE
  Urban legibility and signs / Lance
    Wyman.
    THE WHEEL EXTENDED 1990, v.19,
    no.4, p.8-15, axonometric views,
    ill., maps, photos.

WYN THOMAS AND PARTNERS
  Faculty building, Cardiff.
    The first of six new buildings for
    the Univ. of Wales. Architect: Wyn
    Thomas + Partners.
    BUILDING 1990 Jan.26, v.255, no.4,
    p.63-70, det., photos., plans,
    secns., site plan, table.

WYNGAERT, THIERRY VAN DE
  Force policee: Hotel de Police de
    Douai.
    Police headquarters, Douai.
    Architect: Thierry van de
    Wyngaert. English summary, p.87.
    Spanish summary, p.149.
    TECHNIQUES ET ARCHITECTURE 1990
    Mar., no.388, p.86-87, models,
    plans, secn., site plan, isometric
    dwg.
  La forza tranquilla di un Hotel de
    Police = The calm force of a
    police station.
    Architect: Thierry van de
    Wyngaert.
    L'ARCA 1990 Nov., no.43 suppl.
    l'Arca 2, p.99.

WYSS, MICHAEL
  Un atelier d'orfevre-emailleur
    recemment decouvert a Saint-Denis
    / Olivier Meyer, Nicole Meyer,
    Michael Wyss.
    CAHIERS ARCHEOLOGIQUES; FIN DE
    L'ANTIQUITE ET MOYEN AGE 1990,
    v.38, p.81-94, dwgs., map,
    photos., refs.

XENOPOULOS, SOLON
  Concurso parque Gazi, Atenas,
    Grecia.
    Architects: Rodrigo Perez de Arce,
    Solon Xenopoulos.
    CA: REVISTA OFICIAL DEL COLEGIO DE
    ARQUITECTOS DE CHILE 1989
    Apr.-June, no.56, p.[56]-63,
    dwgs., port., elevs., map, secns.,
    site plans, isometric dwg.

XERISCAPES
  Call me xeriscapable / Karen D.
    Fishler.
    Features a design by landscape
    architect William C. Brigham.
    GARDEN DESIGN 1990 Spring, v.9,
    no.1, p.88-[91], charts, site
    plans.
  Healing the Earth: how 20 years of
    environmentalism have changed
    American gardening / Cheryl Weber.
    GARDEN DESIGN 1990 Spring, v.9,
    no.1, p.30-35, photos.

XERISCAPES--RESEARCH--UNITED STATES--
  PHOENIX (ARIZONA)
  Modeling residential landscape water
    and energy use to evaluate water
    conservation policies / E. Gregory
    McPherson.
    Data derived from computer
    simulations using three types of
    residential gardens, xeriscapes,
    zeroscapes and mesiscapes, in
    Phoenix and Tucson.
    LANDSCAPE JOURNAL 1990 Fall, v.9,
    no.2, p.122-134, photo., plans,
    tables, refs.

XERISCAPES--RESEARCH--UNITED STATES--
  TUCSON (ARIZONA)
  Modeling residential landscape water
    and energy use to evaluate water
    conservation policies / E. Gregory
    McPherson.
    Data derived from computer
    simulations using three types of
    residential gardens, xeriscapes,
    zeroscapes and mesiscapes, in
    Phoenix and Tucson.
    LANDSCAPE JOURNAL 1990 Fall, v.9,
    no.2, p.122-134, photo., plans,
    tables, refs.

XERISCAPES--UNITED STATES
  Regional style: eco-logic at work.
    A brief survey of six
    "environmental" gardens in the
    U.S. Landscape architects: Steven
    K. Domigan, Edith Eddleman, Ron
    Lutsco, Steve Trudnak, James Weht,
    and David Cropp.
    GARDEN DESIGN 1990 spring, v.9,
    no.1, p.46-59, photos., site
    plans, sketch.

XERISCAPES--UNITED STATES--SAN DIEGO
  (CALIFORNIA)
  San Diego: conquering arid obstacles
    / Kathy Day.
    Survey of recent water-conscious
    landscape projects in San Diego.
    LANDSCAPE ARCHITECTURE 1990 Oct.,
    v.80, no.10, p.54,56,58, photos.

XHEDIKU, ELMAZ
  Coping with earthquakes in Albania /
    Elmaz Xhediku.
    EKISTICS 1986 May-Aug., v.53,
    no.318-319, p.162-170, dets.,
    maps, photos, plans.

XIU, WANG
  City profiles: Luo Yang--famous
    capital for nine dynasties / Wang
    Xiu.
    CHINA CITY PLANNING REVIEW 1988
    June, v.4, no.2, p.48-57, plans,
    aerial photos.

XU, CHENGNIAN
  Architects faced with new challenge:
    Beijing's aging trend / Xu
    Chengnian.
    BUILDING IN CHINA 1990 June, v.3,
    no.2 p.41-43,

XU, KEREN
  Investigation on the blind migration
    of rural surplus labor / Xu Keren.
    BUILDING IN CHINA 1990 June, v.3,
    no.2 p.21-23,

XU, RONGLIE
  Construction technology over the
    last forty years in China / Xu
    Ronglie.
    The author is Engineer-in-chief in
    the Ministry of Construction.
    BUILDING IN CHINA 1989 Dec., v.2,
    no.4, p.10-17, port., photos.

XU, YAYING
  A l'ecoute du son: les criteres de
    la perception / Yaying Xu.
    English summary, p.65. Spanish
    summary, p.197.
    TECHNIQUES ET ARCHITECTURE 1990
    Apr.-May, no.389, p.64-65,

YAAKUP, A. B.
The application of geographic
information systems for urban
land-use planning and monitoring:
a case study of low-cost housing
development in Kuala Lumpur,
Malaysia / A.B. Yaakup, R.G.
Healey, C.G. Hughes.
ENVIRONMENT AND PLANNING B 1990
Oct., v.17, no.4, p.385-393, map,
site plans, table, refs.

YABU PUSHELBERG
Capezio: Yabu Pushelberg revitalizes
a Toronto shoe store / David
Lasker.
Located in suburban Bayview
Village Plaza.
INTERIOR DESIGN 1990 Mar., v.61,
no.5, p.210-[211], photos.

YACHT BASINS
See MARINAS

YACHT CLUBS
See also MARINAS

YACHT CLUBS--INTERIOR DESIGN--UNITED
STATES--JACKSONVILLE (FLORIDA)--
EPPING FOREST YACHT CLUB
Epping Forest Yacht Club / Judith
Nasatir.
1926 du Pont mansion converted to
yacht club, Jacksonville, Fla.
Original architect: Harold
Saxelbye. Conversion architects:
Pappa Associates. Interior
designers: Catlin Interiors.
INTERIOR DESIGN 1990 June, v.61,
no.9, p.208-[213], photos., plan.

YACHT CLUBS--UNITED STATES--
JACKSONVILLE (FLORIDA)--EPPING
FOREST YACHT CLUB
Southern traditions: preservation
efforts in today's South show new
interest in 20th-century
landmarks, as well as earlier ones
/ Clifford A. Pearson.
A portfolio of Southeast projects:
Epping Forest Yacht Club,
Jacksonville, Fla. (Pappas
Associates); Freedom Tower, Miami
(Heisenbottle Architects);
Venetian Pool, Coral Gables, Fla.
(H. Carlton Decker & Assoc.);
Howard Memorial Library, New
Orleans (E. Barron, M. Toups); and
Linden Row Inn, Richmond, Va.
(Glave Newman Anderson).
ARCHITECTURAL RECORD 1990 Mar.,
v.178, no.3, p.66-75, photos.,
plans, site plans.

YACHTS
Arks of affluence ... the high-tech
megayacht is taking the sea out of
sailing / Michael Cannell.
METROPOLIS 1990 June, v.9, no.10,
p.[56]-59,85, photos.

YACHTS--INTERIOR DESIGN--BEAUPRE
(BANNENBERG YACHT)
Civilized sailing aboard the Beaupre
/ Elizabeth Lambert.
Interiors of designer Jon
Bannenberg's yacht.
ARCHITECTURAL DIGEST 1990 Oct,
v.47, no.11, p.[230-237], photos.

YACHTS--INTERIOR DESIGN--DOLPHIN
A moveable feast at Mougins: Lane
and Parker Montgomery's Yacht and
villa in the south of France /
Steven M. L. Aronson.
Yacht interiors and the grounds of
their home, La Mougine.
ARCHITECTURAL DIGEST 1990 Sept.,
v.47, no.10, p.[212-217],
240-[241], photos.

YACHTS--SULARA
Sea views: Robin Murrell takes to
the water on a restored Edwardian
motor yacht.
Sulara, designed and built by
Camper & Nicholsons in 1924.
TRADITIONAL HOMES 1990 Aug., v.6,
no.11, p.41, photos.

YALIS
See COUNTRY HOUSES

YAMADA, KOOICH
A study on the restoration of
school-houses in the Omiya Campus,
of the Ryukoku University / Tosheo
Kimura, Kooich Yamada.
Changes made to buildings built in
1879. Text in Japanese; English
summary, p.143.
NIHON KENCHIKU GAKKAI KEIKAKUKEI
RONBUN HOKOKU SHU = JOURNAL OF
ARCHITECTURE, PLANNING AND
ENVIRONMENTAL ENGINEERING 1990
Apr., no.4(410), p.143-153, ill.,
photos., plans, secns., refs.

YAMADA, MAMORU, 1894-1967
Traces of architects early in this
century: Mamoru Yamada / Syuji
Funo.
KENCHIKU BUNKA 1990 Apr., v.45,
no.522, p.165-172, port., model,
photos., plans, aerial photo.

YAMAGUCHI & ESSIG
Wohnungsneubau fur Frankfurt - ein
Ideenwettbewerb.
First prize: Burgstaller, Gebbard,
Klingseisen. Second prize:
Yamaguchi & Essig. Third prize:
Funke & Heinrich.
BAUWELT 1990 Apr.27, v.81, no.16,
p.786, models.

YAMAMOTO, RIKEN, 1945-
The Gully house / Riken Yamamoto.
Located in Kamakura, Kanagawa
Prefecture. Architects: Riken
Yamamoto and Field Shop.
JAPAN ARCHITECT 1990 Feb., v.65,
no.2(394), p.51-57, photos.,
plans, secn., site plan.
Logements Hamlet a Tokyo.
Architect: Rikken Yamamoto.
Includes English summary and
statement by the architect.
TECHNIQUES ET ARCHITECTURE 1990
June-July, no.390, p.142-143,
photos., secn.
Riken Yamamoto / Riken Yamamoto.
Contents: Hamlet, Shibuya-ku,
Tokyo, design: 1986-87;
construction: 1987-88 -- Hotakubo
housing, Obiyama, Kumamoto,
design: 1988-89; completion: Apr.
1991. Text in Japanese and
English.
GA DOCUMENT 1990 Apr., no.25,
p.[184]-191, model, photos.,
plans.

YAMAMOTO, RIKEN, 1945- (CONTINUED)
Special edition I: Sukiya community.
Features Sukiya-Yu, a "community"
composed of nine buildings.
Architect: Kazuhiro Ishii.
Includes dialogue: What is Sukiya,
now? by Arata Isozaki and Kazuhiro
Ishii, and article by Riken
Yamamoto, Generation-Radicalist.
English summary, p.19.
KENCHIKU BUNKA 1990 Feb., v.45,
no.520, p.21-58, ports., elevs.,
photos., plans, secns.

YAMAMOTO, SOTARO
Winners in the Central Glass
International Architectural Design
Competition 1989.
Theme: a terminal for the linear
motor car. Winners: Sotaro
Yamamoto and Kuniaki Takahashi
(1st place). Includes twelve other
winning designs.
JAPAN ARCHITECT 1990 Jan., v.65,
no.1(393), p.61-66, dwgs.

YAMAMOTO, TATSUYA
Analysis of space in Turkish folk
houses / Tatsuya Yamamoto.
Text in Japanese.
SPACE DESIGN 1990 Feb., no.305,
p.45-68, dets., map, photos.,
plans, table.

YAMAMOTO, TERUO
On the types of gates and the
direction and disposition Tennoden
in Obakushu Buddhist temples in
Kyushu district / Teruo Yamamoto.
Four types, from the late 17th
cent. through the 19th cent. Text
in Japanese. Includes English
summary.
NIHON KENCHIKU GAKKAI KEIKAKUKEI
RONBUN HOKOKU SHU = JOURNAL OF
ARCHITECTURE, PLANNING AND
ENVIRONMENTAL ENGINEERING 1990
Sept., no.9(415), p.139-151,
dets., ill., elevs., plans.

YAMANAKA, HIDEO
Measures for traffic calming in
residential areas / Hideo
Yamanaka, Michiyasu Odani.
THE WHEEL EXTENDED 1990, no.73,
p.24-32, axonometric views, chart,
photos., table, refs.

YAMANAKA, MASAYUKI
Competition for "Maison de la
Culture du Japon a Paris":
Masayuki Yamanaka won Grand Prize.
JAPAN ARCHITECT 1990 May, v.65,
no.5(397), p.5, dwgs., models,
photo.
Concours pour la Maison du Japon
[Paris].
Winning team: Mazayuki Yamanaka,
Armstrong Associates. Includes
twelve other entries.
TECHNIQUES ET ARCHITECTURE 1990
Aug.-Sept., no.391, p.17-22,
dwgs., models, plans, secns.
Cultural breaks / John Welsh.
On Armstrong Associates' designs
for the Banco de Portugal, Lisbon
and the Maison de la Culture,
Paris.
BUILDING DESIGN 1990 Apr.6,
no.980, p.28-31, dwgs., elevs.,
models, plans, secns., site plan,
sketches.

YAMANAKA, MASAYUKI (CONTINUED)

Seine perspective: Japanese House of Culture, Paris: exhibition of competition entries [exhibition review] / Peter Wislocki.
Held at the Pavillon de l'Arsenal through 11 Nov. 1990. Exhibition documented all 453 entries. Winners: Masayuki Yamanaka, Kenneth Armstrong, and Jennifer Smith.
ARCHITECTS' JOURNAL 1990 Oct.24, v.192, no.17, p.81-82, elev., model.

Tegenpolen van cultuur: American Center en Maison de la Culture Japon a Paris / Pieter Uyttenhove.
Architects: Frank Gehry; Mazayuki Yamanaka and Kenneth Armstrong.
ARCHIS 1990 Nov., no.11, p.2-3, models, ref.

Winners in the competition for Maison de la Culture du Japon a Paris.
First prize: Masayuki Yamanaka, Kenneth Armstrong, Jenifer Smith.
JAPAN ARCHITECT 1990 June, v.65, no.6(398), p.33-55, dwgs., elevs., models, plans, secns., site plans.

YAMANO, YOSHIRO

A study on similarities between the Seiden of Daijokyu and the Honden of Sumiyoshijinja / Yoshiro Yamano.
Text in Japanese; English summary, p.159.
NIHON KENCHIKU GAKKAI KEIKAKUKEI RONBUN HOKOKU SHU = JOURNAL OF ARCHITECTURE, PLANNING AND ENVIRONMENTAL ENGINEERING 1990 Mar., no.3(409), p.151-159, plan, tables, refs.

YAMASHITA, KAZUMASA, 1937-

Kazumasa Yamashita becomes professor at Tokyo Institute of Technology. Includes short bio.
JAPAN ARCHITECT 1990 Mar., v.65, no.3(395), p.4, port., photo.

Kazumasa Yamashita: recent works and projects / edited by Kazumasa Yamashita.
Contents: Biography of Kazumasa Yamashita -- Essay: Anticipation / Kazumasa Yamashita -- Kazumasa Yamashita's works in the 1980s / Takashi Hasegawa -- Works of firm between 1981-1989 [several indexed seperately]. Text in Japanese and English.
PROCESS: ARCHITECTURE 1989 Dec., no.87, p.[1]-182, port., elevs., models, photos., plans, secns., site plans.

YAMASHITA, MASASHI

The change of distribution about the lots shinfting [sic], utilization of land or shifting right of land ownership and the formation of their owners from the viewpoint of relation between demand and supply land / Hiroshi Aizawa, Masasahi Yamashita.
"A study of planning of land use in rural region from the point of view of forming domain of land use, part 1". English summary, p.92.
NIHON KENCHIKU GAKKAI KEIKAKUKEI RONBUN HOKOKU SHU = JOURNAL OF
(Continued next column)

YAMASHITA, MASASHI (CONTINUED)

The change of...(CONTINUED) ARCHITECTURE, PLANNING AND ENVIRONMENTAL ENGINEERING 1990 Feb., no.2(408), p.81-92, graphs, maps, tables.

YAMASHITA, TOSHIRO, 1888-1983

Traces of architects early in this century: Toshiro Yamashita / Yoshio Uchida.
KENCHIKU BUNKA 1990 July, v.45, no.525, p.137-144, port., photos., table.

YAMASHITA, YASUHIRO

A survey of the actual conditions, preservation and utilization of outdoor stage "playhouse" in Nagano prefecture / Yasuhiro Yamashita, Naoji Matsumoto, Hirokuni Taniguchi.
"A systematic study of the outdoor stage playhouse, 1". Text in Japanese. Includes English summary.
NIHON KENCHIKU GAKKAI KEIKAKUKEI RONBUN HOKOKU SHU = JOURNAL OF ARCHITECTURE, PLANNING AND ENVIRONMENTAL ENGINEERING 1990 Sept., no.9(415), p.39-47, graphs, elevs., maps, photos., plans, secn., tables.

YAMAZAKI, HITOSHI

Applied mapping techniques for ray tracing: study of computer generated architectural perspective drawings (2) / Hitoshi Yamazaki, Masaki Manabe.
Text in Japanese. Includes English summary.
NIHON KENCHIKU GAKKAI KEIKAKUKEI RONBUN HOKOKU SHU = JOURNAL OF ARCHITECTURE, PLANNING AND ENVIRONMENTAL ENGINEERING 1990 June [July], no.7(413), p.11-20, ill., refs.

YAMAZAKI, YASUTAKA

KB topics: preservation and renewal of historical district.
Includes two topics: What is preservation in my designing?, by Yasutaka Yamazaki and International Designing Seminar of "Renewal of Historical District," by Shigeru Iwakiri. Later reports on work done on Piazza Matteotti in Vicenza. English summary, p.27.
KENCHIKU BUNKA 1990 June, v.45, no.524, p.115-126, dwgs., photos., aerial photo.

YANAGISAWA, TAKAHIKO

Isoya Yoshida Award to Takahiko Yanagisawa for Kazumasa Nakagawa Art Museum.
JAPAN ARCHITECT 1990 July, v.65, no.7(399), p.4, port., photo.

YANASE, TAKUKO

An experimental study on visual effects of colours in living rooms / Hiroko Tanaka, Nami Uematu, and Takuko Yanase.
English summary, p.41.
NIHON KENCHIKU GAKKAI KEIKAKUKEI RONBUN HOKOKU SHU = JOURNAL OF ARCHITECTURE, PLANNING AND ENVIRONMENTAL ENGINEERING 1990
(Continued next column)

YANASE, TAKUKO (CONTINUED)

An experimental study...(CONTINUED) Feb., no.2(408), p.33-41, diagrs., graphs, photos., tables, refs.

Influence of floor heating temperature and the human body seated on the floor / Bongae Kim, Norio Isoda, Takuko Yanase.
Includes English summary.
NIHON KENCHIKU GAKKAI KEIKAKUKEI RONBUN HOKOKU SHU = JOURNAL OF ARCHITECTURE, PLANNING AND ENVIRONMENTAL ENGINEERING 1990 Nov., no.11(417), p.19-27, graphs, plan, tables, refs.

YANG, BYOUNG-E

The perception of landscape style: a cross-cultural comparison / Byoung-e Yang, Rachel Kaplan.
Includes Korean, Japanese and Western landscape styles.
LANDSCAPE AND URBAN PLANNING 1990 June, v.19, no.3, p.251-262, photos., table, refs.

YANG, CHUNG-HSIN

The optimal provision of a central park in a city / Chung-hsin Yang.
Chiefly equations.
JOURNAL OF REGIONAL SCIENCE 1990 Feb., v.30, no.1, p.15-36, diagr., graphs, refs.

YANG, MOU

Housing redevelopment in Shanghai's Old City district / Geng Yuxiw, Yang Mou.
BUILDING IN CHINA 1989 June, v.2, no.2, p.26-29, table.

YANG, YANMIN

Old courtyard houses in Beijing / Yang Yanmin.
BUILDING IN CHINA 1990 Dec., v.3 no.4, p.21-24, port., tables.

YAPA, L. S.

Low-cost map overlay analysis using computer-aided design / L. S. Yapa.
Database management techniques and computer-aided design applications for city and regional planning in Third World nations.
ENVIRONMENT AND PLANNING B 1989, v.16, no.4, p.377-391, diagrs., graphs, tables, refs.

YARBROUGH, DAN

The house with a heart of stone / Victor M. Cassidy.
Home near Milwaukee, Wisc., which was constructed around massive stone sculpture, Tower of Babel. Architect: Charles Moore. Artist: Dan Yarbrough.
CONNOISSEUR 1990 May, v.220, no.940, p.104-107,148, axonometric view, port., photos.

YARDS

See also CHURCHYARDS

YARDS--UNITED STATES

Lot, yard, and garden: American distinctions / Paul Groth.
LANDSCAPE 1990, v.30, no.3, p.29-35, diagrs., photos., biblio.

YARNALL, RICHARD
Bucks County manor.
New house which resembles a
Colonial Stone farmhouse, Penn.
Architect: Richard Yarnall.
Interior designers: D'Aquino
Humphreys Interiors.
COLONIAL HOMES 1990 Aug., v.16,
no.4, p.33-[39], dets., photos.

YASHIRO, TOMONARI
Survey on real life span of office
building in Chuuou Ward of Tokyo
City / Tomonari Yashiro...[et
al.].
Text in Japanese. Includes English
summary.
NIHON KENCHIKU GAKKAI KEIKAKUKEI
RONBUN HOKOKU SHU = JOURNAL OF
ARCHITECTURE, PLANNING AND
ENVIRONMENTAL ENGINEERING 1990
June [July], no.7(413), p.139-149,
graphs, tables, refs.

YASUI ARCHITECTS & ENGINEERS
15 Bankan / Nozawa building.
Office building adjacent to Meiji
period western-style home.
Architects: Yasui Architects &
Engineers. English summary, p.19.
KENCHIKU BUNKA 1990 Oct., v.45,
no.528, p.142-148, models,
photos., plans.

YASUI, HIDEO
Una cripta plateada: cementerio de
perros en Tokio / Mercedes Reig.
Architects: Hideo Yashui [sic],
Maroto Araki.
ARQUITECTURA VIVA 1990 Mar.-Apr.,
no.11, p.61-63, ill., photos.,
plan.
Hundegedenkstatte in Tokio, Japan =
Burial chamber for dogs in Tokyo,
Japan.
Architects: Hideo Yasui, Makoto
Araki.
DETAIL 1990 Apr.-May, v.30, no.2,
p.144-145, axonometric view, det.,
photos., plans.

YATES, NIGEL
The mayoral and corporation seats in
Faversham parish church / Nigel
Yates.
Arrangement and position of church
seating, and private seating
arrangements within the church.
ARCHAEOLOGIA CANTIANA 1988, v.106,
p.37-43, refs.

YATSUKA, HAJIME, 1948-
Between architect and producer,
recent works by Hajime Yatsuka.
JAPAN ARCHITECT 1990 Oct., v.65,
no.10(402), p.4, models.
Clinic in Hatano / Hajime Yatsuka.
Architects: Hajime Yatsuka, UPM.
JAPAN ARCHITECT 1990 July, v.65,
no.7(399), p.26-31, photos.,
plans, secn.
Countering clip-on culture / John
Welsh.
On the work of Hajime Yatsuka.
BUILDING DESIGN 1990 May 4,
no.984, p.34-37, photos.
East defines West: Hajime Yatsuka's
dictionary of quotations / Lynne
Breslin.
The architect's Postmodern house
in Tokyo.
ELLE DECOR 1990 Mar., v.1, no.2,
(Continued next column)

YATSUKA, HAJIME, 1948- (CONTINUED)
East defines West:...(CONTINUED)
p.48,52, ports., photos.
Folly 13(3), Expo '90.
Contents: Folly 13 story, by
Hajime Yatsuka.--Martinez Lapena +
Elias Torres, Ryoji Suzuki, Peter
Wilson, Morphosis. Text in
Japanese.
SPACE DESIGN 1990 Apr., no.307,
p.45-53, axonometric views, dwgs.,
elevs., models, plan.
Folly 13: Expo '90.
Contents: Peter Cook + Christine
Hawley, Coop Himmelblau, Andrea
Branzi, Daniel Libskind [sic].--
Folly 13 story, by Hajime Yatsuka.
Text in Japanese.
SPACE DESIGN 1990 Feb., no.305,
p.85-92, elevs., models, plans,
secns., site plans, sketches.
Folly 13 [part 2]: Expo '90.
Contents: Zaha Hadid, Chris
Macdonald + Peter Salter, Hajime
Yatsuka, Eleni Gigantes + Elia
Zenghelis.--Folly 13 story [2], by
Hajime Yatsuka.
SPACE DESIGN 1990 Mar., no.306,
p.129-136, axonometric views,
diagrs., dwgs., models, site
plans.
Koizumi lighting Theater /ISM
[Tokyo].
Office/showroom building.
Architects: Peter Eisenman, Kojiro
Kitayama. Includes interview with
Peter Eisenman entitled Chora and
weak form.
JAPAN ARCHITECT 1990 Nov.-Dec.,
v.65, no.11-12(403-404), p.39-51,
elevs., photos., plans, secns.
Recent works: Daniel Libeskind
[interview] / Hajime Yatsuka,
Ryoji Suzuki.
Extension of the Berlin Museum
with the Jewish Museum, and Urban
Villa Lutzowplatz. Text in
Japanese.
SPACE DESIGN 1990 Feb., no.305,
p.73-84, dwgs., port., models.
Recent works: Elia Zenghelis, Eleni
Gigantes.
Four projects, 1986-1989,
including the Chalkiades villa,
Mytilene. Includes an interview by
Koji Taki and Hajime Yatsuka.
SPACE DESIGN 1990 Mar., no.306,
p.121-128, elevs., photos., plans,
secns., site plans, isometric
dwgs.
Recent works: Peter Wilson.
Projects: Munster City Library,
and ZKM, Karlsruhe. Includes
interviews conducted by Koji Taki,
Hajime Yatsuka, and Ryogi Suzuki.
Text in Japanese.
SPACE DESIGN 1990 Apr., no.307,
p.54-68, dwg., elevs., models,
plans, secns., site plan.

YAZDANI, MEHRDAD, 1959-
Utility by design: two projects by
Ellerbe Becket's Santa Monica,
California, office...
Two buildings for the Los Angeles
Dept. of Water and Power. Project
architect: Mehrdad Yazdani.
ARCHITECTURE: THE MAGAZINE OF THE
AMERICAN INSTITUTE OF ARCHITECTS
1990 May, v.79, no.5, p.50,
axonometric view, elevs., models.

YBARGUENGOITIA, MANUEL
Changing tack / David Redhead.
Interiors of a Barcelona
restaurant, Ticktacktoe. Interior
designers: Manuel Ybarguengoitia,
Maria del Mar Nogues.
DESIGNERS' JOURNAL 1990 Feb.,
no.54, p.64-66, dets., photos.,
plan.
Tienda de complementos en Barcelona:
M. Ybarguengoitia y Ma. del Mar
Nogues.
Spanish, English text.
ON DISENO 1990, no.113, p.158-165,
photos., plans, secn.
Tienda de confeccion para caballeros
en Barcelona: M. Ybarguengoitia y
Ma. del Mar Nogues.
Spanish, English text.
ON DISENO 1990, no.113, p.166-173,
elevs., photos., plans.
Wendeltreppe in einem Schuhgeschaft
in Barcelona, E = Spiral stair
case in a shop in Barcelona,
Spain.
Interior architects: M.
Ybarguengoitia, M. del Mar Nogues.
DETAIL 1990 Apr.-May, v.30, no.2,
p.146-147, det., photos., plan,
secn., elevs.

YE, QISHEN
Xiaoxichang: a veranda market-town
in Sichaun Province / Ye Qishen,
Li Xiankui.
BUILDING IN CHINA 1989 June, v.2,
no.2, p.42-47,inside cover,
diagr., dwgs., photos., plan,
secn., site plan.

YEANG KING-MUN, KENNETH
Exhibition: tropical heights at
Tokyo Designer's Space [exhibition
review] / P.G. Raman.
Exhibition, Jan.8-20, 1990.
Architect: Kenneth Yeang.
ARCHITECTURE AND URBANISM 1990
Apr., no.4(235), p.6-7,
axonometric view, photos.
Paradigms lost in the tropics / Neal
Morris.
"Hairy" office towers in tropical
areas by Ken Yeang; examples in
Kuala Lumpur.
ARCHITECTS' JOURNAL 1990 Apr.25,
v.191, no.17, p.14, axonometric
views.
La tela della tradizione = The web
of tradition: Ken Yeang's
buildings in Malaysia / P.G.
Raman.
Text in Italian and English.
SPAZIO E SOCIETA 1990 July-Sept.,
v.13, no.51, p.96-105, photos.,
plans, secns., site plans, refs.

YEARLEY, STEVEN
Environmentalism and direct rule:
the politics and ethos of
conservation and environmental
groups in Northern Ireland /
Steven Yearley, Kay Milton.
The effect of central government
on conservation in Northern
Ireland.
BUILT ENVIRONMENT 1990, v.16,
no.3, p.192-208, aerial photo.,
refs.

YECK, BUD
   At home in a 1730 gristmill / Rhoda
   Jaffin Murphy.
   Home of interior designers Ed
   Bouchard and Bud Yeck in converted
   Virginia gristmill.
   HOUSE BEAUTIFUL 1990 June, v.132,
   no.6, p.82-89, photos.

YEE, RONALD
   Beating the system [architectural
   competitions] / Callum Murray.
   Examines the success of British
   architects John Pardey and Ronald
   Yee in architectural competitions.
   ARCHITECTS' JOURNAL 1990 Jan.17,
   v.191, no.3, p.30-31, ports.,
   elev., secns.
   British in Genoa / John Welsh.
   Review of four British entries in
   the Piazza Dante competition,
   Genoa. Architects: Alan Power,
   Philippe Faure, Michael Manser
   Associates, Pardey & Yee.
   BUILDING DESIGN 1990 Mar.30,
   no.979, p.20-23, ill., dwgs.,
   models, plans, secns., site plans.
   Pheonix winners [1987,1988] /
   Alistair Macintyre, John Pardey,
   Ronald Yee.
   Features winning crematorium
   projects for 1987, by Alistair
   Macintyre and 1988, by John Pardey
   and Ronald Yee.
   LANDSCAPE DESIGN 1989 Oct.,
   no.184, p.76-77, axonometric view,
   dwgs., site plans.

YEH, A. G. O.
   Applications of geographic
   information systems in urban and
   regional planning / A. G. O. Yeh,
   M. Batty.
   ENVIRONMENT AND PLANNING B 1990
   Oct., v.17, no.4, p.369-374, refs.
   A land information system for the
   programming and monitoring of new
   town development / A. G. O. Yeh.
   ENVIRONMENT AND PLANNING B 1990
   Oct., v.17, no.4, p.375-384,
   chart, map, tables, refs.

YELIN, MAX I.
   A Sanikel cameleon / Beth Dunlop.
   Architects' vacation house, Casa
   Cameleon on Sanibel Island, Fla.
   Architects: Roy J. Solfisburg.
   ARCHITECTURAL DIGEST 1990 Aug.,
   v.47, no.8, p.138-[143], photos.

YELLOW DESIGN
   Die Dusche: Duker-Design-Preis '90.
   First prizewinners: Yellow Design.
   Includes comments by jury
   chairman, Prof. Kurt Weidemann.
   DEUTSCHE BAUZEITSCHRIFT 1990 July,
   v.38, no.7, p.946-949, dwgs.,
   models.

YEMAN--SANAA--VERNACULAR ARCHITECTURE
   Dilder aus dem Jeman / Hridette
   Hellgoth.
   Views of buildings in Sanaa,
   northwest Yemen.
   BAUWELT 1990 Sept.14, v.81, no.35,
   p.1722-1724, 1729-1731, photos.

YEMEN--ARCHITECTURE--MUD--RESEARCH
   Building on the organic / Clare
   Melhuish.
   On the work of Dr. Samar Damluji
   on Yemen's mud-brick architecture.
   BUILDING DESIGN 1990 May 11,
   no.985, p.28-33, elevs., photos.,
   plans, secns.

YEMEN (PEOPLE'S DEMOCRATIC REPUBLIC)--
ARCHITECTURE--MUD--RESEARCH
   Building on the organic / Clare
   Melhuish.
   On the work of Dr. Samar Damluji
   on Yemen's mud-brick architecture.
   BUILDING DESIGN 1990 May 11,
   no.985, p.28-33, elevs., photos.,
   plans, secns.

YEMEN--VERNACULAR ARCHITECTURE
   Cities and villages of the Yemen
   Arab Republic / Satoshi Ueda.
   Includes "The contemporary
   significance of the Islamic city",
   by Nobuhide Jinnai. Text in
   Japanese.
   SPACE DESIGN 1990 Sept., no.312,
   p.077-088, maps, photos., plans,
   secns., refs.

YEMEN--VERNACULAR ARCHITECTURE--MUD
   Building on the organic / Clare
   Melhuish.
   On the work of Dr. Samar Damluji
   on Yemen's mud-brick architecture.
   BUILDING DESIGN 1990 May 11,
   no.985, p.28-33, elevs., photos.,
   plans, secns.

YERBURY, F. R. (FRANCIS ROWLAND),
1885-1970
   Reflejando lo nuevo, la fotografia
   de arquitectura de Frank Yerbury
   1920-1935 = Reflecting the new,
   the architectural photography of
   Frank Yerbury 1920-1935 / Andrew
   Higgott.
   Text in Spanish, Basque and
   English.
   COMPOSICION ARQUITECTONICA, ART &
   ARCHITECTURE 1989 June, no.3,
   p.[5]-38, port., photos, refs.

YIFTACHEL, OREN
   The planning of Perth's changing
   form--invention or convention? /
   Oren Yiftachel, David Hedgecock.
   AUSTRALIAN PLANNER: JOURNAL OF THE
   ROYAL AUSTRALIAN PLANNING
   INSTITUTE 1989 Mar., v.27, no.1,
   p.6-11, chart, site plans, refs.

YIN
   See SHANG

YIZHONG, TAO
   Rehabilitation of leaning tower of
   China / Tao Yizhong.
   The Huqiu (Tiger Hill) Pagoda in
   Suzhou, built in 959 A.D.
   BUILDING IN CHINA 1989 Mar., v.2,
   no.1, p.30-33, chart, photo.,
   plans.

YLIMAULA, ANNA-MAIJA
   Tuusulan sosiaalialan oppilaitos,
   Tuusula = Tuusula School of Social
   Studies.
   Architects: Arkkitehtitoimisto NVO
   KY. Includes essay by Anna-Maija
   Ylimaula and an English
   translation.
            (Continued next column)

YLIMAULA, ANNA-MAIJA (CONTINUED)
   Tuusulan sosiaalialan...(CONTINUED)
   ARKKITEHTI 1989, v.86, no.8,
   p.58-63, elevs., photos., plans,
   site plan.

YNZENGA, BERNARDO
   Parque empresarial Madrid-Las Rozas
   / Bernardo Ynzenga.
   URBANISMO / COAM 1990 Sept.,
   no.11, p.60-67, dwgs., models,
   map, photo., plans.

YOCH, FLORENCE, 1890-1972
   Landscaping the American dream: the
   gardens and film sets of Florence
   Yoch: 1890-1972 [by] James J. Yoch
   [book review] / David Gebhard.
   Discusses the contributions of
   Lucile Council, Yoch's partner.
   SOCIETY OF ARCHITECTURAL
   HISTORIANS. JOURNAL 1990 Dec.,
   v.49, no.4, p.450-452.

YOCH, JAMES J., 1938. LANDSCAPING THE
AMERICAN DREAM
   Landscaping the American dream: the
   gardens and film sets of Florence
   Yoch: 1890-1972 [by] James J. Yoch
   [book review] / David Gebhard.
   Discusses the contributions of
   Lucile Council, Yoch's partner.
   SOCIETY OF ARCHITECTURAL
   HISTORIANS. JOURNAL 1990 Dec.,
   v.49, no.4, p.450-452.

YOH DESIGN OFFICE
   Misumi ferry terminal, pyramid on
   the sea.
   Spiral-shaped marine terminal.
   Architects: Shoei Yoh, Yoh Design
   Office. English summary, p.27.
   KENCHIKU BUNKA 1990 June, v.45,
   no.524, p.149-154, dwg., photos.,
   plan, secn.
   "Pyramid of the sea" / W.
   Nedderhut-Heeschen.
   Spiral-shaped marine terminal,
   Misumi. Architects: Yoh Design
   Office.
   DEUTSCHE BAUZEITSCHRIFT 1990 Nov.,
   v.38, no.11, p.1591-1594, dwgs.,
   photos., plans, secn.
   Shoei Yoh / Shoei Yoh.
   Contents: Wakita Hi-Tecs, Onojo,
   Fukuoka, design: 1988-89;
   completion: Apr.1990.--Matsuchita
   Clinic, Yagami-cho, Nagasaki,
   design: 1989; completion: May
   1990. Text in Japanese and
   English.
   GA DOCUMENT 1990 Apr., no.25,
   p.192-199, dets., elevs., photos.,
   plans, secns.
   Sporthalle in Oguni, Japan =
   Gymnasium in Oguni, Japan.
   Oguni Dome. Architects: Yoh
   Design Office.
   ARCHITEKTUR + WETTBEWERBE 1990
   Mar., no.141, p.5, elev., photos.
   Wakita-Hi-Tecs-Hauptverwaltung / W.
   Nedderhut Heeschen.
   Tensile structure office building,
   Ohnojo. Architects: Yoh Design
   Office.
   DEUTSCHE BAUZEITSCHRIFT 1990 Nov.,
   v.38, no.11, p.1595-1598, dets.,
   dwgs., photos., plan, secn.

YOH, ROBERT
Decorators' private domains / Amy Fine Collins.
The New York apartments of five young interior decorators.
HOUSE & GARDEN 1990 Sept., v.162, no.9, p.[118]-125, ports., photos.

YOH, SHOEI, 1940-
Misumi ferry terminal, pyramid on the sea.
Spiral-shaped marine terminal. Architects: Shoei Yoh. Yoh Design Office. English summary, p.27.
KENCHIKU BUNKA 1990 June, v.45, no.524, p.149-154, dwg., photos., plan, secn.
Oguni dome, una palestra di legno = A wooden gymnasium / Shoei Yoh.
Architect: Shoei Yoh.
L'ARCA 1990 May, no.38, p.12-19, dets., photos., plans, secns.
Shoei Yoh / Shoei Yoh.
Contents: Wakita Hi-Tecs, Onojo, Fukuoka, design: 1988-89; completion: Apr.1990.--Matsushita Clinic, Yagami-cho, Nagasaki, design: 1989; completion: May 1990. Text in Japanese and English.
GA DOCUMENT 1990 Apr., no.25, p.192-199, dets., elevs., photos., plans, secns.
Wakita Hi-Tecs / Shoei Yoh.
Tensile structure office building, Ohnojo. Architect: Shoei Yoh.
JAPAN ARCHITECT 1990 July, v.65, no.7(399), p.[36]-39, dets., elev., photos., plan.

YOHANNAN, KOHLE
Taste of Mexico: haute couture in an East Side duplex / Caroline Rennolds Milbank.
Interiors of Zarela Martinez's New York apartment. Interior designers: Mary McFadden, Kohle Yohannan.
ARCHITECTURAL DIGEST 1990 Nov., v.47, no.12, p.[250]-255, 312, port., photos.

YOKOGAWA, KEN, 1948-
Cosmos: urban house 1990 / Ken Yokogawa.
4-story home, Setagaya Ward, Tokyo. Architects: Ken Yokogawa, Architect and Associates. Includes essay by the architect.
JAPAN ARCHITECT 1990 July, v.65, no.7(399), p.56-62, photos., plans, secns., site plan.

YOKOTA, RYOICHI
For Hong Kong, Ryiochi Yokota proposes major urban restructuring.
Discussion of Ryoichi Yokota's Hong Kong Triple Grand Project.
INTERIOR DESIGN 1990 Jan., v.61, no.1, p.44, ill., elev.
Matsuda / Edie Lee Cohen.
Interiors of Manhattan clothing store, located in the Flatiron district. Interior designer: Ryoichi Yokota.
INTERIOR DESIGN 1990 Sept., v.61, no.12, p.[190-193], axonometric view, photos.

YOKOTA, TAKASHI
A multi-objective approach to location planning of hospitals (Part 1) / Takashi Yokota.
"A case study in K-City". In Japanese; English summary, p.25.
NIHON KENCHIKU GAKKAI KEIKAKUKEI RONBUN HOKOKU SHU = JOURNAL OF ARCHITECTURE, PLANNING AND ENVIRONMENTAL ENGINEERING 1990 May, no.5(411), p.25-34, charts, graphs, maps, tables, refs.
A multiobjective approach to location planning of hospitals [part 2] / Takashi Yokota.
"A case study in K-city". Text in Japanese; includes English summary.
NIHON KENCHIKU GAKKAI KEIKAKUKEI RONBUN HOKOKU SHU = JOURNAL OF ARCHITECTURE, PLANNING AND ENVIRONMENTAL ENGINEERING 1990 Nov., no.11(417), p.43-50, graphs, tables, maps, refs.
On method of predating generation of community facilities in new towns / Han-Su Kim [et al.].
English summary, p.105.
NIHON KENCHIKU GAKKAI KEIKAKUKEI RONBUN HOKOKU SHU = JOURNAL OF ARCHITECTURE, PLANNING AND ENVIRONMENTAL ENGINEERING 1990 Jan., no.1(407), p.97-105, figs., tables, maps, refs.

YOKOUCHI, TOSHIHITO
Atami Refresh Center.
Spa for members of an architectural consulting and engineering union. Architects: Toshihito Yokouchi, Kunio Mayekawa, Architect and Associates. English summary, p.23.
KENCHIKU BUNKA 1990 Mar., v.45, no.521, p.77-86, dets., photos., plans, secns., site plan.

YONDER, AYSE
Informal land and housing markets: the case of Istanbul, Turkey / Ayse Yonder.
AMERICAN PLANNING ASSOCIATION. JOURNAL 1987 Spring, v.53, no.2, p.213-219, photos.

YONE, H. LAW
Physical and environmental determinants of urban deterioration and rehabilitation: a conceptual framework and a case study / H. Law Yone, M. Shechter.
Case study of Haifa, Israel.
ENVIRONMENT AND PLANNING A 1990 June, v.22, no.6, p.763-777, charts, map, tables, refs.

YORK AND SAWYER
Key Bank: an architectural achievement renewed.
Greek revival building at 60 State St., downtown Albany. Original architects: York & Sawyer. Architect for restoration: H.J. Sidford, Jr.
ALBANY PRESERVATION REPORT 1990 Summer, v.9, no.2, p.3, photo.

YORKE, TONY
Scramble for Italian goals [Meazza Stadium] / Tony Yorke.
BUILDING 1990 May 4, v.255, no.18, p.26-27, port., photos.

YORUBA
See SEE "YORUBA" AS A SUBHEADING AFTER SPECIFIC BUILDING TYPES OR OTHER MAIN HEADINGS.

YOSHIDA, TAKAKO
A study of the county carpenter parties in east Omi-country / Takako Yoshida.
During the Edo era. In Japanese; English summary, p.107.
NIHON KENCHIKU GAKKAI KEIKAKUKEI RONBUN HOKOKU SHU = JOURNAL OF ARCHITECTURE, PLANNING AND ENVIRONMENTAL ENGINEERING 1990 May, no.5(411), p.107-114, charts, maps, tables, refs.

YOSHIDA, TETSURO, 1894-1956
Traces of architects early in this century: Tetsuro Yoshida / Satoru Mukai.
KENCHIKU BUNKA 1990 Mar., v.45, no.521, p.145-152, port., photos., table.

YOSHIKAWA, TOHRU
Shirogane Wing.
Tokyo apartment house. Architects: Tohru Yoshikawa, Uniplan. English summary, p.19.
KENCHIKU BUNKA 1990 Feb., v.45, no.520, p.83-90, axonometric view, photos., plans, secns.

YOSHIMURA, DINA YANDO
Motoo Yoshimura: creation of contemporary Japanese gardens / edited by Motoo Yoshimura and Dina Yando Yoshimura.
Contents: Essay: Construction of Japanese landscape gardens in the age of urbanization / Motoo Yoshimura --Works: Shirotori Park --Shirotori Tea House garden --Fukuda house garden, Kyoto --Yoshida Steak House garden --Kyoto Historical Museum garden --Yamamoto Tea Shop & garden, Shigaraki --World Orchid Exhibition grounds, Tokyo --Katsurazaka pedestrian footpath, Kyoto --Osaka International Exposition Memorial Park. Landscape architect: Motto Yoshimura. Text in Japanese and English.
PROCESS: ARCHITECTURE 1990 Sept., no.91, p.[1]-154, dwgs., port., photos., plans, secns., site plans, aerial photos.

YOSHIMURA, HIDEMASA
On method of predating generation of community facilities in new towns / Han-Su Kim [et al.].
English summary, p.105.
NIHON KENCHIKU GAKKAI KEIKAKUKEI RONBUN HOKOKU SHU = JOURNAL OF ARCHITECTURE, PLANNING AND ENVIRONMENTAL ENGINEERING 1990 Jan., no.1(407), p.97-105, figs., tables, maps, refs.

YOSHIMURA, MOTOO, 1937-
Motoo Yoshimura: creation of
contemporary Japanese gardens /
edited by Motoo Yoshimura and Dina
Yando Yoshimura.
Contents: Essay: Construction of
Japanese landscape gardens in the
age of urbanization / Motoo
Yoshimura --Works: Shirotori Park
--Shirotori Tea House garden --
Fukuda house garden, Kyoto --
Yoshida Steak House garden --Kyoto
Historical Museum garden --
Yamamoto Tea Shop & garden,
Shigaraki --World Orchid
Exhibition grounds, Tokyo --
Katsurazaka pedestrian footpath,
Kyoto --Osaka International
Exposition Memorial Park.
Landscape architect: Motto
Yoshimura. Text in Japanese and
English.
PROCESS: ARCHITECTURE 1990 Sept.,
no.91, p.[1]-154, dwgs., port.,
photos., plans, secns., site
plans, aerial photos.

YOSHINO, HIROSHI
Verification of calculation methods
of air infiltration for a detached
wooden house / Hiroshi Yoshino.
Text in Japanese. English summary,
p.19.
NIHON KENCHIKU GAKKAI KEIKAKUKEI
RONBUN HOKOKU SHU = JOURNAL OF
ARCHITECTURE, PLANNING AND
ENVIRONMENTAL ENGINEERING 1990
June, no.6(412), p.19-29, graphs,
elevs., refs.

YOSHINO, SHIGERU
Winners in the 2nd Yokohama Urban
Design International Competition.
Theme: revitalization of the
waterfront - Yokohama Kaigan Dori.
Includes 13 winning entries and
judges' commentary. First prize
winner: Shigeru Yoshino.
JAPAN ARCHITECT 1990 Oct., v.65,
no.10, p.71-76, dwgs., elevs.,
models, plan, secns.

YOSHIRO, IKEHARA
Kitakyushu Prince Hotel / Kensho
Kono.
Architects: Ikehara Yoshiro,
Kenchiku Sekkei Kobo.
JAPAN ARCHITECT 1990 Apr., v.65,
no.4 (396), p.[26]-34, photos.,
plans, secn., site plan.

YOSHITAKE, YASUMI, 1916-
Kobe Institute of Art Technology.
Established in 1989. Architects:
Yasumi Yoshitake, Shigefumi
Suzuki. English summary, p.23.
KENCHIKU BUNKA 1990 Mar., v.45,
no.521, p.111-122, diagr.,
photos., plans, elevs., site
plans, sketches.

YOST, BARBARA
Desert Mansion / Barbara Yost.
A three story "Victorian" house
built 30 miles north of Phoenix in
Cave Creek area. Owner and
builder: Norman Foster.
VICTORIAN HOMES 1990 Fall, v.9,
no.4, p.[33]-38, photos.

YOST, BARBARA (CONTINUED)
The Rosson House [Heritage Square] /
Barbara Yost.
Built in 1895 in Phoenix, Ariz.
Architect: A.P. Petit. Restored in
the late 1970s and now open to the
public.
VICTORIAN HOMES 1990 summer, v.9,
no.3, p.[44]-49, dets., photos.

YOUNG, A. N.
Guidelines for bioclimatic housing
design in Greece / M. Kolokotroni,
A. N. Young.
BUILDING AND ENVIRONMENT 1990,
v.25, no.4, p.297-307, graphs,
plan, map, tables, refs.

YOUNG, AMMI B. (AMMI BURNHAM),
1799-1874
Civic and aesthetic reserve: Ammi
Burnham Young's 1850s Federal
Customhouse designs / Daniel
Bluestone.
For Boston, Cincinnati, Norfolk,
Mobile, Providence, Chicago and
other cities, and dating from the
1830s to 1860.
WINTERTHUR PORTFOLIO 1990 Autumn,
v.25, no.2-3, p.[131]-156, dets.,
elevs., maps, photos., plans,
refs.

YOUNG, BRIAN
Tackling problem estates / Brian
Young.
In Wigan.
HOUSING AND PLANNING REVIEW 1990
Aug.-Sept., v.45, no.4, p.16,18,
photos.

YOUNG, KEN
Toppling the colossus: the LCC and
the historians / Ken Young.
History of the London County
Council.
LONDON JOURNAL 1990, v.15, no.2,
p.d[147]-154, refs.

YOUNG, REGAN
Additions and alterations / Regan
Young, Robert Cerutti.
On the architect's job of adding
to existing structures. Examples
of 12 projects in and near New
Jersey by New Jersey architects:
Katz Novoa Architects and
Planners; John DeFazio; Michael
Burns; Frederick Schmitt; Michael
Ryan Architects; Sykes O'Connor
Salerno Hazaveh; Parette and
Associates; Nadaskay Kopelson;
Michael Graves; Carla Bonacci;
Robert N. Auld; and Albert F.
Zaccone.
ARCHITECTURE NEW JERSEY 1990,
v.26, no.5, p.9-22, axonometric
view, ill., elevs., models,
photos., plans, secn.
Inside a modern icon: Gerrit
Rietveld's Schroderhuis / Regan
Young.
ARCHITECTURE NEW JERSEY 1990 v.26,
no.6, p.28,30, elevs., photo.,
plans.

YOUNG, SAMUEL
Sport and splendor: New Mexico's
spectacular Vermejo Park Ranch /
Samuel Young.
A restored gilded-age wilderness
retreat.
SOUTHERN ACCENTS 1990 July-Aug.,
v.13, no.6, p.110-113, photos.

YOUNG, WILLIAM, 1843-1900
Duncombe Park, Yorkshire - I: the
seat of Lord Feversham / Giles
Worsley.
Architects: William Wakefield,
Charles Barry, and William Young.
COUNTRY LIFE 1990 May 24, v.184,
no.21, p.116-121, dwg., photos.
Duncombe Park Yorkshire - II: the
seat of Lord Feversham / Giles
Worsley.
Architects: William Wakefield,
Charles Barry, William Young.
COUNTRY LIFE 1990 May 31, v.184,
no.22, p.138-143, ill., photo.

YOUNGMAN, PETER
Home ground: Peter Youngman's garden
/ Michael Branch.
LANDSCAPE DESIGN 1990 Mar.,
no.188, p.41-43, elev., photos.,
site plan.
Reflections on landscape: the lives
and work of six British landscape
architects [edited by] S. Harvey
[book review] / David Singleton.
Oral histories from G. Jellicoe,
S. Crowe, P. Shepheard, B.
Hackett, P. Youngman, and B.
Colvin.
ANCIENT MONUMENTS SOCIETY.
TRANSACTIONS 1990, new ser.,v.34,
p.199.

YOUNGREN, RALPH P.
Timeless appeal: Ralph and Ann
Youngren show the virtues of
modern furnishings in their
Bloomfield Hills, Michigan,
residence / Edie Lee Cohen.
Interiors of architects' home.
INTERIOR DESIGN 1990 May, v.61,
no.7, p.278-[285], photos., plan.

YOUNGSON, A. J. MAKING OF CLASSICAL
EDINBURGH
The making of classical Edinburgh
[by] A.J. Youngson [book review] /
K. J. Panton.
Reprint of 1966 ed.
ANCIENT MONUMENTS SOCIETY.
TRANSACTIONS 1990, new ser.,v.34,
p.197-198.

YOUTH AND ARCHITECTURE
See ARCHITECTURE AND YOUTH

YOUTH CENTERS--GERMANY (WEST)--
BREMEN--HAUS ATLANTIS
Ein Denkmal kommt nicht zu Ruhe:
Bremen, Bottcherstrasse, ein
Gesamtdenkmal wird restauriert /
Nils Aschenbeck.
Restoration of the Haus Atlantis,
built 1929-31. Architect: Bernhard
Hoetger.
ARCHITHESE 1990 Sept.-Oct., v.20,
no.5, p.60-66, photos., refs.

YUGOSLAVIA--CITY PLANNING--CITIZEN
PARTICIPATION
Participation in planning: theory
and practice in Yugoslavia / James
Simmie.
THE PLANNER 1989 July, v.75,
no.11, p.19-22, photos, refs.

YUGOSLAVIA--LAND USE--CITIZEN
PARTICIPATION
Participation in planning: theory
and practice in Yugoslavia / James
Simmie.
THE PLANNER 1989 July, v.75,
no.11, p.19-22, photos, refs.

YUGOSLAVIA--LJUBLJANA--CITY PLANNING--
STUDENT PROJECTS
Der Ort der Stadt: eine
Wanderausstellung zur
Wechselwirkung von Topographie und
urbaner Form / Jorg Stabenow.
Student projects at TU Munchen
entitled "Stadt und Topographie,"
directed by Tomas Valena, use
Ljubljana as their basis.
ARCH PLUS 1990 Apr., no.103,
p.32-33, maps.

YUGOSLAVIA--LJUBLJANA--LIBRARIES--
PRESIHOV VORANIC LIBRARY
Igor Skulj: biblioteca a Ljubljana.
Text in Italian and English.
DOMUS 1990 Nov., no.721, p.6-7,
axonometric view, elev., photos.,
plans.

YUGOSLAVIA--SPLIT--PALACES--ROMAN--
PALACE OF DIOCLETIAN
Rilancio plotiniano degli
accorgimenti ottici in due
impianti architettonici
tardo-antichi / Guglielmo De
Angelis d'Ossat.
Discussion of the Palace of
Diocletian in Split, Yugoslavia
and the Villa of Piazza Armerina
in Sicily. Summaries in English,
French, German, and Spanish.
PALLADIO 1989 Jan.-June, no.3,
p.5-18, diagrs., elev., photos.,
plans, site plans, aerial photo.,
refs.

YUILL, DAVID W. B.
The proposed Bloemfontein Civic
Centre / David W. B. Yuill.
ARCHITECTURE SA = ARGITEKTUUR SA
1989 Nov.-Dec., no.11-12, p.43-45,
model.

YUNKER, MARTHA
Contemporary tempo: a new Room &
Board steps to the beat of the
'90s with light, energy and color.
Edina home furnishings store.
Architect: Martha Yunker.
ARCHITECTURE MINNESOTA 1990
Jan.-Feb., v.16, no.1, p.38-39,
photos.
Neoclassical update:
turn-of-the-century house provides
classical charm with a
contemporary twist.
Reinstein House renovation near
Lake of the Isles in Minneapolis.
Architect: Martha Yunker.
ARCHITECTURE MINNESOTA 1990
May-June, v.16, no.3, p.46-49,
photos.

YUNKER, MARTHA (CONTINUED)
Room to breathe: an 83-year-old
Kenwood house rediscovers a
fountain of youth in space and
light.
Additions to Mondale house.
Architect: Martha Yunker.
ARCHITECTURE MINNESOTA 1990
May-June, v.16, no.3, p.54-57,
photos.

YURCO, FRANK J.
3,200-year-old picture of Israelites
found in Egypt / Frank J. Yurco.
Late XIXth Dynasty reliefs
(c.1290s-1180s B.C.) in Karnak.
BIBLICAL ARCHAEOLOGY REVIEW 1990
Sept.-Oct., v.16, no.5, p.[20]-38,
diagrs., dwgs., map, photos.,
refs.

YURDAKUL, A. RENGIN
Patterns of behavior in urban public
spaces / Jack L. Nasas, A. Rengin
Yurdakul.
Includes abstract.
JOURNAL OF ARCHITECTURAL AND
PLANNING RESEARCH 1990 Spring,
v.7, no.1, p.71-85, charts,
diagrs., photos, biblio.

YUTAKA SAITO, ARCHITECT AND ASSOCIATES
Chimenkanoya / Yutaka Saito.
House, Nakano Ward, Tokyo,
nicknamed by architect, "Beaver
House." Architects: Yutaka Saito,
Architect and Associates.
JAPAN ARCHITECT 1990 Jan., v.65,
no.1(393), p.[54]-60, photos.,
plans, secns.

YUU YONEDA + ARCHADIA ARCHITECTS
OFFICE
Tiger house [Hill house].
Apartment house, Japan, located in
an area called "BLUFF."
Architects: Yuu Yoneda + Archadia
Architects Office. English
summary, p.19.
KENCHIKU BUNKA 1990 Oct., v.45,
no.528, p.[131]-141, axonometric
views, dwgs., elevs., photos.,
plans, secns., sketches.

ZAMBONINI, GIUSEPPE, 1942-1990
Giuseppe Zambonini [obituary].
PROGRESSIVE ARCHITECTURE 1990
Nov., v.71, no.12, p.26,

ZAMBRINI, GUGLIELMO
Il museo nella fabbrica = Museum in
a factory / Clara Wick, Davide
Montovani.
Former sugar mill converted to
museum and display facility;
architects for conversion:
Giuseppe Gambirasio, Guglielmo
Zambrini, Loris Macci.
L'ARCA 1990 Feb., no.35, p.62-67,
axonometric view, elevs., photos,
secns.
Politiche per Venezia / Cristina
Bianchetti, Chiara Merlini.
Introduces eight articles on city
planning in Venice. English
summaries, p.124-126. Contents:
Osservare le politiche per
Venezia: perche?; Marittima e
Arsenale nel contesto delle
trasformazioni urbane a Venezia;
Vedute della laguna; Il consorzio
Venezia nuova, concessionario
dello stato per le opere di
salvaguardia di Venezia; La casa a
Venezia; Infrastrutture per la
mobilita (e l'uranistica) nella
nuova dimensione di Venezia;
Appunti sulla questione della
metropolitana a Venezia; Alcuni
limiti alla delegittimazione
sociale delle istituzioni
pubbliche di governo urbano.
URBANISTICA 1990 Mar., no.98,
p.33-86,124-126, graphs, maps,
photos., plans, secn., site plan,
tables, refs.

ZAMIATIN, P.
Il complesso residenziale di
nagatino (Mosca) = Presentation of
the Nagatino residential complex
in Moscow / L. Kozaeva.
Architects: R. Aldominaia, P.
Zapasov, P. Zamiatin. In Italian,
with English summary.
METAMORFOSI 1988, no.11, p.40-41,
photos., elev.

ZAMPINO, GIUSEPPE
Bernini: c'era una volta un castello
= Bernini in the fairytale castle.
A 13th-cent. hunting lodge
(Lagopesole) in Avigliano, Italy,
is being restored and used for
temporary exhibitions. Architect:
Giuseppe Zampino. Installation
designers: Luigi Di Vito,
Antonietta Groia.
OTTAGONO 1990 Dec., no.97,
p.128-[131], photos., plan.

ZANDER, GIUSEPPE
Un singolare capitello
Premichelangiolesco fierldric ul
pontificato di Sisto IV
(1471-1484) / Giuseppe Zander.
Author asserts that the capital
comes from the sepulchral monument
of Paolo II Barbo in the
Constantinian and medieval
Basilica of Saint Peter. Summaries
in English, French, German, and
Spanish.
PALLADIO 1988 Dec., v.1, no.2,
p.137-142, dwgs., photos., refs.

ZANDER, PIETRO
Un inedito fregio con emblema di
Giove reimpiegato nel medioevo in
San Pietro / Pietro Zander.
Frieze discovered in the Holy
Vatican Grottos in 1978; it
belonged originally to the
entablature of a temple dedicated
to Jove. It was then used in the
Middle Ages as a decoration of a
passage in the northern wall of
the Basilica Costantiniana.
Summaries in English, French,
German and Sanish, p.158.
PALLADIO 1990 Jan.-June, v.3,
no.5, p.121-126, dwg., photos.,
plan.

ZANETOV, PIERO
Un architetto romano e lo stile
della Rivoluzione: Giuseppe
Camporesi / Piero Zanetov.
L'URBE: RIVISTA ROMANA DI STORIA,
ARTE, LETTERE, COSTUMANZE 1989
May-Aug., v.52, no.3-4, p.18-26,

ZANETTI, A. M., 1698-1767
Piranesi and the 'Dactyliotheca
Zanettiana' / Diana Scarisbrick.
Miniature engraved hardstones as
sources for illustrations in
Piranesi's "Parere su
l'Architettura" of 1765.
BURLINGTON MAGAZINE 1990 June,
v.132, no.1047, p.413-414, dwg.,
photo., engr., refs.

ZANI, GINO, 1883-1964
Medievale e moderno: Gino Zani e il
rifacimento di San Marino / Guido
Zucconi.
URBANISTICA 1990 Mar., no.98,
p.19-32, ill., dwgs., elevs.,
plans, secns., refs.

ZANI, MAURIZIO
Le circoscirizioni comunali in eta
Napoleonica: La legislazione della
Repubblica Italiana e del Regno
d'Italia / Maurizio Zani.
STORIA URBANA 1990 Jan.-Mar.,
v.14, no.50, p.[33]-75, refs.
Le circoscrizioni comunali in eta
napoleonica: Il riordino dei
dipartimenti del Reno e del Panaro
tra 1802 e 1814 / Maurizio Zani.
In the vicinity of Bologna and
Modena.
STORIA URBANA 1990 Apr.-June,
v.14, no.51, p.[43]-97, maps,
refs.

ZANI, PAOLO
Gli oggetti impenetrabili / Paolo
Zani.
On the theater designs of Robert
Wilson. English summary, p.[8]
MODO 1990 Apr., v.13, no.122,
p.46-49, ill., photos.

ZANINE, JOSE, 1919-
[Jose Zanine Caldas].
CONNOISSEUR 1990 Nov., v.220,
no.946, p.172,174, photos.

ZANINOVICH, GIORGIO
Zaninovich e Trieste: Domus
Itinerario n. 57 / Coop Alea, Eva
Monai.
A guide to building by Giorgio
Zaninovich in Trieste, 1902-1914.
In Italian and English.
(Continued next column)

ZANINOVICH, GIORGIO (CONTINUED)
Zaninovich e Trieste:...(CONTINUED)
DOMUS 1990 May, no.716, p.[4]
folded p. at end of issue.,
elevs., maps, photos., plans,
secns.

ZANIOL, ANGELO
Il restauro dell'organo di Francesco
Merlini (1771) nella chiesa di S.
Samuele a Venezia / Angelo Zaniol.
VENEZIA ARTI 1990, v.4, p.175-176,
photo.

ZANSTRA, GIESEN EN SIJMONS
Retauratie atelierwoningen
Zomerdijkstraat / Mariette van
Stralen.
Renovation of an apartment house
in Amsterdam (built 1932-1934;
architects: Zanstra, Giesen en
Sijmons). Current architect:
Bertus Mulder.
DE ARCHITECT 1990 May, v.21, no.5,
p.30-31, photos., plan, secn.,
refs.

ZANTEN, DAVID VAN
La presse architecturale aux
Etats-Unis, 1870-1910 / David Van
Zanten, Mary Woods.
REVUE DE L'ART 1990, no.89,
p.19-28, photos., plans, engrs.

ZANUSO, FEDERICA
Industrial appeal: nella corte degli
artigiani = Industrial appeal: in
a craft workers' courtyard.
The interior courtyard of
19th-cent. building in Milan has
been renovated as housing and
artists' studios. Architect:
Federica Zanuso.
ABITARE 1990 Dec., no.291,
p.74-81, photos., plans.

ZAPASOV, P.
Il complesso residenziale di
nagatino (Mosca) = Presentation of
the Nagatino residential complex
in Moscow / L. Kozaeva.
Architects: R. Aldominaia, P.
Zapasov, P. Zamiatin. In Italian,
with English summary.
METAMORFOSI 1988, no.11, p.40-41,
photos., elev.

ZAPATA, CARLOS
Dressing for the office: Building
Types Study 679: commercial
interiors / Karen D. Stein.
Three projects: Vogue conference
room (Tod Williams, Billie Tsien);
Spy offices (Chan and Mohney); and
Deloitte & Touche Headquarters
(Peter Pran and Carlos Zapata for
Ellerbe Becket).
ARCHITECTURAL RECORD 1990 May,
v.178, no.6, p.103-115, photos.,
plans, secn.
Espaces en mouvance.
Interiors of offices for company
in Connecticut. Architects: Peter
Pran and Carlos Zapata of Ellerbe
Becket.
ARCHITECTURE INTERIEURE CREE 1990
Aug.-Sept., no.238, p.176-177,
photos., plan.

ZAPPA, ALFREDO
  Case come gioielli: il Neobarocco
  Boemo / Alfredo Zappa.
  Featuring the painted facades of
  houses in the former province of
  Bohemia.
  VILLE GIARDINI 1990 July-Aug.,
  no.250, p.[32]-41, photos.
  A proposito ed intorno ad un muro
  faccia a vista / a cura di Alfredo
  Zappa.
  VILLE GIARDINI 1990 Mar., no.246,
  p.48-53, dets., dwgs., photos.
  Il ritorno della muratura portante /
  a cura di Alfredo Zappa.
  VILLE GIARDINI 1990 Apr., no.247,
  p.[46]-49, diagrs., figs, ill.,
  refs.

ZARDINI, MIRKO
  Barcelona Diagonal / Mirko Zardini.
  Competition projects for new
  buildings along the planned
  extension of the Diagonal.
  Architects: Rafael Moneo and
  Manuel de Sola Morales (winners);
  Richard Plunz and Roberto Collova.
  Text in Italian and English.
  LOTUS INTERNATIONAL 1989, no.64,
  p.86-107, axonometric views,
  elevs., models, plans, secns.,
  site plans.
  Sette finestre su un cortile:
  Umberto Riva: disegno di interni =
  Seven windows on a courtyard:
  Umberto Riva: design of interiors
  / Mirko Zardini.
  Apartment renovation on Via Arena,
  Milan.
  LOTUS INTERNATIONAL 1989, no.63,
  p.16-33, elevs., photos., plans,
  secns.

ZARY, JURAJ
  Kaplnka ceskej kralovnej Zofie
  Bavorskej v Bratislavskom Dome /
  Juraj Zary.
  The chapel of Sophie of Bavaria in
  the Bratislava Cathedral. German
  summary.
  UMENI 1990, v.38, p.1-14, dets.,
  elevs., photos., plan, secns.,
  refs.

ZASCHE, JOSEF, 1871-1957
  Josef Zasche / Zdenek Lukes, Jan
  Svoboda.
  On the work of Czech architect
  Zasche (1871-1957). Includes
  German summary.
  UMENI 1990, v.38, no.6, p.534-543,
  dwg., photos., refs.

ZATLOUKAL, PAVEL
  Architektura let 1850-1950 v Knove /
  Jindrich Vybiral, Pavel Zatloukal.
  Includes German summary.
  UMENI 1990, v.38, no.6, p.521-533,
  elev., photos., refs.

ZATTERA, ARIELLA
  Architettura e religione: note
  critiche a partie dai risidtati
  del concourso "Tre chiese per il
  2000."
  "Significant entries" in a
  competition for 3 new parish
  churches in Italy. Text in Italian
  and English.
  DOMUS 1990 Oct., no.720,
  p.[78]-84, dwgs., elevs., plans,
  secns., site plans, aerial photo.

ZATTERA, ARIELLA (CONTINUED)
  Urban faith / Snjezana Torbarina,
  Bruce Macpherson.
  Two winning designs in the Italian
  competition, three churches for
  2000. Architects: Giangiacomo
  d'Arcia and Ariella Zattera for
  San Romano in Gallaretese, Milan;
  Mauro Galantino for San Ireneo,
  Cesaro Boscone.
  BUILDING DESIGN 1990 Sept.7,
  no.1002, p.20-21, dwgs., elevs.,
  plans, secns., site plan.

ZAVERI, PARUL
  Udaipur, Jaiselmer, Pondicherry,
  Fountainhas.
  Four examples that reflect the
  diversity of conservation issues
  in India, including the
  consequences of tourism and of
  cultural plurality. Authors: Parul
  Zaveri, Nimish Patel; Kulbhushan
  and Minakshi Jain; Deborah
  Thiagarajan, Pierre Richard; Asesh
  K. Maitra.
  ARCHITECTURE + DESIGN 1989
  Nov.-Dec., v.6, no.1, p.45-57,
  ill., elevs., maps, photos, plan,
  secns.

ZAVOTKA, SUSAN
  The integration of entertainment and
  communication technologies within
  home environments / Susan Zavotka.
  HOUSING AND SOCIETY 1990, v.17,
  no.2, p.61-72, charts, graphs,
  tables, refs.

ZBINDEN, UELI
  Trocken gebaut: Einfamilienhaus in
  Daniken SO, 1988/89.
  Architect: Ueli Zbinden. Text in
  German; summaries in German,
  French and English.
  WERK, BAUEN + WOHNEN 1990 Nov.,
  no.11, p.28-35, axonometric views,
  dets., photos., plans, secns.,
  site plans.
  Umbau Traminsel Albisriederplatz,
  Zurich, 1988.
  Architect: Ueli Zbinden.
  WERK, BAUEN + WOHNEN 1990 Apr.,
  no.4, p.46-47, det., photos., site
  plan.

ZDEPSKI, M. STEPHEN
  Computer graphics in architectural
  design / Glenn Goldman, M. Stephen
  Zdepski.
  ARCHITECTURE NEW JERSEY 1990,
  v.26, no.4, p.18-20,27,
  axonometric view, dwgs., elev.,
  model, plan, refs.

ZEBO, JEAN CLAUDE
  Profils: les elus 1989: Albums de
  la jeune architecture.
  Contents: Epinard Bleu, Pascal
  Marchant, Philtre Avant-Travaux,
  Patricia Leboucq, Shinobu Akahori,
  Pascal Quintard Hofstein, and
  Herve Daridan.
  LE MONITEUR ARCHITECTURE AMC 1990
  Mar., no.9, p.55, ports.

ZECHNER + ZECHNER
  EUROPAN-Wettbewerbsergebnisse.
  Five entries by young architects
  for a European housing
  competition.
  ARCH PLUS 1990 Jan., no.102,
  p.13-18, axonometric view, dwgs.,
  models, photos., plans, secns.

ZECKENDORF COMPANY
  Showing the way for large-scale
  urban development: the Zeckendorf
  Company / Patric Dolan.
  New York City real estate firm.
  REAL ESTATE FORUM 1990 Jan., v.45,
  no.1, p.53-78, ports., models,
  photos.

ZEHRFUSS, BERNARD HENRI, 1911-
  Details: Logements: la
  rehabilitation / Jean-Pierre
  Menard.
  Contents: Restoration of Jean Zay
  Universite residence, Antony,
  France, built 1955-1958; original
  architect: Eugene Baudoin;
  renovation architect: Pierre
  Grandveaud-- Renovation of
  apartment complex "Les Buffets",
  Fontenay-aux-Roses, France, built
  1958; original architects: Guy
  Lagneau, Michel Weill, Jean
  Dimitrijevic, Jean Perrottet;
  renovation architect: Jean
  Perrottet-- Renovation of la Viste
  housing complex, Marseille,
  France, built in 1959; original
  architect : Georges Candilis;
  renovaiton architect: Pierre
  Gangnet-- Renovation of apartment
  house, quartier du Haut-du-Lievre,
  Nancy, France, built 1956-62;
  original architect: Bernard
  Zehrfuss; renovation architect:
  Christian Sarfati.
  LE MONITEUR ARCHITECTURE AMC 1990
  Nov., no.16, p.37-44, axonometric
  views, dets., ports., photos.
  Museet som et muldvarpeskud / Jens
  Mollerup.
  The Musee Gallo-Romain, Lyon.
  Architect: Bernard Zehrfuss.
  ARKITEKTEN 1990 May, v.92, no.6,
  p.202-205, model., photos., plans,
  secns., site plans, refs.

ZEIDLER ROBERTS PARTNERSHIP
  Sails in the light / Paul Sandori.
  Lightweight fabric roof at Sherway
  Gardens, Toronto. Architects:
  Zeidler Roberts.
  CANADIAN ARCHITECT 1990 June,
  v.35, no.6, p.26-28, dets.,
  photos., sketch.

ZEIDMAN, FREDERICK H.
  The abc's of waterfront planning /
  Frederick H. Zeidman.
  URBAN LAND 1989 June, v.48, no.6,
  p.11-15, dwg., photos., site plan,
  engr.

ZEIN, RUTH VERDE
  A arquitetura dos anos 80 e as
  tendencias da nova decada.
  An overview of international
  architecture of the 1980s.
  Includes essays by Ruth Verde
  Zein, Marina Waisman, and and
  Franco Purini.
  PROJETO 1990 Jan.-Feb., no.129,
  p.[65]-110, axonometric views,
  (Continued next page)

ZEIN, RUTH VERDE (CONTINUED)
A arquitetura dos...(CONTINUED)
dwgs., model, photos, plans,
aerial photos.

ZEITLER, RUDOLF
Fragor rorande Uppsala domkyrkas
aldsta byggnadshistoria / Rudolf
Zeitler.
Includes German summary.
KONSTHISTORISK TIDSKRIFT 1990,
v.59, no.3, p.[159]-168, dets.,
photos., plans, refs.
Franciscus och Dominicus i en
vaggmalning i Mariakyrkan i
Sigtuna / Rudolf Zeitler.
15th-cent. wall paintings in
13th-cent. Swedish church.
Includes commentary by Jarl Galler
and a German summary.
KONSTHISTORISK TIDSKRIFT 1990,
v.59, no.1-2, p.[144]-150,
photos., ref.

ZEJMA, J. C.
Le nouvel siege social de la Banque
Populaire de la Cote d'Azur.
Architects: J.C. Zejma, L.
Chevalier.
LE MUR VIVANT 1990, no.95,
p.59-62, photos.

ZELINSKY, MARILYN KAY
Translucent treasures / Marilyn Kay
Zelinsky.
Features acrylic accessories
designed by architect/designer
Rand Elliott.
INTERIORS 1990 Dec., v.150, no.5,
p.[88]-91, port., photos.

ZELINSKY, WILBUR
Seeing beyond the dominant culture /
Wilbur Zelinsky.
Discussion with three authors in
this issue on "cultural
landscapes."
PLACES 1990 Fall, v.7, no.1,
p.[32]-37, photo.

ZELLER, CHRISTA
Loos in der Auslage: zur Ausstellung
uber Adolf Loos in Wien
(2.Dez.1989-25.Februar 1990)
[exhibition review] / Christa
Zeller.
At the Graphische Sammlung
Albertina.
WERK, BAUEN + WOHNEN 1990 May,
no.5, p.12-13, port., models,
sketches.
"...as you work, as you play": zur
Ausstellung von
Frank-Lloyd-Wright-Zeichnungen im
Phoenix Art Museum, Phoenix,
Arizona, 13.Januar bis 15.April
1990 [exhibition review] / Christa
Zeller.
WERK, BAUEN + WOHNEN 1990 June,
no.6, p.12-15, dwgs., elevs.,
photos.

ZELLER, JOHN
Iowa tallest buildings: tallest in
town / John Zeller.
IOWA ARCHITECT 1990 Winter, v.39,
no.4, p.20-23, dwgs., elevs.,
photos.

ZEMANKOVA, MARIA
Energy Expert: an expert system for
architects / Bharati Jog, Maria
Zemankova.
COMPUTERS, ENVIRONMENT AND URBAN
SYSTEMS 1989, v.13, no.1, p.29-38,
ill., refs.

ZENGHELIS, ELIA, 1937-
Aduana con peneita: OMA en
Checkpoint Charlie / Jorge Sainz.
Architects: M. Sauerbruch, E.
Zenghelis.
ARQUITECTURA VIVA 1990 July-Aug.,
no.13, p.20-23, dwgs., elevs.,
photos., plans, secns.
Casa a Mitilene, Lesbo = House in
Mitilene, Lesbos.
Architects: Eleni Gigantes, Elia
Zenghelis.
LOTUS INTERNATIONAL 1989, no.63,
p.110-117, elevs., photos., plans,
secns.
Creative influence / Ian Latham.
On the works of Eleni Gigantes and
Elia Zenghelis.
BUILDING DESIGN 1990 Mar.2,
no.975, p.16-21, axonometric view,
ill., photos., plans, secns., site
plans.
Folly 13 [part 2]: Expo '90.
Contents: Zaha Hadid, Chris
Macdonald + Peter Salter, Hajime
Yatsuka, Eleni Gigantes + Elia
Zenghelis.--Folly 13 story [2], by
Hajime Yatsuka.
SPACE DESIGN 1990 Mar., no.306,
p.129-136, axonometric views,
diagrs., dwgs., models, site
plans.
Incursione suprematista nel
Mediterraneo: Therma Hotel, baia
di Gera, Lesbo = Suprematist
incursion in the Mediterranean:
Therma Hotel, Bay of Gera, Lesvos.
Architects: Elia Zenghelis, Ron
Steiner, Elias Veneris, Zoe
Zenghelis.
LOTUS INTERNATIONAL 1986, no.52,
p.30-39, axonometric views,
elevs., models, plans, secns.,
site plans.
Recent works: Elia Zenghelis, Eleni
Gigantes.
Four projects, 1986-1989,
including the Chalkiades villa,
Mytilene. Includes an interview by
Koji Taki and Hajime Yatsuka.
SPACE DESIGN 1990 Mar., no.306,
p.121-128, elevs., photos., plans,
secns., site plans, isometric
dwgs.

ZENGHELIS, ZOE
Incursione suprematista nel
Mediterraneo: Therma Hotel, baia
di Gera, Lesbo = Suprematist
incursion in the Mediterranean:
Therma Hotel, Bay of Gera, Lesvos.
Architects: Elia Zenghelis, Ron
Steiner, Elias Veneris, Zoe
Zenghelis.
LOTUS INTERNATIONAL 1986, no.52,
p.30-39, axonometric views,
elevs., models, plans, secns.,
site plans.

ZENOBI, V.
Techniche di rappresentazione del
piano negli anni Cinquanta e
Sessanta / R. A. Laera, C.
Riccardi, V. Zenobi.
Plans for Bari in the 1950s and
1960s by Alberto Calza Bini,
Marcello Piacentini, and Ludovico
Quaroni.
URBANISTICA 1989 Mar., no.94,
p.17-30, axonometric views, dwg.,
elev., plans, sketches, refs.

ZENTES, JOACHIM
Planning for retail change in West
Germany / Joachim Zentes, Werner
Schwarz-Zanetti.
BUILT ENVIRONMENT 1988, v.14,
no.1, p.38-46, charts, photos,
refs.

ZENTZ, PATRICK
A question of architecture: the work
of Patrick Zentz and Tom Grondona
/ Richard Hansen, Bob Condia.
Both are American artists working
within the context of
architecture.
MONTANA STATE ARCHITECTURAL REVIEW
1990 Spring, v.7, p.8-13, photos.,
model, plans, refs.

ZEPPELINS
See AIR-SHIPS

ZERMANI, PAOLO, 1958-
Paolo Zermani, monumento a S. Polo
di Torrile, Parma / Paolo Zermani.
Design for a war memorial. Text in
Italian and English.
DOMUS 1990 Jan., no.712,
p.12-[13], elevs., models, map,
plans, secns., site plan, sketch.

ZERNIG, MANFRED, 1952-
Graz.
One of three sections in special
feature on "Contemporary Austrian
architecture". Architects
included: Klaus Kada, Michael
Szyszkowitz, Karla
Szyskowitz-Kowalski, Manfred
Zernig, Hermann Eisenkock, Ernst
Giselbrecht, Volker Giencke.
SPACE DESIGN 1990 Mar., no.306,
p.[47]-84, axonometric views,
dets., ports., elevs., models,
photos., plans, secns., site
plans, isometric dwgs.
Wohnbebauung Radegunderstrasse in
Graz, Osterreich = Housing
Radegunderstrasse in Graz,
Austria.
Competition. Winning architect:
Manfred Zernig. Text in German.
ARCHITEKTUR + WETTBEWERBE 1990
June, no.142, p.58-60, dwgs.,
elevs., models, plans, site plans,
isometric dwgs.

ZERVUDACHI, TINO
The model apartment: Jerry Hall
hones in on a stylish London
pied-a-terre. / Guy Nevill.
Interior designers: David
Mlinaric, Jane Rainey, and Tino
Zervudachi.
HOUSE & GARDEN 1990 Feb., v.162,
no.2, p.[88-93],165, ports.,
photos.

ZERWAS, ANDREW
  Nicolau Maria Rubio i Tuduri /
    Andrew Zerwas.
    On the late Spansih architect,
    planner, and garden designer.
    Includes English summary.
    GARTEN UND LANDSCHAFT 1990, v.100,
    no.3, p.37-40, port., photos.,
    aerial photo.

ZETEK, TOM
  Dulwich competition winners / Clive
    Aslet.
    Country Life competition for new
    Dulwich Picture Gallery addition;
    architects: Christopher J. Grasby,
    Brendan T. O'Neill and Tom Zetek
    (winners); Allies and Morrison
    (second prize); Peter Clash (third
    prize). Original architect Sir
    John Soane.
    COUNTRY LIFE 1990 Sept.13, v.184,
    no.37, p.178-179,202-203,
    axonometric views, models, plans,
    secns., site plans.
  Modernism and Soane / Dan
    Cruickshank.
    Competition winners for extension
    to Dulwich Picture Gallery,
    designed by Sir John Soane. First
    prize: Christopher Grasby, Brendan
    O'Neill and Tom Zetek. Two
    additional entries by Allies and
    Morrison, and Peter Clash.
    ARCHITECTS' JOURNAL 1990 Sept.19,
    v.192, no.12, p.26-33, elevs.,
    models, photos., plans, secns.,
    sketches.
  Soane success / Clare Melhuish.
    Features three winning entries and
    one highly commended entry in the
    competition for the addition to
    the Dulwich Picture Gallery,
    designed by Sir John Soane. First
    prize: Christopher J. Grasby,
    Brendan T. O'Neill and Tom Zetek.
    BUILDING DESIGN 1990 Sept.14,
    no.1003, p.13-16, axonometric
    view, dwgs., elevs., model, plans,
    secns., site plans.

ZETTEL, HERBERT
  Grosser Bahnhof: Paketumschlaghalle
    der Post in Munchen / Wilfried
    Dechau.
    Architects: R. Rosenfeld, H.
    Zettel.
    DEUTSCHE BAUZEITUNG 1990 Dec.,
    v.124, no.12, p.78-85, dets.,
    elev., photos., secn.

ZEUS, K.
  Mauerwerk: Stand der Entwicklung /
    W. Manns, K. Zeus.
    DEUTSCHES ARCHITEKTENBLATT 1990
    Sept.1, v.22, no.9, p.1359-1360,
    dwgs., tables.

ZEVI, LUCA
  La ricerca di Paolo Soleri = Paolo
    Soleri's research / Luca Zevi.
    Includes an interview.
    ARCHITETTURA: CRONACHE E STORIA
    1990 Dec., v.36, no.12(422),
    p.[838]-874, ill., dwgs., photos.,
    plans, secns., site plans,
    sketches, aerial photos., biblio.

ZEVON, SUSAN
  Best Small House 1990 / Susan Zevon,
    Katie Ridder.
    Competition sponsored by HB and
    the American Wood Council. Winning
    house in Amenia, N.Y. by Jonathan
    Lanman and Debra Wassman of
    Trumbull Architects, N.Y.C.
    Interior designer: Paul Leonard.
    HOUSE BEAUTIFUL 1990 Nov., v.132,
    no.11, p.81-91, photos., plans.
  Infusion of charm / Susan Zevon.
    Additions to house in Westport,
    Connecticut. Architects:
    Rosenblum/Harb Architects.
    HOUSE BEAUTIFUL 1990 Oct., v.132,
    no.10, p.112-115, dets., photos.,
    plan.
  Merging with the garden / Susan
    Zevon.
    Back addition to Georgian house in
    Washington, D.C. Architects for
    addition: Hartman-Cox; interior
    designers: Oz Interiors.
    HOUSE BEAUTIFUL 1990 Sept., v.132,
    no.9, p.111-118, photos., plan.
  New slant on the small house [New
    Hampshire] / Susan Zevon.
    Architects: Amsler Hagenah
    MacLean, Architects.
    HOUSE BEAUTIFUL 1986 June, v.128,
    no.6, p.[72-75], photos., plans.
  Rebuilding for a bright future /
    Susan Zevon.
    Restoration and additions to 1926
    Colonial revival house in Concord,
    Mass. Architect for addition:
    Frank Adams of Stahl Associates.
    HOUSE BEAUTIFUL 1990 May, v.132,
    no.5, p.121,124,127,[129], ports.,
    photos., plans.

ZHAI, ZONGFAN
  The design of the National Library
    of China / Huang Kewu, Zhai
    Zongfan, Jin Zhishun.
    BUILDING IN CHINA 1989 Mar., v.2,
    no.1, p.37-41,36, photos., plans.

ZHAN, YONGWEI
  Landscape planning and development
    of Suzhou / Zhan Yongwei, Huang
    Wei.
    Covers conservation of classical
    gardens and the restoration and
    exploitation of green spaces.
    BUILDING IN CHINA 1989 Mar., v.2,
    no.1, p.23-29, photos.

ZHANG, JIAQI
  The splendour of the grotto arts of
    the later period in China / Zhang
    Jiaqi.
    ORIENTAL ART 1989 Spring, v.35,
    no.1, p.7-21, dwgs., maps, photos.

ZHANG, QINGYUAN
  Combined effect of earth cooling and
    ventilation on passive cooling of
    dwellings (continued report) /
    Tadahisa Katayama et al.
    English summary, p.83.
    NIHON KENCHIKU GAKKAI KEIKAKUKEI
    RONBUN HOKOKU SHU = JOURNAL OF
    ARCHITECTURE, PLANNING AND
    ENVIRONMENTAL ENGINEERING 1990
    Jan., no.1(407), p.75-83, figs.,
    graphs, tables, refs.

ZHANG, ZHONGYI
  New building for ISTIC in Beijing /
    Zhang Zhongyi.
    The Institute of Scientific &
    Technical Information of China,
    begun in 1984 and completed in
    1988.
    BUILDING IN CHINA 1990 June, v.3,
    no.2 p.31-35, photos., plans,
    aerial photo.

ZHAO, DONGRI
  Studies on Beijing's development
    strategies / Zhao Dongri.
    Covers population structure;
    sub-centers, satellite towns,
    urban region; water shortage;
    traffic.
    BUILDING IN CHINA 1989 Mar., v.2,
    no.1, p.18-22, table.

ZHAO, GUANGIAN
  Three experimental projects for
    housing development / Zhao
    Guangian.
    Focuses on three projects (Qinyuan
    Villa, Wuxi; Yanzishan Estate,
    Jinan; Chuanfu Estate, Tianjin)
    and provides a table of technical
    and economic indices.
    BUILDING IN CHINA 1990 Sept., v.3,
    no.3, p.14-25,[2 p. inserts],
    port., photos., plans, table.

ZHONG JING
  Working at Zhong Jing [Architects
    and Engineers] / Joe Carter.
    A Canadian architect living in
    China for three years discusses
    his work in a Beijing firm during
    1990 and describes the partners'
    work.
    BUILDING IN CHINA 1990 Sept., v.3,
    no.3, p.26-41, axonometric views,
    dwgs., ports., elevs., photos.,
    plans.

ZHOU, MING
  Yu Lu Hotel, Fujian Province / Zhou
    Ming.
    The author's final project at
    Nanjing University, for a Wu Yi
    mountain hotel in the PRC.
    MIMAR: ARCHITECTURE IN DEVELOPMENT
    1990 Sept., v.10, no.3(36),
    p.46-48, dwgs., elevs., map,
    plans, secn., site plan, sketches.

ZHOU, YUANGYANG
  Vernacular dwellings in Huizhou /
    Zhou Yuangyang.
    Houses in Anhui Province with
    white washed walls, small dark
    tiles, decorated gable walls, and
    ornamental carved window frames.
    BUILDING IN CHINA 1990 Mar., v.3,
    no.1, p.27-29, [2 p. photos
    insert], photos.

ZHU, XIULIN
  A "building-blocks" kindergarten /
    Zhu Xiulin.
    Bashu Kindergarten in Chongqing,
    Sichuan province.
    BUILDING IN CHINA 1989 Mar., v.2,
    no.1, p.42-43, photos.

ZHU, YAN
Home-buying, affordable? / Zhu Yan.
Data on Beijing.
BUILDING IN CHINA 1989 Dec., v.2,
no.4, p.43-44, table.

ZHU, ZIXUAN
New exploration into the
conservation and rehabilitation of
old cities / Zhu Zixuan.
BUILDING IN CHINA 1989 Dec., v.2,
no.4, p.18-26,insert, dwgs.,
port., elev., photos., site plans.

ZIEBARTH, ANN C.
Irish-vernacular architecture: an
illustration of semiotic analysis
/ Ann C. Ziebarth.
Studies "the interaction of
culture and design."
HOUSING AND SOCIETY 1990, v.17,
no.1, p.27-34, plans, refs.

ZIEGERT, PAUL
Une lecon d'anatomie berlinoise /
Corinne Jacquand.
Features the winning design in the
competition for Anatomy Institute
at the Freie Universitat, Berlin.
Architect: Paul Ziegert.
ARCHITECTURE D'AUJOURD'HUI 1990
Feb., no.267, p.50-51, dwgs.,
elevs., models, plan, site plan.

ZIETZSCHMANN, ERNST
Uber oder neben den Geleisen? Der
neue City-Terminal in Stockholm,
1989 / Ernst Zietzschmann.
Architects: Anders Tengbom, Ralph
Erskine.
WERK, BAUEN + WOHNEN 1989 Dec.,
no.12, p.12-13, model, photos.,
plans.

ZIGGURATS--ANCIENT--IRAQ--NIPPUR
Ein Zikkurrat - Grundriss aus
Nippur--Addendum / Joachim
Oelsner.
STAATLICHE MUSEEN (EAST BERLIN).
FORSCHUNGEN UND BERICHTE 1989,
v.27, p.51, reconst. dwg.

ZIMMER GUNSUL FRASCA PARTNERSHIP
Accurate reflections: glass,
detailing components / Marc S.
Harriman.
Contents: The Link, Kansas City
(Zimmer Gunsul Frasca
Partnership); 3M Austin Center,
Tex. (CRSS); Dakin Building, San
Francisco (Theodore Brown &
Partners).
ARCHITECTURE: THE MAGAZINE OF THE
AMERICAN INSTITUTE OF ARCHITECTS
1990 Aug., v.79, no.8, p.87-93,
dets., photos., elevs.
Collegamento metropolitano di
superficie per l'area di Portland
= Bahfield Freeway; a light rail
project, Portland, Or. / Silvano
Stucchi.
Architects: Zimmer Gunsul Frasca
Partnership. Includes English
translation. French, German and
Spanish summaries, p.3.
L'INDUSTRIA DELLE COSTRUZIONI 1989
June, v.23, no.212, p.26-33,
elevs., photos., site plans.

**ZIMMER GUNSUL FRASCA PARTNERSHIP
(CONTINUED)**
Frontier justice redefined: Federal
Correctional Institution,
Sheridan, Oregon.
Architects: Zimmer Gunsul Frasca
Partnership.
ARCHITECTURAL RECORD 1990 Sept.,
v.178, no.10, p.142-145,
axonometric views, photos., plans,
secns., site plan.
Plain and fancy: Borders, Perrin &
Norrander Inc., Portland, Oregon,
Zimmer Gunsul Frasca Partnership,
Architects / Donald J. Canty.
Interiors of an advertising
agency.
ARCHITECTURAL RECORD 1990 Sept.,
v.178, no.10, p.[70-77], dets.,
photos., plans.
Role model: Hauser Library, Reed
College, Portland, Oregon: Zimmer
Gunsul Frasca Partnership /
Douglas Gantenbein.
ARCHITECTURE: THE AIA JOURNAL 1990
Nov., v.79, no.11, p.[70-75],
axonometric views, photos., plans,
secns.

ZIMMER, PIERRE
Nouveau siege de la CBC a la Defense
/ Pierre Zimmer.
Office building for the Compagnie
Generale de Batiment et
Construction (1990). Architect:
Andrault et Parat, Architectes.
LE MUR VIVANT 1990, no.97,
p.28-34, det., photos., plans.

ZIMMERMAN, ANNE
Women and Architecture / Anne
Zimmerman.
Report on a conference in San
Diego.
ARCHITECTURE: THE AIA JOURNAL 1990
Apr., v.79, no.4, p.36, photo.

ZIMMERMAN, BERNARD, 1930-
Zimmerman/Stafford, Hamburger
Hamlet, Hollywood / Francesca
Garcia-marquez.
Text in Italian and English.
DOMUS 1990 Mar., no.714, p.[6-7],
axonometric view, dets., photos.,
plan, secn.

ZIMMERMAN DESIGN GROUP
The Milwaukee architect: confidence
at home / Lucia Apostol.
Refers to the work of six firms:
Kahler Slater Torphy Architects,
Inc.; Herbst Epstein Keller and
Chadeck [sic]; Engberg Anderson;
Miller Meier Kenyon Cooper
Architects and Engineers;
Zimmerman Design Group; and
Beckley/Myers Architects.
INLAND ARCHITECT 1990 July-Aug.,
v.34, no.4, p.46-51, axonometric
view, ill., photos.
Wisconsin getaways: urban chic,
rural retreat / Karen E. Klages.
Two interiors: DKC's Armadillo Bar
and Grill, Milwaukee (architect:
Kubala Washatko Architects), and
The Inn at Pine Terrace,
Oconomowoc (designer: Zimmerman
Design Group).
INLAND ARCHITECT 1990 July-Aug.,
v.34, no.4, p.4-[5], photos.,
plan.

**ZIMMERMANN, FLORIAN. SCHREI NACH DEM
TURMHAUS**
Der Schrei nach dem Turmhouse: Der
Ideenwettbewerb Hochhaus am
Bahnhof Friedrichstrasse Berlin
1921-22 [ed. by Florian
Zimmermann] [book review] /
Dietrich Neumann.
KUNSTCHRONIK 1989 Oct., v.42,
no.10, p.593.

ZIMMERMANN, GUNTER
Gneisplatten als Terrassenbelag:
Braunfarbung durch eisenhaltige
Kieskorner / Gunter Zimmermann.
DEUTSCHES ARCHITEKTENBLATT 1990
Oct.1, v.22, no.10, p.1583,
photos.
Marmorplattenbelag im Untergeschoss:
Braunfarbung durch
Grundwasseranstieg / Gunter
Zimmermann.
DEUTSCHES ARCHITEKTENBLATT 1990
Oct.1, v.22, no.10, p.1584,
photos.
Schaden an Belagen und Bekleidungen
aus Naturstein / Gunter
Zimmermann.
DEUTSCHES ARCHITEKTENBLATT 1990
Nov.1, v.22, no.11, p.1737-1742,
photos., det., refs.
Zum Langzeitverhalten von
Umkehrdachern / Gunter Zimmermann.
Maintenance, alterations, and
waterproofing of flat roofs of
various materials.
DEUTSCHES ARCHITEKTENBLATT 1990
Oct.1, v.22, no.10, p.1559-1565,
photos., tables, refs.

ZIMMERMANN, KONRAD
Das Grabungsmuseum -- Struktur und
Funktion / Konrad Zimmermann.
STAATLICHE MUSEEN (EAST BERLIN).
FORSCHUNGEN UND BERICHTE 1989,
v.27, p.257-262, photos, refs.

ZIMMERMANN, YVES
Yiannis Vikelas y la Fundacion
Goulandris de Atenas / Yves
Zimmermann.
Spanish, English text.
ON DISENO 1990, no.108, p.170-188,
photos., plans.

ZINGSHEIM, PATRICIA
The Des Moines Vision Plan Project:
the American City: an
architectural continuum / Patricia
Zingsheim.
Plans by Agrest and Gandelsonas.
IOWA ARCHITECT 1990 Winter, v.39,
no.4, p.10-15, ill., ports.,
photos., site plans.
International Winter Cities 1990,
urban examples competition
enhancing the public realm of
Central Des Moines / Robert A.
Findlay.
An urban design collaboration by
Iowa State Univ. faculty and
students and P. Zingsheim won a
first place award.
IOWA ARCHITECT 1990 Winter, v.39,
no.4, p.16-19, ill., aerial photo.
An interview with Mario Gandelsonas:
"The American City: an
architectural continuum / Patricia
Zingsheim, Gregory Quick
Gandelsonas is heading a 3 year
study of Des Moines, to culminate
in a new master plan.
(Continued next page)

ZINGSHEIM, PATRICIA (CONTINUED)
  An interview with...(CONTINUED)
    IOWA ARCHITECT 1989 Winter, v.38,
    no.5, p.30-33, ill., ports.,
    sketch.

ZINSMEISTER, RAINER
  Futuristische Bau- und Burotechnik:
    Werndls EOS in der neuen
    Hauptverwaltung der EVT / Halina
    Noll.
    Architects: G. Scheffler, R.
    Zinsmeister.
    ARCHITEKTUR, INNENARCHITEKTUR,
    TECHNISCHER AUSBAU 1990 Apr.,
    v.98, no.4, p.108-110, photos.

ZINZENDORF, KARL, GRAF VON, 1739-1813
  The gardens of the British Isles in
    the diary of the Austrian Count
    Karl von Zinzendorf in the year
    1768 / Geza Hajos.
    Archival material which may shed
    light on Zinzendorf's importance
    for the history of garden design
    in Austria.
    JOURNAL OF GARDEN HISTORY 1989
    Jan.-Mar., v.9, no.1, p.[40]-47,
    refs.

ZIVAS, ANTONIO
  Villa Adriana barocca, ouvero le
    antinomie d'avanguardia di Adriano
    architetto, tra la tholos di
    Afrodite Cnidia e l'esedra della
    Piazza d'Oro / Antonio Zivas.
    STORIA ARCHITETTURA 1987
    Jan.-Dec., v.10, no.1-2, p.5-24,
    dets., elevs., photos, plans,
    secns., site plans, recontr. dwg.,
    refs.

ZIVKOVIC ASSOCIATES
  High design, low budget / Angi
    Bates.
    Interiors of New York graphic
    designer recruiting firm, Roshak &
    Co. Architects: Zivkovic
    Associates.
    INTERIORS 1990 May, v.149, no.10,
    p.32, photos., plan.

ZIZKA, JAN
  Cisterciacky klaster v klasterni
    Skalicu u Kourimi / Pavel Kroupa,
    Jan Zizka.
    A 14th-cent. cloister in Kourim,
    Czechoslovakia. Includes summary
    in German.
    UMENI 1990, v.38, no.4, p.312-323,
    elevs., map, photos., plans, refs.

ZIZZUTTO, ROBERT
  Verwaltungsgebaude in Ivrea.
    Office building by Gina Valle in
    "Olivetti City". Includes English
    summary.
    BAUMEISTER 1990 June, v.87, no.6,
    p.46-52, photos., plans, secns.,
    site plans.

ZLONICKY & WACHTEN
  Ludwigshafen - Rheinufer-Sud: ein
    ganz normales
    Stadtentwicklungsprojekt? / Gerd
    Wilhelmus.
    Discusses the site and proposals
    by three firms: Ganz + Rolfes,
    Zlonicky & Wachten, Albert Speer &
    Partner.
    BAUWELT 1990 Sept.28, v.81, no.36,
    p.1793-1808, dwgs., elevs.,
    models, maps, site plans.

ZMEUREANU, RADU
  Assessment of the energy savings due
    to the building retrofit / Radu
    Zmeureanu.
    BUILDING AND ENVIRONMENT 1990,
    v.25, no.2, p.95-103, graphs,
    tables, refs., diagrs.

ZOCHER, KAREL GEORGE, 1796-
  Blikkenburg a Zeist / Heimerick
    Tromp.
    History of the now demolished
    manor house and the county house
    designed on the same site in the
    mid-19th cent. by Karel George
    Zocher.
    MAISONS D'HIER ET D'AUJOURD'HUI =
    DE WOONSTEDE DOOR DE EEUWEN HEEN
    1990 Dec., no.88, p.21-30, ill.,
    map, photos., site plan, biblio.

ZOEGGELER, OSWALD
  Concorso per la riqualificazione
    dell' area di Via Veneto [Trento].
    Presents 10 entries, including 1st
    prize entry by Oswald Zoeggeler.
    FARAMETRO 1990, Nov.-Dec., no.181,
    p.52-69, axonometric views, ill.,
    dwgs., elevs., photos., plans,
    secns., aerial photo.

ZOELLY, PIERRE, 1923-
  Geheimnisse der Lichtpyramide /
    Pierre Zoelly.
    On a project by Zoelly: Atrium
    Rotkreuzmuseum, Geneva.
    DER ARCHITEKT 1990 Sept., no.9,
    p.401-402, dwgs., photos.
  Um- und Ausbau Muhle Tiefenbrunnen
    in Zurich, Schweiz = Conversion
    and extension of Tiefenbrunnen
    Mill in Zurich, Switzerland.
    19th cent. mill buildings now used
    for housing restaurants,
    galleries, offices, etc.
    Architect: Pierre Zoelly.
    ARCHITEKTUR + WETTBEWERBE 1989
    Dec., no.140, p.15, dwg., photos.

ZOFFOLI, PAOLO
  Un nuovo grattacielo a Hong Kong: il
    Bond Centre = A new high-rise
    building in Hong Kong: the Bond
    Centre / Paolo Zoffoli.
    Architect: Paul Rudolph. In
    Italian and English.
    L'INDUSTRIA DELLE COSTRUZIONI 1990
    July-Aug., v.24, no.225-226,
    p.48-54, dwgs., photos., plans.

ZOJAJI, SHOHREH, 1957-
  Gloom hits architects as
    redundancies pile up.
    In Britain. Includes a profile of
    London architect Shohreh Zojaji.
    BUILDING 1990 Oct.5, v.255, no.39,
    p.8-9, ill., table.

ZOLTAN, NAGY
  Temp-rom-ter: a Kiscelli Muzeum uj
    kiallitoterme / Nagy Zoltan.
    MUVESZET 1989 Mar., v.30, no.3,
    p.4-5, photos.

ZOLTOWSKI, EDWARD
  Archives departementales de
    Seine-et-Marne.
    Located in the center of Melun.
    Architects: B. Feypell, E.
    Zoltowski.
    LE MUR VIVANT 1990, no.97,
    p.57-63, photos., elevs., plans,
    secn., site plans.

ZONCA, FRANCK
  Interieurs.
    Contents: Offices of Clan Design,
    61 Rue Servan, Paris; architects:
    Catherine Geoffroy and Franck
    Zonca -- Offices of Cartier, 1,
    Rue Francois ler, Paris;
    architect: Jean Nouvel.
    LE MONITEUR ARCHITECTURE AMC 1990
    Mar., no.9, p.18-20, photos.,
    plans, secns.

ZONING
  See also BUILDING ENVELOPES
  See also BUILDINGS - HEIGHT
    RESTRICTIONS
  See also INCENTIVE ZONING
  See also LINKAGE
  See also ZONING LAW
  How effective is zoning in the
    control of development? / P.
    Booth.
    Compares British and French
    experiences.
    ENVIRONMENT AND PLANNING B 1989,
    v.16, no.4, p.401-415, tables,
    refs.
  Overlay districts as a means of
    resource preservation / Kevin
    Corcoran.
    PLANNING NEWS 1989 May-June, v.55,
    no.3, p.[1],4-5, site plans.
  Why should we revise the zoning
    ordinance? / Leslie S. Pollack.
    AMERICAN PLANNING ASSOCIATION.
    PLANNING ADVISORY SERVICE. PAS
    MEMO 1989 Feb., p.[1]-4, chart.

ZONING--CANADA--SASKATCHEWAN
  The planning system in Saskatchewan
    / Kenneth Palmer.
    PLANNING QUARTERLY 1989 Sept.,
    no.95, p.11-13,

ZONING--HISTORY--UNITED STATES--NEW
    YORK (NEW YORK)
  A reconsideration of the Equitable
    Building in New York / Sally Kitt
    Chappell.
    On ideologies surrounding the 1916
    zoning movement, elevator
    engineering, and management
    techniques used in the 1912-1915
    building, located at 120 S.
    Broadway (architect: E.R. Graham).
    Includes abstract.
    SOCIETY OF ARCHITECTURAL
    HISTORIANS. JOURNAL 1990 Mar.,
    v.49, no.1, p.90-95, dwg.,
    photos., refs.

ZONING LAW
  See also BUILDINGS - ILLEGAL
  See also SOLAR ACCESS RIGHTS
  Euclid v. Ambler: a retrospective /
    Timothy Alan Fluck.
    1926 U.S. Supreme Court decision
    on zoning.
    AMERICAN PLANNING ASSOCIATION.
    JOURNAL 1986 Summer, v.52, no.3,
    p.326-337, ports., maps, tables,
    biblios., refs.

ZONING LAW--UNITED STATES
  Zoning today: a time for reckoning /
    Charles M. Haar, Jerold S. Kayden.
    Succinct, critical analysis of
    zoning.
    PLANNING 1989 June, v.55, no.6,
    p.20-21, ill.

ZONING LAW--UNITED STATES--NEW YORK
(NEW YORK)
Context is everything / Sandy
Hornick.
Amendments to New York City's
zoning resolution allows for
increased lower density areas for
low-rise neighborhood housing.
PLANNING 1990 Dec., v.56, no.12,
p.22-26, diagrs., dwg., photo.,
secn.
A user's guide to Charter process /
Todd W. Bressi.
Effects of the proposed revision
to the City Charter on land use in
New York.
CITY LIMITS 1990 Feb., v.15, no.2,
p.18-19.

ZONING LAW--UNITED STATES--PASADENA
(CALIFORNIA)
Emerald City [Pasadena, Calif.] /
Daniel Solomon, Susan Haviland.
OZ / COLLEGE OF ARCHITECTURE AND
DESIGN, KANSAS STATE UNIVERSITY
1989, v.11, p.42-45, dwgs.,
photos., plans, site plans.

ZONING--NEW ZEALAND--CHRISTCHURCH
Pumping life into central city / Ken
Lawn.
Urban renewal in Christchurch, New
Zealand.
PLANNING QUARTERLY 1989 Sept.,
no.95, p.26-28, map, photo.

ZONING--POLITICAL ASPECTS
Developer as generalist / Gary
Griffith.
The role of neighborhood influence
on rezoning applications.
THE JOURNAL OF REAL ESTATE
DEVELOPMENT 1989 Summer, v.5,
no.1, p.51-55.

ZONING--UNITED STATES
Let the sun shine in: how zoning to
preserve light is significantly
affecting cities across the U.S. /
Terry Jill Lassar.
ARCHITECTURE: THE MAGAZINE OF THE
AMERICAN INSTITUTE OF ARCHITECTS
1990 May, v.79, no.5, p.102-105,
155-156,159, ill., map, diagr.
Zoning today: a time for reckoning /
Charles M. Haar, Jerold S. Kayden.
Succinct, critical analysis of
zoning.
PLANNING 1989 June, v.55, no.6,
p.20-21, ill.

ZONING--UNITED STATES--GEORGETOWN
(TEXAS)
Zoning with intensity [Georgetown,
Texas] / Hildy L. Kingma.
PLANNING 1990 Oct., v.56, no.10,
p.18-21, graph, photos., plan.

ZONING--UNITED STATES--NEW YORK (NEW
YORK)--UPPER EAST SIDE
Oculus Special Feature Committee on
Zoning on the Upper East Side:
Part II.
Shows interpretations for 4 sites,
by James Gauer, Marilyn Taylor,
Peter Samton, and Peter De Witt.
OCULUS 1990 Sept., v.53, no.1,
p.6-10, dwgs., ports., elevs.,
models, map, plans.

ZONING--UNITED STATES--VIRGINIA
Downzoning: an unprecedented
developers' victory.
DEVELOPMENT 1990 Sept.-Oct., v.21,
no.5, p.28-29.

ZONNEVELD, W.
Conceptual complexes and shifts in
post-war urban planning in the
Netherlands / W. Zonneveld.
BUILT ENVIRONMENT 1989, v.15,
no.1, p.40-48, diagrs., plans,
refs.

ZOOK, ROSCOE HAROLD, D. 1949
The Zook look: a suburban fantasy /
Michael J.P. Smith.
Houses and stained glass windows
by Hinsdale, Ill. architect:
Roscoe Harold Zook (d.1949).
INLAND ARCHITECT 1990 Mar.-Apr.,
v.34, no.2, p.26, photos.

ZOOLOGICAL GARDENS
See ZOOS

ZOOLOGICAL MUSEUMS--ALTERATIONS AND
ADDITIONS--SPAIN--BARCELONA--MUSEO
DE ZOOLOGIA
Edificio de servicios para el Museo
de Zoologia de Barcelona: C. Basso
y C. Cirici, arquitectos.
Laboratory addition. Original
architect: Lluis Domenech i
Montaner. Spanish, English text.
ON DISENO 1990, no.114, p.94-103,
elev., photos., plans, site plan.

ZOOMORPHIC STRUCTURES
Porro, rue Paul Eluard a Saint-Denis
/ Marie-Jeanne Dumont.
College Elsa Triolet is shaped
like a dove. Architects: Ricardo
Porro, Renaud de La Noue. English
summary, p.85.
ARCHITECTURE D'AUJOURD'HUI 1990
Sept., no.270, p.82-85, model,
photos., plans, site plans.

ZOOMORPHIC STRUCTURES--DENMARK
"Concetto" / Karin Skousboll.
Organic designs by Danish artists,
including Niels Guttormsen and
Knud Haastrup, such as the
Egebjerggard II projects and
"Vingehuset" in Ballerup.
ARKITEKTEN 1990 Dec., v.92, no.18,
p.574-577,cover, photos.,
sketches.
"Vingehuset" / Niels Guttormsen.
Curved, wooden house at
Egebjergaard, Ballerup by the
author and Colom & Gudmand-Hoyer.
ARKITEKTEN 1990 Dec., v.92, no.18,
p.578-583, dets., photos.,
sketches.

ZOOMORPHIC STRUCTURES--DENMARK--
SILKEBORG--LANGESO--HAMAN -
OVERGAARD GARDEN
Pigen som ligger ved soen / Torben
Schonherr.
Garden for Liselotte Haman and
Henning Overgaard, Langeso,
Silkeborg (1985) in the shape of a
female torso. Article includes a
fictionalized presentation by the
designer. Includes English
translation.
LANDSKAB 1990 Nov., v.71, no.7,
p.118-119, plan.

ZOOS
See also MENAGERIES
See also ZOOLOGICAL MUSEUMS
Environmental theater ... the new
zoo / Elise Vider.
Coe Lee Robinson Roesch, a
landscape architecture firm
specializing in zoo design.
METROPOLIS 1990 June, v.9, no.10,
p.44-49, photos.

ZOOS--ALTERATIONS AND ADDITIONS--
COMPETITIONS--SCOTLAND--EDINBURGH--
EDINBURGH ZOO
Zoo logic [penguin enclosure].
Results of design competition for
new penguin enclosure at the
Edinburgh Zoo. First prize: The
Design Group.
ARCHITECTS' JOURNAL 1990 Feb.7,
v.191, no.6, p.26-29, axonometric
views, port., plans, secns.

ZOOS--ALTERATIONS AND ADDITIONS--
GERMANY (WEST)--FRANKFURT AM MAIN--
NIEDERURSELER HANG
Zooabteilung Niederurseler Hang in
Frankfurt = Zoological district
Niederurseler Hang in Frankfurt.
Competition. Winning architects:
Gottfried Hansjakob, Anton
Hansjakob, Klaus Schmidhuber. Text
in German.
ARCHITEKTUR + WETTBEWERBE 1990
Mar., no.141, p.23-31, axonometric
views, dwgs., plans, secns., site
plans, isometric dwgs.

ZOOS--ALTERATIONS AND ADDITIONS--
NETHERLANDS--AMSTERDAM
Tijgers aan de gracht: Artis breidt
uit / Liesbeth Melis.
Plans for addition to zoo in
Amsterdam.
DE ARCHITECT 1989 Dec., v.20,
no.12, p.55-57, ill., elevs.,
plans.

ZOOS--ALTERATIONS AND ADDITIONS--
SCOTLAND--EDINBURGH--EDINBURGH ZOO
Breaking free of Lubetkin's legacy /
John Welsh.
Entries in a competition for the
penguin pool, Edinburgh Zoo.
Architect for London's pool:
Berthold Lubetkin.
BUILDING DESIGN 1990 Feb.2,
no.971, p.16, plans, dwgs.

ZOOS--ALTERATIONS AND ADDITIONS--
UNITED STATES--NEW YORK (NEW YORK)--
CENTRAL PARK ZOO
Central Park Zoo, New York, New
York, 1988 / Kevin Roche.
Architects: Kevin Roche, John
Dinkeloo and Associates. Text in
Japanese and English.
ARCHITECTURE AND URBANISM 1990
Apr., no.4 (235), p.[26]-39,
photos., site plan.

ZOOS--ALTERATIONS AND ADDITIONS--
UNITED STATES--SAN FRANCISCO
(CALIFORNIA)--SAN FRANCISCO ZOO
Rehabilitating the earth, San
Francisco-style / Kerry J. Dawson.
On the joint-use site of the
Oceanside Water Pollution Control
Plant and the addition to the San
Francisco Zoo. Landscape
architects: Roysten Hanamoto Alley
and Abey, Landscape Architects.
(Continued next page)

ZOOS--ALTERATIONS AND ADDITIONS--
UNITED STATES--SAN FRANCISCO
(CALIFORNIA)--SAN FRANCISCO ZOO
(CONTINUED)
Rehabilitating the... (CONTINUED)
LANDSCAPE ARCHITECTURE 1990 Dec.,
v.80, no.12, p.60-61, elev., site
plan, aerial photo.

ZOOS--ENGLAND--CHESTER--CHESTER ZOO
Zoo masterplanning - a director's
view / Michael Brambell, John
Goodfellow.
Focus on the Chester Zoo.
LANDSCAPE DESIGN 1990 July-Aug.,
no.192, p.22-23, photo., site
plan, tables.

ZOOS--ENGLAND--DUDLEY--DUDLEY ZOO
Arquiteto: Berthold Lubetkin.
Seven projects in England, built
1932-1938.
ARQUITECTURA 1990 Jan.-Feb., v.72,
no.282, p.[79]-103, axonometric
view, photos., plans, secns., site
plan.

ZOOS--SPAIN--BARCELONA
Arquitecturas zoologicas: F. Javier
Aguilar, arquitecto.
Spanish, English text.
ON DISENO 1989, no.104, p.161-166,
dwgs., photos.

ZOOS--SWITZERLAND--BERN--TIERPARK
DAHLHOLZLI
Tierisch gut, od'r?: Erweiterung des
Vivariums im Tierpark Dahlholzli,
Bern.
Architect: Andreas Furrer.
DEUTSCHE BAUZEITUNG 1990 Apr.,
v.124, no.4, p.36-41, elevs.,
photos., plan, site plan.

ZOOS--SWITZERLAND--ZURICH--ZOO ZURICH
Neues Hauptgebaude im Zoo Zurich,
1989.
Architect: Willi E. Christen.
WERK, BAUEN + WOHNEN 1989 Dec.,
no.12, p.36, axonometric view,
photos.

ZOOS--UNITED STATES--PHILADELPHIA
(PENNSYLVANIA)--PHILADELPHIA
ZOOLOGICAL GARDEN--WORLD OF PRIMATES
Special feature: Venturi Scott Brown
and Associates.
Contents: Brief history-- Works:
Primate Center, Philadelphia
Zoological Garden.-- Lewis Thomas
Laboratory for Molecular Biology,
Princeton University, 1986.--
Malcolm S. Forbes Jr. College,
Princeton University, 1984.--
Gordon Wu Hall, Princeton
University, 1983.-- Venturi house,
Philadelphia, 1974-present.--
Izenour house, Stony Creek, Conn.,
1984.-- House in New Castle
County, Delaware, 1983.--
Coxe-Hayden house, Block Island,
R.I., 1981.-- Tarble Student
Center, Swarthmore College,
1985.-- Tree House, Philadelphia
Zoo, 1985.-- Welcome Park,
Philadelphia, 1982.-- Decorative
designs.-- Essay: "Body language"
and artifice: on some recent
designs by Venturi Scott Brown and
Associates. Text in Japanese and
English.
ARCHITECTURE AND URBANISM 1990
(Continued next column)

ZOOS--UNITED STATES--PHILADELPHIA
(PENNSYLVANIA)--PHILADELPHIA
ZOOLOGICAL GARDEN--WORLD OF PRIMATES
(CONTINUED)
Special feature:... (CONTINUED)
June, no.6(237), p.[39]-150,
ports., elevs., photos., plans,
secns., site plans.

ZOOS--UNITED STATES--SAINT LOUIS
(MISSOURI)--SAINT LOUIS ZOO--LIVING
WORLD
The Living World, St. Louis Zoo,
Saint Louis, Missouri, USA, 1989.
Architects: Hellmuth, Obata &
Kassabaum. Text in Japanese and
English.
ARCHITECTURE AND URBANISM 1990
Dec., no.12 extra edition,
p.152-161, photos., plans, site
plan.

ZORDAN, GUIDO
La torre della memoria: il recupero
della torre civica di Mestre = a
tower in search of its past: the
Mestre's public tower renewal /
Guido Zordan.
Architect: Guido Zordan. English
summary.
SPAZIO E SOCIETA 1990 Jan.-Mar.,
v.13, no.49, p.48-57, ill., dwgs.,
port., elevs., models, maps,
secns., site plans.

ZORZI, RENZO
Immagini di architetture di Ivrea /
Renzo Zorzi.
Photographs from the Olivetti
Archives in Ivrea, Italy. Text in
Italian and English.
DOMUS 1990 Feb., no.713,
p.[76-80], photos.
Il patrimonio storico: Venezia, la
Fondazione Cini = Historical
heritage: Venice, the Cini
Foundation / Renzo Zorzi.
The buildings on the island of San
Giorgio Maggiore, owned and
restored by the Cini Foundation.
ABITARE 1990 Nov., no.290,
p.192-[205].256, photos., aerial
photo.

ZOZAYA, JUAN
Las influencias visigoticas en
al-Andalus / Juan Zozaya.
Seminario Internazionale di Studi
su "Archeologia e arte nella
Spagna tardoromana, visigota e
mozarabica"; Ravenna, 4-11 April
1987.
CORSO DI CULTURA SULL'ARTE
RAVENNATE E BIZANTINA 1987, v.34,
p.395-425, photos., biblio.

ZSOLT, JOHN A.
Architectural education: the modern
condition and architecture / John
A. Zsolt.
Art and architecture in modern
society and culture.
CITY MAGAZINE 1990 Fall, v.12,
no.1, p.34-39, model, photos.,
plan, biblio.

ZUAZO UGALDE, SECUNDINO DE
Los nuevos ministerios de Madrid,
una propuesta arquitectonica de
Secundino Zuazo = The new
ministeries in Madrid, and
architectural proposal by
Secundino Zuazo / Lilia Maure
Rubio.
COMPOSICION ARQUITECTONICA, ART &
ARCHITECTURE 1989 June, no.3,
p.[103]-136, dwgs., elevs., maps,
photos., plans, refs.

ZUBE, ERVIN H.
Park-people relationships: an
international review / Ervin H.
Zube, Miriam L. Busch.
Examines relationships of people
living in or near national parks
and reserves to those areas in 38
countries.
LANDSCAPE AND URBAN PLANNING 1990
May, v.19, no.2, p.117-131,
diagrs., tables, refs.

ZUBEL, HENRYK
Vernieuwend plan voor Octrooibureau:
Neutelings-Roodbeen in finale
ontwerpprijsvraag / Egbert Koster.
Proposals by Neutelings en
Roodbeen (winner);
Pysall-Stahrenberg & Partner.
Jouke Post, Daan ter Avest, and
Henryk Zubel; for a new office
building in the Hague.
DE ARCHITECT 1990 Feb., v.21,
no.2, p.40-43, dwgs., models,
secns., ref.

ZUBLENA, AYMERIC
Le avventure del projetto urbano:
Bofill, Grumbach e Zublena a
Montparnasse = The adventures of
urban design: Bofill, Grumbach and
Zublena in Montparnasse / Marc
Bedarida.
LOTUS INTERNATIONAL 1986, no.51,
p.58-77, axonometric views,
elevs., photos., plans, secns.,
site plans.

ZUCCHERI, TONI
Seeiing the light / Justin
Henderson.
On the Reggiani Light Gallery, New
York. Architect: Toni Zuccheri.
INTERIORS 1990 July, v.149, no.12,
p.72-[73], photos.

ZUCCHI, CINO
Cino Zucchi: tra classicismo e
romanticismo = between classicism
and romanticism: Cino Zucchi's
projects and works compared /
Francesco Moschini.
Presents 16 projects since 1979.
In Italian and English; French,
German, and Spanish summaries,
p.3.
L'INDUSTRIA DELLE COSTRUZIONI 1990
May, v.24, no.223, p.6-35,3,
dets., dwgs., models, photos.,
plans, secns., site plans,
sketches.

ZUCCONI, GUIDO
Gustavo Giovannoni: la naissance de
l'architecture integral en Italie
/ Guido Zucconi.
French, English, Spanish and
German summaries, p.247-252.
LES ANNALES DE LA RECHERCHE
(Continued next page)

ZWINKELS, CEES
  Archiprix 1989 [studentenplannen]
    Presents the 19 winning projects
    receiving the annual Dutch awards.
    Introd. by Cees Zwinkels.
    DE ARCHITECT 1990 Apr., v.21,
    no.4, p.83-106, ill., dwgs.,
    elevs., models, photos., plans,
    secns., site plans.
  Architectenregister slaat aan:
    inschrijvingscriteria beinvloeden
    vakonderwijs / Cees Zwinkels.
    The Stichting Bureau
    Architectenregister (SBA) the
    Netherlands.
    DE ARCHITECT 1990 Jan., v.21,
    no.1, p.49-51, diagr., refs.
  Een gebouw als een woonwijk:
    Academisch ziekenhuis Utrecht van
    EGM / Cees Zwinkels.
    DE ARCHITECT 1989 Nov., v.20,
    no.11, p.120-129, photos., plans,
    site plan.
  Houtskeletbouw blijft veelbelovend:
    VSHB zoekt kwaliteitsnorm voor
    stadsvernieuwing / Cees Zwinkels.
    Review several new housing
    projects in the Netherlands in
    conjunction with an international
    conference scheduled for 21-22
    Nov.1989 in Amsterdam (The Urban
    Housing Summit: new solutions to
    inner city redevelopment).
    DE ARCHITECT 1989 Oct., v.20,
    no.10, p.132-137, dwg., model,
    photos., plans, secn., biblio.
  Inspirerende verdichtingsbouw:
    Woningbouwproject De Rade in Den
    Haag / Cees Zwinkels.
    A 74-unit apartment building
    completed Nov.1989. Architect: Van
    Herk en de Kleijn.
    DE ARCHITECT 1990 Jan., v.21,
    no.1, p.70-75, photos., plans,
    secn., site plans.
  Thema: architectuur en macht.
    "Themanummer 41." Seven articles
    indexed separately. Also includes
    Positie architect in bouwproces
    onderzocht, and Is de macht aan de
    ondernemende architect?, both by
    Cees Zwinkels.
    DE ARCHITECT THEMA 1990 Nov.,
    v.21, no.11 suppl., p.3-53, ill.,
    photos., refs.
  Thema: bouwen en milieu.
    "Themanummer 38", with articles on
    energy efficient housing. Authors:
    Cees Zwinkels, Wim Keijsers, Jos
    Verbakel, Hans Groeneveld, Chiel
    Boonstra, Peter Fraanje, Tjerk
    Reijenga, Frans de Haas, Joop
    Niesten.
    DE ARCHITECT THEMA 1990 Mar.,
    v.21, no.3 suppl., p.3-63,
    axonometric views, graph, elevs.,
    models, photos., plans, secns.,
    site plans, tables, biblios.

ZWOCH, FELIX
  Groszstadien 1990.
    Issue features stadiums. In
    addition to several articles
    indexed separately, includes
    essays by Felix Zwoch,
    Heinz-Joachim Fischer, Karl
    Valentin, Mara Pinardi, Marco
    Degl'Innocenti, and Ermanno
    Ranzani, and features the stadiums
    at Bari, Florence, Genoa, Milan,
    Palermo, Rome, Turin, and Udine.
    BAUWELT 1990 June 29, v.81, no.24,
        (Continued next column)

ZWOCH, FELIX (CONTINUED)
  Groszstadien 1990. (CONTINUED)
    p.1202-1246, ill., elevs., models,
    photos., plans, secns., site
    plans, aerial photos.
  Unternehmen Deutschland
    [StadtBauwelt 108] / Felix Zwoch.
    Theme of issue is architecture and
    planning in East German cities.
    Includes essays by Felix Zwoch,
    Stephan Reiss-Schmidt, Rainer
    Krettek, and Hans Heuer, and
    feature sections on Dresden,
    Leipzig, Chemnitz, Rostock, and
    Erfurt.
    BAUWELT 1990 Dec.28, v.81, no.48,
    p.2404-2496, axonometric views,
    dwgs., elevs., models, maps,
    photos., plans, site plans,
    sketches, refs.

ZYKAN, MARLENE
  Der Westbau von St. Stephan /
    Marlene Zykan.
    OSTERREICHISCHE ZEITSCHRIFT FUR
    KUNST UND DENKMALPFLEGE 1990,
    v.44, no.1-2, p.47-52, elevs.,
    photos., refs.

ZZOP, ARCHITEKTEN
  Vendex - driehoek Amsterdam:
    uithuilen en opnieuw beginnen /
    Herman Selier.
    Alterations proposed for
    triangular area between Singel,
    Kalverstraat, and Heiligeweg. Plan
    by ZZOP.
    DE ARCHITECT 1990 May, v.21, no.4,
    p.37-43, ill., models, photos.,
    secns., site plans.